BLOOMSBURY

Guide to English Literature

BLOOMSBURY

Guide to English Literature

The *New* Authority on English Literature
Edited by Marion Wynne-Davies

BLOOMSBURY

First published 1989
This edition published 1992

Copyright © by Bloomsbury Publishing Ltd, 1989
Bloomsbury Publishing Ltd, 2 Soho Square, London W1V 5DE

British Library Cataloguing in Publication Data
A CIP catalogue record for this book is available from the British Library
ISBN 0 7475 1195 0

10 9 8 7 6 5 4 3 2 1

Typeset and printed by Richard Clay Ltd, Bungay, Suffolk

Contents

Acknowledgements

Originator
Christopher Gillie

Editor
Marion Wynne-Davies

Contributors
Janet Barron (18th-century prose)
James Booth (Augustan and Romantic poetry) University of Hull
Catherine Byron (Irish literature) Loughborough College of Art and Design
Edmund Campion (Australian literature) St Patrick's College, Manly, NSW, Australia
Gail Cunningham (19th-century prose) Kingston Polytechnic
John Drakakis (Critical theory) University of Stirling
David Jarrett (Science fiction) Polytechnic of North London
Lesley Johnson (Medieval literature) University of Leeds
Sarah Johnston (19th-century prose) Kingston Polytechnic
David Nokes (18th-century prose) Kings College, University of London
John O'Brien (French literature) University of Liverpool
Valerie Pedlar (Context of literature) University of Liverpool
Andrew Piasecki (Modern drama) Royal Holloway and Bedford New College
Andrew Roberts (20th-century prose) Queen Mary and Westfield College, London
Jonathan Sawday (Renaissance poetry) University of Southampton
Eva Simmons (Restoration and 18th-century drama) Birkbeck College, University of London
Jim Simpson (German literature) University of Liverpool
Mercer Simpson (Welsh literature)
John Thieme (Commonwealth literature) Polytechnic of North London
René Weis (Renaissance drama) University College, London
Linda Williams (Victorian and modern poetry) University of Liverpool

Advisors

Bernard Bealty
Rachel Bowlby
Douglas Brooks-
    Davis
Nick Davis
Simon Dentith
Philip Edwards
Steve Ellis
Lucy Gent
Trevor Griffiths
Andrew Hamer

Mary Hamer
Brean Hammond
Terence Hawkes
Glyn Jones
Anna-Maria Jubb
Peter Lewis
Jon Lopategui
Ann Mackenzie
Robert Miles
David Milles
Brian Nellist

Jocelyn Price
Kay Richardson
David Seed
Paul Simpson
Ann Thompson
Geoffrey Ward
Valerie Wayne
Wendy Wheeler
Helen Wilcox
Sue Wiseman
Katherine Worth

Editorial
Project Editor   Sian Facer
Editorial Assistant   Kate Newman
Editorial Director   Kathy Rooney

Design
Jacket and text design   Fielding Rowinski
Many thanks to:
Anne-Marie Ehrlich; British Library; London Library; Sydney Jones Library, Liverpool;
Tate Gallery; National Portrait Gallery; Clare Dowdy; Brigette Unwin; Alastair Cording;
Carmel Killin; Catherine Carpenter.

Introduction

Reading a book is something like going on a quest, whether for the pleasure it gives, for the resolution of the plot, for information, inspiration or understanding, and *The Bloomsbury Guide to English Literature* is no exception. My intention, when undertaking this edition, was to offer several alternative but intertwining paths of exploration and discovery which are both pleasing in themselves and which lead to the further enjoyment of reading other books. The text is divided into two parts: first, a series of essays ordered generically and chronologically, which provide the reader with approaches to the important literary issues, from Medieval literature to contemporary critical theory. Secondly, there is an alphabetical reference section which is designed to complement and provide more information about the ideas, authors and texts dealt with in the essays. As such the whole supplies a unique combination of animating analyses and specialized contextualization together with detailed, comprehensive and up-to-date material. The wide-ranging cross referencing of both essays and entries allows the reader to follow whichever path, or paths, appear most interesting and profitable.

In addition to the formal literary matter, I have included information of a broader nature in order to offer a material, historical and cultural context for the authors and texts examined. The *Guide* begins with an essay by its originator, Christopher Gillie, which enables the reader to appreciate the relationship of different periods and societies to writers and their works; a chronological table is provided at the back of the book as a supplement to this. The need to look at literature in its context, rather than in a vacuum, has become more relevant at the present time when English is developing in so many diverse and interesting directions, from Commonwealth literature to the writers of non-standard English and women's fiction. I have tried to include as many of these authors as is possible, in addition to those more well-known, although due to the inevitable limitations on space I have been restricted to a predominantly British and Britain-related bias. However, should any reader feel that improvements could be made, I would be happy to receive suggestions for future editions.

Altogether *The Bloomsbury Guide* has been, and will continue to be, a cumulative and democratic production, and my foremost thanks must go to my contributors for their imaginative and careful work. I also wish to acknowledge my debts to Douglas Brooks-Davies for continued inspiration and faith, to Trevor Griffiths for introducing me to this project and to Warwick Gould and Terry Hawkes for their encouragement and capable advice. My colleagues at Liverpool University have been invaluable with their prompt and thoughtful responses to what must have seemed like a never ending stream of queries. Likewise, the departmental secretaries have been unreserved with their time and help. On a personal level, my heartfelt thanks must go to my parents for their unquestioning support and to

Geoffrey Ward for his meticulous scholarship and perceptive criticism which he has exercised on my behalf with a singular degree of care and generosity. Finally, I thank my editors at Bloomsbury, especially Kathy Rooney for her powerful commitment to the project and Sian Facer without whose remarkable dedication and energies I could never have completed this work. I hope that readers of *The Bloomsbury Guide to English Literature* will find their quest as exciting and fulfilling as the creation of the book has been for its writers.

Marion Wynne-Davies
Department of English
University of Liverpool

Editor's Note

Cross references

A liberal use of cross references has been made. In both the essays and the reference entries, names, titles and topics are frequently marked with an arrow ($\triangleright$) to guide the reader to the appropriate entry in the reference section for a more detailed explanation. Cross reference arrows appear both in the text and at the end of entries.

Dates

Dates after the names of people indicate their life spans, except when they follow the names of monarchs when they show the length of the reign.

Essay section

Tom Phillips *The Calligrapher Replies* (*Here We Exemplify*) (1987)

Political history and social context 1066–present day 1

1066–1485

> *Thanne comth oure verray gentilesse of grace;*
> *It was no thyng biquethe us with oure place*
>   Chaucer

British people think of their history as having an unusually distinct beginning: the Battle of Hastings, 1066. This was the victory of ▷ William, Duke of Normandy, Norse by descent and French by culture, over the ▷ Anglo-Saxon king, Harold; William went on to conquer the whole of England, though not the rest of Britain (*ie* ▷ Scotland, ▷ Wales and ▷ Ireland). Such a view of the beginning of formal history is a simplified one. Not all Anglo-Saxon political habits of thought and institutions were extinguished by the Conquest; nor did Anglo-Saxon art and literature, which had been notable, simply expire.

Nonetheless, the Norman Conquest made a profound break in British political and cultural history. Politically, William I and his successors were able, because of the completeness of the Conquest, to reorganize governing institutions, giving them a pattern which is still visible as the basis of those of the present day. Socially, he removed most of the Anglo-Saxon ruling class, replacing it by his own Norman-French followers, bound together by a Norman-French system of relationships. Culturally, this immense social change meant that England became a three-language nation for at least two centuries: the upper class spoke French; English was the tongue of the lower classes; while the educated class (the church men or 'clerks') used Latin – as elsewhere in Europe – for official business and scholarship. Celtic languages were spoken in Scotland, Wales and Ireland.

Another important consequence of the Conquest was that, since the royal families and the nobility were Norman-French or French, England was closely involved in French politics and wars against the kings of France until the middle of the fifteenth century. In the second half of the period this conflict with France led the Norman-French nobility of England to think of themselves as English rather than French, and in the fourteenth century they took to English instead of French as their normal tongue. ▷ Henry IV (1399–1413) is reputed to have been the first of the kings since the Conquest to use English as his native language; ▷ Chaucer (?1340–1400) was the first poet of a royal court to write in English.

The period 1066–1485 is what we think of as 'the English Middle Ages' linguistically, as the 'Middle English' period between the Old English of the pre-Conquest Anglo-Saxons and the Modern English speech and writing of the sixteenth century. It shaped many of the most important political institutions of our own day, and a British culture which is almost as different from the culture of the Anglo-Saxons as it is from the Norman-French culture that succeeded it. Above all, it shaped a sense of nationhood among the British, a sense of identity which intensified their awareness of the identity of the larger civilizations of Europe in which they participated.

The social organization which William the Conqueror established in England was the one known to most of western Europe in the eleventh century; historians call it 'the feudal system'. This kind of society had grown up under the later Roman Empire of the West, when organization was breaking down and social order was maintained by an appeal to self-interest. By this 'system', a landholder held his land as a 'feudum' or 'fee' from a superior lord; in return for protection by this superior, the landholder rendered him some service, such as work on the superior's land or military service. Feudal relationship had grown up spontaneously as a method by which the relatively weak could find defence against forces of disorder, but in few regions besides England after the Conquest was it in any sense systematic. Even in England, the king's government needed its own centralizing institutions for efficient rule; the barons (*ie* the nobility) recognized no interests except their own, evaded service of the king when they could, and regarded themselves as independent rulers within their own territories.

Thus the King's Council (Curia Regis) became a central body of professional officials, who, under efficient kings such as ▷ Henry I (1100–35) and ▷ Henry II (1154–89), worked equally as administrators and as judges ensuring that 'the King's Peace' was kept uniformly throughout the country. The king needed educated men for such tasks, and until the fourteenth century he found them only among men bred to the Church, such as ▷ Thomas à Becket, Henry II's Chancellor, and later Archbishop and the king's enemy. The king's Chancellor was his secretary, and the office was at first overshadowed by that of Justiciar, *ie* chief judge. After 1231, however, the office of Justiciar died out, and the Chancellorship became the most important office of state. The Chancellor came to control not only the administrative machine but also the judicial system, since it was he who handled petitions to the king. The modern Lord Chancellor is the historical descendant of the medieval chancellors; he is the head of the judicial system (equivalent to a Minister of Justice) and, though his political importance diminished greatly after the reign of ▷ Henry VIII (1509–47), he still has high political status as president of the upper house of Parliament, the House of Lords. When he needed the support of his nobles, the king expanded his Curia Regis into the Magnum Concilium (Great Council), of which the modern House of Lords is the historical descendant. Now, as then, the reigning king or queen composes it by summoning to it the lords, lay and spiritual, *ie* the hereditary nobility and the bishops – though the House of Lords also contains other components.

In 1295 ▷ Edward I, following the example of Simon de Montfort, who had ruled England during part of the previous reign of ▷ Henry III, expanded the Great Council by adding to it the ▷ Commons, *ie* elected representatives of the towns and Knights of the Shire from the provincial districts now known as counties. The king was not making a very early experiment in liberal democracy when he formed this Model Parliament; he was merely continuing the policy of previous ▷ Norman and ▷ Plantagenet kings of extending the effectiveness of their central administration. The great administrative problem for governments in the twelfth and thirteenth centuries, when communications were bad, administrators few, and the nobility lacking public spirit, was to establish effective relationships with the people. When the king needed to raise money by taxation, he could not rely on his officials to collect it against the wishes of local interests, until he found means to deal directly with these interests through their elected representatives. Thus the system of government through elected representatives, which by the end of the nineteenth century was the main instrument of democracy, was in the fourteenth century an instrument of monarchy, exercised by kings who never imagined that one day the people would take possession of it and use it against monarchical rule. The process by which this came about was gradual: already in the fourteenth century the Commons presented 'petitions' to the king, which he often found it expedient to grant in order to secure their agreement to taxation more readily; in the fifteenth century this petition became a 'bill' which, when accepted by the king, was called an 'act' or 'statute' and became a law of the land; in the seventeenth century Parliament secured that laws were made in no other way, and in the eighteenth century the king's assent was becoming what it is today – a mere formality concluding a procedure initiated by Parliament.

The use of elected representatives to assist government did not originate with the transformation of the Great Council into Parliament by the addition of the Commons. It was already a habit of the Curia Regis to send for representative Knights of the Shire to give evidence in difficult cases that came before it, and the annual shire courts, presided over by sheriffs ('shire reeves'), were attended by representatives from the subdivisions ('hundreds') of the shires. More important, because it was as central to the development of justice as representatives of the Commons were to the development of government, was the election of 'sworn men' or 'juries' (from French *juré*) to meet judges (Justices of Assize) sent out from the Curia Regis to the shires. These judges tried cases which were too serious for the powers of the local shire courts. In criminal cases, it was at first the main function of the juries to present to the royal judges such people as were accused of serious crimes; the actual trial of criminal cases in the eleventh and twelfth centuries was often conducted by some sort of 'ordeal' undergone by the accused, who was judged guilty or otherwise in accordance with his or her ability to survive it. 'Trial by ordeal' was supposed to reveal the judgement of Heaven which would not allow an innocent person to perish; not until the thirteenth century did public opinion come to accept the judgement of a jury, selected from among neighbours, as a superior means of arriving at the truth. In 'civil cases' of disputes between neighbours, the jury was at first a panel of witnesses who declared the facts (*eg* about the ownership of land) as they knew them. But, like the elected representatives of the Commons summoned by the kings to Parliament, the jury began as an instrument to secure efficient government, and by the seventeenth century it was being used by opponents of the king's government as a safeguard to private liberty.

The office of Sheriff, who stood for the king's interests in every shire, was important in the Middle Ages and still survives, but it began to lose most of its importance in the sixteenth century. He was the principal local authority for law and order; however, he was not a professional official like the members of the king's court, but a local landholder of importance, who occasionally succeeded in making the office hereditary in his family. Justices of the Peace (first known as Guardians of the Peace and nowadays called Magistrates) began obscurely in the twelfth and thirteenth centuries and became supremely important only in the sixteenth century. Like the sheriff, they have never been professional, but were until the nineteenth century members of the middle range of landowner. Nowadays they are commonly drawn from all classes, trades and professions, and their authority is restricted to trial (without jury, but with a professional lawyer called the Clerk to advise them) of petty offences and the examination of more serious charges. At the height of their power (sixteenth to nineteenth centuries) they were the principal local authorities. Sometimes they held office more because of their status in their local communities than because of their competence for the work; equally often, they were responsible men who constituted a very important link between the government and society. The eighteenth-century novelist, ▷ Henry Fielding, himself an admirable representative of the class of magistrates, depicts a worthy and an unworthy example in Squire Allworthy and Squire Western, characters in his novel, ▷ *Tom Jones*.

The history of Britain in the Middle Ages may be seen as the political and legal shaping of society; the chief shaping force was the monarchy, which enforced through its officials a Common Law (*ie* a law which was the same for all members of society) based on custom and precedent. The Common Law was a great force for social liberation, because it freed common men from tyranny by the self-interested nobility. However, the kings sometimes attempted to advance their personal interests against those of society, and it is often difficult to decide when they were doing this and when they were resisting the self-interest of the nobles. An outstanding example of this difficulty is the reign of ▷ King John (1199–1216), who is traditionally regarded as a self-interested king, on whom the barons, in alliance with the Church, were able to impose a charter of rights – the famous ▷ Magna Carta (Great Charter) of 1215. This charter was first given importance as an assertion of human rights against arbitrary government in the seventeenth century, when Parliament came into open conflict with the king, and used it to provide its members with legal support and protection; clauses in it can be interpreted as a basis for the right of trial by jury and for protection against imprisonment without trial. In other respects some modern historians are inclined to interpret Magna Carta as principally a defence of the interests of the barons and of the Church.

The Norman and Plantagenet kings of England and Wales were also French nobles; Henry II (1154–89) indeed controlled more land in France than did the King of France himself; all of it was acquired by inheritance and by marriage. Such preponderance of power in France naturally led to rivalry with the French king, and to intermittent war throughout the twelfth and thirteenth centuries; at the end of this period, the French possessions of the kings of England were greatly reduced.

The second and more important phase of medieval Anglo-French hostility began in 1337 and ended in 1453; it is known as the ▷ Hundred Years' War, and ostensibly it was caused by the claim of ▷ Edward III (1327–77) to be the rightful King of France. The real causes were deeper and more complex; amongst them was the fact that the English national identity had taken shape faster than that of France, and the mood of this new national consciousness was consequently self-reliant and aggressive, particularly among the rich and ambitious nobility. 'The English', wrote the fourteenth-century French chronicler Froissart, 'will never love or honour the king, unless he be victorious and a lover of arms and war against their neighbours ... The king of England must needs obey his people and do their will.' Between 1307 and 1460, the kings who did not engage in successful war in France all had serious trouble with their nobility at home: ▷ Edward II (1307–27), ▷ Richard II (1377–99), Henry IV (1399–1413) and especially ▷ Henry VI (1422–61). The prosperous reigns were those of successful warriors: Edward III (1327–77, especially until 1360) and ▷ Henry V (1413–22).

According to modern value judgments, the Hundred Years' War was an inexcusable war of aggression, but it had the effect of further strengthening the English sense of national unity, as well as creating – by the end – such a feeling among the French. The few great battles (Crécy 1346, Poitiers 1356, and ▷ Agincourt 1415) were victories of English and Welsh common soldiers (archers, using the long bow) over French aristocratic cavalry; the fact indicates radical historical change, since it means that this was the first major European war to be fought (at first only on the English side, but in the end on both sides) by national armies, and not by feudal ones loosely kept together by ties with the feudal lords.

The final defeat of the English resulted in the disbanding by English royalty and nobility of their French dreams. If they had been realized, England, as the smaller and poorer country, would have become a mere appendage to France; instead she became free to shape her own very individual course in the newly arising comity of self-conscious European nations. The immediate effect on England and Wales was disastrous; failure in the foreign war led to extensive civil war amongst the English nobility. The ▷ Wars of the Roses, which opened in 1455 and were finally closed only by the victory of Henry Tudor over ▷ Richard III at the battle of Bosworth in 1485, were remembered as a warning of the hell of national disunity. ▷ Shakespeare's first four history plays ▷ Henry VI, Parts I, II and III and ▷ Richard III, are a tragic epic on the culmination of this disunity.

We have been discussing mainly English history, but it is still important to remember that England is not Britain, though in modern times the names are so often used interchangeably. In 1485 there was, as yet, no Britain. Politically, ▷ Ireland was overrun by Anglo-Norman barons in the twelfth century, and Henry II took the title of Lord of Ireland, but English rule was not effective beyond a strip on the eastern coastline known as the ▷ Pale; Wales was conquered by Edward I in the thirteenth century, but it was not properly assimilated into the English political system until the sixteenth; Scotland defeated English attempts to conquer it early in the fourteenth century, and during the Hundred Years' War it allied itself to France. Both Ireland and Wales had Celtic spoken languages with literatures in those languages, and Scotland was divided between Celtic and a variety of English.

1485–1603

> *The daughter of debate, that eke discord doth sow*
> *Shall reap no gain where former rule hath taught still peace to grow*
> > Elizabeth I

England was one of the first countries in Europe to feel the impact of nationalism, but by the sixteenth century France and Spain had also achieved unity and nationhood. They towered above England almost as the U.S.A. and the U.S.S.R. do today, and constituted a potential – at times an actual – threat to its very existence. Fortunately, they were often hostile to each other. Yet this was not a period of decline for England; its relative inferiority was due to the increase in stature of its neighbours, not to its own diminution. On the contrary, the sixteenth century was that in which the nation developed, consolidated its energies, and found a use for them overseas in seafaring activities. The century was indeed more fortunate for England than for France and Spain, for at the end of it England, unlike Spain, was still advancing economically, and unlike France it had lost none of its representative political institutions.

All this was thanks partly to the reigning family of the ▷ Tudors, the most gifted of the dynasties which have reigned over England. National solidarity elsewhere in Europe had been gained by the consolidation of monarchic power, and in this England was no exception; the period is in fact sometimes described as that of the 'Tudor despotism'. Yet ▷ Henry VIII (1509–47), one of the most despotic of English sovereigns, has also been described by English historians as a great parliamentarian. This seeming paradox is explained by the fact that, whereas the other sovereigns of Europe relied on their professional armies for their authority, and abandoned, as forces for disunity, their representative institutions, the Tudors had no such armies, and, realizing that they could achieve little if they did not carry the nation with them, they found it necessary to keep Parliament alive. So it happened that the political institutions that eventually made for popular government survived in England while they decayed elsewhere; their survival in this period accounts for the difference between the later history of England and that of the other larger nations of Europe.

Although they found it wiser to respect and use Parliament while other

European monarchs found it more convenient to relinquish institutions, the Tudors nonetheless required other institutions of government which were more strengthening to their power.

In the fifteenth century, Parliament, though it had by no means yet become the channel of national feeling, was already an instrument of opposition to the monarchy. The House of Lords was the meeting-place of the great nobles who tore England apart in the Wars of the Roses, and they were able to use the House of Commons as their tool, for the townsmen and smaller landowners who composed it were not yet able to find an independent voice and leadership. To manage so dangerous a body, the Tudors relied upon the old Curia Regis (King's Council), which by this time was known as the ▷ Privy Council. The Privy Council had the acknowledged right to issue ordinances which had the force of law, and when the matter affected the nation too gravely for this to be a wise procedure, the Councillors took their seats in Parliament, much as modern ministers do, and directed the needed Bills through both Houses.

But the Privy Council was put to other purposes as well; subcommittees of it were used to expand the king's administration and justice, just as Henry II in the twelfth century had used the Curia Regis to expand his system of justice by imposing on the feudal nobles the rule of Common Law. The weaknesses of the Common Law courts in the sixteenth century were that their procedure was often slow, and that the juries employed in them could be bribed or intimidated by powerful influences, especially in the wild districts of the north, where the old feudal nobility was still strong, and in Wales. Thus new courts were shaped out of the Privy Council, such as the Council of the North, the Council of Wales, and, most famous of all, the Court of the ▷ Star Chamber, so called from the pattern of stars on the ceiling of the room in which it met. These new courts did not supersede the courts of Common Law; they even revived the prestige of the Common Law courts by restoring public faith in and respect for justice.

However, these new courts had two characteristics which eventually turned public opinion against them: they based their authority on royal prerogative, ie powers peculiar to the king; and they worked without juries. Hence when Parliament once more set itself against the king in the seventeenth century, it saw them no longer as instruments of justice but of tyranny, and it abolished them. The Privy Council, on the other hand, survives today; it is no longer the central instrument of executive power (since the Cabinet is that), but a body which serves a variety of consultative purposes.

The time was well past when the kings depended on churchmen as the only men educated enough to be capable of the art of government; ▷ Cardinal Wolsey was the last priest-statesman in the tradition of Thomas à Becket. Country gentlemen, lawyers, and merchants of the towns were now plentiful in the educated classes, and it was from among these that the Tudors chose their Privy Councillors and Ministers of State. This policy replenished the English aristocracy; not only were the new men of power different in kind from their predecessors, and from different families, but they used their power in a different way. They were politicians and administrators in the modern sense, and they established traditions within their families such that the descendants of some of them, for instance the Cecils, the Russells, the Cavendishes, continue to play an important part in politics.

The former feudal nobility had battered itself into relative weakness during the fifteenth-century Wars of the Roses, and the first Tudor, ▷ Henry VII, eliminated their private armies by fining heavily any nobleman who tried to keep one. The strongholds of this old nobility were in the economically backward north and west, and they did not give way without a struggle; the ▷ Pilgrimage of Grace in 1536 and the rebellion of the northern earls in 1569 were their principal endeavours to re-establish their prestige and the interests of their more conservative society. But the advancing society of the south-east was more numerous, and its interests were strengthened by the inter-relationship of the classes: landed gentry apprenticed their younger sons to merchants of ▷ London – at the end of the century already the largest city in Europe – and both intermarried with the great aristocracy.

The landed gentleman, high in prestige among his lesser farming neighbours who were often bound to him, not by feudal obligations, but as rent-paying tenants, was the successor to the medieval baron, and exerted comparable but very different powers as Justice of the Peace. As such he was responsible for the law and order of his neighbourhood, and if in this he was sometimes unduly mindful of his interests – especially the protection of his 'game', ie animals reserved for ▷ hunting on his land – he was too much in awe of the Privy Council which commissioned his authority to carry tyranny far. The Justices of the Peace, settled men in the upper-middle ranges of society, carried ideas of government and order from the professional administrators of the Privy Council into the intimate world of the village parishes, making justice and politics human, if not always humane.

Since 1066, Britain has never had a reigning family of purely English origins; the Tudors were a Welsh family, which in the fifteenth century connected itself with the Lancastrian branch of the originally French Plantagenets. No other reigning family assimilated so powerfully English ways of thinking and feeling, and this is most apparent in their handling of the great crisis of the century – the crisis that absorbed into itself so many other crises of domestic and foreign concern – that of the religious ▷ Reformation. This movement, which divided Europe in ways that were to prove permanent, was common to most of the northern countries, but in England it took a peculiar form. As elsewhere, the English Reformation had two aspects, political and doctrinal; it also had three phases, corresponding to the reigns of Henry VIII (1509–47), of his son ▷ Edward VI (1547–53), and of his younger daughter ▷ Elizabeth I (1558–1603).

The Church of the Middle Ages had been not only a religious body; it had been a political and legal power as well. Its bishops and greater abbots owned extensive property, which gave them material importance in an age when ownership of land was the measure of influence. Their interests involved them in political games, the prizes of which rewarded the international Catholic Church as well as the English clergy. The Church had its own courts of law, which sometimes competed for authority with those of the Common Law. Taxes, often resented throughout society, were paid to the head of the Church – the Pope in Rome. Nor was the Pope the only international authority of the Church; the heads of the great monastic orders often lived in France or Italy, and the abbots of English monasteries owed obedience and financial contributions to them as well as to the English king. Thus the medieval kings were never full masters of their country, but it often suited them to accept the special position of the Church for the sake of its support against their own barons or some foreign prince, or because they needed churchmen in the running of their governments.

These circumstances which made the Church partly acceptable to the medieval kings no longer applied to the sixteenth-century monarchy. Henry VIII felt only exasperation at the Church's exercise of authority within the English frontiers, at the draining away of money to Church authorities abroad, at the lack of practical value of such institutions as monasteries which had lost many of their social functions and (often) their spiritual vocations. He knew that public opinion was mainly behind him, and his 'Reformation Parliament' (1529–36) supported him in passing the necessary laws to separate the Church of England from Rome, and place it under the supremacy of the King himself. Yet Henry – whom the Pope had rewarded with the title 'Defender of the Faith' for writing against the German reformer ▷ Martin Luther – was conservative in his beliefs, and the Act of Six Articles (1539) reaffirmed the Catholic dogma of Transubstantiation, and such conservative practices as the celibacy of the clergy and the duty of regular confession to and absolution by a priest.

'There are many opinions in England concerning religion', a Venetian ambassador had written early in the century; in the fourteenth century, ▷ John Wycliffe had been a radical reformer of doctrine, and he had died peacefully in his bed instead of being put to death like his contemporary, the Bohemian John Huss. Some of Henry's subjects were more Protestant than himself, and some were more Catholic; his Archbishop of Canterbury, ▷ Thomas Cranmer, was amongst the former. Cranmer led the Protestant movement in the next reign (Edward VI) with his ▷ Book of Common Prayer for use in all English churches; in the reign after he was burnt alive in accordance with the counter-reformation policy of Henry's Catholic daughter, ▷ Mary I (1553–8), who brought England back to allegiance to Rome. Neither reign was popular with the English, perhaps as much for reasons of political feelings as for religious ones. The Protestant reign of the boy King Edward let loose upon the country the more rapaciously self-seeking of the new style of nobleman, and it upset conservative sentiment by the unnecessary destruction of time-honoured religious images in the churches. Mary I was, however, much worse hated for her public burnings of Protestants, and for opening the way to foreign influences by marrying 'His Most Catholic Majesty' Philip II of Spain – a much fiercer persecutor of Protestantism in his own dominions. ▷ Fox's *Book of Martyrs* was revered next to the Bible in many English households for generations later.

So Elizabeth I, last and considered to be the greatest of the Tudors, re-established the ▷ Anglican Church – again by Act of Parliament – in 1559, but characteristically she chose 'a middle way'. Her Settlement was so cautiously worded as to admit the possibility that good Catholics might feel that they could combine their loyalty to the Pope with that to the Queen, and their faith in Catholic dogmas with membership of the Anglican Church. It was not until 1571 that the Pope could bring himself to excommunicate Elizabeth, and the Anglican opinion was that the Church of Rome 'seceded' from the Church of England, not the other way round.

The Elizabethan Settlement established the ▷ Church of England durably; it has remained largely what she meant it to be – a religious body elastic enough to include, to this day, Christians who are Catholic in all points except acknowledgement of the Pope, and Christians who are Protestant enough to resent all but the austerest religious ritual – the High Church and the Low Church as the two extremes came to be called in the nineteenth century. It did not, indeed, do all that she meant: the Roman Catholics did not join it, and the extremer Protestants, first called in her reign ▷ Puritans, remained discontented with it, until they were cast out a century later to make up those numerous dissenting denominations which caused the French writer ▷ Voltaire to describe England as the land of 'many religions and only one sauce'. It is often called the 'Elizabethan Compromise', but it was no mere compromise, as was to be testified by the thinkers of great spiritual dignity which it was to produce in the next hundred years: ▷ Richard Hooker, ▷ Lancelot Andrews, ▷ Jeremy Taylor. Nor did they testify alone, for we have Anglican poets of the same period: ▷ George Herbert, ▷ John Donne and ▷ Henry Vaughan.

The ▷ Renaissance was Rebirth – Europe recovering its supposed origins in the cultures of ancient Greece and Rome. The Reformation was a product of it: people first became critical of the unexamined assumptions of the Middle Ages, and then – in northern Europe – turned against the Church that seemed to embody them. They were disintegrating movements, but also liberating ones, and they were consistently related, by cause and by effect, to liberating movements in politics, commerce and society in every country.

The liberation of English national energies at the end of the century – in trade, seafaring, literature, music – was new; never before had the people cohered in the many-sided activities of nationhood. The English felt that they were experiencing *rebirth* as a nation. The glorious myth of ▷ King Arthur gave them an image of an ancient British golden age, with which the Tudors asserted an astute political connection. King Arthur had been an ancient Briton; the descendants of those Britons were the Welsh; the Tudors were Welsh – ▷ Henry VII had called his eldest son Arthur – and like King Arthur, Henry rescued the country from the darkness of civil war. With less reliance on myth, the English treasured the memory of an earlier Henry – Henry V, who had modelled himself on the pattern of an ideal Christian Prince (like King Arthur himself) and had demonstrated the splendour of national unity by the glorious victory of Agincourt in 1415. There, Henry with his inferior forces was an image of the prince whose personal destiny was identified with the destiny of his people. Whatever the truth of this image of Henry v such identification of princely and national destinies seemed almost very fact in the reign of Elizabeth.

The nation was committed to its own version of Protestantism, and so was the queen; to lose her was to lose Protestantism, and national independence as well. Elizabeth's position was vulnerable, for her mother, Anne Boleyn, had been the cause of Henry viii's divorce of Katharine of Aragon, which had been the occasion for the separation of the Church of England from Rome. Good European Catholics were forced to regard Henry's divorce as illegal, since it had not been allowed by the Pope, and thus to consider Elizabeth an illegitimate child. Legitimacy, in that view, lay with the Catholic ▷ Mary Queen of Scots, and she had the support of the greatest European military power, ruled by Europe's most ardently Catholic sovereign, Philip ii of Spain. His attempted invasion of England in order to depose Elizabeth was defeated in 1588, and England and Elizabeth were saved. The great outpouring of Elizabethan poetry came principally in the last fifteen years of her reign, after this victory over the Spanish ▷ Armada. It was, no doubt, partly the expression of the release of national energies no longer inhabited by foreign menace, and much of it (notably Spenser's ▷ *Faerie Queene*) celebrated the glory of the queen who had become identified with national salvation. But some of this poetry, for instance the verse of ▷ Ralegh and the plays of ▷ Shakespeare written towards the end of the reign, had a more sombre tone, as though anticipating the darker mood of the nation in the more sombre period to come.

1603–1714

All order was confounded
John Bunyan

The theme of this period, which is as coherent as a drama, is the battle for supreme power between King and Parliament, and the eventual supremacy of the latter. How did this struggle arise? The causes were partly economic: the kings never had enough money to pay for government; consequently they went to Parliament – though they sometimes took other courses – to raise taxes. But Members of Parliament looked after their own interests; if they were to pay for government, they wished it to be conducted in accordance with those interests. And here we come to the social causes of the conflict. The centre of power in Parliament had shifted since the fifteenth century. No longer were the Commons the tool of the Lords – it was beginning to be the other way round. The House of Commons represented the merchants and the landed gentry, who were not definitely distinguished, just as the gentry were not clearly distinguishable from the class represented in the Upper House: the sons of the Lords were usually 'commoners', and could and did sit in the House of Commons when they were elected to it. The opposition to the monarchy was more geographical than social; the south and east of England were economically the most developed, and more conscious of disagreement with the policies of the king, who, when the ▷ Civil War eventually broke out in 1642, found that his supporters lived chiefly in the more conservative north and west.

Finally, there are the religious causes of the conflict. Religion, till the second half of the seventeenth century, still affected every department of life, and religious divisions corresponded to economic and social divisions as well. The more extreme kinds of Protestantism known as ▷ Puritanism suited the mentality of the mercantile middle classes, and so the emotional fervour which led to the Civil War was religious fervour, even when the disagreements might in fact be practical issues of politics or economics.

After 1660, when the monarchy was restored, a major change began to affect political behaviour: religion influenced all aspects of experience less and less, and became itself a mere compartment of life. The ▷ Revolution of 1688 was indeed made on account of the Catholicism of ▷ James II – yet chiefly because it was leading him into despotic practices. After 1688, men's ideas were increasingly cast in the mould of the tolerant and sceptical philosophy of ▷ John Locke, the thinker whose ideas were to dominate the eighteenth century.

The term 'Puritan' arose early in the reign of Elizabeth I, as an expression of impatient contempt for those militant Protestants who, discontented with the attempt of the Elizabethan Settlement of 1559 to solve the religious debate, wanted to carry the purification of what they regarded as Catholic abuses of religion to limits beyond compromise. Puritanism covered a wide variety of beliefs, but its outstanding characteristics can be summarized as follows. Firstly, Puritans rejected any spiritual authority save that of the Bible – 'the pure Word of God'. Secondly, they were opposed to the appointment of official Church authorities, such as bishops, regarding the government of the Church as a matter for those whom Puritans considered to be the true believers, though they disagreed among themselves about what form this government should take. Thirdly, in keeping with this objection to temporal authorities imposed from above, they believed that the Voice of God spoke in each man's individual conscience, and that no priest or other intermediary could rightfully come between. Fourthly, they insisted on extreme austerity of worship, believing that images, ornaments, altars, ritual, and embroidered surplices worn by priests were all no better than superstitions. Fifthly, in their insistence on nothing but the pure truth of religion, they tended to regard all fiction such as stage plays as deceiving vanities, tending to divert the minds of men from spiritual devotion, and they were also disapproving of costly clothing, long hair, and even amusements such as dancing.

Not all these characteristics applied to all Puritans: some, for example, were much less severe on worldly amusements than others; on the other hand, something of the Puritan austerity coloured people such as the Elizabethan poet ▷ Spenser who would not have described themselves as Puritans. Again, within the mentioned characteristics, there was plenty of room for disagreement, both in doctrine and in opinions about church organization. But the variations within Puritanism are less important to notice than the kinds of people who were attracted to it, for it was the adoption of the principles by whole classes of society that made it such a formidable political and cultural force.

Its austerity appealed to the businesslike, *ie* those who made work rather than pleasure their chief occupation; so did some of its doctrines, such as predestination, which declared that some people were irremediably damned, and that a sign of Divine Grace being on a person's side was whether he or she prospered in his or her worldly pursuits. Also, the Puritan reliance on the individual conscience tended to encourage independence of political judgement, and Puritan belief in the supremacy of religion over all other considerations accorded with a desire to control the political machine, since Puritans were seldom in doubt that true religion was identical with what they happened to believe. It was thus the hard-working, practical commercial and agricultural classes of south-eastern England that were attracted to Puritanism, and economically as well as religiously, in an age when governments were not yet predominantly commercial, they felt that they had to fight for their interests. When ▷ James I rejected the moderate Puritan appeals to him at the Hampton Court Conference of 1604 with the terse pronouncement 'No Bishop, no King', he was speaking prophetically out of his bitter previous experience as King of Puritanical Scotland; the English Puritans felt that war had been declared upon them.

The ▷ Stuarts had been Kings of Scotland since the fourteenth century. When Elizabeth died, childless, ▷ James VI of Scotland, descended from a sister of Henry VIII, was heir to the English throne; he thus became king of both countries as James VI and I. He insisted on the Divine Right of kings to rule, but the sacredness of a crowned head, which was strong in people's imaginations, was the more respected the less it was proclaimed. He also called his judges 'lions beneath the throne', whereas the English assumption had long been that the king himself was subject to the law. He combined these tactless assertions of royal status with the incompatibility of a timid personality and an ambitious foreign policy which, moreover, since it involved coming to terms with the national enemy Spain, in itself angered Parliament.

▷ Charles I (1625–49) had equally unfortunate qualities, but very different ones. James had lacked personal dignity, whereas his son possessed it notably, and the royal court under James was scandalously conducted, while that of Charles was cultivated and fastidious. On the other hand, Charles was bigoted and unyielding in all his opinions. He quarrelled with his Parliaments by trying to raise taxes without their consent, using imprisonment without trial, and insisting on conformity to the rites of the Anglican Church. After he had tried and failed to rule without summoning Parliament, the breach between himself and the Puritans became too great to be mended. The Parliamentary Puritans (a majority of the House of Commons and a minority of the House of Lords) tried to impose on him a puritan reformation of the Church of England. This finally divided the nation between Royalist ▷ Cavaliers (*ie* courtiers) and Puritan

▷ Roundheads (so called because they wore their hair short): between, that is to say, those who cared less for Parliamentary power than for the Anglican establishment on the one side, and those who saw in Parliament the only protector of religious truth on the other.

The fifteenth-century ▷ Civil Wars of the Roses had been fought with professional soldiers, newly released from the wars in France; the Civil Wars of the seventeenth century were fought by a nation that lacked professional armies, since it had grown accustomed to relying upon its navies for defence. Foreseeably, victory came to the side which succeeded in professionalizing its army first. Thanks to the military genius of ▷ Oliver Cromwell, this was achieved, and the war was won, by Parliament. With Cromwell's Ironsides the English military tradition was renewed; the oldest regiment of the modern British army, the Coldstream Guards, is of Cromwellian origin.

King Charles I was executed in 1649. From that year until 1660 England was a republic, under the rule of the House of Commons and a Council of State until 1653, and then under Cromwell as Protector, a position resembling that of the modern President of the United States. The Protectorate, however, solved no problems; it only brought to light the reality of the English political predicament. This was not, fundamentally, a matter of religious or social differences, none of which were as final as the mismanagement by the first two Stuarts had made them seem; it was a problem of political machinery. Parliament had grown strong enough to insist that governmental policy should accord with its wishes, and the governments – whether of King or of Protector – needed Parliament's financial support. The solution might seem to be that Parliament, the legislative or law-making power, should itself become the executive or policy-making power; but, as Cromwell and the nation discovered in the years 1649–53, a body of several hundred men is altogether too clumsy to devise and execute policy. The dilemma remained, until by slow experiment over the next century and a half the Cabinet system was evolved.

When the great Protector, Cromwell, died in 1658, after finding that he was as unable as Charles I had been to rule either with or without Parliament, the nation recalled the Stuart dynasty. So came about the Restoration of the Monarchy in 1660.

▷ Charles II was a very different man from his father. He had an intelligent, subtle mind, and in contrast to his father's bigotry he was willing to adapt himself to his circumstances to the point of unscrupulousness. He recognized that, as king, he was weaker than his predecessors had been. Parliament, on the brink of the Civil War, had destroyed the weapons forged by the 'Tudor despotism', and he knew that never again could a king raise taxes without Parliament's consent.

On the other hand, the mood of the nation was changing in ways that were helpful to the king. Puritan fanaticism was discredited, and the Anglican establishment was restored. The British were not, though, a tolerant nation: in 1662 an ▷ Act of Uniformity penalized all kinds of Puritan opinion which refused to conform to the Anglican system of belief contained in the ▷ Thirty-nine Articles. This, however, was a political as much as a religious measure, to prevent the revival of a Cromwellian party. In other respects, the Restoration was an unexpectedly mild event; Charles and his chief minister, ▷ Clarendon, who at one time had been a Parliamentary opponent of Charles I, knew better than to embitter public rejoicing by extensive revenge. The spirit of court and Charles II's 'Cavalier Parliament' was no longer that of the doctrinaire 'Martyr King' and his resolute archbishop, ▷ William Laud. Typical of the new age was the ▷ Royal Society, founded for the pursuit of science. It had been started in 1645, but in 1662 it received the king's patronage: the age of philosophic reason was beginning to obliterate the age of religious passion.

But passions were still strong and the differences of creed that had caused the wars of 1642–8 still impressed themselves on Parliament. Two parties resulted: the party of those who inherited the Cavalier sentiment for Church and king, and the party of those who continued the Roundhead support for Parliament and trade. Catholics and Puritans were both excluded from political representation, but those in the Cavalier tradition evoked ideas of Catholic authoritarianism and were called by their opponents 'Tories', a term of abuse for Irish Catholic rebels; in return the Tories called their opponents ▷ 'Whigs', a term of abuse for Scottish Puritanical rebels. So the English 'two-party system' began, and has remained with some challenges till the present day. Even 'Whig' and 'Tory' survived as party names until the middle of the nineteenth century, when they were changed to Liberal and Conservative respectively; Tory still survives as a synonym for Conservative. The interests represented by the different parties, however, have varied at different periods. In the seventeenth and eighteenth centuries, the Tories were mainly the landed gentry, and country squires who provided the majority of the Justices of the Peace, and the Whigs were an alliance of greater landowners and the middle classes of the towns.

The final triumph of Parliament was ensured once more by the ill-judgement of a Stuart king. Charles II had become a Catholic, but he had been careful not to proclaim his conversion, and he died peacefully, a popular king, having frustrated Whig attempts to exclude his brother James, a much more demonstrative Catholic, from succession to the throne. James II accordingly succeeded in 1685, but he quickly antagonized both Tories and Whigs, the former by his evident intention to supplant Anglicanism by Catholicism, and the latter by undermining Parliament's authority in order to do so. The Tories (with misgivings, because James was the legitimate king) allied with the Whigs to summon from Holland William of Orange and his wife Mary, James's Protestant daughter, to reign jointly as ▷ William III and ▷ Mary II. The Revolution succeeded bloodlessly, apart from some resistance from James's supporters in Catholic Ireland and the Scottish Highlands. Parliament had now achieved a decisive victory expressed in law by the ▷ Bill of Rights (1689); it had denied the principle of the Divine Right of Kings by altering the succession, and it confirmed this victory in 1701 (the Act of Settlement) by excluding James's Catholic son from the succession, choosing instead the German Protestant House of Hanover, descended from a daughter of James I.

The Tories indeed, when they were in power just before the death of Mary II's sister, Queen Anne (1702–14), tried to withdraw this act, which was so contrary to their principles, but the Whigs obtained power just in time for George I to succeed peacefully. No longer could the kings openly challenge parliamentary sovereignty, for they themselves were the creations of Parliament. The only king later to attempt revival of monarchical power was ▷ George III (1760–1820), and he did so by trying to turn himself into a parliamentary politician.

The English kings had claimed sovereignty over Ireland since the twelfth century, but they had not succeeded in making their rule effective there. In the sixteenth century, when England and Scotland underwent Protestant Reformations, Ireland remained Catholic, and consequently became a threat to the Protestant establishments in the other two countries. The governments of Elizabeth I and James I were in consequence aroused to subdue the country systematically, both by force of arms and by settling an Anglo-Scottish landowning class upon it. They fully succeeded in their colonizing policy only in most of the northernmost province of Ulster, which still has a Protestant majority. Later Ireland was completely subdued by the armies of Cromwell, and at the opening of the eighteenth century it was an unhappy, subject nation, defended only by the savage indignation of ▷ Jonathan Swift.

The union with Scotland is a very different story. James VI and I had brought about a union of the crowns, but, apart from a brief period of subjugation by Cromwell, Scotland remained an independent country with its own government until 1707. In that year, a Union of Parliaments was negotiated; Scotland lost its own Parliament in return for representation in the English Parliament, but it has kept its independent legal system and its distinct state church. The consequences for Scotland were that from being a poor country, it began to share in English prosperity.

1714–1815

Bliss was it in that dawn to be alive
Wordsworth

The sixteenth century was a formative period; the seventeenth, a period of conflict; the eighteenth century, upon the whole, was a period of stability. There were relatively few great social, political or religious issues to disturb its strongly developed sense of civilization. Culturally, it was the age of classicism: of harmony, proportion, assured taste and balanced statement. Still Puritan Dissenters, like the Catholics and the Jews, were excluded from participation in politics and from education at the universities and this serenity, like much eighteenth-century architecture, was often as shallow as a façade. There were disturbances of spirit within, as the Methodist religious revival showed, and it is significant that the mid-century poets (notably ▷ Collins, ▷ Gray and ▷ Cowper) were characterized by frequent melancholy. Moreover, Swift, ▷ Pope and ▷ Johnson, the great representatives of this ▷ Augustan spirit which felt so assured of the values of civilization, were far from complacent about their time; they were indeed savagely critical of it for falling far below its own standards.

Thus, eighteenth-century culture was relatively stable, but it was not stagnant, and politically, in its peculiar way, it was a constructive period. Politicians went far towards solving the dilemma of how to combine the sovereignty of Parliament with efficient executive government. The process was conducted in a practical spirit, with very little attention to political theory, and it went with a moral cynicism that condoned many political abuses. However, this practical spirit nourished a critical outlook which, in the form of ▷ Utilitarianism, was the eighteenth century's most useful legacy to the reformism of the nineteenth.

The last twenty-five years of the period, from 1790 to 1815, show the latent disturbances of spirit coming to the surface. Politically they emerge as radicalism and culturally as ▷ Romanticism; economically, the ▷ Industrial Revolution deeply affected society. Together, these movements were as decisive for change as the Reformation and the Renaissance had been in the sixteenth century.

Though Parliament was the unquestioned victor in the long struggle with the seventeenth-century kings, Britain was by no means yet a democratic country. It was not democratic electorally, for the system of the election of representatives to the House of Commons had been unreformed since the fourteenth century. Towns (for political purposes called 'borough constituencies') that had flourished then were in some instances no more than villages in the eighteenth century, but they still returned members to Parliament; these were the 'Rotten Boroughs'. Other towns that were still of some importance contained only a tiny minority of citizens with voting rights (the franchise), as in the case of the borough of Onevote in Thomas Love Peacock's novel ▷ *Melincourt* (1817). Furthermore, the country was still undemocratic in its state of opinion: political rights were not yet thought of as the rights of individuals, but as the rights of property owners, and the common people often thought that loyalty to the opinions of their landlords was their principal political duty. Voting, moreover, was public, and voters were in consequence open to bribery and intimidation. It is not surprising that the landed aristocrats who led the Whig party after 1714 saw no need to become electoral reformers, and the system survived the more easily because they were sensitive to commercial interests, in which they often shared; there was as yet little movement from the middle classes for reform.

This is, however, not the whole story of political corruption in the eighteenth century; it would be something in its defence to be able to say that business within Parliament was conducted honestly. This was not so. The political leaders had at their command a number of administrative appointments known as 'sinecures' (*sine cura* = without care or responsibility) because, though they brought the occupiers substantial salaries, they required little or no work. These posts were distributed to Members of Parliament by statesmen holding ministerial office in return for their support. In consequence, politics was apt to become a game for the profit of politicians. The game was played among the 'connexions' of the various statesmen, and genuine political disagreement, though it did not cease, was often subsidiary. Such a state of decadence was caused not merely by the degeneracy of the system, but by the absence of the Tories, whose support of the exiled Catholic Stuarts disqualified them for 50 years from playing any part in politics under the Hanoverians.

The most notoriously corrupt of the Whig statesmen in that half-century was ▷ Robert Walpole. Yet he was in his way a creative statesman, 'the first Prime Minister' (though he refused to admit the description) and a chief inventor of the 'Cabinet system'. If the dilemma of how to combine parliamentary sovereignty with efficient executive government was solved by any one person, this was Walpole, who controlled both the executive and Parliament from 1721 till 1741.

Circumstances assisted him. Firstly, the German kings from Hanover, George I and II, understood little of English politics or even of the English language; they needed English affairs to be 'managed' for them. Secondly, a major financial crisis, the ▷ South Sea Bubble, burst upon the country in 1720, and Walpole had the necessary financial ability to settle it. He continued in Parliament by royal support, and by using the corrupt methods that have been described; he similarly 'managed' the elections to Parliament, which, by the Septennial Act of 1716, had to be held every seven years.

Walpole's management was corrupt, but in his own way he commanded majorities in Parliament, and may justifiably be called the first ▷ Prime Minister, though in fact the title was only used against him by his hostile opponents. One person, however able, cannot rule alone; whether monarch or Prime Minister, he or she has to have ministers to support him or her. The problem therefore remained, for Walpole, of how to keep the support of his ministers and thus preserve unity of policy. To this also he found a solution. He chose his ministers (though officially they were appointed, as they are still, by the reigning monarch) from among his friends in either House of Parliament, and consulted them in his private room or 'cabinet'. In that privacy, he used force of persuasion to secure agreement with his ideas, and if they refused to agree, he tried to secure their resignation. So, today, important policy is framed at meetings of the chief ministers ('Cabinet Ministers') at the Prime Minister's official residence, 10 Downing Street in Westminster; the meetings are never reported in the press, and all the ministers are assumed to agree with the resulting decisions unless any resign.

The crucially important institutions of Prime Minister and Cabinet government were not the work of Walpole alone. Beginnings of these ideas arose even in the reign of Charles II, and they were not fully evolved until Parliament was reformed in the nineteenth century. Walpole is the statesman most distinctly to be associated with them, but even so, his work might have been fruitless because of the disrepute he brought upon politics. The reputation of the political system was fortunately saved by another Prime Minister with an unusually long reign of power, at the end of the century; this was the Tory, ▷ William Pitt the Younger.

The political power game played by the Whigs in the first half of the century could be played by the Tories too, once they could find a way back to power. However, having committed themselves to the Catholic Stuarts, they were regarded as ▷ Jacobites (*ie* supporters of James Stuart, the son of the deposed James II), and the nation stood by the Hanover family, not because it was popular, but because it guaranteed the security of the parliamentary system and the classes that relied upon it. The accession of George III changed the picture. George I (1714–27) and George II (1727–60) were Germans first and British kings only second; it suited both themselves and the Whigs that they should stand back from politics. George III ('Farmer George'), however, felt himself to be an Englishman, with English tastes and outlook; it was natural that such a man should despise a passive role. The Tories by this time, after the defeat of the second Jacobite Rebellion in 1746, had come to recognize that the Stuarts were a lost cause, and began to be attracted to a monarch who was not only secure on the throne but shared so many of their interests. Moreover, both the king and the Tories had an ideology provided for them in *The Idea of a Patriot King* (1749) by the veteran Tory statesman and former Jacobite, ▷ Henry St John Bolingbroke. In this book, Bolingbroke contrasted the demoralization of politics under the Whigs with the idealistic national spirit of the reign of Elizabeth I, and drew conclusions about the capacity of the right kind of monarch to raise the country above the squalor of self-seeking politics.

In the 1760s George III succeeded in forming a party of sympathizers – the New Tories or King's Friends – in Parliament. With the help of these, he fought the Whigs and eventually secured in power for twelve years a Prime Minister congenial to him; this was the ministry of Lord North, 1770–82. George's efforts were finally defeated by two circumstances. The first was that his government was discredited by the success of the rebellious colonists in America – the American War of Independence, 1775–83. This was a crisis which the king and his government seriously mishandled. Possibly the Whigs would not have dealt with it better, for English political assumptions were aristocratic, whereas those of the Americans were already democratic; the old nation spoke the same language as the new, but interpreted it differently, so that there was little common understanding. The second circumstance that defeated George was that, while he had been obliged to fight the Whigs with their own weapons of corruption, when he won power from them he did nothing to reform the political system which invited such conduct. George III lost North, but he was unwilling to submit to the Whigs. This crisis was solved by the appearance of a gifted young man of twenty-three, William Pitt, whose father had brought victory to Britain in the ▷ Seven Years' War (1756–63). Pitt was comparatively independent of party; he kept power for eighteen years (1783–1801), and was Prime Minister again for a short period from 1804 until his death in 1806.

Pitt had financial ability comparable to Walpole's, and he had integrity. He abandoned methods of government by bribery, and relied for his power on genuine votes, both in Parliament and at elections in the country; if his party had supported him, he would have carried out reforms in both. He differed from Walpole in acknowledging that he was Prime Minister, and furthermore he insisted that the office was necessary, and that it implied the collaboration of a Cabinet system as well. He thus not only clarified the atmosphere in which parliamentary politics were conducted, but he transmitted to the nineteenth century much clearer ideas about how to conduct them. Finally, strongly influenced as he was by the ideas of ▷ Adam Smith, he initiated the practice of ▷ Free Trade in foreign commerce – a policy destined to have important effects both politically and economically long after his death.

Pitt's reformism belonged to his early phase of power; in 1789 there broke out the epoch-making ▷ French Revolution, which transformed him into a much more conservative statesman. It transformed, too, the values of English politics. For the Revolution proclaimed ideas of the rights of man which inspired the peoples of all Europe, and in England made democracy for the first time a real issue, so that political thinking was done in new terms. Two influential English books were published while the Revolution was at its height, and typify the opposition of ideas about it. In 1790, the Tory (a former Whig) ▷ Edmund Burke published his *Reflections on the Revolution in France*; he was provoked to write it by a sermon glorifying the Revolution by a Dissenter, that is to say a member of one of the politically unempowered classes in England. Burke, who had understood the case of the American rebels and had written and spoken in their defence, also felt that the politics of revolution were more likely to be destructive than creative and he extolled the English tradition of slow growth as the true way to political and social fulfilment. He underestimated, however, the intolerable distress that a nation may suffer by such patience. His book was thus answered by ▷ Tom Paine's revolutionary testament, *The Rights of Man* (1791–2); 'Burke', said Paine, 'mourns the plumage and forgets the dying bird.'

History in England was to follow Burke's way rather than Paine's, but it moved with a new urgency. This urgency was provoked not only by the French Revolution and the propaganda of its sympathizers, but also by another revolution that happened more slowly. England was developing a new economy of production in factories by power-driven machinery – was, in fact, the first country in the world to experience an ▷ industrial revolution. The process was transforming the north from an empty countryside into a region of populous cities, and the rapidly expanding middle class in them could no longer tolerate a political system run by a landed aristocracy, even though it was a commercially-minded one. The political consequences of the Industrial Revolution will be traced in the next section. The picture was complicated by the development of France into an aggressive military despotism under ▷ Napoleon Bonaparte. The Tories remained in power to fight this despotism. Reactionary at home, they suppressed libertarian movements like the nascent ▷ trade unions, but abroad, in the eyes of Englishmen, they seemed to stand for liberty; the English feared Napoleon as they had feared Philip II of Spain in the sixteenth century, and Nelson's defeat of the Franco-Spanish navies in the ▷ Battle of Trafalgar (1805) was a victory over another Armada. Where was the liberal-minded Englishman to direct his sympathies?

1815–present day

> grunting in gas and air
> they sail to a
> darkness without self
> where no will reaches
>   Elaine Feinstein

Burke, in his *Reflections on the Revolution in France*, argued that true political advance required political continuity with the past. He wrote with the spectacle before him of catastrophic changes in France, and the fear that they might follow in England. His fear might have been even greater if he had been able to discern all the forces making for change in his time.

Modern Britain is one of the most densely populated countries of Europe, where the large majority of the people live in towns. The bigger towns are predominantly nineteenth- and twentieth-century constructions, and recent replanning apart, seem to have been rushed together in the hurry of industrial pressures rather than to be the slow growths of time. Manchester, for example, had a population of 36,000 in 1773; this population had doubled by 1801, and by 1850 it was more than three times the 1801 figure. The fact is that, until the Industrial Revolution, Britain was not an urban nation though it was a trading one; the only large city was London, and much of the industry (especially cloth-making) was conducted in the villages. It is the villages and small country towns that bear the marks of a long, prosperous past.

The biggest social change in British history is the transfer, between 1750 and 1850, of large masses of the population from the countryside to the towns; the basic social classes were transformed from small farmers and rural craftsmen into an urban proletariat and a lower middle class of industrial employers. The movement was hastened by two forces: (i) the agricultural revolution carried out by the landowners (▷ Enclosures) drove the workers off the land, and (ii) they were drawn to the towns by the demand for labour in the factories and mills, operated by machines driven by steam-power. It affected the north of England and parts of the midlands far more than the south, and this, too, was a big transformation; hitherto it had been the south that had been advanced and relatively populous while the north had remained relatively empty, backward and conservative, but now the north was pushing against the conservatism of the south. The evidence of the contrast is frequent in mid-nineteenth-century novels: it is in the title of Elizabeth Gaskell's ▷ *North and South*, and for other examples, ▷ George Eliot's *Silas Marner* appears in a midland village from a northern town like a man from another country, and in ▷ Charles Dickens's *Bleak House* the rich, landed gentleman Sir Leicester Dedlock finds the northern ironmaster Rouncewell a socially incomprehensible figure although he is the son of Sir Leicester's own housekeeper.

The new industrial towns were places of great distress for the workers. The poor were indeed having the worst period of suffering since serfdom had been practically extinguished in the fourteenth century. The prosperous peasant farmer, the yeoman, who had won the battles for the Plantagenet kings in the Hundred Years' War, had long been considered the solid base of English society, but by the nineteenth century he had largely disappeared. If he had not sunk to the level of a labourer on the land of a bigger farmer, or become a factory-worker and little better than a serf, he had turned into an industrial employer. The employers themselves often struggled very hard to get their heads above the level of wretchedness, and they commonly achieved it by a narrow range of human qualities – thrift, industriousness, sobriety – and were apt to conclude that these were the only estimable virtues, because they were the only ones that had proved useful to themselves. Two forces worked for redemption in the industrial towns. One was ▷ Methodism.

Methodism, the religious movement led by the evangelist ▷ John Wesley, was a late outburst of Puritanism, which appealed chiefly to the middle and the lower regions of society; Methodism reached the really poor. Puritanism, which in the eighteenth century was called Dissent and in the nineteenth century, ▷ Nonconformity, lost much of its fighting spirit and passion in the eighteenth century, but these were somewhat restored by the example of Methodism, and together they gave the industrial workers the emotional resistance that they needed to withstand the degradation and harshness of their lives. 'Cleanliness is next to Godliness', Wesley preached, meaning that the circumstances of his audiences made cleanliness the first condition of spiritual survival. The French historian Halévy has suggested ironically, that, by giving the industrial working class something to live for, Methodism diverted them from revolution.

But Methodism and other kinds of Nonconformity did more than provide the poor with psychological resistance to spiritual degradation. The Methodist and other Nonconformist chapels were little communities that educated their members, and trained them in social organization. Nonconformity was a strong contribution to the ▷ Liberal Party in the nineteenth century, and it was Nonconformity rather than ▷ Marxism which inspired the formation of the ▷ Labour Party at the very end of it. By that time, however, the working class had developed a more distinctly political means of education and action; this was Trade Unionism.

Associations of workers for mutual relief in sickness and unemployment began as far back as the middle of the eighteenth century; the oldest British union claims to date from 1747. Until the nineteenth century, however, they were chiefly 'Friendly Societies' for such mutual insurance. In the first quarter of the nineteenth century, they were suppressed by the Tory governments, afraid that any 'combinations' among workers might become centres of revolution. When, after 1824, the ban was removed, Trade Unionism suffered an early setback, owing to the failure of ▷ Robert Owen's ambitious but ill-organized project, the Grand National Consolidated Trades Union. However, during the middle of the century, unionism developed quietly and respectably among skilled workers; one example was the Amalgamated Society of Engineers. When, in the 1860s, unionism was subjected to a government investigation, the verdict was wholly favourable. The result was the establishment of a federation of unions, called the Trades

Union Congress (T.U.C.) in 1868. In the 1870s the Liberal and Conservative Prime Ministers competed with each other to give the Trade Union Movement full legal rights: ▷ Gladstone secured that they could become corporations recognized by the Law, and able to own and acquire property out of the funds provided by their members; ▷ Disraeli took the even more important step of legalizing strike action, so that in future the workers possessed an important weapon (which hitherto they had used illegally) with which to fight the employers.

In the last twenty years of the century, two important advances were made in Trade Unionism; it spread among the unskilled workers, who most needed it, especially through the victory of the Dockers' Strike in 1889, and it became the basis for more direct action through the formation of the Labour Party, of which it has remained the main financial support. By 1920, the working-class part of the nation was able to compete with the rest of the nation politically on equal terms, although in the 1980s Union power has been severely eroded.

By the third decade of the nineteenth century, both the Whigs and the Tories had come to realize that they were faced with a new social landscape, and that political institutions would have to be adapted to conform to it. The Tories were slower, but even they were aware enough to remove the political disabilities from Nonconformists and Catholics by the Emancipation Acts of 1828 and 1829. They resisted the major requirement, however, which was the reform of Parliament, and in 1830 they consequently fell from power, having held it for 50 years. The Whigs passed the First Parliamentary ▷ Reform Bill in 1832.

The Act of 1832, however, was not broadly based enough to be democratic; voting rights, and the right to seek election, were given a systematic property basis, and only the middle classes were enfranchised. Even the Whig party was afraid of the consequences of emancipating the working classes, ignorant and even illiterate – there was as yet no universal system of education – as they extensively still were. The result of this failure to enfranchise the workers led to the working-class ▷ Chartist movement, whose six points of reform included 'manhood suffrage' – that is, the right to vote of every adult male in the country.

But it was the middle classes who were most energetic in their own interests, and most capable of organization. Popular support for the Chartists was drawn off to support a middle-class movement which had nothing directly to do with further parliamentary reform. The new middle classes of the towns were greatly resentful that the sale of British-grown corn was 'protected' by taxes which increased the price of imported corn, since this meant that after bad harvests food was dear for the working classes, and they demanded higher wages. The industrialists, in advance of the rest of the world in the production of factory-made goods, stood to gain by a system of free competition in trade, such as had been advocated by ▷ Adam Smith (in *The Wealth of Nations*; 1777) and already initiated by the Prime Minister Pitt. The working class supported the movement because, more urgently than any political gain sought by the Chartists, they wanted bread. The established leaders of the Whigs and Tories, among whom the agricultural interest was strong, were reluctant to give way, but in 1846 it was a Tory Prime Minister, Robert Peel, who surrendered in the face of a famine in Ireland. He abolished taxes on imported corn by the Repeal of the ▷ Corn Laws.

This step had two important corollaries. The first was that Britain was implicitly declaring herself basically dependent on her industrialists, and not on her food producers. This, of course, meant not that the landed class was ruined, but that it was ceasing to be the dominant class, although it remained for a generation a very prosperous one. The second important corollary was that an industrial nation could not indefinitely keep its industrial workers politically without rights, especially after the middle of the century when they were becoming progressively better informed and organized. It was not, however, until 1867 that a substantial part of the urban working classes got the vote, through the Second Parliamentary Reform Bill, passed this time by a Conservative government. It was followed in 1870 by the establishment of state education; as the politicians said, 'We have to educate our masters.'

The villages had lost much of their vitality by the movement into the towns and by the gradual loss of their crafts by competition with machine production, and their working classes received political rights even later, by the Third Parliamentary Reform Bill of 1884, and this still left some exceptions until 1918. Women everywhere in all classes had to wait longer still. The Women's Suffrage Movement (▷ Suffragette) conducted a fierce agitation in the early years of the twentieth century, but it was World War I that did most to enfranchise them: by doing men's work while the men were fighting, women could no longer be excluded on the baseless ground that they are somehow congenitally unfitted for the conduct of affairs. Women over thirty received the right to vote and seek election in Parliament in 1918; in 1928, women were placed on equality with men over twenty-one. It was not until 1958 that they received the right to sit in the House of Lords, and there are still far fewer women than men in either Parliamentary House.

The social and political changes so far described necessarily produced effects in the composition of Parliament itself, in its organization, and in the parties. But it is first important to notice the continuity, in its social context, of British politics. The medieval social structure was at first fairly clearly stratified, divided into 'castes' rather than 'classes'. Families might advance in course of time, moving from serfs to yeoman farmers, becoming country gentlemen or 'franklins', receiving knighthood, and finally becoming ennobled. Or churchmen might advance the fortunes of their relatives by the road of learning, acquiring power as clerks in noble or royal households. In the later medieval centuries, there was the increasing chance of a merchant becoming a landed gentleman through his acquisition of property. Yet, at a given time, as in Chaucer's Prologue to his ▷ *Canterbury Tales* shows, a man or woman had a recognizable rank and function in society, fairly easily distinguished from other functions and ranks. In the sixteenth century, the decay of feudalism, the rise of the merchants, the Tudor practice of making the fortunes of their servants rather than choosing them from among those who had inherited fortunes, all complicated the social structure and made it much more fluid. Sixteenth-century Englishmen respected 'noble blood', and were keenly sensitive to differences in degree, yet their experience showed them that commoners could be ennobled, and could found noble families. 'Snobbery' is commonly regarded as an English vice and as marking a society of strong social divisions, and both statements are true. Yet snobbery – the feeling that 'I am better than you, because I am your social superior' – flourishes in a fluid society, that is to say, in one in which hopes may exist of improving social status, rather than in a rigidly divided society.

It might be thought that a country whose legislative assembly is divided into a House of Commons and a House of Lords is a country likely to suffer from class conflict in its politics. This has not been especially true of Britain. In the centuries before the Industrial Revolution, both Houses contained land-owners, many of whom had relatives and friends in the other House; similarly, since the Industrial Revolution, both Houses have contained industrialists. Moreover, since the sixteenth century it has been an increasingly common practice for governments to reward Commoners for political services by ennobling them, and a Labour lord today is unlikely even to want to be thought to belong to the aristocracy – he is in the Upper House to serve his party. Thus the members of the two Houses of Parliament have generally had too much in common to wish to quarrel; when they did, the Commons had a decisive weapon in its power: it could persuade the king to threaten the appointment of a sufficient number of Lords to ensure a majority on the Commons side of the dispute. The Lords offered stubborn resistance only once; this was in 1909, when the Liberal Government proposed a Land Tax which would severely penalize the landed proprietors. They had no power to resist the retribution that came upon them in the shape of the Parliament Act 1911, limiting their legal powers to oppose the Commons in future.

Social continuity in English politics has also been remarkable for the persistence of a number of great family names among political leaders: the Churchills, Cavendishes, Cecils and Russells. These have depended on family tradition rather than family privilege, as is evident from their continuance even after the First Reform Bill abolished the rotten and pocket boroughs. Political tradition developed in such families a store of experience to be drawn upon and ambitions to be emulated, and at the same time a pride of independence which made for radical rather than conservative opinions, for instance among the Russells.

Nevertheless, the Reform Bills greatly broadened the social composition of the parties. True, one of the last Prime Ministers of the nineteenth century was a Cecil, of the same family as William Cecil, Elizabeth I's chief statesman; but the most renowned Conservative leader of the century was Benjamin Disraeli, a man of Italian Jewish ancestry who could scarcely have achieved such a position before that time, and the 1980s have seen the advent of a powerful woman Prime Minister, Margaret Thatcher. The parties, also, developed coherent public organizations such as they had never had before, and began to represent particular classes of society in a more distinct and consistent way; But the biggest change resulted from the political rise of the working class.

The Whigs had always stood for the interests of the towns, and for the disfranchised Nonconformists who had their strength there. This meant that they represented both employers and employees. Before the Industrial Revolution, these two classes often shared interests, and even after its inception, the factory workers, though they were more generally and bitterly opposed to the Liberal manufacturing employers, were often unable to organize themselves as a distinct political force: the failure of the Chartist party is evidence of their weakness, and it was often Tories like ▷ Lord Shaftesbury and Disraeli who fought their masters on their behalf. After the workers had gained political rights, however, and had educated themselves for political action through the Trade Unions, they became actively dissatisfied with a party whose leaders were their own employers, and in 1900 the Labour Party was formed. At the same time, the employers came to feel that the Conservatives were more distinctly an upper-class party than the reformist Liberals. Ultimately the result was the collapse, after World War I, of the Liberal Party, and the rise of the Labour Party to its present position. The Conservatives in the meantime had broadened their scope from being above all the party of the squirearchy (country gentry). Disraeli (author of the novel ▷ Sybil, or The Two Nations – the nations of the rich and the poor) had been determined that the working class should see them as a party sympathetic to their plight, and about a third of the English working class votes Conservative even today. But the Conservatives have remained predominantly a party of the middle and upper classes; moreover, they became the Imperial party. At the end of the nineteenth century, Britain ruled the largest empire that the world had ever seen; today that empire has disappeared into the Commonwealth of Nations.

There were two British Empires – that of the eighteenth century, and that of the nineteenth. The most important part of the eighteenth-century empire was the American Colonies, which were lost to Britain by the American War of Independence (1775–83). When she lost these, she had just acquired Canada (which at the time seemed of little value), parts of India (ruled not directly by the Crown but by the East India Company), and some islands in the West Indies. The loss of America gave the British a distaste for colonies, but Britain was now the greatest trader and the greatest sea-power in the world, and in the interests of her commerce she inevitably acquired new territory. Later she felt the competition of other powers, and she became 'empire-conscious', a nation of 'empire builders', and invested much of her national pride in the Empire. Even then, the sentiment was stronger among Conservatives than among Liberals and Labour supporters, who tended to feel guilty about the position. Even among Conservatives, the British Empire was never comparable to the French one – never a 'Britain beyond the Seas' – with the partial exception of such countries as Canada, Australia, New Zealand, which had been colonized principally by British settlers; it was something apart from and extra to Britain. The insularity of the British partly explains this; another explanation is the memory of George III losing

America by trying to hold it too tight. His failure certainly helps to explain the transformation of Empire into Commonwealth by the invention of 'Dominion Status', *ie* the grant of self-government within the Commonwealth, beginning with Canada in 1867. It was the Liberal and Labour parties which were more ready to release these bonds of empire, and in one case the Conservatives held on grimly – Ireland.

Ireland is the country over which Britain has ruled most ruthlessly and unwisely. From the twelfth to the sixteenth centuries, England's sovereignty was chiefly nominal and Ireland was left largely to herself, but in the seventeenth century, owing to the Reformation and English and Scottish fear of Ireland's Catholic majority, the Irish were pitilessly suppressed, and in the eighteenth century the suppression was continued, if less brutally. In the nineteenth century, the British fear of Catholicism lessened, and the British conscience awoke. From 1829, Irish Catholics were able to take seats in the English Parliament, and social reforms were carried out during the next fifty years on behalf of the Irish peasant. These, however, did not satisfy the Irish Members of Parliament (after 1870 called the 'Home Rule Party'); they wanted self-government. The Irish wanted this not merely because of their resentment of past oppression, but because they were divided from England in ways that the Scots and Welsh were not: they not only retained Catholicism (except the northern province of Ulster, which was extensively colonized in the seventeenth century by English and Scots), but they alone lacked a strong middle class able to profit from the expansion of English commerce.

Gladstone, the Liberal Prime Minister, would have given them Home Rule, but the Conservatives and many of his own party opposed him. Conservatives and anti-Home Rule Liberals allied as 'Unionists', and the embittered Irish developed increasing intense nationalist feeling. This attributed to the Irish literary renaissance, one of the most notable contributions to literature in English from outside England. Politically, the consequences were the tragic Dublin Rising in 1916, and the Irish War of Independence of 1919–21. In 1921 the British Government made a treaty with the Irish, according to which the southern three provinces became the Irish Free State with complete self-government, but retaining membership of the British Commonwealth as a Dominion, on equal terms with Canada, Australia and New Zealand. This did not satisfy the more extreme nationalists, who wanted Ireland to become a republic. In 1937, the Irish Prime Minister, De Valera, abolished the title Irish Free State, replacing it by the Erse name Eire; he also abolished the titular head of the Irish Government, the Governor General, and caused the appointment of a President. Ireland kept a shadowy connection with the British Commonwealth, however, until 1949, when, with the consent of the British Labour Government, it separated itself entirely. By the Treaty of 1921 the northernmost province of Ulster remained in the United Kingdom with special rights of self-government. The system of self-government in Northern Ireland has, however, continued the traditional hostility between Protestants and Catholics there, and this hostility, in 1969, sharpened into a new, acute crisis. This has continued with little change until the present day, with vicious hostility and bloodshed on both sides.

In the United Kingdom during the twentieth century however, there have been many radical changes. New demands have been made on governments to ensure a high level of social justice, a healthy minimum standard of social welfare, and the provision of extensive services relatively cheaply. Such demands have imposed unprecedented strains on political institutions. They have been met by the expansion of central government and local government bureaucracies, and by the invention of the public utility corporation. The monarchy has become almost entirely a ceremonial institution; the House of Lords, though it is still recruited by the awarding of noble titles to prominent men and women, is in fact scarcely more medieval or undemocratic than the second chambers of most national assemblies; the Privy Council, though it rarely meets as a body, survives as the instrument of various administrative activities, for which Parliament and the civil service are unsatisfactory.

In its economy, Britain is partly capitalistic and partly socialistic, though basically its structure is still that of capitalist free enterprise. To combine the freedom of capitalist enterprise with the responsibility of state control, certain national industries, services, and means of communication have been organized into public utility corporations. A public corporation is managed by a suitably qualified staff, the members of which are not civil servants; that is to say, they are not members of the bureaucracy which is directly responsible to government ministers, though the government retains the right to interfere with them in certain defined circumstances, and has the duty of ensuring that the corporation fulfils the public function for which it is intended. Thus, within broad limits, the managers of public corporations are free from interference from the government and are able to take such immediate decisions as an efficiently run industry may require. Some of the corporations are required to be economically self-supporting as evidence that they are serving public needs efficiently; some have privately owned enterprises in competition with them; some are assisted by government financial grants.

A few public corporations were already established before World War II, but most of them were established by the Labour Government of 1945–50, or have been established since. The earliest was the British Broadcasting Corporation, incorporated by the ancient expedient of Royal Charter in 1927. It is financed by the payment of broadcasting licences. In 1954 the Conservatives set up the Independent Television Authority in rivalry to BBC television; it is financed by commercial advertising. Other corporations set up later than the BBC are as follows: the British Overseas Airways Corporation (1939) and British European Airways (1946) merged in 1972 as British Airways; the Bank of England (hitherto nominally a private concern – 1945); the National Coal Board (1946); the Atomic Energy Commission (1946 and 1954); the Transport Commission (1947, subsequently divided into five separate authorities in 1962); and boards controlling the supply of electricity (1947); gas (1948); iron and steel. Since the 1980s, however, the public corporations have been steadily privatized by the Conservative government, a policy which has resulted in enormous political controversy.

The Labour Government of 1945–50 also made important innovations in the public care of health and welfare. By a series of Acts passed between 1945 and 1948, the payment of weekly national insurance contributions was made compulsory for most adults, a proportion for each employee being paid by the employer. In return, the individual became entitled to grants in sickness, unemployment, and retirement, to family allowances, and to allowances to help with the expenses of maternity, and for maintenance in widowhood. In addition, national insurance payments entitle individuals to largely free medical attention, made possible by the establishment of the National Health Service in 1948.

The public corporations, national insurance, and the health service are three of the main ingredients of what we call today the Welfare State. To these we should add the system of free education established by the Education Act of 1944, the expansion of the universities, the provision (still far from sufficient) of good housing at low rents by the local authorities, and amenities which have the public assistance of the Arts Council, established (again by Royal Charter) in 1946. Once again, all these services are being eroded by the governmental policies of the 1980s.

The sense of crisis and discontent may be seen in the work of writers (such as the dramatist ▷ John Osborne and the novelist ▷ Kingsley Amis) who were known as the ▷ 'Angry Young Men' of the 1950s, and were succeeded by the more active 'student revolutionaries' of the late 1960s, early 1970s and by the fragmentary nature of ▷ post-modernist literature. The explanations are complex and numerous, and not all of them are yet discoverable. Moreover, while some of them arise from Britain's peculiar situation in the modern world, others concern the crisis shared by all the western nations.

First, Britain is a nation that has lost its former sense of greatness without discovering a new destiny to inspire and unite the people. Britain has surrendered most of her empire since 1945; she no longer has the greatest navy in the world; as an international power she finds herself, for the first time for three hundred years, in a very minor position. Special, though not peculiar, to Britain is the legacy of strong class opposition that descends from the Industrial Revolution. The trade unions arose in the middle of the nineteenth century when the interests of employers seemed to be clearly antagonistic to those of the workers; nationalization has not altered this tradition of opposing, though it is now an opposition more of managers and employees than of proprietors and wage-slaves. The Labour Government of 1945–50 hoped to recruit trade union members among the managers of the public corporations, but on the whole they failed. Since government is part of management, this trade union insistence on preserving an opposition role in society crippled Labour governments in the decades of the 1960s and 1970s.

Beyond this indigenous feature in British politics, there is the instinct of individual protest against the large organizations that have come to dominate the life of modern nations everywhere. In Parliament, party organization has become so closely controlled by party leaders that we now speak of 'party machines'. The party machine of government is thus an instrument of the executive machine, and Parliament, as a body of individuals elected to represent the interests of the people, is in the course of losing the respect of public opinion. The government, in turn, acts through its large impersonal ministries, and 'faceless' coordinating bodies. Even the trade unions have become steadily fewer and larger, in danger of losing the trust of their individual members, with the consequence of numerous 'unofficial' strikes, *ie* strikes unsupported by the unions in the industries concerned.

Significantly at the same time as the social and political organizations grow more fragmented, the media of communication (television and publishing) bring the injustices and conflicts of national and international life to the attention of the individual with unprecedented force, causing recognition of his or her alternatives – deliberate indifference or militant action.

M. C. Escher *Relativity*

Contemporary approaches to literature 2

Introduction

> 'I don't know what you mean by "glory,"' Alice said.
>
> Humpty Dumpty smiled contemptuously. 'Of course you don't – till I tell you. I meant "there's a nice knock-down argument for you!"'
>
> 'But "glory" doesn't mean "a nice knock-down argument,"' Alice objected.
>
> 'When I use a word,' Humpty Dumpty said in rather a scornful tone, 'it means just what I choose it to mean – neither more nor less.'
>
> 'The question is,' said Alice, 'whether you can make words mean different things.'
>
> 'The question is,' said Humpty Dumpty, 'which is to be master – that's all.'

(*Through the Looking-Glass and What Alice Found There*, Lewis Carroll)

The contemporary reader entering the field of critical theory for the first time must often feel a little like Alice passing through the looking-glass. Up until this point he or she has, with few questions, accepted that words have fixed meanings and that language is a simple and accurate reflection of reality. But Humpty's total disregard for commonly accepted practices and his anarchic and subjective use of words presents us with a text so bizarre that we cannot relate it to our own experience. The first thing we must learn, like Alice, is that language cannot mirror reality. As the story continues, Humpty goes on to teach Alice that, contrary to her expectations, language itself can construct meaning. He does this by trying to make sense of the poem 'Jabberwocky' and, at first, his efforts are founded on logical criteria: '"*Brillig*" means four o'clock in the afternoon – the time when you begin *broiling* things for dinner.' It's not long, however, before the words appear almost to provoke their own interpretations:

> '*And* "the wabe" *is the grass plot round a sun-dial, I suppose?*' said Alice, surprised at her own ingenuity.
>
> '*Of course it is. It's called* "wabe," *you know, because it goes a long way before it, and a long way behind it –*'
>
> '*And a long way beyond it on each side,*' Alice added.

'Wabe', a word hitherto without meaning in the text, generates a surprisingly vivid image which simultaneously expands its physical size and solidity of interpretation so as to intrude into Alice's, and the reader's perception of reality. A word has produced a concept rather than the other way about.

The negotiation between the real world and that of the looking-glass, which is produced when Alice undertakes her adventures, is a metaphor for the reader's experience of literary texts. The mirror at first appears to reflect passively and accurately Alice's own drawing room, just as words seem to have fixed and true meanings. But the world behind the glass, like a literary text, destabilizes that certainty, for the language of *Through the Looking-Glass* constructs our world, rather than reflecting it. Much of modern critical theory enacts the same function: to make the reader self-consciously aware that meaning is not passive and universal but produced through the language and contextualization of literary texts. This essay sets out to explore those relationships between literature, criticism, author and reader from different theoretical positions: in other words, it offers an invitation to step through the looking-glass.

F. R. Leavis and evaluation

The history of literary criticism offers many varied ways of reading: as Humpty implies, how you interpret texts depends upon who is 'master'. A productive point at which to start understanding the development of twentieth-century literary theory is with the work of ▷ F. R. Leavis. Although Leavis's ideas have long since been rejected by the critics and schools discussed later in this essay, his importance as one of the first 'masters' remains unchallenged.

In a sometimes acrimonious exchange with the editor of ▷ *Essays in Criticism* whose declared policy was to rival the literary critical review ▷ *Scrutiny* – his own journal – F. R. Leavis asserted that the competent critic's primary concern was with questions of evaluation, that is to discover the universal truth behind the language of the text. Critical judgement was to be clearly distinguished from social processes, since it was founded upon an unexplainable intelligence and sensitivity. Yet, at the same time, Leavis did not wish to concede that literature and criticism had no relevance to life. This problematic serves to focus for us a range of questions which are of a deeply theoretical nature and which move beyond the literature-history debate enacted by the journals *Scrutiny* and *Essays in Criticism* in the early 1950s.

The questions, which will be addressed throughout this essay, concern the ways in which literature and criticism are produced, the values which readers bring to the texts and the freedoms and constraints under which both writers and readers operate. We must also ask about theories of language, the concept of authority, the idea of the individual or human subject and his or her relationship to literature. Finally, we will also need to ask whether literary language may be equated with 'essence' or with 'process', an idea which was explained at the beginning of this essay. Placed within the framework of an idealist criticism, such as Leavis's, the answers can differ radically from when they are located in a materialist, that is, social, set of concerns.

For example, the separation of an essential 'idea' from the way in which language produces meaning can be observed in the approach of another *Scrutiny* critic, L. C. Knights (b 1906). He explains that a Shakespearean tragedy such as ▷ *Macbeth*, can be understood in terms of an essential theme which determines the critical response: 'I have called *Macbeth* a statement of evil; but it is a statement not of a philosophy but of ordered emotion' (*Explorations*; 1946). This theme is the structural motif, which underlies an emotionally charged language, through whose clouded surface the sensitive and intelligent reader may just glimpse the universal idea. This formula also demands the presence of an author whose discriminating consciousness has articulated these ideas and who allows us to see the true meaning. This way of reading and understanding literature is informed by a philosophical position which can be traced back through English literature to ▷ Plato and ▷ Aristotle, and which has accompanied the development of ▷ humanism.

Still, as we have discovered with the aid of Humpty Dumpty, text and context, literature and society, words and meaning are not divorceable oppositions, but mutually determining forces which are caught up in the same process of production. As such, questions of 'mastery' as well as questions about the relationships between author, text, reader and society require radical revision. This revision takes the discussion beyond the boundaries of what has traditionally been thought of as literary history. Today literary criticism is no longer concerned exclusively with either essence or with background, but with the way different histories can interlock to generate ideas, with different reading communities, and most importantly with the complex conditions which determine the reception of individual texts.

Saussure and Structuralism

In the sphere of literary criticism the response to particular texts has usually been built on recognizing that the text is an object of enquiry which has its origin in the writer's creative power. Where matters of history are involved then they are relegated to the category of background. For example, in *A Theory of Literature* (1963) René Wellek and Austin Warren define literature as 'creative, an art', whereas literary study is 'not precisely a science', but is nonetheless, 'a species of knowledge or learning'. The framework within which such statements are possible remains unexamined and, to some extent, not receptive to theory. One of the most influential theorists of the 1980s, the late ▷ Paul De Man, observed that,

> *Literary theory can be said to come into being when the approach to literary texts is no longer based on non-linguistic, that is to say historical and aesthetic considerations.*
>
> (*The Resistance to Theory*; 1986)

and he went on to argue that, 'resistance to theory is a resistance to the use of language about language'.

A fuller understanding of the problem that De Man identifies may be yielded by the analysis of language undertaken in ▷ Ferdinand de

Saussure's *Course in General Linguistics* (published posthumously in 1915), which is at the root of the resurgence of literary theory since the late 1960s. Saussure's work covers a vast area but some of his most influential writing focusses upon the linguistic ▷ sign which he defines as 'not a link between a thing and a name, but between a concept and a sound pattern.' The connection between the signifier (sound pattern) and the signified (its conceptual meaning) is an *arbitrary* one. Saussure's example explains this idea:

> *There is no internal connection, for example, between the idea 'sister' and the French sequence of sounds s-o-r which acts as its signal. The same idea might be represented by any other sequence of sounds.*
>
> (*Course in General Linguistics*)

Saussure suggests then that the signifier and signified are joined or 'cohere' like the recto and verso sides of a sheet of paper:

> *Thought is one side of the sheet and sound the reverse side. Just as it is impossible to take a pair of scissors and cut one side of the paper without at the same time cutting the other, so it is impossible in a language to isolate thought from sound or sound from thought.*
>
> (*Course in General Linguistics*)

If thought, language and social process are mutually interdependent, then meaning itself cannot be unchanging and simple. It therefore follows that the mechanisms used in the construction of utterances and the choices involved in the selectivity of reading determine the ways in which a particular community makes sense of the world. In other words, the means of establishing a hierarchy of values at the conceptual level correspond to those at the material level. A final, essential and enormously influential element of Saussure's investigations is his recognition that each sign is made up of a fixed number of units which are easily distinguished from one another. This leads him directly to the radical observation that in 'language itself, there are only differences'. The importance of ▷ 'difference' to the interpretation of texts is explored more fully later on in this essay, but a simplistic and graphic example would be the drawing of a letter with white chalk on a black surface – the difference of colour produces a meaning. If the same letter had been written with a black crayon, no such interpretation could have taken place.

In practical terms the model proposed by Saussure opened up a form of structural analysis which gave rise to the theory of ▷ Structuralism. Structuralist critics concentrate on the various sets of binary oppositions which 'structure' a text, on the systems which link it to other texts, and thence to the process of cultural production of which both are a part. For example, ▷ Roman Jakobson's formalistic analysis of a ▷ Shakespeare sonnet, 'Shakespeare's Verbal Art in "Th'Expence of Spirit"' (1970) deals with the differences in the poem, such as the tension between centres and margins or couplets and quatrains. Here the structuring of meaning is shown to depend upon a detailed series of 'differences' in the Saussurean sense of the term, which come into play in this particular sonnet, as well as in the sonnet as a poetic form.

What Jakobson calls 'the poetic function' is determined by the activities of selection and combination, that is the establishment of contiguities and similarities respectively. This ▷ dialectic ultimately leads to the preference for either 'metaphoric' or 'metonymic' (▷ metonymy) poles of language and hence to a distinction between poetry and prose. Saussure contended that all systems of signification were structured in accordance with the differential mode of language through which reality is mediated and represented. Thus, beneath each sign system there lies a deep structural affinity with language, thereby rendering them open to structural(ist) analysis. What unites the otherwise disparate group of theoretical writings loosely classified as structuralist – such as the social anthropology of Claude Lévi-Strauss (b 1908) and the 'mythological' investigations of ▷ Roland Barthes – is a commitment to the Saussurean precept that analysis will uncover a series of structural and nonvariable laws. Further, these laws are the basis for the social, political and artistic institutions which sustain cultural values. It is here that both the strengths and weaknesses of Structuralism lie. On the one hand, it reveals the interdependence of all institutions and so brings literature firmly into the social sphere, but on the other, its strict idea of rules denies variation and limits change.

Formalism and Bakhtin

The identification of 'difference' as the principal mechanism in the production of meaning is one that has appealed to a range of theoretical schools. One of the earliest of these was Russian ▷ Formalism which began in 1915–16 with the foundation of the Moscow Linguistic Circle and the Society for the Investigation of Poetic Language (Opoiaz), which included scholars such as ▷ Roman Jakobson (1896–1982) and ▷ Mikhail Bakhtin. Briefly, Russian Formalism was dedicated to the investigation of the 'literariness' of literary language, and to understanding the ways in which it could be distinguished from other forms of linguistic usage. They were particularly interested in poetry because they observed that it subverted 'ordinary speech' with its emphasis on multiple meanings. Secondly, literature was said to distance itself from reality in such a way as to expose the exact manner in which experience could be represented in language. It was this process of 'making strange' that the dramatist ▷ Bertolt Brecht was to use in his development of the 'alienation effect' (▷ *Verfremdungs-effekt*) in his plays.

The Russian Formalists also concerned themselves with larger questions of literary history, seeking to establish the 'literary' nature of certain texts, not as universal and timeless, but in relation to other texts which shared a common body of rhetorical devices. The consequent blurring of the division between the literary canon and other forms of writing, has had a long-term effect. Today genres regarded as 'popular', such as ▷ science fiction are admitted into the canon, and literature as a field of academic study is often integrated into the broader framework of 'Cultural Studies'.

One of Russian Formalism's early founders, and one of its most stringent critics, was Mikhail Bakhtin who argued that, although the 'formalist(s) led the captive word out of prison' (*The Formal Method in Literary Scholarship*, 1928), they sacrificed history for novelty, and thus reduced art to a 'device'. Under the pseudonym of V. N. Volosinov, Bakhtin published a critique of Saussurean Structuralism, *Marxism and the Philosophy of Language* in 1930. Where Saussure had been concerned with the mechanisms which produce meaning within an invariant system, Bakhtin sought to establish a connection between the differential aspects of language and the framework which produces social and political order. Thus language and ▷ ideology – that is a series of beliefs through which people perceive and state their versions of reality – are firmly linked. Consequently, if signs are constructed out of differences then the production of meaning must also involve some measure of social conflict. Moreover, it is through this conflict that a dominant interest group constructs a hierarchy of representations in order to assert its political supremacy.

Another influential and controversial aspect of Bakhtin's legacy is the insistence upon the plurality of voices contained in any one text, which has contributed to the concepts of 'textual polyphony' and ▷ 'intertextuality'. In *Rabelais and His World* (1965) he chronicled the nature of these opposing voices. In fact, in recent literary theory the whole concept of 'voice' with its implied privileging of speech over writing, has been supplanted by the more precise term, ▷ 'discourse'. A discourse is a particular way of talking, writing or thinking which is founded on shared beliefs, for example the discourse of socialism or the discourse of architecture. Also in relation to ▷ Rabelais's ▷ *Gargantua and Pantagruel* (1532–4), he proposed the category of the 'carnivalesque' (▷ Carnival) as a form of festive language which threatens disruption and celebrates the materialist impulse for change in the social order. Bakhtin writes:

> *Carnival was the true feast of time, the feast of becoming, change and renewal.*
> *It was hostile to all that was immortalized and completed.*
>
> (*Rabelais and His World*)

Two contradictory propositions follow from the idea of carnivalesque: firstly, that by identifying class antagonisms it is able to subvert them, and secondly, that by highlighting the distinction between its own and official discourses it can be contained and defused like licensed misrule. Whether a reactionary or radical reading of Bakhtin is preferred, the view that a literary text is structured according to a hierarchy of social differences is one that has had far-reaching effects for literary theory. For example, in the 1960s French theorists, such as the semioticians (▷ Semiotics), developed along diverse lines many of the ideas put forward by Saussure and the Russian Formalists, so that their critiques encompassed cultural anthropology, psychoanalysis and ▷ feminism, as well as literary criticism. Probably the most outstanding of this school, gathered around the journal ▷ *Tel Quel*, was ▷ Roland Barthes whose penetrating investigations of contemporary mythologies, such as the face of Garbo or advertisments for soap powder reveal that what appear to be given truths about a society are instead constructed ideologies through which they sustain their hierarchical systems. However, the most persistent strain of influence was to be seen in Marxist criticism and its fascinating mutations.

Marxism to materialism: Althusser, Macherey and Foucault

The foregrounding of the relationship between literature and ideology occurs in the work of the French theorist, ▷ Louis Althusser. By drawing upon Marxism, psychoanalysis and Structuralism, Althusser was able to propose not only a model for social relations within ▷ capitalism, but also a series of mechanisms whereby individuals or 'subjects' were positioned within the social formation. Althusser's model of society as a series of relatively autonomous structures, each with its own internal contradictions – determined only finally by economic factors – was a controversial departure. He believed that a revolutionary situation would not be brought about by one dominant set of social contradictions, but that each autonomous structure contains and contributes to a diversity of potentially explosive forces. Together with this idea, Althusser developed the concept of a 'destabilized' social formation in which perpetual division and fragmentation were possible. It was within this web of autonomous structures that the individual identity or 'subject' was produced, whose actions, attitudes and feelings were articulated through ▷ ideology. In this context, ideology is not a body of consciously held ideas, but the representation of discontinuous and contradictory human relations in terms of an imaginary unity. Althusser defined ideology as a representation of 'the imaginary relationship of individuals to their real conditions of existence' (*Lenin and Philosophy*; 1971). This system of representations supplements, at the personal and psychological level, the system of freedoms and constraints produced by the dominant structure within the social formation at any one historical moment. The privileging of 'ideology' had far-reaching consequences for the study of literature and artistic production in general. Althusser suggests that art offers us a

> form of 'seeing', 'perceiving', and 'feeling' (*which is not the form of* knowing) . . . *the* ideology *from which it is born, in which it bathes, from which it detaches itself as art, and to which it* alludes.
>
> (*A Letter on Art*)

Thus art is a specific category which is deeply implicated in ideology, but which is, at its best, able to distance itself from it. Following on from a similar argument by the French critic Pierre Macherey in his *Theory of Literary Production* (1978), Althusser argues that the novels of ▷ Balzac and Solzhenitsyn presuppose, *a* retreat, *an internal* distantiation *from the very ideology from which their novels emerged. They make us 'perceive'* [*but not know*] *in some sense* from the inside, *by an* internal distance, *the very ideology in which they are held.*

(*A Letter on Art*)

Althusser's *A Letter on Art* is contentious in that he did not really address issues important to literary critics, such as the question of authorial intention and whether the institution of literature is itself an ideological category. It was Pierre Macherey who, to some extent, followed through the ideas initiated by Althusser. For Macherey the literary text is constructed in difference, and the conflict of which he speaks,

is not the sign of an imperfection; it reveals the inscription of an otherness *in the work, through which it maintains a relationship with that which it is not, that which happens at its margins.*

(*A Theory of Literary Production*)

Consequently the literary text is complex and decentred, and therefore a challenge to ideologically motivated forms of reading which would give more importance to concepts such as 'harmony' and 'centre'.

A Theory of Literary Production is concerned primarily with the historical conditions of the production of literary texts, and the extent to which those conditions are inscribed. Since then, Macherey has turned his attention to the issue of the ideological *effects* which texts produce when they are read. The result of this move is to problematize both the status of the text, and the historical process of its reception, and to raise fundamental questions about the category of 'literature' itself. Here ideology is shown to enter into the dialectical transaction between reader and text so as to shatter the divisions which have traditionally kept the categories of 'literature' and 'history' apart, or preserved their relationship as one of foreground and background.

Althusser and Macherey focussed attention, away from the traditional Marxist notion of society as a single unit, onto the range of social practices and discourses through which ideology operates. This is part of a larger post-structuralist (▷ Post-structuralism) challenge to the metaphysical notion of 'authority', and as such has considerable implications for the literary question of authorship.

In the work of Roland Barthes, and more particularly in the writings of ▷ Michel Foucault, the 'author', traditionally regarded as the origin of meaning, is given a place in language at the point where a range of discourses converge. The writer does not, therefore, occupy a transcendent position, but rather manipulates, and is manipulated by, those discourses which are available at that particular historical moment. Thus questions of the meaning of ▷ Sir Philip Sidney's ▷ *An Apologie for Poetrie*, or ▷ Coleridge's *Biographia Literaria*, or ▷ Matthew Arnold's *Culture and Anarchy*, become secondary to the enquiry into the ways in which these texts intersect with history, the assumptions they make, what they include, what they omit, and the manner in which reality is represented in their language.

Although aware of context, Foucault acknowledges no notion of a continuous or a progressive 'history', but only a series of discourses which determine forms of intellectual enquiry and linguistic representation. Foucault states that his aim,

> ... is most decidedly not to use the categories of cultural totalities (whether world-views, ideal types, the particular spirit of an age) in order to impose on history, despite itself, the forms of structural analysis. The series described, the limits fixed, the comparisons and correlations made are based not on the old philosophies of history, but are intended to question teleologies and totalizations.
>
> (The Archaeology of Knowledge; 1972)

Within this framework 'authority' is shown to be related to power and to desire. Together these insights undermine the traditional grounding of history, and Foucault's emphases on fragmentation, discontinuity and the questions of discourse, knowledge and power, have been eagerly endorsed by more recent criticism. A movement in North America known as 'new historicism', its British counterpart 'cultural materialism' (▷ materialism), and its feminist manifestation 'materialist feminism' have enthusiastically developed Foucault's premises. However, while most critics have responded positively to the focussing on the power of discourse, there remains a concern that what is missing from Foucault's analysis is an emphasis upon the *political* nature of those social conflicts, antagonisms and contradictions which can be found in different discourses.

Lacan and psychoanalytic criticism

▷ Psychoanalytic criticism may at first appear to occupy different territory from that already mapped out by this essay, but there is a significant overlapping of interest. For example, let us take the importation of Saussure on linguistics into psychoanalysis through such writings as those of Emile Benveniste. Benveniste draws a useful distinction between the Saussurean identification of arbitrariness in the linguistic sign, the manner in which it is perceived by its users, and the way in which a system of linguistic values is constructed; he argues that:

> For the speaker there is a complete equivalence between language and reality ... [but that] ... all values are values of opposition and are defined only by their difference. Opposed to each other, they maintain themselves in a mutual relationship of necessity.
>
> (Problems in General Linguistics; 1971)

These two aspects of linguistic theory accord perfectly with what the influential theorist and psychoanalytic critic, ▷ Jacques Lacan designates as the 'imaginary' and the 'symbolic' spheres. The imaginary rests on the fantasy (not that it is perceived as such) of a direct relationship between language and reality, in which the latter as 'absence' can be recalled in its entirety by the former. As Lacan puts it, 'It is the world of words that creates the world of things' (*Ecrits*; 1977). On the other hand, the symbolic designates a differentially derived value structure through which the human subject or individual enters into the social order.

The consequences for the human subject are examined by Benveniste who writes that language is 'so organized that it permits each speaker to *appropriate to himself* an entire language by designating himself "*I*"'. For this 'I' there is an equivalence between language and reality, but for the symbolic self, 'I' is part of a social and material process. The first is the site of the imaginary where the subject is centred, while the second directs attention to *difference* and hence to the decentred nature of the subject. It is to this decentring process that Lacan addresses himself in his analysis of the relationship between the conscious and the unconscious.

Lacan's insistence that, 'the unconscious is structured like a language' (*The Four Fundamental Concepts of Psychoanalysis*; 1977) directs attention to the space between the 'signifier' and 'signified'. This is not an unreasonable claim, since neither the subject nor the unconscious exist in some pre-linguistic realm, but are brought into being through the differential mechanisms which may be said to structure language. This analysis emerges from Lacan's rereading of the works of the founder of psychoanalysis, ▷ Sigmund Freud. For Freud the unconscious is the primal scene of an Oedipal drama (▷ Oedipus complex) whose stages correspond to the growth of the human subject from infancy to maturity, but whose effects must be repressed and redirected in order for successful socialization to occur. If, as Lacan says, the unconscious is structured linguistically then what is repressed must actually be a *representation*. This functions as the 'other' of language, that is a system of desires which language perpetually seeks to recover, but never fully satisfies. The human subject learns to manage this potentially disruptive otherness or system of representations in two ways. Firstly, he or she must learn to recognize himself or herself and to construct an imaginary 'unity' (this is Lacan's famous 'mirror stage'), and secondly he or she must enter the symbolic order where the demands of the other are encountered through the regulating context of ideology. Thus Lacan develops a materialist theory of subjectivity which marks the point at which ideology enters into the subject's consciousness. The result is a direct challenge to any notion of a transcendent relationship between subject and language:

> it is not only man who speaks, but that in man and through man it speaks (ça parle), that his nature is woven by effects in which is to be found the structure of language, of which he becomes the material, and that therefore there resounds in him, beyond what could be conceived of by a psychology of ideas, the relation of speech.
>
> (*Ecrits*)

What 'resounds in him' is the representation of the unconscious where the unstable elements of language, prior to their formation as a fantasy of coherence, reside. The effect is a continuous double play of ▷ condensation and ▷ displacement in the production of the signified. This is the process of 'splitting' which is the price paid at the level of the unconscious for the subject's emergence into the symbolic order of language. It is for this reason that the notion of subjectivity as wholeness is regarded as a fantasy created from the repression of the unstable elements out of which the unconscious is constituted.

For Lacan the unconscious functions as a text whose repetitions, condensations and displacements trace its emergence into the symbolic order, and the process of reading serves to implicate the reader as the one who is analysed (that is, the analysand), rather than the analyst. To this extent the literary text functions as a mirror reflecting back an imaginary order whose images position the reader as 'the subject who is supposed to know', but whose claims to certainty are constantly undercut.

Feminist criticism

An extraordinarily productive area of critical theory which has appropriated Lacanian methods is psychoanalytic ▷ feminist criticism. Nevertheless, in *Feminine Sexuality* the critic Jaqueline Rose demonstrates how Lacan reveals his own phallocentrism through his argument that the phallus is the signifier about which the symbolic order is constructed, and that this symbolic order actually generates 'femininity' as its opposite or other. This echoes concerns expressed by some feminist critics that ▷ gender identity can only ever be produced within patriarchal symbolic structures and that 'woman' is the mirror in which masculinity views itself positively as the power of law, while at the same time identifying her as lack, repression or the space of the unconscious. Entry into the symbolic order, and hence into language, grammar and signifying practices means, as feminist critic Toril Moi points out 'to accept the phallus as the representation of the law of the father' (*Sexual/Textual Politics*; 1985). Thus the way in which theory tends to construct the gendered subject is precisely that which ▷ feminism as a political movement, as well as feminist literary theory, seeks to contest.

There is a contradiction inherent in the aligning of feminist literary criticism with any theoretical position since, in certain manifestations, feminism would resist theory as a form of mastery of knowledge, which articulates those very patriarchal structures from which it seeks emancipation. Indeed, in their pioneering study of the woman writer in the nineteenth century, *The Madwoman in the Attic* (1979), Sandra Gilbert and Susan Gubar take the view that the act of writing itself is a patriarchal gesture. They suggest that in western culture,

> *the text's author is a father, a progenitor, a procreator, an aesthetic patriarch whose pen is an instrument of generative power like his penis.*
>
> (*The Madwoman in the Attic*)

They identify the pen(is) as a metaphor for power, especially political and spiritual control. But they go on to make claims for a distinctly female imagination which seeks to challenge masculine insistence upon the universality of its knowledge and its allegedly neutral value judgements.

Can there be, then, distinctive areas of feminine experience and styles of writing? The French theorist, Hélène Cixous (b 1937) insists that female experience, hitherto repressed, is very different from that of men, and must therefore require a different style of articulation:

> *Time and again, I, too, have felt so full of luminous torrents that I could burst – burst with forms much more beautiful than those which are put up in frames and sold for a stinking fortune. And I, too, said nothing, showed nothing: I didn't open my mouth, I didn't repaint my half of the world. I was ashamed. I was afraid, and I swallowed my shame and my fear. I said to myself: You are mad!*
>
> (*New French Feminism*; 1980)

Cixous's celebration of the female body and female desire represents an attempt to re-state in material terms the positive value of what, in masculine terms, is described negatively as 'other'. She also re-examines the entry of the gendered human subject into the symbolic order of language and discourse, in order to reclaim the ground that Lacan has designated simply as a 'lack'. Cixous asks ironically, 'What's a desire originating in a lack? A pretty meagre desire.' Instead she tries to free feminine language through a new form of writing drawn from the unconscious (▷ Ecriture féminine).

In focussing upon female energy and its repression by the patriarchy, Cixous shares certain concerns with the influential French critic Julia Kristeva. Cixous registers her dissatisfation with the subject position and feelings accorded to her by the phallocentric order, but Kristeva takes the issue further. First, she appropriates Bakhtin's association of the pre-Oedipal phase with the 'feminine', and then goes on to examine exactly how the gendered subject enters into the symbolic order, becoming positioned socially, linguistically and psychologically. She describes entry into the signifying process as the 'thetic phase', by which she means a process which begins when subject and object are recognized as different. This process is completed in the gendered subject through the discovery of castration which, in turn,

> *detaches the subject from his dependence on the mother, and the perception of this lack* (manque) *makes the phallic function a symbolic function* – the *symbolic function.*
>
> (*A Kristeva Reader*; 1986)

However, prior to and still residing beneath that symbolic order is the 'semiotic'. For Kristeva this means a mobile and amorphous feminine force which can distort the masculine chain of signification, and she lays claims to poetic language as especially close to the semiotic. Poetry thus becomes a form of linguistic ▷ subversion that continually threatens those meanings established by the symbolic order. If, at the psychological level, we were to submit fully to these disruptions they would produce 'illness' – hallucination and psychosis. But by incorporating these subversive energies into language we are able to produce artistic creations, and therefore writing ceases to be an authoritarian process. Rather, for Kristeva, writing is dialectical, incorporating both subversion and production into its structures.

The reversal of the values which masculine discourse ascribes to binary oppositions is both philosophical and politically strategic. But some feminists have expressed concern that to situate women's writing in the body and to celebrate the unconscious, as opposed to the masculine symbolic order, risks complicity with the very structures from which women wish to escape. In other words, imprisoned within the dialectic of *difference*, the political and linguistic gains might well be limited. It is true that, at a theoretical level, the critique of a symbolic order has resulted in the interrogation of traditional categories of knowledge, especially those concerned with masculine representations of femininity. But as Toril Moi has argued, the major consequence of feminism as a form of analysis is pre-eminently political, and feminists,

> *find themselves in a position roughly similar to that of other radical critics: speaking from their marginalized positions on the outskirts of the academic establishments, they strive to make* explicit *the politics of the so-called 'neutral' or 'objective' works of their colleagues, as well as to act as cultural* critics *in the widest sense of the word.*
>
> (*Sexual/Textual Politics*)

In other words, in addition to producing analyses of female writing or the masculine representations of women in male-authored texts, feminism must undertake a critique of the mechanisms used by these works in order to transform social and personal relations.

This political programme receives different emphases in different historical situations. The female retreat into 'gyno-criticism' – that is, the study of texts written by women, feminine literary creativity, and the development and form of a female tradition of writing – and the challenge to accepted masculine formulations of subjectivity/subjection, has served to emphasize the personal as the primary area of feminist concern. Clearly though, the logic of its arguments suggest that materialist feminist criticism will have to form a theory of subjectivity which takes into account more fully the political connection between social relations and personal behaviour. A feminism which pursues the personal at the expense of the political is in danger of removing the gendered human subject from history altogether. In her perceptive review of the French 'écriture féminine' Ann R. Jones identifies the danger in pursuing one at the expense of the other:

> *Without making deprecatory psychoanalytic diagnoses feminists may still doubt the efficacy of privileging changes in subjectivity over changes in*

economic and political systems; is this not dangling the semiotic carrot in front of the mare still harnessed into phallocentric social practices?

(*Making the Difference*)

Materialist feminist critics who focus on the political and social formations seek to explore the ideological implications for the female subject within 'difference', but proceed from the assumption that subjectivity is a political space to be contested. The critic Catherine Belsey in *Feminist Criticism and Social Change* (1985) argues that those literary forms which capitalism has sanctioned depend upon the presence of the author as 'authority' and position of the reader as 'subject'. A classic example of this would be the realist novel, which proposes an exact correspondence between itself and reality. Her argument is that the grammatical formulation of mimetic representation enacts the very hierarchical conditions of the symbolic order itself. In this way classic realism may be seen to be founded in an ideology which treats its readers as subjects who are placed in positions of subjection and subjectivity. What Belsey, like both Cixous and Kristeva, focusses on are the ways in which gendered subjects are drawn into a complicity with liberal ▷ humanism which superficially admits differences, only to transform itself into a non-contradictory 'truth', under whose masculine image they are invited voluntarily to live in subjection.

Derrida and deconstruction

If feminism is the most politically challenging of current theoretical innovations, then ▷ deconstruction represents the greatest methodological challenge to traditional knowledge systems. Deconstruction, as advocated by ▷ Jacques Derrida, presents a radical challenge to the entire western tradition of philosophy, from ▷ Plato onwards. As a theory it has developed out of Structuralism, drawing also upon the philosophical scepticism of ▷ Friedrich Nietzsche. The objective of deconstruction is to demystify language's claimed ability to refer outside itself; this is achieved through the disclosure of the rhetorical figures underpinning all systems of thought. However, Derrida does accept that it is not possible to escape metaphysical meaning entirely: a more practicable deconstruction is defined as,

a simultaneous marking *and* loosening *of the limits of the system in which the concept was born and began to serve, and thereby* [*it*] *also represents, to a certain extent, an uprooting of the sign from its own soil.*

(*Positions*)

We may recall Saussure's insistence that in language there were no positive terms, only 'differences', and that particular combinations of sounds or letters (signifiers) produced particular meanings (signifieds). In addition, the rules governing each instance of language (▷ *parole*) were those of a larger and invariant structure (▷ *langue*) to which each 'instance' ultimately referred. Derrida challenges Saussure's signifier/signified principle because it privileges sound, and therefore implies that the voice is synonymous with consciousness itself. Moreover, Derrida rejects the assumption that a linguistic sign constitutes a static unit of reality, derived from a larger structure or system. Rather, he suggests that the sign's construction through difference can never truly recall the totalizing system of which it was a part, and the totality is never available to the reader, who is left instead with a constant 'play' of differences. Derrida explains further that if,

> *totalization no longer has any meaning, it is not because the infiniteness of a field cannot be covered by a finite glance or a finite discourse, but because the nature of the field – that is, language and a finite language – excludes totalization. This field is in effect that of* play, *that is to say, a field of infinite substitutions only because it is finite, that is to say, because instead of being an inexhaustible field, as in the classical hypothesis, instead of being too large, there is something missing from it: a centre which arrests and grounds the play of substitutions.*

> (*Writing and Difference*; 1978)

The status of the centre cannot be fixed any more than the 'play' of the signs about it, for the basic concept of a 'centre' issues from a process of signification which can be shown to be figural and divided, always already in motion, a series of endless substitutions. Clearly, Derrida regards this notion of infinite 'play' as a Nietzschean form of liberation, since he insists notoriously that the loss of the centre should not lead to nostalgia, negativity and guilt, but to a joyous and anarchic 'play', where interpretation is never-ending.

Derrida also develops Saussure's idea of 'difference' through a provocative punning in French: a vowel substitution into *différance* combines the sense of *différence* as substitution with the principle of 'deferral' in time. *Différance* then, is the movement of play which produces differences and as such is the originator of an infinite deferral of meaning. This has repercussions for the notion of subjectivity, for if, as Derrida argues, nothing precedes *différance*, then there can be no uniquely self-founded authorship or mastery and even the human subject itself must become an *effect* of *différance*. The challenge to traditional concepts of metaphysical presence inevitably draws attention to the linguistic mechanisms which allow that challenge. This decentring of the subject has been explained with different emphases by different theoretical positions, but Derridean *différance* directs us to the problems and dangers of attempting to halt a play of substitutions about a supposedly fixed centre.

It is not difficult to see how Derridean deconstruction involves forms of analyses common to all of the theoretical postions described so far in this essay. Marxism, feminism and psychoanalysis are all concerned with human subjects who are in some sense 'alienated' or divided, and all show how this decentring is articulated in language. But deconstruction foregrounds the unending postponement of a point of 'presence', a point which must, of necessity, exist outside the play of *différance*. But Derrida asserts that '*Il n'y a pas de hors-texte*' (there is nothing outside the text) and that any move outside language is a misplaced gesture in the direction of an unattainable transcendence.

As had already been suggested, Derrida attacked Saussure's privileging of speech and the voice, which relegates writing to a subsidiary role. What he locates at the heart of Saussure's language is that very same impulse to organic wholeness and the 'naturalness' of writing which may be seen – transformed into a critique of industrial society – in the work of F. R. Leavis. What Derrida is attacking is the metaphysics of 'presence' and the whole concept of a referential language. He argues that, if we accept the principle of *différance*, then speech must be implicated in the process of writing and bear traces of that involvement. Indeed, he proposes the inversion of the customary hierarchy, that speaking precedes writing, by suggesting that speech could not have existed without being differentially produced by writing. It is this 'arch writing' that Derrida proposes as the basis for his ▷ 'grammatology', that is his investigation of the units of signification produced through *différance*.

It is not difficult to see the implications of this process for traditional literary concepts such as 'mimesis' or 'realism', although the effects reach far more deeply into critical practices than those of genre or style. The charge that Derrida lays against all writing is that its own rhetoricity predicates a deadlock – 'aporia' – at the heart of linguistic activity. This deadlock is detectable both in the representational quality of the text and in the language of criticism. The only way to resolve it would be through an appeal beyond language to some transcendent meaning which, as we have seen, for Derrida has the status of 'prejudice'.

Derrida's challenging theoretical approach appeared on the literary scene at the very moment when American ▷ new criticism and, in Britain, Leavisite practical criticism seemed to reach the point of bankruptcy. Subsequently, the deconstruction of 'master-narratives' and the questioning of boundaries, exclusions, suppressions, and displacements, have been of value to feminists, psychoanalytic critics and Marxists alike. In America it has come as a timely successor to new criticism and has been taken up by the ludic exuberances of the Yale School critics, such as J. Hillis Miller and Geoffrey Hartman. Also at Yale, the more sceptical rigour of Paul De Man's writing gained added impetus from the dialogue with the work of Derrida. This adoption of deconstruction for pedagogic purposes has meant that in America the radical free play of meaning and unsettling consequences of semantic indeterminacy have been denuded of their political implications.

Conclusion

Although this essay has dealt with various schools and critics in a formal order, it would be misleading to think of 'literary theory' in simple chronological terms. The concept of a linear progression cannot encompass the shifts backwards and forwards that have taken place over the last half-century. Perhaps Foucault's notion of 'genealogy' best describes both the complex web of relationships, and the constant debates, between different theoretical positions. Our whole understanding of 'literature' and 'literary criticism' has been unsettled by this unceasing discussion and disruption of traditional boundaries. It seems as if it is no longer enough simply to look at the literary text, nor even to bring a particular theory to bear on that text. Today we are faced with an arresting display of theories, for example we must distinguish between Marxism and feminism and between feminism and psychoanalysis. Moreover, the language used is often difficult for us to understand, although more and more critical terms become current in our everyday speech, 'ideology' for example. But while this is intimidating, it is also exhilarating. No longer do we need to turn to a 'master' author, critic or particular theory, nor do we need to remain constrained by a single interpretation. Rather our practice of literary criticism can become,

> *the joyous affirmation of the play of the world and of the innocence of becoming, the affirmation of a world of signs without fault, without truth, and without origin which is offered to an active interpretation.*
>
> (*Writing and Difference*, Derrida)

First page of Laȝamon's *Brut*

Medieval English literature 3

A context for Medieval English literature?

> For trusteth wel, it is an impossible
> That any clerk wol speke good of wyves,
> But if it be of hooly seintes lyves,
> Ne of noon oother womman never the mo.
> Who peyntede the leon, tell me who?
> By God! if wommen hadde writen stories,
> As clerkes han withinne hie oratories,
> They wolde han writen of men moore wikkednesse
> Than al the marke of Adam may redresse.
> (*The Wife of Bath's Prologue*, 688–696)

When ▷ Chaucer's Wife of Bath recounts her marital experiences with the younger clerk, Jankyn, in her *Prologue* in the ▷ *Canterbury Tales*, her story is focussed on how she confronts the intrusion of his bookish world into her private life. Jankyn, it appears, prefers the company of his book of 'wikked wyves', for him an authoritative source of reference and citation on the subject of marriage, to first-hand marital experience. In fact he substitutes one for the other and gives his wife daily readings from this book, a compilation of anti-matrimonial/anti-feminist writings from medieval and classical Latin sources. For the Wife, the stories reveal less about the experience of marriage and more about the power and prejudices of their (largely) male clerical authors, bound willingly or unwillingly to a celibate life. Her question about who wields the power of the pen is voiced through a quotation from one of ▷ Aesop's fables: 'Who peyntede the leon, tel me who?' In this fable a man tries to use a painting of a man defeating a lion to prove that men are stronger than lions. His lion companion is less impressed with the value of the picture as evidence; the painting itself is a man-made production, and if lions could paint they would offer a different view. The Wife goes on to make a similar point about wives: if they had access to the means of textual representation and production, she points out, they would produce a different image of the 'other' sex. The general point raised by the Wife here, and encapsulated in the question of 'who peyntede the leon', is an important one and applicable to any kind of representation, textual or pictorial, from any period. The answers, though, are rarely as simple and clear-cut as those found in Aesop's fable.

If we were to extend the scope of the Wife's enquiry and consider in a more general way who had access to the means of textual representation in England in the medieval period as a whole, then the Wife's conclusions about those responsible for producing Jankyn's book would still point us in the right general direction. Male clerics were the literate professionals of the time. The Christian Church as an institution controlled access to literate skills, just as, of course, it exerted a pervasive influence over all areas of intellectual activity. Literacy was the privilege of the relatively small percentage of the population who formed the ranks of the clergy, and was the privilege of some members of the civil and social élite in society too. Literate women were in the minority within both these social groupings or estates.

But such generalizations about who wielded the balance of pen-power are only useful in so far as they indicate in a rough and ready way the importance of male clerics as mediators of literary culture during the four centuries or so that are traditionally held to constitute the medieval period in England (1100–1500). This clear-cut picture needs to be qualified because not all the writers in medieval England were male clerics, nor was all the literature produced in England written in English. The case of the twelfth-century writer, Marie (conventionally referred to now as ▷ Marie de France), illustrates both points. The literary signature of one 'Marie', who was probably writing in England, is incorporated into the text of a collection of *Lais*, a collection of *Fables* and a religious narrative about St Patrick, all written in French. Evidently at least one woman did leave her mark on the literary culture of her time, although very little else is known about her. But if the fact that we can identify the work of a medieval woman writer is exceptional, the fact that Marie de France was writing, perhaps in England, in French, for audiences in France and England is not. The answers to the question about who is writing and reading in England would vary to some extent according to which language and which period is under consideration.

Latin, ▷ Anglo–Norman French and English were the principal languages in use in England throughout these centuries but their respective domains of usage (as languages of public and religious ritual, law, record, of high-status culture, as vernaculars) varied considerably. Of these languages, Latin remained the language of the highest cultural authority, of the Church and Christian ritual, of academia, the preserve of the clergy. Yet as the domains of usage of the vernaculars expanded greatly in the 400-year period from 1100 to 1500, the clergy ceased to be the sole mediators of texts and textual traditions. Moreover, access to vernacular texts was not restricted to a reading public. Since textual reception was often a social, aural event rather than a private, silent experience, the question about who was reading texts needs to be reformulated as a question about who formed the audiences of literary works. Nor was access to the means of textual representation wholly restricted to the literate: a point strikingly illustrated by the *Book of ▷ Margery Kempe*, which is the textual record of the spiritual life of a fourteenth-century English mystic who could neither read nor write, but who dictated her story. In fact to address the question of 'who was painting the lion' during this time in a more satisfactory way would involve a consideration of who could commission artefacts, the relationship of patrons to writers, and the different kinds of relationship between writers, their texts and their audiences. This is a highly satisfactory set of questions to which we have, at present, only a partial and fragmentary set of answers.

In the sections which follow some indication is given of the different contexts in which medieval English texts were produced and some sense too of the 'difference' of the literary culture itself. This 'difference' is part of the attraction of medieval literature for modern readers and, paradoxically, part of the modernity of medieval literary studies too. Since medieval literature resists being mapped out in the terms applied to post-Renaissance literary culture, its study has received fresh impetus as those terms have been challenged over the last thirty years or so. Although the organization of this essay on medieval English literature will link up to the focus of subsequent essays in this volume (considering briefly medieval lyric, narrative and dramatic literary traditions), my emphasis throughout will be on the way in which Middle English text cannot be divided up into discrete literary categories and must be seen as part of a continuum of cultural activity that crosses apparent national, linguistic and literary divides. That spectrum of activity itself may be illustrated in the work of the more famous writers of fourteenth-century England. ▷ John Gower's literary corpus, for example, uses the three languages of medieval England as its medium: his story collection in English, the ▷ *Confessio Amantis*, is the final part of a literary triptych of which the first two parts are in French (*Mirour de l'Omme*) and Latin (*Vox Clamantis*). Geoffrey Chaucer's work does not literally cross linguistic divides in this way, but it does challenge any simple notions of separating out categories of literary and non-literary texts. The sheer variety of textual material included in the framework of the *Canterbury Tales* (spanning translations of classical stories, retellings of Christian legends, reworkings of Italian and Old French narratives, stories from 'olde gentil Britouns', performances of sermons and concluding with a prose treatise on penitence) illustrates the range of literary activity at this time and the diversity of the internationaa cultural traditions from which it derives.

The purpose of this essay is not to offer a comprehensive survey, but to illustrate the range of that literary activity and to raise some questions about the terms in which it is discussed. The anomalous position of this essay within the *Bloomsbury Guide* itself indicates some of the problems of fitting a discussion of medieval English literature into a wider context. The literary culture I will be considering neither began in 1100 nor ended in 1500, nor was it exclusively insular, although the emphasis, necessarily, will be on texts produced during this time in England, in English.

Medieval English lyrics?

> *Karolles, wrastlinges, or somour games,*
> *Who so evre haunteth any swiche shames*
> *In cherche, other in cherche yerde,*
> *Of sacrilege, he may be aferd;*
> *Of entirludes, or singinge,*
> *Or tabur bete, or other pipinge –*
> *Alle swiche thing forboden es*
> *Whil the preste stondeth at messe.*
> (Robert Mannyng, *Handlyng Synne*, 8, 991–8)

This general warning against secular diversions from religious observances prefaces a version of the story of the 'Dancers of Colbeck' in ▷ Robert Mannyng's penitential guide *Handlyng Synne*. The story neatly illustrates the dire consequences of sacrilegious distractions, for it concerns a group of carollers who are cursed by their priest for disturbing Mass. As a result of the curse, the group find they cannot stop performing their carol in the churchyard until, having sung and danced for a whole year, they collapse at the end of their ordeal. If this story of the 'Dancers of Colbeck' allows us to glimpse the existence of a popular, secular tradition of song-making (and 'entirlude'-making too), it also illustrates the way in which we have access to that tradition only through clerical mediation of one kind or another. Snatches and fragments of English ▷ lyrics which appear to belong to a popular tradition are preserved in sermons, chronicles and exemplary narratives, but for the most part the short poems and lyrics preserved in manuscripts are the product of learned and literary environments, and not the records of performances in churchyards. Yet that does not mean that the extant texts of poems and lyrics represent a homogeneous body of work. In fact, generalizations about their form and function are very difficult to make, such is the diversity of their range.

First, how do we recognize a medieval lyric text? Is it a literary category composed exclusively of texts designed to be sung to musical accompaniment? Or short, non-narrative texts in verse, or poems with a predominantly personal focus on a secular or religious theme? All of these kinds of texts can be found in modern editions of medieval English lyrics. The diversity of these lyric collections partly reflects the very different ways in which the term lyric can be used now. However, the very act of extracting these short poems from their manuscript text may give the impression that the literary category of 'the medieval English lyric' is more homogeneous than it really is. Some of the earliest Middle English lyrics are religious lyrics embedded as quotations in Latin sermons or are preserved in various kinds of preaching manuals, and seem to have served the ends of preaching and teaching lay audiences (the sermons themselves being preached in English). Some lyrics are collected together in manuscripts which appear to be the medieval equivalents of modern 'literary anthologies' (such as the famous manuscript, now in the British Library, known as ▷ Harley 2253). Others are squeezed as 'space-fillers' into manuscripts containing miscellaneous collections of material or preserved on scraps of parchment, and so survive for us with little indication of any contextual relations. Some musical notations are preserved, but by no means all, and it is not always clear exactly how a text is to be performed or received; in public or in private or perhaps in public and in private. This limpid twelve-line vision of the Crucifixion has some of the features which would fit post-medieval definitions of lyric poetry: it is short, has an emotional focus and a first-person speaker:

> *Quanne hic se on rode* (When I, Cross)
> *Jesu, mi lemman,* (lover)

And besiden him stonden
Marie and Johan,
And his rig iswongen, (back scourged)
And his side istungen, (pierced)
For the luve of man,
Well ou hic to wepen, (ought)
And sinnes forleten, (abandon)
Yif hic of luve kan, (know)
Yif hic of luve kan,
Yif hic of luve kan.

But this text is not so much offering an expression of a personal experience (to adapt ▷ John Ruskin's nineteenth-century definition of a lyric), as providing a model exercise for one. The first seven lines deftly conjure up an emotive image of the Crucifixion, the last five reveal what should be the emotional response of any individual to this sight: the image is offered as a personal test of love (the logic is 'When . . . Then . . . If'). Several versions of this piece survive and one of them is preserved as a quotation in a thirteenth-century sermon text. The use of this poem in a sermon illustrates how medieval lyrics may be used to mediate between private experience and its public expression in different contexts, in different ways. In this case the poem is received, in public, for a performance in private, when the devotional exercise it sketches may be enacted. The sermon context explicitly links the poem to the clerical promotion of a devotional and empathetic kind of spirituality (and the poem itself is a translation of a Latin devotional exercise). This is a spiritual trend which is increasingly in evidence in Middle English religious literature from the twelfth century onwards, and for which the lyric form provided a particularly suitable medium of expression.

More religious lyrics survive in Middle English than secular lyrics: this is a phenomenon which, perhaps, reflects both the 'usefulness' of lyrical texts as ppeaching and teaching devices and the predominance of Anglo-Norman as the medium for sophisticated secular culture for much of the medieval period in England. But it would be wrong to give the impression that the diverse range of Middle English lyric poems which survive can be divided into clear-cut sacred and secular categories. There is a considerable interaction between the language and the conventions of sacred and carnal love-lyrics, as even the short lyric (quoted above) suggests in its address to Jesus as a lover. Indeed, many of the Middle English poems on religious themes use a conventional language of loving drawn from a body of love poetry (a development of French literary culture of the eleventh and twelfth centuries) which celebrates the refined pleasures and pains of 'fin'amur' (▷ Courtly Love) between the sexes. The notion of using a language of carnal love as a way of expressing a spiritual relationship has a precedent in the exegetical convention of reading the Old Testament *Song of Songs* as an account of the relationship between Christ, the bridegroom, and the Church, his bride. Using conventionalized models or refined earthly relationships to recommend (and explore) spiritual relationships is a key strategy employed in many kinds of medieval religious texts including lyrics.

What is interesting about this overlapping use of sacred and secular languages of desire is that conventionalized gender roles may be treated in rather less conventional ways in religious texts. Whereas (as might be expected) male first-person speakers predominate in the secular love lyrics, and women tend to figure more often as objects of desire rather than as desiring subjects, the gender roles in religious texts may be more fluid. Not all first-person religious love lyrics are marked as the expression of male speakers, and there are some examples of female subjects being presented as active lovers (albeit under paternal instruction). In the thirteenth-century 'Love Ron', for example, conventionally attributed to the Franciscan ▷ Thomas of Hales, a young woman is given advice in the art of spiritual loving. Couched in the form of a verse epistle from a male advisor, the twenty-seven stanzas of this text offer advice to a young religious woman on how to choose the best possible lover: the candidate for that role is never explicitly named by the speaker, but is clearly identifiable from his attributes as Christ himself. The self-conscious literary quality of this religious lyric is evident in its use of the art of loving for spiritual ends, and in the way it negotiates between the private and public nature of the instruction it offers. It is both a personal and a public communication, addressed to a single woman and yet sent 'open and with-ute sel' (seal), so other women may have access to it; indeed the recipient is asked to pass it on to other maidens. The last stanza acknowledges the written and performative qualities of this text, as it is a letter for singing in moments of longing:

> Hwenne thu sittest in longynge,
> Drauh the forth this ilke writ; (Draw, same writing)
> Mid swete stephne thu hit singe, (voice)
> & do al so hit the bit. (it bids you)

The 'Love Ron' provides a literary distraction for spiritual instruction and it is one of a group of early English texts, including the ▷ *Ancrene Wisse*, which are produced for, and addressed to, an audience of women who have chosen the religious life.

Our contact with medieval English literature necessarily depends on the vagaries of manuscript survival. This point is underlined by the fact that approximately half the extant texts of English secular lyrics are preserved in a single manuscript, Harley 2253, a literary anthology produced some time in the 1340s, in the Hereford area. But in this context, too, the interplay between sacred and secular literary registers is very clear; indeed some of the lyrics in the collection seem to have been been physically arranged in a way which heightens the interplay between the sacred and secular poems. Thus a lyric on Christ's love for his people beginning 'Litel wot hit any man/ how love hym haveth i-bounde' is followed by one which begins in a similar way, 'Litel wot hit any man/ how derne love may stonde': the addition of the word 'derne' (secret) signals both a change of context and referent as this lyric becomes the complaint of a disappointed male lover. But the language of sacred and carnal desire may also be played off, self-consciously, within a single text, as is the case with 'The Fair Maid of Ribblesdale'. Here, the cumulative effect of a series of religious references is to both elevate and undercut a male speaker's fantasy about a desirable woman.

A range of speaking stances is found within the love lyrics of the Harley collection: there are complaints, petitions, descriptions of reported or imagined encounters in the voice of first-person (male) speakers, but there are dialogue forms too. A wooing game is played out in one lyric (conventionally entitled '*De Clerico et Puella*' – 'About a Clerk and a Girl') between a clerical speaker who has a courtly repertoire of love-sick poses at his command and a young woman who has an equally adept command of deflationary replies. Yet the shorter poems in the collection do not merely address religious and secular emotional subjects: some encapsulate proverbial, monitory material (such as those warning of the last days); one is a poetic rendering of the parable of the vineyard, while a couple address topical, contemporary issues and events (such as the corruption of the consistory courts or the death of ▷ Edward I).

The sheer variety of material and poetic forms in the Harley collection raises questions about how they can best be presented to a modern audience. Not one of the Harley lyrics is attributed to a named poet, and in this respect they are typical of much Middle English literature in general, which is working within a literary tradition that is not concerned with the promotion of literary personalities as such. So if the texts cannot be arranged as the work of particular poets or 'makers', should they then be sorted out according to their material (as love lyrics, as historical and religious poems – as has been the case in past editions), or does the very juxtaposition of diverse poems in the manuscript itself have an interest? The case of the Harley lyrics also illustrates the limitation of approaching medieval English literature solely in terms of the literature written in English, because the collection includes many short poems written in Anglo-Norman; indeed one of the religious lyrics alternates lines in English and Anglo-Norman. If these poems are the product of a bilingual literary culture of some sophistication, then should they not be presented in that context? But the Harley manuscript does not only contain shorter poems in English and Anglo-Norman, but verse narratives too, some religious narratives in Anglo-Norman and Latin prose, and even a collection of recipes in English prose, which have evidently been squeezed on to a blank leaf (including recipes on such matters as how to make iron as hard as steel).

I suggested earlier that the Harley manuscript is a medieval equivalent of a modern literary anthology, but that may be an unhelpful analogy: it is not a book written for national distribution; it is written in one of the 'Englishes' of the time (there being as yet no written standard form of the language); it reflects a regional culture of some sophistication and linguistic plurality, but it is not presented as the work of any single 'maker' or group; its composition shows that poetic form could equally provide the medium for vernacular narrative as prose (a selection of the poetry in the manuscript could include the Middle English romance ▷ *King Horn*). It is a collection which challenges some of the conventional ways in which modern texts may be organized and the terms in which they are discussed, as does that more famous book of medieval narrative poetry and prose, *The Canterbury Tales*.

Narrative poetry?

III   *Hwer is Paris & Heleyne*
       That weren so bryht & feyre on bleo, (of face)
      Amadas & Dideyne,
       Tristram, Yseude and alle theo,
      Ector, with his scharpe meyene, (strength)
       & Cesar, riche of wordes feo?
      Heo beoth i-gliden ut of the reyne
       So the schef is of the cleo. (sheaf, from the cornfield)
                    (Thomas of Hales, 'Love Ron', 65–72)

The connections between the figures of Paris and Helen, Amadas and Idoine, Tristram and Iseult, Hector and Caesar, in the stanza of the 'Love Ron' quoted above is that these figures, drawn from different periods of the past, may illustrate the very transcience of all earthly achievements and pleasures. Presumably, though, the citation is effective because the stories of all these figures are still remembered and retold. It is useful to approach the rich narrative traditions of medieval England with some sense of the important generative story-areas, and ▷ Thomas of Hales's roll-call of names indicates some of these primary narrative subjects drawn from the stories of ▷ Troy, Rome, Gaul and Britain. The reference to Tristram and Iseult perhaps stands out here as being especially resonant of an important subject of medieval narrative (being part of the ▷ Arthurian tradition) and of an important medieval narrative form (the so-called ▷ romance) which deserve to be given special attention as an innovative part of medieval literary culture, and both subject and form will be discussed in due course. There is, however, some critical confusion over the meaning and use of the term 'romance', some of which may be avoided if the genre is approached as part of a wider spectrum of narrative activity, an activity in which stories of Greece, Troy, Britain, and Gaul all have a place.

Translating and reworking Latin classical narratives (such as those of ▷ Thebes, Troy, ▷ Alexander the Great) in the vernacular is an important part of the literary activity of the medieval period. The same is true of English Renaissance literary culture; indeed, one important dimension of English literary culture as a whole is its continual re-engagement with classical texts. But medieval modes of assimilating, transmitting and renewing classical culture may appear rather surprising to a modern audience whose reading habits have been shaped by the Renaissance and post-Renaissance literary ▷ humanist tradition. The medieval versions of these classical stories themselves may be unfamiliar (the medieval Troy story, for example, tends to follow a chronological design, have a strong pro-Trojan slant and focus on Hector as the greatest hero of the war), but more disorientating still for modern readers of medieval 'classics' such as ▷ Chaucer's ▷ Knight's Tale, the alliterative ▷ Destruction of Troy or Kyng Alisaunder is the way in which classical culture is filtered through feudal and chivalric lenses. Theseus, Hector and Alexander don the armour of the knight. In part, the assimilation of the key narratives of the classical past in the medieval period, the act of translating them into the vernacular (into French and Anglo-Norman from the twelfth century, into Middle English from the thirteenth century onwards), involved transforming some aspects of classical culture to reflect the dominant feudal/chivalric ideals of the 'present', and so to endow these ideals with the authority of the 'past'. Medieval narratives relating the Greek, Trojan and Roman past contributed substantially to the establishment of a mythology of chivalry which was developed through the medieval period and continued long after it.

The courtly patina given to medieval versions of the classics was not an unself-conscious action on the part of medieval writers. In Chaucer's Knight's Tale, for example, the narrator both suggests that a continuing chivalric ethos connects the world of classical Athens and that of contemporary England, but also draws attention to the potential incongruity involved in the act of representing this continuous chivalric culture. Such is the splendour of the tournament which Theseus organizes in Athens that every knight 'Were it in Engelond or elleswhere,/They wolde, hir thankes, wilnen to be there' (2,113–4). But the narrator points up the anachronism of this depiction of the 'modern' chivalric world of classical Athens: when some of the knights in Athens set their sights on fashionable gear (Prussians shields!), the narrator wryly remarks on the fact that 'Ther is no newe gyse that it nas old'.

Of course not all aspects of the 'olde gyse' of classical pagan culture could be assimilated to the values and ethos of the Christian present; medieval writers were faced with great interpretative challenges when re-presenting narratives about the classical world (and material drawn from the world of classical learning). Highly elaborate strategies were evolved for reinterpreting pagan structures for contemporary audiences. The pagan framework of the Knight's Tale is part of the 'olde gyse' of the story, which no longer has any place in the 'newe', but it is not used as the occasion for Christian moralizing or denunciation (which is sometimes the case in other medieval versions of classical stories). Rather, the pagan gods in the Knight's Tale are made to function both as representatives of larger forces outside human control and government, and of those human desires and promptings which are potentially controllable by government on both a political and personal level. All the central characters of the narrative, Palamon, Arcite, Emily, Theseus, and Ageus too, have their counterparts in the pagan divinities, and these gods are interpreted as figuring abstracted human passions and powers of some kind. The gods are agents in the narrative and act on the central human figures, but they also provide a means of analysing the actions and desires of the characters themselves when faced with problems of self-government and, in the case of Theseus, the government of others.

The classical, chivalric world of the *Knight's Tale* provides an arena for exploring the interaction between the forces of individual human desire and those of the larger social, political and universal world of which they form a part. Some of the difficulties of putting into practice the conduct-book rules for knights and knight-princes are traced in this narrative, which illustrates the way in which the world of the pagan past may be used to explore, not merely to affirm and exemplify, codes of conduct.

Reworking the narratives of the past offered medieval writers considerable interpretative challenges and innovative possibilities: not only could traditional narratives be refracted through different kinds of generic frames in their retelling, but also new narrative subjects could be opened up within classical, historical frames. The story of ▷ Troilus and Criseyde itself is a medieval 'invention', the story of ▷ Palamon and Arcite in the *Knight's Tale* is another. In both ▷ *Troilus and Criseyde* and the *Knight's Tale*, Chaucer used narratives taken from ▷ Boccaccio to develop a new generic frame for treating classical histories, in which large-scale events were refracted through a microcosmic focus on pairs of lovers. But classical history was not the only prestigious subject for narrative development during the medieval centuries. There is, for example, a large number of Middle English narratives focussed around the activities of ▷ Charlemagne and members of his illustrious court. In these narratives, largely derived from Old French versions, chivalry serves the ends of the Christian faith, and the opposition between pagan and Christian culture (with the transforming possibility of conversion rather than extinction) provides the basic narrative and metaphysical structure of these texts. But it is, perhaps, the opening up of a new history of Britain in the twelfth century that proves to be one of the most striking and productive areas for the creation of vernacular narrative traditions, in verse and later in prose, in the medieval period.

The appearance, some time around 1138, of ▷ Geoffrey of Monmouth's ▷ *Historia Regum Britannie* (*History of the Kings of Britain*) made a significant contribution to opening up the subject of British history for narrative elaboration. This text recounts the sequence of British kings from the foundation of the kingdom of Britain by Brutus, the great-grandson of ▷ Aeneas, to the demise of British rule and the establishment of Saxon control over the island. The reign of ▷ King Arthur marks the high point of British history, for it is during this time that the island is re-established as a unified Christian nation, and becomes a great international power and chivalric centre attracting knights from all over the world. Although Geoffrey of Monmouth was not the first to suggest that British society had classical roots, he was the first to depict the illustrious history of the island in such detail and, in fact, to represent British history in a way that explores some of the political, social and cultural ideals of the twelfth century itself.

Among Geoffrey of Monmouth's academic peers and predecessors, in the early decades of the twelfth century, there was a marked interest in recovering the history of England and in bridging the gap between the narrative history provided by ▷ Bede (and the later Saxon chroniclers) and that of the twelfth-century present. Geoffrey of Monmouth's contribution to this historiographical movement was not to recover the history of Saxon and post-Conquest England but to 'recover' a marvellous pre-history. In developing his account of a relatively undocumented period of insular history, Geoffrey of Monmouth took the opportunity to comment on some aspects of the politics and values of his own, turbulent time. Establishing the political function of this act of historical fabrication (or for that matter the political function of the newly constructed histories of England) is not a simple matter, but, at the very least, a powerful argument for unified rule of the island may be drawn from Geoffrey of Monmouth's history, which is the first requirement if the English kingdom of the 'present' is to live up to the glorious achievements of its British 'past'.

Although the value of Monmouth's account (which considerably disrupted some of the established traditions of English historiography) was challenged by subsequent clerical historians, its influence was immense. Vernacular versions appeared from the mid-twelfth century onwards, and one of the earliest and most substantial verse narratives composed in Middle English, the thirteenth-century *Brut* composed by ▷ Laȝamon, is a reworking of the Monmouth tradition of British history. The way in which retelling the history of the island's past may offer a medium for investigating the cultural politics of its present may be seen in the *Brut*: this very act of retelling insular history in English, with its contrived archaic overtones, seems to be an assertion of a cultural continuity in a land which has 'i-gon from honde to honde', from Brutus's kin to 'Englisce men', and then to 'tha Frensca'.

But if Geoffrey of Monmouth gave Britain a new image and British history a new status, vernacular writers in France and England in the twelfth century opened up other areas of the British cultural heritage for formal literary treatment. The story of ▷ Tristan and Iseult has no place in the design of Monmouth's narrative, which is orientated around regnal history, but it is part of the pre-Saxon British/Celtic narrative store which French writers such as Béroul, ▷ Chrétien de Troyes and ▷ Marie de France drew on for the development of new literary subjects and from which they developed new narrative forms. It is very difficult for us, today, to recreate some sense of this ephemeral, oral, Celtic tradition. However, the range of motifs, themes and subjects which Marie de France, in the late twelfth century, claims to derive from oral British traditions at least suggests that a figure like Arthur did not monopolize this tradition, and probably did not play a large part in it. Rather, vernacular writers from the mid-twelfth century onwards drew on story motifs from British/Celtic traditions to develop a corpus of narratives orientated around the chivalric ▷ Golden Age of Arthur's court, which could be given a historical location too, thanks to Geoffrey of Monmouth's historiographical efforts. Arthurian narrative, like much British historiography itself, is essentially the product of the post-Conquest period.

What seems to happen is that for writers in medieval France and England, Britain becomes a literary landscape where different narrative traditions may be located and where, for example, a historically placed Christian society may encounter otherworldly, magical forces which reflect the remnants of non-Christian cultures. The fourteenth-century verse narrative ▷ *Sir Gawain and the Green Knight* illustrates how brilliantly the narrative potential of the overlapping historical and literary landscapes of Britain may be played off against each other. The impression of Britain rising out of the ashes of Troy, which frames *Sir Gawain and the Green Knight*, offers a resonant image of the way in which new narrative areas are opened up during the period, as material from Celtic and other, hitherto, oral traditions was reworked in literary media and given formal literary status. Aeneas, Brutus, Gawain, and the Green Knight, unlikely as it may seem, form part of a narrative continuum.

I have avoided using the term 'romance' up to this point in favour of the more general term 'narrative'. Partly this is because the term 'romance', like that of 'lyric', has been used in so many different ways – both as a historically specific term and as a literary universal – that its discriminatory value is doubtful at times. The term 'romance' may still perform a useful critical function if, however, it is used of narratives *structured* in certain ways. Chivalric settings are an integral feature of medieval narratives on a wide range of subjects, with the result that the use of a chivalric/feudal setting, and the invocation of the attendant values of that milieu, are intrinsic, but not necessarily distinctive, features of 'romance'.

What is distinctive about the specific category of narratives that I would recognize as romances is that they are focussed around displaced (predominantly male) protagonists, whose social identity and status are threatened in a series of 'adventures', and who survive to reintegrate into society as members of an élite group. The structural pattern is essentially that of estrangement, risk and recovery, which is played out in a providentially ordered world in which all things shall be well, finally, for those who embody the values of the chivalric élite which are theirs by birth. The degree to which Christian providence is recognized explicitly as a controlling force in the fortunes of the protagonists is a variable factor, which is obviously related to the homiletic emphasis of the narrative as a whole.

The romances which are structured around the stories of displaced women, such as *Emaré*, and the ▷ *Man of Law's Tale* of Constance, strongly promote the notion of a providentially controlled world in which a Christian god protects those who have faith and are constant in adversity. Emaré's adventures, as the narrator points out, are firmly under providential direction: when she is put out to sea, because she resists her father's incestuous advances, 'She was dryven into a lond/Thorow the grace of Goddes sond,/That all thyng may fulfylle'. The Amazons of the classical past have few descendants in the female protagonists of medieval romance, whose virtues are predominantly those of suffering and passivity.

While this abstracted romance paradigm may provide a useful starting point for considering the 60 or so extant examples of Middle English romances (such as ▷ *Guy of Warwick* or ▷ *Bevis of Hampton*) which make up such an important part of the vernacular narrative corpus, it is also evident from this corpus that the basic structural paradigm may be developed and refined in various ways. The episodic structure of the form, built up around sequences of adventures, gives it considerable flexibility: sequences may easily be added and interwoven to create more complex narrative structures. Indeed, what is interesting about medieval romances is the way in which variables within and beyond that basic paradigm are played out in particular narratives; the way in which generic frames may be played off against each other; the way in which the form may be used to investigate, not merely affirm, ethical codes. When Guy of Warwick, for example, has earned himself a place in the social structure, and won his wife through his chivalric prowess, the framework of values in which the narrative is working shifts to that of a transcendental Christian ethos. The narrative goes on to chart his displacement from worldly pursuits in general and his actions, thereafter, are entirely in the service of the Christian faith: the genre of romance is contiguous, here, with that of the saint's life.

The possible dimensions of the romance world in general, and the world of Arthurian romance in particular, are well exemplified in the encylopaedia of romance forms, in prose, which constitutes ▷ Malory's ▷ Morte D'Arthur. Here, a sequence of romance narratives is inset within a broader tragic-historic frame. The inset romances are structurally varied (some are longer and interlaced in more complex ways than others), and not all work within the same set of values. In the Quest of the Holy Grail, most notably, two different kinds of chivalric orders confront each other as a transcendent model of chivalric activity subverts the code of behaviour so carefully established through the adventures of the ▷ Round Table knights. The series of adventures radiate out from Arthur's court and yet form part of a sequence, too, with some consequential impetus. The result is the construction of a vast narrative web, which charts the rise, consolidation and, ultimately, the fall of Arthurian society, and which defies any attempt to account for the downfall of Arthur's reign in terms of a single causal structure. In abbreviating and unlocking some of the complex strands of the larger French cycle which formed his principal source, Malory has made the relationship between actions and their consequences much more mysterious. In a world in which any individual has an imperfect knowledge of the circumstances in which she/he is operating, and lacks control over the consequences of their actions, the only measure of action becomes its adherence to a chivalric code of behaviour. But it is precisely the form and scope of that ethical code which are investigated in the epic sequence of Malory's Morte D'Arthur as a whole.

The spectrum of the uses (and perhaps abuses) of romance narratives and their engagement with other kinds of narrative genres (epic, saints' lives, ▷ fabliau) is revealed in the romance collection incorporated in the Canterbury Tales. Alongside the epic-romance structure of the Knight's Tale set in classical Athens (which is set off against the fabliau imitation which follows), there is the embryonic romance-epic of the ▷ Squire's Tale (situated in the marvellous east); the ▷ Man of Law's homiletic Tale of Constance (which moves between the world of Christian Rome and pagan societies in the east and west); Chaucer's burlesque tale of ▷ Sir Thopas which, though nominally set in Flanders, takes the world of romance conventions and motifs as its subject and its setting; and finally the ▷ Wife of Bath's Arthurian romance which provides a provocative analysis of sexual politics.

This Arthurian text opens with a teasing play on the idea of cultural continuity between present and past societies, which may provide both a point of return to the opening subject of this section and a point of transition to the next. The Wife begins her tale with a meditation on the relationship between the inhabitants of Britain in the 'olde dayes of King Artour' and now. The ▷ fairies and elves who once filled the land, she suggests, have been both exorcized and replaced by the wandering friars, who like the fairies can now be found 'in every bussh or under every tree'. It is to the kind of literary material produced by these wandering friars and other clerics that I shall now turn.

Pastoral literature and drama?

> Men yernen gestes for to here
> And romaunce rede in diverse manere:
> Of Alisaunder the conqueroure;
> Of Julius Cesar the emperoure;
> Of Grece & Troye the longe strif
> There mony mon lost his lif;
> Of Bruit that baroun bolde of honde
> Furste conqueroure of Engelonde;
> Of King Arthour that was so riche . . .
> Mony songes of diverse ryme
> As Englisshe, Frensshe, & Latyne –
> To rede & here mony are prest
> Of things that hem liketh best.
> . . . by that thing mon draweth tille,
> Men may him knowe for good or ille.
>   (*Cursor Mundi*, 1–46)

The opening strategy of the narrator of ▷ *Cursor Mundi*, a versified history of the world from Creation to Doomsday, is to suggest that a person's literary tastes (whether for material heard or read) are a sign of their moral and spiritual quality. Reading or hearing the stories of Alexander, Troy, Arthur, etc. is not explicitly criticized by the narrator of the *Cursor Mundi*, but the implication of the opening section is that this monumental account of Christian history offers a morally and spiritually profitable alternative to spending time on 'Stories of diverse thinges', told in 'diverse manere', in 'diverse ryme'. The alternative fare offered by this narrative, which 'courses' over the history of the world (hence its name), is an account of the ▷ Seven Ages of the World, from the first age of creation to the seventh age, which will be heralded by the coming of the 'Antichrist' and end with the Day of Judgement – the 'end' of Christian history as such. Material for this history, first compiled in English around 1300, is drawn not only from the Vulgate version of the Scriptures but from supplementary material in apochryphal sources, from scriptural commentaries in Latin, biblical paraphrases, collections of saints' lives and manuals of Christian doctrine and instruction. A text such as the *Cursor Mundi* gives a literate lay audience access to a body of Christian texts and textual traditions which had been developed and consolidated within the monastic culture of the preceding centuries. It is both the product and a sign of the great pastoral movement which can be traced back to Anglo-Saxon England but which, particularly from the thirteenth century onwards, left an enormous corpus of religious instructional material in its wake.

A wide range of instructional material survives from the medieval period, addressed to different audiences and tackling different areas of Christian teaching: some texts provided the clergy with resources for lay instruction (through the medium of sermons) and guidance for pastoral care; other manuals apparently offered lay audiences direct instruction in how to cultivate their spiritual welfare by explaining the process of penitence (such as in Chaucer's ▷ *Parson's Tale*) or by providing instruction in Christian history (such as the *Cursor Mundi*).

This body of Christian literature (or 'pastoralia') did not exist in a religious vacuum but engaged with the wider spectrum of literary activity of which it formed part and which it influenced in its turn. A dramatic illustration of this engagement can be taken from the *Canterbury Tales*, where figures such as the Friar, the Nun's Priest and the Pardoner deploy the tools of their trade in the construction of tales for a story-telling competition. Though preaching was not, of course, an activity open to medieval women, the Wife of Bath borrows sermonizing techniques to organize the story of her life and lend support to her stance as a secular apologist, thus earning the title of 'noble prechour' from the Pardoner. The Pardoner himself introduces his pilgrim audience to the rhetorical art of sermonizing as he demonstrates the range of linguistic, textual and performance skills that make up his professional routine. According to the Pardoner, lay audiences 'loven tales olde/ Swiche thynges kan they wel reporte and holde' – a point borne out by his own preaching practice and affirmed by the contents of contemporary story collections compiled for preaching purposes.

Such practices of mining all kinds of literary resources for spiritual ends (favoured by the mendicant orders) was not unanimously approved by all sectors of the clergy; indeed, for Chaucer's Parson, literary fictions and 'moralitee and vertuous mateere' are incompatible. His contribution to the *Canterbury Tales* – a prose treatise on the process of penitence – both formally closes the proceedings and actually stops the story-telling game. The Parson's contribution is appropriate, perhaps, for a literary excursion that is nearing the end of the road in all senses. Yet it is clear from considering the *Parson's Tale* within the wider context of the Canterbury collection that the modes and material of spiritual guidance are not necessarily incompatible with those of secular entertainment and instruction. The Parson's rejection of the value of fables and 'swich wreccednesse' represents one position within a wider spectrum of opinion on the value of certain kinds of religious literature in particular and fictionalizing activity in general.

The alliterative poems attributed to the ▷ Gawain poet, composed some time in the later fourteenth century, offer a different view to that of Chaucer's Parson. The poems ▷ *Cleaness* and ▷ *Patience* are both structured in ways which reflect the influence of exegetical practices of reading and interpreting the Scriptures, and use those techniques to explore the interlocking nature of Christian virtues. But whereas *Patience* is focussed around the amplification and explication of a single Old Testament story (that of Jonah and the Whale), the narrative of *Cleaness* draws on more complex sermonizing techniques to investigate the lessons of Christian etiquette, through the retelling of the parable of the Wedding Feast and a further sequence of Old Testament stories. The juxtaposition of these two poems addressing the subject of Christian virtue with the brilliant reworking of Arthurian romance tradition, *Sir Gawain and the Green Knight*, in the same manuscript, suggests that the story of Jonah and the adventures of Gawain do not necessarily belong to mutually exclusive contexts of either literary production or reception.

But it is perhaps the fourth poem in this manuscript, ▷ *Pearl*, which illustrates a merging of Christian and courtly poetics in the most spectacular way. For here the poet uses the fictional frame of a ▷ dream-vision poem as a way of approaching revelation: St John's vision of New Jerusalem in *Revelations* is incorporated into the final sections of this dream poem. The dream-vision genre traditionally offered medieval poets the licence to speculate and explore the interaction between inner and outer worlds in a fictional form. But what is remarkable about this poem is the sheer ambition of its attempt to represent the process by which an individual may come to terms with the prospect of a Christian afterlife, and literally realize and see the vision described by St John in the Bible. The occasion of the poem is one of extreme love-longing, figured in the male narrator's account of his mourning for his pearl, his most precious object, which is described in terms which suggest it represents a female form. The movement of the spiritual 'aventure' which follows is measured by the narrator's ability to see the pearl in different ways, as its possible sphere of reference expands. That expansion is figured in the form of the poem itself, in the concatenating design of every stanza and the linking pattern of the stanzas as a whole, which embodies a pearl shape. The resources of poetic and linguistic artifice, and of Christian techniques for interpreting and explicating the Scriptures, are combined in this poetic narrative, which asserts, in its very form, that fictional making and poetic artifice may serve as a wholly fitting medium for 'virtuous mateere'.

The resources and traditions of Christian teaching and preaching, described above, provide the context for some of the important vernacular dramatic traditions of late medieval England. Most of the surviving evidence for dramatic performances relates to religious drama, and this extant material is generally categorized according to whether its subject is the macrocosmic sweep of Christian history (as found in the ▷ cycle plays, sometimes referred to as 'mystery plays'), or the microcosmic history of an individual human soul (as found in the texts classed as ▷ morality plays). Texts from the first category are the remains of a widespread tradition of Christian urban drama in which select episodes from the cycle of Christian history from Creation to Doomsday were played out in the streets of towns such as York, Chester and Wakefield, which provide the settings for three of the four play cycles which survive. The textual background to this kind of dramatic tradition is provided by works such as the ▷ *Cursor Mundi*, in which a wide range of scriptural, apocryphal and instructional material is merged into a narrative of Christian history.

Considerable resources were required to make Christian history course through the streets of towns, and craft and religious guilds within the towns provided a key organizational structure for play productions. Enacting the play-cycles seems to have served both religious and civic functions: at the same time as the cycle plays celebrate the plan of Christian history, the resources and civic order of these large urban centres are evidently on display too. It is perhaps the community function of cycle drama that helps explain its survival. Performances of the cycles continued even when the religious climate became hostile to some of the doctrinal points they embodied, surviving well into the period traditionally demarcated as that of the 'Renaissance' in England: the last recorded performance of the Coventry plays were in 1579; those of Chester and York in 1569 and 1575, respectively.

If the cycle plays are an enactment of monumental Christian history, the morality plays can be seen as the dramatization of the inner history of a single soul. Whereas cycle drama uses its mundane setting as a prop in recreating a universal, cosmic playing area, the morality plays use dramatic space as an arena for mapping out the history of an inner life, or interior processes, which are less historically specific than typical and exemplary, as the names of their central characters (Everyman, Mankind, Humanum Genus) indicate. The register for morality plays such as the ▷ *Castle of Perseverance* and ▷ *Everyman* echoes that of the penitential manuals designed to provide Christians with a framework for diagnosing and correcting their inner spiritual states, and understanding the mechanics of temptation and sin. This is an analytical vocabulary built of components such as the ▷ Seven Deadly Sins and their corresponding virtues, the World, the Flesh and the Devil. It was not the only register of psychological analysis available to medieval writers: an elaborate descriptive scheme had been developed around the process of falling in love (strongly influenced by ▷ Ovid), and both of these psychological schemes (penitential and amorous) are an important element in the poetic narratives written in the dream-vision mode. But if dream-vision poetry offered a narrative space for the exploration and analysis of inner processes, the morality plays occupied this space in the dramatic tradition of late medieval England, embodying inner life and abstract modes of analysis in dramatic forms.

Although the cycle drama/morality play division offers a starting point for discussing religious drama in English, not all vernacular drama can be neatly slotted into these two categories. The focal points and interests of the cycle drama and morality plays are not mutually exclusive. The so-called ▷ 'N-Town' cycle, for example, combines the representation of Christian history with moral analysis, with the result that personified abstractions, such as 'Mors' (Death) or 'Contemplacio' (Contemplation), occupy the stage alongside figures from Christian history. Unlike the cycle drama of York, Chester and Wakefield, the N-Town sequence of plays seems not to have been designed for processional performance by guild members, and employs a much wider range of dramatic techniques for mediating the literal and symbolic narrative of Christian history.

Historical and moral perspectives could be combined in the 'Saints' Plays' of the period. Few examples of these plays survive, but the text of ▷ *Mary Magdalene* provides an example of how the historical narrative of an individual life may be turned into exemplary drama: Mary's 'fall' into 'wantoness' is represented in this play by the infiltration of the 'Bad Angel' and 'Lady Lechery' into the castle of Maudelyn. The so-called 'Creed' plays and 'Pater-Noster' plays seem to have combined dramatizations of moral analysis and episodes from Christian history, too, in dramatic performances which sought to affirm and explain the power of the Lord's Prayer and the Creed. No scripts of these plays survive, but their contents can be recreated partially from records of their performance in York, Beverly and Lincoln. Clearly our picture of medieval dramatic traditions is very much dependent on the vagaries of the evidence that has survived, and much has been lost.

The spectrum of dramatic activity in medieval England is broader than that represented by plays composed in English. A tradition of Latin Church drama (that is, of acting out parts of the liturgy at key times in the Church year), continues throughout the period, and sophisticated examples of Anglo-Norman religious drama (such as the play known as ▷ *Adam*) survive from the twelfth century. Nor is the drama of medieval England wholly orientated around religious subjects, but as might be expected, far less evidence survives of secular play-making and performing than that of religious drama. Yet of the few English play texts to survive from before the fifteenth century, two of the earliest (the fragmentary account of a meeting between a clerk and a maiden and the text known as ▷ *Dame Sirith*) are humorous and concerned with love problems and tricks.

Records of accounts from noble households suggest that the playing of interludes was an important form of medieval performance art, although little evidence survives of the form and nature of these plays. We have little more idea of the nature of the interlude performed by Jakke Travail in 1427 for ▷ Henry VI than of the popular tradition of interlude-making mentioned by Robert Mannyng in his account of the 'Dancers of Colbeck'. It would be fair to say that a large part of the dramatic activity of medieval England is off the record – or only traceable indirectly through records of civic accounts, household accounts or ecclesiastical prohibitions of various kinds. But it is also fair to suggest that the boundaries between drama and other modes of literary reception were less absolute than now.

The dramatic quality of much medieval narrative, and the dramatic circumstances of its public mediation, undercut distinctions between drama and other literary media, between public and private reading experiences and performances. All kinds of vernacular narratives bear the formalized signals of performance texts ('Herkneth to me'). So the spectrum of medieval performance art is wide and may encompass sermons, readings, recitals, song-making, as well as more conventionally recognized forms of drama. When Chaucer's Pardoner describes his different voice modulations, gestures, props and text, which he deploys when preaching in parish churches, he is providing a script, and stage directions too, for one of the most common and popular forms of medieval performance art.

Chaucer, Gower and Langland

Whylome were lordes in londe that loved in thaire hertis
To here makers of myrthes, that matirs couthe fynde . . .
But now a childe appon chere, withowtten chyn-wedys, (in appearance, beard)
That never wroghte thurgh witt three wordes togedire,
Fro he can jangle as a jaye, and japes telle, (chatter like a jay)
He schall be levede and lovede . . .

(*Winner and Waster,* 19–26)

The narrator of the mid-fourteenth-century ▷ alliterative poem ▷ *Winner and Waster* opens with a lament for a Golden Age when literary 'makers' had status and a duly appreciative audience. Now the decline of society, in all respects, is figured by the preference for entertainment by 'boys' who 'jangle', and this decline is the focus of the rest of the text, which investigates the effects of 'winning' and 'wasting' on social structures. This complaint is a conventional preliminary to the satire which follows.

Yet looking back on the literary activity in English which followed the production of *Winner and Waster*, it may seem that a Golden Age of 'making', far from passing, was just about to begin. The fourteenth century, and the second half of the fourteenth century in particular, is hailed as the time when the English literary landscape opened up; as the time when English became recognized and proven to be a language of literature; as the time when the notion of an English literary *tradition* was born. It is certainly true that there is a massive increase in the use of English as a literary language during this time, and that the status of English – and works produced in English – is firmly established by the end of the century through the work of writers such as ▷ William Langland, ▷ John Gower and, above all, Geoffrey Chaucer. However, this does not constitute a consolidated movement, still less a simple nationalistic endeavour. The distinctive qualities of the work of Chaucer, Langland and Gower, the traditional and innovatory features of their work, derive partly from the diversity of their literary context and their mediation between different models of literary production, between classical and Christian poetics.

By way of conclusion to an essay that has emphasized the plurality of

Middle English literary culture, I will discuss some features of the great encyclopaedic narratives produced by Gower, Chaucer and Langland, and briefly consider the topicality of their work. Though, as we have seen, medieval writers often used stories from the past to investigate the values of the present, these three writers also make the contemporary world a subject of their narratives.

Shared concerns, dramatic techniques, narrative strategies, can be traced between the texts of the ▷ *Confessio Amantis*, the *The Canterbury Tales* and ▷ *Piers Plowman*, although these hardly fall into neat critical patterns. What is striking initially is the way in which Gower, Chaucer and Langland all use penitential occasions, motifs and processes to structure their large-scale narrative compilations. The narrative of the *Confessio Amantis* is organized around a series of confessional and instructional exchanges between a lover (Amans) and a priest (Genius), who are both servants of the Goddess of Love. These exchanges provide the medium for both an encyclopaedic collection of (largely pagan) short stories, organized to illustrate the Seven Deadly Sins, and for a narrative synthesis of other kinds of book learning and lore. Not only does the *Confessio Amantis* contain a collection of classical and Old Testament narratives, but it incorporates sections on the histories of the world, of religion, of culture and instructional material on the governance of self and society. In some respects Gower's text has the quality of a later fourteenth-century manual of culture.

In Gower's earlier works in French and Latin, the narrator assumes the stance of a social prophet and his voice is that of social, ethical and political complaint. Here in the *Confessio* the narrative voice is refracted through that of the Lover and the Priest, and the high stance of Gower's earlier work gives way to a narrative that tries a 'middel weie', between mirth and morality, addressing ethical issues through focussing on the confession and instruction of a lover, a man committed to secular values. But penitential practices are completed both in theory and in practice in this narrative as the focus shifts at the end of the collection from secular ethics to transcendental concerns. The closing stages of the *Confessio Amantis* are marked by the revelation that the Lover is too old to be a follower of Venus, and the gap between his desires and capacities is healed when Cupid's arrow is pulled from his heart. Thus the penitential process of contrition, confession and healing is completed. The state of the Lover and the maker of the *Confessio Amantis* coincide at the end of the narrative: the healing of the lover marks the end of 'love-making' for the figure of the poet, who declares his days of literary composition on the subject of love are over too.

Whereas John Gower uses a personal act of confession as the framework for his story collection, Chaucer makes a public pilgrimage the setting for his narrative drama. The pilgrimage to Canterbury becomes the arena for a tale-telling competition designed to pass the time *en route*. This was not Chaucer's first attempt at constructing a story collection. The occasion for the earlier story collection, the ▷ *Legend of Good Women*, is an act of literary penance for sins against the God of Love, which has obvious parallels with the *Confessio Amantis*. Nor was Chaucer the first writer to use the idea of story-telling as a 'pastime' as a pretext for a framed narrative collection. Before Chaucer the Italian writer ▷ Boccaccio had used a courtly retreat as the setting for a collection of 100 stories in the ▷ *Decameron*. However, Chaucer's choice of a pilgrimage setting allows for a much greater tonal and narrative range. Unlike Boccaccio, Chaucer does not keep within the bounds of a courtly literature tradition, but incorporates a wider panorama of compositional practices and narrative genres, and trades on the social variety of the pilgrim narrators. Diversity is the governing principle of the collection.

Unlike Gower, who uses a relatively stable narrative frame for his story collection, Chaucer makes the framework of the tales a variable factor too, as narratives are generated by different kinds of interaction between the pilgrims and their games-master, the Host. The event is both organized according to certain rules and yet, at the same time, open to unexpected engagements and confrontations. The stories are refracted through a range of narrative voices which defeat any attempt to reconstitute a single, governing authorial stance from the collection. Thus the play between narrators and narrative is much greater than in Gower's *Confessio Amantis* and this ludic quality is one of the singular characteristics of Chaucer's story-collection. Whereas Gower treads a middle way between mirth and morality in the substance and organization of his story-collection, Chaucer conducts a more radical experiment into the morality of mirth at intervals in the *Canterbury Tales*. But this story competition takes place in a setting with moral and spiritual resonances too, and these are invoked at the close of the play by narratives.

The *Canterbury Tales*, though unfinished in parts, was clearly designed to end like the *Confessio Amantis*, with a radical shift of focus and a gesture that marks the end of earthly 'making' and fictionalizing. What begins as a literal and literary excursion ends, with the ▷ *Parson's Tale*, as an occasion for a spiritual journey, a 'parfit, glorious, pilgrymage' to 'Jerusalem celestial'. The time of the maker of the narrative coincides with that of the text itself: most manuscripts of the *Canterbury Tales* close with a leave-taking from the maker of the text in the form of a literary confession and retraction.

In theory and in practice, Chaucer's story-telling collection is a work in progress. Langland's ▷ *Piers Plowman* is very much a poem in progress too, built around a dynamic principle of organization and surviving in at least three different stages of revision and reformulation. If the *Confessio Amantis* and the *Canterbury Tales* bear the signs of being the last works of their respective authors, *Piers Plowman* seems to have been Langland's first and last exercise in literary making. Langland's work is much more the product of a Christian, clerical milieu than that of Gower and Chaucer: the narrative has a pervasive macaronic quality, being suffused with Latin quotations, and the conduct of Christian life in all senses is its central concern. A single penitential action does not provide the setting for the narrative of *Piers Plowman*, but penitential processes and schemes are used to organize the action within the narrative. The first major section of the poem, for example, considers how a Christian society might collectively embark on a process of contrition, confession and pilgrimage. The action of the narrative as a whole might be seen as a pilgrimage of sorts, a spiritual 'chanson d'aventure' by the narrator/dreamer Will, which encompasses a record of a macrocosmic Christian journey through history. The dream framework of the narrative means that all action in the poem is potentially translatable as inner experience, just as all inner experience in the poem may become public history. Through using the dream-vision mode, Langland is able to merge temporal and spatial perspectives, and to combine the diachronic history of Christianity with the synchronic history of an individual human 'will', that of Will, the Dreamer, in his search for Piers Plowman.

Langland's work is not a narrative collection in any obvious sense like that of the *Confessio Amantis* and the *Canterbury Tales*. Yet it has encyclopaedic qualities and synthesizes an enormous tradition of Christian literature, of *pastoralia*. If *Piers Plowman* is encyclopaedic in its scope, its mode of organizing that body of knowledge is very different from that employed by John Gower for example. Langland is concerned not only with what there is to know, but what it is to know. So at the same time as Christian history and doctrine are represented in the narrative, the process of individual assimilation and internalization of that teaching is considered too. The dream mode allows Langland to enquire into the relationship between instruction and understanding. *Piers Plowman* is not, then, a penitential manual, or a Christian handbook, but a poetic venture, committed to the value of fictionalizing as a way of exploring spiritual issues. Yet, in its various versions, *Piers Plowman* exposes the problem of articulating such issues within a fallible medium, through the work of fallible human makers.

Piers Plowman, the *Confessio Amantis* and the *Canterbury Tales* all give the impression of having been produced '*in media via*', '*in medias res*', in the middle of times and traditions, under the shadow of endings which may make all literary labours irrelevant, if not damnable. All three works are given some kind of contemporary placement in late-fourteenth-century society and all three works hold a mirror up to their times, not in the sense of offering a mimesis of events, but in offering a critical assessment of their contemporary political, social and cultural context.

Although Langland opens the first dream-vision of *Piers Plowman* with a paradigmatic picture of Middle Earth, framed by the Tower of Truth and the Dungeon of Falsehood, the sense of a-temporality soon disappears as the contents of the 'fair feeld ful of folk' begin to materialize, and a complex picture emerges of contemporary social and political life. Langland cultivates a greater sense of his narrative unfolding at a particular time in the late fourteenth century than either Gower or Chaucer, and this increases the sense of the pressing urgency of the political and political-ecclesiastical issues addressed in the course of the dream-visions. Gower confronts the political and social issues of his day most directly in his earlier works in French and Latin. However, the *Confessio Amantis*, too, is framed by an extensive prologue and epilogue which places the story collection within a general framework of universal history, and with a specific historical context: the very specificity of Gower's address to his time is underlined by the changes made to parts of the opening and closing frame (notably in its address to ▷ Richard II) as that political context changed.

In comparison to Gower and Langland, Chaucer is much more guarded in his allusions to the turbulent political and social events of his time. Indeed, the topicality of his work is much more orientated towards the world of contemporary European culture. His engagement with the court culture, not only of France, but of Italy too, is unparalleled among his contemporaries. Like Langland, Chaucer opens his encyclopaedic work, the *Canterbury Tales*, with a *Prologue* which gives the story-telling event some sense of historical time and place. As the pilgrims are introduced, an impression is built up of a society in which traditional social bonds are being eroded by materialistic interests. But the pilgrims do not operate within their everyday context in the *Canterbury Tales*. Rather the pilgrims are cut loose from their mundane world to become prime movers in a literary event in which contemporary social and political issues are refracted through an investigation into how literary representations are produced and received. References to such contemporary events as the ▷ Peasants' Revolt or to the deposition of Richard II are rare in Chaucer's work; a concern with the politics of representation, of 'lion painting', is much more pervasive.

When the Elizabethan critic ▷ George Puttenham came to consider the history of the *Arte of English Poesie*, he chose not to delve further back than the time of ▷ Edward III, and mentions only a small group of writers from the fourteenth and fifteenth centuries as worthy of notice, including Chaucer, Gower, Langland, ▷ Lydgate and ▷ John Hardyng. For Puttenham these were not writers from a Golden Age of medieval literature, rather writers from a 'First Age' of a literary tradition which culminates, in his view, in the work of the court poets of his time. It is perhaps not surprising that Puttenham bestows the honorific title of poet on Chaucer, alone, of the writers from this first age. Some of the distinctive qualities of Chaucer's work (such as its poetic self-consciousness, its engagement with an international secular literary tradition) correspond to features of the secular, humanist, literary tradition which Puttenham promotes as *the* tradition of English poetry. But this courtly tradition of literature is part of a much broader spectrum of literary activity: it is not the *only* literary tradition of the time. Puttenham's representation of the 'First Age' of English poetry reveals how the composition of literary history itself reflects the values of its writer and its time, even as the attempt is made to engage with those of another age. Literary history was, is, and continues to be, a contingent construction. Since Puttenham wrote, John Hardyng, the fifteenth-century verse chronicler, no longer occupies a place in the high ground of medieval literary history alongside that of writers such as Chaucer and Langland. The '▷ House of Fame', as Chaucer describes it, is built on a rock of partly melting ice.

In the course of the twentieth century, the study of medieval culture and the retrieval of its artefacts has expanded enormously, with the result that the medieval literary landscape has been opened up in different ways. Its features have been changed quite literally by the mapping out of wider areas of literary activity, as more medieval manuscripts have been edited and made accessible for a modern audience. But at the same time more questions have been raised about the ideological implications of these acts of retrieval, interpretation and cultural assimilation. Medieval literary studies have become the forum for debates about how texts from a half-alien literary culture may be read in a modern context. The engagement with medieval literary culture is a two-way process of critical enquiry and critical self-assessment. Reassessments are currently being made of the interplay between those texts traditionally identified as belonging to the category of 'medieval literature' and the wider spectrum of textual production of which they form a part. If medieval culture no longer speaks to modern audiences with a univocal voice, that is partly because of the greater critical sensitivity, now, to the way in which the tensions and contradictions in the dominant ideological constructions of the time are played out in the texts of the time. Although the Christian Church exerted a pervasive influence over all areas of medieval intellectual, social and political activity, that does not mean that the cultural artefacts which remain project anything like a homogeneous and unified world view. The Wife of Bath is not the only medieval figure to be interested in the politics of 'lion painting'.

My interest in this essay has not been in tracing the origin of an English tradition, so much as giving a broad impression of the range of sacred and secular literary 'making' in Middle English, and raising some questions about who was making it, and in what context. The medieval English tradition cannot be mapped out wholly in terms of individual writers, or in terms of works written just in the 'Englishes' of the time. It has a place within a literary continuum which includes works produced in Latin and French written in England, and on the continent too. This literary continuum does not end in 1500, although from this time on there is an enormous expansion in the productive and receptive contexts of English texts, as the media of page and stage are opened up.

Yet some striking lines of continuity are to be found in the relationship between the sophisticated narrative traditions of the medieval period and the dramatic traditions of the Renaissance. Not only was a great body of medieval narrative material made more readily available for private reading through printed editions, but it was also rendered more accessible through its transformation into dramatic form. Shakespeare's reworking of the medieval Troy stories is but one example of the way in which narratives formerly mediated through public and private readings become the subject of dramatic productions in the Renaissance. ▷ *Troilus and Cressida* is a dramatic innovation which arises out of classical and medieval narrative traditions. Indeed, the homage to Chaucer at the beginning of the ▷ *Two Noble Kinsmen*, or the appearance of Gower as a mediating figure in ▷ *Pericles*, are only the most obvious signs of the deep-seated debt of Renaissance writers to medieval poets and 'makers' of the preceding centuries.

The Distressed Poet: an engraving after William Hogarth

Eighteenth-century prose literature 4

The literary market-place

'No man but a blockhead ever wrote except for money.' ▷ Samuel Johnson's peremptory dictum, though expressed in characteristically provocative manner, highlights a significant development in the prose writing of the eighteenth century. There were, of course, many other motives, apart from the hope of financial gain, which might lead writers to take up their pens: some were inspired by moral or religious convictions; others by the desire to expound a political argument, or the itch for satirical mischief-making; while others still were inspired by the simple authorial vanity of seeing the offsprings of their imagination bound up in folio or octavo volumes. Yet it was the eighteenth century which saw the emergence of the professional writer; the man, or woman, who wrote not as a genteel pastime, or to flatter the self-esteem of a generous patron, but directly for money. For the first time, the spread of literacy, together with the emergence of commercial bookseller-publishers eager to feed the imaginations of an expanding reading public, made the trade of letters a viable, if not always lucrative, profession.

In the early years of the century most of the leading writers still relied more on institutional sinecures, or on a combination of public and private patronage, than on the literary market-place for their support. ▷ Richard Steele was a Commissioner for stamps; ▷ William Congreve was nominally in charge of licensing hackney-carriages; ▷ Daniel Defoe was a government spy; ▷ Jonathan Swift held the livings of two country parishes in Ireland; ▷ Joseph Addison was a career civil servant, finally achieving the position of Secretary of State.

Yet the qualifications required for entry to the professions excluded some authors who had to rely solely on the income from their writing. As a Catholic, ▷ Alexander Pope was unable to hold public office, though he made a virtue of his social exclusion by celebrating his Twickenham retreat as a symbol of independence. His accomplished marketing of the subscription editions of his translations of ▷ Homer netted him an astonishing £10,000 (something in excess of £500,000 in today's terms). It was a commercial coup that other writers could only envy. By contrast, ▷ Swift was paid £200 for ▷ *Gulliver's Travels* (1726), and ▷ Oliver Goldsmith £60 for ▷ *The Vicar of Wakefield* (1761–2).

In recent years critical interpretations of eighteenth-century literature have increasingly questioned the traditional image of the period as an 'age of reason', a peaceful haven of political stability and classical values. Recent studies have revealed the commercial realities that lay behind the classical façade of the eighteenth-century literary pantheon. By exploring the sub-culture of ▷ Grub Street, and by focussing attention on the many previously neglected women writers of the period, modern scholarship has provided a new perspective on this fascinating era in literary history, reminding us of the valuable contributions made by those excluded from the clubs and coffee-houses of the Augustan establishment.

▷ Aphra Behn, debarred from the professions as a woman, attempted to attract state patronage by her political writings. The *Ode on the Coronation* would, she hoped, secure her a pension or a grace and favour house. But no money was forthcoming, and she turned instead to more lucrative markets for her talents in romantic fiction and theatrical comedies.

The career of ▷ Samuel Johnson demonstrates the precariousness of the literary life. Forced by poverty to abandon his studies at Oxford University, he thereby relinquished all hopes of a career in the law or the Church. After an unsuccessful attempt at school-teaching, he arrived in London, virtually penniless, and began to support himself by his writings. Regular contributions to ▷ *The Gentleman's Magazine* provided part of his income, yet his independent projects were also undertaken for commercial reasons. According to legend, ▷ *Rasselas* (1759) was written rapidly to pay the expenses of his mother's funeral; Johnson encouraged such stories as proof of his independence.

In 1755, at the culmination of his labours on the ▷ *Dictionary of the English Language*, Johnson delivered a celebrated epistolary snub to his self-styled patron, the ▷ Earl of Chesterfield: 'Is not a patron, my lord, one who looks with unconcern on a man struggling for life in the water and when he has reached ground encumbers him with help?' His letter is a declaration of literary independence that signals the end of the era of the private patron. Ironically, it was the commercial project of the *Dictionary* which brought Johnson academic recognition, as Oxford awarded him the degree he had been unable to obtain by more conventional means. In 1762, the award of a Crown pension of £300 a year relieved Johnson of some of the drudgery of hack work, though he was careful to insist that this was not a reward for political services, but a recognition of literary achievements.

Just before the start of the century, the lapsing of the Licensing Act in 1695 provided the opportunity for a massive expansion of the printing trade. Entrepreneurial publishers ranging from society figures like Jacob Tonson to Grub Street pirates like Edmund Curll played a vital, though sometimes unrecognized, part in shaping the literary culture of the eighteenth century. The 'Augustan Age' is often, and rightly, portrayed as a period when classical models and formal rules were of paramount literary importance; yet the commercial judgements of men like these were equally influential in promoting and developing the variety of eighteenth-century literature, with works ranging from translations of the classics to lurid Newgate yarns.

It was a time when, according to Martin Scriblerus (alias Pope), 'paper became so cheap and printers so numerous that a deluge of authors cover'd the land'. What is remarkable about the prose writings of the eighteenth century, when compared with those of earlier centuries, is their sheer diversity. The rise of the novel and the development of periodical journalism are only the two most obvious features of this expansion of the literary market. Fabulous adventures, travellers' tales, secret histories, spiritual lives, satires, sermons, pastorals and panegyrics and works of every conceivable style and tone, calculated to appeal to all tastes and pockets, rolled from the presses. The pages of Pope's ▷ *Dunciad* are filled with the names of forgotten Grub Street authors, such as Ned Ward, ▷ Eliza Haywood and Charles Gildon, many of whom eked out a precarious living in the kind of literary sweat-shops hilariously described by ▷ Henry Fielding in his play ▷ *The Author's Farce* (1730).

Establishment authors, like Pope and ▷ Swift, frequently deplored the promiscuous vitality of this new literary world, forseeing the death of civilized values in publishers' lists as the works of classical authors were outnumbered by the ephemeral products of those whom they dubbed the 'moderns' or 'dunces'. The novelists themselves often appeared embarrassed at their own imaginative freedom, prefacing their works with statements which sought to legitimize the seductive appeal of fiction by appealing to some external authority. In referring to his early novels as 'comic epics in prose' Fielding endeavoured to claim a niche for them in the traditional classical pantheon. ▷ Defoe preferred to describe his tales as 'true histories', faking his fictions to read like facts, and filling in the broad sweeps of his adventure stories with minute circumstantial details. To ▷ Samuel Richardson, the only justification for fiction was its clear commitment to moral reform, and he presented his novels as exemplary parables in which vice is routed and virtue rewarded. Yet even the sternest critics of literary self-indulgence found the lure of fictional licence irresistible. ▷ Swift's ▷ *A Tale of a Tub* (1704) is, among other things, a satire on the ephemerality of modern culture. 'I have remarked,' says the *Tale's* narrator, 'that nothing is so very tender as a modern piece of wit'. But, while affecting to deplore this cultural perishability, Swift revels in the world of literary ephemera, turning topical tit-bits into enduring metaphors for human vanity.

Thus to speak of 'the rise of the novel' in the early eighteenth century, as if assuming that by then the novel had attained a clear, recognizable identity, is somewhat misleading. There was no single literary genre which sprang, fully-formed, to life with the publication of ▷ *Robinson Crusoe* in 1719. Instead, a variety of contrasting fictional forms competed for attention, ranging from the vivid ▷ Grub Street pseudo-biographies published in the down-market *Applebee's Journal* (1715–36), to witty anecdotal sketches of the ▷ de Coverley family presented in ▷ *The Spectator* (1712); or from salacious secret histories, such as ▷ Delarivière Manley's *The New Atalantis* (1709) to satiric fantasies, such as Swift's ▷ *Gulliver's Travels* (1726). As late as 1711 ▷ *The Tatler* was still using the word 'novelist' to mean a newspaperman. In much the same way ▷ Johnson's *Dictionary* (1755) continued to define 'journal' as 'any paper published daily', whereas most of the periodicals so described were not in fact daily publications. In both cases it is clear that the regulatory constraints of etymology had little inhibiting influence on the dynamic growth of the genres themselves. For, despite the Augustan predilection for neo-classical rules and critical categories, the novel, like journalism, grew up happily innocent of prescriptive theories. Indeed, the emergence of the novel form in the early eighteenth century, which often appears an inevitable consequence of changing social conditions, can equally well be presented as the result of a series of felicitous accidents. Defoe was almost 60, and nearing the end of an indefatigably varied career during which he had tried his hand at innumerable forms of business enterprise (all failures) as well as journalism and espionage when he published *Robinson Crusoe*. Fielding was a celebrated young playwright until ▷ Sir Robert Walpole's introduction of stage censorship with the new Licensing Act of 1737 forced him to find an alternative outlet for his literary talents. Richardson was a successful printer, whose decision to turn author was partly inspired by a prudent desire to utilize the spare capacity of his press. This process of 'serendipity', a word coined by ▷ Horace Walpole, continued throughout the century, and it was Walpole's own fortuitous success with his fantasy *The Castle of Otranto* (1764) which inspired the later vogue for Gothic fiction.

The career and reputation of ▷ Daniel Defoe offers some useful insights into one type of literary enterprise. The son of a dissenting tallow-chandler, he was a lifelong bankrupt, a tireless entrepreneur and a prolific journalist whose collected works would fill several hundred volumes. For nine years, from 1704 to 1713 he wrote single-handedly his thrice weekly journal *The Review*; for much of the same period he was also one of the government's leading spies, sending back secret reports from Edinburgh on the political manouevring surrounding the negotiations for the Act of Union between England and Scotland in 1707. Simultaneously, he was also striving to extricate himself from massive debts, and contriving to stay out of the hands of his many creditors. In both his business ventures and his journalism one finds the same spirit of brinkmanship, the same flirting with disaster. The energy and excitement of his writings co-exist with a kind of literary carelessness and an apparent impatience with more studied effects which led on occasions to disaster. His ironic pamphlet *The Shortest Way with Dissenters* (1702), which counterfeited the violent language of a High Church zealot, backfired badly when its irony was mistaken for incitement, and Defoe was sentenced to punishment at the pillory. More recently, critics have reassessed the apparent carelessness of Defoe's writing, finding in it the poker-face of a more accomplished literary gamesmanship. The 'failure' of *The Shortest Way* succeeded in exposing the covert menace of High Church policies in a way that more conventional irony could not have achieved. Similar subtleties may be detected in the 'mistakes' and contradictions which abound in Defoe's novels. Generations of readers have noted the glaring contradictions between what characters say in one part of a novel, and how they behave elsewhere. Well on in her narrative Moll Flanders is seized by a sudden maternal instinct and delivers a sober lecture on the depravity of mothers who neglect or abandon their offspring. Yet by this stage she herself has happily abandoned innumerable children of her own without a word or a qualm. Her flair for criminality is accompanied by a constant moral patter as she alternately presents herself as a victim of circumstances and an agent of social education. The unconvincingness of her final 'repentance', which conveniently allows her to retire in comfort on her ill-gotten gains, has often appeared to undermine the novel's moral seriousness. Contradictions like these – and there are many other celebrated examples in all the novels – have often been taken as evidence of a slap-dash journeyman approach to the business of authorship. Yet the pattern of these contradictions, in which characters preach like Puritan moralists yet act like ruthless opportunists, goes to the heart of Defoe's fiction. For all their concentration on mundane details, his novels are fantasies of survival, heroic adventures of social mobility in which individuals single-handedly confront and conquer a host of adverse circumstances. Despite the apparent crudity of their episodic narratives, Defoe's novels are animated by a quality more usually identified with a more self-consciously sophisticated form of fiction, in the characters of his unreliable narrators.

Likewise the unravelling of ▷ Jonathan Swift's ironies has been the key to the twentieth-century reappraisal of his status as a writer. Earlier critics, like ▷ Thackeray, viewed his writings as misanthropic and malign: 'A monster gibbering shrieks, and gnashing imprecations against mankind – tearing down all shreds of modesty, past all sense of manliness and shame; filthy in word, filthy in thought, furious, raging, obscene.'

Judgements like these derive from the tendency to identify Swift with the narrators of his satires, seeing in Gulliver's hysterical reaction to the Yahoos a representation of Swift's supposed alienation from humanity. But Swift is the master of literary disguises, and his chosen narrators are utopians or fanatics, projectors or madmen whose plausible rhetoric of half-truths lead inexorably to such savage conclusions as the eating of babies or the abandonment of human society in favour of life in a stable. As a satirist, Swift's prime target is the irrational utopianism which founds its hopes of progress on a refusal to acknowledge the perversities and flaws of human nature itself. From *A Tale of a Tub* (1704), with its ironic epigraph 'Written for the Universal Improvement of Mankind', to the Academy of Lagado in *Gulliver's Travels* (1726) whose scientists are engaged in projects to produce sunbeams out of cucumbers, Swift ridicules the visionary enthusiasm which finds inspiration in the belchings of a fanatical preacher, and sublime wisdom in the neighing of a horse.

Born and educated in Ireland, Swift took holy orders and became a clergyman in the Church of Ireland. Yet he spent most of Queen Anne's reign in London, pursuing an alternative career as a political journalist. His *Examiner* articles and his pamphlet *The Conduct of the Allies* (1711) provided a magisterial defence of the ▷ Tory government's policy for ending the war with France, and even today offer excellent models of the art of political journalism. Forced to return to his native land on the death of Queen Anne, Swift felt like a virtual exile, and it was several years before he could bring himself to relaunch his journalistic career with a series of powerful pamphlets deploring the miserable economic plight of Ireland. His most celebrated pamphlet, ▷ *A Modest Proposal* (1729), ironically recommends that the people of Ireland should rear their children as food for the tables of their English landlords. The scheme has a savage logic; it is methodically costed, and the arguments are financially flawless. With its plausible phrases and deadpan tone, this satire is a brilliant indictment of a society in which economic exploitation has abnegated the natural ties of humanity and love.

While it is undoubtedly true that Swift's satires dwell on the darker side of human nature, his love of jokes, riddles and *jeux d'esprit* should not be forgotten. From his *Bickerstaff Papers* (1708–9) to his *Directions to Servants* (published posthumously in 1745), a spirit of mischievous and subversive anarchy runs through all his writings. In his most famous poem *Verses on the Death of Dr Swift* (1731), he provided his own obituary, declaring, among other things, that 'fair liberty was all his cry'. The liberty that Swift cherished was less political than intellectual and his satires offer a consistent challenge to our own reasoning powers to find a way through the maze of utopian delusions and political lies.

'The Female Wits'

At one point in her career, ▷ Delarivière Manley worked as Swift's assistant on *The Examiner*, taking over from him as editor in 1711. Manley was already notorious for salacious society scandals: *The Secret History of Queen Zarah* (1705), using the device of a fictional history to avoid prosecution, was an instant success, with its separately published key revealing the code names. In 1709 a further *roman à clef*, *The New Atalantis*, continued this combination of transparent allegory and sexual innuendo. The ▷ Whig ministry, worried by her revelations, issued a warrant for the arrest of printer, publisher and author, and Manley was required to name her informers. Exploiting the ambiguities of fictions-as-facts, Manley declared her only source was divine inspiration. Manley's reputation as an erotic scandalmonger contributed to the stereotype of the immoral female author. Pope's image of the Grub Street hacks and booksellers as literary whores and pimps takes on further implications in the light of Manley's own life; supplementing her income by a series of affairs, she eventually became the mistress of Alderman Barber, her publisher.

Women writers anxious to avoid such notoriety often published their works anonymously, or prefaced them with humble pleas that they were written in distress. And, though scandalous works sold well, novels which conformed to social mores were more widely acceptable as serious literary efforts. The decline of the patronge system made a clear distinction between the aristocratic lady writing as a graceful accomplishment, and the woman who went against the nature of her sex and engaged in disreputable trade.

Even writers with no literary ambitions tailored their products to the changing literary tastes. ▷ Eliza Haywood's early works were titillating confections, and *Love in Excess* (1719) was, with *Robinson Crusoe* and *Gulliver's Travels*, one of the three best-selling works before ▷ Samuel Richardson's ▷ *Pamela* (1740–1). But by the 1740s and 50s, Haywood takes on a new tone of conventional conformity, and the 'women's novel' became increasingly associated with the values of hearth and home. It was a compromise which allowed the critic both to praise women for their delicate understanding, and to confine them to 'feminine' gentility which could be disparaged as frivolous.

Similar arguments were often advanced in condescending appraisal of some of the more chatty periodicals. Swift was in no doubt as to the main audience for ▷ Addison's *Spectator* when he remarked, 'let them fair-sex it to the world's end', and Eliza Haywood exploited this market with the launch of *The Female Spectator* (1744–6). If anything, Addison seems rather to have relished than repudiated his paper's reputation as providing a genteel education of ladies. When he boasted of taking philosophy out of the schools and Colleges, and into 'clubs and assemblies, tea tables and coffee-houses', he made explicit the intention to mingle morality and manners, philosophy and fashion, in an urbane and witty miscellany. And despite a tinge of polite condescension in the tone of its more lightweight contributions, *The Spectator* was remarkably successful in maintaining a style of well-mannered wit. There was, however, a serious side to this endeavour to promote the refined tone and rational debate of coffee-house society to a wider reading public. In the previous century, the Puritan moralist and the fashionable Cavalier had stood on opposite sides in the ▷ Civil War. Addison and Steele endeavoured to heal this breach, by putting a smile on the face of morality, and restraining the more licentious habits of town rakes and courtly roués. In the genial atmosphere of a fictitious Spectator club, the ▷ Whig merchant Sir Andrew Freeport and the ▷ Tory squire ▷ Sir Roger de Coverley could discuss their differences over a glass of port rather than settling them on the battlefield. One form of anti-social behaviour that Addison particularly deplored was the writing of satires, which he described as 'poisoned darts' that gave 'secret stabs to a man's reputation'. In *The Spectator* he promised he would never 'draw a faulty character which does not fit at least a thousand people, or publish a single paper that is not written in the spirit of benevolence, with love to mankind'.

However, it was the growing popularity of the novel rather than Addison's benevolent pieties which gradually killed off the vogue for satire in the middle years of the century. In broad terms, one might say that satire deals essentially with types, whereas the novel presents us with individuals. Eighteenth-century satire is concerned less with the redemption of individual sinners than with the regulation of general standards of conduct. But the novel, particularly under the influence of Richardson, was more interested in questions of moral identity and the expression of individual consciousness. The distinction between the two genres is not always as clear-cut as this might imply. When in ▷ *Joseph Andrews* (1742) ▷ Henry Fielding declares 'once for all, I describe not men but manners; not an individual, but a species', he writes as both satirist and novelist. In the preface to that book, he draws a distinction between comic fiction and satire, and like ▷ *Shamela* (1741), the first ten chapters comprise a burlesque satire on Samuel Richardson's *Pamela*. It is only after this point in the novel that Fielding attempts to transform Joseph's chastity from an absurd parody of Pamela's much vaunted virtue into a mark of fidelity for his beloved Fanny. Similarly, ▷ *Jonathan Wild* (1743), with its consistent ironic attacks on 'greatness', might be regarded more as an extended lampoon than as a novel. It is not until ▷ *Tom Jones* (1749) that Fielding finally achieved his own distinctive form of comic fiction though that novel too contains many incidental satiric and parodic moments.

In Johnson's view there was as great a difference between the literary talents of Richardson and Fielding 'as between a man who knew how a watch was made, and a man who could tell the hour by looking on the dial plate'. Although the terms of the relative judgement has sometimes altered, the temptation to draw comparisons between the literary achievements of these two men has persisted ever since. As authors, they embody two rival traditions of the English novel, appearing as contending 'fathers' of the novel, each disputing the legitimacy of the other's offspring. From Fielding we derive the tradition of comic fiction, a style of writing that revels in its own vivacity and wit, offering its readers a rich and varied diet of social comedy, urbane irony and literary sophistication. From Richardson, we derive the novel of moral introspection and psychological insight; his epistolary style offers a kind of fictional confessional dramatizing the dilemmas of individual moral choice.

The morality of *Tom Jones* is based on a simple antithetical contrast; natural instinct versus social hypocrisy, goodness of heart versus cunning of head. Part of the satisfaction of the book comes from the combination of the formal symmetry of its structure (Coleridge referred to it as one of the three best plots ever written) with the apparent freedom and randomness of its ▷ picaresque episodes. In the same way, Tom's artless and impulsive vitality is made acceptable by the artful manipulations of the narrator's tone.

Pamela (1740–1), Richardson's inspired first person narrative of a young servant girl's triumph over repeated attempts at seduction by her employer, was an immediate commercial success. 'If all the books in England were to be burnt, this book, next the Bible, ought to be preserved', enthused one reader. Nowadays its reputation is less secure. Modern readers are apt to side with Fielding in regarding its notorious subtitle, 'Virtue Rewarded', as evidence that Pamela is a model of policy rather than purity.

Richardson's next novel, ▷ *Clarissa* (1747–8) is an undisputed literary masterpiece. Again using the epistolary form, Richardson interweaves four narrative voices to construct a novel of great psychological complexity. In its treatment of the contradictions between 'virtue' as reputation and virginity as an extension of moral integrity, Richardson highlights the social hypocrisies where the marriage market puts a high price on maidenhood. Anne Howe, Clarissa's friend, urges the conventional solution of marrying the seducer, but Clarissa follows the path of self-imposed martyrdom. The novel escapes any simplistic morality, reverberating beyond a reductive summary.

The distinction which Johnson drew between the novels of Fielding and those of Richardson, was reapplied by Richardson himself to the novels of ▷ Sarah Fielding, Henry Fielding's sister. Johnson and Richardson both encouraged Sarah Fielding to publish her work. Her best-known novel, *The Adventures of David Simple* (1744), provides a notable contrast to the male novelists' treatment of female characters. Where Pamela and Clarissa struggle with threatening seducers, Sarah Fielding's heroines wryly recognize sexual harassment as a part of the social structure.

It was the development of the ▷ circulating libraries in the later decades of the century which provided the largest market for the mass of novelistic fiction. Many critics were alarmed by the proliferation of light romantic fiction which resulted from these cheaper sources of entertainment. 'This branch of the literary trade', one reviewer remarked, 'appears, now, to be almost entirely engrossed by women'. The naive country girl who has her head turned by these frothy fantasies became a stock figure of fictional stereotypes. From ▷ Sheridan's Lydia Languish to ▷ Jane Austen's Catherine Morland, the harmful effects on the uneducated *ingenue* were a favourite topic for literary parody. In ▷ Charlotte Lennox's *The Female Quixote* (1752), the heroine, Arabella, turns from the sterner labours of her father's study to while away her hours with her mother's library, a collection of lengthy French romances which she mistakes for historical accounts. By creating an ironic distance between the heroine and the narrator, Lennox uses this familiar theme to make a social comment on women's education. ▷ Fanny Burney's major novels also focus on the entry of the *ingenue* into a potentially corrupting society. ▷ *Evelina* (1778) uses the epistolary narrative of a woman asking her male mentor for advice. *Cecilia* (1782), her most successful novel, shows an intelligent but naive girl tricked out of her inheritance by an exploitative friend's husband. In drawing attention to the dangers faced by the good-natured but ill-advised heroine Burney contributes to the social debate on the status of women, using the novel as an entertaining medium of discussion.

Sentiment and sensation

In the second half of the century two new styles of writing became suddenly fashionable and all but dominated the fiction market. The first of these was the sentimental novel. 'What, in your opinion, is the meaning of the word *sentimental*, so much in vogue among the polite?' Lady Bradshaigh asked Richardson. 'I am frequently astonished to hear such a one is a sentimental man; we were a sentimental party; I have been taking a sentimental walk.' Some twenty years later the Methodist ▷ John Wesley continued to protest against the word as a meaningless foreign neologism. 'Sentimental? What is that? It is not English; he might as well say Continental. It is not sense. It conveys no determinate idea.' Probably the most celebrated of sentimental novels was Henry Mackenzie's *The Man of Feeling* (1771) in which the tears of the hero, Harley, flow freely throughout the narrative. As a benevolent innocent with the most delicate sensibility, Harley is constantly cheated, deceived and hurt by the more worldly figures he encounters; yet his sufferings carry with them a *tendresse* of pleasure; his humiliations discover the exquisite sensations of injured integrity. Towards the end of the novel his apparently unrequited love for Miss Watson results in his physical decline until, on his deathbed, she reveals her love for him and he dies of sheer happiness. A similar pattern of innocent suffering can be found in ▷ Oliver Goldsmith's novel ▷ *The Vicar of Wakefield* (published 1766) which presents a parallel confrontation between naive benevolence and unscrupulous power. Goldsmith's vicar, Primrose, is a man who takes his 'consummate benevolence' to 'a romantic extreme'. With an authentically sentimental relish for the moral authority of suffering, Goldsmith dwells on the vicar's 'pleasing distress' at the repeated trials and tragedies heaped upon him by Thornhill, the malicious libertine squire.

Mackenzie's novel was an immediate best-seller. ▷ Burns wore out two copies of the work, calling it 'a book I prize next to the Bible'. Johnson was less impressed, commenting scornfully on 'the fashionable whine of sensibility'. In 1773 ▷ Mrs Barbauld offered a psychological justification for this type of fiction in her *Inquiry into the kind of distress which exerts agreeable sensations*, emphasizing the evocation of a sympathetic tenderness on the part of the reader. 'Tenderness,' she wrote, 'is, much more properly than sorrow, the spring of tears'.

For modern readers the best-known fictional example of the cult of sensibility is in fact a partial parody of the genre. ▷ Laurence Sterne's ▷ *A Sentimental Journey through France and Italy* (1768) exploits many features of the sentimental style, yet does so with a tone of ironic self-consciousness that constantly trembles on the brink of satire. Like Mackenzie's Man of Feeling whose face is bathed in tears while listening to another's tale of woe, Sterne's Yorick, hearing of the death of a monk to whom he had behaved uncharitably, 'bursts into a flood of tears'. But whereas Harley's tears are the sign of his refined sensibility, Yorick's tears are produced with a sudden and comic exaggeration. Yorick is a virtuoso of the nervous system, conjuring up both tears and blushes with a facility which testifies less to his goodness of heart than to his incorrigible instinct for self-dramatization. Sterne's masterpiece, ▷ *Tristram Shandy* (1760–7) is another teasing work whose success transformed Sterne from an obscure Yorkshire clergyman into a leading literary celebrity, but whose eccentricities have divided critical opinion ever since. Johnson declared 'nothing odd will do long; *Tristram Shandy* did not last', but a formalist critic in our own century has asserted that '*Tristram Shandy* is the most typical novel of world literature'.

'In a word, my work is digressive, and it is progressive too, – and at the same time', announces Tristram in the book's first volume. It is significant that he puts the word 'digressive' first. With its black and marbled pages, its flash-backs and interpolations, its asterisks, blanks and dashes, *Tristram Shandy* is a novel which denies any conventional notions of narrative development. The first four volumes take place while Tristram, the hero/narrator, is still in the womb, and the book ends before it begins. Yet this work, which seems to break all the rules, and which consistently demonstrates the inability of rules, plans, theories and systems to cope with the accidents and vagaries of human life, is nevertheless held together by a curious pseudo-logic of its own. This is the absurd determinism of the association of ideas, as expressed in ▷ Locke's ▷ *Essay Concerning*

Human Understanding (1690), which Tristram describes as 'a history-book of what passes in a man's own mind'. Each of Sterne's characters, Walter, Toby and Trim, is locked in his own private world of associations; their conversations present the collisions of words rather than the communication of thoughts; their actions are all bounded by accident.

Beside the inventiveness of Sterne, the more conventional comic skills of ▷ Tobias Smollett may seem stolid and predictable. Trained as a surgeon, Smollett published his first, and some would say his best, novel, ▷ *Roderick Random*, in 1748, when he was still only twenty-six. Like all Smollett's novels, this work is a robust ▷ picaresque, episodic in form, slapstick in humour and brisk in pace. Some of its best moments are autobiographical, drawing on Smollett's own experience as a ship's surgeon. His next novel, ▷ *Peregrine Pickle* (1751), also has a nautical flavour, with its collection of old sea-dog characters such as Commodore Hawser Trunnion and the peg-legged Lieutenant Hatchway. His final novel, ▷ *Humphry Clinker* (1771), is epistolary in form though the tone owes more to Fielding than to Richardson. In it a group of assorted characters including the irascible old valetudinarian Matthew Bramble and a Methodist coachman Humphry Clinker (who turns out to be Bramble's son) make a grand tour of Britain from Bristol, Bath and London, to Edinburgh and the Highlands, presenting us with a broad panorama of eighteenth-century society. The idiomatic clashes of the different letter-writing styles provide a constant humorous tone, and the book is rich in comic misadventures, though the plot itself is highly derivative. As one recent critic has written, 'it is as though Tom Jones has given way to Baedeker'.

The other fictional form which enjoyed considerable popularity in the later decades of the century was the ▷ Gothic novel. In terms of the market place, the date at which the Richardsonian novel of moral instruction began to give way to the Gothic novel of crepuscular phantoms can be pin-pointed with some accuracy. In 1777 Clara Reeve published a novel called *The Champion of Virtue*, a title which clearly suggests a continuation of Richardsonian preoccupations. The following year, however, she reissued the same novel in a revised form and with a new title, *The Old English Baron, A Gothic Story*, evidently attempting to exploit the new trend in public tastes. However, the origins of the Gothic novel are usually traced back to ▷ Horace Walpole's ▷ *The Castle of Otranto* (1764), a self-indulgent fantasy of fake medievalism which deliberately revels in its extravagant use of supernatural and 'marvellous' elements. One recent critic (Pat Rogers) has written: '*The Castle of Otranto* is preposterous; its setting is Hollywood-medieval, a Ruritanian version of chivalric times. Its plot is frankly incredible, jumpily constructed and flatly recounted'. Yet much of the novel's overt implausibility is a calculated device to move away from the classical symmetries and rational morality of Augustan literature. Walpole was a fashionable dilettante whose spirit of whimsicality led him to create his 'little Gothic castle' at Strawberry Hill, and also inspired this little Gothic tale. Like the young ill-fated poet ▷ Thomas Chatterton, who passed off his 'Rowley' poems as genuine medieval manuscripts, and the fraudulent

▷ James Macpherson who claimed to be 'translating' his pastiche Celtic epic ▷ *Ossian*, Walpole at first maintained a pretence that *The Castle of Otranto* was an authentic medieval story. For all of these writers, medievalism was a kind of fancy-dress, enabling them to evade the sober responsibilities of neo-classical literary forms and indulge their imaginations in a world of supernatural fantasy. For the Gothic novel entailed a reversal or rejection of many classical values. Instead of Pope's cherished landscape of 'Nature methodiz'd' with its well-proportioned country houses and Palladian villas, the Gothic landscape consists of dark forests and ruined castles, with gloomy dungeons and secret labyrinthine passageways. In place of the daylight world of rational debate and urbane ironies, Gothic fiction presents a nightmare world of torture and fantasies, irrational fears, ancient curses and nameless threats.

Gothic fiction can be divided into two broad categories, the novel of terror and the novel of horror. Practitioners of the novel of terror, from Clara Reeve to ▷ Ann Radcliffe, were interested in using the Gothic form as a means of exploring the psychology of fear. In her most famous novel, ▷ *The Mysteries of Udolpho* (1794), Radcliffe described the effect of terror on the mind. 'A terror of this nature, as it occupies and expands the mind, and elevates it to a high expectation, is purely sublime, and leads us, by a kind of fascination, to seek even the object from which we appear to shrink.' Echoing here some of the sentiments in ▷ Burke's treatise *On the Sublime and the Beautiful* (1759), Radcliffe also demonstrates an affinity with ▷ Wordsworth who, in ▷ *The Prelude* (1799–1805), describes how he 'grew up/Fostered alike by beauty and by fear'. In fact all of the apparently supernatural phenomena in Radcliffe's novels turn out to have perfectly rational, if somewhat contrived, explanations; the ghostly, diabolic presences that haunt her heroines are invariably products of illusionist trickery working on terrified imaginations. Unlike some other Gothic writers, Radcliffe has a perfect control of her plots, and part of the appeal of her novels lies in the ingenuity with which she supplies psychologically convincing explanations for the most apparently mysterious events. Nor is this merely a thriller-writer's gimmick. Radcliffe is interested in the gradations of intimidation and characteristically explores two related levels of fear. The abbeys, castles, dungeons and convents where her heroines find themselves are always reputedly cursed or haunted. Consequently when nocturnal apparitions occur, her heroines are thrown into the kind of superstitious dread satirized by Jane Austen in *Northanger Abbey* (published 1818). But typically, in the morning these imaginary terrors are replaced by a yet more insidious fear, as the heroines gradually realize that they are at the mercy not of ghosts and goblins, but of malevolent human beings. It is some indication of the popularity of Gothic fiction that Radcliffe earned £500 for *The Mysteries of Udolpho*, whereas Jane Austen was paid only £10 for her parody of the genre in *Northanger Abbey*.

A good example of the novel of horror is ▷ Matthew 'Monk' Lewis's *The Monk* (1796), which ▷ Byron described as representing 'the philtered ideas of a jaded voluptuary'. In this extravagant sadistic fantasy Lewis exploits all the charnel-house images that have since become the clichés of Hammer horror films. His heroine, Agnes, having been separated from her lover, is condemned to perpetual incarceration among rotting corpses in the vaults beneath her convent. With undisguised relish Lewis pictures bloated toads and slimy lizards crawling across her flesh, and describes how, on waking, Agnes would often find 'my fingers ringed with the long worms which bred in the corrupted flesh of my infant'. The monk Ambrosio, the villain of the novel, crowns a career of vice by raping and killing Antonia, a fifteen-year-old girl, among these rotting bodies in the vault, having already murdered her mother Elvira. In order to escape the soldiers of the Inquisition, Ambrosio sells his soul to the Devil, who transports him to a mountain peak. There, before being hurled to his death, he is told that Elvira was in fact his mother, and Antonia his sister. Yet this conclusion is less a form of moral retribution, than a final gloating irony in this lurid sensationalist tale.

Loosely based on Arabian sources, ▷ William Beckford's *Vathek* (French edition 1782, English edition 1787) is another orgiastic tale of hedonism, sorcery and murder, that culminates in damnation. Although Beckford's work, like Lewis's, is filled with a self-indulgent horror, this aspect of Gothic fiction also has its serious side. Throughout the Gothic literature of the late eighteenth and early nineteenth centuries, writers as diverse as Beckford, ▷ James Hogg (*The Private Memoirs and Confessions of a Justified Sinner*, 1824) and ▷ Mary Shelley (▷ *Frankenstein*, 1817) explored Faustian themes and Satanic images that represented the dark side of ▷ Enlightenment thought.

Non-fictional prose

Modern critical tastes have tended to value fiction above other kinds of prose writing, but in the eighteenth century this was not always the case. Many of the century's most gifted prose stylists wrote not novels but histories and ▷ biographies, essays, travel books and letters. Apart from the fact that many novels were written in epistolary form and that several of Pope's satires were couched in the form of epistles, the familiar letter was itself a well respected literary genre. Pope felt no more compunction about altering and polishing his personal correspondence for publication than he did about revising and changing his different versions of the ▷ *Rape of the Lock* or the ▷ *Dunciad*. For him, these letters were less autobiographical documents than parts of his literary *oeuvre*, to be edited and revised in the same way as any other work. Among the more notable letter-writers of the period were ▷ Lady Mary Wortley Montagu, ▷ Horace Walpole and the ▷ Earl of Chesterfield. Montagu's letters are witty, jaunty and civilized, with just an edge of malicious satire to give them bite. They reflect a life of rich variety; at the age of seven, Montagu was the infant favourite of the ▷ Kit-Cat Club; during her marriage she travelled throughout Europe and Turkey, finally retiring to live in Italy. Her letters are full of perceptive comments on the customs of the countries she visits, always animated by a tone of self-deprecating irony. Thus to one correspondent she comments, 'this letter is as long and as dull as any of Richardson's!'.

Horace Walpole was a prolific and assiduous letter writer, of whom it has been said that he organized his life to suit the needs of his correspondence. Self-consciously arranging both the occasions and the recipients of each letter, Walpole constructed a correspondence which suggests a life devoted to the delivery of *bon mots* and an experience translated into a seamless sequence of anecdotes. The Earl of Chesterfield's letters have fared least well with later readers. Their complacent tone of worldly wisdom seems designed to recommend a life of superficial elegance at the expense of more serious or humane concerns. Yet Chesterfield's notions of civilized life derive from a tradition initiated by *The Spectator* and his constant stress upon politeness and the social graces offers a useful insight into a significant strand of eighteenth-century thought.

Among biographers ▷ James Boswell still holds pride of place. Although later scholars have revealed his *Life of Samuel Johnson* (1791) to be full of distortions and omissions, its quality of animation, dramatizing Johnson's oracular wit and sober sentiments in a lively series of encounters and anecdotes, captures much of his relish for conversation, for disputation and for life. Boswell's own journals, though full of the vanity of self-display, stand alongside ▷ Samuel Pepys's *Diary* and Swift's *Journal to Stella* as fascinating portraits of the day-to-day excitement of social life; all of these works weave together intimate private dramas with vivid representations of social and public issues.

Perhaps least often read now are the great works of Augustan scholarship; ▷ Edward Gibbon's ▷ *The Decline and Fall of the Roman Empire* (1776–88), the philosophical writings of ▷ Locke and ▷ Hume, ▷ Burke and ▷ Adam Smith. All of these in their different ways share certain humanist assumptions that are common to the literature of the period. Although each pursuing a separate discipline of study, these authors thought of their works not as specialist treatises for students, but as philosophical essays designed for the educated general reader. While never amateurish or condescending, they are works which, in both style and tone, assume the centrality of their concerns to human culture as a whole. As such they are expressions of that Enlightenment spirit which sought to promote the pursuit of knowledge not in the sheltered confines of universities and colleges, but in the coffee-houses, clubs and country houses of a civilized society. Johnson gave memorable expression to such sentiments. At the conclusion of the preface to his *Dictionary of the English Language* he writes: 'it may gratify curiosity to inform it that the *English Dictionary* was written with little assistance of the learned, and without any patronage of the great; not in the soft obscurities of retirement, or under the shelter of academic bowers, but amidst inconvenience and distraction, in sickness and in sorrow'. The name of Johnson has recurred several times throughout this essay, and that is hardly surprising. No one better exemplifies the achievements and anxieties, the triumphs and tribulations of the professional writer of his day. Johnson turned the life of writing into a kind of moral struggle against bigotry and ignorance, against poverty, prejudice and pretensions. Some of his more celebrated utterances may appear dogmatic or prescriptive, but this is a false impression resulting in part from Boswell's creation of him as a man of maxims. In fact, the most enduring characteristic of Johnson's writing is its tolerance in the patient exploration of the complexities and fallibilities of human nature. In his ▷ *Lives of the Poets* (1779–81) he combines balanced judgements with personal pronouncements, in assessing the writers of his own and the previous age. In ▷ *Rasselas* (1759) and in the *Vanity of Human Wishes* (1749), he explores that 'hunger of the imagination' which both fuels the creative impulse, and leads to the inevitable insufficiency of human desires. In his *Preface to Shakespeare* (1765) he articulates literary axioms which lie at the heart of Augustan humanism (and which, incidentally, help to explain his disparagement of *Tristram Shandy*): 'nothing can please many and please long, but just representations of general nature'.

Having begun this essay with Johnson's defence of writing for personal gain, it seems appropriate to end it with his definition of literature's public responsibilities. 'The only end of writing,' he declared, 'is to enable the readers better to enjoy life, or better to endure it.'

William Maw Egley *Omnibus Life in London*

The nineteenth-century novel 5

Background: Authors, readers and publishers

It is a commonplace of modern criticism that the nineteenth century – or perhaps more specifically the Victorian age – was dominated by the novel. 'Fiction' is the word which sits naturally, in literary terms, with ▷ 'Victorian', in the same way that poetry does with ▷ 'Romantic' or drama with ▷ 'Restoration'. It is not only that the century produced a consistent stream of indisputably major practitioners of the form, (a conservative listing of whom would need to include ▷ Jane Austen, ▷ Charles Dickens, ▷ William Thackeray, ▷ Charlotte and Emily Brontë, ▷ George Eliot, ▷ Thomas Hardy and ▷ Henry James, a total difficult to match for a single genre in any other century); more significant, perhaps, is the strength in depth, the immense range and variety of interest to be found amongst novelists of less settled reputation. Fiction in the nineteenth century could and did address every topic, enter every dispute, reflect every ideal of an age perceived by those who lived through it to be one of unprecedentedly rapid change. 'Novels are in the hands of us all; from the Prime Minister down to the last appointed scullery-maid,' wrote ▷ Anthony Trollope in 1870. And of the novels they could have chosen from (an estimated 40,000 titles published in the course of the nineteenth century), an extraordinarily large number have remained in the common currency of popular rather than scholarly reading habits.

The reasons for this enduring popularity are naturally difficult to pin down; and one immediate answer – that such writers as the Brontës and Dickens are still widely read because they are said to have written good novels – must be considered. But this explanation begs the more interesting question of what exactly is a 'good' novel. ▷ Shakespeare and ▷ Wordsworth, for example, both major influences on most nineteenth-century writers, are not read by the general public to the same extent or for the same reasons as Victorian novelists of considerably lesser claims. There is of course a sense in which the novel is more approachable than drama or poetry. It addresses itself directly to 'life', without the intervening artistic medium of verse or dramatic form, in a way which other literary genres do not. It tells stories, reworks the mundane material of everyday life into something significant, and (most nineteenth-century readers would add) it teaches moral lessons. More interestingly, perhaps, it could be argued that the nineteenth-century novel is the first art form to deal explicitly and realistically with issues which speak directly to some of the central concerns of twentieth-century consciousness.

The novels of this period sprang from a society undergoing a more massive upheaval under the influence of industrialization than in any previous era. Not only was the population shifting irrevocably from an agricultural to an urban base, with all the profound changes in social, working and family patterns that this entailed; there were also the dramatic visible changes resulting from technological invention which altered people's perceptions and their world. The railway boom of the 1840s did not merely affect the landscape; its more profound repurcussions lay in revolutionizing expectations of speed, mobility and permanence. When in ▷ *Dombey and Son* (1847–48) Dickens describes 'the first great shock of the earthquake' which the building of the railway brings, he is expressing a now familiar paradox inherent in such change: 'from the very core of all this dire disorder, [the railway] trailed smoothly away, upon its mighty course of civilisation and improvement'. The chaotic but humane little community of Staggs's Gardens has been 'cut up root and branch' to make way for the 'crowds of people and mountains of goods' to be shifted by the railway: the individual and the idiosyncratic have been sacrificed to the corporate and the homogeneous. ▷ Thomas Carlyle's famous definition of this period as 'the Mechanical Age' focussed the anxieties of many contemporaries about the relationship of the individual to society. 'Men are grown mechanical in head and in heart, as well as in hand,' wrote Carlyle, and the development and preservation of individuality within a society dominated by various kinds of mechanistic systems (moral, social, political, economic, even historical) formed a major theme of fiction throughout the century.

However, whereas Carlyle's mechanized individual is tacitly assumed to be a man, the novel of this period belongs in certain crucial respects to women. Not only were women the major consumers of fiction, forming as they did the majority of the readership throughout the century; they were also, to a degree never seen previously, producers as well. Women novelists take equal status with men both as generally acknowledged 'great writers' (fifty per cent of our earlier listing of major novelists were women) and also as part of the huge array of novel writers who produced everything from minor master-pieces to worthless pot-boilers. In the first two decades of the century Jane Austen was writing novels of sophisticated realism, while ▷ Mary Shelley's ▷ *Frankenstein* (1817) was to become the definitive ▷ Gothic romance. Throughout the period, writers like ▷ Charlotte Yonge, ▷ Elizabeth Gaskell, ▷ Harriet Martineau, ▷ Ouida and ▷ Margaret Oliphant were producing novels ranging from serious social comment to wild sensationalism. And in the 1890s the single most popular novelist (though very far from the best) was another woman, ▷ Marie Corelli, whose *The Sorrows of Satan* (1895) sold more copies than any previous English novel. The subject matter of fiction, moreover, fell characteristically into a woman's sphere: even in novels whose thematic interests lie primarily elsewhere, the standard plot and setting were almost invariably domestic and family-orientated, with courtship and marriage providing a major part of the narrative thrust. As George Eliot pointed out, the novel form, more than any other, offered opportunities to women in a society which elsewhere constrained their every activity: 'No restrictions can shut women out from the materials of fiction, and there is no species of art which is so free from rigid requirements.' The nineteenth-century novel was the first art form in which women could take equal status with men.

For George Eliot, though, as for many others, the unusually dominant role of women as both producers and consumers of fiction was not an unequivocally good thing. Her comments are taken from an essay entitled 'Silly Novels by Lady Novelists', in which she draws attention to the self-gratifying and unreal stereotypes which the lady novelists offer to an uncritical female readership. In other respects, too, this female orientation had an unfortunate influence on the sphere of the English novel. The popular picture of the Victorian *pater familias* reading out suitable material to his devoted family was not far from the truth and was felt by many practising novelists to be a major restriction on their art. Dickens's Miss Podsnap in ▷ *Our Mutual Friend* (1864–65), the archetypal 'young person', placed a crippling constraint on the material thought proper for inclusion in the novel: 'The question about everything was, would it bring a blush into the cheek of the young person? And the inconvenience of the young person was, that, according to Mr Podsnap, she seemed liable to burst into blushes when there was no need at all.' As Thackeray lamented in his preface to ▷ *Pendennis* (1848–50): 'Since the author of 'Tom Jones' was buried, no writer of fiction among us has been permitted to depict to his utmost power a MAN'; where ▷ Henry Fielding was at liberty to portray a lovable male libertine, Thackeray and his contemporaries looked constantly over their shoulders for the blushes of the young person and the pursed lips of that mythical guardian of morality, Mrs Grundy. This provided a field of tacit warfare throughout the century: where Trollope recorded complacently that 'no girl has risen from the reading of my pages less modest than she was before', other novelists, such as the popular ▷ feminist writer of the 1890s Mona Caird, chafed furiously against such artificial restraints: 'Mrs Grundy in black silk, with a sceptre in her hand, on the throne of the Ages, surrounded by an angel-choir of Young Persons! Is this to be the end of our democracy?'

Thus for a large part of the nineteenth century the English novel was significantly limited by the necessity to conform to a moral code which aimed to protect a predominantly female readership from exposure to sexual corruption. Extreme circumspection was required in the depiction of any sort of sexual contact, whether in or outside marriage, often with ludicrous results. Jane Eyre's unusually frank accounts of her feelings for Mr Rochester (which included the confession that she had sat on his knee prior to marrying him) brought accusations of coarseness from several critics. The scene in Hardy's ▷ *Tess of the D'Urbervilles* (1891) in which Angel Clare carries the milkmaids across a flooded lane had to be altered to expunge the image of a man lifting a personable young lady in his arms: in the serialized version, Clare had to be equipped with a wheelbarrow. And in broader terms, too, the novel upheld middle-class morality in matters of sexual conduct. Women were to be pure, and morally superior to men; marriage was for life; sex was unmentionable. Where a novel depicted deviation from these values, the appropriate moral lesson had to be firmly underlined, so that the 'fallen woman' who features in so much fiction of the period was invariably seen to be punished. ▷ Mrs Henry Wood's melodramatic and best-selling tale of adultery, *East Lynne* (1861), rammed home these lessons with almost sadistic relish, warning potential adulteresses that their fate 'will be found far worse than death' and proving the point with a story of startlingly ingenious retributive suffering. More commonly, the fallen woman was brought to a dramatic death (like Lady Dedlock in ▷ *Bleak House*) or banished (like ▷ *David Copperfield*'s Little Em'ly). Even in a work which pleaded for the moral rights of the fallen woman, such as Elizabeth Gaskell's ▷ *Ruth* (1853), the sinner had to be removed from society by the end of the novel.

This circumspection had a more profound and potentially damaging effect on the portrayal of women in the nineteenth-century novel than it did on the representation of men. Thackeray was to some extent right to envy Fielding his Tom Jones, but he might have done better to regret his own inability to portray a Moll Flanders. Ironically, it was Thackeray himself who in ▷ *Vanity Fair* (1847–48) encapsulated the Victorian double vision of women which was seen by many nineteenth-century commentators to characterize contemporary attitudes. In Amelia Sedley he satirizes the good woman of conventional ideals, destructively doting and cloyingly sentimental, passive, long-suffering and ultimately parasitical; in Becky Sharp he portrays a woman of wit and initiative, who uses her sexuality and intelligence to exploit a society richly deserving her machinations, but who must finally be condemned as a neglectful mother, adulteress and, possibly, a murderer. Charlotte Brontë's ▷ *Shirley* (1849) explicitly attacks this male polarizing of supposed female attributes: 'Men are often under an illusion about women: they do not read them in a true light: they misapprehend them, both for good and evil: their good woman is a queer thing, half doll, half angel; their bad woman always a fiend.' The bad woman, as we have seen, was habitually disposed of by death; but it was the good woman, half doll, half angel, who forms the common twentieth-century conception of the typical Victorian heroine. Dickens's Agnes Wickfield, who in David Copperfield's image of her is 'forever pointing upward', is a typical role model for the sort of female perfection which is morally impeccable, spiritually uplifting and a well-earned reward for the world-weary hero. It was an ideal whose falsity was under constant attack throughout the period and which was largely discredited by the end of the century: in ▷ Havelock Ellis's phrase, the stereotyped woman was 'a cross between an angel and an idiot'.

How, then, did what now appears such a patently distorted view of women retain such a hold in fictional conventions? We must not dismiss out of hand the notion that Victorian portrayals of women are more reflective of their repression in reality than we would care to believe. ▷ George Gissing argued that women actually were intellectually and developmentally feebler than men, when in typically gloomy mood he stated that 'more than half the misery of life is due to the ignorance and childishness of women. The average woman pretty closely resembles . . . the average male *idiot*.' In a society which, for the greater part of the century, denied women access to higher education and the professions, encased them physically in whalebone and voluminous skirts, and imbued them with the notion that their highest function was to serve and inspire men, it is little wonder that the conformist woman of the time should appear to modern eyes an unacceptably compliant creature – or, as Edmund Carpenter (1844–1929) more waspishly expressed it, 'a bundle of weak and flabby sentiments, combined with a wholly undeveloped brain'. However, there is ample evidence from both the numerous examples of independent and rebellious women of nineteenth-century history, and from the many original and individualized heroines of fiction, that the conventional ideal was not the whole reality. More pervasively influential on characterization, as well as on the form and content of novels, were the actual conditions under which most of them were published.

At the beginning of the nineteenth century, the majority of novels were published in three, or sometimes four, volumes and the 'three decker' retained its popularity until almost the end of the Victorian period. The standard cost of each volume of the novel was half a guinea, a stiff enough price for most middle-class readers and beyond the means of the working class. However, for a subscription of one guinea a year, readers could borrow a volume at a time from one of the ▷ circulating libraries, by far the most influential of which was ▷ Charles Mudie's, opened in 1842. Mudie exercised an influence over the Victorian novel which amounted to a form of ▷ censorship, for he prided himself upon selecting his stock according to its suitability for family consumption. Just as Mudie's moral approval of an author, which could translate into mass buying of copies from the publisher and advance orders for future works, could launch a career in fiction, so his refusal to stock a novel of dubious morality could spell financial disaster. Few novelists could afford the risk of offending the circulating libraries and thus a form of guilty self-censorship constrained the creative freedom of most writers.

Alternatives to publication in three-volume form were initiated by the revival of the monthly serialization of Dickens's ▷ *Pickwick Papers* in 1836. Novels published in this manner were issued as slim volumes appearing at the beginning of each month, continuing as a rule for nineteen numbers. Clearly this form of publication deeply influenced the form of works in a way largely obscured by their subsequent appearance in a single volume. Writers who wished their readers to continue buying their work over a long period had to end each issue with some form of cliff-hanging incentive to purchase the next volume, and needed also to ensure the memorability of characters whose last appearance could have occurred several months earlier. This may in part account for what is now sometimes taken to be a melodramatic form of plotting and exaggeration in characterization on the part of such habitual practioners of the monthly serial as Dickens or Thackeray. On the other hand, publication in parts did allow a writer to adjust his or her work in response to readers' preferences: a popular character could boost sales (as Sam Weller did for *Pickwick*) and a narrative red herring could be expeditiously abandoned. As single volume serialization gradually gave way to part publication in family and literary magazines, the questions of sales and censorship moved from the author's to the editor's domain. Hardy was one of the prime sufferers from editorial restraint in his initial serial publication of novels, and frequently had to wait for one-volume publication before he was able to present his work in the form intended. Both Dickens and Thackeray had experience of the business from both ends, the first as editorial instigator of the family weeklies ▷ *Household Words* and ▷ *All the Year Round*, the second as editor of the prestigious ▷ *Cornhill*. Amongst major Victorian novelists, only the Brontës never published in any sort of serial form.

Development through the century

Given the wealth and variety of nineteenth-century fiction, as well as the inevitable historical shifts in critical judgements, it is hardly surprising to find widely diverging assessments of how the novel developed over the period. ▷ George Saintsbury's *A History of Nineteenth-century Literature*, first published in 1896, gives almost as much space to ▷ Maria Edgeworth as to Jane Austen and George Eliot, and treats ▷ Walter Scott more fully than Dickens: Hardy receives no mention at all. ▷ F. R. Leavis's immensely influential *The Great Tradition* (1948) opens with the character- istically combative statement that 'The great English novelists are Jane Austen, George Eliot, Henry James and Joseph Conrad'; Charlotte Brontë is noted as having 'permanent interest of a minor kind', Dickens as being a 'great entertainer' who lacks 'sustained seriousness'. While few modern critics would wish to eliminate from the canon these four writers, con- temporary interest in the nineteenth-century novel ranges far beyond his vaguely defined but insistently urged criterion of 'significant creative achievement'. Individual writers and sub-genres of the novels which would have been relegated to areas of minor interest by many mid-twentieth- century critics now attract serious study, and the reputations of many well- known novelists have notably shifted. Of those most highly regarded in the nineteenth century itself, Scott and ▷ George Meredith have suffered the most serious depression in critical interest; neither is now much read by the general public or widely taught on literature degrees. Dickens, on the other hand, has been reclaimed from the realm of mere entertainer and praised as an incisive social critic of profound symbolic significance. And Hardy, ignored by Saintsbury and patronizingly dismissed by Leavis, now commands as wide a critical industry on both sides of the Atlantic as any nineteenth- century novelist.

There is no simple way of subdividing the mass of fictional material published during the period, nor, despite Leavis's claim for a great tradition, is there any single line of development which can easily be traced. Conventionally, the pre-Victorian period, where the major figures are Scott and Jane Austen, is seen as having a separate identity, which then gives way to the explosion of talent in the first decades of Victoria's reign, with the emergence of Dickens, Thackerary and the Brontës. The mid-Victorian novel can be seen as dominated by the later Dickens and George Eliot, and the late-nineteenth century by Hardy. These periods will be dealt with separately in conjunction with the major authors within them. However, to identify the major practitioners of the form during the period is very far from finding a consistent train of development. While there is a sense in which James's novels can be seen as a more self-consciously artistic development of Jane Austen's fictional mode, there is no obvious way in which Hardy may be said to emerge from the same tradition. Charlotte Brontë, notoriously, found little to admire in Jane Austen, and Hardy recorded that he was unable to finish reading ▷ *Wuthering Heights* (1847). Arguably, the nineteenth century saw the emergence in the novel of a privileging of 'realism', both in the presentation of psychological depth of characterization and in the depiction of humankind's inevitable inter-relation with the newly perceived complexities of social and historical contexts. There is also a clear change, in the Victorian period at least, in the material thought permissible for inclusion in the novel. The tyranny of the circulating libraries and the family magazines was gradually eroded to allow greater frankness in the fictional portrayal of sexuality. By the 1890s outspokenness on questions of sexual behaviour – particularly in women – had become to some extent fashionable, and a host of popular novels which examined such questions in an overtly polemical manner enjoyed a brief vogue. Even so, the violently antagonistic reception of Hardy's ▷ *Jude the Obscure* (1895), which saw the novel reviled in the press and burnt by a bishop, showed how severely limited this increased tolerance could be.

More importantly, an attempt to treat nineteenth-century fiction as a smoothly developing series of 'great writers' severely distorts the picture of the novel as it would have been viewed by both readers and authors during the period itself. It ignores too much of what was seriously offered and received by contemporary writers and readers, and which is now the subject of increasing critical interest, both as reflections of the nineteenth-century consciousness and as significant and legitimate variations on the novel form. Late-twentieth-century taste is perhaps more open to the claims of romance and fantasy, more sympathetically interested in the overt wrestling with ideas, than was the case when Leavis made high moral seriousness and mastery of form his main criteria of excellence. Minor novelists, and the sub-genres in which they frequently wrote, are an essential and illuminating part of the nineteenth-century fictional scene.

Sub-genres of the novel

During the early decades of the nineteenth century most popular fiction grew out of the traditions of romance and romanticism. The two terms are of course closely linked, but should not be equated. A romance, in David Masson's phrase of 1859, was 'a fictitious narrative . . . the interest of which turns upon marvellous and uncommon incidents', and the debate between romance and realism formed a continuous part of nineteenth-century thinking about the theory of fiction. The influence of the romantic movement was most apparent in the late-eighteenth-century Gothic novel (▷ Gothic revival), a form not lacking in marvellous and uncommon incidents, but which also played on the romantic interest in the supernatural and in the dark and untapped areas of the human psyche. Jane Austen, writing novels of pragmatic realism during the height of the romantic period, mercilessly satirized the implausibility of the Gothic through the credulous Catherine of ▷ *Northanger Abbey* (1818), and neatly pinned down the possible self-indulgence of the romantic sensibility in ▷ *Persuasion*'s Captain Brandon. ▷ Thomas Love Peacock's spoof Gothic novel, ▷ *Nightmare Abbey* (1818), also lampooned the form as well as parodying the romantic excesses of some of that movement's major poets. But the Gothic was still kept vividly alive in Mary Shelley's *Frankenstein* (1817), published in the same year as Peacock's parody, and reappears, subtly transformed, in the works of Charlotte and Emily Brontë. It could also be argued that the historical novel, first popularized by Scott, and continued less successfully in the works of, for example, ▷ Harrison Ainsworth, owed much to the romantic and Gothic preoccupation with the past.

In many ways, though, it was romance rather than romanticism which informed the main sub-genres of the first three decades of the nineteenth century. Writers of popular fiction were concerned to entertain their readers with dramatic incidents and to draw them imaginatively into worlds remote from their own. The historical novel could obviously offer limitless scope here, in terms both of high drama and (often ponderously academic) period detail. Where Ainsworth's novels catered to the contemporary taste for luridly reconstructed English history, one of the other popular practitioners of the form, Edward Bulwer (▷ Lytton), mainly remembered now for *The Last Days of Pompeii* (1834), took the wider sweep of western historical movements as his subject. His historical romances tend to focus on the closing of eras, and may thus be seen as signifying contemporary unease in the face of change and instability. But his writings are too clogged with the fruits of meticulous historical research, and too stilted in the rendering of dialogue, to have lasted well. However, forms of the historical novel continued to be practised throughout the century by major as well as minor writers. George Eliot ventured into historical fiction, not wholly successfully, in ▷ *Romola*, and it is a fact often overlooked by modern readers that large numbers of major Victorian novels are 'historical' in the sense of being set some thirty to forty years before their date of publication.

The historical novel could be both an escape from and a comment on the profound changes which were perceived to be occurring in the contemporary social order. Of less obvious relevance were the other popular sub-genres of the early nineteenth century, the ▷ Newgate novel and the ▷ silver-fork school. The Newgate novel played on morbid tastes for violence and death in ways which relate it to some extent to the Gothic, and in romanticizing its criminals it removed such socially disruptive elements safely into the realm of fantasy. The silver-fork school, on the other hand, displayed the sort of high society life to which increasingly prosperous members of the middle class might hope to aspire and which they could certainly be expected to envy. Novels of this class paraded details of the food, fashions and furniture of the rich and well-bred before a readership which could now begin to dream of emulating such manners. Writers of silver-fork fiction included ▷ Benjamin Disraeli in his early novel *Vivian Grey* (1826), and the now largely forgotten Theodore Hook (1788–1841) and ▷ Catherine Gore. Both Dickens and Thackeray capture and to some degree satirize the mood of envious interest amongst the socially mobile on which these novels played, Thackeray in his portrayal of the *nouveaux riches* Osborne and Sedley families in *Vanity Fair*, Dickens, for example, in his parody 'The Lady Flabella' in ▷ *Nicholas Nickleby* or with the Veneerings in ▷ *Our Mutual Friend*. Interestingly, both the Newgate and silver-fork forms have modern counterparts in popular fiction of the 1980s in what have been neatly designated the 'bodice-ripping' school of historical fiction (in which sex replaces death as the focus) and the 'sex-and-shopping' novel which caters for the emulative dreams of the upwardly mobile.

Of more immediate social relevance, however, as well as in general possessing more lasting literary merit, were the novels which addressed the 'condition of England' question. These works, also known as 'social problem' novels, arose out of the social and political upheavals which followed the ▷ Reform Act of 1832. The 1830s and 1840s marked the beginnings of a conscious effort both by Parliament and by social commentators to address the problems caused by the rapid industrialization of the preceding decades. The first Factory Act and the ▷ Poor Law Amendment Act of 1834 reflected the stirrings of governmental conscience and, from the other side, the rise of ▷ Chartism marked the beginnings of concerted working-class demands for reform. The economic depression of the 1840s produced deprivation amongst the industrial workers of the north on a scale which could not be ignored, and Chartist riots and marches on Westminster made poverty and disaffection visibly threatening to the comparatively untouched middle-class southerner. It was Carlyle who first drew attention to the social effects of the ▷ industrial revolution in his essay 'Signs of the Times' (1829) and who, in coining the phrase 'condition of England question' in *Chartism* (1839), provided a focus for what to many novelists of the early Victorian period seemed to be the central matter for fiction. Writers like Elizabeth Gaskell, Disraeli, ▷ Charles Kingsley and the Dickens of ▷ *Hard Times* (1854), addressed themselves directly to the question and produced novels which dealt realistically and sympathetically with the problems of the industrialized working class.

Probably the major strength of the social problem novel lay in its educational rather than its polemical function. Written by and for the middle classes, these novels laid out with passionate clarity the plight of a section of the community of which most readers, for geographical and social reasons, were simply ignorant. The new cities of the north of England, where industrial workers were herded into hastily erected housing built round smoke-belching factories, were uncharted territory for large parts of the novel-reading public, and the divisive effects of such developments were repeatedly stressed by novelists. In giving his 'condition of England' novel

▷ *Sybil* (1845) the sub-title 'The Two Nations', Disraeli encapsulated his perception of a country tragically and dangerously split between rich and poor, and Elizabeth Gaskell's ▷ *North and South* (1854–5) explores the differences in values and living conditions between the two halves of the country. The vividly realistic descriptions of working-class life provided by many social problem novels were as educative to contemporary readers as to later social historians, and the pressing issues of Chartism, ▷ trade unions, strikes and master-worker relations receive sensitive if rarely revolutionary treatment in such novels as Gaskell's ▷ *Mary Barton* (1848), Kingsley's *Alton Locke* (1850) and Disraeli's *Sybil*. Dickens's *Hard Times*, the only one of his novels to be set exclusively in the north of England, contrasts the mechanistic, and as he sees them, inhuman principles of ▷ utilitarian philosophy with the personal and warm-hearted values of imaginative sympathy, and his handling of the question of solidarity amongst the factory hands is symptomatic of the ambivalence apparently inherent in the genre. His working-class protagonist, Stephen Blackpool, is a saintly victim, his union leader a blustering agitator and the men good-hearted innocents temporarily swayed into an unworthy form of protest against a system portrayed as patently wrong. Blackpool's repeated lament in the face of bafflingly obvious injustice, ''Tis all a muddle', sums up the helplessness of worker and novelist alike in the face of the enormity of the problem.

Indeed, the one major criticism of the genre, levelled by contemporaries as well as by modern critics, was that it proffered inadequate and often sentimental solutions to questions of great social and political complexity. As Thackeray put it, 'At the conclusion of these tales . . . there somehow arrives a misty reconciliation between the poor and the rich; a prophecy is uttered of better times for the one, and better manners in the other . . . and the characters make their bow, grinning, in a group, as they do at the end of a drama when the curtain falls.' This is largely true of the novels mentioned: the symbolic handshake between master and man at the end of *North and South*, Mary Barton's escape to Canada with her newly wed husband, or Stephen Blackpool's martyrdom in the cause of truth and understanding, all substitute reconciliation at a personal level for long-term political solutions. However, there is no reason to expect novelists to be in possession of answers which escaped legislators, whereas in articulating and making imaginatively immediate the social problems of the time, writers of the 'condition of England' novels not only provided a valuable information service but also produced works of significant realism and insight.

The social condition of a newly industrialized Britian was a preoccupation of novelists mainly during the 1840s and 1850s. During the same period the spiritual condition of the country also became of pressing concern and novels dealing with religious questions formed another recognizable sub-genre which retained its currency to the end of the century. In some sense all nineteenth-century novels are 'religious' in so far as they are the product of a society in which Christian observance was the norm amongst the middle classes, and thus the moral and spiritual values of Christianity are necessarily either implicit in or deliberately explored by all writers of fiction. However, the crisis of faith which arose in the middle decades of the nineteenth century predictably gave rise to works which set out to discuss the problems explicitly, in much the same way in which the condition of England novel articulated social and political questions. The three main influences on religious thought during this time were the ▷ Oxford Movement of the 1830s and 1840s, which sought to restore High Church ideals within the Church of England, and culminated in ▷ John Newman's defection to Roman Catholicism in 1845; the new German biblical criticism, first made accessible to English readers with the publication of George Eliot's translation of Strauss's *Leben Jesu* in 1846; and of course the impact of ▷ Charles Darwin's *On the Origin of Species* (1859). Spiritual crises and ecclesiastical quarrellings form the subject of such novels as J. A. Froude's *The Nemesis of Faith* (1849), Disraeli's *Lothair* (1870) and ▷ Mrs Humphry Ward's *Robert Elsmere* (1883), as well as being the basis of Trollope's ▷ Barsetshire novels and Margaret Oliphant's imitations of them, 'The Chronicles of Carlingford'.

Nineteenth-century consumers of fiction were thus very much more receptive to the exposition of ideas in fiction than are most modern readers, who tend to resent being preached at under the guise of fiction. Problem novels, or 'novels with a purpose', tackled issues of all kinds throughout the period. Again, the main beneficiaries of this discursive tendency were probably women, whose problems, lumped under the catch-all phrase 'the woman question', were repeatedly examined. The fallen woman was, as mentioned above, a particularly popular subject, featuring as a dreadful warning in works such as *East Lynne* or as a repentant Magdalen figure in *Ruth*. Charlotte Yonge's *The Clever Woman of the Family* (1865) cautions young women against the temptations of the intellect as memorably as Mrs Henry Wood does against the lure of the flesh. And by the last decade of the century there had arisen a distinct class of novel, the 'New Woman fiction', which dealt with the current feminist questions of sex, marriage and work. Grant Allen's *succès de scandale*, *The Woman Who Did* (1895), marked the culmination of the genre, with its hyperbolic attack on the institution of marriage (a 'temple' where 'pitiable victims languish and die in . . . sickening vaults'). Nor was the problem novel exclusively the province of minor writers: almost all major novelists of the period deal with these ideas in some form or other, and in the 1890s, for example, ▷ George Gissing's *The Odd Women* (1893), Meredith's *Lord Ormont and his Aminta* (1894) and Hardy's *Jude the Obscure* (1895) were all taken by contemporary readers to be variations of the New Woman novel.

There is, then, continuous interaction in terms of themes, issues and genres, between different writers, and between recognizable sub-groups of the novel and what is now regarded as mainstream fiction. The novelists of the period should be viewed within the artistic as well as the social and political context in which they worked.

The pre-Victorian period: Jane Austen

To select ▷ Jane Austen (1775–1817) as the single major writer of this period is at once to make a critical judgement which would not always have been accepted. To later nineteenth-century readers and many earlier twentieth-century ones, Walter Scott would have appeared probably the more influential figure. In initiating the historical romance he popularized a form which retained its appeal throughout the century and he was read with admiration by most subsequent nineteenth-century novelists. Charlotte Brontë, unsurprisingly, much preferred his romantic sweep to Jane Austen's tightly controlled realism, and ▷ Henry James praised his 'responding imagination before the human scene'. Interestingly, though, it was Scott himself who was one of the first to identify and appreciate Jane Austen's particular contribution to the development of the English novel at the time. In his review of ▷ Emma (1816) he discusses at length the limitations and diminishing returns of the predominating romance form, praising her novels for 'presenting to the reader, instead of the striking representation of an imaginary world, a correct and striking representation of that which is daily taking place around him'.

Jane Austen was herself, as is widely known, acutely conscious of the self-imposed restrictions of her range. When she wrote of the 'little bit (two inches wide) of ivory on which I work with so fine a brush as produces little effect after much labour', she was being characteristically both self-deprecating about her limitations and astute about her strengths. As a realist in an age dominated by romance, her fine brush reworked the material of fiction into tones which set standards for the investigation of the individual within a closely observed social framework for later realists to emulate if they could. For a long time her reputation was somewhat distorted by the indulgent cooings of 'Janeites' who praised her 'gentle' irony and indulgent humour, thus creating an impression of a softly female orientation within the safe sphere of domestic concerns, untroubling to the larger issues of life. Nothing could be further from the truth. Her irony, far from being gentle, is habitually savage in its condemnation of the foolish, hypocritical and self-deceiving; her humour is razor-sharp in its exposure of human weakness in a morally flawed society. Her heroines are set painful lessons in personal knowledge and moral self-discipline which entirely deny the possibilities of sentimental or coincidental resolve to which later Victorian novelists often have recourse. If, in keeping with the comic mode, they succeed finally in securing their desirable ends, it is not through a conventional coincidence of circumstance but because moral maturity secures an appropriate partnering. Nor is Jane Austen's world as prim and restricted as is sometimes unguardedly assumed. While never condoning sexual misdemeanour, her treatment of the subject owes more to hard-headed eighteenth-century worldliness than to Victorian repression. Where the Victorian female innocent is habitually seduced, abandoned and condemned to a lonely fate, Lydia Bennet (▷ Pride and Prejudice) bounces exuberantly into Wickham's bed with no thoughts in her head beyond immediate gratification, and after her hastily patched up marriage is received by at least some members of her family.

Jane Austen's values, then, are more eighteenth-century than Victorian, more classical than romantic. She portrays a society in which foolishness, hypocrisy and avarice abound, but where an agreed standard of moral principle may be assumed and where rationality may be invoked to counterbalance the disruptive lure of unbridled emotionalism. Her characters may suffer but they must also understand, and their understanding derives from a proper exercise of rational thought rather than from emotional or subconscious enlightenment. Through Marianne in ▷ *Sense and Sensibility* (1811) she attacks the idea that feeling can be a reliable guide to conduct and in ▷ *Persuasion* (1818) she satirizes, though with more sympathetic indulgence, romantic emotion. But perhaps no single factor marks Jane Austen off more distinctly from the Victorian novelists that followed her than her treatment of children. Amongst her heroines, only Fanny Price in ▷ *Mansfield Park* (1814) is portrayed in childhood, and children in general figure merely as convenient plot devices or as social distractions. By contrast, the Victorian novelist frequently makes the child, often an orphan, and the process of growth to maturity a central thematic focus. After Jane Austen, the influence of romantic thought on ideas about childhood, innocence, imagination and feeling is everywhere apparent.

The mid-nineteenth century: Dickens, Thackeray, the Brontës

It is notable, then, that while biographers of Jane Austen find difficulty in giving dramatic interest to a life of largely uneventful calm, those of the great mid-century novelists have a wealth of misery, neglect and misunderstanding to relate in their subjects' early years. This has the obvious effect of producing answering autobiographical portrayals of children in the novels, but also tends to create a sense of the fictional protagonist as alienated from or at odds with society. In the early Victorian novel the depiction of society generally expands unrecognizably from Jane Austen's little bit of ivory to a consciously panoramic perspective in which the individual is likely to be embattled and forlorn. The figure of the innocent child, often lonely and neglected, becomes a powerful symbol of society's guilt; the education and growth from childhood show the process of adjustment within a largely hostile social structure. While the romantic movement discovered and articulated the moral potency of the child, it was the Victorian novel which produced the first sustained portrayals of children in literature.

Of the major novelists of the period, ▷ William Makepeace Thackeray (1811–63) is probably least directly concerned with children, though his best novel, ▷ *Vanity Fair* (1847–48), does make use of significant incidents from the childhood of his protagonists in order to account for their subsequent development. Though often astute and original in his perception of his characters' psychology, his main strengths as a writer lay in his sharp eye for the particular kinds of human weakness thrown up by a newly complex society and his ability, in *Vanity Fair* at least, to bind all levels of the social structure into a comprehensive vision of moral and spiritual inadequacy. When Charlotte Brontë described him as 'the first social regenerator of the day', she was responding to qualities which were abundantly present in his early work but which faded notably in his later career. *Vanity Fair*, 'A Novel without a Hero', depicts English society in the years surrounding Waterloo as itself a battleground where money and social standing are the criteria for success and where individuals rise and fall according to their skill in playing social games which are as amoral and arbitrary as the values of the ▷ Stock Exchange which determine the fortunes of the Osborne and Sedley families on which the novel centres. Though Thackerary focusses his interest on the newly emerging middle classes, his picture of society extends upwards into the metropolitan aristocracy and the landed gentry, and downwards to the working classes and ▷ Bohemia. What binds them all is the struggle for money and reputation in a cut-throat world where the clever can 'live well on nothing a year' and the weak go to the wall. It is a mark of Thackeray's originality that the character who most successfully exploits the possibilities of his social struggle is a woman, the intelligent and cynical Becky Sharp, whom as we have seen, for all her manifest faults, he can never bring himself thoroughly to condemn. The novel leaves a moral question mark over all its characters and in so doing forces its readers to engage actively in the process of questioning and judgement in a way calculated both to challenge and disturb.

▷ Charles Dickens (1812–70), Thackeray's more successful rival for the affections of the novel-reading public, rarely leaves such moral openness, but develops more consistently towards a bleak view of society in which monolithic institutions (money and commerce in ▷ *Dombey and Son*, the law in ▷ *Bleak House*, the civil service in ▷ *Little Dorrit*) are potentially crushing to the strongly realized goodness of individuals. It was Dickens more than any other Victorian novelist who exploited the possibilities of the child as symbol of innocence amidst corruption, and this is one major factor which has led to accusations of sentimentality in his works. A catalogue of his maltreated but morally reformative children – Oliver Twist, David Copperfield, Paul and Florence Dombey, Jo the crossing sweeper, Little Nell, Sissy Jupe, Little Dorrit (amongst many others) – suggests a preoccupation with the innocence of childhood which could add weight to such an accusation, and it is largely true that Dickens's children are exempt from the barbs of humorous exposure with which he mercilessly illuminates the grotesque flaws in most of his characters' compositions. But his best portrayals of childhood – those in which the child ceases to be a simple symbolic force – uniquely capture the guilts and fears as well as the pathetic helplessness of juvenile innocence.

Modern mainline humanist criticism tends to base its praise for Dickens on a perception of the development in his later novels of a thematically coherent critique of his society which works through imagery and symbolism rather than through the creation of psychologically convincing characters. One can point, for example, to the recurrent images of imprisonment in *Little Dorrit* (1855–57) or to the sustained exploration of legal ramifications in *Bleak House* (1852–53). His world is so richly animated, his descriptive powers so invigoratingly original, as to invest the inanimate objects of his world with a vitality and significance often assumed to compensate for the lack of realism in the people which inhabit it. His women are prime targets for criticism here, since it is generally female characters who, for obvious reasons, carry the sometimes crippling weight of his moral approval. Dickens, while anatomizing the evils of his society with unique imaginative power, had a characteristically Victorian belief in the possibility of unsullied goodness and it is generally the heroines of his novels who provide examples of its morally regenerative force. Sissy Jupe in *Hard Times* (1854) works a change in the harshly utilitarian Gradgrind household 'by mere love and gratitude' and it is her 'wisdom of the Heart' which effectively counteracts the mechanistic values that the novel attacks. Her passive goodness and sweetly self-sacrificing nature exemplify the qualities often taken to be regrettably typical of Dickens's portrayal of women. However, it could also be argued that the twentieth century's automatic suspicion of pure virtue blinds the modern reader to more subtle qualities in Dickens's heroines. His skill in depicting the psychological results of guilt and repression, often noted in his male characters, is present also in his portrayal of many of the women. There is a great deal more to such characters as Florence Dombey, Esther Summerson or Little Dorrit than is usually perceived by an eye habitually prejudiced against the stereotype of the good woman.

Whatever may be reclaimed for Dickens's reputation in the portrayal of women, though, he can never hope to rival the Brontës in this area. ▷ Anne Brontë (1820–49), less talented and original than her sisters, still writes movingly and perceptively about the loneliness of the governess in *Agnes Grey* (1847), and adds new dimensions to the depiction of marital misery in *The Tenant of Wildfell Hall* (1848). Emily Brontë's only novel, *Wuthering Heights*, is generally recognized to transcend normal moral and spiritual expectations. Though Charlotte Brontë (1816–55) felt it necessary in her Preface to apologize for what she felt 'must appear a rude and strange production', the novel is meticulously planned and structured. Its strangeness derives partly from its unaccustomed settings, more perhaps from its extremities of violence and passion, and the central portrayal in Cathy and Heathcliff of a relationship which cannot be assimilated into any conventional framework or concept of character. That Emily Brontë (1818–48) was aware of the difficulties of this structure is shown by the care with which she draws her readers into the story through narrators of familiar social and psychological backgrounds; as their limitations are exposed, so their conventional judgements are progressively rejected and the reader is invited to accept an entirely unfamiliar scheme of values. At the end of the novel, Lockwood's inability to imagine 'unquiet slumbers for the sleepers in that quiet earth' seems more a reflection of his own limitations than an assurance that the grave will provide a final peace for the spirits of Cathy and Heathcliff.

However, the radical nature of Emily Brontë's vision makes her less influenced by social realities. Her main characters, in being largely outside convention, make no direct comment upon it. Charlotte Brontë, on the other hand, in working more within the bounds of recognizable society, produces original depictions of women which are overtly hostile to contemporary ideals. The autobiographical elements in her work create repeated images of women struggling against a world whose expectations they are unable and indeed unwilling to fulfil. Jane Eyre, 'poor, plain and little', and Lucy Snowe, wracked with the pain of unrequited love, obviously call upon Charlotte Brontë's own experiences. Her heroines all struggle in a world whose standards of female behaviour are alien to their own, and their achievements are wrenched painfully from the creation of a personal morality which is frequently at odds with the conventions of their society. Though Lucy Snowe in *Villette* (1953), who in the novel's slightly ambiguous ending is shown as independent mistress of her own school, may seem the most obvious candidate for modern feminist approval, it is really Jane Eyre who is the more impressive figure. Jane's impassioned cry 'I will be myself' summarizes the novel's sustained plea for a morality in which the heroine has the right and indeed the duty to realize her individuality independent of expectations from more familiar moral systems. Both Charlotte and Emily Brontë participate in the romantics' championing of the unique individual, the first within, the second largely outside, contemporary social realities. The poetic intensity of their writing, together with the patent influences of the Gothic and ▷ Byronic traditions, make their works most striking inheritors of romanticism in the fiction of the period.

The mid-Victorian period: George Eliot

It is gratifying to reflect that arguably the first intellectual amongst major English novelists was a woman. In an age when female education was largely limited to the acquisition of 'accomplishments', ▷ George Eliot (1819–80) could read French, Italian, German, Latin and Greek. Deeply involved in and influenced by the philosophical and scientific movements of the time, she lost her religious faith in early womanhood but retained a profound sense of moral imperatives in a secular context. In common with many of her contemporaries, her interests focussed on history and on modern attempts to arrive at systematic descriptions of social, religious and intellectual evolution. Her novels continually show her interest in the relationship between individual and historical change: as the individual is the product of social and historical forces, so society is formed and changed by the apparently inconsiderable lives of the individuals who compose it. Dorothea, who sets out at the beginning of ▷ *Middlemarch* (1871–2) in the view of the narrator as 'a modern Saint Theresa', may be defeated in her youthful objectives of effecting visible or dramatic change in her society but is convincingly displayed at the end as having an effect 'incalculably diffusive' on 'the growing good of the world'. The portrayal of the individual within a complex network of social and historical relationships forms a major part of George Eliot's fictional vision.

The past, and the extent to which her characters are determined by forces contained within it, form a continual theme in her fiction. 'Our deeds determine us, as much as we determine our deeds,' she wrote in ▷ *Adam*

Bede (1859), and her novels repeatedly display what in *Middlemarch* she described as 'the slow preparation of effects from one life on another'. Seeing her characters as largely determined by a meticulously charted individual past, and a socially and historically realized present, she nevertheless insists upon the stern exercise of personal responsibility in moral decision-making. Her characters, or more particularly her narrators, are among the first in English fiction to be consistently portrayed in the process of rigorous *thought*, whether about personal choices or larger intellectual systems. However, George Eliot as narrator remains firmly in control of both her structures and her readers' responses. When in *Middlemarch* she comments on the unknowable significance of future developments in individual lives – 'destiny stands by sarcastic with our *dramatis personae* folded in her hand' – she could have legitimately substituted herself for destiny. George Eliot's authorial voice, omniscient, magisterial and tolerant, constantly controls our reactions and to some extent raises her readers to a level close to her own lofty overview. When ▷ Virginia Woolf described *Middlemarch* as 'one of the few English novels written for grown-up people', she was deftly defining the degree to which George Eliot's fiction makes demands of serious moral response in a readership which could previously have rested happily within the safe bounds of entertaining diversion.

Hardy and the late-nineteenth century

Some contemporary reviewers of ▷ Thomas Hardy's early, anonymously published, work speculated that it might be by George Eliot. Presumably they were misled by the superficial similarities in the portrayal of rural communities and perhaps by Hardy's youthful pretensions to a command of contemporary intellectual issues, imperfectly assimilated. Indeed, an inability to judge his readers' tolerance of progressive moral and intellectual views was a continuing, and to modern eyes endearing, quality of Hardy's fiction, deriving as it did from his unusual combination of a countryman's pragmatism with a self-educated intellectualism. As the creator of the semi-fictional world of ▷ Wessex, Hardy (1840–1928) became the most significant regional novelist of the age and, with his unrivalled knowledge of the local customs and accents of his native land, was in a better position than any other writer to chart the changes in agricultural communities under the various dramatic shocks of nineteenth-century change. Hardy has, moreover, an eye for nature which is at once entirely unsentimental and supremely observant. When in *A Pair of Blue Eyes* (1873) Henry Knight clings desperately to a cliff with a fatal drop beneath him, Hardy notes that his torments are increased by the fact that rain driven against such an obstacle moves upwards not down: and, metaphorically staring death in the face, Knight's eyes actually meet the fossilized gaze of a trilobite embedded for millions of years in the rock before him. The vulnerable human in his extremity meets the indifferent but infinitely varied forces of nature, yet has contact over a gap of several million years with a fellow creature who has similarly suffered the pangs of life and death.

Such an incident is typical of the way in which Hardy's immense imaginative range and habitual preoccupation with the ironies of time are given solidity by observation of the precisely natural. It is also characteristic in that Knight's eventual rescue is effected by an incident at once stimulating and shocking to Victorian sexual tastes. The novel's heroine, Elfride, strips herself of all her undergarments in order to make a rope and, clad merely in a 'diaphanous exterior robe', hauls him to safety. Throughout his career Hardy found himself embroiled in battles against the prudish sensibilities of his readership and as his later novels began to engage more directly with contemporary questions of sexual morality, he was drawn, apparently protestingly, into fervent debates about women, sex and marriage. His views of the human condition, though, are more comprehensively tragic than would be suggested by confining him to immediate social criticism. Frequently accused of being irredeemably pessimistic, he described himself as a meliorist who portrayed the worst in order to point towards the better. But, despite the sharpness of their social criticism, there is little in his last novels – in ▷ *Tess of the D'Urbervilles* (1891) or ▷ *Jude the Obscure* (1895) – to suggest that possible future change could effectively alleviate their essentially tragic vision.

Hardy was in many senses the last of the great Victorian novelists. During the final years of the century it was his reputation, together with the more warily expressed admiration for Meredith, which dominated English fiction. Amongst other novelists, though, the debate about the relationship between romance and realism continued to be waged, with Gissing and Moore as the prime realists vying with the exotic romances of, for example, ▷ Robert Louis Stevenson and ▷ H. Rider Haggard. The vitality of the novel form was undiminished both in its challenge to social and moral convention and in its sheer inventiveness in entertainment. In literary terms, though, it was Henry James, with his infinitely sophisticated narrative and Joseph Conrad's ▷ modernism, which pointed the way forwards into twentieth-century developments of the novel as a form of art.

Georges Braque *Clarinet and Bottle of Rum on a Mantelpiece* (1911)

PART I – 1900 to 1930

Between 1900 and 1930 revolutionary developments took place in the English novel. These developments involved new subject matter, style and technique, and led ultimately to a radical rethinking of the relationship between fiction and reality. This era in the history of the novel, like the corresponding periods in the history of drama, poetry and other arts, is now widely known as modernism. The roots of ▷ modernism are exceptionally diverse, because it was a result of cross-fertilization between cultures, between art forms and between disciplines.

Culture and reality: James and Conrad

▷ Joseph Conrad (1857–1924) and ▷ Henry James (1843–1916), both of whom first published in the nineteenth century, are the earliest of the great modernist novelists writing in English. One form of cross-fertilization is evident at once, in that James was born an American and Conrad a Pole. Each chose to settle in England and to become an English subject and for each the collision of different cultures was an important theme. The relation of America to Europe is a central concern of James's fiction: in major novels such as ▷ *The Portrait of a Lady* (1881) and ▷ *The Wings of the Dove* (1902), as well as ▷ novellas such as ▷ *Daisy Miller* (1879), the moral consequences of the meeting of American innocence and enthusiasm with a sophisticated but corrupt European culture are explored by means of irony, a sustained attention to the nuances of individual consciousness, and a prose style of increasing subtlety and complexity. It was not only in theme that James was cosmopolitan; influences on his work include ▷ Jane Austen, ▷ George Eliot, Nathaniel Hawthorne, ▷ Balzac and Turgenev.

Conrad's life as a merchant seaman, and his upbringing in Poland and Russia, brought him into contact with a wide range of cultures. His prose style owes much to the influences of the nineteenth-century French writers Maupassant and ▷ Flaubert, and in a number of his works he explores what was to become a major concern of the twentieth-century English novel: the experience of the European in Asia, Africa or South America. In ▷ *Heart of Darkness* (1902) a supposedly enlightened colonial programme is revealed as ruthless commercial exploitation and a journey up the Congo becomes symbolic of an exploration of the darkness within man, the atrocities of history, the powerful forces of the unconscious, the mystery of evil. This work epitomizes many features of modernist fiction: the need to confront violence, nihilism and despair; the fascination with, but fear of, the unconscious; the centrality of a dramatized narrator who is not omniscient but rather himself searching for understanding; a symbolic richness which invites multiple interpretations. The last two of these features reflect the influence on modernism of the French symbolist (▷ Symbolism) movement of the nineteenth century, one of whose exponents, Rémy de Gourmont, defined the writer's purpose as being 'to unveil to others the kind of world which he beholds in his own personal mirror'. Conrad's critique of the ideology of Empire also foreshadows the many later works of fiction which use colonial or post-colonial settings to explore the European mind through its contact with what is alien and with what is shared in other cultures, while protesting against bigotry and exploitation. Examples include ▷ E. M. Forster's ▷ *A Passage To India* (1924), ▷ George Orwell's *Burmese Days* (1934), ▷ Graham Greene's *The Heart of The Matter* (1948), and, more recently, the Indian novels of ▷ Ruth Prawer Jhabvala.

But it is in their technique that James and Conrad are most revolutionary. While novelists such as ▷ Arnold Bennett (1867–1931) and ▷ John Galsworthy (1867–1933) continued to write in the accepted realist mode, using an omniscient narrator, a chronologically sequential narrative and the accumulation of details of social and public life, modernist novelists sought radical redefinitions of the real. One such redefinition is based on the view that, since the individual always perceives reality through his or her own consciousness, the contents and structure of consciousness represent the only accessible reality. A number of philosophical influences are relevant here. William James, the brother of Henry James, was an American psychologist and philosopher. In *Essays in Radical Empiricism* (1912) he elaborated the notion of a world of 'pure experience', all reality being described in terms of subjective human experience. (James is also the originator of the term ▷ 'stream of consciousness'.) ▷ Sigmund Freud (1856–1939), whose work began to be known in Britain around 1912, has had an enormous influence on modern literature, though less through direct application of his ideas than as a result of his contribution to the assumptions and preoccupations of modern Western society. One of his most potent ideas is also one of the simplest: that all mental phenomena have meaning. This assumption helped to validate new ways of structuring narrative based on dreams, fantasies, and chains of association. Henri Bergson (1859–1941), the French philosopher of evolution, distinguished between scientific time (a mathematical, abstract, homogeneous medium) and 'real duration' (our direct experience of time as a flowing, irreversible succession of heterogeneous and concrete states). The former, he claimed, is essentially an illusion; it is our subjective experience of time which is 'real'.

The novel was a particularly suitable form for the exploration of such perceptions, because of the possibility of manipulating the reader's experience of time by means of disruption of narrative chronology, and the possibility of representing the nature of consciousness by describing events through the awareness of one or more characters.

In the opening chapters of Conrad's ▷ *Lord Jim* (1900) a sense of foreboding is created so that the reader's expectation and interest are engaged, but at precisely the point of crisis, when an accident occurs to the ship on which Jim is first mate, the narrative jumps forward to the subsequent inquiry. Conrad thus deliberately frustrates the desire for plot satisfaction, diverting our interest from what happens to the moral and philosophical significance of events. The narrative is structured as an investigation; an attempt, largely on the part of Marlow, who befriends Jim, to understand Jim's life. However, Marlow himself obtains much of his information at second hand, through accounts of events given to him by other characters, so that the effect is one of an enigmatic reality seen through a series of consciousnesses.

But it was Henry James above all who, in practice in his novels and in theory in his prefaces, developed the use of an observing consciousness whose viewpoint shapes the narrative. Here we need to distinguish between the narrator (the narrating 'voice' which, if it refers to itself, must do so in the first person) and the focal character or 'reflector' (the character whose point of view orients the narrative perspective). In Conrad's *Heart of Darkness* Marlow is both narrator and focal character, but the two are not identical since they represent Marlow at different points in his life. One of the subtle pleasures of the story is our sense of Marlow the narrator (middle-aged, sitting on a boat on the Thames) reflecting on and reassessing the experience of Marlow the focal character (younger, more idealistic, in the Congo). James's most favoured device is the restriction of the narrative focalization to a reflector who is not the narrator but is referred to in the third person, a prime example being Strether in ▷ *The Ambassadors* (1903). Associated Jamesian techniques include a dominance of 'scene' (the highly detailed account of particular occasions) and long accounts of the nuances of the reflector's sense of events. These reflectors become centres of interest themselves. Viewing events through their eyes, we share the limitations of their knowledge and the distortions of their viewpoint, and this is realistic in the sense that our actual experience of life is always limited in this way; we do not have all the facts, nor access to the thoughts of others. We share in the progressive illumination of Marlow and Strether. Conrad and James inaugurated a form of realism which ▷ Malcolm Bradbury (b 1932) has aptly described as 'not so much a substantiation of reality as a questing for it'.

These various manipulations of narrator and reflector are fruitful sources of irony, a primary characteristic of much modern fiction. Irony can be generated when the reader perceives more, or understands better, than the narrator and/or reflector, and can occur even when our perspective is technically limited to that of this character. James's novella *The Aspern Papers* (1888) is entirely first-person narration, but we gradually realize, through his own words and thoughts, the moral and emotional limitations of the narrator. A different form of irony is developed by Conrad in ▷ *The Secret Agent* (1907) and ▷ *Under Western Eyes* (1911): a pervasive irony of tone and event. The former is produced by a portrayal of human activity as largely futile and human nature as inherently given to self-deception and illusory beliefs. The latter occurs as characters' actions consistently go awry and produce the opposite effect to that intended. The result is a blend of black comedy with a satirical and tragic view of humanity, its pretensions, and its ideals.

A special case of the dramatized central consciousness is the unreliable narrator or reflector. One of the most fascinating examples of the unreliable narrator is Dowell in ▷ Ford Madox Ford's novel *The Good Soldier* (1915). Our initial tendency to accept a first person narrator as an accurate source of information is exploited so that the cruelty, deception and insanity lurking beneath the genteel surface of the lives of two couples emerges with a greater sense of shock. Dowell also reflects on the nature of story-telling and its relation to truth ('I don't know how it is best to put this thing down . . .') and this novel thus anticipates two recurrent features of the twentieth-century novel. The first is the use of narrators or reflectors who are unbalanced, malevolent, of limited understanding or otherwise in an abnormal state of mind. Examples include *The Collector* (1963) by ▷ John Fowles (parts 1 and 3), and *The Spire* (1964) by ▷ William Golding. The second feature is reflexive narrative, in which the nature and purpose of writing becomes a constant secondary theme, or even the primary interest of the work. Examples include ▷ Doris Lessing's *The Golden Notebook* (1962) and William Golding's *Rites of Passage* (1980).

History and art: Lawrence and Woolf

The relationship of history and the novel may be formulated in two ways. On the one hand, we may regard history as an objective series of public events, and the novel as an art form which may represent, ignore or fictionalize them. On the other hand, we may regard history itself as a narrative, and its relation with the novel as more reciprocal, our sense of the nature and significance of narrative influencing our sense of historical pattern and meaning and vice versa. Modernism is sometimes accused of ignoring historical and social realities. But the sense of living in a period of historical crisis is an important aspect of much modernist fiction. The apocalyptic world view which the critic Frank Kermode has identified in the work of ▷ D. H. Lawrence (1885–1930) is at once a reaction to accelerating social change and an expression of a mystical or prophetic view of the role of the artist, influenced by the Bible, and especially the Book of Revelation. ▷ *The Rainbow* (1915) describes the life of three generations of the Brangwen family in the English Midlands, and ▷ *Women In Love* (1921) (originally planned as part of the same work), continues the story of the third generation. In neither novel is there extensive reference to historical events in the conventional sense, though the effect on rural life of progressive industrialization is powerfully felt. Rather, what Lawrence writes is a history of the development of human consciousness and the unconscious life, in which the individual's relation with partner, family, work and the natural and man-made environment reflects large-scale cultural changes.

The harmony achieved by Tom and Lydia, the first-generation couple living at Marsh Farm, is symbolized by the biblical image of the rainbow; by the end of *The Rainbow*, when Ursula, the modern woman, rejects marriage with Skrebensky, the representative of the mechanistic modern society, the rainbow can be only a tentative hope for a future regeneration. Just as James's novels seem to take place in a theatre of consciousness which is his unique discovery, so a considerable part of Lawrence's achievement is his development of a wholly new way of writing about human experience. The aspect of life to which he attends does not fit any of our normal categories; it cannot be summarized as the realm of the instinctual, nor of the unconscious, nor of the physical, nor of the emotional, though it touches all of these. It reflects Lawrence's radically new sense of the nature of the self and his rejection of what he called 'the old stable ego of the character', and is realized by techniques of ▷ symbolism, the repetition of imagery, and the use of sustained passages of highly poetic yet often abstract language to describe the development of the individual. In *Women In Love* contemporary society is unequivocally rejected as mechanistic and destructive, and regeneration is located in personal relations of mystical intensity.

In its apocalyptic view Lawrence's work may be said to subordinate the contingency of history to a typological pattern: that is to say, a pattern of 'types' (events or persons), analogous to, and in many cases based upon, the events and persons of the Old Testament which foreshadow the dispensation of the New Testament. It is a feature of ▷ modernist narratives to order their material by symbol, pattern or metaphor rather than by the linear sequence of history. If the patterns to which history conforms are for Lawrence apocalyptic and typological, for ▷ Virginia Woolf (1882–1941) they are the patterns of art and of human sensibility. ▷ *To The Lighthouse* (1927) was described by Leonard Woolf as a 'psychological poem', and this reflects the privileging of consciousness and the work of art as a made object over the chronological sequence of conventional fiction. The novel is in three sections, of which the first and third describe the life of a family in their holiday home in Scotland on two days, one before and one after World War I. These sections use the ▷ stream of consciousness technique developed in the English novel by Woolf, ▷ James Joyce (1882–1941) and ▷ Dorothy Richardson (1873–1957). So *To The Lighthouse* represents the thought sequences of the Ramsay family and their guests, moving freely in time and space. The middle section of the novel, entitled 'Time Passes', is concerned with the non-human, with change, with history and the ravages of time (the war takes place and several of the characters die; the house decays). An opposition is set up in the novel between, on the one hand, the destructive effect of history and of impersonal nature, and on the other the ordering power of art (represented by the painter, Lily Briscoe) and of human consciousness as a builder of social relationships (represented by Mrs Ramsay's drawing together of family and friends). The novel ends with Lily finishing her painting, completing a pattern in which the past and the dead are not lost, but reconciled in memory and in art. In so far as this painting is an analogue for the novel itself, history is mastered by art.

In Woolf's work the stream of consciousness technique moves towards a radical view of the nature of the self, which is of particular importance for ▷ feminist writing. In ▷ *The Waves* (1931) the lives of six characters are represented, and the close interaction of their consciousnesses is symbolically associated with a pattern of waves on the sea, separate yet part of a greater whole. From her first novel, *The Voyage Out* (1915), Woolf expressed a sense of the fluid nature of the self, its interdependence with the selves of others, and its relation to ▷ gender and class-based power structures. Feminists have increasingly seen the self as socially and politically constructed and have drawn inspiration from Woolf's moves towards ▷ deconstruction of the idea of immutable gender identity. Her interest in androgyny, her sense of the social protest which madness can represent and her satire on repressive psychiatric practices in ▷ *Mrs Dalloway* (1925) have also remained points of reference for feminist writers, although there is disagreement as to how far she tended to withdraw from political issues.

Phases of modernism: Forster and Joyce

It is possible to distinguish an early phase of modernism, ending around the beginning of World War I. In the first decade of the century James's three last great novels appeared, together with most of Conrad's major fiction and the first two novels of ▷ E. M. Forster (1879–1970), whose work is frequently regarded as containing both modernist and Victorian elements. In Forster's novel ▷ *Howards End* (1910) English society is seen as divided between the business world of action and the refined world of culture and the emotions, and a symbolic reconciliation is suggested by the marriage of the chief representatives of each group, and the inheritance of a house (the Howards End of the title), which stands for a threatened continuity in English life. The sense of threat and change is distinctively modernist, as is the location of renewal and reconciliation in the realm of the symbolic and the imagination. But Forster's social comedy, his narrative technique and his ▷ humanism associate him with more traditional strains in the English novel.

▷ *A Passage To India* is at once more symbolic and less schematic than *Howards End*, and, appearing in 1924, belongs to the later post-war phase of modernism. While its satire on the arrogance and narrow-mindedness of British officials in India reflects the same belief in tolerance and liberalism as Forster's earlier work, the novel also explores at a deeper level the philosophical issues arising from the meeting of cultures. This is achieved in part through a symbolic evocation of the Indian landscape, and in particular the mysterious Marabar Caves, which call into question the identity and beliefs of several of the characters by their immitigable otherness. The novel ends with the voice of the landscape itself, on a note of ambivalent hope. While Forster made a contribution to both phases of modernism, the main figures of this post-war phase are Lawrence, Joyce and Woolf. Joyce's ▷ *Dubliners* (1914) is a seminal influence on the modern short story in English. He described his intention as that of writing 'a chapter in the moral history of my culture', using 'a style of scrupulous meanness'. Drawing on French influences, Joyce does indeed inaugurate in English the oblique, laconic short story, later developed by Ernest Hemingway (1899–1961) and *The New Yorker* magazine. But the use of symbol, Joyce's miming of the diction and speech patterns of his Dublin characters, and his idea of the epiphany – a sudden spiritual manifestation in the ordinary – point to a more poetic and symbolic strain which culminates in the powerful yet ironic romanticism of the last story in the collection, 'The Dead'.

▷ *A Portrait of the Artist as a Young Man* (1916) is comparable to Lawrence's ▷ *Sons And Lovers* (1913) in its semi-autobiographical nature. In each the primary interest is in the psychological and intellectual development of a young man, with great concentration on the protagonist. This is most obvious in the *Portrait*, where the other characters remain shadowy and the language and structure of the novel seeks to render the contents of Stephen's mind, but it is important that in *Sons And Lovers* much of what we learn about the other characters is essentially their role in Paul Morel's psychological economy. The protagonists of both novels seek independence, but whereas in Lawrence's work this is primarily emotional independence, in that of Joyce it is predominantly cultural and intellectual, involving Stephen's escape from the restrictions of Irish society and the Catholic Church.

Joyce's ▷ *Ulysses* (1922) is a central text of modernism. A novel of over 600 pages concerned with one day in Dublin, it has an amazing richness of texture, combining mythical and literary allusions, parody and pastiche, punning and humour, with a powerful sense of the infinite complexity and subtlety of the individual's emotional and intellectual life. It is structured around a loose correspondence to the episodes of ▷ Homer's ▷ *Odyssey*, so that the ironic juxtaposition of the ordinary with the heroic generates irony and wit while at the same time drawing on an archetypal level of experience comparable to that which the Swiss psychoanalyst ▷ Carl Jung located in a collective unconscious. The symbolist aspiration to imitate musical form is evident in the use of repeated words, phrases and images as forms of *leitmotif*. The novel encountered virulent opposition at the time of publication, being banned in England until 1936 on grounds of obscenity. Its acceptance into the canon of major works of English literature, together with the successful defence of D. H. Lawrence's ▷ *Lady Chatterley's Lover* at a 1960 obscenity trial, signalled the public endorsement of the principle that all areas of human experience could be valid subjects for the serious artist. It is in part for its combination of mundane details with a vast inclusiveness of reference that *Ulysses* is valued so highly.

The realist tradition: Bennett, Galsworthy, Wells

Despite the genuinely innovative and radical nature of modernist fiction, we should be wary of too schematic an opposition between modernists and traditionalists. We are inheritors of a distinction made by writers such as Woolf and Lawrence in order to define their artistic identity and literary programme. As Frank Kermode has pointed out, modernist programmes have the habit of claiming that they have to 'get out from under something', and ▷ Arnold Bennett (1867–1931), ▷ John Galsworthy (1867–1933) and ▷ H. G. Wells (1866–1946) were cast in the role of that 'something'. Wells himself participated in this process in his well-known comment in a letter to Henry James (8 July 1915): 'To you literature like painting is an end, to me literature is a means, it has a use ... I had rather be called a journalist than an artist'. Nevertheless, there are some affinities between the realists and the modernists in terms of influences and subject matter: Bennett was influenced by French and Russian novelists, and Wells, in his scientific romances, shows a strong sense of the apocalyptic and of the impact of war and technology on twentieth-century society. These writers are also part of important continuities in English fiction. Wells's emphasis on ideas is continued by ▷ Aldous Huxley (1894–1963) and ▷ George Orwell (1903–50) in the 1930s and 40s, while Bennett's regional settings in the Potteries district connect him with the regional realists of the 1950s. Wells, in works such as *The War of the Worlds* (1898) and *The First Men in the Moon* (1901), was also a pioneer of ▷ science fiction, one of the most fruitful of the popular genres in the twentieth-century novel.

Bennett's best work, such as *The Old Wives Tale* (1908) and *Riceyman Steps* (1923), contains telling studies of ordinary lives, with a strong sense of the rich detail of society, and of the passing of time. The limitations of his style include a liability to give information too directly, to 'telling' rather than 'showing'. Like Bennett, Galsworthy was extremely popular and successful during his lifetime, with works such as ▷ *The Forsyte Saga* (1906–21) which are primarily concerned with upper-class society. The most general criticism of his work is that his satire is often lacking in focus and rigour. Wells was an extremely versatile writer of fiction and journalism; his fiction included Dickensian (▷ Dickens, Charles) social comedy such as *The History of Mr Polly* (1910) and studies of contemporary social issues such as *Ann Veronica* (1909), as well as his science fiction or scientific romances. George Orwell, who considered Wells's thinking to be outmoded by the 1940s, nevertheless asserted of his own generation that 'the minds of us all, and therefore the physical world, would be perceptibly different if Wells had never existed.'

1920s satire: Lewis, Huxley and Waugh

Alongside the modernist experimentation of the 1920s a vein of tragicomic satire emerged in the English novel in the work of ▷ Aldous Huxley (1894–1963), ▷ Wyndham Lewis (1882–1957) and ▷ Evelyn Waugh (1903–66). These authors shared a sense of the absurdity of modern society, and one form which this takes in their novels is that of dehumanization and the dissolution of the self. Wyndham Lewis, an artist, philosopher and editor as well as a novelist, was a leading spirit of Vorticism, an anti-realist movement in art, based on jagged, rhythmical, mechanistic forms. Such principles are also reflected in the portrayal of character in Lewis's novels, such as *Tarr*

(1918); he described men as comic because they were 'things, or physical bodies, behaving as persons'. Aldous Huxley's *Crome Yellow* (1921) is primarily a novel of ideas, similar in form to the novels of ▷ Thomas Love Peacock (1785–1866), in which characters carry on debates in the setting of a country house. It is based on a somewhat schematic antithesis between men of thought and men of action. The protagonist, Dennis Stone, an example of the former who wants to be the latter, is a characteristic satirical anti-hero of the period, weak and ineffectual, but both types are portrayed as inadequate. The hero of Evelyn Waugh's first novel, *Decline and Fall* (1928) is described as a shadow; passively enduring a series of outrageous injustices and misfortunes, he ends up precisely where he started. The book describes itself as 'an account of the mysterious disappearance of Paul Pennyfeather'. Paul's adventures, however, bring him up against a large number of eccentrics, so that his shadowiness only serves to emphasize the egregious personalities which surround him.

These works contain images of the modern world as manic, mechanized and incomprehensible; they are essentially about the problem of how to live in a society which seems meaningless. The stance of the implied author (the author as he is manifest in the text) varies: Huxley tends to include some equivalent for himself in the novel, thereby making his own intellectual approach part of the object of his satire; Waugh is detached and invisible; Lewis is outraged, polemical and assertive. Drawing on the tradition of such European writers as ▷ Voltaire, Gogol and ▷ Swift, they represent a powerful alternative vision of the modern condition.

PART II – 1930 to 1950

In the 1930s and 40s political events were felt in English prose writing with a particular directness. The impact of World War I and the associated social changes on the modernist novel tended to take place primarily at the level of the author's general world view, and to filter through into the content of the novel transformed by some principle of artistic shaping. From around 1930, however, there arose in many writers a sense that historical events were of such overwhelming importance in their implications for society that they demanded forms of writing which would attempt to represent, with as much immediacy as possible, the feel of contemporary experience, while also explicitly taking sides in a political or moral debate. In general terms, then, the period was one in which social or documentary realism reasserted itself; that form of realism which is concerned with an outward fidelity to the experience of the mass of individuals and an engagement with public issues. Such a generalization is, however, necessarily an oversimplification. Individual authors continued or commenced their literary careers, responding in a variety of ways to their own experiences, influences and interests as well as to the temper of the times. New works by Joyce and Woolf were still appearing during the early part of the period; Woolf's last novel was *Between The Acts* (1941) while Joyce's final work, ▷ *Finnegans Wake*, was published in 1939. ▷ Ivy Compton-Burnett (1884–1969), whose first novel had appeared as early as 1911, elaborated further her vision of power, pain and obsession in wealthy families of late Victorian and early Edwardian England, rendered almost entirely through dialogue. Evelyn Waugh's novels of the 1930s, including the hilarious *Scoop* (1938), continued and developed the satirical vein begun with *Decline and Fall.* ▷ Elizabeth Bowen (1899–1973), in novels such as *The Heat of the Day* (1949) and short stories such as 'Mysterious Kôr' (from *The Demon Lover*, 1945), combined an evocation of the atmosphere of war-time London with a Jamesian attention to the nuances of personal relations. ▷ Samuel Beckett's unique exploration of man as an isolated being confronting existential despair began with his first novel, *Murphy*, in 1938, which had been preceded by a collection of Joycean stories, *More Pricks than Kicks* (1934).

The approach of war: Orwell and Isherwood

In the public sphere the 1930s were dominated by two factors. The first was the economic depression which, from the collapse of the Wall Street Stock Market in 1929, began to cause widespread unemployment and poverty. The second was the rise of fascism in Europe: Hitler seized power in Germany in 1933; in Italy Mussolini had ruled since 1922; in 1932 Sir Oswald Moseley founded the British Union of Fascists. The most coherent ideological response to both these developments came from the left wing, so that during the 1930s a considerable number of British writers and intellectuals became socialists or communists. The Left Book Club, founded in 1936, provided a focus for this tendency. It is primarily from a left-wing perspective that modernism has been rejected or criticized, both in the 1930s and since. George Orwell, a socialist, though a very independent one, described the 1920s as 'a period of irresponsibility such as the world has never before seen'. Georg Lukács, the Hungarian Marxist (▷ Marx, Karl) critic, writing in 1955 from a more dogmatic perspective, attacked modernism on the grounds that it treated man as a solitary and asocial being, thus denying the reality of history.

Orwell's own writings seek to bring home to readers the human consequences of the economic and political situation: the soul-destroying nature of poverty in *Down and Out in London and Paris* (1933) and *The Road to Wigan Pier* (1937), the miseries of war and the distortions of the press in *Homage to Catalonia* (1938) and the oppressions of British imperialism in *Burmese Days* (1934). The first three of these works blend reportage and autobiography with an element of the fictional, and in each many facts are given, ranging from the minute details of daily life in the trenches of the Spanish Civil War to the income and itemized expenditure of a Yorkshire miner in 1935. This might be seen as a return to the 'materialism' which Woolf objected to in the work of Galsworthy and Bennett, but it gains new force both from Orwell's passionate indignation, and from his imaginative realization of the influence of material conditions on human consciousness and society. However, his individualism and his sometimes sentimental portrayal of the working classes have been criticized by socialist thinkers such as ▷ Raymond Williams.

Orwell's novel *Coming Up For Air* was published in 1939, on the eve of World War II, in the same year as a work by another writer of left-wing views, ▷ Christopher Isherwood's *Goodbye to Berlin*. In each there is a powerful sense of foreboding, of European civilization slipping into violence and chaos. The contrast of narrative techniques illustrates the range of 1930s realism. *Goodbye to Berlin* is a series of linked short episodes set in the decadent atmosphere of Berlin during the Nazi rise to power. The detached quality of the first-person narrator is defined on the first page: 'I am a camera with its shutter open, quite passive, recording, not thinking'; he says relatively little of his own feelings as he moves among a cast of largely manipulative, destructive or self-destructive characters. The narrator's very passivity and neutrality of stance comes to epitomize the failure of the European mind to confront the rise of fascism. Orwell's narrator is George Bowling, a disillusioned insurance salesman approaching middle age who returns to the village of his childhood in an attempt to recapture something of what now seems to him to have been an idyllic Edwardian age. He is an egregiously personal dramatized narrator, who addresses the reader throughout in a conversational tone, masking a highly skilful rhetoric which persuades us to share his vision of an England of petty, narrow lives, a civilization of rubbish dumps and synthetic food, a people with fascist violence hanging over them, 'so terrified of the future that we're jumping straight into it like a rabbit diving down a boa constrictor's throat'. George's anticipation of 'the coloured shirts, the barbed wire, the rubber truncheons', looks forward to Orwell's post-war vision of totalitarianism *1984* (1949) and his political allegory *Animal Farm* (1945).

These post-war works reflect a general disillusionment with communism, resulting from the revelation of the Stalinist show trials, and the Nazi-Soviet pact of 1941. But during the 1930s many writers and intellectuals had become Marxists, and a considerable number fought for the Republicans in the Spanish Civil War. Many novels of the 1930s reflect this commitment, including ▷ Rex Warner's allegory *The Wild Goose Chase* (1937), and Edward Upward's *Journey to the Border* (1938). Both these novels have propagandist Marxist conclusions; in *Journey to the Border* the protagonist's hallucinations and fantasies are associated with a decadent society, and at the end of the novel he decides to regain reality by joining the workers' movement. Thus by the end of the 1930s 'reality' has become for many a politically defined concept, a matter of class commitment rather than of the nuances of consciousness. The experience of working-class life is perhaps most powerfully expressed in the work of writers who grew up in working-class regional communities. Lewis Grassic Gibbon in *A Scot's Quair* (1932–34) and Walter Greenwood in *Love on the Dole* (1933) use dialect to convey social cohesion and social deprivation in north east Scotland and northern England respectively. Gibbon's trilogy is especially remarkable for its sense of community, history and the impact of the Scottish landscape on the consciousness of the characters.

The inner and outer worlds: Greene and Lowry

The dangers of oversimplification inherent in an antithesis between a modernist concentration on the individual inner world, and a politically-committed attention to social relations becomes evident when we consider the work of ▷ Graham Greene (b 1904). His early work of the 1930s, such as *It's a Battlefield* (1934) and *Brighton Rock* (1938) has a sense of the oppressive squalor of areas of modern urban life, a sense which is later translated into the more exotic settings of late colonialism; visions of seediness and corruption in such settings as Africa (*The Heart of the Matter*; 1948), Vietnam (*The Quiet American*; 1955) and South America (*The Honorary Consul*; 1973). He has a long standing, if moderate, left-wing commitment, evident not only in his novels, with their critique of the Western role in the third world, but also in his active friendship and support for those resisting the right-wing dictatorships of Central America, recounted in his memoir *Getting to Know the General* (1984). Yet characters such as the whisky priest of *The Power and the Glory* (1940) confront their moral choices in a condition of existential isolation and Greene himself has associated his use of journeys (he is an inveterate traveller) with the methods of (▷ Psychoanalytical Criticism) psychoanalysis; in the introduction to *Journey Without Maps* (1936) he explains that he sought to give general significance to his travels in Liberia by using 'memories, dreams and word-associations' to suggest a parallel, inner journey. From the time of *Brighton Rock* his ▷ Catholicism became more apparent. Though he does not regard himself as a 'Catholic novelist', his work is informed by a powerful sense of good and evil, and of the sinfulness of human nature, combined with a somewhat determinist tragic irony. In these respects, as well as in his use of extreme situations which test human morality and endurance, he has links to Conrad and Dostoievsky as precursors, and to the post-war English novelist William Golding (b 1911) as a successor. Many of Greene's novels are narrated in the third person in a detached, unemotive style which serves to highlight violence, tragedy, the sordid and the grotesque. This style has affinities with American writers of the 1920s such as Ernest Hemingway and John Dos Passos.

  ▷ Malcolm Lowry's *Under the Volcano* (1947), like Greene's best work, endows a tragic story of human failure with metaphysical overtones. Set in Mexico, where the presence of fascist elements anticipates the approaching world war, the story of the alcoholic British Consul Geoffrey Firmin achieves a wide resonance by means of symbol, an intricate metaphorical structure and a ▷ stream of consciousness technique in which the beautiful but sinister Mexican landscape becomes an equivalent for inner turmoil. This novel belongs to the high modernist tradition in its formal experimentation and literary allusiveness, as well as in its somewhat Laurentian apocalyptic vision of political and cultural crisis. Firmin's story is associated with that of Doctor Faustus (▷ Faust), who sold his soul to the devil, while Mexico is presented as an archetype both of paradise and of hell.

Firmin's inebriation, self-destructiveness and guilt are attributed to contemporary civilization as a whole. The novel, intended as part of a trilogy which was never completed, owes much to Joyce's *Ulysses* in its shifts of consciousness, its concentration on one day, with extended flashbacks, and its intricate, allusive structure.

The complex interplay of modernist experiment and the impulse towards social realism and political commitment was to contribute to a remarkable diversity of modes in fiction of the post-war era.

PART III – 1950 to the present

There has been a tendency among critics to see the post-war English novel as lacking in power and scope compared to the great age of modernism, and essays on the subject frequently begin by acknowledging the lack of either a great genius of the novelist's art or a single dominant movement with techniques and themes which are felt as central to contemporary culture. Gilbert Phelps, for example, in his essay 'The Post-War English Novel' (*New Pelican Guide to English Literature*, 1983), asserts that 'the trend of the English novel since the war has, on the whole, been . . . a turning aside from the mainstream of European literature and a tendency to retreat into parochialism and defeatism'. Several points need to be made about such a view. There is the obvious but important fact that both greatness and cultural significance are more readily detected in retrospect. Furthermore, contemporary critical theory has made us increasingly aware that this retrospective detecting involves an element of construction. A sense of literary history, of the significance of particular works and authors, and of the existence of a canon of recognized major or serious works are necessarily a matter of a subjective, value-loaded and culturally specific process of consensus. This is not to say that such judgments are arbitrary, but only that they represent a characteristically human activity of creating patterns of meaning. Such a conception of cultural process is a powerful aspect of contemporary thought, and it may therefore be claimed that the diversity of contemporary fiction, by encouraging the reader to select from a huge range of available modes and styles, itself characterizes the prevailing *Zeitgeist* more effectively than could any dominant individual or group. Theories of cultural ▷ post-modernism emphasize the transformation of culture into a commodity and the simultaneous availability of many forms, including imitation and pastiche of those of the past. More specifically in terms of the novel, the modernist claim to centrality depended, as we have seen, on a doctrine of experimentation and radical newness, according to which changes in novel technique accompanied changes in the nature of human experience. Works such as Joyce's *Finnegans Wake* (1939) pushed innovation along modernist lines close to the point where the coherence of the novel as a genre seemed in doubt. We have observed one form of reaction against modernism in the politically committed writings of the 1930s. Experimentation did not die out, but it increasingly came to seem one option among many, rather than an essential expression of the times. Furthermore, the shock to the idea of western civilization administered by World War II, the death camps and the atomic bomb rendered the very idea of cultural centrality a dubious one. On the other hand, fictionality itself seemed an increasingly appropriate focus of attention in a culture where clear standards of truth and significance were felt as elusive.

The awareness of fictionality

▷ Samuel Beckett (b 1906) has continued the Joycean line of experimentation, combining a fascination with words with an acute awareness of their limitations, and with a rich vein of parody, irony, imitation and pastiche. His vision is, however, a darker one, although humour is an essential aspect of it. In his trilogy of the 1950s, *Molloy* (1956), *Malone Dies* (1956) and *The Unnamable* (1959), isolated, aged and decrepit social outcasts of obscure identity narrate their own stories with a mixture of black humour and remorseless grimness. They are aware of themselves as story-tellers, making reference to the futility of this activity, yet continuing with the story in order to pass the time, as an act of defiance, or as an obsessive compulsion. As in Beckett's plays, there is a progressive minimalism, in which life is reduced to language, mundane and sordid physical details and the isolated human consciousness. In this respect his novels represent the ultimate breakdown of the classic realist novel, in which character is portrayed in a rich social context. In drawing attention to their own fictionality, and in playing games with language (including the game of teasing the critics by laying false clues) Beckett's narrators anticipate the contemporary fascination with the idea of fiction and of narration. Such concerns are not, of course, the prerogative of the twentieth century, being prominent in, for example, ▷ Laurence Sterne's *Tristram Shandy* (1759–67) and Cervantes's *Don Quixote* (1605–15). However, the current interest in this area reflects ▷ structuralist and ▷ post-structuralist scepticism about the ability of language to refer to a non-linguistic reality, and the sense that fictionality is an attribute of forms of discourse other than fiction, such as history and the social sciences. This has generated an increasing interest in narrative as a model for the structuring both of culture and of individual experience.

Contemporary novelists who explore this model include ▷ John Fowles (b 1926), whose book *The French Lieutenant's Woman* (1969) combines a pastiche of a Victorian novel with passages of social history and statistics about Victorian sexual habits. The author addresses the reader, discussing his own techniques and the reader's likely response, and later, appearing as a minor character, decides to abrogate his authorial power over his characters by providing two alternative endings, even going to the length of tossing a coin to decide their order. The effect is that of an intriguing, if scarcely subtle, consideration of issues of free will, determinism, power and meaning.

Other experimental works which test the limits and nature of fiction include ▷ B. S. Johnson's 1969 novel, *The Unfortunates*, which has twenty-seven loose-leaf sections of which twenty-five may be read in any order, the randomness of the resulting structure serving as a metaphor for the circling and shifting of the mind. Johnson saw 'truth' and 'fiction' as being antithetical terms, and his last work, *See the Old Lady Decently* (1975) employs documents and photographs in an attempt to create a non-fictional novel. This aspiration is paralleled in the documentary style of Alan Burns (b 1929), some of whose novels are structured around news items or press-cuttings. There are therefore two contrary but complementary impulses detectable in the experimental novel: one towards documentary objectivity, and the other towards the recognition of perspectivism. ▷ Lawrence Durrell (b 1912), in his sequence *The Alexandria Quartet* (1957–60) provides multiple perspectives on an intricate series of relationships in a community by means of a diversity of narratives, including third-person and first-person narratives, letters, journals and parts of an inset novel by a character. The reader's understanding of both character and event is subject to revision in the light of new information and perspectives, making the work what has been described as 'a game of mirrors'.

In a sense, experimental novels are particularly dependent upon the traditional qualities of a good novel, such as plot interest and imaginative power in the realization of social context. In the absence of such qualities the reader is unlikely to overcome the difficulties of coming to terms with an unfamiliar form. A novelist who combines imaginative power with a wittily expressed examination of the nature of the fictional is ▷ Dan Jacobson (b 1929). *The Rape of Tamar* (1970) is set in the time of the Old Testament King David, and narrated by Yonadab, who is intensely aware of the philosophical and moral dilemmas of his role as narrator. He has knowledge of our own time as well as that of the story, and shares with us his reflections on the resulting ironies. Thus the act of narrating is a source of interest throughout, generating insights into such issues as hypocrisy, self-deception, voyeurism, the function of art, the pleasures and vicissitudes of speaking, and the culturally specific nature of modes of interpretation. But these sophisticated intellectual concerns are matched and sustained by a powerful poetic evocation of the physical and cultural context, and above all by the sheer vitality of Yonadab's personality as he addresses us with engaging frankness in what he terms 'the simulacrum of time in which you and I have managed to meet'. Self-conscious narrative, which by various means draws attention to its own fictionality, serves to question the nature of reality, and of our understanding of it, and to highlight issues of freedom and control. It has therefore held a strong appeal for writers influenced by French ▷ existentialist thought, including ▷ Christine Brooke-Rose (b 1926) and ▷ David Caute (b 1936). In the post-modernist anti-novel, practised by writers such as ▷ Gabriel Josipovici (b 1940), structures based around repeated scenes or interwoven narratives create a radical uncertainty, and the world evoked by the text disintegrates in order to fulfill the author's aim of, in his own words, 'insisting that his book is a book and not the world' (from *The World and the Book*, a study of modern fiction (1971).

Morality and art

A feature of the work of several considerable post-war novelists is a renewed attempt to present a vision of the world as a battleground of forces of good and evil. William Golding (b1911) has had outstanding success in the construction of moral fables, shaped by Christian archetypes of sin, guilt, purgation and the tentative but precious hope of redemption. His novels, of which the first was *Lord of the Flies* (1954), show a powerful interest in the primitive and the physical, particularly in the examination of extreme conditions or states of consciousness in which human experience is stripped to moral and physical essentials. This description does not, however, do justice to the range of his settings and techniques. *The Inheritors* (1955) attempts to realize the mind and culture of Neanderthal man. This relatively idyllic and innocent culture is used to make us see our own nature (as represented by the arrival of *homo sapiens*) in a new and largely unflattering light; a technique which owes much to Conrad's comparable use of non-European cultures. *The Spire* (1964) renders the tormented consciousness of a fanatical medieval cleric, while *Rites of Passage* (1980) uses pastiche and the ironies arising from a self-confident but mistaken narrator to portray the moral awakening of a gentleman traveller in the early nineteenth century. The limitation of Golding's work is its explicitness. The thrust of his moral vision and his mythic patterning can sometimes seem overbearing, though many readers will feel that this is a small price to pay for its power and authority.

In contrast to Golding's historical and cultural range, most of the novels of ▷ Iris Murdoch (b1919) are set in contemporary English middle-class society, but are informed by a range of philosophical concerns centring on moral responsibility, individual freedom, the nature of love, and the possibility of actively pursuing goodness. They combine a serious, and at times tragic, exploration of these concerns with exciting plots, and elements of the comic, supernatural, and fantastic. These features have been sustained through a prolific career since the appearance of her first novel, *Under the Net* in 1954. Doubts about her work focus on a sense that characters are excessively manipulated in the interest of illustrating abstract ideas, and a dissatisfaction with her use of violence and accident as a plot device. Of her early novels, *The Bell* (1958) is notable for its complex symbolic structure. The moral significance of the lives of a group of characters, brought together in a rather bizarre religious community, is examined by a pattern of interaction centred around the symbol of a convent bell, but using also animal and water symbolism. *The Sea, The Sea* (1978), a Booker Prize Winner, and one of the most acclaimed of her works, is a typically dark comedy about obsession, guilt and egotism, but is remarkable for the richness of its symbols and characters. ▷ A. S. Byatt (b1936) shows the influence of Murdoch in her use of symbolic structures and her portrayal of the inter-relations of a large group of central characters. The latter feature is particularly evident in the opening books of a projected tetralogy: *The Virgin in the Garden* (1979) and *Still Life* (1985). Moral concerns are evident, but less explicit than in Murdoch's work, more attention being given to correspondences between experience and mythic or aesthetic patterns, and to the process of cultural change.

In the work of ▷ Muriel Spark (b 1918), manipulation is less a risk for the author than an explicit theme and, as in Ford Madox Ford's *The Good Soldier* (1915), the manipulative aspects of the narrating activity are exploited as a source of irony in the rendering of patterns of social and psychological control. Thus in the ▷ novella *The Driver's Seat* (1970) the use of the present tense, and an entirely external focalization on one character (the narrative recounting events from her point of view, but with almost no revelation of her feelings, thoughts or intentions) creates a grim and enigmatic vision of a woman with a psychological compulsion and a violent destiny which seem fixed and unchangeable, yet not understood either by author or reader. In *The Prime of Miss Jean Brodie* (1961) humour is more in evidence, but dark shadows of fascism and personal betrayal, evoked particularly through prolepses (jumps forward to later events), lurk around the story of a teacher's charismatic influence on a group of pupils. Spark's Catholic sensibility emerges in her portrayal of diabolic figures, such as the charming, egregiously manipulative Dougal Douglas of *The Ballad of Peckham Rye* (1960).

While Spark is a convert to Catholicism, ▷ Anthony Burgess (b 1917) has a Catholic background, and though not a practising member of the Church, acknowledges the importance of Catholic modes of thought in his work. *A Clockwork Orange* (1962) is concerned with the relation of evil and free-will. The protagonist makes a deliberate choice of a life of horrifying violence and sadistic cruelty, and attempts by a futuristic authoritarian society to reform him by brainwashing can only destroy his human identity. The novel is notable for its use of an invented teenage patois, Nadsat, reflecting Burgess's enthusaism for Joycean linguistic multiplicity and invention. Burgess has stated that he sees the duality of good and evil as the ultimate reality, and in *Earthly Powers* (1980) the history of the twentieth century is portrayed in terms of such a moral struggle, seen through the memories of the narrator, a homosexual writer. As in Murdoch's work, a strong sense of moral patterning underlies and unifies a complexity of events.

In the novels of ▷ Margaret Drabble (b 1939) moral concern is focussed on social justice and the individual quest for identity, particularly on the part of women. Works such as *The Ice Age* (1977) reflect her admiration for ▷ Arnold Bennett in their realist portrayal of the state of contemporary British society.

Feminist writing

The question of what constitutes 'feminist' writing is a contentious issue, but what is certain is that novels concerned with women's experience represent a significant section of the contemporary fiction market, and make rich use of innovations in narrative technique and of a range of styles and genres. An important divide among feminist critics is between those, such as Elaine

Showalter, who see the role of contemporary female writing as that of self-discovery, articulating the nature of women's personal experience within society and revealing structures of oppression, and those such as Toril Moi, who advocate rather the ▷ deconstruction of the idea of the unitary self, and the rejection of the male/female dichotomy in favour of some ideal of androgyny.

The project of articulating women's experience includes the rediscovery of the unrecorded, of what has been omitted from conventional histories and novels. Thus ▷ Eva Figes (b 1932), in *The Seven Ages* (1986), writes a fictional chronicle of the lives of seven generations of women, from pre-history up to the present, concentrating on their struggles with poverty and violence, and their experience of childbirth and child-rearing. An associative, free-floating narrative style suggests a collective female consciousness, transcending the individual self and linking women to natural forces of generation. ▷ Zoe Fairbairns's *Stand We At Last* (1983) also recounts the lives of successive generations of women, though with closer attention to the detailed historical context, while the Manawaka series of novels and stories by the Canadian writer ▷ Margaret Laurence (1926–87) are narrated by women of various ages and generations in such a way as to simultaneously explore the social history of Canada and the dilemmas and achievements of women in the context of a prairie town. ▷ Jean Rhys (1894–1979), in *Wide Sargasso Sea* (1966), writes a feminist complement to ▷ Charlotte Brontë's ▷ *Jane Eyre*, recounting the early life of the mad first Mrs Rochester, from her childhood in the West Indies. Rhys gives consciousness to the character who, in the original novel, is an inarticulate symbolic location for a rejected violence of feeling. Madness is a recurrent theme of feminist writing, because, considered as a refusal to conform to an imposed social identity, it can become a potent symbol of revolt against oppression. ▷ Doris Lessing (b 1919) does not see herself as primarily a feminist writer, but her novel *The Golden Notebook* (1962) has become a seminal feminist text. It is built out of a skeleton narrative, entitled 'Free Women', plus four notebooks kept by Anna, one of the characters of 'Free Women'. This fragmentation reflects her fear of breakdown as she confronts political, literary and sexual problems as an independent woman, but in the fifth and final 'Golden Notebook', a new unity is achieved through a mental breakdown shared with a man, during which the collapse of divisions leads to 'formlessness with the end of fragmentation'.

A number of writers, without adopting an overtly feminist standpoint, attend particularly to women's experience of isolation, betrayal, loss or guilt within the limitations imposed on their lives by social convention or male attitudes and behaviour. They include ▷ Edna O'Brien (b 1932), whose popular and entertaining novels are concerned particularly with the vicissitudes of sexuality and passion, and ▷ Anita Brookner (b 1928), who portrays the disillusionment of her sensitive female characters with an elegant, detached attention to the nuances of human relationships. In one sense these writers are the opposite of feminist, since their work could be held to accept as a premise the view that women seek self-fulfilment largely through relations with men. Yet in representing the tragedy or frustration which may result from such dependence, their novels raise crucial feminist issues, and are part of the context for the debate about the fictional portrayal of women.

▷ Fay Weldon (b 1931) recounts the lives of her women characters with a sort of desperate black humour. In works such as *Down Among the Women* (1971) and *Praxis* (1978), a constant shifting of relationships and roles suggests a terrifying instability of identity; both men and women move between the role of victim and victimizer, but the women are consistently the more disadvantaged, both socially and biologically. Both novels end by suggesting that a new breed of emancipated woman is emerging, but offer little convincing evidence for this hope, and Weldon's work has gradually tended towards disillusion, with an element of biological determinism. Women's sexuality, and sexual politics, have been central feminist concerns. In contrast to Weldon's cynical realism, ▷ Angela Carter (b 1940) approaches these issues through fantasy, myth and fairy-tale. Fantasy and dream can serve as forms of experience emancipated from rational modes of thought which are seen as essentially male, and ▷ Emma Tennant (b 1937), in *The Bad Sister* (1978), employs a split between realist and fantasy modes to develop this opposition. Radical perspectives on sexual relations are also a feature of the work of ▷ Maureen Duffy (b 1933), who explores particularly working-class and lesbian experience.

Realism, satire, social comedy

There is a continuing strain in the English novel which is concerned with the analysis of contemporary English culture by means of satire, humour, or irony, primarily within realistic modes. The satirical strain, building on the earlier work of writers such as Waugh and Huxley, includes ▷ Angus Wilson (b 1913), whose novel, *Anglo-Saxon Attitudes* (1956), set in the late 1940s, is a portrait of academic and London life and the egotism and self-deception of a range of characters. These concerns, however, take on a broader historical and social resonance because of the novel's examination of the effect of the past on the present via the troubled personal life of an historian and the confusion arising out of an historical fraud committed in 1912. *The Old Men at the Zoo* (1961) continues the vein of satirical analysis, but moves into fantasy and allegory in its bizarre tale of the administration of the London Zoo during another war. Wilson is also a writer of short stories, which combine a sharp satirical edge with a considerable emotional charge in their exposure of cruelty, snobbishness and pretension.

During the 1950s a group of writers emerged whose work combined a realist portrayal of provincial communities with a strong sense of social injustice. Some of these writers became known by the label ▷ 'angry young men'; they include ▷ Alan Sillitoe (b 1928), ▷ Stan Barstow (b 1928), ▷ John Wain (b 1925), ▷ John Braine (b 1922) and ▷ David Storey (b 1933), and in their early novels the heroes are working class, or in revolt against the demands of a middle-class background. Novels such as John

Braine's *Room at the Top* (1957), John Wain's *Hurry on Down* (1953), Stan Barstow's *A Kind of Loving* (1960) and Alan Sillitoe's *Saturday Night and Sunday Morning* (1958) seemed to epitomize a post-war sense of futility, discontent and rebellion. Their subsequent careers have developed in various ways, as, for example, towards narrative innovation in the case of Storey, or to a reaction against radicalism in the case of Braine. They were brought up outside London, coming in most cases from working-class backgrounds, and their work continued the tradition of working-class regional writing found earlier in the novels of Walter Greenwood (1903–74) and Lewis Grassic Gibbon (1901–35).

Of those originally seen as 'angry young men', it is perhaps ▷ Kingsley Amis (b 1922) who has most successfully sustained his popular appeal over the succeeding decades. Unlike Angus Wilson, who, influenced by Virginia Woolf, used a range of interior monologues in his sixth novel *No Laughing Matter* (1967), Amis eschews modernist experiment, though working with a number of sub-genres, such as the ghost-story (*The Green Man*; 1969) and the fantasy of an alternative world (*The Alteration*; 1976). His novels are characterized by sharp wit, inventiveness, and a considerable animus against whatever Amis sees as bogus or blameworthy. *Lucky Jim* (1954), his very entertaining first novel, inaugurated the genre of the humorous campus novel, since developed by ▷ Malcolm Bradbury (b 1932) in *Stepping Westward* (1965) and *The History Man* (1975), and ▷ David Lodge (b 1935) in *Changing Places* (1975) and *Small World* (1984). Amis specializes in dislikeable characters, with objectionable attitudes, such as the xenophobia of the protagonists of *I Like It Here* (1958) and *One Fat Englishman* (1963), or the misogyny of Stanley in *Stanley and the Women* (1984). While these attitudes are subjected to a degree of satirical censure, they are not altogether repudiated. Amis's position is now a conservative one, marked by a distrust of the cosmopolitan and the experimental.

The influence of Jane Austen is apparent in the work of ▷ Barbara Pym (1913–80), which enjoyed a revival in the late 1970s, and consists of subtle and ironical studies of middle-class life, combining a shrewd humour with an uncompromising sense of the commonness of frustration, isolation and ennui. The delicacy of her work might be contrasted with the satirical shock-tactics of ▷ Martin Amis (b 1949) who employs black humour to portray human fears, obsessions and desires. Surprisingly, Amis (who is Kingsley Amis's son), claims to be influenced by Jane Austen too; he shares with Pym the use of humour of some sort to reveal human weakness, but they stand at opposite ends of a spectrum stretching from gentle irony to vigorous satire.

Commonwealth writers

This essay started by referring to the cross-fertilization of cultures as essential to the modernist movement at the beginning of the century. Since that time Britain's political and cultural relations with the rest of the world have changed radically. The British Empire has ended; two world wars have

brought enormous social changes; technological developments have transformed the world economic system, and therefore the manner in which
cultural artefacts are circulated. The diversity and plurality which have been
noted as aspects of post-modern society have a particular value insofar as
they promote an attention to the radical otherness of different cultures.
There is thus a new, post-modern form of cross-fertilization taking place.
The difference between the two forms might be epitomized by the difference
between reading ▷ E. M. Forster's ▷ *A Passage to India*, the reaction
of a sensitive and perceptive Englishman to Indian society, and reading the
novels of ▷ R. K. Narayan (b 1906) which, though using the English
language, are written by an Indian who knows that society from within. The
availability of works in translation is also a part of this openness; since the
1970s the English novel-reading public has been less likely to read English
works which somehow attempt to incorporate world culture, and more likely
to read works in translation, such as the Latin American novels of Jorge Luis
Borges (1899–1987), Gabriel García Márquez (b 1928), Carlos Fuentes
(b 1928) or Mario Vargas Llosa (b 1936) and the Eastern European novels of
Alexander Solzhenitsyn (b 1918) or Milan Kundera (b 1929). But a very
considerable contribution to the development of the novel written in English
has been made by Commonwealth writers (▷ Commonwealth literatures).
The term is not satisfactory, being increasingly politically outdated, but
there is not as yet a suitable alternative term for those countries, once part of
the Empire, where English provides a common literary language.

   The novels of ▷ Chinua Achebe (b 1930) articulate the impact on
Nigerian culture of white colonialism and its aftermath, from 1920s tribal
life, the setting of *Arrow of God* (1964), to Lagos in the 1960s in *A Man of
the People* (1966). But the interest of his work is by no means limited to its
political implications. Writing in English, Achebe incorporates African
proverbs and idioms in such a way as to make the cultural context vivid and
compelling for both African and English readers, and characters such as
Okonkwo, the village leader who is the principal character of Achebe's first
novel, *Things Fall Apart* (1958), achieve psychological complexity, and a
considerable tragic status. The continuing oppression of white rule in South
Africa dominates the novels of ▷ Nadine Gordimer (b 1923), but is
addressed obliquely through its impact on private experience. Writing
primarily about the white middle classes, she traces the decay resulting from
their involvement in a brutal and segregated social system.

   ▷ Patrick White (b 1912) is the most accomplished contemporary
Australian novelist. His work draws on the stark polarities of Australian life:
the polite social milieu of suburban Sydney, satirized by White with a dry
wit, and the starkly primitive outback, which in *Voss* (1957) becomes a
spiritual testing ground. The eponymous hero of this novel is a dedicated
German explorer, with a compulsive though enigmatic sense of his own
destiny, who leads an expedition into the Australian interior. In the early
part of the novel the narrative shifts freely between realistic observation of
social mores and poetic evocation of characters' inner worlds of memory,
anticipation and desire. This blend is characteristic of White's idiosyncratic

style, which startles by its immediacy and tonal range. Voss's journey, like those of ▷ Graham Greene's characters, is also an inner journey, and, as in the work of ▷ Joseph Conrad, the confrontation with a harsh and alien landscape is endowed with philosophical and spiritual resonance through the questioning of personal identity; external and internal landscapes function as mutual metaphors. Central to *Voss* is the duality of the physical world and the human imagination; the latter becomes concentrated in the intense and mystical relationship between Voss and a woman he has met in Sydney, a relationship carried on in their thoughts and letters. White is both a social satirist and a visionary and the authority of his work was recognized by the award of the Nobel Prize for Literature in 1973. More recently another Australian novelist, ▷ Peter Carey (b 1943), has achieved considerable popular success with highly inventive works including *Illywhacker* (1985) and *Oscar and Lucinda* (1988).

In both New Zealand and Canada strong traditions of women's writing have grown up. The analysis of New Zealand society by Edith Searle Grossman at the start of the twentieth century, and by ▷ Katherine Mansfield (1888–1923) and Jane Mander in the 1920s has continued since 1950 in the work of writers such as ▷ Janet Frame (b 1924). In Canada ▷ Margaret Laurence (1926–87) and ▷ Margaret Atwood (b 1939) have represented social change and individual quests for identity with a strong sense of the physical and historical context of Canadian life. Just as Laurence uses her fictional prairie town of Manawaka to chart Canadian social history, so ▷ R. K. Narayan has built his work around the fictional South Indian town of Malgudi (based on Mysore), as an epitome of Indian culture, while the work of his fellow countryman ▷ Salman Rushdie (b 1947) employs ▷ post-modernist strategies and the techniques of ▷ magical realism.

Barbadian ▷ George Lamming (b 1927) is notable for his direct treatment of the legacy of colonialism, and in particular of slavery. Some of his works, such as *Water with Berries* (1971), deal with these issues in a British setting: Lamming has lived in England since 1950, contributing to a strong movement of black writing in Britain, along with others such as Samuel Selvan, who came to England from Trinidad at the same time, and the Kenyan Ngugi Wa Thiong'o. Among West Indian writers it is ▷ V. S. Naipaul (b 1932) who has met with the greatest popular success and critical acclaim. His early novels, such as *The Mystic Masseur* (1957) evoke the life of Trinidad with an elegant clarity which emphasizes both its sordid aspects and its vitality. His best known work, *A House for Mr Biswas* (1961) deals with the hero's search for independence combined with the capacity to love and accept responsibility. This search is articulated by the metaphor of the building of a house, a focus of self-respect and growth in the face of the displacement which is the aftermath of colonialism. *A House for Mr Biswas* is a work of considerable scope in the comic realist tradition. As such it exemplifies the role of Commonwealth authors in rediscovering a vitality and power in the existing forms of the English novel, while developing a style and technique appropriate to their distinctive concerns and cultures.

Conclusion

The field of contemporary fiction is large and expanding. This essay attempts to provide an introduction to twentieth-century fiction by examining some perspectives on the major work of the first half of the century, and by suggesting something of the range and variety of writing since 1950, in the hope that the reader will be encouraged to explore further. Traditional features of the novel, such as satire, the pleasure of narrative, the excitement of plot and the rendering of moral distinctions still find new and original exponents. Narrative experiment and the awareness of fictionality provide powerful means for exploring the particular philosophical preoccupations of our age, while genres such as ▷ science fiction and the fantasy novel offer popular alternative modes of writing. At the same time both the language and the techniques of the novel are successfully adapted to various and changing cultures. The diversity of the contemporary English novel is a sign of the vitality of the form and of the continuing ability of fiction to engage at many levels with both intellectual issues and cultural processes.

Claude de Jonge *A London Panorama*

Shakespeare and English Renaissance drama 7

Sixteenth-century drama

Arguably the most productive period of English drama dates from the establishment of the first professional playhouse, The Theatre, outside the City of London in Shoreditch in 1576 and comes abruptly to an end in 1642 when Parliament decreed that 'publike Stage-Playes shall cease, and bee forborne'. The intervening 66 years and particularly the 40 years from the mid-1580s to the death of ▷ James I in 1625 produced some 20 playwrights of distinction and at least half a dozen major theatres. The 'Acte for the Punishment of Vacabondes' of 1572 forced players to constitute themselves into mostly shareholding companies under the protection of patrons such as the Earls of Essex, Oxford, Sussex, Warwick and ▷ Leicester. Leicester's influential patronage resulted in the granting to ▷ James Burbage's company, Leicester's Men, of a royal patent. Burbage duly proceeded to invest in the building of The Theatre as the focus of his company's London activities. Burbage's theatre was succeeded by the Curtain (1577), then ▷ the Rose (1587) and the Swan (1595) – which were both on the south side of the Thames in the 'Liberty of the Clink', beyond the bounds of the City and outside its control – the ▷ Globe (1599), built from the timbers of the dismantled Theatre, the Fortune (1600) and the Red Bull (1605), as well as the small Blackfriars theatre in which ▷ Shakespeare's company would eventually perform during the winter season.

Originally the Blackfriars had housed the Children of the Chapel Royal who, with the boy players of ▷ St Paul's, would regularly perform at Court alongside the adult companies. Unlike the professional theatre, the children's companies were less immediately vulnerable to the opposition of the City Fathers. The mostly Puritan-inspired antagonism to the theatre forced the professional drama to operate largely outside the City walls, except when companies played at Westminster or in the ▷ Inns of Court.

From its early years the history of the Elizabethan theatre is one of a continuous struggle against a hard core of ▷ Puritans who launched several colourful attacks on it, notably ▷ Stephen Gosson's *Playes Confuted in Five Actions* (1582) and ▷ Philip Stubbes's *The Anatomie of Abuses* (1583). In the end it was royal patronage that ensured both the survival and the continuity of the professional companies and theatres. Although the Puritans may well have begrudged the theatre its sheer fun and its ability to draw large crowds – the Globe accommodated nearly 3,000 people – they were also wary of its secular bias. The entertainments written by the first generation of Elizabethan dramatists were a long way from the medieval ▷ Morality and ▷ Miracle Plays, although the Morality form and its favourite character the 'Vice' endured throughout the period in plays like ▷ Marlowe's ▷ *Doctor Faustus* (1592?) and as late as ▷ Jonson's *The Devil is an Ass* (1616).

The earliest extant English comedy, Nicholas Udall's (1505–56) ▷ *Ralph Roister Doister* (1552), shows that the imaginative roots of drama were changing from primarily Christian and native to largely classical ones, in this case the ▷ New Comedy idiom of ▷ Plautus and ▷ Terence, focussed on domestic relationships and involving stereotyped figures such as the wily servant and the swaggering soldier. The impact of classical history, myth and drama through both Latin and other contemporary European literature appears in the titles of some of the better known plays of the 1560s such as Richard Edwards's *Damon and Pythias* (1565), Thomas Preston's *Cambyses* (1569), ▷ George Gascoigne's popular *Supposes* (1566) and George Whetstone's influential *Promos and Cassandra* (1578).

The imprint of the classics is palpable in the writings of the first significant playwright of the period, ▷ John Lyly (1554–1606), who wrote for the children's companies and, like several of his contemporaries, was university-educated. Although Lyly was best known in the sixteenth century as the author of two prose romances, ▷ *Euphues, or the Anatomy of Wit* (1578) and *Euphues and his England* (1580) which bequeathed the most admired and most often parodied style ('Euphuism') to the period, it is his plays that are now more highly regarded. The stylized sophistication of works like *Alexander and Campaspe* (1584), *Sapho and Phao* (1584). ▷ *Gallathea* (1585), *Endimion* (1588) and *Midas* (1589) appeals to an audience steeped in ▷ Ovid and courtly allegory. In them Lyly reveals a remarkable dramatic tact and a unique rhetorical lucidity, which owe much to the anithetically poised style of *Euphues*, as well as to the need to accommodate the limitations of boy actors. *Gallathea* is Lyly's most accomplished play. It integrates native and classical strands in its ▷ pastoral which is set in North Lincolnshire, coloured by ▷ Virgil's *Ecologues* and Ovid's ▷ *Metamorphoses*. The story of the two girls disguised by their father as boys to save them from a virgin sacrifice to Neptune derives from Ovid's tale of Iphis and Ianthe in *Metamorphoses IX*. The girls fall in love with each other and are granted a happy consummation of their love affair through a promise that Venus will transform one of them into a boy.

▷ George Peele (1556–96), ▷ Robert Greene (1558–92), ▷ Thomas Lodge (1558–1625) and ▷ Thomas Nashe (1567–1601) were all ▷ 'University Wits', like Lyly and Christopher Marlowe (1564–93). Nashe and Lodge are remembered mostly for their prose. Lodge's two plays *A Looking Glass for London and England* (1594), and *The Wounds of Civil War* (1594) are now forgotten, whereas his pastoral prose romance *Rosalynde* (1590) is still read, not least because it provided the main source for ▷ Shakespeare's ▷ *As You Like It*. Nashe is the author of the ▷ picaresque and journalist narrative ▷ *The Unfortunate Traveller, or the Life of Jacke Wilton* (1594), as well as of the satire *Pierce Penniless, the Supplication to the Devil* (1592) and the ironic 'pleasant comedy' *Summer's Last Will and Testament* (1592), which for all its poetic inventiveness and wit resembles a procession of seasonal allegorical figures more closely than the vibrant five-act plays of the professional theatre. Peele and Greene follow Lyly in writing romantic comedies; Peele's jewelled idiom, and classical and mythological motifs and pastoral settings reflect his enduring interest in pageantry without sacrificing dramatic plausibility altogether. The titles of his three best known works, *The Arraignment of Paris* (1584), *The Love of King David and Fair Bethsabe* (1587) and *The Old Wives' Tale* (1590) reflect their imaginative preoccupations with mythic, biblical and native pastoral themes, which, in his dramatization of the love affair of King David and the revolt of Absalom, fruitfully interact to produce an impressive and moving play.

Robert Greene is known among others for his scurrilous attack on Shakespeare in *Greene's Groatsworth of Wit bought with a Million of Repentance* (1592) and for the pastoral prose romance ▷ *Pandosto, The Triumph of Time* (1588), which Shakespeare used in ▷ *The Winter's Tale* (1610). But two of Greene's comedies deserve special attention and are still performed: ▷ *Friar Bacon and Friar Bungay* (1589) and *The Scottish History of James IV* (1590). The former dramatizes the medieval philosopher ▷ Roger Bacon's alleged experiment with a head of brass and interweaves this necromantic plot with a gentle romance narrative of the simultaneous wooing by the Prince of Wales and a nobleman of a fair maid. This early formal experiment in the use of double plot is reflected in the narrative perspective of *James IV* which, through its framing device anticipates the stylization of Shakespeare's ▷ *A Midsummer Night's Dream* (1595). Psychologically Greene's drama displays a new realism in understanding human motivation and to that extent it foreshadows Shakespeare's comedies.

If English comedy was well established by the late 1580s, tragedy was in its fledgling stages when ▷ Thomas Kyd (1558–94) wrote ▷ *The Spanish Tragedy* (1587). It was to become the most popular play of the period and marks one of the first Elizabethan attempts at writing a tragedy after ▷ *Gorboduc* (1561), a play by Thomas Norton and ▷ Thomas Sackville which is an artistic failure 'notwithstanding ... it is full of stately speeches and well-sounding phrases, climbing to the height of ▷ Seneca's style, and as full of notable morality' (Sir Philip Sidney, ▷ *Apologie for Poetrie*, 1595). Like the earlier play, *The Spanish Tragedy* reflects a strong Senecan influence in its bloodthirsty plotting and declamatory rhetoric as its protagonist Hieronimo, the Marshal of Spain, labours in vain for justice and has to resort to revenge in the end. Although *The Spanish Tragedy* was largely superseded by the more mature scrutiny of the ethics of crime and punishment in Shakespeare's ▷ *Hamlet*, it retains much of its rhetorical force and manifests a distinct awareness of the moral nefariousness of indiscriminate revenge and its consequences.

A very different note is sounded in the works of Kyd's contemporary and friend Christopher Marlowe (1564–93), who was born the son of a cobbler in Canterbury, where he attended the King's School. Marlowe went up to Cambridge on a scholarship instituted by the former Archbishop of

Canterbury, ▷ Matthew Parker (1504–75). His attendance was erratic, and rumours about his alleged Catholic as well as atheistic leanings were rife. These may have led to the university's decision at first to withhold his degree, but the Queen's Council intervened and overturned it on the basis of Marlowe's good service to the Crown. Marlowe was killed in what was allegedly a tavern brawl in Deptford on 30 May 1593, when he was 29 years old. During this short and turbulent life Marlowe wrote seven plays, translated ▷ Ovid's *Amores* and ▷ Lucan's *Pharsalia* and composed one of the most successful English narrative poems, ▷ *Hero and Leander*, as well as the famous lyric 'Come live with me . . .', the subject of several contemporary imitations and parodies. There is little agreement on the exact dates of the plays other than that they were written between 1585 and 1593, possibly in the following order: *Dido, Queen of Carthage*; ▷ *Tamburlaine the Great, Parts I and II*; *The Tragical History of Doctor Faustus*; ▷ *The Jew of Malta*; *Edward II*; *The Massacre at Paris*. It is on a handful of plays and on his one long poem that Marlowe's reputation as Shakespeare's most talented contemporary rests; and it is a measure of Marlowe's precocious achievement that, although he was born in the same year as Shakespeare, he was already dead when Shakespeare's first great play, *Richard III*, was performed.

Marlowe's choice of subject matter is revealing as much for its diversity as for its unifying vision. To a young man trained in the Elizabethan classical curriculum his adaptation in *Dido* of the central episode from ▷ Virgil's epic poem, the ▷ *Aeneid*, must have seemed part of a natural process. Marlowe does not simply imitate Virgil's stirring account of Dido and Aeneas, but transforms it into a self-contained dramatic vehicle of which the Trojan imperial quest constitutes an ancillary if necessary part. Pyrrhus's spectacular killing of Priam in front of a pleading Hecuba provides Marlowe with an opportunity to indulge his taste for grotesque imagery. The inset narrative of ▷ Troy in an otherwise essentially 'romantic' work contains the shape of things to come. In his ruthless and measured calm ('So, leaning on his sword, he stood still,/ Viewing the fire wherewith rich Illion burnt'), Pyrrhus anticipates Tamburlaine, the Guise (*The Massacre at Paris*), and, to a lesser extent, Barabas (*The Jew of Malta*) and Young Mortimer (*Edward II*). Equally enduring in the later plays is Marlowe's ability to pull out all the stops afforded by lyrical rhetoric and mythopoeia.

Ideologically *Dido* holds out few challenges to established orthodoxies. Notwithstanding its rhetorical resourcefulness it is a light piece compared to *Tamburlaine* and *Doctor Faustus*, Marlowe's most controversial plays. As the Prologue to *Tamburlaine, Part I* boldly announces, the audience will be transported from the 'jigging veins of rhyming mother-wits/ And such conceits as clownage keeps in pay . . . to the stately tent of war'. Consequently, the play traces the emergence of Tamburlaine from obscurity to his victory over the Turks led by Bajazeth and the Egyptians under the Soldan, whose daughter Zenocrate Tamburlaine woos and eventually marries. From the beginning it is clear that *Tamburlaine, Part I* is not at all intended to be an exemplar work in the didactic ▷ *Mirror for Magistrates* tradition in which hubristic aspirations become the means for exemplary punishments. In this play the overreacher is celebrated by the author, however reprehensible he appears. Tamburlaine explodes ordained hierarchy and received wisdom. As he tells us at his first appearance: 'I am a lord, for so my deeds shall prove,/ And yet a shepherd by my parentage'. Against such existentialist convictions the calculated and coercive assertions of Tamburlaine's foes, that he is a mere Scythian thief, are of little avail. On the contrary, Tamburlaine claims to 'glory in the curses of my foes,/ Having the power from the empyreal heaven/ To turn them all upon their proper heads'. As if his self-appointed role as the scourge of God were not enough, Tamburlaine proclaims his desire to scale the heavens to 'become immortal like the gods'. The words 'will' and 'shall' best befit him, he claims, and in a moment of supreme confidence he professes to 'hold the Fates bound fast in iron chains,/ And with my hand turn Fortune's wheel about'. As Marlowe knew from the classics, not even ▷ Zeus controls the Fates. To convey the stature of Tamburlaine, Marlowe endows the character with the most grandiloquent and declamatory style of address. Like a colossus or a ▷ Phaeton at the reins of the chariot of the sun, Tamburlaine bestrides his play and in epic battles defeats the traditional enemies of Christendom, particularly the Turks who had recently been overcome at Lepanto (1571). In spite of this partial concession – in that the enemies of Tamburlaine are the arch-enemies of every European Christian nation in the sixteenth century – Tamburlaine displays no sign of allegiance to any particular faith or political doctrine. He is relentless, ruthless and uncompromising, true only to himself and to his wife Zenocrate. He exists in the public eye, and we are not invited to share his inner thoughts. Soliloquies are beneath Tamburlaine, because they recognize human complexity and the need for reflection, neither of which squares with the image of the man of action. Only once, after the massacre of the virgins of Damascus, does he pause to consider Zenocrate's pleas for her father's life, and momentarily grants us the briefest glimpse of a sensibility which is as responsive to physical beauty as it is to the lure of power. Tamburlaine is a titan whom Zeus is unable or unwilling to defeat, and he ends *Part I* victorious.

Marlowe would not again match the sustained intensity and clear-eyed achievement of *Tamburlaine, Part I. Doctor Faustus* and *The Jew of Malta* have, however, fared better in the theatre. An improved sense of dramatic timing and stage-action, as well as a more moderate and ironic imaginative vision, have superseded the earlier defiant rhetoric addressed to the audience. If the moralizing tenor of the chorus in the 'Epilogue' of *Doctor Faustus* is credited ('Cut is the branch that might have grown full straight . . .') as Marlowe's own work – the textual history of the play is very complex – *Doctor Faustus* would demand to be seen as a late sixteenth-century morality play. Marlowe's reworking of the medieval Faustbook contains all the natural and supernatural ingredients of a work tailored to commercial success.

If the admonitory tone of *Doctor Faustus* perfectly counterbalances *Tamburlaine*, the tone and structure of *The Jew of Malta* suggest that the

Marlovian myth of the overreacher is becoming domesticated and socially accommodated. The famous prologue to the play is spoken by ▷ Machiavelli or 'Machevill' himself, but thereafter the work hardly concerns itself with dramatically disembodied reflections on the nature of power and of good and evil. The stereotyped villain of the piece is the greedy scheming Jew, Barabas. Though he is not a Shylock, Barabas is not wholly undeserving of our sympathy, as he inhabits a virtually unreclaimed world in which Jew and Christian are alike corrupt. Barabas is flexible, inventive, resilient and witty to the point of virtually turning the play into a black farce. He finds his perfect match in the Thracian and Semitic slave Ithamore. Both are capable of the most sublime rhetoric, both delight in mass murder. In its irreverence about religion and those who most profess it, like nuns and friars, *The Jew of Malta* reflects its author's alleged iconoclasm, as in a different way does *Edward II*, the most explicit homosexual play of the period, and the truncated *The Massacre at Paris*.

More than any dramatist of this period, Marlowe emancipated the theatre from the shackles of orthodoxy. His maverick, epic vision and distinct blank verse paved the way not only for Shakespeare but also for ▷ Ben Jonson and ultimately for ▷ John Milton.

Shakespeare and his contemporaries

From the death of Marlowe in 1593 to the ill-fated performance of Shakespeare's ▷ *Henry VIII* in 1613 during which the Globe Theatre burned to the ground, Shakespeare's plays and poems commanded an unchallenged allegiance from his public. In some 20 years of creative activity Shakespeare wrote over a dozen comedies, ten history plays, ten tragedies and four romances, as well as at least two long poems and a cycle of sonnets; and he almost certainly contributed to the work of others.

Of the 37 plays generally attributed to Shakespeare (1564–1616) all except ▷ *Pericles* – which is not wholly his – were printed in the First ▷ Folio of 1623 under the supervision of Heming and Condell, two of Shakespeare's fellow actors. This collection printed plays like ▷ *Macbeth*, ▷ *Antony and Cleopatra*, ▷ *Coriolanus*▷ and ▷ *The Tempest* for the first time and also provided important alternate texts for works which had appeared earlier in ▷ quarto form; ▷ *Hamlet* in 1603 and 1604 and ▷ *Othello* in 1622, sometimes in longer or shorter versions. The qualitative distinctions formerly drawn by editors of Shakespeare between quarto and folio have recently been called into question, and the plays are increasingly perceived as essentially dynamic texts intended for theatrical performance. This challenging process of editorial realignment has occupied the centre stage of Shakespearean studies since the late 1970s, and all the signs are that it will endure as its focus in the closing years of the twentieth century. The textual radicalism pioneered under the auspices of Oxford University Press, and particularly its championing of Shakespeare the reviser, has affected readings in ▷ *Henry IV, Part I*, ▷ *King Lear* and *Pericles*. The restoration in some modern editions of the name 'Oldcastle' for 'Falstaff' (in *Henry IV,*

Part I) and the establishing of a two-text *King Lear* are its most contentious conclusions.

The critical debate about Shakespeare continues vigorously. If ▷ structuralism and ▷ deconstruction have failed to make a major impact, ▷ feminism, on the other hand, has powerfully engaged with Shakespeare and has recently produced some of the most valuable Shakespearean criticism by tapping gender ambiguities deeply embedded in the plays and poetry themselves. Currently, the so-styled '▷ new historicism', with its emphasis on '*Zeitgeist*' and its margins, is the most articulate heir to the traditions of ▷ humanist thinking about Shakespeare.

The 1590s mark the main period of Shakespeare's histories, comedies and poetry. The first tetralogy of history plays was written and performed by 1593, as well as three of the comedies based on models derived from ▷ Plautus (▷ *The Comedy of Errors*, 1592–3), Italian ▷ *commedia dell'arte* (▷ *The Taming of the Shrew*, 1593–4) and native and foreign romance narratives (▷ *Two Gentlemen of Verona*, 1594–5). The imaginative idiom of Shakespeare's early comedies testifies to a searching and essentially open intellect, eager to experiment with the demanding forms of classical comedy and the anarchic energy of sprawling prose texts. The latter had formed the staple theatrical diet throughout the Elizabethan period and had recently been legitimized in ▷ Sir Philip Sidney's *Old Arcadia*. Like the revised *New Arcadia* and ▷ Edmund Spenser's ▷ *The Faerie Queene* it affords a rich seam which Shakespeare mined repeatedly.

The first tetralogy of history plays and particularly ▷ *Richard III* were popular successes for Shakespeare's company at their regular venue, the Theatre. They show him turning to English history through the chronicles of Edward Hall and ▷ Raphael Holinshed. In *Richard III* the hunchbacked Yorkist usurper emerges as a fearsome challenger to both the legitimate powers of the state and to our sympathies. Unlike Marlowe's Tamburlaine, Richard Gloucester is mordantly funny in the chrysalis of evil explored in the last three plays of the tetralogy. In one of the longest soliloquies in the entire works, ▷ *Henry VI, Part III* (III.2.124–95, 'Ay, Edward will use women honourably') Richard promises to 'set the murderous Machiavel to school'. His superb plotting and his triumph against the odds in *Richard III* underline the measure of his intellect. The audience is always privy to Richard's schemes, as he evinces a pathological need almost to confide in us. His soliloquies and asides never convey the impression of true intimacy, but reflect a melodramatic and histrionic concept of stage-character derived from the Vice of the medieval morality play.

The cluster of plays written in the mid-1590s: ▷ *Love's Labour's Lost* (1594–5), ▷ *Romeo and Juliet* (1594–5), ▷ *A Midsummer Night's Dream* (1595–6), ▷ *Richard II* (1595–6) and ▷ *The Merchant of Venice* (1596–7), and the writing of most of the sonnets as well as the narrative poems ▷ *Venus and Adonis* and *The Rape of Lucrece* just before the mid-decade, further confirm Shakespeare's position as the foremost lyrical poet of the age. The stirring language and evocative imagery of Clarence's dream vision in *Richard III* (I.4, 'Methoughts that I had broken from the

Tower . . .') anticipate the tropes of *A Midsummer Night's Dream* and of *Romeo and Juliet*, two plays which are equally stylized in spite of their generic differences.

▷ *A Midsummer Night's Dream* is often now judged to be one of Shakespeare's finest and most atmospheric achievements. The tribulations of the love-struck quartet of young Athenians temporarily at the mercy of the woodland fairies led by ▷ Oberon and ▷ Puck provide the mainspring of the play's action. Woven into this seemingly light and courtly rhetorical fabric is a searching exploration of the relationship between the unconscious world of dreams and the deluded controlling power of reason. The realist anchoring of the play's fiction through the robust comedy of the well-intentioned tradesmen and their burlesque of 'Pyramus and Thisbe' provides not only laughter but wonderment at the poet's skill and tact.

For its tender and generous portrayal of star-crossed young love, *Romeo and Juliet*, which is virtually contemporary with *A Midsummer Night's Dream*, remains a great favourite among the plays. It is Shakespeare's first attempt at writing a romantic tragedy. If in the end its verse does not always rise to the challenge of the tragic idiom, the comic parts of the play and its gallery of unforgettable characters such as ▷ Mercutio and Juliet amply vindicate its popularity. The more formally curtailed and less individuated mode of comedy proved easier for Shakespeare to manage at this point, as is evident from the control in *A Midsummer Night's Dream* and the play which precedes it, *Love's Labour's Lost*, an elegant and sophisticated comedy exploring the limits of the rhetoric of love in expressing true feeling in a mode inspired by the idiom of Lyly's plays.

But from ▷ *The Merchant of Venice* (1596–7) to the 'mature' comedies, ▷ *Much Ado About Nothing* (1598–9), ▷ *As You Like It* (1600), ▷ *Twelfth Night* (1600), and the 'problem plays', ▷ *Measure for Measure* (1600–1), ▷ *Troilus and Cressida* (1601–2) and ▷ *All's Well That Ends Well* (1602–3), Shakespeare increasingly questions the adequacy of the genre and its imaginative legitimacy. Shylock's angry question ('Hath not a Jew eyes?') cannot comfortably be reconciled to the fairy-tale world of Belmont. He leaves the play unreclaimed: 'I pray you, give me leave to go from hence;/ I am not well.' In this he anticipates several later characters who fail to be accommodated into the magic circle where lovers are happily matched to create a future world. The darker side of Shakespearean comedy, already intimated in the 12-month penance exacted from Berowne in *Love's Labour's Lost* and the near rape of Silvia by Proteus in *Two Gentlemen of Verona*, is developed further in *As You Like It* and *Twelfth Night*. The two plays engage with a world of threatened identities in which Rosalind and Viola, the plays' respective heroines, visibly have to disguise their femininity before they can actively involve themselves in their alternative societies. Rosalind quickly realizes the potential of her assumed maleness and buoyantly puts it to good use, whereas Viola becomes trapped by her androgyny in a version of the classic love triangle. Notwithstanding the mellow wistfulness of Illyria in *Twelfth Night* and Feste's melancholy songs, or the sheer resilience of the inhabitants of the wintry forest of Arden who are forever singing songs, doubts about the comic vision prevail in the inability of Jaques in *As You Like It* to leave Arden and in the vengeful exit of Malvolio in *Twelfth Night*.

Shakespeare's ▷ 'problem plays' nearly coincide with the period of the writing of *Hamlet* (1600–1). In ▷ *Measure for Measure* (1600–1) the generic framework barely survives the onslaught of Angelo's treachery, Claudio's fear of death and Isabella's relentless and perhaps uncharitable morality. The moated grange in which, through a bed-trick, Mariana instead of Isabella gives herself to Angelo, is all that remains of the never-never land of the early and later comedies. The play is as rife with real and imaginary diseases and corruption as *Hamlet*, and in its moral probings it appears to be equally cognizant of complexity and despair. Questions about honour and death, crime and punishment are more easily resolved in the abstract than in concrete instances. In his disguise as a friar the Duke eloquently persuades Claudio to 'be absolute for death' on the basis that life is too painful to bear and too prone to casual accidents to be worth living. Isabella argues with equal perception and greater passion that 'the sense of death is most in apprehension', and that her brother Claudio must not surrender to the temptation of asking her to sacrifice her virginity to Angelo to save his life. After initially concurring with the Duke and his sister, Claudio suddenly realizes the full horror of unnatural and premature death:

> Claud. *Death is a fearful thing.*
> Isab. *And shamed life a hateful.*
> Claud. *Ay, but to die, and go we know not where . . .*
>
> *Measure for Measure* (III.1.118–33)

The resonance and poignancy of such plain language almost transcends the more poised rhetoric of *Hamlet* and properly belongs to the imaginative and rhetorical spheres of *Othello* and *Macbeth*.

Towards the end of the sixteenth century Shakespeare completed his second English tetralogy of ▷ history plays, which covers the reigns of ▷ Richard II and those of his successors ▷ Henry IV and ▷ Henry V (▷ *Richard II, Henry IV, Parts I and II,* ▷ *Henry V*). *Henry IV, Part I* (1597–8) introduces one of the favourite characters of English drama, ▷ Sir John Falstaff, who will recur in *Henry IV, Part II* (1597–8) and, in a much diminished and domesticated form, in ▷ *The Merry Wives of Windsor* (1600). Through his corpulence and anarchic manner Falstaff, as the Lord of Misrule in Eastcheap, epitomizes the opposition to the rule of Bolingbroke at Westminster, and the seeming attachment of Hal, the Prince of Wales (and future Henry V), to the lawless *bon-viveur* and his cronies fuels the plot of *Henry IV, Part I*. This play also features ▷ Hotspur ('By heaven, methinks it were an easy leap/ To pluck bright honour from the pale-fac'd moon . . .'),

Hal's flamboyant counterpart who is said to put him to shame by his unquestioned military prowess.

This second tetralogy is partly a study in kingship, as we witness Hal's progress from his conscious disowning of Falstaff (*Henry IV, Part I*; I.2.187 ff.; 'I know you all, and will awhile uphold/ The unyok'd humour of your idleness') to his victory at Shrewsbury, and finally his coronation at the end of the second part of *Henry IV*. Reflections about the sacramental nature of kingship loom large in *Richard II*, providing the imaginative material for the great emblematic scene in the encounter between Hal and his dying father in *Henry IV, Part II* (IV.5) and emphasizing the importance of the play's presentation of the Lord Chief Justice in relation to Falstaff and the new king.

The promise of greatness is fulfilled in *Henry V* at the battle of Agincourt, and the play ends like a comedy in the happy marriage of France (Kate) and England (Henry). Yet the doubt expressed by Williams the Welshman about the 'cause' of the French wars (*Henry V*, IV.1.132 ff.; 'But if the cause be not good, the King himself hath a heavy reckoning to make . . .') refuses to disappear and lingers on in spite of Henry's indignant reply about the nature of delegated responsibility and the hard condition of the king's being 'twin-born with greatness'.

A similar distrust of power enters Shakespeare's first great Roman play, ▷ *Julius Caesar* (1599–1600), written at about the same time as *Henry V*. In dramatizing one of the most famous stories of the classical world, Shakespeare pursued his interest in questions of politics and ethics in a Roman and republican context. The austere quality of the play's verse has at times been interpreted as corroborating politically revisionist readings of it in terms of the prevailing monarchical Tudor doctrine, which strongly condemned dissent from established power through its historiography and pamphlets. This is to underestimate the intelligence of Shakespeare's use of Plutarch's Rome, as well as his portrayal of Brutus. The idealist impulse of Brutus's soliloquy (*Julius Caesar*; II.1.10 ff.; 'It must be by his death . . .'), when he attempts to justify to himself his share in the killing of his friend Caesar ('I know no personal cause to spurn him'), anticipates the *Angst* of Hamlet. It is Brutus's moral integrity which causes him to conspire against Caesar, and which draws from Antony the tribute that Brutus 'only in a general honest thought/ And common good to all made one of them'.

Hamlet (1600–1) remains the most often quoted work of English literature and is Shakespeare's longest play. Its instant fame has not diminished in 400 years, even if its hero has recently been scrutinized more critically. Fewer readers and audiences now project their existential anxieties on to Hamlet, who after all causes at least five people to die. Because so much of the play's action is viewed through Hamlet's eyes, he naturally controls our sympathies; and his Oedipal fears and filial dilemmas have struck a particular chord in post-Freudian audiences, notwithstanding our scepticism about Hamlet's motives. If *Hamlet* thrives on its famous soul-searching soliloquies, it is also the case that their measured intellectual tone at times belies the pressing intensity of the character's emotions, which is why too often *Hamlet* has wrongly been read as a play about a young man who could not make up his mind. Rhetorically *Hamlet* has proved one of the most prolifically inventive of English texts, as if Shakespeare needed to coin a new language to express the predicament of the first tragic hero on the European stage since the Hellenic tragedies of ▷ Aeschylus, ▷ Sophocles and ▷ Euripides. In the play the contemporary worlds of Renaissance and Reformation Europe (Hamlet is a student at Wittenberg University, the seat of the Lutheran breakaway movement) and the universal predicament of man fruitfully interact. The sheer scale of destruction in *Hamlet*, as well as its use of an inset playlet, reflect its indebtedness to earlier revenge dramas such as the lost *Ur-Hamlet*, which was probably by ▷ Thomas Kyd. *Hamlet* outstrips such narrow imaginative moulds by refusing to surrender its intimations of complexity to formulaic resolutions. To the extent that, like his lover Ophelia and her brother Laertes, the play's princely protagonist appears young – in spite of the enduring debate about Hamlet's exact age at the beginning of the play – *Hamlet* is a tragedy of adolescence and political intrigue.

Othello (1604–5) radically differs from *Hamlet*; the sprawling and even leisurely expanse of the earlier tragedy is sharply contracted in the focus on the deterioration of Othello's relationship with Desdemona. This primarily domestic tragedy moves at a precipitate pace, as the middle-aged and exotic Othello is increasingly dominated by his 28-year-old ensign Iago. *Othello* is a brilliant exploration of obsessive erotic passion and its dangers. The Moor destroys the woman he loves, and audiences sympathize with his pathos-ridden predicament. But Othello is not a popular hero. Uniquely among Shakespeare's tragic protagonists, Othello is perceived mostly through the refractive eyes of his detractor. He is never allowed to stand apart from his ritualized action. Through its glamorous tropes and rhythms his intoxicating rhetoric blinds Othello to his more rational self; and as the play moves towards its ineluctable conclusion, the Moor increasingly regresses into the arcane image which Iago projects for him.

From the oppressive privacy of *Othello* Shakespeare moves to the apocalyptic dimensions of *King Lear* (1605–6). The play is set in a storm-swept Britain and relates the story of an old king abdicating most of his duties to his three daughters and their spouses. But the youngest, Cordelia, who is also his favourite, publicly humiliates him by refusing his invitation to flattery. The fairy-tale motif, which opens the play and casts the youngest daughter as a Cinderella figure, underlines its almost archetypal quality. As the country's king, Lear functions in a necessary public role, which he retains and even reasserts in moments of supreme agony. There is no scope for royal soliloquies in the play, and there are none. Lear's ragings against the elements (*King Lear*; III.2.1 ff.; 'Blow, winds, and crack your cheeks; rage, blow . . .') suggest the enduring measure of his stature even after the trappings of kingship have been shed. More than any other Shakespearean text, *King Lear* is passionately committed to the imaginative mediation of profound moral convictions. This is strikingly evident in the encounter between Lear and Gloucester in Act IV Scene 6, when the crazed king lectures his fellow sufferer about the nature of empathy and the need for forgiveness. But such 'poetic' forgiveness as there is is not extended to Cordelia, whose integrity and selfless devotion to her father go unrewarded. The death of Cordelia more than any other aspect of the work proved unpalatable and resulted in ▷ Nahum Tate's rewriting of the end of the play as a tragi-comedy in 1681 in which Lear and Cordelia survive to live happily ever after. *King Lear* has recently been the particular focus of editors and textual scholars because of the crucial differences between its Quarto and Folio texts, which suggest that Shakespeare rewrote it and shortened the original version. The implications for interpreting the play's pace and thematic patterning are significant, as the changes directly affect important characters like Edgar and Albany and long passages like the 'trial' in Act III Scene 6, or the entire scene reporting the French invasion in Act IV Scene 3.

The text of *Macbeth* (1605–6), Shakespeare's shortest tragedy, likewise shows signs of corruption, if not revision, through addition from a later work by ▷ Thomas Middleton. The play tells a story of temptation and damnation as its eponymous hero wrestles with his own better self and finally destroys it. In the process he commits every crime under the sun. Like Hamlet, Macbeth is a great soliloquizer and, like Richard III, he commits premeditated murder. But Shakespeare has come a long way from the exhibitionist antics of Richard and his declamatory verse. *Macbeth* is the married tragedy of Macbeth and Lady Macbeth, and in this mutuality it anticipates *Antony and Cleopatra*. Macbeth retains much of our sympathy through his passionate soliloquies, as in his lines spoken in agony before his wife reaffirms his original decision to murder Duncan:

> *If it were done when 'tis done, then 'twere well*
> *It were done quickly.*
> *Macbeth* (I.7.1 ff.)

He is unable to name the deed. These famous reflections culminate in the apocalyptic images of divine children pleading

> *like angels, trumpet-tongu'd, against*
> *The deep damnation of his taking-off;*
> *And pity, like a naked new-born babe,*
> *Striding the blast, or heaven's cherubin hors'd . . .*
> *Macbeth* (I.7)

Shakespeare's most guilty tragic hero discovers the roots of his moral being in a powerful poetic imagination which, like the play itself, revolves around child metaphors and similes. There is a grim poetic justice operating in the defeat of Macbeth, a childless husband, at the hands of Macduff, born by Caesarean section and the father of the children murdered by Macbeth. Even so Shakespeare's Macbeth, unlike Holinshed's historical figure, revolts from his own evil at the last moment when he warns Macduff off by telling him, 'my soul is too much charg'd/ With blood of thine already'.

The astonishing metaphorical and symbolic depths of *Macbeth* are only matched by *Antony and Cleopatra* (1606–7). Before Shakespeare turned to his new subject matter in ▷ Sir Thomas North's translation of ▷ Plutarch's *Lives* of the Greek and Roman heroes, the story of Antony and Cleopatra had long been an exemplary tale of dotage and sexual folly, resulting in Antony's loss of the Roman empire for a whore, as ▷ Bacon noted in his essay 'Of Love'. But Plutarch had created a fascinating Cleopatra in the pages of 'The Life of Marcus Antonius', and Shakespeare responded to the challenge by turning his queen of Egypt into an even more mysterious creature inhabiting the realms of Isis on the banks of the River Nile. Far from being an exemplar of tragedy about the disgrace of Antony, *Antony and Cleopatra*, as its double title indicates, concentrates on an infinitely rich and varied mutuality. The geo-political conflict of the play is indissolubly linked to its romantic interests. Its politics are now increasingly stripped of their moral momentum and are viewed as part of a wider patterning of the lovers whose aspirations, by their very stature as the eastern and western pillars of the classical world, are apocalyptic. As the play evolves, the lovers' separate male and female, Roman and Egyptian identities are increasingly blurred, as if Shakespeare were intent on exploring not only the dissolution of empire, but also, and above all, the merging of gender, thereby completing an imaginative movement initiated in the early comedies and in the sonnets. *Antony and Cleopatra* is the only Shakespearean tragedy which moves towards a resolution in a cosmic lovers' meeting beyond death. Its action and luminous Mediterranean setting contrast with the brooding darkness and chill winds of the other tragedies. Thematically *Antony and Cleopatra* reaches out naturally to the romances, Shakespeare's 'last plays'. Yet *Coriolanus* and *Timon of Athens* intervene before *Pericles*, the first of the tragicomedies.

Coriolanus (1607–8) is rightly viewed as one of Shakespeare's most enigmatic works. Its eponymous protagonist appears stolid and uncharismatic. Whereas Hamlet insistently relates his fears and dilemmas to whichever audience he has, Coriolanus refuses to make us privy to his inner being. He fiercely insists on his ancient privilege to be a proud patrician and cannot accept a new-found political and social reality. His is the tragedy of archaic values tested and aborted in a world of intrigue and of government by delegation. Like its titan hero, *Coriolanus* is uncompromisingly spartan and yields few of the excitements and luxurious pleasures of *Antony and Cleopatra*. Its interweaving of unrelenting directness and seemingly effortless flexibility conveys a rare sense of Shakespeare's maturest verse.

A despairing vision prevails in *Timon of Athens* (1607–8), to such an extent that scholars have at times claimed to detect evidence of a nervous crisis in the play's author towards the end of the first decade of the new century. Shakespeare is now embarking on the last part of his creative work, the romances: *Pericles*, *Cymbeline*, *The Winter's Tale*, and *The Tempest*. They form the most unified body of works in the canon, even though the Folio of 1623 did not put them in a separate category, but classed *Cymbeline* as a tragedy and the others among the comedies. *The Winter's Tale* and *The Tempest* best illustrate the new and more sanguine direction in which Shakespeare was heading. They constitute the perfectly counterbalanced pair: on the one hand, the sprawling and anarchic pastoral, *The Winter's Tale*, whose action stretches over more than 16 years; on the other hand, the tightly structured and neo-classical *Tempest*, in which the playing time mimetically enacts the three hours of the dramatic action dictated by the magus Prospero.

The *Winter's Tale* (1610–11) shows a Shakespeare reaching back to the idiom of his younger days, particularly the lyricism of ▷ Spenser and the pastoral of ▷ Sidney. In structure and dialogue the play is more ritualized than the earlier romantic comedies; and its imaginative focus rests on parent-child relationships as much as on the youthful loves of a prince and a princess. The visual impact of the pregnant Hermione's presence on the stage during the first half of the play is without parallel and intimates the degree to which this neo-pastoral drama breaks new ground, not least in its theatrical iconography. The pacing of *The Winter's Tale* is leisurely, and enables Shakespeare almost nostalgically to explore traditional themes of innocence and experience.

Both *The Winter's Tale* and *The Tempest* emphasize the urgency of Shakespeare's growing concern with themes of spiritual and specifically Christian recovery: the 'art gallery' of Paulina and the reconciliation of Leontes and Hermione in *The Winter's Tale* are echoed in Prospero's recognition that 'the rarer action is/ In virtue than in vengeance', and more somberly, in his retreat to a Milanese hermitage where every third thought will be his grave. After *The Tempest* Shakespeare wrote *Henry VIII* (1612–13) and contributed to ▷ *The Two Noble Kinsmen* (1612–13).

Jonson and his comedies

In 1616, the year of Shakespeare's death, ▷ Ben Jonson published a folio edition of his plays and called them *Works*, thereby indicating that he regarded his craft and its products with the utmost seriousness. Whereas Shakespeare has struck successive generations as 'the poet of nature . . . that holds up to his readers a faithful mirror of manners and of life' (▷ Dr Johnson, *Preface* 1765), Ben Jonson conveys the impression of great artifice and immense learning. Unlike Marlowe's and Shakespeare's, Jonson's achievement has not gone unchallenged. In T. S. Eliot's words, Jonson's reputation

> has been of the most deadly kind that can be compelled upon the memory of a great poet; to be damned by the praise that quenches all desire to read the book; to be afflicted by the imputation of the virtues which excite the least pleasure; and to be read only by historians and antiquaries.

(Selected Essays, 'Ben Jonson')

Among other things Eliot is alluding here to Jonson's self-appointed task of moral teacher in his works. But Jonson's didacticism is no easy matter. In ▷ *The Alchemist* (1610), for example, he builds up a conventional structure of moral expectation – that the returning master, Lovewit, will set right the abuses perpetrated in his house – only to invert it totally when Lovewit is unmasked as just as unscrupulous and rapacious as the other cozeners.

▷ *Volpone* (1605), ▷ *Epicoene, or the Silent Woman* (1609), *The Alchemist* (1610) and ▷ *Bartholomew Fair* (1614) remain Jonson's most highly regarded plays in prose and poetry and have all seen successful performances in the modern theatre. They best epitomize Jonson's shrewd sense of timing, his use of nomenclature to reflect his characters' essential 'humours', and his uncompromising commitment to portraying the contemporary scene in its local, mostly cockney, idiom. It may be this as much as the plays' moralism – of which it forms a part – which renders Jonson sometimes difficult for modern audiences. The sheer burgeoning in his plays of detailed physical description is not always easy to assimilate, nor are Jonson's many and pugnacious involvements in contemporary controversies which are mirrored in the plays.

Jonson's robust idiom refuses to accommodate romantic love, hence the weakness of his female characters such as Dame Pliant in *The Alchemist* or Celia in *Volpone*. He has no Violas or Rosalinds, let alone Cleopatras or Vittoria Corombonas. But in his last works, which ▷ Dryden famously described as belonging to his 'dotage', Jonson seems to acknowledge the imaginative force of a more romantic idiom. This is true particularly of ▷ The New Inn (1629) which is increasingly acclaimed as a late Jonsonian masterpiece with a Shakespearean transsexual formula. Jonson's two dramatic works on Roman themes, ▷ *Sejanus* (1603) and ▷ *Cataline* (1611), show him experimenting in a new mode, as do the 25 ▷ masques which he wrote between 1605 (*The Masque of Blackness*) and 1625, mostly in collaboration with ▷ Inigo Jones. Jonson is the greatest and most prolific English writer of masques. He was also an impressive critic, sometimes to the detriment of his art, as in the overly discursive and explanatory discussion of the laws of comedy in ▷ *Every Man Out of His Humour* (1599). Jonson's most pungent pronouncements on the responsibilities of literary art are contained in his 'common place' book *Timber; or Discoveries made upon Men and Matter* (1640) and in his reported *Conversations with William Drummond of Hawthornden* (1618, although not published in their entirety until 1833).

In the last act of Jonson's *The Poetaster* (1601) ▷ John Marston (1575–1634) is parodied as Crispinus who, through the administration of emetic pills, is made to vomit up his bilious vocabulary. Marston's reputation as a savage satirist partly belies his genuine achievement which includes his contribution to the politically foolhardy collaborative effort (with Jonson and ▷ George Chapman) ▷ *Eastward Hoe* (1605). In *Antonio and Mellida* (1600) and its sequel, *Antonio's Revenge* (1601) Marston wrote in a heavily derivative idiom about young love and its eventual destruction. There is a strong, if flawed, idealist strain in Marston's work. But unlike Jonson who castigates to reform, Marston's energy is wholly curtailed by the vituperative strain in his writing. His most successful play is the tragicomedy ▷ *The Malcontent* (1604). Although it lacks the single-minded naturalism of the scatalogical *Dutch Courtesan* (1605) and the lyricism of *Sophonisba, Wonder of Women* (1605), *The Malcontent* exhibits a remarkable grasp on moral complexity, as the banished Duke of Genoa Altofronto assumes the disguise of a malcontent to wreak revenge on his successor. After a confrontation with true evil, as opposed to assumed mischief, the play ends happily in a recovery of conjugal relations. Nothing could be more different from Marston's painful vision than the works of Beaumont and Fletcher.

▷ Sir Francis Beaumont (1584–1616) and ▷ John Fletcher (1579–1625) share with Shakespeare and Jonson the accolade of having the fruit of their famous ten-year long collaboration published in a folio volume in 1679. Both also wrote plays independently. Beaumont's first play, *The Woman Hater* (1605), reflects the influence of Jonson, who in turn yoked Beaumont together with ▷ Chaucer and Spenser in his elegy to Shakespeare. Beaumont's burlesque ▷ *The Knight of the Burning Pestle* (1607) is his finest work and is still performed successfully today. It is simultaneously a flamboyant parody of chivalry and of ▷ citizen comedy. By interweaving a main plot with a play-within-the-play, the aspirations of a grocer's family and their apprentice with a romance drama, Beaumont recovers in a Jacobean idiom some of the self-referential dimension of *A Midsummer Night's Dream*.

Fletcher succeeded Shakespeare as the main writer of the King's Men after collaborating with him on *Two Noble Kinsmen* and perhaps earlier on *Henry VIII*. He was prolific and is credited with over 15 plays on his own, as well as an equal number with Beaumont. Best known among his own works is *The Faithful Shepherdess* (1608), a pastoral imitation of Guarini's *Il Pastor Fido* (1589). Through its brief prologue which defines the new mode of tragicomedy, ▷ *The Faithful Shepherdess* announces the advent in England of a new 'old' romance form. The late Shakespeare and Beaumont and Fletcher's joint efforts epitomize the incipient Elizabethan nostalgia which set in during the second decade of the seventeenth century. Three of their works in particular underline the extent to which they are in touch with both the old and the novel: ▷ *Philaster* (1609), ▷ *The Maid's Tragedy* (1610), and ▷ *A King and No King* (1611). In *Philaster* Beaumont and Fletcher explore the romantic motif of transvestism in a mode which borrows its sensibility from Shakespeare's *Twelfth Night*, while providing a paradigm similar to Jonson's *Epicoene* (an exactly contemporary play that is equally secretive to the audience about the true nature of the disguise). The so-called 'female page' in *Philaster*, Bellario, who in reality is a young romantic girl, Euphrasia, is *not* rewarded with a husband, but is left to lead a chaste and solitary life. Similarly redolent of the imaginative world of Sidneian pastoral is *The Maid's Tragedy*, probably the greatest work in the Beaumont and Fletcher canon, whose erotic and psychological charge redeem the tragedy from its melodramatic plotting. Equally suggestive of the period is Beaumont and Fletcher's *A King and No King* which flirts with incest, but allows its characters to resolve their dilemma through a *deus ex machina* intervention. If Beaumont and Fletcher have not lasted as well as they promised, this is partly due to the joint effect of romantic saturation and tortuous plotting in much of their work.

▷ Thomas Dekker (1570–1632), ▷ Thomas Heywood (1575–1641) and ▷ Cyril Tourneur (1575–1626) are each remembered by one play. Although Dekker wrote, or collaborated on, over 50 plays, his reputation rests on ▷ *The Shoemaker's Holiday* (1600), a gentle and forgiving London romance of royal wooing in disguise which treats even its minor characters such as Jane Damport, the wife of a conscripted soldier, with affection and regard. Dekker's comedy straddles the century-divide and marks the accommodation of a romantic idiom to a city setting.

Thomas Heywood, whose comedies such as ▷ *The Fair Maid of the West* (1600 and 1630) and *The Four Prentices of London* (1600) were lampooned by Beaumont, displays a remarkable dramatic intelligence in his domestic tragedy *A Woman Killed with Kindness* (1603), which echoes the powerful anonymous play *The Tragedy of Arden of Faversham* (1592), sometimes ascribed to Shakespeare. The story of Frankford's torturing of his unfaithful wife Anne through banishment from her children and himself is presented by Heywood with poise and insight. On her death bed Anne asks for forgiveness, which is granted. The climax in the play occurs after Frankford has discovered positive proof of Anne's fallibility. He is no Othello, but his agonized response to the shattering of his dreams is impressive:

> *O God, O God, that it were possible*
> *To undo things done, to call back yesterday;*
> *That Time could turn up his swift sandy glass,*
> *To untell the days, and to redeem these hours;*
> *Or that the Sun*
> *Could, rising from the west, draw his coach backward,*
> *. . . that I might take her*
> *As spotless as an angel in my arms.*
>
> *A Woman Killed with Kindness* (Sc. 13)

Jacobean tragedy

The reputation of Cyril Tourneur rests exclusively on ▷ *The Atheist's Tragedy* (1611), as ▷ *The Revenger's Tragedy*, formerly thought to be his, is now attributed to ▷ Thomas Middleton. The play invites comparison with Marlowe's *Doctor Faustus* of which it seems at first a domesticated version, since for Faustus's aggressive Manichean creed it substitutes D'Amville's 'natural philosophy'. But the play quickly abandons its sub-Marlovian ambitions and becomes a story of sexual and material intrigue which results in the atheist's accidentally braining himself with the axe intended to kill his innocent nephew Charlemont.

Whether or not Tourneur was indebted, as is sometimes argued, to ▷ George Chapman (1559–1634) and particularly to his play ▷ *The Tragedy of Bussy D'Ambois* (1604), the fact remains that Chapman was highly regarded by his contemporaries. The learned author of the complex poem *Ovid's Banquet of Sense* (1595) and of the equally demanding continuation of Marlowe's ▷ *Hero and Leander* (1598) also collaborated with other playwrights and wrote a number of comedies as well as tragedies. *The Tragedy of Bussy D'Ambois* tells the story of the meteoric ascendancy of its eponymous hero through a combination of patronage and stamina in a manner reminiscent of Tamburlaine. D'Ambois dies unrepentant and will be partly avenged by his brother Clermont in the sequel *The Revenge of Bussy D'Ambois* (1610), a play which interestingly questions the notion of revenge. Chapman's tragedies are informed by a distinctly metaphysical sensibility. Partly for this reason his comedies work better than his tragedies. *May Day* (1611) for example is contemporary with the second *Bussy* play, but easily transcends it aesthetically by its assured construction, controlled language and multiple ironies as its various characters head for a life-enhancing romantic consummation.

A harsher and more fraught vision informs ▷ *The White Devil* (1612) and ▷ *The Duchess of Malfi* (1613) which constitute the claim to fame of ▷ John Webster (1578–1632). In Vittoria Corombona, the 'white devil' of the play's title, Webster created a tragic female figure who exists unapologetically in her sexual immorality and who thrives on the machinations of her Machiavellian brother Flamineo. In the play's most famous scene, 'The Arraignment of Vittoria' (III.2), Vittoria Corombona is allowed a spirited defence against her accusers whose ethics are hardly preferable to hers. Her refusal to bow to their sentence, and her courage in facing death at the end, leave us with an ambiguous response to her character.

The Duchess of Malfi dramatizes the story of an intelligent and generous widow, the duchess of the title, who secretly marries her steward Antonio in a secular ceremony of binding vows. She bears him several children. Whereas Vittoria's brother is her co-conspirator (Flamineo's part is assumed by the malcontent Bosola), the duchess's brother Ferdinand is incestuously obsessed with his sister's sexuality. He cruelly dupes her with a dead man's hand and with waxen figures of her husband Antonio and their children. Although the good characters in the play are unable to overcome death, their quiet dignity and courage are summed up in the duchess's calm reply to Bosola before she is strangled: 'I am Duchess of Malfi still'. In spite of a sometimes baroque idiom and melodramatic stage-managing of plot, Webster's two great tragedies stand out in this period of ebullient dramatic activity.

Webster's achievement is often compared and contrasted with that of ▷ Thomas Middleton (1580–1627), not least because both dramatists share an interest in tragic female figures. Middleton ranks as one of the most successfully prolific writers of the period. Like Webster he collaborated with several of his contemporaries, notably with ▷ William Rowley (1585–1637) on *The Changeling* (1622). His output is impressive. It includes *The Family of Love* (1602), *A Trick to Catch the Old One* (1604), *Michaelmas Term* (1605), *A Mad World, My Masters* (1606), ▷ *The Roaring Girl* (1606), ▷ *A Chaste Maid in Cheapside* (1613), ▷ *No Wit, No Help like a Woman* (1613), *A Fair Quarrel* (1614), ▷ *Women Beware Women* (1614) and the political, allegorical satire ▷ *A Game at Chess* (1624). Middleton's fascination with the psychology of illicit passion and intrigue manifests itself best in the main plot of *The Changeling*. Instructed by her father to marry Alonzo, a man whom she does not love, the 'heroine' employs the repellent servant ▷ De Flores to murder him so that she will be free to marry Alsemero with whom she has fallen in love. De Flores then blackmails ▷ Beatrice-Joanna into a sexual relationship. She will have to hide the loss of her virginity from Alsemero through a bed-trick. The play ends with the exposure of the guilty couple, who commit suicide. As the main plot evolves, the increasing attraction of the romantic and flawed heroine to the satanic De Flores develops into her claim that he is 'a wondrous necessary man', who has both made and destroyed her. The unresolved pessimism which pervades Middleton's *The Changeling* and *Women Beware Women* is balanced by the sprightly energy of his comedies, as in *No Wit, No Help like a Woman*. The title refers to Kate Low-water, the play's disguised married heroine who at times proclaims her affinity with Middleton's own 'roaring girl', both in her courage and in her ultimate tenderness. Few lines better illustrate Middleton's restrained and lucid language than Kate's soliloquy on 'wit' and 'fate':

> Since wit has pleasur'd me, I'll pleasure wit;
> Scholars shall fare the better. O my blessing!
> I feel a hand of mercy lift me up
> Out of a world of waters, and now sets me
> Upon a mountain, where the sun plays most,
> To cheer my heart even as it dries my limbs.
> What deeps I see beneath me . . .

No Wit, No Help like a Woman (II.3, 250–67)

The four dramatists who see out the ▷ Stuart (1603–25) and ▷ Caroline (1625–42) period are ▷ Philip Massinger (1583–1640), ▷ John Ford (1586–1640), ▷ Richard Brome (1590–1653) and ▷ James Shirley (1596–1666). Massinger took over from Fletcher as the King's Men's main dramatist after the latter's death in 1625. He had earlier collaborated with him on over a dozen plays, and his own writing reflects some of Fletcher's romanticism. His best comedies are ▷ *A New Way to Pay Old Debts* (1625) and ▷ *The City Madam* (1632), while among his tragedies *The Duke of Milan* (1621) and ▷ *The Roman Actor* (1626) are not without imaginative insight. Much of Massinger's work is lost, and his modern reputation rests primarily on the achievement of *A New Way to Pay Old Debts*. The play's popularity in the theatre has never waned. Although its plotting – the overthrow of the mean and cruel Sir Giles Overreach through wit, and his subsequent confinement to Bedlam – is reminiscent of Jonson's *Epicoene* and *Volpone*, Massinger's idiom characteristically reconciles romance with the economic nexus.

John Ford is famous primarily for his one impressive Caroline play, ▷ *'Tis Pity She's a Whore* (1632). Writing towards the end of an extraordinary period, Ford reflects many of its preoccupations, and his work shows the influence of Shakespeare, Beaumont and Fletcher, Greene and others. *'Tis Pity* is a play about taboos, particularly in its treatment of the incest between Giovanni and his sister Annabella, whom he makes pregnant. She marries a rich suitor, Soranzo, but refuses to reveal to him the identity of her child's father. The play ends with Giovanni killing his sister and then Soranzo, before he himself dies at the hands of the latter's servant. The subtle layering of the play's plot, its sympathetic portrayal of the foolish Bergetto, and its masterly control of the tender dialogue between the two lovers who refuse to accept the secular and Christian sanctions against their sin, vindicate the prominent place which *'Tis Pity* has long occupied in the history of English drama.

Richard Brome and James Shirley inhabit the twilight of the Caroline theatre, as the clouds were gathering of the political confrontation between the king and the ▷ Puritans that was to close the playhouses in 1642. Brome was a friend of Jonson's, and the latter's influence is evident in ▷ *The City Wit* (1629), but less so in *The Jovial Crew* (1640). *The City Wit* is an intensely theatrical comedy of manners which in its rapid plotting recalls *Epicoene* and *The Alchemist*, while anticipating the idiom of ▷ Restoration comedy. *The Jovial Crew*, on the other hand, is a rural romantic comedy, in the style of ▷ Sidney's pastoral, about fathers, daughters and prophecies. It is an attractive and big-hearted play, which extends its understanding to beggars and gypsies, a rare occurrence during the period.

James Shirley was the last writer of the King's Men. He was prolific and successful, and some of his works like *The Lady of Pleasure* (1631) and *The Cardinal* (1641) have stood the test of time. But they lack substance and, as ▷ C. S. Lewis pointed out, depend overly on 'variations' on one or two themes. Shirley was a professional whose craft reflects the influence of Jonsonian comedy, but never rises to its imaginative level. One suspects that the social conditions which prevailed in the 1630s in London and at the Court of Queen Henrietta Maria, as mirrored in Shirley's writings, contributed materially to the decadence of the theatre just before it finally closed.

From the courtly, Elizabethan theatre of the pre-Shakespeareans to the darker rhythms of the Jacobean period and the fossilization of both these strains in the Stuart plays, the achievement of English Renaissance drama is distinguished by its buoyancy. Few of the dramatists pursued an active interest in form which, like their ethical intelligence, in the plays is often overridden by a predilection for spectacle, taboo and set speeches. Even if one excepts ▷ Lyly, Shakespeare, Jonson and others to a lesser extent, the fact remains that Elizabethan–Jacobean drama and its Stuart twilight show the symptoms of a rambling and creatively chaotic dramatic culture.

If the theatre was perceived by the City Fathers as spiritually subversive, its political critique was generally negligible. On the few occasions that a politically inspired play escaped the censor's notice, it was either by collusion, as in the case of Middleton's ▷ *A Game at Chess* (1624), or by mistake, as with *Eastward Hoe* (1605) which nearly ruined its authors, fairly mild though its lampooning of the Stuarts was. The most famous example of a play exploited for political capital, and ultimately high treason, were the unlicensed and private performances of Shakespeare's *Richard II* in the period immediately preceding the Essex rebellion in 1601. That Shakespeare's finely honed balancing of Richard's neglect of his duties with the monarchical ambitions of Bolingbroke could lend itself to such distortions does not reflect on the play's politics. If anything *Richard II* is a conservative work. The point is that theatre was potentially a political weapon and one of socio-economic import.

In the best possible sense, the theatre was classless. In the large public London playhouses poor apprentices would hobnob with the lords and ladies of the court during afternoon performances, even though admission prices would stand and seat them in different parts of the buildings. The medium of live theatre ensured that the dramatists never lost touch with a public on whom they depended for their livelihood. Even so the theatre did not degenerate into populist entertainment such as was on offer in the nearby bear gardens or gambling houses. Ben Jonson's strenuous attempts – not always successful – at educating his audience are as significant in this respect as the testimony provided by the long runs of Marlowe's and Shakespeare's plays. The English theatre would never again achieve the degree of social integration, economic success and imaginative integrity that it enjoyed in this period.

William Blake after Hogarth: Act III of the first production of John Gay's *The Beggars' Opera*

Restoration and eighteenth-century drama 8

Introduction

When the theatres re-opened in 1660, it was after an interval of eighteen years, and in very different circumstances from before. Recent criticism has suggested that the Commonwealth Proclamation in the crisis year 1642, ordering the playhouses to be shut down, was not due merely to any ▷ Puritan objections to the theatre as such, but because numerous plays in the preceding years had been openly critical of parliamentary as well as royal policies. Thus closing them was partly what we would now call an act of political repression. The intervening period saw some productions, mostly clandestine – although from time to time the companies attempted open performances, sometimes with severe repercussions.

In the 1650s ▷ Sir William D'Avenant found a legal loophole which permitted the staging of musical performances, and he mounted, openly and successfully, four operas (▷ Opera in England), including ▷ *The Siege of Rhodes* (1656) and *The Cruelty of the Spaniards in Peru* (1658). These were effectively the first entertainments of their kind in England, although they drew on earlier ▷ masques for some techniques. Despite the dearth of public performances, the taste for plays survived throughout the ▷ Interregnum, which saw the publication of large numbers of plays, including dozens of new ones. Some of the readers of these were readily assimilated into the new audiences of the 1660s, and from then on playreading as well as theatre going became an increasingly popular pastime.

The period 1660–1800 is marked by innovation from its outset. The advent of women, both as actresses and as dramatists, had a profound impact on the staging of plays and the responses to them. The shape and layout of the theatres changed, together with the style of acting, and the nature of the audiences. New themes came into prominence in the plays, partly as a reaction to new social and political conditions and, partly in response to the technical changes just mentioned. Within the period also, there were discernible shifts of topic, theme and style of acting. Nevertheless, the theatres continued to operate under varying degrees of ▷ censorship. This encouraged the staging of plays expressing attitudes of loyalty to the reigning monarch and prevailing ethics, and meant that some plays considered politically or socially dangerous were suppressed. Censorship was applied most rigorously during periods of political tension, such as the Popish Plot, resulting in large-scale persecutions of Catholics and the Exclusion crises of the 1680s when unsuccessful attempts were made in Parliament to exclude the Duke of York (later ▷ James II) from the succession, and again in the 1730s, when satirical attacks on the Government contributed to the passing of the Licensing Act of 1737 (▷ Theatres).

In the past, histories of the theatre and drama have tended to focus on so-called canonical texts: those identified by generations of commentators as representing the best in their periods. In the twentieth century the reinforcement of this pattern became known as the Leavisite tradition, after the literary critic ▷ F. R. Leavis, who isolated certain 'great books' which he considered central to civilization. The implication has been that these and only these are worthy of serious study. But the approach has been challenged repeatedly. The Reverend Montague Summers issued new editions of plays by 'lesser' ▷ Restoration dramatists, including ▷ Aphra Behn and ▷ Thomas Shadwell, in the first decades of this century, and Leslie Hotson's *The Commonwealth and Restoration Stage* (1928) broke new ground in research on the theatre of the seventeenth century. More recently, writers including Robert D. Hume, Judith Milhous, Margot Heinemann, Martin Butler, Fidelis Morgan and Dale Spender have contributed to a re-evaluation of many 'forgotten' dramatists and works, including many by women.

The theatres

▷ Charles II loved the theatre, and was from the beginning of his reign an enthusiastic patron of it, but when he officially re-opened the theatres, he sought to ensure political loyalty from that quarter by confirming existing monopolies to two trusted courtiers: Sir William D'Avenant and ▷ Sir Thomas Killigrew, as well as by re-establishing a system of censorship. The pattern of monopolies lasted, with interruptions, for most of the eighteenth century.

On confirmation of their patents, D'Avenant and Killigrew formed two companies, the ▷ Duke's and ▷ King's companies, respectively, and set about finding venues for their performances. For a brief period they used existing theatres which were re-opened for the purpose, including a few dating back to Elizabethan times. In March 1660 D'Avenant began converting Lisle's Tennis Court at ▷ Lincoln's Inn Fields. This introduced the proscenium, or framed stage, to the English theatre for the first time. But although he had extended the property, it was felt that it was still too small, and needed a substitute. D'Avenant died in 1668, and it fell to his widow, Lady Mary D'Avenant, who had inherited the patent, to carry out the work. The new theatre, designed by ▷ Christopher Wren, stood on the river front in Dorset Garden (▷ Dorset Garden Theatre), where it had access both by road and from the water by boat. The Duke's company moved here in 1671, still under Lady Mary's control, until she transferred it to her son Charles in 1673.

Killigrew meanwhile had moved his company to an old riding school in Bridges Street, Drury Lane, which he converted to a theatre – the first Theatre Royal (▷ Drury Lane Theatres). This opened in May 1663, and survived until 1672, when it was destroyed by fire. He then commissioned a new theatre, possibly also by Wren, on a site close by.

The acting area on the ▷ Restoration stage included a deep forestage or apron stage, which projected beyond the proscenium into the pit, past the side boxes. Proscenium doors admitted the actors directly onto the forestage. Here the prologue and much of the dialogue were spoken, clearly audible, and the speakers clearly visible, to the surrounding audience, some of whom might even be seated on the stage itself. The proscenium arch contained a curtain or painted cloth that could be lowered or raised to reveal the interior stage, which had receding rows of painted flats and shutters in grooves on either side. These in turn could be closed or opened, adding further depths to the set or action. Numerous Restoration plays contain 'discovery scenes', indicating that the shutters are opened to reveal behind them other settings or actors, who might then perhaps move forward to join in action nearer the audience. The result was considerable versatility, including the option to change settings in full view of the audience, and with them mood and pace during scenes. Balconies above the stage were also used for some of the action. However there was no naturalistic illusion of landscapes or interiors in the modern sense, but rather a decking of the stage with images and objects to suggest various locations.

A characteristic feature of Restoration drama was its use of elaborate effects – such as cupids or other figures floating on 'clouds' above the stage – aided by mechanical devices. Lighting, for performances were staged mainly in the afternoon, was largely daylight, admitted through the windows, as well as candelabra hung from the centre of the proscenium, and footlights or 'floats' – literally candles, or wicks threaded through corks, floating on troughs of water or oil at the front. Rows of candles and oil lamps, placed in brackets and coloured by strips of stained glass or tinted silk, as well as hand-held candles, lanterns and torches, added light to acting areas further back. Snuffers stood by because of the constant threat of fire.

In addition to the patent theatres were Court theatres, including the Cockpit at ▷ Whitehall, and the Hall Theatre, built in 1665. Two ▷ Inns of Court – the Inner Temple and the Middle Temple – put on plays, sometimes involving Duke's and King's Theatre actors, as part of their festivities. Musical performances took place in private homes and at Court. Several ▷ 'nurseries', training grounds for younger performers, also existed briefly, and mounted their own productions. Killigrew set up one of them in 1667, at Hatton Garden; another was established by Lady D'Avenant after her husband's death, in the Barbican; she was involved in the running of a third at Bun Hill in Finsbury Fields, but this lasted only nine weeks. The nurseries were the butt of opposition from several quarters, but actors sometimes succeeded in 'graduating' from them into the patent companies. Finally, strolling players performed at fairs and other venues from time to time.

Playhouses also proliferated throughout the provinces, as well as in Scotland and Ireland. Today there are only three playhouses surviving from the eighteenth century (the earliest still remaining): the Theatres Royal in Richmond (Yorkshire), Bristol and Margate. Another Georgian theatre, the Theatre Royal at Bury St Edmunds (opened 1819), has the distinction of preserving its original proscenium to this day.

The most important theatres in this context were the two patent houses, and these carried on a fierce rivalry. From the first the ▷ Dorset Garden specialized in staging very elaborate performances, including many operas, while the Theatre Royal concentrated on plays. In 1682 matters came to a head with the failure of the King's Company, which was effectively absorbed into the Duke's to form the ▷ United Company. The United Company continued performances of spectacles at Dorset Garden and plays at ▷ Drury Lane.

Corruption and mismanagement led three of the principal actors, headed by ▷ Thomas Betterton, to secede in 1695, returning to Lincoln's Inn Fields, which they named the 'New Theatre'. In 1705 Betterton left for Her Majesty's Theatre, also known as the Queen's Theatre, Haymarket, or simply, the ▷ Haymarket, a newly opened playhouse designed by the dramatist and architect ▷ John Vanbrugh. The company was managed in turn by Vanbrugh and ▷ William Congreve. But the theatre suffered financial problems; it proved too large for spoken drama, and in due course became the first English opera house, staging many of ▷ Handel's operas. It was burnt down in 1789, and in 1791 a new theatre was built, known first as the King's and later the Queen's.

Theatre construction and alteration continued over the next two decades. In 1714, Lincoln's Inn Fields was refurbished in grand style by the architect and designer Edward Shepherd (1670–1747), with mirrors lining the interior walls, and then run by the actor-manager ▷ John Rich – son of the late ▷ Christopher Rich whose dishonesty and incompetence had contributed to the secession of the actors mentioned above. The theatre became known by different names: sometimes the New Theatre and sometimes the Little Theatre.

In 1720 a new theatre was erected by ▷ John Potter in the Haymarket, almost opposite the Opera House. Confusingly, this was also known variously as the New Theatre, or Little Theatre in the Hay; or even as the French Theatre in the Haymarket. Scenery was still painted onto flats, and lighting was by overhead chandeliers with wax or tallow candles. As in the Restoration period, the curtain rose and fell only at the beginning and end of the play. The Licensing Act of 1737 forced it to close down and it stood empty for ten years, whereupon it was taken over by the actor and dramatist Samuel Foote (1720–77). In 1766 it became a 'Theatre Royal'; it stood until 1820 when the present Theatre Royal, Haymarket, was erected nearby.

In 1732 Shepherd planned the first ▷ Covent Garden Theatre, or Theatre Royal, on the site of the present Royal Opera House, to which John Rich transferred. A contemporary print shows a proscenium with two doors surmounted by balconies, and behind it an inner frame. Another device apparently surviving from the Restoration period is the 'transparent scene': a translucent surface which could be lit from behind to produce special effects. On Rich's death in 1761, the theatre was taken over by his son-in-law, John Beard (?1716–91), who passed the patent to the dramatist ▷ George Colman the Elder, and three partners, in 1767. The theatre was substantially altered in 1784 and rebuilt in 1792, mainly to allow it to hold many more spectators. It was destroyed in a great fire in 1808. A new theatre was built on the same site the following year.

The 1730s saw increasing tensions between the government and the stage. Some in high places were concerned about the rapid and apparently unchecked rise in the number of playhouses, and disputes about who should exercise control were fuelled by a number of satirical performances openly criticising the government. Notable among these were several by ▷ Henry Fielding, who eventually sided with ▷ Sir Robert Walpole's opposition. In 1737 Walpole, precariously clinging to dwindling power, succeeded in bringing in a Licensing Act which re-established a monopoly of theatrical entertainment. This was assigned to two playhouses: Covent Garden and Drury Lane, the latter managed by ▷ David Garrick from 1747. Not surprisingly, the Act was not entirely successful in limiting theatrical activity. For example, the actor-manager James Lacy (1696–1774) defied the law at intervals after its enactment. And the ▷ Goodman's Fields Theatre in Ayliffe Street, despite being ordered like the Haymarket to close in 1737, resumed performances using subterfuges to evade the law until 1742. Here it was that Garrick made his first appearance before London audiences.

Garrick's impact on the theatre was immense not only on methods of acting, but also on the physical conditions of performance. One innovation during his tenure as manager at Drury Lane was precipitated by a number of incidents in which audience rowdiness erupted literally onto the stage, seriously interfering with the performance. In 1763 Garrick announced an increase in the capacity of the auditorium, while prohibiting seating from the area around the stage whose presence had been allowed since the Restoration. The manager of Covent Garden, John Beard, quickly followed suit.

Further, in 1765 Garrick introduced stage lighting concealed from the audience, an effect used in ▷ Richard Brinsley Sheridan's ▷ *The School for Scandal*. He also used naturalistic cut-out scenery designed by ▷ De Loutherbourg, an Alsatian who had already made his name in Paris. In the later years of the century, the ▷ Gothic revival seen in other areas of literature and culture of the period was also reflected on stage in scenes displaying dark and rugged mountains, misty and mysterious lakes, or gloomy ruined castles in the Gothic style. Some of Garrick's changes were ultimately to contribute to an effect of added unreality, as well as a loss of contact between actors and audience.

The efforts to enlarge Drury Lane continued during and after Garrick's tenure. The theatre was extensively altered and expanded by the Adam brothers (▷ Robert Adam) in 1775. In the following year, upon Garrick's retirement, it was taken over by Sheridan, who rebuilt and extended it yet again in 1794, and remained in charge until its destruction by fire in 1809. The removal of spectators from the stage effectively widened the gulf between actors and audience. The last decades of the century saw an increase in the use of the curtain to separate scenes from one another, and doors were added to the side scenes for entrances and exits, ostensibly to aid naturalism. In due course they came to replace the proscenium doors altogether, and eventually the box set, and the limiting of acting to the area behind the proscenium completed the rift between actors and audience. Plays were performed in increasingly large theatres, entirely behind the proscenium frame, and the intimacy and immediacy of drama in earlier eras was lost.

The performers, their companies and their audiences

The period is highlighted by some of the great names of theatre tradition, including some individuals of extraordinary versatility, Thomas Betterton, ▷ Charles Macklin, Samuel Foote, David Garrick and ▷ John Philip Kemble, for example, not only acted in but also wrote plays (although some were merely adaptations of older plays), as well as managing their companies. ▷ Richard Steele, in addition to contributing to and editing or co-editing at various times ▷ *The Tatler*, ▷ *The Spectator*, ▷ *The Guardian*, *The Theatre* (the first English theatrical journal) and other publications, was a theatre manager and also wrote several influential plays ▷ Colley Cibber was a manager as well as actor and dramatist, and in his memoirs made a serious contribution to theatre history. Sir John Vanbrugh designed theatres in addition to writing successful plays. The dramatist Henry Fielding managed the Haymarket during the 1730s until its closure in 1737, after which he became a celebrated novelist; another dramatist, ▷ George Colman the Elder, managed Covent Garden when the plays of ▷ Oliver Goldsmith were first produced there, and took over the Haymarket later. Sheridan, as we have seen, became a manager as well as a dramatist of lasting reputation, ▷ Susannah Centlivre started as an actress, before becoming one of the most successful dramatists of her generation. The actress ▷ Kitty Clive also wrote several plays, including some that were quite successful, and ▷ Charlotte Charke not only acted in dozens of roles, but wrote plays and managed companies as well. However, women dramatists, like other women writers, were subject to attack by men, as in the satire, *The Female Wits* (1696), and ▷ Pope, ▷ Gay and ▷ Arbuthnot's ▷ *Three Hours After Marriage* (1717), which mocks the Countess of Winchilsea through the character of Phoebe Clinket. One character says of her that 'the poor girl has a procidence [prolapse] of the pineal gland, which has occasioned a rupture in her understanding . . . instead of puddings, she makes pastorals, or when she should be raising paste [pastry], is raising some ghost in a new tragedy'.

Other important figures on the Restoration stage include ▷ Michael Mohun, ▷ Edward Kynaston and ▷ Charles Hart, all of whom had begun their careers as boy actors playing largely female roles, as well as ▷ William Smith, William Mountfort (1664–92), ▷ Elizabeth Barry, ▷ Anne Bracegirdle, for whom several of Congreve's parts were written, and of course Ellen or ▷ Nell Gwyn. She retired from the stage after she became Charles II's mistress, but remained its ardent patron and admirer. ▷ Susanna Cibber, ▷ Anne Oldfield, ▷ James Quin, ▷ Spranger Barry, ▷ Peg Woffington and ▷ Sarah Siddons are among major actors and actresses in the eighteenth century. Each era also had its noted comedians, including ▷ James Nokes and Thomas Jevon (or Jevorn, d 1688) during the early Restoration period, and ▷ John Lacy, Thomas Doggett (1670–1721) and ▷ William Penkethman (or Pinkethman) later on.

The most important innovation at the beginning of the period is the introduction of actresses to the stage. Before the Restoration, women had acted occasionally: the casts of court masques included some female members of royalty, and a woman had acted in D'Avenant's ▷ *The Siege of Rhodes* in 1656. But the general rule in England had been for men and boys to act the women's parts. However, on the Continent, actresses had already become common-place, and Charles II during his years of exile had become accustomed to seeing them. In August 1660 he ordered D'Avenant and Killigrew to place women in all female roles, and his subsequent patent suggested that it was indeed improper to do otherwise.

From a modern standpoint, the insistence on having women play women's parts may be considered as a ▷ 'feminist' act. However, there is ample evidence that many male contemporaries saw it chiefly as adding a prurient element to their enjoyment of the theatre, Charles's ostensible views notwithstanding. The diarist ▷ John Evelyn (1620–1706) complained bitterly that 'Foul and undecent women now (and never till now) were permitted to appear and act ... inflaming several young noblemen and gallants ...' More than forty years later, ▷ Sir Richard Steele, in quite a different frame of mind, remarked that a woman's presence was a great help to a dull production, so that 'When a poet flags in writing lusciously, a pretty girl can move lasciviously, and have the same good consequences for the author'. The dramatic motif of woman disguised as man, in order to further some – usually romantic – end, had in ▷ Shakespeare's time relieved the burden on young actors struggling with womanish movements and vocal patterns. After the Restoration it became a means whereby actresses could put on breeches, and show off shapely ankles and calves. ▷ Pepys commented that a woman acting in a man's role 'had the best legs that ever I saw, and I was very well pleased with it'. Many stage directions and lines in the plays, as well as the revealing dresses of the period, also contributed to an emphasis on the women's sexuality. On the other hand, wearing breeches made it possible, at least by the early eighteenth century, for a woman to experience briefly and without censure, freedom from cumbersome skirts in the manner of a man. ▷ Bernard de Mandeville, in *The Fable of the Bees* (1714), wrote that when a woman wore breeches 'Upon the Stage it is done without Reproach, and the most Vertuous Ladies will dispense with it in an Actress, tho' everybody has a full view of her Legs and Thighs; but if the same Woman, as soon as she has Petticoats on again, should show her Leg to a Man as high as her Knee, it would be a very immodest Action, and every Body will call her impudent for it'.

The position of the actress was ambiguous. That many actresses were kept by wealthy lovers, or performed individual sexual favours in return for gain, is undeniable. The acting profession was then, as later, a precarious one, and the temptation to reinforce their incomes in this way must have proved irresistible to many actresses. However, some dramatic historians, such as

John Harold Wilson, have exaggerated the extent to which their function was synonymous with that of courtesan or even prostitute. Many actresses, including those known to be 'unchaste', also gained lasting reputations as artists, ▷ Elizabeth Barry, for example, was said to be ruthlessly promiscuous, and was frequently condemned on this account. Yet she was much admired as both a comic and tragic actress, and as a tragedienne is reported to have performed with great dignity and pathos. It is important to note that male actors also occupied a paradoxical position during much of the period. They were considered to be relatively low down on the social scale (an ▷ Act of ▷ James I had made them, technically, vagabonds). Pepys, visiting the actors at one theatre backstage, remarked that 'the clothes are very poore, and the actors but common fellows'. On the other hand, actors frequently enjoyed close associations with courtiers (including several dramatists), and, in many cases, the respect of other critical theatre goers as well. Gradually during the eighteenth century the status of actors and actresses rose, boosted by Garrick's success and enjoyment of public esteem, as well as the growing popularity of the theatre and interest in the performers generally. But it is clear that for a long time there were conflicts in the attitudes towards all performers, and towards actresses particularly.

The actress ▷ Katherine Corey claimed to be the first woman in her profession: she played the part of Desdemona in a production of ▷ *Othello* in December 1660. Occasionally, as with Thomas Killigrew's *The Parson's Wedding* in 1664 and again for a time during the early eighteenth century, plays were performed by casts made up entirely of women. Some individual women became celebrated for playing particular male roles, notably Peg Woffington as Sir Harry Wildair in ▷ Farquhar's ▷ *The Constant Couple* (1699) and, less famously, Susanna Cibber as Macheath in Gay's ▷ *The Beggar's Opera*. Colley Cibber's talented, versatile and quirky daughter Charlotte Charke, given from childhood to dressing in male attire, became as famous in her performances of men's roles as of women's. She acted the two in rapid succession, sometimes playing a man's part on one night and a woman's on the next, and occasionally, a man's and a woman's in different performances of the same play: for example she was both Macheath and Polly in *The Beggar's Opera*. During a month and half of a single season in 1734 she acted about a dozen men's roles, including Macheath in Roman dress, George Barnwell in ▷ Lillo's ▷ *The London Merchant*, Townly in Vanbrugh and Cibber's *The Provok'd Husband*, and gay Lothario in ▷ Nicholas Rowe's *The Fair Penitent*. And once she played the part made famous by her father, Sir Fopling Flutter, in ▷ Sir George Etherege's ▷ *The Man of Mode*.

Early in the eighteenth century the ratio of men to women in the acting profession was almost two to one. One company listed twenty men and eleven women in the first decade. At Lincoln's Inn Fields account books for the years 1724–25 bear the names of twenty-eight men and sixteen women. Gradually the proportion of women rose, together with the total number of performers employed in the profession, as the number of theatres multiplied. The average for the years 1729 to 1747 was 74, and in a single season, 1729–30, over 250 named performers are listed in the bills.

As for the management structure, during the first years after the Restoration the acting profession was dominated, as already noted, by the two patent companies, which merged into the United Company in 1682. Each company had a core group of performers which shared what was left of the profits after running costs had been paid from general receipts. This group was headed by the largest shareholder, in effect the manager, and augmented by salaried 'hirelings' who might eventually become shareholders, as well as musicians, scene keepers and other non-acting personnel. In the 1690s control of the United Company passed to the unscrupulous Christopher Rich, a profiteer with little or no interest in performers or acting standards, precipitating the secession of Betterton, Barry and Bracegirdle already mentioned, to form another sharing company in 1695.

The double system of management, actor-manager on the one hand and proprietor-manager on the other, persisted into the eighteenth century: Rich in charge of Drury Lane, and Betterton of Lincoln's Inn Fields. After 1705 when Vanbrugh opened the Queen's Theatre in the Haymarket, companies and varieties of organization proliferated until the Licensing Act of 1737 restored the system of two patents. Meanwhile from 1705 opera, developing as an increasingly separate form of entertainment, had its own management structure.

The dominant figure on the stage during the Restoration and early eighteenth century years was undoubtedly Thomas Betterton, both because of his reputation, and his ability. He was equally acclaimed in tragedies and comedies and played mostly leading roles with the Duke's Company, the United Company, and finally his own at Lincoln's Inn Fields. A contemporary portrait shows him as a stout man, quite unlike today's ideal of a romantic actor, but dignified and imposing in a silk robe wrapped and folded round his large body, a cravat loosely tied and the locks of a shiny wig flowing down his back. He excelled in Shakespearean parts, including Hamlet ($\triangleright$ *Hamlet*), Macbeth ($\triangleright$ *Macbeth*), Lear ($\triangleright$ *King Lear*), Othello ($\triangleright$ *Othello*), Mercutio ($\triangleright$ *Romeo and Juliet*) and Sir Toby Belch ($\triangleright$ *Twelfth Night*), but also in contemporary ones such as Heartwell in Congreve's $\triangleright$ *The Old Bachelor*. He married Mary Sanderson (or Saunderson), one of the first English actresses and the first to play a succession of Shakespeare's great female characters, including Lady Macbeth ($\triangleright$ *Macbeth*), Ophelia ($\triangleright$ *Hamlet*) and Juliet ($\triangleright$ *Romeo and Juliet*). They often appeared opposite one another on the stage, setting a precedent to be followed by other couples, from the Mountforts, Cibbers and Bullocks onwards into the twentieth century. Other family members also became involved, and the eighteenth century saw many great acting families and dynasties, including the Bullocks, Mills, Thurmonds, Penkethmans, Kembles and Booths. Early on children also began to feature prominently in stage productions: a Miss Willis, aged five, danced at Lincoln's Inn Fields in 1704, and a ten-year-old girl played Cupid in a masque at Drury Lane later in the same year. In the third quarter of the century it became fashionable to have plays entirely acted by children. Acting became, and remained into the twentieth century, a family business.

Acting styles during the Restoration era can be deduced from contemporary portraits, some written accounts, and largely from the manner of the plays themselves. For comedies it appears to have been more or less an extension of the comportment of gentlemen and women in society, that is, formal and deliberate, involving a large number of elaborate gestures and facial expressions in a curious mixture of flamboyance and decorum. The close links between the theatre and the court must have been reflected on stage, with actors and actresses modelling their performances in many plays on those of well-bred courtiers. The extremes of this style are frequently mocked, as in the characters of Monsieur de Paris, in ▷ William Wycherley's ▷ *The Gentleman Dancing Master* (1672), and Lord Foppington in Vanbrugh's ▷ *The Relapse* (1697). For tragedies the style remained solemn and declamatory, or 'theatrical . . . stiff and affected', according to a contemporary, possibly even involving chanting, until Macklin pioneered and Garrick perfected a more 'natural' approach. Betterton's method has been described as 'dignified, graceful, yet somewhat heavy and florid . . . interpreting admirably those interminable heroic generals who abound in that period of Restoration melodrama'.

Commentators on the period, such as John Harrington Smith, J. H. Wilson, Peter Holland and J. L. Styan, stress the intimate relationship between actors on stage and the audience, as shown in the many asides and direct addresses to the audience in the plays, delivered from the projecting apron. During the eighteenth century acting methods underwent a considerable alteration. In the first decades of the century ▷ Quin and others in his generation continued in the style of Betterton and his contemporaries, but Macklin and then Garrick reacted to Quin's heavy formality, introducing what seemed to theatre goers to be greater naturalism and simplicity, accompanied by a subtle expression of voice, face and gesture. Quin was eventually forced to retire from what had been an outstanding career, including the roles of Othello, Lear and ▷ Falstaff. But alongside this change came an increasing emphasis on performing skills other than acting: dancing, singing, juggling and acrobatics.

The tendency toward greater naturalism, fuelled by the rise of ▷ Romanticism, encompassed a reappraisal of some traditional roles, particularly those of Shakespeare. The part of Shylock in ▷ *The Merchant of Venice* had long been played in a low, buffoonish style. In 1741 ▷ Macklin, later to become Garrick's great rival, appeared as a tragic and dignified, though still villainous, Shylock: 'the Jew that Shakespeare drew', in ▷ Alexander Pope's words. The impact was instant; the audience applauded so much that he had to pause after each speech to allow for the interruptions, and he became famous overnight. Changes in the depiction of Hamlet happened more gradually. From Shakespeare's time he had been portrayed as an heroic 'man of action'. But in the second or third quarter of the eighteenth century, actors including Richard Brinsley Sheridan's father Thomas (1719–88) and David Ross (1728–90) are believed to have begun the trend toward playing him as the irresolute, thoughtful, melancholy personality familiar to audiences in the twentieth century.

Towards the end of the eighteenth century came another change, moving toward the florid acting styles of the nineteenth century, accompanied by a tendency to rant and shout. The enlargement of the theatres and shrinking of the apron now demanded that actors and actresses raise their voices and expand their gestures if they were to be heard and seen from the top gallery. The celebrated tragic actress ▷ Sarah Siddons refused to comply, causing some criticism that she was no longer always audible. But the practice was consistent with her concept of dramatic integrity; she disdained to 'play to the gallery'. She was enormously respected as well as admired for her dignity and grace, the deep beauty of her voice, her consistent professionalism and her capacity to move audiences.

Along with changes in acting methods, came changes in the approach to dress. In 1759 ▷ John Wilkes had pleaded for a return to the Roman tradition whereby actors always dressed 'according to the fashion of the country where their scene was laid'. In 1773 Macklin dressed his *Macbeth* in tartan costumes, and played the title role with a Scottish accent. Garrick responded with a *King Lear* in old English clothing. A famous portrait shows Peg Woffington in quasi-Elizabethan costume as Mistress Ford (▷ *The Merry Wives of Windsor*). And Sarah Siddons attempted to marry authenticity with dramatic propriety, wearing costumes not only true to their historical context but also to the genre employed: thus tragedy demanded heavy garments and simple, natural hairstyles and headgear, in contrast to some of the elaborate creations of her predecessors.

Yet at the same time as Garrick and others were attempting to instil verisimilitude into the trappings and substance of their performances of Shakespeare, they were busy rewriting many of the plays, including some scenes which had escaped onslaught from Restoration revisers. A famous example is Garrick's alteration of *Hamlet* in 1772, omitting 'scenes of low humour' (including the Grave Diggers' scene), 'improving' the character of Laertes, and altering the circumstances of the Queen's death. *King Lear*, given a happy ending by ▷ Nahum Tate in 1681, had been changed again by George Colman the Elder, although he retained much of Tate's action, including the happy ending, as did Garrick in his version. Audiences in the eighteenth century, like their predecessors in the seventeenth, could not bear to see such injustice as was done to Cordelia. ▷ Samuel Johnson wrote that Shakespeare's ending was intolerable. The philosopher ▷ David Hume said that 'An action, represented in tragedy, may be too bloody and atrocious . . . The mere suffering of plaintive virtue, under the triumphant tyranny and oppression of vice, forms a disagreeable spectacle, and is carefully avoided by all masters of the drama'. Most plays were rewritten in one form or another, and several were used as sources for short pieces focussing on just a few characters, in the manner of the time. Garrick's *Florizel and Perdita* (1756) is derived from ▷ *The Winter's Tale*, for example; his *The Fairies* (1755) from ▷ *A Midsummer Night's Dream*; and *Catherine and Petruchio* (1756) from ▷ *The Taming of the Shrew*.

Throughout the period acting was a strenuous and demanding profession, not least because of the size of a company's repertory, with programmes sometimes changing from day to day. During the season of 1721-2 John Mills (d 1736) probably performed in sixty of the seventy plays put on at Drury Lane, including major roles in ▷ Marlowe, Shakespeare, ▷ Jonson, Vanbrugh, Congreve and Farquhar. ▷ Robert Wilks acted at least 170 times, and Barton Booth in at least thirty-five roles, in addition to sharing in the company's management. Mary Porter (d 1765) acted in twenty-eight and Anne Oldfield in twenty-six roles in one season. Rehearsals in such circumstances were almost continuous, and inevitably scanty for any particular play. Furthermore, actors often had to double up, performing several roles in a single play and less frequently, during the eighteenth century, in plays in different theatres on a single night. Kitty Clive, for example, acted in Colley Cibber's *The Lady's Last Stake* at Drury Lane and ▷ Henry Fielding's *The Virgin Unmask'd* at the New Theatre on the Bowling Green on the same evening in January 1747. These factors meant that the actors had to remember huge numbers of lines, which could sometimes lead to complaints about distortions of the text and inappropriate ad-libbing. But some actors took pride in their retentive abilities: Garrick had up to 96 varied roles in his personal repertory and ▷ William Smith boasted that he could perform in any of 52 at a moment's notice.

Training facilities existed throughout the period. The Restoration nurseries have already been mentioned. In addition, senior actors and managers undertook to train the more junior recruits. In 1744 Macklin founded his own school to train actors according to his style of disciplined naturalism. Some performers in the period underwent long apprenticeships, but this did not guarantee that their careers would endure. Charlotte Charke is a prime example of an actress and dramatist who began with the best connections and hopes for her future, but ended up acting mostly in provincial theatres, or managing puppet shows, and living in terrible poverty. Income from acting was often uncertain as it depended largely on receipts. Salaried performers could not always be certain of being paid at all, and indeed payment was not made on days when there were no performances.

However, from the Restoration era onwards, leading performers could earn well: in 1694, Betterton received five pounds a week, plus a present of fifty guineas a year, and Barry received fifty shillings a week. In addition such actors, and later also some other theatre staff, were able to augment their incomes with the proceeds of 'benefits' staged on their behalf. (The profits from the third night of every production – if it survived that long – automatically belonged to the author.) The so-called 'Theatrical Fund', was established in 1765 as a form of insurance whereby a performer could claim from thirty to 65 pounds a year from retirement, or to provide a stipend for an actor's widow and surviving children on his death.

As to the audience, for many years after the Restoration it was far less heterogeneous than it had been in Shakespeare's time, containing a large number of upper-class men and women. Relatively high admission prices, ranging from one to four shillings, kept the poorest members of society away (in 1684 the average labourer's wage was only eight pence a day). But earlier views of the audience as almost exclusively aristocratic, by commentators such as Allardyce Nicoll, ▷ John Wain and A. S. Bear, have now been discounted: at present it is thought that it included a cross-section of middle and upper-class society, including some merchants and 'citizens'. During the Restoration period, these were frequently ridiculed and actually insulted in the plays, and theories vary as to how much they joined in laughing at themselves, refused to identify with the absurd characters on stage and laughed at 'other' citizens shown as bigoted and stupid, suffered in silence, fought back or simply stayed away from plays known or presumed to be particularly offensive. A softening in dramatists' attitudes towards these classes beginning late in the seventeenth century, as well as the campaign to 'clean up' the stage, may represent an increasingly successful rearguard action of such individuals and/or changing social conditions. The economic strengthening and social 'legitimizing' of the bourgeois classes during the eighteenth century encouraged them to exercise their influence on the stage as on other cultural and social ventures. The expansion of the theatres, with the audiences gradually becoming more heterogeneous, coincided with a change in the manner of depicting the middle classes. Merchants and their families ceased to be mere objects of ridicule and were humanized into heroes and heroines, to be admired, criticized, laughed at or laughed with, according to the text.

Life in the theatre was marked by outbursts of violence during much of the period, to an extent that would seem incredible today. In 1669 Edward Kynaston was beaten up by ruffians hired by a rival, and in 1692 William Mountfort was murdered by Lord Mohun and his agents. Elizabeth Barry and ▷ Elizabeth Bowtell, required to struggle in their roles of Roxana and Statira during a revival of Nathaniel Lee's (c 1653–92) *The Rival Queens* (1677), came literally to blows, and the stabbing prescribed by the text became a real assault, with the dagger penetrating flesh. In 1735 Macklin killed a fellow-actor, Thomas Hallam, during a brawl in a green-room – the scene of frequent altercations among members of the acting profession.

Audiences were also often the source of strife. The disturbances caused by Restoration audiences are well-known, but riots often took place in and outside theatres during the eighteenth century. These could cause substantial damage to theatres, and force closures and cancellations of runs by indigenous or visiting performers. In 1744 raised ticket prices at Drury Lane precipitated a riot there. Violent scenes occurred again in 1749, 1755, 1759, 1763, and 1789 over ticket prices and other matters. Competition to gain entry to particularly popular performances often degenerated into bloody fights, and political, religious and personal factions among the spectators also caused many outbursts, including clashes between supporters of rival performers. The riots of 1755, during performances of a ballet called *The Chinese Festival*, spread over several days. They ended with the theatre being torn apart and forced to close. The cause was 'patriotic' hostility to the French performers during a period of high tension with France, which erupted despite Garrick's efforts to pass many of the dancers off as Swiss. In the last years of the century, sentiments ran high over events associated with the ▷ French Revolution; ▷ Thomas Holcroft had to bring out some of his works anonymously, for fear of reaction because of his known links with ▷ William Blake and ▷ Tom Paine.

Apart from the complaints about violence, dramatists were frequently frustrated by their audiences' apparent indifference to their efforts. Some authors ensured applause by packing the audience with friends and even hired 'clapper-men', who would react with suitable enthusiasm to the play. But many plays and players attracted major followings, and some theatre goers were willing to pay large sums to attend particular performances of their choice. The actress ▷ George Anne Bellamy reported that several individuals, including members of the nobility, were willing to pay 100 pounds each to see her perform on a single night, whose proceeds were for her benefit.

The dramatists and the plays

The earliest plays to be performed after the Restoration were, not surprisingly, revivals of plays from earlier periods including many written shortly before the ▷ Civil War and many by Shakespeare. The latter were frequently revised to fit new notions of decorum, poetic justice, and/or French and other concepts of propriety, unity and symmetry, fostered by the ▷ neo-classical revival. For example, an early revision of ▷ *The Tempest* invents a character called Hippolytus, a man who has never seen a woman, to balance the character of Miranda, the woman who has never seen a man, other than her father. Just as, after the chaos of the preceding period, Restoration architects looked back to Greece and Rome for ideal models of order, symmetry, harmony and grace, so many Restoration dramatists looked to the classics, either directly, or via French theorists and practitioners such as ▷ Corneille and ▷ Racine, for models, precepts and subject matter, in composing their plays, rapidly expanding a process begun earlier in the century. A complex body of neo-classical dramatic theory developed, much indebted to ▷ Aristotle and ▷ Horace. This stressed the importance of preserving unities of time, place and action (that is to say, not shifting scenes implausibly through time and space: the ideal scope of action took place inside twenty-four hours, and in locations reasonably close to one another). Theorists also focussed on Aristotle's views that ▷ tragedy's chief task was to arouse pity (for the suffering protagonists) and fear, which the drama was to purge through a process called catharsis; and that dramatic action should imitate life, this process being defined as mimesis.

From Horace dramatists borrowed the view that drama has twin functions; to instruct, and to give pleasure (entertain). They also adopted notions of decorum, that is, a dramatic construction which is appropriate to its subject and to a genteel audience, that excludes obscenity, or anything too distasteful or revolting ('Medea must not butcher her children in front of the audience') and that avoids an awkward mixing of genres. From these theories the neo-classicists derived their own notions of poetic justice; what could be more instructive, they argued, than to reward virtue and punish vice? Shakespeare was censured for his failure to administer poetic justice, as well

as his supposed rough-hewn mingling of tragic and comic elements. One of
▷ Dryden's chief criticisms of ▷ *Troilus and Cressida* was that 'Cressida
is false, and is not punished'. Shakespeare was seen as a flawed genius, who
could only benefit from having his works 'improved' by the present
generation. Many earlier plays, by Shakespeare and others, were re-written
to sanitize or even excise some of the most salacious lines, by authors
conscious of post-Puritan and bourgeois criticism of the drama, and
concerned in this as in other matters to observe at least some trappings of
decorum.

It is important to note, however, that theory and practice often diverged,
and English drama was never as strict in preserving the 'unities', for
example, as was the French. Furthermore, tragedies frequently introduced
scenes of the most ghastly horror onto the stage: a famous engraving of
Elkanah Settle's *The Empress of Morocco* (1673), staged at Dorset Garden,
shows a backdrop with the bodies of several mutilated victims of torture,
stripped and hanging on spikes and hooks upside down, while bones and
dismembered bits of human remains litter the floor. ▷ Delarivière Manley
(1663–1724), in *The Royal Mischief* (1696), shows a character shot from a
cannon, his lover collecting his 'smoking Relicks' and covering them with
burning kisses. ▷ Aphra Behn, one of the foremost adaptors of older
comedy, repeatedly defended herself against charges of immorality in her
plays. Dryden was himself accused of impropriety; in words which look
forward to much of later drama, he wrote, ''Tis charg'd upon me that I
make debauch'd persons . . . my Protagonists, or the chief persons of the
Drama; and that I make them happy in the conclusion of my Play; against
the Law of Comedy, which is to reward virtue and punish vice . . . But, lest
any man should think that I write this to make libertinism amiable . . . I
must farther declare . . . that we make not vicious persons happy, but only as
heaven makes sinners so: that is by reclaiming them first'.

Other elements admitted by neo-classicists to the drama included love and
the idea of 'Admiration', that is, that a character or action should be
admirable. Dryden argued that love itself was admirable. A natural
consequence was the writing of plays about love and honour, and about
conflicts between the two, in which the period abounded. The workings of
neo-classicism, though it influenced some comedy of the period, are seen most
clearly in the so-called heroic plays, as well as non-dramatic poetry,
exemplified in Dryden's verses. Indeed Dryden explained that he 'modelled
[his] heroic plays by the rules of an heroic poem'. Plays, such as Dryden's
Tyrannic Love; or, the Royal Martyr (1669), *The Conquest of Granada* (1670)
and *Aureng-Zebe* (1675), employed the rhymed heroic ▷ couplet as their
medium, with what to modern tastes often seems a ridiculous effect.
D'Avenant, with *The Siege of Rhodes* and other plays, Sir Robert Howard
(1626–98), John Crowne (c 1640–1712), Elkanah Settle (1648–1724),
▷ Thomas Otway, Nathaniel Lee (c 1653–92) and John Banks all contributed to the repertoire of heroic plays as well.

A feature of such plays was their exotic settings. ▷ Elizabethan and
▷ Jacobean tragedy was frequently set in Italy (partly because of its

▷ Italian antecedents in the theatre) and to a lesser extent in Greece. After the Restoration the growing influence of foreign novels and plays placed in distant venues, as well as the growth of trading and other links with hitherto unknown places, contributed to a taste for plays set among Christians and Moors in Spain, Morocco and several countries of the Middle East, and even among the Chinese and the Indians of North and South America. Such settings became the norm for plays of this kind: the popular understanding of the term 'Oriental' (vague and undefined as that was), being almost synonymous with concepts of despotism, cruelty and luxury, made such settings ideal for plays involving spectacle, horror and scenes of high passion and intrigue, until writers such as Dr. Johnson and Goldsmith adopted more cosmopolitan attitudes to their distant fellow-beings.

The altered values and concerns of later generations have meant that today most Restoration tragedies are forgotten, and heroic dramas were mocked even in their own time, notably in George Buckingham's (1628–87) ▷ The Rehearsal (1671), which singles out D'Avenant and Dryden for satiric attack, with devastating wit. Dryden himself recognized the potential for ridicule when he had Nell Gwyn berate an actor who would have carried her 'dead' body off the stage at the end of Tyrannic Love, 'hold, are you mad? you damn'd confounded Dog,/I am to rise and speak the Epilogue', thus undercutting the seriousness of his own preceding action. The modern critic Anne Righter has suggested that Restoration tragedy is 'less serious' than contemporary comedy, even 'essentially frivolous' in its penchant for easy solutions and its intellectual emptiness. A few tragedies, however, would be worthy of more attention than they have been given in recent years, especially some of the political and history plays, such as Nathaniel Lee's ▷ Lucius Junius Brutus (1680), and one or two tragedies of Thomas Southerne. A fine, half-forgotten, blank verse tragedy which focusses strongly on conflicts between love and honour is Thomas Otway's ▷ Venice Preserv'd (1682). The play's urgent intensity, emphasis on character, chronicle of betrayals and mounting atmosphere of despair, link it with Jacobean tragedy. Tracing the failure of a rebellion against the Venetian senate, it has sometimes been viewed as predominantly ▷ Tory propaganda. But the manifest corruption of the authorities which Otway displays, and measure of (however qualified) sympathy which he allows the reluctant plotter Jaffeir, make it a more complex political statement. The play shows the moral turmoil which is produced when rulers are unjust, and that to preserve honour, let alone happiness, under them is impossible. But violent plots require violent plotters whose behaviour even toward their ostensible friends and allies is unpredictable, and whose success could presage a new era of chaos. The play may perhaps be read as ▷ Hobbesian, in that it appears ultimately to discourage rebellion, but it offers no easy solutions, and its strongest message is that the onus is on rulers to do justice by their people. Performed during a time of unrest after the so-called 'Popish Plot', the play had topical relevance.

Not only tragedies have been forgotten. Amongst the hundreds of comedies written during the period, only a handful survive today, in the sense of being widely known and regularly performed. They are the work of no more than half a dozen dramatists, including Etherege, Wycherley, Congreve, Vanbrugh and Farquhar, Dryden, and to a lesser extent Behn, although Dryden is chiefly remembered now for his poetry and non-dramatic prose. From the eighteenth century, the comedies of ▷ Goldsmith and ▷ Sheridan are still well-known; otherwise most drama, from the Jacobeans to the late nineteenth century, is virtually unknown today, even though the period encompasses literally hundreds of plays of immense diversity, including many that were highly successful and acclaimed in their own time. A strange paradox has arisen: many people today have heard of Betterton, Garrick and Sarah Siddons, but few ask what – apart from the handful of Restoration comedies and plays by Shakespeare – they performed.

The reasons for this are manifold: apart from the changes in taste already mentioned, some plays fell victim to circumstances outside their authors' control: for example ▷ Thomas Shadwell, author of many fine comedies and ▷ Poet Laureate after the 'Glorious Revolution' of 1688 (▷ Revolution of 1688), was pilloried by his arch-enemy Dryden who, unfortunately for Shadwell, gained the more lasting reputation. Shadwell's alleged ineptitude and dullness have been proclaimed over the years via the poem ▷ *MacFlecknoe* and kept most people from investigating his work further. Colley Cibber, a tolerable and in his way innovative, if not brilliant, dramatist, experienced the same fate at the hands of Alexander Pope and ▷ *The Dunciad*. Most so-called Restoration dramatists, and not a few that followed, suffered from the Victorian obsession with virtue and propriety. It was not deemed seemly to read, let alone perform, many of the plays from preceding generations; Restoration comedies were vilified most of all. Aphra Behn was subjected to a violently anti-feminist backlash that took hold during her lifetime, mounted in the years following her death, and eventually developed into a concerted campaign to obliterate her memory altogether. ▷ Sir Walter Scott, in a well-known anecdote, related that his grand-aunt returned some of Behn's novels which he had sent her at her own request, saying that she now felt ashamed to read a book which, 60 years before, she had heard read aloud in the best circles in London. Scott attributed the change to the gradual improvement of taste and sense of delicacy in the time leading up to his own. The publisher John Pearson was vilified when, in 1872, he published a collection of Behn's works, along with others by Restoration and early eighteenth-century dramatists including Susannah Centlivre.

This represented the end of a long process of decline in the attitude toward women dramatists: Behn's first play *The Forc'd Marriage*, put on at the end of 1670, has a prologue celebrating its authorship by a woman, as a sort of novelty – though Behn was not the first English woman to have a play peformed (that distinction may belong to the woman better known as a poet, Katherine Philips (1632–64). But opposition gathered during the 1670s, such that Behn soon felt obliged to defend herself in print, not only for the alleged bawdiness of her work, but for the mere fact that she as a woman dared to write at all. In an epilogue she asked, rhetorically, 'What has poor

Woman done, that she must be/Debar'd [*sic*] from Sense and sacred Poetry? . . . pray tell me then,/why Women should not write as well as Men'. She and many of her successors survived the mockery of male contemporaries, only to have their work eclipsed altogether by more narrow-minded subsequent generations. The number of women writing for the stage dwindled from about 1720, although a few prospered in each decade of the eighteenth century.

Behn, the first professional woman dramatist, was also among the most versatile dramatists of the era: she attempted, with varying degrees of success, virtually every genre for the stage, and portrayed almost every comic and perhaps tragic type known in her period. In many ways her plays parallelled those of the significant male dramatists of her time: she excelled at comedy, portraying the intricacies of courtship and marriage with wit and finesse. She was at her best with farcical intrigue comedy, handling multiple and complex plots without ever losing the thread of any individual one. Underlying the humour, however, was a serious vein: unlike many of her male contemporaries, she appears to have sustained a faith in the powers of true romantic love, foreshadowing many dramatists of the next century. Moreover, again unlike many male writers, she viewed the problems of love and marriage from a woman's point of view, idealizing and at the same time satirizing the typical rake character of the period, but also showing the harm which his machinations could inflict on women who took him at face value. Several plays show a sympathetic understanding of the unchaste woman, including the courtesan, or the 'wronged woman' who has rashly forfeited her chastity in the pursuit of love. Ismena in Behn's *The Amorous Prince* (1671) reproaches a suitor, 'as most gallants are,/You're but pleased with what you have not;/And love a Mistress with great Passion, 'till you find/Yourself belov'd again, and then you hate her'. In plays including this one, Behn re-examines the concept of feminine 'virtue', defining it not as virginity like most of her contemporaries, but as something we would now call integrity. Her most sustained theme is the evils of the so-called 'forced marriage': the marriage imposed on unwilling young people by greedy and ambitious relatives. Virtue consists in remaining true to one's own desires, even if that means defying the older generation and, in the case of women, giving up one's virginity to a man truly loved.

Probably the most successful and able of Behn's immediate successors was Susannah Centlivre, two of whose 19 comedies, ▷ *The Busie Bodie* (1709) and *The Wonder: A Woman Keeps a Secret* (1714), remained among the four most ▷ frequently re-printed and performed of any, except for those of Shakespeare, until late in the nineteenth century. Like Behn she excelled at comedy with complex intrigue plots, displaying with vitality and style young people, in pursuit of their own romantic ends, outwitting others functioning as pillars of established authority. But unlike Behn, who was a high Tory, she championed ▷ Whigs and Whig interests in several plays and, again unlike Behn, she fervently opposed Catholicism, which she referred to as 'the Romish Yoke'. Furthermore, in keeping with her more fastidious times, the overt sexual element is omitted from her plays. Two of these, *The Gamester*

(1705) and *The Basset Table* (1705), follow a contemporary convention in exposing current vice – in this case the fashionable one of gambling. She was also a fine craftswoman, creating superb acting roles, including five intended for the same actor in various disguises (▷ *A Bold Strike for a Wife*), which rendered several of her plays favourites of Garrick and Kitty Clive. Garrick chose her play *The Wonder* for the last performance of his career.

From the Restoration onwards, plays were heavily preoccupied with themes of courtship and marriage, treated in ways varying from high comedy including farce, to tragedy. Indeed, the term 'Restoration Comedy' conjures up in people's minds scenes of witty courtship and flirtation, underpinned by conflict: the 'battle of the sexes'. Many plays contain debates, implicit or explicit, about the value or otherwise of marriage as an institution, and discussions concerning the bases on which marriages should be contracted: whether for love or money; according to the choices of parents or lovers; between old and young ('January–May' matches); or lovers of similar age, and so forth. But these themes are not in any sense unique to the drama of the period. They permeate literature of many kinds, including a vast body of ▷ pamphlet material which was digested by increasing numbers of middle-class readers.

The genre has roots in some misogynistic writing of the ▷ Middle Ages, in which marriage was denigrated precisely because it bound men closely to women – the descendants of the flawed Eve. However it was strongly fuelled by the Reformation, with the protagonists dividing along religious lines. Increasingly, the institution of marriage was defended by Protestant Reformers, who accused Catholics of attacking marriage and sanctioning immorality ('whoring') as an alternative, so men could satisfy their sexual needs without having to resort to wedlock. A Reformist priest, Thomas Becon, in his *Boke of Matrimony* (1563), attacks 'Masse and Monckery' and its alleged opposition to matrimony, which is, he says, a state 'holy blessed . . . although counted of the Papistes neuer so Seraphicall . . .' Catholics did not on the whole attack marriage as such, but continued to value celibacy as the highest state for those who could attain it, stimulating further attacks from Protestants for their supposed hypocrisy.

In the seventeenth century the debate over marriage intensified, and at the same time became secularized, erupting through the hundreds of pamphlets written by, and largely appealing to, members of the middle-classes. Marriage was contrasted to whoring as a way of life; many pamphlets also focussed on characters of courtesans or prostitutes, drawing moral conclusions from tales of their prosperity or downfall. Religious attitudes continued to inform many of the pamphlets but, increasingly, pamphlets by women responded to those by men, especially to the satiric ones attacking women. Later, women such as the polemicist poet Sarah Fige Egerton, ▷ Mary Astell and poet and essayist Lady Mary Chudleigh (1636–1710) attacked marriage for its patriarchal enslavement of their sex.

Images of slavery pervade both the pamphlets and the drama, with human and especially sexual relations seen in terms of the enslavement of one partner to another, or the enslavement of both to the oppressive conditions of marriage. The Civil War had heightened public concern with personal freedom, but growing censorship limited the parameters for discussion about the exercise of freedom in the political sphere. After the Restoration, the loosening of the strictures on individual sexual morality permitted a new outlet for debates about freedom, which took the form of a revived focus on the battle of the sexes. The growth of slavery in the New World also contributed to a widespread preoccupation with the metaphoric as well as literal manifestations of this institution.

Together, plays and pamphlets illustrate the debate about marriage and sexual relations in the seventeenth and eighteenth centuries. Indeed on one level, many plays may be seen as dramatized versions of a debate which constitutes a social correlative to the religio-political clash continuing in society, and exploding periodically into overt conflict. Examples are the 'Popish Plot' debacle beginning in 1678, the 'Rye House Plot' a few years later to assassinate Charles II, and Monmouth's Rebellion, culminating with the so-called 'Glorious Revolution' of 1688 – although the latter phenomena had distinct and various ends in view. Several late seventeenth-century pamphlets express concern that because of Catholic influence on society in general and the gentry in particular, marriage as an institution was declining. But the drama shows, on the whole, no such concern. In keeping with dramatic tradition, and the reality of most people's lives, dramatists assumed that most of their characters would marry. But the plays are increasingly preoccupied with the concept of love and/or marriage as slavery, for the man or the woman, depending on the point of view. The metaphoric treatment of these themes in comedies was parallelled by more literal uses in the serious plays, of situations in which individuals are enslaved to one another via imprisonment, although they are also sometimes 'slaves of love'. So-called 'proviso scenes' in which men and women spell out the terms on which they are prepared to submit to the restrictions of marriage, and make bargains to this effect, form the climaxes to some Restoration comedies, the most famous example being the scene between Millamant and Mirabell in Act IV of Congreve's ▷ *The Way of the World* (1700). From 1670 onwards, after the first effective civil divorce, this too became a topic in some plays – seen as the only escape from an impossible union.

In the 1690s came a series of so-called 'marital discord plays', which followed more soberly in the footsteps of Behn. A major figure in this regard is the neglected dramatist, ▷ Thomas Southerne, who borrowed heavily from Behn. In several of his plays he shows the appalling situation of the wife, tied to a philandering and cruel husband, 'this hard condition of a woman's fate', in the words of one of his women characters. Vanbrugh takes up the theme in ▷ *The Relapse* (1697), written as a satiric sequel to Cibber's ▷ *Love's Last Shift*, which showed the husband repenting of his unkindness to his wife, and undergoing a reform.

Today the best-known plays of the Restoration and early eighteenth century periods are some of the so-called wit comedies or comedies of manners (▷ Manners, Comedy of) by Etherege, Wycherley, Congreve, Vanbrugh and Farquhar. The form has an antecedent in the wooing of

Beatrice and Benedick in Shakespeare's ▷ *Much Ado About Nothing*. But after the Restoration, Dryden helped develop it with what some consider the first true 'Restoration Comedy' – ▷ *The Wild Gallant* (1663), in which an impoverished gallant, Loveby, is secretly supplied with money by his mistress, Constance. She articulates the plight of the woman in the period, 'tied to hard unequal laws: The passion is the same in us, and yet we are debarred the freedom to express it'.

Some plays of Etherege and Wycherley illustrate more clearly the inequalities of men and women: in Etherege's ▷ *The Man of Mode* (1676) women mistrust and betray one another. The heroine Harriet wins the appalling Dorimant away from the weak and stupid Belinda and unscrupulous Loveit, but it is clear that her money forms a large part of her attraction in the match, making up for the ruin of his estate, and thus implicitly rescuing him from the slavery of poverty, although this is not stated in these terms. Margery Pinchwife, the title character in Wycherley's ▷ *The Country Wife* (1675), is pathetic and misguided; her denigration comes because she has not learned to guard her true interests in the harsh world of the city. The pursuit of 'interest', meaning both financial and general self-interest, is a frequent theme in plays from a period heavily influenced not only by commercial changes in society, but also the writings of the contemporary social commentators Hobbes and François de la Rochefoucauld (1613–80), and the Greek philosopher ▷ Epicurus as adumbrated by the Roman ▷ Lucretius. Lucretius's works, translated and published during these years, contributed to a flirtation with 'atheism' by some Restoration writers and others. Denying the existence of an after-life implied, so it was thought, making the most of this one – even if that meant ignoring or downgrading the interests of others.

Many critics, such as Nicoll, J. H. Wilson, Bonamy Dobree and Clifford Leech, have attempted to organize Restoration comedies into categories, but this is a thankless task as there are so many overlaps between genres. For example, one frequently mentioned category is the Spanish Romance, such as Sir Samuel Tuke's *The Adventures of Five Hours* commissioned by Charles II (1663), but in the prologue and preface to *The Wild Gallant* Dryden also acknowledges a Spanish origin. The so-called 'split-plot tragi-comedy', exemplified by Dryden's ▷ *Marriage à la Mode* and Behn's *The Widow Ranter*, is another, but here the comic plots have elements from various of the supposed categories. In *Marriage à la Mode*, for example, the lovers Palamede and Doralice exchange banter normally thought of as belonging to the 'comedy of wit', as they arrange a liaison. In another scene Leonidas is identified as the son to the usurper of Sicily, Polydamas, in lines that look forward to a great deal of 'exemplary' and 'sentimental' comedy. In yet another scene illicit meetings and mistaken identities parallel those of comedy of intrigue. Congreve's ▷ *The Double Dealer* (1694), considered among the great comedies of wit because of its sparkling language, also contains many intrigue elements, as shown in its enormously complex and brilliantly managed plot. Shadwell wrote several comedies influenced by Ben Jonson's theory of 'humours' (▷ Comedy of Humours), as suggested in the

Dramatis Personae to *The Sullen Lovers* (1668), which lists characters including 'a morose melancholy man', 'a conceited poet' and 'a familiar loving coxcomb', and in Shadwell's own dedication to the play. But the work has 'witty' and intrigue elements as well. In fact there are often overlaps among intrigue comedy, wit comedy and farce.

Similar problems arise in discussing tragedies, which are sometimes divided into categories including heroic tragedy, horror tragedy – glorying in scenes of torture, such as *The Empress of Morocco* – and pathetic tragedies, including some of Lee and John Banks. But again, there are many overlaps between and among categories; for example, Behn's *Abdelazar* (1676) has both horror and 'heroic' elements. And there have been numerous debates about whether some of Lee's plays really were 'pathetic', and how, in any case, this term should be defined. Happier compromises than those referred to above have been achieved by such authors as Robert D. Hume in *The Development of English Drama in the late Seventeenth Century* and A. H. Scouten in *The Revels History of Drama*. Hume discusses plays according to period, although this too leaves something to be desired, because of the inevitable exceptions and overlaps. But he also discusses some individual plays according to the categories into which they supposedly fit, such as the 'French' Farce, 'Reform Comedy', 'Wit Comedy', 'Sex Comedy', 'City Intrigue Comedy', 'Augustan Intrigue Comedy' and so on. Scouten's categories are much broader ('New Drama', 'Political Plays against the Puritans', and 'Social Comedy', for example), and much of his discussion is according to author.

Behn was one of the earliest to exhibit tendencies toward what has been variously described as 'sentimental', 'exemplary', or 'reform' comedy, the 'comedy of sensibility', and more recently, 'humane comedy'. These are critics' sometimes crude attempts to define a transition between plays dominated by hard wit comic elements of the high Restoration period and the genres that followed. The terms have often been accompanied by a blanket condemnation of the new modes, as representing a loss of wit and humour without any compensatory gain. But as Shirley Strum Kenny (coiner of the term 'humane comedy') has suggested, some of the older drama had much in the way of cynicism and callousness to discredit it, and there were mitigating features of the new.

The change is attended by attacks on the stage – most famously by the Reverend Jeremy Collier in a piece entitled *A Short View of the Immorality and Profaneness of the English Stage*, written in 1698. His tirade on the alleged loose morality and profane language of the plays was the more effective, if perhaps also more puzzling because of his evident knowledge of the texts from reading, if not seeing them performed. But the movement toward reform had been started well before: a long vituperative poem by Robert Gould, *Satyr Against the Playhouse*, written in 1685 and published four years later, is said to have heralded the controversy. Finally, the change is linked with political developments: for example, the ascendancy of the Whigs after the Revolution of 1688, bringing with them a backlash against the supposed immorality and irreligion of the Tory dramatists. Writers such as John Locke, whose works were widely distributed after the Revolution, had far more positive views of human nature than those of his predecessors ▷ Thomas Hobbes and Sir Robert Filmer (c 1590–1653), whose ideas had strongly influenced many Tories. The loss of patronage by the Royal family was also an important factor: as stated above, Charles II was a keen patron of the theatre, and his cultured but wry, satiric personality had a substantial influence on its development during his reign. His brother James II, while less involved in the minutiae of play composition and performance, had also continued the tradition of patronage for the brief period of his reign.

In the 1690s and early 1700s plays began to emerge that were less overtly bawdy and had a more sympathetic and 'moral' attitude toward some of their leading characters and human nature in general. Vanbrugh and Farquhar, although often classed among, and sharing characteristics with, Restoration dramatists, also belong in many ways to this later era. For example, in Farquhar's ▷ The Beaux Stratagem (1707), Aimwell, under the guise of his wealthy brother, spends most of the play courting Dorinda for the sake of her fortune. But at the crucial moment he confesses his poverty, and releases her from her vows. At this she decides to marry him anyway, moved by his 'Matchless Honesty'. This is a far cry from Etherege or Wycherley.

A feature of these plays is their softened attitude to the country, which had been seen as a wasteland of ignorance and dullness by many satiric dramatists, though not by poets, of the Restoration. Many Restoration dramatists associated the country with settled property-based marriages, contrasting them to the 'freedom' of the town. But later dramatists and audiences came increasingly to accept the conventional forms of match-making, and with them, the country seat and its environment where so many wealthy and genteel families made their home. A stock motif of Restoration comedy is young lovers refusing to accept the partners of their parents' choice, and insisting instead upon making their own choices. In the eighteenth century, this is replaced, typically, by situations in which lovers think they are choosing for themselves, but unwittingly become attracted to partners who have in fact been intended for them by their elders all along. Thus at the end conflict is avoided, and the parents are vindicated, indeed revealed as sensible and far-sighted. The effect is an affirmation of the wisdom of the older generation, and by extension, of settled social forms and values. Rebellion against such parents is unjustified, since they have the true interests of the younger generation at heart. The forced marriage motif survives, however, in some plays, including Eliza Haywood's A Wife to be Lett (1723), and several plays by Centlivre.

Another common feature of plays of the period is the reform of a major protagonist. This is in keeping with the more optimistic view of human nature and aspirations espoused not only by Locke, but also by ▷ Shaftesbury and later ▷ David Hume, ▷ David Hartley, Pope and others. For many decades, plays exhibited gamblers, wife-beaters and others deemed guilty of wrongdoing repenting of their ways – though usually not until the last act. Colley Cibber's Love's Last Shift, in which the abandoned wife succeeds in reforming her errant and impoverished husband, is generally agreed to have been a key transitional play in this regard. The husband Loveless, struck by remorse, ends by celebrating the 'chast Rapture of a Vertuous Love'. Meanwhile in a secondary plot, an older man admonishes and successfully disciplines the coquette Hillaria.

Women are also shown repenting, notably by women dramatists including Susannah Centlivre and ▷ Mary Pix. The latter, whose *The Spanish Wives* (1696) had championed women's freedom somewhat in the style of Behn, though less racily, reforms the heroine of *The Deceiver Deceived* (1697) after one bout of adultery. The genre overlaps with the so-called 'exemplary drama' or 'drama of sensibility', epitomized by Steele's ▷ The Conscious Lovers (1722), in which the lovers of the title agonize over the propriety of all their actions. In the second half of the century, parallel with theories about the natural 'benevolence' of human nature, the so-called 'sentimental comedy', epitomized by Hugh Kelly's (1739–77) *The False Delicacy* (1768), developed. Also ▷ Richard Cumberland's *The West Indian* (1771) contains a number of elements typical of the genre, including the reform of a rake, vice exposed and outwitted, virtue rescued from distress and honourable simplicity triumphant.

▷ Sheridan and ▷ Goldsmith reacted against what they saw as a surfeit of pathos and morality: they consciously attempted to revive the spirit of Restoration comedy with plays such as ▷ *She Stoops to Conquer* (1773), ▷ *The Rivals* (1775) and ▷ *The School for Scandal* (1777). So successful were their efforts that many people not too well acquainted with the stage today believe them to belong to the earlier era. And yet in its more 'benign' atmosphere and softened attitude to country life, for example, as well as certain elements of the plot, *She Stoops to Conquer*, at least, belongs to a later period than true Restoration comedy, and has much more in common with Farquhar, let us say, than with dramatists like Etherege, Wycherley, Behn or Congreve.

Along with the changes in comedy came new types of serious drama, although heroic plays remained popular into the eighteenth century. New approaches to Shakespeare have already been referred to, providing in some cases greater authenticity and, in others, fresh distortions, until ▷ Edmund Kean mounted full-scale restorations of Shakespeare's own texts in the nineteenth century. The later eighteenth century may be considered as a transitional period in this regard. John Banks and others developed a variety of tragedy focussing on the sufferings of women, at a time when the numbers of women dramatists were growing, and pamphlets presenting the views and concerns of women were proliferating. Such plays of John Banks include *Vertue Betray'd: or, Anna Bullen* (1682), on Anne Boleyn; *The Island Queens* (1684), on Mary Queen of Scots; and *The Innocent Usurper* (1694), on the execution of Lady Jane Grey. Congreve experimented with the form in the ▷ *The Mourning Bride* (1697), and ▷ Nicholas Rowe took it further with *The Fair Penitent* (1703), *The Tragedy of Jane Shore* (1714) and *The Tragedy of Lady Jane Grey* (1715). There is a link between such plays and some of the comedies of Southerne, Cibber, Vanbrugh and Centlivre, which also focus on the sufferings of women, albeit in less sombre contexts.

Today Banks is usually considered a practitioner of so-called 'pathetic tragedy', encompassing elements of pathos, designed to move rather than thrill or shock the spectator, while Rowe's plays are known as 'she tragedies'. But the two may be seen to overlap. Again negotiating with these, and developing gradually in the period, was the domestic or bourgeois tragedy, characterized by a focus on the lives of ordinary citizens, rather than the kings and queens of the heroic variety. A landmark of this genre is ▷ George Lillo's *The London Merchant: or the History of George Barnwell* (1730), which ends with Barnwell repenting of his crimes before being executed. However, as Allardyce Nicoll points out in *A History of English Drama 1660–1900*, the roots of bourgeois tragedy, like those of so many other 'new' forms, lie in the Restoration period – particularly with Otway.

Burlesque plays and satires, fathered by George Villiers's ▷ *The Rehearsal* (1671), became increasingly popular during the first decades of the eighteenth century. Among the most famous of these were Pope, Gay and Arbuthnot's resentful satire on contemporary women dramatists, *Three Hours After Marriage* (1717), and Fielding's *Tom Thumb* (1730), reworked as *The Tragedy of Tragedies* (1731), again mocking heroic plays. Gay's ▷ *The Beggar's Opera* (1728), technically a ballad-opera, is known to many today mainly as the source for ▷ Brecht's *The Threepenny Opera*. This comedy of low-life has antecedents in the 'rogue literature' of the sixteenth and seventeenth centuries, including some masques by Jonson. But its success was instantaneous: staged by ▷ John Rich, himself a dramatist as well as actor-manager, it is said to have made 'Gay rich and Rich gay'. This and later plays, notably by Fielding, mounted a sustained satiric attack on ▷ Sir Robert Walpole, eventually leading, as we have seen, to the Licensing Act of 1737, whereby the latter was able to subdue his critics and control the stage with a much firmer hand. It resulted in Fielding and others abandoning the stage and contributed, indirectly, to the development of the novel in the eighteenth century, as Fielding and others now concentrated their efforts on this less rigorously controlled, and therefore less risky, form of endeavour.

A dramatic form that developed in the seventeenth century, but became much more popular in the eighteenth, is the 'after-piece', a short pantomime or farce intended to be performed after a more serious play, so the audience would be sent home laughing. Increasingly, these were considered essential to attract audiences to the theatre and, as the demand grew, many earlier plays were re-written in lighter and much abbreviated form. Just as pamphlets on marriage, written in serious or bitingly satiric vein in the seventeenth century were increasingly reworked into light, frivolous pieces in the eighteenth, so full-length, skilfully made comedies and tragi-comedies were later turned into little afterpieces. Garrick altered Wycherley's ▷ *The Country Wife* to *The Country Girl* (1766); a play by Betterton, *The Amorous Widow* (performed c 1670) became a two-act farce, *Barnaby Brittle* (1782); Behn's *The Revenge* (1680), itself a sombre tragi-comic alteration of a savage satire by ▷ John Marston eventually became – via a comic and farcical adaptation by Christopher Bullock (1690–1722) called *A Woman's Revenge*

(1715) – a droll, *The Stroler's Pacquet* (1742). Seventeenth and eighteenth century dramatists were not on the whole concerned with problems of plagiarism let alone copyright. In addition, dancing, singing, acrobatics, juggling and other forms of non-dramatic entertainment – including performances by many visiting companies from the continent – frequently functioned as entr'actes or after-pieces, as well as being staged in their own right, or integrated into plays.

Late in the century the influence of German and, once again, French dramatists became important to the English stage, at a time when the work of German poets and philosophers, in particular, was having a growing impact on the English Romantic poets. Plays of ▷ Kotzebue and René-Charles Guilbert Pixérécourt (1773–1844), for example, translated and reworked by ▷ Thomas Holcroft and ▷ Elizabeth Inchbald, became immensely popular. The translations were to include works known to us now as melodramas, at first literally containing music, from the turn of the century.

In the final years of the period, reaction against the supposed bawdiness of many plays, alluded to above, began to bite in earnest. Readers of ▷ Jane Austen may recall the horrified response of the older generation upon finding the young people in ▷ *Mansfield Park* engaged upon an amateur performance of Inchbald's *Lover's Vows*. Restoration comedy, which had remained part of the repertory throughout most of the century, was attacked once again, in a period marked by the rise of the Evangelical movement. Even Hannah Cowley's (1743–1809) *A School for Greybeards* (1786), itself a 'refined' and 'cleaned-up' version of Behn's genuinely outspoken *The Lucky Chance* (1686), was considered shocking. The stage was set for ▷ Thomas Bowdler's edition of Shakespeare (1818), new plays in the nineteenth century that were even more overtly moral and religiously inspired than their predecessors of the eighteenth, and the disappearance of Restoration plays altogether until the revivals of this century.

Samuel Beckett *Happy Days*

Developments in modern drama: 9
the slow road to change

Early experiments

▷ Henry James lamented the feebleness of English dramatic writing towards the end of the nineteenth century. Whether or not we agree with his judgement the fact is that the theatre itself was thriving, at least in London, the inevitable focus of this survey. For the more popular market there were melodramas, music hall shows and variety entertainments. Meanwhile, the middle classes, the fashionable and the leisured, were being lured back to the theatre by more self-consciously respectable forms of drama. These ranged from the Savoy operas of ▷ Gilbert and Sullivan to the farces and more serious 'problem plays' of ▷ Sir Arthur Wing Pinero and Henry Arthur Jones to the pictorially spectacular productions of ▷ Shakespeare by the great actor-managers of the period, ▷ Sir Henry Irving and Sir Herbert Beerbohm Tree. Apart from historical English insularity, the cultivation of respectability explains the slowness of the English theatre to respond to new developments in drama on the continent. The new drama of playwrights like ▷ Ibsen and Strindberg was critical of complacent bourgeois values and easily identified as politically subverse. Theatre managers, in a competitive commercial business, were hardly likely to promote this kind of dramatic material. After all, English polite society did not go to the theatre to see its moral values attacked. Given the conditions of the English theatre at this time, it is not surprising that it took a long time for Ibsen, Strindberg and ▷ Chekhov to make any serious impact on the English stage.

The new European playwrights initially appealed to a relatively small circle of intellectuals rather than the general theatre-going public. In 1891 ▷ Jack Thomas Grein formed the Independent Theatre Society in an attempt to encourage a native drama comparable to that of France and Scandinavia. The first production was Ibsen's *Ghosts*, which predictably aroused a storm of abuse for openly referring to venereal disease. Unfortunately the Independent Theatre produced little of Ibsen's work thereafter. ▷ George Bernard Shaw (1856–1950) was another campaigner for the new Ibsenite drama and in 1890 he gave a series of lectures on the subject for the ▷ Fabian Society, later published as *The Quintessence of Ibsenism*. This was followed up with a practical project, an experiment in a repertory system at the Court Theatre, between 1904 and 1907, run by the director ▷ Harley Granville Barker and the manager John Eugene Vedrenne. The success of Shaw's plays there enabled the theatre to present Ibsen's *Hedda Gabler* and *The Wild Duck*. Even then there was only a handful of performances, since this new and unfamiliar drama was financially risky. In retrospect it is no surprise that plays at least superficially resembling the drawing-room dramas of Jones and Pinero were favoured above Ibsen's more poetical works like

Brand and *Peer Gynt*, which made much more challenging demands in performance terms. So long as the theatre was run on commercial principles this was bound to be the case. To Fabians like Barker and Shaw it was part of the business of good government to promote the national culture, and of good plays to educate the audience. They yearned for a national subsidized theatre where a new serious drama might be nurtured. Barker actually produced a detailed scheme for such a theatre with the critic William Archer, entitled *The National Theatre: A Scheme and Estimates* (1903). They suggested a policy for encouraging new writers, and provided detailed samples of possible repertory, focussing on world classics; they even laid down principles for actors' training. Unfortunately, such ideals did not impress a government which believed firmly in the principles of free enterprise. Perhaps Henry James should have considered that the dearth of original playwrights was related to the way in which the theatre was financially organized.

Although Shaw claimed to imitate Ibsen, he was shrewd enough not to ignore popular native forms of drama. As he put it, 'my stage tricks and suspenses and thrills and jests are the ones in vogue when I was a boy'. To reject outright the English tradition was to consign oneself to obscurity. This was clearly understood by the other major Irish (▷ Irish literature in English) dramatist of the period, ▷ Oscar Wilde (1856–1900). Wilde openly exploited the devices of melodrama, the implausible plots of farce and the tried and tested theme of 'a woman with a past'. What he added was his own unique wit which gives his plays their distinctive charm and flavour. His most famous play, *The Importance of Being Earnest* (1895), is essentially a light-hearted mockery of aristocratic manners, and derivative of Gilbert's *Engaged*. In his other comedies, such as *Lady Windermere's Fan* (1892) and *A Woman of No Importance* (1893), he used his wit more savagely, particularly to expose the hypocrisy of male double standards. He was himself a victim of the Victorian intolerance he had satirized when his career was ruined by prosecution and imprisonment for homosexuality.

The establishment was just as quick to label Shaw a subversive. In one of his earliest works, *Mrs Warren's Profession*, written in 1893, he adapted the theme of 'a woman with a past' to deal with another taboo subject, prostitution. The reward for his candour was to have the play banned from public performance for thirty years. Though he gained a reputation as a champion of radical causes in the 1890s, it was actually in the Edwardian period that he established his popularity with the British public. The ▷ Court Theatre seasons which gave a modest platform to Ibsen helped Shaw gain a reputation as the leading intellectual playwright in the English theatre of the early twentieth century. Eleven of his plays were produced at the Court, including *Man and Superman* (1903), *You Never Can Tell* (1899), *John Bull's Other Island* (1904) and *Major Barbara* (1905). Shaw's plays were by far the most popular in the Court repertory and thereafter his success continued right up until 1939, with his last memorable full-length play, *In Good King Charles's Golden Days*. His plays depend heavily on witty argument and this idiosyncratic style of propagandist humour has acquired its own term, Shavian. In Shaw's best works, such as the popular *Saint Joan*, first performed in 1924, argument and dramatic action are wholly integrated to produce drama which is both entertaining and thought-provoking.

The longer runs of Shaw's plays at the Court helped to subsidize the work of new writers like ▷ W. B. Yeats, ▷ John Galsworthy, ▷ J. M. Barrie and ▷ Harley Granville Barker. Apart from Ibsen a small sample of the work of the more experimental European authors, ▷ Maeterlinck, Hauptmanm and Schnitzler was presented. Though not exclusively so, there was an Ibsenite emphasis on plays which addressed social issues. Galsworthy's *The Silver Box* (1906) and ▷ Elizabeth Robins's *Votes for Women* (1907) explored the themes of class discrimination and female emancipation in a style combining both innovative and highly conventional features. Thus, *Votes for Women* includes an unusual crowd scene of a mass women's suffrage rally in Trafalgar Square, but elsewhere relies heavily on the conventions of late-nineteenth-century Society drama, as does Granville Barker's *The Voysey Inheritance* (1905), which explores that great Victorian totem, the family. In his play, family wealth and respectability are shown to be based on fraud and deception. He also dealt with corruption and exploitation in his other two major plays from this period, *Waste* (1907) and *The Madras House* (1910). *Waste* was heavily censored for openly dealing with extra-marital sex and laying the blame for an abortion on a senior politician and aspiring prime minister.

Harley Granville Barker (1877–1946) was one of the first true directors in the English theatre, in the sense that he saw the director's role as entirely separate from that of the actor. Between 1912 and 1914 he directed distinguished and highly influential productions of Shakespeare's ▷ *Twelfth Night*, ▷ *The Winter's Tale* and ▷ *A Midsummer Night's Dream* at the Savoy Theatre. Characteristic of these productions were a careful consideration of original performance conditions, an emphasis on ensemble acting and the development of a new aesthetic in theatre design. Inevitably though, there were financial difficulties and shortly after World War I Granville Barker distanced himself from the London theatre scene, disillusioned with its philistinism. He applied his creative talent to the more academic pursuits of translating plays and writing his famous *Prefaces to Shakespeare*. He was less of a pragmatist than Shaw and was ultimately unwilling to compromise his idealism in order to survive the pressures of the commercial market.

At almost the same time as the Court venture, W. B. Yeats (1865–1939) launched his campaign to promote a national Irish culture through drama with the creation of the Irish National Theatre. With the support of like-minded nationalists, notably the benefactress and playwright ▷ Lady Gregory, Yeats established the ▷ Abbey Theatre in Dublin as one of the most experimental European theatres of its time. Its attempt to further the cause of Irish independence by promoting a national cultural identity based on a revival of Celtic mythology was a rather idealistic mission; nonetheless, whatever one might think of the political purpose of Yeats's plays, they were certainly significant experiments in verse dramas. Though they are sometimes criticized for being unstageable, almost all of his plays from *The Countess*

Cathleen (1892) to *Purgatory* (1939) were performed. The Abbey Theatre also provided an audience for the work of ▷ J. M. Synge (1871–1909). Synge preferred a more earthy, if poetic, prose style to the grander mystical verse drama favoured by Yeats. With the exception of *Deirdre of the Sorrows* (published in 1910), based on Celtic legend, he also tended to eschew the Yeatsian spiritual dimension and restricted his subject matter to the lives of the ordinary Irish people. One of his most famous plays, *The Playboy of the Western World* (1907), provides a gentle satirical view of romance and fantasy in a remote Irish community. Its light-hearted and mildly cynical wit was too much for the Abbey Theatre audience which rioted after interpreting the play as an attack on Irish values and the integrity of Irish womanhood. In his short life Synge wrote only six plays, but with these he established himself as an important, if controversial, figure in the Irish dramatic revival. The Abbey continued to flourish under the watchful eye of Yeats long after Synge's untimely death in 1909, and from 1924, shortly after Irish independence, it was granted financial aid by the government, thus making it one of the first subsidized English-speaking theatres.

These attempts to develop a serious intellectual drama on both sides of the Irish Sea made little immediate impact on London's West End. The dominant view of the theatre was summed up by one of the most successful of the Edwardian playwrights, ▷ William Somerset Maugham (1874–1965), when he said that 'its purpose is to afford delight. I do not think it can usefully concern itself with the welfare of humanity or the saving of civilization'. Evidently he did provide delight, for in 1908 he had four plays running simultaneously. He saw himself as an exponent of the comedy of manners, writing in a tradition dating back to the ▷ Restoration period and to ▷ Goldsmith and ▷ Sheridan. His cynical and artificial comedies sometimes shocked and even scandalized, but never really gave serious offence. Maugham's popularity lasted right up until the 1930s, when he decided that he was losing touch with the public and retired.

By the end of World War I the English theatre was as insular as ever. The old actor-manager system was replaced by a few multiple managements which sought quick profits and promoted light musical entertainment as the staple of West End entertainment. Few writers of 'serious' drama found an outlet on the stage. In fact, serious writers were much more likely to turn to the forms of the novel and poetry than drama. The farces of ▷ Ben Travers (1886–1980), written for a popular group of comic actors at the Aldwych Theatre, were a typical product of the 1920s, years of gaiety and frivolity for the affluent in society. Though some of the humour would now appear to be dated, his meandering but well-constructed plots based on implausible coincidence have proved to be surprisingly durable, as a revival of *Plunder* at the National Theatre in 1976 demonstrated. He was a pioneer of the English sex farce, a form which is still dominant in the West End.

The sense of gay abandonment and impending crisis associated with the 1920s and 30s is often captured in the plays of ▷ Noël Coward (1899–1973), who was adept at exploiting the new formulae for commercial success.

Coward followed in the tradition of Wilde, often balancing wit with sentiment and probing beyond the English veneer of respectability. Although his unconventional treatment of sex and social manners did arouse controversy, he was generally a good judge of English tolerance and his knowledge of the theatre from boyhood gave him the experience to know what he could get away with. Admittedly his first staged play, *The Vortex* (1924), gave him a reputation as a radical, despite his adherence to the framework of the old drawing-room drama of Jones and Pinero, and *Sirocco* (1927) was greeted with a first night riot. However, the six comedies written between 1923 and 1942, *Fallen Angels, Hay Fever, Private Lives, Design for Living, Bitter Sweet* and *Present Laughter* did much to establish him as a successful mainstream playwright rather than a critic on the theatrical fringe. Coward was one of those curious English figures who manage to play the role of the rebel whilst being accepted as part of the establishment. The satirical impulse in his plays is generally tempered by his shrewd commercial sense.

In the years just before and just after Irish independence, in 1921, Dublin had little in common with fashionable London. The difference could not be better illustrated than by the three early plays of ▷ Sean O'Casey (1880–1964); *The Shadow of a Gunman* (1923), *Juno and the Paycock* (1924) and *The Plough and the Stars* (1926), which were first performed at the Abbey Theatre during the 1920s. Here the violence of colonialism and misery of poverty is portrayed from the viewpoint of the working-class slum tenement dweller. Bleak as this world may be, it is not devoid of humour. The characters are given a poetic, often flamboyant style of speech, which is frequently used to expose their desire for escapism into a world of fantasy and romance. O'Casey found a means of expression for the lives of the urban Irish, as Synge had done for the Irish peasant communities. The influences for this kind of drama, which extended tragedy to the lives of ordinary people, came from continental political playwrights like the German, Gerhart Hauptmann (1862–1946), as well as from the popular native melodrama. It was also to the continent, and Germany in particular, that O'Casey turned for inspiration for his next play, *The Silver Tassie*, in 1928. In this he experimented with the theatrical devices of ▷ expressionism which had been pioneered by German playwrights around the time of World War I. The play's avant-garde mixture of styles and bitter satire of religion and war made it unacceptable for production at the Abbey. Thereafter O'Casey continued his non-naturalistic experiments in exile. Much of his later work from the autobiographical *Red Roses for Me* (1943) to *Cock-a-Doodle-Dandy* (1949) and *The Bishop's Bonfire* (1955) is only just beginning to be given the recognition it deserves.

Commercial consolidation

During the 1930s, years of the Depression and the growing international threat of fascism, the more interesting experiments in a socially committed and serious drama continued to take place outside the West End, on the theatrical fringe as it were. Again, economic factors contributed to the conservatism of mainstream theatre, as competition from the new forms of radio and film reversed the boom of the early 1920s and discouraged managements from taking financial risks. In London the ▷ Unity Theatre was formed, an amateur company which pursued a policy of dramatizing topical issues, such as the Spanish Civil War and the popular front against ▷ fascism, from a left-wing point of view. This was the first theatre to present ▷ Brecht in English with *Senora Carrar's Rifles* in 1938. The Group Theatre, a private society based at the Westminster Theatre, produced three experimental verse plays by ▷ W. H. Auden and ▷ Christopher Isherwood, *The Dog Beneath the Skin* (1936), *The Ascent of F6* (1937) and *On the Frontier* (1938). ▷ T. S. Eliot's fragmentary and innovatory verse drama, *Sweeney Agonistes*, was also produced here in 1935. Admittedly this was drama for minority audiences, but such activity did provide a welcome alternative to the complacency of the theatrical establishment, and at a time when it was certainly needed. Eliot's contribution in reintroducing verse drama onto the stage is of major significance, although he never quite forced the revolutionary break from prose drama he had hoped for. To him the prosaic was anathema to art; in *The Family Reunion* (1939) and, later, *The Cocktail Party* (1950), he used the conventional drawing-room stage scenario as a starting point to show how 'our own sordid, dreary world would be suddenly illuminated and transfigured' with the power of verse. It was not the traditional English blank verse that he employed, but his own contemporary idiom, sometimes difficult to distinguish from prose. His most assured success was the historical religious play about the martyrdom of Thomas à Becket, *Murder in the Cathedral* (1935). Here the ritualistic style of expression is perfectly suited to the subject matter and the location of Canterbury Cathedral, where it was first performed.

Two new serious, if less unconventional, playwrights, ▷ James Bridie (1888–1951) and ▷ J. B. Priestley (1894–1984), also helped to keep the theatre vital and challenging at a time when it was threatened by frivolity, complacency and commercialism. Both were prolific writers who never quite lived up to early expectations. Bridie was dubbed a second Shaw for his interest in an intellectual drama of ideas. He was by profession a doctor, which perhaps helps to explain the slightly detached concern with the welfare of the world, characteristic of his plays. He also had a tendency to lose inspiration by the final act, for which he had the perfect excuse, 'Only God can write third acts, and He seldom does.' By contrast, Priestly is a recognized master of well-constructed plays. His career was long and varied, beginning with *Dangerous Corner*, in 1932, the first of a series of so-called 'time' plays, and continuing up to 1968 with the television script, *Anyone for Tennis?* He described his prosaic style of dialogue somewhat dismissively as a 'familiar flat thin idiom'. Nonetheless, it was used to good effect to explore major issues, such as the moral nature of mankind and human destiny, subjects which are now accepted as relevant matters for modern dramatists to deal with but at the time were laudably daring.

The 1930s also saw important developments in Shakespeare productions, particularly at the ▷ Old Vic in London and the Memorial Theatre in Stratford. Here were the beginnings of the modern ▷ National Theatre and the ▷ Royal Shakespeare company. The insistence of Granville Barker and ▷ William Poel on a scholarly re-examination of Elizabethan stage conditions was clearly influential on new directors like Tyrone Guthrie, ▷ John Gielgud and ▷ William Bridges-Adams. ▷ Laurence Olivier, Charles Laughton, Ralph Richardson, Edith Evans, Peggy Ashcroft and Sybil Thorndike were all part of a new generation of actors who combined the role of star performer with that of ensemble player. There was inevitably, though, a tension for these actors between the attraction of working for a dedicated but poorly paid company and the financial appeal of the West End and the film industry.

During World War II the Council for the Encouragement of Music and Arts (▷ C.E.M.A.) was formed to provide morale-boosting entertainment on the home front. This was to prove highly significant, for it later evolved into the Arts Council of Great Britain, which was founded in 1946 and which aimed 'to develop a greater knowledge, understanding, and practice of the Fine Arts, to increase their accessibility to the public, and to improve their standard of execution'. Once the principle of government subsidy for the theatre was established, the likelihood of a development of serious drama increased. This did not happen at once; the initial subsidies were small and the immediate post-war years were times of hardship and struggle. The new welfare state era began to make its impact on the theatre in the 1950s and 60s. In the meantime, with little new material available, Shakespeare, the old national stalwart, continued to attract audiences in London and Stratford-on-Avon, as did a profusion of revivals and imports.

Christopher Fry (b 1907) enjoyed an unexpectedly brief period of fame with the success of his verse dramas, *A Phoenix Too Frequent* (1946) and *The Lady's Not For Burning* (1948). His attempts to develop a poet's theatre as pioneered by Yeats and Eliot was considerably helped by the strength of actors like Laurence Olivier, John Gielgud and Edith Evans, who took leading roles in his plays. He seemed to have broken the mould of the commercial theatre but the interest in verse plays was short-lived. Fry was in and out of fashion all too quickly and by the mid 1950s he was already falling out of favour. Typical of the period were the lighter entertainments of Terence Rattigan (1911–77). In his more serious work *The Winslow Boy* (1946), the story of a father's fight to clear his son of a charge of theft, he offered a sophisticated version of the old drawing-room problem play. This won the award for the best play of the year in London. Despite his popularity with the Aunt Ednas, as he called his audiences, his plays hardly qualify as landmarks in English drama. Perhaps had he not been writing at a time when homosexuality could not be openly discussed on stage, this sublimated theme in his work might have been developed into something more interesting. Amongst the others writing at this time only ▷ John Whiting (1917–63) and Peter Ustinov (b 1921) stand out. Whiting died tragically young and Ustinov never developed into the dramatist he was expected to become.

1956 and all that

1956 is often suggested as a starting date for modern political drama in Britain. This was the year of the first visit of ▷ Bertolt Brecht's company, the Berliner Ensemble, to London; it was also the year of ▷ John Osborne's success at the Royal Court with ▷ *Look Back in Anger*, in which the central character, the ▷ angry young man Jimmy Porter, seemed to represent a whole generation of disaffected youth. Like all such apparently seminal dates it can be misleading. One should not overlook the activities of organizations like the Unity Theatre and Group Theatre during the 1930s and the work of ▷ Joan Littlewood and Theatre Workshop which began as early as 1943 (though wider recognition came much later with productions of ▷ Brendan Behan's *The Hostage* in 1958 and Joan Littlewood's improvised piece *Oh, What a Lovely War* in 1963). Still, it is undeniable that from the late 1950s there was an explosion of dramatic activity which has given rise to the most exciting period in British drama since the ▷ Elizabethan and ▷ Jacobean age. A growing interest in international theatre, increased government subsidies and the building of many regional repertory theatres, and changes in the social structure of Britain all contributed to this.

Brecht died in 1956 before the Berliner Ensemble's London visit; but the work of the company which he had set up in East Berlin after World War II exemplified his approach to the theatre. Part of its initial attraction was that it received sufficient subsidy to rehearse at length and develop a genuine ensemble style of performance. Brecht's desire to use the theatre to communicate the need for social change to the working class also had, and still has, its appeal, although it cannot be claimed that theatre-going is a working class activity. Nonetheless, his style of writing and theories of performance assisted a development in the British theatre away from the predominant mode of ▷ naturalism. He trained actors in a method of performing which discourages the audience from suspending disbelief and imagining that what they see on stage is real life. Actors were not to encourage empathy but were to create a critical distance between themselves as performers and the roles they played. The world, and its representation on stage, was to be made available for scrutiny by a technique of 'estrangement', of making the familiar seem strange and the strange seem familiar. Typical 'estrangement' devices were the introduction of songs to interrupt the dramatic action; the juxtaposition of scenes with unexpected shifts of location or viewpoint; and the introduction of scenes with placards explaining the action about to follow. Brecht's was a theatre of reason and political commitment. This did not mean that emotion was banned from the stage but that the ultimate aim was to encourage the audience to think, to look at the world in new ways and understand how it might be changed. As Brecht was a ▷ Marxist it was to be expected that he presented the world and its social relations from a Marxist perspective. Since many of the new British playwrights in the post-war period were themselves politically committed and of the left, it was no surprise that they found in Brecht a model for a new kind of drama, both in terms of subject matter and of form.

Other European influences such as the ▷ Theatre of Cruelty and the ▷ Theatre of the Absurd helped dramatists, directors and actors to explore non-naturalistic techniques. The Theatre of Cruelty conceived by ▷ Antonin Artaud (1896–1948) aimed to communicate with the audience at a primitive, subconscious level by means of symbols, gesture, movement and sound. His most significant impact in the British theatre has been on the director ▷ Peter Brook. The greatest exponent of Absurdist theatre on the English stage has been ▷ Samuel Beckett (b 1906), an Irishman living in France, whose work is heavily influenced by French ▷ existentialist philosophy and who has written many of his plays in French. His rejection of conventional plots and refusal to supply pat explanations of his plays' meanings established him at once as an avant-garde figure. In 1955 ▷ *Waiting for Godot* was performed in London at the Arts Theatre. In this play Beckett created a novel situation in which two tramps in a sparse and inhospitable landscape wait hopefully for help which never comes. The harsh view of life's essential pointlessness is typical of his plays; and his great achievement as a dramatist has been to create sharp and often humorous theatrical images to portray such a bleak philosophy of life. The process of absorbing all these new influences was assisted by one theatre in particular, the ▷ Royal Court. Under the general direction of George Devine, the Royal Court consistently promoted the work of new writers who were given the opportunity to explore a range of theatrical forms of expression which had not been available to preceding generations. Admittedly Brecht's influence on John Osborne was fairly superficial, limited to a few technical devices, but it was certainly profound in the case of ▷ John Arden (b 1930), another product of the Royal Court and one of the most innovatory of the young British dramatists of the 1950s. For Arden, Brecht was one of several models who could help bring back to the theatre the 'noise, disorder, drunkenness, lasciviousness, nudity, generosity, corruption, fertility and ease' which he thought the playwright should provide. It was refreshing for Arden and his contemporaries to be able to experiment with a variety of theatrical techniques, whether they derived from Brecht, Beckett, Artaud or whoever else. Suddenly the days of a theatre characterized by English parochialism and genteel respectability seemed to be over.

Categories such as Theatre of the Absurd and Theatre of Cruelty are useful as rough generalizations about different styles of drama but they do not necessarily say much about the particular qualities of individual authors whose plays fall into these categories. Both ▷ N. F. Simpson (b 1919) and ▷ Harold Pinter (b 1930) could be said to be influenced by the Theatre of the Absurd yet their plays are very different. Much of Simpson's drama, like the commercially successful *One Way Pendulum* (1959), is characterized by a slightly quirky farcical style, very much in an English tradition; Pinter made his reputation via the commercial stage with *The Birthday Party* (1958), originally a stage failure but revived by television, and *The Caretaker* (1960). His plays are certainly less whimsical and more menacing in their portrayal of a hostile and insecure world. Like Beckett, he does not attempt to provide explicit meanings. As he has said, there are 'no hard distinctions between what is real and what is unreal, nor between what is true and what is false. The thing is not necessarily either true or false.' His freedom with dramatic form and precision with language, again characteristic of Beckett, enables him to pinpoint human repressions, anxieties, guilt, struggles for power, primitive desires and behaviour, in a far bolder, more startling manner than was possible within the traditional dramatic conventions. From his earliest plays there was, in effect, a full-scale assault on the decorous drawing-room style drama which rarely probed beyond the surface of English reserve, awkwardness and embarrassment.

The first wave of new writers also included ▷ Ann Jellicoe, ▷ Arnold Wesker and ▷ Shelagh Delaney. As a group they no longer seem as rebellious as they once did and none of them could now be described as shocking. But they all helped in the development of an alternative drama which could be challenging, provocative and socially critical; and they paved the way for dramatists like ▷ Edward Bond, ▷ Joe Orton, ▷ Trevor Griffiths and ▷ Howard Brenton who became known for their radical or iconoclastic tendencies in the late 1960s and early 1970s. A vital quality of the work of these writers and many of their contemporaries is their strong anti-establishment stance. Usually their perspective is political and left-wing; though in the case of Orton the impulse is more anarchic and gleefully outrageous. Orton and Bond both fell foul of censorship laws during the 1960s; Bond's *Saved* (1965) was heavily censored for its realistic street language and relatively explicit sex scenes, and his later play *Early Morning* (1968) was banned for its apparently scurrilous treatment of Queen Victoria. The resulting furore revealed all too clearly just how much the law was out of touch with the times and in 1968 stage censorship was finally abolished. Since then Bond has remained a controversial and outspoken figure; and is now recognized by many as one of Britain's leading political playwrights.

1968, a date which brings to mind student unrest and political agitation, was also the year in which Jerzy Grotowski's *The Poor Theatre* was published in English. Grotowski evolved a detailed training programme for the actor, intended to develop both his or her physical and mental powers; and he also challenged the formal division in the theatre between actor and audience. The emphasis on the adaptability of almost any space for performance and the rejection of the costly paraphernalia of standard theatre was of enormous appeal to those who sought an alternative kind of drama. Again the director Peter Brook was notably receptive to continental developments and applied some of Grotowski's theories to his productions for the Royal Shakespeare Company. By the 1970s the Royal Shakespeare Company was offering more than the traditional large-stage productions by setting up its own low-budget touring group which regularly performed in schools and community centres around the country.

However, many of the new radicals active in the theatre rejected outright the idea of working for such established and relatively well-subsidized theatre companies. They were critical of a policy of capital investment in buildings like the Royal Shakespeare Theatre and the new National Theatre, finally completed in 1976. A plethora of new companies appeared, often with no permanent theatre base, and these attempted to provide entertainment at alternative venues (sometimes quite simply the street or a city square) for alternative audiences. Some companies were overtly political, embracing specific causes like issues of race, gender or class; others concentrated more on experimental avant-garde theatre or performance art. What they all tended to share was the desire to democratize the theatrical process itself and provide an alternative to the standard repertory theatre which had been promoted by the Arts Council since World War II.

Although there is nothing unusual historically about women writing plays it is only really since the late 1960s that female playwrights began to be taken seriously. ▷ Caryl Churchill, Sarah Daniels, ▷ Pam Gems, Susan Todd and Michelene Wandor are just a few of the women writers who contributed in a major way to a widening of dramatic and cultural horizons beyond those traditionally recognized by a male-dominated theatre establishment. Today around fifteen per cent of British playwrights are women, though this figure is certainly not represented in terms of publishing and performance.

Many of the successful playwrights from the post 1956 period, such as John Mortimer, ▷ Robert Bolt, ▷ Tom Stoppard, ▷ Alan Ayckbourn, ▷ Peter Shaffer and Peter Nichols were relatively unaffected by these developments and are not obviously products of an era of radicalism at all. Others like ▷ Howard Brenton, ▷ David Edgar, ▷ David Hare, ▷ Caryl Churchill and Susan Todd wrote regularly for companies which were very much part of this political ▷ fringe movement challenging the values of mainstream theatre. In recent years dramatists have shifted freely between the two camps and transfers from the fringe to the mainstream theatre have been common. An obvious problem for writers and actors working for small touring companies has been the lack of money and annual fight for government subsidy. It is no surprise, therefore, to find both Brenton and Hare now working for the National Theatre and to see plays by feminist writers like Caryl Churchill appearing in the West End. For some, there is still an ideological resistance to the perpetuation of London as the focus of cultural life. ▷ John McGrath, for example, founder of the highly successful touring company 7:84, has resolutely avoided the prestigious London theatres. There has also been an ideological debate about the advantages and disadvantages of writing for television. Trevor Griffiths, who has written for both stage and television, has welcomed the opportunity to reach a mass audience unattainable in the theatre; David Edgar has argued against working for television on the grounds that the writer has little control over his or her product and the form is too heavily dominated by naturalistic conventions. Television is certainly a superior form for providing an imitation of real life and this has had its appeal. One might also argue that this has encouraged the theatre to be more experimental in its use of non-naturalistic forms; since it cannot hope to compete with television it has had to avoid being seen as a poor imitation.

Much has happened in the last thirty years, yet, on the whole, the changes and developments have not been revolutionary. Many influences have been reformed and absorbed by the established theatre in a characteristically British manner, much in the way that the old Fabians Shaw and Granville Barker might have approved of. The general trend has been progressive and liberating although recent events are more ominous. Legislation against the 'promotion' of homosexuality in the theatre heralds the return of direct stage censorship. If the 1960s and 70s were the years of radical experiments, the 1980s are beginning to look like a decade of stagnation and decline, following a period of recession and cutbacks in public subsidies. Funding for theatre companies is severely limited and the emphasis is now on self-sufficiency and private sponsorship rather than public support. The effect of this has been most severe on fringe companies which have always had to survive on extremely low budgets. Without the challenges and provocations of its 'alternative' and experimental practitioners the theatre is always in danger of slipping back into a state of complacency which Peter Brook has so appositely termed 'deadly theatre'.

POLY-OLBION

GREAT BRITAINE

By
Michael Drayton
Esq:

London printed for M Lownes. I Browne. I Iustaue
I Helme. I Busbie. Ihr W Hole

Frontispiece to Michael Drayton's *Polyolbion*

The concealed poet

> Is not this excuse for mere contraries
> Equally strong? Cannot both sides say so?
> That thou mayest rightly obey power, her bounds know;
> Those passed her nature and name is changed; to be
> Then humble to her is idolatry.
> As streams are, power is:
>   (John Donne, Satire 3. 98–103)

We might begin this discussion of ▷ Renaissance poetry with an account of poetry as secrecy. In 1589, ▷ George Puttenham published *The Arte of English Poetry*, a work that was to have considerable influence on Renaissance writers. When, in Book III of his theoretical treatise, Puttenham came to consider 'Ornament' in language, the ornaments which decorate his own prose are metaphors of secrecy and duplicity. Figurative language, in this account, is inseparably caught up in a web of deceit and (to use Puttenham's word) 'doubleness'. So, the writer is:

> ... *occupied of purpose to deceive the ear and also the mind, drawing it from plainness and simplicity to a certain doubleness, whereby our talk is the more guileful and abusing ...*

> (III. ch. VII)

For Puttenham, such doubleness lay at the heart of the courtly aesthetic, and it is not difficult to understand how this awareness of poetic language as a concealing device could have a certain political efficacy. Puttenham continues:

> *And ye shall know that we dissemble, I mean speak otherwise than we think, in earnest as well as in sport, under covert and dark terms and in learned and apparent speeches, in short sentences and by long ambage and circumstance of words, and finally as well when we lie as when we tell the truth. To be short every speech wrested from his own natural signification to another not altogether so natural is a kind of dissimulation, because the words bear contrary countenance to the intent.*

> (III. ch. XVIII)

What Puttenham has observed here is crucial to our understanding of Renaissance writing. In trying to isolate the function of poetic language (an attempt whose result is not dissimilar to the discovery of 'defamiliarization' by the ▷ Russian Formalist critics of the early twentieth century), he has focused attention not simply on the latent 'ambiguity' of all linguistic transactions but also on the struggle which takes place in all discourse. That struggle he expresses through a series of oppositions: speaking/thinking, serious/unserious, dark/apparent, lies/truths.

In reading Renaissance texts, this sense of doubleness, this possibility of concealment, and this understanding of poetic discourse as encompassing contradiction and struggle must be kept in mind. For ▷ Thomas Wyatt, courtier and diplomatic servant of ▷ Henry VIII, doubleness is itself a theme of his writing. 'What 'vaileth truth?' he asks in one of his poems, concluding:

> *True meaning heart is had in disdain.*
> *Against deceit and doubleness*
> *What 'vaileth truth?*

The opposition between truth and deceit here has implications for meaning itself. Wherein can 'meaning' lie if, as Puttenham was to observe some fifty years later, we 'speak otherwise than we think'? 'Meaning', too, becomes of significance in dealing with another of Puttenham's oppositions, that between what is 'dark' or concealed, and what is 'apparent' or open to interpretation. Wyatt's poem 'My galley charged with forgetfulness', itself a version of an earlier poem by ▷ Petrarch – *'Passa la nave mia colma d'obblio'* (*Rime* CLXXXIX) – displays the problem for us:

> *My galley charged with forgetfulness*
> *Thorough sharp seas in winter nights doth pass*
> *'Tween rock and rock, and eke mine enemy alas,*
> *That is my lord, steereth with cruelness,*
> *And every oar a thought in readiness,*
> *As though that death were light in such a case.*
> *An endless wind doth tear the sail apace,*
> *Of forced sighs and trusty fearfulness;*
> *A rain of tears, a cloud of dark disdain*
> *Hath done the wearied cords great hinderance,*
> *Wreathed with error, and eke with ignorance.*
> *The stars be hid that led me to this pain,*
> *Drowned is reason that should me comfort,*
> *And I remain despairing of the port.*

> (XXVIII)

Richard Tottel, the editor of the anthology in which this poem first appeared in published form in 1557, was in no doubt as to the meaning of the sonnet. 'The lover' he headed the poem 'compareth his state to a shippe in perilous storme tossed on the sea' (▷ *Tottel's Miscellany*, sig. E3ʳ). Tottel is reminding the poem's sixteenth-century readers of the tradition of love poetry, stemming from Petrarch, which employs a conventional pattern of metaphors, images and formal metrical and rhythmical devices. Wyatt (together with Surrey, as has been often noted) was instrumental in importing these conventions into English verse. So, the storm-tossed lover might appear as a familiar figure to the Renaissance reader (see, for example, ▷ Edmund Spenser's ▷ *Amoretti* 63, 'After long stormes and tempests' sad assay'). We might compare Wyatt's sonnet to the 'original' (though the very question of originality is a concept to which we shall have to return):

> *My ship full of forgetful cargo sails*
> *Through rough seas at the midnight of a winter*
> *Between Charybdis and the Scylla reef,*
> *My master, no, my foe, is at the helm;*
>
> *At each oar sits a quick and insane thought*
> *That seems to scorn the storm and what it brings . . .*
>   (trans. Mark Musa)

Who are Petrarch's 'master' and Wyatt's 'lord'? The God of love, perhaps, and thus the enemy of reason. Yet, in Wyatt's version of the poem the character of this figure undergoes significant alterations. Where Petrarch suggests a certain unsureness as to the true nature of the helmsman ('My master, no, my foe'), Wyatt is unequivocal: at the helm is 'my enemy, alas,' who, inevitably, is also 'my lord'. And where, in Petrarch, the image was that of a blind and unreasoning steersman, rushing the ship headlong through the storm, in Wyatt he is possessed of intent – steering 'with cruelness'.

Reading Wyatt's sonnet against Petrarch's 'original' (as opposed to reading it in the way in which Richard Tottel asked his sixteenth-century contemporaries to read it), we begin to sense that all is not quite as it appears. Once the 'code', located within conventional Petrarchan imagery, has been identified, we might still feel that there is more than simply a generalized meditation on the pangs of despised love at work in the poem. At this point we might move away entirely from Petrarch, and the overt conventions of sixteenth-century love poetry, to read the sonnet for what it might also be – a profoundly disturbing meditation, not on love, but on the very nature of existence within the ▷ Tudor polity. Wyatt, a diplomat, a justice of the peace, marshal of Calais, ambassador to Spain and to France, M.P. for Kent, and vice-admiral of the Fleet, would appear to represent (and to have gained) all that was most glittering in the establishment of the society in which he found himself. Yet, at the head of that society was a monarch – Henry VIII – with whom conversation, in Stephen Greenblatt's memorable phrase, 'must have been like small talk with Stalin' (Greenblatt, S. *Renaissance Self-Fashioning*; 1980).

The other side of Wyatt's double-existence (and the double-existence of so many Renaissance writers) is what is represented in his ▷ sonnet 'My galley charged with forgetfulness'. That side – which involved, for Wyatt, imprisonment in 1534, further imprisonment and release on parole in 1536, the execution of his patron, ▷ Thomas Cromwell, in July 1540, and a final period of imprisonment in the ▷ Tower in 1541 – is one that might be drawn from any twentieth-century catalogue of existence under the conditions of absolute power. It is the realization of this existence which sends us back to the sonnet and to those key phrases – 'forgetfulness', 'mine enemy . . . my lord', 'cruelness', 'a thought in readiness', 'trusty fearfulness', 'wreathed with error', 'drowned is reason' – with a rather different sense of what this text may encode, and with an understanding, too, of the sonnet's ambiguous air of the sinister. To recall Puttenham again, we are in the presence of a text which possesses a certain 'doubleness'.

From writing to interpretation

For the poets of the ▷ Elizabethan and early ▷ Jacobean period, the contradictions involved in manoeuvring between the 'dark' and the 'apparent' produced, in turn, an awareness that the act of writing could itself be worth writing about. This self-conscious awareness of the writing process (which can be uncovered in the later parts of Petrarch's *Rime*) is the opening theme of ▷ Sir Philip Sidney's ▷ *Astrophel and Stella* (1591), and it was the status of writing, and the relationship *within* writing between meaning and truth, which was to fascinate the sonnet writers of the 1590s – ▷ Samuel Daniel, ▷ Michael Drayton, ▷ Edmund Spenser, ▷ Thomas Lodge and ▷ Shakespeare (to name but a very few). For Astrophel, in Sidney's sequence, the task is to uncover 'fit words' (I. 5) to 'entertaine' his female reader. But where are these words to be found? And once located, what process gives them utterance?

> *Thus great with child to speak, and helplesse in my throwes,*
> *Biting my trewand pen, beating my self for spite,*
> *'Foole' said my Muse to me, 'looke in thy heart and write.'*

This comic self-presentation of the poet conceals an important Renaissance theoretical problem associated with the act of writing. Sidney, here, abandons the conventional notion of male authorship 'begetting' his works upon the world (and we might recall the 'onlie begetter' of Shakespeare's sonnets here). Instead, writing is, once more, a struggle – a painful delivery rendering the author paradoxically helpless. At the same time, writing is a process by which that which was hidden within becomes manifest, and hence it entails an inward scrutiny, promoted by a voice ('my Muse') whose origin is also located within the writing self of the poet. But this inner search should not be understood as a quest for originality in the modern sense. What is at stake here is the Renaissance concept of 'imitation'. 'Imitation', as it was understood by the Renaissance writer, did not entail mere copying, but an assimilation of other voices into the unique voice of the individual poet. Writing, as ▷ Erasmus claimed in the *Ciceronianus* (1527), is therefore not an isolated utterance, but it is the product of other discourses, jostling in the mind. For the poet, working amidst these competing voices, the problem becomes one of establishing a position from which to speak, as

Shakespeare's dramatic denial of other poetic voices in his sonnet 130: 'My mistress' eyes are nothing like the sun' evidences. Here a series of Petrarchan motifs are summoned up, only to be dismissed as not answering to the reality of the woman he addresses. The paradox is, of course, that the very gesture of denial serves to evoke the competing voices of those other poetic discourses.

If writing is a proposition which involves the poet in a search for an authority with which to speak, what of reading? To the modern reader, what may be striking about Renaissance poetry is its determination to both create the reader and control their response to what is read. We might understand this desire to forestall the reader's licence to interpret (for this is what it amounts to) as being a manifestation of a literary culture which is, at once, enclosed (in a social sense) and also profoundly anxious as to the results of unlicensed interpretive power. The freedom to interpret, as Elizabeth's ▷ Protestant divines were never tired of pointing out, could have unfortunate results. Protestant culture may, on the one hand, have championed the right to interpret scriptual texts when that interpretation seemed to support Protestant beliefs against the perceived threat of ▷ Roman Catholic ▷ Counter-reformation, but that did not mean that the right to interpret should be invested in each and every reader. The ▷ Thirty-nine Articles, passed under Elizabeth at the Convocation of 1562, might be thought of, within this context, as an attempt at controlling the interpretation of key doctrinal issues. What the articles set out to establish was 'consent touching true religion' and the 'avoiding of diversities of opinions'. Their end, in other words, was to create a homogeneous reader.

Interpretation was understood as involving the assumption of power over the text and the experience inscribed within that text. Is this, then, the key to understanding the Renaissance poet's constant anxiety as to the way in which his secular verse is to be understood? Are the ▷ Stellas, ▷ Delias, ▷ Dianas, ▷ Licias, ▷ Zephiras, ▷ Fidessas and ▷ Chlorises (the antique names of imagined or real readers to whom sonnet collections are addressed, and whose names are inscribed in their titles) fierce interpretive presences before whom, in true Petrarchan style, the poet-writer trembled? Indeed, they are. But herein lies another paradox of Renaissance writing. The relationship, in ▷ lyric poetry in particular, between the writer and the reader is, above all, sexual. But this sexual connection, though it involves (as we might expect) an active male author confronting a female reader (as the titles to countless sonnet sequences announce), does not position the female reader in a necessarily passive role, since she is not only a reader but an interpreter. As an interpreter she may be threatened, cajoled, persuaded, but never ignored. We can thus understand the female figure, within the dominant masculine codes of Renaissance writing, as one in whom there is invested a network of competing claims and counter-claims. She is the mainspring of the poet's invention, the object of sexual desire, the prize, the besieged fort, the source of religious or quasi-religious consolation or agony, and, most important of all, the reader and interpreter of his verses, So, Stella, in Sidney's *Astrophel and Stella*, is not only the object of Astrophel's verse (whilst his own sufferings and triumphs are the subject), she is also the final reader and interpreter of the verses laid before her. In Spenser's *Amoretti* (1595) the sequence of sonnets opens with an invocation of the reading-presence of his mistress, who is the final interpreter of what is to follow: 'Leaves, lines, and rymes, seeke her to please alone, / whom if ye please I care for other none.' (I. 13–14).

'Politique Devotion'

It would be simple to dismiss this presence of the female reader as no more than a conventional trope of praise – a means of ensuring that the elaborate fiction of the intimacy of the lover's adoration of the beloved is sustained. Thus, the argument would continue, the true object of the sonnet-writer's fascination is himself, and the female subject is evoked only in order that she be marginalized. But to dismiss the importance attached to interpretation on the part of Renaissance poets is not only to dismiss the serious implications of interpretive power discerned by Elizabethan writers in general, but also to ignore the presence of the most important female interpreter of all – that of the queen herself.

It is almost impossible to over-estimate the awareness of late sixteenth-century poets of the abiding presence of the queen. The queen as head of state, head of the Church, and ultimate source of patronage is a figure of real, not merely idealized, power. She is, moreover, a dominating presence in all forms of literary and artistic culture of the period. As such she is a protean figure, paradoxically subject herself to the transforming power of the very verses which sought to confirm her central position in the political hierarchy. But it is in the figure of the queen that the complete identification of aesthetic forms with political power is manifested. Her very name becomes an emblem of power, even whilst it is transformed, literally, through the devices of art:

> E urope, *the Earthes sweete Paradise:*
> L et all thy Kings that would be wise,
> I n Politique Devotion:
> S ail hither to observe her eyes,
> A nd marke her heavenly motion.
>
> B rave Princes of this civill Age,
> E nter into this pilgrimage:
> T his Saints tongue is an oracle,
> H er eye hath made a Prince a Page,
> A nd workes each day a Miracle.
>
> R aise but your lookes to her, and see
> E ven the true beames of Majestie,
> G reat Princes, marke her duly;
> I f all the world you do survey,
> N o forehead spreades so bright a Ray,
> A nd notes a Prince so truly.

These acrostic verses, written by ▷ Sir John Davies and entitled 'To all the princes of Europe', form part of a sequence entitled *Hymns of Astraea*, published in 1599. Elizabeth is addressed as the goddess Astraea, a title bestowed upon her not only by Davies, but by other poets including Spenser and ▷ George Peele. Astraea, associated with spring and with justice, is, in ▷ Ovid's *Metamorphoses* (an important source of poetic mythologizing in the period), a symbol of the former ▷ Golden Age, whilst in ▷ Virgil she is associated with a future Golden Age. The Golden Age, when justice and prosperity rule on earth, of the future and of the past thus meet in the figure of Elizabeth in the present.

To say of these verses thay they are sycophantic or contrived is to miss the fundamental connection between art and political power which poets and the queen herself sought to preserve. We might take Davies's poem as itself emblematic of the queen's presence within art. Her name and title function as the springboard for the poet – the place from which the lines themselves originate. Through her name, she is embedded within the poem – a poem which sets out to admire her, as Davies puts it, with 'politique devotion'. Devotional politics, indeed, are precisely what the poem produces. But the poem memorializes the queen in more than one role. Passively, she is the object of pilgrimage and devotion, moving as does the constellation Virgo (an alternative, and of course immediately appropriate name for Elizabeth/ Astraea) above and beyond the earth. As an object she is, within the poem's structure of images and language, the recipient and bestower of glances and gazings. Her eyes, in a Petrarchan conceit, must be observed, her motion marked, looks raised to her. But her own glances have within them political force, and the Petrarchan conceit is itself transformed in a movement of appreciation of political reality: 'Her eye hath made a Prince a Page'.

For Sir John Davies, lawyer and aspiring politician, later (in 1603) solicitor-general to Ireland, the conjunction between the forms of art and the realities of political power meet in the multiple personnae of the queen. Similarly, for the contemporaries of Davies, and as Elizabeth's reign drew to its close, the queen's continuing presence becomes itself the subject of ever- more elaborate poetic and artistic device. In ▷ Sir Walter Raleigh's poem of devotion 'The Book of the Ocean to Cynthia' (or 'The Ocean's Love to Cynthia'), a text of which only a fragment exists in manuscript form, the queen is Cynthia/Diana, goddess of the moon, hunting and chastity, whilst the poet is the ocean, subject to the moon's transforming power, a power which is absolute and, disturbingly, seemingly arbitrary:

> *No other power effecting wound or bliss,*
> *She gave, she took, she wounded, she appeased.*
> ('Ocean's Love' ll. 55–6)

What can we conclude from this assimilation within art of the realities of power? Reading the poetry of the late sixteenth century, we realize that at the very heart of the literary culture of the period lies the pervasive belief that art and the state must conspire together to affirm a vision of national identity. That it is a vision and not a reality is exemplified by the very urgency with which Renaissance writers pressed home the constantly nation were one. Late Elizabethan culture, rather than appearing 'monumental' (as it has been described) or as the product of a realized sense of national selfhood, begins to appear as a rather more anxious moment of history. That pressing need for unity – whether it be unity of religion, of social practices, of cultural forms, of political expression, or of interpretation (all of these being linked in any case) – like all such calls for national unity, indicates the awareness of what is potentially disuniting and positively disruptive. Within this context the 'monuments' of Renaissance culture, the poets of the late sixteenth century, begin to appear as not only poets but, at one and the same time, ideologues of the first order. Their function was not only to adorn or beautify, but to affirm (sometimes, one feels, for the benefit of Elizabeth as well as her subjects) that the hierarchy was an established reality.

Nowhere is this awareness of the poetic text's power to sanction or authorize a sense of national selfhood more apparent than in what may appear, from the outside, to be the most monumental text of them all – Spenser's ▷ The Faerie Queene. Indeed, it is as a monument that the poem is approached in the first instance. On the dedicatory page of the 1596 edition of the poem appears this inscriptive address:

TO

THE MOST HIGH,

MIGHTIE

and

MAGNIFICENT

EMPRESSE, RENOW-

MED FOR PIETIE, VER-

TUE, AND ALL GRATIOUS

GOVERNMENT ELIZABETH BY

THE GRACE OF GOD QUEENE

OF ENGLAND FRAUNCE AND

IRELAND AND OF VIRGI-

NIA, DEFENDER OF THE

FAITH, &c. HER MOST

HUMBLE SERVAVNT

EDMUND SPENSER

DOTH IN ALL HU-

MILITIE DEDI

CATE, PRE-

SENT

AND CONSECRATE THESE

HIS LABOURS TO LIVE

WITH THE ETERNI-

TIE OF HER

FAME

The queen and her titles are inscribed (together with the poet's name) in the form of a memorial urn whose function is to preserve and consecrate the text which is to follow. The queen's titles, held under God (the teaching of whose works she sanctions as head of His Church in her realm), are titles of monarchy over three nations, and sovereignty over a new entity – the colony of Virginia. The poem which follows (and which will also serve to memorialize the queen and the nation, the two being, once more, inseparable) is thus approached through an elaborate token of royal power.

The Faerie Queene is, however, not only a monument to Elizabeth, but a legendary history of the nation over which she governs. It is important, here, to be fully aware of the circumstances of its composition. When Spenser embarked upon the poem (some time prior to October 1579), he was shortly to gain the position of private secretary to Lord Grey, the newly appointed lord deputy of Ireland. Ireland was to be Spenser's home throughout the period of composition and publication of *The Faerie Queene*, and it was as a diligent servant to the government in Ireland that Spenser was to fashion his own career.

The poem is, therefore, composed not close to the source of political patronage and power, but at the very margins of the Elizabethan polity. Ireland presented, to Elizabethan authority, a continuing source of disruption. A Catholic and unruly nation (in the eyes of Elizabeth's government), it was not until the Battle of Kinsale (1601) where a combined Irish and Spanish force was defeated by the English under Lord Mountjoy, that the Protestant domination of the country was assured. Spenser, whose own colony of English settlers established on confiscated land was destroyed in 'Tyrone's Rebellion' (1598), was an active administrative cog in what is generally agreed to have been a brutalized (and brutalizing) regime. Indeed, Spenser was the author of two important 'policy documents' on Ireland written in the late 1590s. These works are important for what they tell us of the attitude of mind of Spenser and his contemporaries. Informing them is, above all, fear. Fear of the Irish, their alien religion, their customs, their language (which Spenser, though he lived in Ireland for nearly twenty years, never understood), and the threat which they represented to England, determines to a large extent his understanding of the country in which he found himself. They are, in short, documents of colonialism, one of the earliest we possess.

We can perceive this sense of threat, an awareness of an alien alternative to the 'civilizing' culture of the Protestant poet, at work throughout Spenser's text. In the poem we encounter an evocation of a brutal wilderness – a complex psychological state of 'otherness' which it is the task of Spenser's knights to banish both from the fantastic environment through which they move, and, more importantly, from themselves. This fear, or anxiety, which permeates the poem is, it is important to recognize, not simply a fear which can be dispelled through heroic endeavour. It is a fear, rather, of what is uncontrollable within the subject. If we need an analogy in more recent writing, then ▷ Joseph Conrad's Mr Kurtz in ▷ *The Heart of Darkness* might serve. For Conrad's figure of colonial corruption, isolated from any 'civilized' values, it is the discovery that the darkness and horror lie within which is finally destructive of his own sense of integrated selfhood. So, in similar measure, with Spenser's knights. As they progress on their episodic forays into a world of alien values, their discovery of a struggle taking place within themselves is what the poem dramatizes. When, for example, at the climax of Book II (the legend of Guyon, or temperance), Guyon and his guide enter the 'Bower of Blisse' to confront a world of sensuous and artificial luxury (a world rich in images of frozen sexuality), their iconoclastic endeavour is simply to destroy the *representations* of sensuality with which they have been confronted. Yet they themselves are not untainted by what they encounter. Kurtz-like, they creep through the undergrowth to witness the strange rites from which they cannot draw their eyes. The object of their voyeuristic gaze is the enchantress Acrasia:

> Her snowy brest was bare to readie spoyle
> Of hungry eies, which n'ote therewith be fild,
> And yet through langour of her late sweet toyle,
> Few drops, more clear then Nectar, forth distild,
> That like pure Orient perles adowne it trild,
> And her faire eyes sweet smyling in delight,
> Moystened their fierie beames, with which she thrild
> Fraile harts, yet quenched not; like starry light
> Which sparckling on the silent waues, does seeme more bright.
>
> (II. xii. 78)

What, and who is Acrasia? Like the queen, she is the object of a male gaze which is fascinated by what it has alighted upon. Unlike the queen (at least overtly) a world of sensual delight is promised. Acrasia, perceived in a moment of sexual passivity, is offered as a dual object of desire. There to be consumed by 'hungrie eies', thrilling 'fraile hearts', she is also a place of danger and destruction. Just as Ireland, or Virginia, or America itself were represented as female figures in need of mastery, so Acrasia must be captured and her Bower destroyed by the stern masculine (and Protestant) rigour of Spenser's knight.

In externalizing this inward struggle, Spenser's poem is truly a Protestant epic. ▷ Calvinism (the official doctrine of the Church of England under the Elizabethan 'settlement') served to draw attention to the adherent's inner state of mind and promoted a seemingly obsessive curiosity as to the inner health of the individual. But even once this awareness of the poem's Protestant roots has been grasped, we also need to be aware of it as a validating text. *The Faerie Queene* glances back to other epics (to ▷ Tasso and to Virgil in particular) not out of conservatism, or a desire to emulate what previous cultures have produced, but to authorize the present. Spenser himself, in the course of a letter to Raleigh written in 1589, termed the poem a 'darke conceit' – a text which is both apparent and concealed and which might remind us, once more, of Puttenham – but he also described his own method as being that of 'a poet historical'. Within this context, Spenser's epic can be understood as part of an important Elizabethan project. That project entailed nothing less than the active creation, in imaginative culture, of the nation-state as an understandable entity. Together with later texts such as Samuel Daniel's eight books of *The Civil Warres* (1609) and Michael Drayton's vast *Poly-Olbion* (1612–22), Spenser's epic looks back to a past (albeit in Spenser's case a legendary past) to uncover not only 'thinges forepast' but 'thinges to come'. The nation, in other words, must not only have its past created by its poets, but its future mapped out as well.

The deliberate creation of a mythopoeic past was to have enormous influence on the poets who followed Spenser. For one group in particular, the so-called ▷ 'Spenserian poets', Spenser's writing served as a model for their own attempts to create a visionary sense of national and political identity. These writers, who include Michael Drayton, ▷ William Browne and ▷ Phineas Fletcher, discovered in Spenser's writing a readily adaptable means of expressing their own sense of both a mythical past and wished-for future. The past which these poets created, however, was one that was governed by the forms and styles, exploited by Spenser not only in *The Faerie Queene*, but in his autobiographical ▷ *Colin Clout's Come Home Again* (1595), and ▷ *The Shepherd's Calender* (1579). What Renaissance readers uncovered in these poems was a world determined by the conventions, inherited from ▷ classical and continental writers, of ▷ pastoral. It is important to understand that 'pastoral' poetry did not represent simply an idealized retreat into a mythic world of shepherds, shepherdesses and arcadian delight. But it did signal another form of retreat, and one that was predominantly political. The adoption of pastoral personae, the evocation of a vanished 'golden age' became, for the poets of the early seventeenth century, a means of registering their own sense of isolation under the changed conditions of the early Jacobean period. The sense of poetry occupying a central position within the political culture has begun to fragment. Instead, a new kind of poetry begins to emerge – one that we might begin to term 'oppositional'.

Pastoral has been described as an omnipresent metaphor in Renaissance writing rather than a strict genre in its own right. As such it could be endlessly adaptable, but still provide a framework which both the poet and the reader could recognize. For the poets of the seventeenth century (up to and including ▷ John Milton) pastoral forms allowed them a significant freedom. Phineas Fletcher's *The Purple Island* (written c 1614–15, but published in 1633), for example, indicates the adaptability of pastoral forms. This (to modern eyes) strangely incongruous poem – incongruous since its ostensible subject is the anatomized human body – indicates the uses to which pastoral could be put in the years after the death of Elizabeth and the accession of ▷ James I. Fletcher's twelve-canto poem is narrated by a shepherd-poet named Thirsil. Thirsil's task, to which he has been elected by his fellow-shepherds, is to become their poetic spokesman. But what is to be his subject? What role is now alloted to poetry? What kind of audience must the poet create? The answer to these questions involves Thirsil in a literary search for a subject in what he calls 'these iron daies/(Hard daies)' which 'afford nor matter nor reward' for the poet. On the surface, the theme upon which he alights is profoundly apolitical – six cantos of his poem are spent in celebrating the dissected human body. Yet we should remember Puttenham's distinction between the 'dark' and the 'apparent'. For the human body, in Fletcher's poem, is the setting for war. Just as *The Faerie Queene* had dramatized the creation of an individual identity within an alien world of uncivilized values, so *The Purple Island* represents the struggle for the human subject to define itself within a religious and political sphere. The 'Island' of the poem can be understood as the individual (and it thus offers, through allegory, an answer to ▷ Donne's famous observation that 'No man is an island', for in Fletcher's alienated world, everyone is an island) and, at the same time, the potentially saved island which is Protestant England. We can call this island *potentially* saved, since the poem's function is to serve as a warning to its readers that a state of continual armed vigilance against the encroaching forces of Catholic Europe has to be maintained. Poetry, in other words, has begun to stand outside the culture of the court, serving a different function – that of warning, rather than endorsing. It is also worth remarking, in this context, that the creation of the myth with which modern British readers are familiar, of Elizabethan culture as a 'golden age' of national unity to which subsequent generations are to look for political and national definition at moments of crisis, began almost before Elizabeth herself was in her grave.

Constructing identities

If national identity is an important theme in the poetry of the late sixteenth and early seventeeth centuries, what of individual identity? Here we might remember, once more, the figure of Acrasia from *The Faerie Queene*. Acrasia represents a dual object of desire promising both sexual delight and an abyss of destruction which culminates in the loss of masculine identity. For Spenser's contemporaries – those poets of the late sixteenth century who have been celebrated for their evocation of erotic love – the figure of Acrasia seems to return, though appropriately, always in different guises. The key to these texts is not their representation of unproblematic human sexual desire, but, rather, the possibility which they uncover of confusing the boundaries of sexual identity. Shakespeare's sonnets, first published in 1609, might come to mind in this context – poems whose fascinated, and playful, confusion of the boundaries of sexual identity have presented a disturbing problem for those critics and readers who prefer a more tidy, and sanitized, national poet. But Shakespeare was not alone in preferring the confusingly playful to the depressingly ordered. Both he and ▷ Christopher Marlowe were to explore the question of sexual identity in the form of the 'brief epic' which, in the late sixteenth century, emerged as a genre in its own right. Shakespeare's ▷ *Venus and Adonis* (1593), Marlowe's ▷ *Hero and Leander* (1598), and the now largely unread *Scilla's Metamorphosis* (1589) by Thomas Lodge are usually cited as representative of this short-lived genre. Informed by the eroticism derived from the understanding of Ovidian poetry, these texts seem constantly to play with the possibility of a duality of identity. In *Hero and Leander* the opposition between male and female, expressed in the opening opposition of the two cities which are the homes of the lovers, forms a boundary which it is not only Leander's task to cross, but the text's endeavour to confuse. Thus, Hero is at once the chaste devotee of the rites of ▷ Venus, and the tutor of the unskilled Leander. But she is also (and here we might remember Acrasia) both the voyeuristically sought-for object of sexual longing, displayed in a world of sensual (and violent) artifice, and the bestower of glances and gazes charged with erotic power. At the same moment, Leander too becomes the focus of erotic longing – an object of male sexual devotion:

> *Some swore he was a maid in man's attire,*
> *For in his looks were all that men desire . . .*
>
> (I. 83–4)

This sense of confusion, which Shakespeare was to take continual delight in exploiting in the play-house, is sustained throughout that portion of the poem written by Marlowe. But was a fascination with such sexual identities the sole preserve of the male poet? What of Renaissance women themselves?

We have seen that, in the poetry of the sixteenth century, the female presence can be discerned occupying an interpretive role, and as the focus for a conflicting series of messages based on poets' experiments with language, images and forms inherited from continental models, the most important of whom was Petrarch. But this fluid female presence is largely the creation of male poets. Women as patrons are, of course, familiar figures. Not only the queen but others such as John Donne's patron, ▷ Lucy Russell, Countess of Bedford, and (most famous of them all) ▷ Mary Herbert, Countess of Pembroke, were celebrated by writers as diverse as Sir Philip Sidney, ▷ Fulke Greville, ▷ Thomas Nashe, Edmund Spenser, ▷ Gabriel Harvey, Samuel Daniel, Michael Drayton, ▷ John Davies of Hereford and ▷ Ben Jonson. But the question of women's writing in the Renaissance period has increasingly become a subject of urgent debate. The ▷ humanist endeavour of the early sixteenth century, in England, promised women a *theoretical* access to education, but whether such liberal sentiments affected any but a tiny elite is doubtful. The figure of the woman reading in the Renaissance period is one that is, as we have seen, constantly evoked. The figure of the woman writing is another matter. Elizabeth herself was, of course, a poet and scholar of some distinction. So, too, in the earlier period, was ▷ Margaret More Roper. Mary Sidney Herbert and her neice ▷ Mary Sidney Wroth (Lady Wroth) wrote not only poetry, but in the case of the latter, the first full-length work of fiction by an Englishwoman. But these were women whose access to the literary culture of the period was based on considerable fortune and political power in its own right. It is not until the turmoil of the revolutionary period of the 1640s and 1650s that a recognizably female presence begins to emerge to challenge the dominant voices of what is, by and large, an exclusively male preserve.

The question 'Did women have a Renaissance?' is an important one in this context. A powerful conclusion to this problem, on the part of contemporary ▷ feminist scholarship, is that not only was there no such thing as a 'Renaissance' for women, but that women's status and freedom actually declined in the period we are considering. Rather than looking for a female presence in the writing of the period, it is, with significant exceptions, more accurate to speak of a female absence. Absence, at a point when so much writing by men seems devoted to registering the continual presence of the female, alerts us to a further irony as we move from the period of Spenser into the very different world inhabited by the Jacobean and ▷ Stuart poets of the seventeenth century. No poet could be said to be more alive to the possible presence of the female in his writing than John Donne, but then no poet so determinedly ensures that she remains so absent when compared to the true centre of his poetry – the fascinating object of contemplation that the poet's own self presents:

> *Thou at this midnight seest mee, and as soone*
> *As that Sunne rises to mee, midnight's noone,*
> *All the world growes transparent, and I see*
> *Through all, both Church and State, in seeing thee;*
> *And I discerne by favour of this light,*
> *My selfe, the hardest object of the sight.*
> ('Obsequies to the Lord Harrington' ll. 25–30)

Thus Donne, in a meditation addressed to the soul of his dead friend (and brother of his patron, Lucy, Countess of Bedford) Thomas Harrington. These lines, though they speak in a different vein from the more familiar voices heard in the ▷ *Songs and Sonnets* or the *Holy Sonnets*, nevertheless alert us to a voice and a theme with which the reader of Donne's writing soon becomes familiar. Donne, at a moment of still quietness, contemplates the departed soul of his friend, and discovers . . . himself. The world and the poet, rendered transparent in the moment of meditation, merge together to present that 'hardest object' before the enquiring gaze of the imagination.

The urge to render things 'transparent', a desire to peer beyond surface representation, together with the triumphant discovery of the dramatic speaking voice in poetry, and the continual awareness of the poetic self as both the subject and object of his writing, combine to make Donne and Donne's poetry almost inseparable. But which Donne do we read? In an age of poetic self-creation, Donne seems to have been continuously alive to the possibility of re-creating versions of himself in his writing. Indeed, Donne's eight surviving portraits suggest an urge to record all those different variants for the eye of posterity. Dramatically interjecting an image of himself before the reader's gaze, we must also be aware that this poetic Donne is in a state of almost continual flux and fluidity. 'Oh, to vex me, contraryes meet in one' he exclaims in his '*Holy Sonnet XIX*', but the meeting of contraries was hardly a vexing possibility for the poet. In 'A valediction: of my name, in the window' Donne imagines himself to be metonymically reduced to a sign of his absence – his name, scratched in the glass of a window. But even that transparent reminder of Donne can be further reduced – the name itself is no more than a 'ruinous anatomy', waiting to be 'recompacted' at the moment of return to the mistress. In poem after poem, Donne signals his threatened absence from what is happening, imagining himself dead and waiting for dismemberment, or embarked upon a journey which leaves behind both mistress and a unified sense of selfhood, only to remind the reader that this unstable entity is, in its continuous instability, the most constant object in this poetic universe. The multiplicity of 'John Donnes' which first circulated in manuscript for the delight of his contemporaries, and which were, for the most part, first inscribed on the printed page only after his death in 1631 (itself, as ▷ Izaac Walton records, an act of controlled self-presentation) constitute perhaps the most dramatic series of poetically shifting presences of the period.

The language of God

In remarking upon this shifting poetic awareness of a created sense of selfhood, I do not wish to imply that Donne's poetry can somehow be categorized as constantly breaking across a simple binary divide – the 'religious' Donne, for example, and the 'sensual' Donne. Sensual images and language are as much to the fore in his overtly religious poetry as religious images are constantly present in his secular verses. And this was true not only of Donne, but of many of those poets of the seventeenth century who wrote on religious themes. In the writings of ▷ Richard Crashaw, for example, sensuality and eroticism combine to present a religious aesthetic which still possesses the power, within the dominant Protestant culture of Anglo-American criticism, to shock and disturb.

On the surface, Donne's contemporary – ▷ George Herbert – offers a rather different set of poetic values. Herbert's English poetry, all of which is devoted to religious themes, first appeared in printed form in 1633 (the same year that Donne's poetry was published) in a volume entitled *The Temple*. Reading Herbert's verses we appear to have left Puttenham's world of 'doubleness', the conjunction between the 'dark' and the 'apparent', behind. Yet has it entirely vanished to be replaced by the light of ▷ Baconian reason? Certainly, where in an earlier period the Renaissance poet delighted in uncovering a poetic language based on 'ornament', Herbert offers a manifesto for a different kind of poetry:

> *Who says that fictions only and false hair*
> *Become a verse? Is there in truth no beauty?*
> *Is all good structure in a winding stair?*
> *May no lines pass, except they do their duty*
> *Not to a true, but a painted chair?*
>
> ('Jordan I' ll. 1–5)

Fiction, falseness, a 'winding' structure (terms in which the contemporaries of Puttenham would have delighted) are here denied. What is offered, as an alternative, is 'truth' – a kind of poetry which will specifically transcend the ▷ Platonist distinction between representation and object, figured in the opposition between a 'true' and a 'painted' chair.

Yet, reading the complete collection of poems contained in Herbert's *The Temple* (a collection which was to be of profound influence on Herbert's immediate contemporaries, especially Crashaw), we encounter an elaborate structure of metaphor and formal experiment. Take, for example, the careful 'patterning' of the collection as a whole. On the title-page of the 1633 edition we read a quotation from *Psalms:* 'In his temple doth every man speak of his honour', and as we move through the collection we become aware that, in an elaborate architectural conceit, we are indeed placed within a 'temple' where speech – the words of man to God and (more problematically) God to man – is dramatized. But 'speech' is not necessarily open to all. In the opening poem of the collection we read: 'All things are big with jest: nothing thats plain,/But may be wittie, if thou hast the vein' ('Perirrhanterium' ll. 239–40), a statement which not only appears to contradict that poetic manifesto quoted above, but alerts us to a playfully ironic awareness of the resources of interpretation. In other words, beyond the seemingly artless structure of Herbert's verse lies a dense web of poetic device.

However, Herbert's dualistic conception of language – where the seemingly 'plain' may yet conceal the riddlingly 'wittie' – was to echo throughout the later part of the seventeenth century and in contexts which, to modern eyes, seem curiously inappropriate. For example, long after Herbert's collection appeared, ▷ Thomas Hobbes was to argue for a reform of language in all areas of discourse, whilst in the 1660s ▷ the Royal Society was to promote language reform as one of its main objectives. Under-pinning those demands was a belief that it was possible to take control of the words we use, and to uncover the very nature of external reality which (so the argument ran) had been hitherto concealed in the metaphoric (▷ metaphor) labyrinths of poetry. The world, in other words, need no longer be understood as the product of a riddlingly (and fascinatingly) obscure God. Instead, what has been created is a God endowed not only with reason but (unlike Donne's God, and even on occasions, Milton's) reason-ableness.

Retreat or engagement?

We do not, however, have to leap so far forward in time to uncover in poetry a desire to escape out of the world of brittle linguistic ornamentation. Ben Jonson, for example, in his celebration of aristocratic comfort which is depicted in his poem in praise of the Sidney family 'To Penshurst' (published in 1616) calls for an aesthetic which is in direct contrast to that enshrined in the writings of an earlier generation. The house, Penshurst, which is the home of the family his poem celebrates, is not

> *. . . built to envious show*
> *Of touch or marble, nor canst boast a row*
> *Of polished pillars, or a roof of gold;*
> *Thou hast no lantern whereof tales are told,*
> *Or stair, or courts; but stand'st an ancient pile,*
> *And these grudged at, art reverenced the while.*

What is enacted here is just that revolution in taste which Herbert, in a very different context, had called for. And yet, what are the virtues of Penshurst? Essentially they are the virtues of an emergent bourgeois existence. Penshurst is a place of fruitful production, which extends outwards from its walls to embrace the surrounding countryside and its inhabitants. But Penshurst also stands in stark distinction to other houses, and other kinds of social relations, hinted at in the poem as places less benign than that which is contemplated in these verses. At the same time, as the verses quoted indicate, Penshurst represents a different set of aesthetic values. Those values might be characterized as artful without artifice, avoiding of structural complexity, at ease (as the poets of Spenser's generation were plainly not) with the history which surrounds the house and its inhabitants. 'Polished pillars', 'a roof of gold', a 'lantern whereof tales are told', the architectural equivalent, in other words of the world of ornament and allegory which sixteenth-century poets set out to evoke, has been banished to be replaced by a house which is 'ancient' in its own right, no longer needing the mythographic enterprises of Elizabethan culture. It is as though the frenzied *creation* of a past has finally triumphed, and Jonson's house and its inhabitants can relax in a history which has been secured.

Of course, 'To Penshurst' represents an idealized understanding of society and social relations. It is not the case that Jonson has somehow thrown off, in one swift move, the burden of creating identities and histories which Renaissance poets felt. 'To Penshurst' is, in fact, a brilliantly successful deception. It is a performance which manages to unite the present with a past which is discovered in Jonson's enormous reading and imitation (in the Renaissance sense) of classical literature. As such the poem manages to suggest an assimilated sense of past and present working in harmonious unity. But that Penshurst the place may be unique and may, in fact, stand in complete isolation from the society in which it seems to rest so securely is hinted at throughout the poem.

At the same time 'To Penshurst' signalled, for the poets who came after Jonson, a moment of retreat. Nestling in the idealized Kent countryside, Jonson's creation of a secure bourgeois existence was to serve as a place of pilgrimage for poets who, in other respects, seem very different to all that Jonson a peared to stand for in the realm of aesthetics. What these poets were retreating from was, of course, the political and ideological fragmentation of the period of the English ▷ Civil War. What they were retreating to (and whether such retreat was, in fact, possible) is open to question. On the surface, the poets of the late 1630s, 1640s and 1650s are searching for

Jonson's idyll of Horatian retirement. Thus ▷ Andrew Marvell, a poet of avowedly republican sympathies (at least at certain moments), seeks a retirement from a world which appears to have fallen apart. Only behind the walls of the garden of Nun Appleton (the home of the Fairfax family, celebrated in Marvell's 'Upon Appleton House', composed c 1651) can Marvell discover 'more decent Order tame'. But is this order real, or is it an illusion? Can the world, with all its pressing engagement, in reality be fenced in behind (or outside, depending on your point of view) a garden wall? In Marvell's 'An Horatian Ode upon Cromwell's Return from Ireland' – a poem which memorializes the return of the lord protector to England in May 1650 after his bloody campaign against the Irish – the restless figure of ▷ Cromwell is imagined as being urged out of a moment of Horatian retreat into confrontation with political realities. The political reality with which it is Cromwell's task to engage is one in which the state, government, the nexus of social affiliations as a whole, would appear to have broken apart. What Marvell offers in his heroic depiction of Cromwell is an alternative and elemental figure of power – a re-fashioner not only of kingdoms and states, but of the very structures of thinking. It is an alternative, too (though Marvell could not have known it), to that other elemental image of power offered in the 1650s, the ▷ *Leviathan* of Thomas Hobbes. For Marvell, caught up in the turmoil of post-revolutionary thinking, any retreat into a world of disengagement is fraught with difficulties which cannot be negotiated. So, Marvell's figure of pastoral retreat – Damon the Mower – encounters in the fields not an idyll of rural innocence, but his own downfall:

> *While thus he threw his Elbow round,*
> *Depopulating all the Ground,*
> *And with his whistling Sythe, does cut*
> *Each stroke between the Earth and Root,*
> *The edged Stele by careless chance*
> *Did into his own Ankle glance;*
> *And there among the Grass fell down,*
> *By his own sythe, the Mower mown.*
>
> ('Damon the Mower' ll. 73–80)

It is not difficult to understand the self-mown mower as expressing a powerful (even if humorous) image of what seemed to many Englishman to be the self-induced catastrophe of civil war. For Damon is a reflexive figure. He is both the victim of 'edged stele' and the wielder of steel himself – an embodiment of death, lurking in the seemingly innocent fields, and one of death's victims.

The self-destructive double-figure of Damon can be met with again and again, in various guises, in the poetry of the Civil War period. But for other poets, other forms of retreat presented themselves. For the ▷ Cavalier poets (a misleading term since the poets which are usually denoted in the phrase are neither artistically or politically homogenous, though they all shared a general sense of the ultimate value of the rule of kings rather than parliaments or, worse, people), pastoralism, sensuality, drink or the mind itself offered alternatives. Thus ▷ Robert Herrick, in his volume of poetry entitled *Hesperides* (1648), evokes a world of minutely observed detail, which in its fetishistic attention to the elaborate codes of dress and food, offers a form of nostalgic sensuality to counter the breakdown in social structures. But was it possible to evade what Herrick himself in his opening poem of the collection ('The Argument of his Book') termed 'Times trans-shifting'?

For Herrick's close contemporary, ▷ Richard Lovelace, the heroic self-image of the soldier fleeing the 'nunnery' of the 'chaste breast and quiet mind' of his mistress to encounter a new 'faith' composed of 'a sword, a horse, a shield' ('To Lucasta, Going to the Wars') breaks apart when confronted with his own form of the double-figure which Marvell's Damon seemed to represent. That figure appears most memorably in Lovelace's poem 'The Snail', a poem which, on the surface, appears to be no more than an excercise in contrived wit. Yet the poem's object of contemplation, the unlikely figure of the snail itself, is an ambiguously sinister figure – a confusion of geometric order, familial relationships, gender and questions of origin. If the snail is, as the poem claims at the opening, a 'Wise emblem of our pol'tic world', then this world is one which has become a 'deep riddle'. Fluidly mysterious, the world now conforms to no fixed model of social and political stability. By the end of the poem, the snail has dissolved into a jelly, its 'dark contemplation' of its own self no preservative against dissolution. In the directly political 'A Mock Song' Lovelace depicts the universe itself as dissolving, a response to the ultimate political cleavage of the 1640s, that which took place in ▷ Whitehall in the January of 1649:

> *Now the sun is unarmed,*
> *And the moon by us charmed,*
> *All the stars dissolved to a jelly;*
> *Now the thighs of the crown*
> *And the arms are lopped down,*
> *And the body is all but a belly.*
> ('A Mock Song' ll. 15–20)

Social dissolution, the collapse of the body-politic, the transformation of an ordered world into an image of chaotic mis-rule – it is as if that uncivilized wilderness which Spenser and his contemporaries some fifty years earlier had struggled to keep at bay has intruded into the very heart of the culture in which Lovelace is writing.

'Recent liberty recovered'

To express the literary culture of the Civil War and post-Civil War years as a struggle against encroaching forms of social and political fragmentation is to understand the poets of the mid-seventeenth century as engaged in a desperate form of self-preservation. But to other writers (and Marvell comes to mind once more), working in an alternative political tradition – one that might be termed, broadly, republican – other problems seemed to emerge. What the short-lived experiment in a different form of government in the early 1650s represented was the possibility of engagement with a radically altered set of political co-ordinates. Within this new matrix, whose boundaries can be charted in the numberless ▷ pamphlets and ▷ broadsheets of the period, in popular songs, ▷ sermons, prophetic writings, political treatises and poems, and in the ▷ diaries and letters of ordinary men and women, we can locate the most dominating poetic figure of the seventeenth century – ▷ John Milton.

Milton's poetic career is one of linguistic and formal experiment. Almost no poet since Spenser had traversed with such skill such a range of possible genres – which were to include ▷ masque, sonnet, ▷ translation, ▷ elegy, sacred drama, and, of course, ▷ epic. But in understanding Milton's poetic achievement we also need to recognize the continual presence of Milton's political convictions – though that is not to say that those convictions, in themselves, were somehow set in rigid tablets of stone. But for Milton, read by his contemporaries as the prose defender of the great experiment in new forms of government, poetry and politics are inextricably interwoven.

At the centre of Milton's conception of political revolution stands his awareness that language is the key to ordering and understanding the world in which we live. What Milton's poetry represents, therefore, is a recognition that the language in which he is writing – indebted as it is to the language of prophecy and lyric encountered in the ▷ Old Testament, in the patristic authors, and in the classics – is one that has to be re-captured from the determining ideological structures of the moment. It is not, I think, coincidence that, at the very point when a strangely familiar (to modern ears) language of technology and ▷ utilitarian values is being demanded by the supporters of The Royal Society, ▷ *Paradise Lost* (1667) should appear. We can glimpse the revolutionary nature of Milton's struggle on behalf of language in the 1668 preface to the poem, where Milton offers the following justification of his writing:

> *The measure is English heroic verse without rhyme, as that of Homer in Greek and Virgil in Latin, rhyme being no necessary adjunct or true ornament of poem or good verse . . . but the invention of a barbarous age . . . . This neglect then of rhyme so little is to be taken for a defect, though it may seem so perhaps to vulgar readers, that it rather is to be esteemed an example set, the first in English, of recent liberty recovered to heroic poem . . .*
>
> (Preface to *Paradise Lost*)

This, it need hardly be said, is a revolutionary poetic manifesto. And in terming it revolutionary, I have in mind the notion of a cyclical movement. Poetic form and political engagement became linked in Milton's demand for 'a recent liberty recovered'. For both poetry and political expression now seem to exist in an age which is 'barbarous' to both.

Paradise Lost is, above all, the poem of recovered poetic liberty enacted in its very language, and, just as importantly, in what the poem has to say about language. For Adam, in the poem, is the discoverer of a language which not only identifies for himself his position within the world, but initiates his own quest for self-identity. Remembering his own creation, he recalls, that without language he did not know 'who I was, or where, or from what cause' (VIII. 270–1). His response is speech, and in discovering speech, he discovers not only God, but an identity and a world which can be named. Against this ▷ Frankenstein-like fable is set the negative language of a 'barbarous age' – the language of Babel and of Hell, linked, in the final moments of the poem to a 'jangling noise of words unknown' which is the language given by God 'in derision' to the followers of Nimrod: the type of human oppression. The universal history lesson with which the poem closes endeavours to demonstrate that the transgression of human and divine law involves the denial of political equality:

> ... *man over men*
> *He made not lord; such title to himself*
> *Reserving, human left from human free.*
>   (XII. 69–71)

The link between language and identity, which lies at the heart of the experience of both Adam and Eve in the poem, alerts us to Milton's other great theme of *Paradise Lost* and one with which it would be appropriate to end this account of Renaissance poetry. In terming Milton the poet of 'recovered poetic liberty', what we must also acknowledge is that Milton is, at the same time, at one with his contemporaries in seeking to establish a coherent identity for the human subject. Paradoxically, that search for a unified sense of selfhood – the discovery of an identity which has been secured – is dramatized not only in the memories of creation possessed by Adam and Eve and in gender distinctions, but in the figure of ▷ Satan who claims an autonomous position in God's creation. 'Who saw / when this creation was?' Satan asks, before offering his own version of separate identity:

> *We know no time when we were not as now;*
> *Know none before us, self-begot, self-raised*
> *By our own quick'ning power ...*
>   (V. 859–61)

Milton's demonic figure of self-creation – one that entranced that other great poetic visionary and revolutionary ▷ William Blake – stands alongside Marvell's lyrical figure of self-destruction found in the fields and meadows. We do not need, therefore, to place Satan in the simple role of grand adversary, or counter-hero. For Adam, Eve and Satan are bonded to one another in a triangular design which cannot be disrupted. Satan's spiritual home, from which he cannot be excluded by God (into which, indeed, God welcomes him), is neither Heaven, nor Hell, but, disturbingly, ▷ Eden.

'*Et in Arcadia ego*' – that motto of Renaissance mortality – is also Satan's motto, as the ever-perceptive Eve acknowledges in questioning what kind of freedom Eden can represent. And in ▷ Arcadia Satan undergoes the same tormented search for identity which the human figures strive to discover rooted in one another, as, in the most famous exit in English literature, they leave Eden and the poem together, hand in hand.

This account of poetry in the Renaissance period began with Puttenham's description of a 'certain doubleness' which seemed, to the Elizabethan critic, to haunt the language of poetry. It has ended with a description of the creation of a figure of division – Milton's Satan. Doubleness, division and duplicity have become almost the themes of this essay. But I do not want to suggest, in deploying this alliterative trio, that there exists therefore a homogeneity in the writing that we have been discussing. What I would argue, instead, is that in the enormous richness and diversity of literary forms and experience which have reached us, in the twentieth century from the early modern period, we perceive a culture which is neither monumental, nor the product of a mythic golden age of national experience. The lines from Donne's satire on religion quoted at the start of this essay suggest a more complex set of possibilities. What Donne, in these lines, seems to be contemplating is the problematic status of the individual's identity within the boundaries determined by the power relationships within society. The 'nature and name' of power in fact defines, for Donne and for so many other Renaissance writers, the nature of identity itself. But Donne continues:

> . . . *those blest flowers that dwell*
> *At the rough streames calme head, thrive and do well,*
> *But having left their roots, and themselves given*
> *To the streames tyrannous rage, alas, are driven*
> *Through mills, and rockes, and woods, and at last, almost*
> *Consum'd in going, in the sea are lost:*
>
> ('Satire 3, ll. 103–108)

Here is the Renaissance writer's dilemma. To obey, sometimes to celebrate, the nature and name of power is to risk that very loss of identity which so much of Renaissance poetry is designed to preserve.

'Winter' from *The Seasons* by James Thomson, 1726–30

Enlightenment, Sensibility and Romanticism: poetry 1660-1830

Enlightenment

The decades which followed the ▷ Restoration of the monarchy in 1660 saw a rapid transformation of English society. As the ▷ Renaissance gave way to the more confidently secular and scientific spirit of the ▷ Enlightenment, life was becoming more sophisticated and diverse. The absolutism of the ▷ Tudors and early ▷ Stuarts had been effectively defeated during the upheavals of the mid-century. English culture was no longer in the hands of a tiny clique of courtiers and landed aristocrats; it had been inherited by a much larger and more diverse class of merchants, gentry and professional men. The monarch could no longer dictate religious belief and political principle, and in the coffee-houses of the later seventeenth century ideas and 'opinions' were disputed with an unprecedented freedom and security. The political parties, ▷ Whigs and ▷ Tories, emerged at this time, and important national institutions were founded, such as the ▷ Royal Society, Greenwich Observatory and the Bank of England. The dissensions of the ▷ Civil War gave way to a new nationalistic confidence. Britain was felt at last to be becoming a mature, civilized society, which could bear comparison with that of ancient Rome.

The reign of the 'Merry Monarch', ▷ Charles II (1660–85), saw an apparent reinstatement of the old aristocratic court culture. But effectively the period was an uneasy interlude before the establishment of full constitutionality and middle-class cultural hegemony in the 'Glorious Revolution' of 1688. The poetry of John Wilmot, ▷ Earl of Rochester (1648–80), embodies all the contradictions of this time. He upholds many of the old traditions, and one aspect of his writing shows him as a decadent ▷ 'cavalier' poet. He is indeed the last significant lyric writer in English for a century, and his most beautiful lyric is, like so many pieces by ▷ Richard Lovelace, ▷ Sir John Suckling and ▷ Robert Herrick, a seduction poem on the ancient and familiar *carpe diem* ('seize the day') theme. Characteristically, however, it imparts a deeply felt philosophical scepticism to the conventional genre. Beneath its effortless lyricism of tone lies the theory of the materialist philosopher, ▷ Thomas Hobbes (1588–1679), that perception and memory are comprised of fading physical impressions registered on the internal mirror of the mind.

> *All my past life is mine noe more*
> *The flying Houres are gon*
> *Like transitory Dreames giv'n ore*
> *Whose Images are kept in Store*
> *By Memory alone.*
>
> (ll. 1–5)

Rochester's privileged social position gave him a precious ideological irresponsibility, enabling him to avoid the muddled compromises between reason and ▷ Puritan piety which afflict other writers of the period. He is the only important English poet who expresses the ▷ Deist position with unqualified conviction. His translation of lines from ▷ Lucretius's *Concerning the Nature of Things* asserts that humanity is not governed by the caprices of supernatural beings, a view closer to the existentialism of a modern Sartre than the theology of his own day. His version of a chorus from ▷ Seneca's *Troades*, with its tone of bleak certainty, still stands as one of the most effective 'atheist' poems in the language:

> After Death nothing is, and nothing Death,
> The utmost limit of a gaspe of Breath;
> Let the Ambitious Zealout, lay aside
> His hopes of Heav'n, [whose faith is but his Pride] . . .
> Dead, wee become the Lumber of the World,
> And to that Masse of matter shall be swept,
> Where things destroy'd, with things unborne, are kept
>
> (ll. 1–10)

Characteristic of the new poetic spirit here is the carefully controlled impression of the speaking voice: lucid, persuasive, reasonable. The juxtaposition of abstract concepts is eloquent without ornamental fussiness. The antithetical phrase 'whose faith is but his Pride' is almost aphoristically dismissive, while the diction can descend to the spontaneous brutality of 'gaspe' and 'Lumber'.

Rochester's most ambitious philosphical poem, *A Satyr against Reason and Mankind* rejects the growing consensus of the period, which equates Reason with Puritan moral repression, and asserts against this the ancient Epicurean position that the true function of 'right reason' is to direct the senses to their natural, instinctual pleasures. Rochester's libertinism, and his freedom in treating sexual themes, particularly his use of words like 'fuck' and 'cunt', are still a barrier for some readers. But poems such as *A Ramble in St James's Park* and *The Imperfect Enjoyment* are not simply pornographic. The latter indeed offers a profound psychological study of the relationship between lust and love, subjective ideal and objective reality. The poem's comic peroration, in which the poet heaps mock-heroic abuse on his penis, carries undertones of savage obscenity which betray a profound revulsion at the shortcomings of the flesh. Unpleasant though it is at times, Rochester's obscene writing says more about the complexities of eroticism and love than is usually possible within the conventions of the ▷ neo-Platonic courtly tradition.

Rochester was, for all his libertinism, a very learned poet. *The Imperfect Enjoyment* belongs to a tradition going back to ▷ Ovid, and other poems show the same neo-classical tendency, but in more socially acceptable forms. *An Allusion to Horace*, in which Rochester judiciously surveys the literary scene of the day, is the first of the many 'imitations' of ancient works through which poets at this period began to assert the parallel between their own culture and that of the Rome of Augustus, usually in the medium of heroic ▷ couplets. In this sense Rochester could be seen as the first ▷ 'Augustan'.

The more respectable and prolific ▷ John Dryden (1631–1700) was, however, the most influential champion of the new neo-classicism, and his work dominates the final decades of the seventeenth century. It is indicative of the new mood of cultural nationalism that he should be the first English poet to have held the office of ▷ Poet Laureate, created for him by Charles II in 1668. In his official position he set out to establish the parameters of taste under the new dispensation. His prose essays include the first sustained attempts at literary theory in the language. He championed 'polite' ('polished', 'civilized') wit, based on the urbane Latin model, and a favourite butt of his scorn is the 'false' wit of earlier poets, which is patronizingly dismissed in ▷ *MacFlecknoe*:

> *Leave writing Plays, and chuse for thy command*
> *Some peacefule province in Acrostick Land.*
> *There thou maist wings display and Altars raise,*
> *And torture one poor word Ten thousand ways.*
> *Or if thou woued'st thy diff'rent talents suit,*
> *Set thy own songs and sing them to thy lute.*
>
> (ll. 205–10)

The anagram and pattern poems of the ▷ 'Metaphysical' poet ▷ George Herbert, and the punning ingenuity of poets such as ▷ John Donne, seem to Dryden scarcely less puerile and quaint than the hopelessly antiquated lute-songs of John Dowland and ▷ Thomas Campion.

It is important however to distinguish between Dryden the spokesman for the new literary fashion, and Dryden the poet. Poetry did not undergo such a fundamental change at this period as Dryden's theorizing might lead one to assume. His earliest notable poem, *Upon the death of the Lord Hastings* (1649), for all its sinewy couplets, is as decadently 'metaphysical' and rhetorically elaborate as anything in ▷ Abraham Cowley, John Cleveland or ▷ Andrew Marvell. With appalling gusto, the youthful poet compares the pustules of the pox to 'Rose-buds stuck i'th' Lily-skin about'. Then in an elaborate comparison between the microcosm of Hastings's body and the macrocosm of the state, pus becomes tears, and each 'little Pimple', as it 'sprouts', 'wails' at its rebellion against the life of so pure a man. It is tempting to disregard this tasteless brilliance as mere juvenile extravagance, later outgrown when Dryden rejected 'false wit' for 'polite'. But this is not accurate. The loud excessiveness of this poem remains a permanent feature of Dryden's work.

The same poetic spirit can be seen on a broader, more 'Augustan' canvas, eighteen years later in ▷ *Annus Mirabilis* (1667), whose set-piece descriptions emulate the inflated theatricality of some vast ▷ baroque mural painting. The Great Fire, for instance, is described through a string of elaborate epic ▷ similes, which compare it first to 'some dire Usurper', then to a 'rich mighty Murderer' bribing his way out of prison, and finally to an amorous young blade. The winds become 'crafty Courtezans'. teasing the passionate 'flames' of the personified fire, only to 'blow them more'. The young rake leaps at his 'prey' 'with inrag'd desire:/ O'r-looks the neighbours with a wide survey,/ And nods at every house his threatning fire' (ll. 886–8). This comparison of the Great Fire to an angry, engorged penis nodding angrily over London is unforgettable in its ingenious sense of fun and outrageous bad taste.

In keeping with the spirit of the times, Dryden's greatest mature works are ▷ satires, concerned with public figures and events. Here again he is eager to theorize and regulate. In the preface to ▷ *Absalom and Achitophel* he sets out the classic 'Augustan' morality of the satirist:

> *The true end of* Satyre, *is the amendment of Vices by correction.*
> *And he who writes Honestly, is no more an Enemy to the Offendour,*
> *than the Physician to the Patient, when he prescribes harsh*
> *Remedies to an inveterate Disease.*

Once again, however, the reality is more complex than the theory. Dryden himself betrays his awareness of this in *A Discourse concerning the Original and Progress of Satire* (1693), where he describes the master satirist's 'noble trade' as consisting not in 'the slovenly butchering of a man', but rather in 'the fineness of a stroke that separates the head from the body, and leaves it standing in its place'. It is the finesse of the operation which really excites Dryden's enthusiasm, not its moral effect. Clearly such metaphorical decapitation, however elegantly done, is just as fatal as the messiest invective. Indeed its easy contempt could be felt to be even more wickedly (if delightfully) humiliating to the victim. The pure delight in a good joke shown in Dryden's surrealist image here, gives perhaps the most accurate insight into his own best satiric writing.

To understand Dryden's satiric practice it is necessary to look beyond the abstract ▷ didactic theory to the concrete context of the excitingly new and sophisticated practice of polite conversation. Almost all Dryden's best satire tends towards polite insult or raillery, rather than earnest correction. He prides himself on being able to give 'the occasion' for an insult, which his skilful manipulation of wit and irony makes it impossible for the victim to 'take', without appearing foolish. In his *Discourse concerning Satire* he significantly singles out the good-humoured portrait of Zimri, the Duke of Buckingham, in *Absalom and Achitophel* (ll. 543–68) as 'worth the whole poem: 'tis not bloody, but 'tis ridiculous enough'. Dryden notes with pride that 'he for whom it was intended was too witty to resent it as an injury'. This kind of writing Dryden associates with the satire on manners of a ▷ Horace, rather than the moral didacticism of a ▷ Juvenal, a useful distinction of style later taken up by ▷ Alexander Pope and ▷ Samuel Johnson.

Poetry in a more serious vein seems to have come less easily to Dryden's expansive and ebullient temperament. His poems of religious discussion, ▷ *Religio Laici* (1682) and ▷ *The Hind and the Panther* (1687) do not always sustain imaginative interest, and the more serious political passages in *Absalom and Achitophel* suffer from the suspicions of motive which attend all political propaganda. The Achitophel passage (150ff.) is nevertheless a masterpiece of character assassination, turning Shaftesbury's good qualities against him with a magisterial affectation of impartiality: 'Great Wits are sure to Madness near ally'd;/ And thin Partitions do their Bounds divide' (ll. 163–4). But there is an unhappy sourness, an unfairness, about the image which associates Shaftesbury's political ideas with the physical weakness of his son: 'Got, while his Soul did hudled Notions try;/ And born a shapeless Lump, like Anarchy' (ll. 171–2). The image has Dryden's characteristic 'over-the-top' imaginativeness about it, but no matter how witty Shaftesbury may have been, he could scarcely have failed to 'resent' this 'as an injury', and even the modern reader finds it difficult not to wince.

Dryden died in 1700 and his successor, ▷ Alexander Pope, was of a different generation. The new order was now firmly established, and the anxiety and doubt which underlies the works of Rochester and Dryden had been dispelled by a new sense of comfort and security. An important element in Pope's literary development, indeed, is the existence of a number of native 'classic' models, including Dryden, on which he could build. The heroic couplet, for instance, had settled into its familiar 'Augustan' form; balanced, antithetical, self-contained, in keeping with the enlightened rationalism of the age. ▷ Sir John Denham's couplets patriotically comparing his poetry to the River Thames in ▷ *Cooper's Hill* (1642) were frequently cited for their perfection. The pentameter couplets were called 'heroic' by analogy with the epic hexameters of Latin poetry (▷ metre), since it was felt that this was the closest approximation possible in a barbarous language to the spacious dignity of ▷ Virgil and ▷ Homer. Since English lacked the sounding vowels of Latin and the musical pattern of syllable length, rhyme was necessary to impose order. The comparison of rhymed couplet with unrhymed Latin hexameter seems now quite perverse, and indeed even at the time the translations of Virgil by Dryden and of Homer by Pope in this medium were rightly criticized for lacking the spirit of the originals. But the dominant taste swept all before it. Pope became known (preposterously enough) as the 'English Homer', and ▷ Samuel Johnson could later assert that his translation had 'tuned the language'.

At first sight Pope's work presents itself as the self-conscious embodiment of the orthodoxies of his period, both philosophical and literary. Despite his Catholicism, he expresses in his *Universal Prayer* (1738) a moderate, pious sounding version of ▷ Deism, which was acceptable to many undoctrinaire Christians, in a way that the uncompromising scepticism of Hobbes or Rochester never could be. More adventurously, he asserts in ▷ *An Essay on Man* (1733–4) that the 'untutor'd mind' of a 'poor Indian' has access to ▷ natural religion without the benefit of either scripture or science, though admittedly his is 'an humbler heav'n' than that of those whose soul 'proud Science' has 'taught to stray/ Far as the solar walk, or milky way' (I, 101–2). By this time science has ceased to seem a threat to faith, and an easy, unexamined confidence that religion and intellectual inquiry had been reconciled, held sway. Pope sums this up in an aphorism of breathtakingly euphoric facility: 'Nature, and Nature's Laws lay hid in Night./ God said, *Let Newton be!* and All was *Light*'. Enlightenment has become popular orthodoxy – with inevitable simplifications. The now firmly established and prosperous bourgeoisie was only too eager to reassure itself with Pope's optimistic nostrum: 'Whatever *is*, is *right*' (*Essay on Man*, I, 294).

In social and political views, also, Pope is the spokesman of his class. Throughout his writing we see an enthusiasm for the growing wealth and influence of Britain as a trading and imperial nation. In his patriotic landscape poem ▷ *Windsor Forest* (1713), vegetation itself, by an ingenious conceit, naturally embodies the mercantile dynamism of the nation:

> Let India boast her Plants, nor envy we
> The weeping Amber or the balmy Tree,
> While by our Oaks the precious Loads are born,
> And Realms commanded which those Trees adorn.
>   (ll. 28–31)

Similarly in ▷ *The Rape of the Lock* (1712/14), the exotic plunder of the East is domesticated, miniaturized and rendered elegant, for the consumption of the court belle, Belinda:

> This Casket India's glowing Gems unlocks,
> And all Arabia breathes from yonder Box.
> The Tortoise here and Elephant unite,
> Transform'd to Combs, the speckled and the white.
>   (ll. 133–6)

As in the case of Dryden however, it is important not to see Pope's work as the expression of some monolithic ideology of Enlightenment or Augustanism, though in a sense he was deliberately aiming to give this impression. On the more purely literary level, his ideas can more accurately be seen as a defensive screen, behind which he could develop his real talents as a poet. In some ways Enlightenment thinking was, and is, of its very nature antipathetic to poetry. ▷ John Locke, for instance, the respected philosopher of the Enlightenment, considered any non-literal use of language the result of 'wrong and unnatural combinations of *ideas*', and a 'sort of madness'. From a different quarter 'wit' (what we would now call 'imagination') was being attacked by Puritans as an immoral survival from the bad old days of the Restoration. The Society for the Reformation of Manners, founded in 1695, had by 1735 launched 99,380 prosecutions in the courts against immoral or blasphemous behaviour and literature. The early years of the eighteenth century were among the most uncomfortable in English history for an aspiring poet.

Seen in this context Pope's Augustanism can seem to be a brilliantly plausible combination of fashionable ideas designed to disarm all prejudices. He boldly accepts the Enlightenment attack on figurative language, extending Dryden's contrast between true and false wit, in a way which at times seems dangerously close itself to unimaginative philistinism. 'Wit', he says in the ▷ *Essay on Criticism* (1711) must always be balanced by 'judgement', and 'true' wit is no more than the felicitous expression of common wisdom: 'True wit is Nature to Advantage drest,/ What oft was Thought, but ne'er so well Exprest' (ll. 296–7). The dullest of Puritans might be mollified by this marginalization of imagination. And certainly some lines and couplets in this poem seem designed to vindicate this view of poetry as universal platitude: 'A little Learning is a dang'rous Thing' (ll. 215); 'To Err is Humane; to Forgive, Divine' (ll. 525); 'For Fools rush in where Angels fear to tread' (ll. 625). Even when Pope praises the more adventurous flights of the greatest poetry, it is as a kind of 'Lucky Licence', by which 'Great Wits' are allowed to 'rise to Faults true Criticks dare not mend;/ ... And snatch a Grace beyond the Reach of Art' (ll. 153–5). Such breaking of 'the rules' is likened, in a carefully chosen image, to those sublime 'irregular' landscapes 'Which out of Nature's common Order rise', to remind us of God's awesome power.

A key element in Pope's defence of poetry is his constant reference to the classics of antiquity. The earliest poets, he argues, based their work on Nature herself, undistorted by the influence of literary fashion. The best course for the modern poet therefore, is to write according to the 'ancient rules', since 'to copy Nature is to copy them'. In a weirdly far-fetched passage, he pictures the youthful Virgil, scorning poetic precedent in his determination to copy directly from Nature, only to find to his astonishment as he does so, that he is reproducing Homer word for word: 'Nature and Homer were, he found, the same' (*Essay on Criticism*, ll. 135). However, what exactly these 'ancient rules' for copying Nature *are* remains very obscure. Is the only 'natural' ▷ metre unrhymed hexameters, such as both poets use? Is the only 'natural' description of the sea that it is 'wine-dark'? Pope makes no real attempt to define these rules and they remain little more than a propaganda slogan, intended to reassure the philistine or scientific reader that the poet is after all a law-abiding citizen, subject to regulations as strict and invariable as those of Puritan morality, or the natural laws of the scientist.

It is not surprising that Pope's best writing quite fails to answer to his theory. Indeed, far from copying ancient rules, the most inspired passage in *The Essay on Criticism* deliberately perpetrates all the worst faults of contemporary poetic practice (ll. 337–57). And Pope's most original poem is a mock scholarly edition of his own ▷ *Dunciad* (1728) (complete with pages of spoof footnotes) describing the farcical exploits of contemporary hack writers and publishers. We could scarcely be further from 'what oft was thought' in the richly voluptuous description given by one of the Dunces of the Mud-nymphs who 'suck'd him in' after he dived into the Fleet sewer: 'young Lutetia, softer than the down,/ Nigrina black, and Merdamante brown,/ Vy'd for his love in jetty bowr's below' (ll. 309–11). Pope's favourite ▷ mock-heroic technique may appear to satirize disorder and anarchy in contrast with a decorous norm. But the barely controlled nervous vitality and the sheer imaginative *élan* evident in such poems as *The Dunciad*, tell a different story.

Pope was only 4 ft 6 ins tall and progressively crippled with spinal curvature. He referred to himself mock-heroically as 'the little Alexander the women laugh at' (in contrast with Alexander the Great). Throughout his work a jealousy of, and distaste for, the large, the clumsy and the 'macho' reinforces the new bourgeois refinement of his sensibility. He constantly delights in the intricate, the small, the domestic and delicate. Characteristically his most moving evocation of the heroic classical past is his Epistle *To Mr Addison* (1720), concerning the new pastime of coin-collecting. The poem surveys the great cities of antiquity, 'Their ruins ruin'd, and their place no more', and concludes that the most lasting memorial of Rome lies in the tiny simulacra of her triumphs and architecture, cramped into the 'narrow orb' of a coin:

> *Here scantier limits the proud Arch confine,*
> *And scarce are seen the prostrate Nile or Rhine,*
> *A small Euphrates thro' the piece is roll'd,*
> *And little Eagles wave their wings in gold.*
>
> (ll. 27–30)

The awesome grandeur of the past is reduced for the contemplation of the secure, comfortable, modern world. The imaginative strength of this poem lies not in its respectful neo-classicism, but in its picture of the 'pale Antiquaries' who adore 'The sacred rust of twice ten hundred years', and of the young collector, who 'restless by the Fair-one's side,/ Sighs for an Otho, and neglects his bride' (ll. 43–4).

Similarly *The Rape of the Lock* leaves us in no doubt of Pope's preference for the new domestic amenities of Belinda's Hampton Court, over the heat of battle on the plains of Troy. The finest passages in the poem concern the frailty of feminine beauty, the rituals of cosmetics, card-playing or coffee-making. It would be a great mistake to read this poem as an earnest satire against triviality. Indeed the poet's most exquisitely sensuous verse is lavished on the purest and most abstract embodiment of frivolous modernity, the sylphs:

> *Some to the sun their Insect-Wings unfold,*
> *Waft on the Breeze, or sink in Clouds of Gold.*
> *Transparent Forms, too fine for mortal Sight,*
> *Their fluid Bodies half-dissolv'd in Light.*
> *Loose to the Wind their airy Garments flew,*
> *Thin glitt'ring Textures of the filmy Dew.*
>
> (II, ll. 59–64)

Not until ▷ Keats do we again find such concentrated sound-writing employed to so purely sensuous an end.

It is an ironic tribute to Pope's greatness that critics should so often speak as though the early eighteenth century was dominated by an 'Augustan' school of poets, all aiming at the composition of perfect heroic couplets. At the time no such homogeneity would have been apparent. Pope's hyper-correct couplets are personal to him, and quite different from those of his predecessors and contemporaries. ▷ Thomas Parnell's couplets are musical enough, but their effect is vacuous in comparison, and the couplets of ▷ John Gay and ▷ Matthew Prior aim at a quite different, easy-going, conversational tone. Outside the heroic couplet the ferment of new political and aesthetic ideas was reflected in a range of metres and styles. The crude vigour of Hudibrastick tetrameter couplets introduced by ▷ Samuel Butler (1612–80) was imitated by several poets, notably ▷ Bernard de Mandeville. ▷ Miltonic ▷ blank verse was used to superb mock-heroic effect in ▷ John Philips's *The Splendid Shilling* (1701), and more ambitiously in *Cyder* (1708), a long Georgic poem on the apple-growing industry, which was widely imitated. Matthew Prior (1664–1721) expressed a genial social ease in various metres. The popular ▷ ballads of Gay's parody grand ▷ opera, ▷ *The Beggar's Opera* (1728), celebrated the life of London's criminal classes with a distinctly modern ambiguity of moral stance. ▷ James Thomson's *The Seasons* (1726–30) may perhaps stand as a compendium of most of the poetic currents of the period, combining the Georgic tradition of *Windsor-Forest*, with a facile Augustan patriotism, and an innocent enthusiasm for the science of Newton and Linnaeus, all expressed in the flexible and self-consciously literary medium of Miltonic blank verse.

Sensibility

During the middle decades of the eighteenth century English society became increasingly stable, even stagnant. On the death of the last Stuart monarch, Queen Anne, in 1714, the crown passed to the nearest Protestant claimant, George, Elector of Hanover, (George I) who did not even speak English. Under the Hanoverians, and a succession of cautious parliaments, the turbulent ghosts of the old order were laid to rest. The attempts of the son and grandson of James II to regain the throne by force came to nothing in the Jacobite Rebellions of 1715 and 1745, and the larger shifts of thought initiated by the French Revolution were yet to come. Culturally as well as politically this period may seem somewhat dull. The Age of Enlightenment before it and the Age of ▷ Romanticism after it are both periods of ideological assertiveness. Various and contradictory though the views of individual writers might be, their tone gained assurance from a sense of change and possibility. In both Pope's ▷ *Essay on Man* (1733–34) and ▷ Wordsworth's ▷ *Prelude* (completed 1805) we feel that fresh dis-coveries are being made, that the world is being explained. But between public, rationalist Enlightenment, and private, subjective Romanticism there intervenes a period where no such faith as to ultimate direction prevailed.

This does not mean that the poetry of this period is lacking in interest. On the contrary, the very absence of ideological excitement encourages a certain adventurousness and idiosyncrasy, particularly in poetic form. It is, however, a difficult age to classify in terms of a single principle or movement. It has been customary to see the period between about 1740 and about 1790 as 'transitional', its writers being termed either 'late Augustan', or 'pre-Romantic', or both. This approach does at least serve to illuminate the age's paradoxical mix of conservative and individualistic elements. But although some poets of the time employ neo-classical couplets, and others are self-consciously 'romantic', there is something unsatisfactory about seeing them exclusively in terms of an epilogue to the previous age or a prologue to the one which was to follow. It is surely anachronistic to interpret a major poet like ▷ Thomas Gray (1716–71) only in terms of his failure to be someone completely different. More recently therefore, critics have come to character-ize the period in terms of its own most distinctive literary achievements, as an 'Age of Sensibility'. In common with all other literary periods, the Age of Sensibility shows some transitional aspects. But it also possesses a distinctive aesthetic profile of its own.

One element in the poetry of ▷ Sensibility could be described as a new sombre and subdued version of Augustanism. The resounding certainties of Pope's *Essays* are frequently echoed, but the earlier *élan* and excitement have evaporated. In ▷ Thomson's *Spring* (1726) 'Man superior walks/ Amid the glad creation' (ll. 170–1), confident of his place in the world. By the time of ▷ Samuel Johnson's ▷ *The Vanity of Human Wishes* (1749) however, the mood has changed. Man is no longer the measure of all things, and Pope's cheerful confidence that 'Whatever *is*, is *right*', though still essentially unquestioned, has modulated into a resigned acceptance of the human lot:

> *Still raise for good the supplicating voice,*
> *But leave to heav'n the measure and the choice,*
> *Safe in his pow'r, whose eyes discern afar*
> *The secret ambush of a specious pray'r.*
> *Implore his aid, in his decisions rest,*
> *Secure whate'er he gives, he gives the best.*
>
> (ll. 351–6)

For Samuel Johnson (1709–84) personal suffering is not easily to be explained away by enlightened philosophy. Reason is reduced to common sense, and philosophical adventurousness reverts to sincere piety. Such poetry can be intensely moving, its heavy didacticism creating an anxious, troubled effect, even when its content is self-evident truism. But the conservative poet seems afraid to leave the security of the established couplet pattern. Over and over again his lines divide neatly in the middle in balanced parallelism or self-conscious chiasmus ('The golden canopy, the glitt'ring plate'; 'The daughter's petulance, the son's expence'; 'By day the frolick, and the dance by night'). Sometimes the monotonous and hypnotic succession of abstract phrases is emotionally overpowering, but at times it palls into mechanical repetition.

Several poets in this period seek consolation, like Johnson, in piety, sometimes tinged with evangelical fervour. It is no accident that some of the most familiar of English hymns were written at this time, by ▷ Charles Wesley (1707–88) and ▷ William Cowper (1731–1800). Cowper's religious melancholia and nervous, hypersensitive temperament lend psychological interest even to his apparently trivial verses on domestic themes. His delight in the cosy banalities of gardening and village gossip is fostered as a conscious therapy against ▷ Calvinist despair. However, in *The Castaway*, written at the very end of his life in 1799, he is for once psychologically explicit, paralleling his inner sense of sin and spiritual isolation with the anguish of a man drowning at sea:

> *No voice divine the storm allay'd,*
> *No light propitious shone;*
> *When, snatch'd from all effectual aid,*
> *We perish'd, each alone:*
> *But I beneath a rougher sea,*
> *And whelm'd in deeper gulphs than he.*
> (ll. 61–66)

The reflective poems of Thomas Gray (1716–71) share the chastened humility characteristic of the period:

> *The paths of glory lead but to the grave.*
> (*Elegy*, ll. 36)

> *Full many a flower is born to blush unseen,*
> *And waste its sweetness on the desert air.*
> (*Elegy*, ll. 55–6)

But Gray's is a different, perhaps more original, poetic voice than either Johnson's or Cowper's. His terse, personal poetic tone makes his platitudes overwhelmingly poignant, where Johnson's risk lugubriousness, and his poetic diction is less inhibited and dutiful than Cowper's. In the *Ode on a Distant Prospect of Eton College* (1747), for example, we may detect the tones of Sensibility quite uncompromised and assured:

> *To each his suff'rings: all are men,*
> *Condemn'd alike to groan,*
> *The tender for another's pain;*
> *Th'unfeeling for his own.*
> *Yet ah! why should they know their fate?*

> *Since sorrow never comes too late,*
> *And happiness too swiftly flies.*
> *Thought would destroy their paradise.*
> *No more; where ignorance is bliss,*
> *'Tis folly to be wise.*
>
> (ll. 91–100)

Both here and in the ▷ *Elegy written in a Country Churchyard* (1751), Gray's conclusions are distinctly unedifying: stoical if not downright cynical. The predominant emotion is one of resigned endurance. Gray refuses to transcend or explain away the human lot. His insights are, in the words of a similarly reductive twentieth-century poet, ▷ Philip Larkin, 'permanent and blank and true'. Nothing is to be done; life is just like that.

For the poet of Sensibility feeling appears as an end in itself, rather than part of some larger political or aesthetic design. As in the sentimental fiction of the period, the poets cultivate their feelings for their own sake. When they are not expressing the eternal truths of religion or the human lot, they aim to touch the feelings through ornamental elegance or evocative description. And it is this aspect of Sensibility which is most often attacked as timidly 'pre-Romantic'. The mannered personifications of Gray's *Ode on the Spring*, ▷ William Collins's 'How sleep the brave' and *Ode to Evening*, the artificial prettiness of ▷ William Shenstone's *Pastoral Ballad* and the patronizing quaintness of his *The Schoolmistress*, the whimsical humour of Gray's *Ode on the Death of a Favourite Cat* and Cowper's *On Mrs Throckmorton's Bulfinch*, fall within this broad poetic mode. These works are perhaps best seen as the literary equivalent of the rococo music of composers such as Rameau and C.P.E. Bach. At their best they can be fragile and charming, at their worst they seem insipid and trivial.

The ▷ 'romantic' element, which figures prominently in much of the poetry of this period, rests on deep foundations. A tradition of neo-Platonic mysticism subsisted throughout the late seventeenth and early eighteenth centuries as a kind of alternative to Enlightenment. In his *Characteristicks* of 1711 the third ▷ Earl of Shaftesbury boldly rejected moderation, and boasted of his 'enthusiasm' for 'shaggy grots' and wild scenery. In poetic form the irregular ▷ ode became an accepted vehicle for emotional excess, and the unclassically ornamental ▷ Spenserian stanza was used to express sensuous abandon in Thomson's late poem ▷ *The Castle of Indolence* (1748). As Augustanism gave way to Sensibility a restless search began for suitable poetic forms in which to express the new emotionalism. ▷ Robert Blair's popular blank verse poem *The Grave* (1743) painted 'the gloomy horrors of the tomb' with a spine-chilling sublimity imitated from ▷ Jacobean drama. Writers tried to give an exotic cast to their poems. Collins's first works were fashionably termed *Persian Eclogues* (1742). ▷ Thomas Percy translated works indirectly from Chinese and Icelandic. But most significant was the rise of medievalism, and its associated revival of primitive or ▷ 'Gothic' forms and tastes. The oral ballad was given literary respectability by Percy in his influential *Reliques of Ancient English Poetry*

(1765). The scholarly Gray translated Norse and Welsh ballads into English versions (1768). The pseudo-medieval Spenserian stanza style was developed by ▷ Mark Akenside, William Shenstone and ▷ James Beattie, while more suspect forms of medievalism were affected by ▷ Macpherson in his Ossianic prose-poems, and by ▷ Thomas Chatterton in his Rowley concoctions.

But a certain timidity, a failure of nerve, is frequently detectable in this pursuit of novelty. The conviction that serious poetry must be a matter of judgement and decorum was still strong, as can be seen in Johnson's scathing contempt for Gray's ideas of poetic spontaneity:

> *He had a notion not very peculiar, that he could not write but at certain times, or at happy moments; a fantastic foppery, to which my kindness for a man of learning and of virtue wishes him to have been superior.*

> *(Life of Gray)*

It is not surprising then that the more inspirational poems of the time should have a self-conscious feel about them. Gray's Pindaric Ode, ▷ *The Bard* (1757), for instance, treats a romantically medieval theme in a form which, although of classical origin, had long been sanctioned as a vehicle for lyrical elevation. But for all his metrical irregularities and wildness of imagery, the result sounds over deliberate:

> *On a rock, whose haughty brow*
> *Frowns o'er old Conway's foaming flood,*
> *Robed in the sable garb of woe,*
> *With haggard eyes the Poet stood;*
> *(Loose his beard, and hoary hair*
> *Stream'd, like a meteor, to the troubled air)*
> (ll. 15–20)

Any immediacy of effect is undermined by the banks of footnotes which explain the historical context, and worse still, cite the sources of the imagery, which is borrowed from ▷ Shakespeare, ▷ Spenser, Dryden and Milton. It is more of a bookish exercise than an inspired poem. Only with the onset of ▷ Romanticism proper do the new poetic idioms introduced at this time suddenly achieve a new richer tone. The ballad style of ▷ Samuel Taylor Coleridge achieves an originality utterly different from the self-conscious exercises of Gray. And despite the frequent verbal parallels, Keats's *Ode to a Nightingale* (1819) makes ▷ Akenside's *Ode to the Evening Star* (1745) seem excessively literary.

On a more basic level the diction of poetry often suffers from a kind of sclerosis, which inhibits spontaneity and inventiveness. Just as political and social life was stagnating, so the literary decorums of the early part of the century were becoming ossified. At the root of this problem lies the doctrine of kinds, by which each mode of writing – ▷ epic, ▷ pastoral, ▷ Georgic, ▷ elegy – was assigned its own particular language. Such refinement of literary discrimination could easily degenerate into a kind of mechanical class system of language, whereby literary decorum became the mere equivalent of social gentility. The less inventive passages in Thomson's *The Seasons* offer little more than a series of triggers to the reader's literary memory. We are meant to take pleasure in the recognition that 'gelid', 'tepid', 'laughing', and 'enamell'd' are specifically ▷ Virgilian pastoral words, that 'horrid', 'shaggy' and 'freaks' are deliberately 'low' words, with colourful Gothic or rustic associations, and that the poet's constant use of adjective for adverb is a Miltonic echo.

▷ Thomas Warton's poem *The Suicide: An Ode* shows this discrimination at its most diagrammatic. The suicide's grave is described in suitably 'low' words and ▷ Anglo-Saxon alliterations: 'beech', 'branches', 'bare', 'Smit', 'craggy', 'whistle', while the heavenly cherub voice, which corrects the poet's romantic sympathy for the suicide, employs the 'high' vocabulary of a socially elevated speaker: 'Heaven's prerogative', 'thy tributary breath', 'awful expectation'. Until the possibility of real social and political change was opened up in the poets' imaginations, such limitation of diction could not be avoided even by the best of them. It is this which makes such phrases as Gray's 'sable garb of woe' seem so mechanical in their dignity, and the alliterative primitiveness of the Bard's 'hoary hair' so uncomfortably self-conscious. The rejection of this class-based rigidity of language is one of the crucial distinctions between the poetry of the Romantic period and that of the Age of Sensibility which preceded it.

Romanticism

The immediate catalyst which turned the inward-looking literariness of the Age of Sensibility into the more assured movement that we now call ▷ Romanticism, was the ▷ French Revolution, which began in 1789. The first Romantic poets, ▷ Blake, Wordsworth and Coleridge, were inspired by its ideals of social justice, and Wordsworth was present in France during its early days. Although in England any movement towards revolution or social reform was blocked, the events in France nevertheless shifted the foundations of thought. One result was that literature suddenly gained in political content. The bourgeoisie had already demonstrated the relativity of value systems when they overthrew the old aristocracy. Now its more thoughtful members began to question their own enlightened certainties. The roots of modern ▷ socialism and ▷ communism were established during this period. The conception emerged that society is not simply a panorama of various manifestations of human nature, but is divided into social and economic classes, with conflicting interests.

Enlightenment thought had, until now, lacked this sense of social and historical dialectic. It still clung to the security of a stable, unitary universe. Human nature was believed to have been always and everywhere the same. The institutions of society and the distribution of wealth were ordained by God, or were natural. Neither of Pope's two *Moral Essays* concerning 'the use of riches' questions the providence which bestows these riches. The clergyman-poet ▷ John Pomfret (1667–1702), in his popular poem *The Choice* (1700), advocated charity towards the 'Sons of Poverty': 'For what our Maker hath too largely giv'n/ Shou'd be returned in gratitude to Heav'n.' He shows no awareness of the moral and theological problem hidden in the phrase '*too* largely'. And despite their cultivation of personal feeling, the writers of the Age of Sensibility were equally complacent. Both Henry Mackenzie's sentimental novel *The Man of Feeling* (1771), and ▷ Oliver Goldsmith's poem, ▷ *The Deserted Village* (1770), describe the forced eviction of poverty-stricken tenants. But the authors are not concerned with changing the system which promotes such injustice; only with conventional reproaches of the cruel landowner and – most centrally – with their own emotions as sensitive spectators.

It is William Blake (1757–1827) who stands as the prodigious prophet in England of the new political thinking. In a parody of Enlightenment benevolence, using the simple sing-song tone of a children's rhyme, he points out the causal connection between the social structure and personal morality: 'Pity would be no more/ If we did not make somebody Poor'. Many of the ▷ *Songs of Experience* (1794) are indictments of orthodox morality. The lisping urchin in *The Chimney Sweeper* is the perfect subject for sentimental sympathy: 'A little black thing among the snow,/ Crying "weep! weep!" in notes of woe!' But the child's fierce indignation against his parents shames such self-indulgence:

> *And because I am happy, & dance & sing,*
> *They think they have done me no injury:*
> *And are gone to praise God & his Priest and King*
> *Who make up a heaven of our misery.*

It is against institutionalized religion that Blake directs his most seditious logic, asserting the inseparability of religion and politics: 'God & his Priest & King'. The ▷ Deist patriarchal god of the eighteenth-century wealthy classes becomes 'Nobadaddy' or 'Urizen' ('your reason'), a jealous old tyrant inflicting his repressions on society. The loose harmony between Nature, Reason and established Religion, which, despite the questionings of intellectuals like Rochester and Mandeville, had passed current for more than a century, was suddenly shattered. Injustice was now revealed as an inherent part of the social structure, not a mere personal, unChristian aberration. 'Prisons are built with stones of Law, Brothels with bricks of Religion.' In such aphorisms as these Blake shows himself as one of the first writers in English with an awareness of what we would now call 'ideology'.

Blake is the most uncompromisingly religious of poets. But while the religion of his immediate precursors, Johnson and Cowper, was essentially a retreat, a spiritual consolation for the disappointments of the human condition, Blake's is based on a dynamic critique of the human condition itself. It is important to understand that this critique is only in part political. Where the ultimate aim of a secular atheist like ▷ Shelley is to incite the oppressed to revolt against, and change their material circumstances, Blake's moral indignation is part of a metaphysical quest for spiritual harmony beyond the material world:

> To see a World in a Grain of Sand
> And a Heaven in a Wild Flower,
> Hold Infinity in the palm of your hand
> And Eternity in an hour
>
> A Robin Red breast in a Cage
> Puts all Heaven in a Rage.
> (*Auguries of Innocence*, ll. 1–6)

The moral anger of Experience may indeed satirize the spiritual serenity of Innocence. But equally in Blake's transcendant view, the purity of Innocence satirizes the chaos and selfishness of our fallen world of Experience.

Blake's religious views make him quite different from the other Romantics. He is an extreme anti-Enlightenment evangelical, and his original version of Christianity contains strong atavistic elements. 'There is no Natural Religion' he proclaims; only the Gospels can give access to the truth. Materialist thinkers, both ancient and modern, are mockingly dismissed for denying the spiritual essence of matter:

> The Atoms of Democritus
> And Newton's Particles of light
> Are sands upon the Red sea shore
> Where Israel's tents do shine so bright.
> ('Mock on, Mock on Voltaire, Rousseau', ll. 9–12)

Thus, when Blake advocates sexual freedom in *The Garden of Love* (*Songs of Experience*), this is not because he shares the materialist faith in the senses of a Rochester or a Keats, or the humanist idealism of a Shelley. It is part of a transcendant dialectic between the flesh and the spirit, which derives from ancient Christian tradition. In 1801 he added a new poem, *To Tirzah*, to *Songs of Experience*, asserting a transcendance of the flesh by the spirit in the simplistic tones of an evangelical hymn: 'The Sexes sprung from Shame & Pride,/ Blow'd in the morn; in evening died . . . The death of Jesus set me free./ Then what have I to do with thee?' There is no incoherence in Blake's thought here, since his philosophy is fundamentally dialectical. Life is a struggle between opposites, with no middle ground. 'Without Contraries is no progression' (▷ *The Marriage of Heaven and Hell*). Out of the fusion between the otherworldliness of the New Testament and the political radicalism of the French Revolution, he forges a characteristically modern conception of reality, as an unstable flux of relativities.

Blake's intellectual toughness and religious extremism made him an isolated and disregarded pioneer. William Wordsworth (1770–1850) appears at first sight less idiosyncratic, and he exerted far more influence at the time. The mild pantheism which he developed during his lonely but happy childhood in the Lake District can indeed be seen as a Romantic modification of the materialist Deism of Enlightenment. The manner is less formal and public than before, but Nature is still seen (if in a more mystical way) as the direct source of religious and moral illumination:

> *One impulse from a vernal wood*
> *May teach you more of man,*
> *Of moral evil and of good,*
> *Than all the sages can.*
> (*The Tables Turned*, ll. 21–4)

The tone has the same euphorically innocent simplicity about it as Pope's couplet on Newton: 'Nature, and Nature's Laws lay hid in Night./ God said *Let Newton be!* and All was *Light*', which asserts a similar faith that Nature is the sufficient key to all religion and all morality.

The 'forms of Beauty' which he has perceived in Nature, Wordsworth tells us in ▷ *Tintern Abbey* (1798), give him:

> *. . . sensations sweet,*
> *Felt in the blood, and felt along the heart;*
> *And passing even into my purer mind,*
> *With tranquil restoration.*
> (ll. 28–31)

The sentiment is that of a poet of Sensibility, but the language is different. The insistently repeated 'felt', the strangely inventive preposition '*along* the heart', and the confidently vague phrases 'the forms of Beauty', and 'my purer mind', belong to a new, Romantic vocabulary, adventurous and with mysterious metaphysical resonances. We feel we are descending into new realms of consciousness, below those of the common eighteenth-century daylight. The passage culminates, edifyingly enough, in the plain moral lesson that pleasure in natural beauty has 'no trivial influence/ On that best portion of a good man's life;/ His little, nameless, unremembered acts/ Of kindness and of love'. The thought would not be out of place in Pope's *Essay on Man*, but the didactic tone is quite different: intimate, almost 'homespun', rather than magisterial. Most notable of all, however, is the confidence with which the poet refers to himself. Even in the most intimate poems of the previous period, such as Gray's elegiac works, emotion is generalized and the first person is avoided. Wordsworth's poetry, in contrast, is packed with assertions of his own individual feelings, which become the ultimate arbiter of authenticity. 'I have felt' is an insistent refrain, and carries an unquestioned authority. Keats spoke aptly of 'the Wordsworthian or egotistical sublime'.

This Romantic assertion of self goes together with a new interest in realms of experience which were marginalized in the earlier eighteenth century. The authority of age, for instance, disappears during this time of rapid change. In Wordsworth, as in Blake, youth becomes the fount of wisdom: 'The Child is father of the Man'. The ▷ *Ode: Intimations of Immortality* (1807) develops a theology based on the proposition that at birth we come 'trailing clouds of glory ... From God, who is our home'. The youth is 'Nature's Priest' until 'the prison-house' of this world closes around him. It is only by recapturing the bloom of childhood that creativity can be revived. In a similar way the conscious intellect is downgraded in relation to the spontaneous, the instinctual, the subconscious. In an anticipation of later psychoanalysis, dreams are no longer seen as the ravings of an undisciplined fancy during the sleep of Reason. Wordsworth speaks of 'The glory and the freshness of a dream'. And sometimes dreams become in themselves the subject of poetry, as in ▷ *The Prelude* and in Coleridge's ▷ *Kubla Khan*, which is subtitled 'A Vision in a Dream'.

Wordsworth's greatest works concern classes of people generally ignored by earlier writers: children, the very old, the mad and the poor, almost always in a rural context. These poems can be seen as a development from, or revaluation of the ancient pastoral tradition. Like the earlier aristocrat, the modern bourgeois finds spiritual nourishment in contemplating life reduced to the fundamentals of agricultural subsistence. There is an interesting contrast in this respect with ▷ John Clare (1793–1864), a poet who was himself a poverty-stricken agricultural labourer. Clare's unforced and precise diction achieves a far more detailed description of rural life than Wordsworth's, but he lacks Wordsworth's complex interaction with poetic convention and tradition. While Clare is concerned first and foremost to express his intense perception of natural beauty, Wordsworth writes with a missionary intention to change the literary attitudes of his own class. In a letter he attacks a definition of human nature according to the conceptions of 'People in our rank in life ... persons who can afford to buy, or can easily procure, books of half-a-guinea price, hot-pressed, and printed upon superfine paper'. The poet's duty is to 'descend lower, among cottages and fields, and among children'. We must confront basic humanity 'by stripping our own hearts naked, and by looking out of our selves towards men who lead the simplest lives, and those most according to nature'. Class guilt is an essential element in the lessons in humility which Wordsworth receives from downtrodden peasants as Simon Lee and the Leech-Gatherer (▷ *Resolution and Independence*).

Central to the effect of such poems as *We are Seven*, *The Thorn* and *The Idiot Boy* (1798) is a systematic denial of literary pretension. Sing-song rhyme and clumsy repetitions reduce the literary ballad, fashionable since the appearance of Percy's *Reliques*, to its primitive folk origins, while the language seems often wilfully banal:

> *Now Johnny all night long had heard*
> *The owls in tuneful concert strive;*
> *No doubt too he the moon had seen;*
> *For in the moonlight he had been*
> *From eight o'clock til five.*

> *And thus to Betty's question, he*
> *Made answer, like a traveller rold,*
> *(His very words I give to you,)*
> *'The cocks did crow to-whoo, to-whoo,*
> *'And the sun did shine so cold.'*
> *— Thus answered Johnny in his glory,*
> *And that was all his travel's story.*
> *(The Idiot Boy*, ll. 452–63)

Wordsworth's rejection in these poems of the hierarchy of language and subject matter which so clogged poetry of the previous age, is startlingly original, and it is understandable that some readers of the time preferred the work of ▷ George Crabbe (1754–1832), who treats similar social and psychological themes without flouting literary decorum. In this respect Wordsworth is a unique extremist, and unlike any other poet. He possesses that humourless integrity and lack of self-irony which characterize some of the most original artists. *The Idiot Boy* inevitably reduces the reader to laughter, and it must be admitted that the laughter is partly at the poet himself. But it is a tearful laughter, a kind of release from our shame and embarrassment. The common humanity with the idiot and his mother, which Wordsworth asks us to acknowledge, is intensified not dispelled, by our hopeless exasperation at the perverse artifice of his naive style. There is no levity or satire here, except perhaps an implied satire on those who think themselves above such people as Betty and Johnny. Such strenuous moral sympathy, uncompromisingly expressed, is a central element in Wordsworth's poetic achievement.

▷ Samuel Taylor Coleridge (1772–1834), though a close friend of Wordsworth, possessed a fundamentally different sensibility, less secure in its egotism, more intellectual and analytical. Moreover, he was steeped in the philosophical currents of Enlightenment empiricism and Kantian metaphysics. Wordsworth boldly dispelled materialist scepticism by asserting Nature's primitive numinousness:

> *And I have felt*
> *A presence that disturbs me with the joy*
> *Of elevated thoughts; a sense sublime*
> *Of something far more deeply interfused . . .*
> *A motion and a spirit, that impels*
> *All thinking things, all objects of all thought,*
> *And rolls through all things.*
> *(Tintern Abbey*, ll. 94–103)

Coleridge, however, was unable simply to accept his friend's faith in the interfusion of man and nature, as the uneasiness of his insistence on the 'one life' in ▷ *The Ancient Mariner* (1798) shows. Among the Romantics it is Coleridge who engages the most explicitly with this central problem of the relation between 'objective' reality and the 'subjective' perceptions of the individual.

The rejection of the Enlightenment notion that Nature is a fixed objective entity mirrored by the mind had released new imaginative energies. As Coleridge said in ▷ *Biographia Literaria* (1817) even perception itself (or 'primary imagination') must now be seen as an active faculty, without which nothing exists. The poet's role is thus, like God's, a creative one, rather than merely imitative, as in neo-classical theory. In a central passage in this work Coleridge describes how the creative 'secondary imagination' 'dissolves, diffuses, dissipates, in order to re-create; or where this process is rendered impossible, yet still, at all events, ... struggles to idealize and to unify' (XIII). This faculty he opposes to mere 'fancy', which can deal only with 'fixities and definites'. In one sense this merely elaborates, in the new terms of Romanticism, the earlier distinction between 'true' and 'false' wit. But the term 'imagination', as Coleridge uses it here, has a complexity of psychological resonance which is new and distinctively modern.

This stress on the creativity of imagination, however, makes the Romantic poet's relationship with Nature problematic, metaphorical and elusive, as that of his Enlightenment predecessor was not. Coleridge wrestles with this issue in ▷ *Dejection: An Ode* (1802), a poem which shows a characteristically intimate blend between the poet's personal emotions and larger philosophical ideas. In his 'wan and heartless mood' the poet cannot establish the essential creative interaction between the natural scene and his subjective emotion. He finds it impossible to 'feel' its beauty or gain any consolation from it. He describes the sky, with 'its peculiar tint of yellow green' in tones of accurate analytical prosiness, only too aware of the listlessness of his attempts at poetic elevation:

> *I may not hope from outward forms to win*
> *The passion and the life, whose fountains are within.*
>
> *O Lady we receive but what we give*
> *And in our life alone does Nature live.*
>
> (ll. 45–8)

Unless 'A light, a glory, a fair luminous cloud/ Enveloping the Earth' comes out from within ourselves the world must remain inert.

Coleridge's poetic development is dominated by his fear that the 'shaping spirit of Imagination' will be lost to him. And paradoxically his greatest poems, *The Ancient Mariner* and *Kubla Khan* (1816), express this anxiety, and at the same time succeed in the imaginative task of re-creation or idealization. They embody universal human emotions in the most concrete and simple of images. In a characteristically Romantic way their exoticism serves to impart a primal immediacy to the symbols: a sea journey, an albatross, the sun, the moon, a fountain, a river, a dead sea. In Wordsworth, ballad primitiveness of style was used to shame sophisticated readers out of their social prejudices. In *The Ancient Mariner* it performs a quite different function, creating unforgettably stark expressions of inner emotional and spiritual states:

> *All in a hot and copper sky*
> *The bloody sun, at noon,*
> *Right up above the mast did stand,*
> *No bigger than the moon.*

> *Day after day, day after day,*
> *We stuck, ne breath ne motion*
> *As idle as a painted Ship*
> *Upon a painted Ocean.*
> (ll. 107–14)

The ▷ Jungian psychologist will find these poems a rich source of arche-types from the 'collective unconscious' of humankind.

As the promise of the French Revolution was betrayed and reaction hardened in Britain, the first generation of Romantic poets became increasingly conservative and orthodox. Coleridge abandoned political radical-ism and became a spokesman for the Church of England. Wordsworth's pantheism sank into stolid piety. The second generation Romantic poets, ▷ Byron and ▷ Shelley, however, remained true to the progressive ideals of the Revolution, and their work is characterized by a painful sense of opposition to the new conservative mood. They reproached their older contemporaries for betraying their ideals, heaping the greatest contempt on the least poetically gifted of them, ▷ Robert Southey (1774–1843), former revolutionary and co-originator with Coleridge of the ▷ pantisocracy scheme, who now professed a 'dislike of all strong emotion', and in 1813 had achieved the respectability of the laureateship.

The work of George Gordon, Lord Byron (1788–1824), illustrates well the contradictions of the label 'Romantic'. The image of the 'Byronic hero' which sustains his popular reputation, is as much the creation of his life and personality as of his writing: his club foot, his incest, his bisexuality and compulsive promiscuity, his disastrous marriage, his support for revolutionary causes and his early death in Greece. If we turn to the poetry in which he projects the Byronic myth, ▷ *Childe Harold's Pilgrimage* (1812–18), ▷ *The Corsair* (1814), *Lara* (1814), we find a fantasy of adventure and sexual glamour, expressed in old-fashioned poetic diction:

> *There was a laughing Devil in his sneer,*
> *That raised emotions both of rage and fear;*
> *And where his frown of hatred darkly fell,*
> *Hope withering fled, and Mercy sigh'd farewell!*
> (*The Corsair*, I, ll. 223–6)

These works offer a headier version of the adventure romance popularized by ▷ Walter Scott (1771–1832) in ▷ *Marmion* (1808) and ▷ *The Lady of the Lake* (1810). Byron himself did not take his 'Harrys and Larrys, Pilgrims and pirates' seriously, and boasted about the speed with which he dashed them off in the intervals of an active life. When he attempts to modulate from broad rhetoric to a profounder Romantic intensity his tone

can sound very inauthentic. Wordsworth complained that 'the whole third
Canto of *Childe Harold*' was plagiarized from *Tintern Abbey*, the borrowed
sentiments being worked into 'a laboured and antithetical sort of declamation':

> I live not in myself, but I become
> Portion of that around me; and to me
> High mountains are a feeling.
> (*Childe Harold*, III, LXXII)

Byron's feeling for the natural scene was not strong, and though he was a
political radical, he had neither Wordsworth's humility before the lowly and
oppressed nor Shelley's elevated idealism. He is the most socially orientated
of the Romantic poets and the only one who has any serious claim to 'wit'.
The subjects that really interest him and elicit his best writing are public
activity and dramatic human conflict: the crowd watching a gladiatorial
display in ancient Rome, or a ball in Brussels on the eve of the battle of
Waterloo. As a theorist of poetry Byron is an urbane neo-classicist who
rejects almost all of what we now call Romanticism, including his own
contribution to it:

> I am convinced, the more I think of it, that ... all of us, Scott, Southey,
> Wordsworth, Moore, Campbell, I, – are all ... upon a wrong revolutionary
> poetical system, or systems, not worth a damn in itself, and from which none
> but Rogers and Crabbe are free.
> (Letter to John Murray, 15 Sept 1817)

Some of his earliest poems are satires in Popean couplets. In his hands,
however, this medium inevitably sounds clumsy and derivative, and it was
not until he discovered the loose, rattling stanzas of *ottava rima* that Byron
created his distinctive Romantic version of the urbane wit he so admired in
Pope. The coarse-grained rhymes and chiming couplets of ▷ *Beppo: A
Venetian Story* (1818), ▷ *The Vision of Judgement* (1822) and ▷ *Don
Juan* (1819–24), become a source of insouciant humour in themselves, as,
for instance, in his offhand reference to Newton's discovery of gravity:

> And this is the sole mortal who could grapple
> Since Adam, with a fall, or with an apple.
> (*Don Juan*, X, I)

Paradoxically, however, it is in this poetic form that Byron achieves his most
profound writing, since the sudden shifts of mood and the mixed registers
which it encourages, allow him fully to express the contradictory elements of
his personality: Regency man of fashion, libertine, political idealist and
romantic hero. He deals with the great themes of time and decay with a
flippant world-weariness which is genuinely moving:

> *But now at thirty years my hair is gray –*
> *(I wonder what it will be like at forty?*
> *I thought of a peruke the other day –)*
> *My heart is not much greener; and, in short, I*
> *Have squander'd my whole summer while 'twas May.*
> (*Don Juan*, I, CCXIII)

Though Percy Bysshe Shelley (1792–1822) was a friend of Byron, their literary sensibilities were often opposed. ▷ Goethe remarked that as soon as Byron begins to think he becomes a child. Shelley, on the other hand, is preoccupied, sometimes perhaps to a fault, with intellectual issues. Among the Romantics Shelley remains truest to the philosophical scepticism of the Enlightenment tradition. Indeed he was expelled from Oxford for circulating a pamphlet entitled *The Necessity of Atheism* (1811). But paradoxically his very Enlightenment materialism is the source of his most extreme Romantic traits. A materialistic view of the world implies that nothing is unchangeable or taboo: everything is potentially subject to human understanding. It was such rationalist confidence that led Shelley's father-in-law, the philosopher ▷ William Godwin, to the view that correct educational principles would produce perfect human beings. Much of the time Shelley seems to see the poet in this radical light, as a teacher and perfecter of humanity.

Wordsworth had remarked that 'a great Poet ought . . . to a certain degree, to rectify men's feelings, to give them new compositions of feeling'. With less hesitation Shelley argues that poets have wider sympathies than ordinary men; the poet makes 'the pains and pleasures of his species' his own, and is thus a natural leader. 'Poets are the unacknowledged legislators of the world' (▷ *Defence of Poetry*). But the hectic quality of much of Shelley's rhetoric betrays the idealism of a frustrated radical in a time of reaction. Since any possibility of practical alliance between the classes had been frustrated at this time, Shelley can only internalize and abstract his craving for social justice into an insistence on personal selflessness and nobility. The political leaders in *The Revolt of Islam* (1818) are a young man and woman of great beauty, whom the undifferentiated masses follow out of spiritual and aesthetic awe. The politics of the poem are a matter of individual changes of heart, rather than economic or social progress. The fantasy is as self-indulgent as that of Byron, though more refined and idealistic in its narcissism.

In his attitude to Nature, Shelley seeks to reconcile rational scepticism with the metaphorical imagination. The function of poetry is to restore the sense of imaginative wholeness which Enlightenment, for all its practical good works, has destroyed:

> *The cultivation of those sciences which have enlarged the limits of the empire of man over the external world, has, for want of the poetical faculty, proportionally circumscribed those of the internal world; and man, having enslaved the elements, remains himself a slave.*

> (*Defence of Poetry*)

Mont Blanc (1817) expresses awe at the sublime beauty of Nature. But this sublimity cannot be attributed to God. It is the product of 'the human mind's imaginings'. The attempt to replace God by the human imagination in Shelley can produce an overblown floridness of style, and for an atheist his language is peculiarly spiritual, even religiose. Shelley's abstract fervour can sometimes be oppressive. But at his best, in poems such as ▷ *Prometheus Unbound* (1820), ▷ *Adonais* (1821), ▷ *The Masque of Anarchy* (1832), and most impressively in *The Triumph of Life* (1824), whose *terza rima* ▷ metre lends itself to an effect of continuous crescendo, he achieves an intense grandeur unmatched by other poets.

Although, under the influence of ▷ Leigh Hunt, ▷ John Keats (1795–1821) adopted the radical politics of the other second-generation Romantics, his best poetry is not political. It offers a most original treatment of the major Romantic theme of subjective imagination and objective reality. While the union between the individual and nature or humanity, towards which Wordsworth, Coleridge and Shelley strive, is moral or spiritual, Keats's approach is uniquely materialistic and sensuous. His physical empathy is not confined to his own species, nor even to animate creatures. In a letter he speaks of his imaginative compulsion to 'take part in' the existence of a sparrow and 'pick about the Gravel' with it. A friend reported: 'He has affirmed that he can conceive of a billiard ball that it may have a sense of delight from its own roundness smoothness and very volubility, and the rapidity of its motion'. The poet for Keats has no fixed identity, but is a 'chameleon', with the ability to suspend his own egotism by an act of purely physical selflessness: 'O for a Life of Sensations rather than of Thoughts'.

Touch, the most earthy and concrete of the senses, predominates in Keats's poetry. Even eyes become as much agents of feeling as of sight, being described as 'shut softly up alive', or 'muffled'. Madeline in ▷ *The Eve of St Agnes* (1820) dances 'with vague, regardless eyes', and the beauty of the flowers in the ▷ *Ode to a Nightingale* (1819) is intensified by the fact that they can only be guessed at in 'embalmed darkness'. Constant synaesthesia confuses the different senses together, and even the process of thinking is expressed in violently physical terms: 'Sudden a thought came like a full-blown rose,/ Flushing his brow, and in his pained heart/ Made purple riot' (*Eve of St Agnes*, XVI). In *Isabella* (1818) the elegist's commonplace reflection on the dissolution of the flesh is transformed into the strenuous act of burrowing:

> *Who hath not loiter'd in a green church-yard,*
> *And let his spirit, like a demon-mole,*
> *Work through the clayey soil and gravel hard,*
> *To see scull, coffin'd bones, and funeral stole . . .*
> (*Isabella*, XLV)

Significant in this context is Keats's preference, in his letters and also in some of his poems, for the noun 'feel' over 'feeling'. 'Feeling' is often a synonym for 'thought' or 'opinion'. 'Feel' is more intimately a matter of the nervous system and the blood-pressure, as in 'to get the feel of . . .'.

Keats's constant ambition was to embody this response to sensuous beauty in the permanent 'abstract' form of a 'philosophical poem'. In his early work *Endymion* (1818) he takes the simplest way, adopting a tone of bold didactic certainty: 'A thing of beauty is a joy forever:/ Its loveliness increases; it will never/ Pass into nothingness' (I, 1–3). Though the poem acknowledges the pains and limitations of reality, its texture tends simply to evade them in cloying escapist sensuousness. In subsequent works Keats develops a more complex version of his aestheticist faith. In ▷ *Hyperion* (1820), which was left incomplete on his death, he attempts to show the victory of Beauty in terms of an epic struggle between ageing ▷ Titans and youthful Olympian gods. But the narrative's triumphalist message: 'for 'tis the eternal law/ That first in beauty should be first in might' (II, 228–9), is beset by ambiguities. The poetry is at its most immediate and moving in the description of the defeated ▷ Saturn, and the work falters to a stop shortly after the introduction of the victorious ▷ Apollo. There are, it seems, other more profound kinds of beauty than the 'fresh perfection' of healthy youth. The downcast resignation of Hyperion's wife, Thea, Keats tells us, 'made/ Sorrow more beautiful than Beauty's self' (I, 35–6). The projected framework of epic conflict is unable to dramatize such complexities. Keats remained unhappy with *Hyperion* and could not finish it.

It is in the descriptive, reflective mode of *The Eve of St Agnes* and the great *Odes* that Keats most successfully develops this conviction of the interrelationship between pleasure and pain. In these poems Keats achieves a sensuousness whose intensity derives precisely from its vulnerability to 'the weariness, the fever, and the fret' of human life. In the *Ode to a Nightingale*, the natural beauty of the bird's song establishes a subjective moment of epiphany outside time. But then it fades, leaving the poet uncertain whether it was 'a vision, or a waking dream' (VIII). In the *Ode on a Grecian Urn*, artistic beauty, immune from age and disease, bears through the ages its consoling message: 'Beauty is truth, truth beauty'. But though the passion of its painted lovers will not cloy like that of living beings, its purity is earned at the cost of eternal stasis. It is a 'Cold Pastoral'. The great odes are full of images whose beauty derives from an acknowledgement of transience and death.

> *And little town, thy streets for evermore*
> *Will silent be; and not a soul to tell*
> *Why thou art desolate, can e'er return.*
> (*Ode on a Grecian Urn*, IV)

The 'fast-fading violets covered up in leaves' of *Ode to a Nightingale* are beautiful *because* they are fading fast, and the Autumn skies in which 'gathering swallows twitter', will soon be silent (*Ode to Autumn*, III). In such poignant images as these Keats, like Rochester before him, accepts the consequences of the unillusioned materialism which is at the centre of Enlightenment thought. Both the Restoration libertine and the Romantic aesthete celebrate the pleasure of the senses as the ultimate value in life. And both movingly acknowledge their inability to transcend the blows of transience and death.

William Roberts *The Vorticists at the Restaurant de la Tour Eiffel: Spring 1915*

Behind the 'silken-folded mask': Victorian and modern poetry

Victorian poetry

Nay, if there's room for poets in the world
A little overgrown (I think there is),
Their sole work is to represent the age,
Their age, not Charlemagne's, – this live, throbbing age,
That brawls, cheats, maddens, calculates, aspires,
And spends more passion, more heroic heat,
Betwixt the mirrors of its drawing rooms,
Than Roland with his knights at Roncesvalles.

(*Aurora Leigh*; Elizabeth Barrett Browning, 1857)

This essay attempts to trace the key moments in British poetic history since 1830. It is a history which has largely taken place through a series of self-conscious poetic revolutions, or attempts to break old artistic models with new forms. To read this history from the steam age through the machine age to the nuclear age and do justice to poetry's relationship with the convulsive changes of that time span necessarily questions the notion that literature progresses through a series of harmonious organic developments. This century and a half of poetic history vividly resists the idea that it has grown and flowed gracefully from ▷ Wordsworth's pen to the present day. It is a history of fractures, fissures, revaluation and self-conscious re-moulding; each subsequent moment of poetry energetically rewrites history according to its own priorities.

The date at which this discussion begins has often been read as the point of a lamentable Artistic Fall from the grace of romantic insight. From a different vantage point critics such as ▷ F. R. Leavis did not linger with the Victorians on their Grand Tour of an English poetic Great Tradition. For too long we have taken the poets at their own word, believing that the elegaic image their work casts, their nostalgia for finer and surer times, is a necessary reflection upon their own limited possibilities of writing. Certainly, ▷ Matthew Arnold's lament – 'Wordsworth is gone from us' ('Memorial Verses, April 1880') is echoed in a polyphony of poetry written by his contemporaries. Wordsworth had been the living father of poetry, and his grip tightened with the publication of *The Prelude* on his death in 1850.

But need we believe that Victorian poets were so petrified by a combination of anxiety at the enormity of romantic influence (▷ Henry James wrote that Wordsworth 'sterilized' Arnold) and a vertiginous grasp of their complicating opportunities, that nothing of interest could be written? I hope to show that it is the acute anxiety which Victorian poets felt about the task of recapturing the literary magic of the generation who were dead or in decline by 1830 which makes their work most interesting. What animates Victorian poetry is precisely its acknowledgement of crisis, both in its affirmation (in James's words again) of 'the particular ache, or regret, or conjecture, to which poetry is supposed to address itself,' and in its ability to confront more disturbing questions. I shall discuss here particularly those texts which open up and question the problematic nature of the self and its relationship to the material world, a world whose alien(ating) powers were conceived of as profoundly threatening. The most intriguing texts to emerge from this period are those which confront directly the uncontrollable growth and urbanization of the population, the industrial technological infrastructure which seemed to be taking on a life of its own, and Britain's place in a Europe fractured by disunited states and revolutionary possibilities. These texts were not disinterested poetic comments upon a shocking range of social or historical contexts, but rather material elements which *worked within* their chaotic historical framework.

Dusty answers: loss and nostalgia in Victorian poetry

> *Ah, what a dusty answer gets the soul*
> *When hot for certainties in this our life!*
> (*Modern Love*; George Meredith, 1862)

Poetry since 1830 has been written largely in a state of shock. From the shock of electricity to the 'shock of the new' (▷ modernism), currents of difficulty and doubt animate poetic history, fuelled by a crisis of faith and the instability of living in a rapidly growing and urbanizing society within which values were becoming increasingly unstable. This feeling of uncertainty is indulged by the Victorians through the notion that there was once a time, well into the past, when certainty existed. In ▷ Tennyson's words, Victorian poetry is permeated with 'the quiet sense of something lost' (▷ *In Memoriam A.H.H.*).

Tennyson's long elegy, *In Memoriam A.H.H.* (1850), is perhaps the most famous poem of loss to be penned in the nineteenth century. Written almost as therapy over a long period, what is being mourned is not simply Arthur Hallam, the poet's greatest friend; rather his death is a pretext for an extended meditation on absence. What is lost is also a fixed personal identity, certainty of perception and judgement, and the idea of a benign or controlling divinity. Matthew Arnold's elegiac lyric *Dover Beach* (1867) sketches out this sense of loss:

> *The Sea of Faith*
> *Was once, too, at the full, and round earth's shore*
> *Lay like the folds of a bright girdle furled.*
> *But now I only hear*
> *Its melancholy, long, withdrawing roar . . .*

Reading Tennyson's intense lament alongside the passive melancholy of Arnold gives us two perspectives on how this loss, which is of course nothing new, is characterized in a particularly Victorian way. For Tennyson, trust in God must come despite the abysmal fact that,

> *Nature, red in tooth and claw*
> *With ravine, shrieked against his creed*
> (*In Memoriam A.H.H.*)

So if *Dover Beach* is an elegy, who or what has died?

In many ways the most interesting poetry of the period since 1830 can be called 'death of God' poetry, after ▷ Nietzsche's famous proclamation that 'God is dead'. In *Easter Day, Naples 1849* ▷ Arthur Clough writes, 'Ah! "some" did well to "doubt"!', in the midst of a text which repeats an atheist incantation:

> *Christ is not risen, no,*
> *He lies and moulders low;*
> *Christ is not risen.*
>
> *Ashes to ashes, dust to dust;*
> *As of the unjust, also of the just –*
> *Christ is not risen.*

Such a strong statement runs contrary to our cherished notion that the Victorians were a nation of devout church-goers, even if read in the context of the subsequent poem by Clough, 'Easter Day II' which affirms the opposite view. Despite the explosion in church-building which took place up to the 1850s, the Religious Census of 1851 showed that a large proportion of the population did not go to church. This feeling reaches a virulent pitch later in the century with ▷ James Thomson's *The City of Dreadful Night* (1874), a poem which, in its compulsive repetition, is structured like a nightmare. *City* may be the nearest thing in English poetry to Rimbaud's *Une Saison en enfer* (1873), although its invectives against God bring it closer to ▷ Lautréamont:

> *The vilest thing must be less than Thou*
> *From whom it had its being, God and Lord!*
> *. . . I vow*
>
> *That not for all Thy power furled and unfurled, (. . .)*
> *Would I assume the ignominious guilt*
> *Of having made such men in such a world.*
> (*The City of Dreadful Night*)

Thomson's God is alive and actively malicious, but the God who withdraws with Arnold's Sea of Faith is conspicuous only by his absence. Tennyson wrote to fill the absences – 'if there was a blank space I would put in a poem'

– and one such absence has been created by God's departure. *In Memoriam* thus confronts these absences as the grieving self confronts the Victorian 'Unreal city':

> *He is not here; but far away*
> *The noise of life begins again,*
> *And ghastly through the drizzling rain*
> *On the bald street breaks the blank day.*

As with Tennyson's *Maud* (1855), *In Memoriam* shows a self so disrupted and infiltrated that it cannot affirm ▷ Robert Browning's much quoted phrase, 'God's in his heaven – / All's right with the world' (*Pippa Passes*). This is turned inward, for if God does not exist, man cannot exist in his image, and so the self's solidity and its possibilities of self-conscious meaningful action are undermined. Two quotations, the first from *In Memoriam* (LIV), the second from the remarkable poem by ▷ John Clare, 'I Am' (1864), illustrate this:

> *. . . but what am I?*
> *An infant crying in the night:*
> *An infant crying for the light:*
> *And with no language but a cry.*
>
>   *   *   *
>
> *I am – yet what I am none cares or knows,*
> *My friends forsake me like a memory lost;*
> *I am the self-consumer of my woes,*
> *They rise and vanish in oblivions host.*

His 'not being here' renders the urbanized, brave new world of the mid-nineteenth century, the world of cholera and of the Crimean war, all the more ghastly, bald and blank, a world which it seemed, for the most part, God had never visited at all.

In the wake of this appalling possibility, fragments of memory – *In Memoriam* is certainly a fragmented text – are shored up poetically against present fear and ruin,

> *. . . when the sensuous frame*
> *Is racked with pangs that conquer trust;*
> *And Time, a maniac scattering dust,*
> *And Life, a fury slinging flame.*
>   (*In Memoriam A.H.H.*)

The sense that history and technology were advancing out of all rational and moral control was acutely felt by poets, characterized by feelings of alienation from home. 'A wanderer is man from his birth' writes Arnold in 'The Future' (1852), and feelings of loss serve to fill the gap between the self and its long-gone place of safety. In Clare's 'I Am' the world is a 'vast shipwreck', and the 'nothingness of scorn and noise', the 'living sea of waking dreams' renders his loved ones even 'stranger than the rest'. ▷ Anne Brontë laments to herself, 'Sad wanderer, weep those blissful times / That never may return!' ('The Bluebell'; 1840). We could turn to countless verses where this sentiment is repeated, culminating in ▷ Thomas Hardy's double vision of loss and dread right at the end of the century. An image is set up across a wide range of Victorian poems of a lost cherished past – an idyllic pre-industrial England, the innocence of childhood, a place where unproblematic faith was possible. But working in tandem with melancholic lament is the Victorian passion for more positive and elaborate retrospection.

The Victorians had a great talent for nostalgia. This means that their interpretation of the past was double-edged, countering present loss with rosily remembered bygone times. In the face of uncompromising industrial expansion and unprecedented urban squalor a sumptuous pseudo-medieval world was erected, a counter-image of ▷ Gothic grandeur activated by the prose celebrations of ▷ John Ruskin and ▷ Thomas Carlyle. The latter looked to the ▷ Middle Ages as a point of pre-industrial authenticity where 'Antique devoutness, Antique veracity and heroism' were possible (*Past and Present*; 1843); the former's celebration of the Gothic had a profound influence upon the architectural practice of the second half of the nineteenth century. ▷ William Morris's championing of the Arts and Crafts Movement was vehemently anti-capitalist in favouring individual production and handiwork over the mass production of advanced technology. All these were impassioned moral responses to the feeling of contemporary spiritual alienation.

For ▷ Elizabeth Barrett Browning, however, poetic nostalgia was tanta-mount to escapism; shirking the task of producing poetry which engaged with the moment, the nostalgic poet failed to discern 'character or glory in his times, / And trundle(d) back his soul five hundred years' (*Aurora Leigh*). This poetic 'trundling-back' survives in the shadowy ▷ Arthurian world of, for example, Tennyson's ▷ *Idylls of the King* (1859–72) and the archaic images of the ▷ Pre-Raphaelite movement. Pieced into an evocative picture of traditional England, legend-spinning countered the squalid present by con-centrating on a supposedly more authentic yesterday. This sentimental evoca-tion of a mythical past acted, then, rather like what ▷ Freud calls a 'Family Romance', only on a national scale; just as an individual might pretend he or she has more glorious and romantic origins than are in fact the case, so national culture is built upon the wishful creation of images of glorious and graceful past times. By positively forging a myth of the English idyll –

> *Oh, to be in England*
> *Now that April's there*
> ('Home Thoughts From Abroad'; Robert Browning, 1845)

– or of childhood, or of God in His Heaven – personal and national stability is consolidated rather than threatened. By forging an idyllic cultural memory (a sanitized past) which acts as a kind of screen memory, blocking off far more disturbing passages of individual or national history (the dirty materiality of the real past) Victorian verse contributed to glueing together a fracturing present. In the place of what ▷ Chartist poet Gerald Massey (1828–1907) called the 'looming future', a blooming past is constructed.

One way of reading Victorian nostalgia is to assume that the strength of retrospection in a text is an index of the depth of crisis felt at the moment at which it was written. We do find frequent points where crisis is overtly acknowledged; loss in the present is as important a stated element in Victorian verse as the creation of the past. So it is wise to be as suspicious as possible when confronting these images, asking, as Anne Brontë does, why certain things have been remembered and valorized and not others:

> *Sweet memory, ever smile on me;*
> *Nature's chief beauties spring from thee.*

In other words, one remembers what one desires to remember:

> *Is childhood then so all divine?*
> *Or, memory, is the glory thine*
> *That haloes thus the past?*
> ('Memory'; 1846)

What is activated in poetic remembering is, then, highly selective, evading the squalid activity of the past.

Anchors of desire: other voices in the 'double-breasted Age'

> *There cast my anchors of desire*
> *Deep in Unknown eternity,*
> *Nor ever let my spirit tire*
> *With looking for* What is to Be.
> ('Anticipation', Emily Brontë; 1845)

In her suspicious reading of the tricks of memory Anne Brontë comes close to the cynicism of Gerald Massey, whose concern is to scrutinize the 'real present' and the social contexts of idyllic images. In the ironically titled 'All's Right with the World', he shows what occurs when the 'silken-folded mask' of sweet image-making slips,

> *. . . lo, Hell welters at our very feet!*
> *The Poor are murdered body and soul, the Rich*
> *In Pleasure's chalice melt their pearl of life!*
> *Ay, all goes right, and merrily, with the world.*
> ('All's Right with the World')

Perhaps this 'silken-folded mask' is the tapestry woven by Tennyson's *The Lady of Shalott* (1832), which contains scenes of the world she cannot see first hand but only as images in her mirror. Massey's verse asks suspicious questions about who has the power to write and myth-make, and who is excluded from the process of remembering – who says what the mirror reflects? More positively, we might look for other images beneath the mask, and listen to other poetic voices.

The canon has often concealed the tears in the 'silken-folded mask' of bourgeois writing. The poetry of the nineteenth century is, however, extraordinarily heterogeneous. Whilst modernists were able to dismiss Victorian verse as immobile and monolithic, the terms used to discuss it could be much simpler than those which are required to do justice to its plurality and diversity. In this section I wish to point to the cracks in the idea of a Victorian poetic monolith by showing the points at which different voices call from inside the marbling.

The variety of metrical and stanzaic forms in nineteenth-century writing confesses both technical restlessness and openness to development – Clough's verse in parts anticipates ▷ *vers libre*, Browning and Tennyson experimented widely with ▷ metre, and as we shall see ▷ Gerard Manley Hopkins developed rhythmic forms which anticipate modernism. Voices other than that of bourgeois Victorian propriety speak in the dialect poetry of ▷ William Barnes, Thomas Hardy, and even Tennyson, in texts such as Thomas Hood's 'The Song of the Shirt' (1843) (the lament of a labouring woman – 'Would that its tone could reach the rich!'), and in the bizarre sexual delirium of ▷ Algernon Swinburne and some writers of the *fin de siècle*. The ▷ Nonsense verse of ▷ Edward Lear and ▷ Lewis Carroll plays with images from the Victorian unconscious, parodying normality to the point of absurdity, the effect of which is hilarious, provocative and disturbing. Carroll's 'The White Knight's Song' from *Through the Looking Glass* (1872), gives a world of capitalism-turned-upside-down by listing a series of utterly absurd ways of making money, a stream of words which 'trickled through my head, / Like water through a sieve'. The lament of manifest loss in Lear's 'The Dong with the Luminous Nose', (1871) parodies the grander losses of Tennyson and Arnold; 'Dong' is a melancholy pastiche, telling the story of the lost Jumbly Girl in the grandiose tones of the mock-epic:

> But when the sun was low in the West,
>   The Dong arose and said;–
>   –'What little sense I once possessed
>   Has quite gone out of my head!' –
> And since that day he wanders still
> By lake and forest, marsh and hill,
> Singing – 'O somewhere, in valley or plain
> 'Might I find my Jumbly Girl again!
> 'For ever I'll seek by lake and shore
> 'Till I find my Jumbly Girl once more!'

Crucially, too, the mask slips when women take up their pens, especially when they are concerned in their writing, as was Elizabeth Barrett Browning, to inscribe literary history with visions which could not be countenanced by masculine masks. Her desire to 'catch / Upon the burning lava of a song / The full-veined, heaving, double-breasted Age' (*Aurora Leigh*) strongly contrasts with much Victorian poetry's listless return to any age but its own. Her adamant belief that poetry be relevant to its times and contemporary in its material builds up in *Aurora Leigh* into a plea for living verse, since dead images kill poems: 'death inherits death'.

The outstanding texts of this period are, not uncommonly, ways into fear, confrontations of, in Hardy's late-Victorian phrase, 'the growing gloom'. With the revolutionary year of 1848, a turbulent one for much of mainland Europe, vague uncertainties were turned into a radical sense of possibility. This was the year in which Clough published his remarkable *The Bothie of Tober-Na-Vuolich*, which interrogates class and sexual difference through the difficult problem of marriage across class barriers; in the face of a socially volatile moment, Clough asserted the necessity that poetry relate to and guide people in their urban experience. Cultural history registered the shocking dissolution of the solitary and integrated self posited by western rationality. In the British Museum Library ▷ Karl Marx was researching *Das Kapital*; 1848 had seen the publication of his and Engels's *Communist Manifesto*. It is helpful to read Victorian verse in relation to other forms of contemporary writing. Such poetry gathered itself together in the intellectual climate which also produced ▷ Charles Darwin's *On the Origin of Species* in 1859, and since the poets under discussion here never saw themselves as writing in splendid isolation from the intellectual revolutions precipitated by these texts, it would be unwise to treat poetic history as generated by a dynamic solely internal to itself.

In the 'Hungry Forties' many of the young writers which modernism cast as Victorian dinosaurs were only just beginning to reach wide audiences and capitalize most effectively on their poetic energies. The fact that the romantic paradigm was no longer applicable to an acutely altered Britain gradually became a cause for celebration rather than lament. Against a fetishized past, poets countered with a strong vision of the present, even those whose work in other places both celebrates and laments what is in truth a pastiche of medieval England. Tennyson, for instance, also makes use of images of the past to displace 'the woman question' into a space where it can be imaginatively explored. In 1847 he first published ▷ *The Princess*, that extraordinary engagement with 'the woman question' which gives us an image, albeit set up only to be undermined, of strong women of formidable intellect. The certainties of sexual difference are challenged not only by the very existence of a militantly feminist educational institution, but by the humour of the transvestite episode in which the heroes dress as women to infiltrate the enemy camp. Central to *The Princess* is the separatist University, which is both credible and credited only within a context radically different from Tennyson's own, hence his deployment of a vague medieval setting, further displaced by a variety of narrative layers. *The Princess* questions the notion that poetry springs from a singular, unified voice; it is 'A Medley', the construction of many voices, male and female, which together forge 'a sevenfold story'.

In 1855 (during the Crimean War), Tennyson published an even stranger long poem which engaged with the contemporary issues of mental aberration, sexual difference, and the war itself. This was *Maud*, subtitled 'A Monodrama', a self-undermining word since the 'one' who speaks this long complex poem is an extremely fragmented personality; he isn't 'one' – he isn't 'mono' – he speaks with many voices. The drama of the narrative is thus importantly also an effect of the dialogue between his own selves. For the speaker of *Maud* is 'Sick of a nameless fear'; disordered in his senses, he seems to speak from many positions at once. He is precipitated into paranoia, and the synaethesia of the famous 'Come into the garden, Maud' passage, by an erotically intangible heroine who had 'fled on the roses and lain in the lilies of life'. Arnold's phrase 'the dialogue of the mind with itself' takes shape in this mad 'hero' who becomes a figure of the introspective poet, fleeing the foul fiend of horror or doubt: 'I will bury myself in myself'. (*Maud*, Part II, l 75). Tennyson wrote of his character, 'I took a man constitutionally diseased and dipt him into the circumstances of the time and took him out on fire'. Along with Tennyson's more narcotic lyrics, *Maud* shows how a poetry which explored the loss of the rational self could be articulated behind the Laureate mask, even as the mask of civic poetry was held anxiously in place. But *Maud* is also in part a comment upon the circumstances of the time, of modern and mental alienation: its landscape a metaphor for psychiatric derangement, as it was to become in such later poems as Thomson's *City* and ▷ T. S. Eliot's ▷ *The Waste Land* (1922).

Aurora Leigh had a readership as enormous as *The Princess* and *Maud*, and in content deals with the questions of gender and women's power which the Tennyson texts, as well as Clough's *Bothie*, all probe from different angles. Even Queen Victoria read *Aurora Leigh*. Indeed, when the queen was faced with the task of choosing a new ▷ Poet Laureate in 1850, Elizabeth Barrett (as she then was) was a prime candidate. Stepping into Wordsworth's shoes was indeed regarded as an awesome task for any of the young poets who were penning their most interesting work at this time. Whilst no woman has ever become the Poet Laureate, in the middle of a century characterized by such acute patriarchal oppression a woman was seriously considered for the position. She was, indeed, far more popular then than her husband-to-be Robert Browning, appropriate to an age when women wrote poetry prolifically and were highly regarded by their contemporaries, and feminist criticism recently has shown her to be a literary figure worthy of stronger recognition than she has received since her death. *Aurora Leigh* explores the boundaries between biography and fiction, identifying poetic work as a unique space for marking out a woman's relationship to language and creativity. As a feminist interrogation of female friendship and sexual relations it is courageous, 'life-blood' 'wrung . . . / On every leaf . . .' (*Aurora Leigh*, Bk 5, ll. 356–7). As an exploration of how literature creates the self, it deserves its place in a tradition of poets' own critical theories. As a long narrative poem it was indeed hugely popular, fulfilling its own prescription that poetry should not flinch from history, and should partly be the space where women can begin to write their own histories, the story behind the mask. Matthew Arnold wrote that, 'Poetry is at bottom a criticism of life', and Barrett Browning's verse exemplifies this, constructively engaging with rather than retreating from her 'double-breasted Age'. As Cora Kaplan points out in her 1978 introduction to the poem, *Aurora Leigh* is a ▷ feminist bridge between two other overtly political publications, *Casa Guidi Windows* (1851) and *Poems Before Congress* (1860), forming a triptych which perhaps offers the strongest poetic analysis in English of the immediately post-1848 European situation.

As feminist criticism has shown, no mythical past could offer nineteenth-century women a positive image of themselves, so they set to writing it in their own way. The work of ▷ Christina Rossetti presents an intriguing exception. Her 'criticism of life' is uniquely strong in its strange combination of morbidity, painful self-denial and simplicity. Rossetti is undoubtedly ruthlessly hard on herself: much of her work is charged with absence and denial, a will to oblivion and silence, which is repeatedly invoked in a style so sparse it seems to be actively wishing to negate itself. Indeed, the word 'silence' itself is often repeated. Her 'almost Paradise' is a return to absolute equilibrium and desirelessness. In 'Rest' (1862) she calls the earth to

> *Lie close around her; leave no room for mirth*
> *With its harsh laughter, nor for sound of sighs.*
> *She hath no questions, she hath no replies,*
> *Hushed in and curtained with a blessed dearth*
> *Of all that irked her from the hour of birth;*
> *With stillness that is almost Paradise.*

The voice of this poem can only afford to desire the absence of pain; for Rossetti positivity isn't full energy but simply the negation of the negative. Plenitude is, perhaps, asking too much. Is this an instance of woman learning to desire her lot, internalizing the Victorian charge that she 'suffer and be still'?

But when colours and positively charged desires giddily burst into this near-silence, that which 'irked her from the hour of her birth' is quite positively broken open and challenged. Rossetti's sparse verse soars to an unnatural high when suddenly rich detail emerges, the mixture of spartan naïve form with ▷ Pre-Raphaelite decorativeness invoking a strange intoxication of deprivation and excess. The rich erotic language of ▷ *Goblin Market* (1862) pressed into a strict ballad form, or the exultation of 'A Birthday' (1862), are both good examples of this:

> *Raise me a dais of silk and down;*
> *Hang it with vair and purple dyes;*
> *Carve it in doves and pomegranates,*
> *And peacocks with a hundred eyes;*

> *Work it in gold and silver grapes,*
>   *In leaves and silver fleurs-de-lys;*
> *Because the birthday of my life*
>   *Is come, my love is come to me.*

In its privations Rossetti's poetry has a simple beauty, but when it brims over with rich images its singularity and strength are striking.

A more overtly positive woman's poetic voice in the earlier Victorian period is that of ▷ Emily Brontë. Hers is – 'No coward soul . . ., / No trembler in the world's storm-troubled sphere' ('No Coward Soul is Mine'; 1846). The quotation which forms the epigraph to this section is typical of her immediate positivity; she would be a poet of the present moment, evoking earth-bound epiphanies which celebrate the material world rather than striving for the transcendental. Significantly, her 'anchor of desire' is cast forward into 'What is to Be' rather than nostalgically backwards. Across her corpus a theory of human freedom is constructed which needs to be read in the context of her position as a woman writer. In 'The Old Stoic' (1841) she desires only 'a chainless soul', not a heavenly transformation – 'Leave me the heart that now I bear, / And give me liberty'. Freedom is more important than heaven, a sentiment which echoes Catherine Earnshaw's dream in chapter nine of ▷ *Wuthering Heights* (1847):

> *Give me the hills our equal prayer,*
> *Earth's breezy hills and heaven's blue sea;*
> *We ask for nothing further here*
> *But our own hearts and liberty.*
> ('And like myself lone, wholly lone'; 1841)

Unlike the more passive mysticism of Rossetti, Brontë is anything but stoical, and her poetry's affirmation of the earth forms a strong critique of organized religion's promise of better things to come:

> *Let others seek its beams divine*
> *In cell and cloister drear*
> *But I have found a fairer shrine*
> *A happier worship here;*
>
> *By dismal rites they win their bliss,*
> *By pennance, fasts and fear –*
> *I have one rite – a gentle kiss;*
> *One pennance – tender tears.*

Flesh and the Fin de Siècle

Sexuality haunts Victorian poetry as an anxious desire, a force both attractive and repulsive, like the prostitute figure 'Jenny' (1870) in ▷ Dante Gabriel Rossetti's poem of that name. The strict a/a/b/b rhyming scheme of 'Jenny' causes her name to assonate ironically with 'guinea'; she is a fallen goddess, whose access to the 'vile text' of sexual knowledge makes her the object of simultaneous desire and denigration. Jenny's image is distorted by what men desire of her:

> Yet, Jenny, looking long at you,
> The woman almost fades from view,
> A cipher of man's changeless sum
> Of lust, past, present, and to come,
> Is left. A riddle that one shrinks
> To challenge from the scornful sphinx.

From ▷ Coventry Patmore's eulogies to the safe delights of married love in *The Angel in the House* (1858), to ▷ George Meredith's bitter sonnet sequence about estrangement and divorce, *Modern Love* (1862), the Victorians were covertly obsessed with the question of sex. Ahead of Nietzsche's proclamation about God, Meredith declares 'the death of love' and digs its grave with his text (*Modern Love*, (i)).

Through the Victorians' treatment of or silence regarding sexuality we can discover much about what was considered the proper subject matter for poetry. In this section I want to talk briefly about how those norms and rules of propriety gradually broke down as the century closed and as writing itself opened. Tennyson's institutionalization as Poet Laureate caused him to consolidate gradually the shifting selves and voices of his earlier verse, and by the latter decades of the nineteenth century he had become quite firmly the spokesman of decorum over degeneracy. By the time of 'Locksley Hall Sixty Years After' (1886), subterranean rumbles were shifting the ground beneath Tennyson's feet, causing him to castigate vehemently the author's part in inviting a new dark age in which 'Chaos, Cosmos' are interchangeable, and freedom is only 'free to slay herself':

> Authors – essayist, atheist, novelist, realist, rhymster, play your part,
> Paint the moral shame of nature with the living hues of Art. (. . .)
>
> Feed the budding rose of boyhood with the drainage of your sewer;
> Send the drain into the fountain lest the stream should issue pure.
>
> Set the maiden fancies wallowing in the troughs of Zolaism, –
> Forward, forward, ay and backward, downward into the abysm.
>
> Do your best to charm the worst, to lower the rising race of men;
> Have we risen from out the beast, then back into the beast again?

The force with which this sewer imagery is impressed upon us is arguably as blatant and shocking as the kind of literature it would repress; Tennyson is calling for a public health drive to counter poetic corruption as the notorious Contagious Diseases Acts of the 1860s sought to control prostitution. In its utter physical disgust this text reveals much about the bourgeois obsession with cleanliness ('next to Godliness') which psychoanalysis was beginning to encounter in its most extreme and mentally destructive forms: as Tennyson penned these words, ▷ Freud was working toward the publication, with Joseph Breuer (1842–1925), of *Studies on Hysteria* (1895), one of the founding texts of psychoanalysis. But however eloquently this poem speaks of Tennyson's own preoccupations, it is its role as a critical prescription which interests us here. For at stake in this is both the notion that 'dirty writing' messes up a literary tradition in the process of purifying itself, and also that such poetic 'foul passions' can have a profound affect on the moral welfare of the nation.

The decadent writings of the later nineteenth century perversely took such a stance gloriously to heart, actually affirming these powers in an indulgence of the flesh as sin. The period of the 1860s and 1870s, the High Victorian period, was a period of consolidation both politically and poetically, and writing was generally on a grander, surer scale, although this consolidation uneasily co-existed with other tendencies. In the late 1880s and early 1890s Tennyson, Browning and Arnold died, and the emphases of poetry shifted. The artists of what ▷ W. B. Yeats called the 'Tragic Generation' – ▷ Oscar Wilde, Ernest Dowson (1867–1900), Lionel Johnson (1867–1902), ▷ Aubrey Beardsley and Arthur Symons (1865–1943), developed an extreme form of aestheticism, strongly influenced by ▷ Walter Pater's notorious epilogue to *Studies in the History of the Renaissance* (1873). This group of bohemian poets formed ▷ The Rhymers Club in the 1890s, and published their work in a body of journals which reflected their priorities: chiefly ▷ *The Yellow Book* and *The Savoy*. As the century became more ▷ utilitarian, adamantly scientific and technologically precise, poetry turned from the prescription of social relevance and made a virtue of the notion that it was brazenly gratuitous. Perversity, superficiality and hedonism were prioritized over the socially useful, profoundly spiritual and serious. Nineties poetry (▷ Nineties Poets) in particular embraced the idea of poetry as estranged from the real world. The earlier notion of poetry as 'a weapon of strife in the social conflict', or Arnold's celebration of the moral worth of poetry, were reversed by aesthetic doctrine (▷ Aestheticism) – as Wilde wrote, 'The man who could call a spade a spade should be compelled to use one'. Such a shift is, however, most significant in its challenging of the rules of poetic subject matter rather than in any formal innovations which decadent poets enacted. Their work is characteristically sinful rather than amoral, evil rather than atheist. Working within the structures of conventional morality *fin de siècle* writers were anti-Victorian Victorians in that they prioritized beauty over goodness, the aesthetic rather than the ethical, the body over the spirit.

This latter emphasis is what the poet, novelist and dramatist Robert Buchanan (1841–1901) had called (in an essay on D. G. Rossetti) 'the Fleshly School of Poetry'. In the 1860s this 'school' was opened by ▷ Algernon Swinburne under the influence of the ▷ Marquis de Sade and ▷ Charles Baudelaire, and bore its own bizarre progeny in the 1880s and 1890s. Certainly, the earlier obsessions of the Pre-Raphaelites had played an important role in the *fin de siècle's* spectacular materialization of certain lurid themes, particularly in the movement's representation of *femmes fatales* like Jenny or Swinburne's Dolores. Dante Gabriel Rossetti's verse often adorns his paintings of women, so that the woman becomes a fusion of verbal description and detailed visual representation on a gigantic scale.

The painting/sonnet 'Astarte Syriaca' (1877) exemplifies this, representing a woman who combines Venus and Astarte, an embodiment of an ineffable higher knowledge and thus also, an image of Victorian woman worship. Rossetti's power to frame women within a certain range of images could, perhaps, be read alongside Browning's 'My Last Duchess' (1842), the speaker of which gains power over the Duchess in the painted image of her. Together Jenny and Astarte Syriaca – woman as essentially 'Amulet, talisman, and oracle' – offer the double vision of sexual fear and desire with which I began. Christina Rossetti's work supplements this masculine vision, stepping back even further than Browning from the female canvas and sharply disrupting her brother's images of essential femininity.

A more outrageous manifestation of textual fleshiness came, however, with the explosion of Algernon Swinburne onto the relatively conservative poetic scene in the mid-1860s. Swinburne is known about now more for his dissolute lifestyle and sexual excesses. His bloodstained poetry is perhaps best known for its insistence on the themes of lust and violence, not all of which even the most crusading twentieth-century writers on sexuality have thought to legitimize. As *enfant terrible* to High Victorian complacency, his early Dionysian work had an intoxicating effect on his young contemporaries.

The initial impact of Swinburne's poetry stemmed in part from his technical innovation, chiefly an obsessive use of alliteration. As he became a more established literary figure his technique was conservatively consolidated. Intoxicated incantations became simply rhythmically tedious, as Swinburne's outrageous and often blasphemous themes were battered into conventional iambic shapes, just as the bodies of his subjects are, 'Trodden as grapes in the wine-press of lust' ('Laus Veneris'; l 191; 1866). Thus, whilst blood-blotches are symptoms that his figures have been 'trampled' by desire, the purple effect of his writing contained in regular, conservative form signalled for later generations Swinburne's ultimate lack of poetic dynamism.

This late-Victorian prioritization of the body and the beautiful over moral and social worth may have been rebellious, challenging the moralizations of earlier politically engaged poets, but it certainly wasn't revolutionary; it may have broken the rules but it certainly didn't change the structure within which the rules worked. As well as working within a moral economy which still held matter and spirit to be diametrically opposed, the poets discussed so far were also working within a textual economy which held form and content to be separate dimensions of poetry. This, then, brings us onto another important aspect of late-Victorian writing, and in particular the poetry of those key transitional figures who were beginning to question the rules which dictated how a poem was written, just as the 'fleshly school' was questioning what a poem was written about.

The Fruits of unbelief: movements toward modernism

Much of the writing discussed so far is, in its versification and syntax at least, familiar – formally it conforms to what the reader is used to. Victorian poetry of this stylistically conventional type in part has trained our readerly sensibilities. This familiarity, however, breaks down in the more difficult verse of Robert Browning and Gerard Manley Hopkins, whose work looks forward to the formal obscurities and syntactical abnormalities of modernism.

Browning's verse is often convoluted and digressive. ▷ Ezra Pound found *Sordello* (1840) unreadable, and ▷ Jane Welsh Carlyle read the whole of it without discerning whether Sordello was a book, a man or a city. Browning is concerned to show how his verse is constructed, to leave in the traces of the psychological process he went through in writing it, to lay bare the association of ideas which lead to the final full stop. He foregrounds 'The grand Perhaps' ('Bishop Blougram's Apology', l 190 from *Men and Women*; 1855) – the doubts and equivocations of writing and modernity – to such an extent that it takes on some kind of positive identity. In the words of 'Bishop Blougram's Apology', Browning's question concerns the uses of doubt and difficulty, 'how can we guard our unbelief, / Make it bear fruit to us?' Thus he overtly shows the reader the 'perhapses' of poetry writing itself, the process he goes through in trying to get from 'a' to 'b' of a narrative; the fruit that this bears is a highly unusual and difficult type of poetry. He constantly interrupts himself, leaving trails of dots for us to follow as thoughts tail off and into other thoughts. The traces of the process of a poem's construction are left on show as evidence of how it is produced, but because we are used to these traces and half thoughts being edited out, his poems are difficult reading. What aims to be a realistic representation of the flow of mental processes reads as stilted, stuttering parenthesis. In an effort to mimic the patterns of common speech Browning's verse frequently slips from self to self without formal signal:

> *Ay, because the sea's the street there; 't is arched by . . . what you call*
> *. . . Shylock's bridge with houses on it, where they keep the carnival:*
> *I was never out of England – it's as if I saw it all.*
> ('A Toccata of Galuppi's', Men and Women)

So one modernist effect of reading Browning is that he causes us to confront the process through which relevant information is usually selected or omitted, through which different textual registers are signalled. In its obscurity Browning's verse takes on the otherwise thematic problem of a dissolving subject and turns it into a question of form and syntax.

Gerard Manley Hopkins is a Victorian poet in the sense that he wrote mainly from 1875 to 1889, but his work was not published until 1918. There is a certain historical appropriateness to this delay, since his difficulty, and his interest in the ▷ Metaphysical poets, is akin to the modernists who turned to the English Renaissance as part of 'the direct current of English poetry' (T. S. Eliot). 'Difficulty' becomes the catch-word of early twentieth-century writing, a strategy for marking a distinction between modern writing and the nineteenth-century values of the reader-friendly text. Hopkins's contorted versification, syntactic twists, and dictive and rhythmic experimentation have confounded easy readings. His 'grand Perhaps' came at the point at which he started to 'doubt Tennyson', opening up another important emphasis of poetic modernism – its concern is to move away from the preciousness of nineteenth-century poetic diction to something more immediate, to the rhythms of common speech. It is paradoxical, then, that readers had become used to the strict versification of the Victorians, and to a specifically poetic vocabulary and range of images, and it is this faculty which has alienated them from modernism's attempt to deploy the language and images of the everyday. Hopkins's case is highlighted by his innovative rhythmic form – ▷ sprung rhythm – which was designed to bring into his verse the energies of ordinary speech. The syllabic stresses in his lines are syncopated, as they might be in a conversation. In 1877 he wrote to ▷ Robert Bridges,

> *Why do I employ sprung rhythm at all? Because it is the nearest to the rhythm of prose, that is the native and natural rhythm of speech, the least forced, the most rhetorical and emphatic of all possible rhythms, combining, as it seems to me, opposite and one wd.* (sic) *have thought, incompatible excellences, markedness of rhythm – that is rhythm's self – and naturalness of expression . . .*
>
> (21 August 1877)

His use of sprung rhythm is, however, one of the aspects of Hopkins's poetry which was considered most difficult, since difficulty is an indication of unfamiliarity.

In Hopkins's meticulous and characteristically Victorian visual powers, especially regarding the natural world, he prefigures ▷ D. H. Lawrence; he is not a poet of generalization, repeating tiny detail rather than broadly gesturing. But like his later imitator, ▷ Dylan Thomas, words unroll and suggest each other uncontrollably:

> *. . . now, barbarous in beauty, the stooks rise*
> *Around; up above, what wind-walks! what lovely behaviour*
> *Of silk-sack clouds! has wilder, wilful-wavier*
> *Meal-drift moulded ever and melted across skies?*
> ('*Hurrahing in Harvest*', 1877)

There is an (arguably unChristian) exuberance, a vision of excess, in Hopkins's verse, and in his philosophy of 'instresses' and 'inscapes' his Jesuitism becomes almost pantheistic. In touching the inscape of a thing – an image, or complex of images, a natural object or experience – poetry claims access to a vision of that thing's essential existence. This existence is communicated to the individual through an energetic pulse or channel – the 'instress' – which is opened between object and perceiver, if she or he is 'ready'. For Hopkins, poetry exceeds meaning; it is in his impulse to commune with the 'isness' of things, to allow material language to touch the thing itself through a poetic experience of epiphany, that Hopkins's modernity lies.

Hopkins's temptation to visit the dark night of the soul (particularly in the 'sonnets of desolation' of 1884–5) brings his later poems of despair close in their painful intensity to Thomas Hardy's bleakest work. Like Hopkins, Hardy is also a poet known for his use of common language and diction, and is quite literally a *fin de siècle* poet in his uniquely pessimistic and Schopenhauerian stance on passing from the old century into the new. Hardy's hopelessness looks forward and backward; a poem such as 'The Darkling Thrush' (1900) is both a poem of loss and a poem of dread, 'greeting' the twentieth century from a pivotal point which also implicitly glances backwards:

> So little cause for carolings
>   Of such ecstatic sound
> Was written on terrestrial things
>   Afar or nigh around,
> That I could think there trembled through
>   His happy good-night air
> Some blessed Hope, whereof he knew
>   And I was unaware.

Hardy, then, writes at the end point of a process and a century in which the self is gradually and systematically estranged from the familiar. Time is no longer simply the dimension of loss, but also that which brings the 'darkening dankness / The yawning blankness' ('The Going') of the future ever closer. His foreboding about what Yeats called (in 'Coole Park and Ballylee, 1931') the 'darkening flood' indeed prefigures much of late Yeats's feelings about the twentieth century.

The poetry of modernity

> The age demanded an image
> of its accelerated grimace,
> Something for the modern stage,
> Not, at any rate, an Attic grace
> ('Hugh Selwyn Mauberley', Ezra Pound; 1920)

'Less is more': Pound and Imagism

To mark the turn of the century as also a turning point in literature is a rather arbitrary gesture. English modernism established itself slowly, well behind the ▷ French precedent, and the first decade of the twentieth century was dominated by the popular conservatism of ▷ Georgian poetry. People read and enjoyed the poetry of ▷ A. E. Housman, ▷ Rudyard Kipling and ▷ Thomas Hardy, and eagerly bought the Georgian anthologies as they appeared from 1912 onwards. Georgianism perhaps epitomizes the popular notion of English poetry – parochial, solid and unironic, celebrating English rural life, particularly the home counties variety. Its importance lies in the way it fed into the poetry of World War I – many Georgians are better known as ▷ War poets – which sharpened nostalgia into something that could 'draw blood', especially in the later years as the full horror became apparent.

In order to emphasize how shocking modernist poetry was after the technical familiarity of writing up to 1910, I want to focus upon the Imagist (▷ Imagism) movement which, whilst not offering the most powerful or famous texts of the modernist period, certainly exemplifies much of what modernist verse was trying to achieve against Victorianism. '(T)he first heave' of modernism was, in poet Ezra Pound's words, 'to break the pentameter' ('Canto 81'). Pound was a great polemicist against what he called 'the crepuscular spirit in modern poetry' ('Revolt'). Certainly, much poetry of the late-Victorian period was supremely 'crepuscular', languid, pale and dreamy, and in his early so-called ▷ 'Celtic Twilight' period ▷ W. B. Yeats was rather prone to this. He had begun his writing career as a writer of the Victorian *fin de siècle*, and ended it as a key figure of modernist anti-decadence. His early poems are infused with an elegaic quality and peopled with mythological and heroic figures from an 'old Ireland' of ephemeral, supernatural beauty. There is a haunting sense of the inaccessible, characteristic of much Nineties poetry), which rejected earlier Victorians' building of 'brick and mortar inside the covers of a book' (Yeats, 'The Symbolism of Poetry'; 1900). This is Yeats the 'last romantic'.

But Yeats is also arguably the first modernist of poetry, his feeling of alienation from his time strengthening his later apocalyptic poems, which 'sing amid our uncertainty' ('Per Amica Silentia Lunae'; 1917). The cultural crisis of the early twentieth century turned the task of re-thinking the limits and drives of language into one of almost world-historic importance for many poets, impatient that the untenable realist notion of a shared common experience between writer and reader be exposed. If Yeats's early work is marked by a bygone aesthetic, and is metrically and syntactically conventional, his later work – particularly that written from *The Wild Swans at Coole* (1919) until his death in 1939 – would strongly assert his modernity, and was undoubtedly urged towards this point by Pound's influence.

The movement which exploded onto the poetry scene in 1912, of which Pound was initially a key member, sought to counter sloppy diction and to free verse from too much emotion. Later in the war years Imagism developed into the multi-art form movement Vorticism, publishing two polemical texts edited by poet and painter ▷ Percy Wyndham Lewis, *Blast* (1914 and 1915). Vorticism was a movement which brought writing and visual art together in a futuristic celebration of energy and speed. The anti-romantic figures of the 'Great English Vortex' included Wyndham Lewis and Ezra Pound, plus artists David Bomberg (1890–1957), Henri Gaudier Brzeska (1891–1915) and Jacob Epstein (1880–1959). Imagism in its purest form most aggressively countered Victorian versification, producing 'poetry that is hard and clear, never blurred or indefinite' (Preface to *Some Imagist Poets 1915*). Modernist poetry in this form intensifies and condenses; the poetry of modernity is written most strongly in the lyric form, rather than as narrative poems or epic novel-poems favoured by the Victorians. Imagism takes the emphasis on brevity to an extreme, its definitions being heavily reactive (just as its founders were politically reactionary), prescribing the new poetry negatively; in Pound's words modern poetry should be: 'Objective – no slither; direct – no excessive use of adjectives, no metaphors that won't permit examination . . . straight as the Greek!'

Imagism, then, rejected the use of loose simile and, like Hopkins in a different sense, strove to evoke the 'isness' of things: to present reality in a naïvely unmediated sense, avoiding flaccid re-presentation. For the Imagist, brevity is the soul of poetry: 'less is more'. Condensation counters verbiage, and so lyric poetry is put on a strict diet; in Pound's words, it is 'de-suetized':

> *Whirl up, sea –*
> *Whirl your pointed pines,*
> *Splash your great pines*
> *On our rocks,*
> *Hurl your green over us,*
> *Cover us with pools of fir.*
> ('Oread', H. D.)

This is a poem by H.D. (▷ Hilda Doolittle) in its entirety; indeed, 'Oread' (1915) is often tendered as the exemplary Imagist poem, with the complex of sea, pines and nymph fusing as image. Pound had defined the image as 'that which presents an intellectual and emotional complex in an instant of time'; H.D.'s text pares down superfluity to a series of discrete, sparse phrases. What the poem 'is' is the relation between these phrases, how they build up into an image which does not come from individual key words or vague feelings but from the ways in which the component elements of the poem *relate*.

This can be clarified by looking at an even shorter Imagist poem of Pound's, 'In a Station of the Metro':

> *The apparition of these faces in the crowd;*
> *Petals on a wet, black bough.*

It is perhaps hard today to recapture the feelings of shock which hit the first readers of these poems. It is no wonder that at this point in literary history poetry began to become perhaps the most unpopular of art forms. The difficulty of this text lies in its requirement that we simply *accept* it on its own terms, which brings it close to the oriental form of the *haiku*, much admired by Pound.

This text is also exemplary in its peculiar atmosphere and influences. In an effort to achieve delicate clarity, Imagist poetry deployed Japanese motifs, petals, hyacinth and lotus blossoms, and clear contours, and allowed itself to become emotional only in the dexterity with which these evoke feelings. Pound's 'Fan-piece, for her Imperial Lord' (1914) is as much about loss as any Victorian elegy, but is delicately rinsed free of heavy sentiment:

> *O fan of white silk,*
> *clear as frost on the grass-blade,*
> *You also are laid aside.*

Understated, it is also impersonal, a key word at this point and reinforced by T. S. Eliot's notion, in 'Tradition and the Individual Talent' (1919), that: 'Poetry is not a turning loose of emotion, but an escape from emotion; it is not the expression of personality, but an escape from personality'. Thus an Imagist poem may be poignantly posed, but it should not slide into agonized self-reflections or sentiment.

Language speaking: Eliot and the linguistic crisis

Modernist poetry not only demanded intensity, however; crucially it challenged the prevalent philosophy of language with which it was traditionally assumed nineteenth-century verse worked. This philosophy posited language as a transparent medium through which an unproblematic and undistorted 'reality' is represented. For the modernist poet language is emphasized and foregrounded to such an extent that it becomes the most important 'point' of the poem. Poetry scrutinizes the form, the contours, the material of the mask of language. As ▷ Samuel Beckett said of ▷ James Joyce, 'His writing is not *about* something; *it is that something itself.*'

Modernist writing is agonizingly self-conscious, probing its own limits and restrictions, foregrounding itself as text, as the interface of many texts. The process of poetry-writing becomes the object of poetry, so that the way a text is constructed, *how* it connotes many possibilities of meaning and many voices, becomes that which the poem is *about*. We can, perhaps, see why Browning was read with interest by many early twentieth-century poets. Modernism foregrounds form over content, or rather, it opens up for questioning the whole economy of language through which form and content are established as distinct and separate textual dimensions. Pound's later work, especially his long sequence of ▷ *The Cantos*, continually emphasizes its own materiality – the silken-folded mask betrays its own material construction. Alongside their other project of historical synthesis, *The Cantos* expose language as dirty, desirous splashes of ink; echoes of other languages intrude, typographical errors aren't edited out. Sometimes words are 'chosen' not for reasons of sense or meaning but because of the pattern they make on the page, how they sound, or how other words have suggested them. Chinese characters are included, asserting to the uncomprehending eye language's typographic existence. Pound's occasional rantings can seem more like the operation of a multi-lingual machine than a rational mind, reading rather like one enormous Freudian slip. As with many of Gertrude Stein's (1874–1946) texts and ▷ Surrealist automatic writing, words seem to suggest other words because of unconscious drives which are operating on the poem.

All of this has a profound bearing on how the role of the poet and of the reader is understood. A form of writing in which writing itself is so prioritized has also to re-write our understanding of who is 'responsible for' poetry – of who ultimately can guarantee its meaning. Despite the authoritarian postures adopted by particular modernist writers, poetry may be read as acknowledging that the position of both writer and reader is relative, non-omniscient, constructed by the forces of language. Furthermore, this sense of fragmentation has permeated the possibilities of writing to such an extent that the resultant feeling is that *all* possibilities of unity have been lost. Modernist poetry, in the words of Lewis Carroll's *The Hunting of the Snark* (1876), spurned 'merely conventional signs', navigating itself by a map which was: 'A perfect and absolute blank!' It thus affirms – against the desires of its writers, whose quest is still towards the lost home of stable selfhood and meaning – a problematization of the individual subject somewhat analogous to that enacted by Freudian ▷ psychoanalysis and Marxist political theory.

What these breaks in poetic consciousness and linguistic coherence were signalling was the chasm in personal and national identity which World War I brought to crisis point. The War poets, particularly ▷ Siegfried Sassoon, ▷ Wilfred Owen and ▷ Isaac Rosenberg, represented this breakdown thematically, but through pre-war structures of versification and diction. Modernist poetry was more like a linguistic acting-out of the destruction of innocence which took place in the trenches.

Modernism is also identifiable as the point at which writing acknowledges that it doesn't originate purely within the soul of the author; the modernist text plagiarizes shamelessly, building itself up out of a patchwork of unacknowledged quotations from a variety of international cultural sources, fragments 'shored against my ruins' ('What the Thunder Said', from T. S. Eliot's ▷ *The Waste Land*). This is its cosmopolitanism. *The Waste Land*, to the frustration of many an undergraduate reader, straddles eastern and western cultural history in a dazzling and maddening parade of name-dropping and references, which build up into a polemical lament for fallen culture. Geographically, modernism wasn't centred on one cultural-Imperial capital, but danced from London to Paris to Vienna to Berlin to New York to Dublin and back again. It cannot be situated, and this cultural uncertainty is, in *The Waste Land* at least, a symptom of decay:

> *What is the city over the mountains*
> *Cracks and reforms and bursts in the violet air*

> *Falling towers*
> *Jerusalem Athens Alexandria*
> *Vienna London*
> *Unreal*
>
> (*The Waste Land*, ll. 371–6)

Texts jump from 'home' to 'home', emphasizing how they are written 'intertextually' by a wide range of influences, and are a point at which an extraordinarily wide cultural memory is unlocked. Again, *The Cantos* are an extreme example of this in English poetry, as James Joyce's ▷ *Ulysses* is in the modern novel. The wandering poet has become poet-as-exile.

Ezra Pound was an energetic figure, tirelessly championing the modern and collaborating with T. S. Eliot in the preparation of *The Waste Land*, which is dedicated to Pound. Eliot's work is painfully aware of this crisis of the self, and its challenge to nineteenth-century writing is enormous. For Eliot, the lyric poem is 'the voice of the poet talking to himself, or to nobody'. But the manner of his 'talking' is quite bizarre, and shocking to our 'realist' expectations. Eliot's verse plays with and parodies traditional structures, the same poem oscillating in its versification and rhythms. Sometimes it comes near to solidity and fixity of form, only to dissolve into a much more fluid formal structure deploying, in his own words, a 'contrast between fixity and flux', and 'unperceived evasion of monotony'. *The Waste Land* exemplifies this, being an extreme example of formal eclecticism and teasing, a startling series of lyric fragments which jump schizophrenically from the sublimity of dream language to the ridiculousness of pub language and interrogate each through the other.

The problem of who writes is, then, accentuated by Pound's collaboration in the final editorial processing of *The Waste Land*, which caused Eliot to write 'I am never sure that I can call my verse my own'. So just who or what the poet's 'I' is at this stage in literary history is a painful problem, and Eliot's verse highlights this in several aspects. Thematically it often evokes disturbed mental states; in 'Rhapsody on a Windy Night' (1917), for instance, clear perception is distorted, objective reality is twisted to the point of frightening hallucination. A street-lamp tells the 'hero' about women's eyes, twisted 'like a crooked pin', and 'A crowd of twisted things' closes in. When he eventually reaches home, its safety turns out to be 'The last twist of the knife'. The figure of modernity characteristically has no home, wandering nomadically in a world stripped of values, in a shifting reality which confounds fixity in mental states. Many of Eliot's early poems seem close to the knife-edge of madness. 'Morning at the Window' (1917) consists of only two stanzas, the second an ugly, twisted rewriting of the relatively rational first, in which 'I' sits at a window looking on the street. This then becomes an experience subject to 'brown waves of fog' which toss twisted faces and tear smiles from passers by. The 'brown fog of a winter dawn' returns as the climactic condition of *The Waste Land*'s 'Unreal City'.

For Eliot the problem of poetry feeds into the problem of culture and its role in (Christian) society. In 'The Use of Poetry' (1933) he asserts that poetry must be able to account for the sordid and the horrific, the thought that (from Pound's 'Hugh Selwyn Mauberley') 'Caliban casts out Ariel':

> ... the essential advantage for a poet is not to have a beautiful world with which to deal: it is to be able to see beneath both beauty and ugliness; to see the boredom, and the horror, and the glory.

The Waste Land scrutinizes the grand dualism of beauty and ugliness and finds, in the critic and poet I. A. Richards's words, modernity's 'persistent concern with sex', which is then used as the lens through which history is seen as the history of progressive wastage. Just as 'Mauberley' reads the heroes of Victorian culture as the path to modernity's crisis, so The Waste Land re-reads history as a sordid parade, witnessed by the bisexual Tiresias who shuffles across its stage, and which climaxes in a series of sordid liaisons. Tiresias, an 'old man with wrinkled dugs', witnesses and foretells the sterility of heterosexual love. The double edges of Victorian discourse on sex indelibly mark and open up modernist writing. Indeed, pleasure occupies a very warped position in Eliot's corpus, a symptom of the need for a kind of communication and communion which he perceived was no longer possible. The desperate desire for, and the impossibility of, communication, is both a 'truth' of sexual relations and of modernist writing.

However unpalatably, Eliot foregrounded a politicization of writing which aestheticism had repressed in marking out Art for Art's sake against the political engagement of High Victorian writing. His statement, 'I am sojourning amongst the termites', in a letter to Lytton Strachey, speaks eloquently of both the actual immersion of modern poetry in the most sordid aspects of social life, and the depth of his right-wing repulsion. Eliot's treatment of human beings in his poetry can be obsessively cruel and vindictive. Indeed, the extremely reactionary politics of Yeats, Pound and Eliot are problematic, and often make their work painful reading for reasons other than 'difficulty'. Yeats's advocacy of an integrated poetry as 'blood, imagination, intellect, running together' ('Discoveries'; 1906) was undoubtedly informed by the intolerant social pressures which also produced D. H. Lawrence's 'blood conscious' reactionary politics, but it is equally symptomatic of a climate which made possible the more positive politicization of writing in the 1930s. As the 1920s closed, Eliot turned to high-church Anglicanism, and the emphasis in critical theory and poetic practice became that of unity rather than disintegration. For the Eliot of 'The Metaphysical Poets', modern poetry needed to heal the 'dissociation of sensibility' which occurred at the end of the seventeenth century, so that it could 'devour' the plethora of modern experience. In the 1930s this was interpreted as the need for a poetry which countered obscurity and unpopularity with the addressing of relevant social issues, or what ▷ George Orwell called 'the invasion of literature by politics'.

And not before time: as the western world spiralled towards economic breakdown, as unemployment rocketed, as Germany and Italy lurched into fascism, poets recognized that lack of commitment was tantamount to support of the right. ▷ W. H. Auden's poems of the very late 1920s are concerned with psychic landscapes, but in the 1930s his poetry became explicitly politicized and sought again to bridge the gap between theory and praxis in the pursuit of relevance, donning once more the mantle of moral guide. 'Thirties poetry' generally refers to the more politically engaged poetry of Auden, ▷ Stephen Spender, ▷ Louis MacNiece and ▷ C. Day Lewis, the group of left-wing, psychoanalytically informed poets who met in the early 1930s at Oxford. The work of this 'school' is characterized by three collections, all edited by Michael Roberts: *New Signatures* (1932), *New Country* (1933) and the 1936 *Faber Book of Modern Verse*. Through these texts poetry can be seen to become more explicitly concerned not only with diagnosing the world historic disease, but with prescribing a cure. If modernist poetry is antihumanist, showing the human subject as already subverted by desire, the poets of the 1930s re-humanized the subject, as an effective agent of political action.

Poetry since World War II

> Lay the coin on my tongue and I will sing
> of what the others never set eyes on.
>
> ('Desert Flowers', Keith Douglas; 1943)

H.D. and Douglas: seer and soldier

Although H.D. had begun publishing her intense verses when she was part of the Imagist group, her most important work was written during and after World War II. She wrote *Trilogy* (1944) whilst living through the London Blitz. The war had come home; never had British people been so subjected to its extremities of violence and terror as was the urban population in the Blitz. The poets of World War I were fighters at the front; those of World War II didn't have to go to war because the war came to them, and its violence marked texts as different as ▷ Roy Fuller's *A Lost Season* (1944), ▷ T. S. Eliot's *Four Quartets* (1935–42) and ▷ Edith Sitwell's 'Still Falls the Rain' (1940). H.D.'s *Trilogy* opens with a ruined London laid out like a sacrifice, but its tone is positive. Only barriers, boundaries, proprieties are destroyed:

> *there, as here, ruin opens*
> *the tomb, the temple; enter,*
> *there as here, there are no doors:* (. . .)
>
> *ruin everywhere, yet as the fallen roof*
> *leaves the sealed room*
> *open to the air,*
>
> *so, through our desolation,*
> *thoughts stir, inspiration stalks us*
> *through gloom . . .*

The *Trilogy* poems, like many of H.D.'s texts, draw on a wealth of female mythological and historic/heroic figures to spin together a text of new possibilities. H.D. turns destruction into a positive value: the last section of *The Walls Do Not Fall* describes the physical effects of the bombing, but turns debilitating doubt into a clear horizon of possibilities:

> *we know no rule*
> *of procedure,*
>
> *we are voyagers, discoverers*
> *of the not-known,*
>
> *the unrecorded;*
> *we have no map;*
>
> *possibly we will reach haven,*
> *heaven.*

Pessimistic texts have abounded since 1942 when this was written, but H.D. chooses to turn doubt into a possibility of affirmation, to stress the fact that negatives have been blasted away. Indeed, this last quotation could also be a statement about women's writing, which, in its marginalization from the canon and the difficulties of its being written at all, also knows no rule, is unrecorded, and has no map. Many post-war women poets have actively used their exclusion from the English poetic tradition as a fresh breathing space.

One of the most famous poets of World War II is undoubtedly ▷ Keith Douglas (1920–44) who was killed in Normandy, his corpus cut down but his influence disturbing writers in the post-war years. Anxious to make the right mark before it's too late, his perception is fired by the possibility of its termination, and in a clear, precise way is almost extra-sensory. On 'each side of the door of sleep' he finds a nightmare-scape in which sexual desire and unspeakable violence are inextricable. Sexuality comes into Douglas's poetry with cold images of death, corruption and violence. Rather like H.D.'s astonishment that the walls do *not* fall, Douglas finds an intensely positive desire in the midst of blasted desert and mindless military discipline. The murderer has 'a lover's face', and he is one of the:

> *kindly visitors who meant*
> *so well all winter but at last fell*
> *unaccountably to killing in the spring.*
> ('These grasses, ancient enemies'; 1941)

The poetry is in the chilling, clear, simple diction. Words themselves are militarized; poetry has always been in various guises the object of poetry, but in Douglas's case it is viewed as the soldier views his victim. In 'Words' (1943) it is scrutinized, as if (in George MacBeth's words) seen 'through the sights of a rifle':

> *. . . I lie in wait*
> *for them. In what the hour or the minute invents,*
> *in a web formally meshed or inchoate*
> *these fritillaries are come upon, trapped: (. . .)*
> *The catch and the ways of catching are diverse.*

Words are trapped by macabre war-scapes and dead faces;

> *. . . the pockmarked house . . .*
> *whose insides war has dried out like gourds*
> *attract words*

Trap and attraction are interchangeable words for Douglas; an image has already trapped its written description and all it needs is for the poet to close in for the kill.

Dylan Thomas and the Apocalypse

Certainly World War II was a watershed in British life, and in ▷ Charles Causley's words, 'The signature of murder' (in 'I Saw a Shot Down Angel') is scrawled across the history of writing since the war. If certain experiences, cold and macabre for Douglas, actively *attract* words, we need to ask what manner of themes and experiences have words 'found desirable' in the post-war period?

Perhaps the most famous 'forties poet', Dylan Thomas, had produced much of his most interesting and characteristic work before 1940, yet his verve and style exemplify that of the so-called 'New Apocalypse', which was carried through into the dry, sardonic 1950s by Thomas's disciple, ▷ W. S. Graham. 'Apocalypse' writing was unbridled, gloriously undisciplined and heavily emotional. In consequence one can see this moment in poetic history as pitted against Eliot's impersonality, H.D.'s spartan, hard verse, or the political engagement of 1930s poetry. It is important to acknowledge the power of this poetic movement before we can really understand the significance of the philosophies of the more famous and self-conscious movements of the 1950s and 1960s, which were very much, in turn, established in reaction to the Apocalyptics. Thomas's verse is famous for its exuberance and verbal excesses. Like the later poet ▷ Thom Gunn, Thomas often deploys syllabics to convey his sense of the natural world and himself in it rolling out of control. *Fern Hill* (1945) is perhaps typical; just as the 'I' who speaks it recalls roving and falling 'Down the rivers of the windfall light', the poem itself runs its 'heedless ways, / [Its] wishes raced through the house-high hay'; it seems to be driven, polemically and self-consciously, against the repression of formal disciplines, even though Thomas himself was in fact a meticulous and formally tight writer.

The apocalyptic poet would ostensibly free the riches, the thickness, of language from the boundaries of rationality. Thomas himself deploys bizzare juxtapositions to this end in his effort to conjure up unconscious powers; his incessant repetition connotes the power of unconscious rhythmicality when it doesn't simply irritate. In this he can perhaps be compared with Surrealist poets such as ▷ David Gascoyne or the American poet Robert Bly (b 1926), Gascoyne being a figure who continues to represent a certain disturbing undercurrent in English poetry, whose writing analyzes the relationship between language and the unconscious against the empirical grain of 1930s or 1950s poetry. Indeed, it could be said that Gascoyne *is* the unconscious of the English poetic establishment, repressed and marginalized for peculiar obsessions and failure to fit neatly into the ironic moulds of the 1950s, or the passionate egotism of the 1940s and 1960s. In asserting, in a way different from the modernists, that there is nothing common-sensical about reality, he remains resolutely anti-empirical.

In Surrealism obscurity takes on new powers. Dylan Thomas is nothing if not repetitive and obscure, but the Surrealist project is rather different in emphasis from his. Surrealism resists rational explanation; images are peculiarly juxtaposed so as to disrupt common-sense understandings and analogies. Gascoyne's 'Very Image' (1936) gathers a strange exhibition of surreal juxtapositions together:

> *And all these images*
> *and many others*
> *are arranged like waxworks*
> *in model bird-cages*
> *about six inches high.*

Why? Empiricism can do nothing with such incongruity; reading this requires not only a suspension of disbelief but a suspension of rationality – indeed, in 1936 the Surrealist poet Hugh Sykes Davies (b 1909) supplemented the word 'surreal' with the word 'surrational'. Working through every possible permutation of a statement, rearranging its order so as to unhinge sense and cause meaning to self-deconstruct is something which we also encounter constantly in, say, ▷ Samuel Beckett's novel *Watt* (1953). This technique is frequently used to explore the outer reaches of paranoia, and the disturbing meeting of mental illness and political repression, at which point, writes Hugh Sykes Davies, 'ANYTHING YOU SEE WILL BE USED AGAINST YOU' ('Poem' 1938).

To return to Dylan Thomas; his repetitiveness is of a different order, and his relationship with language is both more wilfully erratic than that of Surrealist poetry, and more superficial. If Douglas renders his words corpses with his rifle-pen and his sniper's eye, Thomas consciously throws himself into them as into a fierce alien element. He wants words to seduce him; he wants to be possessed. In 'Especially When the October Wind' (1934) the fact that language has already inhabited the 'I' is particularly clear. .is heart sheds 'syllabic blood' on hearing the raven speak; stick-trees and 'The wordy shapes of women' have a typographical significance; the 'rows' of children are 'star-gestured'. Beeches are 'vowelled', oaks have voices, the water speaks. From this plenitude of verbal nature and life-signs – 'The signal grass', 'the meadow's signs', 'the dark-vowelled birds' – Thomas reads his poem and re-writes it. Indeed, in reading he is also trying to liberate: poetic excess and sexual freedom are inextricable. Thus the incantatory element in Thomas is linked to an attempt to allow words to bleed into a plurality of significance, meanings and connotations, spinning off of their own volition. In the 1950s this verbal free-fall was denigrated as adolescent self-indulgence, and, indeed, on its own terms, there is something inescapably restrictive about Thomas's habit of repetition.

We can, perhaps clarify one of the positions of 1940s poetry through a statement Thomas made about his attitude to the image, in comparison with Pound's notion that an Imagist image is 'an intellectual and emotional complex in an instant of time':

> I let ... animage be 'made' emotionally in me and then apply to it what intellectual and critical forces I possess – let it breed another, let that image contradict the first, make, of the third image bred out of the other two together, a fourth contradictory image, and let them all, within my imposed formal limits, conflict ...
>
> (*Fifty Modern British Poets*, Michael Schmidt)

Such an errant fecundity had to end somewhere, and one ending was a fresh return to the hardness of a confined, complex Poundian image. The re-working of modernism, especially in its American form is, then, one important strand of contemporary poetry. But immediately on Thomas's heels came the ironic self-discipline of the ▷ Movement.

'No Renaissances, please': The Movement and the 1950s

> ... the minipoet is basically safe.
> not well equipped for (but who would think of)
> leaving the highway, he is attuned
> to the temporary surface, balanced,
> reliable, yes, we have few regret
> for the archpoet, who either would not start
> or starting stopped; was temperamental
> wanted to show off, steamed up, was punctured ...
>
> ['minipoet', *Miles Burrows 1966*]

The poetry of the ▷ Movement was, *par excellence*, that of post-war Anglo-Saxon rationalism. Like the famous car of the late 1950s, small but perfectly formed, the Movement poet was repulsed by grand gestures and took on the mask of a 'minipoet', 'slim, inexpensive, easy to discard / nippy rather than resonant, unpretentious' (Miles Burrows). Introducing the Movement anthology of 1956, *New Lines*, Robert Conquest (b 1917) wrote: 'It ... like modern philosophy – is empirical in its attitude to all that comes'. Movement poetry resists 'agglomeration of unconscious commands'; banished at a stroke to the soupy Romantic past are, it seems, all poetic forces which credit unconscious selves with the power to undermine conscious, common-sense control. It has often, then, been seen as the logical reaction to 1940s excesses. Movement poetry met excess with the wisdom of tradition. But which tradition? Certainly the work of 'the Georgians cultivating their gardens' (Stephen Spender); a stable tradition of homely, pre-modernist English writers such as Thomas Hardy and Wilfred Owen, whose descend-ants would include ▷ John Betjeman. Conquest, again, celebrates 'rational structure and comprehensible language' in his choice of verse, as does ▷ D. J. Enright both in his own humanistic, dry, anti-Romantic verse and in the poems he collected in the equally important Movement anthology of 1955, *Poets of the 1950s*. The Bible of the Movement was ▷ Donald Davie's critical work of 1952, *Purity of Diction in English Verse*, which supported stylistic discipline and verbal austerity; words should be rationed and undue extravagance curbed. In Davie's work the obvious parallels between the 1950s and the eighteenth century become concrete, his role being that of the spokesperson of the anti-Bohemian poetic age when he wrote:

> ... there is no necessary connection between the poetic vocation on the one hand, and on the other exhibitionism, egoism, and licence.
>
> (*Purity of Diction in English Verse*)

With the Movement English poetry again scaled itself down, and, clad in the hues of post-war Ealing movies, sardonically stated the primacy of the parochial and the provincial over the eclectic internationalism of modernism. ▷ Philip Larkin exemplifies Movement poetry, in his deflationary, perfectly formed phrases, and in his almost xenophobic stance against other cultures and cultural forms:

> ... to me the whole of the ancient world, the whole of classical biblical and mythology means very little, and I think that using them today not only fills poems full of dead spots but dodges the writer's duty to be original.
>
> ('Four Conversations', *The London Magazine*)

Larkin's provincialism was adamantly rooted in his life in Hull, and his resistance to London's literary elite. The south east's imperialization of other British cultures has since the 1960s found more energetic and positive forms in the growing importance of various regional poetic groups, from Northern Ireland, Newcastle, Scotland and Liverpool in particular. But the adamant Englishness of Larkin in the 1950s is another matter, and is itself beautifully deflated by the poet and critic ▷ Charles Tomlinson:

> Larkin's narrowness suits the English perfectly. They recognize their own abysmal urban landscapes, skillfully caught with just a whiff of English films c. 1950. The stepped-down vision of human possibilities (no Renaissances, please), the joke that hesitates just this side of nihilism, are national vices.

If these are vices, Larkin is an exemplary sinner, melancholically resigning himself to monochrome rather than confront the abyss. His poetic departure from the dominant romantic image of daring and heroism is beautifully epitomized by his poem, 'Poetry of Departures' (1955). The 'audacious, purifying, / Elemental' movements of romantic action are parodied in implicit praise of safety, order and domestic banality which is for Larkin at least genuine:

> So to hear it said
>
> He walked out on the whole crowd
> *Leaves me flushed and stirred,*
> *Like* Then she undid her dress
> *Or* Take that you bastard;
> *Surely I can, if he did?*
> *And that helps me stay*
> *Sober and industrious.*
> *But I'd go today*
>
> *Yes, swagger the nut-strewn roads,*
> *Crouch the fo'c'sle*
> *Stubbly with goodness, if*
> *It weren't so artificial . . .*

Larkin, then, is an ironic conformist; his poetry seems to be always already middle-aged. In 'Church Going' (1955) he responds to the divine by taking off his cycle-clips. Even in his passion for jazz music – he was an important jazz critic as well as poet – his stance is resolutely anti-forties, preferring traditional jazz and his patience ending where the fast pyrotechnics of be-bop begin. Sexual magic is regarded dispassionately:

> *. . . Why be out here?*
> *But then, why be in there? Sex, yes, but what*
> *Is sex? Surely, to think the lion's share*
> *Of happiness is found by couples – sheer*
> *Inaccuracy, as far as I'm concerned.*
>   ('Reasons for Attendance', 1955)

Other sides of nihilism: Gunn, Hughes, Plath

> *He tells you in the sombrest notes,*
> *If poets want to get their oats*
> *The first step is to slit their throats.*
> *The way to divide*
> *The sheep of poetry from the goats*
> *Is suicide.*
>   (James Fenton)

Post-Movement writers strove to break the 'minipoet' mould by formulating a poetics of irrationality and violence, reacting against genteel statements of common-sense experience. This reaction took various forms, particularly towards confessional writing, expressionism, and a further working through of the modernist techniques and internationalism which had been abandoned by the Movement. Georgian moderation was scorned, in favour of more primal passions.

Poetry has had to meet the abysmal possibilities of violence opened up after 1945 in some form or other, one way being an overt thematic acknowledgement of the exponential accumulation of military hardware and the lengthening nuclear shadow of the cold war years. The Movement had responded by consolidating safe images of a humane England for which the violations of tradition by modernists were simply interruptions or moments of forgetting. The latter stance was the consolation of the Movement. Writing 'death of god' poetry becomes a new and darker practice after the Holocaust, Dresden and Hiroshima, events which necessarily violated the pre-war idyll of a safe and sunny England. A. Alvarez, in his seminal introduction to the anthology of 1962, *The New Poetry*, echoes the title of Freud's pathbreaking text on the theory of the death drive (published just after World War I), *Beyond the Pleasure Principle*, when he writes that the new poetry of the early 1960s goes 'Beyond the Gentility Principle'. Alvarez collected together writing which partly reacted against the sobriety of the Movement, took more risks, was more confessional, and again explored pathological states of mind. Poet-as-man-next-door had become poet-as-victim. Alvarez's prescription was taken up particularly in the intense and grotesque work of ▷ Ted Hughes, ▷ Sylvia Plath, ▷ Peter Redgrove, and American expressionists Robert Lowell (1917–77) and John Berryman (1914–72). Both Freud and Alvarez are observing modern forces of disintegration in developing their theories of psychic and poetic development. Alvarez writes:

Theologians would call these forces evil, psychologists, perhaps, libido. Either way, they are the forces of disintegration which destroy the old standards of civilization. Their public faces are those of two world wars, of the concentration camps, of genocide, and the threat of nuclear war.

(The New Poetry)

In the 1960s British poetry begins to affirm more strongly these disturbing aspects of the human psyche and its twentieth-century productions.

Given the clear rational tone of much Movement work, and the at times passionate violence of much post-Movement poetry, one is tempted to superimpose the reaction from Movement to post-Movement onto the old Enlightenment/Romantic binary, especially since Davie's overt championing of Augustan (▷ Augustanism) values. However, the simplicity of such an opposition would be challenged by the work of someone like ▷ Thom Gunn, who uses elements from both poetic worlds. He is something of a bridging figure between the Movement poets, particularly Larkin, and the early 1960s poets, particularly Ted Hughes. On the surface, and from the

point of view of his work in the 1960s, Gunn could not be further from
Larkin, especially when he celebrates the heroes of rock and roll, the
Hemingwayesque swaggerers, 'stubbly with goodness'. When Gunn's poetry
crosses the Atlantic it goes on the road – 'On the Move' (1957), with an
epigram from Marlon Brando and signed just 'California', is typical – and
formally Gunn's work in the 1960s, lavish and energetic, took him towards
more fluid forms and free verse. But in a couplet from his poem of 1955, 'To
Yvor Winters', he anticipates this move from 'Rule' to 'Energy', and unfolds
a Blakean umbrella across his corpus to cover both 1950s reason and 1960s
passion – at its most effective, a twentieth-century marriage of rational
heaven and energetic hell:

> You keep both Rule and Energy in view,
> Much power in each, most in the balanced two.

What, then, of Energy? Ted Hughes is a writer known for his Romanticism,
his evocations of violence and vitalistic cruelty. He is often a very disturbing
writer, showing how the idyll of England reinvoked in the 1950s is already
subverted or betrayed from within by the 'stirrings beyond sense' which
ghost control and self-possession. 'Esther's tomcat' sleeps by day on the mat
but by night 'Walks upon sleep . . . over the round world of men'; Thrushes
aren't safely part of an English country garden but are 'more coiled steel
than living'; a skylark is 'shot through the crested head / With the command,
Not die'. Hughes's verse draws strongly on mythological motifs and can
seem over-written; breaking with the parochialism of the Movement, it
unearths as well as savagery the sinister and harrowing visions of a volume
such as *Crow* (1970).

Hughes's work serves as relief for several comparisons which could be
made at this point. Conceptually it owes much to Freud and Lawrence, who
meet at the point in his verse where it becomes clear that violence and
human repression are inextricably part of the same mechanism, civilization
engendering a more insidious violence bred of repression itself. But he is
quite starkly not a liberationist writer like Dylan Thomas or Lawrence, as he
bleakly emphasizes the closure or inevitability of this mechanism. Other
authorial personae exist, of course, in his children's poetry, his critical essays,
even in his efforts as Poet Laureate, where Hughes the painfully private poet
becomes public property. As part of a new wave in poetry – confessional,
naked, anguished – which looked back in anger at 1950s self-satisfaction,
Hughes exemplified the impolite twist which Alvarez celebrates, and in this
is often compared with the work of Sylvia Plath, primarily because they were
married until 1962 and worked closely together. Hughes was also a strong
champion of Keith Douglas, and marks of disintegration brought to
consciousness by the war are foregrounded by their poetic relation. Finally,
in his Romantic extravagance Hughes's work can be contrasted with that of
those poets who picked up the loose ends of modernism.

These links coalesce at the point at which the 'I' of the poem or poet
needs to be discussed. Again questions of the poet's identity and of his or her

relationship to the text and its context, to writing as public or private are brought to the fore. One way into this problem is to look briefly at the work of Charles Tomlinson, whose resistance to the influences of Thomas in the late 1940s made him turn to the precision of American modernism; he wrote 'here was a clear way of going to work, so that you could cut through this Freudian swamp and say something clearly'. The image of Pound and Eliot cutting through the Georgian 'swamp' and returning to the intellectual hardness of the Metaphysical poets has an uncanny echo in Tomlinson's practice; his 'I' is a problematic entity, rather like Eliot's. It is marginalized but, since something of a process of self-conscious depersonalization is being enacted it takes centre-stage in its impersonality. His attempt to objectify the image, resisting Thomas's emotionalism and surreal obscurity, echoes the austerity of the Imagist project: in his own words he wants to give his images 'The hardness of crystals, the facets of cut glass'. The title of his 1960 volume *Seeing is Believing* emphasizes his attempt to bring together Movement empiricism with Imagism's valuation of visual clarity.

Compare, for instance, Tomlinson's 'Fox' with Hughes's 'Thought-Fox'. Tomlinson's animal is dead in the snow, it has a sharp correctness but in the shifting romantic blizzard gives up its own existence and becomes an image of the hill itself. Tomlinson has to work hard against the drive of his poem to slide into a chaos of white and crosswinds with his mind at the confused centre:

> . . . *the drift still mocked*
> *my mind as if the whole*
> *fox-infested hill were the skull of a fox*

The image of hill-as-skull crystalizes from the blinding blizzard of this text. Hughes's poem begins, however, with fox-as-text; where Tomlinson's fox-skull and hill are 'out there' and the poet's job is to respect and accord them this objective autonomy, Hughes's fox finds his quickness only inside the interior of the poem, the writing of which depends upon a poetic incorporation of the natural world. For Hughes there is no critical distance which gives the image outline; the fox is already inside the self, actually entering the human skull ('the dark hole of the head'), becoming subject to the desire of writing, so that the page can be printed. Similarly, Tomlinson's hawk in 'How still the Hawk' hangs purely 'out there', innocent in its distance from human interpretation, whereas Hughes's 'Hawk Roosting' famously signifies the sinister, cold egotism of the totalitarian personality – Hughes's hawk has a subjective existence, so that it speaks the poems from the point of view of a post-war 'I'. The stillness of the hawk's image is for Tomlinson, then, a challenge to objectivism, for Hughes a point of aberrant control in the maelstrom of modern cruelty, whilst for Dylan Thomas in 'Over Sir John's Hill' it was a moment of emotionally intense poise:

> *Over Sir John's Hill,*
> *The hawk on fire hangs still;*
> *In a hoisted cloud, at drop of dusk, he pulls to his claws.*

The dialogue between these poems, then, serves to illustrate the familiar modern dichotomy in British poetry, that of the privileging of inside or outside. Is poetic writing an attempt to clarify as succinctly as possible the autonomous and the objective, or is it an act of poetic individuation and self-definition? The Romantic question – ▷ Coleridge's notion that poet and poem are indistinguishable – often recurs at this moment in poetic history as the dilemma between confessional, violent, personal writing and a post-war form of Imagism, like Tomlinson's, or like the precise and abrupt decompositional writing of ▷ Christopher Middleton. Who, then, is the poet? Is he or she now dead, like other authors in the ▷ post-structuralist world? And how does the fresh political engagement of the 1980s affect this question? The problem of the self and its relations to writing is intensified as personal subjectivity is viewed increasingly suspiciously in recent times. The question of objectivity, of the subjectivity of the poet and the status of his or her images, which clearly Tomlinson is engaging with, becomes a sharper problem in the 1980s with the increased politicization of radical poetic writing, and, in another form, with the distorted perceptions of 'Martian eye' (▷ Martian poetry) writing. I shall return to this shortly.

Sylvia Plath is, like Keith Douglas, another untimely poet, who wrote four brilliant and disturbing slim volumes of poetry in the early 1960s, three of which were published well after her suicide in 1963. It is hard to read Plath's verse outside the enormous interest in her private life which has burgeoned since her death; in modern mythology she exemplifies the self-consciously tragic poetic genius-figure. The nature of her death also evokes a more disturbing myth, that of the woman writer wracked by neurosis and too weak in body to contain her talent. Whoever Plath was, there is no doubt that her work relentlessly pursues the question of the 'I', of poetry and madness, with all Douglas's desire of words for words. The 'late mouths' of 'Poppies in October' which 'cry open / In a forest of frost' cause her to ask 'O my God, what am I?'; to whom do the poppies come, like a macabre gift, suggesting bleeding in ambulances? There is warfare in her work, a sharp killer's eye and a grotesque but erotic drive. A bleeding, fizzing cut across her thumb is the result of an Indian scalping, a sabotage, a Kamikaze act, a symptom of masochism. The image of blood as the running of 'A million soldiers . . ., / Redcoats, every one' ('Cut') is typically acute, almost humorous, but bites with paranoia as she then asks, 'Whose side are they on?' The sinister possibility that one's own flowing blood could be one's enemy speaks the psychological complexity of Plath's work, which never rests in the notion of anguish as 'authentic'. Cruel humour and ruthless self-suspicion undermine sincerity; arrogance and tragic self-glorification are deflated in 'Lady Lazarus', as suicide is paraded with the grotesque props of concentration camps:

> *Dying*
> *Is an art, like everything else.*
> *I do it exceptionally well.*

> *I do it so it feels like hell.*
> *I do it so it feels real.*
> *I guess you could say I've a call.*

Plath's 'reality' is not that of the every-day Movement, but that is not to say that her work can be marginalized as a depoliticized expression of private agonies; she was acutely aware of the political nature of writing for a woman, and insists on drawing parallels between her experience and disturbing political and historical reality. If she is a personal writer it is because, in the phrase coined by 1960s feminism, 'the personal is the political': 'Daddy' is as much about the powers of horror, opened up by post-war images of death camps and fascist obsession, as it is a text working through a daughter's ambivalent relationship with her father. As Plath said in an interview just before she died, poetry 'should be generally relevant, to such things as Hiroshima and Dachau'. Plath gazes straight at taboo, where a writer like ▷ Peter Porter, in 'Annotations of Auschwitz' for instance, looks satirically sideways at it. Porter's 'Your Attention Please' casts a black-comic nuclear shadow, whilst reminding us of something we meet constantly in Plath's work: 'Death is the least we have to fear'. 'Lady Lazarus' comes back,

> *Out of the ash*
> *I rise with my red hair*
> *And I eat men like air.*

'A dangerous weapon': contemporary poetry

> *I am neither internee nor informer;*
> *An inner émigré, grown long-haired*
> *And thoughtful; a wood-kerne*
>
> *Escaped from the massacre*
> ('Exposure', Seamus Heaney)

The crisis of writing and identity which is traced here as infecting British poetry has recently reached fever pitch. The problems of what constitutes a poem and of who the poet is have more recently become politicized into questions about what constitutes the *British* in 'British poetry'. Poets now, be they black, female or Irish have felt themselves to be 'inner émigrés': as Guyanan-born poet John Agard (b 1949) writes 'I didn't graduate / I immigrate', 'Listen Mr Oxford Don' (1985). The phrase 'poetry in English' is compromised by other voices from Ireland, Scotland, regions of England, and the Commonwealth (▷ Commonwealth literature). From a traditional point of view it seems that English poetry is slowly undergoing an undignified death-process, that the incorporation of other voices into 'Eng. Lit.' constitutes the blowing into oblivion of a much-cherished friend. More energetically and optimistically we could say, rather, that what is gaining prominence is a kind of 'multiverse', a plurality of accents and experiences breaking open the poised egocentric tradition. From going 'Beyond the Gentility Principle' we reach the late 1980s with poet and critic Eric Mottram's assertion that the modern *avant garde* constitutes 'A Treacherous Assault on British Poetry' (*The New British Poetry*; 1988). The literary critic Colin MacCabe writes, 'It is perhaps no longer appropriate to talk of English literature but of a literature in broken English':

> *If the members of the United Kingdom are all nominally British, it is instructive to recall that English as a language has been imposed, often by force, throughout the British Isles. And the peoples of those islands find that along with the imposed language they have acquired a literature to which their relationship is profoundly ambiguous – one need only think of Joyce or MacDiarmid to realise exactly how ambiguous.*
>
> (McCabe, 'Broken English', *Futures for English*, 1988)

This realization began to find some purchase in British poetry in the mid- 1960s, although it is true that in a different way internationalist strains in modernist writing had already undermined the notion of a truly English culture. From the regional focus which constituted much poetic activity during the 1960s, to the broad cultural base of much radical poetry today, British writing now can be defined only as a space within which its vital differences are affirmed. It has many homes: Trinidad-born poet John Lyons now resides in Britain but has left a nomadic trail leading back to his 'Island Muse':

> *I come long years with my pen*
> *and island hauntings*
> *from where my navel string tree*
> *still grows.*

Thus poetry split its focus into a thriving network of regional groups, in the Mordern Tower poets of Newcastle, who found their mentor in the re-discovered ▷ Basil Bunting, and the new renaissance of poetry from Northern Ireland which has emerged as contemporaneous with the troubles, from poets such as ▷ Seamus Heaney, ▷ Paul Muldoon and ▷ Derek Mahon. The emphasis was resolutely anti-London and the cultural imperialism of the south-east. The famous 'Liverpool poets' of the early and mid-1960s – Adrian Henri (b 1932), Henry Graham (b 1930), Roger McGough (b 1937) and Brian Patten (b 1946), collected in the anthologies *The Mersey Sound* (1967) and *New Volume* (1983) – were a British version of American Beat poetry. All four had strong links with the world of pop music, and emphasized poetry as live performance, thus opening up their writing to a wide young audience. Like pop art, Mersey poetry uses the familiar images of throwaway culture in its quick-fire surreal humour, but the effect is ultimately naughty rather than revolutionary. Pop art and pop music found their way into poetry at this time as never before, and the link between rock and writing was kept bubbling underground in the late 1960s largely due to the ministrations of the poet and publisher Michael Horovitz (b 1935) – his magazine *New Departures*, founded in 1959, had long been the organ of the poetic underground, and his anthology *Children of Albion* (1969) exemplifies a late-1960s celebration of liberation politics and poetics, taking ▷ Blake as mentor. Whilst it is true that much *avant garde* writing in the 1960s and 1970s displays the preoccupations of the economically privileged young British middle classes, it also eventually encouraged a certain disrespect – against the gentility principle once more – which opened a space for the more multi-racial and working-class forms of punk, dub, reggae poetry, and New Wave performance in the late 1970s.

The regionalist movement was roughly contemporary with the establishment of a large number of small presses, through which more experimental and *avant garde* work found a space outside the mainstream monolithic publishing houses, just as the high street bookshop's failure to sell marginalized writing urged poets into using local live outlets for their work. The small presses, often set up by poets themselves, have effectively countered the overwhelming influence of the major houses like Chatto & Windus and Faber & Faber – Faber in particular has long dominated poetry publication and in effect established the official canon of post-war and contemporary verse. Aesthetic valuation has seldom walked so nakedly in the profit margins. So the small presses have been vital in countering profitable orthodoxies: names such as Gael Turnbull's Migrant Press, Peterloo Poets, Stuart Montgomery's Fulcrum, Andrew Crozier's Ferry, Desmond Johnson's Akira and Ian Hamilton Finlay's Wild Hawthorn, in conjunction with small magazines like *Stand*, *Poetry Information* and *Agenda*, have over the years given younger and more experimental writers a space within which to work and have access to publishing facilities. In 1971 the champion of experimental and post-modernist work Eric Mottram was made editor of the Poetry Society's *Poetry Review*, an unprecedented move, as a result of which other forms of writing found a voice through the National Poetry Centre, until the scandalous dissolution of the editorial board by the ▷ Arts Council in 1977.

It must be said, however, that these energies remain fired partly by the task of countering the familiar conservatism of the poetic establishment. Two of the larger publishing houses, Anvil Press and Carcanet Press, are indeed open to more obscure and challenging types of modern writing, but Carcanet's statement of its aesthetic policy when it was established in 1969 displays a continued cherishing of bourgeois 'reasonable' traditions. Something of this survived in the compilation of the much criticized 1982 anthology, *The Penguin Book of Contemporary British Poetry*, edited by Blake Morrison (b 1950) and Andrew Motion (b 1952), which collected together a chic, sophisticated body of modern verse, challenging nothing, and punctuated for bizarre effect only by sideways glances from the 'Martian eyes' of ▷ Craig Raine and Christopher Reid.

The modernist question of homelessness has recently been rearticulated by women poets as a problem of one's tradition and one's literary home; women's writing continues to disrupt the smooth contours of the traditional mask. As a woman writer, where does one come from? ▷ Denise Levertov's verse is unsettling in its sense of exile, echoing ▷ Virginia Woolf's '. . . as a woman I have no country'. ▷ Ruth Fainlight's work also knows no fixed identity; a multitude of feminine voices insinuate threats or coaxings from between its lines. Her poems are populated by female 'others' – Sibyls, forgotten sisters, 'Stone-Age' selves, Medusas, 'Sophia, Anima, Kali', 'Gloria', 'Lilith' or the faces in the mirror. They speak to free the texts 'from whomsoever's definition: / Jew, poet, woman'.

Levertov's verse protests strongly against the stench of war and her adoptive America's aggression. Like Douglas, it exults in moments lived as if at 'the last minute', intensified by the consciousness of ending. Death breathes across the still, awestruck poems, 'Living', 'Passage', '. . . That Passeth All Understanding', a finitude which concentrates; if her poetry is spiritual it is so because it exists in the shadow of oblivion:

> *The fire in leaf and grass*
> *so green it seems*
> *each summer the last summer*
> ('Living')
>
> *a day of spring, a needle's eye*
> *space and time are passing through like a swathe of silk*
> ('Passage')

The intense interest in women's writing since the 1960s has, then, been important both to the ▷ women's movement and in opening up literature to a variety of other voices. Indeed, opening up the canon of contemporary poetry has occurred from inside poetry itself. Modernism's amalgamating energies, which brought many other languages and voices forth from the crevices of the silken-folded mask, has been realized in a less authoritarian form since the 1960s. Almost as soon as a new contemporary canon could gather itself, it was eroded by a wave of work penned by black writers, women writers – a self-consciously politicized alternative. Canon challenging has, then, recently been more than an academic exercise, especially since poetry now is written from an acute awareness of the possibilities of academic incorporation and judgement.

MacCabe's punning phrase 'Broken English' suggests both a body terminally injured and broken open, ready for new growth – we are back, perhaps, with H.D.'s celebration of the destruction of restrictive models, which for John Agard again can be achieved armed only 'wit mih human breath / but human breath / is a dangerous weapon'. If the impetus of 1960s poetry was an urge to harmony, that of the 1980s is an affirmation of difference, as the teeming voices of other cultural forms (the language of reggae, for instance) breaks out from the broken body of 'Eng. Lit.':

> *I dont need no axe*
> *to split/ up yu syntax*
> *I dont need no hammer*
> *to mash/ up yu grammar*
> ('Listen Mr Oxford Don', John Agard; 1985)

'Tradition' continues to be a problem, but one which contemporary poetry counters through a strategy of incorporation. Modern poetry uses its marginalization and the elements of literary crisis to form something which has not only a future but many futures, as many futures as there are cultural forms and languages to contribute. What is being affirmed is, then, a process of inoculation; the crisis passes as new forms of writing learn how to grow from that which formerly threatened and marginalized. To paraphrase Nietzsche, what doesn't kill literature makes it stronger. The mask slips – the canon is being opened from within.

Reference section

Aaron

In the ▷ Bible, the founder of the Jewish priesthood; he assisted ▷ Moses in leading the Jews out of Egypt to the frontiers of Canaan, the 'Promised Land'. His rod was a sacred emblem which Moses and he held up above the battle when the Jews were fighting the Amalekites (*Exodus* 17). The novel *Aaron's Rod* (1922) by ▷ D. H. Lawrence, is about a coal-miner who transforms his life with the aid of his flute.

Abbey Theatre, Dublin

The home of the Irish National Theatre Society from 1904 until a fire destroyed the building in 1951. The Society, usually known by the name of its theatre, grew from a fusion of the Irish National Dramatic Company, led by the actor W. G. Fay, and the Irish Literary Theatre founded by the poet ▷ W. B. Yeats, his friend Lady ▷ Gregory and others. The time was propitious: there was an intense national feeling in Ireland and an accompanying literary revival; Europe was undergoing the awakening influences of ▷ Ibsen and ▷ Strindberg; Yeats was a major poet with strong interest in the drama. Consequently the Abbey Theatre was a focus for creative energies which made it a unique institution in the history of the English-speaking theatre. However, the movement was neither the mere mouthpiece of Irish patriotism, nor just a vehicle for European fashions. Though Ibsen was a stimulus and dominated at least one of the Irish dramatists (Edward Martyn), its most outstanding contributor, ▷ J. M. Synge, was in reaction against Ibsen, as was Yeats himself. Neither of them tolerated the prejudices of the more radical nationalists. Synge's masterpiece, ▷ *The Playboy of the Western World*, caused a riot in the theatre when it was produced there in 1907. Yeats used verse of increasing vigour and austerity in a renewal of poetic drama that ranked the Abbey with the most interesting experimental theatres of the time in Europe – the Théâtre Libre in Paris and the Freie Bühne in Berlin. The heroic period of the Abbey Theatre ended with Synge's death and Yeats's retirement from its management in 1909; but under Lennox Robinson the Abbey remained a theatre of distinction. Its most notable playwright after that time was ▷ Sean O'Casey.
▷ Irish literature in English.

Abel

▷ Cain.

Abelard, Peter (1079–1142)

A philosopher in the University of Paris early in the 12th century. At the height of his fame he fell in love with a young girl, Heloise (Eloise), and became her tutor. She bore him a child and to appease the anger of her uncle, Abelard proposed that they should be secretly married; open marriage was out of the question as it would obstruct Abelard's career in the Church. The marriage took place against Heloise's wishes, for she did not want her lover to risk his future prospects for her sake, and she refused to admit to it when challenged to do so. She took refuge in a convent, and her uncle revenged himself on Abelard by causing him to be castrated. Thereafter a famous correspondence took place between them. Abelard continued his career as a teacher but, at the instigation of Bernard of Clairvaux, he was eventually condemned for heresy (1141). The trial broke his health, and he died; his remains were secretly conveyed to Heloise, who died in 1164 and was buried in the same grave. The remains of both are now interred together in Père Lachaise. Their love affair became legendary and the subject of imaginative literature. ▷ Alexander Pope's *Eloisa to Abelard* (1717) is a poem on the subject. ▷ George Moore's novel, *Héloïse and Abélard*, appeared in 1921. There is also a novel by Helen Waddell, *Peter Abelard* (1933).

Abigail

In the Bible (*1 Samuel* 25), the wife of ▷ King David. In addressing him, she calls herself 'thine handmaid'. ▷ Beaumont and ▷ Fletcher gave the name Abigail to a 'waiting-gentlewoman' in their play *The Scornful Lady*. From this, the name came to be used generically in English, for superior women servants.

Abraham (Abram)

In the ▷ Bible (*Genesis* 12–25), the legendary founder of the Jewish nation, and first of the Patriarchs (racial ancestors). He is represented as a nomadic chieftain or 'sheikh' who is directed by God (Yahweh, Jehovah) into the land of Canaan, with promises that in return for his obedience to God's will he is to become the father of a great nation. His only legitimate son is ▷ Isaac, by his wife Sarah; however, he has other sons by his concubines who became the forebears of the hostile tribes which surrounded Israel in the Old Testament. An important episode is that in which Abraham obeys God's command to sacrifice Isaac, for whom a young ram is substituted at the last moment.

Absalom and Achitophel (1681)

A ▷ satire in heroic couplets by ▷ John Dryden, allegorizing the political crisis of the last years of ▷ Charles II in terms of the (▷ Bible) Old Testament story of King David and his rebellious son Absalom (2 *Samuel* 13–19). Charles had no legitimate son and his heir was his brother James, Duke of York, a professed ▷ Catholic, whose succession was feared by many as a menace to the Church of England and the liberty of Parliament. The ▷ Whigs, led by Anthony Ashley Cooper, the ▷ Earl of Shaftesbury, introduced a Bill excluding James from the throne and substituting Charles's illegitimate son, the ▷ Duke of Monmouth. Dryden wrote his poem at the king's suggestion, in order to influence the public against the Whigs. His handling of the biblical story glamorized the king, by paralleling his licentiousness with that of the patriarch David, and represented the Whigs as anarchic enemies of God's anointed. Monmouth becomes Absalom, Shaftesbury becomes the evil tempter Achitophel, the Duke of Buckingham appears as Zimri, and ▷ Titus Oates as Corah. Part II, which was published in 1682, is mainly by ▷ Nahum Tate, but includes a vivid passage by Dryden (ll 412–509) satirizing the poets ▷ Settle and Shadwell under the names Doeg and Og.

Abse, Dannie (b 1923)

Poet. Abse was born in Cardiff, and trained as a doctor in Cardiff and London. His volumes of verse include: *After Every Green Thing* (1949); *Tenants of the House* (1957); *A Small Desperation* (1968); *Selected Poems* (1970); *Way Out in the Centre* (1981); *Collected Poems, 1948–1976* (1977). He has also written novels and plays.

Absurd, Theatre of the

▷ Theatre of the Absurd.

Achebe, Chinua (b 1930)

Nigerian novelist, poet and short-story writer. Born Albert Chinualumogu in Ogidi, East Central State, his mother tongue is Ibo, but he studied English from an early age and in 1953 graduated in English Literature from University College, Ibadan. He has worked in radio, publishing, journalism and as an academic, visiting universities in the U.S.A. In his five novels he has successfully incorporated African idioms and patterns of thought in a lucid English prose style. *Things Fall Apart* (1958), with its title drawn from ▷ W. B. Yeats's poem 'The Second Coming', explores a principal African dilemma; the destruction of the indigenous culture by European influence. It concerns Okonkwo, a village leader whose inflexible adherence to tradition cannot withstand the influence of white missionaries. *No Longer At Ease* (1960) continues the theme of the conflict of African and European values, but in the urban context of Lagos in the 1950s. *Arrow of God* (1964) returns to tribal society, but at an earlier stage of colonialism, in the 1920s, while *A Man of the People* (1966) is again set in Lagos, with direct reference to the turbulent political events following Nigerian independence in 1960. His most recent novel, *Anthills of the Savannah* was published in 1987. He has published two volumes of short stories, *The Sacrificial Egg* (1962) and *Girls at War* (1972) and two volumes of poetry: *Beware Soul-Brother and Other Poems* (1971) and *Christmas in Biafra and Other Poems* (1973). He also writes children's stories.

Bib: Lindfors, B., and Innes, C. L. (ed.), *Achebe.*

Achilles

▷ *Iliad.*

Acrostic

A literary game in which the initial letters of the lines of a poem spell a word when read downwards in order.

> *Kind sister! aye, this third name says you*
>   *are;*
> *Enchanted has it been the Lord knows*
>   *where.*
> *And may it taste to you like good old wine,*
> *Take you to real happiness and give*
> *Sons, daughters and a home like honied*
>   *hive.*

The initial letters spell 'Keats'; and it is the third verse of an acrostic poem to Georgiana Augusta Keats, by her brother-in-law ▷ John Keats. A double acrostic can also be read downwards with the last letters of each line.

Act

In politics: a law which has been passed through both Houses of ▷ Parliament and accepted by the monarch. Until this process is completed, it is called a Bill.

In drama: a division of a play; acts are sometimes subdivided into scenes. The ancient Greeks did not use divisions into acts; the practice was started by the Romans, and the poet-critic ▷ Horace (1st century BC) in his *Ars Poetica* laid down the principle that the number of acts should be five. Since the renaissance of classical learning in the 16th century, most dramatists have used act divisions, and many have obeyed Horace's precepts. All ▷ Shakespeare's plays are divided into acts and scenes in modern editions, but it is certain that he did not write them in labelled scenes, and uncertain whether he thought in terms of acts; some of the first printed versions of his plays show act divisions and some do not.

Acting, The Profession of

Acting began to achieve recognition as a profession in the reign of ▷ Elizabeth I. The important date is the building of The Theatre – the first theatre in England – by ▷ James Burbage in 1576. It was followed by many others in London, and theatres soon became big business. Previously, actors had performed where they could, especially in inn yards and the halls of palaces, mansions, and colleges. They continued to do so, but the existence of theatres gave them a base and (though they still required an official licence) independence such as they badly needed in order to win social recognition.

Until the mid-16th century acting was practised by many kinds of people: ordinary townsmen at festivals, wandering entertainers, boys and men from the choirs of the great churches, and members of the staffs of royal or aristocratic households. It was from these last that the professional actors emerged. They still wore the liveries – uniforms and badges – of the great households, but the connection was now loose (good performers could transfer from one household to another) and was chiefly a means of procuring a licence to perform. This licence was essential because the City of London, around which dramatic activity concentrated, feared the theatre as providing centres of infection for the recurrent ▷ plague epidemics (which from time to time sent the companies away on tour) and disliked acting as a morally harmful and anomalous way of life. Moreover, the royal court, which favoured the stage, was nonetheless on guard against it as a potential source of sedition. Censorship and licensing, however, had the advantage of helping to distinguish the serious performers from the vulgar entertainers.

By the time of Elizabeth's death two great companies were dominant: the ▷ Lord Chamberlain's Men, for whom ▷ Shakespeare wrote, and the ▷ Lord Admiral's Men, headed by the leading actor of the day, ▷ Edward Alleyn. Women did not perform; their parts were taken by boys who enlisted as apprentices. Companies of boy actors from the choirs of St Paul's and the Chapels Royal also had prestige (see ▷ *Hamlet* II.2), especially in the 1570s. The establishment of the profession owed most to the dramatists, but much to the energy of actor-managers and theatre proprietors such as ▷ Philip Henslowe, Edward Alleyn, James Burbage, and his son Richard.

Actresses were allowed to perform after the ▷ Restoration of the monarchy (1660). The status of the profession continued to rise, aided by the theatre's ceasing to be the entertainment of all classes and becoming a fashionable pleasure of the London West End. In the 18th century the genius and culture of ▷ David Garrick greatly enhanced the prestige of the profession. From his time on, there is a long roll of great acting names; the drama, however, declined until the end of the 19th century, partly because the intrinsic value of plays came to be considered secondary to the merit of their performance.

▷ Paul's, Children of St; Puritanism; Theatres.

Adam
▷ Eden.

Adam (*Jeu d'Adam*)
One of the earliest vernacular plays to have survived (also known as *Le Mystère d'Adam* or *Ordo representacionis Ade*), dating from the 12th century and composed in ▷ Anglo-Norman. A dramatization of the story of Adam and Eve, Cain and Abel, is followed by a sequence of prophecies of the coming of Christ from a series of Old Testament figures. It is an early work of great sophistication and it contains extensive stage directions in Latin which illuminate its mode of production.

▷ Eden, Garden of

Adam, Robert (1728–92)
Architect. His work is representative of the middle period of ▷ Augustan taste, as the earlier period of it is expressed in the buildings of ▷ Christopher Wren and ▷ John Vanbrugh. The earlier period is bold and dramatic in its display of shapes and ornaments; the Adam period is graceful and delicate. He was a particularly fine interior designer and is famous for the designs of his ceilings and mantelpieces. His taste was much influenced by ancient Roman architecture in Italy, for instance the ruins of the town of Pompeii and the palace of the Emperor Diocletian (AD 245–313) at Spalato (Split). The last he used as the pattern for a fine urban development (demolished in 1936) overlooking the Thames in London; he carried it out with the help of his brother James, and thus called it the Adelphi from the Greek for 'brothers'. His work in London,

like most good 18th-century architecture there, has been ruined or destroyed, but Edinburgh has preserved some of his best street architecture and a number of country houses survive, either designed throughout by him or ornamented in part. These include Harewood House (Yorkshire), Mersham-le-Hatch (Kent), Syon House (near London) and Kenwood (Hampstead, London).

Adam Bede (1859)

A novel by ▷ George Eliot. The setting is a village in the English Midlands and the events take place at the beginning of the 19th century. Adam Bede is the village carpenter, a young man of stern morals and great strength of character; he is in love with Hetty Sorrel, the vain and frivolous niece of a farmer, Martin Poyser. She is seduced by the village ▷ squire. Another principal character is the young and beautiful Dinah Morris, a Methodist preacher whom Adam marries after Hetty has been transported for the murder of her child. The novel belongs to the early phase of George Eliot's art when her principal subject was the rural civilization which had been the background of her youth; the fine parts of the novel are those scenes, such as the Poyser household, which are directly concerned with this way of life.

Adcock, Fleur (b 1934)

Fleur Adcock

Poet and translator. Born and educated in New Zealand, Adcock has lived in Britain since 1963. Her volumes of poetry include: *The Eye of the Hurricane* (1964); *Tigers* (1967); *High Tide in the Garden* (1971); *The*

Scenic Route (1974) and *The Inner Harbour* (1970). In 1982 she edited the *Oxford Book of Contemporary New Zealand Poetry* and the *Faber Book of 20th Century Women's Poetry*. A volume of her *Selected Poems* appeared in 1983. She has also translated medieval ▷ Latin poetry and ▷ Greek poetry.

Addison, Joseph (1672–1719)

Joseph Addison by Sir Godfrey Kneller

Poet, politician and essayist, Addison is now best known for his contributions to two periodicals, ▷ *The Tatler* (founded by ▷ Richard Steele) and ▷ *The Spectator* (which he co-edited with Steele). *The Tatler* appeared three times a week from 1709–11, and *The Spectator* was issued daily, 1711–12 and 1714. *The Tatler* and *The Spectator* were designed as coffee-house periodicals, aiming to elevate the level of conversation by discussion of manners, morals, literature and philosophy. Addison claimed that they were enormously influential, as each printed copy could be passed around at least 20 people. The character of ▷ Sir Roger de Coverley, a country gentleman, was largely created by Addison.

Addison's first literary success was a poem, *The Campaign* (1705), celebrating the victory of Blenheim the previous year. His classical tragedy *Cato* (1713) was also a contemporary success. In his political career, Addison was a ▷ Whig Member of Parliament, and, briefly, a Secretary of State.
Bib: Samuel Johnson's Life of Addison, in

Lives of the Poets; Smithers, D., *The Life of Joseph Addison*; Otten, Robert M., *Joseph Addison*.

Admiral's Men, The Lord

A company of Elizabethan actors under the protection of Lord Howard of Effingham, who became Lord Admiral in 1585. They are first heard of in 1574, and were at their height in the 1590s, when they were led by one of the two chief actors of the time, ▷ Edward Alleyn, and when their only rivals were the ▷ Lord Chamberlain's Men who were led by the other, ▷ Richard Burbage. As Burbage was ▷ Shakespeare's leading actor, so Alleyn and the Admiral's Men were associated with ▷ Christopher Marlowe. The chief financial management of the company was under Alleyn himself and his father-in-law, ▷ Philip Henslowe, a financier. In the reign of James I (1603–25) the company came under the patronage of his eldest son, Prince Henry; and on his death under that of James's son-in-law, the Elector of the Palatinate. The company came to an end in 1628.

Adonais (1821)

An elegy in ▷ Spenserian stanzas by ▷ Percy Bysshe Shelley, mourning the death of ▷ John Keats, which had been attributed to a violent attack on Keats's poem ▷ *Endymion* in the ▷ *Quarterly Review* (1818). In his preface, Shelley compares the brutal insensitivity of the reviewer to that of the wild boar which killed the mythical Adonis – hence the poem's title. Shelley was not well acquainted with Keats and the inspiration of the poem is fundamentally literary. It is based on the *Lament for Adonis* by the Sicilian-Greek poet, Bion (first century BC), and its style is elaborately rhetorical, Keats being presented as a symbol of poetic creativity in a hostile world.

Adonis

A supremely beautiful youth in Greek myth. Beloved by ▷ Aphrodite, he was cured of a mortal wound by ▷ Persephone on condition that he spent half the year with the latter in the underworld and half with the former on the earth. The myth thus symbolized the change from winter to summer; images of Adonis were surrounded by gardens of flowers; hence the Garden of Adonis in, *eg*, ▷ Spenser's *Faerie Queene*, Bk. III.

Adult education

The scope of adult education has widened and its emphasis changed in recent years. Late educational opportunities, places for mature students at university, evening classes and residential courses of various kinds used to be promoted as desirable for the development of the person as an end in itself. The 1970s and 1980s have seen a more pragmatic approach in the interests of creating a more efficient workforce. Tasks with specific aims have been embraced, such as supplementing an inadequate initial schooling for the illiterate and innumerate, and the updating of workers in their own fields by in-service training. The ▷ Open University's Continuing Education Programme, devoted to vocational updating for community workers, teachers and managers, has received a new emphasis. This shift is matched by the government's investment in PICKUP (1982), a Professional, Industrial and Commercial Updating Programme designed to direct institutions of higher education to provide courses to broaden the skills of white-collar workers in mid-career. REPLAN, for the adult unemployed, was launched in 1984 and in 1987 the first courses of the Open College were begun, providing vocational education and training below degree level. There is provision for mature students at conventional universities, though funding may present problems. Courses, mostly part-time, are also held by a variety of bodies, including further education colleges, extra-mural departments of universities and the Workers Educational Association, the largest of the voluntary bodies.

▷ Williams, Raymond.

Advancement of Learning, The (1605)

A philosophical treatise by ▷ Francis Bacon published in 1605 in English, and expanded in a Latin version entitled *De Augmentis Scientiarium* published in 1623.

The purpose of the book is to suggest ways in which the pursuit of knowledge can be encouraged, and the methods of observation and recording of both natural and human phenomena improved. To this end, Bacon's work proposes nothing less than a taxonomy of all knowledge, a proposition strikingly familiar to that advanced by the French Encyclopaedists of the 16th century.

Perhaps the most influential aspect of *The Advancement* is the methodology which Bacon employs. In surveying all fields of knowledge Bacon offers a form of catalogue of existing fields of enquiry. This attempt at classification, whereby branches of knowledge are grouped together under common headings, relies on a system of particularization. In each subject which is considered, Bacon argues that the first step is the fresh observation of the detail of the phenomena. Once the detail, or particularities, had been assimilated it would become possible, through the process of induction, to assert the general propositions under which groups of phenomena could be considered. This method signalled both a break from what Bacon considered to be the traditional methods of enquiry (which involved deduction from generalized propositions) and the re-examination of observable phenomena through the process of experimentation.

As a theorist of scientific method (rather than as an experimenter in his own right) Bacon was to have considerable influence on the early founders of ▷ The Royal Society, particularly in the area of language reform. On the question of language, and the idea of an appropriate language for scientific discourse, *The Advancement of Learning* is a key text. At the same time, the importance of language to Bacon's project necessitated an exploration of poetic language which was to be influential for poets of the later 17th century, in particular ▷ Abraham Cowley.
▷ Dissociation of Sensibility.

Adventures of Captain Singleton
▷ Captain Singleton, Adventures of.

Adventures of Roderick Random, The
▷ Roderick Random, The Adventures of.

Aelfric (c 955–c 1020)
Scholar and great prose writer who was a monk of Winchester (under Bishop Aethelwold), and taught at Cerne Abbas (987–1002) before being made abbot of a new foundation at Eynsham, near Oxford. His works include two series of homilies, saints' lives, pastoral letters, translations from the Old Testament, and educational aids including a Latin grammar and a Latin text-book in dialogue form. The prose style developed by Aelfric, above all in his *Lives of Saints*, shares some features of ▷ alliterative verse, being patterned around two-stress phrases, often linked by alliteration. The status of his work is reflected in the number of manuscripts which survive (some from the 12th century). His distinctive prose style may have influenced the work of post-Conquest early Middle English writers using the alliterative medium, especially ▷ Laȝamon.

Aeneas
Hero of the Latin epic, ▷ *Aeneid* by ▷ Virgil. Traditions about him had existed long before Virgil's poem. He was the son of Anchises and the goddess ▷ Aphrodite, and the son-in-law of ▷ Priam, king of ▷ Troy. In ▷ Homer's *Iliad* (v) he is

represented as the chief of the Trojans and one of the most formidable defenders of Troy against the Greeks. Other records stated that after the fall of Troy, he set out to seek a new kingdom with some of the surviving Trojans, and eventually settled in central Italy. By Virgil's time, the Romans were already worshipping Aeneas as the father of their race.

Aeneid
An ▷ epic poem by the Roman poet ▷ Virgil (70–19 BC). The poem tells the story of ▷ Aeneas, from his flight from ▷ Troy during the confusion of its destruction by the Greeks to his establishment as king of the Latins in central Italy and his death in battle with the Etruscans. The poem thus begins at a point near where ▷ Homer left off in the ▷ *Iliad*, and its description of the wanderings of Aeneas is parallel to the description of the wanderings of Odysseus in Homer's ▷ *Odyssey*. It is divided into 12 books, of which the second, fourth and sixth are the most famous: the second describes the destruction of Troy; the fourth gives the tragedy of Queen Dido of ▷ Carthage, who dies for love of Aeneas; the sixth shows his descent to the underworld and the prophetic visions of those who are to build the greatness of Rome.

Virgil wished to relate the Rome he knew, a settled and luxurious civilization which threatened to degenerate into complacent mediocrity, to her heroic past, and to inspire her with a sense of her great destiny in world history. The *Aeneid* is thus a central document for Roman culture, and inasmuch as Roman culture is the basis of the culture of Western Europe, it has remained a central document for European culture too.

The most notable English translations of the *Aeneid* are those by the Scottish poet ▷ Gavin Douglas (1553) and by ▷ John Dryden (1697). Henry Howard, ▷ Earl of Surrey translated Books II and III into the earliest example of English blank verse.

Aeolian
From ▷ Aeolus, god of the winds in ancient Greek myth. An Aeolian harp is a stringed instrument, placed across a window or outside a house, so that the wind causes the strings to vibrate and make music. The poet ▷ Samuel Taylor Coleridge possessed one; hence his poem *The Eolian Harp* (1795) and references to the instrument in *Dejection* (1802). For him, it symbolized his conception of the poet 'played upon' by Nature. ▷ Shakespeare's ▷ *Cymbeline* makes reference to and use of an instrument of this kind, and there is one in

▷ Thomas Hardy's *The Trumpet Major* (1880).

Aeolists

In ▷ Swift's satire ▷ *A Tale of a Tub* (1704), a fictional sect of believers in direct inspiration: 'The learned Aeolists maintain the original cause of all things to be wind . . .'. Swift's satire is an attack on all pretensions to truth not in accord with right reason or properly constituted authority, and the Aeolists, in Section VIII, are a kind of climax to the work. He associates them particularly with the ▷ Dissenters, who based their religious faith on belief in direct intimations from the Holy Spirit to the individual soul; Jack, who represents ▷ Presbyterianism in the *Tale*, is a leader of the sect.

Aeschylus (525–456 BC)

With ▷ Sophocles and ▷ Euripides, one of the three great tragic poets of ancient Greece. Only seven of his 70 plays survive; of these the best known are *Agamemnon*, *Choephori* and *Eumenides*, making up the *Oresteia* trilogy. Aeschylus is the great starting point of all European tragedy, but it was the derivative tragedy of the Latin poet ▷ Seneca which influenced the great period of English tragedy between 1590 and 1630. Reacting against this, ▷ Milton deliberately based his tragedy ▷ *Samson Agonistes* (1671) on the Greek pattern. Shelley's masterpiece ▷ *Prometheus Unbound* (1820) was written as a sequel to Aeschylus's *Prometheus Bound*, but without pretensions to Greek form. ▷ T. S. Eliot used the Oresteia myth for his verse drama *The Family Reunion* (1939).

▷ Orestes; Tragedy.

Aesop

A Greek composer of animal ▷ fables of the 6th century BC. He probably did not write them down, but fables purporting to be his were collected by later classical writers, and they and imitations of them have had a wide popularity in European literature. The most notable Aesopian fable in English literature is Chaucer's ▷ *Nun's Priest's Tale* of the Cock and the Fox in the ▷ *Canterbury Tales*.

Aestheticism

A movement of the late 19th century, influenced by the ▷ Pre-Raphaelites and ▷ John Ruskin, but its immediate inspiration was the writings of the Oxford don ▷ Walter Pater. His two most influential books were *Studies in the History of the Renaissance* (1873) and *Marius the Epicurean* (1885). These show him as a ritualistic moralist, laying emphasis on the value of ecstatic experience. Apart from Pater and his predecessors, the aesthetes owed much to the current French doctrine of '*L'Art pour l'Art*' (Art for Art's sake) but they retained, if sometimes not obviously, a typically English concern with moral values and issues. The outstanding aesthete was ▷ Oscar Wilde (1856–1900), and a characteristic aesthetic product was his novel *The Picture of Dorian Gray* (1891). As the movement lacked a programme, writers of very different character were influenced by it: the naturalistic novelist ▷ George Moore; the poet Lionel Johnson who was a Catholic convert; ▷ Swinburne, a main channel for the art for art's sake doctrine, ▷ W. B. Yeats, the Celtic revivalist. A characteristic aestheticist periodical was ▷ *The Yellow Book* (1894–7), so called because French novels, conventionally considered 'daring', were printed on yellow paper. Its main illustrator was ▷ Aubrey Beardsley, whose line drawings were notorious for their sensuality. The excesses and affectations of the movement's adherents were much ridiculed in ▷ *Punch*.

Bib: Aldington, R. (ed.), *The Religion of Beauty: Selections from the Aesthetes*.

Agamemnon

▷ *Iliad*.

Ages, Golden, Silver, etc.

The Greek poet Hesiod (8th century BC) in *Works and Days* writes of an ideal golden age in the past, comparable to the ▷ Garden of Eden; from this period, he considered that there had been a progressive decline through the silver, bronze, and heroic ages until his own time. His classification has been adapted by other writers to describe cycles of history. The terms have also been applied more or less loosely: so one speaks, for example, of the ▷ Elizabethan period as being the golden age of English drama. ▷ Thomas Love Peacock's essay *The Four Ages of Poetry*, is an example of a conscious adaptation of Hesiod's terms.

Agincourt (1415)

A battle in the ▷ Hundred Years' War, in which the English king ▷ Henry V defeated a much larger French army. The victory was the more inspiring because it was especially a victory for English ▷ yeoman archers – humble foot-soldiers – over the aristocratic French cavalry. This allowed ▷ Shakespeare to make use of the battle as part of his creation of the myth of nationhood in his play ▷ *Henry V*: in this Henry is represented as the leader of a whole people, not merely of an aristocracy. The early modern period, in which the play was written, saw the rise of the great nation states and the development of a system of representation that would reinforce a sense of political unity within them. Agincourt became a useful symbol in that project. Another famous account of the battle is ▷ Michael Drayton's *Ballad of Agincourt* (1606–19).

Agnes, St

A Christian martyr in the reign of the Roman Emperor Diocletian (AD 284–313). She became the patron saint of virgins; her day of celebration is 21 January. It was a popular belief that ceremonies performed on the night before this day would cause a girl to dream of the man she was destined to marry. This is the idea behind Keats's ▷ *Eve of St Agnes*.

Agnosticism

The term was invented by the biologist ▷ Thomas Huxley in 1869 to express towards religious faith the attitude which is neither of belief nor of disbelief (▷ atheism). In his own words, 'I neither affirm nor deny the immortality of man. I see no reason for believing it, but on the other hand I have no means of disproving it.' Agnosticism was widespread among writers between 1850 and 1914; it arose from the scientific thought of the time, especially that of Huxley himself, and that of another biologist, ▷ Charles Darwin. Although the term can seem to carry a less polemical change than ▷ atheism in our own time, 19th-century agnostics were often extremely aggressive in their attacks on what they saw as unfounded beliefs.

Ainsworth, William Harrison (1805–82)

Novelist. His best novels are historical: *Jack Shepherd* (1839), *The Tower of London* (1840), *Guy Fawkes* (1841), *Old St Paul's* (1841), *Windsor Castle* (1843). He tended to idealize the heroic criminal, *eg* ▷ Dick Turpin in *Rookwood* (1834) and Jack Shepherd; this was a literary fashion in the 1830s and 1840s and censured by ▷ Thackeray in his early reviews under the designation 'The Newgate School of novelists'. He edited *Bentley's Magazine* 1840–2, *Ainsworth's Magazine* 1842–53 and *New Monthly Magazine* from 1853.
Bib: Ellis, S. M., *W. H. Ainsworth and his Friends*; Worth, G. J., *William Harrison Ainsworth*.

Ajax

In Greek legend, the son of Telamon, king of Cyprus, and one of the principal heroes of the Trojan War. In ▷ Homer's ▷ *Iliad*, he is described as a man of enormous stature

and strength, second only to ▷ Achilles in heroic courage. In ▷ Shakespeare's ▷ *Troilus and Cressida*, Ajax is shown as boastful, brutal and stupid.

Akenside, Mark (1721–70)

Poet. Son of a butcher in Newcastle-upon-Tyne, and a physician by profession. He wrote the influential *The Pleasures of Imagination* (1744), a philosophical poem in Miltonic blank verse. The assured reflective modulations of the poem influenced ▷ William Wordsworth's style in ▷ *The Prelude*, the subject matter of which – childhood impressions, the moral influence of landscape – is often the same. Akenside also wrote lyric poems and Odes.
Bib: Houpt, C. H., *Mark Akenside: A Biographical and Critical Study*.

Albert of Saxe-Coburg-Gotha (1819–61)

Husband (with the title of Prince Consort) of Queen ▷ Victoria. They were cousins. The Queen was devoted to him and the marriage was of considerable political importance; Albert did much to shape the Queen's ideas of her political duties as a constitutional monarch who could not interfere directly in politics but could nonetheless exert great personal influence. The Great Exhibition of 1851 was organized on his suggestion. Unfortunately, his foreign origin caused his influence to be regarded with considerable suspicion in the country. His death was a cause of immense grief to the Queen; it led to her retirement from public appearances between 1861 and the Jubilee of her reign in 1887.

Albion

The most ancient name for Britain, used in Greek by ▷ Ptolemy and in Latin by Pliny. The word possibly derived from Celtic, but it was associated by the Romans with the Latin *albus* = white, referring to the white cliffs of Dover. From the Middle Ages on it has often been used poetically to stand for Britain, notably by ▷ William Blake.

Alcestis

In Greek myth, the wife of Admetus, king of Pherae. The god ▷ Apollo granted Admetus that he should be saved from death if another person would take his place. Alcestis gave herself. She descended among the dead in the underworld, whence she was brought back by ▷ Heracles.

Alchemist, The (1610)

A comedy by ▷ Ben Jonson. The scene is a house in London during a visitation of the plague; its master, Lovewit, has taken refuge in the country, leaving his servant, Face, in charge. Face introduces two rogues: Subtle, a charlatan alchemist, and Dol Common, a whore. Together they collaborate in turning the house into a centre for the practice of ▷ alchemy in the expectation that they can attract credulous clients who will believe that alchemical magic can bring them their heart's desire. Their expectations are realized, and their dupes are representative social types. Sir Epicure Mammon dreams of limitless luxury and the satisfaction of his lust; the Puritans, Ananias and Tribulation Wholesome, hope to enrich their sect; Drugger, a tobacco merchant, wants prosperity for his business; Dapper, a lawyer's clerk, seeks a spirit to guarantee him success in gambling; Kastril, a young country squire, desires a rich husband for his sister (Dame Pliant) and knowledge of the secret of fashionable quarrelling. Only Pertinax Surly, a friend of Mammon, sees the fraudulence of the enterprise, but Face and his colleagues manage to turn the clients against him and he is routed. Each of the clients has to be deceived by a separate technique, depending on his peculiar brand of social credulity, and this requires swift changes of role by the cheats, especially Subtle. They are equal to all emergencies until Lovewit suddenly returns – a crisis which only Face survives. He expels Subtle and Common, and then wins over his master who admires his ingenuity and is satisfied with the plunder, which includes Dame Pliant. The play is one of Jonson's best; it has energetic wit and extraordinary theatrical ingenuity. Moreover the characterization has behind it the force of Jonson's conviction that human folly is limitless and can be cured only by exposure and castigation.

Aldiss, Brian (b 1925)
▷ Science Fiction.

Alexander, Sir William, Earl of Stirling (1567–1640)
Poet, dramatist, statesman, colonialist. Alexander's chief literary work was a collection of sonnets entitled *Aurora* published in 1603. In addition to the composition of dramatic works (*The Tragedy of Darius* appeared in 1603), and his position as Secretary of State for Scotland under ▷ Charles I, Alexander was also an early enthusiast for the foundation of colonies. In 1624 he published a work entitled *Encouragement to Colonies*, which was followed, in 1630, by *The Map and Description of New England*.

Alexander the Great (356–323 BC)
He succeeded to the throne of Macedon in 336 BC after the assassination of his father Philip II. Alexander began by consolidating his father's hegemony. Then he embarked on a rapid career of conquest which took his armies as far as the valley of the Indus in north-west India.

Alexander became a prominent figure in European medieval literature, especially in that of France; a long 12th-century French poem entitled *Li Romans d'Alexandre* was written in lines of 12 syllables, hence originating the term ▷ 'alexandrine' for a line of that length. Diverse accounts of his life, much overlaid by legend, resulted in medieval versions of comparable diversity, depending on whether the writer was secular in his inspiration, using Alexander as a type of chivalric ideal, or morally inspired, seeing him (in contrast to ▷ Diogenes) as a man governed by his will and appetites, or theologically influenced by Orosius as a diabolic type bedevilled by satanic pride. Another line of interest derived from the fact that he had had ▷ Aristotle as a tutor and was supposed to have corresponded with philosophers, so that he could be seen as a type of ▷ Platonic 'philosopher-king'. This diversity was further embroidered by the legend that Alexander was not in fact the son of Philip but of the magician Nectanebus, the last independent king of Egypt, who visited Alexander's mother Olympias, in the shape of a dragon.

An Anglo-Norman poem in French by Thomas of Kent dates from about 1250, and this is the basis of a 14th-century rhymed poem in English, the *Lyfe of Alisaunder*. In addition, two fragments of English ▷ alliterative romances survive, edited by Skeat, and a 15th-century poem in Northumbrian dialect entitled by Skeat *The Wars of Alexander*. In Scots dialect, we have *The Scots Buik of the most noble and vailzeand Alexander the Great* (15th century) based on translations from French sources. ▷ Chaucer's Monk (▷ *Canterbury Tales*) uses the 'storie of Alisaundre' as one of his tragedies; this exemplifies Alexander as a tragic chivalric hero. ▷ John Gower in ▷ *Confessio Amantis* (Bk III) uses him to preach the lesson of self-control, and ▷ John Lydgate in the *Fall of Princes* presents him as an exemplar of excess of pride. In the 17th century a minor ▷ Restoration dramatist, ▷ Nathaniel Lee, wrote a tragedy called *The Rival Queens* on the theme of Alexander's fatal love for two women, Statira and Roxana. In the ▷ Renaissance, Alexander always figures among ▷ 'the Nine Worthies'.

Alexandrine

A 12-syllable line of verse, possibly owing its name to the French medieval work, the *Roman d'Alexandre*. It is common in French poetry particularly of the classical period but unusual in English, where the commonest line length is of ten syllables. ▷ Michael Drayton used it in his long poem *Poly-Olbion* (1613–22), but its most famous use is in the last line of the ▷ Spenserian stanza, invented by ▷ Edmund Spenser for his ▷ *Faerie Queene*.

Alfred, King (849–99)

The greatest of the Anglo-Saxon kings, though he ruled over only the south-western part of England (▷ Wessex). He was famous for his successful resistance to the Danish invaders, and still more for his vigorous encouragement of Anglo-Saxon culture. He raised the standard of learning and religion, spread education among the nobility, laid the foundations of English prose and initiated the ▷ *Anglo-Saxon Chronicle*, the first historical record in the English language. His own writings include translations of ▷ Boethius' *Consolation of Philosophy* and of the *Pastoral Care* of Gregory the Great.
▷ Old English.

Alice's Adventures in Wonderland; Through the Looking-Glass
▷ Carroll, Lewis.

Alienation effect

Term, '*Verfremdungseffekt*', developed by the German dramatist ▷ Bertolt Brecht in his theatrical and theoretical writings. He demanded that his audiences should realize that they were not watching 'life' but a representation, and he urged that actor and audience alike should preserve a critical 'distance' from events on the stage.
▷ Defamiliarization.

All for Love, Or the World Well Lost (1678)

Tragedy in blank verse by ▷ John Dryden, based on ▷ Shakespeare's ▷ *Antony and Cleopatra*, but modified in accordance with Dryden's concern for the principles of neo-classicism. Dryden concentrates on the last stage of Antony's career, after the Battle of Actium. Antony's general Ventidius, his wife Octavia, and his friend Dolabella, all plead with him to leave Cleopatra, and make peace with Caesar. Antony is on the point of complying, but then he is led to believe that Dolabella is his rival for Cleopatra's affections, and he rejects both Octavia and Cleopatra. The desertion of the Egyptian fleet, followed by a false report of Cleopatra's death, lead Antony to take his own life. He falls on his sword and dies in Cleopatra's arms, after which she kills herself with an asp. Dryden stages a meeting between Cleopatra and Octavia which does not take place in Shakespeare's version, and he softens some of Shakespeare's language. His play achieves economy, elegance, and fluency, but lacks the range of Shakespeare's. Nevertheless *All for Love* is a masterpiece of its kind, and generally considered to be Dryden's best play.

All the Year Round

A periodical published by ▷ Charles Dickens from 1859, in succession to ▷ *Household Words*, until his death in 1870. Novels which appeared in it in instalments included Dickens's own ▷ *A Tale of Two Cities* and ▷ *Great Expectations*.

Allegory

From the Greek, meaning 'speaking in other terms'. A way of representing thought and experience through images, by means of which (1) complex ideas may be simplified, or (2) abstract, spiritual, or mysterious ideas and experiences may be made immediate (but not necessarily simpler) by dramatization in fiction.

In both uses, allegory was most usual and natural as a medium of expression in the ▷ Middle Ages, ▷ Catholic doctrine prevailed as deeply as it did widely; even the physical structures of the universe and of man seemed to be living images of spiritual truth. The morality plays, notably ▷ *Everyman* (15th century), were practical applications of this doctrine to ordinary experience. But the tendency to see experience in allegorical terms extended to secular literature, for example the romances of sexual love, such as ▷ *The Romance of the Rose* (14th century) in part translated from the French by ▷ Chaucer. When Chaucer wrote a romance in which there was no overt allegory, *eg* ▷ *Troilus and Criseyde*, the allegorical spirit was still implicit within it (see C. S. Lewis, *Allegory of Love*). Such implicit allegory extended into much ▷ Renaissance drama, *eg* Shakespeare's ▷ *Henry IV, Parts I and II*.

In the Renaissance, however, explicit allegory, though still pervasive, was greatly complicated by the break-up of the dominant Catholic framework; various Christian doctrines competed with one another and with non-Christian ones such as ▷ neo-Platonism, and also with political theories. Thus in a work like Spenser's ▷ *Faerie Queene* religious, political and Platonic allegories are all employed, but intermittently and not with artistic coherence.

Since the 17th century deliberate and consistent allegory has continued to decline; yet the greatest of all English allegories, ▷ *The Pilgrim's Progress* by John Bunyan, is a 17th-century work. The paradox is explained by Bunyan's contact with the literature of the village sermon, which apparently continued to be conducted by a simple allegorial method with very little influence from the ▷ Reformation. Moreover allegory has continued into modern times, partly as an indispensable habit of explanation, partly in a suppressed form (*eg* the names of characters in Dickens's novels), and partly as a resource in the expression of mysterious psychological experience incommunicable in direct terms; here allegory merges with ▷ symbolism, from which, however, it needs to be distinguished.

▷ Fable.

Allegro, L' (c 1631)
A poem by ▷ John Milton, published in 1645 though composed c 1631. The poem is a companion piece to ▷ *Il Penseroso*, and the title can be translated from the Italian as signifying the cheerful or happy individual. The poem's theme celebrates the active life of engagement with the world, as opposed to the reflective life depicted in *Il Penseroso*.

Alleyn, Edward (1566–1626)
Son of an innkeeper, Alleyn rose to become one of the two foremost tragic actors of the great age of English drama. In 1586 he was performing for Lord Worcester's Men; in 1592 he married the step-daughter of the financier ▷ Philip Henslowe, and together they built up the prosperity of the ▷ Lord Admiral's Men. In this company he was celebrated for his performances of ▷ Christopher Marlowe's heroes: ▷ Tamburlaine, Faustus (▷ *Doctor Faustus*), Barabas. He became the main owner of the ▷ Rose and the Fortune theatres, and a wealthy man by his speculation in land. He founded Dulwich College, to this day a leading public school. After the death of his first wife, he married the daughter of ▷ John Donne, the poet and Dean of ▷ St Paul's. His acting was highly praised by contemporary dramatists and other writers – ▷ Thomas Nashe, ▷ Thomas Heywood, and ▷ Ben Jonson among them – and was likened to that of the Roman actor, ▷ Roscius.

▷ Acting, The Profession of; Theatres.

Alliteration
▷ Figures of Speech.

Alliterative revival
The term used to refer to a large group of poems, composed in ▷ alliterative verse between the mid-14th and mid-15th centuries, on a wide range of subjects (histories, romances, contemporary satires, ▷ dream-visions), and employing a wide range of styles. The works of the ▷ Gawain poet and of ▷ William Langland form part of this group. Patterns of poetic and narrative techniques can be established between works using the alliterative verse mode, but it would be too simple to represent these texts as belonging to a single school or to explain the origins of the revival by a single causal model, as has been tried in the past. The production of narrative in alliterative verse seems to have been particularly concentrated in the west and north-west regions of England, though again the 'regional' quality of alliterative poetry, and its opposition to the forms employed in the court poetry of ▷ John Gower and ▷ Chaucer, has been overstressed in the past.
Bib: Lawton, D. (ed.), *Middle English Alliterative Poetry and Its Literary Background*.

Alliterative verse
The traditional verse form of the Germanic people in which pairs of two-stress phrases are bound together by alliteration. All ▷ Old English poetry is written in this prosodic form: usually the stressed syllables of the first phrase (or half-line) and the first syllable of the second are linked by alliteration. Formalized patterns of expression are a characteristic feature of this prosodic mode. From the late Old English period onwards a wider variety of prosodic forms was in use, and the use of rhyme as a binding device for lines increases greatly in post-Conquest English poetry. Traditionally scholars have divided up the corpus of Old English poetry into that written in 'classic' alliterative form (in which a small number of variable stress patterns for phrases can be identified), and a later 'looser' alliterative verse form (in which there are more variable options in the alliterative and stress patterns of the phrases). The alliterative works of the early Middle English period are composed in this looser style which can accommodate rhyme patterns too (as illustrated in ▷ Laȝamon's *Brut*). Conventional distinctions between prose and poetry are undermined by some texts composed in rhythmical, alliterating units. The style of ▷ Aelfric's *Lives of Saints* uses

some of the techniques of alliterative verse, as do a number of later prose works on religious themes (the so-called ▷ Katherine Group of saints' lives and the ▷ *Ancrene Wisse*), composed in the Worcestershire and Herefordshire areas in the late 12th and early 13th centuries. Discussions of the alliterative mode have been hampered by the desire of scholars to formulate a single model which might link classic Old English verse with the later looser traditions, and the increased use of a more disciplined verse medium in the 14th century, in the so-called ▷ Alliterative Revival. But the complex pattern of influences and associations has eluded simple explanatory models and increasingly the trend is to consider the alliterative mode as part of a continuum, as one of a number of forms available to post-Conquest writers in English, rather than as constituting a single poetic tradition.
Bib: Pearsall, D., *Old and Middle English Poetry*.

All's Well that Ends Well (1602–3)

A play by ▷ Shakespeare in which the heroine, ▷ Helena de Narbon, pursues Bertram, Count of Rousillon, whom she loves but who seeks to elude her. He is misled by a dishonourable young courtier, Parolles; she eventually ensnares him by a trick. The plot is taken from Painter's ▷ *Palace of Pleasure* (1566–7) but the play is difficult to date precisely owing to its mixture of styles. ▷ Sir Edmund Chambers dates it 1602–3. This agrees with the kind of difficulty with which it faces critics: uncertainty about Shakespeare's intention; the play seems to be a romantic comedy, but the treatment of the subject is often unromantic and the comedy is often harsh. Thus *All's Well* resembles other ▷ problem plays of Shakespeare written between 1600 and 1604: ▷ *Hamlet*, ▷ *Measure for Measure*, ▷ *Troilus and Cressida*.

Althusser, Louis (b 1918)

One of the most influential French ▷ Marxist philosophers of the 1960s, whose work began to appear in English translation from 1965 onwards: *For Marx* (1965), *Reading Capital* (with Etienne Balibar; 1968), and *Lenin and Philosophy* (1971). Althusser's ideas have been influential in the area of cultural studies, where his particular brand of structural Marxism has led to a radical rethinking of all social institutions, and the place of the human subject within their structures. His essay 'Ideology and Ideological State Apparatuses' (*Lenin and Philosophy*) lays the foundation for a reconsideration of literature and its relationship to ▷ ideology, and has far-reaching effects also in the area of media studies.

Amaryllis

A name used for a shepherdess in Greek and Latin pastoral poetry, *eg* by ▷ Theocritus, ▷ Virgil, and ▷ Ovid, and borrowed by English pastoralists such as ▷ Spenser.

Amazons

A race of female warriors occurring in ancient Greek legend, and said by the historian ▷ Herodotus to live in Scythia, north of the Black Sea. The word is often used to describe aggressive women, women hostile to men, or women in power instead of men.

Ambassadors, The (1903)

A novel by ▷ Henry James. It belongs to his last period, during which he returned to his earlier theme of the interaction of the European and American character.

Lambert Strether, a conscientious, middle-aged American, is engaged to the rich American widow, Mrs Newsome. She sends him over to Paris to bring back her son Chad to run the family business. He arrives to find Chad immersed in Parisian culture, and absorbed in a love affair with the Comtesse de Vionnet, a relationship which Strether mistakenly assumes to be virtuous. Strether, instead of persuading Chad to return, finds his sensibilities released by the freedom and richness of Parisian life, and delays his own return. Chad's sister, Mrs Pocock, and her husband, Jim, are now sent over by Mrs Newsome. Strether urges upon Chad the duty of loyalty to the Comtesse, and Mrs Newsome breaks off her engagement to Strether. After discovering the true nature of Chad's relations with the Comtesse, Strether decides to go back, abandoning his friendship with the intelligent and sympathetic Maria Gostrey, an American expatriate. Chad, however, remains.

Mrs Newsome is an authoritarian American matron, full of rectitude and prejudice. Strether has the highly developed New England conscience (it is his conscience that forces him to return) and a hitherto starved imagination. He is the focal character of the narrative throughout, so that his progressive understanding and development is a rich source of interest and irony. The Pococks stand for American philistinism, without imagination or sensibility. Together with ▷ *The Golden Bowl* (1904) and ▷ *The Wings of the Dove* (1902), the novel shows James's art at its most highly wrought and difficult stage.

Amelia (1751)
A novel by ▷ Henry Fielding. Unlike
▷ *Joseph Andrews* and ▷ *Tom Jones*, *Amelia*
deals with married love, and was Fielding's own
favourite, although fiercely attacked by, among
others, ▷ Johnson and ▷ Richardson.

Set against a background of squalor and
poverty, the novel opens with the
imprisonment of the innocent but careless
husband Captain Booth. In prison Booth
meets the courtesan Miss Matthews, an old
admirer who invites him to share the clean
cell she has been able to afford. Booth
accepts, though feeling guilty about his
virtuous wife Amelia, and the two characters
exchange stories about their past lives.

An old friend Colonel Bath pays Booth's
bail and takes Miss Matthews as his mistress.
Once out of jail, Booth turns to a life of
gambling while trying to curry favour with
the great. An aristocratic acquaintance assures
Amelia that Booth will get his commission,
and invites her to accompany him to a
masquerade. But 'My Lord' is a rake plotting
to seduce Amelia, with the connivance of
Colonel Bath and the Booths' landlady, Mrs
Ellison.

Just as Amelia is about to set out to the
masquerade, a fellow lodger, Mrs Bennet,
warns her that 'My Lord' had ruined her
own life and is now threatening to destroy
Amelia's 'virtue'. After several complications,
the plot ends happily; the Booths are rescued
by their good friend Dr. Harrison, and
Amelia discovers that her virtue is rewarded,
as she will inherit her mother's fortune.

Amis, Kingsley (b 1922)
Novelist and poet. Associated at first with the
▷ 'angry young men' of the 1950s for his
novels, and with the ▷ Movement for his
poetry, he has long outgrown such labelling,
achieving considerable popular success with a
series of sharp, ironic novels notable for
entertaining incident, vivid caricatures and
the comic demolition of pretension. *Lucky
Jim* (1954; filmed 1957) is a hugely enjoyable
novel about a young English lecturer in a
provincial university and his battles against
the academic establishment and a range of
comically infuriating characters. It is not
really a subversive work; it ends with the
hero being given a good job in London by a
wealthy man as well as winning the best girl.
Amis's later novels tend to be less good
humoured; the protagonist of *One Fat
Englishman* (1963) retains some of Jim's
methods, but is fully as unpleasant as his
enemies. Although Amis has remained within
the format of a well-crafted plot and largely

conventional modes of narration, he has
employed a wide range of genres such as the
detective story (*The Riverside Villas Murder*;
1973), the spy-story (*The Anti Death League*;
1966) and the ghost-story (*The Green Man*;
1969). *The Alteration* (1976), one of his most
inventive works, imagines a 20th-century
society dominated by the Catholic Church.

Amis's other novels are: *That Uncertain
Feeling* (1955); *I Like It Here* (1958); *Take A
Girl Like You* (1960); *The Egyptologists*
(1965); *I Want It Now* (1968); *Colonel Sun*
(as Robert Markham; 1968); *Girl, 20* (1971);
Ending Up (1974); *The Alteration* (1976);
Jake's Thing (1978); *Russian Hide and Seek*
(1980); *Stanley and the Women* (1984); *The
Old Devils* (1986); *Difficulties With Girls*
(1988). Story collections include: *My Enemy's
Enemy* (1962); *Dear Illusion* (1972); *The
Darkwater Hall Mystery* (1978); *Collected
Short Stories* (1980). Poetry: *Bright November*
(1947); *A Frame of Mind* (1953); *A Case of
Samples* (1956); *The Evans Country* (1962); *A
Look Around The Estate: Poems 1957–1967*
(1967); *Collected Poems 1944–1979* (1979).
Essays and criticism include: *New Maps of
Hell* (on ▷ science fiction; 1960); *The James
Bond Dossier* (1965); *What Became of Jane
Austen?* (1975); *Rudyard Kipling and His
World* (1975).
Bib: Salwak, D., *Kingsley Amis, A Reference
Guide.*

Amis, Martin (b 1949)

Martin Amis

Novelist. Son of ▷ Kingsley Amis, he was
educated at schools in Britain, Spain and the

U.S.A., and at Oxford University. He has worked for the *Times Literary Supplement*, the *New Statesman* (as literary editor) and the *Observer*. His novels are characterized by black humour, concern with the sordid, violent and absurd, and an apparent misogyny, features which he defends as satire. *The Rachel Papers* (1973) is an account of adolescence through flashbacks and memories; *Dead Babies* (1975) (paperback as *Dark Secrets*) is a tale of decadence and sadism; *Success* (1978) is closer to the hilarity of *The Rachel Papers*, while *Other People* (1981) is an experiment in ambiguity. Other works: *Money* (novel; 1984); *The Moronic Inferno* (essays; 1986); *Einstein's Monsters* (stories; 1987); *Time's Arrow* (1991).

Amoretti (1595)

A sequence of eighty-nine sonnets by ▷ Edmund Spenser, first published, together with the wedding-song ▷ *Epithalamion*, in 1595. The title of the sequence is derived from the term applied to Italian love songs which take the exploits of ▷ Cupid as their subject. *Amoretti* is unusual amongst the ▷ sonnet sequences of the period in that it moves towards an evocation of sexual love within a Christian context, which has, as its end, the sacrament of marriage. Though much of the language and many of the ideas in the sequence are derived from ▷ Petrarch, Spenser nevertheless developed the Petrarchan model in introducing a carefully organized structure to the work. Thus, the events which are described in *Amoretti* follow the course of the Christian year, while the work as a whole evokes the progress of the seasons. It has long been assumed that the sonnets were addressed to Spenser's second wife – Elizabeth Boyle – whom he married in 1594.

Amos Barton, The Sad Fortunes of the Rev. (1857)

The first of the three tales composing ▷ *Scenes of Clerical Life* (1858) by ▷ George Eliot.

Amphibology, Amphiboly

A sentence having two possible meanings owing to the ambiguity of its construction.

Amphibrach

A verse foot composed of a long syllable between two short ones, or an accented foot between two unaccented ones. It is rarely used in English verse.

Ana, -ana

A collection of memorable quotations from a writer, or sayings by a famous person, or anecdotes about him, *eg* Shakespeariana,

Johnsoniana. Usually a suffix at the end of a name, as in these examples.

Anacoluthon

▷ Figures of Speech.

Anacreontics

Any kind of melodious verse, lyrical, and concerned with love and wine. From the Greek poet Anacreon (6th–5th centuries BC). ▷ Byron called his friend ▷ Thomas Moore 'Anacreon Moore', because he translated the Odes of Anacreon into English.

Anacrusis

The use at the beginning of a line of verse of a syllable additional to the number required by the given metrical pattern.

Anagram

A literary game in which a word is disguised by changing the order of its letters so as to make a different word.

Anapaest

A metrical foot having two short or unaccented syllables followed by a long or accented one. It is usually mixed with iambics.

Anatomy of Melancholy, The (1621–51)

A treatise by ▷ Robert Burton (1577–1640) on a topic which was of enduring interest, in particular to Elizabethan and Jacobean playwrights. It was first published in 1621, but by the time that the sixth (posthumous) edition of 1651 had appeared, Burton had expanded the original book of approximately 860 pages by about one-third. Though its ostensible theme is an enquiry into the 'symptomes, prognostickes and severall cures' of the psychological disorder of melancholy, it is also a wide-ranging exposition of the role and function of the human being in the natural order of the universe. Not the least of the work's concerns is the principle of ordering and classification itself, and it thus bears comparison to ▷ Francis Bacon's ▷ *Advancement of Learning* and the work of later scientists associated with ▷ The Royal Society. But in its digressive and allusive pursuit of curious forms of knowledge, and its stylistic delight in the piling up of quotation, modification and qualification, it stands as a work without any immediate precursors or later emulators.
▷ Humour.

Ancien Régime

A French phrase, commonly used in English, to signify the political and social order in France before the Revolution of 1789, and more loosely to indicate a former state of order.
▷ French Revolution.

Ancient Mariner, The Rime of the (1798)
A literary ▷ ballad by ▷ Samuel Taylor
Coleridge (1772–1834) first published in
▷ *Lyrical Ballads.* The mariner kills a
friendly albatross for no stated reason, and he
and the crew of his ship are subjected to
punishment by the Polar Spirit. The members
of the crew die in agonies of thirst, while the
mariner himself lives on in a state of 'life-in-
death', until he 'unawares' blesses some water
snakes and is absolved of his guilt. The dead
albatross which the crew have hung round his
neck falls into the sea, and the ship is
magically driven to the mariner's home port
where he is given absolution by a hermit.
Thereafter he wanders the world,
compulsively telling his story, and
recommending a holy life in communion with
all God's creatures. The story appears naively
didactic: the mariner has sinned against the
'One Life' and has done penance for his sin.
But the poem's moral scheme is deeply
ambiguous. If the theme is one of Christian
sin and redemption, it seems strange that the
destinies of the mariner and the crew are
determined by a game of dice played between
Death and Life-in-Death. And it is unclear
why the rest of the crew are punished so
harshly. The mariner ends with an apparently
orthodox and banal message of religious
consolation: 'He prayeth best who loveth
best/ All things both and small.' But this
consolation is belied by his sinister unease, as
he holds the wedding guest with his 'glittering
eye', preventing him from attending the
marriage ceremony, and leaving him 'A
sadder and a wiser man'. The poem
dramatizes Coleridge's sense of irredeemable
guilt, and his inability at this time to find
consolation in orthodox religion or in the
pantheism of his friend ▷ William
Wordsworth.

Ancrene Riwle
▷ *Ancrene Wisse.*

Ancrene Wisse
A devotional manual, composed in the West
Midlands area, c 1230, for the use of three
sisters who had decided to become recluses.
It seems to have been revised shortly
afterwards, and all of the extant texts
represent revised versions of some kind; the
manual survives in Latin and French versions
too. The influence of this manual can be
traced in other devotional works copied and
adapted down to the 15th century. The text
is referred to as the *Ancrene Riwle* in some
manuscripts, but is introduced as the *Ancrene
Wisse* in one version. It is divided into eight

sections, each dealing with a single division of
the rule for the inner (II–VII) and outer life
(I,VIII) of an anchoress/recluse. The text is
sensitively and evocatively written to serve as
an instructional and meditational aid. One
of its most famous and climactic sections
(VII) considers how the anchoress should
channel her love of God, and presents a
memorable portrait of Christ as a lover-
knight.
Bib: Salu, M. B. (trans.), *The Ancrene Riwle.*
Shepherd, G. (ed.), *Ancrene Wisse: Parts VI
and VII.*

Andersen, Hans Christian (1805–75)
Danish author, known in Britain almost
entirely for ▷ fairy tales of his own
composition, such as 'The Tinder Box', and
'The Princess and the Pea'. They began to
appear in Denmark in 1835 and were
translated into English first in 1846. Their
poetic quality has been much imitated by
English writers, *eg* ▷ Oscar Wilde.
  ▷ Children's Books.

Andreas Capellanus (fl 1175)
Author of *De Arte Honeste Amandi* (*The Art
of Honourable Loving*), a manual of procedures
in love. He claims to be a royal chaplain and
is often said to have been attached to the
court of Marie de Champagne at Troyes, but
there is no evidence for this. His text is
addressed to a young man called Walter and
is divided into three Books which tackle (i)
the nature of love and how it may be
attained, (ii) how love may be retained, and
finally (iii) the rejection of secular love. The
debt to ▷ Ovid's work on the art of loving
and the remedies for secular love is
acknowledged by Andreas. The tone of the
work is open to different interpretations and
its divergent lines on the subject of secular
love are apparent in its tripartite organization.
The text seems to have been read and
interpreted in very different ways by scholars
and writers of subsequent centuries (as a
criticism of secular love values, as a defence
of ▷ courtly love); indeed, the debate about
how to read Andreas's text continues among
20th-century medievalists.

Andrewes, Lancelot (1555–1626)
A bishop and leader of the ▷ Church of
England during the most formative century
(1550–1650) of its thought. His ▷ sermons
were famous in an age when preaching was a
high art; their prose was vivid and condensed,
and an important contribution to the
development of English prose. He took part
in the translation of the King James Bible.
Andrewes is compared to ▷ John Donne,

poet and Dean of St Paul's, whose prose comes near his own poetry. As an intellectual defender of the ▷ Anglican religious position, Andrewes was the successor of ▷ Richard Hooker; but whereas Hooker was mainly concerned to defend Anglicanism against the ▷ Puritans, Andrewes defended it against the Catholics. Both he and Hooker are representatives of Anglicanism as the *via media* between the two.

Bib: Eliot, T. S., 'Lancelot Andrewes' in *Selected Essays*; Higham, F., *Lancelot Andrewes*; Welsby, P. A., *Lancelot Andrewes*.

Androcles and the Lion (1912)
A comedy by ▷ George Bernard Shaw based on a tale by a 2nd-century Latin writer, Aulus Gellius. The lion has a wounded paw which Androcles, a runaway slave, heals; subsequently the lion meets Androcles in an arena combat, and spares his life.

Andromeda
   ▷ Perseus.

Anelida and Arcite
▷ Chaucer's poem of 354 lines, set like the ▷ *Knight's Tale* in Thebes, and drawn from material in ▷ Boccaccio's *Teseida*. The brief story of Queen Anelida's unhappy love experience with Arcite provides the preface to Anelida's epistolary complaint, addressed to her faithless lover (composed of 140 lines of varying and accomplished metrical patterns). The work is influenced by the form and format of ▷ Ovid's *Heroides* and looks forward to Chaucer's collection of stories about wronged women in his ▷ *Legend of Good Women*.

Angel
From the Greek 'messenger' (of God). The best known example of this function of messenger is the annunciation by the Angel ▷ Gabriel to the Virgin Mary of the birth of Christ. Biblical information on angels comes especially from *Revelation*, but there is further detail in the Book of Enoch (not included in the Bible or ▷ Apocrypha).

In general, angels are conceived as a range of beings extending between man and God. The medieval view was that they have a hierarchy in this descending order: seraphim, cherubim, thrones; dominions, virtues, powers; principalities, archangels, angels – the nine orders being grouped into three choirs, of three orders each. A more widespread notion was that angels have as leaders seven Archangels: ▷ Uriel, ▷ Raphael, Raguel, Michael, Sariel, ▷ Gabriel, Jerahmeel. These names derive from the Book of Enoch, but only three of

them are well known: Michael the Warrior, Gabriel of the Annunciation and Raphael, who is sent to warn Adam in Eden in Book V of ▷ John Milton's ▷ *Paradise Lost*.

Earlier, their representation had something in common with the mystical winged warriors of non-Christian traditions, but as in the last three centuries Christian belief has become increasingly rationalized, so angels have been increasingly sentimentalized. Thus cherubs and seraphs are represented in 18th- and 19th-century art as the winged heads of children, and 'cherub' is a common designation for a pretty child; so also we speak of 'a seraphic smile' – often a baby's.

The name 'angel' was also given to a coin (▷ Noble).
   ▷ Angels, Fallen.

Angels, Fallen
The myth of the Fall of the Angels derives from *Isaiah* 14 : 12 'How art thou fallen from Heaven, O Lucifer, son of the morning!' – where ▷ Lucifer was the morning star (planet ▷ Venus) but became identified with ▷ Satan in his unfallen condition. ▷ John Milton in ▷ *Paradise Lost* uses the Lucifer myth and also gives to the angels that fell with him the names of pagan gods.

Angles
The name of one of the three Germanic tribes which invaded the Roman province of Britannia in the 5th century A D. They formed the kingdoms of Northumbria in the north-east, Mercia in the centre (Midlands) and East Anglia in the east. Their dialect was the first to be put into writing and 'English' (derived from Angle) came to be used for the language and people of the large part of the island overrun by the Angles, ▷ Saxons and ▷ Jutes (*ie* excluding Wales and Scotland).
   ▷ English language; Old English.

Anglican
From medieval Latin, *anglicanus* = English. The Catholic Church of medieval Christendom divided Europe into provinces for administrative purposes; England was the 'Anglican' province. Since the separation of the ▷ Church of England from Rome in the 16th century, 'Anglican' has been used adjectively for the Churches in Britain, the U.S.A. and the Commonwealth which are in communion with the Church of England, as well as for that Church itself. The Anglican Church of England has come to be closely associated with the maintenance of establishment values and traditional power relations between classes and between the sexes. Recent moves, particularly towards the

ordination of women, may cause this stereotype to be modified. Anglicanism = doctrine and practices of the Church of England and kindred Churches.

▷ Church of England; Episcopalian; Reformation.

Anglo-Norman
The dialect of French used in the British Isles from the time of the Conquest onwards alongside Latin and English. There were four principal domains of usage of Anglo-Norman: as a spoken vernacular; as a language of legal, administrative and business record; as a language of instruction; as a language of literary culture. It ceased to be used in these various domains at different times in the medieval period in England. From the later 12th century it was no longer a true maternal language and became increasingly a second, acquired language of the social and administrative elite, yet it continued to be learnt and used as a prestige vernacular for a further two centuries. Its function as a language of instruction, as the medium for learning Latin, seems to have been eroded by the later 14th century; its use as a language of law continued into the 15th century; its use as a language of literary culture continued through the 14th century, alongside the increasing use of English in this capacity too. Anglo-Norman literature occupies a major place in the literary culture of medieval England and a large number of English literary works translate, or rework, material from Anglo-Norman texts.
Bib: Legge, D., *Anglo-Norman Literature and its Background*; Short, I., 'On Bilingualism in Anglo-Norman England', *Romance Philology*, 33, 467–79.

Anglo-Saxon
The name is practically identical with ▷ Old English in denoting the language, literature and culture of the English before the Norman-French conquest of 1066, and also after it until it becomes fused (Middle English) in the 13th century with the insular Norman-French; it was later occasionally used *eg* in Disraeli's ▷ *Coningsby* and ▷ *Sybil*, to differentiate the common people from the aristocracy of (supposedly) Norman-French descent.

▷ Angle; English language; Saxon.

Anglo-Saxon Chronicle
A collective term for a corpus of annals, recording events of local and national significance, organized in a more systematic way during the reign of ▷ Alfred. The annals, written in English, were kept up at a number of monastic centres and survive in seven manuscripts (which form four main versions). The subjects and length of entries in the chronicles vary considerably from version to version but collectively they provide a record of events from the beginning of the Christian era to 1154. The continuation of the chronicle for nearly 100 years after the Norman Conquest illustrates the way in which ▷ Old English literary culture did not stop abruptly in 1066, yet the changing form of the language of the later entries in the chronicle also indicates the way in which a standard written form of English could no longer be maintained in post-Conquest literary culture.
Bib: Whitelock, D. W. (ed.), with Douglas, D. C. and Tucker, S. I., *The Anglo Saxon Chronicle*; Gransden, A., *Historical Writing in England, c 550–1307*.

Anglo-Welsh literature
To define Anglo-Welsh literature as that produced in English by Welsh writers is too simplistic. Writers' claims on Welsh ancestry vary enormously. Some even adopt Welshness as, for example, Raymond Garlick (b 1926), an Englishman who identified with Welsh political causes and became founder-editor of the literary magazine *Dock Leaves* (later *The Anglo-Welsh Review*, 1957–88) and a critic and poet firmly within the Welsh context. Thus poet and novelist Glyn Jones's criterion of Anglo-Welshness – expressed in his critical work *The Dragon Has Two Tongues* as involvement in the Welsh situation – seems justifiable. So is ▷ George Herbert, brought up in the Marches (▷ Wales) and an influence on ▷ Henry Vaughan, acceptable? Does ▷ Gerard Manley Hopkins's three-year residence at St Beuno's seminary, during which he learnt Welsh, admit him? His assimilation of *cynghanedd* (▷ Welsh terms) into English poetry transmitted Welsh metric to ▷ Dylan Thomas who could not speak Welsh. For poet and critic Anthony Conran, W. H. Davies qualifies as Anglo-Welsh because his *New Poems* conforms to the thematic divisions of the *bardd gwlad* (▷ Welsh terms). Nevertheless, Conran concedes only two Anglo-Welsh poems to Edward Thomas, who is included on parentage, emotional attachment to Wales, and his belated influence on Anglo-Welsh poets. Richard Hughes and ▷ John Cowper Powys have received the accolade of critical studies in the *Writers of Wales* series through their eventually permanent residence in, and lifelong empathy for Wales. From Powys's Wessex came Jeremy Hooker (b 1941), whose

19 years in Wales made him a leading critic in the Anglo-Welsh field and temporarily changed his poetic direction. Thus a widely debatable area of Anglo-Welsh acceptability exists.

Historically, poetry is the dominant genre of Anglo-Welsh literature, prose a mainly 20th-century growth. The poetic origins can be traced to the 15th century, but excepting George Herbert, Henry Vaughan and John Dyer, all the major work belongs to the present century. What is significant, to cite Anthony Conran, is the 'seepage' from Welsh-language culture into English. For example, the traditional function of the Welsh-language poet was to commemorate the society he lived in whether, as earlier, in 'praise poems' for princes or, later, the local community. In the last-named instance, the *bardd gwlad*'s categories of poems included nature, love, beer, hunting songs, poems to individuals and moral poems. Some were in complex traditional metres, others in less exacting free metres, so form is an overriding concern. In serving his community, the Welsh poet is perceived as a craftsman, cultivating an objectivity that contrasts with English poetry from the ▷ Romantic revival onwards and particularly that of contemporary confessional egocentricity. The formal preoccupations of Welsh-language poetry assimilated by Anglo-Welsh practitioners over four centuries revealed affinities by the early 20th century with the English ▷ Georgians' objective descriptions of nature, in birds, flowers, landscapes, and of people and their working lives in an essentially rural setting. The legacy of this is Anglo-Welsh poetry's perseverance with tighter forms and greater objectivity than English contemporary poetry. Welsh-speaking Anglo-Welsh poets such as Glyn Jones (b 1905), Harri Webb (b 1920) and Anthony Conran (b 1931) have translated Welsh-language poems into English, often following the Welsh metric of the originals, such as *traethodl*, *cywydd*, or *englyn*, sometimes including the internal rhymes and alliterations of *cynghanedd*, and the accretion of comparisons known as *dyfalu* (▷ Welsh terms). As Welsh metric poses almost insurmountable technical problems when grafted onto the English language, any assimilation through the centuries has been gradual, and it is more the common thematic inheritance that unites Welsh and Anglo-Welsh poetry and differentiates the latter from English poetry. However, the growth of Anglo-Welsh literature is a concomitant of the historical process that weakened the influence of the Welsh language.

Anglo-Norman settlements of the Marches and South Wales were followed by Henry I's 12th-century Flemish settlement of South Pembroke, subsequently augmented by English settlements in Gower and around Laugharne. Edwardian castles protected English merchants who were granted privileges within town walls, as at Caernarfon and Conwy. Itinerant drovers and weavers soon forged linguistic links with England. The establishment of the Tudor dynasty brought Welsh influence into England, though Henry VIII's Acts of Union insisted on Welsh office-holders' proficiency in English, eventually producing an anglicized squirearchy. Three centuries later, Victorian government policy further weakened the hold of the Welsh language by encouraging 'The Welsh Not', prohibiting Welsh-language conversation in schools. A piece of wood or slate with the letters 'WN' cut into it was hung round the neck of the last pupil caught speaking Welsh in class – whoever was left wearing it at the end of the school day would be punished. From the early 19th century, the increasing influx into the South Wales valleys not only drained the rural areas of the west and north but brought in labouring or technological expertise for pit-sinking, blast furnace, canal, tramroad, railway and docks construction. The ultimate figure of English-speaking immigrants in the South Wales valleys accounted for at least 40% of the population, swamping the native Welsh speakers. The subsequent foundation of county schools from 1895 onwards provided secondary education in the medium of English. This explains why Glyn Jones, an early pupil at Merthyr's Cyfarthfa Castle Grammar School, though from a Welsh-speaking family, developed into an Anglo-Welsh writer. It was these socio-economic pressures that helped to create the 'first flowering' of Anglo-Welsh literature.

Many young provincial writers departed for London between the wars to find publishers who encouraged them to adapt their work for the metropolitan market. Caradoc Evans (1878–1945), according to the novelist and critic Professor Gwyn Jones the 'first distinctive ancestral voice' of Anglo-Welsh writing, produced the first London published best-seller. In *My People* (1915) and subsequent short-story collections, Caradoc Evans invented grotesqueries of character and speech for his Cardi peasantry whose lust, greed and hypocrisy established a false Welsh stereotype that amused Londoners but gave unmitigated and lasting offence to the Welsh-speaking literary establishment. Notwithstanding, Caradoc Evans's commercial success encouraged a vein of fantasy among the 'first flowering' of Anglo-Welsh writers, Rhys Davies, Glyn Jones and ▷ Dylan Thomas, continued in the post-war period by Gwyn Thomas. Moreover, the eccentric and grotesque provided a diversion from painfully harsh living conditions in decaying rural and unemployment ravaged industrial communities. Beneath this surface, however, industrial realism encapsulates a political message – socialist in the 'first flowering', nationalist in the 'second flowering' in the 1960s. This idealism motivates an inevitably doomed nationalist military uprising in Glyn Jones's ▷ novella, *I Was Born in the Ystrad Valley*, as early as 1937. Communist political activism inspires Lewis Jones's *Cwmardy* (1937) and *We Live!* (1939), Jack Jones paints panoramic historical canvases behind his family epics in *Black Parade* (1935) and *Rhondda Roundabout* (1934), whereas Gwyn Jones employs a briefer time-scale in *Times Like These* (1936) where he examines the social and familial crises precipitated by the General Strike. However, it was Richard Llewellyn's *How Green Was My Valley* (1939) which became the popular stereotype of the Valleys' industrial novel despite its inaccuracies and sentimentality, a far cry from Gwyn Thomas's rejected pre-war novel *Sorrow For Thy Sons* (eventually published in 1986, five years after his death). Gwyn Thomas's post-war hyperbolic wit, farcical situations and eccentric characters create a Valleys' world where laughter is the only antidote to poverty and unemployment. Meanwhile, short stories between the wars mediate between a poetic vision of Welsh-speaking Wales, Lawrentian-influenced in Rhys Davies and Geraint Goodwin, and the realistic depiction of industrial communities, infused with wit and humour. Only one poet identifies with the industrial milieu: Idris Davies, despite a ▷ Georgian vocabulary and the formal strait-jacket of the ▷ Housman quatrain, brings his strike-bound communities to life when he uses local vernacular speech and escapes into free verse.

The two most original poets to appear in the 1930s were very different from Idris Davies in theme and technique. David Jones achieved the critical recognition due to him as a major poet only during the 1980s, shortly after his death. *In Parenthesis*, for example, encapsulated his experiences in World War I but appeared only two years before World War II. His juxtaposition of prose passages with poetry, all loaded with mythopoeic reference, represented an exciting new poetic dimension, though it received scant notice at the time. Very different was the critical reception for Dylan Thomas, who alienated himself from the Welsh concept of community-serving poet and escaped from Swansea to literary London as early as possible to promote his self-advertising poetic image. Nevertheless, his indisputable success and originality gave fresh impetus to Anglo-Welsh writing which found a mouthpiece in Keidrych Rhys's literary magazine *Wales* published in three intermittent series between 1937 and 1960 and in Gwyn Jones's more academically respectable *Welsh Review* published first in 1939 and then between 1944 and 1948. Unlike other Anglo-Welsh poets, Dylan Thomas flowered early because his poetry was self-created. Influenced by his work, some young poets published prematurely shortly after the war, including Leslie Norris and John Ormond, who then waited for 20 years for their individual, mature and successful voices to be heard. Inevitably, the war had limited publishing so that the tragically brief war-time appearance of Alun Lewis's work was all the more remarkable.

In post-war years, attempts to revive *Wales* and the *Welsh Review* were short-lived through lack of funds, though *Dock Leaves* (founded 1949) survived in Tenby, thanks to Raymond Garlick and Roland Mathias. Despite the growing reputation of Vernon Watkins (1906–67) as a poetic visionary, Dylan Thomas's untimely self-destruction left a void that was eventually filled by ▷ R. S. Thomas (b 1913), whose major poetic status was rapidly endorsed by critics in England despite their disregard of most Anglo-Welsh literature. R. S. Thomas's concern for rural and urban poverty in Wales, reflected in his sympathy for the uncouth hill farmer, is revealed in firmly structured, emotionally restrained poems of arresting imagery. For him, nationalism would answer Wales's problems: God he listens for in answer to his own problems as priest-poet. Another major writer of nationalist stance is the novelist and poet Emyr Humphreys (b 1919). Humphreys, of North Walian orientation, examines conscience among the Welsh-speaking professional class, and impartially presents Nonconformity, while never seeking to depart from his fictive high seriousness or to indulge popular taste.

Meic Stephens (b 1938) was the prime mover behind the 'second flowering' which gathered momentum in the 1960s when nationalist ideas were superseding socialist politics. He founded *Poetry Wales* in 1965 with support from Harri Webb, thus providing a nationalist conscious poetic forum, fostering mutual interest between Wales's two languages, especially reinvigorating Anglo-Welsh poetry through John Ormond, Harri Webb, John Tripp, Raymond Garlick, Roland Mathias, Leslie Norris and Gillian Clarke. In 1967 he became Literature Director of the newly constituted *Welsh Arts Council* whose financial support for writers and publishers gave tremendous impetus to Welsh and Anglo-Welsh writing. An unfortunate effect, however, was that London publishers and reviewers disregarded Anglo-Welsh writing when it developed independently from metropolitan influences, leading to a critical undervaluing that still persists in England. In 1968 Meic Stephens led a move to create the English section of *Yr Academi Gymreig*, originally a literary society founded for Welsh-language writers only, but from then on providing invaluable encouragement to Anglo-Welsh writers. Concluding an exciting decade, Ned Thomas launched *Planet* in 1970, a magazine whose political thrust was left-wing and nationalist, and which also published literary material.

Recently, an updated view of Valleys society has informed the short stories and novels of Alun Richards (b 1929) and Ron Berry (b 1920). Alun Richards illuminates social tensions among the migratory professional classes, nuances between the Valleys and Cardiff, and Cardiff and London. His sensitive ear for dialogue contributed to the effectiveness of his work for the theatre (published in *Plays for Players*; 1975) and television. Ron Berry has explored Valleys sexual mores with lively humour. Closely associated with the border country of his upbringing, ▷ Raymond Williams's novels present the tensions of nationalism, social mobility, working-class solidarity and conflicting loyalties, though the political and socio-economic dimensions of his critical *oeuvre* are more familiar. The novelists with Anglo-Welsh connections who have achieved most recent critical acclaim are Bernice Rubens, Alice Thomas Ellis, Stuart Evans and Peter Thomas, a newcomer as a novelist extending Gwyn Thomas's hyperbolic vision.

Anglo-Welsh literature has produced no playwright to emulate Emlyn Williams (1905–1988), though the recent emphasis has shifted from theatre via radio into television, as reflected in the careers of Gwyn Thomas, Alun Owen, Alun Richards and Elaine Morgan.

Although disappointment with the result of the referendum on devolution did not affect the republican nationalist views of some of the younger poets such as Nigel Jenkins and Mike Jenkins, a widening of poetic horizons has been taking place. Its trailblazer ▷ Dannie Abse (b 1923) has exploited a series of fruitful tensions in his work which reflect contrasting life-styles: Cardiff/London; Welsh/Jewish; poetry/medicine. His sympathy for oppressed minorities reveals a humanitarianism and compassion haunted by the horror of the Holocaust. His range of themes ensures his international, as well as Anglo-Welsh, status. Another poet who has broadened his Anglo-Welsh context through exposure to the influence of American 'confessional' poets (such as Robert Lowell, ▷ Sylvia Plath, John Berryman and Anne Sexton), thereby producing many transatlantic poems, is Tony Curtis (b 1946) whose recent work invokes historical perspectives through condemnation of war and nuclear weapons. Peter Finch (b 1947) has experimented with concrete and multilingual, occasionally almost surreal, poetry. John Davies, Steve Griffiths, Robert Minhinnick, Mike Jenkins, Nigel Jenkins, Duncan Bush, Sheenagh Pugh and Chris Meredith are all acutely conscious of their present social reality while rejecting traditional Welsh stereotyping. Moving towards English influences, Oliver Reynolds (b 1957) has embraced the ▷ Martian 'new heartlessness', his poetic incisiveness deriving also from ▷ W. H. Auden. Hilary Llewellyn-Williams's rural, mythopoeic vision owes something to Gillian Clarke and Ruth Bidgood in that it is personal, familial and rooted in the Welsh landscape, its inhabitants and their history.

With a higher concentration of writers in Wales than anywhere else in Britain, the vigorous growth of Anglo-Welsh literature is assured, particularly since, though it has retained its traditionally distinguishing characteristics, it has developed a more outward-looking stance. Happily, as this text proves, there are indications that the Anglo-Welsh literary movement may eventually receive its long overdue recognition from the English critical establishment.

Bib: Stephens, M. (ed.), *The Oxford Companion to the Literature of Wales*; Adams, S. and Hughes, G. R., *Essays in Welsh and Anglo-Welsh Literature*; Conran, A., *The Cost of Strangeness*; Garlick, R., *An Introduction to Anglo-Welsh Literature*; Hooker, J., *The Poetry of Place*; Jones, G., *The Dragon Has Two Tongues*; Jones, G. and Rowlands, R., *Profiles*; Mathias, R., *A Ride Through the Wood*;

Mathias, R., *Anglo-Welsh Literature*; Curtis, T. (ed.), *Wales: the Imagined Nation*.

Angry young men
A term which was loosely applied to novelists and dramatists of the 1950s who expressed a sense of dissatisfaction and revolt against established social mores. ▷ John Osborne's play *Look Back In Anger* (1956) epitomized the mood. Other authors of whom the term was used include ▷ John Braine, ▷ John Wain, ▷ Alan Sillitoe, and ▷ Kingsley Amis.
▷ Realism.
Bib: Allsop, K., *The Angry Decade*.

Anjou, House of
▷ Plantagenets.

Annus Mirabilis (1667)
A poem by ▷ John Dryden dealing with the 'wonderful year' between the summer of 1665 and that of 1666, especially the sea battles against the Dutch, the ▷ Plague and the ▷ Great Fire of London. It is written in 'heroique stanzas', pentameter quatrains rhyming *abab*, which were felt at the time to possess an epic breadth and dignity lacking in the shorter-lined lyric metres of much 17th-century poetry. Its style is public and declamatory, the emphasis being on rapid narrative and imaginative gusto, and its epic hero is a collective one: the English people or London.

Anthology
A collection of short works in verse or prose, or selected passages from longer works, by various authors. Some anthologies lay claim to authority as representing the best written in a given period, *eg* the Oxford Books (of Sixteenth Century Verse, etc.) and others are standard examples of taste at the time of compiling, *eg* Palgrave's *The Golden Treasury of the Best Songs and Lyrical Poems in the English Language*, (1861). Others have had an important influence on taste, or on later literary development: ▷ *Percy's Reliques*; ▷ *Tottel's Miscellany*; ▷ *The Mirror for Magistrates*; ▷ *The Greek Anthology*.

Anthology, The Greek
A collection of poems begun by Meleager of Gadara (about 60 BC) and later expanded, especially by Constantius Cephalas (10th century AD), till it included selections from over 300 writers. Many of the pieces, which number over 4,500, are epigrams. The *Anthology* has been, from the 16th century onwards, an important source of information on Greek culture.

Antichrist
The word occurs in the New Testament, *1 John* 2 and *2 John* 7, and is explained as the being who denied Christ. There was an older Jewish tradition of a mighty ruler at the end of time, the great antagonist of God. In later centuries, Antichrist was identified with various contemporary rulers; some reformers, *eg* ▷ Wycliffe, applied it to the Pope.

Anti-climax
▷ Figures of Speech.

Antigone
In Greek myth, the daughter of ▷ Oedipus, condemned by her uncle Creon, ruler of Thebes, to be buried alive for insisting on carrying out burial rites for her dead brother although he had been a rebel. She is the subject of a tragedy by ▷ Sophocles.

Anti-industrialism
A tradition of writing identified initially by the work of ▷ Raymond Williams in *Culture and Society*. 19th-century observers, the foremost of whom was ▷ Thomas Carlyle, identified a number of threats to what they saw as constructive social living brought by industrialism. When the industrial system was being imposed it could be seen how its pressures obliged the workforce into working in mechanical unison and consequently altered their sense of themselves. The emphasis it brought on material production and material acquisition changed the conditions of life and sapped the individual's powers of resistance. ▷ D. H. Lawrence was its most impassioned 20th-century opponent.
▷ Further education; Capitalism.

Antiquary, The (1816)
A novel by ▷ Walter Scott, the third of his 'Waverley Novels', set in Scotland in the 18th century. The main story is an ordinary romance. A young officer, Major Neville, falls in love with Isabella Wardour, whose father rejects him on account of his supposed illegitimacy. Neville follows the father and daughter to Scotland, where the three have sundry adventures; Neville saves their lives and rescues Sir Arthur Wardour from impending ruin. He also turns out to be the son and heir of a Scottish nobleman. Thus the objections to the union between Neville and Isabella are removed. The distinction of the novel arises from the subsidiary characters: Jonathan Oldbuck, a learned antiquarian scholar (like Scott himself), and Edie Ochiltree, a wandering beggar who epitomizes the feelings and traditions of the Lowland Scottish peasantry. Scott states in

his preface that he agrees with
▷ Wordsworth's opinion (expressed in the
Preface to the ▷ *Lyrical Ballads*) that the
peasantry have an eloquence in expressing the
basic and most universal passions which is
lost to the educated classes.

Antithesis
▷ Figures of Speech.

Antonio and Mellida (1600)
A play in two parts by ▷ John Marston.
Part I is a transvestite, stylized and Italianate
comedy about the loves of its eponymous
protagonists. Part II, usually known as
Antonio's Revenge, portrays the savage
destruction of the same characters in the
idiom of an Elizabethan blood tragedy.
▷ Revenge tragedy.

Antony and Cleopatra (1606–7)
A tragedy by ▷ Shakespeare, probably
written in 1606–7, and first printed in the
First Folio edition of his collected plays in
1623. The source is ▷ Sir Thomas North's
translation (1587 edition) of ▷ Plutarch's
Lives.

Mark Antony, with Octavius Caesar and
Lepidus, is one of the 'triumvirate' (43–31
BC) which rules Rome and its empire, and he
is Rome's most famous living soldier. At the
opening of the play, he is the lover of
▷ Cleopatra, Queen of Egypt, and, to the
disgust of his officers, is neglecting Rome and
his political and military duties. All the same,
he cannot ignore Rome, and from time to
time he reacts strongly against Cleopatra
when he remembers his public position and
his reputation. His strained relations with
Octavius Caesar are temporarily mended
when he marries Caesar's sister, Octavia, but
he soon abandons her and returns to
Cleopatra. Caesar is enraged, and is in any
case anxious to secure sole power over the
empire for himself. Open war breaks out
between them, and Antony is defeated at the
sea battle of Actium, largely owing to
Cleopatra's attempt to participate personally
in the campaign. After Antony's final defeat
on land, he attempts to kill himself, and
eventually dies of his wounds in the arms of
Cleopatra, who has taken refuge in her
'monument'. This is a mausoleum which she
had built so that she and Antony could lie
together in death; it serves as a kind of miniature fortress. After Antony's death, she makes
a bid for survival by pitting her wits against
Caesar's. When she sees that she has failed,
she takes her own life. The two death scenes,
her own and Antony's, are amongst the most
famous scenes in Shakespeare's work.

One of the ironies of the tragedy is that
Cleopatra loves Antony just because he is a
great Roman hero, and yet, in order to get
full possession of him, she has to destroy this
part of him. At a deeper level, Rome and
Egypt are set in dramatic contrast: Rome
stands for the political world, with its ruthless
and calculating manoeuvring for power; Egypt
stands for the heat and colour of passion,
tending always to dissolution and corruption.
The play belongs to Shakespeare's maturest
period. As in his other 'Roman' plays,
▷ *Julius Caesar* and ▷ *Coriolanus*,
Shakespeare shows awareness of writing about
the pre-Christian era, in which the hero
represents the highest human type, instead of
the saint.

▷ John Dryden's ▷ *All for Love* is also
a tragedy about Antony and Cleopatra; a
comparison of the two plays is instructive in
showing the changes that had come about in
English verse in the intervening period.
▷ George Bernard Shaw's play ▷ *Caesar
and Cleopatra* (1901) is about Cleopatra's
earlier relationship with Julius Caesar.

Aphasia
Generally used to designate language
disorder. However, in literary criticism it has
been given a more specific definition by the
linguistician and supporter of the ▷ Russian
Formalist movement, ▷ Roman Jakobson.
Jakobson begins with the observation that
language functions through the *selection* and
combination of its elements into units such as
words and sentences. *Combination* is a term
used to designate the process whereby a
linguistic ▷ sign can generate meaning only
through its relationship with other signs
which provide a context for it. *Selection*
permits the substitution of one element for
another from the total number of elements
that make up the linguistic code as a whole,
and which both speaker (addresser) and
listener (addressee) share. The addresser
encodes a particular message, and the
addressee decodes or interprets it. Any
interference with either the selection or
combination of linguistic units which form an
utterance, such as an unusual use in a literary
work, is designated as aphasia, and this
disordering serves, by contrast, to reveal the
ways in which language operates normally.

Aphorism, apophthegm
A terse sentence, weighted with sense; with
more weight of wisdom than an ▷ epigram
need have, but less elegance.

Aphrodite
In Greek myth, goddess of physical beauty

and sexual love. Her cult was widespread; in Rome she was known as Venus; in Syria, and the Middle East as Astarte, Ashtaroth, Ishtar. She was also called Anadyomene ('sprung from the foam'); and because this occurred near the island of Cythera, she was Cytherean. ▷ Zeus married her to Hephaestus (Lat. Vulcan) but owing to his ugliness she was unfaithful to him with ▷ Ares. She was the mother of ▷ Eros. (Lat. Cupidos) the boy-god of desire and the rival of ▷ Persephone for the love of ▷ Adonis. She competed with ▷ Hera and ▷ Athene for the prize of a golden apple for the greatest beauty, to be awarded by ▷ Paris, and won the contest.

Apocalypse

From Greek 'disclosure'. A kind of visionary literature, especially *Revelation* in the ▷ Bible. The essence of such literature, for instance, the visionary poetry of ▷ William Blake and ▷ W. B. Yeats, is that it expresses in symbolic terms truths and events which surpass the ordinary reach of the human mind.

Apocrypha

1 Books of the Old Testament not counted as the genuine Word of God by the Jews, nor as sacred by Protestants: *Esdras 1* and 2; *Tobit*; *Judith*; the *Rest of Esther*; *Wisdom*; *Ecclesiasticus* (not to be confused with *Ecclesiastes*); *Baruch*; the *Song of the three Holy Children*; *Susanna*; *Bel and the Dragon*; *Manasses*; *Maccabees 1* and 2.

2 Also sometimes used for works alleged on uncertain grounds to be by a given author.

Apollo (Phoebus, Phoebus Apollo)

In Greek and Latin mythology, the son of ▷ Zeus and Leda. Apollo was the god identified with the sun and was regarded as the ideal of male beauty. He was also the god of music and poetry, associated with the founding of states and colonies, and famous for his oracles, especially that at Delphi. More recently he has lent his name to art that emphasizes form, reason, order and harmony.
▷ Delphic Oracle; Dionysus.

Apollyon

In the Bible, *Revelation* 9:11, Apollyon is 'the angel of the bottomless pit'. He is chiefly famous in English literature for his appearance in ▷ Bunyan's ▷ *Pilgrim's Progress*, where he is identifiable with Satan. Apollyon means 'destroying'.

Apologia, Apology

In ordinary speech, *apology* has the sense of an expression of regret for offensive conduct, but as a literary term it commonly has the older meaning still conveyed by *apologia*: defence, *eg* ▷ Sir Philip Sidney's ▷ *Apologie for Poetrie*, or explanation, vindication, *eg* ▷ Cardinal Newman's *Apologia pro Vita sua*.

Apologie for Poetrie, An (1595)

A critical essay by ▷ Sir Philip Sidney, the *Apologie* appeared in 1595, when it was also published under the alternative title *The Defence of Poesie*. Though it has long been assumed that Sidney's treatise was designed to function as a reply to a ▷ pamphlet by ▷ Stephen Gosson entitled *The Schoole of Abuse* (1579), the *Apologie* undertakes to defend imaginative writing from more general objections than those propounded by Gosson. Instead, the *Apologie* undertakes to define the role of both the artist and the literary text in respect of the society and the competing forms of alternative discourses in which they operate and are read. To this end, the *Apologie* explores the classical concept of imaginative writing, arguing that the poet can be considered as a 'creator' or 'maker' rather than a sterile copier of forms located in the real world. The autonomy of the artist is guaranteed against the competing claims of philosophical and historical writing, and, at the same time, Sidney offers a refutation of ▷ Plato's famous condemnation of poetry in his ▷ *Republic*. The essay concludes with a survey of contemporary English writing.

The importance of Sidney's work is that it provides a clear statement of several important themes of Renaissance poetics. In particular, it deals at length with the idea of imitation and with the Platonic objection against poetry – that it is morally questionable, and that the poet is, in producing works of fiction, little better than a liar. In producing a range of arguments to deal with these two points, Sidney offers a synthesis of humanistic arguments derived from his readings in the classics and in the work of continental critics. At the same time, the *Apologie* stands as an example of the ▷ Renaissance use of the art of ▷ rhetoric which determines the work's careful structure. For all its rootedness in late 16th-century debates on poetics, Sidney's treatise was to become, in the 17th century and later, an important statement in its own right on the nature and value of poetic discourse.
▷ *Poetics*; Unities, The Dramatic.
Bib: Shepherd, G. (ed.), *An Apology for Poetry*.

Apologue

A little story, very often a ▷ fable, with a moral.

Apophthegm
▷ Aphorism.

Apostrophe
▷ Figures of Speech.

Apple Cart, The (1929)
A discussion comedy by ▷ George Bernard
Shaw, presenting an imaginary
constitutional crisis in England set in modern
times. '*The Apple Cart* exposes the unreality
of both democracy and royalty as idealists
conceive them' (Shaw in his Preface, 1930).
The title is from the English idiom 'to upset
the apple-cart', *ie* to cause confusion in the
settled order of things. The play is about a
fictional English king, King Robert, who
refuses to conform to the traditional
constitutional role, according to which the
King does not interfere with his ministers in
their conduct of the government. He thus
causes a political crisis, which he cleverly
turns to his own advantage. Shaw's satire is
directed at the idea of responsible democratic
government: this, according to the play, does
not really exist in 20th-century Britain,
because the ministers have to subject
themselves to their bureaucracy, which is
much more experienced in the problems with
which the government has to deal. The King,
on the other hand, is much better qualified to
govern, since, like the bureaucracy, his office
is a permanent one and is not affected by
periodic parliamentary elections which change
the ministers. The play is a good example of
Shaw's genius for transforming political ideas
into witty comedy.

Apprenticeship
A system of training undergone by youths
entering on a trade or craft. The apprentice
was indentured to a master in the craft, *ie*
entered into a contract with him, to serve him
in return for maintenance and instruction for
seven years, usually between the ages of 16
and 23. The apprentice was a member of the
master's household and the master was
responsible for his behaviour before the law.
Thus apprenticeship provided social control,
as well as a form of education, and tended to
maintain standards in manufacture and
professional conduct. It also had the social
advantage of mixing the classes and ensuring
that the landed classes retained interest in
trade, for the smaller landed gentry commonly
indentured their younger sons, who had no
land to inherit, to master craftsmen, especially
in London. Until the 18th century (when the
gentry, grown richer, tended to despise trade)
this mixture of classes, as well as large
numbers, made the London apprentices a
formidable body of public opinion both
politically and, for instance, in the
Elizabethan theatre. Apprenticeship was
systematized by law under the Statute of
Artificers, 1563. It had its beginnings in the
▷ Middle Ages. Usually women were not
permitted to be apprenticed: in this way they
were excluded from skilled paid work,
although wives, daughters and sisters often
helped in the work of their male relatives.
Until the 17th century, apprenticeship was
the only way to enter most trades and
professions.
▷ Craft Guilds; Journeyman; Master
Craftsman.

Aquinas, St Thomas (c 1225–74)
Author of an extensive system of philosophy
and theology, *Summa Totius Theologiae*, on
the principles of ▷ Aristotle. This work
came to be considered the most authoritative
product of scholastic thinking, and, more
than any other, was responsible for Aristotle's
superseding in the ▷ Middle Ages the
philosophy of ▷ Plato.

Arabian Nights Entertainments
Also known as *The Thousand and One Nights*,
this collection of stories supposed to be told
by Scheherazade was probably put together
by an Egyptian story-teller around the 15th
century. The stories became well-known and
popular in Europe early in the 18th century.
English translations have been made by
Edward Lane in 1840 and, with greater
literary merit, by ▷ Sir Richard Burton in
1885–88. They provided, with the Bible, the
chief source of opulent and dramatic reading
approved for and available to 19th-century
children.
▷ Children's books.

Arbitrary nature of the sign
▷ Sign.

Arbuthnot, Dr. John (1667–1735)
Close friend of ▷ Alexander Pope,
▷ Jonathan Swift and ▷ John Gay, with
whom he collaborated in the satiric sallies of
the ▷ Scriblerus Club. Arbuthnot was
physician in ordinary to Queen Anne and a
Fellow of the ▷ Royal Society; he was
widely admired for his medical science and
for his genial wit. His most famous satire is
'The History of John Bull' (1712), a series of
pamphlets advocating an end to the war with
France which turned the arguments of Swift's
Conduct of the Allies into a comic allegory. He
also had a hand in such collaborative
Scriblerian satires as *The Memoirs of Martin
Scriblerus* (1741), *The Art of Sinking in
Poetry* (1727) and *Three Hours after Marriage*

(1717). Among his more important scientific writings are his *Essay on the Usefulness of Mathematical Learning* (1701) and his *Essay concerning the nature of Aliments* (1731).
Bib: Aitken, G. A. (ed.), *The Life and Works of Dr. John Arbuthnot*; Beattie, L. M., *John Arbuthnot, mathematician and satirist*.

Arcades (c 1633)
A short ▷ masque by ▷ John Milton written c 1633. Like all masques, the title of the work indicates the occasion of its production: 'Part of an Entertainment presented to the countess dowager of Derby at Harefield by some noble persons of her family'. The work – an exercise in the ▷ pastoral – is so short that it hardly warrants the description of 'masque', being really little more than a dramatized form of brief tribute. Music for the work was composed by Henry Lawes (1596–1622) who was to write the music for Milton's more elaborate masque ▷ *Comus* when it was performed in 1634.

Arcadia
A mountainous district in Greece, with a pastoral economy, and in ancient times the centre of the worship of ▷ Pan. The country was idealized by ▷ Virgil in his *Eclogues*, and again in the Renaissance in ▷ pastoral works, notably in ▷ Sir Philip Sidney's *Arcadia*. By this time Arcadia was thought of purely as an ideal country of the imagination, uncorrupted by the sophistications of civilization.

Arcadia, The (1578 and 1590)

From the first edition of Sidney's *Arcadia* (1590)

▷ Philip Sidney's ▷ pastoral romance, *The Arcadia* exists in two distinct versions. The 'old' *Arcadia* was begun c 1578, and circulated widely in manuscript form before Sidney undertook to revise it in 1584 – a task which was interrupted by his death in 1586. This revised (though incomplete) version – the 'new' *Arcadia* – was published in 1590. In 1593 Sidney's sister, ▷ Mary Herbert, Countess of Pembroke, to whom the work had been dedicated, undertook to publish a composite version of the text, which combined the two versions in existence together with her own (substantial) emendations. Thus *The Arcadia*, which enjoyed enormous popularity in the 16th and for much of the 17th century, was a curious hybrid.

In its original version the work was a mixture of love and intrigue, but in its revised form, Sidney broadened the scope of his undertaking. The episodic narrative of lovers, derived from Sidney's reading in late Greek romance, was transformed into what Sidney termed 'an absolute heroical poem' the purpose of which, in accordance with the critical precepts which had been established in ▷ *An Apologie for Poetrie*, was to instil 'delightful teaching'. From the first appearance of the work, critical opinion has been divided as to its seriousness. Some of Sidney's contemporaries understood *The Arcadia* as a profound meditation on morals and politics. For other writers, in particular ▷ John Milton, the work was no more than an exercise in escapist fantasy.
Bib: Editions include: Evans, M. (ed.), *The Countess of Pembroke's Arcadia;* Duncan Jones, K. (ed.), *The Old Arcadia*.

Archaeology
This term is commonly used to describe the scientific study of the remains of prehistoric times. However, in the 20th century the French philosopher ▷ Michel Foucault has sought to redefine it in such a way that the focus of attention becomes not objects, or documents, but the very ▷ discourses through which they come to have meaning. In other words, 'archaeology' does not designate the process of returning to some sort of 'origin' or basis which has an existence outside or beyond language (*ie* the bottom layer of a 'dig'); rather it concerns itself with what Foucault himself describes as 'the systematic description of a discourse-object' (*The Archaeology of Knowledge*, 1972). Foucault contends that knowledge is produced within social contexts where questions of power, politics, economics and morality intersect. It is the purpose of

archaeology to rediscover discursive formations in all their complexity as indices of the ways in which society is organized and it is therefore interdisciplinary in its historical concerns. This form of analysis is to be distinguished from a more traditional 'history of ideas' which privileges evolution and development.

Bib: Foucault, M. *The Archaeology of Knowledge* (1969; translated into English, 1972).

Archery

The art of shooting with the bow and arrow. Archery played an important part in English history in the ▷ Middle Ages. Three kinds of bow were used: the short-bow; the crossbow, which fired a metal bolt released by a trigger; the longbow. The first of these was a comparatively primitive weapon, but it was much in use until the 13th century. During the same period, the crossbow became the principal firearm of west European armies, except English ones; it had a longer range than either of the others, although it could not be fired as quickly, nor was it as accurate as the longbow. The virtues of the longbow were proved to the English by the Welsh, who first developed the weapon. It enabled the English to defeat the Scottish commander ▷ Sir William Wallace at the battle of Falkirk (1298), after which it became for two centuries the principal weapon of the English foot-soldiers, bringing them victory again and again in their wars against the French and the Scots. The secret of this success was partly the constant encouragement, and even enforcement, of the practice of archery as a sport by the medieval kings; ▷ Edward III, for instance, in 1363, forbade all sport except archery on Sundays and other holidays. But the English skill with the longbow also resulted from their distinctive way of using it; in the 16th century ▷ Bishop Latimer described how in his youth he was taught 'not to draw with the strength of the arms as . . . other nations do, but with the strength of the body'.

The importance of archery in medieval England is exemplified by the commonness of the surname Fletcher, which means a 'maker of bows and arrows'. The bows were made from wood of the yew-tree, and this timber was imported in quantity. To ensure cheap supplies, the government of ▷ Richard III (1483–5) ordained that merchants had to include yew staves with every ton of other goods imported. The care for a plentiful supply of bows and for widespread training in their use was due to the dependence of the

medieval kings on the peasantry for the defeance of the realm. They had no large standing armies of professional soldiers, and needed to be able to call on the 'militia' of ordinary ▷ yeomen in every shire.

The invention of gunpowder and the spread of muskets and pistols in the 16th century gradually made the longbow obsolete, although 16th-century governments continued to enforce or at least to encourage the practice of archery. The military importance of the longbow, however, was past by 1500; ▷ R. Ascham *Toxophilus* (1545), a defence of archery.

Archimedes (3rd century BC)

Greek mathematician and inventor. He wrote a number of mathematical treatises which survive, and is particularly associated with the Archimedes Principle in the science of hydrostatics.

Arden, Forest of

Formerly an extensive forest in the neighbourhood of Stratford. It gave its name to the important landed family of Arden; ▷ Shakespeare's mother, Mary Arden, may have belonged to a junior branch. The Forest of Arden in Shakespeare's ▷ *As You Like It* is the forest of the Ardennes, but Shakespeare may have had the English forest in mind as well, when he used the name.
   ▷ *Arden of Faversham, The Tragedy of.*

Arden, John (b 1930)

Dramatist. First play: *All Fall Down* (1955). In 1956 he won a B.B.C. drama prize with *The Life of Man*. This brought him to London's best-known theatre for serious modern drama, the ▷ Royal Court Theatre, where his next three plays were produced: *The Waters of Babylon* (1957); *Live Like Pigs* (1958), and *Sergeant Musgrave's Dance* (1959). The last attracted much attention among critics, though it was not a popular success. It is a play about an army sergeant who deserts with three soldiers from his unit which is stationed in a colonial territory. They come to a mining town in the north of England with the mission to inspire the people with a hatred of war; they seek alliance with the miners who are in conflict with the mine-owners. The multiple conflict that arises from this situation is used to propound complex ideas about the nature of conflict and its resolution; but the play ends in tragedy without a solution to the problems. No dramatist in England since ▷ Shaw had used the theatre for such thorough exploration of political and social ideas, but whereas Shaw made the ideas central to his dramas and the characters merely instrumental to them, Arden makes his characters central, presenting them through a dialogue which sometimes achieves poetic intensity without sacrificing truth to the northern idiom. This play is one of the most substantial achievements of the dramatic revival which most distinguishes English literature in recent years. The most important shaping influence on this and others of Arden's plays seems to be that of the German dramatist ▷ Bertolt Brecht, most noticeably in the simple energy of the dialogue and the dramatic use of lyrics. Arden's later plays are: *Soldier Soldier* (1960); *The Happy Haven* (1960); *The Business of Good Government* (1960); *Wet Fish* (1962); *The Workhouse Donkey* (1963); *Ironhand* (1963); *Ars Longa Vita Brevis* (with Margaretta D'Arcy; 1964); *Armstrong's Last Goodnight* (1964); *Left-handed Liberty* (1965); *Friday's Hiding* (1966); *The Royal Pardon* (1966); *The Hero Rises Up* (1968); *Island of the Mighty* (1972); *The Ballygombeen Bequest* (1972); *The Island of the Mighty* (1972); *The Non-Stop Connolly Show* (1975); *Vandaleur's Folly* (1978); *The Little Gray Home in the West* (1978); *The Manchester Enthusiasts* (1984).

▷ Beckett, Samuel; Osborne, John; Pinter, Harold.

Bib: Hunt, A., *Arden: A Study of His Plays*; Gray, F., *John Arden*.

Arden of Faversham, The Tragedy of (1592)

An anonymous Elizabethan tragedy which is sometimes attributed to ▷ Shakespeare and occupies pride of place in the 'Shakespeare Apocrypha'. The play is almost unique in the period in dealing with recent history. Its subject-matter – the murder in Faversham in 1551 of Thomas Arden by his wife Alice and her accomplices – is related in ▷ Holinshed and vividly dramatized in this early domestic tragedy about criminal passion and greed.

Areopagitica (1644)

Title of a ▷ pamphlet, published on 28 November 1644, written by ▷ John Milton. In June 1643 ▷ Parliament had passed an ordinance which attempted to licence the press – in effect it was designed as a form of covert political ▷ censorship, which allowed officers of Parliament to search for, and confiscate, unlicenced books. Milton's *Areopagitica* was offered as a powerful statement on behalf of liberty of the press. In arguing for such liberty, Milton was aligning himself with radicals such as William Walwyn and Richard Overton, and entering a forceful plea for the free dissemination of information

and ideas without which, in his opinion, it was impossible for individuals to make genuine political choices. In discussing this question of choice, *Areopagitica* can be thought of being a precursor of one of the major themes of ▷ Milton's ▷ *Paradise Lost*. The title itself implicitly compares the Parliament of England, to whom Milton was addressing his comments, to the Supreme Court of ancient Athens which met on the hill Areopagos, situated to the west of the Acropolis.

▷ Levellers, The; Milton, John.

Ares

In Greek myth, the god of war, identifiable with the Roman Mars. He was the son of ▷ Zeus and ▷ Hera, symbolizing the rage of war, or blood-thirstiness, and was constantly opposed to ▷ Athene, associated with wisdom and intelligent courage. His love affair with ▷ Aphrodite symbolizes the close connection between love and war.

Aretino, Pietro (1492–1556)

Italian writer, the author of tragedies such as *Orazio* (1546) and comedies such as *La Cortigiana* (1525) – the latter containing his infamous creation Alvigia, a bawd whose speeches are a combination of the obscene and Latin orations. Aretino enjoyed a considerable reputation in England in the late 16th and early 17th centuries, ▷ Thomas Nashe proclaiming himself a particular admirer.

▷ Italian influence on English literature.

Argonauts

In Greek legend, travellers on the ship *Argo* conveying the hero ▷ Jason in search of the golden fleece of a certain sacred ram. The story is told in English in a narrative poem by ▷ William Morris: *Life and Death of Jason* (1867).

Ariadne

Daughter of ▷ King Minos of Crete and Pasiphae, daughter of the sun-god. She fell in love with ▷ Theseus and helped him to guide himself through the labyrinth, where the ▷ Minotaur was kept, with a line of thread. Later, abandoned by Theseus, she was found and married by ▷ Dionysus.

Ariosto, Ludovico (1474–1533)

Italian author of ▷ comedies, ▷ satires, and, most famously, the romantic ▷ epic ▷ *Orlando Furioso* (1532). Ariosto's comedies include *I suppositi* (1509) which was translated by ▷ George Gascoigne in 1572, and used by ▷ Shakespeare in the composition of ▷ *The Taming of the Shrew*.

His satires owe much to ▷ Horace, but it was his *Orlando* which was to have the greatest influence on English writers, in particular ▷ Edmund Spenser.

▷ Italian influence on English literature.

Aristedes the Just (6th–5th century BC)
In Greek history, a statesman and general of Athens, who took a leading part in resisting the Persian invasion of Greece.

Aristophanes (c 448–c 380 BC)
The greatest of the Attic comic poets and the most important writer of Old Comedy which is distinguished by its aggressive, bawdy satire and personalized attacks. Aristophanes's plays evolve against the background of contemporary political, philosophical and literary concerns, such as the Peloponnesian war between Athens and Sparta (*Lysistrata*), or the rivalry between the Greek tragedians (*The Frogs*). His influence on English drama is reflected in ▷ Ben Jonson's comedies, particularly in ▷ *Bartholomew Fair*, although Jonson and his contemporaries are far more dependent on the formal and thematic properties of the ▷ New Comedy idiom of ▷ Plautus and ▷ Terence.

Aristotle (384–322 BC)
A Greek philosopher, born at Stageira, and so sometimes called the Stagirite. He was first a pupil of ▷ Plato, later developing his thought on principles opposed to those of his master. He was tutor to the young ▷ Alexander (the Great). His thought covered varied fields of knowledge, in most of which he has been influential. His best known works are his *Ethics*, *Politics*, and ▷ *Poetics*.

The difference between Aristotle and Plato has been described as follows: Plato makes us think in the first place of an ideal and supernatural world by turning our minds to ideal forms which are the truth in terms of which imperfect earthly things can be known and judged; Aristotle turns us towards the natural world where things are what they are, perfect or imperfect, so that knowledge comes through study and classification of them in the actual world. It can thus be seen that whilst Plato leads in the direction of mysticism, Aristotle leads towards science. Until the 13th century, Christian thought tended to be dominated by Plato, but medieval Christian thought, owing to the work of ▷ Thomas Aquinas, found Aristotelianism more acceptable.

The *Poetics* is based on the study of imaginative literature in Greek from which Italian critics of the 16th century, and French dramatists and critics of the 17th century such as Corneille, ▷ Racine and ▷ Boileau constructed a system of rules. ▷ Sidney knew Aristotle chiefly through the Italians, who had derived from Aristotle some rules not to be found in him – notably the ▷ unities of time and place: ▷ Dryden and ▷ Samuel Johnson, were respectful of and deeply influenced by French neo-Aristotelianism, but they refused to be bound by it, unlike some second-rank critics such as ▷ Thomas Rymer. The 19th century reacted strongly against the attitude, but in this century the elimination of the neo-Aristotelian superimpositions of the ▷ Renaissance has revived interest in the discernment displayed in the *Poetics*.

Armada, The (Spanish), 1588
The fleet dispatched by Philip II of Spain to transport a Spanish army from Flanders to land in and conquer England. The attempt was defeated by the English fleet under Lord Howard of Effingham and his sea-captains, some of whom were already famous for other exploits, such as ▷ Drake, Hawkins, Frobisher. It was written up as part of the nationalist myth of both countries involved and, in consequence, contrasting accounts of it are given in Spanish and English history. For Philip II of Spain it was a holy war against the heretical English who had abandoned Rome and recently put the Catholic ▷ Mary Queen of Scots to death; under Franco the Armada was said to illustrate the Christian fortitude of Philip II and the need for stoicism in adversity. At the time the English represented it as a national triumph, a personal triumph for the queen and an inspiration for the whole people. It did have far-reaching cultural effects both for Europe and for the non-European world that Europe was about to expand into. England was the most important country to have renounced papal authority; her defeat might have been disastrous to the ▷ Protestant side in its struggle against the Catholic powers, of which Spain was then the chief. Instead, the English victory meant a decisive check to the formidable (▷ Counter-Reformation) attempt of Catholicism to recover the northern countries of Europe. The English victory was a milestone in the shift of power from the Mediterranean region to the Atlantic powers of England, France and Holland, which henceforth increasingly led the European expansion over the globe.
Bib: Martin, C. and Parker, G., *The Spanish Armada*.

Armageddon
In the Bible (*Revelation* 16:16), the last battle
that will end the world; the name may derive
from Megiddo, a place associated with
frequent battles in Israelite history.

Arminianism
▷ Predestination.

Arms and the Man (1894)
An early play by ▷ George Bernard Shaw
with the theme that the glamour of war and
of military heroism is essentially a civilian
fiction. The hero, Bluntschli, is a Swiss
mercenary soldier and unheroic 'anti-hero'
such as was to become common in 20th-
century literature, but, with his ironic
intelligence, was a type special to Shaw.

Armstrong, John (1709–1779)
Medical doctor, friend of ▷ James
Thomson, and author of didactic poems in
blank verse, including the mildly erotic
Economy of Love (1736), and *The Art of
Preserving Health* (1744).

Arnold, Matthew (1822–88)

Matthew Arnold

Poet, critic and educationalist, son of
▷ Thomas Arnold. Most of Arnold's verse
was published by the time he was 45: *The
Strayed Reveller* (1849); *Empedocles on Etna*
(1852); *Poems* (1853); *Poems, Second Series*
(1855); *Merope, a Tragedy* (1858); *New Poems*
(1867). From these volumes, the best-known

poems today are *The Forsaken Merman*
(1849), *Sohrab and Rustum* (1853), a narrative
in ▷ epic style; ▷ *The Scholar Gypsy*
(1853), *Thyrsis* (1867) and the famous short
lyric, *Dover Beach* (1867 – perhaps written
much earlier). His poetry is elegiac,
meditative and melancholy; preoccupied with
spiritual alienation and the loss of religious
faith.

As Arnold began to abandon poetry
writing, his essay and prose writing career
took off; as a critic, he was strongly influential
on early 20th-century thought, as a crucial
figure in the development of English studies
as a discipline in its own right. Mediated by
the works of ▷ T. S. Eliot, ▷ I. A.
Richards, Lionel Trilling, ▷ F. R. Leavis
and the journal ▷ *Scrutiny*, his cultural
criticism forms a lynch-pin of traditional
English criticism. This influence does not
come from his studies of individual writers
but from his studies of contemporary culture
and of the relationship, actual and potential,
of literature to industrial civilization. His best
known critical works are ▷ *Essays in
Criticism*, First and Second Series, 1865 and
1888; *On Translating Homer*, 1861; and
Culture and Anarchy, 1869.

Arnold's work as an inspector of schools
and educationist was related to his most
serious critical preoccupations, and the two
worlds meet in such a work as *Culture and
Anarchy*. His educational theories and
absolute valuing of culture were pitted against
the ▷ Utilitarianism of his historical
moment. Arnold posited a system of humane
education under the headship of an ideal,
liberal state, as the means of ensuring the
triumph of culture over social and spiritual
anarchy.

Bib: Trilling, L., *Matthew Arnold*; Jump,
J. D., *Matthew Arnold*; Brown, E. K., *Arnold:
a Study in Conflict*; Tinker, C. B. and Lowry,
H. F., *The Poetry of Arnold*; Honan, P.,
Matthew Arnold: a Life; Carroll, J., *The
Cultural Theory of Matthew Arnold*; Baldick,
C., *The Social Mission of English Criticism*.

Arnold, Thomas (1795–1842)
Influential Broad Church liberal
▷ Protestant, headmaster of ▷ Rugby
School, and an important figure in the
development of the ▷ public school system
and its values. The father of ▷ Matthew
Arnold, he became professor of Modern
History at ▷ Oxford University in 1841.
Famously characterized in Thomas Hughes's
Tom Brown's Schooldays (1857).

Ars Poetica (Art of Poetry)
▷ Horace.

Artaud, Antonin (1896–1948)

French actor, director and poet, associated with the surrealist theatre and founder of the Théâtre Alfred Jarry. He developed an approach to theatre which he named ▷ 'Theatre of Cruelty'. In this he downgraded the written text in favour of a theatrical language based on ritualistic gesture, movement and sound. His aim was to release in the actor and spectator the primitive human forces ordinarily suppressed by social morality and convention. His theories are explained in his collection of essays entitled *Le Théâtre et son double*. He has been a strong influence on French authors, particularly Camus and Genet, and on the English director ▷ Peter Brook. **Bib:** Esslin, M., *Artaud*; Hayman, R., *Artaud and After*.

Artemis (Phoebe, Cynthia)

In Greek myth, the moon-goddess; identifiable with the Roman Diana. She became gradually less associated with the moon, which was given a distinct goddess, Selene. A huntress and virgin, she was regarded by the Greeks as ▷ Apollo's twin sister, like him associated with the light. However, her cult in the Asian city of Ephesus (where her temple was one of the ▷ Seven Wonders of the World) represented her as a fertility goddess with almost opposite qualities to those of the Greek Artemis.

Arthur, King

King Arthur asleep on board ship, illustration from Sir Thomas Malory's *Works*

If there is a historical figure behind King Arthur, it may be that of a British chieftain, active some time in the 5th or 6th century, who resisted Saxon invaders after the Roman garrisons had abandoned Britain. Documentary evidence and archaeological data provide us with only a vague picture of the historical events of these centuries, and so the historical location of an Arthur figure continues to be a subject of great debate. ▷ Gildas, the 6th-century monastic chronicler, records an important British victory over the Saxons at Mount Badon, some time around 500, but there is no mention of Arthur in Gildas's narrative. However, in the 9th-century compilation, the *Historia Brittonum* (*History of Britain*), attributed to ▷ Nennius, Arthur is given responsibility for leading the British side to victory at the battle of Badon, although his role here and in the 11 other battles accredited to him is that of a chieftain or general, not a British king. A 10th-century compilation, the *Annales Cambriae* (*Annals of Wales*), credits Arthur with victory at the Battle of Badon in 518, and also records that in the battle of Camlan in 539, Arthur and 'Medreut' fell.

William of Malmesbury's remarks in his *Gesta Regum Anglorum* (*Deeds of the Kings of the English*) suggest that by 1125 much material had accreted around the figure of Arthur, some of it mere fable and lies according to William. Arthur is credited with great feats at the battle of Badon, but his family connection with Walwen (▷ Gawain) is mentioned later by William, who also comments on the legend that Arthur may yet return. Modern attempts to recreate some sense of early vernacular (Celtic) Arthurian narratives and traditions are fraught with problems. Arthur does figure in early Welsh narratives, as an important chieftain, who in one case goes on an expedition to a Celtic otherworld to obtain a magic cauldron (in the poem known as the *Spoils of Annwfn*), but although this material may be circulating from an early date, the versions that survive are in manuscripts dating from the 13th century onwards. Important Celtic Arthurian narratives, for example, are preserved in the Black Book of Camarthen, c 1200; the White Book of Rhydderch, dating from the early 14th century; the Red Book of Hengest, dating from the late 14th century.

The writer responsible for putting King Arthur firmly on the map of British history was ▷ Geoffrey of Monmouth who, in his ▷ *Historia Regum Britanniae* (*History of the Kings of Britain*), c 1138, provided a continuous account of the British kings from Brutus onwards and made the reign of King Arthur the high spot of this sequence. Under Arthur's rule, Britain regains its status as a unified Christian nation, and gains international power and prestige too. This version of British history, though challenged by some late-medieval historians, appears to have been generally accepted and became a standard feature of accounts of insular history. Notable vernacular versions of Geoffrey's narrative include those by ▷ Wace (in ▷ Anglo-Norman), ▷ Laȝamon and ▷ Robert Mannyng, and material from this chronicle tradition of Arthurian narrative forms the basis for the early 15th-century English poem, the alliterative ▷ *Morte Arthure*. For the development of the tradition of Arthurian romance, we have to turn to the activities of the 12th-century French and Anglo-Norman writers who developed a body of narratives focussed on the adventures of individual members of Arthur's court. Writers such as ▷ Béroul, Thomas of Britain, ▷ Marie de France and ▷ Chrétien de Troyes, drew on Celtic story motifs to develop narratives which explored the interests and tensions of court culture and its ideals. Of these writers, Chrétien de Troyes deserves special attention: his sophisticated vernacular romances seem to have stimulated the creation of a much larger body of texts centred on the court of King Arthur, and some of his works were translated into other European vernaculars (*Yvain*, for example, is reworked in the early 14th-century Middle English verse narrative as *Yvain and Gawain*).

The 13th century sees the development of much longer, interlaced Arthurian narratives, which became organized into the so-called ▷ Vulgate and post-Vulgate cycles of Arthurian romance. A notable addition to the post-Chrétien narrative tradition of Arthurian material is the development of the quest of the Holy ▷ Grail into a narrative which celebrates transcendental Christian ideals and which provides the means for linking Arthurian history to scriptural history.

English translations and reworkings of French Arthurian romances date from the early 14th century onwards (*Sir Tristrem*, *Arthour and Merlin*, and ▷ *Morte Arthur* (stanzaic)), but the alliterative romance of ▷ *Sir Gawain and the Green Knight*, in which Arthurian chronicle and romance traditions are played off against each other, has no French precedent. ▷ Thomas Malory provided English readers with a reworking of the massive Arthurian narrative cycle in the late 15th century (drawn largely from the Vulgate cycle) and his *Works* (or rather ▷ Caxton's printed edition of Malory's text known as the ▷ *Morte D'Arthur*) provides the standard account of Arthurian narrative

for later writers and reworkers of Arthurian topics and themes.

King Arthur thus became an important feature of the English literary and historical landscape, and Arthurian narrative was constantly open in the course of its development for appropriation as a means of expressing and exploring different kinds of political and cultural ideals. ▷ Spenser's epic, ▷ *The Faerie Queene*, has the figure of Prince Arthur as its central protagonist, and later writers such as ▷ Ben Jonson, ▷ Milton and ▷ Dryden all planned major works on Arthurian topics (although only Dryden actually produced an Arthurian text, his dramatic opera *King Arthur*). The history of Arthurian narrative has periods of decline and revival, though the subject of Arthur always seems to have been available as a cultural reference point. Since the 19th century, a major revival of interest in all facets of Arthurian legend, history and culture has been under way. ▷ Tennyson's composite work, ▷ *The Idylls of the King*, reaffirmed the importance of Arthurian narrative as an arena for exploring national, political and cultural values, and provided a major source of stimulation for the Pre-Raphaelite group of painters and writers. An enormous body of 20th-century Arthurian narrative is available to modern readers, including works by ▷ T. S. Eliot, ▷ John Masefield, Charles Williams, ▷ David Jones, T. H. White and Marion Zimmer Bradley (who in *The Mists of Avalon* reworks Arthurian narrative from the perspective of its central female protagonists). **Bib:** Lacy, N. et al. (eds.), *The Arthurian Encyclopedia*; Loomis, R. S. (ed.), *Arthurian Literature in the Middle Ages*.

Arts Council of Great Britain

This body began as the Council for the Encouragement of Music and Art in 1940, to promote theatrical and musical entertainment during World War II. It now provides funding for a great variety of arts projects, including regional and national theatres and touring companies, throughout Britain. Its purpose is 'to develop a greater knowledge, understanding, and practice of the Fine Arts, to increase their accessibility to the public, and to improve their standard of execution'. Although its distribution of funds has often been contentious, its existence has helped the proliferation of theatre companies during the last two decades.
▷ C.E.M.A.

Aryan

A linguistic term derived from the Sanskrit *arya* or noble, coined by the early philologists.

It was applied to the group of languages which includes Sanskrit, Zend, Persian, Greek, Latin, Celtic, Teutonic and Slavonic. Although apparently a convenience of classification, its root-meaning shows how it played a part in creating a hierarchy of languages. Cultural nationalists were quick to appropriate the term and use it to assert that speakers of these languages had a common biological identity. It is now recognized that there is no such thing as common genetic origin within any group, owing to tribal migrations and intermarriages, but the myth of racial purity under the banner of Aryanism promoted the mass killing of Jews under Hitler.

▷ Old English.

As You Like It

A comedy by ▷ Shakespeare. Produced about 1599, and first printed in the ▷ folio of 1623. Its source is ▷ Thomas Lodge's romance, *Rosalynde*.

The story is romantic and ▷ pastoral. A Duke, the father of the heroine, Rosalind, has been turned off his throne by his ruthless brother, the father of Rosalind's devoted friend, Celia. He has taken refuge with a few loyal courtiers in the neighbouring ▷ Forest of Arden. An orphan son, Orlando, is tyrannized by his wicked elder brother, Oliver. Orlando and Rosalind fall in love. Rosalind is banished from court, and goes to the forest in male disguise, calling herself Ganymede; Celia goes with her as Rosalind-Ganymede's sister, Aliena, and they are also accompanied by the court jester, Touchstone. Orlando follows them. He does not discover Rosalind's disguise, however, when, as Ganymede, she makes him 'play-act' courtship with her, episodes which are used by Shakespeare as light satires on the conventions of romantic love. Another pair of lovers in the forest are the shepherd and shepherdess, Silvius and Phebe, a couple who are drawn from the most artifical pastoral mode. Phebe (true to her convention) disdains Silvius, but falls embarrassingly in love with Rosalind (in her disguise) at first sight, and in spite of Rosalind's rudeness to her. Touchstone engages the affections of an unromantic and realistic village girl, Audrey, and thus frustrates her unromantic village lover, William. There is also Jaques, a fashionable and affected young man in the Elizabethan style, attached to the court of the exiled Duke. Rosalind, who is extremely plain-spoken except when she remembers that she is in love, exposes his affectations. In the end the couples are sorted out appropriately,

and Rosalind's father regains his dukedom.

Shakespeare thus plays off real life against literary convention. The play is gay, satirical and romantic, all in one. Together with ▷ *Twelfth Night* it is his best work in the style of romantic comedy.

Ascham, Roger (1515–68)

Humanist, educationalist, tutor to ▷ Elizabeth I and secretary to ▷ Mary I. In 1538 he was made Greek reader at St John's College, Cambridge, and later, in 1546, public orator of the university. His two major works are *Toxophilus* (1545) and *The Schoolmaster* (1570). The latter is an educational manual, addressed to the prospective tutors of the children of the social elite, which sets out the ▷ humanist ideal of creating the harmonious individual. His *Toxophilus* is a dialogue in praise of the sport of archery.

Ash Wednesday

1 The first day of the religious season of Lent, a day of penitence when, in the Catholic Church, the penitents had their foreheads marked with ash.

2 *Ash-Wednesday* is the title of a sequence of poems, 1930, by ▷ T. S. Eliot (1888–1965), marking poetically the conversion of the poet to Christianity.

Astell, Mary (1666–1731)

Now claimed as 'the first English feminist', Mary Astell was a writer and intellectual, who published influential tracts on the duties and injustices of marriage, the most famous being *A Serious Proposal to the Ladies for the Advancement of their true and greatest Interest* (1694), which appeared anonymously as the work of 'a Lover of Her Sex'. With the help of several patrons, most notably William Sancroft, the archbishop of Canterbury, Astell was able to live independently in London and make a career of writing. Her views on the equality of the sexes were, however, modified by her conservative politics and her religious commitment to the Anglican Church. A wife's status in relation to her husband was, she argued, in the nature of a voluntary contract, but: 'It may be any Man's Business and Duty to keep Hogs; he was not Made for this, but if he hires himself out to such an Employment, he ought conscientiously to perform it'.
Bib: Perry, Ruth, *The Celebrated Mary Astell.*

Astraea

In Greek myth, 'the star maiden', usually considered to be the daughter of ▷ Zeus and Themis. During the ▷ Golden Age she lived on earth as the benefactress of humanity. The name was adopted by the playwright, ▷ Aphra Behn.

Astraea Redux ('Astraea Returning', 1660) is a poem by ▷ John Dryden about the restoration of ▷ King Charles II.

Astrophil and Stella (1581–3)

A sequence of 108 ▷ sonnets and eleven songs written by ▷ Sir Philip Sidney and composed c 1581–3. The collection was first published (in a pirated edition) in 1591. The sonnets as a whole take the form of a series of poetic addresses from Astrophil (star-lover) to Stella (star), though it is not difficult to pierce this fiction and associate Astrophil with Sidney himself and Stella with Penelope Devereux, daughter of the Earl of Essex. The sequence should not, however, be taken as a simple disguised autobiographical record. Instead, the sonnets are an investigation of an obsession, a complex depiction of a psychological impasse. Adopting many of the conventions of ▷ Petrarch's poetry, they catalogue not only the cumulative progress of a love affair, but raise important theoretical questions concerning the act of writing and recording a state of mind, whilst also questioning the conventions by which writer and reader are tied to one another. Though sonnet sequences were published before Sidney's collection appeared, it was *Astrophil and Stella* which set the standard by which later sequences were to be judged.

▷ Daniel, Samuel.

Atalanta

In Greek legend, a beautiful girl, famed for her speed. Suitors, to win her, had to beat her in a race, and be killed by her dart if they lost. She was eventually beaten by Milanion, who distracted her from the race by throwing down three golden apples. She is also associated with another legend, of the killing of the Calydonian Boar. *Atalanta's Race* is a poem by ▷ William Morris in *The Earthly Paradise* (1868–70); *Atalanta in Calydon* (1865) is a poetic drama in Greek style by ▷ Algernon Swinburne.

Atheism

Disbelief in God. In the ▷ Middle Ages and the 16th and 17th centuries, atheism was abhorrent; it was equivalent to a denial of conscience – an attitude shown in the play *The Atheist's Tragedy* (1611) by ▷ Cyril Tourneur. There were some who adopted this position and effectively challenged the power of organized religion. ▷ Christopher Marlowe was charged with it in 1593. Nevertheless atheism at this period was different from the systematic belief that man's reason suffices for his welfare. This belief grew in the 18th century and emerged in the ▷ French Revolution, influencing such English intellectuals as ▷ William Godwin and through him ▷ P. B. Shelley, whose atheism caused him to be expelled from Oxford, and for whom ▷ Platonism sufficed. Different, but still 18th-century in its sources, was the atheism of ▷ Utilitarians such as James Mill (1773–1836) and ▷ John Stuart Mill, who were less naïve about Reason than Godwin but, as practical men, saw religion as unnecessary in their scheme for human betterment. The scientific ideas of the ▷ Victorian period, especially those of ▷ Charles Darwin and ▷ Thomas Huxley, were more productive of ▷ agnosticism than of atheism. Modern atheism is exemplified by the Rationalist Press, but it remains a minority attitude among writers, in contrast to agnosticism, which is rather commoner than professed faith.

Atheist, The: or The Second Part of the Soldier's Fortune (1684)

Play by ▷ Thomas Otway; his last. A comedy, with many intrigue elements. Porcia (played by ▷ Elizabeth Barry in the original version) is pursued by an unwanted suitor, her late husband's brother, who tries to force her to marry him. She approaches Beaugard (first played by ▷ Thomas Betterton) in masquerade, to take up her cause and, in effect, marry her instead, although she claims at first to hate him. Beaugard is also pursued by Lucretia, but he remains loyal to Porcia, whereupon Lucretia plots her revenge, disguising herself as a man in the process of attempting to mismate various characters. Meanwhile Courtine and Sylvia, lovers in ▷ *The Soldier's Fortune*, have now married, but the union is unhappy, and he abandons her. Various complications are resolved after an improbable last scene, where numerous characters mistake one another's identities in the dark. It is interesting that the men in the play are largely passive, while most of the action is initiated by women.

Atheist's Tragedy, The (1611)

The only extant tragedy confidently attributed to ▷ Cyril Tourneur, formerly thought to be the author also of ▷ *The Revenger's Tragedy*. The play dramatizes the evil plotting of d'Amville, the atheist, to advance his wealth through marital intrigue, and ends in a grotesque manner with the involuntary suicide of the villain and the safeguarding of true love.

Athenaeum, The

Founded in 1828, it was one of the most
enlightened periodicals of the 19th century. It
was honest and independent in literary
criticism, and a leader of the movement to
spread education among the working classes.
In 1831 it reduced its price by half in order
to reach this wider public, and in consequence
increased its circulation six times. It was also
very progressive in social reform. In 1921 it
was incorporated in the *Nation and
Athenaeum*, which in turn was merged in
1931 with the socialist weekly, ▷ *The New
Statesman*.

Athene (Pallas, Pallas Athene)

(Lat. Minerva). In Greek myth, the goddess
of wisdom, and in general of the intellectual
and active sides of life, *eg* industry and
politics. She sprang fully armed from the
head of her father ▷ Zeus. The city of
Athens was called after her.

Atlantis

A legendary mid-Atlantic island, described
by the Greek philosopher ▷ Plato in his
dialogue *Timaeus*. It is said to have had
immense power and prosperity until it was
submerged by the sea. Its existence was
believed in during the ▷ Middle Ages
partly owing to legends about other
mysterious western lands, such as Avalon
and ▷ Lyonesse, both in Arthurian legend.
Such places were imagined as earthly
paradises, and in the ▷ Renaissance the
myths were used to demonstrate ideal
governments and countries, in the Platonic
style. Hence *The New Atlantis* (1626) by
▷ Francis Bacon.

Atticus (109–32 BC)

T. Pomponius Atticus was a correspondent of
Cicero, learned in Greek literature.
▷ Alexander Pope refers to ▷ Joseph
Addison under this name, in lines which he
originally sent as a reproach to the older man
in a letter in about 1715. They were first
published in 1722 after Addison's death, and
appear in revised form in the *Epistle to Dr
Arbuthnot* (1735).

Attila (d AD 453)

King of the ▷ Huns. His kingdom centred
on Hungary; from it he made devastating
attacks on the Eastern Roman Empire and on
the Germanic kingdoms which had replaced
the Empire in Western Europe. He was
eventually defeated (451). The terror that he
inspired caused him to be known as 'the
scourge of God' and he has remained a
symbol of destruction.

Atwood, Margaret (b 1939)

Margaret Atwood

Canadian novelist, poet and short-story
writer. Born in Ottawa, she spent part of her
early years in the wilds of northern Quebec,
and her poetry makes considerable
metaphorical use of the wilderness and its
animals. Her first two novels are poetic
accounts of the heroines' search for self-
realization, and each has a dominant central
metaphor: emotional cannibalism in *The
Edible Woman* (1969) and drowning and
surfacing in *Surfacing* (1972). *Lady Oracle*
(1976) is a more comic and satirical work,
portraying the limitations of middle-class
Canadian life. Her poetry, which is
unrhymed, shares many themes with her
novels; *The Journals of Susanna Moodie:
Poems* (1970) employs pioneering as a
metaphor for contemporary feminist
questioning of gender roles. Her more recent
novels have broader social themes: *Bodily
Harm* (1981) is a political satire set on a
Caribbean island, while *The Handmaid's Tale*
(1986) is a vision of a futuristic dystopia,
influenced by ▷ George Orwell's *1984*. It
focuses on the exploitation of women in a
state ruled by religious fundamentalism, and
the ambivalent, ironic conclusion promotes a
complex sense of the novel's relevance to our
own times. Atwood's interest in Canadian
nationalism and in feminism have made her
an important figure in contemporary
Canadian culture.

Other novels: *Life Before Man* (1979);
Cat's Eye (1989). Story collections: *Dancing
Girls* (1977); *Murder in the Dark* (1984);
Bluebeard's Egg (1986); *Wilderness Tips*
(1991). Volumes of poetry include:
Selected Poems (1976); *Marsh, Hawk*
(1977); *Two Headed Poems* (1978); *True*

Stories (1981); *Notes Towards a Poem That Can Never Be Written* (1981); *Snake Poems* (1983); *Interlunar* (1984). Criticism: *Second Words: Selected Critical Prose* (1982).
▷ Commonwealth Literature.
Bib: Rigney, B. H., *Margaret Atwood.*

Aubrey, John (1626–97)
Biographer and antiquary. Aubrey was a man of endlessly fascinated speculation on every aspect of the world in which he found himself. Entirely without any form of method, he nevertheless produced (though never published) an invaluable record of people, events and happenings of the period in which he lived. Frequently the record of personalities preserved by Aubrey is highly untrustworthy in terms of its factual content, and yet his *Brief Lives* are still an important document not least because of their often penetrating assessment of his subjects' lives and works. If nothing else, Aubrey has preserved a running critical commentary on many of the figures from the 17th century whose works are read in the 20th century.
▷ Biography.
Bib: Dick, O. L. (ed.), *Aubrey's Brief Lives.*

Auchinleck Manuscript
A famous literary anthology (now kept in the National Library of Scotland, Edinburgh, Advocates' MS 19.2.1), which was probably produced around 1330–40 in a London workshop. It contains a wide range of vernacular texts including an important collection of romances (such as ▷ *Bevis of Hampton*, *King Alisaunder*, *Richard the Lion-heart* and *Sir Tristrem*).

Auden, W. H. (Wystan Hugh) (1907–73)
Poet and dramatist. Born in York, Auden spent much of his childhood in Birmingham, but was educated at Gresham's School, Norfolk, a ▷ public school with liberal ideas about education, and at ▷ Oxford University. The landscape of the industrial Midlands influenced his work throughout his life. Auden began writing poetry at 15, and twice edited the journal *Oxford Poetry* when he went up to Oxford in 1925. As a student he became the central figure in the 1930s group of left-wing intellectuals, which included ▷ Stephen Spender (who printed Auden's first collection of poems on a hand press), ▷ Cecil Day Lewis, ▷ Louis MacNeice and ▷ Christopher Isherwood. His background was a middle-class intellectual one, which produced a sense of social responsibility and a strong didactic tendency in his poetry. He became a teacher and worked both in an English school and in

English and American universities. He married Erika Mann, Thomas Mann's daughter and an anti-Nazi, in 1938, so that she could obtain British citizenship, although Auden was himself a homosexual. He emigrated to the U.S.A. in 1939, becoming an American citizen in 1946. In 1956 he became professor of poetry at Oxford, and died in Austria in 1973.

His first book, *Poems* (1930), was published during the great economic crisis which originated in the U.S.A. in 1929. This was followed by *The Orators* (1932), the 'charade' *The Dance of Death* (1933), *Look, Stranger!* (1936), *Letters from Iceland* (with MacNeice, 1937), *Journey to a War* (with Isherwood, 1939) and *Another Time* (1940). He also wrote plays, often with Isherwood: *The Dog Beneath the Skin* (with Isherwood; 1935); *The Ascent of F6* (with Isherwood; 1936); *On the Frontier* (with Isherwood; 1938).

His verse is full of topical reference to the social and international crises of the time; it gives direct expression to the anxieties of the contemporary intelligentsia as perhaps no other writing has done. Auden was interested in verse technique, and influenced by an extensive range of writing, extending from the ▷ alliterative styles of Old and Middle English to ▷ T. S. Eliot and the late work of ▷ W. B. Yeats. Throughout his life he was interested in ▷ Freud and ▷ psychoanalytic theory, and also absorbed ▷ Marxism, the work of Danish philosopher Søren Kierkegaard, and the 20th-century German-American theologian Niebuhr. After 1940 he became increasingly committed to Anglo-Catholic Christianity.

After his emigration to America, Auden published long poems: *New Year Letter* (1941), *For the Time Being* (1945), *The Age of Anxiety* (1948), and then shorter poems: *Nones* (1952), *The Shield of Achilles* (1955), *Homage to Clio* (1960). He has also written criticism: *The Enchafèd Flood* (1951), *The Dyer's Hand* (1963); libretti for operas, and he has edited a number of ▷ anthologies. Towards the end of his life he became an isolated figure, so unlike the first decade of his writing when he had seemed to be the voice of a generation – although perhaps, in reality, only the generation of the younger middle class. Later works and editions include: *About the House* (1966); *City Without Walls* (1969); *Epistle to a Godson* (1972); *Thank You Fog: Last Poems* (1974); *Collected Poems* (ed. Mendelson; 1976); *The English Auden* (ed. Mendelson; 1977).
Bib: Hoggart, R., *Introductory Essay*; Muir, E. and Daiches, D., *The Present Age*; Drew, E., *Directions in Modern Poetry*; Beach, J. W.,

The Making of the Auden Canon; Spears, M. K., *The Poetry of W. H. Auden*; Everett, B., *Auden* in the Writers and Critics Series; Hynes, S., *The Auden Generation*; Mendelson, E., *Early Auden*.

Augustanism

There are two aspects to 'Augustanism', one political, the other more strictly literary.

1 *Political Augustanism*   In the decades following the Restoration a more or less fanciful parallel between recent English history and that of early imperial Rome was developed, following similar gestures by ▷ Ben Jonson earlier in the century. Both the Emperor Augustus (27 BC–AD 14) and ▷ King Charles II could be felt to have restored order to the state as legitimate successors to rulers who had been assassinated by Republicans (Julius Caesar, Charles I). Both preserved the forms of constitutionality, and kept at least the appearance of a balance of power between Senate or Parliament and the head of state. Both rulers, and their successors, presided over an expansion of imperial power which extended their own civilization over more barbarous peoples, by means of military power – the army in the case of Rome, the navy in the case of Britain. Where there had previously been the *Pax Romana* there would now be a *Pax Britannica*. Both Tories and ▷ Whigs could feel reassured by this parallel, though naturally a Whig would tend to stress the constitutionality of the new order, while a Tory such as ▷ Alexander Pope stresses its Stuart legitimacy: 'And Peace and Plenty tell, a *Stuart* reigns' (*Windsor Forest*, p. 42). Political Augustanism is concerned essentially with society and with public issues, and is optimistic about British civilization and its role in the world as imperial power. It is detectable in such diverse works as ▷ Daniel Defoe's ▷ *Robinson Crusoe* and ▷ James Thomson's *Castle of Indolence*.

2 *Literary Augustanism*   The reign of Augustus coincided with the golden age of Roman culture and literature, and Roman writers of the time, such as ▷ Horace and ▷ Virgil, explicitly celebrate the Roman imperial destiny. During the period of stability and growing prosperity following the ▷ Restoration, the somewhat naive adulation of the classics found in such Tudor writers as ▷ George Chapman and ▷ Ben Jonson, is replaced by a growing understanding of, and sense of equality with, the great Latin writers. At last English literature was coming of age in terms of self-conscious theoretical confidence, technical sophistication and diversity of genre and metrical form. The foundation of the ▷ Poet Laureateship as a regular court office is a sign of this new confidence. In his essays ▷ John Dryden constantly parallels the achievements of modern English writers with their classical ancestors. The young ▷ Alexander Pope picked up the spirit of the age very young and was promoted by his friends as an English Virgil. The true poet, it was vaguely felt, would follow Virgil in writing first ▷ pastorals (which require only technical skill and little experience of life), then would move on to ▷ Georgics, or longer discursive compositions, and would crown his life's work with an ▷ epic. With a little licence this pattern could be read into the careers of the earlier English writers, ▷ Edmund Spenser and ▷ John Milton, who were achieving classic status at this time. Ornamental, courtly forms, such as the ▷ sonnet and Spenserian stanza, were now despised as childishly 'gothic', or employed with a conscious sense of their quaint primitiveness. The 'heroic' ▷ couplet emerged as the most dignified ▷ metre of which English verse was felt to be capable. Since the English language, lacking the sounding mellifluousness of classical Latin, could not support lines the length of the Latin hexameter, nor dispense with the 'barbarous' ornament of rhyme, then the best recourse, it was felt, was to regularize and dignify the pentameter couplet. (Blank verse is of course a much more natural English parallel to the Latin hexameter, but the best poets were wisely unwilling for the time being to risk comparison with the recent example of Milton.) Alongside the cultivation of the couplet a doctrine of 'kinds' grew up which prescribed specific 'high' or noble vocabulary for epic writing, and specific vocabularies for the other genres. This notion, which reflects the class consciousness of the new bourgeoisie, as much as any purely literary doctrine, is seen at its most rigid in ▷ Thomas Parnell's *Essay on the Different Stiles of Poetry* (1713). The neo-classical style which resulted from this regulation of ▷ metre and language could hope to appeal both to the traditional Aristotelian classicist of the time who required an 'imitation' of permanent nature, and the Lockean rationalist who could see ▷ Sir Isaac Newton's 'laws' of nature reflected in the couplet's combination of formal exactitude and infinite variety.

It is important to stress that such Augustanism is, like ▷ Romanticism, the artificial construction of literary historians, and never constituted a systematic programme or manifesto for poetry. The summary above lends it a coherence and exactitude which it never achieved in the work of any poet. Like most literary movements Augustanism was only defined after it was virtually over.

▷ Oliver Goldsmith seems to have been the first to use the adjective 'Augustan' in regard to English literature, applying it in *The Bee* (1759) to the reigns of William III and Queen Anne. The noun Augustanism seems not to have come into use until the early 20th century. In 1904 ▷ Theodore Watts-Dunton accused ▷ Thomas Gray of being 'a slave to 'Augustanism', a judgment that Gray himself would have found quite bewildering. In the later 19th and early 20th century all 18th-century poetry tended to be characterized as overformal and emotionless, and the terms 'Augustan', 'Augustanism' and 'The Augustan Age', frequently served to obscure rather than illuminate the poetry of the period.

Bib: Ford, B. (ed.), *New Pelican Guide to English Literature, Vol. 4: From Dryden to Johnson*; Rogers, P., *The Augustan Vision*; Rogers, P., *Hacks and Dunces: Pope, Swift and Grub Street*; Novak, M., *Eighteenth-Century English Literature*; Sambrook, J., *The Eighteenth Century*; Doody, M. A., *The Daring Muse: Augustan Poetry Reconsidered*.

Aureng-Zebe (1675)

Heroic play by ▷ John Dryden, based on a contemporary account of the struggle between the four sons of Shah Jahan, the fifth Mogul emperor, for the succession to the throne. Dryden makes several crucial changes to his source, notably to the character of Aureng-Zebe, who in Dryden's version remains loyal to his father, even though he is betrayed by him. This morality pays off, in that at the end of the play he receives the crown legitimately. The character of Indamora, a captive queen whom Aureng-Zebe loves, is invented by Dryden. At the end they are united, with the blessings of the emperor who had pursued Indamora for himself.

Aurora Leigh (1857)

One of ▷ Elizabeth Barrett Browning's most important works, and a key text for Victorian debates about the 'woman question', *Aurora Leigh* is a long narrative or 'novel-poem' which has recently been given the critical attention it deserves as an important document of the women's movement (▷ Feminism). On publication it was enormously popular and ran to many editions – three in 1857 alone, 17 by 1882. It is a semi-autobiographical account of the development of a female poet, exploring both the nature of sexual difference and the role of the woman writer. Aurora is brought up in Italy until she is 13, when she is sent to England to live with an aunt. Secretly, she educates herself. At 20 she refuses a marriage proposal from her cousin Romney, who wishes her to give up writing and devote herself to social reform. Left alone and penniless when her aunt dies, she builds herself a reputation as a poet in London. Here she becomes involved with Lady Waldemar who is in love with Romney and wishes to use Aurora to prevent him from marrying the poor sempstress Marian Erle. Marian runs away to the continent before the marriage can take place, where Aurora finds her with an illegitimate child, the product of a rape. The two women live happily together in Italy for some time, before Aurora meets up with the now blinded and politically disillusioned Romney. Aurora and Romney confess their love for each other, as he acknowledges the importance of Aurora's work.

In 1978 *Aurora Leigh* was republished by The Women's Press, edited and introduced by Cora Kaplan.

Austen, Jane (1775–1817)

SENSE

AND

SENSIBILITY:

A NOVEL.

IN THREE VOLUMES.

BY A LADY.

VOL. I.

London:
PRINTED FOR THE AUTHOR,
By C. Roworth, Bell-yard, Temple-bar,
AND PUBLISHED BY T. EGERTON, WHITEHALL.
1811.

Title page of the first edition of Jane Austen's *Sense and Sensibility* (1811)

Novelist. Her novels in order of publication are as follows: ▷ *Sense and Sensibility* (1811), ▷ *Pride and Prejudice* (1813), ▷ *Mansfield Park* (1814), ▷ *Emma* (1816), ▷ *Northanger Abbey* and ▷ *Persuasion* (1818). The last two, published posthumously, are her first and last work respectively in order of composition. Fragments and early drafts include: *Lady Susan* (pub 1871), *The Watsons* (1871) and *Sanditon*, on which she was working when she died, published in 1925.

She restricted her material to a narrow range of society and events: a prosperous, middle-class circle in provincial surroundings. However, she treated this material with such subtlety of observation and depth of penetration that she is ranked among the best of English novelists. A French critic, Louis Cazamian, writes of her method that it is 'so classical, so delicately shaded . . . that we are strongly reminded of the great French analysts'. Her classicism arises from respect for the sane, clear-sighted judgement of the ▷ Augustan age that had preceded her, but its vitality is enhanced by the ▷ romanticism of her own period, so that her heroines acquire wisdom by a counter-balancing of the two. She brought the English novel, as an art form, to its maturity, and the wide range which that form covered later in the 19th century owed much to the imaginative assurance which she had given it.

Her life as a clergyman's daughter was outwardly uneventful but it is probably not true that this accounts for the absence of sensationalism in her novels; her circle of relatives and friends was such as could have given her a wide experience of contemporary society. The restriction of the subject matter of her fiction seems to have been dictated by artistic considerations. D. W. Harding's essay 'Regulated Hatred: An Aspect of the Work of Jane Austen' (*Scrutiny*, 1940) credits her with being a caustic satirist and critic of society.
Bib: Austen-Leigh, J. E., *A Memoir of Jane Austen*; Lascelles, M., *Jane Austen and her Art*; Mudrick, M., *Jane Austen: Irony as Defence and Discovery*; Trilling, L., 'Mansfield Park' in *The Opposing Self*; Leavis, Q. D., *A Critical Theory of Jane Austen's Writings* (*Scrutiny x, xiii*); Southam, B. C. (ed.), *Jane Austen: The Critical Heritage*; Cecil, D., *A Portrait of Jane Austen*.

Authorized Version of the Bible
▷ Bible in England.

Autobiography
The word came into English at the very end of the 18th century. In the 19th and 20th centuries the writing of the story of one's own life has become a common literary activity. However, the practice already had an ancient history, and English autobiography may be divided into three overlapping historical segments: 1 the spiritual confession; 2 the memoir; 3 the autobiographical novel.

1 The spiritual confession has as its basic type the Confessions of St Augustine of Hippo (345–430) who described his conversion to Christianity. Such records of the inner life existed in the English Middle Ages, *eg* the *Book of Margery Kempe* (15th century), but the great age for them was the 17th century, when the ▷ Puritans, depending on the Word of God in the Bible and the inner light of their own consciences, made a practice of intensive self-examination. By far the best known of these records is ▷ Bunyan's ▷ *Grace Abounding to the Chief of Sinners* (1666). It is characteristic of such works that they contain detailed accounts of the emotional life, but little factual description of events.

2 The memoir, on the other hand, of French derivation, originates largely in the 17th century and owes much to the practice of extensive letter-writing which then developed, *eg* the letters of Madame de Sévigné (1626–96). An unusual early example of this class is the autobiography of the musician Thomas Whythorne (1528–96), published in 1964 and entitled *A Book of Songs and Sonetts*. An example from 18th-century England is the fragmentary *Memoirs* (pub 1796) by the historian ▷ Edward Gibbon. But the objective memoir and the subjective confessions came together in the *Confessions* of the French-Swiss ▷ Jean-Jacques Rousseau, and this is the most prevalent form of the outstanding English autobiographies of the 19th century. The varieties of this form are extensive: they may be a record of emotional struggles and experiences, *eg* ▷ *The Confessions of an English Opium Eater* by ▷ Thomas de Quincey; ▷ *Sartor Resartus* by ▷ Thomas Carlyle. They may be essentially a history of the growth of ideas, convictions, and the strengthening of vocation, in the life of the writer, *eg Autobiography* (1873) by ▷ John Stuart Mill; *My Apprenticeship* (1926) by ▷ Beatrice Webb; *Apologia pro Vita Sua* (1864) by ▷ Cardinal Newman. In any case, an autobiographical element becomes prominent in works which are not strictly autobiographies from the early 19th century on; *eg* ▷ Wordsworth's *Prelude, or Growth of a Poet's Mind* (first version 1805); the

periodical essays of ▷ Charles Lamb in
▷ *Essays of Elia* (1820–3) and
▷ Coleridge's mixture of autobiography
with philosophy and literary criticism in
Biographia Literaria (1817). It may be said
that from 1800 on it becomes the instinct of
writers of many kinds to use autobiographical
material, or to adopt from time to time an
autobiographical standpoint.

3 Thus we come to the autobiographical
novel: this begins with the novels of
▷ Charlotte Brontë (▷ *Jane Eyre*, 1847,
and ▷ *Villette*, 1853), and Charles Dickens's
▷ *David Copperfield* (1849–50). This
method of writing a novel really came into its
own however, with ▷ Samuel Butler's
▷ *Way of all Flesh* (1903), which led to
many successors in the 20th century, notably
▷ James Joyce's ▷ *Portrait of the Artist as
a Young Man* (1916), and ▷ D. H.
Lawrence's ▷ *Sons and Lovers* (1913).

Autolycus
A character in ▷ *The Winter's Tale* who is
one of ▷ Shakespeare's most resourceful
rogues. He 'haunts wakes, fairs, and bear-
baitings' in search of victims to fleece.

Avalon
The 'Insula Avallonis' is mentioned in
▷ Geoffrey of Monmouth's ▷ *History of
the Kings of Britain* as the place where
Arthur's sword was forged, and as the place
to which ▷ Arthur is taken after he has been
fatally wounded. More information about
Avalon is given in Geoffrey's poetic account
of the *Life of Merlin* (*Vita Merlini*), where it
is called 'the island of apples', said to be over
the Western waters and the home of
▷ Morgan la Fay. In the course of the
development of Arthurian legend, Avalon has
been given different geographical settings;
▷ Glastonbury, in particular, has been
strongly promoted from the late 12th century
onwards as being Arthur's burial place and,
hence, to be identified as Avalon itself.

Avon
The river of ▷ Shakespeare's birthplace,
Stratford-on-Avon, from which he is called the
'Swan of Avon' by ▷ Ben Jonson in his
poem *To the Memory of Shakespeare*. The
word derives from Celtic *afon* = 'river';
three other rivers with the same name exist in
England.

Awkward Age, The (*1899*)
A novel by ▷ Henry James. Nanda
Brookenham is a young girl brought up in a
smart but corrupt section of London society;
her mother and her mother's circle are willing
to carry on immoral intrigues so long as
respectable appearances are scrupulously
protected. Nanda is in love with Vanderbank,
who, as she learns later, is her mother's lover,
and she feels some affection for Mitchett, a
young man of less charm than Vanderbank,
but with an attractive simplicity of heart.
Unlike the other members of her mother's
circle, she is free and candid in her feelings
and open in her conduct; this alarms
Vanderbank and inhibits him from declaring
his love for her. Her elderly friend, Mr
Longdon, an admirer of her dead
grandmother, gives Nanda a dowry to attract
Vanderbank, but this only increases the
latter's fastidious reluctance to declare
himself. Meanwhile, the Duchess, Mrs
Brookenham's friend and rival, conspires to
capture Mitchett for her own daughter, Aggie,
whose appearance of immaculate innocence
immediately breaks down when it has served
its purpose of qualifying her for the marriage
market. Vanderbank's mixture of
scrupulousness and timidity remains a
permanent barrier between himself and
Nanda. Mr Longdon adopts her, and they
remain together in their love of truthful
feeling, isolated from the sophisticated but
essentially trivial society which has hitherto
constituted Nanda's environment.
    The novel is an example of James's interest
in the survival of integrity in a materialistic
society blinded by its own carefully cultivated
artificiality.

Ayckbourn, Alan (b 1939)
Until recently an underestimated dramatist
whose plays have often been dismissed (or
presented) as light entertainment for
unthinking bourgeois audiences. He often
writes about the middle classes in order to
explore serious issues of modern life. Recent
plays such as *A Small Family Business* (1987)
have illustrated his inclination to use farce as
a weapon of moral force. He has been
commercially very successful and after a long
period at the Stephen Joseph Theatre in
Scarborough he was, until recently, a resident
writer and director at the National Theatre.
His other plays include: *Relatively Speaking*
(1967); *Absurd Person Singular* (1972); *The
Norman Conquests* (1973); *Bedroom Farce*
(1975); *Season's Greetings* (1982); *Way
Upstream* (1982); *A Chorus of Disapproval*
(1984); *Henceforward* (1988); *Man of the
Moment* (1990); *Body Language* (1991).

Ayre
▷ Madrigal.

B

Babes in the Wood
▷ *Children in the Wood*.

Bacchus
▷ Dionysus.

Bacon, Francis, 1st Baron Verulam and Viscount St Albans (1561–1626)

Title page of Bacon's *Instauratio Magna* (1620)

Politician, philosopher and essayist, Francis Bacon rose to the rank of lord chancellor, before being dismissed from that office in the same year in which he attained it – 1621. Bacon's offence was, technically, his conviction for accepting bribes whilst a judge in chancery suits. The cause of his conviction, however, was the ascendency of political enemies he had made in the course of his ambitious career.

It is, however, as an essayist, and, more importantly, as one of the earliest theoreticians of scientific methodology for which Bacon was to become famous. A series of works – which included ▷ *The Advancement of Learning* (1605 expanded into *De Augmentis Scientiarum* in 1623), *De*

sapientia veterum (1609, translated as *The Wisdom of the Ancients* in 1619) and the incomplete ▷ *Novum Organum* (1620) – established his claims to philosophical and methodological pre-eminence amongst his contemporaries. The *De Augmentis* and the *Novum Organum* formed the first two parts of his enormous project, gathered under the title ▷ *Instauratio Magna*, which remained unfinished but which proposed nothing less than a re-ordering of all fields of human enquiry. In addition Bacon wrote a history of the reign of ▷ Henry VIII (published in 1622), a collection of anecdotal stories (1625) and a ▷ utopian work based on the new scientific endeavours of the age – ▷ *The New Atlantis* (1626). His major philosophical works were written in addition to his contribution to the law and his *Essays*, which were first published in 1597 and issued in a final form (much expanded) in 1625.

Until recently, Bacon's reputation tended to rest on his *Essays* which represent a series of terse observations in the style of ▷ Seneca rather than the more fluid meditations to be found in the writings of ▷ Montaigne who is credited with originating the essay as a distinctly modern form. More and more attention is, however, being paid to his theoretical work in the general area of scientific methodology and taxonomy. It was Bacon who, in the later 17th century, was to be celebrated as the true progenitor of the ▷ 'New Science', not least because of his intense interest in the language of science, and in the forms of discourse appropriate to different rhetorical and methodological projects. As a scientist, in the modern sense, his contribution to knowledge was negligible. But as the author of a series of 'manifestos' which set out to establish the basis for inductive or experimental philosophy, his influence on later generations of English philosophers was to be incalculable. The 'Baconian' method was to be the legacy of his work – an adherence, that is, to the importance of observation and definition of the particular, rather than a delight in deduction from the general – and the basis for his reputation in later periods.

Bib: Spedding, J., Ellis, R. L., and Heath, D. D. (eds.), *Works of Francis Bacon* (7 vols.); Rossi, P., *Francis Bacon. From Magic to Science* (trans.) S. Rabinovitch; Vickers, B. (ed.), *Essential Articles for the Study of Francis Bacon*.

Bacon, Roger (1210/14–after 1291)
▷ Franciscan scholar, student at Paris and

Oxford, and author of treatises on sciences such as grammar, logic, physics, mathematics and modern philosophy. He was an acute and independent thinker, and one of the leading philosophers of the ▷ Middle Ages. His originality in devoting himself to experimental methods caused him to be known in Paris as Doctor mirabilis (Wonderful Doctor). He was a vociferous critic of what he saw as the inadequately based scholarship of his time and was placed in confinement at various stages in his career for his heretical propositions. In popular tradition he came to be regarded as a magician and the inventor of a brazen head that could speak. It is in such a role that he is represented in ▷ *Friar Bacon and Friar Bungay* (1594), a romantic comedy by ▷ Robert Greene.

Baconian
   ▷ Bacon, Francis.

***Badman, The Life and Death of Mr* (1680)**
A moral ▷ allegory by ▷ John Bunyan, author of ▷ *The Pilgrim's Progress*, and, apart from the more famous work, the only one of Bunyan's fictions to remain widely known. It is the biography of a wicked man told by Mr Wiseman, and contains vivid and dramatic detail. Its realism of detail and its psychology make it one of the forerunners of the novel.

Baedeker, Karl (1801–59)
The author of famous guide-books, which were carried on by his son and eventually covered most of the civilized world. Their frequent mention in English 19th- and 20th-century fiction shows how indispensable they were to English middle- and upper-class tourists of the last 100 years, especially in visits to countries in which monuments and works of art are plentiful, such as Italy. He wrote in German but English editions were produced after his death, from 1861 onwards.
Bib: Pemble, J., *The Mediterranean Passion.*

Bagehot, Walter (1826–77)
A writer on political and economic affairs, best known for his book *The English Constitution* (1867) which, despite historical change, is still a classic study of the spirit of English politics and notably of the function of monarchy in providing the imaginative appeal of the state and ensuring the dignity of government without hindering desirable conflict of opinion.

Bagehot was also the author of a number of critical essays, the best known of which is *Wordsworth, Tennyson, and Browning or Pure, Ornate, and Grotesque Art in English Poetry* (1864). It is republished in *English Critical Essays* ed. by E. D. Jones (World's Classics).

Bib: Stephen, Leslie in *Studies of a Biographer*; Buchan, A., *The Spare Chancellor*; St John-Stevas, N. A. F., *Life.*

Bailey, The Old
The building that houses the Central Criminal Court in London. A 'bailey' is an outer fortified wall, such as once existed on the site as a medieval defence for the City of London.

Baillie, Joanna (1762–1851)
Friend of ▷ Sir Walter Scott and prolific author of plays based on the ▷ Shakespearean model (*Plays of the Passions*; 1798, 1802, 1812), five of which were acted. She also wrote poems in couplets, and lyrics on sentimental and patriotic themes (*Fugitive Verses*, 1790; *Metrical Legends*, 1821; *Poetic Miscellanies*, 1823).

Bainbridge, Beryl (b 1933)

Beryl Bainbridge

Novelist. Brought up near Liverpool, she worked as an actress before writing her first novel (though not the first to be published), *Harriet Said* (1972), which concerns two girls involved in a murder. Initially seen as a writer of macabre thrillers, she has gained an increasing following and has gradually attracted more serious critical attention. Her novels are characterized by black humour, economy of style and portraits of lower-middle-class manners with a strong element of the ▷ Gothic and grotesque. *The Bottle Factory Outing* (1974) centres on the relationship of two women on an increasingly sinister works outing which leads to the death of one of them. Confused and sordid lives are observed in a detached and ironic manner. *A Quiet Life* (1976) is a partly autobiographical tale of family eccentricities and the tragic precariousness of love, while *Winter Garden* (1980) draws on a visit Bainbridge made to the Soviet Union. Other novels are: *A Weekend with Claude* (1967); *Another Part of the Wood* (1968); *The Dressmaker* (1973); *Sweet William* (1975); *Injury Time* (1977); *Young Adolf* (1978); *Watson's Apology* (1984); *Filthy Lucre* (1986); *An Awfully Big Adventure* (1990).

Bakhtin, Mikhail (1895–1975)

Bakhtin's first major work was *Problems in Dostoevsky's Poetics* (1929), but his most famous work, *Rabelais and His World*, did not appear until 1965. Two books, *Freudianism: a Marxist Critique* (1927), and *Marxism and the Philosophy of Language* (1930) were published under the name of V. N. Volosinov, and a third, *The Formal Method in Literary Scholarship* (1928) appeared under the name of his colleague P. N. Medvedev. Bakhtin's concern throughout is to show how ▷ ideology functions in the process of the production of the linguistic ▷ sign and to develop and identify the concept of 'dialogism' as it operates in literary texts. In Bakhtin's words 'In dialogue a person not only shows himself outwardly, but he becomes for the first time that which he is, not only for others but himself as well. To be means to communicate dialogically.' His work has in recent years enjoyed a revival, particularly among critics. Especially important is the way in which he theorizes and politicizes the concepts of festivity and ▷ carnival. Also one of his concerns is to identify the dialectical relationship between those various 'texts' of which any one literary work is comprised. This notion of ▷ 'intertextuality' is currently used within areas such as ▷ feminism and ▷ deconstruction. Much of Bakhtin's work was suppressed during his life-time and not published until after his death.

Bale, John (1495–1563)

Bishop of Ossory, author of several plays, compiler of a history of English writers and a fervent anti-Papal activist. He promoted the revival of interest in Anglo-Saxon scholarship and was the author of *King John*, regarded as the first English historical play, in which moral analysis and historical representation are combined.

Balin

Balin le Savage and Balan are the two brothers who help ▷ King Arthur in his early struggles to establish power in the first book of ▷ Malory's *Morte D'Arthur*. Balin gives King Pellam the Dolorous Stroke which results in the creation of the Wasteland.

Ball, John (d 1381)

Priest and leader of the ▷ Peasants' Revolt (1381), and the subject of *A Dream of John Ball* by ▷ William Morris.

Ballad

Traditionally the ballad has been considered a folkloric verse narrative which has strong associations with communal dancing, and support for that link has been found in the derivation of the word 'ballad' itself (from the late Latin verb *ballare* – to dance). More recently scholars have viewed the association between ballads and dance forms rather more sceptically. Generally, the term is used of a narrative poem which uses an elliptical and highly stylized mode of narration, in which the technique of repetition with variation may play an important part. Often ballads contain repeated choral refrains but this is not a universal feature.

Ballad forms can be identified in early English texts: the brief narrative about *Judas* in the ▷ Harley manuscript has been hailed as the earliest English example of the form. The so-called ▷ Broadside ballads, sold in Elizabethan times, were narrative poems on a wide range of subjects printed on a single side of a broadsheet. From the 18th century onwards, collections of folk/'popular ballads' began to be made and the form was taken up by some of the most influential poets of the late 18th century as a folkloric form of expression. ▷ Wordsworth's and ▷ Coleridge's collection of poems ▷ *Lyrical Ballads* (1798) does not contain many poems in ballad form (apart from the brilliant balladic composition ▷ *The Ancient Mariner*) but the function of the title seems to be to arouse associations of oral, non-literary poetic forms. In this collection, art is used to conceal art. ▷ Walter Scott produced many adaptations and imitations of traditional Scots ballads and published a collection of ballads entitled *The Minstrelsy of the Scottish Border*. The great ballad collection of F. J. Child, *English and Scottish Popular Ballads*, was published at the end of the 19th century.
Bib: Bold, A., *The Ballad*.

Ballade

A lyrical form favoured by French court

poets of the 14th century (especially
▷ Guillaume de Machaut and ▷ Eustache
Deschamps) and first used in English by
▷ Chaucer (*To Rosemounde*, *Balade de Bone
Conseyl*). The ballade form requires three
stanzas, linked by a refrain and common
rhymes (sometimes the poem being restricted
to three or four rhymes repeated in the same
order in each stanza). 15th-century writers
took up the form following Chaucer, and it
was revived in the late 19th century by poets
such as ▷ Swinburne and ▷ Rossetti.

Ballard, J. G. (James Graham) (b 1930)
▷ Science Fiction.

Ballet
▷ Madrigal.

Balzac, Honoré de (1799–1850)
French novelist. His *La Comédie humaine* is a
panorama of French society from the
▷ Revolution to the July Monarchy (1830).
It is bound together by the use of recurrent
characters (Vautrin is one notable instance,
Rastignac another) and recurrent motifs
(notably the necessity of moral and social
order contrasted with the pressures of the
individual ego). Among the one hundred
novels which Balzac completed, drafted or
projected are *Eugénie Grandet* (1833), *Illusions
perdues* (1837–43), *La Cousine Bette* (1846),
Le Cousin Pons (1847), *Le Père Goriot* (1835),
Splendeurs et misères des courtisanes (1847).

'French society was to be the historian,'
Balzac wrote, 'I had only to be the scribe'.
His ways of depicting French society are
geographical, historical, political and even
geological insofar as all social strata find a
place. These different representations, taken
individually or in combination, bring into
play a dynamic explained in *La Peau de
chagrin* (1831) as the product of desire and
power, with knowledge enlisted to restrain
them. But such a restraint is rare or non-
existent, and society in the *Comédie humaine*
is driven by a restlessness which tends to
exhaustion as it competes for the fulfilment
of desire. Like society, character too is open
to multiple descriptions, as a machine driven
by abstracts (passion, ambition, penury, for
instance) or as a representative of a human or
social type. In that respect, character has a
potential for expansion. It is always ready to
merge into symbol (more than just the
performance of symbolic actions) or be
exaggerated into ▷ melodrama. Indeed,
melodrama is a central Balzacian ingredient
and, just as characters are actors, buildings
and places too are subject to mutation into a
theatre or a scene in which the novelistic

events unfold. In its liking for myth and
melodrama, Balzac's social realism is
correspondingly more than the accumulation
of surface detail, since the detail acts as an
indicator of underlying causes. In turn,
understanding of these causes is open only to
the novelist defined by his capacity for
'second sight', the capacity to perceive pattern
as well as pattern destroyed. And it is
considerations of this kind which distinguish
Balzac from other ▷ *feuilleton* novelists such
as Eugène Sue (1804–57) and help account
for his pervasive influence on 19th century
fiction, particularly in England where Balzac
shaped the already strong vein of social
▷ realism.
Bib: Prendergast, C., *Balzac: Fiction and
Melodrama*; Bellos, D., *Balzac: Le Père
Goriot*.

Bank of England, The
The Bank of England was founded in 1694
on the basis of suggestions by William
Patterson. It first existed as a corporation
with a special charter to raise loans for the
government of ▷ William III to pay for the
wars against France. By degrees, in the 18th
and 19th centuries it became the keeper of
the government's funds, as well as of the
funds of other banks. Thus it grew into the
first 'Central Bank' in the world. Although
nominally a private corporation until 1946,
when it was nationalized, it had long worked
so closely with the Treasury that its
independence of the government had been
only nominal.

Bankside
The south bank of the ▷ Thames in
▷ London. It was famous in
▷ Shakespeare's day for its theatres. The
City of London refused to allow public
theatres within its bounds; hence the famous
theatres such as the ▷ Globe, the ▷ Rose
and the Fortune all had to be built in
▷ Southwark on Bankside.
▷ Theatres.

Bannockburn (1314)
A battle in central Scotland, in which a
Scottish army under ▷ Robert the Bruce
defeated a large invading English force under
▷ Edward II. The battle decided Scottish
independence until the two countries became
united under a Scottish king (▷ James VI
and I, 1603–25). As a heroic episode, it has
had a force of inspiration for the Scots similar
to the victory of ▷ Agincourt for the
English.
▷ Scottish literature in English.

Baptists
An important sect of ▷ Nonconformist
Protestants; originally one of the three
principal branches of English ▷ Puritanism,
the other two being the Independents
(▷ Congregationalists), and the
▷ Presbyterians (Calvinists). Their especial
doctrine is to maintain that the rite of
baptism must be administered to adults, and
not to infants. They began as an offshoot of
the Independents in the first decade of the
17th century, and made rapid progress
between 1640 and 1660 – the period of the
▷ Civil War and the ▷ Interregnum, when
the Puritans usurped the position of the
▷ Church of England. One of the foremost
exponents of the Baptist Church in the
second half of the 17th century was ▷ John
Bunyan (1628–88).

Barabbas
In the ▷ Bible, the robber whom the Roman
governor, ▷ Pilate, released at the demand
of the Jews, instead of Jesus (*Matthew* 27).
Barabbas is the Jew of Malta in Marlowe's
play of that name.

Barbauld, Mrs Anna Laetitia (1743–1824)
Best known as the editor of ▷ Samuel
Richardson's correspondence, Mrs Barbauld
also published several volumes of tales for
children. After the suicide of her husband in
1808, she embarked on a major series of
literary editions, bringing out *The British
Novelists* in 50 volumes. She was also a
prominent member of the ▷ Bluestocking
circle, and a friend of ▷ Mrs Elizabeth
Montagu.

Barbour, John (c 1320–95)
Scottish poet; author of a long verse chronicle
in eight-syllable couplets about the Scottish
War of Independence – *The Bruce* (c 1375).
It tells the story of the defeat of the English
attempts to conquer Scotland (1296–1328),
contains a celebrated account of
▷ Bannockburn and extols the principal
hero of the War – ▷ Robert the Bruce, who
ended his career as king of Scotland. Other
works have been attributed to Barbour,
including *The Buik of Alexander*, but evidence
of his authorship has been disputed.
Bib: McDiarmid, M. P. and Stevenson, J. A.
(eds.), *Barbour's Bruce*, Scottish Text Society
12–13, 15.

Bard
A member of the privileged caste of poets
among the ancient Celtic peoples, driven by
the Romans and then the Anglo-Saxons into
▷ Wales and ▷ Ireland and, legend has it,
exterminated in Wales by Edward I. The
term became known to later English writers
from references in Latin literature. Poets
such as ▷ Shakespeare, ▷ John Milton
and ▷ Alexander Pope refer to any serious
poet as a 'bard'. In the 18th century, partly as
a result of the growing antiquarian interest in
▷ druidism, the term came to designate a
mysteriously or sacredly inspired poet, as in
▷ Thomas Gray's famous ▷ ode ▷ *The
Bard* (1757).

Bard, The (1757)
One of ▷ Thomas Gray's two famous
▷ 'Pindaric Odes' (the other being 'The
Progress of Poesy'). The last surviving Celtic
▷ bard stands on a mountain-top and calls
down curses upon King Edward I and the
English army, as they march below,
prophesying the end of his royal house and
its ultimate replacement by the (Welsh) house
of Tudor. He concludes by throwing himself
into the River Conway beneath. There is a
stagey wildness about the work which irritated
▷ Samuel Johnson, though its failure to
'promote any truth, moral or political' did
not prevent it from being very popular at the
time.

Barker, George Granville (b 1913)
Poet. His first collection, *Thirty Preliminary
Poems*, was published in 1933, along with a
novel, *Alanna Autumnal*. Since then he has
kept up a steady output of visionary and
▷ autobiographical verse that includes
Calamiterror (1937), *Lament and Triumph*
(1940) and the two parts of *The True
Confession of George Barker* (1950 and 1964).
His most celebrated later volume is *Anno
Domini* (1983).
Bib: Fraser, R. (ed.), *Collected Poems*.

Barker, Howard (b 1946)
Modern political dramatist known particularly
for the shocking power of his language and
imagery. His plays deal frequently with
madness, lust, corruption, and despair, so
that although he claims to be a socialist and
presents capitalism as a barbaric and
destructive system there is generally little
hope in his view of contemporary life. He is a
prolific writer and many of his plays have
been produced by the ▷ Royal Shakespeare
Company and the ▷ Royal Court. These
include: *Stripwell* (1975); *Fair Slaughter*
(1977); *The Hang of the Gaol* (1978); *The
Loud Boy's Life* (1980); *Crimes in Hot
Countries* (1983); an adaptation of ▷ Thomas
Middleton's *Women Beware Women* (1985);
Last Supper (1988) and *Bite of the Night*
(1988). *The Poor Man's Friend* (1981), an
account of a hanging in a rope-making town,

was produced in response to an invitation by
▷ Ann Jellicoe to write a community play
for a cast of nearly a hundred. He has also
written a number of plays for television, some
of which have never been transmitted due to
censorship.
Bib: Chambers, C. and Prior, M.,
Playwright's Progress; Craig, S. (ed.), *Dreams
and Deconstructions*.

Barnaby Rudge (1841)
A novel by ▷ Charles Dickens, published as
part of ▷ *Master Humphrey's Clock*. The
only other novel that he published in this
proposed series was ▷ *The Old Curiosity
Shop*; Dickens then abandoned it.

It is set in the 18th century and its central
episodes are descriptions of the fierce anti-
Catholic disorders called ▷ 'the Gordon
Riots', which terrorized London for several
days in 1780. These vivid scenes, and the
characters directly concerned in the riots
(such as the half-wit Barnaby Rudge, the
locksmith Gabriel Varden and his apprentice
Simon Tappertit), constitute the part of the
book which is most memorable and most
representative of Dickens's style. The main
story is a romantic one about the love affair
of Emma Haredale, whose father has been
mysteriously murdered, and Edward Chester,
the son of Sir John Chester, a suave villain
who helps to instigate the Riots. Sir John and
Emma's uncle, Geoffrey Haredale, a Catholic,
are enemies, but they unite in opposition to
the marriage of Edward and Emma. During
the riots, Geoffrey Haredale's house is burnt
down but Edward saves the lives of both
Emma and her uncle, and thus wins his
approval of the match. The murderer of
Emma's father turns out to be the father of
Barnaby.

Barnaby Rudge is one of Dickens's two
historical novels, the other being ▷ *A Tale of
Two Cities*.

Barnes, Julian (b 1946)
Novelist. Born in Leicester and educated in
London and Oxford, Barnes has worked as a
lexicographer on the O.E.D. Supplement
(1969–1972), and in journalism, writing for
the *New Statesman*, *The Sunday Times*, *The
Observer*, and as the notorious gossip
columnist 'Edward Pygge' in the journal of
modern literature, the *New Review*, which ran
from 1974 to 1979 under poet and critic Ian
Hamilton's editorship. Greatly influenced by
French 19th-century novelist ▷ Gustave
Flaubert (the ostensible subject of the
playful and very successful 1984 novel
Flaubert's Parrot), Barnes's work is witty and
parodic. Novels include: *Metroland* (1981);

Before She Met Me (1982); *Flaubert's Parrot*
(1984) – which was shortlisted for the 1985
Booker Prize and won the Geoffrey Faber
Memorial prize; and *Staring at the Sun*
(1986). Barnes also writes crime fiction, and
under the pseudonym Dan Kavanagh
published *Duffy* (1980); *Fiddle City* (1983)
and *Putting the Boot In* (1985). In 1986 he
won the E. M. Forster Award from the
American Academy of Arts and Letters.

Barnes, William (1801–86)
Poet. A clergyman from the West of England
(▷ Wessex), Barnes's most important work
is *Poems of Rural Life, in the Dorset Dialect*
(1844), but he also wrote verse in 'Standard
English'. A champion of ▷ Anglo-Saxon
over the Latinate element in the English
language, he greatly influenced fellow
Dorsetman ▷ Thomas Hardy, who wrote
the poem 'The Last Signal' (1886) on his
death, and prefaced and edited an edition of
his poetry in 1908.
Bib: Jones, B. (ed.), *The Poems of William
Barnes*; Baxter, L., *The Life of Barnes by his
Daughter*.

Barnfield, Richard (1574–1627)
Poet. Barnfield wrote almost all his poetry
before 1600 when he gave up writing to
become a prosperous Shropshire landowner.
Barnfield published three volumes of poetry,
in 1594, 1595 and 1598 respectively. Of these
volumes, *The Affectionate Shepherd,
Containing the Love of Daphnis for the Love of
Gannymede*, which appeared first, is an
exercise in ▷ pastoral. The second volume,
entitled *Cynthia, with Certain Sonnets and the
Legend of Cassandra*, claims to imitate
▷ Edmund Spenser's ▷ *The Faerie
Queene*. The third and final collection
contains ▷ satire, pastoral elegy and a
'debate' entitled 'The Combat Between
Conscience and Covetessnesse'. In this final
collection can be found two poems by
Barnfield ('If music and sweet poetrie agree'
and 'As it fell upon a day') which were
published in the anthology ▷ *Passionate
Pilgrim* (1599) and were not recognized as
being the work of Barnfield.

Barnum, Phineas Taylor (1810–91)
A famous American showman who first made
a success through the exhibition of 'George
Washington's nurse', alleged to be 161 years
old; he later made the American Museum, a
collection of curiosities, one of the most
popular shows in America. He started a
circus in 1871, which, as Barnum and Bailey's
in 1881, became the type and pattern of all
later circuses in England and America, since

he toured in both countries. The name of his famous elephant 'Jumbo' is synonymous with 'elephant' to this day.

Baroque

A term mainly applied to the visual arts, particularly architecture and (with a somewhat different meaning) to music, but now increasingly used in literary contexts also. It derives from the Italian word *barocco* meaning rough and unpolished, and was originally used to denote extravagance or excessiveness in the visual arts. Thence it came to designate the exuberant, florid architecture and painting characteristic of Europe during the period of Absolute Monarchies in the 17th and 18th centuries. The more restrained, constitutionalist climate of Britain prevented baroque architecture from taking firm hold, and the few examples (*eg* Castle Howard and Blenheim Palace, both by ▷ Sir John Vanbrugh) date from shortly after the ▷ Restoration, when French taste was in the ascendant. English ▷ neo-classicism, when it aimed at large-scale grandeur, tended to be more sober and austere, like ▷ Sir Christopher Wren's St Paul's. In domestic contexts the greater economic and political power of the lesser aristocracy and the rising merchant class in England, meant that the modest convenience of the Palladian style was preferred to full blown baroque. ▷ Alexander Pope's patron Lord Burlington was the most prominent advocate of the ▷ Palladian style and Pope wrote his fourth ▷ *Moral Essay*, on the discomforts of baroque magnificence, under Burlington's influence.

In music the term denotes the new, more public, expressive and dramatic style, characterized by free recitative, and most typically seen in the new genre of opera, originating in the Italy of Monteverdi in the late 16th century. It is closely associated with the introduction of new, more expressive and louder instruments, ideal for public performance, such as the transverse flute, the violin and the harpsichord, which at this time began to supplant the softer recorder, viol and virginals, suitable to the intimate, often amateur, music-making of the ▷ Renaissance. The term is now applied to all music between this time and the onset of classicism and romanticism with Haydn and Mozart in the later 18th century. The baroque style in music came to England late, and its first great English exponent is Henry Purcell (1658?–95), who wrote the first English opera, *Dido and Aeneas* (1689; libretto by ▷ Nahum Tate).

The epithet 'baroque' has recently come to be used in literary contexts by analogy with its use in relation to the other arts. Thus the extravagant Italianate conceits of the Catholic poet ▷ Richard Crashaw who ended his life in Rome, can be called 'baroque'. The florid, public quality of ▷ John Dryden's ▷ *Annus Mirabilis*, may also be termed 'baroque', with its innocent celebration of national pride and adulation of the monarch, the literary equivalent of the mural paintings of the Italian baroque artist Verrio, who worked in England, and whose English pupil, James Thornhill, decorated the Painted Hall at Greenwich early in the 18th century. Like 'classical' and 'romantic' the word has also developed a wider application beyond its strict historical period. The exuberant inventiveness of ▷ Dylan Thomas has, for instance, been termed 'baroque'.

Barrie, Sir James Matthew (1869–1937)

A Scots dramatist, nowadays chiefly famous for his creation of ▷ *Peter Pan* (1904). Early in this century he was extremely popular for the theatrical skill and the humour and sentimentality of his plays, which sometimes carried penetrating satire, *eg The Admirable Crichton* (1902).
Bib: Darton, F. J. Harvey, *Barrie*; Hammerton, J. A., *Barrie, the story of a genius*; Mackail, D., *The Story of J.M.B.*

Barry, Elizabeth (1658–1713)

The first well-known English actress, said to have been trained by the ▷ Earl of Rochester, who boasted he could make an actress of her in six months; she became his mistress and later had a daughter by him.

She began by acting at the ▷ Dorset Garden Theatre, probably in 1675, but her career blossomed in 1679–80, with a series of tragic roles which earned her 'the Name of Famous Mrs Barry, both at Court and City'.

Throughout her career she was adored for her acting talents – being admired equally in comic and tragic roles – and sharply satirized for her alleged promiscuity: a contemporary commentary describes her as 'the finest Woman in the World upon the Stage, and the Ugliest Woman off't'. She played Lady Brute in the first production of ▷ *The Provok'd Wife* (1697), Mrs Marwood in the original ▷ *The Way of the World* (1700), and dozens of important roles in plays by contemporary and earlier authors, including many of ▷ Shakespeare's. Succeeding generations of actresses viewed her as an ideal to which they aspired.
Bib: Highfill, P. H. Jr., Burnim, K. A. and Langhans, E. A. (eds.), *A Biographical*

Dictionary of Actors, Actresses, Musicians, Dancers, Managers, and Other Stage Personnel in London 1660–1800.

Barry, Spranger (?1717–77)
Actor, manager. Over six feet tall, and noted for his striking good looks which, added to his natural acting ability, made him one of the leading actors in his generation and a great rival of ▷ David Garrick.

Born in Dublin, he made his early reputation in the Irish theatre, acting with Garrick there and on good terms with him. Barry came to London in 1746, where he performed indifferently, first as Othello and then as Macbeth. However his next role, as Castalio in ▷ Thomas Otway's *The Orphan*, was highly acclaimed, and it became one of his most popular successes.

In 1747 ▷ Drury Lane, where he was acting, came under Garrick's management, and in the following season he and Garrick alternated as Hamlet and Macbeth, drawing large crowds. However, the growing rivalry between them caused Barry to leave for ▷ Covent Garden in 1750, after which a famous 'Romeo and Juliet War' ensued, with the two actors playing Romeo simultaneously at separate performances in the respective houses.

In 1756 Barry began ambitious plans for a theatre of his own in Crow Street, Dublin, which opened in 1758, but the theatre failed and was eventually taken over by a rival.

Barry returned to London and carried on an intermittent association with Garrick until 1774, when he left for Covent Garden, remaining there until his death.

Barsetshire
An imaginary English county invented by ▷ Anthony Trollope for a series of novels some of which centre on an imaginary town in it, the cathedral city of Barchester. It is a characteristic southern English setting. The novels are the best known of his works. Titles: ▷ *The Warden, Barchester Towers, Doctor Thorne, Framley Parsonage, The Small House at Allington, The Last Chronicle of Barset.*

Barstow, Stan (b 1928)
Novelist and short-story writer. His best-known work is his first novel, *A Kind of Loving* (1960), a first-person, present tense narrative of a young man forced to marry his pregnant girlfriend. Barstow came to prominence as one of a group of novelists from northern, working-class backgrounds, including ▷ John Braine, ▷ Alan Sillitoe and Keith Waterhouse. He has retained his commitment to the realist novel (▷ realism)

with a regional setting and his suspicion of metropolitan and international culture. *The Watcher on the Shore* (1966) and *The True Right End* (1976) form a trilogy with *A Kind of Loving*. Other novels are: *Ask Me Tomorrow* (1962); *Joby* (1964); *A Raging Calm* (1968); *A Brother's Tale* (1980); *Just You Wait and See* (1986); *B Movie* (1987). Story collections include: *The Desperadoes* (1961); *A Season with Eros* (1971); *A Casual Acquaintance* (1976); *The Glad Eye* (1984).

Barthes, Roland (1915–80)
Probably the best known and most influential of all the ▷ Structuralist and ▷ Post-structuralist critics. In books such as *Writing Degree Zero* (1953), *Mythologies* (1957), and *S/Z* (1970), Barthes undertook to expose how language functioned, and its relationship with ▷ ideology. Moreover, he was also concerned to uncover the distinctions between literary texts which operated on the basis of a stable relationship between ▷ signifier and ▷ signified, and those for whom the act of signification (establishing meaning) itself was of primary importance. The terms he uses to distinguish between the two types of text are 'readerly' (*lisible*) and 'writerly' (*scriptible*). In later works, such as *The Pleasure of the Text* (1975), he went on to investigate the sources of pleasure which the text affords to the reader, and distinguished between 'the text of pleasure' which does not challenge the cultural assumptions of the reader and which is therefore comforting, and 'the text of bliss' where the reader experiences a '*jouissance*' from the unsettling effect elicited from the text's representation of the crisis of language. In addition to offering penetrating analyses of literary texts, Barthes concerned himself with the structural analysis of all cultural representations, including topics such as advertising, film, photography, music and wrestling.

Bartholomew Fair (1614)
A vigorous prose comedy of ▷ London life by ▷ Ben Jonson. The scene is that of a famous fair held annually in Smithfield, London, from the 12th century till 1855. The cast includes traders, showmen, dupes, criminals, a gambler, and a hypocritical ▷ Puritan – the best-known character, called Zeal-of-the-land Busy. It has very lively surface entertainment, and some of Jonson's characteristic force of satire; the vicious pursue their vices with eloquence but such extravagance that they overreach themselves, and not only produce their own doom but bring ridicule on their own heads by self-caricature.
▷ Humours, Comedy of.

Bastard

A bastard is born out of wedlock, *ie* has no legal parents; in law, he is *filius nullius* = the son of no one. When land, and with it, status, derived from the legal father, the bastard could inherit nothing by his own right. In early medieval times an exception was sometimes made for bastards in ruling families; thus ▷ William 1 of England (1066–87) took the appellation William the Bastard. But in general a bastard was by law something of a social outcast. Hence Edmund in ▷ Shakespeare's *King Lear* (1.ii) 'Why brand they us/With base? with baseness? base, base?' However, a bastard was not debarred from making for himself a position in society, acquiring land, marrying legally and bequeathing his property – all depended on his natural worth, abilities and energies: 'Thou, nature, art my goddess;' says Edmund (I.ii.1) 'to thy law / My services are bound.' In Edmund, as in the bastard Philip of Shakespeare's ▷ *King John*, there is the idea that the bastard is compensated for his lack of rights by unusual natural energies; the same is implicit in ▷ Henry Fielding's ▷ *Tom Jones*. Bastards could inherit by the testament, *ie* legally admitted last wishes of the father. When, by the 18th century, property owning became more varied and flexible, one aspect of the bastard's social problems was relieved. Fatherlessness, however, in a patriarchal society (*ie* one where fathers rule) can hardly avoid being a disabling and alienating condition. Some challenge is being offered to these old patterns by the number of professionally and financially secure people who now choose to have children outside marriage, but for the poorer and weaker members of society the child born outside marriage is still likely to suffer material deprivation.

Bath

A city in the west of England with hot springs with certain mineral properties which afford relief to those with rheumatic diseases. In the 18th century, largely owing to the energies of Richard (▷ Beau) Nash, the city became a brilliant social centre; nearly everyone of eminence in politics, literature or the arts at some time visited or lived there. Hence its prominence in the literature of the time. Nash, who virtually ruled Bath, was a civilizing influence on fashionable society: by his discipline he improved the manners of the rich but ill-bred country gentry, and by refusing to allow the wearing of swords in public assemblies he helped to reduce the practice of ▷ duelling.

▷ Austen, Jane.

Bathos

▷ Figures of Speech.

Battle of Maldon

An Old English commemorative poem, written in imitation of the heroic epics of past Germanic tradition, recounting an incident in the Scandinavian raids against England in 993 at Maldon, Essex. The late-10th-century poem recounts Ealdorman Byrhtnoth's heroic, and disastrous, attempts to oppose the Viking raiders. The text only survives in an 18th-century transcript, made before the manuscript copy was destroyed in a fire.

▷ Old English literature.

Bib: Scragg, D. (ed.), *The Battle of Maldon*.

Battle of the Books, The (1697, published 1704)

(A Full and True Account of the Battel Fought last Friday, Between the Ancient and the Modern Books in St James's Library) A prose satire by ▷ Jonathan Swift, written while he was staying with ▷ Sir William Temple. Temple's essay on 'Ancient and Modern Learning', with its praise of the Epistles of Phalaris, had been attacked by the critics Wotton and ▷ Bentley, the latter proving that the Epistles were false. Swift's *Battle of the Books* satirizes the whole dispute, parodying the scholars' concern with minutiae. The ancients (*ie* the classical writers) are given the stronger claims, but overall the satire leaves the issue undecided.

Baudelaire, Charles (1821–67)

French poet. His best known work, *Les Fleurs du mal* (1857), points the way out of ▷ romanticism towards ▷ modernism. Formally, it draws on the tradition of ▷ sonnet and song which Baudelaire inherited from the ▷ Renaissance. Conceptually, it springs from the perception of 'two simultaneous feelings: the horror of life and the ecstasy of life', periods of heightened sensitivity and sensibility alternating with the monotony of existence without meaning. Baudelaire is rich in suggestion, allowing sensation to transfuse the object as though the object were the source of the sensation rather than the occasion for it; and equally powerful value is bestowed upon the metaphorical expression of sense-experience. When the poet uncovers, invested with desire, an exotic and erotic universe in a woman's hair ('La Chevelure'), this moment is also an uncovering of the possible resonances which the hair triggers in the poet. The contrasting condition of 'Ennui' is a state of torpor which saps intellectual and emotional vigour and induces creative sterility. Everyday objects are here commonly used to embody feelings of failure, dejection, horror and despair. The book's five sections explore these twin conditions, in art and love (*Spleen et Idéal*), in city life (*Tableaux Parisiens*), in stimulants (*Le Vin*), in perversity (*Fleurs du mal*) and in metaphysical rebellion (*La Révolte*), ending (in the poem 'Le Voyage') with man's yearning unsatisfied but finding in death a new journey of discovery.

Baudelaire also wrote fine music and art criticism (he championed Wagner and Delacroix); his translations of Edgar Allan Poe (1809–49) helped confirm, in France, interest in tales of the fantastic; and he was the first to investigate extensively the new genre of prose poetry. In England, his influence has been constant, though at the outset it raised moral controversy. Reviewing *Les Fleurs du mal* in the ▷ *Spectator* of 1862, ▷ Swinburne responded to the sensualism of Baudelaire, and this version of Baudelaire was handed on to the late 19th-century 'decadent' poets. ▷ T. S. Eliot 'rescued' Baudelaire and identified the French poet's sense of sin with 'Sin in the permanent Christian sense', even though Baudelaire himself in a letter to Swinburne warned against easy moral readings of his work.

Baxter, Richard (1615–91)
Theologian, religious writer and autobiographer. Baxter was one of the dominating figures in the period of the English ▷ Civil War. A chaplain to ▷ Oliver Cromwell's army, Baxter served after the ▷ Restoration as chaplain to ▷ Charles II, but he soon fell out with the king on religio-political grounds. Though an initial supporter of the Parliamentarian cause in the Civil War, Baxter's experiences in the New Model Army, in particular his exposure to the thinking of the ▷ Levellers, Seekers, ▷ Quakers and Behmenists, led him to adopt rather more conservative postures. In the 1650s his position changed once more and he emerged as a strong supporter of the Protectorate, dedicating his *Key for Catholics* (1659) to Richard Cromwell. Baxter's stance on religious issues has been defined as one of the earliest examples of ecumenicism or, as he put it in his *A Third Defence of the Cause of Peace* (1681): 'You could not have truelier called me than an *Episcopal – Presbyterian – Independent*.' A prolific writer, Baxter composed over 100 works on religious topics, including *The Saints Everlasting Rest* (1650) and *Call to the Unconverted* (1657). His major work, however, has come to be recognized as

his spiritual autobiography *Reliquiae Baxterianae* (1696). This 800-page folio volume is one of the most important of 17th-century ▷ autobiographies.
Bib: Schlatter, R. B., *Richard Baxter and Puritan Politics*; Keeble, N. H. (ed.), *The Autobiography of Richard Baxter*; Webber, Joan, *The Eloquent 'I': Style and Self in Seventeenth-century Prose*.

Bayes
The name of a character in *The Rehearsal*, a play by the Duke of Buckingham and others, printed in 1672. Bays, or laurels, compose the wreaths with which poets are crowned, and the character is meant as a satire on Sir William D'Avenant, and also on ▷ John Dryden, who was later created official ▷ Poet Laureate. ▷ Alexander Pope uses the same name, in the form Bays, for the Poet Laureate, ▷ Colley Cibber, in *The New Dunciad* (1742), and in the 1743 version of ▷ *The Dunciad*, which has Cibber as hero.

Beaconsfield, Lord
▷ Disraeli, Benjamin.

Bear-baiting, Bull-baiting
In the ▷ Middle Ages and 16th century a popular pastime, in which a bull or bear was tied to a stake and then attacked by bulldogs or mastiffs. Bull-baiting continued longer, and these 'sports' were only made illegal in 1835. In Elizabethan times, bear-baiting was an alternative amusement to drama; 'bear gardens' (notably the Paris Garden) were situated in the same region as the theatres – Southwark, on the south bank of the Thames. The theatres themselves were used for the purpose. Earlier in the century, ▷ Erasmus speaks of herds of bears being kept in the country to supply the bear gardens. The ▷ Puritans disliked the meetings as scenes likely to lead to disorder, but humane disapproval does not come before the middle of the 17th century, when the famous diarist, ▷ John Evelyn, speaks of being 'heartily weary of the rude and dirty pastime'; ▷ Sir Richard Steele attacked the cruelty of the sport in ▷ *The Tatler*. In country places, badgers were often used as cheap alternatives to bulls and bears – see the poem by ▷ John Clare (1793–1864): *Badger*.

Beardsley, Aubrey (1872–98)
An artist famous in the 1890s for his black and white illustrations to writers such as ▷ Oscar Wilde and Ernest Dowson (▷ Nineties Poets). He contributed to the periodicals, ▷ *The Yellow Book* (the first four covers of which he designed) and *The*

'The Dancer's Reward' (1893): illustration
by Aubrey Beardsley for Wilde's *Salome*

Savoy (including his tale, *Under the Hill*),
which were regarded as organs of the aesthetic
movement. The flowing lines and sumptuous
compositions of his illustrations expressed
what was considered most bold and most
daring in the movement.
▷ Aestheticism.

Beatrice and Benedick

Two characters in ▷ Shakespeare's comedy
▷ *Much Ado About Nothing*. They hate
each other and engage in witty exchanges of
repartee. The hatred is only apparent,
however, and they are brought together in
love by a trick. Quarrelsome lovers are often
compared to them.

Beatrice-Joanna

The deeply divided female protagonist of
▷ Middleton's and ▷ Rowley's tragedy
▷ *The Changeling*, whose refusal to marry
her father's choice of a husband leads to
murder and ultimately delivers her into the
arms of the repellent ▷ De Flores.

Beattie, James (1735–1803)

Schoolteacher and later Professor of
Philosophy at Aberdeen University. His
pseudo-medieval poem in Spenserian stanzas,
The Minstrel: or the Progress of Genius (1771–
4), popularized the mystique of the poet as
solitary figure, growing to maturity amid
sublime scenery. He also wrote a prose *Essay*

on Truth, attacking the scepticism of the
philosopher Hume from a position of
orthodox piety.
▷ Bard; Romanticism.

Beau (Brummel, Nash)

'Beau' is a French word which came into use
in the 18th century for an elegant young man,
especially as suitor to a lady. The word also
prefixed the names of certain famous men of
fashion and elegance, notably Beau Nash
(1674–1762) the famous Master of Ceremonies
at ▷ Bath; and Beau Brummel (1778–1840),
friend of George IV in his ▷ Regency days
(1810–20) and leader of London fashion.

Beaumont, Francis (1584–1616)

Dramatic poet and collaborator with ▷ John
Fletcher. They wrote comedies (*eg* ▷ *The
Coxcomb*); tragedies (*eg* ▷ *The Maid's
Tragedy*); romantic dramas (*eg A King and
No King* and ▷ *Philaster*). Fletcher also
collaborated with other writers –
▷ Shakespeare, ▷ Massinger – and wrote
plays on his own. The general superiority of
those he wrote with Beaumont has suggested
to modern critics that Beaumont may have
been the more talented partner. Their plays
were immensely popular in the 17th century,
but they are now regarded as the beginning
of the decadence of the great period of
English drama. The plays have fluent charm
and are theatrically dexterous, but they lack
the force of profound relevance to lived
experience that is characteristic of the great
work of the time.
Bib: Macaulay, G. G., *Beaumont: a critical
study*; Appleton, W. W., *Beaumont and
Fletcher: a critical study*.

Beauty and the Beast

A fairy story, best known in the French
version of Madame de Villeneuve (1744). The
theme is that of a young girl who learns to
love a monster who holds her in his power;
her freely given love transforms him into a
young prince. Before she can go through this
experience, however, she has to surrender her
safe, tender relationship with the father who
dotes on her.
▷ Fairy tales.

Beauvoir, Simone de

▷ De Beauvoir, Simone

Beaux' Stratagem, The (1707)

Play by ▷ George Farquhar, one of his
most successful and popular. Aimwell and
Archer, two impoverished gentlemen, come
to Lichfield in the guise of master and
servant. They go in search of a rich wife for
Aimwell, intending to split the proceeds.
Aimwell courts Dorinda, daughter of Sir

Charles and Lady Bountiful. Archer carries on a flirtation with the landlord's daughter, Cherry, while at the same time, in a separate intrigue, he pursues the unhappily married Mrs Sullen. Aimwell wins Dorinda, but in a fit of honesty, admits his deception. He gives all the money he has gained from the match to Archer, who however remains single. Late in the action, Aimwell finds he has inherited a title and estate, and all ends well for him and his bride to be. The play is vigorous and at times wildly funny, with a partly unconventional ending. Its atmosphere derives largely from ▷ Restoration comedy, but several plot factors link it with the more 'moral' plays of the later 18th century. The play contains a number of incisive comments about women's position in society, particularly in the lines and character of Mrs Sullen.

Becket, St Thomas (?1118–70)

A priest who served ▷ Henry II in various offices, culminating in the highest – that of Lord Chancellor. The period was one of constant disputes between Church and Crown over spheres of power, specially in the courts of justice. When Becket reluctantly became Archbishop in 1162, he became a champion of the very rights of the Church that Henry was trying to curtail. He was exiled on the continent for seven years but, after a brief reconciliation with Henry on his return, he was killed in Canterbury Cathedral on 29 December 1170, on the orders of the King. Henry later claimed that his instructions had been misinterpreted, but he did penance for the assassination. Becket was canonized in 1173 and his shrine at Canterbury became one of the great centres of European pilgrimage, and was the destination of the pilgrims in ▷ Chaucer's ▷ Canterbury Tales. A large number of medieval versions of the life of St Thomas survive and his martyrdom is the subject of ▷ T. S. Eliot's play Murder in the Cathedral (1935).

Beckett, Samuel (1906–89)

Dramatist and novelist. Born in Dublin, he was educated at Trinity College there. He became a lecturer in English at the Ecole Normale Supérieure in Paris (1928–30) and was then a lecturer in French at Trinity College. Since 1932 he has lived chiefly in France, and has written in both French and English. In Paris he became the friend and associate of the expatriate Irish novelist, ▷ James Joyce (1882–1941), whose ▷ stream of consciousness subjective method of narrative has strongly influenced Beckett's own novels; another important

influence upon him has been the French novelist ▷ Marcel Proust (1871–1922).

Poems include: *Whoroscope* (1930); *Echo's Bones* (1935).

Samuel Beckett

Novels and stories include: *More Pricks than Kicks* (1934); *Murphy* (1938); *Watt* (1944); *Molloy* (1951; English, 1956); *Malone Meurt* (1952; trans. *Malone Dies*, 1956); *L'Innommable* (1953; trans. *The Unnamable*, 1960); *Comment C'est* (1961; English, 1964); *Imagination Dead Imagine* (1966, from French); *Nouvelles et Textes Pour Rien* (1955); *Le Depeupleur* (1971; trans. *The Lost Ones*, 1972); *First Love* (1973); *Mercier et Camier* (1974).

Plays include: *En Attendant Godot* (1952; trans. ▷ *Waiting for Godot*, 1954); *Fin de Partie* (1957; trans. *End Game*, 1958); *Krapp's Last Tape* (1959); *Happy Days* (1961); *Play* (1963); *Eh Joe* (1966); *Breath and Other Short Plays* (1972); *Not I* (1973); *That Time* (1976); *Footfalls* (1976); *Ghost Trio* (1976); *. . . But the Clouds . . .* (1977); *Rockaby* (1980); *Ohio Impromptu* (1981); *Quad* (1982); *Catastrophe* (1982); *Nacht und Träume* (1983); *What Where* (1983). Plays for radio include: *All that Fall* (1957); *Embers* (1959); *Cascando* (1964).

Beckett is one of the most singular and original writers to appear in English, or possibly in French, since 1945. Like Joyce an Irish expatriate, he seems to belong to Ireland and to Europe; his characters are commonly Irish, and his cultural background the desolation of European culture. In both narrative and drama, (it is in the second that his achievement is perhaps the more remarkable) his method has been to create art out of increasingly simplified material, reducing his images of humanity to the sparest elements. His particular view of life's absurdity is often expressed through striking theatrical images which reveal a vision of life which is both bleak and grotesquely comic. Thus, in *Happy Days* Winnie appears on stage buried up to her waist in a mound of earth; in *Not I* the audience sees only a mouth on stage struggling to deliver a monologue of reminiscences; and in *Endgame* two elderly characters, Nagg and Neil, are placed in dustbins throughout the play. In so far as he is related to an English literary tradition, it is to the generation between the wars of 1914–18 and 1939–45 when, most notably in the work of James Joyce, communication with an audience was often secondary to experiments in the medium of language. His novels have accordingly had no influence on English fiction. His plays, on the other hand, especially *Waiting for Godot* and the plays for radio, have shown new possibilities in the handling of dialogue, by which speech is used less for communication than for the expression of minds that feel themselves in isolation, or on the point of sinking into it. Such use of dialogue perhaps had its beginnings in the late 19th-century dramatists, the Russian ▷ Chekhov and the Belgian ▷ Maeterlinck, and has superficial parallels with the work of the contemporary English dramatist, ▷ Harold Pinter.

▷ Irish literature in English.

Bib: Kenner, H., *Samuel Beckett, a Critical Study*; Jacobsen, J. and Mueller, W. R., *The Testament of Beckett*; Esslin, M. in *Theatre of the Absurd*; Bair, D., *Beckett: A Biography*.

Beckford, William (1759–1844)
Chiefly remembered for his ▷ Gothic novel *Vathek*, Beckford also wrote travel books, and was an extravagant collector of Gothic curiosities. Son of a Lord Mayor of London, Beckford's substantial family wealth enabled him to create Fonthill Abbey, where he lived in eccentric and scandalous seclusion.

Beddoes, Thomas Lovell (1803–49)
Poet and dramatist. Nephew of the novelist ▷ Maria Edgeworth and son of a physician, Thomas Beddoes. He spent most of his adult life in Germany and Switzerland, repeatedly in trouble for his revolutionary ideas. His first published work was a collection of tales in verse, *The Improvisatore* (1821). He shared

the romantic interest in the ▷ Jacobean dramatists, and sought to revive drama in their spirit with *The Bride's Tragedy* (1822). He continued to revise his second play, *Death's Jest-Book* until his death, and it was published posthumously in 1850, as were his *Collected Poems* (1851). Despite occasional intensities his plays are unexciting dramatically, and his reputation rests chiefly on his lyric verse in the tradition of ▷ Percy Bysshe Shelley, such as *Dream Pedlary*. Beddoes died by suicide.

Bib: Thompson, J. R., *Thomas Lovell Beddoes*.

Bede (673–735)
A native of the Angle kingdom of Northumbria and a lifelong monk in the monastery of Monkwearmouth-Jarrow, Bede was the foremost scholar of the Anglo-Saxon world. His works include scientific and grammatical tracts, a treatise on metrics, scriptural commentaries, saints' lives and a highly influential account of the *Historia Ecclesiastica Gentis Anglorum* (*History of the English Church and its People*) which was later translated into Old English.

Bib: Hunter-Blair, P., *The World of Bede*; Sherley-Price, L. (trans.), *A History of the English Church and its People*.

Bedivere
In ▷ Geoffrey of Monmouth's version of Arthurian history, he is one of ▷ Arthur's principal knights, his cupbearer and governor of Normandy. He has a less prominent role in later French and English Arthurian texts but often he is portrayed as the last knight to remain with the wounded Arthur and who has the task of returning ▷ Excalibur to the Lake (as in ▷ Malory's *Works*).

Bedlam
A famous lunatic asylum. Originally it was a priory, founded in 1247, for members of the religious order of the Star of Bethlehem. Lunatics were admitted to it in the 14th century, and in 1547, after the dissolution of the monasteries, it was handed over to the City of London as a hospital for lunatics. Antonia White's novel, *Beyond the Glass* (1954) gives an account of being ill there and of the primitive treatment used in this century to women in a state of breakdown. The name became shortened to Bedlam, and a Bedlamite, Tom o'Bedlam, Bess o'Bedlam, became synonyms for lunatics; Bedlam itself, a synonym for lunatic asylum. In modern English, 'bedlam' is a scene of uproar and confusion.

Bib: Showalter, E., *The Female Malady*.

Beelzebub

Baal-zebub, 'Lord of the Flies'. In the Old Testament (*2 Kings* 1 : 2) he is a heathen god; in the New Testament, *eg Matthew* 12 : 24 'prince of the devils'. Hence in ▷ Milton's ▷ *Paradise Lost* (Bk. I) he is second only to Satan.

Beer, Patricia (b 1924)

Poet. Beer was educated at Exeter and ▷ Oxford universities, has been a university teacher, and now writes full-time – she is also a novelist and critic. She grew up in Devon and her work draws strongly on West Country images. Her volumes of poetry include: *The Loss of the Magyar* (1959); *The Survivors* (1963); *The Estuary* (1971); *Driving West* (1975); *Selected Poems* (1979); *The Lie of the Land* (1983).

Beerbohm, Max (1872–1956)

Essayist, cartoonist, writer of fiction. When he began his career Beerbohm belonged to the so-called 'decadent' generation of the aesthetic school in the 1890s; this included ▷ W. B. Yeats in his ▷ Celtic Twilight phase, ▷ Oscar Wilde, ▷ Aubrey Beardsley, and the poets Lionel Johnson and Ernest Dowson. He showed his affiliation to this school by the playful fastidiousness of his wit, especially in his cartoons and parodies. *A Christmas Garland* (1912) contains parodies of contemporary writers including ▷ H. G. Wells, ▷ Arnold Bennett, and ▷ Joseph Conrad. But it is in his cartoons that his satirical wit is displayed with most pungency and originality, *eg Caricature of Twenty-five Gentlemen* (1896), *The Poet's Corner* (1904), *Rossetti and his Circle* (1922). As a writer he was above all an essayist; he entitled his first slim volume with humorous impertinence *The Works of Max Beerbaum* (1896), to which he added *More* (1899), *Yet Again* (1909), *And Even Now* (1920). He also wrote stories (*Seven Men*; 1919), and he is probably now most read for his burlesque romance *Zuleika Dobson* (1911), about the visit of a dazzling beauty to the University of Oxford where she is responsible for a mass suicide among the students.

Beerbohm was educated at Charterhouse and Merton College Oxford. He contributed to the ▷ *Yellow Book*, and in 1898 succeeded ▷ George Bernard Shaw as dramatic critic on the *Saturday Review*. From 1910 he lived in Italy, except during the two world wars. He was knighted in 1939. His personal and literary fastidiousness caused him to be known as 'the Incomparable Max', and as such ▷ Ezra Pound commemorates him as 'Brennbaum the Impeccable' in section 8 of *Hugh Selwyn Mauberley*.

Bib: Cecil, D., *Max: A Biography*; Riewald, J. G., *Beerbohm: A Critical Analysis with a Brief Life and a Bibliography*.

Beeton, Mrs (1836–65)

The author of a book on cooking and household management, published serially in *The Englishwoman's Domestic Magazine* (1859–61). The book met the needs of the rapidly broadening Victorian middle class, which was strongly attached to the domestic virtues and satisfactions. It was soon regarded as an indispensable handbook.

Beggar's Opera, The (1728)

By the poet ▷ John Gay, a play with numerous songs to the music of folk tunes. It is the earliest and by far the most famous of the 'ballad operas', which were light entertainment as opposed to the serious Italian operas fashionable in England, and dealt with life in low society. In part it was a political attack on the Prime Minister, Robert Walpole. The daughter of a receiver of stolen goods falls in love with Macheath, a highwayman who is imprisoned in Newgate, where the warder's daughter also falls for him and procures his escape. As a class of literature, *The Beggar's Opera* belongs to the mock heroic; another example from the time is ▷ Fielding's novel ▷ *Jonathan Wild the Great* (1743), which is about a master criminal. The effect of such works was to make their appeal through the lawless zest for life of the characters, coupled with an ironic exposure of their baseness. *The Beggar's Opera* is a classic of the English stage, and its music has been reset by later composers – Arthur Bliss and, more recently, Benjamin Britten. It was adapted by the German dramatist, ▷ Bertolt Brecht in *Die Dreigroschenoper* (*The Threepenny Opera*). *The Beggar's Opera* had an overture by the German musician Pepusch, also arranged from folk tunes.

▷ Opera in England.

Beggars, Sturdy

An expression used in the 16th century for the able-bodied poor who were unemployed and lived by begging. Unemployment was a serious social problem throughout the 16th century for a succession of causes. ▷ Henry VII (1485–1509) disbanded the private armies of the nobles; ▷ Henry VIII (1509–47) dissolved the monasteries, and threw into unemployment the numerous servants and craftsmen who had served them; the nobles enclosed extensive tracts of arable land for sheep-farming, which required less labour, or simply to surround their great houses with ornamental parks; prices rose, and periods of inflation sometimes made it impossible for poor men to support themselves without begging. The beggars were regarded as a serious social threat, since they often moved about in bands and took to robbery with violence. In the reign of ▷ Elizabeth I (1558–1603), the government made serious and fairly successful attempts to deal with the problem: they instituted a succession of ▷ Poor Laws, culminating in the Great Poor Law of 1601, in accordance with which the aged, sick and crippled were given financial relief by the parishes, but the 'sturdy beggars' were forcibly set to work. Not all the 'sturdy beggars' were from the poorer classes; in an age of enthusiastic financial speculation, richer men were sometimes suddenly ruined, and forced to take to the roads.

Behan, Brendan (1923–64)
Irish dramatist. His first play, *The Quare Fellow*, was staged in Dublin in 1954, but made its impact after it was adapted by ▷ Joan Littlewood's company, Theatre Workshop, in 1956, Behan spent time in borstal, and in prison as a political prisoner, and this influenced his play about a British soldier captured by the I.R.A., *The Hostage* (1958). His last play, *Richard's Cork Leg*, was unfinished. Many of his dramatic techniques drawing on popular traditions of entertainment, such as the use of song and dance and direct addresses to the audience, are typical of the style developed by Joan Littlewood's Theatre Workshop company.
Bib: O'Connor, U., *Behan*.

Behn, Aphra (1640–89)
Probably born Aphra (or Afra) Johnson, Behn changed her surname on marriage in 1664. Her husband, who died within two years of the marriage, appears to have been a city merchant, probably of Dutch origins. Behn had already travelled as far as Surinam before her marriage, and in 1666 Charles II recruited her to act as a spy in Antwerp during the Dutch war.

Her first play, *The Forced Marriage*, was staged in 1670, and among the best known of her works is ▷ *The Rover*. Her plays are characterized by sharp social satire focussed on sexual relationships. The hero of *The Rover*, Willmore, is rumoured to be based on the ▷ Earl of Rochester, and *The City Heiress* (1682) contains a caricature of the first ▷ Earl of Shaftesbury. Behn also produced poems and novels. Her novel *Oroonoko, or the History of the Royal Slave* (c 1688), challenges the hypocrisy of Christian slave traders, and was influenced by her experiences in the British colony of Surinam.

As a woman writer Behn was attacked for her lewd language and daring themes, and her own unconventional lifestyle has tended to obscure criticism of her work by moral condemnation. In *A Room of One's Own*, Virginia Woolf praised Behn as the first professional woman writer.
Bib: Spender, D., *Women of Ideas*; Spender, D., *Mothers of the Novel*; Spencer, J., *The Rise of the Woman Novelist*; Duffy, M., *The Passionate Shepherdess: Aphra Behn, 1640–89*.

Belial
In ancient Hebrew means 'worthlessness', but given as a proper name in the ▷ Bible (*Deuteronomy* XIII : 13), it was used by 17th-century ▷ Puritans to describe fashionable and dissipated people – 'sons of Belial'. ▷ Milton makes Belial a fallen angel.

Bell Savage Inn
A famous inn which formerly stood not far from ▷ St Paul's Cathedral in ▷ London, and was used in Elizabethan times for bull-baiting and for dramatic performances.
▷ Inns.

Bellamy, George Anne (?1731–88)
Born at Fingal in Ireland on St George's Day, hence her Christian name, to the actress Mrs Bellamy and her lover, James O'Hara, second Baron of Tyrawley. She made her stage debut at Covent Garden, where her mother was engaged, in 1741, and in 1743 she played for the first time with ▷ David Garrick. In 1745 Bellamy and her mother performed at ▷ Smock Alley in Dublin, alongside Garrick and ▷ Spranger Barry. She soon quarrelled with Garrick, and in 1748 was hired at ▷ Covent Garden, where she became one of the leading actresses. In 1749 she eloped with George Montgomery Metham to Yorkshire, giving birth to a son, George, later that year. Metham, however, reneged on a promise of marriage, and she returned to Covent Garden in 1750. Garrick determined to patch up his dispute with her and, in a famous episode, persuaded her to appear again at ▷ Drury Lane, playing Juliet to his Romeo, in competition with the *Romeo and Juliet* of Barry and ▷ Susanna Cibber. The rival performances lasted 12 nights, until Covent Garden ended its run and Drury Lane triumphed with a 13th. In 1767, now in failing health, Bellamy left the stage and moved in with the actor Henry Woodward. He died in 1777, and she afterwards lived largely off loans and gifts, pursued by creditors. During her years on the stage she played some 96 roles, excelling

in those demanding pathos and grief, including Cordelia, Juliet, Calista in *The Fair Penitent*, Imoinda in *Oroonoko*, and Indiana in ▷ *The Conscious Lovers*. Her autobiography, *An Apology for the Life of George Anne Bellamy* was published in 1785.
Bib: Hartmann, C., *Enchanting Bellamy*.

Bellerophon
In Greek myth, a hero of the city of Corinth. When he was guest of Proetus, king of Tiryns, his host's wife fell in love with him, but Bellerophon scorned her. In revenge, she told her husband that he had tried to seduce her, and Proetus sought ways to put him to death. He was sent on a number of impossibly dangerous tasks, the most famous of which was the slaying of the monster, ▷ Chimaera whom he slew with the aid of the winged horse, ▷ Pegasus.

Belloc, Hilaire (1870–1953)
A versatile writer (novelist, poet, essayist, biographer, historian) now especially remembered for his association with ▷ G. K. Chesterton in Roman Catholic propaganda. The most important phase of his career was before 1914, when he was one of a generation of popular, vivid, witty propagandists; ▷ George Bernard Shaw, ▷ H. G. Wells, and Chesterton were his equals, and the first two (as agnostic socialists) his opponents. With Chesterton, he maintained the doctrine of Distributism – an alternative scheme to socialism for equalizing property ownership. Among his best works is his earliest: *The Path to Rome* (1902), a discursive account of a journey through France, Switzerland and Northern Italy. He is now chiefly read for his light verse, *eg Cautionary Tales* (1907), *A Bad Child's Book of Beasts.* (1896)
▷ Catholicism in English literature; Children's books.
Bib: Hamilton, R., *Belloc: An Introduction to his Spirit and Work*; Speaight, R., *The Life of Hilaire Belloc*.

Belphoebe
A character in Edmund Spenser's ▷ *The Faerie Queene* (1596). Belphoebe, described at some length (Book II, canto iii, stanzas 21–4), is one of the symbolic representations of ▷ Elizabeth I in the poem. Etymologically, her name signifies both beauty and, through the association with ▷ Phoebe, the moon, chastity and hunting.

Belshazzar (6th century BC)
In the ▷ Bible (*Daniel* V) the son of ▷ Nebuchadnezzar and King of Babylon. He gave a great feast where he and his nobles 'praised the gods of gold, and of silver . . .',

when mysterious words suddenly appeared on the wall. Only the Hebrew prophet-in-exile Daniel could interpret that they foretold Belshazzar's overthrow, at the hands of Cyrus, King of Persia. The feast has been the subject of poems and dramas in English, including a poem by ▷ Byron, and an oratorio by William Walton.

Ben, Big
The biggest bell in the clock tower of the Houses of ▷ Parliament; often used as the name of the tower itself. The name commemorates the official under whose authority the bell was cast – Sir Benjamin Hall, Commissioner of Works, 1855–8. The loudness and melodiousness of the chime are well known, and, from the position of the clock high above the Houses of Parliament so as to be a landmark, both the chime and the tower itself have been turned into symbols of corporate national life. They are particularly used to suggest probity, dependability and consensus: for instance, the chimes of Big Ben prefacing the B.B.C. Radio news seem to guarantee its objectivity.

Benedick
▷ Beatrice and Benedick.

Benedictines
▷ Monasteries.

Bennett, Arnold (1867–1931)
Novelist. His principal novels are: ▷ *The Old Wives' Tale* (1908); the Clayhanger trilogy – ▷ *Clayhanger* (1910), *Hilda Lessways* (1911), and *These Twain* (1916) – all three reprinted as *The Clayhanger Family* (1925); *Riceyman Steps* (1923); *The Grand Babylon Hotel* (1902). His distinctive characteristics as a novelist are his regionalism and his ▷ naturalism. His books mainly concern life in the industrial Five Towns of the north-west Midlands (the Potteries), the particular characteristics of which differentiate his fiction considered as an image of English society. Secondly, he was strongly influenced by the naturalism of French fiction-writers such as ▷ Zola and Maupassant. This led him to emphasize the influence of environment on character, and to build his artistic wholes by means of a pattern of mundane details. This importance that he attached to environment caused a reaction against his artistic methods on the part of novelists like ▷ Virginia Woolf (see her essay 'Modern Fiction' in *The Common Reader, First Series*; 1925) and ▷ D. H. Lawrence, who found Bennett too rigid in his notions of form and too passive in the face of environmental influence. Nonetheless, Bennett lacked the ruthlessness of the French

naturalists, and softened his determinism with a sentimentality that recalls ▷ Dickens.
Bib: Drabble, M., *Arnold Bennett, a Biography*; Hepburn, J., *The Art of Arnold Bennett*; Lucas, J., *Arnold Bennett: A Study of His Fiction*.

Benoît de Sainte-Maure

A 12th-century French writer, patronized by ▷ Henry II, who produced a highly influential version of the story of the destruction of Troy (*Le Roman de Troie*) and a verse history of the Dukes of Normandy down to 1135. Benoît's Troy story, amplified from the pseudo-eyewitness accounts of the Trojan war attributed to ▷ Dares and ▷ Dictys, is a rationalized, chronologically ordered history. It presents an account of the first destruction of Troy as a preface to the story of the great Greek siege of Troy, triggered by the abduction of ▷ Helen. Benoît's version was itself translated into Latin in the 13th century by ▷ Guido de Columnis, and this Latin translation superseded Benoît's text as the most popular authoritative medieval version of the Troy story. The story of ▷ Troilus and Criseyde (or Briseida in Benoît's version) appears in Benoît's narrative in an embryonic form and seems largely to have been his invention, based on a few disconnected passages in Dares's text. ▷ Chaucer used Benoît's narrative, as well as ▷ Boccaccio's version of the love story in ▷ *Il Filostrato*, in composing ▷ *Troilus and Criseyde*.
▷ Ovid; Troy.

Bentham, Jeremy (1748–1832)

An extremely influential thinker, founder of the school of thought called ▷ Utilitarianism. The basis of his thought was: 1 that human motives are governed by the pursuit of pleasure and avoidance of pain; 2 that the guiding rule for society should be the greatest happiness of the greatest number; 3 that the test of value for human laws and institutions should be no other than that of usefulness. These views he expounded in *Fragment on Government* (1776) and *Introduction to Principles of Morals and Legislation* (1780). His principal associates were James Mill (1773–1836) and ▷ John Stuart Mill (1806–73); collectively they were known as the Philosophical Radicals, and together they established a practical philosophy of reform of great consequence in 19th-century Britain. But their excessive rationalism frustrated sympathy and imagination in education and the relief of poverty – see ▷ Dickens's novel ▷ *Hard Times* (1854). Bentham's thought derived

from the sceptical 18th-century French 'philosophes' such as Helvetius and 18th-century English ▷ rationalists such as ▷ David Hartley and ▷ Joseph Priestley. It was, in fact, the outstanding line of continuity between 18th-century and 19th-century thinking.
Bib: Stephen, L., *The English Utilitarians*; Pringle-Patterson, A. S., *The Philosophical Radicals and other essays*; Atkinson, C. M., *Life*.

Bentley, E. C. (Edmund Clerihew) (1875–1956)

▷ Detective fiction.

Bentley, Richard (1662–1742)

Distinguished as a classical scholar and noted for his despotic personality as Master of Trinity College, Cambridge. He is satirized by ▷ Jonathan Swift in *The Battle of the Books* and by ▷ Alexander Pope in ▷ *The Dunciad* (Bk. IV, 201–75).

Beowulf

The single extant text of this important ▷ Old English heroic narrative was copied about the year 1000 but there are linguistic traces of an earlier written version dating from the 8th century in the text, and the story material may derive from earlier narratives still. It deals with key events in the life of a 6th-century warrior, Beowulf, from Geatland in south Sweden, who first kills the monster Grendel, which had been ravaging the great hall of Heorot, built by Hrothgar, king of the Danes. Beowulf, nephew of the king of the Geats, slays the monster by wrestling with it and wrenching out its arm. Grendel's mother then seeks vengeance by carrying off one of the Danish nobles, but Beowulf enters the mere beneath which she lives and kills her too. Beowulf returns home and in due course becomes king of the Geats. When he has reigned 50 years, his kingdom is invaded by a fiery dragon which he manages to kill with the aid of a young nobleman, Wiglaf, when all the rest of his followers have fled. However, he receives his own death wound in the fight and as he dies, he pronounces Wiglaf his successor. His body is burnt on a great funeral pyre and the dragon's treasure is buried with his ashes; 12 of his followers ride round the funeral mound celebrating his greatness. This narrative is interlaced with digressions on historical analogues to the action, and asides concerning retrospective and prospective events, which give the poem a dense and complex narrative texture.
Bib: Swanton, M. (ed.), *Beowulf*.

Beppo: A Venetian Story (1818)
A poem in ▷ *ottava rima* by ▷ Lord
Byron. During the Venetian carnival Laura
and her *cavaliere servente* (lover) are
confronted by her long-absent husband,
Beppo, who has turned Turk after being
shipwrecked. The three of them discuss
matters amicably over coffee, and the men
remain friends thereafter. The poem reflects
Byron's own position at the time as *cavaliere
servente* to Theresa Guiccioli.

Berger, John (b 1926)
Novelist, painter and art critic. His novels
reflect both his Marxism (▷ Marx, Karl), in
their attention to the oppressive structures of
society, and his painting, in their vivid
realization of sensual detail. *A Painter Of Our
Time* (1958), through the story of an emigré
Hungarian painter, explores the role of the
artist in a consumer society and the
relationship of art to experience. His best-
known work is *G* (1972), in which authorial
self-consciousness, open-ended, fragmentary
narrative and documentary elements serve to
resist the imposition of order on political
events.

He has collaborated with the photographer
Jean Mohr on a number of works which
address political and social issues by
combining various media and genres,
including photographs, political and social
analysis, poems and fictionalized case studies;
these are *Ways of Seeing* (1972); *A Fortunate
Man* (1967); *A Seventh Man* (1981); *Another
Way of Telling* (1982). Berger has also
published two volumes of a trilogy entitled
Into Their Labours; these are *Pig Earth*
(1979), which comprises short stories and
poems, and *Once In Europa* (1987).
Other novels include: *The Foot of Clive*
(1962); *Corker's Freedom* (1964). A book of
short stories, *Pig Earth* was published in
1979. Drama: *A Question of Geography* (1987;
with Nella Bielski). Volumes of essays
include: *Permanent Red* (1960); *The White
Bird* (1985). Art criticism includes: *The
Success and Failure of Picasso* (1965).

Berkeley, George (1685–1753)
Irish churchman and a philosopher in the
tradition of ▷ Descartes (1590–1650) of
France and ▷ John Locke (1632–1704), but
the opponent of the latter. Locke had affirmed
the independence of matter and mind;
Berkeley held that the reality of anything
depended on its being perceived by a
conscious mind; thus mind (and spirit) had
primacy over matter. Nature is the experience
of consciousness, and the evidence of
Universal Mind, or God. He considered that

Locke's insistence on external matter and
physical causes led to ▷ atheism; but his
own lucid and precise prose is as much the
vehicle of reason as Locke's. While Locke led
towards scientific scepticism, Berkeley's faith,
combined with reason, maintained the
religious vision in an essentially rational
century. His philosophy is expressed in *A
New Theory of Vision*, (1709), and in *Principles
of Human Knowledge*, (1710). His *Dialogues of
Alciphron* (1732) are distinguished for their
grace of style.
Bib: Wild, J., *Berkeley: a study of his life and
philosophy*; Luce, A. A., *The Life of Berkeley*;
Warnock, G. J., *Berkeley*.

Béroul (fl 1190)
Composer of a version of the ▷ Tristan
story (in ▷ Anglo-Norman), of which 4,485
lines survive. The fragment begins with the
scene in which King Mark spies on the lovers
from the tree and breaks off before Tristan
moves away to Britanny. Little is known
about the author.

Berry, James (b 1924)
Poet. Berry comes from the West Indies, but
has lived in Britain since 1948, a prolific
writer and great promoter of multi-cultural
education. Like that of younger poets
▷ Linton Kwesi Johnson, Edward Kaman
Brathwaite and Benjamin Zephaniah, his work
draws strongly on West Indian vernacular
and reggae rhythms, and his volumes of verse
include *Chain of Days* and *Lucy's Letters and
Loving* (1982). He has also edited the poetry
volumes: *Bluefoot Traveller: An Anthology of
West Indian Poets of Britain* (1976); *News
From Babylon* (1984); and a collection from
the 1983 Brixton festival, *Dance to a Different
Drum*. Berry also writes widely for radio and
television, short stories and children's books
– his children's book, *A Thief in the Village*,
won the Grand Prix Prize in 1987. In 1981 he
was awarded the National Poetry Prize.
    ▷ Commonwealth literature.

Bestiaries
Compilations of descriptions of creatures
(natural and fantastic), especially popular in
the medieval period, in which a brief account
of the habits and appearance of the creature
is usually followed by allegorical
interpretations of its significance, and the
moral lessons it may provide. The most
accessible example of a medieval bestiary is
the 12th-century Latin bestiary, translated by
T. H. White, *A Book of Beasts* (1954).

Best-sellers
A transformation of the means of production
in the early years of the 19th century made it

possible for a single text to be printed, advertised, distributed and sold in numbers hitherto inconceivable. ▷ Charles Dickens's ▷ *Pickwick Papers* was the first work of fiction to exploit these new conditions. The financial return on this new mode of production was highly profitable, and a wide market for the commodity was opened up. In our own day the best-seller is associated not only with high sales, however, but also with quick ones. Though there is no agreement on the sales figures which define a text as a best-seller, national newspapers carry weekly charts, showing the titles which are selling most strongly in fiction and non-fiction. This may be seen as a form of advertisement, encouraging further sales of what has been guaranteed as an acceptable product by market success. Writing a best-seller may make a large sum of money for the author and some make it clear (Jeffrey Archer or Shirley Conran for instance) that they gear their fiction to the market with that intention. Recent moves, by publishers as well as authors, to aim writing and publication towards the best-seller lists inevitably threaten to narrow the range of what is published and to discourage publishers from taking chances with new authors and new kinds of writing.

Betjeman, Sir John (1906–84)

Poet and critic of architecture. His poetry is highly nostalgic and written in a style which has given it wide popularity: the 1958 *Collected Poems* was a best-seller. It is largely pastiche and parody, witty and anti-modernist in its form. His works include: *Mount Zion* (1931); *Continual Dew* (1937); *Old Lights in New Chancels* (1940); *New Bats in Old Belfries* (1945); *A Few Late Chrysanthemums* (1954); *Summoned by Bells* (autobiography in verse; 1960); *The Best of Betjeman* (ed. Guest; 1978); *Uncollected Poems* (1982). Betjeman was ▷ Poet Laureate from 1972–84. He was a forceful champion of ▷ Victorian architecture, and editor of the *Shell Guides*. He published some 20 books on architectural subjects.
Bib: Brook, J., *Writers and their Work*, British Council Pamphlet, 153.

Betterton, Mary (1637–1712)

Actress, one of those competing for the title of the first professional actress. She joined ▷ Sir William D'Avenant's company, probably in 1660, and her first known appearance was as Ianthe in D'Avenant's revision of ▷ *The Siege of Rhodes* in 1661. In the same year she played Ophelia to ▷ Thomas Betterton's ▷ Hamlet, and in 1662 the two were married.

Her talents were varied: she played innocent young girls, coquettes, and forceful characters such as Lady Macbeth (▷ *Macbeth*) and the Duchess of Malfi, apparently with equal skill. In the late 1660s, she and her husband took the young actress ▷ Anne Bracegirdle into their home, virtually adopting her as a daughter.

Throughout her career she maintained a reputation for 'virtuous' living: ▷ Cibber described her as leading 'an unblemish'd and sober life'. After her husband's death in 1710, she appears to have suffered some sort of mental breakdown, probably exacerbated by the poverty in which he left her. She was buried in ▷ Westminster Abbey, next to the body of her husband.

Betterton, Thomas (1635–1710)

The greatest English actor of his generation, he probably began acting in the late 1650s. By 1661 he had joined the ▷ Duke's Company, in which he purchased a share, and so was involved in theatrical finances as well as acting for most of his career.

As an actor, he succeeded from the beginning, making a particular impression as Hamlet, coached by ▷ Sir William D'Avenant, who had seen it performed earlier by an actor under ▷ Shakespeare's tutelage, and who had himself been taught by a pupil of Shakespeare's.

In 1662 Betterton was sent by ▷ Charles II to France, on the first of several missions to research the latest developments in French drama and ▷ opera, so as to bring new ideas to the English stage. Returning to England, he proceeded to build on his reputation with a succession of great roles, especially in Shakespeare. Betterton continued acting almost to his death, dying in great poverty. He is buried in ▷ Westminster Abbey.
Bib: Milhous, J., *Thomas Betterton and the Management of Lincoln's Inn Fields 1695–1708*; Highfill, P. H. Jr., Burnim, K. A. and Langhans, E. A. (eds.), *A Biographical Dictionary of Actors, Actresses, Musicians, Dancers, Managers, and Other Stage Personnel in London 1660–1800*; Lowe, R., *Thomas Betterton*.

Beulah, The Land of

In the ▷ Bible, *Isaiah* 62:4. A Hebrew word = 'married'. In Bunyan's ▷ *Pilgrim's Progress* it lies in sight of the Heavenly City and beyond the reach of Giant Despair. It signifies the state in which the soul is 'married' to God.

Bevis of Hampton

A popular metrical romance translated into English sometime in the late 13th/early 14th century. Earlier versions exist in French and ▷ Anglo-Norman. The story-type is one that is found in versions across Europe. Bevis's father has been murdered by his mother's lover, Sir Murdour. Bevis is sold as a slave and has many adventures – with his horse Arundel and his sword Morglay – before the happy ending with Bevis married to Josiane. The story was circulated in the ▷ chapbooks of the 16th century and is retold in ▷ Michael Drayton's *Poly-Olbion*.

Bible in England

The King James Bible, 1611

The Bible falls into two parts.

1 Old Testament

The first and larger part of the Bible, consisting of the sacred writings of the Jews. It concerns the peculiar, divinely ordained destiny of the Jewish race from earliest times, and it is considered by Christians to expound the divine promise which the New Testament fulfils not merely for the Jews but for the whole of mankind. The Old Testament is divided into books which are grouped by Jews into three main sections, as follows:

1 The Torah ('Law', otherwise called the Pentateuch), consisting of five books as follows: *Genesis, Exodus, Leviticus, Numbers, Deuteronomy*. They are called 'the five books of Moses'. The first two are narrative and descriptive, and move from the creation of the world to the escape of the Jews from slavery in Egypt. The remainder contain laws and discourses.

2 The Prophets. This section is divided into two in the Hebrew Bible: the 'Former Prophets', consisting of *Joshua, Judges*, the two books of *Samuel* and the two books of *Kings*; and the 'Latter Prophets', consisting of *Isaiah, Jeremiah, Ezekiel*, and the Minor Prophets. The books of the Former Prophets tell the story of the establishment of the Jews in the kingdom of Israel, and their subsequent history. The Latter Prophets contain history together with prophetic discourses.

3 The Sacred Writings, or Hagiographa, which are divided into three sections: (i) the Poetical books, consisting of *Psalms, Proverbs, Job*; (ii) the five 'Rolls', which are read at special seasons in the Jewish year: *Song of Songs, Ruth, Lamentations, Ecclesiastes, Esther* – of these *Esther* and *Ruth* are narratives; the other three are poetic meditations; (iii) *Daniel, Ezra, Nehemiah*, and *Chronicles*, all consisting mainly of historical narrative.

2 New Testament

The second and shorter part of the Bible, containing the sacred books of the Christians. It is divided into books, on the pattern of the Old Testament, and dates as a whole collection from the end of the 2nd century A D. It is customary to divide the books into four groups.

1 The three Synoptic (*ie* 'summary narrative') Gospels of Saints Matthew, Mark and Luke, and the *Acts of the Apostles*. The Gospels are narratives about Jesus Christ, and *Acts* is the narrative of the missionary careers of the apostles (including St Paul) after Christ's death.

2 The Epistles (letters) of St Paul. The four shortest of these are addressed to individuals: two to Timothy, and one each to Titus and to Philemon. The remainder are addressed to various early Christian communities. These are the Epistles to the Romans, Galatians, Ephesians, Philippians, Colossians, two to the Corinthians, and two to the Thessalonians. The Epistle to the Hebrews has been ascribed to Paul, but is nowadays considered to be by a disciple of his.

3 The Catholic Epistles, so called because they were directed to Christians generally. Two of these are ascribed to St Peter, and one each to James and Jude.

4 The Johannine writings, ascribed to the Apostle John. These are the Gospel of St John, distinguished from the Synoptic Gospels as probably not intended as a

historical narrative, the Epistles of John, and the poetic, visionary narrative called the *Apocalypse*, or *Revelation*.

In the Middle Ages the only version of the Bible authorized by the Church was the ▷ Vulgate, *ie* the translation into Latin by St Jerome, completed in 405. Partial translations were made into Old English before the 11th century. From the 14th century translations were made by reformers, who believed that men without Latin should have the means of seeking guidance from divine scripture without dependence on Church authority. The main translators were these: ▷ Wycliffe (14th century); ▷ Tyndale, and Coverdale (16th century). The last-named was the producer of the *Great Bible* (also called ▷ Cranmer's Bible after the Archbishop of the time), but ▷ Henry VIII, concerned for his intermediate position between Catholics and Protestants, ended by restricting its use. Under the Catholic ▷ Mary I (1553–8) English reformers produced the *Geneva Bible* abroad, with annotations suited to ▷ Puritan ▷ Calvinist opinion; and in 1568 the so-called *Bishops' Bible* was issued by the restored Anglicans to counteract Puritan influence. Finally, in 1611 the Authorized Version was produced with the approval of ▷ James I (1603–25). For three centuries it was to be the only one in general use, and it is still the prevailing version. In the 19th century it was revised (Revised Version) and recently a new translation has been authorized and produced (New Testament 1961; Old Testament 1961; Old Testament Apocrypha 1970). A Catholic translation the (Douai Bible) was issued at about the same time as the Authorized Version.

In spite of various other translations, Catholic and Protestant, in the 19th and 20th centuries the Authorized Version is by far the most important for its literary and social influence. It was based on previous translations, especially that of Tyndale, so that the cast of its prose is characteristically more 16th than early 17th century in style. Nonetheless much of it is of supreme eloquence, *eg* the Book of *Job*, and last 15 chapters of *Isaiah*. It was for many people in the 17th and 18th centuries the only book that was constantly read, and it was familiar to all from its use in church and education. The musical cadence of Authorized Version prose can be often heard in the prose of English writers, whether or not professing Christians. It is conspicuous in John Bunyan's ▷ *Pilgrims Progress* but it can also be heard in the prose of 20th century novelists ▷ T. F.

Powys, *eg Mr Weston's Good Wine* (1927).
▷ Apocrypha
Bib: Daches, D., *The King James' Version of the Bible.*

Bildungsroman
A novel which describes the youthful development of the central character. Prominent examples in English include ▷ James Joyce's ▷ *A Portrait of the Artist as a Young Man* (1916), ▷ Samuel Butler's ▷ *The Way of All Flesh* (1902) and ▷ D. H. Lawrence's ▷ *Sons and Lovers* (1913).

Bill of Rights (1689)
An Act passed by ▷ Parliament, according to which the powers of the king were restricted. In particular, he could no longer suspend laws without the consent of Parliament; nor could he dispense with laws in individual cases. The importance of the Act was less the specific ways in which royal power was limited than Parliament's implicit decision to take over the sovereignty of the government from the Crown. This Bill and the events that led up to it, the flight of ▷ James II (1685–8) and his replacement by ▷ William III and Mary II (the Glorious Revolution), were the real starting-points of 'constitutional monarchy' in England, *ie* a monarchy under which it is accepted by both Crown and people that the representatives of the people are the real sovereigns of the country. Because Britain does not have a written constitution, such historical traces as the Bill of Rights are the major signs of how power has been transferred and located.

Billingsgate
The London fish market, situated by one of the gates of the City by the riverside. In the 17th century the market was famous for the abusive language used in it; hence 'billingsgate' has become synonymous with violent and abusive language.

Biographia Literaria (1817)
A miscellaneous work of ▷ autobiography, philosophy, and literary criticism, by ▷ Samuel Taylor Coleridge. Its psychological approach to creativity, influenced by the German philosophers Schlegel and ▷ Kant, foreshadows the ▷ Freudian concept of the unconscious, and its theory of imagination is central to the development of literary critical theory. The famous distinction between primary imagination, secondary imagination and fancy occurs in Chapter XIII. Primary imagination is seen as 'the living power and prime agent of all human perception'. Secondary imagination is the creative power to synthesize

and re-express experience in new forms: 'It dissolves, diffuses, dissipates, in order to recreate; or where this process is rendered impossible, yet still, at all events, it struggles to idealize and to unify.' Fancy, on the other hand, simply juxtaposes memories and impressions and 'has no other counters to play with but fixities and definites'. Primary perception is thus not the mere passive holding of a mirror up to nature of classical literary theory, but involves an interaction between subjectivity and objective reality.

Much of the literary criticism in the book is devoted to detailed analysis and appreciation of ▷ William Wordsworth's artifice, and to pointing out that his language is not simply, as he asserted in the Preface to the *Lyrical Ballads*, 'the real language of men', but a highly individual artistic construct of his own. The 'critical analysis' of poems by ▷ Shakespeare and Wordsworth which occupies much of the second volume, displays a very modern sophistication in its treatment of metre and diction.

Biography

The chief source of inspiration for English biographers was the Greek, ▷ Plutarch (1st century AD), whose *Parallel Lives* of Greek and Roman great men was translated into English by ▷ Sir Thomas North in 1579 and was widely read. Biography had been practised before in England; there had been the lives of the saints in the Middle Ages, and in the 16th century Cavendish's life of the statesman ▷ Cardinal Wolsey had appeared. The regular practice of biography, however, starts with the 17th century, not merely owing to the influence of North's translation of Plutarch, but as part of the outward-turning, increasingly scientific interest in many kinds of people (not merely saints and rulers) which in the 18th century was to give rise to the novel. Biography is a branch of history, and the art of historical writing advanced with biography: Edward Hyde, ▷ Earl of Clarendon, included fine biographical portraits in his history of the Great Rebellion, written between 1646 and 1670. ▷ Izaak Walton's lives of ▷ John Donne (1640), Sir Henry Wotton (1651), ▷ Richard Hooker (1665), ▷ George Herbert (1670) and Bishop Sanderson (1678) are closer to our modern idea of biography, and they are landmarks, if not originals, in the form inasmuch as the subjects, though eminent men, were humble enough to lead ordinary lives in touch with usual experience. In the 18th century the writing of biographies became habitual; and also biography, or

autobiography, became a way of disguising pure fiction, *eg* in the novels of ▷ Defoe. ▷ Samuel Johnson was a master of biography in his ▷ *Lives of the Poets* (1779–81), most notable among which is his *Life of Mr Richard Savage*, previously published in 1744. The outstanding biography of the century, however, is the life of Johnson himself by ▷ James Boswell, 1791. As an intimate and vivid account of a great man, it was never equalled in the 19th century when so many biographies were written and some classic ones, amongst them and perhaps pre-eminent, ▷ Elizabeth Gaskell's life of her friend, ▷ Charlotte Brontë (1857). The 19th century was, however, more outstanding for its achievements in the largely new form, ▷ autobiography. The 20th century saw a new approach to the art in the work of ▷ Lytton Strachey (1880–1932). His *Eminent Victorians* (1918) sought for the truth in the lives of its subjects in unexpected details, and instead of expounding their greatness exposed the weakness of their mere humanity. The psychological approach and the revolutionary tone of biography has made it, in the last 10 years, one of the fastest growth areas in publishing, Michael Holroyd and Richard Ellman being two of the major biographers of the 1980s.
Bib: Gittings, R., *The Nature of Biography*.

Black Death

An epidemic which struck England in 1348–9 and reduced the population by between one-third and one-half. The economic consequences were far-reaching, especially the shortage of labour. Landowners tended to change from arable to sheep-farming, which required less labour; peasants had better bargaining power and were in a position to commute their serfdom into paid labour; a fierce class struggle resulted from attempts by the landed classes to keep down wages, culminating in the ▷ Peasants' Revolt of 1381.

Black Douglas

▷ Douglas, Black.

Black Friars (Blackfriars)

Dominican ▷ friars, called 'Black' in England owing to the colour of their robes. Their convent in London was dissolved by ▷ Henry VIII (1509–47), but the district has continued to bear their name. Part of the old convent was adapted as a theatre by ▷ James Burbage. The ▷ Blackfriars theatre was at first in the hands of boy actors – the Children of the Chapel – and only came to the Lord ▷ Chamberlain's Company in 1608. It was a 'private' theatre with a more affluent and probably more educated kind of audience than frequented the public theatres such as the ▷ Globe. The change of audience encouraged a change in mode of drama. Never again would the theatre serve the whole society: its present status in this country, as an entertainment for the relatively privileged, is derived from the move from 'public' to 'private' theatres.

▷ Theatres.

Black Hole of Calcutta
Suraj-ud Daula, ruler of Bengal, decided in 1756 to expel the East India Company from its base in Calcutta. He surprised the city and imprisoned 146 Europeans in a small punishment cell in the barracks; only 23 survived till next morning. The incident was followed by the campaign of Robert Clive, the Battle of Plassey of 1757 and the appropriation of Bengal. This story has become a byeword for 'oriental cruelty' and the subsequent takeover of Bengal represented as the moment at which the British started to transform India. Recent scholarship, however, suggests that the wealth of Bengal derived from factors already in place and that the economy was not extensively transformed by British rule.

Black Prince, The (1330–76)
Edward, Prince of Wales, eldest son of ▷ Edward III. He was famous for his military exploits, especially his defeat of a French army at Poitiers, 1356; in consequence he became a national hero comparable to ▷ Henry V. His designation 'Black' seems to originate with 16th-century chroniclers; it probably refers to his reputation as a warrior. His son was ▷ Richard II.

Blackmore, Sir Richard (c 1655–1729)
Poet and physician to Queen Anne. The dullness of his lengthy epic, *Prince Arthur* (1695) and *The Creation: a philosophical poem demonstrating the existence and providence of God* (1712), earned the ridicule of ▷ Alexander Pope in ▷ *The Dunciad* (Bk. II, 370ff). He also wrote a *Satyre against Wit* (1700).

Blackmore, R. D. (Richard Dodderidge) (1825–1900)
Novelist and poet. Born in Berkshire, the son of a clergyman, Blackmore was educated at school in Tiverton, where he was head boy, and at Exeter College, Oxford. His mother had died when he was a baby and he spent much of his youth with an uncle in Glamorgan. A career as a barrister was cut short by epileptic fits and after an unsuccessful period as a schoolteacher,

Blackmore built a house in Teddington where he lived a retired life, dividing his time between writing, and growing and selling fruit and flowers. He married Lucy Maguire in 1852; there were no children and after her death in 1888 he continued to mourn her and keep the house unchanged. He was a shy man, kind but self-centred and determined. He was fond of animals, especially dogs, and deeply absorbed in his gardening enterprise.

He published volumes of poetry, including translations of ▷ Theocritus and ▷ Virgil. His 14 novels include *Lorna Doone* (1869), which was rejected by 18 publishers and is now his most famous novel, *Cradock Nowell* (1866), *The Maid of Sker* (1872), his first attempt at fiction only later finished, *Alice Lorraine* (1875) and *Springhaven* (1887). *Lorna Doone* is said to have done for Devonshire what ▷ Sir Walter Scott did for the Highlands and in general Blackmore's novels abound with carefully observed and detailed descriptions of locations, wildlife and the weather along with exciting incidents, all somewhat loosely structured.

Bib: Burris, Q. G., *R. D. Blackmore: His Life and Novels*; Dunn, W. H., *R. D. Blackmore, The Author of Lorna Doone: A Biography*; Budd, K. G., *The Last Victorian: R. D. Blackmore and his Novels*.

Blackwood's Magazine
Founded in 1817 by the publisher William Blackwood as the *Edinburgh Monthly Magazine*, it was particularly influential in the first 15 years of its existence. Like the ▷ *Quarterly* it was intended as a Tory rival to the liberal ▷ *Edinburgh Review*, but called itself a 'magazine' to indicate a lighter tone than that of the 'Reviews'. It attacked ▷ Lord Byron, and ▷ Percy Bysshe Shelley on political grounds, and was, like the *Quarterly*, particularly hostile to ▷ John Keats, because of his association with the radical journalist ▷ Leigh Hunt. Hunt, Keats, ▷ Charles Lamb and ▷ William Hazlitt were stigmatized as the 'Cockney School' of literature. *Blackwood's Magazine* began with a brilliant group of contributors, especially ▷ Sir Walter Scott, John G. Lockhart (known because of his fierce criticism as 'the Scorpion'), ▷ James Hogg, and John Wilson, who wrote under the pen-name of Christopher North. Between 1822 and 1835 the magazine ran a series of brilliant dialogues, *Noctes Ambrosianae*, 'Nights at Ambrose's' (a well-known inn). In 1857 it published ▷ George Eliot's *Scenes from Clerical Life*.

Blair, Robert (1699–1746)

Scottish clergyman and author of *The Grave* (1743), a ▷ blank verse genre piece blending ▷ Gothic sinisterness, banal piety and a pseudo-Shakespearean sublimity, imitated from ▷ *Hamlet*. Its enjoyable imaginative gusto ensured that it retained its popularity throughout the century, and beyond.

Blake, William (1757–1827)

William Blake's illustration of 'Fire' from *The Book of Urizen* (1794)

Poet and artist. The self-educated son of a London hosier, Blake earned his living by engraving illustrations for books. His own poems are engraved rather than printed, and he wove into his text pictures which elaborated the poetic theme. His earliest poems, *Poetical Sketches* show the influence of earlier lyric writers and ▷ Macpherson's Ossianic writings. His next works, the ▷ *Songs of Innocence* (1789), and ▷ *Songs of Experience* (1794) are startlingly original. Intended, on one level, for children, they are simple but symbolically resonant lyrics 'Shewing the Two contrary States of the Human Soul'. In *Innocence* the world is unthreatening and without morality, and God is trusted implicitly. The *Experience* poems, which often parallel those of the earlier volume in setting or title, depict with fierce moral indignation, a fallen world of repression and religious hypocrisy. There is no simple relation of progression or superiority between the 'contrary states', and Blake makes no attempt to reconcile their contradictions. They remain in unresolved dialectical opposition to each other.

In later works Blake elaborates his revolutionary interpretation of Christian theology using invented characters representing psychological or spiritual forces. In *Thel* (etched c 1789), in rhythmical unrhymed lines, usually of seven stresses, the protagonist, confronted with the interdependence of life and death, creation and destruction, flees back to the shadowy world of the unborn. *Tiriel* was written at about the same time. *The French Revolution* (1791), *America* (1793) and *Visions of the Daughters of Albion* (1793) show Blake's reaction to the American and French revolutions, which he saw as releasing the energies of humanity, so long repressed by the forces of absolutism, institutionalized religion and sexual inhibition. In ▷ *The Marriage of Heaven and Hell* (etched c 1793) Blake expressed in a series of prophetic statements and 'Memorable Fancies', mainly in prose, his contempt for 18th-century rationalism and institutionalized religion.

Because his works remained virtually unknown and he developed no lasting relationship with an audience, his later prophecies became increasingly formless and obscure. He was also unwilling to be too explicit in case he should invite trouble from the authorities. *The Book of Urizen* (1794) focusses on the tyrannical figure of Urizen, ('your reason' or 'horizon'?) who symbolizes the inhibiting powers of control and restriction. Urizen is in constant war with Orc, a Satanic force of revolutionary energy. *The Book of Ahania*, *The Book of Los* (1795) and *Vala* (1797), subsequently rewritten as *The Four Zoas* (1804) develop similar themes with increasing intricacy and elusiveness. His last two prophetic books *Milton* (1804) and *Jerusalem* (1804) are often impenetrable, but include some striking passages. They show a new emphasis on Christian humility and self-sacrifice. In *Milton* he elaborates on his famous observation that ▷ Milton was 'of the Devil's party without knowing it'. Milton is shown returning to earth in the form of Blake himself, in order to correct his earlier mistake. Blake is one of the most intellectually challenging of English poets, with a unique insight into the pieties and ideological deceptions of his time.

Bib: Davis, M., *William Blake: A New Kind of Man*; Bronowski, J., *William Blake and the Age of Revolution*; Glen, H., *Vision and*

Disenchantment: Blake's Songs and Wordsworth's Lyrical Ballads; Bottrall, M. (ed.), *William Blake: Songs of Innocence and Experience* (Macmillan Casebook); Paley, M. D., *William Blake*; Erdman, D. V., *Blake: Prophet Against Empire*; Bloom, H., *Blake's Apocalypse*.

Blank verse

Verse which is unrhymed, and composed of lines which normally contain ten syllables and have the stress on every second syllable, as in the classical ▷ iambic pentameter.

The first user of the iambic pentameter in English was ▷ Chaucer and he used it in rhyming couplets, *eg The Prologue* to ▷ *The Canterbury Tales*. The first user of blank verse was Henry Howard, ▷ Earl of Surrey (1517–47), who adopted it for a translation of the second and third books of ▷ Virgil's *Aeneid* in order to get closer to the effect of the metrically regular but unrhymed Latin ▷ hexameters. The effect in Surrey is that Chaucer's measure is being used but without rhyme:

> *They whisted all, with fixèd face attent,*
> *When prince Aeneas from the royal seat*
> *Thus gan to speak.*

The dramatist ▷ Christopher Marlowe (1564–93) first gave blank verse its distinctive quality. In his plays, he combined the rhythm of the verse with the normal rhythm and syntax of the sentence, so that the effect begins to be like natural speech expressed with unusual music:

> *Hell hath no limits, nor is circumscrib'd*
> *In one self place: for where we are is hell,*
> *And where hell is, there must we ever be . . .*
> (*Dr Faustus*)

Blank verse as used by Marlowe was carried on by ▷ Shakespeare, who employed it with steadily increasing flexibility and power. His contemporaries did the same, but in his immediate successors' work great freedoms are taken with the ▷ metre, and the rhythm of the sentence begins to dominate over that of the line, so that the effect is of rhythmic paragraphs of speech.

The next phase is the epic use of blank verse by ▷ Milton in ▷ *Paradise Lost* (1667), who gave the weight of Latin syntax to the long sentences and accordingly moved away from speech rhythms. ▷ Wordsworth and ▷ Coleridge at the beginning of the 19th century lightened the Miltonic effect back towards colloquialism. 20th-century poets such as ▷ Eliot and ▷ Pound derived from the ▷ Jacobean dramatists new free measures which cannot strictly be described as blank verse at all.

▷ Free verse; Metre.

Bleak House (1852–3)

A novel by ▷ Charles Dickens, published, like most of his novels, in monthly parts. It opens with an attack on the part of the legal system called the High Court of Chancery. The rest of the novel expands this opening into a dramatization, through a wide range of characters, of the various forms of parasitism that society lends itself to, and of the ways in which institutions (especially legal ones) falsify relationships and degrade human beings. Most of the story takes place in London. The telling of the story is shared by two contrasted narrators: the savagely sardonic but impersonal author who uses the present tense and the ingenuous, saccharine, unresentful girl, Esther Summerson, who is ignorant of her parentage, though she knows that she is illegitimate. She is adopted by a philanthropist, John Jarndyce, who also adopts two young orphan relatives, Richard Carstone and Ada Clare, who are 'wards in Chancery' (*ie* legally under the care of the ▷ Lord Chancellor) while the distribution of an estate to which they have claims is endlessly disputed in the Court of Chancery (the case of 'Jarndyce and Jarndyce'). Through Richard, Ada and Mr Jarndyce, Esther becomes acquainted with a large number of characters, some of whom are also despairing participants in Chancery Suits, and others (such as Skimpole, the parasitic man of letters, Mrs Jellyby, a well-meaning but incompetent philanthropist, and Turveydrop, the self-styled model of fashionable deportment) who live off society without giving anything substantial in return. Another focus in the novel is Sir Leicester Dedlock, a simple-minded but self-important land-owner, whose one redeeming feature is his devotion to his wife, the beautiful and silent Lady Dedlock. Lady Dedlock is in fact the mother of Esther Summerson, a fact known to the family lawyer, Tulkinghorn, who blackmails her. Her former lover, Captain Hawdon, is still alive, but lives in destitution and misery. His only friend is the crossing-sweeper, Jo, who resembles Sir Leicester in that they are equally simple-minded and equally capable of one great love for another person. In social respects they are so differentiated, by the lack of any advantages in the one case and by excess of privilege in the other, that it is hard to think of them as belonging to the same species. A large number of other characters contribute to Dickens's panorama of society as mainly constituted by parasites and the victims of parasites. The theme is conveyed partly through the atmosphere of contrasted houses: Bleak House, which is in fact the cordial and life-giving home of Mr Jarndyce; Chesney Wold, the vast but empty mansion of Sir Leicester; Tom-all-alone's, the slum dwelling where Jo finds his sole refuge; the clean and orderly household of the retired soldier, Bagnet; the squalid one of the money-lender, Smallweed, and so forth. For the main characters, the story ends with the corruption of Richard Carstone, the death in despair of Lady Dedlock, the murder of Tulkinghorn and Esther's marriage to the young doctor, Woodcourt. The case of 'Jarndyce and Jarndyce' was based on an actual case centring on a Birmingham millionaire, William Jennings. The character of Skimpole is partly based on ▷ Leigh Hunt, and another character, Boythorn, on ▷ Walter Landor.

Blenheim (1704)
An important battle in the War of the ▷ Spanish Succession in which the forces of ▷ John Churchill, Duke of Marlborough, and Prince Eugene of Savoy defeated the French forces of Louis XIV under Marshal Tallard, near the village of Blindheim (anglicized, Blenheim) in Bavaria.

Blood, Tragedy of
 ▷ Revenge tragedy.

Bloody Assizes
Judicial trials of unusual ferocity held after the failure of ▷ Monmouth's Rebellion against James II. Judge Jeffreys condemned large numbers of the small rebel army to death and sentenced many more to transportation (▷ Botany Bay) to penal colonies.

Bloom, Harold (b 1930)
One of the leading members of the so-called Yale school of literary criticism, along with the late ▷ Paul De Man, Geoffrey Hartman, and J. Hillis Miller. In books such as *The Anxiety of Influence* (1973), *A Map of Misreading* (1975), and *Poetry and Repression* (1976) Bloom seeks to offer a revisionary account of poetry, based especially on a ▷ Freudian model of the relationship between the aspiring poet and his literary predecessors. In this way Bloom moves away from the tenets of American ▷ new criticism in his suggestion that all poetry seeks, but fails, to exclude 'precursor' texts, with which it enters into a struggle, both

destructive and creative, in order to achieve its particular identity.

Bloomsbury Group, The
An exclusive intellectual circle that centred on the house of the publisher, Leonard Woolf, and his wife, the novelist, ▷ Virginia Woolf, in the district of London round the British Museum, known as Bloomsbury. It flourished notably in the 1920s, and included, besides the Woolfs, the economist Lord Keynes, the biographer ▷ Lytton Strachey, the art critics Roger Fry and Clive Bell, and the painters Vanessa Bell and Duncan Grant, as well as others. The group owed much to the Cambridge philosopher ▷ G. E. Moore and the importance he attached to the value of friendship and aesthetic appreciation. Their close relationships which resulted from this, in addition to the fastidiousness which arose from their critical attitude to the prevailing culture of English society, gave them an apparent exclusiveness which made them many enemies. Moore's influence also contributed to their scepticism about religious tradition and social and political conventions; they tended to be moderately left-wing and agnostic. Positively, they were innovators in art and represented an important section of the English avant-garde. Their more constructive opponents attacked them for excessive self-centredness and an aestheticism which was too individualistic and self-regarding to be really creative in social terms.

Blue-coat school
A term used for a number of schools formerly dependent on public subscription; the boys in them wore blue uniforms. Much the best-known example is Christ's Hospital, founded under ▷ Edward VI (1547–53).

Blues, The
1 As dance music, the blues were a jazz setting to melancholy 3-line verse, of American Negro origin (to feel blue = to feel gloomy).
2 An Oxford or Cambridge blue is an athletic distinction, owing its name to the colours (dark and light blue, respectively) representative of these universities.
3 The Regiment of Royal Horse Guards, so called from the colour of its uniform.

Bluestocking
The 'Blue Stocking Ladies' were a group of intelligent, literary women in the mid 18th century who held evening receptions for serious conversation. As a setting for discussions in which both sexes were included, the evenings were a deliberate attempt to challenge the social stereotypes

which confined intellectual debate to male
gatherings and relegated the female sex to
trivial topics. By bringing men and women
together in this atmosphere, it was hoped that
the 'polite' codes of gallantry could be
disposed of. The chief hostesses included
▷ Elizabeth Montagu, Elizabeth Carter,
▷ Mary Delany, and, later, ▷ Hannah
More.

The name 'bluestocking' is thought to
derive from the stockings of Benjamin
Stillingfleet, who, too poor to buy evening
dress, attended in his daytime blue worsteds.
▷ Hannah More's poem *Bas Bleu* (1786)
helped to establish the use of the term as
referring to the society women, although
Admiral Boscawen is traditionally credited
with coining the collective noun.

Blunden, Edmund (1896–1974)
Poet and critic, and author of one of the most
famous books of World War I, *Undertones of
War* (1928). His lyrical poetry produced
during and just after that war is drawn
especially from the English countryside, and
its sincerity and dignity redeemed what was
becoming a hackneyed convention of 'nature
poetry'. His poetry was first published in the
1914 ▷ *Georgian Poetry* anthology. His
literary studies have been important especially
for the 'romantic' period, *eg Life of Shelley,
Charles Lamb and his Contemporaries*; and he
played a great part in editing and raising the
reputation of the poet ▷ John Clare. His
best remembered book now is probably
Cricket Country (1944).
Bib: Hart-Davies, R., *Edmund Blunden*
(British Council).

Boadicea (d AD 61)
A Celtic queen (also Bonduca, Boudicea) who
is a national heroine because of her rising
against the Roman occupying forces. Her
people were the Iceni of what is now the
county of Norfolk; she was defeated by
Suetonius Paulinus and killed herself.
Poetically she has been celebrated by
▷ William Cowper, ▷ Alfred Tennyson,
and in the tragedy *Bonduca* by ▷ John
Fletcher.

Boar's Head Inn
Particularly famous in literature because it is
the setting of some of the scenes in which
▷ Falstaff figures in ▷ Shakespeare's
▷ *Henry IV, Parts I and II*. An actual inn
existed in Eastcheap, ▷ London, in
Shakespeare's day; it was pulled down in
1831.
▷ Inns.

Bobby
A nickname for a policeman. Bobby is an
endearment form of Robert; it was Sir Robert
Peel who first established the London
Metropolitan police – the first of its kind in
the world – in 1828.

Boccaccio, Giovanni (?1313–75)
Italian humanist scholar and writer, born
near Florence. His literary studies began in
Naples where he wrote his first works but he
later returned to Florence and was employed
on diplomatic missions for the Florentine
state. He publicly lectured on ▷ Dante's
▷ *Divine Comedy*, was a friend of
▷ Petrarch and the centre of a circle of
humanist learning and literary activity. His
works included a wide range of courtly
narratives, a vernacular imitation of classical
epic and a number of important encyclopaedic
works in Latin which occupied the last years
of his life. ▷ Chaucer made extensive use of
his work, drawing, for example, on the
Filocolo for the ▷ *Franklin's Tale*, the
▷ *Filostrato* (for ▷ *Troilus and Criseyde*),
the *Teseida* (for the ▷ *Knight's Tale*) and, in
all likelihood, on the ▷ *Decameron* (for a
number of the ▷ *Canterbury Tales*). The
Decameron, like the *Canterbury Tales*, is a
story-collection but it has a rather different
setting. In Boccaccio's collection, the stories
are narrated by a group of ten nobles who
take refuge in the country as the plague
rages in Florence. The company of noble
women and men amuse themselves for two
weeks by telling stories loosely based on a
love theme of some kind, chosen by the
leader of the day. However, the narrators of
the resulting 100 stories are far less
memorable than those of the *Canterbury
Tales* and Chaucer's story-collection, though
shorter than Boccaccio's, has a far greater
tonal range too.

Boccaccio's collection of brief tragic-
narratives in Latin (*De Casibus Virorum
Illustrium*) was reworked in English by
▷ Lydgate in the 15th century and it
provided much material for the Elizabethan
compilation of short tragic-narratives, the
▷ *Mirror for Magistrates*. Tales from the
Decameron were included in William Painter's
anthology, ▷ *The Palace of Pleasure*, and
many Elizabethan dramatists, including
▷ Shakespeare, quarried plots from either
Painter's collection or from the *Decameron*
itself. Boccaccio's vast narrative compilations
in Latin and in the vernacular continued to
provide narrative sources for many later
English writers, including ▷ Dryden,
▷ Keats and ▷ Tennyson.

Boethius, Ancius Manlius Torquatus Severinus (475–524)

Philosopher, scholar and statesman, born in Rome and educated at Athens and Alexandria. He wrote textbooks on logic and music, and was made consul in 510. His illustrious political career, as advisor to the Ostrogothic Emperor Theodoric, ended when he was accused of treason, imprisoned and executed in 524. While imprisoned, he composed his most famous and influential work, the (*Consolation of Philosophy*), *De Consolatione Philosophiae*. Written in prose and verse sections in the voice of a first-person speaker, it recounts how the speaker was tutored by Lady Philosophy to view his imprisonment philosophically and to see his place within a broader universal scheme. It deals with complex issues such as the relationship between divine foreknowledge and individual free will and was one of the most influential philosophical works of the medieval period, being translated into ▷ Old English by ▷ Alfred and later by ▷ Chaucer. The influence of Boethius pervades Chaucer's narratives. Another English translation from the Elizabethan period has been attributed to ▷ Elizabeth I.

Bib: Watts, V. (trans.), *The Consolation of Philosophy*.

Bohemian

Applied to artists and those who live a life supposedly dedicated to the spirit of the imaginative arts, it means living freely, refusing to observe social conventions, especially when they depend on mere habit, snobbery or fear of 'seeming different'. Recently it often carries a slightly mocking tone and is rarely used now without irony. Literally, Bohemian means native to Bohemia, now the western part of Czechoslovakia. In the 15th century ▷ gipsies were supposed to have come from there; in the 19th century, French students were supposed to live like the gipsies and hence to be 'Bohemian'. The word was then introduced into English with this meaning by the novelist ▷ William Makepeace Thackeray. His novel ▷ *The Newcomers* is one of the first studies in English of Bohemianism.

Boiardo, Matteomaria (?1441–94)

Italian poet who reworked the legends of ▷ King Arthur and ▷ Charlemagne. His principal work was the unfinished *Orlando Innamorato*. ▷ Ludovico Ariosto produced a sequel ▷ *Orlando Furioso*.

Boileau, Nicolas (1636–1711)

French critic and poet. The ▷ Earl of Rochester's *Satyre Against Reason and Mankind* broadly follows his Eighth Satire. Through his *Art Poetique* (*The Poetic Art*) (1674), based on ▷ Horace's *Ars Poetica*, and his translation of the Greek treatise *On the Sublime*, attributed to ▷ Longinus, he fostered in ▷ French literature the ideals of classical urbanity and regularity of form. He influenced ▷ John Dryden, who revised a translation of his *Art Poetique*, and ▷ Alexander Pope, whose ▷ *Essay on Criticism* was partly based on it, and whose ▷ *Rape of the Lock* owes something to the French poet's mock-epic, *Le Lutrin*. In the Romantic and Victorian periods Boileau's name became synonymous with stifling (and foreign) neo-classical decadence. The youthful ▷ John Keats abuses the French critic in splendid but callow rhetoric in *Sleep and Poetry*.

Bold Stroke for a Wife, A (1718)

Play by ▷ Susannah Centlivre, the only one for which she claims to have used no sources but her own invention. Anne Lovely has four guardians, all of whom must give their consent before she can marry: Sir Philip Modelove, an 'old Beau', who cares only for French fashions, and loves operas, balls and masques; Periwinkle, a 'silly half-witted Fellow . . . fond of everything antique and foreign', who dresses in the fashions of the previous century; Tradelove, a broker and cheat; and Obadiah Prim, a 'very rigid Quaker'. Colonel Fainwell is in love with Lovely, and sets out to win her by approaching each of the guardians in various disguises, and with various feigned schemes. One of his characters, ▷ Simon Pure, has given the phrase 'the real simon pure' to the English language. The means by which Fainwell succeeds in his plan forms the chief interest of the action. The play provides a wonderful vehicle for a versatile actor: three members of the Bullock family were in the original production, and many other renowned actors, including ▷ John Philip Kemble and Charles Kemble (1775–1854), have played the part of Fainwell. *A Bold Stroke for a Wife* achieved great popularity and became a stock item in the English repertory, surviving until the last quarter of the 19th century. It was acted in command performances before George II and George III.

Bolingbroke, Henry (1367–1413)

In ▷ Shakespeare's ▷ *Richard II* he deposes his cousin, King Richard, to make himself King ▷ Henry IV.

▷ *Henry IV Part I*.

Bolingbroke, Henry St John (1678–1751)
Tory politician, and writer chiefly on political
matters. He favoured the ▷ Stuart (Jacobite)
succession on the death of Queen Anne in
1714, and when the ▷ Whigs took power
and the Hanoverian George I was declared
king, he was impeached. He fled to the court
of the Pretender in France, but in 1723 was
pardoned and returned to England. He
became a friend of ▷ Alexander Pope and
his rationalist, Deist views strongly influenced
the ▷ *Essay on Man*, which is addressed to
him. In 1749 he published *The Idea of a
Patriot King*, which argued that the king's
role should be as a national leader, above the
corruption of politics.
    ▷ Deism.

Bolt, Robert (b 1924)
British dramatist whose first major success
was with the ▷ Chekhovian *Flowering
Cherry* (1957). This was followed by *A Man
for All Seasons* (1960), a play about the life of
▷ Sir Thomas More, which has some
superficial resemblances to the style of
▷ Brecht, such as the use of a common man
figure who plays a variety of roles in the play.
However, the audience is not encouraged to
maintain a critical distance from the action in
the manner of Brecht nor are the particular
historical circumstances of More's life
explored in any detail. Bolt is primarily
concerned with More's conflict between his
commitment to himself, to his own sense of
integrity, and his commitment to society, a
theme which is common in his work. Other
plays include: *The Tiger and the Horse* (1960);
Gentle Jack (1963); *Vivat! Vivat Regina!*
(1970); *State of Revolution* (1977). Film
scripts: *Lawrence of Arabia* (1962); *Dr Zhivago*
(1965); *A Man for All Seasons* (1967); *Ryan's
Daughter* (1970); *Lady Caroline Lamb* (1972);
The Bounty (1984); *The Mission* (1986).
Bib: Hayman, R., *Robert Bolt*.

Bond, Edward (b 1934)
British dramatist and one of the new left-
wing writers to establish themselves at the
▷ Royal Court theatre during the 1960s.
His plays have often aroused controversy; the
early play *Saved* (1965) created a furore for
its scene of a baby being stoned to death and
Early Morning (1968) was banned for
depicting Queen Victoria as a lesbian. He has
written plays regularly on a wide range of
subjects for the past 20 years and is recognized
as a leading modern dramatist. Other major
works are: *The Pope's Wedding* (1962); *Narrow
Road to the Deep North* (1968); *Lear* (1971);
The Sea (1973); *Bingo* (1974); *The Fool*
(1976); *The Bundle* and *The Woman* (both

1978); *Restoration* (1981); *The War Plays*
(1985).
Bib: Coult, T., *The Plays of Edward Bond*;
Hay, M. and Roberts, P., *Bond: A Study of
His Plays*; Hirst, D. L., *Bond*.

Book of the Duchess
▷ Chaucer's dream poem, written in
octosyllabic couplets, which commemorates
Blanche of Lancaster, the first wife of ▷ John
of Gaunt. The date of the poem is uncertain
but it is one of Chaucer's early works and
seems likely to have been composed some
time in the early 1370s. Chaucer drew on the
work of contemporary French poets,
especially ▷ Jean Froissart and
▷ Guillaume de Machaut, for its material
and form. The lovelorn narrator/dreamer
relates how he falls asleep, having read the
story of Ceyx and Alcyone as bedtime reading.
He follows a hunting party in his dreamscape and, in the heart of a wood, meets a
lovelorn knight, dressed in black, whom he
finds lamenting the loss of his lady. In
response to questions from the dreamer, the
Black knight recounts the history of his
courtship of his lady White, and is finally
prompted to reveal, in plain terms, that she
has died. At this point, the dreamer and the
knight begin to move out of the wood
towards the knight's castle; a bell strikes 12;
the dreamer awakes, book in hand, vowing to
preserve his dream experience in a literary
form.
    The name of the lady celebrated in the
poem, 'White', obviously recalls that of
Blanche of Lancaster, and various punning
references are made in the text to John of
Gaunt's position as Earl of Richmond and
Duke of Lancaster. In the Prologue to
Chaucer's ▷ *Legend of Good Women*, this
▷ dream-vision poem is listed among
Chaucer's works as 'the Deeth of Blaunche
the Duchesse'.
    ▷ John of Gaunt; Lancaster, House of.
Bib: Phillips, H. (ed.), *Chaucer: The Book of
the Duchess*; Spearing, A. C., *Medieval Dream
Poetry*.

Booth, Barton (?1679–1733)
Actor, manager, poet: the leading tragic actor
of his generation. Booth became interested in
the theatre while performing in a play at
Westminster School, and afterwards joined
the profession. In 1709 he became the leading
tragic actor at ▷ Drury Lane, but in the
following year, after a quarrel about the
distribution of management duties in the
company, he helped lead a break-in to the
premises which turned into a violent affray.
The dispute was revived in a different form

in 1713, with Booth insisting on sharing in the company's management, a position he won only after action in court. In his new position of power he was able to take on major new roles including King Lear, Jaffeir in ▷ Thomas Otway's ▷ *Venice Preserv'd* and Timon of Athens.

An admirer of ▷ Thomas Betterton, Booth is said to have imitated him – lapsing, at worst, into a monotonous intoning style of delivery; he is reported to have lacked the capacity for humour in his performances. At his best he acted with great dignity and grace, while also possessing fiery qualities enabling him to perform such roles as Othello and Hotspur with passion.

Bib: Highfill, P. H. Jr., Burnim, K. A. and Langhans, E. A. (eds.), *A Biographical Dictionary of Actors, Actresses, Musicians, Dancers, Managers, and Other Stage Personnel in London 1660–1800*.

Booth, Hester (?1690–1773)

Actress and dancer. Hester Booth (née Santlow) began her career as a dancer at ▷ Drury Lane in 1706, moving to the ▷ Queen's Theatre, Haymarket, in 1708. She began acting in the following year, with the role of Prue in ▷ Congreve's ▷ *Love for Love*. Thereafter she played a variety of comic and serious roles, major and lesser. She married ▷ Barton Booth in 1719 and left the stage around 1733, the year of her husband's death. Theatre goers admired her more for her dancing than for her acting, commenting on its smoothness, and her interpretative abilities as a dancer.

Borough

One of the synonyms of 'town', used specifically for a town which has been incorporated and given privileges of limited self-government; also used until the 20th century for a town with the right to elect a Member of Parliament. 'The Borough' is a term for ▷ Southwark, south of the Thames, to distinguish it from 'the City' (of London) to the north.

Borrow, George Henry (1803–81)

Born in Norfolk, Borrow was educated in Edinburgh and Norwich as his father, a recruiting officer in the militia, moved around. Borrow was articled to solicitors in Norfolk 1818–23, then when his father died he moved to London and worked for a publisher. He travelled in France, Germany, Russia, the East and Spain 1833–9, sending letters to the *Morning Herald* 1837–9, blazing a trail as effectively the first newspaper correspondent. In 1835 he published in St Petersburg *Targum*, translations from 30 different languages and dialects. In Russia and Spain he was an agent for the British and Foreign Bible Society. In 1840 he married Mary Clarke, the widow of a naval officer he met in Spain, and bought an estate on Oulton Broad in Norfolk, in which he had already inherited a share. There he allowed gipsies to pitch tents and live, and became friends with them. His books are in part based on his life. *The Bible in Spain* (1834) and *The Zincali or an account of the Gypsies in Spain* (1841) owed as much of their success to public interest in Borrow the man as Borrow the writer. *Lavengro* followed in 1851, losing Borrow much of his popularity due to its strong 'anti-gentility' tone. *The Romany Rye* (1857) and *Wild Wales* (1862) continued the mixture of fact with fiction, vivid portraits and revelations of the personality of the writer. He died largely unknown and little read.

Bib: Knapp, W. I., *Life, Writings, and Correspondence of George Borrow*; Collie, M., *George Borrow, Eccentric*; Williams, D., *A World of His Own: The Double Life of George Borrow*.

Bosola

A hired assassin in ▷ John Webster's play ▷ *The Duchess of Malfi* who belatedly discovers the stirrings of conscience in himself and assumes the role of revenger.

Boswell, James (1740–95)

Best known for his *Life of Samuel Johnson*, whom he met in 1763, Boswell was also a copious diarist. Eldest son of Alexander Boswell, Lord Auchinleck, Boswell studied law at Edinburth, Glasgow and Utrecht, and reluctantly entered the legal profession.

From 1760 onwards, Boswell published many pamphlets, often anonymously. After meeting ▷ Johnson, he travelled in Europe, where he met ▷ Rousseau and ▷ Voltaire. Rousseau fired him with enthusiasm for the cause of Corsican liberty, and he cultivated a lifelong friendship with General Paoli; in 1768 he published an *Account of Corsica*, which attracted considerable international recognition.

In 1769 Boswell, by now a Scottish Advocate, married his cousin Margaret Montgomerie. But Boswell longed to be part of London literary culture, and made journeys to the capital as frequently as he could. Here he was elected a member of ▷ The Club, though his habit of 'scribbling' memoranda of conversations, with the aim of writing Johnson's *Life*, irritated some of its members.

In 1773, Boswell and Johnson made their

tour of the Hebrides (see ▷ *The Journal of a Tour to the Hebrides*). From 1777 to 1783 Boswell wrote a series of articles for the *London Magazine* under the pen-name of 'The Hypochondriack'. In 1782 he inherited the Scottish estate on his father's death, and his last meeting with Johnson was in 1784.

Boswell attempted, unsuccessfully, to make a career in politics, while working on the *Life of Samuel Johnson*, which appeared in 1791.
Bib: Pottle, F. A. (ed.), *Boswell's London Journal, 1762–63*; Hill, G. B. (ed.), revised Powell, L. F., *Life of Johnson and Journal of a Tour to the Hebrides*.

Botany Bay
In New South Wales, Australia, near Sydney. Captain Cook landed there in 1770 and took possession of it for the British Crown. From 1787 Australia was used for convict settlements, *ie* convicted criminals sentenced to transportation were sent there. They were not in fact sent to Botany Bay, but the name was used in common speech to cover convict settlements in Australia generally. The bay received its name from Joseph Banks, a botanist accompanying Cook, because of its rich plant life. The brutality of this system and the suffering it imposed is only now being traced by scholarship and reflected in public opinion. It involved injury not only to the transportees and their families but also to the native peoples whose lands were invaded and appropriated.
▷ Penal system.
Bib: Keneally, T., *The Fatal Shore*.

Bottom, Nick
A comic character in ▷ Shakespeare's ▷ *A Midsummer Night's Dream*. He is a weaver, and the most prominent of the 'Athenian artisans'.

Bow Bells
The church of St Mary-le-Bow in ▷ Cheapside, London, has always been famous for its peal of bells. The church is in the middle of the City of London, so that to be born within hearing of the Bow bells has been the test of being a true ▷ Cockney, *ie* Londoner.

Bow Street
In London, immediately next to Covent Garden Opera House. The chief ▷ Magistrates' Court in London has been situated there since 1735, when it opened in the house of the first Bow Street Magistrate. His successor, the novelist ▷ Henry Fielding, was given a house in Bow Street separate from the court-house. Fielding was exceptionally successful as a Magistrate in

ridding London of its crime. He and his brother established the Bow Street Runners, the predecessors of the London police.

Bowdler, Thomas (1754–1825)
Famous for *The Family Shakespeare*, 1818; an edition in which 'those words and expressions are omitted which cannot with propriety be read aloud in a family'. He later published an edition of ▷ Gibbon's ▷ *Decline and Fall of the Roman Empire* similarly expurgated. From these we get the word 'bowdlerize' = to expurgate.

Bowen, Elizabeth (1899–1973)
Novelist and short-story writer. Born in Dublin and educated in England, she worked in a Dublin hospital during World War I, and for the Ministry of Information in London during World War II. Her novels are concerned with themes of innocence and sophistication, the effect of guilt and of the past on present relationships, and the damaging consequences of coldness and deceit. Her portrayal of the inner life of female characters and her symbolic use of atmosphere and environment show the influence of ▷ Virginia Woolf, as does the structure of her first novel, *The House in Paris* (1935). Her treatment of childhood and youthful innocence owes something to the work of ▷ Henry James, especially in *The Death of the Heart* (1938), where Bowen narrates the story partly through the consciousness of a young girl. Bowen powerfully conveyed the atmosphere of World War II London during the Blitz, and the emotional dislocation resulting from the war, both in *The Heat of the Day* (1949) and in short stories such as 'In The Square' and 'Mysterious Kôr' (in *The Demon Lover*, 1945). Her other novels are: *The Hotel* (1927); *The Last September* (1929); *A World of Love* (1955); *Eva Trout* (1969). Other story collections include: *The Cat Jumps* (1934); *Look at all those Roses* (1941); *A Day in the Dark* (1965).
Bib: Glendinning, V., *Elizabeth Bowen: Portrait of a Writer*; Craig, P., *Elizabeth Bowen*.

Bowles, William Lisle (1762–1850)
Poet and clergyman; ultimately chaplain to the Prince Regent. His *Sonnets* (1789), sentimental effusions delivered in the person of 'the wanderer', were extremely popular, and revived interest in the sonnet form. ▷ Samuel Taylor Coleridge and ▷ Robert Southey were impressed by them. The preface to his edition of ▷ Alexander Pope (1806) took its critical stance from his former

teacher at Winchester, ▷ Joseph Warton, and prompted ▷ Lord Byron's 'Letter on W. L. Bowles's Strictures on Pope' (1821).

Bowtell (Boutell, Bootell), Elizabeth (c1650–97)

Actress. Born Elizabeth Ridley she joined the ▷ King's Company at ▷ Bridges Street Theatre about 1670, afterwards specializing in the playing of 'breeches' parts, although her most famous role was as Queen Statira in *The Rival Queens* (1677). During one performance a quarrel between her and ▷ Elizabeth Barry, who was appearing in the play as Roxana, degenerated into genuine violence on stage. The dispute arose over the possession of a prized prop (a veil). Required to stab Statira on stage, Barry as Roxana lunged at her with such force that she pierced her flesh 'about a Quarter of an Inch', according to a near contemporary. She retired in 1696.

Bracegirdle, Anne (1663–1748)

Actress, singer. She came into the Bettertons' (▷ Betterton, Thomas; ▷ Betterton, Mary) household as a sort of surrogate daughter c1688 and in that year she became a member of the ▷ United Company, playing a succession of roles in contemporary plays, as well as speaking prologues and epilogues for many of them. In 1693 Bracegirdle acted in ▷ William Congreve's first play, ▷ *The Old Bachelor*. By the following year she had become a leading member of the United Company, but in 1695 she joined Betterton and Elizabeth Barry in seceding from the company to form a separate troupe at ▷ Lincoln's Inn Fields. There she played the first Angelica in Congreve's ▷ *Love for Love* and in 1700 Millamant – a part written for her by Congreve – in ▷ *The Way of the World*. Congreve was among a number of prominent men who courted or admired her from a distance.

Throughout her life Bracegirdle was celebrated for her supposed virtue, some of the comments being possibly ironic. She was lauded for her abilities in both comic and tragic acting modes, her style in the latter tending towards pathos, as well as for her beauty, charm, and generosity toward fellow-performers and those in need. She was buried at ▷ Westminster Abbey.

Bib: Highfill, P. H. Jr., Burnim, K. A. and Langhans, E. A. (eds.), *A Biographical Dictionary of Actors, Actresses, Musicians, Dancers, Managers, and Other Stage Personnel in London 1660–1800.*

Bradbury, Malcolm (b 1932)

Malcolm Bradbury

Novelist and critic. His novels are: *Eating People Is Wrong* (1959); *Stepping Westward* (1965); *The History Man* (1975); *Rates Of Exchange* (1983); *Cuts* (1987). These are witty, satirical portraits of the four decades since 1950; the first three use university settings to epitomize the changing moral and political situation of western liberalism. He is often compared to ▷ Kingsley Amis for his hilarious send-ups of academic habits and pretensions, but Bradbury also has a fascination with the idea of fictionality, which he sees as central to the contemporary understanding of reality. His works are therefore informed by current critical theory (a feature which they share with the novels of ▷ David Lodge). *Rates Of Exchange* draws on ▷ structuralist theories, has an eastern European setting, and a somewhat harsher tone than Bradbury's earlier work, in an attempt to register the atmosphere of the 1980s. The title of *Cuts* refers to both cuts in funding and film cutting, and the novel portrays ▷ Tory Britain in the mid 1980s through the story of a collision between an academic and a woman television executive.

Braddon, Mary Elizabeth (1835–1915)

Novelist. Daughter of a solicitor, educated privately, Braddon became an actress for three years to support her mother, before beginning to write. She met publisher John

Maxwell in 1860 and lived with him and his five children, producing six more of their own. They married in 1874 on the death of Maxwell's first wife, who was in a lunatic asylum. She wrote more than 80 ▷ sensation novels; her publisher called her the 'Queen of the Circulating Libraries'. *Lady Audley's Secret* (1862) was first serialized in *Robin Goodfellow* and *The Sixpenny Magazine*, and was immediately successful. Other novels include *Aurora Floyd* (1863), *The Doctor's Wife* (1864), *Henry Dunbar* (1864), *Ishmael* (1884) and *The Infidel* (1900).

Bradley, A. C. (Andrew Cecil) (1851–1935)
Professor of Poetry at Oxford whose books on ▷ Shakespeare, *Shakespearean Tragedy* (1904) and *Oxford Lectures on Poetry* (1909), were inspired by 19th-century idealism and had a considerable influence on the study of character in Shakespeare.

Bradley, F. H. (Francis Herbert) (1846–1924)
Brother of ▷ A. C. Bradley, the literary critic. He was himself an eminent philosopher, author of *Ethical Studies* (1876); *Principles of Logic* (1883); *Appearance and Reality* (1893), and *Essay on Truth and Reality* (1914). His position philosophically was an idealist one, and in this he has been opposed by most British philosophers ever since, beginning with ▷ G. E. Moore. Bradley, however, had a strong influence on ▷ T. S. Eliot, the poet and former philosophy student, whose early thesis on him has recently been published.
▷ Idealism; Realism.

Braine, John (b 1922)
Novelist. His most famous novels are *Room at the Top* (1957; filmed 1958) and *Life at the Top* (1962; filmed 1965). Both of these deal with the new kinds of social mobility and anxiety, characteristic of Britain since World War II, and led to him being thought of as one of the ▷ 'angry young men' of the 1950s. Like the heroes of his novels, however, he has become progressively more conservative in his attitudes. Other novels are: *The Vodi* (1959); *The Jealous God* (1964); *The Crying Game* (1968); *Stay with me till Morning* (1970); *The Queen of a Distant Country* (1972); *The Pious Agent* (1975); *Waiting For Sheila* (1976); *The Only Game in Town* (1976); *Finger of Fire* (1977); *One and Last Love* (1981); *The Two of Us* (1984); *These Golden Days* (1985).
▷ Realism.
Bib: Salwak, D., *John Braine and John Wain: A Reference Guide*.

Brathwaite, Edward Kamau (b 1930)
▷ Commonwealth literatures.

Brecht, Bertolt (1898–1956)
One of the most significant theatre practitioners and theorists this century. His work has had a major influence on British drama since the late 1950s. Brecht's early plays were written shortly after World War I and were influenced by the Expressionist movement. From the mid-1920s he became interested in applying Marxist (▷ Marx, Karl) ideas to plays and performance and developed his concept of '▷ epic theatre'. The essential characteristic of 'epic', as Brecht used the term, was the creation of a critical distance (*Verfremdungseffekt*) between the audience and the performance on stage (and a similar critical distance between the actor/actress and the role he or she performed). The purpose of this was to prevent empathy and encourage audiences instead to reflect on the relationship between social conditions and human action, in such a way that they would recognize their power and agency in the process of history. Brecht was forced to leave his native Germany during the Nazi era and continued writing in exile in Europe and later America. After World War II he returned to Germany and formed the Berliner Ensemble company in East Berlin, where he directed a number of his plays written in exile. The Berliner Ensemble first visited London in 1956 and performed three of Brecht's plays: *Mother Courage and her Children, Drums and Trumpets* and *The Caucasian Chalk Circle*. Other plays include: *Baal* (1918); *Man is Man* (1926); *The Threepenny Opera* (1928; with music by Kurt Weill); *The Measures Taken* (1930); *St Joan of the Stockyards* (1932); *The Seven Deadly Sins* (1933; with Kurt Weill); *The Resistible Rise of Arturo Ui* (1941); *The Life of Galileo* (1943); *The Good Person of Szechwan* (1943). Brecht's influence on dramatists, directors and actors has been profound and is best understood by referring to the following books: Needle, J. and Thomson, P., *Brecht*; Willett, J., *Brecht in Context*.

Brenton, Howard (b 1942)
British left-wing dramatist, strongly influenced by ▷ Brecht, who has worked with both ▷ fringe and mainstream theatre companies since the late 1960s. His iconoclastic plays have frequently caused controversy, particularly when they have been staged at major theatres. He began writing for the Combination, at Brighton, and The Portable Theatre, a touring company.

Recently he has worked at the ▷ National Theatre despite his having expressed doubts in the past about the value of such 'establishment' institutions. Major plays are: *Magnificence*, a ▷ Royal Court success in 1973; *Brassneck* (1973), a collaboration with ▷ David Hare; *The Churchill Play* (1974); *Weapons of Happiness* (1974); *Epsom Downs* (1977); *Romans in Britain* (1978); *The Genius* (1983); *Bloody Poetry* (1984); *Pravda* (1985), also a collaboration with David Hare; *Greenland* (1988).
Bib: Bull, J., *New British Political Dramatists*; Chambers, C. and Prior, M., *Playwright's Progress*.

Breton, André (1896–1966)

French poet, founder of ▷ Surrealism, which he launched in 1924 with the first *Surrealist Manifesto*. Prior to this, Breton had met both the poet Guillaume Apollinaire (during 1917–18) and ▷ Sigmund Freud (in 1921), both of whom provided inspiration for the movement. In 1919, he published his first collection of poems, *Mont de piété*, and in the same year he collaborated with Philippe Soupault (b 1897) on his first properly Surrealist text, *Les Champs magnétiques*, which preceded the official launch of Surrealism. Between 1919 and 1921, he participated in the ▷ Dadaist movement, although it was his initiative to hold in Paris the international congress which led to the break-up of Dada. Believing firmly in the radicalism of Surrealism, Breton resisted any attempt to make the movement subservient to an established political creed. In *Légitime Défense* (1926), he rejected any form of control, even Marxist control, of the psychic life and, by contrast with other members of the movement, this was to lead to his break with communism in 1935. After the war, Breton continued to campaign vigorously on behalf of Surrealist radicalism. He opposed Albert Camus's (1913–60) thesis, as expounded in *L'Homme révolté* (1952) that revolt has its limitations, and a year before his death organized a final Surrealist exhibition, *L'Ecart absolu*, which aimed to challenge the consumer society. Breton contributed to Surrealist writing not only by the three manifestoes (1924, 1930, 1934) and other polemical writing, but also by numerous collections of poetry and prose, the original editions of which were usually illustrated by leading artists connected with Surrealism.

Breton, Nicholas (?1545–?1626)

Poet, miscellanist, pamphleteer. Little is known of the life of Nicholas Breton – a curious irony in that he was one of the most prolific writers of the ▷ Renaissance period. Between 1575 and his death he published over 30 individual collections of verse, three prose fictions and at least 25 ▷ pamphlets and miscellaneous works. From the evidence of the number of times certain of his works were re-printed (in particular his *A Post with a Mad Packet of Letters*, first published in 1602) there is the suggestion that, on occasions, he was able to secure an audience.

Breton Lays

A rather misleading term used by critics to refer to a group of Old French and Middle English verse narratives which claim to derive their story-material from a pre-Saxon, British literary tradition. It would be more accurate to call these texts British lays, rather than Breton lays, for the narratives claim descent from British, not specifically Breton, origins. ▷ Marie de France, writing in the late 12th century for audiences, it seems, in England and France, claims to be the first writer to produce a collection of these verse narratives, and the first vernacular writer to mediate between the old, oral-poetic traditions of the Britons (which Marie suggests had musical accompaniments) and contemporary literary traditions. Some shared themes, settings and protagonists can be traced in her story-collection. Her lays characteristically focus around emotional crises of some kind; the events are often located in Britain or Brittany; and the action tends to involve some interplay between human and otherworldly forces and places. Yet the structural patterns of the narratives vary (and may coincide with those of ▷ romances), so it is the claim to British origins which gives this group of narratives their identity, not their narrative structure. ▷ Chaucer's ▷ Franklin claims to present a British lay as his contribution to the ▷ *Canterbury Tales*.
Bib: Rumble, T. C., *The Breton Lays in Middle English*.

Bridewell

A royal palace until 1555, then a penitentiary. It was largely destroyed in the ▷ Fire of London in 1666. New Bridewell, used for the same purpose, was built in 1829 and pulled down in 1864. The idea of a penitentiary lies behind the more modern idea of the reformatory, *ie* the place to which offenders are sent when they are considered too young to be sent to prison, and in the 19th century 'Bridewell' was used as a synonym for such institutions.

Bridges, Robert Seymour (1844–1930)

Poet and dramatist. He was ▷ Poet Laureate from 1913–30. After medical training and

work as a consultant at Great Ormond Street Children's Hospital, Bridges turned his energies fully to poetry in 1882. His first volume of verse was published in 1873, after which he wrote prolifically: his collected *Poetical Works* (1936), excluding eight dramas, are in six volumes. He was a fine ▷ classical scholar and in his experiments with classical rhythms, was something of an innovator. His most ambitious work was the long, philosophical *The Testament of Beauty*, which appeared in five parts from 1927 to 1929. Other works include: *Shorter Poems* (1890); *The Spirit of Man* (1916) and *New Verse* (1925). He was the chief correspondent and literary executor of the poet ▷ Gerard Manley Hopkins; the latter developed his poetic theories through their letters. A selection of Bridge's work, *Poetry and Prose*, has been edited by John Sparrow.
Bib: Smith, N. C., *Notes on The Testament of Beauty*; Guerard, A. J., *Bridges: A Study of Traditionalism*; Thompson, E., *Robert Bridges*.

Bridges Street Theatre, The
▷ Drury Lane Theatres.

Bridges-Adams, William (1889–1965)
Director of the Shakespeare Memorial Theatre in Stratford-on-Avon from 1919 to 1934, during which time he directed 29 of ▷ Shakespeare's plays. His productions were influenced by the work of ▷ Harley Granville Barker. Unlike his predecessor, Frank Benson, he did not act in his own productions and aimed for: 'The virtues of the Elizabethan theatre without its vices, and its freedom without its fetters: scenic splendour where helpful, but . . . the play to be given as written: the text unmutilated whether in the interests of the stage carpenter or the leading man.'

Bridie, James (1888–1951)
Pseudonym of Dr Osborne Henry Mavor. He was a successful playwright during the 1930s and 1940s and part-founder of the Citizens' Theatre in Glasgow. He wrote 42 plays, many of which were performed on the London stage. He is often compared to ▷ George Bernard Shaw for his prolific output and range of subject-matter. His best-known plays today are *The Anatomist* and *Tobias and the Angel* (both 1930), *Jonah and the Whale* (1932), *A Sleeping Clergyman* (1933), *Colonel Wotherspoon* (1934), *The Black Eye* (1935), *Storm in a Teacup* (1936), *Mr Bolfry* (1943), *Dr. Angelus* (1947) and *Daphne Laureola* (1949).
Bib: Luybem, H., *Bridie: Clown and Philosopher*.

Brighton
An English seaside resort on the south coast, one of the first to become fashionable when, in the 18th century, sea-bathing was first held to be good for health. Early in the next century the Prince Regent (▷ Regency) made Brighton his favourite resort and ordered the erection of the oriental-style Pavilion there. Since then, Brighton has remained one of the largest of a line of seaside resorts extending almost the whole length of the south coast.

Britain, British, Briton
Britain (Latin: *Britannia*) was the name given by the Romans to the island that includes modern England, Wales and Scotland, though the Roman province of Britain (AD 43–410) only reached the south of Scotland. Speaking of pre-Roman times, we call the island Ancient Britain and we call its mixed people Ancient Britons.

Political, rather than descriptive, the term was revived when King James VI of Scotland became also ▷ James I of England (including Wales) in 1603 and called himself King of Great Britain. It was officially adopted by ▷ Parliament when England and Scotland were united in 1707. In 1801 the United Kingdom of Great Britain and Ireland was formed, but most of Ireland became separate again in 1922. Terms now in use are:
British Isles: Great Britain and all Ireland, geographically.
United Kingdom: Great Britain and Northern Ireland.
Great Britain, or *Britain*: England, Scotland and Wales, geographically.
British, referring loosely to the U.K. or to Britain.
Briton: a native of the U.K., but the term is rarely used. A native calls himself an Englishman, Scotsman, Welshman or Ulsterman (N. Ireland).
Britisher: American name for a Briton.
England and *English*: These are often loosely and wrongly used for Britain and British, simply because England is the largest partner and English is the common language.
▷ Ireland; Scotland; Wales.

Britannia
The Latin name for Britain. It became a poetic name for Britain in personification. Since 1672 Britannia has been represented as a woman with helmet, shield and trident on certain coins. It is thus a symbol in which a connection between empire, militarism and the economy is established. The poem *Rule Britannia* by ▷ James Thomson (1700–48)

has been sung to music by Arne as an unofficial national anthem.

British Academy

Founded in 1901 it was intended to complement the function of the ▷ Royal Society by representing 'literary science'; which was defined as 'the sciences of language, history, philosophy and antiquities, and other subjects the study of which is based on scientific principles but which are not included under the term "natural science"'. It derived its authority from the backing of the Royal Society, the grant of a Royal Charter (1902) and the addition of bye-laws by ▷ Order in Council (1903). The British Academy elects its own Fellows, up to a total of 200: candidates have to be nominated by not fewer than three and not more than six existing Fellows. The British Academy publishes its *Proceedings* and certain lectures; research awards are annually made available for competition.

British Council

Established in 1934, it receives three-quarters of its funds, amounting to £260 million pounds in 1987–8, from the Foreign and Commonwealth Office. Its brief is to promote an enduring understanding and appreciation of Britain overseas through cultural, technical and educational exchange. The Council has staff in over 80 countries and is responsible for the implementation of more than 30 cultural agreements with other countries. It has 116 libraries world-wide and its activities include the recruitment of teachers for posts overseas, fostering personal contacts between British and overseas academics, and the placing and welfare of overseas students in Britain. It is exceptionally powerful in determining how Britain represents itself abroad in that the Council decides what is to be presented overseas as 'the best of British arts and culture'. ▷ Graham Greene, ▷ Lawrence Durrell and ▷ Olivia Manning in various novels offer a view of the early years of the Council's work.

Broadside Ballads

Popular ▷ ballads, printed on ▷ folio sheets. They formed a cheap method of publishing songs on topical subjects. The term 'broadside' meant that only one side of the paper was printed. They were a means of issuing news items, political propaganda, religious controversy, travellers' tales, attacks on (or defences of) women, the last words of condemned criminals, etc. Often decorated with wood-cut prints, they were a major source of information in the 16th and 17th centuries. The British Library possesses a unique collection of broadsides amongst the 'Thomason Tracts'.
Bib: Reay, B., *Popular Culture in Seventeenth-Century England.*

Brome, Richard (1590–1653)

The author of two popular ▷ Caroline comedies, ▷ *The City Wit* (1629) and ▷ *The Jovial Crew* (1640). His work reflects the romantic influence of ▷ John Fletcher, but is indebted particularly to ▷ Ben Jonson in whose service Brome spent some time, perhaps as Jonson's secretary.

Brontë, Anne (1820–49)

Novelist and poet. The younger sister of ▷ Charlotte and ▷ Emily Brontë. She was very close to Emily as a child and together they invented the imaginary world of Gondal, the setting for several poems and a prominent feature in their lives. She wrote under the name of Acton Bell, contributing to the volume of poems by all three sisters. Her two novels are *Agnes Grey* (1847) and *The Tenant of Wildfell Hall* (1848).
Bib: Gérin, W., *Anne Brontë.*

Brontë, Charlotte (1816–55)

Novelist; the third among five daughters of Patrick Brontë, a Yorkshire clergyman of Irish origin. All the daughters seem to have been gifted, and all died with their single brother before their father; their mother died in 1821.

In 1846 Charlotte, with ▷ Emily and ▷ Anne Brontë, published a volume of poetry under the pen-names of Currer, Ellis and Acton Bell; only Emily's verse is particularly noteworthy. Charlotte's first novel, ▷ *The Professor*, was not published until after her death; her second, ▷ *Jane Eyre* (1847), was immediately successful. Her third novel, ▷ *Shirley*, came out in 1849, ▷ *Villette*, based on her period of teaching in Brussels, in 1853. *Villette* is her most mature. The impressiveness of her writing comes from the struggle – experienced by herself, related through her heroines in *Jane Eyre* and *Villette* – to preserve her independence of spirit in circumstances which are overwhelmingly adverse. Her novels are often seen to be autobiographical ones. *Jane Eyre* continues to be successful, and *Villette* is increasingly esteemed. *The Professor* is really *Villette* in an earlier and more imperfect form; and *Shirley*, the only one not to have autobiographical form, is less admired. Like Anne and Emily, Charlotte has been the focus of attention for modern ▷ feminist critics and the confined and restless imagery of their novels is often seen as representative of the anger of suppressed and misrepresented women.

Bib: Gaskell, E., *Life*; Cecil, D., *Early Victorian Novelists*; Ratchford, F., *The Brontës' Web of Childhood*; Hanson, L. and E. M., *The Four Brontës*; Gérin, W., *Charlotte Brontë: The Evolution of Genius*; Peters, M., *Unquiet Soul: A Biography of Charlotte Brontë*.

Brontë, Emily (1818–48)

The Brontë Sisters by P. B. Brontë (c 1834)

Novelist and poet. She has been described as the finest woman poet in English literature. It is, however, for her only novel, ▷ *Wuthering Heights* (1847), that she is chiefly famous. The novel is unique in its structure and its vision; the former is so devised that the story comes through several independent narrators. Her vision is such that she brings human passions (through her characters Heathcliff and Catherine Earnshaw) against society (represented by the households of Wuthering Heights and Thrushcross Grange) with extraordinary violence, while at the same time retaining a cool artistic control. This enables the reader to experience a highly intelligent criticism of society's implicit claim to absorb all the energies of the individual, who potentially is larger in spirit than society ever can be. Initially received as morbid and too violent, it has grown in critical stature, particularly with regard to its structure.

Bib: Kavanagh, C., *The Symbolism of Wuthering Heights*; Sanger, C. P., *The Structure of Wuthering Heights*; Gérin, W., *Emily Brontë: A Biography*.

Brook, Peter (b 1925)

One of the most experimental British theatre

directors, renowned for his international outlook and rejection of parochial traditions in the British theatre. By the time he was 20 he was directing at the Birmingham Repertory Theatre and a year later he directed ▷ *Love's Labour's Lost* for the ▷ Royal Shakespeare Company at Stratford-on-Avon. His most famous ▷ Shakespeare production was ▷ *A Midsummer Night's Dream* in 1970, also at Stratford. This was praised for its imaginative interpretation and liberation of the play from traditional ideas of performance, characteristic of his directorial approach. He has been strongly influenced by the work of ▷ Artaud and ▷ Grotowski. Other major productions are: Weiss's *Marat/Sade* (1966); *Orghast* (1971); *The Ik* (1976); *The Mahabharata* (first staged at the Avignon Festival in 1985). Since 1970 he has worked with his own company in Paris at the International Centre of Theatre Research. Brook's ideas about theatre should be read first hand in his publication *The Empty Space*.

Bib: Brook, P., *The Shifting Point*; Williams, D., *Peter Brook: A Theatrical Casebook*.

Brooke, Rupert (1887–1915)

A young poet of exceptional promise, who contributed to the ▷ *Georgian Poetry* volumes, and who died of septicaemia in the Dardanelles during World War I without having taken part in the campaign. His almost legendary physical beauty and the idealistic quality of his work caused him to be represented as the hero of the first phase of the war. *The Soldier* (1915) and *The Old Vicarage, Grantchester* (1912) are much-anthologized poems. Just as it had been patriotically revered, Brooke's work dramatically declined in public opinion as the horror of the war was fully understood, although after World War II his slim and unfinished corpus gained more critical respect.

Bib: Keynes, G. (ed.), *Poems*.

Brooke-Rose, Christine (b 1926)

Novelist and critic. Born in Geneva, of an English father and a Swiss/American mother, she is bilingual, and her best-known works are influenced by the French ▷ *nouveau roman* of Alain Robbe-Grillet and Nathalie Sarraute. *Out* (1964) uses Robbe-Grillet's technique of exhaustive description of inanimate objects. In *Such* (1966) a scientist recalls his past during the three minutes taken to bring him back to consciousness after heart failure, while *Thru* (1975) is a multilingual, playful, Joycean novel, employing typographical patterns and self-referential discussion of its own narrative

technique. More recently, *Xorander* (1986) is
a work of ▷ science-fiction, exploring the
possibilities of a computer-dominated society.
Brooke-Rose lives in France, where she is a
professor at the University of Paris, and her
resolute commitment to modernist
(▷ Modernism) experimental techniques has
led to her relative neglect by English-speaking
readers.

Brookner, Anita (b 1928)

Anita Brookner

Novelist. Since her first novel, *A Start In
Life*, was published in 1981 she has rapidly
achieved popular success, confirmed by the
award of the Booker Prize to her fourth
novel, *Hôtel Du Lac* (1984). Her novels have
an autobiographical element and somewhat
similar heroines; sensitive, intelligent, but not
glamorous, their search for love and fulfilment
leads to disillusionment and betrayal by
attractive but selfish men. Brookner's prose
style is careful, elegant, lucid and mannered
in a way somewhat reminiscent of ▷ Henry
James. She lectures and writes on the
subject of art history.

Her other novels are: *Providence* (1982);
Look At Me (1983); *Family And Friends*
(1985); *A Misalliance* (1986); *A Friend From
England* (1987); *Latecomers* (1988).

Brophy, Brigid (b 1929)

Novelist and critic. The daughter of the
novelist John Brophy, she won immediate
acclaim with her first novel, *Hackenfeller's
Ape* (1953), a fable about imprisonment,

rationality and the instinctive life. During the
1960s she acquired a reputation as a polemical
and aggressive writer, with controversial
libertarian views on sex and ▷ marriage.
She campaigned for animal rights, defended
▷ pornography, and, with ▷ Maureen
Duffy, set up a writers' action group in the
1970s to campaign for Public Lending Right
(the Public Lending Right Bill, which
provides payments to authors out of a central
fund on the basis of library lending, was
passed in 1979). Her novels reflect her
adherence to ▷ Freudian ideas, and to the
evolutionism of ▷ George Bernard Shaw.
Flesh (1962) is a detached yet poetic study of
sexual awakening; *The Finishing Touch* (1963),
described as 'a lesbian fantasy', is stylistically
inspired by the work of ▷ Ronald Firbank;
The Snow Ball (1964) is an artificial, baroque
black comedy of seduction; *In Transit* (1969)
uses a bizarre combination of styles and
characters and is set in an airport. Her works
of criticism include psychological studies of
creative artists: *Mozart the Dramatist* (1964);
*In Black and White: A Portrait of Aubrey
Beardsley* (1968); *Prancing Novelist* (on
Ronald Firbank; 1973); *Beardsley and his
World* (1976). Her other works of non-fiction
include: *Black Ship to Hell* (1962), a Freudian
account of the nature of hate; *Don't Never
Forget* (1966) and *Baroque and Roll* (1987),
collections of her journalism on a wide range
of subjects. Other novels include: *The King of
a Rainy Country* (1956); *Pussy Owl: Super
Beast* (1976); *Palace Without Chairs* (1978).
*The Adventures of God in His Search for the
Black Girl* (1973) is a series of fables. *The
Burglar* (1968) is a play.

Brougham, Henry Peter, Lord (1778–1868)

Lawyer, journalist, and slave-trade
abolitionist. He defended Queen Caroline
brilliantly in the divorce proceedings brought
against her by George IV in 1820, and later
became Lord Chancellor. He was one of the
founders (1802) of the ▷ *Edinburgh Review*,
and may have been the author of the satirical
essay on ▷ Lord Byron's *Hours of Idleness*
which appeared in the *Review* in January
1808 and provoked Byron to write *English
Bards and Scotch Reviewers* (1809).

Browne, Sir Thomas (1605–82)

Physician and author. Sir Thomas Browne
studied medicine at Montpellier, Padua and
Leiden, and began practising medicine in
1633, before moving in 1637 to Norwich,
where he was to spend the rest of his life.
Browne's most influential work was ▷ *Religio
Medici* (1642, re-issued in an authorized

edition in 1643), a title which can be translated as *The Religion of a Physician*. The conjunction between religious meditation and an enduring fascination with observation of the most minute details of the physical world informs the *Religio*, which stands as both a determined act of creation of an authorial persona, and as a disquisition which attempts to reconcile scepticism and belief.

In some ways, Browne can be thought of as a ▷ Baconian in his adherence to the principles of observation, and his determination to refute ideas commonly entertained by the credulous. But his Baconianism is tempered with a vein of mysticism. The two tendencies in his thought are displayed in his later works – *Pseudodoxica Epidemica*, or *Vulgar Errors* (1646); *Hydriotaphia*, or ▷ *Urn Burial* (1658); and ▷ *The Garden of Cyrus* (1658).

Bib: Keynes, Sir G. (ed.), *Works*, 4 vols.; Bennett, J., *Sir Thomas Browne*.

Browne, William (1591–1643)

One of the ▷ 'Spenserian' poets, Browne wrote mainly ▷ pastoral verse. He contributed seven eclogues to *The Shepherd's Pipe* (1614), a work written in collaboration with ▷ George Wither. Browne also composed a ▷ masque, produced in 1614, entitled *The Inner Temple Masque* – a title which was changed to *Ulysses and Circe* when the work was staged again in 1615. In 1613 appeared the first part of Browne's *Britannia's Pastorals*, poetic accounts of familiar pastoral stories derived from Browne's reading in ▷ Edmund Spenser, ▷ Torquato Tasso and ▷ John Fletcher, and placed within an English landscape itself a reworking of Spenser's descriptions. Subsequent parts of the work were published in 1616 and (as a Percy Society edition) in 1852. In 1613, in collaboration with ▷ Fulke Greville, Browne published *Two Elegies*, works commemorating the death of Henry, Prince of Wales.

Browning, Elizabeth Barrett (1806–61)

Poet. Born Elizabeth Barrett, her reputation as a major ▷ Victorian poet was established long before she met ▷ Robert Browning, whom she married in 1846. Her early life as a confined invalid, dominated by her archetypical Victorian father Edward Barrett in Wimpole Street, from which she was rescued by her elopement with Browning, is a favourite and well-documented Victorian legend. Barrett was a formidably intelligent child, who published her first work (anonymously) when she was only 14; *The Battle of Marathon* (1820) was followed by

Elizabeth Barrett Browning by M. Gordigiani (1858)

Essay on Mind, With Other Poems (1826) and *Prometheus Bound: and Miscellaneous Poems* (1833) containing her translation of ▷ Aeschylus. Her reputation was made with *The Seraphim and Other Poems* (1838), and *Poems* (1844), which included *The Cry of the Children*, a famous plea to the social consciences of the Victorian middle classes. Her great friend and distant cousin, John Kenyon (upon whom Romney in ▷ *Aurora Leigh* is based) introduced Barrett to Browning in 1845. After their marriage, which was bitterly opposed by the Barrett patriarch, the Brownings set up home in Florence, and, at the age of 43, Elizabeth gave birth to a son, known as Pen. In 1850 *The Athenaeum*, for whom Barrett Browning was a regular contributor, strongly recommended that she succeed ▷ Wordsworth as ▷ Poet Laureate; the title went to ▷ Tennyson, but the very fact that a woman was considered, in the middle of the 19th century, is indicative of Barrett Browning's high artistic profile at this time. The sequence of 44 sonnets which were still read throughout the period of critical neglect of Barrett Browning (which lasted until relatively recent ▷ feminist re-readings) were published in 1850 as *Sonnets from the Portuguese* in the volume *Poems*. These include the famous and much-anthologized 'How do I love thee? Let me count the ways'. Barrett Browning was a passionate champion of Italian independence, evidenced in her work by *Casa Guidi Windows* (1851) and *Poems Before Congress* (1860). Her

most important work, and enormously popular verse-novel, part autobiography, part discussion of the role of poetry, and a crucial document in the 19th-century 'Woman Question' debate, was ▷ *Aurora Leigh* (1857). Barrett Browning's *Last Poems* were published in 1862. The best edition of her work is *The Complete Works of Elizabeth Barrett Browning* (eds. Charlotte Porter and Helen A. Clarke, New York 1973).
Bib: Moers, E. *Literary Women*; Hayter, A. *Mrs Browning: A Poet's Work and its Setting*.

Browning, Robert (1812–89)
Poet. The son of a clerk in the Bank of England, he married the poet Elizabeth Barrett (▷ Browning, Elizabeth Barrett) in 1846 under dramatic circumstances, and lived with her until her death in 1861 in Italy. He spent the rest of his life in London.

From the first his poetry was exuberant, and he began as an ardent follower of ▷ Shelley: *Pauline* (1833); ▷ *Paracelsus* (1835); *Strafford* (a verse tragedy, 1837); *Sordello* (1840). Between 1841 and 1846 he published seven more plays, the dramatic poem *Pippa Passes*, the collection *Dramatic Lyrics* (including ▷ *The Pied Piper*), and *Dramatic Romances* – all published together under the title *Bells and Pomegranates*. During his married life he produced *Christmas-Eve and Easter-Day* (1850) and, his best-known work, ▷ *Men and Women* (1855). Nonetheless, public recognition only came with ▷ *Dramatis Personae* (1864) and *The Ring and the Book* (1868–9). The latter was his most ambitious work and consists of 10 verse narratives, all dealing with the same crime, each from a distinct viewpoint. It was based on an actual trial, the record of which he discovered in Florence. The period 1850–70 was his best; the later work has endured less well: *Prince Hohenstiel-Schwangau* (1871); *Fifine at the Fair* (1872); *The Inn Album* (1875); *Pacchiarotto* (1876); *La Saisia* (1878); *Dramatic Idylls* (1879–80); *Ferishtah's Fancies* (1884); *Asolando* (1889).

Browning was keenly aware that he was writing poetry in an age of science, of technology and of prose, particularly of prose fiction. He made poetry compete with prose in these conditions, and the curiosity and delight in detail that were part of his temperament fitted him to do so. Where other poets notably ▷ Tennyson, wrote in a style that moved away from and above the preoccupations of daily living, Browning delighted in the idiom of ordinary speech and in the peculiarities of minds and objects. He was not the only practitioner of the

▷ dramatic monologue, but he is especially associated with it; he chose characters out of history or invented them in special predicaments, and made them think aloud so as to display their distinctive mentalities. He was not afraid of obscurity, and both his earlier and his later poems suffer from it (*Sordello* and *Fifine*), although *Sordello* is now increasingly recognized as one of his most extraordinary and important works, influencing, for example, ▷ Ezra Pound in his conception of the ▷ *Cantos*. The influence of his monologues on Pound's and ▷ T. S. Eliot's early poetry should also be noted.
Bib: Griffin, H. W. and Minchin, H. C., *Life;* Miller, B., *Life*; Cohen, J. M., *Robert Browning*; Devane, W. C., *A Browning Handbook*; Duckworth, F. G. R., *Browning: Background and Conflict*; Duffin, H. C., *Amphibian: a Reconsideration of Browning*; Herford, C. H., *Robert Browning*; James, H., in *Notes on Novelists*; Johnson, E. D. H., *The Alien Vision in Victorian Poetry*; Raymond, W. O., *The Infinite Moment*; Litzinger, B. and Smalley, D., (eds.), *Browning: the Critical Heritage*; Langbaum, R., *The Poetry of Experience*.

Brownists
A ▷ Puritan religious sect founded by Robert Browne (1550?–1633?); from about 1640 they were known as Independents, and since the 18th century they have been ▷ Congregationalists. Their best-known doctrine is that on the evidence of the New Testament each religious congregation should be self-governing, so that there should be no over-riding Church, *eg* no government through bishops under a central figure such as the Pope or, in the Anglican system, the Crown.
▷ Congregationalism.

Bruce, Robert the
King of the Scots (1306–29) and hero of the Scottish War of Independence (1296–1328), during which he successfully resisted the efforts of ▷ Edward I and ▷ Edward II to conquer the country. Bruce's decisive victory was the ▷ Battle of Bannockburn (1314).
In about 1375 a Scottish poet ▷ John Barbour wrote an epic poem describing the war, called *The Bruce*.
▷ Scottish literature in English.

Buchanan, George (1506–82)
Scottish poet, classicist, educationalist. George Buchanan's life was a curious mixture of high scholarly endeavour and political intrigue. In this, he can be thought of as

representing that ability, described by
▷ Thomas Browne, to live in 'divided and
distinguished worlds'. As an educationalist
and classicist he was tutor to ▷ Mary Queen
of Scots, and ▷ James VI (later James I of
England). His most illustrious pupil, however,
was the French essayist ▷ Montaigne,
whom Buchanan taught after fleeing to
Bordeaux to escape punishment for writing
▷ satires against the Franciscans. On
returning to Scotland he helped prosecute his
former pupil Mary Queen of Scots for high
treason, and later, under James VI, he held
high office in the Scottish government. The
great majority of his works were written in
Latin, and included love poems,
▷ tragedies, legal works and a history of
▷ Scotland.

Buckingham Palace
The principal residence of the British royal
family in London. The original house
belonged to the Dukes of Buckingham, from
whom it was bought by George III in 1762. It
was rebuilt by the architect John Nash in
1825, who designed Marble Arch as a gateway
to it, but the Arch was removed to its present
position near the entrance to ▷ Hyde Park
in 1851. It was ▷ Queen Victoria (1837–
1901) who first made the palace her principal
residence.

Bunting, Basil (1900–85)
Poet. Bunting's association with the poetry
world began in the 1920s, but he did not
achieve real recognition until the 1960s – the
story of his rediscovery after years of
obscurity is one of the legends of
contemporary poetry. Bunting had been
associated with ▷ Ezra Pound and other
▷ modernists in the 1930s, even to the
extent that ▷ W. B. Yeats called him one of
Pound's 'savage disciples'. *Redimiculum
Matellarum* was published in Milan in 1930,
followed by *Attis* (1931), *The Well of Lycopolis*
(1935), and, later, *Poems* in 1950, but the text
which gave Bunting enormous recognition
after many years of neglect in Britain was
Briggflatts (1966). Undoubtedly Bunting's
most important and challenging work,
Briggflats is a long, intense, mystical synthesis
of Northumbrian legend, ▷ autobiography
and mythology. Other works include:
Collected Poems (1968).

Bunyan, John (1628–88)
Born at Elstow, near Bedford, Bunyan was
the son of a tinsmith, educated at the village
school. Of Baptist sympathies, he fought in
the ▷ Civil War, although little is known of
his military activities. With the persecution of
the ▷ Puritans which followed the
▷ Restoration of Charles II, Bunyan's Non-
Conformist beliefs came under severe censure,
and in 1660 he was arrested for preaching
without a licence.

John Bunyan

For most of the next twelve years Bunyan
was imprisoned in Bedford jail, where he
began to write. His spiritual autobiography,
▷ *Grace Abounding to the Chief of Sinners*,
appeared in 1666, and the first part of his
major work, ▷ *The Pilgrim's Progress*, was
published in 1678. *The Pilgrim's Progress* was
largely written during this period of
imprisonment, though it is probable that
Bunyan completed Part I during a second
spell in jail in 1676; the full text, with the
addition of Part II, was published in 1684. A
spiritual allegory strongly in the ▷ Puritan
tradition, it tells of the pilgrimage of Christian
to reach the state of grace. Bunyan's other
major works, ▷ *The Life and Death of Mr
Badman* (1680) and ▷ *The Holy War*
(1682) are also spiritual allegories.

Burbage, James (d 1597)
Actor and theatre manager. In 1576 he built
the first English ▷ theatre, called simply The
Theatre, in ▷ London's Shoreditch. In 1596
he opened the Blackfriars Theatre, where the
Children of the Chapel performed. He was
the first manager of the ▷ Lord
Chamberlain's Men, to which
▷ Shakespeare belonged as actor and
playwright.

Burbage, Richard (?1567–1619)

Son of ▷ James Burbage. On his father's death, he dismantled The Theatre and rebuilt it as the ▷ Globe on the south bank of the ▷ Thames. As actor-manager of the ▷ Lord Chamberlain's Men he took the leading part in plays by ▷ Shakespeare, ▷ Jonson, ▷ Fletcher and others, using the Globe and (after 1608) the ▷ Blackfriars Theatre. He and ▷ Edward Alleyn were the best actors of the time.

Burgess, Anthony (b 1917)

Novelist and critic. Born John Anthony Burgess Wilson of a Roman Catholic Lancashire family, he was educated at Manchester University. After military service during World War II he worked as a schoolmaster in Oxfordshire, Malaya and Borneo. His experiences in Malaya inspired his *Malayan Trilogy* (1956–9), a rich portrait of the Malayan culture and people, employing words and expressions from Malay, Urdu, Arabic, Tamil and Chinese. A fascination with the textures of language and a ▷ Joycean inventiveness and multilingual playfulness have characterized much of Burgess's work. In 1959 Burgess returned to England with a brain tumour, expecting to survive only a year, yet in that year wrote five novels: *The Doctor is Sick* (1960), *One Hand Clapping* (1961), *The Worm and the Ring* (1961), *The Wanting Seed* (1962) and *Inside Mr Enderby* (1963). During the 1960s he worked as a music and drama critic, and produced plays, T.V. scripts, short stories and numerous book reviews. He has since done a considerable amount of university teaching, and lived in Malta, Rome and Monaco. *A Clockwork Orange* (1962), filmed in 1971 by Stanley Kubrick, is an anti-utopian vision with an appallingly vicious protagonist who deliberately chooses evil, and who is brainwashed by penal techniques based on behaviourist psychology. Its most striking feature is the use of Nadsat, an invented teenage underworld slang largely based on Russian words and English colloquialisms. *Nothing Like The Sun* (1964) is a fictional account of ▷ Shakespeare's love life, told as the parting lecture of a schoolmaster in the Far East, who progressively identifies himself with his subject. An impression of Elizabethan life is conveyed through descriptive detail and imitation of contemporary idiom. *Earthly Powers* (1980) is a large-scale consideration of the nature of evil, with extensive reference to 20th-century literary and political history. Other novels include *1985* (1978) and *The Piano Players*

(1986). Non-fiction includes: *The Novel Today* (1963); *Language Made Plain* (1964); *Ernest Hemingway and his World* (1978); *Flame into Being: the Life and Work of D. H. Lawrence* (1985).

Bib: Aggeler, G., *Anthony Burgess, the Artist as Novelist*.

Burgundy, Duchy of

A province in the south-east of France, with which it was united in 1477. In the phase of the ▷ Hundred Years' War associated with ▷ Henry v of England (1413–22) Burgundy was for the time an important ally of England against France.

The early ▷ Renaissance Burgundian court had a considerable artistic and cultural influence upon the portraiture and court entertainments in England during the reign of ▷ Henry VII.

▷ Masque.

Burke, Edmund (1729–97)

Statesman and political philosopher; described by ▷ Matthew Arnold as 'our greatest English prose-writer'. Born in Dublin, he pursued his political career in England, and was a Member of Parliament for much of his life. Although never attaining high office, his political status was considerable, due mainly to his formidable powers of oratory and polemical argument. His early work *A Philosophical Inquiry into the Origin of our Ideas of the Sublime and the Beautiful* (1756) marks a transition in aesthetic theory from the neo-classicism of ▷ John Dryden and ▷ Alexander Pope. Influenced by ▷ Longinus and ▷ Milton, it emphasizes the sense of awe inspired by both art and nature. His most celebrated work, ▷ *Reflections on the Revolution in France* (1790), argues for the organic, evolutionary development of society, as opposed to the brutal surgery and doctrinaire theories of the French revolutionaries.

Burke's character reveals a number of paradoxes. His writings combine the cautious, pragmatic instincts of a conservative politician with a passionate rhetorical style. He regarded all forms of political innovation with suspicion, yet defended the cause of the American rebels in *On Conciliation with the Colonies* (1775). He attacked the corrupt practice of court patronage and the exploitative activities of the East India Company, yet retained for himself many benefits of the systems he deplored.

Bib: Cone, C. B., *Burke and the Nature of Politics* (2 vols); Stanlis, P. J. (ed.), *Edmund Burke: The Enlightenment and the Modern*

World; Wilkins, B. T., *The Problem of Burke's Political Philosophy*.

Burlesque

A form of satirical comedy (not necessarily dramatic) which arouses laughter through mockery of a form usually dedicated to high seriousness. The word is from the Italian *burla* = 'ridicule'. Burlesque is similar to ▷ parody, but parody depends on subtler and closer imitation of a particular work.
    ▷ Satire.

Burney, Dr. Charles (1726–1814)

Father of novelist ▷ Fanny Burney, Charles Burney was the friend of ▷ Samuel Johnson, ▷ David Garrick and ▷ Sir Joshua Reynolds. An organist and musical historian, he also wrote travelogues of France, Italy, Germany and the Low Countries of the journeys he made to collect material for his *History of Music* (published 1776–89).

Burney, Fanny (Frances, Madame D'Arblay) (1752–1840)

Daughter of ▷ Dr. Charles Burney, Fanny grew up in the distinguished company of ▷ Johnson, ▷ Sir Joshua Reynolds, Garrick and the ▷ Bluestockings. In 1786 she was appointed as an attendant upon Queen Charlotte, wife of George III, and in 1793 she married a French exile, General D'Arblay. From 1802–12, interned by Napoleon, she and her husband lived in France.
    Burney's major novels are ▷ *Evelina* (1778), *Cecilia* (1782) and *Camilla* (1796). Their common theme is the entry into society of a young girl, beautiful and intelligent but lacking experience of the world; during subsequent adventures the girl's character is moulded. Burney was a great admirer of ▷ Richardson, and his influence is apparent in her use, in her first novel, of the epistolary (*ie* letter-writing) form.
    Burney was also well known for her diaries and letters. Her *Early Diary* (1889) covers the years 1768–78, and contains many sketches of Johnson and Garrick; her *Diary and Letters . . . 1778–1840* (published 1842–6) is a lively account of life at court. Amongst her admirers, ▷ Jane Austen shows Burney's influence.
Bib: Simons, J., *Fanny Burney*.

Burns, Robert (1759–96)

Scottish poet. He was born in poverty, the son of a peasant or 'cottar', but nevertheless became well-read in the Bible, ▷ Shakespeare, 18th-century English poetry, and also learnt some French. His best work, in the Lowland Scots dialect, was precipitated by his reading of ▷ Robert Fergusson, and was written between 1785 and 1790, during most of which time he was working as a farmer, an occupation which undermined his health. He intended to emigrate to Jamaica with Mary Campbell, but she died in childbirth in 1787. In the same year his *Poems Chiefly in the Scots Dialect* were published in Kilmarnock, and made him famous. He moved to Edinburgh where a new edition of the volume appeared in the following year, and where he was lionized as a 'natural' genius. He was a hard drinker and womanizer, and two years after Mary Campbell's death he took as his wife Jean Armour, who had already borne children by him. He leased a farm and secured preferment in the excise service in Dumfries, despite his earlier sympathies for the French and American Revolutions. He devoted himself to reworking Scottish songs, which appeared in James Johnson's *The Scots Musical Museum* (1793–1803) and George Thomson's *Select Scottish Airs with Poetry*. But he became further impoverished, and succumbed to persistent ill health.
    Perhaps Burns's best-known poems are sentimental lyrics, such as ▷ *Auld Lang Syne* or love songs like *Ae fond Kiss, Highland Mary*, and 'O my love's like a red, red rose'. His *Cotter's Saturday Night* celebrates Scottish peasant life in Spenserian stanzas, and other poems express a keen sympathy with the downtrodden and oppressed. But it is his comic satires which are now considered his best work: *To a Mouse*; *The Twa Dogs*; ▷ *Tam O'Shanter*; *The Jolly Beggars*. It is significant that those poems which attack Calvinism and the hypocrisy of kirk elders, such as *The Twa Herds* and *Holy Willie's Prayer*, were omitted from the Kilmarnock *Poems* of 1786. Even during his lifetime Burns was beginning to be viewed as a kind of Scottish ▷ Poet Laureate, with all the distortions which this inevitably involved. Over the past two centuries, this status, together with the patriotism of Burns Night, have served to promote a glamorized myth, at the expense of a true appreciation of Burns's poetry.
    ▷ Scottish literature in English.
Bib: Daiches, D., *Robert Burns*; Jack, R. D. S., and Noble, A. (eds.), *The Art of Robert Burns*; Spiers, J., *The Scots Literary Tradition*.

Burton, Sir Richard Francis (1821–90)

Explorer and travel writer. *Scinde, or the Unhappy Valley* (1851); *First Footsteps in East Africa* (1856); *The Lake Region of Central*

Africa (1860); *The Pilgrimage to Al-Medinah and Meccah* (1855). He also translated the ▷ 'Arabian Nights' (*The Thousand Nights and a Night* – 1885–8) and *The Lusiads of Camoens* (1880). For the last 14 years of his life he worked on a translation of *The Perfumed Garden*, which his widow burned after his death.

Bib: Lady Burton, *Life*; Schonfield, A. L., *Richard Burton Explorer*; Wilson, A. T., *Richard Burton*.

Burton, Robert (1577–1640)

Oxford scholar and author. Burton was born in Leicestershire, and entered Brasenose College, Oxford, in 1593, where he was to remain. Besides the anti-Catholic Latin comedy *Philosophaster* (acted in 1618), Burton's one major project was the publication of his ▷ *Anatomy of Melancholy*, a project which occupied him for the majority of his life. He wrote under the pseudonym of 'Democritus Junior', thus emulating the Greek philosopher of the 5th century B C: Democritus.

Bib: Babb, L., *Sanity in Bedlam*; Kiessling, N. K., *The Library of Robert Burton*.

Busie Body, The (1709)

Play by ▷ Susannah Centlivre. Sir George Airy, a wealthy young man, is in love with Miranda, but her old guardian Sir Francis Gripe, intends her for himself. Sir Francis' son, also George's friend, Charles, is in love with Isabinda, whose father Sir Jealous Traffick wants her to marry a Spaniard. Charles's suit is additionally hindered by his impoverishment: his father has tricked him out of his inheritance, while Miranda is being denied her inheritance by Gripe. Another of Gripe's wards, Marplot, does his best to help the lovers, but invariably adds complications because of his bungling naiveté. The action proceeds by means of a series of scenes of deception and intrigue, often frustrated by Marplot. Eventually, Charles disguises himself as the Spanish suitor and marries Isabinda under her father's nose; his fortune is restored by means of writings stolen from Sir Francis by Miranda, while Miranda herself is also united with her lover. The appeal of the well-meaning but witless Marplot helped to make the play so popular that in 1710 it was played simultaneously at both ▷ Covent Garden and ▷ Drury Lane, and it survived well into the 19th century. A sequel, *Marplot in Lisbon, or, The Second Part of the Busie Body* (1710), achieved less success.

Buskin

A long thick-soled boot worn by ancient Athenian actors in Greek tragedy; hence associated with acting or writing in the spirit of tragic drama. Its purpose was to increase the stature of the actor, in keeping with the grandeur of his tragic role. However, it is also a term commonly used in ▷ Renaissance literature, especially romance, to denote archaic dress.

▷ Tragedy.

Bussy d'Ambois, The Tragedy of (1604)

The best-known tragedy by ▷ George Chapman which dramatizes the rise and fall of Bussy d' Ambois at the court of Henri III of France. The play's complex rhetoric reflects the philosophic, particularly neo-Platonic bent of the author's mind and sometimes inhibits its imaginative flow.

Butler, Samuel (1612–80)

Poet. The son of a Worcestershire farmer, he became the friend of ▷ Thomas Hobbes and ▷ Sir William D'Avenant. His ▷ mock-heroic satire on Puritanism, ▷ *Hudibras*, employs deliberately rough and ready tetrameter couplets which were frequently imitated by later poets and became known as 'hudibrasticks'. Butler's other works were neglected, and most of them, including the ▷ Theophrastan *Characters*, and the satire on the ▷ Royal Society, *The Elephant in the Moon* (it is actually a mouse trapped in the telescope), were not published until 1759, when his *Genuine Remains* appeared.

Bib: Johnson, S., in *Lives of the Poets*; Jack, I., *Augustan Satire*.

Butler, Samuel (1835–1902)

Satirist, scientific writer, author of an autobiographical novel, *The Way of All Flesh* (1903) in a form which became a model for a number of 20th-century writers. His satires *Erewhon* (*Nowhere* reversed) and *Erewhon Revisited* (1872 and 1901) are anti-utopias, *ie* instead of exhibiting an imaginary country with ideal customs and institutions in the manner of Sir Thomas More's ▷ *Utopia* (1516), Butler describes a country where the faults of his own country are caricatured, in the tradition of Jonathan Swift's Lilliput (▷ *Gulliver's Travels*). He attacks ecclesiastical and family institutions; in Erewhon, machines have to be abolished because their evolution threatens the human race – a blow at Darwinism.

His scientific work concerned ▷ Charles Darwin's theory of evolution, to which he was opposed because he considered that it left no room for mind in the universe; he favoured the theory of Lamarck (1744–1829) with its doctrine of the inheritability of acquired characteristics. His disagreements and his own theories are expounded in *Life and Habit* (1877), *Evolution Old and New* (1879), *Unconscious Memory* (1880) and *Luck or Cunning?* (1886).

The Way of All Flesh attacks the parental tyranny which Butler saw as the constant feature of Victorian family life (despite much evidence to the contrary); so close did he keep to his own experience that he could not bring himself to publish the book in his own lifetime.

▷ George Bernard Shaw admitted a great debt to Butler's evolutionary theories and to Butler's stand against mental muddle, self-deception and false compromise in society. Writers as different from Butler and from each other as ▷ D. H. Lawrence and ▷ James Joyce wrote autobiographical novels after him in which the facts were often as close to their own experience. **Bib:** Cole, G. D. H., *Butler and The Way of All Flesh*; Henderson, P., *The Incarnate Bachelor*; Furbank, P. N., *Samuel Butler*; Jeffers, T. L., *Samuel Butler Revalued*; Joad, C. E. M., *Samuel Butler*; Muggeridge, M., *Earnest Atheist*; Pritchett, V. S., 'A Victorian Son' in *The Living Novel*.

Button's Coffee-house

Button's was set up in 1712 as a rival to ▷ Will's Coffee-house. It was named after its proprietor Daniel Button, a retired servant of ▷ Joseph Addison, who helped him with the venture.

Byatt, A. S. (Antonia Susan) (b 1936)

Novelist, critic and reviewer. Born in Sheffield and educated at the universities of Cambridge and Oxford, she has worked as a teacher and lecturer in English. The novelist ▷ Margaret Drabble is her sister. Her novels are influenced by the work of ▷ Proust and of ▷ Iris Murdoch (Byatt has published two books on Murdoch), and combine a realistic portrayal of English manners with symbolic structures and a wide range of reference to history, myth and art. *The Shadow of a Sun* (1964) is a feminist ▷ *Bildungsroman* about a girl seeking to escape from a dominating novelist father, while *The Game* (1967), a story of the tragic rivalry between two sisters, has overtones of the Fall of Man. *The Virgin in the Garden* (1979) and *Still Life* (1985) are the first two volumes of a projected tetralogy, intended to trace the lives of a group of characters from the accession of Queen Elizabeth II in 1952 up to the 1980 Post-

Impressionist Exhibition in London. Byatt's later style includes quotation, allusion, narrative prolepses (anticipations of later events) and metafictional reflections on novel writing. Story collection: *Sugar* (1987). *Possession* (1990), winner Booker Prize (1991).

Byrom, John (1692–1763)

Poet. Inventor of a system of shorthand, Fellow of the Royal Society and student of religious mysticism. His posthumous *Miscellaneous Poems* (1773) is notable for its colloquial ease and moderate eloquence of tone.

Byron, George Gordon, Lord (1788–1824)

Lord Byron by R. Westall (1813)

Poet. His childhood was dominated by a sternly ▷ Calvinist mother, a nurse who sexually abused and beat him, and painful medical treatment for his club foot. His incestuous relationship with his half-sister, Augusta Leigh, developed into a close friendship. In compensation for his deformity he prided himself on his physical prowess, particularly in swimming. While at Harrow and Cambridge he gained a reputation for atheism, radicalism and loose-living, keeping a bear as a pet for a time. At the age of 19 he published a collection of unremarkable lyrics, *Hours of Idleness* (1807). *English Bards and Scotch Reviewers*, a vigorous but immature heroic couplet poem in imitation of Pope, followed in 1809.

He travelled across Europe to Greece in 1810, involving himself in self-consciously romantic adventures. He swam across the Hellespont like Leander in the Greek legend, and dressed in Albanian costume. He wrote in a letter, 'I smoke, and stare at mountains, and twirl my mustachios very independently.' After his return in 1811 he published Cantos I and II of *Childe Harold's Pilgrimage* (1812), a moody, self-dramatizing poem in ▷ Spenserian stanzas. It was an immediate success and he followed it with several hastily-written verse tales: *The Bride of Abydos* (1813) and *The Giaour* (1813), mainly in tetrameter couplets, *The Corsair* (1814) and *Lara* (1814), in loose heroic couplets. Each focusses on the characteristic Byronic hero: glamorous, haunted by the guilt of mysterious crimes, which he seeks to forget in violent and dangerous adventure. Lionized in society and pursued by various women, Byron ended by marrying the naive and inexperienced Anne Isabella (Annabella) Milbanke. Her intention to reform him failed, and the marriage broke up shortly after she had given birth to a daughter.

Byron left England for the last time in 1816, and met up with ▷ Percy Bysshe Shelley and Mary Wollstonecraft Godwin in Switzerland. Claire Clairmont, Mary's half-sister gave birth to a daughter by Byron, but she died in infancy. About this time he wrote *Childe Harold* Canto III (1816) which he called 'a fine indistinct piece of poetical desolation', also ▷ *The Prisoner of Chillon* (1816), and the gloom-laden drama, ▷ *Manfred* (1817). He travelled to Italy where, after a period of sexual promiscuity with all kinds of women, he eventually fell in love with Teresa Guiccioli, the 19-year-old wife of an elderly Italian nobleman. His uncomfortable role of *cavaliere servente*, or tolerated lover, is indirectly reflected in *Beppo* (1818), his first poem in *ottava rima*, a form which he made peculiarly its own, employing its rattling rhymes and concluding couplet to superb effect. It is also used in ▷ *Don Juan* (1819–24) and *The Vision of Judgement* (1822). He became restless, and after Shelley had drowned in 1822, he decided to throw himself into the cause of Greek independence.

As he had remarked in a letter of 1820:

When a man hath no freedom to fight for at home,
   Let him combat for that of his neighbours;
Let him think of the glories of Greece and of Rome,
   And get knock'ed on the head for his labours.

In Greece he suffered further frustrations, including a disappointed passion for a Greek youth, Loukas. He began to feel his age, and expressed this poignantly in the lyric 'On this Day I Complete my Thirty-Sixth Year'. He contracted malaria, was bled several times by his doctors, and died at Missolonghi in 1824.

Byron's popular romantic reputation, based on the first cantos of *Childe Harold*, *Manfred* and the verse tales, is important in literary historical terms. On the Continent Byron has been regarded as a significant philosopher of ▷ Romanticism. However, Byron himself was dismissive of his 'Byronic' exercises in 'poetical desolation' He preferred the brilliant wit of Pope to what he called the 'wrong poetical system' of his Romantic contemporaries. The real value of his poetry lies in his evocation of past civilizations in the fourth canto of *Childe Harold*, and in his brilliantly casual poems in *ottava rima*. Byron's letters are often more vivid than his verse. His ▷ autobiographical journal was destroyed after his death, and many of his letters were expurgated before being published by his friend ▷ Thomas Moore in 1830. However the correspondence with his publisher ▷ John Murray has survived intact, and shows the same vitality as the later poetry, but expressed in less inhibited language.
Bib: Marchand, L. A., *Byron: A Portrait*; Quennell, P., *Byron*; Leavis, F. R., 'Byron's Satire' in *Revaluation*; Knight, G. W., *Poets of Action*; Read, H., *Byron*; Rutherford, A., *Byron: A Critical Study*; Rutherford, A. (ed.), *Byron: The Critical Heritage*; Calder, A., *Byron*; Kelsall, M., *Byron's Politics*.

C

Cade, Jack (d 1450)
A leader of a popular rebellion in the counties immediately south of London in 1450, during a time of misrule under the weak king ▷ Henry VI (1422–61). The rebellion had temporary success, but later grew disorganized, and Cade was killed.

Caedmon (fl 650–70)
The first English poet to be known by name. According to ▷ Bede, who provides an account of Caedmon's life in his *Historia Ecclesiastica Gentis Anglorum (History of the English Church and its People)*, Caedmon was a Yorkshire cowherd who had a mystical experience late in life and became an inspired vernacular poet. He joined the monastic community at Whitby, during the incumbency of Abbess Hild (657–80), and produced many English versifications of scriptural works. Various ▷ Old English religious poems have been linked spuriously with Caedmon's name but the only extant text which can be attributed to Caedmon is the 'Hymn of Creation', quoted by Bede, and found in English versions in two manuscripts of Bede's text.

Caesar
The name of an aristocratic ('patrician') family in ancient Rome; the family claimed descent from the legendary ▷ Aeneas, supposed founder of Rome. The name was made famous by the general and statesman Gaius ▷ Julius Caesar, whose adopted son, Octavianus, also called himself Caesar. Octavianus became ▷ Augustus Caesar, the first Roman Emperor, and thereafter Caesar became the adopted name of all the Roman Emperors, until the fall of Constantinople in 1453. The German Holy Roman Emperors, claiming to be the heirs of the Roman Emperors of the West, adopted the title Caesar as 'Kaiser'; similarly the Russian Emperors, claiming to be heirs of the Roman Empire of the East, adopted it as 'Czar'. Thus from the first century the family name of Caesar virtually became a title, 'Emperor'. As Julius Caesar became dictator of Rome, 'Caesarism' has come to mean belief in autocracy.

Caesar, Augustus (Gaius Julius Caesar Octavianus) (63 BC–AD 14)
Great-nephew of Julius Caesar, and his adopted son. He adopted the surname Caesar and was awarded the title of Augustus by the Roman Senate. He overcame the political enemies and assassins of his uncle, Julius, and after defeating his other rivals (notably Mark Antony), he achieved complete power and became first Emperor of Rome.
▷ Horace, ▷ Virgil, ▷ Ovid, Propertius, Tibullus and ▷ Livy were his contemporaries; in consequence, 'an ▷ Augustan age' has become a term to describe a high peak of literary achievement in any culture, whenever such achievement shows similar qualities of elegance, restraint and eloquence. In these qualities, France in the 17th century and England in the 18th century consciously emulated the Augustan age of Rome.

Octavius Caesar, in ▷ Shakespeare's ▷ *Antony and Cleopatra*, is a portrait (based on ▷ Plutarch) of Augustus during his struggle with Antony.
▷ French literature in England.

Caesar, Gaius Julius (?102–44 BC)
Roman general, statesman and writer. He conquered Gaul (*ie* modern France) and in 55 and 54 BC undertook two expeditions to Britain. He described these wars in *De Bello Gallico*, a work long and widely used in English education for instruction in Latin. His victories led to civil war against his chief political rival, Gneius Pompeius, generally known in English as ▷ Pompey, whom he defeated. He then became dictator in Rome, but he was assassinated by other patricians, led by Marcus Brutus, for overthrowing Roman republican institutions. For the Middle Ages, Julius Caesar represented all that was great in Rome. His life was described by the Greek biographer ▷ Plutarch and this with Plutarch's other biographies was translated into English by ▷ Sir Thomas North. ▷ Shakespeare used it as the basis of his play ▷ *Julius Caesar*.

Caesar and Cleopatra (1901)
A play by ▷ George Bernard Shaw, concerning the relationship of ▷ Julius Caesar and the young ▷ Cleopatra, Queen of Egypt. It is an example of Shaw's demonstration of the life force manifesting itself in the great man.

Cain
In the ▷ Bible (*Genesis* 4:1) the eldest child of ▷ Adam and Eve. Cain's sacrifice to God of the fruits of the earth was rejected, while the beast-offerings by his shepherd brother Abel were accepted. In a rage Cain killed Abel, so becoming the first murderer. By tradition, Cain and Judas Iscariot, the betrayer of Christ, both had red hair; hence *Cain-coloured*, to describe such hair or beard, in Elizabethan plays.

In *Cain: A Mystery* (1821), a verse drama by ▷ Lord Byron, the episode was dramatized with Cain in the role of tragic hero, questioning the justice of the Almighty.

Calais
A port on the north coast of France captured by the English under ▷ Edward III in 1347. It was the last of the extensive conquests by the English kings to be regained by the French, in 1558. In the intervening two centuries, Calais was of great commercial importance as the 'wool staple town', *ie* the channel through which wool exports passed into Europe.

Caledonia
Roman name for what is now known as ▷ Scotland; used poetically for that country, as ▷ Albion is for Britain or ▷ Hibernia for Ireland.

Caliban
A character in ▷ Shakespeare's play ▷ *The Tempest*. The word is almost an anagram for 'cannibal', and Caliban represents in part man at his most primitive as reported by travellers of the day. He is also an unnatural monster, child of the witch Sycorax, and as much animal as human. Shakespeare also seems to have intended him to symbolize the mere body, unredeemed by any spark of spirit. Unlike his counterpart, ▷ Ariel, who is composed purely of the element of air, Caliban is mere earth. Both of them are slaves of the magician Prospero, who dominates the play.

Caligula, Gaius Caesar (reigned AD 37–41)
Roman Emperor, famous for his cruelties. He squandered in a single year the huge fortune left by his predecessor and had his favourite horse made a member of the college of priests and consuls. After he declared himself a god he was assassinated.

Callisto
In Greek myth, a ▷ nymph, and companion of the hunting goddess ▷ Artemis. ▷ Zeus loved her, and his jealous queen, ▷ Hera, transformed her into a bear, in which shape she was killed by Artemis.

Calvin, John (1509–1604)
French religious reformer and author of the *Institutes of the Christian Religion* (1535). He settled in ▷ Geneva, which was to become, under Calvin's influence, an important centre of one of the most disciplined and militant branches of ▷ Protestantism.

Calvin's teachings were widely influential in England, Scotland, France and Switzerland in the 17th century and later. Out of the *Institutes* and his book on ▷ predestination (published in 1552) emerged the five chief

points of 'Calvinism', namely its belief in: (1) 'predestination', which holds that God determined in advance who shall be 'elected' to 'eternal life' and who shall be condemned to everlasting damnation; (2) 'particular redemption', or the choosing of a certain predetermined number of souls redeemed by Christ's death; (3) 'original sin', which holds that the infant enters the world in a state of sinfulness, carrying with it the burden of Adam's fall; (4) 'irresistible grace', which argues that those chosen to be of the 'elect' have no means of resisting that choice; and (5) the final perseverance or triumph of the 'elect'.

Taken with Calvin's views on Church government and the relation between state and ecclesiastical power, 'Calvinism' was to be of enormous influence on the ▷ Church of England in the 16th and 17th centuries. From the early 17th century onwards his doctrines became those of the established church. Calvin's *Institutes* became a recognized textbook in the universities, and it was not until the rise of ▷ Arminianism under ▷ Archbishop William Laud in the pre-Civil War (▷ Civil Wars) years that an effective opposition to Calvin's influence was mounted.
Bib: Knappen, M. M., *Tudor Puritanism*; Dickens, A. G., *The English Reformation*.

Calypso
▷ *Odyssey*.

Cambridge Platonists
▷ Platonists.

Cambridge University
One of the two oldest English universities. Its origins are obscure, but it was in existence early in the 13th century, and was probably founded by students emigrating from Oxford. Like Oxford, it is famous for the organization of its students and scholars into colleges, these being independent self-governing bodies whose governing members usually, though not necessarily, hold office in the university as well. It achieved importance equal to Oxford only in the 15th century. From then onwards the two universities have liked to think of themselves as rival leaders of English intellectual life, a habit they retain in spite of the founding of many other universities in the 19th and 20th centuries. In literature, it has been noted for the number of outstanding English poets educated there, *eg* ▷ Spenser, ▷ Donne, ▷ Milton, ▷ Dryden, ▷ Wordsworth, ▷ Coleridge, ▷ Byron, ▷ Tennyson.
▷ Universities.

Campbell, Roy (1902–57)

A South African poet, mainly resident in
England, and well-known in the 1930s for his
opposition to the dominant left-wing school
of poets led by ▷ Auden, ▷ Spender and
▷ Day Lewis whom he satirized under the
composite name of Macspaunday. Much of
his best verse was satirical in heroic
▷ couplets, a form otherwise very rare in
20th-century English verse. He also wrote
eloquent, clear-cut ▷ lyrics. He was
vigorous in all he wrote, but not distinctively
original. Among his best known works are:
The Flaming Terrapin (1924), exalting the
instinctive, vital impulses in man; *The
Waygoose* (1928), a satire on South African
writers; *Adamastor* and *Georgiad*. Amongst
his finest works is his translation of the
poems of San Juan de la Cruz, *St John of the
Cross* (1951). *Collected Poems* in 3 volumes,
1960.

Campbell, The Clan

A Scottish clan, headed by the Duke of
Argyll, which in the 17th and 18th centuries
was one of the most powerful clans in the
▷ Highlands. The heads of the clan became
dukes in the 18th century; their ancient
Gaelic title is Macallum Mhor – the great
Campbell. It was steadfast under its chiefs in
its support of the ▷ Presbyterian Church
and the ▷ Protestant Succession, and in this
it was opposed to other leading Highland
clans who tended to support the Catholic
House of Stuart.

Campbell, Thomas (1777–1844)

Author of the reflective poem *The Pleasures
of Hope* (1799), which includes the well-
known couplet: ' 'Tis distance lends
enchantment to the view,/ And robes the
mountain in its azure hue' (ll 7–8). He also
wrote narrative poems such as *Gertrude of
Wyoming* (1809) in ▷ Spenserian stanzas,
and *Theodoric* (1824) in couplets.

Campion, Edmund (1540–81)

English Catholic. After becoming a fellow of
St John's College, Oxford, in 1557, Campion
enjoyed the patronage of the ▷ Earl of
Leicester before fleeing to Rome in 1572 as
a suspected Catholic. At Rome he joined the
▷ Jesuit order in 1573, before being
ordained a priest in 1578 and being chosen to
return to England as a priest in 1580. In
England he distributed anti-Protestant
material (specifically the *Decem Rationes* in
1581) and was arrested, sent to the
▷ Tower, tortured and finally executed in
1581. His death was said to have been the
cause of many former ▷ Protestants in

England returning to Catholicism. He was
the subject of a hagiographic biography:
▷ Evelyn Waugh's *Edmund Campion*.
    ▷ Catholicism (Roman) in English
literature.

Campion, Thomas (1567–1620)

English lyric poet and musician. He wrote
and composed when the art of English song
was at its height; the words do not exist
merely as a pretext for the music, but are so
composed that the music brings out their
expressiveness. This led naturally to metrical
experiment, and the resulting increase of
rhythmic flexibility no doubt influenced the
playwrights in the great range of expression
which they achieved in blank verse. Campion
wrote ayres, ▷ madrigals and ▷ masques.
Despite his fine command of the rhymed
lyric, he wrote an essay against the use of
rhyme, *Observations in the Art of English
Poesy* (1602). This provoked a reply in one of
the more important Elizabethan critical
essays, ▷ Daniel's *Defence of Ryme*.
    Campion's reputation suffered in the early
part of this century due to the championing
of ▷ Donne and 'metaphysical' poetry
(▷ Metaphysical poets) by critics such as
▷ T. S. Eliot. But his reputation has always
fluctuated considerably – his contemporaries
▷ Ben Jonson and Daniel both having
attacked him in print. The chief difference
between a poet such as Campion and the
styles developed by Donne is that Campion is
concerned with the auditory effects of poetry
rather than concentrating on the striking
effects of images.
Bib: Colles, H. C., *Voice and Verse*;
Kastendieck, M. M., *Thomas Campion,
England's Musical Poet*; Mellers, W., *Music
and Poetry*; Pattison, B., *Music and Poetry of
the English Renaissance*; Warlock, P., *The
English Ayre*; Smith, H., *Elizabethan Poetry*;
Fellows, E. H., *English School of Lutenist
Song Writers*.

Candida (1898)

One of the ▷ *Plays Pleasant and Unpleasant*
by ▷ George Bernard Shaw. Its theme is
the conflict between two views of life: the
lofty, vague one of the poet Marchbanks, and
the narrow but practical one of the Christian
Socialist clergyman Morell. Both men are
rivals for the love of Morell's wife,
Candida.

Canon's Yeoman's Prologue and Tale, The

One of ▷ Chaucer's ▷ *Canterbury Tales*.
Its authenticity as a 'Chaucerian' work has
been questioned because it is not included in
the early Hengwrt manuscript of the *Tales*.

The Prologue recounts how the Canon's Yeoman meets up with the pilgrims *en route* for Canterbury and decides to leave his master, the Canon, and join the company. Although the Canon's Yeoman begins by praising his master, he decides to expose the fraudulence of his alchemical practices in particular and those of alchemy in general in his tale. His description of the alchemical art of the Canon is followed by a story (not about his master, he insists) in which a canon tricks a priest out of £40 by pretending to teach him the secret of making precious metals by alchemical means.

Canterbury Tales, The

KNIGHT. SQUIRE.
Illustration from *The Canterbury Tales*

A famed story-collection by ▷ Geoffrey Chaucer, begun sometime in the later 1380s. The General Prologue gives details of the occasion for the story-telling, relating how a group of pilgrims, bound for the shrine of ▷ St Thomas Becket at Canterbury, meet up at the ▷ Tabard Inn in ▷ Southwark. The pilgrims are introduced in a sequence of portraits which focus on the professional activities of the company (who number 31 in all). The material for these portraits derives partly from a long-standing literary tradition of social analysis and satire, but Chaucer enlarges the scope of the cross-section of society on the pilgrimage by including a broader range of bourgeois professionals in the group. The varied format and style of the descriptive cameos (in which details of dress, character or professional habits are mentioned seemingly at random) enhances the impression of the individuality of the pilgrims, who are introduced by a pilgrim-narrator whose stance is that of a reporter of events.

The list of portraits begins with that of the Knight, a representative of the higher levels of the social élite, who is travelling with his son, the Squire, and their Yeoman. The focus then shifts to the description of members of the clerical elite on the trip, including a Prioress, a Monk and a Friar. There is no clear-cut ordering principle in the sequence of portraits which follows (other than perhaps a broad downward movement through the social scale), describing a Merchant, a Clerk of Oxford, a Lawyer, a Franklin, a group of five Guild members, their wives and their Cook, a Shipman, a Physician, a Wife of Bath, a Parson and his brother, a Ploughman, a Miller, a Manciple, a Reeve and, finally, a Summoner and a Pardoner who pair up as travelling companions. The pilgrim-narrator is described in more detail by the Host, later on the journey. The General Prologue concludes with an account of how the Host of the Tabard Inn, Harry Bailey, devises a story-telling competition to take place on the round trip to Canterbury. The pilgrims agree to tell two stories each on the forward and return journeys; Harry Bailey plans to accompany the pilgrims, act as games-master and reward the pilgrim providing the best story with a meal on return to Southwark.

Diversity seems to be the organizing principle of the collection. The *Canterbury Tales* includes an extraordinarily wide range of material in verse (in rhymed decasyllabic couplets, ▷ rhyme royal verse) and prose, covering a wide range of literary genres and forms: ▷ romances, ▷ fabliaux, an animal fable, saints' lives, exemplary narratives, a moral treatise, a prose treatise on the process of penitence (which concludes the game). The relationship between 'earnest' and 'game', between serious and playful literary material, is one of the running topics of debate within and between the tales.

Judging from the condition of the extant manuscript copies of the *Canterbury Tales*, the project outlined by Harry Bailey in the General Prologue was never completed by Chaucer. The *Canterbury Tales* has the status of a 'work in progress', comprising a series of fragmentary tale-telling sequences, some of which are linked by dramatic interactions between the pilgrims and Harry Bailey, some of which begin and end without any contextual framing, and some of which show signs of being linked to other tellers at an earlier stage in the process of compilation. However, the opening and closing sequences of the *Tales* are provided and from these it seems that the literary plan was designed to change *en route* from a round journey to a one-way trip. The last tale of the sequence, the Parson's prose treatise on penitence, signals not only the end of the journey to Canterbury, but also the end of story-telling altogether, and is followed in most manuscripts by Chaucer's literary Retraction.

None of the 82 manuscripts of the *Tales* was copied during Chaucer's lifetime, and variations in form, style and tale-teller linkage are apparent. Some of the variations seem to reflect the attempts of later scribes and editors to tidy up some of the loose ends of the story-collection and provide more cohesive links for the series of fragmentary sequences left by Chaucer. Modern editions of the *Canterbury Tales* are based on two important early-15th-century manuscripts: the Ellesmere manuscript (E) and the Hengwrt manuscript (H). The form and arrangement of the text in E have provided the basis for the most accessible editions of the *Tales* (by F. N. Robinson, revised and updated by Larry Benson et al.). In E, 22 of the pilgrims mentioned in the Prologue produce a tale, beginning with the ▷ Knight, followed by the ▷ Miller, the ▷ Reeve, the ▷ Cook, the ▷ Man of Law, the ▷ Wife of Bath, the ▷ Friar, the ▷ Summoner, the ▷ Clerk, the ▷ Merchant, the ▷ Squire, the ▷ Franklin, the ▷ Physician, the ▷ Pardoner, the ▷ Shipman, the ▷ Prioress, the pilgrim/ narrator (who tells two tales, ▷ *Sir Thopas*, which is rejected by the Host, and ▷ *Melibeus*), the ▷ Monk, the ▷ Nun's Priest, the ▷ Second Nun, the ▷ Canon's Yeoman (who joins the pilgrimage *en route*), the ▷ Manciple and finally the ▷ Parson. It is now generally accepted that the E text has been quite extensively edited by Chaucer's literary executors and represents a later, tidied-up version of the text represented in H, and more recently the Hengwrt manuscript has been used as the basis for new editions of the *Canterbury Tales* (by N. Blake, by Paul Ruggiers and David Baker). The differences between the two versions are mainly in the ordering and linking of the tales: the E text has more connected sequences of stories and contains the ▷ *Canon's Yeoman's Prologue and Tale*, which is not in H.

Since its publication by Chaucer's literary executors, the *Canterbury Tales* has had an active 'afterlife'. Some new tales were added to the collection by 15th-century editors (notably ▷ Gamelyn), an attempt was made to continue the narrative after the arrival at Canterbury (in the *Tale of Beryn*) and ▷ John Lydgate, the prolific court writer of the 15th century, wrote himself into the literary event of the *Tales* in his work *The Siege of Thebes*, which opens with a description of

Lydgate himself joining the pilgrimage and then contributing his Theban story to the competition. Translations of selected tales were made by ▷ Dryden and ▷ Pope. The attention given to the *Canterbury Tales*, in relation to the rest of the Chaucerian canon, has varied according to the critical temper and tastes of the time, but the enormous attention given by modern scholars and critics to the phenomenon of the *Tales* is only the most recent stage in the long history of their critical reception. The *Canterbury Tales* continues to be a work in progress. **Bib:** Benson, L., et al. (eds.), *The Riverside Chaucer*; Boitani P., and Mann, J. (eds.), *The Cambridge Chaucer Companion*; Cooper, H., *The Structure of the Canterbury Tales*; Howard, D. D. R., *The Idea of the Canterbury Tales*; Pearsall, D., *The Canterbury Tales*.

Canto

Used in Italian literature as a division of a long poem, such as might be sung or chanted at one time (canto = song). The term has been borrowed for some long poems in English.
▷ Pound, Ezra.

Cantos, The

Long poem by ▷ Ezra Pound, unfinished at his death. The latest English collected edition runs to 119 ▷ cantos, and began publication with the first three cantos (later revised) in 1917. Loosely based on the 100 cantos of ▷ Dante's *Divine Comedy*, it attempts a panoramic, encyclopaedic survey of both western and oriental history, dwelling in particular on those rulers and thinkers who had exemplary significance for Pound: Confucius, Sigismondo Malatesta, Duke of Rimini, the early American presidents and Mussolini. Its main targets are usurious international finance and armament manufacturers. However, with the collapse of ▷ Fascism the later stages of the poem became successively more mystical and self consciously explanatory, and it meditates on Pound's vision of the ideal rather than on the possibilities of its earthly realization. **Bib:** Bush, R., *The Genesis of Ezra Pound's 'Cantos'*; Terrell, C. F., *A Companion to the 'Cantos' of Ezra Pound*.

Canute (Cnut) (c 994–1035)

A Danish king of England with a well-documented historical reign, although he has assumed a sort of mythical status in English history. He is especially remembered for the story recorded by the 16th century chronicler ▷ Holinshed about his rebuke to his flatterers. When they declared him all-powerful, he sat down by the seashore and forbade the incoming tide to wet his royal feet. When nonetheless the waves came on, he demonstrated to his courtiers that a king had no more power over nature than an ordinary man.

Capitalism

The system by which the means of production is owned privately. Production is for private profit and productive enterprise is made possible by large-scale loans of money rewarded by the payment of interest.

Before about 1350, in England as in much of the rest of Europe, there was little opportunity for capitalism. On the land, the economic unit was the manor (corresponding approximately to a village) which consumed its own produce and had little left over for sale; the economic relations were feudal, *ie* the landlords provided protection to the peasants in return for economic services, and the peasants were mostly serfs, *ie* they were bound to the land they worked on and were unable to sell their labour freely. The towns were small and manufacture was by ▷ master craftsmen, who worked with their own hands, and employed ▷ apprentices and ▷ journeymen only in small numbers. The masters combined in ▷ craft guilds which regulated trade and limited profits to a communally arranged 'just price'. Moreover, commerce, except for the export of wool, was mainly limited to the districts round the towns. Finally, it was difficult to borrow money for capital investment, partly because the Church disapproved of the taking of interest on money loans, since it regarded this as the sin of usury. The economic bond was not, in fact, a money relationship but a personal one, bound up with an elaborate system of rights and duties; these divided society into something more like castes than the modern social classes, which are differentiated chiefly by wealth.

But already by the lifetime of the poet ▷ Chaucer capitalism was making beginnings. Towns were growing, and they now contained a substantial middle class, as the ▷ *Prologue* to *The Canterbury Tales* illustrates. Master craftsmen were gradually becoming employers of labour rather than workers themselves; this was particularly true in the manufacture of cloth, which required a variety of processes impossible for one man, or even one guild, to undertake alone. The craft guilds were becoming supplemented by the merchant companies, such as the Merchants of the Staple, who had a monopoly of the export of wool to the cloth

manufacturers of Flanders, and later (15th and 16th centuries) the Merchant Adventurers, whose export of cloth became even more important than the older commerce of the export of wool. The economic cause of the ▷ Hundred Years' War was ▷ Edward III's determination to protect the English wool staple towns – *ie* those through which the export of wool was channelled into Flanders – from the threat of France. To sustain the war, Edward III and ▷ Henry V had to borrow extensively from foreign bankers, who were finding methods of escaping the Church's prohibition of usury. Meanwhile, on the land the serfs were becoming independent wage-earners, able to sell their labour freely and where they pleased; this was thanks to the shortage of labour that resulted from the ▷ Black Death epidemics (about 1350). Lack of labour caused many landowners to turn their arable land into pasture and to enclose open land with hedges. This process continued in Tudor times for economic reasons, despite a labour surplus. It weakened the landowners' ties with the peasantry and encouraged the 'drift to the towns' which drained the countryside in the 18th–19th centuries.

The rapid growth of capitalism in the 17th and 18th centuries was aided by the ▷ Reformation, since certain of the ▷ Puritan sects – notably the Calvinist Presbyterians (▷ Calvin, John) – found that religious individualism gave support to and was supported by economic individualism. The dramatists of the period of English drama 1580–1640 found the Puritans to be against them, and they (*eg* ▷ Ben Jonson, ▷ Thomas Middleton, ▷ Philip Massinger) tended to satirize the money-loving, socially ambitious middle classes, among whom the Puritans had their main strength. By the end of the 17th century, however, Puritanism was losing its ferocity; the traditional non-economic bonds of community were by then gravely weakened, and the novels of ▷ Daniel Defoe depict the loneliness of men guided predominantly by economically individualistic motives.

The full triumph of capitalism came only with the fulfilment of the ▷ Industrial Revolution in the 19th century. Workers were, for the first time on a large scale, employed in the mass, in factories. The employers (backed by a number of gifted theorists, such as ▷ Adam Smith, ▷ Jeremy Bentham, ▷ Malthus, Ricardo) developed a ruthless philosophy, according to which their relationship with their workers should be governed entirely by the economic laws of supply and demand, with which the state interfered, in their opinion, only at the cost of wrecking national prosperity, even if the interference were dictated by the need to save the workers from intolerable misery. This stream of opinion among the industrialist employers was, however, progressively opposed by Evangelical Christians among the politicians (*eg* ▷ Lord Shaftesbury), by socialists of the school of ▷ Robert Owen and by the very popular novelists between 1830 and 1860, such as ▷ Elizabeth Gaskell, ▷ Benjamin Disraeli and ▷ Charles Dickens. The most cogent and revolutionary opposition, however, was formulated in the work of Friedrich Engels, *The Condition of the Working Class* (1845) and of ▷ Karl Marx, *Das Kapital* (1867). The two men collaborated, in London, on the *Communist Manifesto* (1848). Gradually industrial capitalism became less inhumane, and in the last twenty years of the 19th century, socialist opinion grew, aided by the leadership of intellectuals such as ▷ George Bernard Shaw and ▷ Beatrice Webb. The principal issue now dividing the main political parties is how much economic activity should be left in private hands and how much freedom this 'free enterprise' should be allowed: the Conservatives support capitalist enterprise and the ▷ Labour Party emphasizes the value of state control. This compromise between capitalism and socialism since the Second World War produced the ▷ Welfare State, where nobody should starve and nobody is supposed to suffer social injustice, though many still do. The Welfare State combined with better education since the war to produce a more articulate working class than has ever been seen in England before; one result of this has been a much larger production of novels, plays and films exploring the experience of social mobility, *eg* the plays of ▷ Arnold Wesker and the novels of ▷ Alan Sillitoe.

▷ Further education; Anti-industrialism.

Capitol, The
In ancient Rome, the hill on which stood the temple to ▷ Jupiter, chief of the gods. Here the chief officers of the Roman Republic, the Consuls, took their vows, and the sacred Sibylline (▷ Sibyl) books were kept.

In the U.S.A., the Capitol is the building where the National Congress meets in Washington.

Captain Singleton, Adventures of (1720)
A novel by ▷ Daniel Defoe. Like the heroes and heroines of Defoe's other novels, the hero has at first no morality and takes to a life of wandering adventure; some of this takes place in Africa (which Defoe knew only from reading and hearsay). Later he becomes a pirate in the Indian Ocean and further east; finally he settles down in England, a respectable married man, converted to a religious life. The story is told in the first person.

Capuchins
▷ Friars.

Capulet
In ▷ Shakespeare's ▷ *Romeo and Juliet*, the name of the family to which Juliet belongs. The inveterate hostility between the Capulets and the ▷ Montagues, the family to which Romeo belongs, causes the tragedy.

Caractacus (Caradoc) (1st century AD)
An ancient British chieftain who resisted the Roman conquest of Britain under the Emperor ▷ Claudius. His courage and dignity before the Emperor, after he had been captured, caused him to be pardoned and released.

Carew, Thomas (1594–1640)
Poet. In the 1630s Carew was a member of the court of ▷ Charles I, and his association with the court and the group of poets moving either within or on the fringe of court circles in the pre-Civil War years, has led him to be grouped as one of the ▷ 'Cavalier' poets. His first important work was his elegy on the death of ▷ John Donne, which appeared in the first edition of Donne's poems in 1633. In 1634 his ▷ masque *Coelum Britannicum* was performed by the king and his gentlemen. His *Poems* were published in 1640 with further editions in 1642 and 1651.

Carew's poetry is remarkable for its combination of eroticism, wit and logical demonstration. His elegy on Donne, as well as representing a tribute to the dead poet, also offers itself as a critical statement in its own right, and an important commentary on the type of verse which came to be known as ▷ 'metaphysical'.
Bib: Miner, E., *The Cavalier Mode from Jonson to Cotton*.

Carey, Peter (b 1943)
Australian novelist and short-story writer. Born in Victoria and educated in science at Monash University, Carey now works part-time in advertising in Sydney. His collection of stories, published in Britain as *Exotic Pleasures* (published as *The Fat Man in History*; 1984, and *War Crimes*; 1979 in Australia) made a great impact when they appeared in 1981, for their extraordinary

mixture of fantasy, ▷ science fiction, and ▷ realism, set in Carey's disturbing evocation of the contemporary Australian landscape. His highly acclaimed novels include *Bliss* (1981); *Illywhacker* (1985); and *Oscar and Lucinda* (1988) which won the 1988 Booker Prize.

▷ Commonwealth literatures.

Carker, James
A character in Dickens's novel ▷ *Dombey and Son*. He is a vicious character and one of Dickens's most successful depictions of villainy, and beautifully tied in with the development of the railways.

Carlyle, Jane (1801–66)
Jane Baillie Welsh displayed early signs of her considerable intelligence while still at school, and was introduced by her former tutor to ▷ Thomas Carlyle in 1821. After their marriage in 1826 her energies were largely channelled into coping with his difficult character and acting as hostess to their large circle of literary friends. Her copious correspondence with many of these, as well as with her relatives and with Thomas, has given her a deserved reputation as a brilliant and observant letter-writer.
Bib: Surtees, V., *Jane Welsh Carlyle*.

Carlyle, Thomas (1795–1881)
Scottish essayist, historian, philosopher. The term 'philosopher' is inappropriate to him if it implies the use of the reason for the logical investigation of truth; his friend ▷ John Stuart Mill, who was a philosopher in this sense, called Carlyle a poet, meaning that he reached his conclusions by imaginative intuition. In his old age he became known as 'the sage of ▷ Chelsea'; this is the kind of admiration that he received in England between 1840 and his death. He hated spiritual mediocrity, mere contentment with material prosperity, moral lassitude and the surrender to scientific scepticism and analytic reasoning. All these he regarded as characteristic of British civilization in the mid-19th century. Part of their cause was the overwhelming technical advances resulting from the ▷ Industrial Revolution; he also considered the immense popularity of the poet ▷ Byron had helped to disintegrate spiritual wholeness because of the cynicism and pessimism of his poetry, and he distrusted equally the influence on the English mind of the coldly logical French philosophers. To counter Byron, he pointed to the spiritual health which he found in ▷ Goethe, and to counter the French he advocated the more emotional and intuitive 18th and 19th century German thinkers like Richter and Goethe.

Carlyle's influence derives even more, however, from his own character and the environment from which he sprang. His father had been a Scottish stonemason, with the moral energy and intellectual interests which comes partly from the influence of Scottish Calvinism (▷ Presbyterianism). This religious tradition in Scotland had much in common with 17th-century ▷ Puritanism which had left such a strong mark on the English character; the resemblance between the two traditions helps to account for the hold which Carlyle established on the English imagination. His own personality was strong and individualistic; this, combined with his intention of counteracting the abstract intellectual thought of writers like ▷ Bentham, caused him to write in an eccentric prose style, distorting natural word order and using archaic language. His ▷ *Sartor Resartus* ('Tailor Repatched', 1833–4) is a disguised spiritual ▷ autobiography in which he faces the tendencies to intellectual scepticism and spiritual denial in himself, and dedicates himself to a life of spiritual affirmation. He is unable to base this affirmative spirit on the traditional religious beliefs that had supported his father, so that he has to base it on his own will, his imaginative response to nature and the inspiration provided by the lives of great men.

History was for Carlyle the storehouse of example of these great men, his 'Heroes' – and it is in this spirit that we have to approach his historical works: *French Revolution* (1837), *On Heroes and Hero Worship* (1841), *Oliver Cromwell's Letters and Speeches* (1845) and *Frederick II of Prussia* (1858–65). In *Signs of the Times* (1829), *Chartism* (1839) and *Past and Present* (1843) he criticized the mechanistic philosophy which he saw underlying contemporary industrial society, and in *Latter-Day Pamphlets* (1850) he attacked the quasi-scientific treatment of social questions by the rationalist political economists. In 1867 *Shooting Niagara – and After?*, written at the time of the Second Parliamentary Reform Bill, reflects his total disbelief in the efficacy of mere political reform.

As a historian, Carlyle wanted history to be related to the life of the ordinary human being; as a social thinker, his advocacy of the imaginative approach to man in society relates him to the thought of ▷ Coleridge, whom he knew through his friend John Sterling (*Life of John Sterling*, 1851), and also to his own disciple, ▷ John Ruskin.

▷ Utilitarianism; Scottish literature in English.

Bib: Trevelyan, G. M., *Carlyle Anthology*; Froude, J. A., *Life*; Neff, E., *Carlyle and Mill*; Harold, C. F., *Carlyle and German Thought, 1819–34*; Symons, J., *Carlyle: the Life and Idea of a Prophet*; Sanders C. R. and Fielding K. J. (eds.), *The Collected Letters of Thomas and Jane Carlyle*.

Carmelites
▷ Friars.

Carnival
The literal meaning of this term is the 'saying good-bye' to meat at the start of Lent. Traditionally it was a period of feasting during the Christian calendar which reached it climax on Shrove Tuesday, and included many forms of festive inversion of normal behaviour, often comic and mocking of authority. To this extent it signifies a spontaneous eruption of those social forces shortly to be restrained by Lent. This sense of disruption of the norm has brought the term 'carnival' into the language of contemporary critical theory. ▷ Mikhail Bakhtin first used the term to describe a form of festive language which threatens disruption and challenges the social order. The association of carnival with popular energies highlights the political tension between official ▷ ideology and potentially subversive energies. In contemporary critical theory, the carnivalesque points to the polyphonic nature of literary texts, identifying in them a series of different and frequently opposing 'voices'.
▷ Deconstruction; Discourse.
Bib: Bakhtin, M., *Rabelais and His World.*

Carol
A hymn of praise, especially associated with Christmas. The origin of the carol may have been pagan, and connected with New Year and spring festivals. Dancing and singing in early medieval churches was common, for instance round the Christmas 'crib' or model of the Christ-child's birthplace in the stable at Bethlehem. English Christmas carols, like those of other nations, are freer of the restricted sentiment of Church piety than other hymns. Examples dating from the 15th century are 'Joseph was an old man' and 'I saw three ships come sailing in'. The earliest collection in English is by ▷ Wynkyn de Worde in 1521.

Caroline Period, The
Term given to the period of the reign of ▷ Charles I (from the Latin *Carolus* = Charles). The 'Caroline poets' (*eg* ▷ Thomas Carew, ▷ Sir John Suckling, ▷ Richard Lovelace) and the 'Caroline divines' (*eg*

▷ William Laud) are all associated with the court culture of the period. The term is thus something of a misnomer, since it represents not so much a period, but rather an ideological and cultural stance which stands in opposition to the popular and emergent republican culture.
▷ Cavalier Poets.
Bib: Sharpe, K., *Criticism and Compliment.*

Carroll, Lewis (Charles Lutwidge Dodgson) (1832–98)

Illustration by Tenniel from *Alice's Adventures in Wonderland*

Writer for children; author of *Alice's Adventures in Wonderland* (1865) and *Through the Looking-Glass* (1872). By profession, a mathematics lecturer at Oxford University. The 'Alice' books describe the adventures of a child in dreams, and owe their distinctiveness to the combination of childlike naivety and an authentic dream atmosphere, so that events succeed and language is used with dream logic instead of daylight logic. Thus these two books mark an epoch in the history of dream literature; the dream state is not merely a pretext for fantasy, but is shown to follow its own laws. Consequently Carroll's two masterpieces have had as much appeal for adults as for children. Dodgson was also a master of ▷ 'nonsense' verse which shows the same characteristics; his most famous poem is *The Hunting of the Snark* (1876). His other book for children, *Sylvie and Bruno* (1889), is less memorable.
▷ Children's books.
Bib: Gardner, M., *The Annotated Alice*; Collingwood, S. D., *The Life and Letters of Lewis Carroll*; Empson, W., 'Alice in Wonderland' in his *Some Versions of Pastoral*;

Green, R. L., *The Story of Lewis Carroll*; Sewell, E., in *The Field of Nonsense*; Hudson, D., *Lewis Carroll*.

Carter, Angela (b 1940)

Angela Carter

Novelist and short-story writer. From her first novel, *Shadow Dance* (1966), her work has been notable for a strain of ▷ surrealist ▷ Gothic fantasy, a fascination with the erotic and the violent, and a blending of comedy and horror. *The Magic Toyshop* (1967) is a ▷ Freudian fairytale seen through the eyes of an orphaned 15-year-old girl, sent, with her brother and baby sister, to live in the claustrophobic and sinister home of her uncle, a sadistic toymaker. Her new family are examples of Carter's ability to create vivid Dickensian caricatures. After *Several Perceptions* (1968) her work became unequivocally Gothic and anti-realist, centring on the reworking of myth and fairytale, and the exploration of aggressive and sexual fantasies. *Heroes and Villains* (1969), *The Infernal Desire Machines of Doctor Hoffman* (1972) and *The Passion of New Eve* (1977) are macabre visions of imaginary worlds, projections of the 'subterranean areas behind everyday experience', with ▷ picaresque and pastiche elements. Carter's interest in the politics of sexuality is reflected in her non-fiction work *The Sadeian Woman* (1979), an analysis of the codes of ▷ pornography. Her other novels are: *Love* (1971); *Nights at the Circus* (1984). Story collections are: *Fireworks* (1974); *The Bloody Chamber* (1979); *Black Venus's Tale* (1980);

Black Venus (1985); *Come Unto These Yellow Sands* (1985).

Cartesianism

The philosophy of ▷ Descartes.

Carthage

A city on the North African coast in the Gulf of Tunis; it was practically destroyed by the Arabs in AD 698. In the 3rd century BC Carthaginian troops invaded Italy under the great general Hannibal and came near to destroying Rome. Rome succeeded in destroying Carthage (Third Punic War) in the 2nd century BC, but the city was rebuilt by the Emperor Augustus (▷ Caesar) (27 BC–AD 14) and remained an important port of the Roman Empire.

Carthusians

An order of monks founded in France in the 11th century. The name derives from Chatrousse (Chartreuse), the village where its first monastery was built. Their monasteries were called Charterhouses in England; the most famous of them, the London Charterhouse, was taken from the monks in 1535 during the ▷ Reformation and in 1611 was turned into a school (now a ▷ public school and moved to Godalming).

Cary, (Arthur) Joyce (Lunel) (1888–1957)

Novelist. He was born in Northern Ireland, where there is a strong tradition of ▷ Protestantism; he was brought up against a background of devout ▷ Anglicanism, lost his faith, and later constructed an unorthodox but strongly ethical faith of his own along Protestant lines. He came late to the writing of novels. He studied as an art student in Edinburgh and Paris before going to Oxford University. In 1912–13 he fought, and served in the Red Cross, in the Balkan War. In 1913 he joined the Nigerian political service, fought against the Germans in West Africa in World War I, and returned to the political service after it. His first novel, *Aissa Saved*, appeared in 1932. His subsequent works were: *An American Visitor* (1933); *The African Witch* (1936); *Castle Corner* (1938); *Mister Johnson* (1939); *Charley is my Darling* (1940); *A House of Children* (1941); the trilogy *Herself Surprised* (1941), *To Be a Pilgrim* (1942) and *The Horse's Mouth* (1944); *The Moonlight* (1946); *A Fearful Joy* (1949); another trilogy, *Prisoner of Grace* (1952), *Except the Lord* (1953), and *Not Honour More* (1955); *The Captive and the Free* (1959). *Spring Song* (1960) is a collection of stories. He also produced three volumes of verse, *Verse* (1908), *Marching Soldier* (1945) and *The Drunken Sailor* (1947), and a number of political tracts – *Power in Men* (1939), *The Case for African Freedom* (1941; revised 1944), *Process of Real Freedom* (1943), and *Britain and West Africa* (1946).

In the first 30 years of the 20th century novelists tended to be open to foreign influences and experimental in expression; Cary was among the first distinguished novelists to return to English traditions and direct narrative, although he here and there uses the ▷ stream of consciousness technique of narration evolved by novelists of the 1920s, notably ▷ James Joyce. He is one of the most eclectic of modern novelists, both in method and in subject. In his comedy and his loose, vigorous narrative he has been compared to the 18th-century novelists – ▷ Smollett and ▷ Defoe; in his characterization, to ▷ Dickens; in his attitude to human nature, to ▷ D. H. Lawrence; in his concern with heroic morality, to ▷ Joseph Conrad; in his endeavour to present experience with immediacy, to ▷ Virginia Woolf and Joyce; in his interlocking of human destiny and social patterns he might be compared with ▷ George Eliot. His first three novels and *Mister Johnson* are products of his African experience; *Charley is my Darling* and *A House of Children* are novels of childhood, and his two trilogies – thought by some to be his major work – are attempts, in his words, to see 'English history, through English eyes, for the last 60 years'.
Bib: Wright, A., *Joyce Cary: a Preface to his Novels*; Mahood, M. M., *Joyce Cary's Africa*; Fisher, B., *Joyce Cary, the Writer and his Theme*.

Casanova De Seingalt, Giacomo (1725–98)

An Italian adventurer, author of scandalous Memoirs. His name has become synonymous in English with a 'man who prides himself on his sexual attractiveness'.

Cassandra

In Greek legend, a daughter of ▷ Priam, King of ▷ Troy. The god ▷ Apollo gave her the gift of prophecy, so that she foresaw the fall of the city. At the end of the war she was made captive by Agamemnon, leader of the Greek forces, and was later murdered by Agamemnon's queen, ▷ Clytemnestra.
▷ *Iliad*.

Castalia, Castalian Spring

▷ Muses.

Castiglione, Baldassare (1478–1529)

Italian ▷ humanist and author of *Il Cortegiano* (1528), translated as *The Courtier*

by Sir Thomas Hoby in 1561. *Il Cortegiano* is based on Castiglione's years spent as a courtier at Urbino under Guidobaldo da Montefeltro, and takes the form of a debate on what features should be possessed by the perfect courtier. Those qualifications include: swordsmanship, nobility, military understanding, virile sports (hunting, swimming, running and riding), dancing, grace, skill at repartee and telling of stories and anecdotes; the possession of the virtues of prudence, justice, temperance, and fortitude; adaptability, literary knowledge, the ability to write prose and verse, musical proficiency, and the gift of charm.

The two important features of Castiglione's book, and the ones that were to become most influential in England in the ▷ Renaissance period, were his description of *sprezzatura* and his ▷ neo-Platonic conception of love and harmony. *Sprezzatura* implies an ease of manner, a suggestion that what has been done has been achieved effortlessly and without art. It was qualities such as these that were to play an important role in the definition of courtly behaviour in the late 16th century in England. The neo-Platonic elements (to be found in Book IV of the work) elevate beauty, together with human and divine love, into an ideal of harmony.

Castiglione was to be of enormous importance to contemporary readers of his work in introducing the idea that individuals can create an identity and a personality for themselves. It is this idea which lies, for example, at the heart of ▷ Edmund Spenser's ▷ *The Faerie Queene*, and in the poetry, in the earlier period, of ▷ Sir Thomas Wyatt.
Bib: Greenblatt, S., *Renaissance Self-Fashioning*.

Castle of Indolence, The (1748)

A poem in ▷ Spenserian stanzas by ▷ James Thomson. Its first canto deals with the 'pleasing land of drowsyhed' governed by the wizard Indolence. The poet himself ('a bard . . . more fat than bard beseems'), his friends Quin the actor, ▷ Lord Lyttelton, and others live a life of sensuous ease in Indolence's castle, until they become bloated and are thrown into a foul dungeon. The second canto depicts the progress of the Knight of Industry from the ancient world to Britain, where he creates the new order of 'social commerce' and imperial expansion, and ends by conquering Indolence and freeing his victims. The poem presents a fascinating mixture of whimsical irony and serious ▷ 'Augustan' didacticism. Lord Lyttelton

wrote the stanza describing Thomson himself (I, stanza LXVIII) and the last four stanzas of Canto I were written by Thomson's friend ▷ John Armstrong.
▷ Augustanism; Bard.

Castle of Otranto, The (1764)
One of the first so-called ▷ Gothic novels, by ▷ Horace Walpole. The fantastic events are set in the Middle Ages, and the story is full of supernatural sensationalism. The story concerns an evil usurper, a fateful prophecy about his downfall, a mysterious prince disguised as a peasant, and his eventual marriage to the beautiful heroine whom the usurper had intended as his own bride.

Castle of Perseverance
A ▷ morality play, dating from the first quarter of the 15th century which is both the longest example of this dramatic genre (3,649 lines) and the earliest to survive in a near-complete form. The play, which is written in an East Midlands dialect, is designed for a large-scale production, with 35 speaking parts. The single extant play text is unusual in that it contains a staging plan that suggests it should be played in the round, with the Castle of Perseverance at the centre and five scaffolds arranged around the perimeter of the circle. The action depicts the life of Humanum Genus (a figure who represents humankind in general), from birth to death, as he resists and succumbs to the forces of temptation to sin. The action continues after his death and follows a debate in Heaven about whether or not Humanum Genus should be admitted.
Bib: Happé, P. (ed.), *Four Morality Plays*.

Castlereagh, Viscount (1769–1822)
Statesman, and Secretary of State for Foreign Affairs during and after the downfall of Napoleon, from 1812 to 1822. This period coincided with a phase of political reaction in Britain, and to the radicals of the time he represented the oppressiveness of the government. Hence the attack on him by ▷ Shelley in the ▷ *Mask of Anarchy*.

Castor and Pollux (the Dioscuri)
In Greek myth, twin sons of ▷ Zeus and Leda, and companions in the voyage of the ▷ Argonauts. They were made into the constellation of Gemini (the Twins). In their divine capacity, they came to be considered as the friends of sailors, with power to calm a storm.

Cathay
The name by which China was known to medieval Europe, still used as a poetic term for the country or, more vaguely, for any exotic and remote place.

Catholic Emancipation, The Act of (1829)
A law by which Roman Catholics in England were awarded full political rights, *eg* to be elected as Members of ▷ Parliament. They had been deprived of these rights by legislation of various kinds since the time of the ▷ Reformation. Of particular importance for the rights of Irish Roman Catholics, who, after they lost the Irish Parliament in 1800, bitterly resented their exclusion from Westminster.
▷ Catholicism (Roman) in English literature.

Catholicism (Roman) in English literature
Until the ▷ Act of Supremacy (1534) by which ▷ King Henry VIII separated the English Church from Roman authority, and the more violent revolution in ▷ Scotland a little later, both countries had belonged to the European community of Catholic Christendom. This community was a genuine culture, allowing great unity of belief and feeling together with great variety of attitude. In the 16th century this community of cultures broke up, owing not only to the ▷ Protestant rebellions but also to the increase of national self-consciousness, the influence of non-Christian currents (especially ▷ Platonism), and the gradual release of various fields of activity – political, commercial, philosophical – from religious doctrine. ▷ The Counter-Reformation after the Catholic Council of Trent (1545–63), even more than the ▷ Reformation, tended to define Roman Catholicism in contrast to Protestantism. Thus, although the dramatists and lyric poets in England from 1560 to 1640 show a plentiful survival of medieval assumptions about the nature of man and his place in the universe, in conflict with newer tendencies of thought and feeling, the Roman Catholic writer in the same period begins to show himself as something distinct from his non-Catholic colleagues. The clearest example in the 17th century is the poet ▷ Richard Crashaw. ▷ Milton's epic of the creation of the world, ▷ *Paradise Lost*, is in many ways highly traditional, but the feeling that inspires it is entirely post-Reformation. By the 18th century, however, religion of all kinds was becoming a mere department of life, no longer dictating ideas and emotions in all fields, even when sincerely believed; it is thus seldom easy to remember that the poet ▷ Alexander Pope was a Roman Catholic.

By the 19th century, writers of strong religious conviction were increasingly feeling themselves in a minority in an indifferent and even sceptical world. They therefore tended to impress their work once more with their faith, and this was especially true of the few Catholic writers, since Catholic faith was dogmatically so strongly defined, *eg* the poet ▷ Gerard Manley Hopkins. The century also saw a revival of Anglo-Catholicism. From the time of the Reformation there had been a school of opinion which sought to remain as close to Roman Catholicism as ▷ Anglican independence allowed. This wing of the Church was important under ▷ Charles I, but lost prestige until it was revived by the ▷ Oxford Movement. Since then it has remained important in the strength of its imprint on literature. Thus in the 20th century the Anglo-Catholicism of the poet ▷ T. S. Eliot is as conspicuous as and more profound than the Roman Catholicism of the novelists ▷ Evelyn Waugh and ▷ Graham Greene. Amongst writers later in the 20th century, Catholicism is noticeable in the work of ▷ Anthony Burgess and ▷ David Lodge.

Catiline (1611)

A tragedy by ▷ Ben Jonson, about the attempt by Lucius Sergius Catilana to overthrow the government of the Republic of Rome in the 1st century BC. It is an example of Jonson's great classical scholarship, but this scholarship impedes the dramatic impact of the tragedy instead of enhancing it as in the case of his other Roman tragedy, ▷ *Sejanus*.

Cato, Marcus Porcius (95–46 BC)

'Cato the younger', great-grandson of ▷ Cato the Censor. He tried to maintain the Republic against the ambitions and popularity of ▷ Julius Caesar. He was noted for his disinterested devotion to duty and disregard for his own personal interests. The later Roman ▷ stoics looked back to him as the pattern of stoic man. He was eventually defeated by Caesar at Utica (46 BC).

Cato the Censor (234–149 BC)

Marcus Porcius Cato, an austere statesman of ancient Rome, famous for his hostility to unnecessary luxury imported from Greece and for his endeavours to maintain traditional Roman simplicity. He was the first important Latin prose writer and the first of the Roman historians. His most important work was *Origines* ('Origins') in which he described the history of Rome and the rise of other Italian states. Later in the Roman Empire, Cato's emphasis on discipline and austerity in private and public life was admired as an ideal from which the sophisticated Romans of the Empire had fallen away.

▷ Cato, Marcus Porcius; Latin literature.

Catullus, Gaius Valerius (?84–54 BC)

A Roman lyrical poet, famous especially for his Lesbia cycle of love poems. He was one of the Latin poets who had an extensive influence over English ▷ lyric poets in the 16th and 17th centuries. For instance, ▷ John Skelton's *Book of Philip Sparrow* (1503–7) echoes Catullus on Lesbia and the sparrow; ▷ Ben Jonson's *Song to Celia* is modelled on Catullus, and so is ▷ Andrew Marvell's *To his Coy Mistress*. Jonson, with his sensitive and profound Latin scholarship, was the most important English follower of Catullus and he transmitted the strength and delicacy of the Latin poet to the ▷ 'Cavalier' lyricists and to Marvell. The most important period for Catullus's influence on English poetry was therefore 1600–50.

Causley, Charles (b 1917)

Poet. Causley is Cornish by birth, and his writing has been compared to his contemporary ▷ John Betjeman in its usage of traditional forms, and to the Spanish poet he admires, Federico Garcia Lorca (▷ Spanish literature), in its usage of the ballad form. He draws his influences from pre-modernist poets, particularly ▷ Victorian, ▷ Georgian and World War I poets (Causley himself fought in World War II in the Royal Navy). His first publication was *Hands to Dance* (1951); this was followed by *Union Street* (1957); *Underneath the Water* (1967); *Figure of Eight* (1969); *Figgie Hobbin* (1970); *Collected Poems* (1975).

Caute, David (b 1936)

Novelist and dramatist. Caute is one of a group of English writers, including ▷ Andrew Sinclair and Julian Mitchell, interested in formal experiment, self-referential narrative strategies and the blending of ▷ realism with elements of fantasy. He admires the work of ▷ Christine Brooke-Rose, and is strongly influenced by ▷ Jean-Paul Sartre. *The Confrontation* is a trilogy consisting of a play, *The Demonstration* (produced 1969), a critical essay supposedly by one of the characters in the play, *The Illusion* (1970) and a novel, *The Occupation* (1971). The questioning of the borders of fiction with other discourses is sustained by the competing narrators and narrative strategies within *The Occupation*. Caute's

works reflect his commitment to Marxism
(▷ Marx, Karl) in their analysis of society
and history, and his novel *The Decline of the
West* (1966) has been criticized as being over-
didactic. He has worked as a lecturer, and as
literary and arts editor of the ▷ *New
Statesman*. Later novels include *News from
Nowhere* (1986).

Cavalier

A word, meaning 'horseman', which was used
for the supporters of ▷ Charles I in the
▷ Civil War. It was first used as a term of
reproach against them by their opponents,
the supporters of ▷ Parliament
(▷ Roundheads); in this sense it meant an
arrogant and frivolous man of the court.
Soon, however, it was accepted with pride by
the Royalists themselves. It is a mistake,
however, to think of the Cavaliers as merely
members of the court and of the aristocracy;
many of the aristocracy supported Parliament
and many of the Cavaliers were fairly modest
country gentlemen who never came near the
court. The Cavalier Parliament sat from 1661
to 1678 after the restoration of ▷ Charles II
and was so called because the king's
supporters won most of the seats.
    ▷ Cavalier poets.

Cavalier Poets

An unhelpful critical term used to encompass
the group of poets associated with the court
of ▷ Charles I (in particular ▷ Thomas
Carew, ▷ Sir John Suckling and
▷ Richard Lovelace) often known as the
▷ Caroline poets. The term is suggestive of
a homogeneity amongst this group of poets,
and also a romanticized implication of their
soldierly and martial prowess.

Cavendish, Margaret, Duchess of Newcastle (?1624–74)

The life and writings of Margaret Cavendish
perfectly illustrate the fate of a woman who
endeavoured to compete on equal intellectual
terms with men. ▷ Samuel Pepys described
her as a 'mad, conceited, and ridiculous
woman' and yet she was much admired for
her erudition. Her chief publications include
scientific and philosophical works such as
Observations upon Experimental Philosophy
(1666) and *Grounds of Natural Philosophy*
(1668), together with poems, plays, and
letters. Her ▷ autobiography is contained in
Natures Pictures (1656) and was followed by a
▷ biography of her husband entitled *The
Life of William Cavendish, Duke of Newcastle*
(1667), which was a considerable success.
Though she was lavishly entertained by the
▷ Royal Society in 1667, it was never

suggested that she be elected to a Fellowship.
Bib: Meyer, G. D., *The Scientific Lady in
England 1650–1760*; Jones, K., *A Glorious
Fame*.

Caxton, William (?1422–91)

Fox and Grapes from Caxton's *Aesop*

The first English printer. He established his
press in Westminster in 1476, and in the
years 1477–91 he issued nearly 80 books,
many of them translations from the French,
and many of these made by himself. Of
English works that he printed, some of the
most important are Chaucer's ▷ *Canterbury
Tales*, ▷ *House of Fame*, and ▷ *Troilus and
Criseyde*, and Sir Thomas Malory's ▷ *Morte
D'Arthur*.

Caxton was a good translator, and has his
place in the development of English prose.
No great writer had set a standard for prose
as Chaucer had for poetry. The language was
in a fluid state, with no accepted standards of
spelling, grammar or style. Caxton had to fix
these for himself, not only as a printer but as
a publisher aiming to be intelligible to the
widest possible public. With few English
prose works available for printing he had to
fall back on producing his own, by
translation.
Bib: Awner, N. S., *Caxton: A Study of the
Literature of the First English Press*; Bennett,
H. S., *English Books and Readers, 1475–1557*.

Cecilia, St

Patron saint of music and the blind; martyred
for her faith, in Rome, AD 230, or possibly in
Sicily rather earlier. Her association with
music depends on a passing reference in the
medieval account of her life. Her legend is
told by ▷ Chaucer in the ▷ *Canterbury
Tales* (▷ *Second Nun's Tale*) and she is
further commemorated by ▷ John Dryden
in one of his most famous poems, *Song for St
Cecilia's Day*, and by ▷ Alexander Pope in
his *Ode for Music on Saint Cecilia's Day*.
▷ Handel set both these poems to music.

Celestial City

The name by which Heaven is denoted in
▷ John Bunyan's ▷ *Pilgrim's Progress*. It
is contrasted with the ▷ City of Destruction,
a typical earthly town standing for
worldliness, from which Christian flees on
hearing that it is doomed.

Celtic Twilight, The

Originally *The Celtic Twilight* was a book of
short stories by the poet ▷ W. B. Yeats,
published in 1893. The book dealt with the
widespread beliefs in magic and the
supernatural which were current among Irish
peasants. Since then, the term Celtic Twilight
has been widely used to describe the idea that
the ▷ Celts, especially in Ireland, preserve a
mystical, imaginative, poetic vision which the
practical and materialistic ▷ Anglo-Saxons
(both in England and in southern Scotland)
have lost. At the end of the 19th century and
beginning of the 20th century Yeats and
other Irish poets used this conception of the
Celtic character as a weapon in the cause of
Irish nationalism, and they cultivated ancient
Irish legends about heroes such as
▷ Cuchulain and heroines such as ▷ Queen
Deirdre so as to build up a distinctively
Irish literary consciousness to replace the
dominant English culture.
▷ Irish literature in English.

C.E.M.A.

The Council for the Encouragement of Music
and the Arts was founded in 1939, and
financed by the Pilgrim Trust and the Board
of Education, to provide entertainments on
the home front and provide employment for
artists during wartime. Its success
strengthened the case for public subsidy for
the theatre and after World War II it became
the ▷ Arts Council of Great Britain.

Cenci, The (1819)

A tragedy by ▷ Percy Bysshe Shelley which
symbolically depicts the political oppression
of his own day in terms of historical events
which took place in 1599. Count Francesco
Cenci, a Roman nobleman, conceives an
incestuous passion for his daughter Beatrice,
and in desperation Beatrice, her brother
Bernard, and her stepmother Lucretia
conspire to kill the Count. They are
discovered, tortured, condemned to death,
and executed on the orders of the Pope. Like
all the dramas of the ▷ romantic poets,
Shelley's play is an artificial, literary
composition. Its ▷ blank verse is highly
derivative from that of the ▷ Jacobean
playwrights, particularly ▷ John Webster.

Censorship and English literature

Systematic censorship has never been an
important restriction on English writing
except in times of war; but English writers
have certainly not always been entirely free.

Until 1640 the monarch exercised
undefined powers by the Royal Prerogative.
Early in her reign, ▷ Elizabeth I ordered
dramatists not to meddle with politics, though
this did not prevent Norton and
▷ Sackville's *Gorboduc* with its warnings on
national disorder; but ▷ Ben Jonson,
▷ Chapman and ▷ Marston found
themselves in prison for *Eastward Hoe* (1605)
because it offended the Scots friends of
▷ James I. In the reign of ▷ Charles I the
term Crop-ears was used for opponents of the
king who lost their ears as a penalty for
criticizing the political or religious authorities.
Moreover, printing was monopolized by the
▷ Stationer's Company, whose charter
might be withdrawn by the Crown, so that
the monopoly would cease.

In the ▷ Civil War, Parliament was in
control of London, and issued an edict that
the publication of any book had to be licensed.
The edict provoked ▷ John Milton's
Areopagitica, an appeal for freedom of
expression. Its influence was not immediate;
after the ▷ Restoration of the Monarchy,
Parliament issued a similar edict in the
Licensing Act of 1663. The Act was only for
a period, however, and in 1696 it was not
renewed. The lapsing of the Licensing Act
was the starting point of British freedom of
the press except for emergency edicts in
times of war in the 20th century, although in
the early 19th century the government
attempted a form of indirect censorship by
imposing a tax on periodicals which restricted
their sale amongst the poor. Nonetheless
there are still laws extant which restrict
freedom of political expression beyond certain
limits.

Also serious are the English laws of libel
and of obscene libel. The first exists to
punish attacks on private reputation, and the
second concerns the defence of sexual morals.
The restrictions are serious restraints on
opinion because they are vaguely defined, so
that it is difficult for a publisher or writer to
know when he is infringing them. Moreover,
prohibition under obscene libel is frequently
reversed, *eg* ▷ D. H. Lawrence's ▷ *The
Rainbow* was suppressed for obscenity, but
by 1965 it was a prescribed text for study in
schools.

Censorship in the theatre has been a
special case since the 18th century. ▷ Henry
Fielding's comedies attacking the Prime

Minister, ▷ Robert Walpole, led in 1737 to the restriction of London theatres to two 'patented' ones – Covent Garden and Drury Lane – and the Court official, the Lord Chamberlain, had to license plays. In 1843 the Theatres Act removed the restriction on the theatres and defined the Lord Chamberlain's powers to the restraint of indecency. The Lord Chamberlain's censorship came to an end in 1968.

Since 1979 there has been a gradual return to the censorship of literature and this has been extended to cover the media. The Official Secrets Act is in the process of being rewritten so as to prevent both former Crown servants from revealing information – especially in autobiographies – as well as the media from printing or broadcasting, sometimes in dramatic form, any of this material. A directive was issued in November 1988 to prevent the broadcasting of statements from people of named organizations; again this may have an effect on drama. Also in 1988, the government emended the 1986 Local Government Act to forbid any Local Authority promoting homosexuality through educational means, printed material or support of gay writers. A non-statutory body (it will become one in 1990), the Broadcasting Standards Council was established, again in 1988, in order to monitor taste and decency in the media. Finally, a non-governmental form of censorship may be found in the effects of the concentration of ownership in publishing houses and the press, which severely limit the range of writing that is commercially encouraged.

Two organizations attempt to alert people to the extent and dangers of these new censorship laws: the Campaign for Press and Broadcasting Freedom and the Writers' Guild of Great Britain.

Centaurs

In Greek myth, a race of beings who were part horse and part man. They are mainly known for their war with a neighbouring race of men, the Lapithae, and for one of their number, Cheiron, famous for his knowledge of medicine, music, and archery.

Centlivre, Susannah (d 1723)

Actress, dramatist, essayist and poet, known in her time as 'the celebrated Mrs Centlivre'. She survived anti-feminist criticism to become the most prolific dramatist, and one of the most successful of either sex, of her day. Two of her comedies, ▷ *The Busie Body* (1709), and ▷ *The Wonder: A Woman Keeps a Secret* (1714), were among the four most frequently performed, apart from those of Shakespeare, in the late 19th century and her ▷ *A Bold Stroke for a Wife* was popular for most of the 18th century. She excelled in writing intrigue comedy, somewhat in the style of ▷ Aphra Behn, but less sexually explicit, and in a softened tone.

Centlivre's origins are obscure, and her birth date has been placed variously between 1667 and 1680. Her plays suggest a knowledge of French acquired, according to contemporaries, from a tutor. One account has her masquerading as a youth and studying at Cambridge University, before coming to London as a strolling actress.

Still in her teens, Susannah married an army officer, Mr Carroll, who died soon afterwards, supposedly in a duel. She began publishing poetry, and copies of her letters, real or fabricated, to ▷ George Farquhar and others. Her first play, a cross between a tragedy and a tragi-comedy, called *The Perjur'd Husband*, appeared at ▷ Drury Lane in 1700. In 1707 she married the 'yeoman of the mouth' to Queen Anne, *ie* the Queen's master cook, Joseph Centlivre, but continued to write for most of her remaining life; her total output was 19 plays. The farcical comedy, *The Busie Body*, immediately became part of the stock repertory, succeeding largely because of the engaging nature of the well-meaning but foolish character, Marplot. A sequel, *Marplot in Lisbon* (1710), was less well received. In other plays, such as *The Gamester* (1705), and *The Basset Table* (1705), Centlivre attacked the fashionable vices of gambling and card-playing. She was closely associated with many of the literary figures of the period, in addition to Farquhar, including ▷ Richard Steele, William Burnaby, ▷ Eliza Haywood, ▷ Delarivière Manley, Catherine Trotter, ▷ Nicholas Rowe, ▷ Mary Pix, ▷ Colley Cibber, and the actress ▷ Anne Oldfield, who played leading roles in several of her plays. Her death came after a prolonged period of ill-health, and she was buried at St Paul's church, in Covent Garden.

Bib: Bowyer, J., *The Celebrated Mrs. Centlivre*; Morgan, F. (ed.), *The Female Wits*.

Cerberus

▷ Hades.

Chamberlain's Men, The Lord

The more important of the two leading companies of actors in the reigns of ▷ Elizabeth 1 and ▷ James 1, and the one to which ▷ Shakespeare belonged as both an actor and playwright. All companies of actors had to have licences in order to perform, and this meant that they had to have the patronage of some leading nobleman, or to be attached to the royal household. The Lord Chamberlain's Men seems to have been formed in 1594 by a regrouping of various companies depleted by a plague epidemic. Its patron was Lord Hunsdon who held the office of Lord Chamberlain at the royal court. After the accession of James I, the King himself became its patron, and the company was known as 'the King's Men'. It was first managed by ▷ James Burbage, builder of the first English theatre (1576), and from 1597 to 1619 by his son, ▷ Richard Burbage, who was one of the leading tragic actors of the day. It played at court, and at a number of theatres in London under the control of the Burbages; its most lasting homes were at the ▷ Globe on the south bank of the ▷ Thames, and at the ▷ Blackfriars on the north bank. No doubt it was the popularity of Shakespeare's plays, both at court and among the general public, which gave the company its commanding position, though the quality of Burbage's acting must also have counted. Its rival was ▷ Edward Alleyn's ▷ Lord Admiral's Men. The King's Men retained their supremacy among the acting companies until the closing of the theatres by ▷ Parliament in 1642.

▷ Acting.

Chambers, Sir Edmund (1866–1954)
Scholar. The exceptional breadth and exactness of his work on English literature make his books indispensable reference works for students of English literature in the medieval and Elizabethan periods. His best-known works are: *The Medieval Stage* (1903); *The Elizabethan Stage* (1923); *William Shakespeare* (1930).

Chancellor, The Lord
The office of Lord Chancellor existed before the Norman Conquest (1066) and has always been one of the most important in the state, although its outstanding political importance diminished after the resignation of ▷ Sir Thomas More in 1532, owing to his disagreement with ▷ Henry VIII's religious policy. In the ▷ Middle Ages the Chancellor was the king's secretary and keeper of the seal which authorized public enactments. This closeness to the centre of power often meant that he was second only to the king himself. In the 14th century he took upon himself the task of hearing appeals from subjects who were unable to get justice through the Common Law Courts. He thus became the head of a new ▷ Court of Law, the ▷ Court of Chancery, operating a new department of law, called the Law of Equity. The Lord Chancellor also presided over meetings of the Great Council of the Barons in medieval times, and he still presides over its historical descendant, the House of Lords, *ie* the Upper House of Parliament. As the House of Lords contains judges who meet as the highest court of judicial appeal in the country, the Lord Chancellor presides over this too, and in this capacity he is the head of the English judicial system. Finally, the Lord Chancellor is *ex officio* a member of every Cabinet and the nearest equivalent in England to a Minister of Justice.

Chandler, Raymond (1888–1959)
▷ Detective fiction.

Changeling, The (1622)
A poetic tragedy by ▷ Thomas Middleton and ▷ William Rowley. Rowley seems in fact to have been responsible for the comic subplot, the value of which is contested; the play is sometimes produced without it, since the connection between the two plots is loose. The main plot, by Middleton, concerns the murder by ▷ Beatrice-Joanna of her prospective husband, Alonso de Piracquo, so that she can marry another man. To execute the murder she employs one of her admirers, the servant ▷ De Flores, a man who physically revolts her, as though by employing such a man she could herself remain free of the guilt and horror of the crime. Instead, De Flores insists that they are now partners and equals in the sin of bloodshed, and blackmails her into becoming his mistress. The play is one of the greatest in English after ▷ Shakespeare; it is written in sober, forceful ▷ blank verse which is one of the finest late ▷ Jacobean examples of this medium. The main plot is taken from *God's Revenge against Murther* by John Reynolds.

Chapbooks
The name for a kind of cheap literature which flourished from the 16th to the 18th century, after which they were replaced by other forms. They were so called because they were sold by 'chapmen' or travelling dealers. Their contents consisted commonly of traditional romances retold, often from the French, in crude form: ▷ *Bevis of Hampton*, *Guy of Warwick*, *Till Eulenspiegel*, ▷ *Doctor Faustus*, are examples. Some of them, such as *Dick Whittington*, about the poor boy who ended up as Lord Mayor of London, have survived as children's stories to the present day, and are often the theme of Christmas ▷ pantomines.

Chapman, George (?1559–?1634)

Poet and dramatist. As a poet he is particularly famous for one of the best-known translations of ▷ Homer's ▷ *Odyssey* and ▷ *Iliad*. It is, however, a very free translation, expressing more of Chapman himself, as an Elizabethan intellectual with strong philosophical interests characteristic of his time, than of the spirit of the ancient Greek poet. He saw the epics as heroic exemplifications of moral greatness, in accordance with ▷ Stoic ethical categories much later than Homer. In his conception, the great man had strong passions, but also strong pride which raised him above the corrupting influences of society; on the other hand, this passion and pride must be tempered by philosophical fortitude and discipline if they are not to be self-destructive. The dramatic conflicts implied in this view of Homer dominate Chapman's tragedies (1603–31): ▷ *The Tragedy of Bussy d'Ambois*; *The Conspiracy and Tragedy of Charles Duke of Byron*; *The Revenge of Bussy d'Ambois*; and *Caesar and Pompey*. Of these the first is acknowledged to be the finest; all of them contain fine passages, and none is without fairly serious imperfections. Bussy is a magnificent portrayal of the heroic man who dominates his morally mean environment but cannot control his passions; Clermont, his brother, in *The Revenge*, is a less successful example of the man of tempered passion and ▷ stoical calm. Chapman also wrote eight comedies including ▷ *May Day* and completed the narrative poem *Hero and Leander*, left unfinished by ▷ Christopher Marlowe.

Bib: Bradbrook, M. C., *George Chapman*; Ide, Richard S., *Possessed with Greatness*.

Characters, Theophrastian

In the early 17th century a form of ▷ essay devoted to the description of human and social types grew up, and collections of such essays were known as 'Characters'. The origin of the fashion is in the brief sketches by one character of another in the comedies of the time – *eg* those of ▷ Dekker and ▷ Jonson – and in the verse satires of such poets as ▷ Donne and ▷ Hall. The tone was always light and often satirical; as a literary form, Characters displaced the satirical ▷ pamphlet popular in the last decade of the 16th century written by such men as ▷ Greene and ▷ Nashe. The basic pattern of the form was the *Characters* of the ancient Greek writer, ▷ Theophrastus (3rd century BC); hence the designation 'Theophrastian'.

The two most famous collections were that of Sir Thomas Overbury – partly by other hands – published in 1614, and *Microcosmographie* by ▷ John Earle, published in 1628. The fashion continued, though it became less popular, throughout the 17th century and into the 18th. It was eventually superseded by the more elaborate and individualized studies by ▷ Addison and ▷ Steele in the *Spectator*, especially the ▷ De Coverley papers, and by the growth of the 18th-century novel.

Charge of the Light Brigade, The

A famous poem by Alfred, ▷ Lord Tennyson about the episode in the battle of Balaclava (1854) in the Crimean War, between the British and the French on one side and the Russians on the other. The charge was of great heroism but an act of folly based on a misunderstood order. Tennyson celebrates the heroism in vivid terms. Curiously enough his poem called *The Charge of the Heavy Brigade*, which occurred in the same battle and was successful, is much less well-known, although it has equal merit.

Charity Schools

▷ Schools in England.

Charke, Charlotte (1713–60)

Actress, manager, puppeteer, dramatist, novelist. Youngest child of the actor, manager, and dramatist ▷ Colley Cibber, and his wife, the former actress Katherine Shore. By the time she was four, Charlotte expressed a preference for masculine clothing, which she resumed at intervals throughout her later career. In 1730 she married Richard Charke, a musician and actor employed at ▷ Drury Lane. She worked as an actress and dancer at Drury Lane and joined her brother ▷ Theophilus Cibber among a group of performers who deserted to the Haymarket Theatre in 1733. There she added more than a dozen male roles to her repertory of female ones, including Macheath in ▷ *The Beggar's Opera*, George Barnwell in ▷ *The London Merchant*, and Lothario in ▷ *The Fair Penitent*. Later she acted Polly in *The Beggar's Opera*, and Millwood in *The London Merchant*. In 1736 Charke joined ▷ Henry Giffard's company at ▷ Lincoln's Inn Fields. From 1737 she managed a succession of businesses, including a puppet theatre. In 1745 she was married again, clandestinely, to John Sacheverell. He died soon afterwards, leaving her penniless, and her subsequent series of odd jobs in London and the provinces did nothing to alleviate her distresses. Estranged from her father for many years, she attempted unsuccessfully to heal the rift in 1755. Her memoirs, *A Narrative of the Life of Mrs Charlotte Charke* were published in eight instalments, in 1755, and again posthumously, in 1775. Her published works also include a play, *The Art of Management* (1735), the novel, *The History of Henry Dumont, Esq., and Miss Charlotte Evelyn* (1756), and two short novels, *The Mercer; Or Fatal Extravagance* (1755), and *The Lover's Treat; Or Unnatural Hatred* (1758).

Bib: Burnim, K. A., and Langhans, E. A., (eds.) *A Biographical Dictionary of Actors, Actresses, Musicians, Dancers, Managers, and Other Stage Personnel in London 1660–1800*; Charke, C., *A Narrative of the Life of Mrs Charlotte Charke*; Todd, J. (ed.), *A Dictionary of British and American Women Writers*.

Charlemagne (742–814)
King of the Franks, son of Pepin the Short and crowned emperor of the western world by Pope Leo III on Christmas day 800. The subject of heroic legends and romances, including ▷ epics by ▷ Boiardo, ▷ Ariosto and ▷ Tasso, and *chansons de geste*, epic poems in Old French, of which the best known is the early 12th-century *Chanson de Roland*. Off the battlefield, he reformed Frankish law, introduced jury-courts and a new coinage, and furthered missionary work and monastic reform. Most important to English literature was the 'Carolingian Renaissance' of learning he established at court, led by the Northumbrian Alcuin, and imitated a century later by ▷ King Alfred.

Charles, Duc d'Orléans (1394–1465)
Poet, and nephew of Charles VI of France, who was captured at the battle of ▷ Agincourt (1415) and spent 25 years as a prisoner in England. During this time he composed the ▷ ballades which form the collection known as the *Livre de Prison*. He is credited with large numbers of English translations of his French poems. On returning to France, he established his court at Blois, which became famous as a literary centre.
▷ Agincourt.
Bib: Steele, R. and Day, M. (eds.), *The English Poems of Charles of Orleans*.

Charles I
King of Great Britain and Ireland (1625–49). He had limited intellectual abilities, and the causes of religious and economic conflict were so strong during his reign that it ended in civil war, his defeat and his execution. He created around him a court of taste, refinement and distinction. His connoisseurship led to a fine collection of pictures later dispersed by ▷ Oliver Cromwell, who sold them to obtain international currency. His patronage of the Flemish artist Van Dyck resulted in some highly flattering portraits which have done the king much good with posterity. His personal qualities, his tragic end and his nobility in its endurance were the basis of a strong sentimental, sometimes even a religious, devotion to his memory. For example, there are churches dedicated to Charles the Martyr in a few places (*eg* Tunbridge Wells) in Britain.
▷ Civil wars.

Charles II
King of Great Britian and Ireland (1660–85). The ▷ Restoration of the monarchy brought him back from exile after the ▷ Interregnum since the execution of his father, ▷ Charles I, in 1649. Politically unscrupulous, he was nonetheless one of the most intelligent kings in English history. His court was a centre of culture and wit as well as of moral licentiousness. His lack of scruple enabled him to raise the monarchy to a new pitch of popularity, in spite of the growing strength of Parliament and its increasing independence of royal authority. His was the last royal court in England to be a centre of cultural vitality.
▷ Cavalier poets.

Charon
In Greek legend, the ferryman who for a fee took the souls of the dead across the River Styx to ▷ Hades.

Charter companies
These were joint stock companies authorized by the Crown to make treaties, to set up trading colonies and to employ armed forces for their protection. The British Empire in India, the Far East and Africa was developed almost entirely by them. The British government only took over their responsibilities when forced to do so by political pressure, *eg* in India (1858), in Nigeria (1900), in Rhodesia (1923).
▷ Companies, Joint Stock; East India Company.

Charterhouse
▷ Carthusians.

Chartist movement
A working-class political movement which flourished between 1837 and 1848. It arose because the ▷ Reform Bill of 1832 had reformed ▷ Parliament in favour of middle-class political rights but had left the working-class without them. The Chartists wanted

Parliament to be closely responsible to the nation as a whole and to reform an electoral system according to which the poor were excluded from membership of Parliament and denied the right to vote others into membership by their lack of the necessary property qualification. Some regions were more heavily represented in Parliament than others and all voting was subject to bribery or intimidation because votes had to be declared publicly. Consequently they put forward their Charter containing Six Points: 1 votes for all males; 2 annually elected Parliaments (instead of general elections every seven years); 3 payment of Members of Parliament (so that poor men could have political careers); 4 secret voting (voting 'by ballot'); 5 abolition of the property qualification for candidates seeking election; 6 electoral districts equal in population. The movement seemed to be a complete failure, but all these points became law between 1860 and 1914 except the demand for annually elected parliaments. The Chartists attracted an ardent following but they were badly led. Allusions are made to them in those novels between 1840 and 1860 which were concerned with 'the Condition-of-the-People Question', *eg* ▷ *Sybil* by ▷ Benjamin Disraeli. This serious discussion of the social crisis of the second quarter of the 19th century was greatly stimulated by ▷ Thomas Carlyle's essay *Chartism* (1839), one of his fiercest and most influential writings.

Chaste Maid in Cheapside, A (1613)

A comedy by ▷ Thomas Middleton. It is one of the ▷ 'citizen comedies' of the ▷ Jacobean period, with a characteristic theme of a merchant (Yellowhammer) scheming against Sir Walter Whorehound, a dissolute landed gentleman, so as to secure marriage with his daughter and entry into the landowning class, while Whorehound in turn tries to marry off his mistress to Yellowhammer's son and thereby gain Yellowhammer's money. These intrigues of the gentry and the citizenry against each other were a common theme of the comedies of the time. The play makes mock of both classes, and has a characteristic robustness in the way in which it uses the social ▷ satire at a deeper level than the merely topical relationships, so as to bring out basic types of human greed, vanity, and lust, in the tradition of ▷ Ben Jonson's 'comedy of humours'.

▷ Humours, Comedy of.

Chatterton, Thomas (1752–70)

Poet. Chatterton's father, a schoolmaster in Bristol, died before he was born, and he was educated at a charity school, then apprenticed to an attorney. He wrote precociously in all the genres of the day: mock-heroic couplets, ▷ Hudibrastics, political satire imitative of ▷ Charles Churchill, African eclogues in the manner of ▷ William Collins and elegiac poetry in the manner of ▷ Thomas Gray. But his most original compositions were pseudo-medieval concoctions concerned with 15th-century Bristol. Influenced by the fashionable medievalism of ▷ James Macpherson, ▷ Thomas Percy, and ▷ Horace Walpole, Chatterton claimed to have discovered lyric poems and a 'tragycal enterlude' by a 15th-century monk, Thomas Rowley, among the documents of the church of St Mary Redcliffe, where his uncle was sexton. The publisher Dodsley rejected the pieces, but they deceived Walpole for a time, and the poet was encouraged to move from Bristol to London. He published some non-medieval poems in journals under his own name, and a burletta (comic opera) by him was accepted for performance at Drury Lane. Then, at the age of 17, in a fit of despondency, he poisoned himself with arsenic.

It was not until seven years later that the Rowley poems were definitively unmasked by the Chaucerian scholar, Thomas Tyrrwhitt. Their language is an artificial amalgam of medieval, Elizabethan and contemporary elements, typical of the omnivorous eclecticism of the period. But occasionally, as in 'An Excelente Balade of Charitie', Chatterton succeeds in evoking a unique exotic world of his own. During the Romantic period Chatterton's reputation lost all associations with hackwork and ▷ Grub Street, and only the 'medieval' lyrics were remembered. His early death took on a mythical quality, making him a symbol, even a stereotype, of youthful poetic genius neglected by a prosaic world. ▷ William Wordsworth referred to Chatterton as a 'marvellous Boy' in *Resolution and Independence*. ▷ Samuel Taylor Coleridge wrote *A Monody on the Death of Chatterton*. ▷ John Keats dedicated his ▷ *Endymion* to his memory, and ▷ Percy Bysshe Shelley compared him with Keats in ▷ *Adonais*.
Bib: Kelly, L., *The Marvellous Boy: The Life and Myth of Thomas Chatterton*.

Chaucer, Geoffrey (c 1340–1400)

Influential poet of the 14th century who occupies a privileged place in the history of English literary traditions because his work has been continuously transcribed, published, read and commented upon since his death.

He was the son of a London vintner, John

Chaucer from the Ellesmere manuscript of
The Canterbury Tales

Chaucer (1312–68), and served in the court of
▷ Edward III's son Lionel (later Duke of
Clarence). In 1359 he was taken prisoner
while fighting in France with Edward III, and
ransomed. His wife, Phillipa de Roet, whom
he married perhaps in 1366, was the sister of
▷ John of Gaunt's third wife, Katherine
Swynford. Substantial records exist of
Chaucer's career in royal service, as a member
of the court and diplomat. He is first recorded
as a member of the royal household in 1367
and he made several diplomatic journeys in
France and Italy, which perhaps gave him
the opportunity to gain access to the work of
important 14th-century Italian writers
(▷ Dante, ▷ Petrarch, ▷ Boccaccio). He
was appointed controller of customs in the
Port of London in 1374, was 'knight of the
shire' of Kent in 1386 (*ie*, represented Kent
in the House of Commons), and was
appointed clerk of the king's works in 1389
and then deputy forester of the king's forest
at Petherton in Somerset in 1391. He returned
to London for the last years of his life and
was buried in Westminster Abbey. His tomb,
erected some time later (1555?) gives the date
of his death as 25 October 1400.

The upward mobility of Chaucer's family
is clear not only from the professional life of
Chaucer himself but also from that of his son
Thomas, who married into the nobility and
became one of the richest men in England at
the time. Thomas's daughter, Alice, married
William de la Pole, Duke of Suffolk, and
their grandson, John, Earl of Lincoln, was
heir designate to the throne of ▷ Richard III.
We may only speculate about the part
Chaucer's literary activities played in
advancing his social status and that of his
family. Although more records survive of
Chaucer's professional life than any other
English writer of the time, the records do not
contain any references to his literary labours.
Thus dating Chaucer's literary works is an
exercise in hypothesis and depends largely on
information provided in Chaucer's own list of
works, notably in the prologue to the
▷ *Legend of Good Women*, and in the
prologue to the ▷ *Man of Law's Tale*.

Chaucer's literary work is notable for its
range and diversity. It explores the
possibilities of a number of different literary
genres, and includes ▷ dream-vision poems
(the ▷ *Book of the Duchess*, the ▷ *House of
Fame*, the ▷ *Parliament of Foulys*, the
▷ *Legend of Good Women*), a classical love-
tragedy (▷ *Troilus and Criseyde*), story-
collections (the *Legend of Good Women*, and
the ▷ *Canterbury Tales*, which itself
encompasses a great range and variety of
genres), as well as shorter lyrical texts,
translations (of ▷ Boethius's *Consolation of
Philosophy* and probably the first part of the
English translation of the ▷ *Roman de la
Rose*) and scientific treatises (on the
Astrolabe, and the *Equatorie of the Planets*,
which is now generally accepted as Chaucer's
work).

A distinctive feature of Chaucer's literary
work is that it engages not only with French
and Latin literary traditions but also with the
work of earlier and contemporary Italian
writers (notably ▷ Boccaccio). His work
became a reference point for later poets in
English, and is frequently discussed in terms
which suggest it played a founding role in the
establishment of an English literary tradition
– a point neatly underlined by the subsequent
establishment of Poet's Corner in
Westminster Abbey, around Chaucer's tomb.
▷ Cecilia, St; Edward III; John of
Gaunt.
Bib: Benson, L., et al. (eds.), *The Riverside
Chaucer*; Boitani, P. and Mann, J. (eds.), *The
Cambridge Chaucer Companion*; Crow, M. C.
and Olsen, C. C. (eds.), *Chaucer Life Records*.

Cheapside

A street in the City of London. In the
▷ Middle Ages it was the site of a busy
market and owed its name to the Old English
word *céap*, 'to buy and sell'.

Chekhov, Anton Pavlovich (1860–1904)
Russian dramatist and short-story writer. In
his last four plays (*Seagull*, *Uncle Vanya*,
Three Sisters, *The Cherry Orchard*) he evolved
a dramatic form and idiom of dialogue which
were highly original and had a great influence
on 20th-century drama. His originality lay in
his combination of faithfulness to the surface
of life with poetic evocation of underlying
experience. This he achieved partly by
exploiting the character of human
conversation when it seems to be engaged in
communication, but is actually concerned
with the incommunicable. This leads on to
the non-communicating dialogue in the work
of playwrights such as ▷ Beckett and
▷ Pinter, when the characters on the stage
alternately baffle and enlighten the audience
by the undercurrents implicit in their words.
The realism of Chekhov's stories is similarly
subtle and original; they have similar
faithfulness to surface combined with delicate
artistic pattern, giving significance to seeming
irrelevance and slightness of incident. An
outstanding exponent of the method in
English is the New Zealand writer
▷ Katherine Mansfield.
Bib: Magarshack, D., *The Plays of Anton
Chekhov*; Styan, J. L., *Chekhov in
Performance*.

Chelsea
A district in the West End of London,
bordering the north side of the Thames, and
well known for its literary and artistic
associations. ▷ Sir Thomas More, author of
Utopia, lived there, and so did ▷ Thomas
Carlyle, the 'Sage of Chelsea'. In the 19th
century it became, and has remained, a centre
for painters. Its most famous architectural
monument is the Chelsea Hospital, designed
by ▷ Christopher Wren and founded as a
home for disabled solders by ▷ Charles II.

Cherub
In the Old Testament of the Bible (pl.
cherubim(s)), angelic beings who in *Genesis*
3:24 guard Paradise; in *Ezekiel* I attend the
divine chariot; in *1 Kings* 1:6 and 8 are
pictured in Solomon's Temple. They are
depicted with the wings of birds and with
human or animal faces. In medieval Christian
tradition they were held to be the second of
the nine orders of ▷ angels. When classical
influence widely affected Christian art in the
16th and 17th centuries, cherubs came to be
represented as winged (bodiless heads of)
children. They lost all grandeur of mystical
and religious symbolism and were chiefly
used as decorative motifs. They even become
closely associated with the classical image of

the child god of love, ▷ Cupid, used in a
similar way as a decorative motif on furniture,
walls, etc.

Cheshire Cheese, The
A tavern off ▷ Fleet Street in London, and
a favourite resort of ▷ Ben Jonson, and,
after it was rebuilt, of ▷ Samuel Johnson
and of ▷ Yeats, who liked to claim it as a
haunt. It still exists.

Chester Cycle
A ▷ cycle of plays, covering episodes from
Christian history from the Creation to the
Last Judgement, performed at Chester in
Whitsun week during the 15th and 16th
centuries (over Monday, Tuesday,
Wednesday), the last recorded performance
being in 1575. The style and themes of its 25
pageants are more homogeneous than those
found in the other major play cycles of
▷ York, ▷ Wakefield and ▷ N-Town.
Bib: Lumiansky, R. M. and Mills, D. (eds.),
The Chester Mystery Cycle.

**Chesterton, G. K. (Gilbert Keith) (1874–
1936)**
An extremely versatile writer of essays,
stories, novels, poems; Chesterton is best
described as a polemicist, since polemics
entered into everything he wrote, whether it
was detective stories (the Father Brown series;
1911, 1914, 1926, 1927), fantasy (*The Man
who was Thursday*, 1908), comic verse, or
religious studies such as *St Francis of Assisi*
(1923) or *St Thomas Aquinas* (1933). He
wrote against life-denial, whether manifested
in the denial of humanity in the Victorian
political economy, or the sceptical withdrawal
into ▷ aestheticism of the 1890s. His basis
of attack was a conviction that life is to be
enjoyed with all the faculties; he also had the
belief that such fullness of life required a
religion large enough to comprehend all the
spiritual and moral potentialities in man, and
he found this religion in Roman Catholicism.
He was not received into the Catholic Church
until 1922, but from *The Napoleon of Notting
Hill* (1904) – a fantasy about a war between
London boroughs – he shows the romantic
medievalism which for him was a large part
of the appeal of Catholicism. The period of
his greatest influence was probably between
1900 and 1914, when he belonged to a group
of vigorous witty polemicists, including
▷ George Bernard Shaw, ▷ H. G. Wells,
▷ Hilaire Belloc. He was from the first an
ally of the Catholic Belloc against the agnostic
socialists, Wells and Shaw. He had in
common with both his antagonists a genius
for vivid particularity strongly reminiscent of

the Victorian novelist, ▷ Charles Dickens; with Shaw he shared a delight in witty and disturbing paradox, which he used as Shaw did, to startle his readers out of the acceptance of platitudes into genuine thinking. In spite of his homely, zestful humanity, one notices nowadays a journalistic superficiality about Chesterton's work, as though he felt that his audience demanded entertainment as the indispensable reward for receiving enlightenment, and this may account for the neglect of his work since his death.

Politically, with Belloc, he preached an alternative to socialism in Distributism, a vision of a society of small proprietors. His critical work perhaps survives better than his other work; it included studies of ▷ Browning (1903), ▷ Dickens (1906), ▷ Thackeray (1909), ▷ Chaucer (1932), and *The Victorian Age in Literature* (1913). He is otherwise perhaps best read in selection, for instance in *Selected Stories* (ed. K. Amis) and *G. K. Chesterton: A Selection from his Non-fictional Prose* (selected by W. H. Auden).

▷ Catholicism in English literature; Detective fiction.
Bib: Belloc, H., *The Place of Chesterton in English Letters*; Canovan, H., *Chesterton, Radical Populist*; Hollis, C., *The Mind of Chesterton*.

Chettle, Henry (1560–1607)
An Elizabethan playwright and printer who collaborated with a number of his contemporaries and is the sole author of a revenge drama, *Hoffman* (1602). He is best remembered for printing ▷ Robert Greene's famous attack on ▷ Shakespeare and ▷ Marlowe, *A Groatsworth of Wit* (1592). He subsequently apologized to Shakespeare in his *Kind-Heart's Dream*, praising Shakespeare's 'uprightness of dealing' and his 'honesty'.

Chevalier of St George
'Chevalier' means literally horseman, and in medieval France was equivalent to knight. After the ▷ Revolution of 1688 and the Act of Settlement of 1701 excluding the Catholic members of the House of ▷ Stuart from the English throne, James Stuart, the son of ▷ James II, was known as the Chevalier of St George as a courtesy title; he was otherwise known as the ▷ Old Pretender (*ie* claimant to the throne) in distinction from his son, Charles Stuart, known both as the Young Pretender and the Young Chevalier.

Chevy Chase, The Ballad of
A famous English ▷ ballad, probably dating from the 15th century. It issues from the border wars which were intermittent between England and Scotland from the 14th to 16th centuries. Lord Douglas, head of the principal Scottish border family, attacks Percy, Earl of Northumberland, who has defied him by coming for a three days' hunt on the Scottish side of the border. Both Percy and Douglas are killed in the ensuing battle. The ballad has been well-known since Bishop ▷ Percy published it in his *Reliques* in 1765, but, earlier, ▷ Joseph Addison praised the poem in the *Spectator* (70), and so did ▷ Sir Philip Sidney in his *Apologie*.
▷ *Otterbourne, the Battle of.*

Child labour
The use of children in agricultural labour was widespread, and not necessarily pernicious, up till the 19th century, but their use in factories and mines after 1800 and during the ▷ Industrial Revolution aroused widespread indignation and led to reform. The Factory Act of 1833 (▷ Factories) limited their working hours in factories and in 1847 their hours were restricted to ten. In 1842 the Mines Act forbade the employment of women and of children under ten underground; this evil was very old, but had become much severer with the expansion of the coal industry in the 18th century after the invention of steam-powered machinery. An old abuse, too, was the employment of little boys to clean chimneys; the boys were made to climb inside the chimneys. Public indignation against the practice was aroused by ▷ Charles Kingsley's ▷ *Water Babies* (1863), but it was only effectively prohibited in 1875. The Victorian age saw the abolition of the worst abuses of children, as well as the establishment of the first universal system of education in England. Since 1939 it has been illegal to employ children under 15.

Childe
Before a name, *eg* Childe Harold, the word is the relic of a medieval title used for young men awaiting the order of ▷ knighthood.

Childe Harold's Pilgrimage (1812–18)
A semi-autobiographical poem in ▷ Spenserian stanzas by ▷ Lord Byron, describing the wanderings of a young man seeking escape from the *ennui* caused by over-indulgence at home. Cantos I and II (1812) describe his wanderings around the Mediterranean, ending with a lament for Greece enslaved by the Turks. The writing is sometimes very slapdash. Cantos III (1816) and IV (1818) are poetically superior, being less concerned with an affectation of solitude and mystery, and focussing on what really

interested the poet: social activity and the stir of great events. In the third canto occurs the famous description of the interrupted ball in Brussels on the eve of the battle of Waterloo (stanzas xxi–xxv). In the fourth canto Byron abandons the fictional protagonist and writes in the first person, evoking the large reversals of history, as he contemplates the great Italian cities of Venice, Rome and Florence. The long meditation in the Coliseum at night, with its evocation of the dying gladiator, is very moving in a broad, rhetorical way. The poem was very popular at the time, not least for its 'Byronic' protagonist – self-regarding, proud and mysterious. Today, with the partial exception of Canto IV, it is less highly regarded than Byron's comic works in *ottava rima*.

Childe Roland to the Dark Tower Came
One of the most famous poems by ▷ Robert Browning. He called it a 'Dramatic Romance' and it was published in ▷ *Men and Women*, 1855. It describes a journey or 'quest' (in the tradition of medieval knightly romances) which has lasted so long that Roland is almost in despair. In the poem, he reaches his destination, the tower, which stands in the middle of a great wasteland full of the signs of death. The poem ends with his sounding his horn to signal his arrival. In spite of its sombreness, the poem has a vigour of style, characteristic of Browning, which communicates itself as the most important part of its otherwise cloudy meaning. Browning, too often associated with facile optimism, is the poet here of courage and energy in the face of desperate circumstances.

The title is a quotation from ▷ Shakespeare's ▷ *King Lear*, where it may be an echo of a still older ballad.

Children in the Wood (Babes in the Wood)
A ballad (1593) well-known for its story, which is often retold in books of children's fairy tales (▷ Children's books). It concerns the plot of a wicked uncle to murder his little nephew and niece, whose property he means to seize. The hired murderers abandon the children in the forest, where they perish and the birds cover them over with leaves. The wicked uncle is then punished by God, with the loss of his son, his wealth and eventually his life.

Children of St Paul's
▷ Paul's, Children of St.

Children's books
Until the 19th century, children were not regarded as beings with their own kind of experience and values, and therefore did not have books written specifically for their entertainment. The literature available to them included popular versions of old romances, such as ▷ *Bevis of Hampton*, and magical folk-tales, such as ▷ *Jack the Giant-Killer*, which appeared in ▷ chapbooks. Children also read such works as ▷ John Bunyan's ▷ *Pilgrim's Progress*, ▷ Daniel Defoe's ▷ *Robinson Crusoe* (1719), and ▷ Jonathan Swift's ▷ *Gulliver's Travels* (1726); ▷ Perrault's collection of French ▷ fairy-tales appeared in English as *Mother Goose's Fairy Tales* in 1729.

During the ▷ Romantic period it was recognized that childhood experience was a world of its own and, influenced, in many cases, by Rousseau's ideas on education, books began to be written especially to appeal to children. Such works as Thomas Day's *Merton and Sandford* (1783–9), ▷ Maria Edgeworth's *Moral Tales* (1801) and Mrs Sherwood's *The Fairchild Family* (1818) usually had a serious moral tone, but showed an understanding of a child's mind that was lacking from Anne and Jane Taylor's cautionary tales in verse (later to be parodied by ▷ Hilaire Belloc in *The Bad Child's Book of Beasts* etc.).

It was not until the Victorian period that writers began extensively to try to please children, without attempting to improve them at the same time. ▷ Edward Lear's *Book of Nonsense* (1846) and ▷ Lewis Carroll's *Alice* books combine fantasy with humour. Romance and magic had a strong appeal to the Victorians, and fairy stories from all over the world were presented in versions for children. The collection of the brothers ▷ Grimm had appeared in 1824 as *German Popular Stories* and ▷ Hans Christian Andersen's original compositions were translated into English in 1846. Andrew Lang's *Fairy Books* were published later in the century. Adventure stories for boys, such as ▷ Captain Frederick Marryat's *Masterman Ready* (1841) and ▷ Robert Louis Stevenson's ▷ *Treasure Island* (1883) became a flourishing genre, but the tradition of moral improvement persisted in such books as ▷ Charles Kingsley's ▷ *Water Babies* (1863). Children's literature is a field to which women writers have made a notable contribution; in the latter half of the 19th century enduring classics were written by Mrs Molesworth (*The Tapestry Room*, 1879), Louisa May Alcott (*Little Women*, 1868), Anna Sewell (*Black Beauty*, 1877) and E. Nesbit (*The Story of the Treasure-Seekers*, 1899, etc.).

Animals have loomed large in children's

books. Beatrix Potter's *Peter Rabbit* appeared in 1902 (doing much to establish the book where text and illustrations were of equal importance), Kenneth Grahame's *The Wind in the Willows* in 1908, the first of Hugh Lofting's *Dr Dolittle* books in 1920, ▷ A. A. Milne's *Winnie the Pooh* in 1926 and the first of Alison Uttley's *Little Grey Rabbit* books in 1929. Charges of anthropomorphism seem to have had little effect on the popularity of these books, and another writer whose lack of critical acclaim has hardly diminished her sales is Enid Blyton. Recently, allegations of racism and sexism have been laid against old favourites, and there have been efforts to bring children's literature into touch with 20th-century problems, such as single-parent families and racial prejudice. As well as writers (*eg* Noel Streatfeild and Nina Bawden) who have concerned themselves with stories about everyday life, there have been others who have continued the tradition of magical fantasy. ▷ Tolkien's *The Hobbit*, Philippa Pierce's *Tom's Midnight Garden*, ▷ C. S. Lewis's *Tales of Narnia*, Ursula Le Guin's stories about *Earthsea* and the work of Alan Garner all fall into this category. In a rather different field, Rosemary Sutcliff has won recognition for the careful research underlying her historical novels. Mention should also be made of Ladybird books, which, in addition to their fiction publications, have done much to introduce children to a wide variety of topics, from music to magnetism. Following Robert Louis Stevenson's *A Child's Garden of Verses* (1885), children's verse has been written by ▷ Belloc, ▷ De La Mare, ▷ A. A. Milne, ▷ Ted Hughes and Charles Causley.

Chiltern Hundreds

A region in the Chiltern Hills north of London belonging to the Crown. It is a rule that Members of ▷ Parliament may not resign between elections, and another rule precludes their holding offices of profit under the Crown. If a Member wishes to resign between elections, he applies for the Stewardship of the Chiltern Hundreds (to which no duties are now attached) and on receiving it, he becomes automatically disqualified from sitting in Parliament. The income from the office is now merely nominal.

Chippendale, Thomas (1718–79)

A famous furniture designer, noted for the combination of elegance and solidity in his designs. His work was very much imitated so that 'Chippendale style' is the most familiar pattern of 18th-century furniture in England.

▷ Furnishings and furniture.

Chloe

In ancient Greek pastoral, a name for a shepherdess, *eg Daphnis and Chloe* (2nd century AD). In 17th- and 18th-century mock-pastoral, the name was sometimes given to disguise actual ladies when they were referred to in poetry or prose, *eg* ▷ Pope uses the name for Lady Suffolk in *Moral Essays* ii.

Cholera

A deadly disease flourishing in dirty living conditions and bad sanitation. The rapid and insanitary growth of industrial towns in England in the first half of the 19th century (the ▷ Industrial Revolution) led to its first occurrence here in 1832; it came again in 1848. The threat of it accelerated the improvement of sanitation in English towns, but slums were not eliminated in the 19th century and it continues to be feared. However the last visitation in 1892–5 caused so few deaths that by then it was clear that the danger had been mastered.

Chrétien de Troyes (fl 1170–90)

French writer of sophisticated and influential courtly narratives. Nothing certain is known of his life but he seems to have had the patronage of Marie, Countess of Champagne (1160–80), and then Phillip of Flanders (c 1180–90). Five of his Arthurian romances survive: *Erec et Enide*, *Cligés*, *Yvain* (later translated into Middle English and other European vernaculars), *Le Chevalier de la Charrette* (which centres on the experiences of ▷ Lancelot and which seems to have been left unfinished by Chrétien), *Perceval* (Chrétien's Grail story which was left unfinished but was continued by later writers). In the prologue to *Cligés*, he claims to have written a number of other poems on Ovidian subjects, including an art of love, and a version of the ▷ Tristan story.
▷ Arthur, King.
Bib: Owen, D. D. R. (trans.), *Chrétien de Troyes: Arthurian Romances*.

Christabel (1816)

An unfinished narrative poem by ▷ Samuel Taylor Coleridge, the first part written in 1797 and the second in 1800. The story derives from the popular folk-ballad tradition. Christabel, daughter of Sir Leoline, finds a distressed lady, Geraldine, in the woods and takes her back to the castle, unaware that she is really an enchantress. Though she discovers Geraldine's nature, Christabel is forced by a spell to keep silent before her father. There is a strange confusion of sympathies in the author's treatment of the relationship between the two women, and between them and Sir Leoline. The poem is in a metrically experimental form reminiscent of Anglo-Saxon alliterative metre, each line having four stresses but a varying number of syllables. Even in its fragmentary state it achieves a compulsively anxious, but at the same time exhilarating, effect.

Christian King, Most (His Most Christian Majesty)
A title assumed by the kings of France from not later than the 15th century. (Compare: 'Most Catholic King' for the kings of Spain, 'Defender of the Faith' for kings of England.)

Christie, Agatha (1890–1976)
▷ Detective fiction.

Christmas Carol, A (1843)
A story by ▷ Charles Dickens, about a miser, Scrooge, who is converted by a series of visions from a condition of mercantile avarice and misanthropy into an embodiment of the Christmas spirit, with its generosity and good will to humankind in general. By no means one of the best of Dickens's works, it nonetheless represents entertainingly his celebration of the virtues associated with Christmas (especially characteristic of his early work). He represented these virtues as the cure for the ▷ puritan narrowness of feeling and inhumanity of outlook which were the dark side of Victorian commerce. Compare the Christmas scenes in his ▷ *Pickwick Papers* (1837) and the comments of Sleary in ▷ *Hard Times*.

Christy Minstrels
Any company of entertainers disguised as negroes, usually singing comic songs. The original band was founded by George Christy of New York (19th century). This may be seen as a form of racism, since blackness was imitated and turned into a spectacle. Although black people did work as entertainers and musicians, their part in theatre history has been obscured and is only now being reconstructed.

Chronicle Plays
▷ History Plays.

Church of England
The history of the Church of England is closely bound up with the political and social history of England. In the ▷ Middle Ages the Church of England was a division of the Catholic Church of Western Europe. Ultimate authority over it, as over the rest of the Catholic Church, was vested in the Pope in Rome. The clergy consisted of an order of priests who, at the humblest level, had in

their charge the village churches and the parishes (each more or less coincident with a village) that surrounded them. The parishes were grouped into regions known as 'sees', each of which was governed by a bishop, and the sees (bishoprics) were grouped into two provinces under two archbishops, those of Canterbury and York, the Archbishop of Canterbury being the senior. The bishops and the archbishops attended Parliament, and the Church had its own assemblies or convocations, attended by the senior clergy and representatives of the lower clergy, *ie* the parish priests. This organization of the Church has survived to the present day, with the important difference that since the 16th century the Pope has ceased to be the Church's supreme authority.

The Church of England became independent in 1534, when ▷ Henry VIII caused Parliament to pass the Act of Supremacy which declared him to be the 'Supreme Head of the English Church and Clergy'. This action was political rather than religious; Henry was conservative in his religious beliefs, and reaffirmed the traditional Catholic doctrines by his Act of the Six Articles (1539). However, a ▷ Protestant party, influenced by the German reformer ▷ Martin Luther, had long been growing in England and was favoured by the Archbishop of Canterbury, ▷ Thomas Cranmer. Under the boy King ▷ Edward VI, the Protestants seized power, and Catholic doctrine was modified by Cranmer's two Books of Common Prayer (▷ Common Prayer, The Book of). These changes were accompanied by the destruction of images and the covering up of holy wall-paintings in village churches; such actions, combined with the rapacity of the nobles who seized church money, were unpopular, and partly reconciled the nation to a return to the Catholic Church under ▷ Mary I. She too became unpopular owing to her persecution of Protestants, and her successor, ▷ Elizabeth I, attempted a compromise Settlement, by means of which she hoped to keep in the Church of England both the Catholics and the extremer Protestants. She succeeded, in so far as her Settlement prevented religious conflict breaking into civil war during her reign.

The Roman Catholics were and remained a small minority, but during the first half of the 17th century the extreme Protestants (now known as ▷ Puritans) grew in strength, especially in London and in the south and east. Their hostility to the monarchy and their dislike of religious direction by bishops led in the end to the ▷ Civil War and the overthrow of ▷ Charles I. Under the Protectorship of the Puritan Oliver Cromwell, the Church of England ceased to exist as a state religious organization, but in 1660 the monarchy and the Church of England were restored, and Puritans were excluded from the Church, from political rights and from attendance at the universities of Oxford and ▷ Cambridge. From this time, the Puritans (increasingly called ▷ Dissenters or Nonconformists) set up their own Churches. Within the Church, religious differences remained and were the basis of the newly emerging political parties, the ▷ Whigs being more in sympathy with the Puritans and the ▷ Tories being closer to, though never identified with, the Roman Catholics.

During the 18th century the apathy into which the Church of England had fallen was shaken by the religious revival led by ▷ John Wesley, who worked mainly among the poorer classes. Although Wesley was forced to form a separate Methodist Church, his example inspired the Evangelical Movement within the Church of England, which by the 19th century was an important force towards social reform. A different sort of revival was led by a group of Anglicans at Oxford University, of whom ▷ John Henry Newman was the most active. The resulting ▷ Oxford (or Tractarian) Movement affirmed the spiritual independence of the Church and its continuity with the medieval Catholic Church. Newman eventually became a Roman Catholic, and the Oxford Movement lost in him its main inspiration. He left behind him, however, divisions of opinion within the Church that exist today: the High Church is composed of Anglicans who are essentially Catholic in belief, though they reject the authority of the Pope, they can be said to be descendants from Henry VIII's Reformation. The Low Church feels itself to be Protestant, and can be said to favour the Reformation of Edward VI. A third group, prominent in the mid-19th century but not to be distinguished now, was the Broad Church; it developed from the Evangelical Movement and was especially active in social and political reform. These have all existed under the common organization of the Church.

Today, the Church of England is the state Church, under the Crown, only in England; in Scotland and Wales, the Commonwealth, and the U.S.A., members of churches originally derived from the Church of England are known as ▷ Episcopalians.

Churchill, Caryl (b 1938)
British feminist (▷ Feminism) dramatist

who has produced some of her best work in collaboration with Joint Stock Theatre Company. *Light Shining in Buckinghamshire* (1976) explored the betrayal of ▷ leveller ideals during the English ▷ Civil War. *Cloud Nine* (1978) used an imperialist context to examine sexuality. Analysis of sexual stereotyping within a clear political context is characteristic of Churchill plays, especially her recent ebullient comedy about stock market swindlers, *Serious Money* (1987). Other plays include: *Owners* (1972); *Vinegar Tom* (1976); *Top Girls* (1982); *Fen* (1982); *Softcops* (1984); *A Mouthful of Birds* (1986; with David Lan).
▷ Royal Court Theatre.
Bib: Keyssar, H., *Feminist Theatre*; Wandor, M., *Carry on Understudies*.

Churchill, Charles (1731–64)
Poet and political writer. A secret ▷ marriage, contracted at the age of 17, brought an end to his academic career at Cambridge. He entered the ministry, but after several years as a curate, separated from his wife, and embarked on a literary and political career, associating himself with the political aspirations of ▷ John Wilkes. In 1763 he eloped with the 15-year-old daughter of a Westminster tradesman, but died suddenly in the following year at the age of 33.

There is a distinctive vigour to Churchill's use of the heroic couplet, though he lacks refinement or nuance. His subject matter in such poems as *The Rosciad* (1761) (by which he made his reputation), *The Prophecy of Famine* (1763), *An Epistle to William Hogarth* (1763) and *The Author* (1763) remains consistently public and ▷ Augustan, at a time when other writers were turning to more intimate themes. He lacks the restraint and poise of ▷ John Dryden and ▷ Alexander Pope however, and his spontaneity anticipates in tone the couplet satires of ▷ Lord Byron. *The Rosciad* parades the theatrical figures of the day before a judgment panel consisting of ▷ Shakespeare and ▷ Ben Jonson, and they award the laurel, predictably, to ▷ David Garrick. In other poems Churchill discusses contemporary politics and the nature of satire. He also wrote less successful works in ▷ Hudibrastic tetrameters (▷ metre), such as *The Ghost* (1762–63), in which he attacked ▷ Samuel Johnson.
Bib: Smith, R. J., *Charles Churchill*.

Cibber, Colley (1671–1757)
Actor, manager, dramatist. His first known role was as a servant in *Sir Anthony Love* in

1690, while his first opportunity at a substantial role came in 1694 in ▷ William Congreve's ▷ *The Double Dealer*. In 1696 he wrote his first play, ▷ *Love's Last Shift*, often seen as a landmark in the transition from 'hard wit' Restoration comedy to the 'comedy of sensibility'. He himself played the first of many fop parts, Sir Novelty Fashion, which he had created for himself; he afterwards played Lord Foppington in ▷ Sir John Vanbrugh's satiric sequel to the play, ▷ *The Relapse* (1696).

In 1730 Cibber was chosen, amid great controversy, as ▷ Poet Laureate. He retired from ▷ Drury Lane in 1733, afterwards writing an opera libretto, poems, essays, more plays, and his ▷ autobiography, *An Apology for the Life of Colley Cibber* (1740), still considered a primary source of information about the theatre in his time.

Throughout his life, Cibber excited controversy, involving himself in quarrels with several prominent men, notably the authors John Dennis and ▷ Henry Fielding and, most damagingly, ▷ Alexander Pope, with whom he kept up a running battle of insults for many years. His ironic misfortune was that Pope, as the better writer, gained a more lasting reputation, so that many students today know of Cibber only through Pope's harsh satires, and his real merit is forgotten.

On the other hand, he made many loyal friends, who praised his wit and good company, and remained loyal to him in extremity. His acting was celebrated and vilified by turns; he was said to be a marvellous comic, but often execrable in tragedy, which he refused to abandon.
Bib: Cibber, C., *An Apology for the Life of Colley Cibber*; Hayley, R. (ed.), *The Plays of Colley Cibber*; Koon, H., *Colley Cibber: A Biography*.

Cibber, Katherine (c1669–1734)
Singer, actress. Born Katherine Shore into a musical family, she studied voice and harpsichord with ▷ Henry Purcell. She married the actor ▷ Colley Cibber in 1693, much against her father's wishes, and with him had seven children, including the actress ▷ Charlotte (later Charke) and actor-manager, ▷ Theophilus.

Katherine Cibber began acting at the ▷ Dorset Garden Theatre in the season of 1693–4, and appeared with the same company (the ▷ United Company) at ▷ Drury Lane in the following year. She specialized in romantic roles, often involving singing.

Cibber, Susanna Maria (1714–66)
Actress, singer, dramatist. Susanna Cibber was the daughter of Thomas Arne, an upholsterer. In 1732 she sang the title role in Carey and Lampe's *Amelia* at the ▷ Haymarket Theatre, and two months later, she performed Galatea in ▷ George Handel's *Acis and Galatea*. In 1734 she married the recently widowed ▷ Theophilus Cibber, with whom she had two children, although both of these died in infancy.

The marriage was a bitter failure: her husband's taste for frequenting brothels, and his general profligacy, meant that he was perpetually in debt, and he soon began to seize his wife's assets, including portions of her salary, as well as her wardrobe and personal effects, in order to satisfy his creditors.

In 1737 she began an affair with a family friend, William Sloper, egged on by her husband, who eventually forced her at gunpoint to spend the night with Sloper. This was part of Cibber's scheme to extract money from the wealthy Sloper, and in 1738 Cibber sued Sloper, but succeeded in winning only ten pounds in damages that year, and only five hundred of the ten thousand he was claiming at the end of another lawsuit in the following year.

In 1741, after a discreet absence, and the birth of her first child by Sloper, Susanna Cibber returned to the stage, both acting and singing with great success. She sang in Handel's *Messiah*, first in Dublin, and then at its London debut in ▷ Covent Garden. Susanna Cibber seems to have been supremely gifted both as a singer and as an actress: she is said to have been Handel's favourite, and he wrote some of his best music expressly for her to perform; as an actress she played mostly in tragedy, eliciting conflicting reports as to the variety of her gestures and tones, but the general agreement was that she could wring tears out of the most hard-hearted audience. Her Juliet and Ophelia were particularly celebrated for their pathos. At her death ▷ Drury Lane stayed closed in honour of its greatest actress. She is also known to have co-authored at least one play, *The Oracle* (1752). She was buried in ▷ Westminster Abbey.
Bib: Mann, D. (ed.), *The Plays of Theophilus and Susannah Cibber*; Highfill, P. H. Jr., Burnim, K. A. and Langhans, E. A. (eds.), *A Biographical Dictionary of Actors, Actresses, Musicians, Dancers, Managers, and Other Stage Personnel in London 1660–1800*.

Cibber, Theophilus (1703–58)
Actor, dancer, dramatist, manager, the fourth child of the actor-manager ▷ Colley Cibber,

and the singer and dancer ▷ Katherine
Cibber. Cibber was educated at Winchester
College, but left at the age of 16 to join the
▷ Drury Lane Theatre, where his father
was co-manager. Still in his teens, in addition
to acting in a range of established plays, he
was already writing or adapting other plays
and appearing in them, including ▷ *Henry
VI* (1723) and *Apollo and Daphne* (1723).

Despite his unscrupulousness as an
individual, Cibber maintained his reputation
as an actor during most of his life: he excelled
as a comedian, specializing in the playing of
fops, but was also compelling in broader
roles, including that of Pistol, whose name he
acquired as a nickname. Less successfully, he
played some serious parts, largely
Shakespeare, including Iago, Othello, Hamlet,
and even (at the embarrassingly advanced age
of 40) Romeo. As a manager he at times
showed considerable common sense and
expertise, but his career was blighted by his
truculence which involved him in personal
conflicts throughout his life. As an author he
was undistinguished, his works showing that
tendency, exhibited in other areas of his life,
to prey upon the efforts of others.
Bib: Mann, D. (ed.), *The Plays of Theophilus
and Susannah Cibber*.

Cicero, Marcus Tullius (106–43 BC)
Roman statesman, and writer on rhetoric,
politics and philosophy. Politically he is
famous for his vigorous resistance to the
conspiracy of Catiline against the government
of the Republic. This is the theme of ▷ Ben
Jonson's tragedy ▷ *Catiline*, of which
Cicero is the hero. Cicero's mastery of
eloquence in his various writings, and his
prestige in ancient Rome, caused him to be
much admired in the ▷ Middle Ages and
afterwards. Cicero's *Somnium Scipionis
(Dream of Scipio)* influenced ▷ Chaucer's
▷ *Parliament of Foulys*, and in the 16th
century the growing body of English prose
writers, such as ▷ Roger Ascham, tended to
take as a model either the rolling, musical
sentences of Cicero or, by contrast, the terse
pointed sentences of ▷ Seneca.

CID
Criminal Investigation Department of a police
force, especially that of the London
Metropolitan Police in Scotland Yard, whose
experts are always available to help other
forces.

Cinderella
A widespread ▷ fairy tale, known in English
from its version by the French collector of
fairy tales, ▷ Charles Perrault, whose work

was translated into English in about 1729.
Cinderella means the 'little cinder girl',
because in the story she is made to do all the
hard work of the house by her cruel elder
step-sisters, and is dirty with the ashes of the
fire. Aided by her fairy godmother, she wins
a prince in marriage. Recent interpretations
of this story focus on the sexual jealousies
and competition it implies.

Circe
▷ *Odyssey.*

Circulating libraries
A library from which books may be borrowed.
Such libraries were in private hands in the
18th century and subsisted on subscriptions
from clients. The first circulating library
started in 1740 and as the institution spread
so the reading habit greatly increased. It was
the more important since, apart from
▷ chapbooks, books were very expensive in
the 18th century.
Bib: Leavis, Q. D., *Fiction and the Reading
Public.*

Citizen comedies
Comedies, especially between 1600 and 1640,
using contemporary ▷ London and its
middle class as their setting, *eg* Ben Jonson's
▷ *Bartholomew Fair* (1614), ▷ Thomas
Middleton's ▷ *A Chaste Maid in Cheapside*
(1611), and ▷ Philip Massinger's *The City
Madam* (1632).

City, The
The customary way of referring to the oldest
and most central part of ▷ London,
occupied now chiefly by commercial offices
and with only a small resident population.
The term is also used to designate collectively
the chief financial institutions of the country,
situated there, such as the ▷ Bank of
England and the ▷ Stock Exchange.
Despite its smallness, the Lord Mayor of the
City of London has outstanding importance
as a ceremonial representative in the nation
for business and commercial interests.

City Heiress, The: or, Sir Timothy Treatall (1682)
Play by ▷ Aphra Behn. Tom Wilding, a
charming Tory (▷ Whig and Tory) rake, is
pursuing the rich and beautiful widow, Lady
Galliard. She is attracted to him but does not
trust him. He is also conducting an intrigue
with the young heiress, Charlot Get-all, as
well as keeping a mistress, Diana. Wilding's
friend, Sir Charles Merriwill, is also
interested in Lady Galliard, and becomes
Wilding's rival for her affections. Meanwhile
Wilding has been disinherited by his uncle,

the 'old seditious Knight' Sir Timothy Treatall. Wilding schemes with Diana to pass her off to his uncle as Charlot, and Sir Timothy marries the mistress, mistaking her for the heiress. In a tempestuous scene Lady Galliard agrees to sleep with Wilding, but regrets it immediately afterwards and rejects him, opting instead for Sir Charles. Wilding turns to the faithful Charlot for solace. Writings stolen from Sir Timothy by Wilding and friends prove the old man to have been involved in treasonable activities, and he is forced to desist from them, and even to make peace with his nephew. The play is one of several with a political bent by Behn, a lifelong staunch Tory herself. A large part of its interest derives from the psychological interplay between Wilding and Lady Galliard, but it contains some hugely farcical scenes, and keeps up an entertainingly rapid pace.

City Madam, The (1632)
A comedy by ▷ Philip Massinger. It is about a London merchant whose wife and daughters grow outrageously extravagant in their tastes. To teach them a lesson, the father, Sir John Frugal, temporarily retires from the world and leaves his affairs in the hands of his hypocritically humble brother, Luke. Once he has power in his hands, Luke throws off his pretence, becomes arrogant and harsh, and humiliates his nieces and sister-in-law. Like so many comedies of the age, *The City Madam* ridicules the extravagance and pretentiousness of the new urban bourgeoisie.

City of Destruction, The
In ▷ Bunyan's ▷ *Pilgrim's Progress* the town from which the pilgrim, Christian, flees to the ▷ Celestial City, *ie* Heaven. The City of Destruction stands for the world divorced from spiritual values, doomed to the destruction that is to overcome all the merely material creation.

City of Dreaming Spires
Oxford, from a description in ▷ Matthew Arnold's poem, *Thyrsis* (1867), an ▷ elegy for ▷ Arthur Hugh Clough.

City of Seven Hills
Rome, said to be built on seven hills, *ie* the Palatine, Aventine, Capitoline, Caelian, Esquiline, Viminal and Quirinal.

City Wit, The (1629)
A fast-moving, intensely theatrical ▷ citizen comedy of manners by ▷ Richard Brome, in which the cash-nexus provides the driving force behind the plot. The play dramatizes the recovery of the fortunes and family-ties of

a young resourceful London prodigal, Crasy, assisted by his wily servant Jeremy.

Civil wars, English and American
England has had two recognized periods of Civil War:

1 The more important, in the 17th century, is also called the Great Rebellion. It was fought between the king (▷ Charles I) and ▷ Parliament, and divided into the First Civil War (1642–6) ending with the parliamentary victory at Naseby (1645) and the capitulation of Oxford (1646), the royalist capital. The Second Civil War (1648–51) also ended with parliamentary victory, this time over the Scots, who had been the allies of Parliament in the First Civil War, but took the king's side in the Second. The issues were complicated; simplified, the economic interests of the urban middle classes coincided with their religious (▷ Puritan) ideology and conflicted with the traditional economic interests of the Crown, correspondingly allied with ▷ Anglican religious belief.

2 The other occurred in the 15th century and is usually known as the ▷ Wars of the Roses.

From outside England, it appears as if the fighting in Northern Ireland, becoming overt in 1968 and still continuing in 1989, constitutes a state of civil war.

The American Civil War, or War of Secession (1861–5), was fought on the issue of whether the southern states of the United States had the right to secede from the Union and establish their independence. Their wish to do so arose from the northern opposition to the slave holding on which the southern landed economy was based.

Clandestine Marriage, The (1766)
Comedy by ▷ George Colman the Elder, and ▷ David Garrick, inspired by the first plate in ▷ Hogarth's ▷ *Marriage à la Mode* series. The play concerns the secret marriage of Fanny Sterling to her father's clerk, Lovewell. Sir John Melvil, who had proposed to marry Fanny's affected older sister, instead falls in love with her, as does his uncle, the foppish Lord Ogleby. Eventually the complications are resolved, with the help of Lord Ogleby, who becomes an ally to the couple, and Fanny and Lovewell are able to disclose their marriage and find happiness. The play was a great success and it was revived frequently throughout the 19th century, and into the 20th.

Clanvowe, John (1341–91)
Diplomat, writer, member of the king's household, who fought in the French wars

and died on a pilgrimage, near Constantinople. He was associated with the so called 'Lollard Knights' (a group of intellectual knights with ▷ Lollard sympathies, apparently known to Chaucer), and was the author of a moralizing treatise, *The Two Ways*, and a ▷ dream-vision debate poem *The Cuckoo and the Nightingale* (which borrows lines from ▷ Chaucer's ▷ *Knight's Tale*).
Bib: Scattergood, V. J. (ed.), *The Works of John Clanvowe*.

Clare, John (1793–1864)

Poet. The son of a farm labourer in the Midlands, he was self-educated, early influences being the ▷ Bible and ▷ James Thomson's ▷ *Seasons*. He was unable to settle down or marry because of his poverty, and hoped that his verse might bring him security. His *Poems, Descriptive of Rural Life and Scenery*, described as being by 'a Northamptonshire Peasant' appeared in 1820, and were a great success. In that year he married, and began work on *The Village Minstrel, and Other Poems*, which appeared in 1821. This volume disappointed his hopes, despite his attempts to adjust his fresh, spontaneous style to the vagaries of literary taste. He visited London several times and made the acquaintance of ▷ Samuel Taylor Coleridge, ▷ William Hazlitt and ▷ Charles Lamb. *The Shepherd's Calendar* was published in 1827, in a version much edited by his publisher, John Taylor. (The original version of the poem, as Clare submitted it to Taylor, was published in 1964.) Under the pressure of apparent literary failure, the demands of his growing family and grinding poverty, Clare became insane in 1837. He spent the remainder of his life in lunatic asylums, periodically imagining that he was Napoleon or ▷ Lord Byron. The works which he wrote during the period of his madness were not published until the 20th century.

Clare is remarkable for his interest in nature for its own sake, rather than, as is the case with most poets, as a key to some philosophical or aesthetic illumination. During his lifetime, and since, this quality has led to the criticism that his work is merely descriptive. In his best poems however, such description conveys, in itself, a celebration of the joy of the natural scene and the changing seasons. Moreover Clare, being a farm labourer, lacks the literary idealization of nature common in other poets. In his anguished poem 'I Am' he abandons description, laments the desertion of his friends, and longs for death.
Bib: Martin, F., *The Life of John Clare*; Storey, M. (ed.), *Clare: The Critical Heritage*; Storey, M., *The Poetry of John Clare*; Howard, W., *John Clare*.

Clarendon, Edward Hyde, Earl of (1609–74)

Statesman and historian; author of *The True Historical Narrative of the Rebellion and Civil Wars in England* about the ▷ Civil War during which he had supported ▷ King Charles I. The published history combines two separate manuscripts: a history written 1646–8 while the events were fresh in his mind, and an ▷ autobiography written between 1668 and 1670 in exile and without the aid of documents. In consequence, Books I–VII are superior in accuracy to Books VIII–XV, with the exception of Book IX, containing material written in 1646. Clarendon's history is a literary classic because of its series of portraits of the participants in the war. His book is a notable contribution to the rise of the arts of biography and autobiography in England in the 17th century and contributed to the development which in the 18th century produced the first English novels.

As a statesman, Hyde was at first a leading opponent of Charles I, but his strongly ▷ Anglican faith led him to take the Royalist side shortly before the war. He became one of the king's chief advisers. He followed the royal court into exile, and was Lord Chancellor and ▷ Charles II's chief minister at the ▷ Restoration (1660). The king's brother, the future ▷ James II, married his daughter, so that he became grandfather of Queen Mary II and Queen Anne. He was made the scapegoat for the unpopularity of Charles II's government in its early years, however, and was driven into exile in 1667. He lived the remainder of his life in France.
▷ Histories and Chronicles.
Bib: Huehns, G., *Selections from the History of the Rebellion and the Life*; Wormald, B. H. G., *Clarendon, Politics, History and Rebellion*; Firth, C., *Essays, Historical and Literary*.

Clarissa (1747–8)

An epistolary novel by ▷ Samuel Richardson. The central characters are Clarissa Harlowe, Anna Howe, Lovelace and John Belford. Clarissa's family wish her to marry the odious suitor, Solmes, a wealthy man whom she abhors. The marriage is proposed to elevate the Harlowes socially, yet in the motives of Clarissa's brother and sister there is also a disturbing undertone of sadistic sexuality. As she refuses to accept Solmes the family ostracize her within their home.

Lovelace, a handsome rake, is initially the suitor of the elder sister Arabella, but his real interest is in Clarissa. When the family ill treat her he poses as her deliverer and persuades her to escape with him to London, promising that he will restore her in the esteem of her relatives. But the apparently respectable house where they stay is in reality a brothel.

Lovelace's attempts at seducing Clarissa are unsuccessful, and he eventually resorts to drugging her and then rapes her. Through this theme Richardson explores the hypocrisy of a society which equates 'honour' with virginity. Clarissa dies after the rape, not from shame but from a spiritual integrity which cannot be corrupted. In the self-martyrdom of the heroine, Richardson achieves a psychological complexity which transcends the limitations of the purported morality.

Bib: Flynn, C., *Samuel Richardson; A Man of Letters.*

Classic, Classics, Classical

These words are apt to cause confusion. The term 'classic' has been used to denote a work about whose value it is assumed there can be no argument, *eg* ▷ *David Copperfield* is a classic. The word particularly implies a changless and immutable quality; it has sometimes been used to deny the need for reassessment, reinterpretation and change. Because only a few works can be classics, it may be argued that the term is synonymous with the best. This is not necessarily the case, especially with regard to changes in literary taste and a constantly moving canon of texts.

'Classics' is the study of ancient Greek and Latin literature. 'Classic' is used as an adjective as well as a noun, *eg* ▷ Dickens wrote many classic novels. 'Classical' is mainly used as the adjective for 'classics', *eg* classical scholarship.

Classical education and English literature

Classical education is based on the study of the 'classics', *ie* the literature of ancient Greece and Rome, principally from ▷ Homer to the great Latin poets and prose writers (*eg* ▷ Virgil, ▷ Ovid, ▷ Cicero) of the 1st century BC – 1st century AD. Latin is more closely bound up with western history and culture, and is the easier language for English speakers to study; consequently it has been more widely used in schools than Greek, and it has been studied at earlier stages of education. Roman literary culture was, however, based on that of the Greeks.

Medieval Europe (Christendom) grew out of the ruins of the western Roman Empire; the Church, like the Empire, was still ruled from Rome; its philosophy was deeply influenced by the Greek philosophers and its language continued to be Latin. The Church controlled the universities and the classics were the basis of medieval university education, especially that part of it known as the 'Trivium' – grammar, rhetoric and logic. Nonetheless, many of the Greek and Roman writers were known principally through inferior versions of their texts and they were valued chiefly in so far as the Church could use them for its own purposes.

The movement known as the ▷ Renaissance started in Italy in the 14th century; it was, first of all, the enthusiastic rediscovery and collection by scholars of ancient classical texts, and the development of new and more accurate methods of studying them. It did not long remain merely a scholarly movement; the scholars influenced the writers and artists, and these in turn, in the 15th and 16th centuries, aroused enthusiasm in the upper classes of all western Europe. The Renaissance practice of studying the classics for their own sake and not under the direction of the Church, brought the discovery of a new principle of growth in literature and the other arts. Knowledge of the classics became a principle of discrimination: those who did not have it were by implication more primitive in their development and often from a lower social class.

The Renaissance first seriously affected England early in the 16th century. The pattern for classical education in the national public schools and the more local grammar schools was formed by such men as John Colet (?1467–1519), High Master of St Paul's School. ▷ Sir Thomas More, author of *Utopia* and Chancellor to ▷ Henry VIII, gave prestige to ▷ humanist values in the royal court. ▷ Erasmus visited England from Holland and made friends among these and other English humanists.

But ancient Greece, and Rome in its greatest days, were pagan; their values were social rather than religious. Thus there was the possibility of divided loyalty between the Rome that was the starting-point of so much European art, thought and politics, and the latter Rome that was the centre of the originally Hebrew and very unclassical religion of Christianity. The Roman Catholic Church in the 15th and early 16th centuries at first responded to the humanists favourably, even when they were critical of its traditions and practices. The thought and outlook of pagan Greece and Rome nevertheless did not agree well with the ancient Hebrew roots of Christianity as shown in the Old and New Testaments of the Bible. The 16th-century Protestant ▷ Reformation was partly the outcome of humanist criticism of the Church, but it was also a return to the Word of God as the Bible displayed it. Thus, from 1560 to 1660, much English imaginative writing has two aspects: the poets ▷ Edmund Spenser and ▷ John Milton, for example, have a Protestant aspect, which is biblical and Hebraic; and a classical aspect, strongly inspired by the classical Renaissance. The poet ▷ Ben Jonson is much more classical than Protestant, while ▷ George Herbert is strongly religious in the moderately Protestant, ▷ Anglican tradition, and despises the kind of subject matter (*eg* 'classical pastoral') which Ben Jonson accepted. Both, however, had an equally classical education.

Another division arose from the difference between native literary traditions, which continued in their non-classical character, and the classical qualities and standards which many writers felt should permeate and regulate the native tradition. This division did not correspond to religious differences: the most Latin of all English poets is the ▷ Puritan, John Milton. ▷ Shakespeare is well-known for his indifference to the classical 'rules' which critics like ▷ Sir Philip Sidney thought necessary to good drama, while his contemporary, Ben Jonson, favoured them, though not slavishly.

Classical and native traditions of literature rivalled and nourished each other until the middle of the 17th century, and so did Protestant biblical and secular classical philosophies of life. But after the ▷ Restoration in 1660, religious passions declined and sceptical rationalism began to take their place. Thus began the most classical period of English art and literature, the so-called ▷ Augustan age of the 18th century. Yet within their neo-classical horizon, the best English writers even of this period retained strong elements of native idiom; this is true of the poets, ▷ John Dryden and ▷ Alexander Pope, and of the prose writers ▷ Jonathan Swift and ▷ Samuel Johnson.

The ▷ French Revolution of 1789 was, at one level, the outcome of 18th century reason, criticism and scepticism, but it challenged the 18th-century classical qualities of order, intellectual proportion and balance, and the view of man as fulfilled only in a civilized structure of society. The English ▷ Romantic

movement was partly an outcome of the French Revolution; it challenged many of the classical values, attaching more importance to the cultivation of the feelings of the individual than to the cultivation of the reason of man in society; it rediscovered the ▷ Middle Ages, which for three centuries had been despised as ▷ 'gothic', *ie* barbarous. At the same time, that part of English society which had always been more biblical than classical in its culture – the commercial middle classes – was now stronger (thanks to the ▷ Industrial Revolution) than it had ever been before. So we find the critic ▷ Matthew Arnold, in his *Culture and Anarchy* (1869), distinguishing between two categories of mind in contemporary society: the majority were the 'Hebraizers', who devoted themselves to the virtues of private conduct and practical achievement; the 'Hellenizers', like himself, valued contemplation, reason and critical discrimination. England, he considered, was becoming barbarous owing to the preponderance of the former over the latter.

Since Arnold, classical education has lost its long-held place in the centre of education. It has retained its privileged status but as education has become available to all, different skills, such as the study of English literature, have been developed as other disciplines.

Classical mythology

Ancient Greek mythology can be divided between the 'Divine Myths' and the 'Heroic Myths'.

The divine myths are known in differing versions from the works of various Greek poets, of whom the most notable are ▷ Homer and Hesiod. Hesiod explained the origin of the world in terms of a marriage between Earth (Ge or Gaea) and Sky (Uranus). Their children were the 12 ▷ Titans: Oceanus, Crius, Iapetus, Theia, Rhea, Mnemosyne, Phoebe, Tethys, Themis, Coeus, Hyperion, and Cronos. Cronos overthrew his father, and he and Rhea (or Cybele) became the parents of the 'Olympian gods', so called from their association with the sacred mountain ▷ Olympus. The Olympians, in their turn, overthrew Cronos and the other Titans.

The chief Olympians were ▷ Zeus and his queen ▷ Hera. The other gods and goddesses were the offspring of either, but as Zeus was usually at war with Hera, they were not the joint parents. They seem to have been seen as male and female aspects of the sky; their quarrels were the causes of bad weather and cosmic disturbances. The principal

offspring of Zeus were ▷ Apollo,
▷ Artemis, ▷ Athene, ▷ Aphrodite
(sometimes represented as a daughter of
Uranus out of the sea), ▷ Dionysus,
▷ Hermes, and ▷ Ares. Zeus had three
sisters, Hestia, ▷ Demeter (the corn
goddess) and Hera (also his wife), and two
brothers, ▷ Poseidon who ruled the sea,
and ▷ Hades who ruled the underworld. In
the 3rd century B C the Olympian gods were
adopted by the Romans, who used the Latin
names more commonly known to later
European writers. Uranus, Apollo, and some
others remained the same. Gaea became
Tellus; Cronos = Saturn; Zeus = Jupiter
(or Jove); Hera = Juno; Athene = Minerva;
Artemis = Diana; Hermes = Mercury; Ares
= Mars; Hephaestus = Vulcan; Aphrodite =
Venus (and her son Eros = ▷ Cupid);
Demeter = Ceres; Poseidon = Neptune.
There were numerous minor deities such as
nymphs and satyrs in both Greek and Roman
pantheons.

The Olympian deities mingled with men,
and rivalled one another in deciding human
destinies. They concerned themselves
particularly with the destinies of the heroes,
ie those men, sometimes partly divine by
parentage, who were remarkable for the kinds
of excellence which are especially valued in
early societies, such as strength
(▷ Heracles), or cunning (▷ Odysseus).
Each region of Greece had its native heroes,
though the greatest heroes were famous in
legend all over Greece. The most famous of
all was Heracles (in Latin, Hercules) who
originated in Thebes. Other leading examples
of the hero are: ▷ Theseus (Athens);
Sisyphus and ▷ Bellerophon (Corinth);
▷ Perseus (Argolis); the Dioscuri, *ie*
▷ Castor and Pollux (Laconia); ▷ Oedipus
(Thebes); ▷ Achilles (Thessaly); ▷ Jason
(Thessaly); ▷ Orpheus (Thrace). Like the
Greek gods and goddesses, the Greek heroes
were adopted by Roman legend, sometimes
with a change of name. The minor hero of
Greek legend, ▷ Aeneas, was raised to be
the great ancestral hero of the Romans, and
they had other heroes of their own, such as
▷ Romulus, the founder of Rome, and his
brother Remus.

After the downfall of the Roman Empire of
the West, classical deities and heroes achieved
a kind of popular reality through the planets
and zodiacal signs which are named after
them, and which, according to astrologers,
influence human fates. Thus in ▷ Chaucer's
▷ *The Knight's Tale*, Mars, Venus, Diana
and Saturn occur, and owe their force in the
poem as much to medieval astrology as to

classical legend. Otherwise their survival has
depended chiefly on their importance in the
works of the classical poets, such as
▷ Homer, Hesiod, ▷ Virgil and ▷ Ovid,
who have meant so much to European culture.
In Britain, important poets translated and
thus helped to 'naturalize' the Greek and
Latin poems; *eg* ▷ Gavin Douglas in the
16th century and ▷ Dryden in the 17th
century translated Virgil's ▷ *Aeneid*;
▷ Chapman in the 16th century and
▷ Pope in the 18th century translated
Homer's epics. In the 16th and 17th centuries,
poets used major and minor classical deities
to adorn and elevate poems intended chiefly
as gracious entertainment, and occasionally
they added deities of their own invention.

While European culture was understood as
a more or less distinct system of values, the
poets used classical deities and heroes
deliberately and objectively. In the 19th
century, however, the deep disturbance of
European beliefs and values caused European
writers to use classical myth more
subjectively, as symbols through which they
tried to express their personal doubts,
struggles, and beliefs. Thus John Keats in his
unfinished epic ▷ *Hyperion* tried to emulate
Milton's great Christian epic, ▷ *Paradise
Lost*, but instead of Christian myth he used
the war of the Olympian gods and the Titans
to embody his sense of the tragedy of human
experience. ▷ Tennyson wrote dramatic
monologues in which personifications of
Greek heroes (*eg* Ulysses, Tithonus, Tiresias
in eponymous poems) recounted the
experiences associated with them in classical
(or, in the case of Ulysses, medieval) legend,
in such a way as to express the emotional
conflicts of a man from the ▷ Victorian age
like Tennyson himself. In the 20th century,
writers have used figures from the classical
myths differently again; they are introduced
to establish the continuity of the emotions
and attitudes characteristic of modern men
and women with emotions and attitudes of
those from the past. It is thus that ▷ T. S.
Eliot uses Tiresias in his poem ▷ *The Waste
Land*, and James Joyce uses the Odysseus
myth in his novel ▷ *Ulysses*. In a
comparable way, modern psychologists have
used the Greek myths as symbolic expressions
of basic psychological conflicts in human
beings in all periods. ▷ Freud's theory of
the Oedipus complex is the most famous of
these reinterpretations.
▷ *Odyssey*; *Iliad*.

Claudius
1 The Roman Emperor (A D 41–54) who

began the systematic conquest of Britain. Subject of the novels by ▷ Robert Graves, *I, Claudius* and *Claudius the God*.

2 King of Denmark in ▷ Shakespeare's *Hamlet*. He mounts the throne after secretly murdering his brother, young Hamlet's father, and he marries Hamlet's mother. At the opening of the play, young Hamlet does not know that his father's sudden death was due to murder, but he is disgusted by the situation on three counts: Claudius's marriage with his sister-in-law is technically illegal according to the law of the time, besides indicating lack of due grief on the part of his mother, and Hamlet himself should naturally have succeeded to the throne, although the law of succession was elective in Denmark.

Claudius differs from most evil men portrayed by Shakespeare and by his contemporaries. We hear of the murder at second hand, from the Ghost; Claudius's own confession of wickedness in the chapel (III.iii) excites the audience's compassion rather than their indignation, since his remorse is so evident; his conspiracies against his nephew are in self-defence, since he knows that Hamlet is plotting revenge. The fact that Claudius is not self-evidently a cruel tyrant is one of the features that differentiates *Hamlet* from other ▷ Revenge tragedies of the period: dramatically, it helps to make intelligible Hamlet's doubt and hesitancy in carrying out his revenge.

Cleanness

One of the four ▷ alliterative poems dating from the second half of the 14th century, conventionally attributed to the ▷ Gawain poet, and preserved along with ▷ *Pearl*, ▷ *Patience* and ▷ *Gawain and the Green Knight* in a single manuscript, British Library Cotton Nero A. x. The poem's structure is influenced by contemporary sermonizing practices, in which a systematic exploration of a given theme would be made using a series of biblical narratives. In this case the narrator investigates the diverse meanings and spiritual resonances of 'cleanness' through a series of New Testament and Old Testament stories (the parable of the Wedding Feast, the story of the Flood, the destruction of Sodom and Gomorrah, Belshazzar's Feast). The poem, which has no title in the manuscript is sometimes referred to as *Purity*.
▷ Bible, The.
Bib: Anderson, J. J. (ed.), *Cleanness*; Davenport, W. A., *The Art of the Gawain Poet*.

Cleland, John (1709–89)

Novelist and journalist, most famous for his novel *Fanny Hill: Memoirs of a Woman of Pleasure*, published in two volumes in 1748 and 1749 and immediately suppressed as pornography. An unexpurgated edition of the book published in England in 1963 was seized by police and became the subject of a trial. Cleland also wrote *Memoirs of a Coxcomb* (1751) and several other novels and dramatic pieces.

Cleopatra of Egypt (51–30 BC)

The last of the dynasty of the Ptolemies. The chief authority for the facts of her life is the Greek historian ▷ Plutarch (1st century AD) in his life of Antony. She was joint sovereign of Egypt with her younger brother Ptolemy Dionysus. Driven out of Egypt, she withdrew to Syria, where she met the Roman general ▷ Julius Caesar while she was preparing to counter-attack. Caesar took her side, re-established her on the throne, and made her his mistress. When Caesar was assassinated, she became the mistress of Caesar's ally Mark Antony, until they were jointly defeated by Caesar's nephew and adopted son, Octavianus. She then committed suicide. Her love affair with Caesar is the subject of ▷ Bernard Shaw's play ▷ *Caesar and Cleopatra*; and that between herself and Antony is the subject of ▷ Shakespeare's ▷ *Antony and Cleopatra* and ▷ Dryden's ▷ *All for Love*. ▷ Samuel Daniel's verse tragedy, *Cleopatra* (1594), has as subject her dealings with Octavian after Antony's death.

Clergy

Collectively the body of men in holy orders in a Church. In the ▷ Middle Ages, 'clergy' was the collective noun of 'clerk' = a man in holy orders; as, in earlier times, only the clergy were learned, 'clerk' was also used for student, intellectual, or scholar. All men not in holy orders are collectively the laity.

Clerihew

A lightweight epigram, usually in four lines of varying length, so called after its inventor E. Clerihew Bentley. For example:

> *Alfred de Musset*
> *Called his cat 'pusset'.*
> *His accent was affected –*
> *That was to be expected.*

Clerk's Tale, The

One of ▷ Chaucer's *Canterbury Tales*. The Clerk begins his tale with a tribute to the Italian poet ▷ Petrarch who has provided him with his story of patient Griselda, who survives and trials and tortures imposed on her by her husband, the higher-born Walter, in his attempt to test the limits of her patience. The story seems to have had considerable appeal for medieval writers, and a number of other versions and analogues survive (including that of Petrarch's source, the hundredth tale of ▷ Boccaccio's ▷ *Decameron*). In producing his version of the story in the *Clerk's Tale*, Chaucer seems to play off the possibilities of interpreting this story as a spiritual allegory and as a literal history, and the resulting narrative has a disquieting effect. Through retelling the story of Griselda, the Clerk takes up and disproves the assertion made by the ▷ Wife of Bath in her *Prologue* (that clerics cannot speak well of wives), and the tale concludes with an 'envoy' considering the lessons of Griselda's story for the Wife of Bath and all her 'sect'.

Cliché
A word borrowed from the French, used to denote a phrase or idiom employed by habit instead of meaningfully, *eg* 'her skin was *as white as snow*'. It is a stock phrase, employed without thought and heard (or read) without visualization.

Climax
▷ Figures of Speech.

Clio
▷ Muses.

Clive, Catherine (Kitty) (1711–85)
Actress, singer, dramatist, and pamphlet-writer. Kitty Clive (née Raftor) joined the ▷ Drury Lane Theatre in 1728 where she spent most of her career, and quickly became one of its leading comic actresses, as well as singing in operas, entr'actes, and afterpieces. Her first major success was as Polly in ▷ *The Beggar's Opera* (1728), followed by roles in *The Old Debauchees* (1732) and *The Covent Garden Tragedy*, (1732) written specially for her by ▷ Henry Fielding.

She herself wrote afterpieces, farces, and a pamphlet attacking the managements of Drury Lane and ▷ Covent Garden theatres, *The Case of Mrs Clive* (1743), and was for many years a close friend of ▷ Horace Walpole. In 1769 she retired and died 16 years later, after frequent bouts of illness. Her admirers praised her for her wit, intelligence, expressive features, and comic sense of timing. She was buried in Twickenham Churchyard.

Bib: Highfill, P. H. Jr., Burnim, K. A. and Langhans, E. A. (eds.), *A Biographical Dictionary of Actors, Actresses, Musicians, Dancers, Managers, and Other Stage Personnel in London 1660–1800*.

For the Benefit of Mrs. CLIVE.
(Being the laſt Time of her Appearing on the Stage.)
At the Theatre Royal in *Drury-Lane*,
This preſent MONDAY, the 24th of *April*, 1769,.
The WONDER.
Don *Felix* by Mr. GARRICK,
Col. *Briton* by Mr. JEFFERSON,
Don *Lopes* by Mr. BADDELEY,
Don *Pedro* by Mr. BURTON,
Liſſardo by Mr. KING,
Frederick Mr. PACKER, *Gibby* Mr. JOHNSTON,
Violante by Mrs. BARRY,
Iſabella by Mrs. STEPHEN'S,
Inis by Mrs. BRADSHAW,
Flora by Mrs. CLIVE,
End of the Play, a Dance called The WAKE,
By Sig. *Giorgi*, Mrs *King*, &c.
To which will be added
LETHE.
Lord *Chalkſtone* (1ſt *time*) Mr. KING,
Æſop Mr. BRANSBY, *Fine Gentleman* Mr DODD,
The *Drunken Man* by Mr. LOVE,
Mercury by Mr. VERNON,
Frenchman Mr. BADDELEY, *Old Man* Mr PARSONS,
The *Fine Lady* by Mrs. CLIVE.
PIT and BOXES laid together.
N. B. No Tickets have been given out, but to thoſe Ladies and Gentlemen who have their Places ſecured, in the Pit or Boxes, and to prevent any Miſtakes, or Confuſion, no Box Tickets will be admitted into the Gallery; Mrs. CLIVE begs the Favour of thoſe who have Places in the Pit, to be there by half an hour after Five and to let their Servants come to keep them a quarter before Four,
To-morrow, The JEALOUS WIFE, with a Farce and Entertainments,
For the Benefit of Mr. BRANSBY, and Mr. BURTON.

The programme for Kitty Clive's farewell, 1769

Cloth manufacture
The export of wool was the foundation of English commercial prosperity, but in the 14th century cloth-making began to overtake it in importance. It was carried on in villages and small towns in East Anglia, in the Cotswold hills and other regions of the west, and in the hill country in the north. Since it required the combination of several crafts – carding, spinning, weaving, fulling, dyeing and finishing – it gave rise to the first great capitalist industrialists, the clothiers, who gave out the work to various craftsmen often in scattered villages, and then marketed the finished product.
▷ Capitalism.

Cloud of Unknowing, The
One of the most admired texts of the medieval English mystical tradition. This spiritual treatise was produced some time in the second half of the 14th century in the north-east Midlands area. The text, which explores the active and contemplative ways of living, is addressed to a young contemplative and is partly presented in dialogue form. The tutor counsels that it is only by experiencing the

cloud of unknowing that God will be felt and seen. Several other spiritual treatises have been attributed to the author of *The Cloud of Unknowing* (who is otherwise unknown).
Bib: Hodgson, P. (ed.), *The Cloud of Unknowing and the Book of Privy Counselling*; Wolters, C. (trans.), *The Cloud of Unknowing*.

Clough, Arthur Hugh (1819–61)

Poet. He was the son of a Liverpool cotton merchant, and was educated at ▷ Rugby School under ▷ Thomas Arnold, and at Balliol College, Oxford. At Oxford he came for a time under the influence of Newman, afterwards a Roman Catholic but at the time one of the leaders of the Anglican religious revival known as the ▷ Oxford Movement; later, when Clough was a senior member (Fellow) of Oriel College, he became a sceptic in religious belief. It was necessary (until 1871) to accept the doctrines of the Church of England in order to be a senior member of an Oxford College; thus Clough's religious doubts caused him to resign. He travelled in Europe, was for a short time Principal of a students' hostel in London University (where no religious restrictions operated) and lectured in America. Finally (1853) he accepted a post under the government in the Education Office. He was the close friend and correspondent of the poet and critic, ▷ Matthew Arnold, who commemorated his death with the elegy *Thyrsis* (pub. 1867). Almost all of Clough's letters to Arnold have disappeared, but Arnold's letters to him (see *Letters to Clough*, ed. H. F. Lowry) are interesting for what they reveal of the minds of the two men. Both were religious doubters, and both were dismayed by the course of 19th century civilization. Arnold was desolated by the loss of his friend, and attributes his death to premature despair ('Too quick despairer, wherefore wilt thou go?').

Clough's long poems, have a light, though scarcely serene, spirit. The best-known ones are the two verse novels, *Tober-na-Vuolich* (1848) and *Amours de Voyage* (1849; pub. 1858), and the uncompleted dramatic dialogue, *Dipsychus* (1850; pub. 1869). The first two are written in a ▷ metre unusual in English, the Latin ▷ hexameter. *Dipsychus* employs a wide variety of metres. The subject of the first poem is a young man of advanced intellectual opinions but emotionally immature, and his love affair with a Scottish Highland peasant girl who has the emotional maturity that he lacks; published in the revolutionary year of 1848, it also explored ▷ Chartism and class differences. *Amours* is

about a self-doubting man who loses the girl he loves through his inability to arrive at conclusions as to the truth of his own feelings. *Dipsychus*, 'the man in two minds', is a colloquy between a self-doubter and the spirit who haunts him, who admits to the name 'Mephistophilis' and yet is not certainly evil. The other poets of the age were as much afflicted by the torments of doubt as Clough was, but Clough differed from them in relating doubt to the conduct of ordinary daily life, and in his use of a kind of irony which is much more characteristic of 20th-century poets than it is of 19th-century ones. He has consequently recently attracted much more critical interest than he has received in the past; see for example the claims made on his behalf in the Introduction to Tom Paulin's *Faber Book of Political Verse* (1986).
Bib: Chorley, K., *Clough: The Uncommitted Mind*; Houghton, W. E., *The Poetry of Clough*; Goode, J., Hardy, B., essays in *The Major Victorian Poets* (ed. Isobel Armstrong).

Clout, Colin

▷ Colin Clout.

Club, The

Later known as the 'Literary Club', an informal group founded in the winter of 1763–4 and meeting at this time in the Turk's Head, Soho. Original members included ▷ Samuel Johnson, ▷ Sir Joshua Reynolds, ▷ Oliver Goldsmith and ▷ Edmund Burke; later, ▷ Thomas Percy, ▷ David Garrick and ▷ James Boswell were amongst those elected.

Clubs

Private associations, organized for a common recreational purpose; sometimes recruited from men of common beliefs or opinions, *eg* the political clubs; sometimes from a particular profession such as the authors' and actors' clubs; sometimes from the casual gatherings of friends. They have been important in English life since the mid-17th cenury, when they first appear by name in association with particular ▷ coffee houses – as important in English social life then as the café in France later. But the principle may be said to go back to the later years of the 16th century, when (according at least to tradition) poets met in taverns. *eg* the Mermaid in London, attended by ▷ Shakespeare, ▷ Ben Jonson, ▷ Sir Walter Ralegh, ▷ John Donne and others. (See ▷ Francis Beaumont's lines *Master Francis Beaumont to Ben Jonson*, describing meetings at this tavern.) In the early years of the 18th century there is frequent mention of clubs in the periodical essays of ▷ Joseph Addison and ▷ Sir Richard Steele; ▷ Jonathan Swift was a leader of the Brothers' Club and founded the Scriblerus. ▷ Dr Johnson founded the Literary Club in 1764; the painter ▷ Joshua Reynolds, the statesmen ▷ Edmund Burke and ▷ Charles James Fox, the writer ▷ Oliver Goldsmith and ▷ David Garrick the actor were all members of it; they met at the Turk's Head Tavern. In the later 18th and early 19th centuries clubs began to leave the taverns and use their own buildings, and the most famous of all literary and artistic clubs, The Athenaeum, was founded in 1824 and moved to its present building in 1831. The Carlton Club (Conservative, 1831) and the Reform Club (▷ Liberal, 1834) are the outstanding political clubs of the 19th century, but Brooks's and White's had been the corresponding bodies in the 18th century, and both still exist. In the 19th century it was usual for men of the middle and upper classes to belong to clubs of some description: this relieved the pressure of compulsory domesticity, promoted in the period as a prime value. There was, however, no parallel form of escape for women of the same class: it was only late in the 19th century that they started their own clubs. The exclusion of women of all classes from sites that have been identified as areas of masculinity, like clubs and even bars, is under challenge in our own time. Working class clubs were usually for education, politics or some other practical objectives. They are still common, especially in the north, but have become more recreational.

Clytemnestra

In Greek myth, wife of ▷ Agamemnon, king of Argos. While her husband was absent, commanding the Greeks in their war against ▷ Troy, Clytemnestra took as lover Aegisthus, Agamemnon's cousin, in whose charge the kingdom had been left. When Agamemnon returned, he was murdered by his wife and her paramour; in retribution she herself was later murdered by her son ▷ Orestes. The story is the subject of several of the greatest ancient Greek tragedies: *Agamemnon*, *Choephori*, and *Eumenides* by ▷ Aeschylus; *Electra* by ▷ Sophocles; *Electra* and *Orestes* by ▷ Euripides.

CND

The Campaign for Nuclear Disarmament, which was launched at a meeting of 5,000 people at the Central Hall, Westminster, in February 1958. Speakers included ▷ Bertrand Russell, ▷ J. B. Priestley and the historian A. J. P. Taylor. A non-party movement (it was not a national organization until 1966), its members rejected the nuclear deterrent on moral grounds and demanded unilateral nuclear disarmament by Britain. Public demonstrations included marches to the atomic research establishment at Aldermaston. After a period of diminished public sympathy in the late 1960s, CND was relaunched in 1980. Opposition to the basing of American Cruise missiles in Britain has swelled its membership: 250,000 people attended a mass meeting in Hyde Park on 6 June 1982.

Cobbett, William (1762–1835)

Journalist and political leader of the working class, especially of the rural labourer. The son of a small farmer and self-educated, he remained identified with country pursuits and interests; he was always a peasant, but a fully articulate one. The work by which he is especially known is ▷ *Rural Rides*, an account of tours through England on horseback, written for the enlightenment of a working-class public, and published between 1820 and 1830 in his periodical ▷ *Political Register*, which he edited from 1802 until his death. The *Rides* are famous for their racy, vigorous description of the countryside. His language is always clear, plain and lively; in an autobiographical fragment he declares that his first inspiration in the writing of prose was the work of ▷ Jonathan Swift, though he is completely without Swift's ironical suavity. His next most famous work is his *Advice to Young Men* (1829); his *Grammar of the English Language* (1818) is an outstanding guide to the writing of vigorous English.

Apart from the still appreciated vividness of his writings, Cobbett has remained a hero of forthright, independent political journalism. When he was in America (1792–1800) his *Porcupine's Gazette* and various pamphlets were in defence of Britain against the prejudices of the newly independent Americans; once back in England, he refused offers of government patronage, and though he started his *Political Register* in support of the Tories, then in power, in a few years he moved over to radical opposition, and spent two years in prison. In 1832 he was elected Member of Parliament in spite of his refusal to use the corrupt methods for influencing electors common at the time; in Parliament he went into opposition to the Whig government as an extreme left radical. He was excessively quarrelsome and prejudiced, but also exceedingly brave and eloquent in support of the cause of justice as, at any given time, he saw it.

▷ Whig and Tory.
Bib: Cole, G. D. H., *Life; Opinions of William Cobbett*; Lobban, J. H. (ed.), *Rural Rides*; Hughes, A. M. D., *Selections*; Hazlitt, W., in *Spirit of the Age*; Carlyle, E. I., *Cobbett*.

Cockney
A native of the old city of London, noted for the 'cockney accent' of his dialect. Country people used the word contemptuously for the typical city-dweller. The word derives from 'cock's egg'; the medieval countryside belief was that small or ill-shaped eggs were laid by cocks.

Cockpit
A small arena where the sport of cockfighting (making one cock fight another) took place. The sport was widely popular in England from the ▷ Middle Ages until the 19th century. The term was extended to describe any region where war often takes place (*eg* Belgium, the 'cockpit of Europe').

Coffee and coffee-houses
Coffee was introduced into England from the east in the mid-17th century, and from the ▷ Restoration until the mid-18th century coffee-houses were fashionable public resorts in London. Certain coffee-houses became acknowledged meeting-places for supporters of particular political parties, or for the members of particular professions. Will's Coffee-house became the centre for men of letters; the Cocoa Tree Chocolate-house became the home of ▷ Tory politicians, while the ▷ Whigs went to St James's Coffee-house; ▷ Lloyd's became popular with merchants; and so forth. In the later 18th century more tea was imported, and as such luxuries were now distributed more widely, ordinary people took to drinking it in their homes. So the flourishing century of the coffee-house was replaced by the domestic tea-party as the typically English social occasion. Some of the coffee-houses survived in other forms; thus Lloyd's became the central office in London for marine insurance, and White's became one of London's most fashionable ▷ clubs.

Cold War, The
Loosely used to describe the power struggle that arose after the end of World War II between the communist and western democratic-capitalist nations. It had no specific beginning but was to be identified in the way each side perceived the other as a political and military threat and as the representative of an alien and menacing ideology. The Korean War (1949–53) intensified this

opposition; its crisis came in 1961 when the Castro regime in Cuba allied itself unequivocally with the U.S.S.R. When it was discovered that Soviet missiles capable of destroying major U.S. targets were being installed on the island, an international crisis ensued in which ▷ nuclear war seemed to threaten. The destruction of the Berlin wall in 1989 and the dissolution of the U.S.S.R. in 1991 has ended the power struggle and opened the way for global understanding.

Coleridge, Samuel Taylor (1772–1834)

Samuel Taylor Coleridge by P. Vandyke (1795)

Poet and critic. Son of a Devon clergyman, he was educated in London and at Jesus College Cambridge. He left Cambridge to enlist in the Dragoons under the pseudonym Silas Tomkyn Comberbache, and although he returned after a matter of months he never completed his degree. His early religious leanings were towards Unitarianism. In 1794 he made the acquaintance of ▷ Robert Southey, with whom, under the influence of the ▷ French Revolution, he evolved a communistic scheme which they called ▷ 'Pantisocracy', and together they wrote the tragedy, *The Fall of Robespierre*. In 1795 he married Sara Fricker, Southey marrying her sister. His *Poems on Various Subjects* were published in 1796, at about the time he met ▷ Wordsworth. The two poets became friends, and lived close to each other for a time in Somerset. ▷ *Kubla Khan* and the first part of ▷ *Christabel* were written at this period, though they were not published until later. The joint publication, *Lyrical Ballads*, which included Coleridge's ▷ *The Rime of the Ancient Mariner*, appeared in 1798. Coleridge expressed his loss of faith in the French Revolution in *France, An Ode* (1798).

In 1798–9 he travelled in Germany and came under the influence of the transcendental philosophy of Schlegel and ▷ Kant, which dominates his later theoretical writing. During 1800–4 he moved near to Wordsworth in Keswick, and fell unhappily in love with his sister-in-law, Sarah Hutchinson, a relationship referred to in ▷ *Dejection: An Ode* (1802). Early in his life he had become reliant on opium and never succeeded in fully controlling the addiction. He began to give public lectures and became famous for his table talk. In 1809 he founded a periodical, *The Friend*, which was later published as a book (1818). In 1817 appeared ▷ *Biographia Literaria*, his autobiographical apologia and a landmark in literary theory and criticism. He quarrelled with Wordsworth in 1810, and in later life he lived in the homes of various benefactors, including the surgeon, James Gillman, who helped him to cope with his addiction. He became increasingly Tory in politics and Anglican in religion, developing an emotionalist conservatism in the tradition of Burke.

Coleridge's poetic output is small, diverse, but of great importance. His ▷ 'conversation poems', such as *Frost at Midnight* (1798), *This Lime-Tree Bower* and *My Prison* (1800), continue and deepen the reflective tradition of Gray and Cowper, culminating in the poignant ▷ *Dejection: An Ode* (1802). On the other hand his major symbolic works, such as *The Rime of the Ancient Mariner* (1798), *Kubla Khan* (1816) and *Christabel* (1816), plumb new psychological and emotional depths, and can be seen to develop along similar lines as his famous theoretical definition of imagination in *Biographia Literaria*, Chapter XIII. His perspectives are consistently more intellectually alert than those of his friend Wordsworth, though the expression of his philosophical ideas is sometimes confused. His sympathetic but discriminating analysis of Wordsworth's work in *Biographia Literaria* is a model of unfussy

analytical method. As both practitioner and theorist, Coleridge is central to ▷ romanticism.
Bib: House, H., *Coleridge*; Lowes, J. L., *The Road to Xanadu*; Coburn, K., *In Pursuit of Coleridge*; Holmes, R., *Coleridge*; Jackson, J. R. de J. (ed.), *Coleridge: The Critical Heritage*; Jones, A. R., and Tydeman, W., *Coleridge: The Ancient Mariner and Other Poems* (Macmillan Casebook); Fruman, N., *Coleridge: The Damaged Archangel*; Cooke, K., *Coleridge*; Hamilton, P., *Coleridge's Poetics*; Wheeler, K. M., *The Creative Mind in Coleridge's Poetry*; Sultana, D. (ed.), *New Approaches to Coleridge*; Magnuson, P., *Coleridge's Nightmare Poetry*.

Colin Clout

The name adopted by ▷ Edmund Spenser in his ▷ pastoral sequence ▷ *The Shepherd's Calendar* and his ▷ allegorical work *Colin Clout's Come Home Again* (1594), written to describe his visit to London and the court in 1589–91. The name became something of a code-word amongst the Spenserian poets, who, in emulation of Spenser, would refer to 'Colin' and adopt their own pastoral personae.

College of Arms

▷ Heralds' College.

Collins, Mr

A character in ▷ Jane Austen's ▷ *Pride and Prejudice*. His combination of pomposity in relation with his social equals, superciliousness to inferiors and servility to his social superiors is comically caricatured, and satirizes the excessive worldliness of the less deserving English clergy of the 18th and early 19th centuries. A 'Mr Collins' came to be a designation for a merely conventional letter of thanks for hospitality, after such a letter written by the fictional Collins.

Collins, Wilkie (1824–89)

Novelist; the first ▷ detective novelist in English. His two famous novels are *The Woman in White* (1860), first published in ▷ *Household Words*, a magazine edited by ▷ Charles Dickens, and ▷ *The Moonstone* (1868). These novels of ▷ sensation established a pattern for English detective fiction. His mastery was especially over plot-construction in which he influenced Dickens. His characterization is less distinguished but in *The Woman in White* he excels in this, too, and in the creation of disturbing atmosphere. He collaborated with Dickens in a few stories in *Household Words* and in ▷ *All the Year Round*: *The Wreck of the Golden Mary, A Message from the Sea, No Thoroughfare*. Collins's other novels include *No Name* (1862) and *Armadale* (1866), which has been praised for its melodrama.

Bib: Robinson, K., *Life*; Phillips, W. C., *Dickens, Reade and Collins: Sensation Novelists*; Ashley, R., *Wilkie Collins*; Eliot, T. S., Preface to *The Moonstone*, World's Classics edition; Lonoff, S., *Wilkie Collins and His Victorian Readers*.

Collins, William (1721–59)

Poet. The son of a hatter in Chichester, he published his *Persian Eclogues* in 1742 while he was still an undergraduate at Oxford. Their elegant exoticism and musical use of the pentameter couplet (▷ metre) made them popular, and they were reissued in 1757 as *Oriental Eclogues*. However his *Odes on Several Descriptive and Allegorical Subjects* (1746), which includes much of his best work, achieved little success at the time. The ▷ romantic *Ode on the Popular Superstitions of the Highlands of Scotland Considered as a Subject of Poetry* was written about 1749 but not published until 1788. In 1750 he suffered a mental breakdown and wrote no more verse before his death nine years later in Chichester. Collins's small output shows a fragile combination of exquisite classical control and intense lyricism. In such poems as *Ode* ('How sleep the Brave'), *To Evening* and *The Passions* he develops his own distinctive rococo idiom, involving the constant use of pretty personifications and classical abstraction, reminiscent of the friezes on Wedgewood pottery. His rhythms and tone are peculiarly original, and often quite haunting, though the influence of ▷ Thomas Gray, ▷ James Thomson and ▷ John Milton is often evident.

Bib: Johnson, S., *Lives of the Poets*; Garrod, H. W., *Collins*; Carver, P. L., *The Life of a Poet: A Biographical Sketch of William Collins*.

Colman, George, the Elder (1732–94)

Dramatist, essayist, theatre manager. He controlled first ▷ Covent Garden, and then the Haymaket Theatre (▷ Haymarket Theatres), and was responsible for staging the earliest productions of ▷ Oliver Goldsmith's plays, as well as writing dozens of plays, masques, and operas himself. He began writing poetry while still a pupil at Westminster School, and after receiving a degree at Oxford University and being called to the bar, he still retained his literary interests. Through his friendship with ▷ David Garrick, he became involved in the theatre, and eventually abandoned law as a career. In 1760 his first play, the farcical *Polly Honeycombe*, billed as 'a dramatic novel',

was produced at ▷ Drury Lane. Six years later he collaborated with Garrick on ▷ *The Clandestine Marriage*, his most successful work.

After inheriting a fortune from his mother, Colman purchased a major interest in the Covent Garden Theatre (▷ Covent Garden Theatres), which came under his joint management in 1767. Among his ventures there were productions of Goldsmith's *The Good-Natur'd Man*, and ▷ *She Stoops to Conquer*. In 1776 Colman acquired the Little Theatre in the Haymarket, where in 1781 he successfully staged ▷ John Gay's ▷ *The Beggar's Opera*, with women cast as the men, and vice versa.

▷ Colman, George, the Younger.

Bib: Burnim, K. A., *The Plays of George Colman the Elder*; Wood, E. R. (ed.), *The Plays of David Garrick and George Colman the Elder*.

Colman, George, the Younger (1762–1836)

Dramatist, miscellany writer, and theatre manager. Son of ▷ George Colman, the elder. He was educated at Westminster School, and at Oxford, like his father. Again like his father, he was intended for the law, but preferred the stage, and had a musical farce, *The Female Dramatist* produced at the ▷ Haymarket Theatre in 1782. In 1784 he underwent a clandestine marriage with the actress Clara Morris, of whom his father disapproved, and re-married her in open ceremony in 1788. In 1789, his father having been stricken with paralysis, and suffering from mental deterioration, he took over management of the Little Theatre in the Haymarket. He proved an effective manager, despite a penchant for personal extravagance which, among other factors, involved him in a series of quarrels and lawsuits. As a dramatist he was prolific, contributing more than 20 plays and musical entertainments, including several which became firm favourites, such as the comic opera, *Inkle and Yarico* (1787). In 1824 he was appointed Examiner of Plays, a title he retained to his death. He proved a fastidious censor, excising all supposedly blasphemous and indecent references, even though some of his own productions skirted close to the margins of propriety.

▷ Censorship; Colman, George, the Elder.

Bib: Tasch, P. A. (ed.), *The Plays of George Colman the Younger*; Sutcliffe, B. (ed.), *Plays by George Colman the Younger and Thomas Morton*.

Colonel Jack (1722)
The History and Remarkable Life of Colonel Jacque, a novel by ▷ Daniel Defoe. Jack is abandoned by his parents, becomes a thief, a soldier, a slave on an American plantation, a planter, and eventually a rich and repentant man back in England. The sequence through crime, suffering and repentance, and from poverty to prosperity, is typical of Defoe's novels.

Colonialism

Although it is known that colonies were established in early history, the term is now taken to refer to nationalistic appropriation of land dating from the ▷ Renaissance period in the west, and is usually understood as perpetrated on black or coloured non-Europeans in Asia, Africa, Australasia, the Americas or the Caribbean by the white western European powers. Colonialism does not have to imply formal annexation, however. Colonial status involves the imposition of decisions by one people upon another, where the economy or political structure has been brought under the overwhelming influence of another country. Western colonialism had its heyday from 1450 to 1900. It began in the Renaissance with the voyages of discovery; the new territories were annexed for their material resources and for the scope they offered to missionary efforts to extend the power of the Church. The last independent non-western territories were parcelled out in 1900. After World War I the growth of nationalism in Africa and Asia started to reverse the process. The establishment of the United Nations (1945), which declared colonial policy a matter of interest to the entire world, helped to spur the relinquishing of former colonies.

Works from Shakespeare's ▷ *The Tempest* to ▷ Joseph Conrad's ▷ *Heart of Darkness* demonstrate the struggle to determine the meaning of colonial power, though there was a strong tradition, founded on the imperialist myth of the Victorian era, of which ▷ Rudyard Kipling and ▷ Rider Haggard were the most famous exponents, that white intervention was made in the interests of the native inhabitants.
▷ Commonwealth literature.
Bib: Memmi, A., *The Colonizer and the Colonized*; Sard, E., *Orientalism*; Spivack, G. C. *In Other Worlds*.

Columba, St (AD 521–97)

Son of an Irish chieftain, he became a Christian evangelist to Scotland, where he founded the monastery of Hy on the Island of Iona. The book of his miracles was written by Adomnan of Iona.

Comedy

▷ Humours, Comedy of; Manners, Comedy of.

Comedy of Errors, The (1592)
An early comedy and ▷ Shakespeare's shortest play, based on ▷ Plautus's *Menaechmi*. The elements of ▷ farce and confusion in the original are enhanced in Shakespeare's taut play – it observes the neo-classical unities of time, place and action – by the addition of a second pair of twins, the Dromios, servants to the lost and separated Ephesian and Syracusan Antipholi. Shakespeare further departs from his source by foregrounding the marriage of Adriana and the Ephesian Antipholus with reference, imaginatively, to St Paul's view on marriage and sexual identity. The play is full of vitality and supersedes the reductive and mercenary view of society propounded in its classical source.

Comical Revenge, The: or, Love in a Tub (1664)
Play by ▷ Sir George Etherege, his first, with a complex and partly tedious series of plots in four different modes: **1** heroic, or mock-heroic, concerning love and honour, and including a duel, in rhymed couplets; **2** witty sparring courtship between Sir Frederick Frollick and the Widow; **3** gulling or trickery, of Sir Nicholas Cully, who is deceived into marrying a whore; **4** farce involving outright clowning, mainly by the absurd Dufoy and his associates. The title derives from the predicament of Dufoy, who has contracted venereal disease, and must sweat in a tub as part of the 'cure'.

Commedia dell'Arte

A kind of Italian comedy, developed in the 16th century, in which the plot was written but the dialogue was improvised by the actors. Certain characters regularly recurred in these plays, and in the 18th century they were adopted in England (by way of France) and became part of the English puppet shows (*eg* ▷ Punch and Judy) and of the ▷ pantomime tradition. Such characters, anglicized, include Harlequin, his mistress Columbine, Pantaloon, Punch.

Common land

Land held in common by the peasantry of a village, and used for the pasturage of their cattle. By the 19th century farms were grouped into fairly large holdings all over the country, and such commons as had not been enclosed were used chiefly for recreation, *eg* cricket and various field sports.
▷ Enclosures.

Common Law

A system of law in use in Great Britain
(excluding Scotland), some parts of the
Commonwealth and the United States, which
retained the system after renouncing English
political authority. The term arose in the
▷ Middle Ages and meant the law common
to the whole people as distinct from law
governing only sections of it, such as the Law
Merchant or local customary law. It is also
distinguished from Statute Law, made by Act
of Parliament, and from Equity, a system
supplementary to Common Law beginning in
the 15th century. Common Law is 'case-
made', *ie* based on precedent judgements, and
originally derived from acknowledged custom.
The Common Law system differs from the
law in most other European countries
(including Scotland) in that the English legal
system did not undergo the influence of the
study of Roman Law in the 16th century.
The difference is important politically, since
Roman law emphasizes the power of the
state, and by its avoidance the English lawyers
of the 17th century were better able to defend
the liberties of the subject against the claims
of the ▷ Stuart kings.
▷ Courts of Law.

Common metre

A four-line stanza with alternating four and
three stresses and alternating rhymes. It is
especially common in ▷ hymns, ▷ carols
and ▷ ballads.

Common Prayer, The Book of

The first *Book of Common Prayer* was
prepared under the supervision of
▷ Archbishop Cranmer and issued in 1549
to meet the needs of the Church of England
for services and prayers in the vernacular. It
is of great importance as a work of literature,
for Cranmer succeeded in combining the
plainness and directness of English with the
dignity and sonority of Latin. Prayer Book
language became a familiar and formative
influence in speech and writing second only
in importance to the Bible itself. There were
revisions in 1552 and 1559. The Prayer Book
authorized in 1662 was substantially the 1559
revision. A fairly extensive revision was
blocked by Parliament in 1928. There are
now alternative forms of the various services
in use.

Commons

As a political term, the 'commons' of England
are all those who do not hold a title of
nobility, or the office of Bishop in the
Church of England. Commoners elect their
representatives to the House of Commons
whereas the lords or peers and the bishops
are entitled to sit in the House of Lords. This
does not mean that the House of Commons
does not include members of the aristocracy:
the sons of peers may hold courtesy titles (*eg*
the eldest son of a duke is called a marquis
but is accorded this title only 'by courtesy')
but politically they are considered to be
commoners and are entitled to vote for
representation in the House of Commons or
to 'stand' for election themselves.
▷ Parliament.

Commonwealth literatures

One of the most abiding consequences of
British imperialism has been the legacy of the
English language bequeathed to the former
colonies of the Empire. It is a legacy that has
at best proved a mixed blessing, but one
which makes it possible to speak of a unity
running through the literary production of
countries as different from one another as
Jamaica and New Zealand, as India and
Canada. The writing of each of these
countries has been strongly influenced by
English cultural norms; at the same time the
fact that English was the language of the
colonizer has always made it a problematic
medium for the Commonwealth writer. The
St Lucian poet Derek Walcott (b 1930)
encapsulates the essence of the problem in a
poem entitled 'A Far Cry From Africa'
which, while on one level dramatizing his
own personal *angst* as a Caribbean person of
mixed racial descent, responding to the Mau
Mau uprising in Kenya in the 1950s, also
addresses the sense of cultural schizophrenia
he feels. He asks how, 'divided to the vein',
he can 'choose/ Between this Africa and the
English tongue I love?'

This dilemma is present, to a greater or
lesser degree, in virtually all Commonwealth
writing in English, and texts from the New
Literatures in English (a term which is often
preferred to Commonwealth Literatures
today, since it imposes fewer political
constraints) are frequently written in hybrid
modes that demonstrate some kind of cross-
cultural fusion between English and the
value-systems of the local culture.

The nature of the local cultures varies
considerably, but it is possible to identify two
main types; those of the disrupted Third
World society and the transplanted New
World society. In the former category belong
the primarily oral ancestral cultures of Africa
and the part-scribal, part-oral cultures of the
Indian sub-continent, as well as a variety of
myth-centred cultures in South-East Asia and
Oceania and other parts of the globe. In all of

these societies there has been a disruption of age-old traditions during the period of colonialism, and in the post-independence era an urge to reconstruct which has had to come to terms with the fact that it is impossible simply to turn back the clock but which nevertheless insists that the age-old traditions become a cornerstone in the process of rebuilding. Thus, in West Africa, writers like the Nigerians Wole Soyinka (b 1934) and ▷ Chinua Achebe (b 1930) have insisted that the artist has a crucial part to play in the process of reconstruction and have seen the author's role as a modern-day equivalent of that of the *griot*, or oral repository of the tribe's history; they have taken the view that he or she must be a spokesperson for the community, not an individualist in the Western Romantic tradition of the artist, and Achebe has particularly stressed the importance of the artist's role as a teacher. In works like *A Dance of the Forests* (Soyinka; 1960) and *Arrow of God* (Achebe; 1964) these two writers, like many of their West African contemporaries, have re-examined the historical past of their societies and, without sentimentalizing it, implied that a dialogue between past and present is a *sine qua non* for progress in the future.

In the latter category, that of the transplanted New World society, belong the cultures of Canada, Australia and New Zealand, where in each case the majority population is of European origin and has had to adapt, transform or subvert Old World cultural forms and genres in order to make them relevant to very different landscapes and social situations. The Canadian writer ▷ Margaret Atwood (b 1939) dramatizes the problem of constructing an identity in a new land in a poem entitled 'Progressive Insanities of a Pioneer' (in *The Animals in That Country*; 1968) in which the eponymous settler finds himself 'a point/ on a sheet of green paper/ proclaiming himself the centre', but finding he has staked his plot 'in the middle of nowhere' is unable even to name the 'unstructured space' of his New World environment. Later, in her novel *Surfacing* (1972), Atwood offers a more positive approach to the same theme in a work which charts the spiritual odyssey of a contemporary Canadian woman who has constructed a false identity for herself as a result of having internalized a set of rationalist values that are particularly identified with the neo-imperialism of American patriarchal and technological society, but seen to be endemic in the modern world. Women and Canadians are represented as suffering from a common

victim syndrome and needing to transform themselves by becoming 'creative non-victims'. The protagonist of *Surfacing* manages to achieve regeneration through reverting to an animal-like identity, regressing to a pre-linguistic mode of existence in which she sees herself as establishing contact with the gods of the original Amerindian inhabitants of Canada and the natural world of the country. Similarly, in ▷ Patrick White's *Voss* (1957) the hero's 19th-century exploration of the interior of Australia, an endeavour which is sharply contrasted with the complacent lives of the country's middle-class coastal dwellers, is only complete once he has died and his blood has seeped into the parched soil of the outback. In both novels the metamorphoses of identity and attitudes to the country that lie at the heart of the texts are complemented on a formal level by a complex metaphorical style that suggests linguistic transformation is crucial to the nationalistic quest. ▷ Peter Carey's writing offers a more nightmarish, post-modern vision of the contemporary Australian landscape, particularly in his collection of fragmentary short stories, *Exotic Pleasures* (1981).

Simply to label Canadian and Australasian cultures as 'transplanted' is, of course, finally simplistic, since it involves a perspective which confines itself to the majority population. In each case an indigenous population (Amerindians in Canada; Aborigines in Australia; and Maoris in New Zealand), which has been the victim of various kinds of brutalization and discrimination, continues to make a very important contribution to the national culture and in recent years has been doing so through the medium of English. For these groups the struggle for social justice and cultural survival has been – and is – the crucial cultural issue, as it is for the Blacks of South Africa. It permeates the writing of Aborigines like Colin Johnson (b 1938), Kath Walker (b 1920), Kevin Gilbert (b 1933) and Jack Davis (b 1917), as well as the prize-winning novels of the Maori writers Witi Ihimaera (b 1944) and Keri Hulme (b 1947). Generally the criterion for Aboriginality has been self-definition and interestingly many writers who are only a small part Maori or Aborigine, like Keri Hulme and, in Australia, Archie Weller (b 1958), have chosen to identify with this aspect of their ancestry and have generally been accepted by the indigenous group in which they have chosen to locate themselves.

The notion of transplantation also comes to be of less value in the contemporary period, when the original phase of settlement is so far in the past that the sense of displacement has long ceased to operate for most of the country's inhabitants. Nevertheless, new waves of migrants (particularly southern European and south-east Asian immigrants into Australia, and middle European, Italian and East and West Indian immigrants into Canada) continue to experience numerous problems occasioned by transplantation. Yet, for the writers of these countries, the twin pulls of the overseas metropolis (the United States as much as Britain in the case of Canada) and the home country – internationalism and nationalism – have continued to be exercised in a variety of ways, not least through the dominance, until recently, of British and American publishing houses and the problem that local publication, when available, frequently meant a far more restricted readership. Place of publication has, of course, in many cases determined the range and nature of writers' references to local culture and their use of non-standard English linguistic forms.

The writing of one Commonwealth region, the West Indies, is the product of *both* disruption and transplantation; the region can be classified as *both* Third World *and* New World. The population of the contemporary Commonwealth Caribbean is almost entirely made up of descendants of peoples transplanted from the Old World (the original Carib and Arawak Indian inhabitants have been almost completely exterminated). The most important population group, the descendants of the slaves who were brought from West Africa to work on the West Indian sugar plantations, underwent a very different experience of transplantation from Europeans who went to the Americas or Australasia, since they were forcibly transported and had their culture systematically destroyed in the New World. Family and tribal groups were generally split up on arrival and this led to the emergence of Creolized forms of English as the *lingua franca* through which the slaves communicated with one another and with their masters. So, while the influence of English culture, imposed through the colonial educational curriculum and a range of other institutions has been dominant until recently, the struggle to throw off this culture and replace it by local folk forms has been of a different kind to similar endeavours in other Anglophone New World societies.

Caribbean writing is characterized by a variety of rhetorical devices that take issue with the norms of English literature. Most prominent among these is a range of oral forms that illustrate the complex ▷ Creole language situation of the various Caribbean territories – in each case the spoken language is a continuum, with a variety of registers ranging from broad Creole at one extreme to something close to Standard English at the other. In recent years oral forms have come to be dominant in West Indian verse, with performers like the 'dub poets' ▷ Linton Kwesi Johnson (b 1952), Michael Smith (1954–83) and Jean Binta Breeze (b 1956) completely isolating themselves from the metrical forms of English poetry in favour of a verse which has its roots in the rhythms of reggae music and has parallels with the protesting affirmative ideology of Rastafarianism. Yet there are many other registers in which Caribbean oral poetry can operate, and in the work of poets like Edward Kamau Brathwaite (b 1930), Louise Bennett (b 1919) and Lorna Goodison (b 1947) one can frequently detect a number of different voices figuring in a single short poem to produce a mode of utterance that illustrates the polyphonic nature of Caribbean speech and the cultural diversity of the region.

Different Caribbean writers have taken a range of stands on the question of Caribbean aesthetics and while writers like Brathwaite have stressed the importance of the African legacy in the West Indies, others like Walcott and the Guyanese novelist Wilson Harris (b 1921) have put the emphasis on the mixed multi-cultural heritage of the region. Harris in particular, in a series of complex and hermetic novels, beginning with *Palace of the Peacock* (1960), which break all the rules of European classic ▷ realism, has argued for a cross-cultural vision of consciousness, which he sees as bringing about both psychic and social integration. Walcott takes a similar view in arguing for a 'creative schizophrenia' and thus turning the fragmented cultural legacy occasioned by colonialism into a source of strength rather than divisiveness. It is a position which has analogues in each of the Commonwealth literatures.

The essence of contemporary Aboriginal writing has been seen to inhere in *bricolage* (a phrase coined by Claude Lévi-Strauss), using the bits and pieces of the various 'means at hand' in a flexible way to produce something new, and this model can be applied to the literary production of most of the Commonwealth countries. While all forms of discourse work in this way – traditional ideas of inspiration functioning in a vacuum have been seriously challenged in recent years – this view of how texts are originated has particular relevance for Commonwealth writing and oral forms, where cross-cultural connections abound and where English almost always functions in an ambiguous way. It is especially marked in the work of a complex, post-modernist writer like ▷ Salman Rushdie (b 1947) whose *Midnight's Children* (1981) draws on a vast range of Hindu, Islamic and Western, classical and modern, 'serious' and 'popular' traditions to produce a highly original collage. This takes on the qualities of a 'Bombay Talkie', the eclectic, decorum-confounding dominant film genre of India, a form that is frequently referred to in *Midnight's Children* and which provides a metaphor for the novel's structure. Yet *bricolage* is also a quality of Indian writing in English, such as the novels of ▷ R. K. Narayan (b 1907) and Nayantara Sahgal (b 1927) or the poetry of Nissim Ezekiel (b 1924) and Kamala Das (b 1954), that exhibits less technical virtuosity on the surface. In the work of each of these writers there is a fusion of traditional and Western elements (the novel itself is not an indigenous genre in India) which produces a hybrid mode of expression that exists at the interface of two or more cultures. Contemporary Indian writing in English is a paradox in that it is written in a tongue that is not the dominant spoken language anywhere in India (as a result Indian drama in English hardly exists) and yet it is perhaps the only modern Indian literature able to cross cultural boundaries and give a sense of pan-Indian identity. This situation is, however, only a particular manifestation of the complex cultural predicament of the various Commonwealth literatures in the post-Independence period. Despite their diversity, they have all had to respond to the alien cultural forms imposed during the period of colonialism and to mediate between these forms and modes of expression that have their origins in local or ancestral traditions.

Bib: Atwood, M., *Survival: A Thematic Guide to Canadian Literature*; Baugh, E. (ed.), *Critics on Caribbean Literature*; Goodwin, K., *A History of Australian Literature*; Gérard, A. (ed.), *European-Language Writing in Sub Saharan Africa* (2 vols.); Mukherjee, M., *The Twice-Born Fiction: Themes and Techniques of the Indian Novel in English*.

Communism

Communism may be interpreted in two ways: 1 the older, imprecise sense covering various philosophies of the common ownership of property; 2 the relatively precise interpretation understood by the Marx-Leninist Communist Parties throughout the world.

1 The older philosophies derive especially from the Greek philosopher ▷ Plato. His *Republic* proposes that society should be divided into classes according to differences of ability instead of differences of wealth and birth; the state is to provide for the needs of all, and thus to abolish rivalries and inequalities between rich and poor; children are to be educated by the state, and women are to have equal rights, opportunities and training with men. In England, one of the most famous disciples of Plato is ▷ Sir Thomas More in his ▷ *Utopia* (1516). More's prescriptions are similar to Plato's in many respects, but though he also requires equal opportunity and training for men, he goes against Plato in keeping the monogamous family intact, whereas Plato wanted a community of wives and children to be brought up by the state. Both Plato and More require for their schemes an all-powerful state in the charge of an intellectual aristocracy; what we should call 'enlightened totalitarianism'. With the growth of the power of the state in the 20th century, however, all forms of totalitarianism were regarded with abhorrence by liberal intellectuals, and so arose the 'anti-utopian' class of literature, for example ▷ Aldous Huxley's *Brave New World* (1932) and ▷ George Orwell's *Animal Farm* (1945) and *Nineteen Eighty Four* (1948), vehemently satirizing totalitarian communism.

In practical experiment, the vows of poverty taken by members of orders of monks and friars and the communal ownership of property in such communities may have kept alight for people in general the ideal of the freedom of the spirit attainable by the renunciation of selfish material ambitions and competition. Protestant sectarian beliefs emphasizing the equality of souls led to such an abortive communistic enterprise as that of the ▷ Levellers in the ▷ Interregnum. In America, a number of experiments were undertaken by immigrant sects such as the Amana community, and under the influence of the English socialist ▷ Robert Owen and the French socialists Fourier and Cabet, but few of them lasted long.

2 Modern so-called scientific communism, based mainly on ▷ Karl Marx and Lenin, differs from certain forms of modern socialism by affirming the necessity for revolutionary, as distinct from evolutionary, method, to be followed by a period of dictatorship. Lenin attempted to implement the communist programme defined by Marx. Between the Revolution of 1917 and 1924, when he was killed, he tried to guide the newly inaugurated

'dictatorship of the proletariat' in Russia. Not all communism is revolutionary, however: the Italian communist party has adopted the parliamentary route to socialism. The collapse of communist hegemony in Eastern Europe and the disintegration of the Soviet Union in the late 1980s and early 1990s has left both an ideological and political vacuum behind the former Iron Curtain.

Companies, Joint Stock

Companies whose profits are distributed among the shareholders. They began in the 16th century and largely superseded the older 'regulated company' whose members traded each on his own account and combined only for common protection. The greatest of the regulated companies was the Merchant Adventurers, founded in the 15th century; the greatest of the joint stock companies was the ▷ East India Company founded in 1600: in the latter half of the 18th century the status of this changed from being a purely commercial concern to being an organ of imperial power, the effective sovereign power in Bengal.

▷ Capitalism; Charter companies; Colonialism.

Complaint

A term used to refer to poems (in a variety of forms), usually in the voice of a first-person speaker, which lament the vicissitudes of life, especially the pangs of disappointed or unrequited love. Used by medieval French poets, it appears to have been employed first by ▷ Chaucer, who intercalated complaints within larger narrative contexts (e.g., in Dorigen's complaint in the ▷ *Franklin's Tale*) but who also produced a number of individual complaint poems. In post-Renaissance literature, the terms elegy or lament are more frequently used to signal complaint-type poetry.

Compleat Angler, The (1653)

A discourse on the sport of fishing (in full, *The Compleat Angler, or the Contemplative Man's Recreation*) by ▷ Isaak Walton, first published in 1653; its 5th edition has a continuation by Charles Cotton (1630–87) and came out in 1676. The book has been described as perhaps the only handbook of art and craft to rank as literature. This is because Walton combines his practical instruction with digressions about his personal tastes and opinions, and sets it in direct, fresh description of the English countryside which may be contrasted with the artificial

pastoralism which had hitherto been characteristic of natural description. The book has the form of a dialogue mainly between Piscator (Fisherman) and Venator (Hunter), which takes place the banks of the river Lea near London. Cotton's continuation is transferred to the banks of the river Dove between Derbyshire and Staffordshire.

Compton-Burnett, Ivy (1884–1969)

Novelist. Her first novel, *Dolores* (1911) is distinguished from all her others by an approach to the method of novel-writing similar to that of the 19th century, in particular that of ▷ George Eliot, and a disposition to accept usual conceptions of moral retribution. From *Pastors and Masters* (1925) both the method and the moral vision change radically. The novels are narrated almost wholly through dialogue; the manner derives from ▷ Jane Austen, but with even less attempt to present visualized environments. In treating occurrences such as matricide, bigamy, betrayal and incest they show affinities with Greek tragic drama, while the novels of ▷ Samuel Butler are another important influence. The period is always 1890–1914; the setting, a prosperous household of the period; the characters include some who are arrogant to the point of evil, and are able, without retribution, to dominate those who are selfless or weak; the plots are melodramatic but never break up the surface of respectability. The dialogue is epigrammatic and pungent, with the consequence that the novels are all exceptionally concentrated structures. The effect is commonly of sardonic comedy with tragic conclusion, although the comic side tends to dominate.

After 1925 the novels are as follows: *Brothers and Sisters* (1929); *Men and Wives* (1931); *More Women than Men* (1933); *A House and its Head* (1935); *Daughters and Sons* (1937); *A Family and a Fortune* (1939); *Parents and Children* (1941); *Elders and Betters* (1944); *Manservant and Maidservant* (1947); *Two Worlds and Their Ways* (1949); *Darkness and Day* (1951); *The Present and the Past* (1953); *Mother and Son* (1955); *A Father and his Fate* (1957); *A Heritage and its History* (1959); *The Mighty and their Fall* (1961); *A God and his Gifts* (1963); *The Last and the First* (1971). Few distinguished novelists have shown such uniformity of treatment and lack of development throughout their career. Probably *A House and its Head* and *A Family and a Fortune* are her two outstanding achievements.

Bib: Hansford Johnson, P., *Ivy Compton-Burnett*; Liddell, R., *The Novels of Ivy*

Compton-Burnett; Spurling, H., *Ivy When Young* and *Secrets of a Woman's Heart*.

Comte, Auguste (1798–1857)

French philosopher. He sought to expound a scientifically based philosophy for human progress, called Positivism which deduced laws of development from the facts of history and excluded metaphysics and religion. His chief works were translated into English. In them he sought to establish a system that would be the scientific equivalent of the Catholic system of philosophy. In this he failed, but his work led to the modern science of sociology. In England, his chief disciple was Frederick Harrison (1831–1923), but he also deeply interested the philosopher ▷ John Stuart Mill and the novelist ▷ George Eliot. The character of his beliefs suited radically reformist and religiously sceptical English intellectuals such as these; on the other hand, his systematization of ideas was alien to English habits of mind, and was criticized by the philosopher ▷ Herbert Spencer.

Comus (1634)

The name now given to the ▷ masque written by ▷ John Milton and performed at Ludlow Castle in 1634. The work's original title was simply *A Maske, presented at Ludlow Castle, 1634, before the Earl of Bridgewater, Lord President of Wales*. This title stresses the important features of any masque – its occasional quality, and the names of those who either witnessed or took part in the masque. Music for the masque was composed by Henry Lawes (1596–1622), and principal parts taken by the children of the Earl of Bridgewater. The masque endeavours to demonstrate the triumph of virtue and chastity over luxury and sensual excess, although generations of readers and critics have found it easier to identify with the anti-hero Comus, rather than with the 'Lady' who opposes his arguments.
Bib: Editions include: Diekhoff, J. S. (ed.), *A Maske at Ludlow*.

Condell, Henry (d 1627)

▷ Heming, John.

Condensation

This term is used by ▷ Freud in *The Interpretation of Dreams* (1900) to describe the compression and selection that takes place during the process of dreaming. When subjected to analysis the details of the dream can be shown to relate to a series of deeper, more extensive psychic connections. Freud distinguishes between the 'manifest content' of the dream, which is what is remembered, and the 'latent content' which can only be arrived at retrospectively through the analytical business of interpretation. Interpretation seeks to reverse the process of condensation and to investigate 'the relation between the manifest content of dreams and the latent dream-thoughts' and to trace out 'the processes by which the latter have been changed into the former' (*The Interpretation of Dreams*). The term has also become part of the language of critical theory. Applied to a literary text it was first used to afford a partial explanation of the energies which bring the text into existence, or to give an account of the unconscious motivations of represented 'characters'. More recently, the analogy between the interpretation of dreams and of texts has been used to suggest the impossibility of arriving at an original 'core' of meaning, prior to ▷ displacement or condensation. Freud speaks of the dream's 'navel' – that knotted point of enigma which indicated that there is always something unresolved, unanalysed.

▷ Displacement; Psychoanalytical criticism.

Confessio Amantis

A story-collection about love and related subjects, in octosyllabic couplets, written by ▷ John Gower in the later 1380s. A confession of a lover (Amans) to Venus's priest (Genius) provides the occasion for the collection; the priest tells exemplary stories to help the lover analyse his own behaviour. Seven of the eight books of the *Confessio Amantis* are organized as illustrations of one of the ▷ Seven Deadly Sins: Book VII is devoted to advice about the government of self and society. The framework and contents of Gower's work draw together traditions of courtly love literature and of religious treatises on the processes of penitence. The collection concludes with the healing of the lover as the penitential process is completed.

The stories themselves are drawn largely from ▷ Ovid, from medieval versions of the ▷ Troy story and from the Old Testament, but large amounts of bookish lore (such as the history of religion, the history of culture) are encompassed in the confessional frame, thus giving the work an encyclopaedic quality. There is some overlap between the stories in the *Confessio Amantis* and those retold in various contexts in ▷ Chaucer's work (notably the stories of Florent, Ceyx and Alcione, Constance, Phoebus and the Crow, Pyramus and Thisbe), and the early version of the text contains complimentary references to Chaucer's work. Undoubtedly each writer knew and read the work of the other.

The Prologue and Epilogue of the *Confessio Amantis* place it in the context of universal and contemporary history. The narrator begins by suggesting that the work was commissioned by ▷ Richard II and concludes with remarks about its value for the English king and the English realm. Although the first version dates from the later 1380s, the opening and closing sections were revised to accommodate the changing political scene in England and the work was re-dedicated to Henry of Lancaster (later ▷ Henry IV). The *Confessio Amantis* was translated into Portuguese, probably in the late 14th century.

▷ Henry IV; Richard III.
Bib: Macaulay, G. C. (ed.), *The English Works of John Gower*; Minnis, A. J. (ed.), *Gower's Confessio Amantis: Responses and Reassessments*.

Confessions of an English Opium-Eater (1822: enlarged ed. 1856)

An autobiography, and the most famous work of ▷ Thomas De Quincey. Like ▷ Coleridge, De Quincey began taking opium to ease physical suffering, and eventually increased the dose until he became an addict. The book contains eloquent, prose-poetic accounts of his opium dreams and also graphic descriptions of his life of poverty in London. In the former aspect the prose evokes the high musical rhetoric of the 17th-century masters – ▷ Thomas Browne, ▷ John Milton, ▷ Jeremy Taylor; in the latter, it is typical of the 19th-century mode of transmitting intimate, minute personal experience, resembling the increasingly close-textured psychology of the novel. In his tenderness for and understanding of childish suffering, De Quincey represents a development that was new in the history of literature, and came to fruition in the Victorian novelists, notably ▷ Charles Dickens.

Congregationalism

Congregationalists differ from other Christians not so much on credal beliefs as on their ordering of church life. For them, Christ rules primarily through the local congregation rather than through the Pope or bishops. In the 16th century, followers of this belief were called Brownists, after their founder, Robert Browne; by the mid-17th century they were known as Independents. It was in this period that the movement had special importance; it became widely influential amongst the Parliamentary opponents of ▷ Charles I and numbered ▷ Oliver Cromwell among its supporters. With other Dissenters they went through

hard times after the ▷ Restoration but survived to be part of the Evangelical Revival. During the 19th century the independent congregations formed county and national unions, but in 1966 there was a breakaway of the Evangelical Fellowship of Congregational Churches, and in 1972 another split resulted in 80% of English Congregational Churches going into the United Reformed Church with English Presbyterian Churches, most of the remaining churches forming the Congregational Federation.

Congreve, William (1670–1729)

Dramatist and poet, born at Bardsey near Leeds, into a military family. He was educated at Kilkenny, and at Trinity College in Dublin, where he was a fellow-student of ▷ Jonathan Swift. In 1690 he entered the Middle Temple, but did not practise as a lawyer. Instead he began writing: his first published work was a novel, *Incognita* (1692), followed by three stage comedies: ▷ *The Old Bachelor* (1693), ▷ *The Double Dealer* (1694), ▷ *Love for Love* (1695). Congreve's one tragedy, ▷ *The Mourning Bride*, was written in 1697. Congreve was a particular target of the Rev. Jeremy Collier's attack on the theatre, *A Short View of the Immorality and Profaneness of the English Stage*, in 1698, and he responded vehemently in his *Amendments of Mr Collier's False and Imperfect Citations* (1698). But the assault may have helped to discourage him from writing: his interest in the stage declined after the performance of his comedy, ▷ *The Way of the World*, in 1700. This, despite its subsequent fame and lasting popularity, into our own time, was not at first a success. Congreve did not depend on the stage for his livelihood, although he retained his involvement in the management of ▷ Lincoln's Inn Fields Theatre until 1705, and managed the new Queen's Theatre in the ▷ Haymarket together with ▷ Vanbrugh after that date. He accepted some government posts, and continued to write intermittently, composing a masque, *The Judgment of Paris* (1701); an operatic piece, *Semele* (1710), which provided part of the libretto for an oratorio by ▷ Handel; a prose narrative, *An Impossible Thing* (1720); and several poems. He brought out an edition of Dryden's works in 1717. Congreve was an admirer of the actress ▷ Anne Bracegirdle, for whom he wrote several of his best roles. His friends included ▷ Steele, ▷ Pope, and ▷ Swift. He went almost blind in his last years, and died following a coach accident at Bath. He is buried in Westminster Abbey. Congreve's comedies are distinguished by their verbal play and wit, in the

▷ Restoration ▷ Comedy of Manners mode. His art is satiric, and he created a number of memorable characters.
Bib: Johnson, S., *Lives of the Poets*; Love, H., *Congreve*; Morris, B. (ed.), *William Congreve*.

Coningsby, or The New Generation (1844)
A political novel by ▷ Benjamin Disraeli. By means of it, the rising politician, Disraeli, expresses his contempt for the lack of principle behind the contemporary ▷ Tory (right-wing) party, whose side he nonetheless took against the expediency and materialism of the ▷ Whigs and ▷ Utilitarians. Against them he advocates a revived, platonically idealized aristocracy with the interests of the people at heart and respected by them as their natural leaders. Such a new aristocrat is the hero of the novel, Coningsby, and he and his friends form a group comparable to the Young England group which Disraeli himself led in Parliament. Coningsby is the grandson of Lord Monmouth, type of the old, unprincipled, predatory aristocracy, whose inveterate enemy is the industrialist Millbank, representing the new and vital middle class. Coningsby falls in love with Millbank's daughter, is disinherited by his grandfather and eventually is elected to Parliament with Millbank's support. The novel is essentially one of propaganda of ideas, but written with great feeling, liveliness and intelligence. Lord Monmouth was based on the actual Lord Hertford, also used as the basis of Lord Steyne in ▷ Thackeray's ▷ *Vanity Fair*. Another excellently drawn character is the detestable Rigby, based on John Wilson Croker, politician and journalist, and author of the notoriously abusive review of ▷ Keats's ▷ *Endymion*.

Conquest, The (Norman)
The conquest of England following the defeat of Harold by the ▷ Norman invading force led by ▷ William I at the Battle of Hastings in 1066.

Conrad, Joseph (1857–1924)
Novelist. His name in full was Józef Teodor Konrad Korzeniowski. He knew hardly any English when he was 20; yet before he was 40 he had completed his first English novel, *Almayer's Folly* (1895), and ten years later he had published one of the masterpieces of the novel in English: ▷ *Nostromo* (1904). The background to Conrad as a novelist is complicated and important for understanding the richness of his art. 1 Early life. His father was a Polish patriot and man of letters, exiled from the Polish Ukraine by the Russian

Joseph Conrad

government, which then ruled it, for his political activity. His mother died when he was seven, and his father when he was 11, and his uncle subsequently became the main family influence in his life. 2 Life at sea. From the tales of sea life (in translation) by the English writer ▷ Captain Marryat, the American Fenimore Cooper, and the Frenchman ▷ Victor Hugo, he became fascinated by the sea and joined the crew of a French ship in 1874, and of an English one in 1878. By 1884 he was a British subject and had qualified as a master (ship's captain). In his voyages Conrad had visited the Mediterranean, South America, the Far East, and Central Africa. 3 Writing life. He began writing in about 1886 with at least as good an acquaintance with French language and literature as English. He brought to the English novel an admiration for the French ▷ realists, ▷ Flaubert and Maupassant. He also had a knowledge of many peoples, and a profound feeling of the contrast between the tightly enclosed communities of ships' crews and the loose egocentric individualism characterizing land societies. In addition, he knew, from his childhood experience in Russian Poland and Russia itself, the tragic impingement of political pressures on personal life, in a way that was unusual in the West until after the outbreak of World War I in 1914. In his preoccupation with the exploration of moral issues he was in the English tradition.

His major work is represented by the novels ▷ *Lord Jim* (1900), ▷ *Nostromo*, ▷ *The Secret Agent* (1907) and *Under Western Eyes* (1911) and the novellas *The*

Nigger of the Narcissus (1898); *Youth* (1902); ▷ *Heart of Darkness* (1902); *Typhoon* (1903); and *The Shadow Line* (1917). *Lord Jim* and *The Nigger of the Narcissus* are concerned with honour, courage and solidarity, ideals for which the merchant service provided a framework. *The Secret Agent* and *Under Western Eyes* deal with political extremism, the contrast between eastern and western Europe, and human folly, cruelty, fear and betrayal. *Nostromo*, set in an imaginary South American state, shares some of the themes of the other work, but is notable for its sense of history and the power of economic forces. *Heart of Darkness* is famous for its ambiguous and resonant portrayal of evil. Conrad's earlier novels, *Almayer's Folly* and *An Outcast of the Islands* (1896) have Far Eastern settings, and a less developed prose style. His later work includes *Chance* (1914), the first to bring him a big public; *Victory* (1915); *The Arrow of Gold* (1919); *The Rescue* (1920); *The Rover* (1923); and *Suspense*, which he was working on when he died. Conrad is one of the most important modern English novelists, both for his concerns and for his techniques. He addressed issues which have come to seem central to the 20th-century mind: the problem of identity; the terror of the unknown within and without; the difficulty of finding a secure moral base; political violence and economic oppression; isolation and existential dread. His technical innovations were particularly in the use of narrators, the disruption of narrative chronology and the employment of a powerful ▷ irony of tone.

His other works are: a number of volumes of short stories and essays, including *Tales of Unrest* (1898) and *Notes on Life and Letters* (1921). *The Mirror of the Sea* (1906) and *A Personal Record* (1912) are autobiographical. Conrad co-operated with ▷ Ford Madox Ford in the writing of two novels: *The Inheritors* (1901) and *Romance* (1903). The first three volumes of his *Collected Letters* were published in 1983, 1986 and 1988.
Bib: Baines, J., *Joseph Conrad: A Critical Biography*; Berthoud, J., *Joseph Conrad: the Major Phase*; Guerard, A. J., *Conrad the Novelist*; Najder, Z., *Joseph Conrad: A Chronicle*; Watt, I., *Conrad in the Nineteenth Century* (1980); Hewitt, D., *Conrad: A Reassessment*.

Conscious Lovers, The (1722)
Play by ▷ Sir Richard Steele, his last, adapted from ▷ Terence's *Andria*, and sometimes considered as an archetype of Augustan (▷ Augustan age) 'exemplary' comedy, in contrast to ▷ Restoration 'wit comedy', and a landmark in the development

of the later 'sentimental comedy'. It is also seen as a vehicle for the expression of Whig (▷ Whig and Tory) attitudes and values, again in contrast to the Tory values espoused in much of Restoration comedy. Young Bevil thinks of himself as consistently virtuous, but this conflicts with his desires. He secretly supports the beautiful but impoverished Indiana, whom he also loves. However, in accordance with his father's wishes, he proposes marriage to Lucinda, while concealing the fact from Indiana. Lucinda is in turn loved by Bevil's friend Myrtle. On the wedding day Bevil regrets his commitment to Lucinda, and offers to help Myrtle to a match with her, describing it as an humanitarian act. In Act V Indiana is revealed as Lucinda's elder half-sister, and therefore heiress to half their father's fortune. She is united with Young Bevil, and Lucinda with Myrtle. The play's title derives from the thought and attention that Bevil Junior and Indiana give to their own emotions. Steele intended them to be admired, and the play as a whole to give moral guidance. But it generated a great controversy, with critics variously pointing to its supposed hypocrisy, its didacticism, and the seriousness of its tone.

Consciousness
In its most general sense consciousness is synonymous with 'awareness'. In a more specifically ▷ Freudian context it is associated with the individual's perception of reality. For Freud, of course, the impression which an individual has of his or her experience is partial, since awareness is controlled by the processes of the unconscious, which are never recognized in their true form. More recently 'consciousness' has been associated with the ▷ Enlightenment view of individualism, in which the individual is conceived of as being distinct from society, and is also held to be the centre and origin of meaning. Following from this, what distinguishes humanity is its alleged capacity for autonomy, and hence freedom of action. The ▷ Romantic equivalent of this philosophical position is that literature is the expression of the pre-existent 'self' of the writer, and that the greatest literature is that which manifests the writer's consciousness most fully. These views of consciousness should further be distinguished from the ▷ Marxist version, in which the self is 'produced' through 'material practices', by means of which social relations are generated. Theories of consciousness affect notions of the relationship between writer and reader, and it

is in working out such relationships that the concept of 'consciousness' is important in current literary critical debate.

Constant Couple, The: Or, A Trip to the Jubilee (1699)
Comedy by ▷ George Farquhar. Angelica is in love with the rake, Sir Harry Wildair, who takes her for a whore. He finds himself in a position where he must marry her or fight; he decides matrimony is the bolder course, and marries her. In the secondary plot, Lurewell has become a coquette after being apparently abandoned by Colonel Standard. The situation is found to have been based on a misunderstanding, and the couple are reunited. The play was so well received that Farquhar followed it up with a sequel, *Sir Harry Wildair* (1701), which proved far less successful.

Constantinople
The name given to Byzantium by the Roman Emperor Constantine when he rebuilt it as his capital in AD 330. It is now a part of Istanbul.

Contemporary Review, The
It was founded in 1866 and has Sir Percy Bunting as its most famous editor. It covered a variety of subjects and in 1955 incorporated ▷ *The Fortnightly Review*.

Contradiction
Used in literary criticism to identify the incoherences in a literary text. Derived from Hegel, Engels and ▷ Marx, contradiction, as applied to literature, implies that artistic representation is not the product of a unifying aesthetic impulse. Contradiction describes patterns of dominance and subordination and thus, in literary terms, points towards divisions within the work which challenge notions of aesthetic coherence.

Conversation poem
A reflective poem, usually in ▷ blank verse, in which the poet meditates aloud, ostensibly talking to a friend. It adopts a more intimate, introspective tone than its predecessor, the 18th-century verse epistle. The term is especially associated with ▷ Samuel Taylor Coleridge, who first used it. His *Eolian Harp* (1795), *This Lime-Tree Bower* (1800), *The Nightingale* (1798) and *Frost at Midnight* (1798) are often termed 'conversation poems'.

Cook's Tale, The
One of ▷ Chaucer's ▷ *Canterbury Tales*. The *Cook's Tale*, set in low-life London, begins a story about 'Perkyn Revelour' before breaking off after only 58 lines. The nature of the Cook's contribution to the story-telling competition seems rather uncertain. Later in

the journey, the Host calls upon the Cook to contribute a story, but the Manciple pre-empts any response from the drunken Cook (in the Prologue to the ▷ *Manciple's Tale*). In some manuscripts of the *Canterbury Tales*, the romance of ▷ *Gamelyn* is inserted and attributed to the Cook.

Cooper, William (b 1910)
Pen name of H. S. Hoff, novelist. Having already published four novels under his real name, Cooper came to prominence in 1950 with *Scenes from Provincial Life*, the story of an unconventional and sceptical schoolteacher living in a Midlands town around the outbreak of World War II. In reacting against the experimental tradition of the ▷ Bloomsbury Group and of ▷ modernism, Cooper's novel initiated the 1950s school of dissentient ▷ realism, which included such writers as ▷ John Braine, ▷ David Storey, ▷ Stan Barstow and ▷ John Wain. *Scenes from Metropolitan Life* (written in the 1950s but not published for legal reasons until 1982) and *Scenes from Married Life* (1961) complete a trilogy. Other novels include: *You Want the Right Frame of Reference* (1971), *Love on the Coast* (1973) and *Scenes from Later Life* (1983).

Cooper's Hill (1642)
▷ Denham, Sir John.

Copernicus (1473–1543)
This was the Latinized form of surname of Nicolas Koppernik, a Polish astronomer. In *De revolutionibus orbium coelestium* (*Concerning the revolutions of the heavenly spheres*) (1543) he expounded for the first time since classical times the belief that the earth and other planets move round the sun. This was contrary to the hitherto accepted theory of the Egyptian astronomer ▷ Ptolemy according to which the earth was the centre of the solar system. The Ptolemaic system suited the traditional Christian conception of the universe and the place of man within it – it is still assumed, for instance, in ▷ Milton's epic of the Creation, ▷ *Paradise Lost* – but the Copernican theory caused little scandal since at the time it was regarded merely as an ingenious hypothesis. Only when ▷ Galileo claimed its validity, on demonstrable grounds, after the invention of his new telescope, did the Church condemn the theory outright, in 1616, and require Galileo to repudiate his findings.

Cophetua, King
A legendary king of North Africa who was indifferent to women until he fell in love with a beggar-maid whom he married. The legend occurs in a traditional ▷ ballad published in

▷ Thomas Percy's *Reliques* and there are several allusions to it in Elizabethan plays and elsewhere.

Coppard, A. E. (1878–1957)

Writer of short stories. He was largely self-educated, and began serving in a shop at the age of nine. Later he began writing while working as an accountant, and his literary interests were nourished when he obtained a post at Oxford where he met and made friends with the intelligentsia. The best of his stories are chiefly in the earlier volumes: *Adam and Eve and Pinch Me* (1921); *Clorinda Walks in Heaven* (1922); *Fishmonger's Fiddle* (1925); and *The Field of Mustard* (1926). Later volumes include: *Pink Furniture* (1930); *Tapster's Tapestry* (1938); *You Never Know Do You?* (1939); and *The Dark-Eyed Lady* (1947). He also wrote poems: *Collected Poems* (1928); *Easter Day* (1931); and *Cherry Ripe* (1935), and an autobiography, *It's Me, O Lord* (1957).

Coppard had a remarkably acute ear for the spoken word, and his best tales have the freshness and simplicity of aural folk-tales. Although his subject matter was often more sophisticated than this suggests, many of his finest stories are about the life of the countryside. He was influenced by ▷ Thomas Hardy's short stories, and he often shows a stoically resigned attitude to human destiny which is similar to Hardy's outlook, but he combined this with a remarkable talent for sharp comedy, again reminiscent of peasant folk-tales.

Copyright, The law of

The right of writers, artists and musicians to refuse reproduction of their works. The right is now established law in every civilized country. The first copyright law in England was passed under Queen Anne in 1709. Before this, it was possible for publishers to publish books without the author's permission, and without allowing him or her any profits from sale, a practice very common during the lifetime of ▷ Shakespeare. Until 1909, the laws of the United States did not adequately safeguard British authors against having their works 'pirated' there, *ie* published without their permission and without giving them suitable financial return. ▷ Dickens was a main sufferer from this state of affairs, and it greatly angered him.

▷ Shakespeare's plays; Stationers' Register.

Corelli, Marie (1855–1924)

Novelist. Born Mary Mackay, illegitimate daughter (though she claimed to be adopted, and born in 1864) of Scottish songwriter Charles Mackay and his second wife. She was educated by governesses and for a while at a convent, and was a gifted pianist, intending to take up a musical career, for which she adopted the name Corelli. In 1885 a psychic experience led her to start writing and her novels are sensational, full of trances, swoons, religious conversions and visions etc. She was very successful around the turn of the century, but her popularity declined into ridicule before her death. Her first novel was *A Romance of Two Worlds* (1886) but her great popularity occurred with *Barabbas: A Dream of the World's Tragedy* (1893), despite unfavourable reviews. *The Sorrows of Satan* (1895) had a greater initial sale than any previous English novel. Other novels include *The Mighty Atom* (1896) and *Boy* (1900).
Bib: Bigland, E., *Marie Corelli: The Woman and the Legend*; Masters, B., *Now Barabbas Was a Rotter: The Extraordinary Life of Marie Corelli*.

Corey, Katherine (?1635–?)

Actress, Katherine Corey (née Mitchell) claimed to be the first professional English actress; she may have played Dol Common in a production of ▷ Ben Jonson's *The Alchemist* in December 1660, and certainly played the part in 1664.

Coriolanus (?1608)

A ▷ tragedy by ▷ Shakespeare about a legendary Roman hero (5th century BC). Shakespeare took the story from the *Lives* by ▷ Plutarch translated into English by ▷ Sir Thomas North. A war is being waged between Rome and the neighbouring city of Corioli, capital city of the Volscians. The hero of the play, Caius Marcius, wins the title Coriolanus for his heroism against the enemy. But Rome is morally at war within herself: the arrogant patricians (aristocrats) despise the plebs, or common people, who in turn are factious and disorderly. Coriolanus differs from his fellow patricians only in being still prouder than they are, in that he cannot stoop to flatter the plebs for their votes. They succeed in expelling him from the city, whereupon he allies himself with the Volscians and returns to destroy it. His mother Volumnia, who embodies the qualities of the arrogant patricians and has herself bred her son to value his pride above all, succeeds in deterring him; he is then assassinated by the Volscians as a traitor. The tragedy has peculiar interest for its study of social influence on the individual. It is less popular than some other tragedies by Shakespeare, but it is certainly among the finest of his plays.

Corn Laws, Repeal of the, 1846
The Corn Laws existed to protect English home-grown corn from competition from imported foreign corn. Their existence made for higher food prices and assumed the superior importance of agricultural interest over urban industrial interests. In the first half of the 19th century the ▷ Tory party derived its main support from landowners, whereas the Whigs owed much of their support to the new industrialists of the rapidly growing industrial towns. The ▷ Whig Anti-Corn Law League consequently represented not merely opposition to a particular measure but rivalry between main segments of society; moreover, the workers, anxious above all for cheap food, supported the urban middle class and the Whigs. It was nonetheless a Tory Prime Minister, Robert Peel, who repealed the Corn Laws under pressure of a severe famine in Ireland. The abolition of the Corn Laws was of historic importance in several ways: 1 it divided the Tory party, sending its younger leader, ▷ Benjamin Disraeli, into opposition, with his supporters, against Peel; 2 it began the era of free trade (*ie* trade unrestricted by import or export taxes); 3 it acknowledged implicitly that industrial interests were henceforth to be regarded as more important than agricultural interests; 4 it relieved the almost revolutionary restlessness of the working class, so that England was one of the few countries in Europe not to undergo upheaval or serious threat of upheaval in the Year of Revolutions, 1848.

Corneille, Pierre (1606–84)
One of the great French classical dramatists whose work exiled Englishmen would have encountered during the ▷ Interregnum. His dramas, *Le Cid* (1636–7), *Horace, Polyeucte* and *Cinna* (between 1640 and 1643), debate the conflict between duty and love, passion and honour, and highlight the difficulties posed by the heroic ethos. They show the influence also of the neo-classical conception of the ▷ unities. Corneille's critical essays (the *Examens* and the *Discours*) were pioneers in serious drama criticism. ▷ Dryden was an admirer, but his heroic dramas did not match Corneille's attainments.

Cornhill Magazine, The
A monthly periodical, at the height of its fame soon after its foundation by ▷ William Thackeray, the novelist, in 1860. Contributors included ▷ John Ruskin, ▷ Matthew Arnold, ▷ Mrs Gaskell, ▷ Anthony Trollope and ▷ Leslie

Stephen, besides Thackeray himself. It continued this century to publish the work of many writers.

Corombona, Vittoria
The tragic female protagonist of ▷ *The White Devil* by ▷ John Webster. Her resilience in the face of adversity combined with her lack of sexual and moral integrity render her a fascinating and emancipated character. This is evident particularly in the famous trial scene when she emerges as morally no more guilty than her accusers, who use the full panoply of the law to pursue their spurious ends against her.

Corpus Christi, The Feast of
A festival of the Roman Catholic Church in honour of the Holy Sacrament. It was ordained in 1264 by Pope Urban IV. By the 15th century it was the principal Church feast in the year, and was particularly celebrated by the performance of ▷ mystery plays.

Corpus Christi Plays
▷ Cycle plays.

Corsair, The **(1814)**
A narrative poem in heroic ▷ couplets by ▷ Lord Byron. Conrad, who has become a pirate for some mysterious reason, disguises himself as a dervish in order to gain entry to the palace of the pasha, Seyd. In the fight which ensues he insists that his men must not invade Seyd's harem ('wrong not on your lives/ One female form'), and Seyd's wife Gulnare, described decorously as 'the trembling fair', consequently falls in love with him. All his men are killed and Conrad is thrown into a dungeon to await a slow death next day. Gulnare sets him free, but when he realizes that she has murdered her own husband, Conrad is filled with revulsion. He returns to his island to find that his faithful consort Medora has died in his absence, upon which he himself mysteriously disappears. The poem's self-indulgent blend of escapist adventure, condescending sexism and glamorous exoticism, made it one of the most popular of Byron's poems.

Cortegiano, Il (*The Courtier*)
▷ Castiglione, Baldassare.

Counter-Reformation
A movement in the Catholic Church to counter the ▷ Protestant ▷ Reformation. It arose from the Council of Trent (1545–63) composed of the ecclesiastical leaders of the Catholic Church. The only important English writer to be influenced by the Counter-Reformation was the poet ▷ Richard Crashaw.

Countess Cathleen, The (1802)
A verse play by ▷ W. B. Yeats. Its theme is
a woman who sells her soul to the devil in
order to save the poor from starvation. It
marks the beginning of Yeats's career as a
poetic dramatist, and was one of the plays
used by the Irish Literary Theatre as a
starting-point.
▷ Abbey Theatre.

Country Wife, The (1675)
Comedy by ▷ William Wycherley. The
irrational jealousy of Pinchwife, instead of
keeping his naive country wife faithful to
him, puts ideas into her head which are
encouraged by the libertine Horner. Horner
has convinced the men of the town that he is
impotent, but secretly seduces several of their
wives. Most treat him merely as a means for
their sexual satisfaction, and in one of the
play's most famous scenes (IV, 3) Horner,
pretending as a cover for his activities that he
is offering china for sale, tells the women that
he has sold out of china, a code meaning that
he has exhausted his energy for sexual
congress. Margery, the country wife of the
title, cares for him more than the others, and
is hurt when he rejects her and forces her to
return to her husband. Meanwhile
Pinchwife's sister, Alithea, is to be married to
Sparkish. The latter pretends to affection but
is interested only in the money which Alithea
will bring as dowry, and takes her for granted.
She is attracted to Harcourt, who really loves
her, but resists his attentions out of duty to
Sparkish. Eventually Sparkish is revealed in
his true colours, and she marries Harcourt.
The play's chief assets are the comedy of its
scenes, heavy with dramatic irony, and the
author's caustic wit. Its free treatment of
sexuality drew condemnation even in its own
time, and there has been critical debate about
whether Horner was intended as a hero, to be
admired for his cleverness, or a vicious object
of Wycherley's satire. It was adapted by
▷ Garrick as *The Country Girl* (1766).

Couplet
A pair of rhymed lines of verse of equal
length. The commonest form is the so-called
▷ heroic couplet of 10 syllables and five
stresses in each line. It was first used in
▷ Chaucer's ▷ *Legend of Good Women*.

> A thousand timës have I herd men telle
> That ther is joye in heven, and peyne in
> helle . . .

The heroic couplet had its most prolific
period between 1660 and 1790 when many
poets from ▷ Dryden to ▷ Crabbe used
it; its master was ▷ Pope:

> Most souls, 'tis true, but peep out once an age,
> Dull sullen pris'ners in the body's cage

> *(Elegy to an Unfortunate Lady)*

▷ Blank verse was a derivative of the
couplet.

The 8-syllable (octosyllabic) couplet gives
a lighter, less dignified rhythm. It was also
used by Chaucer (*The Romaunt of the Rose*,
▷ *The Book of the Duchess*, ▷ *The House of
Fame*) in his earlier work. It is less common
after 1600 than before, but a notable later
user of it is ▷ Jonathan Swift (*eg On the
Death of Dr Swift*). ▷ Keats used it for *The
Eve of St Mark* (1819), and ▷ W. H. Auden
for his *New Year Letter* (1941).

Court of Chancery
A Court of law under the ▷ Lord
Chancellor, head of the English judicial
system. The Court grew up in the 15th
century to deal with cases which for any
reason could not be dealt with efficiently by
the established law courts administering
▷ Common Law. The practice developed a
system of law supplementary to Common
Law, known as Equity. Few things so neatly
demonstrate the disadvantage of women in
English law as the fact that they are treated as
the legal equivalents of orphans and lunatics,
through one of the special fields of jurisdiction
Equity was created to cover. There have been
recent attempts, by means of 'equal
opportunities' legislation, for instance, to
remedy this long-standing disability. By the
19th century Chancery procedure became
excessively complex, its relationship with
other courts of law was ill-defined, and
judgements were often delayed for years –
hence the satire to which ▷ Charles Dickens
subjected the Court in his novel, ▷ *Bleak
House*. The system was reformed by the
Judicature Act, 1873. (The idiom 'in
chancery' means 'remaining undecided
indefinitely'; a 'ward in Chancery' is an
orphan whose interests are in the care of
Chancery.)
▷ Courts of Law.

Court Theatre
▷ Royal Court Theatre.

Courtly Love
Since the 1950s there has been considerable
debate over the historical authenticity of
'courtly love', the term being coined in the
late 19th century to refer to a codified,
stylized expression of the experience of love,
found in medieval European texts. Many of
the problems have arisen from the over-rigid
use of this term by literary critics. What is
clear from considering the literary culture of

Love unto death: Flemish painted shield,
15th century

the 12th century onwards is that the stylized
expression of the lover's experience in texts
cannot be assimilated and organized into a
single code of behaviour or set of procedural
'rules': courtly love is a disparate
phenomenon, arising out of the confluence of
various literary and philosophical traditions,
and its definition would vary, to some extent,
depending on the provenance of the medieval
texts under discussion.

The notion of a refined and ennobling love
experience is not a medieval invention;
scholars have traced Arabic influences in the
modes of expression employed by the
▷ troubadour poets of 12th-century France,
whose work is often taken as the earliest
expression of courtly love sentiments in
medieval Europe. Classical Latin texts,
especially the treatises on the arts and
remedies of loving produced by ▷ Ovid,
exert a great influence on medieval attempts
to formalize and codify the lover's experience.
What is distinctive about medieval
expressions of courtly love is the development
of a range of terms and conventions which
portray the love experience in terms of feudal
models and ethics: the male lover serves his
lady as a member of a court might do his
lord; the relationship is one of love service, in
which the lady has the power to bestow gifts
and rewards to her faithful love-servant. This
love service is frequently represented as a
refining, disciplined experience which has its
own protocol, and there may be a sense of
contiguity between the quality of the love
experience for the female object of desire
and the love of a trascendental, divine
subject (indeed the first may lead to the
second, as it does in ▷ Dante's ▷ *Divina
Commedia* and in ▷ Petrarch's *Rime
Sparse*). 'Fin'amor' is an important term
within the more general conceptual
framework signalled by 'courtly love':
it derives from a tradition of moral
philosophy and denotes a quality of loving
which is not self-seeking, self-gratifying or
possessive.

The relationship between the theory and
practice of this feudalized love ethic is the
subject of literary discussion and debate
throughout the medieval period in a wide
range of texts. The different versions of the
stories of lovers such as ▷ Tristram and
Isolde, ▷ Lancelot and Guinevere,
illustrate how the issue of the rights and
wrongs of loving is a matter for discussion
and debate, and not a clear-cut or rigidly
codified matter. Even those texts which may
appear to offer a more theoretical guide to the
rules of courtly love illustrate the way in
which love remains a subject of discussion
and debate, despite attempts to codify it. One
of the texts frequently cited as offering an
authoritative guide to courtly love, *De Arte
Honeste Amandi* (*The Art of Honourable
Loving*), written some time in the later 12th
century by ▷ Andreas Capellanus, was itself
interpreted in very different ways in
subsequent centuries, as it is by more recent
scholars who hope to find an interpretative
key in this work. Debates about the protocol
of a lover's behaviour constitute a medieval
literary genre in their own right and are often
set in the context of a 'Court of Love' of
some kind. But considering the relationship
between the theory and practice of
heterosexual loving can lead to discussions of
varying dimensions and import. The
influential 13th-century dream-vision poem
▷ *Le Roman de la Rose* shows how the
relationship between the theory and practice
of refined loving can become the focal point
for an exploration of all the resources of
human culture itself. If courtly love is not
seen by modern readers as a monolithic
concept, but rather as an area of discussion
and debate, a nexus point for a wide range of
issues from court etiquette to the principles
of universal ordering, issues trivial and
profound, then the tonal range employed in

such texts as ▷ Chaucer's ▷ *Parliament of Foulys* may be easier to appreciate.

How far the conventionalized modes of representing love experience and ideals in medieval texts influenced and reflected courtly practice at the time is a controversial and complex area, and generalizations are of little profit here. However, the influence of economic and political factors in determining marital arrangements should not be underestimated and, in practice, there seems little room for the exercise of female choice in the arrangements for choosing a legally recognized partner. The conceptual framework offered by the phenomenon of courtly love perhaps served a powerful compensatory function. If this feudalized love ethic arose out of the social circumstances of a specific historic moment, its power to transcend those circumstances and be used as a register for expressing and shaping ideals about loving is demonstrated by its survival through the Renaissance period and beyond.
▷ Ovid.
Bib: Boase, R., *The Origin and Meaning of Courtly Love*.

Couzyn, Jeni (b 1942)
Poet. Couzyn was born and educated in South Africa, which she left in 1965, and has since become a Canadian citizen, although she lives in Britain. Her volumes of verse include: *Flying* (1970); *Christmas in Africa* (1975); *Life By Drowning: Selected Poems* (1985). Couzyn edited the important 1985 ▷ anthology, *The Bloodaxe Book of Contemporary Women Poets*, and she also writes for children.

Covenant and Covenanters
1 When ▷ Charles I tried to impose an ▷ Anglican religious settlement on ▷ Presbyterian Scots, supporters of the Presbyterian system met from all over Scotland and signed the Covenant (1638), by which they solemnly undertook ('covenanted') to defend their common religious belief. Supporters of the Covenant were called Covenanters.
2 The Solemn League and Covenant (1643) was the treaty between the Scottish supporters of the Presbyterian church and the ▷ Puritan Parliamentarian rebels in England to preserve the Scottish Church, reform the Anglican one in England and resist the advances of Catholicism.
▷ Civil wars; Scotland.

Covent Garden Theatres
In 1732 Edward Shepherd (1670–1747) planned the first Covent Garden Theatre, or Theatre Royal, on the site of the present Royal Opera House, to which the actor-manager ▷ John Rich transferred from Lincoln's Inn Fields. The name derives from a convent which had stood on the site previously. Following the Licensing Act of 1737 the Covent Garden Theatre was one of only three theatres in London to be granted a licence. In 1773 Oliver Goldsmith's ▷ *She Stoops to Conquer* was staged here for the first time, and ▷ Charles Macklin mounted his innovative production of ▷ *Macbeth*, dressed for the first time in 'Scottish' costume. The present theatre opened in 1858. Although it is now famous for its internationally distinguished productions of opera it is not often realized that these are funded by the state. Before 1948 Covent Garden was a Mecca *palais de danse* with a two-month opera season. State funding for opera, with massively subsidized seats, was devised by J. M. Keynes as a means of raising the tone of British culture, and, as he hoped, of diffusing it more widely.

Coventry Plays
▷ Cycle plays; N-Town Cycle.

Coverdale, Miles (1488–1568)
▷ Bible in England.

Coverley, Sir Roger de
A fictional character invented by the essayist ▷ Sir Richard Steele for the pages of ▷ *The Spectator*, and developed by his colleague ▷ Joseph Addison. The name was taken from a north country dance, Roger of Coverley. Sir Roger was at first a member of an imaginary club, the Spectator Club, where Steele in his journalist guise of the 'Spectator' purported to be studying human nature. In the hands of Addison, Sir Roger came to take up much more space than the other members; the papers devoted to describing his life (20 by Addison, eight by Steele, and two by Budgell) are much the best known parts of *The Spectator*. In his conservatism, his devotion to the Church of England, and his kindly but despotic control of his tenants, he is a typical ▷ squire of the time, but in his civilized manners he is deliberately made superior to the general run of country squires (compare Squire Western in ▷ Fielding's ▷ *Tom Jones*). In his simplicity and idiosyncrasies he was individual, with a literary relationship to ▷ Don Quixote. Though the 'Coverley Papers' are not a novel, the envisioning of the character is distinctly novelistic, so that they rank among the precursors of the English novel. Addison's especial aim, beyond entertainment, was to civilize the country squire; a secondary aim was the political one of making fun of the Tory English gentry.

Coward, Sir Noël (1899–1973)

British stage and film actor, dramatist and director. He began his theatrical career at the age of 12 acting in a fantasy play called *The Goldfish*. As a dramatist he gained some notoriety with his early works, *The Young Idea* (1923), *The Vortex* (1924), *Fallen Angels* (1925) and *Sirocco* (1927), which was greeted with a riot. However his partnership with the promoter and theatre manager C. B. Cochran proved his ability to work creatively and successfully within the commercial theatre. His reputation rests mainly on the six comedies he wrote between 1923 and 1942: *Fallen Angels* (1925); *Hay Fever* (1925); *Bitter Sweet* (1929); *Private Lives* (1930); *Design for Living* (1932) and *Present Laughter* (1942).
Bib: Gray, F., *Noël Coward*; Kiernan, R. F., *Noël Coward*; Lahr, J., *Coward the Playwright*.

Cowley, Abraham (1618–67)

Poet and essayist. Ever since ▷ Samuel Johnson's disparaging comments on Cowley in his ▷ *Lives of the Poets* (1779–81), Cowley's reputation has suffered, and yet Cowley is one of the most important and influential of the mid-17th-century poets. A Royalist in politics, he accompanied Queen Henrietta Maria into exile in Paris in 1644–6, returned to England in 1654, was imprisoned in 1655 and later released.

His chief works include: *Poeticall Blossoms* (written 1633), a collection of poetry published in 1656 which contained ▷ Pindaric odes and ▷ elegies on William Harvey among others, and an essay on the advancement of science: *A Proposition for the Advancement of Experimental Philosophy* (1661). Cowley's attachment, after the Civil War, to the figures associated with the early ▷ Royal Society is evidenced both in his important ▷ ode, celebrating the Royal Society (first published in Thomas Sprat's *History of the Royal Society*) and his celebration of scientific figures and their works in his poetry.

As well as celebrating the advance of science, Cowley also composed an unfinished ▷ epic, *A Poem on the Late Civil War* (1679), which he abandoned at the point when the war began to turn against the Royalist forces. He also anticipated ▷ John Milton's ▷ *Paradise Lost* in attempting a biblical epic, *Davideis* ('A sacred poem of the Troubles of David', published in the *Poems* of 1656). In the 19th century and through much of the 20th, Cowley was read as a species of inferior ▷ John Donne or ▷ Thomas Carew, yet the range of his writing (which embraced science,

▷ translation and experiments in form and ▷ metre as well as critical statements on the nature of poetic discourse) make him an important figure in his own right.
Bib: Hinman, R., *Abraham Cowley's World of Order*; Trotter, D., *The Poetry of Abraham Cowley*.

Cowley, Hannah (1743–1809)

Dramatist and poet. In 1772 she married Thomas Cowley, a clerk and newspaper writer, and together they moved to London, where she began writing for the theatre. In 1783 her husband went to India with the East India Company, while she remained in London looking after their three children and continuing to write, a total of 11 comedies and two tragedies, as well as several long narrative romances. She also carried on a poetic correspondence with the poet Robert Merry, which was satirized by ▷ William Gifford. Cowley's comedies have a self-conscious morality which stresses the importance of marriage and proper relations between spouses. Her most successful plays include *The Belle's Stratagem* (1780) and *A Bold Stroke for a Husband* (1783). Cowley's *A School for Greybeards* (1786) is a revised and 'sanitized' version of ▷ Aphra Behn's ▷ *The Lucky Chance* (1686), which did not prevent it being attacked for supposed immorality.

Cowper, William (1731–1800)

William Cowper by L. F. Abbott (1792)

Poet and letter-writer. Son of the rector of Great Berkhampstead in Hertfordshire, he was called to the bar in 1754, and through family connections was offered the post of

Clerk of the Journals in the House of Lords. However, the early death of his mother, his experiences of bullying at public school and a thwarted love affair, had caused severe neurosis which led him to contemplate suicide at the prospect of the clerkship examination. He spent a year in an asylum and thereafter led a retired life on his own private income, first in the home of Morley and Mary Unwin in Huntingdonshire and then after Morley's death with Mary Unwin in Olney. They planned to marry in 1773, but Cowper's conviction of his own personal damnation prevented this.

In Olney he came under the influence of the evangelical Rev. John Newton with whom he published *Olney Hymns* (1779), including 'Hark my soul! it is the Lord', and 'God moves in a mysterious way'. In 1780 Newton left Olney for London and Cowper's life became less spiritually strenuous. Mary Unwin encouraged him to write, in order to counteract his religious melancholia. His *Poems* (1782) contain *Table Talk*, and eight moral satires in heroic ▷ couplets which, though uneven in quality, display a distinctive unforced sententiousness which is one of his most attractive poetic characteristics. The volume also includes *Boadicea: an Ode* and *Verses supposed to be written by Alexander Selkirk* ('I am monarch of all I survey'). In the same year Cowper published his famous comic ballad *John Gilpin*. He made the acquaintance of Lady Austen, who suggested the scheme of the ▷ mock-heroic, discursive poem ▷ *The Task: A Poem in Six Books*, which appeared in 1785, and is in the more 'natural' medium of ▷ blank verse, rather than couplets. He followed this with an undistinguished translation of ▷ Homer (1791). In 1794 Mary Unwin died, and Cowper's only subsequent work is the introspective and despairing *Castaway*, published after his death, as were his *Letters* (1803), which are among the most famous in the language.

Cowper's work illustrates the movement away from the public themes of ▷ Augustanism towards a more domestic and personal poetry of sensibility. His work eschews brilliance or technical virtuosity, and can be banal. But at their best his ▷ lyrics are delicately moving, and his ▷ couplet and ▷ blank verse writing achieves an unassuming lucidity of tone, which evokes profound resonances.

▷ Romanticism; Selkirk, Alexander.
Bib: Cecil, D., *The Stricken Deer*; King, J., *William Cowper: A Biography*; Hutchins, B., *The Poetry of William Cowper*; Priestman, M., *Cowper's Task: Structure and Influence*; Newey, V., *Cowper's Poetry: A Critical Study and Reassessment*.

Crabbe, George (1754–1832)
Poet. Crabbe was born at Aldeburgh in Suffolk and his work is intimately associated with the region. He practised medicine before taking orders in 1781. Crabbe's earliest works, *The Library* (1781) and the anti-pastoral *The Village* (1783) have an heroic ▷ couplet metre and public, discursive tone already distinctly old-fashioned at the time. ▷ Samuel Johnson gave advice on the composition of the second poem, and in his grimly stoical vision of life and his distrust of pretension and excess, Crabbe resembles Johnson in temperament. *The Village* is relentless in its rejection of the conventions of literary pastoralism, showing nature with bitter realism as it was known to the poor. In his later works: *The Parish Register*, 1807; *The Borough*, 1810; *Tales in Verse*, 1812; *Tales of the Hall*, 1819, he depicts the diverse lives of his parishioners in a series of highly original short stories in couplets, a form which he made peculiarly his own. His best work treats social outcasts and extreme psychological states, as do a number of poems by ▷ William Wordsworth. But where Wordsworth's approach is transcendental and contemplative, Crabbe's involvement with his characters is compassionate in a more down-to-earth and intimate way. In *Peter Grimes* (Letter XXII of *The Borough*) the landscape of coastal East Anglia becomes an evocative symbol for the protagonist's breakdown and despair. Crabbe's narrative artistry, and uncompromising realism were admired by ▷ Jane Austen who remarked half-seriously that he was the only man she could ever think of marrying.
Bib: Crabbe, G. (junior), *Life*; Pollard, A. (ed.), *Crabbe: The Critical Heritage*; Bareham, T., *George Crabbe*; New, P., *George Crabbe's Poetry*.

Craft Guilds
Medieval societies for the protection and regulation of trade. They grew up in the 13th century out of the already existing merchant guilds, the difference being that the merchant guilds were associations of all the traders in a town, whereas the craft guilds were each limited to a particular craft or line of business. By degrees the craft guilds eliminated the merchant guilds by making them redundant. Each town had its own guilds and part of their function was to protect the trade of that town against competition from 'foreigners'. They gave much-needed security to the exercise of trade in disorderly times, provided

some social security to their members in times of need, and settled standards of work and conditions of sale. The members were ▷ master craftsmen. Guilds declined fairly rapidly in the 16th century as the capitalist, free-enterprise employers became more numerous; the guild system was too restrictive of trade to be compatible with ▷ capitalism. For the study of literature, one of the main interests of the craft guilds was their performance of ▷ mystery plays at festivals, especially ▷ Corpus Christi.

Craig, Edward Gordon (1872–1966)
Son of actress Ellen Terry and designer E. W. Godwin, and one of the most influential of early 20th-century stage designers. He began his theatrical career working with ▷ Henry Irving at the Lyceum, though disillusionment with English theatre led him to spend much of his time on the continent. Most of his highly innovative designs were never actually put into practice, but of those that were his most famous were for a production of ▷ *Hamlet* at the Moscow Art Theatre, in 1912, and ▷ Ibsen's *The Pretenders* at the Royal Danish Theatre, Copenhagen, in 1926. His influential theories on the crucial role of the theatre designer and the importance of expressive, poetic movement are explored in his books, *The Art of the Theatre* (1905); *On the Art of the Theatre* (1911); *Towards a New Theatre* (1907); *The Marionette* (1918); *The Theatre Advancing* (1921); *Books and Theatres* (1925).
Bib: Craig, E., *Gordon Craig*; Innes, C., *Edward Gordon Craig*.

Craik, Mrs Dinah Maria Mulock (1826–87)
Born in Stoke-on-Trent, the daughter of a nonconformist clergyman, she wrote novels, plays, poetry, ▷ biography, ▷ travel books, didactic essays and children's stories (▷ Children's books). After an unsettled childhood, she lived with her brother in London, becoming well-known in literary society and marrying a partner in Macmillans in 1865. She was a shrewd negotiator and businesswoman, but a generous woman, using a pension granted to her in 1864 to help needy authors. Her novels include *The Ogilvies* (1849), *Olive* (1850), *The Head of the Family* (1851) and *John Halifax, Gentleman* (1856), on which her fame largely rests.

Cranford (1853)
A novel by ▷ Elizabeth Gaskell (1810–65), first published in ▷ *Household Words* (ed. ▷ Charles Dickens) 1851–3. It is the best known of her novels. The town of Cranford is actually based on Knutsford, some 17 miles from Manchester. The book describes the life of the predominantly feminine genteel society of the place. Though apparently very slight, it contains graphic description, subtle, ironic humour resembling ▷ Jane Austen's, and acute discernment in discriminating between the vulgar arrogance of the merely rich and the sensitive, humane pride of the gentility. Its most famous characters are the blatant and ostentatious Honourable Mrs Jamieson and, in contrast, the timid, retiring, yet distinguished Miss Matty.

Cranmer, Thomas (1489–1556)
Archbishop of Canterbury, and responsible for the *Book of Common Prayer* (1549 and 1552) containing the liturgy of the Church of England. He was made Archbishop of Canterbury by ▷ Henry VIII during the king's conflict with the Papacy, and supported his rejection of the Pope's authority (▷ Act of Supremacy, 1534), the starting-point of the Church of England. Under Henry's Roman Catholic daughter, ▷ Queen Mary I, Cranmer renounced his opinions, but repudiated his renunciation when he was burnt at the stake in 1556. He is especially important for the literary value of his Prayer Book.
▷ *Common Prayer, Book of.*

Crashaw, Richard (?1612–49)
Poet. He belongs to the ▷ Metaphysical school of English poets, but in a special sense. In 1645 he became a Roman ▷ Catholic, despairing of the survival of the Church of England at that stage of the ▷ Civil War. He earlier came under the influence of the work of the Italian baroque poet, Giovanni Battista Marino (1569–1625) whose extravagance of imagery to some extent resembled the drawing together of unlike ideas into a single image that typified the English metaphysicals. Although Crashaw was perhaps the most sensuous of the English poets of this tendency, his Catholicism and the influence of Marino give to Crashaw's ecstasy an impersonal quality quite different from the direct, very personal devotional poetry of ▷ Donne and ▷ Herbert – the latter of whom had been Crashaw's first master. Crashaw's masterpiece is his *Hymn to Saint Theresa*; the one that shows his extravagances most obtrusively is *The Weeper*. His poems were published in 1646 in one volume under the titles *Steps to the Temple* and *The Delights of the Muses*.
Bib: Warren, A., *Richard Crashaw*; White, H. C., *The Metaphysical Poets*; Williamson, G., *The Donne Tradition*.

Frontispiece of Crashaw's *Steps to the Temple*

Crécy, Battle of (1346)

The first major victory of the English in the ▷ Hundred Years' War. In military history and patriotic sentiment it was important as being brought about by the English ▷ yeomen as archers, using the longbow. For military history, this meant the beginning of the end of the domination of war by the mounted knight in armour, and the beginning of the importance of infantry. In national myths, the English victory was not merely a victory of the English feudal aristocracy over that of the French but one in which the common people shared. The English forces were commanded by ▷ Edward III and the French by King Philip VI.
▷ Archery.

Creoles

British, French and Spanish settlers in South and Central America, Louisiana and the West Indies, and their descendants of any colour.

In English literature it applies especially to British sugar planters in the West Indies, who were very prosperous in the 18th century. Because it was unclear whether place of origin or race was being indicated, the term could be used to hint at or to mask blackness.

Cresseid, The Testament of
▷ Testament of Cresseid.

Cressida

The lover of the Trojan prince Troilus in medieval and post-medieval versions of the Troy story, who is involuntarily separated from Troilus when forced to join her father Calchas in the Greek camp (Calchas, a priest, has previously deserted the Trojan side). In the Greek camp she becomes the lover of Diomedes. She first appears in this role in the 12th-century text, the *Roman de Troie*, composed by ▷ Benoît de Sainte-Maure (in which she is called 'Briseida') and it is possible that the figure of Briseis, a lover of Achilles, whose story features in one of ▷ Ovid's *Heroides*, provides a precedent for the development of the Briseida character. The form of her name changes as the story of her love affair with Troilus is amplified and reworked by a series of writers from Benoît onwards, notably ▷ Boccaccio (Criseida), ▷ Chaucer (Criseyde), ▷ Robert Henryson (Cresseid), and ▷ Shakespeare (Cressida).
▷ Troy.

Cricket on the Hearth, The (1846)

A Christmas book by ▷ Charles Dickens, one of a series started by ▷ *A Christmas Carol*, 1843. It is a tale in which the evil schemes of old Tackleton to injure the married love of Peerybingle and his young wife, Dot, and to marry May Fielding are frustrated by the magic of the Cricket and by a mysterious stranger.

Critic, The: Or, a Tragedy Rehearsed (1779)

Satiric comedy by ▷ Sheridan, using the 'play within a play' technique employed in ▷ *The Rehearsal*, in order to mock contemporary dramatic technique. In the first act Dangle discusses with his wife, a fellow theatre goer called Sneer, and the author, Sir Fretful Plagiary, the fact that a new tragedy, *The Spanish Armada*, is being prepared at ▷ Drury Lane. In the second and third acts, Puff invites the three men to observe a rehearsal of his play, which concerns the approach of the Armada. Tilburnia, daughter of the governor of Tilbury Fort, expresses her love for one of the Spanish prisoners,

Don Ferolo Whiskerandos. As in *The Rehearsal*, the acting of the absurd play is accompanied by the fatuous explanations and instructions of the author, and scathing comments of his guests. The play ends with the destruction of the Spanish fleet, and strains of 'Rule Britannia', ▷ Handel's 'Water Music', and the march in *Judas Maccabaeus*. The tragedy was intended to satirize the works of dramatists such as ▷ Colman and ▷ Cumberland, of whom Sir Fretful Plagiary is a caricature. The play was acted 131 times before 1800.

Critique

A term used in critical theory. Traditional conceptions of 'criticism' have privileged the acts of judgement and comparison but have often anchored them in the unspecified sensitivity of the reader. Criticism presupposes a direct relationship between reader and literary text; the reader responds to the stimulus of particular verbal forms which are evaluated according to their appeal to a universal human condition. The practice of 'critique', in a literary context, however, concerns itself not just with producing readings of primary texts and accounting for those social, cultural, or psychological motivations which are responsible for its appearance in a particular form, but also with appraising critical readings of those texts. Critique addresses itself to questions of why individual texts should be accorded importance at particular historical moments, and implicates 'criticism' in its more traditional guise as a process whereby meanings are constructed, as opposed to being passively discovered.

Cromwell, Oliver (1599–1658)

Chief commander of the Parliamentarian forces in the ▷ Civil War against ▷ Charles I and Lord Protector of the Realm (1653–8) in place of a king. He belonged to the landowning class in the east of England and supported the Independents among the ▷ Puritans. It was his generalship that defeated the forces of Charles I and the Scottish supporters of ▷ Charles II after the execution of Charles I. After his death, his son, Richard Cromwell, succeeded as Lord Protector for some months, after which Charles II was restored by the action of one of Oliver's generals, General Monk, in 1660. After 1660 he suffered the censure of his political opponents and it was not until ▷ Thomas Carlyle published *Oliver Cromwell's Letters and Speeches* (1845) that his stature was generally appreciated.

Cromwell, Thomas (1485–1540)

Chief minister of ▷ Henry VIII; organized the dissolution of the English monasteries in 1536 and 1539. His sister married Morgan Williams; their son adopted the name of Cromwell and was the direct ancestor of ▷ Oliver Cromwell.

Cronos

▷ Classical Myth.

Crotchet Castle (1831)

A novel by ▷ Thomas Love Peacock. The plot is unimportant, and the novel consists mainly of witty talk, burlesquing and satirizing contemporary attitudes and ideas. A crotchet is an eccentric and frivolous notion or prejudice. Some of the characters are representatives of intellectual tendencies, *eg* MacQuedy, a Scots economist whose name suggests 'Q.E.D.' (*quod erat demonstrandum*), stands for the excessive rationalism of the political economists and utilitarians of the age. On the other hand, Mr Skionar stands for the poet, critic and philosopher, ▷ S. T. Coleridge, and burlesques his transcendental mysticism. Mr Chainmail stands for the sentimental cult of the 'Gothic', *ie* the romance and sensationalism of the cult of the Middle Ages, familiar from the historical novels of ▷ Walter Scott and from the ▷ Gothic novels of the previous generation. Sanity is represented by Dr. Folliott, a clergyman, a character of robust and cheerful common sense.

Crowne, John (?1640–?1703)

Dramatist. Crowne published a ▷ romance in 1665, and his first play, *Juliana, or the Princess of Poland*, a tragi-comedy, in 1671. Thereafter, he experimented with various genres: a court masque, *Calisto*, a tragedy, *Andromache*, and a comedy based on a play by Molière (*Le Sicilien ou L'amour peintre*), *The Country Wit*, all appeared in 1675. The heroic verse tragedy, *The Destruction of Jerusalem*, was performed in two parts in 1677. Several political plays followed. Crowne became a favourite of ▷ Charles II, and later Queen Mary (▷ Mary II). His greatest success, *Sir Courtly Nice; Or, It Cannot Be* (1685), modelled on a Spanish play, remained popular for over a century.
Bib: McMullin, B. J., *The Comedies of John Crowne: A Critical Edition*.

Cruelty, Theatre of

▷ Theatre of Cruelty.

Cruikshank, George (1792–1878)

Illustrator, with a strong satirical and

Illustration by George Cruikshank

moralistic bent; famous especially for his illustrations to ▷ Charles Dickens's novel ▷ *Oliver Twist*.

Crusades, The
Military expeditions represented as purely spiritual in motivation to recover the Holy Land, and in particular the Holy City of Jerusalem, from the Muslims. There were eight principal crusades, from the first, proclaimed by Pope Urban II in 1095, which made Godfrey de Bouillon the King of Jerusalem in 1099, to the last on which St Louis (Louis IX of France) died in 1270.

Crystal Palace
▷ Exhibition, The Great.

Cuchulain
In Irish myth the hero of a cycle of prose legends called the Cuchulain or Ulster cycle (9th–13th centuries AD). In English, he is chiefly known by the poems and plays about him by ▷ W. B. Yeats. Yeats's work issued from his support of Irish nationalism, which revived interest in the Irish myths, and led to the publication of English versions of them.
▷ Irish literature in Gaelic.
Bib: Hull E., *The Cuchullin Saga*.

Culler, Jonathan (b 1944)
Academic and critic whose works have done much to introduce English-speaking audiences to the works of ▷ structuralist and ▷ post-structuralist critics. His major studies include *Structuralist Poetics* (1975), *The Pursuit of Signs* (1981) and *On*

Deconstruction (1983). He is Professor of English and Comparative Literature at Cornell University.

Culloden (1746)
A battle in the north of Scotland in the 1745 ▷ Jacobite Rebellion on behalf of the House of ▷ Stuart in the attempt to recover the British throne from the House of Hanover, which had been installed by Parliament in 1714. The Jacobites, consisting mainly of Scottish Highland clans commanded by Prince Charles Edward Stuart ('Bonnie Prince Charlie'), were decisively defeated by the Duke of Cumberland – Butcher Cumberland to his enemies. Not only did Culloden end the rebellion but it practically put an end to the Highland clan system, which remains chiefly in name by force of romantic nostalgia.
▷ Scotland; Scottish literature in English.

Cultural materialism
▷ Materialism.

Cumberland, Richard (1732–1811)
Dramatist, poet, novelist, translator, essayist, associated with the rise of sentimental domestic comedy on the English stage. He began writing poetry while still a pupil at school in Bury St Edmunds. After further education at Westminster School and Cambridge University he published his first play, *The Banishment of Cicero* in 1761. Disappointed in his career aspirations in government, he turned to writing for the stage in earnest. He continued this activity even after his political fortunes improved, eventually completing over 50 plays, operas, and adaptations of plays. His first success of any consequence was with the comedy, *The Brothers*, in 1769. In 1770 he wrote his most famous play, generally considered his best, ▷ *The West Indian*, and ▷ Garrick staged it in the following year. Even so his work was often under attack for its supposed sentimentality, and ▷ Sheridan satirized him as the vain and defensive Sir Fretful Plagiary in *The Critic* (1779). However, Cumberland was sympathetic to the causes of others, especially outcast and vilified groups. He defended the Jews in *The Jew* (1794), which was translated into several languages, including Yiddish and Hebrew, and remained popular well into the 19th century. *The Jew of Mogadore* (1808) again portrays a Jew in a kindly light, and Cumberland also defended Jews in articles in *The Observer*, written under a Jewish pseudonym. His efforts did much to rescue Jews from the villainous antisemitic image hitherto afforded them on

the stage. In addition to plays, he wrote two novels, translations of Greek plays, ▷ epic poetry, and pamphlets expressing his views on controversial topics of the day.

Bib: Borkat, R. F. S. (ed.), *The Plays of Richard Cumberland.*

Cupid
▷ Eros.

Cursor Mundi
An encylopaedic verse narrative recounting Christian history and legend, dating from around 1300 and originating from the north of England. The text survives in seven copies, which vary in length from 24,000 to 30,000 lines.

Cybele
▷ Classical Myth.

Cycle plays
A type of vernacular drama, performed in England from the later 14th century until the latter half of the 16th century, composed of a sequence of episodes, or pageants, dramatizing Christian history. The scope of the sequences characteristically extends from the beginning of Christian history (the fall of the Angels, and the Creation) to the Last Judgement. These plays have been referred to by modern critics variously as 'miracle plays', 'mystery plays', 'Corpus Christi plays': each of these terms has some justification but each may lead to misconceptions of one kind or another. The term 'miracle play' has the advantage of employing a medieval dramatic term but the word 'miracle' was used during the medieval period as a very general term, applicable to any kind of religious drama, not just cycle plays. 'Mystery play' is a term (first used according to the O.E.D. in 1744) deriving from the French word for a trade or craft ('*mystère*') and is applied to the cycle plays because they were very frequently performed by the craft guild of a town, in association with the religious guilds and ecclesiastical authorities. However, not all the extant play cycles appear to be designed for performance by guild members (the so-called ▷ 'N-Town' cycle seems scripted for performance by semi-professionals) and the term 'mystery' may conjure up quite misleading, modern associations. The plays have been called 'Corpus Christi plays' with some justice, for the performance of the plays is associated with the celebration of the feast day of Corpus Christi. This feast day, which is 11 days after Whitsunday, was instituted in 1311 to celebrate the Eucharist, and was marked by a procession. Precisely if, and how, this feast day stimulated the

performance of cycle plays is not clear but there is evidence that by the end of the 14th century at least one major town in England (York) marked the feast day by the performance of a sequence of pageants taken from Christian history. But not all the play cycles were performed on this day: the plays at Chester, for example, were performed over three days in Whitsun week. 'Cycle play' seems the most appropriate term, therefore, for this medieval dramatic phenomenon.

There are four major play cycles extant (the ▷ York, ▷ Chester, ▷ Wakefield, and ▷ N-Town cycles), and fragments survive from play cycles associated with Coventry, Newcastle and Norwich (in addition to three cycle plays in Cornish). The central focus of the cycles is on the events leading up to the Crucifixion and Resurrection, prefaced by selected episodes from O.T. history and followed by the Day of Judgement (the source material being drawn from the Bible, supplemented by legendary and apocryphal narratives). There is some variation in the choice of episodes, as there is in the mode of production of the pageants: those at York and Chester (and probably Wakefield too) were staged on waggons and enacted at fixed points in the streets of the town; the text of the N-Town cycle seems scripted for performance on a fixed set. Necessarily, drama on this scale requires considerable resources, so it is not surprising that the cycles are associated with prosperous provincial towns. Although the efforts of the reformed English Church succeeded in suppressing performances of play cycles in the later 16th century (because they were regarded as idolatrous), the survival of the drama until this time suggests that cycle plays continued to perform a useful municipal function, displaying civic order and wealth, even if their religious function was now outmoded.

Cycle drama is drama in process: the cycles were not static events, their composition continued to change, texts were written and rewritten, pageants inserted and omitted. This process of composition, and indeed the context of cycle production, can only be partially recreated, since most of the play cycles (apart from Chester) exist in single manuscript copies with few indications of production details or even stage directions. However, the intense scholarly interest in the cycle plays, particularly over the last 20 years, has helped to recreate their forms and contexts, resulting in radical reassessments of this major dramatic genre of medieval Europe.

▷ Craft Guilds.
▷ **Bib**: Cawley, A. C., et al., *The Revels History of Drama in English: Vol. 1 Medieval Drama*; Happé, P. (ed.), *English Mystery Plays*.

Cyclops
▷ *Odyssey*.

Cymbeline (1609–10)

A late tragicomedy by ▷ Shakespeare; sometimes called a romance because of its avoidance of realism. Much of the play is set in the court of the ancient British king Cymbeline (1st century AD) and the climax is the defeat of a Roman invasion; on the other hand the love triangle of Posthumus, the British princess Imogen, and the Italian Iachimo is throroughly ▷ Renaissance; Shakespeare has in fact combined a story of ancient British history from the chronicler ▷ Raphael Holinshed with a love-story from ▷ Boccaccio's ▷ *Decameron*. Thus a victory of British patriotism over Roman imperialism is fused with a more up-to-date victory of English single-minded devotion over Italian duplicity. *Cymbeline* has also been called a reconciliation play, because, like ▷ *Pericles* before it, and ▷ *The Winter's Tale* and ▷ *The Tempest* after it, it steadily darkens with murderous conspiracy from the outset to the middle, and then lightens towards a general clarification in candour and love at the end. Also like the other three plays, *Cymbeline* has as a central theme the loss to the world (and, except in *The Tempest*, to the father) of a young girl, whose recovery expresses the recovery of the qualities of youth, purity, beauty, trust and potentiality.
▷ Romances of Shakespeare.

Cynewulf (fl 800)

Old English poet, probably working in the late 8th or early 9th century, who signed his name in runes in four poems, *Christ II*, *Elene*, *Juliana* and *The Fates of the Apostles*. The poems suggest that Cynewulf was a learned writer, familiar with Latin and thus probably a cleric, although nothing more is known about him as a historical personage.
▷ Old English literature.

Cynics, The

A school of ancient Greek philosophers founded by Antisthenes in the 4th century BC. Their belief, that the only realizable aim in life was the fulfilment of the individual by the strict application of reason to practical issues, led them to an extreme individualism, according to which social considerations were irrelevant, ambition was a distraction, pleasure a corruption, and poverty and disrepute were of active assistance in promoting self-reliance. The word 'cynic' seems to derive from the Greek word for 'dog', and they agreed in taking this animal as their emblem. The word has degenerated to imply an attitude of disbelief in the goodness of human motives and in the reality of human values.
▷ Diogenes.

Cynthia
▷ Artemis.

Dactyl
A verse foot consisting of an accented syllable followed by two unaccented ones. It thus gives a light falling rhythm, and is commonly used with ▷ trochees in lines which end in an accented syllable or an iambus.
   ▷ Metre.

Dada
Artistic and literary movement. It arose in two distinct places at about the same time. One group was formed in Zurich in 1916 by three refugees, Tristan Tzara (1887–1968), Hans Arp (1887–1966) and Hugo Ball (1886–1927); another group was formed in New York in the years 1916–19 by Marcel Duchamp (1887–1968), Man Ray (1890–1976) and Francis Picabia (1879–1953). By 1920, both groups had united and made their headquarters in Paris where their journal was *Littérature* (1919–21). The Dada emphasis was on instinctual expression free from constraints and the consequent cultivation of destructiveness, randomness and incoherence; indeed, the very name 'Dada' (= hobby horse) was a random selection from the dictionary. The movement lasted until the mid-1920s. A number of its adherents joined the ▷ Surrealists, a movement which in part evolved out of Dada.

Daedalus
In Greek myth, an artist of wonderful powers. He made wings for himself and his son ▷ Icarus, and flew from Crete to Sicily to escape the wrath of ▷ King Minos, for whom he had built the labyrinth. The fact that he was an artist explains the use of a form of the name by James Joyce – Dedalus – in ▷ *Portrait of the Artist as a Young Man*.

Daisy Miller (1879)
A story by ▷ Henry James. It concerns the visit of an American girl to Europe, and is one of the stories in which James contrasts American freshness of impulse, moral integrity, and naivety with the complexity and deviousness of the European mentality. The girl's innocence and candour is misinterpreted as moral turpitude by the Americans who are long settled in Europe, including the young man who acts as focal character for the narrative.

Dame schools
Schools for poor children in the 18th and 19th centuries, especially in country towns and villages. Unlike the charity schools, they were run by private initiative, especially by single women supplementing their income by teaching reading and writing.

▷ Schools in England.

Dame Sirith
A Middle English verse ▷ fabliau of some 450 lines, dating from the 13th century, which survives in a single manuscript. The narrative, set in dialogue form, relates how a cleric seduces a woman with the help of the tricks of Dame Sirith.

Damon
A shepherd poet in ▷ Virgil's eighth eclogue. Hence the name is sometimes used in English ▷ pastoral poetry for a shepherd and sometimes as a pseudonym for a real person.

Damon and Pythias
In Greek legend, symbols of loyal friendship. Pythias was condemned to death by Dionysius of Syracuse, and asked for temporary release from prison to arrange his affairs. Damon gave himself as pledge for Pythias's return to prison in time for his execution, and Pythias duly returned so that his friend should not be killed in his place. In admiration, Dionysius forgave him. The story is the subject of an early Elizabethan play, *Damon and Pythias* (1564) by Richard Edwards.

Danae
   ▷ Perseus.

Dance of Death
A theme of artistic and literary representation from the later medieval period, in which representative figures from different social estates were taken away to their graves by skeletal, cadaverous corpses. The earliest known representation of the Dance of Death (or *danse macabre*) was made in 1424, in the cemetery of the Innocents in Paris, and was copied in a cloister of Old St Paul's (for which ▷ John Lydgate translated the verse inscriptions).

Danegeld
A tax raised by Anglo-Saxon kings as tribute to the Danes to prevent their invasions of southern England.

Daniel
In the ▷ Bible, a book devoted to a prophet (Daniel) who upheld the Jewish faith during the Babylonian captivity. The book is much referred to in English literature owing to the dramatic character of some of its episodes such as the story of ▷ Belshazzar's feast, and of Daniel in the lions' den. The phrase 'a Daniel come to judgement', used by Shylock in Shakespeare's ▷ *Merchant of Venice* is a reference to the passage in *Daniel* 6, where

Darius is said to have appointed Daniel as one of the three 'presidents' of his empire.

Daniel, Samuel (1562–1619)

Poet and dramatist. After returning from extensive travel in France and Italy (c 1586), he was employed as a tutor to the son of William Herbert, Earl of Pembroke (patron of ▷ Shakespeare). His first publication was 28 ▷ sonnets included in the unauthorized edition of ▷ Sir Philip Sidney's ▷ *Astrophil and Stella* (1591). In 1592 he published his own collection of sonnets under the title of *Delia*. His dramatic work includes *The Tragedy of Cleopatra* (1594), and *Philotas* (1605), which deals with a trial, on a charge of treason, of an ambitious favourite of ▷ Alexander the Great – a theme which the authorities thought uncomfortably close to the events of the Essex rebellion of 1601 and which led to Daniel being summoned before the ▷ Privy Council to explain the play's intentions. His publications also included several ▷ masques, and a philosophical dialogue in verse form, which discusses the conflict between ▷ humanist theory and the value of practical arts, entitled *Musophilus* (1599).

Daniel's major project, however, was his huge unfinished work *The Civil Wars*. This historical ▷ epic, dealing with the ▷ Wars of the Roses first appeared in four books in 1595, and by 1609 eight books in all had been published, which brought his account down to the marriage of ▷ Edward IV. After the project had been abandoned, Daniel turned to writing a prose history of England, which appeared in two parts between 1612 and 1617. In addition to his historical enterprises, Daniel published, in 1603, his answer to ▷ Thomas Campion's *Observations in the Art of English Poesy – A Defense of Rhyme*.

Though Daniel's sonnets represent the major portion of his writings that are read in the 20th century, his attempt at creating a historical epic forms an important part of the late-Elizabethan project (shared in by ▷ Edmund Spenser and ▷ Michael Drayton) to create a firmly realized sense of national identity.

▷ Histories and Chronicles.
Bib: Michel, L. (ed.), *The Civil Wars*; Rees, J., *Daniel: A Critical and Biographical Study*.

Daniel Deronda (1876)

A novel by ▷ George Eliot (Mary Ann Evans). It contains a double story: that of the hero, Daniel Deronda, and that of the heroine Gwendolen Harleth. Daniel is the adopted son of an aristocratic Englishman, and a young man of gracious personality and positive values; he discovers that he is of Jewish parentage, and ends by marrying a Jewish girl, Mirah and devoting himself to the cause of establishing a Jewish homeland. Gwendolen belongs to an impoverished upper-class family and marries (under pressure from her clergyman uncle) a rich and entirely self-centred aristocrat, Henleigh Grandcourt, to redeem their fortunes. Her story is the discovery of the truth of her own nature, just as Deronda's story is the discovery of his origin and vocation. Their stories are linked by the almost casual but entirely beneficent influence of Deronda over Gwendolen, whom he saves from despair after the death of her husband in circumstances that compromise her conscience. (The theme of artistic dedication is central.) Critics have observed that the story of Gwendolen is one of the masterpieces of English fiction, but that that of Daniel is comparatively flat and unconvincing.

Dante Aligheri (1265–1321)

Poet and philosopher. Very little is known about the early life of Dante. He was born in Florence, a member of the Guelf family, and married Gemma Donati in 1285. His involvement in Florentine politics from 1295 led in 1300 to his exile from Florence, to which he never returned. He died at Ravenna in 1321. According to his own report, he was inspired throughout his life by his love for Beatrice, a woman who has been identified as Bice Portinari (d 1290).

It is difficult to date Dante's work with any degree of precision. The *Vita Nuova* (1290–4) is a lyric sequence celebrating his inspirational love for Beatrice, linked by prose narrative and commentary sections. His Latin treatise *De Vulgari Eloquentia*, perhaps begun in 1303–4 but left unfinished, is a pioneering work of literacy and linguistic commentary. Here Dante considers the state and status of Italian as a literary language, and assesses the achievements of earlier French and Provençal poets in elevating the status of their vernacular media. The *Convivio* (1304–7) is an unfinished philosophical work, a 'banquet of knowledge', composed of prose commentaries on allegorical poetic sequences. Dante's political ideas, specifically the relationship between the Pope, Emperor, and the universal Empire, are explored in *De Monarchia* (c 1310). Dante may not have begun his principal work, the ▷ *Divina Commedia*, until as late as 1314. This supremely encyclopaedic work, which encompasses a discussion of every aspect of human experience, knowledge and belief, recounts the poet's journey, with ▷ Virgil as his guide, through Hell (▷ *Inferno*) and Purgatory (▷ *Purgatorio*) and finally, through the agency of Beatrice herself, to Paradise (▷ *Paradiso*).

▷ Boccaccio (1313–75) composed an account of Dante's life and was the first to deliver a series of public lectures on the text of the *Divina Commedia* (1313–14), thus confirming the literary authority, prestige and influence of the work and its author. ▷ Chaucer, the first English poet to name Dante in his work, undoubtedly knew the *Divina Commedia*; quotations from it are scattered through his later work. Dante was read and admired by English poets in the 16th and 17th centuries (including ▷ Milton), and one of the earliest English translations (of part of the *Inferno*) appeared in 1719. 19th-century poets, especially ▷ Byron, ▷ Shelley and ▷ Thomas Carlyle much admired Dante's work and thus revived interest in the medieval poet. Of 20th-century writers, ▷ T. S. Eliot in particular was profoundly influenced by Dante's work. According to Eliot, Dante has the power to make the 'spiritual visible'.
Bib: Holmes, G., *Dante*.

Daphne

In Greek myth, the daughter of a river god and beloved by the god ▷ Apollo. When he pursued her, she was changed by her mother, the earth-goddess, Ge, into a laurel tree. Hence the laurel (or bay tree) became the favourite tree of Apollo, god of the arts, and triumphant poets were crowned with it on his feast-days.

D'Arblay, Madame

▷ Burney, Fanny.

Dares Phrygius

A Trojan priest, mentioned in ▷ Homer's ▷ *Iliad*, who is reputedly the author of an eyewitness acount of the Trojan war, *Troiae Historia* (*The Fall of Troy, A History*), which presents a rationalized, chronologically ordered account of events that ultimately relies on material from Homer. It is likely that Dares's account was originally composed in Greek during the 1st century but it only survives in a Latin version from the 6th century. Together with the other eyewitness account of the war, attributed to ▷ Dictys, Dares's narrative forms the basis for the most influential medieval versions of the Troy story, being used by ▷ Benoît de Sainte-Maure for his 12th-century vernacular narrative of the destruction of Troy. It was not until the beginning of the 18th century that the accounts of Dares and Dictys were conclusively exposed as forgeries.
▷ Troy.
Bib: Frazer, R. M. (ed. and trans.), *The Trojan War: the Chronicles of Dictys of Crete and Dares the Phrygian.*

Dark Ages, The

As late as the early 19th century, 'Dark Ages' was synonymous with ▷ Middle Ages, *ie* the period between the downfall of the Roman Empire in western Europe (about AD 500) and the beginning of the ▷ Renaissance. However, historical studies in the 19th century caused a revision of the idea that the medieval period had as a whole been one of ignorance and intellectual stagnation, and the term is now usually applied to the earlier part of it only, from about AD 500 to about 800.

Darwin, Charles Robert (1809–82)

Contemporary caricature of Charles Darwin

Biologist. His book *On the Origin of Species by means of Natural Selection* (1859) not only expounded the theory of the evolution of natural organisms (which in itself was not new, for it had been held by, among others, Darwin's grandfather, the poet Erasmus Darwin) but presented persuasive evidence for the theory. In brief, this was that species naturally tend to produce variations and that some of these variations have better capacity for survival than others, which in consequence tend to become extinct. Darwin's conviction partly began with his study of ▷ Malthus on population, and it thus belongs to the rationalistic tradition which the 19th century inherited from the 18th. The book greatly disturbed many religious people, since it apparently contradicted the account of the creation of the world of *Genesis* in the Bible; it also raised serious doubts about the existence of the soul and its survival after the death of the body. However, it is possible to exaggerate the importance of the Darwinian theory as a cause of religious disbelief: on the one hand, ▷ Charles Lyell's *Principles of Geology* (1830–3) had already done much to upset traditional beliefs (those, for instance, of the poet ▷ Tennyson) and so had scientific scholarship on biblical texts by men like Charles Hennell (as in the case of the novelist ▷ George Eliot); on the other hand, intelligent believers such as ▷ Coleridge had long ceased to accept the Bible as a sacred record of fact in all its books. The effect of Darwin's ideas was probably rather to extend religious doubt from the intelligentsia (who were already deeply permeated by it) to wider circles. Another kind of effect was to produce in the popular mind a naïve optimism that man was subject to a general law of progress; it thus encouraged an uncritical view of history and society.

Darwin wrote a number of other scientific works, including *The Descent of Man* (1871). His *Journal of Researches into the Geology and Natural History of the various countries visited by H.M.S. 'Beagle'*, a report of his first important scientific expedition (1831–6), is a fascinating travel book. He also wrote a brief but interesting *Autobiography* (edited with additions by Nora Barlow, 1958).

▷ Agnosticism.
Bib: Huxley, L., *Charles Darwin*; Stevenson, L., *Darwin among the Poets*; West, G., *Darwin: the Fragmentary Man*; Darwin, F., *Life and Letters*; Beer, G., *Darwin's Plots*.

Darwin, Erasmus (1731–1802)
Poet and physician; grandfather of the zoologist ▷ Charles Darwin. He wrote a lengthy poem in grotesquely elaborate ▷ couplets, *The Botanic Garden*, on the subject of the scientific classification of plants (Part II: *The Loves of the Plants*, 1789; Part I: *The Economy of Vegetation*, 1791).

Daryush, Elizabeth (1887–1977)
Poet. Daryush was the daughter of poet ▷ Robert Seymour Bridges, and her writing is a continuation and expansion of his experiments in ▷ syllabic metre. She lived for some time in Persia, and syllabically translated some Persian poetry. Publications include: Daryush's own selection of her work, *Selected Poems, Verses I–VI* (1972) and the more recent *Collected Poems* (1976).

D'Avenant (Davenant), Sir William (1606–68)
Theatrical innovator, impresario, dramatist and poet, D'Avenant's career spanned the reign of ▷ Charles I, the ▷ Interregnum and the ▷ Restoration. A pivotal figure in the history of the English theatre, he was involved in most of the developments of this transitional period, including the dissemination of theatrical techniques associated with the aristocratic cultural form of the ▷ masque to the public stage, the creation of new genres (he is credited with the first English ▷ opera), and the introduction of actresses to the professional English stage. He adapted some of ▷ Shakespeare's plays to the new theatrical conditions, including ▷ *The Tempest* with ▷ Dryden (1667) in a version which was the basis of English productions until 1838. During the 1650s, as official Interregnum disapproval of stage plays waned, he openly mounted several musical performances, including ▷ *The Siege of Rhodes* (1656) which is often considered to be the first English opera. When the theatres reopened in 1660 D'Avenant and ▷ Killigrew obtained the only two patents granted by ▷ Charles II allowing them to stage theatrical performances in London. D'Avenant formed the ▷ Duke's Company and began converting Lisle's Tennis Court at ▷ Lincoln's Inn Fields as a theatre. After his death D'Avenant's widow, ▷ Lady Mary D'Avenant, inherited his patent.

D'Avenant, Lady Henrietta Maria (d 1691)
Theatre proprietress, wife of ▷ Sir William D'Avenant: she took over management of the ▷ Duke's Company after his death in 1668, and saw his plans for a new theatre at ▷ Dorset Garden to completion. Lady D'Avenant was born in France, and met William during his stay there, probably in 1646. He returned about ten years later and brought her back to England as his wife in 1655. She had at least nine children by him, and also cared for some of his children by his earlier marriages. As theatre manager she operated effectively, delegating many artistic and technical problems, ensuring the publication of her husband's works, founding ▷ Nurseries for the training of young actors and actresses, and defending the interests of the actor-manager George Jolly after a campaign by ▷ Thomas Killigrew and Lady

D'Avenant's late husband to cheat him and squeeze him out of the profession. In 1673 she ceded control of the company to her son Charles, but held on to her shares in the company and various rights, including income from a fruit concession at the playhouse.
Bib: Hotson, L., *The Commonwealth and Restoration Stage*.

David, King
In the ▷ Bible, the Jewish hero and the second King of Judah; historians believe his reign to have been approximately 1010–970 BC. His story is mainly told in *1 Samuel* from chap. 16, *2 Samuel*, and *1 Kings* 1–2. David seems to have been a poet and musician, and tradition ascribed to him authorship of the *Psalms*, but modern scholarship dissents. It was declared that the Messiah, or Deliverer of the Jewish nation, would be born of the House of David – hence Joseph, earthly father of Jesus Christ, is said in *Luke* 1 to be of this descent.

David Copperfield (1849–50)
A novel in autobiographical form by ▷ Charles Dickens. 'Of all my books I like this the best; like many fond parents I have a favourite child and his name is David Copperfield.' Some commentators have thought that the hero is representative of Dickens himself, and point to the resemblance of initials: C.D. and D.C. It is true that in outline Copperfield's experiences – his sense of early rejection, child labour in a warehouse, experience as a journalist and final success as a novelist – are similar to Dickens's own. But Dickens's purpose was to present an imaginative picture of growth from childhood to manhood in his own period of history, using his own experience as some of its material but without intending a biographical record. The social landscape of this novel is broader than an autobiography would be likely to achieve. It includes the moralistic and sadistic oppressiveness of Copperfield's mercantile step-father, Murdstone, and the intimate study of selfish hedonism in Copperfield's aristocratic friend, Steerforth; the spontaneous cordiality of the humble Yarmouth boatman, Peggotty, and his sister, and the cunning deviousness of Uriah Heap, whose servile humility is disguise for his total ruthlessness in making his way from bleak beginnings to a position of power. The novel is strong in dramatic contrast, and particularly interesting in the counterbalancing of the women characters in a series of feminine archetypes. Copperfield is fatherless, and his gentle, guileless mother (who becomes victim in matrimony to Murdstone) is like an elder

sister to the child; both are children to the motherly, protective servant, Clara Peggotty. She is replaced by the harsh and loveless Miss Murdstone who plays the role of cruel stepmother. Copperfield runs away and takes refuge with his idiosyncratic aunt, Betsey Trotwood, who has shaped for herself an eccentric independence of men, retaining for a harmless lunatic (Mr ▷ Dick) a compassionate tenderness which she now extends to her nephew, in spite of having rejected him at birth because he was a boy. Copperfield's first wife, Dora Spenlow, is a simulacrum of his mother – a child wife, on whom ▷ Ibsen seems to have based Nora in *A Doll's House*. Two other representatives of Victorian womanhood are Agnes Wickfield (whom he eventually marries), the stereotype of defenceless womanly sanctity and nearly a victim of Heap's rapacity, and Little Em'ly who is first under the protection of Peggotty and then becomes 'the fallen woman' when she is seduced by Steerforth. Another very striking portrait is Rosa Dartle, companion to Steerforth's mother and poisoned by vindictive hatred of him because of his cool assumption of social and masculine privilege. Though not the richest and deepest of Dickens's novels, it is perhaps psychologically the most revealing, both of Dickens himself and of the society of his time.

Davidson, John (1857–1909)
Poet. Best remembered for his ▷ ballads and songs, in particular *Thirty Bob a Week*, he also wrote plays, novels and philosophical works. A friend of ▷ W. B. Yeats and fellow member of the Rhymer's Club, a group of ▷ Nineties poets which met to read their poetry from 1890–94 at the ▷ Cheshire Cheese in Fleet Street. Davidson was also influenced by ▷ Nietzsche in his passionate atheism, exemplified by *God and Mammon* (1907), a trilogy of which only two parts were completed when Davidson committed suicide. He contributed to ▷ *The Yellow Book*, and was an important figure in the development of the 20th-century Scottish Renaissance (▷ Scottish Literature).
Bib: Turnbull, A. (ed.), *Poems*; Lindsay, M. (ed.), *John Davidson: A Selection of his Poems* (Preface by ▷ T. S. Eliot).

Davie, Donald (b 1922)
Poet and literary critic. Donald Davie's rational, cool and technically pure poetry perhaps epitomizes the verse of the ▷ Movement; his critical work of 1952, *Purity of Diction in English Verse* was the

Movement's bible. Davie was born in
Barnsley, a place which recurs gloomily
throughout his work, and has taught at
universities in Britain and the U.S.A. His
many publications include: *Brides of Reason*
(1955); *The Forests of Lithuania* (1959); *Events
and Wisdoms 1957–1963*; *Collected Poems
1950–1970* (1972); *In the Stopping Train*
(1977).

Davies, John, of Hereford (?1565–1618)
Very little is known of this prolific writer,
often confused with his better-known
namesake, ▷ Sir John Davies. Davies was a
writing master and the author of numerous
▷ epigrams on his poetic contemporaries.
Perhaps his most ambitious project, however,
was the group of three long poems which
undertook to survey existing areas of human
knowledge, and which cover a vast number of
disparate topics, including English history,
psychology, religion and human anatomy.
These poems are: *Mirum in Modum* (1602),
Microcosmos (1603), and *Summa Totalis*
(1607).
Bib: Rope, H. E. G., 'John Davies of
Hereford: Catholic and Rhymer,' *Anglo-
Welsh Review* 11 (1961), pp. 20–36.

Davies, Sir John (1569–1626)
Poet, lawyer and attorney-general for
▷ Ireland (1606–19). Sir John Davies wrote
virtually all his poetry in the years 1593–9.
After 1603 Davies devoted his career to
advancement within the Jacobean
administration of Ireland, being one of the
architects of the policy of 'plantation' in
Ulster which brought Scots and English to
the northern parts of Ireland: a source of
friction ever since. In 1612 Davies published
an account of Ireland, entitled *A Discoverie of
the True Causes why Ireland was never entirely
Subdued nor brought under Obedience of the
Crown of England Untill his Majesties Happie
Raigne* – a work which can be compared in its
delineation of English misunderstanding of
Irish culture, to ▷ Edmund Spenser's
accounts of Ireland at the end of the previous
century.
    Davies' chief poetic works are the two long
poems *Orchestra* (1596) and *Nosce Teipsum*
(1599), a series of epigrams and the 26
acrostic poems on the name of ▷ Elizabeth
I, *Hymns of Astrea* (1599). Both *Orchestra*
and *Nosce Teipsum* are, in their own ways,
remarkable works. *Orchestra*, composed
c 1594, announces itself as 'A Poem of
Dauncing', and that, in essence, is what it is:
a philosophical account of the physical world
in terms of a universal dance. *Nosce Teipsum*,
on the other hand, develops no over-all

▷ conceit, but is instead a philosophical
poem on human knowledge derived from
Davies' reading in the works of ▷ Cicero,
▷ Montaigne and the two French
philosophers Philippe de Mornay and Pierre
de la Primaudaye. The end of the poem is to
promote self-knowledge, as the title, which
translates as 'Know Yourself', indicates.
Bib: Editions include: Kreuger, R. (ed.),
Poems.

Davis, Jack (b 1917)
▷ Commonwealth literatures.

Day, John (1574–1640)
English dramatist contemporary with
▷ Shakespeare and ▷ Ben Jonson. In his
plays he collaborated with a number of other
dramatists such as ▷ Henry Chettle and
▷ Thomas Dekker. His *Isle of Gulls* (1606),
played by the Children of the Queen's Revels,
lost them royal favour at Court because of the
play's satire on the impact in the country of
the ▷ Jacobean accession. Day's most
acclaimed work is his masque *The Parliament
of Bees* (1609).

Day Lewis, Cecil (1904–72)
Poet and critic. Day Lewis was one of the
small group of poets (with ▷ W. H. Auden
and ▷ Stephen Spender) which made a
considerable impact in the 1930s under the
poetic influence of ▷ T. S. Eliot and the
political influence of ▷ Marx. In some
near-propagandist poetry of that time,
especially on the Republican side in the
Spanish Civil War, he used with effect the
▷ sprung rhythm and ▷ alliteration of
▷ Gerard Manley Hopkins. World War II
broke up the group and tempered Day
Lewis's political aims. His later work shows
the versatility which caused him to be chosen
as ▷ Poet Laureate in 1968. Works include
Collected Poems (1954; reprinted 1970). See
also *Poems 1925–72* (ed. Parsons). Critical
essays include *A Hope for Poetry* (1934), *The
Poetic Image* (1946), *The Lyric Impulse* (1965).
He also translated much of the poetry of
▷ Virgil and wrote ▷ detective fiction
under the pen-name Nicholas Blake.

De Beauvoir, Simone (1908–86)
French novelist, long associated with
▷ Sartre and the ▷ Existentialist
movement, whose views she promoted in a
series of novels: *L'Invitée* (1943); *Le Sang des
autres* (1944); *Les Mandarins* (1954). A play,
Les Bouches inutiles, was performed in 1945.
She contributed greatly to the genre of
autobiography (*Mémoires d'une jeune fille
rangée* (1958); *La Force de l'âge* (1960); *La
Force des choses* (1965); *Tout compte fait*

(1974); all translated); and Sartre declared that anyone seeking the sequel to his own autobiography *Les Mots* could find it in these volumes. *La Cérémonie des adieux* (1984) is invaluable as a record of final conversations with Sartre before his death. Her two-volume study of women, *Le Deuxième Sexe* (1949), has had considerable influence on contemporary feminist writers and thought (*eg* Mary Ellmann, *Thinking about Women*, 1968 and Elaine Showalter, *A Literature of Their Own*, 1977).

De Flores
A tragic villain in ▷ Thomas Middleton's play ▷ *The Changeling* who has fallen in love with his master's daughter and blackmails her into a sexual encounter which leads to the destruction of them both.

De la Mare, Walter (1873–1956)
Poet, novelist, writer of short stories. He was born in Kent, and educated at St Paul's Cathedral Choir School. From 1890 to 1908 he was a clerk in the offices of the Anglo-American Oil Company; he was then given a government ('Civil List') pension to enable him to devote himself to writing. Many of his poems and his stories were addressed to children. Books of verse of this sort were: *Songs of Childhood* (1902); *A Child's Day* (1912); *Peacock Pie* (1913). ▷ Children's stories: *The Three Mulla-mulgars* (1910); *The Riddle* (1923); *The Magic Jacket* (1943); *The Dutch Cheese* (1946). He had conspicuous talent for retelling traditional ▷ fairy tales: *Told Again* (1927); and compiled two unusual anthologies: *Come Hither* (for children, 1923) and *Love* (for adults, 1943). His most remarkable prose fiction for adults is probably *On the Edge* (stories, 1926) and *Memoirs of a Midget* (novel, 1921). His books of verse for adults include: *The Listeners* (1912); *The Veil* (1921); *Memory and other poems* (1938); *The Burning-glass and other poems* (1945); *The Traveller* (1946); *Inward Companion* (1950); *Winged Chariot* (1951); *O Lovely England and other poems* (1953); *Collected Poems* (1979). See also ▷ W. H. Auden's collection, *A Choice of De La Mare's Verse* (1963).

His poems are conservative in technique, with the melody and delicacy of diction characteristic of the poetry of the late 19th and early 20th century, but are unusual in the quiet intensity with which they express evanescent, elusive and mysterious experience. His stories have a singular quietness of tone and are written in an unassuming style, conveying material which is on the borderline of conscious experience. *The Three Mulla-mulgars*, also published

under the title of *The Three Royal Monkeys*, is one of the most original stories for children in English literature. De la Mare's unusual combination of intensity and innocence makes the border line between his work for children and for adults an almost imperceptible one.
Bib: Mégroz, R. L., *De la Mare: A Biographical and Critical Study*; Reid, Forrest, *De la Mare: A Critical Study*.

De Loutherbourg, Philip James (Philippe Jacques) (1740–1812)
Painter, set designer, of noble Polish descent. In 1771 after a successful exhibition in Paris De Loutherbourg moved to London, where he met ▷ David Garrick, and presented him with proposals for co-ordinated improvements to the lighting, scenes, costumes and mechanical effects at ▷ Drury Lane.

Engaged at the theatre, De Loutherbourg 'astonished the audience', according to one observer, by his skilful and innovative use of various translucent coloured silks, lit from behind and mobile, to give changing effects of richness, subtlety, and depth to the sets. His detailed and naturalistic cut-out scenery was likened to fine paintings of contemporary and fantastic views. In 1781 he also became a member of the ▷ Royal Academy.

Admired in his day by Thomas Gainsborough (1727–88), De Loutherbourg is now considered one of the most influential designers for the English stage, bringing both imagination, and technical abilities to bear, so as to create scenes and spectacles of unprecedented realism and magnificence. Much of his work can be seen as an important early contribution to the ▷ Romantic movement in literature and art.

De Man, Paul (1919–83)
Arguably the most rigorous of the so-called Yale School of criticism, and by the time of his death had become the foremost exponent in the U.S.A. of Derridian ▷ deconstruction (▷ Jacques Derrida) in its most unsettling of forms. As Sterling Professor of Comparative Literature at Yale, he was responsible for the first major application of ▷ deconstruction to a variety of primary and critical texts, for example in his book *Blindness and Insight* (1971). His approach was extended in books such as *Allegories of Reading* (1980) and *The Rhetoric of Romanticism* (1984). De Man reflected on the whole of this process, and upon the resistance to certain sorts of theoretical enquiry in a collection of essays, *The Resistance to Theory* published posthumously in 1986.
▷ Rhetoric.

De Quincey, Thomas (1785–1859)

Essayist and critic. Most famous for his autobiography ▷ *Confessions of an English Opium-Eater*. His work was mostly for periodicals and is voluminous, but only a few pieces are now much read. His strong points as a writer were his exceptionally sensitive, inward-turning imagination and his breadth of understanding. The first produced not only his autobiography but a fragment of exceptional literary criticism, *Knocking at the Gate in Macbeth*. *The English Mail Coach* (1849) and *Murder Considered as One of the Fine Arts* (1827) show the quality of an exceptional psychological novelist. His second gift produced studies of German philosophy (▷ Kant, Lessing, Richter) and able translations of German tales, besides some original historical criticism. He was very much a representative of the first generation of English ▷ romanticism and as the poets of that generation found new ranges of expression for their medium, so De Quincey expanded the poetic range of prose, partly by recapturing some of the quality of the early-17th-century prose writers.
Bib: Eaton, H. A., *Life*; Abrams, M. H., *The Milk of Paradise*; Clapton, G. T., *Baudelaire et De Quincey*; Jordan, J. E., *Thomas De Quincey, Literary Critic*; Saintsbury, G., in *Essays in English Literature*; Sackville-West, E., *A Flame in Sunlight*.

Death and Life

An alliterative narrative, dating from the 15th century, in which a dream frame is used as a vehicle for a dramatic debate between Life and Death, over their respective powers. In the course of the debate, the notion of Life is enlarged to encompass that of Eternal Life, and Life herself evokes scriptural authorities to prove she can, therefore, circumvent the power of Death. This technique of analysing abstract concepts through a personified debate can be paralleled in other alliterative poems (including ▷ *Piers Plowman* and ▷ *Winner and Waster*). But whereas ▷ Langland's poem combines a focus on contemporary social satire with an investigation into transhistorical Christian truths, *Death and Life* concentrates on communicating a spiritual truth.
Bib: Gollancz, I., and Day, M. (eds.), *Select Early English Poems 3*.

Decameron, The

A collection of 100 stories in prose, compiled by ▷ Boccaccio in the years 1349–51. The fictional framework of the collection describes how the stories were told by a company of ten gentle-ladies and gentlemen who decide to retreat from plague-ridden Florence and spend two weeks in the country. They spend their weekdays telling short stories to pass the time, and the proceedings are organized by one member of the company who is elected anew every day. Many of the stories concern heterosexual relations of some kind, usually set in the contemporary world, and treated in a variety of serious and comic ways. Many of the short stories have ▷ fabliau-type plots. It seems likely that ▷ Chaucer knew and used the *Decameron* as a resource for the ▷ *Canterbury Tales* (though the connection has not been definitely proved and remains a controversial issue) Boccaccio's work undoubtedly provided many later writers and dramatists (including ▷ Shakespeare) with an important source of narratives. Many of Boccaccio's stories were incorporated into William Painter's ▷ *Palace of Pleasure*, and the first English translation of the *Decameron* itself appeared in 1621.
Bib: McWilliam, G. H. (trans.), *The Decameron*.

Declaration of Independence (1776)

The assertion of independence by the American colonists, starting-point of the United States. It was signed by 13 states.
▷ Colonialism.

Decline and Fall of the Roman Empire, The (1776–88)

By ▷ Edward Gibbon; the most eloquent and imposing historical work in the English language. It begins at the height of the Roman Empire in the 1st and 2nd centuries AD – an age with which Gibbon's own era, so deeply inbued with Latin scholarship, felt strong kinship. He then proceeds to record the successive stage of Roman decline, the rise of Christianity, the struggle with the Eastern Roman Empire (the Byzantine) centred on ▷ Constantinople (Byzantium), and that empire's eventual extinction by the capture of Constantinople in 1453. As an account, it has of course been somewhat outdated in consequence of later research, but as an imaginative epic (still regarded as substantially true) and an expression of the background to modern Europe as understood in the 18th century, it remains a much read and very important work. Its structure is as spacious as the subject, and is sustained by the energy of Gibbon's style. The attitude is one of 18th-century truth-seeking, and of urbane irony towards the Christian religion, whose growth he sees as one of the agents of destruction of classical civilization. Gibbon's sceptical mind is at the same time constantly critical of human pretensions to self-sufficiency, the attainment of wisdom, and integrity of motive; in such respects he is in the tradition of the great satirists of his century – ▷ Alexander Pope and ▷ Jonathan Swift.

Deconstruction

A concept used in critical theory. It has a long philosophical pedigree, but is usually associated with the work of the French philosopher ▷ Jacques Derrida. It is a strategy applied to writing generally, and to literature in particular, whereby systems of thought and concepts are dismantled in such a way as to expose the divisions which lie at the heart of meaning itself. If interpretation is a process designed to reduce a text to some sort of 'order', deconstruction seeks to undermine the basis upon which that order rests. Deconstruction challenges the notion that all forms of mental and linguistic activity are generated from within an autonomous 'centre', advancing the more disturbing proposition that such centres are themselves to be grasped textually only as rhetorical constructions.
Bib: Derrida, J., *Speech and Phenomena*; *Writing and Difference*; *Of Grammatology*; *Positions*; Norris, C., *Deconstruction: Theory and Practice*.

Dedalus, Stephen

Principal character in ▷ James Joyce's novel ▷ *Portrait of the Artist as a Young Man*; he is also a main character in Joyce's ▷ *Ulysses*. The surname derives from the mythical artist of ancient Greece, ▷ Daedalus.

Defamiliarization

In the context of critical theory this term has its origins in Russian ▷ Formalism and in the desire to distinguish between the ▷ Aristotelian view of writing as an image of reality (▷ mimesis) and imaginative literature as a form of writing which deploys images rhetorically. The Russian term 'ostranenie' means literally, 'making strange', rendering unfamiliar that which has hitherto been regarded as familiar. It draws attention to the fact that 'reality' is never depicted in literature in an unprocessed, or unmediated way. Indeed, what literature exposes is the formal means whereby what is commonly taken to be reality itself is, in fact, a construction. In many ways, 'defamiliarization' is a form of ▷ deconstruction, although its objective is to replace one set of epistemological principles (those upon which ▷ capitalism as a particular kind of social formation rests), with other ways of organizing reality. By contrast, deconstruction has the effect of undermining

all assumptions and certainties about what we know.
▷ Alienation effect.

Defence of Poesie, The
▷ *Apologie for Poetrie, An.*

Defence of Poetry, A (1840)

A prose essay by ▷ Percy Bysshe Shelley written as an 'antidote' to *The Four Ages of Poetry* by ▷ Thomas Love Peacock, which appeared in 1821. Shelley sent his *Defence* to Peacock in the same year, but it was not published until 1840. Peacock had argued that with the growth of scientific knowledge, the primitive metaphorical 'visions' of the poet were out of date: 'A poet in our times is a semi-barbarian in a civilized community'. Poetry only wasted time that would be better spent on 'some branch of useful study'. Shelley answered that poetry is not only useful, but essential, in enlarging 'the social sympathies' of humankind. The 'vitally metaphorical' language of the poet is the key to all morality: 'A man, to be greatly good, must imagine intensely and comprehensively; he must put himself in the place of another and of many others; the pains and pleasures of his species must become his own.' In the aftermath of the failure of the ideals of the ▷ French Revolution, Shelley is eager to envisage a political role for the poet, though inevitably this is expressed in rhetoric of an abstract and ideal kind: 'Poets are the unacknowledged legislators of the world'; 'Poetry is a sword of lightning, ever unsheathed'. However, Shelley's analysis of the totalitarian tendency of Peacock's utilitarianism anticipates ▷ Marx and post-Marxist thinking. Only 'anarchy and despotism' he asserts, can be expected from 'an unmitigated exercise of the calculating faculty'.

Defender of the Faith (Fidei Defensor)

A title awarded to King ▷ Henry VIII by Pope Leo X in 1521, in recognition of Henry's *Defence of the Seven Sacraments* written against ▷ Martin Luther. English monarchs have used the title ever since.

Defoe, Daniel (1660–1731)

Son of a London tallow-chandler, James Foe, Defoe changed his name in about 1695 to suggest a higher social status. His writings reflect his ▷ Puritan background: Defoe was educated at Morton's academy for ▷ Dissenters at Newington Green, and his pamphlet of 1702, *The Shortest Way with Dissenters*, landed him in the pillory when its ironic attack on Dissenters was taken seriously.

Daniel Defoe: contemporary engraving

Defoe's attempts to make a living form a colourful picture. Various business enterprises failed dramatically, including the unfortunately timed scheme of marine insurance in wartime, and a disastrous project to breed civet cats. Between 1703 and 1714 he worked as a secret agent for the Tory government of Robert Harley, writing many political (and anti-Jacobite) pamphlets.

Defoe produced some 560 journals, tracts and books, many of them published anonymously or pseudonymously. His reputation today rests on his novels, a genre to which he turned with great success late in his life.

▷ *The Life and strange surprising Adventures of Robinson Crusoe* appeared in 1719, and its sequel, *The Farther Adventures of Robinson Crusoe*, was published some months later. 1720 saw the publication of the *Life and Adventures of Mr Duncan Campbell*, and *Captain Singleton*; 1722, ▷ *Moll Flanders*, ▷ *A Journal of the Plague Year*, *The History of Peter the Great*, and *Colonel Jack*; 1724, ▷ *Roxana*, the *Memoirs of a Cavalier*, and *A New Voyage round the World*; and 1726, *The Four Voyages of Capt. George Roberts*. His guide-book, *A Tour through the Whole Island of Great Britain*, appeared in three volumes, 1724-6.

Among Defoe's later works are *The Complete English Tradesman* (1726), *A Plan of the English Commerce* and *Augusta Triumphans* (1728), and *The Complete English Gentleman*, not published until 1890. Defoe died in

Moorfields, and was buried in the area now called Bunhill Fields.

Bib: Moore, J. R., *Daniel Defoe: Citizen of the Modern World*; Richetti, J., *Defoe's Narratives: Situations and Structures*; Bell, Ian A., *Defoe's Fiction*.

Deism

A form of religious belief which developed in the 17th century as an outcome of the ▷ Reformation. ▷ Edward Herbert evolved the idea that, while the religion revealed in the Gospels was true, it was preceded by ▷ 'natural' religion, according to which by his own inner light a man could perceive all the essentials of religious truth. Herbert's deism was further expounded in the 18th century by others (often in such a way as to suggest that the Christian revelation as presented in the Gospels was redundant), and it suited the 18th-century cool and rational habit of mind which tended to see God as abstract and remote. ▷ Bishop Butler among the theologians and ▷ Hume and ▷ Kant among the philosophers, exposed the unsoundness of deistic arguments in the 18th century, and in the 19th century the growth of the genetic sciences demolished the basic assumptions of deism, *ie* that human nature and human reason have always been constant, in a constant environment.

Dejection: An Ode (1802)

A poem by ▷ Samuel Taylor Coleridge. The earliest version was addressed to Sara Hutchinson ('O Sara'), with whom the unhappily married Coleridge was in love. In a subsequent version this becomes 'O Wordsworth', and in the published text Sara is reinstated, but anonymously ('O Lady'). As these changes suggest, the poem reflects a simple personal unhappiness, but it was also influenced by ▷ William Wordsworth's expression of flagging inspiration in the first part of the ▷ *Immortality Ode*, written at this time. Coleridge watches a beautiful sunset, but finds that in his 'wan and heartless mood' the objective beauty of the clouds, stars and moon, inspire no response in him: 'I see them all so excellently fair,/ I see, not feel, how beautiful they are!' He reflects on the subjectivity of experience, concluding that 'we receive but what we give/ And in our life alone does Nature live'. He thus rejects the idea of the ministering benevolence of nature which was so important to Wordsworth. It is subjective imagination not objective nature which is the 'shaping spirit'. He is ambiguously cheered by reminiscences from other poets, conjured up by the wind blowing

through an Aeolian harp, and the work ends, as midnight approaches, with a poignantly selfless prayer that his beloved be sleeping, safe from the storm. His love for her restores the meaning which nature had lost, but on a strictly metaphorical level: 'May all the stars hang bright above her dwelling,/ Silent *as though* they watched the sleeping Earth!'
▷ Romanticism.

Dekker, Thomas (?1570–1632)
Dramatist and pamphleteer. His best-known play is ▷ *The Shoemaker's Holiday*, based on ▷ Thomas Deloney's *The Gentle Craft* – a narrative about the London crafts. The play celebrates the proud traditions of the citizens, and the romantic zest of its plot and dialogue has kept it alive. His next best known play is *The Honest Whore*, Pt. I (1604). He was essentially a dramatist of middle life. He collaborated with ▷ Rowley in *The Witch of Edmonton* (1623); with ▷ Middleton in *The Roaring Girl* (1611), and with ▷ Massinger in *Virgin Martyr* (1622).

His pamphlets are perhaps more notable than his plays, especially *The Wonderful Year* (1603), a vivid account of an epidemic of plague in ▷ London, and *The Gull's Hornbook*, a satire on the manners of a fashionable young man. He was a master of the racy, vigorous, colloquial prose of his time. Dekker is an example of a minor talent who has survived by sharing in the unusual vitality of an outstanding literary period.
Bib: Bowers, Fredson, *The Dramatic Works of Thomas Dekker* (4 vols.); Bose, T., *The Gentle Craft of Revision in Thomas Dekker's Last Plays*.

Delaney, Shelagh (b 1939)
One of few female dramatists to make an impact during the 1950s. Her best-known play, *A Taste of Honey* (first performed in 1958), was written when she was only 17 and is about a young woman's relationship with her mother, negro lover and a homosexual art student. It was performed by ▷ Joan Littlewood's Theatre Workshop company and transferred to the West End. Other plays include: *The Lion in Love* (1960); *The House That Jack Built* (1978); and for radio: *So Does the Nightingale* (1980); *Don't Worry About Matilda* (1983).

Delany, Mrs Mary (1700–88)
One of the famous letter writers of the 18th century. She had a wide circle of friends among the famous people of her day.

Delia
One of the names of the Greek goddess ▷ Artemis who was said to have been born on the Greek island of Delos.

Delia is also the name of a sonnet sequence by ▷ Samuel Daniel.

Delilah
In the ▷ Bible (*Judges* XVI) a woman beloved by the Jewish hero Samson. She betrayed him to the Philistines by cutting off his hair in which lay his divinely given supernatural strength. In Milton's ▷ *Samson Agonistes* she appears under the name of Dalila, and she is Samson's wife.

Deloney, Thomas (?1543–?1600)
Pamphleteer and balladeer. Little of Deloney's verse can be securely attributed to him, although in the 1590s he was the most popular ballad writer in England. It is, however, Deloney's prose narratives – *The Gentle Craft* (complete version ?1635), *Thomas of Reading* (1612, 12th edition) and *Jack of Newbery* (1619, 8th edition) – which have secured for him a reputation. These works anticipate the kind of novel which ▷ Daniel Defoe was later to write. They mark the end of the tradition of producing courtly romance such as ▷ Sir Philip Sidney's ▷ *Arcadia*, and share, with the writings of ▷ Thomas Nashe, an interest in depicting the life led by those outside the elevated circles of the court.

As well as his fictional works, Deloney produced ▷ translations and ▷ anthologies, which include his *Strange Histories of Kings* (1600). Despite the diversity of his output, it is for the creation of a 'middle-class' fiction that Deloney is of importance.
Bib: Lawless, M. E., *Apology for the Middle Class: The Dramatic Novels of Thomas Deloney*.
▷ Ballad; Pamphlet.

Delphic Oracle
In ancient Greece Delphi was the seat of a temple to ▷ Apollo on the slopes of Mount ▷ Parnassus, and of the most famous oracle of the ancient world. The oracles were spoken by a priestess of Apollo, called the Pythia.

Demogorgon
In early Christian mythology, a terrible deity of the underworld; according to ▷ Boccaccio, a primaeval pagan god. In ▷ Shelley's ▷ *Prometheus Unbound* a spiritual principle superseding false gods.

Demosthenes (4th century)
In ancient Greece, a great Athenian orator; he is often referred to in English literature as the pattern and ideal of all orators. He is especially famous for his speeches warning the Athenians of the danger from the growing

empire of Philip of Macedon, father of Alexander the Great. Hence the word 'philippic' for an aggressive political speech.

Denham, Sir John (1615–69)
Poet and playwright. He took the Royalist side in the ▷ civil war, translated Book II of the ▷ *Aeneid* into pentameter ▷ couplets (*The Destruction of Troy*; 1656) and published a play in blank verse, *The Sophy* (1642). His *Cooper's Hill* (1642; enlarged version, 1655), a topographical poem describing the scenery around Windsor, was much admired and imitated. In it he abandons the *enjambements* of his Virgil translation, preferring a balanced, end-stopped couplet. The passage on the Thames was cited and imitated by poets from ▷ John Dryden onwards as the perfection of heroic couplet writing:

O could I flow like thee, and make thy stream
My great example, as it is my theme!
Though deep, yet clear, though gentle, yet not
* dull,*
Strong without rage, without o'er-flowing full.

The lines are comically parodied in ▷ Alexander Pope's ▷ *Dunciad* (Bk. III, 11. 163–6). ▷ Samuel Johnson, in his *Lives of the Poets* (1781), called Denham 'one of the fathers of English poetry'.
  ▷ Augustanism.

Dennis, John (1657–1734)
Although Dennis's efforts as a poet and playwright are undistinguished, he was one of the foremost literary critics of the ▷ Augustan era. His feud with ▷ Pope, for which he is best remembered, was angry and ill-tempered on both sides, but Dennis's critical views, favouring blank-verse epics on Christian themes, are worthy of more serious attention. Among his most notable works are *The Advancement of Reformation of Modern Poetry* (1701), *The Grounds of Criticism in Poetry* (1704) and *An Essay on the Genius and Writings of Shakespeare* (1712).
Bib: Paul, H. G., *John Dennis, His Life and Criticism*; Hooker, E. N. (ed.), *The Critical Works of John Dennis*.

Dennis, Nigel (1912–89)
Novelist. He is best known for *Cards of Identity* (1955), a satirical fantasy about the nature of individual and cultural identity, influenced by the ▷ existentialism of ▷ Jean-Paul Sartre. It reflects the atmosphere of British life in the early 1950s, but combines this with a self-referential concern with the nature of fiction. His other novels are: *Boys and Girls Come Out to Play* (1949); *A House in Order* (1966).

Depression, The
A 'depression' signifies the slowing of economic activity so that it is at a lower rate than it could be for a considerable period of time. High unemployment and poverty usually accompany economic depression. The most significant such period in Britain was the 1930s, which is currently called 'The Depression'.

Derrida, Jacques (b 1930)
Although he is primarily a philosopher, the influence of Derrida's work on the study of literature has been immense. He is the originator of a mode of reading known as ▷ 'deconstruction', the major stand in what is now regarded as the general area of ▷ post-structuralism. His main works are *Speech and Phenomena* (trans. 1973), *Of Grammatology* (trans. 1974), and *Writing and Difference* (trans. 1978). For Derrida, as for ▷ Saussure, language is composed of differences, that is, a series of non-identical elements which combine with each other to produce linguistic ▷ signs which are accorded meaning. Traditionally, this process is anchored to an organizing principle, a centre, but Derrida questions this concept and rejects the idea of a 'presence' in which authority resides, thereby lifting all restrictions upon the 'play' of differences. But, in addition to the idea that language is composed of 'differences', Derrida also deploys the term '*différance*' to indicate the continual postponement of 'presence' which is located in all signifiers (▷ sign). Thus, signs are produced through a relatively free play of linguistic elements (difference), but what they signify can never be fully present since meaning is constantly 'deferred' (*différance*). Derrida's influence has been greatest in the U.S.A. where after his visit to Johns Hopkins and his teaching at Yale, deconstruction has become the successor to American new criticism.
  ▷ Grammatology; De Man, Paul.

Desai, Anita (b 1937)
Indian novelist and short-story writer. Her novels offer a satirical view of social change in India since Independence, with a powerful sense of waste, limitation, self-deception and failure. *Where Shall We Go This Summer* (1975) and *Clear Light of Day* (1980) are particularly concerned with the problems of Indian women to whom westernization offers an apparent freedom. She uses visual detail and an impressionistic style in an attempt to convey a sense of the meaning underlying everyday behaviour and objects. Her other novels include: *Cry the Peacock* (1963); *Voices*

in the City (1965); *Bye-Bye Blackbird* (1971); *Fire on the Mountain* (1977). Story collections: *Games at Twilight* (1978). She has also written works for children, including *The Village by the Sea* (1982).

Descartes, René (1596–1650)
French philosopher, mathematician. In ethics and religious doctrine he was traditional, but in method of thought he was the starting point of the total reliance on reason – ▷ rationalism – that was pre-eminent in the later 17th and 18th centuries. In his *Discours de la Méthode* (1637) he reduced knowledge to the basic principle of *Cogito, ergo sum* (I think, therefore I am), from which intuition he deduced the existence of God and thence the reality of the external world. He also distinguished mind and matter, finding their source of combination again in God. It was the influence of Descartes's writings that drew the English philosopher ▷ John Locke, the dominant figure in English rationalism, to the study of philosophy.

Deschamps, Eustache (c 1346–1406)
French poet who, like ▷ Guillaume de Machaut his mentor, was interested in developing the technical art of vernacular lyric poetry, and was the author of one of the first treatises on the subject. ▷ Chaucer seems to have read and been influenced by his work (including his narrative poetry) but Deschamps seems to have been very aware of Chaucer's literary skills too: his ▷ ballade addressed to the English poet describes Chaucer as a writer whose learning has illuminated the island.

Deserted Village, The (1770)
A poem in heroic ▷ couplets by ▷ Oliver Goldsmith, written in protest against the enclosure of common land by powerful landowners. The poet recalls his youth in Auburn in the traditional terms of idyllic ▷ pastoral, and laments the present desolation and depopulation. Goldsmith's conventional literary opposition between rural innocence and commercial corruption, prompted ▷ George Crabbe's realistic portrayal of the grimness of peasant life in *The Village* (1783).

Destruction of Troy, The
A Middle English translation, in ▷ alliterative verse, of ▷ Guido de Columnis's account of the first and second falls of Troy. The 14th-century English text was apparently commissioned (though the narrator does not give any precise information about the identity of the patron), and reflects considerable linguistic and metrical skill, sustained for some 14,000 lines.

Bib: Panton, G., and Donaldson, D. (eds.), *The 'Gest Historiale' of the Destruction of Troy.*

Detective fiction
This branch of literature is usually easy to distinguish from the much wider literature of crime and retribution in drama and in the novel. Unlike the latter, detective fiction seldom relies on the presentation of deep emotions or on subtle and profound character creation. Character, emotion, psychological analysis of states of mind, social reflections, will all be present as flavouring, and may even be conspicuous, but the indispensable elements are always a mysterious – but not necessarily horrible – crime, and a detective, who is commonly not a professional policeman, but who has highly developed powers of scientific deduction. It is essential that the surface details should be convincing, and that the author should keep no clues from the reader, who may thus have the satisfaction of competing with the detective at his game. In the detective story proper, as opposed to the crime novel, the criminal's identity is not revealed until the end, and provides the focus of attention. Precursors of the form are ▷ Wilkie Collins's novel *The Moonstone* (1868) and the stories of the American writer Edgar Allan Poe (1809–49), featuring the French detective Dupin. But the widespread popularity of detective fiction began with ▷ Arthur Conan Doyle's Sherlock Holmes stories, of which the first was *A Study in Scarlet* (1887). The staggering perspicuity of the amateur detective from Baker Street, and his superiority to the police and to his companion and foil, Dr Watson, won him a world-wide audience. Another early exponent of the detective short story was ▷ G. K. Chesterton, whose detective, Father Brown, is a modest and intuitive Roman Catholic priest who first appeared in *The Innocence of Father Brown* (1911). From the time of E. C. Bentley's classic work *Trent's Last Case* (1912) the full-length novel became the most popular form. After Conan Doyle, the dominant figure of detective fiction is Dorothy L. Sayers, whose aristocratic amateur detective, Lord Peter Wimsey, appears in works such as *Murder Must Advertise* (1933) and *The Nine Tailors* (1934); she also published a history of crime fiction in 1928 and wrote critical essays on the genre. Other prominent authors of detective fiction include Agatha Christie (the creator of Hercule Poirot and Miss Marple), Michael Innes (pseudonym of the novelist and critic J. I. M. Stewart), H. C. Bailey, P. D. James

and H. R. F. Keating. The American school of tough detective fiction is exemplified by Raymond Chandler (1888–1959) and Dashiell Hammett (1894–1961).

Determination

A Marxist term used in critical theory, it is often confused with 'determinism' whereby a particular action or event is wholly caused by some external agency, and must therefore be assumed to be inevitable. In 'determination', the traditional fatalistic implications of the term 'determinism' are softened considerably, to draw attention to those constraints and pressures which mould human action. Thus a distinction is to be made between a tendency which attributes all movement in the social formation to economic factors, and one which seeks to account structurally for the patterns of dominance and subordination (▷ contradictions) operating at any one moment in history. The concept of determination can also be used to ask questions about particular literary ▷ genres and their historical significance, as well as helping to account for particular elements of the rhetorical structures of texts. Determination helps in seeing texts as part of a larger social context rather than as isolated verbal constructs, and it helps also to raise a number of questions concerning the inter-relationship between literature and the ways in which it represents 'reality'.

Devil is an Ass, The (1616)

A satirical comedy by ▷ Ben Jonson, attacking the speculators, financial tricksters, and their dupes, in contemporary ▷ London. The young dupe, Fitzdottrel, is cheated out of his land by the 'projector' Meercraft with elaborate projects of land reclamation; Pug, an inferior devil trying his hand at deceiving and betraying humanity, finds that he is not the equal in this to human beings themselves.

Diachronic

▷ Synchronic.

Dialectic

Originally used to refer to the nature of logical argument, but in the 19th century this term underwent something of a revaluation, and came to be associated with the work of the German philosophers Kant and Hegel. 'Dialectic' referred to the process whereby the 'idea' (*thesis*) was self-divided, and its internal oppositions (*antithesis*) were resolved in a *synthesis* which opened the way to a higher truth. In ▷ Marxist thinking 'dialectic' refers to the ▷ contradictions present in any one phenomenon, and to their

resolution through conflict. It is the nature of that opposition and that conflict which determines movement and change.

Diana

▷ Artemis.

Diaries

As a form of literature in English, diaries begin to be significant in the 17th century. The spirit of criticism from the ▷ Renaissance and the stress on the individual conscience from the ▷ Reformation combined with the political and social turbulence of the 17th century to awaken people to a new awareness of personal experience and its possible interest for general readers. The private nature of the diary form also led to many women taking up this form of writing. Thus the art of the diary arose with the art of ▷ biography and ▷ autobiography. Diaries may first be divided into the two classes of those clearly meant to be strictly private and those written more or less with an eye to eventual publication. A further division may be made between those which are interesting chiefly as a record of the time in which the writer lived and those which are mainly a record of his personality.

The best known of the English diaries is that of ▷ Samuel Pepys (1633–1703), which was both purely private (written in code) and entirely unself-conscious, as well as an excellent record of the time. His contemporary, ▷ John Evelyn (1620–1706), is less famous partly because his diary is a more studied, self-conscious work. ▷ Jonathan Swift's *Journal to Stella* (covering the years 1710–13) is a personal revelation but unusual in that it was addressed to the woman Swift loved. The diary of the ▷ Quaker, ▷ George Fox (1624–91), is a record of his spiritual experience for the education of his followers. In the 18th and early 19th century the most famous is that of the novelist ▷ Fanny Burney (Madame D'Arblay, 1752–1840), considered as a record of the time ingenuously imbued with her own personality. The diary of the great religious reformer, ▷ John Wesley (1703–91), is comparable to that of Fox as a spiritual record, with a wider outlook on his time. In the 19th century the diaries of Thomas Creevey (1768–1838) and Charles Greville (1794–1865) are famous as records of public affairs, and that of ▷ Henry Crabb Robinson (1775–1867) for impressions of the leading writers who were his friends. In the 20th century the *Journal* of ▷ Katherine Mansfield is an intimate and vivid record of personal experience, and that of ▷ Virginia Woolf is an extremely interesting record of a writer's experience of artistic creation.

Dick, Mr

A character in ▷ Charles Dickens's novel ▷ *David Copperfield*. A harmless lunatic, he has an obsession with King Charles's head (*ie* ▷ Charles I, decapitated in 1649) – hence this is commonly used as synonymous with obsession, like the idiom 'a bee in one's bonnet'.

Dickens, Charles (1812–70)

Charles Dickens by Samuel Lawrence (1838)

The most popular and internationally known of English novelists. His father was a government clerk who liked to live prosperously, and his sudden impoverishment and imprisonment for debt in the ▷ Marshalsea was a drastic shock to the boy Dickens; prisons recur literally and symbolically in many of his novels, which are also filled with attacks on the injustice of social institutions and the inequalities between the rich and the poor. He began his writing career as a journalist, and all his novels were published serially in periodicals, especially in two edited by himself – ▷ *Household Words* started in 1850, and ▷ *All the Year Round*, started in 1859, both of them weeklies.

His first book, ▷ *Sketches by Boz* (1836), was a collection of stories and descriptive pieces written for various papers in the tradition of the essayists – ▷ Charles Lamb, ▷ William Hazlitt, ▷ Leigh Hunt – of the previous generation, with the especial difference that Dickens wrote about the hitherto neglected lower middle class. ▷ *The Pickwick Papers* (1836–7), at first loosely connected but gathering unity as it proceeded, was immensely successful. There followed: ▷ *Oliver Twist* (1837–8), ▷ *Nicholas Nickleby* (1838–9), ▷ *The Old Curiosity Shop* and ▷ *Barnaby Rudge* (1840–1). This concludes the first, comparatively light-hearted phase of Dickens's writing, in which he developed his characteristic comedy and melodrama. ▷ *Martin Chuzzlewit* (1843–4) begins a more impressive style of writing in which the comedy and melodrama deepen into new intensity, though critics observe that the beginning of the novel is still in the earlier manner. In 1843 begins his series of Christmas Books, including ▷ *A Christmas Carol* and ▷ *The Cricket on the Hearth*. Thereafter come his mature masterpieces: ▷ *Dombey and Son* (1846–8); ▷ *David Copperfield* (1849–50); ▷ *Bleak House* (1852–3); ▷ *Hard Times* (1854); ▷ *Little Dorrit* (1855–7); ▷ *A Tale of Two Cities* (1859); ▷ *Great Expectations* (1860–1); ▷ *Our Mutual Friend* (1864–5). Dickens was writing ▷ *Edwin Drood* when he died.
Bib: Forster, J., *Life*; Johnson, E., *Life*; Wilson, E., in *The Wound and the Bow*; Chesterton, G. K., *Charles Dickens*; Gissing, G., *Charles Dickens: A Crucial Study*; House, H., *The Dickens World*; Leavis, F. R., in *The Great Tradition*; Collins, P., *Dickens and Crime; Dickens and Education*; Gross J., *Dickens and the Twentieth Century*; Leavis, F. R. and Q. D., *Dickens the Novelist*; Wilson A., *The World of Charles Dickens*; Carey, J., *The Violent Effigy: A Study of Dickens' Imagination*; Kaplan, F., *Dickens: a biography*.

Dictionary of the English Language, A (1755)

Usually known as *Johnson's Dictionary*, it was compiled by ▷ Samuel Johnson, was published in 1755, and was accepted as authoritative for about a hundred years. The excellence of the work is not so much its scholarship as its literary intelligence. It is weak in etymology, as this was still an undeveloped science, but it is strong in understanding of language, and in particular the English language. In the Preface, Johnson writes a short grammar, but he points out that English simplicity of forms and freedom from inflexions make an elaborate one (as grammar was then understood) unnecessary. He makes clear that the spirit of the English language had been unduly influenced by the spirit of French, and he rejects the idea that correctness should be fixed by the authority of an Academy, since the inherent mutability of language will always cause it to follow its own laws. Johnson thus began the English habit of relying upon current English dictionaries and manuals of usage to discover the best existent expression: Fowler's *Modern English Usage* and the Oxford *New English Dictionary* are 20th-century equivalents of *Johnson's Dictionary*.

Dictys Cretensis

A supposed eyewitness of the Trojan war who kept a diary of events, *Ephemen's Belli Troiani* (*A Journal of the Trojan War*), which, along with the work of the Trojan ▷ Dares, formed the basis for the most influential medieval versions of the Troy story. Dictys, as a warrior on the Greek side, provides a pro-Greek view of events and also includes an account of the homecoming of the Greeks. A small portion of a Greek version of Dictys's work has survived from the early 3rd century but all the rest of the manuscript versions are of Latin reworkings which date from the 4th century. Although the account claims to be that of an eyewitness, the material is basically a rationalized version of events drawn from ▷ Homer's ▷ *Iliad*, organized chronologically. The narratives of Dictys and Dares were shown to be forgeries in the early 18th century.

▷ Benoît de Sainte-Maure; Troy.

Didactic literature

Literature designed to teach, or to propound in direct terms a doctrine or system of ideas. In practice, it is not always easy to identify; so much literature is didactic in intention but not in form; sometimes writers renounce didactic intentions but in practice use didactic forms. Thus ▷ Spenser declared that ▷ *The Faerie Queene* was meant to 'fashion a gentleman . . . in virtuous and gentle discipline', but the poem may be enjoyed for its imaginative vision without much regard to its didacticism, and the same is true of ▷ Bunyan's ▷ *Pilgrim's Progress*. In the 18th century much poetry had at least didactic leanings, such as ▷ Pope's ▷ *Essay on Criticism* and his ▷ *Essay on Man*; minor work by other poets is much more unmistakably didactic. The prevalence of didactic poetry in the 18th century arose from the especially high regard this century had for ancient Greek and Latin literature: Hesiod's *Works and Days* (Greek, 8th century B C) and ▷ Lucretius' *De Rerum Natura* (Latin, 1st century B C) being the major examples of didactic verse. The Romantic poets of the early 19th century

(▷ Wordsworth, ▷ Coleridge, ▷ Shelley, ▷ Keats) reacted against the 18th-century Augustans (▷ Augustanism), and since then there has been a persistent prejudice against explicit didacticism. In fact much of Wordsworth (*eg* ▷ *The Excursion*, 1814) and of Shelley (*eg* ▷ *Queen Mab*, 1813) was highly didactic, though the undisguised passion to some extent conceals the fact. The 19th-century novelists, especially ▷ Dickens and ▷ George Eliot, used didactic digressions, but in the former such passages are especially passionate social invective, and in the latter they are usually more integrated into the imaginative art than is apparent. In the 1930s there was a revival of verse didacticism, especially in the work of ▷ W. H. Auden, *eg New Year Letter* (1941). In general, the view now is that poets and even novelists may be didactic if they choose. True didacticism, however, requires a body of assumptions commonly held by author and reader, as was true of the age of Pope, but is not so today.

Dido (Elissa)

In Roman legend, the daughter of a king of Tyre, and the reputed founder of the city of ▷ Carthage. ▷ Virgil brings her into his epic of the founding of Rome, the ▷ *Aeneid*; she falls in love with ▷ Aeneas when he is shipwrecked on the North African coast, and when he forsakes her to fulfil his destiny, she kills herself. The Romans identified her with the guardian goddess of Carthage.

She is the subject of a tragedy, *Dido* (1594) by ▷ Christopher Marlowe and ▷ Thomas Nashe, and of the opera *Dido and Aeneas* by ▷ Nahum Tate to music by ▷ Henry Purcell, produced in 1689-90.

Difference

A term introduced by ▷ Ferdinand de Saussure in his study of linguistics and used in literary theory. It is the means whereby value is established in any system of linguistic signs whether it be spoken or written. Saussure's *Course in General Linguistics* (1915) argues that in speech it is 'the phonetic contrasts' which permit us to distinguish between one word and another that constitute meaning. In writing the letters used to form words are arbitrary ▷ signs, and their values are therefore 'purely negative and differential' (Saussure). The result is that the written sign becomes important only insofar as it is different from other signs within the overall system of language. The notion of difference as a principle of opposition has been extended beyond the limits of Structuralist thinking laid down by Saussure. For example, the

▷ Marxist philosopher ▷ Mikhail Bakhtin in a critique of Saussurean ▷ Structuralism argued that 'the forms of signs are conditioned above all by the social organization of the participants involved and also by the immediate conditions of their interaction' (*Marxism and The Philosophy of Language*; 1930). Thus the clash of opposites through which meaning and value emerge is determined by the social positions of those who use the language. This means that secreted at the very heart of the form of the linguistic sign is a series of dialectical opposites whose interaction refracts the struggle taking place within the larger framework of society itself. For Bakhtin these oppositions can be defined in terms of the struggle between social classes, but the dialectical structure of these conflicts makes the notion of difference suitable for any situation which can be analysed in terms of binary opposites. For example, for ▷ feminism this would be an opposition between 'masculine' and 'feminine' as the basis upon which sexual identity is constructed. ▷ Jacques Derrida has adapted the term to form the neologism '*différance*', which denotes the deferral of meaning whereby no sign can ever be brought into direct alignment with the object that it purports to recall. This means that meaning is always *deferred*, and can never be final.

Digby Plays
A collection of three medieval plays dating from the 16th century, from the East Anglian region and found with non-literary material in a single manuscript, now kept in Oxford, MS Bodley Digby 133. Two of the plays, *Mary Magdalene* and *The Conversion of St Paul*, are rare survivals of the popular medieval genre of saints' plays. The third play, *The Killing of the Children*, is a self-contained biblical piece written, it seems, for performance on a feast day.
Bib: Baker, Donald et al (eds.) *The Late Medieval Religious Plays of Bodleian MSS Digby 133 and E. Muse 160.*

Dillon, Wentworth (1633?–85)
▷ Roscommon, Fourth Earl of.

Diogenes the Cynic
A Greek philosopher who sought to achieve spiritual independence by renouncing property (even a drinking bowl) and lived in a tub. When the conqueror, Alexander of Macedon, offered to fulfil his wishes, Diogenes asked him to stand out of the way of the sunshine. Whereupon Alexander

declared, 'If I were not Alexander I would choose to be Diogenes'.
▷ Cynics.

Diomedes
A Greek hero in the Trojan war, and king of Argos. In ▷ Chaucer's ▷ *Troilus and Criseyde* and ▷ Shakespeare's ▷ *Troilus and Cressida*, he seduces Cressida (Criseyde) from her devotion to the Trojan prince, Troilus.

Dionysus
In Greek myth, a vegetation god especially associated with wine. He was the son of ▷ Zeus and Semele. His festivals were celebrated by incantations or choruses, which eventually gave rise to Greek tragedy. He is said, like other vegetation gods, to have died and risen again, and the ceremonies by which he was worshipped were orgiastic. He was also known, in both Greek and Latin, as Bacchus. Dionysus is sometimes contrasted with ▷ Apollo: 'Dionysiac' writing is passionate and explosive: 'Apolline' writing is contemplative and serene.

Discourse
A term used in critical theory. Especially in the writings of ▷ Michel Foucault, 'discourse' is the name given to the systems of linguistic representations through which power sustains itself. For Foucault discourse manifests itself only through concrete examples operating within specific areas of social and institutional practice. He argues that within individual discourses a series of mechanisms are used as means of controlling desire and power, which facilitate 'classification . . . ordering [and] distribution' (Foucault). In this way a mastery is exerted over what appears to be the randomness of everyday reality. It is thus possible to investigate those discourses which have been used to master reality in the past *eg* discourses concerned with questions of 'sexuality', criminality and judicial systems of punishment, or madness, as Foucault's own work demonstrates.
Bib: Foucault, M., *The Order of Things*; *Power/ Knowledge: Selected Interviews and Other Writings* (ed. C. Gordon).

Dismal science, The
Political economy; so called by ▷ Thomas Carlyle because the social thought of such writers as ▷ Adam Smith, ▷ Jeremy Bentham, ▷ Thomas Malthus and David Ricardo tended to be pessimistic about the alleviation of poverty and inhumanly indifferent to the consequences of economic laws as they saw them.

Displacement

For ▷ psychoanalytical usage 'displacement' is associated by ▷ Freud (along with ▷ 'condensation') with the mechanisms whereby the conscious mind processes the unconscious in dreams. 'Displacement' is a form of censorship which effectively distorts the ideas which act as the controlling forces of the dream, (what Freud calls 'the latent dream-thoughts') and attaches them to other, more acceptable thoughts or ideas. This complex process is one which involves the omission or re-arrangement of detail, and modification of the dream thoughts. In order to reach the unconscious the 'manifest dream' must be interpreted as a symbolic expression of another text which lies beneath its surface and which is not readily accessible to the conscious mind. This whole mechanism rests on the assumption that psychic energy can attach itself to particular ideas, or objects (cathexis); those ideas or objects are related to the 'latent dream-thoughts', but derive their new-found significance by a process of association. Literature habitually invests objects and ideas with value, and psychic intensity, and the manner in which it does so can be read ▷ psychoanalytically as a manifestation of deeper, more disturbing activities going on in the mind of the writer, or – by analogy – in the 'unconscious' of the society of which the writer is a part.

Disraeli, Benjamin (Lord Beaconsfield) (1804–81)

Statesman and novelist. He was of Spanish-Jewish descent; his grandfather settled in England in 1748. His political career was brilliant; he entered Parliament in 1837; in the 1840s he was the leader in the House of Commons of a small number of Tory (▷ Whig and ▷ Tory) politicians who, as the 'Young England' group, wanted a revival of the party and of the national spirit in an alliance between a spiritually reborn aristocracy and the common people; by 1848 he was leading the Conservatives in the House of Commons; in 1868 and in 1874–80 he had his two periods as one of the most brilliant of English Prime Ministers. Both politically (he secured the vote for the urban working class) and socially (eg his trade union legislation) he at least partly succeeded in securing support for his party from the working class. He was made Earl of Beaconsfield in 1876.

The novels which now chiefly hold attention are his 'Young England Trilogy': ▷ Coningsby (1844); ▷ Sybil (1845) and Tancred (1847). All were written to promulgate his doctrine of Tory Democracy and they all have imperfections, partly because for Disraeli literature was second to politics. On the other hand they have great liveliness of characterization and show keen insight into the structure of society with its cleavage between rich and poor, which Disraeli called 'the two nations'. His other novels are: Vivian Grey (1826); The Young Duke (1831); Alroy and Ixion in Heaven (1833); The Infernal Marriage and The Rise of Iskander (1834); Henrietta Temple and Venetia (1837); Lothair (1870) and Endymion (1880).
Bib: Blake, R., Life; Moneypenny, W. F. and Buckle, G. E., Life; Jerman, B. R., The Young Disraeli; Holloway, J., in Victorian Sage; Dahl, C., in Victorian Fiction (ed. L. Stevenson); Pritchett, V. S., in The Living Novel; Schwartz, D. R., Disraeli's Fiction; Brava, T., Disraeli the Novelist.

Dissenters

A term used for those ▷ Puritans who, owing to their 'dissent' from the established ▷ Church of England, were refused certain political, educational, and (at first) religious rights from the second half of the 17th century. That is to say, they could not enter Parliament, they could not enter a university, and, until 1688, they could not join together in worship. Puritans were not thus formally restricted before 1660. They were released from their political restraints in 1828. In the 19th century it became more usual to call them ▷ Nonconformists or Free Churchmen. The term does not apply to Scotland, where the established Church is ▷ Presbyterian, not the ▷ episcopalian Church of England.

Dissociation of Sensibility

A critical expression made famous by ▷ T. S. Eliot, and used in his essay The Metaphysical Poets (1921, included in his Selected Essays). He states: 'In the seventeenth century a dissociation of sensibility set in, from which we have never recovered; and this dissociation . . . was aggravated by the influence of the two most powerful poets of the century, ▷ Milton and ▷ Dryden.' Eliot's argument is that before 1660 poets, in particular the ▷ Metaphysical poets, were 'engaged in the task of trying to find the verbal equivalent for states of mind and feeling', and that after that date 'while the language became more refined, the feeling became more crude'. Poetry, henceforward, is put to more specialized purposes: ▷ 'Tennyson and ▷ Browning are poets, and they think; but they do not feel their thought as immediately as the odour of a rose. A thought to ▷ Donne was an experience; it modified his sensibility.' The implication behind the argument is that poets (with exceptions) ceased to bring all their faculties to bear upon their art: ▷ 'Racine or Donne looked into a good deal more than the heart. One must look into the cerebral cortex, the nervous system, and the digestive tracts.'

The theory has had great influence. Those who uphold it support it with the evidence provided by the rise of modern prose after 1660, and the gradual displacement of poetry from its centrality in literature thereafter; poetry either subjected itself to the rational discipline of prose (*eg* ▷ Pope), or, in the 19th century, it tended to cultivate areas of feeling to which this rational discipline was not relevant (*eg* ▷ Swinburne). However, the theory has been attacked for various reasons. Eliot himself felt that he had used the expression in too simplified a way (*Milton*, 1974, in *Poets and Poetry*), and that the cause of the process were more complicated than his earlier essay had implied. Other writers have suggested that such a dissociation did not happen; or that it happened in different ways at different periods; or that, if it did happen, no deterioration in imaginative writing can be attributed to it. See Frank Kermode, *Romantic Image* and F. W. Bateson in *Essays in Criticism*, vol. 1.

Dithyramb
A Greek choric hymn in honour of the god ▷ Dionysus (Bacchus), and irregular and vehement in rhythm. 'Dithyrambic' is used to describe verse with similar rhythm.

Divina Commedia (*Divine Comedy*)
The principal work of the Italian poet ▷ Dante (1265–1321). For an account of its contents, see the entries under its major sections: ▷ *Inferno*, ▷ *Purgatorio*, ▷ *Paradiso*.
Bib: Cunningham, G. F., *The Divine Comedy in English, 1090–1966*; Sinclair, J. N. (trans.), *The Divine Comedy*.

Divorce
Until 1857 divorce was possible only through Church courts which had kept their authority over matrimonial relations since before the ▷ Reformation, while losing it in nearly all other private affairs of laymen. Even after a marriage had been dissolved by a Church court, a special ('private') act of Parliament was necessary before the divorce was legalized. In consequence, divorces were rare and only occurred among the rich and influential. Adultery and cruelty were the accepted grounds, and the wife was commonly in an unfavourable position, so that no divorce was granted on account of a husband's adultery until 1801. The law of 1857 added desertion as a ground for divorce, and proceedings were taken out of the hands of the Church courts and put under the courts of the realm. Since 1938, unsoundness of mind may also be pleaded as a cause of divorce, and it has been further facilitated in other ways, perhaps the most important of which is the concept of 'marital breakdown'. This abolishes the idea of one of the partners being 'guilty' and the other, 'injured'.
▷ Marriage; Women, Status of.

Doctor Faustus, The Tragical History of
A tragedy in ▷ blank verse, with comic episodes in prose, by ▷ Christopher Marlowe. The play resembles a medieval ▷ morality play in that its theme is Faustus's sacrifice of his soul to the devil (represented by Mephistophilis) for the sake of unlimited power, glory and enjoyment in this world. On the other hand, it is also thoroughly ▷ Renaissance in its treatment: the conflict of choice is made convincing as it would not have been in a medieval play, and the psychology, not only of Faustus but of Mephistophilis, is presented with moving insight. The medieval and the Renaissance outlooks fuse in *Doctor Faustus*, showing the very important continuity, as well as the contrast, between the two outlooks.

There are two uncertainties about the play. One is about its date. Marlowe uses the material of the German *Faustbuch* (*Faustbook*), which is about an early 16th-century scholar who had claimed powers of black magic, and fuses this historical figure with medieval legends about a man selling his soul to the devil. The earliest surviving English version is dated 1592, and the maturity of the poetry also suggests a date for the play late in Marlowe's life. On the other hand, some critics have found good reason to date *Faustus* at least as early as 1588. The other uncertainty concerns the extent of Marlowe's authorship. Did he have a collaborator for the comic parts? And were some of these added after his death? The edition of 1616 has considerably extended comedy, as compared with the first edition of 1604. The main reason for suspecting a collaborator is that much of the comedy is superfluous as well as trivial. It is, however, a mistake to suppose that the mere presence of comedy is injurious to the highest tragedy; the combination is frequent in Elizabethan serious drama – tragedies and history plays – including ▷ Shakespeare's, and it is one of the inheritances from medieval ▷ mystery and morality plays, with which English Renaissance drama kept a close relationship. Some of the comedy in *Faustus* enriches the tragedy by extending its relevance to common life, *eg* in the parody in which Faustus's servant, Wagner, also tries his hand at summoning the devil.

▷ Faust; ▷ Mephistopheles.

Doctor's Dilemma, The (1906)

A comedy by ▷ George Bernard Shaw. It is simultaneously a satire on the practice of medicine, and a criticism and exploration of the conventional moral code. The immoral artist causes less actual harm by his naked selfishness than do the highly moral doctors in the perfectly lawful discharge of their profession.

Dogberry and Verges

Comic constables in ▷ Shakespeare's play ▷ *Much Ado About Nothing*. Dogberry is famous for his misuse of words – compare ▷ Mrs Malaprop in ▷ Sheridan's *The Rivals*.

Doggerel

Any carelessly made, irregular verse, often of a frivolous nature. The term is used by the host in ▷ Chaucer's ▷ *Canterbury Tales* in regard to the tale of ▷ *Sir Thopas*, told by Chaucer himself as one of the pilgrims: '"This may wel be rym doggerel", quod he.'

Dombey and Son (1847–8)

One of the earliest of the mature novels by ▷ Charles Dickens. Dombey is a proud and heartless London merchant whose sole interest in life is the perpetuation of his name in connection with his firm. For this reason he neglects his deeply affectionate daughter Florence for the sake of his little son, Paul, whom, however, he values not for himself but as the future embodiment of his firm. The boy is motherless, deprived of affection and physically delicate – he dies in childhood. To prevent Florence from marrying a mere clerk in his firm, Dombey sends her lover – Walter Gay – on business to an unhealthy colony in the West Indies. Dombey's pride makes him susceptible to flattery; he is preyed upon by Carker, his manager, one of Dickens's most notable villains, and by Major Joe Bagstock. He is led into marriage with a cold, disillusioned girl, Edith Granger, who runs away from him with Carker. Both his pride and his wealth are eventually taken from him and he finds himself in the end dependent on the forgiving Florence and Walter Gay. A particular interest of the book is that railways play an important part in it just at the time

when they were transforming English life. The sombreness of Dombey's mansion is opposed to the warm-hearted if unbusinesslike environment of the shop of Solomon Gills, Gay's uncle.

Domesday Book

(Dome = doom, *ie* judgement, implying a complete and final record as on the Day of Judgement at the end of the world.) The record of a survey carried out by the order of ▷ William I and completed in 1086. It contains a description of the greater part of the landed property of England and was compiled to assist taxation and other government purposes.

Dominicans

▷ Friars.

Don Juan

The hero of legends from various European countries. His exploits were the subject of the Spanish play *El Burlador de Sevilla* by Tirso de Molina (1571–1641), who gave him his distinctive character of sensual adventurer. Plays and stories were woven round him in French and Italian, and he is the protagonist of an opera by Mozart (*Don Giovanni*). In English literature by far the most important work about him is the satirical epic ▷ *Don Juan* (1819–24) by ▷ Lord Byron; he was also the subject of a forgotten play *The Libertine* (1676) by ▷ Thomas Shadwell, and, in more modern guise, of ▷ George Bernard Shaw's *Man and Superman*.

Don Juan (1819–24)

▷ Lord Byron's unfinished satirical epic in *ottava rima*, based very freely on the legendary figure of ▷ Don Juan. After a love affair in Spain (Canto I), Juan is sent abroad by his mother, but is shipwrecked and washed ashore on a Greek island where he is cared for by a Greek maiden, Haidee. Cantos III and IV describe their love and the destruction of their relationship by Haidee's pirate father, Lambro. In Canto V Juan has been sold as a slave to a Turkish princess who loves him; and in Cantos VI, VII and VIII he escapes and serves the Russian army against the Turks in the siege of Ismail. In Canto IX he attracts the attention of the Russian Empress, Catherine the Great, who in Canto X sends him on a mission to England, the setting for Cantos XI–XIII. Juan's affair with a duchess, and his deeper emotion for an English Catholic girl, are used as foci for a free-ranging satire on contemporary society. Juan has fewer mistresses in Byron's poem than in earlier versions of the legend, and is portrayed essentially as an *ingénu*, more often seduced by women than the seducer. The story-line is however subordinated to the philosophizing commentary of the poet himself, which ranges from flippant witticism ('What men call gallantry, and gods adultery,/ Is much more common where the climate's sultry'), through the moving rhetoric of the inserted lyric 'The isles of Greece', to harsh satire on 'the best of cutthroats', the Duke of Wellington ('And I shall be delighted to learn who,/ Save you and yours, have gain'd by Waterloo?'). The greatness of the poem derives from its flexible and informal metrical form, which, unlike the ▷ Spenserian stanzas of ▷ *Childe Harold's Pilgrimage* and the couplets of his verse tales, allows Byron to give full expression to his complex and contradictory personality.

Don Quixote de la Mancha (1605–15)
A satirical romance by the Spanish writer Miguel de Cervantes (1547–1616). It begins as a satire on the medieval and ▷ Renaissance style of romance about wandering knights and their adventures in the pursuit of the rectification of injustices (▷ the Arthurian cycle). It deepens into an image of idealism perpetually at odds with the pettiness, vulgarity and meanness of the real world. Don Quixote is an impecunious gentleman whose mind has been turned by reading too many romances. He sets out on his wanderings accompanied by his servant, Sancho Panza, the embodiment of commonplace credulity and a shrewd sense of personal advantage. He takes as his patroness a peasant girl, Dulcinea del Toboso, whom he transfigures in his imagination and who is quite unaware of his devotion. The book was translated into English in 1612–20, and again a hundred years later in a more famous version by Peter Motteux. Its influence on our literature has been extensive. In the 17th century the burlesque element is emulated by ▷ Francis Beaumont in his play ▷ *The Knight of the Burning Pestle* and by ▷ Samuel Butler in his mock epic ▷ *Hudibras*. In the 18th century the theme of idealists misunderstanding and misunderstood is followed in ▷ Henry Fielding's ▷ *Joseph Andrews* and ▷ Oliver Goldsmith's ▷ *Vicar of Wakefield*. The influence can likewise be traced in ▷ Lawrence Sterne and ▷ Tobias Smollett, and, in the 19th century, in ▷ Charles Dickens (especially in ▷ *Pickwick Papers*).

Donne, John (1572–1631)
Poet, Dean of St Pauls and prose writer. John Donne is (and was) regarded as one of the most important writers of the ▷ Renaissance period. The early part of his life was spent at the margins of the Elizabethan court. He took part in the expeditions of the Earl of Essex to Cadiz in 1596 and the Azores in 1597, and became private secretary to the Lord Keeper, Sir Thomas Egerton, in 1598. He travelled on the continent in 1605–6 and 1611–12. Originally a Roman ▷ Catholic, he was ordained into the ▷ Anglican Church in 1615, becoming Reader in Divinity at ▷ Lincoln's Inn in 1616, and Chaplain to Viscount Doncaster's embassy into Germany in 1619. In 1621 he was made Dean of St Pauls, and in the following year an Honorary Member of the Council of the Virginia Company.

Donne's works cover an enormous variety of genres and subjects. They include religious works such as the *Devotions on Emergent Occasions* published in 1624 and the *Essays in Divinity* (1651); anti-Catholic works such as *Pseudo-Martyr* (1610) and *Ignatius his Conclave* (1611); a considerable number of sermons (collections appearing in 1625, 1626, 1634 and 1640); a treatise on suicide entitled *Biathanatos* (1646); a collection of paradoxes (1633); and, in poetry, ▷ satires, ▷ lyrics, ▷ elegies, ▷ epigrams, verse letters and divine ▷ sonnets.

As a preacher, Donne was justly famous in an age of famous preachers, as ▷ Izaak Walton, his first biographer, recalled. His poetry, however, with the important exception of the two anniversary poems of 1611 and 1612, did not, for the most part, appear until after his death when a collection was published in 1633. His poetry was, however, well known among his contemporaries, numerous manuscript versions of both his secular and his religious verse being in circulation.
Bib: Grierson, H. J. C. (ed.), *Poems*, (2 vols.); Smith, A. J. (ed.), *John Donne: The Complete English Poems*; Patrides, C. A. (ed.), *The Complete English Poems of John Donne*; Bald, R. C., *Donne: A Life*; Carey, J., *John Donne: Life Mind Art*.
▷ *Songs and Sonnets*.

Doolittle, Hilda ('H. D.') (1886–1961)
Poet. H. D. was born in Bethlehem, Pennsylvania, educated at Bryn Mawr, where she was a contemporary of American poet Marianne Moore, and moved to Britain in 1911. She was an important figure in the ▷ Imagist group, signing her first poems, published in Harriet Monroe's *Poetry* in 1913, 'H. D. Imagiste'. She was a close associate of ▷ Ezra Pound, to whom she

was briefly engaged in 1907. The 'Hellenic hardness' of her work epitomized Imagism. She married fellow writer Richard Aldington in 1913, becoming part of the network sometimes known as the 'Other ▷ Bloomsbury' which was dominated by ▷ D. H. Lawrence, who is characterized in H. D.'s novel *Bid Me To Live* (published 1960). From 1916 she co-edited, with ▷ T. S. Eliot, *The Egoist*, Dora Marsden's originally ▷ feminist journal which had published amongst other texts ▷ James Joyce's ▷ *Portrait of the Artist as a Young Man* in serial form in 1914–5. In 1917 H. D. separated from Aldington, gave birth to her daughter Perdita, and began to travel with her friend Bryher (Winifred Ellerman), with whom she spent much of the rest of her life. Her first collection, *Sea Garden*, was published in 1916, followed by *Hymen* (1921), *Heliodora and Other Poems* (1924) and *Red Roses for Bronze* (1929). The trilogy, *The Walls Do Not Fall* (1944–6) and *Helen in Egypt* (1961), perhaps H. D.'s most important works, have only recently received the critical attention they deserve. Her poetry is intense, difficult, and infused with her passion for classical ▷ Greek culture. Although primarily known as a poet, H. D. wrote novels, and having undergone psychoanalysis with ▷ Freud in Vienna 1933–4, published an account of the process. *Tribute to Freud* is important both as a poetic and visionary text and as a key text in debates about psychoanalysis and feminism.
Bib: Duplessis, R. B., *H. D. The Career of That Struggle*.

Dorset, Lord
▷ Sackville, Thomas.

Dorset, Sixth Earl of (1638–1706)
Poet and patron. Charles Sackville, Lord Buckhurst, and later Earl of Dorset, was a ▷ Restoration courtier and author of ▷ satires and ▷ lyric poems (*Works*, 1714). ▷ John Dryden's *Discourse concerning the Original and Progress of Satire* is addressed to him, and contains high praise for his poetry.

Dorset Garden Theatre, The
The Dorset Garden Theatre, also known as the Duke's Theatre because of its patronage by the Duke of York, later ▷ James II, was designed by ▷ Sir Christopher Wren for ▷ Sir William D'Avenant, and was considered the most magnificent public theatre when it opened in 1671.

The stage had four doors, two on each side, admitting the performers to a deep forestage or apron stage which projected into the pit, past the side-boxes. On this the prologue was spoken, and much of the acting took place, allowing great intimacy between actors and audience when desired. Scene changes were carried out in full view of the audience, the curtain or front 'scene' being moved only at the beginnings and ends of performances; actors could step forward or backward into different, perhaps newly revealed, 'sets', as they were speaking. This made possible fast-paced, fluid action, particularly in comedy. From the first the Dorset Garden specialized in staging the very elaborate performances, including many operas, as distinct from the Theatre Royal, Drury Lane (▷ Drury Lane Theatres), which concentrated on plays. After the ▷ King's Company and ▷ Duke's Company were merged in 1682, Dorset Garden continued for a time to be the main venue for spectacles. In 1689 it was re-named the Queen's Theatre, in deference to Queen Mary (1662–94). It gradually fell out of use, and was demolished in 1709.

Double-Dealer, The (1694)
Busy and rather bitter play by ▷ William Congreve. At its heart is the Machiavellian (▷ Machiavelli) character of Maskwell, an arch dissembler and schemer. Setting himself up as everyone's friend and ally, he contrives to deceive and entrap each character in his single-minded plot to indulge his own lust and greed. His aim is to displace his supposed friend Mellefont, both in the fortune Mellefont is due to inherit from his uncle and aunt, Lord and Lady Touchwood, and in the hand of Cynthia as his wife. The means by which he almost succeeds are shown with infinite skill, as he manipulates other gullible and fallible characters, and situations, with breathtaking credibility. He seduces and then uses Lady Touchwood, and exploits the unhappiness of two other couples. A recurring feature is the ease with which the wives manage to allay their husbands' suspicions of their cuckoldry. Only two characters emerge from this comparatively unstained: Cynthia, and Mellefont – but even he is tainted (as Congreve points out in the preface) by his blind and stubborn adherence to Maskwell. The play's seamy and unpleasant atmosphere is mitigated by scenes of high comedy. It recalls, to some extent, ▷ William Wycherley's ▷ *The Plain Dealer*, and looks forward to ▷ Oliver Goldsmith's *The Good-Natur'd Man*.

Doubting Castle
In Part I of ▷ John Bunyan's ▷ *Pilgrim's Progress*, the castle belonging to the Giant

Despair, where Christian and Hopeful lie prisoners. In Part II the Castle is destroyed by the champion Greatheart.

Douglas, Black

The Douglases were a family of the Scottish medieval border nobility, constantly at war with the English ▷ Percy family on the south side of the border. Two famous Douglases bore the epithet 'Black': James Douglas (?1286–1330), supporter of ▷ Robert the Bruce in the Scottish War of Independence, and eventually killed fighting the Moors in Spain; Archibald Douglas (also called 'the Grim'), another famous warrior, who lived later in the 14th century.

▷ *Chevy Chase, The Ballad of*; *Otterbourne, The Battle of.*

Douglas, Gavin (?1475–1522)

Scottish poet and Bishop of Dunkeld. Unlike many of his contemporaries, he wrote only in the vernacular, and is most famous for his translation of ▷ Virgil's ▷ *Aeneid, Aeneados*, printed in 1533, which seems to have been used by the ▷ Earl of Surrey.

▷ Ezra Pound was a great admirer of this translation. His allegorical poem, the *Palice of Honor* (1501), was influenced by ▷ Chaucer's ▷ *House of Fame*. Douglas, who was heavily involved in ecclesiastical and secular politics, died in exile in England.

Bib: Small, J. (ed.), *Works*; Bawcutt, P., *Gavin Douglas: A Critical Study.*

Douglas, Keith (1920–44)

Poet. Keith Douglas was born in Kent, and educated at Oxford University under the tutorship of poet ▷ Edward Blunden, before enlisting with the British Army when World War II broke out. He is the most famous English poet of that war, although he began publishing his work at the age of 16. His verse is precise, unsentimental and at times chilling, in its treatment of desire and sexuality as well as in its pervasive obsession with death and the relation of death to writing. Douglas was killed in Normandy, having also written about his involvement in the war in North Africa, his slim but intensely powerful corpus concluded at an early age. His work began to receive the acclaim it deserves only when ▷ Ted Hughes, a great admirer, edited and introduced a collection in 1964 (*Selected Poems*). See also the more recent *Complete Poems* (ed. Desmond Graham; 1978).

Doyle, Sir Arthur Conan (1859–1930)

Novelist; chiefly noted for his series of stories and novels about the amateur detective, Sherlock Holmes, a genius in minute deduction and acute observations. His friend, Dr Watson, is represented as the ordinary, ingenuous man, who needs to have everything pointed out to him and explained; and this offsets the ingenuity of the detective. The combination of acute detective and obtuse colleague has been imitated in many detective stories ever since. The stories include: *A Study in Scarlet* (1887); *The Adventures of Sherlock Holmes* (1891); *The Memoirs of Sherlock Holmes* (1893); *The Hound of the Baskervilles* (1902); *The Return of Sherlock Holmes* (1905). Conan Doyle also wrote historical novels of merit; *eg Micah Clarke* (1888), *The White Company* (1891), and *Rodney Stone* (1896).

▷ Detective fiction.

Bib: Lamond, J., *Conan Doyle: a Memoir*; Conan Doyle, A., *The True Conan Doyle*; Carr, J. D., *The Life of Conan Doyle*; Roberts, S. C., *Holmes and Watson*; Pearsall, R; *Conan Doyle: A Biographical Solution.*

Drabble, Margaret (b 1939)

Margaret Drabble

Novelist and short-story writer. Born in Sheffield and educated at Cambridge University. The novelist ▷ A. S. Byatt is her sister. She achieved considerable popular success with her novels of the 1960s, which dealt with the personal dilemmas of intelligent and educated heroines. In *The Millstone* (1965) Rosamund struggles for independence, and achieves relative stability and a sense of moral responsibility through her love for her baby daughter, the result of a casual liaison.

Drabble's later novels broaden their scope, subsuming feminist issues in a general concern for equality and justice, and addressing wider national and international issues. *The Needle's Eye* (1972) established her as a major writer by the moral intensity of its concern with social justice. *The Ice Age* (1977) is a sombre picture of the corrupt and sterile condition of Britain in the mid 1970s. Drabble sees herself as a social historian, and admires the novelist ▷ Arnold Bennett, a biography of whom she published in 1974. The literary allusion which has been a feature of all her work becomes more marked in the 1970s, and her narrative techniques become more adventurous, as in the three points of view, alterations of style and self-conscious authorial voice of *The Realms of Gold* (1975). Her other novels are: *A Summer Bird-Cage* (1962); *The Garrick Year* (1964); *Jerusalem the Golden* (1967); *The Waterfall* (1969); *The Middle Ground* (1980); *The Radiant Way* (1987). Story collections: *Penguin Modern Stories 3* (with others) (1969); *Hassam's Tower* (1980).
Bib: Creighton, J. V., *Margaret Drabble*.

Drake, Sir Francis (?1549–96)

Built up as a national hero for his seafaring exploits at the end of the 19th and early 20th century. He engaged in numerous voyages in which he successfully raided Spain and her American colonies, and circumnavigated the world in his ship the *Golden Hind*, 1577–81. He was one of the commanders of the English fleet against the ▷ Armada during the attempted Spanish invasion of 1588.

Dramatic monologue

A poetic form in which the poet invents a character, or, more commonly, uses one from history or legend, and reflects on life from the character's standpoint. The dramatic monologue is a development from the ▷ conversation poem of ▷ Coleridge and ▷ Wordsworth, in which the poet reflects on life in his own person.

▷ Tennyson was the first to use the form, *eg* ▷ *The Lotos-Eaters* (1833), *Ulysses* (1842) and *Tithonus* (pub. 1860). In these poems, he takes the standpoint of characters in Greek myth and causes them to express emotions relevant to their predicaments. The emotions, however, are really more relevant to those of Tennyson's own age, but the disguise enables him to express himself without inhibition, and particularly without involving himself in the responsibility of having to defend the attitudes that he is expressing. His most ambitious poem in this form is the monodrama ▷ *Maud* (1855).

However it was ▷ Robert Browning who used the form most profusely, and with whom it is most associated, *eg My Last Duchess* (1845); *Fra Lippo Lippi, Andrea del Sarto, The Bishop Orders His Tomb, Bishop Blougram's Apology*, all in ▷ *Men and Women* (1855); *Mr Sludge the Medium* in ▷ *Dramatis Personae* (1864); and *The Ring and the Book* (1869). Browning used it differently from Tennyson: his characters are more detached from his own personality; the poems are attempts to explore a wide variety of attitudes to art and life. His monologues have little to do with drama, though superficially they resemble soliloquies in plays of the age of Shakespeare. They have an even closer resemblance, though still a rather superficial one, to the medieval convention of public confession by characters such as the Wife of Bath and the Pardoner in ▷ Chaucer's ▷ *Canterbury Tales*. Most of all, however, they emulate the exploration of character and society in the novel of Browning's own day, and his *The Ring and the Book* is really an experiment in the novel; the tale unfolds through monologues by the various participators in and spectators of the events. Still another use for the dramatic monologue is that to which ▷ Arthur Clough puts it in his poem *Dipsychus* (*Divided Mind*, 1850). This poem is in the form of a dialogue, but it is a dialogue between the two parts of a man's mind: that which tries to sustain moral principle, and that which is sceptical of principle, seeking only pleasure and material well-being.

A more searching irony was brought to the dramatic monologue by ▷ T. S. Eliot in *The Love Song of J. Alfred Prufrock* (1915) and *Gerontion* (1920).

Dramatis Personae (1864)

A collection of poems by ▷ Robert Browning, including a number of his more famous ones: *Abt Vogler, Rabbi Ben Ezra, A Death in the Desert, Caliban upon Setebos, Mr Sludge the Medium*.

Drapier's Letters (1724)

A series of pamphlets by ▷ Jonathan Swift against a monopoly to issue copper coins in Ireland, granted by the English Government to the Duchess of Kendal (George 1's mistress) and sold by her to William Wood ('Wood's halfpence'). The Irish considered that the monopoly would be economically harmful to them. Swift wrote in their support in the semblance of a Dublin 'drapier' (= draper), *ie* an ordinary shopman. The pamphlets are an example of his apparently moderate, plain style carrying an immense force of irony; they were so effective that the Government had to withdraw the monopoly.

Drayton, Michael (1563–1631)
Poet. Little is known of the life of this prolific writer, whose works encompassed a wide range of ▷ genres and subject matter. His collection of ▷ sonnets, gathered under the title *Idea's Mirror*, first appeared in 1594, and consists of 51 sonnets, mainly in the ▷ Petrarchan mode. The sequence was continuously revised, with additions appearing in the editions of 1602, 1605 and the final version of 1619.

Apart from sonnets, however, Drayton wrote ▷ eclogues indebted to ▷ Edmund Spenser, ▷ Ovidian verses and historical poetry. Of his historical poetry, *Piers Gaveston* (1593, revised in 1596) is remarkable for its combination of the Ovidian and the homoerotic. In 1596, Drayton published the first version of a historical narrative – *Mortimeriados* – an ambitious account, in verse, of the events which ▷ Christopher Marlowe was to dramatize in his play *Edward II*.

In common with Spenser and ▷ Samuel Daniel, Drayton was alert to the importance of celebrating the idea of the nation-state. Drayton's contribution to this late-Elizabethan project was the topographical verse description of England – *Poly-Olbion* (Part I, 1612; Part II, 1622). *Poly-Olbion* sets out to celebrate, in ▷ Alexandrine verse, not only the geographical features of England, but the customs and histories of all the counties of the kingdom. It was an ambitious project which was never to reach completion. But *Poly-Olbion* was only one part of Drayton's desire to celebrate English history. Another aspect of his historiographical enterprise is revealed in the publication, in 1606, of his *Poems Lyric and Pastoral*. The collection contains two verse accounts on themes of considerable national importance – a version of ▷ Richard Hakluyt's 'First Voyage to Virginia', and an account of the battle of ▷ Agincourt based mainly on ▷ Raphael Holinshed's *Chronicles*. The creation of a national past and the formation of a national identity can thus be seen as merging in the work of this writer.
▷ Histories and Chronicles.
Bib: Hebel, J. W., Tillotson, K. and Newdigate, B. H., (eds.), *Complete Works* (4 vols.); Hardin, R. F., *Drayton and the Passing of Elizabethan England*.

Dream of the Rood
A highly sophisticated ▷ Old English dream-vision poem which recounts the dreamer's encounter with a speaking Cross. The Cross recounts its experience of the Crucifixion, its subsequent burial and its resurrection as a Christian symbol. The poem is preserved only in an 11th-century copy but the material seems to have originated much earlier. The 8th-century preaching cross, the Ruthwell Cross preserved in Dumfriesshire has an inscription which closely resembles parts of the Cross's speech in the *Dream of the Rood*.
▷ Old English literature.
Bib: Swanton, M. (ed.), *The Dream of the Road*.

Dream-vision poetry
An important medieval narrative form. What is distinctive about the category of medieval dream-vision poetry is not that a dream sequence is included in the narrative but that a dream sequence offers the framework for a narrative which is presented as the reported experience of the narrator/dreamer. The traditions behind medieval dream-vision poetry are as diverse as the literary dream-experiences themselves: dream-vision poetry is a distinctive, but not homogeneous, literary category. There are numerous classical and biblical precedents for the use of dreams and visions as the mediums for philosophical and/or spiritual truths, but as developed by medieval vernacular poets from the 13th century onwards, the dream-vision form appears to have offered the opportunity for self-conscious literary creation in the guise of unconscious experience. The Old French poem, the ▷ *Roman de la Rose*, provided an especially influential paradigm for later vernacular writers.

The speculative licence of dream-vision poetry is used by medieval writers in many different ways. The frequent appearance of personifications within dream-vision poetry indicates the analytical interest of many of the texts in otherwise hidden processes. Sometimes dream-vision poems investigate the workings of the individual psyche, especially the inner experience of sacred and profane kinds of love (such as in ▷ Chaucer's ▷ *Book of the Duchess*, or the ▷ Gawain poet's ▷ *Pearl*); sometimes the form is used to examine the veiled workings of contemporary society itself and the dream experience becomes the occasion for social satire. In ▷ William Langland's complex visionary narrative, ▷ *Piers Plowman*, the sequence of dream visions (including the experience of dreams within dreams) is the occasion for a highly challenging enquiry into the interaction of inner and outer worlds, personal and public history, in Christian society. A number of Middle English ▷ alliterative narratives, dating from the 14th century, use the dream-vision form for literary debates about issues of personal/public ethics (such as ▷ *Winner and Waster*, ▷ *Death and Life*, the ▷ *Parlement of the Three Ages*). Chaucer's dream-vision poems are especially bookish in their orientation: in the *Book of the Duchess*, the ▷ *House of Fame* and the ▷ *Parliament of Foulys*, the activity of reading a book prompts the narrators' dreams. Vernacular writers from the 15th and early 16th centuries (such as ▷ Robert Henryson, ▷ William Dunbar, ▷ John Skelton) continue to employ the dream-vision mode in their works, but the dream-vision form is less frequently used as the frame for a large-scale narrative thereafter, perhaps because fictional activity no longer required a framing justification. **Bib:** Spearing, A. C., *Medieval Dream Poetry*.

Drinks

Ale was a universal drink in the ▷ Middle Ages, until in the 16th century beer (like ale, brewed from malt) became more popular; a thin brew called 'small beer' was used for children and servants and by the poor. The reason for this general use was the frequent pollution of water. A 16th-century traveller was surprised to be offered, in some parts of the country, milk instead of beer. ▷ Wine was drunk freely by the richer classes from the early ▷ Middle Ages; most of it was imported from France, Germany or the Mediterranean countries, but the grape vine was cultivated in Britain to some extent until the 18th century. In the countryside, wines were made out of local plants and fruits (elderberry, cowslip, dandelion) extensively until the 19th century; cider and perry, from fermented apples and pears respectively, were rivals to ale and beer in some parts. Another very common country drink was the ancient mead, from fermented honey, now seldom found. In the 17th century tea and ▷ coffee were introduced, and for a hundred years (approximately 1650–1750) London enjoyed a flourishing 'cafe' life with its ▷ coffee-houses. Chocolate, as a drink, was also fashionable by the mid-18th century. Tea had become a national drink by the 19th century; the English habit of adding milk was not until then usual. It replaced beer as a normal drink for women, especially in the middle classes. For a short time in the 18th century the working classes, especially in London,

took to gin in preference to beer, with great injury to their health. Even after the imposition of taxes on this spirit (distilled from malt) in 1751, drunkenness, from excessive drinking of comparatively cheap spirits in so-called 'gin-palaces', remained a national problem until the 20th century. This accounts for the extent of teetotalism, *ie* temperance movements, appealing for total abstinence from alcoholic drinks, in working-class religious and political circles in the 19th century. Although, today it is illegal to sell alcoholic beverages to anyone under 18, there is increasing concern about the number of under-age drinkers. This, together with the extension of licensing hours in 1988, has forefronted the debate about alcohol once more.

Druids

The wise and holy men of the ancient ▷ Celts in Gaul, ancient Britain, and ▷ Ireland. We know about them from Roman writers (*eg* Julius Caesar in *De Bello Gallico*) and from Welsh and Irish myth. They held the oak and the mistletoe as sacred, worshipped in oak groves, and believed in the survival of the soul and its transmigration after death into other bodies. There seems to be some doubt as to whether they ever flourished in southern Britain, where in any case they were eliminated by the Roman conquest in the 1st century A D, but they were important in Ireland and in ▷ Scotland, and the early Welsh ▷ bards, or sacred poets, called themselves druids. Caesar does not mention bards but ascribes to the druids a bardic, or sacred, poetic function. In the 18th and 19th centuries an unscientific cult of the druids grew up in England, attributing to them mysterious knowledge and wisdom where modern science finds only superstition.

Drummond, William, of Hawthornden (1585–1649)

Scottish poet. Drummond's first publication was an eulogy on the death of the eldest son of ▷ James I of England – Prince Henry – published in 1613. A volume of poems was published in 1614, and then withdrawn, revised, and re-published as *Poems: Amorous, Funeral, Divine, Pastoral, in Sonnets, Songs, Sextains, Madrigals*, whose title indicates the range of Drummond's interests. A large proportion of the verses contained in the 1616 collection are paraphrases and translations of continental writers. Other volumes of verse followed, including a celebration of the visit of James I to Edinburgh in 1618. Perhaps Drummond's

most famous work, however, is not poetic but is, instead, his record of a series of remarkable conversations with ▷ Ben Jonson, who visited Drummond in 1618. Drummond was careful to keep a record of Jonson's conversation, though much of what was said is the product (one supposes) of a good deal of drink rather than critical insight. Nevertheless, *Conversations with Drummond of Hawthornden*, first published in 1711, does suggest something of Jonson's wit.
Bib: MacDonald, R. H. (ed.), *Poems and Prose of William Drummond of Hawthornden*.

Drury Lane Theatres
The first was an old riding school in Bridges Street, converted by ▷ Thomas Killigrew to form the original Theatre Royal, Drury Lane, also known as the King's Theatre.

In 1682 the ▷ King's Company was absorbed by the ▷ Duke's, and the resulting ▷ United Company continued to stage plays at Drury Lane, and the larger spectacles and operas at ▷ Dorset Garden. After a difficult period under ▷ Christopher Rich, the theatre prospered with ▷ Colley Cibber, ▷ Robert Wilks, Thomas Doggett (c1670–1721), and various other managers jointly in charge, and then again under ▷ David Garrick, who took over in 1747.

In 1776, upon Garrick's retirement, Drury Lane was taken over by ▷ Sheridan, who continued to run it until its destruction by fire in 1809. The present theatre opened in 1812.

Dryads and Hamadryads
▷ Nymphs.

Dryden, John (1631–1700)
Poet, critic, dramatist. By family background and personal sympathies he was on the ▷ Puritan, anti-monarchical side during the Protectorate, and in an early poem, *Heroique Stanzas* (1659) he eulogized ▷ Oliver Cromwell, who had died in 1658. However, like many others, he welcomed the ▷ Restoration, composing *Astræa Redux* (1660) and *Panegyric* (1661) to welcome the king's return. With the ▷ Earl of Rochester he dominated English letters in the reign of Charles II, being appointed ▷ Poet Laureate in 1668 and Historiographer Royal in 1670. On the accession of James II in 1685 Dryden became a Catholic, and refusing to abandon his new faith after 1688, he was stripped of the Laureateship and other royal appointments.

It was in the theatre that Dryden enjoyed the greatest financial success, and between 1663 and 1681 he wrote almost a play a year.

John Dryden by Sir G. Kneller

His best dramatic work, ▷ *All for Love* (1677) is an entirely new version of ▷ Shakespeare's ▷ *Antony and Cleopatra*. *The Indian Empress* (1667), *The Conquest of Granada* (1669–70), and *Aureng-Zebe* (1675) are heroic dramas on the grand model of the French dramatist Corneille. He also wrote comedies such as *Marriage à la Mode* (1673). On the whole his plays are little regarded today.

Dryden's first poetic works, such as his brilliant *Upon the death of the Lord Hastings* (1649), belong to the overblown decadence of 'metaphysical' wit. ▷ *Annus Mirabilis* (1667) looks at the events of 1666, including sea engagements with the Dutch and the ▷ Great Fire. It maintains a ▷ baroque elaboration of imagery, but presented in a new public, ▷ Augustan manner. His greatest works are political ▷ satires in heroic ▷ couplets, a form which his example secured in pre-eminence for several decades after his death. ▷ *Absalom and Achitophel* (1681–2) shows an ironic assurance of tone, a novelist's eye for telling characterization, a complex layering of imagery, and a virtuoso flair for fast-running narrative. Occasionally his satire is biting and cruel, as in the passage on ▷ Shaftesbury (Achitophel). Elsewhere there is good-humoured 'raillery' in the portrait of the Duke of Buckingham (Zimri) ('A man so various, that he seem'd to be/ Not one, but all Mankind's Epitome'), and broad farce in the passage on Settle and ▷ Thomas Shadwell in Part II.

▷ *The Medal* (1682) continues the attack
on the first Earl of Shaftesbury, while
▷ *MacFlecknoe* (1682) shows Dryden in a
more relaxed, uninhibited mood, again
attacking ▷ Thomas Shadwell (the man
who was to succeed him as laureate) in a
burlesque lampoon which is purely, even at
times surrealistically comic. The two long
didactic poems, ▷ *Religio Laici* (1682) and
▷ *The Hind and the Panther* (1687), on the
religious question which at the time divided
his sympathy, contain fine passages, but their
didactic mode makes them difficult to admire
today. Similarly the rhetoric of his ▷ Pindaric
Odes (*eg Alexander's Feast*, 1697) tends to
be regarded now as artificial. Despite its
public and impersonal cast, Dryden's poetry
can on occasion be deeply moving, as in the
elegy on his friend ▷ John Oldham. His last
poetic work *Fables Ancient and Modern* (1699)
is a series of translations from ▷ Homer,
▷ Ovid, ▷ Boccaccio and ▷ Chaucer.

Dryden has been called 'the Father of
English prose'. He set his own stamp on the
new informal, persuasive style, which under
the new constitutional system, replaced the
ornamental court prose of the absolutist
Tudors and early Stuarts. He also produced
the first extended works of literary theory in
the language. *A Discourse concerning the
Original and Progress of Satire* relates the
different classical styles of satire found in
▷ Juvenal and ▷ Horace to modern English
writing, including his own. His celebrated essay
Of Dramatic Poesy discusses the principles of
drama and judiciously compares the qualities of
▷ Ben Jonson and ▷ Shakespeare. The
Preface to the Fables (1700) brings a very
modern sense of historical perspective to the
question of the development and enrichment of
literary language.
Bib: Johnson, S., in *Lives of the Poets*; Ward,
C. E., *Life*; Eliot, T. S., in *Selected Essays*;
Leavis, F. R., in *Revaluation*; van Doren, M.,
The Poetry of Dryden; Bredvold, L. I., *John
Dryden's Intellectual Milieu*; Nichol Smith,
D., *John Dryden*; Kinsley, J. and H., *Dryden:
the Critical Heritage*; Wykes, D., *A Preface to
Dryden*; Rogers, P., *The Augustan Vision*.

Du Bartas, Guillaume de Saluste, Sieur du Bartas (1544–90)

▷ Protestant poet and soldier. The major
work for which Du Bartas became famous in
England in the 17th century was his ▷ epic
on the story of the creation entitled *La
Semaine* (1578), which was followed by a
continuation – *La Seconde Semaine* (1584).
This enormous poem, which celebrates the
first two weeks of the biblical creation of the
world, was to have a considerable influence
on English writers in the period, though it is
now hardly read. The ▷ translation of Du
Bartas's work into English became the major
undertaking of Joshuah Sylvester (1562/3–
1618), though he was not the only English
writer to attempt translations of the work.
▷ Philip Sidney is said to have produced a
translation (now lost), and ▷ James I and
▷ Thomas Lodge both translated small
parts of the text. In the 17th century Du
Bartas's original and Sylvester's translation
became inseparably associated with one
another, and a considerable number of poets
were to praise the work or write under its
influence. 'Divine Bartas', as he became
known, was praised by ▷ Edmund Spenser,
▷ Samuel Daniel, ▷ Michael Drayton and
▷ Edmund Campion. Perhaps the high-
point of the reputation of the work was in the
influence that it had on ▷ John Milton's
▷ *Paradise Lost*. In the 18th century,
however, Du Bartas's reputation underwent a
decline from which it has never properly
recovered.
Bib: Sylvester, J. (tr.), Snyder, Susan (ed.)
*The Divine Weeks and Works of Guillaume de
Saluste, Sieur du Bartas*, 2 vol.

Du Bellay, Joachim (1522–60)

Together with ▷ Ronsard, one of the most
prominent of the French Renaissance group
known as the ▷ Pléiade. His *Deffence &
Illustration de la langue francoyse* (1549) is
often regarded as their manifesto. He was the
nephew of Cardinal Jean du Bellay, the
protector of ▷ Rabelais, and spent the years
1553–7 in Rome in the service of his uncle. It
was here that he composed the sonnet
collection *Les Regrets* (based on Ovid's
Tristia) as well as *Les Antiquitez de Rome* and
the *Songe* of which ▷ Spenser's versions,
Ruines of Rome and *The Visions of Bellay*,
appeared in the 1591 *Complaints*.

Du Maurier, George (1834–96)

Graphic artist and novelist; born in Paris. His
grandparents had been refugees in England
from the ▷ French Revolution; his father
was a naturalized British subject; his mother
was English. In 1865 he joined the staff of
▷ *Punch* and became one of the best known
British humorous artists, satirizing the upper
classes rather in the style of ▷ William
Thackeray. He wrote three novels: *Peter
Ibbetson* (1891), ▷ *Trilby* (1894) and *The
Martian* (posthumous, 1896). The first two
were extremely popular, but their
sentimentality has put them out of fashion.
Bib: Ormond, L., *George du Maurier*.

Dubliners (1914)

A volume of short stories by ▷ James Joyce. Joyce later wrote: 'My intention was to write a chapter of the moral history of my country and I chose Dublin for the scene because that city seemed to me the centre of paralysis. I have tried to present it . . . under four of its aspects: childhood, adolescence, maturity and public life. The stories are arranged in this order.' He adds that he has used in them 'a style of scrupulous meanness', but, in fact, the apparent bare realism of the stories conceals subtle mimetic and symbolic effects which render the spiritual poverty and domestic tragedy of Dublin life through its characteristic colloquial idioms. The stories are based on Joyce's theory of the 'epiphanies', by which he meant that deep insights might be gained through incidents and circumstances which seem outwardly insignificant. Their effect is thus often through delicate implication, like the stories of ▷ Chekhov. However, some of them contain sharp humour, notably 'Grace', and more have very sensitive poignancy, especially the last and longest, 'The Dead'. This story, which moves from ironical satire to a highly poetic conclusion, is often regarded as a masterpiece; it was filmed in 1987 by John Huston.

Duchess of Malfi, The (1613)

With ▷ The White Devil, one of the two famous verse tragedies by ▷ John Webster. The plot is taken from a tale by the Italian writer, Matteo Bandello, in an English version included in William Painter's ▷ Palace of Pleasure. Set in Italy, the drama concerns the vengeance taken upon the young Duchess for marrying her steward, Antonio, against the commands of her brothers, the Cardinal, and Ferdinand Duke of Calabria, who is her twin. Ferdinand employs an impoverished ▷ malcontent soldier, ▷ Bosola, as his instrument for the mental torturing of the Duchess, but Bosola has a character of his own, and is filled with remorse. The Duchess is finally strangled, but Ferdinand goes mad with horror at his own deed, and ends by killing Bosola, who has already killed the Cardinal.

Two main problems arise in assessing the drama. The first is whether the Duchess is purely a guiltless victim. She is a young widow who marries a man of lower status for love: commentators argue that contemporary opinion was against the remarrying of widows, that the Duchess offends against the principle of degree by marrying beneath her, and that her deception of her brothers offends against the principle that a just life must be led in openness. None of these arguments is likely to have force with modern audiences, and those contemporary with the play must have been chiefly impressed by the proud dignity with which the Duchess sustains her cumulative afflictions. The more important problem is that of the brothers' motives. That of the Cardinal is intelligible: he is a cold ▷ Machiavellian who resents his sister's humiliation of the family, and no doubt the fact that by her second marriage she now has heirs to her estate. But Ferdinand's prolonged sadism, and his madness after her death, seem in excess of their ostensible causes. The natural explanation is that he is incestuously in love with his sister, and insanely jealous at her marriage; this is doubted by some critics who point out that incestuous passion is nowhere explicit in the play which was written at a time when such motives were rarely left to the audience's inference. Webster may have preferred to leave the question open, since the bond between a twin sister and brother might itself sufficiently explain Ferdinand's extravagance. Another explanation, since the play is remarkable for its strikingly effective individual scenes, might be that Webster was more interested in opportunities for dramatizing situations than in the exposition of a dominant theme. Even this reductive judgement cannot obscure the grandeur with which Webster dramatizes extreme passion and the horror of its degradation, and in contrast the dignity with which an individual can outface suffering.

Duelling

Two kinds have existed: the judical combat and the duel of honour.

Judicial combat was practised from the 12th century until the 16th century in England, though never so freely as in France. By this practice, a dispute which would now be settled by court of law was decided by combat before a judge or the king, on the assumption that God would defend the right. ▷ Shakespeare, in his play ▷ Richard II, introduces a duel of this kind, between Mowbray and Bolingbroke.

The more familiar 'duel of honour', by which an alleged injury by one gentleman to another was settled by combat privately arranged between them, was never legal and did not become common until the 17th century. Before this, such an injury would more probably be settled by the hiring of assassins. The social code regulated the duel of honour strictly and so long as the regulations were kept, the survivor was likely to escape legal penalty. These duels were fought with either pistols or swords; by degrees, especially when towards the end of the 18th century the wearing of swords by gentleman went out of fashion, pistols became the more usual weapon. The frequency of occurrence can be judged by the frequency with which duels are introduced into 17th and 18th century plays and novels. In the early 19th century the law was used much more severely against duellists, and the religious ('evangelical') revival of the time condemned duels as immoral. After 1840 they ceased to occur, though in ▷ Anthony Trollope's *Phineas Finn* (1867) such a duel is alleged to take place.

Duenna, The (1775)

Comic opera by ▷ Richard Brinsley Sheridan. Don Jerome is attempting to force his daughter, Louisa, to marry the rich but unpleasant converted Jew, Isaac, and locks her up to await the marriage. However, she loves Don Antonio, and uses her duenna as a go-between, to carry messages. Jerome discovers the duenna's role in their affair, and dismisses her, but Louisa escapes disguised as the duenna, while the latter impersonates her mistress and receives Isaac. Meanwhile Louisa's brother and Antonio's friend, Don Ferdinand, has fallen in love with Donna Clara, who is to be forced into a convent. She too escapes from her father, and the two young women join forces. The duenna tricks Isaac into marrying her, and into helping Louisa and Antonio to marry. Ferdinand and Clara are also united, and Jerome is reconciled to both situations. The play was successfully performed at ▷ Covent Garden.

Duessa

Character in Edmund Spenser's ▷ *The Faerie Queene*. She is described as 'clad in scarlot red' (Book I. ii. 13), which associates her with the Catholic Church, ▷ Antichrist and the Whore of ▷ Babylon, as ▷ Protestant commentaries on *Revelation* XVII . 4 make clear.
▷ Catholicism (Roman) in English literature.

Duffy, Maureen (b 1933)

Novelist, poet and dramatist. Her autobiographical first novel, *That's How It Was* (1962) is the account of a childhood of material insecurity and social isolation illuminated by a living relationship between mother and daughter. The themes of her fiction have been the outsider, the oppressions of poverty and class, the varieties of sexual experience and the power of love to transform

and redeem. Her work reflects her socialism, lesbianism and commitment to animal rights. *The Microcosm* (1966) is a study of lesbian society using various modes of narration, including pastiche and ▷ stream of consciousness; it shows the distance between sexual creativity and ordinary life imposed by society. Duffy has lived in London for most of her adult life, and celebrated that city in *Capital* (1975). She employs colloquial language, and a laconic but vivid style. Her play *Rites*, a black farce set in a ladies public lavatory, was produced at the ▷ National Theatre in 1969. *Rites*, *Solo* (1970) and *Old Tyme* (1970) rework the Greek myths of the Bacchae, ▷ Narcissus and ▷ Uranus respectively in terms of modern sexual and public life. Her other plays are: *The Lay Off* (1962); *The Silk Room* (1966) and *A Nightingale in Bloomsbury Square* (1973). Other novels are: *The Single Eye* (1964); *The Paradox Players* (1967); *Wounds* (1969); *Love Child* (1971); *I Want to Go to Moscow* (1973); *Housespy* (1978); *Gor Saga* (1981); *Scarborough Fear* (as D. M. Layer, 1982); *Londoners: An Elegy* (1983); *Change* (1987). Poetry: *Collected Poems* (1985).

Duke of Milan, The (1621)

A tragedy of court intrigue, possessive jealousy and murder by ▷ Philip Massinger.

Duke's Company, The

Acting company formed by ▷ Sir William D'Avenant after the ▷ Restoration of ▷ Charles II. It performed from June 1661 at the former Lisle's Tennis Court in ▷ Lincoln's Inn Fields, which had been converted to a theatre. In November 1671 the company moved to a new playhouse at ▷ Dorset Garden, also known as the Duke's Theatre, where it remained until its union with the ▷ King's Company to form the ▷ United Company in 1682.

Duke's Theatre, The

▷ Dorset Garden Theatre.

Dunbar, William (?1460–?1520)

Scottish poet and priest. Little is known about his life. He was employed at the Scottish court, was involved in a shipwreck off Zeeland while engaged on a diplomatic mission, and was given a pension by James IV in 1500. A relatively large corpus of his poetry survives, which is notable for its wide range of subjects and tone. The 'Thrissil and the Rose', a political allegory about the marriage of James IV to Margaret Tudor, was written in 1503. 'The Dance of the Sevin Deidly Synnis', in which the narrator sees a devil call a dance of unshriven outcasts, dates from 1507. Also dating from around this time are Dunbar's more famous pieces, 'The Golden Targe' (a dream-vision love adventure); 'The Lament for Makaris' (an elegy on life's transience and the passing of great English and Scottish poets such as ▷ Chaucer, ▷ John Gower, and ▷ Robert Henryson); and 'The Tretis of the Twa Mariit Wemen and the Wedo' (a midsummer dream experience in which a male narrator overhears three spirited women revealing their histories and their desires). Dunbar's 'Flyting of Dunbar and Kennedie' is a consummate exercise in poetic abuse.

Bib: Kinsley, J. (ed.), *Poems*; Harvey Wood, H., *Two Scots Chaucerians, Robert Henryson and William Dunbar*.

Dunciad, The (1728–43)

THE
DUNCIAD,
VARIORVM.
WITH THE
PROLEGOMENA of *SCRIBLERUS.*

DEFEROR IN VICVM

VENDENTEM THVS ET ODORES

L O N D O N.
Printed for A. DOB. 1729.

Frontispiece of Pope's *Dunciad*

A ▷ mock-heroic ▷ satire in pentameter ▷ couplets by ▷ Alexander Pope, satirizing his literary enemies. In the earlier three-book version, published anonymously in 1728, the hero is the scholar ▷ Lewis Theobald (spelled 'Tibbald' in the poem), whose *Shakespeare Restored* (1726) had offended the poet by pointing out mistakes and oversights in his edition of Shakespeare's

works (1725). In a brilliantly appropriate stroke, which two centuries later would have been considered daringly modernist, *The Dunciad* itself is presented in a scholarly edition, complete with learned footnotes, as though it were a classic. In the notes Pope and his friends (under the pseudonym ▷ Scriblerus) discuss the knotty textual cruxes of the work, draw attention to its various poetic excellences, and heap straight-faced praise upon the solecisms of other critics and poets. In 1742 Pope issued a fourth book under the title *The New Dunciad*, and in 1743 the whole four-book version reappeared with a new hero, the popular playwright, ▷ Colley Cibber, who to much derision had been made ▷ Poet Laureate in 1730, and thus appears as ▷ Bays.

In Book I Cibber is snatched from his benighted labours by the goddess Dulness and is crowned Laureate in succession to Laurence Eusden, who now 'sleeps among the dull of ancient days'. In Book II the new King of the Dunces presides over a modern ▷ Grub-Street version of the ancient classical games, including a pissing match (to determine 'Who best can send on high/ The salient spout, far-streaming to the sky'), a patron-tickling contest, and a competition to see who can dive deepest into the open sewer of Fleet-ditch. The book ends with the company being read to sleep by the works of John Henley and ▷ Sir Richard Blackmore: 'Soft creeping words on words, the sense compose,/ At ev'ry line they stretch, they yawn, they doze.' In Book III Cibber sleeps in the lap of Dulness and has visions, in true classical style, of the future triumph of the goddess and the destruction of civilization. Book IV traces the pantomimic progress of Dulness through the realms of science and letters ('*Art* after *art* goes out, and all is Night'), and ends in biblical solemnity with a description of the restoration of the ancient Empire of Chaos. Despite its sometimes irritating plethora of topical references, the poem is a unique masterpiece. Its nervous, ironic tone merges raucous vulgarity, exquisite sensuousness, ▷ surrealist fantasy, euphoric farce and sombre despair in strange and original evocative effects.

Dunn, Douglas (b 1942)

Poet. Dunn was born in Renfrewshire, Scotland, and educated in Scotland and Hull, where he lives. His first volume, *Terry Street* (1969) showed him much under the influence of ▷ Philip Larkin in its documentation of everyday provincial life; his later volumes *St Kilda's Parliament* (1981) and *Elegies* (1985)

show more varied subject-matter, meditating on ▷ Celtic history and on his own Scottish ancestry and on the loss of loved ones.
He has trained and worked as a librarian. His other poetry includes: *Backwaters* (1971); *Love or Nothing* (1974); *Barbarians* (1979); *Selected Poems* (1986).

▷ Scottish literature.

Duns Scotus, John (?1265–?1308)

One of the most influential medieval philosophers. He was born at the village of Duns in Scotland, studied at Oxford, and taught at Paris and Cologne. He was the chief opponent of ▷ Thomas Aquinas in the late medieval Church. He opposed Aquinas's belief in the harmony of reason and religious faith by declaring that some doctrines were incapable of proof (*eg* the immortality of the soul); he declared, in opposition to Aquinas, that the will was not necessarily subordinate to the reason; he insisted that individual objects contain a principle of reality distinct from that of the class to which each belongs. The last doctrine was of importance to the Catholic poet ▷ G. M. Hopkins in his formation of the terms 'inscape' and 'instress'. Duns Scotus's philosophy underwent much criticism in the 16th century by both the ▷ humanist scholars influenced by Plato, and the ▷ Protestant reformers. His followers, the Scotists, were regarded as the enemies of the ▷ New Learning, and in consequence a 'Dunsman' or 'Dunce' became eventually, in common speech, synonymous with a stupid person, impervious to education.

Durrell, Lawrence (1912–90)

Novelist and poet. He began writing before the war, and published an experimental novel, *The Black Book* (1938) in France. His present high international reputation is based in particular on the sequence *The Alexandria Quartet* comprising *Justine* (1957); *Balthazar* (1958); *Mountolive* (1958) and *Clea* (1960). *The Alexandria Quartet* has achieved fame partly through its lavishly exotic appeal, and partly through Durrell's experimental technique: a wide range of narrative forms are employed, and the same events are seen, and interpreted quite differently, by the different characters participating in them. *Tunc* (1968) and *Nunquam* (1970) together form *The Revolt of Aphrodite*, which explores the destruction of love and creativity by social pressures, embodied in the 'Firm', a vast and dehumanizing multi-national enterprise. Durrell has followed up the success of *The Alexandria Quartet* with a five-volume novel, *The Avignon Quincunx*,

which also uses exotic settings and multiple narratives, and, combining elements of myth with philosophical speculation, satirizes the values of western society. It is made up of the following volumes: *Monsieur; or, The Prince of Darkness* (1974); *Livia; or, Buried Alive* (1978); *Constance; or, Solitary Practices* (1982); *Sebastian; or, Ruling Passions* (1983); *Quinx; or, The Ripper's Tale* (1985).

As the titles of his two major sequences suggest, the spirit of particular places has always been of importance to Durrell; he has said that in *The Alexandria Quartet* he 'tried to see people as a function of place'. He has published many volumes of travel writing, particularly about the islands of the Mediterranean, including: *Prospero's Cell* (about Corcyra; 1945); *Reflections on a Marine Venus* (about Rhodes; 1953); *Bitter Lemons* (about Cyprus; 1957); *The Greek Islands* (1978). Durrell has also published collections of short stories, including: *Sauve Qui Peut* (1966); *The Best of Antrobus* (1974); *Antrobus Complete* (1985); a number of plays, including: *Sappho* (1959); *Acto* (1961); *An Irish Faustus* (1963) and many volumes of poetry: *Collected Poems* (1960; revised 1968) and *Collected Poems 1931–74* (1980). But his greatest achievement has been to express the indeterminate and multi-faceted nature of experience through the techniques of experimental fiction.

Bib: Fraser, G. S., *Lawrence Durrell: A Critical Study*; Friedman, A. W., *Lawrence Durrell and The Alexandria Quartet*.

Dutch Courtesan, The (1605)

A punitive satirical comedy by ▷ John Marston about deceit and youthful recklessness.

Dyer, John (1700?–58)

Poet and painter. Born in Carmarthenshire, Dyer studied painting under Jonathan Richardson and visited Italy in 1724–5. In 1741 he entered the church. His most important work, *Grongar Hill* (1727), is a topographical landscape poem in the tradition of ▷ Sir John Denham's ▷ *Cooper's Hill* and ▷ Alexander Pope's ▷ *Windsor-Forest*, but its fluent use of tetrameter rather than pentameter (▷ metre) couplets gives it a lyrical *élan* all of its own. Moreover Dyer's painterly eye leads him to focus, in a most original way, on the transient visual effects which succeed each other as he climbs up from the valley of the Towy. Dyer's feeling for the picturesque, rooted in his study of the paintings of Claude and Poussin, was influential on later poetry until well into the Romantic period. In 1740 appeared *The Ruins of Rome*, and in 1757 *The Fleece*, long discursive and didactic poems in Miltonic ▷ blank verse. The second emulates the example of ▷ John Philips's *Cyder*, in its celebration of British scenery and British industry. It attempts to encompass all aspects of the wool trade, from the techniques of sheep-farming, modern and ancient, to the growing prosperity of Leeds and Sheffield and the growth of trade which promises to distribute British woollen manufactures 'over the whole globe'.

▷ Romanticism.

Bib: Humphrey, B., *John Dyer*.

E

Eagleton, Terry (b 1943)
The foremost ▷ Marxist critic writing in
Britain today. Until recently Eagleton was a
Fellow at Wadham College, Oxford, and he
has for some time been a leading force in
Marxism's encounter with a range of
intellectual movements from
▷ Structuralism onwards. His book
Criticism and Ideology (1976) laid the
foundation for the introduction into British
literary criticism of the work of the French
critic Pierre Macherey, and is a clear
development of ▷ Louis Althusser's
understanding of culture. In later works, such
as *Walter Benjamin or Towards a
Revolutionary Criticism* (1981), *The Rape of
Clarissa* (1982), *The Function of Criticism*
(1984), and *William Shakespeare* (1986), he
has sought to develop a sophisticated
▷ materialist criticism which is prepared to
engage with, but which refuses to be overawed
by ▷ Post-structuralism.

Earle, John
▷ Characters, Theophrastian.

East India Company
The most well known of the ▷ Charter
Companies, given a monopoly of eastern
trade by ▷ Queen Elizabeth in 1600.
Competition with the Dutch in the East
Indian islands turned its attention to the
Indian mainland, where in the 18th century
its extensive commercial influence developed
into political power. To protect its Chinese
trade, it gained control of the Burmese and
Malayan coasts down to Singapore, which it
founded in 1819. After the Indian Mutiny of
1857 it was taken over by the British
government, which had shared its rule in
India since the younger ▷ Pitt's Indian Act
of 1784. It was familiarly known as John
Company and its ships as East Indiamen.
▷ Companies, Joint Stock.

Easter Day
The Christian festival of the resurrection of
Jesus Christ, in the spring. The festival
occurs near the spring equinox, when in pre-
Christian England the festival of the Saxon
goddess of the dawn and of the spring,
Eostre, was celebrated.
▷ Festivals.

Eastward Hoe (1605)
A ▷ citizen comedy about London
apprentices and craftsmen written
collaboratively by ▷ George Chapman,
▷ Ben Jonson, and ▷ John Marston.
Modern interest in this play stems not
primarily from its undeniable imaginative

vitality so much as from its foolhardy satire
of the Scots in Act III, which led to the
imprisoning of its authors and nearly lost
Jonson his life and limbs. The play is one of
several works of the period such as ▷ Thomas
Middleton's ▷ *A Game At Chess* and
▷ John Day's *Isle of Gulls* to challenge or
parody the volatile contemporary political
order through the theatre.

Eclecticism
In ancient Greece, a term for the kind of
philosophy that did not follow any one school
of thought (*eg* ▷ Platonism) but selected its
doctrines from a number of schools. The
term is now applied to thinkers, artists and
writers who follow this principle in the
formation of their thought or artistic
methods.

Eclogue
A short pastoral dialogue, usually in verse.
The most famous example is the *Bucolics* of
the Latin poet, ▷ Virgil. The word is often
used as equivalent for ▷ idyll, or
▷ pastoral poem without dialogue.

Ecriture féminine
A term usually reserved for a particular kind
of critical writing by women, emanating from
the radical ▷ feminism of contemporary
French critics such as Luce Irigaray, Hélène
Cixous and Julia Kristeva. What unites this
form of feminist criticism is the belief that
there is an area of textual production that can
be called 'feminine', that it exists beneath the
surface of masculine discourse, and only
occasionally comes to the fore in the form of
disruptions of 'masculine' language. A further
assumption is that woman is given a specific
identity within the masculine structures of
language and power, and that she must strive
to challenge it. This particular brand of
radical feminism takes the view that there is
an 'essential' femininity that can be recovered,
and that it is also possible to distinguish
between a genuine feminine 'writing' and
other forms of language.
Bib: Kristeva, J., *Desire in Language*; Moi,
T., (ed.), *The Kristeva Reader*; Moi, T.,
Sexual/Textual Politics; Marks, E. and De
Courtivon, I., *New French Feminisms*;
Newton, J. and Rosenfelt, D., *Feminist
Criticism and Social Change*; Greene, G. and
Kahn, C. *Making the Difference: Feminist
Literary Criticism*.

Eden, Emily (1797–1869)
The daughter of William Eden, the first
Baron Auckland, Emily Eden was born in
Westminster. She was a close friend of Prime

Minister Melbourne, who appointed her brother George governor general of India in 1835. She went with him and her sister Frances, and acted as his hostess until their return in 1842, and in London till 1849. She was a member of the highest social circles and many celebrities visited her house where she held morning gatherings due to ill health. In 1844 she published *Portraits of the People and Princes of India*, and then in 1866 and 1872 *Up the Country; Letters Written from the Upper Provinces of India*. In 1919 her great-niece edited a further selection of her letters. Her novels, *The Semi-detached House* (1859), published anonymously, and *The Semi-attached Couple* (1860), by 'E. E.', were written some 30 years previously. They portray fashionable society with good-humoured wit and owe something to ▷ Jane Austen whom Eden much admired.

Eden, Garden of

In the ▷ Bible (*Genesis* II and III), the dwelling place of the first man and woman, Adam and Eve. Eden is thought of as a place of perfect bliss where there was no conflict, sickness or suffering, and human needs were satisfied by the fruit of the garden. But it also contained the trees of life and of knowledge; eating the fruit of the latter would give Man the knowledge of good and evil, and so God forbade it to him. Eve succumbed, however, to temptation by the serpent, and Adam followed her example. In consequence, God drove them from the garden. Their disobedience is the symbol of the myth of 'the Fall of Man'. The most famous paraphrase of the story is Milton's ▷ *Paradise Lost* which also includes an account of the fall of the ▷ angels.

Edgar, David (b 1948)

Socialist playwright who has written for a number of ▷ fringe companies, including ▷ John McGrath's 7:84, and also had his work performed by the ▷ Royal Shakespeare Company and the ▷ National Theatre company. *Destiny* (1976) is an exposure of British fascism. This was followed by the documentary works *Mary Barnes* (1977) and *The Jail Diary of Albie Sachs* (1978). His adaptation of *Nicholas Nickleby* (1981) for the R.S.C. was much acclaimed and highly successful. More recent plays are *Maydays* (1983) and *Entertaining Strangers* (1985).
Bib: Bull, J., *New British Political Dramatists*; Chambers, C. and Prior, M., *Playwrights' Progress*.

Edgeworth, Maria (1767–1849)

Novelist. Her tales are commonly set in Ireland. Her work is minor but still read for its vivacity, good sense and realism. *Castle Rackrent* (1800) and *The Absentee* (1812) are two of her works still in print. She was also an excellent writer for children (see *Tales* ed. by Austin Dobson). She collaborated with her father, a noted educationist, in *Practical Education* (1798), influenced by the French-Swiss thinker ▷ Rousseau. She was admired by ▷ Jane Austen, ▷ William Thackeray, ▷ John Ruskin, ▷ Turgenev and ▷ Walter Scott, whom she influenced. She has recently been re-evaluated by ▷ feminist critics as a liberal contributor to women's social history.
Bib: Clarke, I. C., *Life*; Newby, P. H., *Maria Edgeworth*; M. S. Butler: *Maria Edgeworth*.

Edinburgh

Since the middle of the 15th century the capital of Scotland. The union of the crowns in 1603, when James VI of Scotland became also ▷ James I of England, left Edinburgh still with its same political status, since the governments of the two countries remained separate. In 1707, however, the union of the parliaments removed the political capital to London and for half a century greatly reduced Edinburgh's prestige: it was now only the centre of the Scottish legal and Church systems. In the second half of the century, however, Edinburgh had a notable revival. Intellectuals such as the philosopher ▷ David Hume, the historian Robertson, the economist ▷ Adam Smith, challenged the intellectual domination of London; in the early 19th century the poet-novelist ▷ Walter Scott and the very influential ▷ *Edinburgh Review* made it possible to say that, culturally, Britain contained two metropolises. However, this was at the expense of an independent Scottish culture, since before the Scottish Renaissance Scottish writers tended to adopt English styles and standards. More recently Edinburgh has re-emerged as a major cultural centre with the advent of the Edinburgh Festival (▷ Fringe theatre).
▷ Scotland; Scottish literature in English.

Edinburgh Review

A quarterly periodical founded by ▷ Francis Jeffrey, ▷ Sydney Smith and ▷ Henry Brougham in 1802. It introduced a new seriousness into literary criticism and generally took a moderate ▷ Whig position in politics. Jeffrey's literary taste was rigidly classicist and he had little sympathy with the 'Lake Poets', ▷ William Wordsworth, ▷ Samuel Taylor Coleridge and ▷ Robert Southey. The term originates in the

Edinburgh Review, Oct. 1807. Later
contributors were ▷ Thomas Babington
Macaulay, ▷ William Hazlitt, ▷ Thomas
Carlyle and ▷ Matthew Arnold.

▷ Augustanism; *Blackwood's Magazine*;
Romanticism; *The Spectator*; *The Tatler*.

Education

1 *Medieval education: 1350–1500*. Education
in the ▷ Middle Ages followed the division
by the Greek philosopher, ▷ Aristotle, into
mechanical and liberal arts. The former
trained the student in a craft, from the
humblest and most practical trade, such as
shoe-making, to what would now be called the
fine arts of sculpture, painting and
architecture. The main means of mechanical
education was the guild system of the towns,
by which boys began their training as
apprentices (▷ Apprenticeship), achieved
the status of ▷ journeyman half-way
through their course, and became (or might
become) fully recognized master craftsmen at
the end of seven years. The liberal arts were
the training of the mind, and were taught at
the universities, where they were divided into
two stages: the Trivium consisting of
Grammar, ▷ Rhetoric and Logic, and the
Quadrivium, consisting of Arithmetic,
Astronomy, Music and Geometry. There
were two ▷ universities in England
(▷ Oxford and ▷ Cambridge) but to these
we should add the ▷ Inns of Court in
London where law was (and still is) studied.
A third kind of education was provided by
royal and aristocratic households, where boys
of noble and (like ▷ Chaucer) some
merchant families were trained as pages until
later they became squires and were finally
knighted. This training did not, until later,
include much formal education; the page and
the squire learnt to use weapons and to hunt,
to acquire courtly manners and to dance and
sing. They did not necessarily learn to read
and write, but by the time of ▷ King Richard
II (1377–99), when Chaucer was settled as a
court poet and bureaucrat, the English
nobleman was becoming too sophisticated to
remain illiterate.

Liberal education was entirely in the hands
of the Church, and in the middle of the 14th
century, it was not widespread. The idea that
'book-learning', or even mere literacy, was in
itself a desirable acquirement for every man
capable of it became generally accepted only
in the 16th century. The 14th- and 15th-
century clergy, on the contrary, saw liberal
studies as essentially a vocational training for
their profession, and even as that they were
required in very varying degrees – the

medieval parish priest was often barely
literate. However, by the end of the 14th
century, literate laymen became mentioned in
records; after 1415, such mentions cease,
presumably because their large number now
made them commonplace. Among the poor,
the Church tended to discourage literacy
except among those expected to become
clergy; it threatened the Church's authority.

The schools, therefore, were attended
principally by those intending to 'take orders',
although in the 15th century young noblemen
and merchants' sons were to be found in
them. Small schools were sometimes attached
to the monasteries; the monastic almoner,
whose duty it was to relieve the poor,
sometimes included education in his function,
and there were also 'song schools' to provide
for the monastery choirs. More numerous
were the episcopal grammar schools
established by the bishops in their dioceses.
Among these, the most distinguished was
Winchester College, founded in 1382 by the
Bishop William of Wykeham for 'poor
scholars' (usually of the middle classes), but
intended also for noblemen's sons. This was
the first of what became known as the
▷ public schools, distinguishable from the
other grammar schools both by drawing their
pupils from all over the country, and by taking
them from a wider social range. In the 15th
century the laity, from the king downwards,
also founded schools, though the teachers
remained clergy: ▷ King Henry VI founded
▷ Eton College in 1440. Many of these
foundations were established by town guilds
and by 'chantries', *ie* corporations of priests
whose function was to sing masses for the
souls of the dead. At the beginning of the 16th
century, it has been estimated that there may
have been 500 grammar schools in England,
besides a smaller number of almonry and song
schools. In noble households, education began
to be conducted by private tutors, whose
pupils might include a few besides members
of the immediate family of the nobleman.

The principal subject of study in the
grammar schools was Latin (▷ Latin
literature). Religious works were read, but
not the Bible, which was left to interpretation
by the priests. In addition, the pupils read
the works of the great Roman poets, in so far
as they were known, especially ▷ Virgil.
Latin was the language of learning and
administration in daily life, and the pupils
were forced to speak it while they were at
play. By the 15th century, French was no
longer the language of daily speech among
the upper classes; it was sometimes taught in
the grammar schools as a foreign language.

The term 'university' derives from a medieval synonym for 'guild', and the medieval university was in effect a guild of liberal arts, analogous to the town guilds of the mechanical arts. The relationship between the tutor and the student was similar to that between the master craftsman and his apprentice. When the student had completed half of his course he might become a bachelor of arts, analogous to the status of journeyman in the ▷ craft guilds; after this he could complete his course and become a 'Master'. The two universities of Oxford and Cambridge owed their origins to 'custom'; that is to say, they were not royal or church foundations, but arose spontaneously. Oxford originated in the 12th century as a colony from Paris, and Cambridge was the offspring of Oxford early in the 13th century. The teachers were principally secular clergy, like the parish priest and reformer ▷ John Wycliffe (?1320–84), but these had rivals among the teaching order of the ▷ friars – the ▷ Dominicans, from whom the modern term 'don' derives. Until the 15th century, Oxford was the more important of the two, but Wycliffe's criticism of the Church made it suspect as a centre of heresy, so that Cambridge then increased the number both of its students and of the endowments from patrons, the most important of whom was ▷ King Henry VI (1422–61).

In the 14th century, conditions of study in the universities were bad. The students were poor, books were few, and there was constant hostility, sometimes exploding into murderous outbreaks, between students and townsmen. It was in consequence of one of these outbreaks, that students, fleeing from the disorder of Oxford, established the university of Cambridge. The college system arose both as an attempt to discipline the students, and as a means of protecting them against the townsmen, but it was not until the 15th century that it extended sufficiently to be effective. Two of the greatest of the medieval colleges – New College in Oxford and King's College in Cambridge – were founded in conjunction with the great schools, Winchester and Eton respectively.

The Inns of Court in London were begun as colleges of law in the reign of ▷ Edward I (1272–1307). Thereafter they were attended not merely by prospective lawyers, but by numbers of gentry who sought to acquire legal knowledge in order to defend their property in the disputes over land so common in the ▷ Middle Ages. The Inns of Court were the first educational institutions to be used principally by laymen.

2 *The expansion of education: 1500–1800.* The 'discovery of learning' in the ▷ Renaissance was made partly through the activity of the Humanist scholars (▷ Humanism), beginning in Italy in the 14th century, and extending gradually northwards to the rest of Europe. The humanist use of disinterested scholarship awakened men to the importance and potentialities of acquiring knowledge for its own sake. The medieval aristocrat had long formed an image of nobility which far excelled the primitive one of the bloodthirsty warrior; he now began to see that the cultivation of his mind was central to his acquirement of courtly accomplishments and to the aristocratic ideal of the perfected man.

Another cause of the changed attitude to education was the invention of printing, introduced into England late in the 15th century by ▷ William Caxton. The major obstacle to learning so far had been the lack of material; books had had to be copied by hand, and most learning had been conducted by discussion between teacher and student. Printing, however, made books plentiful, and if they were not cheap, at least they were far more accessible than they had been, to both rich and poor.

The humanist passion for education began in the universities and thence extended gradually to the rest of society, through the scholarship and writings of such men as ▷ Grocyn, ▷ Linacre, Colet, ▷ More, and above all, the Dutch humanist ▷ Erasmus, who resided at Cambridge from 1511 to 1514. One of the chief objects of the scholars was to clarify and enlarge Latin culture, out of which the whole civilization of western Europe had grown, but they also taught the universities to extend their studies from Latin to Greek and Hebrew texts, especially those that had constituted the original texts of the ▷ Bible, from which the medieval Latin version, the ▷ Vulgate, had been translated. The critical spirit of the Renaissance easily led to the reforming spirit of Protestantism, and Cambridge soon became and remained a centre of ▷ Reformation ideas. As in literature and philosophy, so, too, in religious thought, this enlargement of understanding and activity of mind extended from the universities throughout society. The translations of the Bible into English, encouraged by Henry VIII (1509–47), and the ▷ Book of Common Prayer, compiled by ▷ Archbishop Cranmer under ▷ Edward VI (1547–53), brought English laymen close to the spiritual texts of Christianity, whereas hitherto the Bible and the liturgies had been mysteries in the control of the priests.

The Reformation, however, was not altogether helpful to the spread of education. Henry VIII dissolved the monasteries and friaries in 1536 and 1539, and since these made important contributions to the universities, Oxford and Cambridge suffered at least financially. A minor ill effect of Henry's action, but minor only because the numbers affected were small, was the closure of the nunnery schools, the only institutions for the education of girls. Much worse was the closing down of many grammar schools under Edward VI. Many of these, established by town guilds and by chantries, had religious affiliations, and Edward VI's Protestant politicians gladly made this the excuse for seizing the funds with which they had been endowed. Some, indeed, were refounded with the title 'King Edward VI Grammar School', with the result that for three centuries this boy king enjoyed the reputation of being a great patron of education, but in fact far more schools were lost than refounded.

These setbacks were, however, temporary. Gradually, from 1560, new schools were opened, including some (for instance, Rugby) which later became famous as public schools. The universities also recovered from their difficulties, and it is in the reign of ▷ Elizabeth I (1558–1603) that we first find them attended by large numbers of the great men of the age, including the poets ▷ Ralegh, ▷ Spenser, ▷ Sidney and ▷ Marlowe, and the philosopher statesman, ▷ Francis Bacon. The college system was now strongly established; it imposed effective discipline and established the relationship between tutor and student as the principal method of instruction which it is to the present day. Young men of the upper classes began to be sent to the universities as a regular practice to complete their education, unless they completed it in the London Inns of Court.

It was not until the 17th century that the well-known public schools – especially Winchester and Eton – became predominantly aristocratic. The young nobleman was more often educated, until he went to the university, by tutors in his home. Gentlemen, however, commonly went to grammar schools. At Repton, later a public school, the first 20 names on the list of pupils in 1564 include the sons of 5 gentlemen, 13 small farmers and 4 tradesmen. There were often entrance fees into the grammar schools, graduated according to the rank of the pupil, but some of the town schools, such as the one probably attended by ▷ Shakespeare in Stratford upon Avon, were free to the sons of burgesses, ie established citizens.

Boys received a predominantly classical education – chiefly in Latin literature – as they were to continue to do until late in the 19th century, though at the universities they might in addition acquire some knowledge of mathematics and the sciences and ▷ Aristotelian philosophy. The universities still followed the medieval pattern of the trivium and the quadrivium, though thinking was much freer and more varied, and no longer subjected to theology. Teaching continued to ignore what were known as the 'mechanical arts'. It was, however, beginning to be a practical age, and in 1597 Sir Thomas Gresham founded Gresham College in London, for lectures which included physic (ie medicine), law and navigation, as well as the more 'liberal' subjects. Gresham College lasted until 1768, by which time other institutions of a similar kind existed. The Inns of Court were attended especially by young men who, like the poet ▷ John Donne, were ambitious but not wealthy, for a legal training was the most useful practical one for a public career in politics and administration as well as the law itself.

Until the later 19th century, upper-class education was commonly pursued for the general cultivation of the mind and manners; it included knowledge of the ancient cultures and the arts; increasingly, it required travel. The lower a boy (or a girl) stood in the social scale, the more practical and vocational his training had to be. It was not, however, until the reign of Queen Anne (1702–14) that much was done, apart from the increasingly expensive apprenticeship system, for the really poor. In that reign, the Church of England began the establishment of large numbers of ▷ Charity Schools which, by the end of the reign, were giving free or nearly free elementary education to about 25,000 children throughout England. The education included religious instruction. At the end of the 18th century, children in industrial areas were employed so extensively in factories that even charity schools were not available to them. For such children, after 1780, there were the Sunday Schools, which again were partly religious and partly concerned to inculcate the beginnings of literacy and numbers.

The Dissenting Academies were started by the large minority of the English ▷ Puritans, who came to be called ▷ Dissenters or ▷ Nonconformists in the 18th century, because they 'dissented from', or refused to conform with, the ▷ Thirty-nine Articles of Anglican belief, and were thus excluded both from the universities and from most of the grammar and public schools. The Academies were often of high quality, since it was natural to the earnestness of the Dissenting mind to take education with deep seriousness. Since the Dissenters were particularly strong among the commercial classes, the tendency of their education was more scientific and technical than that of the public schools and the universities, and capable of throwing up a major scientist, such as the chemist ▷ Joseph Priestley, who attended the Daventry Academy.

The distinction of the Dissenting Academies was the more noticeable because the universities were in a state of decadence. The historian ▷ Gibbon describes in his ▷ autobiography the complete indifference of the Oxford authorities to whether he was present or absent as a student, although they awoke into indignation and expelled him when he underwent his temporary conversion to Catholicism. Both universities developed fine schools of mathematics in the 17th century, and Cambridge produced the most distinguished scientist of the age in ▷ Isaac Newton (1642–1727), but the intellectual complacency which was characteristic of the weaker side of 18th-century civilization reduced them to apathy as teaching centres. The young men of fashion who attended them often learned more from the Grand Tour of Europe which they made after, or sometimes instead of, their university careers, in the company of a tutor.

3 *The growth of national education: 1800–present day*. In the 19th century, partly owing to the breakdown of sectarian restrictions in education, much of which was under Dissenting control, partly owing to the establishment of the non-denominational universities, the Dissenting Academies declined. However, the ▷ Industrial Revolution brought into being a new class of skilled worker: the 'mechanic' of the iron, steel and engineering industries. Such men needed brains for their skills, and their natural intelligence caused them to seek further education to advance their knowledge. This was provided by the growth of the voluntarily established Mechanics' Institutes. They began in ▷ Scotland, where education in general, since the Reformation, was more widely extended and popularly sought than in England. It was the Scottish lawyer, statesman, and man of letters, ▷ Henry Brougham, who brought the movement to England. By 1824, the London Institute had 1,500 artisans subscribing one guinea a year

for their instruction, which was conducted in the evenings. It was the beginning of the movement of education in technology which has led to the enormous expansion of technical colleges under the control of local government authorities in the 20th century, especially since 1945.

In the 19th century, however, the state was much more timid in undertaking national systems of education of any sort, and Britain was well behind the most advanced European countries, especially Prussia, in this respect. The principal reason for this slow development was the religious divisions of public opinion. The medieval assumption that education must fundamentally be the concern of the Church has faded very slowly in England. Even today, 'Religious Instruction', taught non-denominationally, is often the only compulsory subject in state schools. The schools for the children of the mass of the people in the first part of the 19th century were controlled by rival Anglican and Dissenting movements: the National Society for the Education of the Poor, and the British and Foreign School Society respectively. Since the Church of England was the established Church of the state, it claimed that it should have a monopoly of religious instruction in any state system, a claim that was strongly resisted by the Dissenters. In 1833, the government for the first time acknowledged some responsibility independent of the Churches by granting a subsidy of £20,000 for school buildings, whichever society chose to build them. Since Britain was by then the richest country in the world, the sum was contemptibly small. Till 1870, the important advances towards nationwide education remained in private hands.

The most important of these advances, though it affected only a minority, was in the public school system, which had originated in the medieval system of grammar schools. Many of these had been closed in the middle of the 16th century, but others had been established in the later 16th and 17th centuries; in the 18th century they had again been allowed to decline. A few of them, however, had from early times achieved an importance above the rest; they had richer endowments, and drew their pupils from the nation at large and not merely from their immediate localities. These included Winchester (founded 1382), ▷ Eton (1440), Westminster (1560), ▷ Rugby (1567), and ▷ Harrow (1571). Their discipline was bad. By the early 19th century, the pupils were predominantly upper class. They produced some fine teachers and headmasters, but their educational standards varied extensively. However, in the 19th century, the character of these schools greatly changed, largely owing to the influence of one man – ▷ Thomas Arnold, headmaster of Rugby from 1828 to 1842. Arnold believed that his education should provide a boy with a training of the whole character, and not merely the mind. The guiding principle of the public schools became that of the Roman poet ▷ Juvenal, writing at a time when the Roman Empire had a corresponding greatness to the greatness of Britain after Arnold: 'mens sana in corpore sano' – 'a healthy mind in a healthy body'. A consequence of this maxim, though Arnold himself never emphasized it, was that athletics became an essential element in public school education. Hitherto, sport had been discouraged rather than otherwise by educational institutions, as tending to disorderly conduct, but public schools gave it such importance that in many of them it came to exceed the prestige of scholarship. Arnold's Rugby not only introduced new standards into the public schools, but it had two further important results. One was that it gave real significance to boarding school education; the boys lived at the school for three-quarters of the year, not, as before, merely because conditions of travel were difficult, but because the school could thereby educate the boy during his leisure as well as in the classroom, a consideration of importance when it was a question of educating his whole character, and when sport was an essential part of this character-training. The second result was that many new public schools were founded, so that until 1950 a public school education became the normal one, not only for upper-class boys but for the sons of professional men and the more prosperous business men as well. To some extent, the system was also extended to girls, but coeducational public schools, even today, are the exception rather than the rule.

There were special social and political reasons for this adoption of public school education by the middle classes. One was the continuing prestige of the English aristocracy. The middle-class business man, especially if he had raised himself from a lower rank in society, wanted his son to be a 'gentleman', and by this time he could afford the high public school fees. But there was a more important reason. Britian, by 1850, was the centre of the largest overseas empire that the world had ever seen. This great empire required an unprecedented number of

administrators, who had to be men of high moral quality and courage, as well as of good ability. The aristocracy could not provide them all from itself, and would have aroused social resentment had it tried; they came, therefore, from preponderantly middle-class backgrounds, and it was the public schools which gave them the education considered necessary to qualify them for the function.

In some respects, however, the expansion of the public schools had unfortunate influences on the development of English society and education. By giving the governing classes the recruits they needed, the public schools tended to prolong the complacent indifference of the state to its educational responsibilities. Secondly, since the public school tradition was almost entirely an Anglican one, the public schools also prolonged the opposition between the Dissenters and the Anglicans over education. Thirdly but most importantly the public schools made more conspicuous the social gulf between the richer and poorer classes.

Universal elementary education was introduced in 1870 by the provision of state schools wherever the Church schools were inadequate. In 1902, special Local Education Authorities were created with responsibility for both these types of school, and for secondary education as well. It was, however, not until the Education Act of 1944 that the state system was improved sufficiently for the more prosperous middle classes to consent to use it instead of the private system. Even today, the prestige of the public schools is such that most of them continue to flourish (though their fees are now very high) side by side with the state schools.

Yet even the Act of 1944 tended to perpetuate the cleavage between the classes. Education became compulsory between the ages of 5 and 14 (15 in 1947, and 16 in 1972), but at the age of 11, boys and girls were subjected to the '11 + (eleven plus) examination', dividing them into those who were sent to the Secondary Modern Schools (75% of the secondary-school population) and the minority who were sent to the new state grammar schools. The secondary modern school child was expected to leave school at 15, but the grammar school child, though allowed to leave at the same age, was expected to continue to the age of 18, after which he or she could be at least partially supported by the local authority through the university, or some other institution of further education. Some established grammar schools became 'direct-grant' schools which offered scholarships or places to non-fee-paying pupils who were funded through the education authority, as well as taking fee-paying pupils. The system was clearly intended to provide an élite comparable to that of the public schools, but an élite based on real merit, and not on wealth. However, it was often criticized on the grounds that it favoured children who came from materially comfortable, well-educated backgrounds, since these advantages tend to accelerate the mental development of a child. Hence, under the 1964–70 Labour Government, the 11 + selection system was replaced by various forms of comprehensive schools, which do not require selection when children enter the school at 11, though it may divide them according to levels of ability ('streaming') after entry.

During the late 1970s and 1980s problems of lack of funding for schools and teachers, social pressures and consequent low teacher morale meant that comprehensive schools faced extremely difficult problems which were exacerbated by antagonistic government attitudes from 1979 onwards.

From September 1989 government reforms introduced the 'national curriculum' for both primary and secondary schools, as well as reintroducing the notion of formally testing pupils at 11, as well as 16, and, for the first time, testing primary-school children at the age of 7. From September 1989 schools can opt out of local authority control and receive direct funding from central government, becoming grant-maintained schools. Other developments in vocational education and City Technology Colleges still have to prove themselves.

▷ Adult education; Classical education and English literature; Further education; Schools in England; Universities.

Education and the state
The main stages in the growth of state provision of education in Britain are as follows:

1 1833. The government began the practice of making an annual grant of £20,000 for the erection of school buildings. The grant was available to the National Society and the British and Foreign School Society only. The former was controlled by the Church of England and the latter by the ▷ Nonconformist (or ▷ Dissenting) religious denominations.

2 Forster's Act of 1870. This provided state education for all at the primary level, to the age of 11. In 1876 primary education became compulsory for all children.

3 Balfour's Act of 1902. This provided compulsory education up to the age of 14 and placed the secondary schools under the authority of the local government County Councils.

4 The Act of 1944. This paved the way for the raising of the school leaving age to 15 in 1947. Secondary schools were divided into three groups: grammar schools, attendance at which could extend to the age of 18, after which children might continue their education with state financial aid at universities or technical colleges; modern schools, which pupils normally left at 15, though further education might take place at technical colleges; a small number of technical schools, with emphasis on industrial or business training. Children were obliged to enter primary schools at the age of 5, and submitted to a test at the age of 11 to decide the secondary school best suited to their abilities.

This so-called '11 +' examination soon came under heavy criticism and the local authorities often invented other expedients for arranging the secondary education of children. Much the most important of these was the spread of comprehensive schools, which are entered by children of all levels of ability without a preliminary test. The modern educational scene in Britain consequently exhibited much variety: grammar schools, modern schools and the 11 + test remained, but comprehensive schools increased widely in the 1960s with the encouragement of the Labour governments, and most grammar schools were amalgamated within this system. Today most children attend a comprehensive school, although private schooling is a popular alternative for those parents with sufficient financial resources.

The most significant intervention in education in recent years is the Education Reform Bill of November 1987. Its major proposals for primary and secondary schools were that schools be given the right to 'opt out' of local authority control and receive direct grant funding, subject to a simple majority vote, and the introduction of the national curriculum with three core subjects – English, maths, science – and seven foundation subjects. The main areas concerning higher education were that polytechnics were to be established as semi-independent corporations; that commissioners were to review university charters and to abolish academic tenure; and that a University Funding Council should replace the University Grants Committees.

Edward I (1272-1307)

King of England. He is known for the importance of his laws, the conquest of ▷ Wales and the attempted conquest of ▷ Scotland.

Edward II (1307-27)

King of England. His reign is chiefly noted for his decisive defeat by the Scots in the Scottish War of Independence (battle of ▷ Bannockburn, 1314) and for his conflicts with the barons over his excessive indulgence of favourites, especially Piers Gaveston.

  ▷ Christopher Marlowe's play *Edward II* presents him as a decadent sensual prince in ▷ Renaissance style, but pitiable in his horrible death by assassination.

  ▷ Scotland.

Edward III (1327-77)

The king of England under whom the ▷ Hundred Years' War with France began. Up to 1360 he was notably successful, and the English armies won the battles of ▷ Crécy (1346) and Poitiers (1356). He was succeeded on the throne by his grandson, ▷ Richard II, his eldest son, the ▷ Black Prince, having died in 1376.

  The play ▷ *Edward III* (1596) has sometimes been ascribed to ▷ Shakespeare, at least in part.

Edward III (1596)

A historical drama about the perverted courtship of the Countess of Salisbury by the king, and set during the French wars. It is one of the anonymous plays which, it has been argued (by Kenneth Muir, *Shakespeare as Collaborator*, and G. R. Proudfoot, *British Academy Shakespeare Lecture 1985*), on internal evidence should be attributed to ▷ Shakespeare.

Edward IV (1461-83)

First of the kings of England belonging to the House of York; he was victorious in the ▷ Wars of the Roses over the last king of the House of Lancaster, ▷ Henry VI.

  Edward IV plays a prominent part in ▷ Shakespeare's ▷ *Henry VI, Part III*, where he first appears as the Earl of March, and in ▷ *Richard III*, in which he dies and his throne is seized from the rightful heir, his son, by Edward IV's brother, Richard, Duke of Gloucester.

Edward V (1483)

The boy-king, son of Edward IV. He was deposed in the year of his accession to the throne by his uncle, Richard, Duke of Gloucester, who became ▷ Richard III.

Edward and his younger brother were imprisoned by their uncle in the ▷ Tower of London and were never heard of again. Legend (and the 16th century chroniclers) always insisted that he had them murdered there.

Edward VI (1547-53)

The boy-king who succeeded ▷ Henry VIII. Under the regency of the Protectors (the Duke of Somerset and, later, the Duke of Northumberland) Henry's essentially political ▷ Reformation became more ▷ Protestant in doctrine, though the new ▷ *Book of Common Prayer* was a wise compromise. Persecution of Roman Catholics in Edward's reign led to a reaction against Protestantism when his sister ▷ Mary succeeded him.

Edward the Confessor (reigned 1042-66)

The last but one of the ▷ Anglo-Saxon kings. He was not politically efficient but he was very pious and the legend grew up that this had been a very just reign. He is presented in this way, as the royal saint able to work miraculous cures, in ▷ Shakespeare's ▷ *Macbeth* (IV.iii)

Edwardian

A term descriptive of the political, social and cultural characteristics of the early years of the 20th century, roughly corresponding to the reign of King Edward VII (1901-1910). The period is often remembered nostalgically for its luxury and brilliance, soon to be darkened by the horror of World War I (1914-18) and obliterated by the relative austerity of the post-war years. This life of luxury, easy foreign travel, low taxation, etc. is also thought of as being relatively free from the close moral restraint commonly associated with the preceding ▷ Victorian period. It is sometimes remembered, however, that such brilliance was restricted to the upper class and the wealthier members of the middle class, and that life for four-fifths of the population was at best dull and at worst squalid and impoverished. This darker aspect of the time was responsible for the rise of the socialist ▷ Labour party and the prominence of polemical writers, like ▷ George Bernard Shaw and ▷ H. G. Wells. Such writers attacked the social injustice and selfishness of the upper classes in an idiom designed to reach wide audiences. Another critic of the dominant materialism was the novelist ▷ E. M. Forster. ▷ Arnold Bennett was a more representative novelist: his novels were not polemical and convey a materialistic vigour and excitement which were important elements in the harsh but inspiring environments of the more prosperous provincial towns. Thus some aspect of materialism is generally associated with Edwardianism, whether it is being enjoyed, suffered or criticized. Politically, the period was one of disturbance and rapid development: ▷ trade unionism was militant, women fought for political rights (▷ Suffragette Movement), and the social conscience inspired legislation which was later to mature into the ▷ Welfare State of the 1940s.

Edwards, Richard (1523–66)
Master of the children of the Chapel Royal and author of the popular courtly drama about ideal friendship, *Damon and Pithias* (1561), as well as of an influential, posthumously published collection of poets of the early ▷ Elizabethan period, *The Paradyse of Dainty Devises* (1576).

Edwin Drood, The Mystery of (1870)
A novel by ▷ Charles Dickens, unfinished at his death. The novel begins in a cathedral town (based on Rochester); the plot turns on the engagement of Edwin and Rosa Bud, who do not really love each other, and the rivalry for Rosa's love of Edwin's sinister uncle, John Jasper, and an exotic newcomer to the town, Neville Landless. Edwin disappears and Neville is arrested for his murder; Rosa flees to London to escape Jasper; on her behalf the forces for good are rallying in the shape of Rosa's guardian, Mr Grewgious, a clergyman called Crisparkle and a mysterious stranger, Mr Datchery, when the story breaks off. The fragment is quite sufficient to show that Dickens was not losing his powers. The sombreness and the grotesque comedy are equal to the best in his previous works. There have been numerous attempts to end the novel but none of any particular note.

EFL
Teaching English as a Foreign Language: a specialist skill and a profitable enterprise. It covers both the instruction of schoolchildren and their parents whose mother-tongue is not English but who live in Britain, which is a social necessity and prime task in a multi-racial society, as well as the work done in private language schools with older people not permanently resident in Britain. This is where the money lies. The number of these schools continues to increase: overseas the ▷ British Council has also expanded its teaching of English. Material relating to EFL teaching now takes up considerable space in many publishers' lists and is a major export.
▷ Adult education.

Egdon Heath
A gloomy tract of country which is the Dorsetshire setting for ▷ Thomas Hardy's novel ▷ *The Return of the Native*. As often in Hardy's novels, the place is not merely a background to the events but exercises an active influence upon them.

Egoist, The (1879)
One of the most admired novels by ▷ George Meredith. The 'egoist' is the rich and fashionable ▷ Sir Willoughby Patterne, who is intolerably self-centred and conceited. The story concerns his courting of Clara Middleton and her fight for independence from his assertiveness. Willoughby is opposed by Vernon Whitford, who is austere, honest and discerning, the tutor of Willoughby's poor relation, Crossjay, a boy whose vigorous animal spirits are accompanied by deep and spontaneous feeling. Partly owing to Crossjay, Clara is eventually enabled to evade Willoughby's advances, which have been backed by her father whose luxurious tastes Willoughby has indulged. She marries Whitford, a conclusion which is a victory for integrity over deceitful subtlety. The story is told with the brilliance of Meredith's rather mannered wit and is interspersed with exuberant passages of natural description symbolically related to the theme. Though Meredith's mannerism has lost the book some of its former prestige, his analysis of self-deceit and his understanding of the physical components of strong feeling make *The Egoist* an anticipation of kinds of fiction more characteristic of the 20th century.

Eisteddfod
Any festival in ▷ Wales held to encourage literature in the Welsh language, music, and other aspects of Welsh national culture. Its origins are possibly 12th-century; the word is Welsh and means 'a session'. The National Eisteddfod is held annually, alternately in North and South Wales.

Electra
In Greek myth, the daughter of ▷ Agamemnon, king of Argos, who was murdered by his wife, ▷ Clytemnestra. Electra supported her brother ▷ Orestes in avenging their father by killing their mother. She is the main character of plays bearing her name by ▷ Sophocles and ▷ Euripides.

Elegy
An elegy is usually taken to be a poetic

lament for one who has died, or at least a grave and reflective poem. In ancient Greek and Latin literature, however, an elegy was a poem written in a particular ▷ metre (line of six dactylic feet alternating with lines of five feet) and it had no necessary connection with death or gravity; the Latin poet ▷ Ovid used it for love poetry. Following his example, the English poet ▷ John Donne wrote a series of elegies with amorous or satirical themes. Most of the famous elegies in English, however, follow the narrower and more widely accepted definition: ▷ Milton's ▷ *Lycidas* is inspired by the death of his friend Edward King; ▷ Shelley's ▷ *Adonais* laments that of the poet ▷ Keats; ▷ Arnold's *Thyrsis*, that of his friend ▷ Clough. All three of these are in the ▷ pastoral convention, in imitation of a 3rd-century BC Greek elegy called the *Lament of Moschus for Bion*. Contemporary poetry's interest in absence and bereavement has led to a renewed interest in the elegy, *eg* ▷ Douglas Dunn, *Elegies*.

Elegy Written in a Country Churchyard (1751)

A poem by ▷ Thomas Gray, in iambic pentameter quatrains, rhyming *abab* (▷ metre). Its quiet subtlety of tone raises the platitudes of conventional graveyard musing to a unique intensity, and several of its eloquent generalizations and phrases have become proverbial: 'Some mute inglorious Milton', 'the madding crowd's ignoble strife', 'Melancholy mark'd him for her own', 'Full many a flower is born to blush unseen,/ And waste its sweetness on the desert air.' ▷ Samuel Johnson, though contemptuous of Gray's more inspirational experiments such as the ▷ Pindaric Odes, had high praise for this poem: 'The *Churchyard* abounds with images which find a mirror in every mind, and with sentiments to which every bosom returns an echo.'
▷ Elegy; Sensibility.

Elements, The (Four)

The 'four elements' are the ancient Greek and medieval conception of the basic components of matter; they are air, fire, earth and water. It was a division made by ▷ Empedocles of Sicily and adopted by ▷ Aristotle. Aristotle was writing before the beginnings of chemical analysis and considered matter in regard to the 'properties' or qualities that he believed all things to possess; these he found to be 'hotness', 'coldness', 'wetness' and 'dryness'. His four

elements contained these properties in different combinations: air = hot and wet; fire = hot and dry; earth = cold and dry; water = cold and wet. These, therefore, were the basic constituents of nature. Aristotle's great prestige in the ▷ Middle Ages caused his theory to dominate the thought of the time. The medieval alchemists, forbears of the modern analytical chemist, noticed that the properties of various kinds of matter change, *eg* iron becomes rust, and they deduced from Aristotle's theory that materials could be changed, provided that they retained the same basic properties, *eg* lead could be changed into gold. The theory dominated European thought until the 17th century, when the English 'natural philosopher' and chemist, Robert Boyle (1627–91) taught that an element is to be regarded as a substance in itself and not as a substance with certain basic properties. Since Boyle, chemists have discovered that elements are very much more numerous than the original four, and that air, fire, earth and water are not in fact elements at all. Nonetheless, the pervasiveness of these so-called 'four elements' in our environment has caused them to keep their hold on the modern imagination, when it is not engaged in scientific thinking, so that they are still employed as symbols for the basic constituents of our experience of the world in some imaginative literature.

The theory of the 'four elements' was connected in classical and medieval times with the medical and psychological theory of the 'humours', or four basic liquid constituents of the body. The blood humour ('hot and wet') is linked to air; choler ('hot and dry') is associated with fire; phlegm ('cold and wet') corresponds to water and melancholy ('cold and dry') to earth. The preponderance of one or other of these humours in the make-up of a person's character was supposed to determine the temperament.
▷ Humour.

Elf

In old English myth, a tiny supernatural being, neither good nor bad in itself, but commonly responsible for mischief. It is of Teutonic origin but it became increasingly associated with the fairy – of Latin origin – a less malicious kind of creature. ▷ Edmund Spenser, in the ▷ *Faerie Queene* uses the word in places for the Queen's knights. The more mischievous kind of fairy comes to be

called a goblin, *eg* Puck in ▷ Shakespeare's
▷ *Midsummer Night's Dream.*
▷ Fairies.

Elgin Marbles
Greek statues and friezes, once belonging to
the temple of the Parthenon in Athens, by
the sculptor Pheidias (5th century BC). They
are now in the British Museum and were
brought to England by Thomas Bruce, Earl
of Elgin. He was British ambassador in
Constantinople from 1799 to 1802 and it was
then that he conceived the purpose of
removing them. He was accused of vandalism
and defended himself in the pamphlet
*Memorandum on the Earl of Elgin's Pursuits
in Greece* (1810). The collection was
purchased by the nation for £36,000 and
placed in the museum in 1816. Lord Elgin
had spent over £50,000 on removing them.
They are amongst the finest sculptures in
Europe and made a deep impression on
contemporary artists and poets, especially
▷ John Keats and his friend Haydon.
▷ Byron expresses his indignation at
Elgin's action in ▷ *Childe Harold* (II,
st.11–15). The Greek nation continues to
demand their return.

Elia
▷ *Essays of Elia*

Elijah
In the ▷ Bible, a Hebrew prophet whose
career is described in *1* and *2 Kings*. The
stories about him are vivid and dramatic: his
triumph over the prophets of Baal; the ravens
feeding him in the wilderness; God speaking
to him in a 'still, small voice' after the
violence of the whirlwind; the chariot of fire,
witnessed by his successor Elisha, carrying
him up to heaven – these are some of the
most remembered. He was fearless in
condemning the wickedness and failings of
the kings of Israel; in consequence he is often
referred to as the basic type of the relentless
critic of society.

Eliot, George (1819–80)
Pen-name of the novelist, Mary Ann Evans
(at different times of her life she also spelt the
name Mary Anne, Marian and Marianne).
She was the daughter of a land-agent in the
rural midlands (Warwickshire); her father's
work (the management of estates) gave her
wide experience of country society and this
was greatly to enrich her insight and the
scope of her novels. Brought up in a narrow
religious tradition, in her early twenties she
adopted ▷ agnostic opinions about Christian
doctrine but she remained steadfast in the

Etching of George Eliot, from the drawing
by Frederic Burton (1864)

ethical teachings associated with it. She began
her literary career with translations from the
German of two works of religious speculation
(▷ German Influence); in 1851 she became
assistant editor of the ▷ *Westminster Review*,
a journal of great intellectual prestige in
London. Her friendship with ▷ George
Lewes led to a union between them which
they both regarded as amounting to
▷ marriage; this was a bold decision in view
of the rigid opposition in the English society
of the time to open unions not legalized by
the marriage ceremony.

Her first fiction consisted of tales later
collected together as ▷ *Scenes of Clerical
Life*. Then came her series of full-length
novels: ▷ *Adam Bede* (1859), ▷ *The Mill on
the Floss* (1860), ▷ *Silas Marner* (1861),
▷ *Romola* (1862–3), ▷ *Felix Holt* (1866),
▷ *Middlemarch* (1871–2) and ▷ *Daniel
Deronda* (1876). Up till *Romola* the novels
and tales deal with life in the countryside in
which she was brought up; the society is
depicted as a strong and stable one, and the
novelist combines in an unusual degree sharp,
humorous observation and intelligent
imaginative sympathy. *Romola* marks a
dividing point; it is a historical novel about
the society of the Italian city of Florence in
the 15th century. As a work of imaginative
literature it is usually regarded as scholarly
but dead; however, it seems to have opened
the way to the more comprehensive
treatment of English society in her last three
novels, in which the relationship of the
individual to society is interpreted with an

intelligence outstanding in the history of the English novel, and often compared with the genius of the Russian novelist, ▷ Leo Tolstoy. Her critical reputation has varied; it declined somewhat after her death, her powerful intellect being considered to damage her creativity. She was defended by ▷ Virginia Woolf in an essay in 1919, but was really re-established by inclusion in ▷ F. R. Leavis's *The Great Tradition* (1948). With the rapid strides in ▷ feminist criticism in the 1980s, however, Eliot has been reclaimed as a major influence on women's writing and her works have been the focus of numerous feminist critiques, *eg* S. Gilbert and S. Gubar, *The Madwoman in the Attic* (1979).

George Eliot's poetry (*The Spanish Gipsy*, 1868, and *The Legend of Jubal*, 1870) is now little regarded but her essays for the *Westminster Review* include work of distinction and she published a collection, *The Impressions of Theophrastus Such*, in 1879.

In 1880, George Lewes having died, she married John Walter Cross, but she died in the same year.
Bib: Haight, G. S., *Life*; Leavis, F. R., in *The Great Tradition*, Bennett, J., *George Eliot: Her Mind and her Art*; Harvey, W. J., *The Art of George Eliot*; Pond, E. J., *Les Idées Morales et Religieuses de George Eliot*; Hardy, B., *The Art of George Eliot;* Roberts, N., *George Eliot: Her Beliefs and Her Art*.

Eliot, Thomas Stearns (1888–1965)
Poet, critic, and dramatist. Born in St Louis, Missouri, he later settled in England, where his first important long poem – *The Love Song of J. Alfred Prufrock* – appeared in the magazine *Poetry* in 1915; his first book, *Prufrock and Other Observations*, appeared in 1917. From 1917 to 1919 he was Assistant Editor of the magazine *The Egoist*. His most famous poem, ▷ *The Waste Land*, came out in 1922, in which year he established the *Criterion*, one of the most influential literary reviews of this century. In 1927 he became a naturalized British subject, and in the same year he demonstrated his conversion to Christianity by becoming a member of the Church of England. His remaining important volumes of poetry were *Ash Wednesday* (1930) and ▷ *Four Quartets* (1935–42). The total body of his verse is not large, but it is one of the most important collections of the century. His poetic influences were preponderantly the French 19th-century ▷ symbolists (▷ Baudelaire, Mallarmé, Laforgue), and the early-17th-century dramatists

(▷ Middleton, ▷ Webster, ▷ Tourneur, the later ▷ Shakespeare) and their contemporaries the ▷ Metaphysical poets. The great sermon writers of the same period – ▷ John Donne, ▷ Jeremy Taylor, ▷ Bishop Andrewes – exercised a double influence on his style and his thought, and so did the great Italian medieval poet ▷ Dante. The contemporary who influenced him most and, in particular, greatly contributed to his early poetic development, was his fellow American ▷ Ezra Pound. Finally, the idealist philosophy of ▷ F. H. Bradley, whom Eliot studied as a student at Harvard and Oxford, was an important formative influence on Eliot's mind; his early academic thesis on Bradley was published in 1936.

Eliot's importance as a critic is linked with his importance as a poet, inasmuch as his really influential criticism was concerned with a reassessment of the past in such a way as to lead up to his own poetic production. Thus *The Sacred Wood* (1920) came between his first two volumes of verse. The most important of these early essays were republished in *Selected Essays* (1932). His work as a critic of society and civilization, *After Strange Gods* (1933) and *Notes Towards a Definition of Culture* (1948), has been such as to produce less fruitful, more sectarian discussion than his best literary criticism.

Eliot also experimented with verse drama, *Murder in the Cathedral* (1935) and *The Cocktail Party* (1950) being the most commercially and artistically successful. In 1981 his 1939 collection for children, *Old Possum's Book of Practical Cats*, was turned into Andrew Lloyd Webber's hit musical *Cats*, thus reaching an enormous audience.

Eliot's non-dramatic poetry and his early criticism have had the effect in this century of reordering and renewing literary taste both in this country and in America. He was not alone, but he was outstanding, in reviving admiration for the Metaphysical poets, and reducing the relative status of the ▷ Spenserian and ▷ Miltonic strains in the English tradition. His poetry enlarged the range and form of poetic expression as a medium of the modern consciousness.
Bib: Hayward, J., *Selected Prose*; Matthiessen, F. O., *The Achievement of T. S. Eliot*; Kenner, H., *Invisible Poet*; Williamson, G., *A Reader's Guide*; Smith, G., *Eliot's Poetry and Plays*; Drew, E., *T. S. Eliot: The Design of his Poetry*; Gardner, H. L., *The Art of T. S. Eliot*; Moody, A. D., *Thomas Stearns*

Eliot, Poet; Smith, C. H., *Eliot's Dramatic Theory and Practice*.

Elision

The suppression of sounds in words with the effect of drawing words together.

Elizabeth I (1558–1603)

Queen of England. Her reign was an extremely critical one, in which the personal fate of the Queen was unusually bound up with that of the nation and the national Church. As a ▷ Protestant, she broke ▷ Mary's ties with Rome and restored her father's independent ▷ Church of England, but tolerance and compromise won her the loyalty of ▷ Catholics and ▷ Puritans alike. For 30 years she successfully played off against each other the two great Catholic powers, France and Spain. While she remained single, there was always a chance that her Catholic cousin ▷ Mary, Queen of Scots and widow of a French king, might succeed her. Even when Mary, deposed by the Scots, took refuge in England and connived at plots to murder her, Elizabeth avoided reprisals for nearly 20 years. Mary's eventual execution was followed in 1588 by Philip of Spain's attempted invasion of England, which resulted in the defeat of his powerful fleet, the great ▷ Armada. This was represented as a great triumph for Elizabeth personally, and in her person the English nation saw its own triumph.

The reign saw an efflorescence of national spirit in other ways. It was the period of the first great achievements in English seamanship. Elizabeth's court was the focus of the real flowering of the English ▷ Renaissance, expressing itself through music and literature; especially, the age of English poetic drama began. Commerce expanded through the joint stock merchant companies and with it a wealthy upper class, partly landed and partly mercantile, who left their mark in the immense country mansions which they built all over the land. The Queen herself, though cautious in statesmanship, was spirited and highly cultivated and several poems have been acredited to her.

▷ Companies, Joint Stock; Drake, Sir Francis; Elizabethan period of English literature; Ralegh, Sir Walter; Sidney, Sir Philip; Sixteenth-century literature.

Elizabethan novels

The events in a novel or novella are not drawn directly from traditional or legendary sources but are invented by the writer, so that they are new (or 'novel') to the reader. The 'novels' of the Elizabethan period are distinguishable from the long prose romances, such as Sir Philip Sidney's ▷ *Arcadia*, by their comparative brevity, but *Arcadia* is sometimes included among them.

The Italian novella began its history in the 13th century, and one of its best practitioners, ▷ Giovanni Boccaccio, was already well known in England, especially from ▷ Chaucer's adaptation of his work. In the first 20 years of ▷ Elizabeth I's reign, various Italian 'novelle', especially those of Bandello (?1480–1562), were translated into English, notably by William Painter in his collection *The Palace of Pleasure* (1566–7). These translations created a taste for the form, and led to the production of native English 'novels'. John Lyly's ▷ *Euphues* (1578) was the first of these. Best known among those that followed are: Lyly's *Euphues and his England* (1580), Barnabe Rich's (1542–1617) collection *Farewell to the Military Profession* (1581), Robert Greene's ▷ *Pandosto* (1588) and *Menaphon* (1589), ▷ Thomas Lodge's *Rosalynde* (1590), Thomas Nashe's ▷ *Unfortunate Traveller* (1594), and Thomas Deloney's *Thomas of Reading, Jack of Newbury*, and *The Gentle Craft* (all between 1596 and 1600). The style of these works varies greatly. Rich, Greene and Lodge wrote mannered and courtly tales in imitation of Lyly; Nashe's rambling narrative is sometimes strongly realistic, and his style parodies a wide range of contemporary prose styles; Deloney addressed a middle-class public and at his best (in *Thomas of Reading*) anticipates the sober vividness of ▷ Daniel Defoe. The taste for the form lapsed in the early 17th century. There is no continuous development between the Elizabethan novel and the novel form as we know it today: the latter has its beginnings in the work of Defoe in the early 18th century, though it had late-17th-century fore-runners.

Both the Italian and the English novels were used as sources for plots by contemporary English dramatists. Shakespeare's ▷ *Twelfth Night* is drawn from *Apolonius and Silla* in Rich's collection, adapted from an Italian original; his ▷ *As You Like It* is based on Lodge's *Rosalynde*; his ▷ *Winter's Tale* draws on Greene's ▷ *Pandosto*.

Elizabethan period of English literature

The term 'Elizabethan' is used confusingly in regard to literature.

1 It is generally applied accurately to the lyric poetry and prose (*eg* ▷ Elizabethan novels) which flowered during the reign of ▷ Elizabeth I and especially during the last half of it.

2 On the other hand the term 'Elizabethan drama' is sometimes made to cover not only the beginnings of the great poetic drama (roughly 1588–1600) but also the greater period that succeeded this in the reign of ▷ James I and even to include the period of its final decline under ▷ Charles I, *ie* until the closing of the theatres in 1642. But critics usually distinguish the mature phase as ▷ Jacobean and the decline as ▷ Caroline. By this more accurate designation, an Elizabethan dramatist would be such as ▷ Marlowe, the early ▷ Shakespeare, ▷ Greene, ▷ Lyly, or ▷ Peele; the Jacobean drama would include mature and late Shakespeare, ▷ Jonson, ▷ Tourneur, ▷ Webster, ▷ Middleton; and the Caroline drama, the later work of ▷ Massinger, ▷ John Ford and ▷ James Shirley.

3 In literary terminology, 'Elizabethan' has further to be distinguished from Tudor. The Queen was herself the last of the ▷ House of Tudor, but Tudor drama, the Tudor lyric, Tudor prose, etc. commonly refer to work during the previous reigns, *ie* between the accession of ▷ Henry VII in 1485 and her own accession in 1558.

Ellis, Henry Havelock (1859–1939)

Psychologist and essayist. Part of his work was scientific: *Man and Woman* (1894); *Studies in the Psychology of Sex* (1897–1910). Part of it was literary and expressed in reflective essays: *Little Essays in Love and Virtue* (1922); *Impressions and Comments* (1914–23); *The Dance of Life* (1923). In the latter work he exemplified the revival of the ▷ essay as a reflective form early in this century. He was a friend of the novelist ▷ Olive Schreiner.
Bib: Calder Marshall, A., *Life*; Collis, J. S., *An Artist of Life.*

Eloisa to Abelard (1717)

An Ovidian monologue in heroic couplets by ▷ Alexander Pope, based on the tragic love affair between the medieval philosopher Abelard (1079–1142) and Heloise (Eloisa) the daughter of a canon at Notre Dame Cathedral. Eloisa's family, disapproving of the affair, had Abelard castrated, and she became a nun. Their later correspondence on theological and philosophical issues is famous. In Pope's poem Eloisa writes from her convent, expressing her unabated longing, with a mixture of 'romantick' melancholy and theatrical rhetoric. The poem's combination of spirituality and eroticism illustrates the emotional, ▷ Catholic side of Pope's temperament.

Elsinore

A seaport in Denmark (Danish = Helsingør); the castle there is the scene of ▷ Shakespeare's tragedy ▷ *Hamlet*.

Elyot, Sir Thomas (?1499–1546)

Diplomat and scholar. A member of ▷ Sir Thomas More's circle, he was friendly with ▷ humanists such as ▷ Erasmus, ▷ Thomas Linacre and John Colet (1467–1519). His major publication was *A Book Named the Governor* (1531), dedicated to ▷ Henry VIII. The work is similar to the educational and political conduct books such as ▷ Baldassare Castiglione's *Il Cortegiano* and ▷ Machiavelli's *Il Principle*, in that it sets out the humanist ideal of the educated and powerful monarch. Elyot also wrote two other works of political philosophy – *The Image of Governance* (1541) and *The Doctrinal of Princes* (composed c 1534).
Bib: Warren, L. C., *Humanistic Doctrines of the Prince from Petrarch to Sir Thomas Elyot.*

Elysium

In ancient Greek myth, an imaginary island where the souls of the virtuous enjoyed perfect happiness after death. In English literature it is sometimes used synonymously with Heaven.

Emblem-books

Books, very popular in England in the 16th century, containing pictures of ordinary objects (compasses, bottles, flowers, etc.) together with short poems showing how the object could be used to teach a truth applicable to life or conduct. The fashion influenced the imagery of the 17th-century ▷ Metaphysical poets who commonly used simple objects as more or less complex illustrations of human experience, as when the poet ▷ John Donne in *Valediction Forbidding Mourning* compares the relationship of himself and his wife when he goes on a journey to a pair of geometrical compasses whose points can divide but which yet remain united. Poets such as ▷ Francis Quarles and ▷ George Wither wrote verses sometimes shaped like such objects – a bottle, wings, etc. George Wither's *A Collection of Emblems, Ancient and Modern* appeared in four volumes in 1635 ▷ Francis Quarles'

Illustration from 16th-century emblem-book

Emblems also in 1635, and the slightly earlier collection by Peacham entitled *Minerva Britanna* in 1612. Peacham's collection set out to proclaim not so much philosophical truths, but to celebrate English 'worthies' such as ▷ Francis Bacon. It had been argued that poets such as ▷ Richard Crashaw, ▷ George Herbert, and ▷ Henry Vaughan were influenced by emblem books. Such an infuence might possibly be discerned not just in the imagery of individual poems, but in the titles and organization of their collections of poetry

Emerald Isle, The
A poetic name for ▷ Ireland, suggested by the intense greenness of its landscape. Green is also the national colour and appears with white and orange on the national flag.

Emma (1816)
A novel by ▷ Jane Austen. The heroine, Emma Woodhouse, has wealth, social prestige, good looks and intelligence. But her good fortune and the admiration she elicits are in reality her greatest disadvantage: they blind her to the need for self-knowledge and self-criticism. In what she imagines to be pure generosity of heart, she sets about trying to control the fate of her orphan friend of illegitimate birth and insignificant character,

Harriet Smith, imagining her to be the daughter of an aristocrat and deserving a marriage socially worthy of her paternity. Later she also becomes involved with a young man, Frank Churchill, who unknown to her is secretly engaged to a girl, Jane Fairfax, who is superior to Emma in talent but much inferior in worldly fortune. Jane Austen is in fact expanding the theme of the way in which romantic fantasy can blind a character to the realities of experience, more overtly used in earlier novels, ▷ *Northanger Abbey* and ▷ *Sense and Sensibility*. Emma, who has imagination and ability but nothing on which to employ them, is first trying to make a real-life novel with Harriet Smith as heroine and then participating in a mysterious drama, which she misconceives as her own fantasy wants it to be, with Jane Fairfax as main protagonist. But Harriet decides that she is to marry the man, George Knightley, with whom Emma herself has long been unconsciously in love; Emma also discovers that Churchill, with whom she has been conducting a flirtation, has merely been using her as a tool to mask his secret engagement. She realizes, in fact, that she has caused herself to be a victim of the first of her romances and has been made to play an ignominious and unworthy role in the second. Duly repentant, Emma is ultimately rewarded by Mr Knightley's proposal of marriage. The novel is perhaps Jane Austen's finest, displaying her irony at its most subtle.

Empedocles (5th century BC)
A philosopher and statesman of the Greek colony of Agrigentum in Sicily. He is said to have led the people against the tyrannous government of a powerful class and then to have refused to become their king. According to a legend he met his death in the volcano of Etna, though in reality he seems to have died in Greece. There are various allusions to his legendary end in English literature and it is usually ascribed to dangerous curiosity. The most famous account of it is the poem *Empedocles on Etna* (1852) by ▷ Matthew Arnold; in this his death is represented as deliberate suicide by a disillusioned and banished political leader. Arnold uses the poem to express his own scepticism.

Empson, William (1906–84)
Critic and poet. Empson was born in Yorkshire and worked under ▷ I. A. Richards at Cambridge. His main critical works are: *Seven Types of Ambiguity* (1930), *Some Versions of Pastoral* (1935), *The Structure of Complex Words* (1951), and *Milton's God* (1961). Volumes of his verse

include: *Poems* (1940) and *Collected Poems* (1955).

As a critic, he was very influential, especially through his analysis of the nature of language when it is used in imaginative writing, particularly poetry. His approach was influenced by the attitudes to language of 20th-century linguistic philosophers, especially ▷ Bertrand Russell and Wittgenstein, who concentrated on the tendency of language, by the ambiguities inherent in it, to confuse clear thought. Empson's teacher, Richards, in his *Principles of Literary Criticism* (1924), discussed the kinds of truth that are to be found in poetic statements, and how these truths differ from, without being less valuable than, the truths of philosophical and scientific statement. Empson's first book (*Seven Types*) discusses the way in which various kinds of semantic ambiguity can be used by poets, and shows the relevance of this study to the assessment of poems. It has become a major text in what came to be known as ▷ New Criticism. His later books develop the psychological (particularly ▷ Freudian) and philosophical aspects of this approach. More recently post-structuralist and ▷ psychoanalytic critics have become interested in *Seven Types of Ambiguity*. Empson's poetry is difficult, academic – heavily annotated by him – and itself highly ambiguous. Although difficult and obscure, his poetry was greatly influential on the work of the ▷ Movement.

Encyclopaedists
The collaborators in the production of the great French encyclopaedia (▷ *L'Encyclopédie*) of the 18th century. The enterprise began with a translation of the English *Cyclopaedia* by Ephraim Chambers but the French version was intellectually altogether more impressive. Its editors were two leaders of the 'philosophers' – D'Alembert and Diderot – and its contributors were the leading male minds of France, such men as ▷ Voltaire and ▷ Rousseau. The inspiration was faith in reason and the desire to destroy superstition and beliefs thought to arise from it. The movement contributed to the influences which later led to the ▷ French Revolution, and it reinforced ▷ rationalism throughout Europe. In England the movement influenced ▷ Jeremy Bentham and through him the ▷ Utilitarians of the 19th century.
▷ French literature in England.

Encyclopédie, L'
An encyclopaedia published in 35 volumes between 1751 and 1776, under the editorship of Diderot (1713–84) and (until 1758) the mathematician D'Alembert (1717–83). Its contributors included ▷ Voltaire, ▷ Rousseau, Montesquieu (1689–1755), Buffon (1707–88) and Turgot (1727–81). The work originated in a translation of the English *Cyclopaedia* (1728) of Ephraim Chambers (d 1740), but the French version was intellectually more ambitious and more impressive. It was guided by a trust in reason and rationalistic explanation, and the desire to destroy superstition and the beliefs thought to arise from it. The work's fierce attacks on Church and state proved potent criticism of the ▷ Ancien Régime (it was suppressed at various stages of its composition) and heralded the overthrow of the monarchy in the ▷ French Revolution. It reinforced European rationalism and in England influenced ▷ Jeremy Bentham and through him the 19th century Utilitarians (▷ Utilitarianism).

End-rhyme
Rhyme occurring in the usual position, *ie* at the end of a line; internal rhymes occur in the middle of a line, and head-rhymes are the correspondence of the beginnings of words, *ie* alliteration.

End-stopped lines
Lines of verse, especially ▷ blank verse, which end at the end of a sentence or at strongly marked pauses within the sentence. The opposite effect is produced by run-on lines, when the syntax makes the voice go on to the next line without pause.
▷ Enjambment.

Endymion (1818)
Poem by ▷ John Keats. It is based on an ancient Greek myth about a shepherd with whom the moon goddess fell in love. The poem has passages of great freshness and beauty, but, as Keats soon came to realize, it is immature. Its classicism is a resource for the free embroidering of fanciful stories; and the theme, the indulgence of the senses, is one that Keats quickly outgrew.
Endymion is also the title of a play (1591) by ▷ John Lyly and of a novel (1880) by ▷ Benjamin Disraeli.

England's Helicon
An Elizabethan verse anthology, published in 1600 and possibly edited by one Nicholas Ling. The collection mainly comprises ▷ pastoral verse, and contains poems by ▷ Sir Philip Sidney, ▷ Edmund Spenser, ▷ Michael Drayton, ▷ Thomas Lodge and others, as well as 'The Passionate Sheepheards Song' by ▷ Shakespeare. This

last was taken from Act IV of ▷ *Love's Labour's Lost*, first published in quarto in 1598. The poem was republished in ▷ *The Passionate Pilgrim* of 1599. In 1614 a second edition of *England's Helicon* appeared, which included additional verses by Sidney and a poem by ▷ William Browne.

Bib: Macdonald, H. (ed.), *England's Helicon*.

English language

Historically, the language was categorized into three periods: ▷ Old English extending to the 12th century; Middle English, from the 12th to the 16th centuries; and Modern English.

Old English consisted of ▷ Anglo-Saxon and Jutish dialects, and was called English because the language of the ▷ Angles was the earliest discoverable in writing. Old English was strongly modified by Scandinavian elements in consequence of the Danish invasions, and Middle English by an extensive infusion of French vocabulary.

Middle English was divided into a variety of dialects; ▷ Langland, for instance, the author of ▷ *Piers Plowman*, wrote in the West Midland dialect; from the author or authors of ▷ *Sir Gawain and the Green Knight* and of ▷ *Pearl* wrote in a dialect from farther north, and ▷ Chaucer in the East Midland dialect. Because London was the chief city of England and the seat of the royal court, and because ▷ Caxton established his printing press there in the 15th century, East Midland became the forebear of Modern English. Since the 15th century English has not undergone important structural changes; social differences of speech as between the classes have been of greater importance, at least for literary purposes, than regional ones.

Exceptions to this statement have to be made, however, for the form of English spoken and written in southern Scotland, and for those regions of the British Isles where until comparatively recent times Celtic languages were predominant: north-west Scotland, Wales and Ireland. In Ireland especially, a variety of spoken language known as Hiberno English tends to follow the substratum of Irish Gaelic (▷ Irish literature in English). This non-standard idiom of English was exploited by Irish writers such as the dramatist ▷ J. M. Synge and the poet ▷ W. B. Yeats. Irish or Welsh writers may use standard English if they do not adhere to the surviving Celtic languages. In different ways Southern Scots is also important; it is a highly codified variety of non-standard English and has been unusual in

that it has enjoyed a long-established written form (▷ Scottish literature). The literature in Scots (known in the Middle Ages as Inglis and today sometimes as ▷ Lallans, *ie* Lowlands) is considerable, whether one thinks of the late medieval poets such as ▷ Dunbar, ▷ Douglas, or ▷ Henryson; an 18th-century poet such as ▷ Burns, or a 20th-century one like ▷ Hugh MacDiarmid. However, from the 17th century eminent Scottish writers took to writing in standard English, and this became universal amongst prose writers of the 18th century (▷ Hume, Robertson, ▷ Adam Smith).

'The Queen's English' is the term used for the language spoken by the educated classes in England; linguists, however, prefer the term 'Standard English'. The pronunciation most in use among educated people is known as 'Received Pronunciation'.

English vocabulary is basically Germanic, but it also contains a very large number of Latin words. French, of course, developed from Latin, and many of these Latin words entered English in their French form after the ▷ Norman Conquest in the 11th century. For about two and a half centuries the upper classes were French-speaking. Vestiges of this social difference survive in such distinctions as the word 'sheep' used for the live animal, and 'mutton' for the same animal when it is eaten at table; the English shepherds who cared for the sheep ate very little meat, whereas their Norman-French masters were chiefly concerned with the animal when it had been transformed into food. Even after the aristocracy became English-speaking in the 14th century, the adoption of French words continued to be frequent owing to the strong influence of French culture and ways of life on the English educated classes. Latin words, however, have also entered English independently of their French forms; the 'clerks', *ie* the literate class of the earlier Middle Ages, used Latin as a living language in their writings; they were churchmen, and Latin was the language of the Church all over Western Europe. In the 16th century, there was a new and different kind of influx from Latin owing to the fresh interest taken by scholars in ancient Latin culture.

The Latin contribution to the basically Germanic English vocabulary has resulted in a large number of Latin and Germanic synonyms, with important consequences for subtleties of English expression. The associations of Latin with the medieval Church and with ancient Roman literature cause the words of Latin origin to have suggestions of grandeur which the words of Germanic origin do not possess; thus we use 'serpent' in connection with religious and mythological ideas, *eg* the story of the Garden of Eden, but 'snake' will do in reference to the ordinary reptile. On the other hand, the Latinate word is emotionally less intimate than its Germanic synonym; when we wish to lessen the painfulness of death, we say that a man is 'deceased', instead of saying that he has 'died'. This kind of differentiation clearly carries important pragmatic consequences, yielding differences in tone and register. Thus, socially, it is often considered vulgar to use the synonym of French or Latin construction, as suggesting a disposition to speak stylishly rather than truly; many people consider it vulgar to use the French 'serviette' instead of the older 'napkin', the latter is also of French origin, but is more fully anglicized.

Some English writers, *eg* ▷ Milton and ▷ Samuel Johnson, and some periods of literature, especially the 18th century, are often singled out for their preference for the Latin part of the vocabulary, and in the 19th century the preference was sometimes regarded as a fault. Correspondingly, some literature is admired for its reliance on mainly Germanic vocabulary, *eg* the ▷ ballads, and the poems of ▷ John Clare, and ▷ Christina Rossetti, but in this kind of judgement Latin and French words adopted long ago and grown fully familiar are allowed to have the same merit as words of Germanic descent. Language which shows sensitiveness to the value of contrasting Latinate and Germanic vocabulary is always allowed peculiar merit; such is the case with ▷ Shakespeare.

English has borrowed words from many other languages; the chief of these is ancient Greek which contributed extensively during the 16th century ▷ Renaissance, and coloured the language similarly to the Latin contribution at the same time. Borrowings from other languages are more miscellaneous and less distinctive; the most distinctive are the modern borrowings from colloquial American diction.

English has not only borrowed more freely than most languages; it has been spread abroad more than any other world language. It is not only the first language of the larger parts of North America and Australasia, but it is spoken widely, sometimes as a first language in Africa and Asia (especially India), where it is a '*lingua franca*' in countries which have a variety of indigenous languages. This has complicated the study of literature in English; as the various territories of the former British Empire have acquired independence, so they have developed their own literature, which, although in the English language, have distinctive styles and directions (▷ Commonwealth literatures). Only a few 20th-century American writers, for instance, can be included in the truly English tradition; it is now necessary to talk of 'American literature'. It is similarly difficult to think of the Australian ▷ Patrick White or the West Indian ▷ V. S. Naipaul as English writers, in the sense of belonging to the English literary tradition.

In the 20th century the relationship between English language and literature has become theoretical, that is based upon the developments in linguistic techniques as related to the *language* of literature. Today, the teaching of English language with literature is founded on the discipline of literary stylistics and rejects an impressionistic approach to literature, preferring to concentrate on the rigorous analysis of the language texts use. It is the theoretical framework, as for example with the works of ▷ Bakhtin, that form the unifying basis for stylisticians, semioticians, literary theoreticians and linguists, as well as for the simple educational processes of teaching English language and literature.

Bib: Carter, R. (ed.), *Language and Literature: An Introductory Reader in Stylistics*; Fowler, R., *Linguistic Criticism*; Carter, R. and Simpson, D. (eds.), *Language, Discourse and Literature: An Introductory Reader in Discourse Stylistics*.

English Pale, The
▷ Pale, The English.

Enjambment
A term describing the continuing of the sense from line to line in a poem, to the extent that it is unnatural in speaking the verse to make a pause at the line ending. The effect is that of 'run-on' lines.
▷ End-stopped lines.

Enlightenment
The term was originally borrowed into English in the 1860s from German (*Aufklärung*), to designate the spirit and aims of the French philosophers of the 18th century, such as Diderot and ▷ Voltaire. But as historical perspectives have changed the word has come to be used in a much wider sense, to denote the whole period following the ▷ Renaissance, during which scepticism and scientific rationalism came to dominate European thinking. Enlightenment grew out of Renaissance at different times in different countries. In Britain, the empiricism

of ▷ Francis Bacon (1561–1626) and the secular pragmatism of ▷ Thomas Hobbes (1588–1679) mark its early stages. Its golden age began however with ▷ John Locke (1632–1704) in philosophy, and ▷ Sir Isaac Newton (1642–1727) in science, and it reached its height in the first half of the 18th century. Locke argued that 'Reason must be our last judge and guide in everything', and rejected medieval philosophy as superstition. Newton's theory of gravitation seemed to explain the mysteries of the solar system. The fact that Newton had also worked on optics was ingeniously alluded to in ▷ Alexander Pope's couplet: 'Nature, and Nature's Laws lay hid in Night./ God said, *Let Newton be!* and All was *Light* '.

The onset of Enlightenment in Britain coincided with the bourgeois revolution and many of its values reflect the optimistic temper of the newly dominant class, as much as any abstract philosophical system. In contrast to the previous ideology of static hierarchy, appropriate to a landowning aristocracy and its peasant underclass, the new ideology of merchants and professional men, places its emphasis on understanding and dominating the environment. God loses his numinousness, becoming a kind of divine mathematician, and the ▷ Deist thinkers of the time rejected the dogmas of the scriptures in favour of 'natural religion' based on an understanding of God's laws through science. Pope expresses this idea in classic form in his *Essay on Man* (1733–4), cleverly blending it with the older hierarchical idea of the Great Chain of Being. Pope's *Essay* stands as a compendium of popular Enlightenment ideas, expressing the expansive confidence of the middle class that 'Whatever *is*, is *right*.' It was easy for the middle-class reader of the day to feel that British philosophy, science, trade, and imperialism were all working together to advance civilization throughout the world. It is a myth projected in many of the works of Pope, ▷ James Thomson and other writers of the time.

As the 18th century developed, the bourgeoisie's confidence in its progressive destiny faltered, reaching a crisis after the ▷ French Revolution in what we now call the ▷ Romantic movement. ▷ William Blake attempted to restore the pre-Enlightenment numinousness of God and nature, rejecting Newton's 'particles of light', and the idea of inert matter or empty space. Imagination, not science, was for him the key to nature: 'Every thing possible to be believ'd is an image of truth.' ▷ Percy Bysshe Shelley, using politically resonant imagery,

asserted that 'man, having enslaved the elements, remains himself a slave' and warned of the dangers of 'an unmitigated exercise of the calculating faculty' (one of the characteristic institutions of the Enlightenment period was, of course, the slave trade). Even the fundamentally materialist ▷ John Keats complained about the prosaic nature of Enlightenment philosophy:

> There was an awful rainbow once in heaven:
> We know her woof, her texture; she is given
> In the dull catalogue of common things.
> Philosophy will clip an Angel's wings.
> (*Lamia*; 231–4)

More recently 'Enlightenment' has been given a yet wider historical application by the German philosophers Theodor Adorno and Max Horkheimer, whose book, *Dialectic of Enlightenment* (1944) sees the manipulative, calculating spirit of Enlightenment as the identifying characteristic of western civilization. They trace its manifestations from ▷ Odysseus's tricking of the primitive bumpkin Polyphemus, to the treatment of people as means rather than ends which characterizes both modern totalitarian politics and consumer capitalism. Recent ecological movements, which advocate a respect for nature, rather than an exploitation of it, continue the same dialectic.

▷ Augustanism.

Bib: Willey, B., *The Eighteenth-Century Background*; Redwood, J., *Reason, Ridicule and Religion: The Age of Enlightenment in England*.

Enright, D. J. (b 1920)

Poet, novelist and literary critic. Enright was an important figure in the ▷ Movement in the 1950s, and his poetry remains strongly humanistic and anti-romantic. His volumes of verse include: *The Laughing Hyena* (1953); *Bread Rather Than Blossoms* (1956); *Some Men Are Brothers* (1960); *Selected Poems* (1968); *Sad Ires* (1975); and *A Faust Book* (1979).

Ephesians

Inhabitants of the ancient city of Ephesus in Asia Minor, where there was an early Christian community. St Paul addressed to these one of his letters of doctrinal exposition: *Epistle to the Ephesians* in the New Testament. The presiding goddess was ▷ Artemis (Diana), to whom there was a famous temple. Shakespeare (in *Henry IV Part II,* II.2 and *Merry Wives of Windsor* IV.5) uses

'Ephesians' to mean close comrades in pleasure.

Epic

1 A narrative of heroic actions, often with a principal hero, usually mythical in its content, offering inspiration and ennoblement within a particular cultural or national tradition.

2 The word denotes qualities of heroism and grandeur, appropriate to epic but present in other literary or even non-literary forms.

Epics occur in almost all national cultures, and commonly give an account of national origins, or enshrine ancient, heroic myths central to the culture. For European culture at large, much the most influential epics are the ▷ *Iliad* and the ▷ *Odyssey* of ▷ Homer and the ▷ *Aeneid* by ▷ Virgil. ▷ C. S. Lewis in *Preface to Paradise Lost* makes a helpful distinction between primary and secondary epics: primary ones, such as Homer's, are composed for a society which is still fairly close to the conditions of society described in the narrative; secondary epics are based on the pattern of primary epics but written for a materially developed society more or less remote from the conditions described, *eg* Virgil's *Aeneid*. In English literature the ▷ Old English ▷ *Beowulf* may be counted as a primary epic. A number of attempts at secondary epic have been made since the 16th century, but ▷ John Milton's ▷ *Paradise Lost* is unique in its acknowledged greatness and its closeness to the Virgilian structure. ▷ Spenser's ▷ *The Faerie Queene* has many epic characteristics, but, in spite of the important classical influences upon it, the poem's structure is derived from the 'romantic epic' of the 16th-century Italian poets, ▷ Ariosto and ▷ Tasso; moreover, though allegory often plays a part in epics, the allegorical elements in *The Faerie Queene* are so pervasive as to present a different kind of imaginative vision from that normally found in them.

Many other works in English literature have epic qualities without being definable as epics. For example, ▷ Fielding described ▷ *Tom Jones* as a comic epic, and it is this as much as it is a novel: a series of adventures of which Tom is the hero, but of which the consequences are loss of dignity rather than enhancement of dignity. Melville's prose romance *Moby Dick* (1851) has true epic scale, seriousness of treatment and relevance to the human condition. ▷ James Joyce's ▷ *Ulysses* uses the *Odyssey* as the ground plan for a narrative about a day in the life of a Dublin citizen, and though the intention of this and of Joyce's succeeding work ▷ *Finnegans Wake* is in part comic, there is also in both books deep seriousness, such as derives from the authentic epic tradition. In fact, this tradition, in the last three hundred years, has mingled with other literary forms, such as the romance, the comic romance (*eg* ▷ *Don Quixote*), and the novel, and it is in this mixed rather than in its original pure form that it has proved most productive.

Epic, Mock

A form of ▷ satire practised with most success in English by ▷ Alexander Pope. The method is to employ the dignified expression associated with epic about subjects in themselves either trivial or base. Thus ▷ *The Rape of the Lock* describes a family quarrel provoked by a young man robbing a girl of a lock of her hair; it uses a dignity of style appropriate to the Rape of Helen which gave rise to Homer's ▷ *Iliad*, and applies it to the minute detail and obviously trivial scale of emotion appropriate to the slightness of the episode. In Pope's ▷ *Dunciad* the method is rather different, because here Pope is describing what is base rather than what is petty; the contrast is not, as with *The Rape*, an ironic one between grandeur of treatment and pettiness of subject, but between the nobility of the style and the depth of meanness in the subject.

Another form of mock epic is the ▷ mock heroic poem, in which a bad man committing base deeds is described in epic style, without disguising the badness.

The mock epic is especially the product of the century 1660–1760, when admiration for Greek and Latin satire and epic was particularly high.
▷ Epic.

Epic simile

Prolonged similes, commonly used in ▷ epic or heroic poetry, giving the subject described a spaciousness suited to its grandeur. Thus in ▷ *Paradise Lost* Bk. I, ▷ Milton wants to say that the fallen Satan is as big as a whale; this would be to use an ordinary simile. He expands it to an epic simile thus:

> *As huge as . . .*
> *. . . that Sea-beast*
> *Leviathan, which God of all his works*
> *Created hugest that swim th'Ocean stream:*
> *Him haply slumbering on the Norway foam*
> *The Pilot of some small night-founder'd*
>   *Skiff,*
> *Deeming some Island, oft, as Sea-men tell,*
> *With fixéd Anchor in his skaly rind*
> *Moors by his side under the Lee, while Night*
> *Invests the Sea, and wishéd Morn delayes:*

*So stretcht out huge in length the Arch-fiend
    lay . . .*

Epicoene, or The Silent Woman (1609)
A comedy by ▷ Ben Jonson. Epicoene
means having the characteristics of either sex.
The main character Morose, who has an
extreme hatred of noise, wants to disinherit
his nephew and marry a silent woman if she
can be found. A completely silent one is
found, but after marriage she finds the use of
her tongue and is anything but silent. Morose
promises to reinstate his nephew as his heir,
with an additional reward, if he can free his
uncle of the wife who is now the opposite of
what he hoped. The nephew then discloses
that the wife is a boy disguised. Though not
one of the greatest of Jonson's comedies, it
has always been one of his most popular,
owing to a large cast of lively comic
characters. The play is given a close analysis
in ▷ Dryden's ▷ *Essay on Dramatic Poesy*.

Epicurean
▷ Epicurus.

Epicurus (342–270 BC)
Greek philosopher and founder of the
Epicurean school of philosophers. He is best
known for his principle that pleasure is the
beginning and end of the blessed life. This
has commonly been misunderstood to mean
that the purpose of life is pleasure seeking; in
fact Epicurus meant by pleasure the
acquisition of a mind at peace and this
implied, for him, the pursuit of virtue and
hence a life of asceticism rather than excess.
His best-known disciple is the Latin poet
▷ Lucretius, who expounded the philosophy
in his poem *De Rerum Natura* (*Concerning the
Nature of Things*). The Epicureans were
rivals of the ▷ Stoics, who taught that the
end of life was fortitude and liberation from
the passions.

Epigram
For the ancient Greeks the word meant
'inscription'. From this, the meaning
extended to include very short poems notable
for the terseness and elegance of their
expression and the weight and wit of their
meaning. The richest of the ancient Greek
collections is the Greek ▷ *Anthology*; the
greatest Latin masters were ▷ Catullus and
Martial. ▷ Ben Jonson's *Underwoods*
contains epigrams in their tradition. After
him, epigrams became shorter and most
commonly had satirical content; ▷ Pope
was the greatest master of this style, and his
poems include many epigrams.
    ▷ Aphorism.

Epiphany
A Church festival celebrating the showing
('epiphany' means manifestation) of the Christ
child to the ▷ Magi, otherwise known as
the three Wise Men or the Three Kings
(*Matthew* II). The festival is twelve days
after Christmas Day, so it is also called
Twelfth Night. It concludes the season of
Christmas festivities.
    The novelist ▷ James Joyce began his
career by writing what he called 'epiphanies',
ie sketches in which the incident, though
often in itself slight, manifests or reveals the
inner truth of a character. This is the method
he pursues in ▷ *Dubliners*.

Episcopalian
From the Latin 'episcopus' = 'bishop'.
'Episcopacy' is the system of government of
Christian Churches by bishops; an
'episcopalian' is a member of such a Church,
or the supporter of such a system. The belief
on which the system is based is that Jesus
Christ consecrated his apostles in authority
over the first disciples, and that this
consecrated authority has been transmitted
down the centuries to all succeeding bishops.

Episteme
The traditional meaning of the term
'epistemology' is 'the theory or science of the
method or grounds of knowledge' (Oxford
English Dictionary). In the work of the
French philosopher ▷ Michel Foucault,
'episteme' has come to mean something more
specific. He uses the term to describe 'the
total set of relations that unite, at a given
period, the discursive practices that give rise
to epistemological figures, sciences, and
possibly formalized systems,' (*The
Archaeology of Knowledge*; 1972). In short,
the episteme is historicized as the basic unit
used to describe the manner in which a
society represents knowledge to itself.
Foucault conceives of the episteme in
dynamic rather than static terms, since
knowledge is always a matter of the ways in
which 'desire' and 'power' negotiate their way
through the complex ▷ discourses of
society. Foucault is at pains to point out,
however, that the episteme does not establish
a transcendental authority which guarantees
the existence of scientific knowledge, but
rather points towards the fact that different
kinds of knowledge are inscribed in 'the
processes of a historical practice'.
    ▷ Archaeology.

Epitaph
An inscription on a tomb, or a short verse or
prose inscription that might serve such a

purpose. As literary compositions, epitaphs became popular in the ▷ Renaissance, and as the requirement of brevity gives epitaphs a resemblance to ▷ epigrams. The 18th century, the great age of the epigram, was also that in which the epitaph was most cultivated.

Epithalamion (1594)

▷ Edmund Spenser's ▷ ode written in 1594, and published at the end of the ▷ sonnet sequence *Amoretti* (1595). The poem celebrates the marriage of Spenser to Elizabeth Boyle at Cork on 11 July 1594.
  ▷ *Prothalamion.*

Epyllion

A term, now largely unused, to describe the short-lived but popular Elizabethan genre of the minor or brief ▷ epic. It often, though not exclusively, denoted narrative verse which took as its model not the epics of ▷ Homer or ▷ Virgil, but the writings of ▷ Ovid. The genre flourished in England in the late 16th century, and includes works such as ▷ Thomas Lodge's *Scilla's Metamorphosis* (1589), *Ovid's Banquet of Sence* (1595) by ▷ George Chapman (?1559–1634) and ▷ Francis Beaumont's *Salmacis and Hermaphroditus* (1602). The most famous examples of the genre are undoubtedly ▷ Christopher Marlowe's *Hero and Leander* of 1598, to which Chapman and Henry Petowe (fl 1598–1612) appended 'continuations', and ▷ Shakespeare's ▷ *Venus and Adonis* (1593). Invariably, the epyllion's subject matter was erotic myth, but unlike earlier translations of Ovid, there was no attempt at placing the erotic within an ▷ allegorical or moral context.
Bib: Alexander, N. (ed.), *Elizabethan Narrative Verse.*

Erasmus, Desiderius (?1466–1536)

Dutch-born Augustinian monk, translator, ▷ humanist, educationalist, biblical scholar and linguist. Erasmus was one of the most important northern European scholars of the ▷ Renaissance period. The diversity of his interests, the range of his accomplishments, and the weight of his influence on European thought in the 16th century and later are almost impossible to quantify.

Erasmus' chief works are: the *Adages* (first published in 1500), the *Enchiridion* (1503), the *Praise of Folly* (1509) and the *Colloquies* (first published in 1516). But to these popular successes can be added his editions of the Church Fathers, paraphrases, commentaries on the scripture, editions of the classics and a huge correspondence with other European scholars and thinkers, the most important of

whom, in England, was his close friend ▷ Sir Thomas More. The *Praise of Folly*, a satirical work which ranges widely over all aspects of public life in the period, was conceived while Erasmus was travelling to England to see More – a circumstance preserved in the work's punning Latin title: *Encomium Moriae.*

The *Enchiridion*, on the other hand, is a manual of the Christian life which encourages knowledge of pagan (that is ▷ classical) literature as a preparative towards attaining Christian scriptural understanding. The *Adages* – a work which grew from some 800 'adages' or classical sayings into over 4,000 short essays by the time Erasmus died – provided an entry into classical literature, and into humanistic thought generally, for the public at large. Similarly, the *Colloquies* expanded as Erasmus worked at the project until they eventually formed a wide-ranging series of dialogues on a huge variety of topics, which were to include education, games, travel, parenthood, punishment, and social and religious questions.
Bib: *The Collected Works of Erasmus*; Huizinga, J., *Erasmus of Rotterdam.*

Erato

  ▷ Muses.

Erebus

In ancient Greek myth, a god of the underworld, son of Chaos. The word is often used to signify the underworld or hell itself.

Erewhon (1872) and Erewhon Revisited (1901)

Satirical anti-utopias by ▷ Samuel Butler. ▷ Sir Thomas More's *Utopia* is a description of an ideal country as different as possible from England. Erewhon (an anagram of 'Nowhere') represents a country many of whose characteristics are analogous to English ones, caricatured and satirized. Thus Butler satirizes ecclesiastical institutions through the Musical Banks and parental tyranny through the Birth Formulae; machinery has to be abolished before it takes over from human beings. In *Erewhon Revisited*, Higgs, the English discoverer of Erewhon, finds that his previous departure by balloon has been used by Professors Hanky and Panky ('hanky-panky' is deceitful practice) to impose a new religion, according to which Higgs is worshipped as a child of the sun. Butler's method in these satires resembles ▷ Jonathan Swift's satirical technique in the Lilliput of ▷ *Gulliver's Travels.*

Eros

The Greek boy god of love, identical with the

Latin Cupid. He was the son of ▷ Aphrodite (the Greek ▷ Venus) the goddess of sexual beauty. He is always represented with wings, and with arrows and a bow, which he shot into the heart of his victims. He is made use of countless times in English love poetry, especially at the end of the 16th century.

▷ Psyche.

Esmond, The History of (1852)

A historical novel by ▷ William Makepeace Thackeray. It is a very careful reconstruction of early-18th-century English aristocratic and literary society. The hero's father has been killed fighting for ▷ James II, *ie* he was a ▷ Jacobite. The politics of the book are involved with Jacobite plotting by the Roman ▷ Catholic branch of the House of ▷ Stuart to recover the throne of Britain from the Protestant branch. There are portraits of some of the distinguished personalities of the time – the Duke and Duchess of ▷ Marlborough, and the writers ▷ Sir Richard Steele, ▷ Joseph Addison and ▷ Jonathan Swift. The style emulates that of Addison himself. The theme is the devotion of the young Henry Esmond to his relatives, Lady Castlewood, eight years older than himself, and her proud and ambitious daughter, Beatrix. These relationships are complicated by political intrigues and by family mysteries – Esmond is in reality himself the heir to the title and properties inherited by Lady Castlewood's husband. In the end, Esmond marries the widowed Lady Castlewood and emigrates to Virginia; his story continues in *The Virginians* (1857–9).

Essay, The

'Essay' derives from the French *essai*, meaning 'experiment', 'attempt'. As a literary term it is used to cover an enormous range of composition, from schoolboy exercises to thorough scientific and philosophical works, the only quality in common being the implied desire of the writer to reserve to himself some freedom of treatment. But the essay is also a recognized literary form in a more defined sense: it is understood to be a fairly short prose composition, in style often familiarly conversational and in subject either self-revelatory or illustrative (more or less humorously) of social manners and types. The originator of the form was the great French writer ▷ Montaigne.

Montaigne's essays were published in completed form in 1595, and translated by ▷ John Florio into English (1603). His starting-point is 'Que sais-je?' ('What do I know?') and it leads him into a serious inquiry into his own nature as he feels it, and into investigations of facts, ideas, and experiences as he responds to them. In 1597 the first great English essayist, ▷ Francis Bacon, published his first collection of essays, of a very different kind: they are impersonal and aphoristic, weightily sententious. The character writers, ▷ Sir Thomas Overbury and John Earle (?1601–65) use the classical model of the Greek writer ▷ Theophrastus, reminding one that with so indefinite a form it is impossible to be too precise about the dating of starting-points. ▷ Abraham Cowley published the first essays in English closely corresponding to what is now understood by the form, and perhaps shows the first sign of its degeneracy: easiness of tone, which in Montaigne is a graciousness of manner introducing a serious and interesting personality, but which in less interesting writers may be an agreeable cover for saying nothing in particular.

In the early years of the 18th century ▷ Addison and ▷ Steele firmly established what is now known as the 'periodical essay' – a kind of higher journalism, intended often to please rather than instruct, but in their case to instruct through pleasure. In creations such as ▷ Sir Roger de Coverley, they developed the Theophrastian character into a personal, idiosyncratic portrait anticipating the characterization of the novelists a little later in the century. Their graciousness and lightness of tone take point and interest from their serious and conscious social purpose. ▷ Dr Johnson in *The Rambler* and in his essays as ▷ 'The Idler' used the weighty, impressive style soon to be regarded as unsuitable for the medium. ▷ Oliver Goldsmith in *The Citizen of the World* (1762) perfected the graceful, witty manner which came to be considered ideal for it.

If the 18th century was what may be called the golden age of the English essay, the early 19th, in the work of ▷ Charles Lamb, ▷ William Hazlitt, ▷ Leigh Hunt and ▷ De Quincey, was perhaps its silver age. In these writers, social comment combines with a confessional, autobiographical element which had never been so prominent in the English essay before. This was true to the autobiographical spirit of so much 19th-century literature. These essayists were links between the early ▷ Romantic poets – especially ▷ Wordsworth – and the mid-Victorian novelists; they shared the close interest in material surroundings characteristic of those poets, and their essays often contained character delineations related to such environmental settings. The earliest work of ▷ Charles Dickens, ▷ *Sketches by Boz*, is in the essayists' tradition.

After 1830, the periodical essay in the tradition of Addison, Goldsmith, Hazlitt and Lamb dissolved into the morass of constantly increasing journalism; though they had emulators in the 20th century, the form was increasingly despised by serious writers, and the famous essayists of the later 19th century were the more specialized sort, such as ▷ Matthew Arnold and ▷ John Stuart Mill. Yet it is not true to say that the informal essay of serious literary interest has disappeared. In the later 19th and 20th century, essays of natural description of remarkable intensity were produced by ▷ Richard Jefferies and ▷ Edward Thomas. More important still is the use of the essay for unspecialized but serious social and cultural comment by – to take leading examples – ▷ D. H. Lawrence, ▷ George Orwell, and ▷ Aldous Huxley. With the growth in popularity of serious ▷ magazines and the extended articles in the Sunday newspapers, the essay is today having a considerable revival. These informal arguments and 'personality pieces', such as those by Bernard Levin in *The Times*, are very far, however, from the formal essay genre.

▷ Characters, Theophrastian.

Essay concerning Human Understanding (1690)
A philosophical treatise by ▷ John Locke. Locke emphasizes reason as the dominant faculty of man. All knowledge is acquired through experience based on sense impressions; there are no 'innate ideas', *ie* no knowledge arises in the mind independently of impressions received from the outside world. These impressions divide into primary qualities, *ie* the measurable ones such as size, number, form, etc., and secondary ones, such as colour, sound and scent, which are not demonstrably part of the object, but dependent on the observer. Knowledge begins with perception of agreement or disagreement in the qualities observed in the objects or, as Locke calls them, 'ideas'. He distinguishes between rational judgement, which identifies and analyses ideas, and 'wit', which relates them by their resemblances; the distinction is practically one between reason and imagination and gives advantage to reason. Faith, *eg* in religious doctrine, is not distinct from reason, but the assent of the mind to a belief that accords with reason. Thus Locke appeals to clear definition in language and expression; he depreciates the intuitive and imaginative faculties of the mind and elevates the rational ones. His thesis accords with the reaction at the end of the 17th century against the intolerance and fanaticism of the religious conflicts which had prevailed during the first half of it. The influence of his philosophy is impressed on the imaginative prose literature of the first thirty years of the 18th century, for instance in the realism of ▷ Daniel Defoe. Later in the century, the novelist ▷ Laurence Sterne makes ingenious use of Locke's theory of the association of ideas in ▷ *Tristram Shandy*.

Essay on Criticism (1711)
Written when he was only 21 and published when he was 23, ▷ Alexander Pope's compendium of neo-classical poetic theory in ▷ heroic couplets was highly praised by ▷ Joseph Addison, and helped to make his reputation. Pope defends the poetic art by arguing, in the tradition of ▷ Aristotle, ▷ Horace, and more recently ▷ Boileau, that 'true wit' is merely an 'imitation' of nature, and is not startling and original like the 'false wit' of the discredited 17th-century ▷ 'metaphysical' poets. '*True wit* is *Nature* to Advantage drest,/ What oft was *Thought*, but ne'er so well *Exprest*'. Moreover Nature has already been perfectly understood by the revered ancient Greek and Latin poets, and the modern poet need not go to the trouble of copying direct from it since: 'To copy *Nature* is to copy *Them*'. Exception is however made for those of great genius who '*rise* to *Faults* true Criticks *dare not mend*; . . . And *snatch* a *Grace* beyond the Reach of Art'.

The aphoristic quality of some lines in the poem seems to bear out Pope's ideas on true wit: 'To Err is *Human*; to Forgive, *Divine*'; 'For *Fools* rush in where *Angels* fear to tread'. However the best poetry in the *Essay* is as idiosyncratic and figuratively adventurous as anything in the 'metaphysical' poets of the previous century, as for example the description of the blockheads, too dull to perceive that they are being satirized: 'Still humming on, their drowzy Course they keep,/ And *lash'd* so long, like *Tops*, are lash'd *asleep*' (600–1), or the deliberately bad lines, imitating various vices of versification: 'And ten low Words oft creep in one dull Line' (347). Despite its parade of sober respectability Pope's *Essay* is best seen as the protective camouflage of a brilliant poet adapting to the prosaic temper of the times, rather than a seriously pondered theoretical system. It is however important as a summary of neo-classical and 'Augustan' maxims.

▷ Augustanism.

Essay on Man (1733–4)

After the scurrilities of ▷ *The Dunciad* (1728) ▷ Alexander Pope turned to the philosophical poem which he hoped would crown his poetic career. The *Essay* was published anonymously so as to wrong-foot his enemies, who were not sure whether to damn it as Pope's, or to praise it as superior to anything Pope could have achieved. In four heroic-couplet epistles, addressed to the ▷ Tory politician Lord Bolingbroke, the poet attempts with cheerful optimism to 'vindicate the ways of God to Man', arguing that 'Whatever *is*, is *right*'. Pope expounds the medieval and ▷ Renaissance concept of a 'chain of being', with its primitive blend of theology and natural philosophy, and reconciles it uneasily with the modern empirical science of ▷ Sir Isaac Newton. The work became a kind of handbook of popular ▷ Enlightenment notions throughout Europe and was extensively translated.

It expresses the ▷ Deist view that God can be apprehended through nature, and not only through 'revealed' scriptures. 'Lo! the poor Indian, whose untutor'd mind/ Sees God in clouds, or hears him in the wind'. The 'natural religion' of the poem, influenced by ▷ Bolingbroke, and by the ▷ Whig philosopher, the third ▷ Earl of Shaftesbury, incurred a magisterial rebuke from the Swiss professor of divinity Jean Paul de Crousaz, and Pope, a ▷ Catholic, was embarrassed to discover that his work was potentially heretical. Today Pope's facile blend of science and religion appears spiritually trivial in comparison with both the consistent 'atheist' Deism of a ▷ Rochester, and the sense of original sin of an orthodox Christian such as ▷ Jonathan Swift. The poem does however give brilliant poetic expression to a mood of enlightened confidence and *élan* which characterizes the period, even when what is being said is quite unremarkable: 'Know then thyself, presume not God to scan;/ The proper study of Mankind is Man.' And it contains some fine passages and isolated ▷ couplets: 'The spider's touch, how exquisitely fine!/ Feels at each thread, and lives along the line.'
▷ Enlightenment.

Essays, Bacon's
▷ Bacon, Francis.

Essays in Criticism (1865, 1888)

The two volumes (First Series 1865; Second Series 1888) that contain much of the most important of ▷ Matthew Arnold's literary critical work. The first volume opens with 'The Function of Criticism at the Present Time', a discussion of the relevance of criticism both to creative literature and to society and civilization; it is an example of what ▷ T. S. Eliot was later to call Arnold's 'propaganda for criticism', and it has been influential among 20th-century critics. The second essay, 'The Literary Influence of Academies', makes a case for authoritative standards in culture, and constitutes an implicit criticism of the habits of English culture, again in a way that is still relevant. The remainder of the first volume comprises essays on foreign writers and literature. The Second Series opens with a striking essay on 'The Study of Poetry', in which Arnold puts his view that poetry will supply to the modern world the kind of inspiration that was afforded by great religions in the past – a view which has also been put forward in the 20th century, notably by ▷ I. A. Richards in *The Principles of Literary Criticism*, though he expresses the view in other terms. The remainder of the Second Series consists principally of studies of English poets of the 18th and 19th centuries. On the whole, Arnold's fame rests more on the broad themes of the relationships of literature and society than on his particular studies, though some of these, *eg* on the German poet Heinrich Heine in the First Series, are of great interest.

Essays of Elia (1823; 1833)

A series of essays by ▷ Charles Lamb, published in ▷ *The London Magazine* and then in a collected edition. They emulate the essays of ▷ Joseph Addison and ▷ Sir Richard Steele in the ▷ *Spectator* and ▷ *Tatler* of a century before, but depend less on their content than on Lamb's attempt to win the affection and interest of the reader for himself as a person. The style is whimsical and self-conscious, owing something to the musical and humorously eccentric appeal of ▷ Robert Burton's ▷ *Anatomy of Melancholy* which to some extent it emulates. However, there are passages of witty observation and acute character sketches.

Essentialism

Philosophically, the notion of 'essence' refers to the proposition that the physical world embodies in it a range of fixed and timeless essences which precede existence. In Christianity this is exemplified in the division between the soul and the body, where the latter is relegated to the realm of temporal existence. In ▷ materialist accounts essentialism has come to be associated with attempts to deny the primacy of history as a formative influence on human affairs and human personality. It also challenges the emphasis upon the autonomy of the individual as a theoretically 'free' agent who is the centre of meaning. Any questioning of the notion that essence precedes existence deeply affects the issue of what is assumed to be the coherent nature of human identity. It also resists the attempt to reduce material reality to a set of mental images. To remove the human subject from the centre and to re-inscribe him or her in a series of complex historical relations is to challenge, at a theoretical level, human autonomy. It also suggests that those philosophical arguments which place the individual at the centre of meaning and authority are restrictive in that they propose a view of the world which masks the connection between knowledge and particular human interests.

Establishment

A term which has come into use since World War II to describe the institutions which by long tradition have prestige and authority in England. It probably originates in the official description of the ▷ Church of England as 'the Established Church' – *ie* the official state church, having the Queen at its head. The monarchy itself, and ▷ Parliament, are obviously part of the Establishment, and so is the government bureaucracy loosely known as ▷ 'Whitehall'. Beyond this nucleus, the constituents of the Establishment vary according to the point of view of any particular user of the term, but it nearly always includes the following items: the fashionable men's ▷ clubs in London, especially those with long-established intellectual or political prestige, such as the Athenaeum and the Carlton; the older members and leaders of the older political parties – the Conservatives and ▷ Liberals, and sometimes also of the Labour party; the 'ancient universities' of ▷ Oxford and ▷ Cambridge, and within them, certain colleges of special prestige, such as All Souls and Christ Church at Oxford and King's and Trinity at Cambridge; the ▷ public schools, especially the older and more fashionable ones, such as Winchester, ▷ Eton, ▷ Harrow, Westminster and ▷ Rugby; ▷ *The Times* newspaper, with its special prestige; and the officer corps of the fighting services, especially the Navy. Apart from these, the term may be made to include almost anyone or anything that has prestige from tradition or happens to occupy or constitute a position of authority.

The term 'Establishment' is generally used by those who are at least fairly young and by such as are opposed to, or at least critical of, the traditions of existing authority. The war left Britain with reduced importance in the world but without an urgent crisis to absorb social energies. The result was a feeling of restless discontent among the young, who felt – and to some extent still feel – the nation to have become static and dissatisfying. This mood produced the ▷ 'Angry Young Men' of the 1950s who dissented from the traditions of the nation as represented by the 'Establishment'. The playwright ▷ John Osborne and the novelists ▷ Kingsley Amis and ▷ John Braine were prominent among these writers. In the 1980s the term has come to imply a political bias and one which is particularly Conservative.

Etherege, Sir George (?1634–92)

Dramatist, one of those who set the style of ▷ Restoration comedy after the return to the throne of ▷ Charles II. Etherege may have studied at Cambridge University, and is believed to have spent some of his early adulthood in France. He read law at the Inns of Court. His first play, ▷ *Love in a Tub; Or, The Comical Revenge* (1664), composed partly in rhymed couplets, established him in court circles, but his next play, ▷ *She Wou'd if She Cou'd* (1668) was a relative failure. Both these plays show the influence of ▷ Molière. In 1668 Etherege was appointed secretary to the English ambassador to Constantinople. Returning to England in 1671, Etherege continued to write and his last, most famous play, ▷ *The Man of Mode* came in 1676. Some time after 1677 Etherege married a widow, Mary Arnold, it is said for her fortune. In 1685 he was appointed Ambassador at Ratisbon (Regensburg), and abandoned his wife. He had an affair with the actress ▷ Elizabeth Barry, among his many intrigues with women; Barry bore him a daughter. In 1689 he joined the deposed King ▷ James II in Paris, where he died. Known as 'Gentleman George', Etherege epitomized to many of his contemporaries the sort of hell-raising rake depicted in his plays. The part of Bellair in *The Man of Mode* is thought to be a self-portrait, while the flamboyant Dorimant is said to have been modelled on his friend, the Earl of Rochester. His comedy depends primarily on his witty and often cynical dialogue among characters in fashionable society. Several of his comic types were used by later dramatists, such as ▷ Wycherley, ▷ Behn, and ▷ Congreve, and his

fluent, easy style set a precedent for many of
their plays.
Bib: Rosenfeld, S., *The Letterbook of Sir
George Etherege*; Underwood, D., *Etherege
and the Seventeenth Century Comedy of
Manners.*

Ethnography
The term used in the 19th century for what
later came to be known as ▷ anthropology:
it refers to the descriptive studies of customs
of particular tribes or peoples of particular
regions. Pioneered in Britain by J. C. Prichard
(1786–1848), it did not simply study cultural
phenomena but implicitly ranked them in a
hierarchy of degrees of civilization. Philology,
one of the disciplines included in the science,
was also subject to this politicization.
▷ Aryan.

Eton College
Probably the best known of the ▷ public
schools. It was founded by King ▷ Henry
VI in 1440 and was associated with Henry's
other foundation of King's College,
Cambridge, to which the Eton boys could
pass, usually between the ages of 14 and 18.
24 scholarships are still reserved at King's for
Eton boys capable of passing the requisite
examination, though the earliest age of entry
has for some time been 18. Scholarships to
Eton are open to all boys who are British
subjects and between the ages of 12 and 15.
The fall of Henry VI, and the ▷ Wars of the
Roses that brought about his fall, caused
Eton College to take fee-paying boys to make
up for loss of income by royal patronage;
hence the majority of Eton boys were soon
not the 'poor scholars' for whom it was
founded but sons of nobility and other
wealthy families. In this way Eton early
became associated with privilege. It retains,
however, a very high academic reputation, as
does the sister foundation of King's at
Cambridge. The average number of boys
exceeds 1,100.

Ettrick Shepherd, The
▷ Hogg, James.

Euphemism
▷ Figures of Speech.

Euphues (1578–80)
A prose romance by ▷ John Lyly, in two
parts; the first, *Euphues, or the Anatomy of
Wit* was published in 1578; the second,
Euphues and his England, in 1580. The tales
have very little story; they have been
described as 'pattern books' for courtly
behaviour, especially in love. Their most
striking quality is their elaborate style: long
sentences balance clause against clause and

image against image, so as to produce an
effect of ornament taking priority a long way
over sense. Falstaff in *Henry IV Part I* (II.iv)
parodies Euphues when he is burlesquing the
king, *eg* 'for though the camomile, the more it
is trodden on, the faster it grows, yet youth,
the more it is wasted, the sooner it wears'.
Though often parodied as the language of
fops, the style was much imitated especially
by Elizabethan romance writers such as
▷ Robert Greene in *Menaphon* (1589), and
▷ Thomas Lodge in *Rosalynde* (1590). The
name 'Euphues' is from Greek, and means,
generally, 'well-endowed by nature'. Roger
Ascham in *The Schoolmaster* had already used
it to designate a man well endowed for
learning and able to put it to good use.
Ascham was an admirer of ▷ Castiglione's
The Courtier, and Lyly's cult of the courtly
virtues is in the same tradition. Basic to it is
the conception that nature is not to be
imitated but to be improved upon.

Euphuism
▷ Figures of Speech.

Euripedes (480–406 BC)
The last of the three great Athenian writers
of tragedy, the other two being ▷ Aeschylus
and ▷ Sophocles. Like them, he had no
direct influence upon the Elizabethan period
of English drama, though ▷ Gascoigne's
Jocasta (1575) is a translation of an Italian
adaptation of Euripedes's *Phoenissae*. Like
Aeschylus and Sophocles, however, Euripedes
was admired by ▷ Milton, who emulated
the Greeks in ▷ *Samson Agonistes*. Among
Euripides's surviving plays are *Alcestis,
Medea, Hippolytus, Andromache, Hecuba,
Bacchae, Electra, The Trojan Women, Orestes,
Heracles, Iphigenia at Aulis, Iphigenia among
the Tauri, Ion.*

Europa
▷ Zeus.

Eurydice
▷ Orpheus.

Evangelical Movement
A movement for ▷ Protestant revival in the
Church of England in the late 18th and early
19th century. It was stimulated partly by
▷ John Wesley's ▷ Methodist revival and
the activities of other sects (especially among
the lower classes) outside the Church of
England; it was also a reaction against the
▷ rationalism and scepticism of the 18th-
century aristocracy, and against the
▷ atheism of the ▷ French Revolution.
Politically, the movement tended to be
conservative and was therefore strong among
the ▷ Tories, whereas the ▷ Whigs

(especially their aristocratic leaders such as ▷ Charles James Fox) retained more of the 18th-century worldliness and scepticism. In doctrine the Evangelicals were inclined to be austere, to attach importance to strength of faith and biblical guidance, and to oppose ceremony and ritual. Socially they developed a strong sense of responsibility to their fellow human beings, so that one of their leaders, ▷ William Wilberforce, devoted his life to the cause of abolishing slavery and the slave trade in British dominions, and later Lord Shaftesbury (1801–85) made it his life-work to alleviate the social and working conditions of the working classes. The leaders of the movement were laymen rather than clergy, and upper class rather than lower class, amongst whom the ▷ Nonconformist sects were more actively influential. As the Nonconformists were to contribute to English socialism later in the century a religious rather than a ▷ Marxist inspiration, so the Evangelicals later led to generations of highly responsible, independent-minded intellectuals such as the historians Thomas Babington Macaulay and Trevelyan, and the novelist ▷ Virginia Woolf.

Eve
▷ Eden, Garden of.

Eve of St Agnes (1820)
The 18th-century fashion for pseudo-medieval poetry in ▷ Spenserian stanzas culminated in ▷ John Keats's masterpiece of sensuous aestheticism. Madeline retires to bed on St Agnes' Eve hoping to be granted a vision of her lover by the saint. Meanwhile her lover Porphyro, an enemy to her family, steals into her chamber, aided by an aged servant woman, and watches his beloved undress from a closet. When the girl wakes she finds that Porphyro has prepared a sumptuous banquet of 'cates and dainties'. They make love before fleeing into the storm. The poet employs every extreme of verbal artifice to transform this flimsy escapist fantasy into a pattern of archetypal contrasts: youth and age, fire and ice, security and danger. The interwoven rhyme scheme and the final ▷ alexandrine of each stanza are each made to yield the maximum ornamental and musical effect. Dense, tactual imagery abounds ('the tiger-moth's deep-damask'd wings'). There are crowded alliterations ('the silver, snarling trumpets 'gan to chide'); inventive archaisms ('carven imag'ries', 'blue affrayed eyes'); neologisms ('jellies soother than the creamy curd'); transferred epithets ('azure-lidded sleep', 'silken Samarkand'); exotic compounds ('flaw-blown sleet', 'palsy-twitch'd'); and synaesthetic constructions ('warm gules', 'perfume light'), all designed to overwhelm and delight the reader's senses.

Evelina (1778)
A novel in letters by ▷ Fanny Burney. Evelina has been abandoned by her aristocratic father, and her socially much humbler mother is dead. She has been brought up by her guardian, a solitary clergyman. As a beautiful, well-bred, and intelligent young girl, she pays a visit to a friend in London, where she falls in love with a handsome aristocrat, Lord Orville, is pursued by an unscrupulous rake, Sir Clement Willoughby, and is much embarrassed by vulgar relatives, especially her grandmother, Madame Duval. The convincing and delightful part of the novel consists in its acute and lively social observation, in many ways superior to anything of the sort yet accomplished in the 18th-century novel, and anticipating the maturer art of ▷ Jane Austen in the early 19th century.

Evelyn, John (1620–1706)
Chiefly remembered as a diarist. His diary, published in 1818, covers the years 1641–97, and includes impressions of distinguished contemporaries, customs and manners, and accounts of his travels. He published ▷ translations from Greek, Latin and French, as well as essays on the practical arts (gardening, the cultivation of trees, engraving, architecture). He also wrote an interesting ▷ biography of a court lady (*The Life of Mrs Godolphin*, unpublished until 1847).
▷ Diaries.
Bib: *Diary*, ed. E. S. de Beer; Ponsonby, A., *Life*; Hiscock, W. G., *John Evelyn and his Family Circle*; Marburg, C., *Mr Pepys and Mr Evelyn*.

Every Man in his Humour (1598)
The first important play by ▷ Ben Jonson. By ▷ 'humour' is to be understood a passion generated by irrational egotism, and amounting sometimes to a mania. The play – which is better known in its revised form with English characters than in the first version of 1598 with Italian characters – is a comedy of misunderstandings bred largely through the deceitfulness of Brainworm, a mischievous servant, acting on the absurd humours of the other characters: the jealousy of the merchant Kitely, the credulity of his young wife, the susceptibility of her sister, the bullying boastfulness of the cowardly soldier Bobadill, etc.
▷ Humours, Comedy of.

Every Man out of his Humour (1599)
The second of ▷ Ben Jonson's comedies of
▷ humours, with a range of satirical
portraits: Fastidious Brisk, the foppish
courtier with the sharp tongue; Sordido, the
landowner who delights in shortages because
they increase the price of his grain; Deliro,
the infatuated husband; Puntarvolo, the
knight who takes out an insurance on his
pets; Fungoso, the would-be courtier who is
always behind the fashion, etc. The method
of satire is partly through character sketches
in the tradition of ▷ Theophrastus and
partly through the method which Jonson
developed from ▷ Marlowe (in ▷ *The Jew
of Malta*) of making a character carry his
extravagance to the point of self-caricature.
This play is, however, too narrow in the
range and depth of its satire to rank among
Jonson's great ones. The opening scene
includes a speech (by Asper, lines 93–120)
which contains an explicit account of what
Jonson meant by a ▷ 'Humour'.
▷ Characters, Theophrastian.

Everyman

**Cþere begynneth a treatyſe þow þ hye
fader of heuen ſendeth dethe to ſo-
mon euery creature to come and
gyue a counte of theyr lyues in
this worlde/and is in maner
of a morall playe.**

Taken from *Everyman*

A ▷ morality play dating from the end of
the 15th century, which in its extant form is

based on a Dutch play *Elckerlijc*. It dramatizes
the final acts of Everyman's life, when he is
unexpectedly summoned by Death for a
journey beyond this world. Everyman looks
for companions for his journey, but as Goods,
Kindred et al. vanish away, he discovers that
Good Deeds alone will support him. The
play rehearses Church teaching on the
doctrine of penance and provides a vehicle
for a reaffirmation of the importance of the
clergy as mediators between God and the
laity.
Bib: Cawley, A. C. (ed.), *Everyman*.

Examiner, The
  1 A right-wing (▷ Tory) journal, started
by Lord Bolingbroke and continued by
▷ Jonathan Swift. Engaged in controversy
with the left-wing (▷ Whig) writers,
▷ Joseph Addison and ▷ Sir Richard
Steele.
  2 A weekly periodical founded by John
and ▷ Leigh Hunt in 1808, famous for its
radical politics. It had no political allegiance,
but criticized public affairs, in the words of
Leigh Hunt's friend ▷ John Keats, 'from a
principle of taste'. In 1813 the Hunts were
sent to prison for two years for exposing the
gross flattery in another paper of the Prince
Regent (later George IV).

Excalibur
A modification of 'Caliburnus', the name of
▷ King Arthur's sword, forged in
▷ Avalon, in ▷ Geoffrey of Monmouth's
Historia Regum Britanniae. In later versions
of Arthurian narrative, the name Excalibur is
applied to the sword which Arthur receives,
mysteriously, from the hand of the ▷ Lady
of the Lake (as a replacement for his first
sword, drawn from the stone). When Arthur
is mortally wounded, he arranges for
Excalibur to be returned to the lake. One of
his knights (most commonly Bedevere but
sometimes Girflet) is finally persuaded to
throw the sword into the lake, where it is
caught and brandished by a hand, before
disappearing below. Both ▷ Malory and
▷ Tennyson relate this episode in their
respective Arthurian narratives.

Excursion, The (1814)
A long didactic poem in ▷ blank verse by
▷ William Wordsworth. It was intended to
be the middle part of a three-part
philosophical poem, to be called *The Recluse*,
but the other two parts were never written.
▷ *The Prelude*, intended as an introduction
to *The Recluse*, was completed in 1805, but
was not published until after Wordsworth's
death in 1850. Book I of *The Excursion*,

which contains the most enduring poetry in the work, comprises a piece written some years before: ▷ *Margaret or the Ruined Cottage*. Books II–IV contain discussion between the poem's protagonist, the Wanderer, and his friend, the Solitary, who lacks faith in man and God. In Books V–VII a new character, the Pastor, relates the histories of some of his former parishioners buried in the churchyard. The last two books are concerned with the degradation of the poor by industrial expansion, and proposes educational reforms.

Exhibition, The Great

Held in 1851, in Hyde Park in London, it was the first international exhibition of the products of industry and celebrated the peak of the British ▷ industrial revolution. It was regarded as a triumph for British prosperity and enlightenment, though by some critics, *eg* the philanthropist ▷ Lord Shaftesbury, as concealing the scandal of immense urban slums. Its principal building, the Crystal Palace, was a pioneer construction in the materials of glass and cast-iron. The architect was Joseph Paxton.

Existentialism

A modern school of philosophy which has had great influence on European literature since World War II. The doctrines to which the term has been applied are in fact very various, but a number of common themes may be identified. The first is the primacy of the individual, and of individual choice, over systems and concepts which attempt to explain him or her. The second is the absurdity of the universe; reality, it is claimed, always evades adequate explanation, and remains radically contingent and disordered. This absurdity causes anxiety, but also makes freedom possible, since our actions also cannot be causally explained or predicted. Neither the behaviour nor the nature of others can be understood by observation. Existentialism sees freedom of choice as the most important fact of human existence. According to ▷ Jean-Paul Sartre, consciousness of our own freedom is the sign of 'authentic experience', as opposed to the 'bad faith' of believing oneself bound. Investigation of this freedom involves investigation of the nature of being, and this has caused existentialism to form two main streams, the first atheistic, which interprets the free individual existence as self-created, and the second religious, which interprets individual existence as dependent on transcendent Being. The best-known leaders of existentialism have been the philosophers

Martin Heidegger (1889–1976) and Karl Jaspers (1883–1969) in Germany, and Sartre (1905–80) and the philosopher and dramatist Gabriel Marcel (1889–1973) in France. Marcel represents the religious stream whose progenitor was the 19th-century Danish thinker Sören Kierkegaard (1813–55).

Existentialism has had relatively little influence on British philosophy, because of the strong empirical tradition in Britain, although the novelist and philosopher ▷ Iris Murdoch has termed modern British empiricists existentialist in her essay *The Sovereignty of Good*. Correspondingly, existentialism has had a less powerful influence on literature than in France, where authors like Sartre, ▷ Simone de Beauvoir, and Albert Camus have expounded its doctrines in, for example, such works as Sartre's trilogy of novels, *Roads to Freedom* (1947–9) and his play *No Exit* (1944), or Camus's novel *The Outsider* (1942). Nevertheless, these doctrines have been important in two ways. First, they have directly influenced a number of experimental novelists with continental affinities. The most important writer in this category is ▷ Samuel Beckett in whose plays and novels the isolation and anxiety of the characters combine with an awareness of the issues of manipulation and choice implicit in the narrative and dramatic modes, to present existential dilemmas with unrivalled power. Second, existentialist doctrines have contributed much to the general ethos of ▷ post-modernism, and affected a number of major writers, prompting either admiration or resistance. Thus the post-modern concern with the nature of fictionality arises in part from the sense that neither individuals nor reality as a whole can be adequately conceptualized. The author's manipulation of his or her characters has provided a fruitful metaphor for the exploration of issues of freedom, as for example in the work of ▷ John Fowles, ▷ Iris Murdoch and ▷ Muriel Spark. Existentialism speaks powerfully to the sense of the 20th century as a chaotic and even catastrophic era, in which certainties have been lost and man is faced with the abyss of nothingness, or of his own capability for evil. It lays stress on extreme situations, which produce dread, arising from awareness of freedom of choice (according to Sartre) or awareness of original sin (according to Kierkegaard). Extremity and existential dread are important in the work of ▷ William Golding and ▷ Patrick White, and, earlier in the century, ▷ Joseph Conrad, who in this respect as in others anticipates the 20th-century *Zeitgeist*.

Expedition of Humphrey Clinker, The (1771)
▷ *Humphrey Clinker, The Expedition of*.

Experience, Songs of
▷ *Songs of Innocence and Experience*.

Expressionism

Expressionism was originally intended to define an artistic movement which flourished at the beginning of the 20th century in Europe, especially in Germany. The expressionist painters, such as Edvard Munch and Vasili Kandinsky, built upon the departure from realism of Vincent Van Gogh and Henri Matisse, and developed towards the expression of feeling through colour and form. This often led to exaggeration and distortion, which induced unease in the viewing public. Similar haunting and irrational imagery were used in German expressionist cinema, such as Robert Wiene's *The Cabinet of Dr Caligari* (1919) and F. W. Murnau's *Nosferatu* (1922).

The origins of expressionism as a theatrical movement are to be found in the work of a number of German dramatists who wrote between 1907 and the early 1920s. These include Ernst Barlach, Reinhard Goering, Walter Hasenclever, Carl Hauptmann, Franz Kafka, Georg Kaiser, Oscar Kokoschka, Carl Sternheim and Ernst Toller. Even ▷ Brecht was influenced by the movement in his early days. Although their individual styles differ greatly the expressionist playwrights rejected the 'objective' approach of naturalism and developed a highly emotional and subjective form of dramatic expression which aimed to explore the 'essence' of human experience. In their view this could be revealed only by getting beyond the surface appearances of ordinary life and exploring man's subconscious desires and visions. The impulse for this was revolutionary, if politically unclear. ▷ Strindberg, Wedekind, ▷ Freud and ▷ Nietzsche were the idols of the movement. Bourgeois ideology was the enemy and the uniting vision ubiquitously advocated was the rebirth of man (with the emphasis very much on the male) in touch with his spirit and free from petty social restraints. The use of exaggerated gesture, disturbing sound, colour and movement was a vital part of the dramatists' technique of shocking the audience and conveying ecstatic or *Angst*-ridden states of being. Short disconnected scenes replaced carefully constructed plots and scenery was distorted and hallucinatory rather than realistic. Later dramatists, such as Eugene O'Neill, Elmer Rice and ▷ Sean O'Casey, have tended to borrow from the dramatic language of expressionism without necessarily sharing the fervour of their German predecessors.

Extravaganza

Any composition which relies on its fantastic content for its effect. It is usually comic and irregular in its construction. Unlike ▷ farce, however, it is not a defined literary mode; consequently it more often describes a critical reaction to a work than the author's intention in the work.

F

Fabian Society
A large society of socialistic intellectuals, closely bound up with the British ▷ Labour Party. It was founded in 1884 and named after the Roman general Fabius Cunctator – 'Fabius the Delayer' – who in the 3rd century BC saved Rome from the Carthaginian army under Hannibal (▷ Carthage), by using a policy of attrition instead of open battle, *ie* he destroyed the army by small attacks on isolated sections of it, instead of risking total defeat by confronting Hannibal with the entire Roman army. The Fabian Society similarly advocates socialism by piecemeal action through parliamentary reform instead of risking disaster by total revolution; this policy has been summarized in the phrase 'the inevitability of gradualness'. The Fabians were among the principal influences leading to the foundation of the Labour Party in 1900. The years between 1884 and 1900 were those of its greatest distinction; they were led by ▷ George Bernard Shaw and Sidney and ▷ Beatrice Webb, and made their impact through the Fabian Essays on social and economic problems. They always advocated substantial thinking on solid evidence, in contrast to the more idealistic and 'utopian' socialism of such writers as ▷ William Morris.

Fable
In its narrower, conventional definition, a fable is a short story, often but not necessarily about animals, illustrating a piece of popular wisdom, or explaining unscientifically a fact of nature. Animals are commonly used as characters because they are readily identified with simplified human qualities, as the fox with cunning, the lamb with meekness, the wolf with greed, the ass with stupidity. In primitive folklore, fables are worldwide. The tales in ▷ Rudyard Kipling's *Just So Stories* (1902) for children resemble the kind of primitive fable which seeks to explain facts of nature (such as how the leopard got its spots) without the aid of science. Sophisticated literatures favour the moral fable, the leading European tradition for which was established by the Greek fabulist ▷ Aesop. To this tradition belongs the medieval Latin and German beast satire of Reynard the Fox, from which is derived the best strict fable in English – Chaucer's ▷ *Nun's Priest's Tale* of the Cock and the Fox in the ▷ *Canterbury Tales*. Almost equally good are ▷ Robert Henryson's *Thirteen Morall Fabilis*. However, though fables are plentiful in English as in every literature, used

illustratively and ornamentally amongst other matter, English literature is comparatively poor in strict fabulists. ▷ John Gay's *Fables* are usually regarded as pleasant minor works; ▷ John Dryden's *Fables Ancient and Modern* (1699) are mostly not fables. Rudyard Kipling's *Jungle Books* (1894, 5), like his *Just So Stories*, are minor children's classics. ▷ T. F. Powys' *Fables* (1929) are original and beautiful, and ▷ George Orwell's *Animal Farm* (1945) is very well known.

A broader interpretation of the term 'fable' allows a wider range of depiction: a tale which is a comment in metaphor on human nature, less directly figurative than allegory, and less roundabout in reaching its point than parable. In this broader meaning, English literature perhaps produced the greatest of all fables, Swift's ▷ *Gulliver's Travels*. But this broader interpretation admits an aspect of fable into almost any serious fiction; thus critics sometimes speak of a novelist's 'fable' in trying to express the underlying intention implicit in a novel. A modern view of this broader interpretation of the fable is expressed by ▷ William Golding in his essay 'Fable' in *The Hot Gates*, and its practice is exemplified in his own novels.
▷ Allegory.

Fabliau
Derived from 'fable', the term is applied to a medieval genre of short, humorous narratives, particularly popular in Old French poetry of the 13th century, which are usually structured around a battle of wits of some kind. Wit and ingenuity are celebrated in these stories; their outcomes may not conform to the dictates of a Christian morality. Characteristically, fabliaux are located in contemporary settings and many, though not all, have plots centred an adulterous situations. Explicitly sexual, scatological and bawdy terms are frequently employed in these narratives, as befits the kind of action they depict. ▷ Chaucer is one of the first English writers to work in this genre (in the ▷ *Miller's Tale*, the ▷ *Reeve's Tale*, the ▷ *Shipman's Tale*, for example), but from the evidence of the Anglo–Norman fabliaux in ▷ Harley 2253, it is clear that fabliaux were circulating in England before the composition of the ▷ *Canterbury Tales*. Many of the narratives in ▷ Boccaccio's ▷ *Decameron* are reworkings of fabliaux plots.

Factories
In the sense of industrial buildings in which large numbers of men were at work under one roof, as opposed to domestic industry

with the workers in their own homes, factories
existed to some extent in the 16th century. It
was in the 18th century, however, with the
invention of labour-saving machines and then
of steam power to drive them, that the
factory system became general. Pockets of
domestic industry continued well into the
19th century, but it became increasingly the
exception. Large industrial towns grew up
haphazardly to accommodate the new
factories; there is a vivid description of an
extreme example in ▷ Benjamin Disraeli's
novel ▷ *Sybil*. The employment of masses
of labour tended to dehumanize relations
between employer and employees, and
instigated a new kind of class war;
▷ Elizabeth Gaskell's novels ▷ *North and
South* and ▷ *Mary Barton*, and ▷ Charles
Dickens's ▷ *Hard Times* illustrate this.
The first Factory Act to have an important
effect in the improving of conditions was that
of 1833; by then the public conscience was
truly aroused and the Ten Hours Act of 1847
restricted hours of labour. The main intention
of the early Factory Acts was to prevent the
employment of young children and to limit
the hours of employment of women; they
were made effective by the use of Factory
Inspectors. Later Factory Acts have sought to
prevent the use of dangerous machinery and
to ensure that factories were healthy places to
work in. Some employers came to see that it
was in their own interests to make factory
conditions as healthy and pleasant as possible:
Andrew Undershaft in ▷ George Bernard
Shaw's play *Major Barbara* is an example of
an enlightened factory owner of the 20th-
century sort.

Another use of the word 'factory' is to
denote a centre for 'factors', *ie* men of
commerce who transact trade on behalf of
their employers. In the 18th century the
▷ East India Company established such
factories in India, *eg* at Madras.

▷ Anti-industrialism; Industrial
Revolution.

Faerie Queene, The (1590–6)
▷ Edmund Spenser's unfinished
▷ allegorical ▷ romance. *The Faerie
Queene* was first mentioned in correspondence
by Spenser in 1580, and was probably
circulating in manuscript form by 1588.
Books I–III were published in 1590, and a
second edition which contained Books IV–
VI appeared in 1596. In 1609 a folio edition
of the poem appeared, which contained the
first six books of the poem, together with
the ▷ 'Mutabilitie Cantos'. This is all of
the work which has survived, though

The Redcrosse Knight kills Error in Book
One of *The Faerie Queene*

whether any more was written is
doubtful.

The design of the poem, and Spenser's
general conception of what the poem should
set out to achieve, is recorded in a letter from
Spenser to ▷ Sir Walter Ralegh which was
published in the first edition of 1590. Here
Spenser explains that his intention was to
'fashion a gentleman or noble person', and we
can thus understand the poem as forming
part of that ▷ Renaissance desire to create
and sustain a personal identity. But the work
is also a legendary history and celebration of
the emergent British state and its monarch,
▷ Elizabeth I. The urgency of this project
is understandable given Spenser's own
residence in the unstable environment of
Ireland for much of the period of the poem's
composition.

In structure the poem follows the
adventures of six knights, representing
(Spenser claimed in his letter to Ralegh) the
▷ Aristotelian virtues. But the poem is
episodic rather than possessed of a cumulative

narrative structure. At the same time, to mention Aristotle is to mention only one of the poem's many progenitors, which include ▷ Plato, ▷ Ludovico Ariosto's *Orlando Furioso*, ▷ Torquato Tasso, ▷ Virgil and ▷ Arthurian romance.

The Faerie Queene is perhaps best thought of as a rich synthesis of ▷ Protestant and ▷ humanist ideals, and, at the same time, an anxious declaration of faith in the vision of national identity which it is the poem's task to display. Its influence on later writers, especially ▷ John Milton, was enormous.

▷ Arthur, King; Belphoebe; Duessa; Fidessa; Florimell; Gloriana; Orgoglio; Red Cross Knight.

Bib: Hamilton, A. C. (ed.), *The Faerie Queen*.

Fainlight, Ruth (b 1931)
Poet and translator. Born in New York, Fainlight lives in Britain, although she is an American citizen. Her volumes of poetry include: *Cages* (1966); *The Region's Violence* (1973); *Twenty One Poems* (1975); *Another Full Moon* (1976); *Sibyls and Others* (1980) and *Climates* (1983). She has also translated the Portuguese poet Sophia de Mello Breyner.

Fair Maid of the West, The (1600/1630)
A romantic and ▷ picaresque comedy in two parts (1600 and 1630) by ▷ Thomas Heywood. It is set during Essex's expedition to the Azores in 1597 and dramatizes the adventures of the chivalrous Master Spencer and the beautiful Bess Bridges, whom he champions and who rescues him in turn after his capture by the Spaniards.

Fairbairns, Zoe (b 1948)
Novelist. Her novels are: *Live as Family* (1968); *Down: An Exploration* (1969); *Benefits* (1982); *Stand We At Last* (1983); *Here Today* (1984); *Closing* (1987). She uses a range of genres, such as ▷ science fiction (*Benefits*) or the crime thriller (*Here Today*) to explore the development of the ▷ feminist consciousness. *Stand We At Last* recounts the lives of a succession of women from the middle of the 19th century up to the 1970s, and may be compared with *The Seven Ages* by ▷ Eva Figes in its project of rediscovering the unwritten history of women's experience.

Fairies
Supernatural beings such as provide material for folk-tales all over the world. In Britain, as in many other countries, fairies have been regarded as neither good nor evil, but sometimes mischievous and sometimes

beneficient, as human behaviour has given opportunity and invitation (see for instance Mercutio's speech on Queen Mab in ▷ Shakespeare's ▷ *Romeo and Juliet*, I.iv). Belief in them has been thought to be a vestige of pre-Christian beliefs in nature-spirits. Stories about them sometimes include elements of medieval romance and classical myth; thus in Shakespeare's ▷ *Midsummer Night's Dream*, ▷ Oberon derives from a 13th-century French romance, *Huon de Bordeaux*, ▷ Titania is used as a version of Diana the huntress in ▷ Ovid's ▷ *Metamorphoses* and ▷ Puck, also called Robin Goodfellow, is from English folklore. ▷ Spenser's Faerie Queen Gloriana gives Queen Elizabeth I the allure of romance at the same time as identifying her with the Platonic ideal of Glory. Although ▷ witches play a part in fairy stories, witchcraft, as exemplified by 16th- and 17th-century belief and manifested in Shakespeare's ▷ *Macbeth*, is altogether more serious and sinister, and requires separate treatment.

Belief in fairies – or half-belief – may have been widespread among all classes in England until the 17th century, but since then it has steadily shrunk even among country folk. It has persisted longest in Wales, north-west Scotland, south-west England and especially in Ireland; hence the comparatively serious use to which fairies are put in the verse of the Irish poet ▷ W. B. Yeats, *eg The Man Who Saw the Fairies*.

Among popular beliefs about fairies have been these: that they are small, hence sometimes called 'the little people'; they are used to explain natural phenomena such as 'fairy rings' on grass, said to be the traces of their midnight dances; they foretell the fortunes of children (fairy godmothers); they are supposed to steal human babies and leave fairy children ('changelings') in their stead. Many subdivisions of fairy exist, such as elves (▷ Elf), pixies, ▷ gnomes, brownies, goblins.

▷ Fairy tales.

Fairs
The early fairs were large markets held at particular times of the year in or near country towns; they attracted buyers and sellers from a distance. Until this century, every country town held its weekly market day on which the farmers of the district brought their cattle and vegetable produce for sale; a fair was a grand market, attracting trade from a wider region, and lasting for a week or more. They became established institutions after the ▷ Norman Conquest, and the largest, such

as the Stourbridge Fair at Cambridge, were of national and even international importance. Towns found them profitable, not merely because they profited local craftsmen, but because the town corporations were able to collect special payments or 'dues' from the visiting merchants. Apart from commerce, fairs afforded entertainment of many sorts; today their commercial importance is slight and a fair is thought of as merely a travelling collection of roundabouts, swings, peepshows, etc. attractive mainly to children. These would formerly have been regarded as mere 'sideshows'; however they always had prominence and particularly popular were the exhibitions of 'monsters' such as 'the fattest woman in the world', animals with two heads, and other abnormalities.

Fairy tales
Fairy tales have often been seen as simple narratives to amuse children, but their more pervasive significance was noted as early as the 17th century when writers used the stories for a didactic purpose. In the 19th century there was an emphasis on the moral role and related psychological impact of the tales. The major development in the theoretic treatment of fairy tales occurred, however, with ▷ Freud and ▷ Jung: the former saw the narratives as a way in which the subjects could work out their psychic problems, while the latter looked for universal and archetypal patterns. More recently the stories have been linked to a process of socialization as well as the imposition on girls of patriarchal value judgements.
　▷ Women, Status of.
Bib: Zipes, J., *Don't Bet on the Prince*.

Faithful Shepherdess, The (1610)
A ▷ pastoral romance by ▷ John Fletcher which, in a short but influential preface about tragicomedy, acknowledges its indebtedness to the pastoral idiom of G. B. Guarini, the author of the seminal and famous pastoral play, *Il Pastor Fido* (1598), and it thereby contributed to the vogue of English tragicomedies in the 1610s. But, whereas Fletcher's definition of tragicomedy specifically precluded death from its imaginative idiom, the English uses of the genre have tended to weld together the tragic and comic modes in a harsher manner and allowed death its full place in Arcadia.

Falconer, William (1732–69)
Author of a popular poem, *The Shipwreck* (1762; revised 1769), describing the sinking of a ship off the coast of Greece. Falconer himself drowned at sea.

Falstaff, Sir John
A character in ▷ Shakespeare's history plays, ▷ *Henry IV, Parts I and II*, and in the comedy ▷ *The Merry Wives of Windsor*. His death is described in ▷ *Henry V* (II.ii). In the history plays he is a very active comic character, embodying fleshly indulgence, and considered to be the chief injurious influence on Prince Hal (Henry), the heir to the throne. Though a fully realized character in his own right, he clearly carries also some force from medieval ▷ allegory, representing the temptations of physical indulgence or 'riot'. Accordingly Hal, once anointed as King Henry v, casts him off at the end of *Henry IV, Part II*. In *The Merry Wives* he is much less substantial, and plays the role of a comparatively commonplace buffoon.
　▷ Oldcastle, Sir John.

Family
Family has been in most societies the route by which property, wealth and status or their lack have been transmitted. ▷ Marriage, in any formalized sense, according to some authorities did not become established in England until after the 11th century, before which polygamy was practised. The household, which included others beside members related by ties of kin, was the domestic unit of significance and the economically productive unit. Only at the ▷ Reformation did a new ideology of marriage and of the parental role develop, which gave dignity to the wife as her husband's helpmeet and emphasis to the duty of father and mother to raise their children in the fear and knowledge of God. In the 18th century this ideal grew, with an emphasis on the importance of maternal intimacy: suckling her own children, instead of sending them out to nurse, playing with them and instructing them were construed as the proper activities of the mother. The male role throughout was defined in relation to positions held outside the home with which his greater authority inside it was associated. The following century marked the refinement of the concept of 'separate spheres': public life was stringently demarcated from the private world of home, in which children were reared and the wife secluded. Ideas of 'the child' are similarly period-specific.
Bib: Stone, L., *The Family, Sex and Marriage*; Davidoff, L. and Hall, C., *Family Fortunes*.

Far from the Madding Crowd (1874)
A novel by ▷ Thomas Hardy. The title is a quotation from ▷ *Elegy Written in a Country Churchyard* by ▷ Thomas Gray. It is one

of Hardy's ▷ Wessex novels, and the first of real substance, following the comparatively slight ▷ *Under the Greenwood Tree*. The central character is Bathsheba Everdene, who is loved by three men: Farmer Boldwood, a solid but passionate ▷ squire; Gabriel Oak, a shepherd, who loves her with quiet constancy and wins her in the end, and the glamorous soldier, Sergeant Troy, whom she marries first. Troy combines fascinating gallantry with ruthless egoism; he allows his wife-to-be, Fanny Robin, to die in a workhouse, and is capricious and cruel to Bathsheba; he is eventually murdered by Boldwood. A crude outline such as this brings out the ballad-like quality of the story, characteristic of all Hardy's novels but more subtly rendered in later ones. Its distinction of substance is in Hardy's intimate understanding and presentation of the rural surroundings of the characters, and in the contrast between the urbane attractions of Troy and the rough but environmentally vigorous qualities of Boldwood and Oak. Bathsheba herself is a capricious and colourful heroine, not presented with psychological depth but with confident assertiveness which makes her convincing.

Farce
A term used for comedy in which ▷ realism is sacrificed for the sake of extravagant humour. Its derivation is from stuffing used in cookery, and as a literary term it was applied to light and frivolous material introduced by actors into the medieval ▷ mystery plays. Normally it is now applied to lightweight comedies only.

Farquhar, George (1678–1707)
Dramatist, whose topics and style straddle those of the ▷ Restoration period, and of the 18th century, showing some elements of ▷ Reform Comedy. The son of a Church of England clergyman, Farquhar was born in Londonderry, and entered Trinity College, Dublin. Lacking funds, and the ambition to study, however, he left and turned to acting, at the ▷ Smock Alley Theatre in Dublin. There he met ▷ Robert Wilks, who became his friend and acted in several of his subsequent plays. The accidental wounding of another actor during a performance of Dryden's *The Indian Emperor* shocked him profoundly, and he left the stage and turned to writing for the theatre instead. In 1697 Farquhar went to London, where his first play, *Love and a Bottle* was performed successfully at the Theatre Royal, in 1698. With ▷ *The Constant Couple; Or, A Trip to the Jubilee* (1699) he became fully established

as a popular dramatist, Wilks acting the role of Sir Harry Wildair, and ▷ Susanna Verbruggen the part of Lady Lurewell. Sir Harry later became a favourite breeches part for actresses, including ▷ Peg Woffington. The play's sequel, *Sir Harry Wildair* (1701) was less successful. Farquhar obtained a commission in the army, but failed to obtain advancement. He did however travel through various parts of England, recruiting for the military, and used his experiences of army life to satiric effect in ▷ *The Recruiting Officer* (1706). The influence of changing theories about drama which took hold toward the turn of the century is evident in several of Farquhar's plays, especially *The Twin Rivals* (1702) and his last play, ▷ *The Beaux' Stratagem* (1707), which show a more humane and spontaneous attitude to life than the works of some authors of the high Restoration period. The contemporary dramatist ▷ Susannah Centlivre praised him for avoiding the risqué elements which so offended the Rev. Jeremy Collier, prompting him to write his *A Short View of the Immorality and Profaneness of the English Stage*. Centlivre's fulsome appreciation of Farquhar led to a correspondence between them, later published. In 1703 Farquhar married a woman who is said to have deceived him into believing her an heiress. He died in poverty after a lengthy illness.
Bib: Farmer, A. J., *Farquhar*.

Farrell, J. G. (James Gordon) (1935–79)
Novelist. His best work consisted of carefully researched, and powerfully imagined historical novels. *The Siege of Krishnapur* (1973), a fictitious account of the Indian mutiny, won the Booker Prize; *The Singapore Grip* (1978) recounts the collapse of British power in Malaya, culminating in the Japanese capture of Singapore in 1942; *Troubles* (1970) is set in Ireland in 1919. These three novels, which form a kind of trilogy concerned with the long demise of the British Empire, represent an ambitious attempt at historical novel-writing. His career was ended by his early death on a fishing expedition in Ireland. Other novels are: *A Man From Elsewhere* (1963); *The Lung* (1965); *A Girl in the Head* (1967); *The Hill Station* (unfinished, 1981).

Fascist
The fasces, a bundle of rods bound round an axe, were the symbol of the civil power of ancient Rome. The symbol was adopted by Mussolini's Fascist party which ruled Italy from 1922 to 1945. It was right-wing and anti-communist. The National Socialist Party in Germany (1933–45) and the Falangist

Party that helped to bring Franco to power in Spain in 1938 were akin to the Italian Fascist party, and to some extent modelled on it. This is also true of the smaller Fascist parties in other countries, though Oswald Mosley's British Union of Fascists was never politically significant. All such parties favoured strong nationalism, political dictatorship, the suppression of ▷ communism and socialism; under German influence, they were usually marked by racial prejudice.

English writers, especially between 1930 and 1945, were predominantly left-wing in sympathy, and used the term 'Fascist' in the sense of right-wing, despotic, reactionary, brutal, etc. and applied it to any person or body of people whose politics they disliked. This abusive use of 'Fascist', though tiresome and misleading, is not due merely to political prejudice: few political ideas of historical importance have been so closely associated with brutality as Fascism, and few have contributed so little of significance to political thinking. Nonetheless, Fascists' emphasis on leadership and (implicitly) on aristocracy of the sort that requires a trained élite and not hereditary privilege, appealed in varying degree to some leading British and American writers of the period 1920–40, such as ▷ W. B. Yeats and ▷ Ezra Pound. ▷ T. S. Eliot, ▷ Wyndham Lewis and ▷ D. H. Lawrence have also been accused of Fascist leanings. All these writers had right-wing tendencies because they reacted strongly against the simplifications of social theory resulting from the traditions of 19th-century liberalism and from ▷ Marxist Socialism; only Pound became deeply identified with Fascism.

Fathers of the Church
Early Christian writers, important in the formation of Christian doctrine. They included Cyprian (3rd century), Athanasius (4th century), Gregory of Nazianzus (4th century), Augustine of Hippo (4th–5th century), Pope Gregory 1, the Great (end of the 6th century). Those Fathers who were nearly contemporary with the original Apostles of Christ are often called the Apostolic Fathers; they include Clement of Rome, Polycarp of Smyrna, Ignatius of Antioch – all of the 1st century or the 1st and early 2nd centuries.

Fauns
In ancient Roman myth, Faunus was a nature-god. Under Greek influence, he became identified with the Greek nature god ▷ Pan, and is depicted with horns and goat legs. Like Pan, he was credited with a following of merry and mischievous little fauns.

Faust
The Faust myth is much older than those legends which crystallize round the historical figure of Faust and form a part of it. The myth of men seeking great earthly power from demons at the cost of their immortal souls goes back to the ancient Jews at about the time of Christ, and centres on several figures of medieval European Christendom. In the 16th century the myth received new vitality through the influence upon it of various bodies of ideas: ▷ Renaissance humanism, in its sceptical and critical spirit; ▷ neo-Platonic mysticism, in its conception of the potentially immense reach of the human mind; and the Protestant ▷ Reformation, in its adherence to the pure Word of God as opposed to ▷ humanist claims for reason and Catholic claims for authority alike. The historical Faust was an early 16th-century German philosopher who was ridiculed by other intellectuals for his extravagant pretensions to magical powers. Nonetheless, pamphlets and plays built up a widespread, partly comic and partly serious image of him as the pattern of human arrogance eternally damned for his preference of human learning over the Holy Word. ▷ Mephistopheles, the devil with whom Faust made his bargain, was himself condemned to eternal suffering and regarded himself in this light. ▷ Christopher Marlowe's ▷ *Doctor Faustus* is much the most interesting product of this tradition.

▷ Wolfgang Goethe's masterpiece *Faust* (Pt. I 1808; II 1832) gives an entirely new turn to the myth. Mephistopheles is no longer the evil spirit in eternal torment, but 'the spirit that denies', *ie* that refuses to acknowledge the intrinsic reality of any human or spiritual value. Thus Goethe's version of the myth became itself one of the great myths of modern man. The struggle is no longer between earthly power and spiritual holiness: it is between the cynicism of those who deny that there is goodness in the search for goodness, and the dedication of those who make the search.

▷ German influence on English literature.

Faustus
▷ *Doctor Faustus, The Tragical History of.*

Feinstein, Elaine (b 1930)
Poet, novelist and translator. Born in Lancashire and educated at Cambridge, Feinstein has taught literature at Essex University as well as working in publishing. Her poetry is written closely from personal situations, and is deeply experiential. Her volumes of verse include: *In a Green Eye*

(1966) (her first collection); *The Magic Apple Tree* (1971); *The Celebrants* (1973); *Some Unease and Angels: Selected Poems* (1977) and *The Feast of Eurydice* (1980). She has also edited an edition of Marina Tsvetayeva's poetry, and her novels include *Children of the Rose* (1975) and *The Border* (1984).

Felix Holt the Radical (1866)

A novel by ▷ George Eliot. The hero is a talented young working man who makes it his vocation to educate the political intelligence of his fellow-workers. His rival for the love of Esther Lyon, the daughter of a ▷ nonconformist minister, is the local landowner, Harold Transome, also a radical politician though pursuing a more conventional political career. George Eliot makes Holt utter high-minded speeches which weaken the reality he is supposed to possess. On the other hand, a subsidiary theme which concerns Harold Transome's mother, the secret of Harold's illegitimacy, and his hostility to the lawyer, Jermyn, who is really his father, is treated so well that it is among the best examples of George Eliot's art.

Fell, Alison (b 1944)

Poet, journalist and fiction writer. Born in Dumfries, Fell has worked as a sculptor, with women's theatre and for the feminist journal *Spare Rib*, for whom she edited the fiction ▷ anthology, *Hard Feelings*. As well as her volume of poetry, *Kisses For Mayakovsy*, in 1981 she published a children's novel, and two novels for Virago in 1984 and 1987.

Feminism

In literary criticism this term is used to describe a range of critical positions which argues that the distinction between 'masculine' and 'feminine' (▷ gender) is formative in the generation of all discursive practices. In its concern to bring to the fore the particular situation of women in society 'feminism' as a focus for the raising of consciousness has a long history, and can be taken to embrace an interest in all forms of women's writing throughout history. In its essentialist (▷ Essentialism) guise, feminism proposes a range of experiences peculiar to women, which are, by definition, denied to men, and which it seeks to emphasize in order to compensate for the oppressive nature of a society rooted in what it takes to be patriarchal authority. A more materialist (▷ Materialism) account would emphasize the extent to which gender difference is a cultural construction, and therefore amenable to change by concerted political action. Traditional materialist accounts, especially

those of ▷ Marx, have placed the issue of 'class' above that of 'gender', but contemporary feminism regards the issue of 'gender' as frequently cutting across 'class' divisions, and raising fundamental questions about the social role of women in relations of production and exchange. Insofar as all literature is 'gendered', then feminist literary criticism is concerned with the analysis of the social construction of 'femininity' and 'masculinity' in particular texts. One of its major objectives is to expose how hitherto 'masculine' criticism has sought to represent itself as a universal experience. Similarly, the focus is adjusted in order to enable literary works themselves to disclose the ways in which the experiences they communicate are determined by wider social assumptions about gender difference, which move beyond the formal boundaries of the text. To this extent feminism is necessarily the focus of an interdisciplinary approach to literature, psychology, sociology and philosophy.

Psychoanalytic feminism, for example, often overlaps with socialist feminism. It approaches the concept of gender as a problem rather than a given, and draws on ▷ Freud's emphasis on the instability of sexual identities. The fact that femininity – and masculinity – are never fully acquired, once and for all, suggests a relative openness allowing for changes in the ways they are distributed. Literature's disturbance and exploration of ways of thinking about sexual difference have proved a rich source for feminist critics.

▷ Women's movement.

Bib: de Beauvoir, S., *The Second Sex*; Greene, G. and Kahn, C. (eds.), *Making a Difference: Feminist Literary Criticism*; Millett, K., *Sexual Politics*; Spender. D., *Feminist Theorists*; Wollstonecraft, M., *Vindication of the Rights of Women*.

Fenians

An Irish patriotic and revolutionary society founded by Irish immigrants to the U.S.A. in 1858; its aim was to unite Irishmen all over the world to secure the independence of Ireland from British rule. The original Fenians were a semi-legendary band of warriors under the leadership of Finn Mac Coul, said to have lived in the 3rd century AD.

▷ Finn.

Fenton, James (b 1949)

Poet. Educated at Oxford, Fenton has worked as a journalist in Britain (as theatre critic for *The Sunday Times*) and abroad, including in Vietnam. His publications include: *Terminal*

Moraine (1972); *A Vacant Possession* (1978); *A German Requiem* (1980); *The Memory of War* (1982).

Ferdinand

The most conspicuous characters bearing this name in English literature are:

1 the King of Navarre in ▷ Shakespeare's ▷ *Love's Labour's Lost*

2 the son of King Alonso of Naples and lover of Prospero's daughter Miranda in ▷ Shakespeare's ▷ *The Tempest*

3 the Duke of Calabria, villain of ▷ John Webster's play ▷ *The Duchess of Malfi*.

Fergusson, Robert (1750–74)

Poet. A clerk in the Commissary Office in Edinburgh, he died in the local Bedlam after falling ill and becoming prey to religious melancholy. He wrote extensively in English in the usual genres of the day: ▷ lyrics imitative of ▷ William Shenstone, tetrameter (▷ metre) fables and Miltonic ▷ blank verse. But his most important poetry is in the Scots vernacular and builds on the tradition begun by Allan Ramsay, often employing Ramsay's distinctive stanza forms. His *Auld Reekie* and *Hallow-Fair* depict the urban scene with pungent particularity. He intended to translate ▷ Virgil's ▷ *Georgics* and ▷ *Aeneid* into Scots, but the project was never realized because of his early death. The 1782 edition of Fergusson's works helped inspire some of ▷ Robert Burns's best poetry.

Ferrar, Nicholas

▷ *Little Gidding*.

Ferrier, Susan Edmonstone (1782–1854)

Novelist. The youngest of ten children, Susan Ferrier was born in Edinburgh. Her father was a lawyer, a principal clerk of session along with ▷ Sir Walter Scott, so Ferrier was early introduced to literary society. Through visits to Inverary Castle she also became acquainted with the fashionable world. After her mother died in 1797 her three sisters married and she kept house for her father who died in 1829. She later insisted on the destruction of correspondence with a sister, thus destroying much biographical material. Her novels of Scottish life included portraits of known people. *Marriage* (1818) was written in 1810 with a minimal contribution from her friend Miss Clavering, *The Inheritance* in 1824 and *Destiny, or the chief's daughter* in 1831. Her aim was didactic and her method keen observation, comedy and clear writing.

Festivals

Festival days are those regularly set apart every year, either by religious authority for sacred observance, or for the celebration of a change of season by popular tradition. Thus the commonest festival was the weekly Sunday, consecrated by the Church to religious worship and prescribed as a day of rest for all.

The medieval year contained numerous festivals (feast-days) commemorating the saints, but these were abolished at the ▷ Reformation and only the main Christian festivals were retained. Side by side with the Christian festivals were folk festivals, which often showed signs of pagan antecedents.

The main Christian feasts of importance in the past have been the following:

▷ *Epiphany* (Twelfth Night). 6 January. Celebrating the visit of the ▷ Magi to the Child Jesus.

Candlemas. 2 February. Celebrating the presentation of Jesus at the Temple.

▷ *Lady Day*. 25 March. Celebrating Our Lady, the Virgin Mary.

▷ *Easter*. A movable feast, occurring late in March or April. Celebrating the resurrection of Jesus Christ.

Ascension Day. 40 days after Easter. Celebrating the ascension of Christ into Heaven.

Whitsun. 50 days after Easter. Also called Pentecost. Celebrating the descent of the Holy Spirit to the disciples of Christ.

▷ *Corpus Christi*. Celebrating the Holy Sacrament.

Lammas (Loaf-Mass). 1 August. Celebrating the Harvest.

Michaelmas. 29 September. The feast of St Michael and all Angels.

All Saints Day. 1 November. (All Hallows Eve; Hallow E'en 31 October.) Celebrating particularly those saints otherwise omitted from the Church calendar.

Martinmas. 11 November. The feast of St Martin.

▷ *Christmas*. 25 December. Celebrating the birth of Jesus Christ. It corresponded to the pre-Christian feast of ▷ Yule.

Of these, only Christmas and Easter are universally remembered, especially because they coincide with public holidays. Christmas, Easter and All Saints' Day coincide with pre-Christian pagan festivals of the seasons, corresponding to the winter, spring and autumn seasons, respectively. All Hallows, in particular, is associated with the belief that the night before it is one on which ghosts and witches walk abroad.

The main non-religious festivals were as follows:

New Year's Day. 1 January.

Plough Monday. The first Monday after Epiphany. Celebrating the start of ploughing. Folk plays similar to the ▷ Mummers' play performed at Christmas and the New Year were performed on it.

▷ *May Day*. 1 May. A Spring festival, on which ▷ Morris Dances and other revels were performed and has since became treated as Labour Day.

Midsummer. 24 June.

Harvest Home. Coinciding with Lammas (1 August).

Of these, New Year's Day and May Day still have a general importance, the latter chiefly for left-wing political parties. New Year's Day is a public holiday in Scotland.

Feuilleton
In French, a leaflet. Also used in French for that part of a newspaper devoted to literature, non-political news and gossip. In English the term was once used for the instalment of a serial story: it was the French newspaper *Le Siècle* which was the first to commission a serial novel specifically for part publication, in 1836. They were called *romans feuilletons*.

Fidessa
A character in Edmund Spenser's ▷ *The Faerie Queene* (Book I). Though the name Fidessa implies fidelity, she is, in reality, the false ▷ Duessa, and her intention is to lead the ▷ Red Cross Knight, standing for the faith of the ▷ Protestant ▷ Church of England, into captivity.

Field, Nathaniel (1587–1633)
Actor; he was one of the most famous in the lifetime of ▷ Shakespeare. He is mentioned in the first ▷ folio edition of Shakespeare's works as having played parts in them, and he also took leading roles in plays by ▷ Ben Jonson, and the chief one in ▷ George Chapman's most famous play ▷ *Bussy d'Ambois*. He wrote two '▷ citizen comedies' in the style of Jonson: *A Woman is a Weathercock* and *Amends for Ladies*.

Field of Cloth of Gold
The name given to the meeting-place of the English ▷ Henry VIII and the French Francis I, in France. The object of the meeting near Guisnes in 1520 was to arrange an alliance, but the encounter is less memorable politically than it is for characteristically ▷ Renaissance splendour.

Field sports
Sport taking place in the open countryside, consisting of some sort of hunting or racing. The main kinds have been:

▷ *Coursing*. The pursuit of animals (usually hares) with hounds using sight and not scent; a combination of hunting and racing.

Falconry. ▷ Hawking.

▷ *Fowling*. The hunting of birds, by hawking, trapping, shooting.

▷ *Hawking*. The hunting of birds with hawks specially trained for the purpose. Shooting drove this sport out of fashion in the later 17th century.

Horse-racing. This originally took place across country. It became extremely fashionable in the reign of ▷ Charles II and has remained so ever since.

▷ *Hunting*. Usually implies hunting on horseback with hounds.

Shooting. Usually at birds. Until the 17th century the usual weapon was the long bow or the crossbow, but guns called fowling-pieces or bird-pieces came in during the 16th century and in the second half of the 17th century became general. 'Huntin', shootin' and fishin'' were the stereotypical pastimes of the country gentleman and aristocracy.

Fielding, Henry (1707–54)
Born at Sharpham Park in Somerset, the son of a lieutenant. After the death of his mother when he was 11, Fielding was sent to Eton. At the age of 19, after an unsuccessful attempt to elope with an heiress, Fielding tried to make a living in London as a dramatist.

In 1728 his play *Love in Several Masques* was successfully performed at Drury Lane, and Fielding departed for university at Leyden, where he studied classical literature for about 18 months. On his return to London he continued his career as a dramatist, writing some 25 plays in the period 1729–37. His dramatic works are largely satirical, the most successful being ▷ *Tom Thumb* (performed in 1730). Fielding also edited four periodicals, *The Champion* (1739–41), *The Covent Garden Journal* (under the pseudonym Sir Alexander Drawcansir, 1752), *The True Patriot* (1745–6) and *Jacobite's Journal* (1747–8), but his major achievement is as a novelist.

▷ *Shamela*, a parody of ▷ Richardson's ▷ *Pamela*, published in 1741, was developed into the theme of ▷ *Joseph Andrews* (1742), an original and comic creation. In 1743 Fielding published ▷ *The Life of Jonathan Wild the Great*, a satire on the criminal class comparable in its inversion of values to ▷ John Gay's ▷ *Beggar's Opera*. In the same year his lesser known satire, *A Journey*

Henry Fielding; an engraving after Hogarth

From This World to the Next, also appeared.
▷ *Tom Jones*, his greatest work, was
published in 1749, and ▷ *Amelia* in 1751.

In 1748 Fielding was made Justice of the
Peace for Westminster, and pursued a
successful career of social reform. In 1754,
his health failing, he embarked on a journey
to Lisbon in search of a better climate, but
died on the way. *A Journal of a Voyage to
Lisbon*, his final achievement, was published
posthumously the following year.
▷ Fielding, Sarah.
Bib: Alter, R., *Fielding and the Nature of the
Novel*; Rogers, P., *Henry Fielding*; Rawson,
C. J., *Henry Fielding and the Augustan Ideal
under Stress*.

Fielding, Sarah (1710–68)
Sarah Fielding, sister of the novelist ▷ Henry
Fielding, was highly praised by ▷ Samuel
Richardson, who rated her achievements
more highly than her brother's: 'his was but a
knowledge of the outside of a clockwork
machine, while yours was that of the finer
springs and movements of the inside'. Her
first appearance in print consisted of
contributions to her brother's works (see Jill
Grey, 'Introduction' to *The Governess*, OUP;
1968).
Sarah Fielding's first novel, *The Adventures*

of David Simple, began to appear in 1744,
and proved a great success. In its
interpretation of social conventions from a
female point of view, it provides a revealing
contrast with the attitudes expressed by male
writers; the heroine, Cynthia, is subjected to
constant sexual harassment condoned as
socially acceptable behaviour. The second
volume of *David Simple* appeared in 1747,
and the final volume in 1753.
Sarah Fielding's concern for female
education is evident in *The Governess or The
Little Female Academy* (1749). Its success as a
(somewhat pious) moral novel for young
people ensured that it stayed in print for over
150 years.
In 1754, Sarah Fielding published *The
Cry*, a dramatic fable co-written with her
friend Jane Collier. In this allegorical
framework the heroine tells her story to
representatives of truth and justice, malice
and exploitation.
Samuel Richardson was the publisher of
Sarah Fielding's next work, *The Lives of
Cleopatra and Octavia*, in which the two
characters give different versions of their
lives. In 1759 Richardson again helped with
the printing of *The History of The Countess of
Dellwyn*, a further critique of male-dominated
society. Her later works include *The History
of Ophelia* (1760) and a translation of
Xenophon's *Memoirs of Socrates* (1762).

Fifth Monarchy Men
A sect of ▷ Puritans who believed, on the
basis of a prophecy in the Bible (*Daniel* 2),
that ▷ Oliver Cromwell's rise to power was
a preparation for the Second Coming of
Christ, and the establishment of the great
fifth and last monarchy; the previous four
had been the Assyrian, the Persian, the Greek
and the Roman. In disillusionment, they
began to turn against Cromwell and after the
▷ Restoration of the monarchy in 1660 they
tried to raise a rebellion in London. It was
easily suppressed and the leaders were
executed.

Figes, Eva (b 1932)
Novelist and ▷ feminist writer. Born Eva
Unger to a German Jewish family who
escaped to England in 1939 after the
imprisonment of her father by the Nazis.
Educated at London University, she worked
in publishing before writing her first novel,
Equinox (1966), a partly autobiographical and
largely pessimistic account of a woman's
search for meaning and human relationships.
The influence of ▷ Virginia Woolf is
apparent in her exploration of the inner
world of the self and her lyrical sense of the

flux of experience and the continuity of memories. *Days* (1974) and *The Seven Ages* (1986) seek to establish an unrecorded female history, linking many generations of women, while *Waking* (1981) is structured around seven waking moments of a woman or women. These ▷ modernist techniques combine with the influence of ▷ Samuel Beckett in *Winter Journey* (1967), which represents the inner world of an old man dying alone. Figes has a sense of herself as a European, and an awareness of the Holocaust which is a part of her family history, and draws on the work of one of the great European modernists, Franz Kafka. *Konek Landing* (1969) is a Kafkaesque story of victims and executioners in a nameless country. Figes's work rejects the English realist tradition in favour of a ▷ post-modernist commitment to experiment, apparent especially in *B* (1972), a self-reflexive novel about the nature of creativity, and the problematic relations of reality and fiction. She has written short stories, radio plays, children's fiction, criticism, and a classic text of the feminist movement, *Patriarchal Attitudes: Women in Society* (1970). *Little Eden: A Child at War* (1978) is autobiography. Her other novels are: *Nelly's Version* (1977); *Light* (1983); *Ghosts* (1988).

Figures of Speech

Alliteration The beginning of accented syllables near to each other with the same consonantal sound, as in many idiomatic phrases: 'safe and sound': 'thick and thin'; 'right as rain'. Alliteration is thus the opposite of ▷ rhyme, by which the similar sounds occur at the ends of the syllables: 'near and dear'; 'health and wealth'. Alliteration dominated the pattern of Old English poetry; after the Conquest, French influence caused rhyme to predominate. However, in the 14th century there seems to have been an 'alliterative revival', producing such important poems as ▷ *Piers Plowman* and ▷ *Sir Gawain and the Green Knight*. Alliterative verse was accentual, *ie* did not depend on the regular distribution of accented syllables in a line, but on the number of accented syllables in the lines.

After the 14th century, rhyme and the regular count of syllables became the normal pattern for English verse. Alliteration, however, continued to be used unsystematically by every poet.

Anacoluthon From the Greek: 'not following on'. Strictly speaking, this is not a figure of speech, but a grammatical term for a sentence which does not continue the syntactical pattern with which it starts. However, it may be used deliberately with the virtue of intensifying the force of a sentence *eg* by the sudden change from indirect to direct speech.

Anti–climax
    ▷ *Bathos* (below).

Antithesis A method of emphasis by the placing of opposed ideas or characteristics in direct contrast with each other.

Apostrophe A form of direct address often used by a narrator in the middle of his narrative as a means of emphasizing a moral lesson.

Assonance The rhyming of vowel sounds without the rhyming of consonants.

Bathos From the Greek: 'death'. The descent from the sublime to the ridiculous. This may be the result of incompetence in the writer, but ▷ Alexander Pope used it skillfully as a method of ridicule:

Here thou, great ANNA! whom three realms obey
Dost sometimes counsel take – and sometimes tea.

                    (*The Rape of the Lock*)

Pope wrote an essay *Bathos, the Art of Sinking in Poetry*, as a travesty of the essay by ▷ Longinus, *On the Sublime* (1st century AD). Longinus had great prestige as a critic in Pope's time.

Climax From the Greek: 'a ladder'. The climb from lower matters to higher, with the consequent satisfying of raised expectations.

Euphemism A mild or vague expression used to conceal a painful or disagreeable truth, *eg* 'he passed on' for 'he died'. It is sometimes used ironically.

Euphuism A highly artificial quality of style resembling that of ▷ John Lyly's ▷ *Euphues*.

Hyperbole Expression in extreme language so as to achieve intensity.

Innuendo A way of expressing dislike or criticism indirectly, or by a hint; an insinuation.

Irony From the Greek: 'dissimulation'. A form of expression by which the writer intends his meaning to be understood differently and less favourably, in contrast to his overt statement:

It is a truth universally acknowledged,
that a single man in possession of a good
fortune must be in want of a wife.

This opening sentence of ▷ Jane Austen's
Pride and Prejudice is to be understood as
meaning that the appearance of such a young
man in a neighbourhood inspires very strong
wishes in the hearts of mothers of unmarried
daughters, and that these wishes cause the
mothers to behave as though the statement
were indeed a fact.

Dramatic irony occurs when a character in
a play makes a statement in innocent
assurance of its truth, while the audience is
well aware that he or she is deceived.

Litotes Emphatic expression through an
ironical negative, *eg* 'She's no beauty',
meaning that the woman is ugly.

Malapropism A comic misuse of language,
usually by a person who is both pretentious
and ignorant. The term derives from the
character Mrs Malaprop in ▷ Sheridan's
play ▷ *The Rivals* (1775). This comic device
had in fact been used by earlier writers, such
as ▷ Shakespeare in the portrayal of
Dogberry in ▷ *Much Ado About Nothing*.

Meiosis Understatement, used as a
deliberate method of emphasis by irony, *eg*
'Would you like to be rich?' – 'I should
rather think so!'

Metaphor A figure of speech by which
unlike objects are identified with each other
for the purpose of emphasizing one or more
aspects of resemblance between them. A
simple example: 'the camel is the ship of the
desert'.
Mixed metaphor is a confused image in
which the successive parts are inconsistent, so
that (usually) absurdity results: 'I smell a rat,
I see it floating in the air, but I will nip it in
the bud', *ie* 'I suspect an evil, and I can
already see the beginnings of it, but I will
take action to suppress it.' However mixed
metaphor is sometimes used deliberately to
express a state of confusion.
Dead metaphor is one in which the image
has become so familiar that it is no longer
thought of as figurative, *eg* the phrase 'to take
steps', meaning 'to take action'.

Metaphysical conceit
▷ Metaphysical Poets.

Metonymy The naming of a person,
institution or human characteristic by some
object or attribute with which it is clearly

associated, as when a king or queen may be
referred to as 'the Crown';

Sceptre and Crown
Must tumble down,
And in the dust be equal made
With the poor crooked scythe and spade.
('The Levelling Dust', James Shirley)

Here 'Sceptre and Crown' refer to kings, and
perhaps more broadly to the classes which
control government, while 'scythe and spade'
stand for the humble peasantry. Metonymy
has taken on additional meanings since the
advent of ▷ Structuralism. One of the
originators of ▷ Russian Formalism,
▷ Roman Jakobson, draws a distinction
between 'metaphor' – the linguistic
relationship between two different objects on
the grounds of their similarity – and
'metonymy' as a means of establishing a
relationship between two objects in terms of
their contiguity. Where metaphor is regarded
as a major rhetorical device in *poetry*,
metonymy is more usually associated with
prose. The critic and novelist ▷ David
Lodge takes up this distinction in his book
The Modes of Modern Writing (1977), and
suggests that 'metaphor' and 'metonymy'
constitute a structurally significant binary
opposition that enables the distinction to be
made between poetry and drama on the one
hand, and prose on the other. Lodge
emphasizes, however, that these terms are not
mutually exclusive, but rather contribute to 'a
theory of dominance of one quality over
another'. Hence it is possible for a novel to
contain 'poetic' effects and vice versa.

Oxymoron A figure of speech formed by
the conjunction of contrasting terms; it
derives from two Greek words meaning 'sharp
and dull'.

Palindrome A word or sentence that reads
the same backwards or forwards, *eg*

Lewd did I live; evil I did dwel
(Phillips, 1706)

Paradox A statement that challenges the
mind by appearing to be self-contradictory.

Pathetic fallacy A term invented by the
critic ▷ John Ruskin (*Modern Painters*, Vol.
III, Pt. iv, Ch. 12) to denote the tendency
common especially among poets to ascribe
human emotions or qualities to inanimate
objects, *eg* 'an angry sea'. Ruskin describes it
by dividing writers into four classes: those
who do not use it merely because they are
insensitive; superior writers in whom it is a

mark of sensitivity; writers who are better still and do not need it because they 'feel strongly, think strongly, and see truly'; and writers of the best sort who use it because in some instances they 'see in a sort untruly, because what they see is inconceivably above them'. In general, he considers that the pathetic fallacy is justified when the feeling it expresses is a true one.

Personification A kind of metaphor, by which an abstraction or inanimate object is endowed with personality.

Play on words A use of a word with more than one meaning or of two words which sound the same in such a way that both meanings are called to mind. In its simplest form, as the modern pun, this is merely a joke. In the 16th and 17th centuries poets frequently played upon words seriously; this is especially true of ▷ Shakespeare and dramatists contemporary with him, and of the ▷ Metaphysical poets, such as ▷ John Donne and ▷ George Herbert.

This very serious use of puns or plays upon words decreased in the 18th century, when ▷ Samuel Johnson censured Shakespeare's fondness for puns (or, as Johnson called them, 'quibbles'). The reason for this disappearance of the serious 'play upon words' was the admiration of educated men for what Bishop Sprat in his *History of the Royal Society* (1667) called 'mathematical plainness of meaning', a criterion emulated by poets as well as by prose writers. In the 19th century, the play on words was revived by humorous writers and writers for children, such as Thomas Hood, ▷ Edward Lear and ▷ Lewis Carroll (▷ Children's books). Although their use of the pun was ostensibly comic, its effect in their writings is often unexpectedly poignant or even profound, especially in Carroll's 'Alice' books. Puns continued to be despised by the adult world of reason, but they could freely and revealingly be used in what was regarded as the childish world of nonsense and fantasy.

Modern poets and critics have recovered the older, serious use of the play on words. Ambiguity of meaning which in the 18th century was considered a vice of expression, is now seen as a quality of rich texture of expression, though of course 'good' and 'bad' types of ambiguity have to be distinguished. ▷ James Joyce used the technique with unprecedented elaboration in ▷ *Finnegans Wake*; ▷ William Empson revived the serious punning of Donne and ▷ Marvell in his poems, and investigated the whole problem in *Seven Types of Ambiguity* (1930).

Just as admiration for mathematics and the physical sciences caused the decline of the play on words, so the revival of it has been partly due to the rise of another science, that of psychoanalysis, especially the school of ▷ Freud, with its emphasis on the interplay of conscious and unconscious meanings in the use of language.

Pun
    ▷ *Play on words* (above).

Rhyme A verbal music made through identity of sound in the final syllables of words. Several varieties of rhyme exist:
    End-rhyme When the final syllables of lines of verse are rhymed.
    Internal rhyme When one at least of the rhyming words is in mid-line; as in 'fair' and 'air' in the following couplet by ▷ Swinburne:

> *We have seen thee, O Love, thou art*
>   *fair; thou art goodly, O Love;*
> *Thy wings make light in the air as wings*
>   *of a dove.*

Masculine rhymes are single stressed syllables as in the examples already given.
    Feminine rhymes are on two syllables, the second of which is unaccented. As in the following from ▷ Marlowe's *Passionate Shepherd*:

> *And I will make thee beds of roses*
> *And a thousand fragrant posies;*
> *A cap of flowers, and a kirtle*
> *Embroider'd all with leaves of myrtle*

Half-rhymes (pararhymes) are the rhyming of consonants but not of vowels (contrast ▷ *Assonance*). They are sometimes used as an equivalent for full rhymes, since consonants are more noticeable in rhyme music than vowels. Change in pronunciation sometimes has the effect of changing what was intended as full rhyme into half-rhyme, as in the following example from Pope:

> *'Tis not enough, taste, judgement, learning,*
>   *join;*
> *In all you speak, let truth and candour shine:*

In the 18th century, 'join' was pronounced as 'jine'.

Simile Similar to metaphor, but in similes the comparison is made explicit by the use of a word such as 'like' or 'as'.

Syllepsis A figure of speech by which a word is used in a literal and a metaphorical sense at the same time, *eg* 'You have broken my heart and my best china vase'.

Synecdoche A figure of speech by which a part is used to express a whole, or a whole is used to express a part, *eg* 'fifty sail' is used for fifty ships, or the 'smiling year' is used for the spring. In practice, synecdoche is indistinguishable from ▷ metonymy. Like metonymy this figure depends upon a relationship of contiguity, and is regarded as one side of the opposition between 'poetry' and 'non-poetry'. Both metonymy and synecdoche operate by combining attributes of particular objects, therefore they are crucial rhetorical devices for the representation of reality, and are closely related to ▷ realism as a literary style insofar as they function referentially.

Transferred epithet The transference of an adjective from the noun to which it applies grammatically to some other word in the sentence, usually in such a way as to express the quality of an action or of behaviour, *eg* 'My host handed me a hospitable glass of wine', instead of 'My hospitable host handed me . . .'.

Zeugma A figure similar to ▷ syllepsis; one word used with two others, to only one of which it is grammatically or logically applicable.

Filostrato, Il
▷ Boccaccio's version of the love affair between the Trojan prince, Troiolo, and Criseida, written in ▷ *ottava rima* in 1335, which Chaucer used as the principal source for ▷ *Troilus and Criseyde*.
Bib: Havely, N. R. (trans.), *Chaucer's Boccaccio*.

Finlay, Ian Hamilton (b 1925)
▷ Scottish poet and sculptor Finlay works simultaneously in both words and the sculpture of physical objects, exploring the possibility of poetry as a form of visual art. His work is modernistic, and an example of Concrete Poetry, the experimental movement which, since the 1960s, has sought to emphasize poetry's physical, typographical existence. Finlay has created a famous garden at Stonypath, Lanarkshire, which functions as a gallery for his work. His publications include: *The Dancers Inherit the Party* (1961); *Tea Leaves and Fishes* (1966); *Poems to Hear and See* (1971); *Heroic Emblems* (1978).

Finn (Find, Fionn, Fingal)
In Irish myth, a hero of the so-called Ossianic or Fenian cycle of legends; he is supposed to have lived in the 3rd century AD and to have been leader of a band of warriors called the ▷ Fenians. He was the father of Ossian (or ▷ Oisin), the subject of a famous 18th-century poetic forgery.

Finnegans Wake (1939)
A novel by ▷ James Joyce. It is one of the most original experiments ever undertaken in the novel form, and the most difficult of his works to read. It purports to be one night in the life of a Dublin public-house keeper, H. C. Earwicker, and as he is asleep from the beginning to the end of the book, his experiences are all those of dream. The advantage of dream experience is that it is unrestricted by self-conscious logic, and operates by free association unrestrained by inhibitions. The basis of the 'story' is his relationships with his wife, Anna Livia Plurabelle, his daughter, Isobel, and his twin sons Shem and Shaun; it reaches out, however, into Irish and European myths as these are suggested to his sleeping consciousness by objects in his mean little house and neighbourhood. Joyce intends in fact to make Earwicker a type of 'Everyman'. The language is made by fusing together words so as to cause them – as in dreams – to suggest several levels of significance simultaneously; this is a device which had already been used playfully by ▷ Lewis Carroll in his poem 'Jabberwocky' in the dream story for children *Through the Looking-Glass* (1872). Joyce, however, in his desire to universalize Earwicker, freely combines words from foreign languages with English ones, so that Earwicker's mind becomes representatively European while remaining his own. The movement of the narrative is based on the ideas of the 18th-century Italian philosopher Vico, who believed that ages succeed each other – gods, heroes, men – and then recommence; this is followed out in Earwicker's successive identifications (as Adam, Humpty Dumpty, Christ, Cromwell, Noah, The Duke of Wellington etc.), until at the end of the book the final sentence is completed by the first sentence at its beginning. The Christian pattern of fall and resurrection also contributes to the structure of the work. Another important influence on Joyce was the psychological ideas of ▷ Sigmund Freud on the mechanism of repression and the characteristics of dream association. Study necessitates the assistance of such a work as *A Reader's Guide to Finnegans Wake* by W. Y. Tindall.

Firbank, Ronald (1886–1926)
Writer of witty fantasies whose extravagant humour derives from the subtly calculated and highly wrought style. His best-known tales are probably *Vainglory* (1915); *Valmouth* (1919); *The Flower Beneath the Foot* (1923);

The Artificial Princess (1934). His stylistic innovations, including his highly condensed imagery, are regarded by some critics as a major contribution to ▷ modernism.
Bib: Fletcher, I. K., *Memoir*; Forster, F. M., in *Abinger Harvest*; Brooke, J., *Firbank*.

Fire of London, The Great
In 1666 over 13,000 houses, 87 churches and the old St Paul's Cathedral were destroyed. Celebrated accounts of it occur in the contemporary diaries of ▷ John Evelyn and ▷ Samuel Pepys. Owing to disagreements among the citizens, the originalistic and independent architect ▷ Christopher Wren was not allowed to carry out his great plan for rebuilding the City, whose streets accordingly still follow the twisting lines of the old City; but he rebuilt St Paul's and many other churches. A beneficial consequence of the fire was that it ended the terrible epidemic of plague which had devastated London in 1665.
▷ Plague of London, The Great.

First Gentleman of Europe
George IV – so described by his flatterers because of his pursuit of elegant luxury and gaiety. His tutor had predicted of him, at the age of 15, that he would be 'either the most polished gentleman or the most accomplished blackguard in Europe – possibly both'.

Fisher King
The title of the Grail Keeper in Arthurian legendary narrative. The name first appears in ▷ Chrétien de Troyes' romance *Perceval* (where it is not explained), and is given a Christian interpretation in ▷ Robert de Boron's late 12th/early 13th-century version of the ▷ Grail story. In versions of the 'Quest of the Holy Grail' narrative, the Fisher King is not always the same figure as the Grail King.

Fisher, Roy (b 1930)
Poet. Born in Birmingham, Fisher's work is realist in its evocation of the Midlands industrial landscape – this is especially true of his early work, which was generally unknown until the Oxford edition *Poems 1955–1980* (1981) appeared (most of his previous work had been published by the small presses, especially by Fulcrum). Fisher is a prolific poet, and his works include: *City* (1961); *The Memorial Fountain* (1966); *Collected Poems* (1969); *Matrix* (1971); *The Thing about Joe Sullivan* (1978); *A Furnace* (1986).

Fitz-Boodle, George Savage
The pen-name assumed by the novelist ▷ William Makepeace Thackeray for the 'Fitz-Boodle Papers' contributed to *Fraser's Magazine*, 1842–3.

FitzGerald, Edward (1809–93)
Translator and poet; chiefly known for his extremely popular translation of the Persian poem ▷ *The Rubaiyat of Omar Khayyam* (1859). He also published *Euphranor* (1851), a ▷ Platonic dialogue; translations of *Six Dramas of Calderon* (1853), and in 1865, a translation of ▷ Aeschylus's ▷ *Agamemnon*. His delicate praise of a life of pleasure and enjoyment of beauty evident in his *Rubaiyat* countered the moral earnestness of the age and influenced the 'anti-Victorian' ▷ Pre-Raphaelite and ▷ Aesthetic movements later in the century.
Bib: Benson, A. C., *FitzGerald*; Terhune, A. M., *Life*; Campbell, A. Y., in *Great Victorians*, eds. Massingham, A. J. and H.

Flamineo
Brother, and ultimately pimp, of ▷ Vittoria Corombona in ▷ *The White Devil* by ▷ John Webster. Flamineo is presented as an embittered and cynical villain who spurns all the dictates of conscience and duty for self-advancement.

Flaubert, Gustave (1821–80)
French novelist. His first novel, *Madame Bovary*, involved him in a court action for immorality on its publication in 1857. The story of the adultery of a doctor's wife in Normandy, it ironizes not only the ▷ romanticism of the principal character, but also the unappealing bourgeois values of the characters around her and the parochial milieu from which she attempts to escape. The book is equally notable for its contribution to psychological realism in the form of *style indirect libre*, a version of the ▷ 'stream of consciousness' technique regularly employed by ▷ Virginia Woolf and ▷ James Joyce. Flaubert's 1869 novel, *L'Education sentimentale*, intended as the moral history of his generation, portrays the fruitless love of Frédéric Moreau for Mme. Arnoux, against the background of 1840s Paris and the 1848 Revolution; love and politics prove comparable in misdirected and misrecognized opportunities, which defuse both the dynamism of character and the fulfilment of plot. History, together with religion, comes under renewed investigation in *Salammbô* (1862), *La Tentation de Saint Antoine* (1874) and *Trois Contes* (1877). These end in further equivocation, with the reader left uncertain about what values are to be derived from works so pervaded by irony and authorial impersonality. In the unfinished

Bouvard et Pécuchet (1881), the work's eponymous protagonists are composed of the novels, guide books and folk-lore they avidly read, and conversely they take for reality what are only representations of it. In addition to foregrounding fictive processes, this novel also dwells on the stupidity of bourgeois society and the received ideas on which this society feeds, a Flaubertian theme since *Madame Bovary*.

In the 19th century, Flaubert was prized for his ▷ realism (he was also claimed by ▷ Naturalism and rejected both labels), understood as psychological representation or the accumulation of circumstantial detail (called the 'reality effect' by ▷ Roland Barthes). Yet such detail in Flaubert tends to overwhelm rather than sharply define the character. Accordingly, the 20th century has valued him for his challenges to ▷ mimesis, including the traditional privileged ties between author and reader, writer and character, individual and society.

Flecknoe, Richard (17th century)
A poet who was the victim of a satire by ▷ Andrew Marvell, *Fleckno, an English Priest at Rome* (1645). Dryden chose the title ▷ *Mac Flecknoe* (son of Flecknoe) for his satire against ▷ Thomas Shadwell.

Fleet Prison, The
A royal prison in London from the 12th century (▷ Falstaff is sent there at the end of ▷ Shakespeare's ▷ *Henry IV, Part II*), used for debtors after 1641 and demolished in 1848. It is described in ▷ Charles Dickens's ▷ *The Pickwick Papers*. Clergymen imprisoned in the Fleet sometimes conducted secret marriages, *ie* without the formalities of licence or 'banns'. Such marriages were legal though the clergyman was liable to a fine – a penalty which was no deterrent to one already bankrupt.

Fleet Street
A street in London which used to be the headquarters of most of the national newspapers. 'Fleet Street' is often used as a synonym for ▷ 'journalism' although most of the papers have now moved out, to Wapping and elsewhere.

Fletcher, Giles (the Elder) (?1549–1611)
Author of a book on Russia (1591), suppressed by the government at the request of the English joint stock Russia Company (▷ Companies, Joint Stock) as likely to offend the Russian government and hinder trade. He also wrote a sonnet sequence, *Licia, or Poems of Love* (1593) in emulation of ▷ Sir Philip Sidney's ▷ *Astrophil and Stella*.

Fletcher, Giles (the Younger) (1585–1623)
Poet; author of ▷ allegorical religious poems, especially his ▷ epic in ▷ Spenserian stanzas, *Christ's Victorie and Triumph* (1610). He was the younger son of ▷ Giles Fletcher the Elder.

Fletcher, John (1579–1625)
Dramatist; nephew of ▷ Giles Fletcher the Elder. The 1679 edition of his work contains 57 plays – the largest of all the Elizabethan collections – but most of them were collaborations.

Among the works probably by himself alone are: *The Faithful Shepherdess* (1608), a ▷ pastoral; the tragedies *Bonduca* (▷ Boadicea) and *Valentinian* (1614); the tragicomedies, *The Loyal Subject* (1618). *The Humorous Lieutenant* (1619); the comedies, *The Wild Goose Chase, Monsieur Thomas, The Pilgrim* (1621).

It was in collaboration with ▷ Beaumont that Fletcher produced his most famous work; their best plays are commonly held to be the tragicomedy ▷ *Philaster*, and the tragedy ▷ *The Maid's Tragedy*. Another tragedy, *A King and No King* (1611) was greatly admired by ▷ Dryden; the domestic comedy *The Scornful Lady* (1610) has also been highly praised.

Fletcher seems to have ceased collaborating with Beaumont in 1613, and to have joined briefly with ▷ Shakespeare. ▷ *Henry VIII*, formerly attributed to Shakespeare entirely, is now thought to be partly Fletcher's work, and Shakespeare is also thought to have written part of ▷ *The Two Noble Kinsmen*.

Fletcher's name has also been linked with several other dramatists, including ▷ Ben Jonson, but especially with ▷ Massinger between 1619 and 1622. Among these Massinger collaborations are *Thierry and Theodoret* and *The False One*.

Fletcher's reputation stood highest at the ▷ Restoration, when he was ranked with Shakespeare and Jonson. The opinion of most 20th-century criticism is that he was an extremely skilful theatrical craftsman, a master of striking but superficial dramatic effects; his verse, similarly, is admitted to be fluent and musical, but is felt to lack authentic depth and strength of feeling. He is thus felt to be representative of decadence in the great Shakespearean period, and even to be the principal decadent influence.
Bib: Waith, E. M., *The Pattern of Tragicomedy in Beaumont and Fletcher*; Bradbrook, M. C., *Elizabethan Tragedy*; Danby, J., *Poets on Fortune's Hill*; Maxwell,

B., *Studies in Beaumont, Fletcher and Massinger*; Leech, C., *The John Fletcher Plays*.

Fletcher, Phineas (1582–1650)
Elder son of ▷ Giles Fletcher the Elder; ▷ allegorical poet in the tradition of ▷ Edmund Spenser. Principal work: *The Purple Island, or the Isle of Man* (1633), an allegorical representation of the human mind and body.

Flodden, Battle of (1513)
The invading Scottish forces under King James IV, fighting in alliance with France which had been invaded by ▷ Henry VIII of England, were heavily defeated by the English general, the Earl of Surrey. James himself was killed, as well as large numbers of his nobility. The battle was commemorated by a famous dirge *The Flowers of the Forest*, the best-known version of which is by Jean Elliott (1727–1805). ▷ *Marmion, A Tale of Flodden Field* is the most celebrated of the narrative poems by ▷ Sir Walter Scott.

Flora
In Roman myth, goddess of springtime and flowers, later identified with her Greek equivalent, Chloris. She is used in English ▷ pastoral poetry.

Florimell
A character in ▷ Edmund Spenser's ▷ *Faerie Queene* (Books III and IV). She is one of Spenser's representations of chaste love.

Florio, John (?1553–1625)
Translator. Florio published, in 1578 and 1591, two Italian phrase-books, as well as an Italian–English dictionary, *A World of Words* (1598). His best-known work, however, was his ▷ translation of the *Essays* of ▷ Montaigne, which was published in 1603. Bib: Yates, F. A., *John Florio*.

Fluellen
A character in ▷ Shakespeare's history play ▷ *Henry V*. He is a Welsh officer in the army of Henry, fighting in France. He is presented as a brave and fine soldier, but also as a comic character, with the weaknesses of emotional and irritable pride associated with the Welsh in the English mind of Shakespeare's time. The name is a corruption of Llewellyn.

Flyting
A verbal combat, in which the combatants compete against each other in satirical abuse. It may have had its origins in pagan ritual in contests which symbolized the change of the seasons, etc., and is said to have connections with the boasts and abuse hurled at each other by rival heroes and other characters in ▷ epics and ▷ tragedies. The device was particularly common in medieval literature, *eg* ▷ Dunbar's *The Flyting of Dunbar and Kennedy*, and Chaucer's ▷ *The Parliament of Foulys*.

Folio
As applied to books, a folio is one for which the paper has been folded once, and therefore of the largest size. The expression 'the first folio' commonly refers to the first collected edition of ▷ Shakespeare's plays (1623); there were three other folio editions of Shakespeare's plays in the 17th century.

The 1623 volume is edited by two fellow actors of the Lord Chamberlain's Company of Players – Heming and Condell – and contains a preface by them and prefatory poems, notably one by ▷ Ben Jonson. Following the poems there is a list of the 'principal actors in all these plays'; the list includes Shakespeare himself, ▷ Richard Burbage, Nathaniel Field, and of course the editors. The edition opens with the print of a rather inferior engraved portrait of the poet by Martin Droeshout. Thirty-six plays are included; ▷ *Pericles*, included by modern editors, is omitted. Eighteen of the plays had already been published in small ▷ quarto editions (some of them close to the folio version and some differing substantially), and the remainder were being published for the first time. The plays are undated, and grouped into Comedies, Histories and Tragedies; some have divisions into acts and scenes, and some are without them.

Food
1350–1500: ▷ Chaucer's poor widow in the ▷ *Nun's Priest's Tale* (*Canterbury Tales*) lived off 'white and black', *ie* milk and coarse rye bread. Also in the 14th century, another peasant, ▷ Langland's ▷ Piers Plowman, declares that he can afford only green cheese (from thin milk), curds and cream, oat-cake, and bean-loaves. Porridges made out of beans and peas (pease pudding) were also common. Poor peasants probably saw little meat up to the end of the 18th century, though they might have eggs and bacon. By contrast, other 14th-century poems (*eg Winner and Waster*, ▷ *Sir Gawain and the Green Knight*) describe the tables of the nobility as overflowing with meat dishes. Mutton, beef and veal were the common diet of richer peasants, and, as deer abounded, so was venison. Chicken was the most frequent bird-dish, but wildfowl, such as pheasants and partridges, and also small birds such as larks

and linnets, never eaten now, were luxuries for the rich. Great houses and monasteries kept fishponds, and fish was substituted for meat on Fridays and in the Lent fast. Sea-fish was not fresh by the time it reached inland consumers; it had often been dried in the sun without salt and was called 'stockfish'. Meat and fish were often in a tasteless or unpalatable condition, and required a plentiful use of sauces, compounded of vinegar, pepper, salt and garlic. As there were no root crops to feed cattle during the winter, surplus animals were killed off, salted, and eaten with sauces in that season. Herbs and spices were much used for savouring, and honey for sweetening; a foreign observer in the reign of ▷ Elizabeth I mentions bad teeth in the middle and upper classes as a consequence of English addiction to sweet food. Skin infections also seem to have been prevalent, owing to deficiency of vegetables in proportion to meat.

From 1500. Salads ('sallets') began to come into general use among the middle and upper classes in the 17th century. The potato, introduced by Sir Walter Ralegh in the 1580s, spread slowly, and it was not until the 19th century that it became really common, and a staple food among the poor. Sugar was another important innovation; cane sugar was cultivated in the West Indies in the 17th century and took the place of honey and other sweeteners that had gone by the name of sugar in earlier times. (Although sugar continues to be consumed in quantity, it is no longer imported but made from beet; the effect on the economy of the West Indies was severe.) By the 18th century vegetables were extensively cultivated by all classes, and were eaten with meat as plentifully as they are today. Overeating of meat continued to be a chief cause of bad health among the richer classes, hence the frequent apoplexies in 18th-century novels and plays. Lavish orchards were a feature of great houses at least as early as the 16th century, and fruits such as dates, figs and oranges were imported.

Diet greatly expanded in the 18th and 19th centuries with the increase in variety of imports, and it was revolutionized by the invention of canning in the 19th century: canned meat was on show at the ▷ Great Exhibition of 1851, but did not become general until this century. Fruits, such as the banana and pineapple, originally imported cheaply from the Empire as a fashionable novelty, have remained popular to the present time.

In addition to canned food, frozen meals have become extremely popular because they are so easily and speedily cooked. Indeed, 'convenience food' – that which requires little preparation – is now an important staple in the British diet, mainly because of the increasing number of women who have full-time jobs outside the home. This has led to a questioning of dietary patterns and a parallel development of food-consciousness. Health foods are rapidly gaining importance and an increasing number of people are choosing to become vegetarian. Interestingly, these changing patterns in food consumption appear to reaffirm many traditional class and regional associations.

Ford, Ford Madox (Ford Hermann Hueffer) (1873–1939)

Ford Madox Ford

Novelist, critic, poet. His father was of German origin, and became music critic for ▷ *The Times*; his mother was daughter of the ▷ Pre-Raphaelite painter, Ford Madox Brown. Ford was first known as an aesthetic writer of fairy stories, but he became deeply interested in contemporary French writing and culture, and became a propagandist for the rigorous discipline of French art, exercising a strong personal influence on ▷ Joseph Conrad and ▷ Ezra Pound. He co-operated with Conrad on two novels, *The Inheritors* (1901) and *Romance* (1903). He was a prolific writer, but is now chiefly remembered for *The Good Soldier* (1915) and for the four novels known in Britain as *The Tietjens Tetralogy* (after the name of its hero), and in America as *Parade's End*: *Some Do Not* (1924), *No More Parades* (1925), *A Man Could Stand Up* (1926), and *Last Post* (1928). The tetralogy is regarded by some critics as the most memorable fiction about the war of

1914–18 (in which Ford served, although he was 40 on enlistment), and as the most remarkable account of the upheaval in English social values in the decade 1910–20. *The Good Soldier* is a subtle and ambiguous study of the cruelty, infidelity and madness below the respectable surface of the lives of two couples, and is notable for its use of an unreliable narrator.

Ford has an undoubted importance in literary history because of his personal influence. As a poet, he played a significant part in the founding of ▷ Imagism. In 1908–9 he was editor of the brilliant but short-lived *English Review*, to which ▷ Thomas Hardy, ▷ Henry James, ▷ H. G. Wells, ▷ Joseph Conrad and the Russian novelist ▷ Leo Tolstoy all contributed. He was an early encourager of ▷ D. H. Lawrence. Brought up in the relatively narrow Pre-Raphaelite and ▷ aesthetic movements, in the 1900s he was a central figure among the writers who were thinking radically about problems of artistic form, especially in novel-writing. He regarded the 19th-century English novel as too much a product of the accident of genius, and, aligning himself with James and Conrad, was in opposition to ▷ H. G. Wells who preferred the title of journalist to that of artist. After World War I he moved to Paris and became part of a circle of expatriate writers, including ▷ James Joyce, ▷ Ernest Hemingway and ▷ Gertrude Stein. He also founded the *Transatlantic Review*.

After 1930 his imaginative writing was somewhat neglected but he is now recognized as an important figure of the modernist movement. Of present-day novelists, he has perhaps had most effect on ▷ Graham Greene. Apart from *The Tietjens Tetralogy* and *The Good Soldier*, novels selected for praise include the historical trilogy about Tudor England (*The Fifth Queen*, 1906; *Privy Seal*, 1907; *The Fifth Queen Crowned*, 1908). His *Collected Poems* were published in 1936.
Bib: Cassell, R. A. (ed.), *Ford Madox Ford: Modern Judgements*; Green, R., *Ford Madox Ford, Prose and Politics*; Meixner, J. A., *Ford Madox Ford's Novels: A Critical Study*; Mizener, A., *The Saddest Story* (biography); Ohmann, C., *Ford Madox Ford: From Apprentice to Craftsman*.

Ford, John (1586–?1640)
The best of the ▷ Caroline dramatists. He is best known for two tragedies, ▷ *'Tis Pity She's a Whore* and *The Broken Heart* (1633), and a tragic history play, *Perkin Warbeck* (1634). Less well known are *Lover's*

Melancholy (1629) and *Love's Sacrifice* (1633). He collaborated with other dramatists, notably with ▷ Dekker and ▷ Rowley in *The Witch of Edmonton* (1623). In spite of sensational themes and incidents (*eg 'Tis Pity* is about incestuous love) Ford's characteristic tone is the melancholy of private, frustrated passion; pathos rather than tragedy.
Bib: Anderson, Donald K., *John Ford*.

Forest of Arden
▷ Arden, Forest of.

Formalism
School of literary thought which flourished in Russia after 1917. Its main exponents, particularly ▷ Roman Jakobson, focussed on the differentiation between literary language and other forms of written expression. The insights of the Formalists have influenced later critics.
▷ Defamiliarization; Deconstruction.

Forster, E. M. (Edward Morgan) (1879–1970)

E. M. Forster

Novelist. His work is primarily in a realistic mode, and his ideas in the liberal tradition; indeed, much of his work is concerned with the legacy of Victorian middle-class liberalism. He was educated at Tonbridge School (a public school whose ethos is characterized by Sawston in the first two novels) and then at King's College, Cambridge, of which he was later made an honorary fellow. Through contacts made at Cambridge he came to be associated with the ▷ Bloomsbury Group. He travelled in Europe, lived in Italy and Egypt, and spent some years in India, where he was for a time secretary to a rajah after World War I.

Forster's novels are: *Where Angels Fear to Tread* (1905); *The Longest Journey* (1907); *A Room with a View* (1908); ▷ *Howard's End* (1910); ▷ *A Passage to India* (1924); and *Maurice* (1971). The last of these, which has a homosexual theme, was published posthumously, as was *The Life to Come* (1972), a collection of stories, many of which treat the same theme. His other two collections of short stories are: *The Celestial Omnibus* (1914) and *The Eternal Moment* (1928). These are mainly early work; they were published in a collected edition in 1947. His high reputation rests mainly on his fiction, but he has also written biographies and essays which are important for understanding his outlook as an imaginative writer. The biography of his friend Goldsworthy Lowes Dickinson (1934) is about a Cambridge scholar who was an important leader of liberal political opinion; that of his great-aunt, Marianne Thornton (1956), is enlightening about Forster's background. *The Hill of Devi* (1953) is an account of his experiences in India. The essays in *Abinger Harvest* (1936) and *Two Cheers for Democracy* (1951) include expressions of his opinions about politics, literature and society. *Aspects of the Novel* (1927) is one of the best-known critical works on the novel form. He co-operated with Eric Crozier on the libretto for Benjamin Britten's ▷ opera *Billy Budd* (1951).

Forster's dominant theme is the habitual conformity of people to unexamined social standards and conventions, and the ways in which this conformity blinds individuals to recognition of what is true in what is unexpected, to the proper uses of the intelligence, and to their own resources of spontaneous life. Spontaneous life and free intelligence also draw on traditions, and Forster shows how English traditions have on the one hand nourished complacency, hypocrisy, and insular philistinism, and on the other hand, humility, honesty, and sceptical curiosity. In several of the novels, and especially in *A Passage to India*, British culture is contrasted with a foreign tradition which has virtues that the British way of life is without. His style is consistently light and witty, with a use of irony which recalls ▷ Jane Austen and a use of comedy of situation which recalls ▷ George Meredith.

A Passage to India stands out from his work for the subtlety and resonance of its symbolism.

Bib: Trilling, L., *E. M. Forster*; McConkey, J., *The Novels of Forster*; Bradbury, M. (ed.), *E. M. Forster: A Collection of Critical Essays*; Stone, W., *The Cave and the Mountain*; Furbank, P. N., *E. M. Forster: A Life* (2 vols).

Forsyte Saga, The
A sequence of novels constituting a study of ▷ Victorian and ▷ Edwardian society by ▷ John Galsworthy. They comprise: *The Man of Property* (1906); *The Indian Summer of a Forsyte* (1918); *In Chancery* (1920); *Awakening* (1920); *To Let* (1921). A television serialization of the work in 1967 was extremely popular.

Forties, The Hungry
The decade 1840–50, so called because bad harvests caused serious food shortages, leading to mass agitation for abolition of the tax on imported corn (Anti-Corn Law League) and for a more democratic political system (the ▷ Chartist Movement). It was in the years 1845–51 that the Irish Famine took place: about 10 per cent of the population died from hunger and disease, and mass emigration ensued from those remaining.
▷ Corn Laws; Free Trade; Ireland.

Fortnightly Review, The
The Fortnightly Review was founded in 1865 by, among others, the novelist ▷ Anthony Trollope. It was a vehicle of advanced liberal opinion, and included amongst its contributors the scientist ▷ T. H. Huxley, the political scientist ▷ Walter Bagehot, the positivist philosopher Frederic Harrison, the critics ▷ Matthew Arnold and Leslie Stephen, the novelists ▷ George Eliot and ▷ George Meredith, the poets ▷ D. G. Rossetti and ▷ Algernon Swinburne, and ▷ Walter Pater and ▷ William Morris, both of them leaders of social and critical thought.

Forty-five, The
The rebellion or rising of 1745, *ie* the second of the two main ▷ Jacobite attempts in the 18th century to regain the throne of Great Britain for the Catholic branch of the House of ▷ Stuart. It was led by Charles Stuart ('Bonnie Prince Charlie' to his Scottish supporters, the 'Young Pretender' to his enemies), elder son of the claimant James Stuart (the 'Old Pretender'). Charles succeeded in rousing the ▷ Highlands and occupying ▷ Edinburgh. He then advanced into England and reached Derby. He had by then attracted very few English supporters,

and retreated to ▷ Scotland. He was
defeated by the Duke of Cumberland in 1746
at the Battle of ▷ Culloden in northern
Scotland, but escaped abroad.

Forty Shilling Freeholders

The class, outside the towns, who from the
13th century until the ▷ Reform Bill of
1832 possessed the minimum property
qualification to vote for a representative in
▷ Parliament, or to be elected as one.
'Freeholder' implies owning land, not renting
it from another landowner; 'forty shillings' is
the annual value of the land.
    ▷ Franchise; Yeoman.

Foucault, Michel (1926–84)

Along with ▷ Louis Althusser and
▷ Jacques Derrida, Foucault is one of the
most influential of French philosophers whose
work has been taken up by the practitioners
of other disciplines. Foucault rejects the
totalizing explanations of human development
in favour of a more detailed analysis of how
power functions within particular
▷ discourses. In *Madness and Civilization*
(1965) he explored the historical opposition
between 'madness' and 'civilization', applying
▷ Saussure's notion of differentials
(▷ Difference) to the various ways in which
society excludes the behaviour which
threatens it. He later took this issue up in
Discipline and Punish (1977), and *I Pierre
Riviere* (1978). In *The Order of Things* (1971)
and *The Archaeology of Knowledge* (1972) he
investigated the ways in which human
knowledge is organized, and the transition
from discourses which rely upon a notion of
'self-presence', to those which operate
differentially to produce the kind of linguistic
self-consciousness characteristic of ▷ post-
modernism. In essays such as those
translated in *Language, Counter-memory,
Practice* (1977), he sought to clarify specific
areas of opposition through which discourse
is constructed. At the time of his death he
had embarked on an investigation of the
discourses of sexuality through the ages, and
the three volumes of *The History of Sexuality*
(1978–87) have now been published.
    ▷ Archaeology.

Foundling

Used of a child abandoned by its parents,
usually because it was illegitimate or the
parents were too poor to provide for it. Such
children were sometimes left at night on the
doorsteps of the rich and so were 'found' at
daylight. In 1745 a Foundling Hospital was
established in London for such children;
baskets were hung on the outer wall for their
reception, and taken in every morning.

▷ Bastard.

Four P's, The (1568)

One of the amusing ▷ interludes written by
▷ John Heywood. It begins with a
competition between a palmer, a pardoner
and an apothecary, judged by a pedlar, to
find the best liar.

Four Quartets (1935–42)

Four poems written between 1935 and 1942
by ▷ T. S. Eliot, eventually published as a
single work. They are contemplative, religious
poems, each concerned with a distinct aspect
of spiritual experience. Each has as its
symbolic centre a place; each uses
symbolically one of the four '▷ elements' of
medieval physics; each has a structure
analogous to the movements and the
instruments of a musical quartet; the theme
that unites the four is that of the human
consciousness in relation to time and the
concept of eternity. *Burnt Norton* (the element
of air) centres on the rose garden of a ruined
country house (Burnt Norton) in
Gloucestershire and plays on the differences
and relationships between the actual present,
the past in memory, and speculation on what
might have been. *East Coker* (earth) is based
on a village in Somerset, whence the poet's
ancestors derived, and it includes quotations
from *The Governor* (1531) by ▷ Sir Thomas
Elyot; the poem is concerned with man as
part of the process of nature. *Dry Salvages*
(water) is named after rocks off the coast of
Massachusetts; the poem is concerned with
racial time and memory, larger than the time
of history and of the seasons, and embracing
the more unconscious regions of the mind.
▷ *Little Gidding* (fire) derives its title from
the religious community in the reign of
▷ Charles 1, who is supposed to have visited
it when broken by defeat at the battle of
Naseby. Fire in this poem is used as
destruction (with reference to the raids on
London during World War II), purification,
illumination, and as an emblem of Divine
Love.
    Four Quartets was Eliot's last major work
in non-dramatic poetry; the remainder of his
career was devoted to poetic drama.
Bib: Drew, E., *T. S. Eliot: The Design of his
Poetry*.

Fourteenth of July

The French annual national festival, dating
from the storming of the Bastille, a state
prison in Paris, on 14 July 1789. This was the
first triumph of the ▷ French Revolution,
and marked the end of the ▷ Ancien
Régime.

Fourth Estate, The

Traditionally, and for political purposes, English society was thought until the 20th century to have three estates: the lords spiritual, the lords temporal, the commons. ▷ Carlyle alludes to a Fourth Estate, *ie* the press, implying that the newspapers have an essential role in the political functions of society. He attributed the phrase to the 18th-century statesman ▷ Edmund Burke.

Fowles, John (b 1926)

John Fowles

Novelist. Born in Essex and educated at Oxford University. His novels are: *The Collector* (1963); *The Magus* (1965; revised edition 1977); *The French Lieutenant's Woman* (1969); *Daniel Martin* (1977); *Mantissa* (1982); *A Maggot* (1985). He is an experimental writer, interested in the nature of fiction and its interaction with history and reality, but he combines this with a skill in story-telling and an ability to create compelling characters and a vivid sense of social context. Several of his novels have been best-sellers, and three: *The Collector*, *The Magus* and *The French Lieutenant's Woman* have been filmed. His reception by the critics has tended to be more enthusiastic in the U.S.A. than in Britain. The recurrent concerns of his novels are the power of repressive convention and social conformity, the enigmatic nature of sexual relations, the desire to manipulate and control and the problem of individual freedom. The last of these concerns reflects the influence of ▷ existentialism.

The Collector, the story of the kidnapping of an attractive and wealthy girl by an introverted clerk, is in part a study of a pathological desire for possession, and in part a fable about social deprivation. It is in three parts, the first and last narrated by the man,

and the second by the girl. Fowles's novels are highly allusive: *The Magus*, like *The Collector*, employs parallels with ▷ Shakespeare's ▷ *The Tempest*. It also draws on the literary archetype of the quest in its story of a young man who travels to a Greek island where he is lured by a series of magical illusions into a confrontation with existential uncertainty and freedom of choice. *The French Lieutenant's Woman* employs parody of 19th-century novelistic style, quotations from sociological reports, from ▷ Darwin, ▷ Marx, ▷ Arnold and ▷ Tennyson, and authorial interruptions. Fowles's belief in the fundamental uncertainty of existence is reflected in his use of open endings; in *The Magus* the future of the main characters is 'another mystery' and *The French Lieutenant's Woman* has a choice of endings. *Daniel Martin* is more realist than his earlier work, exploiting his descriptive skill in a range of settings: it has less of the element of mystery and a more clearly affirmative ending. He has also written a volume of short stories, *The Ebony Tower* (1974) and works of non-fiction, including: *Islands* (1978); *The Tree* (1979); *The Enigma of Stonehenge* (1980) and *Land* (1985).
Bib: Conradi, P., *John Fowles*; Loveday, S., *The Romances of John Fowles*.

Fowling

Any form of hunting birds. Since the 17th century shooting with guns has been the only common method but previously shooting with the bow and arrow, trapping or ▷ hawking were used. Guns (called bird- or fowling-pieces) began to make their appearance in the 16th century but the crossbow was still the more efficient weapon. Trapping was either by gins (using some kind of net) or by placing lime along the twigs of trees so that the bird's feet stuck to it on alighting. Hawking was deemed the most aristocratic of these sports, until it gave place to shooting in the 17th century.
▷ Hunting.

Fox, Charles James (1749–1806)

Principal leader of the ▷ Whig party from 1775 (the beginning of the American War of Independence) until his death. The crown was not then above politics and the ▷ Tories, almost continuously in power during the same period, had the support of George III. Fox's fearless opposition in the House of Commons to the policies of the government in America, in Ireland and in regard to the ▷ French Revolution caused the king to refuse his offer of participation in the government in 1804, when he became convinced of the rightness of the war against France. Fox was dissolute in private life but set a high standard of political independence of mind. His principal political opponents were the Prime Ministers Lord North during the American war and ▷ William Pitt the Younger during the French one. Though powerful in opposition, he was less effective in office; but his service as Foreign Secretary in the Whig governments of 1782 and 1806 was too brief to show results.

Fox, George (1624–91)
Religious leader. He founded the Society of Friends (▷ Quakers), and left a journal of his spiritual experience, published in 1694. Apart from its religious importance, Fox's Journal is one of the classics amongst the English ▷ diaries.

Fox-hunting
This sport began to reach its outstanding prestige in 18th-century England. Deer, the chief object of hunts in earlier centuries, were less available as land came increasingly under cultivation, but foxes did not diminish and were just as much an enemy to farmers. Special packs of foxhounds were bred and were given names – often taken from the great country houses where they were kept, such as the Quorn, the Pytchley, the Badminton – which became famous far beyond hunting circles. The 18th-century ▷ enclosures of land into hedge-divided fields increased the danger and skill of 'riding to hounds', and this as much as anything steadily enhanced its popularity among the landed aristocracy who hunted for the sport and not merely to protect their poultry, like the farmers. To kill a fox by any method other than the approved one of hunting it with hounds and on horseback came to be regarded as little better than criminal; to be a Master of Hounds was to occupy a great social position; to misuse terminology (eg to call the hounds 'dogs') was to betray not merely laughable ignorance but a shameful sign of ill-breeding.

It was in the 19th century that fox-hunting flourished most. Railways, instead of reducing the sport, encouraged it by making the hunts more accessible from London. ▷ Robert Surtees produced minor classics of hunting-field stories, such as *Hardley Cross* (1843), and 'hunting prints' became a familiar ornament of the walls of English country inns. On the other hand, the urban intelligentsia later in the century sometimes revolted against 'hunting circles'. ▷ Oscar Wilde, leader of the ▷ aesthetic movement at the end of the 19th century, defined fox-

hunting as 'the pursuit of the uneatable by the unspeakable'. Although the practice still continues, there is now vehement protest against such blood sports and the number of hunts has decreased radically.
▷ Field sports; Hunting.

Foxe, John (1516–87)
Author of the *Book of Martyrs*; this was the title under which it was popularly known; the correct title of the 1st edition (1563) was *Acts and Monuments of these latter and perilous days*. Foxe was a Puritan who first set out to write a history of Christian martyrdom in Latin. The first outline dealt chiefly with the 14th-century reformers, the English ▷ John Wycliffe and the Bohemian John Huss. In 1554 he went abroad to escape persecution under the Catholic ▷ Mary, and completed his book there. The English version is fierce and eloquent, and had immense sales; for generations it inspired hatred for Catholicism in Britain, and was read alongside the ▷ Bible by simple folk who read little else. It is a classic of popular prose in the ▷ Elizabethan period.
▷ Reformation.

Frame, Janet (b 1924)

Janet Frame

New Zealand novelist and short-story writer. Her collection of stories, *The Lagoon* (1951) and her trilogy of novels *Owls Do Cry* (1957), *Faces in the Water* (1961) and *The Edge of the Alphabet* (1962) are about childhood innocence and the imagination, both threatened by bereavement and a repressive society. *Scented Gardens for the Blind* (1963) and *The Adaptable Man* (1965) explore the limitations and potentialities of language. Of her later work, *Intensive Care* (1970), written while Frame was in the U.S.A., draws on the horrors of the Vietnam War for a visionary satire on the place of war in the New Zealand consciousness. Her other novels are: *Living in the Maniototo* (1979); *A State of Siege* (1982); *The Carpathians* (1988). Other story collections: *You Are Now Entering the Human Heart* (1983). She has also written three volumes of autobiography.

Franchise
Normally understood as the right to vote for a representative in Parliament. From the reign of ▷ Edward I, when representatives of the ▷ Commons were first summoned to Parliament, until 1832, this right was possessed by landowners whose land was worth at least 40 shillings a year and by the citizens of certain towns (parliamentary boroughs) in which the qualifications varied. The first Parliamentary Reform Bill of 1832 arranged a property qualification which enfranchised the middle classes uniformly throughout Britain. The Reform Bill of 1867 enfranchised the working classes of the towns and the third, in 1884, extended the franchise to include men of all classes everywhere. In 1918 women were enfranchised on reaching the age of 30 and in 1928 they were accorded the vote, like men, at 21. Enfranchisement was one of the main demands made by the ▷ Suffragette movement. The franchise today is said to be 'universal', *ie* it excludes only minors (*ie* people under 18), certified lunatics, criminals serving a sentence or Peers of the Realm (*ie* holders of titles of nobility and bishops, who are entitled to sit in the House of Lords).

▷ Forty Shilling Freeholders; Parliament; Reform Bills, Parliamentary; Women, Status of.

Franciscans
▷ Friars.

Frankenstein, or the Modern Prometheus (1817)
A philosophical romance which is also a tale of terror, by ▷ Mary Shelley. It belongs in part to the 'gothic' tradition of tales of terror popular at the time and partly to a philosophical tradition going back to ▷ Rousseau, concerned with themes of isolation, suffering and social injustice. Mary Shelley originally wrote it to compete with the tales of terror being composed for their

own amusement by her lover and later husband, ▷ P. B. Shelley and their friend, the poet ▷ Lord Byron. Frankenstein is a Swiss student of natural philosophy who constructs a monster and endows it with life. Its impulses are benevolent, but it is everywhere regarded with loathing and fear; its benevolence turns to hatred, and it destroys its creator and his bride.

▷ Gothic Novels.

Franklin's Tale, The
One of ▷ Chaucer's ▷ *Canterbury Tales*. The Franklin suggests that his tale derives from old, insular narrative sources and introduces it as a lay which formerly circulated amongst 'olde, gentil, Britons'. In fact the tale seems to be drawn from Italian sources (from a narrative recounted by ▷ Boccaccio), which have been given a British gloss by Chaucer.

The narrative focusses on the strains placed on the marital vows of Dorigen and Arveragus, when Dorigen, unwittingly, pledges herself to her unwelcome suitor, Aurelius. Aurelius is able to fulfil Dorigen's 'impossible' condition for accepting him as a lover with the help of a clerk-magician, who appears to make the black rocks off Brittany's coast disappear. The chain of interlocking vows is broken when Arveragus and Aurelius cede their claim to exclusive rights over Dorigen's body. The clerk-magician also cedes his claim for payment for his services. The narrator concludes with a question to the audience about who was the most 'free' in the tale.

▷ Breton Lays.

Fraser's Magazine
It started in 1830 as an imitator of *Blackwood's*, but after the mid-19th century it became Liberal. It published Carlyle's ▷ *Sartor Resartus* in 1833–4; at this time it was under the influence of ▷ Coleridge's Conservative philosophy. In 1848 it was publishing ▷ Charles Kingsley's novel of idealistic reform, *Yeast*. The historian J. A. Froude was its editor 1861–74, and tried to publish ▷ Ruskin's radical treatise on the nature of wealth, *Munera Pulveris* (1862–3), but this proved unpopular with the public, and the treatise was left unfinished. The magazine folded in 1882.

Frayn, Michael (b 1933)
British dramatist and novelist. His first plays, *Jamie* (1968) and *Birthday* (1969) were written for television. Since then he has acquired a reputation both as a leading comic writer for the stage, particularly with his production of

Noises Off (1982), and an important translator of ▷ Chekhov's plays. Other plays include: *The Two of Us* (1970); *The Sandboy* (1971); *Alphabetical Order* (1975); *Donkeys' Years* (1976); *Clouds* (1976); *Liberty Hall* (1980); *Make and Break* (1980); *Benefactors* (1984). Translations: *The Cherry Orchard* (1978); *The Fruits of Enlightenment* (1979); *Three Sisters* (1983); *Number One* (1984); *Wild Honey* (1984); *The Seagull* (1986); *Uncle Vanya* (1988). Novels include: *The Tin Men* (1965); *The Russian Interpreter* (1966); *Towards the End of the Morning* (1967); *A Very Private Life* (1968); *Sweet Dreams* (1973).

Frazer, Sir James G. (1854–1941)
Anthropologist. His *Golden Bough* (1890–1915) is a vast study of ancient mythology; it has influenced 20th-century poetry such as ▷ T. S. Eliot's ▷ *The Waste Land*. An abridged edition was published in 1922. Other publications include: *Totemism* (1887); *Adonis, Attis, Osiris, Studies in the History of Oriental Religion* (1906); *Totemism and Exogamy* (1910); *Folklore in the Old Testament* (1918). Frazer was a major influence on the development of 20th-century anthropology and psychology, and in addition edited works by ▷ Cowper and ▷ Addison.

Free-trade
Nowadays the term is understood to mean trade between nations without restrictions either in the form of the prohibition of certain commodities or in duties (taxes) on their importation. The view that trade should be so conducted was expressed most influentially in ▷ Adam Smith's *Wealth of Nations* (1776). In the 19th century free trade particularly suited English industrialists and it became a leading issue between the ▷ Whigs who represented industrial interests and the ▷ Tories who wished to protect agricultural ones. The repeal of the ▷ Corn Laws, which had imposed taxes on imported corn, was a decisive victory for the free-traders, though the policy of governments has always fluctuated, and trade has never been entirely free. Although most countries practise certain trade restrictions, the British Conservative government of the 1980s has encouraged a greater freedom than most.

In the early 17th century the term was used for trade unrestricted by the monopolies granted (for a price) by the Crown to certain individuals. In the 18th century the term was a euphemism for smuggling.

Free verse
A way of writing poetry without use of ▷ rhyme, ▷ stanza pattern, or ▷ metre.

Free verse perhaps had French origins; at all events it is often referred to as *vers libre*. It was practised, especially in the first 30 years of this century, in an attempt to escape from the rather mechanical uses of rhyme and metre by the late ▷ romantics. ▷ T. S. Eliot attacked the whole concept of free verse, declaring that it could only be defined by negatives (*no* rhyme, etc.) and that a genuine form would have a positive definition (*Reflections on Vers Libre*; 1917); 'But the most interesting verse which has yet been written in our language has been done either by taking a very simple form, like the iambic pentameter, and constantly withdrawing from it, or taking no form at all, and constantly approximating to a very simple one.' Eliot himself was as bold as any of his contemporaries in rhythmic experimentation, but his methods are clearly one or other of the two which he here describes.
Bib: Hartman, C., *Free Verse*.

Freemasonry
An international society originating in England in the 18th century and deriving from medieval guilds of building craftsmen. Some of its ritual is secret, and its purposes are obscure, but it is sometimes said to be influential owing to the powerful positions held by some of its membership.
    ▷ Craft Guilds.

French literature in England
Invasion – the Norman invasion of England – may seem a suitably arresting way of establishing a starting point for the initial impact of France upon England. However, in all important senses this is too dramatic and too imprecise. It severely underestimates the degree of contact between Britain and the Continent before and after the Norman Conquest (▷ Conquest, The) with Latin as the *lingua franca*.

Later, in the 12th century ▷ Chrétien de Troyes's romances, as well as ▷ Marie de France's *Lais*, jointly suppose a sophisticated readership acquainted with Arthurian (▷ Arthur, King) background and named settings, usually in southern England and Wales. This period was one of intense literary activity which benefited England through the marriage of ▷ Henry II with Eleanor of Aquitaine. The civilization of the southern French courts became available throughout England and elsewhere in Europe fuelled the revolution in courtly attitudes which was to affect the Italian poets ▷ Dante and ▷ Petrarch. The English vernacular itself resorted to imitation as a means of securing its own achievements. Such imitative activity reaches an apogee with ▷ Chaucer. If his prioress spoke her French 'after the scole of Stratford atte Bowe', Chaucer himself was more fully conversant, as is attested by *The Book of the Duchess*, ▷ *The House of Fame* and ▷ *The Merchant's Tale*, the last itself stimulated by the popularity of the *lai* (▷ Lay). Similar observations could be made about ▷ Sir Thomas Malory's contacts with France. At the same time, Chaucer translated Guillaume de Lorris's ▷ *Le Roman de la Rose* and in the later ▷ Middle Ages there are also adaptations and translations of earlier epic and romance works. Thus the history of the cross-Channel literary flow from France to England is to no small degree the history of the translations and adaptations undergone by French literature.

The influence of Petrarch, felt early on both sides of the Channel, was prolonged by the Italian vogue prevalent in France in the 1550s–70s and compounded by the English admiration for ▷ Pierre de Ronsard. Ronsard's love poetry found favour with the ▷ Renaissance sonneteers, Henry Constable (1562–1613), ▷ Samuel Daniel and ▷ Thomas Lodge among them. ▷ Spenser's cultivation of the 16th-century French poet ▷ Joachim Du Bellay is untypical of his age. However, it is noticeable that poetry is the favoured genre for imitation, possibly because in France itself it is at once the most deeply exploited and the most cohesively organized. Of French drama there is no trace in England; and the fortunes of prose are the fortunes of translation, as represented most momentously in ▷ Shakespeare's recourse to ▷ John Florio for ▷ Montaigne's essay *Des Cannibales* for ▷ *The Tempest*. Yet while Montaigne can unquestionably be said to have had a hand in shaping the English essay form, ▷ Rabelais leaves more elusive traces and to discern his equivalent in English literature, one has to look as close to the Renaissance as Sir John Harington (?1560–1612), ▷ Thomas Nashe and ▷ Samuel Butler, and as far forward as ▷ Laurence Sterne and ▷ James Joyce.

Florio and Sir Thomas Urquhart (1611–60) – Rabelais's 17th-century translator – are authors in their own right. At the same period, Joshua Sylvester's (c 1563–1618) translation of ▷ Guillaume de Salluste Du Bartas was no less influential. In the later 17th and early 18th centuries, translations were supplemented by (undistinguished) adaptations, notably those which represent the barest thread of imitation of French classical drama. One such adaptation was ▷ Ambrose Philips's *The Distrest Mother*

(1712), behind which stands ▷ Racine's *Andromaque* (1667). Its success is recounted in ▷ Samuel Johnson's *Life* of Philips, a success greater than the original would have had in England at that time. This exemplifies a measure of the degree to which the ▷ Restoration was culturally as well as politically out of sympathy with French classical idiom. It was left to ▷ Dryden to put ▷ Corneille back on the literary agenda, while English ▷ comedy of manners was indebted to ▷ Molière. ▷ Alexander Pope and Johnson, in the following century, attended to the criteria of taste laid down by ▷ Nicholas Boileau and René Rapin (1621–87); and with the rise of the novel, Sterne can be found looking back to Rabelais rather than to contemporary French influence. But the important French work in the 18th century was the result of a collective enterprise rather than an individual piece: the ▷ *Encyclopédie*. It provided a focus for the *philosophes*, Diderot, ▷ Voltaire and ▷ Rousseau, and a forum larger than that which Voltaire, for example, enjoyed with ▷ John Locke. More famously, its criticisms of the ▷ Ancien Régime prefigured the French Revolution. It might be possible to see Wordsworth's ▷ *Prelude* as a transposed re-enactment of this yoking of *Encyclopédie* and revolution, the political upheaval described in 'Residence in France' here conducive to 'Imagination and Taste, How Impaired and Restored', politics now harnessed to the service of imagination. The cutting-edge of the early ▷ romanticism occurs in poetry rather than prose, in England rather than in France, with Wordsworth and ▷ Byron rather than with Lamartine (1790–1869) and ▷ Hugo. France was to experience revolution three times in the course of the 19th century, but for a comparable dramatizing of revolution and imagination such as Wordsworth articulates here in the *Prelude*, France needed more than its romantic poets could offer.

The real shift in the fortunes of French poetry in England came in the mid-19th century with ▷ Baudelaire. ▷ Swinburne is the most immediate of his English conquests, with, next in line, those poets influenced by Swinburne, the ▷ Nineties poets, such as Ernest Dowson (1867–1900), and later Arthur Symons (1865–1945) who alternately regarded Baudelaire as deliciously decadent and frankly satanic. Baudelaire's authority is nonetheless most keenly felt as the breadth of his modernity becomes clearer. ▷ W. B. Yeats took that point, as did ▷ T. S. Eliot: 'Baudelaire is indeed the greatest exemplar in *modern* poetry in any language, for his verse and language is the nearest thing to a complete renovation that we have experienced' ('Baudelaire' in *Selected Essays*). Eliot uses Baudelaire potently in ▷ *The Waste Land* (1922). And while Eliot translated Saint-John Perse's (1887–1975) *Anabase* and no Baudelaire, his 1930 essay was occasioned by ▷ Christopher Isherwood's translation of Baudelaire's *Journaux Intimes* and it was Baudelaire again who was placed alongside the ▷ Metaphysical poets as part of Eliot's canon. While the later Eliot moves away from these seminal influences, Baudelaire gave birth to two latter-day recorders of urban experience, poets F. S. Flint (1885–1960) and Richard Aldington (1892–1962). Baudelaire has been a pervasive presence in English poetry; even ▷ Philip Larkin, that arch-enemy of modernism, translated Baudelaire's 'Femmes Damnées' in a version published in 1978.

But Eliot, so sustaining of English literary critical values, could have his blind spots, and wilfully so. When in his 1948 essay 'From Poe to Valéry' he had occasion to reflect on some lines of descent in modern poetry, he ran along the ▷ Symbolist line but made no mention of the impact of ▷ Surrealism. Yet English Surrealism attracted its acolytes: Hugh Sykes Davis, Roland Penrose, ▷ David Gascoyne above all. It was Gascoyne who advertised the movement in England with *A Short Survey of Surrealism* (1935) and performed a valuable service in making its French exponents better known through translation.

Where English poetry since Eliot has become progressively more varied than its still-Mallarmé-haunted French counterpart, the other major genres have developed along a path away from French experimentation. This represents a reversal of the situation one hundred years ago. Throughout the 19th century, French and English prose entertained constant rapport, beginning with ▷ Stendhal whose *Chroniques pour l'Angleterre* were journalistic pieces aimed at a broad literate public. As a novelist, Stendhal beheads (*Le Rouge et Le Noir*) or cloisters away (*La Chartreuse de Parme*) those romantic heroes he had absorbed from a reading of Byron and English romantics. By contrast, ▷ Balzac could stand for a more fully socialized version of the novelist's enterprise. If Stendhal is closer to the romance, Balzac is closer to epic; his individuals are bonded to large-scale social change and evolution, Empire to Restoration, aristocracy to bourgeoisie. The vigour or decay of the individual is analogous to the vigour or decay of the social unit. The individual is not part of, a token for, society and made or unmade by it. He or she absorbs society and seeks to act upon it according to his or her will. Balzac's characters are accordingly all larger than the ▷ realism of which they are taken to be the accredited representatives. As with ▷ Dickens's characters, their fictional representation is constantly extended beyond the terms set for ▷ mimesis alone.

Another version of the social story is followed in ▷ Flaubert. His task was, he said, to demoralize us; and he commences his career as a novelist by poisoning his romantic heroine, Emma Bovary. Flaubert progressively narrates the interwoven failures of individual and society, which are simultaneously a vitiation of historical and emotional plots (*L'Education sentimentale*) and the liquidation of character into cliché (*Bouvard et Pécuchet*) Flaubert's use of irony and his quasi-deconstructionist approach moves him closer to Stendhal than to Balzac, and it may be argued that no English novelist of the period exploited irony to so refined a degree as Stendhal and Flaubert.

Despite Champfleury's (Jules Fleury, 1821–69) manifesto of 1857, realism was never a fixed body of doctrine consciously adhered to by all its supposed exponents. Nonetheless, it was as a realist that Flaubert was most admired in Britain, and the position of French realism was secured when ▷ Emile Zola experimented with veins of psychological determinism traced throughout several generations and several members of two families. Human beings in Zola may seem to be weasels fighting in a hole, yet as the advocate of ▷ naturalism (realism's more exact and scientific successor) Zola helped give impetus to British social and psychological realism explored by ▷ George Gissing and Arthur Morrison (1863–1945), ▷ George Moore and ▷ Arnold Bennett (the latter's *Journal* is based on the brothers ▷ Goncourt, also exponents of naturalism). Arguably, this vein proved consistently richer for the development of the English novel than the experimentation associated in France with the names of ▷ Proust and ▷ André Gide and reflected in the Anglo-Saxon world in the work of ▷ Henry James, ▷ Virginia Woolf and James Joyce. Unreliable protagonists narrating from a restricted angle of vision, disjointed temporal sequences, endings without full resolution – these became familiar devices in the first three decades of this century, but they had their counterparts principally in America rather than in Britain.

In France, this early opening up of the novel proved indispensable to the post-World War II developments – the overlapping of criticism and literature gravitating around the French ▷ Nouveau Roman (New Novel). The trajectory between the two points is admittedly not unilinear, and ▷ Existentialist writing – which dominated the war years and through into the 1950s – projected a more traditional use of the novel (and for theatre) as dramatizing, faced with the absurd, the urgent choices of 'the human condition' (this was ▷ Montaigne's term before it became André Malraux's). The Existentialist idiom caught a public mood and proved popular in Britain. If for Existentialism the world existed to be acted upon and in, for the Nouveau Roman the world simply is. It cannot be colonized by mere human presence or behaviour nor is it open to shaping by intellectual speculation. In the circumstances, the unresponsiveness of things to words throws the attention back on to language itself. The caterpillar which the narrator insistently describes in ▷ Alain Robbe-Grillet's *La Jalousie* (1957) yields a plurality of meanings. Thus the Nouveau Roman anticipates and nurtures as well as illustrates ▷ Roland Barthes's encoded narratives, ▷ Mikhail Bakhtin's carnival, ▷ Jacques Lacan's dispossessed human subject, and ▷ post-structuralism's play of the signifier. As a movement, the Nouveau Roman was a formidable alliance of literature with psychology, philosophy, the human sciences in general.

One crucial result of this activity in France has been the revision of the literary canon: ▷ Marquis de Sade, ▷ Comte de Lautréamont and Mallarmé have long since taken their place alongside ▷ Samuel Beckett, Georges Bataille (1897–1962) and Maurice Blanchot (b 1907) to provide the instrumental forces of disruption which unsettle rather than confirm assumptions about the world (narrative or real). Thus current French objections to realism are not simply objections to a world view taken as paradigmatic for literature, they are equally objections to a type of critical view which sponsors such a world view as natural, co-extensive with the order of things. There is no immediate parallel in Britain for this overall reassessment in theory as well as literature. There are nonetheless equivalents and adaptations. In the novel, these include ▷ John Fowles's experiments most notably in *The Magus* (1966) and *The French Lieutenant's Woman* (1969), William Boyd's (b 1952) splicing of Rousseau and cinema in

The New Confessions (1987), Julian Barnes's (b 1946) witty and humorously ironical recreation of Flaubert in *Flaubert's Parrot* (1984). All of these tend to question realism of character psychology, plot motivation and narrative expectation. Contemporary British ▷ feminism mirrors the coherence of the French position and its iconoclastic thrust, blending theoretical reflection with literary production. It has undoubtedly been stimulated by the work of Julia Kristeva and Hélène Cixous amongst others, and has drawn on the theoretical investigations of Jaques Lacan and ▷ Jacques Derrida.

French Revolution (1789–94)

The immediate effect of the French Revolution was to abolish the French monarchy, to reduce forever the rigid class divisions of French society, and to begin wars (lasting till 1815) which for the time being extensively altered the map of Europe. Its lasting effect was to inspire the European mind with the belief that change is historically inevitable and static order unnatural, and to imbue it with modern ideas of democracy, nationalism and equality at least of opportunity.

The immediate effect on England was confusing, for many of the changes being brought about in France had already occurred here in the 17th century, especially the establishment of the sovereignty of the elected representatives of the people in ▷ Parliament in 1688. Such changes had occurred here, however, without the same upheavals, partly because English society and politics had always been more fluid than in the other larger states of Europe, and though unjustified privileges and inequalities existed, there were few definable between the ▷ Whigs on the left who were neutral or sympathetic to the Revolution, and the Tories on the right who feared it from the start. Only when General Bonaparte took increasing charge of France and became Emperor ▷ Napoleon 1 in 1804 did Britain become united in fear of French aggression. However, ▷ Edmund Burke, published in 1790 his ▷ *Reflections on the Revolution in France*, one of the most eloquent documents of English political thinking, foretelling the disasters which the Revolution was to bring, and condemning it as ruthless surgery on the living organism of society. His opponent ▷ Tom Paine answered him with *The Rights of Man* (1791), and the younger intellectuals agreed with Paine. ▷ Wordsworth wrote later in ▷ *The Prelude* 'Bliss was it in that dawn to be alive', and ▷ William Blake

wore a revolutionary cockade in the streets;
▷ Southey and ▷ Coleridge planned the
ideal communist society, ▷ Pantisocracy;
the philosophic novelist ▷ William Godwin
published *Political Justice* and *Caleb Williams*
to prove that reason was the only guide to
conduct and society needed by man. Later
Wordsworth and Coleridge came round to a
view closer to Burke's, and the younger
generation, ▷ Byron and ▷ Shelley, saw
them as traitors; the more so because the
defeat of Napoleon at Waterloo introduced a
phase of political and social repression
everywhere. But the older generation (except
perhaps Southey) did not so much go back on
their earlier enthusiasms as think them out
more deeply; the philosophical conservatism
of the older Coleridge was as radical in its
thinking as the ▷ Utilitarianism of the
philosophical radicals, ▷ Bentham and the
▷ Mills.

Frere, John Hookham (1769–1846)

Friend of the statesman George Canning and
British envoy in Lisbon and later Madrid in
the first decade of the 19th century. He
collaborated with ▷ Robert Southey on his
translation of *The Chronicles of the Cid* (1808),
contributed extensively to *The Anti-Jacobin*
and was one of the founders of ▷ *The
Quarterly Review*. His mock-romantic
▷ Arthurian poem, *The Monks and the
Giants* (1817–18), written under the
pseudonym 'Whistlecraft' introduced ▷ Lord
Byron to the *ottava rima* style in which he
wrote ▷ *Beppo* and ▷ *Don Juan*. In the
1830s and 40s Frere produced lively verse
translations of four plays by
▷ Aristophanes.

Freud, Sigmund (1856–1939)

The founder of psychoanalysis, and one of
the seminal figures of 20th-century thought.
Born in Moravia, then part of the Austro-
Hungarian Empire, he settled in Vienna. He
began his career as a doctor specializing in
the physiology of the nervous system and,
after experimenting briefly with hypnosis,
developed the technique of free association
for the treatment of hysteria and neurosis.
His work is based on a number of principles.
The first is psychic determinism, the principle
that all mental events, including dreams,
fantasies, errors and neurotic symptoms, have
meaning. The second is the primacy of the
unconscious mind in mental life, the
unconscious being regarded as a dynamic
force drawing on the energy of instinctual
drives, and as the location of desires which
are repressed because they are socially
unacceptable or a threat to the ego. The third

is a developmental view of human life, which
stresses the importance of infantile experience
and accounts for personality in terms of the
progressive channelling of an initially
undifferentiated energy or libido. Important
aspects of ▷ psychoanalytical theory and
practice arising from these principles include
the theory of infantile sexuality and its
development, centred on the ▷ Oedipus
Complex, the techniques of free association
and dream interpretation as means of
analyzing repressed material, and the beliefs
that much behaviour is unconsciously
motivated, that sexuality plays a major role in
the personality, and that civilization has been
created by the direction of libidinous impulses
to symbolic ends (including the creation of
art). Freud regarded neurotic and normal
behaviour as differing in degree rather than
kind.

Despite his scientific orientation, Freud's
thought had affinities with that of the
Romantic poets (▷ Romanticism), and
several features of modern literature which
show his influence also have Romantic
antecedents. These include a particular
interest in the quality and significance of
childhood experience, a fascination with
memory and with what is buried in the adult
personality, and a concern with disturbed
states of consciousness. Such features are
found in the work of ▷ James Joyce and
▷ Virginia Woolf, as well as many later
writers. The ▷ stream of consciousness
technique and other experimental narrative
techniques which abandon external realism in
favour of the rendering of consciousness, of
dreams or of fantasies, owe much to Freud's
belief in the significance of these areas of
experience, which had been relatively
neglected by scientific thought. Furthermore,
the technique of free association revealed a
tendency of the mind, when rational
constraints were lessened, to move towards
points of psychic conflict, and this discovery
helped to validate new means of structuring
literary works, through association, symbol,
and other forms of non-rationalistic
patterning (for example in the work
of ▷ T. S. Eliot). The view that the
individual's unconscious life is as important
as his or her public and social self is crucial to
much 20th-century literature, a notable
example being the work of ▷ D. H.
Lawrence, which rests on the assumptions
that human beings live through their
unconscious, and that sexuality is central to
the personality. The Freudian unconscious is
in particular the realm of fantasy, and
Freudian thought has encouraged the belief

that fantasy is of profound significance in our lives, with considerable consequences for literary forms and modes.

Psychoanalysis has developed very considerably since Freud, and continues to interact with literary practice and theory. In the field of theory, those who have studied but radically revised Freud's ideas, such as ▷ Jacques Lacan and ▷ feminist theorists, have been especially important.
Bib: Brown, J. A. C., *Freud and the Post-Freudians*; Freud, S., *Introductory Lectures on Psychoanalysis*.

Frey, Freya
In Scandinavian myth, brother and sister deities: Frey was associated with fruitfulness, sunshine, rain; Freya, his sister, with love and night.

Friar
The friars were members of the mendicant orders of monasticism that originated in the 13th century. Whereas monks lived in ▷ monasteries which were corporate owners of property, friars were individually self-supporting either by their own labour or by begging – hence 'mendicant'. Friars answered important religious and social needs, since they were, unlike monks, free in their movements to go where they were most needed, working as poor men among the poor. Thus the orders spread rapidly throughout Europe after the deaths of their two main founders, St Dominic (d 1221), founder of the ▷ Dominicans, and St Francis of Assisi (d 1226), founder of the ▷ Franciscans. These remained the dominant orders, though many others were introduced (some including both men and women) such as the ▷ Carmelites, the Augustinian Hermits, and the ▷ Capuchins.

Like other institutions, the friars tended to degenerate from their ideal. Just as the Monk in Chaucer's ▷ *Canterbury Tales* is a bad monk because he refuses to remain bound to his monastery, so the Friar is a bad friar, because as a 'limitor' or licensed beggar, he abuses his spiritual functions for money, and the friar in the ▷ *Summoner's Tale* is worse. The friars in Elizabethan plays, *eg* Friar Laurence in Shakespeare's ▷ *Romeo and Juliet*, are in general depicted from a distance, since England was by then a Protestant country with few friars; they represent 'wise men', often endowed with magical powers.

Friar Bacon and Friar Bungay
A romantic comedy by ▷ Robert Greene, first acted in 1592. The title characters are based on historical figures: ▷ Franciscan

friars of the 13th century whom popular tradition had made into magicians; the play is based on a pamphlet of anecdotes about them. It has a double plot: one action concerns Bacon's manufacture of a brass head endowed (with the help of the devil) with power of speech, and the other is a ▷ pastoral love-story about the rival loves of Prince Edward and Lord Lacy for Margaret, a village maiden. The play is Greene's best; his use of the double plot to present two aspects of a theme, and his treatment of romantic love, have relevance to the later development of ▷ Elizabethan drama, including Shakespeare's.
▷ Bacon, Roger.

Friar's Tale, The
One of ▷ Chaucer's ▷ *Canterbury Tales*. It is an amplified *exemplum* (or moral story) which recounts how a summoner is damned as a result of his corrupt practices, specifically his attempt to extort money from a poor widow. It concludes with the summoner being carried off to hell by a 'summoning' colleague, a devil. This tale, which makes the pilgrim Summoner its butt, provokes the ▷ *Summoner's Tale*, a barbed narrative satire on the corrupt practices of friars.

Fringe theatre
A name which originates from unofficial theatre shows performed on the periphery of the Edinburgh Festival. The term is now used more generally and often refers to an alternative kind of theatre which provides a consciously oppositional entertainment to that on offer at mainstream establishment theatres. One of the typical fringe companies is ▷ John McGrath's 7:84 group which has always pursued a policy of touring plays and performing for working-class audiences away from coventional theatres (a policy which has been more successful in Scotland than in England). The term is useful in as much as it describes a general movement to a politically more radical kind of theatre since the late 1960s (which produced a number of dramatists, such as ▷ Howard Brenton, ▷ David Hare and ▷ David Edgar, who now tend to work within the theatre establishment). However, 'fringe' is now used to describe such a variety of theatrical activity that it no longer has a precise meaning. Other notable groups belonging, or who have belonged, to the political fringe are: Belt and Braces (founded in 1974); The Women's Theatre Group (1975); Gay Sweatshop (1975); Joint Stock Theatre Group (1974); Monstrous Regiment (1976).

Froissart, Jean (c 1337–c 1410)
A French chronicler and poet, who visited
England on several occasions, and recorded
events at the courts of France and England,
from 1325–1400, in the form of a chronicle
narrative, translated into English prose by
Lord Berners in 1523–5. Froissart's lyric and
▷ dream-vision poetry influenced
▷ Chaucer's work.

Fry, Christopher (b 1907)
British dramatist whose first stage success
was with *A Phoenix Too Frequent* (1946). *The
Lady's Not For Burning*, first staged in 1948,
starred ▷ John Gielgud and seemed to
herald a return of verse drama to the stage.
Other notable actors who played major roles
in his plays include: ▷ Laurence Olivier in
Venus Observed (1950), Paul Scofield in an
adaptation of Anouilh's *Ring Round the Moon*
(1950) and Edith Evans in *The Dark is Light
Enough* (1954). His popularity on the
commercial stage was short-lived and by the
mid-1950s he was already out of favour.
Curtmantle (1961) was performed by the
▷ Royal Shakespeare Company but was
only a moderate success. His own particular
brand of religious verse drama was, however,
one of the few notable dramatic developments
in the immediate post-war years. Film scripts
include: *Barabbas* (1952); *Ben Hur* (1959); *La
Bibbia* (1966).
Bib: Stanford, D., *Fry*.

Fuel
Fuel for heating in the Middle Ages was of
course chiefly wood, though in some districts
peat was used, but coal was mined in the
north of England and brought from Newcastle
to London by sea; hence it was called 'sea-
coal'. It was used increasingly in 16th-century
London owing to a shortage of wood. The
great increase of chimneys in Elizabethan
houses was largely due to the need to carry
away the disagreeable fumes from coal. In
both England and Scotland the condition of
coal-miners was wretched and humiliating.
Conditions became in many ways worse in
the 18th century when deep mining became
possible after the steam-pump was invented
(1712) to clear mines of water. Women and
children were employed for hauling
underground; it was not until the Mines Act
of 1842 that this was forbidden. By this time,
danger from explosions was greatly reduced
by the invention of the safety-lamp by Sir
Humphry Davy (1778–1829).
    In transport, the revolutionary change was
brought about by George Stephenson's
invention of the steam locomotive in 1814.
Railways spread rapidly over the country

during the next twenty years. In literature,
▷ Charles Dickens's ▷ *Dombey and Son*
gives an excellent impression of the impact
on contemporary imagination. Today our
domestic and industrial energy comes from
coal, gas, oil and electricity. The production
of the latter is often ▷ nuclear and, as such,
the centre for political contention.
    ▷ Industrial Revolution.

Fuller, Roy (b 1912)
Poet and novelist. Fuller was born in
Lancashire, and trained and worked as a
solicitor. He began writing in the 1930s, and
published two volumes of poetry whilst he
was in the Royal Navy during World War II:
The Middle of a War (1942) and *A Lost
Season* (1944) (his first volume appeared in
1939). Subsequent texts have shown certain
attributes of ▷ Movement irony, but with a
broader technical and emotional scope, as
well as a tendency to experiment with
versification. His more recent publications
include: *Counterparts* (1954); *Collected Poems*
(1962) and *From the Joke Shop* (1975).

**Funds, The; The Funded Debt;
    Fund-holders**
From the reign of ▷ William III the
government sought to finance its wars by
borrowing from private investors, issuing
'bonds' ('debentures') in acknowledgement of
the loan and paying regular interest. This is
the ▷ National Debt. It became the
commonest investment for small investors
and was the source of many 'private incomes'
in the 19th century.
    ▷ Bank of England.

Furies, The
In Greek and Roman myth, the goddesses
who pursued and punished evil-doers. The
Romans called them *Furiae*; the Greeks
Erinyes or, in propitiation, *Eumenides* (= the
Friendly Ones). ▷ T. S. Eliot uses them in
his play *Family Reunion* (1939); they are the
objectifications of the hero's mysterious but
overpowering sense of guilt. When he
discovers the causes of the guilt in his family
history, and is able to accept its burden, his
'furies' become 'friendly'.

Furnishings and furniture
1300–1600. Furniture was sparse and heavy:
benches were the principal seating; chairs at
first were few, and marks of rank. The
commonest light furniture was the backless
'joint-stool', *ie* one put together by a carpenter
or joiner. Heavy chests were used for books
and clothes, and sometimes adapted for
seating as 'settles'. Tables before 1500 were
boards set on trestles, easily movable. Floor-

coverings were commonly of rushes, not often changed. Walls were painted, or had painted cloth hangings, but by the 16th century richer households used embroidered and woven hangings, and these also surrounded the great 'four poster' beds which were also used by the middle classes in the 16th century 'Court-cupboards' were used to store plate (not clothes) and heavy 'buffets' or sideboards were used by the rich for display of dishes and goblets of gold and silver. Cushions were widely used in the 16th century. Display rather than comfort was the objective in all classes that could afford it; the poor were restricted to necessities: straw-stuffed sacks on benches or the earth floor for beds, and perhaps a trestle-table and a few stools.

1600–1800. These two centuries saw a steady advance towards modern standards of comfort. Carpets, formerly used, if at all, as wall-hangings or table coverings, found their way to the floor; walls were panelled in wood; chairs became plentiful in the second half of the 17th century, and the 18th was the great age of English furniture design: furniture of all kinds became light, graceful, adapted to the comfort of the users. Looking-glasses, still uncommon at the beginning of the 17th century, were usual at the end of it. Wallpapers – known since the 16th century – came into general use in the 18th. Even the poor came by then to have the simplest comforts, including 'cottage' versions of 18th-century furniture designs – ▷ Chippendale, Hepplewhite, ▷ Sheraton.

After about 1830, the 19th century saw the spreading of comfort amongst all classes in some degree – with the exception of the poorest agricultural labourers and the overcrowded slum-dwellers of the towns. Comfort rather than display was now the objective; or rather, a display of ornate comfort. Furniture became elaborate and much upholstered; window-curtains were heavy. Only beds became more rational, the four-poster going out of use as houses became better heated by more plentiful coal.

The 20th century has seen some vivid changes in furnishing. The cumbersome Victorian furniture was replaced by the slender, geometric lines of Art Nouveau, exemplified by the work of Charles Rennie Mackintosh. This trend towards simplicity continued in the smooth, straight lines and primary colours of Modernist design. The most influential of the modern developments was the Bauhaus movement, which advocated a basic abstract form in complete harmony with function and comfort. British furniture deviated from European and American design briefly during the 1950s when the post-war Utility programme produced unadventurous and standardized pieces. But in the 1970s and 1980s innovative design has generated two new areas of style: the craft-revival and High Tech. Recently, all these trends, from Chippendale to Utility, have been contained in Post Modernist design, with its radical forms, self-conscious irony and blatant disregard for comfort.

Further education
Term used to refer to education undertaken after leaving school but at a lower level than a degree course; usually of A level standard or below. There are 740 colleges of further education in England, nearly all under the control of local education authorities. Their courses are broadly vocational, in technical and commercial skills. A large proportion of students work only part-time, on day or block release or on evening courses. Two-thirds of the spending of these colleges goes on work-related studies. In the late 1980s, however, the involvement of employers in specifying how future workers should be educated has been officially encouraged: a privately funded body, the Business and Technician Education Council (BTEC), has been established to design syllabuses and validate courses offered at FE colleges; in 1986 the National Council for Vocational Qualifications (NCVQ) was set up by the government as a limited company to design and implement a new national framework for vocational qualifications.

▷ Adult education; Anti-industrialism; Capitalism.

G

Gabriel
Archangel; the heavenly messenger in the
Bible sent to ▷ Daniel to explain a vision
(*Daniel* 8 : 16) and to foretell the births of
John the Baptist and of Christ (*Luke* 1 : 19,
26).

Gael, Gaelic
The Scottish highland branch of the Celtic
race (▷ Celts) and its language. The words
are sometimes used for the Scottish and Irish
Celts together.

Galahad
Galahad is the son of ▷ Lancelot and Elaine
of Corbenic, conceived as a result of a
magical trick played on Lancelot by Elaine's
father, the Grail Keeper ▷ Pelles. When
Galahad comes to ▷ Arthur's court he is
marked out as the knight who will achieve the
Quest of the Grail by marvellous signs: he
alone can sit in the Perilous seat at the
▷ Round Table and draw the sword from
the stone, where it has been fixed by
▷ Merlin. His role is effectively that of a
knight-contemplative, whose values and actions
are directed entirely towards spiritual ends.
In early versions of the Grail narrative, the
role of Grail seeker is played by ▷ Perceval
who becomes a companion of ▷ Galahad's
in later reworkings of the Grail narrative,
including ▷ Malory's *Morte D'Arthur*.
▷ Arthur, King; Grail.

Galatea
In Greek myth, a sea ▷ nymph who loved
the shepherd Acis, and was beloved by the
▷ Cyclops Polyphemus. Polyphemus
crushed Acis with a rock, and Galatea
changed him into a river at the foot of Mount
Etna in Sicily.
A different Galatea was the statue given
life for ▷ Pygmalion.

Galen (Claudius Galenus) (2nd centuryAD)
Greek medical scientist; one of the most
important anatomists and physiologists of the
ancient world, and influential on Medieval
literature.

Galileo Galilei (1564–1642)
Italian astronomer; he was able, by improving
the newly invented telescope, to confirm the
theory of ▷ Copernicus that the earth
revolves round the sun, contrary to the
theory of ▷ Ptolemy that the earth is the
centre of the solar system. The observation
was made in 1610; in 1611 the English poet
▷ John Donne wrote the *Anatomy of the
World*;

> *And new Philosophy calls all in doubt,*
> *The Element of fire is quite put out;*

> *The Sun is lost, and th'earth, and no man's
> wit*
> *Can well direct him where to look for it.*

In fact the Church was disturbed at the
implications of Galileo's discovery in regard
to acceptance of the Holy Scriptures, and
declared it a heresy. Nonetheless Galileo's
view became slowly accepted. ▷ Milton, in
his epic of the Creation of the World,
▷ *Paradise Lost* uses the Ptolemaic theory,
though he had met Galileo and alludes to him
in the poem ('the Tuscan Artist' of Bk. I,
lines 288–91). ▷ Brecht uses Galileo's life
as the subject of an eponymous play.

Gallathea (1585)
A lyrical and courtly transvestite comedy by
▷ John Lyly about a virgin-sacrifice to
Neptune and the ensuing unwitting love-affair
of two disguised girls, one of whom Venus
promises to transform into a boy. The play's
heroine provides an early model for
▷ Shakespeare's Viola in ▷ *Twelfth Night*;
and through its jewelled elegance and
mythopoeia Lyly's play took English comedy
to new heights in the crucial decade preceding
the 1590s.

Galsworthy, John (1867–1933)
Novelist and dramatist. As a novelist, his
reputation was high in the first quarter of this
century for his surveys of upper class English
life, especially the ▷ *Forsyte Saga* sequence
(1906–21) and *A Modern Comedy* (*The White
Monkey*, 1924; *The Silver Spoon*, 1926; *Swan
Song*, 1928). After World War I, Galsworthy
underwent severe criticism by novelists of the
new generation as different as ▷ Virginia
Woolf ('Modern Fiction' in *The Common
Reader*; 1925) and ▷ D. H. Lawrence ('John
Galsworthy', in *Phoenix*; 1927). These
novelist-critics were writing in a period of rich
experiment in rendering the inwardness of
human experience and in testing and
renewing humane values in the social context;
to them, Galsworthy was artistically an
obstructive conservative, severely limited to a
vision of the outside of social phenomena and
to a merely social definition of human beings.
From such attacks, Galsworthy's reputation
has never recovered among the intelligentsia;
however, the popularity of a televised serial
version of the *Forsyte Saga* in 1967 suggests
that he may still be favoured by at least the
older generation of the general public. His
other novels are: *Jocelyn* (1898); *The Country
House* (1907); *Fraternity* (1909); *The Patrician*
(1911); *The Freelands* (1915); *Maid in Waiting*
(1931); *Flowering Wilderness* (1932).

As a dramatist, Galsworthy was one of those in the first decade of the century who restored to the English theatre a substantiality of subject-matter which had long been missing from it. His plays dramatized ethical problems arising from social issues. These too, however, have lost prestige, partly because of weaknesses similar to those that his novels are supposed to suffer from. Another criticism of the plays is that he brought to the theatre a novelist's vision rather than a dramatist's: during the last 50 years, British dramatists have believed that the drama requires an approach to the depiction of character and to the use of dialogue which is different to the vision of the novelist. Plays: *The Silver Box* (1906); *Joy* (1907); *Strife* (1909); *Justice* (1910); *The Pigeon* (1912); *The Eldest Son* (1912); *The Fugitive* (1913); *The Skin Game* (1920); *Loyalties* (1922); *The Forest* (1924).
▷ Realism.
Bib: Barker, D., *A Man of Principle*; Marrot, H. V., *The Life and Letters of John Galsworthy*; Fréchet, A., *John Galsworthy, A Reassessment*.

Galt, John (1779–1839)
Scottish writer of poems, travels, dramas and novels. He is chiefly remembered for his novels, especially *The Ayrshire Legatees* (1821), *Annals of the Parish* (1821), *The Provost* (1822) and *The Entail* (1823). These are vivid, realistic, humorous accounts of Scottish provincial society.
Bib: Gordon, R. K., *John Galt*; Aberdein, J. W., *John Galt*; Parker, W. M., *Susan Ferrier and John Galt* (British Council).

Gambling (Gaming)
A favourite English pastime since the ▷ Middle Ages. The use of dice ('hazard') goes back to pre-Christian times. Playing cards were introduced in the 15th century and were early used for gambling by all classes in the towns. In the reign of ▷ Elizabeth I gambling-houses (gaming-houses) had to be licensed by the Crown, and such licences were granted to courtiers. By the 18th century, upper-class society gambled extensively, and for high stakes. The London ▷ clubs were gambling rooms for men, and fashionable resorts such as ▷ Bath and Tunbridge Wells used their assembly rooms primarily for gambling and dancing. The 18th-century Lord Sandwich is supposed to have invented 'sandwiches' so that he would not need to get up from the gaming-table for a meal. The dramatist ▷ Richard Brinsley Sheridan ruined his finances by his heavy gambling.

Sport, especially horse-racing, has always had gambling as one of its main attractions; horse-races have appealed to rich and poor gamblers since the reign of ▷ Charles II, who first made them fashionable. Fights of all kinds – between cocks, dogs or men – have always been used as pretexts for gambling. Among team games, cricket was such a pretext in the 18th century, and in the 20th century the most popular of all forms of gambling is conducted through 'football pools'.

The English have always been prepared to use any doubtful issue as an excuse for gambling; in the 15th century appeals to the Pope by rival parties of churchmen, especially if these were composed of ▷ friars and of parish priests, were gambling occasions. But the most serious of all forms of gambling has been the kind known as 'financial speculation' and is a product of the capitalist (▷ Capitalism) economic system. Already early in the 17th century, adventurers known as 'projectors' were raising loans for investment in more or less illusory enterprises by encouraging the gambling spirit in country gentlemen; they and their foolish clients, known as 'gulls', were a common subject of ▷ Jacobean comedies such as ▷ Ben Jonson's ▷ *The Alchemist* and ▷ *The Devil is an Ass*. Just over a hundred years later gambling speculations caused the major financial crisis known as the ▷ South Sea Bubble, which brought ▷ Robert Walpole to power as the 'first Prime Minister'. Debtors' prisons such as the ▷ Marshalsea (the scene of much of ▷ Charles Dickens's novel ▷ *Little Dorrit*) were filled with rash speculators until imprisonment for debt was abolished in the mid-19th century.

In present-day Britain, gambling is as widespread as ever. 'Bingo' has led to the establishment of bingo clubs in nearly every town; these, and the widespread practice of gambling on football matches ('football pools'), attract small gamblers in very large numbers, so that occasionally large sums of money are won though only small ones are lost. The government profits from the national gambling instinct by the institution of Premium Bonds, which are similar to state lotteries in other countries. Legal restrictions on the transaction of ordinary bets have been relaxed, so that 'betting shops' are common in the towns of Britain. Whereas in the 19th century gambling was either the fashionable activity of the rich or the disgraceful one of the disreputable poor, it is now, in some of its forms, regarded as a legitimate pastime even for the respectable middle classes.

Game at Chess, A (1624)

A bold political ▷ allegory by ▷ Thomas Middleton. It enjoyed a short but highly successful run in London, because of its imaginative use of the pieces of chess and its appeal to popular sentiment hostile to the proposed Spanish marriage. In the play England is represented by white and Spain by black.

Game laws

'Game' means animals suitable for hunting and protected in the breeding season to ensure that supplies should not fail. Such animals in England have been hares, foxes and deer. Other animals such as rats and rabbits are 'vermin' and may be killed at any time. Certain birds, especially pheasants and partridges, are 'game birds'. Game of all sorts on private estates and in royal forests was protected at all times by severe game laws from depredations by poachers, so that the owner of the land should enjoy the monopoly of hunting the game on his own land. As the ▷ magistrates who enforced the laws were themselves the land-owners who had secured their imposition in Parliament, there was until the 19th century a fierce warfare between the landlords with their gamekeepers on the one side, and the poor who needed the game for food on the other; no part of the English penal system was so disproportionately severe.
Bib: Thompson, E. P., *Whigs and Hunters*.

Gamelyn

An anonymous Middle English verse romance, dating from the mid-14th century. Gamelyn is the youngest of three brothers who is deprived of his heritage and ill-treated by his eldest brother. He takes to the forest and leads the life of an outlaw, with a band of merry men. Eventually he succeeds in overthrowing the forces of the law which side with his unjust brother, retrieves his heritage, and is appointed Chief Justice. The romance appears in some manuscripts of the ▷ *Canterbury Tales* as the tale told by the pilgrim Cook (which is evidently an attempt by a 15th-century editor to fill out the unfinished state of ▷ Chaucer's text). *Gamelyn* was used by ▷ Thomas Lodge for his prose romance *Rosalynde* (1590), which ▷ Shakespeare used as a source for his comedy ▷ *As You Like It*.
Bib: Sands, D. (ed.), *Middle English Verse Romances*.

Gammer Gurton's Needle

A slight but very lively verse comedy of uncertain authorship, first acted in 1566, and printed in 1575. Gammer = old woman. She loses her needle, which she had been using to mend her man's breeches. The whole village is upset, until the needle is found in the seat of the breeches.

Gamp, Sarah

A drunken nurse in ▷ Charles Dickens's novel ▷ *Martin Chuzzlewit*. She always carried an umbrella and her name 'gamp' has therefore come to mean umbrella in colloquial usage.

Ganymede

In Greek myth, a beautiful youth who was carried up to heaven on the back of an eagle and became cup-bearer to the gods and ▷ Zeus's lover.

In Shakespeare's ▷ *As You Like It*, Rosalind takes the name when she dresses as a boy to go to the Forest of Arden.

Garden of Cyrus, The (1658)

A treatise on the quincunx (a shape or pattern composed of five parts) by ▷ Sir Thomas Browne. It was published together with ▷ *Urn Burial*, or *Hydriotaphia*, and is characteristic of Browne's delight in intellectual curiosity and his interest in the relationship between science and faith.

Gardens and Literature

A formal 18th-century garden

In the ▷ Middle Ages, the peasant kept his cottage garden for food, growing cabbages, beans, peas, onion and garlic. Gardens also existed in the towns, and in the 13th century were extensive in the suburbs. ▷ Monasteries had larger gardens, mainly for use rather than ornament, and they included 'stewponds' with stocks of fish. By the 15th century the upper classes were cultivating gardens in a more ornamental style, but it was in the later 16th century that the real enthusiasm for gardening began. ▷ Francis Bacon's essay *Of Gardens* (1625) is the best known of many literary manifestations of it.

The gardens of the period were formal, with straight alleys; plentiful use was made of hedges of box and yew, for dividing flower-beds into ornamental geometrical shapes ('knot-gardens') for flanking alleys, for making 'mazes' such as the one which survives at ▷ Hampton Court, for arbours (sheltered places) in which seats could be placed and for the topiary work (cutting hedges and bushes into the shapes of birds, people, etc) that Bacon despised. Utility was not ignored by rich gardeners and their travel overseas made it possible for them to import new vegetables, such as the potato and the beetroot; these, however, were not cultivated as large crops until much later. Herbs such as marjoram, thyme, rosemary and others were valued both for adding savour to food and medicinally – as the Friar explains in ▷ Shakespeare's ▷ *Romeo and Juliet* II.ii. Rhubarb was also commonly used medicinally. Orchards were important; apples, pears, apricots, almonds, peaches, figs, cherries and currants were all cultivated. Botany and horticulture were studied enthusiastically.

The enthusiasm for gardening, especially during the period 1550–1650, coincided with widespread interest in the literary modes of ▷ pastoral. In these, the garden is commonly used as an emblem for the innocence and freedom of unspoilt nature, in contrast to the corruption and anxiety of life in the towns and at court. Two traditions combined in the literary pastoral: the ▷ Bible-nourished ▷ Puritans recalled the bliss of the original ▷ Garden of Eden before the Fall of Man; and poet-scholars like ▷ Edmund Spenser (the Garden of Adonis in ▷ *The Faerie Queene* III.6) recalled the golden ages of Greek and Latin pastoral myth. Shakespeare uses a garden as an emblem of society in ▷ *Richard II*, III.4 and as an emblem of innocence in ▷ *The Winter's Tale*, IV.3. ▷ Andrew Marvell wrote several of his best poems on gardens as emblems of innocent and lavish happiness; the most famous of these is *The Garden* (about 1650).

The later 17th and the 18th centuries were periods in which comfort and elegance became important civilized values: buildings, to provide shelter from the unreliable British weather began to ornament the grander gardens; orangeries, for instance, containing orange trees in tubs and galleries for sauntering out of the rain, were introduced in the reign of ▷ William III. After 1725, gardens became means of escape from the formality of 18th-century civilization and the old formal garden went out of fashion. Large gardens were designed increasingly with eyes that appreciated the wildness of 'picturesque' landscape, a taste formed partly by 17th-century Italian and French painters such as Salvator Rosa and Claude. Thus gardens became to some extent imitations of pictures; if the landscape were not wild enough, dead trees might be planted, *eg* in Kensington Gardens, London. Imitation Greek temples, such as occur in Claude's pictures, were erected at suitable viewpoints, for instance on an island in a probably artificially created lake. The poet ▷ Alexander Pope was fond of carefully constructed caves ('grottos'). Later in the century, the taste for these architectural ornaments called 'follies' became more exotic: Chinese pagodas were built and imitation ruins of medieval Gothic castles were very common.

The 18th-century taste for 'wild' gardens was closely related to the literature of the period; it was indeed stimulated by ▷ James Thompson's landscape poems the ▷ *Seasons*. Later 18th-century poets, such as ▷ William Collins, ▷ William Cowper, ▷ Thomas Gray and others, wrote landscape poetry; much of it gives the impression of the poet enjoying a landscape from a distance or from a sheltered spot, as the landed gentry enjoyed their landscape gardens from their drawing-room windows. Designers of landscape gardens became artists with great prestige. The poet ▷ William Shenstone (1714–63) devoted his life and his fortune mainly to the landscaping of his property Leasowes. The most famous designer was Lancelot Brown ('Capability' Brown, 1715–83), who refused to allow any merely useful building, such as stables, to remain in sight of the house. But comfort, if not convenience, was maintained: 18th-and early 19th-century novels frequently mention 'shrubberies' – picturesque, sheltered walks, where the ladies could walk out of the weather. At the very end of the century, the books on landscape gardening and on the picturesque in landscape by Repton were widely read and coincided with the rise of the English school of landscape painters such as

Cotman and Crome. Though the novelist
▷ Jane Austen described surroundings very
little, references to the taste for landscape
recur in her books, and the whole fashion for
landscape-gardening is satirized in ▷ Thomas
Love Peacock's witty discussion novel,
▷ *Headlong Hall*.

After 1830, the taste for landscape
gardening on the grand, artificial scale of the
18th century declined. The most interesting
development in the history of gardens in the
19th century is the extension of the possession
of them to all ranks of society; even the poor
in the dense centres of the smoke-blackened
towns commonly had 'allotments' provided
for them at low rents in the suburbs. For
▷ Charles Dickens, the suburban cottage
with its flowery bower or arbour becomes a
setting for a new kind of pastoralism.
Among the rich, the chief new feature was
the large glass 'conservatory' for the
cultivation of exotic plants; even these were
adopted among the poor in the shape of the
modest 'greenhouse'. The 19th century also
saw the triumphant revival of ▷ Kew
Gardens and the Royal Horticultural
Society.

Possibly the most revolutionary
developments in 20th-century gardening
revolve around scientific processes and
mechanization. In a minor way, the rock
garden and the growing of flowers for
the arrangement of cut blooms also
changed British gardens. The triumph of
the small suburban garden continues and
a whole culture, including garden
books, magazines, radio and television
programmes, has developed to feed this
interest.

Public gardens and places of pleasure
became popular after the ▷ Restoration and
allusions to such places, *eg* ▷ Vauxhall, are
common in 17th-and 18th-century literature.
The Victorian period, with its philanthropic
funding, produced the golden age of public
parks. These gardens were not only locations
for scientific exploration, but also sites of
splendour and aesthetic display. The 20th
century has seen a decline in the quality of
parks, especially after the neglect during
World War II and the lack of public
expenditure on gardens in the post-war
economy. The underfunding continued in the
utilitarian eras of the 1950s and 1960s, and
even today, when some efforts towards
reclamation have been made, the public
garden usually remains a characterless and
desolate site.
Bib: Hadfield, M., *A History of British
Gardening*.

Gareth
Gareth is the youngest son of King Lot of
Orkney and Morgause. The fourth book of
▷ Malory's *Morte D'Arthur* recounts how
Gareth (nicknamed Beaumains) becomes
established as a knight of the ▷ Round
Table (he is a protégé of ▷ Lancelot), and
how he finally wins the hand of the lady
Lyones. Lancelot accidentally kills Gareth as
he rescues ▷ Guinevere from the stake.
▷ Gawain, in response, vows to revenge his
brother's death. Thus Gareth's death
provokes the hostilities between Gawain and
Lancelot which form one of the factors
contributing to the break-up of the Round
Table and the end of ▷ King Arthur's
reign.

Gargantua
A ▷ giant, chiefly known as the hero of
▷ François Rabelais's romances *Gargantua*
and *Pantagruel*, though he had a previous
existence in French folk-lore connected with
the Arthurian (▷ Arthur, King) legends. He
is mentioned in ▷ Shakespeare's ▷ *As You
Like It* II.2 before ▷ Rabelais had been
translated into English (1653), though
Shakespeare may have read Rabelais in
French.

Garrick, David (1717–79)

Sketch of David Garrick, March 1771

Actor, theatre manager, dramatist, whose
genius as an actor greatly enhanced the
theatrical profession in social prestige, and
who was also responsible for far-reaching
innovations in the theatre.

In 1737 he came to London with ▷ Samuel
Johnson who had been his tutor at Lichfield,
and entered Lincoln's Inn, but his career

there did not last. He had shown a taste for theatricals early in his youth, and in 1740 he put together a burlesque play based on characters of ▷ Henry Fielding, *Lethe: or Aesop in the Shades*, which was performed at a benefit night for ▷ Henry Giffard.

In 1741 Giffard took a small company including Garrick to Ipswich, and here the actor performed regularly for the first time, making his debut as Aboan in ▷ Thomas Southerne's *Oroonoko*, before returning to Giffard's Theatre at ▷ Goodman's Fields. Garrick, still unknown, played Richard III, to a rapturous reception. In 1742 Garrick travelled to Dublin with ▷ Peg Woffington, who became his mistress, and together they joined the ▷ Smock Alley Theatre. They returned to London and in 1742 Garrick opened his first season at ▷ Drury Lane. Denied their salaries by the irresponsible manager Charles Fleetwood, Garrick, ▷ Charles Macklin, and several other actors rebelled in 1743. Eventually, after a series of further disruptions, including several riots at the theatre, and a season at ▷ Covent Garden (1746–47), Garrick became a joint manager at Drury Lane in 1747. Two years later he married the actress Eva Maria Veigel.

Garrick proved a vigorous and creative manager, reviving the fortunes of Drury Lane, and adding to his own status as the leading actor of his generation. His sensitive and naturalistic acting style, inspired by that of Macklin but perfected by Garrick himself, set a standard for the period, making the previous formal and 'stagey' methods of acting seem outmoded. In 1763, after further rioting at the theatre, Garrick abolished the long practice of allowing spectators on the stage. He introduced lighting concealed from the audience which he had observed during a professional visit to Paris, and engaged the brilliant scene designer ▷ De Loutherberg, who created a series of sets in naturalistic, romantic style that complemented Garrick's own style of acting. He also wrote a number of plays, and rewrote others to conform with the tastes of his time, including *The Lying Valet* (1741), ▷ *Miss in Her Teens* (1747), in which he himself played the part of the fop, Fribble, ▷ *The Clandestine Marriage* (1766) (in collaboration with ▷ George Colman the Elder), *The Country Girl* (1766) (a revision of ▷ William Wycherley's ▷ *The Country Wife*), *The Irish Widow* (1772), *Bon Ton; Or High Life Above Stairs* (1775), and reworkings of several plays of Shakespeare.

Garrick retired in 1776, and died at his home in London after a long and painful struggle with illness. He was buried at Westminster Abbey, near the monument to Shakespeare who had provided him with many of his finest tragic roles, including not only Richard III, but ▷ Hamlet (his most popular part), ▷ Macbeth, and Lear (▷ *King Lear*). Garrick also excelled in comedy, his best parts including Abel Drugger in ▷ Ben Jonson's ▷ *The Alchemist*, Benedick in ▷ *Much Ado About Nothing*, and Bayes in the Duke of Buckingham's ▷ *The Rehearsal*, in which he triumphed when he imitated several well-known contemporary actors.

Bib: Murphy, A., *The Life of Garrick*; Oman, C., *David Garrick*; Kahrl, G. M. and Stone, G. W., *David Garrick, A Critical Biography*; Kendall, A., *David Garrick: A Biography*; Wood, E. R. *Plays by David Garrick and George Colman the Elder*.

Garter, The Order of the

An order of ▷ knighthood instituted by ▷ Edward III about 1344. The order was an imitation of the legendary one established by ▷ King Arthur, and Edward III built the great round tower of Windsor Castle as its meeting-place.

▷ Edward III.

Garth, Sir Samuel (1661–1719)

Doctor and member of the ▷ Whig clique known as the ▷ Kit-Cat club. His ▷ heroic couplet poem *The Dispensary* (1699) is a burlesque attack on the claim of apothecaries to exclusive control over the dispensing of medicines.

Gascoigne, George (1539–77)

Poet and playwright. His chief works include the unauthorized *A Hundreth Sundrie Flowers*, published in 1573; a collection of poems re-published in 1575 as *The Posies*; a ▷ satire entitled *The Steel Glass* (1576); and a number of plays which include *Supposes* (1566), one of the earliest comedies in English. Gascoigne's talents also encompassed fiction, a treatise on prosody and a ▷ masque.

Bib: Johnson, R. C., *Gascoigne*.

Gascoyne, David (b 1916)

Poet and translator. Gascoyne was born in Salisbury, and published his first volume of verse when he was only 16 (*Roman Balcony*; 1932). His poetry is fairly unusual in being strongly influenced by that of French ▷ surrealists, whom he has translated; at the age of 19 Gascoyne wrote *A Short Survey of Surrealism* (1935). His publications include: *Man's Life is this Meat* (1936); *Poems 1937–1942* (1943); *Collected Poems* (1965); *The Sun at Midnight* (1970); and *Collected Verse Translations* (1970).

Gaskell, Elizabeth Cleghorn (1810–65)

Elizabeth Gaskell by George Richmond (1851)

Novelist and biographer. She spent her married life in Manchester. She and her husband, who was a ▷ Unitarian minister, first intended to write the annals of the Manchester poor, in the manner of ▷ George Crabbe and her first novel, ▷ *Mary Barton* (1848), presented the outlook of the industrial workers with justice and sympathy sufficient to anger some of the employers. The novel appealed to ▷ Charles Dickens and she published her best known work ▷ *Cranford* (1851–3) in his periodical, ▷ *Household Words. Cranford* has been compared with the work of ▷ Jane Austen; it is slighter but has some of Jane Austen's ability to endow smallness of circumstance with large implications. It is a study of a small circle in a small town, modelled on Knutsford, Cheshire. *Ruth* (1853) is based on the same place. ▷ *North and South* (1855) is another study of industrial relations, centred this time on a south English heroine who comes to the north as to a foreign country. *Sylvia's Lovers* (1863) is more romantic than her previous work; in the same year appeared *A Dark Night's Work; Cousin Phyllis and other Tales.* Her masterpiece, ▷ *Wives and Daughters,* was not quite completed at her death. It belongs to the *Cranford* strain in her work but has greater richness, substance and variety. Her novels are an interesting connecting link between those of Jane Austen and those of ▷ George Eliot. She lacks the greatness of either and her reputation has unfairly suffered by comparison with them, but her achievement is substantial and enduring.

Her biography of her friend ▷ Charlotte Brontë, published in 1857, is accounted one of the best in English.

Bib: Hopkins, A. B., *Life*; Cecil, D., *Early Victorian Novelists*; Haldane, E., *Mrs Gaskell and her Friends*; Tillotson, K. (on *Mary Barton*) in *Novels of the Eighteen-Forties*; Gérin, W., *Elizabeth Gaskell: A Biography*; Easson, A., *Elizabeth Gaskell.*

Gawain

One of ▷ King Arthur's principal knights, the eldest son of King Lot of Orkney and Arthur's half-sister Morgause (called Anna in ▷ Geoffrey of Monmouth's version of Arthurian history). Gawain is an established member of Arthur's entourage in early accounts of Arthur's reign, and his role as an embodiment of the chivalric ethos is developed in the romances of ▷ Chrétien de Troyes. His reputation seems to have declined in later French Arthurian narratives, especially in the ▷ Grail stories, in which he is portrayed as a knight committed to vain worldly pursuits and ends. He is, however, the central hero of the Middle English romance ▷ *Gawain and the Green Knight*, in which the question of how to judge his performance becomes one of the main issues of the narrative. The variable representation of Gawain in Arthurian narrative is illustrated by his different roles in ▷ Malory's compilation of Arthurian history. In Malory's *Morte D'Arthur* Gawain is an exemplary chivalric figure, a failed knight of the grail quest, a loyal defender of the integrity of the ▷ Round Table who resists attempts by his half-brother Mordred and brother Aggravain to break up Arthur's court, and in the later stages of the narrative, an implacable enemy of ▷ Lancelot who, after the death of ▷ Gareth, promotes Arthur's war against Lancelot and thus plays a major part in the dissolution of Arthur's court. The mysterious link between Gawain's strength and the movement of the Sun, alluded to in Malory, is perhaps a remnant of a distant connection between Gawain and a Sun-god figure of Celtic mythology. According to Malory, Gawain's skull can still be seen at Dover castle.

Gawain and the Green Knight

One of the four later 14th-century ▷ alliterative narratives attributed to the ▷ Gawain poet, which survives, along with ▷ *Patience*, ▷ *Cleanness* and ▷ *Pearl*, in

Sir Gawain from *Gawain and the Green Knight*

a single manuscript. While the other poems address explicitly Christian topics and material, *Gawain and the Green Knight* tackles the traditions and conventions of Arthurian romance in a brilliant and complex narrative, structured around a series of interlocking games which have potentially very serious outcomes.

The story tells how a mysterious Green Knight visits ▷ King Arthur's court on New Year's Eve, offering a game. He offers any knight the opportunity to strike his head with an enormous axe if, in return, the knight agrees to submit to a return blow the following year. Gawain accepts the challenge on behalf of the court, and beheads the Green Knight, who proceeds to pick up his head and leave Arthur's court, reminding Gawain of his promise to come to his Green Chapel in a year for a return blow. The following year Gawain embarks on his quest for the Green Chapel, and takes refuge over the Christmas period in the castle of one Sir Bertilak. There Gawain gets involved in another game: for three days Bertilak is to go hunting and present Gawain with his winnings every evening. In return Gawain is

to give Bertilak whatever he has won during the day at the castle. Over the next three days Gawain is subject to the attentions of Bertilak's beautiful wife as he rests in bed. His chastity, loyalty to his host, and courtesy are tested, for in defending himself against the lady's advances, Gawain has to avoid any offence to her. At the end of every one of the three days Gawain has kisses to exchange for the spoils of Bertilak's hunting expeditions. However, on the final day Gawain does not hand over the green girdle he has accepted from the wife (she has claimed it has magic qualities and will protect Gawain's life against any threat). Gawain, wearing the green girdle, leaves Bertilak's court, and eventually finds the Green Chapel and the Green Knight. There Gawain is made to submit to three feints from the axe of the Green Knight, the last just cutting the flesh of his neck. Although Gawain is overjoyed at having survived his ordeal, his mood changes as the Green Knight reveals his identity and the mechanics of the games which Gawain has played. The Green Knight and Sir Bertilak are the same figure: the outcome of Gawain's experience at the Green Chapel has depended on how honestly he has played the exchange of winnings game at the castle. Gawain's slight wound repays his retention of the girdle, which the Green Knight now excuses. Gawain is mortified, and vows to wear the girdle as a sign of his shame and failure, but is fêted as a great hero on his return to Arthur's court. Henceforth all the members of Arthur's court decide to wear a green girdle.

There are analogues in earlier French romances and Welsh narrative for the beheading game and the exchange of winnings game, but not for their combination. The power and skill of the narrative technique of *Gawain* is reflected in the enormous amount of modern critical interest in the poem, but there is hardly any evidence at all which illuminates its contemporary reception.
Bib: Burrow, J. A., *A Reading of Gawain and the Green Knight*; Tolkien, J. R. R., Gordon, E. V. and Davis, N (eds.), *Gawain and the Green Knight*.

Gawain Poet (or Pearl Poet)
The name given to the hypothetical author of the four Middle English ▷ alliterative poems (▷ *Patience*, ▷ *Pearl*, ▷ *Cleanness*, ▷ *Gawain and the Green Knight*), composed in the second half of the 14th century, in the north-west Midlands area. The poems are all found in a single manuscript, British Library, Nero A. x.

There is no external evidence to suggest the poems are the work of a single writer: the theory of single authorship depends largely on the evidence of shared thematic interests, narrative techniques and sheer poetic skill which can be traced in all four poems.
Bib: Andrew, M. and Waldron, R. A. (eds.), *The Poems of the Pearl Manuscript*.

Gay, John (1685–1732)

Dramatist and poet, born at Barnstaple in Devon, the youngest son of William Gay. In 1708 he published a poem to celebrate the Act of Union between England and Scotland, 'Wine', and in 1711 a pamphlet *The Present State of Wit*. The following year he became a 'domestic steward' to the Duchess of Monmouth, and in 1714 secretary to Lord Clarendon, Tory envoy to Hanover. However, the accession to power of the ▷ Whigs threw him again upon his own resources. His farce, *The What D'Ye Call It*, a burlesque on what he deemed to be the moral and emotional falsity of heroic tragedy, as well as the growing taste for sentiment in comedy, followed in 1715. The play, which also satirized the idealization of country life, became a target for attack by the enemies of ▷ Pope, whom he had befriended. Gay's *Trivia, or the Art of Walking the Streets of London* (1716), on the conditions of life in the capital, is now considered a minor classic. In 1717 he collaborated with Pope and ▷ Arbuthnot on the satirical ▷ *Three Hours After Marriage*, caricaturing a number of contemporary literary figures. This was an initial success, but then lapsed from favour. Gay's *Poems on Several Occasions* (1720) made him some money, which he invested in the South Sea Company. When this failed, he was temporarily ruined.

The work for which Gay is best known is his ballad opera, ▷ *The Beggar's Opera* (1728), the source for ▷ Brecht's *The Threepenny Opera*. An instant success, the piece was said to have made 'Gay rich and Rich (the theatre manager) gay'. The so-called 'Newgate pastoral', with music by the German composer Pepusch, satirized the London underworld, and corruption in general. It was also read as an attack on the ruling party of ▷ Sir Robert Walpole, contributing to the Licensing Act of 1737, which restricted the activities of the theatre. Its sequel, *Polly* (1729), was banned by the Lord Chamberlain, although published by subscription. In his last years Gay lived mainly with two of his patrons, the Duke and Duchess of Queensberry in Wiltshire. He wrote the libretto for ▷ Handel's *Acis and Galatea* in 1731. Gay returned to London in 1732, and there died suddenly. He was buried in Westminster Abbey, where his epitaph, written by himself, is 'Life is a jest, and all things show it; I thought so once, and now I know it'.
Bib: Johnson, S., *Lives of the Poets*; Melville, L., *The Life and Letters of John Gay*; Irving, W. H., *Gay, Favourite of the Wits*; Sutherland, J., *Pope and his Contemporaries*.

Ge (Gaea)

▷ Classical Myth.

Gems, Pam (b 1925)

One of few female playwrights whose work has been performed by the ▷ Royal Shakespeare Company. She established her reputation relatively late in life, only becoming actively involved in the theatre when she was in her 40s. Although her plays deal specifically with female issues she distances herself from direct ▷ feminist polemic. A recurrent theme in her work is the need for women to discover their own identity in a world dominated and defined by men. Major works include: *Dead Fish* (later *Dusa, Fish, Stas and Vi*; 1976); *Queen Christina* (1977); *Piaf* (1978); *Loving Women* (1984); *Camille* (1985).
Bib: Keyssar, H., *Feminist Theatre*; Wandor, M., *Understudies*.

Gender

Originally used to distinguish between the categories of 'masculine' and 'feminine'. In modern ▷ feminist criticism it denotes something more than the different physical characteristics of both sexes. Feminist criticism regards 'masculinity' and 'femininity' as primary social constructions, supported by a range of cultural phenomena. The relationship between men and women is seen in material terms as a process of domination and subordination which functions objectively in material relations, but also subjectively in the ways in which men and women think of themselves. The concept of gender draws attention to the objective and subjective constructions of sexual difference, making possible an understanding of the mechanisms by which they operate, and offering the possibility of change.

There is a difference between the more sociological accounts and those – sometimes psychoanalytically based – which suggest there is something irreducible and specific in the nature of sexual difference. Here 'gender' is not one cultural label among others, but a firmly established basis for identity, as masculine or feminine (and not necessarily according to biological sex).

▷ *Ecriture féminine*; Feminism.

Geneva

City in Switzerland and a canton of the Swiss confederation. In the 16th century it became famous as the centre of the most extreme of the great ▷ Protestant reformers, ▷ John Calvin, founder of Calvinism. It became the centre of the League of Nations (1919) and, since the replacement of the League by United Nations, has remained an important centre of international organizations like the Red Cross, which was founded there in 1864.

▷ Presbyterianism.

Genre

In its use in the language of literary criticism the concept of 'genre' proposes that particular groups of texts can be seen as parts of a system of representations agreed between writer and reader. For example, a work such as ▷ Aristotle's *Poetics* isolates those characteristics which are to be found in a group of dramatic texts which are given the generic label ▷ 'tragedy'. The pleasure which an audience derives from watching a particular tragedy emanates in part from its fulfilling certain requirements stimulated by expectations arising from within the form itself. But each particular tragedy cannot be reduced simply to the sum of its generic parts. It is possible to distinguish between a tragedy by ▷ Sophocles, another by ▷ Shakespeare, or another by ▷ Edward Bond, yet at the same time to acknowledge that they all conform in certain respects to the narrative and dramatic rules laid down by the category 'tragedy'. Each example, therefore, repeats certain characteristics which have come to be recognized as indispensable features of the genre, but each one also exists in a relationship of difference from the general rule. The same kind of argument may be advanced in relation to particular sorts of poetry, or novel. The concept of genre helps to account for the particular pleasures which readers/spectators experience when confronted with a specific text. It also offers an insight into one of the many determining factors which contribute to the formation of the structure and coherence of any individual text.

Gentleman

The French 'gentil homme' meant 'nobleman', man of aristocratic descent. The tradition of courtly love required, however,

Frontispiece of Braithwaite's *English Gentleman* (1633)

that a gentleman's behaviour should correspond to his birth, *eg* in ▷ Chaucer's 14th-century translation of the ▷ *Roman de la Rose*: 'he is gentil bycause he doth as longeth to a gentylman'. By the 15th century, a gentleman did not necessarily own land, and at no time in the ▷ Middle Ages was a coat of arms considered a necessary adjunct to the rank. By the 16th century, however, the connection between the gentleman and the fighting man was established, and coats of arms, whose original function had been to distinguish a man for his followers and friends in battle, were regarded as indispensable. They could be obtained for money from the ▷ Heralds' College (as

▷ Shakespeare's father obtained his in 1596), and as soldiering was not a profession for which there was much opportunity in a peaceful country, they were freely granted. English society was anyway very mixed and the sons of long-established gentlemen became apprentices (▷ Apprenticeship) in the City. By the 17th century the feeling that a gentleman was known by his behaviour more than by his birth was thus more firmly established and ▷ James II is said to have remarked that he could turn a man into a nobleman but God Almighty could not turn him into a gentleman.

By the 19th century the title was allowed to all men of the educated classes, though being occupied in trade was still regarded as a barrier; in this respect the 19th century was perhaps less liberal than the 16th. Frequent explorations of the term in ▷ Anthony Trollope's novels show it as a site of contest: everyone wanted to claim they were a gentleman and its moral connotations were quite unstable. Though in theory it was behaviour that counted, appearances for most people counted still more, as is shown in Magwitch's notions of a gentleman in ▷ Charles Dickens's novel ▷ *Great Expectations* Chap. 39. The ▷ public schools, at least since the 17th century had associated the idea of gentleman with education, especially a classical education in Greek and Latin literature; in the 19th century the public schools were greatly increased in numbers and the association of the rank of gentleman with a public school education persists to the present day.

Gentleman Dancing Master, The (1672)
Play by ▷ William Wycherley, inspired partly by Calderón de la Barca's *El Maestro de Danzar*. 14-year-old Hyppolyta is forcibly betrothed to the stupid fop, Monsieur de Paris, and schemes to evade the watch kept on her and her woman Prue, to keep them in the house and away from men. She is attracted to Gerrard, and tricks her suitor into bringing Gerrard to her window. The pair meet secretly, but are interrupted by her father, Don Diego, alias Mr Formal. Hyppolyta passes Gerrard off as her dancing master, employed to teach her the fashionable dance, the Corant, and gains permission for him to visit her again. Gerrard is confused, but drawn to her beauty, and her fortune. He plans their elopement. After many more farcical episodes, the two are married. Mr Formal reveals that far from being 'of an honourable house', as he has claimed, he is

descended from a long line of merchants. He accepts the marriage, while Monsieur de Paris is obliged to return to Mrs Flirt, a 'common woman of the town', with whom he has had an affair. This is one of Wycherley's least appealing plays, and was not successful.

Gentleman's Magazine, The
Founded in 1731, it was the first to call itself a 'magazine'. It included, as later magazines were to do, a wider variety of material than the Reviews, including political reports which, in 1739–44, were contributed by ▷ Samuel Johnson.

Geoffrey of Monmouth (d 1155)
Author of the highly influential account of British history, in Latin prose, the ▷ *Historia Regum Britanniae* (*History of the Kings of Britain*), completed c 1138, which opened up a new vision of insular history, revealing Britain to be a formerly great European power. Little is known for certain about Geoffrey of Monmouth himself. He was probably born in Monmouth, of Welsh or Breton extraction, and seems to have been a resident of Oxford, probably a canon of the college of St George's, for many years of his life (?1129–51). In 1151 he became Bishop Elect of St Asaph. Before finishing his history of Britain, he produced a version of ▷ Merlin's prophecies, which were then incorporated into the history itself. At a later stage he returned to the subject of Merlin and around 1150 produced a Latin poem, the *Vita Merlini* (*The Life of Merlin*).

His history of Britain is an accomplished and complex exercise in history writing. He claims to have access to a source of British history, 'an ancient book in the British language', which has not been used by his contemporary historiographers, nor their predecessors. His narrative seems less likely to be the product of a single unidentified source, and much more the result of a careful act of compilation (using the work of contemporaries such as William of Malmesbury and earlier authorities on the history of the island, notably ▷ Gildas, ▷ Bede, and ▷ Nennius), and fabrication. In Geoffrey's narrative, a shadowy period of the island's past, covering the period before and after the Roman conquest, up to the beginnings of Saxon control in the 6th century, was given relatively detailed documentation, and a rather startling revision of Roman/British and British/Saxon power relations was advanced which disrupted some of the accepted facts of insular history. Geoffrey not only suggested that at certain stages of British history the power of Britain was a major threat to that of Rome, but that Britain was a unified realm well into the 6th century. His history also presented a picture of Britain as a world famous chivalric centre during the reign of ▷ King Arthur. A powerful argument for unified rule emerges from the history, which is a point of some relevance to the turbulent political context in which Geoffrey was writing.

The historical value of the *History of the Kings of Britain* was a controversial issue, debated and disputed by some historians of the 12th and later centuries. But Geoffrey's formulation of British history was widely used in chronicle histories of the island up to the 16th century and provided a historic foundation for the development of Arthurian narrative during the medieval period. Approximately 200 manuscripts survive of the history, and in addition there are numerous vernacular translations and adaptations extant. Poetic and dramatic versions of early British history, such as ▷ *Gorboduc* (1565), ▷ Spenser's ▷ *Faerie Queene*, ▷ Shakespeare's ▷ *King Lear* and ▷ *Cymbeline*, all use material which derives ultimately from Geoffrey of Monmouth's *History of Britain*.

▷ Laȝamon.

Bib: Thorpe, L. (trans.), *Geoffrey of Monmouth: The History of the Kings of Britain*.

George

The name of six of the kings of England belonging to the Houses of Hanover and Windsor. George I (1714–27) was great-grandson of ▷ James I (1603–25) and ruler ('Elector') of the German principality of Hanover. He was invited to take the throne of Britain, thereby superseding the ▷ House of Stuart, because the surviving members of this family were Catholics. George II, 1727–60; George III, 1760–1820: George IV, 1820–30; George V, 1910–36; George VI, 1936–52.

▷ Windsor, House of.

George, St

The patron saint of England. He is said to have been a native of Asia Minor under the Roman Empire, and to have been martyred as a Christian about AD 300. It is not clear how or why he killed a dragon. He is thought to have come to Britain under the Roman Emperor Diocletian, and to have protested against the persecution of Christians here. ▷ Edward III made him patron of England. St George's festival day is 23 April, but since the Catholic Church demoted him from a place on the universal calendar – due to lack of historical evidence – this is celebrated only in Britain.

Georgian

A term for the architectural style of the period 1714–1810, under ▷ George I, II and III. Georgian architecture was severe but balanced in its proportions. It was influenced partly by the Palladian (▷ Palladio, Andrea) style of ▷ Inigo Jones and partly by the direct experience of English travellers who made the Grand Tour of Italy and admired its classical buildings. The term is not usually applied to 18th-century literature; in other arts its suggestion of elegance and proportion is often modified by a taste for satire and caricature, as in ▷ Hogarth's paintings. It was followed by the ▷ Regency style.

Georgian Poetry

A series of verse ▷ anthologies of which five volumes appeared between 1912 and 1922. It was called 'Georgian' owing to the accession of ▷ George V (1910) and to imply a new start for English poetry, involving a degree of experiment and freshness of approach to the art. The poets represented in it included ▷ Rupert Brooke, W. H. Davies, ▷ de la Mare, ▷ D. H. Lawrence, ▷ John Masefield and ▷ Robert Graves. However, the contemporary work of ▷ W. B. Yeats, ▷ Ezra Pound and ▷ T. S. Eliot, more original and more substantial than the work of the Georgian poets, quickly made their movement seem relatively unexciting. Since 1950 there has been some revival of interest in it. It was lyrical, colloquial, emancipated from some of the dead poetic convention left over from the decadent ▷ romanticism of the previous century, but it lacked the strength and boldness of thought which marked the work of Yeats, Eliot and Pound.

Bib: Vines, S., *Movements in Modern English Poetry and Prose*; Stead, C. K., *The New Poetic*; Ross, R. M., *The Georgean Revolt: The Rise and Fall of a Poetic Ideal 1910–1922*; Rogers, T. (ed.), *Georgian Poetry, 1911–1922: The Critical Heritage*; Reeves, J. (ed.), *Georgian Poetry*.

Georgic

Virgil's *Georgics* (from the Greek word for a farmer) comprise four poems, addressed to the Emperor Augustus, describing the techniques of agriculture. During the 17th and 18th centuries they were extensively imitated in English, in ▷ blank verse or pentameter couplets (▷ metre), examples being ▷ John Philips's *Cyder*, ▷ John Dyer's *The Fleece*, and, in a more general way, ▷ Alexander Pope's ▷ *Windsor Forest* and much of ▷ William Cowper's *The Task*. ▷ John Gay's *Trivia*, set in London, is a humorous 'urban Georgic'.

Georgics, The

A poem on agricultural life by the Latin poet
▷ Virgil; it describes the peasant's year and
contrasts the virtues of life in natural
surroundings with the burdensomeness of
urban luxury. The poem was of great
influence on the tradition of ▷ pastoral
poetry from the 16th to 18th centuries.

German influence on English literature

Unlike other European literatures, such as
French or Italian, the literature of the
German-speaking world did not begin to make
itself felt in Britain to any great extent until
relatively recent times. There are two reasons
for this. The first is that the great flowering
of a literature written in the *modern* form of
the German language did not take place until
the second half of the 18th century; the
second is that German did not begin to
assume the status of a major foreign language
for the English until the second decade of the
following century and even then it remained
far behind French in importance. However,
there are isolated examples of such influence
before the late 18th century, two of which are
particularly interesting because they show
clearly that the structural model of
influencing and influenced literature falsifies
what is a far more complex pattern of
reciprocal interchange between two literary
cultures. For many years it was a matter of
debate whether the anonymous work *Der
bestrafte Brudermord* was derived from one of
the sources of ▷ Shakespeare's ▷ *Hamlet*
or was merely a botched version of the play.
It is now thought that the German play can
teach us nothing about Shakespeare's sources,
but another classic of the Elizabethan stage,
▷ Christopher Marlowe's ▷ *Doctor
Faustus* does draw upon a German source, a
legend which did not give rise to a classic in
its own language until the appearance of
▷ Goethe's ▷ *Faust* over two centuries
later.

In the cultural interchange between the
two literatures Britain has on balance been
the dominant partner. German men and
women of letters during the 18th century
were far more likely to have a lively awareness
of current developments in English literature
than were their English counterparts of
developments in Germany. For example, the
status of ▷ *Paradise Lost* as an epic poem
was debated, ▷ Alexander Pope's ▷ *Rape of
the Lock* was read and discussed, ▷ Oliver
Goldsmith, Edward Young, ▷ Laurence
Sterne and ▷ James Thomson all known
and admired. In this way English literature
was able to play a crucial role in the process

by which German writers of the late 18th
century succeeded in exerting their
independence from the prevailing standards
of neo-classical decorum which French
models seemed to dictate. The writers of the
Sturm und Drang ('Storm and Stress'), as
later the German romantics, looked to Britain
rather than France for support and
justification of their revolutionary project.
Shakespeare's status as a German classic
dates from this time, and the early attempts
of Gothold Ephraim Lessing (1729–81),
▷ Johann Wolfgang von Goethe and
Friedrich Schiller (1759–1805), who also
translated ▷ *Macbeth*, to provide a
repertoire for a German national theatre
owed a great deal to the English dramatist.
So when German theatre first made an
impression in Britain, the new stimulus
contained many, though unrecognized,
indigenous elements. Interest in German
theatre seems to have been kindled by the
Scot Henry Mackenzie who gave an address
on the subject to the Royal Society of
Edinburgh in 1788. During the 1790s the
English stage experienced a vogue for German
plays, but the public's taste was essentially
for the ▷ Gothic, and the most performed
writer was the justly forgotten August von
Kotzebue (1761–1819). It was not in drama,
however, that the first impact of the new
German literature was felt but in the novel.
Goethe's epistolary novel *Die Leiden des
jungen Werthers* (*The Sorrows of Young
Werther*) (1774) was a landmark for it was the
first work of German literature to achieve
European recognition. It was translated into
most European languages and reached Britain
in 1799, significantly via a French version.
The novel's apparent defence of suicide
caused a storm of righteous indignation, but
the huge popularity of the novel, here as
elsewhere, had much to do with the fact that
it appealed to a taste for 'sentimental'
literature which had already been established
in Germany and Britain by, among others,
▷ Samuel Richardson. Other currents made
themselves felt also. Bishop ▷ Percy's
Reliques of Ancient English Poetry (1765) had
stimulated Herder and, through him, Goethe
to explore their own native oral tradition of
'natural' *Volkspoesie*. This interest is reflected
in the novel in Werther's admiration of
Ossian (▷ Oisin), James Macpherson's
collection of supposed fragments of lost Celtic
epics, which had appeared in 1765.

This discovery of German literature by an
English audience unfortunately soon met an
insurmountable obstacle in the form of war.
In the wake of the ▷ French Revolution a

climate of opinion was created which was deeply and indiscriminately suspicious of all mainland European influence as ▷ Jacobin, subversive and unpatriotic. The fashion for German plays was snuffed out almost instantly, and it was not until the ending of the Napoleonic wars, with England and Prussia as victorious allies, that a new climate favourable to the reception of German writers could be created. The publication of Madame de Staël's *De l' Allemagne* (1813) is rightly regarded as a crucial event in this process. When English interest was reawakened, it was once again Goethe who was at the centre of controversy. It is easy to smile now at the response to the first part of *Faust* (1808), but the work was then felt to be deeply shocking. Quite apart from a degree of frankness in sexual matters unthinkable in an English work, there were features which were regarded as highly offensive to orthodox Christian sentiment. Goethe's reputation as an immoral author was revived, and it seems likely that fear for his own reputation played some part in ▷ Samuel Coleridge not undertaking a commissioned translation of the work. It is one of the imbalances in the relations between English and German literature that while English classics found immensely talented translators in Germany – the Tieck-Schlegel version of Shakespeare, for example – many great German works have been either completely overlooked or ill-served by their English translators.

Of the first generation of English romantic poets only Coleridge, if we discount ▷ William Blake's idiosyncratic relationship to the mystic and visionary Jakob Böhme (1575–1624), was deeply influenced by German culture. A cautious admirer of Goethe, translator of Schiller's *Wallensteins Tod* (*Wallenstein's Death*), Coleridge visited Göttingen in 1798. His thought was deeply indebted to ▷ Immanuel Kant, Johann Gottfried von Herder (1744–1803) and the *Naturphilosophie* of Friedrich Schelling (1775–1854). ▷ William Wordsworth, who in his view of nature was far closer to Goethe than he realized, shared the opinion of many in dismissing him as an immoral and irreligious writer, but ▷ Byron and ▷ Shelley had no sympathy with such small-mindedness. Shelley valued *Faust* highly, and it is a loss to English culture that his efforts at translation never extended beyond a few small fragments of the work. As for Byron, his admiration was genuine, if not matched by any great depth of response. His esteem, however, was reciprocated. Sadly Byron, whose works, ▷ *Childe Harold's*

Pilgrimage and ▷ *Don Juan* especially, were widely read and admired in Germany as in the rest of Europe, did not live to see the tribute Goethe paid him in the second part of *Faust* (1832), where the English poet is represented as the child of Faust and Helen. For ▷ Thomas Carlyle, Goethe and Byron signified opposite moral and artistic poles, and it was Carlyle who was the single most important conduit of German literature and thought in the 19th century. He had already published his translation of Goethe's *Wilhelm Meister* when, in 1839, his *Critical and Miscellaneous Essays* appeared, containing the many articles on German literature which he had written for the journals of the day. The work was seminal and inaugurated what was the great age of German influence in Britain. Probably inspired by Carlyle, ▷ Matthew Arnold immersed himself in the works of Goethe and was deeply influenced by him. His discovery and admiration of Heinrich Heine (1797–1856) on the other hand was quite independent and an appreciative essay on the later poet is included in *Essays in Criticism* (1865). For Arnold, Goethe and Heine were great modern spirits in comparison with whom the English romantics were insular and intellectually deficient. Arnold's German culture extends far beyond these two authors however, and, in scope at least, he is like ▷ George Eliot in this regard. It is now appreciated that the profound influence of the so-called 'Higher Criticism' in Britain does not commence with the publication in 1846 of her translation of Strauß's *Das Leben Jesu* (1835) but has roots which reach back into the last quarter of the 18th century, and that Coleridge was ahead of his time in his appreciation of the significance to religion and philosophy of the German school of Biblical criticism. George Eliot is less a beginning than a culmination. Arnold had recognized in Goethe a figure who was working to 'dissolve' the dogmatic Christianity which had once been the bedrock of European civilization. It is now clear, however, that it was the Higher Criticism which, by mythologizing Christianity, undermined its claims more surely even than ▷ Charles Darwin, the geologists and positivist science. From this it is clear that when considering the massive response of English writers to German literature at this time, no sharp line can be drawn between works of imagination on the one hand and works of historical scholarship, cultural history and philosophy on the other. If a novel of ideas such as ▷ *Daniel Deronda* could hardly have been written without

Strauß (1808–74) and Feuerbach (1804–72), then Goethe's *Wilhelm Meister* is scarcely less crucial. The relevance here of ▷ G. H. Lewes, whose *Life of Goethe* appeared in 1855, is obvious. In the last decade of the century another admirer of Goethe, ▷ Oscar Wilde, with inspired flippancy, could show young Cecily earnestly studying her German grammar under the eyes of Miss Prism and the Reverend Chasuble, but for many the loss of religious faith which followed the encounter with German thought brought great anguish before it brought serenity.

It is one of the paradoxes of the Victorian era that, while a series such as Bohn's Standard Library made available to a reading public a large number of German classic texts in translation, there were still many gaps and absences. The imaginative literature of the middle and second half of the century, represented by writers such as the Austrian Franz Grillparzer (1791–1872), E. Mörike (1804–75), A. Stifter (1805–68), Friedrich Hebbel (1813–63), T. Storm (1817–88), Theodor Fontane (1819–98), and the Swiss writers G. Keller (1819–90) and C. F. Meyer (1825–98) did not reach the wider audience it deserved. Because this literature is in a sense provincial, its failure to make much impression in Britain is less surprising than the British blindness to the considerable achievements of important earlier figures such as Heinrich von Kleist (1777–1811) or E. T. A. Hoffmann (1776–1822), though the latter was not unknown and certainly influenced Edgar Allen Poe. Of this generation it was perhaps the figure of Richard Wagner (1813–83), more associated with music than literature, whose work has had most influence on English literature. In some ways he was an important precursor of the Celtic revival, and his aesthetic theories as much as his use of the *leitmotif* influenced subsequent writers throughout Europe. ▷ James Joyce associated the technique with Wagner and, of course, ▷ T. S. Eliot famously quotes *Tristan und Isolde* in ▷ *The Waste Land*.

In the 20th century, however, the European character of modernism in literature, as of romanticism before it, is impossible to mistake, and the German presence is particularly marked even if the complex and contradictory nature of modernism makes generalization hazardous. To study the poetry of Rainer Maria Rilke (1875–1926) and ▷ W. B. Yeats, however, is to be conscious of a broadly similar response to a common cultural situation rather than of indebtedness or influence. Deprived of belief in orthodox religion, both poets satisfied their need for a spiritual sense of existence by creating personal mythologies which display many striking parallels with each other. Rilke is unusual in being perhaps the only German writer to achieve recognition in England solely as a poet. This was certainly made possible by the Leishman, and Leishman-Spender translations, but ▷ Stephen Spender was not alone in his generation in being able to read German literature without the need for translations. ▷ Louis MacNeice himself was a co-translator of *Faust*, both ▷ W. H. Auden and ▷ Christopher Isherwood knew German, Auden translating Goethe's *Italienische Reise* and some works of ▷ Brecht. During the 1930s the rise of ▷ fascism in Germany brought about the exile of nearly every significant writer, and resistance to this evil united many writers of both countries in a sense of common purpose. In the theatre the leading German naturalist playwright Gerhart Hauptmann (1862–1946) may not have had the impact of the Scandinavian dramatists ▷ Ibsen and ▷ Strindberg but in intellectual left-wing circles at least he was read and admired. The presentation of industrial class conflict in *Die Weber* (*The Weavers*; 1892), where Hauptmann succeeds in creating a 'social' drama without individualized heroes, renewed interest in German theatre and in some ways foreshadowed the political commitment associated with the name of Brecht. Hauptmann is rarely performed in Britain now, but this is true of most German dramatists. German expressionist theatre (▷ Expressionism) swiftly found interest in Britain during the 1920s because of its radically experimental approach but only one work, G. Kaiser's (1878–1945) *Von morgens bis mitternachts* (*From Morning to Midnight*; 1916), achieved any success. The number of German plays one is likely to find regularly performed on the English stage now is relatively small in comparison to the presence of English works in German theatres. Goethe's *Faust* or Schiller's *Maria Stuart* are occasionally done, but one is far more likely to see the plays *Woyzeck* and *Dantons Tod* by Georg Büchner (1813–37). As in Germany, Büchner came to be valued only long after his premature death, but the vitality and continuing relevance of his plays and his justified reputation as an early forerunner of modern sensibility ensure continued interest in him. Frank Wedekind (1864–1918) has provided in his *Frühlings Erwachen* (*Spring's Awakening*; 1891) a masterpiece which has triumphantly survived translation, but it was one of Wedekind's admirers, Brecht, who has had the most extensive and long-lasting influence on the theatre of the English-speaking world. His opposition to Hitler and the commitment to peace which informs all his work have made him more acceptable in Britain than in America where his undisguised communist sympathies have told against him. The style of his so-called Epic theatre, particularly in its rejection of naturalism and its use of music, songs and verse, has been widely imitated even where – perhaps especially where – it has been detached from its original political thrust.

As might be expected, it is the modern novelists rather than the poets or dramatists who have reached the widest audiences. During the 19th century the figures of ▷ Walter Scott, ▷ William Thackeray and ▷ Charles Dickens exercised a profound influence on the development of ▷ realist fiction in Germany. Thomas Mann (1875–1955) was closest to this tradition in his novel of the decline of a bourgeois family, *Buddenbrooks* (1901), and for many years was held in high esteem, but, perhaps because his later fiction took a rather different and more philosophical direction, his reputation has waned in recent years. Hermann Hesse (1877–1962), after a period of considerable popularity, has suffered a similar fate, but the fascination of the Czech Franz Kafka (1883–1924) is undiminished. All his writings are fables of alienation and his name has become a byword for the bizarre and nightmarish. His unique vision is too personal for imitation, but it is hard to imagine how Joseph Heller's *Catch 22* (1961) and *Something Happened* (1974) could have been written without Kafka. A very different kind of fantastic realism characterizes the work of Günther Grass (b 1927) and, together with Heinrich Böll (b 1917), he stands out among the writers of the post-war generation as one whose work has spoken most immediately to his English-speaking contemporaries.

There can be little doubt that the profoundest influence on English literature and the literatures of most other countries in the 20th century stems not from the imaginative literature of Germany but from the philosophical. Probably this should not surprise us, since a philosophical tradition from which emerged in the 19th century the towering figures of ▷ Hegel, ▷ Schopenhauer and ▷ Nietzsche had already left its mark. In ▷ Karl Marx (1818–83) and ▷ Sigmund Freud (1856–1939), however, the German-speaking world produced two thinkers who have as decisively and permanently transformed the whole

framework of terms within and by which we conceive society and the human mind, as Darwin and Einstein have transformed our understanding of the physical world. This is no less true for a writer like Vladimir Nabokov (1899–1977), who dismisses Freud as the Viennese witch-doctor, than for ▷ D. M. Thomas. For the British there is, of course, a special poignancy in this, as both these radical thinkers were driven by political circumstances from their native countries and found refuge in Britain.

Goethe foresaw a time when, with the help of translations, national literatures would give way to a *Weltliteratur*. In the bookshops of the Federal Republic, where translations from English abound, one is inclined to feel that the day has arrived, but a visitor to a British bookshop in search of translations from the German is likely to reflect that here at least this consummation has still to come.

Geryon
In Greek myth a triple-bodied monster who owned a herd of oxen guarded by the herdsman Eurytion and the hound Orthrus. The hero ▷ Hercules destroyed them and carried away the oxen. In Dante's ▷ *Inferno*, Geryon is the guardian of the eighth circle of hell. In Spenser's ▷ *Faerie Queene* Geryoneo is a three-bodied monster representing Philip II's power over Spain, Portugal and the Low Countries.

Ghosts
'Ghost' in modern English nearly always denotes a spirit of a dead person appearing to the living, though the older sense remains in the religious use of 'Holy Ghost'. For literary purposes ghosts may be divided into five kinds.

1 Earthbound spirits of popular tradition; they are not allowed to rest in the grave until a wrong done to them or by them has been set right, *eg* vengeance taken for murder. ▷ Hamlet's father is such a ghost.

2 Dream apparitions, commonly sent with a message or a warning to the sleeper, *eg* the murdered man appearing to his friend in ▷ Chaucer's ▷ *Nun's Priest's Tale* (*Canterbury Tales*) and perhaps the ghost of Caesar appearing to Brutus in ▷ Shakespeare's ▷ *Julius Caesar* IV. 3.

3 ▷ Protestant belief in the 16th century was that a ghost might be a disguised emissary of the Devil; this is important in *Hamlet* – 'Be thou a spirit of health or goblin damn'd' etc. (*Hamlet* I. 4. 41) – Hamlet does not know whether the ghost really is his father or a devil with his father's appearance.

4 On the other hand the ghost of Banquo

($\triangleright$ *Macbeth* III. 4) may be regarded as a hallucination both of Macbeth's guilty conscience; another common form of 'ghost'.

5 Finally, there is the comic or melodramatic kind of ghost, a kind of literary caricature of the first type, common in the $\triangleright$ Gothic tales of the 18th and early 19th century, and in more light-hearted Victorian tales, *eg* $\triangleright$ Charles Dickens's $\triangleright$ *Christmas Carol*. Ghosts have rarely been used in serious literature of the last two hundred years; exceptions are $\triangleright$ Emily Brontë's $\triangleright$ *Wuthering Heights* and $\triangleright$ Henry James's $\triangleright$ *The Turn of the Screw*.

Giants

In Greek myth, the children of $\triangleright$ Ge, the Earth, and sprung from the blood of $\triangleright$ Uranus, the Sky. They revolted against the gods under $\triangleright$ Zeus and had to be put down by the hero Hercules ($\triangleright$ Heracles), since the $\triangleright$ oracle declared that they could be overcome only by a mortal. (They are not to be confused with the $\triangleright$ Titans, who preceded them.) They are said to have heaped a mountain on a mountain, Pelion on Ossa, in order to reach the heavens.

Giants are common in other mythology, and frequently occur in folk myth in fairy stories such as $\triangleright$ *Jack and the Beanstalk*.

Giaour, The (1813)

A verse tale by $\triangleright$ Lord Byron in tetrameter couplets ($\triangleright$ metre) interspersed with quatrains. The word was used by the Turks as a general term for non-Muslims, especially Christians. The poem is about the love of a Turkish slave Leila for a giaour; her master causes her to be thrown into the sea, and her lover avenges her death.

Gibbon, Edward (1737–94)

One of the greatest English historians, author of $\triangleright$ *The Decline and Fall of the Roman Empire* (1776–88). His reputation rests almost entirely on this work, but his *Memoirs* (1796), put together from fragments after his death, are one of the most interesting biographies of the 18th century. In 1761 he published in French his *Essai sur l'Etude de la Litteŕature*, translated into English in 1764; it was more successful abroad than at home. He was also a Member of Parliament, 1774–81. **Bib**: Low, D. M., *Edward Gibbon*; Young, G. M., *Gibbon*; Sainte-Beuve, C.-A., in *Causeries dy Lundi* vol viii.

Gide, André (1869–1951)

French novelist. He developed an early preference for the *sotie* or *récit* (short prose piece) and in this form produced *L'Immoraliste* (1902), *La Porte étroite* (1909)

and *La Symphonie pastorale* (1919). These are short, tightly-organized stories which exploit the characteristic weaknesses of first-person narration, in that their narrator-protagonists are without exception blind to the consequences of their words and actions. In all cases, this narrator is sharply distinguished from the author, who distances himself from his characters through $\triangleright$ irony (the title *sotie* denotes strong mockery). *Les Caves du Vatican* (1914) is a longer *récit* which develops the notion of the 'gratuitous act', an unmotivated and unpremeditated act which would constitute an effect without a cause and novelistically represent an unpredictable element altering the course of the narration. The work also portrays the stifling, hide-bound world of marriage, the family and religion, all objects of Gidean criticism. These concerns surface again in the only work which Gide called a novel, *Les Faux-Monnayeurs*, published in 1925. Its theme is moral and literary counterfeiting and the contrasting search for authenticity and openness (*disponibilité*) to experience. The experimental aspect of the novel is striking. Narrative orderliness and momentum are broken up by the plurality of angles of vision and the constant switching from one sub-plot to the next. Moreover, the author himself intervenes in the narrative to rupture any suspension of disbelief by declaring his own lack of control over characters and events. Above all, Gide makes crucial use of what he named the *mise en abyme* technique, a procedure by which the novel debates its own problems. In Gide's novel, this technique is exemplified in the character Edouard. Edouard is a novelist whose diary, 'quoted' by Gide, records his difficulties in writing his own novel, itself called *Les Faux-Monnayeurs*. This self-consciousness, highlighting the literariness of literature, has proved influential in the subsequent development of the novel in France.

Gide also helped found the literary magazine *La Nouvelle Revue française* and certain of his own works first appeared in its pages (*La Porte étroite*, *Les Caves du Vatican*, *Les Faux-Monnayeurs*).

Gielgud, Sir John (b 1904)

English actor and director who first appeared on stage in 1921 at the Old Vic. He is most famous for his performances of leading roles in $\triangleright$ Shakespeare's plays, particularly during the 1930s and 40s. He began directing in 1932 with a production of $\triangleright$ *Romeo and Juliet* for the Oxford University Dramatic Society. His production of $\triangleright$ *Hamlet* at the

▷ New Theatre in 1934 ran for 155 performances and was a landmark in West End productions of Shakespeare. He has continued a distinguished acting career up to the present day.
Bib: Gielgud, J., *Early Stages*; Gielgud, J., *Stage Directions*; Hayman, R., *John Gielgud*.

Giffard, Anna Marcella (1707–77)
▷ Giffard, Henry.

Giffard, Henry (1694–1772)
Actor, manager. The date and place of his first stage performance are uncertain, but by 1720 at the latest he was acting at the ▷ Smock Alley Theatre in Dublin, where he remained for at least seven years, acting in a variety of young romantic lead roles. He married his second wife, Anna Marcella Lyddall, the actress and singer, c1729.

By 1731 Giffard and his wife had appeared at the ▷ Haymarket Theatre, but later that year he took over running ▷ Goodman's Fields Theatre, refurbishing it and engaging a number of new actors. He opened a new theatre, also known as Goodman's Fields, in 1733. In 1737 he took the script of a satiric play to ▷ Sir Robert Walpole, and this was used, in part, by the Government as a pretext for passing the ▷ Licensing Act. Lacking a patent, Giffard was forced out of business, although he subsequently staged some performances at the fringes of the law, including the first performance of ▷ *The Winter's Tale* for over a hundred years.

By 1740 Giffard had successfully petitioned for permission to re-open Goodman's Fields, both managing and acting at the theatre. His reputation later rested not so much on his acting talents, which were not always wholeheartedly received, as on his abilities as a manager. He was also remembered for his encouragement of other actors, not least ▷ David Garrick, to whom he gave his first acting opportunity, in 1741.

Gifford, William (1756–1826)
Journalist. He began as a shoemaker's apprentice, and rose to be an influential writer and editor of the right-wing press. He edited *The Anti-Jacobin* (1797–8) to counteract opinion sympathetic to the ▷ French Revolution, and became editor of the famous Conservative ▷ *Quarterly Review* in 1809.

Gilbert, Sir William Schwenck (1836–1911)
English dramatist most famous for his partnership with Sir Arthur Sullivan. Together they produced the famous ▷ Savoy operas, so called because they were produced at the Savoy Theatre; Gilbert wrote the libretti and Sullivan composed the music. The partnership began with *Thespis*; or, *The God Grown Old* in 1871 and concluded with *The Grand Duke* (1896). The best known of these light operas are *H.M.S. Pinafore* (1878), *The Pirates of Penzance* (1880), *Iolanthe* (1882), *The Mikado* (1885) and *The Gondoliers* (1889). His plays are rarely performed now, although *Engaged* (1887) has received attention recently for its influence on ▷ Oscar Wilde's *The Importance of Being Earnest*.
Bib: Cox-Ife, W., *Gilbert: Stage Director*; Sutton, M., *Gilbert*.

Gildas (d 570)
A British monk, living in the west of England, whose work, *De Excidio Britanniae* (*About the Fall of Britain*), written about 547, provides the only contemporary account of 6th-century Britain. It was written as a polemical piece, aimed at provoking the reform of British ecclesiastics and leaders. Gildas provides a preface to his complaint in which he sketches the course of British history after the Roman withdrawal. No mention is made of ▷ Arthur in his narrative, but the British triumph against Saxon aggressors at Badon (a victory later attributed to Arthur) is noted. Gildas's narrative was later used by ▷ Bede and thus indirectly helped to shape the representation of the British past in all the major insular histories of the medieval period. ▷ Geoffrey of Monmouth reworked parts of Gildas's text in his ▷ *Historia Regum Britanniae*.

Gilfil's Love-Story, Mr
One of ▷ George Eliot's ▷ *Scenes of Clerical Life*.

Gipsies
A nomadic race, dark-skinned, speaking their own language related to the Indian Hindi. They spread across Europe in the 15th century and seem to have reached Britain about 1500. Owing to a belief that they came from Egypt, they were known as Egyptians, corrupted to Gipsies (Gypsies), but they called themselves Romanies. They commonly lived in caravans and moved from place to place, making a living (in the English countryside) as tinkers and by begging. Among country people they had a bad reputation for lawlessness and stealing, including the kidnapping of children; but their exoticism caused them to be romanticized in the 19th century, *eg* the gipsies in the novel ▷ *Guy Mannering* (1815) by ▷ Walter Scott. ▷ George Borrow is the most notable romanticizer of gipsies (of whom he made almost a life study) in his

rambling, often vivid semi-fictional
▷ autobiographical and travel books, such
as *Lavengro* (1851), *The Romany Rye* (1857).
In modern Britain, so-called gipsies are
often merely vagrants with no gipsy
ancestry. Centuries of intermittent
persecution have done less than the modern
▷ Welfare State has done to make the
gipsy existence difficult. They have,
however, in 1988 been officially recognized
as a racial group by the Commission for
Racial Equality. For a 20th-century tale of
a gipsy see *The Virgin and the Gypsy* by
▷ D. H. Lawrence.

Gissing, George Robert (1857–1903)
Novelist; author of: *Workers in the Dawn*
(1880); *The Unclassed* (1884); *Demos* (1886);
A Life's Morning (1888); *The Nether World*
(1889); *The Emancipated* (1890); ▷ *New Grub
Street* (1891); *Born in Exile* (1892); *The Odd
Women* (1893); *The Town Traveller* (1898);
The Crown of Life (1899); *Our Friend the
Charlatan* (1901); *By the Ionian Sea* (1901);
The Private Papers of Henry Ryecroft (1903).
Posthumous: the historical novel *Veranilda*
(1904) and *Will Warburton* (1905). Of these,
much the best known is *New Grub Street*, a
study of literary life in late-19th-century
London. Gissing saw with deep foreboding
the spread of a commercialized culture which
would so oppress the disinterested artist and
so encourage the charlatan that, in his view,
national culture was bound to deteriorate,
with concomitant effects on the quality of
civilization as a whole. The partial fulfilment
of his predictions has given this novel in
particular a greatly revived prestige. His
vision was serious and sombre, and he
depicted the enclosed, deprived world of the
poor of his time in *Demos* and *The Nether
World*. *Thyrza* and *Henry Ryecroft* are other
novels which are singled out from his work.
He was deeply interested in ▷ Charles
Dickens and his study of that novelist
(1898) is among the best on the subject; but
he had also been affected by the austere,
scrupulous artistry of the French 19th-
century novelists ▷ Flaubert and ▷ Zola.
His best work often has a strong
autobiographical content, characteristic of
some of his contemporaries, such as
▷ William Hale White and ▷ Samuel
Butler.
Bib: Donnelly, M., *Gissing, Grave Comedian*;
Korg, J., *Gissing*; Roberts, M., *The Private
Life of Henry Maitland* (novel based on
Gissing's life); Poole, A., *Gissing in Context*;
Collie, M., *The Alien Art: A Critical Study
of George Gissing's Novels*.

Gladstone, William Ewart (1809–98)
One of the principal British statesmen of the
19th century and a leader, first of the
▷ Tories (Conservatives) and later, as Prime
Minister four times, of the Liberals (formerly
▷ Whigs). His strength lay in finance – he
was an advocate of ▷ free trade – and
domestic reform; late in life he advocated and
came near to bringing about self-government
for ▷ Ireland (Irish Home Rule). His
personality was impressive, and his ardour
and energy very great, but he lacked the
intimate charm and subtle wit of his opponent
▷ Benjamin Disraeli, whom he fought with
almost religious dedication. Their rivalry is
often recalled as a golden age of English
parliamentarianism by those who see public
competition and conflict between individuals
as the most productive form of political
activity.
    Gladstone was a man of deep culture, a
classical scholar who published studies of
ancient Greek literature. His reforms were
important in removing abuses and improving
justice and equality in the universities, the
army, the ▷ franchise, the right to form and
maintain ▷ trade unions, and recruitment
to the military and civil services.

Glastonbury
A town in Somerset where there are the ruins
of a great Benedictine abbey. In prehistoric
times it was almost a lake island, being set in
a group of hills surrounded by low-lying
country; the highest of the hills, Glastonbury
Tor, appears to have figured in early myths
as a point of contact with, and entry to, the
Otherworld. Thus the notion of Glastonbury
as a spiritual centre seems to be of great
antiquity.
    Many myths and legends have been
generated about Glastonbury Abbey. It was
the site of an early Celtic Christian
community from the 6th century, but it was
reputed to be the site of the first Christian
church in Britain, founded by Joseph of
Arimathea, the rich man described in the
Gospels who buried Christ in his own
sepulchre. Joseph was reputed to have planted
his staff at Glastonbury, and this miraculously
became the Glastonbury thorn, a tree which
flowers at Christmas. The discovery and
excavation of the graves of ▷ King Arthur
and ▷ Guinevere at Glastonbury in 1191
encouraged the identification of Glastonbury
with the island of ▷ Avalon, and the
connection between Arthurian history and
Glastonbury was further developed in the
Arthurian narratives which recount the
history and quest of the Holy ▷ Grail,

The Globe Theatre

which was reputed to have been brought to Britain by Joseph of Arimathea. At the end of ▷ Malory's ▷ *Morte D'Arthur*, ▷ Lancelot retires from the world to live as a hermit in the Glastonbury area.
Bib: Treharne, R. F., *The Glastonbury Legends*.

Glencoe

A valley in ▷ Scotland, where in 1692 the Campbell clan massacred a branch of the Macdonald clan. The Macdonald chief (out of pride) had delayed taking the oath of allegiance to ▷ William III and this was the pretext for the massacre, the real motive possibly being clan warfare. William III's Scottish administrator shared the guilt because he authorized the action.

Globe Theatre

The theatre used by the Lord ▷ Chamberlain's Men; ▷ Shakespeare's plays were performed there, he acted in it, and was one of the shareholders. It was built by ▷ Richard Burbage in 1599 out of the materials of 'The Theatre' erected in 1576; the new site was at Bankside on the south bank of the ▷ Thames in Southwark. It was built of wood, open in the centre, and the surrounding galleries ('this wooden O' – Prologue, ▷ *Henry V*) were roofed with thatch. It is thought to have held about 3,000 spectators. From the roof flew a flag, depicting Atlas carrying a globe with a Latin inscription equivalent to 'All the world's a stage' (▷ *As You Like It* II.vii.138). The theatre was burnt down in 1613 during a performance of ▷ *Henry VIII*, rebuilt, and finally pulled down in 1644. Much of the information about the Globe comes from the contract for the Fortune Theatre (built in 1599) the structure of which is specified as resembling the Globe, except that the Fortune

was square. A panoramic view of London dated 1616 gives a view of the Globe among other theatres. In the main, the structure of the Globe, like that of its contemporaries, derived from that of the typical inn-yard where plays were commonly performed when theatres were not available.

Under the inspired leadership of Sam Wannemaker and the auspices of the International Shakespeare Globe Centre, the Globe is about to rise again in Southwark, according to its original specifications and on its old site. It will be the first all-timber building licensed in London in the 20th century and will cater for international performances of Shakespeare, lectures and exhibitions. It is expected to open in 1992.

▷ Theatres.

Gloriana

The ▷ Faerie Queene of ▷ Edmund Spenser's poem; she represents ▷ Elizabeth I.

Glover, Richard (1712–85)

M.P. for Weymouth (1761–8), and author of epics and plays. His ▷ ballad, 'Hosier's Ghost', which attacked the naval policy of the Walpole government, was printed in ▷ Thomas Percy's *Reliques*.

Glyndŵr, Owain (?1354–?1416)

A Welsh chieftain who rebelled against ▷ Henry IV of England, and for a time ruled most of ▷ Wales. He was eventually defeated by Henry's son, the future ▷ Henry V. Glyndŵr is a character in Shakespeare's play ▷ *Henry IV, Part I* as an ally of the English rebel Hotspur. He is there presented as a boastful poet and mystic, such being reputed qualities of the Welsh.

Gnome

A kind of fairy, said to live underground; usually represented as hooded and bearded dwarfs; said to guard hidden treasure.

Goblin Market (1862)

Narrative poem by ▷ Christina Rossetti, well known as a children's poem, but its strange, erotic and equivocal fable-like quality renders its status as a classic ▷ Victorian Christian morality tale problematic. The goblins arrive bearing luscious fruit, and try to seduce the sisters Lizzie and Laura. Laura submits to temptation, and pays for the fruit she consumes with a lock of her hair. Having tasted, she wants more, but by this time the goblins cannot be found, and so she sinks into physical and psychological decline. Lizzie, who resisted the fruit, seeks out the goblins but refuses to consume it herself. In their anger at her resistance they press the fruit onto her body – Lizzie seems to sacrifice herself for her sister. When Laura eats and drinks it from Lizzie, the fruit acts strangely as an antidote, the goblin's power is defeated, and she is healed. The simplicity of this powerful poetry at first marginalized it (along with its author), and then opened it up to a wide variety of interpretations, especially ▷ psychoanalytic and ▷ feminist. It is a strong and sinister Victorian evocation of desire, fear and compulsion.

Godwin, William (1756–1836)

Philosopher and novelist. His central belief was that reason was sufficient to guide the conduct, not merely of individuals but also of all society. His principal work was *The Inquiry concerning Political Justice* (1793). Man he believed to be innately good and, under guidance of reason, capable of living without laws or control. Punishments he declared (at a time when the English ▷ penal system was one of the severest in Europe) to be unjust; as were the accumulation of property and the institution of marriage. The Prime Minister, ▷ William Pitt (the Younger), decided that the book was too expensive to be dangerous. Godwin's best-known novel came out in 1794: *Caleb Williams* was written to demonstate the power for injustice accessible to the privileged classes. Godwin was a brave man, not merely with the pen; but his naivety as a thinker would have left him without influence if his opinions had not agreed so well with the more extreme currents of feeling provoked by the contemporary ▷ French Revolution. As it was, he influenced a number of better minds, including, for a very short time, the poet ▷ Coleridge and, for a much longer period,

▷ Shelley, who became his son-in-law. Godwin's wife was ▷ Mary Wollstonecraft, an early propagandist for the rights of women and authoress of *A Vindication of the Rights of Woman* (1792).

Goethe, Johann Wolfgang von (1749–1832)

German poet; the greatest European man of letters of his time. His fame was due not only to the wide scope of his imaginative creation, but to the many-sidedness and massive independence of his personality. From 1770 to 1788 he was an inaugurator and leader of the passionate outbreak known in ▷ German as the *Sturm und Drang* – 'storm and stress' – movement, but from 1788 (after his visit to Italy) he represented to the world a balanced harmony inspired by the ▷ classicism he had found there. But he did not lose his sense that the spirit is free to find its own fulfilment according to its own principle of growth. At the same time, from 1775 he was prominent in the affairs of the German principality of Weimar (whose prince was his friend), concerning himself with practical sciences useful to the state, and thence with a serious study of botany and other natural and physical sciences to the point of making significant contributions to scientific thought. His commanding mind was admired in France, England, and Italy, with whose literatures Goethe was in touch; he corresponded with ▷ Byron; ▷ Walter Scott translated his *Goetz von Berlichingen*, which dated from the romantic phase of Goethe's career; he encouraged the young ▷ Thomas Carlyle. For Carlyle (▷ *Sartor Resartus*) Goethe was the spirit of affirmation that the age needed, to be set against the spirit of denial and withdrawal which he saw manifested in Byron. For ▷ Matthew Arnold, one of the most influential critics of the mid 19th century, Goethe's serene and responsible detachment represented the needed outlook for the practice of criticism.

Goethe is most famous for his double drama of ▷ *Faust*, but other works that became famous in England include the romantic drama already mentioned; the epic *Hermann and Dorothea*; a study in ▷ romantic sensibility *The Sorrows of Young Werther*; the novel *Wilhelm Meister*, an example of the ▷ *Bildungsroman*, and a large body of ▷ lyrical verse.

Gogol, Nikolai Vasilyevich (1809–52)

Playwright, novelist and short story writer, Gogol was born in the Ukraine. He worked as a civil service clerk in St Petersburg, which he hated but made notes for future use in the portrayal of characters. He was a brilliant but unbalanced man, suffering hallucinations and prone to religious extremism. At one stage he walked everywhere sideways, keeping his back to the wall for fear of being stabbed, and he had a pathological fear of eternal damnation. He admired ▷ Shakespeare, ▷ Henry Fielding and ▷ Laurence Sterne among others, and is thought to have greatly influenced Dostoievsky. His first collection of stories was *Evenings at a Farmhouse Near Dikana* (1831–2) which describe Ukranian country life. *Taras Bulba* (1834) has a Cossack tale as its title story, and *Mirgorod* and *Arabeski* followed in 1835. The play, *The Government Inspector* (1836) is a savage satire of civil servants and bureaucracy. His St Petersburg stories, including 'Nevsky Prospekt', 'Notes of a Madman' and 'The Portrait' (1835), 'The Nose' (1836) and 'The Greatcoat' (1842), have a surreal quality. The farce *Marriage* (1842) was successful. *Dead Souls* (1842), begun in Italy, combines satire, humour and brilliant characterization, but during increasing bouts of religious fervour, Gogol burnt the manuscript of the second part, along with further manuscripts. *Selected Passages from Correspondance with Friends* (1847), for which he was rebuked, was an attempt to convey his moral scruples. His work is remarkable for the power of his language and imagination.

Golden Age
▷ Ages, Golden, Silver, etc.

Golden Bowl, The (1904)
A novel by ▷ Henry James. The theme is the relationship of four people: the American millionaire collector, Adam Verver; his daughter, Maggie; the Italian prince, Amerigo, whom Verver acquires as a husband for his daughter; and Charlotte Stant, whom Maggie acquires as a wife for her widowed father. To the grief of the father and the daughter Charlotte seduces the prince into becoming her lover; the story is about the defeat of Charlotte, and Maggie's recovery of the prince's affections.

The novel belongs to James's last phase, which some critics consider to be his best, and others consider to show an excessive obliquity of style. The language of the characters is charged with feeling and yet disciplined by their civilized restraint and their fear of degrading themselves and one another by damaging explicitness. It is a measure of their indirectness that the affair between the prince and Charlotte is never actually mentioned between the father and the daughter. Behind the conflict of personalities there is the theme of the clash

between European and American kinds of value and consciousness; this theme is conspicuous in James's early novels, and he returned to it in his last period after a middle phase in which he was chiefly concerned with the European, and particularly the English, scene.

Golden Fleece, The
1 In Greek myth, the quest of ▷ Jason and the ▷ Argonauts.
2 An order of knighthood instituted by Philip, Duke of Burgundy in 1429.

Golden Legend, The
A medieval collection of lives of the saints, sermons, religious commentaries, etc., begun in the 13th century. It was printed by the first English printer, ▷ William Caxton.

Golden Treasury
▷ Anthology.

Golding, Arthur (?1536–1605)
Translator. Golding's chief work was an important ▷ translation of ▷ Ovid's *Metamorphoses* (1565–67) which was instrumental in promoting knowledge of Ovidian subjects and forms in England.

Golding, William (b 1911)
Novelist. His novels are: *Lord of the Flies* (1954; filmed 1963); *The Inheritors* (1955); *Pincher Martin* (1956); *Free Fall* (1959); *The Spire* (1964); *The Pyramid* (1967); *Darkness Visible* (1979); *Rites of Passage* (1980); *The Paper Men* (1984); *Close Quarters* (1987). *Sometime, Never* (1956) and *The Scorpion God* (1971) are collections of novellas. He has also written a play, *The Brass Butterfly* (1958), and published two collections of essays, *The Hot Gates* (1965) and *A Moving Target* (1982).

No novelist who started his career since 1945 has achieved more prestige, and this was acquired very quickly on the publication of his first book, *Lord of the Flies*. Its fame has no doubt been in part due to its pessimistic vision of human nature as inherently violent, reflecting the mood of the post-war and post-Hitler years; it also epitomizes mid-20th-century disillusionment with 19th-century optimism about human nature. Golding's father (see 'The Ladder and the Tree' in *The Hot Gates*) was a schoolmaster with radical convictions in politics, a belief that religion is outmoded superstition, and a strong faith in science. Golding's own work is strongly, but not explicitly, religious, in the ▷ Puritan tradition which emphasizes Original Sin. In 'Fable' (*The Hot Gates*) he explains how his first novel arose from his insights in the last

war: 'Anyone who moved through those years without understanding that man produces evil as a bee produces honey, must have been blind or wrong in the head.' The book is also meant to counteract what may be called 'the desert island myth' in English literature, deriving from ▷ Daniel Defoe's ▷ *Robinson Crusoe*, and particularly evident in a famous book for boys, *The Coral Island* (1857) by R. M. Ballantyne. This myth nourished the belief that human beings in isolation from civilized restraints will sustain their humanity by innate virtues. Most of the boys in *Lord of the Flies* quickly degenerate into savages, and the process is made more horrifying by the convincing delineation of the characters: Golding, like his father, has been a schoolmaster. His later novels have shown variety of theme and treatment, but similar preoccupation with fundamental corruption and contradiction in human nature. They show, likewise, Golding's most conspicuous literary qualities: great inventiveness in realistic fantasy, and a disposition to use the novel form as fable. For instance, *The Inheritors* is ▷ science fiction about the remote human past: the elimination of innocent Neanderthal Man by the arrival of rapacious Homo Sapiens – a new version of the myth of the Fall. *Pincher Martin* is a dramatization of this rapacity in an individual, and a spectacular example of fantasy presented within the conventions of realism. *The Spire* shows comparable ingenuity used quite differently: it describes the building of the spire of Salisbury Cathedral and dramatizes the conflict between faith and reason. *Rites of Passage* employs a characteristic shift of perspective: the narrow viewpoint of the narrator, a snobbish young aristocrat on a voyage to Australia in the early 19th century, is undermined by his gradual understanding of the devastating experiences of an awkward but sincere clergyman.
Bib: Gregor, I., and Kinkead-Weekes, M., *William Golding: a Critical Study*; Johnston, A., *Of Earth and Darkness*; Medcalf, S., *William Golding*.

Goldsmith, Oliver (1730–74)
Dramatist, novelist, essayist, and poet. Born in Ireland, he studied at Trinity College, Dublin, but ran away to Cork after being disciplined by his tutor. He returned, however, and graduated in 1749. He applied for ordination, but was rejected, then was given 50 pounds to study for the law, but gambled it away. After this, he studied medicine at Edinburgh and at Leyden but it is unclear whether he obtained the medical

Oliver Goldsmith; studio of Sir Joshua Reynolds (c 1770)

degree to which he later laid claim. In 1756 he came to London, penniless, and supported himself with a variety of occupations, including messenger, teacher, apothecary's assistant, usher, and hack writer for a periodical.

In 1758 he translated Marteilhe's *Memoirs of a Protestant, Condemned to the Galleys of France for His Religion*, and in 1759 his *Enquiry into the Present State of Polite Learning in Europe*. His 'Chinese Letters', written for John Newbery's *The Public Ledger* (1760–1) were reissued in 1762 as *The Citizen of the World*, a satiric view of England written from the supposed viewpoint of a Chinaman. His first real success as a writer was with the poem, 'The Traveller', published in 1764. A number of his works are now highly valued, including *The Citizen of the World*; his life of Beau Nash (1762); his novel, ▷ *The Vicar of Wakefield*; a poem, ▷ *The Deserted Village*; and the plays, *The Good Natur'd Man* (1768), and ▷ *She Stoops to Conquer* (1773) written, like the plays of ▷ Richard Brinsley Sheridan, in reaction to the sentiment of many plays of the period, and with the intention to revive the spirit of ▷ Restoration comedy. He wrote much else, including histories of England, Greece and Rome, and biographies of Voltaire, Bolingbroke and Parnell.

Goldsmith was a friend of ▷ David Garrick, and ▷ Samuel Johnson, and figures largely in ▷ James Boswell's *Life of*

Johnson (1791). Johnson praised his writing for its 'clarity and elegance', and later generations have repeatedly praised his literary 'charm', a quality made up of humour, modesty, vitality, and graceful lucidity. These he combined with the ▷ Augustan properties of balance and proportion. He died of a fever, deeply in debt, and the Literary Club which he had helped to found in 1764 erected a monument to him in Westminster Abbey. Garrick wrote an epitaph to comment on his greatness as an author and reputed failings in other areas: 'Here lies Nolly Goldsmith, for shortness called Noll, Who wrote like an angel, but talked like poor Poll'. **Bib**: Forster, J., and Wardle, R. M., *Lives*; Balderston, K. B. (ed.), *Letters*; Ginger, J., *The Notable Man*; Danziger, M. K., *Oliver Goldsmith and Richard Brinsley Sheridan*; Swarbrick, A. (ed.), *The Art of Oliver Goldsmith*.

Goliardic

A descriptive term applied to a satirical and profane kind of Latin poetry, allegedly produced in the 12th and 13th centuries by a class of clerical writers known as goliards, named after a certain 'Golias' (whose own name derives perhaps from the Latin word for glutton '*gula*'). The notion of such a company of poets seems to be a literary myth.

Goliath

The ▷ giant of the Philistines killed by the shepherd boy ▷ David with a stone from his sling in the ▷ Bible, *1 Samuel* 17.

Goncourt, Edmond Louis Antonine Huot de (1822–96) and Jules Alfred Huot de (1830–70)

The brothers, novelists, historians and art critics, of an old Lorraine family, collected books, pictures, manuscripts and furnishings, collaborating on several books of history and art criticism. They wrote novels which are now not much read but helped make literary history, originating the '*roman documentaire*' with its painstaking naturalistic detail, believing novelists should write 'history which might have happened'. After Jules's death, Edmond wrote some further novels and the famous *Journal des Goncourt* which portrayed literary life in Paris 1851–96. The Académie Goncourt was founded under the terms of Edmond's will; it awards the annual Prix Goncourt for imaginative prose. *Germinie Lacerteux* (1864) details the history of their maid, faithfully serving while living a life of vice and debauchery. Other novels include *Soeur Philomène* (1861) and *Madam Gervaisais* (1869). Non-fiction includes *L'Art du dix-*

huitième siècle (1859–75) and *Portraits intimes du dix-huitième siècle* (1857). Novels written by Edmond alone include *Les Frères Zemganno* (1879), *La Faustin* (1882) and *Chérie* (1884).

Goodman's Fields Theatres

The first Goodman's Fields Theatre of which any details survive was opened by theatre manager and dramatist Thomas Odell (1691–1749) in Whitechapel in 1729, and lasted intermittently until 1751; another theatre by the same name was opened by ▷ Henry Giffard in Ayliffe Street in 1733. Like several other theatres this was ordered to close in 1737 under the terms of the Licensing Act, but continued performances at the fringe of the law until 1741, the year of ▷ David Garrick's professional debut at this venue as Richard III (▷ *Richard III*). The theatre became a warehouse, and burned down in 1802. The present building dates from 1812.

Gorboduc, or Ferrex and Porrex

A tragic drama by Thomas Norton (1552–84) and ▷ Thomas Sackville. The story is taken from British legendary history; the immediate source is Grafton's *Chronicle* (1556), but this in turn derives from the 12th-century *Historia Regum Britanniae* (History of the Kings of Britain) by ▷ Geoffrey of Monmouth. It is the first play to be written in ▷ blank verse, and it is modelled on the tragedies of ▷ Seneca.

Gorboduc is a king of Britain. His reign has been a prosperous one, when he decides to retire from government and to divide his kingdom between his two sons, Ferrex and Porrex. He carries out the division against the advice of his wisest councillor. Jealousy and distrust between the two brothers break into civil war, which ends in the death of both, and a rising of the whole people, who slay Gorboduc and his queen. The country is saved from final ruin only by Fergus, Duke of Albany, who, with the aid of other nobles, succeeds in restoring order under single sovereignty.

The drama has slight literary value of its own, but it has considerable historical significance. Sackville and Norton were eminent politicians who foresaw great dangers to the kingdom if Queen ▷ Elizabeth I should die without heirs. The play was first acted before the Queen in 1562, and is plainly designed as a warning to her against leaving her kingdom exposed to disunity. The authors are thus using history (or legend, which was not clearly distinguished from history) as later and greater dramatists were to use it, notably ▷ Shakespeare: that is to say, as a storehouse of political lessons which could be applied to the politics of their own time. The theme of the divided kingdom resembles one of the greatest of Shakespeare's tragedies, ▷ *King Lear*, which deals with the situation in far profounder terms. The Senecan model also anticipates later Elizabethan taste, and the use of ▷ blank verse was the starting-point for the rich development of the medium by ▷ Marlowe and Shakespeare. Apart from Seneca, a literary influence upon the writers is the collection of tragic tales, ▷ *A Mirror for Magistrates* (1559), to which Sackville made the most memorable contribution. This also used legend and history, recounted in a solemn style, to warn and edify contemporary courtiers and public men. The Senecan solemnity and formality of *Gorboduc* gave it peculiar dignity for the contemporary public, raising it above the (often much more lively) style of the familiar ▷ interludes and comedies of the day, and giving it the requisite impressiveness to influence the Queen. It is not known what she thought of it, but ▷ Sir Philip Sidney excepted it from his general condemnation of the English drama of his day, and wrote in his *Apologie for Poetrie*: 'it is full of stately speeches, and well sounding phrases, climbing to the height of Seneca's style, and as full of notable morality . . .' However, he goes on to complain of its failure to observe the so-called Aristotelian ▷ unities of space and time.

Gordimer, Nadine (b 1923)

South African novelist and short-story writer living in Johannesburg. She has won an international reputation and numerous prizes, including the Booker Prize for *The Conservationist* (1974). Much of her work is concerned with the situation of white middle-class liberals in South Africa, privileged by a system to which they are opposed, the relation of the private self to the political, and the failure of liberal compromise. Her work has become progressively bleaker and more disillusioned. In *A World of Strangers* (1958) she uses the perspective of an outsider coming to South Africa, while *The Conservationist* is written from the viewpoint of a rich and conservative capitalist, and employs symbolic elements in its treatment of the struggle for the control of the land. Her other novels are: *The Lying Days* (1953); *Occasion for Loving* (1963); *The Late Bourgeois World* (1966); *A Guest of Honour* (1970); *Burger's Daughter* (1979); *July's People* (1981); *A Sport of Nature* (1987); *My Son's Story* (1990). Story collections include: *Selected Stories* (1975); *Some Monday For Sure* (1976); *A Soldier's*

Embrace (1980); *Town and Country Lovers* (1980); *Something Out There* (1984); *Jump* (1991). She was awarded the Nobel Prize for Literature in 1991.
Bib: Heywood, C., *Nadine Gordimer*.

Gordon riots, The

Riots in London in 1780, led by Lord George Gordon against a law passed in 1778 to relieve the condition of Roman Catholics. The riots form the climax of ▷ Charles Dickens's novel ▷ *Barnaby Rudge*.

Gore, Catherine Grace Frances (1799–1861)

Born Moody, the daughter of a wine merchant in East Retford, Nottinghamshire, Catherine Gore showed literary ability at an early age and was nicknamed 'the Poetess' by her peers. She wrote some 70 novels between 1824 and 1862, of the 'silver-fork school': novels of fashionable and wealthy life. They include *Theresa Marchmont or the Maid of Honour* (1824), *Manners of the day, or Woman as the game* (1830), which was praised by George IV, *Mothers and Daughters* (1830), *Mrs Armytage: or female domination* (1836), possibly her best, *Cecil, or the adventures of a coxcomb* (1841) and *The banker's wife, or court and city* (1843), which was dedicated to Sir John Dean Paul, portrayed as a swindler, as he in fact turned out to be in 1855 when Gore lost £20,000. She also wrote poems, plays – *The School for Coquettes* (1831), *Quid pro Quo or the Days of Dupes* (1844) – and short stories, and composed music. Her writing is characterized by shrewd observation and perceptive insight, together with satire and invention, and gives an interesting portrait of life in a certain class and time.

Gorgons

In Greek myth, three winged sisters – Stheno, Euryale, and Medusa. They had hideous faces, and writhing serpents instead of hair. Of the three, only Medusa was mortal, and she was decapitated by the hero ▷ Perseus. The head turned all beholders to stone.

Gosse, Edmund (1849–1928)

Critic, biographer and poet. He is especially known for his autobiography *Father and Son* (1907) – one of the classic works for interpreting the Victorian age. As a critic, he was one of the first to introduce the Norwegian dramatist ▷ Ibsen to the British public. He also wrote a number of studies of 17th-century literature and a life (1917) of his friend ▷ Swinburne.

Gosson, Stephen (1554–1624)

Preacher and pamphleteer. Stephen Gosson's

chief claim to a measure of literary fame is due to his being the author of *The Schoole of Abuse* (1579) – a ▷ pamphlet attacking poetry and drama which is said to have occasioned ▷ Philip Sidney's ▷ *An Apologie for Poetrie*. Ironically, Gosson's career had begun as a dramatist, but he underwent a religious conversion and became a fierce ▷ Puritan critic of the drama. *The Schoole of Abuse*, if it has a somewhat nebulous relationship to the development of Sidney's critical text, nevertheless did call forth a response from ▷ Thomas Lodge, who replied to Gosson with his *A Reply to Stephen Gosson Touching Plays* (1579). Gosson, in turn, replied to Lodge with his *Plays Confuted in Five Actions* (1582). This interchange, though it added little of substance to dramatic criticism, is itself part of the continuing English debate in the 16th and 17th centuries concerning the corrupting or otherwise influence of drama.

Goth
The Goths were Germanic tribes which invaded the Roman Empire in the 3rd–5th centuries and eventually overthrew it. The western Goths were called Visigoths and conquered Spain; the eastern Goths were the Ostrogoths who conquered Italy. 'A Goth' is a term for an uncultivated person. The Goths had nothing to do with originating the style of architecture known as ▷ Gothic, which began in France in the 12th century when the word was no longer in use as a contemporary racial description.

Gotham, Wise Men of
Gotham is a village near Nottingham in the English midlands. It had a reputation not for wisdom but for folly. The story is that the villagers simulated stupidity when King ▷ John proposed to come and stay among them, since royal courts were burdensome to country neighbourhoods owing to their exactions of provisions and unpaid services from the countryside. When the king's commissioners came to inspect the place, they found the villagers trying to drown an eel in the village pond. King John is said to have seen through the villagers' tactics and to have remarked 'More fools pass through Gotham than live there.'

Gothic
A term for the style of architecture which dominated western Europe in the Middle Ages. Its main features were the pointed arch and the ribbed vault. In England, this period is divided into three: Early English (13th century), Decorated (14th) and Perpendicular

(15th–16th). A fine example of the last is King's College Chapel, Cambridge.
   ▷ Gothic revival.

Gothic novels
A genre of novels dealing with tales of the macabre and supernatural, which reached a height of popularity in the 1790s. The term 'Gothic' originally implied 'medieval', or rather a fantasized version of what was seen to be medieval. Later, 'Gothic' came to cover all areas of the fantastic and supernatural, and the characteristics of the genre are graveyards and ghosts.
   ▷ Walpole's ▷ *The Castle of Otranto* is generally seen as the earliest Gothic novel. ▷ 'Monk' Lewis, ▷ William Beckford and ▷ Mrs Radcliffe are notable exploiters of the genre. The vogue for Gothic novels soon produced parodies; ▷ Thomas Love Peacock's ▷ *Nightmare Abbey* and ▷ Jane Austen's ▷ *Northanger Abbey* are among the best examples.
   In the 19th century, ▷ Mary Shelley, the ▷ Brontës and ▷ Dickens show the influence of the tradition, and the novels of such modern writers as ▷ Emma Tennant and ▷ Angela Carter suggest that tales of the supernatural have undying appeal.

Gothic revival
An architectural style now chiefly associated with the reign of ▷ Queen Victoria (1837–1901). A taste for Gothic had in fact started in the 18th century; its starting point is associated with ▷ Horace Walpole's design of his home, Strawberry Hill (1747). The taste for Gothic spread between 1750 and 1830; as an artistic style it remained a minority cult, but as a sentiment it grew with the popularity of the sensationalism of the ▷ Gothic novels and with the rise of the romantic cultivation of the sensibility. In the 18th century, the taste for Gothic tended to be fanciful and sensational rather than deeply serious, although it gained seriousness from such a publication as ▷ Thomas Percy's *Reliques*; the 19th-century ▷ Romantic Revival, especially the novels of ▷ Walter Scott, produced a deeper and much more genuine feeling for the ▷ Middle Ages. From about 1830, the Gothic revival became a genuine cultural re-direction; in literature it was advanced by ▷ Thomas Carlyle (*Past and Present*) and by ▷ John Ruskin (*The Stones of Venice*); in religion by the ▷ Oxford Movement; in architecture and painting by the Catholic architect Pugin (through his writings rather than his buildings) and the ▷ Pre-Raphaelites. Ruskin, especially in his

The Houses of Parliament; an example of neo-Gothic architecture

famous essay 'The Nature of Gothic', was the most eloquent of these exponents; he used the spirit of Gothic to challenge the materialistic spirit of the time consequent to the mass production methods of the ▷ Industrial Revolution. Nonetheless, in architecture and design the Victorian Gothic Revival was vitiated by the technology of the new industrial methods, which could elaborate Gothic ornament mechanically. In poetry and fiction, ▷ Tennyson's revival of ▷ Arthurian legend in ▷ Idylls of the King, ▷ Browning's delight in elaborate descriptive detail, and ▷ Dickens's vivid idiosyncrasies in the presentation of character and environment, can all be ascribed to a prevailing neo-Gothic appeal to the imagination. But in the 1870s, a reaction set in: neo-Gothic architectural styles were succeeded by a return to ▷ classicism, generally known as the new 'Queen Anne' style, though it was often much more eclectic and exuberant. Eclecticism can be seen to dominate artistic taste in both the plastic arts and literature until the emergence of ▷ Modernism in the 20th century.
   ▷ Furnishings and furniture.

Gower, John (?1330–1408)

Poet. Only a tentative outline can be established of Gower's life. His family had Yorkshire origins and Kent connections (Gower's language bears traces of Kentish influence and he bought lands there in 1378). A reference in one of his works suggests he had a training in law, a point confirmed by other documentary evidence. Gower seems to have been based in London for most of his life. By 1398, and perhaps for some time earlier, he was living in the priory of St Mary Overy (now Southwark Cathedral), where he was buried.
   He wrote extensively in three languages, French, Latin and English. Before 1374 he composed his Cinkante Balades and some

time between 1376 and 1378 he produced the Mirour de l'Omme, another French work, written in octosyllabic 12-line stanzas, tackling the subject of fallen man, his vices and virtues. His Latin poem, Vox Clamantis (The Voice of One Crying), composed c 1379–81, addresses the subject of political governance and, more specifically, the disturbances of the reign of Richard II (notably the ▷ Peasant's Revolt). In his major English poem, the ▷ Confessio Amantis, Gower turned from overtly political and satirical subjects to take a middle way, 'somwhat of lust, somwhat of lore', recounting the experiences of a lover's confession and instruction. But here too Gower's concern with the ethics of government of self and society is very evident. His anti-war sentiments are clearly expressed in his later English poem, addressed to ▷ Henry IV, In Praise of Peace.
   In the colophon added to the Confessio Amantis, Gower suggests that his major works should be seen as a triptych, as 'three books of instructive material'. His evident ambition to figure as a moral commentator and watchman of his times, and to be remembered as such, was fulfilled. His literary reputaton in the century following his death was high, and his name frequently coupled with that of ▷ Chaucer as a founding figure of the English poetic tradition. He is represented as a figure of old poetic authority in ▷ Shakespeare's play ▷ Pericles (which reworks the story of Apollonius of Tyre, drawn from Gower's Confessio Amantis). However, from the 18th century onwards, there seems to have been a decline in interest in his work and his literary reputation has only revived in recent years.
   ▷ Henry IV.
Bib: Fisher, J. H., John Gower: moral philosopher and friend of Chaucer; Macaulay, G. C. (ed.), The Works of John Gower, The English Works of John Gower.

Grace Abounding to the Chief of Sinners
(1666)
The spiritual autobiography of ▷ John
Bunyan, author of ▷ *The Pilgrim's
Progress*. The torments undergone by
Christian in the latter book are substantially
those of Bunyan in the earlier one. Bunyan
had a similar spiritual awakening to
Christian's, being aroused by a book; he
suffers the terrible conviction of sin, like
Christian's; he believes himself to commit the
sin of blasphemy as Christian thinks he does
in the Valley of the Shadow of Death; at last
he achieves confidence in God's mercy. Much
of the narrative is an account of painful
mental conflict; but Bunyan never lost the
sanity of perception into the fanaticism and
mental morbidity of others, such as the old
man who told him that he had certainly
committed the sin against the Holy Ghost
(for which there is no forgiveness). The book
records how he developed that compassionate
understanding of other men's spiritual
conflicts which makes *The Pilgrim's Progress*
the antecedent of the great English novels.

Graham, W. S. (William Sidney) (b 1918)
Poet. Graham was born in Scotland
(▷ Scottish literature) into a working-class
family and grew up on Clydeside where he
trained and worked as an engineer. His early
poetry was immediately associated with
▷ Dylan Thomas and the 'apocalyptic'
poetry of the 1940s – Graham's first collection
was characteristically energetic and vibrant.
He now lives in Cornwall, and its seascapes
have provided a rich source of metaphors and
images for his struggle with language.
Formally, Graham's verse began simply in
terms of syntax and diction, but he has since
developed into more of a ▷ modernistic
writer, especially in his analysis of problems
of personal identity and communication.
Graham's most famous and strongest volume
is *The Nightfishing* (1955). Other works
include: *Cage Without Grievance* (1943); *The
White Threshold* (1949); *Malcolm Mooney's
Land* (1970); *Collected Poems 1942–1977*
(1979).

Grail
A mysterious, sacred object of quest in
Arthurian narratives which is represented and
interpreted in different ways, but always
linked to a conception of completion and
wholeness of some kind. The Old French
word 'graal' means a serving dish or platter,
and in ▷ Chrétien de Troyes's romance of
Perceval, the word is used of a richly

bejewelled dish, carried by a maiden in the
mysterious procession seen by ▷ Perceval in
the castle of the wounded ▷ Fisher King. It
transpires that this dish has life-giving and
healing qualities, and the power to heal the
wounded King and his Wasteland. Perceval,
however, fails to release the healing power of
the dish, because he fails to ask about the
Grail. This dish seems to be related to the
mysterious cauldrons which appear in Celtic
legend and myth, which have the power to
provide never-ending sources of
nourishment.

  ▷ Robert de Boron's reworking of the
Grail story (in the late 12th or early 13th
century) gives an explicitly Christian
interpretation to the key symbolic artefacts of
the story, and provides the means of linking
Arthurian history and Christian history. Here
the Grail becomes the Holy Grail, and is
identified with the chalice used by Christ at
the Last Supper and later used by Joseph of
Arimathea as the vessel to collect the blood
from Christ's body at the Crucifixion. It is
literally part of, and symbolically
representative of, the Eucharist, a source of
physical and spiritual food, and this material
sign of transcendental life is kept by a series
of Grail keepers, beginning with Joseph of
Arimathea. In later developments of the Grail
narrative, the Quest of the Holy Grail is the
last and most marvellous adventure of
▷ Arthur's court, to be achieved by the
Christ-knight ▷ Galahad, and the narrative
becomes the vehicle for a rigorous criticism
of the material values of earthly
▷ knighthood, and a celebration of a
spiritual order of chivalry. Once the Grail
quest has been achieved, neither the Grail
knights nor the Grail itself return to Britain,
and the future for Arthur's court and realm is
only one of decline. The quest of the Holy
Grail forms part of ▷ Malory's *Morte
D'Arthur*, though in his version the criticism
of the ethics and values of secular knighthood
is somewhat modified. The Quest is treated
rather less sympathetically by ▷ Tennyson
in his ▷ *Idylls of the King*. ▷ T. S. Eliot
draws on the multifaceted qualities of the
Grail and its different modes of representation
in Arthurian narrative, in his poetic
exploration of the state of human culture
▷ *The Waste Land*.
Bib: Lacey, Norris J. et al. (eds.), *The
Arthurian Encyclopaedia*.

Grammatology
This term is used by the French philosopher
▷ Jacques Derrida to denote 'a general
science of writing'. As a scientific practice, its

objective is to disturb the traditional hierarchical relationship between 'speech' and 'writing' where the latter is regarded as an instrument of the former. Derrida's 'science of writing' is an attempt to deconstruct (▷ Deconstruction) the metaphysical assumptions upon which the hierarchical relationship between speech and writing is based. He takes to the limit the ▷ Saussurean notion of the arbitrariness of the linguistic ▷ sign, arguing against a natural relationship between the spoken word and what it signifies.

Grand guignol

A term denoting an entertainment relying merely on sensational horror for its effect; after an old French puppet show.

Grand Siècle, Le

The Great Century in France – the 17th, especially the reign of Louis xiv (1643–1715). France was at her most powerful politically (except for the First Empire, 1804–15) and had one of her most productive periods in literature, painting and music.

Granville Barker, Harley (1877–1946)

Actor, producer, director, dramatist, dramatic critic. He began as an actor in 1891, but he achieved fame as a director (1904–21). He favoured the modern drama of ▷ Ibsen, ▷ Shaw and ▷ Galsworthy and did much to educate the public into accepting its often scandalizing themes drawn from contemporary social issues; in this he was much influenced by his close friendship with Shaw. However, his chief fame as a director was in his productions of ▷ Shakespeare. The previous generation of Shakespeare production, dominated by ▷ Henry Irving, had relied on the personalities of star actors, and Irving was continuing a tradition which went back to the 18th century. Granville Barker concentrated on the production of the whole work, transferring the emphasis from the leading roles onto the speech and action of the entire cast. His own plays were in the Ibsen-Shaw tradition; the best known are *The Voysey Inheritance* (1905), *Waste* (which was forbidden by the censor) (1907), and *The Madras House* (1910).

In 1923 he became editor of *The Players' Shakespeare* for which he wrote prefaces to individual plays. The series was discontinued, but the prefaces were published, and because they have Granville Barker's unique stage experience as a basis, they now constitute the crown of his reputation. However he was also a lifelong publicist for the idea of a ▷ National Theatre, which was not to be established until 1976.

Bib: Purdom, C. B., *Harley Granville Barker, Man of the Theatre, Dramatist and Scholar*; Salmon, E., *Granville Barker: A Secret Life*; Kennedy, D., *Granville Barker and the Dream of Theatre*.

Graves, Robert (1895–1985)

Poet, critic, novelist. His poetry belongs to a distinctively English strain of lyrical verse which has been overshadowed by the more ambitious and more massive work of the Anglo-Irish ▷ W. B. Yeats and the American-born ▷ T. S. Eliot. Earlier representatives of this kind of verse were ▷ Thomas Hardy, ▷ Edward Thomas and the war poets such as ▷ Wilfred Owen, ▷ Siegfried Sassoon and ▷ Isaac Rosenburg. The development of Graves's work was decisively affected by his experiences as an officer in World War I, and understanding of it is helped by a reading of Owen and Sassoon. Such poetry was partly a means of preserving sanity in the face of extreme horror, partly a desire to awaken in the reader a distrust of attitudes imposed on him by convention, or adopted by himself to help him preserve his own illusions. Graves published his first poems during World War I, but he is not primarily one of the war poets; he extended the vision aroused by the war into the post-war world of human relations, especially those between the sexes, and into the impulses to self-deceive and to escape the realities of inner experience, especially by choosing to dull its image. He always wrote ▷ lyrics with skilful and precise rhythm and often poignant or pungent rhymes, and an austere yet lively, colloquial diction. A collected edition of his works was published in 1975.

As a critic he was at first a self-conscious ▷ modernist; *A Survey of Modernist Poetry* (1927), written with the poet Laura Riding, educated the public in new kinds of poetic expression by a pioneering critical interest in subtleties and ambiguities of language. His later criticism has been less influential; it includes *The Common Asphodel* (1949), *The Crowning Privilege* (1955).

Graves engaged extensively in historical and anthropological enquiry; this resulted in work on poetry and primitive religion, *eg The White Goddess* (1948), which aroused controversy but was taken up by some ▷ feminists in the 1960s and 70s, and in historical fiction of great popularity, *eg I, Claudius* and *Claudius the God* (1934). By far the most important of his prose works, however, was his ▷ autobiography recounting his experiences in World War I – *Good-bye to All That* (1929).

Bib: Seymour Smith, M., *Swifter than Reason*; Graves, R. P., *Robert Graves*.

Gray, Thomas (1716–71)

Poet and prose-writer. The sole survivor of 12 children, Gray was born in Cornhill, London. His father, a scrivener, was mentally unbalanced and Gray was brought up by his mother, who sent him to ▷ Eton where he made friends with ▷ Horace Walpole. He went on to Peterhouse, Cambridge, and gained a high reputation for his Latin poetry, though he failed to take a degree. In 1739 he embarked on a tour of the continent with Walpole, but in 1741 they quarrelled and Gray returned alone. He turned to the study of law, and began a tragedy *Agrippina*, which remained unfinished. The death of Richard West, a close friend from his Eton days, in 1742, precipitated a period of poetic activity, in which he produced his *Ode on a Distant Prospect of Eton College* (published 1747), *Sonnet on the Death of Richard West* and *Ode to Adversity* (published in Dodsley's *Collections*, 1748). Also in 1742 he began ▷ *Elegy written in a Country Churchyard*, while staying with his mother and aunt at their retirement home in Stoke Poges. The poem was carefully revised over a long period and eventually appeared in 1751, achieving instant recognition as a masterpiece.

From 1742 Gray lived in Peterhouse and later Pembroke College, Cambridge, except for a period (1759–61) in London where he pursued his studies in the British Museum. Relations with Walpole were soon restored and it was the death of Walpole's cat which inspired Gray's delightful ▷ mock-heroic *Ode on the Death of a Favourite Cat* (1748). The *Odes by Mr Gray* (1757), comprising his two Pindaric Odes, *The Progress of Poesy* and ▷ *The Bard*, was the first book published by Walpole's Strawberry Hill press. In the same year he was offered the laureateship on the death of ▷ Colley Cibber, but refused. In 1761 he wrote a number of poems reflecting a mixture of bookish scholarship and romantic primitivism, very characteristic of the period: *The Fatal Sisters. An Ode*, *The Descent of Odin. An Ode* (*From the Norse-Tongue*), *The Triumphs of Owen. A Fragment* (from the Welsh). They were published in 1768 in Dodsley's collected edition of his works, *Poems by Mr Gray*. In the same year Gray was appointed Professor of Modern History at Cambridge, though he never delivered a lecture. In 1769 he travelled in the Lake District and his *Journal* (1775), relates his reactions to its sublime scenery. His letters reveal a profoundly learned, but witty and entertaining personality.

Gray's reflective works, in particular the *Elegy*, are masterpieces of the hesitant, personal poetry of ▷ Sensibility. His odes, although not so successful, reflect the restless experimentalism of his period. It has been too easy to cast Gray either as a half-hearted ▷ Augustan or a timid pre-romantic, both tendencies being encouraged by ▷ William Wordsworth's dogmatic strictures on the language of his *Sonnet on the Death of Mr West*, and ▷ Samuel Taylor Coleridge's corrective follow-up in ▷ *Biographia Literaria*, Chapter XVIII. It is better to see him in his own right. His particular poetic strengths are an ease of personification and abstraction (shared by his contemporaries ▷ William Collins and ▷ Samuel Johnson and emulated by ▷ John Keats in his ▷ *Odes*), and a restrained but eloquent felicity of phrasing, which places some of his lines among the best-remembered in the language: 'where ignorance is bliss/ 'Tis folly to be wise'; 'And Melancholy mark'd him for her own.'

▷ Augustanism; Bard; Romanticism.

Bib: Johnson, S., in *Lives of the Poets*; Arnold M., in *Essays in Criticism* (2nd series); Ketton-Cremer, R. W., *Thomas Gray: A Biography*; Leavis, F. R., in *Revaluation*; Tillotson, G., in *Augustan Studies*; Powell Jones, W., *Thomas Gray, Scholar*; Starr, H. W. (ed.), *Twentieth-Century Interpretations of Gray's Elegy*.

Great Expectations (1860–1)

A novel by ▷ Charles Dickens. Its title refers to expectations resulting from wealth anonymously donated to Philip Pirrip (shortened to Pip) who has been brought up in humble obscurity by his half-sister and her husband, the village blacksmith, Joe Gargery. His 'expectations' are to be made a ▷ 'gentleman' – understood in social terms as holding privilege without responsibility. He supposes his money to be the gift of the rich and lonely Miss Havisham, who has in fact merely used him as an experimental victim on whom her ward, Estella, is to exert her charm with the aim of breaking his heart. Pip's great crisis comes when he discovers his real benefactor to be the convict Magwitch, whom he had helped in an attempted escape when he was a child. Magwitch, who had been made into a criminal by the callousness of society in his own childhood, has built up a fortune in Australia (to which he was deported – ▷ Penal System) and has tried the experiment of 'making a gentleman' out of another child. His assumption is essentially that of society as a whole, that appearances, and the money that makes them, are what matters. Magwitch returns to England illegally to see the fruit of his ambition, and Pip has to decide whether he will be responsible for his unwanted benefactor or escape from him. His decision to protect Magwitch and help him to escape again produces a revolution in Pip's nature: instead of assuming privilege without responsibility he now undertakes responsibility without reward, since he will also divest himself of his money. 'Expectations' are important in other senses for other characters: Estella expects to become a rich lady dominating humiliated admirers, but she becomes enslaved to a brutal husband; Pip's friend, Herbert Pocket, dreams of becoming a powerful industrialist, but he has no capital until Pip (anonymously) provides it; Wopsle, the parish clerk in Pip's village, imagines himself a great actor and becomes a stage hack; Miss Havisham is surrounded by relatives whom she depises and who nonetheless live in expectation of legacies after her death; Miss Havisham herself, and Magwitch also, live for expectations (in Estella and Pip) which are frustrated – in these instances fortunately. In its largest implications, *Great Expectations* is concerned with the futility of a society in which individuals live by desires powered by illusion. This view of the novel gives emphasis to those characters who are free of illusion: the lawyer Jaggers who exerts power by his cynical expectation of human folly; his clerk, Wemmick, who divides his life sharply between the harshness demanded by his profession and the tenderness of his domestic affections; Joe Gargery and his second wife Biddy, survivors from an older social tradition, who remain content with their own naïve wisdom of the heart. Dickens was persuaded by his friend ▷ Bulwer Lytton to change the end of the novel: in the first version Pip and Estella, older and wiser, meet again only to separate permanently; in the revised one, Dickens leaves it open to the reader to believe whether they will be permanently united, or not.

Greek literature

Until Greece was conquered by the Romans in 146 B C, it was a country of small states, mixed racial stock and cultural origins from all round the eastern Mediterranean. These states attained a high level of self-conscious political and artistic culture, which later enriched the Roman Empire and was thence transmitted to medieval and modern Europe.

The beginnings of Greek literature cannot be dated but its first period ended about 500 B C. The period contains ▷ Homer's epics, the ▷ *Iliad* and the ▷ *Odyssey*, and the poems of Hesiod. Homer's epics are the real starting-point of European imaginative literature; Hesiod's *Theogony* is one of the principal sources of our knowledge of the Greek religious system. In English literature since the 18th century, the term ▷ elegy has implied narrower limits of subject and treatment than it had for the Greeks and the Romans, but the Greek evolution of the elegy and the ▷ lyric in this period has shaped our ideas of the character and resources of the short poem. An important variety of the lyric (whose principal characteristic was originally that it was intended to have musical accompaniment) was the 'Pindaric ode', so called after its most famous practitioner, ▷ Pindar; this was much imitated by English poets from the 17th to 19th centuries.

The second period (500–300 B C) is called the 'Attic Period' because it centred on the greatest of the Greek cities, ▷ Athens, capital of the state of Attica. The outstanding imaginative achievement of the Athenians was the creation of dramatic literature. The 'choral lyric', sung by choirs on religious occasions and especially on the festival of the wine-god ▷ Dionysus, was developed into a dialogue by ▷ Thespis in the 6th century. In the 5th century this was further developed into dramatic tragedy by three writers whose works have a fundamental influence on all our ideas of the theatre: ▷ Aeschylus, ▷ Sophocles and ▷ Euripides. The primitive religion of the Greeks, based on the worship of the gods as the all-powerful forces of nature, was the origin of Greek ▷ tragedy; it was also the origin of comedy, of which the greatest Greek writer was ▷ Aristophanes. Athens, in this period, also developed Greek prose literature, in the works of the first of the historians, ▷ Herodotus, in the immensely influential philosophies of ▷ Plato and ▷ Aristotle, and in political oratory, especially that of ▷ Demosthenes.

Demosthenes achieved fame by his efforts to sustain the Greeks in their wars (357–338 B C) against Philip of Macedon, a state to the north of Greece. The war ended with the Macedonians making themselves the dominant power in Greece. They did not actually destroy the independence of the states, but the intensity and many-sidedness of Greek city life diminished. However, Philip's son ▷ Alexander the Great (ruled 336–323 B C) took Greek culture with him in his rapid conquests round the eastern

Mediterranean and as far east as north-west India. The result was the 'Hellenistic Period' (▷ Hellas) lasting until the Roman conquest, after which it did not cease but went into a new phase. The culture of Greece now became a climate of civilization shared by many lands; it was no longer even centred in Greece but in the university city of Alexandria in Egypt. The price paid for this expansion was that without the sustenance of the vigorous Greek city life, the literature lost its force, depth and originality, though it retained its secondary qualities such as grace and sophistication. The best known imaginative works of this period are the '▷ pastoral' poems by ▷ Theocritus and others; they influenced the Roman poet ▷ Virgil, and were extensively used as models by ▷ Renaissance poets in the 16th and 17th centuries.

In the Graeco-Roman period (146 BC–AD 500), the Greeks were the teachers and cultural allies of their conquerors, the Romans. ▷ Latin literature written under Greek influence now excelled what continued to be written in Greek. Yet Renaissance Europe felt so much closer to the Romans than to the Greeks that it was the Greek writers of this period who influenced it more deeply than the earlier Greeks did. The historian and biographer ▷ Plutarch, for instance, was widely read in England in the age of ▷ Shakespeare, who used him as a sourcebook for his plays. The Greek romances, the best known of which is *Daphnis and Chloe* by Longus (2nd century AD), were imitated by 16th-century writers such as ▷ Sir Philip Sidney in his ▷ *Arcadia*. To this period also belongs one of the most influential pieces of Greek literary criticism, the treatise *On the Sublime* by ▷ Longinus.

In considering the influence of Greek literature on European, and in particular on English, literature, we have to distinguish between the influence of Greek philosophy and that of Greek imaginative writing. Plato and Aristotle had profound effects on Christian thought. Plato was made dominant by St Augustine of Hippo (4th–5th century), until ▷ St Thomas Aquinas replaced his influence by that of Aristotle. In the 16th century, Plato again became most important, but now as a source of ▷ humanist as well as of religious ideas. Aristotle remained dominant as the first philosopher of literature for three centuries, and together they are still regarded as the important starting-points of European philosophy. Greek imaginative writing, on the other hand, made its impression on European, and especially

English, imaginative writing chiefly through its assimilation by Roman writers. It was not, for example, the unexcelled Greek dramatists who impressed themselves on the equally unexcelled English dramatists of the age of Shakespeare, but the comparatively inferior Roman ones, ▷ Plautus in ▷ comedy and ▷ Seneca in tragedy. Only in the 30 years of the ▷ Romantic Revival that followed the ▷ French Revolution did English writers (partly under ▷ German influence) really discriminate between Greek and Roman literature, and value the Greeks more highly. Even then, such a poet as ▷ Shelley valued Greek culture as sentiment rather than as a deep influence. For such as him, the Greeks stood for freedom of spirit and of intellect, whereas Latin culture was associated with the pre-revolutionary authoritarian 'old regime' to which he and others of his generation were so much opposed. It must not be forgotten that Greek culture was based on maintaining slaves and that their women were excluded from public life and restricted to the household (▷ Women, Status of). Neither class was considered as capable of full humanity as free Greek males. The extraordinary privilege accorded to Greek culture in western thought has often obscured these details.

▷ Classical education; Classical mythology; Latin literature; Pastoral, Classical; Platonism and Neo-Platonism.

Green, Henry (1905–73)
Pen-name of the novelist H. V. Yorke. His novels are: *Blindness* (1926); *Living* (1929); *Party-Going* (1939); *Pack My Bag* (1940); *Caught* (1943); *Loving* (1945); *Back* (1946); *Concluding* (1948); *Nothing* (1950); *Doting* (1952). Of these, possibly the most distinguished are: *Living*, with an industrial working-class setting; *Loving*, about servants in an anachronistic great house in Ireland during World War II; *Concluding*, set in the future, about an institution for educating women civil servants, and *Party-Going*, a novel in which the events have only a few hours' duration and take place in a fog-bound London railway station. His style is condensed and poetically expressive; events are caught in movement, with a cinematic use of flash-backs to bring the past into relationship with the present. In the autobiographical *Pack my Bag* he wrote: 'Prose should be a long intimacy between strangers with no direct appeal to what both may have known. It should slowly appeal to feelings unexpressed, it should in the end draw tears out of the stone.' Green is set

aside from the ▷ modernist interest in the rendering of consciousness by a belief that the novelist should not attempt to portray the inner depths of characters, but should use their spoken words to capture the opaque and shifting surface of social relations. The later novels show increasing reliance on dialogue, following the example of the novels of ▷ Ivy Compton-Burnett. Green also professed admiration for the work of the French writer, Céline. He wrote no novels in the last 20 years of his life.

Bib: Stokes, E., *The Novels of Henry Green*; Russell, J., *Henry Green*; Bassoff, B., *Towards Loving*; Sarraute, N., in *The Age of Suspicion*.

Green, Matthew (1696–1737)
Author of *The Spleen* (1737), a tetrameter (▷ metre) couplet poem advocating the simple life as a cure for boredom and 'splenetic' irritableness.

Greenaway, Kate (1846–1901)
Born in Hoxton, the daughter of a wood-engraver, Greenaway began nature drawing as a child. She went to the Royal College and the Slade, and became a writer and illustrator of children's picture books in which she portrays an idealized world of sweetly pretty children in floral surroundings. She was encouraged by ▷ John Ruskin, whom she met in 1882 and who lectured on her art at Oxford in 1883, praising its innocent view of childhood and in effect its lack of realism. ▷ George Eliot also admired her art. Greenaway liked the ▷ Pre-Raphaelites and disliked contemporaries such as ▷ James Whistler. A strong, though unorthodox, religious instinct is evident in her search for beauty and goodness. She rejected the women's movement, and enjoyed considerable commercial success, influencing design and children's dress. Her first success was *Under the Window* (1878), a collection of rhymes she wrote and illustrated. Her later work includes *Marigold Garden* (1885) and an illustrated edition of ▷ Robert Browning's ▷ *The Pied Piper of Hamelin*. She also wrote poetry, much of it still unpublished.
Bib: Engen, R. K., *Kate Greenaway*; Holme, B., *The Kate Greenaway Book*.

Greene, (Henry) Graham (1904–91)
Novelist. The son of a schoolmaster. He went to Balliol College, Oxford, and then became a journalist (1926–30) on ▷ *The Times*. He was converted to Catholicism in 1926. His first novel, *The Man Within*, appeared in 1929. It was followed by a steady succession of novels, of which the fourth, *Stamboul Train* (1932) made him well known. It was

Graham Greene

nonetheless one of the books he called 'entertainments', meaning that they were among his less serious works; this group also includes *A Gun for Sale* (1936), *The Confidential Agent* (1939), *The Ministry of Fear* (1943), and *Our Man in Havana* (1958). In 1934 he published *It's a Battlefield*, and in 1935 a volume of stories the title story of which, *The Basement Room*, was later adapted into the film, *The Fallen Idol* (1950). In 1935 came *England Made Me*. In the same year he travelled in Liberia, on which he based his travel book *Journey Without Maps* (1936). He then became film critic for the weekly journal ▷ *The Spectator* (of which he was made literary editor in 1940). His next novel, *Brighton Rock* (1938) was the first in which there was clear evidence of Catholicism. In the same year he was commissioned to visit Mexico and report on the religious persecution there; the result was another travel book, *The Lawless Roads* (1939) and one of his most famous novels, *The Power and the Glory* (1940). During World War II he worked for the Foreign Office, and again visited West Africa. After the war he became a publisher. Later fiction: *Nineteen Stories* (1947; including eight in *The Basement Room* volume); *The Heart of the Matter* (1948); *The Third Man* (1950; also made into a film); *The End of the Affair* (1951); *The Quiet American* (1955); *A Burnt-Out Case* (1961); *A Sense of Reality* (four stories, 1963); *The Comedians* (1966); *Travels with My Aunt* (1969); *A Sort of Life* (1971); *The Honorary Consul* (1973); *The Human Factor* (1978); *Dr Fischer of*

Geneva, or the Bomb Party (1980); *Monsignior Quixote* (1982); *The Tenth Man* (1985); *The Captain and the Enemy* (1988).

He has also written plays: *The Living Room* (1953); *The Potting Shed* (1957); *The Complaisant Lover* (1959); *The Return of A. J. Raffles* (1975), and books of critical essays, *The Lost Childhood* (1951) and *The Pleasure Dome* (film criticism, 1972). His *Collected Essays* were published in 1969 and his *Collected Plays* in 1985. His autobiographical works include *A Sort of Life* (1971), *Ways of Escape* (1981) and *Getting to Know the General* (1984).

Graham Greene's high reputation is partly due to his exploration of emotions that are particularly strong in the middle of the 20th century: the sense of guilt and frustration, impulses to violence and fear of it, pity, including self-pity. He has strong gifts for narrative and for the evocation of atmosphere, especially the atmosphere of squalid surroundings which convey deprivation and despair. His Catholicism counteracts the misery in his books by its implications of spiritual dignity remaining intact even amid degradation and abject suffering.

▷ Catholicism in English literature.
Bib: Allott, K., and Farris, M., *The Art of Graham Greene*; Lodge, D., *Graham Greene*; Pryce-Jones, D., *Graham Greene*; Sharrock, R., *Saints, Sinners and Comedians: the Novels of Graham Greene*; Smith, G., *The Achievement of Graham Greene*.

Greene, Robert (1558–92)
Dramatist and pamphleteer. He was one of the ▷ University Wits, having himself been at Cambridge. Four plays by Greene, apart from collaborations, have survived: *Alphonsus, King of Aragon* (?1587); ▷ *Friar Bacon and Friar Bungay* (1589); *History of Orlando Furioso* (acted 1592); ▷ *The Scottish History of James IV* (acted 1594). Of these the best known are the second and the fourth, and in them both the melodious and fluent handling of the ▷ blank verse and the appealing portrayal of the heroines anticipate ▷ Shakespeare's romantic comedies of the 1590s.

Greene is more notable for his prose. This includes romances written in emulation of ▷ Lyly's ▷ *Euphues* and ▷ Sidney's ▷ *Arcadia*, including *Pandosto*, ▷ *The Triumph of Time* from which Shakespeare derived ▷ *The Winter's Tale* (1610). More distinctive and very lively reading are his 'cony-catching pamphlets' (*ie* booklets about criminal practices in the London underworld), *A Notable Discovery of Cosenage* (*ie* 'cozenage'

or criminal fraud, 1591) and *The Blacke Booke's Messenger* (1591) – both excellent examples of Elizabethan popular prose. A semi-fictional autobiography, *Greene's Groatsworth of Wit bought with a Million of Repentance* (1592) is notorious for containing the earliest reference to Shakespeare as a dramatist and actor, though it is an oblique one. The object of the pamphlet is ostensibly a warning to three others of the University Wits – probably ▷ Peele, ▷ Marlowe and ▷ Nashe – to amend their lives. The allusion to Shakespeare – 'an upstart crow beautified with our feathers . . . in his owne conceyt the onely shake-scene in a countrey' – comes by way of a charge of plagiarism. 35 prose works, most of them short, and many containing lyrics of great charm, are ascribed to Greene.

Greenwich Observatory
Erected by the order of ▷ Charles II in 1675 to advance nautical astronomy. Charles also inaugurated the office of Astronomer Royal. The longitudinal meridian passes through the Observatory from Pole to Pole. Greenwich time is time based on this meridian. In 1946 the observatory was moved to Herstmonceux in Sussex to escape the smoke and bright lights of London.

Gregory, Lady Augusta (1852–1932)
Promoter of Irish drama, she founded the Irish Literary Theatre, with ▷ W. B. Yeats and Edward Martyn in 1898. This became the Irish National Theatre Society in 1902 and led to the establishment of the ▷ Abbey Theatre in Dublin. She wrote several plays for it and collaborated with Yeats in *The Pot of Broth* and *Cathleen ni Houlihan* (both 1902). Of her own plays the best known are *Spreading the News* (1904), *The Gaol Gate* (1906), *Hyacinth Halvey* (1906), *The Rising of the Moon* (1907) and *The Workhouse Ward* (1908). She also translated ▷ Molière into Irish idiom in *The Kiltartan Molière*.

▷ Irish literature.
Bib: Kohfeldt, M., *Lady Gregory: The Woman behind the Irish Renaissance*.

Grein, Jack Thomas (1862–1935)
Playwright, critic and manager who helped introduce the work of European playwrights to English audiences at the end of the 19th century. He founded the Independent Theatre Club in 1891, 'to give special performances of plays which have a literary and artistic rather than a commercial value'. The first production was ▷ Ibsen's *Ghosts* which met with a storm of abuse, and thereafter little of Ibsen's work was shown;

although ▷ George Bernard Shaw's contribution to the controversy, *Widowers' Houses*, his first London production, was put on in 1892. Grein's dramatic criticism has been published in five volumes.
Bib: Orme, M., *J. T. Grein; the Story of a Pioneer*.

Greville, Sir Fulke, 1st Baron Brooke (1554–1628)

Poet, courtier, dramatist, ▷ biographer. Almost all of Fulke Greville's poetic works were published after his death. They include a collection of ▷ sonnets, religious and philosophical poems, and songs gathered under the title *Caelica* which appeared in the collection of his works published in 1633 as *Certaine Learned and Elegant Works*. A life-long friend of ▷ Philip Sidney, Greville wrote a life of Sidney which was published in 1652. A further volume of his work was published much later in the 17th century when *The Remains: Poems of Monarchy and Religion* was issued in 1670. His two plays – *Alaham* (produced c 1600) and *Mustapha* (produced 1603–8) – though set in an exotic and remote world, are valuable attempts at dealing with the important contemporary issues of power and authority in the state. Greville was a member of the brilliant intellectual circle surrounding Sidney at Court, and enjoyed considerable favour from both ▷ Elizabeth I and ▷ James I of England before his death in 1628 when he was murdered by an offended servant.
Bib: Rees, J. (ed.), *Selected Writings*; Rees, J., *Fulke Greville, First Lord Brooke, 1554–1628: A Critical Biography*.

Griffiths, Trevor (b 1935)

British socialist playwright who began writing during the late 1960s. He has since written plays for television as well as the stage and collaborated with Warren Beatty on the script for the film *Reds*. His plays often dramatize a political debate between reformist and revolutionary standpoints. This is most obviously the case in *Occupations* (1970) and *The Party* (1973); it is also true of his comic work about club entertainers, *Comedians* (1975). He has expressed a preference for writing for television because of the wider audiences that can be reached than in the theatre.
Bib: Poole, M. and Wyver, J., *Powerplays: Trevor Griffiths in Television*.

Grimm's Fairy Tales

German folk-tales collected by the brothers Jacob (1785–1863) and Wilhelm (1786–1859) Grimm, and published 1812–15. They first appeared in English in a volume illustrated by ▷ George Cruickshank and containing such stories as 'Snow White', 'Hansel and Gretel' and 'Rumpelstiltskin'. They were the first collectors to write down the stories just as they heard them, without attempting to improve them.
▷ Children's books; Fairy tales.

Grocyn, William (?1446–1519)

English ▷ humanist, and one of the earliest propagators of the study of ancient Greek in England; taught at Oxford.

Grossmith, George (1847–1912) and Weedon (1852–1919)

The brothers were both involved with the theatre, coming from a theatrical family, friends of the Terrys and ▷ Henry Irving. They are remembered, however, for *The Diary of a Nobody* (1852), initially serialized in ▷ *Punch*, written by both brothers and illustrated by Weedon. The nobody in question, Mr Pooter, sensitive to the slightest humiliation, conveys the events and contemporary background detail in a life striving for gentility. The book was immediately successful, with a wide readership, and has remained popular.

Grotowski, Jerzy (b 1933)

Polish director who established the Laboratory Theatre in Wroclaw in the early 1960s, where he developed a training process for actors which emphasized the importance of physical as well as mental skills. His rejection of the expensive paraphernalia of traditional theatre in favour of what he called 'poor theatre', which relies more exclusively on the actor, has been a great inspiration for the British ▷ fringe theatre. He has also been an important influence on the work of the British director ▷ Peter Brook.
Bib: Grotowski, J., *Towards a Poor Theatre*.

Group Theatre

A private play society founded in 1933 and famous for its productions of the experimental poetic plays of ▷ Auden and ▷ Isherwood: *The Dog Beneath the Skin* (1936), *The Ascent of F6* (1937) and *On the Frontier* (1939). Other notable productions include ▷ T. S. Eliot's *Sweeney Agonistes* (1935) and ▷ Stephen Spender's *Trial of a Judge* (1938). Most of its productions were directed by Rupert Doone. Group Theatre was active, apart from an interim during the war years, until 1953.
Bib: Medley, R., *Drawn from Life: a Memoir of the 1930's Group Theatre*; Sidnell, M. J., *Dances of Death: the Group Theatre of London in the Thirties*.

Grub Street
A street in London frequented in the 18th century by hack writers. Hence 'Grub-street' (adjective or noun) indicates literature or journalism of a low order. In the 19th century it was renamed Milton Street.

Grundy, Mrs
A symbol of narrow-minded, intolerant, out-of-date moral censoriousness. The symbol derives from a character in an otherwise forgotten play, *Speed the Plough* (1798) by Thomas Morton. Mrs Grundy herself never appears, but her neighbour, Mrs Ashfield, is constantly worried about what Mrs Grundy's opinion will be about this or that incident or piece of behaviour.

Guelphs and Ghibellines
Rival political parties in medieval Italy, the former supporting the influence of the Popes and the latter that of the German (▷ Holy Roman) Emperor. Hence, sometimes used for any two contending bodies of opinion.

Guido de Columnis (or de Columpnis, or della Colonne)
A Sicilian writer, and a judge at Messina from 1257–80, whose translation of ▷ Benoît de Sainte-Maure's verse narrative of the Troy story into Latin prose (completed around 1287) became the most popular and authoritative version of Trojan history available in the medieval period. ▷ John Lydgate's *Troy Book* is one of the many vernacular translations of Guido's *Historia Destructionis Troiae*, as is the Middle English ▷ alliterative poem, ▷ *The Destruction of Troy*
     ▷ Troy.

Guild
     ▷ Capitalism; Craft Guilds.

Guildhall
In medieval times, the building where the Merchant Guild of a town held its meetings; now, often the name of a building where the town council meets, and especially the 15th-century town hall of the City of London.
     ▷ Apprenticeship; Capitalism.

Guinevere
The wife of ▷ King Arthur in Arthurian narratives. In ▷ Geoffrey of Monmouth's *Historia Regum Britanniae* she is from a Roman family. Mordred takes her for his lover when he usurps Arthur's throne, but the level of Guinevere's complicity in the betrayal is not made clear. In later versions of Arthurian narrative, Guinevere's relationship with ▷ Lancelot becomes the most developed aspect of her story. In ▷ Chrétien

de Troyes's romance, the *Chevalier de la Charrette*, Guinevere is abducted by King Meleagant and rescued by Lancelot, her lover. Her love affair with Lancelot is later linked into the cycles of Arthurian narrative, and represented as one of the factors contributing to the break-up of Arthur's court and reign (ironically the ▷ Round Table is part of her dowry). In ▷ Malory's *Morte D'Arthur*, the quality of the love shared by Lancelot and Guinevere is celebrated, at the same time as its destructive consequences are recounted: Guinevere, in the *Morte D'Arthur* 'is a true lover, and therefore she had a good end'. She dies in the convent at Amesbury.

Gulliver's Travels (1726)
A satirical fable by ▷ Jonathan Swift. It exploits the contemporary interest in accounts of voyages, *eg* William Dampier's *New Voyage* (1697). ▷ Daniel Defoe's fictional account of Robinson Crusoe's voyages had been published in 1719, and had achieved great popularity; this was partly due to Defoe's strictly factual presentation, such that his book could quite well pass for a true account. Swift makes his hero, Lemuel Gulliver, recount his adventures with the same sober precision for the effect of accuracy, causing him, as Defoe caused Crusoe, to follow the philosopher ▷ John Locke in describing only the primary qualities of his strange environments – *ie* the objective, measurable ones – ignoring the secondary qualities of colour, beauty, etc. which are more subjective, less verifiable, and so more likely to arouse a reader's disbelief. Swift's intention in doing this was of course not to deceive his readers into supposing that Gulliver's fantastic adventures were true, but to make them realize the absurdity, and worse, of accepted human characteristics when they are looked at from an unfamiliar point of view. Thus in Part I, ▷ Lilliput, Gulliver is wrecked on an island where human beings are little bigger than insects, and their self-importance is clearly laughable, but in Part II, Brobdingnag, he is himself an insect in a land of giants, and made to feel his own pettiness. In Part III, contemporary scientists of the ▷ Royal Society are held up for ridicule: science is shown to be futile unless it is applicable to human betterment – the science of Swift's day had not yet reached the stage of technology. Part IV is about the land of the ▷ Houyhnhnms, where horses are endowed with reason but human beings are not; the point here is that the horses recognize that Gulliver has reason, unlike the Yahoos of the

island which he so much resembles, but they succeed in demonstrating to him that human reason is woefully inadequate for the conduct of life because of the mischievousness of the human mind. Swift was, after all, a Christian, and believed that Man would destroy himself without divine aid.

Swift was such a good story-teller that his fable became popular for the sake of the narrative, and though it was in no ordinary sense a novel, his close attention to factual detail (the way in which, especially in Parts I and II, Gulliver is continuously under the pressure of his environment) takes a long stride in the advance of novelistic art.

▷ Lagado; Luggnagg.

Gunn, Thom (b 1929)

Poet. Educated at Cambridge and Stanford University in California, Gunn now lives in San Francisco, although he is of British origin. His work was first associated with the ▷ Movement, but gradually it drew away from comparison with ▷ Philip Larkin or ▷ Kingsley Amis through its growing violent energy in the 1960s, although formally his precise, clear style is still akin to 1950s poetry. Gunn's work in the U.S.A. has drawn him close to American beat poets in rhythm and subject matter, motorbikes and rock music, and images of nihilism. He has experimented with syllabic, ▷ iambic and with ▷ free verse forms. His publications include: *Fighting Terms* (1954); *Poems* (1954); *The Sense of Movement* (1957) (which won the Somerset Maugham award); *Moly* (1971); *Jack Straw's Castle* (1976); *Selected Poems, 1950–1975* (1979); and *The Passages of Joy* (1982).

Gunpowder Plot (1605)

A conspiracy by a section of English Roman Catholics to destroy the Protestant government of ▷ James I by blowing up the ▷ Houses of Parliament at a time when the king and the members of the Houses of Lords and Commons were all in the building. The plot was inspired by the ▷ Jesuits and led by Robert Catesby, but undertaken by Guy Fawkes. The date was fixed for 5 November and the explosives were all laid; but the plot was betrayed and Fawkes was arrested on the threshold of the cellar on 4 November. 5 November has since been celebrated annually with fireworks and bonfires on which Guy Fawkes is burnt in effigy.

Guy Fawkes

▷ Gunpowder Plot.

Guy Mannering (1815)

A novel by ▷ Sir Walter Scott. It is set in the south of Scotland near the English border during the 18th century. The plot concerns the attempt of a criminal lawyer, Glossin, to deprive Harry Bertram, the heir to the Scottish estate of Ellangowan, of his property. Bertram is kidnapped as a child by smugglers in Glossin's pay, and carried abroad. He returns to Scotland as a young man and recovers his estate with the help of a gipsy who lives on it, Meg Merrilies. Mannering is an English officer under whom Bertram has served in the army, and with whose daughter Julia he is in love. The novel is notable partly for its romantic scene painting, and partly for the characterization which is markedly more vivid in the lower social orders – the ▷ gipsies, the farmer Dandy Dinmont, the tutor Dominie Sampson – than in its ladies and gentlemen. There are also very good descriptions of ▷ Edinburgh.

Guy of Warwick

A very popular early 14th-century English romance, based on a 13th-century ▷ Anglo-Norman text. It recounts the story of Guy's ultimately successful attempts to prove himself as a knight and win the hand of Fenice, daughter of the Earl of Warwick. He leaves his wife to go on a pilgrimage to the Holy Land, and the narrative tells of his subsequent experiences in the guise of a pilgrim and his efforts, on his return to England, to help King Athelstan resist the Danish invaders (notably by fighting the giant Colbrand). It is only on his deathbed, having been nursed by Fenice, that the hermit, Guy, reveals his identity to his wife. There is a continuation which recounts the history of Guy's son Reinbrun. The combination of romance and saint's life story motifs in a semi-historical setting proved a popular and successful narrative formula. Many versions of the story survive, including one by ▷ John Lydgate, and the story of Guy's fight with Colbrand is retold in ▷ Michael Drayton's *Poly-Olbion*. Guy's story is the subject of several 16th-century ballads and one 17th-century play.
Bib: Barron, W. R. J., *English Medieval Romance.*

Gwynn (Guinn, Guin), Eleanor (Ellen) (Nell) (?1642–87)

Actress, dancer. One account of Gwynn's early years has her hawking herring in the streets of London, before she became an orange seller at the ▷ Bridges Street Theatre, under 'Orange Moll', in about 1663. By 1665 she had graduated to the stage, aided by the actor ▷ Charles Hart, who became the leading actor in the ▷ King's Company, and Gwynn's lover.

Gwynn quickly gained a reputation as a brilliant comic actress, and dancer, 'pretty witty Nell'. By 1667 she had become the mistress of Charles Sackville, Lord Buckhurst, and two years after that, one of the mistresses of King Charles II. She gave birth to a son, later the Duke of St Alban's, in 1670. She resumed acting soon afterwards, but left the stage permanently in 1671, living in a house in Pall Mall provided for her by the king. She continued as an avid patron of the stage, bringing large parties to performances. She also gave away substantial sums to the poor, and used her influence to free some prisoners from gaol. Gwynn remained a favourite of the court circle, and of the people, despite many satiric or even venomous attacks on her.

Bib: Wilson, J. H., *All the King's Ladies: Actresses of the Restoration*; Wilson, J. H., *Nell Gwynn*; Chesterton, C., *Nell Gwynn*; Bevan, B., *Nell Gwynn*.

H

Habeas Corpus
A legal writ which begins with these Latin words (= 'thou shalt have the body . . .'). The purpose is to order that a person should be brought before a judge. It has been most commonly used in instances of persons imprisoned without trial, so that a judge may decide the cause of imprisonment and arrange for a trial to take place. The writ was used in the ▷ Middle Ages as far back as the 12th century, but its use was defined by Parliament in the Habeas Corpus Act of 1679. It has long been considered one of the foundations of liberty.

Hades
In Greek myth, the god of the underworld; his Latin name is Pluto. He was brother of ▷ Zeus, and of ▷ Poseidon. His name is often used for the underworld itself. It was mainly a gloomy world of shadowy existence guarded by the many-headed dog, Cerberus and bounded by the rivers ▷ Styx and Acheron. One region, ▷ Tartarus, was reserved for the punishment of those who had offended the gods, while another, the fields of Asphodel, was reserved for those who deserved neither reward nor punishment. The virtuous dead went elsewhere to ▷ Elysium, though ▷ Virgil regards Elysium too as part of the underworld.
▷ Charon.

Haggard, Sir H (Henry) Rider (1856–1925)
Son of a Norfolk squire, he spent several years in South Africa as a young man, writing books on its history and farming, but he is famous for his numerous adventure novels set in such exotic locations as Iceland, Mexico and ancient Egypt. They are characterized by gripping narrative and strange events, as well as evocative descriptions of landscape, wildlife and tribal society, particularly in Africa. He has had a world-wide readership and some of his stories have been filmed. *King Solomon's Mines* (1886) and *She* (1887) are the most famous novels. *The Days of My Life: an Autobiography* appeared in 1926.
Bib: Haggard, L. R., *The Cloak that I Left*; Ellis, P. B., *H. Rider Haggard: A voice from the Infinite*; Higgins, D. S., *Rider Haggard: The Great Storyteller*.

Hakluyt, Richard (?1553–1616)
Geographer. In 1589 and 1598 he published his *Principal Navigations, Voyages and Discoveries of the English Nation*, being a record of English explorations, which had lagged behind those of the French, Spanish, Portuguese and Dutch until the middle of the century, and then made prodigious progress with the nationalistic energy characteristic of England in the reign of ▷ Elizabeth I.

Hall, Edward (?1498–1547)
Chronicler; author of *The Union of the Noble and Illustrious Families of Lancaster and York* (1542; enlarged 1548, 1550). This tells of the bitter rivalries of the two branches of the House of Anjou (▷ Plantagenets) from the death of the childless ▷ Richard II in 1400, and the accession of ▷ Henry IV, first of the House of ▷ Lancaster, to the death of the last of the House of York, ▷ Richard III, in 1485, and the accession of Henry Tudor as ▷ Henry VII. He idealizes Henry VII and ▷ Henry VIII, partly because they re-established dynastic harmony, and partly because, as a ▷ Protestant, Hall was strongly sympathetic to Henry VIII's reform of the Church. The Chronicle was one of Shakespeare's two main source-books for his English history plays, the other being ▷ Holinshed.
▷ Histories and Chronicles; Wars of the Roses.

Hall, Joseph (1574–1656)
▷ Satirist; 'character' (▷ Characters, Theophrastian) writer; religious controversialist; bishop, 1627–47. He published his *Virgidemiae* (or *Harvest of Rods, ie* for chastisement) in 1597–8; he claimed to be the first English satirist, but ▷ John Donne and ▷ John Marston were writing at the same time, not to mention ▷ Edmund Spenser's *Mother Hubberd's Tale*. He may have considered himself more truly a satirist than his rivals inasmuch as he was stricter in following classical Latin models, notably of ▷ Juvenal. Like Juvenal, he attacked what he saw as contemporary vices. His *Characters of Virtues and Vices* (1608) was likewise in classical tradition, this time modelled on the Greek ▷ Theophrastus, and was also intended for the moral improvement of the age.
Bib: Davenport, A., *The Poems of Joseph Hall*; Huntley, F. L., *Bishop Joseph Hall*.

Hall, Sir Peter (b 1930)
British director whose first major production was ▷ Samuel Beckett's ▷ *Waiting for Godot* at the Arts Theatre in 1955. From 1956 he directed at Stratford-on-Avon and became director of the theatre from 1960, when it became the Royal Shakespeare Theatre (▷ Royal Shakespeare Company). In 1972 he replaced ▷ Laurence Olivier as director of the ▷ National Theatre, from which he retired in 1988.
Bib: Hall, P., *Peter Hall's Diaries: the Stories of a Dramatic Battle*.

Hamlet (c 1601)

A tragedy by ▷ Shakespeare, written in about 1601. Three early versions of it exist: the imperfect ▷ quarto of 1603, the superior quarto of 1604, and the version in the First ▷ Folio of 1623, which omits some of the material in the 1604 quarto. The story was a widespread legend in northern Europe. Shakespeare's immediate source is likely to have been Belleforest's *Histoires Tragiques* (1559), and Belleforest's own version came from a 13th-century Danish chronicler, Saxo Grammaticus. But Shakespeare also had another source: a play of the same name already existed and is thought to have been a lost play by ▷ Thomas Kyd. It is referred to without mention of the author by ▷ Nashe in a letter accompanying ▷ Greene's *Menaphon* (1589), by ▷ Henslowe in his Diary (1594) and by ▷ Lodge in *Wit's Misery* (1596). There are also parallels between Shakespeare's play and Kyd's ▷ *Spanish Tragedy*: both have ghosts and a play within the play; Kyd's tragedy is about a father seeking vengeance for his son, and Shakespeare's is about a son avenging his father. In both plays there are obstacles to the vengeance: in Kyd's play, the obstacle is a straightforward one, of how to bring retribution upon an offender who is so powerful as to be beyond the law; in Shakespeare it is so subtle that Hamlet's hesitations have been among the most discussed subjects in criticism.

Certain features of Shakespeare's play require special attention in assessing the play.

1 The basic situation is that Hamlet's uncle, ▷ Claudius, has married Hamlet's mother, Gertrude, only a month after the death of her husband, old Hamlet. Claudius has, moreover, ascended the throne ignoring the claim of his nephew and with the consent of the court. This thoroughly distasteful situation reflects badly not only on Claudius and Gertrude, but on the court as well, and it has already plunged Hamlet into disgust at the opening of the play. We need also to remember that marriage to a sister-in-law was of at least doubtful validity: it constituted ▷ Henry VIII's legal ground for divorce from ▷ Katharine of Aragon.

2 It is only later that Hamlet learns from his father's ghost that old Hamlet was murdered by Claudius. The revelation does not lead directly to action, but to Hamlet feigning madness, and to the 'play within the play', before which Claudius, in the audience, betrays his guilt.

3 Claudius's self-betrayal, however, is incriminating only to Hamlet and his friend

Horatio, who have already learned the facts. Either Hamlet mistrusts the Ghost who may not have been truly the spirit of his father, or it is part of his vengeance to inform Claudius that his guilt is known. One of the beliefs about ▷ ghosts current in Shakespeare's time was that they were sometimes evil spirits assuming the disguise of dead men.

4 Hamlet's hostility extends not merely to Claudius, but to the whole court, in so far as they are or may be subservient to Claudius. Thus Hamlet behaves brutally to Ophelia (the girl whom he loves) because he suspects (although she is entirely innocent) that she is used as a kind of decoy by Claudius and by her father, Polonius.

5 Laertes, Ophelia's brother, is a contrast to Hamlet in being a straightforward revenger: he immediately seeks the death of Hamlet for causing the deaths of his father and sister. But his impetuosity puts him on the side of evil, for it causes him to connive with Claudius.

6 Claudius is an unusual villain for the drama of the time, for he is not *seen* to be evil on the stage; we know of his guilt indirectly. Even his conspiracy against Hamlet's life can be excused as action in self-defence.

These features of the play suggest that Shakespeare was exposing traditional beliefs about revenge as over-simplified. Revenge is difficult if we do not feel the guilty man to be guilty: 'One may smile, and smile and be a villain' (I. v. 108). Further, revenge does not solve evil, if evil lies in a complex situation: 'The time is out of joint; O cursed spite/That ever I was born to set it right' (V. i. 189–90). Finally, revenge itself may be morally wrong: what *was* the Ghost?

Hammett, Dashiell (1894–1961)
▷ Detective fiction.

Hampton, Christopher (b 1946)
British dramatist, another product of the ▷ Royal Court theatre where he was the first resident dramatist (1968–70), while also working there as literary manager. His most recent play is the much acclaimed adaptation, *Les Liaisons Dangereuses* (1985), performed by the ▷ Royal Shakespeare Company, a dramatization of a novel by Choderlos de Laclos about sexual combat and power in France just prior to the revolution of 1789. Typically of Hampton, the play does not deal explicitly with politics, though it provides a witty and vivid insight into a world of decadence and ruthlessness on the brink of collapse. Other works include: *Total Eclipse* (1968); *The Philanthropist* (1970); *Savages* (1973); *Treats* (1976); *Tales from the Vienna*

Woods (1977); *Don Juan Comes Back From the War* (1978); *Tales from Hollywood* (1983). Hampton has been described as a modern classicist, not least for his translations of plays by ▷ Chekhov, ▷ Ibsen and ▷ Molière: *Uncle Vanya* (1971); *Hedda Gabler* (1971); *A Doll's House* (1971); *The Wild Duck* (1980); *Ghosts* (1983); *Don Juan* (1972); *Tartuffe* (1984).

Hampton Court

A palace on the Thames built by Cardinal ▷ Wolsey and a principal royal residence in the 16th and 17th centuries. It has an addition designed by ▷ Christopher Wren.

Handel, George Frederick (1685–1759)

Composer. Born in Germany, he was appointed chief musician to George, Elector of Hanover, who became ▷ George I of Britain (1714–27). Handel visited England in 1710 and settled there in 1712; he became a naturalized British citizen in 1726. He had studied in Italy and was deeply experienced in French music, but in many respects he was in harmony with the English tradition, whose last great master, ▷ Henry Purcell, had died in 1695. Nonetheless, Handel at first had an uneven career in England. He first attempted to establish ▷ opera in the Italian style; his opera *Rinaldo* was a success in 1711. Yet opera in the end reduced him to bankruptcy and he became the exponent of the art of oratorio, which he transformed from its original religious feeling and setting into a much more theatrical form. His first oratorio, *Esther* (1720), resembled the ▷ masques that had been popular in fashionable circles since early in the previous century. *Semele*, *Susanna* and *Judas Maccabeus*, to mention a few of the 16 oratorios that followed, are choral dramas. His masterpiece was *The Messiah*, first performed in Dublin, 1741. Handel established the oratorio as the most popular English musical form for the next two centuries. Others of his choral works included his choral settings for ▷ John Dryden's poems, *Ode on St Cecilia's Day* and *Alexander's Feast*.
Bib: Deutsch, O. E., *Handel: A Documentary Biography*.

Handlyng Synne

▷ Mannyng, Robert.

Hanover, House of

▷ George; Windsor, House of.

Hansard

The official report of meetings of both Houses of ▷ Parliament, so called after an 18th-century printer employed by the government.

Hard Times (1854)

A novel by ▷ Charles Dickens. It is the only one by him not at least partly set in London. The scene is an imaginary industrial town called Coketown. One of the main characters, Thomas Gradgrind, is based on the ▷ Utilitarian leader James Mill (1773–1836); as such, he is an educationist who believes that education should be merely practical and hence factual, allowing no place for imagination or emotion. He marries his daughter Louisa to a ruthless manufacturer, Josiah Bounderby, who puts Gradgrind's philosophy into practice in that he has no place for humane feeling in the conduct of his business. Louisa accepts him in order to be in a position to help her brother Tom who becomes, under the influence of his upbringing, callous, unscrupulous and meanly calculating. Louisa is nearly seduced by a visiting politician, James Harthouse, who is cynically concerned only to find amusement in a place with no other charms. The opposition to this world of calculating selfishness is a travelling circus called 'the horse-riding' owned by Sleary. Sissy Jupe, a product of the circus and the human fellowship that it engenders, is found ineducable by Gradgrind, whose dependant she becomes, but she has the inner assurance required to face Harthouse and compel him to leave the town. Gradgrind's world falls apart when he discovers that he has ruined his daughter's happiness and turned his son into a criminal. A subplot concerns a working-man, Stephen Blackpool, a victim of the Gradgrind-Bounderby system, and of young Gradgrind's heartless criminality.

Hardy, Thomas (1840–1928)

Novelist and poet, and former architect. He was the son of a village stonemason in Dorset; thus he was close to the country life by his origins, and he never lost feeling for it. As he grew up, he underwent the painful loss of faith so common among intellectuals in England in the second half of the 19th century; this led him to a tragic philosophy that human beings are the victims of indifferent forces. At the same time he witnessed the steady weakening from within and erosion from without of the part of rural England with which he was so much indentified. This region is the six south-western counties of England, approximately coterminous with the 6th-century Saxon kingdom of ▷ Wessex, by which name he calls them in his 'Novels of Character and Environment'. These novels are by far his best known: ▷ *Under the*

Thomas Hardy by William Strang, 1891

Greenwood Tree (1872); ▷ *Far from the Madding Crowd* (1874); ▷ *The Return of the Native* (1878); ▷ *The Mayor of Casterbridge* (1886); ▷ *The Woodlanders* (1887); ▷ *Tess of the D'Urbervilles* (1891); ▷ *Jude the Obscure* (1895). Two volumes of stories are *Wessex Tales* (1888) and *Life's Little Ironies* (1894). Hardy's originality was his discernment of the intimate relationship of character and environment, and his characters nearly always became less convincing when this relationship loses closeness, *ie* in his socially higher, more sophisticated characters. This may account for the fact that the other two groups of his novels have much less prestige. He called them 'Romances and Fantasies' (*A Pair of Blue Eyes*, 1873; *The Trumpet-Major*, 1880; *Two on a Tower*, 1882; *A Group of Noble Dames*, 1891; *The Well-Beloved*, 1897) and 'Novels of Ingenuity' (*Desperate Remedies*, 1871; *The Hand of Ethelberta*, 1876; *A Laodicean*, 1881).

Hardy's poetry is as distinguished as his novels; indeed he regarded himself as primarily a poet. Though he wrote poetry from the beginning of his career, his best verse was chiefly the fruit of his later years when he had abandoned novels. It is in some respects very traditional – ballads such as *The Trampwoman's Tragedy* and tuneful, rhyming lyrics. But though traditional – in touch with

folksong and ▷ ballad – Hardy was never conventional. His diction is distinctive; he experimented constantly with form and stresses, and the singing rhythms subtly respond to the movement of his intense feelings; the consequent poignance and sincerity has brought him the admiration of poets since 1945, who seem especially sensitive to dishonesty of feeling. His ▷ lyrics have the peculiarity that they nearly always centre on incident, in a way that gives them dramatic sharpness. Amongst the most admired are some that he wrote to his dead first wife, included in *Satires of Circumstance* (1914).
Bib: Hardy, E., *Life*; Brown, D., *Thomas Hardy*; Weber, C. J., *Hardy of Wessex*; Stewart, J. I. M., *Thomas Hardy: A Critical Biography*; Gittings, R., *Young Thomas Hardy*; *The Older Hardy*; Millgate, M., *Thomas Hardy: A Biography*; *Thomas Hardy, His Career as a Novelist*; Bayley, J., *An Essay on Hardy*.

Hardyng, John (1378–c 1465)
Compiler of the verse chronicle, covering the period from the foundation of Britain by Brutus to the year 1437, referred to as *The Chronicle of John Hardyng*. The early sections of the *Chronicle* draw material from the framework of British history established by ▷ Geoffrey of Monmouth, but in Hardyng's version ▷ King Arthur is actually crowned Emperor of Rome. The *Chronicle* seems to have been used by ▷ Malory for a few details of Arthurian history in his *Morte D'Arthur*. The interest in validating the claims of the kings of England to overlordship of Scotland, which is evident in the *Chronicle*, perhaps reflects one of the political motivations for its compilation.
Bib: Gransden, A., *Historical Writing in England, Vol. II*.

Hare, David (b 1947)
British left-wing dramatist who established his reputation during the 1970s as a writer for ▷ fringe companies. Since then he has chosen to work from within the establishment as a writer and director at the ▷ National Theatre. Major stage plays include: *Brassneck* (1973), a collaboration with ▷ Howard Brenton; *Teeth 'n' Smiles* (1975); *Fanshen* (1975); *Plenty* (1978); *A Map of the World* (1983); *Pravda* (1985), another collaboration with Howard Brenton; *The Secret Rapture* (1988). Television plays: *Licking Hitler* (1978); *Saigon: Year of the Cat* (1983). Films: *Wetherby* (1985), *Plenty* (1985).
Bib: Bull, J., *New British Political Dramatists*;

Chambers, C. and Prior, M., *Playwrights' Progress*.

Harington, Sir John (1561–1612)

Poet, translator, courtier. Harington's ▷ translation of ▷ Ludovico Ariosto's ▷ *Orlando Furioso* (published in 1591) was undertaken, so it is said, as a punishment exacted by ▷ Elizabeth I for his having translated part of the bawdy sections of that poem. Whatever the circumstances of its production, Harington's work established itself as one of the most important of Elizabethan translations. In addition to his work on Ariosto, Harington also wrote a humorous piece entitled *A New Discourse of a Stale Subject, called the Metamorphosis of Ajax* (1596). This work, with its punning title (Ajax = A 'Jakes' = a water closet) contains diagrams and instructions on the installation of a plumbing system. The queen suspected that the work contained a subtle allusion to the Earl of Leicester and banished Harington from court. During this banishment he put his hydraulic theories into practice, installing the first water closet in England at Richmond Palace. A tendency to overdo a joke is suggested by the publication, again in 1596, of *An Anatomy of the Metamorphosed Ajax*.
Bib: Haughey, R., *Harington of Stepney, Tudor Gentleman: His Life and Works*.

Harley Manuscript

A rich anthology, principally of Middle English and Anglo-Norman poetry and prose (with some ecclesiastical texts in Latin), compiled probably near Ludlow, Shropshire, c 1340; now in the British Library (Harley 2253). The pieces are of considerable literary sophistication, and include a wide variety of genres and literary forms: ▷ lyrics, a ▷ romance, ▷ fabliaux, historical poems, interludes, saints' lives, satires, biblical narratives and a guide to Holy Land pilgrimages. The texts seem to be consciously arranged to produce striking sacred/secular juxtapositions. The manuscript contains an outstanding collection of Middle English lyrics (generally referred to as 'The Harley Lyrics'), and half the extant corpus of Middle English secular lyrics (up to the end of the 14th century) are preserved in unique copies in it.
Bib: Ker, N. R., *Facsimile of BM. MS. Harley 2253*; Brook, G. L. (ed.), *The Harley Lyrics*.

Harpies

In Greek myths, personifications – half bird and half woman – of storm winds. They snatched food from tables and caused hunger, hence Ariel's role as a harpy in ▷ *The Tempest* III. iii.

Harris, Wilson (b 1921)

Guyanese novelist and short-story writer. The landscape and history of Guyana play an important part in his work, which is concerned with such issues as the legacy of the colonial past and the destruction and recreation of individual and collective identity. His novels are visionary, experimental, anti-realist explorations of consciousness, employing multiple and fragmentary narrative structures, and symbolic correspondences between inner and outer landscapes. The later novels use a wider range of geographical settings, including England, Mexico and South America. His volumes of short stories, *The Sleepers of Roraima* (1970) and *The Age of the Rainmakers* (1971) locate a redemptive power in Amerindian myth. His novels are: *The Guyana Quartet: Palace of the Peacock* (1960); *The Far Journey of Oudu* (1961); *The Whole Armour* (1962) and *The Secret Ladder* (1963); *Heartland* (1964); *The Eye of the Scarecrow* (1965); *The Waiting Room* (1967); *Tutamari* (1968); *Ascent to Omai* (1970); *Black Marsden* (1972); *Companions of the Day and Night* (1975); *Da Silva da Silva's Cultivated Wilderness, and the Genesis of the Clowns* (1977); *The Tree of the Sun* (1978); *The Angel at the Gate* (1982); *Carnival* (1985); *The Infinite Rehearsal* (1987).
Bib: Gilkes, M., *Wilson Harris and the Caribbean Novel*.

Harrison, Tony (b 1937)

Poet. His early volumes, *The Loiners* (1970) and *The School of Eloquence* (1978), established his recurrent subject-matter – becoming distanced through education from his working-class, northern upbringing. This intensely felt sense of loss and belonging is still being explored in *V* (1985). Other volumes of poetry include: *Newcastle is Peru* (1974); *Bow Down* (1974); *Continuous* (1982). He has also translated ▷ Aeschylus's *Oresteia* and French drama for the theatre; see *Dramatic Verse 1973–1985* (1985).

Harrow School

▷ Public school. It was founded in 1571 for poor children of the neighbourhood. After 1660 the school took children from the whole country, and in the 18th and 19th centuries it became immensely fashionable. In the 19th century the ▷ Eton v. Harrow cricket match became one of the most fashionable social occasions of the London season.

Hart, Charles (?1630–83)

Actor, manager. He began his career as a boy actor, playing women's parts, at the ▷ Blackfriars Theatre. After the theatres were closed in 1642, he fought in the service of the king, and is said to have acted clandestinely in the late 1640s. Hart resumed acting openly, at the Red Bull Theatre, about the time of the ▷ Restoration and in late 1660 he joined the ▷ King's Company, under ▷ Thomas Killigrew, now performing primarily or wholly in men's roles. He is reputed to have been, during the 1660s, a lover of ▷ Nell Gwynn.

During his lifetime his reputation rested particularly on his abilities in tragic roles: he is said to have acted with great precision and concentration, such that nothing could distract him from his performance; and to have been able to draw full houses. He was for a time the main rival of ▷ Thomas Betterton, who imitated his style on at least one occasion.

Hartley, David (1705–57)

A philosopher best known for his theory of association of ideas, based on the thought of ▷ Sir Isaac Newton and of ▷ John Locke in the 17th century. In his *Observations on Man* (1749) Hartley denied that moral ideas were inborn in man, holding that they derived from associations of pleasure and pain with certain behaviour. The higher pleasures derive from the lower, and culminate in the love of God. This philosophy of mechanistic psychology was very influential in the first half of the 19th century, especially on the ▷ Utilitarian school of thinkers. ▷ Coleridge was at first strongly under Hartley's influence, but later rejected it, asserting that the human personality was active in its growth, not passive as Hartley's theory implied. ▷ Wordsworth, however, based much of his feeling for nature's creative influence on human personality on Hartley.

Hartley, L. P. (Leslie Poles) (1895–1972)

Novelist. His novels and stories are: *Night Fears* (1924); *Simonetta Perkins* (1925); *The Killing Bottle* (1932); a trilogy – *The Shrimp and the Anemone* (1944), *The Sixth Heaven* (1946) and *Eustace and Hilda* (1947); *The Travelling Grave* (1948); *The Boat* (1949); *My Fellow Devils* (1951); *The Go-Between* (1953); *The White Wand* (1954); *A Perfect Woman* (1955); *The Hireling* (1957); *Facial Justice* (1960); *Two for the River* (1961); *The Brickfield* (1964); *The Betrayal* (1966); *Poor Clare* (1968); *The Love Adept* (1968); *My Sister's Keeper* (1970); *The Harness Room* (1971); *The Collections* (1972); *The Will and*

the Way (1973). His reputation rests chiefly on the trilogy (especially *The Shrimp and the Anemone*) and *The Go-Between*. These both contain very sensitive child studies, and relate the influence of childhood experiences on the development of the adult. Hartley was in the tradition of ▷ Henry James, whom he resembles in his presentation of delicate but crucial personal inter-relationships; the influence of ▷ Sigmund Freud intervened to give Hartley a different kind of psychological depth, more concerned with the recovery of the self buried in the forgotten experiences of the past than with the self buried under the false assumptions of society.
Bib: Bien, P., *Hartley*; Mulkeen, A., *Wild Thyme, Winter Lightning*.

Harvey, Gabriel (?1545–1630)

Man of letters and scholar; friend of ▷ Edmund Spenser, who presents Harvey as Hobbinol in ▷ *The Shepherd's Calendar*. Harvey argued vigorously for substituting Latin quantitative metres (based on length of syllables) for the English accentual rhythms which rely on accent. Otherwise he is chiefly known for his violent quarrels (especially with ▷ Thomas Nashe and ▷ Robert Greene) which caused his name to figure prominently in the ▷ pamphlets of the time.

▷ Classical education and English literature; Metre.

Hauptmann, Gerhart (1862–1946)

German dramatist and exponent of a 'naturalistic' style of writing in early plays like *The Weavers* (1892), a play based on factual events relating to social struggle and revolt in the Silesian weaving industry. Much of the play is written in the Silesian dialect. *The Thieves' Comedy* (1904) was shown by ▷ Harley Granville Barker as part of his Court Theatre repertory.
Bib: Sinden, M., *Gerhart Hauptmann: The Prose Plays*.

Havelock

A Middle English verse romance, composed towards the end of the 13th century. Two 12th century ▷ Anglo-Norman versions are extant: one in ▷ Geoffrei Gaimar's *Estoire des Engleis*; the other, the *Lai d'Havelok*, claims descent from a tale told by the Britons (▷ Breton Lays). The romance tells the story of Havelock, the dispossessed heir to the Danish throne, and of Goldborough, the dispossessed heir to her father's kingdom of England. Both suffer as children from the oppression of their respective guardians who have ambitions to establish their own royal dynasties. Havelock only manages to escape from the murderous designs of his guardian, Goddard, through the help of Grim the fisherman. Havelock flees Denmark with Grim and his family, and lives with them in England at the place known as Grimsby. Havelock's marriage to Goldborough is arranged by her guardian, Godrich, as a social slight to the heir to the English throne. However, through the agency of a miraculous light which shines from Havelock's mouth, and the intervention of a divine voice, Goldborough learns that her husband is not a mere kitchen boy but of royal descent. The narrative goes on to relate how Havelock recovers his heritage and that of Goldborough too.

Bib: Barron, W. R. J., *English Medieval Romance*.

Hawking (falconry)

The sport of using birds of prey (hawks, falcons, etc.) for the pursuit of other birds and of small mammals such as rabbits and hares. In England as in every other European country it was both a popular and a fashionable sport until in the 17th century it was driven out by the use of the gun. Different species were considered appropriate to the various ranks of society, *eg* the eagle for emperors, gerfalcons for kings, peregrines for earls, goshawks for yeoman, sparrow-hawks for priests, kestrels for servants. The hawk was kept on the wrist of the falconer and released when the prey or 'quarry' came into view. The training of the hawk, *eg* not to fly away with its prey, is a long and complicated process. A good many hawking terms passed into common speech in the Middle Ages and the 16th century and influenced the literature of those periods, as ▷ Chaucer's ▷ *Parliament of Foulys*.

Haymarket Theatres

The first major theatre in the Haymarket was built in 1705 according to a design by the dramatist and architect ▷ John Vanbrugh, and immediately occupied by ▷ Thomas Betterton and his company. Until Queen Anne's death in 1714 it was known as Her Majesty's Theatre or the Queen's Theatre, and then the King's Theatre, or simply the Haymarket. However, the theatre suffered financial problems since it proved too large for spoken drama, and in due course became the first English opera house, staging many of Handel's operas. After three theatres were destroyed on that site the present theatre, known as Her Majesty's, was built by ▷ Beerbohm Tree (1853–1917) in 1897.

In 1720 another theatre was erected in the Haymarket, which was known variously as the New Theatre, or Little Haymarket, or Little Theatre in the Hay; or alternatively, as the French Theatre in the Haymarket, because of its frequent use by French as well as Italian performers. Eventually, confusingly, it too became known just as the Haymarket. It stood until 1820 when the present Theatre Royal, Haymarket, was erected nearby.

A third theatre in the area was in a converted tennis court built in James Street near the Haymarket in 1634.

The name Haymarket derives from an actual hay market which existed from 1664 to 1830.

Haywood, Eliza (? 1693–1756)

Haywood's literary career spanned some 30 years, from the publication of *Love in Excess or The Fatal Enquiry* (1719) to *Jemmy and Jenny Jessamy* (1753). Haywood was a prolific and highly successful writer: works known to be by her amount to almost a hundred, and she may also have published anonymously.

Like ▷ Delarivière Manley and ▷ Aphra Behn, Haywood's literary reputation has been obscured by the notoriety of her personal life. ▷ Alexander Pope satirized her in ▷ *The Dunciad*, as a 'Juno of majestic size/ With cow-like udders, and with ox-like eyes', her sexual favours offered as the prize in a urinating contest. Yet Pope's vituperative attack, which has been regarded as evidence of misogyny, should be read in the context of the satire on literary hacks; the rival contestants Curll and Chetwood are no less damningly portrayed.

Haywood's novels were widely acclaimed, bringing her something of the status of a 'best-seller'. Their great diversity in tone and scope reflects a period of considerable change in novelistic fashions; the earliest works use romantic names, while the later employ 'character' types such as Trueworth, Saving and Gaylord, and there is an increasing emphasis on the female experience and the heroine as central character.

Haywood was also a prolific journalist, founding, amongst other periodicals, *The Female Spectator*, a women's equivalent to the periodicals of ▷ Addison and ▷ Steele. The articles generally deal with issues of social conduct and moral behaviour, and show an advanced attitude to sexual politics. Haywood also had a brief theatrical career in both writing and acting; her play, *A Wife to Be Let* (1724), was staged at Drury Lane with the author herself as a leading actress, and in the 1730s her frequent stage appearances included roles in *Arden of Faversham* and *The*

Opera of Operas (1733), her own operatic version of ▷ *Tom Thumb*.

Hazlitt, William (1778–1830)
Essayist and critic. He was the son of a ▷ Unitarian minister with strong radical views, and himself took the liberal side in politics throughout his life; though he wrote for many papers and periodicals, he is most associated with John and ▷ Leigh Hunt's radical weekly, ▷ *The Examiner*. He was the early admirer and friend of ▷ Coleridge and ▷ Wordsworth (see one of his best essays, *My First Acquaintance with Poets;* 1823), and though he later resented what he considered their betrayal of the liberal cause, he continued to admire especially Wordsworth's early poetry for its integrity and disinterestedness, qualities which he exemplified in his own life. However, he did not share the simplifying, materialistic outlook of many of the radicals *eg* the ▷ Utilitarians; his best work, *The Spirit of the Age* (1825) – studies of the leading minds of the time, including ▷ Bentham and Wordsworth – shows his feeling that rational theorists like the former were really remoter from reality, though they claimed to base all their thought on experience, than were the poets who gave form to their experience directly. This regard for whole truth shows in his most perceptive criticism, especially of ▷ Shakespeare, (*Characters of Shakespeare's Plays*, 1817–18). Other critical works: *Lectures on the English Poets* (1818–19); *English Comic Writers* (1819); *Dramatic Literature of the Age of Elizabeth* (1820); *Table Talk, or Original Essays on Men and Manners* (1821–2).

Though nowadays best known for his criticism, Hazlitt has always had a larger public for his miscellaneous essays, such as *On Going a Journey, Going to a Fight*, etc. His graphic, terse, energetic style often gives this part of his work strong character.
  ▷ Essay.
Bib: Howe, P. P., *Life*; Baker, H., *Life*; Schneider, E., *The Aesthetics of Hazlitt*; Brinton, C., *The Political Ideas of the English Romantics*; Stephen, L., in *Hours in a Library*; Saintsbury, G., in *Essays in English Literature*.

Headlong Hall (1816)
A novel by ▷ Thomas Love Peacock. It is his first and shows the main characteristics of his maturer work: witty, burlesque conversations and, innovatively, very little plot. The narrative is interspersed with attractive ▷ lyrics and songs. As in his other novels, the characters are caricatures of contemporary types.

Heaney, Seamus Justin (b 1939)
Poet. His early nature poetry, drawing on his upbringing as a farmer's son, is found in *Death of a Naturalist* (1966) and *Door into the Dark* (1969), and shows the influence of ▷ Ted Hughes. The political situation in Northern Ireland begins to be explored in *North* (1975) and *Field Work* (1979), from the standpoint of Heaney's ▷ Catholic background. The strongly individualistic, meditative and solitary vein that marks the distance between his own outlook and that of sectarianism continues to be apparent in subsequent collections: *Station Island* (1984), *The Haw Lantern* (1987).
Bib: Morrison, B., *Seamus Heaney*; Curtis, T. (ed.), *The Art of Seamus Heaney*; Corcoran, N., *Seamus Heaney*.
  ▷ Irish literature in English.

Heart of Darkness (1902)
A ▷ novella by ▷ Joseph Conrad. It is narrated by Marlow, an officer in the Merchant Navy who also appears in Conrad's other works ▷ *Lord Jim, Youth* and *Chance*. Sitting on board a ship anchored in the lower reaches of the River Thames, he tells a group of friends the story of his journey up the Congo River in Africa, in the employment of a Belgian trading company. This supposedly benevolent organization is in fact ruthlessly enslaving the Africans and stripping the area of ivory, and what Marlow sees on his arrival in Africa disgusts him. At the company's Central Station he hears much about Kurtz, their most successful agent, who is apparently lying ill at the Inner Station up river. Marlow's attempts to set out to reach him are delayed by the machinations of the manager and other agents, who are jealous of Kurtz's success. When the steamer which Marlow is to captain is finally repaired, and the party sets off, Marlow experiences a powerful sense of dread as the boat carries them deeper into the primitive world of the jungle, but this is combined with a strong desire to meet Kurtz. After being attacked by natives from the bank, they reach the Inner Station, where an eccentric young Russian adventurer who idolizes Kurtz tells Marlow of his power over the local inhabitants, and the fluency and fascination of his ideas. But Kurtz's hut is surrounded by heads on poles, and it becomes apparent that, in addition to writing a report on the 'Suppression of Savage Customs', ending with the words 'exterminate all the brutes!', he has become compulsively addicted to unspecified barbaric practices, presumably involving human sacrifice. He has also acquired an African mistress. Marlow tries to

get Kurtz away down river, but he dies, his last words being 'The horror! The horror!'. Back in Europe, Marlow tells Kurtz's fiancée that he died with her name on his lips.

The story has come to be regarded as a classic of 20th-century literature, and its ambiguity has made it the subject of numerous interpretations.

Heart of Midlothian, The (1818)

A novel by ▷ Sir Walter Scott. Midlothian is a county in Scotland in which Edinburgh, the Scottish capital, is situated. The title refers to the old ▷ Tolbooth prison in Edinburgh, so nicknamed. The central part of the story is Jeanie Deans's journey on foot to London in order to appeal to the Duke of Argyle – a Scottish nobleman high in royal favour – on behalf of her sister Effie who has been wrongfully charged with child murder. Argyle was a historical character, and the events are linked up with the attack on the Tolbooth – known as the Porteous Riot – which actually took place in 1736. As in other novels by Scott about 18th-century Scotland, the characterization is vigorous, *eg* of Madge Wildfire who has abducted the child whom Effie is supposed to have murdered, and Dumbiedikes, the silent suitor of Jeanie. It is often regarded as the best of Scott's novels.

Heartbreak House (1917)

A play by ▷ George Bernard Shaw. It is set in an English country house, and ends with the outbreak of World War I. The guests are intellectuals, and the mood is one of disillusionment reminiscent of plays of ▷ Chekhov *eg The Cherry Orchard*. But Shaw typically exploits the conventional theatre of the later 19th century, introducing love rivalries which invite expectation of passionate climaxes, but end in calculated anti-climaxes. The Preface discusses the role of the English country house – either hunting or intellectual – in the English scene; the play brings out the frustration and disillusionment which burden the latter.

Hecate

In Greek myth, a goddess of the underworld. She was the queen of magic and witchcraft.

Hector

▷ *Iliad*.

Hecuba

▷ *Iliad*.

Hegemony

Originally used to denote political domination. In its more modern meaning and its use in literary criticism it has come to refer to that process of political control

whereby the interests of a dominant class in society are shared by those subordinated to it. Hegemony depends upon the consent of subordinate classes to their social positions, but the constraints within which that consent operates, and the ways in which it is experienced, are determined by the dominant class. This concept also offers ways of understanding the different kinds of social and personal relationships represented in literary texts. Along with a number of other concepts, it opens the way for an analysis of the different forms of negotiation that take place within texts, and between text and reader, and serves to emphasize the social context of experience, ▷ consciousness and human interaction.

Helen

In Greek myth, daughter of ▷ Zeus, who disguised himself as a swan in order to achieve union with her earthly mother, Leda. Helen has always been regarded as the type of perfect female beauty. She became the wife of Menelaus, king of Sparta, but ran away with ▷ Paris, son of Priam, king of ▷ Troy. She thus occasioned the siege of Troy by the Greeks, the subject of Homer's epic ▷ *Iliad*. After the destruction of Troy, according to Virgil's ▷ *Aeneid*, she returned to Menelaus. Her brothers were ▷ Castor and Pollux.

Hellas

In Greek, the name of Greece. Hellenes were the Greeks. Hellenism: the influence of ancient Hellenic or Greek culture, especially in what was understood as its ideals of intellectual enlightenment and the cultivation of beauty. ▷ Matthew Arnold for example, in *Culture and Anarchy* (1869), contrasted Hellenism, in which he thought Victorian England was deficient, with Hebraism, or primary concern with right and wrong conduct, of which he thought she had quite enough.

Hellas is the title of a poetic drama by ▷ Shelley; it was published in 1822 and inspired by the proclamation of Greek independence in 1821.

Helots

The serfs in the ancient Greek state of ▷ Sparta. They were enslaved by the Dorian invaders, who became the ruling military caste, before 1000 BC.

Hemans, Felicia Dorothea (née Browne) (1793–1835)

Poet. After being deserted by her army captain husband in 1818, Felicia Hemans turned to literature to support her family, living first in Wales and then in Dublin. She published many volumes of verse, including *Translations from Camoens and other Poets* (1818), *Welsh Melodies* (1822), *Records of Women* (1828) and *Hymns on the Works of Nature* (1833). Her combination of liberalism and piety made her very popular. Her best remembered poems today are *Casabianca* ('The boy stood on the burning deck') and *The Homes of England* ('The stately Homes of England,/ How beautiful they stand!').

Heming, John (d 1630) and Condell, Henry (d 1627)

Acting colleagues of ▷ Shakespeare and editors of the first edition of his collected plays, known as the First ▷ Folio, 1623.

Hendecasyllabic

A metrical term meaning a line of verse having 11 syllables; decasyllabic = 10 syllables.

Hengist and Horsa

Brothers who led the ▷ Jutes, invaders of Britain. They were originally summoned by the British king Vortigern after the departure of the Romans (early 5th century) to help him resist the Pictish invaders from the north. They then quarrelled with their British allies and seized what later became the county of Kent.

Henry I (1100–35)

The third ▷ Norman king of England, fourth son of ▷ William I.

Henry II (1154–89)

King of England. Son of Geoffrey Plantagenet, Count of Anjou, and Matilda, daughter of Henry I. Henry II was thus the first king of the House of Anjou or ▷ Plantagenet. By inheritance and marriage with Eleanor of Aquitaine he acquired all western France from Normandy to the Spanish border. In England, he was an extremely efficient ruler, especially in organization of the law courts, but this brought him into his famous conflict with ▷ Thomas à Becket, Archbishop of Canterbury. His relationship with his wife was largely hostile and later romancers made much of his love affair with ▷ Fair Rosamund – Rosamund Clifford – *eg* ▷ Samuel Daniel in his *Complaint of Rosamond*. During his reign the native rulers of ▷ Ireland began to be displaced by Anglo-Norman noble families, authorized by the fact that the Pope, Adrian IV, who was English, had granted Henry power over the whole of Ireland.

Henry III (1216–72)

King of England, fourth of the ▷ Plantagenet line. His reign was much disturbed by internal conflict, especially the rebellion led by Simon de Montfort, who first secured the representation of the towns and the smaller landowners in the Great Council of the kingdom, from which ▷ Parliament has developed.

Henry IV (1399–1413)

King of England. He was called ▷ Bolingbroke from the name of his birthplace. His father, ▷ John of Gaunt, Duke of Lancaster, was a younger son of ▷ Edward III; his cousin ▷ Richard II exiled Henry and confiscated his estates, in retaliation for which Henry succeeded in raising a rebellion and seizing the throne. Richard died mysteriously in prison. Henry thus became first of the three kings of the House of ▷ Lancaster, really a junior branch of the ▷ Plantagenet line. His reign was the subject of two plays by ▷ Shakespeare, ▷ *Henry IV, Parts I and II.*

Henry IV, Part I

A ▷ history play by Shakespeare, performed about 1597 and printed in a ▷ quarto edition, 1598. The central character is Prince Hal, the king's son and later ▷ Henry V. The king is grieved first by the opposition of some of his nobles led by the ▷ Percy family, notably ▷ Henry (Harry) Hotspur, son of the Duke of Northumberland, and secondly by the dissolute conduct of his own son, who wastes his life in taverns instead of emulating Hotspur in a career of military honour. Hal's tavern companion is ▷ Sir John Falstaff, one of the greatest of Shakespeare's comic characters. The contrast between Hotspur and Falstaff is the prominent feature of the play: Hotspur lives only for honour, without relating it to social responsibility; Falstaff, only for pleasure, in equal indifference to social consequences. Hotspur is thus passionate but inhuman, and Falstaff all too human in his passions. At the end of the play, Hal kills Hotspur at the battle of Shrewsbury, but Falstaff manages to steal the credit for Hotspur's death. The play is close to the ▷ Morality tradition in its feeling and structure. Hotspur and Falstaff standing for 'honour' and 'riot' respectively; both in their different ways are rebels, the first in political terms against the state, and the second in spiritual terms against reason. Shakespeare's main sources were the chronicles of ▷ Hall and ▷ Holinshed.
 ▷ *Henry IV, Part II.*

Henry IV, Part II

▷ Quarto edition 1600. A continuation of

▷ Shakespeare's *Henry IV*, *Part I*, though independent in mood and dramatic structure. The Percy rebellion continues, though Hotspur is dead. A sick weariness is over the country, and the king is dying. Hal is still the central character, and again flanked by contrasting types: on the one side, Falstaff, pleasure-loving still but now aging and grasping for the power he expects when Hal becomes King Henry v; on the other side, the scrupulous and fearless Lord Chief Justice, who has faced his responsibilities so far as to send the Prince himself to prison for riot. However, when Hal becomes king at the end of the play, he unexpectedly upholds the Lord Chief Justice and dismisses Falstaff from favour. Again, the ▷ Morality drama tradition is a strong influence: the just king upholds the principle of justice, and sets his face against riot and self-indulgence. Some of the best scenes are still comedy though the mood of *Part II* is grimmer than that of *Part I*; the comedy is chiefly in Mistress Quickly's Boar's Head Tavern in London, and on the country estate of Justice Shallow. Shakespeare's sources were again the 16th-century chronicles of ▷ Hall and ▷ Holinshed.

▷ History plays; ▷ *Henry IV, Part I*.

Henry V
A ▷ history play by ▷ Shakespeare performed in 1599; an imperfect version printed in 1600. It records the battle of ▷ Agincourt, Henry's great victory in France; this is the triumphal conclusion to the series which had so far dramatized national disaster: ▷ *Richard II*, ▷ *Henry IV, Parts I and II*. This play has been censured as too much a patriotic pageant with too little genuine dramatic interest. However, there is drama in the spectacle of a small national army, united in moral purpose under a Christian king, confronting a rich massive array of selfishly disunited nobility. The disintegrative elements on the English side are still present in the traitors Scroop and Grey, and in Falstaff's former cronies, Pistol, Bardolph and Nym. The union of the British Isles is forecast by the presence not only of the prominent Welsh officer, Fluellen, but of Irish and Scottish officers as well, though Scotland was in fact an ally of France at the time. The play is indeed primarily a patriotic drama, but it is by no means an uncritical one. There is, for instance, the obvious element of conflict in Henry between his dual aspects as King and as man, evident especially in his dialogue with Williams and his soliloquy in I V.i; modern critics (*eg* Traversi,

Approach to Shakespeare) find many examples of irony at the expense of Henry in the play.

Henry v (1413–22)
King of England, and second of the House of ▷ Lancaster. His brief reign is memorable for his brilliant victory over the French at ▷ Agincourt. By the Treaty of Troyes (1420) he was recognized as heir to the throne of France, his claim to which had been the cause of the war. His dissolute youth (▷ Shakespeare's ▷ *Henry IV*) was a popular legend but is probably unfounded, though he was on bad terms with his father. He modelled himself on ▷ King Arthur, the heroes of the ▷ Crusades and the ideal of the Christian monarchy (the French war, in English eyes, was a just one) and in English tradition he became a national hero.

▷ Hundred Years' War.

Henry vi (1422–61)
King of England, and last of the House of ▷ Lancaster. He was strongly religious but no man of action, and his reign was darkened by the ▷ Wars of the Roses and by the final defeat of England in the ▷ Hundred Years' War.

Henry VI, Parts I, II and III
Three very early ▷ history plays by ▷ Shakespeare, perhaps written between 1590 and 1592; *Parts II and III* were published in 1594–5 under different titles, but *Part I* not till 1623; it was possibly written, or revised, after the other two. Together they make the first three parts of a tetralogy ending with ▷ *Richard III* in which the spreading feuds, hatreds, crimes and vengeances finally concentrate all their force in the wickedness of one man. *Part I*: the defeat of the English in the ▷ Hundred Years' War, and the beginning of aristocratic feuds; *Part II*: the marriage of Henry to the vigorous ▷ Margaret of Anjou, ▷ Jack Cade's popular rebellion, and the opening of the civil ▷ Wars of the Roses; *Part III*: Henry's final defeat and murder at the hands of the York branch of the ▷ Plantagenets, Edward Early of March (Edward IV, 1461–83) and his brother Richard of Gloucester (Richard III, 1483–5). The Henry VI plays have vivid and poignant episodes but are inferior to the masterly *Richard III*. The 16th-century chroniclers, ▷ Hall and ▷ Holinshed, are the sources of the plays.

Henry vii (1485–1509)
King of England. He was the first of the House of ▷ Tudor, of Welsh origin and related to the House of ▷ Lancaster; he defeated ▷ Richard III, last of the House of

York, at the battle of Bosworth (1485), with a mainly Welsh army. Henry connected his Welsh background with ▷ King Arthur, and gave this name to his eldest son (d 1502). He was a notably able ruler, and was later paralleled with ▷ Henry V as a restorer of national unity and order after civil war. At the end of ▷ Shakespeare's ▷ *Richard III* he makes an appearance as a national redeemer. ▷ Francis Bacon wrote a life of him (1622).

Henry VIII

A ▷ history play written (probably) by ▷ John Fletcher and ▷ Shakespeare in 1612–13. Its main episodes concern the divorce of ▷ Katharine of Aragon, the downfall of ▷ Cardinal Wolsey, and the triumph of ▷ Thomas Cranmer. The play ends with the triumphal christening of Henry's daughter, Princess Elizabeth, the future queen. In 1613 a performance of the play at the ▷ Globe Theatre caused the destruction of the building by fire.

Henry VIII (1509–47)

King of England. He was a powerful and talented man, entitled Defender of the Faith by the Pope for his pamphlet against ▷ Martin Luther, but he replaced Papal authority by his own by the Act of ▷ Supremacy, 1534, an act important for the subsequent development of national identity and sovereign independence. He is notorious for having had six wives, two of whom he executed and two divorced. His personal power was great but he generally exerted it through ▷ Parliament, which has caused a historian to designate him 'the greatest Parliamentarian who ever sat on the English throne'.

▷ Tudor, House of.

Henryson, Robert (c 1425–?1500)

Scottish poet. Little is known about Henryson's life: it appears that he was a master at the Benedictine abbey grammar school in Dumfermline and was evidently a well-educated man with a university training. He composed a number of short poems, mostly on devotional themes, but is best known for his short narrative poetry including a collection of 13 animal fables (the *Morall Fabillis of Esope*), and his continuation of the story of Criseyde (▷ *The Testament of Cresseid*). His characteristic style favours abbreviation rather than amplification and he specializes in saying much in a brief space. His collection of animal fables, drawn from the tradition of ▷ Aesop's fables and from the corpus of stories about Reynard the Fox,

explores the variety of ways in which animals can be read and interpreted according to human schemes of knowledge. Henryson's interest in problems of interpretation and understanding is evident too in the sophisticated rereadings he offers of ▷ Chaucer's ▷ *Nun's Priest's Tale* (in his version of the fable of the Cock and the Fox and its sequel), and ▷ *Troilus and Criseyde* (in his *Testament*).

▷ *Reynard the Fox*.

Bib: Fox, D. (ed.), *The Poems of Robert Henryson*; Gray, D., *Robert Henryson*.

Henslowe, Philip (d 1616)

Theatre owner and builder. The ▷ Rose, the Hope, and the Fortune Theatres were all at least partly owned by him. His son-in-law was the famous actor ▷ Edward Alleyn of the ▷ Admiral's Men, whose finances he looked after. His Diary, 1592–1609, is a main source for the theatrical history of the age.

▷ Theatres.

Hephaestus

▷ Aphrodite.

Heptarchy

From the 5th to 9th centuries England was divided into a number of kingdoms, considered by 16th-century historians to have been seven (hence heptarchy, for seven kingdoms). These were: Northumbria in the north, Mercia in the midlands, East Anglia and Essex in the east, Kent in the south-east, Sussex and ▷ Wessex in the south and south-west. Such kingdoms certainly existed but in fact the number was sometimes larger than seven, sometimes smaller. Essex (= East Saxons), Sussex (= South Saxons) and Kent have survived into modern England as counties. Wessex was a geographical term revived by ▷ Thomas Hardy in his regional novels. East Anglia is still used for the counties of Norfolk (= North folk) and Suffolk (= South folk) together. Northumberland remains as the nucleus of the former much larger Northumbria. The term Mercia is never used, Midlands having replaced it.

Her Majesty's Theatre

▷ Haymarket Theatres.

Hera

(Latin, Juno.) Sister and wife of ▷ Zeus. She was closely associated with the phases of female life and with childbirth: sacred to her were the crow, the cuckoo and the peacock. She was a jealous wife and harried her husband's mortal mistresses.

Heracles

(Latin, Hercules.) In Greek myth, the most
celebrated of all heroes. He was the son of
▷ Zeus and Alcmene, a mortal woman.
Zeus's queen, ▷ Hera, in jealousy, sent two
serpents to destroy him in his cradle but he
strangled them. Later, she succeeded in
driving him mad so that he killed his children.
In penance for this, he undertook the twelve
Labours of Hercules:

1 The killing of the Nemean lion.
2 The killing of a nine-headed serpent
called the Lernaean Hydra.
3 The capture of the wild boar of
Erymanthus.
4 The destruction of the man-eating birds
of Stymphalus.
5 The capture of the hind with the
golden horns and brass hooves on Mount
Ceryneia.
6 The cleansing of the stables of Augeas.
7 The capture of the Cretan mad bull.
8 The capture of the man-eating mares of
Diomedes.
9 The capture of the precious girdle of
▷ Hippolyta, Queen of the Amazons.
10 The destruction of the three-bodied
monster ▷ Geryon and the capture of his
herds.
11 The bringing of the golden apples from
the garden of the ▷ Hesperides, at the
western extreme of the world.
12 The bringing from Hell of the three-
headed dog, Cerberus.

He met his death in a shirt soaked in the
blood of the ▷ Centaur Nessus whom he
had killed; the shirt caused him intolerable
agony, and he caused his friend Poeas to
consume him with flames on his funeral pyre.
He was received by the gods, reconciled to
Hera, and married to her daughter Hebe,
goddess of youth.

Heraclitus (6th century BC)

Greek philosopher. He taught that the
primary element is fire and that all being is,
despite appearances, the process of
'becoming', by the harmonious interaction of
opposites (hot, cold; dark, light; good, evil;
etc.). 'The law of things is a law of Reason
universal; but most men behave as though
they had a wisdom of their own.' His
mysticism and his sombre view of human
nature caused him to be designated 'the dark
philosopher'. ▷ Gerard Manley Hopkins'
poem 'That Nature is a Heraclitean fire . . .'
is an interesting example of the 19th-century's
attempt to found its beliefs in classical
antecedents.
▷ Elements, The Four.

Heralds' College

A royal corporation, also called the College of
Arms, founded in 1483 to regulate coats of
arms, *ie* special formal designs originally
worn by gentlemen in battle (before the days
of military uniforms) to distinguish them for
their followers. By the 16th century the
possession of these 'armorial bearings' was
equivalent to the right to call oneself a
gentleman and their function in battle fell
into disuse. The College grants armorial
bearings for a fee. A modern function of the
College is to trace and record family descent.
▷ Gentleman.

Herbert, Edward, 1st Baron Herbert
of Cherbury (1583–1648)

Poet, philosopher and diplomat. Edward
Herbert (Lord Herbert of Cherbury) was
elder brother of ▷ George Herbert. A friend
of ▷ John Donne, ▷ Ben Jonson and
▷ Thomas Carew, and an ardent Royalist
before the ▷ Civil War, Herbert's major
works were his autobiographical *The Life of
Lord Herbert Written by Himself* (published
by ▷ Horace Walpole in 1765); his
philosophical *De Veritate* (1624) and his
volume of poems *Occasional Verses* (1665).

The *Life*, written when Herbert was in his
60s, recalls his earlier adventures as a younger
man, prior to his return from Paris in 1624,
where he had been ambassador. The *De
Veritate*, which was of considerable influence
in the 17th century, attempts to explore
rationalist positions in the general field of
religious experience. Herbert's own religious
position was that of an orthodox ▷ Anglican,
of a strongly anti-Calvinist persuasion.

Although his poetry was not published
until 1665, the major portion of his verses
was written before 1631. His poetic
contemporaries thus included both his brother
and Donne, of whose verses Herbert's poetry
is strongly reminiscent.
▷ Calvin, Johannes; Deism.
Bib: Herbert, C. A., 'The Platonic Love
Poetry of Lord Herbert of Cherbury', *Ball
State University Forum* 11; Hill, E. D.,
Edward, Lord Herbert of Cherbury.

Herbert, George (1593–1633)

Poet. Herbert shares, with ▷ John Donne,
the distinction of being one of the most
widely read of the 17th century poets in
modern times. Though he was not ordained
as a priest until 1630, and though court
connections ensured that the earlier part of
his life was spent in cosmopolitan circles, all
the extant poems are devotional in nature.

His poetry was first published
posthumously, in 1633, when *The Temple:*

George Herbert from an engraving by R. White

Sacred Poems and Private Ejaculations appeared under the auspices of his friend Nicholas Ferrar shortly after Herbert's death. The collection met with enormous approval, and was a considerable influence on ▷ Richard Crashaw, amongst others. The poems in *The Temple* are deceptively simple at first glance. Yet in his exploitation of the speaking voice, and in the complexity of the complete structure of the volume of poems, Herbert rivals Donne for a fierce logical presence in his verse. Of considerable importance to Herbert's poetic undertaking is his espousal of a direct form of poetic discourse – one that, in many respects, looks forward to the reformist projects of later 17th-century theoreticians of language.

Herbert's other major work was the prose manual *A Priest to the Temple* (1652) which is a form of conduct-guide for the ideal ▷ Anglican priest. ▷ Izaac Walton published a *Life* of Herbert in 1651.
Bib: Hutchinson, F. E. (ed.), *The Works of George Herbert*; Vendler, H., *The Poetry of Herbert*; Summers, J. H., *George Herbert: His Religion and Art*; Strier, R., *Love Known: Theology and Experience in George Herbert's Poetry*.

Herbert, Mary, Countess of Pembroke (1561–1621)

Writer, translator and literary patron. Mary Herbert, Countess of Pembroke, was born Mary Sidney, and was a member of the remarkable family which included ▷ Sir

Philip Sidney, her eldest brother. Her early years were spent at Penshurst Place, in Kent (later to be celebrated in ▷ Ben Jonson's 'To Penshurst') and at Ludlow Castle – the setting for ▷ John Milton's masque ▷ *Comus*. In 1577 she married Henry Herbert, Earl of Pembroke, and took up residence in her husband's great estate of Wilton Place. Wilton was to become, in the words of ▷ John Aubrey, '. . . like a college, there were so many learned and ingenious persons. She was the greatest patroness of wit and learning of any lady in her time.' Amongst her protégés were ▷ Edmund Spenser, ▷ Sir Fulke Greville, ▷ Thomas Nashe, ▷ Gabriel Harvey, ▷ Samuel Daniel, ▷ Michael Drayton, ▷ John Davies of Hereford, ▷ Ben Jonson and ▷ John Donne.

So great was her influence on the writers of the late 16th century that it is easy to forget that she was an accomplished author and translator in her own right. She revised and published an altered version of her brother's ▷ *Arcadia*, completed his translations of the ▷ *Psalms* and translated the French Protestant thinker Philippe de Mornay's *Discourse of Life and Death*, ▷ Petrarch's *Trionfo della Morte* and Robert Garnier's French ▷ neo-classical tragedy *Marc Antoine*.
Bib: Waller, G. F., *Mary Sidney, Countess of Pembroke: A Critical Study of Her Writings and Literary Milieu*.

Hercules
▷ Heracles.

Heresy
▷ Inquisition, The.

Hereward the Wake (11th century)
A half legendary Anglo-Saxon hero who, after the Battle of Hastings (1066), held out against ▷ William the Conqueror in the fen-surrounded town of Ely, which was captured in 1070. His fame depends a good deal on ▷ Charles Kingsley's novel *Hereward the Wake* (1865).

Heritage culture
A term coined to identify the growth and funding, with government backing of institutions devoted to the preservation and representation of Britain's past. This includes, besides the National Trust and English Heritage (The Historic Buildings and Ancient Monuments Commission), such periodicals as *This England* and *Heritage*, *The British Review*, *Heritage Outlook* and *Historic House*. Large sums of money are involved, with serious political implications. The first

National Heritage Act was passed in 1980, the year after Margaret Thatcher came to power. It provides both for the preservation of that range of property which it defines as 'the heritage', and also seeks to ensure its display. It eases the means whereby property can be transferred to the state in lieu of various taxes and indemnifies museums which could not otherwise afford to insure the objects they send out on loan. It also established the National Heritage Memorial Fund, out of the remains of The National Land Fund, a sum realized from the sale of surplus war materials and intended to be used as a memorial to the dead of World War II. The National Heritage Act of 1983 set up English Heritage, a body designed to promote the display of England's history through reanimations aimed at a mass tourist market. Heritage culture, in its many variations, aims to control our idea of the national past, making it more palatable and distinctly nostalgic.

▷ Histories and Chronicles; Tudor myth. **Bib**: Wright, P., *On Living in an Old Country*.

Hermeneutics

Used in literary criticism to denote the science of interpretation as opposed to commentary. Hermeneutics is concerned primarily with the question of determining meaning, and is based upon the presupposition of a transcendental notion of understanding, and a conception of truth as being in some sense beyond language. Hermeneutics also postulates that there is one truth, and is therefore opposed on principle to the notion of 'pluralism' that is associated with ▷ deconstruction and materialist readings.

Hermes

(Latin, Mercury.) In Greek myth, the messenger of the gods; patron of travellers and of trade (honest or dishonest); associated with peace, sleep and healing; bringer of dreams; conductor of the souls of the dead to the underworld. He is commonly depicted with a winged hat, winged sandals, and carrying a winged staff entwined with serpents (his caduceus). He was celebrated for his cunning and trickery.

Hermes Trismegistus

(The thrice greatest Hermes.) The god Thoth of the ancient Egyptians, later identified with the Greek god ▷ Hermes. He was the scribe of the gods and supposed to be the author of certain sacred writings known by the Greeks as the 'hermetic books'. In the 3rd century

AD he was associated with a body of philosophy, partly oriental and partly ▷ Stoic, which greatly interested western ▷ Platonist thinkers in the 16th and 17th centuries.

Hero and Leander

Characters of a Greek myth used by several English writers, especially in a poem so entitled, left unfinished by ▷ Christopher Marlowe and completed by ▷ George Chapman (1598). Hero was a priestess of ▷ Aphrodite, and lived at Sestos on the European shore of the ▷ Hellespont. A youth called Leander, who loved her and lived at Abydos on the opposite shore, used to swim across to her at night, until he was drowned in a storm. Marlowe's poem is one of the finest narrative poems of his period.

Herod the Great

King of Judaea under the Romans in the time of Christ. According to the ▷ Bible (*Matthew* 2), in order to eliminate the infant Christ, he ordered the slaughter of all the young children in the village of Bethlehem. This made him the villain of the medieval ▷ Mystery plays dealing with the subject. In these, he is always shown as an arrogant, boisterous, bullying character. Hence Hamlet's phrase 'it out-herods Herod' (▷ *Hamlet* III.ii), referring to acting in a violent and exaggerated manner.

Herodias

▷ Salome.

Herodotus (5th century BC)

Greek historian. His main theme is the wars of the Persians against the Greeks and other nations.

Heroic Couplet

▷ Augustanism.

Heroic, Mock

A literary mode in which large and important events are juxtaposed with small and insignificant ones for a variety of comic, satirical or more profoundly ironic effects. In its narrow sense mock heroic is the product of the ▷ Augustan, neo-classical age. As the bourgeoisie wrested cultural hegemony from the aristocracy in the late 17th century, a new, more complex attitude to the ancient aristocratic ideals of honour and nobility developed. A new irony infused their literary expression in the ▷ classical forms of ▷ epic and tragedy. Epic retained the respect of the reading public, but it was too archaic and primitive to satisfy the modern imagination in its traditional form. ▷ John Milton's ▷ *Paradise Lost*, the only

significant literary epic in English
(▷ *Beowulf* being an oral poem), has about
it much of the complexity of the novel, and
its more atavistic heroic elements (the war in
heaven, the vision of future history) seem
mechanical. In the generations following
Milton, the major poets, ▷ John Dryden
and ▷ Alexander Pope translated the ancient
epics, but their own original work took the
more complex form of mock epic.

Augustan mock heroic is a development
from the conceit of the Tudor and
▷ 'metaphysical' poets, and its imaginative
appeal derives similarly from far-fetched and
unexpected comparisons and parallels. At its
most basic it can be simply ▷ satirical. The
poet contrasts a contemptible modern person
or event with a respected heroic version.
▷ Samuel Butler's ▷ *Hudibras* works
largely on this level, and there is a strong
element of this kind of satire in ▷ John
Dryden's ▷ *Mac Flecknoe*. The respected
touchstone need not be the classical epic, but
can be any admired model from the past, or
even the present. In ▷ *Absalom and
Achitophel* it is the Old Testament. In parts
of the ▷ *Dunciad* it is Milton and other
'classic' English poets such as ▷ Edmund
Waller and ▷ Sir John Denham. In parts
of the ▷ *Rape of the Lock* it is the pomp of
religious ritual.

Nor need the contrast imply a moral satire
on the modern world, or indeed any satire at
all. At the beginning of *Absalom and
Achitophel* the comparison of Charles II with
King David in the Book of Kings, achieves
the difficult task of aggrandizing the 'merry
monarch' while at the same time slyly
acknowledging his libertinism. The
comparison between Belinda's petticoat-hoops
and Achilles' shield in *The Rape of the Lock*
mocks the heroic model rather than the
modern equivalent, emphasizing the
delightful domestic security of Belinda's
world, as against the primitive *machismo* of
the ancient heroes. Often the comparison
between familiar and modern on the one
hand, and exotic and ancient on the other,
arises from pure imaginative playfulness, as
when Pope, through implied puns, compares
the ceremony of preparing coffee in an
English drawing-room (on 'japanned' tables),
with an awesome religious ceremony in
distant Japan: 'On shining Altars of *Japan*
they raise/ The silver Lamp; the fiery Spirits
blaze' (*Rape of the Lock*, III, 11. 107–8).

Although mock heroic is most closely
associated with the age of Dryden,
▷ Jonathan Swift and Pope, it is found in
all periods. An early example is ▷ Chaucer's
▷ *Nun's Priest's Tale* in which the cock
behaves like a prince, although he is merely
the property of a poor widow. The 'most
Lamentable Comedy' of Pyramus and Thisby,
performed by Bottom and the 'mechanicals'
in ▷ *A Midsummer Night's Dream*, is a
particularly complex example. The low social
status and eager enthusiasm of the actors
contrasts not only with the stilted nobility of
the characters they impersonate, but also with
the unimaginative condescension of the
'audience' within the play. In the Victorian
period, mock heroic can be seen in simple
form in the endearing pomposity of ▷ Charles
Dickens's Pickwick, and also in the more
earnest social satire of such characters as
Pecksniff and Dombey. In the 20th century
the full complexity of 18th-century mock
heroic is again achieved in ▷ James Joyce's
▷ *Ulysses*, whose carefully worked-out
parallels with ▷ Homer's ▷ *Odyssey* are
designed to demonstrate the comic irrelevance
to human existence of any pretension to
order, hierarchy, or even meaning.

Herrick, Robert (1591–1674)
Poet. Robert Herrick's poetry was published
in a collection entitled *Hesperides* (1648)
which appeared together with a companion
volume, *His Noble Numbers*. Numerous
manuscript versions of his poetry circulated
in the 17th century, but the vast majority of
his verse is represented in the 1648
publication.

He has long been associated with the
▷ Cavalier poets, although his writing is of
a quite different kind. Herrick's chief stylistic
models were the ▷ epigrammatic Latin poetic
styles to be discovered in the works of
▷ Catullus and ▷ Horace. His delight in
the epigrammatic style contrasts with his
other memorable poetic achievement – the
creation of fantasies which combine
▷ pastoral motifs with minutely observed
details of nature. The poem which opens the
1648 collection ('The Argument of His Book')
sets out his poetic manifesto, which is revealed
to be one of nostalgic longing for a rural
ideal, probably unobtainable.
Bib: Martin, L. C. (ed.), *Robert Herrick's
Poetical Works*; Rollin, R. B., & Patrick, J.
M. (ed.), *Trust to Good Verses: Herrick
Tercentenary Essays.*

Hesperides
1 In Greek myth, nymphs who guarded
the golden apples in a garden across the
western ocean. The apples had been the gift
of Ge, the earth mother, to ▷ Hera. They
were also guarded by a dragon. It was one of
the Labours of ▷ Hercules to obtain them.

2 A volume of poems by ▷ Robert Herrick.

Hexameter
A line of verse having six metrical feet.
▷ Metre.

Heywood, John (?1497–?1580)
Dramatist. He wrote highly entertaining short plays of the kind known as ▷ interludes, *eg Play of the Weather* (1533), *A Play of Love* (1534), and ▷ *The Four P's* (1568).

Heywood, Thomas (?1574–1641)
Dramatist. His field was especially the drama of sentiment with middle-class characters, and to this belong his best-known plays, ▷ *A Woman Killed with Kindness*, and *The English Traveller*. His ▷ blank verse, though not great poetry, benefits by the influences of a great age, and though plain, sometimes achieves poignancy. His first play may have been *The Four Prentices of London*, obviously appealing to a citizen (as distinct from a court) audience by its combination of romance and idealization of the middle class. This was perhaps acted as early as 1592. He has been admired for his sense of the theatre, *eg* by ▷ T. S. Eliot. His many plays include: ▷ *The Fair Maid of the West*; *Edward IV*; *The Wise Woman of Hogsdon*. He also wrote ▷ pamphlets and non-dramatic verse.

Hibernia
The Latin name for Ireland; used poetically.

Highlands (of Scotland), The
The name given to the north and west of ▷ Scotland. As a region, it is distinctive not merely because it is more mountainous than the Lowlands of the south and east, but for reasons of race, language and history. The Highlands are predominantly Celtic (▷ Celts) and the Celtic language of ▷ Gaelic used to prevail there, although it is now gradually dying out. Socially, the Highlanders until the 18th century lived under the semi-tribal 'clan' system, which again was never characteristic of most of the Lowlands. Economically, the Highlands have always been poorer than the Lowlands, which possess highly developed industry and agriculture. This is the main distinction between the two regions today: the Highlands, despite gradual afforestation, are chiefly given over to sheep and game.

Highwaymen
Robbers on the highways, usually on horseback. They became common in the 18th century, when travel greatly increased, owing to improvements in roads and in vehicles, and policing was still very inadequate. Especially mail coaches were robbed, the practice being for the masked highwayman to stop the coach by pointing a pistol at the coachman. Highwaymen usually acted individually, not in gangs, but often with the assistance of inn-servants who passed on to them information about rich travellers. In the 19th century, as the danger of highwaymen decreased, so they tended to be romanticized as 'gentlemen of the road'; this coincided with a fashion for tales about criminals in the 1830s. Thus ▷ Harrison Ainsworth in *Rookwood* (1834) popularized ▷ Dick Turpin, an 18th-century highwayman, in consequence of which he has become something of a folk-hero like ▷ Robin Hood, though the evidence is that he was a commonplace criminal. Earlier ▷ *The Beggar's Opera* (1728) by ▷ John Gay gives a more challenging and cynical account of the phenomenon.

Hill, Geoffrey (b 1932)
Poet. His first two volumes, *For the Unfallen* (1959) and *King Log* (1968), established the characteristics of his poetry: intense moral seriousness, intellectual complexity and a concern with mythical and historical subjects, most notably with the victims of war or persecution. *Mercian Hymns* (1971), a remarkable sequence of prose poems, added elements of humour and ▷ autobiography; *Tenebrae* (1978) is dominated by the relation of divine and human love, while *The Mystery of the Charity of Charles Peguy* (1978) is a single extended meditation on the life of the French poet. Hill's work shows many continuities with the Modernists, especially ▷ T. S. Eliot, and testifies to the influence of a wide range of European and American thinkers and poets. *The Lords of Limit* (1984); *Collected Poems* (1985).
Bib: Robinson, P. (ed.), *Geoffrey Hill: Essays on his Work*; Sherry, V., *The Uncommon Tongue*.

Hill, Susan (b 1942)
Novelist, short-story writer and radio dramatist. Since graduating from London University, she has worked as a literary journalist and broadcaster. Her novels are sensitive, formal and conventionally structured, and tend to explore loss, isolation and grief. *In The Springtime of the Year* (1974) recounts the gradual adjustment to bereavement of a young widow. She has written effectively of the experience of children (*I'm The King of The Castle*; 1970) and the elderly (*Gentlemen and Ladies*; 1968). Two of her novels deal with intense male friendships; these are *The Bird of Night*

Susan Hill

(1972) and, probably her best-known work, *Strange Meeting* (1971). The latter takes its title from a poem by ▷ Wilfred Owen, and is set in the trenches of Flanders during World War I. Other novels: *The Enclosure* (1961); *Do Me A Favour* (1963); *A Change for the Better* (1969); *The Woman in Black: A Ghost Story* (1983). Story collections are: *The Albatross* (1971); *The Custodian* (1972); *A Bit of Singing and Dancing* (1973).

Hilton, Walter (d 1396)
Mystical writer. Hilton was an Augustine canon of Thurgarton, near Southwell, Nottinghamshire, and the author of *The Scale of Perfection*, an English prose work of spiritual instruction, addressed to a single anchoress, which bears some traces of the influence of the work of ▷ Richard Rolle and ▷ *The Cloud of Unknowing*. It is clear from the numbers of extant manuscripts of *The Scale of Perfection* that it was a relatively popular work, and it was printed by ▷ Wynkyn de Worde in 1494.
Bib: Sitwell, G. (trans.), *The Scale of Perfection*.

Hind and the Panther, The (1687)
A didactic poem in heroic ▷ couplets by ▷ John Dryden, written after his conversion to Catholicism in 1685, and counterbalancing his earlier defence of the Church of England, ▷ *Religio Laici* (1682). It takes the form of a perfunctory allegory, in which the Hind (the Church of Rome) and the Panther (the Church of England) debate at length the merits of their different beliefs.
▷ Prior, Matthew.

Hippocrates (5th–4th centuries BC)
Greek physician – known as 'the father of

medicine'. Reputed author of writings called the Hippocratic Collection, including the Hippocratic Oath whereby confidential information given to doctors is not to be disclosed. The theory of ▷ humours is attributed to him.

Hippocrene
▷ Muses, The.

Hippolyta
In Greek myth, the queen of the ▷ Amazons. ▷ Heracles conquers her and gives her in marriage to ▷ Theseus of Athens. She appears as the bride of Theseus in Shakespeare's ▷ *A Midsummer Night's Dream*.

Historia Regum Britanniae (*History of the Kings of Britain*)
Major work of ▷ Geoffrey of Monmouth, completed around 1138, recounting the history of the kings of the island from its foundation by ▷ Brutus to the loss of British sovereignty in the reign of Cadwallader.
▷ Arthur, King.

Histories and Chronicles
Histories and chronicles are important in the study of literature in two ways: as sources for imaginative material and as literature in their own right. However, with the exception of the ▷ Venerable Bede, it was not until the 17th century that English historians began to achieve the status of major writers.

▷ Geoffrey of Monmouth (d 1154) is the most important amongst a number of medieval historians for originating two national myths in his ▷ *Historia Regum Britanniae*; the myth that Brutus (▷ Brut), great-grandson of Aeneas, was the founder of the British race, and the myth of ▷ King Arthur as the great defender of British Christianity. Both had importance in nourishing nascent English patriotism. When England became a centralized state under the ▷ Tudor monarchs, ▷ Henry VII chose the name Arthur for his eldest son. It was the main task of Tudor chroniclers both to heighten patriotism and to identify it with loyalty to the ruling family. This was the purpose of the Latin history of England by the Italian Polydore Vergil, in the service of Henry VII and ▷ Henry VIII. More important was ▷ Edward Hall's *The Union of the two Noble and Illustrious Families of Lancaster and York* (1548), which showed the House of Tudor to be the saviour of the nation after the civil ▷ Wars of the Roses in the 15th century. ▷ Raphael Holinshed's *Chronicles of England, Scotland and Ireland*

(1578) was a compilation from various sources, including Geoffrey of Monmouth, and begins in ancient biblical times. The belief of the time was that history was useful as the means by which the present could learn from the past as a source of warnings, precepts and examples. The imaginative writers used the material of the chronicles in this spirit. Geoffrey of Monmouth, Hall and Holinshed were sources for many of the historical dramas of the reign of ▷ Elizabeth including those of ▷ Shakespeare, and also for narrative poets such as those who contributed to *A Mirror for Magistrates* (1559), ▷ Samuel Daniel (*Civil Wars*, 1595–1609) and ▷ Michael Drayton (*The Barons' Wars*, 1603). Much of this new interest in history arose from the ▷ Renaissance transference of attention from heavenly destinies to earthly ones; thus the period 1500–1650 also produced the first eminent antiquarians, notably William Camden (1551–1623), and the first historical ▷ biographies: ▷ Thomas More's *Richard III* (written 1513), George Cavendish's life of ▷ Cardinal Wolsey (written shortly after the Cardinal's death but not published in full until 1667), ▷ Francis Bacon's life of Henry VII (1622) and ▷ Lord Herbert's life of Henry VIII (1648).

The True Historical Narrative of the Rebellion and Civil Wars in England by ▷ Edward Hyde, Earl of Clarendon, is the first major historical work to rank as distinguished literature in English. Clarendon began it in 1646 but it was not published until 1702–4. It is told from the point of view of an important participator in the events and is notable especially for its portraits of other participators. Clarendon was a royalist; his younger contemporary, Gilbert Burnet (1643–1715), told the story of the second half of the century from the opposing political viewpoint in his most important work, *The History of My Own Time*. Burnet was more of a professional historian than Clarendon (who was primarily a statesman who took to history partly in self-justification) and he initiated historical writing as a major branch of literary activity and scholarship. The distinguished historical writing of William Robertson (*History of Scotland during the Reigns of Queen Mary and James VI*, 1759, and *Charles V*, 1769), of ▷ David Hume the philosopher (*History of Great Britain*, pub 1754–61) and the lighter histories of England by the novelist ▷ Tobias Smollett (1756) and by ▷ Oliver Goldsmith (1764) have been superseded by later work, but ▷ Edward Gibbon's ▷ *Decline and Fall of the Roman Empire*

(1776–88) is a work not only of history but of English literature and, in the quality of its outlook on civilization, an 18th-century monument.

The 18th century was the one in which antiquarian scholarship became thoroughly established; the antiquarians were interested by the nature of their studies in the detailed life of the past. ▷ Walter Scott was one of them and his historical novels, though very uneven in quality, are important as a new kind of history as well as a new kind of imaginative literature. It was his re-creation of the daily life of the past that was one of the influences upon ▷ Thomas Carlyle, whose historical works (the most notable of which is his *French Revolution*, 1837) are more imaginative than factual. ▷ T. B. Macaulay was a better historian and not inferior as an imaginative writer; ▷ *Macaulay's History of England* is the only historical work which comes near Gibbon's *Decline and Fall* in reputation, and Macaulay was responsible for the so-called 'Whig view of history' as steady progress in material welfare and political advance. Other eminent 19th-century English historians were J. A. Froude, who is, however, notorious for his prejudices in *A History of England from the Fall of Wolsey to the Spanish Armada* (1856–70), and J. R. Green whose *Short History of the English People* (1874) was for some time a popular classic owing to the breadth of Green's social sympathies. It was, however, in the 19th century that the controversy about history as an art or as a science developed, and other distinguished historians of the period tended to become comparatively specialized scholars without the breadth of appeal of such men as Gibbon and Macaulay. The latter's great-nephew, G. M. Trevelyan (1876–1962), continued the broader humane tradition of historical writing, as did Arnold Toynbee's *A Study of History* (1934–61). Recent theoretical developments have led to renewed questioning of the terms of historical knowledge: see for example the work of Hayden White.

▷ Tudor myth; Heritage culture.

History of Rasselas, Prince of Abyssinia, The
▷ *Rasselas, Prince of Abyssinia, The History of*.

History of Sir Charles Grandison, The
▷ *Sir Charles Grandison, The History of*

History plays (chronicle plays)
These are especially a phenomenon of the last two decades of the 16th century, when they may have accounted for more than one-fifth

of the plays written in a very prolific period of the drama. The history play is distinct from what is ordinarily called historical drama, which is a phenomenon of the 19th and 20th centuries, and, like the historical novel of the same period, involves reconstructing another period of history in awareness of its differences in customs, habits, outlook, etc. Absence of 'scientific' history in the 16th century debarred dramatists from a historical sense. On the other hand, they were familiar with the dramatization of biblical events relevant to the Fall and Redemption of Man in the religious ▷ Mystery plays: in a similar way history was to them and their audiences a collection of tales about the past, many of which were relevant to contemporary national predicaments. Thus in the 16th century the English Church and state had cut loose from the Roman Catholic Church, and there was consequent interest in the reign of ▷ King John (1199–1216) when there had been a comparable quarrel between king and pope; in the reign of ▷ Elizabeth I men were alarmed at the possible consequences of the Queen's dying without a direct heir, and this caused them to be interested in the reign of ▷ Richard II, and so on. The ▷ Morality plays also influenced the histories: until the 16th century Moralities had concerned themselves with the spiritual destinies of men in general, but the growth of national consciousness, the splintering off of national churches in the 16th century and the increased importance of the national ruler in deciding human destinies, all caused Morality dramatists to extend their interest to politics and to draw on history for their subject matter. Thus John Bale, supporter of Henry VIII in his emancipation of the English Church from Rome, wrote *King John* (?1547) to make his case for Henry's policy. The Morality content of Bale's play gives it coherent structure, but the chronicles of the 1580s, *eg The Famous Victories of Henry V* (?1588) relied chiefly on the eventfulness of their episodes. It was ▷ Marlowe (*Edward II*, ?1593) and ▷ Shakespeare in his two great tetralogies (*Henry VI, Parts I, II and III* and *Richard III; Richard II, Henry IV, Parts I and II* and *Henry V*) and *King John*, who gave psychological and intellectual substance to the history play form. Marlowe did little more than bring his characters vividly to his audience, but Shakespeare brought deep insights to bear on the nature of political society and its problems. His two tetralogies have been called a great national dramatic epic covering the years 1377–1485; however, it is the second half of the period (from 1422

to 1485; the reigns of Henry VI, Edward IV and Richard III) which constitutes his earlier work (perhaps 1590–93) while the plays concerning the first half (Richard II, Henry IV, Henry V) are relatively mature work (perhaps 1596–99). *King John* (?1596) is between the tetralogies in regard to maturity of style.

It becomes difficult, in the maturer Shakespeare, to draw a clear line between history plays and tragedy. ▷ *Julius Caesar* follows the Greek historian ▷ Plutarch closely, but it is also a tragedy; and ▷ *King Lear* derives from the chronicler ▷ Holinshed as does ▷ *Henry V*, though the former is not history. The history plays and tragedies in fact merge into each other; both contain politics, and both present tragic catastrophe.

Hobbes, John Oliver (1867–1906)
Pseudonym of Mrs Pearl (Mary Teresa) Craigie, Hobbes was born near Boston, Massachusetts, the daughter of a New York merchant. She moved with her family to London as a baby, and was educated in Berkshire and Paris. She read widely and published stories from the age of nine, later writing articles and criticism for journals. She married at 19, but the marriage was unhappy and she left her husband after the birth of their son, of whom she gained custody after a public trial. She became a Roman Catholic and added Mary Teresa to her name. Her first novel, *Some Emotions and A Moral* (1891), established her reputation. Others include *The Sinner's Comedy* (1892), *The Gods, Some Mortals and Lord Wickenham* (1895), *The Scheme for Saints* (1897), *Robert Orange* (1899) and *The Serious Wooing* (1901). Her several plays include *The Ambassador* (1898) and she wrote critical essays on ▷ George Eliot (1901) and ▷ George Sand (1902). She was a figure in London's literary life and entertained at her father's house, was President of the Society of Women Journalists in 1895, but also a member of the Anti-Suffrage League, saying 'I have no confidence in the average woman or her brains.'

Hobbes, Thomas (1588–1679)
Philosopher. Together with the writings of ▷ Francis Bacon and ▷ René Descartes, the political and philosophical theories of Thomas Hobbes dominated thought in late 17th-century England. Yet, unlike Bacon's boundless optimism, Hobbes's philosophy appeared to be determined by an almost cynical view of human nature and society. In his great analysis of the individual and the individual's place in society, *Leviathan* (1651),

Hobbes argued that human society was governed by two overwhelming individual concerns: fear (of death, other individuals, etc) and the desire for power. For Hobbes society is organized according to these two principles, and can be rationally analysed as a 'mechanism' (an important Hobbesian concept) governed by these two concerns.

Leviathan itself emerged out of the turmoil of revolutionary upheaval in England during the ▷ Civil War, and the figure of the 'Leviathan' – the sovereign power, though not necessarily the monarch – expresses a desire for stable government. But in addition to *Leviathan* Hobbes published in various fields of philosophical and social enquiry. His interest in language and the uses of ▷ rhetoric was to be influential amongst post-Restoration thinkers. But it was his analysis of the mechanical laws (as he saw them) of production, distribution and exchange which was to be of profound importance in British economic and philosophical thought in the 18th century and later.

Hobbes's chief works include: *The Elements of Law* (written by 1640, but published ten years later); *De Cive* (1642, translated into English in 1651); *De Corpore* (1655, translated in 1656); and *De Homine* (1658). Hobbes also undertook an analysis of the causes of the English Civil War in composing *Behemoth* (1682), as well as critical work – in particular his *Answer* to ▷ Sir William D'Avenant's *Preface to Gondibert* (1650).
Bib: *The English Works of Thomas Hobbes*, Molesworth, Sir W. (ed.), (11 vols.); Mintz, S. I., *The Hunting of Leviathan*.

Hobbinol
▷ Harvey, Gabriel.

Hobgoblin
A mischievous fairy spirit, or a devil. Hob is a shortened form of Robin, a common name for mischievous fairies, *eg* Robin Goodfellow.
▷ Puck.

Hoccleve, Thomas (1368–1426)
Poet. Hoccleve worked as a clerk for the Office of the Privy Seal in Westminster from c 1387–1423. He suffered a mental breakdown in 1416. His poetry covers a range of courtly topics but has a distinctive interest in the self-presentation and literary representation of Hoccleve himself. His *Letter of Cupid* (1402) is an abridgement of a work by the French writer ▷ Christine de Pisan, in which the God of Love defends women against the slanders of men. Hoccleve's most famous work, the *Regement of Princes* (1405),

is a contribution to the well-established tradition of treatises which offer guides to the right conduct of princes, through a mixture of moralizing advice and exemplary stories. In the text Hoccleve represents himself as a disciple of ▷ Chaucer, whose literary skills he praises; he not only includes a verbal portrait of Chaucer but also a visual portrait of him. Hoccleve's interest in self-portraiture is evident in the Prologue to the *Regement*: rather than cultivating the notion of a fictional first-person narrator (in the manner of Chaucer and ▷ John Gower), he fictionalizes his own identity, and describes his life and work. This interest in self-presentation is seen again in *La Male Regle de Thomas Hoccleve* (1405), where the subject is his own bad conduct and dissolute life. In the *Complaint* (1421–2), an autobiographical frame is given to a collection of narrative and didactic material, in which he alludes to his earlier illness and describes his anxieties about composing the work which follows.
Bib: Seymour, M. C. (ed.), *Selections from Hoccleve*.

Hocktide
From the 12th to 18th centuries, a general holiday held in the week after Easter week. Games were played to raise money for church and parish expenses.

Hogarth, William (1697–1764)
Painter. He excelled in the depiction of social life, especially the heartlessness of the richer classes permeated by social arrogance and commercial greed, with the consequent neglect of the poor. He painted sequences, each following a theme, a technique which is a pictorial equivalent of a stage drama: 'I wished to compose pictures on canvas, similar to representations on the stage; . . . I have endeavoured to treat my subjects as a dramatic writer; my picture is my stage, and men and women are my players. . . .' His art became an extremely popular one, because he made engravings of his oil paintings, and they were to be found on the walls of inns and cottages, not merely in great country houses. In his breadth of appeal and his realism, he is in strong contrast to the fashionable portrait painters of the 18th century, ▷ Joshua Reynolds and Gainsborough, and in the quality of his social indignation and his concern with unprivileged humanity he anticipates the poet-engraver ▷ William Blake. Some of his series of what he called 'pictur'd Morals' are: *A Harlot's Progress* (1731); *A Rake's Progress* (1735); *Marriage à la Mode* (1743–5); *The Four Stages of Cruelty, Beer Street* and *Gin Lane* (1751) (2.2.3) and *Election* (1754–66).

Hogarth's literary connections were close. ▷ Jonathan Swift invokes him as natural collaborator in his own kind of savage satire in his poem *The Legion Club* (1736), and his friendship with the novelists ▷ Samuel Richardson and ▷ Henry Fielding influenced the visual element which gives their novels an advantage over those of ▷ Daniel Defoe (*see* R. E. Moore, *Hogarth's Literary Relationships*). The ordinary people who enjoyed owning and interpreting his engravings, with their satirical edge, were the foundation of the market for later cheap serial fiction, with its engraved illustrations. The importance of the visual element in serials from ▷ Charles Dickens's ▷ *Pickwick Papers* onwards owes a debt to Hogarth and his successors.

Hogg, James (1770–1835)
Poet and novelist. Hogg was nicknamed 'the Ettrick Shepherd' because he had been a shepherd in Ettrick Forest in southern Scotland until his poetic talent was discovered by Sir Walter Scott. He is now best known for his powerful work of Calvinist guilt and ▷ Gothic supernaturalism, *The Private Memoirs and Confessions of a Justified Sinner* (1824).

Hogmanay
A name in ▷ Scotland and the north of England for the last day of the year. Gifts of small cakes are made to children.

Holcroft, Thomas (1745–1809)
Dramatist, novelist, actor, translator, largely associated with the introduction of continental melodrama to the English stage. In 1770 Holcroft obtained a post as prompter in the Dublin theatre and this was followed by a period of acting with strolling companies in England, and in 1778 an engagement at the ▷ Drury Lane Theatre, where his first play was performed. In 1780 his first novel, *Alwyn or the Gentleman Comedian* was published, drawing on his experiences as a strolling actor. His first comedy, *Duplicity*, was staged at ▷ Covent Garden in 1781. In 1784, on a visit to Paris, Holcroft was impressed by a production of Beaumarchais' *Le Mariage de Figaro* and, being unable to obtain a copy, he committed the entire play to memory. On his return, his translation was mounted at Covent Garden, under the title, *The Follies of the Day*. In 1792 Holcroft's most successful play, *The Road to Ruin*, was produced, again at Covent Garden.

An ardent supporter of the French Revolution, Holcroft became active on its behalf in England, and was imprisoned briefly for alleged treason. In 1799 he moved to Paris, where he lived for four years. In his absence his *A Tale of Mystery*, a translation from a play by Pixérécourt, was produced in London. He also published several translations of novels and wrote operas, afterpieces, and polemical essays.
Bib: Rosenblum, J. (ed.), *The Plays of Thomas Holcroft*.

Holinshed, Raphael (d ?1580)

Title page from Holinshed's *Chronicles*

Chronicler: *Chronicles of England, Scotland, and Ireland* (1578). The history of England was written by Holinshed himself but a vivid *Description of England* added to the history is by William Harrison. The history of ▷ Scotland is a translation of a Scottish work written in Latin – *Scotorum historiae* (1527) by Hector Boece, and the account of Ireland is by Richard Stanyhurst and Edward Campion, and others. ▷ Shakespeare and other Elizabethan dramatists used the *Chronicles* as a principal source book for history plays; Shakespeare also used them for ▷ *Macbeth*, ▷ *King Lear* and ▷ *Cymbeline*.
▷ Histories and Chronicles.

Holland House, Kensington
A great mansion to the west of Hyde Park in

London. Built early in the 17th century, in 1767 it was acquired by Henry Fox, Lord Holland, the father of the famous statesman, ▷ Charles James Fox. From then until 1840 it was an important literary centre. The house was destroyed in air-raids in World War II.

Holmes, Sherlock
▷ Detective fiction; Doyle, Sir Arthur Conan.

Holy Roman Empire
Claiming to be the continuance of the Roman Empire of the West, the Holy Roman Empire lasted from the crowning of the Emperor Charlemagne by the Pope in AD 800 to its downfall in 1806 during the Napoleonic Wars. 'Holy' was added in the 12th century to emphasize that the Empire was the political counterpart of the Pope's spiritual authority over Christendom; in truth, much of European history in the 12th and 13th centuries sprang from rivalry between the two. Under Charlemagne, the Empire covered nearly all Europe. Thereafter its frontiers shrank, but its effective core was always the German-speaking lands. The Emperor was supposed to be elected by certain German princes (hence the title Elector, *eg* Elector of Hanover) but from 1493 the Empire remained with the Austrian Habsburg family. Even in Germany the Emperor's authority was by no means always effective; by the 18th century the Holy Roman Empire merited ▷ Voltaire's gibe that it was neither holy, nor Roman, nor an empire.

Holy War, The (1682)
An ▷ allegory by ▷ John Bunyan. Its subject is the fall and redemption of man. The city of Mansoul has fallen into the hands of Diabolus (the Devil) and has to be recaptured by Emmanuel (Jesus Christ), who besieges it.

Home Rule
The term used in the second half of the 19th century and until 1920 for the movement seeking to obtain a separate Irish parliament, to replace Irish representation in the London Parliament.
▷ Ireland.

Homer
Ancient Greek epic poet, author of the ▷ *Iliad* and the ▷ *Odyssey*, basic works for ▷ Greek literature. Ancient traditions exist about Homer, for instance that latterly he was blind and that seven cities claimed to be his birthplace, but nothing is conclusively known about him. Archaeological investigation has disclosed that the destruction of ▷ Troy, following the siege described in the *Iliad*, took place in the 12th century BC; linguistic, historical and literary analysis of the poems show them to date as artistic wholes from perhaps the 8th century BC. That they are artistic wholes is in fact the only evidence for the existence of Homer; efforts to show that they are compilations by a number of poets have proved unconvincing, though it is clear that Homer himself was using the work of other poets between the Trojan war and his own time. The critic ▷ Matthew Arnold in his essay *On Translating Homer* (1861) says that Homer is rapid in movement, plain in diction, simple in ideas and noble in manner; and that the translation of three eminent English poets, ▷ George Chapman (16th century), ▷ Alexander Pope and ▷ William Cowper (18th century), all fail in one or more of these qualities, however fine their verse is in other respects.

Homosexuality
Accorded a marginal place in literary representation, and when it has been shown, usually hedged about with implications of the exotic, the abnormal or at least the exceptional. When Radcliffe Hall published her plea for the recognition and acceptance of lesbianism, *The Well of Loneliness* (1928) – even though it had a sympathetic preface from the sexologist Havelock Ellis, testifying to its scientific accuracy – the book was condemned as obscene and banned. This is in line with official attempts to promote heterosexual activity within marriage as the healthy norm. In the 1950s and 1960s aversion therapy was used in an effort to impose or restore this norm in homosexuals. The Kinsey Reports on *Sexual Behaviour in the Human Male* (1948) and *Female* (1953), however, showed that what had been defined as deviant behaviour was far more widespread than had been believed, thus challenging the 'naturalness' of heterosexuality. Homosexual behaviour in certain circumstances defined as private was decriminalized, but not until ten years after the Wolfenden report recommended it. Meanwhile novelistic discussions of homosexuality tended to promote toleration. It is mostly in works from outside England, by Jean Genet (*Our Lady of the Flowers*) William Burroughs (*The Naked Lunch*) or James Baldwin (*Giovanni's Room*), for example, that one has a more vital vision. Recent scholarship is identifying gay and lesbian communities as potentially important centres of innovation; see Shari

Benstock, *Women of the Left Bank*, an account of women writers in Paris in the early years of this century, which identifies a close connection between the writers' political experience as homosexuals and their readiness to experiment with representation.
▷ Censorship.

Hood, Thomas (1799–1845)
Poet. His serious poetry shows strongly the influence of ▷ John Keats, but he is known chiefly for his comic and topical verse; the latter includes grim but haunting poems about contemporary social abuses, *eg The Song of the Shirt* (1843), a kind of poetic poster art which does not bear close examination but is extremely effective on first reading. In his comic verse, he was notorious for his puns which he used obtrusively but often wittily.
Bib: Jerrold, W., *Life*; Reid, J. C., a critical study.

Hooker, Richard (?1553–1600)
Theologian. His most significant work was *Laws of Ecclesiastical Policy* (1593–7). This was the first outstanding polemic expounding the ▷ Church of England viewpoint, and its main purpose was to defend the Church against attacks by ▷ Protestant reformers. Such reformers (the ▷ Puritans) trusted only the ▷ Bible as authority on matters of religion, since only the Bible was acknowledged to be inspired by God. They criticized the Church of England for being too near the Roman Catholic Church in its organization (*eg* in its retention of the authority of bishops) and for resembling the Roman Church in its excessive reliance on other kinds of authority. Hooker considered that the Puritans were making major issues out of inessentials, and that their attacks were dangerous both socially and religiously, since the state was indissolubly bound up with the Church, and it was essential for both to adapt themselves to historical change and requirement, and to draw upon the law of nature as well as upon the Holy Scriptures for guidance. Law he regarded as inherent in created nature, and as the same principle whether seen in the aspect of natural order, social order or divine order. In this view of law, Hooker is essentially a conservative thinker, inheriting from the Middle Ages the view of the universe as a system of related degrees ranging from God down to the four elements of hot, cold, moist and dry, as the basis of matter. Though conservative, the outlook was not reactionary; it was the most widely accepted assumption of the time, implicit in the imaginative literature, see *eg*

the speech of Ulysses in ▷ Shakespeare's ▷ *Troilus and Cressida* (I.iii.75).

However, for all Hooker's conservatism, in the ▷ Civil War and post-Civil War period his works were widely read by radicals as well as by the more conservative-minded. Hooker's appeal to radicals was based on the posthumous publication, in 1648, of a further three books of his *Laws of Ecclesiastical Polity* – books whose authenticity has long been debated. What recommended Hooker to radicals was the role he assigned to consent in religion, and the fact that, in the later parts of the *Laws*, he offered no defence of divine-right episcopacy.
Bib: Keble, J. (ed.), *The Laws of Ecclesiastical Polity*; Cargill-Thomson, W. D. J., *Studies in the Reformation: Luther to Hooker*.

Hopkins, Gerard Manley (1844–89)
Poet. He was converted to Roman ▷ Catholicism in 1866, and entered the Jesuit Order in 1868. He then gave up poetry, but resumed writing in 1875 with ▷ *The Wreck of the Deutschland*, his first important poem. So unusual were Hopkins's poems that they were not published in his own lifetime; after his death they passed to his friend, ▷ Robert Bridges, who delayed their publication until 1918, and even then Hopkins's fame did not become widespread until the second edition of 1930. The date of his publication, the interest he shared with modern poets in the relationship between poetry and experience and his technical innovation and intense style, has caused him to be thought of as belonging more to the 20th century than to the 19th. His ▷ 'sprung rhythm' is a technical term meaning the combination of the usual regularity of stress patterns with freely varying numbers of syllables in each line. This was not new, but was contrary to the practice that had predominated in English poetry since ▷ Edmund Spenser, which required a uniform pattern of syllabic counts as of stresses. In Hopkins's poetry, the rhythm of the verse could more easily combine with the flow and varying emphasis of spoken language, so that the two kinds of expressiveness unite. A kindred sort of concentration is obtained by his practice – natural to the spoken language but uncommon in writing – of inventing compound words, especially adjectives, *eg* 'dappled-with-damson west' for a sunset, 'lovely-asunder starlight' for stars scattered over the sky.
▷ Keats was a strong influence upon him (as upon so many of the later Victorians) and Hopkins shared Keats's gift for evoking in

words the physical response suitable to the thing they express. This was the more conspicuous in Hopkins because of his intense interest (for which he found support in the 13th-century philosopher ▷ Duns Scotus) in the qualities which give any object its individual reality, distinguishing it from other objects of the same class. For these qualities he invented the term 'inscape'. He also invented 'instress' for the force of these qualities on the mind. This intensity of response to the reality and beauty of objects was akin to the intensity of his feeling about the relationship between God and man. All Hopkins's poetry is religious, and in quality recalls the early-17th-century devotional poets, ▷ John Donne and ▷ George Herbert; in his 'terrible sonnets', for instance, Hopkins engages in direct dialogue with God as does Donne in his *Holy Sonnets*, or Herbert in a ▷ lyric such as *The Collar*. Thus Hopkins unites the rhythmical freedom of the ▷ Middle Ages, the religious intensity of the early 17th century, the response to nature of the early 19th, and he anticipated the 20th century in challenging conventional encumbrances in poetic form.
Bib: Gardner, W. A., *Life*; Hartman, G. H. (ed.), *Hopkins*; Bottrall, M. (ed.), *Gerard Manley Hopkins: Poems*; Bergonzi, B., *Gerard Manley Hopkins*; Roberts, G. (ed.), *Gerard Manley Hopkins: The Critical Heritage*; Oug, W. J., *Hopkins, the Self and God*; Weyland, N. (ed.), *Immortal Diamond: Studies in Gerard Manley Hopkins*.

Horace (Quintus Horatius Flaccus, 65–8 BC)

Roman poet of the ▷ Augustan age. His work divides into three classes; his ▷ Satires, ▷ Odes and Epistles. The last includes the *Art Poetica* or *De Arte Poetica* (Concerning the Art of Poetry) which became an important critical document for Europe – for England particularly in the 18th century. It emphasizes the importance of cultivating art in poetry; he lays down the principle that if you do not understand poetry it is better to leave it alone. Art means above all the cultivation of alert judgement: expression and form must be appropriate to theme; characterization and form must be consistent with the subject and with themselves; conciseness is a virtue in didacticism; adaptation of a writer is allowed but plagiarism is not; the poet must study to be wise as a man, and he must be his own severest critic; a just critic is a severe one. The age of ▷ Alexander Pope and ▷ Samuel Johnson took these principles to

heart and they also liked Horace's cultivation of balance in prosperity between wealth and poverty: he had become the friend of the rich patron of letters, ▷ Maecenas, who had provided him with a small estate in the Sabine hills. The English Augustans' concern was to cultivate proportion and balance. Criticism and satire thus became important to them as correctives of inborn human tendencies, and they cultivated the congenial spirit of Horace as Horace himself had sought to practise the virtues of the Greeks. Thus Pope entitled one of his sequences of poems ▷ *Imitations of Horace*.

Horn Childe
▷ *King Horn*.

Hospitallers of St John of Jerusalem (Knights of St John)

A military religious order associated with the ▷ Crusades. The Hospitallers were founded in 1099 to provide a hostel for pilgrims to Jerusalem. Driven from Jerusalem, they eventually settled in Malta in 1530. They had a branch in England which was suppressed in the 16th century. The modern British order was founded in the 19th century and exists for hospital work similar to that of the Red Cross.

Hotspur (Sir Henry Percy) (1364–1403)

Eldest son of the first Earl of Northumberland. ▷ Shakespeare represented him in *Henry IV, Part I*, where he is shown as the generous, tempestuous warrior, devoted entirely to honour, but failing to relate it to any feeling for human good. He is thus, despite his magnificent qualities, a destructive force.

Hours, Book of

Certain hours of the day, called the Canonical Hours, are set aside for prayers by the Catholic Church. A Book of Hours contained the prayers to be said at the appropriate times; medieval editions were often illustrated ('illuminated') with great art and at great expense. The evidence of their illustrations has allowed some stereotyped ideas about medieval life to be challenged; see *The Medieval Woman. An Illuminated Book of Days* (1985).

House of Fame

One of ▷ Chaucer's ▷ dream-vision poems, in octosyllabic couplets, usually dated to the years 1379–80, in which the narrator records the experience of a December dream which he deems worthy of record. The dream-vision mode is used to great effect in this text, which encompasses very different dream-scapes and explores important poetic-philosophic questions without being tied to providing explanations and answers. It is a speculative work.

Book I is taken up with a retelling of ▷ Virgil's ▷ *Aeneid*, depicted on the walls of the Dreamer's first dream-room, in the temple of Venus. ▷ Dido's unhappy experience is given particular prominence by the narrator, who seems more influenced by ▷ Ovid's sympathetic treatment of her plight (in the *Heroides*) than by Virgil's representation of the incident. In Book II the narrator is given a trip to the heavens, courtesy of a Golden Eagle flown in from ▷ Dante's ▷ *Divina Commedia*. The dreamer, who is called 'Geoffrey' by the eagle, is given a chance to experience metaphysics at first hand, though his preference is for reading about the heavens in books, rather than travelling through them. The whole trip, it transpires, is a reward for the Dreamer's assiduous and bookish service to the God of Love. Book III concerns the Dreamer's visit to the aerial House of Fame (the final destination of all sounds and reports from Earth); his description of this precarious institution, its upholders, and his eyewitness report of the vagaries of Lady Fame's dispensation of her favours. From here the Dreamer is taken to the more volatile environment of the House of Rumour, a whirling house of twigs, in which he sees the generation of the stores which provide the raw material for the House of Fame. The text breaks off as a man of some authority appears on the scene. The poem provides an extremely deft exploration of the nature and scope of Chaucer's cultural heritage and the relationship between different kinds of artistic production, between the literary texts of the past and present.
Bib: Boitani, P. and Mann, Jill (ed.), *The Cambridge Chaucer Companion*.

Household Words

A weekly periodical edited by ▷ Charles Dickens from 1850 to 1859. It emulated the magazine tradition of ▷ *Blackwood's* (started 1817) but aimed at a wider public. Among works published in it were Dicken's novel ▷ *Hard Times* and ▷ Mrs Gaskell's ▷ *North and South*. It was followed by ▷ *All the Year Round*.
▷ Reviews and Periodicals.

Houses of Parliament
▷ Parliament.

Housman, A. E. (1859–1936)
A classical scholar who published two small volumes of ▷ lyrics of enormous popularity:

The Shropshire Lad (1896) and *Last Poems* (1922). They are very pessimistic but have an immediate musical appeal, and several have in fact been set to music by a number of composers, *eg* Vaughan Williams. His lecture *The Name and Nature of Poetry*, in which he described poetic creation as an essentially physical experience, also achieved considerable fame, in his own age.
Bib: Housman, L., *AEH: Some poems, some letters and a personal memoir*; Richards, G., *Housman 1879–1936*; Watson, G. L., *Housman: a divided life*; Graves, R. P., *A. E. Housman: the Scholar-Poet*.

Houyhnhnms, The
The horses endowed with reason in Part IV of ▷ Swift's ▷ *Gulliver's Travels*. The word imitates the whinnying of a horse. The enlightened horses are a purely reasonable aristocracy, inhabiting an island which also contains a race called Yahoos, who, not endowed with reason, typify brutish and degraded behaviour. Gulliver's Houyhnhnm host recognizes that Gulliver is unlike the Yahoos in his possession of the faculty of reason, but proves to him that owing to his other qualities, which are Yahoo-like, he can only use his reason destructively.

Howards End (1910)
A novel by ▷ E. M. Forster. The theme is the relationship between the Schlegel family (Margaret, Helen, and their brother Tibby) who live on an unearned income and are liberal, enlightened, and cultivated, and the Wilcoxes, who work in the commercial world which the Schlegels are inclined to despise but from which they draw their income. The Wilcoxes are snobbish, prejudiced, insensitive, and philistine; in fact they have much in common with the middle classes as described by ▷ Matthew Arnold in his critique of English culture – *Culture and Anarchy* (1869). Mrs Wilcox, however, who has bought her husband the old house, Howards End, belongs to the older, aristocratic continuity of English culture; never understood by her husband and children, on her death she bequeaths the house unexpectedly to Margaret Schlegel. Margaret comes into the inheritance at the end of the book, but only after she has married and subdued to her values Mrs Wilcox's former husband. Meanwhile Helen, moved by sympathy and indignation, has become pregnant by Leonard Bast, a poor bank-clerk who has been the victim of both the Schlegel and the Wilcox social illusions and mishandling. Bast dies after being beaten by one of the Wilcox sons, and Helen and her

child come to live at Howards End with Margaret and Mr Wilcox. The house remains a tentative symbol of hope for the future of English society.

Hudibras (1663, 1664 and 1678)

A ▷ mock-heroic satire in tetrameter ▷ couplets by ▷ Samuel Butler (1612–80). The Presbyterian Sir Hudibras, and his Independent Squire Ralpho, undergo various adventures designed to expose the hypocrisy of the Puritans, interspersed with satire on various scientific and intellectual follies. The poem's structure parodies the 16th-century epic romances of Ariosto and ▷ Spenser, and the hero takes his name from a knight in Spenser's ▷ *Faerie Queene*. In spirit it owes much to Cervantes' anti-romance satire *Don Quixote*. The poem's politics pleased ▷ Charles II who gave Butler £300 and a pension of £100 a year. Though the work fails to sustain narrative interest it establishes its own distinctive vein of rollicking farce and homespun philosophizing:

> *Honour is, like a widow, won*
> *With brisk attempt, and putting on;*
> *With ent'ring manfully and urging;*
> *Not slow approaches, like a virgin.*
> (I,ii, 911–14)

Butler's loose tetrameters with their vigorous colloquial diction and crude rhymes, became an established medium for broad satire, known as 'hudibrasticks', used by, among others, ▷ Jonathan Swift, ▷ John Philips and ▷ Bernard de Mandeville.

Hudibrasticks

▷ *Hudibras*.

Hughes, Richard (1900–76)

Novelist, dramatist and poet. He published four novels: *A High Wind in Jamaica* (1929); *In Hazard* (1938); *The Fox in the Attic* (1961) and *The Wooden Shepherdess* (1971). He was educated at Charterhouse School, and at Oxford University, where he met ▷ W. B. Yeats, ▷ A. E. Coppard, T. E. Lawrence and ▷ Robert Graves. As an undergraduate he wrote a one-act play, *The Sister's Tragedy*, which was staged in 1922 and enthusiastically received, and a volume of poems entitled *Gipsy Night* (1922). In 1924 he wrote the first original radio play, *Danger* and a stage play, *A Comedy of Good and Evil*. Born in Surrey but of Welsh descent, he adopted Wales as his home, but travelled extensively around the world. His travels are reflected in his book of short stories, *In the Lap of Atlas: Stories of Morocco* (1979), as well as in his first two novels, which are set mainly at sea

and are intense studies of moral issues in the context of human crisis. *A High Wind in Jamaica*, his best-known work, is the story of a group of children captured by pirates. It deals with violence, the relation of innocence and evil, and the fallibility of human justice, and takes an unsentimental view of childhood. *In Hazard* describes in great detail the events on board a cargo ship at sea during a hurricane, and has affinities with the work of ▷ Joseph Conrad. After an administrative post in the Admiralty during World War II, Hughes worked as a book reviewer and teacher. His last two novels are part of a projected historical sequence entitled *The Human Predicament*, recounting the events leading up to World War II. Other publications include: *The Man Born to be Hanged* (1923) (stage play); *A Moment of Time* (1926) (short stories); *The Spider's Palace* (1931) and *Don't Blame Me* (1940) (short stories for children); *Confessio Juvenis* (1926) (collected poems).
Bib: Thomas, P., *Richard Hughes*.

Hughes, Ted (b 1930)

One of the liveliest poets writing in Britian since 1945. Hughes was made ▷ Poet Laureate in 1984. His works include: *The Hawk in the Rain* (1957); *Lupercal* (1960); two volumes of verse for children – *Meet My Folks* (1961) and *Earth Owl and Other Moon People* (1963); *Wodwo* (1967); *Crow* (1970); *Poems* (1971); *Eat Crow* (1971); *Prometheus on his Crag* (1973); *Spring Summer Autumn Winter* (1974); *Cavebirds* (1975); *Gaudete* (1977); *Remains of Elmet* (1979); *Moortown* (1979); *River* (1983); *Season Songs* (1985); *Flowers and Insects* (1986). His rather violent poetry appeared when English verse was dominated by the poets of the ▷ Movement (▷ Larkin); these were restrained, disillusioned, ironic and often urban in the setting of their poems. Hughes is remarkable for his evocation of natural life, in particular of animals, presented as alien and opposed to the civilized human consciousness, and for that reason, as in the poetry and prose of ▷ D. H. Lawrence, peculiarly close to sub-rational instinct in the self. Hughes married the poet ▷ Sylvia Plath in 1956.
Bib: Sagar, K., *The Art of Ted Hughes*; Gifford, T. and Roberts, N., *Ted Hughes: a Critical Study*.

Hugo, Victor(-Marie) (1802–85)

French poet, playwright and novelist. Born in Besançon, he lived in Spain and Italy as a child, where his father, a General, followed ▷ Napoleon. Despite nostalgia for the Napoleonic age, Hugo was a confirmed democrat and was elected to the Assembly in 1848 and again in 1870. He lived in exile in the Channel Isles between 1851 and 1870 after the *coup d'état* of Louis Napoleon. As a young man he refused a military career in favour of literature; he gained favour through poetry and was made Chevalier de la Legion d'Honeur by 1825. He read and admired Chateaubriand, a proto-romantic influence, and after the publication of his play *Cromwell* (1827) with its famous Preface, became a spearhead of the French romantic movement. He married Adèle Foucher, and was much affected by the death of his daughter in 1845. He was made a peer and became an important figure, being buried with great ceremony in the Panthéon. His plays have lasted less well than the novels and poetry which are remarkable not for intellectual content so much as beauty, faith and feeling. Hugo's output was prolific: the plays include *Hernani* (1830) and *Ruy Blas* (1838); the novels *Notre Dame de Paris* (1831), the celebrated *Les Misérables* (1862), *Les Travailleurs de la Mer* (1866), *L'Homme qui Rit* (1869). His many collections of poems include *Les Odes* (1822), *Odes et Ballades* (1826), *Les Orientales* (1829), *Les Feuilles d'Automne* (1831), *Les Chants du Crépuscule* (1835), *Les Voix Intérieures* (1837), *Les Rayons et les Ombres* (1840), *Les Châtiments* (1853), *Les Contemplations* (1856) and *La Légende des Siècles* (1859, 1877, 1883).

Hulme, Keri (b 1947)
▷ Commonwealth literatures.

Hulme, Thomas Ernest (1883–1917)
Poet and essayist. His attacks on 19th-century romanticism and the verbosity that often expressed it were an important influence on the theory and practice of ▷ Imagism as a poetry of concentration and verbal compression. His writings in support of a modern classicism that should be austere and authoritarian were also important for ▷ T. S. Eliot. His output as a poet was tiny: *The Complete Poetical Works* were published as an addendum to the *Ripostes* of ▷ Ezra Pound in 1912, but his essays and ▷ translations of writers like the French vitalist philosopher Henri Bergson were of immense significance in the development of ▷ modernism. See *Speculations* (ed. H. Read; 1924); *Further Speculations* (ed. S. Hynes; 1955).
Bib: Kermode, F., in *Romantic Image*; Roberts, M., *T. E. Hulme*.

Humanism
The word has two distinct uses: 1 the intellectually liberating movements in western Europe in the 15th and 16th centuries, associated with new attitudes to ancient Greek and Latin literature; 2 a modern movement for the advancement of humanity without reliance on supernatural religious beliefs.

1 Humanism in its first sense had its beginnings in Italy as early as the 14th century, when its pioneer was the poet and scholar ▷ Petrarch (1304–74), and reached its height (greatly stimulated by the recovery of lost manuscripts after the fall of ▷ Constantinople in 1453) throughout western Europe in the 16th century, when it first reached England. Its outstanding characteristic was a new kind of critical power. In the previous thousand years European civilization had above all been dominated – even created – by the Church, which had put the literatures of the preceding Latin and Greek cultures to its own uses and had directed movements in thought and art through its authority over the religious orders and the universities. The humanists began by criticizing and evaluating the Latin and Greek authors in the light of what they believed to be Roman and Greek standards of civilization. Some of the important consequences of humanism were these: the rediscovery of many ancient Greek and Latin works; the establishment of new standards in Greek and Latin scholarship; the assumption, which was to dominate English education until the present century, that a thorough basis in at least Latin literature was indispensable to the civilized man; the beginnings of what we nowadays regard as 'scientific thinking'; the introduction of the term ▷ Middle Ages for the period between the fall of the Roman Empire of the West (5th century A D) and the ▷ Renaissance, meaning by it a period of partial and inferior civilization. The most prominent of the European humanists was the Dutchman ▷ Erasmus, and the most prominent of the earlier English humanists was his friend ▷ Sir Thomas More. The Church was not at first hostile to humanism; indeed such a pope as Leo x (reigned 1513–21) was himself a humanist. When, in the second 30 years of the 16th century, the critical spirit became an increasingly aggressive weapon in the hands of the religious reformers – the Renaissance branching into the ▷ Reformation – the attitude of the Church hardened, and humanists in the later 16th century found themselves restricted by the religious quarrels of ▷ Protestants and Catholics, or obliged (like ▷ Montaigne) to adopt a retiring and circumspect policy. In the 17th and 18th centuries, humanism hardened into neo-classicism.

2 Modern humanism assumes that man's command of scientific knowledge has rendered religion largely redundant. Its central principle is that 'man is the measure of all things', and elsewhere in Europe it is sometimes called 'hominism' (Lat. *homo* = man).

'Humanism' is also used as a general expression for any philosophy that proposes the full development of human potentiality. In this sense, 'Christian humanism', since the 16th century, has stood for the marriage of the humanist value attached to a conception of humanity based on reason with the Christian value based on Divine Revelation. An example of a Christian humanist movement is that of the Cambridge ▷ Platonists in the 17th century. 'Liberal humanism' values the dignity of the individual and their inalienable right to justice, liberty, freedom of thought and the pursuit of happiness; its weakness lies in its concentration on the single subject and its failure to recognize the power of institutions in determining the conditions of life.

Hume, David (1711–76)

Philosopher. His first major work, *Treatise of Human Nature* (1739–40) did not arouse much interest. His *Enquiry concerning Human Understanding* (1748) and *Enquiry concerning the Principles of Morals* (1751) are revisions and developments of the first work. His theory of knowledge was distinct from those of ▷ John Locke and ▷ George Berkeley. Locke had said that ideas proceeded from sensations, *ie* from experience received through the senses, implying that we know mind only through matter; Berkeley that on the contrary we know matter only through our mental conceptions of it and that this proves the primacy of mind. Hume said that we cannot know of the existence of mind, except as a collective term covering memories, perceptions and ideas. He further argued that there was no necessity in the law of cause and effect, except in mathematics; what we call that law is inferred but not observed, a customary association confirmed by experience but with no provable necessity in it. Thus if Locke had seemed to validate science at the expense of religion and Berkeley the reverse, Hume seemed to drive at the roots of both. The graceful lucidity with which he expounded this extreme scepticism caused a wit to summarize his philosophy in the epigram: 'No mind! – It doesn't matter. No matter! – Never mind.' In his ethics, Hume held that virtue is what makes for happiness, both in ourselves and others, and

that the two kinds of happiness are in accord with each other.

Hume also wrote the first systematic history of England, beginning, at first, with the reign of ▷ James 1, when, as he considered with reasonable justice, the political differences of his own day had their start. His historical view is, however, marked by his political prejudices and, since he was a Scotsman, by his suspicion of English motives towards ▷ Scotland. His *Essays Moral and Political* (1741), and later volumes, contain acute comments on contemporary society. He differed from ▷ Rousseau by arguing against the long-established hypothesis that society is based on a 'social contract'. His economic writings were a stimulus to ▷ Adam Smith.

Bib: Mossner, E. C., *The Life of Hume*; Willey, B., *The Eighteenth Century Background*; Smith, N. K., *The Philosophy of David Hume*; Pears, D. F. (ed.), *Hume: A Symposium*.

Humour

The original meaning was 'liquid'. Ancient Greek and Latin medicine passed on to the ▷ Middle Ages the theory of four liquids (humours) in the human body: phlegm, blood, yellow bile or choler, and black bile or melancholy. Individual temperaments derived their quality from the predominance of one or other 'humour'; thus we still speak of 'phlegmatic' or very calm temperaments, 'sanguine' or ardent temperaments, 'choleric' or easily angered ones, and 'melancholy' or depressive temperaments. In the later 16th century a man's humour was his characteristic disposition, whether or not related to the original four physical humours. It could also have other meanings: his mania or obsession; his caprice or whim; his passing mood.

All these uses can be found in ▷ Shakespeare and his contemporaries; *eg* in ▷ *Julius Caesar* II.i., Portia begs her husband Brutus not to risk his health in the 'humours' (moistures) 'of the dank morning', but in the same scene Decius has declared that he can induce Caesar to go to the Capitol by giving 'his humour the true bent', *ie* by exploiting Caesar's disposition to superstition. In *The Merchant of Venice* IV.i, Shylock suggests that if an explanation is required for his preferring a pound of Antonio's flesh to 3,000 ducats, it should be put down to his caprice – 'Say it is my humour'; in ▷ *As You Like It* IV.i, Rosalind speaks of being in a 'holiday humour', *ie* in a gay mood.

▷ Ben Jonson in ▷ *Every Man in His Humour* III.i speaks of a humour as 'a monster bred in a man by self-love and affectation, and fed by folly' *ie* produced by egotism, encouraged by fashionable ostentation, and not restrained by good sense. This sense is the origin of the principal modern use of the word. ▷ Oliver Goldsmith (*Present State of Learning*, 1759) has already gone beyond 'a humour = that which is ridiculous' to the meaning of a faculty for perceiving the ridiculous, and also the laughter-raising expression of the ridiculous, although this is not one of the definitions found in ▷ Samuel Johnson's ▷ *Dictionary of the English Language*. Goldsmith and ▷ Hazlitt (*English Comic Writers*, 1819) both distinguish this faculty from ▷ wit, though differently.

The novelist ▷ George Meredith (*The Idea of Comedy*, 1877) gives perhaps the most comprehensive definition in accordance with modern use, paraphrasable as an attitude of mind readily responsive to the incongruous and ridiculous, but preserving a feeling of sympathy with, kindliness for, the object of laughter. 'A sense of humour' has, in this sense, become the favourite virtue of the English; and it has often been a singularly limiting one. Its merit has been its identification with a 'sense of proportion' and a refusal to be unduly earnest about secondary matters; its fault is often to confuse seriousness with earnestness, and to ridicule what is original and superior under the impression that it is merely eccentric. The English preference for humour over wit – always distinguished as having an intellectual quality – tends to inhibit recognition of mental mediocrity; and the kindliness supposed to be the concomitant of humour dilutes satire into insipidity.

▷ Humours, Comedy of; Satire; Wit.

Humours, Comedy of

A form of drama especially associated with ▷ Ben Jonson. Starting from the traditional psychology which explained a temperament as the product of its physical constitution, Jonson treats humour as the monstrous distortion of human nature by egotism and the self-regarding appetites, notably some form of greed. Partly timeless satire on human nature, the comedy of humours is also social satire since such personal extravagances are nourished by social tendencies; new prospects of wealth let loose unbounded lusts, as with Sir Epicure Mammon (in Jonson's ▷ *The Alchemist*); the rush of speculation on often fantastic 'projects' (*ie* financial enterprises requiring investment) encourages unlimited credulity in the foolish, *eg*

Fitzdottrel in ▷ *The Devil is an Ass*; the prevalence of avarice causes adventurers to overreach themselves in their contempt for their victims and in their own megalomania (Volpone and Mosca in ▷ *Volpone*). Jonson's world is a jungle of predators and victims, free from the restraint of religion, reason, or respect for tradition. But the passions which Jonson exposes in their excess arise from human energies that are themselves fine and belong to that exhilaration in the scope for human fulfilment which is characteristic of the ▷ Renaissance; Jonson's more massive characters, though they condemn themselves by the exorbitance of their language, make speeches of great poetic splendour and force. The hyperbole of ▷ Christopher Marlowe in ▷ *Tamburlaine* and ▷ *The Jew of Malta* provides the tradition for Jonson's eloquence. Jonson's great comedies are *Volpone* and *The Alchemist*. *The Devil is an Ass* is nearly as fine, and ▷ *Bartholomew Fair* and ▷ *Epicoene, or The Silent Woman* are memorable. The mode was first established by ▷ *Every Man in his Humour*. ▷ *Sejanus* is a satirical tragedy, with similarities to the great comedies.

Among Jonson's followers, ▷ Massinger (▷ *A New Way to pay Old Debts*, and ▷ *The City Madam*) and ▷ Middleton (*A Chaste Maid in Cheapside*) are the best. But Jonson's vision was influential beyond the drama; its detachment, objectivity, and moral emphasis on the need to temper the passions with reason and reverence for virtue, are essentially classical and emerge again in ▷ Pope's ▷ *Essay on Man* Book II.

Humphry Clinker, The Expedition of (1771) ·A ▷ picaresque novel by ▷ Tobias Smollett, written in letters. It describes a tour of England and Scotland made by Mr Matthew Bramble and his family party – his sister Tabitha, his nephew and niece Jerry and Lydia, and the maid Winifred Jenkins. Humphry Clinker is a coachman who joins the party on the way, turns out to be Mr Bramble's illegitimate son, and marries Winifred. Characterization is strongly marked but superficial, the chief object being to characterize the society of the time realistically and with an often coarse humour. This is usually held to be the most successful of Smollett's novels, and shows something of the humane sympathies of the 16th-century Spanish novelist Cervantes, whose ▷ *Don Quixote* Smollett had himself translated in 1755.

Hun
The Huns were Asian tribes which invaded
Europe and ravaged it at the end of the 4th
century. During World War I the word was
used as a term of abuse for the Germans.

Hundred Years' War
The name given to the succession of wars
between the kings of England and France
between 1338 and 1453. The causes were
partly territorial and partly economic. The
territorial causes were especially bound up
with the possession by the English kings of
the large duchy of Aquitaine, first acquired
through marriage by ▷ Henry II of England;
as the French kings grew stronger, they
increasingly coveted this large slice out of
their territory. The economic causes were
connected with Flanders; the Flemish cloth
manufacturing towns were the importers of
English wool, but they owed political
allegiance to the French king; it was largely
to divert this allegiance that ▷ Edward III
first laid claim to the French crown. To these
causes may be added the restlessness of the
English and French nobility, and the
popularity of the war with them as a profitable
and advantageous pursuit – it was the
peasantry who were the main sufferers of the
campaigns. Scotland was much of the time an
ally of France, either sending troops to assist
the French or fighting along her own border.

Militarily, the war was notable for the
great importance of the infantry soldier,
especially in the form of the English
▷ yeoman archer. Hitherto the armoured
knight on horseback had dominated the
battlefield; the victory of the foot-soldiers at
▷ Crécy, Poitiers (1356) and above all
▷ Agincourt not only changed methods of
warfare but looked forward to important
social changes. The aristocracy were in future
more dependent than hitherto on the support
of the common people and this in turn
implied a rise of national feeling.

The outstanding phases of the struggle
were three:

1 The first phase under Edward III until
the Treaty of Brétigny (1360) went strongly
to the English advantage, though Edward
renounced his claim to the French crown.

2 Under ▷ Henry V the English had
another period of brilliant success and by the
Treaty of Troyes (1420) Henry was
recognized as heir to the French throne; his
baby son was acknowledged king of France
and England in 1422. Part of the English
success was due to the assistance provided to
Henry by the French Duke of Burgundy.

3 In the last phase, however, the English

were completely defeated and driven from
France except for the port of Calais, retained
until 1558. This was the phase which has
become memorable for the exploits of the
French peasant patriot, ▷ Joan of Arc
(Jeanne d'Arc), burned for heresy and sorcery
at Rouen in 1431.

Hunt, Leigh (1784–1859)

Leigh Hunt by B. R. Haydon (c 1811)

Journalist and poet. With his brother John,
he edited the boldly radical weekly periodical
▷ *The Examiner* until he gave up his share
in it in 1821. His outspoken attack on the
Prince Regent in 1813 brought two years'
imprisonment for the brothers, but they
continued to edit the journal in prison. He
was joint editor with ▷ Lord Byron of the
short-lived quarterly, the *Liberal*, and he
edited or had a hand in several other
periodicals, doing much to publicize the work
of both ▷ John Keats and ▷ Percy Bysshe
Shelley. His essays, popular at the time, are
mostly effusions on trivial topics, though his
busy and active life makes his autobiography
(1850) one of his most memorable works.
Later in life he was caricatured as the genial
sponger, Mr Skimpole, in Dickens's *Bleak
House* (1852–3).

The Hunt literary circle was nicknamed
the 'Cockney School' by the critic John G.
Lockhart, indicating a certain vulgarity.
Hunt's own poetry does indeed display a
facile cosiness of tone, reminiscent of the
suburban drawing-room. However, its most

prominent technical features: a cloying physicality of imagery, and double or triple rhymes with feminine endings, were enthusiastically adopted by his protégé, Keats. Keats's early poem 'I stood tiptoe upon a little hill' is dedicated to Hunt and closely imitates the manner of Hunt's best work, *The Story of Rimini* (1816), from which it borrows such vocabulary as 'blisses', 'tresses', 'bower', 'blushes'. The characteristic rhyme 'blisses'/ 'kisses' occurs in both poems, and other rhymes of Keats ('posy'/ 'rosy', 'flitting/ quitting', 'ever wrestle'/ 'ever nestle') recall such rhymes as 'flushes'/ 'blushes', 'dissemble'/ 'in a tremble' in *The Story of Rimini*.
Bib: Blunden, E., *Leigh Hunt's Examiner Examined*; Blunden, E., *Life*.

Hunting
In English, the word usually refers to the pursuit of animals on horseback and with hounds, in distinction from shooting, ▷ hawking and other forms of pursuit on foot. The pursuit of deer, for example, is called deer-stalking in the Highlands of Scotland, where it is done on foot, but stag-hunting in the south-west of England, where it is done with horse and hound.

In the ▷ Middle Ages, the wolf, the boar, the stag and the fox were the chief objects of hunting, but the first two were virtually extinct by the 16th century, and by the 18th century improved agriculture restricted the territory of deer. This has left the fox as by far the most important beast of the chase for the last 200 years.
▷ Fox-hunting.

Huxley, Aldous (1894–1963)
Novelist and essayist. His novels are 'novels of ideas', involving conversations which disclose viewpoints rather than establish characters, and having a polemical rather than an imaginative theme. An early practitioner of the form was ▷ Thomas Love Peacock, and it is his novels that Huxley's earlier ones recall: *Crome Yellow* (1921); *Antic Hay* (1923); *Those Barren Leaves* (1925). *Point Counter Point* (1928) is his best-known novel and is an attempt to convey a social image of the age with more imaginative depth and substance, but his polemical and inquisitorial mind was better suited to *Brave New World* (1932), in which a future society is presented so as to bring out the tendencies working in contemporary civilization and to show their disastrous consequences. Fastidious, abhorring what he saw to be the probable obliteration of human culture by 20th-century addiction to

Aldous Huxley

technology, but sceptical of religious solutions – he was the grandson of the great 19th-century agnostic biologist ▷ Thomas Huxley – he turned in the 1930s to eastern religions such as Buddhism for spiritual support. This is shown in *Eyeless in Gaza* (1936). This and his last books – *After Many a Summer* (1939), *Ape and Essence* (1948), *Brave New World Revisited* (1958) – return to the discursive form of his earlier work. His novels and his essays (Collected Edition; 1959) are all concerned with how to resist the debasement of 'mass culture' and to sustain the identity of the human spirit without the aid of faith in supernatural religion of the Christian kind.
Bib: Bowering, P., *Aldous Huxley*; Ferns, C. S., *Aldous Huxley, Novelist*; Woodcock, G., *Dawn and the Darkest Hour*.

Huxley, Thomas Henry (1825–95)
Biologist. He was a supporter of ▷ Darwin's theory of evolution and combined philosophical speculation with technical exposition. His many works, essays, lectures and articles included the influential publications: *Man's Place in Nature* (1863), *The Physical Basis of Life* (1868), *Science and Culture* (1881) and *Science and Morals* (1886). He held that scientific discoveries had neither given support to nor discredited religious faith, and he invented the term ▷ agnosticism for this attitude to religion.

Hydriotaphia
▷ *Urn Burial*, or *Hydriotaphia*.

Hymen (Hymeneus)

In Greek myth, the son of ▷ Dionysus, god
of the vine, and ▷ Aphrodite, goddess of
sexual love; as such, he was a god of
fruitfulness and especially of marriage. He
was sometimes said to be son of ▷ Apollo
and a ▷ muse.

Hymns

The word 'hymn' is of ancient Greek origin;
it meant a song of praise to the gods. Such
songs have been important in all the religions
that have lain behind European culture; Latin
hymns were composed and sung in the
Christian churches from the earliest days of
Christianity, and the Jewish hymns, or
▷ Psalms, are shared by the Jewish and the
Christian religions.

The English hymn began its history in the
religious ▷ Reformation under ▷ Edward
VI when the abandonment of the Latin form
of service produced the need for hymns in
English. The Psalms were the obvious
resource, but they had been translated into
English prose. Accordingly, in 1549, the first
or 'Old Version' of metrical Psalms was
published; the authors were Sternhold and
Hopkins. The most famous of this collection,
and the only one now generally known, is the
'Old Hundredth' (Psalm 100): 'All people
that on earth do dwell'. The Old Version of
the metrical Psalms was replaced by the
'New Version' (1696) by Tate and Brady.
From this book, two psalms are still
familiar: 'Through all the changing scenes
of life' and 'As pants the hart for cooling
streams'.

The majority of hymns in English,
however, were not metrical Psalms, but
specially composed original poems. The great
period of English hymn composition was the
17th and 18th centuries. However, it is
necessary to distinguish between short
religious poems which have been adopted as
hymns, and poems which were composed as
hymns. Some of the best religious poets of
the 17th century, notably ▷ Herbert and
▷ Vaughan, produced work in the first
group. But the first professional hymn writer
(as distinct from the composers of the metrical
Psalms) was the Anglican bishop, Thomas
Ken (1637–1711). His best hymns, *eg* 'Awake
my soul', and 'Glory to thee, my God, this
night', are distinguished poetry.

It was, however, the ▷ Dissenters – the
▷ Puritan movements excluded from the
Church of England by the Act of Uniformity

(1662) – and their ▷ Evangelical
sympathizers within the Church of England,
rather than the orthodox Anglicans, who were
at first most active in hymn-writing. The
Church of England had a set form of worship
in the Book of Common Prayer; hymns (in
addition to the prose versions of the Psalms)
were allowed in this service, but no special
provision was made for them. But the
▷ Dissenting sects had no set form of
worship; hymns for this reason alone were
important to them. They were important also
for three other reasons: Dissent was strong
among classes in touch with traditions of
▷ ballad and folk-song; most forms of
Dissenting faith demanded strong
participation by the congregation in the act of
worship; in the 17th century, Dissenters
underwent persecution, and communal,
militant hymn-singing encouraged their spirit
of endurance. ▷ John Bunyan included
hymns in his ▷ *Pilgrim's Progress*, written
in prison; one of these – 'Who would true
valour see' – is famous. But the greatest of
the Dissenting hymn-writers is ▷ Isaac
Watts. His language combines the
homeliness of the broadside ballads of the
city streets with the dignity and musical
cadence of biblical English. ▷ Charles
Wesley, the brother of the ▷ Methodist
leader ▷ John Wesley, had greater
versatility than Watts, and was very prolific;
his best hymns are impressive though without
the power of the best by Watts. Other
notable 18th-century hymn-writers were John
Newton (1725–1807) and ▷ William
Cowper. All these had at least some of the
force of common speech and spontaneous
emotion in their hymns. Beside them, the
hymns of the orthodox Anglican, ▷ Joseph
Addison, are cold, though dignified and
sincere.

In the 19th century, partly under the
influence of the ▷ Oxford Movement, the
Church of England reversed its policy of
discouraging the use of hymns in its forms of
worship. Hymn-writers became numerous;
220 Church of England hymn-books were
published between 1800 and 1880, including
the official compilation, *Hymns Ancient and
Modern* (1861). It was an age in which strong
religious feeling struggled with bitter doubt,
often in the same mind; the struggle is
exemplified in 'Lead kindly light' by
▷ Cardinal Newman. The 20th century has
produced few hymns in comparison with the
19th, but there has been a small resurgence in
the last 20 years with greater freedom of
language and the introduction of folk-song-
like melodies.

Hyperbole
▷ Figures of Speech.

Hyperion
In Greek myth, a ▷ Titan, son of the sky god Uranus and the earth goddess Ge. He was one of the greatest of the Titans, and often identified with the sun, of whom in the original myth he was the father; the sun-god was Helios.
▷ *Hyperion* by Keats.

Hyperion (1820)
The Fall of Hyperion (1856)
Two fragments of an epic poem in blank verse by ▷ John Keats, written in 1818–19, the second (*The Fall of Hyperion*) unrevised. Keats's aim was to rival ▷ John Milton's philosophical profundity by treating a theme of divine conflict. The Greek myth of the war of the Olympian Gods and the primal Titans is adapted to the aestheticist idea that 'first in beauty should be first in might'. *Hyperion* (published in 1820) opens with a magnificent scene in which Saturn, chief of the Titans, mourns his lost power, while Hyperion, the only Titan as yet unfallen, roams uneasily round his palace. Apollo, the destined Olympian successor to Hyperion is confronted by Mnemosyne who begins to initiate him into godhead. At this point the fragment breaks off, Keats's explanation being that it was too Miltonic: 'I prefer the native music . . . to Milton's cut by feet.' However it is difficult to imagine how the approaching beauty-contest between Hyperion and Apollo could have been related in terms of epic conflict without absurdity, or how the moral difficulties of the theme could have been overcome. It is, indeed, the highly Miltonic passages concerning the suffering of the Titans which are the most poetically moving parts of the surviving fragment.

The Fall of Hyperion (not published until 1856) escapes from narrative problems into personal preoccupations, opening with a dream in which the poet finds himself undergoing a symbolic test of dedication in the temple of (Juno) Moneta, the Counsellor. After a powerful discussion of the nature of the poetic calling, containing some of Keats's most mature verse, the story is retold as before, in the same Miltonic manner, breaking off even earlier than the previous version, as the same narrative problems loomed ahead.

Iambic foot (Iamb, Iambus)

The classical verse foot of a short syllable followed by a long one, which in English is an unaccented syllable followed by an accented one. The ▷ Alexandrine has six such feet.

Iberians

The name originally given by ancient Greek seamen to the population in and around the valley of the Ebro in Spain. Later it was extended to include small dark-haired peoples from Spain to Britain. In Britain the Iberians are thought of as the pre-Celtic population, and the modern Welsh, though Celtic-speaking, are supposed to have their physical characteristics. The race loosely known as 'ancient Britons' are spoken of as their Celtic conquerors. In spite of this 'separating out' of the Celtic element as different, it has been estimated that in fact ▷ Celts form the predominant element in the population of England.

Ibsen, Henrik (1828–1906)

Henrik Ibsen

Norwegian dramatist; his working life (1850–1900) began in a period when the art of the theatre had fallen low everywhere in Europe, and perhaps lowest of all in Britain. By the end of the century Ibsen's example had revived interest in the drama everywhere and had profoundly influenced a number of other important dramatists, such as ▷ Strindberg in Sweden, ▷ Chekhov in Russia, and ▷ Shaw in Britain. Ibsen began by writing romantic and historical dramas. Then, in self-imposed exile, he wrote his two great poetic dramas, *Brand* (1866) and *Peer Gynt* (1867). About 10 years later he started on the prose dramas, the sequence of which continued to 1900. The first group of these treated social problems with startling boldness: *Pillars of Society* (1877); *A Doll's House* (1879); *Ghosts* (1881); *An Enemy of the People* (1882). After this, his work became increasingly psychological, anticipating the 20th century in the handling of inner conflicts, self-deceptions, and frustrations: *The Wild Duck* (1884); *Rosmersholm* (1886); *The Lady from the Sea* (1888); *Hedda Gabler* (1890). So far these plays had been extremely realistic, but the psychological phase showed a new and interesting dramatic use of symbols. In the last group of plays the symbolism takes precedence over the realism: *The Master Builder* (1892); *Little Eyolf* (1894); *John Gabriel Borkman* (1896), and *When We Dead Awaken* (1900). It was the social realist phase which most influenced Shaw, and it was Shaw who was the most eloquent introducer of Ibsen's art to the British public, particularly in his book *Quintessence of Ibsenism* (1891). The English dramatic revival of 1890–1914 (as distinct from the Anglo-Irish one by ▷ Yeats and ▷ Synge happening at the same time) thus consisted predominantly of realist plays dealing with social problems, by such writers as Shaw, ▷ Galsworthy, ▷ Granville Barker. The psychological and symbolical phases of Ibsen's work have had, together with the writing of Chekhov and Strindberg, greater influence since 1920.
Bib: Beyer, E., *Ibsen: The Man and his Work* (trans. Wells, M.); Meyer, M., *Henrik Ibsen: A Biography*, 3 vols.; Williams, R., *Drama from Ibsen to Brecht*.

Icarus

In Greek myth, the son of ▷ Daedalus, the inventor of wings made of wax. Together they took to the air from Crete on the way to Sicily. But Icarus flew too near the sun, which melted his wings, so that he fell into the sea.

Ida

A mountain in Asia Minor, near ▷ Troy, frequently mentioned in ancient Greek myth. From its summit, the gods watched the Trojan war. On its slopes ▷ Paris lived with the nymph ▷ Oenone and passed judgement on the three goddesses, ▷ Athene, ▷ Aphrodite, ▷ Hera. It was the home of the earth-mother ▷ Cybele.

Idealism

In philosophy, any form of thought which finds reality not in the mind of the perceiver (the subject), nor in the thing experienced (the object) but in the idea in which they meet. In its earliest form idealism was developed by ▷ Socrates and his disciple ▷ Plato. Their influence was important in the 16th-century Europe of the ▷ Renaissance, *eg* on ▷ Edmund Spenser. A modern idealist, ▷ F. H. Bradley, had as strong an influence on the poet ▷ T. S. Eliot.

In ordinary usage, idealism means the ability to conceive perfection as a standard by which ordinary behaviour and achievement is to be judged. This view is really an inheritance from Plato, who believed that earthly realities were imperfect derivatives of heavenly perfections. To 'idealize' a thing or person is to present the image of what ought to be, rather than what experience knows in ordinary life. In imaginative art we have come to consider this as a fault, but to a 16th-century critic such as ▷ Sir Philip Sidney poetry existed for just such a purpose. This is not, however, the kind of influence which Bradley had on Eliot; Bradley maintained that no reality existed outside the spirit, and he influenced Eliot towards interpreting the phenomena and dilemmas of his age in religious terms.

In modern critical theory idealism is associated with the anti-materialist impulse to denigrate history and social context. The meaning of this term is complicated by its history within the discipline of philosophy, and by its common usage as a description of human behaviour not susceptible to the 'realistic' impulses of self-interest. The term is sometimes used in critical theory to denote the primacy of thought, and to indicate a particular kind of relationship between writer and text where it is a sequence of ideas that act as the deep structure for events and relationships.

Ideology

This term is defined by ▷ Karl Marx and Friedrich Engels (1800–95) in *The German Ideology* as 'false consciousness'. A further meaning, which ▷ Raymond Williams traces to the usage initiated by Napoleon Bonaparte, denotes a fanatical commitment to a particular set of ideas, and this has remained a dominant meaning in the sphere of modern right-wing politics, especially in relation to the question of dogmatism. The term has come to the fore again in the ▷ post-structural Marxism of ▷ Louis Althusser, where it is distinguished from 'science'. Ideology here is defined as the means whereby, at the level of ideas, every social group produces and reproduces the conditions of its own existence. Althusser argues that 'Ideology is a "representation" of the imaginary relationship of individuals to their real conditions of existence' (*Lenin and Philosophy*; 1971). In order to ensure that political power remains the preserve of a dominant class, individual 'subjects' are assigned particular positions in society. A full range of social institutions, such as the Church, the family and the education system, are the means through which a particular hierarchy of values is disseminated. The point to emphasize, however, is that ideology disguises the real material relations between the different social classes, and this knowledge can only be retrieved through a theoretically aware analysis of the interrelationships that prevail within society at any one time. A ruling class sustains itself in power, partly by coercion (repressive apparatuses), but also by negotiation with other subordinate classes (▷ hegemony; Althusser's ideological state of apparatuses).

Social change occurs when the ideology of the dominant class is no longer able to contain the contradictions existing in real social relations. The function of literary texts in this process is complex. In one sense they reproduce ideology, but also they may offer a critique of it by 'distancing' themselves from the ideology with which they are historically implicated. Since all language is by definition 'ideological', insofar as it is motivated by particular sorts of social relationship, the language of a literary text can very often be implicated in an ideology of which it is not aware. The text's implication in ideology can only be excavated through a critical process which seeks to uncover the assumptions upon which it is based.

▷ Archaeology.
Bib: Althusser, L., *For Marx*; Thompson, J. B., *Studies in The Theory of Ideology*.

Ides

A term used in the Roman calendar for the 15th day of March, May, July and October; and for the 13th day of other months.

Idler, The

Essays contributed weekly by ▷ Samuel Johnson to the *Universal Chronicle*, or *Weekly Gazette* from April 1758 to April 1760. As compared to his ▷ *Rambler* papers, they contain more humour, and more flexible treatment of the fictional characters such as ▷ Dick Minim, but they have the same kind of emotional force and moral gravity which distinguish Johnson as a periodical essayist.

Idyll

In ancient Greek literature, it meant originally a short poem. The Greek poet ▷ Theocritus called his poems about the rural life of Sicily 'idylls'. When the term was revived in the ▷ Renaissance, it was consequently used for a short ▷ pastoral poem, similar to an ▷ eclogue except that an eclogue was more likely to be in dialogue. As pastoral verse commonly presented happiness or virtue in pure and simplified terms, an idyll then came to be used loosely for any piece of writing presenting experience in such a way, often an episode from a longer work.

Idylls of the King, The

A series of poems by ▷ Alfred Tennyson on episodes from the legends of ▷ King Arthur. The earliest and most famous fragment is the *Morte D'Arthur* (1842), but the series really begins in 1859 with *Enid, Vivien, Elaine, Guinevere.* Followed by (1869) *The Coming of Arthur, The Holy Grail, Pelleas and Ettare, The Passing of Arthur;* (1871) *The Last Tournament;* (1872) *Gareth and Lynette;* (1885) *Balin and Balan. Enid* was later divided into *The Marriage of Geraint* and *Geraint and Enid. Morte D'Arthur* was included in *The Passing of Arthur.* The whole series was intended to have a loose ▷ epic structure; single-minded virtue ideally conceived is gradually overcome by evil through the sinful passion of ▷ Lancelot and Arthur's wife, Guinevere. Extremely popular at the time, the *Idylls* have chiefly harmed Tennyson's reputation since. They were written under the influence of the ▷ Pre-Raphaelite movement with its romanticization of the ▷ Middle Ages. Later the poems struck readers as bodiless, with the life neither of the Middle Ages nor of 19th century. However, parts of the *Idylls*, notably *Vivien* with its powerful evocation of unleashed sexuality, and *Morte d'Arthur* with its impotent image of kingship, have recently demanded a less complacent response.

Igraine (Igerne, Ygerna)

Mother of ▷ King Arthur. Igraine, the wife of Gorlois, the Duke of Cornwall, is desired by ▷ King Uther, whose pursuit of her triggers a war with Gorlois. Uther, however, gains access to ▷ Tintagel and to Igraine by means of ▷ Merlin's magical powers which allow Uther to take on the appearance of the Duke of Cornwall. Arthur is conceived as a result of this trick and Igraine becomes Uther's wife after her husband's death. In Malory's *Morte D'Arthur*, Igraine has three daughters by Gorlois, ▷ Morgause, Elaine and ▷ Morgan la Fay.

Iliad

An ▷ epic by the ancient Greek poet ▷ Homer. Its subject is the siege of ▷ Troy by an alliance of Greek states; the occasion of the war is the elopement of ▷ Helen, wife of Menelaus, king of the Greek state of Sparta, with ▷ Paris, a son of Priam, king of Troy. The poem is in 24 books; it begins with the Greeks already besieging Troy. In Book I the chief Greek hero, Achilles, quarrels with the Greek commander-in-chief, Agamemnon, king of Argos and brother to Menelaus. Achilles withdraws from the fighting, and returns to it only in Book XIX after the killing of his friend Patroclus by the chief Trojan hero, ▷ Hector. Achilles kills Hector in XXII, and the poem ends with Hector's funeral in Troy. Hector is the principal hero of the epic, much of which is taken up with his exploits, as well as with those of other Greek and Trojan heroes and with the intervention of the gods on either side. There is much speculation about the date of the historical events and that of the poem respectively. Present opinion seems to be that the historical city of Troy fell early in the 12th century BC and that the poem was written about 300 years later. The surviving text dates from the 2nd century BC.

The *Iliad* has had an enormous influence on the literature of Europe. With Homer's ▷ *Odyssey*, it set the standard for epic poetry, which until the 19th century was considered the noblest poetic form. Its first successor was the ▷ *Aeneid* (1st century BC) by the Roman poet Virgil. The poem has been several times translated into English verse; the most notable versions are those by ▷ George Chapman (1611) and ▷ Alexander Pope (1720).

Ilium

An alternative name for the city of ▷ Troy.

Imaginary

When used in contemporary literary theory, this term originates in ▷ Jacques Lacan's re-reading of ▷ Freud, where it refers generally to the perceived or *imagined* world of which the infant sees itself as the centre. In other words, this is the first opportunity that the child has to construct a coherent identity for itself. But in Lacan's view this image is a myth; it is an imaginary subjectivity that allows the ego to speak of itself as 'I', but which represses those fragmentary energies which constitute the unconscious. ▷ Louis Althusser uses the term 'imaginary', which he takes from Lacan, in a very different way, while retaining the concept of a constellation of forces which contribute to the formation of the human subject. In Althusser the subject *mis*recognizes his or her place in the social order through an ideology which posits as 'natural' a fixed relationship between social classes. What is at issue for both Lacan and Althusser is the way in which individual human subjects are constituted by an order which extends beyond the images through which that order is represented to them. In Lacan's psychoanalytical theory the realm of the 'imaginary' is contained within that of the ▷ 'symbolic order', and it is the function of psychoanalysis to uncover the 'real' relations which exist beneath this series of representations. In Althusser, the 'mirror' phase can be equated with 'ideology' in that this is the means through which individual human subjects *misrecognize* themselves and their position in the social order.

▷ Psychoanalytical criticism.

Imagism

A poetic movement founded by a group led by ▷ Ezra Pound in 1912; it published four anthologies – *Des Imagistes*, 1914; *Some Imagists*, 1915–16–17. The inspiration came from the ideas of ▷ T. E. Hulme (1886–1917) who was an anti-romantic, believing that words were being used by poets to obscure emotions instead of to clarify them. The kind of poet he had in mind was ▷ Swinburne. The Imagist credo may be summarized as:

1 Use the language of common speech, but use it exactly.
2 Create new rhythms for new moods.
3 Allow complete freedom in subject.
4 Present an image, but avoid vagueness.
5 Produce poetry that is hard and clear.
6 Concentration is the essence of poetry.

Pound was an American, though he was then living in England; Imagism was an Anglo-American movement, with an English periodical, *The Egoist* (started 1914), and an American one, *Poetry* (from 1912). Pound was himself the most distinguished of the Imagists, though he separated from the movement in 1914. Notable contributors to the anthologies included ▷ D. H. Lawrence, ▷ James Joyce and H. D. (▷ Hilda Doolittle). The movement was more organized and distinct in its aims than most English literary movements.
Bib: Jones, P., (ed.), *Imagist Poetry*.

Imitation, Renaissance Theories of

Renaissance, like Medieval, theories of imitation were of considerable importance to writers and rhetoricians of the 16th and 17th centuries. However, imitation did *not* mean copying or plagiarism; nor was it suggestive of ▷ translation. Instead, imitation was the process by which Renaissance writers invested their own discourse with authority, aesthetic form and structure by assimilating texts from the ▷ classical past and incorporating them into their own work. A frequently-used ▷ metaphor to describe the process is that of digestion. When ▷ Ben Jonson, for example, sets out to describe an ideal of rural life and aristocratic benevolence in his poem 'To Penshurst', he not only evokes the Kentish countryside and the family who dwell at Penshurst, but he organizes his description according to models found in his reading in ▷ Virgil, ▷ Juvenal, Martial (c AD 40–104) and other classical authors. Imitation is, in this sense, much more than allusion or reference. Rather, it is the means whereby the Renaissance writer could place his/her own work within a tradition of public or private utterance.
Bib: Cave, T., *The Cornucopian Text: Problems of Writing in the French Renaissance*; Greenes, T. M., *The Light in Troy: Imitation and Discovery in Renaissance Poetry*.

Imitations of Horace (1733–78)

Adaptations by ▷ Alexander Pope of the ▷ satires and epistles of the Latin poet ▷ Horace, who had already served as a model for satire by ▷ John Oldham, ▷ the Earl of Rochester and ▷ Jonathan Swift. The aim of the imitation is not merely to translate, but to adapt the Roman model, elaborating the parallel between ▷ Augustan Rome and modern Britain. Sometimes the relation between original and imitation produces ▷ mock-heroic irony as when Pope imitates Horace's verse epistle to Augustus. He addresses the stodgy Hanoverian, George II (who had been christened Augustus), as though he were the great Emperor, and praises 'Your Arms, your Actions, your Repose . . .!' More usually Pope asserts an Horatian detachment from the vices of the city, and praises the self-sufficient retirement of the country gentleman: ' 'Tis true, no Turbots dignify my boards,/ But gudgeons, flounders, what my Thames affords'. The Tiber becomes the Thames, Rome becomes London, and Horace's estate becomes Pope's house with its five acres at Twickenham. Despite, or perhaps because of the Latin parallel, these poems are among Pope's most intimate works.

Imperialism

A desire to build up an empire, that is, to dominate politically and assimilate other countries. It has a long history, from Rome to the present day, although the main period of imperialism began with the 17th-century conquests of the Americas and reached its height in the 1880s and 90s. The British Empire has this century developed into the Commonwealth, but a more ingenious form of imperialism can be seen in the pervasive economic and political influence of the U.S.S.R in the East and the U.S.A. in the West.

▷ Commonwealth literature; Kipling, Rudyard.

In Memoriam A. H. H.

A sequence of poems by ▷ Alfred Tennyson inspired by the death of Arthur Henry Hallam, at 22, in 1833. He was a brilliant young man of great promise and hopefulness; Tennyson, a year or two older, had found in friendship with Hallam a strong resource against his own disposition to despondency and scepticism. Hallam's death crystallized for him the difficulty of spiritual affirmation in an age of upheaval in established ideas. Science was already shaking traditional certainties and contributing to the feeling that the reality of nature itself was perpetual flux: there are echoes in *In Memoriam* of ▷ Lyell's *Principles of Geology* (1830–3).

The poem was written between 1833 and 1850, and is structurally loose or fragmented – it was to be called 'Fragments of an Elegy'. It consists of 130 sections, each section being a ▷ lyric in ▷ stanzas of four eight-syllable lines rhyming *abba* – a form used by ▷ Ben Jonson in his ▷ elegy 'Though Beauty be the Mark of praise'. The sequence is a single poem arranged in three sections divided by Christmas Odes, and the whole concluded by a marriage-song for the wedding of Tennyson's sister; another sister, Emily, had been engaged to Hallam. Various moods of grief are expressed, and a reaching out to restored confidence and hope; in places Tennyson engages in debate between religion and science. Despite much disagreement about the work as a whole, *In Memoriam* is usually acknowledged to be Tennyson's finest achievement.

Inca

A race in Peru which, at the time of their discovery (1533) by the Spanish explorer Pizarro, ruled a large and highly organized empire. The word is also used for the supreme ruler of the Incas.

Inchbald, Mrs Elizabeth (1753–1821)

Novelist, dramatist and actress. Among other plays she translated Kotzbue's *Lovers' Vows* from the German, and this is the play rehearsed in ▷ Jane Austen's ▷ *Mansfield Park*. This, and some of the other 19 plays she wrote or adapted, were popular successes: Jane Austen assumes knowledge of it by the reader. However, her best works are her two novels: *A Simple Story* (1791) and *Nature and Art* (1796).

Bib: Littlewood, S. R., *Elizabeth Inchbald and her Circle.*

Independents

▷ Congregationalism.

Indian Queen, The (1664)

Rhymed heroic drama, the first such play to be staged in London, by Sir Robert Howard (1626–98) and ▷ John Dryden. The Peruvian Montezuma, having defeated the Mexicans, is offered any object of his desire in reward by the Inca. He asks for the hand of Orazia, but is scornfully refused. In a rage, he joins the Mexicans and reverses the victory. The Mexican king's sister Zempoalla is in love with Montezuma, but when she realizes he loves Orazia, she tries to kill her rival. Traxalla, a general who loves Orazia, and who aspires to the throne of Mexico, steps in and threatens to kill Montezuma if Orazia dies. Eventually Zempoalla gives up hope of winning Montezuma's love, and orders the seizure and execution of Montezuma and Orazia, as well as the execution of the now imprisoned Inca, as blood sacrifices on the altar of the gods. Her plan fails, however, and at the end Montezuma is revealed as the son of the Mexican queen, and hence as heir to the throne. He kills Traxalla in a fight, Zempoalla stabs herself, the Inca is appeased by Montezuma's new status, and gives Orazia to him, and the play ends with a speech on the vagaries of fate. Throughout, the heroism of Montezuma is contrasted with Zempoalla's disdain for honour.

Indulgences

Medieval documents bearing the seal of the Pope or of a bishop and granting the recipient remission of punishment in the next world for sins committed in this. They were freely sold in the ▷ Middle Ages by licensed 'Pardoners', and were an easy way for the Church (and also for the pardoners) to raise money. Reformers such as the Englishman ▷ Wycliffe and the German ▷ Luther were fiercely critical of them. ▷ Chaucer made grim comedy of them (▷ *Pardoner's Tale*) and his contemporary Langland regarded them sceptically (▷ *Piers Plowman*, Passus VII).

Industrial Revolution, The

An industrial revolution has been defined as 'the change that transforms a people with peasant occupations and local markets into an industrial society with world-wide connections' (*Encyclopaedia Britannica*). Clearly then many countries have industrial revolutions, and more than one; for example it is currently said that Britain is undergoing a new industrial revolution in high-technology processes. However, we understand *the* industrial revolution to mean the succession of changes which transformed England from a predominantly rural and agricultural country into a predominantly urban and manufacturing one in the 18th and 19th centuries, and especially between 1750 and 1850. It was, moreover, the first such revolution in the modern world.

1 *Causes*. Although not, apart from London, a country of great towns, England at the beginning of the 18th century was already a great trading nation, with much private capital ready for investment. Not only was trade free to move throughout the British Isles but there was considerable freedom of movement between the social classes, which were not rigidly defined almost into caste systems as in other European countries, *eg* France. English middle-class religion had emphasis on the individual conscience as the guide to conduct and also on the moral excellence of sober, industrious employment; these values encouraged self-reliance and enterprising initiative. Although some of this middle class (the Nonconformist or ▷ Dissenting sects which rejected the Church of England) were barred from political rights, and Parliament, controlled by the aristocracy, was far from truly representative, the political leaders of the country were extremely interested in commerce, which they were ready to participate in and profit from. The bent of the whole nation, from the days of ▷ Francis Bacon in the early 17th century, had been increasingly practical and the steadily growing population provided a market which invited exploitation by various methods of improved production. Once the process started, it gathered its own momentum, which was increased by the existence of large supplies of convenient fuel in the country's coalfields. Agriculture also contributed to industrial growth: the landowners were zealous farmers

and their improved methods of cultivation not only freed much labour (▷ Enclosures), which then became available for employment in the town factories, but increased the food supplies available for the towns. Finally, the 18th century (in contrast to 17th) was a time of peace and stability in Britain, undisturbed by the wars in which her armies and money were engaged across the sea.

2 *Process*. In the textile industry, already established since the 15th century as the principal industry, a number of machines were invented which increased production and reduced labour but were too large for the cottages where the processes had hitherto been carried out. They therefore had to be housed in factories and mills where large numbers of employees worked together. These machines were at first operated by water power. In the iron industry, the principal fuel used hitherto had been charcoal, the supply of which was becoming exhausted. However, improved methods of smelting by coal were discovered and ironmasters set up their blast furnaces in the neighbourhood of the coalfields in the north midlands and north of England.

Most important of all, in 1769 ▷ James Watt patented an adaptation of his steam-engine to the machines used in the textile industry; this consequently ceased to depend on water power and concentrated itself in the north of England to be near the coalfields. An important result was the immense expansion in manufacture of cotton cloth. An extensive system of canals was constructed in the 18th century for the transport of goods and fuel, and the modern methods of road and bridge building were introduced, but the decisive advance in communications was the invention of the steam rail locomotive by George Stephenson (1814); by 1850 a railway system covered the country. We cannot understand the process of the British Industrial Revolution if we do not appreciate that it was a period of epic excitement, especially in the development of rail transport. It produced inventors and engineers such as Isambard Brunel (1806–59) who had to force their projects against established prejudice and ignorance. The other side of the epic story was the meteoric emergence of great financial speculators such as George Hudson (1800–71), the 'Railway King', who rose from being a York draper to control of a third of the railway system, and ended in disgrace. The social changes were unprecedentedly dramatic, in the rapid growth of the midland and northern industrial towns and the opening of new opportunities for wealth among humble but ambitious men. This heroic and fantastic aspect of industrialism has to be remembered as a great motive power in Victorian culture.

3 *Consequences*. Britain was by 1850 the 'work-shop of the world'; no other country was yet ready to compete with her in industrial production. The towns were the source of her wealth, though the landowners retained their social prestige and often became much richer by ownership of coalfields, The north of England, until the 18th century a backward region, was now the most advanced in Britain; its towns grew rapidly, unplanned, in ugliness and dirt. The economic motives outran the social conscience and the new urban proletariat worked and lived in evil conditions under employers who had often risen themselves from poverty and had the ruthlessness which was a consequence of the severity of their struggle. England was divided as never before; the industrial north from the agricultural south, the industrial working class from (sometimes) pitiless employers, and both from the long-established gentry, particularly of the south. Victorian novels are eloquent testimony to the social conditions; the title of ▷ Elizabeth Gaskell's novel, ▷ *North and South*, and the subtitle of ▷ Benjamin Disraeli's ▷ *Sybil, or The Two Nations* are evidence in themselves. Josiah Bounderby in ▷ Charles Dickens's ▷ *Hard Times* is a portrait of the unprincipled kind of industrial employer; Sir Leicester Dedlock and Rouncewell the ironmaster in ▷ *Bleak House* exemplify the old order's failure to understand the new.

▷ Anti-industrialism; Cloth manufacture.

Inferno, The

The first part of ▷ Dante's great poem, the ▷ *Divina Commedia*, which describes the poet's journey through Hell, under the guidance of ▷ Virgil, where he speaks to various former friends and enemies. Hell is conceived of as a conical funnel, reaching to the centre of the earth. Various categories of sinners are assigned to the nine gradated circles, where they receive appropriate punishments. The first circle is reserved for pre-Christian pagans who have not had the chance of knowing the true faith. Virgil belongs to these, whose only punishment is the hopeless desire for God. At the very bottom is Satan (Lucifer) himself, and from him Dante and Virgil pass through the earth to its opposite surface, where they arrive at the foot of the Mount of Purgatory (▷ *Purgatorio*).

Innocence, Songs of
▷ *Songs of Innocence and Experience*.

Inns, Taverns, Alehouses

These words went out of common use in the later 19th century; the modern terms are 'hotels' (formerly inns) and 'public houses' or 'pubs' (formerly taverns and alehouses). An inn was especially for travellers, who could eat, drink and sleep there; taverns existed chiefly in London and were drinking resorts; alehouses were a humbler form of tavern such as might be found in any village. From the 16th century tarverns and alehouses had to receive licences for their trade from magistrates, who could withdraw these if they became places of disorder. The word 'hostelry' is equivalent to 'inn' but is an older term still; similarly, 'hospital' originally stood for an institution offering 'hospitality' to travellers, but by the 16th century was reserved for a refuge for the sick and aged; now, merely for the sick.

Until the 14th century travel was comparatively rare and shelter was provided chiefly by the ▷ monasteries, which continued to serve the function of inns until their dissolution in the 16th century. Already in the 14th century, however, travel was becoming more common and inns were growing up independently of monasteries, such as the Tabard Inn in ▷ Chaucer's ▷ *Canterbury Tales;* their number naturally increased after the monastic dissolution. One of the chief functions of the larger inns was to serve as 'post-houses' for mail-coaches which changed horses at them and put down travellers who were using them.

Inns were identified by the coloured signs hanging outside them, still commonly found outside pubs and some hotels. Such signs often showed the coat of arms of the local great family and the inn would be called, *eg* 'the Neville Arms'. Still commoner as a sign was the 'crest' or symbol (often an animal) that usually surmounted a coat of arms; hence the large numbers of inns called the Red Lion, the Black Bull, the White Hart, etc. Sometimes the sign represented a local trade or craft (the Carpenters' Arms, etc.), and the habit of old soldiers turning innkeeper led to many inns and taverns being called after famous generals, particularly if they had been popular, *eg* the Marquis of Granby, the Duke of Wellington.

▷ Pub.

Inns of Court

Institutions belonging to the legal profession, in London. There are now four, all dating from the ▷ Middle Ages: Lincoln's Inn,

Gray's Inn, the Inner Temple and the Middle
Temple. The buildings resemble those of
Oxford and Cambridge colleges, and their
function is to be responsible for the education
of those students of the law who intend to
become barristers, with the right to plead in
the senior courts of law and – in the senior
rank – the qualifications to be appointed
judges. Each Inn is a separate society,
governed by its senior members, called
Benchers. The buildings are not exclusively
occupied by barristers or their students,
however; thus Furnivall's Inn (now pulled
down) was for a time the home of ▷ Charles
Dickens, and one of his characters, Pip of
▷ *Great Expectations*, had rooms in
Barnard's Inn, now part of a school.

Innuendo
 ▷ Figures of Speech.

Inquisition, The
An organization in the Roman Catholic
Church, in the form of a judicial tribunal,
whose task it was to detect and eliminate
heresy, *ie* false religious doctrine. Officially it
was known as the Holy Office, and survives
today only for the identification of heretical
literature. Its beginnings were in the 13th
century and it visited, or had branches in, the
various European countries. In England it
was unpopular even before the
▷ Reformation, but in Spain its function of
heresy hunting was not abolished until 1834.
In the English Protestant mind, from the
16th century, the Spanish Inquisition was
identified with all that was conceived to be
cruel and intolerant in the Catholic Church,
and it was often confused with the Holy
Office in Rome. Nonetheless,
▷ Protestantism in Britain did not itself at
first practise tolerance. The English law of
1401 that heretics must be burned alive was
not abolished till 1676, though the practice
had long ceased; in Scotland a young man
accused of heresy was hanged in 1696.
 ▷ Catholicism (Roman) in English
literature.

Instauratio Magna (The Great Renewal)
The title of the great philosophical work
projected by ▷ Francis Bacon, and left
incomplete. According to Bacon's plan of
1620, it was to have consisted of six parts: I.
A review of existing sciences; *De Augmentis
Scientiarum*, Latin translation of ▷ *The
Advancement of Learning* (1605). II. Outline
of a new inductive method; ▷ *Novum
Organum* (The New Instrument). This exists
in a compressed form, unfinished. III. A
Natural History to be used as a basis for

inductive conclusions. The tract *Parasceve*
(Preparative) and the *Historia Ventorum*
(History of the Winds); *Historia vitae et
mortis* (History of Life and Death); *Sylva
sylvarum* (Forest of Forests), a collection of
facts and observations. IV. Examples of
investigations by the new method, of which
there remains only a small fragment, *Filum
Labyrinthi* (The Thread of the Labyrinth). V.
Hypotheses of Bacon's own, to be tested by
inductive experiment, of which only a preface
exists, though some other writings may have
been intended to belong to it. VI. A synthesis
of conclusions from the inductive method,
none of which remains.

Interlude
A term of disputed origin, in use from the
13th century at least, for dramatic
performances in general. It became the
standard term for plays performed indoors, at
the feasts of rich households or in the halls of
ecclesiastical or educational institutions.

Interludes
Short plays of a kind popular especially in the
16th century before the great flowering of
Elizabethan drama. In general they were
more secular than ▷ Morality plays, still
being performed, but Moralities and
Interludes are not always clearly
distinguishable, and indeed the term
'interlude' was applied to religious plays as
early as the 14th century. Nonetheless there
is no other convenient term for such slight
works as ▷ John Heywood's *Play of the
Weather* (1533) in which an emissary of the
gods tries to find out the ideal weather for
humanity, only to discover that opinions
hopelessly conflict. The function of such a
play seems to have been entertainment after a
banquet in a nobleman's hall or in a college,
or during the intervals of business of a town
council, etc. That it was a performance
during intervals of business or other kinds of
entertainment, or perhaps of long, serious
plays to provide light relief, has been assumed
from the usual meaning of 'interlude' in
ordinary speech; however, the word has also
been surmised to mean merely 'a play
between' performers taking parts. One of the
best known examples is the interlude of
Pyramus and Thisbe played beforeTheseus
and his court in the last act of
▷ Shakespeare's ▷ *A Midsummer Night's
Dream*.

Interregnum
The term used for the period 1649–60,
between the execution of ▷ Charles I and
the accession of his son Charles II – the

▷ Restoration. It is divided into the period 1649–53, when England was ruled by the House of Commons and a Council of State, and the period 1653–8 when ▷ Oliver Cromwell and for a brief time his son Richard were Protectors.

Intertextuality

A term first introduced into critical theory by the French ▷ psychoanalytical writer Julia Kristeva (b 1941), relating specifically to the use she makes of the work of ▷ Mikhail Bakhtin. The concept of intertextuality implies that literary texts are composed of dialectically opposed utterances, and that it is the function of the critic to identify these different strands and to account for their oppositions within the text itself. Kristeva notes that Bakhtin's ' "dialogism" does not strive towards transcendance . . . but rather towards harmony, all the while implying an idea of rupture (of opposition and analogy) as a modality of transformation' (*Desire and Language*; trans. 1980). Similarly, no text can be entirely free of other texts. No work is written or read in isolation, it is located, in Kristeva's words, 'within the totality of previous . . . texts'. This is a second important aspect of intertextuality.
▷ Feminism.

Intimations of Immortality from Recollections of Early Childhood, Ode: (1807)

An ▷ ode by ▷ William Wordsworth in stanzas of varying length. The first four stanzas were composed in 1802; the rest of the poem was completed in 1806, and the whole was published in 1807. The first part laments that nature no longer appears to the poet as it did in his youth: 'Apparelled in celestial light,/ The glory and the freshness of a dream'. Wordsworth explains this in terms of the ▷ Platonic myth that the soul pre-exists the body in a perfect world of oneness with nature. At birth we come 'trailing clouds of glory . . ./ From God, who is our home'. But soon 'Shades of the prison-house begin to close/ Upon the growing Boy'. The poem thus expresses a radical Romantic reversal of accepted values: dream is more real than waking, youth is the period of wisdom and true insight. As the poem progresses, the poet's confidence revives, and he asserts a continuing oneness with nature despite his age: 'To me the meanest flower that blows can give/ Thoughts that do often lie too deep for tears'. The upbeat rhetoric is splendid, but many readers are left with the impression that Wordsworth is unnaturally forcing up

his spirits towards the end of the poem, in a way which ▷ Samuel Taylor Coleridge is unable to do in his related work, ▷ *Dejection: An Ode*.

Iphigenia

In Greek myth, the daughter of ▷ Agamemnon, chief general of the Greeks in the Trojan war. On the way to ▷ Troy, the Greek fleet was windbound, because Agamemnon had offended the goddess ▷ Artemis; Iphigenia had to be sacrificed if the fleet was to be released. Artemis, however, relented and spirited her away to Tauris (Crimea) where she became the goddess's priestess, with the duty of sacrificing all strangers. Faced with the task of sacrificing her own brother, ▷ Orestes, she planned an escape with him, taking with her the statue of Artemis. Plays about her have been written by ▷ Aeschylus, ▷ Sophocles, ▷ Euripides, ▷ Racine and ▷ Goethe.

Ireland

A brief sketch of the confused and tormented history of this country must concentrate on its relations with England, and this account may conveniently be divided into phases.

1150–1600 – Period of Disorder

▷ Henry II was the first English king to be acknowledged sovereign of Ireland, but at no time before 1600 did the English succeed in establishing an efficient central government. In the 12th century Ireland consisted of warring Celtic kingdoms, with a Norse settlement along the east coast. The conquest was not undertaken by Henry but by his Anglo-Norman nobility, notably Richard Strongbow, Earl of Pembroke in alliance with the Irish king of Leinster. By 1500 Ireland was ruled by a mixed English and Irish aristocracy, the former regarded as English by the Irish and as Irish by the English. English law and speech were secure only in a narrow region known as the ▷ Pale, centred on the capital city of Dublin. The first real crisis in relations between England and Ireland arose in the 16th century, when the Irish refused to receive the English Protestant ▷ Reformation. Fierce wars against Spanish armies which landed in Ireland with a view to invading England were followed by fierce suppression under ▷ Elizabeth I, for instance under the governorship of Lord Grey de Wilton. The poet ▷ Edmund Spenser was appointed his secretary (1580) and given a grant of land in the province of Munster as part of a plan to settle the country with Protestant overlords; his castle was burnt down in 1598, a year before his death. Spenser's singularly stern view of Justice in ▷ *The Faerie Queene* (Artegall, Bk. V) is a reflection of his Irish experiences. By 1600 Ireland was a nation of mixed English and Celtic people, with an English-speaking aristocracy, and firm identification with the Roman Catholic faith. The problem as England saw it in the next two centuries was how to subdue the country to effective Protestant rule.

1600–1800 – Irish Protestant Ascendancy
The policy of settling Protstants in Ireland was notably successful in one of the four provinces under ▷ James 1 (1603–25) when Ulster became the Anglo-Scottish Protestant fortress which it has remained to this day. ▷ Oliver Cromwell was savage in subjection of Catholic Ireland to his authority, and by extensive confiscations increased the class of Protestant landlords. In the 18th century, penal laws further disabled Catholic landholders, refused political rights to Catholics, and barred them from most professions and from education. The only Irish university (founded by Elizabeth in 1591), Dublin, was a Protestant one. However, towards the end of the 18th century, partly owing to the Irish patriotism of Anglo-Irish Protestants (including the satirist ▷ Swift and the philosopher ▷ Berkeley), the penal laws were reduced in severity, and in 1782 an Irish constitution was promulgated, by which the Irish Protestants were given political rights and limited powers in an Irish Parliament freed from ▷ Privy Council control. The experiment was a failure, and in 1801 Ireland was united politically and in all other respects with England and Scotland, Irish Protestants receiving for the first time representation in the English Parliament.

1801–1921 – The Union
The 19th century was the age of steady emancipation of Irish Catholics and mounting Irish patriotism. The population at the beginning of the century was four and a half million, fewer than one and a half million being of English or Scottish Protestant descent. The Anglo-Irish were the social leaders of the country; the Scots were a middle class of business men and farmers; the native Irish were largely peasants. In 1829 Catholic Emancipation removed all the important restrictions on Catholics, notably the political ones. Henceforward there was a growing party of Irish Catholics in the English House of Commons, in the last quarter of the century known as the Home Rule Party from its intention to win national

independence for Ireland. In the middle of the century reform was concentrated on land matters; this was the more necessary for the misery of the Irish peasantry whose sufferings were increased by the severe famines of the 1840s, leading to deaths on a massive scale and to massive emigration to the U.S.A. In 1841 the population was over eight million, and it is now about three million; Ireland is thus one of the very few countries in the world whose population has actually diminished in the last 100 years. Attempts to obtain Home Rule through the English Parliament failed. A brief rebellion in 1916 was put down, but a severe one in 1919–21 resulted in independence within the Commonwealth. It was led by the Sinn Fein party, and the great bitterness of the fighting arose in part from their fanaticism and the brutality of the English auxiliary police (called 'Black and Tans' from their uniform) sent to suppress the rebels.

The Irish Free State
This state was formed in 1922 and included the three provinces of Munster, Leinster, Connaught, and three counties of Ulster. The remaining six counties of Ulster, being mainly Protestant and Anglo-Scottish in population have separate status as Northern Ireland with representation in the English Parliament. The Irish Free State took the name of Eire (Ireland) in 1937, and is no longer a member of the Commonwealth. It is a republic with a president and two houses of parliament, the Dáil and the Seanad. The first official language is nominally Gaelic, but it is a minority language, since English has long been the majority language.
  ▷ English language.

Iris
In Greek myth, the messenger between the gods and mortals – an alternative to ▷ Hermes. Her path to earth was the rainbow, with which she became identified.

Irish literature in English
Ireland – England's first and closest colony – presents a recent history of literary movements and concerns that is very differently paced from that of its colonist. From 1171, the year of Ireland's conquest by ▷ Henry II, until the latter years of the 19th century, the history of Irish literature in English is, largely speaking, part of the general history of Engish literature. Since the Irish Literary Revival began in the 1880s, however, the existence and the memory of a literature in Ireland's original tongue, ▷ Gaelic, has interacted with the country's

adopted vernacular at every level: in the detail of syntax; in the choice – or rejection – of subject-matter; and in each writer's wrestle with identity.

Throughout the 18th and 19th centuries – and into the 20th – writers from Anglo-Irish Ireland made a rich and vigorous contribution to English literature: ▷ Jonathan Swift, ▷ William Congreve, ▷ Oliver Goldsmith, ▷ Sheridan, ▷ Oscar Wilde and ▷ George Bernard Shaw are amongst the better known. Their writings were not primarily concerned with the matter of Ireland or their authors' own Irishness. Those who did write of Ireland, like Dion Boucicault (1820–90), who is held by many to be the inventor of the 'stage Irishman', and ▷ Thomas Moore (1779–1852), the purveyor to the drawing-rooms of London of an Ireland sugared by sentiment and exile, capitalized on what looks with hindsight like caricature. All these writers of the Anglo-Irish Ascendancy, coming from their background of landed privilege, seemed to be unaware of the still surviving Gaelic tradition of native Irish literature, with its long ancestry and close connections with mainland Europe – a tradition eloquently evoked in Daniel Corkery's *Hidden Ireland* of 1924, and recently made available anew in Seán Ó Tuama's and Thomas Kinsella's 1981 anthology *An Duanaire: Poems of the Dispossessed*.

Moreover, during this pre-Revival period only a handful of creative writers mirrored the growing interest that folklorists like T. Crofton Croker (1798–1849), travellers (again, many of them from Europe) and diarists were taking in Irish peasant life outside the ▷ 'Pale'. ▷ Maria Edgeworth (1767–1849) and William Carleton (1794–1869) stand almost alone in the seriousness with which they looked at their native land and its inhabitants. Edgeworth's *Castle Rackrent* (1800) and Carleton's *Traits and Stories of the Irish Peasantry* (1830–3) are isolated landmarks; and Carleton, an adopted member of Ascendancy culture who was born a Catholic peasant, has been read in recent years with renewed interest and recognition.

In the decades that followed the devastation of native Gaelic culture by the famine and mass emigration of the 1840s, a new sense of Ireland's nationhood began, paradoxically, to emerge. The poets and dramatists of the Literary Revival of the 1880s and 1890s regarded Standish O'Grady (1846–1928) as its prime mover. His two-volume history of Ireland – *The Heroic Period* (1878) and *Cuchullin and His Contemporaries* (1880) –

sent them back with a new authority to the ancient matter of Ireland. And it was on this material, and on a new attention to the distinctive English actually spoken in Ireland, that the renaissance of Irish letters was founded. Its chief authors – the most notable being ▷ W. B. Yeats (1865–1939), ▷ J. M. Synge (1871–1909) and ▷ Lady Gregory (1852–1932) – were still, to begin with, the sons and the daughters of the Ascendancy, but before long they were joined in their work of forging the soul of the soon-to-be-independent nation by writers who sprang from the native and Catholic population. A common task was perceived.

The history of Irish literature in English is closely linked, then, to the political history of the nation that (except for the six counties in its north-east corner) won its independence from British rule in 1921, and declared its Republican status when leaving the Commonwealth in 1949 (▷ Ireland). The first battle in the war of independence had, after all, been led by a poet, Padraig Pearse (1879–1916), and inspired partially at least by his romantic ideas of blood-sacrifice:

All changed, changed utterly.
A terrible beauty is born.
(Yeats, 'Easter 1916')

Irish writers since the Revival have had to reconsider and redefine ideas of continuity and cultural identity that are quite different from those that face English writers in the post-colonial period, though there are affinities with the experience of the other Celtic nations of Britain – the Welsh and the Scots. (▷ Scottish Literature)

In the hundred-odd years since the poet and translator Douglas Hyde (1860–1949) gave a lecture to the newly formed National Literary Society in Dublin entitled 'The Necessity of De-Anglicising Ireland' (1892), Irish writers have had continually to ask themselves and each other quite how, and to what extent, de-Anglicization is to be carried out – and who they are when they have done it. Questions of national identity cross over with questions of personal identity in this distinctive version of the 20th-century artist's problematic relation to society.

Ireland's writers began by looking to their country's heroic past and its idealized idea of the west, the non-anglicized land of saints, scholars and a noble peasantry; but they also looked, from the very start, to the literatures of Europe, and cast a cold and realist eye at their own urban and rural present. ▷ James Joyce (1882–1941) taught himself enough

Norwegian as a schoolboy to write a letter to his hero, ▷ Ibsen, who was already a profound influence on the playwrights of Dublin's ▷ Abbey Theatre; George Egerton (Mary Dunne, 1859–1945) translated Knut Hamsun's *Hunger* and wrote about the 'New Woman' in her novel *Keynotes* (1893) before the old century ended. Kate O'Brien (1897–1974) and Maura Laverty (1907–66) found inspiration and objectivity by living for a time in Spain, Ireland's old ally. For many Irish writers – Joyce, ▷ Samuel Beckett (b 1906) and Francis Stuart (b 1902) are early examples, followed later to Paris by the poets Denis Devlin (1908–59) and Brian Coffey (b 1905) – this looking outside Ireland necessarily became a longer physical exile: the required distance from which to practise their art – or indeed to have it published and read. For during the first half-century of independence, the Irish state's narrow, inward-looking patriotism and the tight grip of a reactionary Catholic clerisy directly impoverished cultural life within Ireland: ▷ censorship meant that most works of serious literature by Irish men and women were banned in their own country.

Those who stayed, returned, or at least kept a foothold in the place, were able to refine and multiply the means of reclaiming or repairing an Irish heritage. They worked from an intimate knowledge of place, like Patrick Kavanagh (1904–67), who immortalized his townland of Mucker in *The Great Hunger* (1942) and *Tarry Flynn* (1948); others, like Austin Clarke (1896–1974) and later Thomas Kinsella (b 1928), worked from a more scholarly knowledge of the Gaelic-language heritage than was available to the Revivalists. By the mid-20th century poets in particular were recognizing the impossibility of bridging the gap to the past, and were finding that the fractured state of Irish culture itself offered a fruitful area of exploration for the isolated and disillusioned artist/ commentator. Flann O'Brien (Brian O'Nolan, 1911–66) created a comic and fantastic Gaelic/ modernist world in his novel *At Swim-Two-Birds* (1939) as his response to this artistic dilemma.

It tended to be the novelists and short-story writers who recorded the day-to-day reality of life in the young state. ▷ Sean O'Faolain (b 1900) and ▷ Frank O'Connor (Michael O'Donovan, 1903–66) demonstrated, in their short stories of the Troubles and after, not just a consummate art, but a seminal understanding of the why and the how of that wished-for 'de-Anglicization'. Written from the fringes, but courageously central in their concerns, the novels and short stories of the Aran Islander ▷ Liam O'Flaherty (1897–1984) are eloquent accounts of the dignity and constraints of life in the no-longer idealized rural west; and Patrick McGill's *Children of the Dead End* (1914) is a classic account of the reality of land-hunger and migratory labouring.

At home and abroad, then, Irish writers were grappling with the question of identity, and a body of remarkable writing was being assembled into a tradition of its own. But the achievements of three writers in particular placed a burden of success on subsequent generations. In poetry, the novel and drama, the work of Yeats, Joyce and Synge proved difficult to build on directly. Over the years a pattern can be discerned in which Ireland's vigorous – but even in the 1980s essentially naturalistic – tradition of fiction has more in common with the elegiac and story-telling parts of Yeats's *oeuvre* than with Joyce's modernism. Conversely, poets have found in ▷ *Ulysses*' concern with the here and now of life as it is lived – and lived in the city – a more usable language than Yeats' lovely rhetoric or Synge's Gaelic-shadowed experimentalism. It is, perhaps, in drama that writers have found least constraint from the work of their predecessors. Over the years ▷ Sean O'Casey (1880–1964), Samuel Beckett (b 1906), ▷ Brendan Behan (1923–64), and Brian Friel (b 1929) have each developed their own idiosyncratic dramatic structure and voice.

During this first century of a consciously Irish literature in English, Gaelic has continued to be the linguistic bedrock of Irish writers. Whether through translations that are creative works in their own right, from Hyde's *Love Songs of Connacht* (1893) to Kinsella's *The Tain* (1969) and ▷ Seamus Heaney's *Sweeney Astray* (1983), or by regarding all periods of Gaelic literature as a nourishing tradition alongside other literatures, Irish poets have constantly enriched their work in English. A few have decided to write only in Gaelic – two notable poets being Seán Ó Ríordáin (1917–77) and Nuala Ní Dhomhnaill (b 1952) – but such writers are nevertheless an essential part of the English-language writing scene, both in their professional friendships and in creative translation by their peers. One excellent poet, Michael Hartnett (b 1941), publicly dedicated himself in 1975 to writing wholly in Irish; he has recently reverted to writing in both languages.

One half-century into the new state, a

rather less easily accommodated bedrock issue surfaced: the rekindling of violent conflict on a large scale in the Six Counties in 1968. To the chagrin of some writers south of the Border, the work of many poets and playwrights of the North has been received with far more interest and critical acclaim in recent years than has been granted to writing from the South. For a time, all the artistic as well as the political action has seemed to be north of the Border. While the unprecedented prosperity of the 1960s and 70s inclined the South to a certain complacency, in the North it has seemed to both sides 'as though the whole of Anglo-Irish history has been boiled down and its dregs thrown out, leaving their poisonous concentrate on these six counties' (the final sentence of David Thomson's *Woodbrook*; 1974).

With fitting reluctance, and in very different styles, the writers of the North have taken on this new artistic burden. The fortuitous presence of the catalytic English poet and critic Philip Hobsbaum in Belfast in the mid-1960s prepared the ground for a second Irish renaissance. The 'Group' he fostered contained most of the male poets who have become well-known, the youngest of whom is ▷ Paul Muldoon (b 1951). The most impressive to date is ▷ Seamus Heaney, who has in his *oeuvre* explored all the different and conflicting themes and preoccupations of Irish writing, and used his part-time chosen exile in the U.S.A. to enlarge his and Ireland's understanding of poetic possibility.

The North has produced too one of the most exciting women poets of Ireland, Medbh McGuckian (b 1951); she, and Eavan Boland (b 1944) in the South, are the most visible of a new generation of women poets of real distinction. In the field of the novel, Irish women have managed, as women have in English generally, to make a substantial contribution; but the pressures of a conservative and patriarchal society have been less kind to women poets. As Irish women free themselves from the extremes of traditional roles, all the expected fields of women's writings are growing rapidly, and making strong connections with writing in England and the U.S.A. Particularly notable are ▷ Edna O'Brien (b 1930), Julia O'Faolain (b 1932), Jennifer Johnston (b 1930) and the promising Deidre Madden (b 1961).

The great expansion in Irish publishing over the last 20 years, especially of contemporary work, augurs well for the continuing vigour of all areas of Irish literature in English, and in Gaelic too. Another hopeful sign is the Republic's decision not to tax artists' earnings. In recent years writers of all nations, including Seamus Heaney, have moved to voluntary exile in the Republic.
Bib: *Macmillan Dictionary of Irish Literature*; Heaney, S., *Preoccupations: Selected prose 1968–1978*; Kee, R., *The Green Flag: A History of Irish Nationalism*; Garratt, R., *Modern Irish Poetry: Tradition and Continuity from Yeats to Heaney*; Worth, K., *The Irish Drama of Europe from Yeats to Beckett*; Kinsella, T. (trans.), *The Tain*; Brown, T., *Northern Voices: Poets from Ulster*.

Irish literature in Gaelic
Most of this is medieval (1100–1550). Two main cycles of myth are distinguished; the Ulster series, centring on Conchobar and ▷ Cuchulain; that of Leinster and Munster centring on ▷ Finn and Ossian (▷ Oisin). *Ulster Cycle:* Cuchulain was a great warrior in the court of Conchobar king of Ulster. Other characters are Ailill and Medb (Maeve), king and queen of Connaught, against whom Cuchulain defended Ulster; Fergus, the exiled king of Ulster; ▷ Deidre, brought up to be the bride of Conchobar, who killed her lover Naoise. Such legends were versified in the ▷ Middle Ages, but are thought to have originated in pre-Christian times, *ie* before the 5th century A D. *Leinster-Munster cycle:* in their best form ▷ ballads; after 1250 these exceeded the Ulster legends in popularity. The events are supposed to take place in the 3rd–5th centuries A D. Finn was a great warrior when Cormac was king of Ireland, and commanded a band called the ▷ Fenians. He was the father of the hero Ossian, who spent many years in a kind of fairyland, and was at last baptized as a Christian by St Patrick. Such myths were used by poets and dramatists of the Irish Nationalist movement in English, *eg* especially ▷ W. B. Yeats and ▷ J. M. Synge, between 1890 and 1910.

Irony
▷ Figures of Speech.

Irving, Sir Henry (1838–1905)
Actor. His original name was Brodribb, but he adopted the name of Irving when he gave up a commercial career for acting in 1856. For ten years he performed over 500 parts in provincial companies. He made his name in London in 1871 with the part of Mathias in the melodrama, *The Bells* by Leopold Lewis (adapted from *Le Juif Polonais* by Erckmann-Chatrian). This was at the Lyceum Theatre, which later became famous under his management. His reputation grew by his performance in a great variety of roles (including two in plays by the poet

Sir Henry Irving as Macbeth

▷ Tennyson, *The Cup* and *Becket*),
especially ▷ Shakespearean ones: his
performances of ▷ Hamlet and Shylock
became legendary. Irving's style was strongly
romantic and powerfully eloquent; he and
Ellen Terry, with whom he was associated at
the Lyceum from 1878 to 1902, gave English
theatre its main distinction at a time when
contemporary literary contribution to the
drama was undistinguished.
Bib: Bingham, M., *Henry Irving and the
Victorian Theatre*.

Isaac
In the ▷ Bible (*Genesis* XXI–XIII and
XXXV) the second of the Patriarchs, *ie*
ancient founders of the Jewish nation. He
was the sole legitimate son and the heir of the
first Patriarch, ▷ Abraham, and the father
of ▷ Jacob and Esau.

Isaiah
In the ▷ Bible, the greatest of the Old
Testament prophetic books. The majority of it
is dated towards the end of the 8th century BC. It
was a period of conflict among the western
Asiatic powers, and the book includes a
dramatic account of ▷ Sennacherib of Assyria
and his invasion of Judaea. He besieged
Jerusalem, but his army was devastated by an
epidemic of plague, and the city was saved. This
is the subject of one of ▷ Byron's most famous
lyrics – *The Destruction of Sennacherib*. Much of
Isaiah consists of prophecies of great disaster to
the Jews, of recovery, and of the coming of the
▷ Messiah, *eg* Chapter 7.

Iseult (Isoud, Ysolde, Ysoude)
  ▷ Tristan and Iseult.

Isherwood, Christopher (1904–86)
Novelist and dramatist. Born in Cheshire and
educated at Repton School (where he met
▷ Edward Upward), and Cambridge and
London universities. At preparatory school
he met ▷ W. H. Auden, with whom he later
collaborated on three plays, *The Dog Beneath
The Skin* (1935), *The Ascent of F6* (1936) and
On The Frontier (1938). These are primarily
political and psychological parables.
Isherwood's first two novels, *All The
Conspirators* (1928) and *The Memorial* (1932),
employ ▷ modernist styles and techniques.
His experience of teaching English in Berlin
from 1930 to 1933 is reflected in *Mr Norris
Changes Trains* (1935) and *Goodbye to Berlin*
(1939), which employ a more realistic mode.
The latter is a series of linked tales recording
the atmosphere and characters of a decadent
Berlin in the last days of the Weimar
Republic; the narrator is characterized by a
certain passivity and detachment, summarized
in his claim: 'I am a camera with its shutter
open . . .'. The section entitled 'Sally Bowles'
was dramatized in 1951 as *I Am A Camera*
and turned into a stage musical in 1968 as
Cabaret. Isherwood visited China in 1933
with Auden, and together they wrote *Journey
to a War* (1939). In 1939 they both emigrated
to the U.S.A., where Isherwood became
naturalized in 1946. All his major work is
written in the first person, and his American
novels draw extensively on his own
development as a theme. They are: *Prater
Violet* (1945), *The World in the Evening*
(1954), *Down There On A Visit* (1962), *A
Single Man* (1964) and *A Meeting By the
River* (1967). He also wrote numerous
screenplays, and several autobiographical and
travel pieces, including *Lions and Shadows*
(1938), *Christopher and his Kind* (1976) and
*The Condor and the Cows: a South American
Travel Diary* (1950). He translated works
relating to the mystical Hindu philosophy of
Vendanta, a philosophy which is advocated in
A Meeting By the River.
Bib: King, F., *Christopher Isherwood*;
Summers, C. J., *Christopher Isherwood*.

Isis
In ancient Egyptian myth, a nature goddess.
She was sometimes identified with the moon,
and her brother-husband ▷ Osiris with the
sun. Horus, the rising sun, was their son.
The worship of Isis spread all over the
eastern Mediterranean; the Greek historian
Herodotus (5th century BC) identified her
with ▷ Demeter the corn goddess.

Isocrates (436–338 BC)

In ancient Greece, an Athenian orator who advocated a united Greece for war against the states of Asia. He advanced Greek prose style by the care he gave to his speeches.

Italian influence on English literature

Apart from the influence of Italian literature, Italy as a country was particularly important to England in the 16th and early 17th century. The English attitude to Italy was complicated – a mixture of admiration, envy, intense interest and disapproval amounting to abhorrence. The Italian cities were for Englishmen the centres and summits of civilization, and such centres in most periods are supposed to represent not only what is most advanced in thought and behaviour, but also what is most extravagant and corrupt.

Two Italian books of the 16th century were immensely fascinating to Englishmen, and the English response to them explains much of the contradiction in English feeling. The first was ▷ Castiglione's *Courtier* (1528, trans 1561) which offered a model for the virtues and accomplishments of the perfect ▷ gentleman; this was greatly admired by English courtly figures such as the ▷ Earl of Surrey, ▷ Sir Thomas Wyatt, ▷ Sir Philip Sidney, ▷ Sir Walter Raleigh and ▷ Edmund Spenser, and was approved even by such an anti-Italian as ▷ Queen Elizabeth's private tutor, ▷ Roger Ascham. The other was ▷ Machiavelli's *Prince* (1513). This book was not translated into English until 1640, but many educated Englishmen knew Italian in the 16th century; in any case, Gentillet's *Contre Machiavel* (*Against Machiavelli*, 1576) was widely known in England and translated in 1602. Machiavelli's object was to develop a political science capable of uniting Italy; this did not interest Englishmen, but they were deeply horrified by Machiavelli's demonstration that for such politics to be effective they had to disregard ordinary morality and good faith. The work no doubt impressed English statesmen such as Elizabeth's minister Cecil, but it made 'politics' – 'politic' – 'politician' into evil words for those not occupied by statecraft, and a Machiavellian was synonymous with an atheist or with one who had taken the devil as his master. Such a man was ▷ Shakespeare's ▷ Richard III, and it is Machiavelli who speaks the prologue to ▷ Christopher Marlowe's play ▷ *The Jew of Malta*. When Sir Andrew in Shakespeare's ▷ *Twelfth Night* says (III.ii) 'for policy I hate: I had as lief [would as soon] be a ▷ Brownist as a politician' he is coupling a ▷ Puritan sect hated by dramatists and playgoers with Machiavellians hated by the Puritans and anti-Puritans alike. More superficially, travel in Italy was supposed to induce folly and affectation and to corrupt morals. As Roger Ascham put it in *The Scholemaster* (1570) 'what the Italian saith of the Englishman . . . *Englese Italianato, è un diavolo incarnato*, that is to say, you remain men in shape and fashion, but become devils in life and condition.' Italians were poisoners and seducers like Iachimo in Shakespeare's ▷ *Cymbeline*. It was not only because their fiction was popular that so many Elizabethan and Jacobean plays were based on Italian tales ('*novelle*'), but because Italy could be appealed to as the land where human nature was richest, darkest and brightest.

The fact that Rome was the centre of the ▷ Catholic Church was of course bad enough for Protestant Englishmen after 1540; before that date, the image was brighter, and throughout the century Englishmen did not forget that Italy was the nation of such great scholars and philosophers as Pico della Mirandola (1463–94) whose works ▷ Sir Thomas More partly translated. It was the independence of the best Italian minds that attracted the best English minds of the 16th and 17th centuries. The free-thinking Italian philosopher, Giordano Bruno (?1548–99), despised the stale traditions of the English universities on his visit (1583–5), but he admired Queen Elizabeth and made friends with men such as Sir Philip Sidney and Sir Walter Raleigh. The astronomer ▷ Galileo, who, like Bruno, came into conflict with the ▷ Inquisition, was studied by the poet ▷ John Donne, and received visits from the sceptical philosopher ▷ Thomas Hobbes and the Puritan ▷ John Milton. Milton's visit to Italy (1638–9) enriched him with encounters with scholars and patrons of learning, while at the same time he felt in danger from the papal police because of his religious opinions; this is another example of the complicated relationships of Englishmen with Italy.

After 1650 Italy by no means lost its fascination for the English, but it was Italy as a storehouse of the past, rather than a challenging present, that drew Englishmen. In the 18th century the English invented a sort of tourism; what was called the 'Grand Tour' formed part of the education of upper-class young men and Italy was one of its principal objectives. They were drawn to the architectural and sculptural remains of the old Roman Empire, the framework of their literary education in Latin literature. In the second half of the 19th century the art critic ▷ John Ruskin and the ▷ Pre-Raphaelite painters and poets turned their interest to the Italian Middle Ages.

The most important contributors to the Italian romantic novel are probably Alessandro Manzoni (1785–1873), who influenced ▷ Sir Walter Scott, and Ugo Foscolo (1778–1827), who was himself exiled in England. Foscolo's *The Last Letters of Jacopo Ortis* (1802–14) was a major contribution to the novel form, while his poetry, which lays emphasis on his exile, *Of Sepulchres* (1807) participates in the rise of romantic poetry. Another Italian ▷ romantic poet is Giacamo Leopardi (1798–1837) whose international renown, especially for *Canti* (1845) resides in the natural imagery and tones of despair in his poetry.

At the beginning of the 20th century Giosuè Carducci's (1835–1907) ▷ classical, apolitical and solemn poetry won him the Nobel Prize of 1906, but the decadent school was soon to produce two important names in Italian literature: Gabriele D'annunzio (1863–1938) and Luigi Pirandello (1867–1936). D'annunzio's *The Child of Pleasure* (1890) in the novel and *Praises* (1904) in poetry influenced the aesthetic, ▷ symbolist and Pre-Raphaelite schools in England. Pirandello's international reputation is well-known; from the production of *Six Characters in Search of An Author* (1921) his strikingly original tone and characters became immensely influential in drama. The reputation of Italian authors in other countries has continued in the 20th century, often rivalling the golden age of medieval Italianate influence. The works of Italo Calvino (1923–85), Primo Levi (1919–87) and Umberto Eco (b1932) are published in English almost as soon as in the original Italian. Levi's autobiographical accounts of

his experiences in Auschwitz, as for example in *The Periodic Table* (1975), Eco's theoretical works and his best-seller *The Name of the Rose* (1981), and Calvino's neo-realism trilogy *Our Ancestors* (1952–9) have an international readership. Other 20th-century Italian writers of note are the novelist Alberto Moravia (b1907), (the pen name of Alberto Pincherle), who, like Calvino, writes neo-realistic works concerned with socio-political issues, as for example, *Two Women* (1957); Giorgio Bassani (b1916), a confessional novelist aware of the torments of evil and morality, as in his work *The Garden of the Finzi-Contini* (1962); and finally the poet Eugenio Montale (1896–1981), the most renowned Italian poet of the 20th century and winner of the 1976 Nobel prize; his most famous work is *Cuttle-fish Bones* (1925).

Ithaca
An island near Corfu, the kingdom of ▷ Odysseus, the hero of ▷ Homer's epic the ▷ *Odyssey*.

Ivanhoe (1819)
A historical novel by ▷ Sir Walter Scott. It is set in the reign of ▷ Richard I, who is one of the characters; the story concerns rivalry between the king and his wicked brother ▷ John (king, 1199–1216), and between Saxons and the ruling Norman aristocracy. Locksley (the legendary outlaw, Robin Hood) aids Richard against the rebellious Normans, and helps to bring about the union of the Saxon hero, Wilfred of Ivanhoe, and the heroine Rowena. It was the first novel by Scott to deal with an English (as distinct from a Scottish) subject, and was very popular in the 19th century. This popularity is partly due to its being one of the first attempts to write a novel about the Middle Ages with a genuine regard for history.

J

Jack and the Beanstalk
A well-known fairy story based on a myth found all over the world. Jack exchanges his mother's cow for a hatful of beans. When thrown into the garden, the beans rapidly sprout stalks which reach above the clouds. Jack climbs one of the beanstalks and finds himself in a new land near the castle of a man-eating giant. Jack manages by cunning to steal the giant's wealth and when the giant pursues him down the stalk, he fells it so that the giant falls and breaks his neck.
  ▷ Giants.

Jack Horner
A ▷ nursery rhyme usually considered to derive from a study about one of the profiteers who acquired land from the monasteries when these were dissolved by ▷ Henry VIII. Another old rhyme goes:

Hopton, Horner, Smyth and Thynne,
When the abbots went out, they came in.

Jack the Giant-Killer
A traditional fairy tale, set in the time of ▷ King Arthur, about episodes in the career of a boy who had a talent for killing giants by cunning.
  ▷ Giants.

Jack Wilton
  ▷ Nashe, Thomas.

Jacob
In the ▷ Bible, the grandson of ▷ Abraham, son of ▷ Isaac, father of ▷ Joseph, and legendary ancestor of the Jews. He represented the pastoral way of life, while his brother Esau, ancestor of the tribes of Edom to the south of Israel, represented the hunting and raiding existence of the desert Arab.

Jacobean
Used to indicate the period of ▷ James I (1603–25) and applied especially to the literature and style of architecture of his reign. In literature, it is most commonly a way of distinguishing the style of drama under James from the style that prevailed under ▷ Elizabeth. Strictly, Elizabethan drama is experimental, expansive, sometimes ingenuous, in fairly close touch with medieval tradition but energetic with ▷ Renaissance forces. It includes the work of the ▷ University wits – ▷ Christopher Marlowe, ▷ Thomas Kyd, ▷ Robert Greene, ▷ George Peele – and also earlier ▷ Shakespeare. Jacobean drama is thought of as critical, sombre, disillusioned. It includes mature and late Shakespeare, ▷ Ben Jonson, ▷ Cyril Tourneur, ▷ John Webster, ▷ Thomas Middleton, ▷ Francis Beaumont and ▷ John Fletcher. The ▷ Caroline period is associated with such figures as ▷ Philip Massinger, ▷ John Ford and ▷ James Shirley. Courts were the centre of culture, and courts depended largely on the circumstances of monarchs; while the reign of Elizabeth was prosperous at home and (mainly) triumphant overseas, that of James saw increasing disagreement at home, and abroad was negative or even nationally humiliating. The reign of ▷ Charles I was yet more bitter in home dissensions but his court was one of distinction and refinement. The tone of the drama varied with these differences in national fortune and court conduct. However, the labelling of literary periods is always to some extent simplifying and even falsifying.
  The Jacobean period was the first that was really rich in prose, with writers like ▷ Francis Bacon, ▷ John Donne and ▷ Lancelot Andrewes. Their work contrasts especially with ▷ Restoration prose, which sacrificed the poetic qualities of the Jacobean writing for the sake of grace and lucidity.
  ▷ Seventeenth-century literature.

Jacobin
Originally a name given to ▷ Dominican friars in France, because their first convent was in the Rue St Jacques in Paris. The name was transferred to a political society which rented a room in the convent in the first year of the ▷ French Revolution. The society developed into a highly organized political party, led by ▷ Robespierre, who became practically dictator of France in 1793. The club was closed after the fall of Robespierre in 1794. The Jacobins were extreme in asserting the principle of equality and in their opposition to privilege. Later, when conservative reaction had set in, 'Jacobin' was used loosely for anyone with political liberal tendencies in England as well as in France; *eg* the paper *The Anti-Jacobin* was founded to combat English liberal opinion in 1797.

Jacobite
From Jacobus, the Latin form of James. ▷ James II, of the House of ▷ Stuart, was deposed in 1688 because, as a convert to Catholicism, he was considered to be conspiring against the established ▷ Protestant religion and against ▷ Parliament. His supporters were called Jacobites and this name continued for the supporters of his Catholic son and grandsons.

After the crown passed to the House of Hanover, a German Protestant family, in 1714, British Jacobites conspired to restore the House of ▷ Stuart. The Jacobite Rebellions of 1715 and 1745 were the two most formidable attempts; both had principally Scottish support, partly because the Stuarts had originally been a Scottish royal family. The ▷ 'Forty-five' rebellion quickly became a romantic legend chiefly because of the supposed gallantry and charm of its leader, Charles Edward Stuart, grandson of James II – 'Bonnie Prince Charlie' to his Scottish supporters and the 'Young Pretender' to his opponents. After the failure of the 'Forty-five' Jacobitism became increasingly a matter of sentiment which even persists to the present day, though the direct line of the Stuarts died out in 1807.

Jacobson, Dan (b 1929)

Dan Jacobson

Novelist, short-story writer and critic. Born in South Africa, he moved permanently to England in 1954, and is now Professor of English Literature at University College, London. His novels are: *The Trap* (1955); *A Dance in the Sun* (1956); *The Price of Diamonds* (1957); *The Evidence of Love* (1960); *The Beginners* (1966); *The Rape of Tamar* (1970); *The Wonder Worker* (1973); *The Confessions of Joseph Baiz* (1977). His story collections include: *A Long Way From London* (1958); *The Zulu and the Zeide* (1959); *Beggar My Neighbour* (1964); *Through the Wilderness* (1968); *A Way of Life* (1971); *Inklings: Selected Stories* (1973). Up to and

including *The Beginners*, the story of three generations of an immigrant Jewish family, the novels are set in South Africa, and are largely naturalistic in style. *The Rape of Tamar*, which inspired the play *Yonadab* by ▷ Peter Shaffer, is a more experimental work, much concerned with the ambiguities of narration. It has an Old Testament setting, and a self-conscious, and highly characterized narrator. *The Confessions of Joseph Baiz* is the fictional autobiography of a man who can love only those whom he has betrayed, and is set in an imaginary totalitarian country, somewhat resembling South Africa. Recurrent concerns of Jacobson's novels and stories include power, religion, guilt and betrayal, and his work is characterized by its inventiveness and wit. His non-fiction includes: *The Story of the Stories: The Chosen People and its God* (1982); *Time and Time Again: Autobiographies* (1985); *Adult Pleasures: Essays on Writers and Readers* (1988).

Jakobson, Roman (1896–1982)

Born in Moscow where he was educated. He worked in Czechoslovakia for almost 20 years, between 1920 and 1939, and after the German invasion he escaped to Scandinavia, before going to the U.S.A. where he taught in a number of universities, and became Professor of Russian Literature at the Massachusetts Institute of Technology. During his formative years he was heavily influenced by a number of avante-garde movements in the Arts, but in his own work he laid specific emphasis upon the formulation of a 'poetics' which took into account the findings of ▷ structuralism, and the work of the ▷ Russian formalists. He was an active member of the Society for the Study of Poetic Language (OPOYAZ) which was founded in St Petersburg in 1916, and in 1926 he founded the Prague Linguistic Circle. His wife Krystyna Pomorska notes, in a recent collection of his writings, that poetry and visual art became for Jakobson the fundamental spheres for observing how verbal phenomena work and for studying how to approach them (Roman Jakobson, *Language and Literature*, 1987).
Bib: Hawkes, T., *Structuralism and Semiotics*; Jakobson, R., *Language and Literature* and *Verbal Art, Verbal Sign, Verbal Time*; Bennett, T., *Formalism and Marxism*; Erlich, V., *Russian Formalism: History-Doctrine*.

James I, King of Scotland (1406–37)

He was not actually crowned until 1424, owing to a long period of exile in England.

His literary importance is his poetry; he is generally regarded as the author of ▷ *The Kingis Quair*, a love poem which may be autobiographical. It employs the 7-line stanza known as the ▷ rhyme-royal perhaps because of James's use of it, though he derived it from ▷ Chaucer.

James i of England and vi of Scotland
A member of the Scottish House of ▷ Stuart, he ruled over Scotland alone (1566–1603) and then over England as well (1603–25). He was the first sovereign ever to reign over the whole of the British Isles. His accession to the throne of England was due to the death without children of his cousin ▷ Elizabeth i, last of the House of ▷ Tudor. The literature and architecture of his era is known as ▷ Jacobean, a term transferred, especially in architecture, to the greater part of the 17th century.

James ii of England and vii of Scotland (1685–88)
King of Great Britain and Ireland. He was deposed because, as a Catholic, he was threatening the security of the ▷ Church of England and at the same time weakening the power of ▷ Parliament. He was succeeded by his ▷ Protestant daughter ▷ Mary ii in conjunction with her Dutch husband, ▷ William iii.
    ▷ Jacobite; Revolution of 1688, The.

James IV (**1590**)
A romantic transvestite comedy by ▷ Robert Greene which dramatizes the loves of James iv and of his English wife Dorothea against whose life he conspires. The play's main action – which is the stuff of melodrama – is framed by the choric comments of Oberon and Bohan, a misanthropic Scot. In this respect Greene's practice accords with similar dramatic strategies adopted in ▷ Kyd's *The Spanish Tragedy*; and it also anticipates the Chinese-box structure of ▷ *A Midsummer Night's Dream* and, to a lesser extent, Shakespeare's use of an induction in ▷ *The Taming of the Shrew*.

James, Henry (1843–1916)
Novelist. Born in New York; his father was an original writer on philosophy and theology, and his brother, William James, became one of the most distinguished philosophers and psychologists of his day. His education was divided between America and Europe. Europe drew him strongly, and he finally settled in Europe in 1875 after a series of long visits. He was naturalized British in 1915. Towards both continents, however, he had mixed emotions. As to America, he belonged to the eastern seaboard, New England, which had its own well-established traditions originating in English ▷ Puritanism, and he was out of sympathy with the American ardour for commercial enterprise and westward expansion. As to Europe, he was fascinated by the richness of its ancient societies and culture, but he brought an American, and especially a New England, eye to the corruption which such advanced development generated. The conflict was fruitful for his development as an artist, and it was not the only one; he was also aware of the contrast between the contemplativeness of his father's mind and the practical adventurousness characteristic of his brother's outlook and of Americans in general. And in his close study of the art of the novel, he felt the difference between the intense interest in form of the French tradition and the deeper moral interest to be found in the English tradition.

In the first period of his work, his theme is preponderantly the clash between the European and the American outlooks: *Roderick Hudson* (1875); *The American* (1877); *The Europeans* (1878); ▷ *Daisy Miller* (1879); ▷ *The Portrait of a Lady* (1881). To this period also belong two novels about American life: *Washington Square* (1881); *The Bostonians* (1886); and two restricted to English life, *The Tragic Muse* (1890); *The Princess Casamassima* (1886). His second period shows a much more concentrated and difficult style of treatment, and it concerns English society only: *The Spoils of Poynton* and ▷ *What Maisie Knew* (1897); ▷ *The Awkward Age* (1899). Between his first and second periods (1889–95) he experimented in drama; this was his least successful episode, but the experiment helped him to develop a dramatic technique in the writing of his novels. He wrote 12 plays in all. In his last period, the most intensive and subtle in style, James returned to the theme of the contrast of American and European values: ▷ *The Wings of the Dove* (1902); ▷ *The Ambassadors* (1903); ▷ *The Golden Bowl* (1904). On his death he left unfinished *The Ivory Tower* and *The Sense of the Past*. Some of his best fiction is to be found among his short stories, and he was particularly fond of the ▷ 'novella' form – between a story and a usual novel in length; *The Europeans* and *Washington Square* come into this class, and so does his well-known ghost story, ▷ *The Turn of the Screw* (1898).

In his criticism, James is important as the first distinguished writer in English to give the novel and its form concentrated critical attention. His essays have been collected under the title *The House of Fiction* (1957), edited by Leon Edel. He also wrote books of travel, the most notable of which is *The American Scene* (1907), and autobiographical pieces – *A Small Boy and Others* (1913); *Notes of a Son and a Brother* (1914) and *Terminations* (1917). (The last is also the title of a story published in 1895.)

Bib: Edel, L., *Henry James*; Matthiessen, F. O., *Henry James: The Major Phase*; Anderson, Q., *The American Henry James*; Leavis, F. R., in *The Great Tradition*; Dupee, F. W., *Henry James*; Bewley, M., in *The Complex Fate* and in *The Eccentric Design*; Wilson, E., in *The Triple Thinkers*; Krook, D., *The Ordeal of Consciousness in James*; Gard, R. (ed.), *James: The Critical Heritage*; Tanner, T., *Henry James*; Berland, A., *Culture and Conduct in the Novels of Henry James*.

James, P. D. (Phyllis Dorothy) (b 1920)
▷ Detective fiction.

***Jane Eyre* (1847)**
A novel by ▷ Charlotte Brontë. It is in the form of a fictional ▷ autobiography, with some authentic autobiographical experience. The experiences of the penniless, unattractive child at first in the household of her unfeeling aunt Mrs Reed and later at Lowood Asylum – a charitable school – are the subject of the earlier and most generally admired part of the book. Later she becomes governess to the ward of a rich landowner, Mr Rochester, whose terrible secret is his mad wife; this part of the story is a mixture of romantic love, romantic horror and social naivety, together with a truthfulness to feeling which still keeps the heroine convincing and interesting. In the third section, Jane is sought in marriage by a clergyman, St John Rivers, a man of rigorous honour and ideals, whom she refuses after a telepathic communication from Rochester because, unlike the passionate but morally imperfect Rochester, he does not love her. Her marriage to Rochester at the end of the book is again oddly compounded of naivety, romanticism, self-deception and truthfulness. The novel was in more than one respect an innovation: it ran contrary to the puritanic tradition that a good woman did not need to feel physical passion or require it in her lover; it presented a romantic heroine whose nature and appearance it is impossible to sentimentalize or idealize; it is the first novel told in the first person in which the narrator's personality is not just a window through which the events are seen but also defines the quality of the events as we experience them through her mind. *Jane Eyre* was the text which acted as a catalyst in

▷ feminist criticism in the 1980s through the medium of S. Gilbert and S. Gubar's *The Madwoman in the Attic* (1979), in which the unstable female characters in texts written by women were seen as doubles of the sane heroine and products of the suppression of the feminine.

***Jane Shore, The Tragedy of* (1714)**
Play by ▷ Nicholas Rowe, based on a historic character, who was mistress of Edward IV, and afterwards of Thomas Grey, first Marquis of Dorset. Rowe stated on the title page that the play was 'Written in Imitation of Shakespeare's Style'. It traces Jane's descent, from wealth and influence as Edward's mistress, to ignominy and destitution. At her lowest ebb, she is rescued by her husband. The play is numbered among the so-called 'she-tragedies' of Rowe, focussing on the central figure of a suffering woman, and depending largely on pathos for their effect. Jane's story became symbolic of the reversal of fortune.

Janet's Repentance
One of ▷ George Eliot's ▷ *Scenes of Clerical Life*.

Janus
In Roman myth, the god of doorways and guardian of the city during war; he also presided over the first hour of the day, the first day of the month, and the first month of the year (January).

Jason
In Greek myth, son of Aeson, king of Iolchos; the kingdom was seized by his uncle Pelias, and he was brought up by the ▷ centaur, Cheiron. His uncle agreed to return the kingdom if he brought back the Golden Fleece, which he obtained with the help of the princess ▷ Medea of Colchis. He married her, but later abandoned her for Glauce (or Creusa). In revenge, Medea slew his children.
    ▷ Argonauts.

Jefferies, Richard (1848–87)
Essayist and novelist. He wrote about the English countryside and its life and presented it plainly, without affection but with force. This has caused his reputation to rise in the 20th century, with its intensified interest in preserving natural surroundings and in understanding their environmental influence on society. He is well known for his volumes of essays: *Gamekeeper at Home* (1878); *Wild Life in a Southern County* (1879); *Round about a Great Estate* (1880); *Wood Magic* (1881); *The Life of the Fields* (1884). His novels are

Greene Ferne Farm (1880); *The Dewy Morn* (1884); *Amaryllis at the Fair* (1887); *After London, or Wild England* (1885). His best-known books are probably *Bevis* (1882), a children's story (▷ Children's books), and his autobiography, *The Story of my Heart* (1883).
▷ Essay.
Bib: Taylor, B., *Richard Jefferies.*

Jeffrey, Francis (1773–1850)
Critic and editor (1803–29) of the influential ▷ *Edinburgh Review* which he helped to found in 1802. His poetic taste was conservative, and he was unsympathetic to the ▷ Lake Poets, ▷ Wordsworth and ▷ Coleridge. However, in 1820 he judiciously encouraged ▷ Keats for his ▷ *Endymion*, which had been condemned by ▷ *Blackwoods* and the ▷ *Quarterly*. His weakness as a critic was not his conservatism but his susceptibility to verse of second-rate appeal such as that of Thomas Campbell and of Samuel Rogers.
    As editor, Jeffrey gave the ▷ *Edinburgh* authority proportionate to its intellectual independence, and its sales reached nearly 14,000 in 1818 – a high figure at any time for a periodical of such intellectual seriousness. In politics, Jeffrey was ▷ Whig and his journal was the mouthpiece of responsible Whig opinion.
    His profession was the law, in which he excelled and was eventually made a judge.
    ▷ *Edinburgh Review*; Reviews and Periodicals.

Jeffreys, Judge
▷ Bloody Assizes; Sedgemoor, Battle of.

Jekyll and Hyde
From a novel *The Strange Case of Dr Jekyll and Mr Hyde* (1886) by ▷ Robert Louis Stevenson. Dr Jekyll discovers a drug that can reduce his personality to an embodiment of his merely evil impulses – *ie* Mr Hyde.

Jellicoe, Ann (b 1927)
One of few women to break into the theatre business as a writer and director during the 1950s and 60s. She was a ▷ Royal Court writer and a member of the Theatre Writers' Group organized there between 1958 and 1960, which also included ▷ John Arden, ▷ Edward Bond and ▷ Arnold Wesker. Her early plays include *The Sport of My Mad Mother* (1958), about teddy-boy violence, and *The Knack* (1961), about sexual competition. The written text of both these plays only gives a slight impression of their effect in performance since she writes in a non-literary style with clear ideas for direction in mind. Later plays such as *Shelley* (1965) and *The*

Giveaway (1969) are less unconventional. More recently she has become renowned for her productions of community plays in which she has drawn on the talents of large numbers of people from single communities, bringing together professionals and amateurs, adults and schoolchildren. An example of such work is *Entertaining Strangers* written by ▷ David Edgar and originally performed in Dorset (later re-written by him for a ▷ National Theatre production in 1987).
Bib: Jellicoe, A., *Community Plays: How to Put Them on.*

Jennings, Elizabeth (b 1926)
Poet. Published her first collection, *Poems*, in 1953, and was initially associated with the ▷ Movement, although the mystical quality of her work (Jennings is a Roman ▷ Catholic) makes this categorization problematic. She writes prolifically, generally using traditional verse techniques, but she has also experimented with ▷ free verse. Jennings has spent much of her life living and working in Oxford. Her second book, *A Way of Looking* (1955), won her the Somerset Maugham Award, and her most important collections to date are: *A Sense of the World* (1958); *Song for Birth and Death* (1961); *Recoveries* (1964); *The Mind Has Mountains* (1966); *Growing Points* (1975); *Moments of Grace* (1979); and *Celebrations and Elegies* (1982). A *Collected Works* and a *Selected Works* appeared in 1967 and 1979 respectively.

Jeremiah
In the Old Testament of the ▷ Bible, a prophet in a particularly disastrous period of Israelite history, culminating in the temporary destruction of the Jewish kingdom (585 BC). His book is full of lamentations and warnings, from which comes the word 'jeremiad' *ie* a sorrowful complaint.

Jerusalem
The chief city of the ancient Jews, and a holy city for Jews, Muslims and Christians. In medieval geography, which, like medieval cosmology, was governed by theology, Jerusalem was regarded as the centre of the land mass of the earth. Its capture by the Muslims led to the ▷ Crusades. All the more for being in the power of an alien religion, Jerusalem represented a spiritual reality for medieval Europe, and in *Revelation* in the ▷ Bible the New Jerusalem had already been used as a term for Heaven. The most famous imaginative work concerned with the Crusades is the Italian romantic ▷ epic *Jerusalem Delivered* (1581) by

▷ Torquato Tasso. ▷ William Blake wrote a prophetic poem *Jerusalem*, using it as a symbol of mankind redeemed by the spiritual energies of the imagination; he did so again in his conception of a redeemed England in his famous lyric 'And did those feet in ancient time'.

Jesuit

A member of the Society of Jesus, a religious order founded by Ignatius Loyola, and approved by the Pope in 1540. The Jesuits were in the forefront in combating ▷ Protestantism. In the reign of ▷ Elizabeth I they led, or were reputed to lead, the various conspiracies against her on behalf of the ▷ Catholic claimant to the English throne, ▷ Mary Queen of Scots; they were therefore regarded as national as well as religious enemies. Their advanced training made them skilled debaters and subtle negotiators. In the 18th century, when religious conflicts had subsided, Jesuits were no longer feared in England; but their activities in Europe led to their expulsion even from Catholic lands like France and Spain, and for 41 years they were totally suppressed by the Pope. Of later members of the order the most celebrated in English literature is the poet, ▷ Gerard Manley Hopkins.

Jevon (Jevorn), Thomas (1652–88)

Actor, dancer, singer, dramatist. Jevon started his career as a dancing master, and joined the ▷ Duke's Company, possibly before 1673. He had an irreverent sense of humour, and specialized in low comic parts. He was a favourite speaker of prologues and epilogues, and also wrote the highly successful *The Devil of a Wife* (1686), which was adapted several times in the 18th century.

Jew of Malta, The

A ▷ blank verse drama by ▷ Christopher Marlowe, written and performed about 1590; published 1633. An actor impersonating the Italian political philosopher ▷ Machiavelli speaks the prologue and thereby sets the tone of the play, since to the English of Marlowe's time Machiavelli, who had sought to conduct politics amorally by scientific methods, was a godless monster. We thus expect a play dominated by evil. However, a comic tradition for the presentation of godless monsters had come down to Marlowe from the medieval ▷ Mystery plays which had presented such figures as ▷ Herod and Satan as grotesque caricatures, frightening but funny at the same time. So the Machiavellian central character, Barabas the Jew, boasting that his wealth has been acquired iniquitously, is made too impressive to be taken lightly and yet too extravagant to be taken soberly. His only philosophy is the art of gaining advantage. In the first half of the play he tries to outwit the Christians of Malta, who, scarcely less Machiavellian than himself, try to deprive him of his wealth. He eventually betrays the island to the Turks, and proceeds to try to outwit them, but he falls victim to his own plot. In a famous essay on Marlowe (*Selected Essays*) ▷ T. S. Eliot described the play as an example of 'the farce of the old English humour, the terribly serious, even savage comic humour'; in his essay on ▷ Ben Jonson Eliot points to *The Jew of Malta* as the forebear of Jonson's Comedy of ▷ Humours.

Jews in England

The Jews first settled in England after the ▷ Norman Conquest and, as elsewhere, undertook the occupation of lending money on interest which in the earlier ▷ Middle Ages was forbidden to Christians. They were expelled from England by ▷ Edward I in 1290. Neither in the Middle Ages nor later was anti-semitism as strong in England as in some other countries, but the baseless myth that the Jews made ritual sacrifices of Christian boys is exemplified by the ▷ *Prioress's Tale* in ▷ Chaucer's ▷ *Canterbury Tales*. Between 1290 and 1655, when they were readmitted by ▷ Oliver Cromwell, a few Jews were admitted by special licence, and a number of rich Jews were living in London in the reign of ▷ Elizabeth I.

Jews returned to England after 1655 in fair numbers; by the end of the 18th century there were about 20,000 living in London. Anti-semitism was inconspicuous – this fact has been attributed to the assiduous Bible-reading of the English middle classes – but unless they renounced their religion they suffered restrictions on political rights and entry into certain professions (*eg* the Law) similar to those of other denominations outside the ▷ Church of England. These restrictions were not entirely removed until the middle of the 19th century, although by that time ▷ Benjamin Disraeli, a Jew who had been received into the Church of England, was already one of the country's leading statesmen. In 19th-century fiction Jews are commonly depicted in extremes of good or bad; as against the evil criminal Fagin of ▷ Charles Dickens's ▷ *Oliver Twist* there is his Riah of ▷ *Our Mutual Friend*, ▷ George Eliot's idealized Daniel

Deronda, the godlike Sidonia in Disraeli's
▷ *Coningsby* and Rebecca, the secondary
heroine of ▷ Walter Scott's ▷ *Ivanhoe*.
Some of ▷ Anthony Trollope's novels
portray a confirmed anti-semitism in
established society. In the 20th century,
Leopold Bloom in ▷ James Joyce's
▷ *Ulysses* is partly a representation of the
myth of the ▷ Wandering Jew.
   ▷ Zionism.

Jewsbury, Geraldine Endsor (1812–80)
Daughter of a merchant from Manchester,
Geraldine Jewsbury was born, the fourth of
six children, in Measham, Derbyshire. Her
elder sister, also a writer, cared for the family
until her marriage, when Geraldine took over,
caring for her father until his death in 1840
and her brothers till her marriage in 1853.
Her ill-health prevented her becoming a
journalist, but she contributed to and was a
reader for *Bentley's*, influencing the choice of
books in ▷ Mudie's Circulating Library:
novels were to have moral tone and nothing
'unpleasant'. An intimate friend of the
▷ Carlyles, Jewsbury was known for
brilliant wit and conversation, and the houses
in Manchester and London were visited by
many celebrities. She published articles in,
among other magazines, ▷ *The Athenaeum*
and the ▷ *Westminster Review*, and wrote
six novels, including *Zoe* (1845), *The Half
Sisters* (1848), *Marian Withers* (1851), *The
Sorrows of Gentility* (1856), and two stories
for children. *A Selection from the letters of
Geraldine Jewsbury to Jane Carlyle* was
published in 1892 (ed. Mrs A. Ireland).
▷ Virginia Woolf wrote an article about
this: 'Geraldine and Jane' (*TLS* 28 Feb.
1929). The women had wanted the letters
destroyed.
Bib: Howe, S., *Geraldine Jewsbury*.

Jezebel
In the ▷ Bible, the fierce and arrogant wife
of Ahab, king of Israel, and his accomplice in
opposing the worship of ▷ Jehovah. She
persecuted the prophets of Jehovah (*1 Kings*
18) and caused ▷ Naboth to be put to death
in order to obtain his vineyard for Ahab (*1
Kings* 21). Her equally fierce opponent was
the prophet ▷ Elijah; in fulfilment of his
curse, she was destroyed by Jehu (*2 Kings* 9).
Before encountering Jehu she is described as
adorning herself and painting her face; 'a
painted Jezebel' thus became a term for a
shameless woman.

Jhabvala, Ruth Prawar (b 1927)
Novelist, short-story writer, and writer of

Ruth Prawar Jhabvala

screenplays. She was born in Germany of
Polish parents who came to England as
refugees in the year of her birth. She studied
at London University and in 1951 married
the Indian architect C. S. H. Jhabvala. From
1951 to 1975 she lived in India, and since
then has lived in New York. Many of her
novels are based on her own ambiguous
position in India as a European with an
Indian family. They explore the tensions of
contemporary Indian society, such as the
conflict of ancient and modern ideas and the
interaction of westernized and non-
westernized Indians. They are based on witty
but sympathetic observation of social
manners, largely in domestic settings. Some
of the sharpest satire is reserved for the naive
and superficial enthusiasm of certain visiting
Europeans, who are frequently exploited by a
manipulative swami. *Heat and Dust* (1975)
employs a double narrative consisting of the
experiences of a contemporary English girl in
India, and the love affair of her grandfather's
first wife with an Indian prince in 1923. *In
Search of Love and Beauty* (1983) reflects
Jhabvala's change of home; it is a story of
German Jewish emigrés in 1930s New York.
Her other novels are: *To Whom She Will*
(1955); *The Nature of Passion* (1956); *Esmond
in India* (1958); *The Householder* (1960); *Get
Ready For Battle* (1962); *A Backward Place*
(1965); *A New Dominion* (1972); *Three
Continents* (1988). Story collections are: *Like
Birds, Like Fishes* (1963); *A Stronger Climate*
(1968); *An Experience of India* (1971); *How I
Became A Holy Mother* (1976). She has

written a number of screenplays, some of which are based on her own works, as part of a highly successful film-making team with James Ivory as director and Ismail Merchant as producer: *The Householder* (1963); *Shakespeare Wallah* (with Ivory; 1965); *The Europeans* (1979) (based on the novel by ▷ Henry James); *Quartet* (1981) (based on the novel by ▷ Jean Rhys); *Heat and Dust* (1983); *The Bostonians* (1984) (based on the ▷ Henry James novel); *A Room with a View* (1986) (based on the novel by ▷ E. M. Forster).

Jig

A country dance, with equivalents in many countries. In England at the end of the 16th century comic actors introduced the jig to the London theatre, where it was combined with singing and miming to make up a dramatic performance amounting to comic opera. Jigs were often performed at the ends of plays, particularly to lighten the effect of ▷ tragedies.

Joan of Arc (Jeanne d'Arc) (1412–31)

A French national heroine for the leading part she played in turning the ▷ Hundred Years' War finally against the English invaders of France.

Politically the position was that ▷ Henry v of England had succeeded by the Treaty of Troyes (1420) in getting his son recognized as the next king of France in succession to Charles VI (1380–1422). His son was in fact proclaimed king of France in 1422 in Paris, but the English controlled only the north and east of France, and the French were still fighting, although Charles VI's son, Charles the Dauphin, had no appetite for war. The English, in alliance with the Burgundians, continued to win victories.

In 1429 Joan, daughter of a French farmer, came forward declaring that heavenly voices had directed her to relieve the city of Orleans, besieged by the English, and to lead the Dauphin to Rheims to be crowned King Charles VII. She carried out both promises and attempted to relieve Paris, which was in English hands. She was, however, taken prisoner by the Burgundians, who delivered her to the English. She was by this time regarded as a heaven-sent inspiration to the French, and the English were determined to discredit her; accordingly they secured that she was condemned for heresy by a Church court, and then burnt alive in Rouen. The war continued to go against them, however, and by 1453 they were driven from France. In 1456 the condemnation of Joan for heresy was annulled by the Church, and in 1920 she was declared a ▷ saint.

For some time the English continued to remember her as a witch, and she is so represented in the early play by Shakespeare, ▷ *Henry VI, Part I*, where she appears under her French nickname of 'La Pucelle' – the Maid. By far the most striking representation of her career in English is the play *Saint Joan* (1924) by ▷ George Bernard Shaw.

Job

In the ▷ Bible, the central character of a book of the same name in the Old Testament. Much of the book consists of dialogues with his friends, who declare that his misfortunes must be the consequence of his sins; hence the expression 'Job's comforters'. Job, however, continues to affirm his innocence. Finally God speaks out of a whirlwind, justifies Job, and restores his fortune.

John

King of England, 1109–1216. His reign was particularly disturbed; he succeeded in raising against him both his own nobles and the Church, as well as losing his father's French possessions. In 1215 the alliance of nobles and Church successfully imposed on him the ▷ Magna Carta by which he agreed not to infringe the rights of the Church or of his subjects.

His quarrel with the Church caused him to be regarded favourably in the 16th century when the Tudors were occupied in reducing the Church from a supranational into a national institution; thus he is idealized in the play *King John* (1547) by Bishop Bale. In Shakespeare's play ▷ *King John*, his crime is the death of his nephew Arthur, and sympathy is still with him against the Church; there is no mention of Magna Carta. It was in the 17th-century quarrels between the kings and parliaments that this document became important, as seeming to justify parliamentary resistance to the Crown.

John Bull

A personification of England, dating from a political allegory *The History of John Bull* (1712) by John Arbuthnot. The character is there described as honest but quarrelsome, his temper depending on the weather; he understands business and is fond of drinking and the society of his friends. He is intended to represent the national character.

John of Gaunt, Duke of Lancaster

Fourth son of ▷ Edward III. He derived the name 'Gaunt' from his birthplace, the town of Ghent in Flanders. By marrying the only daughter of the Duke of Lancaster he inherited the title and became the most

powerful lord in England. He is chiefly remembered; 1 as the ancestor of the Lancastrian line of kings, beginning with his son ▷ Henry IV; 2 as the protector of the religious reformer ▷ John Wycliffe; 3 as the patron of the poet ▷ Geoffrey Chaucer, whose wife's sister he married; 4 for the representation of him by Shakespeare in ▷ *Richard II*.
▷ Lancaster, House of.

Johnson, B. S. (1933–73)
Novelist, poet and dramatist. His novels were highly experimental, taking as their main subject his own life as a novelist and the nature of the novel. He employed a whole range of ▷ post-modernist narrative devices for questioning the boundaries of fact and fiction. He claimed to write, not fiction, but 'truth in the form of a novel'. *Travelling People* (1963) uses a different viewpoint or narrative mode for each chapter, including a film scenario, letters and typographical effects. In *Alberto Angelo* (1964) the 'author' breaks into the narrative to discuss his own techniques, aims and sources. *The Unfortunates* (1969) is a loose-leaf novel of 27 sections, 25 of which can be read in any order. Johnson committed suicide at the age of 40, soon after completing *See the Old Lady Decently* (1975), which is based around the death of his mother in 1971, and incorporates family documents and photographs. His other novels are: *Trawl* (1966); *House Mother Normal* (1971); *Christie Malry's Own Double Entry* (1973). He also wrote plays, screenplays, T.V. scripts and several collections of poems.

Johnson, Linton Kwesi (b 1952)
Poet and recording artist. Johnson was born in Jamaica and has lived in Britain since 1961; he read sociology at London University and is now a Fellow at Warwick University. The most famous of the young Anglo-Jamaican poets to emerge since the mid 1970s (others include Benjamin Zephaniah and the older ▷ James Berry), influenced by reggae, dub and Rastafarian rhythms, his live performances and recordings with Virgin records have done much to open other forms of contemporary British poetry to a wide young audience. His three volumes of poetry have been extremely popular: *Voice of the Living and the Dead* (1974); *Dead Beat An' Blood* (1975); *Inglan is a Bitch* (1980).
▷ Commonwealth literature.

Johnson, Pamela Hansford (1912–81)
Novelist. Perhaps her best-known work is the trilogy composed of *Too Dear for my*

Possessing (1940), *An Avenue of Stone* (1947) and *A Summer to Decide* (1949). These extend from the late 1920s to the late 1940s, and combine observation of events and society with the study of intricate relationships arising from the attractions for each other of unlike characters. The formal quality reflects the influence of ▷ Marcel Proust, on whom Pamela Hansford Johnson composed a series of radio programmes, *Six Proust Reconstructions* (1958). Some of her later novels were more comic and satirical (*eg, Who is Here?*, 1962 *Night and Silence*, 1963; *Cork Street*, 1965 and *Next to the Hatter's*, 1965) but *An Error of Judgement* (1962) concerns the problem of apparently motiveless evil in modern society, and relates to her non-fictional investigation of the Moors Murder case which raises the problem of dangerous assumptions in our so-called 'permissive society': *On Iniquity* (1961). Pamela Hansford Johnson was married to the novelist ▷ C. P. Snow. Her other novels are: *The Survival of the Fittest* (1968); *The Honours Board* (1970); *The Holiday Friend* (1972); *The Good Listener* (1975); *The Good Husband* (1978); *A Bonfire* (1981).
Bib: Allen, W., in *Tradition and Dream*; Burgess, A., *The Novel Now*.

Johnson, Samuel (1709–84)

Samuel Johnson by J. Barry

Critic, poet, lexicographer, essayist. Born at Lichfield to elderly parents, Johnson's childhood was marred by ill health; a tubercular infection from his wetnurse affected both his sight and hearing, and his face was scarred by scrofula or the 'King's Evil'. He was educated at Lichfield Grammar School, and in 1728 went up to Pembroke College, Oxford; his studies at the university were, however, cut short by poverty, and in 1729 he returned to Lichfield, affected by melancholy depression.

After a brief period as a schoolmaster at Market Bosworth, Johnson moved to Birmingham, where he contributed articles (now lost) to the *Birmingham Journal*. In 1735 he married Elizabeth Porter a widow greatly his senior, and using her money attempted to start a school at Edial, near his home town. The school quickly failed, and in 1737 Johnson set off to London accompanied by one of his pupils, the actor ▷ David Garrick. Lack of a university degree hindered him from pursuing a profession, and he determined to make a living by writing.

Edward Cave, the founder of *The Gentleman's Magazine*, allowed him to contribute articles, and for many years Johnson lived by hack writing. His *Parliamentary Debates* were published in this magazine, and were widely believed to be authentic. In 1738 the publication of his poem, *London*, revealed his literary abilities. But the project of compiling the ▷ *Dictionary of the English Language* which was to occupy the next nine years testifies to Johnson's concern to produce saleable material. Lacking a patron, he approached ▷ Lord Chesterfield with the plan; the resulting snub is a notorious episode in the decline of the patronage system. In 1749, the poem ▷ *The Vanity of Human Wishes* was published, and his play *Irene* staged by Garrick. In 1750 he began the twice-weekly periodical ▷ *The Rambler*, to add to his income but also as a relief from the *Dictionary* work.

The death of his wife in 1752 returned Johnson to the melancholy depression he had suffered after leaving Oxford. However, he continued to contribute to periodicals, and in 1755 the *Dictionary* was published, bringing him wide acclaim which also included, by the intervention of friends, an honorary degree from Oxford. From 1758–60 he wrote the ▷ *Idler* essays for the *Universal Chronicle*, and in 1759 ▷ *Rasselas* was published. In 1762 a crown pension relieved some of the financial pressure, and the following year he met ▷ James Boswell, who was to become his biographer.

In 1765 Johnson's spirits were much lifted as he made the acquaintance of the ▷ Thrales, and over the next few years he spent much time at their home in Streatham. In the same year, his edition of Shakespeare, for which he wrote a famous Preface, appeared.

Johnson's desire to travel was partly fulfilled by journeys made in his later years. In 1773 he and Boswell made their ▷ *Journey to the Western Islands of Scotland* (1775), and in 1774 Johnson went to Wales with the Thrale family. The following year he accompanied the Thrales to Paris, his only visit to the Continent.

In 1777 Johnson began work on ▷ *The Lives of the Poets* (1779–81), at the request of booksellers. In 1784, estranged from his friend Mrs Thrale by her remarriage, he died in his home in Bolt Court. He is buried in Westminster Abbey.

Bib: Boswell, J. (ed. Hill, G. B.; revised Powell, L. F.), *The Life of Samuel Johnson*; Bate, W. J., *Samuel Johnson*; Hardy, J. P., *Samuel Johnson: A Critical Study*.

Johnson, The Life of Samuel (1791)
▷ Boswell.

Johnson's Dictionary
▷ *Dictionary of the English Language, A.*

Jonah
In the Old Testament of the ▷ Bible, a Jewish prophet and hero of the narrative in the book of *Jonah*. Jonah is ordered by God to go and preach to the wicked city of Nineveh. He tries to evade the order by taking ship to Tarshish; on the way a storm arises, and to appease God's wrath he asks to be thrown into the sea, where he is swallowed by a whale. Three days later, the whale vomits him safely on to dry land, and Jonah proceeds to Nineveh to obey God's will.
▷ *Patience.*

Jonathan Wild the Great, The Life of (1743)
A satirical romance by ▷ Henry Fielding. His purpose was to ridicule 'greatness' by telling the story of a 'great' criminal in apparently admiring terms. The subject makes clear that the admiration is ironical, but the reader is reminded that eminent statesmen and other 'respectable' men of power – all those, in fact, who are normally regarded as great – commonly pursue their aims with as little scruple. Wild was a historical character who had been executed in 1725, and made the subject of a narrative by ▷ Defoe.

In Fielding's fictional satire, Wild begins his career by being baptized by ▷ Titus Oates – also a criminal character – and takes to a career of crime in childhood. He becomes the leader of a gang of thieves, among whom

St Paul's Church, Covent Garden by Inigo Jones

he keeps discipline by threatening them with denunciation, while himself avoiding incrimination. The vilest of his crimes is the systematic ruin of his former schoolfriend, the jeweller Heartfree, whom he nearly succeeds in having executed. In the end it is Wild who is executed, but he is sent to his death with the same mock-heroic impressiveness as has characterized Fielding's treatment of him throughout.
▷ Picaresque.

Jones, David Michael (1895–1974)
Poet and artist. His paintings, engravings and woodcuts are probably now better known than his writing, with the exception of *In Parenthesis* (1937), an account of his experiences in World War I that combines verse and prose. See also *The Anathemata* (1952), Jones's most important work, and *Epoch and Artist* (selected writings), (1959).

Jones, Henry Arthur (1851–1929)
Dramatist. He wrote some 60 plays, and is notable for beginning an English dramatic revival in the later years of the 19th century along with ▷ T. W. Robertson, ▷ Arthur Pinero and ▷ Shaw. For instance *Saints and Sinners* (1884) was not only a dramatic success, but aroused controversy by discussing religious issues in a study of middle class provincial life. Other plays of comparable note: *The Middleman* (1889) and *Judah* (1890). His lectures and essays on drama were collected in *The Renascence of the English Drama* (1895).
Bib: Jones, A. D., *Life*; Archer, W., *The Old Drama and the New*; Cordell, R. A., *Henry Arthur Jones and the Modern Drama*.

Jones, Inigo (1573–1651)
Architect and stage designer. He is sometimes called 'the English ▷ Palladio' because he was strongly influenced by the Italian architect of that name, and he was in fact the first important classical (Palladian) architect in English architecture. Outstanding buildings of his design include the Banqueting Hall in Whitehall and St Paul's church in Covent Garden, both in ▷ London. He also designed sets for ▷ masques, to which words were contributed by ▷ Ben Jonson, ▷ Samuel Daniel and other poets among his contemporaries. Scenery and music were as important in the masque as was poetry, and the fusion led to bitter rivalry between Jones and Jonson, who satirized him as In-and-In Medlay in ▷ *The Tale of a Tub*.

Jonson, Benjamin (1572–1637)
Dramatist and poet; always known as Ben Jonson. In drama, he was ▷ Shakespeare's most distinguished rival, but they differed greatly in gifts and achievement. 16 of his plays, not including ▷ masques, have survived; 14 comedies and two tragedies. Their merits vary greatly: his universally acknowledged masterpieces are the comedies ▷ *Volpone* (1605 or 1606) and ▷ *The Alchemist* (1610), to which some distinguished critics add the satirical tragedy ▷ *Sejanus* (1603). In the second rank of importance, the following are usually included: ▷ *The Devil is an Ass* (1616), of great satirical power but less dramatic concentration: ▷ *Epicoene, or The Silent Woman* (1609) and ▷ *Bartholomew Fair* (1614), slighter in content but vigorous entertainments; and ▷ *Every Man in his Humour* (1598), the first of the comedies of ▷ humours with which his name is identified. Although all of Jonson's work

Title page of Ben Jonson's *Works*, 1616

contains passages of interest, his remaining plays have faults (such as excessive academicism, diffuseness of treatment, or narrowness of satirical range) which usually restrict their interest to scholars. They are: ▷ *Every Man out of his Humour* (1599), *Cynthia's Revels* (1600); *The Poetaster* (1601); ▷ *Catiline* (a tragedy, 1611); *The Staple of News* (1625); ▷ *The New Inn* (1629), *The Magnetic Lady* (1632); ▷ *The Tale of a Tub* (1633); *The Case is Altered* (an early work, before he had discovered his characteristic comic medium, 1597). He left unfinished a ▷ pastoral drama *The Sad Shepherd*.

Jonson was both very much a man of his age and a strong traditionalist. Society was undergoing radical changes; the unsettlement of accustomed moral values gave scope to extravagance and folly. He himself was a man of strong appetites and vitality, but he understood and deeply cared for the restraining and directing qualities of civilization. His conception of civilization derived partly from his typically ▷ Renaissance admiration for ancient Roman culture, which he thoroughly assimilated through ▷ Latin literature, and partly from the traditional virtues of English society, which economic and religious changes

were challenging. He was thus a moral satirist, who delighted in animal vitality and human aspiration but made it his business to chasten the ▷ 'humours' (or, as we might say, 'manias') to which society was liable when it escaped the control of civilized discipline and reason. This made him a self-conscious artist in matters of literary form, and his plays, his prose miscellany (*Timber: or Discoveries made upon Men and Matter*, published 1640), and his conversations reported by the Scottish poet ▷ Drummond, contain much critical comment on the virtues of poetic and dramatic discipline – often at the expense of his contemporaries including Shakespeare. At the same time he was a highly independent writer who showed no disposition to subject his work to the restriction of a code of rules.

In his non-dramatic poetry, Jonson produced a body of fine poetry which influenced the form of later lyric verse. His poems have neither the emotional extravagance of the idealizing love poets of the age, nor the rough texture of a realist like ▷ Donne; they combine the grace of manner of the former with the masculine strength of the latter, and fuse a vitality which is personal to Jonson with an intellectual control which he learnt from Latin poets such as ▷ Catullus. ▷ Andrew Marvell was to learn from Jonson an incisiveness to temper the imaginative ingeniousness he learnt from Donne, and the school of ▷ Cavalier Poets of the reign of ▷ Charles I got from him much of their grace and poise.

Jonson had considerable importance as a personality who exercised influence by his talk. He was not born into the aristocratic circles of a poet like ▷ Philip Sidney, and his proud and independent attitude to his noble patrons helped to enhance respect for the independence of the literary profession. His meetings and discussions with other poets at the ▷ Mermaid Tavern were commemorated by ▷ Francis Beaumont in *Francis Beaumont to Ben Jonson* and much later by ▷ John Keats in *Lines on the Mermaid Tavern* (1818) and in his old age he had a school of disciples who called themselves 'the sons of Ben'. They included such poets as ▷ Thomas Carew and ▷ Robert Herrick.

Bib: Knights, L. C., *Drama and Society in the Age of Jonson*; Eliot, T. S., in *Selected Essays*; Barish, J. A., on Jonson's dramatic prose and (ed) critical essays; Partridge, E. B., *The Broken Compass: A Study of the Major Comedies*; Barton, A., *Ben Jonson, Dramatist*; Duncan, D., *Ben Jonson and the Lucianic Tradition*; Leggatt, A., *Ben Jonson:*

His Vision and His Art; Orgel, S., *The Jonsonian Masque*.

Joseph

1 The husband of Mary the mother of Jesus, and betrothed to her at the time of the birth. 2 In the Old Testament of the Bible, the son of Jacob and Rachel, and one of the principal ancestors of the twelve tribes which were later to make up the kingdoms of Israel and Judaea. His story is told in *Genesis* 37–50.

Joseph, Jenny (b 1932)

Poet and prose writer. Joseph has been writing since 1961 (her first publication was *The Unlooked-for Season*, a volume of poetry). In 1974 she won the Cholmondely award for *Rose in the Afternoon*. Other volumes include: *The Thinking Heart* (1978) and *Beyond Descartes* (1983). She also writes for children.

Joseph Andrews (1742)

A novel by ▷ Henry Fielding. It was begun as a parody of ▷ Samuel Richardson's novel ▷ *Pamela*. In Richardson's novel the heroine, Pamela Andrews, is a chaste servant girl who resists seduction by her master, Mr B, and eventually forces him to accept her in marriage. Fielding ridicules Richardson by opening his novel with an account of the resistance by Pamela's brother Joseph to seduction by his employer, the aunt of Mr B, whose name Fielding maliciously extends to Booby (= clumsy fool). Joseph is dismissed for his obstinate virtue, and sets out in search of his own sweetheart. On the journey he is befriended by his old acquaintance, a clergyman, Parson Adams. At this point Fielding seems to have changed the plan of his novel; Adams, instead of Joseph, becomes the central character on whom all the interest centres. With the change, the novel becomes something like an English ▷ *Don Quixote*, since Adams is a learned but simple-hearted, single-minded Christian whose trust in the goodness of human nature leads him into constant embarrassments.

Joseph of Arimathaea

In the New Testament, according to all four of the Gospels, the rich Jew who provided a tomb for Jesus Christ after the Crucifixion. According to a medieval English tradition (found in the works of William Malmesbury, 12th century, but possibly inserted by someone else) he later came to Britain to preach Christianity, founded ▷ Glastonbury Abbey, and was buried there; his planted staff became the miraculous 'Glastonbury thorn' which flowered at Christmas. Later Arthurian legend attributes to him the ▷ Holy Grail (in earlier legend a pagan symbol) as a vessel in which he caught the blood of Christ at the Crucifixion.
▷ Arthur, King.

Josipovici, Gabriel (b 1940)

Novelist, short-story writer and critic. Born in France, educated in Cairo, Cheltenham and at Oxford University, Josipovici is a lecturer and (since 1984) Professor of English at the University of Sussex. His novels are ambiguous and experimental works of ▷ post-modernist fiction, conveying a sense of fragmentation and uncertainty. *The Inventory* (1968), *Words* (1971) and *The Echo Chamber* (1980) are almost entirely in dialogue; *The Present* (1975) uses a present tense narration and interweaves a number of stories: *Migrations* (1977) and *The Air We Breathe* (1981) are structured by the repetition of scenes and images. His other novels are: *Conversations in Another Room* (1984); *Contre-Jour* (1986); *In the Fertile Land* (1987). Story collections are: *Mobius the Stripper: Stories and Short Plays* (1974); *Four Stories* (1977). Plays include: *Evidence of Intimacy* (1972); *Echo* (1975); *Marathon* (1977); *A Moment* (1979); *Vergil Dying* (broadcast 1979). Criticism includes: *The Lessons of Modernism and Other Essays* (1977); *Writing and the Body* (1982); *The Book of God: An Essay on the Bible* (1988).

Journal of a Tour to the Hebrides, The (1785)

▷ James Boswell's account of the tour to the Hebrides which he made with ▷ Samuel Johnson in 1773 (cf. ▷ *A Journey to the Western Islands of Scotland*). The tour gave Boswell the opportunity to encourage Johnson's consideration of many topics, and the narrative, which he showed to Johnson, records Johnson's opinions and perorations on many matters. Boswell was partly motivated in undertaking the tour by the desire to show Johnson his homeland, but he also saw it as a good occasion to collect material for his ▷ *Life of Samuel Johnson*.

Journal of the Plague Year, The (1722)

Written by ▷ Daniel Defoe, the *Journal* purports to be the record of 'H.F.', a survivor of the plague in London of 1664–5. The initials have suggested to critics that Defoe's uncle, Henry Foe, may have provided some of the first-hand information.

The narrative tells of the spread of the plague, the suffering of the Londoners, and the attempts by the authorities to control the disease. Defoe incorporates statistical data, some of which is taken from official sources, to demonstrate the extent of the plague and its effects on the life of the capital. The 'factual' nature of the statistics stands in grim juxtaposition to the vivid recreation of death and disease, the inhabitants imprisoned in their own homes by danger and terror, and the mass burial sites and death-carts which became a familiar part of everyday existence.

Journalism

The distinction between journalism and literature is not always clear, and before the rise of the modern newspaper with its mass circulation in the second half of the 19th century, the two forms of writing were even more difficult to distinguish than they are today. The most superficial but also the most observable difference has always been that journalism puts immediacy of interest before permanency of interest, and easy readability before considered qualities of style. But of course what is written for the attention of the hour may prove to be of permanent value; a good example is ▷ William Cobbett's ▷ *Rural Rides* in his weekly *Political Register* in the early 19th century.

The ▷ 'pamphlets' of writers such as ▷ Thomas Nashe and ▷ Thomas Dekker in the 1590s, and those on the controversial religious matters of the day such as the Marprelate pamphlets, are no doubt the earliest work with the stamp of journalism in English. However, the profession began to take shape with the wider reading public and the regular periodicals of the early 18th century. In that period we can see that it was the attitude to writing that made the difference – at least on the surface – between the journalist and the serious man of letters. ▷ Addison considered himself a serious man of letters, whereas ▷ Defoe, writing incessantly on matters of practical interest without concerning himself with subtleties and elegance of style, is more our idea of a journalist. The 18th century was inclined to disparage such writing as ▷ Grub Street, though this term included all kinds of inferior, merely imitative 'literature', that we would not accept as journalism. The trade of journalism taught Defoe the realism that went into his fiction. A good example of the combination of facts and fiction is his ▷ *A Journal of the Plague Year* (1722) which is both a fine example of journalistic reporting (from other people's accounts) and a fine achievement in imaginative realism.

Defoe in the 18th century and Cobbett in the 19th century both assumed that the main function of their writing was to *enlighten* their readers. In the 1890s, however, the 'popular press' arose in which the desire to entertain was as strong as the desire to inform, and

profitability was a major concern. The distinction between the popular and serious press is still current. There has been a strong division in the 1980s especially between newspapers such as *The Times* and *The Guardian* and the tabloid press papers such as *The Sun* and *The Mirror*.

▷ Newspapers; Reviews and Periodicals.

Journey to the Western Islands of Scotland, A (1775)

▷ Samuel Johnson's account of the tour which he and ▷ James Boswell made in 1773 (cf. ▷ *Journal of a Tour to the Hebrides*). The tour gave rise to Johnson's meditations on the life, culture and history of the Scottish people, as well as on the Scottish landscape. Its publication aroused the wrath of Macpherson, whose work *Ossian* (or ▷ *Oisin*) Johnson rightly regarded as inauthentic.

Journeyman

A trained craftsman, originally one who worked by the day (French: *journée*). In the Middle Ages, a journeyman worked under a master who owned the business, and who also employed apprentices, *ie* craftsmen undergoing training. In the 13th century, master, apprentices and journeymen were socially equal and all members of the craft guild; by the later 14th century the richer masters were drawing away from the journeymen, most of whom, in the richer guilds, could no longer hope to become masters. A social cleavage thus developed between the class of masters and the class of journeymen, and this grew sharper as modern ▷ capitalism developed (especially in the clothing industry) during the 15th and 16th centuries.

▷ Apprenticeship; Craft Guilds; Master Craftsman.

Jove

▷ Zeus.

Joyce, James (1882–1941)

Novelist. He was Irish, and born at a time when Irish ▷ nationalism was moving into its fiercest, most desperate phase. Joyce was born into a Catholic family, was educated by the ▷ Jesuits, and seemed destined for the Catholic priesthood, yet he turned away from the priesthood, renounced Catholicism, and in 1904 left ▷ Ireland to live and work abroad for the rest of his life. But although he took no part in the movement for Irish liberation, he did not renounce Ireland; the setting for all his fiction is the capital city (and his home town) of Dublin. This and his own family relationships were always his centres, and from them he drew increasingly

James Joyce by J. E. Blanche (1935)

ambitious imaginative conceptions which eventually extended to the whole history of European culture.

His first important work was a volume of stories, ▷ *Dubliners*, published after long delay in 1914. The collection has artistic unity given to it by Joyce's intention 'to write a chapter of the moral history of my country . . . under four of its aspects: childhood, adolescence, maturity and public life'. The method combines an apparent objective realism with a subtle use of the symbolic and the mimesis of Dublin speech idiom and is based on Joyce's idea of 'epiphanies' – experiences, often apparently trivial, presenting to the observer deep and true insights. His first novel, ▷ *A Portrait of the Artist as a Young Man* (1916), is largely autobiographical and describes how, abandoning his religion and leaving his country, he discovered his artistic vocation. Its original method of narration causes the reader to share the hero's experience by having it presented to him with a verbal equipment which grows with the hero's development, from infancy to young manhood.

The next novel, ▷ *Ulysses* (1922), is still more original in the use of language. Its subject is apparently small – a single day in the life of three Dubliners – but Joyce's treatment of it makes it vast. The characters are made to correspond to the three main characters of ▷ Homer's ▷ *Odyssey*, and the 18 episodes are parallels to the episodes in that epic. The past is thus made to reflect forward on to the present, and the present back on to the past, revealing both with comic irony and endowing the apparently trivial present with tragic depth. In this book, modern man in the modern city is presented with unprecedented thoroughness and candour.

In his last book, ▷ *Finnegans Wake* (1939), Joyce attempts an image of modern 'Everyman' with all the forces of his experience released – in other words it concerns one night of a character who, because he never fully wakes up, is not restricted by the inhibitions of normal daylight consciousness. To express this night consciousness Joyce uses a special dream language by which words are fused together to give instantaneous multiple allusiveness; the same technique had been used by the mid-19th-century children's writer ▷ Lewis Carroll in the poem called 'Jabberwocky' (*Through the Looking-Glass*; 1872). However, because Joyce wishes to use the public-house keeper who is his hero as the representative of modern European man, he often fuses English words with those of other European languages, thus increasing the difficulty for the reader. Critics have pointed out that in *Finnegans Wake* the dream comes mainly through the ear; Joyce, like ▷ Milton with whose mastery of language his own has been compared, had poor sight, and his imagination worked especially through the sense of hearing.

He published three volumes of poetry, which show his sense of poignant verbal beauty: *Chamber Music* (1907); *Gas from a Burner* (1912); *Pomes Penyeach* (1927). His *Collected Poems* appeared in 1936. His single play, *Exiles* (1918) is interesting chiefly for showing his admiration for the Norwegian dramatist, ▷ Ibsen. An early version of his *Portrait of the Artist* was published in 1944 (enlarged 1955) as *Stephen Hero*.

▷ Catholicism in English literature; Irish literature in English.
Bib: Ellmann, R., *James Joyce* (biography), *Ulysses on the Liffey* and *The Consciousness of Joyce*; Burgess, A., *Joysprick*; Peake, C. H., *James Joyce: the Citizen and the Artist*; Kenner, H., *Joyce's Voices* and *Ulysses*; Tindall, W. Y., *A Reader's Guide to Finnegans Wake*; Joyce, S., *My Brother's Keeper*; Levin, H., *Joyce: a Critical Introduction*; Budgen, F., *James Joyce and the Making of Ulysses*; Gilbert, S., *James Joyce's Ulysses: a Study*; Denning, R. H. (ed.), *Joyce: The Critical Heritage*.

Judas Iscariot
The disciple of Jesus who betrayed him to
the Jewish authorities (*Matthew* 26) for thirty
pieces of silver. He later repented, returned
the money, and hanged himself (*Matthew* 27).

Jude the Obscure (1895)
The last novel by ▷ Thomas Hardy. In
Hardy's words the theme is the 'deadly war
. . . between flesh and spirit' and 'the contrast
between the ideal life a man wished to lead
and the squalid real life he was fated to lead'.
Jude Fawley is a village mason (like Hardy's
father) who has intellectual aspirations. He is
seduced into marriage by Arabella Donn;
when she abandons him, he turns back to
learning, but falls in love with Sue Bridehead,
whose contradictory nature seeks freedom
and yet frustrates her own desire. She runs
away from her schoolmaster husband,
Phillotson, who disgusts her, and joins with
Jude in an illicit union. Their children die at
the hands of Jude's only child by Arabella,
who takes his own and their lives because he
believes that he and they had no right to be
born. Sue returns in remorse to Phillotson,
while Jude is beguiled back by Arabella, who
deserts him on his deathbed.

The setting and the four main characters
are so representative that the novel is almost
an allegory. Jude's native place is Marygreen,
a run-down village which is a kind of emblem
of decayed rural England. His ambition is to
enter the university of Christminster, which
is ▷ Oxford, but so named as a reminder by
Hardy that the way of learning had once also
been a goal of the spirit. Jude uproots himself
from Marygreen but is unable to enter the
university because of his social origins, though
he lives in the town (where he meets Sue)
and works there as a mason. Hardy's point is
not so much the social one that the old
universities of Oxford and Cambridge were
all but closed to working-men; he is more
concerned to show that the decay of spiritual
goals in the England of his day matches the
decay of the countryside. Jude himself is a
complete man – physically virile as well as
spiritually aspiring; it is his very completeness
which the modern world, both Marygreen
and Christchurch, is unable to accept. Sue
Bridehead represents the 'new woman' of the
day, emancipated in her own theory but not
in body. Sue is all mind; Arabella all body,
and Phillotson a kind of walking death – a
man of the best intentions who is nonetheless
helplessly destructive in consequence of his
lack of both physical and spiritual vitality.
The novel epitomizes Hardy's longing for
spiritual values and his despair of them; its

pessimism has strong poetic quality, and after
completing it he gave himself entirely to
poetry. Like many of Hardy's novels, *Jude
the Obscure* is set in the recent past – about
20 years before the time of writing.
Publication of the book caused an uproar;
after its hostile reception Hardy wrote no
further novels.

Julian of Norwich (c 1343–after 1416)
English mystic and recluse whose name
derives from the church of St Julian of
Norwich, to which her cell was attached. Her
work, the *Revelations of Divine Love*,
describing her 16 visionary experiences, is
extant in two versions. The short version was
written first, perhaps not long after her
visionary experience; the longer text was
composed after some 20 years of meditation
and reflection on her visions. Little is known
about her life apart from the few details
which appear in the *Revelations*. Her visions
came, in answer to her prayer, not long after
she was 30. By the time ▷ Margery Kempe
visited her (around 1413–15), Julian was
established as a spiritual authority, and
although she refers to herself as an unlearned
woman (perhaps a reference to a lack of skills
in Latin, rather than a lack of literate skills),
Julian's work reveals a detailed knowledge of
a wide range of scriptural and mystical texts
and traditions. Her exploration of the notion
of Jesus as Mother has attracted much
interest, and her formulation of God's
assurance to her that 'all shall be well . . . all
manner of things shall be well' is one of the
more famous passages of her work.
Bib: Petroff, E. A. (ed.), *Medieval Women's
Visionary Literature*; Wolters, C. (trans.),
Revelations of Divine Love.

Julius Caesar (c1599)
A historical tragedy by ▷ Shakespeare based
on the events of 44 BC, when Caesar was
assassinated on suspicion of seeking to
overthrow the Roman republic and make
himself king. The conspiracy against him is
led by Brutus, descendant of the Brutus who,
according to legend, had first established the
republic by throwing out the Tarquin line of
kings in the 6th century. Brutus is a friend of
Caesar, and his motive in organizing Caesar's
assassination is his disinterested love of Rome;
his chief associate, Cassius, on the other
hand, is motivated by personal envy and
resentment. The third outstanding character
in the drama is Caesar's friend Mark Antony,
who, after the assassination, treacherously but
most successfully turns the Roman mob
against Brutus and Cassius and drives them
out of Rome. Acts IV and V show the defeat

of Brutus and Cassius at the battle of Philippi
(42 BC). Caesar himself plays a comparatively
small part although he is, alive and dead, the
centre of the drama. The dramatic interest
arises from the interplay between the
characters of Brutus, Cassius and Antony,
and from the conflicts in the mind of Brutus
who, as a good man, finds himself in the
tragic dilemma of having to commit a horrible
crime against a man he loves for the sake of
the nation. Shakespeare based the events,
with some interesting alterations, on
▷ Plutarch whose *Lives* had been translated
into English by ▷ Thomas North (1579).
The play dates from about 1599.
    ▷ Caesar, Gaius Julius.

Jung, Carl (1875–1961)

Swiss psychiatrist. He was part of the group
surrounding ▷ Sigmund Freud between
1907 and 1913, but because of disagreements
with Freud, he left to form his own school of
'Analytical Psychology'. Jung attributed less
importance to the sexual, and saw the
unconscious as containing, not only repressed
material, but also undeveloped aspects of the
personality, which he divided into thinking,
feeling, sensuous and intuitive aspects. The
personal unconscious he held to be the reverse
of the persona, or outer self, and to perform a
compensatory function. Furthermore, beneath
the personal unconscious lay the racial and
collective unconscious, the repository of the
beliefs and myths of civilizations, which at
the deepest level were all united. Jung termed
the themes and symbols which emerged from
this collective unconscious, archetypes, and
Jungian therapy uses dream interpretation to
connect the patient with the healing power of
these archetypes. Jung saw the libido as a
non-sexual life force, and neuroses as
imbalances in the personality. He made a
comparative study of the myths, religions and
philosophies of many cultures, and his
thought has a religious and mystical tenor.
He is also the originator of the terms
'introvert', 'extrovert' and 'complex'.

    His influence on 20th-century literature
results particularly from the importance he
gave to myths and symbols as universal and
creative modes of understanding. The
creation, or reworking, of myths is a feature
of the work of writers such as ▷ James
Joyce (in ▷ *Ulysses*, about which Jung
wrote an essay; 'Ulysses: A Monologue',
1932), ▷ T. S. Eliot, ▷ David Jones,
▷ Ted Hughes and ▷ Geoffrey Hill.
    ▷ Psychoanalytical criticism.
Bib: Jacobi, J., *The Psychology of C. G.
Jung.*

Junius

The pen-name of a political polemicist who
published celebrated letters attacking the
government of the day in the London
newspaper *Public Advertiser*, 1769–72. The
letters were fiercely satirical against the
ministers of George III, and were notable for
their unusual eloquence. The name 'Junius'
was chosen from Lucius Junius Brutus, who,
in legend, overthrew the Tarquin kings of
Rome in the 6th century BC. Their style
shows the influence of ▷ Swift and of the
Latin historian ▷ Tacitus. The real author
has long been a mystery, but is now generally
considered to have been Sir Philip Francis
(1740–1818), a politician of the ▷ Whig
party who supported the rights and privileges
of Parliament against what they considered to
be dangerous encroachments by the king and
his supporters.

Juno
    ▷ Hera.

Jupiter
    ▷ Zeus.

Jury system

A body of citizens without legal training who
are summoned before a court of law and
given the task, under the guidance of a judge,
of ascertaining the facts of a case. If the case
before the court concerns a crime, the most
important fact for them to ascertain is whether
the accused is guilty or not guilty. Hence it is
the jury, not the judge, that tries the accused
('trial by jury') and its decision is called ' the
verdict', in accordance with which the judge
has to release the prisoner or decide the
penalty appropriate to his offence.

    The system originated in the 12th century
and reached its present form by the 15th. It
was often a defence against tyranny, although
juries can be prejudiced (*eg* the jury in the
town of Vanity Fair, in Bunyan's ▷ *Pilgrim's
Progress*) or 'packed', *ie* deliberately made
up from enemies of the accused man; or they
can be intimidated.

    Juries trying criminal or civil cases were
technically called Petty Juries; Grand Juries
(no longer in use) had the function of
presenting men suspected of crime before the
royal judges on their visits to the region.
Small crimes have never been tried by juries
but (since the early 14th century) by Justices
of the Peace (Magistrates).
    ▷ Courts of Law; Magistrates.

Justices of the Peace
    ▷ Magistrates.

Justinian I (AD 527–65)

Emperor of the Byzantine (Eastern Roman)
Empire whose capital was ▷ Constantinople.
He arranged the codification of Roman law,
which became the basis of law all over
Europe, including Scotland but not England.

Jutes

The earliest of the three Germanic tribes to
invade Britain after the downfall of the
Roman Empire. They were summoned by the
Britons in the 5th century (according to
tradition) to help them resist the Pictish
invasions from the north. Their leaders are
said to have been ▷ Hengist and Horsa.
They established themselves permanently in
Kent in the south-east, and in Hampshire
and the Isle of Wight in the south. The other
two invading tribes were the ▷ Angles and
the ▷ Saxons.

Juvenal (Decimus Junius Juvenalis) (AD?60–?130)

Roman satirical poet. His sixteen satires
describe the society of his time and denounce
its vices. ▷ Satire, as a literary form, is
usually regarded as being a Roman invention,
but Juvenal was the first of the Romans to
associate it altogether with denunciation; his
predecessor, ▷ Horace, had used it for
ironic comment and discussion but was only
intermittently denunciatory with the moral
conviction associated with Juvenal. Like
Horace, Juvenal had a strong influence on
English poetry from 1590 until 1800; during
these two centuries satire was increasingly
practised, and Horace, Juvenal, or Horace's
disciple ▷ Perseus were taken as models.
Both ▷ Thomas Nashe and John Oldham
(1653–83) have been described as 'the English
Juvenal', but the most distinguished of his
conscious followers is probably ▷ Samuel
Johnson in his two poems ▷ *London* and
The Vanity of Human Wishes, imitations of
Juvenal's third and tenth satires respectively.
It is interesting to compare these with Pope's
▷ *Imitations of Horace*, which Johnson was
emulating. The spirit of Juvenal is also
strongly present in the satirical comedies of
▷ Ben Jonson who used Juvenal in his
satirical tragedy ▷ *Sejanus*. ▷ John
Dryden translated Juvenal (1692).

K

Kant, Immanuel (1724–1804)

German philosopher of Scottish descent. His most important works include: *Critique of Pure Reason* (1781 and 1787); *Prolegomena to every future Metaphysic* (1783); *Foundation for the Metaphysic of Ethic* (1785); *Critique of Practical Reason* (1788); *Critique of Judgement* (1790). He counteracted Leibnitzian rationalism and the scepticism of ▷ David Hume by asserting the 'transcendence' of the human mind over time and space (hence 'transcendental philosophy'). Time and space are forms of our consciousness: we can know by appearances but we cannot know 'things in themselves'. On the other hand, it is in the nature of our consciousness to have inherent in it an awareness of design in nature, and of moral and aesthetic value under a Divine moral law. His philosophy, continued and modified by other German philosophers (Fichte, Schelling, Hegel), profoundly influenced the poet and philosopher ▷ Coleridge; through Coleridge, it provided a line of thought which, in 19th century England, rivalled the sceptical materialistically inclined tradition stemming from ▷ Locke, ▷ Hume and ▷ Bentham.

▷ German influence on English literature.

Katherine Group

A term used by modern critics to refer to a group of early English religious works (spiritual meditations, saints' lives, didactic treatises), dating from the late 12th/early 13th century, which have affinities of language and style. At times this term is used more specifically to refer to a group of five religious texts found in the Bodleian Library Oxford MS Bodley 34, which includes the lives of three heroic female saints (*Seinte Katerine*, after whom the group is named; *Seinte Iuliene*; *Seinte Margerete*), a vivid treatise recommending the benefits of living a chaste, religious life and pointing out the drawbacks of living the life of a married woman and mother (*Hali Meidenhad*), and an allegorical narrative on the 'safeguarding' of the soul (*Sawles Warde*). These five texts are all written in a rhythmical ▷ alliterative style and are highly accomplished prose works. They have linguistic, stylistic and thematic affinities with the manual for anchoresses, the ▷ *Ancrene Wisse*, and seem particularly, though not exclusively, to cater for a specialized audience of religious women.
Bib: Ker, N. R., *Facsimile of MS Bodley 34*; Millett, B. and Price, J. (eds.), *Medieval English Prose for Women*.

Kavanagh, Julia (1824–77)

Novelist. Born in Thurles and educated at home, Julia Kavanagh was the daughter of a writer who later claimed to have written her novels and that his own worst work was hers. She lived with her parents, remaining single to care for her invalid mother. Much of her youth was spent in France, and French character and way of life are reflected in her novels. On the death of her mother she returned to France and lived in Nice until her death. Her first novel, *The Montyon Prizes* (1846) was very popular. The best known are perhaps *Madeleine* (1848), *Nathalie* (1850) and *Adèle* (1858). Her biographical sketches, *French Women of Letters* (1862) and *English Women of Letters* (1863), have been much praised. Her other publications include a volume of short stories, *Forget-me-nots* (1878).

Kay

Kay (Cai/Kei) is one of ▷ King Arthur's principal followers, along with ▷ Bedivere, in Welsh Arthurian narratives. In ▷ Geoffrey of Monmouth's treatment of Arthurian history he has the role of chief steward of King Arthur's household, and is killed while fighting against the Romans. In later French and English Arthurian narratives, Kay becomes a more degenerate figure, assuming the role of a knight who is a slanderer and vain boaster. In ▷ Malory's *Morte D'Arthur*, Kay is the son of Sir Ector and thus Arthur's foster-brother.

Kean, Edmund (?1787–1833)

One of the greatest actors of the early 19th century. He was the illegitimate son of a hawker and itinerant actress, Anne Carey. He began acting as an infant, and trained at ▷ Drury Lane so vigorously, it is said, that he had to wear irons to prevent deformity. This disadvantage was aggravated by a later fall during a circus performance in which he broke both his legs. He remained small in stature, and the actress ▷ Sarah Siddons once referred to him as 'a horrid little man'. He received some education through the charity of a Jew, at a school in Leicester Square, and again at a school in Soho, paid for by an aunt. Despite some early recognition as an actor, Kean long led a precarious existence, as strolling actor, singer, and tumbler, during which period he married Mary Chambers, an actress.

In 1814 Kean made his famous debut as Shylock (▷ *The Merchant of Venice*), discarding the traditional red wig and playing

him as a violent and tragic figure, after which his career blossomed, bringing him fame and financial reward. He followed his first success with other triumphs as Macbeth, Othello, Iago, Richard III, Lear, Barabas in ▷ Marlowe's ▷ *The Jew of Malta*, Jaffeir in ▷ *Venice Preserv'd*, and Sir Giles Overreach in ▷ Massinger's ▷ *A New Way to Pay Old Debts*. He toured America and Canada, receiving tumultuous acclaim. Much of his personal behaviour attracted gossip and censure; he had numerous love affairs, and drank excessively. At one time he appears to have been locked up as a lunatic. In 1829 he broke down during a performance of *Henry V*, and apologized to the audience for losing his memory. His last performance was as Othello, with his son Charles as Iago, at ▷ Covent Garden and he died a few weeks later. The most famous judgment of Kean is ▷ Coleridge's: 'To see him act, is like reading Shakespeare by flashes of lightning'.
Bib: Cornwall, B., *Life of Edmund Kean* (2 vols); Hawkins, F. W., *Life of Edmund Kean* (2 vols); Hillebrand, H. N., *Edmund Kean*; Fitzsimmons, R., *Edmund Kean: Fire from Heaven*.

Keats, John (1795–1821)

John Keats by C. A. Brown (1819)

Poet. The son of a livery-stable keeper in London, he was apprenticed to an apothecary, and for a time intended to be a surgeon, but abandoned this career in his determination to be a poet. He became the protégé of ▷ Leigh Hunt, and adopted many of the older man's attitudes and literary mannerisms, though he was never, like Hunt, politically active. Through Hunt he met ▷ Percy Bysshe Shelley who helped him with the publication of *Poems by John Keats* (1817), which include his exhilarating if callow statement of poetic ambition, *Sleep and Poetry*. The volume was not a success and Keats set himself to improve his art by writing a long poem in couplets – almost as a kind of technical exercise. *Endymion*, appeared in 1818, and though its rambling allegory fails to sustain narrative interest and its poetry is of uneven quality, it performed its function in developing Keats's style and ideas. It was severely criticized in the ▷ *Quarterly Review* and ▷ *Blackwood's Magazine*, partly with justification and partly because of their opposition to Hunt's radicalism. Its first lines show in an early immature form the aesthetic creed which preoccupied Keats throughout his short career: 'A thing of beauty is a joy forever:/Its loveliness increases'.

Early in 1818 Keats composed *Isabella*, a macabre Italian romance in ▷ *ottava rima*, superficially similar to Hunt's work but with a sensuous complexity of Keats's own. In the same year he began work on ▷ *Hyperion*, a 'philosophical' poem in Miltonic ▷ blank verse, which remained unfinished at his death. During much of 1818 Keats was nursing his brother Tom as he died of consumption, an experience which complicated his later expressions of faith in the permanence of beauty. Towards the end of 1818 he fell in love with Fanny Brawne, and from this point on his work shows a leap in emotional depth and maturity. ▷ *The Eve of St Agnes* (1820), is a 'medieval' romance fragment in ▷ Spenserian stanzas. In 1819 Keats wrote his ▷ Odes, *To Psyche, To a Nightingale, On a Grecian Urn, On Melancholy, On Indolence, To Autumn*, and ▷ *Lamia*, a narrative romance in pentameter couplets (▷ metre). On 3 February 1820 Keats began coughing blood, and at once realized its meaning: 'That drop of blood is my death warrant. I must die.' He had consumption and knew that he would soon follow his brother. It seems that he wrote nothing from this point onwards. He travelled to Italy in September 1820 with his friend Joseph Severn and died in Rome in February 1821, directing that the epitaph on his grave should read 'Here lies one whose name was writ in water.'

Keats felt that the deepest meaning of life lay in the apprehension of material beauty, and his works are the most important embodiment in poetry of the philosophy of Aestheticism. His mature poems confront the implications of this belief in a world of disease and decay, and their most characteristic effect is the evocation of poignant transience. He is remarkable also for his intelligent awareness of his own poetic development, which enabled him to reach maturity so early in his short career. His letters are among the finest in English, not only for their discussion of his aesthetic ideas ('negative capability', 'the chameleon poet') but also simply for their human quality, their spontaneity and humour.

Bib: Gittings, R., *John Keats*; Leavis, F. R., in *Revaluation*; Ridley, M. R., *Keats's Craftsmanship*; Hill, J. S. (ed.), *Keats: Narrative Poems. A Selection of Critical Essays*; Fraser, G. S., *Keats: Odes. A Selection of Critical Essays*; Jones, J., *John Keats's Dream of Truth*; Ricks, C., *Keats and Embarrassment*; Van Ghent, D., *Keats: The Myth of the Hero*; Hirst, W. S., *John Keats*; Allott, M., *John Keats*.

Kemble, John Philip (1757–1823)

Actor, singer, manager, dramatist. Kemble was the son of the theatrical manager Roger Kemble and actress Sarah (née Ward). His sister became known as the actress ▷ Sarah Siddons, and six other siblings also went onto the stage.

In 1777 he began acting at Liverpool, and the following year his first play, *Belisarius; or Injured Innocence* was staged there.

He began the first of many seasons at ▷ Drury Lane in 1783, where his roles included Hamlet, Richard III, Shylock, and King John. Three of his sisters acted there during this time, and he played Othello to Sarah Siddons' Desdemona in 1785. In 1788 he took over management of Drury Lane, whose patent was held by ▷ Richard Sheridan, and soon introduced elements of 'theatrical realism' into his productions, such as providing what he considered authentic Roman costumes for some of ▷ Shakespeare's Roman plays.

After 1791 when Drury Lane was declared unsafe, Kemble moved his company to the ▷ King's Theatre in the Haymarket, ▷ Covent Garden and several provincial theatres. In 1816 the advent of ▷ Edmund Kean to the stage drew from Kemble much of the public respect and admiration he had enjoyed throughout his career and he retired the following year.

Throughout his life, Kemble was admired for his good looks, elegance, and charm, and respected for his forceful professional abilities as an actor and as a manager. He had a rigorous, classical approach to acting, excelling in parts, especially those of Shakespeare, to which a grand manner and style were suited, and, like many of his period, had a prodigious memory enabling him to retain many long roles in his repertoire. He lacked the emotional range of ▷ David Garrick, and later Edmund Kean, and suffered from a tendency to drink to excess, which occasionally interfered with his ability to perform. Some 58 plays, most of them alterations, are attributed to his authorship.

Bib: Baker, H., *John Philip Kemble*; Child, H., *The Shakespearean Productions of John Philip Kemble*; Donohue, J., *Dramatic Character in the English Romantic Age*; Joseph, B., *The Tragic Actor*; Kelly, L., *The Kemble Era: John Philip, Sarah Siddons and the London Stage*.

Kemp, William (fl. 1600)

A famous comic actor, contemporary with ▷ Shakespeare. He acted parts such as Peter, the comic servant of the Nurse in ▷ Shakespeare's ▷ *Romeo and Juliet*, and the muddle-headed constable ▷ Dogberry in ▷ *Much Ado About Nothing*, and excelled at ▷ jigs. His most famous exploit was dancing from London to Norwich (over a hundred miles) for a bet. He and ▷ Richard Tarlton established a national reputation for themselves as comic actors, as ▷ Richard Burbage and ▷ Edward Alleyn did as tragic ones.

Kempe, Margery (c. 1373–after 1438)

A mystic, who lived in Norwich, and whose spiritual biography is the subject of the *Book of Margery Kempe*, which Margery claims to have dictated to an amanuensis. Unlike ▷ Julian of Norwich, whom she consulted for spiritual advice at one stage, Margery was not a recluse but a married woman with 14 children who attempted to live a life devoted to Christ, and sought official Church recognition for her status as a spiritual woman, while continuing to live in the secular world. She experienced intense emotional visionary encounters with Christ, which have at times a strikingly homely quality, and the *Book* not only records these visions but also her travels in Europe and pilgrimage to Jerusalem. Her special spiritual trial, according to her book, is to be misrepresented and rejected by many of her clerical and lay peers. The recording of her spiritual life, despite severe difficulties and her own illiteracy, becomes a symbolic act in itself, representing both her claim to spiritual status and evidence of her special relationship with God.

Bib: Petroff, E. (ed.), *Medieval Women's Visionary Literature*; Windeatt, B. (trans.), *The Book of Margery Kempe*.

Ketch, Jack (John) (d 1686)
A public executioner who made a name for himself in popular folklore, so that later executioners bore his name as a nickname. He was notorious for the clumsy brutality of his executions, which took place in public.

Killigrew, Thomas (1612–83)
Dramatist, actor, manager. Born in London to Sir Robert Killigrew, he became a page of honour to ▷ Charles I, possibly from 1625. Killigrew wrote his first play, *The Prisoners*, in 1635 and in the following year he married Cecilia Crofts, a maid of honour to Queen Henrietta Maria, by whom he had at least one son, before she died in 1638. Killigrew remained loyal to the king after the outbreak of the ▷ Civil War, and was imprisoned for a time. He afterwards travelled as an exile on the Continent during the 1640s, serving first the Duke of York, later ▷ James II, and then Prince Charles, later ▷ Charles II. His exploits during that period are romanticized in his play *Thomaso; Or, The Wanderer* (published 1664).

After the ▷ Restoration he was granted one of the two royal patents to form a theatre company which became known as the ▷ King's Company. In 1667 Killigrew set up a ▷ nursery to train young actors, in Hatton Garden, and in 1673 he became Master of the Revels, after the death of Sir Henry Herbert (1596–1673). This made him responsible for supervising theatrical entertainment and licensing theatres and he held the post for four years before resigning in favour of his son Charles. In 1682 the King's Company, having foundered for several seasons, was effectively absorbed by the ▷ Duke's Company, but by then Killigrew had little to do with it. He was buried at ▷ Westminster Abbey, near his first wife and a sister.

Kilt
The heavily pleated skirt-like garment worn by Highland Scotsmen and reaching from the waist to the knees. Before the 17th century it was the lower part of the plaid, or large woollen cloth in which the Highland Scotsmen wrapped themselves; the kilt was the part that hung down below the belt. Plaid and kilt are now separate. The term 'kilt' is often used for the whole costume, and is regarded as the Scottish national dress. In fact, it was only worn by Highlanders of the lower classes, and was forbidden in the middle of the 18th century as part of a policy of destroying Highland ways of life by the British government. Since then, apart from its use in Highland regiments, the kilt has been revived for romantic and sentimental reasons, and is worn by Scotsmen of all classes, especially on ceremonial occasions.
▷ Scotland; Tartan.

Kilvert, Robert Francis (1840–79)
Diarist. He was curate in the village of Clyro, Radnorshire. His candour and responsiveness to people and environment make his diaries valuable records of rural environment in the mid-Victorian era. Selections were published in 1938–40, edited by William Plomer.
▷ Diaries.

Kim (1901)
A novel by ▷ Rudyard Kipling. Kim, whose real name is Kimball O'Hara, is the orphan son of an Irish soldier in India, and he spends his childhood as a waif in the city of Lahore. He meets a Tibetan holy man in search of a mystical river, and accompanies him on his journey. Kim falls in with his father's old regiment, and is adopted by them, eventually becoming an agent of the British secret service under the guidance of an Indian, Hurree Babu. In spite of the ingenuousness of Kipling's British chauvinism, conspicuous in the later part of the book, the earlier part is an intimate and graphic picture of the humbler reaches of Indian life.

King, Henry (1592–1669)
Poet and Bishop of Chichester. King, himself the son of a bishop, was prebend of St Pauls until his appointment as Bishop of Chichester in 1642. A year later he was expelled from his bishopric by the ▷ Puritans, but was reinstated after the ▷ Restoration. The major poetic influences on King were ▷ John Donne (with whom he was friendly) and ▷ Ben Jonson. The majority of his poetry was published in 1657, when his *Poems, Elegies, Paradoxes and Sonnets* appeared. A large proportion of King's poetic output consisted of responses to public occasions, obituaries and ▷ elegies: these included two separately published elegies on ▷ Charles I (1648 and 1649).
Bib: Berman, R., *Henry King and the Seventeenth Century*.

King and No King, A (1611)
A tense and melodramatic tragicomedy by ▷ Beaumont and ▷ Fletcher, which explores and tests the limits of courtly and romantic psychology.

King Horn
One of the earliest extant English verse romances, dating from the first half of the 13th century, which has an earlier ▷ Anglo-

Norman analogue. The narrative recounts the story of Horn, dispossessed from his heritage, the kingdom of Sudene, by Saracen invaders; his experiences in Westernesse and Ireland which allow him to establish his identity as a knight of skill and valour; his eventual triumph over the wicked designs of his evil companion Fikenhild, who attempts to sabotage Horn's relationship with Rymenhild, daughter of the king of Westerness; his recovery of the kingdom of Sudene and his eventual return there as king with Rymenhild as his queen. The principle of repetition with variation provides the key to the narrative structure of *Horn*, and Horn's voyages themselves, narrated in a formulaic way, function as section-markers for the narrative. The story of Horn's loss and recovery of identity is told in a highly stylized, paratactic mode which enhances the memorability of the narrative. *Horn Childe* is a later Middle English version of the Horn story (dating from the early 14th century and written in ▷ tail-rhyme verse), which has the same plot structure as *King Horn* but differs in many points of detail. The story of Horn evidently had a wide currency during and after the medieval period. There are many balladic versions of the story, and versions of the narrative are extant in other European vernaculars too.
Bib: Barron, W. R. J., *English Medieval Romance*.

King John

A ▷ history play (*The Life and Death of King John*) by ▷ Shakespeare, perhaps derived from the anonymous *Troublesome Reign of King John*, and written before the great history plays *Henry IV, Parts I and II*, which first exhibit his genius in maturity. Anticipations of this maturity show themselves in the central character, Philip Faulconbridge, illegitimate son of the previous king, ▷ Richard I. The reign of the historical King ▷ John (1199–1216) was very unsettled; in the play, the disturbance arises from John's having usurped the throne from his nephew Arthur, whose cause is taken up by the king of France, the Church, and his nobles. Philip, 'the Bastard', is excluded by his illegitimacy from the privileges and status of the class into which he is born, and he at first enters the king's service in a spirit of cynicism, like that of Shakespeare's other bastard, Edmund in ▷ *King Lear*. By degrees he takes to heart the dangers to the nation of the disorderly passions among the great men, and he acquires a political conscience. He is

presented substantially, and stands out from the relatively flat background of the rest of the characters. However the theme that has given the play most of such popularity as it possesses centres not on the Bastard but on the child Arthur, whose pathos persuades his gaoler Hubert to spare his life. Arthur later dies from a fall in an attempt to escape.

Historically, the best-known factor about the reign of John is ▷ Magna Carta, the Great Charter which the nobles and Stephen Langton, Archbishop of Canterbury, forced the king to accept as a guarantee against tyrannical interference with the rights of the subject. Shakespeare does not mention this; it came into prominence for the national imagination only in the next reign during the quarrels between King ▷ James I and his Parliaments.

King Lear (1605)

A tragedy by ▷ Shakespeare. The play survives in two substantially different source texts: the 'Pied Bull' ▷ quarto of 1608 and the ▷ folio edition (1623). The quarto edition contains some 300 lines which are missing from the folio, and the folio has 100 lines not in the earlier text. Most modern editions of the play conflate the two sources to make them yield a composite text which contains all the missing lines. This accommodating editorial policy has been challenged persuasively by one of the most exciting Shakespearean ventures of the second half of the 20th century, the publication of a radical edition of the complete works by Oxford University Press under the general editors Gary Taylor and Stanley Wells. Their conclusion, that Shakespeare revised and shortened *King Lear* for the folio edition, can no longer be ignored in critical discussions of the play.

The main plot of *King Lear* proceeds from the division of the kingdom of England and Lear's ill-judged rejection of his daughter Cordelia who refuses to conform to her father's demand for a public expression of her love for him. The subplot traces the rise and fall of Edmund, the bastard and ruthless son of the Earl of Gloucester who, at Edmund's instigation, wrongfully persecutes his loyal and legitimate heir Edgar. The double plot of the play widens its imaginative treatment of parents and alienated children and portrays a society fallen from the bias of nature, in which the old, though guilty, are more sinned against than sinning. The play offers an almost unmitigated, dark and apocalyptic vision of a universe in which good characters, particularly Cordelia, perish as well as bad ones like Goneril, Regan and Edmund. For this reason, and because Shakespeare's play contravenes poetic justice, ▷ Samuel Johnson preferred it in its mutilated, rewritten version by Nahum Tate (1681), which ended happily as a tragicomedy with the marriage of Edgar and Cordelia. Modern audiences have responded with empathy to the play's bleak vision.

King, William (1663–1712)
Author of satirical and ▷ burlesque works in both prose and verse, including (with Charles Boyle) *Dialogues of the Dead* (1699) and *The Art of Cookery* (1708), imitating ▷ Horace's *Art of Poetry*.

King-maker, The
The nickname of Richard Neville, Earl of Warwick (1428–71). He was one of the most powerful English nobles during the civil wars known as the ▷ Wars of the Roses. In the early 1460s he was from time to time in a position to control the destinies of the rival claimants to the throne – ▷ Henry VI (of the ▷ House of Lancaster) and ▷ Edward IV (of York).

Kingis Quair
A narrative in ▷ rhyme royal, written c 1422, and attributed to ▷ James I of Scotland. The *Kingis Quair* (*King's Book*) is greatly indebted to the work of ▷ Chaucer, especially to the ▷ *Knight's Tale*. The narrative (some 1,379 lines long) recounts the experiences of a knight-prisoner who falls in love with a lady walking in the garden below his cell and in a dream-vision visits the realm of Venus, the palace of Minerva, and encounters Fortuna, and finally is assured that his suit for the lady will be successful.
▷ James I, King of Scotland.
Bib: Norton-Smith, J. (ed.), *The Kingis Quair*.

King's Company, The
Acting company formed by ▷ Sir Thomas Killigrew after the ▷ Restoration of ▷ Charles II. It performed from November 1660 at the former Gibbons' Tennis Court in ▷ Vere Street, near Lincoln's Inn Fields, which had been converted to a theatre. In May 1663 it moved to a purpose-built theatre at Bridges Street, ▷ Drury Lane, also known as the Theatre Royal. In January 1672 that theatre was destroyed by fire and in March 1674, after a temporary sojourn at ▷ Lincoln's Inn Fields, the company moved to a new King's Theatre, or Theatre Royal, designed at Drury Lane by ▷ Sir Christopher Wren. Here it remained until its union with the ▷ Duke's Company to form the ▷ United Company in 1682.

King's Evil, The
A skin disease: scrofula. An ancient tradition maintained that kings could cure it by 'touching' the sufferer. In England the tradition goes back to ▷ King Edward the Confessor; his miraculous healing power is described by the English Doctor in Shakespeare's ▷ *Macbeth* (IV. iii). The poet and critic ▷ Samuel Johnson suffered from the disease, and was 'touched' for it as a child in 1712 by Queen Anne, the last reigning sovereign to practise the rite. Her nephew Prince Charles also used it during the ▷ Jacobite Rebellion of 1745: since the power was supposed to inhere in the true royal line, the exercise of it was of propaganda value to him in his campaign for the English throne.

King's Friends
George III (1760–1820) tried to revive the power of monarchical government in England against the ▷ Whig aristocracy which, since the accession to the throne of the House of Hanover in 1714, had controlled the country through Parliament. Since the institution of Parliament was too strong for the king to ignore it, he tried to carry his purpose by securing (largely through various forms of bribery) a party to support his policies and ministers from within Parliament. These became known as the King's Friends or the New Tories.

King's Men, The
▷ Chamberlain's Men, The Lord.

King's Theatre
▷ Drury Lane Theatres; Haymarket Theatres.

Kingship
The British tradition of kingship has two sources: the Germanic view was that the king was the father of his people, with no particular sacredness about the authority he exercised; the Latin tradition was that the king's powers were sacred, and after Christianity became the official religion of the Roman Empire (in the 4th century AD) the Emperor represented the earthly side of the authority delegated by God to the Holy Church. The two aspects became united when the Frankish king ▷ Charlemagne was crowned Emperor of the West in 800. Medieval English kings only nominally recognized the authority of the Holy Roman Emperors who succeeded Charlemagne, but they took to themselves the same status; a king on being crowned was anointed by holy oils, and a crime against him was a crime against God. In early times kings were elected, though the elected king

was traditionally of the same family as the dead king, but by degrees the nearest surviving relative assumed the crown as a matter of course and eventually by right. (In Shakespeare's ▷ *Hamlet* and ▷ *Macbeth* neither young Hamlet nor Malcolm is the inevitable heir to the Danish and the Scottish thrones respectively.)

Until the 17th century, peace, law and order depended on the king's authority. In the reign of ▷ Henry II, for example, the king's judges imposed a universal 'Common Law' over the selfish interests of the competing barons, and the peace of the country was called 'the king's peace'. Everything depended on the king being universally acknowledged and respected; every kind of disaster followed when the king lost his authority like ▷ John, ceased to be respected like ▷ Richard II, was a tyrant like ▷ Richard III, was a usurper like ▷ Henry IV, or died without direct heir, leaving the succession uncertain, as seemed likely to happen after ▷ Elizabeth I. The ▷ House of Tudor had brought England stability and prosperity after a century of civil wars between the competing families of York and ▷ Lancaster, and of kings (Richard II, Henry IV, Henry VI, Richard III) who had almost all exhibited one or another of the disadvantages mentioned. The reign of Elizabeth, last of the Tudors, was particularly prosperous, but her childlessness and the changefulness of the times caused the nation to look to the future with foreboding.

James VI of Scotland, however, succeeded peacefully as ▷ James I of England, but almost at once his quarrels with Parliament and with the country began. James exaggerated the sacredness of kingship into the doctrine of 'the Divine Right of Kings', according to which the King was responsible to God alone; this made adjustment between royal policy and national interests difficult, and Parliament raised up Magna Carta from the reign of King John to prove the right of the people to restrain royal power. No method had yet been discovered, however, of securing stable government except through a strong king, and under James's successor, ▷ Charles I, ▷ civil war broke out, culminating in the execution of the king. It took the remainder of the 17th century and the whole of the 18th to work out the modern system of 'constitutional monarchy', in accordance with which the king or queen reigns but does not rule, and government is conducted through an elected and truly representative parliament to which, and not to the crown, the ministers are responsible. The office of kingship remained sacred, but became symbolic.

Kingsley, Charles (1819–75)
Novelist; clergyman; reformer. He belonged to a movement known as Christian Socialism, led by F. D. Maurice. He is now remembered chiefly for his ▷ children's book, ▷ *The Water Babies* (1863). His novels *Yeast* (1848) and *Alton Locke* (1850) are concerned with the theme of social injustice. *Hypatia* (1853), *Westward Ho!* (1855) and *Hereward the Wake* (1865) are historical novels. His retelling for the young of Greek myths, *The Heroes* (1856) is well known.
Bib: Pope-Hennessy, U., *Canon Charles Kingsley*; Martin, R. B., *The Dust of Combat: A Life of Kingsley*; Thorp, M. F., *Life*; Barry, J. D., in *Victorian Fiction* (ed. L. Stevenson); Chitty, S., *The Beast and the Monk: A Life of Charles Kingsley*; Collom, S. B., *Charles Kingsley: The Lion of Eversley*.

Kipling, Rudyard (1865–1936)
Poet, short-story writer, novelist. He was born in India, educated in England, and returned to India at 17 as a journalist. In 1889 he came to England to live.

Kipling's poetry is striking for his success in using, vividly and musically, popular forms of speech, sometimes in the ▷ Browning tradition of the ▷ dramatic monologue, *eg McAndrew's Hymn*, or in the ▷ ballad tradition, *eg Barrack-Room Ballads* (1892). He was also able to write poetry appropriate to public occasions and capable of stirring the feelings of a large public, *eg* his famous *Recessional* (1897). His poetry is generally simple in its components but, when it rises above the level of doggerel, strong in its impact. It needs to be read in selection: *A Choice of Kipling's Verse* (ed. ▷ T. S. Eliot), with a very good introductory essay.

Kipling's stories brought him fame, and, partly under French influence, he gave close attention to perfecting the art of the ▷ short story. The volumes include *Plain Tales from the Hills* (1887), *Life's Handicap* (1891); *Many Inventions* (1893); *The Day's Work* (1898); *Traffics and Discoveries* (1904); *Actions and Reactions* (1909); *A Diversity of Creatures* (1917); *Debits and Credits* (1926) and *Limits and Renewals* (1932). The early stories in particular show Kipling's capacity to feel with the humble (common soldiers, Indian peasants) and the suffering. But he admired action, power, and efficiency; this side of his character brought out much of the best and the worst in his writing. Some of his best stories show his enthusiasm for the triumphs of technology, and are about machines rather than people, *eg* in *The Day's Work*. On the other hand he was inclined to be crudely

Illustration by W. H. Drake from Rudyard Kipling's *The Jungle Book*

chauvinistic, and to show unpleasant arrogance towards peoples ruled by or hostile to Britain, though he also emphasized British responsibility for the welfare of the governed peoples. Yet again, he sometimes engaged in delicate if sentimental fantasy, as in *They* and *The Brushwood Boy* (1925); some of his later stories show a sensitive and sometimes morbid insight into abnormal states of mind, *eg Mary Postgate* (1917). The stories, like the poems, are best read in selection: *A Choice of Kipling's Prose* (ed. Somerset Maugham).

Kipling is not outstanding as a full-length novelist. His best novel is ▷ *Kim* (1901), based on his childhood in India; *Stalky and Co* (1899) is well-known as a tale about an English public school, and is based on Kipling's own schooldays at the United Services College. *The Light that Failed* (1890) shows his more sensitive and sombre aspect. An autobiographical fragment, *Something of Myself*, was published in 1937.

Kipling's children's stories are minor classics of their kind: *The Jungle Books* (1894–5); *Just So Stories* (1902); *Puck of Pook's Hill* (1906). *Rewards and Fairies* (1910) is less celebrated.

▷ Children's books; Imperialism.
Bib: Birkenhead, Lord, *Rudyard Kipling* (biography); Page, N., *A Kipling Companion*; Carrington, C. E., *Life*; Dobree, B., *Kipling*; Orwell, G., in *Critical Essays*; Wilson, E., in *The Wound and the Bow*; Green, R. L. (ed.), *Kipling: The Critical Heritage*.

Kipps (1905)

A novel by ▷ H. G. Wells. It describes the social rise of a shop-assistant through an unexpected legacy, his engagement to a vulgarly snobbish young lady who has hitherto been out of his reach, and his painful acquisition of the false standards and cares which are forced upon him. He escapes the marriage by marrying suddenly a girl of his own former class, but he only escapes his worries when he loses his money. The book contains acute social observation and comedy in the Dickens tradition, though Wells's style is quite his own.

Kit-Cat Club

Founded early in the 18th century by leading ▷ Whig men of letters and politicians; its members included ▷ Marlborough, ▷ Walpole, ▷ Steele, ▷ Addison, ▷ Congreve and ▷ Vanbrugh. It met at the house of a pastry-cook called Christopher Cat. Their portraits by Sir Godfrey Kneller hang in the National Portrait Gallery.
▷ Clubs.

Knight of the Burning Pestle, The (1607)

A comedy by ▷ Francis Beaumont. It mocks the London middle-class taste for extravagant romances in the Spanish tradition about the adventures of wandering knights ('knight-errantry'). It also parodies a contemporary play, *The Four Prentices of London* by

▷ Thomas Heywood, who flattered this taste. It seems to owe something to Cervantes' ▷ *Don Quixote* (Pt I, 1605), itself a parody of the Spanish romances; this, however, was not translated until 1612 (▷ Spanish influence on English literature).

The play at first purports to be called *The London Merchant* but a grocer and his wife, sitting in the audience, become worried that this may turn out to be a ▷ satire on London citizens. They are determined to have something to flatter their vanity, and force their apprentice, Ralph, up on to the stage to perform the role of a 'grocer errant'; he wears on his shield the sign of a burning pestle, *ie* an implement used by shopkeepers. The play of *The London Merchant* proceeds together with Ralph's Quixote-like adventures, and the grocer and his wife, still in the audience, interpose appreciative comments.

The comedy shows the great theatrical dexterity achieved by English dramatists at the height of the Shakespearean period. A main part of this dramatic skill is the intermingling of styles – song, comic rhyme, serious ▷ blank verse, and colloquial prose.

Knighthood

A term which covers a complex historical and cultural phenomenon, referring both to members of a social estate whose role and status evolved in different ways in medieval Europe, and to a more abstract ethos, a framework of values and a code for behaviour, which is promoted in various kinds of medieval and post-medieval artistic representations and social rituals (in manuals of chivalric activity, in rituals of state and Church, in visual media, etc.), but which is perhaps more honoured in the breach than in the observance by those who claim the title of 'Sir'.

Knighthood (or chivalry – the term more favoured by modern historians of culture) cannot be summed up in a few words because it is not a homogeneous phenomenon. It seems that the role of the knight, which was defined as a military function in the early medieval period (as an armed, mounted warrior who rendered military service in return for a fief), came by the 13th century to be a socially prestigious role to which members of the nobility aspired (the military function being rendered, it seems, by financial payment). Tracing the history of that evolution requires attention to the specific power structures in operation in different countries, in different regions, during this time: the role of the knight-figure in post-

Conquest England (in which Anglo-Norman and Saxon institutions were intermeshed) is not the same as that of the knight in the regions of France. However, tracing the history of the institution of knighthood also requires attention to how the cultural concept of knighthood evolved, and how a body of material on knighthood, in theory and in practice, came about. The Church had an important part to play in this: necessarily, if knights are given a role to play as defenders of the faith (and the faithful), some examination of the codes and limits of justifiable martial action is required. But all kinds of secular literature too, from romances to classical histories and conduct books, played a part in cultivating the mythology of knighthood and developing the notion of chivalry as a transhistorical phenomenon which may encode the values of the social elite of different historical times.

Attempts to generalize about medieval chivalric literature may be as misleading as attempts to generalize about knighthood. Some of the chivalric narratives most familiar to modern English audiences, such as ▷ *Gawain and the Green Knight* or ▷ Chaucer's ▷ *Knight's Tale*, are far from simple manifestos promoting the interests of chivalric culture: these texts are as much concerned with exploring the tensions in the chivalric ethos as celebrating the panoply of knightly adventure and its civilizing effects. The trio of Knight, Squire, Yeoman, as presented in the *General Prologue* of the ▷ *Canterbury Tales*, provides both an image of the idealized structure of a feudal/chivalric hierarchy bound by notions of service, and embodies a recognition of the different models of chivalry, embodied in the single term. The Knight and the Squire represent different 'ages of Man' *and* different kinds of chivalric models: the crusading defender of the faith provides a contrast to the figure of the Squire, immersed in a world of courtly and amorous accomplishments and values. Chaucer's single foray into the world of Arthurian romance, ▷ *The Wife of Bath's Tale*, clearly shows how definitions of knighthood might be opposed: in this tale the definition of 'courtoisie' as a moral virtue, not a 'natural' attribute of class origin, voiced by the Old Woman in the narrative, is potentially at odds with the notion of knighthood as a quality of class, voiced by the central knightly protagonist who finds it difficult to accommodate marriage to a social inferior. Many of the anonymous Middle English romances are concerned with negotiating between these two different approaches to defining knighthood. Many of their central chivalric heroes serve an 'apprenticeship' in disguise, or are dispossessed in some way from their heritage, and thus demonstrate, finally, that their membership of a social elite is justified by birth and by the moral quality of their performance as in ▷ *King Horn* or ▷ *Havelock*.

Unravelling the interrelation between the literary theory and the social practice of chivalry is no simple matter. There is no doubt, for example, that Edward III's institution of the Order of the ▷ Garter in 1348 was influenced by a model of chivalric life developed in Arthurian narratives, among others. But it is also the case that this tradition of Arthurian literature itself developed as a literary arena in which examinations of the theory and practice of the values of a social elite could take place. The chivalric world offered, and continues to offer, writers and artists an arena for the exploration of codes of behaviour and modes of social organization, even when the social and historical context of the artist's culture is far removed from the world of knights and ladies.

▷ Crusades, The.
Bib: Keen, M., *Chivalry*.

Knight's Tale, The
One of ▷ Chaucer's ▷ *Canterbury Tales*, which is a reworking of the *Teseida* by ▷ Boccaccio, and recounts the story of ▷ Palamon and Arcite's love for Emily, sister of Hippolyta (wife of Theseus, Duke of Athens). The two Theban knights fall in love with Emily while held as Theseus's prisoners and eventually compete for Emily in a public tournament in Athens. Although Arcite wins the tournament, he is subsequently thrown from his horse and dies. After an interval of many years, Theseus arranges the marriage of Palamon and Emily, prompted by the desire for a political alliance with Athens. The gods play an active part in the narrative, reflecting the powers and desires of the earthly characters, and partly shaping the lives of the earthly protagonists too. In Chaucer's version of the narrative, questions about how order can be achieved on a personal and political level are very much to the fore. A Chaucerian version of the story of Palamon and Arcite appears to pre-date the composition of the *Canterbury Tales*: in the prologue to the ▷ *Legend of Good Women*, composed around 1386-7, the story is mentioned as one of Chaucer's 'makyngs'. Chaucer also tackled the story of Arcite from a rather different

angle in his unfinished work ▷ *Anelida and Arcite*.
▷ Theseus.

Knights of the Shire
A term used in the 14th and 15th centuries for small landowners who elected representatives to ▷ Parliament. They were not necessarily knights in the usual sense of having had ▷ knighthood conferred on them.
▷ Forty shilling freeholders.

Knox, John (1505-72)
Scottish religious reformer. More than anyone else, he was responsible for the conversion of Scotland from Catholic to ▷ Calvinist Christianity, and the eventual establishment of the national ▷ Presbyterian Church there. This brought him into conflict with ▷ Mary Queen of Scots, but he was out of the country when rebellion forced her to abdicate in 1567 and seek the protection of ▷ Elizabeth I. His *History of the Reformation of Religion within the realme of Scotland* includes an account of his celebrated controversy with the queen. Knox's vehement antagonism towards the concept, as well as the actuality, of female sovereign power has recently been highlighted by ▷ feminist critics.

Koestler, Arthur (1905-83)
Novelist and philosopher. He was born in Hungary and educated at the University of Vienna. From 1932-8 he was a member of the Communist Party (▷ Communism). He went to Spain as a correspondent during the Spanish Civil War, and was imprisoned by the Nationalists. Subsequently imprisoned in France during 1939-40, he joined the Foreign Legion before escaping to Britain in 1941. After World War II he became a British subject. From the 1930s to the 1950s his work was primarily concerned with political issues; his novel *Darkness At Noon* (1940) exposed Stalinist methods through the story of the imprisonment and execution of a former Bolshevik leader. From the 1950s onwards his writings were more concerned with the philosophical implications of scientific discoveries. His non-fiction trilogy, *The Sleepwalkers* (1959), *The Act of Creation* (1964) and *The Ghost in the Machine* (1967) considered the effect of science on man's idea of himself, and defended the concept of mind. A persistent feature of his work was a sense of horror at the barbarities of 20th-century Europe. Koestler, who had advocated the right to euthanasia, and who was suffering from leukaemia and Parkinson's disease,

committed suicide together with his third wife, Cynthia Jefferies, in 1983. His other novels are: *The Gladiators* (1939); *Arrival and Departure* (1943); *Thieves in the Night* (1946); *The Age of Longing* (1951); *The Call Girls* (1972). Autobiographical writings include: *Arrow in the Blue* (1952); *The Invisible Writing* (1954). Other prose writings include: *The Yogi and the Commissar* (1945); *The Roots of Coincidence* (1972).
Bib: Hamilton, I., *Koestler: A Biography*; Pearson, S. A., *Arthur Koestler*.

Kubla Khan: or, A Vision in a Dream: A Fragment (1816)

An ▷ ode by ▷ Samuel Taylor Coleridge, written in 1797, when he was living in Somerset. Coleridge recorded that he fell asleep after reading a description in *Purchas his Pilgrimage* (1613) of the pleasure gardens constructed in Xanadu by the 13th-century Mongol king of China, Khan (king) Kublai. While he was asleep 'from two to three hundred lines' came to him, which upon waking he hastened to write down. However he was interrupted by 'a person on business from Porlock', and afterwards could recall nothing of the remainder, 'with the exception of some eight or ten scattered lines and images'. It is difficult to know how much of this account to believe. One element Coleridge suppresses is his addiction to opium, which is certainly relevant to the hallucinatory clarity of the poem's exotic images. Because of the oddness of Coleridge's account 'a visitor from Porlock' has become a byword for any kind of intriguing, possibly evasive, excuse.

Despite its designation 'A Fragment' the work is artistically complete. The first three sections rework phrases from the ▷ Jacobean travel book, to describe a strangely primal landscape. An awesome 'mighty fountain' forms the source of the 'sacred river' Alph, on the banks of which Kubla has built a 'stately pleasure-dome' surrounded by orchards and gardens. After watering the garden the river continues its course, entering 'caverns measureless to man' and sinking 'in tumult to a lifeless ocean'. The clarity and primitiveness of these images gives the poem an archetypal resonance. The river can be seen as the river of life or creativity; the fountain symbolizes birth (of an individual, civilization, poetic inspiration), and the 'lifeless ocean' death or sterility. The dome stands for the precarious creative balance between. It is possible that the final fourth section of the poem, which seems to be a commentary upon the preceding lines, were 'the eight or ten lines or images' written after the departure of Coleridge's visitor, if he or she ever existed. The poem ends by imputing magical qualities to the poem itself and its bardic author: 'Weave a circle round him thrice,/ And close your eyes with holy dread,/ For he on honey-dew hath fed,/ And drunk the milk of Paradise.'
▷ Bard; Romanticism.

Kyd, Thomas (1558–94)

Dramatist. He is associated with the group known as the ▷ University Wits. His only known and important contribution to the output of the group is ▷ *The Spanish Tragedy* (1587), extremely popular in its own time and the first important ▷ revenge tragedy. He was probably also the author of a lost play on ▷ Hamlet, used by ▷ Shakespeare as the basis of his own; even without this, it is clear that Shakespeare developed the revenge theme from Kyd's first handling of it. Kyd's own starting-point was the tragedies of the Roman dramatist ▷ Seneca whose *Ten Tragedies* had been published in translation (1559–81). He was not interested in Senecan form, but in Seneca's mingling of dramatic horror and the stern restraints of ▷ Stoic philosophy, both of which were congenial to the Elizabethan age. Kyd's other surviving tragedies are only attributed to him and are much less important: *Soliman and Perseda* (?1588) and *Cornelia* (?1593), an adaptation of a Senecan tragedy by the French dramatist Robert Garnier.

Kyd was a friend of ▷ Marlowe, and was arrested in 1593 on the accusation of atheistic pronouncements which he declared, under torture, to be really Marlowe's; he was released after Marlowe's death by murder in the same year, and seems to have died soon afterwards in poverty.
Bib: Murray, P. B., *Thomas Kyd*.

Kynaston, Edward (1643–1712)

Actor. Kynaston began his theatrical career as a boy actor in women's roles, in 1660, when he was considered 'a Compleat Female Stage Beauty', by the prompter, John Downes.

Kynaston soon transferred to ▷ Killigrew's ▷ King's Company, acting first at the Red Bull Playhouse, and then at the ▷ Vere Street Theatre. He began playing men's parts in addition to women's, but with the full advent of women to the stage, and his own growing maturity, he took on men's roles exclusively.

Labour Party

Since 1923, one of the two main political parties in Britain, the other being the Conservative Party. The Labour Party was founded in 1900, and was called the Labour Representation Committee until 1906, when it took its present name. It claims to represent the interests of the working classes, and it favours state ownership of the means of production and distribution (state socialism) but it is not committed to complete socialization of the economy. The majority of its supporters are working-class, but it also has fairly extensive middle-class support among intellectuals.

It was under the Labour government of 1945–50 that the ▷ Welfare State was set up and under Harold Wilson's Labour administration (1966–70) that important legal reforms were made, including the facilitating of birth control and divorce, the permitting of homosexuality and abortion, the abolition of hanging and theatre ▷ censorship.

Origins of the Labour Party:

1 The 19th-century working-class movements. The most important of these was the growth of ▷ trade unions, which began a process of confederation in 1866; it was in consequence of a resolution by the Trades Union Congress (TUC) in 1899 that the Party was founded. Earlier movements which contributed to the origins of the party were those of the socialist ▷ Robert Owen; the ▷ Chartist Movement which, though it failed in its objectives, educated the working class in political consciousness; the Philosophical Radicals or ▷ Utilitarians, led by ▷ John Stuart Mill, who appealed to intellectuals among the workers, and elsewhere.

2 The Liberal Party. Throughout the 19th century the ▷ Liberals (formerly the ▷ Whigs) claimed to be the party of reform, although important social reforms were often initiated by Conservatives (Tories) such as ▷ Shaftesbury and ▷ Disraeli. It was in alliance with the Liberal Party that the workmen Members first entered Parliament in the last 20 years of the 19th century. The Liberals, however, received much support and money from employers of labour in the towns, so that a split caused by workers leaving the Liberal Party became inevitable.

3 The ▷ Nonconformist sects. The Protestant churches which refused conformity with the Church of England included ▷ Baptists, ▷ Congregationalists, ▷ Presbyterians, ▷ Quakers, ▷ Unitarians and ▷ Methodists. Most of their support was from the lower social classes, and, though they were predominantly non-political, they inevitably encouraged thoughtful discussion of political questions, especially social justice; they also assisted by helping to educate their members in social co-operation.

4 ▷ The Fabian Society. This was a society of socialist intellectuals, founded in 1884. It was led by some brilliant minds, including ▷ Bernard Shaw and ▷ Beatrice Webb, and became very influential.

5 ▷ Marx and the growth of Social Democracy in Europe. The European Social Democratic Federation was founded in 1881. However, although the British Labour Party has always had affinities with Social Democracy, in its origins it was not predominantly Marxist; its socialism derived more from earlier thinkers such as Owen.

6 The leadership of the Scottish Labour Movement – Keir Hardie. ▷ Scotland was not so bound by tradition to the existing political parties as England was, and the Scottish working class was on the whole better educated. The Scotsman Keir Hardie was one of the finest leaders of the British Labour Party at the time of the foundation of the party.

▷ Parties, Political.

Lacan, Jacques (1901–81)

French psychoanalyst whose re-readings of ▷ Freud have become influential within the area of literary criticism. Lacan's *The Four Fundamental Concepts of Psychoanalysis* (trans. 1977), and his *Ecrits: A Selection* (trans. 1977) outline the nature of his revision of Freudian psychoanalytic method. A further selection of papers has appeared under the title of *Feminine Sexuality* (trans. 1982). It is to Lacan that we owe the terms ▷ 'imaginary' and ▷ 'symbolic order'. Similarly, it is to his investigation of the operations of the unconscious according to the model of language – 'the unconscious is structured like a language' – that we owe the notion of a 'split' human subject. For Lacan the 'imaginary' is associated with the pre-Oedipal (▷ Oedipus complex) and pre-linguistic relationship between mother and child (the 'mirror' stage) where there appears to be no discrepancy between identity and its outward reflection. This is succeeded by the entry of the infant into the 'symbolic order', with its rules and prohibitions centred around the figure of the father (the phallus). The 'desire of the mother' is then repressed by the child's entry into language and the 'symbolic order'. The desire for 'imaginary' unity is also repressed to form the unconscious, which the interaction between analyst and patient aims to unlock. Some of the fundamental divisions that Lacan has located in the 'subject' have proved highly adaptable for a range of ▷ materialist literary criticisms, including (more controversially) ▷ feminism.

Lacy, John (?1615–81)

Actor, dancer, choreographer, manager, dramatist, Lacy came to London in 1631, probably to join the Cockpit Theatre, and became a dancer, before his career was interrupted by the ▷ Interregnum. In 1660 he joined Killigrew's ▷ King's Company, acting first at ▷ Vere Street Theatre, and soon acquired shares in the company's new building at ▷ Bridges Street, becoming a co-manager in 1663.

His first play, *Sauny the Scot* (1667), was a free adaptation of ▷ *The Taming of the Shrew*, written largely to provide a comic vehicle for himself in the part of Sauny, which became one of his major triumphs on stage. He wrote at least three other plays, all adaptations of earlier works.

His reputation was based primarily on his abilities as comedian, with a special talent for mimicry. He was the first to play Bayes in the Duke of Buckingham's ▷ *The Rehearsal*, and became a favourite of Charles II.

Lady Bountiful

A character in ▷ Farquhar's play ▷ *The Beaux' Stratagem*. She is a rich country lady who devotes her time to helping her less fortunate neighbours. She has become a proverbial figure. Farquhar portrays her satirically.

Lady Chatterley's Lover (1928)

▷ D. H. Lawrence's last novel. Constance Reid ('Connie') is the daughter of late-Victorian, highly cultured parents with advanced views. She marries Sir Clifford Chatterley in 1917, when he is on leave from the army; soon afterwards he is wounded, and permanently crippled from the waist down. Connie finds herself half alive, as though she has not been fully awakened; her dissatisfaction, however, does not proceed merely from her husband's disability, but from the impotence of civilization which the disability symbolizes. She is rescued from it by her husband's gamekeeper, Mellors, who fulfils her as a lover and as a human being. For Lawrence, the sexual relationship was potentially the profoundest human relationship: to treat it lightly was to trivialize

the whole human being, and to regard it with shame was to repress essential human energies. He saw that 'advanced' young people took the former attitude, and that the older generation took the latter; he regarded both attitudes as leading symptoms of decadence in our civilization. He did not suppose that the sexual relationship could in itself constitute a renewal of civilization, but he considered that such a renewal depended on the revitalization of relationships, and that this revitalization could never take place without the recovery of a true and healthy sexual morality. 'I want men and women to be able to think sex, fully, completely, honestly and cleanly.' (*Apropos of Lady Chatterley's Lover*, 1930.)

This aim led Lawrence to use unprecedentedly explicit language in conveying the love affair between Connie and Mellors, and the novel thus acquired unfortunate notoriety. In Britain, the full version was suppressed for immorality, but an expurgated version was published in 1928. An unabridged edition came out in Paris in 1929; the first British unabridged edition was published by Penguin Books in 1959. This led to an obscenity trial, the first test of the 1959 Obscene Publications Act, at which many distinguished authors and critics (including ▷ E. M. Forster) testified in defence of the novel. The acquittal of Penguin had important consequences for subsequent ▷ publishing. Lawrence's defence of the novel, *Apropos of Lady Chatterley's Lover*, is one of the finest of his essays.

▷ Censorship and English literature.

Lady Day

In the Church calendar, the feast of the Annunciation to the Virgin Mary, celebrating the prediction of the Birth of Christ by the ▷ Angel Gabriel (*Luke* 1). It is observed on 25 March, which is also a ▷ Quarter Day, *ie* it marks the end of the first quarter of the year on which bills, etc. have to be paid. In the ▷ Middle Ages there were other Lady Days commemorating other events in the life of the Virgin Mary.

Lady of Shalott, The (1832)

One of the best-known poems by ▷ Alfred Tennyson. The story is an episode from the ▷ Arthurian legend of ▷ Sir Lancelot, and is to be found in Malory's ▷ *Morte d'Arthur* and in the 13th-century French romance *Lancelot*. Tennyson's poem is popular as an example of his extremely musical verse; it is also an example of his recurrent theme of withdrawal from deathly reality into a world of reverie. He expanded the story in his *Lancelot and Elaine* (1859), one of the ▷ *Idylls of the King*.

Lady of the Lake

The name refers to an important role in Arthurian narratives, in origins perhaps that of an otherworldly enchantress, which may be filled by different women (including ▷ Morgan la Fay, Nimue/ Viviane). In ▷ Malory's ▷ *Morte D'Arthur* the Lady of the Lake provides Arthur with ▷ Excalibur. The Lady seems to preside over a group of 'damsels of the Lake' who may take over the central role when necessary, as does the 'damsel' Nimue (or Viviane), the woman who entraps ▷ Merlin, and becomes Lady of the Lake after Balin has beheaded the previous Lady. She is one of the company of women who appear, mysteriously, in a boat to take Arthur to ▷ Avalon. In the ▷ Vulgate version of the story of ▷ Lancelot, the 'Dame du Lac' steals Lancelot away as a child and rears him until he is ready to be knighted at Arthur's court.

Lady of the Lake, The (1810)

A narrative poem by ▷ Sir Walter Scott set in the Scotland of James V (1513-42).

Lagado

In ▷ Swift's ▷ *Gulliver's Travels* (Part III) capital of the island of Balnibarbi, and its neighbouring flying island Laputa.

Lake Poets

A term coined by ▷ Francis Jeffrey in the ▷ *Edinburgh Review* (October 1807) to describe ▷ Samuel Taylor Coleridge, ▷ Robert Southey and ▷ William Wordsworth, who for a time lived in close association in the Lake District. The community of literary and social outlook in their earlier work made it natural to speak of them as a group, but in fact only Wordsworth was profoundly identified with the locality.

Lamb, Lady Caroline (1785–1828)

Novelist and poet. The only daughter of the 3rd Earl of Bessborough, she was taken to Italy at the age of three and brought up mostly in the care of a servant. Educated at Devonshire House School, she was then looked after by her maternal grandmother, Lady Spencer, who worried about her instability and 'eccentricities'. She married the statesman William Lamb (later the 2nd Viscount Melbourne), but in 1812, just after her marriage, became desperately infatuated with ▷ Byron, of whom she wrote in her diary that he was 'mad, bad and dangerous to know'. After he broke with her, she became increasingly unstable and violent-tempered,

and her husband sued for separation, becoming temporarily reconciled, however, on the day fixed for the execution of the deed. Meeting Byron's funeral cortège seems to have hastened her disintegration and she ended up living with her father-in-law and only surviving son, an invalid. Her first novel, *Glenarvon* (1816), had a significant, though brief success, due no doubt to its portrayal of Byron and herself in a wild and romantic story. It was published anonymously, though she courted notoriety, being impulsive, vain and excitable to the point of insanity, as well as highly original. She wrote two further novels, *Graham Hamilton* (1822) and *Ada Reis* (1823), and poetry, some of which has been set to music.
Bib: Jenkins, E., *Lady Caroline Lamb*.

Lamb, Charles (1775–1834)

Essayist and critic. His best-known work is his two volumes of the ▷ *Essays of Elia* (1823 and 1833), in which he discourses about his life and times. His *Specimens of English Dramatic Poets who lived about the Time of Shakespeare* directed interest towards ▷ Shakespeare's contemporaries, who had been somewhat neglected in the 18th century, although perhaps not so much ignored as Lamb thought. His friends included many writers of his time, and this fact gives a special interest to his letters. He collaborated with his sister Mary in adapting Shakespeare's plays into stories for children – *Tales from Shakespeare* (1807). His poems are unimportant but one or two, *eg The Old Familiar Faces* (1798) and the prose-poem, *Dream Children*, recur in anthologies. Lamb seems to have been a man of unusual charm and of gifts which he never allowed himself to display fully and energetically, perhaps because he was haunted by the fear of insanity, to which both he and his sister were subject.
    ▷ Children's books.
Bib: Lucas, E. V., *Life*; Tillyard, E. M. W. (ed.), *Lamb's Criticism*; Blunden, E., *Charles Lamb and his Contemporaries*; Cecil, D., *A Portrait of Charles Lamb*.

Lamb, Mary Ann (1764–1847)

Sister to ▷ Charles Lamb and daughter of a lawyer, she was brought up in poor circumstances, helping her mother, who worked as a needlewoman. In 1796, overworked and stressed, she pursued her mother's apprentice round the room with a knife in a fit of irritation, and when her mother interposed she killed her. The verdict was one of insanity and she was given into the custody of her brother Charles who took

charge of her, finding suitable accommodation for her during her periodic bouts of illness and maintaining a close and affectionate relationship. With Charles, she wrote *Tales from Shakespeare* (1807), designed to make ▷ Shakespeare's stories accessible to the young; *The Adventures of Ulysses* (1808), which was an attempt to do the same for ▷ Homer; and *Mrs Leicester's School* (1809), a collection of short stories.
　　▷ Children's books.

Lamia (1820)

A poem in pentameter couplets (▷ metre) by ▷ John Keats, based on a story in ▷ Robert Burton's ▷ *Anatomy of Melancholy*. In ancient myth a lamia was a female demon, one of whose practices was to entice young men in order to devour them. In Keats's poem a serpent is transformed into a beautiful girl who fascinates a young Corinthian, Lycius. He takes her into his home and makes a bridal feast which is attended by the philosopher Apollonius. Apollonius recognizes the lamia and calls her by her true name, whereupon she vanishes and Lycius dies. The poem, with its rich, fluently enjambed ▷ couplets, is an ambiguous plea in favour of aestheticism and sensual escapism. Lamia should be the villain of the poem, but in fact it is Apollonius. The world to which she introduces the young Greek is one of ravishing beauty and magic, and the final triumph of philosophical truth is accompanied by the death of the imagination: 'Do not all charms fly/ At the mere touch of cold philosophy?'

Lammas

In Old English, 'loaf mass'; used formerly in the Church as a thanksgiving for harvest, or harvest festival, celebrated on 1 August. It was also (and in Scotland still is) a ▷ Quarter Day for the payment of bills, etc.

Lamming, George (b 1927)

Barbadian novelist. After teaching in Trinidad he moved to Britain in 1950. His novels are concerned with the West Indian identity, both individual and collective, and the aftermath of colonialism and slavery. *The Emigrants* (1954) is a bleak portrayal of identity sought and lost among black emigrants to England in the 1950s; *Season of Adventure* (1960) represents the awakening to a new and more liberal consciousness of the daughter of a West Indian police officer; *Water with Berries* (1971) uses parallels with the colonial symbolism of ▷ Shakespeare's ▷ *The Tempest* to represent the historical consequences of colonialism through the

personal crises of three West Indian artists living in London. His other novels are: *In the Castle of my Skin* (1953); *Of Age and Innocence* (1958); *Natives of my Person* (1972); *The Pleasures of Exile* (1984).
Bib: Paquet, S. P., *The Novels of George Lamming*.

Lampoon

A personal attack in the form of a verse ▷ satire, usually motivated by mere malevolence. It was common in the later 17th and 18th centuries.

Lancaster, House of

A branch of the ▷ Plantagenet family, or House of Anjou. The Lancastrian branch ruled over England from 1399 to 1461. It acquired the throne owing to a successful rebellion by Henry Bolingbroke, son of John Duke of Lancaster (John of Gaunt), against the reigning king, ▷ Richard II, Henry's cousin. Henry became ▷ Henry IV, and was succeeded by his son ▷ Henry V, and his grandson ▷ Henry VI. Henry VI was, in turn, deposed by his cousin, Edward, first king of the House of York.
　　▷ Wars of the Roses.

Lancelot

One of the most famous of the knights of the ▷ Round Table and lover of Queen ▷ Guinevere. Although Lancelot has no place in ▷ Geoffrey of Monmouth's version of Arthurian history (1138), by the end of the 12th century he was established as an important figure in vernacular Arthurian narratives. It is possible that an ▷ Anglo-Norman narrative about his life and adventures once existed (for it is used as the source of the late-12th-century German narrative *Lanzelet*). But the earliest extant romance about Lancelot is ▷ Chrétien de Troyes's *Chevalier de la Charrete* (c 1175), which recounts how Lancelot rescues Guinevere after her abduction by King Meleagant, as well as other episodes in Lancelot's chivalric career in her service. Chrétien does not provide many details of Lancelot's background but his profile is developed considerably in the 13th-century prose *Lancelot* and in other sections of the ▷ Vulgate cycle of romances (from which ▷ Malory draws much of his material for his ▷ *Morte D'Arthur*).
　　Lancelot is the son of King Ban of Benoic (in western France), who is carried away as a baby and brought up by the ▷ Lady of Lake (hence his full name Lancelot du Lac), who eventually presents him to ▷ Arthur's court. There he establishes himself, through

many adventures, as a knight of superlative status. Though he is a faithful lover of Guinevere, he is induced by a trick to spend the night with Elaine, daughter of King ▷ Pelles, and ▷ Galahad is conceived from their union. He fails to achieve the Quest of the Holy Grail because of his adulterous sin, though he pledges reform. His continuing affair with Guinevere is exploited by Mordred and his company to stir up the trouble in Arthur's court which leads, in part, to the downfall of the kingdom and the court. Lancelot's accidental killing of ▷ Gareth provides a further catalyst. He spends the last years of his life as a hermit (after he has taken his leave of the penitent Queen).

Lancelot is the emotional centre of Malory's reworking of Arthurian narrative, which substantially moderates the criticism he attracts in the ▷ Grail Quest. Indeed the whole structure of Malory's narrative affirms Lancelot's superlative status: after he has returned from the Grail Quest and resumed his affair, he nevertheless achieves the miraculous healing of Sir Urry, a feat which can only be performed by 'the beste knyghte of the worlde'. Ector's lament for Lancelot is structured around a litany of the superlative qualities of this 'hede of al Crysten knyghtes'.

Landor, Walter Savage (1775–1864)
Poet. Of upper-class background he was expelled from Oxford University for his intemperate radicalism, and lived for many years in Florence. He wrote the ▷ blank verse epic, *Gebir* (1798), the tragedy *Count Julian* (1812), and collections of verse: *Hellenics* (1847), *Italics* (1848), *Heroic Idylls* (1863). He was a fine classical scholar, producing a Latin version of *Gebir*, and his imagination was essentially literary in its inspiration. He is now chiefly remembered for his prose *Imaginary Conversations* (1824, 1828, 1829) between such figures of the past as Dante and Beatrice, and Elizabeth and Mary Tudor. His quarrelsome but generous personality was caricatured by ▷ Charles Dickens as Boythorn in ▷ *Bleak House*.
Bib: Pinsky, R., *Landor's Poetry*.

Lanfranc (d 1089)
Archbishop of Canterbury, 1070–89, under ▷ William I, first of the Norman kings. Lanfranc, an Italian by origin, corrected and reformed the English church, and yet helped the king to resist papal interference.

Langhorne, John (1735–79)
Poet, private tutor, clergyman and Justice of the Peace. He wrote sermons, translated ▷ Plutarch and edited the poems of ▷ William Collins (1765). His own poems include exercises in the numerous genres current in the 18th century: topographical verse, animal fables, ▷ pastorals, ▷ elegies and didactic epistles. His most important work, *The Country Justice* (1774–7), in pentameter couplets (▷ metre), mixes didacticism and sentimental anecdote. Its satire on the Poor Laws imitates ▷ Oliver Goldsmith's ▷ *The Deserted Village* (1770).

Langland, William (?1330–?81)
Little is known for certain about the life of William Langland, author of ▷ *Piers Plowman*, other than what can be gleaned from his literary portrait, refracted through the fictional persona of the dreamer/narrator Will. From this, especially from a passage inserted into the C text of *Piers Plowman* (Passus 6), Langland seems to have been a cleric in minor orders, originally from the West Midlands area, who made a living by saying prayers for the dead. In one manuscript of the C text there is a biographical note which identifies him as the son of Stacy de Rokayle of Shipton-under-Wychwood, in Oxfordshire. Although some other alliterative poems have been attributed to him in the past, there is no evidence for his composition of any other poems than *Piers Plowman*, which seems to have been the work of a lifetime in its own right.

Langue
This term appears throughout ▷ Ferdinand de Saussure's *Course in General Linguistics* (1915) to denote the system of ▷ signs which makes up any language structure. According to Saussure, individual utterances (▷ parole) are constructed out of elements which have no existence 'prior to the linguistic system, but only conceptual and phonetic differences arising out of that system'. This observation is fundamental to ▷ Structuralism, which is concerned with the positioning of particular elements within a nonvariable structure. 'Langue' is the term used to denote the linguistic structure itself, that is the rules which lie behind particular linguistic events.

Laodicean
In the ▷ Bible (*Revelation* III : 15–16) a reference to the weakness of the Church of Laodicea, one of the oldest of the Christian communities; they were accused of indifference – 'I know thy works, that thou art neither cold nor hot: I would thou wert cold or hot.' The term is thence applied to indifferentism in politics or religion.

A Laodicean is a novel by ▷ Thomas Hardy.

Laputa
In ▷ Jonathan Swift's ▷ *Gulliver's Travels*, the flying island in the satire against the ▷ natural philosophers of Part III.

Larkin, Philip (1922–85)

Philip Larkin

Poet. He was the most eminent of the group known as the 'New Lines' poets (from an anthology of that name, 1956, ed. by Robert Conquest) otherwise called the ▷ Movement. Many of them held posts in universities, and their work is characterized by thoughtfulness, irony, self-doubt, humility, and the search for completely honest feeling. These qualities are in accord with the imaginative temper of ▷ Thomas Hardy's poetry; Larkin, who greatly admired Hardy, has also been compared to ▷ W. H. Auden, though his political conservatism and concern to proclaim the pathos and humour of everyday experience rather than address the 'academic' reader represent a turning away from the technical radicalism of writers like Auden and ▷ T. S. Eliot. Publications: *The North Ship* (1945); *The Less Deceived* (1955); *The Whitsun Weddings* (1964); *High Windows* (1974); Editor *Oxford Books of Twentieth Century English Verse* (1973). Larkin also wrote two novels, *Jill* (1946) and *A Girl in Winter* (1947); see also his book of essays *Required Writing* (1983). Larkin was also known for his passion for jazz music; see *All*

What Jazz?: A Record Diary 1961–1968 (1970).
Bib: Thwaite, A. (ed.), *Larkin at Sixty*; Motion, A., *Philip Larkin*.

Last Chronicle of Barset, The (1867)
The last of the ▷ Barsetshire novels, about the politics of the imaginary cathedral town of Barchester, by ▷ Anthony Trollope. It centres on one of Trollope's best characters – the Reverend Josiah Crawley, the curate of Hogglestock. A poor, proud, isolated man with rigorous standards, he is accused of theft and persecuted by the arrogant Mrs Proudie, wife of the bishop. A minor theme is the engagement of Major Grantly to Mr Crawley's daughter, Grace, in defiance of the wishes of his father the Archdeacon. It is often considered to be the best of Trollope's novels.

Latimer, Hugh (?1490–1555)
One of the chief English ▷ Protestant reformers. He was favoured by ▷ Henry VIII and supported the king's separation of the ▷ Church of England from papal authority. However, he went further than Henry in his independence of thought, and in 1539 he resigned the bishopric of Worcester because he could not accept Henry's conservative statement of doctrine, the Act of Six Articles. Under the more Protestant regime of ▷ Edward VI he became a very popular preacher, but in 1555 he was burnt alive as a heretic under the Catholic ▷ Mary I. Among his memorable works is his letter to Henry VIII (1530) urging the free circulation of the ▷ Bible in translation.
▷ Reformation.

Latin literature
Rome began as a small Italian city state, and grew to an empire that surrounded the Mediterranean and extended as far north as the borderland between England and Scotland. Politically, it established the framework out of which modern Europe grew. Culturally, in part by native force and in part by its assimilation and transmission of the older and richer culture of Greece, its literature became the basis of European values, and especially those values that arise from the individual's relationship to his society.

Between 300 and 100 BC, Rome began to produce literature, and at the same time, after its conquest of the rich Greek colonies in southern Italy, to expand its imaginative and intellectual vision and to increase and refine the expressiveness of the Latin language through the study of ▷ Greek literature.

Primitive Roman literature had been of two kinds: that of the recording and examination of public life and conduct in annals of eminent men and in oratory, and that of the distinctively Roman art of ▷ satirical comedy. These centuries saw the production of the comic dramas of ▷ Plautus and of ▷ Terence. The orator and historian ▷ Cato the Censor upheld the virtues of Roman severity against Greek sophistication and luxury; the dominant figure, however, was the poet Ennius (239–169) who preserved a balance between Greek and Latin values by emulating ▷ Homer in a patriotic epic in Latin idiom and Greek metre, the *Annales*.

The first half of the first century B C was the last great period of the Roman Republic. Active participation in politics was still one of the principal concerns of Roman aristocrats, and by this time Romans had studied and profited from lessons in depth and force of thinking from Greece. ▷ Cicero was the great persuasive orator of public debate; such was the power of his eloquence that the period is often known as the Ciceronian age. ▷ Julius Caesar's terse, practical account of his wars in Gaul and invasion of Britain shows a different kind of prose excellence, and the vividness of ▷ Sallust's histories of episodes in recent Roman history is different again. It was thus an age of prose, but it included one of the finest of all philosophical poems, the *De Rerum Natura* ('Concerning the Nature of Things') of ▷ Lucretius, who expounded the thought of the Greek philosopher ▷ Epicurus. It included also the passionate love poems of ▷ Catallus, who gave new vitality to Greek mythology.

Julius Caesar's great-nephew, ▷ Augustus Caesar, became the first Emperor in 27 B C, and he ruled till his death in A D 14. The Republic ended, and with it the kind of moral thought and eloquence which had made Cicero so famous. Roman literature, however, entered upon its most famous period – the ▷ Augustan Age. If the Empire had not quite reached its greatest extent, its power was nonetheless at its peak; the old traditions of austerity and energy were not yet extinct; civilization, wealth and sophistication had not yet overbalanced into decadence resulting from excessive luxury. Augustus himself was a patron of letters. In prose, the outstanding writer was the historian ▷ Livy, but it was above all an age of poetry. The most famous of Roman poets, ▷ Virgil, celebrated great traditions, looked back to by a stable society, in which active political participation had become difficult or unimportant. His contemporary, ▷ Horace, celebrated the values of civilized private life. Tibullus, Propertius, and above all ▷ Ovid were poets of pleasure appealing to the refined taste of an elegant society.

The last period of Roman literature lasted approximately a hundred years from the death of Augustus. The Emperors were bad, the idea of Rome was losing much of its force, society was showing symptoms of decadence. The best writers became more detached from and more critical of Roman society. In the philosophy and drama of ▷ Seneca, the heroic poetry of ▷ Lucan, the satire of Persius (34–62), the Greek philosophy of ▷ Stoicism seemed the strongest defence of human dignity against social oppression and distress. The most powerful work, however, was the savage satire of ▷ Juvenal and the sombre history of his time by ▷ Tacitus.

Literature in Latin did not of course end here, nor did it end with the Roman Empire in the 5th century A D. Latin became the language of the Roman Catholic Church, and therefore of the early medieval educated classes. It remained a living, growing language till its style was fixed by ▷ Renaissance scholars in the 16th century. Even in the 17th century, ▷ Francis Bacon wrote much of his philosophy in Latin, and ▷ Milton wrote Latin poetry. Classical Latin was read and admired in medieval England, but knowledge of it was incomplete and inaccurate; much of this knowledge was obtained (for instance, by ▷ Chaucer) from contemporary French and Italian writers whose traditions were closer to classical Latin. Virgil retained great prestige, and Terence was studied in the monasteries for the purity of his style. After 1500, the Renaissance caused English writers to study and emulate the classical writers. Writers modelled themselves on styles of classical prose; the terse manner of Seneca and Tacitus was imitated by Bacon, whereas the eloquent flow of Cicero was emulated by ▷ Edmund Burke. More important than the study of styles was the way in which English writers again and again measured themselves against their own society by placing themselves in the position of Roman writers, and then assessed their society from a Roman standpoint. So, in the late 16th century ▷ Donne modelled his elegies on those of Ovid, and a little later ▷ Ben Jonson rewrote the lyrics of Catullus; in the 17th century Milton emulated Virgil as Virgil had once emulated Homer; in the 18th century ▷ Pope took the standpoint of Horace, and ▷ Samuel Johnson adopted that of Juvenal.

▷ Classical education.

Laud, William (1573–1645)
Archbishop of Canterbury under ▷ Charles
I. He firmly resisted the desire for further
reform among the religious extremists, and
even tried to impose religious uniformity
upon Scotland. His rigour was partly
responsible for the discontent which led to
the outbreak of the ▷ Civil War in 1642.
Parliament, which had already secured his
imprisonment in 1641, ordered his execution
in 1645.

Laura
▷ Petrarch.

Laurence, Margaret (1926–87)
Canadian novelist and short-story writer. She
wrote a series of novels and short stories
centred on Manawaka, Manitoba, a fictional
small town on the Canadian prairies: *The
Stone Angel* (1964); *A Jest of God* (1966); *The
Fire Dwellers* (1969); *A Bird In The House*
(stories; 1970); *The Diviners* (1974). These
works explore the social history of Canada,
through the lives of several generations of
women, dealing with themes such as the
claustrophobia of small town life, the force of
social inhibitions, the quest for identity and
the importance of a sense of the past.
Laurence's earlier work reflects the seven
years which she spent in Somalia and Ghana
between 1950 and 1957. *A Tree For Poverty*
(1954) is a translation of Somali oral poetry
and prose; *This Side Jordan* (1960) is a novel
about racial tension in the Gold Coast (now
Ghana); *The Tomorrow Tamer* (1963) is a
collection of stories; *The Prophet's Camel Bell*
(1963) is a travel narrative; *Long Drums and
Cannons: Nigerian Dramatists and Novelists
1952–66* (1968) is literary criticism.
▷ Commonwealth literature.
Bib: Thomas, C., *Laurence*.

**Lautréamont, Comte de (pseudonym of
Isidore-Lucien Ducasse) (1846–70)**
French writer of lyrical prose pieces which
appeared under the title *Les Chants de
Maldoror* in 1868, with a slightly expanded
posthumous version in 1890. The hero,
Maldoror, is a demonic figure and his world
is one of delirium and nightmare interspersed
with blasphemy and eroticism. The
hallucinatory quality of this work attracted
the interest of the Surrealists
(▷ Surrealism), who claimed Lautréamont
as one of their own and promoted his work.
Their interest has been carried forward into
contemporary French criticism.

**Lawrence, D. H. (David Herbert) (1885–
1930)**

D. H. Lawrence

Novelist, poet, critic. The son of a coal-
miner, he passed through University College,
Nottingham, and for a time worked as a
teacher. He eloped to Italy with Frieda
Weekley, the German wife of a Nottingham
professor, in 1912, and married her in 1914.
His hatred of World War I, together with the
German origins of his wife, caused them
unhappiness in 1914–18; after the war they
travelled about the world, visiting especially
Australia and New Mexico. Lawrence died of
tuberculosis at Vence in France in 1930. His
reputation has grown gradually, and he is
likely always to remain a controversial figure.
   Lawrence's life, art, criticism, poetry, and
teaching were all so closely related that it is
unusually difficult to distinguish one aspect
of his achievement from all the others.
Misunderstandings about his supposed
obsession with sexuality and the needless
legal action for obscenity in connection with
two of his novels (▷ *The Rainbow* and
▷ *Lady Chatterley's Lover*) initially distorted
judgement of his work, but he is now firmly
established as a major ▷ modernist novelist.
On the other hand, he has been the subject of
irrelevant hero-worship which is equally
distorting, and which he would have
repudiated. He was a deeply religious –

though not a Christian – writer who believed that modern man is perverting his nature by the wilful divorce of his consciousness from his spontaneous feelings. He has been accused of social prejudice. It is true that he was keenly critical of society; but he was the first major English novelist to have truly working-class origins, and this, together with his wide range of friendships with men and women of all classes, gave him unusual perceptiveness into the contradictions of English society. His attitude to women has been severely criticised (see K. Millett, *Sexual Politics*; 1970), as have the general political implications of his ideas (see J. Carey 'D. H. Lawrence's Doctrine' in S. Spender (ed.), *D. H. Lawrence: Novelist, Poet, Prophet*; 1973).

Novels: *The White Peacock* (1911); *The Trespasser* (1912); ▷ *Sons and Lovers* (1913), an autobiographical novel, was his first distinguished work, and it was followed by what are generally regarded as his two masterpieces, ▷ *The Rainbow* (1915) and ▷ *Women in Love* (1921); *The Lost Girl* (1920); *Aaron's Rod* (1922); *Kangaroo* (1923) about Australia; *The Plumed Serpent* (1926) about New Mexico; *Lady Chatterley's Lover* (1928), banned except for an expurgated edition until 1959. The unfinished *Mr Noon* was published in 1984. He also wrote several volumes of short stories and novellas which include much of his best fiction. Among the best known of these are *St Mawr, The Daughters of the Vicar, The Horse Dealer's Daughter, The Captain's Doll, The Prussian Officer, The Virgin and the Gipsy*.

One of Lawrence's most distinguishing features as an artist in fiction is his use of natural surroundings and animals realistically and yet symbolically, to express states of experience which elude direct description. This 'poetic' element in his fiction is reflected in much of his verse; some of this is in rhymed, metrical stanzas, but a great deal of it is free of verse conventions and close to the more condensed passages of his prose. Lawrence began writing poetry at the time when ▷ Imagism was seeking more concrete expression, and he contributed to Imagist anthologies. Some critics (*eg* A. Alvarez, *The Shaping Spirit*) are inclined to see his poetry as among the most important produced in the century, deserving to be set alongside the work of ▷ T. S. Eliot and ▷ W. B. Yeats.

Lawrence's descriptive, didactic, and critical prose is also important. His psychological essays, *Psychoanalysis and the Unconscious* (1921) and *Fantasia of the Unconscious* (1922) are imaginative, not scientific works, and contribute to the understanding of his creative mind. His descriptive volumes, *Sea and Sardinia* (1921), *Mornings in Mexico* (1927) show his outstanding powers of presenting scenes with sensuous immediacy, and his characteristic concentration of all his interest – moral and social, as well as aesthetic – on to natural environment. The same concentration is to be seen in his critical and didactic writing; he brought moral, aesthetic, and social judgements into play together. Much of his best critical writing is contained in the posthumous volumes *Phoenix* I and II; the *Study of Thomas Hardy* is of particular importance for the understanding of Lawrence's own work. His letters are being published in 7 volumes (vols 1–3, 1979–84).

Lawrence wrote eight plays including: *The Widowing of Mrs Holroyd* (1920); *Touch and Go* (1920); *David* (1927); *A Collier's Friday Night* (1965); *The Daughter in Law* (1967); *The Fight for Barbara* (1967). These have never received the attention accorded the rest of his work. He was an excellent letter-writer: *Letters* (ed. Aldous Huxley).

Bib: Leavis, F. R., *D. H. Lawrence, Novelist*; E. T., *D. H. Lawrence, a Personal Record*; Lawrence, F., *Not I, but the Wind*; Moore, H. T., *The Intelligent Heart*; Nehls, E., (ed.) *Lawrence: a Composite Biography*; Spilka, M., *The Love Ethic of D. H. Lawrence*; Draper, R. P., *Lawrence: The Critical Heritage*; Hough, G. G., *The Dark Sun*; Kermode, F., *Lawrence*; Burgess, A., *Flame Into Being*; Sagar, K., *The Life of D. H. Lawrence* and *D. H. Lawrence: Life Into Art*.

Lay

A term in use from the medieval period for a lyrical or narrative composition, especially one recited or sung to music. The 19th-century revival of interest in the Middle Ages stimulated a revival of the lay form, which may be exemplified in poems such as ▷ Walter Scott's *Lay of the Ancient Minstrel*.

Laȝamon

Composer of the *Brut*, a history of Britain from its foundation by Brutus to the establishment of Saxon control over the island in Middle English ▷ alliterative verse, based on ▷ Wace's *Roman de Brut* (completed 1155). Laȝamon's text is difficult to date precisely: it was composed some time between 1189 and 1275 (the date of the two extant manuscripts). Most of what is known about Laȝamon himself derives from the highly stylized prologue to the *Brut*, which introduces the writer as a priest, who lives at Arley Kings (in Worcestershire) and as which describes his process of composition (his search for books and his act of compilation from at least three sources).

The *Brut* is of great interest, not only because it contains the earliest account of Arthurian history in English (and its depiction of ▷ Arthur's reign is considerably amplified from the *Roman de Brut*), but because of its approach to the act of commemorating the past as a whole. It is composed in a style which echoes that of earlier English poetry and seems to have self-consciously archaic touches built into the text. Laʒamon's work goes against the grain of most vernacular historical narrative, in so far as it appears to cultivate a sense of the 'pastness' of the history being related, through its use of a deliberately archaic style which enhances the memorability of the history itself. Some of the archaisms of vocabulary and the stylization of descriptive passages in the British Library Cotton Caligula A ix manuscript have been revised in the text contained in the Cotton Otho C xiii manuscript: the difference between the two versions is not one of date but of literary style. The *Brut*'s regional point of origin helps provide some context for this interesting literary experiment. Worcester is the centre of an area where the greatest continuity can be traced between pre- and post-Conquest literary traditions: the copying and studying of ▷ Old English works seems to have been actively fostered there for some time after the Conquest. There are echoes of phrases and expressions drawn from Old English homilies (notably by ▷ Aelfric), written in rhythmical ▷ alliterative prose, and these seem to have provided Laʒamon with some of the resources for his creation of an archaistic literary medium.
▷ Round table.
Bib: Brook, G. L., and Leslie, R. F., (eds.), *Laʒamon's Brut*; Brook, G. L. (ed.), *Selections from Laʒamon's Brut*.

Le Fanu, J. (Joseph) S. (Sheridan) (1814–73)
Novelist and journalist. Born in Dublin of an old Hugenot family related by marriage to ▷ Sheridan's family, he wrote poetry as a child, including a long Irish poem at the age of 14. After education by his father and tutors, he went to Trinity in 1833, writing for the *Dublin University Magazine* and in 1837 joining the staff. He later became editor and proprietor. In 1837 he published some Irish ▷ ballads and in 1839 was called to the bar, although he did not practise, soon turning to journalism. He bought *The Warden, Evening*

Packet and part of the *Dublin Evening Mail*, later amalgamating the three into the *Evening Mail*. In 1844 he married Susan Bennett and withdrew from society after her death in 1858, when he wrote most of his novels, many in bed, on scraps of paper. His writing is ingeniously plotted, shows an attraction to the supernatural and has been increasingly well received this century. The novels include *The House by the Churchyard* (1863), *Wylder's Hand* (1864), *Uncle Silas* (1864), *Guy Deverell* (1865), *The Tenants of Malory* (1867), *A Lost Name* (1868), *The Wyvern Mystery* (1869), *Checkmate* (1871), *The Rose and the Key* (1871) and *Willing to Die* (1873), which was finished a few days before his death. The short stories, *In a Glass Darkly*, appeared in 1872 and a collection of neglected stories, *Madam Crowl's Ghost and Other Tales of Mystery*, in 1923.

Lear, Edward (1812–88)
Comic poet. He wrote *The Book of Nonsense* (1846) and *Nonsense Songs, Stories, and Botany* (1870) for the grandchildren of the Earl of Derby. Like ▷ Lewis Carroll, who wrote the *Alice* books for children, Lear's poems for children show remarkable freedom of fantasy; in consequence, the 20th century, with its new science of psychoanalysis, has seen in them unsuspected depths of interest. The poems combine grotesque comedy with haunting melancholy. He did much to popularize the ▷ limerick. He illustrated the poems himself with extremely witty line drawings. Lear was by profession a landscape painter, but his elaborate landscape paintings have much less distinction and interest than his drawings and sketches.
▷ Nonsense literature; Psychoanalytical criticism; Children's books.
Bib: Davidson, A., *Life*; Noakes, V., *Life*; Sewell, E., *The Field of Nonsense*.

Leavis, Frank Raymond (1895–1978)
Critic. From 1932 till 1953 he edited ▷ *Scrutiny*, a literary review with high critical standards, and pervaded by his personality. It maintained that the values of a society in all its activities derive from its culture, and that central to British culture is English literature; that a literature can be sustained only by discriminating readers, and therefore by a body of highly trained critics working together, especially in the collaborative circumstances of a university (*Education and the University*; 1943). The need for the testing of judgements by collaborative discussion is important in Leavis's view of criticism. Unfortunately, collaboration may become uncritical

There was an Old Man who said, "Hush! I perceive a young bird in this bush!"
When they said, "Is it small?" he replied, "Not at all!
It is four times as big as the bush!"

Illustration typical of Edward Lear's humorous verbal and visual style

discipleship, and this was one of the two unfortunate consequences of the exceptional force of Leavis's personality. The other unfortunate consequence was the hostility which this force of personality aroused in many critics who were not among his collaborators and followers. He maintained that true critical discernment can be achieved only by a total response of the mind – intellectual, imaginative and moral; thus a critical judgement reflects not only the work of literature being judged, but the worth of the personality that makes the judgement, so that Leavis's censure of critics with whom he strongly disagreed was sometimes extraordinarily vehement, as in his *Two Cultures?: The Significance of C. P. Snow* (1962). However this vehemence was a price he paid for his determination to sustain a living tradition of literature not only by assessing contemporary writers with the utmost rigour, but also by reassessing the writers of the past, distinguishing those he thought had a vital relevance for the modern sensibility from those that stand as mere monuments in academic museums. Such evaluative treatments caused him to be widely regarded as a destructive critic; his attack on the three-centuries-long prestige of ▷ Milton (*Revaluation* 1936 and *The Common Pursuit* 1952) gave particular offence.

Leavis's intense concern with the relationship between the kind of sensibility nourished by a literary culture and the quality of a society as a whole has a historical background that extends to the beginning of the 19th century. It first appears in ▷ Wordsworth's ▷ *Preface to the Lyrical Ballads* (1800), is to be felt in the writings of the 19th-century philosopher ▷ John Stuart Mill (see *Mill on Bentham and Coleridge*, ed. by Leavis, 1950), and is explicit in ▷ Matthew Arnold's writings, especially *Culture and Anarchy* (1869). Later the theme is taken up by the novelists, *eg* in ▷ Gissing's ▷ *New Grub Street* and, both in his novels and in his criticism, by ▷ D. H. Lawrence. The outstanding importance of novels in connection with the theme has caused Leavis to be foremost a critic of the novel; perhaps his most important single book is *The Great Tradition: George Eliot, Henry James, Joseph Conrad* (1948), but this should be read in conjunction with his books on Lawrence and (with Q. D. Leavis) on *Dickens the Novelist* (1971). Although still influential, Leavis must now be considered together with more contemporary literary theory, such as ▷ post-structuralism which has tended to challenge radically and contradict vehemently his criticism.

Lee, Nathaniel (?1653–92)

Dramatist. After an unsuccessful acting career Lee turned to writing plays. He became popular for his extravagant tragedies which included *Nero* (1674), *Sophonisba* (1675), and *Gloriana* (1676), and his *The Rival Queens* (1677) heralded a return to the use of blank verse for tragedy. His most serious play, ▷ *Lucius Junius Brutus*, was considered too politically dangerous and was banned after only a few performances. Towards the end of his life Lee spent five years in ▷ Bedlam and died after a drinking bout.

Leech-Gatherer, The
Sometimes used as an alternative title for ▷ William Wordsworth's poem ▷ *Resolution and Independence*.

Legend of Good Women, The
A story-collection composed by ▷ Chaucer, probably not long after ▷ *Troilus and Criseyde*, but revised some time later (the Prologue exists in two versions known as 'F' and 'G'). Dating the poem is difficult, but it seems to be Chaucer's earliest work using the decasyllabic couplet form, the staple of the ▷ *Canterbury Tales*. The story-collection is framed by a ▷ dream-vision narrative in which Chaucer, as writer, is tried in a ▷ pastoral court of love as a sinner against the God of Love. The intervention of a legendary good woman, Alceste, helps the poet/narrator, who promises to do penance for his literary misdeeds (one of which is having written about the infidelity of Criseyde) by writing a work composed of exemplary stories of good women who are true lovers. The work is to be a secular legend, in effect, not containing stories of the lives of those who have suffered for the Faith, but of those who have suffered for their love.

Although the Prologue suggests that the *Legend* is to be a large narrative project, only nine stories are extant (including those of Cleopatra, Thisbe, Dido, Hypsipyle and Medea, Lucrece, Ariadne, Philomela, Phyllis, Hypermestra). Narrating the stories themselves is an exercise in the art of abbreviation, for only cameo narratives are provided of their lives. But the art of abbreviation has a greater thematic point in some of the stories: it is only by abbreviating half of the story of Medea, for example, that she can be given a place in the company of good women. The construction of the dream-frame is influenced by the work of French love vision poets (especially ▷ Guillaume de Machaut) and the form of the stories themselves owes much to ▷ Ovid's *Heroides*. Although the collection has not always been very sympathetically received by modern readers, it seems to have been much read and admired in the 15th century.
Bib: Frank, R. W., *Chaucer and the Legend of Good Women*.

Lehmann, Rosamond (1901–90)
Novelist and short-story writer. The poet and critic John Lehmann was her brother. Her novels depict the experience of educated and sensitive women, focussing in particular on infatuation, betrayal and the contrast between the relative safety of childhood and the disillusionment of adolescence and adulthood. They make considerable use of memories and impressions, rendered in a lyrical prose style. She was initially associated with ▷ Virginia Woolf and ▷ Elizabeth Bowen for her rendering of the consciousness of women, but her work is generally regarded as narrower in scope. Her novels are: *Dusty Answer* (1927); *A Note in Music* (1930); *Invitation to the Waltz* (1932); *The Weather in the Streets* (1936); *The Ballad and the Source* (1944); *The Echoing Grove* (1953); *A Sea-Grape Tree* (1976). Story collection: *The Gipsy's Baby* (1946). She has also written her autobiography, *The Swan in the Evening* (1967).

Leicester, Robert Dudley, Earl of (?1531–88)
One of the principal favourites of ▷ Elizabeth I and for some time expected to become her husband. He was also the uncle of ▷ Sir Philip Sidney, killed at Zutphen during Leicester's campaign to assist the Netherlands in their resistance to Spain. Leicester had the brilliance which Elizabeth liked in her personal favourites, although for her statesmen she preferred more sober types such as Cecil and Walsingham. Scandalous stories were rumoured about his relationships with women, and in particular about his early marriage with Amy Robsart, but ▷ Sir Walter Scott's treatment of him in his novel ▷ *Kenilworth* is fiction.

Lemnos
One of the largest islands off the coast of Greece in the Aegean Sea. In Greek myth, ▷ Hephaestus, the artificer of the gods, was hurled down upon it by ▷ Zeus, from Mount Olympus. In the legend of the ▷ Argonauts, it was said to be peopled by women who had slain their husbands. Their queen was ▷ Hypsipyle.

Lennox, Charlotte (?1727–1804)
Charlotte Lennox was probably born in America, and grew up in New York. From an early age she is known to have been in London trying, unsuccessfully, to make a career on the stage. In 1747 she published *Poems on Several Occasions*, and in 1750, the year in which her appearance on the stage is last reported, she brought out her first novel, *The Life of Harriot Stuart*.

Lennox's literary talent was enthusiastically supported by ▷ Samuel Johnson and

▷ Henry Fielding. In 1752 *The Female Quixote* established her name as a writer; the novel tells of a naive heroine, Arabella, whose view of the world is foolishly filtered through the romances she reads. Lennox uses this framework to satirize sexual stereotypes and the social conventions of courtship.

Johnson's help in finding publishers for Lennox was probably partly motivated by his knowledge of her circumstances as well as her literary achievements. Her husband, Alexander, was a constant drain on the family's finances, and Lennox's writing provided their only support. She worked on translations and adaptations to supplement their income, and produced three volumes of Shakespeare's sources, with Johnson's encouragement. Her final novel *Euphemia* (1790) explores the position of women in marriage, reflecting her own experience with the spendthrift husband she eventually left.

Leprechaun
In Irish folklore, a shoemaker to the ▷ fairies, and one who knows the secrets of hidden treasure.

Lesbos
An island off the coast of Greece, famous in the 7th–6th centuries B C for its school of poets, the chief of whom was a woman, ▷ Sappho.

Lessing, Doris (b 1919)
Novelist and short-story writer. Born in Persia (now Iran) and brought up in Southern Rhodesia (now Zimbabwe), she settled in London in 1949. Her writing spans an exceptionally wide range of genres, settings and narrative techniques, but is unified by certain persistent concerns: the analysis of contemporary culture and of social process; a sense of 20th-century history as catastrophic and an attempt to link this to personal unhappiness; a mystical and sometimes utopian emphasis on higher states of consciousness; an intense anger at social injustice; an interest in radical revisions of the self and of personal and sexual relations.

Her first novel, *The Grass is Singing* (1950) is the story of a relationship between a white woman and a black man in Rhodesia, and was followed by the *Children of Violence* series, a *Bildungsroman* about a young Rhodesian girl in revolt against the establishment, ending in England with a vision of future chaos and a tentative hope for a utopian future. The series consists of: *Martha Quest* (1952); *A Proper Marriage* (1954); *A Ripple from the Storm* (1958); *Landlocked* (1965); *The Four Gated City* (1969). *The Golden Notebook* (1962) exemplifies the element of ▷ post-

modernist experiment in Lessing's work, in its use of multiple narratives and its concern with fiction and the reconstruction of the self, but it also addresses social issues of the 1960s: the crisis in radical politics, women's liberation, the value of psychoanalysis. During the 1970s Lessing started to write ▷ science fiction, and has remained a fierce exponent of its value as a literary form. Her series *Canopus in Argus: Archives* comprises: *Shikasta* (1979); *The Marriages Between Zones Three, Four and Five* (1980); *The Sirian Experiments* (1981); *The Making of the Representative for Planet 8* (1982); *The Sentimental Agents* (1983). These novels attempt to set human history and human relationships in the context of a battle between good and evil in the universe and an evolutionary quest for a higher state of being. Lessing has continued to show her inventiveness and flexibility with *The Diary of Jane Somers* (1984), a critique of society's treatment of the old, *The Good Terrorist* (1985), a study of the making of a terrorist, and *The Fifth Child* (1988), which uses elements of the horror story genre to explore problems in liberal ideals. Her other novels are: *Briefing for a Descent into Hell* (1971); *The Summer Before Dark* (1972); *Memoirs of a Survivor* (1974). Story collections include: *This Was the Old Chief's Country* (1951); *Five: Short Novels* (1953); *The Habit of Loving* (1957); *A Man and Two Women* (1963); *African Stories* (1964); *Winter in July* (1966); *The Black Madonna* (1966); *The Story of a non-Marrying Man* (1972).

Her other works include: *Going Home* (1957), a study of Southern Rhodesia; *In Pursuit of the English* (1960), a study of England in 1960; *A Small Personal Voice: Essays, Reviews, Interviews* (1974). *The Making of the Representative for Planet 8* has been turned into an opera, with music by Philip Glass (1988).
Bib: Sage, L., *Doris Lessing*; Sprague, C., and Tiger, V. (eds.), *Critical Essays on Doris Lessing*.

Lesson of the Master, The (1892)
A story by ▷ Henry James. Its theme is the barrier set up against the true artist by supposedly cultivated society, which can understand nothing about the artist's dedication and can therefore only hinder him by its unintelligent praise based on false standards.

Letter-writing
This is clearly an important branch of literature even when the interests of the letters is essentially historical (*eg* the ▷ Paston

Letters) or ▷ biographical. Letters may also be, by intention or by consequence of genius, works of intrinsic literary value. The 18th century (the age of the epistolary novel) was more than any other the period when letter-writing was cultivated as an art: see, above all, the letters of ▷ Horace Walpole and those to his son by ▷ Lord Chesterfield – the former a record of events and the latter consisting of moral reflections. Earlier than the 18th century, postal services were not sufficiently organized to encourage regular letter-writing, and the art of familiar prose was inadequately cultivated; by the mid-19th century, communications had improved enough to make frequent and full letter-writing redundant. By then letters had intrinsic, literary interest chiefly by virtue of the writers' talent for literary expression in other modes of writing, added to the accident that they found letters a congenial means of communication. The letters of the poet ▷ Gerard Manley Hopkins and the novelist ▷ D. H. Lawrence are examples. In the first 30 years of the 19th century the romantic habit of introspection resulted in a quantity of extremely interesting letters: those of ▷ Keats, ▷ Byron, ▷ Coleridge and ▷ Lamb are outstanding.

Levellers

An important political party during the period of the ▷ Civil War and the Commonwealth. It first became prominent in 1647; the term was first found in a letter of November of that year, describing them as people who wanted to 'rayse a parity and community in the kingdom'. Mainly found among the soldiers and opposed to kingship, the Levellers feared the Parliamentary leaders were insufficiently firm. Two documents were composed by them, *The Case of the Army Truly Stated* and *The Agreement of the People*, asking for a dissolution of ▷ Parliament and change in its future constitution. They were at odds with ▷ Oliver Cromwell, who suppressed the mutinies they engineered; Parliament declared other Leveller writings by John Liburne treasonable and in March 1649 their leaders were arrested. A public meeting in London in their support, and risings at Burford and Banbury were suppressed. Associated with them were the 'True Levellers' or 'Diggers' of April 1649, who took possession of some unoccupied ground at Oatlands in Surrey and began to cultivate it. The leaders, arrested and brought before Fairfax, denounced landowners.
▷ Civil wars; Cromwell, Oliver; Utopianism.

Lever, Charles James (1806–72)

Irish novelist. Famous in the 19th century for his vigorous comic novels about Irish country life and life in the army, *eg Harry Lorrequer* (1837), *Charles O'Malley* (1841), *Tom Burke of Ours* (1843). He was criticized for perpetuating the Englishman's comic notion of the Irish character – the 'stage Irishman' caricature, but ▷ William Makepeace Thackeray, who was a friend of Lever and parodied him in *Novels by Eminent Hands*, declared (in *A Box of Novels*) that Lever was true to Irish nature in being superficially humorous but sad at heart.
Bib: Stevenson, L., *Dr. Quicksilver: The Life of Charles Lever.*

Levertov, Denise (b 1923)

Poet and prose writer. Levertov was born and grew up in Britain but has lived in the U.S.A. since 1948. Her first publication was *The Double Image* (1946), and her work was also included in Kenneth Rexroth's *The New British Poets* (1948). Her most recent work is published in Britain by Bloodaxe, and she also features in the important *Bloodaxe Book of Contemporary Women Poets* (1985). Her volumes of verse include: *Collected Earlier Poems 1940–1960*; *Poems 1960–1967*; *To Stay Alive* (1971); *Life in the Forest* (1978); *Candles in Babylon* (1982): *Selected Poems* (1985); *Oblique Prayers* (1985). Her volumes of prose essays include: *The Poet in the World* (1973) and *Light up the Cave* (1982).

Leviathan

In the ▷ Bible, the name of a vast marine animal of varying character; in *Job* 41:15 it seems to be the crocodile, in *Isaiah* 27:1 a sea-serpent, in the *Psalms* 104:26 a dragon.

Leviathan (1651)
▷ Hobbes, Thomas.

Lewes, George Henry (1817–78)

Philosopher and critic. He wrote on a wide variety of subjects but his most remembered work is his *Life of Goethe* (1855), researched with ▷ George Eliot's help. Other works include *The Biographical History of Philosophy* (1845–6), studies in biology such as *Studies in Animal Life* (1862), two novels, *Ranthrope* (1847) and *Rose, Blanche and Violet* (1848), critical essays on the novel and the theatre, and, his most important philosophical book, *Problems of Life and Mind* (1873–8), the last volume of which was completed by George Eliot after his death. He collaborated with ▷ Thornton Leigh Hunt in founding the *Leader* and was first editor of the *Fortnightly Review* 1865–6. In 1854 he left his wife, who had had three sons by Hunt, and lived with

Mary Ann Evans ($\triangleright$ George Eliot) until his death.
Bib: Kitchell, A. T., *George Lewes and George Eliot*.

Lewis, C. S. (Clive Staples) (1898–1963)
Novelist, critic, poet and writer on religion.
Born in Belfast, Lewis served in France
during World War I. From 1925 until 1954
he was a Fellow of Magdalen College, Oxford
and tutor in English, and from 1954 was
Professor of Medieval and Renaissance
Literature at Cambridge. His fiction reflects
an interest in fantasy, myth and fairytale with
an underlying Christian message. He wrote a
$\triangleright$ science-fiction trilogy: *Out of the Silent
Planet* (1938); *Perelandra* (1943) (as *Voyage to
Venus*, 1953); *That Hideous Strength* (1945).
The Lion, The Witch, and The Wardrobe
(1950) was the first of seven fantasy stories
for children. His popular theological works
include: *The Problem of Pain* (1940); *Miracles*
(1947) and *The Screwtape Letters* (1942),
which takes the form of letters from an
experienced devil to a novice devil. *A Grief
Observed* (1961) is a powerful autobiographical
work, an account of his grief at the death of
his wife. He also wrote such classics of
literary history as *The Allegory of Love* (1936)
and *A Preface to Paradise Lost* (1942).
$\triangleright$ Children's books.

Lewis, Matthew Gregory (1775–1818)
$\triangleright$ 'Monk' Lewis.

Lewis, Percy Wyndham (1882–1957)
Painter, novelist, critic and polemical
journalist. Before 1914 he was leader of the
Vorticist movement in painting, which,
drawing on the French Cubist movement and
the Italian Futurist movement, advocated
dynamic, semi-abstract representation of
angular, precise and rhythmical forms. Lewis
carried over this predilection for vigour and
energy into literature, taking a boldly
independent attitude to modern culture,
rather like that of the poet $\triangleright$ Ezra Pound
with whom he edited the review *Blast* (1914–
15), and asserted the right and the power of
the intellect to take command in the cultural
crisis. He was opposed to domination by
political ideology (though he wrote favourably
of Hitler in 1931), by psychological cults and
by the bureaucratic and welfare state; he
made it his principal aim to expose the
confusion of mind which he considered to be
overwhelming 20th-century man, and the
hollowness of humanity which he believed to
be the consequence of encroaching
mechanization. He had something in common
with his friend $\triangleright$ T. S. Eliot (see $\triangleright$ *The*

Waste Land) but never became a Christian;
with $\triangleright$ D. H. Lawrence (see $\triangleright$ *St Mawr*)
whose mysticism he nevertheless despised;
with $\triangleright$ James Joyce, though he was strongly
opposed to his subjective $\triangleright$ stream of
consciousness technique; with $\triangleright$ F. R.
Leavis and the other $\triangleright$ *Scrutiny* critics,
who, however, rejected him as brutally
negative. He prided himself on his very
distinctive style of expression, which is
energetic and concentrates on presenting the
externals of human nature with icy clarity.

His outstanding writings are probably his
novels and stories: *Tarr* (1918); *The Wild
Body* (stories; 1927); *The Apes of God* (1930 –
a satire); *Snooty Baronet* (1932); *The Revenge
for Love* (1937 – considered by some critics to
be his best novel); *The Vulgar Streak* (1941);
Rotting Hill (stories; 1951); *Self Condemned*
(1954); and the four-part fable *The Human
Age – The Childermass* (1928), *Monstre Gai*
(1955), *Malign Fiesta* (1955) to have been
completed by *The Trial of Man* which he did
not live to finish.

His ideas are expounded in his
philosophical work *Time and Western Man*
(1927) and his autobiographies *Blasting and
Bombardiering* (1937) and *Rude Assignment*
(1950). He wrote notable literary criticism in
*The Lion and the Fox: the Role of Hero in the
Plays of Shakespeare* (1927), *Men without Art*
(1934) and *The Writer and the Absolute*
(1952).
Bib: Grigson, G., *A Master of Our Time*;
Kenner, H., *Wyndham Lewis*; Meyers, J., *The
Enemy*; Materer, T., *Wyndham Lewis: the
Novelist*; Meyers, J. (ed.), *Wyndham Lewis: a
Revaluation*; Jameson, F., *Fables of Aggres-
sion: Wyndham Lewis, the Modernist as Fascist*.

Liberal Party
The Liberals were the successors of the
former $\triangleright$ Whig Party; the change of name
came about gradually after 1830 owing to a
change in the composition of the party's
supporters. In its political sense, the word
'Liberal' was an importation from Spain and
France. After the end of the Napoleonic
Wars (1815) it was first applied to what were
considered to be extreme or even
revolutionary reformers. $\triangleright$ Byron and
$\triangleright$ Leigh Hunt, both famous for the boldness
of their policies, collaborated to found the
short-lived *Liberal* magazine in 1822. In the
meantime, the Philosophical Radicals, led by
$\triangleright$ Bentham and the $\triangleright$ Mills, were
collaborating with the Whigs to secure the
passing of the first Parliamentary $\triangleright$ Reform
Bill, which was to extend the right to vote to
a larger proportion of the population. When

this Bill was passed into law (1832) the Whigs, who had formerly consisted preponderantly of landed aristocracy, found themselves supported by the newly enfranchised industrial middle class, and it became increasingly clear that a new name had to be adopted to cover the former Whigs, the Radicals, and the industrialists. By the end of the 1830s the Whigs were increasingly calling themselves Liberals, and it became the accepted name for the party by the 1860s. Until 1923 the Liberals and the Conservatives were the principal political parties in Britain. The differences between them changed from decade to decade, but the Liberals were always more representative of town and industrial interests, and more inclined to strive for reform, whereas the Conservatives stood more for the countryside and sought stability. The disastrous decline of Liberal strength since 1923 has been due to a realignment of social interests.

In the 1970s the Liberal Party regained some strength. The general disillusionment with the polarized party system of Conservative and Labour also produced another political group in the Parliamentary arena. In 1981 a number of MPs broke away from the Labour party and formed the Social Democratic Party, which was intended to 'break the mould' of British politics. The growing power of the Conservative government in the 1980s and the lack of proportional representation, however, sapped the energies of the centrist groups, and in 1988 the two parties merged to form the Social and Liberal Democrats.

Liberty, On (1859)
A political essay by ▷ John Stuart Mill, in which he discusses how far and in what ways the state is entitled to interfere with the liberty of individuals. He concludes that in general this interference should be restricted to the protection of other individuals, and of individuals collectively considered as society. Mill was mainly alarmed lest a new tyranny should arise from democratic majorities who might be indifferent to minority rights.

Licensing Act
▷ Theatres.

Life and Death of Mr Badman, The (1680)
▷ Badman, The Life and Death of Mr.

Life of Jonathan Wild the Great, The (1743)
▷ Jonathan Wild the Great, The Life of.

Life of Samuel Johnson, The (1791)
▷ Boswell.

Lilliput
The island in Part 1 of ▷ Swift's ▷ Gulliver's Travels; the Lilliputians are diminutive in body, and their corresponding pettiness of mind is intended as satirical comment on the pettiness of contemporary English politics and society.

Lillo, George (1693–1739)
Dramatist. Lillo owned a jewellery shop in Moorgate Street, writing plays after hours, and contemporary descriptions of his character talk of him as a modest and moral man. His first piece, *Silvia, or the Country Burial*, a ballad-opera in the style of ▷ *The Beggar's Opera*, was staged at ▷ Drury Lane in 1730, and in 1731 Lillo produced *The Merchant*, afterwards renamed *The London Merchant, or the History of George Barnwell*, based on an old ballad. *The Merchant*, with its focus on a middle-class character led astray by temptation, and the depiction of his suffering, distress, and eventual penitence and execution, helped to establish the so-called domestic or bourgeois tragedy on the English stage, and was also influential in Germany and France via Lessing and Diderot. Lillo's other plays include *The Christian Hero* (1734), *Fatal Curiosity* (1736), again based on an old ballad about a murder, and ▷ *Arden of Feversham* (1736), drawing, like its Elizabethan predecessor, on an account by ▷ Holinshed.

Lily, William (?1468–1522)
Scholar; a pioneer of Greek studies, and part-author with Colet of a famous textbook on Latin; it was still in use in the 19th century.

Limbo
In medieval tradition, a region on the borders of Hell, supposed to be inhabited by the unbaptized: the souls of those who died before the coming of Christ and infants who died too soon for baptism.

Limerick
A kind of comic verse ▷ epigram which hardly ever varies from the following form:

> There was a faith-healer of Deal
> Who said, 'Although pain isn't real,
> If I sit on a pin
> And it punctures my skin
> I dislike what I fancy I feel!'

The form was popularized by the comic poet ▷ Edward Lear, though he was not its inventor. Whatever the derivation of its name, it seems to have no traceable connection with the town and county of Limerick in Ireland.

Linacre, Thomas (?1460–1524)
Physician, and a pioneer in Greek and Latin scholarship. He was chiefly responsible for founding the College of Physicians in 1518, and translated into excellent Latin some of the works of the Greek physician ▷ Galen. He is, however, less famous for his literary work than for the nobility of his character and for his zeal in promoting the study of medicine at Oxford and Cambridge.

Lincoln's Inn Fields Theatre
In March 1660 ▷ Sir William D'Avenant began conversion of Lisle's Tennis Court, built between 1656 and 1657 at Lincoln's Inn Fields, in order to house the ▷ Duke's Company under his newly confirmed patent from the king. The resulting theatre introduced the proscenium, or framed stage, to the English theatre for the first time. But increasingly the building was felt to be too small, and in 1671 the company moved to ▷ Dorset Garden. It was occupied by various companies until, in 1714, it was refurbished in grand style by Edward Shepherd, with mirrors lining the interior walls, and reopened under the auspices of the actor-manager ▷ John Rich.

Lindsay (Lyndsay), Sir David (c 1490–1555)
Scottish poet, courtier to James IV and 'Usher' of the infant James V. He was entrusted with various overseas diplomatic missions and knighted in 1542. He is most famous for his satirical work, especially his verse morality play, the *Satyre of the Thrie Estates* (1540), which analyses the corruption of Church and State. His other works include 'The Dream' (1528), an allegorical lament on the mismanagement of the realm; *The Complaynt and Testament of the Papyngo* (Parrot) (1530), in which a parrot is used as the mouthpiece for advice to the king and warnings to courtiers; and his narrative about a Scottish laird in two parts, the *Historie of ane Nobil and Vailzeand Squyer, William Meldrum* (1550).
Bib: Hamer, D. (ed.), *Poetical Works*; Kinsley, J. (ed.), *A Satire of the Three Estates*.

Linton, Eliza Lynn (1822–98)
Novelist and critic. Born in Keswick, Cumberland, she was a baby when her mother died. She did not agree with the ideas of her family and moved to London in 1845, entering the London literary scene with two historical novels, *Azeth the Egyptian* (1846) and *Anymone* (1848). She wrote for the ▷ *Morning Chronicle* 1848–51, publishing *Realities* in 1851, when she moved to Paris

until 1854. She married a widower with children, William James Linton, in 1858, adding his name to hers; but they were incompatible and separated in 1867. Her fiction changed from being romantic and imaginative; well-constructed and vigorous, it lacked both the early enthusiasm and sentimentalism. She had friends in the literary world including ▷ Walter Landor, and sold the house she inherited at Gad's Hill to ▷ Charles Dickens. From 1866 she wrote for the *Saturday Review* and offended many women with her attacks on ▷ feminism and the ▷ New Woman in an article called 'The Girl of the Period' (1868). Her other works include *Ourselves: essays on women* (1869), *Rebel of the Family* (1880), *The True History of Joshua Davidson, Christian and Communist* (1872) and *The Autobiography of Christopher Kirkland* (1885), which contains much of her own autobiography but portrayed through a masculine persona. Her own memoir, *My Literary Life*, appeared posthumously in 1899, showing her generosity, but also her acid tendency in an attack on ▷ George Eliot.
Bib: Layard, G. S. (ed.), *Mrs Eliza Lynn Linton. Her Life, Letters and Opinions*.

Lion, The British
The national emblem, perhaps from its representation on the coats of arms of medieval kings. The first literary mention of the British Lion is in ▷ John Dryden's poem ▷ *The Hind and the Panther*.

Lisle's Tennis Court
▷ Lincoln's Inn Fields.

Litotes
▷ Figures of Speech.

Little Dorrit **(1855–7)**
A novel by ▷ Charles Dickens. It centres on the theme of imprisonment, both literal and symbolic. William Dorrit (with his children and his brother Frederick) has been so long in the ▷ Marshalsea Prison for debtors that he is known as 'the Father of the Marshalsea' – a title that gives him a spurious social prestige. Arthur Clennam, who befriends him in the belief that the Dorrit family has been victimized by the commercial interests of his own family, is eventually confined in the same prison. But outside, the characters inhabit prisons without visible walls: William Dorrit inherits a fortune, and he and his family are constricted by social ambition under the gaolership of Mrs General who instructs them in fashionable ways; Mrs Clennam, Arthur's supposed mother, inhabits a gloomy house, confined to her chair and her bad conscience, under the gaolership of her

servant Flintwinch who knows her guilty secrets; Merdle, the financier of reputedly enormous wealth, is the prisoner of his false position, and his gaolers are his fashionable wife and his arrogant butler; the servant girl, Tattycoram, is at first the prisoner of the well-intentioned but misguided Mr and Mrs Meagles, and then escapes to the worse prison of Miss Wade, herself a prisoner of her self-inflicted loneliness. The nation is under the imprisoning control of a government department, the Circumlocution Office, which exists to gratify the interests of the enormous Barnacle family. Three characters stand out in independence of this conspiracy to confine and frustrate: Frederick Dorrit, who lives out an existence of passive misery by refusing to share (in or out of the Marshalsea) the self-deceptions of his brother William; Amy ('Little Dorrit') who consistently follows the compassion of her affections and the duties this imposes on her; and Daniel Doyce, the engineer whose enterprise is baffled by the Circumlocution Office but who perseveres in his vocation with humble and disinterested reverence for the demands that it makes on him. The self-interested Circumlocution Office at the top of society is balanced by the inhabitants of Bleeding Heart Yard, people who are themselves prisoners of the exorbitant property owner, Casby, but who live in the freedom of their own equal and open-hearted society. The blackmailer Rigaud is a figure of menacing evil and a dramatic counterpart to Mrs Clennam's hypocrisy and pretence, which is at the heart of the imaginative scheme of the novel. *Little Dorrit* is often regarded as Dickens's finest work, both in dramatic impressiveness and in richness of psychological insight.

Little Gidding

A small religious community founded by the Anglican theologian Nicholas Ferrar (1592–1637) at a manor house in Huntingdonshire in 1625. It was dispersed, and the buildings were destroyed, by Parliamentary soldiers at the end of the ▷ Civil War (1646).
▷ Charles I visited the community in 1633 and according to tradition he came again after his final defeat at the battle of Naseby (1645). The community is the starting point of one of ▷ T. S. Eliot's poems which takes its title from it (in ▷ *Four Quartets*), and an account of it comes into the historical novel *John Inglesant* (1881) by J. H. Shorthouse.

Little John

In the ▷ Robin Hood cycle of legends, the principal lieutenant of the popular outlaw, Robin Hood. Originally John Little, his names were reversed ironically, owing to his great size and strength.

Little Theatre

▷ Lincoln's Inn Fields.

Little Theatre in the Hay

▷ Haymarket Theatres.

Littlewood, Joan (b 1914)

British director and founder of Theatre Union in the 1930s with her husband Ewan MacColl. The company reformed after the war as Theatre Workshop, based firstly in Manchester and, from 1953, in East London at the Theatre Royal, Stratford East. Littlewood developed a method of working with actors which encouraged collaboration and improvisation. Her two most famous productions were ▷ Brendan Behan's *The Hostage* and *Oh, What a Lovely War*, the latter accredited to Theatre Workshop, Charles Chilton and the members of the original cast. Her aim was to provide a 'fun palace' for working-class audiences, though commercial pressures meant that the company had to rely heavily on West End transfers for survival, which destroyed her attempts to create a genuine ensemble.
Bib: Goorney, H., *The Theatre Workshop Story*.

Lives of the Poets, The (1779–81)

By ▷ Samuel Johnson; originally entitled *Prefaces biographical and critical to the Works of the English Poets*. Johnson began work on the project at the request of a number of booksellers, who required essays on the poets which could be prefaced to editions of their works. The essays developed so successfully that it was decided to issue them in their own right. The essays are interesting both for their critical insight and because they embody the literary tastes of the time. They are idiosyncratic and prejudiced, but always lively; Johnson's bias against the ▷ metaphysical poets in particular has been challenged by changing literary tastes.

Livy (Titus Livius) (59 BC–AD 17)

Roman historian. He wrote the history of Rome in 142 books, 35 of which have survived, with summaries of most of the rest. His aims were partly to ensure that the achievements of 'the chiefest people of the world' should be remembered and partly to provide material for future political guidance.
▷ Latin literature.

Lloyd's

An association of shipowners and other business men concerned with shipping. Its activities are primarily the insurance of ships and cargoes, and the dissemination of shipping information. It arose from a ▷ coffee-house kept by an Edward Lloyd in London early in the 18th century; this was frequented by merchants and insurers of ships who eventually formed their own association.

Locke, John (1632–1704)

Philosopher. He follows ▷ Thomas Hobbes in his sceptical ▷ rationalism, but he is the direct opposite of Hobbes in his optimistic view of human nature and in the moderation and flexibility of his social and political ideas. Hobbes was born in the year of the attempted invasion by the ▷ Armada and was painfully aware of the human propensity to violence from the decade of ▷ civil wars (1642–52); Locke's sympathies were identified with the moderation of the bloodless ▷ Revolution of 1688 and the climate of reasonableness which followed it.

In his two *Treatises of Government* (1690), Locke, like Hobbes, presupposes a state of nature preceding a social contract which was the basis of political society. But whereas Hobbes saw the state of nature as a state of war, Locke saw it as a peaceful condition in which the Law of Nature and of Reason was spontaneously observed; his idea of the social contract was not, as for Hobbes, that human existence was intolerable without it, but that it merely provided additional assurance that life and property would be respected. For Hobbes sovereignty had to be single and absolute, but for Locke it was merely a public service always responsible to society, which may at any time remove it. Similarly, in his *Letters concerning Toleration* (1689, 1690, 1692 and a fourth published posthumously) Locke, unlike Hobbes, held that the state has no right to interfere in religious matters and that oppression of religion by governments caused religion to spark civil violence.

Locke's advocacy of religious toleration was consistent with his sceptical attitude to faith and knowledge. Man must first discover what he can know before he persecutes others for publishing false beliefs, and this inquiry he conducts in his ▷ *Essay concerning Human Understanding* (1690). This shows man's capacity for knowledge to be distinctly limited, but the existence of God turns out to be a necessary hypothesis discoverable by reason. Christianity therefore is inherently reasonable (*Reasonableness of Christianity*, 1695) and faith by revelation is indispensable only because the use of reason is unavailable to the majority of mankind; 'nothing that is contrary to . . . reason has a right to be urged or assented to as a matter of faith' (*Human Understanding*, Bk. IV).

In his *Thoughts on Education* Locke extols reason at the expense of imagination and therefore (by implication) of the imaginative arts. When he applies his philosophy to politics or education, Locke is always guided by standards of practical utility, and in his abstract speculation he refrains from carrying his reasoning so far (as ▷ David Hume was to seem to do) that the logical basis for the conduct of practical life by the light of reason was undermined. His philosophy dominated the 18th century and is at the back of such 19th-century rationalist movements as ▷ Utilitarianism.

Bib: Cranston, M., *Life*; MacLean, K., *John Locke and English Literature in the Eighteenth Century*; Willey, B., *The Seventeenth Century Background; English Moralists*; James, D. G., *The Life of Reason: Hobbes, Locke, Bolingbroke*.

Lodge, David (b 1935)

David Lodge

Novelist and critic, born in London and educated at London University. Since 1976 he has been Professor of Modern English Literature at the University of Birmingham. *His novels are: The Picturegoers* (1960); *Ginger, You're Barmy* (1962); *The British Museum is falling Down* (1965); *Out of the Shelter* (1970); *Changing Places* (1975); *How Far Can You Go?* (1980); *Small World* (1984);

Nice Work (1988). His earlier novels are views of English society in a light, realistic mode, but *The British Museum is Falling Down* introduces extensive use of parody and a farcical element. He is best known for *Changing Places* and *Small World*, inventive, humorous tales of academic life, full of jokes, puns, allusions, parodies and reflexive comments on the nature of narrative which reflect his interest in critical theory. They have affinities with the campus novels of ▷ Malcolm Bradbury. *Out of the Shelter* is a ▷ *Bildungsroman*, and *How Far Can You Go?* explores the personal struggles of a group of Catholics from the 1950s to the 1970s, concentrating in particular on the issue of contraception. Criticism includes: *Language of Fiction* (1966); *The Novelist at the Crossroads* (1971); *The Modes of Modern Writing* (1977); *Working With Structuralism* (1981).

Lodge, Thomas (1558–1625)

Poet and man of letters. He was one of the group now known as the ▷ University Wits; university scholars who used their learning to make a career as professional writers for the expanding reading public of the late 16th century. In many ways his career is representative of this new kind of ▷ Elizabethan professional writer.

He was the son of Sir Thomas Lodge, a Lord Mayor of London, and was educated at Merchant Taylors School and Trinity College, Oxford. He then became a student of law at Lincoln's Inn, London, in 1578. The law students of the ▷ Inns of Court in the reign of Elizabeth were a leading element of the literary public, and others besides Lodge found these law colleges a nursery for literary rather than legal talent. During the next 20 years he practised all the kinds of writing which were popular at the time. His first work (1580) was a ▷ pamphlet entitled *A Defence of Plays*, written in answer to ▷ Stephen Gosson's attack on theatrical literature, *Schoole of Abuse* (1580). Besides other pamphlets, he wrote prose romances interspersed with lyrics (*eg Rosalynde, Euphues Golden Legacy*, 1590, and *A Marguerite of America*, 1596), verse romances (*eg Scilla's Metamorphosis*, 1589, reissued as *Glaucus and Scilla*, 1610), a sonnet sequence (*Phillis*, 1593), and a collection of epistles and satires in imitation of the Roman poet ▷ Horace, *A Fig for Momus* (1595). He also wrote plays, or at least collaborated with playwrights, *eg* a chronicle play *The Wounds of Civil War* (printed 1594), and, probably with ▷ Robert Greene, *A Looking Glass for London and England* (1594). Besides this writing activity,

he joined two piratical expeditions against Spain, the first to the Canary Isles in 1588, and the second to Brazil in 1591. It was on the first that he wrote his most famous work, the romance ▷ *Rosalynde*, later used by Shakespeare as the story for ▷ *As You Like It*, and on the second that he wrote *A Marguerite of America*. After 1596, when he published the penitential and satirical pamphlets (*Wit's Misery* and *World's Madness*), he became converted to Roman Catholicism and took to the study of medicine, receiving the degree of M.D. from Oxford University in 1603. His literary works during the remainder of his life were serious and chiefly translations, (*eg* of Josephus (1602) and ▷ Seneca (1614)), and religious and medical treatises.

Bib: Sisson, C. J., *Lodge and Other Elizabethans.*

Logres

In ▷ Geoffrey of Monmouth's version of the history of Britain (completed c 1138), 'Loegria' is the name of a part of Britain, ruled by Brutus's son Locrine, which corresponds to the domain of England. The name is used in some medieval Arthurian romances and becomes associated with a legendary landscape that cannot be located in a precise historical time or place. It appears as 'Logris' in ▷ Spenser's ▷ *Faerie Queene*.

Loki

In Scandinavian myth, one of the gods, though evil and mischievous. He is both friend and enemy of the other gods, and this twofold nature has led him to be associated with fire. He has been compared to the Greek god ▷ Hephaestus, to the Titan ▷ Prometheus, and to ▷ Lucifer.

Lollardism

Lollard was the name (of disputed origin) given to the English followers of ▷ John Wycliffe. Their movement was widespread by the end of the 14th and beginning of the 15th century, continuing down to the ▷ Reformation. The wealth of the Church and its readiness to take money from starving peasants was what Lollardism attacked, though nobles and country gentlemen were among its supporters. It was at its most flourishing in the ten years after Wycliffe's death. In 1382 ▷ Richard II issued an ordinance requiring every bishop to arrest all Lollards. They formed an association of poor preachers to go about England preaching in the vernacular and talking privately with the faithful. Their literature was widely circulated in spite of proscription and in 1395 Lollards petitioned ▷ Parliament to reform the Church on Lollard principles. They were against celibacy, the doctrine of transubstantiation and ritual, like vestments, which they described as magical. There was to be no praying for the dead; confession they defined as the root of clerical arrogance; war was murder and plundering of the poor for the sake of kings and rich men intolerable; nuns' vows of chastity led to infanticide. There were some Lollard martyrs at the beginning of the 15th century. In 1408 Convocation issued various decrees designed to control Lollard activities: a bishop's licence to preach would henceforth be necessary; preachers addressing the laity were not to rebuke the sins of the clergy; Lollard books and bibles were to be destroyed. Under ▷ Henry v they endured further persecution and in 1418 preaching in the open air was banned. In 1428, however, they were said to be as numerous as ever. Lollardism did much to shape the English Reformation: subord-ination of clerical to lay jurisdiction, the reduction of Church possessions and making the ▷ Bible available to ordinary people in their own language were all Lollard goals.

▷ Utopianism.

Lollards

A term (originally abusive, deriving from the Dutch word '*lollaerd*' or mumbler) used of the followers of the Wycliffite reform movement of the later 14th century onwards. The programme of the movement was aimed at reforming the materialistic corruption of the clergy, creating a ministry closer to the Gospel ideal and promoting greater access to vernacular versions of scriptural texts. The Lollards seem to have enjoyed the patronage of certain knights who appear to have sponsored a scriptorium where Lollard texts could be copied and corrected.

▷ Wycliffe, John.
Bib: Coleman, J., *1350–1400. Medieval Writers and Readers.*

Lombard Street

In the City of London; for centuries a centre for finance and commerce. Its name derives from the settlement of Italian merchants from Lombardy (north Italy) in the ▷ Middle Ages. To bet 'All Lombard Street to a China orange' would show great confidence.

London

The capital of Great Britain and, in particular, the capital of England. The original core of London is called 'the City'; it is the financial capital of Britain and now has only a small residential population. Its Lord Mayor is still a figure of prestige, as a kind of symbolic representative of the financial and commercial power of the country. From the early 18th century, London expanded rapidly outwards from the City so as to absorb the surrounding villages which until 1965 retained their identity as districts within the administrative county of Greater London.

London has always had a great cultural dominance in England, partly because from the 12th century its neighbourhood was the main centre of the royal court and partly because of its great superiority in size and wealth over other English towns. In the ▷ Middle Ages the chief royal residences were the Palace of ▷ Westminster and the ▷ Tower (respectively to the west and east of the City); in the 16th century, ▷ Hampton Court; in the 17th century, ▷ Whitehall in Westminster and (at the end of the 17th century) Kensington Palace; since the middle of the 18th century, Buckingham Palace. ▷ Windsor Castle, a royal palace and stronghold since the 14th century, is not far to the west of London. London's superiority in size can be shown by the fact that in 1700 it had a population of about 600,000, whereas the cities next to it in size, Norwich and Bristol, had only about 30,000 each. A century before, in the time of ▷ Shakespeare, London's estimated population was a quarter of a million, and it was already one of the largest towns in Europe.

Districts west of the City (the 'West End') such as Westminster, ▷ Kensington, ▷ Chelsea, have always tended to be rich and fashionable; those to the east (the 'East End') the poorer areas.

The neighbourhood of the royal court was not the only cause of London's importance as the literary centre of national life. The ▷ Inns of Court – colleges of legal education originating in the 13th century – were equivalent to a university in fostering intellectual life, especially from the 15th to 17th centuries. In the later 15th century, the proximity of lawyers, courtiers, politicians, merchants and churchmen, at a time when every aspect of English society was in a critical phase of growth, gave London a peculiar vitality which expressed itself in the Elizabethan drama and in the building of the first ▷ theatres. London had virtually a monopoly of the drama until the 18th century; it was not until then that other towns began to build their own theatres. In the same century, the importance of the court as a cultural centre markedly declined. Intellectuals and men of letters met in the ▷ coffee-houses – equivalent to the cafés of

London: about 1660 (*above*); about 1860 (*below*).

19th-century Paris – and in the town mansions of the aristocracy and richer merchants. By the 19th century the population of London had enormously enlarged, and in consequence artistic and intellectual activity tended to concentrate in certain districts of it. Thus the British Museum Library made Bloomsbury (part of Holborn) a centre of scholarship, and London University (founded 1828) has its Senate House nearby; Chelsea became a home of painters, and ▷ Fleet Street the erstwhile base of journalism. (▷ Newspapers).

London (1738)

A poem by ▷ Samuel Johnson in heroic ▷ couplets, written in imitation of the *Third Satire* by ▷ Juvenal. In the spirit of Juvenal, Johnson satirizes (through the character of Thales) the degenerate sophistication, the social injustice, and the crime and licence of the so-called civilization of London. The style has Johnson's typical compression and force, and the ▷ satire is more impersonal than that of his chief predecessors, ▷ Dryden and ▷ Pope who followed the more relaxed and personal style of ▷ Horace. Juvenal is not imitated slavishly but interpreted with discernment and used as a criterion for emulation.

London Bridge

The famous bridge of this name, between the ▷ City and ▷ Southwark, was completed in 1209 and until 1750 it was the only bridge across the Thames at London. It was built of stone and had 20 piers; the narrow arches caused the river to flow through them in violent and dangerous currents. The bridge was 20 feet (6·1 m) wide with a 12 ft (3·7 m) roadway between houses and shops projected over the water on each side. Over the widest, centre arch there was a chapel dedicated to ▷ St Thomas à Becket of Canterbury. It was the approach to the ▷ City from the south and it bore two gates, on the northernmost of which the heads of traitors were exposed. The bridge was a source of civic pride, but a real inconvenience to shipping. In the second half of the 18th century two more bridges were built and the houses on London Bridge were taken down; in 1831 the bridge itself was demolished and replaced.

London Cuckolds, The (1681)

Comedy by ▷ Ravenscroft. Three old citizens, Doodle, Dashwell, and Wiseacre, are married to three young women: Arabella, Eugenia, and Peggy. Each of the men believes he has made the best choice, but the play shows how the women conspire to outwit their husbands, in order to carry on liaisons with their lovers. The atmosphere is one of farcical intrigue, with scenes of concealment, duplicity, and mistaken identity. Despite contemporary attacks on its supposed indecency, the play was staged each year on the Lord Mayor's Day until 1751. It was revived in 1979 at the ▷ Royal Court Theatre, and more recently, at the Lyric Theatre, Hammersmith.

London Magazine, The

Three periodicals of this name have existed: the first ran 1732–85; the second, 1820–29; and the third, founded in 1954, still exists. The second is the most famous. It was founded as the political opponent of the right-wing ▷ *Blackwood's Magazine*, and its first editor, John Scott, was killed in a duel in consequence of the rivalry. It had unusual literary distinction, with ▷ Lamb, ▷ Hazlitt, ▷ Hood and ▷ De Quincey on its staff; it published the first version of De Quincey's ▷ *Confessions of an English Opium-Eater*.

London Merchant, The (1731)

Tragedy by ▷ Lillo, based on an old ballad. First named *The Merchant*, and afterwards renamed *The London Merchant, or the History of George Barnwell*. The play focusses on the fortunes of the apprentice Barnwell, led into crime by the courtesan, Millwood. He robs and murders his uncle, but repents before being hanged. The play, with its emphasis on Barnwell's suffering and distress, helped to establish the so-called domestic or bourgeois tragedy on the English stage, and Lillo's stated purpose was corrective. *The London Merchant* is dedicated to a wealthy merchant, Sir John Eyles, and comments on the usefulness of merchants to the nation.

Long Parliament, The

A parliament which was summoned by ▷ Charles 1 in 1640 and continued until 1653, when it was dissolved by ▷ Oliver Cromwell. It was this parliament that broke with the king and started the ▷ Civil War in 1642. In 1648 those of its members who were disposed to come to terms with the king were expelled by Colonel Pride (Pride's Purge') and the remainder continued to sit under the nick-name of 'the Rump'. After dissolving it, Cromwell called parliaments of his own but after his death in 1658 it reassembled and in 1660, the year of the ▷ Restoration of the Monarchy, it dissolved itself to make way for a new parliament under the restored king, ▷ Charles 11. His government did not recognize the legality of Cromwell's parliaments, so that the law in the Long Parliament was considered to have sat continuously from 1640 to 1660.

Longinus, Dionysius Cassius (1st century AD)

Greek critic. Most of his works have perished but he is the reputed author of the extremely influential treatise *On the Sublime*. This is about literary style; 'the Sublime', though the traditional rendering of the Greek title, is usually regarded as misleading. The author is concerned with the qualities of expression that make for true impressiveness, relates them to distinction of mind in the writer and discusses faults that arise from fallacious ideas of eloquence. The French critic, ▷ Boileau, made a famous translation of the treatise in 1674, and through him it influenced 18th-century English ideas on style.

Look Back in Anger (1956)

A play by ▷ John Osborne, first performed at the ▷ Royal Court theatre where it immediately made a major impact. The plot and dramatic structure are fairly conventional: Jimmy Porter, from a working-class background, lives in cramped conditions with his upper-middle-class wife Alison. Alison's friend persuades her to leave Jimmy only to fall for him herself. When Alison has a miscarriage her friend obligingly makes way for her to return to her former husband. The story and subsidiary characters are really a vehicle for Jimmy's tirades against the class-ridden nature of British society in the post-war period. For many amongst the original audiences Jimmy was a kind of modern ▷ Hamlet figure, even though a modern audience would be more likely to focus on the sexist manner in which he hectors and bullies his wife. Nonetheless, the fact is that the play captured a particular mood of disillusionment in the period and established the Royal Court as a venue for drama of social protest.
▷ Angry young men.

Lord Chamberlain's Men, The
▷ Chamberlain's Men, The Lord.

Lord Jim (1900)

A novel by ▷ Joseph Conrad. It is narrated by Marlow, an officer in the Merchant Navy who also appears in Conrad's other works, ▷ *Heart of Darkness*, *Chance* and *Youth*. The first 35 chapters we are to suppose recounted to companions after dinner; the rest is in the form of a letter and written narrative subsequently posted to one of these friends. Jim is a young sailor, the son of an English country parson, who dreams of being a hero. He becomes chief mate of the *Patna*, a decrepit ship with second rate officers, carrying pilgrims from Singapore to Jeddah. When the ship seems about to sink he loses his nerve and, at the last moment, jumps into a small boat with the other officers. When they reach land they discover that the *Patna* has stayed afloat and been towed to safety. The other officers disappear, but Jim stays to face disgrace at the official enquiry. He meets Marlow, to whom he tells his story and subsequently, persecuted by his sense of lost honour, Jim takes up humble employment as a water clerk in various Eastern ports (it is thus that Marlow introduces him to us at the start of the novel). Through the intervention of Marlow, Jim is sent by Stein, a benevolent trader, to a remote trading post in the jungle called Patusan. There, in alliance with a local chief called Doramin, who is Stein's friend, Jim defeats in battle the forces of Sherif Ali, a half-caste Arab bandit leader, and becomes a venerated figure. However, when a party of European adventurers led by the scoundrelly Gentleman Brown appears in Patusan, the memory of his past dishonour fatally weakens Jim's resolve. He asks Doramin to let them go free, pledging his own life for their good behaviour. They massacre a party of the villagers, including Doramin's son, and Jim allows himself to be shot by Doramin.

Lords, House of

Technically the Upper House of the two Houses of Parliament, the British legislature. It sits under the presidency of the ▷ Lord Chancellor, who is minister for justice and the head of the judicial system. When he sits alone with seven specially appointed judges, the Lords of Appeal in Ordinary, the House of Lords constitutes the highest court of appeal in Britain.

The House of Lords is the direct descendant of the medieval Great Council, to which the king summoned his chief landholders (the nobles or 'peers of the realm') and the leaders of the Church. The House still consists of heriditary peers in a majority, though a small number of life peers (created under the Life Peerages Act of 1958) have been added to the number of non-hereditary members, the Lords of Appeal and the Lords Spiritual (the two Archbishops and 24 other bishops of the ▷ Church of England). In theory this makes the House of Lords a very large body with about 1,060 members; in fact only those peers who are politicians normally attend, so that in practice it is a smaller body than the House of Commons.

Until 1911 the legal power of the House of Lords was about equal to that of the House of Commons, though the latter had become politically the more important as early as the 17th century. The Parliament Act of 1911 greatly reduced its powers, however, and it rarely shows opposition to the majority decisions of the Lower House. A Bill for reform of the House of Lords was dropped by the Labour government in 1968–69.
▷ Parliament.

Lotos-Eaters, The
A poem by ▷ Alfred Tennyson, first published in the 1833 volume, which contains much of his most distinguished work. Its subject is the ancient Greek myth of the *lotophagi* ('lotus-eaters' – Tennyson used the Greek spelling, 'lotos') who occur in ▷ Homer's ▷ *Odyssey*. Those who visit the land where the lotus fruit grows and eat some of it lose all desire to return home. The theme of Tennyson's poem is the temptation to reject the world of activity, change and stress, in favour of a trancelike existence measured only by the more languorous rhythms of nature. It is in the tradition of ▷ Spenser and the more luxuriant ▷ Keats: the rhythms have hypnotic music, and the imagery is strongly and unsettlingly sensuous.

Love for Love (1695)
A comedy by ▷ William Congreve. The plot centres on an intrigue to frustrate an uncharitable father, Sir Sampson, who wishes to disinherit his extravagant elder son, Valentine, in favour of the younger brother, Ben, a hearty but ludicrous sailor. The intrigue is managed by Angelica, a rich and spirited girl in love with Valentine. A minor plot concerns Sir Sampson's attempt to marry Ben off to an equally awkward country girl, Miss Prue, the daughter of a superstitious astrologer, Foresight. The rustic embarrassment of Ben and Prue, neither of whom wants to marry the other, nicely contrasts with the wit and grace of Valentine and Angelica. The play succeeds particularly because of its skilful and witty prose dialogue.

Lovelace, Richard (1618–58)
Poet. One of the so-called ▷ 'Cavalier poets', Lovelace fought on behalf of the king during the ▷ Civil War. The majority of his poetry was written before 1649, when his collection of poems entitled *Lucasta* appeared. *Lucasta* is prefaced with a commendatory poem by ▷ Andrew Marvell, and his work might be thought of as anticipating themes expressed in Marvell's poetry – in particular the search for a form of

disengagement from the world. It is not, however, with the more republican Marvell that Lovelace is associated, but with aristocratic codes of love and honour embraced by the literary and military circles in which Lovelace moved. Of special note are the series of 'bestiary poems' (*eg* 'The Snail' or 'The Grasshopper') which seem often to offer themselves as a form of disguised, or encoded, commentary on the political crisis of the pre-Civil War period.
Bib: Wilkinson, C. H. (ed.), *The Poems of Richard Lovelace*; Weidhorn, M., *Richard Lovelace*.

Lovers' Vows (1798)
Play by ▷ Elizabeth Inchbald, adapted from *Das Kind der Liebe* by ▷ August von Kotzebue. Agatha has been seduced and abandoned by Baron Wildenhaim, who has married another woman. Agatha has given birth to a son, Frederic, but become separated from him. He finds her sunk in deep poverty, and learns about his birth for the first time. Eventually he persuades his father, now widowed and elderly, to marry his mother, and to allow his daughter Amelia to marry the man of her choice, instead of the wealthy man her father had chosen for her. The play is featured in ▷ Austen's ▷ *Mansfield Park*.

Love's Labour's Lost (1594–5)
A comedy by ▷ Shakespeare, published in a ▷ quarto edition in 1598. It is a play for court taste, recalling the comedies of ▷ John Lyly; the plot is light and fantastic, and a pretext for dextrously witty dialogue and poetic flights of fancy. But the graceful artificiality is enriched by freshness that arises from elements of rural life, both in the imagery employed by the courtiers and in some of the characters. As in later comedies written by Shakespeare in the decade 1590–1600 (▷ *A Midsummer Night's Dream*, ▷ *As You Like It*, ▷ *Twelfth Night*) the witty courtiers end by making fools of themselves in their own way, much as the clowns and simple-minded pedants do – predictably – in theirs.

The king of Navarre and three of his lords vow to shut themselves away from pleasure and ladies in order to devote themselves to study. They quickly find excuses to break the vow when the king is visited by the princess of France and three of her ladies on an embassy. A subplot concerns a group of ludicrous characters – the proud but seedy Spaniard, Don Armado; the pedantic schoolmaster Holofernes; Sir Nathaniel, the country clergyman, and Costard the rustic – who attempt to entertain the lords and ladies with a performance of the ▷ interlude of 'the Nine Worthies'. The courting of the princess and her ladies by the king and his lords is abruptly ended by the announcement of the death of the princess's father. The play ends with the ladies imposing a year's ordeal on their suitors.

Some scholars have seen in the play a light satire on the ▷ School of Night. Some of the characters are identified with living contemporaries, for instance Armado with ▷ Sir Walter Ralegh, who is said to have been one of the key members of the School.

Love's Last Shift (1696)

Comedy by ▷ Colley Cibber, often said to have set the stage for 18th-century '▷ Reform Comedy'. Loveless, having abandoned his wife Amanda and gone abroad, returns to England deeply in debt. She has inherited a fortune, and remained loyal to him. Amanda seduces him in disguise, then reveals her true identity. Shaken by remorse, Loveless embraces the 'chast Rapture of a Vertuous Love', and the two are reunited as a couple. The ending is said to have reduced the audience to tears, and the play was a great success. Sub-plots concern the courtships of Young Worthy and Narcissa, and of the Elder Worthy, a reformed rake and the teasing woman, Hillaria. ▷ Sir John Vanbrugh's *The Relapse* (1696) was written as a sequel and sardonic 'comment' on Cibber's play, showing that Loveless' reformation is only temporary. Cibber himself performed in both plays, as Sir Novelty Fashion, who later assumes the title of Lord Foppington.

Lowry, Malcolm (1909–57)

Novelist. He was educated in England, but spent most of his later life in Mexico, the United States, and British Columbia. His first novel, *Ultramarine*, was published in 1933. His reputation chiefly rests on his second and only other novel, *Under the Volcano* (1947). The central character, Geoffrey Firmin, is British Consul in a Mexican city situated under two volcanoes, just as in ancient times the Underworld, Tartarus, was supposed to be situated beneath the Sicilian volcano, Etna. Firmin is an alcoholic who has rejected the love of his wife and his friends and taken to drink as escape from the inhumanity of the modern world (the events take place in 1938) and his own sense of guilt and failure. The novel is highly allusive and symbolic, with metaphysical and mythical overtones, and the narrative is partly ▷ stream of consciousness. It shows the influence of ▷ Joseph Conrad and ▷ James

Joyce and it has been described as the most distinguished work of fiction produced by an English novelist since 1945. A number of works were published posthumously, including: two novels entitled *Dark as the Grave Wherein My Friend is Laid* (1968) and *October Ferry to Gabriola* (1970), which were put together from Lowry's drafts by his widow; *Selected Poems* (1962) and a volume of short stories, *Hear Us, O Lord, from Heaven Thy Dwelling Place* (1961).
Bib: Woodcock, G., *Lowry: the Man and His Work*; Day, D., *Lowry, a Biography*; Cross, R. K., *Malcolm Lowry: a Preface to His Fiction*.

Lucan (Marcus Annaeus Lucanus) (AD 39–65)

A Roman poet; author of the poem *Pharsalia* about the struggle for power between ▷ Julius Caesar and ▷ Pompey. ▷ Christopher Marlowe translated the first book (1600). The translation by Rowe (1718) was greatly praised by ▷ Samuel Johnson. In ancient times Lucan was noted for his florid style, and for his gift for ▷ epigram.

Lucian (2nd century AD)

Greek satirist. He is especially known for his satirical dialogues and for his *True History*, an account of imaginary voyages which ▷ Jonathan Swift may have used as a model for his ▷ *Gulliver's Travels*.

Lucifer

A Latin name meaning 'the light-bearer'. 'Lucifer' became one of the names for Satan, the brightest of angels before his fall.

Lucius Junius Brutus (1680)

Tragedy by ▷ Nathaniel Lee, based on the historic overthrow of Tarquin and establishment of a republic in Rome, using ▷ Livy as a major source. It contains strong libertarian and egalitarian speeches, as when Brutus accuses Tarquin of arbitrary rule (Act II) and looks forward to a time when 'no man shall offend because he's great' (Act V). Staged at a time of high political tension in England, with the ▷ Whigs pressing the Exclusion Bill, the play was considered too dangerous, and was suppressed.

Lucky Chance, The (1686)

Comedy by ▷ Aphra Behn. The title plot concerns the fortunes of Julia, Lady Fulbank, married to an old man, Sir Cautious Fulbank, but in love with the poverty-stricken Gayman. She secretly conveys money to Gayman, and then visits him disguised as an old crone. Later Sir Cautious gambles with Gayman, and stakes a night with his wife as the prize.

Gayman wins, and is brought to Julia's chamber, where he makes love to her in the guise of her husband. In the secondary plot, Bellmour, having killed a man in a duel, flees to Brussels, leaving behind his fiancée Leticia. In his absence Sir Feeble Fainwou'd, an old alderman whose name describes his condition, convinces Leticia that her lover is dead, and she agrees to marry Sir Feeble, but the wedding is forestalled when Bellmour returns, and manages to thwart his rival's plans. The play ends with Lady Fulbank announcing that she is leaving her husband, and both women being united with the men of their choice. In an extended and vivid speech, Lady Fulbank defends the right of women to love where they please, even if it means cuckolding their husbands. The play was successfully staged at ▷ Drury Lane, and formed the source of ▷ Hannah Cowley's *School for Greybeards* (1786). It was revived at the ▷ Royal Court Theatre in 1984.

Lucrece (Lucretia)
A Roman lady of outstanding virtue and beauty. She was the wife of Tarquinius Collatinus but Sextus, the son of Tarquin, king of Rome, tried to seduce her and, when she resisted, raped her. She told her father and her husband of the outrage and exacted an oath of vengeance from them, after which she killed herself. In consequence, a relative of her husband, Lucius Junius Brutus, led a rebellion against the Tarquin monarchy and expelled them from the city. Lucrece was thus traditionally the occasion for the foundation of the ancient Roman Republic. The tale has been reworked many times because it poses questions about guilt and innocence that are of enduring concern.
Bib: Donaldson, I., *The Rapes of Lucrece*.

Lucretius (Titus Lucretius Carus) (1st century BC)
Roman poet; author of the great didactic poem *De Rerum Natura* ('Concerning the Nature of Things'). It outlines the philosophy of the Greek thinker ▷ Epicurus, which is based on the atomic theory of Democritus. The poet seeks to expound that all reality is material. The gods exist but they also are material, though immortal, and they are not concerned with the affairs of men; the soul exists but it, too, is material and mortal like the body, dissolving into its original atoms after death. Lucretius is not, however, a cynical poet; he testifies to the beauty of the natural world and the poem opens with an eloquent invocation to Venus, the conception of whom is followed by ▷ Edmund Spenser in ▷ *Faerie Queene* Bk. IV, x, stanza 44

onwards. Lucretius' love of the natural world and his reverence for reason caused him to be greatly admired during the ▷ Renaissance and the succeeding two centuries; parts of the poem were finely translated by ▷ Dryden.

Lucretius is a late ▷ dramatic monologue by ▷ Tennyson, in which the poet philosopher expounds his dying vision of the world.

Lucy Poems
A group of five ▷ lyrics by ▷ William Wordsworth, composed between 1799 and 1801. There is no clear evidence that the figure of Lucy represents any actual person, though her ambiguity may be an expression of the poet's intense relationship with his sister Dorothy. In 'Strange fits of passion I have known' the lover approaches Lucy's cottage as the moon sinks behind it, and suddenly imagines, for no apparent reason, that she might be dead. In 'Three years she grew' Lucy is a child who has died young, and in 'A slumber did my spirit seal' the poet consoles himself with the idea that the dead Lucy is now part of inanimate nature, 'Rolled round in earth's diurnal course,/ With rocks, and stones, and trees'. The sublime, almost mystical, simplicity of style of these poems has incurred parody. The poem which begins 'She dwelt among the untrodden ways/ Beside the springs of Dove,/ A Maid whom there were none to praise/ And very few to love', was delightfully rewritten by ▷ Samuel Taylor Coleridge's son, Hartley, to apply to the poet himself: 'He lived amidst th'untrodden ways/ To Rydal Lake that lead;/ A bard whom there were none to praise,/And very few to read'.

Lud
A mythical king of the ancient Britons, originally a god. He was supposed to have been the first to build walls round the City of London, and one of the medieval gates – Ludgate, still the name of the street that once led to it – was perhaps called after him.

Luddites
A name used for destroyers of machines, 1811–16. They were craftsmen who feared unemployment if the machines became established and were so called after a mythical leader, Ned Ludd. Nowadays the term 'new Luddites' is sometimes misleadingly used for those who fear modern technological development, for whatever reason.

Luggnagg
A country in Part III of ▷ Swift's ▷ *Gulliver's Travels*. It is inhabited by the Struldbrugs who have immortality, and find it a curse.

Luther, Martin (1483–1546)
German religious reformer, and the chief
figure in the European movement known as
the ▷ Reformation. The beginning of this is
often dated from 1517, when Luther fixed on
the church door at Wittenberg his 95 'Theses'
against the sale of 'indulgences'; a
consequence of this was his condemnation by
the Pope at the Diet of Worms (1521).

Luther's influence on the English
Reformation is a matter of dispute. Before he
separated the English church from the
authority of the Pope, ▷ Henry VIII wrote a
treatise against Luther, for which the Pope
awarded him the title of Defender of the
Faith (*Fidei Defensor*), still used by English
monarchs. Lutheran influences were felt by
humanists such as John Colet and ▷ Sir
Thomas More, and inspired ▷ William
Tyndale's translation of the ▷ Bible, the
first of several in the 16th century. They
certainly operated on the doctrines
represented by the second Prayer Book,
introduced by ▷ Archbishop Cranmer
under ▷ Edward VI. However, reformist
influences had been current in England since
▷ John Wycliffe in the 14th century.

Luther is the subject of a play, *Martin
Luther* (1961), by the English playwright,
▷ John Osborne.

Lycidas (1637)
A ▷ pastoral ▷ elegy by ▷ John Milton,
written in 1637. It is in the form of a
monody, *ie* modelled on the ▷ odes sung by
a single actor in ancient Greek ▷ tragedy.
Line lengths vary between three and five feet,
and the rhymes follow no regular pattern, but
the mournful, majestic sonority is consistently
sustained. Milton is lamenting the death of
his college friend Edward King, a gifted
young man who was drowned at sea, but it is
not a poem of personal loss. The theme is the
tragic loss of promise: King is seen as a
young man of talent and serious endeavour in
an age whose spiritual laxity requires the
reforming zeal of such a spirit. Greek pastoral
imagery is used – gods, ▷ muses,
▷ nymphs, including Camus, invented for
the occasion as the god of the river that flows
through Cambridge where Milton and King
had studied. More important, however, is the
pastoralism of the ▷ Bible: King was a good
shepherd; the clergy are spiritual shepherds
by their function but mostly bad ones.

Lycurgus (?9th century BC)
In ancient Greek history, the reputed founder
of the political system of the state of
▷ Sparta. He is often referred to as the type
of the lawgiver.

Lydgate (c 1370–1449/50)

John Lydgate at his desk, from Pynson's
print of *The Testament*

A prolific 15th-century writer who seems to
have enjoyed a higher contemporary literary
reputation than he does now. He was born in
Lydgate, Suffolk, and entered the famous and
well-endowed monastery of Bury St Edmunds
c 1385. He successfully aspired to noble and
royal patronage, and his vast literary output
provides a cultural 'barometer' of his time.
He translated a number of key texts on
classical, historical and moralizing subjects,
including his monumental *Troy Book*
(composed over 18 years, 1412–20), which is
a translation of ▷ Guido de Columnis's
Troy story; the *Siege of Thebes* (1420–2),
which he presents as a contribution to the
▷ *Canterbury Tales*; the *Pilgrimage of the
Life of Man* (1426–30); and the *Fall of Princes*
(1431–8), which is a translation of a French
version of ▷ Boccaccio's compilation of
tragedies (*De Casibus Virorum Illustrium*). He
also composed ▷ dream-vision poems
(including the *Temple of Glass*, modelled on
▷ Chaucer's ▷ *House of Fame*), large
numbers of lyric poems and a selection of
dramatic pieces (including ▷ Mummings),
designed for performance on various
ceremonial occasions or to mark court
festivities. His development of a Latinate,
aureate poetic register influenced the style of
court poetry in the 15th century.

Lydgate styled himself as a follower of
Chaucer, and his reputation as a leading man
of letters was evidently established during
and after his lifetime: from the later 15th
century onwards, his name is coupled with
that of Chaucer's as a founding figure of the
English literary tradition. Although his
enormous output finds less favour with
modern readers, he is undoubtedly a writer of
monumental dimensions, who assimilated

some of the important, authoritative narratives of medieval European court culture and made them available to a prestigious English audience. The scale of his work is daunting but that is also his strength.
Bib: Norton-Smith, J. (ed.), *Poems*; Pearsall, D., *John Lydgate*.

Lyell, Sir Charles (1797–1875)
Geologist. His principal work, *The Principles of Geology* (1830–33) revolutionized ideas about the age of the earth, and was a challenge to current theological thinking as ▷ Darwin's *Origin of Species* (1859) was to be. He also contributed the idea of change as continuous and ceaseless instead of sudden, intermittent and catastrophic, which had been the prevailing view. This added to the sense of flux and instability which haunted such contemporary imaginative writers as ▷ Matthew Arnold, ▷ Clough and ▷ Tennyson, whose ▷ *In Memoriam* shows traces of Lyell's influence.

Lyly, John (1554–1606)
Poet, writer of romances, dramatist. He was a popular writer for the cultivated society of court and university circles.

His prose romances, ▷ *Euphues, or the Anatomy of Wit* (1578) and *Euphues and his England* (1580), contain little story and are mainly pretexts for sophisticated discussion of contemporary manners and modes in a style whose graceful ornateness is really an end in itself. Its artificiality, now regarded as its fault, was at the time regarded as a virtue of high cultivation. It was much imitated in the last 20 years of the 16th century, and it was also parodied *eg* by ▷ Shakespeare in his early comedies and, through Falstaff, here and there in ▷ *Henry IV, Part I*.

Lyly's comedies are in the same elaborately sophisticated style, and are in fact the first *socially* sophisticated comedies in English. The plays were performed by boy actors in private theatres; they were not intended for the socially mixed audiences of the public theatres such as the ▷ Globe. *The Woman in the Moon* (before 1584) was the only one of these in verse. He followed it with prose plays interspersed with graceful lyrics: *Sapho and Phao* (1584); *Alexander and Campaspe* (1584); ▷ *Gallathea* (1585); *Endimion* (1588); *Midas* (1589); *Mother Bombie* (1594), and *Love's Metamorphosis* (published 1601). The best-known of these are *Alexander and Campaspe*, *Endimion* and *Mother Bombie*. They have grace and wit, and were closer to popular taste than was ▷ Restoration comedy a century later.
▷ Theatres.
Bib: Hunter, G. K., *John Lyly*.

Lyonesse
A legendary country in Arthurian narratives which came to be identified with a tract of land extending westwards and southwards from Cornwall, now submerged under the sea, according to the legends. ▷ Tristan is the son of the king of Lyonesse.

Lyric
In Ancient Greece the name given to verse sung to a lyre (from the Greek *'lurikos'* – 'for the lyre'), whether as a solo performance or by a choir. In English usage, the term has had different associations in different historical/literary periods. Elizabethan critics first used the term in England: ▷ George Puttenham, for example, describes a lyric poet as someone who composes 'songs or ballads of pleasure to be sung with the voice, and to the harpe'. From the illustrative quotations in the O.E.D. (sv. lyric), it is clear that in later usage musical accompaniment was no longer considered essential to the definition of the form. By the 19th century Ruskin defined lyric poetry as 'the expression by the poet of his own feelings': a definition which has the virtue of drawing attention to the personal and emotional focus of many lyric poems, but rather obscures any recognition of the highly stylized modes of mediating between personal experience and its public expression employed in lyric texts, which, like all literary conventions, may change over time. In modern English, the term lyric has a very general range of reference: it may be used to cover most forms of short poetry, especially that which has a personal focus of some kind, or is non-narrative. But the very generality of its reference undermines its value as a critical term since it may refer to many different kinds of poetic genres and sub-genres (as modern collections of lyric poetry reveal). The term 'lyrics' now describes verbal arrangements for musical accompaniment.
Bib: Lindley, D., *Lyric*.

Lyrical Ballads, with a Few other Poems (1798)
A collection of poems by ▷ William Wordsworth and ▷ Samuel Taylor Coleridge, often seen as the starting point of the Romantic movement, the term 'lyrical ballad' indicating the combination of primitive simplicity (▷ ballad) and literary elevation (▷ lyric) at which Wordsworth in particular aimed. The volume first appeared anonymously in 1798. Most of the poems were by Wordsworth, Coleridge's contributions being *The Rime of the Ancient Mariner*, *The Foster Mother's Tale*, *To the*

Nightingale, and *The Dungeon*. The second
edition (1800) appeared under Wordsworth's
name only, and included the famous *Preface*
and his poem ▷ *Michael*. Coleridge's poem
Love was added in place of Wordsworth's
The Convict. In the third edition of 1802 the
Preface was enlarged. The fourth and final
edition appeared in 1805.

In Chapter XIV of his *Biographia Literaria*,
Coleridge describes how the collaboration
came about. He and Wordsworth had been
discussing 'two cardinal points of poetry, the
power of exciting the sympathy of the reader
by a faithful adherence to the truth of nature,
and the power of giving the interest of
novelty by the modifying colours of the
imagination'. They projected a volume in
which Coleridge should direct himself to
characters 'supernatural' or at least romantic;
yet so as to transfer from our inward nature a
human interest . . . sufficient to procure . . .
that willing suspension of disbelief for the
moment, which constitutes poetic faith'.
Wordsworth's object would be to 'excite a
feeling analogous to the supernatural' for
everyday things the beauty of which was
normally concealed by the 'film of
familiarity'.

Wordsworth's *Preface* (1800) is a poetic
manifesto attacking the 'gaudiness and inane
phraseology' of poets such as ▷ Thomas
Gray, who attempt to separate the language
of poetry as far as possible from that of real
life. Wordsworth proposes instead to fit 'to
metrical arrangement a selection of the real
language of men in a state of vivid sensation'.
'Humble and rustic life' is the chosen subject
'because in that condition, the essential
passions of the heart find a better soil in
which they can attain their maturity, are less
under restraint, and speak a plainer and more
emphatic language'. It is important not to
oversimplify Wordsworth's aims or practice
here. His language in the volume does
sometimes affect the flat plainness of prose
(in *The Thorn* for example), and at other
times he employs the sing-song metre and
artless repetitions of the primitive ballad
('Her eyes were fair, and very fair,/ – Her
beauty made me glad.'). Sometimes however,
as in the non-ballad ▷ blank verse poem
*Lines Written a Few Miles Above Tintern
Abbey*, the philosophical, literary vocabulary
of earlier reflective verse is in evidence
('tranquil restoration', 'somewhat of a sad
perplexity'). At first Coleridge felt entirely at
one with Wordsworth's *Preface*, but later, in
Biographia Literaria, Chapters XVII–XX, he
subjected Wordsworth's theories of poetic
language to incisive analysis.

▷ The Lake Poets.

Lyttelton, George, Lord (1709–73)
Politician and poet. Opponent of ▷ Sir
Robert Walpole and for a time in 1756
Chancellor of the Exchequer. ▷ James
Thomson apostrophizes him in ▷ *The
Seasons* and he was a friend of ▷ Alexander
Pope, ▷ Henry Fielding and ▷ William
Shenstone. His own poems include *The
Progress of Love* (1732), *Monody to the
Memory of a Lady* (1747), and *Dialogues of
the Dead* (1760–5). He also published a
History of Henry II (1767).

**Lytton, Edward George Earle Lytton
Bulwer-(1st Baron Lytton) (1803–73)**
Novelist. He was the son of General Bulwer
and added his mother's surname of Lytton on
inheriting her estate in 1843. He was educated
at Trinity and Trinity Hall, Cambridge, and
was made a Baron in 1866. His novels were
very famous in his lifetime, and their range is
an indication of the literary variety and
changes in the Victorian period. His political
outlook was radical when he was young; he
was then a friend of the philosopher
▷ William Godwin, whose influence is
evident in his early novels, *Paul Clifford*
(1830) and *Eugene Aram* (1832). On the other
hand, he was a member of fashionable society
and his first success (*Pelham*, 1828) is closer
to ▷ Benjamin Disraeli's political novels of
high society, for example ▷ *Coningsby*. Then
in mid-career, under the influence of the
strict Victorian moral code, he wrote domestic
novels such as *The Caxtons – A Family
Picture* (1848). He showed the influence of
▷ Sir Walter Scott on the Victorians in his
historical novels such as *The Last Days of
Pompeii* (1834), *Rienzi* (1835) and *The Last of
the Barons* (1843), and the current
▷ German influence in the didacticism of
his early novels and in fantasies such as *The
Pilgrims of the Rhine* (1834). Bulwer-Lytton
was a friend of ▷ Charles Dickens (see the
biography of Dickens by Jack Lindsay) and
satirized ▷ Lord Tennyson in his poem *The
New Timon* (1846). He wrote some successful
plays – *The Lady of Lyons* (1838), *Richelieu*
(1838) and *Money* (1840). Like Disraeli, he
combined his literary with a political career,
for which he was rewarded with a peerage as
Baron Knebworth (his mother's estate), but
in his case literature had priority. His work is
now little respected (he is considered as
neither sincere nor original) but he is
interestingly representative of his period.
Bib: Sadleir, M., *Bulwer: A Panorama*;
Christensen, A. C., *Edward Bulwer-Lytton:
The Fiction of New Regions*.

Mabinogion

A collection of medieval Welsh tales, some from the 14th-century *Red Book of Hergest*. A *mabinog* was a bard's apprentice. 11 tales were translated by Lady Charlotte Guest (1838); four of these are versions of still older Celtic myths and are called the 'Four Branches of the Mabinogi'. These are the true *Mabinogion*. The others are old British tales of Roman times, British tales of ▷ King Arthur, and later tales of medieval romance.
▷ Wales.

Mac Flecknoe, or a Satyr upon the True-Blew-Protestant Poet, T. S. (1682)

A ▷ mock-heroic satire by ▷ John Dryden in pentameter couplets, written about 1678 and published in 1682. The poem attacks ▷ Thomas Shadwell, who is designated as the successor, or 'son' of Flecknoe, a ▷ Catholic poet previously the butt of a satire by ▷ Andrew Marvell. Shadwell had replied to Dryden's attack on Lord Shaftesbury in ▷ *The Medal*, with *The Medall of John Bayes*, accusing the Laureate (hence ▷ 'Bayes') of atheism. Dryden countered by attacking Shadwell in ▷ *Absalom and Achitophel*, Part II, and in this poem. It is a masterpiece of high-spirited lampoon, in which Dryden mocks Shadwell by making Flecknoe eulogize his 'son's' literary ineptitude and corpulence: 'The rest to some faint meaning make pretence,/ But Shadwell never deviates into sense . . . Besides his goodly Fabrick fills the eye,/ And seems design'd for thoughtless Majesty.' Its conclusion, in which two specialists in the new theatrical gimmicks of pantomime send 'the yet declaiming Bard' through a trapdoor, is purely farcical, and helps to make this one of the best comic poems in the language.

Macaulay, Thomas Babington (1800–59)

Historian, ▷ essayist, politician and poet. He was actively on the ▷ Whig side politically; that is to say, without being a radical reformer, he had strong faith in the virtue of British parliamentary institutions. He was, from the publication of his essay on ▷ Milton in 1825, a constant contributor to the main Whig periodical, the ▷ *Edinburgh Review*, and his *History of England* (1848 and 1855) is strongly marked by his political convictions. He was trained as a lawyer and became an eloquent orator; his writing has corresponding qualities of persuasiveness and vividness. As a historian he was best at impressionistic reconstruction of the past, and the same gift served him in his biographical essays on ▷ John Bunyan,

▷ Oliver Goldsmith, ▷ Samuel Johnson, ▷ Fanny Burney and the younger ▷ Samuel Pitt. He represented the most optimistic strain of feeling in mid-19th-century England – its faith in the march of progress.

Macaulay's *Lays of Ancient Rome* (1842) were an attempt to reconstruct legendary Roman history in a way that might resemble the lost ▷ ballad poetry of ancient Rome. Though not major poetry, they are very vigorous verse with the kind of appeal that is to be found in effective ballad poetry.

Macaulay was raised to the peerage in 1857.
▷ Histories; *Macaulay's History of England*.
Bib: Trevelyan, G. M., *Life and Letters*; Bryant, A., *Macaulay*; Firth, C., *A Commentary on Macaulay's History of England*; Trevelyan, G. M. in *Clio: a Muse*; Stephen, L., in *Hours in a Library*; Clive, J., *Thomas Babington Macaulay: The Shaping of the Historian*.

Macaulay's History of England from the Accession of James II

The history (Vols. 1 & 2, 1848; 3 & 4, 1855; 5, 1861) is a thorough, detailed account of two reigns: ▷ James II and ▷ William III. It is unfinished and was originally intended to extend to the time of George I (1714–27) and further. The period covered was perhaps the most crucial for English political development. James II, a ▷ Catholic, tried to enforce his will in the Catholic interest against Parliament, which frustrated him and expelled him from the throne in the ▷ Revolution of 1688. Parliament then summoned William from Holland to reign jointly with his wife, who was also James's daughter, Mary II (1689–94). William was the champion of the Protestant cause in Europe, and Mary was also Protestant.

Macaulay's politics were strongly in the ▷ Whig parliamentary tradition and his history is an epic of the triumph of the ideas which to him gave meaning to English history. Considered as history, the work is accordingly one-sided, much more a work of historical art than of historical science; it represents what historians have come to call 'the Whig interpretation of history'.

Macbeth (1605–6)

A tragedy by ▷ Shakespeare; it probably dates from 1605–6, and was first printed in the first ▷ folio edition of Shakespeare's collected works, 1623.

The material for the tragedy comes from ▷ Raphael Holinshed's *Chronicle of Scottish*

History (1578). Macbeth was an historical king of ▷ Scotland who reigned approximately 1040–58. He seems to have been a capable and beneficent sovereign in spite of his usurpation of the throne and sundry acts of cruelty, and Holinshed so records him. Shakespeare blackens his character, elevates his predecessor Duncan into a kind of saint, and makes a virtuous figure out of Macbeth's associate Banquo. Banquo was the legendary ancestor of James VI of Scotland, who ascended the English throne as ▷ James I in 1603. The relative idealization of Banquo, the prominence of witchcraft – a subject which was one of King James's hobbies – and other indications show that the play was written to appeal to the king's interest. They are all put to artistic purpose by Shakespeare, however, and enhance rather than deflect from his imaginative intention.

The tragedy is the conversion of a good man into a wholly evil one. Macbeth begins as the heroic warrior who defends Scotland against a triple enemy: the king of Norway has invaded Scotland in alliance with the open rebel Macdonwald and the secret rebel Cawdor. After his victory, Macbeth is confronted by a triple enemy assailing his own soul: the witches; his own evil desires; and his wife, who reinforces these desires. He first encounters the witches, who predict that he is to be king of Scotland, after being made Thane (Lord) of Cawdor. As Macbeth knows nothing of Cawdor's part in the rebellion and invasion, both prophecies are to him equally incredible. The second is, however, immediately confirmed by emissaries from Duncan, king of Scotland. Macbeth is now also lord of Cawdor and finds himself haunted by thoughts of bloodthirsty ambition: he becomes his soul's own secret enemy. The witches and his own desire would not in the end have been sufficient to cause him to murder the king, but Lady Macbeth dedicates herself to reinforcing his ambition. Macbeth is thus brought to murder Duncan, though in a state of horror at the deed, and becomes king on the flight of Duncan's son Malcolm. After the murder, however, he becomes a hardened man though a restless and desperate one; he proceeds to the murder of Banquo, whose children the witches have predicted will succeed him on the throne, and then degenerates into massacre and tyranny. The play exemplifies one of the beliefs of Shakespeare's time: that the soul of man is the pattern of the state, and that where evil breaks into the soul of a king it will extend over the state he rules.

Macbeth was written in Shakespeare's maturest period; together with ▷ *Othello*, ▷ *King Lear*, and ▷ *Antony and Cleopatra*, it is accounted one of his greatest tragedies.

MacCaig, Norman (b 1910)
Poet. A Scottish writer, educated at Edinburgh University, and often compared to fellow-Scot ▷ Hugh MacDiarmid, MacCaig uses mainly traditional poetic forms for his witty verse, although he has also been drawn towards ▷ free verse. His publications include: *Far Cry* (1943); *Riding Lights* (1955); *A Common Gate* (1960); *Surroundings* (1967); *Selected Poems* (1971); *Tree of Strings* (1977); *The Equal Skies* (1980); *A World of Difference* (1983); *Voice-Over* (1988).
▷ Scottish literature in English.

MacDiarmid, Hugh (Christopher Murray Grieve) (1892–1978)
Poet and critic. A ▷ Marxist, and a leading Scottish nationalist. His outstanding contribution has been the revival of the Lowland Scottish branch of English (once called Inglis, now for literary purposes, ▷ Lallans, and still the medium of speech) as a poetic medium. The language had a distinguished literary phase about 1500, and reached another peak in the work of ▷ Robert Burns in the 18th century, but thereafter was overwhelmed by southern English. In the earlier and greater period, Scots poetry was part of the wide European tradition; Burns's excellence drew from the surviving vigour of Lowland Scots culture. MacDiarmid's success has arisen from his ability to follow the example of Burns in far less promising conditions, and to resist southern English modes by his awareness of the wider context of Europe. His best-known poem in Lallans is *A Drunk Man Looks at the Thistle*. He has also written in southern English. *Complete Poems 1920–1976*, ed. M. Grieve and W. R. Aitken.
▷ Scottish literature in English.
Bib: Glen, D., *Hugh MacDiarmid and the Scottish Renaissance*.

Machaut, Guillaume de (c 1330–77)
French poet and musician. Machaut was a prolific and influential composer of lyric poems and songs, using and developing a number of poetic forms (eg ▷ ballade, ▷ rondeau). His narrative poetry includes several ▷ dream-vision poems, exploring problems of love and its literary representation, which influenced the form and structure ▷ Chaucer's dream-vision poetry, especially the ▷ *Book of the Duchess*.
Bib: Wimsatt, J., *Chaucer and the French*

Love Poets: the Literary background of the 'Book of the Duchess'; Windeatt, B. (trans.), *Chaucer's Dream Poetry: Sources and Analogues.*

Machiavelli, Nicolo di Bernardo dei (1469–1527)

Italian political theorist and historian. Machiavelli can be thought of as having two discrete existences. One is that of the Florentine diplomat, author of a comedy *La Mandragola* (1518) and of a series of important treatises on politics and statecraft: *The Prince* (1513), *Art of War* (1520) and *The Discourses* (1531). The other existence, however, is that which haunted the imagination of English writers in the 16th century and later, when Machiavelli's reputation as a cynical, cunning and diabolic figure emerges. In fact, Machiavelli's own works were very little known in England (other than by unreliable report) until a translation of *The Prince* appeared in 1640, though translations of his *Art of War* and portions of his historical works had been translated and published in 1560 and 1593, respectively. Nevertheless, it is the image of Machiavelli which became influential in England as is evidenced by ▷ Christopher Marlowe's creation of the stage-figure Machevill in his play ▷ *The Jew of Malta*. We can perhaps best understand this image of the Italian thinker in England as the embodiment, or focus, of a network of anxieties experienced within the emergent ▷ Protestant state, and directed outwards on the threatening presence of continental (and Catholic) Europe.
Bib: Gilmore, M. P. (ed.), *Studies on Machiavelli.*

Mackenzie, Compton (1883–1972)

Novelist. Son of a British actor-manager and an American actress. A very prolific writer of great popularity; his best-known novels are probably *Sinister Street* (1913–14) and *The Four Winds of Love* – a sequence composed of *The East Wind* (1937), *The South Wind* (1937), *The West Wind* (1940), *West to North* (1940), *The North Wind* (1944–5). When he began writing, ▷ Henry James regarded him as one of the most promising of younger novelists, and ▷ Ford Madox Ford thought *Sinister Street* perhaps a work of genius. However, serious critics have rarely given him extensive attention.
Bib: Dooley, D. T., *Mackenzie.*

Macklin, Charles (1699–1797)

Actor, manager, singer, dancer, dramatist. Macklin began employment as a scout at Trinity College Dublin, and came to London as a waiter before 1720. Some of his early stage performances were at ▷ Lincoln's Inn Fields, and in the next few years, he acted at ▷ Goodman's Field Theatre, the ▷ Haymarket Theatre, and ▷ Drury Lane.

In 1741 he astonished audiences with a radical new interpretation of the role of Shylock (▷ *The Merchant of Venice*), hitherto played for many years in low buffoonish style. Macklin presented him as a harsh, stern character, dressed 'authentically' with a red Venetian-style hat and red beard, and a long black gown. The response was repeated thunderous applause, such that he had to stop at the ends of several speeches to allow it to die away. His performance was recalled in detail by some spectators for decades afterwards. Its naturalism helped to render ▷ James Quin's elaborate and stylized methods obsolete, and set a precedent for the ultimately more successful actor, ▷ David Garrick, whom Macklin then began to sponsor and coach.

Subsequent years of Macklin's career were mainly divided between Dublin and London, but in 1773 he caused another sensation by creating a ▷ Macbeth in 'the old Caledonian habit', instead of the scarlet coat and wig worn, for example, by Garrick in the role. By the 1780s, Macklin's advanced age and failing health began to interfere seriously with his performances and he was finally forced to retire in 1789, after a career lasting nearly 70 years.

Macklin's achievements, and his reputation, have been somewhat obscured by those of his younger, more personable and physically attractive contemporary, David Garrick, who perfected the acting style which Macklin initiated. Macklin trained a generation of actors and actresses in his methods, and he is credited with turning acting into a 'science', a tribute to the seriousness with which he took his profession, and to his imaginative abilities. His career was constantly interrupted by squabbles with other actors and managers, fuelled by his notorious temper.
Bib: Appleton, W., *Charles Macklin an Actor's Life*; Kirkman, J. T., *Memoirs of the Life of Charles Macklin*; Congreve, F., *Authentic Memoirs of the Late Charles Macklin.*

Macmillan's Magazine

It was founded in 1859 and published a variety of material, including pieces by ▷ Tennyson, ▷ Arnold , ▷ Henry James and ▷ Thomas Hardy. It folded in 1907.

MacNeice, Louis (1907–63)

Poet. He was born in Northern Ireland, the son of an Anglican clergyman who became a bishop. During the 1930s he was associated by the reading public with a group of left-wing poets led by ▷ W. H. Auden. They were certainly his friends, but, although he had socialist sympathies, he never committed himself politically; in politics, as in religion, he was ▷ agnostic. He excelled in witty, sensuous verse of rhythmical versatility and with a strong element of caustic pessimism. He also wrote criticism, notably *The Poetry of W. B. Yeats* (1941), numerous plays for radio, and translated the *Agamemnon* of ▷ Aeschylus (1936) and ▷ Goethe's *Faust* (1951). He collaborated with Auden in *Letters from Iceland* (1937). *Collected Poems*, ed. E. R. Dodds (1979).
Bib: Fraser, G. S., in *Vision and Rhetoric*; Thwaite, A., *Essays on Contemporary English Poetry*.

Macpherson, James (1736–96)

The son of a farmer, educated in Aberdeen and at Edinburgh University. In 1760 he published 16 prose poems under the title *Fragments of Ancient Poetry, Collected in the Highlands of Scotland, and translated from the Gaelic or Erse Language.* He attributed them to the 3rd-century poet Ossian (▷ Oisin), an attribution which was accepted by most readers at the time, though some scholars were sceptical. After travelling in the Western Isles in 1760–1 at the expense of his supporters in Edinburgh, he published 'translations' of two complete epics by Ossian: *Fingal* (1762) (▷ Finn) and *Temora* (1763), which he claimed to have similarly 'collected'. The cloudy rhetoric and dramatic character simplification of Macpherson's prose-poetry caught the mood of the moment. ▷ Thomas Gray was enraptured by 'the infinite beauty' of the *Fragments*, ▷ William Blake was adulatory about them, and Macpherson's *Ossian* retained its popularity throughout the Romantic period, particularly on the continent. ▷ Goethe admired it; Napoleon carried a copy of Macpherson on his campaigns and took it into exile with him to St Helena. ▷ Samuel Johnson was amongst those who attacked the authenticity of Macpherson's sources, replying when asked if he believed that any modern man could have written such works: 'Yes Sir, many men, many women, and many children.' The indignant poet threatened him with physical violence. In later years Macpherson became a political journalist, wrote history with a Jacobite bias, and was elected M.P. for Camelford. After his death the Highland Society of Scotland undertook an inquiry into his work and in 1805 declared it to be an amalgam of freely adapted Irish ballads and original compositions by Macpherson himself.
▷ Percy, Thomas.

Madrigal

A poem composed to be sung, with or without instrumental accompaniment. It derived from the Italian 'canzone', and flourished in England especially between 1580 and 1630. It was sung chorally, and had three forms:
1 The Ayre. This had a melody composed for the top voice, which was accompanied by the other voices to the same melody.
2 The Ballet. This resembled the ayre, but was distinguished by its dance-like melody and refrain.
3 The Madrigal proper. This had different 'parts', *ie* melodies, for the individual voices, and was so composed that the melodies interwove. The parts were sometimes composed with the effect of dramatic contrast, *eg* by Thomas Weelkes (?1575–1623). Great attention was paid by composers to bringing out the meaning of the words, so that poets and musicians worked in close collaboration. Only ▷ Thomas Campion is known to have composed music for his own words, but others are believed to have done so. Ayres and madrigals are common in the plays of the period, and most of the poets wrote them.

Maeterlinck, Maurice (1862–1949)

Belgian symbolist (▷ Symbolism) dramatist, influential in the development of 'serious' drama at the end of the 19th century. His most famous work is *Pelleas et Melisande*, produced in London in 1898, and again in 1904 with Sarah Bernhardt as Pelleas and Mrs Patrick Campbell as Melisande. His plays were admired by ▷ W. B. Yeats and ▷ Harvey Granville Barker; *Aglavaine and Selysette* was given six performances at the ▷ Court Theatre in 1904.
Bib: Knapp, B., *Maurice Maeterlinck*.

Magazine

Originally meaning 'storehouse', the word has also denoted, since the 18th century, a periodical containing miscellaneous material, *eg* the *Gentleman's Magazine* (founded 1731): 'a Monthly Collection to store up, as in a Magazine, the most remarkable pieces on the subjects above-mentioned' (from the introduction to the first number). In the 18th and early 19th century magazines only differed from other serious periodicals (*eg* the

▷ *Edinburgh Review* and the ▷ *Quarterly*) in having greater variety of content and being open to imaginative writing. Distinguished magazines of this kind include ▷ *Blackwood's* and the second ▷ *London Magazine* (1820–29). Later in the 19th century, magazines became predominantly popular periodicals devoted principally to fiction. However, serious magazines still exist, *eg* the current *London Magazine*, the third to bear the name. Since World War II magazines have often been seen as synonymous with reading matter specifically directed at women. See *Wellesley Index to Periodicals*.

▷ Reviews and Periodicals.

Magi

1 A priestly caste in ancient Persian religion.

2 Supremely wise men or magicians, according to 16th-century neo-Platonic mysticism.

3 In the Bible (*Matthew* 2) the three wise men from the east who came to worship at the cradle of the child Jesus; they are also traditionally known as the Three Kings and bear the names of Caspar, Melchior and Balthazar.

Magic realism

A term applied in literature primarily to Latin American novelists such as Jorge Luis Borges (1899–1987), Gabriel García Márquez (b 1928) and Alejo Carpentier (b 1904), whose work combines a realistic manner with strong elements of the bizarre, supernatural and fantastic. This technique has influenced novelists such as ▷ John Fowles, ▷ Angela Carter and ▷ Salman Rushdie.

▷ Spanish influence on English literature.

Magistrates

In England and Wales, magistrates (also known as Justices of the Peace or J.P.s) are primarily minor judges who try small offences and examine more serious charges in order to decide whether they should be taken to a senior court. Most magistrates are private citizens and the ordinary Magistrates' Court is composed of a panel of J.P.s, never fewer than two; they are assisted by a Clerk who is a qualified lawyer but they themselves are unpaid. Their meetings are Petty Sessions and appeal from them lies to Quarter Sessions. There are also Stipendiary Magistrates' Courts, originally set up to cover the Metropolitan Police District of London and therefore known popularly as Police Courts, a term now commonly applied to any Magistrates' Court. Stipendiary magistrates are qualified lawyers and receive a salary; they may sit alone.

In the past, however, magistrates have had much wider functions and they have played an important part in English social and political life. The office dates from the 13th century, when petty landowners were appointed as magistrates to help the sheriffs maintain order in their districts, but until the 16th century their importance was comparatively slight. The feudal lords and the abbots of the monasteries were the real powers outside London and the districts adjacent to it. But by the 16th century the feudal nobility were weakened, displaced, or overthrown and in 1536–39 ▷ Henry VIII closed the monasteries. The ▷ Tudor sovereigns relied on the magistrates to enforce governmental policy in their districts and supervised them carefully through the ▷ Privy Council. Not only did the magistrates have to execute the ▷ Poor Laws, maintain the roads and enforce law and order, but they had to carry out functions formerly exercised by the town trade ▷ guilds (now greatly weakened) such as the regulation of wages, prices, and the rules of ▷ apprenticeship. The middle class of landed gentry, from which magistrates were appointed, was the class most loyal to Tudor policies and therefore provided the most effective allies of the ruling family. These magistrates were often to some extent qualified for the legal parts of their functions by education in law at one of the ▷ Inns of Court; law was more a field for general (as distinct from professional) education than it is in modern England.

Magistrates continued to be drawn from the same class, and to have comparably wide functions, throughout the 17th, 18th and much of the 19th century, but their relationship to the Crown changed in political fact, although not in nominal allegiance. ▷ James II lost the support of the class to which they belonged by his policy of re-establishing Roman Catholicism, and the ▷ Revolution of 1688 was carried out bloodlessly in England largely for this reason. In the 18th century they were only nominally servants of the Crown; in reality, they and their class controlled the government through ▷ Parliament. However, it was in this century that the legal authority of the amateur magistrate first met competiton from professional lawyers in the function of suppressing crime.

The ▷ Reform Bill of 1832 put an end to much of the political influence of the magistrates and their class, and the Local

Government Act of 1888, which set up County Councils, deprived them of their governing functions in their districts. In this century, magistrates have been chosen more democratically from all social classes; they are appointed by the ▷ Lord Chancellor on advice from local committees.

Magistrates were satirized at the height of their power, *eg* by ▷ Shakespeare (Justice Shallow in ▷ *Henry IV, Part II*) and by the 18th-century novelists ▷ Henry Fielding and ▷ Tobias Smollett. They were often regarded as inefficient, untrained in social as well as legal experience and selfish in their interests, especially in their stern penalizing of offences against the ▷ game laws. It is clear, however, that they exercised their functions with considerable responsibility and that the magisterial function was itself valuable training in public affairs for the class which, by its preponderance of wealth; was in any case the most influential body in the country.

In the 16th century the term 'Magistrate' was sometimes synonymous with 'Prince' or 'Ruler'; the anthology ▷ *A Mirror for Magistrates* shows this use.

▷ Courts of Law.

Magna Carta

The Great Charter which ▷ King John was forced by his barons to accept in 1215. It has long been popularly regarded as the foundation of English liberties, guaranteeing such rights as freedom from arbitrary imprisonment. However, 16th-century plays on King John, *eg* ▷ Shakespeare's, omit mention of the Charter, which came to have its modern symbolic importance only in consequence of the conflicts between kings and parliaments in the 17th century.

Mahon, Derek (b 1941)

Poet. Mahon was born in Belfast and educated at Dublin, and has lectured at the universities of Sussex and Ulster. Along with fellow poets James Simmons, ▷ Paul Muldoon and Michael Longley, he is an important figure in the Northern Irish renaissance in contemporary poetry, his work being strongly influenced by that of ▷ Seamus Heaney.
See *Night Crossing* (1968); *Beyond Howth* (1970); *Lives* (1972); *The Snow Party* (1975); *Light Music* (1977); *Poems 1962–1978* (1979).
▷ Irish literature in English.

Maid Marian (1822)

▷ Thomas Love Peacock's parody of medieval romances (such as ▷ Scott's ▷ *Ivanhoe*, 1819) fashionable in the early 19th century. It contains very good songs in comic opera style.

Maid's Tragedy, The (1610)

A play by ▷ Francis Beaumont and ▷ John Fletcher. It takes place in the town of Rhodes, and the story concerns the attempt of the king to conceal his relationship with his mistress, Evadne, by forcing one of his most loyal courtiers, Amintor, to marry her. Aspasia, the 'maid' of the tragedy, is the girl whom Amintor has to give up. Evadne's brother, Melantius, discovers the unhappy secret and compels his sister to murder the king; she then commits suicide on finding that Amintor will not forgive her.

The tragedy is generally considered to be Beaumont and Fletcher's masterpiece. It is typical of later ▷ Jacobean tragedy in relying for its effectiveness on individual scenes rather than on its totality, which is unconvincing. It is typical of Beaumont and Fletcher in the accomplished melody of its ▷ blank verse and the skill of its theatrical craftsmanship.

Malaprop, Mrs

A character in ▷ Sheridan's comedy ▷ *The Rivals*. She is the aunt and guardian of the heroine, Lydia Languish. Her principal comic effect is her habit of misusing words; this has given rise to the term 'malapropism'.

Malcontent, The (1604)

A tragicomedy by ▷ John Marston, with additions by ▷ John Webster. An intrigue

Derek Mahon

engineered by the villainous lord Mendoza has caused the deposition of Giovanni Altofronto, the noble Duke of Genoa, and substituted the weak Pietro Jacomo, who is married to Aurelia, daughter of the Duke of Florence. Altofronto, however, has returned to his own court in disguise as Malevole (the 'malcontent'). He is tolerated as a witty though sour court jester and commentator on the times and its corrupt manners. Meanwhile he awaits his chance for revenge and the recovery of his dukedom. Mendoza continues to conspire against the new Duke, whose wife is Mendoza's mistress, and Malevole in turn conspires against Mendoza. In the end, Mendoza is exposed, and Pietro and Aurelia penitently resign the duchy back to the rightful Duke.

The play is part ▷ satire and part ▷ revenge play, midway between ▷ Ben Jonson's comedies of ▷ humours (eg ▷ Volpone) and ▷ Tourneur's ▷ Revenger's Tragedy. The malcontent role of bitter commentator on society is a common one in ▷ Jacobean drama; Bosola in ▷ Webster's ▷ Duchess of Malfi is a well-known example, but ▷ Hamlet, Iago (in ▷ Othello) and Thersites in ▷ Troilus and Cressida all have some aspects of the malcontent in their parts. The essence of the role is that the malcontent is somehow frustrated from satisfying his ambitions or being accepted by the rest of society; such exclusion gives him the motives (morally acceptable or otherwise) and the detachment for his satire.

Mallarmé, Stéphane
▷ Symbolism.

Mallet (Malloch), David (1705?–65)
Poet. On moving from Edinburgh to London he expunged the Scotticisms from his speech and changed his name from the Scottish Malloch to the English Mallet. He is remembered for his collaboration with ▷ James Thomson on the ▷ masque Alfred (1740), and also for his ▷ ballad William and Margaret (1724), which anticipates the ▷ gothic fashion in popular taste, and was reprinted in ▷ Thomas Percy's Reliques under the title Margaret's Ghost.

Mallock, W. H. (1849–1923)
A ▷ Catholic controversialist now best known for his satirical novel The New Republic, portraying leading members of the Victorian intelligentsia, including ▷ John Ruskin, ▷ Matthew Arnold, ▷ Walter Pater and ▷ Thomas Huxley. He wrote a number of books on social questions against socialism. His Memoirs of Life and Literature was published in 1920.
Bib: Adams, A. B., The Novels of W. H. Mallock; Wolf, R. L., Gains and Losses: Novels of Faith and Doubt in Victorian England.

Malone, Edmund (1741–1812)
The greatest early editor of ▷ Shakespeare's works, many of whose textual emendations and editorial principles are still widely used. His greatest work remains his posthumously published edition of the complete Shakespeare (1821) and his research on the order in which Shakespeare's plays were written. He was also the first to denounce the Shakespearean forgeries of William Henry Ireland (1775–1835), one of whose fake plays, Vortigern and Rowena, was performed as Shakespeare's at Drury Lane.

Malory, Thomas
Identifying which Thomas Malory produced the work known as the ▷ Morte D'Arthur in around 1469/70 remains a controversial issue. Sir Thomas Malory of Newbold Revel (c 1446–71) is the most generally accepted candidate for the role. He was in the service of the Earl of Warwick in the French wars (c 1414), and by 1440 was established as a country gentleman, being knighted in 1442. After 1450 his public standing seems to have radically declined. His extensive spells in prison (on a range of charges including rape) after 1450 may have provided the opportunity for his literary labour. Although it is possible to recreate the public life of this Sir Thomas Malory, there is no documentation which sheds any light on his literary career.
Bib: Lacy, N. et al. (ed.), The Arthurian Encyclopaedia; Takimiya, T. and Brewer, D. (ed.), Aspects of Malory.

Malthus, Thomas Robert (1766–1834)
Economist; particularly famous for his Essay on Population (1798), which he reissued in an expanded and altered form in 1803. Its original title was: An Essay on the Principle of Population as it affects the Future Improvement of Society, with Remarks on the Speculations of Mr Godwin, M. Condorcet, and other Writers.

The essence of his view was that social progress tends to be limited by the fact that population increases more rapidly than means of subsistence, and always reaches the limits of subsistence, so that a substantial part of society is doomed to live beyond the margin of poverty. The 'natural checks' which prevent population increase from exceeding the means of subsistence are war, famine, and pestilence, to which he added human misery and vice. In the second edition he added a further possible check by 'moral restraint', *ie* late marriages and sexual continence. These arguments made a strong impression on public opinion; an important practical consequence of them was the replacement of the existing haphazard methods of poor relief by the harsh but reasoned and systematic ▷ Poor Law system of 1834.

Malthus's relentless and pitiless reasoning led to political economy becoming known as the 'gloomy science'. His conclusions were contested by humanitarians, and later seemed belied by factors he did not foresee, such as cheap imports of food from newly exploited colonies like Canada. Since 1918 'Malthusian' theories of the dangers of over-population have revived.

Mammon
In the Bible, an Aramaic word for 'riches' – *Matthew* 6:24; *Luke* 16:9–13. In the Middle Ages, Mammon was personified as the devil of covetousness, and is so used by ▷ Spenser in the Cave of Mammon episode (▷ *Faerie Queene* II, vii) and by Milton in ▷ *Paradise Lost* (i, 678 and ii, 228).

Man in Black, The
A character in the collection of essays by ▷ Oliver Goldsmith entitled *The Citizen of the World* (1762). He is prodigiously generous, but his sensibility causes him to conceal this virtue by pretending to be mean.

Man in the Moon, The
In English folklore, a tradition that the marks on the moon represent a man with faggots on his back; he was supposed to have been banished there for gathering sticks on the Sabbath day – see Bible, *Numbers* 15:32.

Man of Law's Tale, The
One of ▷ Chaucer's *Canterbury Tales*, written in ▷ rhyme royal, recounting the story of Constance, daughter of a Christian emperor, whose adventures are triggered by her marriage to the Sultan of Syria (who agrees to convert to the religion of his wife). Constance becomes the victim of a plot organized by the Sultan's mother, a confirmed pagan, and is cast adrift on the sea. She is providentially protected on her journey but becomes a victim of yet another plot by a pagan mother-in-law, after her conversion of, and marriage to, the King of Northumberland. After further ordeals she is eventually reunited with all members of her family in Rome. The basic narrative paradigm has analogues in other examples of pious romances which have a constant woman at their centre (notably the Middle English romance *Emaré*), and ▷ John Gower tells a version of the story of Constance in Book II of the ▷ *Confessio Amantis*. The tale is prefaced by a wry complaint from the Man of Law, who claims to have difficulty in finding a story to tell because Chaucer has told them all before.

Man of Mode, The: Or Sir Fopling Flutter **(1676)**
Third and last play by the ▷ Restoration dramatist, ▷ Sir George Etherege, written in the ▷ Comedy of Manners style, and generally held to be his best. It concerns the amours of Dorimant, a rake whose character is probably based on that of the ▷ Earl of Rochester. He pursues, and then rejects, first the infatuated Mrs Loveit and then her supposed friend, the weak and stupid Belinda, who intrigues with him in secret. He ends up with the wealthy and beautiful Harriet, who has held out against his wiles until he has promised to marry her. A subplot concerns the wooing of Young Bellair and Emilia. The title derives from the foolish Sir Fopling Flutter, a minor figure who personifies slavery to fashion. Dorimant's chief charm is his acerbic wit; otherwise he is a portrait of a misogynist, who takes as much delight in hurting women as in seducing them. The play's tone is cynical rather than satirical, and the overall effect one of brilliance, but with a deeply disturbing note.

Manchester Guardian, The
It was started in 1821 as a weekly paper, becoming daily in 1855. As the leading Liberal publication outside London, it was edited from 1872 to 1929 by C. P. Scott. Its title was changed to *The Guardian* in 1959, and since 1961 it has been published from London. It is considered to be one of the more liberal papers of the 1980s.

Manchester Massacre, The
▷ Peterloo Massacre, The.

Manchester School, The
A group of politicians in the 1840s, led by Richard Cobden and John Bright; they advocated the reduction or abolition of import duties (▷ Free Trade) and the prevention of all political interference in the development of commerce ('Laissez-faire'). The heart of the movement was in the rapidly growing industrial towns of the north, of which Manchester was one of the chief. The name was first applied to the group by their opponent, the Conservative politician ▷ Benjamin Disraeli.

Manciple's Tale, The

One of ▷ Chaucer's ▷ *Canterbury Tales*, an animal fable which tells the story of the metamorphosis of a tell-tale crow (based primarily on ▷ Ovid's *Metamorphoses* ii, though ▷ John Gower also tells the story in the ▷ *Confessio Amantis*). The Manciple recounts how Phoebus fosters a white crow whom he teaches to speak and through whom he learns of his wife's adultery. In his rage, Phoebus kills his wife, and then blames the crow for his action. He plucks out all its feathers, deprives it of the faculty of speech and throws the bird to the Devil: from that time onwards, the narrator explains, all crows are black. The *Tale* concludes with a moralizing rant about the need to keep 'mum' and never to pass on stories.

Mandeville, Bernard de (1670?–1733)

Of Dutch birth, Mandeville made his career in London as a doctor. His satire in ▷ Hudibrastic couplets *The Grumbling Hive, or Knaves turn'd Honest* (1705) was reissued with accompanying prose essays in 1714 as *The Fable of the Bees; or Private Vices, Public Benefits*. Mandeville followed through the economic implications of the new bourgeois individualistic ethic with enthusiastic gusto, arguing that the greatest social good was generated by allowing the individual the maximum freedom to pursue private self-interest. The hive thrives so long as this principle is respected: 'Thus every Part was full of Vice,/ Yet the whole Mass a paradise'. But once the Puritan moralist camp among the bees takes control, demand for luxuries and corrupt pleasures disappears, enterprise declines and the hive is ruined. The prose essays defend public brothels, argue that without the wasteful luxury of the rich the poor would starve, and doubt the utility of Christian morality in the conduct of war. Mandeville delighted in driving uncomfortable wedges between the economic and religious components of the new bourgeois consensus, and, like a kind of conservative ▷ George Bernard Shaw he expounded unpalatable truths with unabashed vigour. His pungent intellectual honesty offended optimistic ▷ Deists and pious Puritans alike, and it proved easier for writers such as ▷ William Law to attack him as a scoffing blasphemer, than to answer his impressive logic.

Manfred (1817)

A dramatic poem in ▷ blank verse by ▷ Lord Byron, set in the Alps. It focusses on the typical Byronic hero, outcast from society and haunted by the guilt of unnamed crimes. Manfred conjures up the Spirits of earth and air, the Witch of the Alps, the Destinies and Nemesis, and beseeches them in vain for oblivion. He eventually dies absolved, however, saved from the clutches of the evil spirits who claim his soul by the intervention of Astarte, the spirit of the woman whom he had loved. The poem, reminiscent of ▷ Goethe's *Faust*, was very popular throughout the 19th century, Schumann and Tchaikovsky basing major musical compositions upon it. Byron himself referred to it in a letter as 'a sort of mad drama'.

Mankind

A ▷ morality play, dating from c 1465–70, seemingly designed for performance by a small professional or semi-professional group (the collection of money for performance is built into the play text). The plot recounts an exemplary incident in the life of its central character, Mankind, who allows himself to be distracted almost to damnation by a rowdy, bawdy trio (New-Guise, Now-a-Days, Nought) directed by the devil Titivellus (a demonic figure traditionally associated with loose speech). Mankind's repentance brings the aid of Mercy. The play draws attention to the pleasures and dangers of the dramatic medium itself, and toys with its own audience's commitment to dramatic distraction.

Bib: Eccles, M. (ed.), *Macro Plays*.

Manley, Delarivière (? 1663–1724)

Playwright and novelist. Manley's unconventional lifestyle led to many scandalous strictures. She married her cousin John Manley at an early age, only to find he was already married, and on making this discovery left him, although she was pregnant and had no means of support. For some months she lived in the household of the Duchess of Cleveland, acting as secretary and companion, but left her patronage after rumours of an affair with the Duchess's son.

For some time she seems to have lived in the country, returning to London in 1696, when two of her plays were performed: *The Lost Lover or the Jealous Husband* and *The Royal Mischief*. At this time she became the mistress of John Tilly, the Warden of Fleet Prison.

In 1705 Manley's novel *The Secret History of Queen Zarah* appeared, and proved an enormous success. In its use of a mythical society to satirize contemporary English life, it set the pattern for her later *roman à clef, The New Atalantis* (1709). In 1711 Manley succeeded ▷ Jonathan Swift as editor of

The Examiner, and in the course of her writing career produced many political pamphlets. In 1714 *The Adventures of Rivella*, apparently a fictionalized autobiography, appeared. Her final achievement was a series of novels, *The Power of Love*, published in 1720.

Manners, Comedy of

A form in which laughter is provoked by exaggerations of fashionable behaviour, absurdities in fashion itself, or departures from what is considered to be civilized normality of behaviour. Thus a comedy of manners can only arise in a highly developed society, in which there is a leisured class which not only has standards of politeness and good sense in human relationships but tends to give such standards first importance in social life. The ▷ Comedy of Humours of ▷ Ben Jonson and his younger contemporaries dealt with fundamental human appetites, and was therefore concerned with much more than what was regarded as civilized behaviour by fashionable society, though that was often included in their purview. In the court of the French king Louis XIV in the second half of the 17th century, a highly civilized society held to a code of behaviour which was also a code of morals; the comedies of ▷ Molière were the first true examples of the Comedy of Manners, and had profundity as well as surface brilliance. His comedy influenced dramatists in England. The Comedy of Manners in England is not so much a pure variety of drama, as a framework for plays with a witty, satiric atmosphere, and social comment, which may also contain other elements, such as ▷ Spanish Intrigue, ▷ Humours, ▷ Reform, etc. The best-known comedies of this type were written after the ▷ Restoration of ▷ Charles II in 1660. Many involve a critique of marriage, and re-assessment of relations between the sexes, and of women's role in society. The plays are often sexually explicit, contributing to a growing reaction against them in the 18th and 19th centuries when, as standards of polite and rational behaviour extended through society, and audiences became more heterogeneous, drama tended to become more middle class, and to show more propriety. ▷ Goldsmith and ▷ Sheridan reacted to what they considered excessive sentimentalism in the works of some of their contemporaries, and consciously revived the spirit of Comedy of Manners in their plays, though these were never as bawdy as those of any of their predecessors. The plays of

▷ Oscar Wilde owe a large debt to the Manners tradition, and ▷ George Bernard Shaw incorporated some of its elements in his comedies.

Manning, Olivia (1915–80)

Novelist and short-story writer. Her major work is *The Balkan Trilogy*, set in Romania, Greece and Egypt during the early stages of World War II, and which consists of: *The Great Fortune* (1960); *The Spoilt City* (1962) and *Friends and Heroes* (1965). It is told primarily through the consciousness of a newly married Englishwoman, and builds up a strong sense of place and of history through the portrayal of a wide range of characters and the accumulation of details of daily experience. The story is continued in *The Levant Trilogy: The Danger Tree* (1977); *The Battle Lost and Won* (1978); *The Sum of Things* (1980). Other novels: *The Wind Changes* (1937); *Artist Among the Missing* (1949); *School for Love* (1951); *A Different Face* (1953); *The Doves of Venus* (1955); *The Rain Forest* (1974). Story collections: *Growing Up* (1948); *My Husband Cartwright* (1956); *A Romantic Hero* (1967).

Mannyng, Robert (fl 1288–1338)

Writer and chronicler. Robert Mannyng is one of the few Middle English writers to offer autobiographical details in their work. From the information he provides in the prologues of his two works, it seems Mannyng (a native of Bourne in Lincolnshire) entered the Gilbertine order at an early age, was sent to Cambridge and then began his translation (*Handlyng Synne*) of the ▷ Anglo-Norman *Manuel de Pechiez* in 1303. Some time later, at the Gilbertine house of Sixhills, he produced a chronicle history of England, which he finished in 1338. *Handlyng Synne* is a book of doctrinal instruction, describing and illustrating the Ten Commandments/ Seven Deadly Sins/ Sacrilege/ Seven Sacraments/ Shrift; it follows the model of its Anglo-Norman source but Mannyng adds new exemplary narratives which liven the text considerably. His expanded story of the 'Dancers of Colbeck' appears in the Sacrilege section.

Mannyng's *Chronicle* covers the foundation and history of Britain (following ▷ Wace's *Roman de Brut* with additions from ▷ Geoffrey of Monmouth and ▷ Bede) and the history of England up to 1307 (following the Anglo-Norman *Chronicle* of Pierre de Langtoft). In both works he comments on the sources he uses, acknowledges his additions and remarks on the function of his translations into English.

In the *Chronicle* he adds some interesting comments on the paucity of Arthurian material available in English and defends the historicity of ▷ King Arthur.
Bib: Sullens, Idelle (ed.), *Handlyng Synne*; Furnivall, F. J. (ed.), *The Story of England by Robert Mannyng of Brunne*.

Mansfield, Katherine (1888–1923)

Katherine Mansfield

Short-story writer. Born (Katherine Mansfield Beauchamp) in Wellington, New Zealand; married the critic ▷ John Middleton Murry in 1913. Her story collections are: *In a German Pension* (1911); *Je Ne Parle Pas Français* (1918); *Bliss* (1920); *The Garden Party* (1922); *The Dove's Nest* (1923); *Something Childish* (1924); *The Aloe* (1930); *Collected Stories* (1945). Her *Journal* (1927, enlarged edition 1934) and *Letters* (1928) were edited by Murry. The stories resemble in their form those of the Russian writer ▷ Chekhov, and ▷ James Joyce's ▷ *Dubliners*; they do not have a distinct plot with a definite beginning and ending and a self-sufficient action, conveying instead an impression of continuity with ordinary life, and depending for their unity on delicate balance of detail and feeling. She contributed to the development of the ▷ stream of consciousness technique, and to the ▷ modernist use of multiple viewpoints.
Bib: Alpers, A., *The Life of Katherine Mansfield*; Hanson, C., and Gurr, A., *Katherine Mansfield*.

Mansfield Park (1814)
A novel by ▷ Jane Austen. The theme is the conflict between three different styles of moral feeling. The first is that of Sir Thomas Bertram, owner of Mansfield Park; it stands for a system of conservative, orderly principle, a tradition inherited from the 18th century, emphasizing stability and discounting the feelings. The second style of moral feeling is embodied in Fanny Price, Sir Thomas's niece whom he takes into his household because her parents are poor and their family too large; although she is timid, withdrawn and overawed by her new surroundings, she possesses a highly developed sensibility and capacity for affection both of which are foreign to the Bertrams, except to the younger son, Edmund, who to some degree appreciates her. The third style is represented by Henry and Mary Crawford, half-brother and half-sister to the wife of the village parson. They are rich, independent, attractive; they do not share Sir Thomas's cold theories, and they do possess Fanny's capacity for ardent feeling; on the other hand, they are without Sir Thomas's dedication to conscience and without Fanny's reverence for consistency of moral with affectionate and aesthetic sensibilities. The difference between the three styles of life becomes overt while Sir Thomas is absent in the West Indies; the Crawfords virtually take over Mansfield Park in order to rehearse, with the Bertram children and two guests, a performance of Kotzebue's *Lovers' Vows*. Henry Crawford is by this time conducting a flirtation with Maria Bertram, who is engaged to one of the guests, Mr Rushworth, and Mary Crawford is in love with Edmund; these relationships are in effect parodied in the play (popular in Jane Austen's time) so that the characters can perform on the stage what they desire to enact in real life. Fanny, knowing that Sir Thomas would disapprove of amateur acting, refuses to take part, but the situation is painful to her because she is secretly in love with Edmund herself. The rehearsals are stopped by Sir Thomas's sudden return, but a new crisis occurs in Fanny's life when Henry, awakened to the reality of her diffident charms, proposes marriage to her. She refuses him, much to Sir Thomas's uncomprehending disapproval, and is not in a position to explain to him the grounds of her refusal: that she disapproves of Henry morally and is in love with his son. She is exiled to her own family at Portsmouth, where disorder and strong emotion, often reduced to callous bad temper by poverty and overcrowding, are the rule. Henry is for a time constant, but he disgraces himself, the

Bertrams and his sister by eloping with Maria after she has married. By degrees, both Sir Thomas and Edmund came to appreciate Fanny at her true value, and at the end of the novel she is to become Edmund's wife.

Of Jane Austen's completed works *Mansfield Park* is the most direct criticism of the ▷ Regency style of sensibility (represented by the Crawfords), with its tendency to reject continuity with the best elements of the past; at the same time the criticism is balanced by a recognition of the importance of the sensibility if morality is to receive true life from the feelings. It is also a bold challenge to the romantic style of fiction: Mary Crawford, antagonist to the heroine Fanny, is not only shown as friendly to her and in all but the deepest sense appreciative of her; she is also the possessor of genuine social attractions which Fanny lacks. The reader is made to like both her and her brother, and at the same time obliged to acknowledge Fanny's ultimate human superiority.

Margaret of Anjou (1430–82)

The queen of ▷ King Henry VI. Owing to the weakness of her husband, it was she who was the effective leader of the Lancastrian party in the ▷ Wars of the Roses. As a woman with exceptional power and responsibilities she posed problems for representation: she became famous for her determined leadership, the ferocity with which she defended the rights of her husband and son, and her pitiless vengefulness. She is a prominent character in the three ▷ *Henry VI* plays by Shakespeare, and reappears in his ▷ *Richard III* IV. iv, where she joins with the Yorkist ladies in a common lament for the dead of both families, since Richard has now laid waste his own, as well as contributing to the destruction of the Lancastrians.

Mariana

A character in ▷ Shakespeare's ▷ *Measure for Measure*; she was betrothed to Angelo, the deputy of the Duke of Vienna and after being cast off by him she lives forsaken in 'the moated grange' until the Duke compels Angelo to marry her. She is the subject of one of the most famous poems by ▷ Alfred Tennyson – *Mariana*.

Marie de France (fl. c 1180)

One of the earliest known women writers of vernacular poetry, working in French, some time during the years 1160–1215, for, it seems, audiences in France and England (judging by the provenance of the extant manuscripts of her work). Little is known about her life; indeed the principal record of her existence derives from the signatures built into her work: her collection of *Lais*, her collection of *Fables*, and her version of *Espurgatoire S. Patrice* (*St Patrick's Purgatory*) all contain references to their composition by one 'Marie' who is, according to the epilogue of the *Fables*, from France. She was clearly an educated woman, acquainted with Latin and likely, therefore, to have had an ecclesiastical training of some kind. The image she develops in her work is of something of a cultural polymath, mediating between British/English/Latin culture of the past in the production of her poetry: she claims to have taken material for her *Lais* from British sources; claims to be translating her collection of *Fables* from an Old English work of ▷ King Alfred; and translates her account of St Patrick's Purgatory from Latin. She remains something of a literary enigma, despite scholarly hypotheses about her life and her possible connection with the court of Henry II.
Bib: Burgess, G. and Busby, K. (trans.), *The Lais of Marie de France*; Wilson, K. (ed.), *Medieval Women Writers*.

Marina

A character in ▷ *Pericles, Prince of Tyre*, a play written wholly or in part by ▷ Shakespeare. She is the daughter of King Pericles, who loses her at sea and later recovers her (V.i) in a scene described by ▷ T. S. Eliot as one of the most beautiful by Shakespeare. She is the subject of one of Eliot's Ariel Poems, *Marina*.

Marlborough, John Churchill, Duke of (1650–1722)

Son of Winston Churchill, a minor country gentleman. At fifteen he became a page of honour to James, Duke of York, and in 1667 he received an officer's commission in the Guards. In 1672 he showed distinction in various sieges in the Netherlands in a campaign in which the English were allied with the French against the Dutch, and in 1685 he was made a Baron and promoted to the rank of Major General. It was largely due to his efficiency that the ▷ Monmouth rebellion against ▷ James II (formerly the Duke of York) was defeated at the ▷ Battle of Sedgemoor. When William of Orange landed in England in 1688, however, Marlborough deserted James, and thus facilitated the bloodless Revolution by which William became ▷ King William III. Churchill was made Duke of Marlborough on the accession of Queen Anne in 1702, and his wife, Sarah, was the Queen's chief favourite. On the outbreak of the War of the Spanish Succession in the same year, Marlborough commanded the armies of the allied states against France, and won victories at ▷ Blenheim (1704), Ramillies (1706), Oudenarde (1708) and Malplaquet (1709). The country was tiring of the war, however, and the Queen was tiring of the Duchess. Marlborough was relieved of his command in 1711. In the meantime the great mansion of Blenheim Palace had been built for him in honour of his first and most remarkable victory in the war. The architect was ▷ Sir John Vanbrugh.

Marlowe, Christopher (1564–93)
Dramatist and poet. Son of a Canterbury shoemaker; educated at King's School, Canterbury, and Corpus Christi College, Cambridge. He most likely began writing plays on leaving Cambridge. They were produced by the Earl of Nottingham's Company (the Lord ▷ Admiral's Men). Marlowe probably became a government agent, and his mysterious death in a fight in a tavern at Deptford – nominally about who should pay the bill – may have had a political cause. When he died, he was under shadow of charges of ▷ atheism on the evidence of his fellow dramatist, ▷ Thomas Kyd.

His four major plays were written between 1585 and 1593; ▷ *Tamburlaine the Great, Parts I and II*; ▷ *The Jew of Malta*; ▷ *The Tragical History of Doctor Faustus*; *Edward II. Dido, Queen of Carthage* (with ▷ Nashe, 1594) and ▷ *The Massacre at Paris* (1593) are attributed to him. His non-dramatic poetry is famous for the narrative, ▷ *Hero and Leander*, based on the Greek of Musaeus (5th century AD) and completed by ▷ Chapman, and the lyric *The Passionate Shepherd*. Little else has survived, apart from his translation of ▷ Ovid's *Amores* (printed 1596) and of *The First Book of Lucan* (printed 1600). It has been suggested without evidence that he had a share in the writing of a number of other plays, including ▷ Shakespeare's ▷ *Henry VI*, ▷ *Titus Andronicus*, and ▷ *Richard III*.

Marlowe was much the greatest dramatic writer in the 16th century after Shakespeare, and much the most important influence upon Shakespeare. His importance is due to the energy with which he endowed the ▷ blank verse line, which in his hands developed an unprecedented suppleness and power. His plays have great intensity, but they show a genius which is epic rather than dramatic – at least in *Tamburlaine* and *Doctor Faustus* which

are his acknowledged masterpieces; his best constructed piece of theatre, *Edward II*, is also the least typical of his poetic genius. On the other hand the final scene of *Doctor Faustus* is one of the most intensely dramatic in English literature. In the musical handling and control of the ten-syllable line, he learned from ▷ Spenser, and contributed to ▷ Milton as well as to Shakespeare.
▷ Faust.
Bib: Boas, F. S., *Christopher Marlowe*; Levin, H., *The Overreacher*; Steane, J. B., *Marlowe: a critical study*; Leech, C. (ed.), *Essays on Marlowe*; Eliot, T. S., in *Selected Essays*; Kelsall, M., *Christopher Marlowe*; Masington, C. G., *Christopher Marlowe's Tragic Vision*; Robinson, J. H., *Marlowe, Tamburlaine and Magic*.

Marmion, A Tale of Flodden Field (1808)
An historical romance in tetrameter couplets (▷ metre) by ▷ Sir Walter Scott, set in 1513, the year of the catastrophic defeat of James IV of Scotland by the English. The story concerns the attempts of Lord Marmion to marry the rich Lady Clare, and to dispose of her lover by making false allegations of treason against him. Marmion is eventually killed in the battle and the lovers are reunited. The poem contains the famous lyrics 'Where shall the lover rest', and 'O, young Lochinvar is come out of the west'.

Marprelate, Martin
The pen-name for an anonymous author or authors of a series of ▷ pamphlets which appeared 1588–90. They were written from a ▷ Presbyterian stand-point denying the validity of bishops, and they attacked the religious establishment, by which the Church was governed by crown-appointed bishops. The bishops were satirized so vigorously in such expressive, popular prose that the authorities were alarmed into commissioning such gifted writers as ▷ Thomas Nashe, ▷ John Lyly and ▷ Robert Greene to reply to them. The leaders of the movement were arrested in 1593, and the government of ▷ Elizabeth I imposed severe restrictions on sermons and on the press. (Marprelate: mar = damage, ruin; prelate = bishop.)

Marriage
According to Laurence Stone, in England marriage only gradually acquired its function of regulating sexual chastity in wedlock: up to the 11th century polygamy and concubinage were widespread and divorce was casual. Even after that time divorce by mutual consent followed by remarriage was still widely practised. In the 13th century,

however, the Church developed its control, asserting the principles of monogamy, defining and outlawing incest, punishing fornication and adultery and ensuring the exclusion of ▷ bastards from property inheritance. In 1439 weddings in church were declared a sacrament and after 1563 in the Roman Catholic Church the presence of a priest was required to make the contract valid. In this way, what had been a private contract between two families concerning property exchange – Claude Lévi-Strauss was the first to point out in 1948 women's universal role in such transactions between men – became regulated. Ecclesiastical law always recognized the formal exchange of oral promises (spousals) between the parties as a legally binding contract; as the Church got more powerful it exerted greater control over the circumstances in which those promises were made. In 1604 the hours, place and conditions of church weddings were defined and restricted; notice and publicity (the calling of the banns) were required, as a guard against bigamy and other abuses. One effect of this was to create a demand for clergymen willing to perform weddings outside the specified conditions. In 1753 Lord Hardwicke's Marriage Act was designed to close these loopholes: weddings had to be in church, duly registered and signed, verbal spousals would not be legally binding and marriages already contracted in breach of the 1604 conditions were declared invalid. No-one under 21 could marry without parental consent and there were heavy penalties for clergymen who defied these injunctions. After this, the Civil Marriage Act of 1836 was passed to regulate all marriages solemnized other than in accordance with the rites of the Church of England. Divorce, with the option of remarriage, was not available except by private Act of Parliament, which only the rich could afford: there were only 131 cases between 1670 and 1799. The poor used a ritualized wife-sale (as in ▷ Thomas Hardy's ▷ *The Mayor of Casterbridge* – the last recorded example was in 1887) or desertion. In 1857 the Matrimonial Causes Act introduced civil divorce for adultery: again only the rich could afford it and only men could do the divorcing. Wives were not permitted to divorce their husbands for adultery until 1923. In 1937 three additional grounds for divorce were introduced, cruelty, desertion and insanity. Further liberalization of the divorce laws took place in the 1960s: recognition of the concept of marital breakdown has allowed a less punitive and accusatory procedure.

▷ Divorce; Women, Status of.

Marriage à la Mode (?1671)

Play by ▷ John Dryden, sometimes described as a 'split-plot tragi-comedy', setting a serious unrhymed 'heroic' plot against a witty love plot. In the serious plot, Polydamas has usurped the throne of Sicily from the rightful prince, Leonidas, who is unaware of his rights. Leonidas is in love with Palmyra. She is courted by Argaleon, while he is loved by Argaleon's sister, Amalthea. The comic plot concerns the adulterous love between Rhodophil, a captain of the guards, and Melantha, 'an affected lady', and Rhodophil's wife Doralice and Palamede. Palamede is also a suitor to Melantha. The play's action essentially revolves round the complications arising from these situations, and has scenes of mistaken identities, including women disguised as men. A factor unifying the two plots is the theme of longing for the apparently unattainable. The play represents an attempt by Dryden to resist what he saw as the coarsening and cheapening of contemporary comedy. In his dedication he claimed to have preserved the 'Decencies of Behaviour', but this did not prevent him from inserting a number of very bawdy songs between some serious scenes.

Marriage of Heaven and Hell, The (c 1793)

Blake's design for the cover of *The Marriage of Heaven and Hell*

A composition mainly in poetic prose by ▷ William Blake. It was engraved, with designs woven into the text in the early 1790s, at the time he was working on ▷ *The Songs of Experience*. The text consists of a series of symbolic, caustically humorous anecdotes, and terse aphorisms. Blake's thesis, influenced by the thought of the mystic ▷ Emanuel Swedenborg, is that the rationality of ▷ John Locke and ▷ Sir Isaac Newton, and the piety of established hierarchical religion, are repressive and sterile. He thus presents Hell as a region of dangerous but vital energies, and Heaven, without them, as a lifeless, ▷ Deistic abstraction. The most famous section of the work is the 'Proverbs of Hell', 70 aphorisms asserting flux and creativity against the stasis and hierarchy of Heaven: 'The road of excess leads to the palace of wisdom', 'The tygers of wrath are wiser than the horses of instruction', 'Sooner murder an infant in its cradle than nurse unacted desires.'

▷ *Songs of Innocence and Experience*.

Marryat, Frederick, Captain (1792–1848)
Novelist. He was a Captain in the Royal Navy and his novels are chiefly about the sea. The best known of them are: *Frank Mildmay* (1829); *Peter Simple* (1834); *Jacob Faithful* (1834); *Mr Midshipman Easy* (1836). *Japhet in Search of a Father* (1836) is the story of a child of unknown parents who eventually achieves prosperity. Others of his books were intended for boys; the best-known of these is *Masterman Ready* (1841). Marryat continued the 18th-century realistic tradition of narrative, the most famous examples of which are the novels of ▷ Tobias Smollett.

▷ Realism.
Bib: Marryat, F., *Life and Letters of Captain Marryat*; Conrad, J., 'Tales of the Sea' in *Notes on Life and Letters*; Warner, O., *Captain Marryat: a Rediscovery*.

Mars
▷ Ares.

Marshalsea
A prison in Southwark, London. It was opened in the 13th century as a prison for the Marshalsea Court, which dealt with cases involving a member of the royal household. After the ▷ Restoration it was kept for petty debtors. Dickens's father was imprisoned there for debt, and it is described in ▷ *Little Dorrit* (1858). The prison was abolished in 1849.

Marston, John (?1575–1634)
Satirist and dramatist. His father was a lawyer. John Marston was educated at Brasenose College, Oxford; lectured in the Middle Temple (one of the ▷ Inns of Court); entered the Church in 1609. His writing life runs from 1598 to 1607. During this period he engaged in literary warfare with ▷ Ben Jonson ('the war of the theatres') who satirized Marston and ▷ Dekker in *The Poetaster* (1601) and elsewhere. The two men were, however, intermittently friends, and collaborated (with Chapman) in writing ▷ *Eastward Hoe* (1605) for which they were imprisoned for offending the king's Scottish friends.

In 1598 Marston published *The Metamorphosis of Pygmalion's Image* and, under the pen-name of W. Kinsayder, a collection of satires entitled *Scourge of Villainie*. The satires are modelled on those of the Roman poet Persius. Their language is coarse and vigorous, and the violence and disgust they exhibit become a feature of Marston's dramatic writing. His plays are his most successful work, but they are very uneven. ▷ *Antonio and Mellida* and *Antonio's Revenge* (1599 – *Antonio*) are ▷ revenge plays in the tradition of Kyd's ▷ *The Spanish Tragedy*, and exhibit a mixture of ▷ stoic idealism and melodramatic sensationalism, with passages of intense poetry. ▷ *The Malcontent* is a tragicomedy and usually considered to be Marston's most effective work; its satirical qualities and the role of the central character suggest comparisons with ▷ Shakespeare's ▷ *Measure for Measure* and ▷ *Hamlet*. ▷ *The Dutch Courtesan* (1605), *The Parasitaster, or the Fawne* (1606) and *What You Will* (1607) are comedies; *Sophonisba, Wonder of Women* (1605) and *The Insatiate Countess* (?1606) are tragedies.

It was Marston's lack of critical control and the bad taste of his extravagance which caused the satirical attacks on him by Jonson. His violent revulsion from sensuality and worldly vice inspired some of his best passages as well as his worst ones. ▷ T. S. Eliot (*Selected Essays*) remarks on Marston's 'positive, powerful and unique personality', which asserts itself even through his faults.
Bib: Ellis-Fermor, U. M., *The Jacobean Drama*; Caputi, A., *John Marston, Satirist*.

'Martian' poetry
The name of the so-called 'Martian' school of poetry derives from the second collection of ▷ Craig Raine, *A Martian Sends a Postcard Home* (1979). Everyday objects are described in an unusual, often highly striking manner, as if being seen for the first time by an alien

visiting earth. The poet attempts to write from a position of innocence, radically outside of the society he or she observes, reading things from a position of exile, or as an anthropologist. The ordinary or common-sense world is twisted, often by an outrageous use of simile (▷ Figures of speech):

> *Rain is when the earth is television.*
> *It has the property of making colours darker.*
> (*Raine*, 'A Martian Sends a Postcard Home')

Much contemporary poetry makes use of 'Martian eye' techniques, but the chief poets of the school are Raine and Christopher Reid (b 1949).

Martin Chuzzlewit, The Life and Adventures of (1843–44)

A novel by ▷ Charles Dickens. The Chuzzlewit family includes old Martin, a rich man grown misanthropic owing to the selfishness and greed of the rest of his family; young Martin, his grandson, who begins with the family selfishness but is eventually purified by hardship and the good influence of his servant, Mark Tapley; Anthony, old Martin's avaricious brother, and Jonas, Anthony's son, who, by the end of the book, has become a figure of the blackest evil; Pecksniff, at first a trusted friend of old Martin, is one of Dickens's most effective hypocrites; ▷ Mrs Gamp, the disreputable nurse, is one of his most famous comic creations. The novel is divided rather sharply by the episode in which young Martin temporarily emigrates to America. This episode is a self-sufficient satire on American life; moreover, not only is young Martin's character radically changed by it but the story thereafter takes on a denser substance. Pecksniff, Jonas and the fraudulent financier Tigg Montague cease to be merely comic and become substantially evil. These changes mark the transition from the earlier Dickens, the comic entertainer, into the later Dickens, of sombre power. The novel is thus a transitional work but it is also, as his comic masterpiece, the climax of Dickens's first phase.

Martineau, Harriet (1802–76)

Critic and ▷ essayist; also ▷ biographer and novelist. The sixth of eight children of a manufacturer of camlet and bombazine, she was born in Norwich where she was educated, at home and later in school. She had no sense of taste or smell and was a sickly child, gloomy, jealous and morbid, suffering from her parents' discipline and domestic scrimping, necessitated by their desire to educate their children to earn their own living. She supported herself initially partly by needlework and partly by writing reviews for the *Monthly Repository*. A devout ▷ Unitarian, she first published *Devotional Exercises* (1823), and in 1830 and 1831 won all three prizes in a competition set by the Central Unitarian Association for essays intended to convert the Roman ▷ Catholics, Jews and Mahommedans. Between 1832 and 1834 she wrote *Illustrations of Political Economy*, social reformist stories influenced by ▷ Jeremy Bentham and ▷ John Stuart Mill, along with stories for 'Brougham's Society for the Diffusion of Useful Knowledge', of which some 10,000 copies were sold. She became a celebrity, living with her mother and aunt in Westminster, dining out every day except Sunday with friends such as ▷ Malthus, Sydney Smith, Milnes and politicians whom she advised; she suggested and managed ▷ Thomas Carlyle's first course of lectures in 1837. In 1834 she visited the U.S. partly for her health, supporting the Abolitionists despite threats and difficulties, publishing in 1837 *Society in America* and, a lighter and more popular product of her trip, *A Retrospect of Western Travel*. In 1839 she toured abroad again, but had to return quickly from Venice and was ill for some six months. In 1843 she published *Life in the Sick Room*, which she came to despise when her views on religion developed. She was cured of a serious illness by mesmerism in 1844 and went on to practise it herself, giving an account in *Letters on Mesmerism* (1845). She travelled in Egypt and Palestine in 1846–7. By now she had rejected all religion.

She wrote numerous articles in the *Daily News* and some for the ▷ *Edinburgh Review*. Her other works include: *Deerbrook* (1839), her first novel and her favourite, *The Hour and The Man* (1840) on Toussaint l'Ouverture, a popular volume of children's stories (▷ Children's books) *The Playfellow* (1841), *The History of England During the Thirty Years' Peace* (1849) and *Laws of Man's Social Nature*. She was influenced by ▷ Comte, of whose philosophy she produced a free translation and condensation, *The Philosophy of Comte* (1853). She wrote a hurried autobiography in 1855 when diagnosed terminally ill, *An Autobiographical Memoir*, published eventually in 1876. She attributed her power to 'earnestness and intellectual clearness within a certain range', although she had 'no approach to genius' due to her lack of imagination.

Bib: Pichanick, V. K., *Harriet Martineau, the*

Woman and Her Work; Webb, R. K., *Harriet Martineau, a Radical Victorian.*

Marvell, Andrew (1621–78)

Poet. He was educated at Hull Grammar School (where his father was master) and Trinity College, Cambridge. He travelled in Europe, and in 1650 became tutor to the daughter of Lord Fairfax, the ▷ Civil War Parliamentary general. In 1653 he became tutor to ▷ Cromwell's ward, and in 1657 ▷ John Milton's assistant in the foreign secretaryship. In 1659 he became Member of ▷ Parliament for Hull, which he continued to represent after the ▷ Restoration of the monarchy in 1660, apart from a period in which he was secretary to Lord Carlisle.

The main body of Marvell's lyric poetry is to be found in *Miscellaneous Poems* of 1681, which contains his best known verse. He published, in addition to the lyric poetry for which he is famous, a number of ▷ satirical works and, in 1672–3 the curious amalgam of theological controversy and prose satire which is *The Rehearsal Transprosed* – the work for which he was most famous in the 17th century. But it is the lyric poetry that has attracted most modern critical attention. Of enduring fascination to modern criticism has been the question of the relation of Marvell's poems of the 1650s to the poet's own political sympathies. Is, for example, his celebration of the return of Cromwell from Ireland ('An Horatian Ode upon Cromwell's Return from Ireland') enlisting sympathy for Cromwell, or ▷ Charles I? Or is it, as some modern critics have argued, simply disinterested? Similarly, to what extent does his poetry represent a struggle to escape out of the turmoil of civil war? More radically, does the poetry dramatize the impossibility of any such retreat?

Together with the poetry of ▷ John Donne and ▷ George Herbert, Marvell's poetry has come to be appreciated as some of the most important to have been written in the 17th century. But modern criticism has, itself, not been disinterested in championing Marvell's work. For both ▷ T. S. Eliot and ▷ F. R. Leavis, Marvell became an ideological touchstone, while for ▷ Marxist literary historians Marvell's work represented a continually fascinating test-case of the relationship between literature and history.
Bib: Legouis, P. (ed.), *The Poems and Letters of Andrew Marvell*; Patterson, A., *Marvell and the Civic Crown*; Chernaik, W., *The Poet's Time.*

Marx, Karl (1818–83)

Born in Trier of German-Jewish parentage,

Karl Marx

and attended university in Berlin and Bonn where he first encountered Hegelian dialectic. He met Friedrich Engels (1820–95) in Paris in 1844, and in 1848, the Year of Revolutions, they published *The Communist Manifesto* together. In that year Marx returned to Germany and took part in the unsuccessful revolution there before fleeing to Britain where he was to remain until his death in 1883. In 1867 he published *Capital*, the voluminous work for which he is best known. Marx is justly renowned for his adaptation of the Hegelian dialectic for a materialist account of social formations, which is based upon an analysis of the opposition between different social classes. He is, arguably, the most prolific thinker and social commentator of the 19th century whose work has had far-reaching effects on subsequent generations of scholars, philosophers, politicians and analysts of human culture. In the political ferment of the 1960s, and especially in France, his work has been subject to a series of extraordinarily productive re-readings, especially by philosophers such as ▷ Louis Althusser which continue to affect the understanding of all aspects of cultural life. In Britain Marx's work is what lies behind a very powerful literary and historical tradition of commentary and analysis, and has informed much work in the areas of sociology, and the study of the mass media. *Capital* and a range of earlier texts, have come to form the basis of the materialist analysis of culture.
▷ New historicism.

Mary [in the Bible]

Four women named Mary are mentioned in the Gospels:

   1 Mary, the Mother of Jesus. The chief

mentions of her are in *Matthew* 1 & 2, *Luke* 1 & 2, *John* 2 & 19. Three doctrines about her were especially held: she was regarded as being perpetually virgin; she was absolutely sinless; she had supreme powers of intercession with God on behalf of man. Often referred to as 'the Holy Virgin', 'Our Lady' and 'Mother of God', she is constantly mentioned in medieval literature. As such the Virgin Mary became the archetype of feminine docility and suffering – the opposite to the sexual and corrupting figure of Eve. Her role in literature has been evaluated by feminists as the masculine ideal of womanhood and as a stereotype of female repression by the male-dominated hierarchy of the Church.

2 Mary Magdalene. One of the women disciples of Jesus. She was frequently identified with the unnamed woman who washed the feet of Jesus with her tears, in *Luke* 7:37, and thus tradition held her to be a repentant prostitute.

3 Mary of Bethany, sister of Martha (*Luke* 10:38–42) and of Lazarus, whom Jesus raised from the dead (*John* 11).

4 Mary the mother of James and Joses, mentioned in *Matthew* 27 & 28, *Mark* 16, *Luke* 24 as accompanying Mary Magdalene to the tomb.

▷ Bible.

Bib: Warner, M., *Alone of all her sex: the myth and the cult of the Virgin Mary*.

Mary I (1553–58)
Queen of England. She was the eldest child of ▷ Henry VIII who had used his divorce from her mother, Katharine of Aragon, as a pretext for taking the control of the English Church out of the hands of the Pope and into his own. Under her brother ▷ Edward VI England had swung further into ▷ Protestantism but Mary restored the Roman Catholic religion of her mother. In 1554 she married the most fanatically Catholic sovereign in Europe, Philip II of Spain; this involved her in wars with France and the loss of the last English possession there – the town of Calais. Her reign, not bloodthirsty by comparison with that of Philip in his own dominions, was nonetheless severely repressive of Protestantism, and some 300 English Protestants were burnt alive, including ▷ Cranmer and the eloquent ▷ Bishop Latimer. ▷ John Foxe's *Book of Martyrs* (1563) consigned her memory to national hatred, and she has come down in school books as 'Bloody Mary'. Her sister and successor ▷ Elizabeth I restored a moderate form of Protestantism.

▷ Tudor, House of.

Mary II (1689–94)
Queen of Great Britain. She was the daughter of ▷ James II by his first wife, and was educated in Protestant doctrine, which she retained when her father became converted to Catholicism. She married William of Orange, ruler of the Netherlands, in 1677. When James was removed from the throne in the ▷ Revolution of 1688 Mary was summoned to rule the nation jointly with her husband, who assumed the throne as ▷ William III.

▷ Stuart, House of.

Mary Barton (1848)
The first novel by ▷ Elizabeth Gaskell. Written while she was in deep distress over the death of her infant son, it is a plea for greater understanding between the employing class and the industrial proletariat of the north. It is set in Manchester in the decade in which she wrote; this was known as 'the hungry forties' because of the distress among the working classes. The most interesting character creation is John Barton, a sober and intelligent workman, whose perception of the social injustice which surrounds him and of which he is a victim drives him into bitter resentment. A group of workers draw lots to assassinate Henry Carson, one of the younger and most callous of the employers, as a warning to the rest of the class. The lot falls on Barton, who commits the murder. Suspicion, however, falls on his daughter's lover, Jem Wilson, who is brought to trial and saved from the death penalty only by Mary Barton's strenuous efforts. John Barton confesses to the murder to Henry Carson's father, who forgives him on his deathbed. Despite implausibilities, the novel is one of the most sensitive studies of industrial working-class life in Victorian fiction; as such, it suffered angry criticism from some of the employing class whom it was intended to convert. It was admired by ▷ Thomas Carlyle and ▷ Charles Dickens.

Mary Magdalene
▷ Digby Plays.

Mary Queen of Scots (1542–67)
Queen of ▷ Scotland. She was born a few days before the death of her father, James V. In 1548, when she was five years old, she was betrothed to Francis, heir to the French throne, and was sent to France. She returned to Scotland only after the death of her husband in 1560; she was Catholic, but in the meantime the Scottish Protestants with English help had overthrown the Catholic establishment in their country. Mary in

consequence found herself opposed to her people, led by the reformer ▷ John Knox. She was dangerously involved in English politics, both because she would be heir to the English throne should Elizabeth of England die childless, and because in the eyes of Catholics she was already legitimate Queen of England, since the Catholic Church did not recognize the legality of the marriage between Elizabeth's father, ▷ Henry VIII, and her mother. For diplomatic reasons, Mary married her cousin, Lord Darnley, a worthless young man who treated her abominably. In 1567 Darnley was murdered. The evidence for Mary's complicity in the murder is in the so-called 'casket letters', but their authenticity is uncertain. However, three months later she married his murderer, Lord Bothwell. Her subjects rebelled, and Mary was imprisoned but escaped and fled to England. Elizabeth gave her shelter, but the succession of plots against her on Mary's behalf eventually drove the English Queen to authorize the Scottish Queen's execution. Her son, already recognized as James VI in Scotland, became in 1603, on the death of Elizabeth, ▷ James I of England as well.

Owing to her charm, beauty, intelligence and misfortune, Mary became a legend in Europe. The greatest imaginative work about her is the tragedy *Maria Stuart* by the German poet Schiller; in English literature she is the subject of a dramatic trilogy by ▷ Swinburne and of ▷ Walter Scott's novel, *The Abbot* (1820).

Masefield, John (1878–1967)
Poet and novelist. He went to sea in 1893, and published his first volume of poems, *Salt-Water Ballads* in 1902. He was a prolific poet; the first edition of his *Collected Poems* came out in 1923, and the collection increased steadily until 1964. His work has immediate appeal, and is strongest in narrative verse: *The Everlasting Mercy* (1911); *The Widow in the Bye Street* (1912); *Dauber* (1913); *The Daffodil Fields* (1913); *Reynard the Fox* (1919). He was chosen as ▷ Poet Laureate in 1930. His novels have romantic charm, *eg Sard Harker* (1924); *Odtaa* (1926). *The Midnight Folk* (1927) is a classic of children's literature.
▷ Children's books.
Bib: Babington Smith, C., *John Masefield, a Life*; Spark, M., *John Masefield*.

Mask of Anarchy, The (1832)
A poem by ▷ Percy Bysshe Shelley, written in 1819, after he had heard news of the ▷ 'Peterloo Massacre' in Manchester, when soldiers fired on a peaceful demonstration in

favour of parliamentary reform. He sent the poem to ▷ Leigh Hunt for publication in his radical periodical ▷ *The Examiner*, but Hunt dared not print it at the time, and withheld publication until 1832. The poem was intended for popular reading, and Shelley used quatrains and five-line stanzas, similar to those of the popular ▷ ballad. He identifies Anarchy with the lawless tyranny of the British government, and exhibits its leaders in a garish pageant of Anarchy's minions: 'I met Murder on the way –/ He had a mask like Castlereagh –/ Very smooth he looked, yet grim;/ Seven blood-hounds followed him.' Shelley ends with a magnificent address to the 'Men of England, heirs of Glory', exhorting them to throw off their chains: 'Ye are many – they are few.' Its rough, angry style and passionate rhetoric give the poem a prophetic resonance which anticipates the *Communist Manifesto* of ▷ Karl Marx and Friedrich Engels (1848).

Masque
A form of dramatic entertainment which combined verse, music, dancing and scenic effect in about equal proportions. In England it flourished between 1580 and 1630, and was essentially an aristocratic style of entertainment, especially popular at the royal court. The performers were commonly professional actors, while the masquers themselves, who remained silent, were played by ladies and gentlemen of the court. The subject was often symbolic – a conflict between virtue and vice (as in ▷ John Milton's ▷ *Comus*) – or ceremonial, celebrating a great personage, *eg* Milton's ▷ *Arcades* in honour of the Countess of Derby. The masque was often preceded by an anti-masque, the content of which was comic and often satirical; the anti-masque was always performed by professionals.

Masques were sophisticated entertainments for carefully selected audiences. They were in keeping with many forms of imaginative expression of the age, and may be regarded as a synthesis of them. First of all, the visual sense had been highly developed by the great ▷ Renaissance schools of painting and architecture in Italy and France, and a favourite activity of artists was to translate into visual terms the allegorical vision that the Renaissance had inherited from the Middle Ages. This visual ▷ allegory influenced the poets; much of the best of ▷ Edmund Spenser's ▷ *The Faerie Queene* consists of brilliantly visualized allegorical scenes, such as the House of Busirane (Book III, canto 12). Secondly, the age attached

great importance to spectacles such as
▷ pageants (*ie* ceremonial processions)
which often contained symbolic, masque-like
features; a famous example (which still
survives) was the annual Lord Mayor's
Pageant in the ▷ City of London, for which
the dramatist ▷ George Peele was more
than once employed as designer. Thirdly,
masques appealed to the contemporary taste
for imaginative extravagance, delighting in
the fairytales of English folk-lore and in
classical mythology as well as in grand
pageantry. Fourthly, the fantastical styles of
many Elizabethan plays – attributable partly
to popular taste and partly to the explorations
of ▷ humanist scholars – made them either
akin to masques (*eg* ▷ Robert Greene's *James
IV*, Peele's *The Old Wives' Tale*, ▷ John
Lyly's *Mother Bombie*), or capable of
including masques as part of the dramatic
ingredient, eg ▷ Shakespeare's ▷ *Love's
Labour's Lost* and ▷ *The Tempest*. Finally,
it was an age of close musical and literary
collaboration, and masques provided
opportunities for musicians and poets to
collaborate on a large scale, just as they
already did on a small scale in the ▷ madrigal.

   Dramatists who were eminent for their
composition of masques included ▷ George
Chapman, ▷ John Fletcher and ▷ James
Shirley, but the greatest of them – in his
own estimation and probably that of others –
was ▷ Ben Jonson. He collaborated with
the composer Alfonso Ferrabosco the
younger, and the great architect ▷ Inigo
Jones; with the latter he had bitter quarrels
as to which of them had artistic control of the
production. Amongst Jonson's most
celebrated masques are *Masque of Blackness*
(1606), *Masque of Beauty* (1608) and *Masque
of Queens* (1609). The most famous of all
masques, however, is Milton's *Comus*,
composed for the Earl of Bridgewater, whose
children acted the main parts, when he was
installed as Lord President of Wales. Part of
the fame of *Comus* is due to its untypical
quality of containing much larger speaking
parts than most masques did; thus Milton
allowed himself more poetic scope than was
usual. For this reason, some critics prefer to
call *Comus* a ▷ pastoral drama, like Jonson's
The Sad Shepherd (1637) and Fletcher's *The
Faithful Shepherdess* (1610). However,
pastoral dramas and masques had much in
common; both were spectacular and symbolic
rather than dramatic.

   Though designed as a form of lavish court
entertainment, it is also true that, in the
1630s especially, the masque also played a
significant political role in the culture of the
court. It existed to legitimate, through
spectacle and pageantry, the authority of the
monarch and the central position of the court
in the affairs of the nation. At the same time,
however, the masque form is implicated in
the cultural break-down which preceded the
▷ Civil War. Not only were masques
extravagantly expensive to produce (as critics
of the court pointed out), but they may also
have served to suggest to the monarch and
those around him that a harmony pertained
in the affairs of the nation, and in the court's
relationship to the world outside, when no
such harmony, in fact, existed.
Bib: Lindley, D. (ed.), *The Court Masque*.

Massinger, Philip (1583–1640)

Dramatist. His father was in the service of
the great Herbert family. He left Oxford
University without a degree in 1607. He has
been suspected of Catholic sympathies, largely
on the strength of four plays: *The Virgin
Martyr* (1620), ▷ *The Duke of Milan* (1621),
The Maid of Honour (1621), and *The Renegado*
(1624). He collaborated extensively with other
dramatists, especially ▷ Fletcher, but 16 or
18 plays are attributed to him alone; of these,
the two usually regarded as being of the most
enduring value are the comedies, ▷ *A New
Way to Pay Old Debts* (1625) and ▷ *The
City Madam* (1632). He himself regarded
his tragedy ▷ *The Roman Actor* (1626) as
his masterpiece. The dates of these plays
show them to belong to the last, or
▷ Caroline, phase of what is commonly
called Elizabethan drama because it started in
the reign of ▷ Elizabeth I. They belong,
therefore, to the decadence, and tragedy
declined faster than comedy. The comedies
mentioned still show a lively influence from
▷ Ben Jonson, whereas Massinger's
tragedies have been accused of a lack of that
intensity which gave grandeur to the work
not only of ▷ Shakespeare but of
▷ Chapman, ▷ Tourneur and
▷ Webster. Massinger's ▷ blank verse is
in the late Shakespeare tradition, but grown
so flexible as almost to have lost its rhythms
into prose. However, he handled his sustained
periods skilfully and sometimes impressively,
anticipating ▷ Milton.
Bib: Eliot, T. S., in *Selected Essays*; Knights,
L. C., *Drama and Society in the Age of
Jonson*.

Master Craftsman

In the ▷ Middle Ages, a full member of a
▷ Craft Guild and usually an employer of
▷ apprentices and ▷ journeymen.
Originally every apprentice could theoretically

hope to become 'a master' after a specified period of 'apprenticeship' or training and the production of a 'masterpiece' to prove his skill in the craft. By the 14th century, however, the master craftsmen of the guilds were already becoming a comparatively rich class of employers, which the apprentices could not hope to enter unless they themselves had money, or married the master's daughter. Most apprentices could by then only hope to become trained journeymen.

▷ Capitalism; Women, Status of.

Master Humphrey's Clock

The title of what ▷ Charles Dickens intended to be an inclusive serial linking distinct tales – ▷ The Old Curiosity Shop and ▷ Barnaby Rudge. Master Humphrey is the narrator of the early pages of the former, but Dickens abandoned the idea.

Master of the Revels

▷ Revels, Master of the.

Materialism

The philosophical theory that only physical matter is real and that all phenomena and processes can be explained by reference to it. Related to this is the doctrine that political and social change is triggered by change in the material and economic basis of society.

▷ Marx, Karl.

Matura, Mustapha (b 1939)

Trinidadian dramatist. One of the few black playwrights as yet to have made a major impact beyond the ▷ fringe world of community theatre. His plays deal with both personal and institutional forms of racism. Matura has been an important influence on new black British playwrights such as Tunde Ikoli and Hanif Kureishi. Major works: Nice (1973); Welcome Home Jacko (1981); Play Mas, Independence and Meetings (1982); Trinidad Sisters (1988).

▷ Commonwealth literatures.

Maturin, Charles Robert (1782–1824)

Irish novelist and dramatist. Like ▷ 'Monk' Lewis and ▷ Mrs Radcliffe he belonged to the school of writers who exploited the emotions of terror and love of mystery among readers in the late 18th and early 19th centuries. The Fatal Revenge, or The Family of Montorso (1807), The Wild Irish Boy (1808) and The Milesian Chief (1812) were ridiculed but admired for their power by ▷ Walter Scott. Scott and Byron secured the production of Maturin's tragedy Bertram in 1816, which was a great success. His other tragedies were less successful, and he returned to the novel. The best of his later novels is

Melmoth (1820), to which the French novelist ▷ Balzac wrote a sequel Melmoth réconcilé à l'église (1835).

Maud (1855)

One of the best-known poems by ▷ Alfred Tennyson. It is called 'A Monodrama', and is in fact an example of the ▷ dramatic monologue, a form particularly characteristic of ▷ Victorian poetry, especially in the work of ▷ Browning and Tennyson.

It is in three parts. Part I tells of the mysterious death of the narrator's father, who has been ruined by the contrivances of 'that old man, now lord of the broad estate and the Hall'. But the narrator gradually falls in love with the old lord's daughter, and here occurs the famous lyric 'Come into the garden, Maud'. The young lord, her brother, treats him with contempt, however, and Part II opens with their duel and the death of the brother. The narrator flies abroad, and falls into the depths of morbid despair. In Part III he recovers, and seeks salvation through the service of his country in war: the poem was written in the year in which the Crimean War broke out.

Maud exemplifies the versatility of Tennyson's craftsmanship by the variety of its ▷ metrical and ▷ stanzaic form, and the brilliant distinctness of his vision in some of the imagery. It contains bitter criticism of the temper of the age. The poem has been held to betray Tennyson's confusion about his age; criticizing it, yet swimming with its tide. Maud is a ▷ Gothic conflation of images of disease, mental aberration and sexual repression.

Maugham, William Somerset (1874–1965)

Novelist, short-story writer and dramatist. Educated at King's School, Canterbury, and Heidelberg University; he then studied medicine in London. His first novel, Liza of Lambeth (1897) shows the influence of ▷ Zola, an example of the growing importance of French influence on English fiction at the end of the 19th century. His semi-autobiographical novel Of Human Bondage (1915) made his name. Other novels include: The Hero (1901); The Moon and Sixpence (1919); The Painted Veil (1925); The Casuarina Tree (1926); Cakes and Ale (1930). The professional accomplishment of his novels gave him a wide foreign public, and after 1930 his reputation abroad was greater than at home, though interest in him revived here towards his 80th birthday. He celebrated his 80th year by the special republication of Cakes and Ale, a novel which satirizes the English propensity for admiring the 'Grand

Old Men' among their writers. Some of his best fiction is in his short stories, in volumes such as *The Trembling of a Leaf* (1921), *The Mixture as Before* (1940). His plays were successful, but have lost interest now. They include: *Our Betters* (1917); *Caesar's Wife* (1919); *East of Suez* (1922); *The Constant Wife* (1926); *The Letter* (1927); *The Breadwinner* (1930); *Sheppey* (1933).
Bib: Maugham, R., *Somerset and All the Maughams*; Morgan, T., *Somerset Maugham*; Brander, L., *Somerset Maugham: A Guide*.

May Day (1611)
A complex, multiple-plot comedy by ▷ George Chapman which skilfully interweaves a wealth of ▷ romance and native ▷ pastoral motifs with stock characters from Plautine (▷ Plautus) and Terentian (▷ Terence) comedy. Unlike Chapman's tragedies, *May Day* is unimpeded by an overly inflated and abstract rhetoric.

Mayflower, The
   ▷ Pilgrim Fathers.

Mayor of Casterbridge, The (1886)
A novel by ▷ Thomas Hardy. Its hero is the country labourer, Michael Henchard. At the beginning of the book, when times are hard, he gets drunk at a fair and sells his wife and child to a sailor called Newson. He bitterly repents and renounces strong drink for 20 years. His wife returns after 18 years, supposing Newson to be drowned, and by this time Henchard has prospered so far as to have become Mayor of Casterbridge (Dorchester). At the same time as her return, Henchard takes on as his assistant in his business of corn-dealing a wandering Scotsman, Donald Farfrae. The rest of the novel is the story of the rivalry between Farfrae and Henchard. Farfrae is never deliberately his enemy, yet merely by virtue of living in the same town he deprives Henchard of everything, and the latter leaves the place at the end of the novel as poor as when he started, and far more wretched. Hardy seems to have intended a kind of Darwinian study of the survival of the fittest among human beings. Henchard is a monolithic character, who puts all his energy and passion into every relationship and activity; Farfrae has a flexible personality and is able to devote to every predicament exactly what it demands, without excess. Henchard's crowning sadness is the loss of the girl he has supposed to be his daughter but who is in fact Newson's; he loves her nonetheless but Newson returns and claims her.

McEwan, Ian (b 1948)
Novelist and short-story writer. His first collection of stories, *First Love, Last Rites* (1975) gained immediate notoriety for its erotic, perverse and macabre, concerns which also figure in *In Between the Sheets* (1978). His first novel, *The Cement Garden* (1978) is a story of adolescent guilt, while *The Comfort of Strangers* (1981) is a dream-like narrative set in Venice and ending in violence. His most recent novel is *The Child in Time*, published in 1987. He has also written a T.V. play, *The Imitation Game* (1981) and a screenplay, *The Ploughman's Lunch* (1983).

McGrath, John (b 1935)
One of the foremost writers of the political ▷ fringe during the 1970s and 80s. In 1971 he founded the 7:84 company (the name is based on a statistic which revealed that 7% of the population owned 84% of the country's wealth). The company was divided in two, between Scotland and England, in 1973. One of McGrath's most successful works was the popular entertainment *The Cheviot, the Stag and the Black, Black Oil* (1973), written for 7:84 Scotland. In this he compared the plundering of Scottish oil assets with the Highland Clearances. He has consistently insisted on disassociating himself from the theatre establishment and once said he would 'rather have a bad night in Bootle' than write a play for the ▷ National Theatre. His radical ideas about the politics of entertainment are recorded in his book, *A Good Night Out* 1981. Other plays are: *The Game's a Bogey* (1974); *Fish in the Sea* (1977); *Little Red Hen* (1977); *Yobbo Nowt* (1978); *Joe's Drum* (1979); *Blood Red Roses* (1981); *Swings and Roundabouts* (1981).

McKerrow, R. B. (Ronald Brownlees) (1872–1940)
Editor and bibliographer who was co-founder of the Malone Society (1906), dedicated to the study and editing of early and often neglected English drama. He wrote the seminal *An Introduction to Bibliography for Literary Students* (1927). He was one of the driving forces behind the 'New Bibliography' and is the author of the important *Prolegomena* (1939) for an Oxford edition of ▷ Shakespeare's works. This latter, which aimed at discovering an editorial methodology from ten selected texts, has proved an important milestone on the road to the new and revisionary Oxford University Press Shakespeare edited by Gary Taylor and Stanley Wells.
   ▷ Shakespeare – history of textual study.

Measure for Measure (1603–4)
A play by ▷ Shakespeare. It was probably written in 1603–4, and was first printed in the First ▷ Folio of 1623. Its plot derives from *Promos and Cassandra* (1578), the translation by ▷ George Whetstone of a tale by the Italian Cinthio. In the Folio it is grouped with the comedies, but modern critics are inclined to call it a ▷ problem play, a modern classification that includes ▷ *Troilus and Cressida*, ▷ *All's Well that Ends Well*, and sometimes ▷ *Hamlet*.

Vincentio, Duke of Vienna, is faced with the difficulty of enforcing severe laws against unchastity after they have fallen into disuse; he finds that the claims of justice and virtue conflict with those of mercy and compassion. He makes the experiment of pretending to leave the country so as to depute the task to Angelo, a man of austere life and rigid principle. In fact, the Duke remains on the scene, disguised as a friar, to watch the experiment. Angelo condemns Claudio to death for seducing his betrothed before marriage. Claudio's sister, Isabella, a novitiate nun, comes to plead for her brother's life, urged on by Lucio, a man of loose life but a friend of Claudio's. Angelo is appalled to find that his lust is aroused for Isabella. His strict principle is transformed into brutal hypocrisy when he attempts to blackmail Isabella into surrendering herself in return for her brother's life. The disguised Duke induces her to pretend to consent, while he substitutes for her ▷ Mariana, whom Angelo has cold-heartedly discarded in spite of his engagement to her. Even after Isabella's apparent consent, Angelo orders Claudio's execution, in order that no witness of his brutal conspiracy shall survive. Finally the Duke reveals himself, and exposes his deputy, but spares his life on the appeals of Isabella and Mariana.

It is necessary to remember the biblical text (*Matthew* 7:1) from which the title is taken: 'Judge not that ye be not judged. For with what judgement ye judge, ye shall be judged: and with what measure ye mete, it shall be measured to you again.' The three main problems that perplex critics are:

1 The Duke is evidently intended to be a virtuous ruler, who even plays the role of God, the invisible witness of our most secret thoughts and actions. Viewed realistically, however, he escapes from his duty and then plays the role of a mean spy on Angelo's actions. The mistake here is to confuse the conventions of modern, realistic drama with the conventions of Shakespeare's drama. The latter saw character in terms of role, or social function, first, and in terms of individual psychology only second. Vincentio is a ruler as God is the Ruler; by taking on the role of the omnipresent witness who has ultimate power of judgement, he is extending his function, not escaping from it.

2 Isabella is presented as a virtuous woman, and yet she seems inexcusably callous in her refusal to put her brother's life before her own chastity. This is not a problem if we understand that Isabella's religious vocation is the meaning of life to her (I.iv); she has to be educated into seeing that virtue can never retain its value if it is segregated from life, just as law can never operate widely if it is isolated from knowledge of the human heart; this is Angelo's mistake.

3 Although the death penalty on Claudio is cruel, no one disputes that he has committed an offence, and yet later Angelo (by the contrivance of the Duke) is made to commit the same offence with Mariana, for which neither of them is held guilty. An answer to this is the difference between Claudio's and Angelo's actions. Claudio had offended against the law, but not against his betrothed, Juliet, whereas Angelo had previously offended against Mariana by renouncing his engagement to her, though not against the law. Morally, the play shows that Angelo's offence is the worse, and is in fact made good by his 'sin' of the Duke's contrivance.

For an adverse view of the play, see A. P. Rossiter in *Angel with Horns*; for favourable ones, see F. R. Leavis in *The Common Pursuit* and Wilson Knight in *The Wheel of Fire*.

Mecca
The birthplace of the Prophet Muhammad, and the chief goal of pilgrimage for Muslims. In English, the word is also used for any place that one is determined to reach.

Medall, The. A Satyre against Sedition (1682)
A satire in ▷ heroic couplets by ▷ John Dryden. The ▷ Earl of Shaftesbury, leader of the ▷ Whig party which opposed the succession of the Catholic James, Duke of York, to the throne, had been acquitted on a charge of treason. Dryden found an ideal focus for his mock-heroic ridicule in the medal struck to celebrate the Whig victory, which shows Shaftesbury's head on the obverse, and on the reverse the sun rising over the Tower of London (where Shaftesbury had been imprisoned), with the legend *Laetamur* ('Let us rejoice').

Medea
In Greek myth, a celebrated sorceress. She

was the daughter of Aeetes, king of Colchis, possessor of the ▷ Golden Fleece. She helped ▷ Jason of Iolchos to steal it, and fled with him to Corinth. There, Jason abandoned her for Glauce, daughter of the king. In revenge, Medea destroyed her own two children by Jason, and Glauce as well. She was worshipped as a goddess in Corinth. Other tales about her show her as destroyer or renewer of life.

Medes

Inhabitants of ancient Persia; the Persians subjugated them in the 6th century BC. A reference in the Bible (*Daniel* 6:8) has caused the Law of the Medes and Persians to stand proverbially for that which is unalterable.

Medusa

▷ Gorgons.

Meiosis

▷ Figures of Speech.

Melibee, The Tale of

The second of ▷ Chaucer's own contributions to the ▷ *Canterbury Tales*, which follows the narrative of ▷ *Sir Thopas* rejected by the Host. This allegorical prose narrative concerns the counselling of the impetuous Melibeus, by his wise wife Dame Prudence. The treatise derives from a French source, itself a translation of an earlier 14th-century Latin composition.

Melincourt, or Sir Oran Haut-ton (1817)

A novel by ▷ Thomas Love Peacock. Sir Oran Haut-ton is an orang-outang of delightful manners and a good flute-player for whom the young philosopher, Mr Sylvan Forester, has bought the title of baronet and a seat in Parliament. 'Haut ton' is a French phrase then used in English for 'high tone', *ie* fashionable, refined, and aristocratic. Peacock is developing the idea of Lord Monboddo (1714–90), an early anthropologist, who describes such a creature in his books, as an example of 'the infantine state of our species'; Peacock's ape, however, compares favourably with the aristocracy. The book is a satire on the right-wing (Tory) establishment, and especially those writers who had once been Radicals but now favoured it: ▷ Southey (Mr Feathernest); ▷ Wordsworth (Mr Paperstamp); ▷ Coleridge (Mr Mystic). Mr Vamp and Mr Killthedead are Tory reviewers, and Mr Fax may represent ▷ Malthus. Sylvan Forester may be the poet ▷ Shelley; and Simon Sarcastic, Peacock himself.

Melodrama

The prefix 'melo-' derives from the Greek 'melos', music. Originally, melodrama was a play in which there was no singing but the dialogue had a musical accompaniment; the first example is said to be ▷ Rousseau's *Pygmalion* (1775). The musical accompaniment gradually ceased; the word came to denote romantic plays of extravagantly violent action, and it is now applied to sensational action without adequate motivation, in any work of fiction.

The word has also been used to denote popular ballad operas in which spoken dialogue is used extensively. This use, however, is much less common.

Melpomene

▷ Muses.

Memoirs of a Cavalier (1724)

A work of fiction by ▷ Daniel Defoe, but it was thought that the memoirs were possibly genuine. They describe the career of a professional soldier, Colonel Andrew Newport, born in 1608. He sees military service in Europe during the ▷ Thirty Years War, and then joins the English Royalist army in the ▷ Civil War.

Men and Women (1855)

A volume of poems by ▷ Robert Browning. It contained 50 pieces, nearly all in ▷ dramatic monologue, a form in which a character soliloquizes about himself, his predicament or his relationship with another. The book contains much of Browning's best-known work, such as *Any Wife to Any Husband, Andrea del Sarto, Fra Lippo Lippi*. In the *Collected Works* of 1868, the poems were dispersed, and only 13 remained under the title *Men and Women*.

Menander (342–293 BC)

An Athenian comic poet whose plays were popular in the classical world and provided the characteristic matrix of ▷ New Comedy, which became the model for both ▷ Plautus and ▷ Terence. Menander is widely acknowledged by the Roman dramatists as their mentor, but it was not until the 20th century (1905) that substantial parts of manuscripts of his plays and one complete work (*Dyskolos*, 1955) were discovered. These confirmed the high regard in which Menander was held by his contemporaries.

Menelaus

▷ *Iliad*.

Mephistopheles

An evil spirit whose name first occurs in the German *Faustbuch* (1587), a collection of tales about the necromancer ▷ Johann Faust. He is one of the seven great princes of hell. As

Mephostophilis he is best known in English through Marlowe's ▷ *Dr Faustus* (1592).

Mercantile system
A term used by the economist ▷ Adam Smith (*Wealth of Nations*, 1776) and later writers to denote the assumptions behind the practice of commerce from the later ▷ Middle Ages until the 18th century. In its extreme form, it identified wealth with money so that the main object of governments was to accumulate large stocks of precious metals. Smith advocated a contrary theory of free trade, which became the dominant policy by the middle of the 19th century.
Bib: Foucault, M., *The Order of Things*.

Mercer, David (1928–80)
British dramatist renowned for his television work as much as his stage plays, some of which have been performed by the ▷ Royal Shakespeare Company. He was one of the first to write serious plays for television dealing with the working class. Mercer's treatment of this subject has been accused of being excessively nostalgic and only his middle-class, not his working-class, characters are generally given any intellectual depth. Social alienation and madness are commonly the fate of those who move away from their class origins. Although he wrote from a (▷ Marx, Karl) Marxist perspective there is little optimism about the modern world in his plays. Television plays include: *The Generations* (1961–3); *Morgan, A Suitable Case for Treatment* (1962); *For Tea on Sunday* (1963); *In Two Minds* (1967); *On the Eve of Publication* (1968); *The Cellar and the Almond Tree* (1970); *Emma's Time* (1970). Stage plays include: *Ride a Cock Horse* (1965); *Belcher's Luck* (1966); *After Haggarty* (1970); *Duck Song* (1974); *Cousin Vladimir* (1978); *The Monster of Karlovy Vary* (1979); *Then and Now* (1979).
Bib: Trussler, S. (ed.), *New Theatre Voices of the Seventies*.

Merchant Adventurers
▷ Companies, Joint Stock.

Merchant of Venice, The (1596–7)
A comedy by ▷ Shakespeare. It is dated by external evidence 1596–7. Its two outstanding incidents – the winning of a bride by undergoing a test, and the demanding of a pound of human flesh by the usurer – occur in a number of earlier narratives, but Shakespeare seems to have depended principally on a collection of Italian novels called *Il Pecorone* (*The Blockhead*) and the *Gesta Romanorum* (Tales of the Romans).

▷ Quarto edition, 1600; included in the First ▷ Folio (1623).
The play has a double plot.
1 An impoverished young Venetian, Bassanio, seeks to marry a wealthy heiress, Portia of Belmont. For the expense of the courtship he has to borrow 3,000 ducats from his friend, the merchant Antonio. When Bassanio and Portia meet, they fall in love at first sight, but before she can surrender herself, Bassanio has to pass the test of the caskets, ordained by her dead father. The test is to choose between a gold, a silver, and a lead casket; the right casket contains her portrait. He passes the test, but their rejoicing is interrupted by the arrival of a letter from Antonio.
2 Antonio's money is all invested in mercantile expeditions, so that to help Bassanio he has had to borrow from the Jewish usurer, Shylock. Shylock has made the strange stipulation that Antonio will have to surrender a pound of flesh in default of repayment. Antonio's letter now relates that his voyaging ships have all been lost, he is penniless, and will have to pay the pound of flesh. The two plots join in the trial scene of IV.i. The issue has come before a court of law at which Portia appears disguised as a young lawyer instructed to judge the case. She appeals to Shylock to show mercy, but when he insists on the letter of the law she lets him have it: he may take his pound of flesh, but there is no mention of blood in the bond; if he sheds any, the law of Venice is clear: his lands and goods are to become the property of the state. Antonio is saved, and Shylock has to undergo certain severe penalties, including compulsory conversion to Christianity. Act V concludes the play with light comedy and the lyrical union of several pairs of lovers.
Like others of Shakespeare's earlier comedies, the play is a mixture of courtly sophistication, light fantasy, and moving realism. The plot belongs to fable and fairy story, and the love affairs to the tradition of courtly romance. On the other hand, Shylock is a very powerful, sombre figure. His revolting bond is conterbalanced by Antonio's arrogant treatment of him and the eloquent irony with which Shylock protests against it. The trial scene is one of the elements of fable in the play: in real terms, Shylock is being treated with gross unjustice, but the real theme is the contrast between Mercy and the Law. It is the function of mere Law to be merciless; he who refuses mercy and insists on law must abide by the consequences.
▷ Usury.

Merchant's Tale, The
One of ▷ Chaucer's ▷ *Canterbury Tales*.
Prompted by the *Clerk's Tale* of patient
Griselda, the Merchant tells a contrasting
story of married life, set in Italy, involving
the tricking of an old jealous husband,
January, by his young wife, May, and her
lover, Damian (who is January's squire). The
tale is built up from a mixture of different
styles, registers, and generic conventions. It
begins in a debate mode with a long discussion
about the theory and practice of married life,
which injects a tone of Christian idealism into
the narrative; the relationship between May
and Damian is described using the register of
a courtly romance (although the two lovers
hardly live up to romance role models); the
characters' names give the narrative a semi-
allegorical quality; the intervention of the
classical gods in January's garden endows the
action with an epic touch (since the gods
function as a domestic *deus ex machina*); while
the plot structure itself is basically that of a
▷ fabliau. The climax of the tale comes
when the old, now blind, knight January
miraculously recovers his sight, only to see
his wife making love with Damian in a pear
tree. This climactic scene has many European
analogues but none has the elaborate build-
up which distinguishes Chaucer's version.

Mercia
One of the ancient ▷ Anglo-Saxon
kingdoms from the 6th to the 9th centuries.
From the 10th century to the ▷ Norman
Conquest (1066) it was an earldom in the
kingdom of England. It roughly corresponded
to the modern Midlands.
▷ Heptarchy.

Mercury
▷ Hermes.

Mercutio
The friend of Romeo and related to the
Prince in ▷ Shakespeare's tragedy ▷ *Romeo
and Juliet*. He makes the celebrated speech
about Queen Mab in I. iv. His
quarrelsomeness leads to his death at the
hands of Tybalt, the cousin of Juliet, followed
by Romeo's fatal duel with Tybalt.

Meredith, George (1828–1909)
Novelist and poet. Born at Portsmouth, the
son of a tailor and naval outfitter; his
grandfather, Melchizedeck, had had the same
business and is the basis of the character Old
Mel in the novel *Evan Harrington* (1861).
George Meredith was educated
in Germany and his writings were influenced

Illustration from George Meredith's *The
Shaving of Shagpat*

by ▷ Germans, especially the novelist Jean
Paul Richter (1763–1825), who stimulated his
conception of comedy. Meredith was even
closer to ▷ French culture, especially the
radical thinking of the 18th-century
Philosophes (▷ Encyclopaedists). On his
return to England he began to study law but
soon took to journalism and serious literature.
   He began by publishing verse: *Poems*
(1851). In 1855 he published his eastern
romance *Shaving of Shagpat*, and in 1857 a
romance in German style, *Farina, a Legend of
Cologne*. ▷ *The Ordeal of Richard Feverel*
(1859) was his first real novel, followed by
Evan Harrington, which is now regarded as
one of his best. In 1862 he produced his most
famous volume of poems, *Modern Love*. Other
publications included: *Sandra Belloni* (1864;
originally called *Emilia in England*); *Rhoda
Fleming* (1865); *Vittoria* (1867 – a sequel to
Sandra); *The Adventures of Harry Richmond*
(1871); *Beauchamp's Career* (1875 – his own
favourite); *The Idea of Comedy* (1877 – a
critical essay, important for understanding his
work); ▷ *The Egoist* (1879 – one of his best
known novels); *The Tragic Comedians* (1880);
Poems and Lyrics of the Joy of Earth (1883);
Diana of the Crossways (1885 – the first of his
novels to reach a wide public); *Ballads and
Poems of Tragic Life* (1887); *A Reading of
Earth* (1888 – verse); *One of Our Conquerors*
(1891); *The Empty Purse* (1892 – a poem);
Lord Ormont and his Aminta (1894); *The*

Amazing Marriage (1895). His concluding works were all poetry: *Odes in Contribution to the Song of French History* (1898); *A Reading of Life* (1901); *Last Poems* (published in 1910 after his death). His unfinished novel, *Celt and Saxon*, was also published posthumously.

Meredith's reputation at present rests chiefly on his novels but, like ▷ Thomas Hardy, he seems to have been a novelist who preferred poetry. His prose is poetic in its use of ▷ metaphor and ▷ symbolism, and both his poetry and his prose are often expressed in concentrated and difficult language which invites comparison with ▷ Robert Browning. The impulsiveness and ruggedness of his prose also recalls ▷ Robert Carlyle, whom Meredith resembled in his hostility to the mechanistic qualities of his age. Of all the Victorian novelists who ever had a major reputation, his has perhaps sunk the lowest in this century: both his prose and his poetry tend to be regarded as intolerably mannered and he is accused of fixing his attention on style as an end, instead of using it as a medium. Nonetheless, his intense interest in psychological exploration (again recalling Browning), his use of metaphor and symbol from the natural world to express states of mind and the freshness of some of his characters (especially women) were all original in his own time and keep him from being forgotten.
Bib: Stevenson, L., *Life*; Lindsay, L., *Life*; Trevelyan, G. M., *Poetry and Philosophy of George Meredith*; Sassoon, S., *Meredith*; Sitwell, O., *Novels of Meredith*; Lees, F. N., in *Pelican Guide 6: Dickens to Hardy*; Cline, C. L., *Letters*; Woolf, V., in *Common Reader*; Williams, D., *George Meredith: His Life and Lost Love*.

Meres, Francis (1565–1647)
Author of *Palladis Tamia, Wit's Treasury* (1598), a book of moral and critical reflections. One chapter is an account of English writers, and his comments are interesting for estimating their reputations at the time.

Merlin
Prophet and enchanter who comes to play a central role in directing the early stages of Arthurian history. Merlin first appears in the guise of prophet of British history and magic worker in ▷ Geoffrey of Monmouth's version of British history (completed c 1138). There, a whole book is devoted to his veiled predictions about the future shape of British history; he is also responsible for the removal of Stonehenge from Ireland to Britain, and he engineers ▷ King Arthur's conception

by allowing ▷ Uther to take on the guise of ▷ Igraine's husband. His name, 'Merlinus', is an adaptation of 'Myrddyn', the bard who features in Welsh legendary narratives, and is credited with the prophecy of a future Celtic revival. So although Merlin first appears in Geoffrey's work, there are earlier precedents for his role. In Geoffrey of Monmouth's poetic account of the *Vita Merlini* (the *Life of Merlin*), completed c 1150, the seer is presented as a former battle leader who has gone mad after a great defeat, and lives as a man of the woods, endowed with prophetic insight.

In ▷ Robert de Boron's version of Arthurian narrative, which gives a pronounced Christian bias to the history, Merlin is conceived as part of the Devil's plot to oppose Christ; however, the goodness of his mother ensures that his magical powers are used for positive ends. He is credited with the founding of the ▷ Round Table and with the arrangements for Arthur's fostering. In ▷ Malory's *Morte D'Arthur* Merlin has a key role to play in setting up the Arthurian kingdom and mapping out the shape of later events but he is prevented from playing any further part in the history because he is entrapped in a rock by Nimue (or Viviane), after he has taught her his magical secrets.

Mermaid Tavern
A 16th-century tavern in ▷ London's Bread Street. According to legend the Bread Street, or Friday Night, Club was founded by ▷ Sir Walter Ralegh, and was one of the earliest English clubs and meeting-place of writers.

Mermaids and Mermen
In the folklore of many races, half-human creatures of the sea, able to live above its surface. In British folklore, they always have fish-tails, but this is not universal. They often had supernatural powers, and beguiled men down to their submarine world. They resemble, among other such creatures in ancient myths, the ▷ sirens and the tritons of Greek myth.

Merry Wives of Windsor, The (1600–1)
A comedy by ▷ Shakespeare, probably written 1600–1; an imperfect edition came out in 1602, and a corrected version was published in the ▷ First Folio of 1623. The critic John Dennis (1657–1734) states that it was written at the request of ▷ Queen Elizabeth I, who wanted a play about ▷ Sir John Falstaff in love. Falstaff had been a great popular success in the two ▷ *Henry IV* plays. It has also been suggested that Shakespeare was emulating the realistic

comedy of ▷ Thomas Dekker
(▷ *Shoemaker's Holiday*, 1600) and ▷ Ben
Jonson (▷ *Every Man in his Humour*,
1598; ▷ *Every Man out of his Humour*,
1599). *The Merry Wives* is the only play by
Shakespeare to be written mainly in prose.

Falstaff makes love to two married women,
the wives of Ford and Page; but the wives
and their husbands finally expose him in
Windsor Forest, after he has been beset by
neighbours disguised as fairies. A subordinate
plot concerns the wooing of Anne Page by
three suitors, and how she and Fenton, the
suitor she prefers, contrive their elopement.

Apart from Falstaff, other characters recur
from the Henry IV and V plays: Nym, Pistol,
Slender, Mistress Quickly. Falstaff in
The Merry Wives, bears little resemblance to
the creation of the earlier plays.

Messiah
In Hebrew, the title – meaning 'the anointed'
– of the great deliverer who was expected, and
who would raise up the Jewish nation: *Daniel*
9:25–6. In the New Testament, the Messiah
(Messias) is identified with Jesus Christ (*John*
1:41).

Metafiction
This term is applied to fictional writing
which questions the relationship between
reality and fiction through deliberately and
self-consciously drawing attention to its own
status as a linguistic construct. Examples
would include ▷ John Fowles' *The French
Lieutenant's Woman*.

Metalanguage
A term coined by the linguist L. Hjelmslev to
describe a language which refers to *another
language* rather than to non-linguistic objects,
situations or events. In the words of
▷ Roland Barthes it is 'a second language in
which one speaks about the first'
(*Mythologies*). In this sense, metalanguage
can be used as a means of reflecting on
language itself.
    ▷ Metafiction.

Metamorphoses
Poems in Latin by ▷ Ovid. They are a
series of mythological tales whose common
subject is miraculous transformation of shape,
beginning with Chaos into Cosmos, ending
with ▷ Julius Caesar into a star, and
including such tales as Baucis and Philemon,
the peasants who unawares gave hospitality to
the gods, who granted them immortality as a
pair of trees. They were popular in medieval
Europe and afterwards, up till the 19th
century, and have often been translated, in
whole or in part, into English, *eg* by ▷ Arthur

Golding in the 16th century, George Sandys
and ▷ John Dryden in the 17th, and
▷ Pope in the 18th.

Metaphor
    ▷ Figures of Speech.

Metaphysical conceit
    ▷ Figures of Speech.

Metaphysical Poets
The accepted designation of a succession of
17th-century poets, of whom the following are
the principal names: ▷ John Donne,
▷ George Herbert, ▷ Richard Crashaw,
▷ Andrew Marvell, ▷ Henry Vaughan,
▷ Abraham Cowley. The term came to be
applied to them in a special sense; that is to
say, they were not so described because their
subject was the relationship of spirit to
matter or the ultimate nature of reality; this is
true of ▷ Lucretius, ▷ Milton and
▷ Dante, who have little else in common. It
is true that some of them – Donne, Herbert,
Vaughan and Crashaw especially – were
metaphysical in this generally accepted sense,
but the adjective is applied to them to
indicate not merely subject matter, but
qualities of expression in relation to subject
matter.

    ▷ Samuel Johnson was the first so to
classify these poets: 'The metaphysical poets
were men of learning, and to show their
learning was their whole endeavour' – essay
on Cowley, in ▷ *Lives of the Poets*. The
sentence shows that he is using the term
disparagingly, and this disparagement had
already been expressed by ▷ John Dryden:
'Donne affects the metaphysics not only in
his satires but in his amorous verses . . . [he]
perplexes the mind of the fair sex with nice
speculations of philosophy' (*Discourse
concerning the Original and Progress of Satire*,
1693). Dryden and Johnson were antagonistic
to Donne and his followers because they
valued above all the assurance, clarity,
restraint and shapeliness of the great
▷ Augustan poets of ancient Rome. Critics
and poets of the 20th century have on the
contrary immensely admired Donne, Herbert
and Marvell, but they still use 'Metaphysical'
as the term under which to group them.
H. J. C. Grierson (Introduction, *Metaphysical
Poetry: Donne to Butler*) justifies it because it
indicates 'the peculiar blend of passion and
thought, feeling and ratiocination which is
their greatest achievement.' However, they
have also been labelled '*The Fantasticks*' (an
anthology edited by W. S. Scott) and
Professor Martz has suggested *The Poetry of
Meditation* (the title of his book). The first of
these alternative designations suggests

resemblance between the English poets and their so-called 'baroque' contemporaries in Italy (Marino), Spain (Góngora) and France (Théophile de Viau and Saint-Amant); the second emphasizes the difference – the greater balance and control among the English poets; it may be said that Crashaw, at one extreme, belongs more to the former, and Herbert, at the other extreme, is much better described as 'meditative'.

The distinctiveness of the Metaphysicals was their use of the so-called 'metaphysical ▷ conceit' – *ie* paradoxical metaphor causing a shock to the mind by the unlikeness of the association, *eg* Donne's

> *her pure and eloquent blood*
> *Spoke in her cheeks, and so distinctly wrought,*
> *That one might almost say her body*
> *　　thought.*
> 　　　　　　　(*Second Anniversary*)

or Herbert's

> *Only a sweet and virtuous soul,*
> *Like season'd timber, never gives;*
> *But through the whole turn to coal*
> *　　Then chiefly lives.*
> 　　　　　　　(*Virtue*)

In most respects, therefore, the term is so broad, and embraces poetic styles and forms so disparate, that its use is nearly meaningless, being little more than an anthologist's convenience.

Methodism

A religious movement founded by ▷ John Wesley. The name was at first applied derisively to himself and his associates when he was a student at Oxford in 1729, referring to the strict rules that they made for themselves in order to follow a religious life; however, he early accepted the designation. From 1739 a time when the Church of England was particularly apathetic, the movement spread rapidly among the poor all over England, and it became especially strong in the industrial towns. Wesley himself had no desire to separate Methodism from the Anglican Church, but the demands on his energies forced him to ordain preachers whom the Church felt it could not accept as clergymen; consequently the Methodists developed an independent organization.

The later movement divided into a number of distinct organizations. It spread abroad, especially to the U.S.A. where the membership numbers about 13 million, as compared with rather more than half a million in Britain.

Metre

From the Greek word meaning 'measure'. In poetry, metre is the measure of the rhythm of a line of verse, when the line is rhythmically systematic, *ie* can be divided into units of 'metrical feet'. The names for these feet all derive from ancient Greek verse. The commonest feet in use in English are as follows:

Iambus　*eg* the words 'again', 'revenge', 'delight'.

> 'Iambics march from short to long.'

Trochee　*eg* the words 'never', 'happy', 'heartless'.

> 'Trochee trips from long to short.'

Anapest　*eg* the words 'entertain', 'supersede', 'engineer'.

> 'With a leap and a bound the swift anapaests throng.'

Spondee　*eg* the words 'maintain', 'heartbreak', 'wineglass'

> 'Slow spondee stalks, strong foot . . .'

Dactyl　*eg* the words 'melody', 'happiness', 'sorrowful'.

> '. . . yet ill able
> Ever to come up with dactyl trisyllable.'

The illustrative lines are taken from ▷ Coleridge's mnemonic rhyme 'Metrical Feet' (the dactyl example in particular being a joke).

It is important to remember three points when analysing ('scanning') English verse:

1 Despite Coleridge's use of 'long' and 'short' for iambic and trochaic feet, these words are inappropriate to English metrical feet, which are composed of accented and unaccented syllables (two accented ones in the case of the spondee) irrespective of their length.

2 Except in the case of the iambus, it is unusual to find lines of verse composed entirely of the same foot; this is especially true of the spondee and the dactyl.

3 It is unwise to think of metre at all when reading a great deal of English verse. Old and Middle English ▷ alliterative verse was not

metrical. ▷ Chaucer's is metrical, but not consistently so; his verse depends more on the natural rhythms of the English speaking voice. This is also true of ▷ Sir Thomas Wyatt in the early 16th century, of the mature dramatic verse of ▷ Shakespeare and his contemporaries, of ▷ John Donne, of ▷ Gerard Manley Hopkins in the 19th century, and of many 20th-century poets.

Verse lines have names according to the number of feet they contain; much the commonest English line is the iambic pentameter (five feet). The hexameter has six feet, and is called an ▷ Alexandrine when they are iambic. Other lengths: monometer = one foot; dimeter = two feet; trimeter = three feet; tetrameter = four feet; heptameter = seven feet; octameter = eight feet. Some minor 16th-century poets used lines of 14 syllables known as 'fourteeners'; a couplet consisting of a fourteener and an Alexandrine, first used by Wyatt, is known as the ▷ poulter's measure.

▷ Blank verse; Free verse; Ode; Sonnet.

Mew, Charlotte (1869–1928)
Poet. Mew lived in London in the shadow of her oppressive family, and having had little educational advantages, published her first poems in ▷ *The Yellow Book*. Her small corpus of poetry was very well received by ▷ Thomas Hardy, ▷ John Masefield, Harold Monro and ▷ Walter de la Mare, whose influence secured her a civil list pension in 1923. Her most famous poem, 'The Farmer's Bride' (1916), deals with a difficult marital relationship, and is characteristic of the strength of her work in analysing suffering and loss. 'Madeleine in Church', a ▷ dramatic monologue, is perhaps Mew's most powerful text. She committed suicide after the death of her sister. The best recent edition of her work is the 1982 Virago collection, *Collected Poems and Prose*.

Michael (1800)
A poem in ▷ blank verse by ▷ William Wordsworth concerning the austere life of a shepherd in the Lake District, whose only son Luke goes away to work in town, meets disgrace, and then disappears. The emptiness of Michael's life without his son is symbolized, in an image of characteristic simplicity, by the unbuilt sheepfold, whose first stone Luke had laid before his departure as a covenant between them. Michael spends the last seven years of his life brooding over it and leaves it still unfinished at his death.

▷ Lake Poets.

Michael, St
In the ▷ Bible (*Revelation*, 12:7) the leader of the ▷ angels against the dragon, *ie* the Devil. In Milton's ▷ *Paradise Lost* (vi, 44) he is the Prince of the heavenly armies.

Michaelmas
The feast of St Michael, 29 September. Also, the name for a term (September to December) in law-courts and universities. 29 September is a ▷ quarter day from which leases are dated, servants used to be hired, etc.

Microcosmographie
▷ Characters, Theophrastian.

Midas
In Greek myth, a king of Phrygia, of whom two particularly well-known tales are told:

1 For a service to the god Dionysus, he was able to turn all he touched into gold.

2 Asked to judge between Apollo, god of the arts, and Pan, god of shepherds, as flute players, he preferred Pan. To punish him, Apollo gave him ass's ears.

Midas is also the name of a prose play by ▷ Lyly, written in 1592.

Middle Ages, The
A term used by historians to cover the period between the fall of the Roman Empire of the West (end of the 5th century) and the beginning of the ▷ Renaissance, conventionally dated from the extinction of the Roman Empire of the East (Byzantine Empire) in 1453. The expression dates from the 16th century when it is found in the Latin writings of a number of ▷ humanists – 'media aetas', 'medium aevum'. The conception in the 16th century was that civilization was renewing itself by rediscovery of the ancient civilizations of Greece and Rome; scholars considered that the centuries between the 5th and 15th were a relatively dark period of ignorance and cultural backwardness. For long after the 16th century modern history was commonly assumed to have begun with the 15th-century Renaissance. Some scholars are inclined to think this view mistaken; many of them also consider that the so-called Middle Ages had much more continuity with classical history than the men of the Renaissance supposed. The term Middle Ages is thus a misleading and erroneous one but its use has become habitual and cannot be dispensed with. Moreover the Renaissance of the 15th–16th centuries did herald an important change, however one interprets it, and it is still useful to have a term to designate the centuries which preceded it.

In English history, it is common to think of the Middle Ages as extending from the ▷ Norman Conquest of 1066 until the end of the ▷ Wars of the Roses and the accession of ▷ Henry VII (first of the House of ▷ Tudor) in 1485. The period from the 5th to the 11th century is called loosely the ▷ Old English period. The term Middle Ages was first used by ▷ John Donne in a sermon in 1621.
▷ English language.

Middlemarch, a Study of Provincial Life (1871–2)

A novel by ▷ George Eliot. The events it describes occur just before the ▷ Reform Bill of 1832 but its content of ideas is more relevant to the mid-Victorian period when it was written. The material was originally intended for two novels, one centred on Dorothea Brooke and the other a study of provincial life in the town of Middlemarch, based on Coventry. Unity is achieved by the fusion of the two senses of 'provincial': the geographical sense of 'situated outside the capital' and the cultural one of 'ignorant of the central current of ideas'. Dorothea, the daughter of a country gentleman, aspires to a high spiritual conduct of life; she is however isolated geographically, socially and intellectually, like most females of her time, and she finds no scope for her ambitions. In consequence she is led into an infatuation with Mr Casaubon, an elderly parson-scholar whose life-work is the writing of his 'Key to all Mythologies', in which he expects to demonstrate the centrality of the Christian scriptures among human beliefs. Unfortunately, his work is reduced to futility by his ignorance of the leading (German) scholarship in his field, and his egotism and narrowness of human experience prevent him from appreciating the quality of Dorothea's ardour and potentiality. Dorothea finds her marriage a total disillusionment. This marital failure runs parallel to that of Tertius Lydgate and Rosamund Vincy. Lydgate, a young medical scientist, is engaged in equally radical research into the possible existence of a 'basic tissue'. Unlike Casaubon, he is alert to the intellectual centre of his thought (Paris) and he has chosen to live in a provincial town only because he supposes that by so doing he can escape the social involvements and professional rivalries of the metropolis. But Rosamund, the daughter of a Middlemarch manufacturer who has the typically provincial ambition to raise his family to the level of metropolitan fashion, has been attracted to Lydgate only because he has aristocratic

relations. Rosamund has no understanding of her husband's intellectual promise and does nothing but frustrate it. Moreover, he has been beguiled into the marriage by his own emotional immaturity, which has misled him into assuming that a beautiful wife is a mere ornament to the life of an intellectual man, without a will of her own; his mistake, in fact, is a youthful equivalent of Casaubon's when the latter marries Dorothea. Lydgate is also mistaken in supposing that the provincialism of Middlemarch will leave him free to conduct his own affairs: he becomes unwittingly involved in the intrigues of the chairman of the Hospital Board, Nicholas Bulstrode, a banker and a bigoted ▷ Dissenter who supposes himself to have a divine mission to direct the lives of others and a heavenly dispensation which enables him to balance his moral accounts with God, as his clients balance their financial accounts with himself. Bulstrode is ruined by the consequences of his own criminal past and his ruin nearly drags down Lydgate, already faced with financial disgrace by the expensive tastes of his wife.

These are the novel's themes of public failure arising from individual inadequacies which are a result of a personal blindness in the characters and their failure to discern the central truths of their life and work. The themes of failure are counter-balanced by those of fulfilment. Dorothea loses her spiritual arrogance by learning from her own mistakes; after the death of her husband, she acquires a capacity for humble and open-minded human sympathy, which helps to save Lydgate and even momentarily redeems Rosamund. Her frustration is released by the gradual awakening of sexual love between herself and Casaubon's young relative, Will Ladislaw, who differs from the other characters by being essentially cosmopolitan in his background and outlook. Another centre of judgement is that of the Garth family, who acknowledge their provinciality and by avoiding illusions achieve balanced insights and clear directions for their energies in ways that are really less provincial than those of their superiors in wealth and social status. Mary Garth manages to rescue Fred Vincy, Rosamund's brother, from the unreal values which obsess his family. A minor character but one central to George Eliot's valuations is the free-thinking parson Farebrother, condemned to a life of self-sacrifice by external causes and yet able to live it not only without either bitterness or unctuousness but also without any narrowing down of his capacity for human sympathy.

At first sight *Middlemarch* seems to be as narrow in its environmental setting as it is complex in its structure, but George Eliot touches upon so many aspects of 19th-century experience as to make it one of the richest and most spacious of all English novels.

Middleton, Christopher (b 1926)

Poet, literary critic and translator. Middleton was born in Cornwall, educated at Cambridge and became a university lecturer in Germany, England and then America. He teaches German studies, and his work is influenced by German and French literature, although it is notoriously eclectic, drawing also on English ▷ Victorian poets, ▷ Dada and ▷ Spanish poetry. Middleton's work is both technically precise and extremely difficult – it employs highly disruptive techniques, disturbing conventional syntax and rhythm and in this lies its obscurity. His texts include: *Torse 3: Poems 1949–1961* (1962); *Our Flowers & Nice Bones* (1970); *The Lonely Suppers of W. V. Balloon* (1975); *Pataxanadu* (1976).

Cartoon of Thomas Middleton

Middleton, Thomas (1580–1627)

Dramatist. Little is known about his life; he may have been a student of law in London and in the 1590s he was at Oxford University. Later he was often employed to write ▷ pageants to celebrate civic occasions, and in 1620 he was appointed city chronologer (historian).

His masterpieces were two tragedies: ▷ *Women Beware Women* (1614) and ▷ *The Changeling* (1622) with a subplot by ▷ William Rowley. The latter play is one of the finest tragedies in English since ▷ Shakespeare. In his comedies he was one of the two notable successors to ▷ Ben Jonson, the other being ▷ Philip Massinger. His best are probably: *A Trick to Catch the Old-one* (1604), ▷ *The Roaring Girl* (with ▷ Dekker, 1606), and above all ▷ *A Chaste Maid in Cheapside* (1613). These, like others of his comedies are ▷ citizen comedies, *ie* about London middle-class life like the comedies of Dekker, but presented with more substantial realism. ▷ *A Game at Chess* (1624) was a political satire provoked by the king's failure to marry his son to a Spanish princess; its performance was stopped by the protest of the Spanish ambassador. *The Witch*, a ▷ revenge play of uncertain date, may have influenced Shakespeare's ▷ *Macbeth* but was more probably influenced by it, and Middleton has been thought by some to have contributed Act III, Sc. v in *Macbeth*.

With Rowley, Middleton also wrote *A Fair Quarrel* (1614); *The World Tost at Tennis* (1620); *The Spanish Gipsy* (1623). Plays ascribed to Middleton alone: *The Old Law* (1599); *Blurt, Master-Constable* (1601–2); *The Family of Love* (1602); *Michaelmas Term* (praised by ▷ Swinburne – 1605); *The Phoenix* (1607); *A Mad World, my Masters* (1606); *Your Five Gallants* (?1607); ▷ *No Wit, No Help like a Woman's* (?1613); *Anything for a Quiet Life* (?1617); *More Dissemblers besides Women* (before 1622); *The Widow* (uncertain date). Eleven of his ▷ masques have survived. He also wrote some minor poetry and prose ▷ pamphlets.

Bib: Bradbrook, M. C., *Elizabethan Tragedy*; Knights, L. C., *Drama and Society in the Age of Jonson*; Barker, R. H., *Thomas Middleton*; Heinemann, M., *Puritanism and Theatre*; Mulryne, J. R., *Thomas Middleton*.

Midsummer Night's Dream, A (1595)

A comedy by ▷ Shakespeare. From internal evidence it has been dated about 1595; it was printed in 1600. The title refers to the fantastic quality of events, resembling a dream on Midsummer night, when fantastic dreams were supposed to be commonly experienced.

The characters are in four distinct groups. The background is the court of a character from Greek mythology, King ▷ Theseus of Athens, on the eve of his marriage to ▷ Hippolyta, queen of the Amazons. The four lovers whose confusions form the bulk of the action, Helena and Demetrius, Hermia and Lysander (as they are eventually paired), have classical names, but their story is a typical comedy of ▷ Renaissance romantic love, in which they are all victims of blind passion. The third group is made from the Athenian artisans whose names – Bottom, Quince, Snout, Flute and Starveling – show them to be English types of Shakespeare's own day. They celebrate Theseus' wedding night (and that of the other lovers) by performing the interlude ▷ 'Pyramus and Thisbe' – intended to be tragic but, as they carry it out, decidedly comic. The fourth group is the ▷ fairies. In general (especially Puck, or Robin Goodfellow) these are drawn from English folklore, but their king, Oberon, comes from *Huon de Bordeaux* (a medieval French romance) and Titania from ▷ Ovid's ▷ *Metamorphoses*. Oberon, through Puck, confuses the lovers as they wander through the wood near Athens, and causes Titania to fall in love with Bottom, who, for the night, is given an ass's head. The fantasy is deftly contrived.

Mill, John Stuart (1806–73)

Writer on economics, politics, psychology, logic and ethics. He did not invent the word ▷ Utilitarian, but was the first to apply it to the reform movement which had been started by his father's friend ▷ Jeremy Bentham and of which his father, James Mill, was one of the leaders. The movement derived from 18th-century ▷ rationalism and the group was known as 'the philosophical radicals' because of the intellectual thoroughness with which they reasoned out their political and social standpoints. James Mill educated his son strenuously from a very early age but the education, wide as it was, ignored the imaginative and emotional needs of his son's character. J. S. Mill describes in his *Autobiography* (1873) how this neglect produced in him a spiritual crisis when he was 21, after he had already made a brilliant start to his career. He discovered that he was emotionally indifferent to the ends for which he was working. He recovered partly through his discovery of the poetry of ▷ Wordsworth and the crisis enabled him to develop a far more sympathetic and balanced outlook on human needs than had been possessed by his father or Bentham.

Mills's literary output was very large and his influence on his time was great, though much of his writing (for instance his psychology, which he based on 18th-century associationism – ▷ David Hartley) has now been superseded by subsequent thinking.

However, his *Autobiography* and a number of his essays have permanent value, for instance his essay ▷ *On Liberty* (1859) and those on Bentham (1838) and ▷ Coleridge (1840), whom he described as the two great formative influences of his age. His most massive work was his *Principles of Political Economy* (1848). He was an early leader of the movement for the emancipation of women and published *The Subjection of Women* (1869). His *Utilitarianism* (1863) was a reasoned defence of his philosophy.

A peculiarity of his upbringing, considering its period, is that that he was educated against the Christian faith.

▷ Women, Education of.

Bib: Packe, M. St J., *Life*; Leavis, F. R., *Mill on Bentham and Coleridge*; Wishy, B., *Preface to Liberty*; Halévy, E., *The Growth of Philosophic Radicalism*; Abrams, M. H., *The Mirror and the Lamp*; Anschutz, R. P., *The Philosophy of J. S. Mill*; Bain, A., *J. S. Mill: a Criticism*; Stephen, L., *Utilitarianism*; Neff, E., *Carlyle and Mill*; Britton, K. W., *Mill*.

Mill on the Floss, The (1860)

A novel by ▷ George Eliot. It is set in the English midlands and its central character is Maggie Tulliver, the daughter of a miller. She is intelligent and richly imaginative beyond the understanding of her relatives and in particular of her brother, Tom, a boy of limited intelligence and sympathies to whom she is devoted. The novel is divided into seven parts; the first three lead up to Mr Tulliver's bankruptcy and make a rich and comic study of English country life in the mid-19th century with deep insights into the psychology of the rural middle class. The last three deal with the tragic love of Maggie for Philip Wakem, the deformed son of the lawyer through whom Mr Tulliver has been ruined, the compromising of her reputation by the educated and agreeable Stephen Guest and her alienation from her brother, with whom she is, however, reconciled by means of the flood which drowns them both. The earlier chapters contain some of Eliot's best writing, though not sustained in the later part. It is one of her most popular novels.

Miller's Tale, The

One of ▷ Chaucer's ▷ *Canterbury Tales*. Following the ▷ Knight's story about competing lovers, set in classical Athens, the Miller insists on 'quiting' this story with a tale of love rivalry set in Oxford. Double trickery is at the heart of this ▷ fabliau. An old jealous husband, John, a carpenter, is deceived as a result of believing his lodger's prediction about the coming of a second flood, and gullibly accepting the chance offered to play the role of Noah. His lodger, the clerk Nicholas, thus plots a means of spending the night with the young Alison, John's wife. In the course of the evening, Alison spontaneously plays a trick on another of her admirers, Absolon, and gets him to kiss her 'nether eye'. Nicholas is branded with a ploughshare as a result of attempting to repeat the trick. Echoes of the *Knight's Tale* abound in the *Miller's Tale*.

Milne, A. A. (Alan Alexander) (1882–1956)
Novelist, dramatist, children's writer. He was for many years assistant editor of *Punch*, and he became widely popular as the author of light comedies and novels. His earliest play is *Wurzel-Flummery* (1917) and his best known *Mr Pim Passes By* (1919). However he achieved fame by four ▷ children's books, centring on his son, Christopher Robin. Two of these are verse: *When We Were Very Young* (1924) and *Now We Are Six* (1927). The other two are prose stories, with Christopher Robin's teddy bear Winnie the Pooh as hero: *Winnie the Pooh* (1926); *The House at Pooh Corner* (1928). They have been translated into many languages; *Winnie the Pooh*, rather to its advantage, into Latin.

Milton, John (1608–74)

John Milton, aged 62. From the frontispiece of his *History of Britain*

Poet and prose polemicist. Milton was born in London, the son of a scrivener and musician, and educated at St Paul's School and Christ's College Cambridge. After leaving Cambridge, in 1632, Milton lived for the next five years at his father's house in Horton. During this, his early poetic career, he wrote the companion pieces ▷ *L'Allegro* and ▷ *Il Penseroso*, two ▷ masques ▷ *Arcades* and ▷ *Comus*, and the ▷ elegy ▷ *Lycidas*. From 1638 to 1639 Milton travelled abroad, chiefly in Italy. His Italian journey was to have a lasting influence on his later development, not least in the contact he established amongst Florentine intellectuals. But more than that, it re-affirmed his distaste – loathing even – for Roman Catholicism, and focussed his intense opposition to the Laudian (▷ Laud, William) regime in England.

Milton's continental journey was interrupted early in 1639 at Naples, where he claims to have first heard news of the political crisis in England. He was later to claim that he thought it 'base that I should travel abroad at my ease for the cultivation of my mind while my fellow citizens at home were fighting for liberty' (*Defensio secunda*). Returning to England, Milton embarked upon what has now come to be seen as the second phase of his career – that of a political prose writer, and propagandist for the anti-Royalist cause in the English ▷ Civil War. Between 1640 and 1655, Milton was to write little poetry. His energies and his sympathies were now to be engaged fully on the side of the republican forces in England – though he was a not uncritical supporter of the new experiment in government. From this period can be dated the series of great prose declarations dealing with political and religious questions – *Of Reformation* (1641), his attack on episcopacy in the *Apology for Smectymnuus* (1642), his statement on personal liberty contained in *The Doctrine and Discipline of Divorce* (1643). These works were followed by ▷ *Areopagitica* (1644), *Tenure of Kings and Magistrates* (1649), *Eikonoklastes* (1649), the two 'defences' of the English people (1651 and 1654), *A Treatise of Civil Power* (1659) and, almost at the moment when ▷ Charles II returned to England to re-establish the claims of monarchy, *A Readie and Easie Way to Establish a Free Commonwealth* (1660). The list of topics upon which Milton wrote in this period is bewildering, but running through all his prose writings is a stable belief that the English people have been chosen, by God, to perform a necessary political act – the establishment of a state based on principles of choice and, within certain bounds, freedom.
▷ *Paradise Lost*, Milton's great religious

and political poem, was begun at some point in the mid-1650s – perhaps in the growing awareness that, though political choices had been made in England, the wrong choice had been made. The poem was not published, however, until 1667, with a second (revised) edition appearing in 1674, shortly before Milton's death in November of that year. But the period after 1660 is usually recognized as the third and final phase of Milton's career. It is the period of the publication of ▷ *Paradise Regained* and ▷ *Samson Agonistes*. Though it has long been claimed that Milton's absorption in the task of writing these works marked an end to his career of political engagement, it is probably truer to say that these works signal a renewed, and possibly deeper, investigation of the themes which had occupied him for most of his life – the questions of political and religious liberty, the problems associated with choice and rule, and the problematic nature of government and obedience.

Bib: Carey, J. and Fowler, A. (ed.), *The Complete Poems of John Milton*; Wolfe, D. M. (ed.), *Complete Prose Works of John Milton*; Parker, W. R., *Milton: A Biography*; Hill, C., *Milton and the English Revolution*; Nyquist, M. and Ferguson, M. (ed.), *Re-membering Milton*.

Mimesis

In ▷ Plato's *Republic* 'mimesis' is used to designate 'imitation', but in a derogatory way. The term is given a rigorous, positive meaning in ▷ Aristotle's *Poetics* where it is used to describe a process of selection and representation appropriate to tragedy: 'the imitation of an action'. Literary criticism from ▷ Sir Philip Sidney onwards has wrestled with the problem of the imitative function of literary texts, but after ▷ Structuralism with its questioning of the referential function of all language, the term has taken on a new and problematic dimension. Mimesis has frequently been associated with the term ▷ 'realism', and with the capacity of language to reflect reality. At particular historical moments, *eg* the ▷ Renaissance, or the present time, when reality itself appears to be in question, then the capacity of language to represent reality is brought to the fore. The issue becomes even more complex when we realize that 'reality' may be something other than our experience of it. The debate has been carried on most vigorously at a theoretical level in the exchanges earlier this century between the Hungarian critic Georg Lukács, and the dramatist ▷ Bertolt Brecht. The nub of the

debate between these two ▷ Marxist thinkers was how best to represent 'the deeper causal complexes of society' (Brecht). Brecht rejected the view propounded by Lukács that the novel was the literary form which pre-eminently represented social process, arguing that realism was a major political, philosophical and practical issue and should not be dealt with by literature alone. Such a view rejected the metaphysical implications which lay behind the Aristotelian notion of mimesis, in favour of a more historical analysis which saw literature as part of the process of social change.

Minerva
▷ Athene.

Minim, Dick
A character in ▷ Samuel Johnson's ▷ *Idler* essays for the *Weekly Gazette*. Dick Minim is a satirical representation of the kind of person who seeks a reputation for critical acumen by praising what is in fashion and sneering at what is unfamiliar.

Minos
▷ Theseus.

Minotaur
▷ Theseus.

Miracle plays
▷ Cycle plays.

Mirror for Magistrates, A (1559)
A collection of verse monologues, spoken by characters in English history and legend. The collection was inspired by ▷ John Lydgate's *The Fall of Princes* (1494), and written by William Baldwin, George Ferrers and others. Nineteen verse monologues are spoken by historical figures from the reign of ▷ Richard II to ▷ Edward IV, and in the main the intention of these verse accounts is to warn rulers and subjects against (respectively) tyranny and rebellion. After the first edition of 1559, numerous editions appeared throughout the 16th century, and well into the 17th. With each edition, the work expanded, though the edition of 1563 (with contributions by ▷ Thomas Sackville) is claimed to be, artistically, the most satisfactory. The edition of 1610 (the last, though there were reissues of 1619, 1620 and 1621) is the largest of what had become a series rather than a sequence of editions.

Though the *Mirror* was perhaps not an artistically distinguished enterprise, it nevertheless exerted a considerable thematic influence on the writing of history plays in the period, and on the conception of ▷ tragedy pursued by ▷ Elizabethan and ▷ Jacobean writers. It partakes, too, in that

Elizabethan attempt at creating a sustained account of national history of which the work of ▷ Samuel Daniel, ▷ Michael Drayton and ▷ Edmund Spenser is also, in part, representative.

▷ Histories and Chronicles.
Bib: Campbell, L. B. (ed.), *A Mirror for Magistrates*.

Misrule, Lord of

Title given to the master of revels for the 12 days of the Christmas festivities, which mark a licensed period of disorder and which may be celebrated in medieval noble and royal households.

Miss in Her Teens (1747)

A shortened (two-act) comedy by ▷ David Garrick, one of the first of its type (also known as 'petite pièce' or 'petite comédie'), adapted from D'Ancourt's *La Parisienne*, and staged as an 'afterpiece' at Covent Garden. The main plot concerns Captain Loveit's competition with his miserly father, Sir Simon Loveit, for the hand of the 16-year-old country girl and heiress, Biddy Bellair. She is also courted by two other suitors: a braggart and a fop. The Captain is assisted in his plans by the girl's own cunning and determination, and by two clever servants. A sub-plot concerns the rivalry between two of the servants for the attentions of a third. The Captain chases away the absurd rivals and confronts his father, who gives up his claim to Biddy voluntarily. The play has various patriotic elements referring to the contemporary War of the Austrian Succession: its last line, spoken by Biddy, is, 'Who fails in honour, will be false in love'. Garrick himself played the effeminate suitor, Fribble, who has some of the wittiest lines in the play; it was one of his most popular roles. The rest of the dialogue, and the action, is simple but very funny, and the piece was staged repeatedly.

Mistletoe

A small bush with white berries which grows on other trees and shrubs. In pagan times it was widely regarded as sacred in Europe, especially when it grew on the oak (see J. G. Frazer, *The Golden Bough*). According to the Roman historian ▷ Pliny the ▷ Celtic Druids ceremonially cut it at the beginning of the year with a golden sickle. It is one of the pagan symbols which has survived into the celebration of the modern Christmas.

Mnemosyne

▷ Muses.

Modern Love (1862)

A series of 16-line poems resembling ▷ sonnets, by ▷ George Meredith. The poems tell the story of the breakdown of a marriage ending in the suicide of the wife. The tone is strongly emotional and the attitude to the emotions is self-scrutinizing; in these ways Meredith's *Modern Love* suggests comparison with the ▷ dramatic monologues of ▷ Robert Browning and ▷ Alfred Tennyson, for example Browning's *Any Wife to Any Husband* and Tennyson's ▷ *Maud*.

Modernism

Since the term 'modernism' was first used earlier in the 20th century, its meaning has developed and been revised. It now is agreed to mean the influential international movement in literature, drama, art, music and architecture which began in the latter years of the 19th century and flourished until at least the 1920s. Modernism was felt to be a reaction to ▷ Realism and ▷ Naturalism, undermining the representationalism (▷ mimesis) associated with those movements. In fiction the ▷ stream of consciousness novel was a prime example of modernism. In critical terms, modernist writing challenged the approaches of students and critics alike and so contributed to the development later in the century of new approaches to literature and reading.

▷ Post-modernism; Deconstruction; Symbolism.

Modest Proposal, A (1729)

A satirical ▷ pamphlet by ▷ Jonathan Swift, written when he was Dean of St Patrick's Cathedral, Dublin. The full title is *A Modest Proposal for Preventing Children of Poor People from being a Burden to their Parents or the Country*. Indignant at the extreme misery of the Irish poor under English government, Swift, in the guise of an economic 'projector', calmly recommends that it would be more humane to breed up their children as food for the rich. The pamphlet is an example of the controlled but extreme savagery of Swift's irony, and the fierceness of his humanitarianism.

Mohammed (?570–632 AD)

(Sometimes 'Mahomet', but more correctly Muhammad.) Founder of the Islamic religion. He was born at ▷ Mecca in the Arabian peninsula; this is consequently the principal holy place of the Islamic religion. He established monotheism (the worship of the one God, Allah) in Arabia, and the religion rapidly spread through the Middle East and across North Africa. In particular, the Muslims captured ▷ Jerusalem, the Christian Holy City, in 637. They constituted

A MODEST

PROPOSAL

For preventing the

CHILDREN

OF

POOR PEOPLE

From being a Burthen to their PA-
RENTS or the COUNTRY,

And for making them Beneficial to the
PUBLICK.

The THIRD EDITION.

DUBLIN,
Printed: And Reprinted at *LONDON,* for
WEAVER BICKERTON, in *Devereux-Court*
near the *Middle-Temple.* M.DCC.XXX.

Title page of *A Modest Proposal* by Jonathan
Swift

the principal threat to Christendom
throughout the ▷ Middle Ages, and it was
against them that the ▷ Crusades, or holy
wars, were organized. They ruled southern
Spain until 1492 and south-east Europe (the
Balkans) until the 19th century. Meanwhile
Muslim pirates, the Barbary corsairs, preyed
on Mediterranean trade. ▷ Chesterton's
poem *Lepanto* describes a famous sea-battle
between Christian and Muslim forces. Since
the fall of the Turkish Empire, the two faiths
have existed together in relative peace.
   ▷ Rushdie, Salman.

Mohocks
The nickname for disorderly and violent
young aristocrats who roamed London early
in the 18th century. It derives from Mohawk,
a warrior tribe of North American Indians.

Mohun, Michael (?1616–84)
Actor, manager. Mohun trained as a boy
actor under Christopher Beeston (?1570–
1638) at the Cockpit Theatre, in Drury Lane,
and graduated to adult roles before the
theatres closed in 1642. He joined the army
on the royalist side during the ▷ Civil War,
reaching the rank of major. Shortly after the
theatres reopened, he became the leading
actor of the newly formed ▷ King's
Company under ▷ Killigrew. He created

several roles in tragedy and comedy, and his
Iago (▷ *Othello*) was especially admired.

Molesworth, Mary Louisa (1839–1921)
Children's writer and novelist. Born Stewart,
in Rotterdam where her father was a
merchant, she was educated at home by her
mother in Manchester where they moved in
1841. In 1861 she married Major Richard
Molesworth, and first told stories to her own
seven children, writing stories for and about
them from a child's viewpoint, in which she
portrayed a disciplined but loving world. In
1878 she separated from her husband, whose
personality had been changed by a head
wound sustained in the Crimean War, and
from then on wrote to support her family.
Using the pseudonym Ennis Graham, she
wrote a large number of novels and stories.
Her own childhood is described in *The
Carved Lions* (1895) but perhaps the most
famous and popular children's book is *The
Cuckoo Clock* (1877). Others include *The
Tapestry Room* (1879), *Tell Me a Story*
(1875), *Carrots* (1876) and *Two Little Waifs*
(1883).
   ▷ Children's books.
Bib: Avery, G., *Nineteenth-Century Children*;
Lancelyn Green, R., *Tellers of Tales*.

**Molière (pseudonym of Jean Baptiste
   Poquelin) (1622–73)**
French dramatist. Born in the middle class,
the son of an upholsterer, he became one of
the most favoured playwrights at the court of
Louis XIV. With one exception his plays are
comedies, and a basic influence behind
English comedy from 1660 to 1800. His *Les
Précieuses ridicules* (1659), a satire upon an
extremely fashionable, excessively
sophisticated circle in contemporary Paris,
marks the beginning of the ▷ comedy of
manners tradition in which the English
dramatists ▷ Etherege, ▷ Wycherley,
▷ Vanbrugh, ▷ Congreve and
▷ Sheridan all worked. He wrote over 30
plays, of which the best known are:
Sganarelle (1660); *L'Ecole des maris* (The
School for Husbands, 1661); *L'Ecole des
femmes* (The School for Wives, 1662);
Tartuffe (1664); *Le Festin de Pierre* (Don
Juan, 1665); *Le Misanthrope* (The
Misanthropist, 1666); *Le Médecin malgré lui*
(The Reluctant Physician, 1666); *L'Avare*
(The Miser, 1668); *Le Bourgeois Gentilhomme*
(The Middle-Class Nobleman, 1670); *Les
Femmes savantes* (The Learned Women,
1672); *Le Malade imaginaire* (The
Hypochondriac, 1673). His nearest
equivalent on the English stage is ▷ William
Congreve, but the only achievement in

English literature comparable with Molière's kind of excellence is in the Augustan ▷ satire of ▷ Dryden (▷ *Absalom and Achitophel*) and ▷ Pope, and the novels of ▷ Jane Austen.

Moll Flanders (1722)

A novel by ▷ Daniel Defoe, and his most famous, after ▷ *Robinson Crusoe* (1719). Its full title was *The Fortunes and Misfortunes of the Famous Moll Flanders*, and its substance is the adventures of an orphan girl from her early seduction through her various love affairs and her career of crime, to her transportation to Virginia and her final prosperity there. It is a realistic, episodic narrative with keen social and psychological perception in certain incidents. The book has no unifying structure, however, and none of the characters is fully established imaginatively. The conclusion is an example of Defoe's crude and superficial morality, ▷ Puritan in its tradition, but much less profound and subtle than that of his predecessor ▷ John Bunyan. The Puritanism has become simplified to commercialism, especially evident in Moll's final 'repentance'.

▷ Picaresque.

Moloch

In the Bible, the name of a deity to which the people of Israel occasionally sacrificed their children: *Leviticus* 18:21; *2 Kings* 23:10. In Milton's ▷ *Paradise Lost* (i. 392) Moloch is one of the fallen ▷ angels.

Monasteries and Monasticism

The practice of monasticism arose in the lands about the eastern Mediterranean in the early centuries of Christianity, and was inspired by the belief that the holy life could be lived only in isolation from the practical interests of worldly society. This early monasticism consisted of hermits each living in his own cell, and Irish monasticism of the 6th–8th centuries had similar characteristics. However, in the 6th century St Benedict founded in Italy the ▷ Benedictine order which, during the ▷ Middle Ages, dominated western Europe including the British Isles, and had immense consequences for Western civilization; the monks lived in community, and followed a regular rule of life which included a great deal of practical activity. They were artists, architects, scholars and writers – especially historians, such as the ▷ Venerable Bede, ▷ Geoffrey of Monmouth, and Matthew Paris (13th century); monasteries such as the Cathedral

Priory at Canterbury were seats of learning which rivalled universities such as Paris and Oxford. Corporately, the monasteries were great landowners, and some of the abbots managed these estates with great constructive efficiency; an example is the 12th-century Abbot Samson of Bury St Edmund, – see ▷ Carlyle's fine study of him in *Past and Present* Bk II (1843). The Cistercian Order, a reformed version of the Benedictine, planted their monasteries in the wild places in England, and set up sheep farms. In medieval England the monasteries were the only source of poor relief, and they were the only inns and hospitals until the 14th century. Politically, the great abbots ranked with the Bishops in the Great Council of the realm; in the 12th and 13th centuries monks were the intelligentsia, owners of at least 10% of the national income, and the largest employers.

By the 14th century monasteries were losing their value, and monks were often useless parasites like the Monk in Chaucer's ▷ *Prologue*. When ▷ Henry VIII dissolved the monasteries (1536–9) the measure met with no resistance in the south-east but it provoked the rebellion known as the ▷ Pilgrimage of Grace in the north.

There were no monasteries in Britain after the middle of the 16th century, but since the second half of the 19th century some have been re-established.

'Monk' Lewis (1775–1818)

Matthew Gregory Lewis, whose sensational novel *The Monk* (1796) had such success in its day that he was nicknamed after it.

▷ Gothic novels.

Monk's Tale, The

One of ▷ Chaucer's ▷ *Canterbury Tales*. The Monk produces a collection of short verse narratives recounting the fall of individuals from high estates, spanning subjects as diverse as Adam and Ugolina of Pisa. The shape of the narratives corresponds to that of the '*de casibus*' model of tragedies in which the falls of individuals are attributed either to moral weakness or to fortune, or to both, and is modelled on ▷ Boccaccio's collection of tragic exemplum in his *De Casibus Virorum Illustrium* (*Concerning the Falls of Famous Men*). The Monk does include a few examples of the fall of famous women too. His sequence is halted by the intervention of the Knight, who objects to the tone and subject of the Monk's contribution.

Monmouth, James Scott, Duke of (1649–85)

An illegitimate son of ▷ Charles II. Charles

had no legitimate son, and the heir to the throne was consequently James, Duke of York, his brother. James, however, was an open Catholic, and fear of Catholicism in England and Scotland was still very strong. Thus a movement arose in both countries to persuade Charles to exclude James from the succession, and to recognize Monmouth, who had been educated a ▷ Protestant. Exclusion Bills to secure this change were introduced into Parliament, where the Exclusionists were led by ▷ Lord Shaftesbury. Charles, however, resisted the movement, and in 1681 a reaction of opinion in the country came to the support of the King and his brother. In 1685, Charles died, and James succeeded him as ▷ James II. Some of his more fanatical Protestant opponents, such as the Scottish Duke of Argyll, persuaded Monmouth to attempt rebellion. The Monmouth Rebellion was defeated at the single ▷ Battle of Sedgemoor (1685) and Monmouth himself was executed.

▷ *Absalom and Achitophel*; Bloody Assizes.

Montagu, Elizabeth (1720–1800)
An eminent ▷ Bluestocking and famous epistolarist, Montagu's early intellectual abilities were widely remarked upon, and ▷ Samuel Johnson hailed her as 'Queen of the Blues'.

Montagu began to hold her formal receptions in the early 1750s, and she boasted to ▷ David Garrick that, whatever the social status of the guests, 'I never invite idiots'. Her patronage of young authors aided James Beattie and Richard Price.

In 1769 her *Essay on the Writings and Genius of Shakespeare*, challenging ▷ Voltaire's theories, was widely admired, though Johnson perceived its critical failings.

Montagu, Lady Mary Wortley (1689–1762)
Poet and letter-writer. In 1716–18 her husband was Ambassador to Constantinople, where she came across the practice of inoculation against smallpox, which she popularized in England. In 1716 the publisher Edmund Curll produced an unauthorized edition of her poems, from a manuscript which she had dropped in the street, under the title *Court Poems by a Lady of Quality* (the authorized edition of 1747 was entitled *Town Eclogues*). ▷ Alexander Pope took her side against Curll but they later quarrelled for some reason, and she appears in *Moral Essay II* as Sappho in her 'dirty smock' (pp.

24–8). She lived in Italy during her later years and her lively and informative *Letters* were published in 1763–7.

Montague
The family of which Romeo is a member, and the sworn enemies of Juliet's family the ▷ Capulets, in ▷ Shakespeare's play ▷ *Romeo and Juliet*.

Montaigne, Michel de (1533–92)
French essayist, and inventor of the ▷ essay form. His life was lived partly at court, or performing the office of magistrate in the city of Bordeaux, and partly in retirement. During retirement, he wrote his *Essais* ('experiments'), the first two volumes of which were published in 1580, and the third in 1588. He was a scholar, well-read in ▷ humanist literature and in the works of the ancient Greeks and Romans. His favourite author was ▷ Plutarch.

The Essays seem to have been begun as commentaries on his reading, perhaps to assist his exceptionally bad memory. From this grew a desire to arrive at a complete image of man; as a means to this, he tried to develop a portrait of himself, since 'each man bears the complete stamp of the human condition'. The sentence shows the still-prevailing view of his time, that human beings followed general principles in the structure of their personalities – a view quite unlike the view that grew up in the 18th century and came to predominate in the 19th, that each individual is unique (see ▷ Rousseau). He recognized, however, the difficulties in arriving at conclusive ideas about human nature, and the essays are characterized by the scepticism with which he weighs contradictions and opposing views.

Montaigne was translated into English by ▷ Florio in 1603. The essays had an extensive influence upon English literature. Whether the long essay entitled *Apologie de Raimond de Sebond* had an important influence on Shakespeare's ▷ *Hamlet* is a controversial question; but Gonzalo in Shakespeare's ▷ *Tempest* quotes from Montaigne's *Des Cannibales* in II.i.143–60 ('I' th' commonwealth . . .'). More important were the emulators of Montaigne in the essay form. Montaigne's sceptical, searching, flexible mind resembles those of ▷ Robert Burton (▷ *Anatomy of Melancholy*) and ▷ Sir Thomas Browne (▷ *Religio Medici*). These, however, were not essayists; the Montaigne tradition of essay writing was taken up later in the century by ▷ Abraham Cowley (*Essays in Verse and Prose*, 1668), ▷ Sir William Temple (*Miscellanea*, 1680,

1692, 1701) and, after the more formal period of the 18th century, Charles Lamb's ▷ *Essays of Elia* (1823).

Montrose, James Graham, Marquess of (1612–50)

Scottish patriot, general and statesman. He was one of the noblest and most gifted of ▷ Charles I's supporters in and after the ▷ Civil War. After spasmodic but brilliant successes, he was caught by Parliament forces and executed. ▷ Walter Scott's novel *A Legend of Montrose* (1819) concerns his career. John Buchan wrote a biography of him.

Moonstone, The (1868)

A novel by ▷ Wilkie Collins. It is one of the earliest stories of detection and concerns the mysterious disappearance of a valuable diamond, formerly sacred to the Moon-god in one of the Indian temples. The novel is told in the first person by various participants in the events; it is plotted with skill, psychological ingenuity and a typically Victorian delight in characterization. Sergeant Cuff, the first detective in English fiction, appears in it.
▷ Detective fiction.

Moore, G. E. (1873–1958)

Philosopher. He lectured on philosophy at Cambridge from 1911 to 1925, when he became Professor. His principal book is *Principia Ethica* (1903); he also wrote *Ethics* (1912) and *Philosophical Studies* (1922). His philosophy was that of the 'New Realism', in opposition to the idealism of ▷ F. H. Bradley who was in the tradition of ▷ Hegel. Where the ▷ Idealists tended to a poetic conception of truth and ethics, rhetorically expressed and appealing to the emotions as much as to the reason, Moore appealed to the reason only, basing his arguments on common sense, and holding it to be the function of philosophy to clarify statements and arrive at fully intelligible definitions. At the same time, he argued that all experience is to be enjoyed, and that the richest possessions are aesthetic experience and personal friendship. He consequently had two kinds of influence, philosophical and literary. Philosophically, he was one of the starting points of ▷ Russell and the Logical Positivists such as A. J. Ayer, but in literary circles he had considerable personal influence on the ▷ Bloomsbury Group, centred on the novelist ▷ Virginia Woolf and her husband Leonard. The Bloomsbury Group owed its cohesiveness to a cult of personal relations such as Moore advocated, and some of its members regarded the state of mind of perfect aesthetic appreciation as one of the aims of life.
Bib: Schilpp, P. A., *The Philosophy of Moore*; Johnstone, J. K., *The Bloomsbury Group*.

Moore, George (1852–1933)

Irish novelist. He combined an ▷ aestheticism in tune with the aesthetic movement at the end of the 19th century, and the Celtic revivalism that went with a part of it, with a ▷ naturalism which showed the influence of late 19th-century French literature, especially from the novelist ▷ Zola. His most famous novels are: *A Mummer's Wife* (1885); *Esther Waters* (1894); *Evelyn Innes* (1898); *Sister Theresa* (1901); *The Brook Kerith* (1916); *Héloise and Abélard* (1921). He was equally well known for his autobiographical studies: *Confessions of a Young Man* (1888); *Avowals* (1919, 1926); *Hail and Farewell* (1911–14) and *Conversations in Ebury Street* (1924). His carefully worked style was more admired in his own day than it is now.
▷ Celtic Twilight.
Bib: Korg, J., in *Victorian Fiction* (ed. L. Stevenson); Brown, M. J., *Moore: a Reconsideration*; Sechler, R. P., *George Moore: 'a Disciple of Walter Pater'*; Yeats, W. B., in *Dramatis Personae*; Hough, G., in *Image and Experience*.

Moore, Thomas (1779–1852)

Born in Dublin, Moore studied law at the Middle Temple and became a popular drawing-room singer. Later he was for a time Admiralty Registrar in Bermuda. His early pseudonymous volume, *The Poetical Works of the late Thomas Little Esq.* (1801) was referred to by ▷ Lord Byron in *English Bards and Scotch Reviewers* (1809), and the two poets became close friends. Moore received many letters from Byron, though he shamefully expurgated them after Byron's death, and agreed to destroy the *Memoirs* which Byron had left to him. Moore's own writings range from lyric to satire, from prose romance to history and biography. The extremely popular *Irish Melodies*, which contain his most enduring work, appeared in ten parts between 1807 and 1835, and in 1813 he published a group of satires aimed at the Prince Regent, *The Twopenny Post Bag*. His long narrative poem in the Byronic mode, *Lalla Rookh: An Oriental Romance* (1817), achieved an international reputation, but in his next work *The Fudge Family in Paris* (1818) he returned to satire, aiming his shafts against the Englishman abroad. His *Loves of the Angels* (1823) became notorious for its eroticism. He also wrote a prose romance set in 3rd-century Egypt, *The Epicurean* (1827), a *History of*

Ireland (1835–46), and biographies of
▷ Thomas Sheridan (1825), and (ironically
in view of his destruction of his friend's own
autobiographical work) of Byron (1830).
Bib: White, T. de V., *Tom Moore: The Irish
Poet.*

Moral Essays (1731–5)

Four epistles in heroic ▷ couplets by
▷ Alexander Pope, concerned with large
ethical and philosophical issues. Epistle I
elaborates a simplistic philosophy of 'the
ruling passion' as an explanation of human
psychology, and its poetic value lies in the
occasional witty vignette of human folly,
rather than in any profundity of thought.
Epistle II, *To a Lady*, concerns the characters
of women, and is addressed to Pope's close
friend Martha Blount. Though the work has
many memorable lines it is little more than a
series of crudely sexist jibes at particular
women, or at women in general: 'Nothing so
true as what you once let fall,/ "Most Women
have no Characters at all"'; 'ev'ry Woman is
at heart a Rake'. Epistle III treats the right
use of riches, and ends with an idealized
portrait of John Kyrle, the 'Man of Ross', a
celebrated philanthropist. Epistle IV,
addressed to Lord Burlington, was the first to
be published (1731) and is the most
impressive. It again satirizes the wrong use of
wealth, but focusses specifically on
architecture, Burlington being an active
promoter of the convenient decency of the
▷ Palladian style as opposed to the large
scale exuberance of ▷ baroque, so much in
vogue in absolutist France. Pope follows his
patron also in advocating a 'natural' style of
garden rather than the artificial geometricality
of continental taste. The description of the
discomfort of Timon's villa brilliantly satirizes
such un-English grandiosity as Blenheim
Palace, or Castle Howard, both recently built
by ▷ Sir John Vanbrugh.

Morality plays

A term used by modern critics to distinguish
plays expounding points of moral doctrine,
extant from the 15th century, from other
kinds of contemporary vernacular drama
which commemorate the events of Christian
history (such as the ▷ cycle plays or saints'
plays). The plots of morality plays are
allegorical narratives of one kind or another;
the human protagonists tend not to be
individualized or given a historical identity.
The scope of the plays may vary: whereas the
▷ *Castle of Perseverance* dramatizes the epic
story of 'Humankind's' life from birth to
beyond the grave, and requires great dramatic
resources, ▷ *Mankind* focuses on an

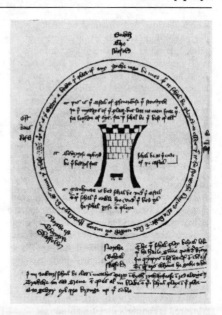

From *The Macro Plays*, named after their
18th-century owner

exemplary episode in Mankind's life, and
seems designed as an itinerant production by
a smaller acting group. Generally, however,
the genre is associated with plays like
Mankind, which can be performed in halls by
smaller acting groups. Behind plays such as
Castle of Perseverance, *Mankind* and
▷ *Everyman* is a long tradition of Christian
instruction and teaching: sermons addressed
to lay audiences and manuals of instruction
may employ similar devices of analysis and
instruction to those dramatized in these
morality plays, which endow abstract notions,
concepts, processes, with a tangible form.

But this kind of drama is not confined to
expounding points of religious doctrine. In
the morality plays dating from the late 15th
century (such as Henry Medwall's *Fulgens
and Lucres*), or from the 16th century (such
as John Rastall's *Of Gentilness and Nobility*),
issues of social order (in these cases the
relationship between social rank and moral
virtue) come under scrutiny. The
instructional impetus of this kind of drama
can be used for secular as well as religious
ends. This dramatic form has had more
impact on the drama of the Renaissance than
the ▷ cycle plays, due to the flexibility of its
form and the use of allegory for ethical and
moral analysis.

Although the term 'morality' play is useful
for locating a distinctive dramatic form which
seems popular in the 15th and 16th centuries,
it should not be regarded as a fixed and

wholly distinctive dramatic genre. Allegorical personages appear in the cycle drama, and saints' plays too, and many plays confound rigid generic categories: ▷ John Bale's play, *King John* (c 1536), for example, presents a historical narrative and an allegorical commentary on the action at the same time.
Bib: Cawley, A. C. et al., *The Revels History of Drama in English: Vol. 1 Medieval Drama*; Davenport, W. A. *Fifteenth Century English Drama: the Early Moral plays and their Literary Relations*.

Mordred

In the 10th century *Annals of Wales* (*Annales Cambriae*), a figure called Medraut is reported as having fought and fallen in a battle against ▷ King Arthur in 539. In ▷ Geoffrey of Monmouth's version of British history, Mordred is Arthur's nephew, who usurps the throne and takes ▷ Guinevere for his lover while Arthur is fighting against the Romans. In later developments of Arthurian narrative, Mordred is Arthur's illegitimate son, conceived through a brief, incestuous relationship with ▷ Morgause. He provokes trouble over the affair between ▷ Lancelot and ▷ Guinevere.

More, Hannah (1745–1833)

Hannah More, by Opie 1786

An eminent ▷ Bluestocking, More settled in London in 1774, where she became the friend of ▷ Garrick, ▷ Johnson, ▷ Burke, ▷ Richardson, ▷ Reynolds, ▷ Percy and ▷ Montagu. She was a conservative Christian feminist who opposed ▷ Mary Wollstonecraft on women's rights. Her tragedy *Percy* was produced by Garrick in 1777, and established both her literary reputation and her social status. A tragedy, *The Fatal Falsehood*, appeared in 1779.

▷ Horace Walpole became her great admirer, printing *Bishop Bonner's Ghost* at the Strawberry Hill press in 1789. In 1784 her earlier poem *Bas Bleu* was published.

More used her writing to express concern about social reform. *Village Politics* appeared in 1793, and the *Cheap Respository Tracts* of 1795–8 sold two million copies. *Thoughts on the Importance of the Manners of the Great* (1788) also ran into several editions. In 1809 More published *Coelebs in Search of a Wife*, a novel which, despite hostile reviews, proved an immense success. Her correspondence is lively and entertaining.
Bib: Jones, M. G., *Hannah More*.

More, Sir Thomas (St Thomas More) (1478–1535)

Scholar, thinker and statesman. He was the leading ▷ humanist of his day, and a friend of ▷ Erasmus. For some time he was a particular favourite of ▷ Henry VIII, who raised him to the Lord Chancellorship, the highest office in the state. However, More firmly refused to recognize the king's divorce from Queen Katharine and the ▷ Act of Supremacy (1534). For this the king executed him, and the Catholic Church canonized him exactly 400 years later.

More's *History of King Richard III* (1513) has been called the first masterpiece of ▷ history and biography in English, but his principal work ▷ *Utopia* (1516) was in Latin, translated into English in 1551. Famous as a patron of letters and the arts, he invited the painter Holbein to England.

▷ Catholicism (Roman) in English literature; Roper, Margaret More.
Bib: Surtz, E. (ed.), *Selected Works*, Sylvester, R. S., Harding, D. P. (eds.), *The Life of Sir Thomas More*; Hexter, J. H., *More's 'Utopia': The Biography of an Idea*; Greenblatt, S., *Renaissance Self-fashioning*.

Morgan La Fay

In ▷ Geoffrey of Monmouth's account of the life of ▷ Merlin, Morgan is introduced as a ▷ Lady of the Lake figure, who has magic powers and is in charge of nine women who live on ▷ Avalon and who receive ▷ King Arthur after he has been wounded. She is perhaps a literary form of a much older Celtic goddess. Her role becomes much more ambiguous in later versions of Arthurian narrative (including ▷ Malory's version), in which she both assists and obstructs the foundation of Arthurian society. She becomes identified as Arthur's half-sister, wife of Lucan and daughter of ▷ Igraine, and is portrayed as a frustrated woman who uses her magical powers to ensnare men. But she continues to be one of the women who escort Arthur away to Avalon, after his last battle. In recent Arthurian fiction, Morgan has become a more complex figure; she has been used by some writers as the focus of feminine power and independence in the legends.

Morgause
Half-sister of ▷ King Arthur in Arthurian narratives (post ▷ Geoffrey of Monmouth's version of Arthurian history), who marries King Lot and is the mother of ▷ Gawain, Gaheris, Agravain and ▷ Gareth. She conceives ▷ Mordred as a result of a brief affair with Arthur (who is unaware of his familial connection with her), and she is killed by Gaheris when discovered in bed with Lamorak.

Morning Chronicle
A London ▷ Whig ▷ newspaper founded in 1769; its contributors included ▷ Sheridan, ▷ Lamb, James Mill, ▷ John Stuart Mill, ▷ Dickens, and ▷ Thackeray. It came to an end in 1862.

Morning Herald, The
A London ▷ newspaper, 1780–1869. It had a large circulation, and published police cases, illustrated by the famous artist ▷ George Cruikshank, illustrator of Dickens's novel ▷ Oliver Twist.

Morning Post, The
A conservative but highly independent London newspaper, founded 1772, ceased 1936. ▷ Wordsworth, ▷ Coleridge and ▷ Southey contributed to it.

Morris, William (1834–96)
Poet, socialist thinker, designer and printer. He was one of the leading artists of his day, associated with, though not a member of, the ▷ Pre-Raphaelite Brotherhood, which sought to recover the cultural unity of medieval society. It is as a designer of textiles and wallpapers that he is most admired today. His aim was to counteract the industrial squalor of ▷ Victorian England, and to correct the major social injustice by which the proletariat were cut off from beauty of any sort by the nature of their environment: 'I don't want art for a few, any more than education for a few,

William Morris 1834–1896.

Caricature of William Morris

or freedom for a few.' Paradoxically his campaign against aesthetic barbarism went with rejection of the machine and insistence on handwork, which cut him off from the economic realities of his age.

This withdrawal from social and political complexities is in keeping with his poetry which expresses withdrawal into the romances of the ▷ Middle Ages (Defence of Guinevere, 1858; Earthly Paradise, 1868–70); into ancient Greek ▷ epic (Life and Death of Jason, 1867; translation of ▷ Virgil's ▷ Aeneid, 1875, and of ▷ Homer's ▷ Odyssey, 1887); and into Icelandic epic (Sigurd the Volsung, 1876). His verse (the majority of it translation) was voluminous, fluent, decorative and musical in the ▷ Spenserian tradition current in the Victorian period.

Nonetheless, his socialism was a reality. He was one of the founders of the Socialist League (1884) and edited its monthly periodical Commonweal, until in 1890 the anarchist wing of the movement drove him out. His News from Nowhere (1891 – previously contributed to Commonweal) is a prose 'utopia' describing England at a future date after the establishment of socialism. It is one of the most read of his works today. Another work of socialist inspiration, in mixed prose and verse, is A Dream of John Ball (1888).

Morris had some influence on the young ▷ W. B. Yeats, who remarked 'The dream-

world of Morris was as much the antithesis of daily life as with other men of genius, but he was never conscious of the antithesis and so knew nothing of intellectual suffering.' (*Autobiographies*, 1955).
Bib: Henderson, P., *Life*; Mackail, J. W., *Life*; Hough, G., *The Last Romantics*; Jackson, H., *Morris: Craftsman-Socialist*; Thompson, E. P., *Morris: Romantic to Revolutionary*; Lewis, C. S., in *Rehabilitations*.

Morris dance

A kind of dance popular in England from the 14th to the 16th century. It is said to have been introduced from Spain ('Morris' from 'Morisco' or Moorish). By the 16th century it played a major part in village festivities. It was danced by a group accompanied by two musicians; the dancers adopted the characters of the ▷ Robin Hood legends. The ▷ Puritans abolished the dance in the mid-17th century and it never flourished after the ▷ Restoration.
   ▷ May Day.

Morte Arthur (stanzaic)

Stanzaic poem, dating from the mid/late 14th century, which recounts events from the later stages of Arthurian narrative, specifically those leading up to the break-up of the ▷ Round Table. This narrative follows the framework of the 13th-century Old French Arthurian narratives in which the love affair between ▷ Lancelot and ▷ Guinevere, and the enmity between ▷ Gawain and Lancelot are important catalysts in the destruction of Arthurian society, in addition to the treachery of Mordred. It was used by ▷ Malory in the final books of his *Morte D'Arthur*.
   ▷ Arthur, King.
Bib: Benson, L (ed.), *King Arthur's Death*.

Morte Arthure (alliterative)

▷ Alliterative poem, dating from c 1400, recounting events in the second half of ▷ King Arthur's career, from his campaign against Rome to his final battle against ▷ Mordred, concluding with his death. The narrative follows the basic frame ultimately provided by ▷ Geoffrey of Monmouth's version of Arthurian history but events are elaborated and a remarkable dream sequence is added (just before Arthur returns to fight Mordred) which features a vision of the ▷ Nine Worthies, organized around Fortune's wheel. The dream, in effect, provides a meditation on the nature of the forces which shape Arthur's history. The *Morte Arthure* was used by ▷ Malory in

Book 2 of his *Morte D'Arthur*
Bib: Benson, L. (ed.), *King Arthur's Death*.

Morte D'Arthur

The *Morte D'Arthur* is the conventional title for a highly influential prose narrative, completed in 1469/70 by a Sir Thomas ▷ Malory, which recounts the foundation, history and destruction of ▷ King Arthur's court and the knights of the ▷ Round Table. Until 1934 Malory's narrative was known only through ▷ Caxton's edition (first printed in 1485) entitled the *Morte D'Arthur*, but the discovery of a manuscript version of the text in 1934, and its publication in 1947 as Malory's *Works*, revealed the extent of Caxton's editorial intervention. Whereas Caxton's text is divided into 21 books, the *Works* is composed of eight narratives (called 'Tales', or 'Books'), which are relatively self-contained, but taken together form an overall history of Arthur's reign. The first recounts the founding of Arthur's kingdom and the Round Table; the second concerns Arthur's campaign for Rome; the third is devoted to the adventures of ▷ Lancelot; the fourth is taken up with the romance of ▷ Gareth; the fifth is predominantly concerned with a version of ▷ Tristan's history; the sixth recounts the Quest of the Holy ▷ Grail; the seventh relates the events which follow Lancelot's return to court and his love affair with ▷ Guinevere; the eighth recounts events leading up to the break-up of the Round Table and the end of all Arthur's knights. This organization into eight Tales/Books helps point up Malory's narrative strategy: he has not chosen to present events in a continuous narrative sequence, organized chronologically. Rather he has cultivated a looser structure that enables his reader to follow a number of narrative lines, which make up the sequence of Arthurian history.
   Malory drew material for his work principally from the massive cycles of Arthurian narrative which had been compiled in France in the 13th century and in which accounts of the adventures at Arthur's court were organized in interlaced narrative forms (▷ Vulgate Cycle). Malory has abbreviated and reorganized this material, drawing out some of the narrative threads from the interlaced sequences, and reordering some of the adventures. His narrative is structured as an investigation into the meaning of the codes and ethos of that world. The institution of the Round Table is meant to introduce a civilizing code of behaviour to Arthur's kingdom, but the stories of the knights' adventures reveal the difficulty of working

out a chivalric ethos in practice. The narrative explores and celebrates chivalric values, but it does not present a narrow moralizing account of Arthurian history, nor a simple explanation of why the brave new world of Arthur's court eventually collapses in such disarray. Malory's narrative is structured in such a way that no single chain of actions 'causes' the breakdown of the Round Table: the relationships between events and actions are more mysterious than in the Old French sources.
Bib: Vinaver, E. (ed.), *Malory: Works*; Cowen, J. (ed.), *The Morte D'Arthur*.

Moses

The great Jewish lawgiver, prophet and judge who led the Israelites out of slavery in Egypt and through 40 years' wandering in the wilderness. References in English literature include his adoption by Pharaoh's daughter, who found the infant Moses floating in an ark on the Nile; his demand for freedom for the Jews, and the plagues which afflicted the Egyptians on their refusal; his leading the Jews to safety through the Red Sea; his striking the rock for water; his receiving from God the Ten Commandments, and his promulgation of a complete code of laws as contained in the first five books of the ▷ Bible, the ▷ Pentateuch.

Mother Hubberd's Tale, or Prosopopeia (c 1579)

A verse ▷ satire by ▷ Edmund Spenser, in 10-syllable ▷ couplets, presented in the form of a fable; 'Prosopopeia' means 'endowing things or animals with personalities'. It was published with other poems in *Complaints* (1591) but written at about the same time as ▷ *The Shepherd's Calendar* (1579). It was written at a time when ▷ Elizabeth I seemed inclined to marry the Duke of Anjou, brother of Henry III of France. He was hated by the more convinced ▷ Protestants in England (of whom Spenser was one) because he was a Catholic, and a member of the family responsible for the Massacre of St Bartholomew, 1572, in which French Protestants had been slaughtered. The fable tells how the ape and the fox steal the lion's crown while he sleeps. The ape is Anjou, and the fox is William Cecil, Lord Burleigh, Spenser's enemy.

Mothering Sunday

A festival derived from the worship of ▷ Cybele (Rhea), Great Mother of the Gods, in ancient Rome. Under Christianity it was converted into worship of the 'Mother Church', and it was also set aside as a day on which children paid special tribute to their mothers. It occurred in Mid-Lent (*ie* some time in March) but its secular descendant in America is on the second Sunday in May. Commercialism has added father's days, etc.

Mourning Bride, The (1697)

Congreve's only play with a tragic action, though a happy ending, set in Granada. Almeria, Princess of Granada, has secretly married Alphonso, Prince of Valentia, when she was a captive in the Valencian palace. In battle the King of Valentia, Anselmo, dies, and Alphonso disappears and is presumed dead. While mourning at his tomb, Almeria is interrupted by the prisoner Osmyn, who turns out to be Alphonso in disguise. Meanwhile the captive queen Zara has fallen in love with 'Osmyn' but, failing to win him, plots to have him killed. Belatedly she tries to save him, but unknown to her, he escapes, and the tyrant King of Granada, Manuel, is mistakenly murdered in his place. Zara, finding his headless body, believes it to be that of Osmyn, takes poison and dies. Almeria is about to do the same when Alphonso enters, and the couple are reunited. The play ends with the assurance that 'blessings ever wait on virtuous deeds'. *The Mourning Bride* was hugely successful, and survived well into the 18th century. It contains two quotations which remain famous: 'Music has charms to soothe a savage breast' and 'Heav'n has no rage, like love to hatred turn'd,/Nor Hell a fury, like a woman scorn'd'.

Movement, The

One of the most important 'movements' in post-war British poetry, *the* Movement was really made into a coherent poetic body with the publication of three important anthologies: ▷ D. J. Enright's *Poets of the 1950s* (1955), Robert Conquest's *New Lines* and G. S. Frazer's *Poetry Now* (both 1956). As with any poetic school all of the prominent members of the Movement can be linked only very problematically, and indeed by 1957 its cohering impulse was dissolving. Some of its major figures are generally understood to be ▷ Kingsley Amis, Conquest and Enright, ▷ Donald Davie, ▷ Thom Gunn, ▷ Elizabeth Jennings, ▷ Philip Larkin and ▷ John Wain. The work which is covered by this umbrella term is sardonic, lucid and self-consciously ironic. Opposed to the romantic and apocalyptic tone of much 1940s poetry, especially that of ▷ Dylan Thomas and ▷ W. S. Graham, Movement poetry is meticulously crafted and witty, controlled and common-sensical.
Bib: Morrison, B., *The Movement*.

Mrs Dalloway (1925)
A novel by ▷ Virginia Woolf. Set in
London, it is the story of one day in the life
of Clarissa Dalloway, the wife of Richard
Dalloway, a Member of Parliament (the
Dalloways appeared in Woolf's earlier novel,
The Voyage Out). Clarissa spends the day
preparing for a party she is to give that
evening, a party which provides the
culmination of the novel. The ▷ stream of
consciousness narrative represents the
thoughts of Clarissa and a range of other
characters with whom she is acquainted, or
connected by chance occurrences of the day.
Throughout the novel memories of the past
are blended with present sensations, and the
narrative builds up a highly poetic evocation
of the atmosphere of London and of the
interaction of different lives. The principal
characters, apart from the Dalloways, are:
their daughter Elizabeth and her embittered
and envious tutor, Miss Kilman; Peter Walsh,
with whom Clarissa was in love during her
youth; Sally Seton, Clarissa's girlhood friend,
and Lady Bruton, a society hostess. In
contrast to this group, whose lives are
linked, are Septimus Warren Smith and his
wife Rezia; Septimus is in a highly
disturbed state after his experiences during
World War I and the news of his suicide
intrudes on Clarissa's party, brought by Sir
William Bradshaw, a manipulative
psychiatrist whom Septimus had consulted.
The novel ends with the affirmation of life
with an awareness of loss and death.

Much Ado about Nothing (1598)
A comedy by ▷ Shakespeare. It was acted
in 1598, and printed in 1600. The main plot
is drawn from ▷ *Orlando Furioso* (Bk V)
and from a novel by Bandello. The scene is
Messina, at the court of the governor,
Leonato, who receives a visit from the Prince
of Aragon, his evil-minded brother, Don
John, and the Prince's friend, Claudio. The
main plot concerns Claudio's indirect
courtship of Hero, Leonato's daughter, the
frustration of their marriage plans by Don
John who plants a slander on Hero, the
eventual exposure of the slander, and the
reconciliation. A sub-plot concerns the
relationship between Benedick and Beatrice,
who are famous in the court for their war of
wits in which they declare mutual detestation;
a plot is devised which enables each to
recognize that their war is really a mask
disguising their real love, and they
acknowledge this to each other. The subplot
joins the main plot when Beatrice tests
Benedick's feelings for her by demanding that

he challenge Claudio (his friend) to a duel for
slandering Hero. The play is more famous for
its subplot (and for ▷ Dogberry and Verges,
the comic constables) than for its main plot,
owing to the vividness of the characters in the
former and the comparative colourlessness of
those in the latter. However the comedy has
more unity and impressiveness once the
reader sees in it a strong current of satire.
The court, like other ▷ Renaissance courts,
is an environment in which witticism is
valued without regard to true feeling, disguise
of some sort is normal, artifice has more
prestige than nature, and carefully cultivated
appearances take the place of reality. In such
a world, it is natural that Claudio should be a
superficial lover easily deceived by a
stratagem and that a mere game played in
mockery of Beatrice and Benedick should
lead to their stumbling on the truth. Their
moment of truth stands out with dramatic
poignancy. Similarly, Dogberry's naïve
stumbling over language is a contrast to the
courtiers' artificial perversion of it.

Mudie, Charles Edward (1818–90)
Son of a bookseller, Mudie founded Mudie's
Circulating Library, which loaned books to
the public for a fee. Beginning in Bloomsbury,
he expanded to Oxford Street where the
business ran for many years. Along with
other ▷ circulating libraries, Mudie's
exercised a noticeable moral censorship in the
selection of books.

Muir, Edwin (1887–1959)
Autobiographer, critic, poet, and novelist. He
spent his childhood on a farm in the Orkney
Islands, from which his father was compelled
by economic hardship to move to Glasgow.
For several years Muir struggled to earn his
living in Glasgow as a clerk in various
businesses; he became interested in socialism,
and started writing. In 1919 he married,
moved to London, and became a journalist.
Thereafter, he travelled widely in Europe,
and held a number of teaching posts. In 1940
he produced the first version of his
autobiography, *The Story and the Fable*,
expanded, revised and republished as
Autobiography in 1954. The experiences of
his own lifetime afforded him deep insight –
social, cultural, spiritual. He had moved from
a pre-industrial society in Orkney to 20th-
century industrialism at its grimmest in
Glasgow. He was deeply aware of the Scottish
roots of his culture, and was liberated from
their limitations partly through ▷ German
literature and thought – ▷ Nietzsche, Heine,
Hölderlin; in the 1930s he and his wife Willa

Mummers from an illuminated Medieval manuscript

translated Kafka. Experience of psychoanalysis liberated the deeper levels of his
imagination, and led him, through
illumination about the relationship of man to
his natural environment, to strong and
unusually lucid religious feeling. His
Autobiography is a modern classic.

His birthplace, Orkney, has had some
measure of detachment from the history of
the rest of ▷ Scotland, and it is partly this
that enabled him to show some of the most
penetrating perceptions about modern
Scottish culture in *Scottish Journey* (1935)
and *Scott and Scotland* (1936). His critical
works include: *Latitudes* (1924); *Transition*
(1926); *The Structure of The Novel* (1928);
The Present Age (1939); *Essays on Literature
and Society* (1949).

Poetry: *First Poems* (1925); *Journeys and
Places* (1925); *Chorus of the Newly Dead*
(1926); *Variations on a Time Theme* (1934);
The Narrow Place (1943); *The Voyage* (1946);
The Labyrinth (1949); *Prometheus* (1954); *One
Foot in Eden* (1956); *Collected Poems 1921–
1958* (1960). He came to writing poetry late,
through urgency of personal feeling rather
than a professionally poetic concern with the
medium. Nonetheless his later volumes
embody some of his most moving insights, *eg*
'The Combat' from *The Labyrinth*.

His novels are: *The Marionette* (1927); *The
Three Brothers* (1931); *Poor Tom* (1932).
Biography: *John Knox* (1929).

▷ Autobiography; Scottish literature.
Bib: Knight, R., *Edwin Muir; an Introduction
to His Work*; Butter, E., *Edwin Muir, Man
and Poet*.

Muldoon, Paul (b 1951)

Poet. Born in County Armagh and educated
at Queen's University, Belfast, Muldoon is
one of the younger generation of poets to
emerge from Northern Ireland in the last two
decades (see also ▷ Seamus Heaney and

▷ Derek Mahon). He works for the B.B.C.
His publications include: *Names and Addresses*
(1978); *New Weather* (1973); *Mules* (1977)
and *Why Brownlee Left* (1980).

▷ Irish literature in English.

Mummers' Plays/Mumming

Although many Mummers' plays survive from
various parts of the country, all of the texts
date from the 18th century or later.
Characteristically they take the form of a
fight between a Champion (often St George)
and an Antagonist, who is killed but
resurrected at the end through the agency of
a Doctor. The plays often conclude with a
Dance and the opportunity for a collection of
money. Archetypal patterns are ritually
enacted within these plays, though the texts
as we have them may themselves be the
product of folkloric revivals. Access to folk-
drama and rituals of the past is necessarily
difficult because by its very definition this
kind of cultural activity does not depend on
written records or texts. Information about
medieval folk-drama is derived from the
records of attempts by ecclesiastical
authorities to ban, curb, or suppress it.

Mummings, as their name suggests, are
dumb-shows, particularly masquerades and
disguisings associated with the festivities of
the New Year and Shrove-Tide. Again,
though there are records of prohibitions on
mummings from the early medieval period,
the texts that survive from the 15th century
are of mummings contrived as occasions of
civic and aristocratic entertainment, such as
those composed by ▷ John Lydgate (in
which a dumb-show is accompanied by a
verse commentary).
Bib: Brody, A., *The English Mummers and
their Plays*.

Murdoch, Iris (b 1919)

Novelist and philosopher. Her novels are:
Under the Net (1954); *Flight from the*

Iris Murdoch by Tom Phillips (1986)

Enchanter (1955); *The Sandcastle* (1957); *The Bell* (1958); *Bruno's Dream* (1960); *A Severed Head* (1961; dramatized 1963); *An Unofficial Rose* (1962); *The Unicorn* (1963); *The Italian Girl* (1964; dramatized 1967); *The Red and the Green* (1965); *The Time of the Angels* (1966); *The Nice and the Good* (1968); *A Fairly Honourable Defeat* (1970); *An Accidental Man* (1971); *The Black Prince* (1973); *The Sacred and Profane Love Machine* (1974); *A Word Child* (1975); *Henry and Cato* (1976); *The Sea, The Sea* (1978); *Nuns and Soldiers* (1980); *The Philosopher's Pupil* (1983); *The Good Apprentice* (1985); *The Book and the Brotherhood* (1987).

Iris Murdoch is one of the most prolific and the most popular of serious contemporary novelists. Born in Dublin and educated at Somerville College Oxford and Newnham College Cambridge, she has lectured in philosophy. Her husband is the critic John Bayley. Her profession as a philosopher is reflected in many aspects of her fiction. She has written a study of the work of Jean-Paul Sartre (*Sartre, Romantic Rationalist*, 1953) and her interest in, and dissent from Sartre's ▷ existentialism is evident in her first two novels, which treat existential issues of identity and freedom. These concerns have persisted in her work, but *The Bell* and *The Time of the Angels* introduce religious themes, while since *The Nice and the Good* many of her novels have directly addressed ethical questions. *The Good Apprentice*, for example, explores the idea of a character who, without explicit religious faith, sets out to be good.

Although her works are novels of ideas, they combine this with exciting and sometimes macabre plots, elements of the grotesque and supernatural and touches of social comedy. They are highly structured, both by the use of symbolism, and by the patterning of shifting personal relationships.

Her plays include: *The Three Arrows* (1970); *The Servants and the Snow* (1973); *Art and Eros* (1980). Other works are: *The Sovereignty of Good* (1970); *The Fire and the Sun: Why Plato Banished the Artists* (1977); *Acastos: Two Platonic Dialogues* (1986).
Bib: Byatt, A. S., *Iris Murdoch*; Conradi, P., *Iris Murdoch: the Saint and the Artist*; Johnson, D., *Iris Murdoch*; Todd, R., *Iris Murdoch*.

Murray, John (1778–1843)
Publisher. He founded the ▷ *Quarterly Review* in 1809, and published works by ▷ Lord Byron, ▷ Jane Austen and ▷ George Crabbe, among others. Alone among Byron's correspondents he refused to cooperate with the conspiracy to destroy the poet's *Memoir* and expurgate his letters after his death. Byron's correspondence with Murray thus provides our best insight into Byron's actual language in informal contexts. Murray's father (1745–93) and his son (1808–92), both named John, were also publishers of note.

Murry, John Middleton (1889–1957)
Critic. His own struggles to achieve personal integration, his close relationship with ▷ D. H. Lawrence, and his marriage to the story-writer ▷ Katherine Mansfield, led him to write about a number of writers relating their personal lives to their art: *Dostoevsky* (1916), *Keats and Shakespeare* (1925), *Studies in Keats* (1930), *William Blake* (1933), *Shakespeare* (1936), *Jonathan Swift* (1954). He is perhaps best known for his controversial study of D. H. Lawrence, *Son of Woman* (1931), and for *The Problem of Style* (1922). He was editor of the ▷ *Athenaeum* from 1919 to 1921, and published the work of a number of major writers, including ▷ T. S. Eliot and ▷ Virginia Woolf.
Bib: Lea, F. A., *The Life of John Middleton Murry*.

Muses, The
The nine daughters of Zeus and Mnemosyne (Memory) in Greek myth. Each presided over a separate art: Clio – history; Euterpe – lyric poetry; Thalia – comedy; Melpomene – tragedy; Terpsichore – the dance; Erato – love poetry; Polyhymnia – sacred songs; Urania – astronomy; Calliope (who ranked

first) – epic poetry and eloquence. They may
have originally been water deities, and various
springs were associated with them – Castalia,
Hippocrene, Aganippe. Water has always
been associated with inspiration, and hence
their later role as inspirers of the artist. They
were also originally 'the mindful ones'
through association with their mother, the
goddess of Memory. Variations through the
centuries have caused writers to attribute to
them functions differing from the above list.

Musgrove
Charles, Henrietta, Louisa – characters in
▷ Jane Austen's novel ▷ *Persuasion*.
Charles is husband to the heroine's sister,
and Louisa temporarily distracts Captain
Wentworth from the heroine, who loves him.

'Mutabilitie Cantos', The (1609)
When the 1609 folio edition of ▷ Edmund
Spenser's ▷ *The Faerie Queene* was
published, two further cantos of the poem,
and two stanzas of a fragmentary third canto,
were printed. These, the putative cantos vi,
vii, and a fragment of viii of Book VII of the
poem were described in the 1609 edition in
the following way: 'TWO CANTOS of
Mutabilitie: Which, both for Forme and
Matter, appear to be parcell of some
following Booke of the *FAERIE QUEENE*
under the legend of Constancie'. The precise
relationship between these cantos and the
main body of the poem has been a subject of
dispute ever since their first appearance. The
fragmentary nature of the material, together
with the theme of the verses (not simply
constancy, but a dispute between mutability
or 'change' and nature) might, it has often
been thought, provide a key to the
interpretation of Spenser's complete project
which is *The Faerie Queene*. Whatever the
theological or artistic nature of these final
cantos, in reading them after the main body
of the poem many modern readers have
concluded that they are evidence for the
resistance of Spenser's text to any form of
'closure'.

Myers, Leopold Hamilton (1881–1944)
Novelist. His father, F. W. H. Myers (1843–
1901) was a characteristic product of the
19th-century ▷ agnosticism so prominent
among the educated classes; his reaction
against it took the form of attempts to prove
the existence of the soul by scientific
experiment; he was one of the founders of the
Society for Psychical Research. The son's
concern with the spiritual life took the form
of seeking answers to the question 'Why do

men choose to live?'. His chief opponents in
his pursuit of the answer were not scientific
rationalists in the tradition of ▷ T. H.
Huxley, but aesthetes of the Bloomsbury
tradition, who left moral experience to look
after itself while they cultivated enjoyment of
'states of mind'. He also regarded the great
influence on English writing of the French
novelist, ▷ Marcel Proust (1871–1922) as
pernicious, because Proust likewise esteemed
experience aesthetically and not morally.
Myers considered that this led to the
trivializing of life, and his novels dramatize
the opposition between those who interpret
experience through moral discrimination and
those who vulgarize it by regarding it as a
means to aesthetic experience only; from the
latter evil arises. He regarded civilized society
as corrupted by its moral indifference.
   His first novel, *The Orissers* (1922) presents
the issue in bare terms, but his principal work
was the sequence of novels about 16th-century
India, published together as *The Near and the
Far* in 1943. Myers chose the remote setting
of India under the Emperor Akbar because he
wanted to escape from the secondary
preoccupations of daily life in modern
England, and to treat moral and spiritual
issues with the large scope which the India of
that date, with its multiplying religions and
philosophies, afforded him. Evil is represented
in the novel through Akbar's son Prince
Daniyal, intelligent, artistic, but morally
nihilistic, and rival of his merely stupid
brother Salim for succession to the throne.
Good is expressed through the character of
the Guru (teacher) of the last section (*The
Pool of Vishnu*): 'All communion', he says, 'is
through the Centre. When the relation of
man and man is not through the Centre it
corrupts and destroys itself.' In his later years
he became a ▷ Communist. He committed
suicide in 1944. Other novels include: *The
Clio* (1925); *Strange Glory* (1936).
   ▷ Bloomsbury Group.
Bib: Bantock, G. H., *L. H. Myers: A Critical
Study*.

Mysteries of Udolpho, The (1794)
A novel by ▷ Mrs Ann Radcliffe. It
achieved great fame in its own day, and is
often cited as the typical ▷ Gothic novel. It
is mainly set in a sombre castle in the
Apennine mountains in Italy. The atmosphere
is of secret plots, concealed passages,
abductions, and the supernatural. ▷ Jane
Austen satirized the taste for such sensational
literature in ▷ *Northanger Abbey*.

Mystery plays
   ▷ Cycle plays.

N

N-Town Cycle
A ▷ cycle of plays, recounting episodes from Christian history, formerly called the *Ludus Conventriae Cycle* because it was mistakenly linked to the town of Coventry. But unlike the other examples of cycles from the late medieval period in England (such as ▷ York, ▷ Chester), this sequence of plays cannot be linked to any specific town. The Banns of the play announce that it will be performed at 'n town'; which suggests the cycle was scripted to be performed at different towns, using a fixed stage setting, not pageant waggons. The text seems to have originated from the East Midlands area but there are no records of its performance.
Bib: Block, K. S. (ed.), *Ludus Conventriae, or The Plaie called Corpus Christi.*

Nabob
In its original sense, a Muslim government official in 17th-century India, akin to 'Nawab'. In English 19th-century usage, it was a term for a rich man who had made his fortune in India.

Naiads
▷ Nymphs.

Naipaul, V. S. (Vidiadhar Surajprasad) (b 1932)
Trinidadian novelist of Indian descent. Educated at Queens Royal College, Port of Spain, Trinidad, and Oxford University, he settled in England in 1950. His brother was the novelist Shiva Naipaul (1945–85). V. S. Naipaul is the most admired of contemporary Caribbean novelists writing in English and has won many literary awards. His work is concerned with personal and political freedom, the function of the writer and the nature of sexuality, and is characterized by fastidiousness, clarity, subtlety, and a detached irony of tone. His earlier novels, *The Mystic Masseur* (1957), *The Suffrage of Elvira* (1958) and *Miguel Street* (1959) convey both the vitality and the desolation of Trinidadian life. *The Mimic Men* (1967) is a satirical examination of the economic power structure of an imaginary West Indian island. *A House for Mr Biswas* (1961), often regarded as his masterpiece, tells the tragicomic story of the search for independence and identity of a Brahmin Indian living in Trinidad. His other novels are: *Companion* (1963); *In A Free State* (1971); *Guerillas* (1975); *A Bend in the River* (1979). Naipaul has also produced criticism, journalism, autobiography and travel writing, including: *The Middle Passage* (1962); *An Area of Darkness* (1964); *A Congo Diary* (1980); *Finding the Centre* (1984).
Bib: Hamner, R. D. (ed.), *Critical Perspectives on V. S. Naipaul.*

Napoleon I (Napoleon Bonaparte, originally Buonaparte, 1769–1821)
A Corsican whose unique career began in the ▷ French Revolution, when he joined the French army defending the first French Republic against European alliances. His military successes brought him to dictatorship in 1799, with the title of First Consul, and in 1804 he became Emperor. His armies dominated the greater part of Europe until 1812, when his campaign against Russia failed. His final defeat at the hands of the British and the Prussians under ▷ Wellington and Blucher at ▷ Waterloo (1815) led to his exile on the Atlantic island of St Helena, where he died.

His unprecedented success aroused contrasted feelings amongst the British. For the great majority he was a nightmare figure; mothers used his name to frighten naughty children into discipline. To a man like ▷ Wordsworth he was the tyrant who revealed the illusoriness of the ideals of universal freedom which the Revolution had seemed to express. For ▷ Byron and ▷ Shelley he was the first man in Europe to have risen to the summit of power by intrinsic merit and not at least partly through privilege; his downfall and the restoration of the traditional kinds of government that he had overthrown was for them a defeat of the new hopes for mankind. Byron described him memorably in ▷ *Childe Harold* Canto iii, stanzas 36–44.
▷ French literature in England.

Napoleon III (lived 1808–73)
The nephew of ▷ Napoleon I. He became Emperor of the French in 1852, after previously being elected to the office of President of the second French Republic in 1848. His revival of the Napoleonic title caused him to take the title of Napoleon III, out of respect for his uncle's dead son who had in fact never succeeded to the title. He was without his uncle's genius in war and statecraft, but among the British the mere fact of his succession to power renewed fears of French aggression. His regime was overthrown by the Germans in the Franco-Prussian war of 1870, and he died in England.

Narayan, R. K. (Rasipuran Krishnaswami) (b 1906)
Indian novelist and short-story writer. His

novels are: *Swami and Friends* (1935); *The Bachelor of Arts* (1937); *The Dark Room* (1938); *The English Teacher* (1945); *Mr Sampath* (1949); *The Financial Expert* (1952); *Waiting for the Mahatma* (1955); *The Guide* (1958); *The Man Eater of Malgudi* (1961); *The Vendor of Sweets* (1967); *The Painter of Signs* (1976); *A Tiger for Malgudi* (1983); *Talkative Man* (1986). His novels are set in the imaginary southern Indian community of Malgudi, based on the town of Mysore, which he uses to epitomize Indian culture from the days of the Raj to the present. The early novels show the continuing influence of British culture, in particular on the education system, and contain elements of ▷ autobiography. His work attains a new seriousness with *The English Teacher*, which is based on his own marriage and the early death of his wife. His mature work deals with spirituality and with human weakness, corruption, failure and lack of fulfilment in an ironic and sceptical manner, supported by the vivid realization of the life of the town. *The Guide*, the story of a con man who becomes a saint, is one of his outstanding works, while *A Tiger for Malgudi* represents an excursion into a fantasy mode; drawing on the Hindu doctrine of reincarnation, it has a tiger as its hero and narrator. Story collections are: *Malgudi Days* (1943); *Dodu* (1943); *Cyclone* (1944); *An Astrologer's Day* (1947); *Lawley Road* (1956); *A House and Two Goats* (1970); *Old and New* (1981); *Malgudi Days* (1982) (not the same as the 1943 volume); *Under The Banyan Tree* (1985). Narayan has also written travel literature, memoirs, essays and versions of the Indian epics *The Ramayana* and *The Mahabharata*.
Bib: Walsh, W., *R. K. Narayan: a Critical Appreciation.*

Narcissus
In Greek myth, a youth of exceptional beauty. He rejected the love of the nymph Echo, and to punish him ▷ Aphrodite caused him to fall in love with his own reflection in water. He was changed into the flower which bears his name.

Nashe, Thomas (1567–1601)
Pamphleteer, poet and playwright. He spent six years at St John's College, Cambridge, and is numbered among the ▷ University Wits who made the decade 1590–1600 an unusually lively period in literature. Two features of this liveliness were ▷ satire and prose romance (sometimes misleadingly called 'the Elizabethan novel'). Nashe contributed to both: his best known work, ▷ *The Unfortunate Traveller, or the Life of Jack*

Wilton (1594), is one of the outstanding romances of the decade, and it includes some of his best satire, often in the form of ▷ parody of some of the contemporary styles of fine writing. Most of the rest of his satire was also in prose. *Pierce Penniless, His Supplication to the Devil* (1592) is a satire in the tradition of the allegorical ▷ Morality plays; an attack on the qualities that made for success in the London of his day, and a denunciation of them as new versions of the ▷ Seven Deadly Sins; the method looks forward to ▷ Ben Jonson's Comedy of Humours (▷ Humours, Comedy of). His last work, *Lenten Stuff* (1599), is a comic extravaganza on Yarmouth, a fishing town, and the red herring. Other prose work includes his early ▷ pamphlets attacking the ▷ Puritan side in the ▷ Marprelate controversy and vigorous disagreement with ▷ Gabriel Harvey on literary and moral questions between 1593 and 1596. His *Christ's Tears over Jerusalem* (1593) records his repentance for religious doubts.

Nashe was sent to prison in 1597 for an attack on abuses in his play *The Isle of Dogs*, which has been lost. The only play of his sole authorship which survives is *Summer's Last Will and Testament* (1592). This defends the traditional festivities of the countryside against Puritan condemnation of them, and at the same time attacks the useless extravagance of courtiers. It includes some very fine lyrics, especially *In Plague Time* and *Autumn*.

Nashe is chiefly known as a prose writer; his prose is notable for the abundance of its energy which compensates for the confusion of its organization. His gift for parody and the rapidity and vividness of his expression show that the greater coherence and lucidity which English prose was to achieve in the 17th century was not all gain. The freedom and zest of his comic writing owe something to earlier ▷ Renaissance writers – the Italian poet and comedian ▷ Pietro Aretino and the great French satirist ▷ François Rabelais.
Bib: McKerron, R. B. (rev.), *The Works of Thomas Nashe*, 5 vol; Hibbard, G. R., *Nashe: A Critical Introduction.*

National Anthem, The British
'God Save the King', sung as a national anthem, dates back to 1745, when the throne of ▷ George II was threatened by the second ▷ Jacobite Rebellion in ▷ Scotland on behalf of the ▷ Stuart claimant. It consists of four verses of which the first only is normally sung, and the last (calling for suppression of the Scots) has been entirely

forgotten. The tune has commonly been attributed to the composer John Bull (?1563–1628); alternatively, the words and the tune are said to have been the composition of the poet Henry Carey (d 1743), but there is no certainty. ▷ Wales has its own separate national anthem, 'Land of my Fathers'.

National debt
The system by which a government finances itself by borrowing money from its citizens, in addition to taxing them; the lenders in effect invest money in the state as in a business enterprise. In Britain this system originated in the reign of ▷ William III and the ▷ Bank of England was founded in order to operate it.

National Theatre, The
The idea of a national theatre in London had existed since the 18th century. Serious efforts to create such an institution began early this century with the publication in 1903 of *The National Theatre: A Scheme and Estimates*, by William Archer and ▷ Harley Granville Barker. Enthusiastic lobbying of governments continued after World War I and by 1938 a fund of £150,000 had been raised. However, it was not until 1962 that a National Theatre Board was established. This body created a National Theatre company led by ▷ Sir Laurence Olivier, which was based at the ▷ Old Vic whilst a new theatre was built for it on the South Bank at Waterloo. This was finally completed in 1976; the theatre has three auditoria: the Lyttelton, Olivier and Cottesloe theatres, providing a proscenium stage, an open stage and a workshop studio. The first general director was ▷ Sir Peter Hall, who was replaced by Richard Eyre in 1988. Current associate directors are Bill Bryden, Howard Davies, William Dudley and Peter Gill. The company policy is to present a diverse repertoire, embracing classic, new and neglected plays from the whole of world drama and to give audiences a choice of at least six different productions at any one time.
Bib: Elsom, J. and Tomalin, N., *The History of the National Theatre*.

Nationalism
The emotion or the doctrine according to which human egotism and its passions are expanded so as to become identical with the nation state. As a widespread phenomenon it is usually dated from the American War of Independence (1775–83) and from the ▷ French Revolution and the wars that followed it. This makes it an especially 19th- and 20th-century phenonemon, which it

undoubtedly is, but on the other hand intense national self-consciousness existed among the older European nations before, though without the fanaticism which has been characteristic of it since 1790. Thus strong national feeling arose in England and France, in consequence of the ▷ Hundred Years War in the 15th century; it arose again in the 16th and 17th centuries under the English queen ▷ Elizabeth I and the French king Louis XIV respectively. Possibly these earlier emotions should be distinguished as patriotism, but the distinction is vague.

Natural History and Antiquities of Selborne
▷ White, Gilbert.

Natural Law
According to theologians (*eg* ▷ Richard Hooker), that part of the Divine Will that manifests itself in the order of the material world: distinguishable from but of a piece with human and divine law. Modern scientists define it as the principles of uniformity discernible in the behaviour of phenomena, making such behaviour predictable. For the 18th century, the existence of Natural Law was important as the basis for ▷ Natural Religion.

Natural Philosophy
In the 17th and 18th centuries, the study of physics and kindred sciences. Interest in Natural Philosophy became organized and heightened with the establishment in 1662 of the ▷ Royal Society, which took the whole of knowledge as its province. The natural philosophers included such eminent persons as ▷ Isaac Newton, the chemist Robert Boyle (1627–91), and the naturalist John Ray (1627–1705). They were religious men and made their religion accord with their science. However, in spite of the respect accorded to some of them, especially Newton, intellectuals in the period 1660–1730 tended to react against natural philosophy with angry contempt. They were provoked not so much by the fear of the injury such thought might do to religious faith – this was much more a 19th-century reaction – as by disgust at the triviality of much scientific inquiry, the technical fruits of which were slow to appear. The most notable satire was Swift's 'Laputa' in Part III of ▷ *Gulliver's Travels*. Other examples were Samuel Butler's *Elephant in the Moon*, some of the ▷ *Spectator* essays of Addison and Steele, and the *Memoirs of Martinus Scriblerus*, published with the works of ▷ Pope in 1741, though the principal author seems to have been John Arbuthnot (1667–1735).

Natural Religion

A belief first taught by ▷ Lord Herbert of Cherbury; according to him, belief in God and right conduct are planted in human instincts. This Christian doctrine was the basis for deistic thought (▷ *Deism*) in the later 17th and 18th centuries, and contributed to the growth of religious toleration, though also to passivity of religious feeling and hence to indifference. Herbert's aim was to resolve the doubts arising out of the religious conflicts of his time – see *eg* ▷ Donne's *Third Satire*. For the reaction against Deism, see ▷ William Blake's propositions *There is No Natural Religion* (1788).

Naturalism

In literature, a school of thought especially associated with the novelist ▷ Emile Zola. It was a development of ▷ Realism. The Naturalists believed that imaginative literature (especially the novel) should be based on scientific knowledge, and that imaginative writers should be scientifically objective and exploratory in their approach to their work. This means that environment should be exactly treated, and that character should be related to physiological heredity. Influential in France and Germany, the movement counts for little in Britain; the novelists ▷ George Gissing and ▷ Arnold Bennett show traces of its influence in the treatment of environment in relation to character.

▷ French literature in England.

Nature

The word is used throughout English literature with meanings that vary constantly according to period or to mode of expression, *eg* philosophic, religious or personal. This note is intended to guide the student by showing some of the basic approaches to the idea.

1 *Creation and the Fall*. Fundamental to all conceptions of Nature is traditional Christian doctrine. This influences English writers even when they are using a more or less agnostic or atheistic approach. The doctrine is that Nature is God's creation, but by the fall of man, symbolized by the story of ▷ Adam's disobedience in the book of *Genesis*, earthly nature is self-willed and destructive though not to the extent that the Divine Will and Order is obliterated in it.

2 *All-embracing Nature*. Nature is sometimes seen as the whole of reality so far as earthly experience goes. For instance, the opening 18 lines of ▷ Chaucer's ▷ *Prologue to the Canterbury Tales* show Nature as the great reviver of life. This use of the word has a different kind of significance in the 18th century when scientific Reason has replaced the religious imagination as the familiar vehicle for the interpretation of reality. See 4 *Nature and Truth*.

3 *Nature and God*. In line with traditional Christian doctrine, Natural Law is linked to Human Law and Divine Law as a manifestation of the Divine Will, in such works as ▷ Hooker's *Laws of Ecclesiastical Polity* (1597). However, from the beginning of the 17th century, there was a new interest in the function of human reason as an instrument for the acquisition of knowledge independently of religious feeling. Men like ▷ Ralegh (*History of the World*, 1614) and ▷ Bacon (▷ *The Advancement of Learning*) began to ask what, given that God was the Primary Cause of Nature, were the Secondary, or Immediate, Causes of natural phenomena. ▷ Newton's work on gravitation (*Principia Mathematica*, 1687) and ▷ Locke's ▷ *Essay Concerning Human Understanding* seemed to solve the problem, causing people to see God as the Divine Artificer whose Reason could be discerned in the government of even the smallest phenomena, as well as in the great original act of Creation.

4 *Nature and Truth*. Nature is in the 18th century Truth scientifically considered. 'To follow Nature' (*eg* in works of imaginative literature) may mean: (i) to present things and people (*eg* an imagined character) as they really are; (ii) to reveal truths that lie beneath appearances; (iii) to follow rational principles. It was the attempt to 'follow Nature' in these ways that constituted the main discipline of the novelists ▷ Defoe, ▷ Richardson, ▷ Fielding, ▷ Smollett.

5 *Nature as Moral Paradox*. The Christian conception of Nature as both God-created and spoilt by the fall of man led at various times to the problem that Nature is both good and evil. According to the medieval conception, maintained until the middle of the 17th century, human society was itself the outcome of the Divine Natural Order, so that it was by Natural Law that children should honour their parents, subjects their sovereigns, etc. On the other hand, the natural passions of men and beasts, unrestrained by reason, were the source of rapacity and ruin. Thus ▷ Shakespeare's King Lear begins by relying on the former conception of Nature, but he is exposed to the reality of the latter.

19th-century natural science revived the feeling that Nature was essentially destructive, and hostile or at best indifferent to men; this is the 'Nature red in tooth and claw' image of ▷ Tennyson's ▷ *In Memoriam*, set against the idea of the love of God. The atheistic ▷ Thomas Hardy saw men as subjected to the irony of indifferent fates, and the natural environment as governed in the same way.

6 *Nature for Man's Use*. Implicit in Christian doctrine was the belief that Nature was created *for* man; that it was his birthright to exploit and use it. This begins with the conception of Nature as the Great Mother, originating in pre-Christian times but pervasive in medieval verse and later, *eg* in much Elizabethan ▷ pastoral poetry. It took a more active significance when the 17th- and 18th-century 'natural philosophers' from ▷ Bacon onwards sought methods by which man could increase his power over Nature; 18th-century poetry commonly shows Nature as beautiful when she is productive under the ingenuity of human exploitation.

7 *Nature and Art*. 'Art' in earlier contexts often includes technology, *eg* in Polixenes' remarks on cultivation to Perdita in *The Winter's Tale* IV. iii; here art is seen as itself a product of nature. But art was often set against nature in Shakespeare's time and afterwards, *eg* in Sidney's ▷ *Apology for Poetry*: 'Her (*ie* Nature's) world is brazen; the Poets only deliver a golden'; here the function of imaginative art seems to be the opposite of the 18th-century poets' and novelists' conception of 'truth to nature', but Sidney meant that poetry should improve on Nature, not falsify it; the creation must be ideal but consistent with Nature.

8 *Nature opposed to Court and City*. 'Art', however, was not necessarily an improvement. The city and the court, in Shakespeare's time, were the centres of new financial forces generating intrigue and 'unnatural' (*ie* inhuman) behaviour. There was also a kind of pastoral made by idealizing the life of the great country houses, *eg* ▷ Ben Jonson's ▷ *Penshurst*. In the 18th century poets like ▷ James Thomson wrote about natural surroundings for their own sake, and sometimes included wild nature as their subject, but it was ▷ Wordsworth who gave to wild nature its importance as the principal subject of what later came to be known as 'nature' poetry.

9 *Nature in Communion with the Individual*. Wordsworth was to some extent anticipated in the 18th century by such a poet as ▷ William Cowper, and his teacher was especially ▷ Jean-Jacques Rousseau. It was Wordsworth above all, however, who gave to Nature its modern most familiar sense – as the non-urban, preferably wild environment

of man, to which the depths of his own nature always respond. Here he finds a communion which refreshes the loneliness of his spirit in a relationship which underlies and gives meaning to his human relationships.

Nebuchadnezzar

King of Babylon, 605–562 B C. He conquered Israel. The first four chapters of the book of *Daniel* in the Bible tell of his dream that was correctly interpreted by Daniel; of his erection of a golden image which he ordered the people to worship; of the refusal of Shadrach, Meshach and Abednego to obey, and their survival from the fiery furnace into which they were cast by his orders; and of his eventual madness, in which he is said to have gone on all fours.

Nelson, Horatio, Viscount (1758–1805)

English admiral, and a national hero. His naval successes against ▷ Napoleon culminated in the ▷ Battle of Trafalgar (1805) at which he lost his life in gaining victory over the combined French and Spanish fleets, thus saving England from French invasion. As an officer he was strongly independent and unconventional; one of the famous anecdotes about him tells how he put his telescope to his blind eye at the battle of Copenhagen in 1801 in order not to see his superior officer's signal ordering him to withdraw. Equally famous are the signal to his ships before Trafalgar: 'England expects every man to do his duty', and his dying words: 'Now I am satisfied; thank God I have done my duty.' His love affair with the beautiful Lady Hamilton was a notorious romance. In 1813 the poet ▷ Robert Southey published his life, one of the best known of the English ▷ biographies.

▷ Nationalism.

Nennius

Welsh monk and reputed compiler of a 9th-century *Historia Brittonum* (*History of the Britons*), which provides an outline of British history, from the founding of the island by ▷ Brutus, used by ▷ Geoffrey of Monmouth as a framework for his historical narrative. ▷ Arthur is mentioned as a British battle leader (not a king), who fights 12 battles, culminating in the battle of Badon, in which he fells 960 men at one charge.

▷ Arthur, King.

Neo-classicism

This term can be understood for the purposes of English literary culture in two senses: (1) the broad sense, which refers to the ▷ Renaissance of Classical culture and its influence on English literature down to the end of the 18th century. This influence operated mainly by the cultivation of Latin culture, and was mediated first by Italy and later by France. (2) The narrow sense of neo-classicism refers to a European artistic movement which originated in Germany and lasted approximately from 1750 until 1830.

In the first sense, neo-classical culture affected English literature in two phases:

1 In the 16th century England developed a fine school of classical scholars, of whom the best known was ▷ Thomas More. Through travellers and scholars such as ▷ Sir Thomas Wyatt and Henry Howard, ▷ Earl of Surrey, poetry and prose received strong influences from Italian writers such as ▷ Petrarch and French ones such as ▷ Ronsard who already belonged to the classical revival. A critic like ▷ Sidney showed the influence of Italian critics who in turn were developing 'rules' out of classical writers for dramatic construction, etc. All these influences matured in the last decade of the 16th century but their effect was uneven; the greatest of the rising dramatists, ▷ Shakespeare, ignored the neo-classical rules for dramatic construction, whereas ▷ Ben Jonson, his chief rival in the theatre by 1600, was deeply affected by classical principles and classical culture generally. ▷ Pastoral poems, deriving from Italian influences and more directly from Virgil, were numerous from Spenser's ▷ *The Shepherd's Calendar* (1579) onwards, and in the 1590s there was a widespread production of ▷ sonnets under the influence of Petrarch. Much of the classical influence was on the level of ornament, however, as it was in English architecture in the same period. Jonson was outstanding in his absorption of classical influence to a deep level, and it was deeper in his lyrical work than in his drama. He is, in fact, an important link with the next phase of English neo-classicism – that which began in 1660 and lasted throughout the 18th century.

2 The second phase was much influenced by contemporary French literature, which was marked by distinguished achievement. English culture was entering a relatively aristocratic period by reaction from the Republican decade of the 1650s; it was also undergoing an increasingly strong revulsion against religious and political passions such as produced the ▷ Civil War. The result was admiration for philosophy, reason, scepticism, ▷ wit and refinement – all qualities conducive to neo-classic culture. Significantly this was also the first important period of English criticism. Yet thoroughly neo-classic critics like ▷ Thomas Rymer were the exception. The restlessness of English society, the increasing importance of the middle class, the difficulty of making such a large exception to neo-classical principles as Shakespeare, and the hostility the English literary tradition has always shown to authoritative doctrines, all help to explain the refusal of the leading critics, ▷ Dryden and ▷ Samuel Johnson, to adopt neo-classic theory unquestioningly. Nonetheless, such a figure as the French neo-classicist ▷ Boileau was deeply respected, and the best poets and essayists (though hardly the novelists) – ▷ Addison, ▷ Swift, ▷ Pope, Johnson – all exhibited the neo-classic virtues of clarity, order, reason, wit and balance.

Neo-classicism in the narrow sense was the cultivation of Greek culture in opposition to Roman culture, and originated partly in the German movement to emancipate German culture from France. It can be said that whereas Renaissance classicism sought to emulate the culture of Rome, this 'New Humanism' sought inspiration in the originality of the Greeks. This difference enabled the new Neo-Classicism to merge with ▷ Romanticism, whose progenitor was above all ▷ Rousseau. In England, it is thus impossible to distinguish Neo-classic from Romantic writers in the period 1790–1830. It is clear, however, that ▷ William Blake shows neo-classic inspiration in his graphic art, and that the poems by ▷ Keats on classical themes (▷ Endymion and the two ▷ Hyperions) are in a romantic-classical style, very different from ▷ Augustan classicism of the previous century. Neo-classicism is more distinguishable in the architectural style known as ▷ Regency, and in the sculpture of an artist such as Flaxman (as well as in ▷ costume), than in imaginative literature.

▷ Classic, Classics, Classical; Unities; French literature in England; Italian influence in English literature.
Bib: Honour, H., *Neo-classicism.*

Neo-Platonism
  ▷ Platonism.

Neoptolemus (Pyrrhus)
  ▷ *Iliad.*

Neptune
  ▷ Poseidon.

Nereids
  ▷ Nymphs.

Nero (AD 37–68)

Roman Emperor 54–68, and notorious for his tyrannous cruelty, the result of insane suspicion. In 64 Rome was burnt, according to many accounts by his secret orders. Legend says that he enjoyed the spectacle, and played music while he watched the conflagration – hence the proverb 'to fiddle while Rome burns', *ie* to be frivolous during a disastrous happening. At all events he had a highly developed aesthetic sensibility. Eventually his subjects revolted against his tyranny and he is reported to have died by his own hands with the words: 'What an artist dies with me!'

New Atlantis, The (1626)

A philosophical tale by ▷ Francis Bacon, in the tradition of ▷ Sir Thomas More's ▷ *Utopia* (1615). It was left unfinished at Bacon's death, and published in 1626. The title is an allusion to the mythical island described by ▷ Plato in his dialogue *Timaeus*. Bacon's island is called Bensalem (*ie* an analogous place to Salem or ▷ Jerusalem, the holy city) and its chief glory is its university, 'Solomon's House'. Unlike the English ▷ universities of Bacon's day, this is devoted to scientific research – 'the knowledge of causes, and secret motions of things; and the enlarging of the bounds of human empire, to the effecting of all things possible'. The boundless optimism of this Baconian ideal was to be reflected in the work of 17th-century science in general.

New Comedy

Unlike ▷ Aristophanes's Old Comedy, New Comedy as extant in the writings of ▷ Menander, ▷ Plautus and ▷ Terence does not address specific and topical issues so much as focussing on general moral and imaginative motifs. Its formulae consist of stock characters like the young rake, the wily servant (*servus dolosus*), the courtesan, the braggart soldier (*miles gloriosus*) and the irascible old man (*senex*). The plays are populated by lost children and siblings. The genre of New Comedy proved highly influential for English literature. It could more readily accommodate the neo-classical, Horatian moral stance which distinguishes much Elizabethan drama, and its generalized approach proved politically safe in a theatre where every play needed a licence for performance from the Lord Chamberlain's office.

New criticism

This term is given to a movement which developed in the late 1940s in the U.S.A., and which dedicated itself to opposing the kind of criticism that is associated with ▷ Romanticism, and 19th-century realism. The 'practical criticism' of ▷ I. A. Richards was an influential stimulus to this movement in which emphasis was placed upon the self-contained nature of the literary text. In the work of 'new' critics such as Cleanth Brooks, W. K. Wismatt, John Crowe Ransom, Allen Tate, and R. P. Blackmur, concern with the 'intention' of the writer was replaced by close reading of particular texts, and depended upon the assumption that any literary work was self-contained. New criticism placed a particular emphasis upon poetry, and asserted that the individual poem 'must not mean but be'.

New Grub Street (1891)

A novel by ▷ George Gissing. The title refers to ▷ Grub Street, which was inhabited in the 18th century by journalists of a low order, who wrote to gain a living without seriousness of intention or artistic standards. The living they earned was generally a mean one, but since 1875 the new periodicals and newspapers had found a way to achieve massive circulations by printing material which had an immediate appeal although its intrinsic quality was trivial or merely sensational. This commercialization of journalism had spread to the production of books. Gissing's novel is about the difficulties of the serious literary artist faced by successful competition from the now very well rewarded commercial writer without scruples, either moral or artistic. The serious writer in the book is Edwin Reardon (a self-portrait) and his successful competitor is Jasper Milvain. Commercial success is also illustrated by Whelpdale, editor of the magazine *Chit-Chat* (based on the actual magazine *Titbits* founded in 1881) which never publishes articles longer than two inches in length. At the other extreme is the novelist Biffen, who has the artistic fastidiousness of the French novelist ▷ Flaubert and writes the same kind of book. Biffen and Reardon both end in failure but Gissing's novel was fairly popular, which perhaps argues against the extreme pessimism of his thesis.
▷ Journalism; Newspapers.

New historicism

▷ Materialism; ▷ Critical theory.

New Inn, The (1629)

A late play by ▷ Ben Jonson which attempts to work native romance motifs into the fabric of a contemporary ▷ citizen comedy. More than any Jonson play, *The New Inn* has been the particular discovery of the 1970s, when several leading Jonson scholars championed its claim to being a masterpiece of mixed genre and a Jonsonian tribute to ▷ Shakespeare.

New Learning, The
Study of the Bible and the Greek ▷ classics in the original languages instead of through Latin versions. This study in the 15th–16th centuries was an important influence in the ▷ Renaissance and the ▷ Reformation.

New Model Army, The
Formed by Parliament in 1645 towards the end of the ▷ Civil War between itself and King ▷ Charles I. The war had so far been indecisive owing to the amateurish soldiering on both sides. Parliament now secured that its own army should be highly professional. The result was the decisive victory of Naseby in June 1645. The commander was Sir Thomas Fairfax, but its most gifted general was ▷ Oliver Cromwell, who between 1646 and 1660 made the English army one of the most formidable in Europe. Cromwell's special contribution was his highly trained force of cavalry, the Ironsides.

New Monthly Magazine
It started in 1814 and had editors of considerable literary note such as the poets ▷ Thomas Campbell and ▷ Thomas Hood, the novelists ▷ Harrison Ainsworth and ▷ Bulwer Lytton, and the essayist Theodore Hook. It gave considerable space to criticism. It closed in 1884.

New Philosophers, The
▷ Nouveaux Philosophes, Les.

New Science
The term 'New Science' or 'New Philosophy' is something of a catch-all phrase, but one which usually is used to suggest the revolution in scientific understanding in Europe generally in the 16th and 17th centuries. On the continent, the work of ▷ Galileo in the field of astronomy and Andreas Vesalius (1514–64) in the area of human anatomy signalled a reassessment of the study of the natural world. In England the influence of ▷ Francis Bacon in the area of scientific methodology was to be of considerable importance. English science in the 16th century, however, lagged behind the work that was taking place on the continent. But, with the publication of William Harvey's discovery of the circulation of the blood (1628), an age of remarkable scientific innovation began in the British Isles.

The influence of the 'New Science' of the age on literature is a much-debated topic.

Certainly poets such as ▷ John Donne and ▷ Henry Vaughan were aware of the changes taking place in the ordering and understanding of the natural world – and this awareness is reflected in their writings. Others, such as ▷ Abraham Cowley, were enthusiastic in promulgating ideas and experimental attitudes associated with new scientific methodology. ▷ Thomas Traherne, on the other hand, found himself in the paradoxical situation of being fascinated with the products of scientific enquiry while being deeply suspicious of the anti-fideistic tendency of much of the work that was undertaken.
Bib: Debus, A. G., *Man and Nature in the Renaissance*.

New Statesman and Society, The
The leading left-wing weekly periodical of the intelligentsia. It was founded in 1913; its Conservative counterpart is ▷ *The Spectator*. In politics it has always followed a general line of ▷ Fabian socialism.

New Theatre, The
The present Albery Theatre in St Martin's Lane was known as the New Theatre from its opening in 1903 to 1973.
▷ Lincoln's Inn Fields; Haymarket Theatres.

New Way to Pay Old Debts, A (1625)
The best-known comedy by ▷ Philip Massinger. The main character is Sir Giles Overreach, a man of powerful energy and unlimited rapacity, who has no scruples in his schemes to increase his own wealth and social greatness. He is, however, outwitted by those very social superiors, Lord Lovell and Lady Allworth, whom he attempts to flatter and use; they take the side of the young people whom he tries to victimize, his nephew Wellborn and his daughter Margaret. Overreach thus 'overreaches' himself, in the manner of ▷ Ben Jonson's characters, and he is in fact the last vigorous representative of the Comedy of ▷ Humours tradition. The weakness of the play is that Overreach's opponents are colourless characters, so that the play is artistically unbalanced in Overreach's favour. Massinger's use of ▷ blank verse is extremely flexible to the point sometimes of insipidity although in the best passages it regains much of the concentrated force of Ben Jonson himself. Overreach is based on a contemporary profiteer, Sir Giles Mompesson.

New Woman, The
A term popularized in the 1890s by journalists and literary reviewers, it was used in a

general and often ill-defined way to describe the modern ▷ feminist figure who was emerging in the press and in novels (though to a lesser extent in real life) and who caused considerable shock to conventional opinion by the radicalism of her ideas. Although there was never any identifiable single movement with which she was associated, the New Woman was thought to embody all that was most advanced in feminist ideology. Broadly, her beliefs included rejection of marriage, a more honest and direct approach to female sexuality, and a demand for the reorganization of society so as to give women economic and personal independence. During the 1890s a type of novel known as 'The New Woman Fiction' enjoyed considerable notoriety, several of its kind becoming best-sellers. Amongst these were Sarah Grand's *The Heavenly Twins* (1893), George Egerton's *Keynotes* (1893) and Grant Allen's *The Woman Who Did* (1895). Several established novelists were also accused of embodying New Woman figures in their novels of the 1890s, including ▷ Thomas Hardy in ▷ *Jude the Obscure* and ▷ George Gissing in *The Odd Women*. The New Woman as a popular stereotype did not outlast the Victorian age and early 20th-century feminism concentrated its energies more on the suffrage movement than on the New Woman's ideals of personal integrity and sexual freedom.

Bib: Cunningham, G., *The New Woman and the Victorian Novel.*

Newcomes, The (1853–5)
A novel by ▷ William Makepeace Thackeray; it was published in instalments. The characters are drawn from the middle and upper classes, and the book is a study of the vices and virtues of such mid-19th-century society. The vices are shown in the worldly cynicism of Lady Kew who seeks a fashionable marriage for her grand-daughter Ethel Newcome; in the mean snobbery of Ethel's brother Barnes, who frustrates her marriage with her cousin Clive Newcome; in the hypocrisy, intrigue and viciousness of Clive's eventual mother-in-law Mrs Mackenzie, and in the philistinism and arrogance of the social world as a whole. The virtues are less successfully presented. Clive Newcome's father, Colonel Newcome, is the honourable, single-minded soldier who loses his fortune and is subjected to the tyranny of Mrs Mackenzie. Thackeray was inclined to see decency as overwhelmed by materialism.

Newgate
In the ▷ Middle Ages, the principal west gate of the City of London. The gate-house was a prison from the 12th century, enlarged in the 15th century and burnt down in the ▷ Gordon Riots in 1780. Its destruction is described in ▷ Dickens's novel ▷ *Barnaby Rudge*. It was rebuilt and finally demolished in 1902, when the present Central Criminal Court (Old Bailey) was built on its site.

The 'Newgate school of novelists' in the 1830s and 1840s were such writers as ▷ Harrison Ainsworth and ▷ Bulwer Lytton, who tended to idealize famous criminals such as the highwayman ▷ Turpin. They were attacked by ▷ Thackeray who satirized the mode in his novel *Barry Lyndon* (1844).
▷ *Oliver Twist.*

Newman, John Henry (1801–90)
Writer on religion and education. From 1833 to 1842 he was one of the most influential and controversial leaders of the Church of England, but in 1845 he was received into the Roman Catholic Church. As a Catholic convert he was even more influential, and he was made a Cardinal in 1879.

His first period of activity (1833–42) was as leader of the Tractarian Movement – more or less identical with the ▷ Oxford Movement – whose aim was to defend the Church of England against encroachments by the state on the one hand, and against adulteration of its doctrines by the Broad Church tendencies on the other. The Church of England was founded in the 16th century on a central position between the Catholicism of Rome and the whole-hearted ▷ Protestantism of ▷ Luther and ▷ Calvin. This had always been both its strength and its weakness; it was able to accommodate a variety of believers, but it was inclined to lose itself in vagueness and become subserviant to the state. Newman's *Tracts for the Times* tried to secure a firm basis for Anglican doctrine and discipline, as against supporters of the Broad Church party (such as ▷ Thomas Arnold) who cared less for doctrine than for social ethics. Newman's tracts led him steadily towards Roman Catholicism, however, until his *Tract XC* went so far as to say that the Anglican 39 Articles – which all clergy had to accept – were not incompatible with essential Roman Catholic beliefs, but only with distortions and exaggerations of them.

As a Roman Catholic, Newman's first valuable literary work was *The Scope & Nature of University Education* (1852), a collection of lectures to the new Catholic University of Dublin, of which he became Rector in 1854. These were combined with further lectures delivered in 1859 to make *The Idea of a University Defined* (1873). His spiritual autobiography, defending the sincerity of his Catholic beliefs against the accusations by the Broad Churchman, ▷ Charles Kingsley, came out with the title *Apologia pro Vita sua (Defence of his Life)* in 1864. It was not only very persuasive in convincing the public of the genuineness of his faith; it was also an eloquent and lucid presentation of the nature of religious belief at a time when much religious thinking in English was muddled, superficial and entangled in irrelevant controversies with scientific agnostics such as ▷ T. H. Huxley. His *Grammar of Assent* (1870) was a more strictly philosophical account of religious belief.

Newman also wrote some minor poetry, including the famous hymn *Lead Kindly Light*, and the ▷ dramatic monologue *The Dream of Gerontius*, better known for the music set to it by Elgar. He also wrote two religious novels – *Loss and Gain* (1848) and *Callista* (1856).

As a writer he is famous for the lucidity and grace of his style. His wide influence, still very powerful, arose from his ability to understand the tragic extremity of the emotional and intellectual bewilderment of his contemporaries, while refusing to compromise his beliefs.

▷ Agnosticism.
Bib: Harold, C. F., *Newman: an Expository and Critical Study of his Mind, Thought and Art.*

Newspapers

Periodicals resembling newspapers began in a small way in the reign of ▷ James I; in the decades of the ▷ Civil War and the ▷ Interregnum they increased in number owing to the need of either side to engage in propaganda. From 1695 press ▷ censorship was abandoned; newspapers and weekly periodicals began to flourish.

The first English daily, the *Daily Courant*, a mere news-sheet, began in 1702, but in the earlier part of the 18th century papers more nearly resembling what we now know as the weekly reviews were of greater importance, and leading writers conducted them, *eg* ▷ Defoe's *The Review* (thrice weekly – 1704–13); ▷ Steele's ▷ *Tatler* (thrice weekly – started 1709); Steele and ▷ Addison's ▷ *Spectator* (daily – started 1711); and the ▷ *Examiner* (started 1710), to which the chief contributor was ▷ Jonathan Swift. ▷ Samuel Johnson's ▷ *Rambler*

Example of an 18th-century periodical

(1750) was of the same kind. Of these men, only Defoe resembled fairly closely what we nowadays regard as a journalist as distinct from a man of letters.

The first attempt to reach a mass circulation was made through this kind of periodical by ▷ William Cobbett with his *Weekly Political Register* (started 1802), and in 1808 ▷ Leigh Hunt's weekly *Examiner*, directed to a more educated public though with less remarkable literary merit, began to rival Cobbett's paper as a medium of radical comment and criticism.

Of daily papers founded in the 18th century, the ▷ *Morning Post* (started 1772) survived until 1936, and ▷ *The Times* (started 1785) is today the daily with the greatest prestige, though it has a comparatively small circulation. Other important dailies with a shorter life were the ▷ *Morning Chronicle* (1769–1862), and the ▷ *Morning Herald* (1780–1869). Both reached peak circulations of about 6,000. To reach the very large circulations of today, newspapers had to await the abolition of the stamp duty – a tax on newspapers – in 1855. The Stamp Tax was started in 1712. It was a method of restricting circulations by raising the prices of newspapers. The government of the day resented criticism of its policies but did not dare revive the Licensing Act, the lapsing of which in 1695 was really the start of the British freedom of the press. The abolition of the tax, together with the advent of cheap paper and a nationwide potential public thanks to universal literacy, led to a new kind of newspaper at the end of the 19th century. Alfred and Harold Harmsworth, later Lord Northcliffe and Lord Rothermere, founded the *Daily Mail* in 1896; by 1901 it was selling a million copies. Other popular newspapers followed it with steadily increasing circulations.

Several unfortunate consequences have followed this development:

1 Much ▷ journalism has degenerated into mere commerce, so that news is regarded as what is most saleable, *ie* what appeals most readily to the baser and more easily roused human appetites.

2 Newspapers, in order to keep their prices down, have come to rely on advertising revenue, which is attracted chiefly to those with very large circulations so that some with smaller circulations have been eliminated.

3 The British newspapers have divided rather sharply into the serious ones with a large influence but a small circulation, and the popular ones or tabloids, which often achieve their large circulations by irresponsible appeals to the baser public tastes. Finally, modern newspapers, as great capitalistic enterprises, tend to be right wing politically, so that left-wing opinion is under-represented in the daily press. However, British newspapers are jealous of their independence: they are quick to resist any tendency by the government to check their freedom of expression. Since the war, the Press Council has been established for the purpose of limiting the abuse of this freedom by, for instance, the infringement of personal privacy; however, its powers are limited to public rebuke, and it has no power to penalize or censor newspapers.

The 20th-century weekly reviews have seldom been able to compete with the daily papers in the size of their circulations. However, the strong tradition of weekly journalism inherited from the 18th and 19th centuries ensures that the 'weeklies' have large influence among the intelligentsia. The oldest of the influential weeklies is the *Spectator* which has no connection with Addison's periodical, but was founded in 1828. It is conservative and is counter-balanced by ▷ *The New Statesman and Society* on the left. The most authoritative literary periodical in Britain is *The Times Literary Supplement*, a weekly which is published by *The Times* newspaper.

Newton, Sir Isaac (1642–1727)

Mathematician and natural philosopher. He entered Trinity College, Cambridge, in 1661, became a fellow of the college in 1667, and Professor of Mathematics in the university in 1669. He resigned the professorship in 1701; in 1703 he was made President of the ▷ Royal Society, and was re-elected annually until his death. Queen Anne knighted him in 1705.

His principal work was *Philosophiae Naturalis Principia Mathematica* (1687), written in Latin. By the application of mathematical calculation, it explained the force of mathematical calculation, it explained the force of gravity in its operation through the solar system. His book on *Optics* (1704) was less important, but it aroused new interest in vision and colour and influenced descriptive writing throughout the 18th century. His scientific and mathematical discoveries did not shake his religious convictions, which were very strong, and he also wrote on theology and biblical chronology. On the other hand, he did not understand and had no use for the imaginative faculty, and, like ▷ Locke (whose ▷ *Essay concerning Human Understanding* was published in 1690) he dismissed poetry as an unimportant and irrelevant activity.

Despite this indifference to poetic literature, Newton's discoveries, combined as they were with his religious piety, had a great influence on 18th-century poets. He caused them to revere Reason in both Man and God, who, seen through Newton's writings, became the Divine Artist of the Universe. Pope's *Essay on Man* was a restatement of the traditional vision of the natural order newly shaped to accord with Newton's rational harmony, and it was Pope who composed for Newton the famous epitaph:

> *Nature and Nature's laws lay hid in night:*
> *God said, 'Let Newton be!' and all was Light.*

The most famous poet of the natural scene in the 18th century, ▷ James Thomson, wrote his ▷ *Seasons* in accordance with Newtonian principles. In the revised ▷ *Prelude* (1850) ▷ Wordsworth wrote of the statue in Trinity College:

> *Of Newton with his prism and silent face,*
> *The marble index of a mind for ever*
> *Voyaging through strange seas of Thought, alone.*

Wordsworth thus chooses to emphasize the mysteriousness of science, whereas Pope had emphasized its power to clarify mystery. In general, 19th-century poets, having discovered the force of the irrational in human experience, lost respect for Newton;

for ▷ William Blake he stood for a deathly narrowing of experience:

May God us keep
From Single vision & Newton's sleep!
(Letter to Butts 1802)

Bib: Nicholson, M. H., *Newton Demands the Muse.*

Nicholas, St

An early Christian bishop (early 4th century AD) of Myra in Asia Minor. His festival is celebrated on 6 December. Very little is known of him, but legends accumulated round him, and in the ▷ Middle Ages he became an extremely popular saint. He is supposed to have restored three youths to life after they had been murdered and concealed in a salting tub by an innkeeper. He is also said to have secretly found dowries for three impoverished girls, thus enabling them to marry. The practice grew of secretly giving presents on the eve of his festival. This practice was in time transferred to ▷ Christmas, and St Nicholas was always supposed to be the mysterious giver. In the United States, the Dutch form of his name 'San Nicolaas' was corrupted to 'Santa Claus', but in the England he is identified with 'Father Christmas', although 'Santa Claus' is also used.

Nicholas Nickleby (1838–9)

A novel by ▷ Charles Dickens; like his other novels, it was first published in serial parts. Nicholas, his sister Kate and their mother are left penniless and struggle for a living under the oppressive guardianship of Ralph Nickleby, an avaricious financier, the dead Mr Nickleby's brother. Morally, the tale is in black and white; Nicholas stands for ardent and youthful virtue, Ralph for meanness and cruelty. Nicholas is sent to teach at Dotheboys Hall, an iniquitous school run by Wackford Squeers to whom Nicholas gives a vigorous thrashing. Kate is apprenticed to Madame Mantalini, a dressmaker, where she is exposed to the vicious advances of Ralph's associate, Sir Mulberry Hawk. Nicholas beats him too. Ralph's evil intentions are eventually exposed by his eccentric but right-minded clerk, Newman Noggs, and the Nickleby family are befriended by the Cheeryble brothers. The novel is in Dickens's early, episodic and melodramatic style but many of the episodes are presented with great vividness and comedy. It was dramatized, with huge success, by the ▷ Royal Shakespeare Company in 1980.

Nichols, Grace (b 1950)

Poet and novelist. Born in Guyana, and educated at the University of Guyana, Nichols came to live in Britain in 1977. Her publications include, *I is a Long Memoried Woman* (1983) (which won the Commonwealth Poetry Prize), and *The Fat Back Woman's Poems* (1984). She also writes ▷ children's books.
▷ Commonwealth literature.

Nichols, Peter (b 1927)

British dramatist whose first major success was with *A Day in the Death of Joe Egg* in 1967, a serious comedy about the struggles of a family with a spastic child. This was first seen at the Glasgow Citizens' Theatre and later transferred to London. In 1969 *The National Health* was produced at the ▷ National Theatre. Again Nichols used comedy to dramatize a serious subject, in this case terminal illness and undignified death. His more recent plays are: *Passion Play* (1980); *Poppy*, a musical, (1982); *A Piece of My Mind* (1986).

Nietzsche, Friedrich Wilhelm (1844–1900)

German philosopher. He challenged the concepts of 'the good, the true, and the beautiful' as, in their existing form of abstract values, a decadent system at the mercy of the common man's will to level distinctions of all kinds. He set his hope on the will to power of a new race of men who would assert their own spiritual identities. Among his more famous works are a book on the philosopher Schopenhauer and the composer Wagner, whom he regarded as his own teachers: *Unzeitgemässe Betrachtungen* ('Thoughts out of Season'; 1876); *Die Fröhliche Wissenschaft* ('The Joyful Wisdom'; 1882); *Also sprach Zarathustra* ('Thus spake Zarathustra'; 1891).

Nietzsche was one of the important progenitors of ▷ Existentialism, and he had a considerable influence on some of the major English writers in the first quarter of this century. His ideas inspired ▷ George Bernard Shaw in the latter's belief in the Superman-hero as the spearhead of progress, *eg* his conception of ▷ Joan of Arc in his play *Saint Joan*, and ▷ D. H. Lawrence wrote in Nietzsche's spirit in his affirmation of spontaneous living from deep sources of energy in the individual – human 'disquality' (see ▷ *Women in Love*, ch. 8) as opposed to democratic egalitarianism. The Irish poet ▷ W. B. Yeats also affirmed a natural aristocracy of the human spirit, and saw in Nietzsche a continuation of the message of the poet ▷ William Blake, who preached the transcendence of the human 'identity' over the 'self', which is defined and limited by the material environment. After 1930, Nietzsche's influence declined because he was seen as a prophet of the more vicious forms of ▷ fascism. However, in recent criticism Nietzsche's work has been re-evaluated by ▷ post-structuralist theory, especially with regard to his discussion of ▷ metaphor and ▷ metonymy and the privileging of a rhetorical reading of philosophical texts. ▷ German influence on English literature.

*Night Thoughts on Life, Death, and
   Immortality, The Complaint or*
   ▷ Young, Edward.

Nightingale, Ode to a
   ▷ Odes, Keats's.

Nightmare Abbey (1818)
A novel by ▷ Thomas Love Peacock. It is a satire on the current taste for ▷ Gothic mystery and romantic despair. Mr Glowry and his son Scythrop own the Abbey; Scythrop is in love with two girls, like Peacock's friend, the poet ▷ Shelley. Mr Flosky is a satirical portrait of ▷ Coleridge in his aspect as a transcendental mystic, and Mr Cypress represents ▷ Byron's self-centredness. There are other characters of cheerful temperament to counteract the romantic sombreness of these. The plot is slight, but the comic fantasy is sustained by it and by the conversations which are always the greater part of a Peacock novel.

Nine Worthies
The subject of literary, artistic and dramatic representation from the later medieval period onwards, the so-called 'Nine Worthies' is a group representing the best knights of all time, made up of three figures drawn respectively from the periods of pagan, Old Testament and Christian history. Composition of the list, especially the Christian representatives, may vary somewhat but most of the versions found in England include Hector, ▷ Alexander, Julius Caesar, Joshua, David, Judas Maccabeus, ▷ King Arthur, ▷ Charlemagne, Godfrey of Bouillon. The 'Nine Worthies' theme promotes the notion of chivalry as a transhistorical phenomenon and is part of the developing mythology of ▷ knighthood, in evidence throughout the medieval period (and after). The list of Nine Worthies is first recorded in an Old French Alexander narrative of the early 14th century; it features in the Middle English poem, the alliterative ▷ *Morte Arthur*, and in ▷ Caxton's preface to the ▷ *Morte D'Arthur*. A

dramatized pageant of the 'Nine Worthies' is included in ▷ Shakespeare's ▷ *Love's Labours Lost*.

Nineteenth century in English literature
The period opened with a great revival of poetic expression. The first generation of the new poets – ▷ William Blake, ▷ William Wordsworth, ▷ Samuel Taylor Coleridge – all began under the inspiration of deep spiritual and social disturbances, the historical manifestation of which was the ▷ French Revolution. Against this Wordsworth and Coleridge reacted in disillusionment when they saw it transformed by ▷ Napoleon Bonaparte. On the other hand, the second generation of poets – ▷ Lord Byron, ▷ P. B. Shelley, ▷ John Keats (he was the least touched by politics) felt the bitterness of anticlimax after the overthrow of Napoleon in 1815 and intensely resented the restoration of the old oppressive regimes. These six poets differed from one another greatly, although all except Blake felt the influence of Wordsworth, and they were not, except for Byron, amongst the most popular. Several of the more popular ones are now almost forgotten, *eg* ▷ Thomas Moore; ▷ Walter Scott is more remembered for his novels but his poetry is important in that he did most to express the new liberation of feeling through old ▷ ballad styles and in medieval settings. ▷ George Crabbe continued 18th-century poetic style with a 19th-century awareness of the common people and sensitiveness to the influence of environment.

But a sharp change occurred in the dominant form of literary expression after 1830. Despite the popularity of the poetry of ▷ Alfred Tennyson in the mid-century and (later) that of ▷ Robert Browning, it was the novel, particularly adapted as it was to the rapid social transformations of the ▷ Industrial Revolution, which became the representative medium. 1830 marks the beginning of the career of ▷ Charles Dickens and his lifetime was almost to coincide with the first phase of the English novel; in addition to himself, the leading names are ▷ George Eliot, ▷ Emily Brontë, ▷ Charlotte Brontë and ▷ William Makepeace Thackeray. Novelists of marked talent but lesser rank include ▷ Elizabeth Gaskell, ▷ Anthony Trollope and ▷ Benjamin Disraeli. The last quarter of the century saw the second phase of the novel in ▷ Henry James and ▷ Joseph Conrad, who wrote with much more awareness of foreign influences; with their more radical questioning of social and cultural assumptions they became also the first important figures of the 20th-century novel. ▷ Thomas Hardy is almost as prominent a figure but as a regional novelist he stands apart from the other two, who were notably cosmopolitan: his insight is profound but, in his best work, it is expressed through a specific environment.

An important aspect of 19th-century literature is its autobiographical inclination. Some outstanding works during the century were autobiographies (*eg* ▷ Thomas De Quincey's ▷ *Confessions of an English Opium-Eater*) but the tendency was even more important as a diffused approach to imaginative art, in poetry (*eg* Wordsworth's ▷ *Prelude*) and in the novel (*eg* Charlotte Brontë's ▷ *Villette*). This may account for the increase in women novelists of the period; ▷ feminist criticism often argues for the attraction of autobiography to women writers as an expression of freedom. It was, if anything, even more important in non-fictional prose, both that of the early 19th-century periodical essayists such as ▷ William Hazlitt and ▷ Charles Lamb, and that of the Victorian 'sages' – the polemicists of the middle and later century, who commonly expressed their deep concern with society (its changes, and its dangers and potentiality for the human consciousness) in autobiographical and semi-autobiographical form. Examples are Carlyle's ▷ *Sartor Resartus*, ▷ John Newman's ▷ *Apologia* and ▷ John Stuart Mill's *Autobiography*. The autobiographical habit of mind is bound up with great changes in prevailing attitudes to the nature of the human personality but the literary practice derives from a French 18th-century work, the *Confessions* of ▷ Rousseau.

19th-century literary criticism also shows urgent concern with the social and spiritual questions of the age. The most important critics are Wordsworth, Coleridge (whose chief critical work is characteristically in part autobiography – ▷ *Biographia Literaria*) and ▷ Matthew Arnold. By the end of the century, Henry James had become the first important systematic critic of the novel.

It is common to think of the 19th century as the century of ▷ Romanticism in contrast to the 18th century as the 'Age of Reason'. This is too simple, however. Firstly, Romanticism had its beginnings in the 18th century; secondly, continuity with 18th-century ▷ rationalism was an important aspect of 19th-century thought and feeling, *eg* in ▷ Utilitarianism; and finally, Romanticism is a difficult term in relation to English literature and needs separate treatment.

▷ Autobiography; Victorian period.

Nineteenth Century, The
A monthly review founded in 1877 by J. T. Knowles, its first editor. It was renamed *The Nineteenth Century and After* in 1900, and *The Twentieth Century* in 1950. It was distinguished for bringing together leading antagonists of opposing views. Contributors included ▷ Ruskin, ▷ Gladstone, ▷ T. H. Huxley, ▷ Beatrice Webb, ▷ William Morris, ▷ Ouida and ▷ Oscar Wilde.

Nineties Poets
The group of poets centred around the Rhymer's Club in the 1890s, including Lionel Johnson (1867–1902), Ernest Dowson (1867–1900) and Arthur Symons (1865–1945). The Rhymer's Club met at the Cheshire Cheese café in Fleet Street, immortalized by ▷ W. B. Yeats in *The Trembling of the Veil* and 'The Grey Rock,' and published two volumes of its members' verse in 1891 and 1894. Nineties poetry was part of the *fin-de-siècle* ▷ Aesthetic movement. Strongly influenced by French (▷ French literature in England) culture and particularly French ▷ Symbolist poetry, it was also a development of the work and ideas of ▷ Algernon Swinburne, ▷ Walter Pater and the ▷ Pre-Raphaelite Brotherhood. The confessional and decadent quality of their work, together with the incidence of untimely death in their lives, led Yeats to label them 'The Tragic Generation' in his *Autobiographies*. They were important in their influence on poets like Yeats and ▷ Ezra Pound. Much of their work was published in the journals ▷ *The Yellow Book* and *The Savoy* (which Symons edited). **Bib**: Stanford, D., *Poets of the Nineties*; Thornton, R. K. R., *Poetry of the 'Nineties*.

No Wit No Help Like a Woman (1613)
A high-spirited comedy by ▷ Thomas Middleton which evolves on a complex double-plot level and reworks material from ▷ Ben Jonson's ▷ *Epicoene* and ▷ Shakespeare's ▷ *Twelfth Night*. The play's heroine, Kate Low-water, a disguised married woman intent on recovering her lost fortune, is one of the most charismatic female characters in the drama of the period. The extent to which the play's idiom of mercenary ▷ citizen comedy becomes submerged in Shakespearean romance depends largely on Kate's magnetic personality.

Noble (coin)
A former gold coin first issued in the 14th century. It was engraved with the image of the king (originally ▷ Edward III) in a ship. Its value was 33p. Edward IV reissued it with

'The Queen's Croquet Party', Carroll's original sketch from *Alice's Adventures Underground*

the new design of the archangel Michael killing a dragon, and it became known as the Angel-noble or Angel. He also issued a new coin, worth 50p, adding a Yorkist rose to the old design of the king and ship; this was called the Rose-noble.

Noh plays
A kind of drama practised in Japan since the 15th century. It is highly formal, austere, and ritualistic, making a great part of its effect through ▷ symbolism. Its artistic economy and symbolism have greatly interested some Western writers in the 20th century – see the book *Noh, or Accomplishment* by Fenollosa and ▷ Pound. The poet ▷ W. B. Yeats imitated the form in some of his experiments to revive the verse drama, *eg At the Hawk's Well* (1917).

Nokes, James (d 1696)
Actor. Nokes performed briefly at the Cockpit in Drury Lane, largely in women's roles, before joining the ▷ Duke's Company under ▷ William D'Avenant in 1660 as actor and shareholder. He usually played in low and crude comic roles, specializing as foolish old husbands, nurses, and fops.

Nominalism
One of the two main schools of late medieval philosophy, the other being ▷ Realism. The nominalists argued that terms naming things according to their kinds ('animal', 'vegetable', etc) and abstract terms ('beauty', 'goodness', etc) are merely names describing the qualities of things and do not refer to things that have

reality in themselves. The realists argued that on the contrary such 'universals' alone have an ultimate reality and that the reality of individual objects depends upon them. The nominalist viewpoint is represented in modern philosophy by such thinkers as ▷ John Stuart Mill and other 'empiricist' philosophers who reason that reality can only be known by particular experience of it, and argue against any theory of implanted ideas such as the Deists believed in.
Bib: Knowles, D., *The Evolution of Medieval Thought*; Leff, G., *Medieval Thought: St Augustine to Ockham*.
▷ Deism; Ockham, William of.

Nonconformists
▷ Dissenters; Puritanism.

Nonsense literature
This covers several kinds of literature, which have in common that they all in some way deliberately defy logic or common sense, or both. In English folk literature, many ▷ nursery rhymes come into the category. The most important kind, however, is undoubtedly in ▷ children's literature, especially the poems of ▷ Edward Lear and the *Alice* stories by ▷ Lewis Carroll, both of which are to be taken seriously as literature. Both writers are ▷ Victorian and this perhaps accounts for their imaginative depth; they wrote in a period of intense mental restlessness before the time of ▷ Freud and thus they gave themselves wholly to their fantasies, undisturbed by the idea that they might be betraying secrets of

their own nature. Modern writers, *eg* ▷ James Joyce in his ▷ *Finnegans Wake*, will as fearlessly reveal their depths, but it will not be to children. Another reason why nonsense literature reached its peak in the Victorian period is perhaps that this was almost the earliest period when intelligent minds considered that children were worth writing for merely in order to amuse them, and not to elevate their minds. 20th-century writers in plenty have thought children worth amusing but the child-public is now a recognized one, whereas Lear and Carroll wrote for a few young friends; they were thus as much concerned with their own interest and amusement as with that of their audience.

Norman Conquest, The
    ▷ Conquest, The (Norman).

North and South (1854–5)
A novel by ▷ Elizabeth Gaskell published serially (1854–5) by ▷ Charles Dickens in his periodical ▷ *Household Words*. The heroine, Margaret Hale, moves from the rural south of England to the industrial north, Lancashire. The sharp contrast between the two halves of England is equalled by the misunderstandings and savage opposition between employers and employees in the northern town. Margaret becomes involved in the affairs of one of the employers, John Thornton, with whom she too has deep misunderstanding. Suffering eventually brings them together and teaches Thornton the necessity of treating his workers as human beings and not merely as factors in industrial calculation. Like her earlier ▷ *Mary Barton*, this novel is a courageous penetration of the industrial jungle which she knew at first hand; both are attempts, like Dickens's ▷ *Hard Times*, to modify the harshness of the industrial world with humane values.

North Briton, The
It was a radical political weekly, started in 1762 by ▷ John Wilkes and Charles Churchill. It opposed the government of ▷ George III and his Prime Minister, the Scotsman Lord Bute, and was aimed particularly against Bute's journal *The Briton*, edited by the Scottish novelist, ▷ Tobias Smollett. After 45 issues it was suppressed.

North, Sir Thomas (?1535–?1601)
Translator. He is especially known as the translator of ▷ Plutarch's *Lives* of the ancient Greek and Roman heroes. The translation was from the French of Amyot, and was published in 1579. It was not close, but very clear and vigorous, and constituted one of the masterpieces of English prose. It was widely read in ▷ Shakespeare's day, and was used by Shakespeare himself as the basis for his plays ▷ *Julius Caesar*, ▷ *Antony and Cleopatra*, and ▷ *Coriolanus*. Other translations by him were: the *Dial of Princes* (from *Reloj de Príncipes* by Guevara) published in 1557, which set the fashion for ornate writing culminating in ▷ Lyly's ▷ *Euphues*; and ▷ *The Moral Philosophy of Doni* (1570), an Italian collection of eastern fables.

Northanger Abbey (1818)
A novel by ▷ Jane Austen. It was started in 1798 and incompletely revised when it was published (in 1818 after her death) with her last completed novel ▷ *Persuasion*.

The book is in part a satire on the sensational and sentimental literature of the time, particularly of the enormously popular ▷ *Mysteries of Udolpho* by ▷ Mrs Radcliffe. The heroine is an ingenuous young girl, Catherine Morland, who visits the fashionable resort of Bath and afterwards, with some friends she has made there, the country house of Northanger Abbey. She is healthy-minded and trusting but very suggestible; on the one hand she is entirely deceived by the worldly flattery of her scheming friend, Isabella Thorpe, who tries to marry Catherine's brother under the mistaken impression that he is very rich, and on the other hand she suspects (under the influence of Mrs Radcliffe's novel) that Northanger Abbey conceals terrible secrets. Its owner, General Tilney, is the father of the man she loves and is in fact almost as cold-hearted and inhumane as she suspects him of being, but in quite a different way; he has not, as she at first suspected, murdered his wife, but he turns Catherine out of the house at very short notice from purely mercenary motives. The theme of the book is partly the danger of confusing literature and life, a theme to which Jane Austen returns in ▷ *Sense and Sensibility* and ▷ *Emma*; it is also that life is as surprising and remorseless as the most romantic literature but in quite a different way.

Northcliffe, Alfred Harmsworth, Viscount (1865–1922)
One of the principal founders of the 'popular press' with its very large circulation, and in particular of the *Daily Mail* (1896).
    ▷ Newspapers.

North-West Passage
In the reign of ▷ Queen Elizabeth I English trade with Eastern Asia through the Indian and the Pacific Oceans was made difficult by

opposition from England's national enemies, especially Spain. It was believed that a practicable passage existed by sea to the north of North America. Several attempts were made in Elizabeth's reign without success. When the route was discovered in the 19th century it was found to be commercially useless.

Nostromo (1904)

A novel by ▷ Joseph Conrad. The setting is an imaginary South American state called Costaguana, intended to be typical of that continent; all the events occur in or near Sulaco, capital city of the Occidental Province in Costaguana. At the beginning of the novel, Costaguana is ruled by a brutal and corrupt dictator after a short period of enlightened and liberal rule. The Occidental Province, however, remains a refuge of enlightenment and comparative prosperity, thanks partly to its geographical isolation from the rest of the country, and mainly to the existence of a large silver mine, run by an Englishman, Charles Gould, who secures the financial support of an American millionaire. In outline, the story is the history of how the Occidental Republic establishes its independence of the rest of the country, but at the same time loses the ideals which inspired it in the struggle.

Each of five main characters serves as a focus for a strand of narrative:

1 Charles Gould (nicknamed 'King of Sulaco'), in his struggles to save the mine from ruin by the corrupt government, becomes the centre of the party of freedom and justice; but he becomes increasingly dehumanized by his preoccupations, and estranged from his wife, whose values of humaneness and compassion are betrayed, despite the eventual triumph of her husband's party.

2 Captain Mitchell, the Harbourmaster, is another Englishman; stupid, but honest and courageous, he is unable to see beneath the surface of events, and is used by Conrad to record these deceptive appearances.

3 Gian'Battista Fidanza, the Italian chief of the dockworkers, is universally known as 'Nostromo' ('Our Man'). He has a romantic pride in the devotion of his men, and in the knowledge that Mitchell, Gould, and their associates have complete confidence in his integrity. His spiritual downfall, unknown to any but himself, is due to his desire to preserve the appearance of integrity while yielding to secret dishonesty.

4 Martin Decoud is the journalist of the Sulacan revolution; he is totally French by education and culture, though not by descent. He is cynically entertained by the spectacle of Costaguaneran politics, but romantically attached to Antonia Avellanos, daughter of José, a Sulacan scholar and liberal politician. He dies of the physical isolation brought upon him by circumstances, since his highly cultivated consciousness is incapable of sustaining a sense of his own reality when the spectacle of events and the woman he loves are removed from him.

5 Dr Monygham is an Irishman, embittered by his self-contempt arising from his betrayal, under torture, of his political associates. His humanity is preserved by his devotion to Mrs Gould, who is for him the uncontaminated embodiment of what is good in human nature.

These are only the chief characters, and they do not exhaust the novel's large cast. They are united by the theme of individual isolation even in co-operation with one another, and by a discrete pattern of symbols, of which the chief is the silver of the mine. This operates at first as an instrument of liberation, and later as a force of corruption; all the time it is a symbol of the illusiveness of human idealism. The novel depicts the pervasive and debasing effects of 'material interests' (primarily the economic power of U.S. business). The narrative structure is highly complex, and uses shifts of chronology and retrospective narration to combine a detailed account of 17 days of crisis with a sense of the broad sweep of historical events.

Nouveau roman (new novel)

A French literary movement originating in the late 1950s and associated principally with Nathalie Sarraute (b 1902), Claude Simon (b 1913), Michel Butor (b 1926), Robert Pinget (b 1919) and Alain Robbe-Grillet (b 1922). Their common concern was a challenge to narrative assumptions based on strictures of the orderly unfolding of plot and life-like characters moving in a recognizable universe. These assumptions, however widely held, suppose that literature is mimetic, that it imitates life. The *nouveau roman* set out to challenge the illusion of reference (that the novel 'refers' to life) insofar as reference is tied to representation. It held that the so-called naturalness of narrative was a set of artifices to which we had become accustomed and that narrative order and significance were an illusion fostered by the omniscient author. For the 'new' novelists, representation is not an *a priori* given; it is produced. Drawing on the work of ▷ André Gide and ▷ Marcel Proust, notably Gide's *mise en abyme* technique, the *nouveau roman* will therefore expose its own means of production and raise the problem of its own narrative existence. Correspondingly, the role of the reader is also revised. He or she is called upon to co-author the text, to act not as a passive recipient of information, but as an active producer of meanings. Indeed, given the fragmentary or elliptical nature of *nouveau roman* narrative presentation, the reader's active endeavours are an inevitability. The author is thus not the final guarantor of meaning and the reader's search for meaning is often thematized as an (impossible) attempt to solve an enigma (the *nouveau roman* frequently adopts the detective story format).

The impact of the *nouveau roman* was greatly magnified by the fact that the practice of novel writing was accompanied by thorough-going critical reflection on that practice. The novelists themselves were also heavily engaged in theory and frequently worked alongside professional academic theoreticians or were allied to magazines such as ▷ *Tel Quel*. Of the original group of new novelists, Robbe-Grillet and Simon are still strong practitioners. While the mainstream of the English novel has been little affected, the techniques of the *nouveau roman* have influenced writers such as ▷ Christine Brooke-Rose and ▷ Brigid Brophy. In the 1970s there emerged the new new novel (*nouveau nouveau roman*), centring on the novelist and theorist Philippe Sollers (b 1936) and displaying many of the traits of ▷ deconstructive and post-structuralist principles.

Bib: Robbe-Grillet, A., *Pour un Nouveau Roman*.

Nouveaux Philosophes, Les

A title coined by the magazine *Les Nouvelles littéraires* in June 1976 to describe a group of writers among whom the most prominent are André Glucksmann (*Les Maîtres penseurs*, 1977; reviewed by Michel Foucault) and Bernard-Henri Lévy (*La Barbarie à visage humain*, 1977; *L'Idéologie française*, 1981). The group combined certain traits of Foucault and ▷ Jacques Lacan (often simplified and distorted) with right-wing views – hostility to ▷ Marxism, vague spiritual yearning and finding the source of all value in the individual. As a group, their influence was at its height in the late 1970s and is now played out (it was in any case media-promoted), but Glucksmann and Lévy are still well-known.

Novella

A long short story or short novel, such as ▷ Joseph Conrad's ▷ *Heart of Darkness* (1902), or ▷ Henry James's *The Aspern Papers* (1888).

Novum Organum (1620)

A philosophical treatise by ▷ Francis Bacon, the *Novum Organum (New Instrument)* was written in Latin, and published in the ▷ *Instauratio Magna* (1620) in an incomplete form. His aim was to describe a method of gaining power over nature through a complete and correctly founded system of knowledge. Knowledge must be acquired by experience and experiment, *ie* inductively. The obstacles to true knowledge are false assumptions which Bacon calls 'Idols'. These are of four kinds: the Idols of the Tribe are common human weaknesses such as allowing the emotions to interfere with the reason; the Idols of the Cave are individual weaknesses arising from individual upbringing; Idols of the Market-place arise from erroneous uses of language, such as using names for non-existent things, or for concepts which have been inadequately defined; Idols of the Theatre are caused by false philosophical principles and by incorrect reasoning. The object of speculative science must be to discover the true 'forms' of things, beginning with the forms of 'simple natures', *ie* the true manifestations of the most elemental phenomena such as heat and light. By inductive experiment certain axioms will be made of increasing generality and abstractness. Thus Bacon sought a method of recognizing what he called 'an alphabet of nature' so that a reliable language could be built up from it. The method of discovery proved too slow to be scientifically useful in the coming centuries, but his approach was a development from the too exclusively deductive methods of medieval thought towards the modern scientific combination of deduction and experiment.

Nuclear energy and weapons

The first half of the 20th century saw a series of stupendous discoveries in physics. Albert Einstein (1879–1955) was perhaps the most famous of many great people involved. The discoveries altered many of the ideas formerly considered definite and immutable; time could be altered with speed, mass could be changed into energy, and so on. This was merely abstract theory to most of the population until 1945 when atom bombs were exploded over Hiroshima and Nagasaki. The atom bombs were regarded as a great development by some, by others as a terrible warning of the future. Initially the U.S.A. and Britain had a monopoly of the technology but it was only a few years before the U.S.S.R. had exploded its own atomic bombs and then the more advanced and powerful hydrogen bombs. Gradually it came to be realized that the bombs created more than energy: radioactive contamination was released, capable on the one hand of affecting people in the first few days or weeks and on the other of creating long-term genetic damage or cancers which would not be revealed for many years.

Nuclear power

After World War II there was enormous enthusiasm for the utilizing of nuclear energy, the turning of swords into ploughshares, and Britain and the U.S.A. rapidly became involved in this, with the ancillary aim of creating the correct materials for their bombs. The use of nuclear energy was expected to be cheap and clean; the reality is less clear. Costs are hard to determine, being inextricably connected with weapon programmes and also with the governments' wish to promote a new technology. Little thought was given until quite late in the development of nuclear power about how to dispose of the waste products: far from being clean it produces extremely hazardous by-products. The shortage of conventional fuel in the mid-1970s led to rapid building programmes in many parts of the world, not least in the U.S.A., and although the technology attempted to meet every contingency, it was, almost inevitably, flawed. After a well publicized accident in the U.S.A. at Three-Mile Island in 1979 (in which no one was seriously hurt and little if any radioactive material escaped) the American programme of nuclear building was doomed: the incident revealed that despite all the care, accidents could still happen. Other countries did not respond to the incident with the same decisiveness and outside the U.S.A. the building of nuclear power plants continued, even in countries where there is no reason to believe safety standards will be high. In 1986 a reactor in Chernobyl in the U.S.S.R. exploded, releasing vast amounts of radioactivity into the atmosphere and causing certain produce to be unsafe for human consumption as far away as Britain. Although it was possible to point to special failings in the Soviet designs and operating procedures, it nevertheless incurred widespread doubts about nuclear power throughout the world. It was also instrumental in revealing hitherto suppressed facts: it was learned that the British nuclear programme had had a serious fire and release of nuclear radiation in the 1950s but at that time official secrecy had hidden

from the public the true scale and seriousness of the event.

The threat of nuclear war and the guilt associated with the capacity to produce such destruction have been powerful influences on imaginative writing since 1945. Fear, too, of a governmental secrecy which jeopardizes the lives of its citizens and of the world in the interests of power politics, as well as fantasies of life after the Bomb, are common themes. See Nevil Shute's *On The Beach* (1957), Russell Hoban's *Riddley Walker* (1980) and the films *Silkwood* (1983) and *Defence of the Realm* (1985).

Nuns and Nunneries

Monastic orders in the Middle Ages had female as well as male branches; most English nuns belonged to the ▷ Benedictine Order. They lived in 'nunneries', later increasingly known as 'convents', though originally a convent might house either sex. They were ruled by elected prioresses or abbesses. Until the 14th century nuns were usually from aristocratic families; among the lower classes it was generally possible for a woman to work; but in the upper classes, a nunnery was the only alternative to marriage. Before the ▷ Norman Conquest (1066) nunneries compared with monasteries as places of learning, but afterwards the nuns were seldom learned, though they excelled in such accomplishments as embroidery. From the 14th century merchants' daughters as well as girls from noble families were increasingly admitted. Nunneries were sometimes used as places of confinement for girls who refused to marry the husbands of their parents' choice, etc. Manual work was neglected from the 13th century and conducted by lay servants, as in monasteries, but nunneries sometimes ran small schools for the children of well-to-do families. Nuns who wished to live a life dedicated to solitary meditation were called 'anchoresses'; such was the mystical writer ▷ Juliana of Norwich. The number of nuns probably never exceeded 2,000.

Nun's Priest Tale, The

One of ▷ Chaucer's ▷ *Canterbury Tales*. The Nun's Priest, who is barely mentioned in the General Prologue, contributes a brilliant animal fable to the competition which greatly amplifies the traditional story of the cock who is captured by the fox, but who manages to escape by exploiting the fox's pride in his achievement. The story has analogues in ▷ Marie de France's collection of fables, and in the 13th-century beast epic, the *Roman de Renart* (▷ Reynard the Fox), but Chaucer's version is distinguished by its

Simon was sent to market,
To buy a joint of meat,
He tied it to his horse's tail,
To keep it clean and sweet.

He went for water in a seive,
But soon it all run through,
And went all o'er his clothes,
Which made poor Simon rue.

He went to slide upon the ice,
Before the ice would bear,
Then he plunged in above his knees,
Which made poor Simon stare.

He washed himself with blacking ball,
Because he had no soap,
And then said to his mother
I'm a beauty now I hope.

He went to shoot a wild duck,
But the duck flew away,
Says Simon I can't hit him,
Because he would not stay.

He went to eat some honey,
Out of the mustard pot,
It bit his tongue until he cried,
That was all the good he got.

Then Simple Simon went a hunting,
For to catch a hare,
He rode an ass about the street,
But could not find one there.

Simple Simon cutting his mother's bellows open to see where the wind lay.

Illustrated nursery rhymes

enormous build-up to the fox's assault. Much of the early section of the *Tale* is taken up with an argument over the value of dreams between Chauntecleer, the cock, and his hen-consort, Pertelote, which is prompted by the cock's dream of being attacked by a large red animal. Problems about how to extract meaning from dream narratives, raised in their debate, are relevant to the *Tale* as a whole, which ends with a challenge to the reader to extract the moral 'fruit' from this brilliantly inflated, mock-heroic animal fable.

Nurseries
Training establishments for actors and actresses in the ▷ Restoration period.

Nursery Rhymes
A body of folk verse, some of it very ancient, some of it being concealed comment on political events, some of it apparently never having had any meaning.

Nut-Brown Maid, The
A 15th-century anonymous poem, first printed in 1502. It is in 30 12-line stanzas, spoken by a young man and woman alternately, with the respective refrains 'Alone a banished man' and 'I love but you alone', and their debate focusses on the faithfulness of women. Although the woman believes her lover to be an outlaw, she remains true. The poem was included in ▷ *Percy's Reliques*, and later paraphrased by ▷ Matthew Prior, in a very different poetic style, in *Henry and Emma*.

Nymph
In Greek myth the nymphs were a race of minor female deities, often attendant on the major deities of both sexes. The word derives from the Greek for marriageable woman, and nymphs seem to have been associated with fertility. They were subdivided according to their various habitats: Naiads belonged to rivers, springs and lakes; Oceanids or Nereids lived in the sea; Oreads inhabited mountains and rocky places; Dryads and Hamadryads, forests and trees.

O

Oates, Titus (1649–1705)

An English conspirator. He was the son of a ▷ Puritan preacher, and himself professed to stand for the defence of ▷ Protestantism against supposed Catholic dangers, but he was really a disreputable adventurer who used the religious passions of the time for his personal advantage. In 1678 he fabricated the Popish Plot, by which he pretended without factual basis to expose a Catholic conspiracy against the ▷ Church of England. Popular suspicion of ▷ Charles II, and the fact that the Queen and his brother James were avowed Roman Catholics, caused a national panic, and a large number of Catholics were put to death. His evidence was eventually proved false, and he was imprisoned. He is satirized under the name of Corah in Dryden's ▷ *Absolom and Achitophel* and occurs in ▷ Scott's novel *Peveril of the Peak* (1822).

Oberon

In Germanic myth, king of the elves, or fairies. A French 13th-century Romance, *Huon of Bordeaux*, in which he occurs, was translated into English in 1534. From this ▷ Robert Greene introduced him into his romantic play ▷ *James IV* (1594), and ▷ Shakespeare into his comedy ▷ *A Midsummer Night's Dream*. He was used thereafter in a number of works, including a ▷ masque by ▷ Ben Jonson and the poem ▷ *Nymphidia* by ▷ Michael Drayton.
▷ Fairies.

Objective correlative

An expression first used by the critic and poet ▷ T. S. Eliot, in his essay on ▷ *Hamlet* (1919). Eliot describes Shakespeare's play as an artistic failure because it 'is full of some stuff that the writer could not drag to life, contemplate, or manipulate into art'. He goes on: 'The only way of expressing emotion in the form of art is by finding an "objective correlative"; in other words, a set of objects, a situation, a chain of events which shall be the formula of that *particular* emotion; such that when the external facts . . . are given, the emotion is immediately evoked'. He then instances the sleep-walking scene in ▷ *Macbeth* as a successful 'objective correlative', and adds: 'The artistic "inevitability" lies in this complete adequacy of the external (*ie* the event on the stage is witnessed by the audience) to the emotion; and this is precisely what is deficient in *Hamlet*.'

Eliot's adverse judgment of *Hamlet* has not been widely accepted, but the term 'objective correlative' has passed into critical currency.

O'Brien, Edna (b 1932)

Edna O'Brien

Novelist and short-story writer, born in County Clare, Ireland. Novels include: *The Country Girls* (1960); *The Lonely Girl* (1962) (as *Girl With Green Eyes*, 1964); *Girls in Their Married Bliss* (1964); *August is a Wicked Month* (1965); *Casualties of Peace* (1967); *A Pagan Place* (1970); *Night* (1972); *Johnny I Hardly Knew You* (1977); *The High Road* (1988). Her novels are concerned primarily with women's experience of loss, guilt and self-division; they are characterized by a certain lyricism and nostalgia, combined with a detached humour which has become more bitter as her work has developed.

Her first three novels form a trilogy about the lives of two contrasted women, and use a realistic mode which is replaced by internal monologues in some of her later work. Her style is very effective in the short-story form: *The Love Object* (1968); *A Scandalous Woman* (1974); *Mrs Reinhardt* (1978); *Returning* (1982); *A Fanatic Heart: Selected Stories* (1984). She has also written plays, screenplays and T.V. plays.

Observer, The

A ▷ newspaper published only on Sundays, started in 1792. It is central in its politics, and aims to appeal to the thoughtful, better-educated public.

O'Casey, Sean (1880–1964)

Irish dramatist best known for his three plays about tenement life in Dublin around the time of Irish independence in 1921. These were first performed at the ▷ Abbey Theatre: *The Shadow of a Gunman* (1923), *Juno and the Paycock* (1924) and *The Plough and the Stars* (1926). The last of these was greeted with a riot on its opening night. His next play, *The Silver Tassie* (1928), was an anti-heroic piece which experimented with expressionistic techniques. The play was rejected for performance at the Abbey by ▷ W. B. Yeats. After this O'Casey lived in England in self-imposed exile until his death. With *The Star Turns Red* (1940), *Purple Dust* (1940), *Red Roses for Me* (1943), *Oak Leaves and Lavender* (1947), *Cock-a-Doodle Dandy* (1949) and *The Bishop's Bonfire* (1961), he continued experimenting with non-naturalistic theatrical devices. These later plays deserve greater recognition than they have been given to date.

▷ Irish Literature.

Bib: Kosok, H., *O'Casey the Dramatist*; Krause, D., *Sean O'Casey: The Man and His Work*.

Ockham (Occam), William of (?1300–?1349)

Philosopher and ▷ Franciscan friar. He was one of the leaders of the Nominalist school of philosophy, according to which individual things were considered to be real, but the names for kinds and classes referred to qualities of individuals only, and not to independent realities. This prepared the way for the thought of ▷ Francis Bacon which was in itself the starting point of modern scientific thinking, since Ockham's ideas implied building generalizations from the knowledge of individual objects instead of arguing from pre-established generalizations, as the more typically medieval Realists had reasoned.

The principle known as 'Ockham's Razor' lays down that 'entities' must not be unnecessarily invented, implying that abstractions must be somehow proved to have a necessary relationship with known realities. The principle makes for exact thinking, and also for scepticism. He went so far as to say that the existence of God could not be proved, though he did not mean by this that God did not exist.

▷ Nominalism; Realism.

O'Connor, Frank (pen name of Michael O'Donovan) (1903–66)

Irish writer, especially famous for his short stories. He was born in Cork, received little education, and for some time worked as a librarian in Cork and Dublin. He was encouraged to write by the Irish poet A E (George Russell), and his publisher, Harold Macmillan (later the English Conservative Party leader) influenced him in deciding for a literary career. He participated in the Irish

Rebellion after World War I. His first volume of short stories, *Guests of the Nation*, was published in 1931. Other volumes are: *Bone of Contention* (1936), *Three Tales* (1941), *Crab Apple Jelly* (1944), *The Common Chord* (1948), *Traveller's Samples* (1951), *My Oedipus Complex* (1963). His translations of poetry and legends from the Irish are also famous: *A Golden Treasury of Irish Poetry* (1967). He wrote two novels which have less repute than his short stories: *The Saint and Mary Kate* (1932) and *Dutch Interior* (1966). His critical works include one of the best studies of the art of the short story, *The Lonely Voice*, and a study of the novel, *The Mirror in the Roadway*. He also published two volumes of an uncompleted autobiography, *An Only Child* and *My Father's Son*. From 1952 he taught in an American university.

O'Connor's stories are remarkable for their insight, comedy, pathos and compassion. His field was the lower ranges of Irish society, which he understood profoundly, and which he universalized by his generous intelligence and sympathies in a way that recalls Chekhov's treatment of Russian life.

Bib: Sheehy, Maurice (ed.), *Michael/Frank*.

Octavia

Half-sister of Octavius Caesar, who became the first Roman Emperor, ▷ Augustus (ruled 27 BC–AD 14) She married her brother's rival, Mark Antony, and occurs as a character in ▷ Shakespeare's tragedy ▷ *Antony and Cleopatra* and in Dryden's tragedy ▷ *All For Love*.

Ode

The Pindaric Ode is modelled on the works of ▷ Pindar, a Greek poet of the 5th century BC, best known for his odes celebrating the victors at the Olympic games. These were accompanied by music and dance, and were disposed in a threefold pattern corresponding to the movements of the Greek dramatic chorus (*strophe*, *antistrophe*, *epode*). From the 17th century onwards English poets took Pindar as a model for lyric and declamatory verse expressive of high-wrought emotion. ▷ Thomas Gray's *Progress of Poesy* follows Pindar's stanza forms with scholarly exactness, but ▷ Abraham Cowley had earlier established the more usual 'irregular ode', which sanctions unpredictable variations in line-length, rhyme and ▷ metre within each stanza. Early examples of this form are ▷ John Dryden's *Alexander's Feast* and *Ode to the Memory of Anne Killigrew*. 'Pindarics' remained popular throughout the 18th century and became a natural vehicle for the new ▷ 'romantick' sensibility. Gray's use of them in ▷ *The Bard* and *The Progress of Poesy*, for all its scholarly meticulousness, is intended to sound bold and inspirational. The form remains essentially the same in such ▷ romantic works as ▷ William Wordsworth's ▷ *Ode: Intimations of Immortality* and ▷ Samuel Taylor Coleridge's ▷ *Dejection*, though by now it has lost its classical, 'Pindaric' associations, and is fully naturalized.

The Roman poet ▷ Horace imitated Pindar, but his odes employ unvarying stanza forms. The 'regular' Horatian ode was imitated by ▷ Andrew Marvell in his *Horatian Ode upon Cromwell's Return from Ireland*, and by ▷ William Collins in *How Sleep the Brave* and *To Simplicity*. ▷ John Keats's Odes, with their long and complex, but regular stanzas, lie somewhere between the Pindaric and Horatian form.

Odes, Keats's

▷ John Keats's six Odes: *On Indolence, On a Grecian Urn, On Melancholy, To Psyche, To a Nightingale,* and *To Autumn,* were all written in 1819. They are in regular stanzaic form, but the length of stanza and complexity of rhyme-scheme recalls the freer Pindaric tradition of the ▷ ode. They constitute the most complex expression of Keats's aestheticist approach to life. In each poem a celebration of sensuous beauty of the material world is rendered the more intensely poignant by an acknowledgement of transience and decay.

On a Grecian Urn and *To a Nightingale* are companion pieces, one concerned with Art, the other with Nature. Both urn and bird persuade the poet for a while that their beauty is permanent. The urn's message to Man is 'Beauty is truth, truth beauty', and the Nightingale seems an 'immortal bird', 'not born for death'. However the urn's comfort remains on its beautiful surface. Though a 'friend to man' it is a 'Cold Pastoral'. The beautiful figures depicted upon it, preserved from time by art, can never reachieve the trembling elusive life which they possessed when really alive. Their death and distance is paradoxically only accentuated by Keats's ecstatic, even hectic, celebration of its artistic immortality. Similarly, the nightingale's song, though unchanged through history, fades as the particular bird to which he is listening flies away, and Keats is returned to his 'sole self', admitting that 'the fancy cannot cheat so well/ As she is fam'd to do, deceiving elf'.

The Ode to Autumn contains no explicit philosophizing, and seems purely descriptive. It provides, however, an emotional answer to the problems of the previous odes. The images of the poem are beautiful precisely because the scene described is a transient moment in the flux of time. The poignant pleasure they give derives from their lack of permanence or stability: 'And gathering swallows twitter in the skies'. Keats is here expressing in his own way the paradox of the great prophet of ▷ Romanticism, ▷ William Blake: 'He who binds to himself a joy/Does the winged life destroy;/ But he who kisses the joy as it flies/ Lives in eternity's sun rise.'

Odin

The principal god of the pagan religions of northern Europe; he presided over war and wisdom. In England he was called 'Woden', and his name is preserved in 'Wednesday'. The Angles and Saxons, before their conversion to Christianity, believed him to be the ancestor of their kings.

Odysseus

The Greek hero and king of Ithaca in the ▷ *Odyssey*, an epic by Homer. In Latin he was known as Ulixes, which has been converted into Ulysses. He also occurs in Homer's ▷ *Iliad*, where he is famous among the Greek leaders for his wise advice. In the dramas of ▷ Sophocles and ▷ Euripides his wisdom shows as mere cunning, but Shakespeare (in ▷ *Troilus and Cressida*) shows him as the sane politician, making the best of a bad world. For ▷ Tennyson (*Ulysses* 1842) he is the heroic wanderer, setting out for a final voyage after his return to Ithaca; Tennyson got this conception of him from Dante's ▷ *Inferno*. See Stanford, W. B., *The Ulysses Theme*.

Odyssey

An ▷ epic by the ancient Greek poet ▷ Homer. The hero, ▷ Odysseus King of Ithaca, is on his way home after the Trojan war, but he is blown off course and the return journey takes him ten years. The principal episodes of his voyage are as follows:

1 The land of the Lotus-Eaters. Those who eat of the lotus plant forget their homeland.

2 The land of the ▷ Cyclops. These are a race of one-eyed giants. Odysseus puts out the eye of the Cyclops Polyphemus, who is son of ▷ Poseidon, god of the sea; it is to punish him for this that Poseidon sends him wandering for ten years.

3 The Isle of Aeolus, king of the winds. Odysseus steals from him the bag in which

the winds are contained, but his companions open it too soon, and the winds escape.

4 Telepylus, the city of the cannibal Laestrygonians. They destroy his fleet except one ship, in which he escapes.

5 The Isle of ▷ Circe. She transforms his men into swine, but with the aid of the god ▷ Hermes, he resists her enchantments, compels her to restore his men, and remains in the island as her lover for a year.

6 He visits the Underworld, ▷ Hades, to learn from the prophet ▷ Tiresias the way home. Tiresias warns him against harming the cattle of the sun-god, Helios.

7 He evades the enchanting songs of the ▷ Sirens, who try to lure him on to the rocks.

8 He passes through the strait of Scylla and Charybdis – a treacherous rock and a whirlpool.

9 He comes to the Island of Thrinacia (Sicily) where the cattle of Helios live, which the ghost of Tiresias has warned him not to harm, but overcome by hunger, his companions devour them.

10 In punishment, his ship is wrecked and all his men perish, but Odysseus reaches the island of the goddess ▷ Calypso, who keeps him prisoner for seven years as her lover. He eventually escapes, with the aid of the goddess ▷ Athene, and reaches the lands of the Phaeacians where Nausicaa and her father, the king of the country, befriend him. The narrative of all the above events comes to the reader through Odysseus, who tells them to the king. The king helps him back to Ithaca. There, with the help of his son Telemachus, he kills the suitors who have been pestering the chaste Penelope, his queen.

Oedipus
In Greek myth, a character first mentioned by ▷ Homer as having (unknown to himself) killed his own father and married his own mother. In later versions the story was filled out: his father, King Laius of Thebes, was warned by an ▷ oracle that his son would kill him, and ordered that the child Oedipus should be destroyed; he was accordingly exposed in a waste place, but a shepherd rescued him; ignorant of his parentage, he later returned to Thebes, and on the way there, killed his father in consequence of a wayside quarrel; on his arrival at Thebes, he saved the city from the ▷ Sphinx and married his mother, Jocasta. ▷ Sophocles' *Oedipus the King*, tells of his subsequent discovery of his parentage and the consequences of this discovery; Sophocles also dramatized Oedipus' death in *Oedipus at Colonus*.

The 'Oedipus Complex' is the name for a discovery by the psychoanalyst ▷ Sigmund Freud that children tend to feel sexual attraction to the parent of the opposite sex, and corresponding jealousy towards the parent of the same sex.
▷ Psychoanalytical criticism.

Oedipus complex
In ▷ Freudian psychoanalysis ▷ Sophocles's story of Oedipus who killed his father and married his mother, is used as a model of the way in which human desires and feelings are structured during the passage from infancy to adulthood. The triangular relationship modelled on Sophocles's text can be used to explain relationships within the family which is the model of socialization available to the child. In order for successful socialization to occur, the child must emerge from the position of desiring an incestuous relationship with individual parents – for which in the case of the male, the penalty would be castration – and to transfer the affections for the mother onto another. The difficulties which this sometimes causes are illustrated in novels such as ▷ D. H. Lawrence's ▷ *Sons and Lovers* where Paul Morell is faced with having to transfer his affections for his mother onto other women. The Oedipus complex, and the model of triangulated desire upon which it is built, must be overcome in order for individual gendered human subjects to take their place in a world of which they are not the centre. This process of 'decentring' is explained by ▷ Jacques Lacan as an acceptance of the repression of desire imposed upon the subject by the father, an acceptance of a 'symbolic castration'. This raises a number of difficulties in the case of the gendered *female* subject who can never break free of the castration complex imposed upon her by a phallocentric ▷ symbolic order. Basically the Oedipus complex is used to account for a particular hierarchy of relationships within the family unit. It is a process through which the male is expected to pass in order to reach mature adulthood, and it seeks to offer an explanation of the ways in which authority operates as a system of constraints and laws.

Oenone
▷ Paris.

O'Faolain, Sean (b 1900)
Irish novelist and writer of short stories. He was born in Dublin and attended the National University of Ireland and Harvard University in the U.S.A. He participated in the Irish Rebellion following World War I, and later

lived in England as a teacher. His novels include *A Nest of Simple Folk* (1933) and *Bird Alone* (1936). His first volume of stories, *Midsummer Night Madness* (1932), vividly reflects the atmosphere of the Irish disturbances. A collected edition of the stories was published in 1958, and in 1966 he published a further volume, *The Heat of the Sun*. Among his other writings are two biographies which are studies of Irish leaders, one on Daniel O'Connell entitled *King of the Beggars* (1938), and *The Great O'Neill* (1942). His critical work includes *The Short Story* (1948). His autobiography *Vive Moi!* appeared in 1965. He was made Director of the Arts Council of Ireland in 1957.

O'Flaherty, Liam (1897–1984)

Irish novelist and writer of short stories. Born in the Aran Islands he was educated for the Roman Catholic priesthood, but did not enter it. He fought in World War I, and settled in England in 1922. His first volume of stories, *Spring Sowing*, was published in 1926; it contains stories of Irish peasant life and wild nature. At his best, his stories have the intensity of fine lyric poetry, and he is peculiarly gifted at representing the exhilaration and poignancy of life directly exposed to natural forces. Other volumes of stories include: *The Mountain Tavern* (1929), *The Wild Swan* (1932), *Two Lovely Beasts* (1948). His novels include *The Informer* (1925 – made into a film in 1935) and the historical *Famine* (1937). His autobiography is entitled *Shame the Devil* (1934).

Og, king of Bashan
▷ *Absalom and Achitophel.*

Oisin

Also known as Ossian. In 1760–3, ▷ James Macpherson published a series of blank verse epics which he attributed to Ossian and claimed to have translated from the Gaelic. His version had an immense success and a wide influence; however, Macpherson was later proved not to have translated the poems, but to have synthesized them from a number of genuine Celtic legends, in which the hero Oisin occurs. ▷ Dr Johnson was among the earliest sceptics; when asked whether he thought any man 'of the modern age' could have written the poems, he replied: 'Yes, Sir, many men, many women, and many children.'

▷ W. B. Yeats wrote a narrative poem *The Wanderings of Oisin* (1889), the earliest of his attempts to create a new literature out of Celtic mythology. In the ancient legends Oisin bridged the gap between the heroic pagan age and Irish Christianity; his longevity was due to a long sojourn in Fairyland.
▷ Celtic Twilight; Irish Literature; Finn.

O'Keeffe, John (1747–1833)

Actor and dramatist, who wrote many popular comedies and comic operas in the late 18th century. O'Keeffe was drawn to the stage by reading ▷ Farquhar and he wrote his first play, *The Gallant*, at the age of 15, later obtaining a post as an actor. In 1773 he took up writing seriously, and his farce, *Tony Lumpkin in Town*, based on ▷ Goldsmith's ▷ *She Stoops to Conquer*, was staged in Dublin, and afterwards at the ▷ Haymarket Theatre in London. His *Wild Oats, or the Strolling Gentleman* (1791) was revived by the ▷ Royal Shakespeare Company in 1976, with great success, largely because of the magnificent acting vehicle provided in the character of Rover. O'Keeffe's autobiography was published in 1826.

Old Bachelor, The (1693)

Comedy by ▷ Congreve. After being seduced and abandoned by Vainlove, Silvia sets out to marry, pretending to be sexually inexperienced. Heartwell, the aged and surly 'old bachelor' of the title, falls in love with Silvia, and marries her. He later discovers to his relief that the marriage is a sham, as the parson was only Vainlove's friend Bellmour in disguise. Afterwards Silvia traps Sir Joseph Wittol into a genuine marriage. Bellmour loves Belinda, but at first she keeps him at a distance, knowing him to be a rake: eventually they marry. In another intrigue, Bellmour is attracted to the uxorious Fondlewife's wife Laeticia, whom Vainlove has wooed, as he woos any pretty woman. In this instance Vainlove allows Bellmour to reap the fruit of his labours: Bellmour goes to Laeticia's house, disguised as a Puritan preacher, and seduces her in her husband's absence. Fondlewife returns, but the lovers convince him that she has remained chaste. Araminta, another woman whom Vainlove pursues, loves him but resists him. At last they seem near to marrying, but the ending of their plot-line remains ambiguous. The play is lively and entertaining, but cynical in tone.

Old Comedy
▷ Aristophanes.

Old Curiosity Shop, The (1840–1)

A novel by ▷ Charles Dickens; it was serialized as part of ▷ *Master Humphrey's Clock* in 1840–1 (published in book form in 1848).

The Curiosity Shop (a shop which sells second-hand goods of ornamental or rarity value) is kept by the grandfather of little Nell Trent. The old man has been impoverished by the extravagances of his son-in-law and those of Fred Trent, Nell's brother. He is forced to borrow money from Quilp, a grotesque and malevolent dwarf, who believes the old man to be a miser with a hidden store of wealth. Quilp gets possession of the shop, and Nell and her grandfather take to wandering about the countryside. Eventually Nell dies, too late to be saved by her grandfather's brother, who has returned from abroad and finds them after a long search. Quilp is drowned while attempting to escape arrest. Other characters include Sampson Brass, Quilp's unscrupulous lawyer, his sister Sally and 'the Marchioness', a child whom the Brasses keep as a servant in vile conditions.

The novel shows Dickens's extraordinary vitality of imagination and also exemplifies the vulgarity which was part of his vitality. This vulgarity tended to display itself in melodrama and in sentimentality, here exhibited in the characters of Quilp and Little Nell respectively. The death of Little Nell is often regarded as Dickens's most notorious sentimental indulgence.

Old English

The name is practically identical with Anglo-Saxon in denoting the language, literature and culture of the English before the Norman-French conquest of 1066, and also afterwards until it becomes fused (Middle English) in the 13th century with the insular Norman-French; it was later occasionally used to differentiate the common people from the aristocracy of (supposedly) Norman-French descent.

▷ English language; Saxons.

Old English literature

The four centuries preceding the Norman Conquest of 1066 were a period during which the Teutonic tribes who invaded Britain in the 5th century, after the fall of Roman dominion, achieved a level of organization capable first of resisting, then assimilating, the 8th-century invaders from Scandinavia. The conversion to Christianity of the Angles in the north and east of England, the Saxons in the south and the Jutes in Kent, partly by Irish, partly by Continental missionaries, led to the establishment of monasteries which became centres of learning and literate culture. Partly as a result of initiatives taken by ▷ Alfred to cultivate the use of English as a literary medium (to compensate for the decline in Latin learning during the period of the Danish invasions), partly as a result of the

pastoral impetus of the ▷ Benedictine Revival, English achieved a status as a literary language surpassing that of any other European vernacular. By the 11th century a standard written form of English (West Saxon) was being cultivated as a medium for pastoral instruction, for literary culture, for the purposes of administration and record (although Latin remained the language of the highest cultural authority and scholarship). Old English literary culture may be roughly classified as follows:

1 The Latin work of monastic scholars. Monastic, Latin culture occupied a central and crucial position within Anglo-Saxon, and European, culture as a whole. From this context, the Latin work of ▷ Bede, Alcuin, and Aldhelm deserves special recognition. Bede (673–735) was the foremost scholar of Anglo-Saxon culture and the most enduringly influential of this group. Alcuin (735–804) was the most famous Saxon scholar of his time, as a result of his important position in the court of the Emperor Charlemagne (from about 781) as an educational reformer and pioneer. His works cover a range of topics (historical, grammatical, and scientific) in Latin verse and prose. Aldhelm (640–709) was Abbot of Malmesbury and later Bishop of Sherbourne. His works include florid treatises in verse and prose in praise of virginity, and a treatise on metrics. His English poetry, apparently admired by Alfred, is lost.

2 Old English poetry. The bulk of this is preserved in just four manuscripts, dating from the second half of the 10th century (the so-called Junius ms, the Vercelli Book, the Exeter book and the ▷ Beowulf ms). The prosodic form of Old English poetry is ▷ alliterative verse, and the extant poetic corpus is one of considerable formal sophistication. The blend of traditions and values from Germanic and Christian culture gives it a distinctive quality. The heroic narratives rework material from a historical-legendary Germanic past, preserved through the efforts of literate Saxon monks. Most of the material cannot be attributed to a single writer, nor dated with any degree of precision. A list of the subjects will give some idea of its range:

i Heroic narratives about the legendary-historical past (such as ▷ *Beowulf, Deor, The Battle of Finnsburh, Waldere, Widsith*).
ii Commemorative historical poems (*The Battle of Brunanburh* and the ▷ *Battle of Maldon*).
iii Poems on biblical and scriptural themes (retelling O.T. narratives such as *Genesis A,*

Genesis B, Judith, Exodus; retelling N.T. events such as ▷ Cynewulf's *Christ II* or those contained in apocryphal gospels, such as *Andreas*; meditations on Christian iconography, such as the ▷ *Dream of the Rood*, the *Phoenix*; hymns of praise, such as the famous, earliest extant example of O.E. poetry, ▷ Caedmon's 'hymn').

iv Lives of saints (such as *Guthlac A and B*, *Juliana, Elene*).

v Short elegies (complaints written from the stance of a first-person speaker on the hardships of separation and isolation of one kind or another, such as *The Wanderer, The Seafarer, The Wife's Lament*).

vi Riddles and gnomic verse (the riddles, such as those collected in the Exeter Book, are characteristically in the voice of objects who pun on their identity, using clever metaphorical and metonymical twists).

3 Old English prose. There was a well-developed prose tradition in Old English, stimulated by the initiatives taken by Alfred to produce translations of those books 'most necessary for men to know': translations by Alfred, or attributed to the Alfredian school, include Gregory the Great's *Pastoral Care*, ▷ Boethius's *Consolation of Philosophy*, Augustine's *Soliloquies*, ▷ Bede's *Ecclesiastical History*. Prose was used as the medium for homiletic instruction (most notably by ▷ Aelfric and Wulfstan, and in the *Blickling Homilies*), and for translations from the Old and New Testaments. Classical narratives, such as the story of Apollonius of Tyre and parts of the ▷ Alexander legend, also survive in vernacular prose translations. The ▷ *Anglo-Saxon Chronicle* illustrates the use of Old English prose as a medium of historical record, and there are also extant examples of laws, charters, wills, scientific and medical writings in O.E. prose.

A number of factors contributed to the demise of English as a prestige vernacular in the later 11th century. With the Conquest, the English administrative, ecclesiastical and social elite was replaced by Norman personnel. The effect was to confirm Latin as the language of official administration and record, and to encourage the use of Norman-French (▷ Anglo-Norman) as a vernacular of status. There seems to have been no attempt to prevent English being used in official contexts: it simply was no longer practical to do so in many cases. But Latin culture underwent an enormous renaissance from the late 11th century onwards, as did French culture from the mid-12th century, which influenced their use across Europe as cultural and literary mediums. The tradition

of O.E. learning was kept up at some monastic centres through the 12th century, particularly at Worcester, but a standard written form of the language could no longer be maintained. The early written forms of English which survive from the 12th century reflect regional variations in usage and the enormous changes in the spoken forms of the language that had not permeated the standard written forms of O.E.. Thus the so-called Middle English period begins. The study of O.E. texts never entirely died out through the medieval period in England, but it increasingly became an area of antiquarian scholarship. The revival of substantial scholarly interest in Anglo-Saxon culture in the 16th century (reflected in the work of scholars such as ▷ John Bale and ▷ Matthew Parker) was stimulated in part by religious-political issues, and the desire to find evidence of an autonomous national, ecclesiastical tradition in the pre-Norman era that could be used to refute Papal claims to ecclesiastical and spiritual authority. In the next century, Anglo-Saxon traditions and culture became a reference point for pro-Parliamentarians anxious to locate the roots of English political institutions firmly in the Saxon past. The subsequent history of Anglo-Saxon scholarship reflects a similarly complex merging of academic, political, national and racial interests.

▷ Alfred, King; Heptarchy.
Bib: Mitchell, B. and Robinson, F., *A Guide to Old English*; Shippey, T., *Old English Verse*; Swanton, M., *English Literature before Chaucer*.

Old Pretender, The
James Francis Edward Stuart (1688–1766), son of ▷ King James II who had been deposed for reasons connected with his Catholicism. He was a pretender to (*ie* he claimed) the British throne on the death of his half-sister Queen Anne in 1714, but his claim was rejected because like his father he was a Catholic. Instead, George of Hanover became king as George I. In 1715, James led a rebellion on his own behalf in ▷ Scotland, but this failed. His followers were called ▷ Jacobites from the Latin Jacobus = James, and he was termed the 'Old' Pretender to distinguish him from his son, Charles Edward Stuart, the Young Pretender, who attempted a similar Scottish rebellion in 1745.
▷ Stuart, House of.

Old Testament
▷ Bible.

Old Vic Theatre, The

The Old Vic

Situated in Waterloo Road, this is one of London's most famous theatres. Built in 1816–18, during the 19th century it drew on the local working-class population for its audiences, with productions of popular melodramas. In 1880 it was converted into a temperance amusement-hall. From 1881 to 1883 it was managed by the ▷ Shakespearean actor and director ▷ William Poel. Under the management of Lillian Baylis, from 1912 to 1937, it became famous for its popular productions of Shakespeare's plays financed on a shoe-string budget. Her great achievement was to attract some of the best actors and directors of the time when they could have earned far greater salaries working in the West End. The theatre was damaged during World War II but reopened in 1950 and continued the tradition of performing Shakespeare plays along with other classics. Between 1963 and 1976 it served as the home for the ▷ National Theatre company before the new National Theatre was built. It is now managed by Ed Mirvish, a Canadian entrepreneur, who has restored it and attempted to re-establish it as a venue for neglected classics with Jonathan Miller as his artistic director.
Bib: Roberts, P., *The Old Vic Story*.

Oldcastle, Sir John (1378–1417)

Sir John Oldcastle became Lord Cobham and died a martyr for Wycliffite (▷ Wycliffe, John) heresy which rejected the transubstantiation. There is cogent evidence to suggest that ▷ Falstaff in ▷ *Henry IV* was originally called Oldcastle, notwithstanding ▷ Shakespeare's explicit disclaimer of this in the 'Epilogue' to *Henry IV, Part II*. The complete works of Shakespeare edited by Gary Taylor and Stanley Wells retains (uniquely) Oldcastle for Falstaff in *Henry IV, Part I*, on the basis that the name was changed for reasons of political accommodation, not for aesthetic ones.

Oldfield, Anne (?1683–1730)

Actress. She served in a tavern where, according to tradition, her talents as an actress were recognized by the playwright ▷ George Farquhar, who heard her reciting some lines behind the bar. She was engaged at ▷ Drury Lane from 1699 where apart from a brief sojourn at the Queen's Theatre (▷ Haymarket Theatres), she remained to the end of her career. She gradually supplanted the previous leading actress, ▷ Anne Bracegirdle.

Throughout her career Oldfield preferred comic to tragic roles, excelling in the performance of coquettes and women of fashion such as Lady Betty Modish in ▷ Colley Cibber's *The Careless Husband* (1704).
Bib: Robins, E., *The Palmy Days of Nance Oldfield*; Melville, L., *Stage Favourites of the Eighteenth Century*.

Oldham, John (1653–83)

Poet. Some of his early poems were written under the influence of the ▷ Earl of Rochester, and his *Ode, Suppos'd to be spoken by a Court-Hector at Breaking of the Dial in Privy-Garden*, also known as *A Satyr against Vertue*, concerns one of Rochester's drunken exploits. His *Satyrs upon the Jesuits*, in heroic ▷ couplets (1681), ridicule Catholic superstition. He was a pioneer of the 'imitation' form, writing versions of poems by ▷ Horace, ▷ Juvenal and ▷ Boileau in urbane couplets, adapting the original to an English contemporary context. His *Poems and Translations* appeared in 1683. He died early from smallpox, and ▷ John Dryden wrote an elegy to his memory.
Bib: Zigerell, J., *John Oldham*.

Oliphant, Margaret (M.O.W.) (1828–97)

The daughter of a Scots Customs clerk named Wilson, Margaret Oliphant was born in Wallyford, near Musselburgh. The father was somewhat indifferent to his family, the mother energetic, eager and sarcastic, with a similarity to ▷ Jane Carlyle recognized by her daughter. She went to London in 1851 to take care of an 'unsatisfactory' brother and in 1852 married her cousin, an artist. From 1852 she wrote novels in ▷ *Blackwood's Magazine* and reviewed for them. Her

husband died of consumption in 1859, three months before the birth of their third child, leaving her dependent on her writing. After the death of her daughter in 1864 she took on her widowed brother and his three children and provided for their education and maintenance as well as that of her own sons. She produced a constant stream of writing: ▷ biography, fiction and reviews, and published nearly 100 different works. She wrote vividly and inventively, with pathos and humour, but the struggle to meet her financial obligations, her disappointments and griefs constantly oppressed her and she expressed regret at having to write such quantities. Her works include: *Passages in the Life of Mrs Margaret Maitland* (1849), *Caleb Field* (1851), a historical novel, *Merkland* (1851) which was a great success, *The Athelings* (1857), one of several domestic romances. Her 'Chronicles of Carlingford' series perhaps owes something to ▷ George Eliot, comprising *Salem Chapel* (1863), *The Rector and the Doctor's Family* (1863), *The Perpetual Curate* (1864), *Miss Marjoribanks* (1866) and *Phoebe Junior* (1876). *Stories of the Seen and Unseen* deal with experiences of death and matters of the soul, including elements of mysticism, and include *A Beleaguered City* (1880) and *A Little Pilgrim* (1882). Her *Literary History of England* (1882) was much praised. *Annals of a Publishing House*, about *Blackwood's* was published in 1897 and a posthumous ▷ autobiography in 1899.
Bib: Coghill, A. L. (ed.), *The Autobiography and Letters of Mrs M. O. W. Oliphant*; Colby, V. & R., *The Equivocal Virtue: Mrs Oliphant and the Victorian Literary Market Place*; Cunningham, V., *Everywhere Spoken Against: Dissent in the Victorian Novel* (chapter).

Oliver Twist (1837–9)

A novel by ▷ Charles Dickens, published in instalments in 1837–9. Oliver is a child of unknown parents, born in a ▷ workhouse where he leads a miserable existence under the tyranny of Bumble, a beadle, *ie* a parish council official. He runs away to London and becomes mixed up in a gang of thieves led by Fagin and including the brutal burglar, Bill Sikes, Nancy his whore and a young pickpocket called the 'Artful Dodger'. He is temporarily rescued by the benevolent Mr Brownlow but a mysterious character called Monks, who has an interest in keeping Oliver's parentage a secret, induces the gang to kidnap him. He is finally rescued through the action of Nancy, who in consequence is brutally murdered by Sikes.

The novel shows the mixture of sentimentality and melodrama characteristic of early Dickens but in Bumble especially he exhibits keen social satire, and the London underworld is presented vividly. It was written at a time when a number of novelists (*eg* the 'Newgate School', especially ▷ Harrison Ainsworth) had written romances about crime but Dickens dissociated it from these in the preface to the 3rd edition, and was realistic enough to startle the educated public into a new consciousness of the unprivileged and the criminal level of society, and to show how lack of compassion in the more privileged helped to make poverty a nursery of crime.

Olivier, Laurence (1907–89)

Actor and producer, knighted in 1947, and created a life peer in 1970. He established his reputation at the ▷ Old Vic theatre during the 1930s, especially with his performance of ▷ *Hamlet* in 1937. The range and success of his career on stage and in films mark him as the leading English actor of this century. In 1961 he was appointed director of the Chichester Festival Theatre and made the first director of the ▷ National Theatre.
Bib: Gourlay, L. (ed.), *Olivier*; Olivier, L., *Confessions of an Actor*.

Olney Hymns (1779)

A collection of religious poems by the Rev. John Newton and ▷ William Cowper, so called from the village of Olney where they lived.

Olympus

The name of a number of mountains in Greece and Asia Minor, but especially of one which the ancient Greeks considered to be the home of the gods. It is situated on the border of Thessaly and Macedonia in Greece, and is about 10,000 feet (3,000 metres) high, with a massive and precipitous appearance.

Ombre

A card game introduced from Spain into England in the 17th century, and very popular throughout the 18th century. Its appeal lay in its demand on the intelligence of the players, and it was later superseded in popularity by whist and then bridge, games which make a similar demand. The name is from the Spanish for 'Man'. Ombre is the game played in Pope's famous poem, ▷ *The Rape of the Lock*.

Onomatopoeia

The use of verbal sound to evoke the sound of what the word represents. Thus a cuckoo is a bird whose song resembles the two syllables of its name, which is therefore onomatopoeic.

Open field system

That system of land use especially typical of medieval English agriculture. Land under cultivation was divided into strips, and distributed among the peasants of the village or manor. The strips were not surrounded by hedges or fences, so that good farmers suffered from the effects of the bad farming of their immediate neighbours. The system began to be replaced in the 16th century, when landowners preferred sheep-farming, and it was effectually abolished in the 18th century when, in the course of 'the agricultural revolution', the open fields were enclosed in larger arable units by the landlords.
▷ Enclosures.

Open University

The Open University was established in 1969, began teaching in 1971 and is now based at Milton Keynes. Its aim to provide degree courses for those students who do not have formal qualifications, who are not of a standard, and who do not have the opportunity or the finance to enter for full-time university degrees. The courses are based at home and the teaching is done mainly through television and radio. It's popularity continues to increase.

Opera in England

Opera, in the sense of a staged drama in which the words and music are of equal importance, began in Italy at the end of the 16th century. It was an integral part of the ▷ Renaissance, arising out of the attempt to revive what were thought to be the performance practices of Greek drama. Subjects, therefore, were tragedies drawn from classical mythology and the words were set to a declamatory style of singing known as recitative. The first English opera was *The Siege of Rhodes*, with a libretto by ▷ William D'Avenant and music (now lost) by Matthew Locke and others. It was first produced in 1642, at a time when the ▷ Puritans had closed the theatres, and seems to have been an attempt to circumvent the ban on plays. The convention of recitative, however, does not seem to have been to the English taste, so that, apart from Blow's *Venus and Adonis* and ▷ Purcell's *Dido and Aeneas*, the main contribution of composers in the 17th century was in the genre now known as dramatic or semi-opera. After the theatres reopened in 1660, many plays were given with musical interludes, ▷ Shakespeare being adapted for this purpose by ▷ D'Avenant and ▷ Dryden. Two sets of ▷ *Tempest* music exist, one by Locke, the other sometimes thought to be by ▷ Purcell. *The Fairy Queen* (1693), an adaptation of ▷ *A Midsummer Night's Dream*, is Purcell's best-known work in this field.

In the 18th century Italian opera was imported, as well as the German composer, Handel, who wrote operas in the Italian style, but the fashion for such entertainment proved to be short-lived. ▷ Addison, amongst others, ridiculed the conventions of opera in the ▷ *Spectator*. Nor, despite its popularity at the time, did ▷ Gay's ▷ *The Beggar's Opera* (1728) lead to a significant tradition of ballad opera. The romantic operas that held the stage in the first half of the 19th century are, apart from Balfe's *The Bohemian Girl*, little known nowadays. More lasting fame, however, has attached to the comic operas written by ▷ Gilbert and Sullivan between 1875 and 1896.

Until the 20th century, London had a virtual monopoly of opera performances, the only touring company that lasted for any time being the Carl Rosa Opera Company. In recent years the establishment of regional companies who tour, as well as performing at their home base, has brought opera to a much wider public, although cuts in public subsidies are now threatening this expansion. Improved standards of production and a general policy of singing in English if possible have helped to make it a more popular art form. Two English composers in particular have enriched the repertoire: Benjamin Britten and Sir Michael Tippett. Britten tended to find inspiration in classic texts, as, for instance, in ▷ *Peter Grimes* (▷ George Crabbe), *Billy Budd* (Herman Melville), ▷ *The Turn of the Screw* (▷ Henry James), *A Midsummer Night's Dream* (▷ Shakespeare), *Death in Venice* (Thomas Mann), whereas Tippett writes his own, very individual, libretti. Of the younger composers, Harrison Birtwhistle has contributed a variety of dramatic pieces (including *Punch and Judy*, *Down by the Greenwood Side*, *The Mask of Orpheus* and *Yan Tan Tethera*) which are largely concerned with re-working myth, whilst Peter Maxwell Davies has written several chamber and children's operas, as well as the large-scale *Taverner* and *Resurrection*.

Oracle

In ancient Greek religion, a place where an inspired priest gave answers to the questions put to him by worshippers about their destinies or the outcome of a crisis. The most famous was the oracle of Delphi, sacred to ▷ Apollo. Here the mouthpiece of the oracle was a priestess known as the Pythia, who gave ambiguous replies in verse.

Orange, House of; Orange Free State; Orangemen

The town of Orange in southern France was originally an independent principality. Philibert of Orange (1502–30) was rewarded by the Emperor Charles v (who ruled the Netherlands amongst his other territories) with large estates in the Netherlands for his help in statesmanship and war. The Princes of Orange thus became Dutch nobles, and later William 'the Silent' of Orange established the Dutch (Netherlands) Republic by defeating the armies of the territory's former ruler, Philip II of Spain. William's leadership, and the importance of the Orange family in the Netherlands, gave the House of Orange special eminence in the Republic, and successive members of it held the high office of Stadtholder. They twice married into the ▷ Stuart family reigning in Britain: William II married Mary, daughter of ▷ Charles I, and in 1677 their son, William III, married Mary, daughter of ▷ James II. William and Mary became joint sovereigns of Britain in 1689 after the expulsion of James II. After William III's death in 1702, the family continued to be pre-eminent in Dutch politics, and were kings of Holland (the Netherlands) from 1814. In the same year the Dutch colony in South Africa was ceded to Britian; in 1836 some of the Dutch colonists, fleeing from British sovereignty, set up the Orange Free State Republic to the north of the colony.

Throughout the 17th century the House of Orange were champions of ▷ Protestantism against the Catholic powers, first of Spain and then of France; the religious conflict was also a fight for Dutch national survival, and from 1690–1700 it was in addition one for the survival of the British system of politics. The issue was then felt most keenly in ▷ Ireland, where the northern province of Ulster was Protestant, and the southern three provinces were Catholic. Religious hostility between the north and the south continued throughout the 18th century, when it died down in most of Europe, and it is still a political issue at the present day. In 1795 'Orange Societies' were founded in Ulster, in memory of the great Protestant king William III, who had saved Ulster from being overrun by the Catholic south by defeating James II's army at the Battle of the Boyne (1690). Orangemen (*ie*

members of these societies) are still an important political force in Northern Ireland, although the societies are nominally religious and not political.

Oranges and Lemons
A ▷ nursery rhyme based on the church bells of London. Each chime is given its distinctive utterance – *eg* 'Oranges and lemons say the bells of St Clement's' – culminating in 'the great bell of Bow'. The earliest record of the rhyme is 1744. It is also the basis of an old children's game.

Ordeal of Richard Feverel, The (1859)
A novel by ▷ George Meredith. Sir Austin Feverel prides himself on the 'system' which he has devised for the upbringing and education of his motherless son, Richard; he is, however, a self-satisfied egotist who lacks disinterested understanding of his son's character. The 'system' breaks down in Richard's adolescence, when the boy falls in love with Lucy Desborough, a girl of lower social background than Sir Austin's ideal for his son's bride. They are secretly married but Sir Austin manages to separate them by egotistically exploiting Richard's love for him. Richard becomes involved with a beautiful woman of loose morals; he begins this new relationship with characteristically romantic and idealistic motives of redeeming her but he partly falls under her spell. Lord Mountfalcon, who is interested in permanently separating Lucy and Richard, is chiefly responsible for Richard's betrayal of her, and in remorse for his infidelity Richard fights a duel with him and is wounded. Lucy has meanwhile become reconciled with Sir Austin but the shock of the duel kills her. The novel – Meredith's first important one – exemplifies his combination of romantic intensity with psychological analysis.

Orders in Council
Laws or regulations made by the king or queen in conjunction with the ▷ Privy Council; in practice this means that the Prime Minister and his Cabinet advise the sovereign to issue them, and they are then accountable to ▷ Parliament for the action. Orders in Council were often used in emergency, especially in wartime. Modern Orders in Council are usually administrative regulations limited by relevant Acts of Parliament.

Orestes
In Greek legend, the son of ▷ Agamemnon and ▷ Clytemnestra. He is the hero of the *Oresteia* – three tragedies by ▷ Aeschylus: *Agamemnon, Choephori, Eumenides*. In the

second, Orestes kills his mother in vengeance for her murder of his father. The legend was further developed by ▷ Sophocles and by ▷ Euripides with emphasis on the roles of Orestes' sister ▷ Electra and his friend Pylades.

Orfeo, Sir

An early Middle English narrative, dating from the 13th century, which claims to be a reworking of a lay composed by British harpers (▷ Breton Lays). In *Sir Orfeo*, the classical story of ▷ Orpheus and Euridice is translated into a feudal/chivalric Celtic world in which Orfeo is a former British king whose court is at Winchester (which, the narrator explains, was formerly called Thrace). The Underworld of the classical story becomes an Otherworld, presided over by the King of the Fairies. Heurodis is eventually rescued by Orfeo, who enters the Otherworld disguised as a minstrel, and after an absence of many years from their kingdom, the couple return and resume their positions as king and queen. **Bib:** Barron, W. R. J., *Medieval English Romance.*

Orgoglio

A character representing Arrogance in ▷ Edmund Spenser's ▷ *Faerie Queene*. He occurs in Book I, canto vii, viii; he captures the ▷ Red Cross Knight and is slain by Prince Arthur (▷ Arthur, King). The name derives from the Italian for pride.

Oriana

A name sometimes used for ▷ Elizabeth I by Elizabethan poets. It comes from the 15th-century Spanish-Portuguese romance *Amadis de Gaula*, in which Oriana is a British princess beloved by the hero, Amadis.
   ▷ Spanish influence on English literature.

Origin of Species, The

   ▷ Darwin, Charles.

Orlando

The Italian form of the name ▷ Roland, hero of the Old French *Chanson de Roland* (*Song of Roland*). From the Italian 16th-century romantic epics by ▷ Ariosto, the name passed into English romance narratives, being used, for example, for the hero of ▷ Shakespeare's romantic drama ▷ *As You Like It*.

Orlando (1928)

A fantasy by ▷ Virginia Woolf in which the evolution of poetic genius is traced through the Sackville family and their country mansion of Knole from ▷ Thomas Sackville (1536–1608) to the poet Victoria Sackville-West (1892–1962). This is done through an immortal character Orlando, representing the poetic genius of the family; he changes sex in the 17th century and throughout he meets a number of the great poets of English literature. The book is a combination of historical novel and biographical fantasy which parodies the changing styles of English literature and explores the themes of androgyny and women's creativity.

Orlando Furioso (1532)

A romance epic by the Italian poet ▷ Ludovico Ariosto. It is in a tradition of Italian developments of the legends centring on the French hero Roland, who in the reign of Charlemagne (768–814) repelled the Muslim invasion of Europe. Ariosto invents fantastic episodes and complicated romantic intrigues and adventures. Orlando goes mad because his lady, Angelica, marries a Moorish youth, but he is cured in time to defeat Agramante, king of Africa, who has been besieging Paris. Many linked tales and episodes accompany this central theme, as is usual in the 16th-century romantic ▷ epic, of which Ariosto is the master, and ▷ Edmund Spenser (▷ *The Faerie Queene*) one of his chief emulators.

Orpheus

In Greek myth, the son of the ▷ muse Calliope and ▷ Apollo, from whom he received a lyre on which he played so beautifully that the wild beasts came to listen to him. When his wife, Eurydice, was killed by a snakebite, he descended to the underworld to bring her back. His music charmed the deities there so much that they permitted him to return to earth with her on the condition that he never looked back at her during the journey. When they were nearly at the gates, however, he could not resist the temptation to see whether she was following him, and so she was lost to him for ever. Orpheus was the centre of an ancient religious cult, Orphism. He is also connected with the ▷ Argonaut legend; his singing subdued the various natural and supernatural dangers which threatened the ship Argo, and it lulled into acquiescence the dragon that guarded the Golden Fleece.
   ▷ Orfeo, Sir.

Orton, Joe (1933–67)

British dramatist renowned for his black humour, witty and savage verbal dialogue in the tradition of ▷ Oscar Wilde, and iconoclastic attacks on social conventions. He was murdered by his homosexual partner when his career had barely begun. His first play, *Entertaining Mr Sloane* (1964), is a comedy about suburban sex. In this, as in his other plays, much of the humour is derived from the disparity between what characters say and what they actually mean or do. This was followed by two farces, *Loot* (1966) and *What the Butler Saw* (produced in 1969); the former about money, death and police corruption and the latter about sex and institutionalized corruption. Other plays are: *The Ruffian on the Stair* (staged 1966), *The Erpingham Camp* (staged 1967) and *Funeral Games* (staged 1970).

Bib: Bigsby, C. W. E., *Joe Orton*; Lahr, J., *Prick Up Your Years.*

Orwell, George (pseudonym of Eric Blair) (1903–50)

George Orwell

Novelist, journalist and critic. Born into a poor but proud middle-class family, he was sent to a private school, from where he won a scholarship to Eton. His snobbish upbringing, and the uneasiness he felt in living with boys richer than himself, gave him a distaste for middle-class values and, in relation to the working-classes, a sense of guilt which was intensified by the large unemployment of the 1930s. He served in the Burma Police (1922–7), and then resigned from dislike of what he interpreted as ▷ imperialist oppression – *Burmese Days* (1934). He then tried to appease his sense of social guilt by living for 18 months in the utmost destitution – *Down and Out in Paris and London* (1933). At the height

of the economic ▷ depression in the 1930s, he was commissioned by a left-wing publisher, Gollancz, to make a personal investigation of conditions in the north of England – *The Road to Wigan Pier* (1937). By the time of its publication, Orwell was fighting for the Republicans in Spain, where he was wounded in the throat – *Homage to Catalonia* (1938). He came to regard himself as an independent and democratic socialist. During World War II, he was rejected for the army on medical grounds, and worked for the Indian service of the B.B.C. In 1945 he published his masterpiece, the fable *Animal Farm*, a satire on Stalinism. After the war he wrote his most famous work, *1984* (1949), a vision of a world ruled by dictatorships of the Stalinist style, taken to an extreme in which private life and private thought are all but eradicated by surveillance, propaganda, and the systematic perversion of language.

His other novels are: *A Clergyman's Daughter* (1935); *Keep the Aspidistra Flying* (1936); *Coming Up For Air* (1939). Among his best works are his social and literary critical essays: *Inside the Whale* (1940); *The Lion and the Unicorn* (1941 – subtitled *Socialism and the English Genius*); *Critical Essays* (1946); *Shooting an Elephant* (1950). Recurrent themes in his work are the effect of poverty on the spirit, the difficulty of reconciling public demands with private desires and conscience, and the danger of corrupted language. He was literary editor of *Tribune* 1943–5. His *Collected Essays, Journalism and Letters* were published in 1968 (ed. S. Orwell and I. Angus).

Bib: Woodcock, G., *The Crystal Spirit*; Williams, R., *Orwell*; Crick, B., *George Orwell, a Life*; Meyers, J., *George Orwell: the Critical Heritage.*

Osborne, Dorothy (1627–95)

Wife of ▷ Sir William Temple, statesman, diplomatist and author. Their marriage was delayed for seven years owing to the disapproval of her family, and her letters to him during a part of this time are famous social documents.

Osborne, John (b 1929)

Dramatist. He is widely thought of as the leader of the dramatic revival which started in the 1950s, through the great popular success of *Look Back in Anger* (1956), which found an infectious contemporary idiom for the frustration of the younger British generation since World War II, and for their rejection of the traditional values of 'the Establishment'. The play gave currency for a decade to the term 'the ▷ angry young men'. His later plays include: *The Entertainer* (1957); *Epitaph for George Dillon* (1958); *The World of Paul Slickey* (1959); *Luther* (1961); *The Blood of the Bambergs* (1962); *Under Plain Cover* (1962); *Inadmissible Evidence* (1965); *A Patriot for Me* (1965); *A Bond Honoured* (1966); *Time Present* (1967); *West of Suez* (1972); *A Sense of Detachment* (1972); *A Place Calling Itself Detachment* (1972); *The Picture of Dorian Grey* (1973); *Watch It Come Down* (1975); *The End of Me Old Cigar* (1975). For television: *A Better Class of Person* (1985); *God Rot Tunbridge Wells* (1985).

Bib: Allsop, K., *The Angry Decade*; Banham, M. *Osborne*; Trussler, S., *The Plays of Osborne*.

Osiris

In ancient Egyptian myth, at first a nature god who died with the harvest and was reborn with the sprouting grain; later the god of the dead. The Greeks identified him with ▷ Dionysus, their vine god, and with ▷ Hades, their god of their dead; Osiris used music to subdue violence. He was assassinated by his evil brother Set; his sister-wife ▷ Isis brought him to life again, but he preferred to reign over the dead and the souls of the just.

Osmond, Gilbert

A principal character in ▷ Henry James's novel, ▷ *Portrait of a Lady*; he is a poor, expatriate American dilettante living in Italy, and secures in marriage the rich young heroine, Isabel Archer, whose life he then ruins by his moral triviality and cold-heartedness.

Ossian

▷ Oisin.

Othello (1604)

A tragedy by ▷ Shakespeare, first acted in 1604. It was based on an Italian tale in *Hecatommithi* by Giraldi Cinthio (1565 – translated into French 1584).

The full title of the play is *Othello, the Moor of Venice*: the extended title emphasizes Othello's position as commander of Venetian forces against the Turks, and it is a clue to the understanding of his tragedy. Othello is highly valued by the Venetians for his military prowess, but he is not a member of Venetian society; he is first and last a soldier, a member of a military community, trusting and trusted by his brother officers. Consequently it is as astonishing to him when Desdemona, a conventional Venetian aristocratic girl, leaves her home to marry him, as it is outrageous to her indignant father, Brabantio. Venice urgently needs Othello to defend Cyprus against the Turks, so that Brabantio is forced to accept the match; however he warns Othello that a girl who has behaved so unpredictably once may prove as unreliable a wife as she has been a daughter. Othello is in rapture; his bliss is the greater for its incredibility, so that he naïvely imagines himself transported into a heaven on earth. But his junior officer, Iago, has motives of resentment against him; the most concrete of these is that the Florentine, Cassio, has been promoted over his head. Moreover, he is himself a cynic who has a low opinion of human nature and of the scope for genuine happiness. Partly as a double revenge against Othello and against Cassio, partly as a cynical game the object of which is to bring Othello down to his own level of reality, he contrives first to disgrace Cassio temporarily, and then to insinuate into Othello's mind the suspicion, mounting by degrees to certainty, that Cassio and Desdemona are conducting a secret love affair. In Othello's mind the circumstances make this affair more than plausible: he has the habit of trusting Iago as his confidential officer; Desdemona has come to him out of a foreign society; Cassio is the sort of man who would have been considered an eligible husband for her. Until their marriage, Othello had had a single-minded dedication to his military vocation; the marriage has enriched this dedication, since it was Desdemona's admiration for him as a soldier that attracted her to him; he now finds that his jealousy has divided his single-mindedness and is destroying his integrity. Accordingly he murders her, in the belief that heavenly justice is on his side. Desdemona, however, has been presented as one of the most innocent of all Shakespeare's heroines, for whom adultery is unimaginable, and her innocent goodness has won the heart of her lady companion, Emilia, who is Iago's wife. Emilia, who has been ignorant of Iago's plot but has unintentionally assisted him in it, realizes his guilt and publicly exposes him; Othello, restored to his dignity, makes a final speech of self-assessment, and kills himself.

Othello follows ▷ *Hamlet* in the sequence of Shakespeare's tragedies and is another masterpiece in the tradition of ▷ Revenge Tragedy. It is psychologically much more lucid, though perhaps not a greater play, than *Hamlet*, and one of the most eloquent of Shakespeare's poetic dramas.

Ottava rima

An Italian stanza of 8 lines rhyming *a b a b a b c c*. It was used by ▷ Boccaccio in the

14th century. Pulci in the 15th century used it for the ▷ mock-heroic, ironic style with which the ▷ stanza is chiefly associated in English through ▷ Byron's ▷ *Don Juan* and his *Vision of Judgement*.

Otterbourne, The Battle of

A famous medieval ▷ ballad about a battle fought in 1388 between the English and the Scots near the English castle of that name. The English commander was ▷ Henry Hotspur, Lord Percy, and the Scottish one, James Earl of Douglas. The ▷ Percy family and the Douglases were the chief rival familes on either side of the Scottish-English border in the later Middle Ages. The battle was a Scottish victory but Douglas was killed; Hotspur was taken prisoner. Another version of the battle is the ballad ▷ *Chevy Chase*.

The Hotspur of the ballad is the same as the character in ▷ Shakespeare's ▷ *Henry IV, Part I*; the Douglas in that play is another member of that family, whom Hotspur had just taken prisoner in the battle of Homildon Hill (1402).

Otway, Thomas (1652–85)

Dramatist and poet. He made a single attempt as an actor, when ▷ Aphra Behn gave him an opportunity as the old King in her *The Forc'd Marriage* (1670). Paralysed with stage fright, he broke down, and the next night the part had to be given to another actor. Otway turned instead to writing, he made an immediate success with his tragedy, *Alcibiades* (1675), in which ▷ Elizabeth Barry made her first appearance. Otway is said to have fallen in love with her at that time, though she did not reciprocate his feelings. Otway nevertheless wrote several of his finest parts for her.

Otway followed his first play with the rhymed tragedy *Don Carlos* (1676); adaptations of a comedy by ▷ Molière as *The Cheats of Scapin* (1676) and ▷ Racine's tragedy *Titus and Berenice* (1677); and another comedy, *Friendship in Fashion* (1678). In 1678 Otway went to Flanders as a soldier, and drew on his experiences for ▷ *The Soldier's Fortune* (1681) and its sequel, ▷ *The Atheist* (1684). His best-known and most admired plays are two blank verse tragedies, *The Orphan; Or, The Unhappy Marriage* (1680), and ▷ *Venice Preserv'd; Or A Plot Discovered* (1682). Otway also wrote prologues and epilogues, and a few poems. He died in poverty.
Bib: Taylor, A. M., *Next to Shakespeare*; Ham, R. G., *Otway and Lee*; Summers, M. (ed.), *The Complete Works of Thomas Otway*; Ghosh, J. C. (ed.), *The Complete Works of Thomas Otway*.

Ouida (1839–1908)

The pseudonym of Marie Louise de la Ramée, 'Ouida' originates in a childish failure to say 'Louise'. She was born in Bury St Edmunds of an English mother and French father, was educated in local schools and then in Paris, where her father disappeared during the Paris Commune of 1871. From 1860 she lived mostly in Italy, an expensive and affected life with dogs and frequent hopeless infatuations. She had a high opinion of her own genius, writing 45 novels of an unreal fashionable world, rebelling against the moral tone of contemporary literature. Her powerful novels were very popular for a time, despite their extravagance and inaccuracies, and her ridiculous portrayals of men. However, she became less popular from 1890 and ultimately died in destitution in Viareggio. Her stories appeared in *Bentley's Miscellany* 1859–60. Her first success was *Held in Bondage* (1863) but *Strathmore* (1865) really established her reputation. Her other novels include *Under Two Flags* (1867), *Folle-Farine* (1871), *Two Little Wooden Shoes* (1874), *A Village Commune* (1881) dealing with peasant life, *In Maremma* (1882) and the animal stories, *A Dog of Flanders* (1872) and *Bimbi, Stories for Children* (1882).
Bib: Ffrench, Y., *Ouida: A Study in Ostentation*; Bigland, E., *Ouida: The Passionate Victorian*; Stirling, M., *The Fine and the Wicked: The Life and Times of Ouida*.

Our Mutual Friend (1864–5)

The last complete novel by ▷ Charles Dickens, published serially 1864–5.

The principal plot starts from the will of a deceased refuse-collector, Old Harmon, who bequeaths his fortune to his son, John Harmon, on condition that he marries a certain girl, Bella Wilfer. Young Harmon wishes to discover what she is like before he discloses himself. He intends to adopt a disguise but his identity is obscured beyond his intention when circumstances point to his death by murder. Since he is believed dead, the father's property goes instead to Mr Boffin, old Harmon's foreman. Boffin adopts Bella, and young Harmon, disguising himself as John Rokesmith, becomes engaged as Boffin's secretary. Bella becomes spoilt by wealth and contemptuously rejects Rokesmith-Harmon as a lover; she is, however, reformed by Boffin, who pretends himself to undergo complete debasement of character through his accession of wealth and thus gives Bella, who has been devoted to him, a violent distaste for the evils of money. Rokesmith's true identity as young Harmon is at length brought to light. With this main plot goes a minor story of Silas Wegg's attempt to blackmail Boffin. In addition there is a parallel main plot concerning the rival lovers of Lizzie Hexam, daughter of a Thames boatman; one of her lovers is the aristocratic young barrister, Eugene Wrayburn, and the other the embittered schoolmaster of low social origins, Bradley Headstone. Headstone tries to murder Wrayburn and nearly succeeds, but he is drowned in a struggle with Rogue Riderhood, another waterman who is also a blackmailer. Wrayburn, physically wrecked, marries Lizzie for whom he at last comes to have a real need. The two main plots are linked through the waterside characters who are connected with young Harmon's supposed murder at the beginning of the book. The novel extends through the Wrayburn–Lizzie story into upper-middle-class circles which include the arrogant Podsnaps, the Veneerings who attempt to climb into wealthy society and fall out of it again, the fraudulent social adventurers Mr and Mrs Lammle, the mean and ruthless financier Fledgeby. Through Fledgeby on the one side and Lizzie on the other, the lower social circles include Riah, the benevolent Jew, and Jenny Wren, the bitter-sweet doll's dressmaker. The book is thus given an unusually wide variety of character and social environment, even for Dickens, and it is pervaded by a rich symbolism arising from the use made of the River Thames and the dust-heaps out of which the Harmon fortunes have been made. The motive of special social reform, more characteristic of early Dickens (eg ▷ *Oliver Twist*, 1838) is evident in the episode of Betty Higden, the poor woman who dies by the roadside sooner than enter a workhouse.

Overbury, Sir Thomas (1581–1613)
Essayist and poet; as a writer he is chiefly remembered as the author of one of the most widely read collections of ▷ 'Theophrastian' character-sketches, published in 1614; ▷ John Webster, ▷ Thomas Dekker, ▷ John Donne and others made additions to subsequent issues of the collection between 1614 and 1622.

Overbury was also the victim of one of the most sensational murders in English history. He tried to oppose a love intrigue between ▷ James I's royal favourite, Thomas Carr, Earl of Somerset, and the young Countess of Essex. The lovers conspired to have Overbury poisoned; the crime came to light, and the prosecution was conducted by ▷ Francis Bacon. Carr and the Countess were

convicted and disgraced, but their agents who actually administered the poison were hanged.

Ovid (Publius Ovidius Naso) (43 BC-AD 17)
Roman poet, and the last of the greatest period of Latin poetry, the ▷ Augustan Age. He wrote for the sophisticated and elegant society of the capital of the Empire, but the immorality of his *Ars Amatoria* ('Art of Love') offended the Emperor ▷ Augustus who (for this and some other more mysterious offence) exiled him to the Black Sea about AD 9. The works by which Ovid is principally known are: the *Amores*, love poems in what is called the 'elegiac' couplet; the *Ars Amatoria*; the *Remedia Amoris*, in which he tries to redeem himself for the offence he caused by the *Ars Amatoria*; the *Heroides*, in which he makes the heroines of myth give tongue to their misfortunes; the ▷ *Metamorphoses*, a collection of tales about miraculous transformation of shape; the *Fasti*, a poetic account of the Roman calendar; and the *Tristia*, verse epistles lamenting his exile.

Ovid was one of the most read and influential poets in later centuries; in England this is especially true from the 16th to 18th centuries. His most popular work was the *Metamorphoses*; these were repeatedly imitated and translated, memorably by ▷ Golding in the 16th century and by Sandys and ▷ Dryden in the 17th. ▷ Shakespeare was called in 1598 'the English Ovid' because the source of his *Venus and Adonis* was the *Metamorphoses* and that of *The Rape of Lucrece* was the *Fasti*; moreover the quality of these two poems was felt to be Ovidian. ▷ Marlowe translated Ovid's love elegies, and the freedom and vigour of his kind of love poem influenced ▷ Donne in his Elegies. As early as the 14th century ▷ Chaucer got the tales in his ▷ *Legend of Good Women* from the *Heroides*, and these poems set a tradition in 'Heroic Epistles' which began with ▷ Drayton in the early 17th century and culminated in Pope's *Eloisa to Abelard*. Ovid's influence is traceable repeatedly in the work of ▷ Spenser and touched ▷ Milton. Thus he may be said to have affected, either in subject matter or in style, almost all the major poets from Chaucer to Pope, and his influence was equally extensive among lesser figures. The influence was not always deep, however, and it can be ascribed partly to his being the liveliest and most beguiling of the Roman poets who were regarded as the basis of a cultured understanding of literature.
▷ Elegy; Latin literature.

Owen, Robert (1771–1858)

Social reformer, and a leading socialist thinker
in the early 19th century. He became part-
owner of the New Lanark Cotton Mills in
1800, and found that its workers were living
in the degraded and nearly desperate
conditions common in the earlier phase of the
▷ Industrial Revolution. He set about
improving their housing and working
conditions, and established infant schools.
His reforms were a success, but his
expenditure on them caused resentment
among his partners, and in 1813 he
established a new firm, with ▷ Jeremy
Bentham as one of his partners. In the same
year he published a volume of essays, *A New
View of Society*, in which he sought to prove
that the human character is entirely created
by its environment. In 1817, in a report to
the House of Commons, Owen pointed out
that the existing social misery was caused by
men competing unsuccessfully with machines,
and he recommended the establishment of
socialist working communities in the country;
they were to vary from 500 to 3,000 in size,
and were to be partly industrial. His views
were received favourably by, among other
people, the Duke of Kent, the father of
Queen Victoria, but Owen spoilt his case
with public opinion in general by mixing his
proposals with anti-religious propaganda.
Nonetheless two experiments were attempted
in 1825, one in England and one in America;
both failed in under two years. Owen now
became the leader of a socialist-secular
movement, through which he sought to
replace the emphasis on political reform by
emphasis on economic action. His influence
led to the Grand National Consolidated
Trades Union in 1833 (▷ Trade Union),
but this also failed owing to bad organization.
The word 'socialism' originated through
discussions centred on the Association of all
Classes of all Nations, which Owen founded
in 1835. The only permanent success among
Owen's experiments was his establishment of
the Cooperative Movement, which nowadays
is affiliated to the ▷ Labour Party.

Owen, Wilfred (1893–1918)

The best known of the so-called 'War Poets'
of World War I: *Poems* (1920). He served as
an infantry officer, was awarded a decoration
for bravery, and was killed a week before the
armistice. Before the war he was already
writing mildly sensuous poetry influenced by
▷ Keats; for some time during the war he
continued to write in this late romantic
tradition. But he then adapted his technique
so as to express the intensity of the suffering
of the Western Front, deliberately introducing
elements of discordance and harshness into
his style especially by the use of 'para-rhyme',
ie the repetition of consonants but changing
the vowels, as in the words 'hall'-'hell'. The
best known of his poems is *Strange Meeting* –
a dream about an encounter with an enemy
soldier who is, humanly, a friend, in
surroundings which are both those of the war
and of hell. Owen's poems have been used by
the composer Benjamin Britten in one of his
major musical compositions, *War Requiem*.
    ▷ War Poets.
Bib: Owen, H., *Life*; critical study by D. S.
R. Welland; Hibberd, D., *Owen the Poet*.

Owl and the Nightingale, The

A Middle English anonymous debate poem,
dating from the early 13th century. It is a
sparkling, highly sophisticated piece in which
the two birds take opposing views first on
their respective arts of song-making, but then
on a wide range of religious and moral issues.
The natural song-making ability of the birds
is used to represent the clash between
different kinds of lyrical literary traditions;
indeed the question of whether literature
should be used as a medium of entertainment
or instruction becomes part of the grounds of
their quarrel. The author makes full use of
the range of shifting symbolic and figural
associations of owls and nightingales, and
plays with the possibilities of their
anthropomorphic and naturalistic
representation. Neither of the two birds is a
wholly positive or negative figure, neither is
clearly right or wrong, though generally the
nightingale takes the lighter role whereas the
owl espouses a more solemn stance. Their
dispute is not resolved: the narrative
concludes with their departure to seek
judgement from one Master Nicholas of
Guildford.
Bib: Stanley, E. G. (ed.), *The Owl and the
Nightingale*.

Oxford Groups (Buchmanism)

A religious movement in Britain during the
1930s, inspired and led by the American
evangelist Frank Buchman. It was organized
in small groups, whose members met to
discuss their problems under Divine
Guidance received in answer to prayer, a
procedure similar to that employed by the
18th-century ▷ Methodists and the 17th-
century ▷ Quakers. Opponents alleged that
Divine Guidance was unduly right wing; the
movement was concerned about the spread of
▷ atheism through ▷ Communist cells
throughout Europe. It was largely despised

by intellectuals, but had wide influence especially among the upper classes. Since World War II the movement has been re-formed under the title MRA – Moral Rearmament. MRA seems to have many of the same characteristics as the Groups, but to be more international in its scope. To left-wing intellectuals, both the Groups and MRA represent a kind of ▷ 'Fascism'.

Oxford Movement (Tractarian Movement)

A religious movement within the ▷ Church of England; it had its origin and main centre in Oxford and ran from 1833, when it began with a sermon by ▷ Keble, until 1845 when its most eloquent leader, ▷ John Newman, entered the ▷ Roman Catholic Church. Some of the leaders of the Church of England realized (especially after the Act of Catholic Emancipation, 1829) that the Church was by its constitution largely at the mercy of the state, and was in danger of becoming in essentials a department of the state. The Oxford Movement preached that the Church had its independent, spiritual status, was in direct descent from the medieval Catholic Church, and represented a 'middle way' between ▷ post-Reformation Catholicism and ▷ Protestantism. The movement's propaganda was conducted through ▷ tracts, many of them by John Newman, and culminated in *Tract XC* which asserted that the ▷ Thirty-Nine Articles, on which ▷ Anglican doctrine is based, are compatible with Roman Catholic doctrine. The tracts divided Anglican opinion severely, and Newman's secession to the Church of Rome, followed by the secession of other High Anglican clergy, brought the movement into discredit with the majority of Anglican opinion. Edward Pusey, Professor of Hebrew at Oxford, was the leader of the Oxford Movement, which was in consequence often called Puseyite. An indirect result of the movement was to focus attention on the medieval background of the Church, and to encourage that reification of the ▷ Middle Ages which emerged in much Victorian literature, in the artistic movement known as ▷ Pre-Raphaelitism and in Victorian neo-Gothic architecture.

Oxford University

The oldest of the English Universities. It was started by students from the still older University of Paris in the 12th century, and the colleges which give it (and Cambridge) its distinctive character began to be founded in the 13th century, as a means of housing students and keeping order among them. The colleges are not controlled by the University, but are self-governing institutions, though their members usually (always in the case of senior members) hold university appointments as well. Oxford provided the students who early in the 13th century started ▷ Cambridge University, but Oxford remained of superior importance until the 15th century, by which time it was infected by ▷ Wycliffite heresies, and the major patrons (especially the Crown) began to distribute to Cambridge at least an equal share of the wealth in endowments.

Oxford produced some of the intellectual leaders of medieval Europe: in the 13th century ▷ Roger Bacon and ▷ Duns Scotus, in the 14th century ▷ Wycliffe. The ▷ New Learning of the ▷ Renaissance began in the 16th century, under the leadership of ▷ Erasmus, ▷ Thomas More, ▷ Grocyn and Colet to oust medieval ▷ scholasticism. Since then Oxford has retained its status as one of the main channels through which persons who attain positions of power in public life receive their education.

▷ Universities.

Oxymoron

▷ Figures of Speech.

Ozymandias (1818)

A witty sonnet by ▷ Percy Bysshe Shelley concerning the vanity of human ambition. An ancient statue stands broken and isolated in the desert, its boastful inscription now carrying an ironically different meaning from that first intended: 'My name is Ozymandias, king of kings:/ Look on my works, ye Mighty, and despair!' The ancient Greek historian Diodorus Siculus (1st century BC) calls the tomb of the great Egyptian Pharoah Rameses II the tomb of Ozymandias.

P

Paean
In ancient Greece, a hymn of thanksgiving, obscurely linked with the god of health (or perhaps ▷ Apollo in one of his aspects), perhaps through the practice of chanting sacred healing spells.

Pageant
The word derives from the name of a kind of stage used in medieval ▷ Mystery plays which moved in procession to prearranged positions in the town and exhibited scenes from the Bible dramatizing the fall of man and his redemption by Christ. In modern England, a pageant is a display, commonly in the form of a procession, celebrating a historical or legendary event, usually with patriotic significance. This sense of the word 'pageant' has a clear relationship with the Mystery plays, and illustrates a particular dramatic viewpoint. The Mysteries were dramatic inasmuch as they represented conflicts between good and evil, but the stories and their outcome were fully known to the audience, so that there was small place for the unexpected. The modern pageant is an undramatic spectacle, and such pageants existed in the 16th century, symbolizing non-biblical legends of patriotic significance like the story of ▷ St George and the Dragon. Thus the traditions of the pageant are twofold: in one sense it is purely spectacle, but in another it may be a spectacle combined with the narrative of a conflict, which is dramatic only because the conflict is seen as symbolic of a permanent truth of human experience. The second sense of the pageant tradition is important for understanding ▷ Elizabethan ▷ history plays, especially those of ▷ Shakespeare. Thus, in ▷ *Henry IV, Part I* the modern audience is inclined to see the drama as a conflict for the soul of Prince Hal, who on the one hand is faced with the temptations of self-indulgence through Falstaff, and on the other with the task of winning 'honour' from Hotspur. Yet the audience is misled by this approach, since in I.ii Prince Hal declares that he is in no danger of yielding to Falstaff, and his acquisition of honour is also foreknown through the historical fact of the battle of ▷ Agincourt; Hal is thus not the hero of an inner moral and an outer physical conflict, at least in the sense that there is the smallest uncertainty in the audience's mind about the outcome. On the other hand, Falstaff and Hotspur – the self-indulgent favourite and the self-centred politician – are dangers to which any nation is everlastingly exposed. Thus the dramatic interest of the play is not Hal but the nation, and the play is essentially the re-enactment of a conflict to which the nation is perpetually exposed – a dramatic pageant in the Mystery and ▷ Morality tradition. Pageants even informal ones continued to be important in the social life of communities: ▷ Virginia Woolf's *Between the Acts* is based on one.

Paine, Thomas (1737–1809)
Political author. The son of a small farmer, his early career in England as an official ended in failure, and he sailed for America in 1774. In 1776 he published the republican pamphlet *Common Sense*, which set the colonists openly on the road to independence. After the start of the American War of Independence, he maintained the morale of the rebels with a series of pamphlets called *The Crisis* (1776–83). The opening sentence was 'These are the times that try men's souls' – words which became a battle-cry.

In 1787 he returned to Europe to carry on his fight for republican democracy. When ▷ Burke published his ▷ *Reflections on the Revolution in France* in 1790, Paine replied with Part I of his *Rights of Man* (1791). The Government was making the preparations for his trial for treason in 1792 when the poet ▷ William Blake got him out of the country to France, where the French revolutionary government had elected him a member of the republican Convention. In France he published his *Age of Reason* (1793) which defended a rational, abstract form of ▷ deism against orthodox Christianity. This caused him to lose his popularity in England and in America. He also lost favour with the French for his injudicious criticisms, and for a time he was imprisoned, though he was later restored to his seat in the Convention. In 1802 he returned to America to find that he had lost his influence there and he died at his farm in New Rochelle in 1809. Ten years later the English radical ▷ William Cobbett returned to England with Tom Paine's bones. For some time his works remained a text-book for English radicalism.

Palace of Pleasure
An anthology of tales translated from the Italian and Latin, compiled by William Painter (?1540–94) and published 1566–7. Writers include Bandello, ▷ Boccaccio, ▷ Herodotus and ▷ Livy. It was used as a source-book for plots by ▷ Elizabethan dramatists, including ▷ Shakespeare who drew on it, at least to some extent, for ▷ *All's Well that Ends Well*, and perhaps some other plays.

Palamon and Arcite
Rivals for the love of Emily in ▷ Chaucer's
▷ *Knight's Tale*, the first of the
▷ *Canterbury Tales*. ▷ Dryden
paraphrased Chaucer's tale as *Palamon and
Arcite*, published in his *Fables Ancient and
Modern* (1699).

Pale, The English
An area round Dublin on the eastern coast of
Ireland in which, from the 12th to the 16th
centuries, English authority was well
established; the rest of the country, though
nominally under the English Crown, was not
governed effectively by it. The Pale was
larger or smaller according to the degree of
English strength, and its importance lessened
in the reign of ▷ Elizabeth I when Ireland
was for the first time thoroughly subdued.
The idiom 'beyond the Pale' means
'uncivilized', or merely 'unacceptable in
civilized society'.

Palindrome
▷ Figures of Speech.

Palinode
The withdrawal in a piece of writing of ideas
or attitudes expressed in another by the same
writer; or the expression in one work of ideas
which are in direct opposition to those which
the author has expressed in a previous one.

Palladio, Andrea (1508–80)
Italian architect. Palladio's villas, public
buildings and churches – built between 1540
and 1580, and to be found in Venice, Vicenza
and the countryside around these two
important ▷ Renaissance Italian cities –
were to have a lasting effect on English and
American architectural styles. The first great
English classical architect – ▷ Inigo Jones –
was strongly influenced by Palladian ideals of
design. These ideals – usually manifested in
symmetrical fronts and applied half-columns
topped by a pediment – were themselves
derived from Palladio's intense study of
architectural styles to be found in the
surviving antiquities of ancient Rome. Indeed,
Palladio was himself the author of one of the
earliest guidebooks to the city's remains when
he published his *Le Antichita di Roma* in
1554. This work, together with his *Quattro
Libri dell' Architettura* (1570), served to
publicize the classical forms of architecture
which came to dominate design in the 17th
and 18th centuries.
The 'Palladian' style expresses key
Renaissance aesthetic ideas. Those ideas,
which encompass proportion, harmony and
balance, were to become of great importance
during the 18th century when Palladio's

designs, and studies of his works, were much
in vogue.
Bib: Wittkower, R., *Architectural Principles
in the Age of Humanism*; Ackerman, J. S.,
Palladio.

Pamela (1740–1)
Subtitled 'Virtue Rewarded', *Pamela* is an
epistolary novel by ▷ Samuel Richardson.
The story of a young servant girl who evades
her master's attempts at seduction,
Richardson's novel was a great contemporary
success, yet sophisticated readers were quick
to see its ambiguous message. By her
insistence on her country simplicity, Pamela
persuades the squire to marry her; yet her
self-conscious parade of 'artless' virtue
suggests a level of sexual innuendo of which
Richardson may or may not have been aware.
▷ Henry Fielding's *Shamela* and ▷ *Joseph
Andrews* parody this element of *Pamela*.

Pamphlet
Any short treatise published separately,
usually without hard covers. It is usually
polemical, *ie* written to defend or attack some
body of ideas, especially religious or political
ones. In the 16th century and especially
towards the end of the reign of ▷ Elizabeth
I pamphleteering became a widespread
literary industry, the beginning of journalism.
▷ Thomas Nashe and ▷ Thomas Dekker
were amongst the most famous pamphleteers,
and the ▷ Marprelate controversy was the
most famous of the 'pamphlet wars'. In the
17th century Milton was the most famous
writer of pamphlets, and his ▷ *Areopagitica*
is his masterpiece. In the 18th century some
of ▷ Swift's finest prose was in pamphlet
form, *eg* ▷ *A Modest Proposal* (1729), and
▷ Defoe was a prolific pamphleteer. The
18th century, however, saw the rise of the
weekly periodicals, which reduced the need
for the pamphlet form of literature.
▷ Journalism.

Pan
In Greek myth, the god of shepherds and
huntsmen, and therefore associated with
animals and wild places. He is represented
with horns, with the legs and feet of a goat,
and as playing on the seven-reed shepherd's
pipe. He was worshipped chiefly in the
pastoral state of ▷ Arcadia.
The ▷ nymph Syrinx was turned into a
reed so that she could escape pursuit by Pan.

Pandora
In Greek myth, the first woman. She was
sent as a calamity to men by ▷ Zeus, who
was enraged by the theft of fire by
▷ Prometheus, acting for mankind. Zeus

sent her as a gift to Epimetheus, the brother of Prometheus, and she brought with her a vase ('Pandora's box'). When she opened the vase, all the calamities from which mankind suffers spread over the world; only Hope remained in the vase to comfort mankind.

Pandosto (1588)
A prose romance by ▷ Robert Greene, used by Shakespeare as the basis for his late play, ▷ *The Winter's Tale*.

Panjandrum
The word first occurs in a sentence devised by the actor-playwright Samuel Foote (1720–77) to test the memory of another actor-playwright, Charles Macklin (d 1797): '. . . and there were present the Picninnies, and the Joblillies, and the Garyulies, and the Grand Panjandrum himself, with the little round button at top.' The word came to be used for any pompous person, or for someone of supposed power.

Pantagruel
A comic romance by ▷ François Rabelais, published in its first version in 1532. Pantagruel is the son of ▷ Gargantua.

Pantaloon
A character in old Italian popular comedy. He represented a Venetian, and the name derived from the Venetian saint, San Pantaleone. He became a popular figure in international ▷ pantomime, and appears as a stupid old man wearing spectacles, slippers, and clumsy trousers or pantaloons, from which comes 'pants'. Pantaloon used also to be a term for any feeble-minded old man, *eg* in ▷ Shakespeare's ▷ *As You Like It*.

Pantheism
A term used to cover a variety of religious and philosophical beliefs, which have in common that God is present in Nature, and not separable from it in the sense in which a cause is separable from its effect, or a creator from his creation. Pantheism is implicit in doctrines derived from ▷ Plato, *eg* in some of the neo–Platonists of the 16th century, and in some poetry inspired by the natural environment. Amongst English poets, the most famous example is ▷ Wordsworth in his earlier phase (1797–1807), notably in the first two books of his 1805 version of ▷ *The Prelude*. In his revised version of this autobiographical poem, Wordsworth tried to eliminate the pantheistic tendencies, since they are not in accordance with most forms of Christian doctrine.

Pantisocracy
The name given by ▷ Samuel Taylor Coleridge and ▷ Robert Southey to the ideal anarchistic society which preoccupied them in 1794–5 during the first phase of the ▷ French Revolution (from the Greek: *pan* = 'all', *isos* = 'the same', *cratos* = 'power'). They hoped to establish a community on the banks of the River Susquehanna in the United States in which motives of gain would be replaced by brotherly love. They were unable to raise money, however, their ideas changed, and they abandoned their plan.

Pantomime
Originally, in ancient Rome, a representation by masked actors, using gestures and dance, of religious or warlike eposodes. One actor played many parts, male and female, with changes of mask and costume. It was often accompanied by music. It was used for episodes in medieval religious drama, and as the 16th-century Italian ▷ *commedia dell 'arte* it became a form of popular drama that spread all over Europe together with a number of traditional characters such as Harlequin and the Clown. In the 18th century it established itself in England. Nowadays the children's pantomimes performed in Britain after Christmas are usually musical plays representing traditional folk-tales (*Puss in Boots, Dick Whittington*, etc.) in a vulgarized form, but sometimes introducing traditional characters from the *commedia dell'arte*. Certain conventions are peculiar to it: the hero of the story or 'principal boy' is always performed by an actress, and a comic character known as the 'pantomime dame' is performed by an actor.

Paolo and Francesca
Lovers who lived in 13th-century Italy and who are famous largely through their appearance in the fifth Canto of ▷ Dante's ▷ *Inferno*. Francesca was married to Giovanni Malatesta of Rimini but fell in love with Paolo, his brother. When the affair was discovered, the lovers were both killed. In the *Inferno*, Francesca tells Dante how she and Paolo first realized and communicated their love while reading the love story of ▷ Lancelot and ▷ Guinevere. ▷ Leigh Hunt recounts their love affair in his poem, *The Story of Rimini* (1816).

Paphos
A city in Cyprus and, in the period of ancient Greece, a centre for the worship of ▷ Aphrodite (originally of a similar goddess who became identified with her). As she was the goddess of sexual love, a 'Paphian' became a synonym for a prostitute.

Paradise Lost (1667)

Illustration from *Paradise Lost*

An ▷ epic poem by ▷ John Milton, first
published in ten books in 1667, but
reorganized and published in 12 books in a
second edition of 1674. The composition of
Paradise Lost was possibly begun in the mid-
1650s, but the idea for an epic based on
scriptural sources had, in all probability,
occurred to Milton at least as early as 1640,
when the four drafts of an outline ▷ tragedy
were composed. These drafts, contained in a
Trinity College, Cambridge, manuscript,
indicate that, in original conception, *Paradise
Lost* (or, to give the poem its draft title –
Adam Unparadized) was to have been a
sacred drama, rather than an epic. This hint
at a dramatic origin, on the lines of classical
Greek tragedy, helps to explain the
undoubtedly dramatic qualities to be found in
the poem – for example the soliloquizing
habits of Satan, and the *perepeteias*, or
discoveries, where new ironies in the narrative
are allowed to unfold.

The chief source of the poem is the
▷ Bible, but the Bible as glossed and
commented upon by the Patristic (early
Christian) authorities, and by ▷ Protestant
theologians. But also important to Milton's
project were the classical writers – ▷ Homer
and ▷ Virgil – from whom Milton's

conception of 'epic' was principally inherited.
▷ Edmund Spenser's ▷ *The Faerie Queene*
was also vital to Milton's handling of language
and imagery. To these principle sources can
be added the epics of ▷ Ludovico Ariosto
and ▷ Torquato Tasso, ▷ Ovid's
Metamorphoses, the *De rerum natura* of
▷ Lucretius, and the once popular, though
now little read, *La Semaine* by ▷ Guillaume
de Saluste du Bartas. Once these sources
have been remarked upon, however, the
possible progenitors of Milton's poem still
remain numberless, since *Paradise Lost* draws
upon the whole field of intellectual endeavour
open to a classically trained European scholar
in the 17th century.

For all that it is a poem rooted in Milton's
literary experience, it is also a poem of, and
for, its times. The poem's chief theme is
rebellion – the rebellion of Satan and his
followers against God, and the rebellion of
Adam and Eve against divine law. Within
this sacred context, Milton sets himself the
task of justifying God's creational will to his
17th-century readers. But, in confronting
questions such as choice, obedience and forms
of government, Milton also raises the issues
of freedom, social relationships and the
quality and definition of power – whether
almighty, satanic or human. We can thus
understand the poem as confronting political
questions which, in the moment of its
composition and eventual publication
following the English ▷ Civil War and the
▷ Restoration of the monarchy, were of real
urgency both to the republican Milton and
his readers. That is not to say that, as some of
Milton's commentators have claimed, the
poem operates as a veiled ▷ allegory of
events in mid-17th-century England. But the
issues which the protagonists in *Paradise Lost*
face are also issues which were at the heart of
contemporary political debate. To entwine
matters of theology and political theory was
by no means a strange grafting to Milton's
contemporaries. Religion and politics were
inseparably twinned, and *Paradise Lost*
confronts that conjunction at every point.

The history of the poem's critical reception
since the date of its publication is itself a
commentary on the history of English literary
'taste'. For all that 18th-century writers
admired Milton's grand scheme, their
admiration was tinged by a certain uneasiness.
Both ▷ Joseph Addison and ▷ Samuel
Johnson felt that Milton's achievement was
undoubtedly immense, but that it was also an
achievement which could not and should not
be replicated. For the poets of the
▷ Romantic period – ▷ William Blake,

▷ Percy Bysshe Shelley, ▷ John Keats, and the ▷ William Wordsworth of ▷ *The Prelude – Paradise Lost* was read as a significant text in the history of the individual's struggle to identify him or herself within the political and social sphere. But rather than understand the poem as a theological epic, they tended to read it as a text of human liberty, with Satan, rather than God, as the focus of the poem's meaning. In the 20th century, following the re-evaluation in poetic taste prompted by ▷ W. B. Yeats, ▷ T. S. Eliot and ▷ F. R. Leavis, *Paradise Lost* was seen, once more, as a masterpiece of questionable stature. Was it, perhaps, removed from what Eliot and Leavis in particular cared to identify as the 'English tradition'? The debate initiated by Leavis and his followers was to be answered in a series of important accounts of the poem by ▷ C. S. Lewis, ▷ William Empson and ▷ Christopher Ricks. In the 1970s and 1980s attention has been refocussed, by ▷ Marxist and ▷ feminist critics especially, on what have long been unexamined aspects of the poem: its treatment of patriarchal authority and its relationship to the continuing historical debate on the intellectual culture of the revolutionary period. At the same time, Milton's themes of language and identity have rendered the poem a fruitful text for ▷ psychoanalytic criticism. We might conclude, then, that, if perhaps the greatest achievement of the English literary ▷ Renaissance, *Paradise Lost* is also a text open to continuous re-reading and revision.
Bib: Carey, J. and Fowler, A. (eds.) *The Complete Poems of John Milton.*

Paradise Regained (1671)

An ▷ epic poem by ▷ John Milton in four books, it was first published (together with ▷ *Samson Agonistes*) in 1671. Begun after the publication of ▷ *Paradise Lost* in 1667, the poem can, in some sense, be thought of as a sequel to *Paradise Lost*. In particular, the poem's treatment of Christ, his resistance to temptation, and the redeeming nature of his ministry on earth, cast him in the theologically traditional role of the 'Second Adam' – a regenerative and redeeming force in the world.

Where *Paradise Lost*, however, was conceived of along lines inherited from classical epic, *Paradise Regained* is in the form of the 'brief epic' in the style of the book of ▷ *Job*. The chief subject matter of the poem is the temptation of Christ in the wilderness, described in the gospel of *St Luke*.

Paradiso

The third and final section of ▷ Dante's great poem, the ▷ *Divina Commedia*. Dante has been led through the Inferno and the Purgatorio by the spirit of the Roman poet ▷ Virgil. Now his guide is Beatrice, the woman who had inspired Dante's love. As the Inferno had been divided into circles, so Paradise is divided into spheres: the sphere of the Moon, of Mercury, Venus, the Sun, Mars, Jupiter, Saturn, the Fixed Stars, and the Primum Mobile, or First Mover. Each sphere contains the kind of spirit which the ancient Greek and Roman myths had caused to be associated with it: Mars, the Christian warriors and martyrs; Jupiter, the just rulers; Saturn, the holy contemplatives, etc. The spheres are in ascending order of merit, and culminate in Dante's remote, ecstatic vision of God Himself. In each, Dante has conversations on philosophical and spiritual matters with the men and women from history whom he conceives to have been assigned there.
▷ *Inferno; Purgatorio.*

Paradox
▷ Figures of Speech.

Pardoner's Prologue and Tale, The

One of ▷ Chaucer's ▷ *Canterbury Tales*. As his contribution to the storytelling competition, the Pardoner offers an exposé of his standard preaching routine in theory and in practice. His performance may be compared to that of Faus Semblant (False Seeming) in the ▷ *Roman de la Rose*. His prologue outlines the range of techniques he employs to persuade his lay audiences to buy his (self-confessedly) worthless relics, and contains verbatim extracts from his routine. The theme of his performance as a whole is '*Radix malorum est cupiditas*' ('covetousness is the root of all evil'), but the maxim is graphically illustrated in his tale of the three 'riotoures' who set out to kill Death (who has killed one of their companions). They meet a mysterious old man on their quest, who directs them to a spot where they might find Death, but when they arrive they simply find a pile of gold. As a result of their plotting to cheat each other out of their shares in the gold, all three are killed. Although the Pardoner has exposed his mercenary motives to the pilgrim audience, he ends his performance apparently with a serious attempt to sell them his relics. His invitation to the Host to have the first choice is violently and abusively rejected. The game limits have been transgressed and the Knight steps in to heal the breach so that the *Canterbury Tales* may continue.

Paris

In Greek myth, the son of ▷ Priam, king of ▷ Troy, and his queen, ▷ Hecuba. Because Hecuba dreamed that Paris would bring destruction on Troy, Priam ordered the baby to be exposed on Mount Ida. However, he was found and brought up by shepherds. He fell in love and lived happily with the nymph ▷ Oenone until called upon to award the golden apple to the fairest goddess. ▷ Hera, ▷ Athene and ▷ Aphrodite disputed for its possession, each trying to bribe him to decide in her favour, but Aphrodite won the prize by promising him the most beautiful woman in the world. Paris abandoned Oenone and went to ▷ Troy where Priam acknowledged him as his son. He then visited ▷ Menelaus, king of Sparta, whose wife, ▷ Helen, was the most beautiful woman in the world. Paris and Helen eloped to Troy, thus starting the Trojan War. Paris was mortally wounded by an arrow shot from the bow of ▷ Philoctetes and sought out Oenone, who alone could cure him. She refused to treat him until it was too late, when she took her own life from grief.

Parker, Matthew (1504–75)

Became Archibishop of ▷ Canterbury on the accession of ▷ Elizabeth I, and her main ally in her policy of keeping the ▷ Church of England on its unique midway course between the Roman Catholic Church and the more decidedly ▷ Protestant sects such as the ▷ Lutherans and ▷ Calvinists, represented in England by the ▷ Puritans. He was a notable scholar, and promoted the 'Bishops' Bible' (1568) which became the basis for the 'Authorized Version' of 1611.

▷ Anglican; Bible in England; Reformation; Catholicism (Roman) in English literature.

Parlement of the Three Ages, The

A 14th-century alliterative poem, recounting a ▷ dream vision experience in which the narrator witnesses a debate between Youth, Middle Age, and Old Age. These figures describe the different occupations and preoccupations of the successive stages in a man's life (the focus is on masculine pursuits); the pursuit of courtly pleasures advocated by Youth, gives way to the materialistic concerns which obsess Middle Age, and finally the *contemptus mundi* views of Old Age are ushered in. Old Age eclipses the views of Youth and Middle Age, because for him any engagement in worldly pleasures or materialistic gains is vain and futile. There is a correlation between the different attitudes and interests of the figures and different kinds of literary traditions, so the narrative offers a summary view of a range of literary themes and subjects at the same time as it epitomises the stance of Youth, Middle Age and Old Age.

Bib: Offord, M. Y. (ed.), *The Parlement of the Thre Ages.*

Parliament

The name of the supreme law-making body of Great Britain and Northern Ireland. It has two parts – the House of Commons, whose members are elected, and the House of Lords, the majority of whose members still sit by hereditary right. 'House' in these expressions does not refer to a building, but is equivalent to 'assembly'; the Lords and Commons meet in different chambers of the same building, officially called the ▷ Palace of Westminster but colloquially known as the Houses of Parliament.

Parliament is a direct descendant of the medieval Magnum Concilium or Great Council, composed until the end of the 13th century of the chief landowners (nobility) of the realm, together with the bishops and principal abbots. To these ▷ Edward I added representatives of the Commons, *ie* elected members from the towns and smaller landowners; his purpose was to facilitate the imposition and collection of taxes. At first the Commons assembled with the nobility or lords, but in the 14th century they began to sit as separate assemblies.

In the 16th century the great nations of western Europe became despotisms; the kings of France and Spain ceased to summon their national assemblies, which under different names were equivalent to the English Parliament. In England, ▷ Henry VIII, though no less a despot, found his Parliament useful as an instrument in asserting the independence of the ▷ Church of England, since the authority of the Pope had long been unpopular in England. The growth in wealth of the English middle class and the financial weakness of the Crown combined with religious disagreements inherited from the ▷ Reformation to make the 17th century a period of epic struggle for power between Parliament and the kings. The successive stages of this conflict – open disagreement on policy under ▷ James I, the ▷ Civil Wars under ▷ Charles I, the republican interregnum followed by the restoration of the monarchy – culminated in the complete victory for Parliament (in which the Commons were now taking the leading role) following the deposition of ▷ James II in the ▷ Revolution of 1688.

This did not mean, however, that England became a parliamentary democracy; methods of election were corrupt, and the system did not correspond to the distribution of the population, with the result that throughout the 18th century power remained in the hands of the landed aristocracy, which controlled both Houses and usually tied the hands of the kings, but retained an alliance and close connections with the middle class. In the 19th century steady movements were made towards democracy through the succession of laws widening and modernizing the electoral system: the passing of the ▷ Reform Bill of 1832 extended the vote to all the richer middle class; the Act of 1867 gave it to industrial workers, and the Act of 1884 to agricultural workers. Women had to wait for laws passed in 1918 and 1928 to receive the vote. These changes in the 19th century were brought about by the ▷ Industrial Revolution, which enormously increased the populations of the towns, some of which had hitherto been unrepresented in Parliament, and brought about a cleavage of interest between the urban industrialists and the land-owners; the same set of causes encouraged the working classes to organize themselves so that they could no longer be ignored as a separate body of opinion.

▷ Scotland had her own Parliament until the Union of Parliaments in 1707, since when she has sent representatives to Westminster; ▷ Ireland sent members from 1801, when her own parliament was abolished; ▷ Wales never had her own parliament but has sent members to Westminster since union in 1535. In 1922, Irish representation at Westminster was reduced to Ulster, or Northern Ireland, since the rest of the country became an independent republic.

Since the 17th century, the Commons has been unquestionably the more important House; since the Parliament Act (1911) the legal powers of the House of Lords have been severely reduced, by that law and by later legislation.

Parliament of Foulys, The

A ▷ dream-vision poem by ▷ Chaucer, in ▷ rhyme royal, which concludes with an account of a bird parliament, held on St Valentine's Day, when the birds meet to decide their mates for the year. The poem begins with an account of the melancholic narrator's reading matter, ▷ Cicero's *Dream of Scipio*, and then proceeds to recount a marvellous dream-experience in which the narrator is taken into a garden of love by Africanus, an important guide figure of the *Dream of Scipio*. Inside the garden, the narrator first explores Venus's temple and then moves on to witness the bird parliament, presided over by Dame Nature. Proceedings are delayed by a debate over which of three tercel eagles is the most fitting mate for a formel eagle. Representatives from the three bird estates offer their views, but the decision is finally given to the formel eagle herself, who defers making a choice for another year. The rest of the birds are then free to choose their partners and the dream ends with a bird song (a ▷ roundel) welcoming Spring. The dreamer awakes and returns to his books, still hoping to learn something of value from them.

In just 699 lines, Chaucer explores the continuum of love and its literary expression, evoking the philosophical and ethical dimensions of love as a literary subject, yet keeping the tone of this *tour de force* light and comic, through using a slightly ineffectual narrator, and giving floor space to the down-to-earth views of geese and cuckoos on the subject. It is a poem which wittily negotiates quotations from ▷ Dante and from ducks.

▷ Courtly Love.
Bib: Brewer, D. S. (ed.), *The Parliament of Foulys*.

Parnassus

A mountain near Delphi in Greece. Originally sacred to Dionysus, it was later regarded as the dwelling of ▷ Apollo and the nine ▷ Muses, and hence particularly associated with poetry. The ▷ Castalian spring rises there, and drinking from it was said to give inspiration.

Parnell, Charles Stewart (1846–91)

Irish political leader. He entered Parliament in 1875, and led the ▷ Home Rule party in its fight for Irish self-government. He converted ▷ Gladstone and the ▷ Liberal Party to the support of Home Rule, but was politically ruined by becoming involved in a scandal with the wife of Captain O'Shea in 1890. His success was the more remarkable because he was a ▷ Protestant; the scandal finally turned the Catholic Church in Ireland against him. His downfall caused a deep split among the Irish nationalists.
▷ Ireland.

Parnell, Thomas (1679–1718)

Member of the ▷ Tory clique associated

with the ministry of Harley and
▷ Bolingbroke and participant with
▷ Jonathan Swift, ▷ Alexander Pope,
▷ John Gay and ▷ John Arbuthnot, in
the shortlived ▷ Scriblerus Club. He
translated a comic epic then attributed to
▷ Homer, *Battle of the Frogs and Mice*, into
heroic ▷ couplets (1717). He also composed
moral and allegorical ▷ fables including *The
Hermit*, and the drearily sexist *Hesiod: or,
The Rise of Woman*, 'A creature fond and
changing, fair and vain,/ The creature woman,
rises now to reign.' His versification has a
facile elegance which was greatly overvalued
at the time. In *A Night-Piece on Death*, first
published in his posthumous *Poems* (1722),
the characteristic tetrameter (▷ metre)
couplet of 17th-century reflective poetry is
smoothed out and polished, transforming
religious intensity into conventional piety:
'There pass with melancholy State,/ By all
the solemn Heaps of Fate,/ And think, as
softly-sad thou tread/ Above the venerable
Dead,/ Time was, like thee they Life possest,/
And Time shall be, that you shalt Rest.'
Later graveyard musings in the 1740s and
1750s add ▷ gothic or sentimental
elaborations to Parnell's model. Parnell's
Essay on the Different Stiles of Poetry (1713)
gives a rigid exposition of the ▷ Augustan
doctrine of literary kinds.
Bib: Woodman, R., *Thomas Parnell*.

Parody

A literary form which constitutes a comic
imitation of a serious work, or of a serious
literary form. Thus ▷ Fielding's ▷ *Joseph
Andrews* is partly a parody of
▷ Richardson's ▷ *Pamela*, and ▷ Pope's
▷ *Rape of the Lock* is a parody of grand
▷ epic in the style of ▷ Homer and
▷ Virgil. It is difficult to draw a line
between parody and ▷ burlesque; the latter
is more obviously comic in its style of
imitation.

Parole

In the work of ▷ Ferdinand de Saussure,
the founder of ▷ Structuralism, this is
usually translated as 'speech' or 'speech act'.
It refers to a particular instance of speech.
'*Parole*' is to be distinguished from ▷ '*langue*'
(language) which is the linguistic system
which underpins every utterance (*parole*).
Speakers of a language (*langue*) avail
themselves of parts of that system and
reactivate it each time they engage in speech
(*parole*).
    ▷ Sign.

Paronomasia
    ▷ Figures of Speech.

Parson's Tale, The

The last of ▷ Chaucer's ▷ *Canterbury
Tales*. It is prefaced by a call from the Host
for the Parson to complete the sequence with
a 'fable'. Although the Parson rejects this
request (indeed he rejects the value of literary
fictions altogether), he offers instead a 'myrie
tale in prose', which will complete the journey
by showing the pilgrims the way to that
'parfit, glorious pilgrimmage that highte
Jerusalem celestial'. What he presents is a
treatise on the art of penance (drawn in fact
from two well-known penitential handbooks
of the 13th century), which includes a review
of the ▷ Seven Deadly Sins and concludes
with an emphatic call for repentance.
Chaucer's 'Retraction' follows the Parson's
treatise (in most manuscripts). In this the
'maker' takes leave of his book, and asks
forgiveness for any literary sins he may have
committed in his writing career. In
concluding the *Canterbury Tales* in this way,
Chaucer is both affirming the ultimate values
propounded in *The Parson's Tale* (the
Parson's call for repentance is followed by an
act of repentance) and following a long
tradition of literary endings in which writers
distance themselves from the non-religious
aspects of their work.

Parthenon

(Literally 'Temple of the Maiden'.) The
ruined temple to the ancient Greek goddess
▷ Athene in Athens. It is one of the noblest
examples of ancient Greek architecture.

Parties, Political

The English political scene has been
dominated by political parties since the mid-
17th century. It was not till the 19th century
that political parties became highly organized,
and though there have seldom been more
than two important ones, these have not
always been the same. Nonetheless, there has
been a continuity in the history of parties
sufficient to give a long history to political
loyalties. The principal phases of party
development are summarized as follows:
    1 *1640–1660: the* ▷ *Civil War and*
▷ *Interregnum.* ▷ Parliament, especially
the ▷ House of Commons, successfully led
a rebellion against the king, and established a
republic. The division was partly religious
(▷ Puritan against ▷ Anglican), and partly
economic (the commercially progressive south
and east against the more traditional north
and west). A minority of the House of
Commons and a majority of the House of

Lords sided with the king against the rest of
Parliament; the supporters of the former were
known as Royalists or ▷ Cavaliers, and the
supporters of the latter as Parliament Men, or
▷ Roundheads.

2 *1660–1714: rivalry of Tories and Whigs.*
The basic opposition represented by the Civil
War continued after the ▷ Restoration. The
Tories were strong upholders of the monarchy
and of the Church of England; the Whigs,
without opposing the continuance of either as
institutions, laid emphasis on the rights of
Parliament and the dangers of a re-
establishment of Roman Catholicism with
monarchical despotism. The Whigs were
twice victorious – at the bloodless
▷ Revolution of 1688 when they succeeded
in deposing ▷ James II in consequence of
his Roman Catholicism, and in 1714 when
they prevented the succession of his son as
James III, on the same grounds. (▷ Whig
and ▷ Tory – for the origin of these
names.)

3 *1714–1832: the Whig Oligarchy and the
Tory Revival.* Tories virtually disappeared
from the political scene until the accession of
George III in 1760. During this period
Parliament dominated the monarchy, but the
Whigs divided up into a number of family
alliances and political coteries. After 1760,
George III tried to revive royal power by
creating a party in Parliament to support it;
these were called the King's Friends or New
Tories. The victory of the colonists in the
American War of Independence (1776–83)
and the king's insanity destroyed his
ambitions for reviving royal power, but other
issues confirmed the Tories in power from
1783 to 1830. Chief among these new issues
dividing the nation were: (i) the ▷ French
Revolution, which influenced the Whigs in
the direction of political reform and the
Tories in the direction of resistance to change;
(ii) the English ▷ Industrial Revolution,
which was rapidly expanding an urban middle
class which lacked political rights owing to
the anachronistic parliamentary electoral
system; and (iii) new social problems arising
from the growth of a large urban proletariat.
▷ The Reform Bill of 1832 was another
Whig victory, greatly increasing the power of
the urban middle class.

4 *1832–1918: the evolution of the modern
parties;* ▷ *Liberals, Conservatives and,
finally,* ▷ *Labour.* The parties became more
self-conscious and closely organized; Whigs
came to call themselves Liberals, and Tories
changed their name to Conservatives. Until
1840, the division was between the
agricultural interest (Conservative) and the
industrial interest (Liberal), and the old
religious divisions survived, so that the
Conservatives were the guardians of the
Church of England, and the more decidedly
Protestant sects – now called ▷ Nonconformists – voted Liberal. In the second
half of the 19th century the upper classes of
both towns and countryside tended to vote
Conservative, and the Liberals depended
increasingly on the urban working-class vote.
However, the Liberals, by their traditions,
could never become a predominantly
working-class party; hence the Labour Party
was founded in 1900. The chief issue over
which Liberals and Conservatives fought in
the mid-19th century was ▷ Free Trade
against Protection (by import taxes) of
English agriculture. Later the Tories became
the imperialist party, resisting Irish and South
African Dutch nationalism – issues on which
some Liberals took a more liberal view.

5 *1918–Present Day.* After World War I,
social discontents caused the Labour Party to
succeed the Liberal Party as one of the two
largest in the country. Since 1923, the
Liberals have been reduced to a small though
not insignificant Parliamentary body and now
form part of the Social and Liberal
Democratic Party. The Labour Party, on the
other hand, owes as much to the great 19th-
century Liberal traditions as to the doctrinaire
socialism of ▷ Marx. In the 1980s, due to a
reworking of constituency boundaries and the
trend towards right-wing politics, the
Conservative party has achieved an almost
unassailable position. Moreover, the divisions
in the opposition parties have added to the
overwhelming success of the Tory party.

Pascal, Blaise (1623–62)

French religious philosopher and
mathematician. In 1646 he became a devout
adherent of the Jansenist movement which
had its headquarters at the nunnery of Port-
Royal near Paris. Jansenism (started by
Cornelius Jansen, 1585–1638) maintained, like
the Protestant predestinarians, that salvation
through the love of God was possible only for
those whom God pleased to love, *ie* an
individual was predestined to salvation or to
damnation; however it also emphasized the
necessity of belonging to the Roman Catholic
Church. The movement was strongly attacked
by the ▷ Jesuit Order, and when its leading
exponent, Antoine Arnauld, was being
threatened with dismissal from his academic
post, Pascal wrote *Provincial Letters* (1656) in
his defence. This was his first important
work, a masterpiece of lucid, ironical
controversy; in particular, Pascal advocated

moral austerity and criticized Jesuit libertinism. His *Pensées* ('Thoughts' – pub. 1670) is his more famous work; it consists of notes for a book on religion intended to demonstrate the necessity of the religious life. Though fragmentary, the notes have great aphoristic power; with an intellect as powerful and a style as lucid as that of ▷ Descartes, Pascal criticizes the earlier philosopher's notion of the supreme power of human reason, and shows the limitations of reason in dealing with ultimate mysteries.

Passage to India, A (1924)

A novel by ▷ E. M. Forster. It had originally been planned ten years earlier, and its picture of India belongs partly to that period. The scene is the city of Chandrapore on the banks of the Ganges, and India is under British rule. The background characters consist mainly of the British officials and their wives, and the local Indian intelligentsia. The main characters are as follows: Aziz, a Muslim Indian doctor; Godbole, a Hindu professor; Fielding, the headmaster of the Government College; Ronald Heaslop, another of the British officials; and two visitors from Britain, Mrs Moore, the mother of Heaslop by her first marriage, and Adela Quested, who is engaged to him. Both women have strong liberal principles, and make friends easily with Fielding, the only liberal in the resident British colony. Fielding is also a friend of Aziz, and a colleague of Godbole. Aziz issues an impulsive invitation to the British visitors to visit the local Marabar Caves; these have a strong significance for the Hindus, although Godbole, when he is asked about them, is unable to explain it. The climax of the book occurs when this visit takes place. Heat, discomfort, and the caves themselves cause Mrs Moore and Adela to suffer traumatic experiences. Mrs Moore loses all her faith and idealism; Adela has an attack of hysteria which temporarily convinces her that Aziz has attempted to rape her. This supposed rape brings the already strained relations between the British and the Indians to a crisis, but the crisis is resolved (not without disgracing the more reactionary British officials) by Adela's return to sanity in the witness-box. Mrs Moore, although she is now selfish, hard and disillusioned, whereas before she had been generous, kind and idealistic, is in touch with a new kind of truthfulness which helps Adela's restoration. Only Mrs Moore and Godbole understand the true nature of Adela's experience in the caves, and they understand it from opposite, though

complementary, points of view.

The novel has psychological, political, and religious dimensions, and it is the last of these that is the most important. The Christianity, or the sceptical liberalism, of the more enlightened of the British is shown to be adequate for normal relationships and practical affairs, but they have become too shallow for the interpretation of deeper human experience; Aziz's Muslim faith is stronger, but it is more an aesthetic and cultural tradition than a binding spiritual faith. Godbole's Hinduism, on the other hand, is profound and intelligent, though it is no guide to the daily conduct of affairs. This religious dimension is presented by constant symbolism, ranging in character from unobtrusive (though often important) details, to the conspicuous and suggestive image of the caves themselves. *A Passage to India* is usually regarded as Forster's masterpiece, and is certainly one of the finest English novels of the 20th century.
▷ Imperialism.

Passionate Pilgrim (1599)

An anthology of poetry containing odes by Richard Barnfield (1564–1627) formerly attributed to ▷ Shakespeare.

Passover

A Jewish religious feast held in the spring; it commemorates the event narrated in the ▷ Bible (*Exodus* 12) when the angel of the Lord passed over the houses of the Jews but slew the eldest child of each Egyptian family as a punishment to Pharaoh for not releasing the Jews from captivity. Pharaoh then released the Jews.

Paston Letters

The general name for a large collection of correspondence by, or to, members of the Paston family of Norfolk, dating from 1422–1509. The letters, written at times with great vigour, provide an interesting insight into the political and domestic life of this rising Norfolk family, during the turbulent reigns of Henry vi, Edward iv, and Richard iii.
▷ *Edward IV; Henry VI; Richard III.*
Bib: Davis, N. (ed.), *The Paston Letters.*

Pastoral

A form of literature originally developed by the ancient Greeks and Romans in the ▷ idylls of the former (*eg* ▷ Theocritus's) and the ▷ eclogues of the latter (*eg* ▷ Virgil's). Ancient pastoral idealized the Greek state of ▷ Arcadia which had a rustic population of shepherds and herdsmen. The ▷ Renaissance of the 16th century, deeply interested in the literature of the Greeks and Romans, revived the pastoral mode; the

earliest forms of it date back in Italian
literature to the 15th century, but it was the
romance *Arcadia* (1504), by the Italian poet
Sannazaro, which was particularly influential
throughout Europe. The appeal of the
pastoral kind of literature was partly to
human wishfulness – the desire to conceive of
circumstances in which the complexity of
human problems could be reduced to its
simplest elements: the shepherds and
shepherdesses of pastoral are imagined as
having no worries, and they live in an ideal
climate with no serious physical calamities;
love and death, and making songs and music
about these experiences, are their only
preoccupations. Another function of pastoral,
however, was as a vehicle of moral and social
criticism; the shepherds and shepherdesses
sought the pleasures of nature and despised
or were innocent of the corrupting luxury of
courts and cities. Finally, pastoral presented a
means of offering, allegorically, thinly
disguised tributes of praise and flattery to
real people whom the poet admired or wanted
to please. The satirical, moral and eulogistic
functions of Renaissance pastoral all tended
to make it allegorical, since it was through
▷ allegory that the poet could most safely
make his criticisms felt, and could most
eloquently convey his praise. Allegory also
suited the ▷ neo-Platonic, idealizing cast of
mind so characteristic of 16th-century writers.
When we remember that the tradition of
romantic love was one of the most ardently
pursued inheritances from the ▷ Middle
Ages, and that the circumstances of pastoral
lent themselves to its expression, it is not
surprising that the pastoral mode was so
extensively cultivated in 16th-century Europe.
To England it came late, by way of influences
from France, Spain and Italy, but it lasted
longer; it was especially pervasive in the last
quarter of the 16th century, and continued
till the mid-17th; there was a minor revival
early in the 18th century.

The first important English pastoral poem
is ▷ Edmund Spenser's ▷ *The Shepherd's
Calendar* which consists of an ▷ eclogue
for each month of the year; the tone is
morally didactic in some, satirical in others,
and eulogistic of the queen in a third group.
▷ Philip Sidney's ▷ *The Arcadia* is a
pastoral romance whose purpose is
entertainment, but it idealizes the courtly
virtues, as does Book VI of Spenser's ▷ *The
Faerie Queene*, about Sir Calidore, the
Knight of Courtesy. ▷ The University Wits,
▷ Peele, ▷ Lyly, ▷ Greene and
▷ Lodge, wrote pastoral dramas in verse
and romances in prose, and one of the best

pastoral works of the 1590s is Shakespeare's
▷ *As You Like It*, based on Lodge's
romance *Rosalynde* (1590). Shakespeare
dramatized the pastoral mode, however, with
a difference: the fanciful world of pastoral
romance is contrasted with the world of
common sense, and the fairyland pastoral
country of shepherds and shepherdesses with
Greek names is juxtaposed to the real English
countryside and its commonplace peasants, so
that his pastoral romance is also antipastoral.
It was not unusual, however, to salt pastoral
with elements from real country life – Spenser
does it in *The Shepherd's Calendar*, and
Shakespeare does it most skilfully in ▷ *The
Winter's Tale* IV. iii. More conventional
pastoral dramas were ▷ John Fletcher's
Faithful Shepherdess (1610) and ▷ Ben
Jonson's *The Sad Shepherd* (1635). The
artificiality of pastoral lent itself to the
▷ masque form which combined music,
poetry, dancing and the decor in equal
proportions; Jonson, the master of masque,
wrote a number of pastorals for it, but by far
the most famous pastoral masque is
▷ Milton's ▷ *Comus*.

Of the various forms of pastoral, the prose
romance had the shortest life, and ended with
the 16th century; the last pastoral drama was
Elkanah Settle's *Pastor Fido* (1677). In non-
dramatic poetry, pastoral lasted much longer.
▷ Michael Drayton is the next pastoral poet
of note after Spenser with *Idea: The
Shepherd's Garland* (1593) and *Endimion and
Phoebe* (1595); ▷ Marlowe's famous pastoral
lyric *Come Live With Me* was first printed in
1599, and pastoral lyric writers in the tradition
of Spenser were numerous from 1590 up to
1650; they included Nicholas Breton (?1545–
?1626), ▷ George Wither (1588–1667),
▷ William Browne (1591–1643), and above
all ▷ Robert Herrick. However, the most
famous poems in 17th-century pastoral are
Milton's: ▷ *L'Allegro* and *Il Penseroso* and
his ▷ elegy ▷ *Lycidas*. In the 18th century,
▷ Pope's early *Pastorals* (1709) were a small
masterpiece influenced by Virgil, but his
▷ *Windsor Forest* (1713) is a more
impressive work, using pastoral to extol the
Peace of Utrecht (1713) which ended the long
War of the Spanish Succession, and to
celebrate peace, prosperity and civilization.

Classical pastoral has not been practised
notably since the first half of the 18th
century. However ▷ William Empson (*Some
Versions of Pastoral*, 1935) sometimes uses the
term more widely than classical pastoral
denotes. Even so, pastoral – even of the non-
classical kind – is not synonymous with
'nature poetry' or poetry of country life:

▷ Wordsworth, ▷ Clare, ▷ Hardy, ▷ Blunden, and ▷ Heaney are not writers of pastoral in any usually accepted sense.

Pater, Walter Horatio (1839–94)
Scholar, essayist and critic. He was elected to a fellowship in Brasenose College, Oxford, in 1864. He was connected with the ▷ Pre-Raphaelite group, shared their idealistic worship of beauty and became an important influence in the cult of art which led to the ▷ Aesthetic Movement at the end of the century. His most important work was *Studies in the History of the Renaissance* (1873), a collection of essays on Italian painters and writers from the 14th to 16th centuries; the Conclusion to these essays, in which he advocates a fusion of psychic, moral and sensuous ecstasy, became a kind of manifesto of the aesthetic movement. His next most famous work is the philosophic romance *Marius the Epicurean* (1885). Other works: *Imaginary Portraits* (1887); *Appreciations with an Essay on Style* (1889); *Plato and Platonism* (1893); *The Child in the House* (1894); *Greek Studies* and *Miscellaneous Studies* (1895); an unfinished romance, *Gaston de Latour* (1896). Pater wrote with immense care for beauty of style, which became for him an end in itself.
Bib: Levey, M., *The Case of Walter Pater*; Monsman, G., *Walter Pater*.

Pathetic fallacy
▷ Figures of Speech.

Patience
The conventional title given to a 14th-century ▷ alliterative poem, found in the same manuscript as ▷ *Gawain and the Green Knight*, ▷ *Cleanness* and ▷ *Pearl*, and so attributed to the ▷ Gawain poet. This relatively short composition explores the active and passive meanings of patience, through a reworking of the story of the Old Testament prophet, ▷ Jonah.
Bib: Anderson, J. J. (ed.), *Patience*.

Patmore, Coventry Kersey Dighton (1823–96)
Poet. He contributed to the ▷ Pre-Raphaelite periodical *The Germ*; in 1864 he became a ▷ Catholic. The two books by which he is most remembered are *The Angel in the House* (comprising *The Betrothed*, 1854; *The Espousals*, 1856; *Faithful for Ever*, 1860; *The Victories of Love*, 1862) and *The Unknown Eros* (1877). The former is about his first marriage and celebrates married love; the latter, consisting of 42 irregular ▷ odes, is on a similar theme but more mystical. Both poems are examples of philosophizing in verse characteristic of ▷ William

Wordsworth's famous ▷ *Prelude*. Patmore had independent ideas on poetic technique, and has been considered by some critics to bear resemblance to the 17th-century ▷ Metaphysical poets. As much as for his own poetry, he is known today for being the friend and correspondent of the poet ▷ Gerald Manley Hopkins, whose work, however, he seems not to have properly appreciated. Other works include: *Amelia* (1878), which was his own favourite among his poems; the critical essays *English Metrical Law* (1878); *Principle in Art* (1879); *Religio Poetae* (1893); the religious meditations *Rod, Root and Flower* (1895).
Bib: Patmore, D., *Life*; Oliver, E. J., *Life*; Page, F., *Patmore: a Study in Poetry*; Reid, J. C., *The Mind and Art of Coventry Patmore*; Hopkins, G. M., (ed. Abbott, C. C.) *Further Letters*.

Patrick, St
The patron saint of ▷ Ireland; he seems to have been of Welsh birth, and was born about 389. He was early carried off to Ireland by Irish raiders, but later he escaped and for a few years studied at the French monastery of Lérins. He then returned to Britain, and was there inspired with the vocation to convert Ireland to Christianity.

Patroclus
▷ *Iliad*.

Patronage in literature
A system by which the king or a nobleman afforded protection and livelihood to an artist, in return for which the artist paid him special honour, or returned him service in the form of entertaining his household and his guests. The great period for this system was the 16th century, but patronage continued to be an important cultural and social institution until the end of the 18th century. In the ▷ Middle Ages the writer or scholar might work under the protection of a religious order, but already ▷ Chaucer was dependent on the patronage of ▷ John of Gaunt. After the 18th century, through ▷ circulating libraries and wide circulation of periodicals, writers could rely on support from the general public; from the 16th to 18th centuries failure to secure a patron might mean oblivion, or at least starvation, as in the case of ▷ Chatterton. In the 16th century patronage was a natural institution since noblemen still kept large households and it was assumed that these would include entertainers (such as a band of actors) and scholars who performed educational and secretarial functions. In this century actors ('players') who were not

attached to some household were regarded as vagabonds liable to punishment or shutting up in houses of correction by the public authorities; by the end of the century, however, the ▷ Lord Chamberlain's Men, the ▷ Lord Admiral's Men etc. were attached to their patrons only in name, and they performed in public theatres or at court. The Earl of Essex (patron of ▷ Ben Jonson), the Earl of Southampton (patron of ▷ Shakespeare), and ▷ Sidney's sister, ▷ Margaret Countess of Pembroke, were among the great patrons in the reign of ▷ Elizabeth I, but the most valuable patron was the sovereign. Disagreeable results of patronage were the flattering 'dedications' which commonly preceded works of literature, and poems written specially to honour or gratify the patron, such as ▷ Donne's *First* and *Second Anniversary* commemorating the death of Elizabeth Drury, daughter of his patron Sir Robert Drury – though Donne's poems are evidence that such work was by no means necessarily bad or insincere. The status of men of letters steadily gained in esteem, moreover, freeing the writer of the necessity of servility, and Ben Jonson was one of the most vigorous in upholding its dignity and independence. Nonetheless, it tended to be true under Elizabeth and her successor, ▷ James I, that writers were either 'gentlemen amateurs' like Sidney and ▷ Ralegh, able to work independently, or professional writers like Jonson and Shakespeare, for whom patronage was important, if not indispensable. By the 18th century, thanks largely to the increased reading public and the growth of periodicals like Addison's ▷ *Spectator* and Jonson's ▷ *Rambler*, patronage was obsolescent, and chiefly required when a writer of slender means, such as ▷ Samuel Johnson, attempted a major task, such as his Dictionary. Johnson's famous letter to Lord Chesterfield is a classic example of rebuke to a neglectful patron. Political parties and leaders by this time provided extensive patronage, *eg* Harley and the ▷ Tories to ▷ Defoe. Many writers gained a livelihood through the system by which the universities and landlords inherited from the monasteries (dissolved in the 1530s) the right to appoint parish priests; one example among many is the poet ▷ Crabbe whose verse tale *The Patron* (*Tales* of 1812) illustrates the unhappy side of patronage.

Patterne, Sir Willoughby
The character referred to in the title of ▷ George Meredith's novel ▷ *The Egoist*.

The name is an ironical reference to his conception of himself as the 'pattern' of gentlemen; he is a parody of ▷ Samuel Richardson's Sir Charles Grandison.

Paul's Cathedral, St
The cathedral of the City of London, and its principal church. The old cathedral was burnt down in the ▷ Great Fire of London (1666) and the present one was built according to the design of ▷ Sir Christopher Wren. Until the 18th century not only the churchyard but the building itself was a public meeting-place for much besides Christian worship; news was exchanged there, servants were hired, and business was conducted. The central aisle was called Paul's Walk, and a Paul's Man was a term for one of its frequenters.

Paul's, Children of St
A company of boy actors, chosen from the choirboys of ▷ St Paul's Cathedral, who were very popular with audiences at the end of the 16th century. Their chief rivals among boy actors were the Children of the Chapel Royal. Both were to some extent serious rivals of the adult actors (see ▷ Shakespeare's ▷ *Hamlet* II, ii). The boy companies were used especially for ▷ pastoral plays, such as those of ▷ John Lyly and ▷ George Peele.
  ▷ Acting, The Profession of.

Peacock, Thomas Love (1785–1866)
Novelist and poet. After unsuccessful attempts in poetry and the theatre, he found his special form in the 'discussion novel': *Headlong Hall* (1816); ▷ *Melincourt* (1817); ▷ *Nightmare Abbey* (1818); ▷ *Maid Marian* (1822); *The Misfortunes of Elphin* (1829); ▷ *Crotchet Castle* (1831); ▷ *Gryll Grange* (1861). These consist almost entirely of conversation and have very little plot; the characters represent outlooks, ideas, and attitudes such as arouse Peacock's derision, and the prevailing tone is comic and satirical. The conversations are interspersed with songs, often of great charm, and hilarious and extravagant episodes. His sceptical essay *The Four Ages of Poetry* (1820) provoked ▷ Shelley's famous *Defence of Poetry* (1821).
Bib: Van Doren, C., *Life*; Priestley, J. B., *Life*; Able, A. H., *Meredith and Peacock – A Study in Literary Influence*; House, H., in *All in Due Time*; Brett-Smith, H. F. B. (ed.), *Life* in *Works*, Vol I; Mayoux, J. J., *Un Epicurien Anglais: Peacock*; Jack, I., Chap VII in *Oxford History of English Literature*.

Peake, Mervyn (1911–68)

Novelist, dramatist, poet and painter. Peake was born in China, but his family returned to England in 1923, where he subsequently trained as an artist. He is best known for his trilogy *Gormenghast*, a fantasy epic set in a grotesque world, consisting of *Titus Groan* (1946), *Gormenghast* (1950) and *Titus Alone* (1959). In form it is a ▷ *Bildungsroman* with multiple subplots, and it is distinguished by a rich vocabulary and by the effects of Peake's strong visual imagination. Peake's work met a mixed critical reception, but gained a considerable cult following, aided by the increasing popularity of fantasy fiction associated with the work of ▷ J. R. R. Tolkien.

Pearl

A 14th-century ▷ dream-vision poem attributed to the ▷ Gawain poet, preserved in the same manuscript as ▷ *Gawain and the Green Knight*, ▷ *Patience* and ▷ *Cleanness*. It draws on the diverse traditions behind this literary form (as a medium for analysing abstract concepts, secular and religious, as a medium for insight into higher truths) and literally incorporates a scriptural vision into the narrative: the vision of New Jerusalem in *Revelation* becomes part of the personal experience of the Dreamer in *Pearl*. This translation of material from the Bible to the personal experience of the Dreamer, the realization of a prospect of an afterlife, epitomizes the subject of the narrative as a whole, which explores how spiritual truths may be represented by necessarily imperfect material means.

The pearl is the central object of meditation in the poem, providing both the means and end of the dream-vision. The movement of the narrative is shaped by the process of revealing layers of meaning in the form of a pearl. It opens with the narrator lamenting the loss of his prize possession, a pearl. But as he meets his lost pearl in his dream, the relationship between the man and his pearl is reinterpreted as that between a father and a daughter who has died in infancy. Retrospectively, the garden spot where the dreamer lost his pearl, and fell asleep, takes on the aspect of a grave. But the Pearl-maiden in the dream tries to redefine their relationship again and to convince the Dreamer that she is not lost, rather she has found a much better setting in New Jerusalem. In a series of exchanges she tries to tutor the Dreamer out of his materialistic values. The Dreamer finally sees his Pearl as one of the 144,000 virgin companions of Christ in New Jerusalem, but breaks his visionary experience when he tries to get closer and join the maiden.

The poem is itself pearl-shaped: the opening line is reworked as the closing line and this overall linking structure is repeated in the organization of the stanzas into groups of five, which are linked by echoing first and last lines. Each stanza is structured by a combination of alliterative lines and an elaborate rhyme scheme. It is an exercise in formal artifice of the highest order, and suggests that poetry may serve the ends of spiritual vision, but some recognition of the limitations of art are also built into the poem's structure, for one of its 12 sections contains six not five stanzas. The poem appears to be constructed as a pearl with a flaw of the most self-conscious literary kind.
Bib: Gordon, E. V. (ed.), *Pearl*.

Peasants' Revolt

A popular uprising in 1381, which attempted to force the reform of an outmoded manorial system. The immediate stimulus of the revolt was an attempt to levy a further poll tax (on every head of the population), but it is clear from the demands finally presented to ▷ Richard II that the grievances arose from injustices in the manorial system, and from the 1370s onwards there had been growing signs of unrest with the restrictions of villeinage (the system whereby a tenant held land in return for manorial services). ▷ John Ball and ▷ Wat Tyler were among the leaders of the protest movement which mobilized disaffected labourers and peasants in 1381. The protesters, gathered from the counties around London, finally entered the city (having had no answer to their demand to meet the king), and opened prisons and attacked the property of nobles and civic administrators. ▷ John of Gaunt's palace of Savoy, in the Strand, was gutted, and the Archbishop of London and several councillors were later executed. Risings occurred outside London at the same time, notably in the eastern counties. Richard II met the protesters, discussed their grievances, and agreed to their demands to abolish villeinage, to allow labour services to be engaged on the basis of free contract, and to the right to rent land for 4d an acre. At a later meeting with the king, Wat Tyler was killed by the Lord Mayor of London. The promises made by the king were not honoured and subsequently the Chief Justice toured the disaffected areas dispensing severe punishments to those involved in the uprisings.
Bib: Hilton, R., *The English Peasantry in the*

Later Middle Ages; McKisack, M., *The Fourteenth Century*.

Peele, George (1556–96)

Poet and dramatist and one of the
▷ University Wits, Peele was educated at
Christ's Hospital and Oxford University. His
work comprised various forms of dramatic
entertainment characteristic of the taste of the
time. His best-known plays are the ▷ pastoral
play *The Arraignment of Paris* (?1584), acted
by the Children of the Royal Chapel, and *The
Old Wives' Tale* (1590), which is something
like a dramatized folk-tale. He also wrote a
biblical play, *The Love of King David and
Fair Bethsabe* (1587), and patriotic history
plays, *The Famous Chronicle of King Edward
I* (printed 1593) and *The Battle of Alcazar
with the Death of Captain Stukeley* (?1588),
and a number of other plays have been
attributed to him. In 1585 and 1591 he
designed pageants for the London Lord
Mayor's Show. As a precursor of
▷ Shakespeare he has a similar importance
to ▷ Robert Greene; he helped to give
greater smoothness and flexibility to the use
of the ▷ blank verse line, and to combine
elements appealing to popular taste with
qualities of courtly refinement. He can thus
be regarded as a contributor to the rich
variety of tone which is unique to the best
Elizabethan drama.
Bib: Prouty, C. T., *Life and Works*; Cheffaud,
P. H., *George Peele*.

Peerages

▷ Titles of nobility.

Pegasus

In Greek myth, a winged horse which sprang
from the body of Medusa (▷ Gorgons)
when ▷ Perseus had beheaded her. ▷ Ovid
makes Perseus ride Pegasus when he slays the
monster that threatens ▷ Andromeda. It
was with the aid of Pegasus that
▷ Bellerophon slew another monster, the
▷ Chimaera. The spring ▷ Hippocrene,
on Mount Helicon, sacred to the ▷ Muses,
is said to have sprung from the hillside at a
blow of his hoof, and Pegasus is hence
associated with the Muses and especially with
poetry.

Pelagian

The adjective from Pelagius, the Latin name
of an early British theologian (4th–5th century
AD). He is associated with a doctrine ('the
Pelagian heresy') held to be false by most
branches of the Christian Church – that it is
within human power to be good; this is
contrary to the Christian doctrine of 'Original
Sin', according to which human beings

relying on their own efforts must inevitably
sooner or later do wrong, since moral
goodness depends on the aid of Divine
Grace.

Pellam

A Grail-keeper in the Quest of the Holy
▷ Grail narratives, the father of ▷ Pelles
and Pellinore, who is wounded by ▷ Balin
(with the Dolorous Stroke) but healed much
later by his great-grandson ▷ Galahad.

Pelleas, Sir

In ▷ Malory's version of Arthurian
narrative Pelleas first appears in hopeless
pursuit of Ettard. ▷ Gawain promises to
assist Pelleas in his quest but becomes
Ettard's lover himself. Pelleas is helped by
Nimue's spell to recover from his love
sickness and subsequently marries this
▷ Lady of the Lake.

Pelles, Sir

A ▷ Fisher King, Lord of Corbenic,
descended from Joseph of Arimathea. Sir
Pelles engineers the conception of
▷ Galahad, the knight who is to achieve the
▷ Grail Quest.

Peloponnesian War

Between the ancient Greek states of
▷ Athens and ▷ Sparta (431–404 BC). It
ended with the victory of Sparta, which
succeeded Athens as the leading state of
Greece. The Peloponnese is that part of
Greece south of the Isthmus of Corinth; in
the ▷ Middle Ages it was known as the
Morea.

Pembroke, Mary Herbert, Countess of (1561–1621)

Sister of the poet ▷ Sir Philip Sidney and a
famous patroness of literature. Sidney wrote
his prose romance ▷ *The Arcadia* for her,
and she edited this and prepared it and his
poems for publication in 1590–1. ▷ Edmund
Spenser refers to her under the name of
Clorinda in his poem in honour of the dead
Sidney, *Astrophel*, and he dedicated to her his
Ruins of Time. She assisted the poet
▷ Samuel Daniel who was tutor to her son,
as well as other poets including ▷ Ben
Jonson.
▷ Patronage in literature.

Penal system

As in most societies without efficient police
forces, punishments were severe in England
until the establishment of the Metropolitan
Police by Robert Peel and his reform of the
penal system between 1823 and 1827. They
tended to become more severe as society
became more settled and prosperous, in order

to deter crime, especially robbery, by terror, so that by 1800 there were 200 offences punishable by hanging. However, the penal laws were not consistently formulated or applied. Until the reign of ▷ Henry VIII the privilege known as 'Benefit of Clergy', according to which those in any kind of priestly orders could not be punished by lay courts, was apt to be interpreted in such a way that educated people were treated leniently. Later, juries would return verdicts of 'Not Guilty' when they were moved to compassion, or magistrates would interpret the accusation mercifully. The normal form of capital punishment was by hanging, though decapitation, as more dignified, was used for the aristocracy. In the 17th century, when the colonies in America had become established, transportation was often used instead; after the loss of the colonies in 1783, Australia was substituted (▷ Botany Bay). Transportation was finally abolished in 1864. Execution was public, and watching it a favourite amusement, until in the mid-19th century public hanging was abolished. In the 16th century burning was used for religious heretics and for ▷ witches; for a short time boiling was used as a capital punishment for poisoning.

For minor offences, whipping was a common punishment, and it too was public until the 19th century, to increase the disgrace. Confinement in the stocks or the ▷ pillory – wooden structures with holes for the head, the legs and the arms – was used for some offences, and there were also, of course, imprisonment and fines. Ducking in a pond or river was reserved for women who had given offence by their speech.

By 1861, crimes punishable by hanging had been reduced to four (murder, treason, piracy, arson) and in 1965 capital punishment was abolished. Corporal punishment was abolished in 1948.

Torture was legal to extract evidence until it was abolished in the 18th century. Mutilation – cutting out the tongue or cutting off the ears, nose or hand – was a penalty for certain offences, especially of a treasonable nature, and it survived in law until 1870, but was not used after the 17th century.
▷ Prisons.

Pendennis, The History of
A novel by ▷ William Makepeace Thackeray, published serially 1848–50. It is about worldly upper-class society in London and the fortunes of a young man, Arthur Pendennis, whose 'bad angels' are his cynical, materialistic uncle, Major Pendennis, and the

pretty but selfish Blanche Amory whom he nearly marries. Blanche's father, an escaped convict who is thought to be dead but is in fact – as Major Pendennis knows – still alive, haunts the book in the guise of Colonel Altamont. Arthur's 'good angels' are his widowed mother, Helen; Laura Bell, whom he eventually marries and whom his mother has adopted; and George Warrington, a friend with whom he shares rooms. The good influences are, however, less imaginatively presented than the bad ones, and the distinctiveness of the novel depends on its amusing portrayal of the vulgarity, intrigue, and materialism of London society and the journalistic and literary world of ▷ Fleet Street.

Penelope
In ▷ Homer's ▷ *Odyssey* the wife of ▷ Odysseus king of ▷ Ithaca. During his long absence, she is pestered by numerous suitors who seek her in marriage on the assumption that he will never return. She puts them off by telling them that they must wait until she has woven a winding-sheet for Laertes, the father of Odysseus. She weaves all day, but every night she unweaves the day's work, so that it never draws to completion. Eventually the trick is exposed by her maids. Odysseus returns after an absence of 20 years, and slays the suitors.

Penkethman (Pinkethman), William (?–1725)
Actor, singer, dancer, manager. Penkethman is believed to have begun acting in about 1692 with the ▷ United Company at ▷ Drury Lane where he remained for most of his career. Penkethman's forte as an actor was comedy, and he was often asked to speak prologues and epilogues. Much of his humour was conveyed through clowning and mobile facial expression, although he was accused, on numerous occasions, of over-acting, and ad-libbing to excess.

Penseroso, Il (c 1631)
A poem by ▷ John Milton, published in 1645 though composed c 1631. The poem is a companion piece to ▷ *L'Allegro*. The title can be translated, from the Italian, as signifying the thoughtful or reflective individual. The poem celebrates the retired life of thought and contemplation.

Pentameter
In English verse, usually five iambic feet, *ie* with the stress coming on every second syllable. The line has been the commonest in use since ▷ Chaucer, *eg* the *Prologue to the Canterbury Tales*:

He knew the taverns well in every town.

The commonest English uses of the iambic pentameter are in ▷ blank verse and in ▷ heroic couplets (as in the *Prologue*).
▷ Metre.

Pentateuch
In the Bible, the first five books of the Old Testament: *Genesis, Exodus, Leviticus, Numbers, Deuteronomy*. They were traditionally ascribed to the authorship of ▷ Moses.

Pepys, Samuel (1633–1703)

Excerpt from Pepys' diary

Diarist. He was an industrious and highly efficient official in the Admiralty Office, and a man who had musical culture and persistent, if amateurish, scientific and literary interests. As secretary to his cousin, Edward Montagu, Earl of Sandwich, he was aboard the fleet which brought ▷ Charles II back to England at the ▷ Restoration in 1660. His official position in the Admiralty gave him the confidence of the king's brother, James Duke of York, who was Lord High Admiral, and an opportunity for direct observation of court life. He was elected to Parliament and knew the world of politics, was a friend of a number of leading writers and musicians, and held distinguished appointments in the City of London. He was thus centrally placed to observe his age, and with all his seriousness he was pleasure-loving and witty.

His diary (kept 1660–9) is a unique document not only because he brought to it these qualities and advantages (many of which were shared by his friend the diarist ▷ John Evelyn) but because he kept it for his eye alone, and consequently wrote with unusual candour and objectivity. To prevent his servants and family from prying into it, he used a kind of shorthand cypher, which was not interpreted until 1825, when part of the diary was first published. The first more or less complete edition was in 1896. Of all diaries in English, it has the greatest appeal to the general reader, as well as having outstanding value for the historian.
▷ Diaries.
Bib: Lives by J. R. Tanner, A. Bryant, and J. H. Wilson. Letters edited by J. R. Tanner, A. Bryant, and J. H. Wilson. Marburg, C., *Mr Pepys and Mr Evelyn*; Latham, R. and Mathews, W., (eds.), *Diary*.

Perceval
One of the members of the court of ▷ King Arthur. There is some variation in the treatment of Perceval's adventures and achievements in the Arthurian narratives of medieval Europe: Perceval is the hero of the ▷ Grail Quest before ▷ Galahad takes over his role. The earliest extant Perceval narrative is that composed by ▷ Chrétien de Troyes (left unfinished but the subject of later continuations). The basic story of Sir Perceval is that of a child of noble origin who is brought up outside a court context but becomes fascinated with chivalry (despite his mother's attempts to keep him away from the world of knights). He is gradually educated in the chivalric code through a series of blunders, caused by his literal-minded application of helpful advice about how to be a knight. One of his missed opportunities involves his failure to heal the ▷ Fisher King because he does not ask any questions about the mysterious Grail procession at the Fisher King's castle. Perceval attempts to make up for this mistake by searching for the Grail castle, and is successful in some versions of his story. In *Parzival*, composed in the 13th century by Wolfram von Eschenbach, Parzival is the knight who finally achieves the mystical Grail quest. In ▷ Malory's version, he becomes a companion of Galahad and dies as a hermit in Sarras after Galahad has achieved the Quest. The 14th-century Middle English romance *Sir Perceval* concentrates on Perceval's over-literal attempts to follow the advice of his mother and others, and exploits the comic possibilities of Perceval as a non-ideal hero.

Percy

The name of a noble family closely connected with ▷ Northumberland and famous in history, ▷ ballad, and Shakespeare's dramas ▷ *Henry IV, Parts I and II*. They are especially famous for their border warfare with the Scots, and in particular with the Scottish border family of Douglas.

The English history of the family originates with William de Perci, a follower of ▷ William I. A descendant, Henry Percy, was one of the English commanders in the attempt of ▷ Edward I to conquer ▷ Scotland, but he was driven out by the Scottish leader ▷ Robert the Bruce; he built the great family fortress of Alnwick in the north of England. His son captured the Scottish king David II at the battle of Neville's Cross (1346).

Later in the 14th century come the two Percies who are famous in ballad and Shakespeare's drama – Henry Percy, 1st Earl of Northumberland, and his son Sir Henry, nicknamed Hotspur. The ballads ▷ *Chevy Chase* and ▷ *Otterbourne* describe the battle of Hotspur and his brother against the Scots under Douglas by the River Otterbourne in 1388; Douglas was killed, but the Percies were taken prisoner. Later Hotspur and his father assisted Henry Bolingbroke to seize the throne from ▷ Richard II in 1399 – the theme of Shakespeare's ▷ *Richard II*. In 1402, Hotspur fought the battle of Homildon Hill against the Scots under another Douglas, and it was now Douglas who was taken prisoner. In the meantime, relationships with Henry IV had been deteriorating, and Hotspur broke into open rebellion over rights to possession of the Scottish prisoners. In 1403, in alliance with the Welsh chieftain Glendower and the Scottish Douglas, he met the king's forces at the Battle of Shrewsbury, and was defeated and killed; this is the subject of Shakespeare's *Henry IV, Part I*. His father, the Earl, was killed at the battle of Bramham Moor (1408). The Percies were deprived of their lands, but these were restored to them by the next king, ▷ Henry V.

The Percies continued to be important in English history, but they cease to have prominence in literature. In the 18th century the male line died out, but the name of Percy was taken by the family which succeeded to the lands and titles.

Percy, Thomas (1729–1811)

Clergyman and antiquarian; he became Bishop of Dromore in 1782. Along with ▷ James Macpherson, ▷ Horace Walpole and ▷ Thomas Gray, Percy was a pioneer of the literary exoticism which flourished in the later 18th century. In 1761 he published *Hau Kiou Choaan*, a translation of a Portuguese version of a Chinese romance, and in 1763 *Five Pieces of Runic Poetry*, translated from Latin versions of Old Icelandic texts. His most influential work, ▷ *Reliques of Ancient English Poetry* (1765), includes poems from a 17th-century manuscript now in the British Museum and known as 'The Percy Folio'. This manuscript contains many ballads of ancient origin which Percy edited according to 18th-century taste, adding also some modern compositions in the archaic style. Although his editorial approach was not that of a modern purist, the volume marks a significant phase in the revival of interest in early poetry, and exerted a strong influence on later poets such as ▷ Thomas Chatterton, ▷ Sir Walter Scott, ▷ William Wordsworth and ▷ Samuel Taylor Coleridge.

Bib: Davis, B. H., *Thomas Percy*.

Peregrine Pickle, The Adventures of (1751)
A novel by ▷ Tobias Smollett. The hero is an adventurer seeking his fortune in England and on the Continent. Its form is a succession of episodes without a uniting structure, depending for its interest on the vigour of depiction of the characters and incidents. It contains famous eccentric characters, especially the retired sailor and his associates, Commodore Trunnion, Lieutenant Hatchway, and Tom Pipes. The episodes give opportunity for much social and political satire, from English village life upwards, and show an awareness of social structure like that found in the novels of ▷ Henry Fielding. Trunnion and his circle were an inspiration to ▷ Laurence Sterne's Uncle Toby in ▷ *Tristram Shandy*.

Perfectibilism

The optimistic doctrine that individuals and society are capable of achieving perfection in living. The ▷ French Revolution, with its reliance on reason for the solution of all human problems, encouraged perfectibilism, and the philosopher ▷ William Godwin was an English example. ▷ Peacock, in *Headlong Hall* (1816), presents a humorous version of a perfectibilist in Mr Foster.

Pericles

In Greek history, a leading statesman of ▷ Athens in the 5th century BC. His period of power (460–429) was that when Athens was at her greatest, politically and artistically. The ▷ Peloponnesian War, which ended in her defeat by ▷ Sparta, began in 431. At the end of that year Pericles made his great funeral oration, which included a survey of Athenian greatness and appealed to the national pride of the Athenians. It is recorded by the 5th-century Athenian historian ▷ Thucydides.

Pericles, Prince of Tyre (1608–9)
A play, Acts III–V of which are considered to be by ▷ Shakespeare; Acts I–II are mainly or entirely by another writer. The play was published in 1609 in an untrustworthy edition, but it was not included in a collected edition of Shakespeare's works until (in the same version) the third ▷ folio of 1664. The story is based on a well-known late classical romance, Apollonius of Tyre, used by ▷ John Gower in his 14th-century cycle of poems ▷ *Confessio Amantis* (Book VIII). Gower appears in the play to speak the chorus, but the play does not follow his version in all respects; another source book was Lawrence Twine's *The Pattern of Painful Adventures*, first published in 1576.

In the first two acts, the play has a very rambling structure, but from Act III it follows a pattern characteristic of Shakespeare's last four plays; though in each the pattern is varied, they have in common a central relationship between a prince and his daughter – in this case Pericles and ▷ Marina. Pericles is separated from her and is led to believe that both she and her mother Thaisa are dead. By the end of the play, however, he recovers them both, and the recovery restores him to happiness and health. The scene (V. i) in which Marina, at first unrecognizing of and unrecognized by her father, restores him from his stupor of sorrow, is of remarkable beauty, and recalls the scene in *King Lear* (IV. vii) in which Cordelia restores her father.

Periodicals
▷ Reviews and Periodicals.

Perrault, Charles (1628–1703)
French author, known in England chiefly for his collection of ▷ fairy tales published in 1697, *Histoires et Contes du Temps Passé* ('Stories and Tales from the Past') subtitled *Contes de ma Mère l'Oie* ('Tales of Mother Goose'). They were translated into English by Robert Samber (1729), and have remained the best known fairy tales among English children. They were retold by Perrault from popular sources, and are as follows:
▷ *Sleeping Beauty*; ▷ *Red Riding Hood*; *Blue Beard*; ▷ *Puss in Boots*; *The Fairy*; ▷ *Cinderella*; *Riquet with the Tuft*; *Hop o'*

my Thumb. Several of them provide the themes for modern Christmas ▷ pantomimes.
▷ Fairies.

Persephone (Proserpine)
In Greek myth, the daughter of the corn-goddess, ▷ Demeter, and ▷ Zeus. ▷ Hades, god of the underworld, carried her off while she was gathering flowers, and Demeter wandered in search of her while the earth went barren. To save the life of the earth, Zeus persuaded Hades to surrender Persephone for six months of the year. Persephone is thus the spring and autumn goddess: the spring announces her return, and the autumn, her departure.

Perseus
In Greek myth, the son of Danae and the god ▷ Zeus. The legend about him has the following episodes:

1 Zeus caused Danae to conceive him by pouring into her as a shower of gold. Acrisius, father of Danae, learnt that her son was destined to kill him; to prevent the fulfilment of this prophecy he caused the mother and son to be launched into the sea in a chest. They were rescued by Polydectes, king of Seriphos.

2 Polydectes fell in love with Danae, and tried to rid himself of Perseus by sending him to fetch the head of ▷ Medusa, the sight of whom turned men to stone. Perseus discovered the whereabouts of the ▷ Gorgons, of whom Medusa was one, from the Graeae. These were three ancient women who shared a single eye and a single tooth among them; by stealing the eye and the tooth, Perseus persuaded them to give him the information he needed. He also stole from the Graeae a magic bag and a helmet that made him invisible. In some versions of the story, the goddess ▷ Athene gave him a shield as highly polished as a mirror, the god ▷ Hermes gave him wings for his shoes and a sword, and he got the helmet from ▷ Hades, god of the underworld.

3 With the aid of this equipment, Perseus beheaded Medusa, from whose body sprang the winged horse, ▷ Pegasus. He passed through the country of Ethiopia, where he learnt that Andromeda, daughter of King Cepheus, was in the act of being sacrificed to a sea-monster sent by the sea-god Poseidon, whom Cepheus' queen, Cassiopeia, had offended. He rescued Andromeda by slaying the monster, and married her.

4 In some versions, another adventure on his return from slaying the Medusa was to turn into stone the giant ▷ Atlas, who

supported the heavens, or perhaps the world, on his shoulders; Atlas thus became the great mountain chain (in North Africa) which bears his name today.

5 Perseus then returned to Seriphos, where he rescued his mother from the undesired attentions of Polydectes by petrifying him with Medusa's head. He then offered the head to the goddess Athene, who henceforth wore it on her shield.

6 He next returned to his birth-country, Argos, where the prophecy was fulfilled that he would one day kill his grandfather. This happened accidentally when Perseus was throwing the discus at funeral games. Unwilling to succeed to the throne of the man whom he had killed, Perseus reigned over Tyryns and Mycenae, where he established the family which was destined to produce ▷ Heracles.

Personification
   ▷ Figures of Speech.

Persuasion (1818)
The last completed novel by ▷ Jane Austen; it was published, incompletely revised, in 1818, the year following her death. The theme is the coming together of the heroine, Anne Elliott, and the hero, Captain Wentworth, in spite of social obstacles, the selfishness and foolishness of her father (Sir Walter) and sisters, and the rival attraction of the more obviously seductive Musgrove sisters. Anne, before the novel begins, had already refused Wentworth on the counsel of Lady Russell, who stands in place of mother to her; Lady Russell had misunderstood Wentworth's character and feared his poverty. Anne's personality is diffident and humble but at the opening of the story she has begun to realize that the refusal was a mistake, likely to ruin her happiness. The renewal of Wentworth's love and his eventual marriage to Anne is a victory: their strong and distinctive but quiet and reticent qualities overcome the cruder and shallower social characteristics of their circumstances.

Peter Bell: A Tale (1819)
   Peter Bell the Third (1839)
The first is a 'lyrical ballad' by ▷ William Wordsworth, written in 1798 but not published until 1819. Peter, a hard-hearted hawker of earthenware, finds an ass gazing down at its drowned master in the River Swale. He seeks out the man's widow, and on his journey is reformed by the spiritual influence of nature. The poem possesses that deliberate flatness which characterizes some of Wordsworth's most original early works.

▷ Percy Bysshe Shelley, in his *Peter Bell the Third* (1819; published 1839), having read a review of the poem, used its title (somewhat inappropriately) in a ▷ satire on the older poet's descent into respectability and conservatism. As Shelley says in his Dedication: 'He was at first sublime, pathetic, impressive, profound; then dull; then prosy and dull; and now dull – oh so very dull! it is an ultra-legitimate dulness.'

Peter Grimes
A tale in heroic couplets (▷ metre) by ▷ George Crabbe, Letter XXII in the series composing *The Borough* (1810). Peter is the son of a poor fisherman who tries to bring him up kindly and religiously. However, the boy is violent and wilful, and causes the death of his father by ill-treatment. He then lives a solitary life, distrusted and feared by the neighbourhood, with only a boy from an orphanage for company. He treats the boy brutally and finally causes his death, after which he misuses two other boys in the same way. The magistrates forbid him to employ any more pauper boys as apprentices, and his life becomes increasingly solitary, until he is found drifting distractedly along the desolate coast in his boat. As he dies he tells how he has been haunted by the ghosts of his dead father and the three boys, who never leave him, and ceaselessly condemn him to an eternity of lonely drifting. The poem is remarkable for its social realism and psychological power. It was made into an opera by Benjamin Britten (1945).

Peter Pan (1904)
A children's play by ▷ J. M. Barrie, originally called *Peter Pan, or the Boy who wouldn't grow up*. It became, and remains, extremely popular for its whimsical charm and its ingenious use of some traditional features of children's romances, such as Red Indians, the pirate Captain Hook who lives in fear of a crocodile which has already consumed one of his arms, and the fairy Tinkerbell.
   ▷ Children's books.

Peter's Pence
A medieval tax paid by England to the Pope until it was abolished by ▷ Henry VIII in the 16th century. Its origins are obscure. It survives as a voluntary contribution by English Roman Catholics.

Peterloo Massacre, The
At a political meeting advocating the reform of parliamentary elections at St Peter's Field, Manchester, in 1819, the magistrates took

alarm and ordered soldiers to attack the crowd. A small number of people were killed, and a large number were injured. The event caused intense resentment against the government of the time, and was nicknamed 'Peterloo' in ironic reference to the Anglo-Prussian victory over Napoleon at ▷ Waterloo in 1815. It provoked ▷ Shelley's fierce poem ▷ *The Masque of Anarchy*. It was also one of the causes of the establishment of the Metropolitan Police Force by Robert Peel in 1829, so that there should be a possibility of keeping order among crowds without the use of soldiers and firearms.

▷ Reform Bills, Parliamentary.

Petition of Right
A demand leading to a law forced on ▷ King Charles I by ▷ Parliament in 1628; it ended imprisonment without trial, the raising of taxes without parliamentary authorization, martial law (*ie* legal judgements enforced under military authority), and the billeting of troops in private houses as an indirect means of forcing political obedience. It was the first major clash between Charles and Parliament in the conflict which ended in the ▷ Civil War of 1642–6.

Petrarch (Francesco Petrarca) (1304–74)
Italian poet and scholar. Petrarch's influence on English ▷ Renaissance poetry is incalculable. Petrarch's early years were spent in the Papal court at Avignon, but his life was one of constant movement – he described himself as *peregrinus ubique*, a wanderer everywhere. He travelled throughout Provence and Italy, living for eight years in Milan (1353–61) but visited, in that time, centres as far afield as Prague and Paris.

Travelling was to become a central metaphor in Petrarch's writing. The idea of the journey in his own life seemed to imitate great journeys of the past – those of the Apostles, St Augustine of Hippo (345–430), and the ▷ Homeric heroes. Life itself could be represented as a journey, or pilgrimage, or, on occasion, a flight. This metaphor of transience was to be one of the many 'Petrarchan' motifs which English poets were to assimilate with such delight (cf ▷ Sir Thomas Wyatt's sonnet 'My galley charged with forgetfulness').

Petrarch's chief works are his *Africa* (a Latin ▷ epic on *Scipio Africanus*), the *Secretum* (a self-analytical dialogue) and his collection of poetry – the *Canzoniere*. The *Canzoniere* (also known as the *Rime* or *Rime sparse*) contained, by the end of his life, some 366 poems in all, the majority of which deal with the poet's love for 'Laura' – the unobtainable ideal of womanhood – whom Petrarch claimed to have first seen in church on 6 April 1327. In addition to the *Canzoniere*, he composed imitations of ▷ Virgil's *Eclogues* and the six *Trionfi* (Triumphs) poems – the triumphs of Love, Chastity, Death, Fame, Time and Eternity.

The *Trionfi* and the *Canzoniere* were medieval best-sellers. Both circulated widely in manuscript form before their first publication in 1470. The *Trionfi* were to have a huge influence upon all forms of Renaissance representation – poetry, painting, tapestry, medals, emblems, pageants and theatre. At the same time, the introspective self-analysis, and the depiction of a female ideal who is both mistress and saint in the *Canzoniere*, were to influence European poets of the 16th and 17th centuries. The ▷ sonnet sequences of ▷ Sir Philip Sidney, ▷ Samuel Daniel, ▷ Michael Drayton and others, as well as the poetry, in an earlier period, of ▷ Sir Thomas Wyatt and ▷ Henry Howard, Earl of Surrey, all took Petrarch as a starting point. Similarly, the anti-Petrarchism of some of ▷ Shakespeare's sonnets, or ▷ Donne's poetry, is, in its vigorous denial of Petrarchan modes, a tribute to the pervasive influence on the Renaissance sensibility of the Italian poet's work.
Bib: Durling, R. M. (ed.), *Petrarch's Lyric Poems; Minta, S., Petrarch and Petrarchism.*

Phaedra
In Greek myth, the daughter of ▷ Minos and the wife of ▷ Theseus of Athens. She fell in love with Theseus' son Hippolytus; when he rejected her, she accused him to Theseus of trying to seduce her, thus causing his death. She is the subject of tragedies by ▷ Euripides, ▷ Seneca and ▷ Racine.

Phaeton
In Greek myth, son of the sun-god Helios and the nymph Clymene. The sun was envisaged as a burning chariot that drove round the earth; Phaeton took charge of his father's chariot, but, losing control of his father's horses, he drove it too near the earth. To save the earth from being consumed by fire, ▷ Zeus slew Phaeton with a thunderbolt, and he fell into the river Eridanus (the Po in Italy). He was buried by the ▷ nymphs, and his sisters, who came to weep at his tomb, were changed into poplar trees. Their tears were said to form the amber which was plentiful by this river.

In the 19th century the name 'phaeton' was given to a kind of light carriage.

Philaster, or Love lies a-bleeding (1611)
A romantic play by ▷ Francis Beaumont
and ▷ John Fletcher; it was produced in
1611, and is in ▷ blank verse. It is the first
in a style of ▷ tragicomedy which became
characteristic of the English theatre during
the next 30 years. Of all Beaumont and
Fletcher's collaborations, it is perhaps the
most famous; it derives from the prose
romances of chivalry popular in France and
Spain, and to some extent (*eg* ▷ Philip
Sidney's ▷ *The Arcadia*) in England. The
plot is characteristic: Philaster is rightful king
of Sicily, but his throne has been usurped by
the king of Calabria, with whose daughter,
Arethusa, he is in love. He keeps
communication with her through his page,
Bellario. Her father wants her to marry
Pharamond of Spain, and to avoid this she
reveals to him the love affair between
Pharamond and Megra, a lady of her father's
court. In revenge Megra makes out that
Arethusa has been having an affair with
Bellario, whom Philaster accordingly
dismisses. It then turns out that Bellario is a
girl disguised as a page for love of Philaster.
This situation seems to be borrowed from
▷ Shakespeare's ▷ *Twelfth Night*, but
Shakespeare combined poignant truth to
natural feelings with the romantic
extravagance of the plot. Beaumont and
Fletcher's emotion is obviously 'poetic' but
not convincing.

Philemon and Baucis
A tale by the Roman poet ▷ Ovid, from the
eighth book of his ▷ *Metamorphoses*. They
are an aged peasant couple and very poor, but
they give hospitality to the gods ▷ Zeus and
▷ Hermes, disguised as travellers. In
reward, their cottage is transformed into a
temple, of which they are made priest and
priestess; they are also permitted to die in the
same hour, and after death they are
transformed into trees with intertwining
boughs. ▷ Dryden's version (1693) of
Ovid's poem is one of his best
▷ translations; ▷ Swift also wrote a poem
on the subject (1709).

Philips, Ambrose (1675?–1749)
Poet. Associate of ▷ Joseph Addison and
▷ Richard Steele, and member of the
▷ Whig clique which frequented
▷ Button's Coffee-house. His ▷ couplet
epistle, describing a snow scene addressed
from Copenhagen to the ▷ Earl of Dorset,
is a brilliantly evocative work, which was
admired by ▷ Alexander Pope. His *Pastorals*
(1709) were published in the same year as
those of Pope, and the coincidence prompted

a theoretical debate, which now seems quite
arid, concerning the correct understanding of
the form. Philips, it was felt, preserved the
authentic rusticity of the ancient genre, while
Pope polished it into a modern elegance.
When the Buttonian, ▷ Thomas Tickell,
pointedly praised Philips's pastorals in ▷ *The
Guardian*, Pope submitted an anonymous
piece *On Pastorals* to the same journal, in
which with straight-faced irony he prefers
Philips's poems to his own. The irony was so
fine that, as ▷ Samuel Johnson relates,
'though Addison discovered it, Steele was
deceived, and was afraid of displeasing Pope
by publishing his paper'. Philips also edited a
periodical, *The Freethinker* (1718–21), wrote
several plays, Pindaric ▷ odes, and poems
addressed to children, whose archness led his
contemporary Henry Carey to attack him in
Namby-Pamby (1725), from which the epithet
in current use derives.

Philips, John (1676–1709)
Poet and physician. A pioneer of poetry in
▷ Miltonic ▷ blank verse. *The Splendid
Shilling* (1701), described by ▷ Joseph
Addison as 'the finest burlesque poem in
the British language' presents a rueful self-
portrait of the down-at-heel poet, without a
shilling to his name. 'But I, whom griping
penury surrounds,/ And Hunger, sure
Attendant upon Want,/ With scanty Offals,
and small acid Tiff/ (Wretched Repast!) my
meagre Corps sustain:/ Then Solitary walk,
or doze at home/ In Garret vile, and with a
warming puff/ Regale chill'd Fingers'. The
poet hides in a cupboard from a dun, then
writes moody poems about disappointed love,
and the work ends with an ▷ epic simile
comparing the splitting of his ageing breeches
to a shipwreck in the Aegean. Philips's
obvious delight in self-dramatization gives
the poem permanent appeal. He also wrote a
serious epic, *Blenheim* (1705), but his most
influential work was *Cyder* (1708), a
▷ Georgic poem in two books blending
landscape description (often focussed on
Hereford, where he practised medicine),
historical and philosophical reflection, and
detailed advice on orchard-management. Its
assured handling of blank verse, and its easy
discursiveness of tone, were emulated and
developed further by ▷ James Thomson in
his *Seasons*.

Philistines
In the original sense, a race inhabiting the
coast of Palestine in biblical times.
    In a secondary meaning, the term is applied
to those who are indifferent or actively hostile
to artistic and cultural values. This common

use was introduced by ▷ Matthew Arnold (*Culture and Anarchy* 1869; ▷ *Essays in Criticism* I – essay on Heine). Arnold divided the English society of his day into three classes of cultural indifference: the upper class were barbarians; the middle class, philistines; the working class, the populace. By this he meant that the upper class underestimated cultural values, the middle class ignored them, and the populace was ignorant of them. Arnold had derived this use of 'philistines' from the Germans, who applied it to townspeople as opposed to students in university towns.

Philoctetes
In Greek legend, a great archer and the possessor of a deadly bow and arrows given to his father by ▷ Heracles. During the siege of ▷ Troy, he was abandoned on the isle of Lemnos owing to a snakebite that refused to heal. However, the Greeks were told by an ▷ oracle that victory was impossible for them without the weapons of Philoctetes. ▷ Odysseus and ▷ Diomedes, accordingly, brought him to Troy where he was cured of his wound and slew ▷ Paris. He is the subject of a tragedy, *Philoctetes*, by the Greek poet, ▷ Sophocles.

Philosophes
▷ Encyclopaedists.

Phiz (Browne, Hablot Knight) (1815–82)
Illustrator. He was the principal illustrator for the novels of ▷ Charles Dickens (especially ▷ *David Copperfield*, ▷ *The Pickwick Papers*, ▷ *Dombey and Son*, ▷ *Martin Chuzzlewit*, ▷ *Bleak House*). He also illustrated the works of other Victorian novelists, notably ▷ Harrison Ainsworth and ▷ Charles Lever.

Phoebe
▷ Artemis.

Phoebus
▷ Apollo.

Phoenix
A mythical bird. Belief in it seems to have been widespread both in Greece and all round the eastern Mediterranean in the centuries before Christ. It was the only one of its kind, and was always male; it had an immensely long life – according to most accounts 500 years. It met its death by consuming itself by fire, and from its ashes a new phoenix was born.

Phoenix and the Turtle, The
A poem by ▷ Shakespeare included in an anthology *Love's Martyr* (1601) assembled by

Robert Chester. The book includes other poems on the love and death of the phoenix and the turtle (turtle-dove); some of these are anonymous and others (including Shakespeare's, and verses by ▷ Ben Jonson, ▷ George Chapman and ▷ John Marston) are signed.

Shakespeare's poem consists of 13 quatrains followed by five triplets (stanzas of three lines) as a concluding 'threnos' (*ie* threnody, or song of lament). The phoenix represents Beauty, and the turtle, Truth; they are united by love; by their death, Reason (personified as the singer of the threnos) declares that the world has been deprived of real truth and real beauty:

> *Truth may seem, but cannot be;*
> *Beauty brag, but 'tis not she;*
> *Truth and beauty buried be.*

Beauty and Truth, the poem says, have therefore no meaning separable from Love. The poem is idealist in the style of ▷ Renaissance ▷ Platonism, it is also metaphysical in its concepts, but not in the style of the ▷ Metaphysical Poets who owe their name to ways of thinking rather than to the concepts they invoke.

Physician's Tale, The
One of ▷ Chaucer's ▷ *Canterbury Tales*. It is an exemplary narrative, set in the Roman past, recounting the history of Virginia, a beautiful young woman who is beheaded by her father Virginius. He chooses to murder his daughter, rather than allow her to be placed in the care of a corrupt and lascivious judge, Appius. The judge is later publically executed for his corruption of the law: Virginius is publically reprieved. Several other versions of this disturbing narrative were available to Chaucer (in ▷ John Gower's ▷ *Confessio Amantis*, in the ▷ *Roman de la Rose*), but the version in the *Physician's Tale* is distinctive for its emphasis on the pathos of Virginia's murder, subversive of the apparent lesson of the narrative, which purports to show how sin has its rewards.

Picaresque
From the Spanish *picaro*, 'rogue'. The term is especially applied to a form of prose fiction originating in Spain in the 16th century, dealing with the adventures of rogues.

The first distinctive example in English is ▷ Thomas Nashe's *Unfortunate Traveller*, 1594. In the 18th century, examples include ▷ Daniel Defoe's ▷ *Moll Flanders*, ▷ Henry Fielding's ▷ *Jonathan Wild* and ▷ Tobias Smollett's *The Adventures of*

Ferdinand Count Fathom. Other traditions combine with the picaresque: the mock romance in the tradition of ▷ *Don Quixote*, and the tradition of religious pilgrimage (cf. ▷ *The Pilgrim's Progress*).

Pickwick Papers, The (1836–7)
The first novel by ▷ Charles Dickens, published serially 1836–7. The story is the adventures of Mr Pickwick and his friends Tupman, Snodgrass and Winkle, who go on a journey of observation of men and manners on behalf of the Pickwick Club, of which Mr Pickwick is the founder and the chairman. The episodes are predominantly comic and Mr Pickwick seems at first to be intended as a mere figure of fun, destined always to be made a fool of owing to his extreme innocence of the ways of the world. Fairly early on, however, he acquires a servant, Sam Weller. Sam is the ideal servant; he is practical, good-humoured, resourceful and devoted. Pickwick now begins to be endowed with a new dignity; still very innocent, he is no longer a mere figure of fun, for he is also shown to have positive moral qualities, such as a determination to stand by the values of truth and justice. He becomes, in fact, a kind of 19th-century English middle-class Don Quixote with Sam Weller as a Sancho Panza, without any of the ridiculousness of Sancho, but with a great deal of comedy derived from his highly developed and typically Cockney sense of humour. At first there is a story but no plot; about half-way through, however, a semblance of a plot develops with Mrs Bardell's conspiracy to obtain £750 from Mr Pickwick for breach of promise of marriage. Assisted by a firm of unscrupulous lawyers, she is at first successful and Mr Pickwick goes to prison. This is the beginning of Dickens's constant preoccupation with prison and with the parasitic qualities of the legal profession. Various episodes illustrate the kinds of social viciousness which Dickens was to enjoy ridiculing or dramatizing – the cheerful roguery of Mr Jingle; the hypocrisy of the 'shepherd', Mr Stiggins; the demagogic Mr Potts in the parliamentary election at Eatanswill, etc. By contrast, Mr Wardle represents the opulent philanthropy and cordial 'religion of Christmas' which were also to figure in Dickens's novels to the end but especially in the earlier ones. In the outcome, Mr Pickwick and Sam Weller emerge as a kind of ideal alliance between the middle and working classes – complete sincerity and integrity in moral guidance on Pickwick's part, total devotion and most useful practical capacity on Weller's side.

The values of the book are representative of the older rural England; Dickens has not yet entered the darkness, mystery and dramatic evil of 19th-century urban civilization.

Picturesque, The Cult of the
A term used in the late 18th and early 19th centuries to describe a certain kind of scenery, where cultivation was employed to produce artificially 'wild' nature. Landscape gardeners incorporated 'wildernesses' into their prospects, often with fake ruins suggesting the decay of classical civilization. The writer most identified with the 'picturesque' was William Gilpin (1724–1804), who wrote a series of illustrated picturesque tours. ▷ Jane Austen in ▷ *Mansfield Park* parodies the cult, and ▷ Thomas Love Peacock's *Headlong Hall* satirizes a contemporary dispute about its qualities.

Pied Piper of Hamelin, The (1845)
A poem by ▷ Robert Browning. It retells an ancient legend: a piper promises to rid the town of Hamelin in Germany of its plague of rats in return for a thousand guilders from the Council. The rats follow the music of his pipe as far as the river Weser, where they are drowned. The Council, however, refuse to pay the piper, whereupon he similarly plays the children out of town and into the side of a mountain which opens to receive them. The origin of the legend may be the Children's Crusade of 1212, when thousands of young people were persuaded to join an expedition to the Holy Land, and many of them perished on the journey.

Pierrot
A character in French ▷ pantomime plays, familiar also in English pantomimes and similar entertainments. His face and dress are always white, and the dress is loose like that of a circus clown. Originally he was a comic, playful figure, but he is often made to perform pathetic or romantic roles.

Piers Plowman
Attributed to ▷ William Langland, *Piers Plowman* is a major ▷ alliterative narrative poem, composed in the later 14th century and extant in three versions, conventionally known as the A, B and C texts. It is now generally accepted that Langland is responsible for each of these versions, and it seems the composition of the poem must have occupied some 25 years of his life: the A text, consisting of a Prologue and 12 Passus (the 'steps' or divisions of the poem), dates from c 1367–70; the B text, which reworks and develops material from A and is about three times as long, dates from c 1377–9; the

Piers Plowman; farmworkers from an illustrated Medieval manuscript

C text, a partial revision of B, dates from c 1385–6.

The ▷ dream-vision mode frees medieval poets from the conventional time and space limitations of other narrative genres, and facilitates literary speculations of all kinds. Langland uses these possibilities to the full in *Piers Plowman*, which is made up of a series of dream-vision sequences (ten in all in the B and C texts, two of which occur as dreams within dreams). The dreams of Will, the narrator, provide the medium for a wide-ranging investigation into the theory and practice of Christian conduct – in Christian society as a whole, and in the life of its individual members. The current corrupt state of clerical and ecclesiastical practice is an insistent topic of the text. The dreamscapes shift from overviews of a whole society (as seen in the 'field ful of folk' with which the poem opens) to a more introspective landscape (as when Will encounters other personified faculties such as Wit and Thought in later Passus) to a visionary experience of major events in Christian history (such as Will's vision of the Crucifixion and Resurrection sequence in the B and C texts). The context of Will's dreams shifts too in the course of the poem: he begins dreaming alone in the Malvern hills but after a later dream he wakes up to call his wife and daughter to church.

Through using the dream medium Langland is able to locate the events of his poem in different times as well as places: attention is focussed on the status quo of 14th-century English society (in the Prologue), on a projected future state of its reform, on the stages in the life of an individual member of that society (in the history of Will, the Dreamer/ narrator), on the history of the Church itself and on the place of the individual and society within the overarching framework of Christian history (Will witnesses a replaying of events leading up to, and following, the Crucifixion). In fact Langland progressively complicates the temporal dimension of the action in the B and C texts, so that individual, social and Christian history intermesh. By the end of the narrative, the end of the Dreamer's life approaches, as the institution of the Christian church itself seems set to crumble as the time of Antichrist draws near.

The poem does not however end with universal collapse, but with the Dreamer renewing his quest for Piers Plowman, the linking character of the narrative, who appears in different roles (as leader of social reform, as a model for the spiritual life), and who seems able to make the connections between the divisions the Dreamer sees all around him (between Christian theory and practice, between knowledge and understanding, between the different stages of Christian life, Do-wel, Do-bet, Do-best). In *Piers Plowman* the dream medium is used not only as a means of analysis and debate (as it is in many other dream-vision poems of his time) but also as a medium for experiences of insight and integration when manifold connections can be made, although not sustained.

The language of the Church and the Bible (Latin) is woven together with the language of the laity (English): the question of how the former should be translated into the latter creates one of the crisis points in the B text (Passus 7), when Piers Plowman and a priest debate how the text of a pardon should be interpreted. Partly the issues at stake in the poem come down to questions of semantics, as the Dreamer tries to find out what words mean, and is sometimes enlightened, but is often confused. The result is a text which pays extraordinary attention to the resources of verbal expression, and in which puns, metaphors and word-play of all kinds abound, as Langland explores ways of making the spiritual visible.

Over 50 manuscripts are extant, which suggests that Langland's work enjoyed considerable popularity in the 15th century among clerics and members of the educated middle classes. An edition of the B text was printed in 1550. George Puttenham's response to Langland's work (in the *Art of English Poesy* c 1589) suggests he read it less as 'poesy', more as social satire, and that view has tended to predominate in critical studies of Langland's work until very recently.
Bib: Alford, J. (ed.), *A Companion to Piers Plowman*; Pearsall, D. (ed.), *Piers Plowman by William Langland: An Edition of the C text*;

Schmidt A. V. C. (ed.), *William Langland: the Vision of Piers Plowman.*

Pilate, Pontius
Roman Governor of Judea, AD 26–36. His action of handing over Jesus Christ to the Jews is mentioned in each of the Gospels: *Matthew* 27; *Mark* 15; *Luke* 23; *John* 18 and 19. Each account suggests that he acted with reluctance, and the degree of his responsibility for the Crucifixion has been much debated throughout the Christian Churches. The early Church tended to exonerate him, and he is even held a saint by the Abyssinian Church. The Medieval Church regarded him much more severely; see for instance the ▷ Wakefield play of the Crucifixion.

Pilgrim Fathers, The
The earliest settlers in the 'New England' section of the east coast of America. They left England in 1620 in the ship *Mayflower* in order to escape political persecution for their faith. This was the Independent (▷ Congregational) kind of ▷ Protestantism, which in England resisted the authority of the Bishops of the Church of England.

Pilgrim's Progress, The
A prose ▷ allegory by ▷ John Bunyan. *The Pilgrim's Progress from this World to that which is to come* is in two parts: Part I (1678) tells of the religious conversion of Christian, and of his religious life – conceived as a pilgrimage – in this world, until he comes to the River of Death, and the Heavenly City which lies beyond it; Part II (1684) describes the subsequent conversion of his wife Christiana and their children, and their similar journey with a group of friends.

Both parts contain episodes which symbolize real life experiences: thus, Christian, soon after the way has been pointed out to him, falls into the ▷ Slough of Despond – a bog which represents the depression which overcomes the new convert when he has passed the stage of first enthusiasm; later he has to pass through phases of spiritual despair and terror, symbolized by the ▷ Valleys of Humiliation and the Shadow of Death; he has to face the derision and anger of public opinion in the town of Vanity Fair, and so on. Christiana and the children have an easier time; perhaps Bunyan wished to show that God in his mercy shields the weaker pilgrims, or perhaps that public opinion is harsher to pioneers than to those that follow them.

The 'pioneer pilgrims' – Christian and his

Frontispiece of the fourth edition of Bunyan's *Pilgrim's Progress*, 1680

associates – belong to the ▷ Puritan sects, of one of which Bunyan was himself a member, who were undergoing persecution in the reign of ▷ Charles II, especially during the earlier years, when English society was in strong reaction against the previous Puritan regime of ▷ Oliver Cromwell. Yet *The Pilgrim's Progress* is much more than merely a dramatization of the Puritan spirit. By its allegorical content, it is related to the tradition of the allegorical sermon which, in village churches, survived the ▷ Reformation of the 16th century, and some of the adventures (Christian's fight with Apollyon, the Castle of Giant Despair, the character of Greatheart) are related in spirit to popular versions of medieval and 16th-century romances, surviving in the ▷ chapbooks. These aspects give it a close relation with popular traditions of culture to an extent unequalled by any other major literary work. Another element of popular culture shows in Bunyan's assimilation of the English translation of the ▷ Bible, and this reminds us that for many households the Bible was the only book constantly read, and that during the next century Bunyan's allegory took its place beside it. Still more important than these links with the past is Bunyan's anticipation of the kind of vision of human nature which in the 18th and 19th centuries was to find its scope in the novel: his allegorized characters do not, as in past allegories, merely simplify human virtues and vices, but reveal how an individual destiny can be shaped by the predominance in a personality of an outstanding quality, good or bad; the adventures of the pilgrims are conditioned by the differences of these qualities. Thus, Christian and Faithful, fellow pilgrims, have radically different temperaments and correspondingly different experiences.

▷ Celestial City; City of Destruction; Doubting Castle; Vanity Fair.

Pilgrimage of Grace, The

A rebellion provoked by the closing of the ▷ monasteries in 1536. It arose in and was chiefly supported by the north of England, and this fact shows that it had a social and political basis, as well as a religious one. The south of England was economically and socially much more advanced, and more closely in touch with movements of religious reform on the continent of Europe; in consequence, monasteries were not only becoming redundant there in their social functions, but were to some extent actively resented. In the north of England they were more respected on religious grounds, and still served social functions of poor relief and large employment of labour. In addition to these causes which were directly related to monastic institutions there were other social causes bound up with the resentment of the old landed nobility of the north for the newer nobility of the south who were encouraged and advanced in public service by ▷ King Henry VIII; the closing of the monasteries was a pretext for rebellion such as the northern nobility had been looking for. The rebellion was formidable, and the government, through its representative the Duke of Norfolk, had to come to terms; the terms, however, were not kept, and once the rebel army had dispersed, its leaders were executed.

Pillory and stocks

The pillory was a form of punishment in use for small offences from the early Middle Ages until its abolition in 1837. It consisted of a rectangular wooden frame raised above the ground; the pilloried man stood behind the frame, and his head and hands were thrust through holes in the horizontal bar at the top. He was often made to stand in the pillory

throughout the day, and was the target for insults and missiles.

The stocks were a similar instrument. The victim was seated behind the frame, and his legs were thrust through holes in a bar along the bottom of it. Sometimes his head and his hands were also exposed through holes in another horizontal bar higher up. The stocks survived longer than the pillory; they were last used in 1865.

▷ Penal system.

Pindar (5th century BC)

Greek poet. He is famous for his lyrical ▷ odes, *ie* poems to be sung to the accompaniment of musical instruments and dancing. The odes had a strong religious tone and were designed for solemn occasions, including sporting celebrations. The fact that their composition was influenced by their musical and dance accompaniment gives the odes an appearance of irregularity. This, and the loftiness of their emotion, made them tempting models, from the 17th to 19th centuries, for English poets when they were writing on themes of deep emotional power and felt the need of an ample form which would allow them considerable licence in the treatment of the subject. Pindar's odes were not really as unsystematic as they seemed, however, and many English poems in 'Pindarics' have only a superficial resemblance to the kind of ode that Pindar wrote. Notable examples are ▷ Dryden's *Alexander's Feast*, and *Ode to the Memory of Anne Killigrew*.

Pindaric Ode

▷ Ode.

Pindarics

▷ Pindar.

Pinero, Sir Arthur Wing (1855–1934)

Dramatist. His earliest plays were farces, but in 1889 *The Profligate* showed a great advance in seriousness over earlier plays in the century, when the English theatre had been practically bankrupt of contemporary drama of interest. At about this time, largely owing to the influence of ▷ Ibsen, drama was being revised radically in Europe. Pinero's *The Second Mrs Tanqueray* (1893) was at the time of its production a conspicuous contribution to the new movement; it was translated into French, German and Italian, and attracted the leading European actress of the age, Eleonora Duse. Pinero followed this success with other plays which sustained his reputation in Britain at least, such as *Trelawny of the 'Wells'* (1898) and *The Gay Lord Quex* (1899). He was, in fact, a prolific writer, publishing 39 plays between 1891 and 1930.

Caricature of Sir Arthur Pinero by H. Furniss

His plays are now seldom produced and little studied: in wit and dramatic ingenuity he was soon excelled by ▷ George Bernard Shaw. Like ▷ Tom Robertson before him, his brilliance was like that of a candle in the dark: he was conspicuous in contrast to the dullness that preceded him.

Bib: Dunkel, W. D., *Life*; Boas, F. S., *From Richardson to Pinero*; Lazenby, W., *Pinero*.

Pinter, Harold (b 1930)

British dramatist. Major works are: *The Room* (1957); *The Birthday Party* (1958); *The Dumb Waiter* (1957); *A Slight Ache* (radio 1958, stage 1961); *A Night Out* (1960); *The Caretaker* (1960); *The Homecoming* (1964); *Old Times* (1971); *No Man's Land* (1975); *Betrayal* (1978); *A Kind of Alaska* (1982); *Mountain Language* (1988); *Party Time* (1991).

His distinctiveness among contemporary dramatists, among whom he is perhaps the most remarkable, arises from his use of dialogue. Words are used less for communication than for justification by the speaker's self to himself, and as weapons against others who exist not for relationship but in order that each may find assurance that he exists himself. The characters live in constant mistrust and fear, requiring refuge and assurance from their physical environment, and expecting mysterious invasions. When strong emotion actually brings about relationship through words, however inarticulately, the effect is dramatically poignant. Pinter's characters have been compared to ▷ Samuel Beckett's, but the resemblance is probably superficial; Beckett's characters exist in dissolving relationship, whereas Pinter's require social bond. The idiom, however, of both dramatists derives in part from dramatists working at the end of the 19th century – the Swedish Strindberg, the Russian ▷ Chekhov, and the Belgian ▷ Maerterlinck.

Bib: Esslin, M., *The Theatre of the Absurd* and *Pinter: A Study of his Plays*; Taylor, J. R., *Anger and After*; Quigley, A. E., *The Pinter Problem*; Bull, J., *Stage Right: The Recovery for the Mainstream*.

Pitt (the Elder), William, Earl of Chatham (1708–78)

English politician. He led the government during the major part of the ▷ Seven Years' War, during which the British won Canada from the French, and established themselves as the dominant political influence on the subcontinent of India. The successes of this war are usually attributed to Pitt's statesmanship.

Pitt (the Younger), William (1759–1806)

Politician. The son of William Pitt, Earl of Chatham. He led the government from 1783 to 1801, and again in the years 1804–6. He first became Prime Minister when he was only 24, at a time when George III's government had been deeply discredited by defeat in the American War of Independence, brought to an end by the Treaty of Versailles, 1783. Moreover, politics were thoroughly corrupted by various systems of bribery, and Parliament represented only the interests of various sections of the privileged classes. Pitt was as prudent a statesman as his father had been a dynamic one, and he was famous for his strict integrity. His first ministry was one of cautious reconstruction such as Britain needed for the long wars with France (War of the French Revolution, 1793–1801, and the Napoleonic War, 1803–15). Politically he was conservative ('Tory'), but he was the first political leader to rely on public opinion as expressed in the electoral constituencies instead of on more or less bribed backing among Members of Parliament.

Pix, Mary (1666–1709)

Dramatist and novelist, one of the so-called 'Female Wits' satirized in a play of that name in 1696. Pix's first play, a heroic tragedy called *Ibrahim, the Thirteenth Emperor of the Turks*, was produced at ▷ Drury Lane in 1696, the same year as her novel, *The Inhuman Cardinal, Or: Innocence Betrayed*, and a comedy following ▷ Aphra Behn, *The Spanish Wives*. Another comedy, *The Innocent Mistress*, was staged at Lincoln's Inn Fields in the following year. Later plays include *The Deceiver Deceived* (1697), *The False Friend* (1699), *The Beau Defeated* (1700), *The Double Distress* (1701), and *The Conquest of Spain* (1705); Pix wrote a dozen plays in all, of which the comedies are generally considered far superior to the tragedies.

Bib: Steeves, E. L. (ed.), *The Plays of Mary Pix and Catharine Trotter*; Clark, C., *Three Augustan Women Playwrights*; Morgan, F. (ed.), *The Female Wits*.

Plague of London, The Great

A particularly severe epidemic of bubonic plague which struck London in 1664–5. Epidemics had been frequent, either of the bubonic plague or of equally deadly diseases, ever since the ▷ Black Death of the 14th century, and several times caused the compulsory closing of theatres (for fear of infection) during the lifetime of ▷ Shakespeare, but this epidemic, at its height, killed over 68,000 of London's population of 460,000 in one year. It was already declining when the ▷ Great Fire of London in 1666 helped to end it.

▷ *Journal of the Plague Year, A.*

Plain Dealer, The (1676)

Dark comedy by ▷ William Wycherley, based on ▷ Molière's *Le Misanthrope*. Manly, an 'honest' but dour sea captain, has put his trust in the duplicitous Vernish, and brittle Olivia, to whom he has been betrothed. In his absence the two have secretly married, and she has appropriated the fortune that he had entrusted to her care. Manly returns from the Dutch Wars and, on learning of her marriage to an unknown man, determines to revenge himself on her by seducing her, with the help of his page. Also unknown to him, the page is a woman in disguise, Fidelia, who has loved him and gained employment with him in order to be near him. The 'youth' reluctantly agrees to address Olivia on Manly's behalf, but Olivia becomes attracted to Fidelia, and attempts to make love to her, in a scene recalling the one between Viola and Olivia in ▷ Shakespeare's ▷ *Twelfth Night*. Manly overhears Olivia's acknowledgement that she deceived him deliberately. Later Vernish witnesses an assignation between the women and on discovering Fidelia's sex, attempts to rape her, but is interrupted. In the final scene, Fidelia is wounded in a skirmish, defending Manly from Vernish, who is revealed as Olivia's husband. Fidelia's true identity, and status as an heiress, are also made known, and she and Manly are united. A subplot involves the litigations of the Widow Blackacre and her doltish son Jerry. The play was considered by ▷ Dryden to be Wycherley's best, and from it he derived the frequent appellation, 'Manly Wycherley'. The play survived to the late 18th century, when it disappeared from the stage, but has been revived (several times) in the 20th century, including the 1988–89 production by the ▷ R.S.C.

Plantagenet (Anjou), House of

A medieval royal family which reigned over England from 1154 until 1399; ▷ Henry II 1151–89; ▷ Richard I 1189–99; ▷ John 1199–1216; ▷ Henry III 1216–72; ▷ Edward I 1272–1307; ▷ Edward II 1307–27; ▷ Edward III 1327–77; ▷ Richard II 1377–99. The first of the line, Henry II, succeeded to the English throne through his mother, Mathilda, daughter of the last ▷ Norman king, Henry I. Henry II's father was Geoffrey, Count of Anjou, a province in France; hence the family was known either as the House of Anjou or as Plantagenet, from the plant broom (in Latin, *planta genista*) which Geoffrey used to wear in his cap. The families of ▷ Lancaster and York, which ruled England successively in the 15th century, were junior branches of the Plantagenet family.

Plath, Sylvia (1932–63)

Poet and novelist. She was brought up in the United States; her father, who died when she was nine, was of Prussian origin and her mother Austrian. Her university education was at Smith College, Massachussetts, and Newnham College, Cambridge. She married the English poet, ▷ Ted Hughes, in 1956. For a time she taught at Smith College, but in 1959 she settled in England. In 1960 she published her first volume of poetry, *The Colossus*, and in 1963 her only novel, *The Bell Jar*, under the pen-name of Victoria Lucas. Her reputation was established on the posthumous publication of her book of poetry, *Ariel* (1965). This volume aroused more interest in Britian than any other since ▷ Dylan Thomas's *Deaths and Entrances* (1946). The poems combine bold imagery and original rhythms with strenuous artistic control; their themes concern states of mind in extremity. In a commentary recorded for the ▷ British Council, she declared: 'One should be able to control and manipulate experiences, even the most terrifying . . . with an informed and intelligent mind.' Plath committed suicide in 1963. Other important posthumous publications are *Crossing the Water* (1971) and *Winter Trees* (1972); Plath also wrote a radio play, *Three Women*, broadcast in 1962. *Collected Poems* (ed. Ted Hughes; 1981); *Letters Home* (1978). **Bib**: Alvarez, A., in *Beyond All This Fiddle* and *The Savage God*; Uroff, M. D., *Sylvia Plath and Ted Hughes; The Art of Sylvia Plath: A Symposium* (ed. Charles Newman) contains a bibliography.

Plato (?428–?348 BC)

Greek philosopher. He was a follower of the Athenian philosopher ▷ Socrates, and his dialogues represent conversations in which Socrates takes the lead. The most famous of these 'Socratic' dialogues are *Protagoras, Gorgias, Phaedo, Symposium,* ▷ *Republic, Phaedrus, Timaeus*. His longest work, the *Laws*, does not include Socrates as a character. His central conception is that beyond the world of transient material phenomena lies another eternal world of ideal forms which the material world represents in the form of imitations. His figure for this in the *Republic* is that men in the material world are like people watching shadows moving on the wall of a cave; they see only these shadows and not the realities which cast the shadows. Plato is one of the two most influential philosophers in European thought, the other one being ▷ Aristotle, who was at first his pupil.
  ▷ Platonism.

Platonic Love

A term which has come to possess three distinct, if related, senses: **1** A love between individuals which transcends sexual desire and attains spiritual heights. This is the most popularly understood sense of the term. **2** The complex doctrine of love which embraces sexuality, but which is directed towards an ideal end, to be found discussed in ▷ Plato's *Symposium*. ▷ John Donne's poem 'The Extasy' explores this form of love. **3** A reference to homosexual love (cf ▷ W. H. Auden's suppressed poem 'The Platonic Blow'). This third sense is derived from the praise of homosexual love to be found in the *Symposium*.

Platonism and Neo-Platonism

The term 'Platonism' is applied to the school

of thought derived immediately from the Greek philosopher ▷ Plato. 'Neo-Platonism' names schools of thought which adapted his philosophy by adding to or modifying it. Two main periods of revival of Plato's thought are described as neo-Platonism: **1** that initiated by the pagan Plotinus (3rd century AD) in Rome, and at first a revival of Christianity, into which it was to some extent carried by St Augustine of Hippo (345–430) when he was converted; **2** that which Marsilio Ficino initiated by his studies of Platonic philosophy in Florence (15th century). The 17th-century group known as the ▷ Cambridge Platonists were true Platonists rather than Neo-Platonists.
  1 Plato had taught that beyond the world of transient phenomena that surrounds us is that of permanent and imperishable ideas, but he relied on logical reason for the development of his philosophy. Neo-Platonism added a religious aspect which depended on revelation; it derived this influence from other philosophies and from eastern religions. The elements that St Augustine transferred to Christianity remained dominant until the 13th century when Platonic influence was succeeded by that of ▷ Aristotle.
  2 Sixteenth-century neo-Platonism in Italy revived the ancient neo-Platonist conception that the universe was peopled by many supernatural beings, and maintained that these existed in addition to the angels and devils allowed by Christian doctrine. It also taught that men, being essentially spirits, could, by the acquisition of wisdom and virtue, immensely increase their power and knowledge, and could control for their good and wise purposes the non-human supernatural spirits. Thus arose the idea of 'the Mage', or master of high magic; in ▷ Shakespeare's ▷ *The Tempest*, Prospero is such a neo-Platonic Mage, and Ariel is a spirit such as the neo-Platonists believed could be controlled and used. Neo-Platonism also influenced poetic conceptions, such as that the beloved lady of a sonnet sequence (*eg* ▷ Sir Philip Sidney's ▷ *Astrophil and Stella*) was a sublime image of her ideal soul, and that the virtues (*eg* those allegorized by ▷ Edmund Spenser in ▷ *Faerie Queene*) could exist as ideal realities. In criticism, Sidney shows neo-Platonic influence in his conception that poetry should not merely represent but improve on nature, in accordance with the Platonic idea that the world of ordinary realities was an inferior imitation of the eternal idealities. This outlook emphasized the importance of the

imagination, as the faculty that could create ideal images and not merely imitate the general qualities common to classes of actual objects, in accordance with Aristotle's critical theory.

Platonists, The Cambridge

A group of thinkers at Cambridge University in the mid-17th century. Their aim was to combine reason with revealed religion, and to counteract the religiously destructive tendencies of the thought of ▷ René Descartes and ▷ Thomas Hobbes. Their concern with true religion was combined with a care for clarity of thought and for religious tolerance. Their chief representatives were Henry More (1614–87), Ralph Cudworth (1617–88), Benjamin Whichcote (1609–83) and John Smith (1618–52).
▷ Platonism and Neo-Platonism.
Bib: Patrides, C. A. (ed.), *The Cambridge Platonists*.

Plautus, Titus Maccius (?254–184 BC)

Roman comic dramatist. His comedies are based on situation and intrigue; they had a high reputation in his own time, but unlike the other outstanding Roman comedian, ▷ Terence, he was ignored during the Middle Ages. In the 16th century his reputation revived, and his style of comedy was emulated throughout Western Europe. The play which is often called the first English comedy, Nicholas Udall's ▷ *Ralph Roister Doister*, is based on Plautus' *Miles Gloriosus* ('The Boastful Soldier') and Shakespeare's ▷ *Comedy of Errors* on Plautus' *Menaechmi*, which, using a confusion between twins, may also have influenced Shakespeare's ▷ *Twelfth Night*. Again, Shakespeare's ▷ *Taming of the Shrew* may be partly based on Plautus' *Mostellaria*, and the last act of Jonson's ▷ *The Alchemist* is also indebted to it. Certain of Plautus' comic characters, such as that of the boastful soldier as in Udall's play, started a tradition, exemplified by Captain Bobadill in Jonson's ▷ *Every Man in his Humour* and Parolles in Shakespeare's ▷ *All's Well that Ends Well*. These are the most important examples, but traces, at least, of Plautus in the background of English plays can be found in other works of Ben Jonson, and in plays by ▷ Thomas Heywood, ▷ Dryden and ▷ Fielding.

Play on words
▷ Figures of Speech.

Playboy of the Western World, The (1907)

A play by ▷ John Millington Synge. The scene is a remote part of rural Ireland. The hero, Christy Mahon, arrives at a village inn in flight from the law, since he believes himself to have killed his tyrannical father. Instead of being handed over to the police or regarded with abhorrence, he is treated with admiration, and the innkeeper's daughter, Pegeen Mike, falls in love with him. He is at first a miserable youth with no belief in himself, but the universal admiration and Pegeen's love build up his confidence, until he behaves like a true hero. This fiction is destroyed momentarily when his father, who has merely been injured, suddenly appears on the scene. The assault on the father is then suddenly removed from fiction into fact, and the village, including Pegeen, turn against Christy. However, Christy turns into yet a third type of person; he defies the village, through sheer desperation at the idea of sinking back into subservience to his father, and makes his departure in the bullying style which has always been his father's character. The play is thus a mixture of ironic comedy, poetic tragedy, and exuberant farce.

The language is that of the superstitious Irish peasantry, musical and imaginative in its idiom, and though the dialogue is prose, it reaches an intensity that is unique in drama in the English language since the days of ▷ Shakespeare. Irish nationalist opinion was deeply angered by Synge's refusal to idealize the Irish character, and its early performances at ▷ W. B. Yeats's ▷ Abbey Theatre in Dublin caused riots.
▷ Irish literature in English.

Plays for Puritans (1901)

The title for a volume of three plays by ▷ George Bernard Shaw: *The Devil's Disciple*; ▷ *Caesar and Cleopatra*; *Captain Brassbound's Conversion*. Shaw was himself a declared ▷ Puritan in the sense that he shared the Puritan insistence on the importance above all of a sensitive conscience, but he was concerned that the public should be clear-thinking about it. Hence each of these plays treats the conscience and its workings from an original and ironic angle.

Plays Pleasant and Unpleasant (1898)

A collection of seven plays by ▷ George Bernard Shaw. The four 'pleasant' plays are comedies with serious themes (the character of the true soldier, what constitutes moral strength, the nature of greatness, etc) but nothing likely to dismay or shock the conventional moral sense of the audiences of the day. These are: ▷ *Arms and the Man*, ▷ *Candida*, ▷ *The Man of Destiny*, *You Never Can Tell*. The three 'unpleasant' plays dealt with social topics (sexual morality and the ownership of slum property) such as were generally felt to be unsuitable for presentation in the theatre. These are: *Widowers' Houses, The Philanderer, Mrs Warren's Profession.*

Pléiade
The name given to the group of 16th-century poets led by ▷ Ronsard and ▷ Du Bellay, supposedly seven in total, although early mentions of poet comrades are far in excess of this number. Du Bellay's *Deffence & Illustration de la langue francoyse* (1549) sets out a credo common to the group as a whole: wholehearted promotion of the vernacular, imitation of the Ancients, rejection of medieval forms of ▷ lyric verse such as the *ballade* or *rondeau*, establishment of the 12-syllable ▷ Alexandrine as the staple of French verse. Their cultivation of the ▷ sonnet stimulated the major English writers of the last decade of the 16th century such as ▷ Sidney, ▷ Spenser and ▷ Shakespeare.

Pleiades
In Greek myth, the seven daughters of the Titan, ▷ Atlas.

In French literature the name Pléiade was used more than once for a brilliant group of writers. The most famous of these is the group of 16th-century poets led by ▷ Ronsard and ▷ Du Bellay; they abandoned medieval forms of ▷ lyric verse such as the ▷ ballade and the ▷ rondeau, and cultivated the ▷ sonnet, thus stimulating the great English writers of the sonnet – ▷ Sidney, ▷ Spenser, ▷ Shakespeare etc. – in the last decade. They also established the twelve-syllable ▷ Alexandrine as the staple of French verse.

Pleonasm
The use of unnecessary words in the expression of a meaning, *eg* in the phrase 'a deceitful fraud', 'deceitful' is pleonastic, since a fraud is by definition a kind of deceit.

Pliny
There were two Roman writers of this name, Pliny the elder (1st century AD) was the author of a famous *Natural History*, in which fantastic myths about animals are mixed up with some sound early science. His nephew, Pliny the younger, was the author of letters which are an interesting source of information on the ancient Roman world under the Emperor Trajan, especially about the treatment of Christians.

Plotinus
▷ Platonism and Neo-Platonism.

Plutarch (AD 46–?120)
Greek biographer and moralist. He is chiefly famous for his 46 *Parallel Lives* in which he matches 23 famous men from Greek history with 23 famous Romans. The *Lives* were presented in an English version by ▷ Sir Thomas North in 1579; North did not translate them from the original Greek but from the French version by Jacques Amyot. North's book was as popular and influential in England as Amyot's was in France; Plutarch's conception of the great and many-sided man was in harmony with the 16th-century conception of the public virtues and personal accomplishments that should go to make the full man and the perfect courtier. The *Lives*, in North's version, were used as a source-book by dramatists – notably by Shakespeare in ▷ *Julius Caesar*, ▷ *Antony and Cleopatra* and ▷ *Coriolanus*. Plutarch also wrote a number of treatises on moral and physical subjects known as the *Moralia* – a precedent for the essays of ▷ Bacon as well as the very different ones of the great French essayist, ▷ Montaigne.
▷ Translation.

Pluto
▷ Hades.

Plymouth Brethren
A Christian community founded in Plymouth in 1830. It is in the ▷ Puritan tradition, and more famous for the narrow strictness of its moral teaching than for its doctrines.

Poe, Edgar Allan (1809–49)
▷ Detective fiction.

Poel, William (1852–1934)
Actor, director and ▷ Shakespeare scholar. He founded the Elizabethan Stage Society in 1894. Poel's influential productions of the plays of Shakespeare and his contemporaries rejected the traditional techniques of stage realism dominant at the end of the 19th century. Characteristic of his productions was an attempt to recreate Elizabethan stage conditions by performing on a bare apron stage. He also pursued a policy, not always successfully, of restoring full uncut texts for production. Though it is now accepted that he overstressed the notion of the 'bare' Elizabethan stage, he was, with ▷ Harley Granville Barker, a great influence on the development of Shakespeare productions in this century.
▷ Old Vic Theatre.
Bib: Speaight, R., *William Poel and the Elizabethan Revival.*

Poet Laureate
The laurel, also known as the bay (*Laurus nobilis*), was sacred to Apollo, the god most

associated with the arts. The Greeks honoured Olympic victors and triumphant generals, by crowning them with a wreath of laurel leaves. In the 15th century the universities of Oxford and Cambridge gave the title 'laureate', meaning worthy of laurels, to various poets including ▷ John Skelton, and it was later given to court poets like ▷ Ben Jonson. In 1668 the title gained its modern status when ▷ John Dryden was granted a stipend as a member of the royal household charged with writing court odes and celebrating state occasions in verse. Since the time of Dryden the laureateship has been awarded to a few poets of lasting worth and to many of mediocre talent, chosen for reasons of fashion or political acceptability. The list is as follows: ▷ Thomas Shadwell, ▷ Nahum Tate, ▷ Nicholas Rowe, Laurence Eusden, ▷ Colley Cibber, William Whitehead, ▷ Thomas Warton, Henry James Pye, ▷ Robert Southey, ▷ William Wordsworth, ▷ Alfred Tennyson, Alfred Austin, ▷ Robert Bridges, ▷ John Masefield, ▷ Cecil Day Lewis, ▷ John Betjeman and ▷ Ted Hughes. Poets who were offered the laureateship but declined it include ▷ Thomas Gray, ▷ Sir Walter Scott, ▷ Samuel Rogers, ▷ William Morris and ▷ Philip Larkin. Wordsworth was the first Poet Laureate to make his acceptance of the office conditional on his not being obliged to honour official occasions with specially composed poems, though some later laureates have continued the practice, notably Tennyson, Betjeman and Hughes.

Poetics

In ▷ Aristotle's *Poetics* the rules of ▷ 'tragedy' are abstracted from a collection of specific instances to form a theoretical model. The function of 'poetics', therefore, has always been to organize formally details of poetic structures, and to this extent it is both prescriptive and descriptive. This Aristotelian usage persists, though in considerably extended form, in the titles of works of critical theory, such as Jonathan Culler's *Structuralist Poetics* (1975). The theoretical works also address the issue of an organized system of analytical methods, as well as aesthetics of artistic construction. More recently, for example in the work of ▷ new historicist critics such as Stephen Greenblatt, the phrase 'cultural poetics' is used to designate an investigation into 'how the boundaries were marked between cultural practices understood to be art forms and other, contiguous, forms of expression' (*Shakespearean Negotiations*; 1988). Such

investigations seek to explain how particular aspects of general cultural life are given artistic expression. Whereas Aristotle's Poetic can be said to have a ▷ formalist bent, one of the ways in which the term has come to be used today locates the formal aspects of literary texts within a social context.

Poetics

A treatise on poetry by the Greek philosopher ▷ Aristotle. He had already written a dialogue *On the Poets*, which has only survived in fragments, and a treatise on Rhetoric; knowledge of both is to some extent assumed in the *Poetics*. The *Poetics* is considered to have been an unpublished work, resembling notes for lectures addressed to students rather than a full worked-up treatise for the general public, like the *Rhetoric*. This accounts for its fragmentary character. Thus Aristotle distinguishes Tragedy, Epic and Comedy as the chief kinds of poetry, but Comedy is practically omitted from fuller discussion. Lyric, though it is referred to, is not included among the chief kinds, either because Aristotle considered it to be part of music or because he considered it to be taken up into Tragedy. The main part of the work is therefore concerned with Tragedy and Epic – the former more extensively than the latter. Aristotle's method is essentially descriptive rather than prescriptive; that is to say, he is more concerned with what had been done by acknowledged masters such as ▷ Homer and ▷ Sophocles, than with what ought to be done according to so-called 'rules'.

Nonetheless, the *Poetics* became the most authoritatively influential of all critical works. Its dominance in European critical thought from the 16th to the 18th centuries was partly due to its influence on the most widely read of the Roman critics, ▷ Horace, and partly because it was rediscovered at the end of the 15th century when the ▷ Renaissance was at its height, and the spirit of the Greek and Latin writers was felt to be civilization itself. Critics such as the 16th-century Italian Scaliger took what are mere hints in Aristotle and erected them into important rules of art, such as the 'neo-Aristotelian' ▷ unities of time and place. In England, the important critics, such as ▷ Dryden and ▷ Jonson, regarded Aristotle and neo-Aristotelianism with strong respect rather than total reverence, but the complete submission of minor critics such as ▷ Thomas Rymer is exemplified by his obtuse treatment of Shakespeare's *Othello* in the essay *Short View of Tragedy* (1692). Neo-Aristotelianism was set aside by the Romantics, who cultivated literary virtues which are different from Aristotelian shapeliness and order, but the influence of the *Poetics* is still evident in Wordsworth's Preface to the ▷ *Lyrical Ballads*.

Today the *Poetics* remains one of the most outstanding works of European thought. Critics still use Aristotle's terminology in classifying poetic forms; his theory of art as imitation (different from ▷ Plato's) is still the starting-point of much aesthetic discussion; such terms as 'harmatia', for the element in human nature which makes it vulnerable to tragedy, 'peripeteia' for the reversal of fortunes common in tragic narrative, and 'katharsis' for the effect of tragedy on the mind of the audience, have been useful for a long time.

Political Register, The
A weekly journal started by ▷ William Cobbett in 1802, and continued until the year of his death, 1835. It was singularly bold and independent in opinion, and had a wide circulation especially among the poor of rural England. In 1803, Cobbett was fined £500 for his criticism of the government's Irish policy, and in 1809 he was sent to prison for two years for his criticism of military punishments. He continued to edit the paper from prison. From 1821 it included serial publication of ▷ *Rural Rides*.
▷ Journalism.

Pollard, A. W. (1859–1944)
Influential bibliographer and ▷ Shakespearean scholar who is best known for his work on the *Short-Title Catalogue of Books Printed In England . . . 1475– 1640* (1926), which was revised by Katharine Pantzer and others in 1976 (Vol. II) and 1985 (Vol. I).

Polo, Marco (?1254–?1324)
Italian traveller. At a time when Europe was in almost total ignorance of the majority of Asia, he travelled from Venice across central Asia as far as China where he remained for 17 years. On his return to Italy after an absence of 24 years, he wrote an account of his journeys. This became very popular, particularly in the 16th century, when contacts with eastern Asia were renewed. The book was first translated into English in 1579.

Polyhymnia
▷ Muses.

Pomfret, John (1667–1702)
Rector of Maulden in Bedfordshire and author of *Poems on Several Occasions* (1699),

a collection of Pindaric ▷ odes, narrative poems, pastorals, and epistles. His most important poem, *The Choice* (1700) treats the ▷ Horatian theme of rural retirement with a bland cosiness which exactly hit the popular taste of the time. 'Near some fair Town I'd have a private Seat,/ Built uniform, not little nor too great'. He eschews aristocratic splendour in favour of comfortable amenity: 'I'd have a Clear and Competent Estate,/ That I might live Genteelly, but not Great', and advocates benevolent charity towards 'the Sons of Poverty'. *The Choice* presents an ideal of the private life to which both the aristocrat and the successful new bourgeois could subscribe, and it was immensely popular. ▷ Samuel Johnson remarked in his ▷ *Lives of the Poets* (1781): 'Perhaps no composition in our language has been oftener perused'.

Pompey (Gnaeus Pompeius) (106–48 BC)
A Roman general in the period when the republican system of government was weakening. In the social struggles he was a leader of the aristocratic party, and he was very successful in wars of Roman expansion on the eastern seaboard of the Mediterranean. At the height of his power he was, with Crassus and ▷ Julius Caesar, a member of the triumvirate which ruled the Empire. Later, Pompey and Caesar quarrelled, and Caesar decisively defeated him at the Battle of Pharsalus in 48. Soon after the battle he was assassinated by one of his officers.

Poor Laws
Laws which gave public relief to those among the poor who could not earn their own living and were not supported by others. The first great Poor Law was that of 1601, under ▷ Elizabeth I. The dissolution of ▷ monasteries and other Church institutions which had undertaken the care of the destitute, together with a number of causes of unemployment (*eg* ▷ enclosures) caused a series of poor laws to be passed in the 16th century, of which the law of 1601 was the climax. Every parish was required to appoint overseers, whose task it was to provide work for the able-bodied unemployed, and relief (through a local tax called a 'poor rate') for those who were unable to work. The law survived until the 19th century, when problems of poor relief had become too great for it to be an efficient solution. Local magistrates employed a method known as the 'Speenhamland System', from the place of its origin, by which the unemployed were given enough money to enable them to survive; the disadvantage of this system was that it

demoralized those who were employed in very hard labour but unable to earn more than the unemployed who were given relief. In 1834, the New Poor Law was passed. Parishes were grouped into Unions under Boards of Guardians. The main principle of this was that the able-bodied poor were only given relief in ▷ workhouses and that these were not to be so agreeable as to make them inviting to such unemployed as were merely lazy and unwilling to work. The workhouses were in consequence often very disagreeable places, and bitterly unpopular. The law was replaced in 1925 by a more complicated and humane system. In the 1930s, when there was extensive unemployment in Britain, the most unpopular feature of relief to the unemployed was the 'Means Test', involving detailed investigation into whatever means a family might possess to support itself without state aid. The system of National Insurance, set up by the Labour Government of 1945–50, avoided this cause of resentment by making relief available to everyone whatever their income, in return for a universal weekly payment. What is an appropriate level of relief continues to be a matter of debate.

Pope, Alexander (1688–1744)

Alexander Pope

Poet. The son of a ▷ Catholic linen-draper in London, born significantly in the year of the 'Glorious Revolution' of 1688, which heralded the new era of optimism and national confidence reflected in much of his work. In childhood his father encouraged him to produce 'rhymes', insisting that they be perfect, and by his early teens he was already writing polished imitations of such diverse models as ▷ Chaucer, ▷ Edmund Spenser,

▷ Edmund Waller and ▷ Abraham Cowley. His *Pastorals* (1709) established his reputation, followed by the ▷ *Essay on Criticism* (1711), and ▷ *Windsor-Forest* (1713). The last line of this poem is virtually identical with the first line of his *Pastorals*, indicating an ▷ Augustan parallel with Virgil, the last line of whose ▷ *Georgics* is the same as the first line of his *Eclogues*. The ▷ mock heroic ▷ *Rape of the Lock* appeared in 1712, and in an enlarged form in 1714. The characteristic miniaturizing effect of Pope's use of mock heroic can be related to the fact that he was only 4 ft 6 ins high, and suffered from curvature of the spine.

During the early years of his career he had associated with ▷ Joseph Addison, the magisterial arbiter of the new moderate bourgeois taste. But Pope's volatile temperament and ▷ Tory leanings drew him towards the more heady intellectual circle of ▷ Jonathan Swift, ▷ John Gay and ▷ John Arbuthnot, with whom in 1713 he formed the ▷ Scriblerus Club, whose object was to 'ridicule all false tastes in learning'. In 1717 Pope produced a collected volume of *Works*, in which appeared ▷ *Eloisa to Abelard* and *Elegy to the Memory of an Unfortunate Lady*, which shows a bold and unorthodox sympathy for a suicide.

Meanwhile he capitalized on his growing reputation by inviting subscriptions for a translation of ▷ Homer's ▷ *Iliad*, a new practice at the time. The work, published in instalments between 1715–20, served to make him financially secure. Several commentators remarked at the time on the failure of his brisk pentameter ▷ couplets (▷ metre) to capture the rugged grandeur of Homer's unrhymed hexameters, but most were happy to have an 'English Homer', adapted to contemporary taste. He followed up his success by an advertisement 'undertaking' a translation of the ▷ *Odyssey*, which appeared in 1725–6. It leaked out, however, that much of the labour had been subcontracted to two minor poets, Elijah Fenton and William Broome, and for a time Pope was nicknamed 'the undertaker'. Unlike his original compositions, his Homer has not outlived its age. In 1725 he published an edition of the works of ▷ Shakespeare, based on textual comparisons between Quarto and Folio versions, and is thus one of the earliest editors to apply the scholarly techniques previously reserved for ancient ▷ classical literature to an English 'classic'.

In ▷ *The Dunciad* (1728), itself a parody of a scholarly edition, Pope attacked his literary enemies, including the Shakespeare scholar Lewis Theobald, who had corrected errors in his edition. In 1733–4 he turned away from translation and editing and the squabbles in which these had involved him, and published his philosophical poem ▷ *An Essay on Man* and the four ▷ *Moral Essays* (1731–5). Between 1733 and 1737 he produced his ▷ *Imitations of Horace*, and in 1735 appeared the *Epistle to Dr Arbuthnot* which contains some of his most polished satire. In 1742 he produced the *New Dunciad*, a continuation of the earlier poem, and in 1743 this was added as Book Four to a new edition of *The Dunciad*, the hero being changed from Theobald to ▷ Colley Cibber, the ▷ Poet Laureate.

Pope's last years were spent in a rented riverside house at Twickenham, where he played out his own version of ▷ Horatian retirement. Imitating a landed gentleman, he indulged in a ▷ mock heroic, miniaturized version of landscape-gardening, designing a whimsically romantic 'grot' in a tunnel which linked the waterfront with his back garden. It was walled with shells and pieces of mirror, so as to reflect fragments of the river scene in the day, and after dark the light of a flickering lamp which was hung from the roof. Before his death he received the last sacrament, never having abandoned his Catholic religion, despite his ▷ Deist leanings and the double taxation which his recusancy incurred. He left his property to his lifelong friend Martha Blount.

All Pope's important poetry, with the exception of the Deist *Universal Prayer* (1738), is in heroic ▷ couplets, a form which he used with an idiosyncratic perfectionism, not attempted by any other poet of the period. He refined his own personal 'rules': on the exact positioning the caesura, on the choice of diction and on perfection of rhymes (monosyllabic nouns or verbs containing long vowels are preferred). The reader's ear quickly adapts to this hyper-regularity and thus any variation in tone or rhythm, or any deliberate 'irregularity' has an explicit precision of effect virtually unknown in other poets. This characteristic is found cloying by some readers. But, particularly in his more flexible, later verse, it creates one of the most expressive and versatile literary media in the English language.

▷ Augustanism.

Bib: Johnson, S., in *Lives of the Poets*; Mack, M., *Alexander Pope: A Life*; Leavis, F. R., in *Revaluation*; Tillotson, G., *On the Poetry of Pope*; Rogers, P., *An Introduction to Pope*; Gooneratne, Y., *Alexander Pope*; Hill, H. E., and Smith, A. (eds.), *The Art of Alexander*

Pope; Bateson, F. W., and Jukovsky, N. A. (eds.), *Pope* (Penguin Critical Anthology); Hunt, J. D. (ed.), *The Rape of the Lock* (Macmillan Casebook).

Popish Plot
▷ Oates, Titus.

Pornography
This is generally understood to mean representations or literature which is intended to produce sexual excitement. There is, however, a considerable degree of dispute about pornography and it has become the subject of legal cases and public campaigns. The most notorious of these must be the trial concerning ▷ D. H. Lawrence's ▷ *Lady Chatterly's Lover* in 1960. On the right-wing are those moralists who wish to police public standards and ban all sexual material, arguing that it depraves and corrupts. ▷ Feminists also attack pornography at all levels, saying that it is male violence against women; they have particularly broad categories, including advertising. The liberal viewpoint, summed up by the Williams Committee of 1979, draws a distinction between public and private pornography, and if it is not hurting anyone will not interfere legally.

▷ Censorship.

Porter, Peter (b 1929)
Poet. Born in Brisbane, Australia, Porter has lived in Britain since 1951. His work is most famous as an acutely satirical, witty analysis of the decadence of post-war society, and was

Peter Porter

included in A. Alvarez's 1960 ▷ anthology *The New Poetry*. His volumes include: *Once Bitten, Twice Bitten* (1961); *Poems Ancient and Modern* (1964); *A Porter Folio* (1969); *The Last of England* (1970); *Living in a Calm Country* (1976); and *English Subtitles* (1981).

Portrait of a Lady, The (1881)

A novel by ▷ Henry James. The heroine, Isabel Archer, is brought from America to England by her aunt, Mrs Touchett, the wife of a retired American banker. Isabel has the candour and freedom conspicuous among American girls of the period; she also has beauty, intelligence, and a spirit of adventure and responsiveness to life. She refuses offers of marriage from both Lord Warburton, a 'prince' of the English aristocracy, and Caspar Goodwood, a 'prince' of American industry. In the meantime her cousin, Ralph Touchett, has fallen in love with her, but he is slowly dying of consumption and dare not become her suitor. Instead, he tries to play the 'fairy godmother' by persuading his father to leave her the money which would have been due to himself. His action has two unfortunate results: it awakens Isabel's New England Puritan conscience through the sense of responsibility which the possession of wealth entails, and it attracts the rapacious Madame Merle, whose guilty secret is that she is looking for a rich stepmother for her daughter by her former lover, Gilbert Osmond. Osmond (like Madame Merle herself) is an artistic but cold-blooded and totally self-centred expatriate American. Isabel in her humility is easily made to feel her own cultural inferiority to the exquisite exterior qualities of Osmond, whom she sees as the prince she has been looking for – a man deprived of noble potentialities by the unjust circumstance of his poverty. She marries him, only to discover his hollowness, and that her marriage is imprisonment in the ogre's castle.

The novel, sometimes regarded as James's masterpiece, shows his conception of the relationship of the American and European consciousnesses; the Americans have integrity, the will to live, and good will towards humanity, but they lack richness of tradition and are restricted by the limitations of the New England puritan inhibitions; the Europeans (especially some of the American expatriates) have rich cultural awareness but this commonly corrupts their integrity, and instead of good will they have immense rapacity. On the other hand the best kind of American expatriate (Ralph Touchett) combines the best of both worlds.

Portrait of the Artist as a Young Man, A (1916)

An autobiographical novel by ▷ James Joyce. The theme is the life of a middle-class Irish boy, Stephen Dedalus, from his infancy in the strongly Catholic, intensely nationalistic environment of Dublin in the 1880s to his departure from Ireland some 20 years later. In his boyhood he sees his elders bitterly divided in consequence of the Church's rejection of ▷ Parnell, the nationalist leader, owing to the scandal of his private life. As he grows up he is repelled by the pettiness, treacheries and vindictiveness of Irish nationalism, and for a time is drawn towards the rich spirituality of the Catholic tradition. The Irish Catholic Church, however, also suffered from provincialism and narrowness, and a moment of revelation on the seashore shows him that the largeness of an artistic vocation will alone suffice for him to harmonize the spiritual and fleshly sides of his nature, and enable him to rise above the vulgarity of his environment; but the choice brings with it the decision to leave Ireland.

The originality of the novel consists in its presentation of the hero's experience from within his own consciousness. The language gradually expands from the fragmentary diction of an infant on the first page through the connected but limited range of expression characteristic of a schoolboy to the sophistication of a fully articulate university student.

▷ Irish literature in English.

Poseidon

In Greek myth, the god of the sea, identifiable with the Roman Neptune. He was the son of Cronus and Rhea, and brother of ▷ Zeus and ▷ Hades. His character was generally wild and cruel, and his symbol was the trident with which he lashed the sea into storm; he was also supposed to cause earthquakes. Like another violent god, ▷ Ares, he was the enemy of the goddess of wisdom, ▷ Athene.

Positivism

▷ Comte, Auguste.

Post-modernism

The break away from 19th-century values is often classified as ▷ modernism and carries the connotations of transgression and rebellion. However, the last twenty years has seen a change in this attitude towards focussing upon a series of unresolvable philosophical and social debates, such as race, gender and class. Rather than challenging and destroying cultural definitions, as does modernism, post-modernism resists the very idea of boundaries. It regards distinctions as undesirable and even impossible, so that an almost ▷ Utopian world, free from all constraints, becomes possible.

It must be realized though, that post-modernism has many interpretations and that no single definition is adequate. Different disciplines have participated in the post-modernist movement in varying ways, for example, in architecture traditional limits have become indistinguishable, so that what is commonly on the outside of a building is placed within, and vice versa. In literature, writers adopt a self-conscious ▷ intertextuality sometimes verging on pastiche, which denies the formal propriety of authorship and genre. In commercial terms post-modernism may be seen as part of the growth of consumer ▷ capitalism into a multi-national and technological identity.

Its all-embracing nature thus makes post-modernism as relevant to street events as to the *avant garde*, and as such is one of the major focal points in the emergence of interdisciplinary and cultural studies.
Bib: Jameson, F., *Post-modernism and Consumer Society*; Lyotard, J.-F., *The Post-modern Condition*.

Post-structuralism

At first glance, the term post-structuralism seems to imply that the post-structuralists came after the structuralists and that post-structuralism was the heir of ▷ structuralism. In practice, however, there is not a clear-cut division between structuralism and post-structuralism. Although the two have different focuses of interest and preoccupations, many of their concerns bind them together. Structuralism encompasses approaches to criticism which use linguistic models to enable critics to focus not on the inherent meaning of a work but on the structures which *produce* or generate meaning. Post-structuralism focuses on the ways in which the texts themselves subvert this enterprise. Leading post-structuralists include ▷ Derrida, ▷ Lacan, J. Hillis Miller and ▷ Paul de Man.

▷ Deconstruction; Feminism; Reader-response criticism.
Bib: Culler, J. *On Deconstruction.*

Potter, John (?–1749)

Theatre proprietor, and craftsman. Potter entered the theatre in or after 1708, probably as a carpenter and/or scene painter. He erected a playhouse known as the French Theatre as well as the Little Theatre in the Hay (▷ Haymarket Theatres), and eventually, the Haymarket Theatre (▷ Haymarket Theatres).

Poulter's Measure

A verse ▷ metre used by some 16th-century poets; it consisted of a 12-syllable line (▷ Alexandrine) alternating with a 14-syllable one. 'Poulter' = 'poulterer' – an allusion to variations in the number making up a dozen in the poultry trade. It was used by ▷ Thomas Wyatt, ▷ Henry Howard Surrey and less distinguished poets.

> When Dido feasted first the wand'ring Trojan knight,
> Whom Juno's wrath with storms did force in Lybic sands to light,
> That mighty Atlas did teach, the supper lasted long,
> With crispéd locks, on golden harp, Jopas sang in his song.
>
> (Wyatt: 'Jopas' Song')

Pound, Ezra (1885–1972)

American poet. He came to Europe in 1907, and made London his home during the period 1908–20. His influence on English poetry during this period, especially on that of his fellow-American, ▷ T. S. Eliot, was very great. English poets had become insular, and they tended (with some exceptions) to occupy themselves with a marginal field of experience left over to them by the novelists, abstaining from the issues that were central to the destiny of their thoroughly industrialized society. They also restricted themselves to a limited diction, consecrated as 'poetic', with an obvious emotional appeal. The recent British poets who interested Pound were ▷ Robert Browning for his direct and 'unpoetic' address to the reader, and the Irish poet ▷ W. B. Yeats, for his austere seriousness and energy. In his campaign to reform diction he became the leader of the ▷ Imagist Movement, though he later abandoned it; this phase is illustrated by his *Ripostes* (1912) and *Lustra* (1916). It also drew him to Chinese poetry, from which he made excellent English verse, although his are not such accurate translations as those of his contemporary Arthur Waley.

In his campaign to free English poetry from insularity, Pound accepted the concept, which he shared with some other American writers (eg ▷ Henry James and T. S. Eliot), that European culture is a whole, not segmented into national cultures. Thus he offered fresh insights into ▷ French and ▷ Italian poetry back to the ▷ Middle Ages (see his critical essays, *Make It New*) and into the Latin classics. In his poetry he used the diction of everyday speech with a subtle ear for its rhythms. Like Eliot, he abandoned the logical continuity of prose in favour of a juxtaposition of ideas and images whose continuity appears through their psychological association. Also like Eliot, he used quotation frequently, thereby relating his treatment of his themes with the treatment accorded by past poets to similar themes, and thus illuminating the fundamental alterations in outlook and assumption brought about in the course of history. This technique of quotation is conspicuous in Eliot's poem ▷ *The Waste Land*, which Pound heavily revised. A comparable poem by Pound is *Hugh Selwyn Mauberley* (1920), which heralded his departure from Britain by offering an assessment of the state of culture there at the time. He moved to Paris, and in 1924 to Italy, where he became increasingly sympathetic to ▷ Fascism, partly in consequence of his strongly held and eccentric economic theories (see his *ABC of Economics*).

From this time onwards, his poetry output consisted almost entirely in working on his extended poem ▷ *The Cantos*, which was not finished at his death. The *Pisan Cantos* (1948) are the most famous section, recording his incarceration in Pisa by the American forces at the end of World War II, while waiting to stand trial for treason. Found unfit to plead at his trial in 1948, he was committed to St Elizabeth's Hospital, Washington D.C., from where he was released in 1958, spending the rest of his life in Italy. See also his *Literary Essays* (ed. T. S. Eliot), and *The Translations of Ezra Pound* (ed. H. Kenner).
Bib: Kenner, H., *The Poetry of Ezra Pound* and *The Pound Era*; Davie, D., *Ezra Pound: Poet as Sculptor*; Bush, R., *The Genesis of Ezra Pound's 'Cantos'*.

Powell, Anthony (b 1905)
Novelist. He writes sophisticated comedy of upper-class life in England since 1920; his approach may be compared with the different treatment of the same society by ▷ Aldous Huxley, ▷ Evelyn Waugh, and by ▷ D. H. Lawrence in *St Mawr*. Early novels are: *Afternoon Men* (1931); *Venusberg* (1932); *From a View to a Death* (1933); *Agents and Patients* (1936); *What's Become of Waring* (1939).

In 1948 he produced a study of ▷ John Aubrey, the 17th-century anecdotal biographer, author of *Brief Lives*. He then began his major work which, it has been suggested, owes something to Aubrey as it clearly does to the sequence *A la Recherche*

du Temps Perdu by the French novelist ▷ Marcel Proust. Powell's sequence of novels is called *A Dance to the Music of Time*. The narrator, whose personality is kept in detachment but not eliminated, is an upper-class young man with whose life various circles of friends intertwine in a kind of dance, and in a way that is only conceivable in the upper levels of any society. The characters make a pattern of contrasts, the most serious and interesting being that of the man of distinction – Stringham – who evokes the high style of an Elizabethan courtier such as ▷ Ralegh, but who is in the worldly sense a failure, and Widmerpool, the man of grotesque and crude manners and feeling, who is yet a worldly success owing to his insensibility and the force of his ambition. *A Dance to he Music of Time* consists of: *A Question of Upbringing* (1951); *A Buyer's Market* (1952); *The Acceptance World* (1955); *At Lady Molly's* (1957); *Casanova's Chinese Restaurant* (1960); *The Kindly Ones* (1962); *The Valley of Bones* (1964); *The Soldier's Art* (1966); *The Military Philosophers* (1968); *Books Do Furnish a Room* (1971); *Temporary Kings* (1973); *Hearing Secret Harmonies* (1975). The sequence begins in 1921 at the narrator's public school; it ends after the war with the death of Widmerpool in circumstances of sinister pathos. Powell has followed up his novel sequence with a sequence of memoirs entitled *To Keep The Ball Rolling: Infants of the Spring* (1978); *Messengers of Day* (1978); *Faces in My Time* (1980); *The Strangers All Are Gone* (1982). Other novels: *O, How the Wheel Becomes It!* (1983); *The Fisher King* (1986).
Bib: Bergonzi, B., *Anthony Powell*; Spurling, H., *Invitation to the Dance*; Tucker, J., *The Novels of Anthony Powell*.

Powys, John Cowper (1872–1963)
Novelist, poet and essayist. Principal novels are: *Wolf Solent* (1929); *A Glastonbury Romance* (1932); *Weymouth Sands* (1934); *Maiden Castle* (1936); *Owen Glendower* (1940); *Porius* (1951). Works of criticism and thought: *Visions and Revisions* (1915; revised 1935); *Psychoanalysis and Morality* (1923); *The Religion of a Sceptic* (1925); *The Meaning of Culture* (1929); *In Defence of Sensuality* (1930); *The Art of Happiness* (1935); *The Pleasures of Literature* (1938). One of his most famous books is his *Autobiography* (1934), developed from his contribution to the *Confessions of Two Brothers* (1916) written with Llewelyn Powys.

Like his brother, ▷ T. F. Powys, his fiction is influenced by his background in the English west country, but his prose is

contrasted with his brother's by its
expansiveness and diffuseness. His writing
combines a strongly physical sensationalism
with a fascination for the intangible and
mysterious reaches of human experience. He
is concerned with the transformation of
ordinary life by a contemplative intensity
which generates a mythical sense of the
individual's relation to his natural
environment. His work shows the influence
of ▷ Thomas Hardy, with whom he was
acquainted. Critics are divided as to whether
Powys is an overrated or an underrated
novelist.
Bib: Graves, R. P., *The Brothers Powys;*
Cavaliero, G., *John Cowper Powys, Novelist*;
Churchill, R. C., *The Powys Brothers.*

Powys, Theodore Francis (1875–1953)
Novelist and short-story writer; brother of
▷ John Cowper Powys. His novels and
fables were set in the rural south-west of
England; the characters are presented with a
simplicity and poetry resembling the style of
the Old Testament of the Bible, but the
individuality of the expression is too distinct
for the resemblance to be obvious, and the
tone is naïve on the surface but sophisticated
in its pagan, often cynical implications. At its
best, *eg* in *Mr Weston's Good Wine* (1927) and
Fables (1929), Powys's art rose to exquisite
tragic poetry; at its worst it descended to
brutality and cruelty. His fiction is a very late
and unusual example in English of a writer
using purely rural traditions and environment;
the tragic pessimism, less humane and more
sophisticated than ▷ Thomas Hardy's, is
perhaps a reflection of the disappearing
vitality of that way of life. Some other works:
Mark Only (1924); *Mr Tasker's Gods* (1925);
Kindness in a Corner (1930). *Fables* was
republished as *No Painted Plumage* in
1934.
Bib: Coombes, H., *T. F. Powys*; Hunter, W.,
The Novels and Stories of T. F. Powys.

Predestination
A theological doctrine which holds that, since
God in his eternal wisdom has foreknown the
events of time since before the creation of the
world, he has foreseen and chosen those
individuals who are damned and those who
are saved for eternal life after death. Those
who are saved are called 'the elect', and those
who are damned 'the reprobate'.

Prelude, or Growth of a Poet's Mind, The
(1850)
A ▷ blank verse ▷ autobiographical poem
by ▷ William Wordsworth. The first
version, in 13 books, was written between
1799 and 1805, but remained unpublished.

Wordsworth continued to revise the poem at
intervals throughout his life, and a version in
14 books appeared in 1850, after his death.
With the encouragement of ▷ Samuel Taylor
Coleridge, Wordsworth originally hoped to
achieve a great philosophical poem
(provisionally entitled *The Recluse*) 'on man,
on nature, and on human life', to which *The
Prelude* was intended as an introduction.
Only one further part of the project, the
vastly inferior ▷ *Excursion*, was completed.
In *The Prelude* Wordsworth takes stock of his
experience and resources, and traces the
events of his early life. Books I–II, which
concern 'Childhood and School-Time'
contain some of his best-known work,
illustrating the interaction between his
growing mind and nature, as he climbs up to
a raven's nest, rows a boat out on to a lake at
night, or skates under the stars. Later books
concern his time at Cambridge, in London
and in revolutionary France (▷ French
Revolution). The heading of Book VIII
sums up a constant theme: 'Love of Nature
Leading to Love of Man'.
 In a sense the work is a continuation of the
▷ epic tradition in a bourgeois form, the
heroic adventures of the aristocratic
warrior hero being replaced by the inner
adventures of the individual poet. This helps
to explain the epic grandeur of the poem's
tone and scope, though this is not always
sustained in practice. The revisions in the
1850 version, though they frequently
improve the phrasing and pace of the 1805
text, impose upon it a Christian orthodoxy
which muffles the immediacy of
Wordsworth's original idiosyncratic
▷ pantheism.

Pre-Raphaelite Brotherhood
A movement of painters and poets which
began just before 1850; it was more important
in painting then in poetry, but one of its
leading members. ▷ Dante Gabriel Rossetti,
was equally famous in both arts. The essence
of the movement was opposition to technical
skill without inspiration. This made it anti-
Victorian, inasmuch as industrial techniques
(illustrated by the ▷ Great Exhibition of
1851) were producing vast quantities of
work which were products of engineering.
Technical skill without inspiration was
deemed to be an aspect of the neo–classical
art of the 18th century, against which the
▷ Romantics had already protested, and
behind neo–classicism lay the 16th century
▷ Renaissance of Greek and Roman art,
and the paintings of the Italian artist Raphael
(1483–1520), who had produced religious
pictures of extraordinary perfection

Typically Pre-Raphaelite illustration

in technique but (in the opinion of the Pre-Raphaelites) with an almost cynical disregard of spiritual feeling. This tenderness of the spirit had existed in medieval art; hence the Brotherhood, by no means hostile to highly polished technique, cultivated the artistic spirit of the ▷ Middle Ages. The principal painters of the Brotherhood were Rossetti, John Millais and Holman Hunt; its poets were Rossetti and his sister ▷ Christina Rossetti, and, a little later, ▷ William Morris.

The movement drew for its poetical inspiration on the ardour of the romantic poet, ▷ John Keats, who had also cultivated the Middle Ages, and it greatly revered the contemporary poet, ▷ Alfred Tennyson, whose art owed much to Keats. But Pre-Raphaelitism was not merely an aesthetic movement; a great influence upon it was the work of the art critic ▷ John Ruskin, who had a strong social conscience about the duty of art to society, and especially of the duty of redeeming the squalid life of the urban working classes. Less close to the movement, but still in harmony with it, was the poet and critic ▷ Matthew Arnold, with his attack on the philistinism of the middle classes and the barbarism of the upper classes. Finally, the ground of Pre-Raphaelitism had been prepared by the ▷ Oxford Movement in the Church of England; this had rejected the interfering state, and by its cultivation of ritual in religous worship asserted that it had brought beauty back into religion.

However, Keats had not been dismayed by the world of his time so much as by the inevitability of desperate suffering as part of the human lot in every age. Arnold and Tennyson, in their poetry, were dismayed by the surface hideousness and the apparently irremediable injustices of their society. They had tended to write a 'poetry of withdrawal', creating an inner world of unassailable dreams (Tennyson) or a transcendent fortress of lofty feeling (Arnold). The Pre-Raphaelites followed this example. The poetry of Rossetti and of Morris is a 'literary' art, *ie* it depends on the proved poetic stimulus of a special 'poetic' language and imagery which was alien to the ordinary man of the age, and had no relationship to the economically productive genius of the age itself. (The intensely pious Christina Rossetti had a more authentic, religious inspiration, but even in her work the feeling is subjectively personal as compared to the work of a 17th-century religious poet such as ▷ George Herbert, whom in some respects she resembled.) Thus, whatever the social consciences of Rossetti and Morris, they tended to take poetry to be an autonomous activity, largely independent of the political and social issues of the time. The poet ▷ Algernon Swinburne had the courage to take this autonomy seriously; with him, 'art for art's sake' was born, and the aesthetic movement (▷ Aestheticism). The only poetry which was moving strongly in another direction was that of ▷ Gerald Manley Hopkins from 1865 to 1889, and he was regarded as unpublishable. Another poet, ▷ W. B. Yeats, owed much to the Pre-Raphaelites and especially to Morris, but the bitter realities of Irish politics made him, in the next century, one of the leaders of the reaction against the whole direction of art as the worship of Beauty. This reaction has lasted to the present day. The Pre-Raphaelites had their own periodical – *The Germ*; it first appeared in January 1850, and ran for only four numbers.
Bib: Stanford, D. (ed.), *Pre-Raphaelite Writing.*

Presbyterianism
A doctrine of church organization maintained by an important group of ▷ Protestants. 'Presbyter' comes from a Greek word meaning 'elder', and Presbyterianism is a system of church government by councils of elders. The system was devised by ▷ Calvin; it became dominant in Scotland under the leadership of ▷ John Knox and had wide support in England from about 1570. It is still the national Church of Scotland, but in England it seceded extensively to ▷ Unitarianism during the 18th century. In 1972 the English Presbyterians joined with

the Congregationalists to form the United Reformed Church.

Press Council, The
A body recently established by the British Government to maintain good and responsible standards of ▷ journalism. When newspapers seem to abuse their powers by interfering with private life and liberty, complaints may be made to the Council which can then, if it thinks the abuse is genuine, administer a public rebuke to the newspaper concerned. It has no powers of censorship.

Preston, Thomas (1537–98)
Author of the early Elizabethan tragicomedy *Cambyses, King of Persia* (1569). He may also have written the popular and influential romance *Sir Clyomon and Sir Clamydes*.

Pretender
    ▷ Old Pretender, The: Jacobite.

Pride and Prejudice (1813)
A novel by ▷ Jane Austen. Mr and Mrs Bennet belong to the minor gentry and live at Longbourne near London. Mr Bennet is witty and intelligent, and bored with his foolish wife. They have five daughters, whose marriage prospects are Mrs Bennet's chief interest in life, since the estate is 'entailed' – *ie* by the law of the period it will go on Mr Bennet's death to his nearest male relation, a sycophantic clergyman called ▷ Mr Collins. The main part of the story is concerned with the relationship between the witty and attractive Elizabeth Bennet and the haughty and fastidious Fitzwilliam Darcy, who at first considers her beneath his notice and later, on coming to the point of asking her to marry him, finds that she is resolutely prejudiced against him. His friend Charles Bingley is in love with the eldest daughter, Jane, but they are kept apart by the jealous snobbishness of his sisters and (at first) the fastidious disapproval of Darcy. Meanwhile, Elizabeth is subjected to an insolent offer of marriage by Mr Collins and the arrogant condescension of his patroness, Lady Catherine de Bourgh, Darcy's aunt. Those who regard the Bennet family as foolish and vulgar have their opinion justified when Lydia Bennet elopes with an irresponsible young officer, George Wickham. By this time, however, Darcy and Elizabeth have been chastened by finding in one another a fastidiousness and pride that equal their own and, despite the family scandal, they are united.

The novel has always been one of the most liked of Jane Austen's, and it contains excellent social comedy, but in some respects it stands apart. She herself said of it 'The work is rather too light, and bright, and sparkling; it wants to be stretched out here and there with a long chapter of sense.' Elizabeth Bennet was, however, her own favourite heroine.

Priestley, J. B. (John Boynton) (1894–1984)
British novelist and playwright, whose first success was with *Dangerous Corner* in 1932, a thriller dealing with the theme of time. This was followed by two other 'time' plays, *Time and the Conways* and *I Have Been Here Before*, in 1937. He is notable for experimenting with a variety of dramatic subjects and styles from the popular thrillers such as those mentioned above and *An Inspector Calls* (1945), to conventional comedies like *Laburnum Grove* (1933) and *When We are Married* (1938), the ▷ Chekhovian *Eden End* (1934) and the expressionistic *Johnson over Jordan* (1939). One of his later works was a dramatization with ▷ Iris Murdoch of her novel, *A Severed Head* (1963).
Bib: Evans, G. L., *Priestley the Dramatist*.

Priestley, Joseph (1733–1804)
A nonconformist minister, scientist and teacher. He was partly educated at a nonconformist academy at Daventry; such academies existed in the 18th century to give a university education to non-conformists, who for their religious views were not admitted to the recognized universities of Oxford and Cambridge. They were commonly more advanced scientifically than the real universities; Priestley eventually became the first chemist to isolate oxygen. In 1768 he published his *Essay on the First Principles of Government*, advocating 'the happiness of the majority' as the criterion by which government must be judged. This line of thought was developed by ▷ Jeremy Bentham and his 19th-century followers, the ▷ Utilitarians. Priestley's house in Birmingham was destroyed by the mob in 1791 owing to his well-known sympathy with the ▷ French Revolution, and in 1794 he emigrated to the United States.

Prime minister
Since the 18th century the office of greatest power in the British political system. It arose in consequence of the struggles for power between king and parliament in the 17th century. Parliament was victorious, inasmuch as it became difficult for the king to lead the

country politically without the approval of Parliament at every major step. This could be managed only by a politician who was himself a member of the parliamentary body, as the king was not; moreover George I (1714–27) and George II (1727–60), the first two kings of the House of Hanover (▷ George) had the additional disadvantage of being foreigners in the nation they were supposed to govern. Thus the 18th-century art of 'managing' parliaments grew up; the first politician to be a master of the art was ▷ Robert Walpole, whose period of power ran from 1721–42. He is usually regarded as 'the first Prime Minister' in English history, though he objected to the title. Walpole's 'management' was politically unsatisfactory, however, since it depended too much on the bribery of Members of Parliament. After his downfall, the parliamentary system went through an unsatisfactory period of about 40 years during which aristocratic coteries intrigued for power, and George III (1760–1820) made an ultimately unsuccessful attempt to recover royal political initiative. Then ▷ William Pitt the Younger took over the government with the king's approval, and retained power from 1783 to 1801. He insisted that he should have complete control; his personal integrity placed him above the suspicion of exercising it dishonestly; he based his authority on public opinion. For these three reasons he did more even than Walpole to establish the office of prime ministership, although Parliament had to undergo the reform of 1832 before this office could achieve a strong basis in national acceptance.

A Prime Minister now usually has a seat in the ▷ House of Commons and is in the first place elected as an ordinary Member of Parliament, but it is nearly always understood that they are the leader of one of the contending parties, and that the sovereign will call on them to 'form a government' if the party in question has a majority of members in the House of Commons.

Primrose League

A Conservative political society founded in memory of ▷ Benjamin Disraeli, Lord Beaconsfield, whose favourite flower was said to be the primrose. The society was founded in 1883 and achieved large membership; it was one of the earliest successful attempts at permanent organization of public opinion in support of a political party.

Princess, The (1850)

Poem by ▷ Alfred Tennyson, originally titled *The Princess, A Medley* (1847), enlarged

and revised in 1850. Despite bad reviews, *The Princess* was immensely popular and sold well on publication. Like ▷ Elizabeth Barrett Browning's ▷ *Aurora Leigh*, it was a key text in the so-called 'woman question' debate, displaced onto a pseudo-medieval scene. The tale of Princess Ida, champion of women's rights who rejects ▷ marriage and sets up a women-only university, is collectively told by a group of friends entertaining themselves. Ida was betrothed in infancy to the Prince who narrates the tale, of how he defies 'the inscription on the gate, LET NO MAN ENTER IN ON PAIN OF DEATH'. He and two friends dress as women and infiltrate the university. The men's identities are discovered by the women, and the university is attacked by the prince's father, who demands that they be released unharmed. In the ensuing battle between Ida's father and the Prince's, the three young men fall. Ida calls for the women to nurse them, and the women's university is turned into a hospital. When the Prince recovers he proposes a progressive marriage of equality to Ida, to which she yields:

> *My bride*
> *My wife, my life. O we will walk this world,*
> *Locked in all exercise of nobel end . . .*

▷ Women, Education of; Feminism.
Bib: Killham, J., *Tennyson and 'The Princess'*.

Prior, Matthew (1664–1721)

Poet and diplomat. The son of a joiner, Prior was educated under the patronage of the ▷ Earl of Dorset. While an undergraduate at ▷ Cambridge he collaborated with the Earl of Halifax on a parody of ▷ John Dryden, *The Hind and the Panther transvers'd to the Story of the Country Mouse and the City Mouse* (1687), and in 1700 he celebrated the arrival of William III from Holland in *Carmen Saeculare*. After a period as secretary to the ambassador at the Hague he allied himself to the Tory camp of Harley and Bolingbroke and was involved in secret negotiations with the French government over the Treaty of Utrecht (1713), which was nicknamed 'Matt's Peace' after him. When Queen Anne died in 1714 and the ▷ Tories fell from power he was impeached and imprisoned for two years. His *Poems*, published by his friends in 1718, helped to restore his fortunes. His best work is marked by an easy-going humour. *Alma: or the Progress of the Mind* (1718), a long poem in loose ▷ Hudibrastics, mocks the systematic philosophy of ▷ Aristotle and ▷ Descartes and elaborates the proposition, borrowed from ▷ Montaigne's essay 'On Drunkenness', that the mind begins in youth in the toes, and rises by degrees until it reaches the head in old age. It is in his shorter, occasional poems that Prior achieves his most satisfying poetic effects. 'Jinny the Just' (published in 1907), an elegy for his housekeeper and mistress, employs an unheroic ▷ metre of anapaestic triplets to characterize its uneducated subject, and to create a moving personal tribute:

> Tread Soft on her grave, and do right to her
> honour
> Lett neither rude hand nor Ill tongue light
> upon her
> Do all the Small favours that now can be don
> her.

Other poems of importance are *Solomon on the Vanity of the World* (1718), in heroic ▷ couplets; *Henry and Emma* (1707), a travesty of the old ballad *The Nut-Brown Maid*; and *Down-Hall, a Ballad* (1723). Prior was a brilliant exponent of the epigram, a memorable example being 'A True Maid':

> 'No, no; for my Virginity,
>   When I lose that, says Rose, I'll dye:
> Behind the Elmes, last Night, cry'd Dick,
>   Rose, were you not extreamly Sick?

Bib: Johnson, S., in *Lives of the Poets*.

Prioress's Tale, The

One of ▷ Chaucer's ▷ *Canterbury Tales*, which derives from the popular tradition of devotional narratives celebrating the miraculous interventions of the Virgin Mary. It is an anti-Semitic story, set in Asia, which recounts how a young Christian boy is murdered by Jews as he walks through their quarter singing a Christian hymn. His body is discovered because he continues to sing the hymn, miraculously, even after his death. The narrative, written in ▷ rhyme royal, is narrated in an emotive and pathetic style.

Prisoner of Chillon, The (1816)

A poem by ▷ Lord Byron in tetrameter ▷ couplets (▷ metre) interspersed with quatrains. It is based on the story of François de Bonnivard (1496–1570), prior of the monastery of St Victor, near Geneva, who participated in a revolt against the Duke of Savoy and attempted to set up a republic in Geneva. He was imprisoned from 1530 to 1536 in the castle of Chillon. Byron's work is prefaced by a facile sonnet extolling Liberty as the 'Eternal Spirit of the chainless Mind!' The poem itself, however, contradicts this optimism, describing the slow pining away of the narrator's two brothers, and the disintegration of his own mind under the strain of solitude: 'It was at length the same

to me,/ Fetter'd or fetterless to be,/ I learn'd to love despair.' The historical Bonnivard was given a pension after his release, and was married four times.

Prisons

In the 11th and 12th centuries dungeons (underground cells) in castles were the prisons of those who displeased powerful barons or the king, and for long afterwards the Tower of London – fortress, palace and prison – was used for important political prisoners. In London there were the royal prisons of ▷ Newgate, the ▷ Marshalsea and the ▷ Fleet, which all lasted till Victorian times. In the 16th century houses of correction were set up for the incarceration of vagrants, who were regarded as a menace to the peace; these were modelled on the first to be established at ▷ Bridewell, London, in 1552, and were called 'Bridewells' after it. They were at first intended as 'workhouses' for the unemployed, but they became prisons in all but name. Prisoners were also kept in prison ships or 'hulks'.

Conditions in the prisons were very bad until the 19th century. Three principal reasons for this were:

1 Prisons were not considered to be the responsibility of the authorities but of the gaolers; there was thus no supervision or maintenance of even the lowest standards of decency and hygiene, or of other aspects of living conditions.

2 The gaolers were not regarded as officials, but as though they kept lodging-houses as tenants of the local or central authorities; they were paid no salaries, and drew their incomes from the prisoners who had to pay for privileges, and from whom the gaolers often extorted money by abominable treatment.

3 Public attention to the necessity of a secure but humane prison system was delayed by the practice of 'transporting' criminals convicted of the more serious crimes to the American colonies or, after 1783, to Australia; transportation only ceased in the 1840s.

John Howard in the 18th century and Elizabeth Fry in the 19th were the leaders of the movement of reform in the prison system, which only made real advances after 1850. ▷ Jeremy Bentham was also influential in making prison organization more efficient and rational. The best known of all the writers who publicized the need for reform was ▷ Charles Dickens; he repeatedly used prison themes and episodes in his novels.

▷ Penal system.

Pritchard, Hannah (1709–68)

Actress, singer. She joined ▷ Theophilus
Cibber and other performers who seceded
from the company at ▷ Drury Lane, and
opened at the ▷ Haymarket Theatre in
1733, only to return to ▷ Drury Lane in the
following year. By now she was frequently
cast in major roles, including Phaedra in
▷ Dryden's *Amphitryon* (1690), Isabella in
▷ Sir Richard Steele's ▷ *The Conscious
Lovers*, and Dol Common in ▷ Jonson's
▷ *The Alchemist*.

In 1740 Pritchard played Desdemona to
▷ James Quin's Othello (▷ *Othello*), but
her performance as Rosalind in ▷ *As You
Like It* from the end of that year is said
finally to have established her as one of the
leading actresses of her generation. She
appeared as Nerissa in the production of
▷ *The Merchant of Venice* in which
▷ Charles Macklin revolutionized the
portrayal of Shylock, and later acted in
several plays with ▷ Garrick.

In 1749 her popularity forced a change in
the ending of ▷ Samuel Johnson's *Mahomet
and Irene*, to the author's chagrin: she was to
have been strangled on stage, but the audience
would not have it, and the action was modified
so that she was 'killed' away from their view
instead. She was noted for the intelligence of
her interpretations, her versatility, and her
dedication to her profession.
Bib: Vaughan, A., *Born to Please: Hannah
Pritchard, Actress*.

Pritchett, V. S. (Victor Sawdon) (b 1900)

Novelist, short-story writer, critic and travel
writer. He left school at 15 to work in the
leather trade, and also worked in the
photographic trade in Paris before becoming
a journalist. Since 1926 he has been a regular
critic for the ▷ *New Statesman*, and since
1946 a director. He is best known for his
short stories, which are economical and
understated, employing colloquial dialogue.
His work is primarily in a ▷ realist mode,
and consists of ironic observation of society
and human eccentricity. Story collections are:
Collected Stories (1982); *More Collected Stories*
(1983). His novels are: *Clare Drummer* (1929);
Shirley Sanz (1932); *Nothing Like Leather*
(1935); *Dead Man Leading* (1937); *Mr
Beluncle* (1951). Criticism includes: *The
Living Novel* (1946); *Balzac: A Biography*
(1973); *The Myth Makers: Essays on
European, Russian and South American
Novelists* (1979).

Privy Council

With a history going back to the king's
council which in the 13th century gave the
sovereign private ('privy') advice on the
government of the country, this is now a
body with largely formal work, mainly carried
out by committees since the membership –
now conferred as a special honour – is large.
The former powers of the Privy Council are
now exercised by the Cabinet.
▷ Orders in Council.

Problem plays (of Shakespeare)

A term first used in the late 19th century by
critics of ▷ Shakespeare to designate a
group of his plays written between 1600 and
1604. These are: ▷ *Troilus and Cressida*,
▷ *All's Well that End's Well* and ▷ *Measure
for Measure*. What makes these all 'problem
plays' in the view of some critics is that it is
difficult to discern the author's intention.
Troilus and Cressida is regarded as a problem
because, while the Trojans are shown to be
intrinsically nobler than the Greeks, they are
also shown to be wrong, although the Greeks
are not conclusively shown to be right in
their outlook. Thus no positive value is
preached by the play, nor does it seem to be
light-hearted enough to be a mere comedy.
All's Well, the slightest of the three, is a
problem because the noble heroine uses
means which we should nowadays despise to
gain her lover, who does not, in any case,
seem to be worth her trouble. The play is
thus a 'romantic comedy' but one in which
the romance has gone sour. *Measure for
Measure* is a comedy which, in the opinion of
some critics, is both too serious and too
cynical in some of its characteristics to be
successful either as a comedy or as a serious
critique of society. Not every critic agrees
that all these plays or any of them, are really
'problematic'.
Bib: Tillyard, E. M. W., *Shakespeare's
Problem Plays*.

Professor, The (1857)

The first novel by ▷ Charlotte Brontë. She
offered it for publication in 1846 but it was
refused and not published until 1857 after
her death. In the meantime she recast the
material, which was based on her experience
as a teacher in Brussels in 1843, and made it
into ▷ *Villette*, which came out in 1853.
The Professor has a man, William Crimsworth,
for its central character, whereas *Villette* has
a young woman, Lucy Snowe. William
Crimsworth has a love affair with an Anglo-
Swiss woman teacher analogous to Lucy's
with Monsieur Paul Emmanuel but the
relationship is less intricate and profound.

Prologue to The Canterbury Tales

▷ *Canterbury Tales, The*.

Prometheus

In Greek myth, one of the ▷ Titans.

In the war between the gods and the Titans, he remained neutral, and was still on terms with ▷ Zeus when the gods were victorious. He was, however, very cunning, and skilful.

According to legend Zeus was angry at a deception practised on him by Prometheus and deprived mankind of fire. Prometheus, however, stole fire from the gods, and gave it to man. Zeus then tried to punish man by sending the first woman (▷ Pandora) with her jar of misfortunes; Hope, however, was left to man when the misfortunes were released to plague humanity. Zeus now tried to drown the human race in a great flood, but again Prometheus came to the rescue. To punish Prometheus for repeatedly outwitting him, Zeus had him bound to Mount Caucasus, and sent an eagle which gnawed incessantly at his liver. Prometheus, however, refused to ask pardon, and withheld a secret affecting Zeus's destiny. Eventually, Zeus allowed ▷ Heracles to free the Titan, who told the secret, and enabled Zeus to save himself. Prometheus was mortal, and on his death descended to the underworld. However, at the prayer of the centaur, Cheiron, he was eventually released, and permitted by Zeus to join the company of the gods.

Prometheus Unbound (1820)

A 'lyrical drama in four acts' by ▷ Percy Bysshe Shelley, written to correspond to the final lost play of the Promethean trilogy by the Greek poet, ▷ Aeschylus. The demigod Prometheus, having stolen the secret of fire from the gods and given it to man, is punished by being chained to a rock and subjected to everlasting torture. Nevertheless, comforted by his mother, the Earth, and consoled by thoughts of his bride, Asia, the Spirit of Nature, he remains defiant against Jupiter, king of the gods. At the appointed hour Demogorgon, the primal life-force, defeats Jupiter, frees Prometheus, and an era of love dawns, in which all cruelty and oppression are banished: 'the man remains/ Sceptreless, free, uncircumscribed, but man/ Equal, unclassed, tribeless, and nationless,/ Exempt from awe, worship, degree, the king/ Over himself'. The original Greek myth in which Zeus (Jupiter) and Prometheus are reconciled, is thus transformed into a political allegory of modern revolution. The style is elaborately abstract, and the play is to be read rather than acted. In his Preface the poet refers to his desire 'to familiarize the highly refined imagination of the more select classes of poetical readers with beautiful idealisms of moral excellence'. Despite its cloyingly consistent elevation of tone, it is a strangely powerful work.

Proserpine

▷ Persephone.

Protestant succession

The belief that the throne should not pass to a Roman Catholic. The arguments about the royal succession became bitter when ▷ Charles II was succeeded by his brother ▷ James II. James's Catholicism was only one reason for the ▷ Revolution of 1688 but the fear of a return of James or of later succession by other Catholics caused further controversy and led to the Act of Settlement of 1701 and later Acts which made it impossible for a Catholic to succeed to the throne.

▷ Protestantism.

Protestantism

A term used for all varieties of Christian belief which broke away from Roman Catholicism during the ▷ Reformation in the 16th century, or for religious communities not in agreement with Roman Catholicism but originating since the Reformation. It was first used in regard to those who protested against the Emperor Charles V's condemnation of the reformers in Germany at the Diet of Spires, 1529. Protestants in Britain include ▷ Anglicans, ▷ Presbyterians, ▷ Methodists and ▷ Baptists.

Proteus

In Greek myth, a sea spirit, whose task it was to care for the herds of the sea (ie seals, etc.). He had prophetic power, but those who wished to consult him had to catch him and bind him when he came ashore for his midday sleep. This was no easy task, since Proteus could turn himself into any shape.

Prothalamion (1596)

A wedding song, written by ▷ Edmund Spenser and published in 1596. Prothalamion is roughly half the length of Spenser's other wedding song – ▷ Epithalamion. The ▷ ode celebrates the double wedding of two sisters – Lady Elizabeth and Lady Katherine Somerset in August 1596.

Proust, Marcel (1871–1922)

French writer. Early in his career, he was the author of critical works, Les Plaisirs et les jours (1896; translations from Ruskin), Pastiches et mélanges (1919) and two posthumously published works Contre Sainte-Beuve (1981), and the incomplete novel

Jean Santeuil (1952). Proust is nonetheless known for one book, his major work, *A la recherche du temps perdu*. It runs to 3,000 printed pages and was originally published in eight parts between 1913 and 1927. The novel was first translated by C. K. Scott-Moncrieff under the title *Remembrance of Things Past*, but a recent and much improved version has been completed by Terence Kilmartin.

A la recherche is the story of an artistic vocation, the attempt to write a novel which is similar to (though not the same as) that which the reader has before him. The novel itself is full of artist-figures, and the narrator's own endeavours to perceive pattern in disorder and fragmentation centre crucially on a discovery, a discovery about time and memory. The attempt to resurrect and recapture time past through voluntary memory cannot but fail, for voluntary memory is sifted for its relevancies. The past can consequently only be reached by involuntary memory, itself triggered by the most apparently innocuous and circumstantial of objects: a madeleine dipped in tea, a starched napkin, an uneven paving-stone. These objects are associated with forgotten events in the past, and those instants when the bond between past and present is recovered and the past reborn are 'privileged moments' (*moments privilégiés*). The novel jettisons a unilinear plot, while the central focus for narration is restricted to that of Marcel (not to be confused with Proust himself); impressions and sensations are fed through his consciousness which evolves over time and constitutes a devolved, perceptually-limited human subject. Proust's portrayal of social and above all sexual relations, moreover, intensify the sense of a self unable to know others, until the narrator realizes that only art gives access to others, since only in art is there the 'real residue' of the personality.

Proust's novel aroused two kinds of reactions. His minuteness in rendering human consciousness, for example, recalls both ▷ Henry James and ▷ James Joyce. His perception that the insignificance of an incident at the time of experiencing it contrasts with the importance it may come to have in the memory anticipates ▷ Virginia Woolf. The design by which relationships amplify through a lifetime into a pattern evocative of musical composition was emulated by ▷ Anthony Powell in *A Dance to the Music of Time*. On the other hand, other 20th-century novelists, such as ▷ D. H. Lawrence and ▷ L. H. Myers, have rejected Proust on the grounds that his principles are merely aesthetic.

Proviso scene
Scene in a play showing bargaining between lovers, typically those featured in so-called ▷ Comedies of Manners, of the Restoration, wherein they set their terms before agreeing to be married. The most famous such scene is that between Millamant and Mirabell in ▷ William Congreve's ▷ *The Way of the World* (1700), in which they guarantee one another independence within marriage, before announcing their engagement (IV, 2).

Provok'd Wife, The (1697)
Play by ▷ Sir John Vanbrugh. The drunken, boorish and misogynistic Sir John Brute, married but hating marriage, conducts a deliberate campaign to abuse and humiliate his wife and her niece Bellinda. In revenge, Lady Brute determines to cuckold him with the amorous Constant, who has been courting her for the past two years. In a parallel plot Heartfree, another misogynist, at first woos the affected Lady Fanciful, then falls in love, for the first time in his life, with Bellinda. A series of intrigues brings the pairs of lovers together in amorous assignations, although Lady Brute refrains from adultery with Constant. In the final scene Lady Fanciful attempts, but fails, to defame the reputations of both Bellinda and Heartfree, with whom she is now in love. Bellinda and Heartfree are united, while Sir John undergoes a supposed but unconvincing change of heart, and vows to be a better husband in future. The play's comedy barely sweetens its bitter comments on marriage, and especially, the vulnerability of women in marriage. But it affirms the value of true love: Constant says, 'Though marriage be a lottery, in which there are wondrous many blanks, yet there is one inestimable lot in which the only heaven on earth is written'. Ironically, however, he, the only admirer of women, apparently remains unmarried at the end, while the misogynists are matched.

Psalms, The
A book of the Old Testament composed of the sacred songs of the ancient Jewish religion. In ancient Hebrew, they were called 'praise-songs', indicating the predominant function of the collection, though other functions – lament, meditation imprecation etc. – were included. Authorship was traditionally attributed to ▷ King David, but it is evident that the psalms either date from after the Babylonian Captivity (6th century BC) or were re-edited then; in any case they originated at different periods.

In the 16th century under the inspiration of the ▷ Protestant Reformation, the psalms were translated into English. There are two prose versions in official use in the ▷ Church of England: that of the Authorized Version of the ▷ Bible of 1611, and the older translation in the Book of ▷ Common Prayer dating from 1549. Both include some of the well-known masterpieces of English prose of the ▷ Renaissance. In addition, there are the metrical and rhymed versions especially favoured by the more extreme Protestants. The so-called 'Old Version' by Sternhold and Hopkins was published in its complete form in 1562. Another version, principally the work of Francis Rouse, came into general use in Scotland in the mid-17th century, and in 1696 Nicholas Brady and ▷ Nahum Tate produced the so-called 'New Version'. More distinguished attempts to versify the prose psalms were made in the 16th century by ▷ Sir Philip Sidney and his sister the ▷ Countess of Pembroke; in the 17th, by George Sandys, ▷ George Wither and ▷ John Milton; in the 19th, by John Keble.

▷ Bible in England.

Psyche
In Greek myth, a personification of the human soul. ▷ Eros fell in love with her, and kept her in a magnificent palace where he visited her only at night, warning her that should she try to see him or discover who he was, he would leave her for ever. However, one night she lit a lamp to see him; he awoke, and departed. The palace vanished, and Psyche became the victim of a series of terrible ordeals imposed on her by ▷ Aphrodite – which she survived, thanks to the invisible protection of Eros, who finally persuaded ▷ Zeus to allow Psyche to be admitted among the gods. Psyche has been the subject of a number of poems in English, the most famous of which is the *Ode to Psyche* (1819) by ▷ John Keats.

▷ Odes, Keats's.

Psychoanalytical criticism
Psychoanalysis and literary criticism both seek to interpret their respective objects of enquiry, and both involve the analysis of language. In its early manifestations psychoanalytical criticism (*eg* Ernest Jones's *Hamlet and Oedipus*; 1949) sought to apply the methods of psychoanalysis to particular texts, in order to uncover their 'unconscious'. Jones's claim was to reveal the causes of Hamlet's behaviour beginning from the assumption that 'current response is always compounded partly of a response to the actual situation and partly of past responses to older situations that are unconsciously felt to be similar'. The French psychoanalyst ▷ Jacques Lacan's re-reading of ▷ Freud

has sought to render problematical this relationship between patient and analyst, and, by implication, between text and reader. Lacan's description of the unconscious as being structured 'like a language' raises fundamental questions for the authoritative role usually ascribed to the literary critic. To this extent the 'unconscious' of the literary text is brought into confrontation with the unconscious of the critic.

Many of the terms taken from psychology which are associated with Lacan's reading of Freud have been incorporated into the language of literary criticism; for example, the decentred subject of psychoanalysis, ▷ condensation, ▷ displacement, the realm of the ▷ 'imaginary', the ▷ symbolic order, all refer in some way to textual mechanisms.

Bib: Laplanche, J. and Pontalis, J-B., *The Language of Psychoanalysis*; Lacan, J., *The Four Fundamental Concepts of Psychoanalysis*; Wright, E., *Psychoanalytical Criticism*.

Ptolemy (Claudius Ptolemaeus) (2nd century AD)
Astronomer, geographer and mathematician. He was a native of the Egyptian city of Alexandria, and may have been of Greek origin. His theory of the structure of the universe, according to which the planets, sun and stars all revolved round the earth, remained the accepted opinion until replaced by the theory of ▷ Copernicus in the 16th century and the observations of ▷ Galileo in the 17th. This is the Ptolemaic System summarized in the *Almagest*, his treatise on astronomy.

'Pub' (Public house)
A house which is licensed to sell intoxicating drinks to be enjoyed on the premises, essentially the same as a 'tavern' – a word which is now seldom used but is sometimes assumed by a pub which wishes to appear picturesque. Licensing laws controlling the sale of drink go back to 1551, when it first became necessary to obtain permission from a ▷ magistrate to open a tavern. This long history is not so much evidence of English Puritanism as of the reputation the nation had, and kept until the 20th century, for the vice of drunkenness. In 1910 restrictions were introduced limiting the hours when pubs were allowed to open. These were relaxed in 1988 with the introduction of 'all day opening' with landlords being able to choose to open for up to 12 hours a day (11am to 11pm, except Sundays). Socially, the English pub has the peculiarity that it is commonly divided into different bars: the 'public bar' where the beer is usually slightly cheaper, and the

'saloon bar'. Some pubs, especially the old-fashioned ones, are further divided into the 'lounge bar', the 'private bar', the 'jug and bottle' (where patrons are served when they wish to take drink to their homes), and even a 'ladies' bar'. This segmentation probably derives from the time when drunkenness was more common, and some customers did not wish to associate with drunken working-men. Most pubs are 'tied houses', *ie* they are owned by particular brewers who stock them with their own beers; a 'free house' is one not so owned, and free to buy its beer where it chooses. Beer is the principal drink consumed in pubs, but they also sell distilled spirits and wines.

▷ Inns, Taverns, Alehouses.

Public schools

In Britain these are not and have never been either schools under the state, or entirely non-feepaying schools. They are distinguished from 'private' schools in not being run for private profit by individual owners; like the colleges of Oxford and Cambridge, they were founded and endowed for the public good, often for poor scholars. Until the Education Act of 1944, they were often hard to distinguish from endowed Grammar Schools; the latter were, however, more likely to draw on the immediate locality for their pupils, whereas the public schools drew on the whole nation, with varying provision for 'poor scholars'. Since, until the 19th century, education was largely restricted to study of the classics – ancient Greek and Latin language and literature – they tended to attract, in the ▷ Middle Ages, those who were to enter the Church and the learned professions; from the 16th century it became increasingly regarded as indispensable to 'a gentleman' that he should possess a firm classical culture, and from the 18th century, public schools began to be aristocratic educational institutions. The middle classes often had little use for the education they provided, or they were excluded as Dissenters and went to a Dissenting Academy instead, where in any case the education was wider and more practical. A change came in the 19th century when the middle classes had enormously increased in wealth and numbers and many of them aspired to be or regarded themselves as 'gentlemen' and required a 'gentleman's education' for their sons. Several other causes extended public school education to much of the middle class: Dissenting Academies declined and public school education broadened; ▷ Thomas Arnold as headmaster of ▷ Rugby (1828–42) imbued

it with strong religious and moral feeling, suited to the traditions of the middle classes, in which Puritanism was a large element; the country needed a large governing class for its rapidly growing empire. Now that this empire has gone, various motives, creditable and less creditable, cause the English upper and middle classes to maintain the public schools; sometimes the motive may be snobbery, but it is often the educational prestige that some public schools have acquired. The nature of this prestige varies greatly, since 20th-century public schools do not conform to a model. In the 19th century the inspiration of Arnold tended to make the public schools somewhat narrow; leadership and fair-mindedness were cultivated at the expense of wide culture and intellectual flexibility. When Arnold's son, the poet and critic ▷ Matthew Arnold, described the English upper classes as 'barbarians', he was thinking of the products of the public schools.

Some public schools date from the 19th century, but those with most prestige are usually much older: Winchester (founded 1382); Westminster (1560); Eton (1440); Harrow (1571); Rugby (1567). The public school system is 'English' rather than 'British', since it has flourished mainly in England, and has never become characteristic of Scotland, Wales or Ireland, though distinguished public schools exist in those countries. It was at one time a predominantly masculine system, although there are now a large number of girls' public schools and a number of boys' schools have begun to admit girls, especially into their sixth forms.

▷ Education; Schools in England.

Puck

In Old English, an evil spirit; from the 16th century a mischievous fairy, as in ▷ Shakespeare's ▷ *A Midsummer Night's Dream.*

▷ Fairies.

Punch

A weekly comic periodical, founded in 1841. ▷ Hood and ▷ Thackeray were early members of its staff, and it employed a number of distinguished illustrators in the 19th century including Leech, Tenniel, Keene, and ▷ Du Maurier. From 1849 for a century it kept the same cover picture – of Punch of the puppet-shows. It was at first a radical paper, but as it became more and more an upper class 'institution', so in politics, tone and taste it began to represent an influential but increasingly narrow section of the upper middle class. It has published the work of many famous cartoonists,

JOHN LEECH'S PICTURES

PUNCH

HOTEL METROPOLE
LONDON, S.W.

Cover of Punch: April 24, 1886

including, in recent years, Ronald Searle, Michael Heath, Bill Tidy and Gerald Scarfe.

Punch and Judy
The principal characters of a popular puppet-show. There are allusions to Punch in the diaries of ▷ Pepys and ▷ Evelyn, and the show can still be seen, especially at seaside resorts. Punch is hooknosed, humpbacked, violent and cunning; he is always represented with his wife Judy, who is not particularly grotesque, and a little dog Toby – often real. Punch kills his wife and the dog, beats the doctor who comes to visit him, hangs the hangman who is supposed to execute him, and eventually outwits the devil.
▷ Mime; Pantomime.

Purcell, Henry (1658–95)
Composer. His father and uncle held musical appointments at the Chapel Royal, and his father was also master of the choristers of Westminster Abbey. He himself became a chorister in the Chapel Royal as a young boy, and as a young man was made 'composer in ordinary to the king' and organist at the Abbey. He composed some instrumental pieces, but is expecially famous for his choral compositions. Some of these were church music, eg the Te Deum and Jubilate (1694), which was the first English religious work to be scored for both strings and brass. His official appointments also caused him to set choral odes written for official occasions, such

as the odes to St Cecilia. In addition, he collaborated with a number of ▷ Restoration dramatists in writing for the theatre, including a musical setting for a ▷ masque in ▷ Betterton's drama Diocletian and musical numbers in several dramas by ▷ Dryden: Tyrannic Love (1687), Amphitryon (1690), King Arthur (1691). This work for the theatre included a musical version of Shakespeare's A Midsummer Night's Dream, entitled The Fairy Queen (1693), and his opera Dido and Aeneas (1689), with a libretto by ▷ Nahum Tate.

Purcell's career concluded the period of English music which had begun in the mid-16th century. In his youth one of his principal teachers had been the English composer John Blow, but he was also a close student of French and Italian musical development. As a composer he had great freedom of imagination and strong gifts for dramatic writing. The poet ▷ Gerard Manley Hopkins composed a work in his honour.
▷ Opera in England.

Purgatorio
The second book of the ▷ Divina Commedia by ▷ Dante. Having emerged from the Inferno, the poet, still accompanied by ▷ Vergil, follows a spiral up to the Mount of Purgatory, where the souls of the dead are purged of the stains of their sins as they await release into Heaven. They encounter various groups of repentant sinners on the seven circular ledges of the mountain, who suffer punishments and pain, but do so more willingly, knowing the suffering will pass in the end. On its summit is the Earthly Paradise where the poet meets Beatrice, who is to guide him through the spheres of Heaven.
▷ Inferno; Paradiso.

Purgatory
According to Catholic faith, a state in which the souls of the dead undergo purification from their sins on earth. These sins must be 'venial' not 'mortal', ie not so serious as to cause the soul damnation in Hell, yet too serious for them to attain the spiritual perfection that enjoys the eternal bliss of Heaven. It is believed that the prayers of the living on earth can shorten the duration of Purgatory. The Protestant Churches, with the exception of Anglo–Catholic members of the Church of England, do not accept the doctrine of Purgatory.

Puritanism
The term is used in a narrow sense of religious practice and attitudes, and in a

broad sense of an ethical outlook which is much less easy to define.

1 In its strict sense, 'Puritan' was applied to those Protestant reformers who rejected Queen Elizabeth's religious settlement of 1560. This settlement sought a middle way between Roman Catholicism and the extreme spirit of reform of ▷ Geneva. The Puritans, influenced by Geneva, Zurich, and other continental centres, objected to the retention of bishops and to any appearance of what they regarded as superstition in church worship – the wearing of vestments by the priests, and any kind of religious image. Apart from their united opposition to Roman Catholicism and their insistence on simplicity in religious forms, Puritans disagreed among themselves on questions of doctrine and church organization. The principal sects were: ▷ Presbyterians, Independents (at first called ▷ Brownists, and later ▷ Congregationalists), ▷ Baptists, and (later) ▷ Quakers. They were strong in the towns, especially in London, and in the University of Cambridge, and socially they were widespread, and included members of the aristocracy and of the working classes, as well as the middle, commercial classes where they had their chief strength. Puritanism was very strong in the first half of the 17th century and reached its peak of power after the ▷ Civil War of 1642–6 – a war which was ostensibly religious, although it was also political. Matters of church government were much involved with matters of state government, since Presbyterians and Independents, who believed in popular control of the church, were not likely to tolerate royal control of Parliament's political affairs. Puritanism was both religiously and politically supreme in the decade 1650–60, but on the ▷ Restoration of the monarchy Puritans were denied participation in the Church of England, and refused rights of free religious worship. The last was granted them by the Toleration Act of 1689, and during the 18th century both Puritanism and the official attitude to it were modified under the influence of Rationalism. Nonetheless, the ▷ Methodist movement of that century had many of the characteristics of the older Puritan sects. It was, moreover, only in 1829 that Nonconformists (as they were now called) were allowed to offer themselves as candidates for seats in Parliament, and only in 1871 did the Universities of Oxford and Cambridge cease to be the monopoly of the Church of England.

2 In the broader sense of a whole way of life, puritanism has always represented strict obedience to the dictates of conscience and strong emphasis on the virtue of self-denial. In this sense individuals can be described as 'puritan' whether or not they belong to one of the recognized Puritan sects, or even if they are atheists.

The word 'Puritan' is often thought to imply hostility to the arts, but this is not necessarily true. In the reign of ▷ Elizabeth I poets such as ▷ Spenser and ▷ Sidney combined a strong puritan moral tone (without any Puritan doctrine in the sectarian sense) with an intense delight in artistic form; in the 17th century John Milton was an ardent Puritan, but his poetry is one of the climaxes of English ▷ Renaissance art. However, it is true that the strict Puritans of the age of Shakespeare were commonly opponents of the art of the theatre; this was partly because the theatres were sometimes scenes of moral licentiousness and disorder, and partly because the strict Puritan, in his intense love of truth, was very inclined to confuse fiction with lying. Thus in the later 17th century Bunyan was criticized by some of his Puritan comrades for writing fiction in his allegory, ▷ Pilgrim's Progress, and in the early 18th century ▷ Defoe had to defend his ▷ Robinson Crusoe against similar charges. Nonetheless, in the 18th and 19th centuries, Puritanism, or attitudes derived from it, did tend to encourage 'philistinism', or contempt for culture. This was because Puritanism had always encouraged an essentially practical attitude to worldly affairs, and when religion slackened as a driving force, the practical virtues came to be regarded as the principal, if not the only ones. Art, on the other hand, encourages the contemplative virtues, which the practical man of Puritan tradition was inclined to regard as unnecessary, therefore frivolous, and so, in a puritan sense, 'sinful'. There is continuity of development from Priestley, the 18th-century scientist and preacher, through the practical philosophy of ▷ Bentham, to James Mill, the ▷ Utilitarian leader, who was an atheist.

What is called the 'Puritan conscience', on the other hand, had an important influence on one kind of art form – the novel. Puritans believed that the good life could only be lived by 'the inner light' – the voice of God in the heart – and to discern this light it was necessary to conduct the most scrupulous self-enquiry. This produced the kind of spiritual autobiography that was common in the mid-17th century, and of which the best example is Bunyan's ▷ Grace Abounding. Such self-knowledge had two important

consequences: it increased interest in, and understanding of, the human heart in others as well as the self, and the first results of this are apparent in Bunyan's *Pilgrim's Progress*; but it also encouraged a sense of the loneliness of the individual – a sense that was supported by the growing economic individualism of the later 17th century. These are important constituents of the novelist's vision, and when one adds to them the preoccupation with moral values with which Puritanism is so bound up, and which are such a permanent feature of the English novel, it is possible to think that without Puritanism the novel form would never have developed indigenously in England.
▷ Reformation.

Purity
▷ *Cleanness.*

Puss in Boots
A folk tale, translated into English in 1720 from the French collection by ▷ Charles Perrault. The cat is the property of a poor man, the third son of a miller. By the animal's ingenuity, the miller's son marries the king's daughter. The story is a popular theme of Christmas ▷ pantomimes.

Puttenham, George (d 1590)
The reputed author of *The Art of English Poesy* (1589). The book is a thorough treatise on English poetic technique at the time, on the threshold of one of the great decades of English short poems. It discusses the various forms of metrical verse, discusses – without deciding between them – the rival merits of metrical and non-metrical forms (▷ Metre), and presents an enlightened review of English verse. With Sidney's ▷ *Apologie for Poetrie*, Puttenham's book is one of the two most important critical works of the Elizabethan period. It is more scholarly, if less eloquent, than Sidney's essay, but like Sidney, Puttenham is trying to establish civilized standards for the composition of poetry, and is opposed to the 'vulgar', popular traditions of a poet such as Skelton.

Pygmalion
In Greek myth, a king of Cyprus famous for his sculpture. He made an ivory statue of a woman, so beautiful that he fell in love with it, and was in despair because the statue could not return his love. ▷ Aphrodite took pity on him, and brought the statue to life.

Pygmalion (1912)
A play by ▷ George Bernard Shaw. The theme is the transformation of Lizzie, an impoverished, illiterate and wretchedly

neglected London girl, into the image of a fashionable lady who can make an imposing appearance at an ambassador's reception. The transformation is contrived by the phonetician Higgins, who undertakes it as a scientific experiment; he resembles the sculptor
▷ Pygmalion in bringing into existence a being of great beauty, but, like Pygmalion's statue, Lizzie possesses no life, in this case because Higgins has invested no feelings in her, merely using her as an instrument of his research. The play has always had great success, though it is one of the least convincing of Shaw's plays: the real transformation of Lizzie could not have been made by changing Lizzie's speech sounds, and Shaw falls a victim to the same fallacy that he exposes in Higgins, inasmuch as he, too, fails to understand the true nature of his own creation. The plot was later used as the basis for the musical *My Fair Lady*, first staged in 1956.

Pym, Barbara (1913–80)

Barbara Pym

Novelist. Educated at Oxford University, she served with the W.R.N.S. during World War II, and subsequently worked at the International African Institute in London. Between 1950 and 1961 she published six novels: there then followed 16 years during which she could not find a publisher. After praise from Lord David Cecil and the poet ▷ Philip Larkin in 1977 her work received renewed attention, and she published a further three novels. Since then her work has

enjoyed considerable popularity. Her novels are sensitive, shrewd, ironical portraits of English middle-class life, with a particular focus on the lives of women; the social contexts are frequently academic and clerical. She is often said to write in the tradition of ▷ Jane Austen. A further three novels were published posthumously. Her novels are: *Some Tame Gazelle* (1950); *Excellent Women* (1952); *Jane and Prudence* (1953); *Less Than Angels* (1955); *A Glass of Blessings* (1958); *No Fond Return of Love* (1961); *Quartet in Autumn* (1977); *The Sweet Dove Died* (1978); *A Few Green Leaves* (1980); *An Unsuitable Attachment* (1982); *Crampton Hodnet* (1985); *An Academic Question* (1986).
Bib: Benet, D., *The Life and Work of Barbara Pym.*

Pyramus and Thisbe

The hero and heroine of a love story by the Roman poet ▷ Ovid (▷ *Metamorphoses* iv). The lovers are forbidden marriage by their parents, but they exchange vows through a hole in the wall that separates their respective houses. They agree to meet outside Babylon at the tomb of Ninus, but Thisbe, who arrives first, is frightened by a lion and hides in a cave, the lion meanwhile covering her dropped veil with blood. When Pyramus arrives and finds the bloody veil, he supposes Thisbe to be dead, and kills himself; Thisbe follows his example. In Shakespeare's play ▷ *A Midsummer Night's Dream* the artisans give a comically bungled performance of the tragedy before King Theseus of Athens.

Pyrrhus (318–272 BC)

A King of Epirus, in northern Greece. He made war against the Romans, the Greeks of Southern Italy, and the Carthaginians. After a victory over the Greeks and Romans at Heraclea, his own losses were so heavy that he declared: 'One more such victory, and we are lost.' This is the origin of the phrase 'a Pyrrhic victory', meaning one gained at too great a cost.

Pythagoras (6th century BC)

Greek philosopher. He is important in the histories of religion, mathematics and astronomy. In religion he founded the Pythagorean brotherhood, which believed in the immortality of the soul and its migration into another body, perhaps that of an animal, after death; for this reason they practised vegetarianism. In mathematics, he discovered the mathematical relations of musical intervals; he or his followers believed that the sun and the planets were divided by comparable intervals – hence the tradition of 'the music of the spheres' inaudible to earthly hearing. In geometry, he is credited with the theorem called after him, that the square on the hypotenuse of a right-angled triangle is equal to the sum of the squares on the other two sides. In astronomy, he discovered that day and night are caused by the revolution of the earth about its own axis.

Many legends grew up round Pythagoras, amongst others that he was of extraordinary beauty and had golden thighs. Historically, his ascetic philosophy, based on the belief that the body was the tomb of the soul and that denial of the flesh was the way to its final release, is considered to foreshadow ▷ Platonism.

Quadrille

1 A game of cards which replaced ▷ ombre in fashion about 1726, to be succeeded about 20 years later by whist.

2 A dance of French origin; it was first used in ballet, and then became popular in the ballroom. Introduced into England in the late 18th century.

Quadrivium and Trivium

In the medieval educational syllabus the 'seven liberal arts' were divided into the Trivium – grammar, rhetoric, logic – followed by the Quadrivium – arithmetic, geometry, astronomy, music.

Quakers

Originally a derisive name for the members of a religious society properly called the Society of Friends; the Friends are still known as Quakers, but the term has lost its contemptuous significance. The Society was founded by ▷ George Fox, who began his preaching career in 1647. He preached that the truth came from an inner spiritual light, and declared that no special class of men (*ie* priests) or buildings (*ie* churches) should be set apart for religious purposes. This individualism at first attracted a number of mentally disturbed followers whose ecstasies are perhaps responsible for the nickname 'Quaker', though Fox himself declared that it was first used in 1650 because he taught his followers to 'Tremble at the Word of the Lord'. They held a view, unusual among ▷ Puritans, that it was possible to gain complete victory over sin in this life. Such a doctrine, in addition to their refusal to accept those religious institutions that the other Puritans accepted, made them intensely unpopular for the first ten years of their existence. Later they became influential far beyond their numbers, which have remained comparatively few. Owing to the freedom of mind which is the essence of the movement, it is difficult to define their doctrine, which seems to vary greatly among individuals. On the other hand they are well known for a range of characteristic virtues: humanitarianism (they were amongst the first to protest against slavery – 1688); non-resistance to violence; respect for individuals regardless of race, sex, or religion; sobriety of conduct and tranquillity of mind. One of the most important of their early members was William Penn (1644–1718), the founder of the American colony of Pennsylvania. Like other Puritans, they were prominent in commerce, but took care to engage in activities that were not harmful; in consequence Quaker names are particularly well known in connection with the manufacture of chocolate. However, in the 18th century their outstanding importance was in banking: their sober-mindedness and strictness of morality counteracted the speculative manias of the time, and did much to establish secure financial foundations for the rapid expansion of British trade.

Quarles, Francis (1592–1644)

Poet, emblematist, pamphleteer. Francis Quarles was a prolific author, producing not only a number of verse collections, but a play, biblical paraphrases, a ▷ romance and two remarkable ▷ emblem-books: *Emblems* (1635) and *Hieroglyphics of the Life of Man* (1638). His earlier verse publications, such as *A Feast for Worms* (1620), *Hadasa; or, The History of Queen Esther* (1621) and *Sion's Elegies* (1624), were, in the main, adaptations of biblical themes. In the 1630s his attention was devoted to the production of his emblem-books and to occasional pieces. With the outbreak of the ▷ Civil War, Quarles published a series of anti-Puritan ▷ pamphlets. But it is for his emblematic work that Quarles is chiefly remembered: indeed, *Emblems* is said to have been the most popular book published in the 17th century. **Bib:** Grosart, A. B. (ed.), *Complete Works in Verse and Prose*, 3 vol.; Hasan, M., *Quarles: A Study of his Life and Poetry*.

Quarterly Review, The

Founded by ▷ John Murray in 1809 as a moderate Tory rival to the ▷ *Edinburgh Review*. The first editor was the irrascible traditionalist William Gifford, and later editors included ▷ Samuel Taylor Coleridge's nephew, Sir J. T. Coleridge, and John Lockhart. ▷ Sir Walter Scott, ▷ Robert Southey, and ▷ Samuel Rogers were early contributors. Scott's approving review of ▷ Jane Austen's ▷ *Emma* appeared in the *Quarterly* in March 1816, and a hostile article by John Wilson Croker on ▷ John Keats's ▷ *Endymion* (Sept. 1818) provoked ▷ Lord Byron's squib (written in 1821):

> Who kill'd John Keats?
> '*I*,' says the Quarterly,
> So savage and Tartarly;
> '*Twas one of my feats.*'

Quarto

A term used in publishing to designate a size of volume, made by folding the standard paper twice instead of only once (▷ folio size). The quarto editions of

▷ Shakespeare's plays are those published in his lifetime, as distinct from the folio collected editions after his death. 18 of his plays appear in separate quarto editions.

Quatrain
A stanza of four lines, usually rhyming *a b a b* or *a b c b*.

Queen Mab
A name for the queen of the fairies used in ▷ Shakespeare's ▷ *Romeo and Juliet* (I. iv), ▷ Drayton's ▷ *Nymphidia*, and ▷ Shelley's polemical poem *Queen Mab* (1813).

Queen of Hearts, The
1 A character in an English ▷ nursery rhyme based on the figures in a pack of cards.

2 A character in *Alice's Adventures in Wonderland* by ▷ Lewis Carroll, based on the nursery-rhyme character.

3 A nickname of Elizabeth of Bohemia, daughter of ▷ King James I and grandmother of George I.

Queen's Theatre, The
▷ Haymarket Theatres.

Quin, James (1693–1766)
Actor, manager, singer. Born in London, Quin was the product of a bigamous union between James and Elizabeth Quin, and grandson of a former Lord Mayor of Dublin.

After 1713 he began acting at the ▷ Smock Alley Theatre in Dublin, and by early 1715 he had reached the ▷ Drury Lane Theatre in London, where he later helped to manage the company. In 1746 and 1747 Quin acted together with ▷ Garrick at Covent Garden (▷ Covent Garden Theatres), and the two became friends despite their ostensible rivalry. But Garrick's light, naturalistic style made Quin's acting appear absurdly formal, pompous, and monotonous to many observers, and the older man gradually retired from the stage, to Bath.

Quin was noted for his 'strong passions', including a violent temper, but also a good humour and dignity. He was a friend of ▷ Pope and ▷ Swift, admired by ▷ Horace Walpole and the Prince of Wales (later George III). He held his own in parts ranging from ▷ Othello, ▷ Macbeth, ▷ Richard III, ▷ Coriolanus, ▷ Comus, Bajazet in ▷ Rowe's *Tamerlane*, and Pierre in ▷ Thomas Otway's ▷ *Venice Preserv'd*, to his most celebrated role as ▷ Falstaff. Garrick's innovations hurt his reputation more substantially, perhaps, than that of any leading actor of the period, quite suddenly making him seem outmoded. But even at the end of his career, Garrick and other colleagues continued to respect him, and he was still able to draw large crowds.
Bib: Taylor, A. M., *Life of Mr James Quin, comedian.*

Rabelais, François (?1495–1553)

French comic writer. He was successively a
▷ Franciscan friar, then ▷ Benedictine
monk, before abandoning the religious life
and turning to the study of medecine (he
became a Batchelor of Medecine at
Montpellier in 1535). He was protected by
the powerful ▷ Du Bellay family in his
censorship disputes with the ▷ Sorbonne.
His famous works are all in prose, but
difficult to classify because of their
kaleidoscopic forms of narrative and plot.
▷ *Pantagruel* (1533) and ▷ *Gargantua*
(1535) were later reversed in sequence,
Gargantua being the father of Pantagruel.
Ten years and more later come *Tiers Livre*
(*Third Book*, 1545) and *Quart Livre* (*Fourth
Book*, first version 1548, expanded version
1552). The authenticity of the *Cinquiesme
Livre* (1564) remains disputed, though the
opening section, *L'Isle Sonnante* ('Ringing
Island'), was published separately in
Rabelais's lifetime and is accepted by some as
his work.

There is in Rabelais an exuberant
command of linguistic mechanisms which
underpin the entire range of comedy he
deploys, from simple pun to obscenity, and
slapstick and absurdity to invective and satire.
Among English writers consciously indebted
to Rabelais, Sir John Harington's (?1560–
1612) *Metamorphosis of Ajax* and *Anatomy*
follow his style, using coprological humour
and mock encomia; the Elizabethan journalist
▷ Thomas Nashe has much of Rabelais's
vitality; ▷ Robert Burton's ▷ *Anatomy of
Melancholy* has a comparable amplitude of
language; and ▷ Samuel Butler's bitter
attack on the Puritans (▷ Puritanism), the
mock-epic ▷ *Hudibras* is more-than-
Rabelaisian in its bitter humour. ▷ Swift
shares Rabelais's indignation, but his
disgust is un-Rabelaisian, while ▷ Sterne
has a similar expansiveness, yet the
prurience of his humour has no counterpart in Rabelais. Rabelais was notably
translated by the Scotsman, Sir Thomas
Urquhart (c 1611–60) (Books I–II, 1653;
Book III, 1693), with continuations by Peter
Motteux (1663–1718) (Books IV–V, 1693–
94).

Racine, Jean (1693–99)

French dramatist. His principal sources of
inspiration were either classical (the larger
group of his works, including *Andromaque*
(1667), *Britannicus* (1669), *Bérénice* (1670),
Mithridate (1673), *Iphigénie* (1674) and *Phèdre*
(1677)) or biblical (*Athalie*, (1690)). Racine
examines the nexus of passion and power,
and the distorting effect these invariably have
upon the heroic values which his characters
inherit or purport to represent. He delineates
the moral and political blindness which can
all too easily sway human judgement and
conduct and he highlights with particular
force the destructiveness of passion from
which tragedy will proceed. His dramas are
tightly constructed according to classical
criteria of the ▷ unities and display a
virtuoso command of the ▷ Alexandrine
line combined with a strong sense of rhyme
and rhythm and a lucid, economical style.
Racine was admired in England by ▷ John
Dryden and ▷ Thomas Otway, whose
'heroic drama' is nevertheless no serious rival
to its French counterpart. ▷ Roland
Barthes's essay, *Sur Racine* (1963), with its
▷ structuralist approach to its topic, aroused
the antagonism of the Sorbonne professor
and critic Raymond Picard, who published a
hostile retort, *Nouvelle Critique ou nouvelle
imposture?*. The Barthes-Picard dispute
marked the strong emergence of the French
new criticism (*nouvelle critique*) in the public
domain.

Radcliffe, Mrs Ann (1764–1823)

Novelist. She was one of the most famous of
the writers of ▷ Gothic novels, which
sought to gain their effect through mystery
and the supernatural in a setting of grand
scenic description. She was immensely
popular in her own day for her four novels:
The Sicilian Romance (1790); *The Romance
of the Forest* (1791); ▷ *The Mysteries of
Udolpho* (1794), and *The Italian* (1797).
Udolpho is the most remembered, owing to
satirization through an account of its effect
on a young girl in ▷ Jane Austen's
▷ *Northanger Abbey*.

Radicalism

The political views of Radicals, who believe
in the need for thorough reform going right
to the roots (the meaning of 'radical') and
origins of undemocratic abuses. The term
probably originated in 1797 with the
declaration of Charles James Fox that 'radical
reform' was necessary. In the early 19th
century it had the pejorative connotation that
'extremist' has today.

Rainbow, The (1915)

A novel by ▷ D. H. Lawrence. It is set in
Lawrence's own background, the English
Midlands; the subject is three generations of
the Brangwen family extending from the
middle of the last century to the early years
of the present one.

The Brangwens are a family of farmers and have for generations lived on their own land which, by the time at which the novel begins, is near an encroaching industrial area. The men of the family are depicted as concentrating their minds earthwards, on their work and surroundings; the women have tended to look outwards to society, and to emulate their social superiors. Tom Brangwen, the first of the main characters, is sent to a grammar school by his ambitious mother; the experience both frustrates him and arouses him. His awakened need for what is strange and mysterious attracts him to Lydia Lensky, an aristocratic but impoverished Polish exile, a widow, and the mother of a small daughter. They marry and although their marriage meets difficulties it becomes a happy one. Lydia and Tom remain ignorant of much in each other's nature, but Lydia finds confidence in Tom's established way of life, while he finds enlargement precisely in what, for him, is mysterious in his wife. Tom's stepdaughter, Anna, is attracted to his nephew, Will Brangwen, who has had an urban upbringing and has a strong artistic imagination and profound religious instincts inherited from his forefathers. This marriage is much less happy. Anna is suspicious and jealous of her husband's religious spirit, and since he himself cannot relate it to a way of life, she succeeds in destroying it. In doing so, she unintentionally transforms him from an original artist into a mere craftsman in the ▷ William Morris style. They are united in a passionate night-time sensuality, but have no daylight union. Their daughter, Ursula, belongs to the first generation of the modern woman: she sets out to be a teacher, and after an intense struggle in one of the characteristically inhuman English board schools, she succeeds in affirming her independence. But her love affair with Skrebensky, a thoroughly Anglicized descendant of another Polish exile, ends in frustration. She inherits from her mother a capacity for passion which expresses her full nature, whereas his nature is divided between a dead conformity to society and a sensuality which is incapable of real passion. Ursula tries to compromise by suppressing her instincts, but a concluding scene, in which she is exposed at night to the menace of restless horses, on to which she projects her disturbed emotions, shows that she is wrong in attempting this solution. The story of Ursula and her sister Gudrun is continued in ▷ *Women in Love*, originally conceived as part of the same novel. The title of the novel refers to its central symbol of a rainbow, or

arch. This symbol signifies an ideal which modifies with time, from the stability of an achieved relationship in the first generation to the transcendant hope of a collective rebirth at the end of the novel.

The novel was for a time suppressed on grounds of immorality, but is now regarded as one of Lawrence's greatest achievements.

Raine, Craig (b 1944)

Poet. His first two collections, *The Onion, Memory* (1978) and *A Martian Sends a Postcard Home* (1979), established a vogue for ▷ 'Martian' poetry in this country. *Rich* (1984) shows him extending his work into areas such as prose ▷ autobiography. He has also written an opera libretto and work for the theatre.

Raine, Kathleen (b 1908)

Poet and critic. Raine has been prolifically publishing poetry since the 1930s; in 1943 *Stone and Flower: Poems 1935–1943* appeared. In 1956 *Collected Poems* appeared, followed by *The Hollow Hill* (1964). The 1981 *Collected Poems, 1935–80* gathered together much of her important work. Raine is also well-known as a scholar of ▷ William Blake, and has also written on ▷ Yeats and ▷ Coleridge. Recent collections include: *The Lost Country* (1971); *On A Deserted Shore* (1973); *The Oracle in the Heart* (1980), and *World Within a World* (1982), as well as three volumes of her ▷ autobiography.

Ralegh (Raleigh), Sir Walter (1552–1618)

Poet, historian, courtier, explorer, colonist. The career of Sir Walter Ralegh has been taken as almost symbolic of the 'Renaissance ideal' of the complete individual – one who, with an easy grace, excels in all forms of endeavour. In addition to the pursuits listed above, for example, one might add: seaman, soldier, chemist, philosopher, theologian and even pioneer in naval medicine and dietetics, diplomat and (somewhat unsuccessful) politician. Ralegh's military experience included soldiering in France (1569) and Ireland (1580). As an explorer and colonist, Ralegh was the driving force behind the project to found a colony on the eastern seaboard of the North American continent in 1585. The project was abandoned in 1586 and, after several unsuccessful expeditions, the patent for what had become the Virginia settlement lapsed to the Crown in 1603. In 1595, following a period of imprisonment in the ▷ Tower due to the queen's displeasure at his relationship with a member of her court, Ralegh led an expedition to South America – an enterprise which was to be

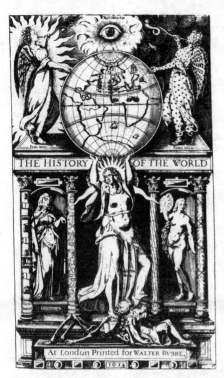

Title page of Ralegh's *History of the World*, 1614

repeated in a further unsuccessful expedition to the Orinoco in 1616. Ralegh's South American exploits were directed chiefly towards gaining treasure at the expense of the Spaniards, and it was as a member of the expeditions to Cadiz (1596) and the Azores (1597) that his military reputation in fighting the Spanish was established. With the accession of ▷ James I in 1603, however, Ralegh's brand of vigorous expansionism became unfavourable. With the exception of the Orinoco expedition, the period between 1603 and his execution in 1618 was spent in confinement in the Tower, to which he had been committed following his being found guilty of conspiring against the king in November 1603. His execution, on the charge for which he had been sentenced in 1603, was in fact due to his pursuit of an anti-Spanish policy when such attitudes were no longer favourably perceived at court.

Ralegh's life was, in some measure, his greatest achievement – for it became one of the foundation stones of the myth of Elizabethan accomplishment. The fact that almost every project in which he was involved

(exceptions being the Cadiz and Azores expeditions) failed was conveniently ignored. As a myth-maker, however, Ralegh was a potent force: not only his own life, but his earlier written works served to underline the Elizabethan self-image. In particular *A Report of the Fight about the Azores* (1591) and *The Discovery of the Large, Rich, and Beautiful Empire of Guiana* (1596) can both be read as attempts at promoting an ideal of national endeavour. Ralegh's poetry also contributes to the romantic legend, tinged as it is with a melancholic awareness of the transitory nature of existence. Perhaps his most significant poetic achievement, though, is the fragmentary 'Ocean's Love to Cynthia' – a brooding, obscure and allusive text of loss and longing. A rather different proposition is his *History of the World* (1614), which, in its all-inclusiveness, might stand as an apt commentary on its author. The *History*, though it draws veiled comparisons between the present and the past, concludes at the date 130 BC. It is yet another unfinished enterprise.

▷ School of Night.
Bib: Oldys, W. and Birch, T. (ed.), *Works*, 8 vol.; Greenblatt, S., *Ralegh: The Renaissance Man and His Roles*.

Ralph Roister Doister (1552)

A comedy by Nicholas Udall, printed in 1566, and written in about 1552. It is sometimes called 'the first English comedy', presumably because the earlier 'comic interludes' notably by ▷ John Heywood (*eg The Play of the Weather* and *The Four P's*) were too slight to count, whereas Udall's play, which may have been written for the boys of Westminster School, is an adaptation of the *Miles Gloriosus* ('The Boastful Soldier') by ▷ Plautus. The basic situation is the same in both plays: vain but foolish and boastful soldier makes love to a respectable woman (Christian Custance in Udall's play) who is betrothed to a merchant, Gawin Goodluck, and Ralph is encouraged in his misguided enterprise by a mischievous associate, Matthew Merygreek. But the play has a kind of farcical humour, which has more in common with the popular ▷ Interludes and even the May Games of English country life, and it reads as a thoroughly native product. The rhymed verse is rather primitive, but the dialogue has realistic freshness. The comedy is an example of humanistic learning married to popular entertainment, a union which 40 years later was to give rise to the beginnings of the great period of English drama.

Rambler, The

A twice-weekly periodical produced by ▷ Dr
Samuel Johnson from March 1750 to March
1752. All except five were written by Johnson
himself. The papers were in the tradition of
The Tatler, and *The Spectator* essays by
▷ Addison and ▷ Steele 40 years before.
The essays cover a wide variety of subjects,
including eastern tales, criticisms and
allegories. Johnson's moral seriousness in the
work is indicated by the prayer that he wrote
on its commencement. *The Rambler* was
pirated and copied, evidence of its great
popularity, and in Johnson's lifetime ran to
ten reprintings.

Ramsay, Allan (1686–1758)

Edinburgh wig-maker and father of the
portrait painter of the same name. He was a
prolific poet in both English and Scots, using
a variety of ▷ metres, from intricate stanzas
to pentameter and tetrameter couplets. His
marriage of ▷ Scottish and English literary
traditions, together with his earthy realism of
language and dramatic flair, laid down the
foundations on which ▷ Robert Fergusson
and ▷ Robert Burns were later to build.

Rape of the Lock, The (1712/1714)

A ▷ mock heroic poem in pentameter
couplets by ▷ Alexander Pope. Its
immediate occasion was a quarrel between
two families with whom Pope was acquainted,
caused by Lord Petre cutting off a lock of
Miss Arabella Fermor's hair. Pope hoped to
place this act of sexual harrassment in a
trivial light by his comic and burlesque
treatment, which owes something to the
example of ▷ Nicolas Boileau's *Le Lutrin*
(*The Lectern*, 1674), a mock epic concerning
an ecclesiastical quarrel over the placing of a
lectern. However Pope only succeeded in
giving further offence. The first published
version (1712) comprised two ▷ cantos, but
Pope continued to work on it after the
immediate occasion had passed, and in 1714
it was issued in a much enlarged five canto
version, incorporating the epic machinery of
the sylphs.

   The work has been interpreted as a severe
moral satire. By describing this transient
quarrel in the heroic language of ▷ Homer's
▷ *Iliad*, Pope could be said to be ironically
mocking the selfish vanity of fashionable
society. However, the sensuous beauty of the
verse and the elaborateness of the poem's
imagery suggest that the young Pope was no
Puritan moralist. The most vivid passages in
the poem celebrate the new ease and amenity
of the English middle class in its first
confident phase of capitalist imperialism. The
heroine's exotic cosmetics and beauty aids,
brought from the farthest corners of the earth
by British ships, are described with delight.
The sylphs, fanciful projections of the secular
drawing room, are substituted for the
awesome gods of the ancient Greeks, and the
primitive *machismo* of Hector and Achilles
becomes the feminine 'armour' of stays and
petticoats, or the elegant 'triumph' of a game
of cards. Counterpointing this delight in
social life is an elegiac lament over its
transience, and the poem is at its most
moving when it laments the imminent decay
of Belinda's 'frail beauty', 'When those fair
Suns shall sett, as sett they must,/ And all
those Tresses shall be laid in Dust'.

Raphael the Archangel

▷ Angels.

Raphael the Painter

▷ Pre-Raphaelite.

Rasselas, Prince of Abyssinia, The History of (1759)

A prose work by ▷ Samuel Johnson.
Tradition has it that Johnson composed the
work rapidly to pay for the cost of his
mother's funeral. Its theme has often been
compared by critics to that of Johnson's
poem *The Vanity of Human Wishes*.

   The theme of *Rasselas* is 'the choice of
life', a phrase which occurs repeatedly. The
prince, son of the emperor of Abyssinia, is
tired of the pleasant life in the 'happy valley',
and in the company of his sister Nekayah, her
attendant Pekuah, and the philosopher Imlac,
escapes to Egypt.

   Imlac's advice demonstrates to the youth
the transient nature of human happiness, a
state which is in any case unobtainable. Imlac
also voices Johnson's views on 'the business
of a poet', which is to 'examine not the
individual, but the species'. The poet should
aim to be 'the interpreter of nature, and the
legislator of mankind', not to 'number the
streaks of the tulip'. *Rasselas* often parallels
▷ Voltaire's *Candide*, published in the same
year, and when Johnson later read this work
he commented on the similarities.

Rationalism

1 In philosophy, the belief that reason,
rather than sensation, is the only certain
guide to knowledge.
2 In religion, the practice of seeking
explanations which satisfy reason for what
had been accepted as supernatural.

Rattigan, Sir Terence (1911–77)

British dramatist whose first stage success

was with the light comedy *French Without Tears* (1936). This was followed by such plays as *Flare Path* (1942), *While the Sun Shines* (1943), and *Love in Idleness* (1944), the last of these a modern treatment of Hamlet and ▷ Claudius (▷ *Hamlet*). *The Winslow Boy*, a play about a father's struggle to defend his son on a charge of theft, won the Ellen Terry Award for the best play of the year in 1946. *The Browning Version* received the same award in 1948. *The Deep Blue Sea* (1952), a piece about passion and suicide, might have been more interesting had Rattigan been able to deal openly, in the play, with his own tragic homosexual love which inspired him to write it. But English repression is a subject which he knows and writes about well. Rattigan was well aware that his commercial success depended on the appeal of his plays to 'Aunt Edna', as he called the middle-brow members of his audience. His sound judgment of the market ensured continued success with *Separate Tables* (1955), *Variations on a Theme* (1958), *Ross*, a dramatization of the life of T. E. Lawrence (1960), *A Bequest to the Nation* (1970) and *Cause Célèbre* (1977).
Bib: Darlow, M. and Hodson, G., *Rattigan: The Man and His Work*.

Ravenscroft, Edward (?1650–97)
Dramatist, popular mainly for his farces. A lawyer by training, he was a member of the Middle Temple in 1671, where he composed his first play, *Mammamouchi, or the Citizen Turn'd Gentleman*, based on ▷ Molière's play, *Le Bourgeois Gentilhomme*; Ravenscroft was to use Molière as a source several more times. *The Careless Lovers* followed in 1673, and *The Wrangling Lovers* in 1676, again using French as well as Spanish sources. A play inspired by the ▷ *commedia dell'arte*, *Scaramouch a Philosopher, Harlequin a Schoolboy, a Bravo, Merchant and Musician*, and a play based on George Ruggle's 1615 Latin comedy, *Ignoramus, or the English Lawyer*, were produced in 1677, and *Titus Andronicus, or the Rape of Lavinia*, an alteration of the play by ▷ Shakespeare, in 1678. His most celebrated play, ▷ *The London Cuckolds*, another farce in the French manner, was staged in 1681. It became a tradition to perform this at both Drury Lane and Covent Garden on the Lord Mayor's Day (9 November) every year; the play was revived in 1782 and again by the ▷ Royal Court Theatre in 1979. Ravenscroft's great rival, Dryden, referred to his works with great contempt.

Reade, Charles (1814–84)
The seventh of 11 children, Reade was born in Oxfordshire and educated largely at home; he excelled in sports and was self-motivated in study. In 1831 he went to Oxford and in 1843 was called to the bar, but preferred music and the theatre. In 1845 he was made Dean of Arts at Magdalen where he upset some members by wearing a green coat with brass buttons. In 1846 he tried medicine in Edinburgh, and in 1847 obtained a D.C.L. and began to deal in violins. In 1851 he was made vice-president of his college, and began a long and prolific career as writer and dramatist. He met the actress Mrs Seymour in 1854 and they lived together until her death in 1879, after which he wrote little, turning to religion. He was a philanthropic man, helping the poor, distressed gentlefolk, lunatics, and waifs and strays; both impulsive and impatient, he was generous, boisterous and kept dogs, horses and other animals. He remained a theatre manager to 1882.

His writing career began with a stage version of ▷ Tobias Smollett's *Peregrine Pickle* in 1851. He co-wrote and produced *Masks and Faces* in 1852, turning it into the novel *Peg Woffington* the following year, when the 'reforming' novel about prisons, *Christie Johnstone*, also appeared. *It is Never Too Late to Mend*, in similar vein, followed in 1856, as well as the play *Gold!*; the novel was later dramatized and the play rewritten as the novel *Foul Play* (1869). He wrote short stories, pieces of journalism and plays at the same time. In 1858 he published *The Autobiography of a Thief* and *Jack of all Trades*, and in 1859 *Love Me Little, Love Me Long. The Cloister and the Hearth* was published in 1861. *Hard Cash* (1863) tackled the disgrace of lunatic asylums and in 1866 *Griffith Gaunt* triggered scandal and litigation by its frank attitude to sexual problems. From this time on, Reade was a controversial and litigious figure. *Put Yourself in His Place* (1870) attacked enforced ▷ trade union membership; *The Simpleton* (1873) gave rise to a libel action and a quarrel with ▷ Anthony Trollope. Other novels and plays include *The Wandering Heir* (1873) and *A Woman Hater* (1877). Reade was both famous and successful, being regarded as the natural successor to ▷ Charles Dickens, and by ▷ Henry James and ▷ Swinburne as superior to ▷ George Eliot. He commented on himself, 'I am a painstaking man, and I owe my success to it.' His writing is now considered overburdened with detail, melodramatic and superficial in characterization. His most successful work is

The Cloister and the Hearth, for which he is largely remembered.

Bib: Elwin, M., *Charles Reade: A Biography*; Burns, W., *Charles Reade: A Study in Victorian Authorship*; Hughes, W., *The Maniac in the Cellar: Sensation Novels of the 1860s*.

Reader-response criticism
▷ Reception theory.

Realism
A term used in various senses, both in philosophy and in literary criticism. Three principal meanings, two of them philosophical and one literary, are particularly worth distinction.

1 In medieval philosophy, the realists were opposed to the ▷ nominalists. Realism here means that classes of things ('universals') have reality whereas individuals have not, or at least have less: *eg* individual birds take their reality from the classification 'bird'. The nominalists considered that only the individual bird has reality, and that the classification 'bird' is only a formulation in the mind.

2 Since the Middle Ages, realism has become opposed to ▷ idealism. Here realism means that reality exists apart from ideas about it in the mind, and idealism represents the view that we can know nothing that is not in our minds.

3 Literary realism is a 19th-century conception, related to 2 and coterminous with industrial capitalism. In general, it means the use of the imagination to represent things as common sense supposes they are. It does not apply only to 19th-century literature; ▷ Defoe is commonly called a realist because of his factual description and narration. 19th-century realism in literature arose, however, from a reaction against 19th-century romanticism, and it is related to naturalism; for a discussion of late 20th-century critiques of realism as a vehicle of ▷ ideology, see Catherine Belsey, *Critical Practice*. Realism is also used in modern literature in opposition to what is regarded as sentimentalism – the disposition to represent feelings (*eg* the various forms of love) as nicer than we know them to be; an illogical extension of this use of the term is sometimes to apply it to literature that represents experience as nastier than we know it to be. Finally, realism in literature is sometimes related to nominalism, *ie* the realist writer is he who represents individuals rather than types; in this sense, modern literary realism is the opposite of the realism of medieval philosophy.

Rebellion, The Great
▷ Civil Wars.

Reception theory
This movement is associated pre-eminently with the German contemporary literary theorists Wolfgang Iser and Hans-Robert Jauss, and is often linked with reader-response criticism. Reception theory emphasizes the reader's consumption of the literary text over and above the question of the sum total of rhetorical devices which contribute to its structure as a piece of literature. The work of reception (*Rezeptionästhetik*) causes the reader constantly to rethink the canonical value of texts, since it involves noting the history of a text's reception as well as the current value which it may possess for the critic. Insofar as reception theory concerns itself with larger historical questions, it emphasizes histories of response which help to account for the reception of particular texts in the present. The approach to 'history' outlined here is pragmatic, and the emphasis is laid firmly on the matter of the interaction between text and reader and on the way cultural context is required to make sense of literature.

Recluse, The
▷ *Excursion, The*.

Recruiting Officer, The (1706)
Comedy by ▷ George Farquhar. Captain Plume recruits men to the army by courting the women with whom they are in love, and his sergeant, Kite, poses as an astrologer to lure men into service. Sylvia, the daughter of Justice Ballance, loves Plume but has promised not to marry him without her father's consent. She disguises herself as a man and contrives to get herself arrested for scandalous conduct. She appears before her father, who hands her over to Plume as a recruit, and eventually the two are married. In a secondary plot, Captain Brazen seeks to marry the wealthy Melinda but is deceived into almost marrying her maid, while Melinda herself marries Mr Worthy. The play draws on Farquhar's own experiences as a recruiting officer at Lichfield and Shrewsbury in 1705–6, and there is some amusing satire on the law in the courtroom scenes. The play captures much of the spirit of the ▷ Restoration, but its realism, rural setting (unlike the urban settings of most Restoration comedies), and broader humour, give it the hallmark of its later period.

Recusancy
A term used under ▷ Elizabeth 1 for refusal, usually by Roman Catholics, to attend

religious worship in the ▷ Church of England. The recusancy law continued to exist until the Toleration Act (1689) which permitted freedom of worship.

Red Cross Knight, The
The central figure of Book I of ▷ Edmund Spenser's ▷ *The Faerie Queene*. He represents Holiness, the ▷ Church of England and ▷ St George, whose red cross on a white ground is the national emblem of England. His adventures are connected with two women: Una, the true religion from which he is separated, and ▷ Duessa, the Roman Catholic Church, which beguiles him. He is eventually united to Una with the assistance of Prince Arthur (▷ Arthur, King) who rescues him from the House of Pride.

Red Riding Hood, Little
A popular fairy tale, originally derived from the French version by ▷ Perrault, translated into English in 1729. The little girl is so called because of the red hood that she wears. A wolf meets her in the forest while she is on her way to her grandmother. Having discovered the purpose of her journey, he goes on ahead and eats the grandmother and takes her place in bed; when Red Riding Hood arrives he eats her as well. In modern versions, she and her grandmother are subsequently cut out of the wolf's stomach, alive and well, by her father, a woodcutter.

Redgrove, Peter (b 1932)

Peter Redgrove

Poet and novelist. Redgrove is a prolific writer whose work straddles many forms – he

has worked as a scientific journalist, and has written many novels, poems, plays (he won the Italia prize in 1981) and non-fiction (including *The Wise Wound* with poet Penelope Shuttle, with whom he lives in Cornwall). His poetic work was originally associated with that of the Group, the 'school' of post-Movement (▷ Movement) poets which included his contemporaries at Cambridge in the late 1950s, ▷ Ted Hughes and ▷ Sylvia Plath. Redgrove is now also a lay psychoanalyst. His poetry publications include: *The Collector* (1960); *The Force* (1966); *Sons of my Skin* (1975); *The Weddings at Nether Powers* (1979); *The Applebroadcast* (1981) and *The Man Named East* (1985).

Reeve's Tale, The
One of ▷ Chaucer's ▷ *Canterbury Tales*, it is told by the Reeve to 'quite' the Miller for the personal insult he perceives in the ▷ *Miller's Tale* about a cuckolded carpenter (the Reeve being a carpenter by trade). So the Reeve replies with a tale about a cuckolded Miller, set just outside Cambridge (whereas the *Miller's Tale* had been set in Oxford). This ▷ fabliau charts a battle of wits between a thieving miller and two northern clerks, students at Cambridge University. Neither side displays much intellectual vigour but the clerks manage to sleep with the Miller's wife and daughter in order to avenge the theft of their corn. The Miller emerges as the loser in the contest, although the clerks only narrowly escape from a physical battle with the Miller through the chance, and mistaken, intervention of the Miller's wife. Several analogues to this tale are extant in French and Italian (one in the ▷ *Decameron*) but Chaucer's version is distinctive for its detailed development of the setting of the story and for the number of verbal puns built into the text. Chaucer is one of the earliest writers to present a conscious imitation of another English dialect: the clerks in this tale are characterized by their use of northern English forms.

Reflections on the Revolution in France (1790)
A political treatise by ▷ Edmund Burke. Burke attacks the principles on which the ▷ French Revolution was being conducted, denies that the English ▷ Revolution of 1688 was based on the same principles, and insists that a society is an organic growth like a tree, requiring the same kind of careful surgery in accordance with its principles of growth. The book was provoked by a sermon in praise of the French Revolution, preached by a Nonconformist minister, Dr Price; Burke

is in effect not merely attacking the French revolutionaries, but the reverence for abstract, rational, scientific enlightenment which, during the 18th century, had increasingly transformed the 17th-century Puritans into the 18th-century rationalistic Dissenters or Nonconformists, and had found disciples among many others of the educated classes. The *Reflections* is a great work of conservative political philosophy, as well as a masterpiece of polemical prose. It represents the French Revolution as a turning-point in history: 'The age of chivalry is gone. That of sophisters, economists and calculators has succeeded; and the glory of Europe is extinguished for ever.'

Reform Bills, Parliamentary
In English history, a succession of laws passed in the 19th and 20th centuries for the reform of the system of election of Members of Parliament. The system has always been based on towns and rural districts, grouped into constituencies, each electing one or (until recently) sometimes more than one candidate as Member. The most important Reform Bill was the first, passed through Paraliament in 1832, because it reduced the electoral confusion into a rational system. Most constituencies had remained unchanged since the ▷ Middle Ages; in consequence, some towns had grown to great size with inadequate representation in Parliament, or none at all, while others were represented by more than one Member although they had sunk into insignificance or even, in a few cases, had ceased to exist. This meant great power for the landed aristocracy, and great deprivation of power for the large and growing middle class. Some boroughs ('towns' – but often mere villages) were called 'pocket boroughs' because they were virtually owned by one landlord, who had them 'in his pocket', *ie* caused them to elect the Members of his choice; others were called 'rotten boroughs' because few inhabitants possessed the right to vote, and they were easily and habitually bribed. The law of 1832 redistributed Members of Parliament so as to correspond to the great centres of population, but limited the franchise (right to vote) to those who possessed a level of income such as ensured that electors belonged at least to the middle class.

The Reform Bill of 1867 extended the franchise to all male members of the working class in the towns, and that of 1884 to the rural working class. The delay in extending the franchise to the working class was bound up with the absence of any official state

system of education; this was introduced in 1870. The town working classes received the vote before the rural ones owing to their greater experience in organization gained through ▷ trade unions and the running of Nonconformist (▷ Dissenting) chapels.

The vote was now possessed by all men over 21 (with few exceptions, such as lunatics, criminals, and peers who had seats in the House of Lords) but not by women. Women over 30 were enfranchised in 1918 thanks to the campaigning by ▷ Suffragette movements and the services performed by women in World War I. Women over 21 received the vote in 1928. The same laws enabled women to stand for Parliament. A 1969 Act lowered the voting age for both men and women to 18.

Much of the intimidation and corruption of voters was a consequence of votes being made openly; secret voting or 'voting by ballot', was introduced in 1872.
  ▷ Parliament.

Reform comedy
Comedy whose *dénouement* is dominated by a major character repenting some wrong-doing, and promising to reform. The type became prominent toward the end of the 17th century, especially after ▷ Colley Cibber's ▷ *Love's Last Shift* (1696), in which the central figure of Loveless repents, after leading a debauched life and abandoning his wife, leaving his debts unpaid. Attacks on the supposed immorality and profanity of the stage by the Rev. Jeremy Collier and others encouraged the writing of more such plays. Other early exponents, besides Cibber, include ▷ Steele, ▷ Centlivre, Wilkinson, and ▷ Pix. ▷ Farquhar also incorporates some elements of the type in a few of his plays. Reform comedy became more prevalent during the 18th century, eventually overlapping with Sentimental Comedy, in which didactic considerations are paramount.
Bib: Loftis, J., *Comedy and Society from Congreve to Fielding*; Hume, R. D., *The Development of English Drama in the Seventeenth Century*.

Reformation
An important religious movement in the 16th century; its aim was to protest in a variety of ways against the conduct of the Catholic Church, which had hitherto remained undivided. The outcome was division: the Roman Catholics remained dominant in the countries bordering on the western Mediterranean and in south Germany; the new ▷ Protestant churches became supreme in northern Europe. The causes of the

movement were political (the rise of the new nation-state); moral (resentment at the low example set by many of the clergy); and doctrinal (disagreement, stimulated by the new critical spirit of the ▷ Renaissance, over points of doctrine hitherto imposed by the authority of the Church).

The reformation in England proceeded in three phases.

1 ▷ Henry VIII carried out the first in merely political terms. His desire to divorce Katharine of Aragon was merely a pretext; he himself sought complete control over the Church of England, and needed money; he resented the authority of the Pope in Rome and the internationalism of the monastic orders; he welcomed the opportunity to increase his wealth by confiscating their property. He declared himself Supreme Head of the Church of England by the ▷ Act of Supremacy, supported by Parliament and passed by it in 1533; he dissolved the monasteries in 1536–39. On the other hand, his ▷ Six Articles of 1539 tried to keep the Church fully Catholic on all points except that of papal sovereignty. As the support by Parliament showed, he had popular opinion behind him, at least in southern England; the English Church had long been restive against the sovereignty of the Pope, particularly when, in the 14th century, he had reigned from Avignon in France, the home of the national enemy.

2 The second phase, under his son ▷ Edward VI, went further and aroused more national disagreement. The clergy were permitted to marry, and the ▷ *Book of Common Prayer* included 42 articles of faith (later reduced to 39) which defined the doctrine of the Church of England in Protestant terms; there was extensive destruction of religious images in churches throughout the country. Henry's daughter ▷ Mary I undertook a complete reaction back to Catholicism, but her persecution of the Protestants and her subservience to her husband, Philip II of Spain, the most fanatical of the Catholic sovereigns, confirmed the country in a Protestant direction.

3 Henry's remaining daughter ▷ Elizabeth I contrived a religious settlement that was a compromise between the reforms of her father and those of her brother. The intention was to be inclusive: Catholics were not to be driven out of the Church of England if she could help it, and she wanted to keep as many of her Protestant subjects within it as possible. The result, however, was disunion: Catholics could not subscribe to the Church of England after the Pope had

excommunicated the Queen in 1571, and the more extreme Protestants were constantly pressing for further reforms, especially in the structure of church government (they mostly wanted the abolition of rule through bishops) and in the conduct of worship, which they wanted in full austerity. These ▷ Puritans, as they were called by their enemies, eventually established their own religious organizations, but not until after 1660. The vagueness of the Elizabethan settlement also gave rise to disagreement within the Church of England, and this has lasted unil the present day: the High Church is the section which emphasizes the more Catholic interpretation of the settlement (*ie* more in keeping with Henry VIII's intentions), and the Low Church is the section which insists that the Church of England is essentially Protestant. This disagreement, however, has never disrupted the organization of the Church, which, under the headship of the sovereign, is still that of the Catholic church of medieval England.

The reformation in Scotland proceeded side by side with the Elizabethan phase in England, and helped to bring about a reconciliation of the two nations which had been hostile to each other for three centuries. The Scottish reformation, however, was extreme, under the leadership of ▷ John Knox, a disciple of the French reformer ▷ Calvin. The national Church of Scotland has remained Calvinist (▷ Presbyterian) to this day. Ireland remained Catholic, and in consequence suffered severe persecution by its English rulers in the 16th and 17th centuries. The only excuse for this tyranny was the real danger that Ireland might become a base for one of England's more powerful Catholic enemies – France or Spain.

Regency
In English history, the period 1811–20 when George, Prince of Wales, later George IV (1820–30), took the title of Prince Regent during the final illness of his father, George III (1760–1820). In British cultural history, the term is often applied to cover the first 20 years of the 19th century during which a certain style of taste in art and architecture prevailed. It was inspired by the taste of the first French Empire (▷ Napoleon I) which itself arose from French revolutionary cultivation of ancient Greece, especially the republic of Athens. Architecture was austerely classical (the 'Greek style'), and dress was similarly modelled on long, graceful lines suitable for men and women with slender figures.

In literature, the term covers the working life of the second generation of romantic poets (▷ Byron, ▷ Shelley and ▷ Keats), the work of the essayists ▷ Lamb and ▷ Hazlitt, and that of the novelists ▷ Jane Austen and ▷ Walter Scott. The best work of the essentially Augustan poet ▷ Crabbe also comes into the Regency period. The word is applied, however, more to architecture, dress and furniture than to literature, the principal architects being John Nash (1752–1835) and John Soane (1753–1837), architect of the Bank of England.

Regicides

(From Latin, meaning 'king killers'.) In English history, the group of men responsible for the execution of ▷ King Charles I. The king was tried on a charge of treason, a distinction being made between the institution of the Crown and Charles himself, who was king. Eighty-four people, including the executioners, were said to be responsible for his trial and death. When his son was restored to the throne in 1660 as ▷ Charles II, the regicides were tried, and ten of them were executed; some of them, however, had already escaped abroad.
        ▷ Restoration.

Rehearsal, The (1671)

Burlesque play attributed to George Villiers, Duke of Buckingham, satirizing the heroic tragedies of the day. Bayes (a name implying that he is ▷ Poet Laureate) takes two friends, Johnson and Smith, to see a rehearsal of his latest play, which concerns the struggle for the Kingdom of Brentford. Most of the action consists of scenes from the absurd play within a play, punctuated by the two spectators' incredulous, sardonic, or contemptuous questions and comments, and Bayes's ridiculous explanations to them and instructions to the players. Finally, the two observers, and then the actors themselves, steal off before the play is finished, and the piece ends with Bayes vowing to revenge himself on 'the Town' for its ill-use of him and his plays. ▷ D'Avenant and ▷ Dryden are thought to have been the main targets of the satire; the figure of Drawcansir has been viewed as a parody of Almanzor in ▷ Dryden's The Conquest of Granada. His name became symbolic of blustering, bragging characters.

Rejected Addresses (1812)

When the ▷ Drury Lane theatre was rebuilt after having been destroyed by fire, the committee in charge, which included ▷ Lord Byron, advertised for an address to be recited at the reopening. None of those submitted was judged suitable, and Byron himself composed the lines which were actually delivered. Rejected Addresses, by James and Horace Smith, purports to include the unsuccessful submissions of all the major poets of the day. It contains often brilliant parodies of ▷ William Wordsworth, ▷ Samuel Taylor Coleridge, ▷ Robert Southey, ▷ Lord Byron, ▷ George Crabbe and ▷ Sir Walter Scott, among others.

Relapse, The: Or, Virtue in Danger (1696)

Play by ▷ Sir John Vanbrugh, written as a sequel to, and gentle satire on, ▷ Colley Cibber's ▷ Love's Last Shift (1696), in which the central character stages a repentance which Vanbrugh found unbelievable. This did not prevent Cibber himself from acting the part of Lord Foppington in The Relapse, with relish and to great acclaim. Loveless is now living quietly in the country with his faithful and virtuous wife Amanda, whom he had abandoned and then rejoined in Love's Last Shift. They return to the town for the winter season, whereupon he falls in love with Amanda's gayer cousin, Berinthia. Meanwhile, Worthy, an old flame of Amanda's, begins a new pursuit of her. Berinthia becomes an accomplice in his plan to seduce Amanda, so as to clear the path for her affair with Loveless. The latter is consummated, but Amanda summons her resources to resist Worthy's advances. A separate plot involves the impoverished Young Fashion's scheme to impersonate his older brother Lord Foppington, so as to marry the wealthy and lustful country girl, Miss Hoyden. At the end Worthy is shown unfulfilled and now in love with Amanda, while she achieves another uncertain reunion with her husband. The play's humour resides more in comic action than in witty dialogue, and there is a good deal of crude farce. Amanda's sobre virtue is somewhat at odds with the rest of the play, while the consequences of Loveless' intrigue with Berinthia are left unclear.

Religio Laici (1682)

A poem in heroic ▷ couplets by ▷ John Dryden, defending the tenets of the Church of England against the extremes of ▷ Deism and Roman Catholicism. It is frequently compared with ▷ The Hind and the Panther which Dryden published five years later after becoming a ▷ Catholic.

Religio Medici (1635)

(The Religion of a Physician). A work of

*A true and full coppy of that which was most
unperfectly andSurreptitiously printed before
vnder the name of : Religio Medici.
Printed for Andrew Crooke 1645.*

Frontispiece of the reissue of Browne's
Religio Medici

spiritual and autobiographical reflection by
▷ Sir Thomas Browne. It was written
c 1635, and seems not to have been intended
for publication but for circulation among
the author's friends. After its publication
without Browne's permission in 1642,
however, an authorized text was issued in
1643 which was subsequently translated into
Dutch, German, Latin and French. As a
form of ▷ autobiography, the work
presents the image of a relaxed, sceptical,
philosophic and endlessly self-intrigued
author. Informed by a desire to reconcile
religious belief with the kind of scepticism
associated with the ▷ 'New Science' of the
mid-17th century, Browne's work became
something of a ▷ best-seller. Stylistically,
in its engaging enjoyment of digressive,
curious and highly intellectualized
speculation, the work can be compared to
the poetry of ▷ John Donne or, later,
▷ Henry Vaughan. But it also forms part
of the trend towards sceptical enquiry which
was to be fostered by ▷ Thomas Hobbes
and ▷ John Locke.

Reliques
    ▷ Percy, Thomas.

Renaissance in England, The
'Renaissance' (or 'Renascence') derives from
Latin 'renascentia' = 'rebirth'. The word was
first used by Italian scholars in the mid-16th
century to express the rediscovery of ancient
Roman and Greek culture, which was now
studied for its own sake and not used merely
to enhance the authority of the Church.
Modern scholars are more inclined to use the
term to express a great variety of
interdependent changes which Europe
underwent politically, economically and
culturally between 1450 (although the
starting-points were much earlier) and 1600.
The religious outcome of these changes is
expressed through the terms ▷ Reformation
and ▷ Counter-reformation, a sequence of
events which were closely bound up with the
Renaissance.
  In England, the Renaissance is usually
thought of as beginning with the accession of
the ▷ House of Tudor to the throne in 1485.
Politically, this marks the end of the period of
civil war amongst the old feudal aristocracy
(the ▷ Wars of the Roses) in the mid-15th
century, and the establishment of something
like a modern, efficient, centralized state;
technically, the date is close to that of the
introduction of printing into England – an
invention without which the great cultural
changes of the Renaissance could not have
occurred. Culturally, the first important
period in England was the reign of the second
Tudor monarch, ▷ Henry VIII. This was
the period of the English ▷ humanists
▷ More, ▷ Grocyn, ▷ Linacre and the
poet ▷ Sir Thomas Wyatt.
  Several distinctive features characterize the
English Renaissance. The first is the lateness
of its impact; Italian, French, German, Dutch
and Spanish scholars had already worked on
the ancient Greek and Latin writers, and had
produced works of their own inspired by the
classics; in consequence, English culture was
revitalized not so much directly by the classics
as by contemporary Europeans under the
influence of the classics. ▷ Castiglione's
The Courtier, ▷ Machiavelli's *The Prince*,
▷ Ariosto's *Orlando*, were as important in
the English Renaissance as Virgil's ▷ *Aeneid*
or the plays of ▷ Seneca, and it was
characteristic that ▷ North translated
▷ Plutarch's *Lives* not from the original
Greek but from a French version. Such an
influx of foreign influences, both
contemporary and ancient, might have
overwhelmed the native English literary

tradition but for two more distinctive features: England as an insular country followed a course of social and political history which was to a great extent independent of the course of history elsewhere in Europe, for example in the peculiarity of the English Reformation, and this assisted the country in preserving its cultural independence; and owing to the example of the works of the 14th-century poet ▷ Chaucer, the native literature was sufficiently vigorous and experienced in assimilating foreign influences without being subjected by them. A fourth characteristic of English Renaissance literature is that it is primarily artistic, rather than philosophical and scholarly, and a fifth is the coinciding of the Renaissance and the Reformation in England, in contrast to the rest of the Europe where the Reformation (or, in countries that remained Roman Catholic, the Counter-reformation) succeeded the Renaissance.

The English Renaissance was largely literary, and achieved its finest expression in the so-called Elizabethan drama which began to excel only in the last decade of the 16th century and reached its height in the first 15 years of the 17th; its finest exponents were ▷ Christopher Marlowe, ▷ Ben Jonson and ▷ William Shakespeare. Non-dramatic poetry was also extremely rich, and reached its peak in the same period in the work of ▷ Edmund Spenser, ▷ Philip Sidney, Shakespeare and ▷ John Donne, but it is typical of the lateness of the Renaissance in England that its most ambitious product, John Milton's epic ▷ *Paradise Lost*, was published as late as 1667. Native English prose shaped itself more slowly than poetry; More wrote his ▷ *Utopia* in Latin, which was the vehicle of some other writers including ▷ Francis Bacon (in much of his work) owing to its advantages (for international circulation) over English, at a time when the latter was little learned in other countries. Nonetheless English prose developed with vigour in native English writers such as ▷ Roger Ascham, Thomas North, ▷ Richard Hooker, in the English works of Francis Bacon, and in the translators of the ▷ Bible.

Republic, Plato's

A philosophical dialogue by the Greek philosopher ▷ Plato. ▷ Socrates discusses with his friends the nature of justice, and the conversation leads to an outline of the ideal state. Public life must exhibit the highest virtues of private life, and justice is achieved if the classes work together to contribute to society the virtues in which each excels. Democracy (the rule of the people), oligarchy (the rule of a small powerful group), and timocracy (the rule of men of property) are in turn rejected, in favour of aristocracy – the rule of the best, trained by an exacting system of education. The aristocrat will seek wisdom, whereas the man of action seeks honour, and the merchant gratifies his appetites. Wisdom is a direct apprehension of the good conceived as a system of ideal forms; Book VII contains the famous parable of men sitting with their backs to these forms (the only substantial reality) watching the shadows on the wall of the cavern – *ie* phenomena apprehended by the senses – and supposing these shadows to be the only reality. Book X contains Plato's notorious rejection of poetry: poets must be expelled, though with honour, because they frustrate the pursuit of true wisdom by extolling the illusory phenomena of this world, and weaken the mind by stimulating wasteful sympathy with the misfortunes of men.

Resolution and Independence (1807)

A poem by ▷ William Wordsworth, sometimes known as *The Leech-Gatherer*, composed in 1802, published in 1807, and subsequently revised. It uses a reduced version of ▷ Spenserian stanzas, rhyming *ababcc*, the first six lines being pentameters and the last an Alexandrine (▷ metre). Travelling across the moor the poet finds that the freshness of nature fails to raise his spirits. He reflects on ▷ Thomas Chatterton and ▷ Robert Burns, and the 'despondency and madness' to which the poetic vocation seems to lead. In his reverie he encounters the portentous figure of 'a Man', 'in his extreme old age', standing 'Beside a pool bare to the eye of heaven'. At first he seems part of inanimate nature, like a 'huge stone', but when approached he explains that he earns 'an honest maintenance' by roaming from pond to pond collecting leeches (much in demand by doctors of the day for blood-letting). The man's equanimity dispels the poet's moodiness: 'I could have laughed myself to scorn to find/ In that decrepit Man so firm a mind'. Despite its elements of conventional piety, the poem is remarkable for its sense of awe and spiritual humility before a man who in social terms is of no account.

Restoration, The

The word is used in two senses: the re-establishment of the Stuart monarchy in the person of ▷ King Charles II after the republican experiment of 1649–60; and as a period designation, often to cover the last 40 years of the 17th century, *ie* not only the reign of ▷ Charles II but that of his brother ▷ James II, and that of ▷ William III and Mary II. This period was marked by special cultural characteristics which were promoted by the political fact of the restoration of the monarchy. In this sense the term is most commonly used to identify three principal literary products: 1 Restoration prose; 2 Restoration drama (especially comedy); 3 Restoration poetry.

1 Restoration prose is marked by a very conscious determination by leading writers to use prose as a vehicle of reason. It had of course already been used in this way by, for instance, Francis Bacon, but even Bacon did not distinguish the virtues of prose for such a vehicle. It was one of the aims of the new ▷ Royal Society to cultivate these virtues, which were described by Thomas Sprat in his *History of the Royal Society* (1667): 'a close, naked, natural way of speaking; positive expressions; clear senses; a native easiness; bringing all things as near the Mathematical plainness, as they can: and preferring the language of Artisans, Countrymen, and Merchants before that of Wits, or Scholars'. Sprat thus describes what have been considered the normal qualities of good prose ever since, and the Restoration period is indeed the first age of modern English prose writing. Its master was the poet, ▷ John Dryden, in his prose criticism, for instance his *Essay on Dramatic Poesy* (1668).

2 Restoration drama. This period is sometimes described as 'the silver age' of English drama, by comparison with the 'golden' age of Shakespeare. Owing to the hostility of the ▷ Puritans to drama, the art had practically ceased to be practised in the period of their power, 1642–60 when the public theatres were closed; it was then continued with ardour, but in less promising circumstances than in the 'golden' age. The decline had indeed already been evident before the close of the ▷ theatres in 1642, and a dramatist such as ▷ James Shirley, writing in the 1630s, exhibits many of the characteristic virtues and weaknesses of the Restoration. The audience had already ceased to be one drawn from all classes, and was restricted to people of fashion and refinement; wit, elegance of speech, skilful stage technique were the qualities which were sought after, and they implied a drama different from that of Shakespeare and his contemporaries, which had been intended to please alike the learned and the simple, the profound and the frivolous. After 1660, the French drama of

▷ Molière in comedy and of ▷ Corneille and ▷ Racine in tragedy were the dominating influences of the English stage, but English society was not so constructed as to be able to emulate the French 'golden' age. English 'heroic' tragedy, with the exception of a few plays by Dryden and ▷ Otway, lacked the conviction of French tragedy in a comparable style, and the comedy of ▷ Etherege, ▷ Wycherley, ▷ Vanbrugh, ▷ Farquhar, and even of ▷ Congreve, is slight and superficial by comparison with that of Molière. However, Restoration comedy is in prose, unlike most of the tragedy, and the virtues of Restoration dramatists are especially in the wit, grace and poise of their prose dialogue; the comedies are still successful and even popular on the English stage, whereas few of the tragedies are ever performed.

3 Restoration (non-dramatic) poetry. This, especially the poetry of Dryden, is really the beginning of ▷ Augustan poetry. The virtues admired in the prose of the time reigned also over the poetry, so that a 'close, naked, natural way of speaking' is as evident in the verse as in the prose of Dryden. Besides him, ▷ Samuel Butler and the ▷ Earl of Rochester are the principal names classifiable as 'Restoration poets', but the foremost poet of the reign of Charles II, ▷ John Milton, cannot be so classified. The Restoration poets excelled in satire whereas Milton, in his epics and his one tragedy in so different a style from the neo-classic French tragedies, is a late product of the English Renaissance, profoundly modified by Puritanism.

Resurrection man; Resurrectionist
A term in use in the late 18th and early 19th centuries for one who made a living by digging up dead bodies and selling them to anatomists to use for dissection; such a person is Jerry Cruncher in Dickens's novel about the French Revolution, ▷ *A Tale of Two Cities.*

Return of the Native, The (1878)
A novel by ▷ Thomas Hardy. Its setting is Egdon Heath, a wild tract of country in Dorset, in the south-west of England. The atmosphere of the Heath prevails over the whole book; as an environment, it repels some characters and absorbs others; those who are absorbed achieve a sombre integration with it but those who are repelled and rebel suffer disaster. The central character – 'the Native' – is Clym Yeobright, a Paris diamond merchant who has returned to the Heath in revulsion from the futility of his urban life and occupation. He intends to

become a schoolmaster and marries the restless, self-seeking Eustacia Vye who is unfaithful to him; her affair with the unscrupulous Damon Wildeve leads to the death of both. Other characters include Thomasin Yeobright whom Wildeve marries, to her misfortune and the grief of Diggory Venn, the travelling sheep-dyer (or 'reddleman') who represents a primitive sincerity and truthfulness, and Mrs Yeobright, Clym's mother, whom Eustacia estranges from her son. Clym becomes a furze-cutter on the Heath and eventually a travelling preacher. The novel is an example of Hardy's preoccupation with the relationship of characters with natural environment but it suffers from a weak conception of the central character, Clym.

Revels, Master of the

An official at the royal court in the 16th and 17th centuries; his function was responsibility for court entertainments, *eg* ▷ masques.

Revenge tragedy

A kind of tragedy which was particularly popular during and just after the lifetime of ▷ Shakespeare, *ie* 1590–1620. The plot of such plays was commonly the murder by a person in power of a near relative, wife, or husband of the central character, who is then faced with the problem of how, or sometimes whether, to carry out revenge against a murderer who, because of his social importance, is out of reach of ordinary justice. The literary inspiration for this kind of play came from the plays of the Roman poet ▷ Seneca whose *Ten Tragedies* were translated into English between 1559 and 1581. Seneca's plays would doubtless have been insufficient in themselves, however, to get going the great English series of revenge tragedies, if the theme had not been relevant to English society. This society was in a stage midway between primitive lawlessness, in which justice is beyond the reach of the weak and unprivileged, and the modern state, in which justice is impartial and police are numerous and efficient. The tradition that revenge for an injury to a member of his or her family was a duty for the individual was still widely maintained; against it, the state maintained that revenge not carried out as due punishment through a court of law was a crime, and the Church taught that it was a sin. On the other hand, the law was unreliable, though not helpless, against the powerful and the powerfully protected, and in the face of the religious prohibition, the revenger might consider himself to be the instrument of Divine Vengeance.

This state of conflict in the Elizabethan conscience made for different styles of revenge play. The first of those offering straightforward treatment of the theme was ▷ Thomas Kyd's ▷ *The Spanish Tragedy*; ▷ Shakespeare's early ▷ history plays ▷ *Henry VI, Parts I, II and III* and ▷ *Richard III*, are revenge plays as well, and another early example by Shakespeare is his ▷ *Titus Andronicus*. Later examples: *The Revenger's Tragedy* by ▷ Cyril Tourneur (or perhaps ▷ Thomas Middleton) and Thomas Middleton's ▷ *Women Beware Women*, to mention only plays of distinction. Another style might be called the 'anti-revenge' drama, in which the hero is too enlightened to seek revenge – examples are Tourneur's *The Atheist's Tragedy* and ▷ Chapman's *Revenge of Bussy d'Ambois*, both about 1611. The greatest of all tragedies of revenge, Shakespeare's ▷ *Hamlet*, is between the two styles, inasmuch as the hero both accepts the obligation to revenge and has to fight against his revulsion from it. A third style might rather be called the tragedy of retribution, inasmuch as a crime is avenged but the drama is not centred on a specific avenger; such plays include ▷ Webster's ▷ *The White Devil* and ▷ *The Duchess of Malfi* and Middleton's masterpiece ▷ *The Changeling*. Revenge and retribution are of course akin, and the importance of revenge tragedy, apart from its intrinsic interest, is that it is the starting point for the development of some of Shakespeare's greatest tragic themes, *eg* his ▷ *Othello* and ▷ *Macbeth*, though these are not usually placed in the same category.

Revenger's Tragedy, The (1607)

A drama in ▷ blank verse attributed to ▷ Cyril Tourneur, although modern scholars incline increasingly to attribute it to ▷ Thomas Middleton. The scene is a dissolute ▷ Renaissance court in Italy. The sensual Duke has a vicious legitimate son, Lussurioso, by his first wife; the Duchess, his second wife, is in love with his illegitimate son, Spurio, who uses his bastardy as a pretext for general sensual rapacity; her own sons, Ambitioso and Supervacuo, are consumed with envy, and she herself is totally without moral restraint. This evil family is not so much a group of characters in the ordinary, realistic sense as an array of allegorical representations of the fleshly vices; their Italianate names suggest their ▷ allegories – Lussuriosis = Luxury, Spurio = falseness, etc. They are predatory on one another, and the downfall of the whole family is plotted by Vindice (= Revenger), whose betrothed has been poisoned by the Duke; he is assisted by his brother Hippolito. Disguised, Vindice enters the service of Lussorioso, and pretends to procure his own sister, Castiza (= Chastity) as mistress for his master; he finds to his horror that their own mother is prepared to sell her for the price of becoming a court lady. Vindice carries out his revenge on the Duke in a scene of great emblematic ferocity, and eventually contrives the bloodthirsty destruction of the whole family. He himself, however, is sent to his death by the Duke's virtuous successor: a Revenger, in however just a cause, is a criminal too dangerous to leave alive.

The violence of the action is redeemed from crudity by the energy, compression, and conviction of the language, and by the way in which Tourneur fuses three modes of feeling into original art. One of these is the tradition of medieval allegory, which was becoming diluted and abstract in much Renaissance poetry, but in this play keeps its old power of condensing emotion into powerful images. Tourneur uses the allegorical form to substantiate ▷ Puritan detestation of sensual vice, which was the evil extreme of the Renaissance liberation of the physical appetites. At the same time, both these vices and Vindice's vindictiveness are expressed with an energy that is itself a rich manifestation of Renaissance feeling. In uniting these disparate resources, the play is one of the masterpieces of ▷ Jacobean drama.

▷ Revenge tragedy.

Review, The
It was written by ▷ Daniel Defoe and published three times weekly from 1704 to 1713. Politically impartial; it expressed Defoe's opinion on current political events, and also on literature and manners. Defoe has been called the inventor of the leading article, a feature of modern newspapers.

Reviews and Periodicals
The English periodical press arose gradually from the controversial religious and political pamphleteering of the late 16th and 17th centuries. It became established as a recognized institution early in the 18th century, and it was also in the 18th century that the review, which expresses opinion, became distinguished from the newspaper, which gives priority to information on current events. The great age for the periodical press was, however, 1800–1914; this was the period when the quarterlies and the monthlies had their widest influence, and the weeklies their largest circulation proportionately to the size of the reading public. Since 1914, the influence of the quarterlies and monthlies has declined; the weeklies have remained important, but they have had to compete on the one side with the tendency of newspapers to include a large amount of material originally restricted to reviews, and on the other with the medium of broadcasting.

Revolution of 1688, The
A name given to the removal by ▷ Parliament of ▷ King James II (1685–88) and the substitution of his daughter ▷ Mary II and her husband ▷ William III. The reason for the quarrel between James and Parliament was not so much that James was a Catholic as that he was using every means in his power to assert the superiority of royal power (in the name of his religion) over the power of Parliament. His policy united the whole nation against him, except for a very small minority of Catholics, and the success of Parliament finally settled the question of whether sovereign power lay with the king or with Parliament; this problem had been left unsolved when the period of republican rule (1649–60) had been succeeded by the ▷ Restoration of the monarchy. In 1688 the Revolution was a bloodless one, though there was subsequently some fighting in Ireland and Scotland. The consequences of the event were that the passionate religious and political disagreements which had so divided the nation since the beginning of the 17th century were greatly lessened, and a new temper of reasonable debate took their place; the change is typified by the *Letters concerning Toleration* (begun 1689) by the philosopher ▷ John Locke.

Reynard the Fox
The hero of a cycle of animal fables or ▷ bestiaries, begun about 1200, and very popular during the Middle Ages. The animals stand for basic characteristics of human nature, especially as it betrays itself in social relationships. Reynard is the cunning self-seeking individualist who betrays everyone and preys on society, always escaping justice. ▷ Caxton published an English translation of a Flemish version of the tales in 1481, but there is no native version of the cycle in English. The most famous work in which Reynard makes an appearance is Chaucer's ▷ *Nun's Priest's Tale*, one of the *Canterbury Tales*.

Reynolds, John Hamilton (1796–1852)
Recipient of some of ▷ John Keats's

most important letters, and of the verse epistle *To J. H. Reynolds Esq.* He published several volumes of poetry, including *The Garden of Florence and Other Poems* (1821).

Reynolds, Sir Joshua (1723–92)

One of the leading portrait painters of the 18th century, the age of English portrait painting. He was the first President of the ▷ Royal Academy, and the author of *Discourses, ie* lectures, delivered to its students between 1760 and 1790, on the principles of art. The friend of ▷ Samuel Johnson, he was a founder-member of the Literary Club of which Johnson was the centre. Reynolds was strongly representative of 18th-century aristocratic taste, and in the opinion of ▷ William Blake, writing about 1808, ▷ 'This man was Hired to Depress Art'. However, his *Discourses* were admired by the greatest 19th-century English art critic, ▷ John Ruskin.

Rhea

▷ Classical Myth.

Rhetoric

Rhetoric in the medieval period was a formal skill of considerable importance. It was taken to mean the effective presentation of ideas with a set of rules or style, and was founded in the classical tradition of ▷ Aristotle and ▷ Cicero. It was taught in monastic schools as part of the *trivium*, Rhetoric, Logic and Grammar, which used as its basic text Geoffrey de Vinsauf's *Poetria Nova* (1200). Rhetoric not only formed patterns in which texts should be written, but it also governed how the works should be received and allocated them to particular categories, *eg* epic, debate or sermon. The system of rhetoric was paramount to the operation of literature in the medieval period.

Similarly, almost all of the practice or theory of writing in the ▷ Renaissance period was touched by what became known as the 'Art of Rhetoric'. Rhetorical theory formed an important part of the educational syllabus at the universities, and almost every major writer of the 16th and 17th centuries would have undergone some training in rhetoric. Rhetoric was learned first through reading the classical text-books on rhetoric, in particular the works of Quintilian (especially the *Institutio Oratore*) and Cicero. Secondly, practical rhetorical exercises were performed by the student in which a particular topic was debated. In these debates, the student was expected to be able to organize an argument according to set formulae, producing examples with which to sustain the analysis

which themselves would be derived from a suitable store of words, images, fables and metaphors discovered in reading classical texts.

But the production of arguments was only one part of the rhetoricians' skills. Rhetoric also involved the classification of language – in particular the classification and analysis of ▷ figures of speech. Further, it was understood as an enabling tool by which ▷ discourse could be reproduced. In essence, therefore, it offered a system for producing both speech and writing. This system can be considered under five distinct parts: 1 'invention', which signifies the discovery of arguments applicable to a given case; 2 'arrangement' or 'disposition', which governed the ordering of the arguments to be used; 3 'style' or the actual choice of words and units of expression; 4 the important area of 'memory', which helped the rhetorician develop skills in recalling the order and substance of the argument being deployed; 5 'delivery', which was applicable mainly to spoken discourse but which governed such details as the appropriate facial expressions or gestures which might be used.

Whilst rhetoric was understood as a way of facilitating the classification of the various parts of an argument it was also a powerful tool in the analysis of discourse and it can thus be understood as a form of literary criticism. It was, however, in its abiding influence on stylistic forms that it was of most importance to the Renaissance writer. Numerous text-books on rhetoric were published throughout the 16th century in England. Perhaps the most important were: Leonard Cox, *The Art or Craft of Rhetoric* (1624); Richard Sherry *A Treatise of Schemes and Tropes* (1550); Thomas Wilson, *Art of Rhetoric* (1553); Henry Peacham, *The Garden of Eloquence* (1577); and Abraham Fraunce, *Arcadian Rhetoric* (1584). But many other texts were written with the art of rhetoric either governing the structure or informing the language. ▷ Sir Philip Sidney's ▷ *An Apologie for Poetrie*, for example, is structured according to rhetorical principles of organization.

Recent developments in critical theory have sought to re-emphasize rhetoric as a form of critical practice, particularly in relation to the *effects* that any verbal construction may have on those to whom it is addressed. In this respect rhetoric is closely associated with some of the larger issues which surface in relation to the theory of 'discourse'. The recent emphasis upon the *structure* of discourse draws attention away from language as a means of *classifying* to one of examining the way discourses are constructed in order to achieve certain effects. Here the emphasis would be on the different *ways* in which particular figures are presented in language, and what that presentation may involve. This form of rhetorical analysis has been undertaken by ▷ Jacques Derrida in volumes such as *Of Grammatology* (1974), by ▷ Paul De Man in his *Blindness and Insight* (1971), by ▷ Terry Eagleton in *Criticism and Ideology* (1976), and in a whole range of texts by ▷ Michel Foucault.

Rhyme
▷ Figures of Speech.

Rhyme Royal
▷ Chaucer seems to have been the first English poet to use the rhyme royal form in his narrative poetry but it is conventionally named after its use in the ▷ *Kingis Quair*, attributed to ▷ James 1 of Scotland. In rhyme royal, seven decasyllabic lines form a stanza, rhyming ababbcc. Chaucer's use of this form suggests that it was used for narrative subjects of a sophisticated courtly or devotional kind (the ▷ *Second Nun's Tale* and ▷ *Troilus and Criseyde* are both composed in rhyme royal). It became an extremely popular form in the 15th century for courtly poetry.

Rhys, Jean (1894–1979)

Jean Rhys

Adopted name of novelist, born Jean Williams on the West Indian island of Dominica.

Brought up speaking both English and the Dominican French dialect, she lived in Europe from the age of 16, moving between London, Vienna and Paris before finally settling in Devon. *The Left Bank* (1927), a series of sketches of Bohemian life in Paris, was followed by four novels which tell the stories of isolated, poor, victimized women, adrift in London or Paris, in a laconic, lucid style which combines the tragic and the absurd. These are: *Postures* (1928) (in the U.S.A. as *Quartet*; 1929); *After Leaving Mr Mackenzie* (1931); *Voyage in the Dark* (1934) and *Good Morning, Midnight* (1939). After a considerable period of critical neglect, *Wide Sargasso Sea* (1966) reawakened widespread interest in her work, especially among ▷ feminists. It recounts the early life of the first Mrs Rochester from ▷ Charlotte Brontë's ▷ *Jane Eyre*, rendering the alienation and suffering of an isolated consciousness with great power. Set mostly in the West Indies, it is richer in imagery and symbolism than her earlier work, combining lyricism and psychological insight with an exploration of political, racial and sexual oppression. She has written two books of short stories: *Tigers Are Better Looking* (1968) and *Sleep It Off Lady* (1976). *Quartet* was made into a film (with a screenplay by ▷ Ruth Prawer Jhabvala) by the director James Ivory in 1981.
Bib: Stanley, T. F., *Jean Rhys: A Critical Study*.

Rich, Christopher (1657–1714)
Theatre manager. Rich assumed full control of the ▷ United Company in 1693, but his mismanagement contributed to the defection of the leading actors, including ▷ Thomas Betterton, ▷ Elizabeth Barry, and ▷ Anne Bracegirdle, in 1695. Even so, he succeeded in building up an able company in their place, including the young ▷ Colley Cibber, William Bullock, Joe Haines, ▷ John and ▷ Susannah Verbruggen, ▷ Anne Oldfield, and ▷ William Penkethman, as well as bringing in foreign performers as attractions.

In 1701 Rich weathered an attempt to oust him from control of ▷ Drury Lane, but he continued to invite conflict with both actors and dramatists, and in 1709 he was forced to close Drury Lane on an order from the Lord Chamberlain, after his attempt to deny his actors their full profits from benefit performances. Rich was not allowed to form a new company until 1714, but he died just six weeks before the scheduled opening.
Bib: Highfill, P. H. Jr., Burnim, K. A. and

Langhans, E. A. (eds.), *A Biographical Dictionary of Actors, Actresses, Musicians, Dancers, Managers, and Other Stage Personnel in London 1660–1800.*

Rich, John (1692–1761)

Actor, manager, dancer, dramatist, son of ▷ Christopher Rich. John inherited the largest share of the theatrical patent owned by his father, and took over the new ▷ Lincoln's Inn Fields Theatre built by his father before his death in 1714. He soon began acting and dancing at the theatre, and built up its repertory of dance, variety, and pantomime programmes, for whose growing popularity he was largely responsible.

During the following years he gained a mixed reputation for, on the one hand, allegedly degrading the stage, and on the other hand, providing popular entertainment by talented performers in settings of great magnificence. He was also complimented for reviving the best of the old plays, and encouraging new authors. It was under his auspices that ▷ John Gay's ▷ *The Beggar's Opera* was first staged in 1728, making (according to a well-known quotation) 'Gay rich and Rich gay'. The profits from *The Beggar's Opera* helped finance a new theatre in Covent Garden (▷ Covent Garden Theatres), on the site of the present Royal Opera House, which opened in 1732 with a cast headed by ▷ James Quin. A fierce rivalry developed between Covent Garden and ▷ Drury Lane under ▷ Garrick's management, highlighted in 1750–51, when the theatres staged ▷ *Romeo and Juliet* simultaneously. For decades after his death, theatres continued to honour Rich in tributes on stage, or by borrowing devices from his shows.

Bib: Highfill, P. H. Jr., Burnim, K. A. and Langhans, E. A. (eds.), *A Biographical Dictionary of Actors, Actresses, Musicians, Dancers, Managers, and Other Stage Personnel in London 1660–1800.*

Richard I Coeur de Lion (Lionheart) (1189–99)

King of England. He spent most of his reign out of the country, engaged in various wars, especially the third ▷ Crusade. His exploits made him into a figure of romance and legend, and as such he appears in two very popular novels by ▷ Walter Scott: ▷ *Ivanhoe* and *The Talisman* (1825). He belonged to the ▷ House of Plantagenet (Anjou) and was the son of his predecessor ▷ Henry II and the brother of his successor, ▷ John.

Richard II (1377–99)

King of England, and last of the direct line in the ▷ House of Plantagenet (Anjou). He was the son of the ▷ Black Prince and the grandson of his predecessor, ▷ Edward III. His neglect of the war against France, his youthfulness (he came to the throne at the age of 11), and his capricious, inconsistent character all helped to make his reign a period of disorder; the throne was eventually usurped by his cousin, Henry Bolingbroke, who became first king of the ▷ House of Lancaster as ▷ Henry IV. Richard had an expensive court, and was a patron of the arts in so far as he intermittently showed favour to the poets ▷ Chaucer and ▷ Gower.

Richard II, King

A historical drama in ▷ blank verse by ▷ Shakespeare, based on the Chronicles of ▷ Holinshed. First performed in 1595, and published in a 1st ▷ Quarto in 1597, it is the first of the second tetralogy of ▷ history plays by Shakespeare, the other three being ▷ *Henry IV, Parts I and II* and ▷ *Henry V*.

The theme of all four is kingship; ▷ Richard II is treated as a king whose sacred claim to the throne is beyond doubt, but tragically unaccompanied by any capacity to rule. The leading story is about his relationship with his cousin, ▷ Henry Bolingbroke; he drives Henry (not altogether without justification) into exile, and then quite unlawfully confiscates Henry's land. Henry returns to England to defend his right, and receives so much support that he is driven to making himself king. Usurpers, however, were considered to be opposing God, since kings held the throne by God's authority, and so Henry does his best to persuade Richard to abdicate publicly. Richard does so, but he skilfully makes it clear to all the witnesses that his abdication is involuntary (IV, i), so that the public abdication only emphasizes, instead of relieving, Henry's guilt. Concerned as it is with the ritualistic aspect of monarchy – the ceremonies that are the signs of the sacredness of the office – the whole play has been observed by critics to have a ritualistic style, in the formal patterning of much of the verse and the pageant-like ceremony of a number of the important scenes. Richard is imprisoned in the Tower, and is later assassinated; thus the effect of criminality in Henry's action in seizing the throne is confirmed.

Richard III (1483–85)

Last King of England in the House of York,

which seized the throne from the ▷ House of Lancaster in 1461. The first of the short line was ▷ Edward IV (1461–83), Richard's brother; he was succeeded by his son, the boy king ▷ Edward VI, whose throne Richard usurped. He was himself defeated and killed at the Battle of Bosworth (1485) by Henry Tudor, who succeeded as ▷ Henry VII the first sovereign of the ▷ Tudor line. It was very much in the Tudor interest to blacken the character of Richard III, and 16th-century historians (Polydore Vergil, ▷ Thomas More, ▷ Holinshed) depict him as satanically evil. Modern historians have found it difficult to discover whether this account is just, and there have been some attempts to rehabilitate his character. One of the chief charges against him is the murder of his two nephews Edward V and Richard of York, the 'princes in the Tower'. That they were murdered is almost certain, but there is no proof that Richard was guilty.

▷ Histories and Chronicles.

Richard III (?1593)

Anthony Sher as Richard III

A historical drama in ▷ blank verse by ▷ Shakespeare based on ▷ Holinshed's Chronicles, and the last of Shakespeare's first historical tetralogy, the other plays in which are the three parts of ▷ *Henry VI*. The Henry VI plays are about the ▷ Wars of the Roses, and the accumulation of hatred, vengefulness and crime which those wars brought about. *Richard III* opens in the reign of ▷ Edward IV, Richard's brother, and

shows the attempts of the king to induce his nobles to be reconciled. Fear and war-weariness make them comply, but Richard is still filled with ambition and cold-blooded cruelty. In spite of his appearance – he is a hunchback and has a withered arm – he has a magnetic personality and manages to win friends to help him in his conspiracies. By consistent treachery and ruthlessness he acquires the throne, but is shortly after defeated and killed by Henry Tudor (▷ Henry VII), who is shown in the play to have right and divine aid on his side. Though totally evil, Richard is presented as a character of energy and wit, the source of much sardonic comedy. Dramatically he is both in the tradition of ▷ Machiavelli's ▷ *The Prince* – a treatise of evil for Englishmen of Shakespeare's day – and in that of ▷ Herod in the medieval ▷ Mystery plays. The play is the masterpiece of the earliest group of Shakespeare's plays, *ie* those probably written before 1594.

▷ History plays.

Richard Feverel
▷ *Ordeal of Richard Feverel, The.*

Richards, I. A. (1893–1979)
Critic. His approach to poetry was philosophic, linguistic and psychological. One of his important insights was that we are inevitably influenced by some kind of 'poetry', even if it is only that of bad films and magazine covers, or advertisements. In *Principles of Literary Criticism* (1924) and *Science and Poetry* (1926) he discusses what kind of truth is the subject-matter of poetry, the place of poetry in the context of the rest of life, and what is the nature of critical judgements of poetry. He worked to his conclusion on Benthamite (▷ Utilitarian) lines, of asking what is 'the use' of poetry, but his conclusion was not far from that of ▷ Matthew Arnold, that poetry's function in the modern world is that formerly provided by religion – to provide a 'touchstone' of value, and hence, if only indirectly, a guide to living (see Arnold's 'Study of Poetry', in ▷ *Essays in Criticism*, 2nd Series, 1888). This view resembles the judgements of other writers of the 1920s and 30s, such as ▷ Pound, ▷ Wyndham Lewis, ▷ Eliot, ▷ Leavis, though each of them arrives at his judgement by a different approach. Richards's *Practical Criticism* (1929) is a teaching manual for the study of poetry with the aim of training students to judge poems presented anonymously, without being influenced by the author's reputation; its ideas have been

extensively followed in English and American schools and universities. Much of his later work has been purely linguistic, *eg Basic English and its Uses* (1943). Other works: *The Meaning of Meaning* (with Ogden, 1923); *Coleridge on Imagination* (1934); *The Philosophy of Rhetoric* (1936); *Speculative Instruments* (1955); *Goodbye Earth and other poems* (1959); *The Screens* (1961).

▷ New criticism.

Bib: Hyman, S., *The Armed Vision*.

Richardson, Dorothy (1873–1957)
Novelist. Born in Abingdon, Berkshire, she worked as a governess from the age of 17, before moving to London where she became an intimate of ▷ H. G. Wells and part of a circle of socialists and intellectuals. She took up journalism, and for the rest of her life earned a meagre living by this means, while dedicating herself to her long novel, *Pilgrimage*, which consists of the following volumes: *Pointed Roofs* (1915); *Backwater* (1916); *Honeycomb* (1917); *The Tunnel* (1919); *Interim* (1919); *Deadlock* (1921); *Revolving Lights* (1923); *The Trap* (1925); *Oberland* (1927); *Dawn's Left Hand* (1931); *Clear Horizon* (1935); *Dimple Hill* (1938); *March Moonlight* (1967). It is a semi-autobiographical work, recounting the life of the heroine, Miriam Henderson, through concentration on her continuous subjective experience of the present moment. Richardson, together with ▷ Virginia Woolf and ▷ James Joyce was responsible for the development of the ▷ stream of consciousness technique (though she disliked this term) which was an important aspect of the ▷ modernist revolution in narrative.

Bib: Rosenberg, J., *Dorothy Richardson: the Genius They Forgot*.

Richardson, Henry Handel (1870–1946)
Pseudonym of Australian novelist and short-story writer Ethel Florence Lindesay Richardson Robertson. She studied music in Leipzig from 1887–90, lived in Strasbourg 1895–1903, and in England from 1903. Her trilogy *The Fortunes of Richard Mahony* uses elements of her father's life, and is the sombre tale of an emigrant doctor's rise to riches and unexpected loss of fortune. It consists of *Australia Felix* (1917); *The Way Home* (1925); *Ultima Thule* (1929). Her work shows the influence of ▷ Goethe and the German Romantic tradition. Her other novels are: *Maurice Guest* (1908); *The Getting of Wisdom* (1910); *The Young Cosima* (1939). Story collections include: *The End of Childhood and Other Stories* (1934).

Bib: Mcleod, K., *Henry Handel Richardson: A Critical Study*.

Richardson, Samuel (1689–1761)

Samuel Richardson by J. Highmore (1750)

Novelist. Richardson was the son of a furniture-maker, born near Derby, though most of his childhood was spent in London as the family returned to live there. Little is known of his education, though by the age of 13 he is known to have written love letters on behalf of his friends, an activity relevant for his later choice of the epistolary genre.

In 1706 Richardson was apprenticed to a printer, and in 1715 became a freeman of the Stationers' Company. In 1721 he began his own business, which proved successful for the rest of his life. In the same year he married the daughter of his former master, though his wife died ten years later, and in the early 1730s he suffered the deaths of all the six children born to the marriage.

In 1733 he remarried, again to the daughter of a colleague, and four of their daughters survived. In the same year he published *The Apprentice's Vade Mecum*, a conduct guide to moral behaviour. In 1739 his own, deliberately moral, version of *Aesop's Fables* appeared.

The moral intention of his early works is evident in his fiction, though the creations of his imagination frequently escape any strict schemata. ▷ *Pamela*, begun in the same year as *Aesop's Fables* appeared, began as a series of conduct guides or 'Familiar Letters', which his friends encouraged him to write. Richardson's professional life, meanwhile, was proving rewarding. In 1723 he had begun to print *The True Briton*, an influential ▷ Tory journal, and in 1733 the House of Commons was using his presses. In 1742 he gained a lucrative contract as printer of the Parliamentary Journals.

His social life was proving equally enjoyable. He particularly relished the company of young women, whom he referred to as his 'honorary daughters', and while writing ▷ *Clarissa* (probably begun in 1744) he frequently asked them for their comments and teased them with speculations about the fate of his heroine. The first two volumes appeared in 1747 and were widely acclaimed; five more followed in 1748. The novel was praised, but readers were uneasy about its sexual elements, and its popularity proved less than that of *Pamela*.

About 1750 Richardson embarked on a new project, which was to be centred on the 'good man'. In 1752 ▷ Samuel Johnson read the draft manuscript of the work, ▷ *The History of Sir Charles Grandison*, and the novel appeared in seven volumes in 1753–4. Again, there was some doubt about the morality of the book, an ironic fate for a writer with Richardson's intentions.

In 1755 Richardson published a volume of selections from his three novels, in a form which he considered contained the essence of his writing; he was constantly concerned about the length of his fictions, and continually worked on revisions. His novels develop the epistolary style to a great degree of psychological subtlety, and he has long been regarded as one of the chief founders of the English novel.
Bib: Eaves, T. C. D. and Kimpel, B. D., *Samuel Richardson*; Kinkead-Weekes, M., *Samuel Richardson, Dramatic Novelist*; Flynn, C. H., *Samuel Richardson, A Man of Letters*.

Ridley, Nicholas (?1500–55)
One of the leading religious reformers in the reign of ▷ Henry VIII and, with ▷ Cranmer and ▷ Latimer, one of the three principal martyrs in 1555 under the Roman Catholic reaction of Mary I. He helped Cranmer compile the ▷ Book of Common Prayer of 1549 and 1552, and thus contributed to one of the first English prose masterpieces. He became Bishop of London in 1549.

Ridolfi plot (1570)
Organized by an Italian Roberto di Ridolfi against ▷ Elizabeth I. He planned to marry the Catholic ▷ Mary Queen of Scots to the Duke of Norfolk, and place her on the throne of England with Spanish help. The plot was discovered by Elizabeth's spies, but Ridolfi was himself in safety in Paris.

Ridotto
A kind of public social gathering, with dancing and music, introduced into England in 1722, and very popular in the 18th century.

Rights of Man
▷ Paine, Thomas.

Risorgimento
Italian for 'resurrection'. The name given to the movement for the unification of Italy in the mid-19th century, led by Victor Emmanuel, king of Sardinia, his Prime Minister Cavour, the agitator Mazzini, and the soldier Garibaldi. In 1847 Cavour founded a newspaper called 'Risorgimento'. The movement appealed to English sympathies, which were strongly liberal at that time; references to it are common in mid-19th-century literature.

Rivals, The (1775)
A prose comedy by ▷ Richard Brinsley Sheridan. It is set in the fashionable city of Bath, and the plot concerns parents and guardians at cross purposes with their children. The central situation is that the young and sentimental Lydia Languish, a great novel reader, prefers the idea of marrying a young, penniless officer to the possibility of a rich young heir as a husband. Captain Absolute is such an heir and genuinely in love with her, but to win her affections he disguises himself as the penniless Ensign Beverley. His father, Sir Anthony Absolute, a rich baronet, is determined to make an unromantic marriage of convenience between his son and Lydia, but the Captain dare not disclose his disguise and so seems to be disobeying his father's wishes. Mrs Malaprop, Lydia's guardian, is equally anxious for the worldly match and disapproves of Beverley, but at the same time she is making love by letter to the aggressive Irishman, Sir Lucius O'Trigger, who supposes that the letters come from Lydia, and is one of her suitors. An additional complication is that the so-called Beverley and Sir Lucius have as another rival an absurd young country squire, Bob Acres. A sub-plot is another love affair between Julia Melville and the morbidly jealous Faulkland.

Sheridan's comedies – of which *The Rivals* is the first – are, like those of ▷ Goldsmith at about the same time, above all a reaction against the sentimental tradition, and recall the wit and theatrical deftness of ▷ Restoration drama without its sexual explicitness.

Roaring Girl, The, or Moll Cut-Purse (1606)
A buoyant and big-hearted comedy of gender
ambiguity by ▷ Thomas Middleton,
structured around the benevolent figure of
Moll Cutpurse whose function in the play it
is to smoothe the course of true love. She is
described by her detractors as a 'woman more
than man,/ Man more than woman,' and
becomes the play's moral centre of reference.
More than anything Middleton's Moll
Cutpurse seems to be conceived of as a
▷ Jacobean ▷ citizen comedy version of
▷ Shakespeare's Rosalind from ▷ *As You
Like It*.

Rob Roy (1817)
A novel by ▷ Sir Walter Scott, giving a
picture of Scotland just before the first
▷ Jacobite rebellion of 1715. The plot
concerns the rivalry in love of the cousins
Francis and Rashleigh Osbaldistone for Diana
Vernon. Rashleigh, the villain, is involved in
Jacobite intrigue. Their adventures are
interwoven with the fortunes of Rob Roy
Macgregor, a historical character whom Scott
romanticizes. He is the chief of the Clan
Macgregor in the Scottish Highlands, and a
convicted outlaw who lives by plunder. In
the novel he acts on the side of the hero,
Francis, at Diana's earnest appeal. As usual
in Scott's novels, the notable parts are those
which concern Scottish common life, and
such characters as Bailie Nicol Jarvie and
Francis's servant Andrew Fairservice.

Robert de Boron
French writer, working in the late 12th/early
13th century, who substantially developed the
early history of the ▷ Grail (in his *Roman
de Graal/ Joseph d'Arimathie*), giving it a
Christian interpretation as the vessel used by
Christ at the Last Supper and by Joseph of
Arimathea to collect Christ's blood at the
Crucifixion. He thus provided the means
whereby Arthurian history could be seen as
another key chapter in Christian history.
Robert seems to have taken the Grail story
further in his narratives of *Merlin* (of which
only a fragment survives) and *Perceval*, which
is not extant. Both verse narratives stimulated
further reworkings and continuation. The
13th-century continuation of *Merlin* (known as
the *Suite de Merlin*) provides the basis for
▷ Malory's version of the foundation of
Arthur's court. The prose reworkings of
Robert's work (the prose *Joseph*, the prose
Merlin, and the so-called *Didot Perceval*)
were used substantially in the later
composition of the ▷ Vulgate Cycle.

Roberts, Michèle (b 1949)
Poet, short-story writer and novelist. Roberts
is a prolific writer, has appeared widely on
television, radio and in anthologies, and
regularly gives readings of her work. She has
been very influential on the development and
recognition of contemporary poetry in her
capacity as poetry editor of the London
listings magazine, *City Limits*. Her recent
publications include *The Mirror of the
Mother* (1986), a volume of poetry, and *The
Book of Mrs Noah* (1987), her most recent
novel.

Robertson, T. W. (1829–71)
Dramatist. Plays include: *Society* (1865), *Ours*
(1866), *Caste* (1867), *Play* (1868), *M.P.*
(1870). He is memorable chiefly for restoring
to the drama some degree of relevance to
contemporary social life at a time when
contemporary plays had very little serious
interest. His best-known play is the social
comedy *Caste*.
Bib: Nicoll, A., in *A History of Late
Nineteenth Century Drama 1850–1900*;
Rowell, G., *The Victorian Theatre*.

**Robespierre, Isidore Maximilien de
(1758–94)**
A leader of the extremist ▷ Jacobins during
the ▷ French Revolution. He exercised
virtual dictatorship from July 1793 to July
1794, during which he conducted the Reign
of Terror and tried to establish the worship
of the deistic Supreme Being in opposition to
Catholicism on the one side and atheism on
the other. His reputation for fanatical
integrity caused him to be known as the
Incorruptible. Represented in Trollope's *La
Vendée*, where considerable emphasis is placed
on the fact of his integrity.
   ▷ Deism.

Robin Goodfellow
   ▷ Fairies.

Robin Hood
The hero of popular ▷ ballads from the
14th to 16th centuries. The earliest surviving
reference to him is in Langland's ▷ *Piers
Plowman* (Passus 5) where Sloth, seventh of
the ▷ Seven Deadly Sins, says:

> *I can noughte perfitly my pater noster as the
>   prest it syngeth
> But I can rymes of Robin Hood and Randolf
>   erle of Chestre*

As a popular hero, he was to some extent the
counterpart of ▷ King Arthur, the ideal of
the noble class. Robin Hood lived in the

forest of Sherwood near Nottingham in the Midlands; he was an expert archer and huntsman, stole from the rich in order to give to the poor, was the enemy of the rich churchmen but not a pagan. He is sometimes represented as a ▷ Saxon hero resisting the Norman-French aristocracy, but the period at which he was supposed to live varies from the 12th to 14th centuries; Scott's novel ▷ *Ivanhoe* sets him (as Locksley) in the reign of ▷ Richard 1 which is also the time of the Randolf Earl of Chester in Langland's reference.

The ballads about him do not have great literary merit, and the surviving texts do not date further back than the 15th century; the most important is *A Lytell Geste of Robyn Hode* (1510). He and some other characters in the legends (▷ Friar Tuck, ▷ Maid Marian, ▷ Little John) were enacted in the ▷ morris dances and May games performed until the mid-17th century. The stories, however, have had vitality enough to survive into modern children's versions and films.

Robins, Elizabeth (1862–1952)

American actress and novelist whose play *Votes for Women* was performed at the Court Theatre in 1907. In this she introduced an innovatory crowd scene of a (▷ Suffragette Movement) suffragette rally at Trafalgar Square; the rest of the play is written within the conventions of society drama. She worked mainly in London and belonged to the group of Ibsenites encouraging the development of an English drama of ideas. She performed in the first productions of several of ▷ Ibsen's plays during the 1890s, including *Pillars of Society* (1889), *A Doll's House* and *Hedda Gabler* (both 1891).
Bib: Robins, E., *Ibsen and the Actress*; Robins, E., *Both Sides of the Curtain*.

Robinson, Henry Crabb (1775–1867)

Diarist. Robinson studied at Jena University where he met ▷ Goethe and Schiller. He was one of the first foreign ▷ newspaper correspondents, becoming foreign editor of ▷ *The Times*. In later life he practised as a barrister, and helped found the Athenaeum Club and University College London. His extensive diaries and correspondence throw much light on the literary scene of his time, in particular on ▷ William Blake, ▷ William Wordsworth, ▷ Samuel Taylor Coleridge, ▷ Charles Lamb and ▷ William Hazlitt. They were partly published in 1869, and since then further selections have appeared.

Robinson Crusoe, The Life and strange surprising Adventures of (1719)

A novel by ▷ Daniel Defoe. The first part

Engraving illustrating Defoe's *Robinson Crusoe* (1719)

was based on the experiences of a sailor, ▷ Alexander Selkirk, who went ashore on the uninhabited island of Juan Fernandez in 1704, and remained there until he was rescued in 1709. Crusoe runs away to sea (as Selkirk had done) and after a number of adventures is wrecked on an uninhabited island, where he remains for 20 years. Defoe describes the industrious and methodical way in which he builds up a life for himself, how he is endangered by the periodic visits of a race of cannibals, how he tames one of them into an ideal servant, Man Friday. The island is eventually visited by a ship in the hands of mutinous sailors; he subdues the mutineers and rescues the officers, who take him back to England, leaving the repentant mutineers behind as a colony, together with some Spaniards whom he had previously rescued from the cannibals.

In *The Farther Adventures of Robinson Crusoe*, published in the same year, Crusoe revisits the colony and relates its fortunes; he also travels elsewhere, visits China, and returns to England across Siberia and Russia. The third part, *The Serious Reflections of Robinson Crusoe* (1720), consists of moral essays in which Defoe represents the book as an ▷ allegory of his own life. This was partly a defence against the disapproval of his fellow ▷ Puritans who regarded fiction as hardly distinguishable from lies; on the other hand, Defoe's tale is certainly an image of the loneliness and arduousness of the life of individual economic enterprise which was becoming increasingly typical of society; Crusoe is made to say that he has been more lonely since his return to London than he ever was on his island.

Modern critics have noticed how Crusoe sees human beings merely in terms of their economic virtues. The book has always been praised for its detailed verisimilitude, which caused it to be received at first as an authentic account; the descriptions are almost entirely in terms of what the philosopher ▷ John Locke had distinguished as the objectively discernible 'primary qualities' (▷ *Essay Concerning Human Understanding*) as opposed to the subjectively experienced 'secondary qualities' (colour, beauty, etc.) which it is difficult to verify. The style of the writing is extremely plain, in keeping with the principles that Thomas Sprat had laid down for the ▷ Royal Society in 1667 (*History of the Royal Society*): 'the language of Artisans, Countrymen, and Merchants'. That Crusoe appears much less religious than Defoe means him to is also often remarked; on the other hand, if there is a principle of unity in the long, episodic narrative, it is the function of God as the basic Providence, subjecting chaos so that man may use his constructive virtues for the building of an orderly world.

Rochester, John Wilmot, Second Earl of (1647–80)

Poet and libertine. His father had been ennobled by Charles II for his support during his exile and he enjoyed a privileged position at the ▷ Restoration court, being more than once banished (and later pardoned) for his unruly behaviour and verses. His reputation among his contemporaries can be gauged from the portrait of the elegant and witty Dorimant in ▷ Sir George Etherege's ▷ *The Man of Mode* (1676) which is based on the poet. He showed conspicuous courage in battle during sea-engagements with the Dutch. Later, however, he was suspected of acting less honourably in having ▷ John Dryden set upon in an alley, believing him to be the author of an anonymous satire in a poem by the Earl of Mulgrave. Rochester's motive for refusing to fight a duel with Mulgrave is unclear. It is unlikely to have been the simple lack of courage which his enemies attributed to him at the time,

though he did recommend cowardice in his poetry.

Rochester's combination of aristocracy and rigorous intellectual honesty set him at odds with the emergent bourgeois ethos of the time. He followed ▷ Hobbes and the ancient philosophers ▷ Lucretius and ▷ Seneca in consistent philosophical materialism. He was a ▷ Deist who believed that God, if He existed, could take no interest in petty human affairs, that there was no life after death and that the soul was merely a function of matter. His translation of lines from Seneca's *Troades* dismisses Hell and the afterlife as 'senselesse Storyes, idle Tales/Dreames, Whimseys, and noe more.'

Also he wrote freely about sexual intimacy, both in its pleasurable and disgusting aspects, flouting bourgeois prudery and linguistic censorship. There is sometimes a trivial, unpleasant tone to his writing in this vein, for example in *Signior Dildo* and the Chloris lyrics. But his obscenity is more often psychologically profound and philosophically disturbing, as in *A Ramble in St James's Park* and *The Imperfect Enjoyment*. Moreover, as an aristocrat, he was contemptuous of the proprietorial sexism of the new bourgeoisie. His friend Gilbert Burnet, later bishop of Salisbury, showed the orthodox attitude when he argued that Rochester's libertinism amounted to 'theft' by one man from another: 'men have a property in their wives and daughters, so that to defile the one, or corrupt the other, is an unjust and injurious thing'. In contrast, though Rochester could scarcely be called ▷ feminist, his ambiguous satire on the Earl of Mulgrave, *A Very Heroical Epistle in Answer to Ephelia*, shows an insight into what we would now call male chauvinism, which is most unusual for the period.

Rochester's puritan mother and his friend Burnet refused access to his libertine friends as he lay dying of syphilis, and apparently persuaded him to turn to orthodox religion. After the poet's death Burnet published *Some Passages of the Life and Death of the Earl of Rochester* (1680), and over the next two-and-a-half centuries Rochester's poetry (much of it suppressed) was overshadowed by the edifying legend of the atheist's death-bed repentance. The argument over whether he 'really' repented as he lay in his syphilitic delirium is, however, irrelevant to his poetry, all of which is consistently materialist and libertine. The pious poems attributed to his last days are not by him and lack the quality of his genuine work.

His poetry is diverse, reflecting the social

and cultural transitions of his time. He wrote some exquisite lyrics in the ▷ cavalier tradition, including the movingly philosophical *carpe diem* poem 'All my past life is mine noe more' (sometimes called *Love and Life*). Much of his best work, however, is in the new medium of heroic ▷ couplets, a form which he uses, in such poems as *A Satyr against Reason and Mankind*, *Timon*, and *Tunbridge Wells*, with a conversational ease and freedom much admired and imitated by later ▷ 'Augustans'. His *An Allusion to Horace, the Tenth Satyr of the First Book* is the first example of the characteristically Augustan genre of the 'imitation', also adopted about this time by ▷ John Oldham.
Bib: Johnson, S., in *Lives of the Poets*; Pinto, V. de S., *Enthusiast in Wit*; Adlard, J., *The Debt to Pleasure*; Treglown, J., *Spirit of Wit: Reconsiderations of Rochester*; Farley-Hills, D., *Rochester's Poetry*.

Roderick Random, The Adventures of (1748)
A novel by ▷ Tobias Smollett. It is based on Smollett's own experience as a naval doctor at the siege of Cartagena in 1741; it is episodic in form, and vivid but somewhat brutal in manner. In the Preface, the author pays tribute to the comic genius of ▷ Cervantes, author of ▷ *Don Quixote*.

Rogers, Samuel (1763-1855)
Poet. The wealthy son of a banker from Stoke Newington, he wrote an *Ode to Superstition* (1786) and the popular reflective poem, *The Pleasures of Memory* (1792). *Columbus*, a fragment of an epic, appeared in 1810, and a narrative poem, *Jacqueline*, was published together with ▷ Lord Byron's *Lara* in 1814. He was offered the ▷ Poet Laureateship on the death of ▷ William Wordsworth in 1850, but declined.

Roland
Hero of the Old French *chanson de geste*, the *Chanson de Roland*, dating from the first half of the 12th century, an epic account of the battle between the rearguard of ▷ Charlemagne's army, led by his nephew Roland, and the large Saracen forces who ambush the rearguard in the valley of Roncevaux. The ambush is arranged with the treacherous connivance of Roland's stepfather, Ganelon. Roland takes up the challenge to fight against the odds and refuses to summon help from Charlemagne, as his companion, Oliver, advises. When many of the French side have been slaughtered, Roland finally summons Charlemagne's aid. The French king returns to find his rearguard massacred but goes on to rout the pagan army and avenge his nephew's death. The narrative is structured around a series of binary oppositions, the most obvious being that between the forces of the west and east, between righteous Christians and sinful pagans. Yet within that clear-cut antagonism, the heroic ethos of the narrative is made more complex, not only by Gamelon's perfidy, but by the juxtaposition of Roland and Oliver's response to the prospect of fighting against the odds: the necessary rashness which constitutes heroism is contrasted with a more pragmatic response to the prospect of a hopeless, if glorious, battle. The earliest extant copy of the text was copied in England (1125-50). Roland is the hero of ▷ Boiardo's *Orlando Innamorato* and ▷ Ariosto's *Orlando Furioso*.
Bib: Sayers, D. (trans.), *The Song of Roland*; Whitehead, F. (ed.), *La Chanson de Roland*.

Rolle, Richard (1300-49)
One of the most prolific of the English mystical writers, who lived as a hermit in Yorkshire and became a spiritual advisor to a group of nuns at Hampole. He composed devotional works in Latin, and his English work includes a commentary of the Psalter, meditations on the Passion and a guide to the spiritual life, *The Form of Living*, written for a single recluse but circulated more widely. His prose style makes frequent use of alliteration. Although never canonized, he was widely regarded as a saint until the time of the Reformation.
Bib: Allen, H. E., *The English Writings of Richard Rolle*; Riehle, W., *The Middle English Mystics*.

Roman Actor, The (1626)
A blood tragedy by ▷ Philip Massinger set at the time of the emperor Domitian. The play dramatizes Domitian's marriage to the resourceful Domitia, whose husband he has executed. During a play-within-the-play he kills the actor Paris with whom she has fallen in love, which leads to her conspiring against him and his assassination.

Roman de la Rose
An immensely influential French ▷ dream-vision narrative, composed during the 13th century. The first 4,058 lines of the poem were written by Guillaume de Lorris, c 1237; the remaining 17,622 lines were a later addition of Jean de Meun (le Clopinel), c 1277. The whole narrative is framed as an allegorical account of a love affair, reported as a dream-vision experience by the narrator/lover. Guillaume de Lorris's section

provides an exemplary account of the protocol of loving, from the viewpoint of a male lover who courts the object of his desire, a beautiful Rosebud, in the garden of Love, presided over by Mirth. The love garden is the arena of courtly society itself; the dreamer, appropriately, is ushered in by Oiseuse (Leisure), for leisure is a necessary prerequisite for the refined courting which goes on in the garden, as is Richesse; Poverty and Old Age figure among the undesirable qualities kept out by the garden wall. The desired woman is represented as an object to be plucked, but aspects of her response to the lover's advances are represented in a series of personified figures (including Fair Welcoming, Shame and Danger) which surround the Rose, just as some aspects of the Lover, notably Reason, are figured in personified forms. Guillaume's poem ends, unfinished, with the lover in an impasse, having only kissed the Rose which now is protected in a castle by Jealousy. As it stands, the poem provides a manual of the art of ▷ courtly loving in a narrative form, and this dreamscape and mode of working out love's protocol through an allegorical narrative were imitated and reworked in many courtly love poems in French, and in English too (including ▷ Chaucer's dream-vision poems).

Jean de Meun's continuation remains set within the garden but substantially expands the subject of the narrative, and its philosophical and moral dimensions. The expansion comes in the form of a new cast of personified figures (including a Friend, an Old Woman, Nature and Genius her priest) who step in to advise, and assist, or to educate the Lover. The precious and rarified atmosphere of the garden is subverted, as the Lover's desire is subjected to a rigorous appraisal by Reason (who assumes a far larger role in the action), and made into a much more pragmatic quest for satisfaction, though the intervention of the Friend and the Old Woman (who brings a temporal perspective to the action which Guillaume de Lorris deliberately excluded). Rather than being a delicate embodiment of love theory in practice, the narrative beomes an arena for large-scale debates about social organization in theory and in practice, including what part sexual desire has to play in society and how it is being abused. In the end the Lover gets the chance to pluck his Rose and the narrative concludes with a barely disguised description of a sexual assault. Jean de Meun's section of the poem provides a different kind of cultural handbook: it subverts the 'givens' in the structure of Guillaume's love garden and embarks on a broader, more intellectual and philosophical discussion, which considers different kinds of loving (including divine love), but it does so through dramatized debates and monologues. It provides an example of how the clash of opposing ideas can be given dramatic expression but not necessarily a resolution (a point which seems to have profoundly influenced the construction of much of Chaucer's narrative poetry).

The poem as a whole was immensely influential throughout the 14th, 15th and even the 16th centuries. It provoked controversy as well as literary imitation and was the subject of a public debate in France at the end of the 14th century in which ▷ Christine de Pisan was a leading figure (who objected to its misogynistic polemic and its blatant representation of a sexual attack). Chaucer translated the poem into English but his relationship to the extant Middle English translation (▷ *The Romaunt of the Rose*) is not clear. There are three extant fragments (two translating sections from Guillaume's section, the third an excerpt from Jean de Meun's) and most critics seem to accept that fragment A (covering the first 1,700 lines of the poem) is Chaucer's work.
Bib: Dahlberg, C. (trans.), *The Romance of the Rose*.

Roman wall
A wall built across the north of England by the Roman Emperor Hadrian (reigned AD 117–38) and strengthened or reconstructed by the Emperor Severus in the 3rd century. Its purpose was to provide a line of fortifications against the tribes of Picts and Scots to the north, and hence to protect the province of Britannia (corresponding to modern England and Wales) from invasion. Substantial sections of the wall, which runs south of the Scottish border, still survive.

Romances of Shakespeare
A term often used to express the character of four of the last plays by Shakespeare: ▷ *Pericles* (1608–9); ▷ *Cymbeline* (1609–10); ▷ *The Winter's Tale* (1610–11); ▷ *The Tempest* (1611).

The following are some of the qualities that distinguish these plays:
1 Extravagance of incident. Shakespeare abandons the comparatively realistic presentation characteristic of his tragic period, 1604–8. Events are extraordinary, and in *Pericles* and *The Winter's Tale* they are widespread in place and time; in *Pericles* and *Cymbeline* they are loosely related in plot. In

Cymbeline and *The Winter's Tale* there is no consistency of period, and classical history mingles with 16th-century social settings. In *The Tempest* Shakespeare makes a freer use of magic than in any of his other plays, but in its strict unity of time and place this play is otherwise in contrast to the other three plays of the group.

2 Although *The Tempest* is again here to some extent a contrast to the others, the group belongs to a category known as 'tragicomedy'; that is to say *Pericles, Cymbeline, The Winter's Tale* each deepen into tragedy which reaches climax midway in the story, and then lighten towards a happy conclusion. *The Tempest* is different in that the tragedy has all taken place before the play has begun; the whole play is thus devoted to restoring happiness out of tragedy already accomplished.

3 In each play the theme concerns an ordeal undergone by the main character; in this respect, however, the plays show a progression. Pericles does no wrong; he is a passive sufferer, with no power of his own to relieve his suffering. Cymbeline commits errors, and the tragedy arises from them, but he is not called on to act in order that the errors shall be redeemed. In *The Winter's Tale* Leontes' error amounts to terrible crime, and this has to be expiated by a long period of unremitting repentance. Prospero, in *The Tempest*, has committed no error beyond severing himself from his worldly responsibilities; he is a powerful and virtuous man who could wreak vengeance on his enemies but chooses instead to reconcile himself to them by acts of godlike mercy.

4 In the first three plays, the ordeal of the hero is characterized by the loss of his family, and in each of them it is a daughter who is chiefly instrumental in bringing about the reunion which constitutes the happy ending. *The Tempest* is again somewhat different from the others; here father and daughter remain together, but they are both cast off from the rest of the world; it is again the daughter who is instrumental in the final reunion.

In the romances the imaginative emphasis is on reconciliation. Prospero's statement in *The Tempest* that 'the rarer action is/In virtue than in vengeance' epitomizes the distance Shakespeare has travelled since ▷ *Hamlet* and the other tragedies, all of which are to some extent reworked in the late plays.

Romantic poets
▷ Romanticism.

Romanticism
Two phases in the development of this concept need to be distinguished:

1 *'Romantick' taste* (c 1650–c 1789) The adjective 'romantic' came into use in the mid-17th century, at the point when the romance form, which had dominated secular literature during the Middle Ages and the ▷ Renaissance, fell from prominence. As ▷ Enlightenment philosophy and neo-classical taste developed, the romance form was subjected to self-conscious analysis and criticism. In its early stages the word took various forms: 'romancy', 'romancical', 'romantique', 'romantick'. Its meaning, 'like a romance', carried a number of different connotations, related to the various features of romance: the archaic rituals of chivalry, magic, superstition, improbable adventures, idealistic love, and wild scenery. ▷ Samuel Pepys used the word in 1667: 'These things are almost romantique, and yet true'. And the *Oxford English Dictionary* cites a 1659 reference to 'An old house in a romancey place'.

During the 18th century romantic wildness was disapproved of by the more puritanical, rational and enlightened reader. Some thinkers, however, such as the third ▷ Earl of Shaftesbury, self-consciously boasted of their emotional idealism and enthusiasm for wild scenery. Also most readers enjoyed the 'romantick' alternatives to neo-classicism indulged in at times by the poets and prose writers. Sometimes poets employed imitations of ornamental, medieval or ▷ 'gothic' forms, such as the ▷ Spenserian stanza and the ▷ ballad, though romantic sensibility could also be expressed in the heroic ▷ couplet. ▷ Alexander Pope's ▷ *Eloisa to Abelard* and *Elegy to the Memory of an Unfortunate Lady*, ▷ James Thomson's ▷ *Castle of Indolence*, ▷ Thomas Gray's translations of Norse and Welsh ballads and his ode, ▷ *The Bard*, and ▷ James Macpherson's Ossian, illustrate the range of romantic taste in the 18th century. The subjects of these works: passionate love, religious enthusiasm, laziness, medieval history, suicide, lie outside the mainstream of ▷ Augustanism, and they all share (with different degrees of seriousness) a sense of daring literary excess.

2 *The Romantic Movement* (1789–1824) The six great poets of what is now generally called the Romantic Movement, are in many ways extremely diverse. ▷ William Blake, the pioneer of the group, was broadly speaking a fundamentalist Christian, who felt that ▷ William Wordsworth's ▷ pantheistic 'natural piety' made him 'a Heathen Philosopher at Enmity against all true Poetry'. ▷ Lord Byron emulated the wit and urbanity of ▷ Alexander Pope, whereas

▷ John Keats was contemptuous of neo-classical couplet writers who 'sway'd about upon a rocking horse,/ And thought it Pegasus'. ▷ Percy Bysshe Shelley was an atheist, ▷ Samuel Taylor Coleridge became an apologist for the Church of England. However, despite their differences, these poets show essential similarities in their response to the same historical situation, and do form a coherent group. It will be best to begin by describing their characteristics, leaving the label, 'Romanticism', to be explained afterwards.

The ▷ French Revolution dispelled the literary self-consciousness of the period of ▷ Sensibility. On the political level, the bourgeois complacency of the earlier period was suddenly lost. Even conservative writers at this time, such as ▷ Edmund Burke and ▷ Sir Walter Scott were forced to find new arguments in favour of the *status quo*, based on appeals to ancient tradition and emotional prejudice, rather than the authority of Reason and the natural order. The major poets were less inhibited. Blake was morally indignant about the institutions of State and Church. Wordsworth and Coleridge began their careers as fervent proponents of social revolution, while the second generation Romantics, Byron, Shelley, and (less prominently) Keats, remained true to the original revolutionary spirit through the succeeding period of reaction. The Romantics rejected the rigid social and literary hierarchy of the 18th century. Where Pope in the ▷ *Essay on Man* condescendingly conceded 'the poor Indian' his Natural Religion, Wordsworth feels profoundly shamed by that of the lowly leech gatherer in ▷ *Resolution and Independence*. The feelings of the individual take precedence over Reason and social convention, and particularly in the works of Wordsworth, outcasts, the very young, the very old, the poor and the mad, are seriously attended to. In the work of both Blake and Wordsworth youth becomes the fountain of wisdom rather than age. In a similar way dreams take on a new significance as the key to the unconscious depths of our being. Coleridge in his ▷ *Biographia Literaria*, gives a new, more complex meaning to the key Romantic term 'imagination'.

Fundamental to romanticism is a new attitude towards the role of man in nature. The writers of the ▷ Enlightenment period, ▷ the Earl of Rochester, ▷ John Dryden and Pope had shared with the ancients a certainty as to what nature was, and a confidence about their place in it. For them *human* nature was an integral part, even the greatest glory, of 'Nature', and (like gravity) obeyed 'Nature's laws'. In the early stages of Enlightenment it seemed easy to reconcile the new exploitative science and technology with a traditional piety about God's creation. But by the end of the century a crisis had developed. Enlightenment had finally robbed nature of its authentic, primitive awesomeness. More practically its manipulative exploitation by man seemed in danger of destroying nature itself. ▷ William Cowper expressed this new mood of diffidence and alienation in his aphorism: 'God made the country, and man made the town', while Shelley declared more boldly that 'man, having enslaved the elements, remains himself a slave'. Newton's light had reduced nature to a manipulable material system. It had become either a useful recreational facility (Wordsworth wrote a guidebook to the picturesque Lakes), or – in atavistic reaction – a mystical substitute for religion. Shelley's proposed answer to the crisis of Enlightenment, like that of all the Romantic poets, was to cultivate the 'imagination' and 'the poetical faculty'.

Nature thus ceases to be an objective intellectual concept for the Romantics, and becomes instead an elusive metaphor. The brisk clarity of Pope's: 'First follow *Nature* . . . which is still the same', is replaced by the anxious emotive rhetoric of Wordsworth's: 'And I have felt/A sense sublime/ Of something far more deeply interfused'. Nature is often approached indirectly – seen from afar, or not *seen* at all: 'I cannot see what flowers are at my feet,/ Nor what soft incense hangs upon the boughs,/But, in embalmed darkness, guess each sweet' (▷ *Ode to a Nightingale*, stanza V). The relation between the poet and nature becomes ambiguous and insecure: 'I see, not feel, how beautiful they are!' (▷ *Dejection: An Ode*, stanza II); 'Whither is fled the visionary gleam?/ Where is it now, the glory and the dream?' (▷ *Ode: Intimations of Immortality* , ll. 56–7); 'The wilderness has a mysterious tongue/ Which teaches awful doubt' (Shelley, *Mont Blanc*, ll. 76–7). From being the middle term in the Great Chain, 'The glory, jest, and riddle of the world!' (▷ *Essay on Man*, II, l. 17), or – less buoyantly but equally definitively – a 'reas'ning *Engine*' inevitably destined for the dirt (Rochester, *Satyr on Reason*, ll. 29–30), the human being has become a dubious subjectivism, constantly redefining his or her identity.

The Romantic poets continued to employ the 'romantick' forms of the earlier period:

Spenserian stanzas, ▷ ballad, and irregular ▷ ode. They cultivated medievalism and imitated Elizabethan and ▷ Jacobean playwrights. They also revived the neglected ▷ sonnet form. However, their designation 'Romantic Poets' derives less from their development of previous romantic taste, than from the growing popularity of German aesthetic categories in England. In the late 18th century ▷ Goethe and Schiller had developed the contrast between romantic (emotional, inspirational) art, and classical (serene, balanced) art, into a theoretical opposition between aesthetic absolutes, and the German critic Schlegel and the French essayist Mme de Stael had popularized this distinction. At first, observers in England saw this debate as a strictly foreign phenomenon. Byron in a letter of 1820 remarked 'I perceive that in Germany as well as in Italy, there is a great struggle about what they call *Classical* and *Romantic*', and he went on to hope that such disputes would not spread to England. However, such a polarity does seem to underlie some of Keats's work. His ▷ *Hyperion*, and his *Ode on a Grecian Urn* (written after he had seen the Parthenon or 'Elgin' marbles in London), can be seen as 'classical', while his ▷ *Eve of St Agnes* and *Ode to a Nightingale* are 'romantic' (▷ Odes, Keats's).

The abstract noun 'Romanticism', did not come into use in England until the mid 19th century; early citations in the *Oxford English Dictionary* are in reference to the music of Liszt, and in the phrase 'German Romanticism'. By the time readers began to see these six English poets as forming a single 'movement' it seemed natural to simplify their work in accordance with this categorization. Romanticism thus stands as an emotional reaction against the rational classicism of 18th century ▷ Augustanism. It is important to remember that all these terms embody large simplifications. If they are used without a sense of the historical complexities which lie behind them, they can distort the literature to which they refer, rather than illuminating it.
Bib: Abrams, M. H., *The Mirror and the Lamp*; Praz, M., *The Romantic Agony*; Ford, B. (ed.), *New Pelican Guide to English Literature, Vol. 5: From Blake to Byron*; Bloom, H., *The Visionary Company*; Watson, J. R., *English Poetry of the Romantic Period: 1789–1830*; Butler, M., *Rebels and Reactionaries: English Literature and its Background: 1760–1830*; McGann, J., *The Romantic Ideology*; Mellor, A. K., *Romanticism and Feminism*.

Romany
  ▷ Gipsies.

Romaunt of the Rose, The
The Middle English translation of the ▷ *Roman de la Rose*, which has been attributed, in part, to ▷ Chaucer.

Romeo and Juliet (1597)
A romantic tragedy by ▷ Shakespeare. It was published in ▷ quarto in a corrupt form in 1597, and in a better edition in 1599. The story is an old one; Shakespeare's version is based on a poem *Romeus and Juliet* (1562) by Arthur Brooke, itself based on a French version of an Italian tale by Bandello (1554). The story is of the romantic love of Romeo, belonging to the family of ▷ Montague, and Juliet, of the ▷ Capulet family, both living in the Italian city of Verona. The affair has to be kept secret owing to the bitter hostility of the two families, and only Juliet's nurse and Friar Laurence, who marries them, know of it. Even so the affair is not allowed to continue peacefully; Juliet's cousin Tybalt provokes an affray which leads not only to his own death but to that of Mercutio, friend of Romeo and relative of the Prince of Verona, with the result that Romeo is exiled from the city. Moreover, Juliet's father, in ignorance of his daughter's secret marriage, proposes to marry her off in haste to a young nobleman, Paris. To enable her to escape this, Friar Laurence gives Juliet a potion which sends her into a profound sleep and causes her family to suppose her dead; the Friar's design is that she shall be placed in the family burial vault, and that meanwhile a message is to be sent to Romeo directing him to come by night and steal her away. However, by an accident the message is not sent, and Romeo hears only of her death; he returns to Verona, but only to take poison and die by her side. A moment later, the effect of the potion wears off and Juliet recovers; she sees her lover dead beside her, and kills herself in turn.

The play is one of Shakespeare's early masterpieces, and is famous for its exquisite poetry and the dramatic excellence of some of its scenes (*eg* II. i where the lovers declare their love to each other in the 'balcony scene') and of three of its characters, namely Juliet, her nurse, and Romeo's friend Mercutio. It is not, however, a tragedy in the sense in which we understand the term 'Shakespearian tragedy', in regard to the plays written after 1600. In these plays, tragedy is the outcome of the nature and situation of the central character (*eg* ▷ *Othello*) whereas in *Romeo and Juliet* the unhappy ending is more the result of accident

– notably the failure to send the message to Romeo. On the other hand, it is possible that the usual response to the play is more sentimental than Shakespeare intended: Brooke's poem is puritanical and reproves the lovers for their passion; Shakespeare presents them sympathetically, but there are signs – *eg* the Friar's soliloquy opening II. iii – that he intended the passion to be regarded as a misfortune in itself. Whatever one's views on this, the excellence of the play arises above all from the actuality with which Shakespeare presents Juliet: the tradition of courtly romance is brought, as in ▷ Chaucer's ▷ *Troilus and Criseyde*, closely into relationship with real life.

▷ Courtly love.

Romola (1863)

A historical novel by ▷ George Eliot, serialized in ▷ *Cornhill Magazine* (1862–3). It is set in late-15th-century Florence at the time of the predominance of the reforming monk ▷ Savonarola. Romola is a high-minded girl who marries a self-indulgent and unscrupulous Greek, Tito Melma. Repelled by her husband and disillusioned by the course of Savonarola's career, she eventually finds her salvation in self-denial. In writing the novel, George Eliot was putting forward the principle that it is as important to actualize the society in which the characters move as to give reality to the characters themselves. The novel has been praised for the thoroughness of research which established the Florentine scene; on the other hand, by comparison with the later novels (▷ *Middlemarch* and ▷ *Daniel Deronda*) set in England, modern readers feel that medieval Florence did not touch the author in the sense that she participated imaginatively in its life, with the result that of all her novels, *Romola* is probably the least read.

Romulus
▷ Classical Myth.

Rondeau
A form of short poem originated in 16th-century France. It consisted of 13 eight- or ten-syllable lines, divided into stanzas of unequal length, with the addition of short refrains, and only two rhymes throughout. The form was little used in England until the late 19th century when a taste developed for the more artificial forms of short poem among poets like ▷ Swinburne *eg* his *Century of Roundels*.

Rondel
A form of short poem similar to the rondeau, but consisting of 14 lines instead of 13, and with a somewhat different rhyme scheme. It was not much used in English until the end of the 19th century in the work of such poets as ▷ Bridges, Dobson and Henley. It originated in France in the 14th century.

Ronsard, Pierre de (1524–1585)
French poet, leader of the ▷ Renaissance group known as the ▷ 'Pléiade'. His output was wide-ranging (▷ odes, ▷ hymns, ▷ epic, elegies), but he is particularly famous for his love ▷ sonnets, Petrarchan (▷ Petrarch) in style, and it was in this form that Ronsard was influential among English sonneteers of the Renaissance, *eg* Henry Constable (1562–1613) and ▷ Samuel Daniel.

Roper, Margaret More (1505–44)
Margaret Roper, the daughter of ▷ Thomas More, became renowned in England for her learning. As a member of More's household, her education was of great importance, indeed she was perhaps the intellectual star of what has been sometimes termed the 'School of More' which included More's children, wards, relatives and friends. In a letter, written in 1521, ▷ Erasmus records that it was the education and intellectual capacities of Margaret Roper which convinced him of the value of education for women in general. Indeed, Margaret Roper may well have formed the basis for Erasmus' sympathetic portrait of the learned woman in one of his *Colloquies*. Many of Margaret Roper's works are now lost, but what is known of her is derived mainly from the letters she and her father exchanged while he was in prison prior to his execution and from her husband's account of More's life which is also an account of his wife. Her major surviving published work is her ▷ translation of Erasmus' commentary on The Lord's Prayer, which was published (though its translator was not acknowledged) as *A Devout Treatise Upon the 'Pater Noster'*, probably in 1524.
Bib: McCutcheon, E., 'Margaret More Roper: The Learned Woman in Tudor England', *Women Writers of the Renaissance and Reformation* (ed.) K. M. Wilson.

Rosalind, Rosalynde
1 The central character in ▷ Shakespeare's comedy ▷ *As You Like It*. She is based on the heroine of ▷ Thomas Lodge's romance *Rosalynde, Euphues Golden Legacy* (1590).

2 A character in *January*, the first month of Spenser's ▷ *Shepherd's Calendar*; she has been thought to represent Rosa Daniel, the sister of the poet ▷ Samuel Daniel, and

wife of ▷ John Florio, translator of the Essays of ▷ Montaigne.

Rosamund, Fair

Rosamund Clifford, the mistress of ▷ Henry II and the subject of a number of later legends, These relate that Henry built a labyrinthine house for her at Woodstock, and guided himself to her chamber by a clue of thread; Henry's queen, Eleanor of Aquitaine, is said to have found her way by the same thread, and to have poisoned Rosamund. The legend has a clear basis in the ancient Greek myth of the labyrinth of Crete, where ▷ Theseus, guided by ▷ Ariadne's thread, found and killed the ▷ Minotaur. The story, baseless in fact, is used by ▷ Samuel Daniel in his poem *The Complaint of Rosamond* (1592) and by ▷ Thomas Deloney in a ballad.

Roscius (Quintus Roscius Gallus) (?126–62 BC)

A famous Roman comic actor. He wrote a treatise comparing acting and oratory, and the great orator Cicero took lessons from him. It became a habit to praise actors by comparing them to Roscius; thus ▷ Ben Jonson compared ▷ Edward Alleyn to him.

Roscoe, William (1753–1831)

Poet. Famous for his ▷ children's book, *The Butterfly's Ball and the Grasshopper's Feast* (1806). He also wrote other poems, and biographies of Lorenzo de Medici (1796) and Pope Leo the Tenth (1805).

Roscommon, Wentworth Dillon, Fourth Earl of (1633?–85)

Critic and ▷ Restoration courtier. His translation of ▷ Horace's *Art of Poetry* (1680) in blank verse, and his *Essay on Translated Verse* (1684), in heroic couplets, were greatly admired at the time, and his versification was praised by ▷ Alexander Pope.

Rose Theatre

Opened by the theatre manager, ▷ Philip Henslowe, in 1587 on ▷ Bankside in Southwark. ▷ Shakespeare was a member of his company at the time. Henslowe managed the theatre together with his son-in-law, Edward Alleyn, until 1603.

▷ Theatres.

Rosenberg, Isaac (1890–1918)

Poet. He was born in Bristol, and educated at an elementary school in London. He then became apprenticed to an engraver, and entered the Slade School of Art in 1911. He joined the army in 1915, serving as a private

soldier, and was killed in action. He was the most original of all the 'war poets'. His work is full of rhythmic energy, less sombre than ▷ Wilfred Owen's, and bolder in imagery. Owen reacted with indignation and compassion against the war; in the Preface to his poems he wrote: 'Above all I am not concerned with Poetry. My subject is War, and the pity of War. The Poetry is in the pity.' Rosenberg wrote in a letter (1916): 'I will not leave a corner of my consciousness covered up but saturate myself with the strange and extraordinary new conditions of this life, and it will all refine itself into poetry later on.' Works include: *Night and Day* (1912); *Youth* (1915); *Poems* (ed. G. Bottomley, with a Memoir by L. Binyon; 1922). *Collected Poems* (ed. G. Bottomley and D. Harding, 1937).

▷ War Poets.

Roses, Wars of the

▷ Wars of the Roses.

Rosetta Stone

A stone bearing an inscription in Egyptian hieroglyphics, and in the simplified form of hieroglyphics known as 'demotic', and in Greek. The combination made it possible to interpret Egyptian hieroglyphics. It was found by the Nile by soldiers of Napoleon, and is now in the British Museum, London.

Rosicrucianism

A system of philosophical and mystical beliefs professed by an organization known as the Ancient Mystic Order of Rosa Crucis (the red cross). Its origins are obscure; it is first mentioned in 1614. Part of its doctrine has consisted in the belief that the universe contains a hierarchy of spirits governing the various elements. Pope, in his second version of ▷ *The Rape of the Lock*, used this system for satirical purposes; he needed for his mock ▷ epic a supernatural system comparable to the ancient Greek gods and goddesses of Homer's ▷ *Iliad*, but adapted, as they would not be, to the pettiness of his theme. He used the Rosicrucian system because it provided spirits of all degrees of importance.

Rossetti, Christina Georgina (1830–94)

Poet. She was the youngest child of Gabriele Rossetti, an Italian political refugee who came to England in 1824. Her brothers were the poet and painter, ▷ Dante Gabriel Rossetti, and the critic William Michael Rossetti; her sister, Maria Francesca, entered an Anglican convent, and is known for a book on ▷ Dante. Christina was also a deeply religious Anglo-Catholic, and her poetry is painfully subjective; she modelled herself on the 17th-century spiritual poet ▷ George Herbert in this respect. She was also associated with the ▷ Pre-Raphaelite Brotherhood led by D. G. Rossetti, contributing to its journal *The Germ* edited by her other brother, William Michael; she shared the Pre-Raphaelite taste for beautiful but sad and rather languid imagery, but her diction is remarkable for its simplicity. This simplicity attracted her to children as an audience, and her poems have a nursery-rhyme quality which belies their psychological complexity (▷ Children's books). Her religious appeal, in contrast to Herbert, is also limited by the narrowness of High Anglicanism in relation to the rest of the society of her time. Her most famous book of verse, ▷ *Goblin Market and other Poems* came out in 1862. Other volumes: *The Prince's Progress* (1866); *Sing-Song* (1872); *A Pageant and other Poems* (1881); *New Poems* (1896). She also published works of religious prose, and *Time Flies, a Reading Diary* (1883) combines prose and verse. Christina Rossetti was one of the finer products of the ▷ Oxford Movement, and her work is admired by 20th-century critics for simplicity and sincerity unusual in poetry of the second half of the 19th-century. More recently, she has been credited by ▷ feminist criticism as one of the most important women writers in English.

▷ Church of England.
Bib: Bell, M., *Life*; Sandars, M. F., *Life*; Bald, M. A., in *Women Writers of the Nineteenth Century*; Birkhead, E., *Christina Rossetti and her Poetry*; Zativenska, M., *Christina Rossetti: a Portrait with a Background*; Packer, L. M., *Christina Rossetti*.

Rossetti, Dante Gabriel (1828–82)
Poet and painter; the son of an Italian political refugee and an English mother. In 1848 he started the ▷ Pre-Raphaelite Brotherhood with a number of fellow-painters, but the inspiration of his painting as of his poetry was essentially literary. The poetry is a continuation of the English ▷ romantic movement, particularly the work of ▷ Keats, inasmuch as its central impulse is the sensuous response to beauty, and the inspiration of the Pre-Raphaelites was the direct appeal of detail in medieval painting. Rossetti also inherited, however, the feeling for the mysteriousness of the ▷ Middle Ages which both he and Keats shared with the taste for ▷ 'Gothic' which was an aspect of romanticism at the beginning of the century. In addition, he inherited some of the feeling for ▷ aestheticism in sanctity which had

been part of the ▷ Oxford Movement in the Church of England during the 1830s and 40s. The triumph of English industrialism, with its admiration for technology, tended to disregard values which were not practical ones. Thus poets like Rossetti were tempted to use their poetry as a dream world of refuge from external squalor and commercial struggle and this led to a self-regarding nostalgia. This meant that fields of inspiration such as the Middle Ages and religion are not so much expressed in their own vitality as used as a defence against other, objectionable realities; Rossetti is accused of being 'religiose' rather than 'religious', and of having falsified the past. On the other hand, Rossetti's poetry, within these limitations, is sumptuous and melodious. He was at first much better known for his paintings, but his poem *The Blessed Damozel* was published in the Pre-Raphaelite journal *The Germ* in 1850. Later came his translations from ▷ Dante, *The Early Italian Poets* (1861); *Poems by D. G. Rossetti* (1870); *Ballads and Sonnets* (1881), including a sonnet sequence, *The House of Life*, which was expanded from a version in the 1870 volume, and is sometimes called his masterpiece.
Bib: Doughty, O., *A Victorian Romantic*; Winwar, F., *Poor Splendid Wings*; Holman Hunt, W., *Pre-Raphaelitism and the Pre-Raphaelite Brotherhood*; Boas, H. O. B., *Rossetti and his Poetry*; Cary, E. L., *The Rossettis*; Pater, W., in *Appreciations*; Hough, G., in *The Last Romantics*; Rees, J., *The Poetry of Dante Gabriel Rossetti*.

Round Table, The
The Round Table is first mentioned in ▷ Wace's *Roman de Brut* (1155), where it is described briefly as a construction devised by ▷ King Arthur, to pre-empt rivalry for a place at the hall table among members of his fast-expanding entourage. ▷ Laȝamon amplifies the story of how a marvellous table was introduced to Arthur's hall: after a riot breaks out at one of Arthur's feasts, a witty Cornish woodworker devises a table which can be expanded to accommodate any number of guests (it is not specifically round). In later Arthurian narrative, the Round Table frequently provides a way of demarcating the elite members of Arthur's court (as the Knights of the Round Table) but the significance and size of the table itself may vary considerably: it is not a fixed artefact by any means.

In the Christianized version of the ▷ Grail legend (first formulated by ▷ Robert de Boron), the Round Table is invested with a mystical significance, as a successor to the earlier Holy Tables of the Last Supper and the Grail Table (of Joseph of Arimathea). Its round shape is symbolic of the universe, and one place at the Table is reserved only for the knight who will achieve the Grail quest (known as the 'Perilous Seat'). ▷ Merlin constructs this Table for ▷ Uther, who passes it on to ▷ Guinevere's father; Arthur receives it as part of Guinevere's dowry.

In ▷ Malory's version of Arthurian narrative, the Table (Guinevere's dowry) can accommodate up to 150 knights, and it becomes symbolic of the chivalric ethos itself, and Arthur outlines the rules for its members in the first tale of Malory's *Morte D'Arthur*. The import of its round shape is later explained by ▷ Perceval's Aunt in the course of the Grail Quest but it is not identified as a successor to the Grail Table, which is made of silver and found in ▷ Pelles's castle.

The Round Table still preserved at Winchester, though identified by ▷ John Hardyng in his *Chronicle* as *the* Round Table, is a manufactured relic: it was built some time around the mid-13th century and repainted sometime in the mid-16th century. It is largely responsible for the popular modern notion of the Round Table as one which has a strictly fixed number of places. It is, however, just one of the many shapes which the Round Table assumes in medieval Arthurian narratives.

Roundel
▷ Chaucer seems to have been the first English poet to compose roundels in imitation of the French ▷ rondeau form. Roundels have a varying number of lines (8–14), but use only two rhymes. The opening line recurs as the refrain. The bird song at the end of the ▷ *Parliament of Foulys* is in the form of a roundel.

Roundheads
A name for ▷ Puritan supporters of the ▷ Parliamentary party in the ▷ Civil Wars of 1642–51. They were so called because they habitually cut their hair close to their heads, whereas the Royalists (▷ Cavaliers) wore their hair ornamentally long. This Cavalier habit was regarded by the Puritans as a symptom of worldliness. The word has been traced back to 1641, when a Cavalier officer was quoted as declaring that he would 'cut the throats of those round-headed dogs that bawled against bishops'. Earlier than this, a pamphlet against long hair was published under the title of 'The unloveliness of lovelocks'.

Rousseau, Jean-Jacques (1712–78)
French-Swiss thinker. His chief works were: *Discourse on the Influence of Learning and Art* (1750), in which he argues that progress in these has not improved human morals; *Discourse on Inequality* (1754), in which society is considered to have spoilt the liberty and virtue natural to primitive peoples; a novel, *The New Héloise* (1761), in which the return to primitive nature is considered in relation to the relationships of the sexes and the family; ▷ *The Social Contract* (1761), a political treatise with the theme that the basis of society is artificial, not binding on individuals when society ceases to serve their interests; *Emile* (1762), advocating education through the evocation of the natural impulses and interests of the child, and the *Confessions*, an autobiography which was self-revealing without precedent, published after his death.

Rousseau was immensely influential, not only in France but throughout Europe. His praise of nature and protests against society were significant contributions to the creation of a revolutionary state of mind, culminating in the ▷ French Revolution of 1789. Education from nature, his conception of nature as a life-giving force, was of great importance in the background of ▷ Wordsworth, and through Wordsworth, of much of English 19th-century imaginative thinking, and linked with his devotion to nature was his equally influential reverence for childhood. As an autobiographer, Rousseau was one of the first to base the importance of individual experience on its uniqueness, not on its moral excellence or intellectual attainment. This was quite contrary to the characteristic 18th-century view, expressed in works like Samuel Johnson's ▷ *Rasselas*, in which the valuable experience was conceived to be only that which was true of and for humanity at large.

Rover, The (1679)
Comedy by ▷ Aphra Behn, reworked from ▷ Thomas Killigrew's play *Thomaso* (1663–64). The play concerns four cavaliers, exiled in the cause of the future Charles II, and the women whom they meet during a sojourn in Naples. Penniless Willmore (the Rover) is accompanied by the English Colonel Belville, his friend Frederick, and an English country gentleman called Blunt. Hellena, a 'gay young woman design'd for a Nun' is determined to avoid her fate and find a husband, while her sister Florinda is equally determined to avoid marrying the man intended for her by her brother. She has fallen in love with Belville, while Hellena, attending a carnival in disguise

with her sister and two other women, falls in love with Willmore. He, however, is attracted by the wealthy and beautiful courtesan Angelica Bianca, and determines to gain her services without payment. Hellena pursues him, at one time disguised as a boy, while he woos Angelica Bianca, whom he eventually manages to bed. No sooner has this happened when he loses interest in her, while she is now painfully in love with him. She plans to kill him, but at the last moment is interrupted, and then finds herself unable to pull the trigger. Willmore marries the wealthy and virtuous Hellena, while Florinda, after a series of incidents, is united with Belville. Frederick marries Florinda's and Hellena's kinswoman Valeria, and the foolish Blunt, after being deceived and robbed by the prostitute Lucetta, remains unattached. The play takes place at carnival time, and there are colourful scenes of dancing and singing, wit and clowning. But the anguished character of Angelica Bianca adds a solemn note to the action, which also contains some ugly episodes, as when the enraged Blunt attempts to revenge himself for Lucetta's perfidy by raping Florinda. The other men join him, and only the appearance of Valeria saves her. The play achieved great success, and remained popular until late in the 18th century. It generated a sequel, *The Rover, Part II*, and some imitations, including ▷ John Kemble's *Love in Many Masks* (1790).

Rowe, Nicholas (1674–1718)

Poet and dramatist, known today chiefly for his so-called 'she-tragedies' in which the distresses of female victims are displayed, and for his edition of ▷ Shakespeare. Rowe was initially a barrister in the Middle Temple, but gave this up for the theatre when his father died leaving him an inheritance, in 1692. He became in due course a friend to ▷ Pope and ▷ Addison. Rowe's ▷ blank-verse tragedy, *The Ambitious Stepmother*, was staged successfully at Lincoln's Inn Fields in 1700, with ▷ Betterton, ▷ Barry and ▷ Bracegirdle in the cast. His *Tamerlane* (1702), a tragedy whose figures of Tamerlane and Bajazet were modelled on those of William III and Louis XIV, became a stock play. *The Fair Penitent* (1703), based on ▷ Massinger's *The Fatal Dowry* followed, to great acclaim. The heroine Calista, abandoned by the 'gallant, gay Lothario', and eventually committing suicide, drew enormous sympathy from audiences; she was played first by ▷ Elizabeth Barry and later by ▷ Sarah Siddons. The characters formed part of ▷ Richardson's inspiration in his writing of ▷ *Clarissa* (1747–8). Rowe's edition of Shakespeare (1709; reissued in 1714) is often considered the first attempt to edit Shakespeare in the modern sense, dividing the plays into acts and scenes according to fixed principles, marking actors' entrances and exits, clarifying the texts, and supplying lists of characters. ▷ *The Tragedy of Jane Shore* (1714), was written 'in Imitation of Shakespeare's Style', although as Odell and others have pointed out, many would barely discover Shakespeare among the lines. Both this and *The Tragedy of Lady Jane Grey* (1715), continued Rowe's tradition of suffering heroines. The former, like *Tamerlane* and *The Fair Penitent*, lasted into the 19th century, and all three became well-known in translation, in France. In 1715 Rowe became ▷ Poet Laureate.

Bib: Canfield, J. D., *Nicholas Rowe and Christian Tragedy*.

Rowley, William (1585–1637)

English actor and dramatist who collaborated with ▷ Thomas Middleton on several plays, including ▷ *The Changeling* to which he almost certainly contributed the subplot.

Roxana, or the Fortunate Mistress (1724)

A novel by ▷ Daniel Defoe presented as a fictional autobiography. 'Roxana', the daughter of French Protestant refugees, is deserted and left destitute by her first husband, and, with a taste for the finer things in life, sees prostitution as her only lucrative profession. A second marriage to a Dutch merchant leaves her widowed, but she climbs to a state of social importance by a series of increasingly grand affairs, one of which is hinted to be with the king. As in ▷ Defoe's ▷ *Moll Flanders*, the whore repents; but the penitence of Roxana is also ambiguous, and her thoughts are haunted by the illegitimate daughter whose death is on her conscience.

Royal Academy of Arts

Founded with the approval of King George III in 1768 'for the purpose of cultivating and improving the arts of painting, sculpture and architecture'. The first President (P.R.A.) was the portrait painter ▷ Sir Joshua Reynolds. Angelica Kauffmann was a founding member, although women were not permitted to study in the life classes. An elected council of 40 Royal Academicians are entitled to place R.A. after their names, and a further number of Associates bear the letters A.R.A. The Royal Academy runs schools of art to which women have been admitted since 1867 and holds an annual exhibition of about

1,000 works submitted to it and approved by it; the opening is an important social occasion. The Academy is further the manager of financial trusts on behalf of artists, and organizes exhibitions of foreign artists. Until the mid-19th century the Academy included distinguished artists amongst its number, such as the landscape painter, Turner, but for the last 100 years its policy has been conservative to the point of mediocrity, so that the livelier movements of English art have occurred without its patronage. Nonetheless, apart from the ▷ Royal Society, it is the only official institution in the arts to have achieved national prestige. It has occupied its present site, Burlington House, Piccadilly, London, since 1869.

Royal Court Theatre

A theatre of this name has existed in Sloane Square since 1871. The first outstanding period of its history was between 1904 and 1907 when, under the management of J. E. Vedrenne and ▷ Harvey Granville Barker, the work of new writers such as ▷ Shaw and ▷ Galsworthy was presented, as well as works by ▷ Euripides, ▷ Ibsen, ▷ Hauptmann and ▷ Maeterlinck. Since 1956, when ▷ John Osborne's ▷ *Look Back In Anger* was performed by George Devine's company, the English Stage Company, the theatre has consistently supported the work of new writers, helping to establish, amongst others, the reputations of John Osborne, ▷ John Arden, ▷ Edward Bond, ▷ Christopher Hampton, ▷ Caryl Churchill, Bill Gaskill, Peter Gill and Max Stafford-Clark.
Bib: Browne, T., *Playwright's Theatre*; MacCarthy, D., *The Court Theatre*; Roberts, P., *The Royal Court Theatre 1965–1972*.

Royal Martyr, The

▷ Charles I, so called by his supporters in consequence of his trial and execution by the revolutionary ▷ Parliament of 1649. Charles was devout, and the ▷ Civil Wars broke out for reasons which were partly and ostensibly religious; the victory of Parliament was also that of the ▷ Puritans, and entailed the temporary overthrow of the ▷ Church of England. Charles was consequently not only regarded as a martyr for the Anglican Church, but even by some as a saint, and a few churches exist dedicated to King Charles the Martyr.
The Royal Martyr is also the subtitle of a play otherwise called *Tyrannic Love* (1669) by ▷ John Dryden.

Royal Shakespeare Company

The resident company at the Royal Shakespeare Theatre (formerly the Memorial Theatre) in Stratford-upon-Avon since 1960. The first general director was ▷ Peter Hall who was replaced by Trevor Nunn in 1968. Recent directors for the company include Bill Alexander, John Barton, Terry Hands, Barry Kyle and Adrian Noble. Although the company mainly produces ▷ Shakespeare's plays, there is a policy of showing the work of his contemporaries and encouraging new modern writers. The company now has a second theatre in Stratford, The Swan, which contains a scaled-down imitation of an Elizabethan stage. It also has two theatres for large- and small-scale productions in the Barbican Centre in London.
Bib: Beauman, S., *The R.S.C., A History of Ten Decades*; Chambers, C., *Other Spaces: New Theatre and the R.S.C.*

Royal Society, The

Founded with the authority of ▷ Charles II in 1662; its full name was 'The Royal Society of London for Promoting Natural Knowledge'. It grew out of a philosophical society started in 1645 and was composed of 'divers worthy persons, inquisitive into natural philosophy and other parts of human learning, and particularly of what hath been called the New Philosophy or Experimental Philosophy', in other words, of men whose minds were moving in the way opened up by ▷ Francis Bacon. The Society took the whole field of knowledge for exploration; one of its aims was to encourage the virtue of intellectual lucidity in the writing of prose, and Thomas Sprat, writing the *History of the Royal Society* in 1667 defined the standards which writers were to emulate. The Royal Society was thus central in the culture of its time; it was promoted not only by scientists such as the chemist Boyle, but by poets – ▷ Cowley, ▷ Dryden, ▷ Waller – the biographer ▷ Aubrey, and the diarists ▷ Evelyn and ▷ Pepys. Since its foundation, the Society has become increasingly scientific; the title Fellow of the Royal Society is today much esteemed by scientists. Part of its functions is to advise the government on problems which require scientific elucidations. Its original meeting place was Gresham College, which since its foundation by Sir Thomas Gresham in 1597 had always served more practical branches of knowledge than the universities of Oxford and Cambridge; since 1857 it has been situated at Burlington House, premises which it shares with the ▷ Royal Academy.

R.S.C.
▷ Royal Shakespeare Company.

Rubaiyat of Omar Khayyam, The
Verses by Omar Khayyam, a Persian scholar
and poet who died in 1123. He was an
outstanding mathematician and astronomer,
but is still more famous for his verse epigrams
written in 'rubai', *ie* four lines the first,
second and fourth of which have the same
rhyme while the third is usually rhymeless.
The rubai had been invented for the
epitomizing of subtle thoughts on Islamic
belief, but Omar used them to satirize
religious bigotry with a free-thinking irony.
This has caused him to be referred to as 'the
Voltaire of the East'.

The English poet ▷ Edward FitzGerald
published a translation of the Rubaiyat in
1859 (75 verses); he enlarged this to 110
verses in a new edition in 1868, and issued
other versions (101 verses) in 1872 and 1879.
FitzGerald emphasizes the pleasure-loving
aspect of the Persian poet, and the poem was
extremely popular in ▷ Victorian England
both for its musicality and for its expression
of a liberated way of life which contrasted
with the narrow and bigoted codes of mid-
Victorian respectability. The poet ▷ Robert
Graves has published a new translation of
the Rubaiyat.

Rudkin, David (b 1936)
British dramatist whose first major play,
Afore Night Come (1962) explored mysterious
dark forces affecting apparently ordinary life
in the modern British countryside. This, and
later plays, have been performed by the
▷ Royal Shakespeare Company. For some
years Rudkin turned his back on the stage
and worked for television, his two best-known
plays during this time being *Children Playing*
(1967) and *Blodwen Home from Rachel's
Wedding* (1969). *Cries from Casement as His
Bones Are Brought to Dublin* (1973) and *Ashes*
(1975) marked his return to the stage with
dramatizations of events in Northern Ireland
(a subject often avoided by modern British
dramatists). Rudkin is clear about the political
purpose behind his work: 'I believe the
dramatist's function in a society to be to
transmute the idiosyncrasies of personal life
experience into metaphors of public, political
value to mankind.' Other plays include: *The
Sons of Light* (1977); *The Triumph of Death*
(1981); a translation of *Peer Gynt* (1983); *The
Saxon Shore* (1986).

Rugby School
One of the most famous of the English
▷ Public Schools. It was founded in 1567,
but its importance begins with the
headmastership of Thomas Arnold (father of
the poet and critic ▷ Matthew Arnold)
from 1828 to 1842. Hitherto, the ancient
Public Schools had imparted education
(chiefly in the Greek and Latin languages and
literatures) but without any consistent moral
instruction. Rugby became a pioneer of
'character-building', which came to be
regarded as the most typical quality of the
English 'public school tradition'. The virtues
were supposed to be those of physical and
moral discipline, leadership and fair-
mindedness. A large number of public schools
were founded in the second half of the 19th
century, and they were modelled on Arnold's
ideals. Since the large Empire of which
Britain was the centre required an extensive
class of administrators, these ideals were
eminently useful in producing them. A once
popular novel, *Tom Brown's Schooldays* (1857)
by Thomas Hughes, describes life at Rugby
under Arnold.

There is a tradition that the game of rugby
football was invented at Rugby in 1823.

*Ruined Cottage, The, or The Story of
    Margaret* (1814)
A poem in ▷ blank verse by ▷ William
Wordsworth, written in 1797, and included
in Book I of ▷ *The Excursion* (1814). It tells
the poignant story of a woman whose husband
is driven by grinding poverty to join the
army. He never returns, and eventually grief
and poverty take Margaret's life.
Contemplating her cottage, now derelict and
overgrown, the narrator is overcome by 'the
impotence of grief', and reflects on:

*That secret spirit of humanity
Which 'mid the calm oblivious tendencies
Of nature, 'mid her plants, and weeds, and
flowers,
And silent overgrowings, still survived.*

Rule Britannia (1740)
A patriotic poem by ▷ James Thomson,
occurring in the ▷ masque *Alfred* (1740) by
Thomson and ▷ David Mallet. The
universally known musical setting is by
Thomas Arne (1710–78).

Rumpelstiltzkin
One of ▷ Grimm's fairy tales, about a
dwarf who enables a girl to become a king's
bride by undertaking a number of impossible
tasks for her. In return she has to guess his
name. When she succeeds in this most
unlikely task of all through hearing him say
it, he tears himself in two with rage.

Runnymede

The place on the south bank of the Thames, where the Barons forced ▷ King John to accept ▷ Magna Carta in 1215.

Rupert, Prince (Count Palatine of the Rhine, and Duke of Bavaria) (1619–82)

Son of Frederick of the Palatinate and ▷ James I's daughter Elizabeth. Rupert was an able cavalry commander on the Royalist side in the ▷ Civil Wars, and after the ▷ Restoration, an enthusiastic supporter of the ▷ Royal Society.

Rural Rides (1820–30)

Reports of rural conditions by ▷ William Cobbett. He disapproved of certain remedies proposed by an official body to the Government for agricultural distress resulting from the Napoleonic War. He decided to make a number of tours on horseback in order to find out the facts for himself, and published his impressions in his journal, the ▷ *Political Register*, between 1820 and 1830, when they were collected into book form. The essays are in vivid, direct prose, full of acute comments, lively incident, and strong if prejudiced argument. They are early examples of direct journalistic reporting and are raised to permanent value as literature by the energy of Cobbett's conviction and the simplicity and vigour of his prose, which he had modelled on the writings of ▷ Jonathan Swift.
  ▷ Journalism.

Rushdie, Salman (b 1947)

Salman Rushdie

Indian novelist. Born in Bombay and educated at Cambridge University, he now lives in London. His second novel, *Midnight's Children* (1981) won the Booker Prize and became a best-seller. It is a voluminous work, ranging in time from World War I to 1977, and combining a realistic portrayal of poverty and suffering with magic, fantasy, farce, symbolism and ▷ allegory in a manner which associates it with ▷ magic realism. Its many narrative strategies compete with, and undermine, each other, and serve to question the relation of history to fiction; in this respect Rushdie is a ▷ post-modernist writer. In particular, narrative multiplicity functions in his work as a form of resistance to the unitary nature of ▷ Imperialist ideology and political control. He is an inventive, self-conscious and versatile writer, with a flamboyant style which at times verges on the self-indulgent. His other novels are: *Grimus* (1975); *Shame* (1983), and ▷ *The Satanic Verses* (1988) which aroused worldwide controversy and criticism from Muslims for its alleged blasphemy. Travel writing: *The Jaguar Smile: A Nicaraguan Journey* (1987).

Ruskin, John (1819–1900)

Writer on art and on its relationship with society. His central inspiration was that great art is moral and the corollary that the working men of industrial England were spiritually impoverished. Like the ▷ Pre-Raphaelites (he was a patron of ▷ D. G. Rossetti, their leader), he found the contrast to the England of his day in the freedom of individual response to environment among the medieval artists, and he expressed this view in the famous chapter called 'The Nature of Gothic' in *The Stones of Venice*. In the field of design, Ruskin, like ▷ William Morris, advocated a return to handicrafts and to medieval conditions of production.
  The latter part of his life was much concerned with attacks on the social philosophies of political economists, such as ▷ John Stuart Mill, to whom he did less than justice, and in endeavours to awaken the working classes to the nature of their combined artistic and moral impoverishment. He wrote his artistic books in a style of elaborate but precise and delicate eloquence but his social gospel had more concentrated and direct fervour. His puritanical mother (he was an only child) had given him a concentrated education in the Bible and though his religious views as an adult were not explicit, his conception of art as

fundamentally spiritual arose out of the intensity of his early religious training. Though a supporter of the Pre-Raphaelites, Ruskin did not lean like them towards 'art for art's sake' but towards 'art for the spiritual health of man'. In his campaign against the mediocre aspects of industrial culture, he was a disciple and admirer of ▷ Thomas Carlyle but he extended Carlyle's vision of greatness and has proved to be a writer of more permanent interest. Nonetheless, he wrote so voluminously that, like Carlyle, he is best read in selections.

His principal works are: *Modern Painters* (1843–60) in which he champions Turner, one of the greatest of English painters and at the time one of the most controversial; *The Seven Lamps of Architecture* (1849) leading to *The Stones of Venice* (1851–3) in which he makes his discovery of 'the Nature of Gothic'; this took him towards problems about the nature of civilized society in *The Political Economy of Art* (1857), *The Two Paths* (1859) and, one of his most famous books, ▷ *Unto This Last* (1862). *Sesame and Lilies* (1865), *Ethics of the Dust* (1866), *The Crown of Wild Olive* (1866) are essays in criticism on the age, and *Fors Clavigera* (1871–84) is composed of 96 letters to an educated artisan in which he shows himself distrustful of liberal democracy. *Praeterita* (1885–9) is one of the celebrated ▷ autobiographies in English, although it is fragmentary and incomplete. Its most famous section is the first, in which Ruskin describes his unusual, in some ways unnatural, yet fertilizing childhood.

▷ Gothic.

Bib: Selections by Quennell, P.; Clark, K.; Rosenberg, J. D.; Leon, D., *Life*; Evans, J., *Life*; Ladd, H., *The Victorian Morality of Art*; Rosenberg, J. D., *The Darkening Glass*; Wilenski, R. H., *John Ruskin*; Lippincott, B., *Victorian Critics of Democracy*.

Russell, Bertrand Arthur William, Lord (1872–1970)
Philosopher. He belonged to one of the aristocratic families elevated by the ▷ Tudors in the 16th century, which in large measure took over power from the English feudal aristocracy of the Middle Ages. Such families, by their control of ▷ Parliament, became effective rulers of the country in the 18th century; the 19th-century politician-novelist ▷ Disraeli called them a 'Venetian Oligarchy'; to the present day, they retain prestige and influence. Their importance raised them above fear and insecurity, and individual members have sometimes been ▷ radical in their social and

political thinking; an example is the Prime Minister Lord John Russell, Bertrand Russell's grandfather. Bertrand Russell was a founder member of the Campaign for Nuclear Disarmament (▷ C.N.D.).

Russell, Lucy, Countess of Bedford (d. 1627)
Together with ▷ Mary Herbert, Countess of Pembroke and ▷ Mary Wroth (Lady Wroth), Lucy, Countess of Bedford was one of the most important patrons of poetry in the early 17th century. Herself a poet, she was also the patron of ▷ Ben Jonson, ▷ George Chapman, ▷ Samuel Daniel and ▷ Michael Drayton. Perhaps the poet who benefitted most from her interest, however, was ▷ John Donne. Donne addressed seven of his verse letters (published in 1633) to the Countess, who had been godmother to Donne's second daughter, Elizabeth.

Bib: Byard, M. M., 'The Trade of Courtiership: The Countess of Bedford and the Bedford Memorials – A Family History from 1585 to 1607', *History Today* (January, 1979), pp. 20–28; Hannay, M. P., *Silent But for the Word: Tudor Women as Patrons, Translators, and Writers of Religious Works*.

Russian Formalism
▷ Formalism.

Russian influence on English literature
The international importance of Russian literature belongs chiefly to its achievements in the 19th century. Until the middle of the 19th century, the influence was chiefly from Britain upon Russia: ▷ Laurence Sterne, ▷ Walter Scott, ▷ Lord Byron and, later, ▷ Charles Dickens all made an important impression on Russian writers. Since about 1850, however, the balance of influence has been in the opposite direction, although Russian literature has chiefly been known in translation, which has limited extensive public knowledge to prose works, especially the novels. These have been widely read, especially in the famous translations by Constance Garnett, who translated ▷ Tolstoy, ▷ Dostoevski, ▷ Turgenev, ▷ Chekhov and ▷ Gogol in the decades before and after 1900.

Tolstoy and Turgenev were the first Russian novelists to receive wide acclaim in Britain and Tolstoy is still considered the supreme novelist. His reputation in Britain owed much to ▷ Matthew Arnold, whose essay in praise of Tolstoy appeared in 1887, and is included in ▷ *Essays in Criticism, Second Series*, 1888. His tribute is the more noticeable because he otherwise ignored novelists in his criticism, and it made its mark because he was the most influential critic of his day. However, other critics contributed their admiration for the Russians in the last quarter of the 19th century. This interest was awakened by the feeling that the Russians, besides the French, were the only nation to produce a range of major novelists comparable to those writing in English and that, unlike the French, they shared with the British and Americans a moral concern with human nature in society. There was also the feeling that the Russian novelists went beyond the British and Americans, excelling in their rendering of religious experience, though the full force of this was not felt until Constance Garnett produced her translation of Dostoevski's *Brothers Karamazov* in 1912.

In America, interest in Russian writing seems to have gone deeper, because of a feeling that these two great continental nations shared comparable experiences in the disorderly variety of their rapid growth. It was not merely this, however, that made the great Anglo-American novelist ▷ Henry James a lifelong admirer of Turgenev. Turgenev was already well known in England from the middle of the century when he became the friend of ▷ George Eliot. These two novelists were the predominant influences on James's own work. He admired both for the depth of their moral insights but he admired Turgenev for what he saw as his superior artistic strictness in handling the elusive novel form. Turgenev thus combined for James the virtues of the French novelists with those of the English novelist he most admired. Gilbert Phelps, in *The Russian Novel in English Fiction* (1956), traces Turgenev's influence in some of the detail of James's novels and suggests his further influence on ▷ George Gissing, ▷ George Moore, ▷ Arnold Bennett, ▷ John Galsworthy and ▷ Joseph Conrad. Conrad is the most doubtful instance of these writers showing the Russian influence; as a Pole, he felt antagonistic to Russia and he did not know Russian, and yet it is impossible not to think of both Turgenev and Dostoevski when reading ▷ *Under Western Eyes*.

Chekhov's influence on the short story and on the drama seems evident, although it may be that the distinctive development of the ▷ short story in English (for instance in ▷ James Joyce's ▷ *Dubliners* and in

▷ Katherine Mansfield) is as much an example of parallel development in the form as owing to Chekhov's initiation. In the drama, Chekhov's original handling of human speech as a medium has been developed in the works of ▷ Samuel Beckett and ▷ Harold Pinter.

The prestige of Russian literature in the mid-20th century remains very high in Britain, especially Boris Pasternak's *Doctor Zhivago* (1957) and the works of Alexander Solzhenitsyn. What is admired is the rendering of human experience and suffering on an heroic scale, and the courage and vitality of literary productivity in the face of adverse and repressive conditions. Recently, however, with the more liberal regime in Russia, more, possibly dissident, literature has become available to the west.

Ruth
1 A book of the Old Testament of the ▷ Bible which tells how Ruth began by gleaning corn in the fields of the rich landowner, Boaz, and eventually married him, thus becoming the ancestress of ▷ King David.
2 The title of a novel by ▷ Elizabeth Gaskell. Her *Ruth* (1853) is based, like her more successful ▷ *Cranford*, on the small town of Knutsford.
3 The title of a poem by ▷ Wordsworth in the ▷ *Lyrical Ballads* (1800).

Rutherford, Mark
▷ White, William Hale.

Rye House plot (1683)
A plot led by the ▷ 1st Earl of Shaftesbury, the leader of the ▷ Whig Party, to kidnap ▷ Charles II and force him to summon a parliament. The plot was discovered, and the consequent discredit of the Whigs, together with Charles II's popularity, caused a public reaction against them, and enabled ▷ James II to succeed peacefully in 1685, in spite of his open Roman Catholicism.

Rymer, Thomas (1641–1713)
A rigidly neo-classical critic, chiefly known for his obtuse though witty and amusing *Short View of Tragedy* (1692) in which he condemned ▷ Shakespeare's tragedy ▷ *Othello* for a barbaric failure to observe the classical ▷ unities.

S

Sabines
A tribe of central Italy, noted for their frugality and hardihood, contemporary with the ancient Roman Republic. In legend, they made war on the Romans, who took revenge by carrying off the Sabine women.

Sackville, Thomas, 1st Earl of Dorset (1536–1608)
Poet, statesman, diplomat; created 1st Earl of Dorset in 1604. He contributed the *Induction* and the *Complaint of Buckingham* in the verse compilation ▷ *Mirror for Magistrates*; the *Induction* is the main basis for his fame as a poet. He also collaborated with Thomas Norton in writing the first ▷ tragedy in ▷ blank verse, ▷ *Gorboduc*.
Bib: Berlin, N., *Thomas Sackville*.

Sade, Donatien Alphonse, Marquis de (1740–1814)
French novelist and poet. His belief that his destructive impulses were part of his nature, and yet uncontrollable, counterbalanced the doctrine of ▷ Rousseau, according to whom man undistorted by social forces was naturally good. Sade's ideas profoundly influenced the dark side of ▷ romanticism but, with the exception of ▷ Swinburne, were less pervasive in England. Sade has recently received renewed attention in France (*eg* ▷ Roland Barthes, *Sade, Fourier, Loyola*; 1971), where he has fed into a ▷ Nietzschean strain of literary and theoretical thinking.

Sadler's Wells
Originally a health resort in north London, on account of its mineral spring. A theatre was built there in the 18th century, and in the 19th century this became – like the ▷ Old Vic in south London – famous for its productions of Shakespeare. Since 1931 it has been used principally for ballet and ▷ opera. Both theatres are in unfashionable parts of London, and their policy of appealing to poorer and less educated people caused them to become the starting-point for a ▷ National Theatre.

Saga
An old Norse word meaning 'oral story'. The sagas were a body of Norwegian and Icelandic prose epics (11th–13th centuries).

Saintsbury, George Edward Bateman (1845–1933)
Literary historian and critic. His works include: *A Short History of French Literature* (1882); *A Short History of English Literature* (1898); *A History of Criticism* (1900–4); *A History of English Prosody* (1906–21); *The History of English Criticism* (1911); *A History of the French Novel* (1917–19). He also wrote studies of ▷ Dryden, ▷ Walter Scott, and ▷ Matthew Arnold. His treatment of literary study was historical; that is to say, principles of evaluation or critical theory were for him secondary to coherent narration.

Saladin (1138–93)
Sultan of Egypt. His conquest of the Christian Latin Kingdom of Jerusalem (1187) provoked the Third Crusade under ▷ Richard I of England and Philip II of France, with whom he made a truce. He was famous for his fierce piety compounded with chivalrous generosity; in English history and legend these qualities are made to represent him as a suitable antagonist to Richard, himself a legend for his courage and chivalry. Their rivalry is the subject of ▷ Scott's novel *The Talisman* (1825). Historically, Saladin is important for halting the invasion of the East by the Christian West, and starting a counter-movement against the West which lasted until the 17th century.
▷ Crusades.

Salic Law
A body of early French laws which include a prohibition against women inheriting property and attacked on this account by contemporary women writers. This prohibition was once supposed to be the ground for disallowing the claims of English kings (from ▷ Edward III in the 14th century onwards) to have inherited the French throne through the female line; hence in the first act of Shakespeare's play ▷ *Henry V*, the Archbishop of Canterbury is made to refute the validity of the Salic Law at some length. Historically, however, the Salic Law seems not to have been invoked against the English claim.

Sally Lunn
A kind of sweet bun, apparently called after a young woman who sold them in Bath in the late 18th century.

Salome
1 In the New Testament of the Bible, one of the women present at the crucifixion of Christ (*Mark* 15:40) and afterwards at the tomb (*Mark* 16:1).
2 The woman who danced before Herod and afterwards demanded the head of John the Baptist (*Matthew* 14:6–8 and *Mark* 6:17–25) is referred to as the 'daughter of Herodias' – another Salome. The latter was the subject of a drama by ▷ Oscar Wilde – *Salome* (1893).

Salvation Army

Founded in the slums of the East End of London as the Christian Mission by William Booth in 1865; the organization took its present name in 1880, and was organized like an army, with military ranks. Its success in penetrating the most deprived areas of the big English cities caused it to spread widely throughout Britain and to other countries. Its meetings often take place in the open air to the accompaniment of brass bands, and the Army provides hostels for the destitute. The idiom and glamour of the Army had a strong appeal to the slum-dwellers of the big London boroughs, and influenced even the most brutalized of that population to an extent that excelled every other organization. In many ways its influence was parallel to that of the ▷ Methodists of the 18th century.

▷ George Bernard Shaw's play *Major Barbara* (1905) analyses the virtues and limitations of the Salvation Army approach to the problem of poverty, by comparison with the organization of material welfare by the 'social conscience'.

Samson Agonistes (1671)

A ▷ tragedy in ▷ blank verse by ▷ John Milton, published (with ▷ *Paradise Regained*) in 1671. It is an example of Milton's blended ▷ Puritan-biblical and ▷ Renaissance-classical inspiration: the subject is drawn from the Old Testament (*Judges* 16) and the form from the ancient Greek tragedies of ▷ Aeschylus and ▷ Sophocles.

Samson, the Jewish hero, has been betrayed by his Philistine wife, Dalila (spelt ▷ Delilah in the Authorized Version of the ▷ Bible, where she is not his wife) to her people, who are the foes of the Jews. His hair, on which depended his exceptional, God-given strength, has been cut off; he has been blinded, and cast into prison in Gaza; here his hair is allowed to recover its former length and he is subjected to slavery by his enemies. The play opens while he is resting from his enormous labours and he is approached by a chorus of lamenting Jews. In his mood of extreme despair, he is visited by his father Manoa, who hopes to negotiate his release from the Philistines; Samson, however has the moral strength to refuse Manoa's suggestions, on the grounds that his lot is a consequence of his own moral weakness in betraying the secret of his strength to his wife. His next visitor is Dalila herself, who seeks his forgiveness in return for alleviation of his sufferings; he replies, however, that if he cannot pardon himself, her crime is still more unpardonable. This double moral victory heartens him enough to enable him to frighten away his third visitor, the Philistine giant Harapha, who comes to mock at him. Next a messenger arrives with an order that he is to come before the Philistine lords in order to entertain them with feats of his strength. To the dismay of the chorus, he accepts the order, but we learn from a messenger that it is only to destroy the entire assembly (including himself) by rooting up the two pillars which support the roof of the building. The chorus is left to chant praise of the hero and of the wisdom of God, who sustains his people.

It has long been assumed that *Samson Agonistes* was written after Milton had finished *Paradise Lost* (*ie* between 1667 and 1671). This traditional dating reinforces the connection between the blind and defeated hero of the work, and the blind and (ideologically) defeated figure of Milton after the ▷ Restoration. However, strong reasons have now been advanced for dating Milton's drama to a much earlier period of his career, between 1647 and 1653. The two principle themes of modern criticism of the work have centred on the question of 'structure' (▷ Samuel Johnson initiated the debate by claiming that the play has a beginning, an end, but no middle), and the question of whether the guiding spirit of the play is 'Hellenic', 'Hebraic' or 'Christian'. In essence, both of these questions address a problem that *Samson Agonistes* has long posed to readers – that interpretation of the work rests on locating it in relation to other texts (Greek ▷ tragedy or the ▷ Old Testament, for example) and to a specific historical moment.

Samuel

In the Old Testament of the ▷ Bible, an early prophet, after whom are named the two books which cover the history of Israel to the death of ▷ David, the second king of the Jews. Samuel heard the voice of God calling him while he was a young child in the temple, and he was dedicated to the priesthood from then on. He became the ruler of the Jews as a national leader against the Philistines, and appointed the first king of Israel, ▷ Saul, who was later replaced by David.

Sand, George (1804–76)

Pseudonym of Amandine-Aurore Lucille Dupin, baronne Dudevant, she was born in Paris and brought up at her paternal grandmother's country property at Nohant (later hers), following the death of her father, in an atmosphere of quarrels between her mother and grandmother. After a convent education in Paris, she ran wild again at Nohant, reading avidly ▷ Rousseau, ▷ Byron, ▷ Shakespeare and Chateaubriand among others. She married the baron Dudevant, a retired army officer, and had two children, but by 1831 was living an independent life in Paris, writing to earn her living. Her work reflected the men and ideas in her personal life, and her catholic enthusiasm for humanitarianism, Christian socialism, Republicanism, etc. She also wrote idealized romances of rustic life, set around Nohant. *Indiana* (1832) was the first of many successes and was followed by *Valentine* (1832), *Lélia* (1833), *Jacques* (1834) and *Mauprat* (1837). These championed the rights of women to follow their desires and ignore convention. *Spiridion* (1839) and others reflect her ideas, and the country tales include *La Mare au Diable* (1846) and *La Petite Fadette* (1848). Her relationship with the poet Alfred de Musset is fictionalized in *Elle et lui* (1859) and incidents in her nine-year liaison with the composer Chopin are portrayed in *Un hiver à Majorque* (1841). She also wrote some political articles, biographical and critical essays, unsuccessful drama and an autobiography in four volumes, *Histoire de ma vie* (1854–5).

Sandhurst

The popular name for the Royal Military Academy, founded in 1802 as the Royal Military College, for the training of officers for the British Army. The small town of Sandhurst in Berkshire, to which the College moved in 1813, gave its name to the establishment.

Sanger, John (1816–89)

The founder of the most famous of the British travelling circuses. He began with a conjuring exhibition in Birmingham in 1845, and reached the height of his fame as a circus proprietor in the 1870s and 80s. In his later years he was known as Lord John Sanger, though he never received a peerage.

Sangreal

A name for the Holy ▷ Grail.

Sansculottes

The name for recruits from the poorer classes to the ▷ French Revolutionary army. The word means 'without breeches' – knee-breeches being then the wear of all but the poorest. The sansculottes wore loose trousers or 'pantalon'.

Sansom, William (1912–76)

Short-story writer, novelist and travel writer. He served in the London Fire Brigade in World War II, an experience which gave rise to *Fireman Flower* (1944), a volume of short stories, which was the form in which he was most successful. His work covers a wide range of subject matter and styles, from documentary realism to macabre fantasy. In *The Body* (1949) the mental stability of the first-person narrator gradually disintegrates as a result of obsessive jealousy.
Bib: Michel-Michot, P., *Sansom: A Critical Assessment.*

Sappho of Lesbos

Greek woman poet of the 6th century BC. The fragments that have survived are famous for their passion and simplicity. The term 'lesbian', for homosexual love among women, derived from her passionate poems referring to her women friends. The poet, Katherine Philips (1631–64) was known as the 'English Sappho' partly because of the many poems she addressed to women.

Saracens

A term used, chiefly in the ▷ Middle Ages, for the Muslim Arabs against whom the ▷ Crusades were waged. Its origin is obscure, but the ancient Greeks and Romans used 'Saraceni' as a name for nomadic Arabs.

Sardanapalus (7th century BC)

In Greek legend, the last king of Assyria, famous for his luxury and effeminacy. He threw off his self-indulgence to defeat formidable rebels in a succession of battles. Eventually he had to face total defeat, and burnt up his wives and himself in his palace. This (with variations) is the subject of ▷ Byron's tragedy *Sardanapalus* (1821).

Sargasso Sea

A region of the North Atlantic, covered by floating seaweed from which it is named. It was once believed that ships could be embedded in the weed and immobilized.

Sargeson, Frank (b 1903)

New Zealand novelist, short-story writer and dramatist. His stories tend to deal with a small group of characters and to be narrated from within the consciousness of one of them, often a character with limited powers of self-expression, like the narrator of ▷ novella *That Summer* (1946). His novels are more various in tone, but render the sense of a claustrophobic and somewhat Puritan New Zealand society by means of irony, comedy and a skilful rendering of idiom. His novels are: *I Saw In My Dream* (1949); *I For*

One . . . (1954); *Memoirs of a Peon* (1965);
The Hangover (1967); *Joy of the Worm* (1969);
Sunset Village (1976). Story collection:
Collected Short Stories (1965).
Bib: Copland, R. A., *Frank Sargeson*.

Sarmatia

In ancient Roman geography, the name of a
region of eastern Europe, extending from the
River Vistula to the River Volga. In English
poetry it is used as a name for Poland.

Sartor Resartus: The Life and Opinions of Herr Teufelsdröckh

A disguised spiritual ▷ autobiography by
▷ Thomas Carlyle. It was serialized
(1833–4) in *Fraser's Magazine* and published
in book form in Boston, U.S.A., in 1836 and
in Britain in 1838. Carlyle was under the
influence of the ▷ German romantics, *eg*
Jean Paul Richter. The title is Latin for 'the
tailor re-patched': Carlyle offers the fable that
human beliefs and institutions are like clothes
and need renewing. Against ▷ Byron's
attitude of doubt, isolation and suffering,
Carlyle calls for the affirmativeness of the
German poet ▷ Goethe; heroic qualities
such as sacrifice and devotion to duty must
redeem the inner man and, through men, the
directionless age in which Carlyle felt himself
to be living – the age of flux and the decay of
unquestioning religious faith. Besides the
drive of German influence, Carlyle felt the
force of the old-fashioned Scottish Calvinism
such as had animated his father. The three
crucial chapters are 'The Everlasting No',
'Centre of Indifference' and 'The Everlasting
Yea'. Despite the difficulty he had in getting
the book published in Britain, it marks the
beginning of his exposition of the creed of
heroism, which made Carlyle an inspiring
figure in commerce-dominated mid-19th-
century Britain.

Sartre, Jean-Paul (1905–80)

French writer. His areas of activity and
influence covered philosophy, the novel,
drama, literary criticism and political
commitment. He was the major exponent of
atheistic ▷ Existentialism in France and
made an early impact with his novels *La
Nausée* (1938) and *Les Chemins de la liberté*, a
projected tetralogy of which only three
volumes were published: *L'Age de raison*
(1945), *Le Sursis* (1945) and *La Mort dans
l'âme* (1949). In *La Nausée*, the central
character, Roquentin, discovers that far from
being central to the nature of things, man is
metaphysically superfluous (*de trop*) in the
universe. *Les Chemins de la liberté* are set at
the outbreak of World War II and portray

the urgent necessity of commitment,
especially in the form of political action, to
secure personal and collective freedom. The
same themes run through Sartre's drama,
which is more accessible than the fiction and
has proved more enduringly popular (*Les
Mouches*, 1943, a version of the ▷ Orestes
story; *Huis Clos*, 1945; *Les Mains sales*, 1948).
The philosophical background to
Existentialism was expounded in *L'Etre et le
néant* (1943) and *Critique de la raison
dialectique* (1960).

Satre also wrote a number of Existentialist-
orientated biographies, of ▷ Baudelaire, of
Jean Genet (1910–86) and of ▷ Flaubert.
His volumes of *Situations* contain mainly
essays on politics, literature and society and
in 1945 he founded the important literary and
political review, *Les Temps modernes*. In 1964
he published his autobiography, *Les Mots*,
which seeks to expose the ideology of the
autobiographical genre and views with irony
his years of childhood under his grandfather
Charles Schweitzer (Sartre was the cousin of
Albert Schweitzer (1875–1965)). In the same
year, Sartre was awarded and refused the
Nobel Prize for Literature.

Sassenach

A Gaelic word, used by Gaelic-speaking
Irishmen and Scottish highlanders for
Germanic (▷ Saxon) inhabitants of
Britain.

Sassoon, Siegfried (1886–1967)

Poet and autobiographer. His *Memoirs of a
Foxhunting Man* (1928) and *Memoirs of an
Infantry Officer* (1930) are accounts of his life
as a country gentleman before World War I,
and of his experiences during it. He also
became famous for his savagely satirical
poems written during his military service, his
first and most famous volume of anti-war
poems being *Counter-attack* (1918). He was a
friend of ▷ Wilfred Owen, and influenced
Owen's writing. The two volumes of memoirs
were put together as *The Complete Memoirs of
George Sherston* (1937), which includes an
addition section, *Sherston's Progress*. His
poems, including volumes published since
World War I, are in a collected edition
(1961).
    ▷ War Poets.

Satan

A Hebrew word meaning 'adversary'; in the
Christian tradition, one of the habitual names
for the Devil. In ▷ *Job* (Old Testament), an
older tradition is evident in I:6–12 and II:1–
6. Satan is a servant of God, and his special

function is to test the virtue of men by trials and suffering.
▷ Lucifer.

Satanic Verses, The (1988)

Novel by ▷ Salman Rushdie which received mixed reviews on its publication in 1988. Controversy erupted when Muslims protested that the book was blasphemous. Copies were burned in Bradford and demonstrations took place there and elsewhere in Britain, Pakistan and the U.S.A. In Iran mass demonstrations against the author, book and publisher caused international tension to rise. The Ayatollah Khomeni passed a death sentence on Rushdie, who went into hiding. The novel returned to the ▷ best-seller lists in the wake of the controversy, which raised many issues of freedom of speech and expression, and the freedom to publish.

Satire

A satirical playing card

A form of attack through mockery; it may exist in any literary medium, but is often regarded as a medium in itself. The origins of the word help to explain the manifestations of satire. It derives from the Latin 'satura' = a vessel filled with the earliest agricultural produce of the year, used in seasonal festivals to celebrate harvest; a secondary meaning is 'miscellany of entertainment', implying merry-making at such festivals, probably including verbal warfare. This primitive humour gave rise to a highly cultivated form of literary attack in the poetry of ▷ Horace, Persius (1st century AD) and ▷ Juvenal. Thus from ancient Roman culture two ideas of satire have come down to us: the first expresses a basic instinct for comedy through mockery in human beings, and was not invented by the Romans; the second is a self-conscious medium, implying standards of civilized and moral rightness in the mind of the poet and hence a desire on his or her part to instruct readers so as to reform their moral failings and absurdities. The two kinds of satire are inter-related, so that it is not possible to distinguish them sharply. Moreover, it is not easy to distinguish strict satire in either of its original forms from other kinds of comedy.

1 Strict satire, *ie* satire emulating the Roman poets. This was one of the outcomes of ▷ Renaissance cultivation of ancient Latin literature. Between 1590 and 1625 several poets wrote deliberate satires with Juvenal, Persius and Horace in mind; the most important of these were ▷ Donne and ▷ Ben Jonson, but ▷ Joseph Hall claimed to be the first, and another was ▷ Marston. The great age of the strict satire was the 18th century, notably in the work of ▷ Pope who emulated the relatively genial satire of Horace, and ▷ Samuel Johnson, who emulated the sombre style of Juvenal. Satire of this sort makes its object of attack the social forms and corruptions of the time, and its distinctive medium is the 10-syllable rhymed couplet, perfected by Pope and used with different force by Johnson.

2 ▷ Comedy of Humours and ▷ Comedy of Manners. These are the most easily distinguishable forms of dramatic satire. The former is associated chiefly with Ben Jonson, and has its roots in the older ▷ Morality drama, which was only intermittently satirical. The 'humours' in Jonson's conception are the obsessions and manias to which the nature of human beings invites them to abandon themselves; they have a close relation to the medieval ▷ Seven Deadly Sins, such as lust, avarice and gluttony. The Comedy of Manners belongs to the period 1660–1800, and, especially, to the first 40 years of it. Its most notable exponents are ▷ Congreve at the end of the 17th century and ▷ Sheridan at the end of the 18th. This comedy is less concerned with basic human dispositions and

more with transient social ones; rational social behaviour is the standard in the mind of the dramatist. Both these forms of satire were taken over by novelists; the 18th-century novelist ▷ Fielding began as a writer of dramatic comedies of manners, but Dickens in the 19th century writes more distinctly in the tradition of the comedy of humours, with a strong addition of social stagnation. Satire in the theatre has, since the 1960s, been replaced by television satire, with radical programmes such as *Beyond the Fringe* and more recently, *Spitting Image*.

3 Satire of ▷ Parody and ▷ Irony. This includes the most skillful and powerful satire in the language; its most productive period is between 1660 and 1750. Parody at its most powerful implies the writer's complete respect for the serious form which he is using in a comic way; thus in this period (which included the very serious ▷ epic ▷ *Paradise Lost*) the prestige of the epic form was still high, and ▷ Dryden (▷ *Absalom and Achitophel*) and ▷ Pope (▷ *The Rape of the Lock* and ▷ *The Dunciad*) used their appreciation of epic to make ironic contrast between the grandeur of its style and the pettiness, meanness and destructiveness of their chosen subject. Similarly ▷ Samuel Butler used the mode of romantic epic to attack the ▷ Puritans in ▷ *Hudibras*.

Irony does not necessarily use parody, but even when it does not, it operates in a similar way, by addressing the reader in terms which he has learnt to receive as acceptable at their face value, and then shocking him into recognition that something quite unacceptable is the real subject.

4 ▷ Flytings, and other traditional forms. The ▷ Middle Ages took from its popular festivals a strong tradition of verbal combat (flytings) and sardonic criticism of the established social order. One aspect of this emerges in popular ▷ ballads (especially in the printed form of broadsides which developed after the medieval period) and in the work of educated writers such as ▷ Langland and ▷ Chaucer – grimly in the former's ▷ *Piers Plowman*, and genially in the latter's ▷ *Canterbury Tales*. Dunbar was another eminent practitioner of flytings, *eg* his *Flyting of Dunbar and Kennedy*.

5 Novelistic satire. Much satire in novels from the 18th to the 20th century cannot be summed up under comedy of manners. The novels of ▷ Peacock, for example, establish a tradition of comic discussions mocking at contemporary trends of thought; Peacock's example was partly followed by

▷ Meredith and ▷ Aldous Huxley. Another variant is the 'anti-utopia', using an imaginary country to satirize actual tendencies in contemporary Britain. The most notable examples of this are ▷ *Erewhon* by ▷ Samuel Butler and *Brave New World* by ▷ Aldous Huxley. Apart from these examples, it is difficult to find a novelist who does not use satire at least intermittently, usually as social comment. Eminent examples are: Fielding, ▷ Jane Austen, ▷ Thackeray, ▷ Dickens, ▷ Wells, ▷ Forster, and more recently ▷ Angus Wilson, ▷ Evelyn Waugh, ▷ George Orwell, and the 'campus novels' of ▷ Kingsley Amis and ▷ David Lodge.

Saturday Review
It was founded in 1855 and noted for the brilliance of its contributors and the severity of its criticism. Later it took a greater interest in literature and included contributions from ▷ Thomas Hardy, ▷ Max Beerbohm, Arthur Symons and ▷ H. G. Wells. ▷ George Bernard Shaw was dramatic critic from 1895 to 1898 and Agate from 1921 to 1923.

Saturn
▷ Classical Myth.

Satyr
A woodland nature spirit or minor deity in Greek myth; the satyrs were companions of the wine god ▷ Dionysus (Bacchus). They had goatlike legs, horns and ears.

Saussure, Ferdinand de (1857–1913)
Swiss linguist, generally regarded as the founder of ▷ Structuralism. Saussure's *Course in General Linguistics*, was published two years after his death, in 1915, and represents a reconstruction of three series of lectures which he gave at the University of Geneva during the years 1906–7, 1908–9, and 1910–11. It was Saussure who pioneered the distinction between ▷ 'langue' and ▷ 'parole', and who sought to define the operations of language according to the principles of combination and ▷ difference. Although ▷ deconstruction has done much to undermine the Structuralist base of Saussure's thinking, the concept of 'difference' as a determining principle in establishing meaning ('signification') remains one of the key concepts in modern critical theory. Moreover, Saussure's work provided the foundation for the methodological analysis of ▷ sign systems (▷ semiotics), and the types of linguistic investigation which he undertook have been successfully appropriated by literary critics, as well as by

social anthropologists such as Claude Lévi-Strauss (b 1908).

Savage, Richard (1697?–1743)

Poet. Savage claimed to be the illegitimate son of the Countess of Macclesfield, and spent his life in petulant complaint against her, and in cultivating wealthy patrons. He was accused of being ▷ Alexander Pope's spy at the time of the composition of ▷ *The Dunciad*, and after his death was the subject of an intimate biography by ▷ Samuel Johnson. His monologue in heroic ▷ couplets, *The Bastard* (1728) dramatizes his situation following the death sentence passed on him after he had killed a man in a brawl. It contains some vigorous lines:

Blest be the Bastard's *birth!* . . .
No sickly fruit of faint compliance he;
He! stampt in nature's mint of extasy!
He lives to build, not boast, a gen'rous race:
No tenth transmitter of a foolish face.

On the intervention of his friends he was pardoned and a long poem, *The Wanderer*, appeared in 1729. Savage also wrote satirical poems in couplets, including *The Progress of a Divine* (1735).

Savonarola, Fra Girolamo (1452–98)

In Italian history, a Florentine monk who led a revolt against the worldly excesses of the ▷ Renaissance. His own reforms went to excess, and he was eventually condemned and executed as a heretic. George Eliot's novel ▷ *Romula* deals with his period of power.

Savoy

A 13th-century London palace, between the Strand and the river. It was burnt down in the ▷ Peasants' Rebellion and replaced, in ▷ Henry VIII's time, by a hospital. The site is now occupied by a famous hotel and restaurant and by the Savoy Theatre. Here the ▷ Gilbert and Sullivan operas were produced from 1882 on, and were therefore called the Savoy Operas. The royal chapel of the Savoy, built by ▷ Henry VII, is still in use.

Saxons

The name of a Germanic people which invaded southern Britain from their homeland around the mouth of the Elbe in the 5th and 6th centuries, after the departure of the Roman occupying forces. They eventually shared what came to be known as England (Angle-land) with the Angles and the Jutes. Their principal kingdom was Wessex (*ie* West Saxons) in the south-west. Other Saxon kingdoms are commemorated in the names of modern English counties: Sussex (South Saxons); Middlesex (Middle Saxons, in London and to the immediate north of it); and Essex (East Saxons). ▷ Wessex itself has disappeared as a geographical name, except in the novels of ▷ Thomas Hardy.
▷ Anglo-Saxon.

Sayers, Dorothy L. (Leigh) (1893–1957)

▷ Detective fiction.

Scenes of Clerical Life (1857)

Three tales by ▷ George Eliot, and her earliest work in fiction: *The Sad Fortunes of the Rev. Amos Barton*; *Mr Gilfil's Love-Story*; and *Janet's Repentance*. The hero of each is a clergyman. They were published first in ▷ *Blackwood's Magazine* in 1857 and collected as *Scenes of Clerical Life* in 1858.

Schism, The Great

The state of division in the Western Church owing to the election of rival Popes. The Schism was ended by the Council of Constance in 1417, though it was not properly healed until 1448. The papacy had been forcibly transferred from Rome to Avignon in 1305, but in 1378 the Italians elected their own Pope in Rome. He was supported by Germany and England, while the French Pope was supported by Spain as well as by France.

Scholar Gipsy, The

A poem by ▷ Matthew Arnold, first published in 1853. He took the subject from a legend reported by Joseph Glanvill in *The Vanity of Dogmatizing* (1661). The Scholar of the legend renounced the anxiety of seeking a career through his scholarship, and took to wandering with the ▷ gipsies, dedicating himself to learning their lore. Arnold regards him as an immortal figure, and uses him as the type of a man who has happily escaped the anguish of the 19th-century intellectual's loss of faith and controlling convictions. The poem is not always considered to be Arnold's best, but it is one of his most famous, since it expresses the distress and doubt that is widely evident in mid-Victorian writing. It is written in 25 10-line ▷ stanzas resembling those of ▷ Keats's ▷ Odes. It is like the Odes too in its sensuous evocation of natural surroundings, though Arnold's tone is often nostalgic and insular. In 1867 Arnold published a companion-piece to *The Scholar Gipsy* entitled *Thyrsis*, an elegy to his friend ▷ Clough who died in 1861.

Scholasticism

A term covering a variety of philosophical and theological forms of thought, dominant in the Western Church between 1100 and 1500. The name derives from the episcopal schools (*ie* schools under bishops) first set up under the French emperor Charlemagne in the 8th century; followers of the philosophy taught in these schools were called 'schoolmen'. Their aim was to reconcile the logic of ancient Greek philosophy (especially ▷ Aristotle) with the teachings of the Christian faith; thus human reason was not conceived as being able to operate independently of theology, which explains the contempt into which scholasticism fell during the ▷ Renaissance. The first of the major scholastics was the 9th-century Irish philosopher, Scotus Erigena, who found Christian theology perfectly in keeping with thought in the tradition of ▷ Plato, but ▷ St Thomas Aquinas preferred the tradition of Aristotle. His contemporary, ▷ Duns Scotus, however, began a process of challenging the possibility of achieving perfect harmony between faith and reason, and the 14th-century William of Occam (▷ Ockham) carried the process further. This began the decay of scholastic philosophy; one of the characteristics of the Renaissance was to liberate philosophy from its status as 'the handmaid of theology'. At the same time interest in the philosophy of Plato greatly revived, but now for its own sake.

School for Scandal, The

A comedy by ▷ Richard Brinsley Sheridan, first produced in 1777. Two of the central characters are brothers: Charles Surface, whose character is open-hearted but reckless and extravagant, and Joseph Surface, a mean-hearted hypocrite. The principal women are Lady Teazle, the young, gay wife of the elderly Sir Peter Teazle, and Maria, his ward, with whom Charles is in love and whom Joseph is trying to marry for her money, while he also makes love to Lady Teazle. Sir Oliver Surface, rich uncle to the two brothers, returns from India in disguise in order to spy on his nephews, thereby to discover their true characters. In the background, a group of scandal-lovers (Lady Sneerwell, Mrs Candour, Sir Benjamin Backbite) do their worst to damage as many reputations as possible. Sir Oliver satisfies himself, in scenes of extremely successful theatrical comedy, about which of his nephews truly deserves his affection: Charles marries Maria, and the deceitfulness of Joseph is exposed.

The comedy is Sheridan's masterpiece, and the last notable play in the tradition of the English ▷ Comedy of Manners until ▷ Oscar Wilde at the end of the 19th century.

School of Night

A term used to designate a circle of intellectuals which centred on ▷ Sir Walter Ralegh in the early 1590s. It derives from ▷ Shakespeare's play ▷ *Love's Labour's Lost* (IV. 3. 251–2). The courtier Berowne has just been praising the lady Rosaline who has a dark complexion: 'No face is fair that is not full so black', whereupon the king breaks in –

> *O paradox! Black is the badge of hell,*
> *The hue of dungeons and the School of*
> *Night.*

'School of Night' has puzzled editors, who have variously emended it to 'scowl' and 'stole'. Some modern scholars, however (see especially the Cambridge Shakespeare edition, and M. C. Bradbrook's *The School of Night*), consider that Shakespeare was alluding to Ralegh's dark complexion and to the reputation of himself and his circle for atheism. At about the time the play was written (1594–5), Ralegh, in disgrace at court, had retired to his country house and declared his preference for a life of study over the active and public life. The rival claims of the studious and retired and the active and public life is the theme of *Love's Labour Lost*.

Ralegh's circle seems to have consisted of himself, the famous mathematician Thomas Harriot, the poets ▷ Christopher Marlowe and ▷ George Chapman, the Earls of Northumberland and Derby, and a few others. Marlowe and Harriot shared Ralegh's atheistic reputation, Chapman had highly developed philosophical interests, and Northumberland and Derby had esoteric interests in ▷ alchemy.

Schools in England

The following is an alphabetical list of most kinds of school mentioned in English literature.

Almonry schools. One of the forms of grammar schools (see below) in the ▷ Middle Ages; they were usually attached to ▷ monasteries, and the boys followed the rules of monastic life.

Board schools. These got their names from the School Boards, *ie* committees responsible for education in a neighbourhood, set up by the Education Act of 1870, which provided for universal elementary education to the age of 11. The boards were abolished by the Education Act of 1902 and were replaced by the usual local authorities (County Councils, etc.).

Boarding schools. Schools where the pupils live during their terms of study, as opposed to Day schools from which they return each evening.

Charity schools. Set up in the 18th century for children (of both sexes) of the very poor. The schools were endowed or maintained by the churches, and gave only elementary education. They were widespread but their distribution was uneven, so that many villages were without one.

Comprehensive schools. A large school giving secondary education of all types in one complex of buildings so that in theory there is equality of educational opportunity given to all pupils, there being no selection (as by an examination at the age of 11 or later) for grammar school, modern school, etc. (see below). The most popular form of state education at the present time.

Dame schools. Characteristic of the 18th and early 19th centuries, and so called because they were commonly owned and run by poor, single women to make a small income. Only reading and writing and the beginnings of arithmetic were taught.

Dissenters' schools and academies. In the 18th century, Protestants who did not belong to the ▷ Church of England (*ie* Dissenters or Nonconformists) were not allowed to attend its schools. They could enter Scottish but not English universities. They therefore set up their own educational institutions which provided efficient education, often more up-to-date than that in the schools attended by ▷ Anglicans. Dissenting schools and academies became steadily less important in the 19th century, especially after London University was opened in 1828. (The last restrictions on non-Anglicans at Oxford and Cambridge were removed in 1871.)

Elementary schools. This is either a general term for schools of any period which taught nothing more than reading, writing and arithmetic, or for the state schools established by the the Act of 1870 providing for education up to the age of 11. The term 'Elementary' was abandoned by the Education Act of 1944, and 'Primary' was substituted.

Finishing schools. Schools for girls, fairly common in the 19th and early 20th centuries. They cater for the richer classes and take adolescents. Emphasis is commonly laid on behaviour and artistic accomplishments, though the education is sometimes more thorough. They are often situated in France, Germany, Switzerland or Italy, to facilitate · the learning of a foreign language.

Girls' schools. Until the dissolution of the monasteries in the 1530s, many convents of nuns ran schools for girls. In the 16th and 17th centuries girls' schools for the wealthier classes were rather rare, and such girls received their education at home from private teachers, *ie* governesses. This was still usual in the 18th century, though private boarding schools for girls were increasing in number. By the mid-19th century girls were in theory approaching equality with boys in opportunities for education in all classes.

Grammar schools. In the Middle Ages the various kinds of monastery school for older children had Latin grammar as their principal subject. This continued to be true when such schools were taken out of the hands of the Church between 1530 and 1560 and endowed by public funds or placed in the hands of town councils etc. An example is the Grammar School at Stratford-on-Avon, probably attended by the young Shakespeare. As time went on, the educational curriculum changed, but the term 'grammar school' remained for all schools providing an academic education up to university entrance standard, unless they were called 'public schools' – which were usually richer and drew their pupils from a wider area. Now largely merged with other secondary schools in the Comprehensive system.

High schools. Until 1944, equivalent to grammar schools, but usually for girls. Nowadays the term is merely a survival.

Modern schools. Set up in 1944 to provide for education of children who were not attending a grammar school, attendance at one or other type of secondary school being then made compulsory till the age of 15.

National schools. Schools founded in the 19th century by the Church of England 'National Society for Promoting the Education of the Poor in the Principles of the Established Church'. From 1833 it received a small grant from the government. The National Society had its complement in the British and Foreign School Society, which founded schools on behalf of the Dissenters. Until 1870, the National Society was responsible for most of the schools for the poor in 19th-century England. It gave a fairly intensive education in the Bible as well as elementary education of a general description.

Preparatory schools. In the 19th and 20th centuries, schools which prepared the sons of the wealthier classes for public schools. They were and are nearly all privately owned. Boys pass from them to public schools at the age of 13.

Private schools. Used either for schools under private ownership (*ie* not endowed, and not run by public subscription or by the state), or as an alternative term for 'preparatory schools'.

Public schools. See separate entry. Here, it is relevant to point out that they are schools neither run by the state nor under private ownership.

State schools. Applicable to all schools, since 1870, run under the authority of the state but the term is used to distinguish those which do not make a direct charge to parents and are most closely regulated by the state.

Secondary schools. Applicable to state schools providing education over the age of 11.

Sunday schools. Started in 1780 for the education of poor children on the one day in the week on which they were likely to be free from employment. They are now wholly religious in their instruction.

Technical schools. In the second half of the 19th century, places for training youth in industrial and craft skills; schools called 'polytechnics' and technical colleges became common. Since 1944, while polytechnics and technical colleges have continued and increased, the term 'technical school' has been restricted to alternatives to grammar schools and modern schools, providing a more technical education than either. Technical colleges receive only students over the age at which compulsory education ceases.

Voluntary schools. A term applicable to all schools supported by voluntary contributions.

Schreiner, Olive (Emilie Albertina) (1855–1920)

Daughter of a ▷ Methodist missionary of German descent and an English mother, Olive Schreiner was born in Basutoland, the sixth of 12 children. Self-educated, she became governess to a Boer family at the age of 15 and began to write. She came to England in 1881 to seek a publisher and in 1884 met ▷ Havelock Ellis with whom she developed a close friendship. Ten years later she returned to South Africa and married the politician Samuel Cron Cronwright who became her literary assistant and later literary executor. They took trips to England and travelled around Africa together. Her first and most acclaimed work is *The Story of an African Farm* (1883), which was published under the pseudonym Ralph Iron. Its unorthodox religious views and ▷ feminist standpoint caused a considerable stir. She wrote most after her return to South Africa: *Trooper Peter Halket of Mashonaland* (1897), *From Man to Man* (1926) and *Undine* (1929),

all with feminist themes, and short stories, *Dreams* (1891), *Real Life* (1893) and *Stories, Dreams and Allegories* (1920). She also wrote *Woman and Labour* (1911). See also: *Letters* (1924).

Bib: Schreiner, S. C. C., *The Life of Olive Schreiner*; First, R. & Scott, A., *Olive Schreiner*.

Science Fiction

The term 'science fiction' was coined in the mid 19th century, though it was 'reinvented' and given wider currency in the late 1920s by the American magazine editor Hugo Gernsback, who popularized the stories deriving from, pre-eminently, ▷ H. G. Wells and Jules Verne. To Gernsback a science fiction story was 'a charming romance intermingled with scientific fact and prophetic vision' (editorial, *Amazing Stories*, 1926). Wells had called what would now be dubbed his science fiction 'scientific romances', and the relation between romance, particularly Gothic romance (▷ Gothic novels), and science fiction has often been remarked on by definers of the form. ▷ Kingsley Amis in *New Maps of Hell* (1960), a work which did much to encourage serious critical attention to this branch of popular literature, allows for a broadening of the speculative base of science fiction through reference to sciences, or 'pseudo-sciences', like sociology, psychology, anthropology, theology and linguistics.

Darko Suvin (*Metamorphoses of Science Fiction*, 1979) remarks that 'cognition' would be a more appropriate word than science in defining this literary genre, and his emphasis on estrangement, or alienation, provides a useful direction for the discussion of science fiction in terms of recent critical theory, which has given new life to the ▷ Russian Formalist assertion that literature 'defamiliarizes' conventional assumptions. Science fiction, which is a product of and response to an era of rapid scientific and technological development, has often been concerned to promote new ways of seeing appropriate to, for example, the human consequences of industrialization, the implications of Darwinian (▷ Charles Darwin) evolutionary theory, Einstein's theory of relativity, and the second law of thermodynamics concerning the ultimate entropy of a closed system like the universe. Though the popularity of science fiction may result from the withdrawal of much modern mainstream fiction from traditional forms of storytelling, its concerns as speculative, defamiliarizing literature set it apart from

Science fiction writer Isaac Asimov

the conventions of classic realism with its emphasis on, for example, characterization. Critics hostile to the science fiction genre have complained that its presentation of human character compared unfavourably with that of realist fiction, whereas others have argued that this represents a response to a world dehumanized by technology, or a radically different viewpoint for asking the question 'What constitutes the human?'

▷ Mary Shelley's ▷ *Frankenstein, Or The Modern Prometheus* (1817) is centrally concerned with this question of defining the human through its treatment of artificially created life and offers the polar opposites of the human as idealist romantic hero and as mere mechanism. This duality is figured in a wide range of subsequent science fiction, most obviously in the genre's obsession with robots and other forms of artificial life and intelligence. In constructing a nameless 'other', Frankenstein's creation or 'monster', *Frankenstein* deals with another obsessively pursued theme of science fiction – confrontation with the alien. Mary Shelley's text, in its repeated patterns of dualism, of attempted completion of incomplete individuals, suggests the possibility, dear to much recent science fiction, that Earth is the alien planet and 'otherness' is the repressed in the human psyche or in human society.

Frankenstein may be regarded as a significant root work of science fiction, but it is the scientific romances of ▷ H. G. Wells which established the genre in the 1890s. Many of these share with *Frankenstein* an

unsettling pessimism deriving from a perception of the destructive and alienating uses to which technological development might be put, while much American science fiction, at least in the period before World War II, suggested an optimistic faith in the possibilities of scientific and technological development, springing, perhaps, from a culture defining itself through reference to an expanding frontier. Wells established an influential British tradition of bleaker Darwinism, emanating from an imperial culture already in decline.

Wells's *The Time Machine* (1895) provides a model for a range of subsequent science fiction. It introduces, in almost comic pseudo-scientific discourse, a technological means of travel through time; it facilitates sociological criticism and prediction through the use of utopian and dystopian discourses; it treats the theme of confrontation with the alien, of the last man on earth, of the entropic death of the world; it provides new contexts for old myths; and it defamiliarizes the cosy certitudes of the late Victorian male world in which it starts. *The War of the Worlds* (1898), repeatedly adapted and imitated in the 20th century, may be regarded as the genesis of the bulk of science fiction treatments of interplanetary war or invasion by the alien. *Mr Blettsworthy on Rampole Island* (1928), which employs the traditional device of the dream as a means of transport in place of a time-machine, involves an inversion of dream and reality of a kind familiar in a wide range of science fiction. *The Shape of Things to Come* (1933), widely known through the Alexander Korda film version, represents a more optimistic element in Wells's science fiction in that it suggests the possibility of redemption through an enlightened, technologically oriented élite; yet images of global disorder and collapse are, perhaps, most vividly projected in this text.

Mark Rose, in *Alien Encounters: Anatomy of Science Fiction* (1981), approaches the definition of science fiction through its phases of development. Thus the scientific romances of such as Wells transform earlier kinds of romance, like the Gothic, and fill a gap left by the predominance of realistic fiction. Later phases manifest a generic self-consciousness, in that science fiction texts come to be based on an explicit form. Rose provides the example of ▷ C. S. Lewis, whose science fiction output is in part a response to the fiction of Wells. The settings of Lewis's space trilogy, *Out of the Silent Planet* (1943), *Perelandra* (1943) and *That Hideous Strength* (1945), are respectively Mars, Venus and

Earth, but Lewis's preference for angels rather than space-ships as a means of interplanetary travel has led to some questioning of their status as science fiction. The trilogy evinces an attachment to supernatural Christianity rather than to science, in opposition to the element of pessimistic materialism in Wells; but some variant of such mysticism is not uncommon in the genre. For example, Lewis's near-contemporary, Olaf Stapledon, in works like *Last and First Men* (1930), *Last Men in London* (1932) and *Star-Maker* (1937), projected what he called 'myths' of future history on a scale that goes beyond beyond Wells's scientific romances.

▷ Aldous Huxley acknowledged that his *Brave New World* (1932) started out as a parody of H. G. Wells's *Men Like Gods*, and it has become, in the words of Brian Aldiss (b 1925) (*Billion Year Spree*, 1973) 'arguably the Western World's most famous science fiction novel'. The status accorded this satirical dystopian text, like that enjoyed by the still controversial *Nineteen Eighty-Four* (1949) by ▷ George Orwell, may result from the fact that, in the context of the author's novel output outside the field of science fiction, it can be regarded as somehow 'mainstream' fiction. Both of these works have been regarded as more 'serious' than most science fiction, though this may be based on questionable assumptions about intrinsic literary merit.

A number of British writers were regular contributors to the pre-World War II American science fiction magazine which did much to create a persistent downmarket image for the genre in the popular imagination. The first magazine devoted entirely to science fiction was Hugo Gernsback's *Amazing Stories* (published from 1926), which made an effort to appear respectably scientific and educational in a market which often relied upon lurid presentation. It was followed by such titles as *Science Wonder Stories, Wonder Stories* and *Astounding Stories* in the late 1920s and early 1930s. Besides Wells, British contributors included John Russell Fearn, Eric Frank Russell and John Beynon Harris. Fearn, whose work appeared in *Amazing Stories* first in 1933, produced a staggering quantity of novels and short stories under no less than 25 pseudonyms as well as editing two British science fiction magazines. Russell, whose output was modest compared to Fearn's, began publishing in *Astounding Stories* in 1937 and went on to contribute to British magazines like *Tales of Wonder* and *Fantasy*. Harris is better known as ▷ John

Science fiction writer Ray Bradbury

Wyndham, though he also wrote as John Beynon, J. B. Harris and Johnson Harris. He published short stories and novels from 1930 on, though his reputation rests on the novels he produced as John Wyndham from 1951, the year in which *The Day of the Triffids* was published.

'Exiles on Asperus' (in *Wonder Stories Quarterly*, 1933) by John Beynon Harris demonstrates how Wyndham was not temperamentally drawn to the 'space-opera' conventions of the American magazines or to their attachment to science fiction 'gadget' stories. He was happier, and more successful, developing the Wellsian tradition of science fiction in novels centring on an imagined disaster arising from the upsetting of the natural and social orders generally through the agency of technology. His catastrophe stories, including *The Day of the Triffids, The Kraken Wakes* (1953) and *The Midwich Cuckoos* (1957), belong to a class of British science fiction stretching from Wells to the present, including New Wave science fiction which in some ways represented a reaction against Wyndham's formulae. *The Day of the Triffids* makes use of the traditional science fiction theme of the Last Man/ Last Woman, a new Adam and Eve faced with the arduous complexities of an unfamiliar world. The treatment evokes a characteristically English romantic nostalgia, reminiscent of ▷ Richard Jefferies's vision of the ruined capital in *After London* (1885). The remaking of a new world out of the scraps of the old in *The Day of the Triffids* also suggests a debt to ▷ Daniel Defoe's ▷ *Robinson Crusoe*

(1719), but Wyndham's novel is predominantly Wellsian, though it retains a safe, genteel quality not so typical of Wells.

Arthur C. Clarke (b 1917), one of the most celebrated science fiction writers of the 20th century, combines meticulous attention to the scientific and technological aspects of the genre, in the tradition of Jules Verne, with a lyrically didactic commitment to the benign evolutionary potential of technology that owes much to the impact of Clarke's early reading of Stapledon. Both were powerfully expressed in Stanley Kubrick's film *2001* (1968), for which Clarke wrote the screenplay. The kind of wondering transcendence conveyed at the end of that film is characteristic of Clarke's work, encountered in, for example, one of his most popular novels, *Childhood's End* (1953); while *The Deep Range* (1957) develops into a lesson in respect for the non-human creatures of the earth as the prospect of contact with beings from other worlds approaches.

The first novel of Brian Aldiss, *Non-Stop* (1958), gave an indication of the exhilarating variety which has proved a feature of his subsequent fictional output. *Hothouse* (1962) and *Greybeard* (1964) treat the well-established theme of imagined catastrophe, but combine a playful abundance of exotic science fiction invention with romantic nostalgia. A Swiftian satirical mode characterizes *The Dark Light Years* (1964), while the alienating detachment of *Report on Probability A* (1968) draws the techniques of the French ▷ *Nouveau roman* into the orbit of science fiction. *Frankenstein Unbound* (1973) and *Moreau's Other Island* (1980) reinvent seminal science fiction texts for a new context, while the abundance of Aldiss's Helliconia trilogy (1982–5) defies brief categorization. The epilogue to the third volume, *Helliconia Winter* (1985), a translated extract from ▷ Lucretius, *De Rerum Natura*, might be applied to Aldiss's *oeuvre*: 'Everything must pass through successive phases. Nothing remains forever what it was.'

Aldiss's commitment to science fiction, his urge to experiment and enjoy, and to extend the possibilities of the genre, gave him a respected place in the so-called New Wave science fiction writing associated with the magazine *New Worlds* under the editorship of Michael Moorcock (b 1939) from 1964. Until then *New Worlds* had been edited by E. J. Carnell, who was also responsible for *Science Fantasy*. Carnell's magazine published a wide range of British science fiction, including the work of such prolific authors as Kenneth Bulmer, who employed 15 pen-names in addition to his own name, and John Brunner,

who began publishing science fiction at the age of 17. The scale of Brunner's output may have resulted in his work being critically underrated, though his dystopian novels *Stand on Zanzibar* (1968), *The Jagged Orbit* (1969) and *The Sheep Look Up* (1972) achieved critical acclaim. Like Brunner, Moorcock is a prolific author who started young; he was editing *Tarzan Adventures* at the age of 17. His 'sword and sorcery' fantasies embody the apocalyptic theme which runs through much of his later science fiction, in which he reconstructs the past as well as imagining the future; this kind of reconstruction may be seen as a way of deconstructing the present. Works like *War Lord of the Air* (1971) and *The Land Leviathan* (1974) present a past manufactured from a range of literary reference, to, for example, Verne, Wells and ▷ Joseph Conrad, and demonstrate Moorcock's attachment to the concept of the 'multiverse', which proposes a variety of separate realities which can sometimes interact. His fondness for series of novels and a modernist tendency to fragment his narratives are particularly evident in his Jerry Cornelius novels, including *The Final Programme* (1969), *A Cure for Cancer* (1971), *The English Assassin* (1972) and *The Condition of Muzak* (1977).

New Worlds under Moorcock represented a spirited reaction against the continuing influence of American pulp science fiction, and a number of American authors were attracted to its programme. But it was a British author, J. G. Ballard (b 1930), who was championed most consistently by the magazine. The Conradian tone of much of Ballard's science fiction contrasts with the racier products of some *New Worlds* writers, influenced by the current 'rock' culture; he has never been much interested in the traditional science fiction fare of space travel and the distant future, preferring to focus on something challengingly closer to the present, defamiliarizing the familiar earth into the alien planet, and insisting that the outward thrust of science fiction be matched by an inward journey. The estranging, detritus-strewn landscapes of much of his fiction indicate Ballard's fascination with surrealist art, though his *Empire of the Sun* (1983), a novel drawing on his boyhood experience of World War II in the Far East, reveals a source closer to home for his images of collapse and desolation. Ballard's catastrophe novels, like *The Drowned World* (1962), *The Drought* (1965) and *The Crystal World* (1966), bear some relation to the disaster stories of John Wyndham and John Christopher, though there is little in the way of romantic nostalgia in his treatment of 'biospheric' disasters. What might be seen as his post-imperial pessimism has not generally endeared Ballard to an American audience. His experimental 'condensed' novels, which first began appearing in *New Worlds*, were published together in *The Atrocity Exhibition* (1970) and, again, did not find favour in the U.S. The disturbing presentation of perverse urban nightmares in *Crash!* (1973), *Concrete Island* (1974) and *High Rise* (1975) bring the concept of the science fiction catastrophe even closer to our own time, as if the irreversible disaster had already occurred in our culture.

▷ Doris Lessing, who turned to science fiction in the early 1970s when her reputation as a mainstream novelist was already established, is also drawn towards visions of the decline and breakdown of society. The last volume of the 'Children of Violence' novels, *The Four-Gated City* (1969), ultimately projects into the future, but from the publication of *Briefing for a Descent into Hell* (1971) Lessing has shown a firm commitment to the exploratory, speculative potential of science fiction, with particular reference to questions of gender and the theme of spiritual awakening. The evocations of collapse and depletion in Lessing's science fiction, which, in the 1980s, turns to space fiction on the grand galactic scale, are set against the possibility of a utopian alternative, and its emphasis is more mystical than scientific. In *Briefing* and *Memoirs* the alternative might amount to no more than dreams; but in *Shikasta* (1979) utopian society is destroyed by a malign galactic empire, while in *The Marriages between Zones Three, Four, and Five* (1980) it is confirmed that the project of utopian evolutionary development, through, for example, the use of psychic powers, lies within the province of women.

A number of ▷ Angela Carter's novels may be classed as science fiction, though, like Lessing, she tends not to focus primarily on science. *Heroes and Villains* (1970) is set in the familiar terrain of a post-catastrophe world and, using the structure of romantic fantasy, explores a variety of dualities, including fantasy/reality, beauty/barbarism, love/hate, male/female. Carter's particular skill, evident in *The Infernal Desire Machines of Dr Hoffman* (1972), *The Passion of New Eve* (1977) and *Nights at the Circus* (1983), lies in her exuberantly self-conscious, inventive storytelling in which romance, satire, horror and comedy interact exotically.

Ian Watson is also adept in exotic narrative,

for example, *Whores of Babylon* (1988), but his reputation has been for intellectual, speculative brilliance. His texts, like Lessing's, have a tendency to the mystical and transcendent, and approach the possibility of such transcendence through the discourses of science, linguistics, mysticism and myth, as is impressively demonstrated by his first four novels: *The Embedding* (1973), *The Jonah Kit* (1976), *The Martian Inca* (1977) and *Alien Embassy* (1977).

Christopher Priest also built up during the 1970s a reputation as a thoughtful and inventive science fiction author through such works as *Inverted World* (1974) and *A Dream of Wessex* (1977).

The next new wave of science fiction is already upon us. Science fiction might be said to have begun with the work of a woman and, looked at one way, Mary Shelley's *Frankenstein* is a coded analysis of female experience. The women's movement of recent years, with a strong lead from the United States, has led to a powerful reaction against science fiction's traditional marginalization of women, and Lessing is not unique in turning to science fiction from a different novel tradition. Michèle Roberts, for example, adopts the dystopian mode in *The Book of Mrs Noah* (1973), while ▷ Zoë Fairbairns uses science fiction's speculative resources to consider the issue of wages for housework in *Benefits* (1979). The Women's Press boasts a growing list of feminist science fiction, and one of the editors responsible for this, Sarah Lefanu, has written a study of feminism and science fiction, *In the Chinks of the World Machine* (1988). Commenting on the value of science fiction, Lefanu has said: 'It deals with the possibility of change, and allows the investigation of radical ideas.'

Scone

A town in Scotland, at which Scottish kings were crowned. 'The stone of destiny' or 'stone of Scone' on which they sat, was by ancient tradition that on which in the Bible (*Genesis* 28) Jacob rested his head and dreamt of the ladder ascending to Heaven. The English king ▷ Edward I captured it, and ever since it has been kept under the English coronation chair in ▷ Westminster Abbey.

Scotland

The northern kingdom of Great Britain. Geographically, racially, linguistically and culturally, it has two parts.

The northern and north-western half, known as the ▷ Highlands and the Islands, is Celtic in race, with a Norse admixture. The native language was originally the Celtic one called ▷ Gaelic, but this is now spoken only by a small minority. Until the middle of the 18th century its social structure was of the semi-tribal clan system under hereditary chieftains. Its culture was chiefly oral and Gaelic-speaking, and much of it has been lost. The so-called Scottish national dress, of the ▷ kilt woven into chequered designs known as ▷ tartans, was peculiar to this region; it was forbidden after the second ▷ Jacobite rebellion of 1745, when the British government started its policy of colonizing the Highlands, but it was revived in the 19th century as a sentimental fashion for the upper classes and is now an extremely profitable export item. This region of Scotland, though extremely beautiful, has had a torn history; centuries of clan warfare were followed by a century and a half of economic neglect and depopulation, during which the small farms or 'crofts' were steadily replaced by 'grouse moors', preserved by rich landlords for hunting and shooting. In the 20th century the economy has to some extent revived, thanks to the tourist industry and efforts by successive governments to cultivate forests.

The southern and eastern half of the country is called the Lowlands, and contains all the important cities including the capital, ▷ Edinburgh, and the largest, Glasgow. These two cities are respectively at the east and west ends of the narrowest part of the country, and the plain between them is a rich coal-mining area. The Lowlands are geographically hilly, in spite of their name. Racially, the population is as Germanic in origin as that of most of England, and with small exceptions it has always been English-speaking. It has never been subjected to the clan system of the Highlands, although the great families along the border with England had, until the 17th century, an influence comparable to that of the clan chieftains of the Celtic north. Economically and politically, the Lowlands have always been the richer and more important part of the country. When we speak of Scottish culture, we are nearly always thinking of the literature of the Lowlands; this has had its distinctive tradition, but it has become increasingly absorbed into English culture since the 16th century.

Scott, Paul (1920–78)

Novelist. He served in India, Burma and Malaya during World War II and subsequently worked in publishing. His major achievement was *The Raj Quartet*, a tetralogy consisting of: *The Jewel in the Crown* (1966); *The Day of the Scorpion* (1968); *The Towers*

of Silence (1971); *A Division of the Spoils* (1975). A portrait of Indian society at the time of Independence in 1947, it uses a range of narrative forms, including letters, journals, reports and memories. The story is built around the consequences of the rape of an English girl; consequences which serve to reveal corruption and racism in the Raj administration and the roots of the political unrest and intercommunal violence at the Partition of India. Scott was accorded little critical recognition until *Staying On* (1977), a gentle satire set after Independence, won the Booker Prize. His work is notable for its combination of complex narrative technique with historical accuracy. *The Raj Quartet* was televised as *The Jewel in the Crown* in 1984 and *Staying On* was adapted for television in 1981. Scott's earlier novels include *The Birds of Paradise* (1962).

Scott, Sir Walter (1771–1832)

Sir Walter Scott

Scottish poet and novelist. The son of an Edinburgh lawyer, he was descended from famous families on the Scottish side of the border with England. This ancestry early attracted him to the drama and tragedy of Anglo-Scottish border history; he became an antiquarian, and a very romantic one. His ▷ romanticism was stimulated further by reading the poetry of the contemporary Germans, Bürger and ▷ Goethe; he hoped to do for the Scottish border what they had done for the German Middle Ages, and make its past live again in modern romance. A widespread taste was already developed for the ▷ Middle Ages and was manifesting itself in the ▷ Gothic novel. He collaborated with the most famous of the Gothic novelists – ▷ 'Monk' Lewis – in producing *Tales of Wonder* in 1801. A little later Coleridge's poem ▷ *Christabel*, inspired him to write poems in the same metre, and between 1805 and 1815 he produced the succession of narrative poems which made him famous. He began to feel himself outdone as a narrative poet by ▷ Byron, however, and from 1815 he devoted himself to the novels for which he is now better known. Publishing enterprises in which he had begun to involve himself in 1809 left him with a debt of £130,000 to pay off, when the London publisher Constable went bankrupt. Scott was immensely proud, and determined to pay off the debt by his own literary efforts. By writing very prolifically for the rest of his life, he nearly succeeded; he was by then a very sick man, and his efforts are a legend of literary heroism.

Scott's most famous poems are *The Lay of the Last Minstrel* (1805); ▷ *Marmion* (1808), and *The Lady of the Lake* (1810). The first two are from Anglo-Scottish border history and legend; the third is about the equally bitter enmity of Scottish Highlander for Scottish Lowlander. The readability of these poems makes it easy to account for their popularity, but the kind of interest they offer – the dramatization of the life of a whole society – was not such as Scott was able to work out in the verse-narrative medium.

His novels show a double interest: he was the first novelist in English to present characters as part of a society, and not merely against the background of a particular society, the nature of which is taken for granted; he was also the inventor of the true historical novel. His best work is contained in the Waverley novels and in the first three series of *Tales of My Landlord*: ▷ *Waverley* (1814), ▷ *Guy Mannering* (1815), *The Antiquary* (1816), *Old Mortality* (1816), ▷ *Rob Roy* (1817), ▷ *The Heart of Midlothian* (1818), *The Bride of Lammermoor* and *The Legend of Montrose* (1819). All these concern 17th- and 18th-century Scotland, and the religious and dynastic struggles that shaped the nation as Scott knew it. From then onwards he was writing with excessive haste in order to pay off his debts, and he commonly chose English and medieval subjects, *eg* ▷ *Ivanhoe* (1819), *Kenilworth* (about English Elizabethan times – 1821), *Quentin Durward* (1823) and some 16 others,

only one of which, *St Ronan's Well* (1823), was set in Scott's own time.

Not only was Scott's influence, both in Britain and Europe, very large in shaping literary taste, but he had an extensive influence in encouraging non-literary taste, such as that for wild landscape (especially of the Highlands) and more intelligent interest in the past. As a critic he was among the first to recognize the genius of ▷ Jane Austen. In politics he was strongly right wing (Tory), and he helped to found the great Tory review, the ▷ *Quarterly*, in 1809.
Bib: Buchan, J., *Life*; Davie, D., *The Heyday of Sir Walter Scott*; Hayden, J. O., *Scott: The Critical Heritage*; Hillhouse, J. T., *The Waverley Novels and their Critics*; Lewis, C. S., in *They Asked for a Paper*; Lockhart, J. G., *Memoirs*; Muir, E., *Scott and Scotland*.

Scottish Chaucerians

A rather over-generalized term, applied to a diverse group of Scottish poets of the 15th and 16th centuries (including ▷ William Dunbar, ▷ Robert Henryson, ▷ Gavin Douglas, and James I of Scotland, author of the ▷ *Kingis Quair*), on the grounds that their work shows signs of Chaucerian influence.

Scottish literature in English

This belongs above all to the Lowlands (▷ Scotland); it is a distinctive branch of literature in the English language, the Lowland Scottish form of which had originally a close resemblance to that spoken in the north of England. Racially, linguistically and culturally, Lowland Scottish ties with England were close, despite the constant wars between the two countries between the late 13th and mid-16th centuries. In contrast, until the 18th-century destruction of Highland culture, the Lowlanders had little more than the political bond of a common sovereign with their Gaelic-speaking fellow-countrymen of the north. While it is not true to say that Scottish literature is a branch of English literature, the two literatures have been closely related.

One of the first notable works was ▷ John Barbour's *The Bruce* (1375–8), an ▷ epic in 8-syllable ▷ couplets about the war of independence against England (1296–1328). Written at a time when Scottish political fortunes were low, its intention is to inspire the national spirit, not by rhetorical eloquence but by the facts of the heroic struggle; it is one of the least fanciful of the more important medieval poems. Barbour was writing at the same time as ▷ Chaucer in his early work. The next notable Scottish poem was strongly under Chaucer's influence – ▷ *The King's Quair*, perhaps by James I of Scotland, part of whose reign was spent in imprisonment in England, where it was no doubt written. It is a tale of romantic love, echoing Chaucer's ▷ *Knight's Tale*. In Scotland, the 15th century saw the beginning of a golden age, covering the careers of ▷ Robert Henryson, ▷ William Dunbar, ▷ Gavin Douglas, and David Lindsay. The climax of this period was the reign of the exceptionally able King James IV (1488–1513), who produced an unusual state of order and civilization in the country. Henryson's masterpiece is the ▷ *Testament of Cresseid*, a continuation of Chaucer's ▷ *Troilus and Criseyde*, but with a tragic quality which is quite un-Chaucerian. Dunbar wrote in contrasting styles – the courtly and the colloquial; his finest work is perhaps in the latter, notably, the *Tretis of the Tua Mariit Wemen and the Wedo* (Treatise of the Two Married Women and the Widow). Douglas's finest work is his translation of Virgil's ▷ *Aeneid*, and Lindsay is best known for his *Satire of the Three Estates* – a political morality play.

The flowering of high Scottish poetry was halted by the Scottish religious ▷ Reformation, and all the political troubles attendant on it from 1550 till 1700. Such poets in this period as deserve attention (*eg* ▷ Drummond of Hawthornden, 1585–1649) were thoroughly anglicized. The native culture remained alive at popular level, however, especially in its fine ballad and folksong tradition of which ▷ *Sir Patrick Spens* is one of the most notable examples. In the 18th century a revival took place, the first noteworthy example being Allan Ramsay's *The Gentle Shepherd* (1725). ▷ Robert Burns is perhaps the first famous Scottish poet since the 16th century. By now, however, the tide of English influence had moved strongly into Scotland; ▷ Walter Scott collected Scottish ▷ ballads, and produced a few fine examples in the ballad tradition, but his longer poems belong to the history of English verse narrative, though their subject was often Scottish history and legend. Patriotic sentiment still seized on opportunities to resist the English pressure, however, and the 20th century has seen a reassertion of the national idiom in the Lallans (Lowland) renaissance, the most vigorous example of which is the work of ▷ Hugh MacDiarmid. This idiom can also be seen in the work of Henryson, Dunbar, Douglas and Burns; it is concrete, sardonic, realistic, harsh and physical.

Gaelic literature of the Highlands had what is said to be a 'golden age' in the later 18th century, just at the time when Gaelic culture was being destroyed by the English and the Lowland Scots for political reasons. The work in it (*eg* that of Alexander Macdonald, Dugald Buchanan) is little known outside the comparatively small number of Gaelic speakers in the Highlands, and does not belong to English literature. For the alleged translations of the Ossianic poems by ▷ James Macpherson (1736–96) see under Oisin.

Scottish prose literary tradition may be seen in Medieval philosophers such as ▷ Duns Scotus and Renaissance ▷ humanists such as ▷ George Buchanan (16th century) who wrote principally in Latin. Thereafter the great Scottish writers (especially from the 18th century) were mainly anglicized in their prose expression; ▷ David Hume and ▷ Adam Smith in the 18th century, Walter Scott and ▷ Thomas Carlyle in the 19th. Apart from Scott, other writers participated in the adventurous prose narrative, such as ▷ Robert Louis Stevenson and R. M. Ballantyne (1825–94) who are both well known for their escapist fantasies often read as ▷ children's fiction. In a similar supernatural vein ▷ Margaret Oliphant produced several novels with Scottish backgrounds.

The 20th century has seen what is often described as the Scottish Renaissance, which suggests a revival in cultural production and political identity. There have been three waves in this redevelopment, the first, in the early part of this century with a growth in nationalistic sentiment. In this period the work of Hugh MacDiarmid is most seminal, from his early Scottish propaganda in the *Scottish Chapbook* (started 1922) to his most famous poem *A Drunk Man Looks at the Thistle* (1926) and later poetical works. MacDiarmid rejected the earlier nostalgic approach and placed Scottish literature firmly in the European ▷ modernist movement. Other important writers of the first wave include the poet ▷ Edwin Muir, and the novelists Lewis Grassic Gibbon (1901–35) and Neil M. Gunn (1891–1973). Muir adopts a mythopoeic discourse which Gibbon and Gunn take up as a sense of Celtic inheritance, although while Gibbon uses myth fatalistically, Gunn sees in it a possibility for Scottish self-regeneration. Like MacDiarmid, all actively reject nostalgia and evoke social and political themes.

The second wave which occurred during the 1940s and 1950s saw a continuation, but rejuvenation of the earlier themes. George Mackay Brown (b 1921), for example, takes up the mythic patterns, while Edwin Morgan's (b 1920) contemporary idiom, such as ▷ science fiction, and ▷ Ian Hamilton Finlay's concrete poems strongly assert their identification with European ▷ modernism.

The third period in the Scottish Renaissance is still happening and takes the broadest sense of national literary identity to its utmost limits. For example, 7:84, the dramatic company founded by ▷ John McGrath has an avowedly ▷ Brechtian and international socialist purpose, but at the same time is located unquestionably in a Scottish political scene – as with his *The Cheviot, the Stag and the Black, Black Oil* (1973) – and determinedly retains its ▷ fringe status. Novelists, such as William McIlvanney (b 1936) similarly focus upon the political unrest and tension of modern urban life in Scotland. Like McIlvanney, the novelists ▷ Muriel Spark and Robin Jenkins (b 1912), the poets ▷ Douglas Dunn and Liz Lochhead (b 1947), and the dramatists Tom McGrath (b 1940) and John Byrne (b 1940), have taken advantage of the expansion of publishing in the 1980s to reach a wider and more international market.
Bib: Watson, R., *The Literature of Scotland.*

Scriblerus Club
Formed in 1713 by ▷ Alexander Pope, ▷ Jonathan Swift, ▷ John Gay, ▷ Thomas Parnell, ▷ John Arbuthnot, and the Tory politician, Lord Oxford. The aim was to satirize 'false tastes' through the fictional memoirs of a conceited and arrogant 'modern' writer, Martinus Scriblerus. The club's members were scattered when the Tories fell from power after Queen Anne's death in 1714. Only the first volume of the memoirs was completed, and this was published in Pope's works in 1741. However, the ideas initiated at this time saw fruit in various later works, in particular Pope's ▷ *Dunciad*, many of the notes of which are signed 'Scriblerus', and in the satire on science and learning in the third book of Swift's ▷ *Gulliver's Travels.*

Scrutiny
A literary critical review published in Cambridge from 1932 to 1953; its principal editor was ▷ F. R. Leavis. *Scrutiny* was famous for its intellectual energy, the coherence of outlook among its contributors, and the urgency and purposefulness of its tone. This purposefulness was a response to a Leavisite analysis of the contemporary

cultural scene which may be summarized as follows. The quality of Western (more particularly, British) civilization was deteriorating because of the influence upon it of commercial vulgarization. Such vulgarization could only end in the complete loss of those standards by which life in any organized society can be seen and felt to be valuable. The importance of a great literary tradition is that it constitutes a form of spiritual life that sustains high values and withstands vulgarization. However, such a tradition must itself be sustained by constant, sensitive and scrupulous critical activity carried on by alert and active intellects within the society. But the British literary tradition no longer possessed this kind of cultural leadership; the leading men of letters, on the contrary, with a few exceptions, regarded literature as an elegant pastime for a fashionable elite (such as the ▷ Bloomsbury Group) and they employed slack and inadequate standards in their judgements. *Scrutiny*, therefore, was intended to demonstrate the exacting standards which are required of criticism if a lively and effective literary tradition is to be sustained. The example to be followed was that of the recently defunct review, *The Calendar of Modern Letters* (1925–27) edited by Edgell Rickword.

The strongest part of *Scrutiny*'s critical attack was directed towards literary education. It sought to counteract the kind of academic inertia which tends to the passive acceptance of some literary reputations and the equally passive neglect of other writers. This policy led to an extensive revaluation of the writers of the past. In regard to poetry, this revaluation took the direction already pursued by ▷ T. S. Eliot (*Selected Essays*, 1932); in regard to the novel, the dominant influences were those of F. R. Leavis himself, and his wife Q. D. Leavis. *Scrutiny* had a pervasive influence in Britain and the U.S.A., especially among teachers at all levels of education.

Scylla and Charybdis
▷ *Odyssey.*

Seasons, The (1726–30)
Four ▷ blank verse poems by ▷ James Thomson. *Winter* was published in 1726, followed by *Summer* (1727), and *Spring* (1728). *Autumn* first appeared in the collected *Seasons* in 1730, which also contained a concluding *Hymn on the Seasons*. The work blends numerous strands: the classical spirit of ▷ Virgil's *Pastorals* and ▷ *Georgics*, a self-conscious sublimity which comes from ▷ John Milton, and the topographical genre

Illustration from James Thomson's *The Seasons*, quarto edition, 1730

popularized by ▷ Sir John Denham's ▷ *Cooper's Hill* (1642) and ▷ Alexander Pope's ▷ *Windsor-Forest* (1713). Thomson's blank verse is an extremely flexible and capacious medium, though always affecting a somewhat mechanical Miltonic dignity. On the one hand there are charming descriptions of the natural scene, such as the famous snow scenes in *Winter*, the nest-building passage in *Spring*, and the *Summer* thunderstorm. There are discussions of philosophy and morality, such as the condemnation of blood-sports in *Autumn*, and the expression of 'natural religion' in the concluding hymn. There are celebrations of British history, industry and commerce in *Summer* and *Autumn*, and sentimental vignettes of rural life, such as the man dying in the snow in *Winter* and Amelia struck by lightning as she is embraced by her astonished lover in *Summer*.

An important element is Thomson's scientific and practical approach to nature. In *Summer* he describes the beginning of the Newtonian universe, as the 'unwieldy planets' are 'launched along/ The illimitable void'. In *Autumn* he speculates on the migration of birds, and throughout the poems he is concerned to use a kind of poetic version of Linnaean taxonomy, stressing the generic qualities of animals and plants: 'plumy people' (birds) 'the finny drove' (fish) and 'woolly people' (sheep). Typically nature is seen as providing a livelihood to man. Despite their

influence on later more romantic 'nature poets', such as ▷ Mark Akenside, ▷ William Collins, ▷ William Cowper, ▷ Thomas Gray, and ▷ William Wordsworth, the *Seasons* in themselves are peculiarly smug and inert in their ▷ Augustan optimism. Thomson's is a world in which, without a qualm, 'Man superior walks/ Amid the glad creation', where farm labourers are picturesque adjuncts of the landscape, and where British industry and commerce subject the world. Its ideal for living smacks of bourgeois self-congratulation:

> *An elegant sufficiency, content,*
> *Retirement, rural quiet, friendship, books,*
> *Ease and alternate labour, useful life,*
> *Progressive virtue, and approving Heaven!*

Second Nun's Tale, The
One of ▷ Chaucer's ▷ *Canterbury Tales*. A saint's life, written in ▷ rhyme royal, recounting the life and martyrdom of ▷ St Cecilia, a noble Roman maiden, who publically affirms the power of the Christian faith and opposes the pagan practices of the Deputy, Almachius. Her husband and brother become martyrs for the faith but Cecilia defies Almachius's attempts to kill her by boiling her in a bath. Even when her throat is cut, Cecilia miraculously manages to continue preaching for three days before dying. Her testimony converts many to Christianity, both during her lifetime and afterwards. The story of her life follows the outline of her life in the ▷ *Golden Legend*.

Secret Agent, The (1907)
A novel by ▷ Joseph Conrad. The subject is revolution and counter-revolution in western Europe; the scene is London; the 'secret agent' is Mr Verloc, of mixed nationality. He is employed by the embassy of an unnamed foreign power (Czarist Russia) to mix with anarchist conspirators who have taken refuge on British soil, and to report their activities. Between the embassy and the conspirators are the London police, represented by Chief Inspector Heat, whose work is to watch the anarchists but not to interfere with them until they commit crimes. The embassy wishes to force the British government and its police to suppress the anarchist colony, and uses Verloc to organize a bomb outrage (against Greenwich Observatory) so as to incriminate them. Verloc's seedy shop in Soho is a meeting place for the motley group of political fanatics, including Karl Yundt, a malevolent old terrorist, Ossipan, a scientific materialist who

lives off women, Michaelis, a utopian Marxist and the Professor, the most ruthless of the anarchists, who always carries with him a bomb to prevent arrest. The Professor is disquieted by the inability of the British masses to see politics in terms of violence; if violence were used by the government, the masses would believe that counter-violence was their only hope, and a revolutionary situation would exist in Britain. In addition to this political level, the novel has a psychological one: if either revolution or counter-revolution is to be accomplished successfully, the human instruments must be disinterested, but in fact both the revolutionaries and their opponents are dominated by self-regard. The only characters capable of full disinterest are those who are so wretched as to be incapable of reflecting on their own condition. Mrs Verloc's half-witted brother Stevie rises to one idea only: 'bad life for poor people'. He thus becomes the willing tool of Mr Verloc, who charges him with the task of placing the bomb. In the event, Stevie causes no damage to the Observatory but he is himself blown up. Mrs Verloc, who has married Mr Verloc solely to provide support for Stevie, though her husband supposes her entirely devoted to himself, murders him from rage and grief. She tries to flee the country with Ossipan and, when he deserts her, she throws herself overboard from a Channel ferry. In contrast to Winnie Verloc and Stevie, characters simplified by misery and elementary development, is the Assistant Commissioner of Police, who neither acts disinterestedly nor has any belief that he can, but lives by the awareness that self-knowledge is the only antidote to the poison of self-regard. He solves the mystery of the outrage, and thus frustrates the destructive folly of Mr Vladimir, the ambassador. The novel is distinguished by the use of a pervasive irony to expose the futility of political extremism, the strength of human illusions, and the suffering and chaos prevailing in a supposedly civilized society.

Sedan chair

A portable covered chair, carried on two poles by chairmen, and with a trap in the roof so that the passenger could stand. It was introduced into England in 1634, and was much used as a way of getting about towns in the 18th century.

Sedgemoor, Battle of (1685)

The culmination of a rising of west-of-England ▷ Puritans against Charles II's openly Catholic brother ▷ James II. It was led by Charles's illegitimate son, the Duke of Monmouth. The battle was won by the government troops, and was followed by the ferocious punishment of the rebels by Judge Jeffreys in his notorious ▷ Bloody Assizes. Sedgemoor was the last battle fought on English (as distinct from British) soil.

Sejanus (1603)

A satirical tragedy by ▷ Ben Jonson. The central character is a historical figure, a favourite of the Roman emperor Tiberius (reigned AD 14–37). The play is a study of a man driven by extreme ambition; he first eliminates all his rivals to power in the Senate, and then, exploiting the emperor's love of luxurious indolence and inclination for retirement, he conspires to murder Tiberius' heirs in order to occupy the throne himself. Tiberius, however, is too cunning for him; he employs Macro, a new favourite, to bring about the downfall of the old, and Sejanus ends up being torn to pieces by the Roman mob, leaving Macro, equally ambitious and unscrupulous, in his former seat of power. The sensuality of Tiberius and his court, and the violence of the politicians, are contrasted with a group of grim commentators led by Arruntius, remnants of the old stoical (▷ Stoics) Romans whose austere virtues had made Rome great. Ben Jonson presents through Sejanus one of the ▷ Renaissance 'men of power', glorying in the consciousness of unlimited resources, the pattern for whom is ▷ Christopher Marlowe's ▷ Tamburlaine. Sejanus is also the diabolical ▷ Machiavellian politician, without conscience and capable of any crime, such as recurs in many Elizabethan and ▷ Jacobean dramas. Yet in his unbounded appetites, he is almost a grotesque figure, like the ludicrous sensualists in Jonson's great comedies, ▷ Volpone and ▷ The Alchemist. The play may have been an attempt to rival ▷ Shakespeare's ▷ Julius Caesar of a few years before; it is much more learned in its use of ancient authors, and dramatically it is perhaps the more impressive work.

Selborne, Natural History and Antiquities of
▷ White, Gilbert.

Selkirk, Alexander (1676–1721)

A sailor, whose experiences on the uninhabited island of Juan Fernandez, where he was landed at his own request and remained from 1704 to 1709, are the basis of the desert island part of ▷ Daniel Defoe's ▷ Robinson Crusoe.

Semele
▷ Dionysus.

Semiology, Semiotics
The term 'semiology' was used in
▷ Ferdinand de Saussure's *Course in
General Linguistics* (published 1915) to
describe 'a science of ▷ signs', whose
objective is 'to investigate the nature of signs
and the laws governing them'. The more
current term, semiotics, was associated
originally with the American philosopher C.
S. Peirce. Peirce's tripartite division of signs
into 'icon' (a sign possessing a similarity to its
object), 'symbol' (a sign arbitrarily linked to
the object), and 'index' (a sign physically
associated with its object), has more recently
been revised in Umberto Eco's *A Theory of
Semiotics* (1976) where the emphasis
throughout is upon the complex mechanisms
and conventions which govern the production
of signs.

Semiramis (about 800 BC)
Historically, an ancient queen or princess of
Assyria, about whom little is known. In
legend, she is said to have built great cities
including Babylon, to have had wonderful
beauty and many lovers. More than one
queen has been nicknamed after her, notably
Catherine II of Russia (1729–96).

Seneca, Lucius Annaeus (?4 BC–AD 65)
Roman philosopher and dramatist. He
belonged to the ▷ Stoic school of
philosophy, which taught that men should
seek virtue, not happiness, and that they
should be superior to the influences of
pleasure and pain. As an orator, he was
famous for the weight and terseness of his
expression – the 'Senecan style'. He was tutor
to the emperor ▷ Nero during the latter's
boyhood, but later was suspected of being
involved in a conspiracy against him; Nero
accordingly ordered him to end his life which
he did with true stoical dignity. His nine
tragedies were modelled on those of
▷ Aeschylus, ▷ Sophocles and
▷ Euripides, but there is much doubt
whether they were ever intended to be
performed in a theatre; they seem to be
designed for declamation to small circles.
They contain no action, though the subjects
are of blood-thirsty revenge. Their titles:
Hercules Furens; *Thyestes*; *Phoenissae*; *Phaedra
(Hippolytus)*; *Oedipus*; *Troades (Hecuba)*;
Medea; *Agamemnon*; *Hercules Oetaeus*. A
tenth, *Octavia*, has proved to be by another
author.
   Neither as a philosopher nor as a dramatist
was Seneca one of the most important figures

of the ancient Mediterranean world, but he
had great importance for the 16th-century
▷ Renaissance in Europe, and particularly
for English poetic drama between 1560 and
1620. This influence was of three kinds: 1
Seneca's dramas provided inspiration for
Elizabethan ▷ revenge tragedy or 'tragedy
of blood'; 2 at a time of English literature
when there was keen interest in modes of
expression but no settled standards about
them, Senecan style was one of the favourite
modes, both inside and outside the drama; 3
at a time when inherited ideas about the
ordering of society and the ethical systems
that should control it were undergoing
alarming transformations, Senecan stoicism
had an appeal for thoughtful men that
harmonized with ▷ Protestant strictness and
individualism of conduct. The three
influences were more related than might
appear. The translator of Seneca's *Ten
Tragedies* (1559–81) declares in his preface
that their effect was 'to beat down sin', and
Protestants were familiar with the
vengefulness of Old Testament religion.
Sensational drama could unite with serious
social purpose, and thus mingle learned,
sober conceptions of drama (*eg* ▷ *Gorboduc*)
with the demands of popular taste. Outside
the drama, the terse sententiousness of
Senecan style is best found in the *Essays* of
▷ Francis Bacon.

Sennacherib
King of Assyria, 705–681 BC. He made
extensive conquests, but one of the most
eloquent narratives of the Old Testament of
the Bible describes how his attempt to capture
Jerusalem from Hezekiah, king of the Jews,
was prevented by a sudden pestilence among
his army (*2 Chronicles* 32). This is the subject
of ▷ Byron's poem, 'The destruction of
Sennacherib' in *Hebrew Melodies* (1815).

Sensation, Novel of
Popular from about 1860, sensation novels
included extravagant, often horrible events,
and may be considered the precursors of the
modern thriller. Examples are ▷ Wilkie
Collins's *The Woman in White*, ▷ Mrs
Henry Wood's *East Lynne*, ▷ Mary
Elizabeth Braddon's *Lady Audley's Secret*
and even some of ▷ Charles Dickens. See
also **Bib** to ▷ Charles Reade.

Sense and Sensibility (1811)
A novel by ▷ Jane Austen. A youthful
version, *Elinor and Marianne*, has been lost.
The revised novel was published in 1811.
   The two heroines, Elinor and Marianne
Dashwood, are fatherless sisters who live with

their mother in comparative poverty, having been defrauded of more substantial income by their stepbrother, John Dashwood, and his arrogant and selfish wife. The title of the novel indicates the difference between the sisters: Elinor is practical and watches after the family affairs with sober good sense, and Marianne prides herself on the strength of her feelings and her contempt for material interests. Elinor is in love with a depressed and apparently dull young man, Edward Ferrars (brother of Mrs John Dashwood), while Marianne loves the handsome and glamorous John Willoughby. The superficial contrast between the sisters and their lovers is shown to be deceptive: Elinor's feelings are as deep as Marianne's but her sense of responsibility is greater and she keeps her sorrows to herself, whereas Marianne makes almost a virtue of the public exhibition of her grief, thus becoming a burden on her sister and her mother. In the end, the romantic-seeming Willoughby turns out to have given up Marianne from fear of losing a legacy, while the prosaic Edward gladly sacrifices the favour of a rich relative for the sake of marriage to Elinor.

Sensibility
The term 'sensibility', indicating the tendency to be easily and strongly affected by emotion, came into general use in the early 18th century. At this time writers and thinkers, such as the third ▷ Earl of Shaftesbury, in reaction against the practical, materialist philosophy of ▷ Hobbes, began to promote an idealistic, spiritual alternative, based on personal feeling. ▷ Joseph Addison in 1711 defined modesty as 'an exquisite Sensibility', 'a kind of quick and delicate Feeling in the Soul'. By the middle of the 18th century the word 'sensibility' had grown in stature, indicating the capacity for compassion or altruism, and also the possession of good taste in the arts. ▷ Joseph Warton in 1756 declines to explain a subtle point since 'any reader of sensibility' will already have taken it. ▷ Laurence Sterne in his ▷ *Sentimental Journey* (1768) eulogizes 'Dear Sensibility! source unexhausted of all that's precious in our joys or costly in our sorrows!' The word remained fashionable in this sense in the early 19th century when ▷ Jane Austen used it in the title of her novel *Sense and Sensibility* (1811).

Recently critics have begun to refer to the period from about the time of the death of ▷ Alexander Pope in 1744 until the publication of ▷ *Lyrical Ballads* in 1798 as the 'Age of Sensibility'. This label is preferred to 'late Augustanism' or 'pre-Romanticism', since it stresses the distinctive characteristics of the period rather than relating it by negative contrast to a different one. The poets of this time, ▷ Thomas Gray, ▷ William Collins and ▷ William Cowper, share a distinctive emphasis on feeling as an end in itself, rather than as part of some larger philosophical scheme. This can be seen both in the resonant truisms of Gray's ▷ *Elegy* and *Eton College Ode*, and in the descriptive delicacy of Collins's *To Evening* or Cowper's *The Poplar-Field*. Even the conservative neo-classicist ▷ Samuel Johnson shows something of this sensibility in the emotional intensity of his Christian stoicism.

However, the cultivation of sensibility also led to experiment and restlessness in poetic form. Emotional novelty was sought in exoticism and medievalism. The oral ▷ ballad was given respectability by ▷ Thomas Percy's *Reliques*, while ▷ James Macpherson, ▷ Thomas Chatterton, and ▷ Thomas Warton all adopted various medieval, ▷ 'Gothic' tastes or literary forms. These developments in poetry were paralleled in the 'Gothic story', ▷ *The Castle of Otranto* (1765) by ▷ Horace Walpole. The new intensity of feeling took a less exotic form in the profuse sentiment of ▷ Samuel Richardson's novels, and also in the cult of sentimentalism promoted by Sterne's *A Sentimental Journey* and Henry Mackenzie's ▷ *The Man of Feeling* (1771).
Bib: Todd, J., *Sensibility*; Hilles, F. W., and Bloom, H. (eds.), *From Sensibility to Romanticism*; Frye, N., *Towards Defining an Age of Sensibility*.

Sentimental Journey through France and Italy, A (1768)
A narrative, part novel and part travel book, by ▷ Laurence Sterne (under the pseudonym of 'Mr Yorick' – the name of a character in Sterne's ▷ *Tristram Shandy*), based on his stay in France, 1762–64. It was intended to be longer, but Sterne died after the publication of the first two volumes in 1768.

September Massacre
An episode of the ▷ French Revolution, when fear of foreign invasion caused revolutionaries to massacre political prisoners between 2 and 5 September 1795.

Septuagint
The oldest Greek translation of the Old Testament of the Bible, so called from the

tradition that 72 translators were employed on it ('septuagint' derives from the Latin for 70). According to this tradition, the translation was made on the orders of Ptolemy II of Egypt (3rd century BC) on behalf of the Jews of the Egyptian city of Alexandria.

Serapis

In ancient Egyptian myth, a fusion of Apis, the bull-god of the sun, with ▷ Osiris, king of the underworld. Serapis eventually came to be worshipped as god of the underworld, or world of the blessed dead, in preference to Osiris.

Serf

▷ Village, The English.

Sermons

The word 'sermon' is used in English to denote a speech from a church pulpit for the edification of the audience, always in this context called a 'congregation'. The sermon considered as a means of communication had a central importance in English life until the 19th century, when universal literacy and the rise of the mass-circulation newspaper tended to eclipse it. At a popular level, it reached a larger audience than any other form of public communication. ▷ Chaucer's Pardoner in the ▷ *Canterbury Tales* demonstrates the power that a medieval preacher felt that he had over an ignorant and superstitious audience, but ▷ *The Pardoner's Tale* is partly a satire about how the sermon could be abused. The sermon was a means of religious and governmental (*eg* Elizabethan *Book of Homilies*) propaganda. Doctrine, speculative philosophy, social criticism, and ethical problems of daily life were all within the sphere of the sermon, and interested all ranks of society in one way or another.

The sermons of ▷ Hugh Latimer, who lived through the most dramatic phase of the English Reformation, are some of the earliest examples in English of vivid prose in the popular and spoken idiom. Three famous preachers of the golden age of Anglicanism in the first half of the 17th century have left sermons addressed to the Court or to other highly educated audiences. The best known of these is the poet ▷ John Donne, who became Dean of St Paul's in 1621. His sermons have massive learning, but his style is richly personal and persuasive, with a depth of feeling comparable to that of his great religious verse. ▷ Lancelot Andrewes was a subtle and elaborate analyst in language, and appealed more exclusively to the intellect, and ▷ Jeremy Taylor was described by ▷ Coleridge as the 'Spenser of prose'

because of his command of musical cadence and linguistic flow.

The change that came over English in the middle of the century emphasized flexibility, control, and lucidity at the expense of poetic emotive power. It is heralded by John Wilkins's book on preaching, *Ecclesiastes* (1646), which teaches the virtue of strict method in organizing a sermon. The main Anglican preachers of the next hundred years, were Robert South (1634–1716), notable for his succinctness and ▷ satire, Isaac Barrow (1630–77), whom ▷ Charles II called 'the best scholar in England', John Tillotson (1630–94), famous for the elegance of his prose, and Joseph Butler (1692–1752), an acute thinker. The virtues of this kind of sermon, and the vices that it sought to combat, are tersely expressed by ▷ Swift (whose own sermons are exemplars of the ideal) in his *Letter to a Young Gentleman entered into Holy Orders* (1721). The best of the ▷ Puritan preachers followed a similar course in a more popular idiom, for instance the Presbyterian Richard Baxter (1615–91) who declared 'The Plainest words are the profitablest oratory in the weightiest matters', and this is a criterion which ▷ Bunyan exemplifies at its noblest.

During the 18th century there was a tendency for sermons to lose touch with the common people. The sermons of William Paley (1743–1805) owed their fame to his talents as a teacher, but they show mediocrity of thought and tepidity of feeling. Those of the novelist ▷ Laurence Sterne (*Sermons of Mr Yorick*, 1760) and of the poet ▷ George Crabbe have merit (especially Sterne's) as literary essays in ethics, but that is what they are, rather than spiritual discourses. It was left to those outside the Anglican tradition, ▷ John Wesley, the founder of ▷ Methodism, and George Whitefield (1714–70) to address themselves to the less educated.

In the 19th century there were still preachers of great influence, some on the popular level, such as the enormously popular ▷ Baptist clergyman, ▷ Charles Spurgeon. But ▷ J. H. Newman, the leader of the ▷ Oxford Movement who later became a Catholic and a cardinal, was perhaps the last preacher to be also a major literary figure. It was not merely the competition of the Press that displaced the sermon from its central influence in English life by the end of the 19th century, but the growth of agnosticism among the intelligentsia and the corresponding decline in the prestige of the pulpit.

Bib: Henson, H. (ed.), *Selected English Sermons* (World's Classics); Sampson, A. (ed.), *Famous English Sermons*.

Setebos
A god of the Patagonians in South America at the time when Shakespeare wrote ▷ *The Tempest*. In the play, he is the god worshipped by the witch Sycorax, mother of Caliban. Shakespeare may have known of Setebos from Francis Fletcher's account of ▷ Drake's voyage round the world, 1577–81. In his poem 'Caliban upon Setebos' (*Dramatis Personae*, 1864) ▷ Robert Browning presents a savage's meditation on the creation of the world.

Seven Ages of the World
A scheme of universal, Christian history, frequently represented in pictorial form in the medieval period. the chief figures of the first three 'ages of the world', the time of natural law, are Adam, Noah, ▷ Abraham and ▷ Isaac. The time of written law, the fourth and fifth 'ages of the world', are devoted to Moses and the Prophets. The time of Christ's birth to the present constitutes the sixth 'age of the world', the time of grace. The time of Doomsday is the time of the seventh age.

Seven Champions of Christendom
A collective term for the guardian saints of European countries: St George of England, St Andrew of Scotland, St Patrick of Ireland, St David of Wales, St Denis of France, St James of Spain and St Anthony of Italy.

Seven Deadly Sins
The sins for which, as the Church taught, the punishment was spiritual death (*ie* not a venial sin for which it was possible to obtain forgiveness). The list usually given is: Pride; Envy; Sloth; Gluttony (or intemperance); Avarice (or covetousness); Anger (ire, wrath); Lust. These sins were frequently personified, *eg* in the medieval ▷ morality plays and in ▷ *Piers Plowman*, the Parson's Tale in Chaucer's ▷ *Canterbury Tales*, Spenser's ▷ *The Faerie Queene* and Marlowe's ▷ *Doctor Faustus*.

Seven Sisters, The
A name for the group of stars called the ▷ Pleiades. Also, a line of high chalk cliffs on the south coast of England, near Newhaven.

Seven Sleepers of Ephesus, The
A Christian legend dating from the 6th century. In the 3rd century, seven young Christians, fleeing persecution by the Emperor Decius, took refuge in a cave. When they were discovered asleep there, the emperor ordered that the cave should be walled up. Their sleep was miraculously prolonged, and 187 years later they emerged to find Christianity everywhere triumphant. They told their story to the Christian emperor, Theodosius II, and then returned to their slumbers.

Seven Wonders of the World, The
A list dating from the 2nd century BC of what were then considered to be the most remarkable productions by man in the known world: the Egyptian pyramids; the Mausoleum at Halicarnassus; the hanging gardens of ▷ Babylon; the temple of ▷ Artemis at Ephesus; the statue of ▷ Zeus by ▷ Pheidias at Olympia; the ▷ Colossus of Rhodes, and the Pharos at Alexandria (for which the Walls of Babylon was substituted in another list).

Seven Years' War, The (1756–63)
Frederick the Great of Prussia, in alliance with Great Britain and Hanover, fought an alliance of France, Austria and Russia. Frederick kept his dominions by the Treaty of Hubertusberg. The importance of the war for Britain was that it left her predominant in North America and in India (Treaty of Paris, 1763). An indirect consequence of this was that the American colonists, no longer afraid of conquest by the French, now felt free to resist the British policy of taxing them without allowing them representation in Parliament; this led to the American War of Independence (1775–83) and the establishment of the United States.

The Seven Years' War produced three war-leaders: in India, Robert Clive, victor of the battle of Plassey, 1757; in America, James Wolfe, captor of Quebec, 1759; and ▷ William Pitt the Elder, Earl of Chatham, the minister who controlled the strategy of the Franco–British struggle.

Seventeenth-century literature
The 17th century was one of the richest periods in the history of English literature, both for achievement and for variety. It also saw a revolution in the human mind, not only in Britain but elsewhere in Europe – a revolution which constitutes the birth of modern outlook. The century begins with writers like ▷ William Shakespeare and ▷ John Donne, whose language fused thought and feeling in both poetry and prose; it ends with ▷ John Dryden and ▷ John Locke, writers whose language was shaped by a new ideal of prose, who opposed 'judgement' to 'wit' – that is to say, the

analytic to the synthetic powers of the mind. Another way of putting it is to say that the century opens with one of the most exciting periods of poetic drama in the whole history of Europe, and it closes with the most influential period of English ▷ satire, and the prose of fact which in the next century was to find its most ample form of expression in the ▷ novel.

We are in the habit of using the term 'Elizabethan drama' for this period of the English theatre, but in fact it was in the reign of ▷ James I, the ▷ Jacobean period, that this type of drama came to fruition. By 1600, Shakespeare was only approaching his best work, ▷ Ben Jonson was just beginning his career, and the plays of the other important dramatists – ▷ Chapman, ▷ Webster, ▷ Tourneur and ▷ Middleton – were as yet unwritten. The finest of this drama was the result of a precarious balance, which kept the long medieval past in mind together with the social and intellectual changes of the present, and communicated with the populace as well as with the court. Already by 1610, this balance was being upset; the elegant but superficial taste of the younger dramatists, ▷ Beaumont and ▷ Fletcher, was turning a national drama into an upper-and middle-class London theatre, which has remained dominant to the present day. By the time of the ▷ Caroline drama of the reign of ▷ Charles I, this transformation was nearing completeness in the plays of ▷ Massinger, ▷ Ford and ▷ Shirley. But in the meantime, the peculiar genius of the best dramatists, especially Shakespeare, had helped to produce among the lyric poets the school now so much admired under the name of the ▷ Metaphysicals. The great Metaphysical poets (notably John Donne, ▷ George Herbert, and ▷ Andrew Marvell) owe their name to the possession of a quality which is central to Shakespeare's genius: the capacity to unite oppositions of thought and of feeling under the control of a flexible, open, but poised intelligence; their poetry, like Shakespeare's work, thus expresses a peculiarly rich body of experience, united from different levels of the mind.

But the Metaphysicals were not the only fertile school of poets in the first half of the century, nor was Shakespearean drama the only kind from which poets could learn. Shakespeare's rival, Ben Jonson, was, as a dramatist, in isolated opposition to the Shakespearean drama. The difference lay partly in conceptions of form. Jonson imposed his form upon his matter; the confusion and

violence of experience is shaped by a selective process which is a disciplining of the mind as well as a critical analysis of the subject. In his lyric poetry as well as in his dramas, this discipline shows itself in irony, proportion, and a union of strength with elegance. Jonson's example influenced the later Metaphysicals, notably Marvell, but it also led to a different school, not always to be sharply distinguished, which we know as ▷ the Cavalier Poets, such as ▷ Carew, ▷ Herrick and ▷ Lovelace. Above all, Jonson's criteria anticipated the 'classicists' of the later part of the century, especially Dryden.

But yet another poet left an important legacy to the 17th century. This was ▷ Edmund Spenser who had perfected those qualities of musical cadence and sensuous imagery which many readers think of as essentially 'poetic'. He had his followers in the first 30 years of the 17th century, though none of note, but it is to him that ▷ John Milton owes most among his predecessors. In Milton, we have two very different 17th-century outlooks uneasily united: the love of all that is implied by the ▷ Renaissance, that is to say the revaluation of classical literature and the discovery of the glories of earthly civilization as opposed to those of a heavenly destiny, and devotion to ▷ Puritanism, implying the extreme Protestant belief that not only is all truth God's truth, but that the sole ultimate source of it is the Bible. This uneasy union produced in Milton the determination to impose on his society a Judaic-Christian conception of human destiny so grand that it compelled acceptance, and to use as his medium what was considered to be the grandest of all the ancient artistic forms, the ▷ epic.
▷ Paradise Lost (1667) was so impressive as an attempt to realize this impossible ambition, and so imposing in its union of the classical form and the biblical subject, that it has won the reverence of three centuries. But Milton's sonorous eloquence, like Spenser's sensuous music, was a kind of magic that subdued the intellect rather than persuaded it. The unfortunate consequence was the common belief among 18th- and 19th-century poets that 'sublime' poetry should elevate the emotions while passing the intellect by. This Miltonic influence no doubt encouraged the exponents of reason like ▷ Locke (▷ Essay concerning Human Understanding, 1690) to believe that poetry belongs to an immature stage of mental development, before the mind has acquired reason and respect for facts, the best medium for which is prose.

From the beginning of the century, prose writers showed signs of seeing their function as clarifying the reason as opposed to enlarging the imagination. This turning away from the imagination went naturally with a gradual relegation of religion. ▷ Francis Bacon, in his ▷ *Advancement of Learning* (1605), treats religion with respect and then ignores it, and he ends his few remarks on poetry with the sentence: 'But it is not good to stay too long in the theatre.' ▷ Shelley (in his *Defence of Poetry*, 1821) was nonetheless to consider Bacon himself to be a poet, but the vivid imagery which strikes out of his terse style is more functional than that of earlier prose writers. Bacon's main theme is the inductive method of acquiring knowledge through experiment, and all his prose, including his ▷ *Essays*, is essentially practical. Although the imaginative connotations are preserved, the dominant tendency in the first half of the century (*eg* in the ▷ 'character' writers such as John Earle, and ▷ Robert Burton's treatise on psychology, ▷ *The Anatomy of Melancholy*) is to use prose descriptively and analytically. Thomas Browne's ▷ *Religio Medici* is written, like his other works, in the most sonorous prose in the English language, but Browne is defending his religious faith just because it exceeds his reason, and his poetic style (in contrast to that of the great sermon writers like John Donne) is partly a conscious contrivance.

In the middle of the century, Thomas Hobbes published his treatise on political philosophy, ▷ *Leviathan* (1651) in which, with pungent ruthlessness, he forced his readers to face the 'facts' of human nature in their grimmest interpretation. After the ▷ Restoration of the Monarchy (1660), the historian of the ▷ Royal Society, Bishop Sprat, laid down the new standards that were to guide the prose writer: 'a close, naked, natural way of speaking; positive expressions; clear senses; a native easiness'. This is the prose we find in the dialogue of Restoration comedy (▷ Etherege, ▷ Wycherley, ▷ Vanbrugh and ▷ Congreve), in the literary criticism of Dryden, and above all in the sceptical, reasonable philosophy of Locke. However, the spiritual life of the middle and lower classes was not yet permeated by this rationalism. The spirit of Puritanism, still biblical and poetic, is expressed in the spiritual autobiographies of the Puritan leaders, such as the Quaker ▷ George Fox (*Journal*, 1694), and, at its most impressive, that imaginative work ▷ *The Pilgrim's*

Progress, by the Baptist tinsmith, ▷ John Bunyan. In this work, the old ▷ allegories of the Middle Ages reach forward into the field of the novel, the new form which was to come into being in the 18th century.

▷ Dissociation of Sensibility; Humours, Comedy of; Manners, Comedy of; Elizabethan period of English literature.

Seward, Anna (1747–1809)
Poet and letter-writer. She was nicknamed 'The Swan of Lichfield', and ▷ James Boswell consulted her in the composition of his ▷ *Life of Samuel Johnson*. Her poetical works were published by ▷ Sir Walter Scott in 1810, and her *Letters* appeared in 1811.

Sewell, Anna (1820–78)
Famous for the one book she wrote, *Black Beauty* (1877), whose success was largely posthumous. Sewell was paid only £20 for the book, which was published just before her death. The story, of a black mare's unhappy adventures, ending happily, has remained a children's classic.
▷ Children's books.
Bib: Chitty, S., *Life*.

Shadwell, Thomas (?1642–92)
Dramatist and poet. Born in Norfolk. Shadwell was educated at Bury St Edmunds and at Cambridge and entered the Middle Temple in 1658. However, he decided on a literary career instead of the law. He travelled on the Continent, and married Ann Gibbs, an actress in the ▷ Duke's Company. Shadwell was a disciple of ▷ Ben Jonson and admirer of ▷ Molière, on whose play *Les Facheux* he based *The Sullen Lovers* (1668). Shadwell wrote 17 plays, of which the best known are *Epsom Wells* (1672), ▷ *The Virtuoso* (1676), an engaging satire on the Royal Society, and *The Squire of Alsatia* (1688) (the latter refers to Whitefriars, a London district where those liable to arrest took sanctuary, and the play makes free use of the cant language of thieves and their associates).

A convinced ▷ Whig, unlike most of his leading contemporaries in the theatre, Shadwell incurred the fierce enmity of the Tory ▷ John Dryden. At first the two men were on good terms, but they took opposite sides when ▷ Lord Shaftesbury clashed with ▷ Charles II on the issue of the Protestant succession to the throne. Dryden attacked Shaftesbury in ▷ *Absalom and Achitophel* and *The Medal*; Shadwell retorted with *The Medal of John Bayes: A Satire*

Against Folly and Knavery (1682). Dryden then stigmatized Shadwell in *MacFlecknoe, Or A Satire on the True Blue Protestant Poet, T. S.* (1682) as one who 'never deviates into sense', and as Og in the second part of *Absalom and Achitophel*. Shadwell attempted counter-attack in an adaptation of ▷ Juvenal's tenth satire, but Dryden's proved the more lasting reputation, and Shadwell has retained an unfair image as a dull author. However, he had some revenge by superseding Dryden as ▷ Poet Laureate after the Protestant triumph in the Revolution of 1688. A regular user of opium, Shadwell died suddenly, supposedly after an overdose. His daughter Anne became an actress, the celebrated ▷ Anne Oldfield, and a son, Charles, became a dramatist.

Bib: Dobree, B., *Restoration Comedy*; Summers, M. (ed.), *Works*; Borgman, A. S., *Thomas Shadwell: His Life and Comedies*.

Shaffer, Peter (b 1926)

British dramatist who has established his reputation with a number of major successes: *The Royal Hunt of the Sun* (1964); *Black Comedy* (1965); *Equus* (1973); *Amadeus* (1974); and *Lettice and Lovage* (1987). The first is a spectacular play about the Spanish conquest of Peru; the second a short farce; the third an exploration of the disturbed psyche of a violent youth who puts out the eyes of a horse; *Amadeus* looks at the court composer Antonio Salieri's jealousy (and possible murder) of Mozart; Shaffer's most recent play is a comedy written especially for the actress Maggie Smith.

Bib: Klein, D., *Peter Shaffer*.

Shaftesbury, Lord (Anthony Ashley Cooper, 1st Earl of Shaftesbury, 1621–83)

Politician. He first took the side of the king in the ▷ Civil War of 1642–46, but changed sides because he considered that Royalist policy threatened the Protestant religion. He later became a parliamentary opponent of ▷ Cromwell, however, and after the ▷ Restoration he became one of ▷ Charles II's chief ministers. Charles II, however, was Catholic in sympathy, and Shaftesbury again went into opposition in 1673. By the Exclusion Bill, he tried to exclude Charles's openly Catholic brother, James, Duke of York, from succession to the throne, advancing the claims of Charles's illegitimate son, the ▷ Duke of Monmouth, in James's place. The alliance of Shaftesbury and Monmouth is satirized in Dryden's ▷ *Absalom and Achitophel*, one of the best-known satirical poems in the English language. Charles II's statesmanship outwitted Shaftesbury, who fled to Holland and died in exile.

Shaftesbury, Lord (Anthony Ashley Cooper, 3rd Earl of Shaftesbury, 1671–1713)

A moral philosopher, with great influence in the first half of the 18th century. His main beliefs are contained in his *Characteristics of Men, Manners, Opinions, Times* (1711; revised edition, 1713). He was a Deist (▷ Deism), a Churchman, and a Platonic idealist. His optimistic philosophy was in direct oppositon to that of ▷ Thomas Hobbes, author of ▷ *Leviathan*. He believed that men have 'natural affections' which are capable of going beyond self-interest. The cultivation of disinterested affection for others will produce virtue and the true social morality. His concept of these 'natural affections' seemed to make the supernatural elements of Christian doctrine unnecessary to the acquirement of true religion. On this ground he was opposed by Bishop Butler in his *Analogy of True Religion* (1736). On a purely theoretical level, Shaftesbury anticipated the beliefs about Nature of the poet ▷ William Wordsworth, and he encouraged the growing emphasis on sentiment and sensibility in criticism and poetry in the 18th century.

Bib: Willey, B., in *Eighteenth-century Background* and *The English Moralists*; Brett, R. L., *The Third Earl of Shaftesbury: a Study in Eighteenth-century Literary Theory*.

Shaftesbury, Lord (Anthony Ashley Cooper, 7th Earl of Shaftesbury, 1801–85)

Statesman and philanthropist. His politics were right wing, but he devoted his career to improving the condition of the working classes. It was largely owing to him that the Ten Hours Bill, restricting hours of work in factories became law in 1847, and in the same decade his efforts led to improvement in the mines. After 1846, he gave his attention to the London slums; clearance of the squalid district of ▷ Seven Dials led to the building of Shaftesbury Avenue, called after him; the statue of Eros in Piccadilly Circus also commemorates him. Shaftesbury was an adherent of the religious revival known as the ▷ Evangelical Movement, working against the ▷ Utilitarian theories of the political economists (▷ Adam Smith, ▷ Jeremy Bentham, ▷ Thomas Malthus) in the shaping of the industrial changes and urban expansion of the mid-19th century.

▷ Industrial Revolution. Anti-industrialism.

Shakespeare, William (1564–1616) – biography

William Shakespeare's signature

Dramatist and poet. He was baptized on 26 April 1564; his birth is commemorated on 23 April, which happens also to be St George's Day, the festival of the patron saint of England. His father, John Shakespeare, was a Stratford-on-Avon merchant who dealt in gloves and probably other goods; his grandfather, Richard Shakespeare, was a yeoman, *ie* small farmer, and his mother, Mary Arden, was the daughter of a local farmer who belonged to the local noble family of Arden, after whom the forest to the north of Stratford was named. John Shakespeare's affairs prospered at first, and in 1568 he was appointed to the highest office in the town – High Bailiff, equivalent to Mayor. A grammar school existed in Stratford, and since it was free to the sons of burgesses, it is generally assumed that William attended it. If he did, he probably received a good education in the Latin language; there is evidence that the sons of Stratford merchants were, or could be, well read and well educated. He married Anne Hathaway in 1582, and they had three children: Suzanna, born 1583, and the twin son and daughter, Hamnet and Judith, born 1585.

Thereafter Shakespeare's life is a blank, until we meet a reference to him in *A Groatsworth of Wit* (1592), an autobiographical pamphlet by the London playwright ▷ Robert Greene, who accuses him of plagiarism. By 1592, therefore, Shakespeare was already successfully embarked as a dramatist in London, but there is no clear evidence of when he went there. From 1592 to 1594 the London theatres were closed owing to epidemics of plague, and Shakespeare seems to have used the opportunity to make a reputation for himself as a narrative poet: his ▷ *Venus and Adonis* was published in 1593, and ▷ *The Rape of Lucrece* (▷ *Lucrece*) a year later. Both were dedicated to Henry Wriothesley, ▷ Earl of Southampton. He continued to prosper as a dramatist, and in the winter of 1594 was a leading member of the ▷ Lord Chamberlain's Men with whom he remained for the rest of his career. In 1596 his father acquired a coat of arms – the sign of a ▷ Gentleman – and in 1597 William bought New Place, the largest house in Stratford. There he probably established his father, who had been in financial difficulties since 1577. In 1592, John Shakespeare had been registered as a recusant (▷ Recusancy); this might mean that he was a Catholic, but is more likely to show that he was trying to escape arrest for debt.

In 1598, ▷ Francis Meres, in his literary commentary *Palladis Tamia, Wit's Treasury*, mentions Shakespeare as one of the leading writers of the time, lists 12 of his plays, and mentions his ▷ sonnets as circulating privately; they were published in 1609. The Lord Chamberlain's Men opened the ▷ Globe Theatre in 1598, and Shakespeare became a shareholder in it. After the accession of ▷ James I the company came under royal patronage, and were called the King's Men; this gave Shakespeare a status in the royal household. He is known to have been an actor as well as a playwright, but tradition associates him with small parts: Adam in ▷ *As You Like It*, and the Ghost in ▷ *Hamlet*. He may have retired to New Place in Stratford in 1610, but he continued his connections with London, and purchased a house in Blackfriars in 1613. In the same year, the Globe theatre was burnt down during a performance of the last play with which Shakespeare's name is associated, ▷ *Henry VIII*. His will is dated less than a month from his death. The fact that he left his 'second-best bed' to his wife is no evidence that he was on bad terms with her; the best one would naturally go with his main property to his elder daughter, who had married John Hall; his younger daughter, who had married Thomas Quiney, was also provided for, but his son, Hamnet, had died in childhood. His last direct descendant, Lady Barnard, died in 1670.

Owing to the fact that the subject-matter of biography was restricted until mid-17th century to princes, statesmen and great soldiers, the documentary evidence of Shakespeare's life is, apart from the above facts, slight. His contemporaries, ▷ Christopher Marlowe and ▷ Ben

Jonson, are in some respects better documented because they involved themselves more with political events. Many legends and traditions have grown up about Shakespeare since near his own day, but they are untrustworthy. He was certainly one of the most successful English writers of his time; his income has been estimated at about £200 a year, considerable earnings for those days. After the death of Marlowe in 1593, his greatest rival was Ben Jonson, who criticized his want of art (in *Discoveries*, 1640), admired his character, and paid a noble tribute to him in the prefatory poem to the ▷ First Folio collection of his plays (1623).

Bib: Chambers, E. K., *William Shakespeare: A Study of Facts and Problems*, 2 vols.; Schoenbaum, S., *Shakespeare's Lives; William Shakespeare: A Documentary Life*.

Shakespeare – criticism

As with any author of the first greatness, different ages have appreciated different aspects of Shakespeare. In his own day, popular taste, according to ▷ Ben Jonson, particularly enjoyed ▷ *Titus Andronicus*, now regarded as one of the least interesting of his plays. ▷ John Dryden (▷ *Essay on Dramatic Poesy*), picked out ▷ *Richard II*; ▷ Samuel Johnson (*Preface to Shakespeare*, 1765) admired the comedies. It is possible to understand these preferences: *Titus* is the most bloodthirsty of all the plays, and suited the more vulgar tastes of an age in which executions were popular spectacles. Dryden and Johnson both belonged to ▷ neo-classical periods. Johnson, like Dryden, was troubled by the differences in Shakespeare's tragedies from the formalism of ancient Greek and 17th-century tragedy which the spirit of their period encouraged them to admire, and Johnson's warm humanity caused him to respond to the plays which displayed wide human appeal while their mode permitted some licence of form. Both Johnson and Dryden rose superior to the limitations of their period in according Shakespeare such greatness. The inheritor of ▷ Johnson's mantle as the most perceptive critic of Shakespeare in the 19th century is ▷ S. T. Coleridge, whose seminal lectures on Shakespeare were inspired by German Romanticism. In his letters ▷ John Keats offers some of the most enduringly valuable comments on Shakespeare's works before A. C. Bradley published *Shakespearean Tragedy* in 1904, which was to prove the most influential text on Shakespeare for two generations.

If the 20th century has not produced a Johnson, or Coleridge or Bradley in Shakespeare studies, Wilson Knight (*The Imperial Theme, The Crown of Life*), ▷ Harley Granville-Barker (*Preface to Shakespeare*) and others such as D. A. Traversi (*An Approach to Shakespeare*) and H. C. Goddard (*The Meaning of Shakespeare*) have all contributed to our deeper understanding of the plays and poetry. Shakespeare's education has been closely scrutinized by T. W. Baldwin in two volumes, *Shakespeare's Smalle Latin and Lesse Greeke*, and Geoffrey Bullough's eight volumes on Shakespeare's sources, *Narrative and Dramatic Sources of Shakespeare*, are indispensable to Shakespearean critics. Increasingly the critical debate has been conducted in a number of specialized journals, particularly the long established *Shakespeare Jahrbuch, Shakespeare Survey, Shakespeare Studies*, and *Shakespeare Quarterly*. A few books are outstanding in their focus on particular aspects of Shakespeare, such as C. L. Barber's influential essay on Shakespearean comedy and the rituals of English folklore and country customs, *Shakespeare's Festive Comedy*, and Northrop Frye's archetypal study of comedy and romance, *A Natural Perspective*. Howard Felperin's distinguished book on Shakespeare's last plays, *Shakespearean Romance* and Janet Adelman's thought-provoking study of *Antony and Cleopatra* and its mythopoeic imagery in *The Common Liar*, both reflect the influence of Frye in their sober and formally predicated approaches.

Of a more radical bent is Jan Kott's famous essay on *King Lear* in '*King Lear*, or *Endgame*' (1964) which argued the case for Shakespeare as our contemporary, with his finger imaginatively on the pulse of a dark, modern human predicament. On the same lines Peter Brook's famous production of *A Midsummer Night's Dream* in 1970 emancipated the play from its putative operatic and conformist frame and irretrievably altered our perception of it. By thus indicating the extent to which the theatre can influence interpretation of plays, Brook materially contributed to redirecting critical attention back to the stage.

Modern social and critical movements have made their impact felt in the field of Shakespeare studies: deconstruction, in the guise of a creative disintegration of the texts' organic status, and feminism provide the impetus for some of the most controversial writing on Shakespeare in the 1980s, as do 'cultural materialism' and particularly 'new historicism'. The latter in particular seems set to command a wide audience in the works of Stephen Greenblatt and Louis Montrose, whose work combines the scholarly scruples of the older tradition with an acute sceptical and self-critical awareness of the historical and epistemological contexts of literary criticism in society.

Bib: Bradley, A. C., *Shakespearean Tragedy*; Barber, C. L., *Shakespeare's Festive Comedy*; Coleridge, S. T., *Shakespearean Criticism*; Dollimore, J., *Radical Tragedy*; Dryden, J., *Essays*; Frye, N., *A Natural Perspective*; Greenblatt, S., *Renaissance Self-Fashioning*; Jardine, L., *Still Harping on Daughters*; Johnson, S., *On Shakespeare*.

Shakespeare – history of textual study

MR. WILLIAM

SHAKESPEARES

COMEDIES,
HISTORIES, &
TRAGEDIES.

Published according to the True Originall Copies.

LONDON
Printed by Isaac Iaggard, and Ed. Blount. 1623.

Frontispiece to first folio of Shakespeare's works, 1623

Apart from a scene sometimes ascribed to Shakespeare in the play *Sir Thomas More* (1596), none of Shakespeare's work has survived in manuscript. In his own lifetime, 18 of his plays were published in separate volumes (the ▷ Quartos), but this was probably without the author's permission, and therefore without his revisions and textual corrections. His non-dramatic poems,

including the ▷ sonnets, were also published during his lifetime. After his death, his fellow-actors, Heming and Condell, published his collected plays (except ▷ *Pericles*) in the large, single volume known as the ▷ First Folio, and this was succeeded by the Second Folio (1632), and the Third (two editions), and Fourth in 1663, 1664 and 1685. The Second Folio regularized the division of the plays into Acts and Scenes, and the second issue of the Third added *Pericles*, as well as other plays which are certainly not by Shakespeare. In several important respects the Folio editions were unsatisfactory:

1 The texts of some (though not all) of the smaller quarto volumes of the plays published during the poet's lifetime differed materially from the text of even the First Folio, which in turn differed from the later folios.

2 The First Folio arranged the plays according to their kinds (Comedies, Histories, or Tragedies) and gave no indication of the order in which the plays were written.

3 There was no evidence that even the first editors had had access to the best manuscript texts, and there were evident errors in some passages, the fault of either the editors or their printers, and editors of the later Folios made alterations of their own. Consequently, there was plenty of work during the next two centuries for scholars to re-establish, as nearly as possible, Shakespeare's original text. Work also had to be done on the chronological order of the plays, discovery of the sources of their plots, philological investigations of linguistic peculiarities, and research into the conditions in which the plays were originally acted.

Two of the most eminent 18th-century writers published editions of the plays; these were ▷ Alexander Pope (in 1725 and 1728), and ▷ Samuel Johnson (in 1765). Neither, however, was a sound scholarly edition, though Johnson's was important for its critical Preface and annotations. Lewis Theobald (1688–1744) attacked Pope's poor scholarship in his *Shakespeare Restored* (1726), and published his own edition in 1734. He was the first enlightened editor, and did permanently useful work both in removing post-Shakespearean additions and alterations and in suggesting emendations of corrupt passages. After him came Steevens and Capell, who compared the original Quarto texts with the Folio ones, and ▷ Edmond Malone (1741–1812), the most eminent of the 18th-century Shakespeare scholars. In 1778 he made the first serious attempt to establish the chronological order of the plays, and in 1790 he brought out the best edition of them yet established.

Shakespearean scholarship in the 18th century was more the work of individuals than a collaborative enterprise. They saw many of the problems involved in estimating the relative values of the early texts, the possibilities of scholarly emendation of corrupt passages, and the necessity of eliminating the errors of unscholarly 17th- and 18th-century editors. This work culminated in the publication of 'Variorum' editions of the plays, 1803–21. But the establishment of a really sound text required the study of wider subject-matter: Shakespeare's work had to be estimated as a whole so that his development could be understood; philological study of the state of the language in his time was needed; historical events had to be examined for their possible relevance; many sources for the plots remained to be discovered; theatrical conditions and the relationship of Shakespeare to dramatists contemporary with him needed exploration; even handwriting was important, for the detection of possible misprinting. All this was the work of the collaborative scholarship of the 19th century. It was carried out by German scholars, by the English Shakespeare Societies led by Halliwell and Furnivall, and by the universities.

In the later 18th century Shakespeare became an inspiration to the movement in Germany for the emancipation of German culture from its long subjection to French culture, represented by the very different genius of ▷ Racine. A. W. Schlegel's remarkable translations (1797–1810) were fine enough to enable Germans to adopt Shakespeare as something like a national poet. German scholars such as Tieck, Ulrici, Gervinus and Franz adopted Shakespearean studies with thoroughness and enthusiasm. They stimulated the foundation of Shakespeare Societies in England, and in 1863–6 the Cambridge University Press was able to publish an edition of Shakespeare's works, which, in its revised form (1891–93), is substantially the text now generally in use.

There has been considerable editorial activity in the 20th century, and it was to be expected that the 'New Bibliography', spearheaded by A. W. Pollard, ▷ R. B. McKerrow and W. W. Greg would produce a major reconsideration of the Shakespearean text. In the end the fruit of their research, and particularly of McKerrow's brilliant *Prolegomena for the Oxford Shakespeare* (1939), needed to wait for nearly 40 years

before they were put to use by the editors of the *Oxford Shakespeare*, Gary Taylor and Stanley Wells. In the meantime Charlton Hinman produced two seminal volumes on the collations of the extant Folios in *The Printing and Proof-Reading of the First Folio* and incorporated his findings in *The Norton Facsimile: The First Folio of Shakespeare*, which remains a standard work of reference. All the major university and other presses turned their attention to re-editing Shakespeare in the late 1960s and early 1970s. At a time when Oxford University Press were printing two complete one-volume Shakespeares (one old spelling and another modern spelling) as well as a huge textual companion and the entire works in separate editions for the Oxford English Texts, Cambridge University Press published the first volume of Peter Blayney's exhaustive survey of the 'origins' of the First Quarto of ▷ *King Lear; The Texts of 'King Lear' and their Origins*. Cambridge, Methuen (New Arden), Macmillan and Longman have pursued similar goals: updating and editing afresh Shakespeare's works, each bringing to the canon a different approach. Whereas most of the editions have followed basically conservative principles, most have embraced to a greater or lesser degree the Oxford view of the plays as primarily works for the theatre. Increasingly Oxford's view of Shakespeare as a dramatist who regularly reshaped his plays in line with theatrical and aesthetic demands is gaining ground. The particular focus for this hypothesis has become the two-text (Quarto and Folio) *King Lear* which most editors now agree reflects two different versions of the play. The same editorial principles are being applied to other texts which reflect similar source situations such as ▷ *Richard III*, ▷ *Hamlet* and ▷ *Othello*. Among Oxford's most radical proposals are the printing of two versions of *King Lear*, the calling of Falstaff 'Oldcastle' in ▷ *Henry IV, Part I*, as well as boldly recreating the text of ▷ *Pericles*.

The history of Shakespeare editing in Britain towards the end of the 20th century is ultimately one of the creative disintegration of the shibboleths of traditional editorial policy, even if all the changes proposed by contemporary scholars do not find favour with posterity.

Bib: Bowers, F., *On Editing Shakespeare*; Greg, W. W., *The Shakespeare First Folio: Its Bibliographical and Textual History*; Honigmann, E. A. J., *The Stability of Shakespeare's Text*; McKerrow, R. B., *Prolegomena for the Oxford Shakespeare*;

Wells, S., *Re-Editing Shakespeare for the Modern Reader*.

Shakespeare's plays

Earliest publications. The first collected edition was the volume known as the First ▷ Folio (1623). This included all the plays now acknowledged to be by Shakespeare, with the exception of *Pericles*. It also includes *Henry VIII*. ▷ Stationers (the profession then combining bookselling and publishing) were glad to bring out individual plays in ▷ quarto editions in his lifetime, however, and since there was no law of copyright these were often 'pirated', *ie* published without the permission of the author. On the whole, Shakespeare's company (the Lord ▷ Chamberlain's Men) did not want such publication, since printed editions enabled other acting companies to perform the plays in competition. 18 of Shakespeare's plays were published in this way, sometimes in more than one edition, and occasionally in editions that varied considerably. Since none of the plays has survived in the original manuscript, the task of modern editors is often to reconcile different quartos (where they exist) with each other, and any quartos that exist with corresponding versions in the First Folio. The following is a list of the separate editions of the plays, published while Shakespeare was alive or soon after his death, with dates of different editions where they substantially disagree with one another:

Titus Andronicus (1594)
Henry VI, Part II (1594)
Henry VI, Part III (1595)
Richard II (1597, 1608)
Richard III (1597)
Romeo and Juliet (1597, 1599)
Love's Labour's Lost (1598)
Henry IV, (Part I) (1598)
Henry IV, (Part II) (1600)
Henry V (1600)
A Midsummer Night's Dream (1600)
The Merchant of Venice (1600)
Much Ado About Nothing (1600)
The Merry Wives of Windsor (1602)
Hamlet (1603, 1604)
King Lear (1608)
Troilus and Cressida (1609)
Pericles (1609)
Othello (1622)

Order of composition. The First Folio does not print the plays in the order in which they were written. Scholars have had to work out their chronological order, on three main kinds of evidence: 1 external evidence (*eg*

records of production, publication); 2 internal evidence (*eg* allusions to contemporary events); 3 stylistic evidence. The following is an approximate chronological arrangement, though in some instances there is no certainty:

1590–91	Henry VI, Parts II and III
1591–92	Henry V, Part I
1592–93	Richard III
	The Comedy of Errors
1593–94	Titus Andronicus
	The Taming of the Shrew
	Two Gentlemen of Verona
1594–95	Love's Labour's Lost
	Romeo and Juliet
1595–96	Richard II
	A Midsummer Night's Dream
1596–97	King John
	The Merchant of Venice
1597–98	Henry IV, Parts I and II
1598–99	Much Ado about Nothing
	Henry V
1599– 1600	Julius Caesar
	The Merry Wives of Windsor
	As You Like It
	Twelfth Night
1600–1	Hamlet
	Measure for Measure
1601–2	Troilus and Cressida
1602–3	All's Well that Ends Well
1604–5	Othello
	King Lear
1605–6	Macbeth
1606–7	Antony and Cleopatra
1607–8	Coriolanus
	Timon of Athens
1608–9	Pericles
1609–10	Cymbeline
1610–11	The Winter's Tale
1611–12	The Tempest

Shakespeare is now believed to have written all of *Henry VIII* and to have collaborated with ▷ Fletcher on *Two Noble Kinsmen*.
▷ Romances of Shakespeare; Problem plays (of Shakespeare).

Shakespeare – Sonnets

First published in 1609, but there is no clear evidence for when they were written. They are commonly thought to date from 1595–9; ▷ Francis Meres in *Palladis Tamia* (1598) mentions that Shakespeare wrote sonnets. There are 154 sonnets; numbers 1–126 are addressed to a man (126 is in fact not a sonnet but a 12-line poem) and the remainder are addressed to a woman – the so-called 'dark lady of the sonnets', since it is made clear that she is dark in hair and complexion. There has been much speculation about the dedication: 'To the only begetter of these ensuing sonnets Mr W. H. all happiness and that eternity promised by our everliving poet Wisheth the well-wishing adventurer in setting forth T.T.' 'T.T.' stands for Thomas Thorpe, the stationer (*ie* bookseller and publisher of the sonnets); speculation centres on what is meant by 'begetter' and who is meant by 'W.H.' W.H. may stand for the man (William Hughes?) who *procured* the manuscript of the sonnets for Thorpe, if that is what 'begetter' means. But if 'begetter' means 'inspirer', it has been conjectured that W.H. may be the inverted initials of Henry Wriothesley, ▷ 3rd Earl of Southampton, to whom Shakespeare had dedicated his ▷ *Venus and Adonis* and *The Rape of Lucrece*, or they may stand for William Herbert, Earl of Pembroke, or for someone else. Guesses have also been made as to the identity of the 'dark lady', who has been thought by some to be Mary Fitton, a Maid of Honour at Court who was a mistress of William Herbert. There is too little evidence for profitable conjecture on either subject.

Critics and scholars disagree about the extent to which the sonnets are autobiographical (and if so what they express) or whether they are 'literary exercises' without a personal theme. A middle view is that they are exploratory of personal relations in friendship and in love, and that some of them rehearse themes later dramatized in the plays – for instance 94 suggests the character of Angelo in ▷ *Measure for Measure*, and the recurrent concern with the destructiveness of time seems to look forward to ▷ *Troilus and Cressida* and the great tragedies. Since it is unknown whether the edition of 1609 is a reliable version, there is also some doubt whether the order of the sonnets in it is that intended by Shakespeare; most scholars see little reason to question it.

One of the most valuable recent editions of the *Sonnets* is Stephen Booth's which uses the 1609 text, rightly accepting its ordering of the poetry as binding. Booth's edition compares the modern text with the ▷ Quarto versions at each stage. But if his extensive notes are instructive, they also tend to be too comprehensive in their suggestions of infinite and ultimately meaningless ambiguities in the text. John Kerrigan's edition of *The Sonnets and A Lover's Complaint* provides a sensitive text, informative notes and does justice to the often neglected *A Lover's Complaint*. Kerrigan

authoritatively attributes the poem to Shakespeare and offers the best commentary on it to date.

Bib: Leishman, J. B., *Themes and Variations in Shakespeare's Sonnets*; Schaar, C., *Elizabethan Sonnet Themes and the dating of Shakespeare's Sonnets*; Smith, Hallett, *The Tension of the Lyre: Poetry in Shakespeare's Sonnets*.

Shalott
▷ *Lady of Shalott.*

Shamela (1741)
An Apology for the life of Mrs Shamela Andrews, published pseudonymously by ▷ Henry Fielding, parodies ▷ Samuel Richardson's, ▷ *Pamela* of the preceding year. The plot and characters are taken from Richardson's novel, yet the tone reveals what Fielding saw as Richardson's hypocritical morality, where virtue is rewarded by worldly wealth and status.

Shamrock
A plant whose leaf is divided into three segments; the leaf is used as the national emblem of Ireland. Legend says that ▷ St Patrick, who converted Ireland to Christianity early in the 5th century, used the leaf to exemplify the doctrine of the Trinity.

Shaw, George Bernard (1856–1950)
Dramatist, critic, social thinker. His family belonged to the Irish Protestant gentry. His father was an unsuccessful business man; his mother was a musician of talent. Apart from the musical education he received from her, he was practically self-educated. He came to London in 1876, and set to work as a novelist. The novel proved not to be his medium, but his efforts in the form were an apprenticeship for dramatic writing in which he excelled. He wrote five novels in all: the best known are *Cashel Byron's Profession* (pub. 1885–6) and *The Admirable Bashville* (pub. 1901). In 1884 he joined the newly formed socialist ▷ Fabian Society, of which he became a leading member; he edited *Fabian Essays* (1887) which was influential in forming socialist opinion in Britain. Between 1885 and 1898 he wrote much criticism for a number of papers; he was probably the most astute music and dramatic critic of his time.

His career as a dramatist began in 1892 and lasted substantially until 1939, though he wrote his last play when he was over 90. Through Joseph Archer, the translator, he had come to know the work of the Norwegian dramatist ▷ Henrik Ibsen and was profoundly impressed especially by Ibsen's plays of social criticism such as *A Doll's*

House. In 1891 came his study *The Quintessence of Ibsenism*, and then he embarked on plays of social purpose on his own account. Shaw's art is, however, very different from Ibsen's; whereas for Ibsen the characters are always more important than the ideas in a play, and the characters engage in convincing talk, in Shaw's plays it is the ideas that really matter, and his characters don't talk – they make speeches. The speeches are composed in the operatic tradition of Mozart; Shaw once said that it was Mozart who taught him to write. As a dramatic critic and a student of Ibsen, he had learnt stage-craft thoroughly, and he knew how to achieve theatrical effect, to which his unique talent for wit, surprise, and paradox strongly contributed. In regard to ideas, he was concerned to shock his audiences out of their unthinking acceptance of social conventions, but he was careful (unlike Ibsen) never to scandalize them beyond their willingness to listen. Apart from socialism, his leading doctrine (derived partly from the French philosopher Bergson and partly from the German philosopher ▷ Nietzsche) was his belief in the 'Life Force' – that the progress of humanity depends in every generation on the evolution of geniuses, who comprise the spearheads of advance but inevitably arouse the hostility of their contemporaries. He was the first dramatist to realize that the reading public for plays was now larger than the theatre-going public; accordingly he published his own plays with long prefaces, which are commonly as famous as the plays themselves, and with elaborate stage directions intended not only for stage producers but for readers accustomed to the kind of detail provided by novels.

His most famous plays are probably: *Man and Superman* (1903); *Major Barbara* (1905); ▷ *Pygmalion* (1912); ▷ *Heartbreak House* (1917); *Back to Methuselah* (1921); *Saint Joan* (1924). Other plays: in ▷ *Plays Pleasant and Unpleasant* (1898) – *Widowers' Houses* (first staged 1892); *The Philanderer*; *Mrs Warren's Profession;* ▷ *Arms and the Man;* ▷ *Candida*; *The Man of Destiny*; *You Never Can Tell*. In ▷ *Plays for Puritans* (1901) – *The Devil's Disciple*; ▷ *Caesar and Cleopatra*; *Captain Brassbound's Conversion*. Other plays before 1914: *John Bull's Other Island*; *How He Lied to Her Husband*; *Press Cuttings*; ▷ *The Doctor's Dilemma*; *Getting Married*; *The Showing up of Blanco Posnet*; *Misalliance*; *Fanny's First Play*; ▷ *Androcles and the Lion*; *Overruled*; *Great Catherine*. After 1918: ▷ *The Apple Cart*; *In Good King Charles's Golden Days*.

Among Shaw's extensive political writings are his attack on the British government, *Common Sense about the War* (1914) and *The Intelligent Woman's Guide to Socialism and Capitalism* (1928).
Bib: Pearson, H., *Life*; Henderson, A., *Life;* Chesterton, G. K., *George Bernard Shaw*; Bentley, E., *George Bernard Shaw*; Meisel, M., *Shaw and the Nineteenth Century*; Morgan, M., *The Shavian Playground*.

She Stoops to Conquer

A comedy by ▷ Oliver Goldsmith, first acted in 1773. The basic comedy is that of a morbidly shy man misled into a situation in which he behaves in a way such as to horrify him when he awakes to the true circumstances. The young man is Marlow, sent by his father to court in marriage the daughter of his friend Hardcastle. Marlow loses his way, and is deceived into supposing the Hardcastle house to be an inn. In a gentleman's house he is horribly embarrassed, but in an inn he is at ease; he proceeds to behave off-handedly to old Hardcastle as to a landlord, and to make love to his daughter, as to a waiting maid. The arrival of his father clears up the situation, and the mistake turns out to Marlow's advantage. The play is one of Goldsmith's best works, and an example of the brief revival of the ▷ Comedy of Manners in the 1770s.

She Wou'd If She Cou'd (1668)

Play by ▷ Sir George Etherege, with a cynical and bawdy atmosphere. Two gallants, Courtall and Freeman, are out to seduce and ruin women, but fall in love with Gatty and Ariana in spite of themselves, and are united with them after several scenes of bantering flirtation. The character referred to in the title is Lady Cockwood who, being badly treated by her despicable husband, longs to cuckold him. Courtall and Freeman make sport with her, openly leading her on, but privately mocking and insulting her. The play is derogatory of marriage, despite its endings in espousal, and heavy with race-course imagery, with women seen as horses for men to ride.

Shelley, Mary Wollstonecraft (1797–1851)

The only daughter of feminist ▷ Mary Wollstonecraft and radical philosopher ▷ William Godwin, her mother having died a few days after her birth. Her father remarried in 1801 but Mary found her stepmother unsympathetic and remained rather close to her father despite his cold manner. She idolized her own mother, and educated herself through contact with her

Mary Shelley by R. Rothwell (1841)

father's intellectual circle and her own hard study. She met ▷ Percy Bysshe Shelley in 1812 and on return from an extended visit to friends in 1814 became very close to him. He was in the midst of separating from his wife Harriet, and within a couple of months he and Mary left England together, marrying in 1816 after Harriet's suicide. They had a devoted but difficult relationship, only one of their children surviving childhood, Godwin pressing them for loans and Shelley's father Timothy making only a small allowance for the child, Percy. After Shelley's death in 1822 Mary stayed a short while in Italy, then returned to London where she continued to write novels, produced an account of her travels with Percy in Europe and edited Shelley's poetry and prose, but proved too exhausted to write his biography, which she abandoned. ▷ Frankenstein, or the Modern Prometheus (1817) was her first and most famous novel, apparently inspired by a dream. The Last Man (1826) has characters based on Shelley and ▷ Byron, and Lodore (1835) contains much that is autobiographical. Mathilda (1819) and Valperga (1823) are among her other novels; Rambles in Germany and Italy (1844) was well received; she also published many short stories in annuals like The Keepsake.
Bib: Jones, F. L. (ed.), Mary Shelley's Journal and The Letters of Mary Shelley; Lyles, W. H., Mary Shelley: An Annotated Biography; Nitchie, E., Mary Shelley; Poovey, M., The Proper Lady and the Woman Writer; Gilbert, S. and Gubar, S., The Madwoman in the Attic; Fleenor, J., The Female Gothic.

Shelley, Percy Bysshe (1792–1822)
Poet. He was born into an aristocratic family in Sussex, and was educated at ▷ Eton and ▷ Oxford, from which he was expelled in 1811 for circulating a pamphlet, The Necessity of Atheism. He eloped with and married Harriet Westbrook, who was then only 16, and whom he left after three years. He travelled abroad in 1814 with Mary Wollstonecraft Godwin, daughter of the ▷ feminist ▷ Mary Wollstonecraft and the philosopher William Godwin, whose extreme ▷ rationalism had attracted the young poet. At one point, in accordance with his idealistic notions of free love, Shelley proposed that both Harriet and Mary should live together with him. Accompanied by Mary's step-sister, Claire Clairmont, he and Mary travelled to Switzerland where they joined ▷ Lord Byron, with whom Shelley made a close friendship. Harriet drowned herself in the Serpentine in 1816 and Shelley married Mary, though he continued to develop intense platonic relationships with other women. They moved to Lerici in Italy and in 1822 he was drowned while sailing, in circumstances which suggested that he made no attempt to save himself.

Shelley's earliest writings, produced while he was at Eton and Oxford, are ▷ gothic romances in the style of ▷ Matthew 'Monk' Lewis. His first important poem was the atheistic Queen Mab (1813) in the tradition of the irregular ▷ ode. In 1816 appeared the ▷ blank verse Alastor; or the Spirit of Solitude, in which an exquisitely sensitive young poet is drawn by a highly erotic vision, representing 'truth and virtue . . . And lofty hopes of divine liberty', across exotic eastern landscapes, only to die, disappointed. The Revolt of Islam (1817) in ▷ Spenserian stanzas, preaches bloodless revolution, and has a similar beautiful youth as its protagonist. Mont Blanc, published in the same year, is a less self-indulgent work, in which Shelley turns his intellectual scepticism on the conventional piety of such poems as ▷ Samuel Taylor Coleridge's Hymn Before Sun-rise in the Vale of Chamouni (1802), which describes the same landscape. Where Coleridge attributes the sublime beauty of nature to a 'Great Hierarch', the atheist Shelley attributes it (like Coleridge himself in ▷ Dejection: An Ode) to 'the human mind's imaginings'. In Julian and Maddalo (written 1818, published 1824), he describes in irregularly rhyming ▷ couplets a visit to a madhouse in Venice in the company of Byron, who appears in the guise of an Italian nobleman.

In 1819 Shelley published *The Cenci*, a play in the Elizabethan style, and composed the 'lyrical drama', ▷ *Prometheus Unbound* (1820). He also wrote the *Ode to the West Wind* in which his abstract symbolism is, for once, brilliantly controlled, and makes the natural force of the wind into a convincing metaphor for political revolution. The news of the ▷ 'Peterloo Massacre' in Manchester on August 16, 1819, prompted ▷ *The Mask of Anarchy* (published 1832), a poem of superb rhetoric, calling upon the men of England to overthrow their oppressors. This was followed by *To a Skylark* (1820), the famous elegy on ▷ John Keats, ▷ *Adonais* (1821), *The Witch of Atlas* (published 1824), and another 'lyrical drama', *Hellas* (1822), inspired by the struggle for Greek independence from Turkey. He was working on *The Triumph of Life* when he died, a grimly garish dream-allegory in *terza rima* in which the poet contemplates the gory but awesome pageant of history, in company with the spirit of ▷ Jean-Jacques Rousseau. Shelley's prose ▷ *Defence of Poetry* (written 1821; published 1840) was written in answer to *The Four Ages of Poetry* by his friend ▷ Thomas Love Peacock, who argued that poetry was an obsolete art. Shelley retorts boldly that poets are 'the unacknowledged legislators of the world'.

Shelley can be an extremely irritating poet, particularly when congratulating himself on the exquisiteness of his own sensibility, or indulging in dreamy abstraction and elaborately theatrical symbolism. In his best work, however, he actually achieves the sublimity about which he talks so much, and when dealing with intellectual or political issues he can be eloquently lucid and incisive.
Bib: Blunden, E., *Life*; Barcus, J. E., *Shelley: The Critical Heritage*; Rogers, N., *Shelley at Work*; Webb, T., *Shelley: A Voice Not Understood*; Leighton, A., *Shelley and the Sublime*; Foot, P., *Red Shelley*; Dawson, P. M. S., *The Unacknowledged Legislator: Shelley and Politics*; Swinden, P. (ed.), *Shelley: Shorter Poems* (Macmillan Casebook).

Shenstone, William (1714–63)
Poet and landscape gardening enthusiast. He wrote *The Schoolmistress* (revised version 1742), a ▷ Spenserian ▷ burlesque, celebrating Sarah Lloyd, the schoolmistress of a village near Shenstone's family estate. The condescending sentimentalism of this poem, and the facile lyricism of such works as *A Pastoral Ballad*, in anapaestic ▷ quatrains (*Poems on Various Occasions*, 1737), make Shenstone an important

representative of the new post-Augustan sensibility of the time. ▷ Thomas Percy consulted him in the preparation of his *Reliques*, and he wrote several essays on landscape gardening. His estate at the Leasowes near Halesowen, Staffordshire, became famous for its ingenious 'natural' effects.

Shepherd's Calendar, The (1579) [by Edmund Spenser]
A ▷ pastoral poem by ▷ Edmund Spenser in 12 parts, one for each month of the year, published in 1579. The series is written in the tradition of the ▷ 'eclogues' of ▷ Virgil, *ie* verse dialogues in a rural setting, with shepherds and shepherdesses with classical, French or (more frequently) English peasant names, *eg* ▷ Colin Clout (for Spenser himself) and Hobbinol (for his friend ▷ Gabriel Harvey). The intention is not that of 19th-century nature poetry (contrast ▷ John Clare's ▷ *Shepherd's Calendar*) to give a description of the countryside as it acually is at any particular time of the year, but to use the simplified conditions of an ideal rural setting as a standpoint for commenting on life, often that of the court. Four of the dialogues ('January', 'June', 'November' and 'December') are ▷ complaints, *ie* laments for such things as lost love ('January') or advancing age ('December'). Three of them are cheerful: 'March', in praise of love; 'April' in praise of ▷ Elizabeth I, and 'August', a shepherds' song competition, again in praise of love. 'February', 'May', 'July', 'September' and 'October' are 'moral' eclogues on such topics as respect for age ('February') or a ▷ Protestant attack on Roman Catholicism ('May'). The three main themes are love, poetry and religion. The verse is sophisticated and varied, owing much to the examples of Virgil and ▷ Theocritus, and also to the French 16th-century pastoralist Clement Marot, but paying tribute to ▷ Chaucer as well and following the free rhythms of medieval English poetry. The poem set a fashion for pastoral in England, and inaugurated the great lyrical period of the last 20 years of the 16th century.

Shepherd's Calendar, The (1827)
▷ Clare, John.

Sheraton, Thomas (1751–1806)
Next to ▷ Chippendale the most famous English furniture designer. His reputation, which began about 1790, was built up on his severe and graceful style; later, under the influence of French Empire furniture, his

designs became much more elaborate. He had many imitators, and the name 'Sheraton' is usually associated with a general style rather than with the works of the original master.

Sheridan, Richard Brinsley (1751–1816)
Dramatist and politician. Like many dramatists of note writing in English during the 18th and 19th centuries, he was of Irish extraction, born in Dublin. His courtship of his future wife, Elizabeth Linley, began with his carrying her off to a French nunnery to save her from the attentions of a suitor to whom she objected; he returned to fight two duels with his rival; in 1773 his secret marriage to her in France was publicly recognized. In 1776 he became principal director and, a little later, sole proprietor of the ▷ Drury Lane Theatre in London; it was twice burnt down and rebuilt during his proprietorship. He entered Parliament in 1780, and was famous for his oratory there; his opposition to the American War of Independence caused the American Congress to offer him £20,000, which he refused. His most famous oratorical exploit was his impeachment of Warren Hastings in 1787. During the ▷ French Revolution, he supported the ▷ Whig leader, ▷ Fox, in opposing military intervention against France. Later he held an independent position politically, but he was influential, partly owing to his friendship with the Prince Regent (later George IV). He ended his life deeply in debt.

His memorable plays are ▷ *The Rivals* (1775), ▷ *The School for Scandal* (1777), and *The Critic* (1779); they show a reaction against the sentimental comedy which had dominated the English theatre for much of the 18th century, and the first two belong to a revival of the ▷ Comedy of Manners which had been dominant at the beginning of it. They are still appreciated for the freshness of their dialogue and the ingenuity of their comic situations. Other plays: *St Patrick's Day* (1775); *The Duenna* (a comic opera, 1775); *A Trip to Scarborough* (1777), an adaptation of ▷ Vanbrugh's ▷ *Relapse* (1696), and the tragedy *Pizarro* (1799). **Bib:** Sichel, W., *Life*; Nicoll, A., *A History of Late Eighteenth-century Drama*; Sadleir, T. H., *The Political Career of Sheridan*; Danziger, M. K., *Oliver Goldsmith and Richard Brinsley Sheridan*.

Ship Money
An ancient tax for providing ships to defend the country in time of war. ▷ Charles I revived it in 1634 in time of peace and without the consent of ▷ Parliament. His action caused great resentment, but 12 judges gave their verdict that it was legal. Nonetheless, repeated revivals of the tax aroused positive resistance, notably from John Hampden, and it was one of the contributory causes of the ▷ Civil War that broke out in 1642. In 1641 Parliament passed a law declaring Ship Money an illegal tax.

Shipman's Tale, The
One of ▷ Chaucer's ▷ *Canterbury Tales*. This ▷ fabliau, set in Flanders, involves marital and financial trickery on the part of a wife and a monk, at the expense of the husband, a merchant. A series of bargains between different pairs of the three central protagonists makes up the plot sequence, which concludes with the wife offering sexual credit to her husband, in order to cover his lost loan to the monk. An analogue to the story is found in the ▷ *Decameron* (8.1) but Chaucer's version is distinctive for its detailed development of the mercantile backdrop to this story of a domestic economy.

Shirley, James (1596–1666)
Dramatist. He was one of the last dramatists of the great Elizabethan–Jacobean–Caroline period of English drama, a period which lasted from 1580 to 1640 and included the career of ▷ Shakespeare. Shirley wrote fluent, graceful ▷ blank verse and is at his best in social comedy; in many ways he anticipates the ▷ Restoration writers of comedies of ▷ manners after 1660. His audience, as in Restoration comedy, was that of the elegant, refined court; it was not drawn from all social classes like the audiences for Shakespeare and ▷ Ben Jonson, so that his plays have a comparatively narrow, though sophisticated, range of interests. He wrote over 40 plays, of which the best known are the tragedies *The Traitor* (1631) and *The Cardinal* (1641); and the comedies *The Lady of Pleasure* (1631) and *Hyde Park* (1632).

Shirley (1849)
A novel by ▷ Charlotte Brontë. It is set in the north of England and deals with the bad labour relations of the time of the Napoleonic Wars (1803–15). A mill-owner, Robert Gérard Moore (half Belgian and half English), introduces labour-saving machinery against the opposition of his workers, who threaten to destroy the mill. He attempts to gain money by marrying the rich and proud Shirley Keeldar, who refuses him and eventually marries his brother Louis, opposed to Robert. The end of the war releases Robert from his financial difficulties and he

marries Caroline Helstone, whom he really loves and who loves him. The novel was characteristic of a number written during the 1840s and early 1850s (by ▷ Charles Dickens, ▷ Benjamin Disraeli, ▷ Mrs Gaskell) on the social problems of class hostility. It is also much concerned with the need for useful employment for women. In the character of Shirley Keeldar, Charlotte portrayed her sister ▷ Emily Brontë as she might have been.

Shoemaker's Holiday, The

A comedy by ▷ Thomas Dekker, published in 1600. It is a ▷ citizen comedy, *ie* designed to appeal to the taste and sentiment of the London merchant class, with a strong romantic flavour. The time of the story is mid-15th century, and the principal character is Simon Eyre, shoemaker and, at the end of the play, Lord Mayor of London. The story concerns the courtship by the young nobleman, Rowland Lacy, of Rose, the daughter of the existing Lord Mayor. The courtship is opposed both by his uncle, the Earl of Lincoln, and by Rose's father. Lacy disguises himself as a shoemaker, takes employment with Simon Eyre, and eventually, with the support of the king, they are successfully married. The play is mainly in prose, with blank verse interspersed; it has no profundity but its happy mood has kept it popular.

Shoreditch

A district of east London; it was the first to have a theatre (1576–7). According to legend, its name derives from Jane Shore, the mistress of ▷ Edward IV; she is supposed to have died in a ditch there. In fact the name is older.
▷ Theatres.

Short Story

This very early kind of fiction was first taken seriously in the 19th century as an independent literary form, making different demands on the writer and the reader from the demands of longer works of fiction such as the novel. Three writers originated this serious practice of the art of the short story: the American, Edgar Allan Poe (1809–49); the Frenchman, Poe's disciple, Guy de Maupassant (1850–93); and the Russian, ▷ Anton Chekhov. These writers evolved the qualities especially associated with the short story: close texture, unity of mood, suggestive idiom, economy of means. Such qualities associate the short story with the short poem, and we find that in English the verse story anticipated the prose story in

works such as the tales of ▷ George Crabbe and ▷ Arthur Hugh Clough's *Mari Magno* (1862). However, no relationship can be established between the verse of such writers and the prose of ▷ Rudyard Kipling, with Maupassant behind him, or that of ▷ Katherine Mansfield, who was strongly influenced by Anton Chekhov. These two wrote little else in prose except stories (Kipling wrote two novels), but the greatest masters of the short story form – ▷ Henry James, ▷ Joseph Conrad, ▷ James Joyce, and ▷ D. H. Lawrence – were predominantly novelists. Their stories were perhaps formed less by the example of the foreign writers mentioned than by the structure of their own novels. These had a less distinctly marked plot line than those of earlier novelists, and yet a closer coherence; chapters from them can be extracted showing many of the essential qualities of short stories (*eg* 'Rabbit' in Lawrence's ▷ *Women in Love*, or the Christmas dinner in Joyce's ▷ *Portrait of the Artist*) in spite of their relationship to their respective novels as wholes. It seems therefore that the best stories of these writers were by-products of their novels, which by their structure suggested the evolution of stories as separate entities.

It is difficult to make a clear distinction between the short story and the *nouvelle* (novella or long story); it is difficult also to say at what point a *nouvelle* stops short of being a novel; on the whole the *nouvelle* or 'long short story' seems to share with the short story as generally understood a unity of mood, which is not so likely to be found in a true novel, however short. All the masters of the short story who have been mentioned were also masters of the *nouvelle*, but not necessarily (*eg* Chekhov) of the novel form.

The period 1880–1930 was the flowering time of the short story in English; besides the English writers already mentioned, it included the early and best work of ▷ A. E. Coppard, who was one of the few English fiction-writers of any note (Katherine Mansfield being another) who have restricted themselves to the short-story form. Later short-story writers have been numerous, but they have mostly practised the art as an alternative and often subsidiary form to that of the novel. In Ireland, where the art of the novel has scarcely taken root, the art of the short story has flourished more distinctively. It begins with the stories of ▷ George Moore (*The Untilled Field*, 1903), but the Irish tradition becomes really outstanding in the first books of ▷ Liam O'Flaherty (*Spring Sowing*, 1926), ▷ Sean O'Faolain

(*Midsummer Night Madness*, 1932), and
▷ Frank O'Connor (*Guests of the Nation*,
1931). In his book on the art of the short
story, *The Lonely Voice* (1964), O'Connor
offers an explanation as to why the short
story should be the more natural form of
fiction for Irish literary culture.

Since O'Connor, William Trevor has
continued the Irish connection with the short
story. Other contemporary writers who excel
at the form include ▷ Peter Carey, whose
early stories are collected in *Exotic Pleasures*
(1980) and Ian McEwan, whose collections
First Love, Last Rites (1975) and *In Between
the Sheets* (1977) attracted great critical
attention. ▷ Angus Wilson, ▷ Muriel
Spark, ▷ Nadine Gordimer, ▷ Margaret
Atwood, Desmond Hogan and Shena
Mackay have also used the genre to interesting
effect.
Bib: Bates, H. E., *The Modern Short Story*;
O'Connor, F., *The Lonely Voice*; O'Faolain,
S., *The Short Story*.

Shrovetide, Shrove Tuesday
The period, and in particular the day before,
the six weeks of fast called Lent, which
precedes Easter. The name derives from the
verb 'to shrive', *ie* to absolve a person from
his sins after he has confessed to a priest.
Traditionally, it was a period of festivity
before the period of fast; in England this
festivity is now reduced to the eating of
pancakes on the last day of shrovetide, *ie*
Shrove Tuesday. The following day, Ash
Wednesday, is the first day of Lent, during
which luxuries are supposed to be renounced.

Sibyl
A proper name used, especially in ancient
Greek myth, for women who were divinely
inspired by the god ▷ Apollo with the gift
of prophecy. The original Sibylla is said (by
▷ Heraclitus) to have lived at Marpessus,
near ▷ Troy. She was supposed to be the
author of the Sibylline Books which were
kept in the temple of Jupiter Capitolinus at
Rome. Apollo loved her, and granted her not
only the gift of prophecy but as many years
of life as grains of dust she could hold in her
hand. However, she forgot to ask for eternal
youth, and when, long after, some boys asked
her what she wanted, she said that she
wanted to die.

Sick Man of Europe, The
In the second half of the 19th century, a way
of referring to Turkey, regarding that country
as one which was too large to ignore, yet too
weak to be able to control its own conquered

territories, so that it had become a subject of
chronic international crisis. The phrase was
originated by Tsar Nicholas I of Russia, in
conversation with the British ambassador.

Siddons, Sarah (1755–1831)

Sarah Siddons by G. Stuart

Actress. The most celebrated woman on the
stage in the 18th century. She was the eldest
child of the actor-manager Roger Kemble
and Sarah (née Ward), and was born into
what became an important acting dynasty.
Siddons began acting as a child, including the
part of Ariel in a performance of the
▷ Dryden/▷ D'Avenant version of
▷ *The Tempest*, in which her future
husband, William Siddons (1744–1808),
played Hyppolito. She fought her parents'
disapproval in order to marry him, in 1773,
and the couple continued acting in the
provinces. ▷ Garrick engaged her for a
season at ▷ Drury Lane, 1775–76, but her
first appearances there were poorly received.
Her fortunes turned during a visit to
Manchester, and her reputation as an actress
was consolidated at Bristol and at Bath. In
1782 she appeared again at Drury Lane,
playing Isabella in Garrick's version of
▷ Thomas Southerne's *The Fatal
Marriage*. Her triumph was immediate, and
she went on to play a succession of major
roles with the company, including Belvidera
in ▷ Otway's ▷ *Venice Preserv'd*. It is
said that people breakfasted near the theatre,
so as to be first in the queue for tickets to see

her, some coming from as far away as Newcastle, and prices rose to as much as a hundred guineas. Contemporaries commented on her beauty, stately dignity, and expressiveness, as well as her articulacy, so that not a word was lost. Her capacity to convey passion and grief was legendary. But she was sometimes criticized for her lack of variety, was poor in comic roles, and although she had many friends in high places, she had a reputation for being difficult to work with, and mean with money.

In 1785 Siddons played her most famous part, Lady Macbeth (▷ *Macbeth*), for the first time, later performing it on occasion by royal command. She added to her repertoire Cordelia, Cleopatra, Desdemona, Rosalind in ▷ *As You Like It*, other major Shakespearian roles and many other roles, some written especially for her. Her career was interrupted only for brief intervals by the births of her seven children. In 1803 she followed her brother ▷ John Philip Kemble to Covent Garden. In old age she became fat and had to be helped out of a chair, the fact disguised by other actresses being similarly treated. Widowed in 1805, Siddons retired in 1812, afterwards appearing only at special benefits.

Bib: Boaden, J., *Memoirs of Mrs Siddons* (2 vols); Campbell, T., *Life of Mrs Siddons*; Manvell, R., *Sarah Siddons*; Kelly, L., *The Kemble Era: John Philip and the London Stage*.

Sidney, Sir Philip (1554–86)

Poet, courtier, soldier and statesman. A member of a distinguished noble family, he was a fine example of the ▷ Renaissance ideal of aristocracy in his ability to excel in all that was regarded as fitting for a nobleman. He thus became a pattern for his age, as is shown by the numerous elegies to him, including one by ▷ Edmund Spenser (*Astrophel*) and one by ▷ James I of England. He was wounded at the battle of Zutphen in Flanders in characteristic circumstances, having discarded leg armour on finding that a comrade in arms had neglected to wear any; as he lay mortally wounded in the leg, he is reputed to have passed a cup of water to a dying soldier with the words, 'Thy need is greater than mine.'

Sidney's writings date mostly from the period 1580–83, when he was temporarily out of favour with ▷ Elizabeth I for political reasons, and was living with his sister, ▷ Mary Herbert, Countess of Pembroke at Wilton House near Salisbury; they were

Sir Philip Sidney, miniature by Isaac Oliver

published after his death. His most famous poetry, the ▷ sonnet sequence, ▷ *Astrophil and Stella*, was published in 1591, and inspired the numerous other sonnet sequences of the 1590s, including ▷ Shakespeare's.

Apart from his sonnets, Sidney's poetic reputation rests on the verse interludes in ▷ *The Arcadia*, Sidney's prose romance, started in 1580 and published in 1590. His prose work also includes the most famous piece of Elizabethan criticism, ▷ *An Apologie for Poetrie* published in 1595. A collaboration with his sister, the verse paraphrase of the *Psalms*, was not published till 1823. He also wrote two ▷ pastoral poems published in Davison's *Poetical Rhapsody* (1602) and partly translated from the French Du Plessis Mornay's *A Work Concerning the Trueness of the Christian Religion* (1587).

Bib: McCoy, R. C., *Sir Philip Sidney: Rebellion in Arcadia*; Hamilton, A. C., *Sir Philip Sidney*; Waller, G. F. and Moore, M. D. (eds), *Sir Philip Sidney and the Interpretation of Renaissance Culture*.

Siege of Rhodes, The (1656, revised in 1661)

Opera–cum–heroic drama by ▷ Sir William D'Avenant, thought to have been written originally as a play, with music added later in order to circumvent the Commonwealth law against purely dramatic entertainment, and gain the Government's permission to mount it at Rutland House. The performance helped pave the way for the re-opening of the theatres, and for D'Avenant's own receipt of one of the monopoly patents as theatre manager. The action concerns the siege of Rhodes by Soleyman the Magnificent, and Duke Alphonso's unreasonable jealousy of his wife, the virtuous Ianthe, who eventually saves her husband and the island. D'Avenant said he wrote it partly to illustrate 'the Characters of Vertue in the shapes of Valor and Conjugal Love'. The staging as with the earlier court ▷ masque was accompanied by lavish spectacle.

Sign

This is the term used by ▷ Ferdinand de Saussure in his *Course in General Linguistics* (1915) to refer to any linguistic unit through which meaning is produced. In Saussure's theory, the *sign* is the combination of two discrete elements, the *signifier* (form which signifies) and the *signified* (idea signified). In the phrase 'A rose by any other name would smell as sweet', the word 'rose' is the signifier and the 'concept of a rose' is the signified.

Signifier and signified are distinct aspects of the sign, but exist only within it. One important aspect of Saussure's definition of the sign is that any particular combination of signifier and signified is *arbitrary*. So a 'rose' could be called a 'chrysanthemum' or a 'telephone', but would still be as aromatic. Saussure's perceptions have been extremely influential in the development of ways of discussing the processes through which meaning is achieved.

▷ Langue; Parole; Structuralism; Post-structuralism; Discourse; Barthes, Roland; Derrida, Jacques.

Signified

▷ Sign.

Signifier

▷ Sign.

Silas Marner (1861)

A novel by ▷ George Eliot. Silas is a weaver who has been driven out of a small community of ▷ dissenters in a northern industrial town, in consequence of false information that he has stolen some of the community's funds. He emigrates to a midland village where he is in all essential respects 'a foreigner'. He sets up again as a weaver but he has no relationship with his neighbours beyond the commercial one; having also lost his religious faith, he lives only for money and acquires a store of it.

This is stolen from him by Dunstan Cass, son of the local ▷ squire, but Silas's despair is later obliterated by the mysterious arrival in his cottage of a little girl, whom he adopts, calls Eppie and devotes himself to. His love for her gradually brings to him the affection and respect of his neighbours. It turns out that Dunstan, who had vanished after the theft, had drowned immediately afterwards and that Eppie is really the daughter of Dunstan's elder brother, Godfrey, by a low-class, drunken woman, now dead, to whom Godfrey was secretly married. Godfrey, now happily married but childless, claims Eppie when she is nearly grown up but she refuses to part from Silas. The plot of the novel thus resembles a fable about living and deathly attachments.

Silenus

In Greek myth, a minor woodland deity, usually depicted as drunk. He was generally represented as the son of ▷ Hermes (sometimes ▷ Pan) and Earth; the oldest ▷ satyr, he was also tutor to the wine god ▷ Dionysus and one of his principal followers. He is usually depicted as a bald-headed fat old man riding on a donkey.

Sillitoe, Alan (b 1928)

Novelist and poet. The son of a labourer in a cycle factory, he left school at 14 to work in a similar factory. His birthplace was the Midlands town of Nottingham, near which ▷ D. H. Lawrence also grew up. Sillitoe, like Lawrence, writes from the standpoint of one whose origins are outside London and the middle classes, and he is the best known of a group of post-war novelists from similar backgrounds, including ▷ Stan Barstow, ▷ John Braine and ▷ David Storey. The influence of Lawrence on these writers is inevitably strong, and especially so in the case of Sillitoe, but he presents a narrow spirit of social rebellion from which Lawrence is free. At present, his fame rests chiefly on his first novel, *Saturday Night and Sunday Morning* (1958), which has been filmed. The novel's hero, Arthur Seaton, has become a type-figure of the post-1945 industrial, welfare state working man, born into an economic fabric against which his strong impulses rebel. More original and equally well known is the tale *The Loneliness of the Long-Distance Runner* (1959), a kind of fable of anarchic social rebellion. He has also written stories: *The Ragman's Daughter* (1963); *Guzman Go Home* (1968); *Men Women and Children* (1973); *Down to the Bone* (1976); *The Second Chance* (1980); and poems: *The Rats* (1960); *A Falling Out of Love* (1964); *Snow on the North Side of*

Lucifer (1979); *Sun before Departure: poems 1974 to 1982* (1984); *Tides and Stone Walls* (1986); and more novels: *The General* (1960), about the war in Malaya, in which Sillitoe served; *Key to the Door* (1961); *The Death of William Posters* (1965); *A Tree on Fire* (1967); *A Start in Life* (1970); *Travels in Nihilon* (1971); *Raw Material* (1972); *The Flame of Life* (1974); *The Widower's Son* (1976); *The Storyteller* (1979); *Her Victory* (1982); *The Last Flying Boat* (1983); *Down From the Hill* (1984); *Life Goes On* (1985); *Out of the Whirlpool* (a novella; 1987). In 1978 he published three plays: *This Foreign Field* (1970), *Pit Strike* (1977), *The Interview* (1978).

▷ Realism.

Bib: Atherton, S., *Alan Sillitoe: a Critical Assessment.*

Silver-Fork School
▷ Gore, Catherine.

Simile
▷ Figures of Speech.

Simnel, Lambert (?1477–1525)
An impostor, used by Yorkist opponents of ▷ Henry VII, first king of the ▷ Tudor family; they declared Simnel to be Edward, Earl of Warwick, whose father, George, Duke of Clarence, was the younger brother of ▷ Edward IV. The true Earl of Warwick (1475–99) had been imprisoned by Henry VII. Simnel received extensive foreign support, but his army was defeated by Henry VII at Stoke-on-Trent in 1487. Henry spared Simnel's life, and made him a humble servant in the royal household.

Simon Pure
Character in ▷ *A Bold Stroke for a Wife* (1718), comedy by ▷ Susannah Centlivre, who is described in the list of *Dramatis Personae* as 'a Quaking Preacher'. He is impersonated by Colonel Fainwell, as part of the latter's plot to impress the guardians of Mrs Lovely, and gain their permission to marry her. The scene in which this occurs is interrupted by the arrival of Simon Pure himself, giving rise to the expression, 'the real Simon Pure', meaning the real, genuine, or authentic person or thing.

Simpson, N. F. (Norman Frederick) (b 1919)
British dramatist sometimes classified as an absurdist writer, although his work is strongly influenced by a bizarre and zany humour in the English tradition of ▷ Lewis Carroll and the Goon Show. He wrote several short plays before his more famous *One Way*

Pendulum in 1959, in which 500 weighing machines are taught to sing the Hallelujah Chorus. This was followed by a spy comedy, *The Cresta Run* (1965). Although he is not considered a major dramatist his work helped the development of drama away from conservative conventions during the 1950s and early 60s.

▷ Theatre of the Absurd.

Sinbad the Sailor
The hero of one of the eastern tales called ▷ *Arabian Nights*. His best-known adventure is that with the huge sea-bird called the Roc. (Also spelt Sindbad.)

Sinclair, Andrew (b 1935)
Novelist. Like ▷ David Caute, Sinclair is interested in ▷ post-modernist experimental narrative. *Gog* (1967), the epic journey through England of an alienated, semi-mythical character, blends realism and fantasy, and employs a variety of narrative forms, including critical essay, comic strip and film script. Sinclair's work has affinities with that of American writers such as Kurt Vonnegut. Other novels include: *Magog* (1972); *A Patriot for Hire* (1978).

Sir Charles Grandison, The History of (1753–4)
The last of the three novels presented through letters by ▷ Samuel Richardson. It is an attempt to present the type of the perfect gentleman, just as its predecessor, ▷ *Clarissa* had represented the perfect woman. It prescribes the kind of behaviour which ▷ Addison had preached in his periodical ▷ *The Spectator*. However, it suffers much more than does *Clarissa* from the excessive idealization of its central character. The theme is right conduct in acute sentimental and ethical dilemma; Grandison is in love with Harriet Byron (whom he rescues from the vicious Sir Hargrave Pollexfen), but has obligations to Clementina Porretta, member of a noble Italian family. Among other lessons, Sir Charles shows how a gentleman can avoid fighting a duel without losing his honour. The book has some good minor characters, and is an interesting study in manners, though Richardson did not understand the Italian aristocracy of his period. As a psychological study, it is much inferior to *Clarissa* but it influenced the work of ▷ Jane Austen.

Sir Patrick Spens
An old Scottish ▷ ballad describing the loss at sea of a Scottish ship, its commander Sir Patrick and all the crew. It exists in several versions; in the shortest, the ship puts to sea

in bad weather at the order of the king and Sir Patrick foresees the disaster – brought about, apparently, by royal vanity. In the longest version, the ship goes to Norway to bring back a princess, who may be based on the Maid of Norway who died at sea in 1290, or may be the Scandinavian queen of James VI (16th century); the Norwegian lords complain about the behaviour of the Scottish nobility, who leave suddenly, in bad weather, having taken offence. Both versions are fine examples of the art of the ballad, but the shortest exhibits that form at its most economical and dramatic. The first printed version is in ▷ *Percy's Reliques*. The best-known version is probably ▷ Walter Scott's.

Sir Thopas
    ▷ *Thopas, Sir*.

Sirens
    ▷ *Odyssey*.

Sitwell, Edith (1887–1964), Sir Osbert (1892–1969), Sir Sacheverell (1897–1988)
An eminent literary family, of whom Edith is best known as a poet, and her brothers (both of whom were also poets) as an autobiographer and a writer of travel books respectively.

Edith is the most celebrated of the three. Born of repressive and disapproving aristocratic parents, Edith's eccentric beauty and unconventionality set her apart. As an adolescent she encountered the work of Rimbaud, who influenced her greatly. Her first volume of poems was *The Mother and Other Poems* (1915). Her poetry is distinctive for her interest in elaborately contrived sound effects, experiments in rhythm, and startling imagery. Her sequence *Façade* (1923) is her most popular work; it was set to music by the composer William Walton. Osbert Sitwell indicates its character in his autobiography, *Laughter in the Next Room*: 'The idea of *Façade* first entered our minds as the result of certain technical experiments at which my sister had recently been working: experiments in obtaining through the medium of words the rhythm of dance measures such as waltzes, polkas, foxtrots. These exercises were often experimental enquiries into the effect on rhythm, on speed, and on colour of the use of rhymes, assonances, dissonances, placed outwardly, at different places in the line, in most elaborate patterns'. The tone of *Façade* is lighthearted or satirical. From *The Sleeping Beauty* (1924) a more romantic tone predominated, and in 1929 *Gold Coast Customs* opened her most ambitious phase of

philosophic verse with majestic themes. These include *Street Songs* (1942), *The Song of the Cold* (1945) and *The Shadow of Cain* (1947). Her prose works and criticism include a biography of ▷ Alexander Pope (1930). From 1916 to 1921 she edited *Wheels*, a magazine which represented a resistance to the ▷ Georgian poets.
Bib: Glendinning, V., *Edith Sitwell* ; Pearson, J., *Façades*.

Six Articles
A law passed through Parliament on the authority of ▷ Henry VIII in 1539. Having removed the English Church from the authority of the Pope and abolished the ▷ monasteries, Henry was concerned to prove himself a true Catholic 'without the Pope'. He therefore ordained that the traditional doctrines should be reaffirmed, especially 'the real presence' of Christ in the bread and wine taken in Holy Communion. ▷ Protestants, by then numerous in southern England, disliked the law, which they called 'the whip with six strings'.
    ▷ Reformation.

Sixteenth-century literature
In the 16th century changes in English society produced an extraordinary release of radical energies, particularly in the last decade. The powerful feudal system gave place to a new aristocracy and the growth of a new class, that of the country gentlefolk and of the city merchants. The Church ceased to be part of an international organization and became part of the national polity, under the authority of the Crown. The ▷ Renaissance secularized learning and after a struggle for survival, the nation became succinctly nationalistic.

Yet in some respects the ▷ Middle Ages died slowly in England. Lord Berners's translation (1525) of the 14th-century *Chronicles* of ▷ Froissart belongs with the prose of ▷ Malory's ▷ *Morte d'Arthur*, and ▷ Sir Thomas More's principal work in English, *The History of King Richard III* (written 1513?), is medieval in spirit.

The language of prose made notable advances in the 16th century. It is significant that much of the finest prose was about education, such as ▷ Sir Thomas Elyot's *Governor* (1531) and ▷ Roger Ascham's *The Schoolmaster* (pub 1570), and some of it arose out of the religious changes, notably ▷ William Tyndale's version of the New Testament, the Sermons of ▷ Latimer, and ▷ Cranmer's noble ▷ *Book of Common Prayer*.

In poetry, the same tentative movement

away from the Middle Ages occurred.

▷ John Skelton has more vitality than the English (as distinct from Scottish) poets of the 15th century. ▷ Thomas Wyatt's poetry has a strong individuality and his rhythms, though often subtle, seem to be suspended between the roughness of the 15th century and the smoothness which ▷ Chaucer had introduced, thereby creating a tension redolent of the changing social position of the Tudor courtier. ▷ Henry Howard, Earl of Surrey and ▷ Thomas Sackville are less interesting than Wyatt, but their work is moving closer to the smooth handling of language which the Elizabethans prized so much in the ▷ sonnets of ▷ Sir Philip Sidney (pub 1591) and in ▷ Spenser from ▷ *The Shepherd's Calendar* (1579) to ▷ *The Faerie Queene* (1596).

The ▷ Morality Play style of drama continued into the 16th century although its content became less religious and more secular, as in Skelton's *Magnificence* (1516?) and the *Satire of the Three Estates* (1540) by the Scots poet ▷ David Lindsay. A lighter kind of play called the ▷ Interlude (*eg* the plays of ▷ John Heywood) moved towards the first pure comedies, ▷ *Ralph Roister Doister* (written 1551?) and ▷ *Gammer Gurton's Needle* (1556). Meanwhile the Morality Play could be said to have become secular and (often) political, and tended to evolve into the historical drama, such as ▷ *Gorboduc* (1561) by Sackville and Norton, and *Cambyses* (1569) by Preston. Preston was a scholar; Sackville was an aristocrat. Now that the drama had lost its roots in the Church and the town rituals, it needed thoroughly professional writers to give it a fully developed form and life of its own. A group of just such writers – ▷ Thomas Kyd, ▷ John Lyly, ▷ George Peele, ▷ Robert Greene and ▷ Christopher Marlowe, collectively known as the ▷ University Wits – began work in the 1580s. They evolved among them a self-confident art of the theatre, and ▷ Shakespeare in his first decade (from ▷ *Henry VI* to ▷ *Hamlet*) was indebted to them.

These new writers, including Shakespeare himself, formed a new social phenomenon: the professional man of letters, who was not a nobleman like Wyatt, Surrey or Sidney, practising literature as part of the aristocratic life, nor a scholar or churchman like Ascham or Tyndale, practising it as a by-product of his profession, nor a court poet as Chaucer had been and Spenser was, practising it

partly with a view to receiving court emoluments, but a writer who depended on monetary 'takings' from the public theatre. They contributed to the extraordinary vitality of the 1590s, not only in the drama but in prose pamphleteering and the kind of romance known as the ▷ Elizabethan novel, in which ▷ Thomas Nashe, ▷ Thomas Lodge and ▷ Thomas Deloney were among the foremost practitioners.

In the 1590s the drama, non-dramatic poetry of all kinds but notably the ▷ sonnet and the ▷ lyric, and prose including not only pamphleteers but the great philosophical writing of ▷ Richard Hooker (▷ *Laws of Ecclesiastical Polity*) developed in new ways. The poetry has an extraordinary range of style, from the highly wrought music of Spenser's *Faerie Queene* to the involved and complex thought of ▷ Donne's ▷ *Songs and Sonnets*. Literary criticism has also made its beginnings with ▷ Puttenham's *Art of English Poetry* (pub 1589) and Sidney's ▷ *Apologie for Poetry* (pub 1598). There were also a number of ▷ translations in the period; ▷ Italian and ▷ French writing and thought, as well as the ancient classics (above all, the philosophy of ▷ Plato and the critical theory of ▷ Horace and, through the Italians, ▷ Aristotle) contributed a large part of the English literary Renaissance.

Skelton, John (c 1460–1529)

Poet; awarded the title of ▷ 'poet laureate' by the universities of Oxford and Cambridge; tutor to Prince Henry, later Henry VIII (1494–1502); ordained in 1498 and Rector of Diss from 1502. Skelton composed poetry in Latin but is most famous for his satirical English poetry, in which the corruption and corrupting influence of Cardinal Wolsey are a frequent target. He is a brilliant stylist, who seems to delight in the juxtaposition of learned and popular registers (often inserting Latin verses or tags into his work). He developed the 'skeltonic' verse form: lines containing 2/3 accented syllables which often alliterate, linked in couplets or sometimes longer rhyme runs of up to 14 lines. His work is highly self-conscious, playful, sometimes parodic, and reveals a wide acquaintance with the work of late 14th- and earlier 15th-century court poets. The *Bowge of Court* (1498) is a barely veiled attack on court corruption through a reworking of the 'ship of fools' convention.

His *Phyllype Sparrow* (c 1505) is in two parts: the first represents an attempt by a young convent girl to compose a fitting

Contemporary woodcut of John Skelton

memorial for her dead sparrow, using the resources of classical and Christian culture, which includes a parodic bird Mass; the second is a lengthy praise poem outlining the attractions of Jane herself, and the fantasies she arouses in the speaker. The *Tunnyng of Elinour Rummyng* (c 1517) is an exercise in creating the female grotesque, which describes the establishment and the female patrons of Elinour's ale house. Skelton's later satires, *Speke Parrot, Colin Clout, Why Come Ye Nat to Court,* (all written c 1521–2) attack Wolsey's abuse of power in particular, and state and ecclesiastical corruption in general. The *Garlande or Chapelet of Laurell*, heavily indebted to ▷ Chaucer's ▷ *House of Fame*, is Skelton's witty projection of his place, as a poet laureate, in the Hall of Fame. He is also the author of a ▷ morality play, *Magnyfycence* (c 1515–16), which examines the dangers of materialistic corruption at court.
Bib: Carpenter, N., *John Skelton*; Fish, S., *John Skelton's Poetry*; Scattergood, J. (ed.), *John Skelton: The Complete Poems.*

Sketches by Boz (1836)
Early journalism by ▷ Charles Dickens. The sketches, 'Illustrative of Everyday Life and Everyday People', were begun in 1833,

published in various magazines, and collected into book form in 1836.

Sleeping Beauty, The
A famous fairy story in the collection made by ▷ Charles Perrault, translated into English in 1729. A baby princess is doomed by a wicked fairy to prick herself on the finger and die, but a good fairy changes death into a hundred years' sleep, from which the princess is awakened by the kiss of a prince.

Slough of Despond
A boggy place in ▷ John Bunyan's allegory ▷ *Pilgrim's Progress*. Christian sinks into it immediately after taking flight from the ▷ City of Destruction. It signifies the period of depression into which a convert is liable to fall after the first enthusiasm of his conversion.

Smart, Christopher (1722–71)
Poet. He showed early poetic gifts, and received support from the aristocratic Vane family, on whose estates his father was a steward. He made a precarious living through his early poems, which followed the fashions of the time. His *Poems on Several Occasions* (1752) include *The Hop-Garden*, a blank-verse ▷ Georgic in the manner of ▷ John Philips's *Cyder*, and a satirical poem, *The Hilliad* appeared in 1753. In the 1750s he developed a religious mania which drove him to continuous prayer, and he was for a time locked up in an asylum where he developed the original poetic style for which he is now best known. After his release he published *A Song to David* (1763), an ecstatic poem in praise of David as author of the Psalms. It is written in six-line stanzas rhyming *aabccb*, and owes something to the biblically inspired poetry and hymns of such writers as ▷ Isaac Watts and ▷ Charles Wesley. Smart's work was ignored at the time and much of it, including *Jubilate Agno, A Song from Bedlam*, was not published until 1939.
Bib: Ainsworth, E. G., and Noyes, C. E., *Life.*

Smectymnuus
A name under which five ▷ Presbyterian writers wrote against episcopacy – rule of the Church by bishops – in the 17th century. The name was suggested by the initial letters of the names of the writers: Stephen Marshall, Edward Calamy, Thomas Young, Matthew Newcomen, and William Spurstow. Their ▷ pamphlet was attacked by ▷ Bishop Joseph Hall, and was defended in two pamphets by ▷ John Milton in 1641 and 1642. ▷ Samuel Butler, in his poetic satire *Hudibras*, written against the ▷ Puritans, calls the Presbyterians the 'Legion of Smec'.

Smiles, Samuel (1812–1904)

Journalist: philosopher of 'self-help'. Born at Haddington in Scotland, one of eleven children, his early life was a struggle, dominated by the vigour of his widowed mother. He graduated in medicine at Edinburgh University in 1832, and began practising as a doctor in his home village. Competition was severe however, and he exchanged medicine for ▷ journalism, becoming editor of the *Leeds Times*. He also became secretary to railway companies, and in this capacity he made acquaintance with George Stephenson (1781–1848), inventor of the steam railway engine. His *Life of Stephenson* was published in 1857, and was followed by the lives of other famous 19th-century engineers: *James Brindley* (1864); *Boulton and Watt* (1865); *Telford* (1867). But the book that made him famous was *Self-Help* (1859); it sold 20,000 copies in the first year, and was translated into at least 17 languages. He followed it by similar books, all demonstrating the worldly advantages of certain moral virtues: *Character* (1871); *Thrift* (1875); *Duty* (1880). The success of these books was due to their optimism, and to the simple, practical expression of his ideas. His international prestige is illustrated by his reception of the Order of St Sava from the King of Servia in 1897. Smiles represents the vigorous and hopeful aspect of the ▷ Industrial Revolution, as it affected ordinary people, in contrast to the sceptical view of it taken by many other writers.

Smith, Adam (1723–90)

Political economist. His important work was *An Enquiry into the Nature and Causes of the Wealth of Nations* – always referred to as *The Wealth of Nations* – published in 1776, at the outbreak of the rebellion of the American colonists, who, he predicted, 'will be one of the foremost nations of the world'. The especial influence of this book comes from his discussion of the function of the state in the degree and kind of control it should exercise over the activities of society, and in particular, of trade. He concluded that the traditional ▷ mercantile system (nowadays called 'protection') was based on a misunderstanding of the nature of wealth, and that nations prospered to the extent that governments allowed trade to remain freely competitive, unrestrained by taxes intended to protect the economy of a nation from competition from other nations. His opinions became increasingly influential and eventually dominant in British economics during the first half of the 19th century; his opposition

to *unnecessary* interference by the government in trade and society became harmful in that it was interpreted by later governments as an excuse not to remedy social abuses arising from industrialism.

▷ Free Trade.

Smith, Stevie (Florence Margaret) (1902–71)

Poet and novelist. Her 'unpoetic' life as an office worker who cared for her elderly aunt in a London suburb is well-known as the context for the production of her concise but anarchic poetry. Much of her work is animated by themes of sexual anxiety and an ambivalence towards Christianity which belies its popular image of comic whimsy. Of her novels, *Novel on Yellow Paper* (1936) is the most widely known, her several collections of witty, understated poems being accompanied by her own drawings. Works include: *Collected Poems* (1975); *Me Again: Uncollected Writings* (ed. Barbera, J. and McBrien, W.; 1983).

Smith, William (d1696)

Actor. Smith joined the ▷ Duke's Company under ▷ Sir William D'Avenant in 1662, where he became one of its leading actors, and created many prestigious roles of the period, including Sir Fopling Flutter in ▷ Sir George Etherege's *The Man of Mode*, Pierre in ▷ Thomas Otway's ▷ *Venice Preserv'd*, a part written for him, and Willmore in ▷ Aphra Behn's ▷ *The Rover* (*Parts I and II*). Tall and handsome, Smith was viewed by his contemporaries as a gentleman, of high moral reputation. He is said to have acted in both comedy and tragedy with dignity and flair.

Smock Alley Theatre, Dublin, The

This was important not only in its own right, but also to the London theatre as a venue for preview performances. In addition, many of the great names in the English theatre began their careers in Dublin, including ▷ Spranger Barry, ▷ Kitty Clive, Thomas Doggett (c 1670–1721), ▷ George Farquhar, ▷ Charles Macklin, ▷ James Quin, ▷ Richard Brinsley Sheridan (whose father Thomas acted at Smock Alley for many years), ▷ Robert Wilks, and ▷ Peg Woffington. Others like ▷ David Garrick and ▷ Barton Booth acted in Dublin on various occasions.

Smollett, Tobias George (1721–71)

Born near Dumbarton, the son of a Scots laird, Smollett studied at Glasgow University and was then apprenticed to a surgeon. In 1739 he moved to London, trying to stage his

Tobias Smollett pictured in Hogg's *New Novelist's Magazine*, 1794

play *The Regicide*, but the attempt was unsuccessful, and he joined the navy as a surgeon's mate, sailing for the West Indies.

In 1744 Smollett returned to London and set up a medical practice in Downing Street, though never making a living out of medicine. His first publication, a poem entitled *The Tears of Scotland* appeared in 1746, and later that year he published a satire on London life, *Advice*. In 1747 a further satire, *Reproof*, appeared, and he wrote the novel ▷ *The Adventures of Roderick Random*, published to great acclaim in 1748. Further novels, which draw on his experiences in the navy and his continental travel, include ▷ *The Adventures of Peregrine Pickle* (1751) and *The Adventures of Ferdinand Count Fathom* (1753).

Smollett, now married and a father, struggled to support his family by editorial work, working on *The Critical Review* from 1756–63, and publishing his translation of ▷ *Don Quixote* in 1755. Finally, his *Complete History of England* proved a commercial success, and was followed by *Continuation* volumes. In 1760 Smollett began *The British Magazine*, where *The Life and Adventures of Sir Lancelot Greaves* was run as a serial; in the same year he was fined and imprisoned for a libellous article in the *Critical Review*.

Smollett had been suffering from ill health for several years, and in 1753 he began to show symptoms of consumption. In 1763 his daughter died, and he abandoned literary

work to travel with his wife in Italy and France. On their return in 1765 he wrote the epistolary work *Travels through France and Italy*, which drew from ▷ Sterne the nickname 'Smelfungus'. His final major work was ▷ *The Expedition of Humphry Clinker*, published shortly before his death in 1771.
Bib: Knapp, L. M., *Tobias Smollett: Doctor of Men and Manners*; Boucé, P. G., *The Novels of Tobias Smollett*.

Snobs, The Book of (1848)
A collection of satirical sketches by the novelist ▷ William Makepeace Thackeray, first published in the periodical ▷ *Punch* in 1846–7 as *The Snobs of England by one of themselves*. The title is based on a Cambridge student paper, *The Snob*, to which he contributed as an undergraduate in 1829.

Snow, C. P. (Charles Percy 1905–80)
Novelist; author of the sequence *Strangers and Brothers* comprising *Strangers and Brothers* (1940), *The Light and the Dark* (1947), *Time of Hope* (1949), *The Masters* (1951), *The New Men* (1954), *Homecomings* (1956); *The Conscience of the Rich* (1958), *The Affair* (1960), *Corridors of Power* (1964); *The Sleep of Reason* (1968); *Last Things* (1970).

He also played a large part in public affairs; he was created Baron (Life Peerage) in 1964, and served as a junior minister (Ministry of Technology) from 1964 till 1966. Trained as a scientist, he held strong views about the intellectual cleavage between men trained in the sciences and those trained in liberal studies in the modern world. His Rede Lecture at Cambridge, *The Two Cultures and the Scientific Revolution* (1959) became famous, partly because it provoked an exceptionally ferocious retort from the critic ▷ F. R. Leavis. Other novels include: *The Malcontents* (1972); *In Their Wisdom* (1974).
Bib: Cooper, W., *C. P. Snow*; Leavis, F. R., *Two Cultures? The Significance of C. P. Snow*.

Social and Liberal Democratic Party
▷ Liberal Party.

Social contract
A doctrine about the origins of society especially associated with the English thinkers ▷ Thomas Hobbes and ▷ John Locke, and the French thinker ▷ Jean-Jacques Rousseau. Hobbes (in ▷ *Leviathan*) argued that people were naturally violent and rapacious, and that they contracted to put themselves under strong government in order to make the continuance of life and property possible. Locke (*Treatise on Government*)

thought the social contract was a convenience rather than a necessity, arguing that private property could have existed in pre-social humanity, but that people contracted to accept government to make themselves secure. Humanity for Locke was not necessarily violent, and government should be tolerant and humane. Rousseau (*Social Contract*) argued that primitive peoples were above all timid, and that they contracted to form governments which rested on the consent of the people, who should overthrow them if they were inefficient or tyrannical. Rousseau's view supported the action of the French revolutionaries and encouraged the growth of democratic ideas in the 19th century. All three opposed the beliefs maintained until the mid-17th century everywhere, that rulers owed their authority to the will of God.

Social Democratic Party
▷ Liberal Party.

Society for Promoting Christian Knowledge (S.P.C.K.)
Founded in 1698; it was then an unusual collaboration of all the ▷ Protestant sects to help in the education of the poor by founding 'charity schools', and to extend religious education by the circulation of inexpensive Bibles and other religious literature. A subsidiary was the missionary Society for the Propagation of the Gospel in Foreign Parts, in the 19th century a channel for the movement against slavery and the slave trade.
▷ Schools in England.

Socinianism
A theological doctrine associated with two 16th-century Italian theologians, Lelio and Fausto Sozzini (latinized to Socinus). They regarded Jesus Christ as wholly human (*ie* not a member of the Holy Trinity) but as divinely inspired. They were thus representative of that side of the ▷ Protestant Reformation that sought to simplify and rationalize Christian doctrine; in Britain in the 17th century 'Socinians' were substantially what in the 18th century became known as ▷ Unitarians.

Socrates (?470–399 BC)
Greek philosopher. He taught entirely by word of mouth, the so-called 'Socratic method' being the discovery of the truth by putting appropriate questions. Because he wrote nothing, all information about him depends on the writings of two contemporaries – the historian ▷ Xenophon (*Memorabilia*) and the philosopher ▷ Plato, who stands in relation

to Socrates somewhat as St Paul does to Jesus Christ, except that Plato was personally taught by Socrates. Plato puts his own ideas into the mouth of Socrates in his philosophical dialogues, and it is of course difficult to know just how much and in what ways he expanded the Socratic philosophy. This philosophy declared that the true end of philosophy was not to discover the nature of the world but the nature of goodness and how to lead the good life; related to this is the doctrine of Forms, according to which reality is seen as fundamentally spiritual, and the real in a person is their soul.

Socrates is said to have had a beautiful soul in an ugly body; he was married to a woman called Xanthippe. He fell out of favour with the ruling party of Athens, his native city, because he befriended enemies of the party; he was accordingly made to put himself to death by drinking hemlock.

Soldier's Fortune, The (1681)
Comedy by ▷ Thomas Otway. Beaugard and Lady Dunce have loved one another for seven years, but during his absence in France, she has been prevailed on by her family to marry Sir Davy Dunce. Aided by the unpleasant pander, Sir Jolly Jumble, the former lovers plot to cuckold Dunce, duping him into carrying their messages and even facilitating their adulterous liaison unwittingly. This intrigue is offset against the witty courtship of Sir Jolly's adopted daughter Sylvia and the impoverished Courtine. She quite literally snares him in a noose, in order to win him. In a comical ▷ 'proviso scene', full of *double entendre*, he undertakes to farm her lands and keep other tenants away, unless he finds the property 'too common' already. The play is fast-moving, but rather episodic in structure. It is expressly royalist, but there are elements of social comment, as in the references to the poverty of the king's loyal soldiers and servants (▷ Charles II was notoriously bad at paying his debts to those whom he employed). A sequel, ▷ *The Atheist*, appeared in 1684.

Somerset House
A building on the north bank of the Thames, which was used to house state departments concerned with records of births, deaths, wills, marriages and income tax. The General Register Office for births, marriages and deaths, formerly at Somerset House, became part of the Office of Population Censuses and Surveys in 1970 and moved to St Catherine's House on the Strand. The present building dates from the 18th century; its name derives

Blake's design for 'The Blossom' from *Songs of Innocence and Experience*

from a 16th-century palace on the same site, belonging to the Duke of Somerset.

Somerville, William (1675–1742)
Author of *The Chace* (1735), a poem in Miltonic ▷ blank verse celebrating the various branches of hunting. He followed this in 1740 with *Hobbinol*, a ▷ mock heroic piece set in rural Gloucestershire and a poem on hawking, *Field Sports* (1742).

Songs and Sonnets (Donne) (c 1633–5)
A heading given to 55 love poems by ▷ John Donne. Though the poems themselves first appeared in the 1633 edition of Donne's *Poems* (with the exception of 'Breake of Day' and 'The Expiration', which had been published earlier), the category of 'Songs and Sonnets' did not appear until the publication of the second edition of Donne's poetry in 1635. Despite the title, very few of the poems gathered under the heading are songs, or, in the technical sense ▷ sonnets. Modern editors have questioned the authorship of two of the poems attributed to Donne (though not published either in 1633 or 1635), these being 'The Token' and the poem known as 'Self-Love'. Again, some modern editors have felt the need to add to the category by transferring other poems of Donne's into the group. Various attempts at arranging the poems into a sequence according to their presumed date of composition have been made, but with little real success.

Songs and Sonnets (Tottel)
▷ *Tottel's Miscellany*.

Songs of Innocence and Experience (1789/1794)
Two collections of lyric poems by ▷ William Blake, engraved and illuminated by hand. The *Songs of Innocence* were completed in 1789, and The *Songs of Experience* were added in an enlarged edition in 1794. They were intended to be read by children, and although frequently profound and complex, are perfectly lucid and easy to comprehend. They present 'the Two Contrary States of the Human Soul', and are thus complementary, since in Blake's dialectical view 'Without Contraries is no progression'. The world of Innocence is without morality, repression or fear, and in Blake's dynamic interpretation of Christian mythology, unFallen. Inevitably some of the *Innocence* poems, such as *The Lamb* and *A Cradle Song*, seem sentimental and oversweet to the adult, Fallen reader, while others, such as *Holy Thursday* and *The Chimney Sweeper* can seem highly ironic in their trusting attitude towards corrupt parental and political authority. But irony is no part of Innocence, and the *Experience* counterparts to these poems are in no sense a debunking of the *Innocence* versions. However it must be admitted that the bitter social criticism and moral indignation of *Experience* produce more memorable verse (though again perhaps this is more the case for the adult reader than the child). *The Tyger*, *The Clod and the Pebble*, and *The Sick Rose*, are the most concentrated symbolic poems in the language, remarkable for their combination of emotional complexity and intellectual clarity. It is characteristic of Blake's dialectical approach that the later poem *To Tirzah*, added to *Experience* in the 1801 edition, flatly contradicts the sexual libertarianism of the other poems in the *Experience* collection, depicting the freeing of the soul from its physical bonds.

Sonnet
A short poem of 14 lines, and a rhyme scheme restricted by one or other of a variety of principles. The most famous pattern is called the 'Petrarchan sonnet', from its masterly use by the Italian poet ▷ Petrarch. This divides naturally into an eight-line stanza (octave) rhyming *abba abba*, and a six-line stanza in which two or three rhymes may occur; the two stanzas provide also for

contrast in attitude to the theme. The origin of the sonnet is unknown, but its earliest examples date from the 13th century in Europe, although it did not reach England until the 16th century. The immense popularity of the form perhaps derives from its combination of discipline, musicality and amplitude. The subject-matter is commonly love, but after the 16th century it becomes, at least in England, much more varied.

The first writers of sonnets in England, were ▷ Sir Thomas Wyatt, and ▷ Henry Howard Surrey; the popular anthology ▷ *Tottel's Miscellany* (1559) made their experiments widely known. The first really fine sonnet sequence was ▷ Sir Philip Sidney's ▷ *Astrophil and Stella*. Its publication in 1591 set an eagerly followed fashion for its distinctively English form. This consisted of a single stanza of 14 lines concluding in a ▷ couplet; it is thought that the comparative scarcity of rhyming words in the English language may be the explanation of the greater number of rhymes and freedom in the rhyming scheme in contrast to the Petrarchan form. The greatest of the succeeding sequences was undoubtedly ▷ Shakespeare's (▷ Sonnets, Shakespeare's), but notable ones were produced by ▷ Samuel Daniel, ▷ Michael Drayton, and ▷ Edmund Spenser.

The sonnet form continued to be used after 1600, notably by ▷ John Donne and ▷ John Milton, but much less for amorous themes and more for religious ones (*eg* Donne's *Holy Sonnets*) or by Milton for expressions of other forms of personal experience (*eg On his Blindness*) or for political declamation (*On the Late Massacre in Piedmont*). Milton used the Petrarchan rhyme scheme, but he kept the English form of using a single stanza. From the mid-17th to mid-18th century the different style of thought and feeling suggested by the heroic couplet kept the sonnet out of use; the cult of sentiment by poets such as ▷ Thomas Gray and ▷ William Cowper then brought it back, but a real revival had to wait for the first 30 years of the 19th century in the work of the ▷ 'romantics' – especially ▷ William Wordsworth, who used it freely, ▷ John Keats, who wrote few but some of them among his best short poems, and ▷ Percy Bysshe Shelley whose ▷ *Ozymandias* sonnet is one of the best of all his poems. The romantic poets tended to follow the Miltonic example both in form and subject-matter. After 1830, the form continued to be popular in the 19th century, notably in the work of

▷ Christina Rossetti, ▷ Dante Gabriel Rossetti, ▷ Elizabeth Barrett Browning (*Sonnets from the Portuguese*, 1847). ▷ G. M. Hopkins experimented very boldly in the form, and produced some of his best work in what he claimed to be sonnets, though they are often scarcely recognizable as such. Though in the earlier part of the 20th century the sonnet form appeared to have lost favour, in the later part of this century there has been a revival of interest in the form. The most notable example of this re-awakening of interest is perhaps the two 'sonnet sequences' by John Berryman (1938–68) published in 1952 and 1967.

Sonnets, Shakespeare's
  ▷ Shakespeare – Sonnets.

Sons and Lovers (1913)
The first of ▷ D. H. Lawrence's major novels. It is based on his own early life in the Midlands coal-mining village of Eastwood (Nottinghamshire), on his relationships with his mother and with his father who was a mineworker, and on those with his early women friends.

Eastwood is called Bestwood in the novel; the character who corresponds to Lawrence himself is Paul Morel. The strongest relationship is the close tie between Mrs Morel and Paul, who has two brothers and a sister. Mrs Morel comes of a proud, ▷ Dissenting middle-class family with memories of ancestors who fought against ▷ Charles I. She inherits the uncompromising traditions of English Dissent, and, though her family has been impoverished, she has an inherent aristocracy of temperament derived from her family tradition of high standards. The father, Walter Morel, a miner, is a contrast to his wife, both in his background (he is the grandson of a French refugee and an English barmaid) and in his easy-going, pleasure-loving, spontaneous temperament. The marriage is an unhappy one: Mrs Morel's strictness and truthfulness are outraged by her husband's slackness and deceitfulness. In the war between them, the children take the side of the mother.

The closeness between Mrs Morel and Paul develops after the death of her eldest son, William, and Paul's own serious illness. He goes to work in a Nottingham factory, but he has his mother's intellectual seriousness and artistic sensitivity, and has ambitions to become an artist. Mrs Morel invests in him all her pride of life and the hopes and passions that her marriage has disappointed. She finds a rival in Miriam Leivers, the shy and intensely serious daughter of a local farmer, and bitterly opposes her friendship with Paul. He is affected by his mother's opposition, and at the same time he resents what he considers to be Miriam's emotional demands upon him, since he believes them to be a barrier to the sensual release for which he craves. He reacts against Miriam by engaging in a sensual love affair with Clara Dawes, a married woman who has quarrelled with her husband. This relationship is not opposed by Mrs Morel, since it is a physical one and does not compete with her own emotional possessiveness. Paul, on the other hand, finds that Clara affords him no more release than Miriam had done; he is unconsciously subjected, all the time, to his mother. The mother's protracted illness and death, and Paul's fight with Baxter Dawes, Clara's husband, are complementary climaxes of the novel. Both together constitute his release, although the death leaves him with a sense of complete dereliction: he has to face the choice of willing himself to live or surrendering to his own desire for death.

The book was early regarded as a vivid presentation of the working of the ▷ Oedipus Complex. Lawrence was not acquainted with ▷ Freud's theories when he started work on the novel in 1910, but had come into contact with them before completing the final version in 1912. It is in its own right a major novel, but it certainly constitutes Lawrence's attempt to release himself from the problems of his own early development. He later declared that his study of his father had been unfair and one-sided. Jessie Chambers, the woman on whom Miriam was based, wrote a study of Lawrence as a young man: *D. H. Lawrence, A Personal Record* by E. T. (1935)

Sophists

In ancient Greece of the 5th century B C, professional educators, who claimed to train men for civic life, but not for any particular trade or profession. They differed from philosophers in that they professed to teach, whereas philosophers professed to know; it is the difference between victory by argument and discovery through argument. By degrees the Sophists fell into disrepute, and today the term 'sophistry' means an ingenious argument deliberately intended to mislead the audience.

Sophocles (495–406 BC)

One of the three foremost ancient Greek dramatists, the other two being ▷ Aeschylus and ▷ Euripides. He wrote about 100 dramas, of which only seven survive: *Oedipus the King*; *Oedipus at Colonus*; *Antigone*;

Electra; *Trachiniae*; *Ajax*; *Philoctetes*. His poetic language shows more flexibility than that of Aeschylus – their relationship in this respect has been compared to that of ▷ Shakespeare and ▷ Marlowe – and he used three actors on the stage instead of only two (not counting the Chorus). In his relationship to Euripides, he is quoted by ▷ Aristotle as saying that he depicted men as they ought to be whereas Euripides depicted them as they were. The Irish poet ▷ W. B. Yeats made free English renderings of his *Oedipus the King* (1928) and *Oedipus at Colonus* (1934).

Sophy, The

Originally the surname of the ruling family of Persia (16th–18th centuries) and later adopted as a title of the ruler.

Sorbonne

Originally the name of a college founded in Paris by Robert de Sorbon in 1256, then used for the theological faculty in the university of Paris, and finally extended to the whole university.

South Sea Bubble

The name given to a series of extensive speculations in 1720 involving the South Sea Company, founded in 1711. In 1720 individuals who had lent money to the government through the Bank of England were invited to exchange their claims for shares in the Company, which had a monopoly of trade with Spanish America and was very prosperous. This project led to irresponsible financial speculation in a number of dishonest companies, financial scandals in which ministers of the Crown were involved, and a major financial collapse in which thousands were ruined. The South Sea Company survived until the 19th century. Its headquarters, South Sea House, was for a time the place of employment of the essayist ▷ Charles Lamb, and is the subject of one of his essays.

Southampton, Henry Wriothesley, 3rd Earl of (1573–1625)

Chiefly famous as a patron of letters, and particularly as a patron of ▷ Shakespeare. He was educated at St John's College, Cambridge, from 1585 to 1589, where he made friends with the chief favourite of ▷ Elizabeth I, the Earl of Essex, and was shown special favour by the Queen herself. Shakespeare dedicated to him his poems ▷ *Venus and Adonis* (1593) and (in terms of warm devotion) *The Rape of Lucrece* (1594). There has long been much speculation about whether the young man in the ▷ Sonnets is

Southampton, and whether the initials of 'Mr W. H.' in the dedication ('To the Onlie Begetter of These Insuing Sonnets') stand for 'Henry Wriothesley' reversed. Southampton accompanied Essex on his two naval expeditions against Spain in 1596 (to Cadiz) and 1597 (to the Azores), and distinguished himself by his daring on the second of them. In 1598 he had to make a hasty marriage with Essex's cousin, Elizabeth Vernon, and this angered the Queen against him. He was later concerned in Essex's conspiracy against Elizabeth, and is thought to have arranged a special performance of Shakespeare's ▷ *Richard II* on the eve of the rebellion. In 1601 he was sentenced to death; however the sentence was commuted to life imprisonment, and when ▷ James I acceded in 1603, Southampton returned to court. He died of a fever when serving, with his son, as a volunteer on the side of the Dutch in their war with Spain. Other writers with whom he was associated as patron included ▷ John Florio, the translator of Montaigne, and ▷ Thomas Nashe, who dedicated ▷ *The Unfortunate Traveller* to him.

Southcott, Joanna (1750–1814)
A religious fanatic who attracted a following of about 100,000 early in the 19th century. She is particularly known for her sealed box, which she declared should be opened in the presence of the assembled bishops at a time of national crisis. It was opened in 1927, but was found to contain unimportant objects, perhaps because only one bishop was present.

Southerne, Thomas (1659–1746)
Dramatist. A ▷ Tory, Southerne wrote his first play, *The Loyal Brother; Or, the Persian Prince* (1682), to honour the Duke of York, later ▷ James II, and satirize ▷ Shaftesbury and the ▷ Whigs. Southerne found his path to an intended military career blocked because of his political sympathies, and he turned more seriously to writing plays. He became a friend of ▷ Dryden, whose tragedy, *Cleomenes*, he was asked to complete in 1692, and of ▷ Aphra Behn, whose work he used repeatedly for source material. His *The Fatal Marriage; Or, the Innocent Adultery* (1694) and *Oroonoko* (1695) are based on two of her novels, with added material from one of her plays, and several other works drew on plays attributed to her, or sources used by her. Southerne is identified with a wave of so-called 'marital discord comedies' of the 1690s (other writers include ▷ Vanbrugh and ▷ Farquhar) which focussed on the

problems of marriage, as much as on courtship. Southerne had a capacity for seeing difficulties from a woman's point of view; for example, his ▷ *The Wives Excuse: Or Cuckolds Make Themselves* (1691) presents the dilemma of the woman trapped in an unhappy marriage to a shamelessly unfaithful husband, while she restrains herself from accepting the advances of another man.
Bib: Root, R. L., Jr., *Thomas Southerne.*

Southey, Robert (1774–1843)
Poet and historian. He was a friend of ▷ Samuel Taylor Coleridge (they married sisters) and also of ▷ William Wordsworth. Southey shared their revolutionary ardour in the 1790s, but his opinions, like theirs, became conservative at about the turn of the century, and when the ▷ Tory ▷ *Quarterly Review* was founded in 1809 he became one of its leading contributors. He was made ▷ Poet Laureate in 1813. Southey wrote long heroic ▷ epics (*Thalaba*, 1801; *Madoc*, 1805; *Roderick*, 1814) which at the time were much admired. The best known of his shorter poems is *The Battle of Blenheim*. He wrote several historical works in prose, including *The Life of Nelson* (1813) and *A History of the Peninsular War* (1823–32). His change in political opinion, and in particular his position as Poet Laureate, drew the fire of the second generation of Romantic poets, and he lacked the poetic originality which partially redeemed Wordsworth and Coleridge in their eyes. In 1821 his poem ▷ *A Vision of Judgement*, describing the admission of George III into heaven, provoked ▷ Byron's ▷ *The Vision of Judgement*, with its brilliant caricature of Southey as servile turncoat and bumbling hack: 'He had written much blank verse, and blanker prose,/ And more of both than anybody knows.' He also features as Mr Feathernest in ▷ Thomas Love Peacock's satirical novel ▷ *Melincourt* (1817).
▷ Pantisocracy.
Bib: Curry, K., *Southey*; Madden, L. (ed.), *Robert Southey: The Critical Heritage.*

Southwark
A district of London south of the Thames, opposite the City, in distinction from which it is often referred to as 'the Borough'. In literary history it is famous for its ancient inns (*eg* the Tabard Inn of Chaucer's ▷ *Canterbury Tales*, and the White Hart of Dicken's ▷ *Pickwick Papers*) and still more for the theatres that existed in it in Shakespeare's day – the ▷ Globe, the Hope and the Rose.

Southwell, Robert (?1561–95)
Poet and Roman Catholic priest. He worked
in England as a member of the ▷ Jesuit
Order at a time when this was illegal; in 1592
he was arrested and tortured for evidence of
other priests, which he did not disclose. He
was executed after three years in prison,
where he wrote some fine religious poems (*St
Peter's Complaint with Other Poems* and
Maconiae, 1595). His most famous poem is
The Burning Babe. He also wrote a long poem
Fourfold Meditation of the Four Last Things
(1606) and a number of religious tracts, one
of which, *Mary Magdalen's Tears*, was
imitated by ▷ Thomas Nashe in his *Christ's
Tears over Jerusalem*.
Bib: Devlin, C., *The Life of Robert Southwell:
Poet and Martyr.*

Soyinka, Wole (b 1934)
▷ Commonwealth literatures.

Spanish influence on English literature
The earliest translation of a Spanish
masterpiece into any language was that of
▷ Cervantes' ▷ *Don Quixote* (1605–15)
by Thomas Shelton in 1612 (Part I) and 1620
(Part II). Of all Spanish texts, *Don Quixote*
was to have the most profound influence on
English literature: in the 17th century
▷ Francis Beaumont's ▷ *The Knight of
the Burning Pestle* (1607) and ▷ Samuel
Butler's ▷ *Hudibras* (1663) utilize the
comic elements of the novel, while ▷ Philip
Massinger's *The Renegado* (1624) combines
material from *Don Quixote* together with
Cervantes' play, *Los Baños de Argel* (1615).
In the 18th century ▷ Henry Fielding's
Don Quixote in England (1734) and
▷ Laurence Sterne's ▷ *Tristram
Shandy* (1760–7), and in the 19th century
the novels of ▷ Walter Scott and
▷ Charles Dickens perpetuate English
indebtedness to Cervantes.
   The 16th and 17th centuries in Spain are
known as the ▷ Golden Age, which
paralleled in quality, but greatly exceeded in
abundance of texts, the creativity of the
Elizabethan and Jacobean ages in England.
The plays of Pedro Calderón de la Barca
(1600–81) have often been compared to those
of ▷ Shakespeare, for example by
▷ Shelley, who learned Spanish in order
to read Calderón's dramas and partially
translated into English Calderón's famous
religious drama, *El mágico prodigioso* (*The
Wonder-Working Magician*, 1637). Shelley also
admired *La cisma de Inglaterra* (*The Schism
of England*, perf. 1627), a play dealing with
the same subject as Shakespeare's ▷ *Henry
VIII*. Spanish Golden Age influence on

contemporary English drama can be seen in
▷ James Shirley's *The Young Admiral*
(1633) and *The Opportunity* (1634), as well as
in Beaumont and ▷ Fletcher's *Love's Cure*
(1629). (▷ Spanish intrigue comedy).
   The 17th-century translations of James
Mabbe further facilitated Spanish literary
influence in England; works translated by
Mabbe include Cervantes' *Novelas ejemplares*
(1613; *Exemplary Novels*, trans 1640); the late
medieval novelesque play *La Celestina* (c
1499) by Fernando de Rojas (c 1465–1541);
and Mateo Alemán's (1547–?1614)
▷ picaresque novel, *Guzmán de Alfarache*
(trans 1622). The latter text, with *Don
Quixote*, formed part of the broader, generic
development of the picaresque novel in Spain,
England and elsewhere in Europe, while *La
Celestina* was one of the earliest medieval
texts to be translated into English. The
tradition of translating Iberian masterpieces
into English continues through to the 20th
century: Joan Martorell's novel, *Tirant lo
Blanc* (1490), was translated in 1984 by D. H.
Rosenthal.
   Translation has inevitably played an
important role in the interrelationship
between Spanish and English literatures, but
occasionally the two cultures actually
converge, as in the English poetry of the
Spanish romantic poet and intellectual,
Joseph Blanco White (1775–1841) whose
sonnet, 'To Night', appears in *The Oxford
Book of English Verse 1250–1918* (ed. A.
Quiller-Couch). In the 20th century Spanish
texts in English have become more readily
available, for example, the works of Federico
García Lorca (1898–1936), especially his
dramas *Blood Wedding* (perf. 1933) and *The
House of Bernada Alba* (perf. 1945), enjoy
regular revivals in Britain. His socialist
sympathies, together with an almost openly
acknowledged homosexuality, ran parallel to,
although surprisingly did not influence, the
English poets such as ▷ W. H. Auden and
▷ Stephen Spender who were involved in
the Spanish Civil War. Lorca's work has had
far greater impact on post-war American
fiction than on English literature. Perhaps
fittingly, in recent years it is Latin-American
literature which has had the most pronounced
effect on English writing and on the reading
public in England. The ▷ 'magic realism'
novels of Gabriel García Márquez (b 1928),
such as *Cien Años de Soledad* (*One Hundred
Years of Solitude*, 1967), and the novels,
essays and criticism of Carlos Fuentes
(b 1928), such as *Terra Nostra* (1975), are
now internationally famous in English as
well as Spanish.

Spanish intrigue comedy

English comedy influenced by, or using as its source, a type of Spanish play known as the 'comedia de capa y espada' (comedy of cape and sword). The originals include works by Pedro Calderón de la Barca (1600–81), Lope de Vega (1562–1635), and Tirso de Molina (1571–1648). The plays frequently turn on conflicts of love and honour and are dominated by busy intrigue plots involving problems of mistaken identity, duelling, and concealment. One of the first of this variety was Sir Samuel Tuke's *The Adventures of Five Hours* (1663), based on a play by Calderon, and commissioned by ▷ Charles II. Other elements of the type include rigid fathers, brothers and uncles attempting to force young relatives into unwelcome marriages, and high-spirited women active in determining their own fates. This helped to make the form popular with women dramatists, including ▷ Aphra Behn, ▷ Susannah Centlivre, and ▷ Mary Pix.
▷ Spanish influence on English literature.
Bib: Loftis, J., *The Spanish Plays of Neoclassical England*.

Spanish Tragedy, The

A drama by ▷ Thomas Kyd, probably written around 1587. It is the earliest important ▷ revenge tragedy, and both by date and by influence it is one of the principal starting-points of the great age of Elizabethan drama. The plot has no known source and is presumably Kyd's invention. The scene is Spain, just after the Spanish-Portuguese war of 1580. Andrea, a Spanish nobleman, has been unchivalrously killed in a battle by Balthazar, a Portuguese prince, who in turn is captured by Lorenzo, nephew of the King of Spain, and Horatio, son of Hieronimo, Marshal of Spain. The ghost of Andrea and the spirit of Revenge sit above stage and watch the action throughout: Andrea is to witness how his death is to be avenged. This process is most intricate, and centres on Bel-imperia, Lorenzo's sister. She and Andrea have been lovers, and in consequence she detests Balthazar, who nonetheless seeks her in marriage with Lorenzo's support. She deliberately slights Balthazar by cultivating the affections of Horatio, who is in consequence murdered by Lorenzo and Balthazar. Hieronimo – hitherto a background figure – discovers the identity of his son's murderers; half crazed with grief, he seeks justice, but his pleading is brushed aside by the king. He eventually secures it by

contriving a play (within the play) in which the guilty parties suffer real deaths instead of simulated ones. Hieronimo then takes his own life after biting out his tongue. Thus Andrea (after displaying some impatience) watches how his own death is avenged. The audience sees how justice is brought about when it is left to mere human motives: not as Heaven would bring it, cleanly and economically, but wastefully and brutally, hatred breeding hatred, and callous contrivance countered by contrivance still more ruthless. Only Lorenzo can be described as an evil character – a ▷ Machiavellian schemer; the other characters are driven out of their natural virtue by vindictive bitterness. Hieronimo himself is momentarily checked by biblical authority – 'Vindicta mihi': 'Justice is mine, saith the Lord' (*Romans* 12:19), but he is driven on by the energy of his grief.

Kyd's poetry is undistinguished, but the play is theatrically so effective that it remained popular for a generation. In 1602 the play was expanded by some more effective verse, probably by ▷ Ben Jonson, whom the theatre manager ▷ Philip Henslowe paid for additions. However, these obscure rather than enhance Kyd's essential drama.

Kyd was certainly influenced by the plays of ▷ Seneca, for instance in his use of ▷ stichomythia and in the role of the ghost. Kyd's own influence was great, and can be seen in ▷ *Hamlet*. The dilemma of revenge, in one aspect seen to be a duty and in another an acknowledged sin, deeply preoccupied the Elizabethans. At the lowest level it was a pretext for the violence that appealed to them in the theatre – the 'tragedy of blood'; at a higher level is presented the problem of how it could be executed against evil-doers who were men of power or protected by such men; at a higher level still it was a natural vehicle for dramatizing the theme of the corrupted conscience which both ▷ Renaissance and ▷ Reformation ideas brought to the forefront of social attention. *The Spanish Tragedy* was effective on all these planes.

Spark, Muriel (b 1918)

Before becoming a novelist, she was a poet (*Collected Poems*, 1967). Her first novel was *The Comforters* (1957), which she has described as 'a novel about writing a novel' *ie* an experiment in, and exploration of what it means to write fiction. At about the same time she became a convert to Roman Catholicism, and her novels since have tended

Muriel Spark

to take a parabolic form (characteristic of other contemporary novelists, *eg* ▷ Iris Murdoch, ▷ William Golding) combining overt, often wittily satirical ▷ realism with implications of an extra-realist, spiritual dimension. One of her best-known works is *The Prime of Miss Jean Brodie* (1961), the story of the influence over a group of schoolgirls of a progressive spinster schoolteacher in Edinburgh. It is characteristic of Spark's work in its combination of the comic and the sinister, and the skilful use of anticipations of later events. Her three ▷ novellas, *The Public Image* (1968); *The Driver's Seat* (1970) and *Not to Disturb* (1971) exemplify the economy, precision and hardness of her work; they invite little sympathy for their characters, but rather convey a strong sense of pattern and fate underlying an apparent contingency of event. Her other novels are: *Robinson* (1958); *Memento Mori* (1959); *The Ballad of Peckham Rye* (1960); *The Bachelors* (1960); *The Girls of Slender Means* (1963); *The Mandelbaum Gate* (1965); *The Hothouse by the East River* (1972); *The Abbess of Crewe* (1972); *The Takeover* (1976); *Territorial Rights* (1979); *Loitering with Intent* (1981); *The Only Problem* (1984); *A Far Cry From Kensington* (1988).

Other writings include a stage play *Doctors of Philosophy* (1962), radio plays collected in *Voices at Play* (1961), a further volume of poetry, *Going Up to Sotherby's* (1982) and short stories in *Collected Stories 1* (1967); *The*

Stories of Muriel Spark (1985).
Bib: Stanford, D., *Muriel Spark: A Biographical and Critical Study*; Stubbs, P., *Muriel Spark* (Writers and their Work series); Kemp, P., *Muriel Spark*; Bold, A., *Muriel Spark*.

Sparta

One of the two principal states of ancient Greece, the other being ▷ Athens. Whereas Athens was famous for its material, artistic and intellectual civilization, Sparta cultivated the austere, warlike virtues. The two states were allies against the Persian invaders at the beginning of the 5th century BC, but they fought against each other in the ▷ Peloponnesian War of 431–404 BC, which ended in the downfall of Athens as the greatest power of the Greek world. The Spartans have always been considered as exemplars of the virtues of courage, endurance and austerity of life.

Spectator, The

The name of two periodicals, the first appearing daily (1711–12 and 1714), and the second a weekly founded in 1828 and still continuing. The earlier is the more famous of the two, owing to the contributions of its famous editors, ▷ Addison and ▷ Steele; it had an important influence on the manners and culture of the time. The later *Spectator* has also had a distinguished history, however; it began as a ▷ radical journal, but is now the leading intellectual weekly periodical of the right.

▷ Reviews and Periodicals.

Spencer, Herbert (1820–1903)

Philosopher. He was representative of one aspect of the Victorian period in his faith in ▷ Darwin's theory of evolution and his trust in scientific progress. Politically he was individualist, and ethically ▷ utilitarian. Some of his more influential works were: *First Principles* (1862); *Principles of Biology* (1864); *Principles of Psychology* (1870–2); *Principles of Sociology* (1877–96); *Principles of Ethics* (1893).

Spender, Sir Stephen (b 1909)

Poet and critic. Son of a distinguished journalist, J. A. Spender, who was editor of the liberal *Westminster Gazette*. Educated at University College School, London, and University College, Oxford. At Oxford, he became friendly with the poets ▷ W. H. Auden, ▷ C. Day Lewis, and ▷ Louis MacNiece. The four, together with the novelist ▷ Christopher Isherwood, formed an influential group of left-wing writers in the 1930s. Spender was and is a passionately political poet, working as a propagandist for

the Republicans in the Spanish Civil War
and, in *The Destructive Element* (1935), partly
defending poetry's addressing of political
subjects through a discussion of fellow-poets
▷ W. B. Yeats and ▷ T. S. Eliot. As
his career has progressed Spender's political
orientation has changed; though briefly a
member of the ▷ Communist Party, in
1950 he contributed to the anti-Communist
collection of essays, *The God that Failed* (ed.
R. H. S. Crossman). His volumes of verse
include *Nine Entertainments* (1928), *Twenty
Poems* (1930), *The Still Centre* (1939), *Ruins
and Visions* (1942). As a critic he has written
two studies of modern literature: *The
Destructive Element* (1935) and *The Creative
Element* (1953). His ▷ autobiographical
writings include *World within World* (1951).
In 1953 he became co-editor of *Encounter*, a
monthly review of culture and world affairs.
In 1969 he published a study of student
politics: *The Year of the Young Rebels*. In
1970 he became Professor of English
Language and Literature at University
College, London. Later works include *Love-
Hate Relations* (1974), *The Thirties and After*
(1978) and a critical study of T. S. Eliot and
Collected Poems 1928–85 (1985). Spender is
also an important translator, particularly of
▷ German literature, and has collaborated
with painter David Hockney in the 1982
account of their trip to China, *China
Diary*.

Spens, Sir Patrick
  ▷ *Sir Patrick Spens.*

Spenser, Edmund (?1552–99)
Poet. Spenser's poetry, and in particular
▷ *The Faerie Queene*, was possibly the
single most influential body of writing to
appear in the ▷ Renaissance period in
England. Throughout the 17th century his
influence was immense, not least on ▷ John
Milton. In the 20th century, however, his
reputation began to decline – readers
preferring the so-called ▷ 'metaphysical'

school of writing represented by ▷ John
Donne. Yet, in recent years, there has been
a revival of interest in Spenser, particularly
among ▷ 'New Historicist' critics for
whom *The Faerie Queene* has become an
endlessly fascinating text.
  Spenser was born in London, but lived for
most of his adult life in ▷ Ireland. He first
visited Ireland in 1577, becoming in 1580
private secretary to Lord Grey, the newly-
appointed lord deputy of Ireland. From 1580
onwards Spenser's fortunes were connected
with his progress through the ranks of the

Edmund Spenser, from an original
engraving

colonial administration of Ireland, and by
1588 Spenser had occupied the forfeited
estate of the Earl of Desmond. The estate, at
Kilcolman in County Cork, Spenser
developed as a small 'colony' of six English
householders and their families. Kilcolman
was to be Spenser's home until 1598 when, in
October of that year, the castle of Kilcolman
was destroyed in the course of 'Tyrone's
Rebellion'. Following the upheaval, Spenser
returned to London for the last time, where
he died, according to ▷ Ben Jonson 'for
lack of bread' in 1599.
  Spenser's first published works were
anonymous translations from ▷ Petrarch
and the French poet ▷ du Bellay which
appeared in a violently anti-Catholic
collection in 1569. It was not, however, until
the publication of ▷ *The Shepherd's
Calendar* (1579, with five editions by 1597)
that Spenser's poetic reputation became
established. In 1580 he published a
correspondence with ▷ Gabriel Harvey, an
old friend from his Cambridge days, which
set out his views on ▷ metrics and
▷ prosody. The correspondence is not,
perhaps, of startling critical force. Further
collections of poetry appeared in 1591,
followed by his sonnet sequence ▷ *Amoretti*,
together with ▷ *Epithalamion* in a single
volume in 1595. The autobiographical
▷ *Colin Clout's Come Home Again* (1594)
was followed by the ▷ Platonic *Fowre
Hymnes* of 1596 and his celebration of the

marriage of the daughters of the Earl of Worcester, ▷ *Prothalamion*, also in 1596. Spenser's major poetic work, *The Faerie Queene*, begun prior to 1579, appeared first in 1590 when the first three books of the poem were published. The second edition of Books I–III appeared together with Books IV–VI in 1596, and the final version (as we have it) of the poem after Spenser's death when a folio edition including the ▷ 'Mutabilitie Cantos' was published in 1609.

In the late 16th century, Spenser was the dominating literary intellect of the period, and his reputation was sustained throughout the 18th century, reaching an apotheosis amongst the ▷ romantic poets. To the modern reader he presents a complex set of problems and responses. As a 'source' for wide areas of Renaissance intellectual culture he has been continuously explicated and re-explicated, his texts being examined for their Platonist, numerological, Lucretian (▷ Lucretius) and ▷ Calvinist elements. But he is also a writer whose engagement with the creation of a national myth of identity was part of a vital Elizabethan project.

Bib: Greenlaw E. *et al.* (eds), *Works of Edmund Spenser*, 10 vol.; Nohrnberg, J., *The Analogy of 'The Faerie Queene'*; Sale, R., *Reading Spenser*; Goldberg, J., *Endlesse Worke: Spenser and the Structures of Discourse*.

Spenserian stanza

A verse form devised by ▷ Edmund Spenser for his poem ▷ *The Faerie Queene*. It consists of eight ten-syllable lines, plus a ninth line of 12 syllables (▷ Alexandrine), an iambic rhythm and a rhyme scheme as follows: *a b a b b c b c c*. Example from *The Faerie Queene*:

> *And as she looked about, she did behold,*
> *How over that same door was likewise writ,*
> *'Be bold, be bold,' and everywhere 'Be bold',*
> *That much she mused, yet could not construe it*
> *By any riddling skill, or common wit.*
> *At last she spied at that room's upper end,*
> *Another iron door, on which was writ,*
> *'Be not too bold'; whereto though she did bend*
> *Her earnest mind, yet wist not what it might intend.*
>
> (Book III, Canto xi, 54)

The stanza was used by Spenser's poetic disciples, ▷ Giles and ▷ Phineas Fletcher, early in the 17th century. It was revived in the 18th century by reflective poets such as

▷ James Thomson (▷ *The Castle of Indolence*), ▷ Mark Akenside (*Virtuoso*, 1737), ▷ William Shenstone (*Schoolmistress*, 1742), ▷ James Beattie (*Minstrel*, 1771). The romantics used it more notably, *eg* ▷ Lord Byron in ▷ *Childe Harold*, though he was never quite at home with it; ▷ Percy Bysshe Shelley in his elegy on Keats, ▷ *Adonais*; and ▷ John Keats himself in his *Eve of St Agnes*. Since then it has been rarely used; its use and disuse are a fair index of the periods of rise and decline in Spenser's influence.

Sphinx

A mythical monster of ancient Egypt, Assyria, and Greece. It may have originated in Egypt, where the most famous effigy of a sphinx survives, near the Great Pyramid of Giza; it is male, with the body of a lion and the head of a man, and it represents the pharaoh identified with the sun-god Ra. Assyrian sphinxes are also male, but Greek sphinxes are female and winged. The most famous legend about a sphinx is the Greek one about the monster that laid waste the neighbourhood of the Greek city of Thebes. The ▷ Muses had taught her a riddle which was at last answered by ▷ Oedipus, whereupon the Sphinx destroyed herself.

Spitalfields

A district in east London, so called because from the 12th to 16th centuries, it belonged to the religious foundation called the Hospital of St Mary. Later the district was colonized by French Protestant refugee silk weavers.

Spondee

In ancient Greek and Latin poetry, a unit of verse measure composed of two long syllables; in English verse, two accented syllables. Words like 'maintain'

and 'wineglass' in English may be spondees, just as

'again' is an iambus, and 'only' is a trochee. It is possible to find whole lines of verse in trochee (falling) rhythm, and usual to find lines in iambic (rising) rhythm, but whole lines in spondaic rhythm have to be artificially contrived, *eg*

> *Slow spon/dee stalks; / strong foot.*

▷ Metre.

Sporus

A homosexual favourite of the Emperor Nero. His name was used by ▷ Alexander Pope for the sexually ambiguous Lord Hervey, politician and adviser to the Queen, in *Epistle to Dr. Arbuthnot* (ll. 305–333).

Sprung Rhythm

A term used by the poet ▷ Gerard Manley Hopkins to denote the method by which his verse is to be scanned. In his time most English verse was written in Running Rhythm, *ie* ▷ metres with regular stresses in the line:

> *Tonight the winds begin to rise*
> *And roar from yonder dropping day*
>   (Tennyson – *In Memoriam*)

Hopkins wished to free English verse from this rhythm, so as to bring verse into closer accord with common speech, to emancipate rhythm from the linear unit, and to achieve a freer range of emphasis. His theory of Sprung Rhythm (contained in the Preface to his Poems) is complicated, perhaps because he felt he had to justify himself to rather academic metricists like his friend ▷ Robert Bridges. In fact he was reviving the rhythm of ▷ Old English ▷ Alliterative Verse (he cites Langland's ▷ *Piers Plowman* as being in Sprung Rhythm) and in folk poetry including many ▷ ballads and ▷ nursery rhymes. In Sprung Rhythm the number of stresses in each line is regular, but they do not occur at regular intervals, nor do the lines have a uniform number of syllables. The rhythm also drives through the ▷ stanza, and is not basically linear. The following is an example:

> *Summer ends now; now, barbarous in beauty,*
>   *the stooks rise*
> *Around; up above, what wind-walks! what*
>   *lovely behaviour*
> *Of silk-sack clouds! has wilder,*
>   *wilful wavier*
> *Meal-drift moulded ever and melted across*
>   *skies?*
>   (Hopkins–*Hurrahing in Harvest*)

Spurgeon, Charles Haddon (1834–92)

An extremely popular ▷ Baptist preacher, for whom the Metropolitan Tabernacle, Newington, London, was built to hold audiences of 6,000. His sermons were in the old ▷ Puritan tradition, with strong appeals to the emotions and the conscience, but also varied by a bold and unusual kind of humour. In doctrine he was thoroughly traditional, and eventually he left the Baptists because of his distrust of the new biblical criticism.

Squire

▷ Knighthood.

Squire's Tale, The

One of ▷ Chaucer's ▷ *Canterbury Tales*. It is set in the exotic east and begins with an account of how Cambyuskan, King of Tartary, receives magic gifts on his birthday, including a magic ring for his daughter Canace. The ring allows her to understand the language of birds and through it she hears the sad lament of a female falcon who has been deserted by a faithless tercelet. The tale is unfinished but from the plot résumé given before it breaks off, it seems that the Squire was embarking on a romance of epic length, involving several major narrative lines in an interlaced structure (of the kind found later in the works of ▷ Boiardo, and ▷ Ariosto).

Both ▷ Spenser and ▷ Milton admired the tale, which is related in a highly self-conscious manner by its narrator. The Franklin follows on with praise for the Squire's contribution and there is no indication that the Franklin's response is designed to interrupt the Squire, although the *Squire's Tale* is left unfinished.
    ▷ *Franklin's Tale, The*.

St James's Palace

One of the royal palaces in London, built in the 16th century by ▷ Henry VIII. In the 18th century it superseded ▷ Whitehall as the official royal residence; hence foreign ambassadors have ever since been officially accredited to 'the Court of St James', meaning the British government, although in the reign of ▷ Victoria it was in turn superseded by ▷ Buckingham Palace close by.

Stanislavsky, Konstantin (1863–1938)

Russian actor and director, and founder of the Moscow Art Theatre in 1898 with Nemirovich-Danchenko. He rejected the declamatory acting style of the Imperial Theatres and developed a rigorous actors' training which explored, among other things, character psychology and motivation. These ideas about acting can be studied in his published works: *My Life in Art*; *An Actor Prepares*; *Building a Character*; *Creating a Role*. He has been a great influence for the American Method and other naturalistic approaches to acting. However he did not restrict his directing to naturalistic plays for which the so-called Stanislavskian approach was relevant.

Bib: Benedetti, J., *Stanislavski: An Introduction*; Magarshack, D., *Stanislavsky on the Art of the Stage*.

Star Chamber

A room in the old ▷ Palace of Westminster with a ceiling ornamented with stars. From

the 14th century to 1641, it was used for meetings of the royal council, sometimes for judicial purposes. Judicial meetings of the Council came to be known as the Court of the Star Chamber; it was used to try accused men who were too powerful to be tried by an ordinary court of law with a jury. However it was 'a prerogative court', *ie* it depended directly on royal authority, unlike the ▷ Common Law courts with which the king had very little, if any, power to interfere. Its oppressive role under ▷ James 1 and ▷ Charles 1 led to its abolition by ▷ Parliament just before the outbreak of the ▷ Civil War.
▷ Courts of Law.

State funding
This is an important source of income for much of the 'arts' in Britain. Theatre, as for example the ▷ R.S.C, and ▷ opera, like the Royal Opera at Covent Garden, are subsidized by the state, while on a smaller scale local authorities provide grants for writers, bookshops and courses.
▷ Arts Council of Great Britain; Censorship.

Stationers
In modern English, sellers of writing materials. In the ▷ Middle Ages and until the mid-17th century, however, they were booksellers, and were so called from their practice of taking up stalls or 'stations' at suitable places in cathedral towns (*eg* against the walls of St Paul's Cathedral in London) and universities. In the 16th and early 17th centuries they not only sold books, but printed and published them as well. The absence of a law of ▷ copyright (until 1709) made it lawful for stationers to publish author's manuscripts whenever and however they could procure them, without the authors' permission. This kind of unauthorized publishing is now called 'pirating'. 18 of Shakespeare's plays were possibly pirated before the publication of the first collected edition of his plays in the First Folio of 1623, and the fact has caused some difficulties to scholars; there is no assurance that their publication was authorized by the poet, that he had revised the plays for publication, or even that the stationer had procured a reliable version.

The Stationers' Company was formed in 1557 by royal charter; by this charter, no one not a member was entitled to publish a book except by special privilege, and all stationers had to record the titles of books they published; the Company's record of books is thus an important source of information for the literary historian, and particularly valuable evidence in dating many Elizabethan plays. The Company gradually lost its publishing monopoly in the 17th century.

The modern institution, Her Majesty's Stationery Office, publishes official government documents.
▷ Stationers' Register.

Stationers' Register
An important source of bibliographical information for the 16th and 17th centuries. In 1557, ▷ Mary I granted the Worshipful Company of ▷ Stationers and Papermakers of London the monopoly of printing. Under the charter granted to the company, all printers were enjoined to record the titles of any works intended for publication for the first time in a register. Once a title had been recorded, no other member of the company was allowed to publish the book. The Stationers' Register thus *should* include the titles of all books intended for publication between 1554 and 1709. In practice, however, the record is incomplete. First, records for the years 1571–6 have been lost. Secondly, titles were sometimes entered but the book never published. Thirdly, on occasion a book was published without being entered. Finally, though titles were usually entered shortly before the actual publication of a book, there are cases where a period of years elapsed between the entering of a title and the final publication of a work. Nevertheless, the Stationers' Register is an important record of the English book trade in the period. Not least, it provides a valuable indication of what works were being considered for publication at a particular moment.
Bib: Arber, E. (ed.), *A Transcript of the Register of the Company of Stationers of London, 1554–1640*, 5 vol.; Eyre, G. E. B. (ed.), *A Transcript of the Register of the Worshipful Company of Stationers from 1640 to 1709*, 3 vol.

Stead, Christina (1902–83)
Australian novelist. Educated at Sydney University Teachers' College, she moved to Europe in 1928, and to the U.S.A. in 1935, travelling with the American political economist William James Blake, whom she married in 1952. She worked as a Hollywood screen-writer before moving to England and, in 1968, returning to Australia. Many of her novels are concerned with the experience of women, and in particular the quest for love. They are notable for their stylistic power, richness of observation, and vivid characterization, and contain an element of the fantastic. Her first works were collections

of stories: *The Salzberg Tales* and *Seven Poor Men of Sydney*, both published in 1934. Of her novels, *House of All Nations* (1938) reflects her left-wing views in its account of a glittering, amoral world of financial speculation, while *The Man Who Loved Children* (1940), a novel of American family life, shows an interest in the causes of genius. In *For Love Alone* (1944) a girl escapes to Australia in search of love and freedom.

▷ Commonwealth literature.

Steele, Sir Richard (1672–1729)
Essayist and journalist. He was educated (with ▷ Addison) at Charterhouse School and at Oxford University. On graduation he entered the army. His prose treatise *The Christian Hero* (1701) attracted the favour of ▷ King William III, but caused Steele the inconvenience of finding that he was expected to live up to his own precepts. This his pleasure-loving nature did not find convenient, and he redressed the balance by his comedy *The Funeral* (1701). He wrote other comedies: *The Lying Lover* (1703); *The Tender Husband* (1705), an imitation of ▷ Molière's *Sicilienne*; *The Conscious Lovers* (1722). It is not, however, for his comedies that he is now read, but for a new kind of periodical ▷ essay of which he was practically the inventor, and which he published in ▷ *The Tatler*, started in 1709, and appearing three times weekly. Although since the lapsing of the Licensing Act in 1695 there was no active ▷ censorship of political opinion, Steele found it safer to avoid politics, at least after the ▷ Tory party came to power in 1710, since he was a consistent ▷ Whig. His essays treated daily life, manners and behaviour, in a way calculated to educate middle-class readers and win the approval of people of virtue, and yet always to entertain them. These motives, and the kind of interest that his essays inspired, anticipate the character of later 18th-century novels, especially those of ▷ Samuel Richardson. *The Tatler* was already a success when ▷ Joseph Addison started to collaborate with Steele, but they closed it down in 1711, and started the still more famous ▷ *Spectator* (1711–12). The crisis of succession to the throne grew intense in 1713–14: the Whigs favoured the Protestant House of Hanover and a powerful Tory faction was ready to support Anne's half-brother James if he would turn Protestant, though other Tories remained loyal to the Act of 1701 in favour of Hanover. Steele was consequently attacked by the Tory journalist, ▷ Jonathan Swift, both for his conduct of

his next paper, *The Guardian* (1713), and for his ▷ pamphlet in favour of the Protestant succession, *The Crisis* (1714). In 1714 the Whigs returned to power and Steele's political fortunes revived; he was knighted in 1715, and received various official posts. In 1714 he produced his autobiographical *Apology for Himself and his Writings*; he also edited a number of other periodicals, all of them short-lived, and none with the fame of *The Tatler* and *The Spectator*: *The Englishman*, *The Reader*, *Town Talk*, *Tea-Table*, *Chit Chat*, *Plebeian*. The last, a political paper, led to a quarrel with Addison in 1718.

▷ Coverley, Sir Roger de.
Bib: Aitken, G. A., *Life*; Hazlitt, W., *The English Comic Writers*; Dobree, B., *Variety of Ways*; Bateson, F. W., *English Comic Drama, 1700–50*.

Stella
1 The name used by ▷ Sir Philip Sidney for Penelope Devereux in his ▷ sonnet sequence ▷ *Astrophil and Stella* ('Star-lover and star') published in 1591; she married Lord Rich.
2 The name used by ▷ Jonathan Swift for Esther Johnson in his *Journal to Stella*, published in 1768.

Stendhal (pseudonym of Henri Beyle) (1788–1842)
French writer, known for his novels *Armance* (1822), *La Chartreuse de Parme* (1839), *Le Rouge et le Noir* (1830) and *Lucien Leuwen* (unfinished and published posthumously in 1894). Considered the first of the French realists (▷ Realism), Stendhal is renowned for his exact depiction of milieu and for his close attention to psychological verisimilitude and motivation. However, his realism is neither a simple fidelity to detail nor does it underwrite the values and representations which aristocratic and bourgeois society makes of itself. Stendhal depicts indeed the conflict of social verisimilitudes with narrative inventions which contravene such verisimilitudes; so the mainspring of *Le Rouge et le Noir* is the socially unacceptable love of the aristocratic Mathilde and the commoner Julien, while *Armance* raises the 'shocking' issue of homosexuality before its Byronic (▷ Byron) conclusion. On the author's side, ▷ irony is his means of refusing to endorse such values. Irony here is not as a purely corrosive negativity. It discreetly raises the issue of the ethics of representation itself, moving outwards from the hero and society to ask whether the novel can hold together

that encounter of social and individual forces it narrates.

Stendhal's interests were wide and he was likewise the author of travel books, journalism and controversial literary pamphlets (*Racine et Shakespeare*, 1823 and 1825, in which he declared his support for the romantics (▷ Romantic Revival)). Three volumes of autobiographical writing were published after his death: his *Journal* (1888), *La Vie de Henry Brulard* (1890) and *Souvenirs d'égotisme* (1892).

Stephen, Sir Leslie (1832–1904)

Critic and biographer. He began his career as a tutor at Trinity Hall, Cambridge, and university rules demanded that he should be in orders as an Anglican clergyman. His philosophical studies led him to the religious scepticism so frequent among intellectuals of the middle and later 19th century, and he renounced his orders in 1875. From 1866 he contributed critical essays to the ▷ *Cornhill Magazine* and political ones for the *Nation*; he also wrote for the *Saturday Review* and helped to found the *Pall Mall Gazette* (1865). In 1871 he became editor of the *Cornhill*; the 11 years of his editorship made it one of the most distinguished literary reviews of the later 19th century. His critical essays were published in book form in *Hours in a Library* (1874–9). He wrote philosophical essays, defining his agnostic position: *Essays on Free Thinking and Plain Speaking* (1873). He contributed a number of ▷ biographies to the *English Men of Letters* series: *Johnson* (1878); *Pope* (1880); *Swift* (1882); *George Eliot* (1902), and *Hobbes* (1904). His most distinguished work is firstly his editorship of the *Dictionary of National Biography*, started in 1882, to which he contributed many of the articles, and his book on *The English Utilitarians* (1900). His last book, *English Literature and Society in the Eighteenth Century*, was published on the day of his death.

Today, Stephen is one of the most respected among critics of the later 19th century; the rigour and sincerity of his thinking make him a link between the Victorians and 18th-century rationalist traditions of thought which continued into the 19th century in the ▷ Utilitarian school of thinkers. He has twice been used as the basis of a character in the masterpieces of distinguished novelists: Vernon Whitford in ▷ *The Egoist* by ▷ Meredith, and Mr Ramsay in ▷ *To the Lighthouse* by ▷ Virginia Woolf, his daughter by his second wife. His

first wife had been a daughter of the novelist ▷ William Makepeace Thackeray.

▷ Agnosticism; Reviews and Periodicals.
Bib: Lives by F. W. Maitland; Noel Annan.

Sterne, Laurence (1713–68)

Sterne was born at Clonmel in Ireland, the son of an improvident army officer. After leaving Cambridge University he became an Anglican priest near York, where his great-grandfather had been Archbishop. His celebrated novel ▷ *The Life and Opinions of Tristram Shandy* appeared in successive volumes from 1760 until 1767. Opinions have always been divided about the qualities of this book, although Sterne's reputation rests principally upon it. ▷ Samuel Johnson found it eccentric and shallow, declaring, 'Nothing odd will do long. *Tristram Shandy* did not last'; but in the 20th century the critic Viktor Schlovsky has argued that '*Tristram Shandy* is the most typical novel of world literature.' ▷ *A Sentimental Journey through France and Italy*, which demonstrates many of the same stylistic idiosyncrasies, appeared in 1768, the last year of Sterne's life. His *Journal to Eliza*, published posthumously, is a curious, quasi-autobiographical work that hovers uneasily between fact and fiction, tragedy and farce. The same blend of seriousness and whimsicality is evident in Sterne's sermons, he published under the name of one of the characters from *Tristram Shandy* as *The Sermons of Mr Yorick*. A contemporary review took offence at this jesting allusion. 'We have read of a Yorick likewise in an obscene romance,' it thundered. 'But are the solemn dictates of religion fit to be conveyed from the mouths of buffoons and ludicrous romancers?'

Sterne's characteristic blending of sentimentality and farce, although distinctive in style, is not without precedent. His main literary influences can be found in ▷ Rabelais, ▷ Cervantes, and ▷ Montaigne, although there are also debts to ▷ Burton's *Anatomy of Melancholy*, ▷ Locke's *Essay on Human Understanding*, and ▷ Swift's *Tale of a Tub*. From Rabelais Sterne derived not only his bawdy humour, but also his fascination with exuberant word-play, his love of lists and puns, his delight in the sonorous malleability of words and his absurd parodies of learned debates. From Locke he borrowed and parodied the theory of the association of ideas, a theory which allows him to present each of his characters trapped in a private

world of allusions. ▷ Thackeray objected
to the self-indulgence of Sterne's wit; 'He is
always looking on my face, watching his
effect, uncertain whether I think him an
impostor or not; posture-making, coaxing and
imploring me.' Yet it is precisely this fictional
virtuosity that has recommended Sterne as a
model to later writers keen to assert not only
that all art is artifice, but that history and
biography too are merely varieties of elaborate
fiction.
Bib: Cash, A. H., *Laurence Sterne*; New, M.,
Laurence Sterne as Satirist.

Stevenson, Anne (b 1933)

Anne Stevenson

Poet. Stevenson was born in Britain, and now
lives here, but was brought up and educated
in the U.S.A. She has written critical texts as
well as poetry, and has worked as a teacher.
Her publications include: *Living in America*
(1965); *Travelling Behind Glass: Selected
Poems* (1974); *Enough of Green* (1977); *Minute
by Glass Minute* (1982); *The Fiction-makers*
(1985); *Selected Poems* (1986).

Stevenson, Robert Louis Balfour (1850–94)
Novelist, essayist, poet. The son of an
engineer, he intended to take up the same
profession, for which he showed early talent,
but bad health prevented this. Partly because
of his health and partly for love of travel, he
spent much of his life abroad and some of his
best writing is in essays of travel, *eg An
Inland Voyage* (1878) and *Travels with a
Donkey in the Cevennes* (1879). His most
famous works, however, are the fantasy, so
often used as an emblem of divided

Robert Louis Stevenson by W. B. Richmond
(1887)

personality, *The Strange Case of Dr
Jekyll and Mr Hyde* (1886 - ▷ Jekyll and
Hyde) and his adventure story ▷ *Treasure
Island* (1883). Still well known are his
Scottish historical romances, in the tradition
of ▷ Walter Scott: *Kidnapped* (1886), *The
Master of Ballantrae* (1889), and *Catriona*
(1893); it has been said that *Weir of Hermiston*,
also in this style but left unfinished, would
have been his masterpiece. Other works of
fiction: *New Arabian Nights* (1882); *Prince
Otto* (1885); *The Black Arrow* (1888); *The
Wrong Box* (1889); *The Wrecker* (1892); *Island
Nights Entertainments* (1893); *The Ebb Tide*
(1894); *St Ives*, also left unfinished at his
death. Essays: *Virginibus Puerisque* (1881);
Familiar Studies of Men and Books (1882);
Vailima Letters (1895). His *A Child's Garden
of Verses* (1885) was for long considered a
minor children's classic (▷ Children's
books), and he published other poetry in
Underwoods (1887). Stevenson was strongly
influenced by French ideas of literary style
and his preoccupation with style apart from
the substance that is being expressed was
characteristic of the ▷ aestheticism of the
later 19th century although he had too much
love of the world of action and simplicity of
mind to make it possible to class him with the
aesthetes. He has had a wide popular
readership which has perhaps denied him
critical attention; critics have detected a
darker side to his writing beneath the

swashbuckling, and dualism is a theme in evidence.

Bib: Balfour, G., *Life*; Daiches, D., *Robert Louis Stevenson*; Elwin, M., *The Strange Case of Stevenson*; Furnas, J. C., *Voyage to Windward* (life); Eigner, E. M., *Robert Louis Stevenson and Romantic Tradition*; Calder, J. (ed.), *Stevenson and Victorian Scotland*.

Stichomythia

A terse but artificial style of dramatic dialogue, used in disputes between two characters, each speaking in turn a single line of verse. It originated in ancient Greek tragedies; from them it passed to ▷ Seneca whose influence caused it to be used by some of the early Elizabethans.

Stock Exchange

An institution in London for the purchase and sale of investments in the form of shares, stocks and bonds. London stockbrokers once met at the Royal Exchange and elsewhere for the transaction of their business, but in 1802 they formed themselves into a society and built their own premises on a site between Throgmorton Street and Old Broad Street.

Stoics

A school of philosophy founded by the Greek Zeno of Citium, in the 4th century BC. It later extended to Rome, where its leaders became Epictetus and ▷ Seneca (both 1st century AD) and the Roman Emperor Marcus Aurelius (2nd century AD). They reasoned that all being is material, and therefore the soul is, and so are the virtues. The soul, however, is an active principle which sustains the body, and proceeds from God; only the active principle has significance, and the wise person is therefore indifferent to material suffering and cares only for virtue governed by judgement which is in accordance with the principles of wisdom. Some of the ethical principles of Stoicism were in accordance with Chrisianity (which Marcus Aurelius nevertheless persecuted) and, abstracted from religious doctrine, they appealed to the ▷ Renaissance ideal of the noble soul; hence the recurrence of Stoic attitudes in the drama of ▷ Shakespeare and his contemporaries.

Stonehenge

Concentric circles of standing stone, some of them very large, situated on the chalk plateau called Salisbury Plain in central southern England. They are prehistoric, dating perhaps from the second millenium BC, but their purpose is unknown.

Stoppard, Tom (b 1937)

Czech-born British dramatist and something of an eclectic who has experimented with a variety of forms in his writing for stage and television. Characteristic of his plays is a heavy reliance on intellectual wit and allusion, which would appear to make his appeal rather esoteric, yet he has had several West End successes and is now established as a leading comic playwright. His major works include: *Rosencrantz and Guildenstern Are Dead* (1966); *The Real Inspector Hound* (1968); *Jumpers* (1972); *Travesties* (1974); *Dirty Linen* (1976); *Every Good Boy Deserves Favour* (1977); *Night and Day* (1978); *On the Razzle* (1981); *The Real Thing* (1982); *Rough Crossing* (1985); *Hapgood* (1987). Television plays include: *Professional Foul* (1977); *Squaring the Circle* (1984).

Bib: Bigsby, C. W. E., *Tom Stoppard*; Hunter, J., *Tom Stoppard's Plays*.

Storey, David (b 1933)

Novelist and dramatist. His novels include: *This Sporting Life* (1960); *Flight into Camden* (1961); *Radcliffe* (1963); *Pasmore* (1972); *A Temporary Life* (1973); *Saville* (1976); *A Prodigal Child* (1982); *Present Times* (1984).

Before he became a novelist and playwright Storey was an art student, and to pay for his studies in London he played at weekends in professional Rugby League football for a northern team. The son of a miner, Storey is the most interesting of a number of novelists in modern Britain who have in common that their social viewpoint is outside the middle class and centred geographically outside London; they include ▷ Alan Sillitoe, ▷ John Braine and ▷ Stan Barstow. Their obvious antecedent is ▷ D. H. Lawrence. Storey is distinguished from his contemporaries with a similar background by the absence of social belligerence and an ability to reach across from a provincial-industrial world denuded of art to a world of highly cultivated sensibility without playing false to the social experience that shaped him. His first novel, which has been filmed, is about his background world, in which sport is the principal cultural force; the next two are in different ways more ambitious and less successful, but their faults are interesting as the price paid for their serious experimental boldness. *Radcliffe* modifies 1950s' ▷ realism with elements of the ▷ Gothic, allegorical and fantastic, while retaining a concern with class and social mobility; *Pasmore* continues this development by linking social instability to a personal crisis of identity. His plays often explore class antagonism and

social dislocation. In *The Contractor* (1969) the process of manual work is presented dramatically as the action centres around the construction of a huge marquee on stage. This bold if somewhat sentimental gesture about the worth of work originally made a strong impression. Yet Storey's plays tend to avoid simplistic idealization of the working class or indeed any kind of simple obvious 'meaning'. The ▷ Chekhovian *Home* (1970) is set in a mental hospital, perhaps a metaphor for modern Britain, whose communication is painfully reserved. Much is hinted at but little is directly expressed. The later plays, *Mother's Day* (1976) and *Sisters* (1978), both have working-class settings and deal with what Storey termed the 'delusions, illusions and fantasies' of domestic life. Other plays include: *The Restoration of Arnold Middleton* (1966); *In Celebration* (1969): *The Changing Room* (1971); *The Farm* and *Cromwell* (both 1973): *Life Class* (1974); *Early Days* (1980).
Bib: Taylor, J. R., *David Storey*.

Strachey, (Giles) Lytton (1880–1932)
Biographer. His best-known works are *Eminent Victorians* (1918) – short biographical studies of Cardinal Manning, Florence Nightingale and General Gordon – and *Queen Victoria* (1921). He also wrote *Elizabeth and Essex* (1928), and criticism: *Landmarks in French Literature* (1912) and *Books and Characters* (1922). Strachey regarded most biographies of the 19th century as dull monuments to the subject, whereas he considered biography to be an art form, presenting the subject as a human being and showing him or her from unexpected aspects. Strachey was a prominent member of the ▷ Bloomsbury Group.
  ▷ Biography.
Bib: Sanders, C. P., *Strachey: His Mind and Art*; Johnstone, J. K., *The Bloomsbury Group*; Holroyd, M., *Lytton Strachey*.

Strafford, Sir Thomas Wentworth, first Earl of (1593–1641)
Statesman, and one of ▷ Charles I's chief ministers. He began his career as an opponent of the king; as Member of Parliament for Yorkshire in 1625, he opposed the attempt of Charles's minister, the Earl of Buckingham, to raise taxes for war against Spain, and in 1627 he was imprisoned for refusing to contribute a forced loan to the king. His opposition to Charles was different in motive from that of other members; theirs was based on the desire to assert the power of ▷ Parliament, whereas Wentworth's motive was to secure efficient government.

Consequently when in 1628 Parliament asserted itself by forcing on the king the ▷ Petition of Right, he changed sides. Charles in 1632 sent him to Ireland to reform the administration there. He was never consulted on English affairs until the major crisis brought about by the defeat of the royal troops by the Scots in 1639. Wentworth was then recalled, and made Earl of Strafford in 1640; events, however, had gone so far that he could no longer help the king, and merely focused public hostility upon himself. Parliament condemned him to death by an Act of Attainder (*ie* a law effecting death of a subject without using the normal judicial process), and he was executed accordingly.

Strawberry Hill
  ▷ Walpole, Horace.

Stream of consciousness
A term which was used by William James in his *Principles of Psychology* but was first applied to literature in a 1918 review by May Sinclair of volumes of ▷ Dorothy Richardson's *Pilgrimage*. Since then it has been used for the narrative technique which attempts to render the consciousness of a character by representing as directly as possible the flow of feelings, thoughts and impressions. The term 'interior monologue' is also sometimes used. The classic exponents of the technique, apart from Richardson, are ▷ Virginia Woolf, ▷ James Joyce and the American novelist William Faulkner (1897–1962).

Strindberg, August (1849–1912)
Swedish dramatist and novelist. His bad relations with his father were the beginning of a psychologically tormented life for Strindberg; he was married and divorced three times, and had a mental breakdown in 1895–6; described in *Inferno*, one of several autobiographical fragments and a vivid document. Intellectually he was immensely versatile: a student of Chinese, botany, chemistry, alchemy and painting. He had comparable literary versatility, and wrote radical journalism (1872–80), prose fiction (notably *The Red Room*, 1879), and his varied, original dramas. He is chiefly famous, at least outside Sweden, for the last. He wrote historical dramas (*Master Olof*, 1872; *Saga of the Folkungs, Gustavus Vasa, Eric XIV*, 1899) which show the influence of Shakespeare's ▷ history plays; tragedies influenced by ▷ Zola's ▷ naturalism and the philosophy of ▷ Nietzsche; fantasies (*Easter*, 1900; *Dream Play*, 1902) under the influence of the Belgian dramatist, Maurice

Maeterlinck (1862–1949); and, at the end of his career, highly symbolic dramas often called ▷ 'expressionist', of which the best known is *The Ghost Sonata* (1907). Two partly autobiographical works, *To Damascus* (1898) and *The Great Highway* (1909–12) can also be termed 'expressionist'.

Strindberg's dramatic inspiration was to epitomize human experience as the experience of conflict. This shows most clearly in his naturalist phase, especially the two plays by which he is best known in Britain: *The Father* (1887) and *Lady Julia* (1888). To these may be added the double play *The Dance of Death* (1901), a naturalist tragedy verging towards the expressionist symbolism of his later work. One of his strongest preoccupations at the time was the theme of conflict in relationships between women and men. He was also aware of the possibilities of visual experiment on stage, and was also experimental in dialogue, though not with such decisive success as his Russian contemporary, ▷ Anton Chekhov.

In Britain (in contrast to America), Strindberg did not have an influence comparable to that of ▷ Henrik Ibsen until after World War II. Since then, the outspokenness of such dramatists as ▷ John Osborne and ▷ John Arden, and the dialogue and stage experiments of ▷ Harold Pinter and ▷ Samuel Beckett, as well as new freedoms shown by many dramatists in the handling of stage sets and dramatic plots, all show his impact.

Strophe
A Greek word meaning 'turn'. It is used as a term in Greek versification, for example, the ▷ Pindaric Ode, for a passage which is sung and danced (or 'turned') by a chorus. When another passage succeeds it, to be danced and sung by another part of the chorus, this second passage is known as an 'antistrophe'.
▷ Ode.

Structuralism
This influential school of criticism grew out of the ideas of ▷ Ferdinand de Saussure as they appeared in his *Course in General Linguistics* (1915). Saussure established the role of ▷ difference, the relationship between linguistic elements (▷ signs), as the major determining principle in the establishment of meaning (signification). Thus structuralism encompasses approaches to criticism which use linguistic models to enable critics to focus not on the inherent meaning of a work, but on the structures which produce or generate that meaning or meanings.

As a critical method Saussure's insights were developed subsequently in a wide range of areas, from anthropology, especially by the social anthropologist Claude Levi-Strauss (b 1908), to language, in particular by the Russian ▷ Formalists such as ▷ Roman Jakobson and Tzetvan Todorov (b 1940). In addition, Saussure's insights into sign systems were applied to phenomena as varied as folk tales by the Russian critic Vladimir Propp and menus and traffic lights, in the work of the French critic ▷ Roland Barthes.
▷ Post-structuralism and ▷ deconstruction have developed from the basis of structuralism.
Bib: Culler, J., *Structuralist Poetics*,
▷ Derrida, Jacques; discourse; Foucault, Michel.

Stuart (Stewart), House of
The family from which came the sovereigns of Scotland between 1371 and 1603, and the sovereigns of Scotland, England and Ireland between 1603 and 1714. In 1603 ▷ Elizabeth I of England died childless, and James VI of Scotland inherited the crown of England by virtue of his descent from Elizabeth's aunt Margaret, who had married James IV. James VI thus became also ▷ James I of England, and ruled over the two countries until 1625. The succession continued as follows:
▷ Charles I (1625–49), after whom there was an ▷ interregnum until 1660 when the monarchy was restored in his son, ▷ Charles II (1660–85); ▷ James II (1685–88); ▷ Mary II and ▷ William III (1688–1702); Anne (1702–14).

Stubbes, Philip (?1555–?1611)
▷ Puritan author of *The Anatomie of Abuses* (1583) who censured stage plays and wrote a strong and colourful prose. He may have been involved in the ▷ Martin Marprelate controversy, and was attacked in pamphlets by both ▷ John Lyly and ▷ Thomas Nashe. He is most valued now for his contribution to our understanding of the popular customs and festivals of the time.

Styx
▷ Hades.

Subjectivity
In its use in the language of literary criticism this concept is not to be confused with the notion of 'individual response' with which it has customarily been associated. ▷ Louis Althusser and ▷ Jacques Lacan develop the notion of human beings as 'subjects', that is points at which all of those social, cultural,

and psychic forces which contribute to the construction of the individual, come together. Implicit in the concept of the 'subject' is the idea of the grammatical positioning of the personal pronoun in a sentence: the 'I' being referred to as 'the subject of discourse'. Also, implicit in the concept of 'subjectivity' is the notion of 'subjection', which raises fundamental questions about the ways in which the behaviour of individual 'subjects' is conditioned by external forces. Within the boundaries of critical theory the 'subject' is never unified (except through the functioning of an ▷ ideology which is designed to efface contradiction), but is, in reality split, or 'decentred'. This is part of a movement away from the kind of philosophical ▷ humanism which would place the individual at the centre of attention. It would attribute to him or her an autonomy of action as well as an authority arising out of the suggestion that he or she is the origin and source of all meaning. 'Subjectivity' is an indispensable category of analysis for ▷ feminism, ▷ psycho-analytical criticism and for the various kinds of ▷ materialist analysis of texts.

Sublimation

This term is used in ▷ Freudian psychoanalysis to describe the process whereby activities which have their origins in the unconscious, and which can be traced to primal issues of sexuality, are diverted and surface in other areas of human endeavour, as something else. This concept is of particular use to literary criticism, not only because it can provide an explanation of the mechanisms of artistic creation itself, but because it assists in the analysis of literary representations of human motives and actions. Implicit in sublimation is the notion of an unconscious whose operations, distorted as desires, rise to the level of the conscious.

Subversion

This is a term usually associated with the sphere of political action, but applied to literary texts it points towards the relationship between a particular text, or even a part of a text, and what is generally regarded as the prevailing order. Individual texts are capable of challenging dominant orthodoxies (eg ▷ James Joyce's ▷ Ulysses or ▷ D. H. Lawrence's Lady Chatterley's Lover), either at the level of literary form, or at the level of discernible content. Thus, they may be said to subvert expectations or dominant values. A more complex kind of subversion may take place within the boundaries of a particular text which otherwise would be accepted as conforming to prevailing values and attitudes. Where this happens, negotiation takes place (which can be analysed as part of the text's structure) whereby that which is dominant in the text seeks to contain and control those forces which could subvert it. Such a process is particularly evident in relation to sexual difference, where a potentially subversive 'femininity' is often seen to threaten the dominant masculine discourses which seek to contain it. Very often potentially subversive energies are only ever permitted to enter a text in marginalized forms, eg female promiscuity, as various forms of 'evil' all of which are shown to be a danger to the status quo. An acceptance of the judgements implied in these moral categories is usually a precondition of a reading which is complicit with its dominant discourses and structures. A more critical reading will seek to reinstate the text's 'subversive' elements in order to show precisely how certain values, and the literary structures which sustain them, are produced.

Suckling, Sir John (1609–41)

Poet and dramatist. Suckling has been grouped with the ▷ 'Cavalier' poets who were associated with the Royalist cause during the ▷ Civil War. Closely associated with the court, his military career was marked by an ostentatious delight in appearance rather than the reality of a campaign: he is said to have paid £12,000 from his own pocket to have 100 cavalrymen decked out in striking uniforms for the war against the Scots in 1639. The king's army, of which Suckling and his troops were a part, were routed. Following the abortive attempt to rescue the king's favourite, the Earl of Strafford, from the ▷ Tower, Suckling, who took part in the plot, fled abroad where he died, possibly committing suicide and probably in the autumn of 1641.

Although the author of four plays, the most successful of which was *Aglaura* (first produced in 1637 as a ▷ tragedy, and revised and produced as a comedy in 1638), Suckling's reputation rests on his short ▷ lyric poems, written in an anti-Petrarchan style and calculated to strike the pose of a cynical rake.

Suffragette Movement

Colloquial term for the Women's Suffrage Movement which pursued violent action to secure political rights for women before and during the first World War. Specifically they wanted equal rights with men to have the vote (suffrage) in parliamentary elections and to be candidates for election. Among the famous leaders of the movement were Mrs Pankhurst and her two daughters, Sylvia and Christabel. The movement ended in 1918 when votes were given to woman at the age of 30; in 1928 they received equal rights with men.

▷ Women, Status of.

Bib: Tickner, L., *The Spectacle of Women*.

Summer's Last Will and Testament (1592)
A lyrical ▷ allegory and pageant by ▷ Thomas Nashe, and his only surviving dramatic work.

Summoner's Tale, The
One of ▷ Chaucer's ▷ *Canterbury Tales*. It is delivered as a riposte to the ▷ *Friar's Tale*, has a strong scatological emphasis and contains a devastating picture of the corrupt practices of Friar John, who uses his profession and professional skills to procure material comforts for himself and his colleagues. The basic plot follows a ▷ fabliau structure, and recounts the gulling of Friar John by one of his lay clients, who appears to promise him a significant gift, but this turns out to be no more than sound and wind (and provides a fitting comment on the Friar's principal qualities). However, the Friar has promised to distribute the gift among his colleagues, and the tale closes with an investigation into how the offensive gift might be divided into 12: a squire of the local lord solves this difficult problem of 'arsmetrike' and thus completes the total humiliation of the Friar.

Supremacy, Acts of
1 The law passed through ▷ Parliament on the initiative of ▷ King Henry VIII in 1534; it established the King as Supreme Head of the Church in England, and thus displaced the sovereignty of the Pope. The Act was the immediate consequence of Henry's dispute with the Pope over his attempt to divorce his Queen, Katherine of Aragon; however, this immediate cause was insufficient by itself to bring about the break. Deeper causes include the growth of national feeling; longstanding resentment against some forms of papal taxation; distrust of Roman Catholic doctrine, first roused by ▷ Wycliffe and now reawakened by the German reformer, ▷ Luther; growing dislike of the international religious orders of monks and friars who were ultimately subject to the Pope. Nonetheless, Henry was a conservative in doctrine, and the act did not entail doctrinal reformation.

2 The similar law passed through Parliament on the initiative of ▷ Elizabeth I in 1559. Since the act of 1534, the English nation had undergone ▷ Protestant doctrinal ▷ reformation in the reign of ▷ Edward VI and had reverted to full Roman Catholicism under headship of the Pope in the reign of ▷ Mary I. In consequence Elizabeth's Act of Supremacy was deliberately vague, so as to gain the widest possible national support, from both Protestant and Roman Catholic sympathizers. Elizabeth abandoned the title 'Supreme Head' and adopted that of 'Supreme Governor'.

Surrealism
Inaugurated in Paris in 1924 by ▷ André Breton's first *Surrealist Manifesto* (two further manifestos were to follow in 1930 and 1934), its founding members included Louis Aragon (1897–1982), Robert Desnos (1900–45), Paul Eluard (1895–1952), Benjamin Péret (1899–1959) and Philippe Soupault (b 1897). The movement's ambition was a radical programme, extending beyond art and literature to embrace social and political reform. To advertise and propagate their aims, the Surrealists created a 'Bureau de recherches surréalistes' and a number of reviews: *Littérature* (1919), *La Révolution surréaliste* (1924), *Le Surréalisme au service de la Révolution* (1930) and *Minotaure* (1932). Purely within France, Surrealism's roots lay in Guillaume Apollinaire's (1880–1918) experiments with poem-objects and in the cubist poetry of Pierre Reverdy (1889–1960). More broadly, as the first *Manifesto* made clear, it was especially indebted to Freudian (▷ Freud) theories of dream and sought to overthrow rationalism in favour of unconscious mental states, so giving rise to an expanded sense of the psychic life. Such unconscious processes could best be liberated by activities such as 'automatic writing'. By this technique, a writer's faculty of conscious censorship is laid aside, allowing the chance encounter between two otherwise unrelated elements which might produce the surreal image and intimate the incursion of dream into reality.

Just as Surrealism travelled easily between forms of artistic production and ostensibly external forms such as psychology and philosophy, so its own artistic manifestations span poetry, prose and painting, though it is best known for and possibly most representatively manifested in the first and last of these. Max Ernst (1891–1976), René Magritte (1898–1967) and Joan Miró (1893–1983) helped establish the movement in art and Salvador Dali (1904–89) provided greater impetus still when he associated himself with Surrealism in 1929; his dream-like work was plainly inspired by Freud, while his surreal objects such as the lobster-telephone amuse and shock our sense of the everyday propriety of such objects. Louis Aragon (1897–1982), the foremost of Surrealism's several communists (Eluard was another), made an early contribution with his *Feu de joie* (1920) and *Le Mouvement perpétuel* (1925) as well as major novels. However, Aragon's commitment to communism from 1927 onwards finally led to his break with Surrealism in 1932, even though Breton's *Second Manifesto* of 1930 had called for the harmonization of Freud and ▷ Marx. World War II caused an hiatus in Surrealism's activities and despite the success of the various Surrealist Exhibitions (eg London, 1936; Paris 1938, 1947, 1959), by the 1950s the movement's force was to all intents and purposes spent.

The widespread influence of French Surrealism between the Wars gave rise to two corresponding movements, Belgian Surrealism and English Surrealism.

Surrey, Henry Howard, Earl of (?1517–47)
Poet. He was the son of the Duke of Norfolk, the senior nobleman of England. Surrey and his father were both arrested by ▷ Henry VIII on a ridiculous charge of high treason. Surrey was executed, Henry's last victim; his father, also condemned to death, survived Henry and was reprieved. In character Surrey was a man of the ▷ Renaissance, with the Renaissance conception of the courtier as the complete man in all worthy things – art, learning and action. His poetry was thus a cultivation of poetic ideals on the model of the poets of the Italian Renaissance, and he shares with his older contemporary, ▷ Sir Thomas Wyatt the distinction of being the first poet to naturalize Renaissance poetic modes in English; their work was published by ▷ Tottel in his *Miscellany* of 1557. Like Wyatt, Surrey cultivated the ▷ sonnet, and he was the first poet to use ▷ blank verse, in his translation of Virgil's ▷ *Aeneid*, Books 2 and 3. However, Surrey was respected for these contributions more by modern critics, who point out that the merit of his poetry is much slighter than Wyatt's, and that the flowering of the English short poem in the 1590s owed more to the ▷ sonnets of ▷ Sir Philip Sidney (*Astrophil and Stella*) and to ▷ Edmund Spenser's pastorals (▷ *The Shepherd's Calendar*) than to the work of either Wyatt or Surrey.
Bib: Jones, E. (ed.), *Poems*.

Surtees, Robert Smith (1805–64)
Novelist. In 1832 he helped to found the *New Sporting Magazine*, which he edited for five years and to which he contributed sketches collected in 1838 under the title of *Jorrocks's Jaunts and Jollities*. It was this book which suggested to the publishers, Chapman and Hall, the idea that ▷ Charles Dickens might write a similar series of sketches about a Nimrod Club of amateur sportsmen. Dickens adapted this idea to the Pickwick Club and thus started ▷ *The Pickwick Papers*, issued in 20 parts in 1836–7 and published in book form in 1837. Surtees's most famous fox-hunting novel is probably *Handley Cross* (1843), still regarded as a minor classic. He published eight novels in all.
Bib: Cooper, L., *R. S. Surtees*; Welcome, J., *The Sporting World of R. S. Surtees*.

Swedenborg, Emanuel (1688–1772)
Swedish scientist, philosopher and theologian. The earlier part of his life was dedicated to the natural sciences, and his theories anticipate important discoveries in geology, cosmology, and especially in the physiology of the brain. Later he devoted himself to religion and had mystical experiences: his religious beliefs led to the founding of the New Jerusalem Church and the English Theosophical Society. According to Swedenborg's beliefs, God is Divine Man, whose essence is infinite love; there are correspondences between spiritual nature and material nature, but the former is alive and the latter is dead; both in God and in man and nature there are three degrees, those of love, wisdom and use, or end, cause and effect; by a love of each degree man comes into relation with them, and his end is to become the image of his Creator, God. Swedenborg's *Heaven and Hell* and *True Christian Religion* were translated into English in 1778 and 1781, and amongst his followers were the father of the poet ▷ William Blake, and Blake's friend, the sculptor, John Flaxman. Swedenborg's doctrines are the starting point of much of Blake's thinking. But Blake, who wrote comments on Swedenborg's doctrines, came to disagree with the philosopher in important respects.

Swift, Jonathan (1667–1745)
Satirist. He was of an old English family, but his grandfather seems to have lost his fortune on the Cavalier side in the ▷ Civil Wars of the mid-17th century. The poet ▷ Dryden was his cousin. Swift was educated in Ireland, where he had the future playwright ▷ Congreve as a schoolfellow, and took his

Jonathan Swift, from an original engraving

degree at Trinity College, Dublin. He began his working life as secretary to the statesman and writer ▷ Sir William Temple in 1689, left him to take orders as a priest in the Church of England in 1694 (receiving a small ecclesiastical office in Ireland), and returned to remain in Temple's service until Temple's death in 1699. Throughout the reign of Queen Anne (1702–14) he played a large part in the literary and the political life of London, though he was dividing his time between England and Ireland. He contributed some numbers to ▷ Addison and ▷ Steele's journals, ▷ *The Tatler* and ▷ *The Spectator*, and together with ▷ Pope and Arbuthnot founded the ▷ Scriblerus Club. Politically he at first served the ▷ Whig party, but in 1710 he changed over to the Tories, led by Edward Harley, Earl of Oxford, and the brilliant but unreliable ▷ Bolingbroke. He served the Tories by his ▷ pamphlet *The Conduct of the Allies* (1711) advocating peace in the War of the ▷ Spanish Succession, and by his conduct of the journal *The Examiner* (1710–11). His assistance was invaluable to the Tory party, who held power from 1711 until the death of the Queen; in 1713 Swift was rewarded by being made Dean of St Patrick's Cathedral, Dublin, an office which he at first held as an absentee. By this time, however, the Queen was dying, and Harley and Bolingbroke, divided over the succession to the throne, were opponents: Bolingbroke offered Swift

great rewards for his support, but Swift preferred to remain with Harley, who had lost power and for a time was even in danger of losing his life. In 1714 the Queen died, the Whigs returned to power, Bolingbroke fled, and George I came over from Germany as King. Swift left England for his Deanery in Ireland. At first he had few friends there, but between 1720 and 1730 he wrote a number of eloquent ▷ pamphlets in the interests of the oppressed Irish, and ended by achieving great popularity. The same decade saw the crisis of his relationships with the two women who loved him: Esther Johnson, the 'Stella' of his *Journal to Stella*, compiled 1710–13, and Esther Vanhomrigh, whom he called 'Vanessa'. The relationship with the latter was tragically concluded with her death in 1723; Stella died in 1728. Swift lived as a conscientious and efficient Dean almost to the end of his life, unselfishly disposing of most of his wealth for the poor, but he went out of his mind in 1742.

Swift wrote a great deal of prose, chiefly in the form of pamphlets, and not all of it is satire; *The Conduct of the Allies* is not, for instance, nor are his ▷ sermons. However, his great reputation rests principally on his prose satire, and he is especially admired for the very subtle and powerful form of his irony. The surface of his prose is limpidly clear and beguilingly placid, but his use of it is to enforce by close logic an impossible and often very shocking proposition, which is driven home with distinct and startling imagery. His position is that of a sincere Christian who advocates reason; he despises alike the emptiness of the ▷ Deists and the emotionalism of ▷ Puritans. He is at the same time a strong humanitarian, who is revolted by injustices leading to so much suffering, but despairs of the capacity of the human race to rid itself of its tendency to bestiality and heartlessness. Though a believer in reason, he despised the pedantry of so many scholars, and the irrelevances of the 'natural philosophers' in their pursuit of science. He has been censured on two grounds: first, the minor but undoubted one that his disgust at some aspects of human existence derived from his own morbidity, and secondly, the much more controversial one that his vision is in the end negative and destructive. His most famous works are as follows: ▷ *The Battle of the Books* (written 1697, published 1704), a contribution to the dispute between the relative merits of the ancients and the moderns in literature; ▷ *A Tale of a Tub* (1704), a satire on 'corruption in religion and learning' and one of his masterpieces;

Argument against Abolishing Christianity (1708), a satire on the irreligion of the time; ▷ *Drapier's Letters* (1724), against the monopoly granted by the English government to William Wood to provide the Irish with a copper coinage; ▷ *Gulliver's Travels* (1726); and ▷ *A Modest Proposal* (1729), a most forceful exposure of the conditions of the Irish poor. Swift's poetry has only recently received the critical attention that it deserves. His most admired poem is *Verses on the Death of Dr Swift* (1731), a partly satirical poem in which he imagines public reaction to the news of his death, and then gives his own deliberately deceptive assessment of his life and achievements. *Cadenus and Vanessa* is an equally deceptive poem which purports to give an account of his love affair with Esther Vanhomrigh. It was published, at her request, after her death in 1723. ('Cadenus' is an anagram of 'Decanus' = Dean.)

Bib: Ehrenpreis, I., *Swift, The Man, His Works and The Age*; Nokes, D., *Jonathan Swift, A Hypocrite Reversed*.

Swinburne, Algernon Charles (1837–1909)
Poet and critic. His family background was aristocratic: his father was an admiral and his grandfather a baronet. He was educated at ▷ Eton and at Balliol College, Oxford. The style of his poetry is very distinctive, and his literary sympathies were wide. Swinburne led a dissolute, wild life (his predilection for flagellation is infamous), and produced poetry which shocked those who read it carefully, and intoxicated his youthful contemporaries, especially ▷ Thomas Hardy and the ▷ Pre-Raphaelites. He read eclectically, absorbing classical literature, the ▷ Elizabethans, Walt Whitman, ▷ William Blake, the ▷ Marquis de Sade and ▷ Baudelaire. In his first book, the dramas *The Queen Mother* and *Rosamond* (1860), he was, like most English 19th-century verse dramatists, in the Elizabethan tradition, but his more famous *Atalanta in Calydon* (1865) as well as his much later *Erectheus* (1876) were in the style of the ancient Greek tragedy of ▷ Sophocles. The eroticism of his lyrics in *Poems and Ballads* (1866) owed something to the Latin poet, ▷ Catullus, and more to Pre-Raphaelite poetry of his own day, chiefly that of ▷ Dante Gabriel Rossetti. In this book he is rebelling against the moral repressiveness of the dominant middle-class attitude to sex; in the *Song of Italy* (1867) and *Songs before Sunrise* (1871) he is siding with Italian political revolt against oppression in the spirit of the French 19th-century poet ▷ Victor Hugo. *Chastelard*

(1865) and *Bothwell* (1874) are the first two plays, again in Elizabethan style, on ▷ Mary Queen of Scots, and were completed by ▷ *Mary Stuart* in 1881. A second series of *Poems and Ballads* in 1878 contains tributes to the contemporary French poets, ▷ Baudelaire and Théophile Gautier and translations of the medieval French poet François Villon. *Songs of the Springtides* and *Studies in Song* (1880) show the strong inspiration he drew from the sea, and the ▷ Arthurian legend *Tristram of Lyonesse* (1881) is a romance of the ▷ Middle Ages comparable to those of ▷ William Morris and ▷ Alfred Tennyson, amongst other mid-Victorians. In *Marino Falieri* (1887) he produced a drama on a theme drawn from medieval Venice already used by ▷ Byron (*Marino Falieri*, 1821); it was published with another drama, *Locrine*. His later works are: the dramas *The Sisters* (in prose, 1892) and *Rosamund, Queen of the Lombards* (1899); poems – *Poems and Ballads*, 3rd series (1889); *Astrophel* (1894), *A Tale of Balen* (1896), *A Channel Passage* (1904), *The Duke of Gandia* (1908).

Swinburne was thus a poet who drew on a wide range of influences and interests, and was prolific in output. Against the prejudices of his time, which declared that poets should be morally serviceable, he asserted the right to pursue the poetic vocation to express beauty, but this in itself isolated him from contemporary English culture, especially the novel, which emphasized the search for deeper moral experience. Swinburne's influence was strong on his younger contemporaries of the ▷ aesthetic movement.

In his criticism, Swinburne is notable for studies of dramatists who were contemporaries of ▷ Shakespeare as well as of Shakespeare himself: *Study of Shakespeare* (1880); *The Age of Shakespeare* (1990). He also wrote a study of William Blake (1868), *A Note on Charlotte Brontë* (1877), *A Study of Victor Hugo* (1886), amongst other criticism.

Swinburne also wrote novels, which are very little known; they have been praised by the distinguished American critic Edmund Wilson in *The Bit between my Teeth*. One of them, *Love's Cross-Currents*, was published in 1905. They show yet another influence upon him – that of the French 18th century writer the Marquis de Sade.

Bib: Gosse, E., *Life*; Lafourcade, G., *La Jeunesse de Swinburne*, literary biography (in English); Chew, S. C., *Swinburne* (critical study); Nicolson, H., *Swinburne*; Welby, T. E., *A Study of Swinburne*; Winwar, P., *The*

Rossettis and their Circle; Eliot, T. S.,
'Swinburne as a Poet' in *Selected Essays*;
Hyder, C. K., *Critical Heritage*.

Swithin, St

A bishop of Winchester who died in 862.
William of Malmesbury (12th century) states
that he requested to be buried 'where the
rains of heaven might fall on him and he be
trodden underfoot by those who entered the
church'. This has led, obscurely, to a tradition
expressed by the following lines:

> *St Swithin's day if thou dost rain*
> *For forty days it will remain;*
> *St Swithin's day if thou be fair*
> *For forty days 'twill rain na mair*

St Swithin's day is 15 July.

Sybaris

An ancient Greek town in southern Italy. In
the 6th century BC it was unrivalled among
the Greek cities of the Mediterranean for its
wealth, luxury and splendour – hence the
term 'sybarite' for one who is addicted to
luxury.

Sybil, or The Two Nations (1845)

A novel by ▷ Benjamin Disraeli. The 'two
nations' are the rich and the poor. The
country is shown to be governed by the rich
in the interests of the rich – *ie* the landlords
and the employers. Sybil is the daughter of
Gerard, a ▷ Chartist leader; she is loved by
an enlightened young aristocrat, Charles
Egremont, younger brother of an oppressive
landlord, Lord Marney. Disraeli gives
romantic historical background to his theme
by causing Sybil to belong to the same family
as the last abbot of Marney, whose lands
Lord Marney's ancestors had seized at the
time of the dissolution of the monasteries
under ▷ Henry VIII. The poor nation is
likewise identified with the ▷ Anglo-Saxons,
despoiled of their land by the ▷ Norman
conquerors of the 11th century. This novel,
like ▷ *Coningsby* (1844) is part of Disraeli's
campaign to renew the ▷ Tory party
through the Young England movement by
inspiring it with a true and disinterested
ideology. The novel combines a rather comic
element of operatic romanticism with shrewd
observation and social satire.

Sylphs

According to the 16th-century Swiss
physician, Paracelsus, they were spirits of the
air, something between pure spirit and
material being.

Symbolic order

A psychoanalytical term now frequently used
in literary criticism. 'Symbolic' in this context
refers initially to the notion that language
itself is comprised of symbols which stand for
things. But, the French psychoanalyst
▷ Jacques Lacan observes that: 'It is the
world of words that creates the world of
things', and in so doing introduces an 'order'
into what would otherwise be disparate units.
That process of ordering is motivated by a
series of impulses and desires which are not
usually available to the conscious mind. Thus,
the symbolic order is that order of
representations through whose organization
the child enters into language and the social
order as a gendered human 'subject'. In the
case of ▷ Freudian psychoanalysis each
symbol refers back to an Oedipal stage
(▷ Oedipus complex) which the infant
passes through on the way to maturity. In
Lacan, the 'unconscious' is said to be
structured like a language, already a system
of representations through which the
individual gendered subject realizes his or her
identity. In some respect all literary texts
traverse the realm of the symbolic order in
that they represent and articulate those images
through which reality is grasped discursively.

Symbolism

A name primarily associated with a school of
French poets writing in the second half of the
19th century. The movement grew out of the
work of ▷ Baudelaire (1821–67) and is
above all associated with Paul Verlaine
(1844–96), Arthur Rimbaud (1854–91) and
▷ Stephane Mallarmé (1842–98). In
addition to Baudelaire, the American writer
Edgar Allan Poe (1809–49) and the German
music-dramatist Richard Wagner (1813–83)
contributed to the shaping of Symbolism. It
constituted a development from
▷ Romanticism inasmuch as it was poetry
of the feelings as opposed to the reason, but it
was a reaction against it inasmuch as it was
more intellectual in its conception of the way
poetry operates. This intellectualism did not
imply that the content of poetry should be
one of what is ordinarily called ideas:
Mallarmé's affirmation was that 'Poetry is not
made with ideas; it is made with words'. This
looks forward to much 20th-century thought
in all the arts, requiring that the artist should
above all have respect for the medium in
which he has chosen to work; it also
anticipates ▷ T. S. Eliot's praise of the
English 17th-century ▷ Metaphysical poets
that 'they were, at best, engaged in the task of
trying to find the verbal equivalent for states
of mind and feeling'. Since 'states of mind
and feeling' are ultimately mysterious and
elusive, the Symbolists emphasized the

suggestiveness of poetic language, but though this emphasis on suggestiveness makes much of their poetry obscure, their care for the organization and operation of language kept it from vagueness, in the sense in which the poetry of their English contemporary, the late Romantic ▷ Algernon Swinburne, is very commonly vague. Swinburne is also much concerned with the poetic medium of words, but in such a way that his verse subdues the reader into a state of passive receptivity, whereas the French Symbolists evoke active participation; Swinburne relies for his effect on stimulating emotions already latent in the reader, whereas the Symbolists incite extension of these emotions. T. S. Eliot's essay on Swinburne (in *Selected Essays*) is a help in elucidating the distinction.

The French Symbolists are particularly important in English literature for their decisive influence on the two most important poets writing in English in the first half of the 20th century: T. S. Eliot and ▷ W. B. Yeats. Eliot's understanding of them was much the more intimate and profound, but A. Symons's *The Symbolist Movement in Literature* (1899) acted on them both.

Synchronic
Adjective used by ▷ Ferdinand de Saussure to describe the analysis of the meaning of a ▷ sign in relation to the other current elements of the language system ▷ *langue*. Saussure juxtaposes the synchronic study of language with the *diachronic* study of language which looks at the historical development of language. This is one of the important polarities in Saussure's theories.
▷ Parole.

Synecdoche
▷ Figures of Speech.

Synge, John Millington (1871–1909)
Irish dramatist. He belonged to the Protestant Anglo-Irish segment of Irish society, but at the suggestion of ▷ W. B. Yeats in 1899, he devoted his career to interpreting Irish Celtic peasant life. From this proceeded his remarkable series of dramas which were the chief glory of the drama of the Irish literary renaissance, and of the ▷ Abbey Theatre

in Dublin (under the direction of Yeats) through which this movement expressed itself. Part of the Irish dramatic endeavour was to revive poetic drama; Synge wrote in prose, but he exploited with great sensitivity the poetic suggestiveness of the rhythms, diction, and imagery of Irish peasant speech. At the same time he avoided the sentimentalities of late-19th-century romanticism and the falsifications which Irish nationalistic vanity required; the result was that his masterpiece, ▷ *The Playboy of the Western World* (1907) was received with rage and uproar. His other plays are: *The Shadow of the Glen* (1903); *Riders to the Sea* (1904); *The Well of the Saints* (1905); *The Tinker's Wedding* (1907), and his last play – drawn unlike the others from Irish myth – *Deirdre of the Sorrows*, published in 1910 after his death.

Synge also wrote descriptions of Irish peasant life in *The Aran Islands* (1907) and *In Wicklow* and *In County Kerry* (both published 1910).
▷ Irish Literature.
Bib: Greene, D. H. and Stephens, E. M., *Life*; Price, F., *Synge and Anglo-Irish Drama*; Thornton, W., *J. M. Synge and the Western Mind*.

Synoptic Gospels
In the New Testament of the ▷ Bible, the Gospels of St Matthew, St Mark, and St Luke, so called because in their content and its treatment they have much in common so that they can be considered together, *ie* 'synoptically'. The Gospel of St John, on the other hand, is different in important respects from the other three, and requires separate study.

Syrinx
In Greek myth, a maiden pursued by the god ▷ Pan; she threw herself into the river Ladon, where she was changed into a reed, from which Pan made his pipe. Her legend is retold by ▷ Pope in his pastoral poem ▷ *Windsor Forest* (1713). In ▷ Spenser's ▷ *Shepherd's Calendar* for the month of April, Syrinx represents Anne Boleyn, mother of ▷ Elizabeth I.

T

Tabard Inn
An inn on the south bank of the Thames, in the borough of ▷ Southwark. It was here that ▷ Chaucer's pilgrims assembled before setting out to Canterbury in the ▷ *Canterbury Tales*. The inn was pulled down in 1875.

A tabard was a sleeveless coat worn by heralds and by knights over their armour. The coat was painted or embroidered with armorial bearings, *ie* the crest and emblems of the knight's family or the king whom the herald represented.

Tacitus, Cornelius (AD ?55–?120)
Roman historian. He was eminent in Roman political and social life, and the son-in-law of Gnaeus Julius Agricola, the governor of Britain who effectively transformed the island into an orderly Roman province. His surviving works are the *Dialogue on Orators*, consisting of conversations about the decay of Roman education; the *Life of Agricola*, including an account of Britain under the rule of his father-in-law; *Germany*, an account of the characteristics of the land and its people, contrasting their freedom and simplicity with the degeneracy of Rome; the *Histories*, a fragment of an account of the Roman Empire during the last 30 years of the 1st century; the *Annals*, a fragment of a history of the Empire in the first half of the century.

Tacitus was a contemporary of the satirical poet ▷ Juvenal; together they represent the last significant phase of classical ▷ Latin literature; both have a strong ethical concern with the condition of Roman civilization, and Tacitus reveres the austere virtues of the pre-imperial republic, though he accepts the Empire as a political necessity. His style is distinguished for its brevity, and his works were an outstanding constituent of English education from the 16th to 19th centuries.
▷ Classical education.

Tail-Rhyme
A verse form used in a number of Middle English romances, which is structured around the repetition of a 'tail' line (often shorter than the rest), after at least two rhyming lines. In ▷ Chaucer's ▷ *Sir Thopas*, for example, the stanzas are built up from a pattern of six lines rhyming aabaab.

Tale of a Tub, A (1704)
A prose satire by ▷ Jonathan Swift. The title is the same as that of one of the last and least interesting comedies by ▷ Ben Jonson, but Swift ironically explains it in his Preface as derived from the practice of sailors of

tossing a tub to a whale in order to divert it from attacking the ship. The ship, Swift explains, is an image of the state, and the whale is ▷ *Leviathan*, ▷ Hobbes's political treatise, from which the wits of the age drew their dangerous armament of scepticism and satire; he pretends that he has been employed to divert these attacks by his engaging nonsense. For the next edition (1710), Swift added *An Apology*, in which he discloses his true aim – to satirize 'the numerous and gross corruptions in Religion and Learning'. The real meaning of the title is that Swift is beguiling readers so as to expose them the more effectively to the ferocity of irony. The central fable of the *Tale* is the story of three brothers, Martin, Peter and Jack, who inherit three simple coats from their father, whose will enjoins that the coats must in no way be altered. Under the leadership of Peter, however, the brothers find it convenient to alter the coats beyond recognition to comply with fashion. Peter's authority eventually becomes so insanely domineering that Martin and Jack revolt against him; Martin tears off the ornaments on his coat, but stops before he altogether disfigures it; Jack, however, reduces his to a squalid rag. The fable is an allegory of the ▷ Reformation: Peter represents the Church of Rome, Martin the Church of England, in which Swift was a priest, and Jack the extremer Protestants, or ▷ Dissenters; the coat is the Word of God as expressed in the New Testament. Swift's main object of attack is Jack, since he regarded the Dissenters, with their claim to receipt of divine inspiration and their resistance to authority, as the principal threat to the rule of right reason, true religion, and fine civilization in his time. The fable is interspersed with digressions, satirizing the arrogance of those who set up their private intellects or privileged inspiration as guides to their fellow-men; by Section XI the digressions come together with the fable, and Jack is declared to be the leader of the ▷ Aeolists, who expound their doctrines through 'wind', from Aeolus, Greek god of the winds. The satire is essentially an attack on the 'windiness' that Swift discerned in the more pretentious philosophical and religious teaching of his time.

Tale of Two Cities, A (1859)
A novel by ▷ Charles Dickens. The cities are London and Paris, and the tale is a romance of the ▷ French Revolution. The hero is a young French nobleman, Charles Darnay, who has renounced his status as

nephew of the Marquis de St Evrémonde from hatred of the pre-revolutionary aristocratic oppression, exemplified by his uncle. He marries the daughter of Dr Manette, who at the beginning of the novel has just been released from the Paris prison of the Bastille, where he was confined 18 years before by the secret influence of the Marquis. Darnay, owing to his aristocratic descent, nearly falls victim to the ▷ Terror but he is saved by the dissolute Englishman, Sydney Carton, who redeems himself by sacrificing his life for Darnay; this is made possible because Carton and Darnay exactly resemble each other, so that the former is able to substitute himself for the latter. The novel is notable for its scenes of revolutionary violence, for which Dickens was indebted to ▷ Thomas Carlyle's *History of the French Revolution* (1837). The revolutionaries Monsieur and Madame Defarge, and the English body-snatcher Jerry Cruncher, who makes a living by stealing corpses and selling them for medical dissection, are memorable characters.

Taliesin

A Welsh poet of the 6th century AD whose Welsh name translates as 'bright brow'. Various poems are attributed to him, of which the tales of Urien and Owain (in the legends of ▷ King Arthur called Ryence and Yvain) may be genuine. Taliesin is a half-legendary figure. ▷ Thomas Love Peacock introduces him into his parody of Arthurian romance, *The Misfortunes of Elphin* (1829), and ▷ Tennyson includes him as one of the Knights of the Round Table in his ▷ *Idylls of the King* (1859–72).

Talmud

A collection of Jewish religious law and teaching, developed from the scriptural law of the ▷ Old Testament. It was codified in the 2nd–6th centuries AD.

Talus

In Greek myth, a man of brass made by ▷ Hephaestus, the smith of the gods. He protected the island of Crete, and received the ▷ Argonauts with a shower of rocks.

In Book V of ▷ Spenser's ▷ *Faerie Queene* Talus is a character who acts as an instrument of punitive justice, represented by Sir Artegall. He disposes of criminals with an iron flail.

Tam O'Shanter (1791)

A poem by ▷ Robert Burns in Lowland Scots dialect. Tam, a drunken farmer, riding home late at night, passes 'Aloway's old haunted Kirk' which he sees lighted up. He creeps nearer to find witches and warlocks dancing to the tune of the bagpipes played by Old Nick. He admires one of the prettiest of the witches and in his excitement cries out: 'Weel done, cutty-sark!' ('short-shirt'). The witches come rushing after him, but he is able to reach the middle of the bridge over the River Doon, beyond which they cannot follow him, though they wrench off his horse's tail. The work shows an effortless adaptation of the ▷ mock heroic pentameter ▷ couplet to the vigorous and earthy Scots language.

Tamburlaine the Great, Parts I and II

Two dramas in ▷ blank verse by ▷ Christopher Marlowe, published in 1590. The subject is the life of the 14th-century central Asian, Timur, who rose by his conquests from obscurity to become one of the most powerful men in Asia. A life of Timur by Pedro Maxia was translated into English and published in 1571.

Part I is a drama of conquest. Tamburlaine is an obscure shepherd chieftain who defeats Mycetes, king of Persia, and subsequently the king's brother, Cosroe, as well. He is next victorious over Bajazet, Emperor of Turkey, and finally captures Damascus from the Soldan (Sultan) of Egypt. His victories are a triumph of immense natural energy and of ruthlessness over equally cruel but weak and decadent civilizations; however, Tamburlaine's barbarity is not merely brutish – he worships the potentialities of the human mind, and he falls passionately in love with his bride, Zenocrate, the daughter of the Soldan. Tamburlaine is, in fact, a product of Marlowe's characteristically ▷ Renaissance imagination, fascinated by the earthly magnificence available to men of imaginative power who have the energy of their convictions. The play is essentially non-moral; Tamburlaine is not judged, but presented as though he were a natural force.

Part II was probably written in consequence of the success of Part I, rather than foreseen as a sequel, though critics differ in their opinions about this. Tamburlaine is forced to face the truth that, though he feels his energies to be inexhaustible, he cannot triumph over death – first that of Zenocrate, and then his own. This play is therefore a tragedy, that man feels himself to be infinite but is nonetheless mortal.

The plays are a most important advance in the use of blank verse as a medium of drama. Hitherto it had been used stiffly and unimaginatively; Marlowe, for the first time in these plays, made blank verse eloquent.

Taming of the Shrew, The

An early comedy by ▷ Shakespeare; probably written 1593–4, and first published in the first ▷ folio of 1623. It may be partly a recasting of an anonymous play, *The Taming of a Shrew* (of uncertain date), and both are based on ▷ George Gascoigne's comedy *Supposes* (1566), itself a translation from the Italian of Ariosto's *Suppositi* (1509).

In a prologue or 'induction', a drunken tinker, Christopher Sly, is subjected to a practical joke; a nobleman picks him up in his stupor, brings him to his mansion, and causes his servants to explain to him that he is himself a great lord who has for some time been out of his wits. The play is then performed by the nobleman's actors for Sly's benefit. The scene is Verona, and the plot concerns the successful attempts of a gentleman, Petruchio, to tame into obedience and love the wilful and ferocious Katharina, thought to be unmarriageable because of her shrewishness. A subplot concerns the courting of Katharina's sister, Bianca, by Lucentio (who is successful) and by Hortensio, who marries a widow instead. At a feast that concludes the play, Petruchio proves that he has, after all, the most affectionate and docile wife of the three. The play is essentially a comedy of situation, and may be regarded as one of several experiments in different kinds of comic form by Shakespeare in the years 1592–95.

Tantalus

In Greek myth, a king of Phrygia or of Lydia, condemned for crimes against the gods to an eternity of thirst and hunger in the underworld. He stood in water up to the chin, with a bough of delicious fruits within his reach; when he stooped to drink or stretched out his arm to pluck, the water or the branch always receded. This punishment is the origin of the word 'tantalize'.

Tarlton, Richard (d 1588)

A famous comic actor, mentioned in 1583 as one of the Queen's Players, and a favourite clown of ▷ Elizabeth I. He dressed as a rustic ('a clown' was originally a term for a simple-witted country peasant) and was gifted at composing the rough, comic kind of verse known as 'doggerel'; he popularized on the London stage the mixture of song and dance, something like light opera, called country ▷ jigs. He wrote a comedy, *The Seven Deadly Sins*, for the Queen's Players, and after his death a number of volumes of popular humour – not necessarily his – were published under the title of *Tarlton's Jests*. He was one of the first actors to become a national figure. He was probably an innkeeper before he became an actor.

▷ Acting, The Profession of; Yorick.

Tarot cards

Playing cards bearing emblems such as sun, moon, hanged man etc. instead of the effigies of kings, queens, and knaves of usual cards. They were used in the ▷ Middle Ages; today they are associated chiefly with fortune-telling. The emblems may be vestiges of ancient myths.

Tarquin

The family of seven legendary kings of ancient Rome; the last, Lucius Tarquinius Superbus, was expelled by a rising of the citizens in consequence of the rape of ▷ Lucrece by his son in 510 BC.

Tartan

Cloth woven into chequered designs; this cloth was formerly the regional dress or 'plaid' in the Scottish ▷ Highlands. The plaid was draped about the body and hung down below the belt as a skirt or ▷ kilt. It is commonly believed that each Highland clan has always had its own tartan of distinctive colour and weave. The evidence that this was true before the prohibition of Highland national dress (which followed the ▷ Jacobite Rebellion of 1745 and lasted until 1782) is uncertain. Undoubtedly many existing tartans ascribed to clans are the invention of 19th-century romanticism (especially stimulated by ▷ Sir Walter Scott) and the tourist industry. However, tartan weaves certainly varied from region to region of the Scottish Highlands, and to this extent there must have been some degree of distinction among the clans.

Tartars (Tatars)

An Asian Mongol race which overran Asia and Eastern Europe in the 13th century under the leadership of ▷ Genghis Khan. They came to represent the essence of barbarism and ferocity for civilized Europeans.

Tartarus

In Greek myth, an underworld of punishment for the dead. Homer in the ▷ *Iliad* describes it as being as far below ▷ Hades as Hades is below the earth. ▷ Virgil describes it as surrounded by impenetrable walls and the burning waters of the Phlegethon. The ▷ Titans, and others who defied ▷ Zeus were confined there. In the oldest myths, Tartarus was the son of the sky-father and the earth-mother.

Task, The (1785)

A long ▷ blank-verse poem by ▷ William
Cowper, combining ▷ mock heroic with
▷ Georgic and sentimental elements. It
begins in heavily Miltonic vein with an
account of the history of Cowper's own sofa.
Later passages concern the joys of rural
retirement, gardening, the peculiarities of
various local characters, and the moral and
religious corruptions of the day, which are
condemned at great length. The poem
manages to achieve a distinctive and engaging
tone, despite the miscellaneousness of its
literary elements, and its simplicity of diction
foreshadows that of ▷ William Wordsworth
in ▷ Lyrical Ballads.

Tasso, Torquato (1544–95)

Italian poet. He continued the tradition of
the ▷ romance epic, already made famous
by ▷ Ludovico Ariosto's ▷ Orlando
Furioso (1532), in his two major works,
Rinaldo (1562) and Jerusalem Delivered (1581).
Tasso's imagination was romantic but in his
literary ideal he was ▷ classical, and the
thought of the second poem is elevated by the
high seriousness of the Catholic ▷ Counter-
Reformation. His seriousness made his work
very attractive to the English romance epic
poet, ▷ Edmund Spenser, whose very
▷ Protestant ▷ The Faerie Queene is also
an attempt to rival Ariosto by a poem of
similar form but imbued with strong religious
feeling. Tasso's impress is strong on parts of
The Faerie Queene, especially in its
▷ Platonism. Jerusalem Delivered was finely
translated by Sir Edward Fairfax and
published under the title of Godfrey of
Bulloigne or the Recovery of Jerusalem in 1600.

Tasso was locked up for insanity by
Alphonso II, Prince of Ferrara, between
1579–86; subsequent legend attributed his
imprisonment to a love affair with the
Princess Leonara d'Este. This supposed love
affair was the subject of a poem by ▷ Lord
Byron, The Lament of Tasso (1817).

▷ Translation; Italian influence on
English literature.

Tate, Nahum (1652–1715)

Educated in Dublin. He assisted ▷ John
Dryden with the second part of ▷ Absalom
and Achitophel, and wrote the libretto of
Purcell's opera Dido and Aeneas (performed
1689). His metrical version of the psalms,
written with Nicholas Brady, appeared in
1696, and his revised version of ▷ King
Lear, with a happy ending, was that
performed through most of the succeeding
century. His Panacaea – a Poem on Tea
appeared in 1700.

Tate Gallery, The

A public gallery for modern paintings and
sculpture on the north bank of the Thames in
London. It was established by a sugar-
merchant, Sir Henry Tate, and opened in
1897.

Taylor, Jane (1783–1824) and Ann (1782–1866)

Authors of popular children's books in verse:
Original Poems for Infant Minds (1804),
Rhymes for the Nursery (1806), in which
appears 'Twinkle twinkle, little Star', and
Hymns for Infant Minds (1810).

Taylor, Jeremy (1613–67)

Clergyman and religious writer. He was one
of the representatives of ▷ Anglicanism in
its most flourishing period, and his career
shows the vicissitudes of the Church of
England in the 17th century. The son of a
barber, he was educated at a Cambridge
grammar school and in the University of
Cambridge. His talent for preaching attracted
the favour of ▷ Archbishop Laud, to whom
and to ▷ King Charles I he became
chaplain. In 1645 he was captured by
Parliamentary troops, and until 1660, while
the Church of England was in abeyance, he
was private chaplain to the Earl of Carbery.
It was during this period that he wrote much
of his best work. Later, he was made Bishop
of Dromore in Ireland, where, contrary to his
inclination, he was obliged to discipline clergy
who were hostile to the Anglican
establishment. He thus stands in contrast to
his former patron, the authoritarian
Archbishop Laud, and the change marks not
merely a difference in personalities but the
growth in the spirit of Anglican tolerance in
the later 17th century. His A Discourse of the
Liberty of Prophesying (1646) was a plea for
religious toleration; his other outstanding
works were his The Rule and Exercises of Holy
Living (1650) and The Rule and Exercises of
Holy Dying (1651).

▷ Sermons.

Bib: Stranks, C. J., Jeremy Taylor; Gosse, E.,
Jeremy Taylor; Smith, L. P., The Golden
Grove: Selected Passages from Jeremy Taylor.

Taylor, John (c 1580–1653)

Poet and miscellanist. John Taylor was
apprenticed, in early life, to a London
waterman (ferryman). He enlisted in the
Navy, making several voyages, and then
returned to London to ply his trade as a
waterman. Hence he became known as 'The
Water Poet'. Taylor was an extraordinarily
prolific writer. His large collected edition –
All the Works of John Taylor the Water Poet

(1630) – though it contains over 60 separate works, does not begin to represent his complete *oeuvre*. Almost any topic attracted his attenion, and almost every topic did. He was famous for proposing preposterously difficult travel-projects, such as travelling from London to Edinburgh and back without spending any money, or rowing a paper boat. On the strength of these proposals, he would solicit subscriptions from the curious, who would then read his accounts of his difficulties and dangers. His death, at the age of 75 followed his last trip from London to Gravesend and back: a journey made all the more difficult by the fact of his being lame.

Tel Quel

A magazine, for many years the leading French *avant-garde* journal. Its name was taken from a work by Paul Valéry (1871–1945) and it was edited by Philippe Sollers (b 1936), novelist, theorist and husband of the feminist writer, Julia Kristeva. In political terms, the magazine's sympathies were Marxist-Leninist-Maoist. It welcomed the student demonstrations of May 1968 with an issue entitled 'The Revolution, here and now' and its programme for a French 'Cultural Revolution' was backed by figures such as the composer Pierre Boulez (b 1925) and the novelist and theoretician Jean Ricardou (b 1932). *Tel Quel* provided a forum for left-wing intellectuals and gave rise to the *Tel Quel* group. Their joint publication, *Théorie d'ensemble* (1968), contained *inter alia* ▷ Jacques Derrida's essay 'La Différance', ▷ Michel Foucault's piece 'Distance, aspect, origine' (discussing Alain Robbe-Grillet and Sollers) and ▷ Roland Barthes's 'Drame, poème, roman' (on Sollers). Alongside its support for radical political and theoretical positions, the magazine did much to promote the cause of a literary counter-orthodoxy, represented by ▷ Sade, ▷ Lautréamont, Georges Bataille and Robbe-Grillet.

In the late 1970s, *Tel Quel* began to lose its radical impetus. Sollers renounced his theoretical persuasions, sympathized with the right-wing group, ▷ Les Nouveaux Philosophes, and embraced ▷ Catholicism. From 1982, the magazine changed its name to *L'Infini* and found itself a new publisher.

Tellus

▷ Classical mythology.

Tempest, The (1611)

A play by ▷ Shakespeare probably written in 1611, and regarded by some as the last completely by his own hand. The plot does not derive from any known principal source. The setting of the island with its aboriginal inhabitant Caliban, and the shipwreck with which the play opens, owe details to travel books of the time, especially a ▷ pamphlet by Sir George Somers (1609) about his voyage to and shipwreck on the Bermudas.

Prospero, Duke of Milan, with his daughter Miranda, has been expelled from his duchy, where he had avoided the task of government for the sake of devoting himself to secret learning, by his wicked brother, Antonio. At the opening of the play Prospero and Miranda have lived on a lonely island for many years, served by the brutish savage Caliban, and the sprite Ariel. By his magic powers, Prospero contrives the shipwreck on the island of his enemies – his brother Antonio, Alonso king of Naples who had conspired with Antonio, Alonso's wicked brother Sebastian and a few courtiers. Also shipwrecked, but separated from the others, is Ferdinand, the virtuous son of Alonso; each believes the other to be drowned. The situation is such that Prospero, if he wishes, can use his supernatural powers to execute vengeance on his enemies; instead, he uses it to bring about reconciliation and forgiveness. Ferdinand, after a brief trial in which he is subjected to austere labours, is united with Miranda. Alonso's company is also subjected to trials, but finally reunited with Ferdinand and reconciled to Prospero, who discloses himself. A subplot concerns the farcical attempt of Trinculo and Stephano, Alonso's servants, to rob Prospero of his instruments of magic, with the aid of Caliban.

The play is the most symbolic of Shakespeare's plays. Prospero is in the tradition of the ▷ Platonic mage, who, according to one line of ▷ Renaissance thought, could achieve extraordinary power by uniting exceptional wisdom with exceptional virtue. Miranda unites the innocence of nature with the nobility of high breed; her union with Ferdinand and their restoration to a corrupt world symbolize the renewal of vital forces. Caliban, on the other hand, represents the unredeemably brutal side of nature, and also the inherently vicious propensities of the body: he can be forced to serve, but he cannot be elevated. The other characters represent degrees of redeemability: the 'good old lord' Gonzalo has always been virtuous though he has been made to serve evil ends; Alonso has done evil but is capable of repentance; Antonio and Sebastian do not repent and can only be intimidated; the rest are merely passive and, in Antonio's words 'take suggestion as a cat laps milk'.

The Tempest is the last of four plays sometimes called ▷ romances, the others being ▷ *Pericles,* ▷ *Cymbeline,* ▷ *The Winter's Tale.* An interesting feature of it is that while the other plays in the group are very loosely constructed in terms of time and place, *The Tempest* has the greatest unity in these respects of all Shakespeare's plays: the action is restricted to the island, and occupies only three hours.

Templars, The
The Knights Templars, or Poor Knights of Christ and the Temple of Solomon, were a religious military order founded in the 12th century to protect pilgrims to the Holy City of Jerusalem, to defend the city itself, and to wage war against the Muslims who either threatened it or occupied it. They owed obedience to the Pope, and took vows of poverty and humility, but in the course of time they became powerful, rich and arrogant. This caused them to be suppressed early in the 14th century – the English branch in 1308. The Grand Master of the Order, Jacques de Molay, was burnt as a heretic by the King of France in 1314.

Temple, Sir William (1628–99)
Statesman, diplomatist, essayist. In English literature he is especially known as the patron of ▷ Jonathan Swift, who lived at his house (Moor Park) as Temple's secretary from 1689 to 1694, and again from 1696 till Temple's death. Temple's most famous ▷ essay was his contribution to the controversy about the relative merits of ancient (*ie* Greek and Latin) and modern literature. Entitled *Of Ancient and Modern Learning*, it praised the *Letters of Phalaris* as a notable example of ancient work. Unfortunately the great scholar ▷ Bentley exposed the Letters as a forgery. Temple's embarrassment provoked Swift to come to his aid with his first notable essay, ▷ *The Battle of the Books.* Temple was a model of the cultivated aristocracy of his time, and his essays (chiefly on political matters) were regarded as setting standards for correctness and elegance of expression. His wife was ▷ Dorothy Osborne and her letters to him before their marriage (in 1655) were first published in 1888; her position resembled that of ▷ Samuel Richardson's heroine in his novel ▷ *Clarissa,* inasmuch as her parents were opposed to the marriage. Temple's memoirs were published by Swift in 1709.
Bib: Lives by C. Marburg and H. E. Woodbridge.

Temple, Solomon's
The main centre of worship of the ancient Jews in Jerusalem. Erected by King Solomon in the 10th century B C, it was several times destroyed and restored in the course of Jewish history; its final destruction by the Romans took place in A D 70. Its original form is described in the Bible, *2 Chronicles* 3.

Temple Bar
Originally a gateway between the City of London and the City of Westminster, now marked by the effigy of a griffin on a pedestal, situated opposite the Law Courts, at the junction of Fleet Street and the Strand, near the Temple Church. A stone gateway was designed and erected by ▷ Sir Christopher Wren in 1672; this was removed in 1878 and later re-erected at Theobald's Park, Hertfordshire. The heads of traitors used to be displayed on spikes on Temple Bar.

Tennant, Emma (b 1937)
Novelist. Her work combines a ▷ feminist perspective with a ▷ post-modernist use of allusion, parody, and fantasy, and in these respects has some affinity with that of ▷ Angela Carter. *The Time of the Crack* (1973) and *The Last of the Country House Murders* (1974) are both set in the future; the former is an apocalyptic satire, while the latter is a black comedy which parodies country house detective fiction. *The Bad Sister* (1978) satirizes the divisive effect upon women of social roles and expectations: the heroine finds herself inhabited by a demented other self, and the book itself is split between a prosaic account of contemporary society and a realm of dreams and fantasy. The expression of feminist revolt through a disturbed mental state has antecedents in *The Golden Notebook* by ▷ Doris Lessing, and in the work of ▷ Virginia Woolf. Tennant's other novels are: *The Colour of Rain* (1964); *Hotel de Dream* (1976); *Wild Nights* (1979); *Alice Fell* (1980); *Queen of Stones* (1982); *Woman Beware Woman* (1983); *Black Marina* (1985); *The Adventures of Robina, by Herself* (1986); *The House of Hospitalities* (1987).

Tennyson, Alfred (1809–92)
Poet, usually known, after he was made a baron in 1884, as Alfred, Lord Tennyson. Fourth of 12 children (two others of whom, Frederick and Charles, were also poets) of a Church of England clergyman. The family was long-established among Lincolnshire landowners, but the poet's father had been disinherited by his grandfather, and Alfred's

Alfred Tennyson, engraving from a
daguerrotype

childhood and youth were spent in
comparative poverty; he was partly educated
by his father but later he went to Trinity
College, Cambridge. Tennyson's family
background does not conform to the 20th-
century ideal of the family in the 19th
century. He was one of 12 children, his father
was a violent alcoholic rector, his mother was
distressed and wretched, two of his brothers
became insane and a third was also an
alcoholic. Images of mental illness, doubt and
conflict thus naturally fracture Tennyson's
work, especially the most interesting and
intense poems. His earliest work (*Poems by
Two Brothers*, in which his brother
collaborated) is unimportant, and he did not
begin to win fame until the 1840s. Thereafter
he achieved popularity unequalled by any
other English poet in his own lifetime. In
1850 he was made ▷ Poet Laureate (in
succession to ▷ Wordsworth) and in 1884
he was made a Baron – the only English poet
ever to have been ennobled purely for his
poetry. This popularity arose from two facts:
he had, on the one hand, exquisite poetic
skill; he was, on the other hand, in his mental
and emotional outlook, very representative of
his age. He had a characteristically
▷ Victorian insular patriotism; he was both
exhilarated and disturbed, like so many of his
contemporaries, by the social and industrial
changes of the age, and he was distressed by
the shaking of traditional religious beliefs by
the scientists – in his youth, the geologist
▷ Charles Lyell (*The Principles of Geology*,

1830–33), and in his middle age, the biologist
▷ Charles Darwin (*The Origin of Species*,
1859). He countered this threat from the
intellect by an emotional, sometimes
sentimental, idealism which was extremely
acceptable to the middle-class reading public.
His idiom was that of the Romantics –
Wordsworth, ▷ Shelley, especially
▷ Keats – but his formal technique was as
meticulous as that of the 18th century poets;
the combination was both beguiling and
reassuring. Physically and in his dress, he was
imposing and romantic, and with this
appearance he typified the poet for the nation.

The first three books of his sole authorship
(1830, 1832, 1842) include much of what is
now considered his best, most disturbing and
challenging work – *eg* ▷ *Mariana*, ▷ *The
Lady of Shalott, Ulysses, Morte d'Arthur*,
▷ *The Lotos-Eaters*. In 1833 his great friend,
Arthur Hallam, died, and the great grief of
this loss produced the series of ▷ elegies
which are usually considered to be his
masterpiece - ▷ *In Memoriam A.H.H.*,
eventually published in 1850. Queen Victoria
declared that she valued it next to the Bible;
however, it was the mixture of picturesque
romanticism and acceptable idealism in
▷ *The Princess* (1850) which greatly
extended Tennyson's popularity with the
general public. In 1852 he produced the most
impressive of his public poems, *Ode on the
Death of the Duke of Wellington*, and in 1854,
the most popular of English patriotic poems,
the ▷ *Charge of the Light Brigade*. ▷ *Maud*
(1854) is one of the most singular of his
works, evoking mentally deranged states, and
written at the time of the Crimean War.
Other works: his immensely popular cycle of
tales, ▷ *Idylls of the King* (1859–72); dialect
poems, *eg The Northern Farmer* (1864);
narrative, in the tradition of Wordsworth,
Enoch Arden (1864); ▷ ballads, notably *The
Revenge* (1880), and a number of verse
dramas, of which the most successful is
Becket (1884).

Taste in the early 20th century on the
whole turned against his poetry; the
accusation of one of his earliest critics,
▷ John Stuart Mill, (reviewing the 1832
volume) that Tennyson's poetry is deficient
in power of thought anticipated modern
opinion, which has been, until recently,
attuned to ▷ T. S. Eliot and the 17th-
century ▷ Metaphysical poets. It was still
admitted that he had an extraordinary ear for
cadence and rhythm, but it was implied that
this virtue did not compensate for the
mediocrity of his intelligence. However, this
tribute to his 'fine ear' amounted to

acknowledgement that Tennyson was a fine artist. His first three books and *In Memoriam* contain poems in which some of the deeper emotional conflicts of his time are beautifully articulated. In recent years readings of Victorian poetry have freed themselves from modernist valuations, and Tennyson's work has been re-read with interest for its strong acknowledgement and analysis of problematic areas of psychic and social existence; questions of mental health, the role of women, war and economic conditions.

Bib: Sinfield, A., *Alfred Tennyson*; Nicholson, H., *Tennyson: Aspects of his Life, Character and Poetry*; Palmer, D. J. (ed.), *Tennyson*; Killham, J., *Tennyson and The Princess*; Killham, J. (ed.), *Essays on Tennyson*; Ricks, C., *Tennyson*; Ricks, C. (ed.), *Poems*.

Terence (Publius Terentius Afer, ?190–?159 BC)

Latin dramatist. His six comedies are adaptations of older Greek comedies, especially those of Menander (342–291 BC). They have been praised for the purity of their Latin and criticized for their deficiency of comic power. They were known, read and imitated throughout the Middle Ages and afterwards, *eg* his *Heautontimorumenos* (163) was adapted by ▷ Chapman into *All Fools* (1605), and his *Andria* (166) was adapted by ▷ Steele into *The Conscious Lovers* (1722). Other dramatists such as ▷ Ben Jonson used some of his themes and his comic devices such as the role of the crafty slave (*eg* in ▷ *Volpone*).

Terpsichore
▷ Muses.

Terror, The (Reign of)
The period in the ▷ French Revolution from June 1793 to July 1794 under the dictatorship of ▷ Robespierre, when many people were executed without trial merely because they were suspected of opposition to the Revolution. The term has since been applied to similar regimes in other periods and countries.

Terza rima
The pattern used by the Italian poet ▷ Dante in his long poem the ▷ *Divine Comedy*. Each line is of 11 syllables, the last syllable unaccented, and the rhyme scheme follows the pattern *aba bcb cdc ded* etc. Examples in English are rare, and consist of 10-syllable lines. One reason for the scarce use of *terza rima* in English is the paucity of rhyming words in the language, by comparison with Italian. The form was first used in English by ▷ Thomas Wyatt in his *Satires* and paraphrases of the ▷ Psalms.

Tess of the D'Urbervilles, A Pure Woman (1891)
A novel by ▷ Thomas Hardy. The heroine is Tess Durbeyfield, daughter of a poor west-country peasant who learns that he may be a descendant of the aristocratic D'Urbervilles. The novel is about her tragic predicament between her brutal seducer, Alec Stoke D'Urberville, and her husband Angel Clare. Both Alec and Angel are intruders into Tess's environment; Alec (who has no proper title to his aristocratic surname) is the son of a north-country businessman who has bought his way into the class of gentry; Angel is the son of a conventional clergyman and has dissociated himself from his background by acquiring vague liberal ideas. When Tess confesses to him her seduction, his old-fashioned prejudices overcome him and he casts her off, repenting when it is too late. Forsaken by her husband, Tess is faced by renewed assaults from Alec, whom she eventually murders. After a period of hiding with Angel, Tess is tried, condemned and executed for murder. The finest passages of the book are the episodes set in the peaceful environment of Talbothays Dairy Farm, where Tess meets Angel, and the grim surroundings of Flintcomb Ash, where she works when Angel has forsaken her. Tess is represented as the victim of cruel chance – an example of Hardy's belief that the world is governed by ironical fate – but as usual in his work it is the intruders who are the instruments of the destructive force.

Testament of Cresseid, The
A poem by ▷ Robert Henryson (late 15th century), which provides an ending to Criseyde's story. In ▷ Chaucer's ▷ *Troilus and Criseyde*, there is little account of Criseyde's life in the Greek camp, after her affair with Diomede has begun: the narrative focus in Book V is on ▷ Troilus's history and his end. However, the old narrator of Henryson's poem, who finds his pleasures in books, discovers another 'quair' (book) containing 'the fatall destenie/ Of fair Cresseid, that endit wretchitlie' (61–2).

The contents of that 'quair' form the substance of Henryson's poem, which relates how Cresseid is abandoned by Diomede, is stricken with leprosy and has a final meeting with Troilus, in which neither wholly recognizes the other. Something about the leper's glance triggers a memory of Cresseid for Troilus (and he throws her a purse of money) but Cresseid does not discover the identity of her generous patron until he has left. She has time only to compose a testament (a will), leaving a ring to Troilus, before she dies.

The poem is a consummate exercise in the art of abbreviation: it is only 616 lines long and contains a collection of short poetic forms, being called a 'ballet' and encompassing a visionary sequence (in which the classical gods descend to judge Cresseid), two formal complaints and an epitaph. The significance of Cresseid's affliction with leprosy is open to a number of interpretations, and in the poem final endings and definitive judgements about Cresseid are juxtaposed with speculation and hearsay about her life and death. The *Testament* does not end Cresseid's life as a narrative subject. Although Henryson's poem disrupts rather than continues Chaucer's text, it was printed in the 1532 edition of Chaucer's work as if it formed the sixth book of *Troilus and Criseyde*: thus it was well known to subsequent readers of Chaucer's work, including ▷ Shakespeare.

▷ Troy.

Bib: Fox, D. (ed.), *The Poems of Robert Henryson*.

Thackeray, William Makepeace (1811–63)

William Makepeace Thackeray by F. Stone (c 1839)

Novelist. He had a conventional upper-class education at a public school – Charterhouse – and Cambridge University, which he left in 1830 without taking a degree. For the next 16 years he worked as a comic illustrator and journalist, writing satirically humorous studies of London manners in *The Yellowplush Correspondence* (*Fraser's Magazine* 1837–8), and *Snob Papers* (▷ *Punch* 1846–7) – later published as ▷ *The Book of Snobs*; parodies of the contemporary fashion for the criminal-hero (*Catherine*, 1839, and *Barry Lyndon*, 1844); humorous travel books (*The Paris Sketch-Book* and *The Irish Sketch-Book*, 1840 and 1843), tales of humour and pathos (*The Great Hoggarty Diamond*, 1841).

His first major novel, ▷ *Vanity Fair*, came out in the year 1848 (it was published serially, as were most of his novels, and the date given is that of completion); it was a social panorama of the English upper-middle classes, satirizing their heartlessness and pretentiousness at the height of their prosperity; it was followed by novels in a similar field: ▷ *Pendennis* (1850), and ▷ *The Newcomes* (1853–5). ▷ *Esmond* (1852) is a historical novel set in the reign of Queen Anne (1702–14) and represents Thackeray's strong taste for the 18th century; *The Virginians* (1859) is its sequel in 18th-century England and America. The same taste for 18th-century England is expressed in his historical lectures, *The Four Georges*, published in 1860. In 1855 he published his comic-romantic ▷ children's story, *The Rose and the Ring*. In 1860 he became editor of the famous ▷ *Cornhill Magazine*, and contributed to it *The Adventures of Philip* (1861–2), his essays *Roundabout Papers* and the novel, unfinished at his death, *Denis Duval*.

Thackeray was once considered the great counterpart to ▷ Charles Dickens in the mid-Victorian novel (the years 1850–70). Dickens conveyed a panorama of the lower half of society and Thackeray of the upper half; both were great humorists, with a strong bent for satire and a capacity for social indignation. Thackeray is now chiefly remembered for *Vanity Fair*. His imaginative intensity is seen to be less than that of Dickens and the sentimentality with which he counterbalanced his satire is the more conspicuous. Like Dickens, he opposed the ▷ utilitarianism of his age by an appeal to spontaneous affection and he tried to counterbalance it by an appeal to 18th-century proportion and elegance, but he also felt impulses of ▷ romanticism, which in Dickens are far more uninhibited.

Bib: Ray, G. N., *Life*; Tillotson, G., *Thackeray the Novelist*; Stevenson, L., *The Showman of Vanity Fair*; Stevenson, L., ed. in *Great Victorians*; Studies by J. Dodd, L. Ennis, J. Y. T. Greig and G. N. Ray; Tillotson, G., and Hawes, D. (eds.), *The Critical Heritage*; Carey, J., *Thackeray: Prodigal Genius*.

Thalia
▷ Muses.

Theatre of Cruelty
A style of theatre developing out of the work
of ▷ Antonin Artaud, introduced to English
audiences in 1964 by a 'Theatre of Cruelty'
season at the LAMDA Theatre arranged by
▷ Peter Brook and Charles Marowitz.
These experiments were developed in Brook's
productions of Peter Ulrich Weiss's
Marat/Sade in 1964 and the improvised play
US in 1966. Theatre of Cruelty aims to
shock the audience out of its complacency
and restricted conventional behaviour into an
awareness of the primitive forces within
human nature. To do this it requires a
committedly non-rationalistic approach to
acting.
Bib: Artaud, A., *The Theatre and its Double*;
Styan, J. L., *The Dark Comedy*.

Theatre of the Absurd
A name given by the critic Martin Esslin to
describe the work of a number of dramatists,
including Ionesco, Genet, ▷ Beckett and
▷ Pinter. These and other authors did not
belong to any 'school' as such but their plays
often have in common the sense that human
existence is without meaning. The idea is
reflected in the form as well as the content of
the plays, by the rejection of logical
construction, and the creation of meaningless
speeches and silences. Such devices helped to
develop new forms of theatre during the
1950s and 60s no longer reliant on outmoded
dramatic conventions.
Bib: Esslin, M., *The Theatre of the Absurd*.

Theatres
No special buildings were erected in England
for dramatic performances until late in the
16th century. The earliest form of regular
drama in England was the ▷ Mystery Plays,
which began as interpolations in religious
ritual in the churches. By the 15th century
these plays were being performed at religous
festivals in towns on movable stages or
▷ pageants, conveyed from point to point
on wagons. In country districts at seasonal
festivals such as ▷ May Day, primitive
dramas of pagan origin – jigs, May games,
Morris dances – were performed in the open
air. The absence of theatres did not indicate
scarcity of drama, but its wide pervasion of
ordinary life.

Secular dramas of entertainment, such as
we know today, grew up in the 16th century;
they were performed in the courtyards of
inns and in the great halls of country
mansions, royal palaces, Oxford and
Cambridge colleges, and the ▷ inns of court
of London. The performers were professional
actors who were usually incorporated in
companies attached to noble or royal
households, but by degrees this attachment
became increasingly nominal, and actors
required places where they could work
independently and permanently. Hence the
first playhouse, known as The Theatre, was
erected by ▷ James Burbage in Shoreditch,
outside the City of London, in 1576–7. It was
followed by many others, including the
▷ Globe (1598) which is the most famous
owing to its association with Shakespeare.
None of these theatres survived the middle of
the 17th century, but a contemporary sketch
of one of them (the Swan) exists, and there is
a detailed description in the contract for the
Fortune (1600).

The designs owe nothing to those of
ancient Greece and Rome (unlike
contemporary Italian theatres) but seem to be
based on a mixture of the typical inn-yard
and the bear-pits, *ie* the arenas for fights
between animals. The structures were usually
of wood, and round or hexagonal, though
they might be rectangular. The centre was an
arena exposed to the open air, where the
poorer spectators stood; the richer ones sat in
galleries surrounding the arena. The stage
was probably divided into two or three parts;
the main ('apron') stage projected into the
arena, so that spectators surrounded it on
three sides. The wall at the back of this stage
was flanked by doors for exits and entries,
between which there was probably a rear
stage, though the sketch of the Swan does not
include this. Above the rear stage there was
probably an upper stage (to represent *eg* a
castle wall); above this again, possibly a
musicians' gallery. A canopy may have
extended partly across the apron stage. The
projection of the apron stage – upon which
spectators sometimes actually sat – shows
that the theatre of Shakespeare's day was not
adapted to convey illusion like the typical
modern theatre; scenery was scarcely used,
though 'props' (*ie* thrones, objects
representing flowery banks, etc.) were
brought on and off.

Such were the 'public theatres'; there were
also 'private theatres' such as the
▷ Blackfriars which came into the hands of
Shakespeare's company in 1608. Pictures or
accounts of these do not survive, but they
were roofed, probably used some kind of
artificial lighting, and may have provided
more opportunity for scenery. Scenic
spectacle was certainly not unknown or

The Swan Theatre, London, 1596

despised by Shakespeare's contemporaries; in the reign of ▷ James I there was a pronounced fashion for ▷ masques, an early form of opera, in which a poet such as ▷ Ben Jonson and a designer such as ▷ Inigo Jones collaborated.

It was only after the ▷ Restoration of the Monarchy in 1660 that the theatre began to assume its modern shape, with a proscenium arch dividing the audience from the stage, thus providing greater scope for scenery and illusion. One of the earliest English theatres of this style was ▷ Drury Lane, which had already been a theatre in the reign of James I and was rebuilt in 1662. From this time the theatre became the special entertainment for the middle and upper classes, largely cut off from the mass of the people, and it has, on the whole, remained that way. It was still, however, a place of influence, and in 1737 the government found it convenient to pass a Licensing Act which had the effect of restricting the theatres in London to three – the Haymarket opera house, Drury Lane, and Covent Garden – until the act was repealed in 1843, though licences were issued for a few theatres in the provinces, at Bath, Bristol and Liverpool. The law greatly hindered the development of a creative drama in 18th-century England, though it was a period of great actors and actresses.

The repeal of the Licensing Act in 1843 was followed by widespread building of theatres, but there was no live taste for intelligent new plays until ▷ George Bernard Shaw, in the last decade of the 19th century, began to create one. In the 20th century there has been a sharp division between the commercial theatres which provide intellectually commonplace entertainment, and the theatres of the intelligentsia. Two companies of the latter kind have an official national status, ▷ The Royal Shakespeare Company and the ▷ National Theatre. The Royal Shakespeare Company produces Shakespeare's and other dramatists' plays at Stratford-on-Avon and, formerly, at the Aldwych theatre in London. Since 1982 the Royal Shakespeare Company have performed at their new base in the Barbican Centre near ▷ St Paul's, where they are spaciously accommodated in a London home of their own, similar to that of the National Theatre which, after opening at the Old Vic Theatre in 1963 transferred to a new site on the South Bank in Waterloo in 1976–77. Under the guidance of Trevor Nunn and Sir Peter Hall respectively, the two national companies have inventively produced the English repertoire from Shakespeare and his contemporary dramatists to classical and modern European and American drama. They have increasingly benefited from funding by the Arts Council whose key role in freeing the British theatre since World War II from the shackles of economic success at the expense of art cannot be underestimated. To the extent that both the great companies have enjoyed a certain artistic franchise, the gap between them and the more radical theatrical groupings has narrowed.

Of these the English Stage Company, founded in 1955 and housed for years in the Royal Court Theatre in London, is the most important. It pioneered new modes of dramatic expression and encouraged new dramatists by giving them a space for their writings. ▷ John Osborne's *Look Back in Anger* (1956) was launched at the Royal Court and went on to become a milestone in the history of modern British drama. The 1960s saw the blossoming in London and in Britain of ▷ fringe theatre which corresponded to the New York Off Broadway and Off-Off Broadway. It was associated with Americans such as Charles Marowitz and Jim Haynes, mostly working at different improvised venues in London. Their work, and that of many of the dramatists of the 1960s and 1970s, above all shows the influence of ▷ Brecht and ▷ Artaud. The theatrical scene in 1980s Britain is bleak, as resources are dwindling and funding bodies like the Arts Council are increasingly reluctant to underwrite commercially non-viable plays. The re-emergence in the metropolis of a new theatre of farce and social comedy is an indication that the age which was once hailed as that of the new radical Elizabethans is on the wane, as new norms of quietist conformism are endorsed in the theatre.

Thebes (Egypt)
The Greek name for an ancient capital of Egypt, on the site of which Luxor now stands.

Thebes (Greece)
In ancient Greece, the capital of Boeotia. It was the setting of many famous Greek legends, *eg* those associated with ▷ Cadmus, ▷ Oedipus, ▷ Dionysus, ▷ Heracles.

Theocritus
A Greek poet of the 3rd century BC. Little is known about him, but his importance is that he originated ▷ pastoral poetry in his 'idylls' – short poems about shepherds and shepherdesses living in primitive simplicity in the rural parts of Sicily. He may have written these in the Egyptian city of Alexandria for urban readers; one of the characteristics of pastoral has been that it has expressed the town-dwellers' fantasy of the beauty of country surroundings, the simplicity of country living and the purity of country air. Theocritus was emulated by the Roman poet ▷ Virgil, and both Theocritus and Virgil were taken as models by the 16th-century ▷ Renaissance poets in Western Europe, of whom the most notable English example is ▷ Edmund Spenser.

Theophrastus
A Greek philosopher, follower of ▷ Aristotle, of the 4th century BC. Amongst other writings, he composed a series of descriptions of moral types called *Ethical Characters*. These were the original pattern for the minor literary form of character-writing, widely practised in England in the early 17th century. The most notable example is John Earle's *Microcosmography* (1628). Other examples: ▷ Joseph Hall's *Characters of Virtues and Vices* (1608); ▷ Thomas Overbury's *Characters* (1614).
  ▷ Characters, Theophrastian.

Thermopylae
A pass between the mountains and the sea in Greece; in 480 BC a force of 300 Spartans under Leonidas defended it against a large army of Persians under ▷ Xerxes until not one Spartan was left alive.

Thersites
In Homer's ▷ *Iliad* (ii) the ugliest and most disagreeable of the Greek host besieging Troy. In Shakespeare's play ▷ *Troilus and Cressida* he is a kind of clown, with extraordinary powers of vituperation.

Theseus
In Greek myth, the principal hero of Athenian legend. His mother, Aethra, was jointly loved by Aegeus, king of Athens, and Poseidon, god of the sea; Theseus was thus credited with double, and partly divine, paternity. His principal adventures were as follows:

1 Before leaving Troezen, the home of Aethra, Aegeus hid his sword and sandals under an enormous rock. At the age of 16, Theseus lifted the rock single-handed, put on his father's sword and sandals, and set out for Athens.

2 On the way to Athens he accomplished a number of feats, ridding the countryside of various terrorizers.

3 His father, Aegeus, had married the witch, ▷ Medea; jealous of Theseus, who was unrecognized, she tried to poison him. His father recognized him by his sword, however, and Theseus drove Medea and her children away from the court. He next overcame Aegeus's nephews, the Pallantids, and destroyed the great wild bull that was devastating the land of Attica.

4 His next, and most famous, adventure, was to slay the ▷ Minotaur, the monster inhabiting the Labyrinth of Crete. He was guided through the Labyrinth by a thread provided by Ariadne, Minos's daughter, who had fallen in love with him. On his return to Athens he unintentionally caused his father's death by forgetting to substitute a white sail, the sign of victory, for the black one, the sign of defeat. When Aegeus saw the black sail approaching, he threw himself over the cliff in his grief.

5 Theseus was now king of Athens; he instituted its basic social structure and established its principal religious festival in honour of the goddess ▷ Athene, the Panathenaea.

6 In his wars against the race of women warriors, the ▷ Amazons, Theseus carried off Antiope, who bore him a son, Hippolytus. Later he repudiated Antiope, and married ▷ Phaedra, who fell in love with her stepson. When Hippolytus rejected her, she made accusations against him to Theseus, who caused the death of his son.

7 In grief at these tragedies, Theseus retired to the island of Scyron, whose king

Notes for Dylan Thomas's 'Poem on his Birthday'

treacherously killed him from jealousy at his fame.

Thespis (6th century BC)
A Greek poet of the 6th century BC; he is usually regarded as the originator of tragic drama. Choric songs were already sung at festivals; Thespis is said to have introduced an actor who engaged in dialogue with the leader of the chorus.

Third Estate
From the 13th century, three classes of society were said to participate in the work of politics in ▷ Parliament: the Lords Spiritual (leaders of the Church) or first estate; the Lords Temporal (nobility) or second estate; and the Commons (common people) or third estate. This organization is still shown in modern Parliaments: Bishops of the Church of England and peers with the rank of baron and above sit in the House of Lords; the rest of society is represented by Members of Parliament who sit in the House of Commons.

Thirty Years' War
A European religious war, lasting from 1618 to 1648, between nearly all the Catholic and Protestant nations of Europe. It was fought principally in Germany to the ruin of that country, and was concluded by the Peace of Westphalia. Britain was one of the few important countries which took hardly any part in it.

Thirty-nine Articles
The code of religious doctrine which all clergy of the ▷ Church of England have to accept. In 1553 42 articles were laid down; these were reduced to 39 in 1571.

Thomas (fl c 1170)
Composer of an influential version of the ▷ Tristan story, which only survives in fragmentary form (totalling about 3,150 lines). Little is known about the author, although modern scholars have suggested he was writing for the royal household of ▷ Henry II. The Middle English version of the Tristan story, *Sir Tristrem*, reworks material deriving from Thomas's poem.

Thomas, D. M. (Donald Michael) (b 1935)
Novelist and poet. His best-known work is *The White Hotel* (1981), a fictional account of the life of one of ▷ Freud's patients, making extensive use of fantasy. It also contains poetry and a pastiche of a case study by Freud. His other works include *Ararat* (1983); *Swallow* (1984); *Selected Poems* (1983).

Thomas, Dylan Marlais (1914–53)
Poet. He was born in the Welsh town of Swansea; much of his work shows the impression on his early life of grim Welsh religious ▷ Puritanism contrasting with the equally Welsh characteristic of strong emotion combined with his own sensuality.
His *18 Poems* (1934) and *Twenty-five Poems* (1936) bring together conflicting images in startling association, with pronounced and emotive verbal rhythms. The method has superficial resemblances to those of the 19th-century poet ▷ Gerard Manley Hopkins and the 17th-century ▷ Metaphysicals, but it presents less access than they do for the analytical intellect. Thomas's theme is characteristically the relationship between the disorderliness of sexual impulses and the forces of growth in nature. *The Map of Love* (1939) is mixed prose and poetry; it includes one of his most remarkable poems, *After the Funeral*, in which the striking rhythm and images cohere round the figure of the woman for whose death the poem is an ▷ elegy. *Deaths and Entrances* (1946) contained most of Thomas's most famous work. The poems show the impression made on him by World War II (during which he remained a civilian) in *A Refusal to Mourn*, a more overt use of religious emotion in *The Conversation of Prayer*, and delight in natural environment (*eg Poem in October, Fern Hill*). These poems are often less obscure than earlier ones, but the method remains a strong attack on the

emotions, achieved by the shock of the imagery and the sweep of the rhythm.

Thomas also wrote prose works – notably the stories entitled *Portrait of the Arist as a Young Dog* (1940) and the play *Under Milk Wood* published after his death (1954). The prose has no obscurity and exhibits, as the poems do not, Thomas's strong humour. The play shows a mastery of the medium of drama for sound broadcasting which remains unexcelled.

Thomas's wide fame derives especially from three qualities: his unashamed appeal to latent emotionalism in the common reader, on whom he made a direct impact perhaps greater than that of other modern poets except ▷ W. B. Yeats; his remarkable talent as a public reader of verse; his personality, which became a legend during his own lifetime, especially in America. On the other hand, his exuberance ran counter, before the war, to the intellectual fastidiousness of ▷ T. S. Eliot and the emotional scepticism of ▷ W. H. Auden, the two poets with the greatest prestige amongst the intelligentsia in England during the 1930s; again, he has been regarded with suspicion since 1945 by younger poets who have cultivated scrupulous honesty of feeling.

▷ Wales.

Bib: Jones, T. H., critical study in *Writers and Critics* series; Fraser, G. S., in British Council *Writers and their Work* series; Holbrook, D., *Llaergyb Revisited*.

Thomas, Philip Edward (1878–1917)
Poet and essayist. He was educated at St Paul's School and Lincoln College, Oxford, and was killed at the battle of Arras during World War I. He made his living by writing a long series of prose works, beginning with *The Woodland Life* (1897) and including ▷ biography, criticism and essays on natural surroundings. The last are in a tradition that extends back through ▷ Richard Jefferies, about whom Thomas wrote a critical assessment (1909), to the poetry of ▷ William Wordsworth. It was not until 1914 that Thomas began to write poetry, under the influence of the American poet Robert Frost, whom he first met the year before. His poems are continuous with his prose studies of ▷ nature, but it is by the poems rather than the prose that his reputation has grown since his death. English 'nature poetry' at its best has never been merely descriptive, but has concerned the power of the natural environment to elicit the purest human responses, not only to the environment but to elemental human relationships, including the

relationship of the poet with himself. Thomas's poems show integrity of responsiveness and sensitivity to the language of his day; they are without the weakening nostalgia and sensibility which showed the decadence of the nature poetry tradition in some of his contemporaries. After his death, his poetic achievement was at first overshadowed by the reaction against the decadence of his contemporaries. ▷ Ezra Pound and ▷ T. S. Eliot led public taste away from the whole tradition, in both its good and its bad aspects, in which Thomas wrote. However, *New Bearings in English Poetry* (1932) by ▷ F. R. Leavis contains an intelligent reassessment of his work. Since 1945, Thomas's austere honesty and delicacy of perception have caused his work to appeal strongly to English poets striving for the same virtues; with ▷ Thomas Hardy, he is seen as representative of distinctively English sensibilities in contrast to the partly alien sensibilities of Pound and ▷ W. B. Yeats.

Bib: Lives by Eckert, R. P., Moore, J., and Farjeon, E.; Thomas, H., *As It Was* and *World Without End*; Coombes, H., *Edward Thomas*; 'Hardy, De la Mare and Thomas' in *The Modern Age* (Pelican Guide); Leavis, F. R., *New Bearings in English Poetry*; Day Lewis, C., in *Essays by Divers Hands* (Transactions of the Royal Society of Literature Vol. XXVIII, 1956; Motion, A., *The Poetry of Edward Thomas*.

Thomas, R. S. (Ronald Stuart) (b 1913)
Poet. Since his first volume, *The Stones of the Field* (1946), he has maintained a regular and substantial output, including *Song at the Year's Turning* (1955), *Laboratories of the Spirit* (1975) and *Experimenting With an Amen* (1986). He is best known as a recorder of the rigorous beauty of the Welsh landscape, and of the duress of farming-community life there and the religious sensibility that evolves in such a context. In 1936 Thomas was ordained as a Church of Wales clergyman. *Selected Poems 1946–68* (1973), *Later Poems: a Selection* (1983), *Selected Prose* (revised ed. 1986).

▷ Wales.

Bib: Dyson, A. E., *Riding the Echo: Yeats, Eliot and R. S. Thomas*; Phillips, D. Z., *R. S. Thomas*; Ward, J. P., *The Poetry of R. S. Thomas*.

Thomas Becket
▷ Becket, St Thomas.

Thomas of Hales (fl 1250)
A Franciscan preacher, possibly from Hailes, Gloucestershire, who composed at least one Anglo-Norman sermon and is identified as the

author of the poem known as the 'Love-Ron' (which survives in a single manuscript version, dating from the late 13th century). The 'Love-Ron' is a verse epistle, addressed ostensibly to a young religious woman who has requested spiritual advice. It offers a guide to the art of spiritual 'fin'amor' and recommends Christ as the best lover of all.
Bib: Brown, C. (ed.), *English Lyrics of the Thirteenth Century*.

Thompson, Francis (1859–1907)

Poet. He gave up the study of medicine in Manchester to seek his fortunes in London, where he nearly starved. He published his *Poems* in 1893. Thompson was a ▷ Catholic; the most famous of his poems (included in the above volume) was the intensely religious *Hound of Heaven*. It's bold, extravagant style recalls the work of the 17th-century Catholic poet, ▷ Richard Crashaw, one of the English ▷ Metaphysicals. On the other hand, Thompson was more in the tradition of his immediate predecessors in his employment of sensuous, ornate symbolism; in this he resembles the ▷ Pre-Raphaelites of the mid-19th century, and another Catholic poet – one of the first of his admirers – ▷ Coventry Patmore. In this respect, a comparison of the *Hound of Heaven* with *The Wreck of the Deutschland* (1875) by yet another Catholic, ▷ Gerard Manley Hopkins, is instructive; Hopkins shows equal emotional intensity with much more of the intellectual rigour of the 17th-century poets. Thompson's other volumes were *Sister Songs* (1895) and *New Poems* (1897). His prose work includes his *Essays on Shelley* (1909).
Bib: Lives by Meynell, E., Meynell, V., and Thompson, P. van K. Critical study by Reid, J. C.

Thomson, James (1700–48)

Poet. Born in the Scottish border country, the son of a minister. He studied divinity at Edinburgh University, but in 1725 sought his fortune in London, where he became tutor in an aristocratic family. His poem *Winter* was published in 1726 and its success encouraged him to write poems on the other three seasons during the following years, the ▷ *Seasons* being completed in 1730. Thomson's artificially dignified ▷ Miltonic ▷ blank verse, and his miscellaneousness of subject-matter, struck the new bourgeois taste exactly, and the *Seasons* were extremely popular. He possesses a facility, almost amounting to genius, for holding together in loose, artificial suspension all the characteristic elements of the popular culture of his day: ▷ Augustan patriotism,

classicism in diction and tone, ▷ gothic excess, sentimentalism. His most original passages elaborate ▷ Virgilian pastoral into a pleasantly self-indulgent enthusiasm for the natural scene. Rhetorical patriotism, of which he is the period's most unembarrassed exponent, features also in his next large-scale poem, *Liberty* (1735–6), and also in the ▷ masque *Alfred*, written and produced with ▷ David Mallet in 1740, which contains the song ▷ *Rule Britannia*. Thomson also wrote tragedies, which were very successful at the time, but are now forgotten (*Sophonisba*, 1730; *Agamemnon*, 1738; *Edward and Eleanora*, 1739; *Tancred and Sigismunda*, 1745; *Coriolanus*, 1749). His Spenserian imitation, ▷ *The Castle of Indolence* (1748) is far more successful, eclectically combining ▷ mock heroic ▷ burlesque, sensuous description, whimsical self-mockery, patriotism and didactic moralizing.
Bib: Johnson, S., in *Lives of the Poets*; Grant, D., *Thomson, Poet of the Seasons*; Cohen, R., *The Art of Discrimination*; Cohen, R., *The Unfolding of the Seasons*.

Thomson, James (1834–82)

Poet. He was the son of a sailor in the merchant navy, and of a deeply religious woman who belonged to one of the narrower Protestant sects. He was an army schoolmaster, 1850–62, during which period he had a tragic love affair, and made friends with Charles Bradlaugh, who became a well-known atheist radical. Thomson is chiefly known for a long, sombre, ▷ atheistic poem, *The City of Dreadful Night* (1880), which expressed in the most uncompromising terms the darkest aspect of the loss of religious belief common among ▷ Victorian intellectuals. He was also capable of gaiety (*Vane's Story and Other Poems*, 1881). *A Voice from the Nile and other Poems* was published posthumously in 1884. He commonly wrote under the initials B.V. (Bysshe, from Percy Bysshe Shelley, and Vanolis, anagram for the German poet, Novalis).
Bib: Dobell, B., *The Laureate of Pessimism*; Walker, E. B., *James Thomson*.

Thopas, Sir

One of ▷ Chaucer's ▷ Canterbury Tales. Chaucer's own contribution to the tale-telling competition is a burlesque ▷ tail-rhyme romance, which the Host stops after only 200 lines or so. Although nominally set in Flanders, the narrative is placed in the world of romance conventions and motifs itself, and its orientation is signalled by the cast list of romance heroes with whom Sir Thopas is compared in the second 'fitt' (a conventional name for the sectional division of a poetic narrative). *Sir Thopas* is built up from a series of anti-climaxes, both in terms of action and style. When the Host steps in to halt proceedings, Sir Thopas has neither found a fairy lover nor fought the giant who challenges him, and though he has contemplated the possibility of doing both, has actually achieved very little in the course of his furious ride across the meadows. For the Host, this tale with its 'drasty rymyng' is 'nat worth a toord'. Chaucer's own contribution to his own tale-telling contest is thus a brilliant anti-climax: it is the only tale of the whole collection which is rejected on aesthetic grounds.

He counters with a second tale, ▷ *Melibee*, a prose moral treatise which could not be more different to *Sir Thopas*.

Thor
An ancient god of the Germans, Scandinavians, Icelanders, and possibly the ▷ Anglo-Saxons. The name means Thunder and his sign was a hammer. He has given his name to the day of the week, Thursday.

Thrale, Hester Lynch (1741–1821) (later Hester Thrale Piozzi)
Born Hester Salusbury, she married Henry Thrale in 1763. Thrale was a wealthy brewer with political ambitions, and when in the following year they made the acquaintance of ▷ Samuel Johnson, Johnson assisted Thrale by writing election addresses. The friendship between Johnson and Hester Thrale became very close, and at various times Johnson lived with the family in their home at Streatham. When Thrale died in 1781, Hester Thrale remarried. Gabriel Piozzi, her second husband, was an Italian musician, and her friends and family vociferously disapproved. The marriage ended the friendship with Johnson, who sent her an anguished letter on the subject.

Hester Thrale's biography of Johnson, *Anecdotes of the late Samuel Johnson*, was strongly contested by ▷ Boswell when it appeared in 1786; his motives in challenging her account probably stem from literary rivalry. Hester Thrale was also an energetic letter writer, and *Thraliana*, a selection of anecdotes, poems, jests and journal entries, covers the period 1776–1809.
Bib: Clifford, J. L., *Hester Lynch Piozzi*.

Threadneedle Street, The Old Lady of
A familiar term, dating from the 18th century, for the ▷ Bank of England, which stands in

a street of that name. The name of the street seems to derive from its original occupation by tailors.

Three Hours After Marriage (1717)
Burlesque comedy by ▷ Pope, ▷ Gay, and ▷ Arbuthnot, satirizing several contemporary literary figures, including John Dennis (Sir Tremendous), ▷ Colley Cibber (Plotwell), and the Countess of Winchilsea (Phoebe Clinket). The play was at first a success, but its production occasioned a furious hostility between Gay and Cibber, and it was not revived for another 20 years.

Through the Looking-Glass
▷ Carroll, Lewis.

Thucydides (5th–4th centuries BC)
Greek historian of the ▷ Peloponnesian war. It is one of the earliest historical works in European literature in its distinct care for accuracy. Nearly a quarter of the book however, is devoted to political speeches, including the great Funeral Oration by ▷ Pericles; these give an important insight into Greek attitudes to politics. Thucydides has been a principal text for English ▷ classical education.

Thyrsus
In ancient Greece, a rod or staff, tipped with a pine cone and wreathed with vine leaves or ivy, carried by the worshippers of the god ▷ Dionysus.

Tickell, Thomas (1686–1740)
Member of the clique which frequented Button's Coffee-house and whose leader was ▷ Joseph Addison. He contributed to ▷ *The Guardian* and ▷ *The Spectator*.
▷ Alexander Pope suspected that Addison had attempted to spoil his success by inciting Tickell to publish his translation of the first book of ▷ *The Iliad* just before the appearance of Pope's translation of the first two books (1715). Tickell edited Addison's works after his death, his edition being prefaced by a moving ▷ elegy in heroic ▷ couplets (1721).

Timber
A collection of commentary, paraphrase, and translation by ▷ Ben Jonson, *Timber* was first published in the two-volume edition of Jonson's works which appeared after his death. As a record of Jonson's reading in the ▷ classics, it is invaluable. More than this, however, is the insight it provides into questions which inform Jonson's own aesthetic theories, in particular his use of ▷ 'Imitation'.

Times, The
British newspaper. It was founded in 1785 as

The Daily Universal Register, and took its present name in 1788. In the 19th century it took the lead in contriving new methods of collecting news (notably through the employment of foreign correspondents), and its succession of distinguished editors and contributors gave it an outstanding status among British newspapers. Though always in private ownership, it has always claimed to be an independent newspaper rather than a party one. The literary style of one of its staff writers caused it to be nicknamed 'The Thunderer' in the 19th century; the novelist ▷ Anthony Trollope consequently refers to it as *The Jupiter* in his novels, since this king of the gods was known as the Thunderer by the ancient Romans. *The Times* publishes *The Times Literary Supplement* and *The Sunday Times* weekly. Its outlook is traditional and often conservative in political terms.

▷ Newspapers.

Timon

A rich citizen of Athens of the 5th century BC; he was celebrated for his hatred of mankind. He is referred to by a number of ancient Greek writers including ▷ Aristophanes, and notably by ▷ Plutarch, in his life of Mark Antony, and by ▷ Lucian in his dialogue *Misanthropos*. Shakespeare (▷ *Timon of Athens*) makes him a rich, ostentatious philanthropist who becomes a misanthropist through disillusionment at men's ingratitude. Pope, in his ▷ *Moral Essays* (iv–1734) described a rich Timon of his own day – perhaps the Duke of Chandos – laying emphasis on tasteless ostentation and indifference to people rather than hatred of them.

Timon of Athens (1607)

A tragedy by ▷ Shakespeare, written about 1607. The material is probably taken from ▷ Plutarch's life of Mark Antony (written 1st century AD), ▷ Lucian's dialogue *Misanthropos* (2nd century AD), and an anonymous play of Shakespeare's own day.

Timon is an Athenian nobleman who delights in the prodigal entertainment of his guests. In spite of his great wealth, he presently finds himself in debt; he is then outraged to discover that none of those to whom he has been so generous is prepared to help him. He invites his friends to one more banquet, but the steaming dishes, uncovered, contain only hot water; throwing the dishes and water at them, he drives his guests out of the house. In a frenzy of hatred, he then takes to a life of solitude in the wilderness, where he is visited by the cynical philosopher Apemantus, his devoted steward Flavius, the

general Alcibiades who is rebelling against the meanness of the Athenian government, and other characters from his past life of opulence. This part of the play consists of a series of dialogues which leave Timon resolute in his hatred of humanity, though he is obliged to make an exception of his disinterestedly loyal steward. The dialogue with Apemantus is the most striking: Apemantus has always foreseen that Timon would be deceived by his friends, since he has a low opinion of human nature; Timon, however, retorts that Apemantus's cynicism is groundless except for the mean motive of jealousy, whereas he, Timon, has proved that humanity is inferior after testing it on the opposite hypothesis. Alcibiades is afflicted by the public meanness of the Athenian state, as Timon has been afflicted by private ingratitude; thus he regards Timon as an ally though he cannot persuade him to join forces with the rebels. The rebellion of Alcibiades is successful, and when Timon dies, the Athenian rulers penitently acknowledge their ill-treatment of him.

Tintagel

In ▷ Geoffrey of Monmouth's version of British history, Tintagel features as the castle where ▷ King Arthur is conceived. In later Arthurian romances it is identified as the castle of King Mark, overlord of Cornwall and uncle to ▷ Tristan. Today there are remains of a medieval castle on the headland, but archaeological evidence suggests that there may have been a stronghold on the site in the late 5th century.

Tintern Abbey

One of the most famous remains of the medieval abbeys, dissolved by ▷ Henry VIII in 1536–39. It stands in a particularly beautiful natural setting, in the valley of the River Wye, near the border of England and Wales. The poet ▷ William Wordsworth used this setting for one of the best known of his early poems, *Lines Composed a Few Miles Above Tintern Abbey* (in ▷ *Lyrical Ballads*), in which he meditates on the influence of natural surroundings on the formation of his mind.

Tintern Abbey, Lines Composed a Few Miles Above (1798)

A reflective poem in ▷ blank verse by ▷ William Wordsworth, not itself a lyrical ballad but one of the 'few other poems' included in ▷ *Lyrical Ballads* (1798). The poet returns to a spot on the river Wye visited five years earlier, and reflects upon the moral influence its beauty has exerted upon him in the meantime, inspiring 'little, nameless, unremembered, acts/

Of kindness and of love'. He goes on to describe himself as 'A worshipper of Nature', and this is his most ▷ pantheistic work.

Tiresias (Teiresias)
In Greek myth, a sage of Thebes whom the gods afflicted with blindness but then compensated with the gift of prophecy. In the most familiar form of the legend, he spent part of this life as a woman.

▷ Tennyson's poem *Tiresias* is one of those ▷ dramatic monologues which are now among the most admired of his poems; here, Tiresias speaks with the voice of the lonely, timeless sage. He also occurs in Part III of ▷ T. S. Eliot's poem ▷ *The Waste Land*; here he is more the impartial witness of the crises of the human mind, and is described in a note as 'the most important personage in the poem, uniting all the rest'.

'Tis Pity She's a Whore (1632)
▷ John Ford's greatest tragedy which treats the passionate and incestuous love-affair between the siblings Giovanni and Annabella – and their relationship's inevitable progress towards destruction – with remarkable empathy and tact. When Annabella finds she is pregnant by her brother she marries a suitor, Soranzo, who discovers the truth about the child's paternity and conspires to revenge his own humiliation. The play concludes in a mass killing after a grotesque scene during which Giovanni enters with his sister's heart on the point of his dagger.

Titania
In ▷ Shakespeare's ▷ *A Midsummer Night's Dream*, the Queen of the Fairies and wife of Oberon, the king. The name derives from ▷ Ovid, who used it in his ▷ *Metamorphoses*, for a variety of female deities, especially woodland ones.

Titanic, The
The name of a great Atlantic liner which sank with the loss of over 1,500 lives in consequence of striking an iceberg on 15 April 1912. ▷ Thomas Hardy described the event, which exemplified his fatalistic philosophy, in one of the finest of his narrative poems, *The Convergence of the Twain* (1914).

Titans
In ancient Greek myth, the first divine race, the children of ▷ Uranus, the sky, and Ge (Gaea) the earth. The six male Titans were Oceanus, Coeus, Crius, Hyperion, Iapetus and ▷ Cronos; the six females – Thea, Rhea, Themis, Mnemosyne, Phoebe and Tethys. The brothers and sisters inter-married; for instance Iapetus and Themis

produced ▷ Prometheus and Epimetheus, and Cronos and Rhea produced ▷ Zeus and the other gods of Mount ▷ Olympus; Hyperion and Thea produced Helios, later the Sun, Selene, the Moon, and Eos, Dawn.

In the two versions of his unfinished epic ▷ *Hyperion*, Keats described the overthrow of the Titans to symbolize the replacing of old orders by new, and the consequent tragedy which he felt to be intrinsic to experience. Keats mingled Roman deities with Greek, giving Cronos the Roman name of Saturn; he opposed Hyperion to Apollo, instead of to Helios. Shelley invented an associated myth in ▷ *Prometheus Unbound*: Prometheus, son of the Titan Iapetus, witnesses, on behalf of Man, the downfall of the tyrant Zeus. Prometheus is represented as the child of Earth.

Tithes
A system for the maintenance of the parish clergy of the ▷ Church of England, consisting, originally, of one-tenth of the produce of the parish farmers. It was replaced during the 18th century by an annual rent and was abolished altogether by Parliament in 1936.

Tithonus
In Greek myth, the son of Laomedon, king of Troy. Such was his beauty that Eos (Aurora), goddess of the dawn, fell in love with him and made him her husband. She secured for him from ▷ Zeus the gift of immortal life, but forgot to require also immortal youth.

▷ Tennyson's poem *Tithonus* is a ▷ dramatic monologue representing Tithonus in the agony of his eternal old age.

Titles of nobility
The main titles of nobility, or peerages, in Britain are as follows, from lowest to highest in order of seniority:
Baron. A title originating with the Norman aristocracy after the Conquest.
Viscount. Originating in 1440.
Earl. As old as the title of baron, and equivalent to the title of Count in other countries of Europe. An earl's wife is known as a countess.
Marquess. Originating in 1385.
Duke. Originating in 1337, when the title Duke of Cornwall became a title regularly awarded to the heir to the throne. The title of duke was restricted to the royal family until the end of the 14th century.

All the above-mentioned titles are hereditary, with the exception of life peerages (always Baron or Baroness) originally awarded for political purposes. Whether inherited or awarded for the life of the holder, such a title carried with it the right to sit in the ▷ House of Lords.

The title of knight or baronet (hereditary ▷ knighthood) is not a title of nobility; the holder is, politically speaking, a commoner, *ie* represented in accordance with his vote in the House of Commons, and entitled to seek election as a member of it.

Titus Andronicus (1594)

A tragedy by ▷ Shakespeare, published in 1594. The origin of the plot is not known; it may owe something to ▷ Ovid's Procne and Tereus, one of his ▷ *Metamorphoses* translated by Golding, 1565–7, and to ▷ Seneca's drama *Thyestes* translated between 1559 and 1581. It is in any case a violent ▷ revenge tragedy of the kind that Shakespeare and his contemporaries derived from Seneca. The setting is imperial Rome; the plot concerns the revenge of Titus, a Roman general, for the atrocities committed by Tamora, the Queen of the Goths, against his family. She is aided by a villainous slave, Aaron the Moor. Much doubt has been expressed by scholars as to whether the play is entirely by Shakespeare, by Shakespeare in collaboration, or not by Shakespeare at all; the last opinion arises partly from the low esteem in which the play is usually held, although, according to ▷ Ben Jonson, it was popular among the contemporary public.

To the Lighthouse (1927)

A novel by ▷ Virginia Woolf. The setting is a house used for holidays by Mr and Mrs Ramsay. The household consists of themselves, their eight children, and a number of their friends, of whom the most important is the painter Lily Briscoe. The novel dispenses with plot and is organized into three parts, dominated by two symbols – the lighthouse out at sea, and Lily's painting of the house, with Mrs Ramsay sitting in the window with her son James. The parts are entitled 'The Window', 'Time Passes', and 'The Lighthouse'. The first part is dominated by Mrs Ramsay, who is intuitive, imaginative, and possesses a reassuring and vitalizing influence upon people and their emotions. The mysterious lighthouse flashing through the darkness is associated with her. In the interval represented by the second part of the novel, corresponding to the war years 1914–18, she dies, and the third part is dominated by Mr Ramsay who is intellectual, philosophical, and lonely. The lighthouse seen as a practical instrument, close at hand and by daylight, is associated with him. The middle section concerns the empty house,

subject to the flux of time and its changes. Lily Briscoe, the artist, stands aloof from Mrs Ramsay's embracing influence and seeks to fix the constantly changing relationships of people and objects in a single composition; she completes the picture in the last sentence of the book, when the Ramsay son, James, achieves reconciliation with his father and with the lighthouse seen as fact. Mrs Ramsay, in her role as wife and mother, and Lily, single and an artist, represent alternative possibilities for a woman's way of life.

The story is told through the ▷ stream of consciousness technique – in the minds of the characters, especially James, Lily, and Mrs Ramsay. The novel, one of the most original of the many fictional experiments in the 1920s, is partly autobiographical, and based on Virginia Woolf's own family. Mr and Mrs Ramsay are her father and mother, ▷ Leslie Stephen and his second wife.

Tolbooth

Originally, a stall where tolls, *ie* taxes on merchandise, were collected. This then became identified with a town hall, perhaps with prison cells beneath it, and finally the term was applied, in Edinburgh, to the town prison.

Tolkien, J. R. R. (John Ronald Reuel) (1892–1973)

Novelist, philologist and critic. From 1925 to 1945 he was Professor of Anglo-Saxon at Oxford University, and during the 1930s belonged to 'The Inklings', a literary society whose other members included ▷ C. S. Lewis. From 1945 to 1959 he was Merton Professor of English Language and Literature at Oxford. His large scale fantasy of another world *The Lord of the Rings* (1954–6) has gained enormous popularity. His other novels are: *The Hobbit* (1937) and *The Silmarillion* (1977).

Tolpuddle Martyrs

In 1834 six farm labourers from Tolpuddle in Dorset were transported to Australia for swearing men into a trade union lodge. The men were respectable – five were ▷ Wesleyans – and were returned home after three years of the seven-year sentence. But the lack of ▷ Whig support revealed the limits of common interest between the middle and working classes. The event nourished the ▷ Chartist movement and the men were seen as martyrs to the cause of unskilled-labour ▷ trade unions.

Tolstoy, Count Leo Nikolaevitch (1828–1910)

Russian novelist, dramatist and moral

philosopher. What are usually considered his two greatest novels, *War and Peace* (1865–9) and *Anna Karenina* (1875–7), have a spaciousness, profundity and balance of sanity which have caused them to be used as a standard by which the achievements of other novelists can be measured. The scale of greatness is to be accounted for not only by the depth of Tolstoy's mind but by the breadth of his experience, which in turn owes something to Tolstoy's position in Russian society and the critical phase of history through which Russia was passing during his lifetime. He belonged to the class of Russian landed gentry and was partly educated by French tutors, a fact which, taken with the sensitivity of the Russian intelligentsia to West European culture, gave him a broader understanding of the issues of civilization in his time than was characteristic of most Western novelists. Tolstoy frequented the intellectual and fashionable classes of Russian society, travelled abroad and spent the years 1851–7 in the Russian army, seeing service in the Crimean War against Britain, France and Turkey. Two other absorbing aspects of his experience were the problems of Russia's vast peasantry, emancipated from serfdom in 1861, and the prominence of religion in Russian life.

Tolstoy was early influenced by the thought of ▷ Jean-Jacques Rousseau and this, combined with his own direct experience of peasant life, developed in him a strong faith in spontaneous, simple living in contrast to the sophisticated, fashionable, educated society which he also knew well. From 1876, disillusioned by worldliness and inspired by the example of the peasants, he thought increasingly about the religious interpretation of experience, but his thinking turned him away from the Russian Orthodox Church to a religion of his own, based on the words of Christ (in *Matthew* 5 : 39) 'that ye resist not evil'. Tolstoy's religion was thus pacifistic and on the side of self-abnegation; it did not admit the existence of life after death nor a personal God, his belief being that the kingdom of God is within man. He described his religion in *What I believe in* and *A Short Exposition of the Gospels*; a complete account of his conversion is given in *A Confession* (1879–82), and in the same year he published stories inspired by his inner life at the time, *The Memoirs of a Madman* and *The Death of Ivan Ilyich*. In *What is Art* (1896), he expounded his doctrine that good art works by re-creating in the reader the fine emotions of the writer, bad art by similarly conveying the bad ones. Tolstoy's influence may be seen in the works of ▷ G. B. Shaw, ▷ E. M. Forster and ▷ D. H. Lawrence.

▷ Russian influence on English literature.

Tom Brown's Schooldays
▷ Rugby School.

Tom Jones, a Foundling (1749)
A novel by ▷ Henry Fielding. The central character begins life as a baby of unknown parentage (*ie* 'a foundling') who is discovered in the mansion of the enlightened landowner, Squire Allworthy. Allworthy adopts him, and he grows up a handsome and generous-hearted youth, whose weakness is his excess of animal spirits and inclination to fleshly lusts. He falls in love with Sophia Western, daughter of a neighbouring landowner, Squire Western, who is as gross, ignorant and self-willed as Allworthy is refined and enlightened. Western intends Sophia for Blifil, Allworthy's nephew, a mean and treacherously hypocritical character, who is supported against Tom by two members of Allworthy's household, the pedantic chaplain Thwackum and the pretentious philosopher, Square, who counterbalance each other. They succeed in disgracing Tom, whom Allworthy is persuaded to disown. The central part of the novel describes his travels and amorous adventures in the company of a comic follower, Partridge. Sophia also leaves home, to escape from Blifil, and nearly falls victim to a plot by Lady Bellaston, with whom Tom has become amorously entangled, to place her in the power of Lord Fellamar. Tom is eventually identified as the son of Allworthy's sister; the plots against him are brought to light; he is received again by Allworthy, and marries Sophia.

The novel, like its predecessor by Fielding, ▷ *Joseph Andrews*, is a 'comic epic', offering a wide range of social types of the age, all of whom are presented as permanent human types rather than as unique individuals, as 19th-century novelists would show them. Fielding's method is expository; he does not attempt to create illusions of characters with interior lives of their own, but expounds behaviour, with the aid of prefatory essays to his chapters, always light-heartedly, but always with a view to exhibiting basic human motives as they have always existed, rather in the manner of the 17th-century comedies of ▷ humours and of ▷ manners. He owes much to ▷ Cervantes' comic romance ▷ *Don Quixote* and to the studies of contemporary morals and manners by the painter ▷ William Hogarth. To some extent the book was written in rivalry to ▷ Samuel

Richardson's ▷ *Clarissa*, a novel written in a tragic spirit and in a strenuous and idealistic moral tone. It was Fielding's tendency to 'correct' Richardson's idealism and partly self-deceiving moral rigour by reducing events to more usual human experience and interpreting this in the light of tolerant comedy instead of grand tragedy; for instance, Lovelace, in *Clarissa* is a human fiend (though also an interesting psychological study) where Tom is merely a healthy young man whose licentiousness is bound up with his virtue of outgoing sympathy and generosity. Thus, *Tom Jones* is both one of the first important English novels, a new kind of imaginative work, and one that embodies highly traditional values.

Tom Thumb

An old folk-tale, several versions of which exist in northern Europe. Tom is (in the English version) the son of a ploughman living in the days of the legendary ▷ King Arthur; he is Tom Thumb because he is no bigger than the ploughman's thumb. He has a number of absurd adventures consequent on his diminutive size, including being carried off by a crow, swallowed by a cow, and swallowed again by a giant.

Tom Thumb the Great (1730)

Burlesque play by ▷ Fielding, expanded and performed as *The Tragedy of Tragedies, or, The Life and Death of Tom Thumb the Great* in 1731. The piece satirizes heroic tragedy, somewhat in the manner of ▷ *The Rehearsal*, but in ▷ blank verse rather than ▷ heroic couplets. In addition, the satire works entirely through the absurdity of the lines, and the device of having the tiny Tom Thumb as 'hero', without the benefit of commentary from sources outside the 'tragic' action. Fielding acknowledged his debt to ▷ Pope's *The Art of Sinking in Poetry* by attributing the play to 'Scriblerus Secundus'.

Tomlinson, Charles (b 1927)

Poet and literary critic. Tomlinson has been a university lecturer since 1956, and he also paints and translates. His work is precise and aspires to technical objectivity, influenced by both ▷ Donald Davie (who taught him at Cambridge and introduced Tomlinson's 1955 volume *The Necklace*), and by ▷ imagists and American ▷ modernists, especially William Carlos Williams and Marianne Moore. He has experimented with ▷ free verse and rhythmic irregularities, and is constantly expanding his technical range. His later volumes include: *The Way of a World* (1969); *The Shaft* (1978); *Selected Poems 1951–1974* (1978); *The Flood* (1981).

Torquemada, Tomas de (1420–98)

A Dominican friar who was appointed in 1483 as the first Inquisitor-general to investigate religious heresies in Spain. His zeal has made him a symbol of cruelty in England.

▷ Inquisition, The.

Tory

▷ Whig and Tory.

Tottel's Miscellany (1557)

An influential ▷ anthology of verse published by Richard Tottel, a bookseller, and Nicholas Grimald, a translator and scholar. It was originally entitled *Songs and Sonnets*, and included the work of the ▷ Earl of Surrey and ▷ Sir Thomas Wyatt. Their poems, the first of any distinction in English to show characteristics of ▷ Renaissance style, had never before been printed though they had circulated in manuscript, and the great popularity of the anthology helped to shape the short poem so much cultivated in the last 20 years of the century; their success led to the publication of many similar anthologies.

Tournaments

A 12th-century English chronicler described tournaments as 'military exercises carried out, not in the spirit of hostility, but for the practice and display of prowess'. Tournaments appear to have originated sometime between the mid-11th to mid-12th century (perhaps in France), as part of the social institutionalization of ▷ knighthood, and provided a forum where the military function of a knight could be displayed, even as knights ceased to have a functional role in the conduct of medieval warfare (for which mercenaries were employed increasingly from the 12th century onwards). The martial engagements in tournaments (melees and jousts) were highly formalized combats, in theory at least. Rule books codifying conduct in the arena are extant from the 13th century, although the fact that both the Church and the monarchy in England took steps to ban, or at least to restrict tournaments, reflects the frequent failure of such events to live up to the rule books, or their idealized literary representations (such as the one described in ▷ Chaucer's ▷ *Knight's Tale*).

Tournaments continued to be held well into the 16th century, although they came increasingly to be occasions for the display of pageantry and the promotion of a mythology of chivalry. The 19th-century revival of interest in the medieval period stimulated a revival of tournaments: ▷ Benjamin

Disraeli's novel *Endymion* (1880) contains a description of a tournament held at Eglinton Castle in 1839.

Tourneur, Cyril (?1575–1626)
Dramatist. Not much is known of his life, except that he was employed abroad in military and diplomatic service, and died in Ireland on the return of the unsuccessful naval expedition under Buckingham to capture Cadiz. He is well known for two plays, one of which, ▷ *The Revenger's Tragedy* (1606–7), is regarded as one of the finest achievements of the period, and is attributed by most scholars to another dramatist, ▷ Thomas Middleton. The other, *The Atheist's Tragedy* (1611), an interesting anti-revenge play, is much less esteemed. The case for Tourneur being the author of the more admired of the two plays is partly based on the resemblance to an obscure religious poem by him, *The Transformed Metamorphosis* (1600). He also wrote a number of ▷ elegies.
    ▷ Revenge Tragedy.
Bib: Murray, P. B., *Tourneur*; Eliot, T. S., in *Selected Essays*; Bradbrook, M. C., in *Themes and Conventions of Elizabethan Tragedy*.

Tower Hill
A slight hill near the ▷ Tower of London on the north bank of the Thames. It was used as a place of execution for aristocratic or otherwise eminent political prisoners, including ▷ Sir Thomas More (beheaded there in 1535), the poet ▷ Earl of Surrey (1547), the ▷ Earl of Strafford (1641), and ▷ Archbishop Laud (1645).

Tower of London
A medieval fortress, the central part of which – the White Tower – was built after the ▷ Norman Conquest by ▷ William I to subdue the City of London; it stands by the Thames at the south-east corner of the old City, and counterbalances the ▷ Palace of Westminster (now the Houses of Parliament), also on the river, at the western end of the City. The Tower was extended later in the ▷ Middle Ages, and incorporated a royal palace, which was pulled down in the 1650s by the order of ▷ Oliver Cromwell. The frequent mention of the Tower in English history and literature is due to the imprisonment there (and often execution there or on the adjacent ▷ Tower Hill) of numerous eminent men and women. For instance ▷ Edward V and his brother were imprisoned in it by ▷ Richard III and probably murdered there; other victims include two of the queens of ▷ Henry VIII,

Anne Boleyn and Catherine Howard, Sir Thomas More (beheaded in 1535), Sir Walter Ralegh (1618), and Charles II's illegitimate son, the Duke of Monmouth (1685). The Tower continued to be used as a prison until the 19th century. It is now a museum, and contains 'the Crown Jewels', *ie* the regalia of the British monarchy. It is guarded by the Yeoman of the Guard (known as 'Beefeaters' – ▷ Yeoman) who wear 16th-century uniforms.

Towneley Plays
    ▷ Wakefield Cycle.

Tract
An ▷ essay or treatise, usually short but published singly and usually on a religious subject. The most famous in English are the *Tracts for the Times* (1833–41) by a group of devout Anglicans, Hurrell Froude, Pusey, Keble, and ▷ Newman. Their purpose was to increase the spiritual dignity and independence of the ▷ Church of England by the revival of doctrines stressed in the 17th century but since then largely neglected, with the consequence, as the authors believed, that the Church was losing its spiritual identity and was exposing itself more and more to secular ▷ utilitarianism and domination by the state. Newman's was the predominating spirit in the group; he started the series, and he wrote *Tract XC*, which caused scandal by emphasizing the closeness of the Anglican to the older Catholic tradition, and thus ended it.
    ▷ Oxford Movement.

Tractarian Movement
    ▷ Oxford Movement; Tract.

Trade Union
The history of British trade unionism may be divided into four main phases.

1 Impulses to start trade union associations arose from the early development in England of capitalist industrialism and the congregation of workers in factories in the later 18th century. At first workers associated chiefly in small ways for such purposes as mutual insurance against unemployment in what were known as 'Friendly Societies'. Nonetheless the movements were regarded with suspicion by the government as possible centres of revolution, especially after the ▷ French Revolution of 1789–93. Consequently ▷ Parliament passed the Combination Acts of 1799–1800 to forbid the formation of unions. These laws were repealed in 1824, and thereafter the activity of forming

associations amongst employees was a lawful one, but this did not include striking.

2 The next phase was a brief one, and ended in failure. An attempt was made, at first successfully, to form a national union of workers called the Grand National Consolidated Trades Union; this came to nothing after the trial and transportation of six Dorsetshire agricultural labourers in 1834 on the charge of administering false oaths; they are the so-called ▷ 'Tolpuddle Martyrs' whose memory is still revered.

3 For 30 years industrial relationships remained stormy, but until 1890 working-class energies were taken up with other movements such as the ▷ Chartist Movement and the Anti-Corn Law League. A respectable kind of Trade Unionism developed among skilled workers, such as the Amalgamated Society of Engineers. In the 1860s a number of outrages in the industrial north of England again alerted public suspicion of trade unions, and the government appointed an inquiry into their activities. This was so reassuring that unionism began to prosper. In 1868 the Trades Union Congress (T.U.C.) was started; thus began a new phase in which trade unionism again had a national organization capable of coordinating the interests of industrial workers.

4 The last phase, since 1870, has been the development of Unionism to its present state: for a time it was one of the most powerful factors of national life. Two laws gave the movement new legal security; that of 1871 legalized action through strikes, and that of 1876 gave unions the right to exist as corporations, able to own property and to defend their rights corporatively (*ie* not as mere collections of individuals) in courts of law. Two important developments followed in the last 20 years of the century: the growth of unions where they were most needed, among unskilled workers; and the formation of a political party, the ▷ Labour Party, which had union interests at heart and strong financial support from the T.U.C. Modern unions federated in the T.U.C. have a membership of around 9 million, and unions have tended to amalgamate, so that, while they are much larger than in the 19th century, they are fewer in number. The Industrial Relations Act, which came into force in 1972, was a move towards bringing the question of industrial action within a legal framework. By the late 1980s Union power was severely diminished, owing to opposition by the Tory government.
▷ Industrial Revolution.

Trafalgar, Battle of (1805)

The chief sea-battle of the war against ▷ Napoleon, in which the British fleet under ▷ Nelson defeated a joint French and Spanish fleet under Villeneuve. The victory made impossible an invasion of Britain by the French army, but Nelson was killed in the action.

Tragedy

Tragedy as it is understood in Western Europe has its origins in the Greek dramas by the Athenian dramatists ▷ Aeschylus, ▷ Sophocles and ▷ Euripides, in the 6th–5th centuries BC. Essentially the spirit of this writing was that inevitable suffering overwhelms the characters, and yet the characters maintain their dignity in the face of this suffering, and prove their greatness (and the capacity of human beings for greatness) by doing so. Greek tragedy arose out of their religious interpretation of the nature of human destiny. When Christianity prevailed over Western Europe, a much more hopeful interpretation of human destiny dominated the thought of writers, and tragedy, in the Greek sense, became difficult to imagine and unnatural: if good men suffer in this world, they are rewarded in Heaven, and this is not tragic; wicked men who happen to suffer in this world may be damned in the next, but this is also not tragic because they are wicked. Hence medieval tragedy was on the whole reduced to the conception of the Wheel of Fortune – that chance in this world is apt to take men from prosperity to misfortune, whatever their spiritual merits.

In the late 16th century the tragic vision of human experience was rediscovered by some English dramatists, notably by ▷ Marlowe and ▷ Shakespeare. Insofar as it had a literary ancestry, this was not the tragedy of the ancient Greeks, which was scarcely known, but the comparatively debased imitation of it by the Roman poet ▷ Seneca, which helped to give rise to Elizabethan ▷ Revenge Tragedy or 'Tragedy of Blood'. More interesting was the growth of conceptions of human destiny which did not usurp the Christian conception, but existed side by side with it, as an alternative, or perhaps rather as a complementary, vision. Thus perhaps the first important English tragedy is Marlowe's ▷ *Doctor Faustus* in which the hero forgoes eternal happiness after death for the sake of earthly ecstasy; Marlowe sets in opposition the Christian doctrine of the soul and ▷ Renaissance delight in earthly experience. ▷ *Hamlet*, in which

Shakespeare for the first time makes the task of revenge a genuine moral dilemma, is perhaps the next. The best known achievements of English tragic drama are Shakespeare's five plays: ▷ *Othello*, ▷ *Macbeth*, ▷ *King Lear*, ▷ *Anthony and Cleopatra* and ▷ *Coriolanus*. These cannot be summed up in a phrase, but they have in common that the hero's hope of some form of supreme earthly happiness collapses into terrible misery, brought about less by the hero's character than through the nature of earthly reality of which his character forms a part. Among Shakespeare's later contemporaries and his successors, several dramatists wrote distinguished plays in the tragic style *eg* ▷ Middleton's ▷ *The Changeling* and ▷ Webster's ▷ *The Duchess of Malfi* and ▷ *The White Devil*.

This period, from 1590 till about 1625, was the only one in English literature in which there were more than isolated examples of distinguished theatrical tragedy. The single important example of a work written in the Greek style is Milton's *Samson Agonistes*, but critics disagree as to whether it can be called truly dramatic. Numerous attempts were made to write tragedy in the Greek style, or in the neoclassical French style of ▷ Corneille and ▷ Racine, after 1660, but they lacked conviction; perhaps the best is ▷ Dryden's *All for Love*. Various attempts were made by 19th-century poets to revive the Shakespearean mode of tragedy. Of these, Shelley's ▷ *The Cenci* is the only noteworthy example, but even that was only a minor success.

Some of the plays of ▷ Synge and ▷ Yeats were genuinely remarkable and original tragedies, but their scale is unambitious. However, in the 1960s the work of such dramatists as ▷ Pinter, ▷ Osborne and ▷ Arden has revived dramatic tragedy in a more recognizable form.

Tragedy of Arden of Faversham, The
  ▷ *Arden of Faversham, The Tragedy of.*

Tragical History of Doctor Faustus, The
  ▷ *Doctor Faustus, The Tragical History of.*

Tragicomedy
Drama in which the elements of both ▷ tragedy and comedy are present. Examples are the ▷ romances of ▷ Shakespeare, particularly ▷ *Pericles*, ▷ *Cymbeline*, and ▷ *The Winter's Tale*, each of which reaches a tragic climax half way through and then lightens towards a happy conclusion. A peculiarly English form

of tragicomedy developed in the years 1610 to 1640, particularly in the works of ▷ Beaumont and ▷ Fletcher.

Traherne, Thomas (c 1638–74)
Poet and religious writer. In the 17th century, the only works published by Traherne were three religious pieces, all of them in prose. In 1896, however, the Victorian editor A. B. Grosart discovered a collection of manuscripts in a London bookshop which he believed to be by ▷ Henry Vaughan. The manuscripts were identified as being those of Traherne, and comprised religious poems and the remarkable mystical prose work *Centuries of Meditation*. This latter constitutes a spiritual autobiography, tracing the author's progress towards 'felicity' (a key term for Traherne). Criticism of Traherne's poetry has in the 20th century, concentrated on his affinity with ▷ George Herbert, and on his visionary delineation of childlike experience. Understood as a mystic, and as an intellectual conservative in comparison to the rationalism of 17th-century science, Traherne has been closely linked with the ▷ Cambridge Platonists – almost as though he were the poetic 'voice' of that group. Yet, for all Traherne's concern with 'the inward eye', in fact his approach to language, his undoubted fascination with the possibilities of rational science (particularly as it had unfolded a new perspective in which to understand the human body) and his experimental verse forms make him one of the most remarkable of later 17th-century writers.
Bib: Margoliouth, H. M. (ed.), *Traherne's Centuries, Poems, and Thanksgivings*; Clements, A. L., *The Mystical Poetry of Thomas Traherne*.

Transference
This is the term used in ▷ Freudian psychoanalysis, along with others such as ▷ 'condensation' and ▷ 'displacement', to describe one of the mechanisms whereby unconscious desires enter into ▷ consciousness. It is given a more specific meaning in the relationship between analyst and patient (analysand) in psychoanalysis, as part of the process of removing those impediments to the recollection of repressed impulses on the part of the latter. Situations and emotions are relived during the treatment and these ultimately express the indestructibility of unconscious fantasies. In the structure of a literary work, repetitions of particular situations and events, and even the duplication of 'character', can be explained as kinds of transference of the 'unconscious fantasies' of the writer. In this way desires and feelings which in psychoanalysis occur in

the life of the patient, are *transferred* onto the analyst/reader, producing a repetition or re-enactment of them. For example, in Shakespeare's ▷ *Hamlet* 'madness' is transferred from the hero onto Ophelia, and an analysis of that process situates the reader/spectator within a complex process of the construction of male/female subjectivity as a result. The issue can be complicated further if the writer 'Shakespeare' is taken to be the 'analysand' projecting unconscious desires and feelings through his 'characters' onto the 'analyst' (reader/spectator).

Transferred epithet
▷ Figures of Speech.

Transgression
As a term used in contemporary literary criticism, it is generally associated with the concept of ▷ 'subversion' insofar as it denotes the act of crossing accepted boundaries. Applied to literary texts it is usually taken to refer to any form of behaviour or representation which challenges the dominant values encoded within that text. A classic example of the process might be the introduction of the act of 'cross-dressing' in a number of ▷ Renaissance drama texts, and the resultant challenge which is posed to the issue of a stable sexual identity. Here, the practical constraints of the ▷ Elizabethan or ▷ Jacobean theatre, involving the impersonation of female roles by male actors, serve to highlight what in the world outside the theatre was becoming a controversial issue as the relative positions of men and women in 17th-century society underwent re-evaluation.

Translation
The life of English literature has always issued from a combination of strong insular traditions and participation in wider European traditions. Translation has always been the principal means of assimilating European literatures into the English idiom, and it was particularly important before the 18th century, when the main streams of European cultural life were flowing through other languages. The aim of translators was then less to make an accurate rendering than to make the substance of foreign work thoroughly intelligible to the English spirit; the character of the translation thus proceeded as much from the mind of the translator as from the mind of the original writer. If the translator had a strong personality, the translation often became a distinguished work of English literature in its own right. Translators with less individuality often

produced work of historical importance because of its contemporary influence on English writing.

From the 14th to the 18th centuries, English writers were constantly absorbing the ancient and contemporary Mediterranean cultures of Europe, and worked on the literatures of France, ancient Rome, Italy, ancient Greece, and Spain. There is no distinct boundary between translation and adaptation; ▷ Chaucer brought English poetry into accord with French and Italian poetry partly by freely adapting work in those languages. His outstanding work of translation is his version of Guillaume de Lorris's *Roman de la Rose*. French ceased to be the first language of the English upper classes in Chaucer's lifetime, but the English nobility continued to have strong ties with French aristocratic culture, and thus translations from French prose were in demand in the 15th and 16th centuries. ▷ Caxton, the first English printer, published many English versions of French romances. The outstanding 15th-century work of English prose was ▷ Malory's ▷ *Morte d'Arthur*, which Caxton published, and which is partly a translation and partly an adaptation. The work of translation was an important influence on the development of a fluent English prose medium, and this is evident in the difference between ▷ Wycliff's 14th-century translation of the Latin Bible and ▷ Tyndale's version of the New Testament from the Greek (1525). Lord Berner's translation of ▷ Froissart's *Chronicles* is another distinguished example of English prose development in the 15th and early 16th centuries.

Printing, the ▷ Renaissance, and the rise of new educated classes, all helped to expand translation in the 16th century, which was the first major period for translation of classical writers. These had been of central importance in the ▷ Middle Ages too (King Alfred and later Chaucer had translated ▷ Boethius's *De Consolatione Philosophiae*) but knowledge of them had now widened and standards of scholarship had advanced. The first important rendering in English of a great classical poem is that of ▷ Virgil's ▷ *Aeneid* by the Scots poet, ▷ Gavin Douglas (1553). ▷ Chapman's *Iliad* (1611) and *Odyssey* (1615) are impressive, but have less intrinsic merit as English literature. ▷ Ovid had long been a favourite poet, and translations were made of his poems by ▷ Arthur Golding (1565–67) and ▷ Christopher Marlowe (pub 1597). But in the 17th and 18th centuries the best-known English version of Ovid was

George Sandys's version of
▷ *Metamorphoses*, completed in 1626. Ovid
had an extensive influence on poets, including
▷ Shakespeare; ▷ Seneca's influence on
the poetic drama, both as a philosopher and
as a dramatist, was equally conspicuous, and
it was no doubt helped by the historically
important but otherwise undistinguished *Ten
Tragedies*, translated by various hands and
published between 1559 and 1581. Among
the most distinguished prose translators of
ancient literature in this period was Philemon
Holland, remembered especially for his
version of ▷ Pliny's *Natural History*, which
he published in 1601. The best known of all,
especially for his value to Shakespeare but
also for the quality of his writing, is
▷ Thomas North, whose version (1579) of
▷ Plutarch's *Lives* was made not from the
original Greek but from the French of Jacques
Amyot.

Translations from the contemporary
European languages were also numerous in
the 16th and early 17th centuries, and indicate
the constant interest of English writers in
foreign literatures. ▷ Sir John Harington
translated ▷ Ariosto's ▷ *Orlando Furioso*
in 1591: ▷ Tasso's *Jerusalem Delivered* was
translated as *Godfrey of Bulloigne* or *The
Recovery of Jerusalem* (1600); ▷ Castiglione's
very influential ▷ *Il Cortegiano* was
translated by Sir Thomas Hoby (1561). The
best known of all these contemporary works
is ▷ John Florio's rendering of the
▷ *Essays* of ▷ Montaigne, published in
1603. Part I of Cervantes's ▷ *Don Quixote*
was translated in 1612 before Part II was
written; the whole work was three times
translated in the 18th century, by Motteux
(1712), Jarvis (1742) and ▷ Smollett (1755).
The first three books of ▷ Rabelais's
Gargantua and Pantagruel were translated
notably by Thomas Urquhart; two were
published in 1653, and the third in 1694. The
fourth and fifth books were added by Motteux
in 1708.

Many of the translations made before 1660,
especially those in prose, were marked by a
super-abundance of words, characteristic of
much English writing in the 16th and 17th
centuries; the originals tended to be amplified
rather than closely rendered. After the
▷ Restoration in 1660, writers attached
importance to discipline and control, and to
emulating these virtues as they were
exemplified in the old Latin poets and in
contemporary French writers of verse and
prose. In consequence, ▷ John Dryden
accomplished some of his best work in
translating Latin poetry, especially Ovid (*eg*

▷ *Philemon and Baucis*) and the *Aeneid* of
Virgil, whose works he translated entire,
completing them in 1697. ▷ Pope's
translations of Homer's *Iliad* and *Odyssey*,
which appeared in 1720 and 1726, greatly
enhanced his reputation, but despite the
skill of the versification, they are obviously
much further from the spirit of Homer than
Dryden's renderings are from the Latin
poets; the British Augustans
(▷ Augustanism) were much closer in
feeling to the Roman Augustans than they
were to the ancient Greeks. As the century
went on, writers became restless under
Augustan restraints, and became interested
in literatures that had hitherto been ignored
or despised; ▷ Thomas Gray imitated
Icelandic and Celtic verse. Macpherson's
versions of Gaelic legends, which he alleged
to be by the legendary poet ▷ Ossian,
were more inventions and adaptations than
translations, but they probably had a wider
influence in other countries than any other
English work going under the name of
translation, with the exception of the
English Bible. Sir William Jones (1746–94),
the first important British Oriental scholar,
published in 1783 a version in English of
the ancient Arabic poems called *Moallakat*,
as well as other work from Persian and
from Sanskrit.

Some of the more distinguished translations
of the first 30 years of the 19th century, such
as Cary's translation in ▷ blank verse of
Dante's *Divine Comedy* (1805–12),
▷ Coleridge's version of Schiller's
Wallenstein (1800), and ▷ Shelley's
fragments of ▷ Goethe and Calderón
(▷ Spanish influence on English literature),
show the new kinds of influence on the
Romantic writers. After 1830, translation
became a kind of net for hauling in exotic
writings, and its field became very wide, *eg*
▷ Fitzgerald's version of the Persian poem,
The Rubaiyat of Omar Khayyam (1859),
▷ Richard Burton's ▷ *Arabian Nights*
(1885–88), ▷ William Morris's translation
of the Icelandic Sagas (beginning in 1869),
▷ Swinburne's versions of Villon, as well as
many new versions of the ancient Greek and
Latin authors. Two vices of the period were a
tendency to make a foreign work express
essentially English 19th-century sentiment (*eg*
FitzGerald's *Rubaiyat*), and to use
peculiarities of style under the mistaken
impression that because they gave strangeness
to the work, therefore they gave the
translation an air of authenticity – a fault
which ▷ Matthew Arnold criticizes in his
fine essay *On Translating Homer* (1861). The

really influential translations were more often of contemporary writers, such as those by Constance Garnett of the Russian novelists ▷ Tolstoy and ▷ Turgenev (▷ Russian influence on English literature); William Archer's translations of ▷ Ibsen; and Scott Moncrieff's fine rendering of ▷ Proust's great novel under the title of *Remembrance of Things Past*. These works bring us into the 20th century, in which translation has been cultivated with a new sense of its importance and difficulties. Among the most eminent of modern translations are ▷ Ezra Pound's *Cathay* (from the Chinese) and his version of the Old English *The Seafarer* (1912), and Willa and ▷ Edwin Muir's translations of Kafka (1930–49). In the 20th century translation has become more widespread, making texts in many languages readily available, and this has included critical as well as fictional works. However, while providing us with an international ▷ best seller list, regularly including writers such as Umberto Eco (▷ Italian influence on English literature) and Gabriel Garcia Márquez (▷ Spanish influence on English literature), there is a danger that a new saleable canon will be created and more marginal texts will remain trapped by linguistic barriers.

Travel and transport
The Middle Ages: 1350–1500. The extent of travel in any period of history depends not only on the availability of means, but on the existence of motives and on what facilities are offered or refused by governments.

In the ▷ Middle Ages, the means of travel were bad, but pilgrimages (▷ *Canterbury Tales*) and trade supplied an important motive. Consequently, above the level of the very poorest class, there was more travel than one might expect when one considers the obstacles to movement. It is true that the very poor – the largest segment of the population – did not travel. The mass of the peasantry and many town artisans remained locked within the horizons of the small town or village and barely emerged from them until the age of railways. Those who could afford pilgrimages, however, often undertook at least a few short ones, for a pilgrimage was in the eyes of the Church a deed of virtue and was frequently imposed as a penance. There were professional pilgrims, called Palmers, who dedicated their lives to pilgrimage, and ▷ Crusaders were really a military variant of the Palmer. The destinations were places of reputed holiness: Jerusalem, the Holy City; Rome, the capital

of Christendom; or the shrine of some great saint, like that of St James of Compostella in northern Spain. In England, there were many places of pilgrimage, but three were outstanding: Glastonbury, the legendary starting-point of Christianity in Britain; Walsingham, which possessed a miraculous statue of the Holy Virgin; and Canterbury, the shrine of the most famous English saint, ▷ Thomas à Becket, the 12th-century martyr. Besides pilgrimage, trade, war and diplomacy were the most important motives. Some men were travellers in the course of business, such as pedlars and chapmen who carried their goods on their backs or on pack-horses from village to village. Although the conditions were bad, there was in some respects more freedom of movement than in modern Europe, where passports and sometimes visas are now required by almost every country with an independent government; national frontiers were not yet the barriers of prejudice that they sometimes are now. Language, too, was less of a problem for many travellers, since Latin was an international tongue for the learned and ▷ French, until the 15th century, was spoken by the English upper class.

The conditions, however, must often have been formidable. The Romans, before their organization collapsed in Britain early in the 5th century, created a great system of paved roads; these may have survived to some extent into the Middle Ages, though they were probably sometimes pillaged for building material. Until the 18th century, hard roads were seldom constructed, apart from a few causeways which merchants sometimes arranged for over marshy places. There were not only the problems of impassability in bad weather, but also the dangers of highway robbery. A law of 1285 ordained that roads should be widened to 200 feet by the destruction of bushes and trees, so that there should be no cover for robbers lying in ambush. Travel was by foot or on horseback; heavy carriages were used by the rich, but they were very rare until the 16th century; the sick, the old, and great ladies were carried in litters supported by their servants; goods were transported in large wagons or by packhorse.

The badness of roads made water transport preferable; rivers were used whenever they were navigable. Heavy goods were transported by sea; hence the expression 'sea coal' for coal brought from Newcastle to London.

By later standards, trade was necessarily much restricted, but many traders would risk one journey a year for the sake of gain; hence the importance of the annual ▷ fairs. From the 14th to the 19th century, there were numerous fairs throughout England, and many survive today, although their purpose is now often entertainment rather than trade. The size of the region from which fairs drew traders varied greatly; it might consist of a few neighbouring villages, or – like the Stourbridge Fair at Cambridge – it might draw traders from the extremities of the country and even from foreign lands.

1500–1800. The Protestant ▷ Reformation in the 16th century put an end to pilgrimage; it forbade the reverence hitherto paid to the bones of the saints and Rome was no longer the capital of Christendom for Britain. But the pilgrims were replaced by students and writers seeking enlightenment at the sources of ▷ Renaissance culture, especially in Italy. Already in the 14th century ▷ Chaucer had learnt much from meeting French and ▷ Italian writers on his diplomatic journeys, and ▷ Sir Thomas Wyatt (?1503–42) was to renew this experience as a diplomatist; later ▷ John Donne (1572–1631) and ▷ John Milton (1608–74) travelled on their own account. The idea of travel as a means of education became normal among the educated classes of the 17th century, and in the 18th century it became an enthusiasm, until in 1785 40,000 Englishmen were said to be doing the 'Grand Tour'. Besides travel for education, there was the constantly increasing travel for trade. By far the most important technical advance in the 16th century was the adoption of a new structure of sail enabling ships to voyage much farther: this made possible the great voyages of discovery which, in the last 30 years of the century, enormously expanded trade.

Overland transport, however, was difficult. The increasing movement of goods about the country in huge carrier's wagons drawn by teams of six or more horses caused the bad roads to deteriorate still further. In the 16th century the care of the roads was in the charge of the country parishes under the supervision of the magistrates, but the work was neglected, since it was not the countrymen who were the chief users of the roads. In the second half of the 17th century, the 'turnpike system' was introduced, to transfer the cost of road repairs on to the road users. The turnpikes were barriers across the roads at suitable places, where travellers were compelled to pay tolls before they were allowed to proceed. The system worked with unequal success, and extended to remote regions only slowly, but in the 18th century it improved. In the second half of the 18th century roads were immensely improved by the great engineers Macadam, who invented the method of building road surfaces from broken stone, and Telford, who was also a great bridge-builder. By the end of the century, foreign observers acknowledged English roads to be the best in Europe.

The improvement naturally affected ways of travel and styles of vehicle. A system of post-horses for royal messengers already existed in the 16th century: relays of horses were established about the country to expedite their journeys. As early as 1660 stage coaches, which changed horses at fixed stages, were available; a century later the improvement of the roads made this the usual way of travelling on long journeys. The system of 'post-horses' was by then at the disposal of people who could afford to travel in privately owned or hired post-chaises; these light vehicles made it possible to accomplish in a day journeys of a hundred miles which had taken three days at the beginning of the century. By the beginning of the 19th century, various styles of vehicle existed.

For heavy transport, water was still more convenient than land, and in the 16th and 17th centuries, rivers were deepened, locks were built and the first canals were dug. But it was again the second half of the 18th century that was the great period for the improvement of water transport. By his wealth and political influence, the Duke of Bridgewater was largely responsible for the construction of a system of canals throughout England. His enterprise was very important in advancing the ▷ Industrial Revolution, since it not only facilitated the distribution of heavy manufactures but enabled large supplies of corn and other foodstuffs to be brought to the new population centres.

1800–present day. In 1840, England had 22,000 miles of good roads, maintained by 8,000 turnpikes; it also had a magnificent canal system for industrial use. But in 1843 it had, in addition 2,000 miles of railway, which increased to 5,000 miles by 1848, and was to exceed 23,000 by the end of the century. The first steam-railway had been opened in 1825, a distance of 11 miles. Thus, no sooner had the 18th-century system of transport reached perfection than it was superseded by the 19th-century one. The great canal system decayed and the road system lost most of its long-distance traffic. Railways could move passengers and goods more economically, in far greater quantities, at hitherto unimagined speeds, and perhaps not even the motor car has caused such marked changes in the economic and social life of Britain. They were the more marked, of course, because of the swiftness of the spread of railways. Steam made much slower progress at sea: in 1847, steamships represented only 116,000 tons out of a total of three million tons of British merchant shipping. Not until the end of the century did steamships completely supersede sailing ships on long voyages.

The effect of railways was to bring all the regions of the country into close relation with one another and to make extensive travel possible for all the social classes for the first time. They had, in fact, an effect on single countries comparable to that which air travel has had on the entire world in the 20th century. The formerly enclosed, regional cultures lost their self-sufficiency, so that British civilization in the 20th century has become much more uniform than it once was. The railways were breakers of social barriers, too; they were a comparatively democratic mode of travel. Hitherto only the rich and leisured had been able to afford the money and time to travel extensively, but now the poor could manage it too; and trains mixed the social classes, despite the provision of first, second and third class coaches. Perhaps the most important effect of all was that railways greatly increased the movement of population from the countryside into the towns, although this had already begun in the 18th century. Many industrial towns in the north owed their rapid enlargement to railways, so that railways are one of the most important explanations for England becoming the first thoroughly urbanized country in the world.

Railways naturally extended the habit of foreign travel from the upper to the middle class, which visited foreign countries in the second half of the 19th century in far greater numbers than ever before.

But humbler kinds of travel also became common in the 19th century for the first time, for reasons that had nothing to do with the invention of the steam engine. Until the later 18th century, Britain was too rural for people to have much curiosity about the countryside, and travel for pleasure was chiefly limited to friendly visits and journeys to pleasure resorts such as ▷ Bath and – when sea bathing became fashionable in the reign of George III – the seaside towns such as ▷ Brighton. In every century from the 16th there were individuals who had the curiosity to make surveys of the entire country – Leland and Camden in the 16th century,

Fynes Morrison in the 17th, ▷ Daniel Defoe in the 18th and ▷ William Cobbett in the early 19th – but they were interested in economic and social facts, not landscape. However, the romantic writers who were contemporary with Cobbett (▷ Walter Scott, ▷ Samuel Coleridge, ▷ William Wordsworth and ▷ John Keats) awakened a new interest in scenery as part of their new kind of attention to nature, and they walked about the countryside merely for the pleasure it gave them. Such an activity would have been incomprehensible to a medieval man, but by the middle of the Victorian period it had become an accepted one. When the pedal cycle came into popular use at the end of the century, touring the countryside for its fresh air and natural beauty extended to women as well as men.

The two greatest travel developments of the 20th century have of course been aircraft and the motor car. Since Britain is relatively small in area, aircraft have been chiefly important in foreign travel and transport, but aeroplanes have dramatically changed Britain's relationship to other countries, not only by closer communications with them, but by causing her to lose much of the defensive protection of insularity. In the war against Spain in the 16th century, the wars against France in the 18th and early 19th centuries, the war against Germany of 1914–18, Britain was made safe by her navies; but in World War II she depended, like every other modern country, on her air force. The change is important not only politically but psychologically; it has changed the attitude of the British to their own nation, causing them to see it, for the first time, as just one among many nations and not as a privileged exception to the depredations of history.

The first cars appeared on the roads of Britain in 1894, but it was not until after 1918 that they became widespread, and not until after 1945 that ownership of a car extended to all but those on the lowest income levels. Since then motor transport has superseded rail transport for passenger travel; not only have the roads had their revenge on the railways but road construction has not been able to keep pace with the increase of motor traffic. The mobility of the population has been intensified and people no longer commonly die in the place in which they were born. Cars have also changed the relation of living-place to working-place, and it is now quite usual to drive every day to and from one's work over a distance which, even in the 18th century, would have been a long day's journey. Meanwhile, rural Britain continues to perish under the weight of urbanization which this increasingly dense traffic has produced. In trade and transport, as in some other important matters, the movement has been from the oppression of one extreme to the oppression of another: from confinement to one place in the 14th century to the confinement of belonging nowhere in particular in the 20th.

Travel literature

This large branch of English literature may be conveniently discussed under these headings: 1 fantasy purporting to be fact; 2 factual accounts; 3 travel experiences regarded as material for art.

1 *Literature of fantasy purporting to be fact.* So long as extensive travel was rarely undertaken, it was possible for writers to present accounts of fantasy journeys and to pass them off as fact without much fear of being accused of lying. Thus a 14th-century French writer wrote the *Travels of Sir John de Mandeville*, which is a work of fiction or compilation from narratives by other travellers, but purporting to be an account of genuine journeys written by Mandeville himself. The work was translated into English in 1377, became extremely popular, and was long regarded as genuine. Long after the extravagances of the story were seen to be falsehoods, Mandeville, a purely fictional English knight, was thought to be the genuine author.

2 *Literature of fact.* By the second half of the 16th century, the great Portuguese, Spanish and Italian explorers had discovered the Americas and greatly extended knowledge of eastern Asia. Liars could still find large, credulous audiences, but the facts were marvellous enough to require no distortion. Writers also began to feel strong motives for publishing truthful accounts. Thus ▷ Richard Hakluyt published his *Principal Navigations, Voyages and Discoveries of the English Nation* in 1589, partly for patriotic reasons. The English had been slow to start on exploratory enterprises, although by this time they were extremely active. Hakluyt, finding that the reputation of his nation stood low among foreigners in this field, wanted to demonstrate the reality of the English achievement, and at the same time to stimulate his fellow-countrymen to further endeavours. His book is really a compilation of accounts by English explorers; an enlarged edition came out in 1598, and a still further enlarged edition was published under the title of *Hakluytus Posthumus, or Purchas his*

Pilgrims by Samuel Purchas in 1625. The accounts vary from those by accomplished writers like ▷ Sir Walter Raleigh to others by writers with little or no experience of writing; they constitute an anthology of early English descriptive writing in which the writers are concerned with the truthfulness of their accounts rather than with entertaining or deceiving the reader. Other examples of this new kind of honest and truthful handling of descriptive language are Captain John Smith's history of the founding of the colony of Virginia, *General History of Virginia, New England, and the Summer Isles* (1624). The contrast between this newer, plainer style and the extravagant and whimsical style more characteristic of the ▷ pamphleteers can be seen in accounts of travels in Europe by Thomas Coryate (?1577–1617), author of *Coryate's Crudities*, and Fynes Morison (1556–1630), author of *Itinerary*: Coryate is deliberately strange and fanciful, though an acute observer, but Morison is much more straightforward.

The steady growth of English overseas trade kept alive a taste for accounts of great voyages throughout the 17th and 18th centuries. At the end of the 17th century Captain William Dampier published three books which included the imaginations of ▷ Defoe and ▷ Swift: *New Voyage Round the World* (1697), *Voyages and Descriptions* (1699), and *Voyage to New Holland* (1703). Dampier was an excellently direct and clear writer of his own books, but Lord George Anson's voyage round the world (1740–44) was written up from his journals by his chaplain, R. Waters, and depends on the singularly dramatic events for its force of interest. The last of these outstanding accounts of great voyages were the three undertaken by Captain James Cook, *A Voyage Round Cape Horn and the Cape of Good Hope* (1773), *A Voyage Towards the South Pole and Round the World* (1777), and *A Voyage to the Pacific Ocean* (1784). With the discovery of the coastlines of Australia and New Zealand, the main outlines of world geography became known, and the interest of both explorers and their readers passed to the mysteries of the great undiscovered interiors of the continents. With this change in subject matter, a change also came over the style of travel literature.

3 *Travel literature as material for art.* Mungo Park's *Travels in Central Africa* preserves the plain, unaffected style of 18th-century travel literature, but subsequent work, for instance ▷ Richard Burton's book about India, *Scinde or the Unhappy Valley*

(1851), and his later books about his exploration of East and Central Africa (*First Footsteps in East Africa*, 1856; *The Lake Region of Central Africa*, 1860) bear more of the stamp of the author's personal feelings and reactions. Partly, no doubt, this arose from the new importance attached to authorial personality due to ▷ Romanticism; also the contact with strange physical environments and peoples (in contrast to the emptiness and impersonality of the ocean) inevitably drew out authorial response. At all events, travel literature began to draw nearer to autobiography. Not only 'darkest Africa', but the Arabian peninsula fascinated writers. Burton was one of the first Englishmen to visit the holy city of Mecca, and wrote an account of it in *Pilgrimage to Al-Medinah and Mecca* (1855). Later Charles Doughty tried to restore the vividness of 16th-century language to 19th-century prose in his *Arabia Deserta* (1888), and ▷ T. E. Lawrence's *Seven Pillars of Wisdom* (1926), an account of the Arab struggle against the Turks in World War I belongs to the same tradition of art made from travel in Arabia. George Borrow (1803–81) did not go so far for his material, but he went a stage further than these writers in combining travel literature and imaginative art, so that it is difficult to know whether or not to classify his books with the novel. They are full of personal encounters with individuals, chiefly among the common people; he was particularly interested in the ▷ gipsies (*The Gypsies in Spain*, 1841; *Lavengro*, 1851; *Romany Rye*, 1857) and he was talented at conveying the intimate texture of the life of a country (*The Bible in Spain*, 1843; *Wild Wales*, 1862). James Kingslake's account of his travels in the lands of the Eastern Mediterranean, *Eothen* (1844), and Lafcadio Hearn's *Glimpses of Unfamiliar Japan* (1894) are two other examples of travel literature which owe their classic status as much to the author's art and personality as to their subject matter. Thus travel literature became a natural subsidiary form for the novelists; it is among the best writing of ▷ R. L. Stevenson and ▷ D. H. Lawrence. ▷ Joseph Conrad, who, as a sailor, was a professional traveller during the first part of his adult life, may be said to have completely assimilated the literature of travel into the art of the novel.

Increasing ease of travel since World War II has greatly increased the amount of travel writing. Eric Newby's *A Short Walk in the Hindu Kush* (1959) has became a classic. Other important contemporary travel writers include Bruce Chatwin (1940–89).

Travers, Ben (1886–1980)
British dramatist famous for his 'Aldwych farces', performed at the Aldwych Theatre by casts which included Mary Brough, Robertson Hare, Ralph Lynn, and Tom Walls. The first of these was *A Cuckoo in the Nest* (1925), followed by several others including *Rookery Nook* (1926), *Thark* (1927), and *Plunder* (1928). At the age of 89 he wrote the 'sex comedy' *The Bed Before Yesterday*, which was first performed in 1975, by which time Travers was able to deal explicitly with matters which he had previously only written about implicitly.
Bib: Smith, L., *Modern British Farce: a Selective Study*.

Treasure Island (1883)
A romance by the novelist ▷ Robert Louis Stevenson, perhaps his best known work. It is set in the 18th century and the plot concerns the search for hidden treasure buried in a desert island by an actual 18th-century pirate, Captain Kidd. The story contains the basic elements of a traditional English romance – treasure, pirates, adventure, a desert island – and belongs to a line of desert island literature descending from ▷ *Robinson Crusoe*.

Treatise of Human Nature
▷ Hume.

Tree, Sir Herbert Beerbohm (1853–1917)
English actor-manager famous for his productions at the Haymarket and Her Majesty's theatres, and for founding the Royal Academy of Dramatic Art. Productions at the ▷ Haymarket included ▷ Oscar Wilde's *A Woman of No Importance* (1893), ▷ Shakespeare's ▷ *The Merry Wives of Windsor* (1889) and ▷ *Hamlet* (1892). Most successful was an adaptation of a George Du Maurier novel, *Trilby* (1895), the proceeds from which enabled him to build Her Majesty's. The repertoire at Her Majesty's was dominated by Shakespeare and historical verse drama. His Shakespeare productions were illustrative of the fashion of the period for spectacular 'romantic realism'. Detailed ostentatious sets, busy stage action and sometimes bizarre stage additions were all characteristic of these productions, disparagingly referred to by designer ▷ Gordon Craig as 'beautiful copies of Irving'. Tree combined the qualities of the showman and pioneer. The Shakespeare festivals at Her Majesty's from 1905 to 1913 matched those being given by actor-manager Frank Benson at Stratford. He also championed the cause of ▷ Ibsen, by

running matinée performances of *An Enemy of the People*.
Bib: Bingham, M., *The Great Lover*.

Tricoteuses

The 'knitters', from the French tricoter = to knit. A name given to the women who brought their knitting to the debates in political assemblies during the ▷ French Revolution. In English fiction, Madame Defarge in Dickens's novel ▷ *A Tale of Two Cities* knits the names of those who are to meet death by the guillotine into an endless scarf.

Trilby (1894)

Novel, written and illustrated by ▷ George du Maurier. It tells the story of Trilby O'Ferrall, an artists' model in Paris with whom all the art students fall in love. She comes under the mesmeric influence of Svengali, a German-Polish musician who makes her famous. His spell is so strong that when he dies she loses her voice, fails and dies herself. The novel enjoyed enormous popularity and was dramatized in 1895. Trilby's soft felt hat with an indented crown is the original 'trilby'.

Triolet

A graceful verse form of 8 lines and two rhymes with a rhyme scheme *abaaabab*. It was invented in France in the 13th century, and was not used in England till the 17th century. Like other verse forms which have little merit beyond their gracefulness, it has seldom been used in English except by minor poets, and those chiefly of the late 19th and early 20th centuries.

Triplet

In verse, three lines rhyming together, occasionally used among ▷ couplets to introduce variety.

Tristan and Iseult

There are many medieval and post-medieval versions of the tragic love affair between Tristan (Tristram/Tristrem) and Iseult (Iseut/Isolde/Isolt/ Isode); however, if the lovers' tragedy is a fixed element in their history, details of why and how it happened are not. It seems likely that their love story has a source in early Celtic legendary narrative: Tristan seems to be a transfiguration of the 8th-century Pictish Prince Drust, and there are Irish analogues to the story of the erotic triangle which forms the basis of the Tristan and Iseult narrative. But there are no Celtic versions of the love story which pre-date the French versions, composed in the later 12th century.

In the mid-12th century Tristan is mentioned as an ideal lover in the lyrics of the ▷ troubadours, which suggests some version of his story was circulating at this time. Fragments of longer vernacular narratives about Tristan and Iseult are extant by ▷ Thomas (c 1175) and ▷ Béroul (c 1190). ▷ Marie de France also included an episode from the lovers' history in her collection of *Lais*, and ▷ Chrétien de Troyes claimed to have produced a version of the story too, though no trace of the text has survived (his romance, *Cligés*, contains many references to the affair between Tristan and Iseult). From the fragments by Thomas and Béroul, and from their subsequent reworkings (especially in early medieval German versions), some idea of the overall story-line may be established.

Tristan is the son of Rivalen and Blancheflor (the sister of King Mark of Cornwall). Blancheflor dies the day her son is born, and he is brought up as an orphan until he is old enough to go to Mark's court, where he kills the Irish champion, Morholt. Later he is given the task of finding a bride for Mark. Tristan travels to Ireland, is wounded in a fight against a dragon, and is nursed by the king of Ireland's daughter, Iseult. She manages to identify Tristan as the killer of her brother Morholt; however, she saves Tristan's life on condition that he rescue her from an unwanted marriage. Tristan takes Iseult back to be Mark's wife, but on the voyage to Cornwall they accidentally drink a love potion which had been designed for Iseult and her future husband, and so they fall passionately in love. Their love affair continues after Iseult's marriage to Mark (with the help of Iseult's maid), but rumours about their adultery finally reach Mark. Later, after the affair has been exposed, Tristan goes into exile in Brittany, and marries another Iseult (of the White Hands), although the marriage is never consummated. When, at a later stage, he is wounded by a poisonous weapon, he calls for Iseult of Ireland to come to heal him: if she consents, the ship which carries her is to have white sails; if not, her message is to be carried in a ship with black sails. Although Iseult comes to Tristan's aid, Iseult of the White Hands tells Tristan that a ship with black sails is approaching. At this news Tristan dies. Iseult, realizing she has come too late, dies of grief beside Tristan.

The status of the love potion (whether it is a permanent or temporary spell, whether it is a metaphor for their love, rather than a literal love potion) is a variable element in the love story. So too is the means by which the lovers are exposed and punished by Mark: in some versions the lovers are condemned, but Tristan manages to escape and rescue Iseult from a group of lepers to whom she has been given for their pleasure; in some versions Iseult survives a truth ordeal by swearing an equivocal oath, and the lovers subsequently run away to live together for a time in a forest. The story of frustrated and passionate love arouses very different ethical responses, too, from medieval poets and prose writers: Tristan and Iseult have an equivocal status as exemplary lovers, being famous and infamous, a subject for praise and blame. Gottfried von Strassburg's *Tristan* (c 1210) provides one of the most celebratory versions of the story, which strongly affirms the metaphysical status of the bonds between these two lovers (and this, in turn, is the source for Wagner's opera of 1865, *Tristan und Isolde*).

The experience of Mark, Iseult and Tristan clearly offers a parallel to, and perhaps a prototype for, the other major erotic triangle of Arthurian romance involving ▷ King Arthur, ▷ Guinevere, and ▷ Lancelot. And in the later French prose versions of the Tristan story (dating from the 13th century), the friendship between Tristan and Lancelot is developed: in these versions, substantial accounts are added of Tristan's adventures as a Knight of the Round Table, and in these versions he is killed, finally, by King Mark himself. ▷ Malory's long 'Book of Sir Tristram' is a reworking of the French prose *Tristan* (c 1225). The 13th-century English verse romance, *Sir Tristrem* (in the ▷ Auchinleck manuscript), provides an incomplete reworking of Thomas's 12th-century *Tristran*.

▷ Tennyson, ▷ Matthew Arnold, and ▷ Swinburne are among the later poets to take Tristan and Iseult as their subjects, and of these, Tennyson presents the least sympathetic, and most critical interpretation of the lovers' experience.
Bib: Ferrante, J., *The Conflict of Love and Honour: The Medieval Tristan Legend in France, Germany, and Italy*; Lacy, N. et al (eds.), *The Arthurian Encyclopaedia*.

Tristram Shandy, The Life and Opinions of (1760–7)
A novel by ▷ Laurence Sterne, published in successive volumes, 1 to 1x from 1760 to 1767. Any attempt to paraphrase the 'plot' of this eccentric materpiece would be doomed, like trying to net the wind. Sterne deliberately flaunts his freedom to tease and surprise the reader with his interruptions and digressions. 'If I thought you was able to form the least

judgement or probable conjecture to yourself, of what was to come in the next page,' he writes, 'I would tear it out of my book.' Tristram, the nominal hero, plays little part in the action of the book, though as the authorial voice of the narrative his random associations determine its form. As a character he is not born until volume iv, and never gets beyond infancy. The bulk of the novel is taken up with the theories and hobby-horses of Tristram's father, Walter Shandy, and his uncle Toby; these two brothers appear like comic caricatures of ▷ Locke's theory of the association of ideas. Each of them is trapped in his own private world of associations; for Walter these centre on his obsessions with noses and names; for Toby they are based on military science and his quest to determine the circumstances of the wound in the groin which he suffered at the seige of Namur. The other characters, Dr. Slop, Corporal Trim, parson Yorick, Mrs Shandy and the Widow Wadman are swept up in the general associations – many of them sexual – of noses and wounds, breeches and ballistics.

'Shandy' is an old Yorkshire dialect word meaning crackbrained, odd or unconventional, and it suits this book perfectly. With its black and marbled pages, its flash-backs and interpolations, its asterisks, blanks and dashes, this novel defies any attempts to unscramble a straightforward narrative theme. The effect on the reader is to suggest that the conventional notion of a biographical narrative, with a distinct beginning, sequence of events and ending, is untrue to human experience which finds that beginnings do not really exist, and orderly sequences are frustrated by every kind of distraction. Tristram Shandy has been called 'the greatest shaggy-dog story in the language' and a satiric essay on human misunderstanding. It is a joyous, exuberant cock-and-bull story, in which the juggler Sterne shamelessly leads the reader by the nose on an endless quest for the elusive copula that links cause and effect, intention and achievement.

Trochee
▷ Metre.

Troilus and Cressida (1601–2)
A play by ▷ Shakespeare, written 1601–2, and first printed in 1609. Its position in the first collected edition of Shakespeare's plays, the ▷ folio of 1623, is curious, inasmuch as it was placed by itself and not in one of the three groups of histories, tragedies and comedies. Shakespeare used as sources ▷ Caxton's *Recuyell of the Histories of Troy*

(1474), translated from the French of Raoul le Febvre, ▷ Chaucer's *Troilus and Criseyde*, especially for Pandarus and the love story, ▷ Chapman's translation of the ▷ *Iliad* (for Thersites) and possibly ▷ Lydgate's *Troy-book*.

Troilus, son of King Priam of Troy, woos Cressida, with the help of her uncle, Pandarus. Meanwhile the war continues between the Trojans and the Greeks; the latter are doing badly, because their chief warrior, Achilles, is sulking in his tent. The subtle Ulysses contrives a plan to rouse Achilles by provoking his vanity; he chooses the brutishly stupid Ajax to fight the Trojan champion, Hector; the ruse is successful. A pact is made for an exchange of prisoners, and the Trojans consent to hand over Cressida, whose father has deserted to the Greeks; she and Troilus part, with many promises of fidelity, but she quickly becomes the mistress of the Greek Diomed, to the bewildered disillusionment of Troilus who sees her in Diomed's arms during a truce. The end of the play is a chaos of fighting, in which all higher emotions are lost in a rage of murderous hatred, and Hector, the noblest character in the play, is treacherously murdered by Achilles.

What bewilders critics is the hopelessness of the play. Two of the finest episodes are debating scenes, during the first of which (I. iii) the Greeks discuss their failure in the cold light of reason; in the second (II. ii) the Trojans defy reason for the sake of emotional dedication to 'honour'. But the play shows that reason alone conduces to ignobility and treachery, while honour alone is defeated by the facts of human nature. The voice of truth seems to be the mocking one of the Greek clown Thersites, who despises everybody and respects nothing. A possible view is that the much prized virtue of honour, so cultivated by ▷ Renaissance courtiers, is an idealistic value, a literary growth in terms of which real life cannot be evaluated, whereas the 'reason' of politicians by itself destroys the value of living. This interpretation makes the play more an affair of lighthearted mockery than it is commonly taken to be; it is frequently interpreted as a grim and despairing satire.

▷ Problem plays (of Shakespeare)

Troilus and Criseyde

▷ Chaucer composed *Troilus and Criseyde* some time in the 1380s (before 1388). His contribution to the medieval Troy story was not to produce an English version of the history of Troy, from beginning to end (in the tradition of ▷ Benoît de Sainte-Maure

and ▷ Guido de Columnis), but to refract the the Troy story through that of the relationship between Troilus ('little Troy') and Criseyde, organized as an epic love-tragedy, with a five-book division and elaborate apostrophes and a palinode. The siege of Troy and past Trojan and Greek history form a significant backdrop to, and determining influence on, the conduct and outcome of their affair.

The outline of Chaucer's narrative is taken from ▷ Boccaccio's ▷ *Il Filostrato* but in addition to developing the background to their story, Chaucer changes some aspects of the presentation of its key characters, not least in the role of the narrator himself, who no longer presents Troilus's experience as a cipher for his own but adopts the familiar 'ineffectual' Chaucerian role. Pandaro, the go-between figure in Boccaccio's version, is a cousin of Criseida and a peer of Troilus; in Chaucer's version, Pandarus is Criseyde's uncle and, though still a lover himself, plays the role of an avuncular confessor to Troilus. His engineering power is increased on a local domestic scale and his role as stage-manager of their affair is enhanced, but his controlling powers are markedly circumscribed at the same time: he may be on hand literally to help Troilus into bed with Criseyde but his resources diminish as the larger context of the siege intervenes in the lovers' lives. Criseyde is more vulnerable, naive and sensitive to the pressures around her than her counterpart in Boccaccio; there is no precedent for her presentation as a woman under siege within a siege. Troilus is a more bookish lover in Chaucer's version, who has a lyrical tradition of love sentiments at his command, and his songs and monologues in Book III celebrate his relationship with Criseyde in metaphysical terms. However, Chaucer is not presenting a Divine Comedy in this narrative but a pagan history, and one in which human love is subject to the forces of time and change.

The organization of the poem into five books reflects the progress of the love affair: the broad opening panorama of Book I gives Troilus and Criseyde a place in the wider history of Troy; the focus narrows in Books II and III, which chart the increasing self-involvement of the lovers as they create their own private world within Troy. Book IV marks the interruption of the historical world into their affairs, with the plan to exchange Criseyde; and the final Book sketches the 'changing' of Criseyde, her transferral to the Greek camp and engagement with Diomedes, Troilus's reluctant perception of her change,

and his final change, as he ascends the spheres after his death and laughs at the behaviour of mortals, their loves and longings, on little earth. The book ends with its 'maker' committing it to the care of his peers 'Moral ▷ Gower', and 'philosophical Strode'.
  ▷ Troy.
Bib: Windeatt, B. (ed.), *Troilus and Criseyde*; Salu, M. (ed.), *Essays on Troilus and Criseyde*.

Troilus and Criseyde: the legend
The love affair between the Trojan prince, Troilus, and Criseyde, the daughter of the Trojan Priest Calchas, is not included in classical versions of the Troy story, but first appears in the work of the 12th-century French writer, ▷ Benoît de Saint-Maure. In his *Roman de Troie*, details of the love affair emerge as the Criseyde figure (Briseida) is handed over to join the Greeks at the request of her father (who deserts the Trojan side at the beginning of the war). Following the separation of the lovers, Troilus learns that Briseida has taken the Greek prince, Diomedes, for her lover, and denounces her infidelity, publicly, on the battlefield.
  ▷ Boccaccio considerably amplified details of the early stages of the love affair in his poem ▷ *Il Filostrato*, which is ▷ Chaucer's principal source for ▷ *Troilus and Criseyde*. In Chaucer's text, the relationship between the lovers and their wider historical context is more developed, and larger philosophical issues about the historical determination of their lives are opened up (notably by the injection of material derived from ▷ Boethius). By Chaucer's time, the Criseyde figure had become a proverbial figure of infidelity, but his text works against this proverbial grain and makes her betrayal a much more interesting and complicated phenomenon.
  ▷ Robert Henryson took up the opportunity to go beyond Chaucer's text (and pick up a loose thread of the narrative), by pursuing the end of Criseyde in his ▷ *Testament of Cresseid*: it is here that the notion of Cresseid's end as a leper is developed, though the 'cause' of her final state is a topic of debate and speculation within the poem.
  ▷ Shakespeare used both *Troilus and Criseyde* and the *Testament of Cresseid* in the composition of ▷ *Troilus and Cressida*, in addition to other medieval versions of the full-scale Troy story (descending from Benoît de Saint-Maure) and ▷ Homer's version of events too.
  ▷ Troy.

Bib: Benson, C. D., *The History of Troy in Medieval English Literature*.

Trollope, Anthony (1815–82)

Anthony Trollope by S. Laurence (1865)

Novelist. The unbusinesslike qualities of his father, a barrister who forsook the law and ruined himself in farming, caused his childhood to be poverty-stricken, although his mother, ▷ Frances Trollope kept her family from the worst hardships by writing. Trollope himself was a prolific novelist, and though he worked seriously his *Autobiography* (1883) deeply offended the taste of the time by his frank statement that the writing of novels was a craft and a business, like making shoes, with nothing exalted or inspired about it. He was a strong admirer of the novels of ▷ Thackeray and shared Thackeray's contempt for the commercial arrogance of the British upper-middle classes. On the other hand, unlike Thackeray, Trollope had also strong faith in the traditional virtues and values of the English gentry, and several of his novels are about how the gentry class opened its ranks (through marriage, and after a struggle) to the best elements of less-privileged classes. His first novel was published in 1847, but it was in 1855 that he published the first of his most famous series, the Barsetshire novels – ▷ *The Warden*. The series continued with *Barchester Towers* (1857); *Dr Thorne* (1858); *Framley Parsonage* (1864); *The Small House at Allington* (1864); ▷ *The Last Chronicle of Barset* (1867). It is in these books that he displays his very conservative values most winningly and convincingly; they present a world of very

solidly portrayed church dignitaries and
landed gentry and show a loving care for
fully-rounded characterization. The world he
shows with such conviction was perhaps
already passing, and in presenting it Trollope
does not forget the weaker side of its values
nor the assaults and encroachments upon it of
political adventurers and the more vulgar of
the middle class. His later work became more
political, for instance *Phineas Finn* (1869);
The Eustace Diamonds (1873); *Phineas Redux*
(1874); *The Way We Live Now* (1875); *The
Prime Minister* (1876); *The Duke's Children*
(1880). Some critics consider that this group
of his novels is unduly neglected; the setting
is commonly London, which Trollope
thought a source of evil, and the tone is more
critical of society. *The Way We Live Now*
reflects his disillusionments most strongly; it
includes a powerful portrait of a fraudulent
tycoon in Melmotte, and is not so much
political as a devastating social study.

Trollope lost favour after his death, but
regained strong popularity in the mid-20th
century. This was because this period of
insecurity and war made Trollope's world of
traditional values seem very reassuring. Yet
critics seldom allow him rank equal to his
contemporary ▷ George Eliot; he does not
even pretend to insight as deep, or tragic
vision, though he is often subtle and fond of
pathos.
Bib: Sadleir, M., *Life*; Bowen, E., *Trollope: a
new Judgement*; Cockshut, A. O. J., *Anthony
Trollope: a Critical Study*; Gerould, W. G.
and J. T., *Guide to Trollope*; Smalley, D.
(ed.), *The Critical Heritage*; Wall, S., *Trollope
and Character*.

Trollope, Frances (1780–1863)
Born Frances Milton in Somerset, the
daughter of a vicar, she married in 1809 and
had six children, including the future novelist
▷ Anthony Trollope. She began writing
when she was over 50 to support the family
in the face of her husband's financial disasters
and published in all some 114 books on
travel, and novels. Despite the financial
success of her first book she worked extremely
hard, from before dawn each day, writing and
caring for her family. She visited America for
an extended period and lived in France,
Austria and Italy (meeting the ▷ Brownings,
▷ Dickens and ▷ Walter Landor) for a
few years. Her writing owed its popularity
perhaps to her scathing views of Americans,
also to its exuberant quality and her rather
coarse, humorous women. *Domestic Manners
of the Americans* (1832) brought her fame and
popularity; *Paris and the Parisians* (1835),

Vienna and the Austrians (1838) and *A Visit
to Italy* (1842) were also successful. Her
novels include *The Vicar of Wrexhill* (1837),
portraying a mixture of vice and religion, *The
Widow of Barnaby* (1838) and *The Life and
Adventures of a Clever Woman* (1854).
Bib: Trollope, F. E., *Frances Trollope: Her
Life and Literary Work from George III to
Victoria*; Johnston, J., *The Life, Manners
and Travels of Fanny Trollope: A
Biography*.

Troubadours and Minstrels
Court poet-composers of southern France
(*trouvères* is the term for their northern
French counterparts), who produced a
sophisticated poetic corpus which reflected
and promoted an emerging secular court
culture in early medieval France. The
troubadours are renowned for their love
poetry, and their highly formalized
descriptions of the experience of love and
desire, often expressed in terms of a
relationship of feudal service between the
male speaker and his desired lady (▷ Courtly
Love). But their work is far from
homogeneous: it includes a wide variety of
lyrical genres and sub-genres (laments, dawn-
songs, ▷ pastoral poems and debates), may
be satirical (▷ Satire) as much as
celebratory, and is always highly self-
conscious about the literary nature of the
experience it provides.

Some of the early poet-composers (as
opposed to *jongleurs*, who performed the work
of others) were from the ranks of the social
elite: the earliest poet whose name and work
has survived is that of Guilhelm IX, Duke of
Acquitaine (fl 1071–1127), but although their
milieu was undoubtably that of the court,
most troubadour poets were not aristocrats
themselves but professionals who made their
living from their art. Some work by women
troubadours has survived too, though this has
attracted less attention than that of their male
counterparts.

The legendary status of some of the 12th-
century poets in particular was promoted by
the appearance in the 13th century of prose
'Lives' (*Vidas*), which provided idealized
histories of the poets to match the substance
of their poems. But the high status of these
court poets also derives from their influence
on later medieval writers, including ▷ Dante
and ▷ Petrarch.
Bib: Bogin, M., *The Woman Troubadours*;
Dronke, P., *The Medieval Lyric*; Press, A.
(ed. and trans.), *Anthology of Troubadour
Poetry*; Patterson, L., *Troubadours and
Eloquence*.

Troy
Ancient capital city of the Troad, a region on
the north-west coast of Asia Minor; strictly, the
capital was Ilium (in Homer's ▷ *Iliad*) and
Troy and Ilium have become alternative names
for the same city. Troy is the subject of legends
which began in ancient Greek times and were
added to by the Romans, and further expanded
by medieval writers in Western Europe.
Somewhere behind the legends is a background
of historical fact, but this is very obscure.

1 *Historical background*. Archaeologists and
historians doubted whether a real city of
Troy ever existed, until the German
archaeologist Heinrich Schliemann discovered
its remains near the modern Hissarlik, very
near the traditional site. Subsequently,
excavations uncovered nine cities in successive
levels; the earliest (Troy 1) dates from 3000–
2500 BC, and the latest (Troy 9) faded away
in about the 5th century AD. Opinion has
been divided about whether the Trojan war
was fought against Troy 6, which in fact was
destroyed by earthquake and fire about 1800
BC, or the rebuilt city known as Troy 7A,
destroyed by similar causes in about 1200 –
nearer the traditional date of the Trojan War
in which the city is supposed to have been
destroyed by the alliance of Greek princes.

2 *Greek myths of the founding of Troy*.
These recount a succession of mythical
princes, the earliest being of divine or semi-
divine origin: Teucer, Dardanus, Ericthoneus,
and Tros – from whom the name of the
country and its people originated. Tros's son
Ilus was the founder of the city of Ilion
(Ilium) or Troy. In the reign of Laomedon,
son of Ilus, the walls of Troy were built by
the ocean god Poseidon, to whom Laomedon
refused the agreed reward; he was in
punishment killed, together with most of his
family, by the hero ▷ Heracles. One of his
two surviving children was ▷ Priam, who
was king of Troy in the Trojan war and met
his death after the capture of the city. Priam's
children included: ▷ Hector, the Trojan
hero of Homer's *Iliad*; ▷ Paris, whose
elopement with ▷ Helen was the cause of
the war; ▷ Cassandra, the sombre
prophetess; and ▷ Troilus, around whom
legends were to be constructed in medieval
times. Ilus' brother Assaracus was ancestor of
another line of heroes who were to become
more important in Roman and medieval
European myth: this line of descent went
through Capys, Anchises and Aeneas, who
according to the Roman poet ▷ Virgil was
the ancestor of the Roman people.

3 *Troy epic*. The legendary Trojan war led
to three epics: Homer's *Iliad*, about the siege;

Homer's ▷ *Odyssey* about the wanderings
of Odysseus after the siege; and Virgil's
▷ *Aeneid*, about the wanderings of Aeneas
until he finds his destination in Italy. Homer's
epics arise out of still more ancient legends,
but their own date is uncertain, as, to some
extent, is their authorship; scholars do not
think that they can be later than the 7th
century BC. Virgil's poem dates from the 1st
century BC, and is a deliberate attempt to
emulate Homer. The three poems are the
pattern of a tradition of European ▷ epic –
eg Milton's ▷ *Paradise Lost*.

4 *Trojan myth in western Europe to AD
1500*. The prestige of Homer and Virgil kept
Trojan myth alive and growing in the
▷ Middle Ages of Europe, but these poets
were not the only source of its growth. Two
collections of writing, alleged to be records of
the Trojan war, and to be by Dictys the
Cretan and Dares the Phrygian, date from
the 4th–6th centuries AD, and are the source
of new legends, including Troilus and
Cressida. Virgil's view that the Romans were
descendants of the Trojan Aeneas led to
legends that other European nations have
similar ancestry. For instance, *The History of
the Britons* by the Welsh chronicler Nennius
(8th–9th centuries) declares the ancestor of
the British race to have been Brutus
(▷ Brut), the great-grandson of Aeneas: this
is repeated by the 12th-century ▷ Geoffrey
of Monmouth.

Tudor, House of
The name of a family that ruled over England
and Wales from 1485 until 1603. The
succession was as follows: ▷ Henry VII; his
son, ▷ Henry VIII; Henry VIII's three
children, ▷ Edward VI, ▷ Mary I and
▷ Elizabeth I. Elizabeth died childless, and
the throne passed to the Scottish family of
▷ Stuart, one of whom (James IV) had
married a daughter of Henry VII.

The Tudors were of Welsh origin; Henry
VII was the grandson of Owen Tudor, who
married a member of the Lancastrian branch
of the royal ▷ Plantagenet family; Henry
thus acquired the claim of the ▷ House of
Lancaster to the English throne, which he
won at the Battle of Bosworth, the concluding
battle of the ▷ Wars of the Roses, where he
defeated ▷ Richard III of the House of
York.

The Tudor family was notable for its
abilities. Henry VII was a cautious ruler, who
reconstructed the government's finances.
Henry VIII started the ▷ Reformation in
England by founding the ▷ Church of
England, and this became distinctively

▷ Protestant under the boy king Edward VI. Mary I was a Catholic, married Philip II of Spain, and re-established Catholicism in England, but she died childless, and Protestantism was restored by her sister Elizabeth, possibly the most successful sovereign ever to sit on the English throne. The last ten years of Elizabeth's reign saw the beginnings of the literary flowering known as the 'Elizabethan age'. Her reign was also remarkable for victory over Spain and the beginnings of English overseas enterprise.

Tudor myth
A term used by historians to express the 16th-century belief, encouraged by the royal ▷ House of Tudor, that the Tudors were national saviours from the horrors of the ▷ Wars of the Roses and restorers of legendary national greatness. The first Tudor, ▷ Henry VII, took the throne from ▷ Richard III in 1485 by force of conquest, and since usurpation of a kingdom from its rightful king was a deadly sin, it was important for the Tudors to prove that they had not been guilty of it. Henry maintained that his was the rightful claim, but this was too clearly open to doubt; on the other hand if Richard III was a proved tyrant, the usurpation was justified. 16th-century historians made it their business to blacken Richard's character, not only to please the Tudors, but in reflection of national relief that they had brought the civil wars to an end, with the consequence that Richard is the legendary evil man of English history. Such is the picture given by ▷ Thomas More's *Richard III* (1513), ▷ Hall's *Union of the Noble and Illustrious Families of Lancaster and York* (1548), and ▷ Holinshed's *Chronicles* (1578). The Tudors also encouraged the belief that, as a Welsh line of princes, they could trace themselves back to ▷ King Arthur, the hero of the mythical British golden age; Henry VII called his eldest son Arthur, but he did not live to succeed to the throne. The impress of the Tudor myth is strong on ▷ Shakespeare's ▷ history plays.
Bib: Anglo, S., *Spectacle, Pageantry, and Early Tudor Policy.*

Turgenev, Ivan Sergeevich (1818–83)
Novelist and playwright. Born in Orel, central Russia, educated at Moscow and St Petersburg Universities and Berlin, Turgenev, after a brief spell in the civil service, devoted himself to literature. In 1852 he was imprisoned for a month for his article on the death of ▷ Gogol and was

subsequently banished to his estate. He left Russia in 1861 and, apart from a few visits, remained in self-imposed exile, largely in Baden Baden and Paris, where he died, although he continued to write of Russia and his own class, which he perhaps sensed was doomed. The novels have something of an autumnal character. He fell in love with the singer Pauline Garcia Viardot who did not give him an easy life, and this is also reflected in the novels in the theme of a strong woman and rather weak man. He knew ▷ Flaubert, ▷ George Sand and other French writers, and from 1847 visited England. He was widely read in English, admiring ▷ Shakespeare greatly; he knew and valued ▷ Charles Dickens and ▷ George Eliot, and was acquainted with ▷ William Thackeray, ▷ Anthony Trollope, ▷ Thomas Carlyle, ▷ Robert Browning, ▷ Alfred Tennyson, the ▷ Rossettis and others. He admired, met and influenced ▷ Henry James, and influenced many writers including ▷ George Moore, ▷ Joseph Conrad and ▷ Virginia Woolf. He published a little poetry in 1838 but his first published prose was *A Hunter's Notes* (1847–51). He wrote a series of novels illuminating social and political issues: *Rudin* (1856), *A Nest of Gentlefolk* (1859), *On the Eve* (1860), *Fathers and Sons* (1862), *Smoke* (1867) and *Virgin Soil* (1877). His short stories include 'Asya' (1858), 'First Love' (1860) and 'Torrents of Spring' (1870); his most famous and critically acclaimed play is *A Month in the Country* (1850).
▷ Russian influence on English literature.

Turn of the Screw, The (1898)
A ▷ novella by ▷ Henry James, published in *The Two Magics*. It is a ghost story, about a governess given sole charge of two children, Miles and Flora, in a country house named Bly. She comes to believe that she has to contend with the evil, ghostly influence of two dead servants, Peter Quint and Miss Jessell, over the children, who are ostensibly angelic but invisibly corrupted. Flora is taken away to London by the housekeeper, but Miles, when confronted by the governess with her belief, dies in her arms. The possibility that the governess is an hysteric who hallucinates the ghosts and herself manipulates the children provides a second layer of meaning. This layer is, however, absent in Benjamin Britten's ▷ opera of the same title. James's story, which he described as 'a trap for the unwary', is a masterpiece of ambiguity throughout.

Turnbull, Gael (b 1928)

Poet. Born in Edinburgh, Turnbull has long
been passionate champion of contemporary
writing, especially visible since he set up the
small but influential Migrant Press in the late
1950s. He has also been important in bringing
▷ Basil Bunting's work to prominence in
Britain. His works include: *A Trampoline,
Poems 1952–1964* (1968); *Scantlings* (1970); *A
Gathering of Poems 1950–1980* (1983); and *A
Winter Journey* (1987).

Turpin, Richard (Dick) (1706–39)

A famous English highwayman and thief,
hanged at York for horse-stealing. He was
greatly romanticized by the novelist
▷ Harrison Ainsworth in his novel
Rookwood (1834), in which Turpin's famous
ride from London to York on his mare, Black
Bess, is described. The ride, like other
romantic episodes told about him, is fictional.

Twelfth Night, or What You Will (1599–1600)

A comedy by ▷ Shakespeare, probably
written 1599–1600 or possibly a little later.
Its main source is a prose tale, *Apolonius and
Silla* (1581) by Barnabe Rich, an English
version of an Italian tale by Cinthio
(▷ Elizabethan Novels.) The comic
situations arising from confusion between
twins come down from *Menaechmi* by the
Roman playwright ▷ Plautus; Shakespeare
had already adapted this play into ▷ *The
Comedy of Errors*. Two 16th-century Italian
plays, *Inganni* (Deceits) and *Gl' Ingannati*
(The Deceived) have also been suggested as
possible sources.

The setting is the court of Orsino, Duke of
Illyria, and the house of the wealthy Countess
Olivia, whom he is courting. He uses as a go-
between his page Cesario, really a girl, Viola,
disguised as a boy. The page has already
fallen in love with Orsino, and expresses
sentiments on love so eloquently to Olivia
that the Countess believes herself in love, but
with the page, not with the Duke. Meanwhile
Viola's twin brother, Sebastian, turns up,
wearing the same style of clothes that his
sister has chosen to wear as Cesario; he has
been rescued from shipwreck by a sea-captain,
Antonio, who feels a deep affection for him.
The possibility of confusion is clearly various
and great, and every possible confusion
occurs. A subplot centres on Olivia's drunken
kinsman, Sir Toby Belch, and her conceited
steward, Malvolio; Sir Toby takes revenge on
Malvolio for an insult, and incidentally gets
mixed up in the confusions occurring round
Viola and Sebastian by playing a trick on his
friend, Sir Andrew Aguecheek, who is also
courting Olivia. Sir Toby's interference ends

in a clearing-up of the confusions of identity,
and a subsequent suitable pairing off of
Orsino and Viola, Sebastian and Olivia.

The comedy can be regarded as being
about different forms of love, or imagining
oneself to have fallen in love, and though the
plot is bewildering in summary, it is deftly
worked out theatrically and beautifully
balanced, with finely cadenced poetry and a
more unifying theme than any earlier comedy
by Shakespeare. The title, like ▷ *A
Midsummer Night's Dream* and ▷ *The
Winter's Tale*, indicates the sort of occasion for
which the story is suitable; Twelfth Night was
the last night of the Christmas festival and a
time of licensed disorder presided over by a
▷ Lord of Misrule, such as Sir Toby Belch.

Twentieth-century literature

Twentieth-century English literature may be
divided into two phases: ▷ modernism and
▷ post-modernism. In both phases, changes in
literary technique and subject matter are
closely linked with comparable
transformations in music, art and architecture.
Modernism and post-modernism were also
inspired by, and contributed to, social
changes, and developments in philosophy,
psychology, anthropology and science.
Literary modernism in England started
during the first decade of the century, but
World War I played a major part in its
development, contributing especially to the
sense of radical newness, of the apocalyptic
and of destruction and desolation. The
prolonged and massive slaughter of the war
put paid to the Victorian sense of progress.
Post-modernism remains a controversial term,
but may be linked to a second transformation
of European culture at the end of World war
II. This war produced the death camps and
the atomic bomb, and thus generated a new
sense of man's propensity to evil, of the
destructive potential of scientific knowledge,
and of the perils of political totalitarianism.
The end of Empire and the post-war changes
in the world economy and power-structure
involved new relationships between Britain
and other cultures.

Modernism. In poetry, it was ▷ T. S. Eliot
and ▷ Ezra Pound who were the leading
spirits of modernism, Eliot through his poetry
and his criticism; Pound to some extent in his
poetry, but even more through his role as
man of letters, theorist, starter of movements
and champion of artists and writers. Reacting
against the Romantics, and against the
conventions of Edwardian poetry, these
writers introduced ▷ free verse, fragmentary
and innovative structures and allusive and

eclectic modes of thought. The best-known example of these developments is Eliot's ▷ *The Waste Land* (1922). Powerful accounts of the experience of war are found in the work of the ▷ War Poets, in particular ▷ Isaac Rosenberg, ▷ Wilfred Owen, ▷ Siegfried Sassoon, ▷ Edmund Blunden, Ivor Gurney and Charles Sorley, and later in David Jones's *In Parenthesis* (1937). Some of the War Poets had also been associated with the ▷ Georgian Poets, whose work appeared in Edward Marsh's five anthologies of 1912–22 and who, in technical terms, represented a relatively traditional strain in poetry. Three poets are best considered independently of movements (which are anyway somewhat arbitrary and temporary phenomena): ▷ W. B. Yeats, ▷ Thomas Hardy and ▷ Gerard Manley Hopkins. Yeats, the greatest of modern Irish poets, followed a unique line of development, from the aestheticism of his early work to the eloquent symbolic power of his major poetry of the 1920s and 30s. Hardy, though born in 1840, did not publish his poetry until 1898 (it appeared in eight volumes between 1898 and 1928). His idiosyncratic diction and metrical experiment were to influence, among others, ▷ Philip Larkin. Hopkins had died in 1889, but his lyrical and visionary work had appeared only in anthologies prior to 1918. Other poets who published major work before 1930 included ▷ D. H. Lawrence, ▷ Robert Graves and the Scottish poets ▷ Hugh MacDiarmid and ▷ Edwin Muir.

In the novel the modernist period is dominated by six major figures: ▷ Henry James, ▷ Joseph Conrad, ▷ James Joyce, ▷ Virginia Woolf, ▷ D. H. Lawrence and ▷ E. M. Forster. Each made a distinctive contribution to the modernist transformation of fiction. James's work is notable for a fine moral sense, a complex style, and subtle studies of human consciousness (▷ *The Ambassadors*; 1903); Conrad's for narrative experiment, irony, sense of history and tragic moral vision (▷ *Nostromo*; 1904); Joyce's for linguistic exuberance, broad humanity and structural richness (▷ *Ulysses*; 1922); Woolf's for the representation of the texture of consciousness and for symbolic and poetic qualities (▷ *To The Lighthouse*; 1927); Lawrence's for the exploration of the unconscious and a unique and unrelenting vision of human nature and history (▷ *The Rainbow*; 1915); Forster's for a blend of liberalism with human insight and symbolic power (▷ *A Passage to India*; 1924). Other writers who made significant contributions to modernism include ▷ Ford Madox Ford

and ▷ Dorothy Richardson. Alternative modes of fiction were the popular, realistic, relatively conventional works of ▷ Arnold Bennett and ▷ John Galsworthy, the ▷ science fiction and social realism of ▷ H. G. Wells, and the tragi-comic satire of ▷ Evelyn Waugh, ▷ Wyndham Lewis and ▷ Aldous Huxley.

In the theatre the early decades of the century were dominated by ▷ George Bernard Shaw, who created a drama of ideas which questioned prevailing assumptions and expounded his socialist views. The concern with contemporary social and moral problems in Shaw's work reflected the influence of the Norwegian dramatist ▷ Henrik Ibsen. In Ireland the ▷ Abbey Theatre, Dublin, became the centre of an Irish dramatic revival. In the first decade of the century the theatre staged ▷ J. M. Synge's poetic dramas of Irish peasant life, and in the 1920s the more naturalistic and overtly political tragi-comedies of ▷ Sean O'Casey. In the 1930s, and again in the 1950s, ▷ T. S. Eliot attempted to revive verse drama in English, while ▷ W. H. Auden and ▷ Christopher Isherwood co-operated on plays which, while mixing verse and prose, owed something to the early expressionist work of the German dramatist ▷ Bertolt Brecht.

In the 1930s political concerns predominated in both fiction and poetry. A group of poets led by W. H. Auden employed the ideas of ▷ Marx and ▷ Freud and dealt directly with contemporary social issues such as unemployment, class conflict and the approach of war, as well as exploring psychological states. The main members of this group were ▷ Stephen Spender, ▷ Cecil Day Lewis and ▷ Louis MacNeice. In the 1940s the Welsh poet ▷ Dylan Thomas achieved considerable popularity with his lyrical and rhetorical style of poetry. Novelists of importance who emerged during the 1930s and 40s included ▷ Graham Greene, ▷ George Orwell, ▷ Christopher Isherwood, ▷ Elizabeth Bowen, ▷ Joyce Cary and ▷ C. P. Snow. *Post-modernism.* Since 1945 two tendencies have been evident in English literature. One of these is identifiable with post-modernism considered as a phase of western culture, and is characterized by a continuing interest in experimental techniques, the influence of philosophy and literary theory (in particular ▷ existentialism, ▷ structuralism and ▷ post-structuralism) and a creative interchange with continental, American, Latin-American and other literatures. The second tendency is a reaction against aesthetic and philosophical radicalism in favour of the reassertion of more traditional modes: this tendency has an English and anti-cosmopolitan streak. This division does not necessarily entail a polarization into opposed camps; both tendencies are sometimes found in the work of the same writer.

The reassertion of traditional modes was especially evident in the 1950s. The group of poets who became known as the ▷ Movement favoured clarity, irony, scepticism and a no-nonsense tone: these included ▷ Philip Larkin, ▷ Donald Davie and ▷ John Wain. Just as the Movement was a reaction against the influence of symbolism, of Ezra Pound and of Yeats, so the modernist novel provoked a comparable reaction. The value of the realistic and satirical novel was reasserted by the work of the so-called ▷ 'angry young men', (such as ▷ John Osborne, ▷ John Braine, ▷ Alan Sillitoe and ▷ Kingsley Amis) who expressed a mood of alienation and revolt. Both these movements are, however, partly journalistic inventions, and of less importance than the individual bodies of work which emerged from them: Philip Larkin's sceptical, poignant and witty poetry; ▷ Kingsley Amis's entertaining and often acrimonious tales of English life. In the satirical and realistic vein, ▷ Angus Wilson is one of the most considerable post-war novelists, while ▷ Iris Murdoch, another writer who emerged in the 1950s, combines intricate tragi-comic plots with philosophical and artistic concerns. Murdoch's sense of life as a battle of good and evil is shared by ▷ William Golding, ▷ Muriel Spark and ▷ Anthony Burgess; these writers blend elements of realistic narrative with post-modernist techniques such as intertextuality (sustained allusion to another literary work) and devices which draw attention to the contingency of narrative and its interpretation. In the novel, post-modernism has taken the form of a foregrounding of fictionality which undermines the mimetic illusion, or a multiplication of perspectives which emphasizes uncertainty and subjectivity. Such features are found particularly in the work of ▷ John Fowles, ▷ Lawrence Durrell, ▷ Bryan S. Johnson and ▷ Salman Rushdie. Rushdie also employs the mode of ▷ magic realism, developed primarily by Latin American novelists like Gabriel García Márquez (b 1928). The prose writings of ▷ Samuel Beckett have a Joycean linguistic playfulness, but their experimentalism is dominated by a relentless and progressive minimalism. Other notable areas of development in the post-war novel have been

the feminist novel, science fiction and the fantasy novel.

During the 1960s a number of major poetic talents emerged: ▷ Ted Hughes, ▷ Sylvia Plath, ▷ Charles Tomlinson, ▷ Geoffrey Hill and ▷ Seamus Heaney. All of these poets except Heaney were included in the anthology *The New Poetry* (1962). In the polemical introduction, Al Alvarez championed the cause of poetry which, absorbing the implications of psychoanalysis and World War II, abandoned the gentility of the Movement. Hughes's poetry of extremity, physicality, anthropomorphism and the creation of myth rapidly gained him popularity and a place on the school syllabus. Plath, like Eliot and Pound, came to England from the U.S.A.; she is best known for her powerfully sensuous and symbolic explorations of disturbed states of mind, which associate her with fellow Americans such as Robert Lowell and John Berryman. Charles Tomlinson and Geoffrey Hill are poets with smaller, but devoted followings. Tomlinson is very much a cosmopolitan poet, influenced by American and continental models, and by the painting of Cézanne; his poems render the process and significance of visual perception with an unerring subtlety. Hill's work combines religious and historical subject matter and an almost overpowering sense of tradition with an intensely physical imagination and a post-modernist scepticism about the ability of language to engage with reality. Heaney's work, with its sensuous precision, its involvement with Irish political issues and its deeply personal yet highly accessible concerns, has made him one of the most popular and admired of contemporary poets, pre-eminent among a flourishing group of Ulster poets, including ▷ Paul Muldoon, John Montague, ▷ Derek Mahon and Michael Longley.

The power of English drama to confront contemporary experience was revived in the 1950s by a new generation of dramatists who employed colloquial speech with an expressive and symbolic power which showed the influence of the leaders of modern European drama: ▷ Ibsen, ▷ Strindberg, ▷ Chekhov and Brecht. Foremost among them was ▷ Samuel Beckett, whose play *Waiting For Godot* (first published in Britain in 1955) initiated a new era with its existentialist preoccupations and anti-realist techniques. The ▷ Theatre of the Absurd of Beckett and Eugene Ionesco influenced the work of another of this generation, ▷ Harold Pinter, whose plays explore the ambiguities and failures of everyday communication through terse, minimalist dialogue and significant silences. Blending realism and sinister fantasy, they suggest the fear and violence underlying mundane experience. The dramatists of the 1950s reacted against the upper-middle-class milieu of the work of ▷ Noël Coward and ▷ Terence Rattigan. In the work of ▷ John Osborne and ▷ Arnold Wesker this took the form of so-called 'kitchen-sink drama', which deals with working-class life and social conflict. Since 1950 it has been the drama, more than any other form of English literature, which has directly addressed public issues and exhibited political commitment, frequently of a radical nature. These features were evident in the 1950s and 60s in the work of Wesker, ▷ John Arden and ▷ Edward Bond, and more recently in that of ▷ Howard Brenton, ▷ Howard Barker, ▷ Trevor Griffiths and ▷ David Edgar. Many of the dramatists mentioned here have been brought to public notice by the productions of the English Stage Company, whose home at the ▷ Royal Court Theatre in London has been a centre for innovatory drama since 1956. Another important development has been the success of ▷ fringe theatre in exploiting the dramatic potential of small, open performing spaces. Feminist drama has flourished, prominent exponents being ▷ Anne Jellicoe, ▷ Shelagh Delaney and ▷ Caryl Churchill. Three of the most popular of contemporary dramatists are ▷ Peter Shaffer, ▷ Alan Ayckbourn and ▷ Tom Stoppard. Shaffer's work has a wide range, embracing comedy, studies of obsession and of creativity, and historical epic. Ayckbourn and Stoppard both make use of humour; Ayckbourn in farces of middle-class life, pervaded by a lurking desperation; Stoppard in witty, playful, parodic and allusive dramas which explore political and metaphysical issues.

Across the range of literary forms an increasing contribution is being made by writers from India, Africa, Australia, New Zealand, Canada, and the West Indies (▷ Commonwealth literatures). A primary characteristic of post-modernism as an era is the diversity and rapid circulation of culture, evident not only in the multi-cultural nature of contemporary literature in English, but also in the success of ▷ fringe theatre and small poetry presses and in the sheer range of styles and modes of literature currently available to a large public. But theories of post-modernism also suggest that cultural artefacts function increasingly as commodities, and this emphasizes the extent to which such diversity is dependent upon economic forces and political decision-making, and in these respects the future of literature is highly unpredictable.

Two Gentlemen of Verona, The (1594)
An early romantic comedy by ▷ Shakespeare, probably written about 1594.

Shakespeare's source seems to have been a Spanish tale, Montemayor's *Diana*. The plot is a double love affair with complications; Proteus is in love with Julia, and Valentine with Silvia, but Proteus plays both Valentine and Julia false in his efforts to win Silvia. Julia follows Proteus, disguised as a page, while Valentine, by the contrivance of Proteus, has to flee and takes refuge as the captain of a band of robbers. Proteus in the end is confronted by both Valentine and Julia, and happiness is restored by his suitable repentance. In plot, poetry and characterization the play is clearly very immature, though it has a limpid charm. There is an element of low-life comedy in the role of Launce, servant to Proteus, accompanied by his dog. Julia's disguise and the sentiment of the play look forward to the much more interesting ▷ Twelfth Night.

Two Noble Kinsmen, The
A play of romantic love chiefly by ▷ John Fletcher, perhaps in collaboration with ▷ Shakespeare. It was probably written in 1612–13, and was printed in 1634. The plot derives from ▷ Chaucer's ▷ Knight's Tale about the tragic rivalry in love of Palamon and Arcite.

Tyburn
The site of public executions by hanging until 1783. The gallows stood somewhere near the modern Marble Arch, at the end of Oxford Street and on the edge of Hyde Park, about three miles north-west of the old City of London.

Tyler, Wat
The leader of the ▷ Peasants' Revolt of 1381. He was killed in the street by the Lord Mayor of London in the presence of ▷ Richard II.
▷ Ball, John.

Tyndale, William (?1492–1536)
A translator of the Bible; his version was a principal basis for the Authorized Version of 1611. He was a convinced ▷ Protestant. His other works include: *Parable of the Wicked Mammon* (1528), *Obedience of a Christian Man* (1528), and *Practice of Prelates* (1530). These works influenced the forms that extreme Protestantism, ▷ Puritanism, took in England. While on a visit to the Netherlands, he was arrested in 1535 and burned as a heretic.
▷ Bible in England; Reformation.

U

Udall, Nicholas (1505–56)
The writer of ▷ *Ralph Roister Doister*.

Ulysses
A novel by ▷ James Joyce. It was first
published in Paris in 1922, but was banned in
England for its alleged obscenity until 1936.
In a number of ways the book is an innovation
in methods of presenting human experience
through the novel form, and it is also the
most ambitiously comprehensive attempt to
do so, except perhaps for Joyce's next book,
▷ *Finnegans Wake* (1939). 1 It is an attempt
to present a character more completely than
ever before. The story shows in immense
detail the life of a man during a single day of
24 hours. The man is Leopold Bloom, a Jew
of Hungarian origin living in Dublin; the day
is 16 June 1904. 2 To do this requires a
method of conveying the process of thinking;
Joyce's method has become known as the
▷ stream of consciousness technique,
suggested to him by the work of a French
novelist, Dujardin. 3 At the same time as
seeking to create imaginatively 'a whole
individual', Joyce seeks to make this
individual representative, by setting him
against the background of the oldest
extended portrait of a man in European
literature. He does this by making Bloom
analogous with ▷ Homer's Odysseus, and
by dividing the book into episodes, each of
which corresponds to one in the
▷ *Odyssey*, though not in the same order.
4 Joyce varies the technique of written
expressions so as to make his language as
close an analogy as possible to the modes of
modern human experience. Thus in the
fierce drunken episode 15 (Circe), the
method is dramatic dialogue; in the fatigued
anti-climax of 17 (Ithaca), the questionnaire
is used; in the final episode 18 (Penelope),
the stream of consciousness is used to the
full, without punctuation.

No human experience is complete without
relationship; Bloom is a lonely man, with
numerous casual acquaintanceships. However,
two deeper relationships dominate his story:
there is the physical relationship with his
wife, Molly, whose fidelity he more than
mistrusts, and a spiritual affinity with
Stephen Dedalus, whom he does not meet till
near the end, but who is a lonely young man
unconsciously seeking a father, as Bloom is a
lonely middle-aged man wanting a son. Molly
is analogous to Penelope in the *Odyssey* and
Stephen relates to Telemachus, the wife and
son respectively of Odysseus.

In some respects Joyce is carrying the
artistic devotion of the French novelists to an
extreme: *Ulysses* is an elaborate formal
construction of immense seriousness, showing
a dedication to art for its own sake comparable
to that of the novelist ▷ Flaubert; it is also
a realistic exercise, carrying to extreme the
naturalism of ▷ Zola.

Ulysses
▷ Odysseus.

Uncommercial Traveller, The
A collection of tales, sketches and essays,
descriptive of places, society and manners, by
▷ Charles Dickens. They were published in
▷ *All the Year Round* and reissued in book
form in 1861 and 1868.

Under the Greenwood Tree (1872)
The first of the ▷ Wessex novels by
▷ Thomas Hardy. The story is a village
love affair between a schoolmistress, Fancy
Day, and Dick Dewy, son of a 'tranter' or
carrier of goods. It includes the theme of the
rivalry of the village orchestra, who have
hitherto played the music in church services,
with Fancy, who takes over from them by
substituting the harmonium. The story is
thus slight and idyllic compared to Hardy's
later Wessex stories but it is written with
delicacy and insight. The title is the first line
of a song in ▷ Shakespeare's ▷ *As You
Like It*.

Under Western Eyes (1911)
A novel by ▷ Joseph Conrad. It is set in
pre-revolutionary Russia and in Switzerland,
and is told through the character of the
English-language teacher, who witnesses many
of the events in Switzerland, and reconstructs
those in Russia from the notebooks of the
central character, Kyrilo Sidorovitch
Razumov. Razumov is the illegitimate son of
a Russian nobleman, and has been brought
up in the household of a Russian priest. He is
given to understand that if he behaves well,
his real father will assist him in his career;
accordingly he is studious at the university,
and keeps himself rigorously isolated from
student politics. His enigmatic silence on
political subjects, however, is misinterpreted
by the radical students as signifying that he is
a strongly committed supporter of
revolutionary activity; thus, when one of
them, Victor Haldin, commits a political
assassination and takes refuge with him,
Razumov tries to disembarrass himself by
betraying Haldin to the police. The police,
however, will not allow him to return to his
solitary studies; instead they send him to
Switzerland, ostensibly as a revolutionary

emissary, but actually to spy on the Russian
revolutionaries in exile there. He finds them
to be a circle composed partly of flamboyant
or brutal self-seekers, such as Peter
Ivanovitch, Madame de S., and Nikitin
(nicknamed Necator, the killer). But there are
also idealists of complete integrity, including
Victor Haldin's sister, Nathalie Haldin.
Nathalie is a pupil and friend of the English
language teacher, who thus becomes involved
in the story. She welcomes Razumov as a
revolutionary hero, and the friend of her
brother, for whose death he has in fact been
responsible. Razumov is tormented by his
guilt, his love and admiration for Nathalie,
his horror and contempt of the debased
elements among the revolutionaries, and the
seeming impossibility of recovering his
integrity and living otherwise than by false
appearance. Eventually he confesses the truth
to Nathalie and to the revolutionaries, and is
reduced to total deafness by two blows from
Nikitin. Nathalie is appalled, but understands
him. She has told her English friend: 'You
belong to a people which has made a bargain
with fate, and wouldn't like to be rude to it.'
The western (British and Swiss) attitude to
politics and the individual is such that fateful
choices such as the one forced on Razumov
are not demanded. His drama 'under the
Western eyes' of the English language teacher
is the drama of a nation where the individual
is not permitted to withdraw from political
decision into private life. Razumov spends
the rest of his days as a sick man in Russia,
respected by the best of the revolutionary
circle whom he has known in Switzerland,
and cared for devotedly by one of them.

Underhill, Cave (1634–?1710)
Actor. Underhill joined John Rhodes's
company before the ▷ Restoration, and
afterwards became a member of the ▷ Duke's
Company under Sir William D'Avenant,
specializing in comic roles, including the
eponymous Cutter, in ▷ Abraham Cowley's
Cutter of Coleman Street, the first
Gravedigger in ▷ *Hamlet*, and the Clown in
▷ *Twelfth Night*. Tall, with a large face, flat
nose, and 'unwandering eye', coupled with an
apparently stolid, stupid, or lugubrious
manner, he is said to have inclined people to
laugh, merely by looking at him.

Underwoods (1640–1)
Title of a collection of poems by ▷ Ben
Jonson published in the second folio edition
of his *Works* in 1640–1. In the first edition of
his works (1616) a collection of his poems had
been given the title 'The Forest'.

**Unfortunate Traveller, or the Life of Jack
  Wilton, The (1594)**
A ▷ romance by ▷ Thomas Nashe,
published in 1594. Wilton begins as a page in
the court of ▷ Henry VIII, and then travels
through Europe as adventurer, soldier of
fortune, and hanger-on of the poet ▷ Henry
Howard Surrey. It is one of the first notable
▷ picaresque tales in English. Among other
historical figures, apart from Surrey, Wilton
meets ▷ Sir Thomas More, ▷ Erasmus
and ▷ Pietro Aretino; he witnesses historical
events, such as the struggle between the
Anabaptists of Munster and the Emperor
Charles V, and describes a plague in Rome.
The book is extremely episodic, and Jack
himself has no consistent character. The
narrative begins as a sequence of mischievous
pranks in the manner of the popular 'jest-
books' of Nashe's time, and at the other
extreme goes into brutally realistic
descriptions of rape and of the plague in
Rome. Nashe's story is remarkable for its
creation of a self-conscious narrative voice,
and in its awareness of its status as a text
which is created by the activity of a reader.
At the same time, its delight in the grotesque,
and in a constantly re-iterated discourse of
bodily distortion and pain, serves to make the
work one of the most vivid attempts at
linguistic refashioning in the 16th century.
Bib: Rhodes, N., *Elizabethan Grotesque*.

Unicorn
A mythical beast, with a history that goes
back to the ancient Greeks. It is commonly
represented as a white horse with a straight,
spiral horn projecting from its forehead. In
the ▷ Middle Ages the unicorn was
supposed to possess great strength and
ferocity, perhaps owing to misunderstanding
of the Hebrew word for wild ox in the Bible.
It was also symbolic of chastity, and the horn
was said to be an antidote to poison. In
heraldry, the unicorn was used often as a
'supporter' of a shield bearing a coat of arms;
until 1603, the Scottish royal coat of arms
had two unicorns to support it; in that year
the union of the kingdoms led to the modern
coat of arms of Great Britain, bearing a lion
(for England) on the right, and a unicorn (for
Scotland) on the left. The old folk-rhyme
(▷ nursery rhyme), 'The Lion and the
Unicorn', obviously relates to the conflicts
between the two nations, though it may
earlier have had a seasonal symbolism.

Uniformity, Acts of
Laws passed by Parliament during and after
the ▷ Reformation to secure religious union
in England. The first was that of 1549 (under

▷ Edward VI) and the second and more important in 1559, under ▷ Elizabeth I. Both required the common use in church worship of the ▷ Book of Common Prayer. In 1662, under ▷ Charles II, another Act of Uniformity insisted on its use by all clergy and schoolmasters, and marks the beginning of the ▷ dissenting sects as formally separate religious bodies, distinct from the ▷ Church of England.

Union Jack

Flag of the United Kingdom of Great Britain and Ireland, combining the crosses of St George (▷ George, St) (patron saint of England), St Andrew (patron saint of Scotland), and St Patrick (▷ Patrick, St) (patron saint of Ireland). The St George's cross was rectangular, red, on a white ground. James VI of Scotland added the St Andrew's cross (diagonal, white, on a blue ground) after he became ▷ James I of England in 1603. St Patrick's cross (diagonal, red, on a white ground) was added in 1801 when Ireland was for the first time represented in Parliament at Westminster. 'Union' clearly originates in the uniting of the separate kingdoms; 'Jack' probably derives from the name of James I (Latin – Jacobus).

Unionist

A name used by politicians from 1886 to express opposition to ▷ Home Rule for Ireland, ie a separate Parliament for that country. The word at first united Conservatives with a number of Liberals who resisted the Home Rule policy of their leader, ▷ Gladstone. Later 'Unionist' became synonymous with 'Conservative', and it is still used by members of that party, though it officially accepts the existence of the Irish Republic.

Unitarianism

A doctrine of religion that rejects the usual Christian doctrine of the Trinity, or three Persons in one God (the Father, the Son, and the Holy Ghost), in favour of a belief in the single person of God the Father. It originated in Britain in the 18th century and was in accord with the rationalistic approach to religion of that century. The first Unitarian church opened in London in 1774; many English ▷ Presbyterians (in the 16th and 17th centuries one of the largest sects outside the Church of England) became Unitarians.

United Company, The

Acting company formed by the union of the ▷ King's Company with the ▷ Duke's Company in 1682. In effect the stronger Duke's Company absorbed what had been its rival for 21 years, because of the latter's ailing state. The United Company lasted until 1695, when its leading players, including ▷ Thomas Betterton, ▷ Elizabeth Barry, and ▷ Anne Bracegirdle, defected, because of a dispute with the theatre management, and moved to the remodelled ▷ Lincoln's Inn Fields Theatre. Until that time the United Company occupied both the Theatre Royal at ▷ Drury Lane and the ▷ Dorset Garden Theatre, using the Theatre Royal mainly for plays and Dorset Garden for the larger spectacles and musical performances.

Unity Theatre

A left-wing amateur theatre group founded in London in 1936, with the aim of dramatizing current affairs such as the Spanish Civil War, the popular front against war and Fascism, and the problems of unemployment. The use of theatrical documentary and group composition were innovatory at the time. The company was influenced by European developments in the theatre, but more so by the Living Newspaper method developed in America, 'a method which makes a continual claim to observed truth, to verified fact, whilst at the same time ordering and shaping these facts dramatically so they are charged with emotion'. Notable productions were: Clifford Odets's *Waiting for Lefty* (1936); ▷ Brecht's *Senora Carrar's Rifles* (1938); *Busmen* (1938), a collectively written piece; and ▷ Sean O'Casey's *The Star Turns Red* (1940). A left-wing amateur company of the same name was formed in Glasgow in 1941. **Bib:** Chambers, C., *The Story of Unity Theatre.*

Universities

Until 1828, England possessed only two universities, those of ▷ Oxford, founded from Paris in the 12th century, and of ▷ Cambridge, founded largely by an emigration from Oxford in the early 13th century. Scotland's first university was St Andrew's (1411), followed by Glasgow (1451), Aberdeen (two – 1494 and 1593) and Edinburgh (1582). That of Dublin (Trinity College) was opened in 1591. Medieval universities were in the hands of the clergy, which mattered little when the Church was undivided and Christian belief was almost universal. After the ▷ Reformation in the mid 16th century, Catholics were excluded, and from 1660 (the ▷ Restoration) all Protestants who were not members of the ▷ Church of England were excluded from the English universities, though not from the Scottish ones, since the Anglican Church was not established there.

▷ Dissenters established their own academies in the 18th century, and in the early 19th century a movement was started among prominent Dissenters to establish the University of London, which opened in 1828.

Since then, numerous universities have been founded, many of them since 1945; there is one in Wales, and there are forty-one in England, eight in Scotland, and two in Northern Ireland. The university population in 1985–6 was 310,000.

This rapid rise of new universities has reduced the pre-eminence of Oxford and Cambridge (sometimes referred to jointly as 'Oxbridge') which preserved their superior prestige at least until 1945. The universities of the 19th and earlier 20th centuries were disdainfully designated 'provincial', and were popularly known as 'red-brick' in allusion to their architecture.

Oxford and Cambridge, which became open to the members of all religious sects in 1871, represented an aristocracy of intellect, but their students were also drawn disproportionately from the richer classes, since, until 1945, state grants of money to poorer students were relatively few, and life at these ancient universities was comparatively expensive. Attendance at prestigious colleges, especially when preceded by attendance at one of the more important ▷ public schools (*eg* ▷ Eton, ▷ Harrow, Winchester, ▷ Rugby) was regarded by many people as of even greater social than intellectual importance. It was not uncommon for commercial families (like the Vincys in George Eliot's ▷ *Middlemarch*) to send their sons to Oxford and Cambridge to acquire no more than the manners of their social superiors. In the 1960s, however, the prevailing radicalism among students led them to react violently against this kind of 'Oxbridge' appeal, and some elements in Oxford and Cambridge are themselves seeking to free their reputations from the suggestion of social privilege and conservatism.

Before 1945, British universities were singularly independent of state control; this independence is now threatened by their extensive and growing dependence on government finance. In the 1980s severe cutbacks and even departmental closures have been enforced, though it is still felt politically unacceptable to force the closure of a whole institution.

University Wits
A group of young men in the reign of ▷ Elizabeth I who were educated at either Oxford or Cambridge Universities, and then embarked on careers as men of letters. Their names were ▷ John Lyly, dramatist and writer of the kind of romance known as the ▷ Elizabethan novel; ▷ George Peele, dramatist; ▷ Robert Greene, dramatist; ▷ Thomas Lodge, who tried most of the branches of contemporary literature; ▷ Thomas Nashe, novelist and ▷ pamphleteer; ▷ Christopher Marlowe, dramatist. To these, the name of ▷ Thomas Kyd is sometimes added, although he is not known to have attended a university. Lyly was a writer for court circles, but the others were representative of a new kind of writer (of which ▷ Shakespeare was also an example) who sought his fortune with the general public. Most of them had some kind of influence on, or relationship with, Shakespeare: Lyly used the kind of sophisticated diction which Shakespeare partly emulated and partly parodied in ▷ *Love's Labour's Lost* and elsewhere; Greene wrote a mellifluous ▷ blank verse which anticipates some qualities in the earlier verse of Shakespeare, and was the author of the 'novel' *Pandosto*, source of ▷ *The Winter's Tale*; Lodge wrote *Rosalynde*, the source of ▷ *As You Like It*; Marlowe was the greatest architect of the dramatic blank verse medium; Kyd possibly wrote the first version of ▷ *Hamlet*.

Unto This Last (1860–2)
Four essays on political economy by ▷ John Ruskin. They were intended to be part of a larger treatise, but their publication in the ▷ *Cornhill Magazine* aroused so much hostility that the editor (▷ William Thackeray) discontinued them. The reason for the anger was that Ruskin (an art critic) was, as it seemed to the public, stepping out of his professional function in order to attack the predominant economic theory of trading relationships, which he was considered by the middle-class public unqualified to do. The middle classes were inclined to believe that the subject had been reduced to the clear elements of a science by the political economists and ▷ utilitarian thinkers of the first half of the 19th century – men such as ▷ Jeremy Bentham, Ricardo, ▷ Malthus, James and ▷ John Stuart Mill. Ruskin pointed out that what was called 'political economy' was really 'commercial economy' and that it was untrue since it omitted facts of human nature, unjust since it unduly favoured the employing middle class and uncivilized since it omitted the cultural values that ought to underlie wealth. He found space to praise ▷ Charles Dickens's novel

▷ *Hard Times*, itself an attack on
Utilitarianism. In spite of the hostility and
scorn of Ruskin's contemporaries, much of
his thinking in these essays has been accepted
by later sociologists and economists. The
Indian leader Mahatma Gandhi admitted a
debt to *Unto This Last*, as did a number of
the early leaders of the British ▷ Labour
Party.

Upward, Edward (b 1903)
Novelist. He was educated at Repton School
and Cambridge University with
▷ Christopher Isherwood, with whom he
invented a fantasy world, Mortmere, a setting
for bizarre and anarchic stories which survives
only in Upward's *The Railway Accident*
(1969). *Journey to the Border* (1938) reflects
Upward's commitment to ▷ Marxism; it
ends with the neurotic protagonist rejecting
his fantasies in favour of the 'real world' of
the Worker's Movement. *In the Thirties*
(1962), which ▷ Stephen Spender described
as 'the most truthful picture of life in that
decade', is the first part of a trilogy, *The
Spiral Ascent*, which examines the conflict
between private fulfillment and political
activism. The trilogy concludes with *The
Rotten Elements* (1969) and *No Home But the
Struggle* (1977). Story collection: *The Night
Walk* (1987).

Urania
▷ Muses.

Uranus
▷ Classical mythology.

Uriel
In Christian and Jewish myth, one of the
seven archangels; in Milton's ▷ *Paradise
Lost*, the Regent of the Sun.
▷ Angels.

Urizen
▷ Blake, William.

Urn Burial, or Hydriotaphia (1658)
A treatise by ▷ Sir Thomas Browne,
published in 1658. Its starting point is the
discovery of ancient burial urns in Norfolk;
this leads to an account of various ways of
disposing of the dead, and meditations on
death itself.

Usury
Nowadays, demanding excessive interest in
repayment of a loan. In the ▷ Middle Ages,
any charging of interest was at first considered
wrong in principle, and was forbidden by the
Church; since it was not forbidden by Jewish
law, and Jews were in general forbidden to
compete with Christians in other forms of
trade, money-lending as a business became a
Jewish speciality. The Christians soon found
it convenient to relax their practice, however,
and by the 13th century Christians were
competing with Jews in money-lending. The
more commerce developed, the more
necessary it was for capital to become fluid so
that investment could increase, and
investment could only increase if the payment
of increase on loans became normal practice.
Yet the feeling that *any* taking of interest was
usurious remained, and it continued to be
condemned on principle. The change to the
modern view that demanding interest on
loans is legitimate, and that it is only wrong
to demand excessive interest, is illustrated by
two laws passed by the English Parliament in
the 16th century: in 1552 an Act of Parliament
forbade interest as 'a vice most odious and
detestable'; in 1571 a new Act permitted the
taking of interest up to 10%.
▷ Capitalism; Jews in England.

Uther Pendragon
King of Britain, father of ▷ King Arthur.
In ▷ Geoffrey of Monmouth's version of
British history, his title 'Pendragon' (lit.
'head of dragon') derives from his commission
of two dragon banners, which commemorate
the dragon-shaped portent which appeared to
him at the moment of his father's death.
▷ Merlin is on hand to explain the
significance of the dragon sign, which
anticipates both Uther's and Arthur's great
achievements.

Utilitarianism
A 19th-century political, economic and social
doctrine which based all values on utility, *ie*
the usefulness of anything, measured by the
extent to which it promotes the material
happiness of the greatest number of people.
It is especially associated with ▷ Jeremy
Bentham, at first a jurist concerned with
legal reform and later a social philosopher.
Followers of the movement are thus often
called 'Benthamites' but Bentham's disciple
▷ John Stuart Mill used the term
'Utilitarians'. Owing to their habit of
criticizing social concepts and institutions on
strictly rational tests, the leaders of the
movement were also known as Philosophical
Radicals.
Utilitarianism dominated 19th-century
social thinking, but it had all its roots in
various forms of 18th-century ▷ rationalism.
In moral philosophy, ▷ David Hume had a
strong influence on Bentham by his
assumption that the supreme human virtue is
benevolence, *ie* the disposition to increase the
happiness of others. Psychologically,

Bentham's principle that humans are governed by the impulses to seek pleasure and avoid pain derives from the associationism of ▷ David Hartley. But Bentham and his associates believed that the virtue of benevolence, and human impulses towards pleasure, operate within social and economic laws which are scientifically demonstrable. Bentham accepted ▷ Adam Smith's reasoning in *The Wealth of Nations* (1776) that material prosperity is governed by economic laws of supply and demand, the beneficial operation of which is only hindered by governmental interference. ▷ Malthus, in his *Essay on the Principle of Population* (1798), maintained that it is mathematically demonstrable that population always tends to increase beyond the means of subsistence and Ricardo, a friend of Bentham's, applied Malthus's principle to wages, arguing that as the population increases wages will necessarily get lower, since the increase is more rapid than that of the wealth available to support the workers. Smith, Malthus and Ricardo were masters of what was called the science of Political Economy, and the inhuman fatalism with which they endowed it caused it to be known as the ▷ dismal science. However, it was not dismal for the industrial middle class of employers, whose interests it suited; they were already 'utilitarians' by self-interest and thus willing converts to the theory.

Thus the operation of Utilitarianism in the 19th century was paradoxical. It liberated society from laws which were inefficient survivals from the past (the Elizabethan ▷ Poor Laws) but it replaced them by laws that often operated with cold inhumanity (*eg* the Poor Law of 1834). It reduced senseless government interference with society but its concern with efficiency encouraged a bureaucratic civil service. It liberated the employers but it was often unsympathetic to the interests of the employees. Its principle was benevolence but its faith in reason often made it indifferent to individual suffering. The inhumanity of the creed, and its indifference to cultural values unless they could be shown to be materially useful, caused it to be vigorously attacked by leading writers between 1830 and 1870, including ▷ Thomas Carlyle, ▷ Charles Dickens, ▷ John Ruskin and ▷ Matthew Arnold. But perhaps its sanest and most lucid critic was John Stuart Mill; though himself a Utilitarian to the end of his life, he saw the philosophical limitations of the movement and exposed them in his essays in 1838 on Bentham, and on ▷ Samuel Taylor Coleridge whom he admired as the father of the opposing tendency of thought. Mill's essay *Utilitarianism* (1863) emphasized that some kinds of pleasure are better than others – a distinction Bentham failed to make – and that the highest virtue in humanity is 'the desire to be in unity with our fellow creatures'. Mill was aware, as Bentham had not been, of the importance of the artistic imagination, in particular of poetry, in a civilization.

Our society is still in many ways utilitarian but as a systematic philosophy Utilitarianism did not outlast the 19th century. The last important figures connected with the movement are the philosophers ▷ Herbert Spencer and ▷ Leslie Stephen.

▷ *Unto This Last*.

Utopia (1516)

Woodcut illustration from More's *Utopia*

A political and philosophical treatise by ▷ Sir Thomas More, in the form of an account of an imaginary, newly discovered country. It was written in Latin, and translated into English (after More's death) in 1551; it had already been translated into French (1530), and such was the European fame of the book that Italian, Spanish and German versions also appeared.

The idea of a fictional country was no doubt stimulated by recent Italian, Portuguese, and Spanish exploration, and in particular by ▷ travel literature such as ▷ Amerigo Vespucci's account of his travels (1507). Philosophically, the book is a pure product of ▷ Renaissance ▷ humanism, and like other products of that movement, it was inspired by the ancient Greek philosopher

▷ Plato. The land of Utopia is the Platonic ideal of a country, only to be realized on the assumption that man is basically good. Private property is replaced by communal ownership; there is complete freedom of thought; war is regarded as abominable, and to be used only in the last resort, when it should be waged as effectively as possible, even, if necessary, by unscrupulous means. Earthly happiness is glorified; the good life is the life of mental and physical fulfilment, rather than the medieval Christian life of self-denial and asceticism, but the Utopians are humane and benevolent, not self-indulgent. There is perfect mutual respect, and women receive the same education as men.

Utopian literature

More's ▷ *Utopia* introduced into the English language the word 'utopian' = 'imaginary and ideal', and started a succession of 'utopias' in English literature. The idea of inventing an imaginary country to be used as a 'model' by which to judge earthly societies did not, however, originate with More, but with his master the Greek philosopher ▷ Plato, who did the same in his dialogues *Timaeus* and the *Republic*. *Utopia*'s most notable successors in the 17th century were ▷ Bacon's unfinished ▷ *New Atlantis* (1626), in which science is offered as the solution for humanity, and James Harington's *Oceana* (1656), which put forward political ideas that were to have a powerful influence in America. In the 20th century, ▷ H. G. Wells was, in his earlier days, a vigorous Utopian: *Anticipations* (1901), *A Modern Utopia* (1905), and *New Worlds for Old* (1908). Just before Wells, ▷ William

Morris's *News from Nowhere* (1890) is a noteworthy socialistic utopia.

However, from the 18th century, much utopian literature is satirical, intended to give warning of vicious tendencies of society rather than to exemplify ideals. An example of this is Bernard de Mandeville's (1670–1733) *Fable of the Bees* (1714), about the downfall of an ideal society through the viciousness of its inhabitants; and Swift's ▷ *Gulliver's Travels* (1726) can be put in the same class. In the 19th century the best known examples are Samuel Butler's ▷ *Erewhon* (1872) and *Erewhon Revisited* (1901). In the 20th century, fears for the future of mankind have predominated over the optimism about inevitable progress which was more typical of the 19th century, and this has led to a new kind of utopian writing, portraying our own society set in the future, showing our fears realized. For this kind of work, the term 'dystopia' has been invented. The first striking example was ▷ Aldous Huxley's *Brave New World* (1932), about the deadness of a civilization which has come to be dominated by scientific technology; ▷ E. M. Forster's tale *The Machine Stops* has a similar theme, and both are written in reaction against H. G. Wells's optimism about technology. ▷ George Orwell's *1984* is a nightmare about 20th-century political totalitarianism, the grimmer because Orwell brought the date of his anticipated society so close to the time of writing.

▷ Science Fiction.

Utrecht, Treaty of (1713)

▷ Spanish Succession, War of the.

Vagabonds and vagrants

Generally known today as 'tramps'; men and women who have no settled residence or work, but live by begging or 'casual labour', wandering from place to place, finding shelter where they can or in ▷ Salvation Army hostels or 'casual wards' in the towns. Accommodation for the single homeless is however critically short, due to a combination of factors including rent protection and cutbacks on funding.

The vagrant class probably began in the 14th century owing to the breakdown of the status of serfdom. A ▷ serf was not a slave, but his labour was due to a specific employer – probably a landowner – and his residence was fixed to one place; that is to say, he could not 'sell' his labour wherever he could get the best wages, nor was he free to move about as he wished. The epidemic of ▷ Black Death in the mid 14th century reduced the population so much that there was a shortage of labour, and landowners were forced to find their labourers wherever they could. Nonetheless, wandering labourers were regarded with suspicion, and the government tried to stabilize the working population and relationships with them by the law known as the Statute of Labourers, which sought to fix wages regardless of economic change, and ensure that labourers did not move about. Any who did so became known as 'vagabonds', and were regarded as potential criminals.

The 16th century was a period when vagrancy was a critical problem, for special causes: the dissolution of the ▷ monasteries (1536–9) caused unemployment among monastic servants and tradesmen; ▷ enclosures of land for sheep-farming and parks evicted peasants from their farms. Some of the vagabonds (also called 'rogues') were wandering entertainers, including actors ('players') unattached to noble households; some were pedlars (like Autolycus in Shakespeare's ▷ The Winter's Tale) with goods for sale; a special class were the ▷ gipsies who appeared in England early in the 16th century. Many, more or less inevitably, became part of the underworld of crime, for which a large slang language of 'cant' grew up: Abraham men = pretended lunatics (Mad Tom, in Shakespeare's ▷ King Lear); 'hookers' or 'anglers' = thieves who extracted goods from houses with a hooked stick; 'rufflers' = highway robbers; 'priggers of prancers' = horse thieves. 'Prig' was at this time a common word for thief. This underworld was the subject of a class of popular literature known as 'rogue pamphlets', the most notable examples of which are ▷ Robert Greene's 'conny-catching' ▷ pamphlets, 1591–2.

The government tried to deal with the problem of vagrancy by constructive legislation (eg the ▷ Poor Law of 1601) and by severity – imprisonment, whipping, and, in the 17th century, branding. The Poor Law of 1834 dealt with vagrants (such as were not proved criminals) by regulating workhouses, which were hated more than prison, so that Betty Higden in Dickens's ▷ Our Mutual Friend prefers to die by the roadside. Begging in modern England is illegal, and the tramp population is much reduced and treated, on the whole, humanely, but tramps are still suspected and may find themselves arrested for 'loitering with intent' to commit a crime. ▷ George Orwell assumed the identity of a tramp in order to participate in their world and wrote of his experiences in Down and Out in Paris and London (1933).

Valentine's Day, St (14 February)

St Valentine is the name of two early Christian martyrs. It is also a festival of lovers, and has been this at least since the 15th century. There appears to be no connection between lovers and either of the saints, and the association is probably an example of a Christian feast by chance coinciding with a pre-Christian, pagan one. 14 February is at the end of winter, when animals and birds begin to think of mating. 'A Valentine' was originally a chosen lover of either sex, but is nowadays a card or other token sent, often anonymously, to someone of one's choice.

Valhalla

In Germanic myth, a great hall of ▷ Odin, the chief of the gods, where he received the souls of brave warriors killed in battle.

Valkyries

In Germanic myth, female messengers in the service of ▷ Odin; they decided the issues of battles, and selected the heroes suitable for ▷ Valhalla.

Valley of Humiliation; Valley of the Shadow of Death

Two places of trial through which pilgrims had to pass in ▷ John Bunyan's ▷ Pilgrim's Progress. The Valley of the Shadow of Death is a reference to Psalm 23 in the Bible (Authorized Version).

Vanbrugh, Sir John (1664–1726)

Architect and dramatist, who designed

Blenheim Palace for the Duke of
Marlborough, the Queen's Theatre in the
▷ Haymarket, and (with Nicholas
Hawksmoor) Castle Howard. He also wrote
several plays of distinction. The son of a
London tradesman whose father was a
Protestant refugee from Ghent, Vanbrugh
became a captain under Marlborough, and
was imprisoned from 1690 to 1692 in the
Bastille, where he wrote parts of his play,
▷ *The Provok'd Wife*, eventually staged in
1697. His first performed play was ▷ *The
Relapse: Or Virtue in Danger* (1696), a
satiric response to ▷ Colley Cibber's
▷ Reform Comedy, ▷ *Love's Last Shift*.
He wrote several other lively comedies, mostly
adaptations from the French, including *The
False Friend* (1701), *The Country House*
(1703), *Squire Trelooby* (1704), and *The
Confederacy* (1705), performed by Thomas
Betterton's company at the newly opened
Queen's Theatre, which Vanbrugh managed
for a time with ▷ William Congreve.

Vanbrugh was one of the dramatists singled
out for attack by the Rev. Jeremy Collier in
his *A Short View of the Immorality and
Profaneness of the English Stage* (1698), to
which he responded vigorously in *A Short
Vindication of the 'Relapse' and 'The Provok'd
Wife' from Immorality and Profaneness* in
1698. He was knighted and became
Clarencieux king-of-arms in 1705, and was
made comptroller of royal works in 1714. His
last play, *A Journey to London*, was left
unfinished at his death, and completed by
Cibber as *The Provok'd Husband* (1728).
▷ Sheridan reworked *The Relapse* as *A Trip
to Scarborough* (1777). The original version
was revived in 1947 and again by the ▷ Royal
Shakespeare Company in 1967.
Bib: Whistler, L., *Sir John Vanbrugh,
Architect and Dramatist*; Berkowitz, G. M.,
*Sir John Vanbrugh and the End of
Restoration Comedy*; Beard, G., *The Work of
John Vanbrugh*; Downes, K., *Sir John
Vanbrugh: A Biography*.

Vandals
A Germanic group of tribes which in the
4th–5th centuries AD overran Gaul, Spain, and
North Africa, capturing Carthage, the third
city of the Roman Empire, in 439, and Rome
in 455. They took from Rome all its movable
wealth, and this has led to their reputation
for barbarous destructiveness, though they
were not more destructive than other
Germanic invaders of the Empire.

Vanessa
▷ Jonathan Swift's name for Esther

Vanhomrigh who was in love with him
between the years 1708 and 1723.

Vanity Fair
A town through which the pilgrims pass in
▷ John Bunyan's ▷ *Pilgrim's Progress*. It
is a vivid representation of the pleasure-loving
worldliness of society in the reign of
▷ Charles II, seen from a ▷ Puritan point
of view. 'Vanity' in the biblical sense is
equivalent to triviality and worthlessness, and
it includes all the good things of this world,
when compared to the values of the heavenly
world of the spirit: 'Vanity of vanities, saith
the Preacher, vanity of vanities; all is vanity.'
(*Ecclesiastes* 1:2). The town is a great market
(fair) for these vanities; the townsmen are not
only trivial but heartless, and also bitterly
resentful when the pilgrims despise their
vanities. Faithful is martyred there, but in
Part II he has left disciples behind him and
they are to some extent tolerated. Perhaps
this is Bunyan's way of acknowledging that
the spirit of his age was becoming more
tolerant of the Puritans.

Vanity Fair (1874–8)
A satirical historical novel by ▷ William
Thackeray published in monthly issues. The
title, borrowed from ▷ John Bunyan's
▷ *Pilgrim's Progress*, shows that Thackeray's
subject matter is the worldly, materialistic
society of his time. He shows his men of
religion to be either hypocrites or deluded.
▷ Dissenters, the descendants of Bunyan,
include old Osborne, the arrogant, sombre
and unfeeling businessman;
▷ evangelicalism is represented by the
hypocritical Bute Crawley.

The novel is subtitled 'A Novel without a
Hero' and there is in fact nothing heroic
about the society that Thackeray presents.
However, its heartlessness and snobbery are
skilfully manipulated by the central character,
Becky Sharp, an ingenious and vigorous
adventuress of poor parentage. She begins
her socially ambitious career with a friendship
with Amelia Sedley, the soft-hearted, weakly
sentimental heroine of the book. Becky tries
to marry Jos Sedley, Amelia's brother, a
foolish but rich ▷ 'nabob'. Frustrated in
this, and reduced to being a governess, she
then makes love to the mean and avaricious
Sir Pitt Crawley, but makes the mistake of
marrying his second son, Rawdon, a gallant
but ignorant and dissolute man who, despite
his incapacity, is later made Governor of the
unhealthy Coventry Islands. Her marriage
does not prevent her from pursuing her social
ambitions still further by becoming the
mistress of the aristocratic and degenerate

Lord Steyne. Her ambitions are eventually defeated but she manages to end up as a respected member of society.

Amelia Sedley first marries the worthless young officer, George Osborne, who is killed at the battle of Waterloo. The only fine human values are characterized by his friend, Dobbin, an English ▷ gentleman in the moral rather than the social sense, who eventually becomes Amelia's second husband. The novel is an impressive, if negative, landscape of upper-class society in the first half of the 19th century; its best parts are those that concentrate on Becky Sharp and are written with a keen, sardonic humour. The novel is commonly regarded as Thackeray's most successful work.

Vanity of Human Wishes, The (1749)
An imitation of ▷ Juvenal's Tenth Satire in heroic ▷ couplets by ▷ Samuel Johnson. Where the tone of the imitations of ▷ Horace by other poets is detached and urbane, Johnson's poem affects the moral earnestness and ruggedness of Juvenal. The poet reflects upon the vanity of ambition as illustrated by the lives of various historical figures, including Cardinal Wolsey the statesman, a number of famous scholars, and the 'warrior' Charles XII of Sweden. The poem is remarkable for its sonorous authority of tone, exemplified by the famous first lines: 'Let observation with extensive view,/ Survey mankind, from China to Peru'. It is packed with memorable generalizations, expressing a kind of Christian stoicism. All human activity ends in disappointment and all life ends in death: 'From Marlb'rough's eyes the streams of dotage flow,/ And Swift expires a driv'ler and a show.' The universality of the poem can descend to mere platitude, and its unremittingly emphatic gloom risks lugubriousness. It has consequently been felt to embody a decadent, mechanically inauthentic ▷ Augustanism. In fact, it shows a morally hypersensitive poet taking refuge from despair in satisfyingly rhetorical pessimism and pious abjection: hence its surprisingly moving, personal intensity. It is as much a product of the age of ▷ Sensibility as a 'late Augustan' work.

Vaughan, Henry (1622–95)
Poet. Henry Vaughan, together with his brother Thomas Vaughan (1622–66) the alchemist and poet, was born at Newton-by-Usk in Wales. Vaughan's Welsh roots were to feature prominently in his writing. He termed himself 'The Silurist' after a local Welsh tribe termed the Silures by ▷ Tacitus, and

his third published collection of poems was entitled *Olor Iscanus* (1651), which can be translated as 'The Swan of Usk', a reference to Vaughan's native river. In addition to *Olor Iscanus*, three collections of Vaughan's poetry appeared in his lifetime: *Poems with the Tenth Satire of Juvenal Englished* (1646), *Silex Scintillans* (1650, revised ed. 1655), and *Thalia Rediviva* (1678).

Silex Scintillans perhaps provides a clue as to Vaughan's intellectual identity. The title means 'The Flashing Flint' – an image which was given ▷ emblematic significance on the title-page of the collection where a hand, issuing from a cloud, is shown striking fire from a flintstone, fashioned in the shape of a heart. The image, which signifies a 'stony' heart surrendering flames of divine love when struck by God's spiritual force, suggests ▷ George Herbert's influence on Vaughan. But the image, with its conjunction of stone and fire suggestive of a religious awakening (a theme explored in the collection of poems as a whole), also alerts us to another side of Vaughan's writing. In 1655 Vaughan published a translation of an 'Hermetic' work entitled *Hermetical Physick* and in 1657 appeared his *The Chymists Key*. Hermeticism – the linking of ▷ alchemy, magic and science –might also be thought of as represented in the physical image of the flint flashing with fire. These two elements in Vaughan's intellectual life combine in his poetry in a way which is reminiscent of ▷ Thomas Traherne's concern for expressing the physical and spiritual worlds.
▷ Hermes Trismegistus.
Bib: Martin, L. C. (ed.), *Works*; Hutchinson, F. E., *Henry Vaughan: A Life and Interpretation*; Post, J., *Henry Vaughan: The Unfolding Vision*.

Vehicles
The development of ways of travelling by vehicle in Britain may for convenience be divided into three phases.

1 *Until 1550.* Travelling overland in the ▷ Middle Ages was chiefly on foot (for the poor) or on horseback. The sick and aged would be carried by a portable bed known as a 'litter', suspended between horizontal poles; heavy goods went by ox- or horse-drawn wagons, of a design similar to the farmers' wagons still in use in the first half of the 20th century, and light goods went by packhorse. Travel by barge along the rivers was common.

2 *1550–1830.* The first coach in England was built in 1555, and in the next century

and a half coaches came more and more into use among the nobility; in the 17th century hackney coaches (*ie* coaches for hire) were already beginning to put the Thames watermen out of business. By the 18th century the stage-coach was in use for general travel; it was so called because horses were changed at fixed 'stages' on the journey. More rapid travel was undertaken by privately hired post-chaises. Movement about towns was by sedan-chair, resembling a light litter except that the traveller was seated. The great improvement in roads towards the end of the 18th century led to a great increase in light private carriages of various designs; gigs and curricles were the lightest, favoured by young men.

3 *1830–Present Day*. The first major revolution in transport was the invention of steam railways shortly before 1830; they spread rapidly over the country by 1850, soon eliminating stage coaches except in remoter districts. Private travel was still by carriage; a new style was invented in 1838 for ▷ Lord Brougham and was called after him. In towns, the old kind of hackney carriage and the sedan chair were alike superseded by the hansom cab, invented in 1834. It resembled a more spacious sedan on wheels, with the driver seated above and behind the passengers. The pedal-bicycle came into general use in the 1870s, although primitive forms of it had been invented a hundred years before; it was the first private vehicle available to even the humblest. The motor car made its entry in the last decade of the 19th century. By the next century the best makes – notably the Daimler and the Rolls-Royce – were becoming symbols of high social status. Since the 1950s air travel has become increasingly popular both for long international journeys, such as to America, and for internal flights.

Venice Preserv'd: or, A Plot Discovered (1682)

Tragedy by ▷ Thomas Otway, his sixth and last, set in Venice, and based on an original work by Cesar Vischard, Abbé de Saint Real. Jaffeir, married to Belvidera, pleads with her father Priuli, a wealthy Venetian senator, to make peace with him. Priuli adamantly refuses; he is outraged because Jaffeir, having been made welcome in Priuli's house after saving Belvidera's life, 'stole' her from him, and married her secretly. Jaffeir's friend Pierre enters, and privately they commiserate over the tyranny of the Senate. Pierre's beloved Aquilina has been taken from him by

the rich, elderly senator Antonio, and Pierre tells Jaffeir his property is being confiscated by Priuli, leaving him and his wife destitute. The two plot rebellion and revenge, but the conspiracy fails, and Jaffeir betrays Pierre, who is taken and condemned to death. But at the end Jaffeir repents, stabs Pierre to preserve him from a shameful death, then stabs himself. Belvidera is driven mad and dies. The tragedy was topical: the character of Antonio is a satire on the Earl of Shaftesbury, and the 'plot' referred to in the sub-title was related by many to the 'Popish plot' to murder Charles II and reinstate Catholicism, in which Shaftesbury played a large part. The play has been seen as transitional in the move toward the domestic tragedy of the 18th century.

Venus
▷ Aphrodite.

Venus and Adonis (1593)

A narrative poem in six-lined stanzas by ▷ William Shakespeare. It is dedicated to Henry Wriothesley, ▷ Earl of Southampton. It is based on the Romano-Greek myth of the love of Venus (▷ Aphrodite), the goddess of sexual beauty, for the beautiful youth ▷ Adonis. The poem probably emulates the love poem ▷ *Hero and Leander* by ▷ Marlowe (completed by ▷ Chapman) and is Shakespeare's earliest published work. The poem reflects the extent to which Shakespeare was indebted to Ovid, particularly the *Metamorphoses*.

Verbruggen, John (?–?1707)

Actor, singer, dancer, manager, dramatist. He joined the ▷ United Company in 1688, acting at first under the name of Alexander.

A handsome man, Verbruggen was often in trouble because of his fiery temperament: on one occasion he got into a brawl with the Duke of St Albans behind the scenes at ▷ Drury Lane, and afterwards apologized publicly for hitting and insulting the Duke. He created many important roles, including Loveless in ▷ Colley Cibber's ▷ *Love's Last Shift*, and ▷ Sir John Vanbrugh's ▷ *The Relapse*; Constant in Vanbrugh's ▷ *The Provok'd Wife*; the King of Granada in ▷ William Congreve's ▷ *The Mourning Bride*, and Mirabel in his ▷ *The Way of the World*.

Verbruggen, Susanna (?1667–1703)

Actress. Susanna Verbruggen (née Percival) acted at the Theatre Royal, and later at ▷ Dorset Garden, with the ▷ United Company, and in 1686 married the popular actor and dramatist William Mountfort (1664–92). By 1690 she was recorded as being one of the leading actresses of the company. Two years after Mountfort's death, she married the actor John Verbruggen, and died in childbirth.

Susanna Verbruggen excelled in comedy, was a superb mimic, and according to ▷ Cibber 'gave many heightening touches to Characters but coldly written, and often made an Author vain of his Work, that in it self had little merit.' She was famous for her special talents in men's parts, playing Bayes in George Buckingham's (1628–87) ▷ *The Rehearsal* to great acclaim, and in the roles of hoydens and female fops. Cibber described her performance as Melantha in ▷ Dryden's ▷ *Marriage à la Mode* as '(containing) the most compleat System of Female Foppery, that could possibly be crowded into the tortur'd Form of a Fine Lady'.

Vere Street Theatre, The
One of the first venues used for stage performances after the ▷ Restoration, before the construction of purpose-built theatres, and, like ▷ Lincoln's Inn Fields, it involved conversion of a former tennis court.

Verfremdungseffekt
▷ Alienation effect.

Verges
▷ Dogberry and Verges.

Vergil, Polydore
▷ Histories and Chronicles.

Vers de Société
A kind of poetry originating in France in the 17th century, distinguished by its content, and the treatment of it: light, graceful, witty comment on current manners. In England it was particularly characteristic of early 18th century – much of the work of ▷ Prior, ▷ Gay and ▷ Swift. An example is Swift's *A Soldier and a Scholar* (1732).

Vers Libre
▷ Free Verse.

Versailles
A town near Paris where Louis XIV of France (1638–1715) built the most splendid of all the European royal palaces. It was also the scene of two important treaties: the Peace of Versailles (1783) which ended the American War of Independence, and the Treaty of Versailles (1919), concluding World War I.

Vicar of Bray, The
The title of an anonymous 18th-century song in which a parish priest boasts of having changed his views to fit every political and religious regime from the time of ▷ Charles I to that of ▷ George I. The figure may be based on Simon Aleyn, who actually belongs to an earlier period. He was vicar of Bray in Berkshire from about 1540 to 1588, and changed his religion several times to suit the policies of ▷ Henry VIII, ▷ Edward VI, ▷ Mary I, and ▷ Elizabeth I. 'Vicar of Bray' has become a byword for a time-server.

Vicar of Wakefield, The (1761–2)
A novel by ▷ Oliver Goldsmith written 1761–2 but not published until 1766. Dr Primrose, a good-natured and innocent vicar, lives in comfortable circumstances with his wife and six children. Then their life is overturned by a series of disasters, reducing them to poverty and disgrace; the vicar endures his troubles with sweetness and stoicism. Eventually, they are restored to prosperity by the friendship of a benefactor, Mr Burchill, who turns out to be Sir William Thornhill, whose nephew had originally caused their misfortunes. The novel has conventionally been interpreted as a simplistic moral fable, the chief virtue of which is its sentimentality. Recent critics however suggest an element of satiric irony, drawing parallels with Goldsmith's complex creations in other genres.

Vice, The
A 16th-century term for a type of tempter found in 16th-century Interludes, used for the first time in ▷ John Heywood's *Play of the Wether* (1533), in which Merry-report is called the 'vice of the play'. The figure has precedents in the devil-tempters which appear in earlier medieval drama, and descendants in the individualized tempters in Elizabethan drama.

Victoria
Queen of Britain, 1837–1901. She came to the throne at 17, and had the longest reign in British history. It was also a highly successful reign, for it re-established the prestige of the monarchy, which at her accession was neither popular nor respected. The political conflicts between the monarchy and Parliament between 1603 and 1714 had concluded with the victory of Parliament, and England was a constitutional monarchy, with the king reduced to symbolic status. However, Victoria's grandfather, George III (1760–1820) was insane for the last ten years of his life; her uncle George IV (1820–30) had disgusted the nation by his immoral conduct, thus leaving a bad impression which the reign of

his successor and brother, William IV (1830–37), had been too short to redeem. The other members of the royal family, including Victoria's father, the Duke of Kent, were also in low esteem. Yet when Victoria died in 1901, the monarchy was more popular and respected than ever before, and she succeeded in establishing a model of behaviour for the sovereign which has preserved the popularity of royalty to the present day.

Victoria had dignity and a fine sense of behaviour on public occasions; moreover, she could be pointed to as setting a standard for the domestic virtues of rectitude of personal conduct and devotion to her husband and family, virtues greatly esteemed by the middle classes at the period when these classes dominated national life. She married ▷ Prince Albert of Saxe-Coburg-Gotha in 1840; he died in 1861, by which time they had had nine children. Their court was dull, but it was dignified and decorous.

Victoria was able to perform the role of a monumental symbol for the nation during the 60 years of the greatest prosperity, power and influence that it had ever known. During her reign the British Empire was built up to its greatest extent, and for an empire a monarchy is a much more effective symbolic head than a president. This her Prime Minister, ▷ Benjamin Disraeli, well understood when he induced Victoria to adopt the title Empress of India in 1877. Her relationships with her ministers were not always as happy as they were with Disraeli, but the disagreements were mainly behind the scenes. Her jubilees of 1887 and 1897 were great national occasions, on which the sovereign was identified with the nation as never before since the reign of ▷ Elizabeth I.

▷ Victorian period.

Victorian period

The period coinciding with the reign of Queen Victoria (1837–1901) is commonly divided into three.

1 *1837–1851: the Early Victorian period.* This was a time of struggle and growth; the age of the ▷ Chartist Movement and the Anti-Corn Law League (▷ Corn Laws), but also of the building of railways. The ▷ 'hungry forties' ended with the ▷ Great Exhibition in 1851, the culmination of the ▷ Industrial Revolution, which Britain achieved earlier than any other nation.

2 *1851–1870: the Mid-Victorian period.* Britain had passed the time of the worst popular discontents, and was at her height in wealth, power, and influence.

3 *1870–1901: the Late Victorian Period.* A less fortunate period, when other nations (especially Germany and the United States) were competing with Britain industrially. Britain had acquired much territory in consequence of her pursuit of trade; she now became imperialist in her jealousy and mistrust of other imperialist nations, and the period ended with the imperialist South African War (Boer War) of 1899–1901. Economically, Britain was becoming less the 'workshop of the world' than the world's banker. Domestically, partly in consequence of the second Parliamentary ▷ Reform Bill (enfranchising the town workers – 1867) and the Education Act (establishing a state system of education – 1870) it was a time of popular political and social movements which included the building up of ▷ trade unions and the formation of the ▷ Labour Party.

Culturally, the Victorian period was the age when change rather than stability came first to be accepted as normal in the nature of human outlook. Ancient foundations of religious belief were eroded, among intellectuals, by scientific advances, especially the biological discoveries of ▷ Darwin (▷ Agnosticism). The educated classes and their leaders sought to establish guiding values for living; it was the period of the 'Victorian Sage' – ▷ Carlyle, ▷ Mill, ▷ Arnold, ▷ Ruskin, and ▷ Tennyson – educating the social conscience. The relationship of the individual to himself, to other individuals, and to society at large is the study to which the ▷ novel is admirably adapted; the English novel developed in the works of ▷ Gaskell, ▷ Thackeray, ▷ Trollope, the ▷ Brontës, ▷ Dickens, ▷ George Eliot and ▷ Henry James into the art form of the age. Culturally and in many ways socially, the Victorian period saw the outset and display of the problems which the 20th century has had to solve.

▷ Agnosticism; Corn Laws; Chartism; Exhibition; Gothic Revival; Victoria, Queen; Williams, Raymond.

Vienna, The Congress of (1814–15)

A conference of governments at the end of the Napoleonic War to settle the national frontiers in Europe. Britain, Russia, Prussia and Austria were represented on the side of the allies, and Talleyrand was the French representative. The spirit of the Conference was such as to ignore or repress the nationalistic and democratic emotions aroused all over Europe by the ▷ French Revolution and by ▷ Napoleon; on the other hand, great attention was paid to the Balance of

Power and the preservation of international peace. The consequence was a period of 40 years' international peace, but much popular unrest culminating in the civil wars of 1848, from which Britain was one of the few countries to be exempt.

Vikings

The name by which are known the Scandinavian (especially Danish and Norwegian) invaders of western Europe from the 9th to 11th centuries; they are also called 'Norsemen'. They overran the northern and western coasts and islands of ▷ Scotland, and established a kingdom, centred on Dublin, on the east coast of ▷ Ireland. They also conquered northern, central, and eastern England, but were then defeated by ▷ Alfred of Wessex (reigned 871–901). In northern France they settled in what became known as the province of Normandy at about the same time; from this, two centuries later, they set out (no longer as Vikings but as ▷ Normans) to conquer England. In neither England nor France did the Vikings make a strong original contribution to culture; they became absorbed by the ▷ Anglo-Saxon and French (▷ French Literature in England) cultures respectively, and in the 11th century they imported their Norman French culture to England.

Village, The English

Before the ▷ Norman Conquest of 1066, the Anglo-Saxon rural communities were the 'vils'; these became more or less identified with the Norman manor, the basic social and economic unit of the ▷ Middle Ages. Each manor usually had a 'lord of the manor', or principal landowner, but it was common for one lord to hold several manors and his authority in the village was then exercised (through the manor court or 'court leet') by his 'reeve' or steward. Most of the peasants were 'serfs'; that is to say, in return for their lord's protection, they were compelled to work on his land, owed him certain gifts on such occasions as the marriage of a daughter or the death of the head of a family, and were not allowed to leave their settlements. Their own land consisted of large open fields which were divided into strips for cultivation, each husbandman being awarded particular strips in the manor court. This is known as the ▷ open field system of agriculture. Beyond the arable fields was another area of pasture for grazing the peasants' cattle; this was held in common by all the villagers and was known as 'common land'.

The status of 'serf' could be 'commuted',

if the lord agreed, by the payment of a sum of money in consequence of which the serf might become a landless labourer, free to work for wages, or a tenant farmer, paying rent. There were many degrees and kinds of serfdom, but in no case was the serf a mere slave; he owed his services to the lord, but the lord had no rights over his person. The lord could not usually impose his own will over the manor court which decided the domestic affairs of the village; its law was 'customary', *ie* decided by tradition and precedent, much as the ▷ Common Law of England was. There were even cases when the lord was fined by the manorial court, like any of his serfs, for infringing the customary law. In addition to the lord and his steward or reeve, an important person in each village was the priest or parson (such as Chaucer describes in the ▷ *Canterbury Tales*), supported by 'tithes' or tenths of the agricultural produce of the villagers.

The first important change in this system came as a result of the devastations of the Black Death epidemic of about 1348–49, which greatly reduced the population of serfs and the available labour on the manors. Lords found it convenient to hire labour, and by the 16th century serfdom, with a few exceptions, had gone from England. The peasants were now tenant farmers paying rents to the lord of the manor, who farmed his own land by hired labourers. The next important change was the enclosure of land by the landlords in the 16th century. The profitability of sheep-farming was such as to make it worth the lord's while to deprive the peasants of their holdings in order to turn arable land over to grazing. Enclosures of land continued until the 19th century for different motives, with the consequence that the small farmer ('▷ yeoman' or 'smallholder') ceased, at least from the mid-18th century, to be typical of English rural society in the sense that he is typical, for instance, of French society. They remained, nonetheless, a substantial class, represented by Tom Brangwen in D. H. Lawrence's novel ▷ *The Rainbow*, which begins in mid-19th-century England.

The final important change in the English village was brought about by the rapid growth of towns in the 19th and 20th centuries. The percentage of the population now directly engaged in agriculture is about 5%; the inhabitants of the villages are often town workers who go to their employment in the neighbouring town daily, and others are owners of 'weekend cottages' who live in the town and use the village merely as a holiday resort; farms are commonly large but so mechanized that they employ comparatively little human labour. The traditional pattern of village life, so often described in 18th- and 19th-century novels, has gone. Redistribution of wealth has created a new set of village-dwellers and ways of life, drawing their interest, if not their income, from the countryside.

But running concurrently with this trend is the growing use of villages as bases for commuting to the large financial centres, especially ▷ London.

Villanelle
Originally a rustic song; made into a regular form of courtly grace and sweet tunefulness by the French poet Passerat (d 1602). The form was not much used in England until the period 1880–1910, when a fashion developed – chiefly among minor poets – for all such graceful forms (the ballade, rondeau, ▷ triolet, etc.). It consists of five three-line stanzas and a final four-line one; the first and third lines of the first stanza recur, alternately, as refrains and make a concluding couplet to the last stanza.

Villette (1853)
A novel by ▷ Charlotte Brontë. The title is the name by which the author disguises Brussels, capital of Belgium, where she had been employed as a teacher in a school kept by Monsieur and Madame Héger. The novel is based on her experiences and is told in the first person by the central character, Lucy Snowe. Lucy is a young girl who begins life in secure circumstances and then, as the result of disasters, finds herself deprived of family and means of financial support. After a period of living as companion to an old lady, who dies, she sets forth to seek her fortune in the foreign city of Villette, where she is first nursery governess to the children of Madame Beck, who keeps a school, and then one of the teachers. The main part of the novel is the story of her stormy relationship with Paul Emmanuel, Madame Beck's cousin and her colleague in running the school. She ends up with her own school, established by Monsieur Paul, and as his fiancée, but the conclusion is left uncertain. The novel is remarkable in three respects. First, like Charlotte Brontë's ▷ Jane Eyre, it is ▷ autobiographical in a new and interesting sense: the reader experiences the events entirely through the mind and feelings of Lucy, who thus provides the psychological atmosphere, while at the same time allowing the reader to make judgements of events

independently of Lucy's prejudices. Secondly, the love affairs are so presented that they are shown to be a process of self-discovery by which the lovers learn to know themselves and thus enlarge their personalities. This is especially true of Lucy and Paul but it is also true of secondary affairs in the book; only the trivial personalities fail to undergo this development and are proved trivial by their failure. Thirdly, the novel shows the clash of two cultures – the Protestant ▷ Anglo-Saxon culture of Lucy Snowe and the Latin, ▷ Catholic culture of Paul Emmanuel – and the ways in which the personalities of each transcend their differences so as to achieve mutual admiration and love, although their cultural opposition remains as strong at the end as at first.
Bib: Newton, J., 'Villette' in *Feminist Criticism and Social Change* (ed. Newton and Rosenfelt).

Virgil (Publius Vergilius Maro) (70–19 BC) Roman poet. He was born on a farm not far from Mantua in northern Italy, and is often referred to as 'the Mantuan'. He greatly esteemed the farming section of society to which he belonged, and valued the farming way of life. He was not, from the place of his origin, of Roman descent, but belonged to the first generation of Italians who felt a consciousness of nationhood, with Rome as their capital. By 40 BC he was in Rome, under the patronage of the wealthy Roman patrician (nobleman), Maecenas. He wrote the first work for which he is famous, the *Eclogues* or *Bucolics* (▷ Eclogue), between 42 and 37 BC; their title merely means short, selected pieces, but his intention was to praise the Italian countryside as the Greek poet, ▷ Theocritus had praised the countryside of Sicily. The ▷ *Georgics* (37–30 BC), written at the instigation of Maecenas to encourage a sense of the value of a stable and productive society, is devoted to the praise of the farming way of life. The ▷ *Aeneid* written during the remainder of his life, is an ▷ epic about the travels of Aeneas the Trojan, and emulates Homer's ▷ *Odyssey*. Its purpose is not merely this, but to relate the Romans to the great civilization of the Greeks, on which their own civilization was so much based, by making Aeneas the ancestor of the Roman nation. The *Aeneid*, with the epics of Homer, is one of the basic poems in the culture of Europe and is taken as a standard for what was, perhaps until the 19th century, regarded as the noblest form of literature.

Not even Homer exceeds Virgil in the extent of his influence and prestige in the 20 centuries of European culture. He did not, like all the Greek poets and many of the Roman ones, have to wait for the ▷ Renaissance to 'discover' him, for he was esteemed in the ▷ Middle Ages, when, indeed, he became a legend. This was partly owing to his *Fourth Eclogue* which celebrated the birth of a child who was to restore the Golden Age (▷ Ages, Golden, Silver), a poem which in the Christian centuries was supposed to be a prophetic vision of the birth of Christ. He was thus regarded as more than merely a pagan poet, and ▷ Dante chose him as his guide through Hell and Purgatory in his 13th-century Christian epic, the *Divine Comedy* (▷ Divina Commedia). In direct literary influence, he was, even more than Theocritus, the pattern for ▷ pastoral poetry, and even more than Homer, for the epic, although he was himself a student of both.

Virgin Queen
A name for ▷ Elizabeth I of England, on account of the fact that she never married. The title enabled poets and other writers to associate her with Diana, the Roman goddess of chastity (▷ Artemis). The first English colony in America was called Virginia by ▷ Sir Walter Raleigh in her honour. The iconography associated with the public persona of Elizabeth is elaborate: see Frances Yates *Ashaea: The Imperial Theme in the Sixteenth Century*, and Roy Strong, *Gloriana: the Portraits of Elizabeth I* and *The Cult of Elizabeth I*.

Virtuoso, The (1676)
Comedy by ▷ Shadwell, which satirizes contemporary scientific endeavour, and the efforts of the Royal Society in particular. The virtuoso of the title, Sir Nicholas Gimcrack, conducts absurd experiments on respiration, for example, which mock researches carried out by the physicists Robert Boyle, Robert Hooke, and other members of the Royal Society. In the same famous scene, Gimcrack demonstrates swimming upon a table, without the use of water, which he abhors and considers unnecessary to the purpose. The episode ridicules excessive reliance on scientific theory. There is also some serious romantic action involving two pairs of lovers: Longvil and Clarinda, and Bruce and Miranda, as well as scenes which involve the aged Lady Gimcrack's attempts to flirt with the young lovers. An historically interesting element is the besieging of Sir Nicholas's house by weavers, enraged by his purported invention of a mechanical loom.

Vision of Judgement, A (1821)
Vision of Judgement, The (1822)
▷ Robert Southey's poem *A Vision of Judgement*, which shows the soul of the dead king George III being received into heaven, provoked ▷ Lord Byron's comic masterpiece *The Vision of Judgement*. Byron's poem changes Southey's ponderous classical hexameters (▷ metre) into racy ▷ *ottava rima* stanzas, and reduces George's ascent into heaven to the familiar genre of a 'Saint Peter sat at the celestial gate' story. George arrives, 'an old man/ With an old soul, and both extremely blind' and has to wait at the gate while Satan and St Michael argue over his immortal destiny. Satan claims him, since despite his 'neutral virtues' he was the constant enemy of political liberty: 'The New World shook him off; the Old yet groans/ Beneath what he and his prepared, if not/ Completed'. The debate is interrupted by the arrival of the devil Asmodeus who, hovering over Skiddaw, has caught the ▷ Poet Laureate scribbling away at 'some libel' (Southey's *Vision*) and snatched him up to heaven to give an account of himself. After offering to write both Michael's and Satan's biographies for a good profit ('Mine is a pen of all work'), Southey insists on reading his 'grand heroics' to the assembled throng, and in the ensuing desperate scramble to escape, King George slips into heaven unnoticed.

In his poem Byron finally achieved his ambition to rival his literary idol ▷ Alexander Pope, and the imaginative *élan* and iconoclastic inventiveness of the earlier poet's ▷ *Dunciad* are brilliantly emulated. Byron's *ottava rima* form however, generates a freer, looser tone than Pope's ▷ couplets, allowing for some touches of magnificent political rhetoric. Moreover, Byron's wittily blasphemous treatment of religion shows a characteristically ▷ Romantic insight. Theology is converted into politics: the angels 'all are Tories', Peter is jealous of Paul as a *parvenu*, and Satan is compared to an impoverished Castilian nobleman, wary of the 'mushroom rich civilian', Michael, who has supplanted him. Though Southey's gauchely painstaking poem is now quite unread, Byron's parody remains one of the most imaginative comic works in the language.

Vision of Piers Plowman, The
  ▷ Piers Plowman.

Volpone
A comedy in ▷ blank verse by ▷ Ben Jonson; it was first acted in 1605 or 1606 and was printed in 1607, and is often considered Jonson's masterpiece. The names

of the principal characters signify their roles in the comedy: Volpone = fox; his servant Mosca = fly, since he is a parasite who tries to take advantage of the vicious natures of everyone; the lawyer Voltore = vulture, Corbaccio = crow, and Corvino = raven, because all three birds feed on dead bodies, and all three men hope to gain from Volpone's will when he dies. Volpone is well aware of this, and pretends to be very ill in order to extract gifts from his so-called friends; Corvino, a jealous husband, is even prepared to sacrifice his wife, the pure-hearted Celia. Mosca tries to outdo his master by blackmailing Corvino, and this leads Voltore the lawyer to bring them both to judgement. A subplot concerns an absurd Englishman and his wife, Sir Politick and Lady Would-Be, who are on a visit to Venice (the scene of the play) and are satires on the contemporary English enthusiasm for financial speculation through fantastic 'projects'. The concentrated satire in the ▷ morality tradition of the main plot rises to heights of great poetry: the play is not, as it first seems, a piece of savage cynicism, because the characters, especially Volpone, have a vivid zest for living which is morally condemned only because they carry it to the point of mania. The manias are what Johnson means by ▷ 'humours', and what ▷ Pope in ▷ *The Essay on Man* was to call 'the Ruling Passion'.

Voltaire (pseudonym of François Marie Arouet, 1694–1778)

French writer. He wrote prolifically, and in his own day was regarded as above all a poet and a philosopher, but his international fame rests more on his prose work – satirical essays, and the ironical romance, *Candide* (1759). He is even better known as the pattern of humane intellectuals: he was the determined opponent of beliefs and institutions sanctified by tradition but really disguising the selfishness and inhumanity of privileged classes of society. His dictum *'Ecrasez l'Infâme'* (Crush the Evil) is not, as it has often been thought to be, a slogan against religion as such, but against intolerance, superstition and unjustified privileges supported by religious institutions. He gained immense prestige all over Europe, and corresponded with Frederick II of Prussia and Catherine II of Russia. *Candide* was published very near in date to ▷ *Rasselas* by ▷ Samuel Johnson, and Johnson himself remarked on the extraordinary similarity of their themes, although there was no direct exchange of ideas between the two men. In general, Voltaire had strong sympathies with English trends of thought, and his long visit to England (1726–9) was an important episode in his development. In his *Lettres sur les Anglais* he used his English experiences as a basis for his attack on the French establishment. Correspondingly, Voltaire was admired in England and his influence is pervasive in English 18th-century writing.

Vulcan
▷ Aphrodite.

Vulgate, The
From the Latin 'vulgatus' = 'made public or common'. The name of St Jerome's Latin version of the ▷ Bible, completed in AD 405. For a long time it was the only authorized text for the Catholic Church. The ▷ Protestants in the 16th century insisted on extending Jerome's principle of making the Word of God common to all, by translating it into other languages, a principle now accepted by the Catholic Church itself.
   ▷ Catholicism (Roman) in English literature.

Vulgate Cycle
The conventional modern name for a 13th-century compilation of Arthurian prose narratives which collectively provide an encyclopaedic account of Arthurian history, quests and adventures, comprising the *Lancelot en prose* (which is nearly half the length of the cycle as a whole), the *Queste del Saint Graal*, the *Morte (le roi) Artu*, and two Arthurian pre-histories which recount the early history of the ▷ Grail, going back to its place in the Last Supper, the *Estoire del Saint Graal*, and the early history of ▷ Merlin and the foundation of ▷ Arthur's kingdom, the *Estoire de Merlin*. A matrix of cross-references and prophecies gives cohesion to this massive narrative cycle, and allows access to the comprehensive scope of the material through any one of its parts. The cycle is sometimes called the 'Lancelot-Grail' cycle, or the 'Pseudo-Map cycle' (because parts are attributed to the 12th-century writer Walter Map).

Wace (c 1100–c 75)

Composer of one of the most influential vernacular versions of the history of Britain, the *Roman de Brut* (completed 1155), which is a close reworking of ▷ Geoffrey of Monmouth's ▷ *Historia Regum Britanniae*. In Wace's version, however, the sophisticated court environment over which ▷ Arthur presides is particularly developed. The earliest record of Arthur's ▷ Round Table appears in Wace's text too. What little is known about Wace derives largely from comments included in his other major work of vernacular history, the *Roman de Rou* (an unfinished verse history of the Dukes of Normandy). It seems that he was born in Jersey, had a clerical education, and was made canon of Bayeux by ▷ Henry II. He aspired to court patronage, but he complains in the *Rou* of too little material support for his literary labours. The *Roman de Brut* was reworked in Middle English by ▷ Laȝamon.

Wain, John (b 1925)

John Wain

Novelist, poet and critic. Prose fiction: *Hurry on Down* (1953); *Living in the Present* (1955); *The Contenders* (1958); *A Travelling Woman* (1959); *Nuncle and Other Stories* (1962); *The Young Visitors* (1965); *Death of the Hind Legs and Other Stories* (1966); *The Smaller Sky* (1967); *A Winter in the Hills* (1970); *The Life Guard* (1971); *The Pardoner's Tale* (1978), *Young Shoulders* (1982). Criticism: *Preliminary Essays* (1957); *Essays on Literature and Ideas* (1963); *The Living World of Shakespeare* (1964). His first novel showed him to be a leading member of the school of novelists who concern themselves with the changed surface and social texture of the post-war world. His novels are distinguished by unusual narrative force and economy, and his criticism by the clarity and forthrightness of his judgements. As a poet, Wain's work has been associated with that of the ▷ Movement and with later 'movements' of the 1960s, publishing *A Word Carved on a Sill* (1956); *Weep Before God* (1961); *Wildtrack* (1965); and *Feng* (1975).

Waiting for Godot (1953)

A play by ▷ Samuel Beckett which could be categorized as a modern tragi-comedy. The plot is utterly absurd, which is the point of the play, since it is implying that life itself is absurd (▷ Theatre of the Absurd). Two tramps, Estragon and Vladimir, wait for the mysterious Godot who never arrives. Their only visitors are Lucky and Pozzo, who are locked in a sadomasochistic bonding of master and servant from which there seems to be no escape. Despite its bleak view of life the play has great wit, drawing on the traditions of music hall and popular clowning. It was first performed in Britain in 1955 and is an undisputed landmark in British drama.

Wakefield Cycle

A ▷ cycle of 32 plays (commonly referred to as the *Towneley Cycle* after an 18th-century owner of the manuscript), which was performed at Wakefield, Yorkshire in the 15th and 16th centuries, and which is indebted for some of its plays to an early form of the ▷ York cycle. Parts of the cycle were rewritten and revised in a distinctive nine-line stanzaic form, and modern critics have discussed this revision as the work of a so-called 'Wakefield Master', a dramatist of considerable skill with an interest in the possibilities of black comedy. Six plays, including the 'Second Shepherd's play' are wholly in his distinctive stanzaic form, but traces of his influence can be seen in several other plays too. The cycle exists in a single manuscript copy, dating from the mid to late 15th century. Performance of the plays was prohibited in 1576.
Bib: Cawley, A. C. (ed.), *The Wakefield Plays in the Towneley Cycle*; Pollard, A. (ed.), *The Towneley Plays*.

Walcott, Derek (b 1930)

▷ Commonwealth literatures.

Wales

A mountainous country to the west of
England; it has been united to England
politically since 1536, but it has preserved a
national individuality and its native Celtic
language, though this is now spoken by only
about 20% of its 2.8 million population. The
geography of the country has always been a
hindrance to its unity, and before the English
conquest it tended to divide into separate
northern and southern regions. Just before
the ▷ Norman Conquest of England (1066),
however, Gruffudd ap Llywelyn, a Welsh
prince, succeeded in briefly uniting the
country, and Wales in consequence seemed
formidable enough for the first Norman king
of England, ▷ William I, to establish three
strong earldoms for the defence of England
along the Welsh frontier. These earldoms
correspond to the former English counties of
Hereford, Shropshire and Cheshire, long
known as the Marches.

After his conquest of Wales, ▷ Edward I
in 1301 gave his eldest son the title of Prince
of Wales, a custom which has been followed
by many English monarchs since then.
However, until the 16th century, they did
very little else to govern Wales. The Welsh
have twice been influential in English history
: once they rebelled with considerable success
under ▷ Owain Glyndŵr against ▷ Henry
IV (see ▷ Shakespeare's play *Henry IV,
Part I*), and it was a mainly Welsh army that
won the Battle of Bosworth (1485) and thus
established on the English throne a dynasty
of Welsh descent – the ▷ Tudors. The
second king of this dynasty, ▷ Henry VIII,
passed an Act of Union in 1536 which united
Wales administratively with England. Since
then, the most notable differences between
the two countries have been in language and
religion.

The ▷ Reformation made slower
headway in Wales than in England, but it was
effectively established by the end of the 16th
century. In the 18th and 19th centuries,
▷ Methodism became very strong in Wales,
to the extent that the Church of England was
disestablished (*ie* it ceased to be the state
Church) by a law passed in 1914. The Welsh
▷ Nonconformist churches are thus not
'nonconforming' in the English sense; the
country is divided among a number of
religious denominations (of which
▷ Anglicanism is only one), none of which
have any official pre-eminence over the
others. The Methodist churches in particular
have done much to keep the Welsh language
alive and vital. Education is conducted in the
Welsh language mainly in state schools in
those regions where families are
predominantly Welsh-speaking: one or more
subjects are taught in the medium of Welsh
in 20% of primary and 16% of secondary
schools, whereas Welsh is taught as a language
in 80% of primary and 88% of secondary
schools (these statistics relate only to the state
system throughout Wales). The S4C
television channel began transmitting late in
1982, its Welsh-language programmes being
concentrated in peak-viewing times. The
annual cultural festival of the National
▷ Eisteddfod exists to keep literature in the
Welsh language alive and healthy. The chief
opponent of this nationalism is not English,
but industrialism; the main industrial regions
are in the south-east, around the capital city
of Cardiff, and in the south, around the port
of Swansea. In this area, once dominated by
coal mining, where steel still plays an
important though reduced role, light
industries, especially electronics, (sometimes
through Japanese and American investment)
have relieved some of the problems of
unemployment created by post-war pit
closures. Historically, however, where there
are large towns and urban ways of life, the
essential rural and working-class
characteristics of Welsh life have tended to
anglicization.

Whereas, since 1350, the principal output
of literature in ▷ Scotland and ▷ Ireland
has been in English, though with Scottish
and Irish national colouring, Welsh literature
has chiefly been in the native Welsh language.
It is thus scarcely possible to say that English
literature has been distinctively modified by
the literature of Wales, as can be said of the
literatures of Scotland and Ireland.
Occasionally a writer of English arises with a
distinctively Welsh personality, and this is
true of two 20th century poets, though they
are of very different character: ▷ Dylan
Thomas (1914–53) and ▷ R. S. Thomas
(b 1913), the former rejecting Wales's
language, religion and society, the latter
embracing it, learning Welsh as his second
language, becoming an Anglican priest, a
convinced nationalist and a powerful upholder
of Welsh cultural identity. Nor is it common
for an English writer to learn Welsh so as to
receive influence from Welsh literature,
though this is to some extent true of
▷ Gerard Manley Hopkins (1844–89).
Unfortunately the strength of Welsh literature
is especially its poetry, and poetry is never
fully translatable. Its best period was the
Middle Ages. The majority of Arthurian
legend (▷ Arthur) as we know it is of
French, not Welsh, creation, but the oldest

parts (*eg* the figure of ▷ Gawain) have their roots in Welsh myth.

▷ Anglo-Welsh literature.

Walker, Kath (b 1920)

▷ Commonwealth literatures.

Wallace, Sir William (?1270–1305)

A Scottish national hero of the Scottish War of Independence (1296–1328). He cleared most of the country of the English and then gained a major victory over them at the Battle of Stirling (1297), but he was defeated by ▷ Edward I at Falkirk in 1298. Taken prisoner in 1305, he was brought to trial by the English as a traitor; he replied to this charge that he owed no allegiance to the English king and therefore could not be a traitor to him. He was executed. Wallace was one of the first patriots in a nationalistic sense in British history; he received comparatively little help from the Scottish nobility, who wanted to stand well with Edward. He is the subject of a long poem by Henry the Minstrel ('Blind Harry') written about 1461.

▷ Scotland.

Waller, Edmund (1606–87)

Poet. As with so many of his contemporaries, Waller's career reflects the vicissitudes of public life in the revolutionary period of the mid-17th century. As a member of ▷ Parliament prior to the ▷ Civil War, he opposed the bishops, but, on the outbreak of hostilities, he was on the Royalist side. In 1643 he was found guilty of plotting to surrender London to the Royalist armies, and was banished. In exile in Paris he became friendly with ▷ Thomas Hobbes, before returning to England (having secured permission) in 1651. On his return he wrote a 'Panegyric to my Lord Protector' (1655) addressed to ▷ Oliver Cromwell, but with the ▷ Restoration in 1660 Waller was fully restored to the king's favour, and proceeded to write a second panegyric, this time to ▷ Charles II.

Waller's chief verse collections were his *Poems* of 1645 (a second part being published in 1690) and his collection of religious verse *Divine Poems* (1685). After 1660 he produced numerous occasional verses, including *To the King, Upon His Majesty's Happy Return* (1660) and *To the Queen, Upon Her Majesty's Birthday* (1663). But it is as a transitional figure that he has attracted critical comment. Waller's poetry can be seen as marking the transition from the 'witty' ▷ conceits of poets such as ▷ John Donne to the smoother ▷ neo-classicism of 18th-century poetry. Indeed, ▷ John Dryden, ignoring figures

such as ▷ Robert Herrick and ▷ Ben Jonson, claimed that, if Waller had not written, 'none of us could write'.
Bib: Thorn-Drury, G. (ed.), *Poems*, 2 vol.; Chernaik, W. L., *The Poetry of Limitation: A Study of Waller*.

Walpole, Horace (1717–97)

Letter-writer, antiquarian, connoisseur. He was son of the powerful statesman, ▷ Robert Walpole, and for a short time followed a political career, but he abandoned it, though he continued his interest in politics. His father's influence procured for him three sinecures (*ie* posts under the government which carried salaries though they required very little work) and these enabled him to pass his life as an assiduous spectator and man of pleasure. He developed a strong taste for the Gothic style in all its forms, converting his house (Strawberry Hill, Twickenham, where he settled in 1747) into what he called 'a little Gothic castle', and writing the first of the ▷ Gothic novels, ▷ *The Castle of Otranto* (1764). He is chiefly famous for his letters, however, and is regarded as one of the best correspondents in the best period of ▷ letter-writing. Their main quality is their liveliness, humour, and vividness of observation.
Bib: Lives by Ketton-Cremer and Lewis, W. S.; Stephen, L., in *Hours in a Library*.

Walpole, Sir Robert (1676–1745)

Statesman. He is sometimes called 'the first Prime Minister', meaning that he was the first statesman to hold chief power in the state and at the same time to base this power on the ▷ House of Commons. His practice of consulting his ministers in a private office or 'cabinet' and of insisting that they should comply with his policies or resign their posts has also caused him to be credited with the invention of the Cabinet system of government. In both, he is a figure of importance in the history of the development of the British constitution. He held power continuously from 1721 to 1742, and was enabled to do so partly by his financial ability (he came to office at the time of the ▷ South Sea Bubble crisis), and partly by the incapacity of the German-born kings, ▷ George I (1714–27) and George II (1727–60), to manage English politics.

Walsh, William (1663–1708)

Minor poet, called by ▷ John Dryden the best critic in the language. The youthful ▷ Alexander Pope was encouraged by his advice that 'though we had several great poets, we never had any one great poet that was correct; and he desired me to make that my study and aim'.

Walton, Izaac (1593–1683)

Biographer. Izaac Walton's popular reputation has rested on his *The Compleat Angler* (1653, with revised editions in 1658 and 1661) – ostensibly a fishing manual. The comprehensive nature of the work is, however, hinted at in its subtitle: *The Contemplative Man's Recreation* – an evocation of an idyllic, reflective, ▷ pastoral nostalgia. As a biographer Walton was the author of a series of important 'lives' of 17th-century poets and divines. His *Life of John Donne* was published in 1658, and was followed by lives of ▷ Richard Hooker (1665), ▷ George Herbert (1670) and Robert Sanderson (1678). *The Life of Sir Henry Wotton* first appeared appended to a posthumous edition of Wotton's poetry in 1640 and was published separately in 1651. The two biographies of ▷ Donne and Herbert are the most renowned. Walton is concerned with recording his subjects' piously ▷ Anglican Christian virtue, but they are, nevertheless, important statements concerning the contemporary perception of these major writers and instances of a 17th-century art of hagiographic ▷ biography.
Bib: Keynes, G. L. (ed.), *The Compleat Walton*; Novarr, D., *The Making of Walton's Lives*.

Wandering Jew, The

An old legend, first found in England in 13th-century chronicles by Matthew Paris. The story is that a Jew, following Christ when he was bearing his cross to the place of crucifixion, struck him and cried, 'Go faster, Jesus; why dost thou linger?' whereupon Christ replied, 'I indeed am going, but thou shalt tarry till I come.' The Jew thereafter was condemned to wander the earth, waiting for the Second Coming of Christ.

War Poets

A group of poets who served in the army in World War I, and made poetry out of the experience. The three who are most commonly thought of as 'war poets' are ▷ Wilfred Owen, ▷ Siegfried Sassoon and ▷ Isaac Rosenberg. ▷ Rupert Brooke, who wrote with feeling about the outbreak of war, died before he saw much action; his poetry does not in consequence reflect the shock and violence so evident in the other three. ▷ Edward Thomas was killed in action, but little of his poetry is about the war. ▷ Edmund Blunden and ▷ Robert Graves both survived to write memorable prose works about the war, but their poetry was only indirectly affected by it.

The effect of the war on the verse of Owen, Sassoon and Rosenberg was to cause them to turn away from the rather tepid ▷ romanticism of much pre-war poetry, and to adapt their language to the new and terrible experiences. They thus played a significant part in the renewal of poetic language.

Warbeck, Perkin (1474–99)

The son of a poor citizen of Tournai in Flanders, he pretended to be Richard, Duke of York, one of Edward IV's two sons whom ▷ Richard III had imprisoned in the Tower of London, and whose fate was unknown. He was supported by a number of enemies of ▷ Henry VII, including Charles VIII of France and James IV of Scotland. Eventually he landed in the west of England in 1497, but was soon captured by Henry's troops and hanged. The dramatist ▷ John Ford wrote a moving play about him, *Perkin Warbeck* (1634).

Ward, Edward ('Ned') (1667–1731)

Tavern-keeper and ▷ Grub Street writer, specializing in doggerel verses and humorous sketches of London life. His prose work *The London Spy* (1698–1709) takes us on a tour of the sights of London, and is full of humorous anecdotes and eccentric characters. His *Hudibras Redivivus* was published 1705–7.

Ward, Mrs Humphry (Mary Augusta) (1851–1920)

Novelist. Her most famous novel, *Robert Elsmere* (1888), was a study of religious conflict. Elsmere is a clergyman who loses his faith through a study of the 'higher criticism' of Bible texts. (The novelist ▷ George Eliot lost her faith in Christianity by the same influence.) The purport of the book is that the revitalization of Christianity required more attention to the social obligations of the Church and the abandonment of its supernatural – or at least its miraculous – constituents of belief. The book was very widely read in Britain and America, partly in consequence of a review of it in the *Nineteenth Century* by the statesman, W. E. Gladstone. In accordance with the ideas expressed in the novel, Mrs Ward was a very active philanthropist. She was also an active opponent of the Women's Suffrage Movement (the ▷ Suffragettes). She wrote a number of other novels, and translated Amiel's *Journal Intime* into English.

Bib: Trevelyan, J. P., *The Life of Mrs Humphry Ward*; Jones, E. H., *Mrs Humphry Ward*; Peterson, W. S., *Victorian Heretic: Mrs Humphry Ward's Robert Elsmere*.

Warden, The (1855)

A novel by ▷ Anthony Trollope, the first to be a success with the public, and the first of his ▷ Barsetshire series.

The theme of the novel is the two aspects of the problem of the reform of public abuses. It shows how an office which brings to its holder an income much in excess of his duties may nonetheless be conducted usefully and with integrity, so that to abolish the office may be an act of personal injustice although the abolition may be justifiable on public grounds.

The novel is set in the cathedral city of Barchester in Barsetshire. A clergyman, the Reverend Septimus Harding, is Warden of Hiram's Hospital, a long-established charitable institution for maintaining 12 poor old men in comfort. For this he draws an income which in the course of time has increased to £800 a year, although his actual duties are almost non-existent. However, he maintains with the old men affectionate relationships which are inestimable financially. The wardenship is attacked as a public abuse by John Bold, a Barchester surgeon, although Bold is in love with Harding's daughter Eleanor. Bold is opposed (on the wrong grounds) by the worldly churchman Archdeacon Grantly, who is Harding's son-in-law. Harding resigns his office as a matter of conscience, but the Bishop refuses to appoint a new Warden, and the old men of the Hospital lose the chief solace of their old age.

Wardour Street

A street in London, formerly taken up by dealers in antique and imitation antique furniture. From this arose the expression 'Wardour Street English', for the diction of some historical novelists when they try to imitate the language of the past, and thus produce a kind of linguistic equivalent of imitation antique furniture. The street is nowadays associated with the film industry.

Warner, Rex (b 1905)

Novelist, poet and translator. He was educated at Oxford University, where he met ▷ W. H. Auden and ▷ Cecil Day-Lewis. His allegorical first novel, *The Wild Goose Chase* (1937) examines the political issues of the 1930s through a fantastic imaginary world and concludes with a ▷ communist ▷ Utopia. *The Professor* (1938) and *The Aerodrome* (1941) are similarly concerned with political power, and the conflict of love and personal integrity with totalitarianism. Warner's work is frequently compared with that of Kafka, but also shows the influence of classical literature, of which he made many translations. He also wrote several historical novels, including *The Young Caesar* (1958) and *Imperial Caesar* (1958), which are written in the form of supposed autobiography.

Wars of the Roses, The

A name for the civil wars that were waged intermittently between the two branches of the ▷ Plantagenet family, the ▷ House of Lancaster and the House of York, between 1455 and 1485. The name derives from the emblems chosen by either side: the Lancastrians chose the red rose, and the Yorkists chose the white. The ▷ Tudor rose was a red and white emblem, to signify the reconciliation of the two sides by the marriage of Henry Tudor on the Lancastrian side (▷ Henry VII) with Elizabeth of York, daughter of ▷ Edward IV.

The immediate causes of the war were dynastic; the underlying ones were social. ▷ Richard II, the last Plantagenet king by direct succession, died without heirs, having lost his throne by usurpation to ▷ Henry IV, his cousin and the first king of the Lancastrian line, so called because Henry was the son of John Duke of Lancaster (▷ John of Gaunt). There was always some doubt whether the descendants of another of Richard's uncles, Edmund Duke of York, had not a better claim to the throne, and the disagreement broke into open war in 1455 owing to the drop in Lancastrian prestige when England was at last defeated in the ▷ Hundred Years' War against France (1453). It is here that the social causes become important. In the first place, power in England was in the hands of a number of rich, self-interested and ambitious nobles, whose energies were now no longer taken up by the wars in France. They sought new outlets for their ambition by an attempt to dominate the government at home. Secondly, the ending of the French wars let loose upon England a mass of unemployed soldiers who urgently needed occupation. The interests of the majority of the common people were not deeply engaged, though the towns were disposed to be Yorkist and the rural areas to be Lancastrian. Consequently the Wars of the Roses were felt to be a profitless evil by the majority of the nation. The reign of ▷ Elizabeth I was haunted by the fear that civil wars might recur because the queen (like Richard II) had no direct heirs.

The House of Tudor was correspondingly revered because it brought the wars to an end. An important social consequence was that the medieval nobility which was responsible for their outbreak was much weakened and discredited at the end of them. The Tudor sovereigns raised up their nobility from men of lesser family, from whom the aristocratic families of modern England, *eg* the Cecils and the Russells, commonly descended.

▷ Shakespeare used the Wars of the Roses as the material for his first tetralogy of historical dramas, the three plays on ▷ Henry VI and one on ▷ Richard III. The first three are national tragedies of mounting conflict and destructive hatred; the last shows the evil which has afflicted the country concentrated in one king of diabolic proportions, with Henry Tudor presented in religious terms as the saviour of the people at the conclusion.

Warton, Joseph (1722–1800)
Critic and poet; headmaster of Winchester School and the brother of ▷ Thomas Warton. His *Essay on the Genius and Writings of Pope* (vol. I, 1756; vol. II, 1782) distinguishes the 'true poet' from the mere 'man of wit' and is often seen as a 'pre-Romantic' document, though Warton himself admired ▷ Alexander Pope and edited his works (1797).

Warton, Thomas (1728–90)
Professor of Poetry at Oxford (1757–67) and later (1785–90) ▷ Poet Laureate. His *Poems* (1777) include several ▷ sonnets, a form neglected in previous decades. His *The Suicide: An Ode* and *Verses on Sir Joshua Reynolds' Painted Window*, toy with ▷ 'romantick' excess and ▷ gothic medievalism, without ever having the courage of their convictions, and his comic verse is perhaps more successful. He edited the humorous miscellany, *The Oxford Sausage* (1764). It is in his criticism, with its scholarly approach to early literature that his real importance lies. His *Observations on the Fairie Queene of Spenser* (1754) shows a sensitive historical perspective, and his *History of English Poetry* (1774–81), conveys his fascination with the 'gothic' Middle Ages more convincingly than the dilettantism of his poems. Breaking off at the death of Elizabeth I, it complemented ▷ Samuel

Johnson's ▷ *Lives of the Poets,* and despite their aesthetic differences the two men were on friendly terms. In 1785 he published an edition of ▷ John Milton's early poems.
▷ Romanticism.
Bib: Pittock, J., *The Ascendancy of Taste: The Achievement of Joseph and Thomas Warton*; Rinacker, C., *Thomas Warton: A Biographical and Critical Study.*

Washington, George (1732–99)
Leader of the American rebel forces in the War of Independence (1775–83); president of the American convention, 1787; first President of the United States, 1789. He served in the British forces during the wars against the French and Indians in the 1750s and was a rich and efficient tobacco planter, but he did not play a leading part in American politics until relationships with Britain became critical in the 1770s. He was however noted as 'a young man of an extraordinary and exalted character'. Washington's great-grandfather had emigrated from Britain in 1657.

Waste Land, The **(1922)**
A poem by ▷ T. S. Eliot. It is 433 lines long, and is divided into five parts: I. *The Burial of the Dead*; II. *A Game of Chess*; III. *The Fire Sermon*; IV. *Death by Water*; V. *What the Thunder Said.* There is no logical continuity between the parts, or within each part except for the very short Part IV. The lines vary in length and rhythm and are usually unrhymed, but the poem is not written in ▷ 'free verse'. The author contributed his own (often cryptic) explanatory notes.

The theme is the decay and fragmentation of Western culture, conceived in terms of the loss of natural fertility. Despite the absence of logical continuity, *The Waste Land* possesses artistic coherence brought about by four closely related methods.

1 The use of symbols derived from two anthropologists: Jessie L. Weston (*From Ritual to Romance*) and ▷ James Frazer (*The Golden Bough*). These books relate to ancient myths about the alternation of fertility and barrenness. Although study of them undoubtedly helps the reader to understand the poem, it is not entirely necessary; Eliot intended the symbols to be imaginatively convincing, by their own force, to a sufficiently responsive reader.

2 The juxtaposition of passages with contrasting rhythms, diction, and imagery to accomplish 'a music of ideas . . . arranged not that they must tell us something, but that

their effects in us may combine into a coherent whole of feeling and attitude'. (See ▷ I. A. Richards. Compare Eliot in *Shakespeare and the Stoicism of Seneca*: 'The poet who "thinks" is merely the poet who can express the emotional equivalent of thought.')

3 The use of past history in contrast to the present time, as a means of demonstrating the peculiarities of the present. This method is paralleled by ▷ James Joyce in ▷ *Ulysses* and ▷ Ezra Pound in his ▷ *Cantos*.

4 The use of literary quotation and parody in order to bring out the contrasts of past and present states of culture. At least 35 writers are quoted or parodied in *The Waste Land*.

The poem caused great controversy when it was published, and is often considered to mark the effective beginning of a distinctively 20th-century style of verse, although Eliot had already published verse in the new idiom with *The Love Song of J. Alfred Prufrock* (1915) and *Gerontion* (1920). *The Waste Land* is dedicated to ▷ Ezra Pound, whose extensive revisions of the poem can be seen in the facsimile of the original drafts edited by Valerie Eliot and published in 1971.
Bib: Williams, H., *T. S. Eliot: 'The Waste Land'*.

Water Babies, The (1863)

A moral fantasy for children, by ▷ Charles Kingsley, subtitled *A Fairy Tale for a Landbaby*. The little boy Tom is employed as a chimney-sweep by the brutal Mr Grimes; he falls into the river, gets turned into a water baby and is carried down to the sea. He meets a number of fabulous creatures and undergoes ordeals which effect moral instruction. He emerges purified, on equal terms with Ellie, the little girl in whose house he once swept the chimneys. Grimes is sent away to a penance of sweeping out Etna. The book is partly an attack on the exploitation of child labour and on the brutalization of the poor, and partly a fable about their moral education. Some of the moralizing is offensive, socially and psychologically, to modern readers but the book remains a children's classic for the sake of the ingenuity of its fantasy.
▷ Child labour; Children's books.

Waterloo, Battle of (1815)

An army of British, Dutch, Belgians and Germans under the ▷ Duke of Wellington and the Prussian army under Blücher finally defeated a French army under ▷ Napoleon and thus ended the Napoleonic War (1803–15). Waterloo is a village in Belgium to the south of Brussels. Wellington's army took up its position in squares, which the French attacked unavailingly all day, until Blücher's army came to Wellington's assistance. Wellington's own comment on the battle was that 'it was a damn near thing', and Napoleon's defeat is partly attributable to his failing health. He surrendered to the British and was exiled for the remainder of his life to the island of St Helena. English history represents this as a victory for the English army: in Germany it is seen as an occasion retrieved by the Prussian force from defeat.

Watt, James (1736–1819)

Scottish engineer, inventor, and scientist. His outstanding achievement was the improvement of the steam engine, the principles of which (apart from ancient Greek experiments) had been discovered in the 17th century. Newcomen's improvements on existing models in 1705 enabled it to be put to practical use, but it was Watt in 1763 who made it commercially successful and one of the main instruments for the ▷ Industrial Revolution, the beginnings of which are sometimes dated from his time. Watt's engine made deep mining for coal possible when it was applied to pumping; it could be used for driving machines in factories, and it led in the 1820s to the invention of railway locomotives.

Watts, Isaac (1674–1748)

Poet and hymn writer. He was minister of an Independent church in London until in 1712 ill health forced him into an early retirement in the household of the Whig merchant Sir Thomas Abney in Hertfordshire. His verse appeared in *Horae Lyricae* (1706), *Hymns* (1707), *Divine Songs for Children* (1715), *Psalms of David* (1719). Later in life he turned to prose tracts on theology. Much of his work is charged with a Puritan dogmatism, but sometimes more literary instincts prevail. Watts experimented with classical ▷ metres, and wrote bold Pindaric ▷ odes and distinctive ▷ blank verse. Some of his hymns, for instance 'O God, our help in ages past' and 'When I survey the wondrous cross' are famous. His songs for children became a part of popular British culture, and form the basis of some of ▷ William Blake's ▷ *Songs of Innocence and Experience*.

Waugh, Evelyn (1903–66)

Novelist. Born in London and educated at Hertford College Oxford, he worked for a

Evelyn Waugh

commercialization of death, and *The Ordeal of Gilbert Pinfold* (1957), a pseudo-autobiographical caricature of a 50-year-old Catholic novelist. His post-war work expresses a distaste for, and rejection of, modern civilization, and a pervasive sense of the vanity of human desires. All Waugh's work is marked by an exquisite sense of the ludicrous and a fine aptitude for exposing false attitudes. His comedy is closely dependent on the carefully calculated urbanity of his style. Other novels are: *Vile Bodies* (1930); *Black Mischief* (1932); *A Handful of Dust* (1934); *Scott-King's Modern Europe* (1947); *Tactical Exercise* (1954); *Basil Seal Rides Again* (1963). Story collections are: *Mr Loveday's Little Outing* (1936); *Work Suspended* (1949).

Waugh also wrote travel books, selections from which have been collected under the title *When the Going Was Good* (1946), and biographies of the 19th-century poet and painter ▷ D. G. Rossetti (1928), and of the 16th-century Catholic martyr, ▷ Edmund Campion (1935).

▷ Catholicism in English literature.

Bib: Bradbury, M., *Evelyn Waugh* (Writers and Critics Series 1964); Stannard, M., *Evelyn Waugh: the Critical Heritage*; Sykes, C., *Evelyn Waugh: a Biography*.

while as an assistant schoolmaster, an experience which provided the basis for his first novel, *Decline and Fall* (1928). His satires of the late 1920s and 1930s up to and including *Put Out More Flags* (1942), present the modern world as anarchic and chaotic, and are a blend of farce and tragedy. His technique included the extensive use of dialogue, and rapid changes of scene. Many of the early novels recount the ▷ picaresque and outrageous experiences of a naive central character, such as Paul Pennyfeather in *Decline and Fall*, and William Boot in *Scoop* (1938), a hilarious story of western journalists in Africa. Waugh became a Catholic in 1930; this was initially reflected in his work only in a sense of the transience and emptiness of worldly concerns. But World War II, during which Waugh served with the Royal Marines in Crete and Yugoslavia changed the character of his work; it became more explicitly Catholic, serious to the point of sombreness, and more three-dimensional in his portrayal of his characters. The first novel to show these qualities was *Brideshead Revisited* (1945). In 1961 he completed his most considerable work, a trilogy about the war entitled *Sword of Honour*. Among others of his novels that have achieved fame are *The Loved One* (1948), a satire on American commercialism, extending to the

Waverley (1814)

The first of ▷ Sir Walter Scott's novels, subtitled *'Tis Sixty Years Since*. The hero, Edward Waverley, is a young English officer who visits the Highlands of Scotland just before the ▷ Jacobite Rebellion of 1745. Here he falls in love with Flora, the Jacobite daughter of a Highland chieftain. He joins the Jacobite forces. When these are eventually defeated, Waverley is saved from execution by a senior English officer on the other side, whom he has saved in a battle. *Waverley* is the first historical novel of distinction in English literature, and Scott's vivid description of Scottish society and scenery caused it to be received with great enthusiasm.

Waves, The (1931)

A novel by ▷ Virginia Woolf. It is the story of six characters, each of whom tell his or her own story in monologue, and reflects images of the others in his or her own mind. The monologues occur in groups, at different stages of their lives, and each group is preceded by a passage describing a time of day, from dawn to nightfall. It is a poetic, lyrical and highly patterned work, and presents human existence as an organic process, uniting individuals like waves on the sea. *The Waves* is the climax of Virginia Woolf's experiments in fictional form.

Way of All Flesh, The (1903)

A novel by ▷ Samuel Butler, written 1873–5 and published after his death, in 1903. It is one of the few purely satirical works of distinction of the ▷ Victorian period; the satire is directed against the Victorian cult of the family as the sacred and blessed nucleus of society, and (as so often in ▷ Charles Dickens) the refuge from the harshness of the world. The arrogant, self-righteous, intolerant and stupid kind of Victorian parent is exemplified in the clergyman Theobald Pontifex, father of Ernest Pontifex. Victorian authoritarianism and repressiveness is also attacked in Theobald, seen as a religious humbug, and in Dr Skinner, headmaster of the ▷ public school that Ernest attends. The first 50 chapters of the book are autobiographical; Butler even includes actual letters in the text. The narrative is not told through Ernest (Butler as a boy) but in the first person through his friend the middle-aged Overton, who represents a more tolerant aspect of Butler; by this means, Butler conveys criticism of his intolerant younger self, in the person of Ernest. The book was much praised, especially by ▷ G. B. Shaw.

▷ Autobiography.

Way of the World, The (1700)

A comedy by ▷ William Congreve, produced in 1700. The plot is a complicated succession of intrigues which surround the love affair between the sparkling young rake, Mirabell (a hero in the tradition of ▷ Etherege's Dorimant in ▷ *The Man of Mode*), and the urbane and witty heroine, Millamant. Mirabell's aim is to trick or persuade Millamant's aunt, Lady Wishfort, into consenting to their marriage; and his efforts include pretending to make love to Lady Wishfort herself. This intrigue is frustrated by Mrs Marwood, embittered against Mirabell because he has previously rejected her. Mirabell then attempts further intrigue, and this leads to counter-intrigues by Mrs Marwood in alliance with Mirabell's treacherous friend Fainall, who combines them with conspiracies against his wife, a former mistress of Mirabell's, and blackmail of Lady Wishfort. Mirabell finally succeeds in defeating his enemies and saving Lady Wishfort from the threats against her; in gratitude, she consents to his marriage to Millamant. The intrigues serve as a framework for theatrically very successful comic scenes and imaginatively witty dialogue. Millamant and Mirabell set out the conditions on which they agree to relinquish their freedom and submit to marriage, in a famous ▷ Proviso scene (IV, vi).

Millamant's charm and independence have made her role a star part for great actresses, and supply a main reason for the play's lasting reputation.

▷ Manners, Comedy of.

Weak ending

In ▷ blank verse an unstressed syllable in the place of the normally stressed one at the end of a line; also, a word such as a conjunction or preposition which may bear metrical stress but cannot bear speech stress.

Wealth of Nations

▷ Smith, Adam.

Webb, Beatrice (1858–1943)

Beatrice Webb

Sociologist. She was the daughter of Richard Potter, a railway director and friend of the philosopher, ▷ Herbert Spencer, who exercised a guiding influence over her education. Her mother was a product of the 19th-century ▷ Utilitarian school of thought. She early developed a strong social conscience, which led her to choose as her career the almost unprecedented one of 'social investigator'. Victorian sensitiveness to social abuses was strong amongst the intelligentsia, but she realized that constructive action was hampered by lack of exact information: 'The primary task is to observe and dissect facts.' In order to do so, she took bold steps for a

Victorian girl of the prosperous middle class, such as disguising herself as a working girl and taking employment under a tailor in the East End of London. She and her husband were among the early members of the ▷ Fabian Society, and among the founders of the ▷ Labour Party. Her autobiographies *My Apprenticeship* (1926) and *Our Partnership* (1948) are in the tradition of ▷ John Stuart Mill's *Autobiography* (1873) in being essentially histories of the growth of opinions and ideas; *My Apprenticeship*, however, is very enlightening about social backgrounds in the 1880s, and a valuable addition to the Victorian novels, which, she said, were the only documents for the study of society available in her youth. She and her husband were among the founders of the weekly journal ▷ *New Statesman*, still a leading left-wing journal.

Webster, John (1578–1632)

English dramatist about whom little is known, although his father's life is well documented. He is the author of two of the most famous ▷ Jacobean tragedies, ▷ *The White Devil* (1612) and ▷ *The Duchess of Malfi* (1613), and collaborated with ▷ Dekker, ▷ Fletcher, ▷ Ford and others on a number of plays. Webster excels in constructing richly metaphorical passages and iconographic scenes, but he is less satisfactory on form and in overall conception. His works have been accused of lacking moral fibre in their pursuit of grotesque and titillating images of death.

Wedgwood

The name of a firm of distinguished manufacturers of china. The founder of the firm, Josiah Wedgwood (1730–95), was the son of a potter of Burslem. He perfected an English style of pottery called cream ware, and later Queen's ware. He then developed a new style of classical designs, inspired by contemporary interest in ancient Greek pottery and by the discovery of the Roman city of Pompeii in southern Italy. The most famous of the Wedgwood designers in this style was the friend of the poet ▷ William Blake, John Flaxman. The Wedgwood factory near Hanley is called Etruria; the firm continues in production at the present day. Josiah's son, Thomas Wedgwood (1771–1805), was a generous patron to the poet ▷ Coleridge.

The ceramics industry established by the Wedgwoods in Staffordshire is the basis of the industrial area known as the ▷ Five Towns, and was to constitute the principal setting for the novels of ▷ Arnold Bennett.

Weldon, Fay (b 1931)

Novelist, dramatist and television screenwriter. Her novels are: *The Fat Woman's Joke* (1967); *Down Among the Women* (1971); *Female Friends* (1975); *Remember Me* (1976); *Words of Advice* (1977); *Praxis* (1978); *Little Sisters* (1978); *Puffball* (1980); *The President's Child* (1982); *The Life and Loves of a She-Devil* (1983); *The Shrapnel Academy* (1986); *The Rules of Life* (1987); *The Heart of the Country* (1987); *Leader of the Band* (1988). Story collections are: *Watching Me, Watching You* (1981); *Polaris* (1985). The ▷ feminism of her work is concentrated in the portrayal of the exploitation of women by men in domestic situations, and in relationships. Her tragicomic novels are powerful stories of pain, loss and betrayal, and their desperation is accentuated by the sense of a controlling social and biological pattern which negates the characters' attempts to make choices about their lives. The endings of her books, however, often hint at the emergence of a new and more liberated woman.

Welfare State

A term currently in use to describe the national system of social security brought into being by the ▷ Labour government of 1945–50 and based on W. A. Beveridge's *Report on Social Insurance and Allied Services* (1942). The system depends on National Insurance payments which are obligatory for all adult members of the community apart from Old Age Pensioners and family dependants. It is also funded from general taxation. In return for these payments, made weekly, the state grants financial assistance in the form of family allowances, payments made during sickness and unemployment and to maintain those who have been permanently incapacitated by injury, and pensions for the old. Medical attention is partly free and partly assisted. State education, from the nursery school level for children under five to university level, is also frequently assumed in the concept of the Welfare State.

The Welfare State is thus the opposite of the *laissez faire* concept of the state which prevailed in the 19th century. According to the latter, the state was expected to allow society to develop freely according to 'natural' economic forces. Its function was merely to prevent interference with these in the shape of crime or insurrection. The *laissez faire* concept was never quite supreme; the state always assumed some responsibility for the very poor, for instance in the provision of ▷ workhouses. Nevertheless, *laissez faire* ideas prevailed to the extent that the state was assumed to have no basic responsibility for the individual material welfare of its citizens. The opposite 'Welfare' concept of the state's duties arose partly from the 19th-century religious thinking about society, and partly from the growth of socialist philosophies. The modern Welfare State is generally considered to have had its beginnings under the ▷ Liberal government of Campbell Bannerman and Asquith (1905–14); this introduced old-age pensions, some Unemployment and Health Insurance, and other measures. In the 1980s *laissez faire* concepts of the state have been reasserted and responsibility for individual welfare repudiated as the market economy is encouraged.

Wellington, Arthur Wellesley, 1st Duke of (1769–1852)

General and statesman. By origin, of Anglo-Irish aristocracy. He joined the army in 1787, and between 1796 and 1805 he had a distinguished military career in India, where his eldest brother was Governor-General. Arthur Wellesley then returned to Britain. Between 1808 and 1814 he gained fame for his resistance to the French armies of ▷ Napoleon on the Spanish Peninsula. In 1815, with the Prussian general Blücher, he inflicted the final defeat on Napoleon at ▷ Waterloo. He was created Duke in 1814.

He took part in the ▷ Congress of Vienna, which made the peace treaty with France, and his influence did much to prevent the partition of the country. Thereafter, his career was in British politics, where he was one of the principal leaders of the ▷ Tory (Conservative) party. He gave way, however, over one issue, that of Catholic Emancipation (*ie* granting Catholics full political rights) because he understood its political inevitability; he was less clear-sighted about Parliamentary reform, and was forced to resign in 1830. He again held ministerial posts, though not that of Prime Minister, in 1834, and 1841–6, under the leadership of Robert Peel. After his death, ▷ Tennyson commemorated him with one of his best poems, his *Ode on the Death of the Duke of Wellington*. He was popularly known as 'the Iron Duke', and used proudly to call his London mansion at Hyde Park Corner, 'Number One, London'.

Wells, H. G. (Herbert George) (1866–1946)

Novelist and journalist. He was brought up in the lower middle class, the son of a professional cricketer; in 1888 he took an

H. G. Wells

excellent degree in science at London University. His social origins and his education explain much of his approach to life as a writer. The great novelist of the 19th-century lower middle classes is ▷ Dickens, and some of H. G. Wells's best fiction is about the same field of society; novels such as ▷ *Kipps* (1905) and *The History of Mr Polly* (1910) are of this sort, and they have the kind of vigorous humour and sharp visualization that is characteristic of early Dickens. On the other hand, rising into the educated class at a time of rapid scientific and technical progress, he ignored the values of traditional culture and art, and became fascinated with the prospects that science offered, for good as well as for ill. This side of him produced a different kind of writing: Wells was one of the inventors of ▷ science-fiction. *The Time Machine* (1895), *The Invisible Man* (1897), *The War of the Worlds* (1898) and *The First Men in the Moon* (1901) are examples of his fantasies. But his social experience and his interest in technology also drew him to writing fictional-sociological studies in which he surveyed and analysed, often with the same Dickensian humour, the society of his time; *Tono–Bungay* (1908) is perhaps the best of these. Other examples are *Ann Veronica* (1909) about the problems connected with newly emancipated women, *The New Machiavelli* (1911) about socialist thinking – Wells had joined the ▷ Fabians in 1903 – and *Mr Britling Sees It Through* (1916) about World War I seen from the point of view of the 'Home Front'. But the interest in science also made him a ▷ utopian optimist, and this point of view caused him to write such didactic works as *A Modern Utopia* (1905) and *New Worlds For Old* (1908). There was always a great deal of naivety in Wells's optimism, and later in his life he paid the penalty by reacting into excessive gloom, in *Mind at the End of its Tether* (1945). He declared that *The Open Conspiracy* (1928) contained the essence of his philosophy. He was never a deep thinker, however; his work lives by the vitality of his humour and by the urgency with which he pressed his ideas. This urgency necessarily made him a popularizer, and his most notable work of popularization was *The Outline of History* (1920).

In some ways Wells resembles his contemporary, the dramatist ▷ George Bernard Shaw; both were socialists, both felt the urgency to enlighten mankind as quickly as possible, and both cared more that their works should have immediate effect than that they should be works of art – Wells told the novelist ▷ Henry James that he would rather be called a journalist than an artist. Possibly the most penetrating remark on Wells was that addressed to him by the novelist ▷ Joseph Conrad: 'You don't really care for people, but you think they can be improved; I do, but I know they can't.'
Bib: Mackenzie, N. and J., *The Time Traveller: Life of H. G. Wells*; Bergonzi, B., *The Early H. G. Wells* and *H. G. Wells: Twentieth-Century Views*; Parrinder, P. (ed.), *H. G. Wells: the Critical Heritage*.

Welsh terms
bardd gwlad Country poet or folk poet. There were instances of their skills being practised in the English language, as, for example, in Gower, which was predominantly English-speaking.
traethodl Seven syllable lines with rhymed couplets, an accented syllable usually rhyming with an unaccented one.
cwywydd Traethodl with the addition of a form of *cynghanedd*.
cynghanedd Internal rhymes with alliteration in a fixed metrical pattern.
englyn The most common is a four-line stanza of ten, six, seven and seven syllables. There is a break, like a caesura, after the seventh syllable of the first line, and it is on this syllable that the rhyme usually occurs with the end syllable of the second, third and fourth lines. Thus each line rhymes with the others, though the first-line rhyme is internal. Most commonly occurring on the seventh syllable, it may occur on the eighth or ninth.

dyfalu A series of comparisons.
   ▷ Anglo-Welsh literature.

Werewolf
According to an ancient superstition, a person capable of transforming himself into a wolf – sometimes into another animal, such as a hare, *eg* in Scotland. The superstition may have connection with a widespread belief that the corn-spirit sometimes embodied himself as a wolf. The superstition existed in England at least until the 18th century.

Wesker, Arnold (b 1932)
British dramatist, born in London's East End and son of a Russian Jewish tailor. After military service, he became a professional pastry-cook, and then entered the London School of Film Technique. ▷ John Osborne's ▷ *Look Back in Anger* (1956) influenced him to concentrate on the theatre. In 1961, he became Director of Centre Forty-two, intended to break down such barriers to popular appreciation of the arts as commercialism and intellectual and social snobbery, or social fragmentation due to restricted ways of life and inarticulacy in the shaping of goals. These obstacles to communication in the mass of society are the subject matter of his plays which are pervaded by a search for cordial understanding and sympathy. His plays include: *Chicken Soup with Barley* (1958); *Roots* (1959); *The Kitchen* (1960); *I'm Talking about Jerusalem* (1960); *Chips with Everything* (1962); *The Four Seasons* (1966); *Their Very Own* and *Golden City* (1966); *The Friends* (1970); *The Old Ones* (1972); *The Wedding Feast* (1974); *The Merchant* (1976); *Love Letters on Blue Paper* (1977); *Caritas* (1981).   •

Wesker was one of the leaders of the post-war dramatic revival, together with ▷ John Osborne, ▷ Harold Pinter, and ▷ John Arden.
Bib: Taylor, J. R. *Anger and After;* Ribalow, H. U. *Arnold Wesker*; Leeming, G., *Arnold Wesker* (Writers & their Work series).

Wesley, Charles (1707–88)
Hymn writer. Brother of the evangelist, ▷ John Wesley, he was the poet of the ▷ Methodist movement. He wrote about 6,500 hymns of unequal merit. Some of them, such as 'Hark the herald Angels Sing', 'Jesu, lover of my soul', and 'Love divine all Love's excelling' show genuine poetic feeling, and are well known.

Wesley, John (1703–91)
Evangelist, and founder of the ▷ Methodist religious movement. At Oxford, with his brother Charles, he became the centre of a

society which regulated the lives of its members; this led to their being described as 'Methodists'. He was at first a strict ▷ Anglican, conforming rigidly to Church of England liturgies and doctrines, but on a voyage to America in 1735 he became deeply impressed by the purity and undogmatic spirit of fellow-passengers belonging to the German sect known as the Moravians. On his return to England, Wesley preached up and down Britain. Both the Church of England and the ▷ Dissenters who were heirs of the 17th-century ▷ Puritans had by now relatively little to offer to the minds of the simple people; reaction against the violent conflicts of the previous century had caused the clergy of all denominations to obscure the sense of religion as a power in individual lives. Wesley taught both that every man was naturally a sinner, and that the power of God was available to all for spiritual salvation. In this he followed the Arminian (▷ Arminianism) tradition of religious belief, instead of the belief in ▷ Predestination more prevalent among the 17th-century Puritans. Wesley's direct challenge to the hearts and the wills of his hearers caused deep psychological disturbances, and the Methodists were despised by many for the hysteria and emotionalism of their meetings. Nonetheless, the influence of Wesley was extensive and profound, and bore fruit in other religious revivals in the 19th century. He was courteous and had a pleasant wit. When confronted by an arrogant opponent in a narrow street who declared 'I never make way for fools!', Wesley stood aside politely, replying: 'I always do.'

▷ Sermons.

Wessex
The kingdom of the West Saxons from the 6th century till the reign of ▷ Alfred at the end of the 9th, after which it developed into the kingdom of England. The capital was the town of Winchester in Hampshire, and the area also included Dorset, Somerset, Wiltshire, and Berkshire. The name of Wessex was revived by the novelist and poet ▷ Thomas Hardy for his regional novels.

▷ Barnes, William.

West Indian, The (1771)
Comedy by ▷ Richard Cumberland. Belcour has been brought up in the West Indies; he is honest but unsophisticated. Arriving in London, he falls in love with Louisa, the daughter of the impoverished Captain Dudley, but is deceived into thinking her the mistress of Charles, who is in fact her brother. He makes advances to her as if she were a whore and she repels him with the classic phrase, 'Unhand me, sir!'. Meanwhile, Charles loves his wealthy cousin Charlotte, but will not acknowledge the fact because of his own poverty. Belcour comes to the aid of Captain Dudley. Eventually Charles and Louisa are revealed as heirs, Belcour and Louisa become reconciled and are married, and Charles marries Charlotte. The play contains references to the workings of Providence in refusing to allow 'innocence to be oppressed', or cruelty and cunning to prosper; it has often been cited as an archetypal example of sentimentality in the drama of the period.

Westminster, The Palace of
Though it still officially bears this title, the building is more familiarly known as the ▷ Houses of Parliament. It already existed as a palace under ▷ Edward the Confessor. As such, it was the meeting-place of the ▷ House of Lords and the ▷ House of Commons in the ▷ Middle Ages. In 1512, the palace was damaged by fire and it has not been a royal residence since. In 1834, it was further and more seriously damaged, and all that now remains of the medieval palace is the great Hall built by William II in 1097 and reroofed by ▷ Richard II in 1399, and the crypt to the chapel of St Stephen's, under the present House of Commons. The rest of the present building dates 1840–67; it contains the two chambers of the House of Lords and the House of Commons. The latter was destroyed by a bomb during World War II, but it was afterwards reconstructed identically in every detail.

Westminster Hall has been the scene of many famous state trials including those of the Scottish patriot ▷ William Wallace; the kings ▷ Richard II and ▷ Charles I; the Catholic martyrs ▷ Sir Thomas More and Edmund Campion; George IV's queen Caroline (1820), and the Governor-General of India, Warren Hastings (1788–95).

Westminster Abbey
Originally an abbey of monks on the bank of the Thames and to the west of the City of London. The abbey was dissolved by ▷ Henry VIII in 1539, and the present building is the old abbey church. It was built by ▷ King Edward the Confessor in 1065 and rebuilt by ▷ Henry III, whose structure still stands. It has long been the state church of England; since ▷ William I the sovereigns have been crowned in it, and many have been buried there. To be buried in Westminster Abbey is a national honour, and the church is in consequence lined with monuments. The

Poets' Corner contains monuments to eminent writers, not all of whom are buried in the Abbey; they include ▷ Chaucer, ▷ Spenser, ▷ Shakespeare, ▷ Ben Jonson and ▷ Milton.

Westminster Review

It was founded in 1823 as a vehicle for the Benthamite (otherwise known as the Utilitarian (▷ Utilitarianism)) school of thought, and at first kept severely to its principles. Its politics of ruthless, scientific institutional reform made it not only a strong opponent of the Tory *Quarterly Review* but put it well to the left of the *Edinburgh Review*. It appealed to a narrower public, and tended, in the Utilitarian manner, to regard the arts with disdain. In 1836 it combined with the now livelier Utilitarian *London Review*, and continued as the *London and Westminster Review*, under the editorship of the distinguished Utilitarian ▷ John Stuart Mill. Mill wanted to broaden Utilitarian thinking, and writers who were not followers of the movement were brought in, such as ▷ Carlyle and the novelist ▷ George Eliot, who was assistant editor 1851–54. Later contributors varied as greatly as ▷ Walter Pater, father of the ▷ Aesthetic movement, and the positivist Frederic Harrison. It continued to advocate scientific progress, and by the end of the century it ceased to be literary.

What Maisie Knew (1897)

A novel by ▷ Henry James. Its theme is the survival of innocence in a world of adult corruption, the influence of adults on a child, and her influence on them.

Maisie Farange is a small girl whose parents have divorced each other with equal guilt on both sides. The parents are heartless and indifferent to their daughter, except as a weapon against each other and in their farcical, though not wholly vain, struggles to maintain acceptable social appearances. Maisie is passed from one to the other, and each employs a governess to take responsibility for her welfare. Both parents marry again, and eventually relinquish Maisie herself. By the end of the book Maisie finds herself torn between two prospective 'step-parents', each formerly married to her real parents, divorced from them, and about to marry each other, Maisie herself having been the occasion of their coming together. Her 'stepfather', Sir Claude, is charming and sweet-natured, but weak and self-indulgent; her 'stepmother', Mrs Beale, is genuinely fond of Maisie (as Sir Claude is) but is basically selfish and rapacious. In addition,

the child has a simple-minded, plain and elderly governess, Mrs Wix, who is herself in love with Sir Claude, and devoted to Maisie. The affection of none of them, however, is single-minded, as hers is for each one of them. The pathos of the novel arises from the warm responsiveness, deep need, and pure integrity of Maisie, from whose point of view all the events are seen. Its irony arises from the way in which the child's need for and dependence on adult care and love is transformed into responsibility for the adults themselves, who become dependent on her decisions. In the end these decisions lead her to choose life alone with Mrs Wix, who naively hopes to imbue her with a 'moral sense', unaware that beside Maisie's innocence her own idea of a moral sense represents modified corruption.

The novel is written in James's late, compressed and dramatic style, and is one of his masterpieces.

Wheatley, Phillis (1753?–1784)

The first black poet in English. As a child she was sold as a slave to the Wheatley family in Boston, who treated her well and encouraged her inclination to write. Her *Poems on Various Subjects, Religious and Moral*, published in London in 1773, comprises derivative and conventional verses on didactic themes: 'Remember, *Christians*, *Negroes*, black as *Cain*,/ May be refin'd, and join the angelic train.'

Whetstone, George (1550–87)

English poet and dramatist who is mostly remembered for the comedy *Promos and Cassandra* (1578) which ▷ Shakespeare used in ▷ *Measure for Measure*.

Whig and Tory

Political terms distinguishing the two parties which were the forebears of the present ▷ Liberal and Conservative parties respectively. They were originally terms of abuse, provoked by the attempt of ▷ Lord Shaftesbury in 1679 to exclude James Duke of York (later ▷ James II) from succession to the throne because he was a Catholic. Shaftesbury and his party were called Whigs because their preference for the ▷ Protestant religion over the law of hereditary succession caused their opponents to liken them to the Scottish ▷ Presbyterian rebels of the time – called derisively 'whigs' from the nickname given to Scottish drovers. They retaliated by calling the supporters of James, 'tories', from the Irish term for robbers, implying that they no more cared about safeguarding the Protestant religion than did the Irish Catholic rebels. The

Exclusion question was settled in favour of James, but not for long, since the Tories did in fact care greatly about the maintenance of the ▷ Church of England, and when James II was clearly seen to be acting in Catholic interests, the Tories united with the Whigs in deposing him in 1688. The political terms remained because, though not very consistently, the parties remained; and the parties survived because they represented distinct social interests in the country, though also not very consistently. The Whigs were especially the party of the landed aristocracy, who cared less for the institutions of the Crown and the Church of England than for their own power; since this was allied to the commercial interests of the country, they tended to gain support from the merchants of the towns, many of whom were ▷ Dissenters opposed to the Church of England. The principal Tory support came from the smaller landed gentry, or squirearchy, whose interests were conservative, and whose fortunes seemed best protected by introducing as little change in the established institutions, whether of Church or of State, as possible. In the major crises the Tories were generally defeated, but they had extraordinary survival capacity by virtue of their willingness to accept changes once they had become inevitable. Their first major defeat was in 1714 when the Tory party was split between ▷ Bolingbroke's anti-Hanoverian faction and those loyal to the 1701 Act of Settlement by which the throne went to the House of Hanover and not to Anne's Catholic half-brother.

Whigs were then supreme for 40 years (though they disintegrated into rival groups), until after the accession of George III in 1760. George tried then to revive the power of the throne by securing supporters for his politics in Parliament; these supporters were known as 'the King's Friends' or 'New Tories'. This policy was also defeated, however, by their loss of prestige as a result of the victory of the American rebels in the War of American Independence (1775–83). The country was not then in a mood to see the return of the restless and corrupt Whigs, and Tory governments continued in power until 1832.

About 1830 the names Liberal and Conservative began to replace Whig and Tory in popular use, and these terms were officially adopted some 30 years later. 'Tory' survives, to some extent, as interchangeable with Conservative (it is shorter for newspaper headlines), but 'Whig' has been altogether superseded.

Whit-Sunday
The religious ▷ festival of Pentecost, commemorating the descent of the Holy Ghost upon Christ's disciples – in the Bible, *Acts* 2. Whit = white, perhaps from the white garments of those who underwent baptism on the night before. Whit-Sunday occurs on the 7th Sunday after Easter. Pentecost was originally a Jewish feast, when thanks were given for the first fruits of the earth, after the return of spring.

White, Gilbert (1720–93)
Writer on natural history. He was born at Selborne, a village in Hampshire. After spending some years as a Fellow of Oriel College, Oxford, he became a country curate, and spent the last nine years of his life in the village of his birth. His *Natural History of Selborne* (1789) is a record of the plant, animal, and bird life there, inspired by genuine scientific curiosity and showing great delicacy and charm of expression. The book has been described as the first to raise natural history to the level of literature, and is the fruit of the development of 17th- and 18th-century natural science, partly initiated by the greatest of English naturalists, John Ray (1627–1705), author *The Wisdom of God Manifested in the Works of his Creation* (1691), a scientist who shared ▷ Newton's intellectual curiosity and his religious awe at the spectacle of divine organization in the universe. Another tradition leading to White was the newly awakened sensibility for natural surroundings in the poetry of ▷ William Collins, ▷ Oliver Goldsmith and ▷ William Cowper. The poetic movement culminated in the 19th century in the work of ▷ Wordsworth and ▷ Clare.
Bib: Holt-White, R., *Life and Letters.*

White, Patrick (1912–90)
Australian novelist, dramatist and poet. Born in London, educated in Australia, and at Cheltenham College and Cambridge University. He travelled widely in Europe and the U.S.A., served in the Royal Air Force during World War II, and then returned to live in Australia. His work combines an intense spirituality with social comedy and a distaste for human pretension and egotism. His first novel, *The Happy Valley* (1939), set in remote New South Wales, shows the influence of ▷ Joyce, while *The Living and the Dead* (1941) is primarily a condemnation of English society of the 1920s and 1930s. White established his reputation with *The Tree of Man* (1955) and *Voss* (1957). Both concern man's confrontation with the inhuman forces of

Patrick White

nature in Australia, the former through the struggles of a young farmer, the latter through the journey among the Aborigines of a mid-19th-century German explorer. White's most recent works of fiction have been two collections, each containing three short pieces: *Memoirs of Many in One* (1986) and *Three Uneasy Pieces* (1988). His other novels are: *The Aunt's Story* (1948); *Riders in the Chariot* (1961); *The Solid Mandala* (1966); *The Vivisector* (1970); *The Eye of the Storm* (1973); *A Fringe of Leaves* (1976); *The Twyborn Affair* (1979). Drama includes: *Return to Abyssinia* (1947); *Four Plays* (1965) (*The Ham Funeral*, 1961; *The Season at Sarsaparilla*, 1962; *A Cheery Soul*, 1963; *Night on Bald Mountain*, 1964); *Big Toys* (1977); *Signal Driver* (1983). Story collections are: *The Burnt Ones* (1964); *The Cockatoos* (1974). Verse: *The Ploughman and Other Poems* (1935). He was awarded the Nobel Prize for Literature in 1973.
▷ Commonwealth literature.
Bib: Walsh, W., *Patrick White's Fiction*.

White, William Hale (1831–1913)
(pseudonym: Mark Rutherford)
Novelist. His father was a ▷ Dissenter and intended his son to be a Dissenting clergyman. However, he could not reconcile his ideas and the religious doctrines that he was required to believe, and instead he had a civil service career in the Admiralty. His three famous novels were *The Autobiography of Mark Rutherford* (1881), *Mark Rutherford's Deliverance* (1885) and *The Revolution in Tanner's Lane* (1887). The first two are

▷ autobiographical and concerned with loss of faith. White makes Rutherford more outwardly unfortunate than he was himself, since he had a successful career both as a writer and as a civil servant; the reason seems to be that he makes his character represent not only his own loss of Christian faith but the sense of impoverishment that accompanied it. In his study of ▷ John Bunyan (1905), he makes the statement: 'Religion is dead when imagination deserts it.' White's own questioning of his belief started from reading ▷ Wordsworth in ▷ *Lyrical Ballads* (1798–1800) and the subsequent feeling that nature stirred him as 'the God of the Church' could not. As studies of spiritual loss and contention with it, the Mark Rutherford novels have wide human relevance. The third novel is concerned with radical movements in the early 19th century and shows White's political intelligence, which comes out directly in his pamphlet on the political franchise. His other novels are *Miriam's Schooling* (1890), *Catherine Furze* (1893) and *Clara Hopgood* (1896). Other works: *Pages from a Journal* and *More Pages from a Journal* (1900 and 1910); *Last Pages* (1915).
▷ Agnosticism.
Bib: Maclean, C. M., *Life*; Stone, W., *Life*; Stock, I., *William Hale White*; Lucas, J., *The Literature of Change: Studies in the Nineteenth-Century Provincial Novel* (chapter).

White Devil, The (1608–9)
A tragedy by ▷ John Webster, published in 1612 with the subtitle ▷ *Vittoria Corrombona*, written in 1608–9. It is based on the story of the actual murder of Vittoria Accoromboni (1585) as told in William Painter's ▷ *Palace of Pleasure*. Vittoria is the wife of Camillo. The Duke of Brachiano, husband to Isabella, the sister of the Duke of Florence and of Cardinal Montecelso, falls in love with her and is assisted in winning her by her brother, Flamineo. Flamineo causes the death of Camillo, and Brachiano poisons his own wife. In Act III, Vittoria is on trial before Cardinal Montecelso for adultery and murder; she is proudly defiant, and condemned to confinement in a convent, where Brachiano continues to visit her, and whence he eventually steals her away and marries her. In Act V, Flamineo kills his brother, Marcello, who is upbraiding him for his wickedness, and their mother sings over her dead son the lovely dirge 'Call for the robin redbreast and the wren'. The Duke of Florence's hireling, Lodovico, avenges the death of Isabella by killing Flamineo and

Vittoria. 'My soul, like to a ship in a black storm, is driven, I know not whither;' the spirit of the stormy play is expressed by this line spoken by the dying Vittoria. The play contains many passages of intense poetry, no virtuous characters among the outstanding ones, and a number of fine theatrical episodes which are difficult to perform because they are long drawn out. The unifying tone is of desperation produced by destructive and self-destroying passions.

Whitehall

A street in London that runs between Trafalgar Square and Parliament Square. It is mainly occupied by the buildings of government ministries, so that 'Whitehall' is often used as a term for the state bureaucracy. The name derives from the royal palace that formerly stood there, of which only ▷ Inigo Jones's Banqueting Hall (erected under ▷ James I) now remains. Until the fall of ▷ Cardinal Wolsey (1530) it was called York Place, since he built the palace when he was Archbishop of York:

IST GENTLEMAN: *Sir,*
> *You must no more call it York-place, that's past;*
> *For, since the cardinal fell, that title's lost:*
> *'Tis now the king's, and call'd Whitehall.*
>   (*Henry VIII* IV. i.94)

It was outside the Banqueting Hall that ▷ Charles I was executed in 1649.

Whiting, John (1917–63)

British dramatist and actor. Although his plays are now rarely performed, he is important as a pioneer of serious drama during the immediate post-war period. Plays include: *A Penny for a Song* (1951), *Saint's Day* (1951), *Marching Song* (1954) and *The Devils* (1961), based on ▷ Aldous Huxley's *The Devils of Loudun*. Both *A Penny for a Song* and *The Devils* were performed by the ▷ Royal Shakespeare Company.
Bib: Salmon, E., *The Dark Journey*.

Whittington, Richard (d 1423)

A rich and famous Lord Mayor of London in 1397–8, 1406–7, and 1419–20. He made substantial loans of money to the kings ▷ Henry IV and ▷ Henry V, and used his wealth for public works, including a legacy for improving ▷ Newgate Prison. His almshouses for the poor are still maintained. According to popular legend, he was originally a poor orphan and became the ill-treated servant of a rich merchant. He ran away from London, with his cat, until he heard Bow bells calling him back:

> *Turn again, Dick Whittington,*
> *Lord Mayor of London.*

The legend is a popular subject of Christmas ▷ pantomimes, in which the cat plays a principal part.

Who's Who

An annual biographical dictionary of eminent contemporary men and women. First published in 1849.
    ▷ Biography.

Wife of Bath's Prologue and Tale, The

Part of ▷ Chaucer's ▷ *Canterbury Tales*. The Wife of Bath contributes both the story of her life and an Arthurian (▷ Arthur, King) romance to the story-telling collection. Her *Prologue*, of some 856 lines, gives an account of her marital career, spanning five marriages, and borrows sermonizing techniques for its thematic organization, structure and mode of argument. The Wife's history outlines the economic laws of the marriage market: it is only after three marriages to old, but financially well-endowed men that the Wife has gained the economic independence to find more pleasing partners. She challenges some of the clerical attitudes to marriage both in theory (in her opening comments) and in practice (in her physical confrontation with her fifth husband Jankyn, the clerk, and his book, an anti-feminist compilation). The Arthurian narrative which follows is a version of the 'Loathly Lady' story (which has parallels in ▷ Gower's ▷ *Confessio Amantis*, and the *Weddynge of Sir Gawen and Dame Ragnell*), and offers an equally complex view of power relations between the sexes, but refracted through the lens of the romance genre.

Unlike the analogues, the Wife's story begins with a rape of a young woman by a knight. The female members of King Arthur's court agree to commute the knight's death sentence for the offence, if he can answer the question 'What do women most desire?'. The winning answer (sovereignty) is supplied by a mysterious old woman whom the knight meets on his quest. In return for saving the knight's life, the old woman demands that the knight should marry her. He does so, but she is transformed into a beautiful woman (after the knight has ceded sovereignty to her over the choice she offers him between a wife who is beautiful or one who is faithful), and they enjoy, according to the narrator, a happy harmonious life together. No explanation is offered for the mechanics of this transformation in the Wife's version of events (again, unlike the other analogues). The Wife's contribution provides a catalyst for further tales, a debating point for the pilgrims, and a subject of modern critical controversy. A debate between the Friar and the Summoner is provoked in the course of her tale, which continues after she has finished; she is referred to an authority on marriage in the ▷ *Merchant's Tale*; and the clerk explicitly replies to her criticism of the clerical representation of secular women in his tale.

Wilberforce, William (1759–1833)
Philanthropist and politician. He devoted much of his life to the campaign to abolish the slave trade and slavery in overseas British territories. In 1807, the slave trade was made illegal, and so was slavery itself in the year of his death. He was leader of the ▷ Evangelical movement, particularly of a group known as the Clapham Sect because it met in his house at Clapham.

Wild Gallant, The (**1663**)
Play by ▷ John Dryden, which has been seen by some as the first ▷ Restoration ▷ Comedy of Manners. Constance, a rich heiress, is in love with the charming but penniless Loveby. She steals money from her father in order to supply her lover secretly; he, however, thinks it is a gift from the devil. He expresses his appreciation of the devil in a number of lines bordering on blasphemy. Eventually, by pretending to be pregnant Constance gains leave to wed the man of her choice, and marries Loveby. In a separate but linked plot Isabella, a witty and charming relative of Constance's, wants to marry a man with money and chooses the wealthy Timorous, to whom she is somewhat attracted, although she does not love him. She wins him by means of various intrigues and disguises, including passing herself off as Constance. The play has some farcical comic business: in one sequence Constance persuades the men in the play that they too are pregnant. There is also some feminist comment, as when Constance complains that 'Women are tied to hard unequal laws: the passion is the same in us, and yet we are barred the freedom to express it'.

Wilde, Oscar Fingal O'Flahertie Wills (1856–1900)
Dramatist, poet, novelist and essayist. He was the son of an eminent Irish surgeon and a literary mother. At Oxford University his style of life became notorious; he was a disciple of ▷ Pater, the Oxford father of ▷ aestheticism, and he carried the doctrine as far as to conduct his life as an aesthetic disciple – a direct challenge to the prevailing outlook of the society of his time, which was inclined to regard overt aestheticism with

suspicion or disdain. In 1888 Wilde produced a volume of children's fairy tales very much in the melancholy and poetic style of the Danish writer ▷ Hans Christian Andersen – *The Happy Prince*. He followed this with two other volumes of stories, and then the novel, *The Picture of Dorian Grey* (1891), whose hero is an embodiment of the aesthetic way of life. More commonly known were his comedies, *Lady Windermere's Fan* (1892), *A Woman of No Importance* (1893), *An Ideal Husband* (1895), and above all the witty *Importance of Being Earnest* (1895). The plays are apparently light-hearted, but they contain strong elements of serious feeling in their attack on a society whose code is intolerant, but whose intolerance is hypocritical. In 1895, by a libel action against the Marquis of Queensberry, he exposed himself to a countercharge of immoral homosexual conduct, and spent two years in prison. In 1898 he published his *Ballad of Reading Gaol* about his prison experience, proving that he could write in the direct language of the ▷ ballad tradition, as well as in the artificial style of his *Collected Poems* (1892). His *De Profundis* (1905) is an eloquent statement of his grief after his downfall, but modern critics are equally as impressed by the intelligence of his social essays, such as *The Critic as Artist* (1891) and *The Soul of Man under Socialism* (1891). The paradox of Wilde is that, while for his contemporaries he represented degeneracy and weakness, there is plenty of evidence that he was a brave man of remarkable strength of character who made an emphatic protest against the vulgarity of his age and yet, artistically, was himself subject to vulgarity of an opposite kind.
Bib: Critical studies by Roditi, E., Ransome, A.; Lives by Lemmonier, L.; Ervine, St. J.; Pearson, H.; Bentley, E. R., in *The Playwright as Thinker*; Beckson, K. (ed.), *The Critical Heritage;* Bird, A., *The Plays of Oscar Wilde*; Worth, K., *Oscar Wilde*.

Wilkes, John (1727–97)
Journalist and politician. He was dissolute, and notorious for his membership of the scandalous Hell-Fire Club at Medmenham Abbey, with its motto 'Fay ce que voudras' = 'Do as you will'. Politically he was radical and courageous, and a popular hero. In 1762 he attacked ▷ George III's administration under Lord Bute in *The North Briton*, a periodical which countered *The Briton* edited by the novelist, ▷ Tobias Smollett. As an M.P., he was twice expelled from the House of Commons for libel, and in 1769 he was three times elected to Parliament by the

county of Middlesex, the election each time being annulled. He was allowed to sit in 1774, in which year he was Lord Mayor of London. His character was such as to win the respect of ▷ Dr Johnson, a man of opposite moral and political principles: 'Jack has great variety of talk, Jack is a scholar, Jack has the manners of a gentleman.' (Quoted in ▷ Boswell's *Life of Johnson*.)

Wilks, Robert (?1665–1732)

Actor, manager. Wilks made his first public appearance, as ▷ Othello, at the ▷ Smock Alley Theatre in Dublin in 1691, and in the following year he was employed as an actor by ▷ Christopher Rich in London. He became noted for his gentlemanly style of acting, and was the original Sir Harry Wildair, in his friend, ▷ George Farquhar's, ▷ *The Constant Couple*.

Wilks became co-manager first of the ▷ Haymarket, and then, from 1709, of ▷ Drury Lane, in combination with several others including, at various times, Owen Swiney (1675–1754), ▷ Colley Cibber, Thomas Doggett (c1670–1721), Richard Estcourt (1668–1712), ▷ Sir Richard Steele, ▷ Barton Booth, and ▷ Anne Oldfield. He shared control for the rest of his career, while at the same time continuing to strengthen and build up his repertoire as a leading actor, succeeding more in comedies than in tragedies.

Throughout his life Wilks maintained a reputation for sobriety and conscientiousness. Cibber also speaks of his superb memory which, coupled with his diligence, meant that he was almost invariably word-perfect, in an age when ad-libbing on stage was common. However, he could be unduly exacting of others, and at times, quarrelsome. Wilks is generally credited with a large share of responsibility for Drury Lane's prosperity during the 1710s and 1720s.

Will's Coffee-house

Named after its owner William Unwin, it was the haunt of such authors as ▷ John Dryden, ▷ William Wycherley, ▷ Joseph Addison and ▷ Alexander Pope. It became dominated by the older, mainly Tory set in the early years of the 18th century and ▷ Button's Coffee-house was set up as a fashionable rival, with a more Whiggish clientele.

William I (1066–87) the Conqueror

As Duke of Normandy he came to power in 1035, and proved himself an effective soldier and ruler. In 1051, he may have received some sort of promise from ▷ Edward the Confessor, his relative, that the English throne should pass to him, and Harold Earl of ▷ Wessex promised his support in 1064. When, nonetheless, Harold himself succeeded Edward, William invaded England and defeated Harold near Hastings in Sussex, 1066. By 1070 he had reduced the whole country. The invasion had behind it the authority of the Pope, since the English Church was in a decadent and heretical condition. William's government was remarkably thorough and efficient. There was an extensive redistribution of land, with the result that the ▷ Anglo-Saxon nobility were largely dispossessed and England was subjected to a Norman-French aristocracy, French-speaking until the 14th century when it became anglicized. At the same time, William so managed this redistribution that the royal authority could be more effectively maintained throughout the country than was usual in 11th-century western Europe.

▷ Domesday Book; Lanfranc; French literature in England.

William II (1087–1100)

King of England. His nickname William Rufus arose from the reddish colour of his complexion and hair. He continued the policy of his father, William I, but was much more unpopular owing to his wilful tyrannies. According to legend he was killed while hunting in the New Forest by an arrow shot by Walter Tirel.

William III (1689–1702)

King of Britain, reigning jointly with his wife Mary until her death in 1694. As William of Orange, Stadtholder of Holland, he was leader of the European opposition to the power of Louis XIV, which also menaced Britain. His wife was the daughter of ▷ James II, deposed for his Catholicism and his threat to the liberty of ▷ Parliament. His reign was largely taken up with war against France. The political power of Parliament was further increased by his foreign preoccupations, and by the fact that, as a foreigner, he lacked experience of English political affairs.

William IV (1830–37)

He was brother of his predecessor, ▷ George IV, and uncle to his successor, ▷ Victoria. He was a well-meaning man of small ability, but the most popular member of a royal family which was otherwise very unpopular.

Williams, Raymond (1921–87)

The most influential of all radical thinkers in Britain in the 20th century. Williams's work spans literary criticism, cultural studies, media studies, communications and politics, and he also wrote plays and novels. In *Culture and Society 1780–1950* (1958) and *The Long Revolution* (1961) he laid the foundation for a wide-ranging analysis of modern cultural forms, and can justly be accredited with the foundation of cultural studies as an interdisciplinary field of enquiry. In books such as *Modern Tragedy* (1966) and *Drama from Ibsen to Brecht* (1968), which was a revision of his earlier *Drama from Ibsen to Eliot* (1952), he challenged accepted ways of evaluating drama and dramatic forms, and in 1968 he was a guiding spirit behind the New Left's *Mayday Manifesto* (1968). For Williams writing was always and primarily a social activity, deeply implicated in politics. Through books such as *The Country and The City* (1973), *Marxism and Literature* (1977), *Politics and Letters* (1979), *Problems in Materialism and Culture* (1980), *Writing in Society, Towards 2000* (1983) and his *John Clare's Selected Poetry and Prose* (1986), he pursued these themes with an intellectual rigour which refused easy formulations. His was the intellectual force behind the current movement of cultural ▷ materialism, the British equivalent of American ▷ new historicism.

Wilmot, John (1647–80)

▷ Rochester, Second Earl of.

Wilson, Sir Angus (1913–91)

Novelist and short-story writer. Born in Durban, South Africa, Wilson was educated at Westminster School in London and at Merton College, Oxford. He worked for many years in the British Museum Reading Room, served in the Foreign Office during World War II, and, from 1963, taught English literature at the University of East Anglia. He is primarily a satirist, with a particularly sharp ear for the way in which hypocrisy, cruelty and smugness are betrayed in conversation. His first published works were short stories, *The Wrong Set* (1949) and *Such Darling Dodos* (1950), depicting English middle-class life around the time of World War II. His early work was traditional in form, inspired by his respect for the 19th-century English novel and a reaction against the dominance of post-Jamesian narrative techniques in the ▷ modernist novel. *Hemlock and After* (1952), *Anglo-Saxon Attitudes* (1956) and *The Middle Age of Mrs Eliot* (1958) deal with such issues as responsibility, guilt and the problem of loneliness. The surface is satirical, and at times highly comic, but, as the protagonist of *Anglo-Saxon Attitudes* comments, 'the ludicrous was too often only a thin covering for the serious and the tragic'. *The Old Men at the Zoo* (1961) represents a considerable change of mode: it is a bizarre fable concerning personal and political commitment, set in the London Zoo at a time of international crisis. From this point on Wilson's work became more experimental: *Late Call* (1964) makes use of pastiche, while *No Laughing Matter* (1967) reflects the influence of ▷ Virginia Woolf, employing multiple interior monologues, as well as parodic dramatic dialogue and stories by one of the characters. It has a broad historical and social sweep, setting the story of a family between 1912 and 1967 in the context of British society as a whole. Like *Anglo-Saxon Attitudes* and *Late Call* it traces personal and public concerns back to the period immediately before World War I. *Setting the World on Fire* (1980) is another new departure in form; it is a complex and highly patterned work in which the myth of ▷ Phaeton is re-enacted in modern London. His other novels are: *As If By Magic* (1973). Story collections: *Death Dance* (1969); *Collected Stories* (1987). Travel writing: *Reflection in a Writer's Eye* (1986). Critical works include: *Emile Zola* (1952); *The World of Charles Dickens* (1970); *The Strange Ride of Rudyard Kipling* (1977). **Bib:** Cox, C. B., *The Free Spirit*; Halio, J. L. (ed.), *Critical Essays on Angus Wilson*; Gardner, A., *Angus Wilson*; Faulkner, P., *Angus Wilson, Mimic and Moralist*.

Wilson, Colin (b 1931)

Novelist and critic. He is known primarily as the author of the ▷ existentialist work *The Outsider* (1956), which was much acclaimed at the time of its publication. He is the author of 15 novels, and over 50 works of non-fiction. His novels feature violence, sexuality and the idea of the outsider in society, and seek to acknowledge fictionality by using genres such as the detective story with a deliberate incongruity.

Wilson, John (1785–1854)

Scottish journalist, chiefly known under the pseudonym 'Christopher North' which he used when writing for ▷ *Blackwood's Magazine*, for which he was the principal writer from 1817. He wrote very lively, semi-dramatic discussions called *Noctes Ambrosianae* which became famous. In 1820 he was elected to the professorship of moral philosophy in Edinburgh University. He had no special qualifications for the post, but was backed by ▷ Walter Scott. Nonetheless he filled the post very effectively. He contributed much other journalism to *Blackwood's*, and was also a poet: *The Isle of Palms* (1812) and *The City of the Plague* (1816).

Bib: Swan, E., *Christopher North – John Wilson*.

Winchilsea, Anne Finch Countess of (1661–1720)

Poet, and maid-of-honour at the royal court. Her occasional and reflective verse was collected in *Miscellany Poems* (1713), and her *Nocturnal Reverie* has been frequently anthologized.

Windsor, House of

Since 1917, the official designation of the British royal family, which, previously, had been known as the House of Hanover. The change was made by George v, in deference to British hostility to Germany during World War I.

▷ George.

Windsor Castle

The principal residence of the English royal family since the 11th century. Its most conspicuous feature is the huge round tower at the summit of the hill on which the castle is built; it was constructed by ▷ Edward III on the site where, according to the contemporary French chronicler Froissart, ▷ King Arthur had sat surrounded by his Knights of the Round Table; Edward, who had founded the knightly Order of the Garter, still the most distinguished order of knighthood, built the tower as a meeting-place for it, in emulation of Arthur.

Windsor Forest (1713)

A poem by ▷ Alexander Pope in heroic ▷ couplets describing the landscape around his home, and reflecting on its history and economic importance. It blends ▷ Georgic, ▷ pastoral and topographical elements in an engaging expression of ▷ Augustan optimism.

Wine

This was previously a rich man's drink in England, though in the 17th and 18th centuries, because beer and ale were considered low class, it was more frequently and widely drunk. Home-grown British wines existed at least until the 18th century, but as early as the 14th century ships were sent in convoy to Bordeaux in south-west France to import claret. Spanish wines such as sherry and canary were drunk in the 16th and 17th centuries; French burgundy is mentioned in 1672 in a play by ▷ Wycherley; champagne is first mentioned in 1700, and the sweet Portuguese wine, port, in 1711. For a hundred and fifty years the last was above all the gentleman's drink, taken among the men as they sat round the table after dinner when the ladies had departed to the 'withdrawing room'. Rhenish wines from Germany were popular from the 16th century. Until the 18th century, wine was not allowed to mature, nor, until the mid 17th century, were glass bottles used, and wine glasses were often imported from Venice. By the 19th century, taste was much more sophisticated; gentlemen 'laid down' bottles to be drunk by their sons, and such a legacy was much prized. Since Britain's accession into the European Economic Community (E.E.C.) wine has become more readily available at a much lower cost and consequently a popular drink for all classes.

▷ Drinks.

Wings of the Dove, The (1902)

A novel by ▷ Henry James. The scene is principally London and Venice. Kate Croy and Merton Densher, a young journalist, are in love, but without the money to marry. Kate's rich aunt, Maud Lowder, takes into her circle Milly Theale, a lonely American girl of great single-mindedness, eagerness for life, and capacity for affection, and also a millionairess. Milly is travelling in Europe with Susan Stringham, an old friend of Mrs Lowder's. Mrs Stringham learns from Milly's doctor that the girl is suffering from a fatal illness, that her death cannot be long delayed, and that it can only be delayed at all if she achieves happiness. Mrs Stringham communicates this to Kate, who conceives a plot with a double purpose: Merton is to engage Milly's love, thus bringing her the happiness that she needs, and at the same time securing her money when she dies, so that Kate's own marriage to Merton can at last take place. Milly's love for Merton is very real; because of it, however, she refuses another suitor, Lord Mark, who knows Kate's plot and in revenge betrays it to Milly. She dies, broken-hearted, but she leaves Merton her money. Merton and Kate, however, find that they are for ever separated by the shadow of the dead Milly between them.

The story is an example of James's 'international theme': in this case, the openness and integrity which he saw as strengths of the American personality are opposed to the selfishness and deviousness which he saw as part of the decadent aspect of European culture. It is written in the condensed, allusive style which is characteristic also of ▷ *The Ambassadors* and ▷ *The Golden Bowl*.

Winner and Waster

An ▷ alliterative ▷ dream-vision poem, composed in the mid to later 14th century, which investigates the relationship between the earning (winning) and dispending (wasting) forces in a society, by dramatizing a confrontation between the martial forces of Winner and Waster. The narrator describes how, in his dream, he sees the two sides in full martial array, drawn up before a king (whose emblems suggest he is ▷ Edward III). The two leaders from either side embark on a war of words, attacking the principles of the other and defending their own position, and present their respective cases for the judgement of the king (and thus defer physical combat). The debate is the vehicle for a wry assessment of various kinds of materialistic corruption in contemporary society, and of the injustices which result from the misuse of money. The last lines of the poem are missing so the king's judgement, if he offered one, is not known. It may have influenced the techniques of social satire developed by ▷ Langland in ▷ *Piers Plowman*, but Langland's poem takes the debate very much further.

Bib: Gollancz, I. (ed.), *Winner and Waster*.

Winter's Tale, The (1610–11)
A play by ▷ Shakespeare; one of his ▷ romances, dated 1610–11, and based on ▷ Robert Greene's *Pandósto*. Leontes, king of Sicilia, is married to Hermione, whom he deeply loves, and at the opening of the play is receiving a visit from Polixenes, king of Bohemia and the intimate friend of his childhood. Leontes becomes consumed by an insane jealousy, and is convinced that the child with which Hermione is pregnant has been fathered by Polixenes. He orders Camillo, a courtier, to poison Polixenes, but instead Camillo and Polixenes flee the country together. Leontes orders the trial of Hermione for adultery, and, to appease his indignant courtiers, he sends to the oracle of Delphi in order to obtain what he believes will be confirmation of her guilt. The baby is born, but Leontes orders another courtier, Antigonus, to leave it in a desolate place to perish. At this point a succession of catastrophes is heaped on Leontes: he learns from the oracle that his wife is innocent, from Paulina, wife of Antigonus, that Hermione has died, and that his little son has also died, of grief at the suffering of his mother. The last scene of Act III shows Antigonus depositing the baby on the coast of Bohemia and her discovery by two shepherds. Thus far the play is tragic; Acts IV and V show recovery. The baby grows up into a beautiful girl, Perdita, who believes herself to be a shepherd's daughter. Florizel, son of

Polixenes, courts her at the shepherds' sheepshearing feast, but they have to flee to Sicilia to escape the anger of his father. Polixenes follows them, and at Leontes' court once more a great reconciliation takes place. Paulina discloses that Hermione is not dead, but has been kept in hiding until the return of Perdita, in accordance with the prediction of the oracle; in the last scene she is shown to Leontes as a statue of her supposedly dead self, but at the command of Paulina the statue gradually comes to life to the sound of music.

The summary shows that the play has no pretence to external realism; it is a fable about the destructiveness of the passions and the healing power of time. The symbolism is especially of the seasons: 'a winter's tale' is about deprivation, but the play ends in autumn, the season of recovered fulfilment, while the sheep-shearing scene (IV. 3) has springlike qualities, with Perdita reminding one of ▷ Persephone in her lines about the spring flowers. The ▷ pastoral aspect of the play shows pastoralism in a new light – not as an escape into daydream from change and decay, but as a phase of development which must be outgrown if capacity for growth is to be fulfilled. The process of growth implies desire, fear, and possessiveness which are the state of mind of the jealous Leontes at the beginning of the play, when he finds that he has outgrown his pastorally innocent friendship with Polixenes. From this false development, he can recover only by repentance.

Wit
This word has a number of distinct, though related, meanings. 1 The oldest meaning is identical with 'mind', as in ▷ Wycliffe's 14th-century translation of the Bible: 'Who knew the wit of the Lord?' (*Romans* 11:34). This use of 'wit' rarely occurs in the literature of the last hundred years. 2 Another long-established meaning is 'a faculty of the mind'. This is still in use today, as when we speak of someone having 'lost his wits', *ie* lost the use of his mental faculties. 3 A common meaning in the 17th and 18th centuries was the capacity to relate unlike ideas, as in ▷ Locke's definition: 'Wit lying in the assemblage of ideas, and putting these together with quickness and variety wherein can be found any resemblance or congruity, thereby to make up pleasant pictures in the fancy' (▷ *Essay concerning Human Understanding*, 1690). ▷ Cowley, in his poem *Of Wit* (1656) wrote 'In a true piece of wit all things must be./Yet all things there

agree'. ▷ Samuel Johnson, in his *Life of Cowley* (1779), wrote: 'It was about the time of Cowley that Wit, which had been till then used for Intellection, in contradistinction to Will, took the meaning, whatever it be, which it now bears.' Johnson here refers to the original meaning of wit as 'mind' or 'understanding', and points to the complex and important suggestiveness of the word in his own day. **4** During the same period, but chiefly in the 'Age of Reason' (about 1660–1800), wit was also thought of as meaning fine and clear expression: ▷ Dryden's 'propriety of thoughts and words elegantly adapted to the subject' (*Heroic Poetry and Poetic Licence*, 1677), and ▷ Pope's 'what oft was thought but ne'er so well expressed' (▷ *Essay on Criticism*). Johnson went some way to reconciling interpretations **3** and **4** in his own definition: 'that which is at once natural and new, and that which though not obvious is upon its first production acknowledged to be just . . . that which he that never found it wondered how he missed it'. **5** Definition **3** points to the element of surprise in wit; this often induces laughter. Thus wit has also been considered, since 1600, to be one of the principal sources of comedy, and it is in this sense that it is chiefly used in 20th-century English. **6** In the personal sense, in the later 17th and 18th centuries a wit was a man with clear insight into many aspects of life and manners, capable of summarizing and relating these aspects lucidly and forcefully. The term is often used disparagingly, however, for pretentious young people who try to achieve reputations for themselves by their superficial but fashionably clever talk. Nowadays, a wit is often seen as a person capable of expressing him- or herself in concise and memorably amusing language.

Witches

People supposed to be in league with the devil, who gives them supernatural powers. The name 'witch' was sometimes used for both sexes, though those accused of being witches were usually women. They commonly had 'familiars' in the form of spirits disguised as animals of bad or sinister reputation – toads or cats of certain colours. To work their magic, witches uttered 'spells' of specially devised words, or they used objects ('charms') supposed to have magical properties; witches used to gather in small communities known as 'covens', and they assembled on one day of the year (a 'witches' Sabbath') to worship the Devil.

The common explanation of witchcraft is that, in Europe at least, it represents the long survival of pre-Christian pagan religions in which the gods were the embodiments of the powers of nature, usually in the forms of animals, often a goat, but in Britain commonly the bull, the dog, or the cat. More recently witchcraft, or the accusation of witchcraft, has been regarded as a 17th-century mechanism of social control, used to discourage women from living alone outside the authority of a male-dominated household.

That witchcraft was common in the ▷ Middle Ages is not surprising; it is at first sight surprising that it was conspicuous in the later 16th and early 17th centuries, and that not merely the ignorant and uneducated but some of the learned believed in it. ▷ James VI of Scotland and I of England, who has been called 'the greatest scholar who ever sat on the English throne', was himself deeply interested in it and wrote a denunciation of it – his *Daemonologie* (1599). The pamphlet *News from Scotland* (1591) describes his conversion from scepticism to belief in it, and seems to have been used by ▷ Shakespeare in the portrayal of the witches in ▷ *Macbeth*. James later, however, moved to a more sceptical position again. The first law making witchcraft an offence punishable by death in England was passed in 1603 (though causing death by witchcraft had been so punishable since 1563) and it was not repealed until 1736. Sir Thomas Browne declares his firm belief in it in ▷ *Religio Medici* (1643); the last learned defence of the belief was *Saducismus Triumphatus* (1681) by the scholar and clergyman Joseph Glanville. The belief seems to have been particularly strong among ▷ Puritans and in Puritan countries, for instance in Scotland, 17th-century New England, and England under the ▷ Long Parliament. Rare survivals of it have been found in 20th-century England. It has been suggested that the prevalence of the belief in the 17th century and among Puritans is that their superstitious impulses were no longer satisfied by the Catholic system of mysteries (miracles, lives of the saints, etc.) which they had expelled from their faith by its 'purification'.

In the reign of James I, a number of plays besides *Macbeth* dealt with witchcraft, *eg* ▷ Dekker and ▷ Ford's *Witches of Edmonton* (1623) and ▷ Middleton's *The Witch* (1615). ▷ William Golding's *The Spire* (1964) deals with medieval pagan survival.

Wither, George (1558–1667)

Poet. Between 1612, when Wither's first publication appeared, and the poet's death in

1667, there were very few years which were not marked by the publication of at least one volume of verse or prose from this prolific author. Wither was possibly the most imprisoned writer in the history of English literature. In 1613 his ▷ satiric work *Abuses Stripped and Whipped* earned him a period of imprisonment, a punishment which he earned once more, in 1621, when *Wither's Motto* appeared, and which was to befall him again in 1646 (on publication of his ▷ pamphlet *Justiarius Justificatus*) and in 1660 (appearance of unpublished satire: *Vox Vulgi: A Poem in Censure of Parliament*). His later works were written in the belief that he was God's prophet. Of note, however, are several volumes of earlier verse, and his collection of emblems (▷ Emblem-books) which appeared in four volumes in 1635.

Wives and Daughters (1864–6)
A novel by ▷ Mrs Gaskell, published serially in the ▷ *Cornhill Magazine* and not completed at her death. It is a study of two families, the Gibsons and the Hamleys, in a small country town and the relationships of the parents and the children in each. The central character is Molly Gibson, whose liberal, frank, sincere and deeply responsible nature is painfully tested by the marriage of her widowed father (a country doctor) to a silly, vain widow. The widow brings with her, however, her own daughter, Cynthia, a girl with her mother's outward charm but without her silliness and with feelings guided more by her discerning intelligence than by spontaneous loyalties. Cynthia at 16 has become engaged to a coarse but astute man, Mr Preston, who is a local land-agent. The two girls become involved with the two sons of Mr Hamley, the local squire. The elder boy, Osborne, is superficially brilliant and charming, and much overestimated by his father. The younger son, Roger, has much less showy qualities but a deeper nature and eventually wins the academic success expected of but not achieved by the elder, who makes an unfortunate marriage, is cast off by the father and dies young. The novel thus brings out the differences between superficial and deep natures, and the perils that result from consequent false estimates of character, made even by the intelligent.

Wives Excuse, The: Or Cuckolds Make Themselves (1691)
Play by ▷ Thomas Southerne, identified with a wave of so-called 'marital discord comedies' of the 1690s by writers including ▷ Vanbrugh and ▷ Farquhar, which focussed on the problems of marriage, as much as on those of courtship. Southerne concentrated on showing up the sexual double standard and its effects on women. *The Wives Excuse* bleakly presents the dilemma of the woman trapped in an unhappy marriage to a man whose shameless infidelity goes unpunished, while she stands to lose her dignity, reputation, and remaining peace of mind if she succumbs to the advances of her would-be lover. Mrs Friendall wrestles with temptation in the form of the attractive but unscrupulous Lovemore, while Mr Friendall pursues an affair with Mrs Wittwoud. At the end, the couple agree to separate. Southerne implies that Mrs Friendall will eventually give in to Lovemore, only to be abandoned when he tires of her. The play was unsuccessful, but is now considered one of the great plays of the period, its polish and sophistication serving only to point up the hypocrisy underlying the situation which it portrays.

Woffington, Margaret (Peg) (?1714–60)
Actress. At the ▷ Smock Alley Theatre, Dublin, in 1740, she played the first of many performances as Sir Harry Wildair in ▷ George Farquhar's ▷ *The Constant Couple*. She repeated the role at ▷ Covent Garden and at ▷ Drury Lane, and became so celebrated in it that even ▷ Garrick could not equal her when he took on the same part.

The rest of her career from 1741 was spent largely at Drury Lane, but with further appearances at Covent Garden and in Dublin. She became the mistress of Garrick, and a theatrical rival of ▷ Kitty Clive, and ▷ George Anne Bellamy, whom she literally stabbed during a performance of Nathanial Lee's (c1653–92) *The Rival Queens*, just as ▷ Elizabeth Barry had done to ▷ Elizabeth Bowtell more than half a century before.

Peg Woffington was described as the most beautiful woman to have appeared on the stage in her own day. She was said to be full of vitality, elegance, and wit. During a career lasting over 30 years, she took on major roles in well over a hundred plays, sometimes acting different parts in the same play, at different periods in her life. She was especially famous for her talent in men's roles.
Bib: Daly, A., *Life of Peg Woffington*; Molloy, J. F., *The Life and Adventures of Peg Woffington*.

Wolcot, John (1738–1819)
Poet. After a career as a doctor in Jamaica and Cornwall, Wolcot accompanied the painter Opie to London, intent on a career in literature. His poems, published under the

pseudonym Peter Pindar are crude if vigorous
▷ satires on respectable public figures and
institutions: *Lyric Odes to the Royal
Academicians* (1782–5), *The Lousiad* (1785),
Instructions to a Celebrated Laureat (1787).
His *Bozzy and Piozzi* (1786) is a whimsical
poem in which ▷ James Boswell and
▷ Hester Thrale are shown reminiscing
about ▷ Samuel Johnson, who had died two
years earlier.

Wollstonecraft, Mary (1759–97)
Pamphleteer and novelist. Wollstonecraft is
notable for her outspoken views on the role of
women in society, and on the part played by
education in woman's oppression. After
running a school in London with her sister,
she set out her ideas in the early pamphlet
Thoughts on the Education of Daughters (1787).
The following year her novel, *Mary*,
developed this theme, together with a satirical
perspective on the manners of the aristocracy,
possibly based on her own experiences as
governess with the family of Lord
Kingsborough in Ireland.

Wollstonecraft's most famous work, *A
Vindication of the Rights of Woman* (1792)
now stands as one of the major documents in
the history of women's writing. Attacking the
'mistaken notions of female excellence' which
she recognized in contemporary attitudes to
'femininity' and the cult of the sentimental,
Wollstonecraft argued that women were not
naturally submissive, but taught to be so,
confined to 'smiling under the lash at which
[they] dare not snarl'. Although widely
caricatured by critics for her own 'immoral'
life – an affair with Gilbert Imlay, and
subsequent marriage with ▷ William
Godwin – Wollstonecraft's ideas are closely
related to the moralist tradition of writing
addressed to young women. Arguing that the
true basis of marriage must be not love but
friendship, she continues the rational
proposals outlined by the 17th-century
pamphleteer ▷ Mary Astell in such works
as *A Serious Proposal to the Ladies*. The most
radical of her thoughts concern the treatment
by society of unmarried mothers, whom she
believed were worthy of the respect and
support of their families and lovers. Her
novel *Maria: or, The Wrongs of Woman*
(1798) remained unfinished and was
published posthumously, but develops the
ideas of *A Vindication* in a more complex and
experimental context. The philosophical
tradition behind her writings is evident in *A
Vindication of the Rights of Man* (1790), a
reply to ▷ Burke, and in the dedication of
Rights of Woman to Talleyrand.

Bib: Tomalin, C., *The Life and Death of
Mary Wollstonecraft*.

Wolsey, Thomas (?1475–1530)
Statesman and churchman. He was born of
comparatively humble parents in Ipswich,
but with the aid of various patrons he
received rapid promotion in the Church. In
1507 he became chaplain to ▷ King Henry
VII who employed him on diplomatic affairs.
In the next reign he was for 20 years
practically the sole ruler of the country,
having the full confidence of ▷ Henry VIII.
He became Bishop of Lincoln, Bishop of
Tournai in France, Archbishop of York,
Cardinal, within reach of becoming Pope. At
home he was a firm and able administrator.
His foreign policy was skilful, but his personal
ambitions led to its ultimate failure. In his
anxiety to become Pope, he sought the favour
of the Emperor Charles V and allowed him to
become too powerful in Europe. Charles was
nephew to Henry VIII's queen, Katherine of
Aragon, whom in 1528 Henry wanted to
divorce. Since Charles had Rome in his
hands, the Pope could not consent, and in
1529 Wolsey lost the favour of the king; his
downfall was the more complete because he
had no other powerful supporters in the
country. His life was written by a member of
his household, George Cavendish, but it was
not published until 1641. His downfall was
dramatized by ▷ Fletcher and
▷ Shakespeare in ▷ *Henry VIII*.

Woman Killed with Kindness, A (1603)
A powerful domestic tragedy by ▷ Thomas
Heywood, which explores the marriage,
adultery and death of Anne Frankford, the
wife of a gentle and upright man, who kills
her with his 'kindness' by refusing her his
and her children's company. The seduction
of Anne by Frankford's friend Wendoll and
the subsequent husband's discovery of the
lovers are presented with great sympathy and
understanding. The play's subplot is informed
by a similar range of domestic detail and is
not without tenderness.

Women, Education of
In medieval convents, nuns often learned and
received the same education as monks.
Thereafter, women's intellectual education
was not widely provided for until the later
19th century, though much would depend on
their social rank, their parents, or their
husbands. Thomas More in ▷ *Utopia*
advocated equal education for both sexes;
▷ Swift in the 'Land of the Houyhnhnms'
(▷ *Gulliver's Travels*) causes his enlightened
horse to scorn the human habit of educating

only half mankind, and yet allowing the other half (*ie* women) to bring up the children. On the other hand, in the 16th century the enthusiasm for education caused some highly born women to be very highly educated; this is true of the two queens, ▷ Mary I and ▷ Elizabeth I, of the 'ten-days queen' Lady Jane Grey (whose education is described in ▷ Ascham's ▷ *Schoolmaster*, 1570), and of the ▷ Countess of Pembroke, Sidney's sister. In the 17th century we see from ▷ Pepys's Diary how he tried to educate his French wife, and ▷ Evelyn, the other well-known diarist, describes his highly educated daughter. Rich women were expected to have some social and some artistic accomplishments, but Pepys, for example did not expect his wife to share his scientific interests.

It is often difficult to interpret the evidence from the past as it is sometimes based on assumptions or fears about women's education that enlightened people do not now share.

Boarding schools for girls came into existence in the 17th century and became more numerous in the 18th, but either they were empty of real educational value or they were absurdly pretentious, like Miss Pinkerton's Academy described in Thackeray's ▷ *Vanity Fair* (1848); Mrs Malaprop in Sheridan's comedy ▷ *The Rivals* (1775) is a satire on the half-educated upper class women. Upper class girls had governesses for general education, music masters, dancing masters, and teachers of 'deportment', *ie* in the bearing of the body; lower class women were illiterate, unless they learned to read and write at 'charity schools'. On the other hand they had a much wider range of domestic skills than is usual with modern women, and among the poor, a rich store of folklore. However, in the 18th century there was already a shift in values. Swift, in his letter to a young lady about to enter marriage, points out that the way to keep a husband's affections was to grow in maturity of mind, and the ▷ blue stocking women of the middle of the century were entertainers of the intellectual elite of their society.

The big change dates from the mid-19th century. ▷ Tennyson's ▷ *The Princess* (1850), for example advocates educational opportunities for women and the eponymous heroine's actually founds a university for this purpose. Actual colleges were founded for the higher education of women (beginning with Queen's College, London, 1848), and schools (*eg* Cheltenham Ladies' College) comparable to the ▷ public schools for boys were founded. The women's colleges Girton (1869)

and Newnham (1875) were founded in Cambridge, and others followed at Oxford. Societies were also founded for the advancing of women's education. All this in spite of warnings from medical men that cerebral development in the female must be at the cost of physiological, *ie* child-bearing, aptitude. Since the commencement of state education in 1870, the status of women teachers has been brought equal to that of men teachers, and since 1902 equal secondary education has been provided for both sexes.

▷ Schools in England.

Women, Status of

Unmarried women had few prospects in Britain until the second half of the 19th century. In the ▷ Middle Ages they could enter convents and become nuns, but when in 1536–9 ▷ Henry VIII closed the convents and the monasteries, no alternative opened to them. Widows like Chaucer's Wife of Bath in ▷ *The Canterbury Tales* might inherit a business (in her case that of a clothier) and run it efficiently, or like Mistress Quickly in Shakespeare's ▷ *Henry IV, Part II* they might run inns. The profession of acting was opened to women from the ▷ Restoration of the Monarchy in 1660, and writing began to be a possible means of making money from the time of ▷ Aphra Behn. Later the increase of interest in education for girls led to extensive employment of governesses to teach the children in private families; such a position might be peaceful and pleasant, like Mrs Weston's experience in the Woodhouse family in Jane Austen's ▷ *Emma*, but it was at least as likely to be unpleasant, underpaid, and despised, as the novelist ▷ Charlotte Brontë found. Nursing was also open to women, but nurses had no training and were commonly a low class of women like Betsey Prig and Mrs Gamp in Dickens's ▷ *Martin Chuzzlewit* until Florence Nightingale reformed the profession.

Wives and their property were entirely in the power of their husbands according to the law, though in practice they might take the management of both into their own hands, like the Wife of Bath. A Dutch observer (1575) stated that England was called the 'Paradise of married women' because they took their lives more easily than continental wives. Nonetheless, a middle-class wife worked hard, as her husband's assistant (probably his accountant) in his business, and as a mistress of baking, brewing, household management and amateur medicine.

The 19th century was the heroic age for women in Britain. No other nation before the

20th century has produced such a distinguished line of women writers as the novelists ▷ Jane Austen, ▷ Elizabeth Gaskell, Charlotte and ▷ Emily Brontë and ▷ George Eliot (Mary Ann Evans). In addition there was the prison reformer, Elizabeth Fry; the reformer of the nursing profession, Florence Nightingale; the explorer, Mary Kingsley; the sociologist, ▷ Beatrice Webb, pioneers in education, and the first women doctors. The Married Women's Property Act of 1882 for the first time gave wives rights to their own property which had hitherto been merged with their husbands'. Political rights came more slowly, and were preceded by an active and sometimes violent movement, led by the Suffragettes (▷ Suffragette Movement), who fought for them. Women over 30 were given the vote in 1918 as a consequence of their success in taking over men's work during World War I, but women over 21 (the age at which men were entitled to vote or stand for Parliament) had to wait until 1928. Now most professions are nominally open to women, including the law; a notable exception is the priesthood of the ▷ Church of England and some other religious denominations but there are signs of change even there.

The position of women at work is still generally subordinate to men: the success of a few women does not alter the fact that the average wage of women is about three-quarters that of men. Women are disproportionately under-represented in positions of security and power, for example in high level management jobs or tenured university posts.

▷ Nuns and Nunneries.

Women Beware Women (1614)
A baroque and vindictive tragedy of misdirected desire by ▷ Thomas Middleton, which ends in a bloodbath. Like ▷ *The Changeling* the play features a skilfully integrated subplot which dramatizes the incestuous love of Hippolito for his brother's daughter Isabella, whom he hopes to seduce with the help of her aunt. The most famous scene in the play concerns the seduction of Bianca by the Duke of Florence in a series of moves which parallel those of a game of chess played simultaneously between Bianca's mother-in-law and a corrupt go-between, Livia. Like ▷ Webster's ▷ *The White Devil*, *Women Beware Women* evinces a cynical and erotic awareness of the role of power and money in human relationships, and their ability to destroy even marriage.

Women in Love (1921)
A novel by ▷ D. H. Lawrence. It continues the lives of two of the characters in ▷ *The Rainbow*. Ursula Brangwen is a schoolteacher, and her sister Gudrun is an artist. The other two main characters are Gerald Crich, a mine-owner and manager, and Rupert Birkin, a school-inspector. The main narrative is about the relationships of these four: the union of Rupert and Ursula after conflict, the union of Gerald and Gudrun ending in conflict and Gerald's death, the affinities and antagonisms between the sisters and between the men. The settings include Shortlands, the mansion of the mine-owning Crich family; Breadalby, the mansion of Lady Hermione Roddice, a meeting-place of the leading intellectuals of the day; the Café Pompadour in London, a centre for artists, and a winter resort in the Austrian Tyrol. The theme is human relationships in the modern world, where intelligence has become the prisoner of self-consciousness, and spontaneous life-forces are perverted into violence, notably in Gerald, Hermione, and the German sculptor Loerke. Symbolic episodes centred on animals and other natural imagery are used to present those forces of the consciousness that lie outside rational articulation, and personal relationships are so investigated as to illuminate crucial aspects of modern culture: the life of industry, the life of art, the use and misuse of reason, and what is intimate considered as the nucleus of what is public. Rupert Birkin is a projection of Lawrence himself, but he is objectified sufficiently to be exposed to criticism.

Women's movement, The
The women's movement – under many names – is dedicated to the campaign for political and legal rights for women. It wishes to prevent discrimination on the grounds of gender and is, generally, a movement for social change.

There is no single source, although the history of women's quest for equality is a long one. The ▷ *Querelle des Femmes* in the medieval period, ▷ Aphra Behn and Mary Astell in the 17th century, and ▷ Mary Wollstonecraft in the Romantic Age all furthered women's rights. In the Victorian period ▷ feminism became linked with other social movements such as anti-slavery campaigners, evangelical groups and ▷ Quakers. The ▷ suffragette movement (1860–1930) united women and this solidarity was to re-emerge in the radicalization of the 1960s. The important works of this later stage in the women's movement are

▷ Simone de Beauvoir's *Le Deuxième Sexe* (1949), Kate Millett's *Sexual Politics* (1969) and Germaine Greer's *The Female Eunuch* (1970). The 1970s and 1980s have witnessed the second stage of the women's movement and seen its dismemberment into separate pressure groups – *eg* lesbianism, Third World – and its partial metamorphosis into post-feminism. This latter term has become popularized and takes for granted that women now have equality with men, but the mainstream of the women's movement denies this emphatically and perseveres with its campaign.

▷ Women, Status of.

Bib: Mitchell, J. and Oakley, A. (eds.), *What is Feminism?*; Eisenstein, H., *Contemporary Feminist Thought*.

Wonder, A Woman Keeps a Secret, The (1714)

Comedy by ▷ Susannah Centlivre, partly based on ▷ Ravenscroft's *The Wrangling Lovers* (1677), and often considered Centlivre's best play. It is set in Lisbon, where Don Felix, son of a Portuguese grandee, Don Lopez, wounds Antonio in a duel, after refusing to marry Antonio's sister. He goes into hiding, but secretly visits Donna Violante, a young woman intended for a nun, with whom he is in love, and who loves him. In the secondary plot, Don Lopez wants his daughter, Isabella, to marry the wealthy but foolish Don Guzman, and locks her into a room to await her suitor. She escapes into the arms of Colonel Britton, a Scotsman on his way back to England. He takes her to another house, which turns out to be Violante's, and asks for her to be cared for. Violante recognizes her and agrees to hide her and keep the secret. In fact she conceals not only Isabella, but Felix as well, and, further, hides Isabella from Felix. All the lovers are united at the end. The title is gently ironic for in the play's final triplet Felix remarks that Violante's steadfastness has shown 'That Man has no Advantage but the Name'. *The Wonder* was first produced at ▷ Drury Lane with ▷ Robert Wilks as Don Felix and ▷ Anne Oldfield as Violante, to whom Centlivre paid tribute as being largely responsible for its success. But it was revived numerous times during the 18th and 19th centuries, notably with ▷ Garrick as Felix, from 1756 onwards, and ▷ John Philip Kemble in the part afterwards. Garrick chose the play to end his theatrical career in 1776. It survived to 1897.

Wood, Ellen (Mrs Henry), 1814–87

Novelist. Daughter of a glove manufacturer of scholarly tastes, Ellen Price was born in Worcester and lived as a child with her maternal grandmother. Curvature of the spine affected her health all her life and she wrote her novels in a reclining chair. In 1836 she married Henry Wood, head of a banking and shipping firm, and they lived in France until 1856 when they returned and remained in London. She was a very orthodox churchwoman and strongly conservative. Her first novel, *East Lynne* (1861), was enormously successful and has been much dramatized, translated and filmed. She wrote numerous other novels, though none other so famous, including *Mrs Halliburton's Troubles* (1862), *The Channings* (1862), *The Shadow of Ashlydyat* (1863), *Lord Oakburn's Daughters* (1864), *Within the Maze* (1872) and many more. The *Johnny Ludlow* series of stories (1868–89) drew on local and family history from her early life, and lacked some of the melodramatic and sensational elements of many of her other novels. Despite the heavy moralizing as well as careless and inaccurate writing, her novels were immensely popular, especially at first. She also took on contemporary issues: *A Life's Secret* (1867) portrayed a negative side of ▷ trade unionism and caused her publisher's office to be mobbed by a hostile crowd.

Bib: Wood, C. W., *Memorials of Mrs Henry Wood*; Hughes, W., *The Maniac in the Cellar: Sensation Novels of the 1860s* (chapter).

Woodlanders, The (1887)

A novel by ▷ Thomas Hardy. The setting is Dorset in the south-west of England and the human relationships are a kind of movement upwards, downwards and upwards again from the primitive rural base. The primitive peasant girl, Marty South, is in love with the young cider-maker, Giles Winterbourne, who is as simple in his background as she is herself but has great natural delicacy of feeling. Giles is himself in love with Grace Melbury, the daughter of a local timber merchant, who has had a 'lady's' education. She has not been spoiled by this but her sensibilities have spoiled her for the primitive environment to which Giles belongs. Her parents marry her to the young doctor, Edred Fitzpiers, who, however, is enticed away by the great lady of the district, Felice Charmond. Grace takes refuge in the woods with Giles, who, though a sick man, abandons his cottage to her and lives in a hut nearby, where he dies. Grace and Marty South mourn together over his grave but Grace becomes reconciled to Fitzpiers and Marty is left to mourn alone. Neither

Fitzpiers nor Mrs Charmond belongs to the rural background and their intrusion into it is disruptive of its values, embodied above all in Giles Winterbourne.

Woolf, Virginia (1882–1941)

Virginia Woolf

Novelist and critic. She was the daughter of ▷ Leslie Stephen, the literary critic; after his death in 1904, the house in the Bloomsbury district of London which she shared with her sister Vanessa (later Vanessa Bell) became the centre of the ▷ Bloomsbury Group of intellectuals, one of whom, the socialist thinker Leonard Woolf, she married in 1912. Together they established the Hogarth Press which published much of the most memorable imaginative writing of the 1920s. She experienced recurrent bouts of depression, and during one of these took her own life by drowning herself in the River Ouse, near her home at Rodmell, Sussex.

Her first two novels, *The Voyage Out* (1915) and *Night and Day* (1919), are basically ▷ realist in their technique, but in the next four – *Jacob's Room* (1922), ▷ *Mrs Dalloway* (1925), ▷ *To the Lighthouse* (1927) and ▷ *The Waves* (1931) – she became increasingly experimental and innovatory. Her attitude was formed by three influences: the negative one of dissatisfaction with the methods and outlook of the three novelists who, in the first 20 years of this century, dominated the contemporary public, ▷ H. G. Wells, ▷ Arnold Bennett, and ▷ John Galsworthy (see Woolf's essay 'Mr Bennett and Mrs Brown', 1923), the outlook of the Bloomsbury circle, with their strong emphasis on the value of personal relations and the cultivation of the sensibility; the sense of tragedy in the 19th-century Russian novelists, ▷ Tolstoy and Dostoievsky, and the short-story writer ▷ Chekhov. She sought to develop a technique of expression which would capture the essence of the sensibility – the experiencing self – and to do this, she reduced the plot-and-story element of novel-writing as far as she could and developed a ▷ stream of consciousness narrative to render inner experience. The last two of the four experimental novels mentioned are usually considered to be her most successful achievements, especially *To the Lighthouse*. In her later novels, *The Years* (1937) and *Between the Acts* (1941), she again used a more customary technique, though with stress on symbolism and bringing out the slight incident as possibly that which is most revelatory. She is now generally regarded as one of the greatest of the modernist innovators, and is also an important focus for feminist debate.

▷ *Orlando* (1928) is a composite work, ostensibly a biography of a woman poet (Victoria Sackville-West), but in part a brilliantly vivid historical novel (though her subject was her contemporary) and in part literary criticism. Her more formal literary criticism was published in two volumes *The Common Reader* (1925) and *The Common Reader, 2nd Series* (1932). In these she expressed her philosophy of creative writing (for instance in the essay *Modern Fiction*, 1925) and her response to the writers and writings of the past that most interested her. She had a partly fictional way of re-creating the personalities of past writers which is sensitive and vivid. In her social and political attitude she was feminist, *ie* she was much concerned with the rights of women and especially of women writers. This is one of the basic themes of *Orlando* but it comes out most clearly in *A Room of One's Own* (1931). *Flush* (1933) is another experiment in fictional biography (of ▷ Elizabeth Barrett Browning's spaniel) and she wrote a straight biography of her friend the art critic Roger Fry (1940). Apart from *The Common Reader*, her volumes of essays and criticism include: *Three Guineas* (1938); *The Death of the Moth* (1942); *The Captain's Death Bed* (1950); *Granite and Rainbow* (1958). Her *Collected Essays* were published in 1966, her *Letters* between 1975 and 1980 and her diaries (*The Diary of Virginia Woolf*) between 1977 and 1984. *Moments of Being* (1976) is a selection of autobiographical writings. Her stories are collected in *A Haunted House* (1943).

Bib: Woolf, L., *Autobiography*; Bell, Q.,
Virginia Woolf, A Biography; Gordon, L.,
Virginia Woolf: A Writer's Life; Clements,
P., and Grundy, I. (eds.), *Virginia Woolf:
New Critical Essays*; Daiches, D., *Virginia
Woolf*; Johnstone, J. K., *The Bloomsbury
Group*; Marcus, J. (ed.), *New Feminist Essays
on Virginia Woolf*; Naremore, J., *The World
Without a Self*; Rosenthal, M., *Virginia
Woolf*.

Wordsworth, William (1770–1850)

Poet. He was born in Cumberland, the son of
a law-agent. His mother died when he was
only eight, and when his father died five
years later, he was sent to school at
Hawkshead, where he led a life of solitary
freedom among the fells. In 1787 he went to
Cambridge, but more inspiring in their
influence were his two visits to revolutionary
France: the first in 1790, and the second,
lasting a year, from November 1791. During
the second visit his love affair with a surgeon's
daughter, Annette Vallon, resulted in her
pregnancy, and she later bore him a daughter.
Forced to leave Annette behind on his return
Wordsworth underwent a period of turmoil,
intensified when England went to war with
France in 1793. The emotional trauma of this
period in his life seems to have been displaced
into the searching anxiety which underlies
much of his early poetry. The love affair is
not mentioned explicitly in his work but is
recounted at one remove in the story of
Vaudracour and Julia (written c. 1804;
published 1820).

Wordsworth's relatives intended him for
the Church, but his religious views at this
time tended towards an unorthodox
▷ pantheism, evolved during his strangely
lonely but happy childhood. Moreover, the
writings of the extreme rationalist philosopher
▷ William Godwin influenced him still
further against the possibility of a career in
the Church of England. Fortunately in 1795 a
friend left him a legacy sufficient to keep him
independent, and he settled down in Somerset
with his sister Dorothy, one of the most
sustaining personal influences of his life. By
1797 he had made the friendship of ▷ Samuel
Taylor Coleridge, who came to live nearby,
and in 1798 the two poets collaborated in
producing ▷ *Lyrical Ballads*. In 1799
William and Dorothy moved to Dove Cottage,
Grasmere, and in 1802 Wordsworth married
Mary Hutchinson. By this time, he was
disillusioned with France, now under
dictatorship, had abandoned Godwinism, and
was beginning to turn back to orthodox
religion. He also became more conservative in

politics, to the disgust of younger men such
as ▷ Byron and ▷ Shelley. The great
decade of his poetry ran from 1797 to 1807.
Thereafter it declined in quality while his
reputation slowly grew. By 1830 his
achievement was generally acknowledged, and
in 1843 he was made ▷ Poet Laureate.

Wordsworth's first volumes (*Descriptive
Sketches*, *An Evening Walk*, 1793) show the
characteristic tone and diction of 18th-century
topographical and nature poetry. They were
followed by a tragedy, *The Borderers* (not
published until 1842). The *Lyrical Ballads*
collection marks a new departure however, in
the uncompromising simplicity of much of its
language, its concern with the poor and
outcast, and its fusion of natural description
with inward states of mind. These qualities
have caused the volume to be viewed as the
starting point of the ▷ Romantic
Movement. The *Preface* to the 1800 edition
of *Lyrical Ballads* also contained
Wordsworth's attack on the 'gaudiness and
inane phraseology' which he felt encumbered
contemporary verse. With the encouragement
of Coleridge, he planned a long philosophical
poem to be called *The Recluse*, and in
preparation for it, wrote ▷ *The Prelude*.
This was completed by 1805, but not
published until 1850, and then in a revised
form. In 1807 Wordsworth published *Poems
in Two Volumes*, and in 1814 ▷ *The
Excursion*, the only part of *The Recluse* to be
completed besides *The Prelude*. These were
followed by *The White Doe of Rylstone* (1815);
Peter Bell (1819); *The River Duddon* (1820);
Ecclesiastical Sketches (1822); *Sonnets* (1838).

Wordsworth's greatness lies in his
impressive, even stubborn authenticity of
tone. Sometimes this is achieved through the
use of primitive or simplistic literary form as
in such lyrical ballads as *We are Seven* and
The Thorn, and also the ▷ Lucy poems.
Sometimes Wordsworth develops the
discursive ▷ blank verse manner of the
18th-century ▷ Georgic into an original,
profoundly introspective vehicle for what
▷ John Keats called his 'egotistical sublime',
as in *The Prelude*, ▷ *The Ruined Cottage*
and ▷ *Tintern Abbey*. Frequently he
succeeds in convincing the reader that subject
matter which in other poets would be merely
banal or even comic, is in fact of mysterious
portentousness. This technique is particularly
impressive in poems which treat the poor, the
mad, the senile, members of humanity
generally disregarded in earlier poetry. In
these works his diction and tone brush aside
the class-based doctrine of kinds, and the
related conceptions of 'high' and 'low'

language which dominate much 18th-century verse. Such poems as *Simon Lee, The Idiot Boy*, and ▷ *Resolution and Independence* (1807) seem to challenge the reader's humanity, by their empathy with the wretched, the abject, and the poverty-stricken.

Another characteristically Romantic idea, that 'the child is father to the man', that youth is essentially richer in wisdom and insight than age, is developed into a full-scale philosophy in the early books of *The Prelude*. It is significant however that the illustrative reminiscences of the poet's own youth are far more effective as poetry than the passages of explicit theorizing. The ▷ *Ode: Intimations of Immortality from Recollections of Early Childhood* (1807) is often thought to show Wordsworth's uneasy recognition that his inspiration was leaving him. It is a mistake, however, to suppose that he wrote no good poetry after 1807, though his spiritual earnestness increasingly declines into orthodox piety, and his bold austerity of tone into mere banality.

Bib: Moorman, M., *Life*; Bateson, F. W., *Wordsworth, A Reinterpretation*; Knight, G. W., in *The Starlit Dome*; Sherry, C., *Wordsworth's Poetry of the Imagination*; Beer, J., *Wordsworth and the Human Heart*; Wordsworth, J., *William Wordsworth: The Borders of Vision*; Watson, J. R., *Wordsworth*; Hartmann, G., *The Unremarkable Wordsworth*; Jacobus, M., *Tradition and Experiment in Wordsworth's Lyrical Ballads* (*1798*); Jones, A. R., and Tydeman, W. (eds.), *Wordsworth: Lyrical Ballads* (Macmillan Casebook); Harvey, W. J., and Gravil, R., *Wordsworth: The Prelude* (Macmillan Casebook).

Workhouses

Institutions to accommodate the destitute at public expense, and to provide them with work to ensure that they were socially useful. They were first established under the ▷ Poor Law of 1576; they increased in number, but by the 18th century the administration of them, the responsibility of the parish, had become seriously inefficient, and ▷ magistrates were more inclined to administer financial relief to the paupers in their homes. This 'outdoor relief' – the 'Speenhamland System', so called from the parish in which it was first used – tended to be demoralizing to the working poor, who earned very little more than the workless paupers. The whole system was remodelled by the New Poor Law of 1834, by which workhouses were established regionally and administered by Boards of Guardians. The philosophy behind the Poor Law was that most destitution was due to laziness and vice, so that workhouses ought to be practically penal institutions. Consequently, though they ceased to be places of brutality and vice as they had been in the 18th century, they became coldly inhuman, providing only the barest necessities of existence. Their inhumanity aroused ▷ Dickens to his indignantly satirical picture of them in ▷ *Oliver Twist*; in his last complete novel, ▷ *Our Mutual Friend*, Dickens returned to the theme by portraying the old woman, Betty Higden, as dying by the roadside sooner than enter a workhouse. Workhouses were indeed bitterly hated by the poor, and in the 20th century they have been gradually eliminated, partly by the reinstitution of assistance in the home, and partly by gradual modification into institutions chiefly for the aged poor.

Wreck of the Deutschland, The

A poem by ▷ Gerard Manley Hopkins, written in 1875, but not printed until the first editions of his collected poems (edited by ▷ Robert Bridges) was published in 1918, apart from a short extract in Bridges's anthology *The Spirit of Men* (1918). Hopkins had ceased writing poetry when he entered the Jesuit Order in 1868. He broke his silence in consequence of being deeply moved at the news of the loss of the ship *Deutschland* at the mouth of the Thames in the winter of 1875, and of the drowning of five German nuns, who were passengers and exiles on account of Bismarck's anti-Catholic legislation (the Falk Laws).

It is the first of Hopkins's important poems to be written in what he called ▷ Sprung Rhythm, which he employed for most of his subsequent poetry; the lines have a regular count of rhythmic stresses but a varying count of syllables. This rhythm enabled Hopkins to combine the emphasis and syntax of the spoken language with the musical devices of the verse, and his use of it illustrates his statement that the language of poetry is 'that of current speech heightened'. The technique was very foreign to 19th-century ideas of poetic decorum, and explains why the poem was not published until much later: Hopkins offered it to the Jesuit journal *The Month*, but the editor declared that he dared not publish it.

Wren, Sir Christopher (1632–1723)

Architect. He was also a distinguished mathematician and astronomer, a member of the circle which in 1662 became the ▷ Royal

Christopher Wren by Godfrey Kneller
(1711)

Society. He was in fact a representative of
his age, which regarded the great cultural
tradition of Europe as descending from
ancient Rome and Greece and immensely
valued the scope and power of the human
reason. His masterpiece is St Paul's
Cathedral in London; even before the old
Cathedral was burnt down in 1666, he
proposed to remodel it 'after a good Roman
manner' not following 'the ▷ Gothic
rudeness of the old design'. Wren's
cathedral is an example of an English
version of the classical style known as
Baroque elsewhere in contemporary Europe.
He also proposed a replanning of the City
of London, in an arrangement of wide
streets radiating from a central space, but
difficulties in agreeing about property
valuations with the existing landowners
prevented this. He did, however, rebuild 52
London churches after the ▷ Fire of 1666,
giving them towers and spires of ingeniously
varied and graceful designs in white stone
that stood out against the black dome of the
cathedral – an effect now entirely ruined by
the alteration of the skyline by commercial
buildings. Wren also contributed fine
buildings to Oxford and Cambridge.

Wriothesley, Henry
    ▷ Southampton, Henry Wriothesley, 3rd
Earl of.

Wroth, Mary (Lady Wroth) (?1586–?1652)
The niece of ▷ Philip Sidney and ▷ Mary
Herbert, Countess of Pembroke, Mary
Wroth was a member of court, where she

danced in ▷ Ben Jonson's ▷ masque, *The
Masque of Blackness*. Jonson was a particular
admirer of her talents, dedicating his play
▷ *The Alchemist* to her and enthusiastically
acclaiming her poetry. In 1614, following the
death of her husband, Sir Robert Wroth,
Mary Wroth was left with over £20,000
debts, which she undertook to pay off.
Financial difficulties stalked her for most of
her life, a factor which may have induced her
to publish the first part of her work *Urania* in
1621. The second part of this work, together
with a ▷ pastoral tragi-comedy entitled
Loves Victorie, circulated in manuscript.
Urania is the first prose romance written in
English by a woman. Soon after its
publication it was withdrawn, because various
passages touched upon court intrigues. Like
Philip Sidney's ▷ *Arcadia*, *Urania* contains
poetry, including a sequence of songs and
▷ sonnets entitled *Pamphilia to
Amphilanthus* – this title being derived from
the names of the two protagonists of *Urania*.
The sequence is important because, while
participating in the ▷ Petrarchan tradition,
it is also written from the perspective of a
woman.
Bib: Roberts, J. A. (ed.), *The Poems of Lady
Mary Wroth*; Hannary, M. P., 'Mary Sidney:
Lady Wroth' in *Women Writers of the
Renaissance and Reformation*, (ed.) Wilson,
K. M.

Wuthering Heights (1847)
The sole novel by ▷ Emily Brontë. The
title of the book is the name of an old house,
high up on the Yorkshire moors, occupied by
the Earnshaw family. The period is the very
end of the 18th century. Into this house Mr
Earnshaw brings a child who has been living
the life of a wild animal in the slums of
Liverpool. His parents are quite unknown
and Earnshaw adopts him, giving him the
single name of Heathcliff. However, Mr
Earnshaw treats him less like a human being
than like an over-indulged pet animal; this
arouses the fierce resentment of his son
Hindley and it is only with the daughter
Catherine (Cathy) that Heathcliff has a
human relationship. After Mr Earnshaw's
death, Heathcliff is maltreated by Hindley,
now master of the house, and lives like a
despised animal instead of a spoilt one; his
strong bond with Cathy, however, remains.
But Cathy marries Edgar Linton from the
'civilized' household of Thrushcross Grange
in the valley. Heathcliff runs away and is
heard of no more for three years. During this
period Cathy and Edgar are contented
together, though she has fits of depression.

When Heathcliff returns, he has become a rich man but is as socially excluded as ever, as deeply identified with Cathy, and full of hatred for the Linton and the Earnshaw families, which he sets about to destroy, especially after the death of Cathy in giving birth to a daughter. He nearly succeeds in doing so but has to withhold harm from Hareton Earnshaw, the son of Hindley, and Catherine Linton, the daughter of Cathy, who are deeply in love. Heathcliff becomes detached from external reality and lives only for his union with Cathy in death. On the last page a weeping little boy declares that he has seen the ghosts of the dead Heathcliff and Cathy walking on the moor.

Emily Brontë's aim seems to have been to present an image of the feminine personality under the social constrictions of the civilization of the time. Cathy rather than Heathcliff is the central character. Women were not supposed to possess the wilder, instinctive feelings which were acknowledged in men; and girls' training, among the middle and upper classes, was a systematic inhibition of anything of the sort. Cathy, however, has this element in herself awakened by her early association with Heathcliff and though her marriage with Edgar Linton is in many ways ideal both personally and socially, she can never afterwards be fully herself: 'Nelly, I *am* Heathcliff.' Heathcliff, on the other hand, represents the savage forces in human beings which civilization attempts vainly to eliminate, whereas it should somehow assimilate them. Much of the interest of the book lies in the brilliant complexity of the structure, the dual narrative, time shifts and flashbacks, as well as the original handling of Gothic and Romantic elements, and how they colour the evocation of houses and landscapes.

Wyatt, Sir Thomas (1503–42)

Poet, courtier, diplomat. Wyatt's life, with its changes in fortune, perfectly represents the uncertain conditions of existence in the court of ▷ Henry VIII. Imprisoned several times (once because he was suspected of being the lover of Anne Boleyn), he brought to his writing an awareness of continental European styles and manner to which his life as a diplomat exposed him. His best-known poems appeared in ▷ *Tottel's Miscellany* (1557) together with poems by ▷ Henry Howard, Earl of Surrey, though his first printed works were his translations and adaptations of the *Psalms* (1549). His complex, ambiguous lyrics with their development of ▷ Petrarchan motifs and images, are not

only some of the earliest attempts at writing in a recognizably 'modern' (that is, non-medieval) style, but are important statements in their own right on the uncertain quality of life in the ▷ Renaissance polity.
Bib: Daalder, J. (ed.), *Collected Poems*; Greenblatt, S., *Renaissance Self-Fashioning*.

Wycherley, William (1640–1716)

Dramatist of the ▷ Restoration period. Born at Clive near Shrewsbury, the son of a lawyer, and educated first in France, where he became a Catholic, and then at Oxford. He studied law at the Inner Temple, but preferred to write for the stage, and to mix in courtly literary circles, associating with such individuals as the ▷ Earl of Rochester, ▷ Sir George Etherege, and Sir Charles Sedley (1639–1701). His first play, *Love in a Wood; Or St James's Park* (1671), is dedicated to one of ▷ Charles II's mistresses, the Duchess of Cleveland, who later became his mistress as well. After this he served for a time in the fleet, and was present at a sea-battle. His second play, ▷ *The Gentleman Dancing Master* (1672) is an adaptation of a play by Calderón, and written in the ▷ Spanish Intrigue style.

It is for his last two plays that Wycherley is now best remembered: ▷ *The Country Wife* (1675) and ▷ *The Plain Dealer* (1676), in which his deep cynicism lends savagery to his wit. ▷ Dryden praised the 'satire, strength and wit of Manly Wycherley', punning on the name of Manly, the chief character in *The Plain Dealer*, and Wycherley was often referred to in this way thereafter. In 1676 he stopped writing for the stage, and in 1679 married the Countess of Drogheda, a wealthy widow. She died in 1681, leaving him her fortune, but the bequest involved him in litigation, and he was reduced to poverty and imprisoned for debt for four years (1682–86). During this period he wrote *Epistles to the King and Duke* (1683), expressing his need. James II secured his release from prison, paid his debts, and awarded him a pension.
Bib: Nicoll, A., *Restoration Comedy*; Dobree, B., *Restoration Comedy*; McCarthy, E. B., *William Wycherley: A Biography*; Thompson, J., *Language in Wycherley's Plays: Seventeenth Century Language Theory and Drama*.

Wycliffe, John (?1320–84)

Religious reformer. He was distinguished at Oxford for his ability in disputes; in 1374, he became Rector of Lutterworth, and soon afterwards he started attacking the Pope and the papal court, at first chiefly on political grounds. He attacked the wealth of the senior

John Wycliffe

clergy, and contrasted it with the poverty of the parish priests. This suited a party of the nobility headed by John of Gaunt who became Wycliffe's patron and protector; they hated the rivalry of the upper clergy, and the powers possessed by the Pope to interfere in national affairs. His opposition to the Papacy grew and was accompanied by opposition to

the international religious orders such as those of the friars; this divided Oxford into rival camps. He then went on to attack some of the central doctrines of the Church such as Transubstantiation, *ie* the conversion of the bread and wine of the Sacrament into the actual body and blood of Christ. He also preached direct communion between the individual and God, and wanted an English translation of the ▷ Bible; in fact he made one, which is regarded as one of the foundation works of English prose. In all this he anticipated the ▷ Reformation which divided the Church across Europe in the 16th century; yet such was the power of his protectors that he died safely in his bed. Although Wycliffe thus anticipated the 16th-century reformers, no independence could come to the ▷ Church of England until it suited the interests of the kings; the cause of Wycliffe's success was partly that ▷ Richard II was little more than a boy, and unable to decide on religious policy.

▷ Bible in England.

Wynkyn de Worde (d 1534)
Jan van Wynkyn moved to England with ▷ Caxton in 1476, and took over Caxton's press in 1491, which he ran until his death c 1534. He published the first illustrated edition of ▷ Malory's ▷ *Morte D'Arthur* in 1498.

Xanadu
▷ *Kubla Khan.*

Xenophon
Ancient Greek (Athenian) historian and
philosopher, born about 430 BC. He was a
disciple of ▷ Socrates, and greatly
embittered against ▷ Athens, which had
put his master to death. Because of this,
although he had been an Athenian general, he
left the city and served the ▷ Spartans. His
writings on Socrates, the *Memorabilia* and the
Symposium, are the principal records we
possess of Socrates besides those of ▷ Plato.
Xenophon's *Anabasis* is an account of the war
against Artaxerxes; his *Hellenica* is a
continuation of the history by ▷ Thucydides
down to 362 BC. He wrote other works on
household management, history, the duties of
a cavalry officer, and on the elder Cyrus,
founder of the Persian monarchy.

Xerxes (5th century BC)
King of Persia. He invaded Greece in 480 BC,
crossing the ▷ Hellespont between Asia
Minor and Greece by a bridge of boats, and
at first had great success. He captured the
Pass of ▷ Thermopylae, and drove the
Greeks allied against him to the Isthmus of
Corinth. Fortunately for the future of Europe,
he was induced to fight on disadvantageous
terms at sea, and was defeated at Salamis
(480 BC). Xerxes also occurs in the ancient
Jewish romance of *Esther* (Old Testament of
the Bible) where he bears the name of
Ahasuerus.

Y

Yankee
A slang term used by the British for an American from any part of the United States. In America, it was originally used for an American from the east coast region known as New England. The term arose in the 18th century, perhaps from an American Indian word for English colonists, perhaps from an American Indian corruption of the French 'Anglais' = 'English'.

Yeats, W. B. (William Butler) (1865–1939)

W. B. Yeats

Anglo-Irish poet. He was of ▷ Protestant family, a fact of importance in 19th-century Ireland where patriotism was so bound up with Roman Catholicism. His father was an eminent painter. He spent his boyhood between school in London and his mother's native county of Sligo, a wild and beautiful county in north-western Ireland which is a background to much of his poetry. His youth was passed during the upsurge of Irish political nationalism represented by the ▷ Home Rule movement led by ▷ Parnell. He shared the antagonism felt by English writers of ▷ Pre-Raphaelite background – notably ▷ William Morris – to the urban and industrial harshness and materialism of contemporary English culture. He sought a basis for resistance to it in Irish peasant folk traditions and ancient Celtic myth. His first work was on a theme from this mythology – The Wanderings of Oisin (▷ Oisin). Yeats

was indeed fortunate in having such a cultural basis at hand for his anti-materialistic poetry, while his English contemporaries had further to look. His carreer divides naturally into four phases:

1 *1889–99*. During this period he was a leading member of the ▷ Aesthetic Movement in London, an outcome of ▷ Pre-Raphaelitism, but especially indebted to the Oxford scholar, ▷ Walter Pater. In its revolt against ▷ Victorian materialism, it tended to ▷ Catholicism and to mysticism. Its meeting-place was the Rhymers' Club, and its public voice the ▷ *Yellow Book*. Yeats shared its mystical sympathies, which in his case brought together Celtic and Indian mythology; these come out in his works of the period: prose – ▷ *The Celtic Twilight* (1893), *The Secret Rose, The Tables of the Law, The Adoration of the Magi* (1897); verse – *Crossways* (1889), *The Rose* (1893), *The Wind Among the Reeds* (1899); verse plays – *The Countess Cathleen* (1892) and *The Land of Heart's Desire* (1894).

2 *1899–1909*. Yeats, with the help of ▷ Lady Gregory, built up the Irish National Theatre, which found a home in the ▷ Abbey Theatre, Dublin. Until 1909, he was its manager, and he wrote plays for it, predominantly based on Irish myth. The period was disillusioning for him so far as his hopes for Irish culture went, but it was formative in his development as a major poet. He hoped to make the theatre the voice of a distinctively Irish modern culture, and at least he succeeded in creating one of the most interesting dramatic movements in contemporary Europe. In personal terms, the theatre business brought out new strength and realism in his character and in his writing; he was the first poet writing in English since the 17th century to seek intelligently and purposefully for an effective dramatic idiom and for new methods of dramatic production. His only volume of verse during these ten years was *In the Seven Woods* (1904); amongst his plays are *Cathleen ni Houlihan* (1902), *The King's Threshold* (1904), *Deirdre* (1907).

3 *1910–18 – the Period of Transition*. He had begun his career in the tradition of ▷ Spenser, ▷ Shelley and the Pre-Raphaelites, and he had always been interested in the mysticism of ▷ Blake, but he now became one of the poets, including ▷ Ezra Pound (whom he met at this time) and ▷ T. S. Eliot, drawn to the intellectually more vigorous tradition

associated with the 17th-century
▷ Metaphysicals, especially ▷ Donne. He
was no longer a ▷ romantic, at least in the
decadent sense of a dreamer, but though his
mood was harsher and he had lost some of his
faith, he searched no less assiduously for
symbols which could give meaning to history
and life. At first he turned away from Ireland,
but the Irish Rebellion of 1916 turned him
back to the country which was after all the
human context of his emotions. His books
The Green Helmet (1910) and *Responsibilities*
(1914) represent the new austerity of his
poetry.

4 1919–39: It is in this period that Yeats
grows into one of the most important poets of
the 20th century, with the publication of *The
Wild Swans at Coole* (1919), *Michael Robartes
and the Dancer* (1921), *The Tower* (1928) and
The Winding Stair (1933). This work is
marked by strong rhythms, by ▷ stanza and
rhyme patterns which enforce thought, by
severe diction with few adjectives, and by a
range of symbols each of which is a nucleus
of meanings. The symbols are part of an
elaborate theory of history (explained in the
prose *A Vision*, 1925) derived from the
Italian philosopher Vico (1668–1744) and the
▷ neo-Platonism of ▷ Plotinus (3rd century
AD). Whatever the faultiness of the system
considered apart from the poetry, it
constituted for Yeats a mythology which he
could use poetically to embody human
experience widely and deeply. It is scarcely
helpful to try to 'learn' this mythology in
order to understand Yeats's poetry; it is
elucidated by the poetry itself, if it is read in
bulk. With these symbols (the tower, the
moon, etc.) Yeats had a wide mythology of
persons, some drawn from his own friends,
some from history and myth, and some
invented, *eg* Crazy Jane in *Words for Music
Perhaps*. This, like *A Woman Young and Old*,
A Full Moon in March (1935) and *Last Poems*
(1936–39), has more bitterness and less richness
than the previous volumes of this period.
Yeats continued to write plays and to improve
his dramatic idiom, partly under the influence
of the Japanese ▷ Noh drama; his best play
is nearly his last – *Purgatory* (1939). After
1910, Yeats's prose is also distinguished,
notably his *Autobiographies* (1915 and 1922),
some of his critical essays, *eg Per Amica
Silentia* (1918) and his essays on drama, *Plays
and Controversies* (1923).

▷ Irish literature in English.
Bib: Hone, J. M., *Life*, Ellmann, R., *Yeats,
the Man and the Masks; The Identity of
Yeats*; Henn, T. R., *The Lonely Tower*; Stock,
W. B. *Yeats*; Rudd, M., *Divided Image: a*

Study of Blake and Yeats; Unterecker, J., *A
Reader's Guide to Yeats*; Kermode, F.,
Romantic Image; Hall and Steinmann (eds.), a
collection of essays; Leavis, F. R., *New
Bearings in English Poetry*; Raine, K., *Yeats
the Initiate*; Dorn, K., *Players and Painted
Stage*; Ure, P., *Yeats the Playwright*.

Yellow Book
An illustrated quarterly review, 1894–7. It
was a main organ of the arts during the
period, and though it was especially the voice
of the ▷ Aesthetic Movement, it also
published writers who did not belong to this
movement, *eg* ▷ Henry James.
▷ Nineties Poets.

Yellow peril
A phrase used at the end of the 19th century,
expressing the fear that the Mongolian races
might sweep across Asia and destroy the
European ones. The fear is partly based on
previous events, such as the invasion of the
West by the ▷ Huns, and that of eastern
Europe by the ▷ Tartars, and partly because
of the rise of Japan and hostility to Europeans
among the Chinese at the end of the 19th
century.

Yeoman
Originally the word probably meant
'countryman', but by the 14th century it was
used for a peasant freeholder, *ie* a man below
the class of gentry, but an independent owner
of land, or at least 'a tenant at will', *ie* a man
who owed rent for his land but who could
abandon his tenancy when he pleased.
Yeomen thus formed a class between the
gentry and the hired labourers or serfs (who
were few after the 14th century). The younger
sons of yeomen would be landless, and
commonly took service with the gentry, often
bearing arms for them, like the Yeoman who
follows the Squire in Chaucer's ▷ *Canterbury
Tales*. As a class they were substantial and
independent; their skill as archers caused
them to be invaluable to the 14th- and 15th-
century kings (especially ▷ Edward III and
▷ Henry V) engaged in wars with the
French, who relied on cavalry. The success of
the yeoman archers at the battles of ▷ Crécy
(1346), Poitiers (1356) and ▷ Agincourt
(1415) indeed brought about a military
revolution; from the 15th century the
cavalryman declined in importance and the
importance of the infantryman increased.

The ▷ Wars of the Roses and the policy
of the ▷ Tudor sovereigns reduced the
power of the old nobility and encouraged the
prosperity of the yeomen, who flourished
throughout the 16th and 17th centuries, and

often improved their condition so as to rise into the class of the gentry. In the 18th century the tide ran the other way; the richer landowners were anxious to enclose land into large farms, and to buy out the freeholding yeomen whose small farms stood in the way. This freeholding class thus declined, or joined the ranks of the tenant farmers under the big land-owners. Often they went to work in the rapidly growing industrial towns. By the mid-19th century, the term 'yeoman' practically disappeared but it is now used for a nostalgic concept of the sturdy independent Englishman, full of common sense and natural patriotism.

The Yeomen of the Guard were established in 1485, and now guard the ▷ Tower of London; they are popularly known as Beefeaters. Yeomanry Regiments were regiments of volunteers who in peacetime trained as soldiers in their spare time; after 1920 they were known as the Territorials.

Yeoman's Tale, The Canon's
▷ *Canon's Yeoman's Tale, The.*

Yonge, Charlotte Mary (1823–1901)
Novelist. She was a prolific writer with strong High Church beliefs which permeate her writing. Religiously she was influenced by the ▷ Oxford Movement and artistically, to some extent, ▷ Pre-Raphaelitism. Among the novels which brought her fame, perhaps the best known were *The Heir of Redclyffe* (1853) and *The Daisy Chain* (1856). She wrote a number of historical romances, of which at least one, *The Little Duke* (1854), became a famous children's book.
Bib: Battiscombe, G., *Charlotte Mary Yonge*; Battiscombe, G. and Laski, M., (ed.) *A Chaplet for Charlotte Yonge*; Woolf, R. L., *Gains and Losses: Novels of Faith and Doubt in Victorian England* (chapter); Foster S., *Marriage and Freedom in Victorian Women's Fiction*.

Yorick
1 In ▷ Shakespeare's ▷ *Hamlet*, the former king's jester whose skull the gravedigger turns up in V. i, giving Hamlet a subject for meditation. It has been conjectured that Shakespeare may have been alluding to ▷ Tarlton, or some other famous jester of the time.
2 In ▷ Sterne's novel ▷ *Tristram Shandy* the witty parson who, Sterne suggests, is probably a descendant of Shakespeare's Yorick. Sterne also used Yorick as the pen-name under which he published his ▷ sermons, and as his pen-name in his ▷ *Sentimental Journey*.

York Cycle, The
A ▷ cycle of plays performed on pageant waggons, at stations in the streets of York, on Corpus Christi day from the late 14th century until performances were suppressed in the late 16th century. The earliest record of the performance of plays on Corpus Christi day comes from York (1378), and if it was one of the oldest cycles, it seems also to have been one of the longest. There are 48 plays in the single extant manuscript of the cycle, but there are signs that texts of more plays in the cycle have not survived. The cycle underwent several revisions, and the work of some distinctive revisers (the 'York metrist', the 'York realist' have been identified by critics).
Bib: Beadle, R. and King, P. (eds.), *York Mystery Plays: A Selection in Modern Spelling*; Beadle, R. (ed.), *The York Plays*.

Yorkshire Tragedy, A
A domestic tragedy published in 1608, and based on actual murders occurring in 1605. The play was ascribed to ▷ Shakespeare on its publication but he is not now thought to have had any hand in it. It is, however, a forceful work, in a tradition of domestic tragedy that is an important subordinate line of the drama of Shakespeare's time: ▷ *Arden of Faversham*; *Warning for Fair Women* (Anon., 1599), and ▷ Thomas Heywood's *A Woman Killed with Kindness* (1603). They have in common that they deal with men and women of the middle classes (not, like the grand tragedy of the age, with the courts of princes), that they are realistic, and that they convey a strong moral warning.

Young, Edward (1683–1765)
Royal chaplain and later Rector of Welwyn in Hertfordshire. He wrote three tragedies which were successfully acted in Drury Lane, and a series of didactic satires: *The Force of Religion* (1714) in ▷ couplets, and *The Love of Fame* (1725/8), *The Vindication of Providence* (1728) and *Resignation* (1762), all in Miltonic ▷ blank verse. His most important work, the melancholy and reflective poem, *The Complaint or Night Thoughts on Life, Death and Immortality* (1742–5), consisting of 10,000 lines of blank verse, was considered by ▷ Samuel Johnson to display 'the magnificence of vast extent and endless diversity', and became immensely popular both in Britain and on the continent. As their titles suggest, Young's poems are marked by a crushing orthodoxy of religious sentiment, and their turgid rhetorical dogmatism makes them very difficult to read today. Young's influential prose essay *Conjectures on Original Composition* (1759), focusses on the nature of

artistic 'genius' and marks an important stage in the development of pre-romantic literary theory.

Bib: Wicker, C. V., *Edward Young and the Fear of Death.*

Yvain

One of the Knights of the ▷ Round Table, the son of King Urien, who appears in early Welsh legendary narratives as Owein. His story is the central focus of ▷ Chrétien de Troyes's 12th-century romance *Yvain*, which charts events by which Yvain wins, loses, and regains his chivalric identity. He wins a wife and a rich court as a result of his encounter with the Knight of the Fountain; but forfeits his wife and reputation when he fails to return, as promised, from more than a year away in the company of the Round Table. A period of madness ensues, but he gradually builds up a reputation through his adventures as the Knight of the Lion (so called because his companion and aide is a Lion). The Lady of the Fountain reluctantly accepts him back finally, largely as a result of the plotting of her maid. Chrétien's narrative forms the basis for the 14th-century Middle English romance, *Yvain and Gawain.*

Z

Zany
A court ▷ fool or jester, from the Italian
'zani' for actors or clowns in the ▷ Commedia
dell'Arte.

Zeal-of-the-land Busy
A hypocritical ▷ Puritan in ▷ Ben
Jonson's comedy ▷ *Bartholomew Fair*. It
was common for Puritans of the period to
give themselves names that were phrases
derived from biblical texts.

Zeugma
▷ Figures of Speech.

Zeus
In Greek myth, the king of the gods,
identified with the Roman Jupiter (Jove). He
was first of all associated with day and sky;
his weapons were thunder and the
thunderbolts. Zeus was all-powerful and all-
knowing, and gradually developed qualities of
compassion. The temple of Olympia
contained the great statue of him by Pheidias,
one of the ▷ Seven Wonders. His queen
was ▷ Hera, also originally a sky deity; she
was constantly jealous and with good reason –
their frequent quarrels were possibly a way of
accounting for bad weather.

Before his union with Hera, his wives were
Metis = wisdom; Themis = law, mother of
Dike (Justice), Eirene (Peace) and the Fates;
▷ Mnemosyne, mother of the ▷ Muses;
Eurynome, mother of the three graces or
charities – Aglaia, Euphrosyne, Thalia. He
violated ▷ Demeter (the fertile earth), who
thus gave birth to ▷ Persephone.

After union with Hera, Zeus had affairs
with various ▷ Titanesses and ▷ Nymphs,
including Leto, mother of ▷ Apollo and
▷ Artemis; Maia, mother of Hermes. By
other relationships, Zeus was made the
ancestor of various Greek races, including the
Arcadians and the Lacedaemonians
(Spartans).

In his affairs with mortal women, he
frequently disguised himself to gain access to
them: thus to Europa he came as a bull, to
Leda as a swan, to Danae as a shower of gold,
and to Alcmene he assumed the most effective
disguise of all – that of her own husband. All
such unions were in some way attempts to
symbolize truths of nature, or attempts to
find divine ancestry for human races. Thus
the legend of Danae is thought to be an
image of the fertilizing rays of the setting
sun. The union with Hera remained, and
Zeus was the protector of monogamous
marriage and of the home.

The Roman Jupiter has many of the same
characteristics as Zeus, but is perhaps more
civic and political; he is the protector of the
city and stands for the power of empire.

Zimri
▷ *Absalom and Achitophel*.

Zionism
A Jewish nationalistic movement for the
return of the Jews to Palestine. The Jews of
Europe preserved their sense of national
identity throughout the ▷ Middle Ages,
and in the 16th and 17th centuries there was
a succession of movements among them for a
return to Zion – a synonym for Jerusalem. In
the 19th century the increase of anti-Semitism
in various countries of Europe intensified the
longing, and the movement received more
coherent organization. ▷ George Eliot's
novel *Daniel Deronda* (1876) was an
inspiration to the movement. During World
War I, an English Jew, Chaim Weismann,
proposed that Britain should provide for a
home for the Jews in Palestine. In February
1918 Britain in association with France issued
the Balfour Declaration (Balfour was British
foreign secretary) declaring their support for
the policy. In 1920 Palestine became a British
mandate, and the policy was carried out. It
was not originally intended that the Jewish
community should turn itself into a Jewish
state, nor that the rights of Arabs in Palestine
should suffer.

**Zola, Emile Edouard Charles Antoine
(1840–1902)**
French novelist. He carried the ▷ realism of
▷ Flaubert a stage further into the doctrine
of ▷ naturalism. He believed that the
biological sciences (notably the discoveries of
▷ Darwin) had changed the conditions
under which the human character should be
presented and interpreted, and that in future
the novelist should present his characters in
relation to the influences of heredity and
environment. This he carried out in the
succession of novels about the Rougon and
Macquart families (1871–93) including *La
Fortune des Rougon* (1871), *La Curée* (1874),
Le Ventre de Paris (1874), *La Conquête de
Plassans* (1875), *La Faute de l' Abbé Mouret*
(1875), *Son Excellence Eugène Rougon* (1876),
L'Assommoir (1878), *Nana* (1880), *Germinal*
(1885), *La Terre* (1888), *La Débâcle* (1892)
and *Docteur Pascal* (1893). Zola's influence
was healthy in England inasmuch as his
doctrine counteracted an English prejudice
against the ugly, the 'indecent' and the
horrible in art. He had English imitators, *eg*
▷ George Moore, and he influenced such

realists as ▷ George Gissing, ▷ H. G. Wells and ▷ Arnold Bennett; James Joyce's ▷ *Ulysses* takes Zola's art (but not his pesudo-scientific theory) to the furthest limit.

Zoroaster

The Greek form of the Persian name Zarathustra. A Persian philosopher of the 6th century BC, about whom there are many legends. He preached twin deities – Ormazd, who is light and good, and Ahriman, who is darkness and evil. They are in conflict, and their conflict is the history of the world; it centres on man, created by Ormazd, but brought to grief by Ahriman. Zoroastrianism has kinship with the dualistic religions of Mithraism and Manichaeism, rivals to Christianity in its early centuries. He originated the Magi (▷ Magi [1]).

Chronology

This chronology gives a breakdown of important dates, both literary and historical. The literary dates are listed in the left hand column and the historical events in the right hand column. The listing is necessarily selective.

1066
Battle of Hastings. Victory of William, Duke of
Normandy
1086
Doomesday Book compiled

c. 1136
Geoffrey of Monmouth: *History of the Kings of
Britain*
c. 1155
Wace: *Brut*

c. 1209
After riots at Oxford some students move to
Cambridge
1215
The Magna Carta signed
1231
Establishment of the Chancellorship as most
important office of state
1295
Edward I forms the Model Parliament

c. 1220
Laȝamon: *Brut*

1337
Beginning of the Hundred Years War
1349
The Black Death

c. 1360
Gawain and the Green Knight, Patience and *Pearl
Morte Arthure*
c. 1367
Piers Plowman (A Text)
c. 1369
Chaucer: *Book of the Duchess*
1375–99
Chaucer: *Canterbury Tales* (? 1373–93)
House of Fame
Legend of Good Women
Troilus and Criseyde
Gower: *Confessio Amantis* (?1393)
Langland: *Piers Plowman* (B Text, 1377–79)
Wycliffe: Trans. of the Bible (1380)
Piers Plowman (C Text, 1385–86)

1377
Richard II
1381
The Peasants' Revolt: Wat Tyler's rebellion
1399
Henry IV

1400–24
James I of Scotland: *King's Quair*
Paston Letters (1422–1507)
Townley Mystery Plays
Lydgate: *Fall of Princes*
Caxton: *Recuyell of the Histories of Troy* (? printed
1474)
Malory: *Morte d'Arthur* (printed 1485)
Caxton: trans. of Aesop's *Fables*
Henryson: *Moral Fables of Aesop*
Skelton: *The Tunning of Elynor Rummyng*

1413
Henry V
1415
Battle of Agincourt
1422
Henry VI

1429
Joan of Arc raises the Seige of Orleans
1461
Edward IV
1475
Richard III
1476/7
Establishment of Caxton's printing press in
England
1485
Henry VII
1492
Columbus discovers America
1498
Erasmus in England

1507
Dunbar: *Dance of the Seven Deadly Sins*
Skelton: *Book of Philip Sparrow* (? written)

1509
Henry VIII succeeds as King of England on
  death of Henry VII

1513
Gavin Douglas: trans. of Virgil's *Aeneid* (written;
  printed 1553)
1514
Barclay: *Eclogues* (completed)
1516
Sir Thomas More: *Utopia*

1517
Luther's '95 Theses': start of the Reformation
1520
Meeting at the Field of Cloth of Gold between
  Henry VIII and Francis I
1521
Henry VIII Defender of the Faith
Luther appears before the Diet of Worms

1525
Tyndale: trans. of the New Testament

1526
Burning of Tyndale's trans. of the New
  Testament
1531
Henry VII declared Head of the Church in
  England
1532
Submission of the clergy (to Henry VIII; begins
  English Reformation)

1533
Skelton: *Magnificence* (posthumous)

1533
Jan. Henry VIII secretly married to Anne Boleyn
Apr. Divorce of Henry VIII from Catharine of
  Aragon
June Coronation of Anne Boleyn
July Henry VIII excommunicated by the Pope
Sept. Birth of Princess Elizabeth to Anne Boleyn
1534
England's final break with Rome
More's refusal to take oath to the succession
Parliament passes Act of Supremacy: Pope's
  powers in England taken over by Henry VIII

1535
Coverdale: trans. of the Bible

1535
Henry VIII named 'Supreme Head of the
  Church'
Trial and execution of Sir Thomas More
1536
Execution of Anne Boleyn
1539
Act of the Six Articles passed, 'abolishing diversity
  of opinions'
Marriage treaty between Anne of Cleves and
  Henry VIII
1540
Annulment of Henry VIII's marriage to Anne of
  Cleves
Marriage between Henry VIII and Katharine
  Howard
1542
Execution of Katharine Howard
Mary Queen of Scots accedes on death of James
  V of Scotland
1543
Marriage of Catharine Parr and Henry VIII

1545
Sir Thomas Elyot: *Defence of Good Women*

1545
The Council of Trent: beginning of the Counter
  Reformation

1547
Death of Henry VIII: succeeded by Edward VI
(aged 9)
Repeal of Act of Six Articles (1539)

1548
Book of Common Prayer

1549
New Book of Common Prayer to be used from
this date

1553
Gavin Douglas: trans. of Virgil's *Aeneid* (written
1513)
Wilson: *Art of Rhetoric*

1553
Death of Edward VI
Lady Jane Grey proclaimed queen
Mary proclaimed queen in place of Lady Jane
Grey

1554
Roman Catholicism re-established in England by
Parliament

1556
Stationers' Company gains monopoly of English
printing

1557
Earl of Surrey: trans. of Virgil's *Aeneid* (Books II
and IV)
Tottel's Miscellany (poems by Surrey, Wyatt, *et
al.*)

1558
Knox: *First Blast of the Trumpet*

1558
Death of Mary; accession of Elizabeth I

1559
Mirror for Magistrates (first edition)

1559
Coronation of Elizabeth I
Act of Supremacy and Act of Uniformity

1561
Thomas Sackville (and Norton): *Gorboduc* (acted)

1563
Foxe: *Acts and Monuments* (Foxe's Book of
Martyrs)

1563
The Plague in London kills many thousands

1565
Golding: trans. of Ovid's *Metamorphoses* (Books
I–IV)

1566
Birth of James VI of Scotland

1567
Abdication of Mary Queen of Scots

1570
Ascham: *The Schoolmaster*

1572
St Bartholomew's Day massacre in Paris

1577
Holinshed: *Chronicles*

1577
Francis Drake starts his circumnavigation of the
globe

1578
Lyly: *Euphues, the Anatomy of Wit* Part One

1578
James VI takes over government of Scotland

1579
North: trans. of Plutarch's *Lives* (from French)
Spenser: *Shepherd's Calendar*

1580
Lyly: *Euphues and his England*
Sidney: *Apologie for Poetrie*

1580
Performance of plays on Sunday forbidden
Francis Drake returns to England

1581
Joseph Hall: *Ten Books of Homer's Iliads*

1581
Laws against Roman Catholics passed

1583
Discovery of the Somerville plot to assassinate
Elizabeth I
Discovery of the Throgmorton plot for Spanish
invasion of England

1584
Greene: *Mirror of Modesty*
Knox: *History of the Reformation in Scotland*
Peele: *Arraignment of Paris*

1586
Camden: *Britannia*

1587
Marlowe: *Dr Faustus* (acted; published 1604)

1589
Puttenham: *Art of English Poesie*
1590
Marlowe: *Tamburlaine* Parts I and II printed; Part
I acted 1586/7
Sidney: *Arcadia*
Spenser: *Faerie Queene* (Books I–III)
1591
Sir John Harington: trans. of Ariosto's *Orlando
    Furioso*
Shakespeare: *Henry VI* (Parts II and III)
            The Two Gentlemen of Verona
Sidney: *Astrophel and Stella* (posthumous)
Spenser: *Complaints*
1592
Shakespeare: *Henry V* Part I
Lyly: *Galatea*
Marlowe: *Edward II* (acted)
1593
Henryson: *The Testament of Cresseid* (published)
Shakespeare: *Comedy of Errors*
            Richard III
            Venus and Adonis
1594
Hooker: *Ecclesiastical Polity* (Books I–IV)
Shakespeare: *Lucrece*
            Titus Andronicus
1595
Shakespeare: *Love's Labour's Lost*
            Midsummer Night's Dream
            Richard II
            Romeo and Juliet
Spenser: *Amoretti*
        Epithalamion
        Colin Clout's Come Home Again
1596
Jonson: *Every Man in his Humour* (acted)
Shakespeare: *Merchant of Venice*
            King John
Spenser: *Faerie Queene* (Books IV–VI)
        Four Hymns
1597
Bacon: *Essays*
Joseph Hall: *Virgidemiarum* (Books I–III)
Shakespeare: *Richard II*
1598
Chapman: trans. of Homer's *Iliad* (Books I–II;
    VII–XI)
Marlowe: *Hero and Leander*
Shakespeare: *Henry IV* Parts I and II
1599
Jonson: *Every Man out of his Humour*
Shakespeare: *Julius Caesar* (acted 21 Sept.)
            Henry V
            Much Ado about Nothing

1585
Raleigh establishes his first colony at Roanoke,
    Virginia
1586
The Star Chamber condemns Mary Queen of
    Scots to death
1587
Mary Queen of Scots executed
1588
19 July Spanish Armada sighted off the Cornish
    coast
29 July The Battle of Gravelines: the Armada
    defeated

1592
Establishment of the Presbyterian Church in
    Scotland

1595
Death of Sir Francis Drake

1599
Birth of Oliver Cromwell

1600
Dekker: *The Shoemaker's Holiday* (first quarto)
Fairfax: trans. of Tasso's *Jerusalem Delivered*
Shakespeare: *The Merry Wives of Windsor*
    As You Like It
    Twelfth Night

1601
Shakespeare: *Hamlet*

1602
Marston: *Antonio's Revenge*
Shakespeare: *Troilus and Cressida*

1603
Jonson: *Sejanus*
Shakespeare: *All's Well that Ends Well*

1604
Marlowe: *Dr Faustus* (earliest surviving edition)
Shakespeare: *Hamlet* (second quarto)
    Othello (? acted)

1605
Drayton: Poems
Jonson: *Volpone* (acted; published 1607)

1606
Shakespeare: *King Lear* (acted)
    Macbeth (probably written by this date)

1607
Shakespeare: *Antony and Cleopatra* (probably
 written; Stationers' Register 20 May 1608)
Tourneur: *Revenger's Tragedy*

1608
Thomas Heywood: *Rape of Lucrece*
Shakespeare: *Coriolanus* (probably written)
    King Lear (two quartos)
    Timon of Athens (probably written)

1609
Jonson: *Epicene, or the Silent Woman* (Stationers'
 Register 20 Sept. 1610)
Shakespeare: *Pericles* (Stationers' Register 20 May
 1608)
    Sonnets
    Troilus and Cressida (two quartos)

1610
Beaumont and Fletcher: *Knight of the Burning
      Pestle* (? acted)
      The Maid's Tragedy
      (probably written)
Chapman: trans. of the *Iliad* Books I–XII
Jonson: *The Alchemist* (Stationers' Register 3 Oct.)
Shakespeare: *Cymbeline* (perhaps written)
    Winter's Tale (perhaps written)

1611
Authorised Version of the Bible
Chapman: trans. of the *Iliad* Books XIII–XXIV
Dekker and Middleton: *Roaring Girl* (printed)
Shakespeare: *Macbeth* (first recorded performance
    20 Apr.)
    The Tempest (perhaps written)
    Winter's Tale (acted by 15 May)

1612
Drayton: *Poly-Olbion* Part One
Webster: *The White Devil* (printed)

1613
Shakespeare: *Henry VIII* (acted 2 July)

1601
The execution of Earl of Essex

1602
Bodleian Library founded
Re-conquest of Ireland begun

1603
Queen Elizabeth I dies and is succeeded by James
 VI of Scotland as King James I of England
 and Ireland

1604
The Hampton Court conference: James supports
 new translation of Bible
James VI and I proclaimed king of 'Great Britain,
 France and Ireland'

1605
The Gunpowder plot

1606
Suppression of Roman Catholics by English
 Parliament

1607
English colony founded in Virginia

1611
The colonisation of Ulster

1613
Globe Theatre burns down
Poisoning of Sir Thomas Overbury

1614
Chapman: trans. of *The Odyssey* Books I–XII
Jonson: *Bartholomew Fair* (acted; published 1631)
1615
Chapman: trans. of the *Odyssey* Books XIII–XXIV
1616
Jonson: *The Devil is an Ass* (acted)
    Underwoods
Webster: *Duchess of Malfi* (acted; printed 1623)

1619
Drummond of Hawthornden: *Conversations with Ben Jonson*

1621
Burton: *Anatomy of Melancholy*
1622
Drayton: *Poly-Olbion* Part Two
Middleton and Rowley: *The Changeling*
1623
Shakespeare: *Comedies, Histories and Tragedies* ('The First Folio')
Webster: *Duchess of Malfi* (printed)
1624
Middleton: *A Game of Chess* (acted 6 Aug.)

1626
Sandys: trans. of Ovid's *Metamorphoses*
1631
Herbert: *The Temple*
Jonson: *The Devil is an Ass* (printed)
    The Staple of News (printed)
1633
Donne: Poems (posthumous (d. 1631))
Ford: *'Tis Pity She's a Whore* (printed)
1634
Thomas Carew: *Coelum Britannicum*
Milton: *Comus* (acted)
1637
Milton: *Lycidas*
1641
Milton: *Of Reformation Touching Church Discipline in England*
1642
Sir Thomas Browne: *Religio Medici*
Denham: *Cooper's Hill*
Milton: *Apology for Smectymnuus*
1644
Milton: *Areopagitica*

1646
Vaughan: Poems

1614
'The Addled Parliament'

1618
Start of Thirty Years War
Execution of Sir Walter Raleigh

1620
Freedom of worship granted to Roman Catholics in England in terms of marriage treaty between England and Spain
Pilgrim Fathers depart from Plymouth, England, in Mayflower

1625
Accession of Charles I
Marriage of Charles I and Henrietta Maria

1633
William Laud appointed Archbishop of Canterbury

1642
Civil War starts
Battle of Edgehill

1645
Prohibition of the Prayer Book by Parliament
Execution of Archbishop Laud

1648
Herrick: *Hesperides and Noble Numbers*

1649
Execution of Charles I
Abolition of the monarchy
Declaration of the Commonwealth
1651
Battle of Worcester

1651
Cleveland: Poems
D'Avenant: *Gondibert*
Hobbes: *Leviathan*
1653
Izaak Walton: *Compleat Angler*

1653
Long Parliament expelled by Cromwell
Establishment of the Protectorate: Oliver Cromwell
    Lord High Protector
1654
Union of England, Scotland and Ireland

1656
Cowley: Works (includes 'Davideis' and 'Pindaric
    Odes')
1657
Middleton: *No Wit, No Help Like a Woman's*
Two New Plays (includes *Women Beware Women*)

1658
3 Sept. Death of Oliver Cromwell: succeeded by
    Richard Cromwell, his son, as Lord Protector
1660
16 Mar. Dissolution of the Long Parliament
Charles II invited to return to England by
    Convention Parliament
1661
Corporation Act: magistrates' oath of allegiance
1662
Act of Uniformity: revises Prayer Book; Licensing
    Act forbids import of anti-Christian literature
1665
The Great Plague
1666
2 Sept. Great Fire of London

1660
Pepys: *Diary* (begun 1 Jan.)

1667
Milton: *Paradise Lost*
1668
Aphra Behn: *Oroonoko*
1671
Aphra Behn: *Forced Marriage*
Milton: *Paradise Regained*
        Samson Agonistes
1672
Dryden: *Marriage à la Mode*

1674
Rebuilding of the Theatre Royal, Drury Lane

1675
Wycherley: *Country Wife*
1676
Etherege: *Man of Mode*
1677
Aphra Behn: *The Rover* (Part One)
Wycherley: *Plain Dealer* (acted 1674)
1678
Bunyan: *Pilgrim's Progress* (Part One)
Dryden: *All for Love*
1681
Aphra Behn: *The Rover* Part Two
Dryden: *Absalom and Achitophel* Part One (Part
    Two 1682)
Marvell: *Miscellaneous Poems* (posthumous)
1682
Dryden: *Macflecknoe*

1678
The Popish Plot: the Pope, France and Spain are
    accused of conspiracy to defeat Charles

Dryden and Tate: *Absalom and Achitophel* Part
   Two
Otway: *Venice Preserv'd*

1683
Rye House plot to kill Charles II and his brother,
   James, Duke of York

1684
Bunyan: *Pilgrim's Progress*

1685
Death of Charles II; succeeded by James II
The Monmouth rebellion

1687
Dryden: *The Hind and the Panther*
           A Song for St Cecilia's Day

1688
The Glorious Revolution
William of Orange invited to England by Whig
   lords
1689
Abdication of James II declared by Parliament
Coronation of William and Mary
Act of Toleration (for Dissenters)
1690
Battle of the Boyne
1693
The National Debt established
1694
Congreve: *Double Dealer*   Establishment of the Bank of England
1695   1695
Congreve: *Love for Love*   End of press censorship
1698
Vanbrugh: *The Provoked Wife*

1700
Congreve: *The Way of the World*

1701
Protestant succession to British throne established
   by the Act of Settlement
1702
Death of William III. Accession of Queen Anne
1704
Swift: *Battle of the Books*   1704
        Tale of a Tub   Marlborough achieves victory over the French at the
1707   Battle of Blenheim
Farquhar: *The Beaux' Stratagem*   1707
                                    The Union of England and Scotland as Great
                                       Britain
1709
Pope: trans. of part of Books XII and XVI of
   Homer's *Iliad*
Steele: *The Tatler* (Apr. 1709–Jan. 1711)
1711
Addison (and Steele): *The Spectator* (1 Mar.
   1711–6 Dec. 1712)
Pope: *Essay on Criticism*
1712
Pope: *The Rape of the Lock* (first version)
1713
Pope: *Windsor Forest*
1714
Pope: *The Rape of the Lock* (final version)   1714
                                    1 Aug. Death of Queen Anne: succeeded by George
                                       I (Elector of Hanover)
                                    1715
                                    Jacobite up-rising

1719
Defoe: *Robinson Crusoe*

1720
South Sea Bubble

1721
Robert Walpole becomes Prime Minister

1724
Defoe: *Journal of the Plague Year*
         Moll Flanders
1725
Pope: trans. of Homer's *Odyssey* (Volumes I–III;
    completed 1726)
         The Plays of Shakespeare (an edition)
1726
Swift: *Gulliver's Travels*

1727
Death of George I: succeeded by his son
    George II

1728
Gay: *The Beggar's Opera* (first acted 29 Jan.;
    published 14 Feb.)
Pope: *The Dunciad* (in three books)
1730
The Grub Street Journal (–1737)
1733
Pope: *Essay on Man* (Epistles I–III)
1734
Pope: *An Essay on Man* (Epistle IV)
Theobald: *The Plays of Shakespeare* (an edition)
1735
Pope: *Epistle to Dr Arbuthnot*
1740
Richardson: *Pamela* (Volumes I-II)
1741
Fielding: *Shamela*
Hume: *Essays Moral and Political* (Volume I)
Richardson: *Pamela* (Volumes III–IV)
1742
Fielding: *Joseph Andrews*
1747
Richardson: *Clarissa* (Volumes I–II)
1749
Cleland: *Fanny Hill*
Fielding: *Tom Jones*

1752
Adoption of the Gregorian calendar: 2 September
    followed by 14 September
1753
Apr. Charter granted for the foundation of the
    British Museum

1755
Johnson: *Dictionary of the English Language*
1760
Sterne: *Tristram Shandy* (Volumes I–II)

1760
25 Oct. Death of George II. Accession of George
    III.

1761
Sterne: *Tristram Shandy* (Volumes III–IV and
    V–VI)

1763
16 May Boswell meets Johnson

1764
Horace Walpole: *The Castle of Otranto*
1765
Johnson: *The Plays of Shakespeare* (an edition)
Percy: *Reliques of Ancient English Poetry*
Sterne: *Tristram Shandy* (Volumes VII–VIII)
1766
Goldsmith: *The Vicar of Wakefield*
1767
Sterne: *Tristram Shandy* (Volume IX)

1768
Chatterton: *Rowleyan Writings* (composed)
Gray: Poems

1769
Opening of the Royal Academy
1770
Lord North becomes Prime Minister
Import duties on all goods except tea removed
1772
Start of Captain Cook's second voyage of
    discovery

1773
Goldsmith: *She Stoops to Conquer* (produced)
1774
Thomas Warton: *History of English Poetry*
    (Volume I; completed 1781)
1775
Sheridan: *The Rivals* (produced)

1773
The Boston Tea Party

1775
Defeat of the British at the Battle of Lexington:
    start of the American War of Independence
George Washington becomes Commander-in-Chief
    of American forces

1776
Gibbon: *Decline and Fall of the Roman Empire*
    (Volume I)
1777
Sheridan: *School for Scandal* (first acted)
1778
Fanny Burney: *Evelina*
1779
Johnson: *Lives of the Poets* (Volume I)
Sheridan: *The Critic* (first acted)
1780
Bentham: *Principles of Morals and Legislation*
    (privately printed)
1781
Johnson: *Lives of the Poets* (Volume II)
1782
Fanny Burney: *Cecilia*
Cowper: Poems

1782
Resignation of Lord North
Preliminaries for peace between Britain and
    America
1783
Pitt's first ministry (−1801)
1784
John Wesley founds Methodism
William Pitt becomes Prime Minister

1785
Cowper: *The Task*
1786
Burns: *Poems Chiefly in the Scottish Dialect*
    (Kilmarnock)

1788
First colony founded in Australia
The Times first published
1789
The Storming of the Bastille: Start of the French
    Revolution

1789
Blake: *Songs of Innocence* (composed)

1790
Burke: *Reflections on the Revolution in France*
Malone: *The Works of Shakespeare* (an edition)
1791
Boswell: *The Life of Johnson*
Tom Paine: *The Rights of Man* (Part I)
1792
Tom Paine: *The Rights of Man* (Part II)

1792
Paris Commune established
Trial of Tom Paine
1793
Louis XVI executed

1793
Godwin: *Political Justice*

1794
Blake: *Songs of Innocence and Experience* (first combined volume)
Ann Radcliffe: *The Mysteries of Udolpho*
1796
Fanny Burney: *Camilla*
Coleridge: *Poems on Various Subjects*
M. G. Lewis: *The Monk*
1797
Coleridge: *Kubla Khan* (probably written)
1798
Wordsworth: *The Prelude* (begun)
         (and Coleridge): *Lyrical Ballads*

1799
Hannah More: *Modern Female Education*

1798
The Irish rebellion
Nelson beats the French fleet at the Battle of the Nile
1799
Newspaper Act

1800
Bill of Union of Great Britain and Ireland

1802
Scott: *Ministrelsy of the Scottish Border* (Volumes I and II)
1803
Scott: *Ministrelsy of the Scottish Border* (Volume III)

1804
Napoleon crowned emperor
1805
Battle of Trafalgar: Nelson defeats French fleet

1805
Wordsworth: *The Prelude* (completed)
1806
Scott: *Ballads and Lyrical Pieces*
1807
C. and M. Lamb: *Tales from Shakespeare*

1809
Battle of Corunna: death of Sir John Moore
1811
The Regency Act makes the Prince of Wales Prince Regent (George III insane)
Luddite riots

1811
Jane Austen: *Sense and Sensibility*

1812
Byron: *Childe Harold* (Cantos I and II)
1813
Jane Austen: *Pride and Prejudice*
Shelley: 'Queen Mab'
1814
Jane Austen: *Mansfield Park*
Fanny Burney: *The Wanderer*
Maria Edgeworth: *Patronage*
Scott: *Waverley*
Wordsworth: 'The Excursion'
1815
Wordsworth: Poems

1815
Passage of Corn Law prohibiting imports when price low
Battle of Waterloo: Wellington defeats Napoleon

1816
Jane Austen: *Emma*
Byron: *Childe Harold* (Canto III)
Coleridge: *Kubla Khan* (published)
Scott: *Old Mortality*
1817
Blackwood's Magazine (established)
Coleridge: *Biographia Literaria*
Mary Shelley: *Frankenstein*
1818
Jane Austen: *Northanger Abbey*
           Persuasion
Byron: *Childe Harold* (Canto IV)

1818
5 May Birth of Karl Marx

Hazlitt: *Lectures on the English Poets*
Keats: *Endymion*
Peacock: *Nightmare Abbey*
Scott: *Heart of Midlothian*
1819
Byron: *Don Juan* (Cantos I and II)
Keats: 'Hyperion' (written; published 1856)
Scott: *Bride of Lammermoor*
Shelley: 'The Cenci'
1820
Keats: 'Eve of St Agnes'
Lamb: *Essays of Elia* (begun)
Scott: *Ivanhoe*
Shelley: 'Prometheus Unbound'
1821
Byron: *Don Juan* (Cantos III and V)
    'Sardanapalus'
De Quincey: *Confessions of an English Opium Eater*
Scott: *Kenilworth*
1822
Shelley: 'Hellas'

1823
Byron: *Don Juan* (Cantos VI–XIV)
Hazlitt: *Liber Amoris*
Scott: *Quentin Durward*

1824
Byron: *Don Juan* (Cantos XV–XVI)
Lamb: *Essays of Elia* (second series)
Westminster Review (established)
1825
Carlyle: *Life of Schiller*
1826
Elizabeth Barrett Browning: *Essay on Mind and other Poems*
1828
The *Spectator* (established)
1830
Cobbett: *Rural Rides*
Tennyson: *Poems Chiefly Lyrical*
1831
Peacock: *Crotchet Castle*
1832
Tennyson: 'The Lady of Shalott'

1833
Carlyle: *Sartor Resartus* (in *Frazer's Magazine*; completed 1834)
Tennyson: Poems
1834
Dickens: *Sketches by Boz*

1836
Dickens: *Pickwick Papers* (completed 1837)
1837
Dickens: *Oliver Twist* (completed 1838)

1819
The Peterloo Massacre: Manchester reform meeting broken up
Parliament passes the Six Acts to suppress possible disorder
1820
Death of George III: succeeded by George IV (the Prince Regent)

1821
Greek War of Independence
Legislation regarding free trade

1822
George Canning becomes Leader of the House of Commons and Foreign Secretary
1823
Catholic association established in Ireland by Daniel O'Connell
Robert Peel permits transportation of convicts
The Monroe doctrine: United States refuses to tolerate European political intervention in American states

1828
Tory administration formed by Wellington
1830
26 June Death of George IV: William IV comes to the throne

1832
The Reform Bill becomes law (start of electoral reform process)
1833
29 Aug. Controls placed upon child labour by passage of Factory Act

1834
Formation of the Grand National Consolidated Trades Union
The Tolpuddle Martyrs sentenced to transportation
Abolition of slavery in territories governed by Britain
1836
Chartist movement founded
1837
Death of William IV; Queen Victoria succeeds to the throne

1838
Elizabeth Barrett Browning: *The Seraphim and Other Poems*
Dickens: *Nicholas Nickleby* (completed 1839)
1840
Browning: 'Sordello'
Dickens: *Old Curiosity Shop*
1841
Browning: 'Pippa Passes'
Dickens: *Barnaby Rudge*
1842
Browning: 'Dramatic Lyrics'

1843
Carlyle: *Past and Present*
Dickens: *Martin Chuzzlewit* (completed 1844)
Macaulay: *Essays* (reprinted from *Edinburgh Review*)
Ruskin: *Modern Painters* (Volume I)
Wordsworth (becomes Poet Laureate)
1844
Elizabeth Barrett Browning: Poems
1845
Browning: *Dramatic Romances and Lyrics*
Benjamin Disraeli: *Sybil, or The Two Nations*
1846
C., E. and A. Brontë: Poems
Dickens: *Dombey and Son* (completed 1848)
1847
A. Brontë: *Agnes Grey*
C. Brontë *Jane Eyre*
E. Brontë: *Wuthering Heights*
1848
Elizabeth Gaskell: *Mary Barton*
Thackeray: *Vanity Fair* (completed)
1849
C. Brontë: *Shirley*
Dickens: *David Copperfield*
Thackeray: *Pendennis* (completed 1850)
1850
Elizabeth Barrett Browning: *Sonnets from the Portuguese*
Ruskin: *Pre-Raphaelitism*
Tennyson: 'In Memoriam' (becomes Poet Laureate)
'The Princess'
Wordsworth: 'The Prelude' (written 1805)

1852
Dickens: *Bleak House*
1853
Matthew Arnold: 'The Scholar Gypsy'
'Sohrab and Rustum'
C. Brontë: *Villette*
Elizabeth Gaskell: *Cranford*
1854
Dickens: *Hard Times*

1841
Conservative ministry formed by Robert Peel

1842
Parliament rejects Chartist petition
Mines Act: regulates employment of women and children underground
Chartist uprisings

1846
May Repeal of the Corn Laws

1849
Benjamin Disraeli becomes Conservative leader

1851
Palmerston resigns
1852
Lord John Russell resigns
1853
Free Trade budget introduced by Gladstone

1854
Britian and France declare war on Russia (Crimean War)
The Battle of Balaclava: the charge of the Light Brigade

1855
Browning: 'Men and Women'
Dickens: *Little Dorrit* (completed 1857)
Tennyson: 'Maud'
Trollope: *The Warden*
1857
C. Brontë, *The Professor*
Elizabeth Barrett Browning: 'Aurora Leigh'
Trollope: *Barchester Towers*
1858
William Morris: *Defence of Guinevere and other Poems*

1859
Darwin: *Origin of Species*
Dickens: *Tale of Two Cities*
George Eliot: *Adam Bede*
Tennyson: *Idylls of the King*
1860
Wilkie Collins: *Woman in White*
Dickens: *Great Expectations* (completed 1861)
George Eliot: *Mill on the Floss*
1861
George Eliot: *Silas Marner*
D. G. Rossetti: *Early Italian Poets*
Swinburne: *The Queen Mother Rosamund*

1862
Elizabeth Barrett Browning: *Last Poems*
J. S. Mill: *Utilitarianism* (in *Frazer's Magazine*)
Christina Rossetti: *Goblin Market and Other Poems*
1863
George Eliot: *Romola*
Thomas Huxley: *Man's Place in Nature*
Kingsley: *Water Babies*
1864
Browning: *Dramatis Personae*
1865
Matthew Arnold: *Essays in Criticism*
Lewis Carroll: *Alice's Adventures in Wonderland*
Dickens: *Our Mutual Friend* (completed)

1866
Elizabeth Gaskell: *Wives and Daughters*
Swinburne: *Poems and Ballads*
1867
Matthew Arnold: *The Study of Celtic Literature*

1868
Wilkie Collins: *The Moonstone*
George Eliot: *The Spanish Gypsy*
William Morris: *Earthly Paradise* (Volumes I and II)
1869
Blackmore: *Lorna Doone*

1870
Dickens: *Mystery of Edwin Drood*
D. G. Rossetti: Poems
1871
George Eliot: *Middlemarch* (completed 1872)
Swinburne: *Songs before Sunrise*

1859
Benjamin Disraeli's Reform Bill
Liberal administration formed by Palmerston

1861
American Civil War starts

1865
The Confederate army surrenders at Shreveport:
  end of the United States Civil War
Palmerston dies; Lord John Russell becomes Prime
  Minister

1867
Fenian disturbances
The Dominion of Canada established by the
  British North America Act
Suffrage extended by Parliamentary Reform Act
1868
Benjamin Disraeli becomes Prime Minister
Liberal victory in General Election: Gladstone
  forms ministry

1869
Opening of the Suez Canal
Birth of Gandhi

1871
Religious tests for entry to universities of Oxford
  and Cambridge abolished by the Universities
  Tests Act
Trades Unions legalised by Act of Parliament

1872
Hardy: *Under the Greenwood Tree*

1873
Pater: *Studies in the History of the Renaissance*
1874
Hardy: *Far from the Madding Crowd*
Swinburne: *Bothwell*

1876
George Eliot: *Daniel Deronda*
1877
Henry James: *The American*
1878
Hardy: *The Return of the Native*
Swinburne: *Poems and Ballads*
1879
Browning: 'Dramatic Idylls'
Henry James: *Daisy Miller*
Meredith: *The Egoist*
1880
Browning : 'Dramatic Idylls' (second series)
Benjamin Disraeli: *Endymion*
Swinburne: *Songs of the Spring Tides*
1881
Hardy: *A Laodicean*
Henry James: *Portrait of a Lady*
Christina Rossetti: *A Pageant and Other Poems*
D. G. Rossetti: *Ballads and Sonnets*
1882
Matthew Arnold: *Irish Essays*
Swinburne: 'Tristram of Lyonesse'
1883
Burton: trans. of *Arabian Nights Entertainments*
Stevenson: *Treasure Island*

1886
Henry James: *The Bostonians*
Stevenson: *Dr Jeckyll and Mr Hyde*
          Kidnapped

1888
Matthew Arnold: *Essays in Criticism* (second
   series)
1889
Yeats: 'The Wanderings of Oisin'

1891
Gissing: *New Grub Street*
Hardy: *Tess of the D'Urbervilles*
William Morris: *News from Nowhere*
Shaw: *The Quintessence of Ibsenism*
Wilde: *The Picture of Dorian Gray*
1892
Wilde: *Lady Windermere's Fan*
Yeats: *The Countess Cathleen*
1893
Gissing: *The Odd Woman*
Wilde: *Salome*
1894
Kipling: *The Jungle Book*
William Morris: *The Wood beyond the World*

1872
Voting by secret ballot introduced by the Ballot
   Act
1873
Judicature Act, reforming courts of law
1874
Conservative victory in General Election
Benjamin Disraeli forms ministry
1875
Public Health Act

1877
Queen Victoria becomes Empress of India

1880
Liberal administration formed by Gladstone

1883
Karl Marx dies

1885
General Gordon dies at Khartoum
1886
Gladstone brings in Home Rule Bill for Ireland
Second reading of Home Rule Bill brings Liberal
   defeat
1887
The Golden Jubilee of Queen Victoria
1888
Local Government Act (establishes local councils)

1890
Parnell resigns as Irish Nationalist leader

1893
Jan. Independent Labour Party formed by Kier
     Hardie at Bradford conference

1895
Hardy: *Jude the Obscure*
H. G. Wells: *The Time Machine*
Wilde: *The Importance of Being Earnest*
Yeats: Poems
1897
Henry James: *What Maisie Knew*
H. G. Wells: *The Invisible Man*
Yeats: 'The Secret Rose'
1898
Conrad: *The Nigger of the Narcissus*
Hardy: *Wessex Poems*
Henry James: 'The Turn of the Screw'
Shaw: *Arms and the Man*
　　　Mrs Warren's Profession
H. G. Wells: *The War of the Worlds*
Wilde: *Ballad of Reading Gaol*
1899
Henry James: *The Awkward Age*
John Cowper Powys: Poems (published)

1898
19 May Gladstone dies

1899
Boer War begins

1900
Conrad: *Lord Jim*
Saintsbury: *History of Criticism*
1901
Kipling: *Kim*
Shaw: *The Devil's Disciple*
1902
Conrad: *Heart of Darkness*
Hardy: *Poems of the Past and the Present*
Henry James: *Wings of a Dove*
Yeats: *Cathleen ni Houlihan*
1903
Henry James: *The Ambassadors*
Shaw: *Man and Superman*

1904
Bradley: *Shakespearean Tragedy*
Henry James: *The Golden Bowl*
Yeats: *The King's Threshold*
　　　Stories of Red Hanrahan
1905
Shaw: *Major Barbara*
Wilde: *De Profundis*
1906
Yeats: *Poetical Works* (two volumes – 1907)
1907
Conrad: *The Secret Agent*
　　　Nostromo
1908
Forster: *A Room with a View*

1910
Forster: *Howard's End*

1911
Rupert Brooke: Poems
Conrad: *Under Western Eyes*
Lawrence: *The White Peacock*

1900
British Labour Party founded
Commonwealth of Australia proclaimed
1901
Queen Victoria dies and Edward VII accedes to
　　the throne
1902
Boer War ends
Secondary schools established by Education Act
　　for England and Wales

1903
Emmeline Pankhurst founds the Women's Social
　　and Political Union
Orville and Wilbur Wright's first flight
1904
Entente Cordiale between Britain and France

1905
Unrest in Russia

1909
Institution of a system of old age pensions for all
　　persons over 70 years of age
1910
Death of Edward VII; accession of George V
Commons resolution to reduce the life of
　　Parliament from seven to five years with
　　restrictions on the power of the Lords' veto
1911
Passage of the Copyright Act: copies of all British
　　publications go to the British Museum and five
　　other copyright libraries
National Insurance Bill introduced by Lloyd
　　George
Suffragette riots in London

1912 R. Bridges: *Poetical Works* Shaw: *Androcles and the Lion* **1913** Lawrence: *Sons and Lovers*	**1912** Commons reject Women's Franchise Bill **1913** Commons pass Irish Home Rule Bill, rejected by the Lords Suffragette demonstrations in London 'Cat and Mouse' Act
1914 Joyce: *The Dubliners*	**1914** Germany declares war on Russia: start of the First World War Britain declares war on Germany

1915
Buchan: *The Thirty-Nine Steps*
F. Madox Ford: *The Good Soldier*
Lawrence: *The Rainbow*
Somerset Maugham: *Of Human Bondage*
Virginia Woolf: *The Voyage Out*
1916
Joyce: *A Portrait of the Artist as a Young Man*
Shaw: *Pygmalion*
1917
T. S. Eliot: *Prufrock and Other Observations*
Henry James: *The Ivory Tower*
Shaw: *Heartbreak House*
Yeats: 'The Wild Swans at Coole'
1918
Rupert Brooke: *Collected Poems*
G. M. Hopkins: Poems (published)
Katherine Mansfield: 'Prelude'
 	
1919
T. S. Eliot: Poems (published)
Hardy: *Collected Poems*
Sassoon: *The War Poems* (published)
1920
Katherine Mansfield: 'Bliss'
Wilfred Owen: Poems
Pound: *Hugh Selwyn Mauberley*
	1915
	Second Battle of Ypres
	English and French forces land at Gallipoli
	
	1916
	The Battle of Verdun
	Lloyd George becomes Prime Minister
	1917
	Abdication of Czar Nicholas II
	United States declares war on Germany
	The October revolution: Lenin leads Bolsheviks
	  agains Kerensky in Russia
	1918
	Second Battle of the Somme
	Second Battle of the Marne
	Execution of Nicholas II
	Women over 30 given the vote
	1919
	Peace conference at Versailles adopts Covenant of
	  the League of Nations
	The Treaty of Versailles signed
	1920
	The League of Nations formed
	The Government of Ireland Act passed: providing
	  for North and South to have their own
	  Parliaments

1921 Lawrence: *Women in Love* **1922** T. S. Eliot: *The Waste Land* Galsworthy: *The Forsyte Saga* A. E. Housman: *Last Poems* Aldous Huxley: *Mortal Coils* Joyce: *Ulysses* Yeats: *Later Poems*	**1922** Proclamation of the Irish Free State Mussolini joins Fascist government in Italy

1924
Forster: *A Passage to India*
Shaw: *St Joan*
Mary Webb: *Precious Bane*
1925
I. A. Richards: *Principles of Literary Criticism*
Virginia Woolf: *Mrs Dalloway*
1926
Lawrence: *The Plumed Serpent*
Sassoon: *Satirical Poems*
1927
R. Graves: Poems
Virginia Woolf: *To the Lighthouse*
	1923
	Establishment of the USSR
	Equality in divorce proceedings given to women
	  by the British Matrimonial Causes Act
	1924
	Ramsay MacDonald forms first Labour
	  government
	
	1925
	British Unemployment Insurance Act
	
	1926
	May General Strike
	Germany joins the League of Nations
	1927
	German financial and economic crisis
	Rise of Stalin: expulsion of Trotsky

1928
Lawrence: *Lady Chatterley's Lover*
    Selected Poems
Evelyn Waugh: *Decline and Fall*
Virginia Woolf: *Orlando*
Yeats: 'The Tower'
1929
R. Graves: *Good-bye to All That*
I. A. Richards: *Practical Criticism*

1930
Hardy: *Collected Poems*
Lawrence: *The Virgin and the Gypsy*
Masefield (becomes Poet Laureate – 1967)
Shaw: *The Apple Cart*
1931
Virginia Woolf: *The Waves*

1932
T. S. Eliot: *Sweeney Agonistes*
Aldous Huxley: *Brave New World*
F. R. Leavis: *New Bearings in English Poetry*
Evelyn Waugh: *Black Mischief*
1933
A. E. Housman: *The Name and Nature of Poetry*
Orwell: *Down and Out in Paris and London*
H. G. Wells: *The Shape of Things to Come*
1934
Evelyn Waugh: *A Handful of Dust*

1935
Auden (and Isherwood): *The Dog Beneath the
    Skin*
T. S. Eliot: *Murder in the Cathedral*
Empson: *Some Versions of Pastoral*
Spender: 'The Destructive Element'
1936
Aldous Huxley: *Eyeless in Gaza*
Dylan Thomas: *Twenty-five Poems*
Yeats: *Modern Poetry*

1937
Orwell: *The Road to Wigan Pier*
1938
Auden (and Isherwood): *On the Frontier*
Beckett: *Murphy*
G. Greene: *Brighton Rock*
Macneice: *Modern Poetry*
Evelyn Waugh: *Scoop*
Yeats: *New Poems*
1939
G. Granville Barker: 'Elegy on Spain'
T. S. Eliot: *The Family Reunion*
Isherwood: *Goodbye to Berlin*
Joyce: *Finnegans Wake*
Spender: 'The New Realism'
    Poems for Spain
1940
T. S. Eliot: 'East Coker'
G. Greene: *The Power and the Glory*
Dylan Thomas: *Portrait of the Artist as a Young
    Dog*

1928
Minimum voting age for women reduced to 21
    from 30 years

1929
General Election victory for Labour Party
The Wall Street Crash: collapse of the US Stock
    Exchange
1930
Gandhi begins his campaign of civil disobedience
Nazis win seats from moderates in German
    elections

1931
The New Party formed by Oswald Mosley
National government formed by Ramsay
    MacDonald
Invergordon naval mutiny
1932
Hunger marches in Britain
Nazis gain majority in German parliament

1933
Adolf Hitler becomes Chancellor of Germany
Persecution of the Jews in Germany begins

1934
The British Union of Fascists addressed by
    Oswald Mosley
Adolf Hitler becomes Führer
Purge in the Russian Communist Party

1936
Penguin Books founded
Accession of Edward VIII on death of George V
Spanish Civil War starts
The abdication of Edward VIII
1937
Irish Free State becomes Eire
1938
Munich Conference

1939
Franco secures the surrender of Madrid: end of
    the Spanish Civil War
Britain and France declare war on Germany: start
    of the Second World War

1940
National government formed, Churchill becomes
    Prime Minister
Evacuation of Dunkirk
Battle of Britain
Start of the Blitz: German night-time raids on
    London

1941
T. S. Eliot: 'Burnt Norton'
Virginia Woolf: *Between the Acts*
1942
T. S. Eliot: 'Little Gidding'
Sassoon: *The Weald of Youth*
Spender: 'Ruins and Visions'
1943
T. S. Eliot: 'Four Quartets'
G. Greene: *The Ministry of Fear*
Kathleen Raine: *Stone and Flower: Poems 1935–1943*
Dylan Thomas: *New Poems*
1944
Macneice: *Springboard: Poems 1941–1944*

1945
Isherwood: *Prater Violet*
Larkin: 'The North Ship'
Orwell: *Animal Farm: A Fairy Story*
Evelyn Waugh: *Brideshead Revisited*

1946
Orwell: *Collected Essays*

1947
Larkin: *A Girl in Winter*
Lowry: *Under the Volcano*
Spender: *Poems of Dedication*
1948
G. Greene: *The Heart of the Matter*
F. R. Leavis: *The Great Tradition*
Pound: *Cantos 1–84*
Rattigan: *The Browning Version*
Evelyn Waugh: *The Loved One*

1949
T. S. Eliot: *The Cocktail Party*
Christopher Fry: *The Lady's Not for Burning*
Stevie Smith: *The Holiday*

1950
G. Greene: *The Third Man*
Doris Lessing: *The Grass is Singing*
1951
Larkin: Poems

1952
Beckett: *Waiting for Godot*
Doris Lessing: *Martha Quest*

1953
Orwell: *England, Your England*

1941
Japanese bomb Pearl Harbor
United States declares war on Germany and Italy

1943
Germany surrenders at Stalingrad
Surrender of Italy

1944
Butler's Education Act
'D Day' landings on the Normandy beaches
1945
The Yalta conference: meeting between Churchill, Roosevelt and Stalin
Mussolini dies
Death of Hitler
'VE' day
The Potsdam conference: meeting between Churchill and Atlee, Stalin, Truman
The United States drops atomic bombs on Hiroshima and Nagasaki
The surrender of Japan; end of Second World War
Labour win General Election
1946
United Nations General Assembly holds its first meeting
Arts Council founded
National Insurance comes into effect
1947
Nationalisation of the Coal Industry
Independence of India and Parkistan founded

1948
National Health Service founded
Nationalisation of British Railways
Berlin blockade and airlift
British Citizenship Act: Commonwealth citizens granted subject status
UN convention on human rights and genocide
1949
Beginning of South African apartheid
North Atlantic Treaty signed by Britain, France, Belgium, Netherlands, Italy, Portugal, Denmark, Iceland, Norway, United States and Canada
Proclamation of the Republic of Eire
Proclamation of the Communist People's Republic of China
1950
Korean War begins

1951
The Festival of Britain
Conservatives win British General Election
1952
Death of George VI; accession of Elizabeth II
British atomic bomb announced
Mau Mau troubles in Kenya
1953
Death of Stalin
Coronation of Elizabeth II

1954
Kingsley Amis: *Lucky Jim*
Golding: *Lord of the Flies*
Thom Gunn: Poems
Dylan Thomas: *Under Milk Wood*
1955
Empson: *Collected Poems*
G. Greene: *The Quiet American*
1956
J. Osborne: *Look Back in Anger*

1957
Beckett: *Endgame*
Iris Murdoch: *The Sandcastle*
Patrick White: *Voss*

1958
G. Greene: *Our Man in Havana*
C. Achebe: *Things Fall Apart*
Alan Sillitoe: *Saturday Night and Sunday Morning*
1959
John Arden: *Serjeant Musgrave's Dance*
Beckett: *Krapp's Last Tape*
Alan Sillitoe: *The Loneliness of the Long-Distance Runner*
Muriel Spark: *Memento Mori*
Wesker: *Roots*
M. Horovitz founds *New Departures*
1960
Pinter: *The Birthday Party*
       The Caretaker
       The Dumb Waiter
1961
G. Greene: *A Burnt-out Case*
Thom Gunn: 'My Sad Captains'
Ted Hughes: 'Meet My Folks!'
Elizabeth Jennings: 'Song for a Birth or a Death'
Iris Murdoch: *A Severed Head*
John Osborne: *Luther*
Muriel Spark: *The Prime of Miss Jean Brodie*
V. S. Naipaul: *A House For Mr Biswas*
1962
Anthony Burgess: *A Clockwork Orange*
Margaret Drabble: *A Summer Bird-Cage*
Ted Hughes (and Thom Gunn): *Selected Poems*
Doris Lessing: *The Golden Notebook*
David Storey: *This Sporting Life*
Wesker: *Chips with Everything*
1963
Nell Dunn: *Up the Junction*
Iris Murdoch: *The Unicorn*
C. P. Snow: *Corridors of Power*

1964
Bellow: *Herzog*
Ann Jellicoe: *The Knack*
Peter Shaffer: *The Royal Hunt of the Sun*

1965
John Fowles: *The Magus*

1954
Nasser becomes Egyptian Premier

1955
West Germany admitted to NATO
Universal Copyright Convention
1956
Suez crisis
Russian invasion of Hungary
1957
The Common Market founded when Treaty of
   Rome signed
The Wolfenden report on homosexuality and
   prostitution
Launch of Sputnik I
Independence of Ghana (formerly Gold Coast)
1958
The appearance of Beatniks

1959
Obscene Publications Act

1960
'Wind of Change' speech made by Macmillan
Kennedy wins US Presidential election from
   Nixon
1961
Yuri Gagarin becomes first man in space
Britain applies for membership of the EEC
East Germany closes the border between East and
   West Berlin
The Berlin Wall
Mass CND rally in Trafalgar Square

1962
The United States blockades Cuba: the 'Cuban
   missile crisis'

1963
The Beatles become popular
Britain refused Common Market entry
The Profumo scandal: Profumo resigns
The assassination of President Kennedy
1964
Harlem race riots in US
Martin Luther King awarded Nobel peace prize
Wilson forms Labour administration on resignation
   of Alec Douglas-Home
Fighting in Vietnam
1965
Edward Heath becomes Leader of the
   Conservative Party
Death penalty abolished

1966
G. Greene: *The Comedians*
Tom Stoppard: *Rosencrantz and Guildenstern are Dead*

1967
Angela Carter: *The Magic Toyshop*
Nell Dunn: *Poor Cow*
Peter Nichols: *A Day in the Death of Joe Egg*
Pinter: *The Tea Party and Other Plays*
David Storey: *The Restoration of Arnold Middleton*
1968
C. Day-Lewis (becomes Poet Laureate – 1972)
Roy Fuller: *New Poems*

1969
John Fowles: *The French Lieutenant's Woman*
G. Greene: *Travels with My Aunt*
Pound: *Cantos CX–CXVII* (published)
Booker Prize first awarded
1970
Ted Hughes: 'Crow'
Larkin: 'All What Jazz?'
1971
Edward Bond: *Lear*
Forster: *Maurice*
Thom Gunn: 'Moly'
Roger McGough: *After the Merrymaking*
Iris Murdoch: *An Accidental Man*
1972
John Betjeman becomes Poet Laureate
Margaret Drabble: *The Needle's Eye*
Ted Hughes: 'Crow' (enlarged edition)
Elizabeth Jennings: 'Relationships'
1973
Iris Murdoch: *The Black Prince*

1974
Auden: *Thank You Fog: Last Poems*
Beckett: *Not I*
Thom Gunn: 'Mandrakes'
                     'Song Book'
Doris Lessing: *The Memoirs of a Survivor*
1975
Bradbury: *The History Man*
Lodge: *Changing Places*
1976
New National Theatre completed
1977
National Poetry Centre dissolved
Tom Stoppard: *Professional Foul*
1978
David Hare: *Plenty*
Iris Murdoch: *The Sea, The Sea*
Emma Tennant: *The Bad Sister*
Fay Weldon: *Praxis*
1979
S. Heaney: *Field Walk*
C. Raine: *A Martian Sends a Postcard Home*
1980
Anthony Burgess: *Earthly Powers*
William Golding: *Rites of Passage*

1966
Labour win British General Election
Cultural Revolution in China

1967
Legalization of homosexuality and abortion

1968
Assassinations of Bobby Kennedy and Martin Luther King
Civil Rights Bill passed in the United States
United Nations adopts Nuclear Non-proliferation treaty
Richard M. Nixon elected President of the United States
1969
First American moon landings

1970
Lowering of the voting age in Britain to 18
Conservative win in British General Election
1971
Anti-Vietnam War demonstration in Washington

1972
Direct rule by British government in Northern Ireland

1973
Signing of Vietnam peace agreement
Britain joins the EEC
1974
Solzhenitsyn's expulsion from the USSR
General Election in Britain with no overall majority
Labour wins General Election
The 'Watergate' scandal: Nixon resigns
1975
End of the Vietnam War

1979
Winter of discontent
Conservatives win General Election
1980
Soviet invasion of Afghanistan
American hostages in Iran

1981
Edward Bond: *Restoration*
Salman Rushdie: *Midnight's Children*

1983
William Golding wins the Nobel Prize for
   Literature
Fay Weldon: *The Life and Loves of a She-Devil*
1984
Kingsley Amis: *Stanley and the Women*
Anita Brookner: *Hôtel Du Lac*
Angela Carter: *Nights at the Circus*
Seamus Heaney: *Station Island*
Ted Hughes becomes Poet Laureate
David Lodge: *Small World*
Craig Raine: *Rich*
1985
Peter Ackroyd: *Hawksmoor*
Peter Carey: *Illywhacker*
Douglas Dunn: *Elegies*
David Hare: *Pravda*
Fay Weldon: *Polaris*
1986
Kingsley Amis: *The Old Devils*
Margaret Atwood: *The Handmaid's Tale*
Wole Soyinka wins Nobel Prize for Literature
1987
Peter Ackroyd: *Chatterton*
Caryl Churchill: *Serious Money*
Seamus Heaney: *The Haw Lantern*

1988
Ayckbourn: *Henceforward*
Peter Carey: *Oscar and Lucinda*
Douglas Dunn: *Northlight*
David Lodge: *Nice Work*
Marina Warner: *The Lost Father*
Salman Rushdie: *Satanic Verses*
1989
Margaret Atwood: *Cat's Eye*
Peter Ackroyd: *First Light*
Anthony Burgess: *Any Old Iron*
Elizabeth Jennings: *Tributes*

1981
Riots in London, Liverpool and Manchester

1982
The Falklands War
1983
Conservative victory in General Election
Anti-nuclear protests at Greenham Common
The Ballykelly Bombing
1984
Miners' strike

1985
Famine in Ethiopia – Live Aid concerts raise
   money for famine relief

1986
Chernobyl nuclear power station explosion –
   radioactive cloud over much of Europe

1987
Conservative party wins third term of office
British government attempts to ban publication of
   Peter Wright's *Spycatcher*
'Black Monday' – British stock market crash
1988
Bicentenary of Australia

1989
Russian troops complete withdrawal from
   Afghanistan
Controversy over *Satanic Verses*

Picture Acknowledgements

Jerry Bauer – Ruth Prawer Jhabvala, Malcolm Bradbury; Jane Bown – Beryl Bainbridge; British Library, London – First page of Laȝamon's *Brut*, *The Seasons* by James Thomson, Quarto Edition; reproduced by courtesy of the Trustees of the British Museum – William Blake after Hogarth *The Beggars' Opera*; Julian Calder – Salman Rushdie; Donald Cooper – *Happy Days*, Antony Sher as Richard III; Andrew Douglas – David Lodge; © M. C. Escher Heirs/Cordon Art, Baarn, Holland – *Relativity*; Fay Godwin – Margaret Drabble; Trevor Leighton – Anita Brookner; London Borough of Tower Hamlets – Claude de Jonge, *A London Panorama*; Tom Miller – John Fowles; John Minihan – Samuel Beckett; National Portrait Gallery, London – M. Gordigiani – Elizabeth Barrett Browning, P. B. Brontë – The Brontë Sisters, J. E. Blanche – James Joyce, Tom Phillips – Iris Murdoch, R. Rothwell – Mary Shelley, W. B. Richmond – Robert Louis Stevenson, J. Barry – Samuel Johnson, R. Westall – Lord George Byron, P. Vandyke – Samuel Taylor Coleridge, L. F. Abbott – William Cowper, S. Laurence – Charles Dickens, Henry Fielding, G. Richmond – Elizabeth Gaskell, Oliver Goldsmith, B. R. Haydon – Leigh Hunt, C. A. Brown – John Keats, H. Furnino – Arthur Pinero, J. Highmore – Samuel Richardson, G. Stuart – Sarah Siddons, F. Stone – William Makepeace Thackeray, S. Laurence – Anthony Trollope, G. Kneller – Christoper Wren; Axel Poignant – Patrick White; Franta Provanznik – Susan Hill; Philip Sayer – Philip Larkin; Christopher Smith – Martin Amis; Tate Gallery, London – William Maw Egley – *Omnibus Life in London*, Georges Braque – *Clarinet and Bottle of Rum on a Mantelpiece* (1911), William Roberts – *The Vorticists at the Restaurant de la Tour Eiffel: Spring 1915*; William Wain – John Wain.

While every effort has been made to contact the copyright holders of all illustrations, and to make full acknowledgement for their use, if any errors or omissions have occurred, please contact the publishers who will correct these in subsequent editions.

Contributors' biographies

Janet Barron (BA, King's College, London) is a freelance writer who reviews regularly for *The Literary Review* and *New Statesman and Society*. Her books include *An Annotated Critical Bibliography of Augustan Poetry* (Harvester Press, 1989, co-author), and *A Study of Fanny Burney* (forthcoming, Longman). She is co-author of the essay on eighteenth-century prose literature.

James Booth graduated from Oxford and is a lecturer in English at the University of Hull. He is author of *Writers and Politics in Nigeria* (1981) and various articles on British and African literature, and on numismatics. He contributed the essay on Augustan and Romantic poetry and reference entries in the same area.

Catherine Byron (MA, M Phil) was born in 1947 of an Irish mother and English father. She was educated in Belfast and at Somerville College, Oxford. A writer and poet on Irish themes (*Settlements*, 1985; *Samhain*, 1987; *Station Island Journal*, forthcoming), she is a member of the British Association of Irish Studies and contributed the entries on Irish literature.

Gail Cunningham is Senior Lecturer in English at Kingston Polytechnic. She took her first degree and doctorate at Oxford, and has published widely on nineteenth- and twentieth-century fiction. Works include *The New Woman and the Victorian Novel*. She contributed the essay 'The Nineteenth-Century Novel'.

John Drakakis (BA, MA, Wales; PhD, Leeds; Dip Ed, Exon) is senior lecturer in English Studies, University of Stirling. He is General Editor of *Routledge English Texts* series, and General Editor of the revised *Critical Idiom* series. He was editor of *British Radio Drama* (Cambridge, 1981), and *Alternative Shakespeares* (Routledge, 1985). He has contributed articles and reviews to journals on the subjects of radio drama, Elizabethan and Jacobean drama and critical theory, and is currently working on a volume of essays on *Shakespeare's Tragedies*, a full-length study of *Shakespearian Discourses* and an edition of Marlowe's *Doctor Faustus*. He wrote the essay 'Contemporary Approaches to Literature' and reference entries on critical theory.

Christopher Gillie (MA, Cambridge). His books include *Character in English Literature* (Chatto, 1965); *Longman Companion to English Literature* (1972); *A Preface to Jane Austen* (Longman, 1974); *English Literature 1900–1940* (CUP, 1975); *A Preface to Forster* (Longman, 1983).

David Jarrett lectures in the School of Literary and Media Studies at the Polytechnic of North London. He contributed the entry on science fiction.

Lesley Johnson teaches in the School of English, University of Leeds. Her publications include articles on Old French fabliaux, *The Testament of Cresseid*, 'Feminist Options', Anglo-Norman historiography, and she is currently working on a major study of the history of Britain in Medieval narratives. She wrote the essay and reference entries on Medieval English literature.

Sarah Johnston lectures at Kingston Polytechnic and elsewhere. She has a first class BA, and an MA from London University, writes fiction, and has published a book on boats. She is largely responsible for the nineteenth-century prose entries.

David Nokes (MA, PhD, Cambridge) is Reader in English Literature at King's College, London. His books include *Jonathan Swift, A Hypocrite Reversed* (OUP, 1985) and *Raillery and Rage, a Study of Eighteenth-Century Satire* (Harvester Press, 1987). He is co-author of the essay on eighteenth-century prose literature.

John O'Brien (BA, Cambridge; D Phil, Oxford) teaches at the University of Liverpool, where he specialises in French Renaissance literature and critical theory. He has published articles and reviews in *MLR, French Studies* and *Renaissance Studies*, and has books currently with Princeton University Press and Routledge. He contributed reference entries on French literature.

Valerie Pedlar (MA) is working for her PhD at Liverpool University and teaches part-time for the Open University. She took her first degree in sociology before taking another in English and music. She has written on John Clare for the *John Clare Society Journal*. She contributed context entries to the reference section.

Andrew Piasecki (BA, MA in Drama and Theatre Art) teaches drama at Royal Holloway and Bedford New College, London University. He has a special interest in Renaissance and modern European theatre, has published a chapter in the *Shakespeare Handbook* (1987) on Elizabethan and Jacobean theatre, and contributes regularly to theatre magazines, including *Plays International*. He is currently producing a *Theatre File* on the playwright Lorca. He wrote the essay and the reference entries on modern drama.

Andrew Roberts (MA, London) is a lecturer in English at Queen Mary and Westfield College, University of London. He has published articles on modern fiction and contemporary poetry, and contributed the essay and reference entries on twentieth-century prose.

Jonathan Sawday is a lecturer in Renaissance literature and critical theory at the University of Southampton. His publications include studies of seventeenth-century literature and science. He is the author of the essay and reference entries on Renaissance poetry.

Eva Simmons (BA, Cambridge) is completing a PhD on Restoration drama and non-dramatic prose at Royal Holloway and Bedford New College, London University. Her research has a special emphasis on the dramatist Aphra Behn. Ms Simmons has taught at Cambridge and London. She also works as a journalist and has published articles in academic and non-academic journals and newspapers. She wrote the essay on Restoration and eighteenth-century drama, as well as entries relating to the drama of the period.

Jim Simpson (BA, PhD) lectures in German at the University of Liverpool. He has written on Goethe and Matthew Arnold and is currently working on Bertolt Brecht. He contributed the entry 'German Influence on English Literature'.

Mercer Simpson (MA, Cambridge; MA, Wales; Cert. Ed, Bristol) was formerly senior lecturer at the Polytechnic of Wales, and is now a freelance literary journalist. He was also judge, Welsh Arts Council's Annual Literature Prizes, 1987 and has been editor, *BWA*, since 1986. He contributed the 'Anglo-Welsh literature' entry and other Welsh-related entries.

John Thieme lectures in the School of Literary and Media Studies at the Polytechnic of North London. He contributed the material on Commonwealth literature.

René J. A. Weis (BA, PhD) is a lecturer in English at University College, London. He is the editor of a forthcoming edition of *The Plays of John Webster* (OUP), and of *King Lear* (Longman). He wrote the essay on Shakespeare and English Renaissance drama and the reference entries relating to the period.

Linda Williams lectures in English at Liverpool University. She has also taught at the universities of Exeter, Manchester and Sussex, where she completed her doctoral research on gender and epistemology in D. H. Lawrence, Freud and Nietzsche. She contributed the essay and reference entries on Victorian and modern poetry.

Marion Wynne-Davies lectures in English at the University of Hull. She has a PhD on Arthurian literature in Spenser's *Faerie Queene* and seventeenth-century poetry from the University of London. She has published essays on *The Post Spenserian Romance Epic*, *Yeats and Arthur*, *Women in the Court Masque* and *Titus Andronicus*, and an edition of Chaucer's *Wife of Bath* and *Clerk's Tale* (Routledge). She is working on a study of women in Arthurian literature from the medieval period to the present day.